Benelux

2004

■ *Sélection d'hôtels et de restaurants*

Selectie van hotels en restaurants ■

■ *Auswahl an Hotels und Restaurants*

Selection of hotels and restaurants ■

Benelux

Cher lecteur

Le Guide Michelin vous propose, dans chaque catégorie de confort et de prix, une sélection des meilleurs hôtels et restaurants. Cette sélection est effectuée par une équipe d'inspecteurs, professionnels de formation hôtelière, qui sillonnent le pays toute l'année pour visiter de nouveaux établissements et ceux déjà cités afin d'en vérifier la qualité et la régularité des prestations. Salariés Michelin, les inspecteurs travaillent en tout anonymat et en toute indépendance.

Les équipements et services sont signalés par des symboles, langage international qui vous permet de voir en un coup d'œil si un hôtel dispose, par exemple, d'un parking ou d'une piscine. Pour bien profiter de cette très riche source d'information, plongez-vous dans l'introduction. Un texte décrivant l'atmosphère de l'hôtel ou du restaurant complète ces renseignements.

L'inscription dans le guide est totalement gratuite. Chaque année, les hôteliers et restaurateurs cités remplissent le questionnaire qui leur est envoyé, nous fournissant les dates d'ouverture et les prix pour l'année à venir. Près de 100 000 informations sont mises à jour pour chaque édition (nouveaux établissements, changements de tarif, dates d'ouverture).

Une grande aide vient aussi des commentaires des lecteurs avec près de 45 000 lettres et Email par an, pour toute l'Europe.

Merci d'avance pour votre participation et bon voyage avec le Guide Michelin 2004.

Consultez le Guide Michelin sur
www.Viamichelin.fr
et écrivez-nous à :
leguidemichelin-Benelux@be.michelin.com

Sommaire

Le choix d'un hôtel, d'un restaurant

Ce guide vous propose une sélection d'hôtels et restaurants établie à l'usage de l'automobiliste de passage. Les établissements, classés selon leur confort, sont cités par ordre de préférence dans chaque catégorie.

Catégories

	XXXXX	*Grand luxe et tradition*
	XXXX	*Grand confort*
	XXX	*Très confortable*
	XX	*De bon confort*
	X	*Assez confortable*
sans rest.		*L'hôtel n'a pas de restaurant*
	avec ch.	*Le restaurant possède des chambres*

Agrément et tranquillité

Certains établissements se distinguent dans le guide par les symboles rouges indiqués ci-après. Le séjour dans ces maisons se révèle particulièrement agréable ou reposant.
Cela peut tenir d'une part au caractère de l'édifice, au décor original, au site, à l'accueil et aux services qui sont proposés, d'autre part à la tranquillité des lieux.

à	*Hôtels agréables*
XXXXX à X	*Restaurants agréables*
« Parc fleuri »	*Élément particulièrement agréable*
	Hôtel très tranquille ou isolé et tranquille
	Hôtel tranquille
< mer	*Vue exceptionnelle*
<	*Vue intéressante ou étendue.*

Les localités possédant des établissements agréables ou très tranquilles sont repérées sur les cartes placées au début de chaque pays traité dans ce guide.
Consultez-les pour la préparation de vos voyages et donnez-nous vos appréciations à votre retour, vous faciliterez ainsi nos enquêtes.

L'installation

Les chambres des hôtels que nous recommandons possèdent, en général, des installations sanitaires complètes. Il est toutefois possible que dans la catégorie 🏠, certaines chambres en soient dépourvues.

30 ch	*Nombre de chambres*
	Ascenseur
	Air conditionné
TV	*Télévision dans la chambre*
	Établissement en partie réservé aux non-fumeurs
	Chambres accessibles aux personnes à mobilité réduite
	Repas servis au jardin ou en terrasse
	Wellness centre : bel espace de bien-être et de relaxation
	Balnéothérapie, Cure thermale
	Salle de remise en forme
	Piscine : de plein air ou couverte
	Sauna – Jardin de repos
	Location de vélos
	Tennis à l'hôtel
25 à 150	*Salles de conférences : capacité des salles*
	Garage dans l'hôtel (généralement payant)
P	*Parking (pouvant être payant)*
	Ponton d'amarrage
	Accès interdit aux chiens (dans tout ou partie de l'établissement)
Fax	*Transmission de documents par télécopie*
mai-oct.	*Période d'ouverture, communiquée par l'hôtelier En l'absence de mention, l'établissement est ouvert toute l'année.*
✉ 9411 KL	*Code postal de l'établissement (Grand-Duché de Luxembourg et Pays-Bas en particulier)*

La table

Les étoiles

Certains établissements méritent d'être signalés à votre attention pour la qualité de leur cuisine. Nous les distinguons par **les étoiles de bonne table***.*

Nous indiquons pour ces établissements, trois spécialités culinaires et, au Grand-Duché de Luxembourg des vins locaux, qui pourront orienter votre choix.

✿✿✿ **Une des meilleures tables, vaut le voyage**

On y mange toujours très bien, parfois merveilleusement. Grands vins, service impeccable, cadre élégant... Prix en conséquence.

✿✿ **Table excellente, mérite un détour**

Spécialités et vins de choix... Attendez-vous à une dépense en rapport.

✿ **Une très bonne table dans sa catégorie**

L'étoile marque une bonne étape sur votre itinéraire. Mais ne comparez pas l'étoile d'un établissement de luxe à prix élevés avec celle d'une petite maison où à prix raisonnables, on sert également une cuisine de qualité.

Le nom du chef de cuisine figure après la raison sociale lorsqu'il exploite personnellement l'établissement. Exemple : XX ✿ **Panorama** (Martin)...

Le "Bib Gourmand"

Repas soignés à prix modérés

Vous souhaitez parfois trouver des tables plus simples, à prix modérés ; c'est pourquoi nous avons sélectionné des restaurants proposant, pour un rapport qualité-prix particulièrement favorable, un repas soigné.

Ces maisons sont signalées par le "Bib Gourmand" ☺ *et* Repas *(environ 33 euros).*

La carte des vins

Carte offrant un choix particulièrement attractif.

Parmi les restaurants que nous avons sélectionnés, dans toutes les catégories, certains proposent une carte des vins particulièrement attractive. Mais attention à ne pas comparer la carte présentée par le sommelier d'un grand restaurant avec celle d'une auberge dont le patron se passionne pour les vins de sa région.

Consultez les cartes des étoiles de bonne table ✿✿✿, ✿✿, ✿ *et des* "Bib Gourmand" ☺ *placées au début de chaque pays et les listes signalées au sommaire.*

Voir aussi ⊜ *page suivante.*

Les prix

Les prix que nous indiquons dans ce guide ont été établis à l'automne 2003 et s'appliquent à la **haute saison**. *Ils sont susceptibles de modifications, notamment en cas de variations des prix des biens et services. Ils s'entendent taxes et services compris. Aucune majoration ne doit figurer sur votre note, sauf éventuellement une taxe locale.*
Les hôtels et restaurants figurent en gros caractères lorsque les hôteliers nous ont donné tous leurs prix et se sont engagés, sous leur propre responsabilité, à les appliquer aux touristes de passage porteurs de notre guide.
Les week-ends et dans les grandes villes, certains hôtels pratiquent des prix avantageux, renseignez-vous lors de votre réservation.
Les exemples suivants sont donnés en euros.
Entrez à l'hôtel le Guide à la main, vous montrerez ainsi qu'il vous conduit là en confiance.

Repas

	Établissement proposant un menu simple à moins de 22 euros.
Repas *Lunch 18*	*Repas servi le midi et en semaine seulement.*
	Menus à prix fixe :
Repas 25/50	*Minimum 25 et maximum 50 des menus servis aux heures normales (12 h à 14 h 30 et 19 h à 21 h 30 en Belgique – 12 h à 14 h et 17 h à 21 h aux Pays-Bas).* *Certains menus ne sont servis que pour 2 couverts minimum ou par table entière.*
bc	*Boisson comprise (vin)*
	Vin servi au verre
	Repas à la carte :
Repas carte 40 à 75	*Le premier prix correspond à un repas normal comprenant : entrée, plat garni et dessert.* *Le 2e prix concerne un repas plus complet (avec spécialité) comprenant : deux plats et dessert.*

Chambres

☕ 12	*Prix du petit déjeuner (supplément éventuel si servi en chambre).*
ch 70/85	*Prix minimum* (70) *pour une chambre d'une personne prix maximum* (85) *pour une chambre de deux personnes.*
suites	*Se renseigner auprès de l'hôtelier.*
29 ch ☕ 75/105	*Prix des chambres petit déjeuner compris.*

Demi-pension

½ P 90/110	*Prix minimum et maximum de la demi-pension (chambre, petit déjeuner et l'un des deux repas) par personne et par jour, en saison. Il est indispensable de s'entendre au préalable avec l'hôtelier pour conclure un arrangement définitif.*

Les arrhes

Certains hôteliers demandent le versement d'arrhes. Il s'agit d'un dépôt-garantie qui engage l'hôtelier comme le client. Bien faire préciser les dispositions de cette garantie.

Cartes de crédit

AE ① MC VISA JCB	*Cartes de crédit acceptées par l'établissement : American Express – Diners Club – MasterCard (Eurocard) – Visa – Japan Credit Bureau*

Les villes

1000	Numéro postal à indiquer dans l'adresse avant le nom de la localité
✉ 4900 Spa	Bureau de poste desservant la localité
P	Capitale de Province
C Herve	Siège administratif communal
531 T 3 716 E 3	Numéro de la Carte Michelin et carroyage ou numéro du pli
G. Belgique-Lux.	Voir le guide vert Michelin Belgique-Luxembourg
4 283 h	Population (d'après chiffres du dernier recensement officiel publié)
BX A	Lettres repérant un emplacement sur le plan
18	Golf et nombre de trous
※, ≤	Panorama, point de vue
✈	Aéroport
🚗 ☎ 02 45 52 14	Localité desservie par train-auto Renseignements au numéro de téléphone indiqué
⛴	Transports maritimes
⛴	Transports maritimes pour passagers seulement
i	Information touristique

Les curiosités

Intérêt

★★★	*Vaut le voyage*
★★	*Mérite un détour*
★	*Intéressant*

Situation

Voir	*Dans la ville*
Env	*Aux environs de la ville*
Nord, Sud, Est, Ouest	*La curiosité est située : au Nord, au Sud, à l'Est, à l'Ouest*
②, ④	*On s'y rend par la sortie ② ou ④ repérée par le même signe sur le plan du Guide et sur la carte*
2 km	*Distance en kilomètres*

La voiture, les pneus

En fin de guide figure une liste des principales marques automobiles pouvant éventuellement vous aider en cas de panne.
Vous pouvez également consulter utilement les principaux automobiles clubs du Benelux :

Belgique *Royal Automobile Club de Belgique (RACB),*
FIA, rue d'Arlon 53 – Bte 3,
1040 Bruxelles
☏ 0 2 287 09 11 fax 0 2 230 75 84
Royal Motor Union
boulevard d'Avroy 254 – Bte 1,
4000 Liège
☏ 0 4 252 70 30 fax 0 4 252 83 01
Touring Club Royal de Belgique (TCB)
AIT, rue de la Loi 44, 1040 Bruxelles
☏ 0 2 233 22 02 fax 02 286 33 23
Vlaamse Automobilistenbond (VTB-VAB)
Sint-Jakobsmarkt 45, 2000 Antwerpen
☏ 0 3 253 63 63

Luxembourg *Automobile Club du Grand Duché de Luxembourg (ACL)*
FIA & AIT, route de Longwy 54,
8007 Bertrange
☏ 45 00 45 1 fax 45 04 55

Pays-Bas *Koninklijke Nederlandse Automobiel Club (KNAC)*
FIA, Wassenaarseweg 220,
2596 EC Den Haag
☏ (070) 383 16 12
fax (070) 383 19 06
Koninklijke Nederlandse Toeristenbond (ANWB)
AIT, Wassenaarseweg 220,
2596 EC Den Haag
☏ (070) 314 71 47
fax (070) 314 69 69

Vitesse : Limites autorisées (en km/h)

	Autoroute	*Route*	*Agglomération*
Belgique	*120*	*90*	*50*
GD Luxembourg	*120*	*90*	*50*
Pays-Bas	*100/120*	*80*	*50*

Les cartes de voisinage

Avez-vous pensé à les consulter ?

Vous souhaitez trouver une bonne adresse, par exemple, aux environs de Arnhem ? Consultez la carte qui accompagne le plan de la ville.

La « carte de voisinage » (ci-contre) attire votre attention sur toutes les localités citées au Guide autour de la ville choisie, et particulièrement celles situées dans un rayon de 30 km (limite de couleur).

Les « cartes de voisinage » vous permettent ainsi le repérage rapide de toutes les ressources proposées par le Guide autour des métropoles régionales.

Nota :

Lorsqu'une localité est présente sur une « carte de voisinage », sa métropole de rattachement est imprimée en BLEU sur la ligne des distances de ville à ville.

Exemple :

Vous trouverez EDE sur la carte de voisinage de ARNHEM.

EDE *Gelderland* 715 *I 5 – 101 700 h.*
Env. *Parc National de la Haute Veluwe****
Amsterdam 81 – Arnhem 23 – Apeldoorn 32 – Utrecht 43.

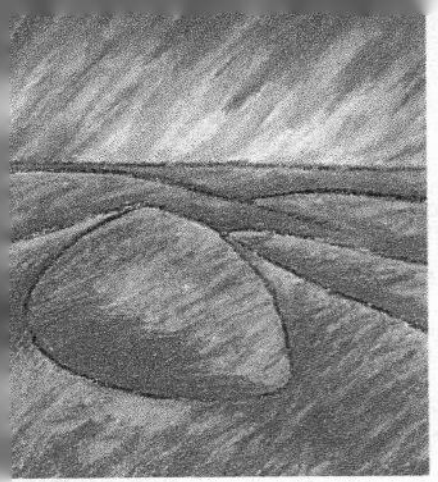

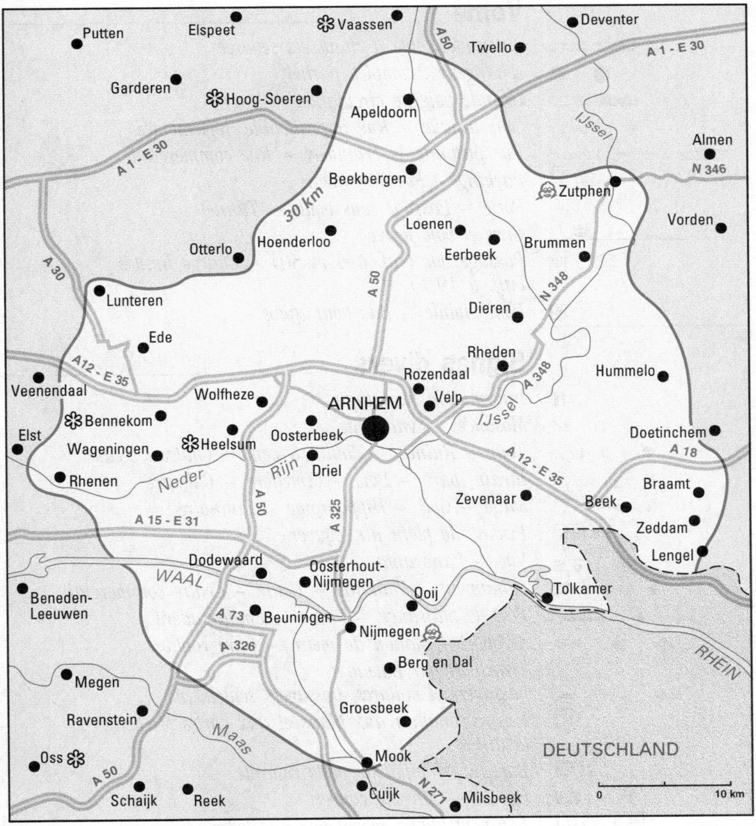

Putten
Elspeet
Vaassen
Deventer
Twello
A 50
A 1 - E 30
Garderen
Hoog-Soeren
Apeldoorn
IJssel
Almen
N 346
A 1 - E 30
Beekbergen
Zutphen
30 km
Vorden
Loenen
Hoenderloo
Eerbeek
Brummen
Otterlo
A 30
A 50
N 348
Lunteren
Dieren
Ede
Rheden
A 12 - E 35
Hummelo
Rozendaal
A 348
Veenendaal
Wolfheze
ARNHEM
Velp
IJssel
Bennekom
Doetinchem
Elst
Heelsum
Oosterbeek
Wageningen
A 12 - E 35
A 18
Rijn
Driel
Neder
Braamt
Rhenen
A 50
A 325
Zevenaar
Beek
A 15 - E 31
Zeddam
Lengel
Dodewaard
Oosterhout-
Nijmegen
WAAL
Tolkamer
Ooij
Beneden-
Leeuwen
A 73
Beuningen
Nijmegen
RHEIN
A 326
Berg en Dal
Megen
Groesbeek
Ravenstein
Maas
DEUTSCHLAND
Mook
Oss
A 50
0
10 km
N 271
Schaijk
Reek
Cuijk
Milsbeek

Les « Cartes de voisinage » sont localisées sur la carte thématique de chaque pays respectif.

Les plans

Hôtels
Restaurants

Curiosités

Bâtiment intéressant
Édifice religieux intéressant

Voirie

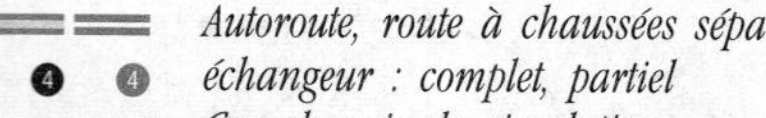

Autoroute, route à chaussées séparées
échangeur : complet, partiel
Grande voie de circulation
Sens unique – Rue impraticable, réglementée
Pasteur *Rue piétonne – Tramway – Rue commerçante*
Parking – Parking Relais
Porte – Passage sous voûte – Tunnel
Gare et voie ferrée
Passage bas (inf. à 4 m 50) – Charge limitée (inf. à 19 t.)
Pont mobile – Bac pour autos

Signes divers

Information touristique
Mosquée – Synagogue
Tour – Ruines – Moulin à vent – Château d'eau
Jardin, parc – Bois – Cimetière – Calvaire
Stade – Golf – Hippodrome – Patinoire
Piscine de plein air, couverte
Vue – Panorama
Monument – Fontaine – Usine – Centre commercial
Port de plaisance – Phare – Embarcadère
Aéroport – Station de métro – Gare routière
Transport par bateau :
passagers et voitures, passagers seulement
③ *Repère commun aux plans et aux cartes Michelin détaillées*
Bureau principal de poste restante
Hôpital – Marché couvert
Bâtiment public repéré par une lettre :
H P - *Hôtel de ville – Gouvernement Provincial*
J - *Palais de justice*
M T - *Musée – Théâtre*
U - *Université, grande école*
POL. G - *Police (commissariat central) – Gendarmerie*

- ☐ a. ***Baie de Palerme (Sicile)***
- ☐ b. ***Rade de Toulon (Côte d'Azur)***
- ☐ c. ***Baie de San Francisco (Californie)***

E. Baret / Michelin - (06 - Roubion)

☐ a. ***Departementale weg D17***

☐ b. ***Rijksweg N202***

☐ c. ***Departementale weg D30***

U weet niet hoe u hier moet komen ?
Sla dan snel een Michelinkaart open !

De Michelinkaarten in de reeksen NATIONAL, REGIONAL, LOCAL en ZOOM en de atlassen van Michelin zijn erg duidelijk en nauwkeurig; daarmee kunt u een route uitstippelen, de weg makkelijk vinden en op elk moment bepalen waar u bent.

Beste lezer

De Michelingids biedt in elke categorie van comfort en prijs een selectie van de beste hotels en restaurants. Onze inspecteurs zijn opgeleid in de horecasector en reizen het hele jaar door het land om nieuwe en reeds vermelde etablissementen te bezoeken en te beoordelen of deze voldoen aan de kwaliteitseisen en een constant niveau van dienstverlening. Zij zijn in vaste dienst bij Michelin en werken anoniem en onafhankelijk.

De voorzieningen en geboden diensten zijn aangegeven met symbolen zodat iedereen in een oogopslag kan zien of een hotel bijvoorbeeld een parking of een zwembad heeft. Lees de inleiding om zo goed mogelijk te profiteren van deze rijke informatiebron. Deze gegevens worden aangevuld door een korte beschrijving van de sfeer van het hotel of restaurant.

Vermelding in de gids is kosteloos. Ieder jaar ontvangen de eigenaren van hotels en restaurants een vragenlijst waarin zij opgave doen van hun openingsperioden en prijzen voor het komende jaar. Voor elke nieuwe editie worden ongeveer 100 000 gegevens bijgewerkt (nieuwe etablissementen, prijswijzigingen, openingsperioden).

Een grote bijdrage wordt geleverd door lezers uit heel Europa die ons jaarlijks ongeveer 45 000 brieven en e-mails met commentaar sturen.

Bij voorbaat hartelijk dank voor uw medewerking en goede reis met de Michelingids 2004.

Raadpleeg de Michelin Gids op
www.Viamichelin.be.
en schrijf ons per :
leguidemichelin-benelux@be.michelin.com

Inhoud

Keuze van een hotel, van een restaurant

De selectie van hotels en restaurants in deze gids is bestemd voor de automobilist op doorreis. In de verschillende categorieën, die overeenkomen met het geboden comfort, worden de bedrijven in volgorde van voorkeur opgegeven.

Categorieën

Hotel	Restaurant	
⌂⌂⌂⌂⌂	XXXXX	*Zeer luxueus, traditioneel*
⌂⌂⌂⌂	XXXX	*Eerste klas*
⌂⌂⌂	XXX	*Zeer comfortabel*
⌂⌂	XX	*Geriefelijk*
⌂	X	*Vrij geriefelijk*
sans rest.		*Hotel zonder restaurant*
	avec ch.	*Restaurant met kamers*

Aangenaam en rustig verblijf

Bepaalde bedrijven worden in de gids aangeduid met de onderstaande rode tekens. Een verblijf in die bedrijven is bijzonder aangenaam of rustig. Dit kan enerzijds te danken zijn aan het gebouw, aan de originele inrichting, aan de ligging, aan de ontvangst en aan de diensten die geboden worden, anderzijds aan het feit dat het er bijzonder rustig is.

⌂⌂⌂⌂⌂ tot ⌂	*Aangename hotels*
XXXXX tot X	*Aangename restaurants*
« Parc fleuri »	*Bijzonder aangenaam gegeven*
🐎 (rood)	*Zeer rustig of afgelegen en rustig hotel*
🐎	*Rustig hotel*
< mer	*Prachtig uitzicht*
<	*Interessant of weids uitzicht*

Voorin elk gedeelte van de gids dat aan een bepaald land gewijd is, staat een kaart met de plaatsen met aangename of zeer rustige bedrijven. Raadpleeg deze kaarten bij het voorbereiden van uw reis en laat ons bij thuiskomst weten wat uw ervaringen zijn. Op die manier kunt u ons behulpzaam zijn.

Inrichting

De hotelkamers die wij aanbevelen, beschikken in het algemeen over een volledige sanitaire voorziening. Het kan echter voorkomen dat deze bij sommige kamers in de hotelcategorie ontbreekt.

- 30 ch — *Aantal kamers*
- *Lift*
- *Airconditioning*
- *Televisie op de kamer*
- *Bedrijf dat gedeeltelijk gereserveerd is voor niet-rokers*
- *Kamers toegankelijk voor minder mobiele personen*
- *Maaltijden worden geserveerd in tuin of op terras*
- *Wellness centre : Innerlijke en uiterlijke lichaamsverzorging in een aangenaam kader*
- *Balneotherapie, Thalassotherapie, Badkuur*
- *Fitness*
- *Zwembad : openlucht of overdekt*
- *Sauna – Tuin*
- *Verhuur van fietsen*
- *Tennis bij het hotel*
- 25 à 150 — *Vergaderzalen : aantal plaatsen*
- *Garage bij het hotel (meestal tegen betaling)*
- *Parkeerplaats (eventueel tegen betaling)*
- *Aanlegplaats*
- *Honden worden niet toegelaten (in het hele bedrijf of in een gedeelte daarvan)*
- Fax — *Telefonische doorgave van documenten*
- mai-oct. — *Openingsperiode ; door de hotelhouder opgegeven. Het ontbreken van deze vermelding betekent, dat het bedrijf het gehele jaar geopend is*
- 9411 KL — *Postcode van het bedrijf (in het bijzonder voor Groothertogdom Luxemburg en Nederland)*

Keuken

Sterren

Bepaalde bedrijven verdienen extra aandacht vanwege de kwaliteit van hun keuken. Wij geven ze aan met één of meer sterren.

Bij deze bedrijven vermelden wij meestal drie culinaire specialiteiten en voor Luxemburg lokale wijnen. Wij adviseren u daaruit een keuze te maken, zowel voor uw eigen genoegen als ter aanmoediging van de kok.

❁❁❁ **Uitzonderlijke keuken : de reis waard**

Het eten is altijd zeer lekker, soms buitengewoon, beroemde wijnen, onberispelijke bediening, stijlvol interieur... Overeenkomstige prijzen.

❁❁ **Verfijnde keuken : een omweg waard**

Bijzondere specialiteiten en wijnen... Verwacht geen lage prijzen.

❁ **Een uitstekende keuken in zijn categorie**

De ster wijst op een goed rustpunt op uw route. Maar vergelijk niet de ster van een luxueus bedrijf met hoge prijzen met die van een klein restaurant dat ook een verzorgde keuken biedt tegen redelijke prijzen.

De naam van de chef-kok staat vermeld achter de naam van het bedrijf als hij zelf het etablissement uitbaat.
Voorbeeld : ✕✕ ❁ **Panorama** (Martin)...

De "Bib Gourmand"

Verzorgde maaltijden voor een schappelijke prijs

Soms wenst u iets eenvoudiger te eten, voor een schappelijke prijs. Om die reden hebben wij eetgelegenheden geselecteerd die bij een zeer gunstige prijs-kwaliteit verhouding, een goede maaltijd serveren.

Deze bedrijven worden aangeduid met de "Bib Gourmand" ☺ Repas *(ongeveer 33 euro's).*

Wijnkaart

Interessante wijnkaart

In alle categorieën hebben wij in de selectie van restaurants naar merkwaardige wijnkaarten gezocht. Deze zijn niet onderling te vergelijken, een sommelier van een groot restaurant en een aubergist die van regionale wijnen spreekt hebben dezelfde passie maar niet dezelfde middelen. Bekijk ze dus niet op dezelfde wijze.

Raadpleeg de kaarten van de sterren ✿✿✿, ✿✿, ✿ en van de "Bib Gourmand" ☺ *voorin elk gedeelte van deze gids dat aan een bepaald land gewijd is en de lijsten vermeld in de inhoud.*

Zie ook ⚭ *op de volgende pagina.*

Prijzen

De prijzen in deze gids werden in het najaar 2003 genoteerd en zijn geldig tijdens **het hoogseizoen**. *Zij kunnen gewijzigd worden,*
met name als de prijzen van goederen en diensten veranderen. In de vermelde bedragen is alles inbegrepen (bediening en belasting).
Op uw rekening behoort geen ander bedrag te staan, behalve eventueel een plaatselijke belasting.
De naam van een hotel of restaurant is dik gedrukt als de hotelhouder ons al zijn prijzen heeft opgegeven en zich voor eigen verantwoording heeft verplicht deze te berekenen aan toeristen die onze gids bezitten.
Talrijke hotels hebben tijdens het weekend voordelige prijzen (grote steden). Informeer U.
Onderstaande voorbeelden zijn in euro's gegeven.
Als u met de gids in de hand een hotel of restaurant binnen gaat, laat u zien dat wij u dat bedrijf hebben aanbevolen.

Maaltijden

ꝏ	*Bedrijf dat een eenvoudig menu serveert van minder dan* 22 *euro's.*
Repas *Lunch 18*	*Deze maaltijd wordt enkel 's middags geserveerd en meestal alleen op werkdagen.*

Vaste prijzen voor menu's :

Repas 25/50	*laagste* (25) *en hoogste* (50) *prijs van menu's die op normale uren geserveerd worden (12-14.30 u. en 19-21.30 u. in België – 12-14 u. en 17-21 u. in Nederland).* *Sommige menu's worden alleen geserveerd voor minimum 2 personen of per tafel.*
bc	*Drank inbegrepen (wijn)*
🍷	*Wijn per glas*

Maaltijden « à la carte » :

Repas carte 40 à 75	*De eerste prijs betreft een normale maaltijd, bestaande uit een voorgerecht, een hoofdgerecht en een dessert.* *De tweede prijs betreft een meer uitgebreide maaltijd (met een specialiteit) bestaande uit : twee gerechten, en een dessert.*

Kamers

☕ 12	*Prijs van het ontbijt (mogelijk wordt een extra bedrag gevraagd voor ontbijt op de kamer).*
ch 70/85	*Laagste prijs* (70) *voor een eenpersoonskamer en hoogste prijs* (85) *voor een tweepersoonskamer.*
suites	*Zich wenden tot de hotelhouder*
29 ch ☕ 75/105	*Prijzen van de kamers met ontbijt.*

Half pension

½ P 90/110	*Laagste en hoogste prijs voor half pension (kamer, ontbijt en één van de twee maaltijden), per persoon en per dag, in het hoogseizoen. Het is raadzaam om van tevoren met de hotelhouder te overleggen en een goede afspraak te maken.*

Aanbetaling

Sommige hotelhouders vragen een aanbetaling. Dit bedrag is een garantie, zowel voor de hotelhouder als voor de gast. Het is wenselijk te informeren naar de bepalingen van deze garantie.

Creditcards

AE Ⓓ MC VISA JCB	*Creditcards die door het bedrijf geaccepteerd worden : American Express – Diners Club – MasterCard (Eurocard) – Visa – Japan Credit Bureau*

Steden

1000	*Postcodenummer, steeds te vermelden in het adres voor de plaatsnaam*
✉ 4900 Spa	*Postkantoor voor deze plaats*
P	*Hoofdstad van de provincie*
C Herve	*Gemeentelijke administratieve zetel*
531 T 3 716 E 3	*Nummer van de Michelinkaart en graadnet of nummer van het vouwblad*
G. Belgique-Lux.	*Zie de groene Michelingids België-Luxemburg*
4 283 h	*Totaal aantal inwoners (volgens de laatst gepubliceerde, officiële telling)*
BX A	*Letters die de ligging op de plattegrond aangeven*
18	*Golf en aantal holes*
✳, ⋞	*Panorama, uitzicht*
✈	*Vliegveld*
☎ 02 45 52 14	*Plaats waar de autoslaaptrein stopt. Inlichtingen bij het aangegeven telefoonnummer.*
⛴	*Bootverbinding*
⛴	*Bootverbinding (uitsluitend passagiers)*
ℹ	*Informatie voor toeristen - VVV*

Bezienswaardigheden

Classificatie

★★★	*De reis waard*
★★	*Een omweg waard*
★	*Interessant*

Ligging

Voir	*In de stad*
Env.	*In de omgeving van de stad*
Nord, Sud, Est, Ouest	*De bezienswaardigheid ligt : ten noorden, ten zuiden, ten oosten, ten westen*
②, ④	*Men komt er via uitvalsweg ② of ④, die met hetzelfde teken is aangegeven op de plattegrond in de gids en op de kaart*
2 km	*Afstand in kilometers*

Auto en banden

Achter in deze gids vindt u een lijst met de belangrijkste auto-importeurs die u van dienst zouden kunnen zijn.
U kunt ook de hulp inroepen van een automobielclub in de Benelux :

België

Vlaamse Automobilistenbond (VTB-VAB)
Sint-Jakobsmarkt 45, 2000 Antwerpen
☎ 0 3 253 63 63
Koninklijke Automobiel Club van België (KACB)
FIA, Aarlenstraat 53 – Bus 3, 1040 Brussel
☎ 0 2 287 09 11 fax 0 2 230 75 84
Royal Motor Union
boulevard d'Avroy 254 – Bte 1, 4000 Liège
☎ 0 4 252 70 30 fax 0 4 252 83 01
Touring Club van België (TCB)
AIT, Wetstraat 44, 1040 Brussel
☎ 0 2 233 22 02 fax 02 286 33 23

Luxemburg

Automobile Club du Grand Duché de Luxembourg (ACL)
FIA & AIT, route de Longwy 54, 8007 Bertrange
☎ 45 00 45 1 fax 45 04 55

Nederland

Koninklijke Nederlandse Automobiel Club (KNAC)
FIA, Wassenaarseweg 220, 2596 EC Den Haag
☎ (070) 383 16 12
fax (070) 383 19 06
Koninklijke Nederlandse Toeristenbond (ANWB)
AIT, Wassenaarseweg 220, 2596 EC Den Haag
☎ (070) 314 71 47
fax (070) 314 69 69

Maximumsnelheden (km/u)

	Autosnelwegen	Wegen	Bebouwde kom
België	120	90	50
Luxemburg	120	90	50
Nederland	100/120	80	50

Omgevingskaarten

Sla ze erop na!

Bent u op zoek naar een hotel of een restaurant in de buurt van bijvoorbeeld Arnhem ?

Gebruik dan de kaart die bij de stadsplattegrond hoort.

Deze kaart (zie hiernaast) geeft de in de Gids vermelde plaatsen aan die zich in de buurt van de geselecteerde stad bevinden.

De plaatsen die binnen een straal van 30 km liggen, bevinden zich binnen de blauwe lijn.

Aan de hand van deze kaarten kan men dadelijk de in de Gids geselecteerde bedrijven in de buurt van de verschillende regionale hoofdplaatsen terugvinden.

N.B. :

Wordt een gemeente of dorp op een kaart van de omgeving in de buurt van een stad aangegeven, dan wordt deze stad in het blauw vermeld.

Voorbeeld :

EDE staat vermeld op de kaart van de omgeving van ARNHEM.

EDE *Gelderland* **715** *I 5 – 101 700 h.*
Env. *Parc National de la Haute Veluwe*★★★
Amsterdam 81 – Arnhem 23 – Apeldoorn 32 – Utrecht 43.

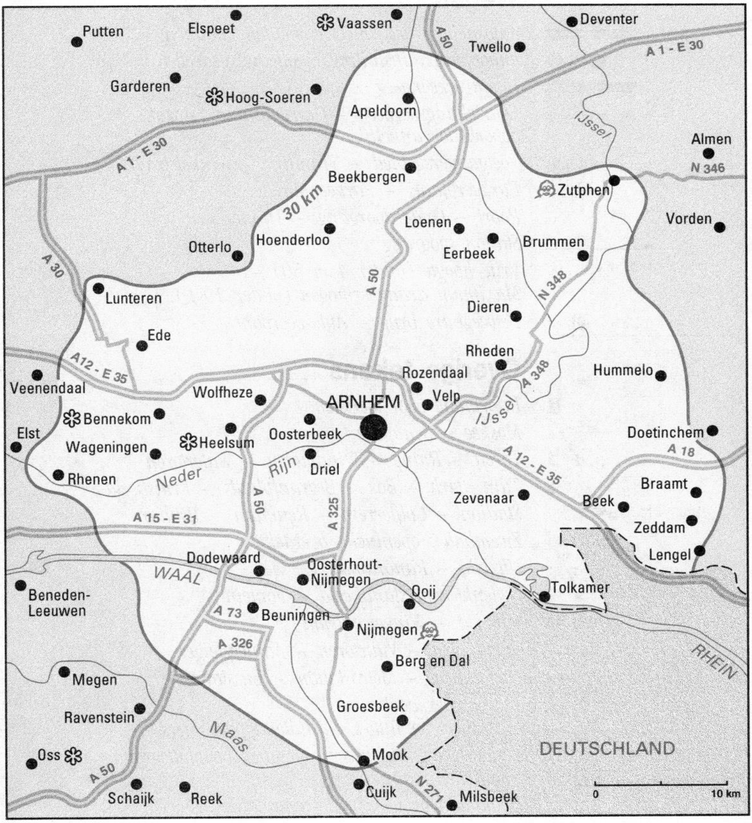

*De omgevings-
kaarten staan
vermeld op
de thematische
kaart van elk
respectievelijk land.*

Plattegronden

Hotels
Restaurants

Bezienswaardigheden

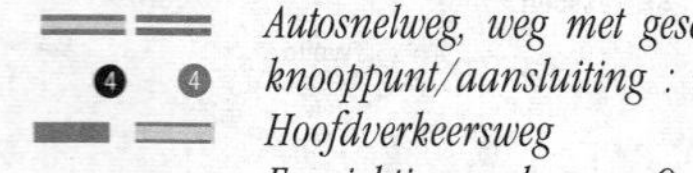

Interessant gebouw
Interessant kerkelijk gebouw

Wegen

Autosnelweg, weg met gescheiden rijbanen
knooppunt/aansluiting : volledig, gedeeltelijk
Hoofdverkeersweg
Eenrichtingsverkeer – Onbegaanbare straat, beperkt toegankelijk
Pasteur — Voetgangersgebied – Tramlijn – Winkelstraat
Parkeerplaats – Parkeer en Reis
Poort – Onderdoorgang – Tunnel
Station spoorweg
18 — Vrije hoogte (onder 4 m 50) – Maximum draagvermogen (onder 19 t.)
B — Beweegbare brug – Auto-veerpont

Overige tekens

Informatie voor toeristen
Moskee – Synagoge
Toren – Ruïne – Windmolen – Watertoren
Tuin, park – Bos – Begraafplaats – Kruisbeeld
Stadion – Golfterrein – Renbaan – IJsbaan
Zwembad : openlucht, overdekt
Uitzicht – Panorama
Gedenkteken, standbeeld – Fontein
Fabriek – Winkelcentrum
Jachthaven – Vuurtoren – Aanlegsteiger
Luchthaven – Metrostation – Busstation
Vervoer per boot : passagiers en auto's, uitsluitend passagiers
3 — Verwijsteken uitvalsweg : identiek op plattegronden en Michelinkaarten
Hoofdkantoor voor poste-restante
Ziekenhuis – Overdekte markt
Openbaar gebouw, aangegeven met een letter :

H P - Stadhuis – Provinciehuis
J - Gerechtshof
M T - Museum – Schouwburg
U - Universiteit, hogeschool
POL. - Politie (in grote steden, hoofdbureau) –
G - Marechaussee/rijkswacht

Lieber Leser

Der Michelin-Führer bietet Ihnen in jeder Komfort- und Preiskategorie eine Auswahl der besten Hotels und Restaurants. Diese Auswahl wird von einem Team von Inspektoren mit Ausbildung in der Hotellerie erstellt, die das Jahr hindurch das ganze Land bereisen. Ihre Aufgabe ist es, die Qualität und die Leistung der empfohlenen und der neu aufzunehmenden Hotels und Restaurants zu überprüfen. Als Angestellte bei Michelin arbeiten die Inspektoren anonym und völlig unabhängig.

Die Einrichtung und der gebotene Service der Betriebe wird durch Symbole gekennzeichnet – eine internationale Sprache, die auf einen Blick erkennen lässt ob ein Hotel beispielsweise einen Parkplatz oder ein Schwimmbad besitzt. Um diese umfangreiche Information voll nutzen zu können, werfen Sie einen Blick in die Einleitung. Der Text, der die Atmosphäre eines Hotels oder Restaurants beschreibt, ergänzt die Symbole.

Die Empfehlung im Michelin-Führer ist absolut kostenlos. Alle empfohlenen Hotel und Restaurant füllen jedes Jahr einen Fragebogen aus, in dem uns die Schließungszeiten und die aktuellen Preise für das nächste Jahr genannt werden. Nahezu 100 000 Veränderungen für jede Ausgabe ergeben sich daraus (neue Betriebe, veränderte Preise und Schließungszeiten).

Eine sehr große Hilfe sind jedoch auch Sie, unsere Leser –mit beinahe 45 000 Briefen und E-Mail aus ganz Europa.

Wir bedanken uns im Voraus für Ihre Hilfe und wünschen Ihnen eine gute Reise mit dem Michelin-Führer 2004.

*Die Auswahl des Michelin-Führers finden Sie auch im Internet unter : **www.Viamichelin.be***
*Sie erreichen uns unter : **Leguidemichelin-benelux@be.michelin.com***

Inhaltsverzeichnis

Wahl eines Hotels, eines Restaurants

Die Auswahl der in diesem Führer aufgeführten Hotels und Restaurants ist für Durchreisende gedacht. In jeder Kategorie drückt die Reihenfolge der Betriebe (sie sind nach ihrem Komfort klassifiziert) eine weitere Rangordnung aus.

Kategorien

Hotel	Restaurant	
		Großer Luxus und Tradition
		Großer Komfort
		Sehr komfortabel
		Mit gutem Komfort
		Mit Standard Komfort
sans rest.		*Hotel ohne Restaurant*
	avec ch.	*Restaurant vermietet auch Zimmer*

Annehmlichkeiten

Manche Häuser sind im Führer durch rote Symbole gekennzeichnet (s. unten.) Der Aufenthalt in diesen ist wegen der schönen, ruhigen Lage, der nicht alltäglichen Einrichtung und Atmosphäre sowie dem gebotenen Service besonders angenehm und erholsam.

Symbol	
bis	*Angenehme Hotels*
bis	*Angenehme Restaurants*
« Parc fleuri »	*Besondere Annehmlichkeit*
	Sehr ruhiges, oder abgelegenes und ruhiges Hotel
	Ruhiges Hotel
mer	*Reizvolle Aussicht*
	Interessante oder weite Sicht

Die den einzelnen Ländern vorangestellten Übersichtskarten, auf denen die Orte mit besonders angenehmen oder sehr ruhigen Häusern eingezeichnet sind, helfen Ihnen bei der Reisevorbereitung. Teilen Sie uns bitte nach der Reise Ihre Erfahrungen und Meinungen mit. Sie helfen uns damit, den Führer weiter zu verbessern.

Einrichtung

Die meisten der empfohlenen Hotels verfügen über Zimmer, die alle oder doch zum größten Teil mit Bad oder Dusche ausgestattet sind.
In den Häusern der Kategorie
kann diese jedoch in einigen Zimmern fehlen.

30 ch	*Anzahl der Zimmer*
	Fahrstuhl
	Klimaanlage
TV	*Fernsehen im Zimmer*
	Haus teilweise reserviert für Nichtraucher
	Zimmer die für körperlich beeinträchtigte Personen leicht nugänglich sind
	Garten-, Terrassenrestaurant
	Wellness centre : schöner Bereich zum Wohlfühlen und Entspannen
	Badeabteilung, Thermalkur
	Fitneßraum
	Freibad – Hallenbad
	Sauna – Liegewiese, Garten
	Fahrradverleih
	Hoteleigener Tennisplatz
25 à 150	*Konferenzräume (Mindest- und Höchstkapazität)*
	Hotelgarage (wird gewöhnlich berechnet)
P	*Parkplatz (manchmal gebührenpflichtig)*
	Bootssteg
	Hunde sind unerwünscht (im ganzen Haus bzw. in den Zimmern oder im Restaurant)
Fax	*Telefonische Dokumentenübermittlung*
mai-oct.	*Öffnungszeit, vom Hotelier mitgeteilt Häuser ohne Angabe von Schließungszeiten sind ganzjährig geöffnet*
✉ 9411 KL	*Angabe des Postbezirks (bes. Niederlande und Großherzogtum Luxemburg)*

Küche

Die Sterne

Einige Häuser verdienen wegen ihrer überdurchschnittlich guten Küche Ihre besondere Beachtung. Auf diese Häuser weisen die Sterne hin.

*Bei den mit « **Stern** » ausgezeichneten Betrieben nennen wir drei kulinarische Spezialitäten (mit Landweinen in Luxemburg), die Sie probieren sollten.*

✲✲✲ **Eine der besten Küchen : eine Reise wert**

Man ißt hier immer sehr gut, öfters auch exzellent, edle Weine, tadelloser Service, gepflegte Atmosphäre... entsprechende Preise.

✲✲ **Eine hervorragende Küche : verdient einen Umweg**

Ausgesuchte Menus und Weine... angemessene Preise.

✲ **Eine sehr gute Küche : verdient Ihre besondere Beachtung**

Der Stern bedeutet eine angenehme Unterbrechung Ihrer Reise.

Vergleichen Sie aber bitte nicht den Stern eines sehr teuren Luxusrestaurants mit dem Stern eines kleineren oder mittleren Hauses, wo man Ihnen zu einem annehmbaren Preis eine ebenfalls vorzügliche Mahlzeit reicht.

Wenn ein Hotel oder Restaurant vom Küchenchef selbst geführt wird, ist sein Name (in Klammern) erwähnt.
Beispiel : XX ✲ **Panorama** (Martin)...

Der "Bib Gourmand"

Sorgfältig zubereitete, preiswerte Mahlzeiten

Für Sie wird es interessant sein, auch solche Häuser kennenzulernen, die eine etwas einfachere Küche zu einem besonders günstigen Preis/Leistungs-Verhältnis bieten.

Im Text sind die betreffenden Restaurants durch das rote Symbol ⛑ "Bib Gourmand" *und* Repas *(ungefähr 33 euro) vor dem Menupreis kenntlich gemacht.*

Die Weinkarte

Weinkarte mit besonders Angebot attraktivem

Einige der von uns empfohlenen Restaurants bieten eine besonders interessante Weinauswahl. Aber bitte vergleichen Sie nicht die Weinkarte, die Ihnen vom Sommelier eines großen Hauses präsentiert wird, mit der Auswahl eines Gasthauses, dessen Besitzter die Weine der Region mit Sorgfalt zusammenstellt.

Benützen Sie die Übersichtskarten für die Häuser mit ✿✿✿, ✿✿, ✿ *und* "Bib Gourmand" ⛑. *Sie befinden sich am Anfang des jeweiligen Landes. Eine zusammenfassende Liste aller Länder finden Sie in der Einleitung.*

Siehe auch ⛓ *nächste Seite.*

Preise

Die in diesem Führer genannten Preise wurden uns im Herbst 2003 angegeben, es sind **Hochsaisonpreise**. *Sie können sich mit den Preisen von Waren und Dienstleistungen ändern. Sie enthalten Bedienung und MWSt.*
Es sind Inklusivpreise, die sich nur noch durch eine evtl. zu zahlende lokale Taxe erhöhen können.
Zahlreiche Hotels im großen Städten bieten sehr günstige Wochenendtarife.
Die Namen der Hotels und Restaurants, die ihre Preise genannt haben, sind fettgedruckt. Gleichzeitig haben sich diese Häuser verpflichtet, die von den Hoteliers selbst angegebenen Preise den Benutzern des Michelin-Führers zu berechnen.
Die folgenden Beispiele sind in Euro angegeben.
Halten Sie beim Betreten des Hotels den Führer in der Hand. Sie zeigen damit, daß Sie aufgrund dieser Empfehlung gekommen sind.

Mahlzeiten

⊛	*Restaurant, das ein einfaches Menu unter* 22 *euros anbietet.*
Repas *Lunch 18*	*Menu im allgemeine nur Werktags mittags serviert.*
	Feste Menupreise :
Repas 25/50	*Mindest-* 25 *und Höchstpreis* 50 *für die Menus (Gedecke), die zu den normalen Tischzeiten serviert werden (12-14.30 Uhr und 19-21.30 Uhr in Belgien, 12-14 Uhr und 17-21 Uhr in den Niederlanden). Einige Menus werden nur tischweise oder für mindestens 2 Personen serviert.*
bc	*Getränke inbegriffen (Wein)*
🍷	*Offene Wein*
	Mahlzeiten « à la carte » :
Repas carte 40 à 75	*Der erste Preis entspricht einer einfachen Mahlzeit und umfaßt Vorspeise, Tagesgericht mit Beilage, Dessert. Der zweite Preis entspricht einer reichlicheren Mahlzeit (mit Spezialität) bestehend aus: zwei Hauptgängen, Dessert.*

Zimmer

☕ 12	*Preis des Frühstücks (wenn es im Zimmer serviert wird kann ein Zuschlag erhoben werden).*
ch 70/85	*Mindestpreis* (70) *für ein Einzelzimmer, Höchstpreis* (85) *für ein Doppelzimmer.*
suites	*Auf Anfrage*
29 ch ☕ 75/105	*Zimmerpreis inkl. Frühstück.*

Halbpension

½ P 90/110	*Mindestpreis und Höchstpreis für Halbpension (Zimmer, Frühstück und 1 Hauptmahlzeit) pro Person und Tag während der Hauptsaison. Es ist ratsam, sich beim Hotelier vor der Anreise nach den genauen Bedingungen zu erkundigen.*

Anzahlung

Einige Hoteliers verlangen eine Anzahlung. Diese ist als Garantie sowohl für den Hotelier als auch für den Gast anzusehen. Es ist ratsam, sich beim Hotelier nach den genauen Bestimmungen zu enkundigen.

Kreditkarten

AE ⓓ MC VISA JCB	*Vom Haus akzeptierte Kreditkarten : American Express – Diners Club – MasterCard (Eurocard) – Visa – Japan Credit Bureau*

Städte

1000	*Postleitzahl, bei der Anschrift vor dem Ortsnamen anzugeben*
✉ *4900 Spa*	*Postleitzahl und zuständiges Postamt*
P	*Provinzhauptstadt*
C *Herve*	*Sitz der Kreisverwaltung*
531 *T 3* 716 *E 3*	*Nummer der Michelin-Karte mit Koordinaten bzw. Faltseite*
G. Belgique-Lux.	*Siehe Grünen Michelin-Reiseführer Belgique-Luxembourg*
4 283 h	*Einwohnerzahl (letzte offizielle Volkszählung)*
BX A	*Markierung auf dem Stadtplan*
18	*Golfplatz und Lochzahl*
✻, ≤	*Rundblick, Aussichtspunkt*
✈	*Flughafen*
🚗 ✆ 02 45 52 14	*Ladestelle für Autoreisezüge. Nähere Auskünfte unter der angegebenen Telefonnummer*
⛴	*Autofähre*
⛴	*Personenfähre*
i	*Informationsstelle*

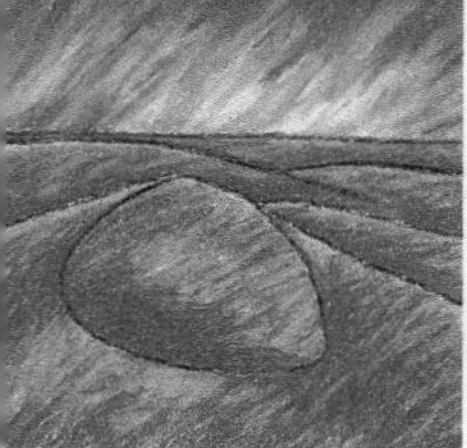

Sehenswürdigkeiten

Bewertung

★★★	*Eine Reise wert*
★★	*Verdient einen Umweg*
★	*Sehenswert*

Lage

Voir	*In der Stadt*
Env.	*In der Umgebung der Stadt*
Nord, Sud, Est, Ouest	*Im Norden, Süden, Osten, Westen der Stadt*
②, ④	*Zu erreichen über die Ausfallstraße ② bzw ④, die auf dem Stadtplan und auf der Michelin-Karte identisch gekennzeichnet sind*
2 km	*Entfernung in Kilometern*

Das Auto, die Reifen

Am Ende des Führers finden Sie eine Adress-Liste der wichtigsten Automarken, die Ihnen im Pannenfalle eine wertvolle Hilfe leisten kann. Sie können sich aber auch an die wichtigsten Automobilclubs in den Beneluxstaaten wenden :

Belgien

Royal Automobile Club de Belgique (RACB)
FIA, rue d'Arlon 53 – Bte 3,
1040 Bruxelles
☎ 0 2 287 09 11 fax 0 2 230 75 84

Royal Motor Union
boulevard d'Avroy 254 – Bte 1,
4000 Liège
☎ 0 4 252 70 30 fax 0 4 252 83 01

Touring Club Royal de Belgique (TCB)
AIT, rue de la Loi 44, 1040 Bruxelles
☎ 0 2 233 22 02 fax 02 286 33 23

Vlaamse Automobilistenbond (VTB-VAB)
Sint-Jakobsmarkt 45, 2000 Antwerpen
☎ 0 3 253 63 63

Luxemburg

Automobile Club du Grand Duché de Luxembourg (ACL)
FIA & AIT, route de Longwy 54,
8007 Bertrange
☎ 45 00 45 1 fax 45 04 55

Niederlande

Koninklijke Nederlandse Automobiel Club (KNAC)
FIA, Wassenaarseweg 220,
2596 EC Den Haag
☎ (070) 383 16 12
fax (070) 383 19 06

Koninklijke Nederlandse Toeristenbond (ANWB)
AIT, Wassenaarseweg 220,
2596 EC Den Haag
☎ (070) 314 71 47
fax (070) 314 69 69

Geschwindigkeitsbegrenzung (in km/h)

	Autobahn	*Landstraße*	*Geschlossene Ortschaften*
Belgien	*120*	*90*	*50*
Luxemburg	*120*	*90*	*50*
Niederlande	*100/120*	*80*	*50*

Umgebungskarten

Denken sie daran sie zu benutzen

Die Umgebungskarten sollen Ihnen die Suche eines Hotels oder Restaurants in der Nähe der größeren Städte erleichtern.

Wenn Sie beispielsweise eine gute Adresse in der Nähe von Arnhem brauchen, gibt Ihnen die Karte schnell einen Überblick über alle Orte, die in diesem Michelin-Führer erwähnt sind. Innerhalb der in Kontrastfarbe gedruckten Grenze liegen Gemeinden, die im Umkreis von 30 km sind.

Anmerkung :

Auf der Linie der Entfernungen zu anderen Orten erscheint im Ortstext die jeweils nächste größere Stadt mit Umgebungskarte in BLAU.

Beispiel :

Sie finden EDE auf der Umgebungskarte von ARNHEM.

EDE *Gelderland* **715** *I 5 – 101 700 h.*
Env. *Parc National de la Haute Veluwe*★★★
Amsterdam 81 – Arnhem 23 – Apeldoorn 32 – Utrecht 43.

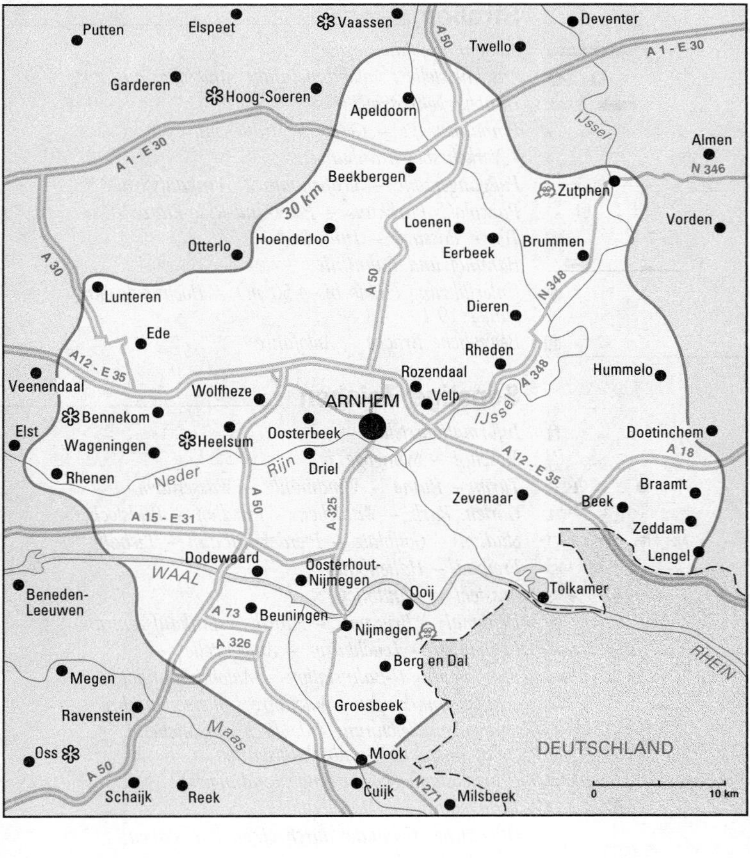

Putten
Elspeet
Vaassen
Deventer
Twello
A 50
A 1 - E 30
Garderen
Hoog-Soeren
Apeldoorn
IJssel
Almen
N 346
A 1 - E 30
Beekbergen
Zutphen
30 km
Vorden
Loenen
Hoenderloo
Brummen
Otterlo
Eerbeek
A 30
A 50
N 348
Lunteren
Dieren
Ede
Rheden
A12 - E 35
Rozendaal
Hummelo
Veenendaal
Wolfheze
Velp
A 348
ARNHEM
IJssel
Bennekom
Oosterbeek
Doetinchem
Elst
Heelsum
Wageningen
A 18
Driel
A 12 - E 35
Rijn
Rhenen
Neder
Braamt
A 50
A 325
Zevenaar
Beek
A 15 - E 31
Zeddam
Lengel
Dodewaard
Oosterhout-
Nijmegen
WAAL
Tolkamer
Beneden-
Leeuwen
Ooij
A 73
Beuningen
Nijmegen
A 326
RHEIN
Berg en Dal
Megen
Groesbeek
Ravenstein
Maas
DEUTSCHLAND
Oss
Mook
A 50
N 271
0
10 km
Schaijk
Reek
Cuijk
Milsbeek

Die Umgebungskarten finden Sie auf der Themenkarte des jeweiligen Landes.

Stadtpläne

Hotels
Restaurants

Sehenswürdigkeiten

Sehenswertes Gebäude
Sehenswerter Sakralbau

Straßen

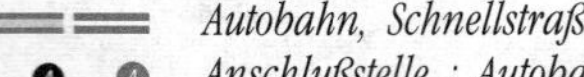

Autobahn, Schnellstraße
Anschlußstelle : Autobahneinfahrt und/oder-ausfahrt,
Hauptverkehrsstraße
Einbahnstraße – Gesperrte Straße, mit
- Verkehrsbeschränkungen
Pasteur Fußgängerzone – Straßenbahn – Einkaufsstraße
Parkplatz, Parkhaus – Park-and-Ride-Plätze
Tor – Passage – Tunnel
Bahnhof und Bahnlinie
Unterführung (Höhe bis 4,50 m) – Höchstbelastung (unter 19 t.)
Bewegliche Brücke – Autofähre

Sonstige Zeichen

Informationsstelle
Moschee – Synagoge
Turm – Ruine – Windmühle – Wasserturm
Garten, Park – Wäldchen – Friedhof – Bildstock
Stadion – Golfplatz – Pferderennbahn – Eisbahn
Freibad – Hallenbad
Aussicht – Rundblick
Denkmal – Brunnen – Fabrik – Einkaufszentrum
Jachthafen – Leuchtturm – Anlegestelle
Flughafen – U-Bahnstation – Autobusbahnhof
Schiffsverbindungen : Autofähre – Personenfähre
Straßenkennzeichnung (identisch auf Michelin Stadtplänen und – Abschnittskarten)
Hauptpostamt (postlagernde Sendungen)
Krankenhaus – Markthalle
Öffentliches Gebäude, durch einen Buchstaben gekennzeichnet :

H P - Rathaus – Provinzregierung
J - Gerichtsgebäude
M T - Museum – Theater
U - Universität, Hochschule
POL. - Polizei (in größeren Städten Polizeipräsidium)
G - Gendarmerie

Dear Reader

The Michelin Guide offers a selection of the best hotels and restaurants in many categories of comfort and price. It is compiled by a team of professionally trained inspectors who travel the country visiting new establishments as well as those already listed in the guide. Their mission is to check the quality and consistency of the amenities and service provided by the hotels and restaurants throughout the year. The inspectors are full-time Michelin employees and their assessments, made anonymously, are therefore completely impartial and independant.

The amenities found in each establishment are indicated by symbols, an international language which enables you to see at a glance whether a hotel has a car park or swimming pool. To take full advantage of the wealth of information contained in the guide, consult the introduction. A short descriptive text complements the symbols.

Entry in the Michelin Guide is completely free of charge and every year the proprietors of those establishments listed complete a questionnaire giving the opening times and prices for the coming year. Nearly 100,000 pieces of information are updated for each annual edition.

Our readers also contribute through the 45,000 letters and e-mails received annually commenting on hotels and restaurants throughout Europe.

Thank you for your support and please continue to send us your comments. We hope you enjoy travelling with the Michelin Guide 2004.

Consult the Michelin Guide at ***www.Viamichelin.be***
and write to us at : ***Leguidemichelin-benelux@be.michelin.com***

Contents

Choosing a hotel or restaurant

This guide offers a selection of hotels and restaurants to help motorists on their travels. In each category establishments are listed in order of preference according to the degree of comfort they offer.

Categories

🏨🏨🏨🏨🏨	✗✗✗✗✗	*Luxury in the traditional style*
🏨🏨🏨🏨	✗✗✗✗	*Top class comfort*
🏨🏨🏨	✗✗✗	*Very comfortable*
🏨🏨	✗✗	*Comfortable*
🏨	✗	*Quite comfortable*
sans rest.		*The hotel has no restaurant*
	avec ch.	*The restaurant also offers accommodation*

Peaceful atmosphere and setting

Certain hotels and restaurants are distinguished in the guide by the red symbols shown below. Your stay in such establishments will be particularly pleasant or restful, owing to the character of the building, its decor, the setting, the welcome and services offered, or simply the peace and quiet to be enjoyed there.

🏨🏨🏨🏨🏨 to 🏨	*Pleasant hotels*
✗✗✗✗✗ to ✗	*Pleasant restaurants*
« Parc fleuri »	*Particularly attractive feature*
🪑	*Very quiet or quiet, secluded hotel*
🪑	*Quiet hotel*
« mer	*Exceptional view*
«	*Interesting or extensive view*

The maps preceding each country indicate places with such very peaceful, pleasant hotels and restaurants.
By consulting them before setting out and sending us your comments on your return you can help us with our enquiries.

Hotel facilities

In general the hotels we recommend have full bathroom and toilet facilities in each room. This may not be the case, however for certain rooms in categorie 🏠.

30 ch	*Number of rooms*
	Lift (elevator)
	Air conditioning
TV	*Television in room*
	Hotel partly reserved for non-smokers
♿	*Bedrooms accessible to those with restricted mobility*
	Meals served in garden or on terrace
	Wellness centre : an extensive facility for relaxation and wellbeing
	Hydrotherapy
	Exercise room
	Outdoor or indoor swimming pool
	Sauna – Garden
	Cycle hire
	Hotel tennis court
25 à 150	*Equipped conference hall (minimum and maximum capacity)*
	Hotel garage (additional charge in most cases)
P	*Car park (a fee may be charged)*
	Landing stage
	Dogs are excluded from all or part of the hotel
Fax	*Telephone document transmission*
mai-oct.	*Dates when open, as indicated by the hotelier Where no date or season is shown, establishments are open all year round*
✉ 9411 KL	*Postal code (Netherlands and Grand Duchy of Luxembourg only)*

Cuisine

Stars

*Certain establishments deserve to be brought to your attention for the particularly fine quality of their cooking. **Michelin stars** are awarded for the standard of meals served. For such establishments we list 3 speciality dishes (and some local wines in Luxembourg). Try them, both for your pleasure and to encourage the chef in his work.*

✲✲✲ **Exceptional cuisine, worth a special journey**
One always eats here extremely well, sometimes superbly. Fine wines, faultless service, elegant surroundings. One will pay accordingly !

✲✲ **Excellent cooking, worth a detour**
Specialities and wines of first class quality. This will be reflected in the price.

✲ **A very good restaurant in its category**
The star indicates a good place to stop on your journey. But beware of comparing the star given to an expensive « de luxe » establishment to that of a simple restaurant where you can appreciate fine cuisine at a reasonable price.

The name of the chef appears between brackets when he is personally managing the establishment. Example : XX ✲ **Panorama** (Martin)...

The "Bib Gourmand"

Good food at moderate prices

You may also like to know of other restaurants with less elaborate, moderately priced menus that offer good value for money and serve carefully prepared meals.

In the guide such establishments bear the "Bib Gourmand" *and* Repas *(approximately 33 euros) just before the price of the meals.*

Wine list

A particularly interesting wine list

Some of the restaurants we have chosen, across all categories, offer a particularly interesting wine list. Beware, however, of comparing the list presented by the sommelier of a grand restaurant with that of a simple inn where the owner has a passion for wine.

Consult the maps of star-rated restaurants ✿✿✿, ✿✿, ✿ *and* "Bib Gourmand" *preceding each country and lists indicated in the summary.*

See also ⚭ *on next page.*

Prices

Prices quoted are valid for autumn 2003 and apply to ***high season****.*
Changes may arise if goods and service costs are revised. The rates include tax and service and no extra charge should appear on your bill, with the possible exception of a local tax.
Hotels and restaurants in bold type have supplied details of all their rates and have assumed responsibility for maintaining them for all travellers in possession of this Guide.
Many hotels offer reduced prices at weekends (large towns).
The following examples are given in Euros.
Your recommendation is self evident if you always walk into a hotel Guide in hand.

Meals

Establishment serving a simple menu for less than 22 *euros.*

Repas *Lunch 18* — *This meal is served at lunchtime and normally during the working week.*

Set meals

Repas 25/50 — *Lowest price* 25 *and highest price* 50 *for set meals served at normal hours (noon to 2.30 pm and 7 to 9.30 pm in Belgium – noon to 2 pm and 5 to 9 pm in the Netherlands).*
Certain menus are only served for a minimum of 2 people or for an entire table.

bc — *Wine included*

Wine served by glass

« A la carte » meals

Repas carte 40 à 75 — *The first figure is for a plain meal and includes hors-d'œuvre, main dish of the day with vegetables and dessert.*
The second figure is for a fuller meal (with « spécialité ») and includes 2 main courses and dessert.

Rooms

☕ 12	*Price of continental breakfast (additional charge when served in the bedroom).*
ch 70/85	*Lowest price* (70) *for a single room and highest price* (85) *for a double.*
suites	*Ask the hotelier*
29 ch ☕ 75/105	*Price includes breakfast.*

Half board

½ P 90/110	*Lowest and highest prices (room, breakfast and one of two meals), per person, per day in the season.* *It is advisable to agree on terms with the hotelier before arriving.*

Deposits

Some hotels will require a deposit, which confirms the commitment of customer and hotelier alike.
Make sure the terms of the agreement are clear.

Credit cards

AE (D) MC VISA JCB	*Credit cards accepted by the establishment* *American Express – Diners Club – MasterCard (Eurocard) – Visa – Japan Credit Bureau*

Towns

1000	*Postal number to be shown in the address before the town name*
✉ *4900 Spa*	*Postal number and name of the post office serving the town*
P	*Provincial capital*
C *Herve*	*Administrative centre of the "commune"*
531 *T 3* 716 *E 3*	*Michelin map number, co-ordinates or fold*
G. Belgique-Lux.	*See Michelin Green Guide Belgique-Luxembourg*
4 283 h	*Population (as in publication of most recent official census figures)*
BX **A**	*Letters giving the location of a place on the town plan*
18	*Golf course and number of holes*
✳, ⩽	*Panoramic view, viewpoint*
✈	*Airport*
☎ 02 45 52 14	*Place with a motorail connection ; further information from telephone number listed*
⛴	*Shipping line*
⛴	*Passenger transport only*
ℹ	*Tourist Information Centre*

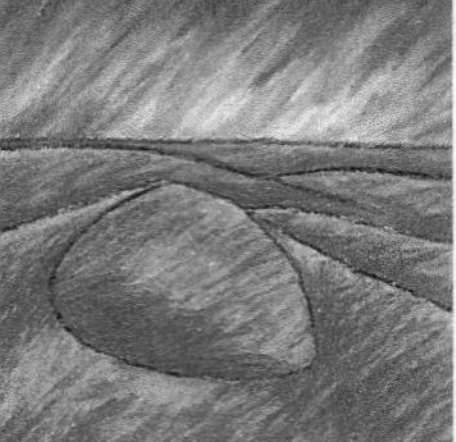

Sights

Star-rating

★★★	*Worth a journey*
★★	*Worth a detour*
★	*Interesting*

Location

Voir	*Sights in town*
Env.	*On the outskirts*
Nord, Sud, Est, Ouest	*The sight lies north, south, east or west of the town*
②, ④	*Sign on town plan and on the Michelin road map indicating the road leading to a place of interest*
2 km	*Distance in kilometres*

Car, tyres

A list of the main Car Manufacturers with a breakdown service is to be found at the end of the Guide.
The major motoring organisations in the Benelux countries are :

Belgium

Royal Automobile Club de Belgique (RACB)
FIA, rue d'Arlon 53 – Bte 3, 1040 Bruxelles
☎ 0 2 287 09 11 fax 0 2 230 75 84

Royal Motor Union
boulevard d'Avroy 254 – Bte 1, 4000 Liège
☎ 0 4 252 70 30 fax 0 4 252 83 01

Touring Club Royal de Belgique (TCB)
AIT, rue de la Loi 44, 1040 Bruxelles
☎ 0 2 233 22 02 fax 02 286 33 23

Vlaamse Automobilistenbond (VTB-VAB)
Sint-Jakobsmarkt 45, 2000 Antwerpen
☎ 0 3 253 63 63

Luxembourg

Automobile Club du Grand Duché de Luxembourg (ACL)
FIA & AIT, route de Longwy 54, 8007 Bertrange
☎ 45 00 45 1 fax 45 04 55

Netherlands

Koninklijke Nederlandse Automobiel Club (KNAC)
FIA, Wassenaarseweg 220, 2596 EC Den Haag
☎ (070) 383 16 12
fax (070) 383 19 06

Koninklijke Nederlandse Toeristenbond (ANWB)
AIT, Wassenaarseweg 220, 2596 EC Den Haag
☎ (070) 314 71 47
fax (070) 314 69 69

Maximum speed limits

	Motorways	*All other roads*	*Built-up areas*
Belgium	*120 km/h (74 mph)*	*90 km/h (56 mph)*	*50 km/h (31 mph)*
Luxembourg	*120 km/h (74 mph)*	*90 km/h (56 mph)*	*50 km/h (31 mph)*
Netherlands	*100 km/h (62 mph)* *120 km/h (74 mph)*	*80 km/h (50 mph)*	*50 km/h (31 mph)*

Local maps

May we suggest that you consult them

Should you be looking for a hotel or restaurant not too far from Arnhem, for example, you can now consult the map along with the town plan.

The local map (opposite) draws your attention to all places around the town or city selected, provided they are mentioned in the Guide. Places located within a range of 30 km are clearly identified by the use of a different coloured background.

The various facilities recommended near the different regional capitals can be located quickly and easily.

Note :

Entries in the Guide provide information on distances to nearby towns. Whenever a place appears on one of the local maps, the name of the town or city to which it is attached is printed in BLUE.

Example :

EDE *Gelderland* **715** *I 5 – 101 700 h.*
Env. *Parc National de la Haute Veluwe★★★*
Amsterdam 81 – Arnhem 23 – Apeldoorn 32 – Utrecht 43.

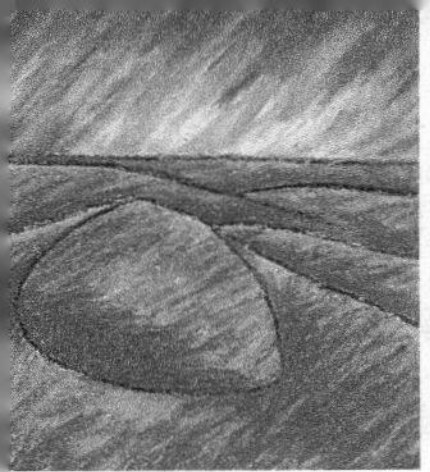

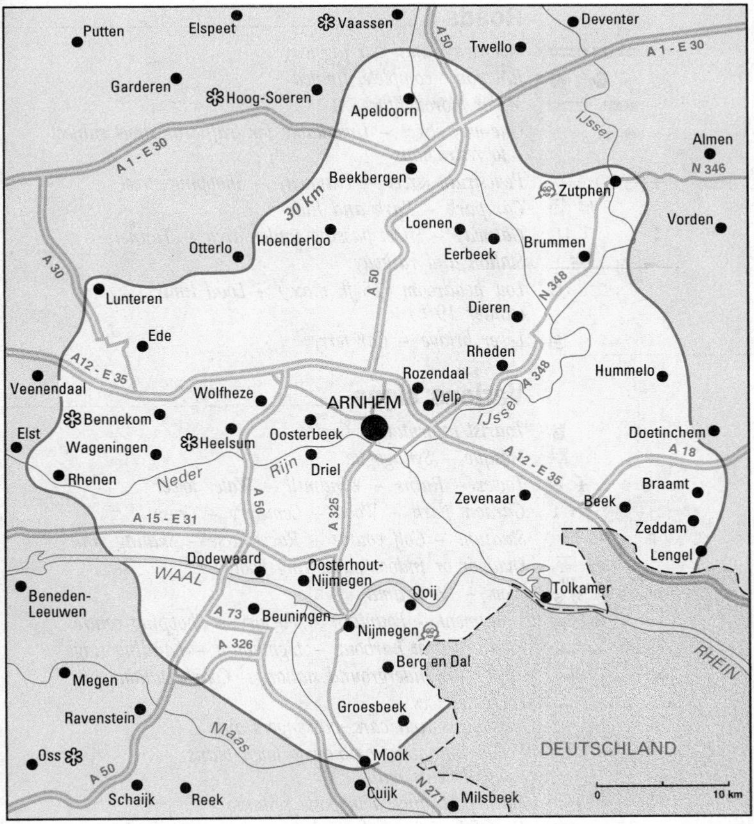

The local maps are indicated on the thematic map preceding each country.

Town plans

Hotels
Restaurants

Sights

Place of interest
Interesting place of worship

Roads

Motorway, dual carriageway
Junction : complete, limited
Major thoroughfare
One-way street – Unsuitable for traffic or street subject - to restrictions
Pasteur *Pedestrian street – Tramway – Shopping street*
Car park – Park and Ride
Gateway – Street passing under arch – Tunnel
Station and railway
4m4 18 *Low headroom (15 ft. max.) – Load limit (under 19 t.)*
B *Lever bridge – Car ferry*

Various signs

Tourist Information Centre
Mosque – Synagogue
Tower – Ruins – Windmill – Water tower
Garden, park – Wood – Cemetery – Cross
Stadium – Golf course – Racecourse – Skating rink
Outdoor or indoor swimming pool
View – Panorama
Monument – Fountain – Factory – Shopping centre
Pleasure boat harbour – Lighthouse – Landing stage
Airport – Underground station – Coach station
Ferry services :
passengers and cars, passengers only
3 *Refence number common to town plans and Michelin maps*
Main post office with poste restante
Hospital – Covered market
Public buildings located by letter :
H P *- Town Hall – Provincial Government Office*
J *- Law Courts*
M T *- Museum – Theatre*
U *- University, College*
POL. *- Police (in large towns police headquarters)*
G *- Gendarmerie*

Les langues parlées au Benelux

Située au cœur de l'Europe, la Belgique est divisée en trois régions : la Flandre, Bruxelles et la Wallonie. Chaque région a sa personnalité bien marquée. Trois langues y sont utilisées : le néerlandais en Flandre, le français en Wallonie et l'allemand dans les cantons de l'Est. La Région de Bruxelles-Capitale est bilingue avec une majorité francophone. La frontière linguistique correspond à peu près aux limites des provinces. Ce « multilinguisme » a des conséquences importantes sur l'organisation politique et administrative du pays, devenu État Fédéral depuis 1993.

Au Grand-Duché, outre le « Lëtzebuergesch », dialecte germanique, la langue officielle est le français. L'allemand est utilisé comme langue culturelle.

Aux Pays-Bas le néerlandais est la langue officielle. Néanmoins dans la province de Frise, le frison se parle encore couramment.

De talen in de Benelux

In het hartje van Europa ligt België, verdeeld in Vlaanderen, Brussel en Wallonië. Elke regio heeft zijn eigen karakter. Er worden drie talen gesproken : Nederlands in Vlaanderen, Frans in Wallonië en Duits in de Oostkantons. Het Brussels Hoofdstedelijk Gewest is tweetalig met een meerderheid aan Franstaligen. De taalgrens komt ongeveer overeen met de grenzen van de provincies. Het feit dat België een meertalig land is, heeft belangrijke gevolgen voor de politieke en bestuurlijke organisatie. Dit leidde tot de vorming van een Federale Staat in 1993.

In het Groot-Hertogdom wordt het « Lëtzebuergesch », een Duits dialect gesproken. De officiële taal is het Frans. Het Duits is de algemene cultuurtaal.

De officiële taal in Nederland is het Nederlands. In de provincie Friesland wordt ook Fries gesproken.

Die Sprachen im Benelux

Belgien, ein Land im Herzen von Europa, gliedert sich in drei Regionen : Flandern, Brüssel und Wallonien. Jede dieser Regionen hat ihre eigene Persönlichkeit. Man spricht hier drei Sprachen : Niederländisch in Flandern, Französisch in Wallonien und Deutsch in den östlichen Kantonen. Die Gegend um die Haupstadt Brüssel ist zweisprachig, wobei die Mehrheit Französisch spricht. Die Sprachengrenze entspricht in etwa den Provinzgrenzen. Diese Vielsprachigkeit hat starke Auswirkungen auf die politische und verwaltungstechnische Struktur des Landes, das seit 1993 Bundesstaat ist.

Im Grossherzogtum wird ausser dem « Lëtzebuergesch », einem deutschen Dialekt als offizielle Sprache französisch gesprochen. Die deutsche Sprache findet als Sprache der Kultur Verwendung.

In den Niederlanden wird niederländisch als offizielle Sprache gesprochen. Das Friesische wird jedoch in der Provinz Friesland noch sehr häufig gesprochen.

Spoken languages in the Benelux

Situated at the heart of Europe, Belgium is divided into three regions : Flanders, Brussels and Wallonia. Each region has its own individual personality. Three different languages are spoken : Dutch in Flanders, French in Wallonia and German in the eastern cantons. The Brussels-Capital region is bilingual, with the majority of its population speaking French. The linguistic frontiers correspond more or less to those of the provinces. The fact that the country, which has been a Federal State since 1993, is multilingual, has important consequences on its political and administrative structures.

In the Grand Duchy, apart from « Lëtzebuergesch », a German dialect, the official language is French. German is used as a cultural language.

In the Netherlands Dutch is the official language. However, Frisian is still widely spoken in the Friesland province.

La bière en Belgique

La Belgique est le pays de la bière par excellence. On y brasse environ 400 bières différentes, commercialisées sous plus de 800 appellations. Une partie se consomme à la pression, dite « au tonneau ».

On distingue trois types de bières, selon leur procédé de fermentation : les bières de fermentation spontanée (type Lambic), haute (type Ale) et basse (type Lager).

Suite à une deuxième fermentation en bouteille, le Lambic devient ce qu'on appelle la Geuze. La Kriek et la Framboise ont une saveur fruitée due à l'addition de cerises et de framboises. Ces bières sont caractéristiques de la région bruxelloise.

En Flandre, on trouve des bières blanches, brunes et rouges, en Wallonie on brasse des bières spécifiques à certaines saisons. Partout en Belgique, on trouve des Ales, des bières Trappistes et des bières d'abbayes. Parmi les bières belges, les fortes dorées et les régionales aux caractères typés occupent une place spéciale. La Pils belge, une bière blonde, est une excellente bière de table.

Amères, aigrelettes, acides, fruitées, épicées ou doucerettes, les bières belges s'harmonisent souvent avec bonheur à la gastronomie locale.

Het Belgische bier

België is het land van het bier bij uitstek. Men brouwt er ongeveer 400 verschillende biersoorten. Zij worden onder meer dan 800 benamingen op de markt gebracht. Sommige bieren worden "van het vat" gedronken.

De bieren kunnen volgens hun gistingsproces in 3 groepen worden onderverdeeld: bieren met een spontane gisting (type Lambiek), hoge gisting (type Ale) en lage gisting (type Lager). Geuze is een op flessen nagegiste Lambiek. Kriek en Framboise hebben hun fruitige smaak te danken aan de toevoeging van krieken (kersen) en frambozen. Deze bieren zijn typisch voor de streek van Brussel.

Vlaanderen is rijk aan witte, bruine en rode bieren. In Wallonië bereidt men seizoengebonden bieren. Overal in België brouwt men ales, trappisten- en abdijbieren. De sterke blonde bieren en de zogenaamde streekbieren nemen een speciale plaats in onder de Belgische bieren. De Belgische pils, een blond bier, is een uitstekend tafelbier.

Het Belgische bier met zijn bittere, rinse, zure, zoete smaak of kruidig aroma, kan zonder problemen bij een gastronomisch streekgerecht worden gedronken.

Das belgische Bier

*Belgien ist das Land des Bieres schlechthin.
In Belgien werden ungefähr 400 verschiedene Biersorten gebraut, die unter mehr als 800 Bezeichnungen vermarktet werden. Ein Teil davon wird vom Faß getrunken.
Man unterscheidet drei Biertypen nach ihrer Gärmethode: Bier mit spontaner Gärung (Typ Lambic), obergärig (Typ Ale) und untergärig (Typ Lager). Nach einer zweiten Gärung in der Flasche wird das Lambic zu Geuze. Das Kriek und das Framboise haben einen fruchtigen Geschmack, der durch den Zusatz von Kirschen und Himbeeren entsteht. Diese Biere sind typisch für die Brüsseler Gegend.
In Flandern findet man helles, braunes und rotes Bier, während die Saisonbiere typisch für Wallonien sind. Überall in Belgien gibt es verschiedene Sorten Ale, Trappistenbier und Klosterbier. Unter den belgischen Biersorten nehmen die goldbraunen Starkbiere und die Biere mit speziellem regionalen Charakter einen besonderen Platz ein. Das belgische Pils, ein helles Bier, ist ein exzellentes Tafelbier.
Mit den Geschmacksrichtungen herb, leicht säuerlich, fruchtig, würzig oder süßlich kann das belgische Bier ein deftiges regionales Menü begleiten.*

The beers of Belgium

*Belgium is the country for beer "par excellence".
There are over 800 different brands on sale there today. The breweries produce approximately 400 different beers. In the flat country of the Ardennes beer is served in 35,000 cafes. Some of it is on draught – "from the barrel".
There are three different types of beer dependent upon which fermentation process is used: spontaneous fermentation (Lambic), high (Ale) and low (Lager).
Following a second fermentation in the bottle, the Lambic becomes what is called Geuze. Kriek and Framboise have a fruity taste due to the addition of cherries and raspberries. These beers are characteristic of the Brussels region.
In Flanders, pale ale, brown ale and bitter are found.
In Wallonie beers are brewed which are particular to each season. Throughout Belgium there are Ales, Trappist beers and Abbey beers. Of all the Belgian beers, the strong golden ones and the regional ones with their own individual characters are held in special regard.
Belgian Pils, a light ale, is excellent to have on the table.
Whether bitter, vinegarish, acidic, fruity, spicey or mild, Belgian beers are the perfect accompaniment to local specialities.*

Le vin au Luxembourg

Le vignoble luxembourgeois produit essentiellement du vin blanc. Depuis l'époque romaine, l'Elbling, cultivé sur les bords de la Moselle, donne un vin sec et acidulé. Ce cépage a été progressivement remplacé par l'Auxerrois, le Pinot blanc, le Pinot gris, le Gewurztraminer ou le Rivaner. Habitué des sols calcaires, le Riesling atteint ici la finesse qui le caractérise. C'est le cépage le plus tardif qui occupe +/- 13 % du territoire. Actuellement, le Pinot gris est le cépage le plus demandé. Il donne le vin le plus moelleux et le plus aromatique et permet une consommation jeune.

Le vignoble luxembourgeois couvre environ 1 345 ha. dans la vallée de la Moselle. Quelques 850 viticulteurs sont groupés en 5 caves coopératives, qui représentent 70 % de la production. L'autre partie est vinifiée par une vingtaine de viticulteurs indépendants. Les vins luxembourgeois sont toujours vendus sous le nom du cépage ; l'étiquette de ceux bénéficiant de l'Appellation d'Origine Contrôlée (A.O.C.) mentionne en outre le nom du village, du lieu et du producteur. Le canton de Remich (Schengen, Wintrange, Remich) et le canton de Grevenmacher (Wormeldange, Ahn, Machtum, Grevenmacher), ont droit à l'appellation "Moselle Luxembourgeoise" et sont considérés comme étant les plus réputés. Au Grand-Duché, on produit également des vins mousseux et des crémants en quantité importante et quelques vins rosés à partir du cépage Pinot noir. Pratiquement partout, ces vins jeunes, servis au verre, en carafe ou à la bouteille, vous feront découvrir un "petit" vignoble qui mérite votre considération.

De Luxemburgse wijn

In Luxemburg wordt vooral witte wijn verbouwd. De Elbling, die sinds de oudheid wordt verbouwd langs de oevers van de Moezel, is een droge en lichtelijk zurige wijn. Deze wijnstok werd geleidelijk aan vervangen door de Auxerrois, de Pinot blanc, de Pinot gris, de Gewurztraminer en de Rivaner. De Riesling, die goed gedijt op kalksteenbodems, bereikt hier zijn kenmerkende finesse. Deze wijnstokvariëteit heeft een late rijping en beslaat ongeveer 13 % van het gebied. De Pinot gris is voor het ogenblik de meest gevraagde wijn. Het is de meest volle en zachte wijn, die jong kan worden gedronken. Het Luxemburgse wijngebied beslaat in de Moezelvallei ongeveer 1345 ha. Ongeveer 850 wijnbouwers zijn gegroepeerd in 5 coöperatieve wijnkelders. Zij nemen 70 % van de productie voor hun rekening. Een twintigtal onafhankelijke wijnbouwers verbouwt de rest van de wijnproductie. De Luxemburgse wijnen worden steeds onder de naam van de wijnstok verkocht; het etiket van de wijnen, die de benaming "Appellation d'Origine Contrôlée" (gecontroleerde herkomstbenaming) dragen, vermeldt bovendien de naam van het dorp, de plaats en de wijnbouwer. Het kanton Remich (Schengen, Wintrange, Remich) en het kanton Grevenmacher (Wormeldange, Ahn, Machtum, Grevenmacher) mogen de naam "Moselle luxembourgeoise" dragen. Deze kantons worden beschouwd als de meest beroemde.

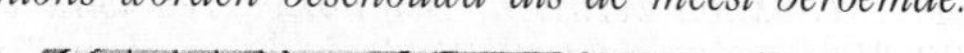

In het Groot-Hertogdom wordt ook een grote hoeveelheid mousserende en licht mousserende wijnen bereid, evenals enkele roséwijnen op basis van de wijnstok Pinot noir. Deze jonge wijnen zijn praktisch overal per glas, karaf of fles verkrijgbaar. Op die manier ontdekt u een "kleine" wijnstreek, die meer dan de moeite waard is.

Services et taxes

En Belgique, au Grand-Duché de Luxembourg et aux Pays-Bas, les prix s'entendent service et taxes compris.

Der luxemburgische Wein

Im luxemburgischen Weinbaugebiet wird im wesentlichen Weißwein angebaut. Seit der Zeit der Römer ergibt der Elbling, der an den Ufern der Mosel wächst, einen trockenen und säuerlichen Wein.

Diese Rebsorte wurde nach und nach durch den Auxerrois, den Pinot blanc, den Pinot gris, den Gewürztraminer oder den Rivaner ersetzt. Auf Kalkbödem erhält der Riesling die Fenheit die ihn charaktrisiert. Es ist die Rebsorte mit der längsten Reifezeit, +/- 13 % der Rebfläche sind damit bepflanzt. Zur Zeit ist der Pinot gris die gefragteste Rebsorte. Sie ergibt den lieblichsten und aromatischsten Wein, der schon jung getrunken werden kann.

Das luxemburgische Weinbaugebiet umfaßt zirka 1345 Hektar im Moseltal. Ungefähr 850 Winzer haben sich zu 5 Weinbaugenossenschaften zusammengeschlossen, die 70 % der Produktion vertreten. Der übrige Teil wird von etwa 20 Winzern produziert. Die luxemburgischen Weine werden immer unter dem Namen der Rebsorte verkauft, die besondere Appellation d'Origine Contrôlée (geprüfte Herkunftsbezeichnung) nennt auch das Dorf, die Lage und den Produzenten.

Nur das Gebiet des Kantons Remich (Schengen, Wintrange, Remich) und des Kantons Grevenmacher (Wormeldange, Ahn, Machtun, Grevenmacher) haben wegen ihrer besonderen Lage das Recht auf die Bezeichnung "Moselle Luxembourgiose".

Im Großherzogtum werden auch Sekt und Crémant in bedeutenden Mengen sowie einige Roseweine auf der Basis von Pinot noir produziert.

Fast überall lassen diese jungen Weine – im Glas, in der Karaffe oder in der Flasche serviert – Sie ein "kleines" Weinbaugebiet entdecken, das eine größere Bekanntheit verdient.

Halten Sie beim Betreten des Hotels oder des Restaurants den Führer in der Hand
Sie zeigen damit, daß Sie aufgrund dieser Empfehlung gekommen sind.

The wines of Luxembourg

Luxembourg is essentially a white wine producer. The Elbling grape, grown on the banks of the Moselle, has been yielding a dry acidic wine since Roman times.

However, this grape has been gradually replaced by the Auxerrois, the Pinot blanc, the Pinot gris, the Gewurztraminer and the Rivaner. Well adapted to chalky soil, the Riesling grown here develops a distinctive flavour. These late maturing grapes occupy around 13 % of the land. The Pinot gris is currently the most popular. It gives the most mellow, aromatic wine and can be drunk whilst still young.

Vineyards cover approximately 1345 hectares of the Moselle valley. Some 850 wine growers are grouped into 5 cooperative "caves", which overall produce 70 % of the wine, the remainder being made up by another 20 independent wine growers. Wines from Luxembourg are always sold under the name of the grape. The label, which bears the AOC ("Appellation d'Origine Contrôlée), also gives the vintage, producer and location of the vine.

Wine produced in the cantons (districts) of Remich (Schengen, Wintrange, Remich) and Grevenmacher (Warmeldange, Ahn, Machtum, Grevenmacher) is the most reputed and has the right to be called "Moselle Luxembourgeoise".

Sparkling wines and a large number of Crémants are also produced in the Grand Duchy, as well as some rosés based on Pinot noir.

These young wines, served by the glass, carafe or bottle, will usually give you a taste of a little known wine which is well worth trying.

Le fromage en Hollande

La Hollande produit 11 milliards de litres de lait par an dont la moitié est transformée en fromage par environ 110 laiteries. Dans les provinces de Zuid-Holland et d'Utrecht, quelques fermiers préparent encore de façon artisanale le fromage. La fabrication du fromage est le fruit d'une longue tradition, plusieurs musées en retracent l'histoire (Alkmaar, Bodegraven, Arnhem, Wageningen).

Au moyen-âge déjà, le fromage aux Pays-Bas faisait l'objet d'un commerce actif comme en témoignent encore aujourd'hui les marchés pittoresques d'Alkmaar, Purmerend, Gouda, Bodegraven, Woerden et Edam.

On peut distinguer plusieurs catégories de fromages : Le Gouda, parfois aux grains de cumin, l'Edam, le Maasdam, le Leidse, la Mimolette, le Friese aux clous de girofle et le Kernhem.

Selon la durée de la maturation qui va de 4 semaines à plus de 3 ans, on distingue du fromage jeune, mi-vieux et vieux. Quelques fromages de brebis (en général sur les îles) et de chèvre complètent la gamme.

La majorité de ces fromages vous fera terminer un repas en beauté.

De Hollandse kaas

Nederland produceert 11 miljard liter melk per jaar. De helft wordt door zo'n 110 melkerijen bereid tot kaas. In de provincies Zuid-Holland en Utrecht maken nog enkele boeren op ambachtelijke wijze kaas. Het kaasmaken kent een lange traditie, waarvan verschillende musea de geschiedenis illustreren (Alkmaar, Bodegraven, Arnhem, Wageningen).

In de Middeleeuwen werd in Nederland reeds druk kaas verhandeld. Ook nu nog worden er in Alkmaar, Purmerend, Gouda, Bodegraven, Woerden en Edam schilderachtige kaasmarkten gehouden.

Er zijn verschillende soorten kaas: Gouda, soms met komijn, Edam, Maasdam, Leidse kaas, Mimolette, Friese kaas met kruidnagels en Kernhem.

Naargelang de duur van het rijpingsproces (van 4 weken tot meer dan 3 jaren) onderscheidt men jonge, belegen en oude kaas. Enkele schapenkazen (vooral op de eilanden) en geitenkazen vervolledigen het assortiment.

Met de meeste van deze kazen kan u op passende wijze de maaltijd beëindigen.

Der holländische Käse

Die Niederlande produzieren jährlich 11 milliarden Liter Milch, wovon die Hälfte in zirka 110 Molkereien zu Käse verarbeitet wird. In den Provinzen Zuid-Holland und Utrecht bereiten einige Bauern den Käse noch auf traditionelle Weise zu. Die Käseherstellung hat eine lange Tradition, die in mehreren Museen vergegenwärtigt wird (Alkmaar, Bodegraven, Arnhem, Wageningen).

Schon im Mittelalter wurde in den Niederlanden mit Käse gehandelt, wovon auch heute noch die folkloristischen Märkte in Alkmaar, Purmerend, Gouda, Bodegraven, Woerden und Edam zeugen.

Man unterscheidet verschiedene Käsearten: den Gouda, den es manchmal auch mit Kümmelkörnern gibt, den Edamer, den Maasdamer, den Leidse, den Mimolette, den Friese mit Nelken und den Kernhemer.

Je nach Reifezeit, die von 4 Wochen bis über 3 Jahre dauern kann, unterscheidet man jungen, mittelalten und alten Käse. Einige Sorten Schafs– (meist von den Inseln) und Ziegenkäse ergänzen die Palette.

Die meisten dieser Käsesorten werden für Sie der krönende Abschluß einer gelungenen Mahlzeit sein.

The cheeses of Holland

Holland produces 11 billion litres of milk a year, half of which is made into cheese by approximately 110 dairies. In the provinces of Zuid-Holland and Utrecht, some farmers still make cheese in the old-fashioned way. Cheese-making stems from an age-old tradition, the history of which is documented in several museums (Alkmaar, Bodegraven, Arnham, Wageningen).

In the Middle Ages there was already an active cheese trade in Holland and this can still be seen today in the quaint markets of Alkmaar, Purmerend, Gouda, Badegraven, Woerden and Edam.

There are several different categories of cheese: Gouda, sometimes made with cumin seeds, Edam, Maasdam, Leidse, Mimolette, Friese with cloves and Kernham.

According to the length of maturing, which varies from 4 weeks to more than 3 years, a cheese is identified as young, medium or mature. A few sheeps cheeses (generally on the islands) and goats cheeses complete the selection.

Most of these cheeses will round your meal off beautifully.

Les établissements à étoiles
De sterrenrestaurants
Die Stern-Restaurants
Starred establishments

Belgique / België

Brugge Q. Centre *De Karmeliet*
Bruxelles *Comme Chez Soi*

Nederland

Rotterdam Q. Centre *Parkheuvel*
Zwolle *De Librije*

Belgique / België

Antwerpen
– Env. à Kapellen *De Bellefleur*
Bruxelles *Sea Grill (H. Radisson SAS)*
– Ganshoren *Bruneau*
– Ganshoren *Claude Dupont*
– Env. à Groot-Bijgaarden *De Bijgaarden*
Ellezelles *Château du Mylord*
Kruishoutem *Hof van Cleve*
Namur à Lives-sur-Meuse *La Bergerie*
Paliseul *Au Gastronome*
Tongeren à Vliermaal *Clos St Denis*
Waregem *'t Oud Konijntje*
Zeebrugge *'t Molentje*

Grand-Duché de Luxembourg

Echternach à Geyershaff *La Bergerie*

Nederland

Amsterdam Q. Centre *La Rive (H. Amstel)*
– *Vermeer (H. NH Barbizon Palace)*
Haarlem à Overveen *De Bokkedoorns*
Kruiningen *Inter Scaldes (H. Le Manoir)*
Maastricht Q. Centre *Beluga*
Sluis *Oud Sluis*

Belgique / België

Antwerpen Q. Ancien *'t Fornuis*
– *De Kerselaar*
– Env. à Boechout *De Schone van Boskoop*
– Env. à Edegem *La Cabane*
Beaumont à Solre-St-Géry *Host. Le Prieuré Saint-Géry*
Berlare *'t Laurierblad*
– aux étangs de Donkmeer *Lijsterbes*
Blaregnies *Les Gourmands*
Bornem *Eyckerhof*
Braine-l'Alleud *Jacques Marit*
Brugge *Den Gouden Harynck*
– Périph. à Sint-Andries *Herborist*
– Env. à Varsenare *Manoir Stuivenberg*

Bruxelles
– Q. des Sablons *L'Écailler du Palais Royal*
– Q. Palais de Justice *Maison du Bœuf (H. Hilton)*
– Q. Bois de la Cambre *Villa Lorraine*
– *La Truffe Noire*
– Anderlecht *Saint Guidon*
– *La Brouette*
– Ganshoren *San Daniele*
– Ixelles Q. Boondael *Marie*
– Schaerbeek *Senza Nome*
– Uccle *Bon-Bon*
– Q. St-Job *Le Passage*
– Watermael-Boitsfort *Au Vieux Boitsfort*
– Woluwe-St-Lambert *De Maurice à Olivier*
– Woluwe-St-Pierre *Les Deux Maisons*
– Env. à Groot-Bijgaarden *Michel*
– Env. à Nossegem *L'Orangerie Roland Debuyst*
– à Overijse *Barbizon*

Charleroi
– à Loverval *Le Saint Germain des Prés*
– à Montigny-le-Tilleul *L'éveil des sens*

Dendermonde *'t Truffeltje*
Dinant à Sorinnes *Host. Gilain*
Eghezée à Noville-sur-Mehaigne *L'Air du Temps*
Elewijt *Kasteel Diependael*
Fauvillers *Le Château de Strainchamps*
Gent Q. Centre *Jan Van den Bon*
Habay-La-Neuve *Les Forges*
Hamme *De Plezanten Hof*
Hasselt
– à Lummen *Hoeve St-Paul*
Heure *Le Fou est belge*
Houthalen *De Barrier*
Hulsthout *Hof ter Hulst*
Ieper à Elverdinge *Host. St-Nicolas*
Keerbergen *The Paddock*
Knokke-Heist à Albertstrand
– *Esmeralda Jardin Tropical*
– à Heist *Bartholomeus*
Kortrijk *St Christophe*
Leuven *Belle Epoque*
– à Heverlee *Arenberg*
Liège
– Périph. à Rocourt *La Petite Table*
– Env. à Neuville-en-Condroz *Le Chêne Madame*
Malle à Oostmalle *De Eiken*
Mechelen *D'Hoogh*
– *Folliez*
Mol *'t Zilte*
Namur à Temploux *L'Essentiel*
Ninove *Hof ter Eycken*
Noirefontaine *Aub. du Moulin Hideux*
Oignies-en-Thiérache *Au Sanglier des Ardennes*
Opglabbeek *Slagmolen*
De Panne *Host. Le Fox*
Pepinster *Host. Lafarque*
Profondeville à Arbre *L'Eau Vive*
Reet *Pastorale*
Reninge *'t Convent*
Roeselare *Bistro Novo*
Sankt-Vith *Zur Post*
Spontin à Dorinne *Le Vivier d'Oies*
Virton à Torgny *Aub. de la Grappe d'Or*
Westouter *Picasso*
Zeebrugge *Maison Vandamme*

Grand-Duché de Luxembourg

Esch-sur-Alzette *Fridrici*
– *Aub. Royale*
Frisange *Lea Linster*
Gaichel *La Gaichel*
Luxembourg – Centre *Clairefontaine*
– *Le Bouquet Garni Salon*
– *Saint Michel*
– *Speltz*
– Grund *Mosconi*
– Env. à Hesperange *L'Agath*
Mondorf-les-Bains *Les Roses (H. Casino 2000)*
Schouweiler *La Table des Guilloux*

Nederland

Amsterdam Q. Centre *Christophe*
– *Sichuan Food*
– *Van Vlaanderen*
– Q. Sud et Ouest *Yamazato (H. Okura)*
– Env. à Ouderkerk aan de Amstel *Ron Blaauw*
Apeldoorn à Hoog Soeren *De Echoput*
Beetsterzwaag *De Heeren van Harinxma (H. Lauswolt)*
Bennekom *Het Koetshuis*
Blokzijl *Kaatje bij de Sluis*
Borculo *De Stenen Tafel*
Castricum *Apicius*
Delft *De Zwethheul*
Drachten *Koriander*
Driebergen-Rijsenburg *Lai Sin*
Eindhoven *De Karpendonkse Hoeve*
– *Avant-Garde*
Ermelo *De Roggebot*
Etten-Leur *De Zwaan*
Giethoorn *De Lindenhof*
Groningen *Muller*
– à Aduard *Herberg Onder de Linden*
Gulpen *Le Sapiche*
Den Haag Q. Centre *Calla's*
– Env. à Rijswijk *Paul Van Waarden*
– *Imko's*
– Env. à Voorburg *Savelberg*
Haarlem *Chapeau !*
Hardenberg à Heemse *De Bokkepruik*
Harderwijk *Olivio*
– *'t Nonnetje*
Heelsum *De Kromme Dissel*
Heerlen *De Boterbloem*
Heeze *Boreas*
's-Hertogenbosch *Chalet Royal*
Hilversum *Spandershoeve*
Houten *Kasteel Heemstede*
Leens *Schathoes Verhildersum*
Maasbracht *Da Vinci*
Maastricht Q. Centre *Toine Hermsen*
– *Tout à fait*
– au Sud *Château Neercanne*
Nuenen *De Lindenhof*
Nuth *In de'n Dillegaard*
Ootmarsum *De Wanne (H. De Wiemsel)*
Oss *Cordial (H. De Weverij)*
Purmerend à Neck *Mario Uva*
Rijsoord *Hermitage*
Roermond *Onder de Boompjes in Kasteeltje Hattem*
Rotterdam Q. Centre *La Vilette*
Schoorl *Merlet*
Sint-Oedenrode *Wollerich*
Ubachsberg *De Leuf*
Vaassen *De Leest*
Valkenburg *Juliana (H. Prinses Juliana)*
Vreeland *De Nederlanden*
Waddeneilanden / Terschelling à Oosterend *De Grië*
Wittem à Wahlwiller *Der Bloasbalg*
Yerseke *Nolet-Het Reymerswale*
Zeist à Bosch en Duin *de Hoefslag (H. de Hoefslag)*
Zweeloo *Idylle*

"Bib Gourmand"

Repas soignés à prix modérés

Verzorgde maaltijden voor een schappelijke prijs

Sorgfältig zubereitete, preiswerte Mahlzeiten

Good food at moderate prices

Repas

Belgique / België

Antwerpen
– Q. Centre *La Luna*
– Périph. à Berchem *Brasserie Marly*
– *De Troubadour*
– Périph. à Ekeren *De Mangerie*
Barvaux *Le Cor de Chasse*
Bastogne *Léo*
Bellevaux-Ligneuville *Du Moulin*
Blankenberge *Escapade*
Borgloon *Ambrozijn*
Bornem à Mariekerke *De Ster*
Bouillon *La Ferronnière*
– à Corbion *Ardennes*
Brugge Q. Centre *'t Stil Ende*
– Périph. à Sint-Kruis *Ronnie Jonkman*
Bruxelles
– Q. Grand'Place *Aux Armes de Bruxelles*
– Q. Ste-Catherine *La Belle Maraîchère*
– *François*
– *Le Loup Galant*
– Q. des Sablons *La Clef des Champs*
– Q. Palais de Justice *JB*
– Q. Atomium *La Balade Gourmande*
– Ganshoren *Cambrils*
– Ixelles *Le Yen*
– Q. Louise *De la Vigne ... à l'Assiette*
– Jette *Rôtiss. Le Vieux Pannenhuis*
– *French Kiss*
– St-Josse-ten-Noode Q. Botanique *Les Dames Tartine*
– Uccle *Villa d'Este*
– Q. St-Job *Les Menus Plaisirs*
– *Le pré en bulle*
– Watermael-Boitsfort *Le Grill*
– Woluwe-St-Pierre *Medicis*
– *La Tour d'Argent*
– Env. à Itterbeek *De Ster*
Court-Saint-Etienne *Les Ailes*
Deerlijk *Severinus*
Deinze à Astene *Au Bain-Marie*
Dinant *Le Jardin de Fiorine*
– à Falmignoul *Les Crétias*
Durbuy *Le Moulin*
Ecaussinnes-Lalaing *Le Pilori*
Gent Q. Ancien *De 3 Biggetjes*
Genval *L'Amandier*
De Haan à Klemskerke *De Kruidenmolen*
– à Vlissegem *Vijfweghe*
Jodoigne à Mélin *La Villa du Hautsart*
Knokke-Heist à Knokke *'t Kantientje*
– à Heist *Old Fisher*
Kortrijk *Huyze Decock*
Lasne à Plancenoit *Le Vert d'Eau*
Leuze-en-Hainaut *Le Châlet de la Bourgogne*
Liège – Vieille Ville *Enoteca*
– *Le Bistrot d'en face*
– Env. à Herstal *La Bergamote*
– Env. à Liers *La Bartavelle*
– Env. à Tilleur *Chez Massimo*
Lier *Numerus Clausus*
Ligny *Le Coupe-Choux*
Malmédy à Bévercé *Plein Vent*
Marche-en-Famenne *Les 4 Saisons*
Marcourt *Le Marcourt*
Marenne *Les Pieds dans le Plat*
Mirwart *Aub. du Grandgousier*
Mons à Baudour *Le Faitout*
Mouscron *Madame*

nur direction Citadelle *Au trois Petits Cochons*
ssogne *La Gourmandise*
rpelt *De Landerije*
tduinkerke-Bad *Eglantier (H. Hof ter Duinen)*
tende *Petit Nice*
lenaarde à Mater *De Zwadderkotmolen*
Panne *@De Braise*
Le Flore
ondeville *La Sauvenière*
Roche-en-Ardenne *Host. Linchet*
hefort à Belvaux *Aub. des Pérées*
St-Hubert *Le Cor de Chasse*
Sint-Martens-Latem *Sabatini*
Soheit-Tinlot *Le Coq aux Champs*
Spa *La Tonnellerie*
Stoumont *Zabonprés*
Verviers à Petit-Rechain *La Chapellerie*
Vielsalm à Hébronval *Le Val d'Hébron*
Vresse-sur-Semois *Le Relais*
Walcourt *Host. Dispa*
Waregem à Sint-Eloois-Vijve *bistro desanto*
Watou *Gasthof't Hommelhof*
Wavre *La Table du Marché*

nd-Duché de Luxembourg

vaux à Roder *Manoir Kasselslay*
ange à Hellange *Lëtzebuerger Kaschthaus*
Luxembourg-Grund *Kamakura*
– Périph. à l'Aéroport *Le Grimpereau*
Mullerthal *Le Cigalon*

erland

aar *Bios*
en *Bunga Melati*
terdam
Q. Centre *Café Roux (H. The Grand Sofitel Demeure)*
Le Relais (H. de l'Europe)
Q. Rijksmuseum *Le Garage*
Q. Sud et Ouest *Pakistan*
Q. Est et Sud-Est *VandeMarkt*
nv. à Amstelveen *De Jonge Dikkert*
Erwijk *'t Gildehuys*
Bijl *Hof van Sonoy*
Ba *de Stadstuin*
Bn *Brasserie Floris*
Daen *De Witte Gans*
De *L'Orage*
Draten à Boornbergum *Het Spijshuys*
Enuizen *Die Drie Haringhe*
Go *Het Binnenhof*
Grongen *De Pauw*
Gulpn *L'Atelier*
DenHaag env. à Voorburg *Papermoon*
Haarlem à Bloemendaal *Terra Cotta*
– à Heemstede *Cheval Blanc*
Harlingen *De Gastronoom*
Heerenveen *Sir Sèbastian*
Heeze *Host. Van Gaalen*
Hindeloopen *De Gasterie*
Hoek van Holland *Sand*
Holten sur le Holterberg *Bistro de Holterberg*
Hoorn *Hendrickje Stoffels*
Houten *Coco Pazzo*
Leiden *Anak Bandung*
Middelharnis *Brasserie 't Vingerling*
Nijmegen *Het Savarijn*
Noorden *De Watergeus*
Norg à Westervelde *De Jufferen Lunsingh*
Ossenzijl *Klokzicht*
Purmerend à Middenbeemster *Het Heerenhuis Beemster*
Rinsumageest *Het Rechthuis*
Rotterdam
– Q. Centre *Foody's*
– *Rosso*
– Env. à Schiedam *Bistrot Hosman Frères*
Tilburg *Sprakeloos*
Tubbergen *Droste's*
Wamel *D'Oude Weeghbrug*
Warmond *De Moerbei*
Wateringen *'t Raethuys*
Weert *Les Deux Charmes*
Yerseke *Nolet's Vistro*
Zeist à Bosch en Duin *Bistro de Ruif (H. De Hoefslag)*
Zierikzee à Schuddebeurs *Host. Schuddebeurs*
Zutphen *'t Schulten Hues*
Zweeloo à Aalden *Adema*
Zwolle *'t Pestengasthuys*

Hôtels agréables
Aangename Hotels
Angenehme Hotels
Particularly pleasant Hote

Nederland

Amsterdam Q. Centre — *Amstel*

Belgique / België

Bruxelles
- Q. Léopold — *Stanhope*

Nederland

Amsterdam Q. Centre — *'Europe*
Beetsterzwaag — *auswolt*
Ootmarsum — *Wiemsel*
Valkenburg à Houthem — *Château Gerlach*

Belgique / België

Antwerpen Q. Ancien — *De Witte Lelie*
Brugge Q. Centre — *de tuilerieën*
- *Relais Oud Huis Amsterdam*
- *Die Swaene*
- *Pandhotel*

Bruxelles Q. Louise — *Hyatt Regency*
- St Gilles Q. Louise — *Manos Premier*
- Woluwe-St-Pierre — *Montgomery*

Comblain-la-Tour — *Host. St-Roch*
Genval — *Le Manoir du Lac*
Habay-la-Neuve à l'Est — *Les Ardillières*
Knokke-Heist à Het Zoute — *Manoir du Dragon*
Noirefontaine — *Aub. Du Moulin Hideux*

Grand-Duché de Luxourg

Luxembourg
- Périph. à Belair — *rt Premier*

Nederland

Amsterdam Q. Centre — *Blakes*
Kruiningen — *Le Manoir*
Leeuwarden à Aldtsjerl — *Land De Klinze*
Oisterwijk — *De Swaen*
Ootmarsum à Lattrop — *De Holtweijde*
Valkenburg — *inses Juliana*
Zeist à Bosch en Duir — *de Hoefslag*

Belgique / België

Antwerpen Q. Sud — *Firean*
Brugge Q. Centre — *Prinsenhof*
Crupet — *Le Moulin des Ramiers*
Poperinge — *Manoir Ogygia*

Grand-Duché de Luxembourg

Luxembourg
Périphérie à Dommeldange — *Host. du Grünewald*

Nederland

Amsterdam Q. Centre — *Ambassade*
- *Seven one Seven*

Amsterdam Env. Ouderkerk aan de Amstel — *'t Jagershuis*
Den Haag Q. Centre — *Haagsche Suites*
Wijk aan Zee — *De Klughte*

Belgique / België

Rance à Sautin — *Le Domaine de la Carrauterie*

Restaurants agréables
Aangename Restaurants
Angenehme Restaurants
Particularly pleasant Restaurants

XXXXX

Belgique / België

Bruxelles
- **Env. à Groot-Bijgaarden** *De Bijgaarden*

Tongeren à Vliermaal *Clos St. Denis*

XXXX

Belgique / België

Bruxelles
- **Q. Grand'Place** *La Maison du Cygne*
- **Q. Palais de Justice** *Maison du Bœuf*
- **Q. Bois de la Cambre** *Villa Lorraine*
- **Env. à Overijse** *Barbizon*

Ellezelles *Château du Mylord*
Habay-la-Neuve à l'Est *Les Forges*
Kortrijk à Marke *Marquette (avec ch)*
Namur à Lives-sur-Meuse *La Bergerie*
Reninge *'t Convent (avec ch)*
Verviers *Château Peltzer*
Waregem *'t Oud Konijntje*

Grand-Duché de Luxembourg

Gaichel *La Gaichel (avec ch)*
Luxembourg Q. Centre *Clairefontaine*

Nederland

Amsterdam Q. Centre *La Rive (H. Amstel)*
- *Excelsior (H. Europe)*

Beetsterzwaag *De Heeren van Harinxma*
Eindhoven *De Karpendonkse Hoeve*
Den Haag
- **Env. à Voorburg** *Savelberg (avec ch)*

Haarlem à Overveen *De Bokkedoorns*
Kruiningen *Inter Scaldes (H. Le Manoir)*
Valkenburg *Juliana (H. Prinses Juliana)*
Zaandam *De Hoop Op d'Swarte Walvis*
Zeist à Bosch en Duin *de Hoefslag (H. de Hoefslag)*

XXX

Belgique / België

Anhée *Host. Henrotte – Au Vachter (avec ch)*
Bornem *Eyckerhof*
Brugge Q. Centre *De Snippe (avec ch)*
- **Env. à Varsenare** *Manoir Stuivenberg (avec ch)*

Bruxelles *Comme Chez Soi*
- **Watermael-Boitsfort** *Au Vieux Boitsfort*
- **Woluwe-St-Pierre** *Des 3 Couleurs*

Diest *De Proosdij*
Elewijt *Kasteel Diependael*
Habay-la-Neuve à l'Est *Les Forges*
Hasselt *Figaro*
Hasselt à Lummen *Hoeve St. Paul*
Keerbergen *The Paddock*
Knokke-Heist
- **à Westkapelle** *Ter Dycken*

Kortrijk *St-Christophe*
- **au Sud** *Gastronomisch Dorp (avec ch)*

Kruishoutem *Hof van Cleve*
Menen à Rekkem *La Cravache*
Namur à Temploux *L'Essentiel*
Olen *Doffenhof*
Opglabbeek *Slagmolen*
De Panne *Host. Le Fox*
Pepinster *Host. Lafarque (avec ch)*
Ronse *Host. Shamrock (avec ch)*

✗✗✗

Grand-Duché de Luxembourg

Echternach à Geyershaff *La Bergerie*
Luxembourg-Grund *Mosconi*

Nederland

Aalst *De Fuik*
Amsterdam Env. à Amstelveen *De Jonge Dikkert*
Apeldoorn à Hoog Soeren *De Echoput*
Delft *De Zwethheul*
Groningen à Aduard *Herberg Onder de Linden (avec ch)*
's-Hertogenbosch *Chalet Royal*
Leiden à Oegstgeest *De Beukenhof*
Meppel à De Wijk *de Havixhorst (avec ch)*
Ootmarsum *De Wanne (H. De Wiemsel)*
Roermond *Onder de Boompjes in Kasteeltje Hattem*
Sluis *Oud Sluis*
Vreeland *De Nederlanden (avec ch)*
Waalre *De Treeswijkhoeve*
Wittem *Kasteel Wittem (avec ch)*
– Wahlwiller *Der Bloasbalg*
Wolphaartsdijk *'t Veerhuis*
Zwolle *De Librije*

✗✗

Belgique / België

Aalst *'t Soethout*
Bouillon *Le Ferronnière (avec ch)*
Brugge
– Périph. au Sud-Ouest *Herborist (avec ch)*
Bruxelles
Q. des Sablons *Trente rue de la Paille*
Crupet *Les Ramiers (H. Le Moulin des Ramiers)*
Dilsen à Lanklaar *Host. La Feuille d'Or (avec ch)*
Geel *De Cuylhoeve*
Gent Q. Centre *Waterzooi*
Heure *Le Fou est belge*
Knokke-Heist à Albertstrand *Jardin Tropical*
– à Heist *Bartholomeus*
Profondeville à Arbre *L'Eau Vive*
Tielt *De Meersbloem*
Virton à Torgny *Aub. de la Grappe d'Or (avec ch)*
Zeebrugge *'t Molentje*

Grand-Duché de Luxembourg

Luxembourg Périph. à Clausen *Les Jardins du Président*
Schouweiler *La Table des Guilloux*

Nederland

Blokzijl *Kaatje bij de Sluis*
Borculo *De Stenen Tafel*
Leens *Schathoes Verhildersum*
Oud-Loosdrecht *Zin*
Ubachsberg *De Leuf*

✗

Nederland

Holten sur le Holterberg *Bistro de Holterberg*
Waddeneilanden / Terschelling à Oosterend *De Grië*

Belgique
België
Belgien

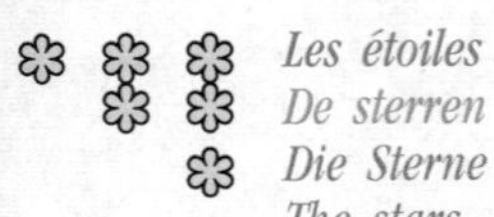

Les étoiles
De sterren
Die Sterne
The stars

"Bib Gourmand"

Repas 33

Repas soignés à prix modérés
Verzorgde maaltijden voor een schappelijke prijs
Sorgfältig zubereitete preiswerte Mahlzeiten
Good food at moderate prices

L'agrément
Aangenaam verblijf
Annehmlichkeit
Peaceful atmosphere and setting

Carte de voisinage : voir à la ville choisie
Kaart van de omgeving in de buurt van grote steden
Stadt mit Umgebungskarte
Town with a local map

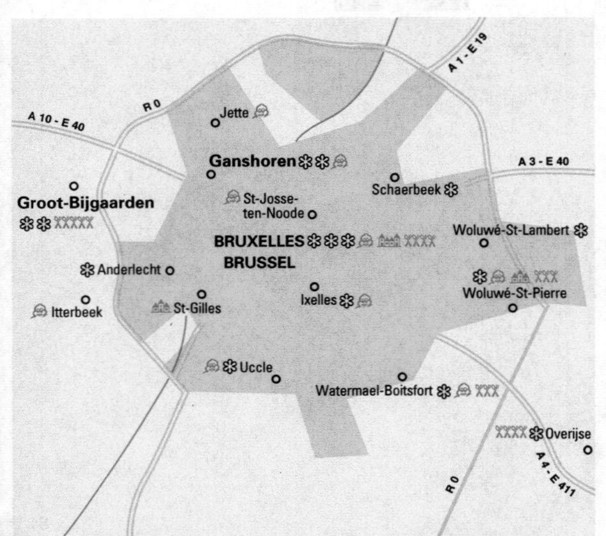

NEDERLAND
A 16 - E 19
A 58 - E 312
A 58 - E 312
A 58 - E 312
N 62
A 4
A 12
Kapellen
A 1 - E 19
Oostmalle
Ekeren
A 21 - E 34
Antwerpen
Berchem
Albert Kanaal
A 14 - E 17
Edegem
Boechout
A 13 - E 313
Geel
Hamme
Bornem
Reet
Lier
Olen
Mariekerke
Mechelen
Hulshout
Gent
Donkmeer
Keerbergen
Berlare
Dendermonde
Demer
Sint-Martens-Latem
Schelde
A 1 - E 19
Diest
A 14 - E 17
Astene
A 10 - E 40
Aalst
Elewijt
Kruishoutem
R 0
Nossegem
Waregem
Leuven
Ninove
Heverlee
Escaut
Mater
BRUXELLES / BRUSSEL
Ronse
Mélin
Ellezelles
Genval
Wavre
Braine-l'Alleud
A 8
R 0
A 4 - E 411
Plancenoit
Court-St-Etienne
Leuze-en-Hainaut
Ecaussines-Lalaing
Noville-sur-Meha
Dendre
A 54
A 16 - E 42
Ligny
Baudour
A 15 - E 42
Meuse
Temploux
Lives-s
Namur
A 7 - E 19
Fosse-le-Ville
Wierde
Mons
Charleroi
Profondeville
A 2
Arbre
Blaregnies
Montigny
Crupet
Loverval
Sambre
Anhée
Dorinne
Nalinnes
Lisogne
Walcourt
Dinant
Sorinne
Solre-St-Géry
N 5
Falmignoul
Soumoy
Sautin
Meuse
FRANCE
Frasnes
Boussu-en-Fagne
Oignies-en-Thiérache
Vresse-sur-Semois

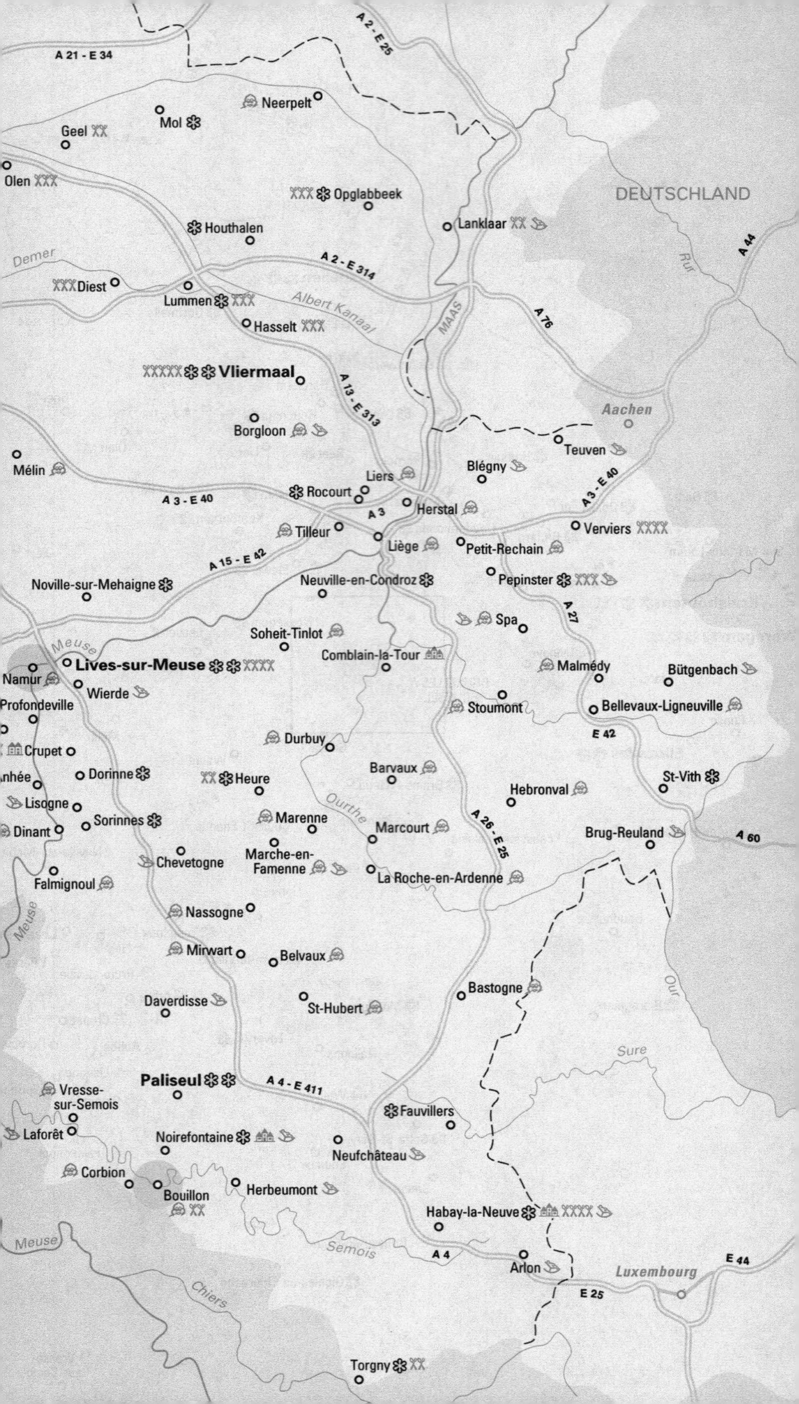
A 21 - E 34
A 2 - E 25
Neerpelt
Mol
Geel
Olen
Opglabbeek
DEUTSCHLAND
Houthalen
Lanklaar
A 44
Demer
Rur
A 2 - E 314
Diest
Lummen
Albert Kanaal
MAAS
A 76
Hasselt
Vliermaal
A 13 - E 313
Aachen
Borgloon
Teuven
Mélin
Blégny
Liers
Rocourt
A 3 - E 40
A 3 - E 40
A 3
Herstal
Tilleur
Verviers
Liège
Petit-Rechain
A 15 - E 42
Neuville-en-Condroz
Pepinster
Noville-sur-Mehaigne
A 27
Spa
Soheit-Tinlot
Meuse
Comblain-la-Tour
Lives-sur-Meuse
Malmédy
Bütgenbach
Namur
Wierde
Stoumont
Bellevaux-Ligneuville
Profondeville
E 42
Crupet
Durbuy
Barvaux
St-Vith
Dorinne
Heure
Hebronval
Lisogne
Ourthe
Marenne
A 26 - E 25
Sorinnes
Marcourt
Dinant
Brug-Reuland
A 60
Chevetogne
Marche-en-Famenne
Falmignoul
La Roche-en-Ardenne
Nassogne
Meuse
Mirwart
Belvaux
Our
Bastogne
Daverdisse
St-Hubert
Sure
Paliseul
A 4 - E 411
Vresse-sur-Semois
Fauvillers
Laforêt
Noirefontaine
Neufchâteau
Corbion
Bouillon
Herbeumont
Habay-la-Neuve
Meuse
Semois
A 4
Arlon
E 44
Luxembourg
E 25
Chiers
Torgny

AALBEKE *West-Vlaanderen* 533 E 18 *et* 716 C 3 – *voir à Kortrijk.*

AALST (ALOST) *9300 Oost-Vlaanderen* 533 J 17 *et* 716 F 3 – *76 382 h.*

Voir *Transept et chevet★, tabernacle★ de la collégiale St-Martin (Sint-Martinuskerk)* BY **A** – *Schepenhuis★* Y **B.**

Grote Markt 3 ✆ *0 53 73 22 70, aalst@toerismevlaanderen.be,* Fax 0 53 73 22 73.

Bruxelles *29* ④ – *Gent 33* ⑦ – *Antwerpen 52* ①

AALST

Street	Grid	No.
Albrechtlaan	AZ	2
Alfred Nichelsstraat	BZ	3
Burgemeesterspl.	BZ	5
Brusselsesteenweg	AZ	6
Dendermondsesteenweg	AZ	8
Dirk Martensstraat	BY	9
Esplanadepl.	BY	10
Esplanadestraat	BY	12
Frits de Wolfkaai	BY	13
Gentsesteenweg	AZ	15
Geraardsbergsestraat	AZ	16
De Gheeststraat	BZ	17
Graanmarkt	BY	19
Grote Markt	BY	20
Heilig Hartlaan	AZ	21
Houtmarkt	BZ	23
Josse Ringoirkaai	BY	24
Kapellestraat	BY	25
Kattestraat	BY	
Korte Zoutstraat	BZ	26
Van Langenhovestraat	BZ	28
Lange Zoutstraat	BY	29
Leopoldlaan	AZ	30
Molendries	BY	31
Molenstraat	BY	32
Moorselbaan	AZ	33
Moutstraat	BY	34
Nieuwstraat	BY	
Priester Daensplein	BY	35
Schoolstraat	BY	37
Vaartstraat	BY	38
Varkensmarkt	BY	39
Vlaanderenstraat	BY	41
Vredeplein	BY	42
Vrijheidstraat	BY	43
1 Meistraat	BY	45

Keizershof sans rest, Korte Nieuwstraat 15, ✆ 0 53 77 44 11, *info@keizershof-hotel.com, Fax 0 53 78 00 97,* – 25 à 100. AE VISA. BY x

71 ch ☐ 145/205.

◆ Un atrium lumineux, où s'étagent de belles plantes vertes, dessert les chambres de cet hôtel résolument moderne. Le petit-déjeuner se prend sous une agréable verrière.

◆ De kamers van dit moderne hotel komen uit op een atrium met groene planten, waar veel licht naar binnen valt. Het ontbijt wordt geserveerd onder een mooie glaskoepel.

Royal Astrid, Keizersplein 27, ✆ 0 53 66 66 06, *info@royalastrid.be, Fax 0 53 67 02 26,* – – 25 à 100. AE VISA. BY f

Repas *(fermé 15 juil.-8 août, sam. midi et dim.)* Lunch 30 – carte 40 à 63 – **14 ch** ☐ 77/114 – ½ P 90/139.

◆ Hôtel mettant à profit une ancienne maison de notable (1812) au bord d'une esplanade arborée. Chambres de bonne ampleur, pourvues d'un mobilier de style. Salle de restaurant classique où l'on vient faire des repas au goût du jour.

◆ Dit hotel is gevestigd in een herenhuis uit 1812 aan een esplanade met bomen. De kamers zijn goed van formaat en met stijlmeubelen ingericht. In de klassieke eetzaal worden eigentijdse gerechten geserveerd.

Station sans rest, A. Liénartstraat 14, ☎ 0 53 77 58 20, *bart-quintijn@proximedia.be, Fax 0 53 78 14 69*, – AE VISA. BY c
15 ch 64/83.
◆ À un jet de vapeur des quais de la gare, petite affaire au cachet bourgeois aménagée dans une demeure ancienne. La clientèle d'affaires y a ses habitudes.
◆ Klein hotel in een fraai patriciërshuis in de buurt van het station. Zeer geliefd bij zakenlui vanwege zijn gunstige ligging en bourgeoischachet.

Ibis, Villalaan 1, ☎ 0 53 71 18 19, *h3155@accor-hotels.com, Fax 0 53 71 07 11* – 25 à 120. AE VISA A b
Repas *(fermé sam., dim. et jours fériés)* (ouvert jusqu'à 23 h) Lunch 17 – carte 26 à 39 – 9 – **76 ch** 75 – ½ P 63/101.
◆ Établissement de chaîne hôtelière nouvellement implanté au Sud de la Ville, dans le voisinage de l'autoroute. Chambres fonctionnelles conformes aux standards de l'enseigne.
◆ Dit hotel is onlangs geopend aan de zuidkant van de stad, vlak bij de snelweg. De kamers zijn functioneel en voldoen aan de normen van de Ibisketen.

't Overhamme, Brusselsesteenweg 163 (par ③ : 3 km sur N 9), ☎ 0 53 77 85 99, *overhamme@skynet.be, Fax 0 53 78 70 94*, – AE VISA.
fermé 1 sem. Pâques, 15 juil.-15 août, sam. midi, dim. soir et lundi – **Repas** Lunch 36 – 52/82 bc.
◆ Demeure agrémentée d'un jardin et d'une terrasse. Cuisine créative et élaborée. Cave cosmopolite. L'intimité des lieux plaira aux couples romantiques comme aux businessmen.
◆ Dit pand heeft een tuin en een terras. Creatieve, verzorgde keuken. Kosmopolitische wijnkelder. De intieme sfeer zal zowel verliefde paartjes als zakenlui aanspreken.

Kelderman, Parklaan 4, ☎ 0 53 77 61 25, *Fax 0 53 78 68 05*, , Produits de la mer – AE VISA JCB. BZ e
fermé août, merc. et jeudi – **Repas** Lunch 38 – carte 43 à 115.
◆ Cette résidence cossue a plus d'un atout pour séduire : appétissantes recettes littorales, cave digne de Bacchus et Neptune réunis, belle terrasse estivale et jardin bichonné.
◆ Dit restaurant in een luxueus pand heeft heel wat te bieden : heerlijke visgerechten, mooie wijnkelder, zonnig terras en weelderige tuin.

La Tourbière, Albrechtlaan 15, ☎ 0 53 76 96 10, *restaurant.la.tourbiere@pandora.be, Fax 0 53 77 25 44*, – AE VISA A a
fermé du 22 au 26 fév., 15 août-6 sept., merc., sam. midi et dim. soir – **Repas** Lunch 28 – 57/105 bc.
◆ Jolie villa début 20e s. reconvertie en plaisante maison de bouche. Salle à manger d'esprit classique, claire et élégante. Carte alléchante, cave de même.
◆ Fraaie villa uit de vroege 20e eeuw die tot restaurant is verbouwd. De klassieke eetzaal is licht en elegant. Aantrekkelijke menukaart en lekkere wijnen.

't Soethout, Priester Daensplein 7, ☎ 0 53 77 88 33, *Fax 0 53 77 88 33*, – VISA BY n
fermé sem. carnaval, 2e quinz. août, mardi, merc. et sam. midi – **Repas** Lunch 25 – 36/75 bc.
◆ À l'ombre de la collégiale St.-Martinus, vous goûterez des plats relevés d'un zeste d'innovation plutôt heureux, dans un décor à l'audace non moins convaincante.
◆ Op een steenworp afstand van de St.-Martinuskerk staat een innovatieve chef-kok achter het fornuis. De inrichting van de eetzaal is al even gedurfd.

Borse van Amsterdam, Grote Markt 26, ☎ 0 53 21 15 81, *borsevanamsterdam@skynet.be, Fax 0 53 21 24 80*, , Taverne-rest – AE VISA BY b
fermé sem. carnaval, 11 août-2 sept., merc. soir, jeudi et dim. soir – **Repas** Lunch 10 – 28/38 bc.
◆ Taverne-restaurant de tradition établi dans un fier édifice (17e s.) typiquement flamand où se réunissait la chambre de rhétorique. Terrasse d'été à l'ombre des arcades.
◆ Traditioneel eethuis in een typisch Vlaams pand uit de 17e eeuw, waar vroeger de rederijkerskamer bijeenkwam. 's Zomers terras onder de arcaden.

Tang's Palace, Korte Zoutstraat 51, ☎ 0 53 78 77 77, *Fax 0 53 71 09 70*, Cuisine chinoise, ouvert jusqu'à 23 h – AE VISA. BZ h
Repas Lunch 10 – 22/40.
◆ Cet honorable "pavillon" de l'Empire du Milieu propose un bel éventail de saveurs dépaysantes. Le vin est le péché mignon du patron. Parking aisé.
◆ Dit paleisje uit het Chinese Rijk biedt een keur van Aziatische specialiteiten. De eigenaar heeft duidelijk een zwak voor wijnen. Groot parkeerterrein.

Grill Chipka, Molenstraat 45, ☎ 0 53 77 69 79, *grill.chipka@proximedia.be, Fax 0 53 77 69 79*, , Grillades – AE VISA. BY r
fermé carnaval, 1 sem. après Pâques, 15 août-début sept., sam. midi, dim. soir et lundi – **Repas** carte 32 à 53.
◆ Envie d'une belle côte à l'os ou de poisson grillé ? Le Chipka et ses portions "pantagrueliques" combleront vos petits creux. Dives bouteilles gouleyantes.
◆ Wie zin heeft in een sappige entrecote of vis van de grill wordt hier op zijn wenken bediend. De royale porties kunnen worden weggespoeld met een lekker wijntje.

à Erondegem *par ⑧ : 6 km* 🄲 *Erpe-Mere 19 043 h. – ✉ 9420 Erondegem :*

Host. Bovendael, Kuilstraat 1, ✆ 0 53 80 53 66, *info@bovendael.com, Fax 0 53 80 54 26,* – rest, – 25 à 40.
Repas *(fermé 2 sem. en juil., merc. et dim. soir)* (dîner seult sauf dim. et lundi) *Lunch 20* – carte 30 à 49 – **20 ch** 55/100 – ½ P 70/120.
◆ Près de l'église, aimable hôtel tenu en famille dont les chambres, assez simples et équipées de meubles fonctionnels, promettent des nuits sans histoire. Resto "couleur locale" où les vedettes du cyclisme ont leur rond de serviette.
◆ Dit vriendelijke familiehotel bij de kerk is eenvoudig, maar de kamers zijn rustig en praktisch ingericht. Hier zult u goed uitgerust weer uit de veren stappen ! Traditioneel restaurant waar wielervedetten klant aan huis zijn.

à Erpe *par ⑧ : 5,5 km* 🄲 *Erpe-Mere 19 043 h. – ✉ 9420 Erpe :*

Cottem, Molenstraat 13 (direction Lede), ✆ 0 53 80 43 90, *Fax 0 53 80 36 26,* ←, – *VISA*. – *fermé 1 sem. en fév., 3 sem. en juil., dim. soir, lundi soir et mardi* – **Repas** *Lunch 28* – carte 35 à 44.
◆ Une carte classico-traditionnelle vous sera soumise dans cette imposante villa dont la salle à manger s'ouvre sur un parc arboré et son étang où s'ébattent les cygnes.
◆ Restaurant in een imposante villa, waar klassieke gerechten op tafel worden gezet. De eetzaal kijkt uit op een grote tuin met bomen en een vijver met zwanen.

Het Kraainest, Kraainestraat 107 (Ouest : 2 km, direction Erondegem), ✆ 0 53 80 66 40, *Fax 0 53 80 66 38,* – – 25 à 50. *VISA*
fermé carnaval, du 15 au 31 août, lundi et mardi – **Repas** *Lunch 30* – 45.
◆ Ce restaurant disposant de quelques tables sous véranda et d'une plaisante terrasse estivale a été aménagé dans une villa moderne entourée d'un jardin soigné.
◆ Dit restaurant in een moderne villa beschikt over enkele tafeltjes in de serre en een goed onderhouden tuin. 's Zomers kan op het terras worden gegeten.

AALTER *9880 Oost-Vlaanderen 533 F 16 et 716 D 2 – 18 607 h.*
Bruxelles 73 – Brugge 28 – Gent 24.

Memling, Markt 11, ✆ 0 9 374 10 13, *Fax 0 9 374 70 72,* – . *VISA*.
fermé fin déc.-début janv. – **Repas** *(fermé mardi soir sauf en juil.-août et sam.) Lunch 10* – carte 22 à 39 – **17 ch** 60/80.
◆ Au centre-ville, établissement abritant des chambres confortables. La moitié d'entre elles se trouvent à l'annexe, quelques-unes disposent d'une kitchenette.
◆ Comfortabel hotel in het centrum. De helft van de kamers bevindt zich in de dependance en sommige zijn voorzien van een kitchenette.

Bacchus, Aalterweg 10 (Nord : 5,5 km sur N 44), ✆ 0 9 375 04 85, *brasserie-bacchus@mail.be, Fax 0 9 375 04 95,* – *VISA* – *fermé prem. sem. avril, 2 dern. sem. juil., vacances Noël, mardi soir, merc. et sam. midi* – **Repas** 37/62 bc, ♀.
◆ Restaurant officiant dans une ancienne ferme entourée de dépendances. Carte classique-actuelle et cave mondialiste effectivement digne de Bacchus. Belle terrasse.
◆ Restaurant in een oude boerderij met bijgebouwen. De kaart is klassiek-eigentijds en de wijnkelder met flessen uit de hele wereld doet Bacchus eer aan. Mooi terras.

à Lotenhulle *Sud : 3 km par N 409* 🄲 *Aalter – ✉ 9880 Lotenhulle :*

Den Ouwe Prins, Prinsenstraat 9, ✆ 0 9 374 46 66, *Fax 0 9 374 06 91,* – *VISA*. – *fermé du 1er au 18 juil., lundi et mardi* – **Repas** *Lunch 40 bc* – 50/70 bc.
◆ Un vaste jardin borde cette villa dont l'intérieur, intime, est décoré de tableaux et d'une collection de balances. Agréable salon invitant à prendre l'apéritif ou le café.
◆ Het interieur van deze villa met grote tuin is verfraaid met schilderijen en een collectie weegschalen. Prettige salon voor een aperitiefje of kopje koffie.

AARLEN *Luxembourg belge – voir Arlon.*

AARSCHOT *3200 Vlaams-Brabant 533 O 17 et 716 H 3 – 27 663 h.*
18 au Sud : 10 km à Sint-Joris-Winge, Leuvensesteenweg 252 ✆ 0 16 63 40 53, Fax 0 16 63 21 40.
Bruxelles 43 – Antwerpen 42 – Hasselt 41.

De Gouden Muts, Jan Van Ophemstraat 14, ✆ 0 16 56 26 08, *geert.ieven@belgacom.net, Fax 0 16 57 14 14,* – . *VISA*.
fermé du 2 au 25 août, 26 déc.-6 janv., mardi, merc. et sam. midi – **Repas** *Lunch 28* – carte 44 à 55, ♀.
◆ À deux pas de la collégiale Notre-Dame, discrète demeure ancienne fréquentée par nombre de "batteurs de pavés" (les habitants d'Aarschot). Terrasse sur l'arrière.
◆ Dit etablissement in een oud pand ligt vlak bij de O.-L.-Vrouwekerk en wordt vooral bezocht door "kasseistampers", d.w.z. de plaatselijke bevolking. Terras aan de achterkant.

BELGIQUE

De Geloofte, Begijnhof 19, ✆ 0 16 57 36 75, *rest.degelofte@pi.be, Fax 0 16 57 36 76* – ▤. MC VISA. ✂
fermé sem. carnaval, 2 dern. sem. août, merc. et dim. – **Repas** *Lunch 25* – 35.
◆ Table à dénicher au cœur d'un béguinage fondé au 13e s. Salle de restaurant contemporaine, assez sobre. Petite carte actuelle. Attention : nombre de couverts limité !
◆ Dit sober ingerichte restaurant staat midden in een begijnhof uit de 13e eeuw. Kleine kaart met hedendaagse gerechten. Let op : beperkt aantal couverts !

à Langdorp *Nord-Est : 3,5 km* C *Aarschot* – ✉ *3201 Langdorp* :

Gasthof Ter Venne, Diepvenstraat 2, ✆ 0 16 56 43 95, *info@tervenne.be, Fax 0 16 56 79 53* – ▤ P – 25 à 250. AE ⓓ MC VISA. ✂
fermé mardi, merc. et dim. soir – **Repas** *Lunch 28* – 40/90 bc.
◆ Les banqueteurs apprécient cette maison à toit de chaume "perdue" au milieu des bois. Salle à manger rustico-bourgeoise avec poutres et murs de briques. Beau jardin d'hiver.
◆ In dit huis met rieten dak in de bossen worden ook feestmalen georganiseerd. Rustieke eetzaal met houten balken en bakstenen muren. Mooie wintertuin.

AARTSELAAR *Antwerpen* 533 L 16 *et* 716 G 2 – *voir à Antwerpen, environs.*

AAT *Hainaut – voir Ath.*

ACHEL *Limburg* 533 R 15 *et* 716 J 2 – *voir à Hamont-Achel.*

ACHOUFFE *Luxembourg belge* 534 T 22 – *voir à Houffalize.*

AFSNEE *Oost-Vlaanderen* 533 H 16 – *voir à Gent, périphérie.*

ALBERTSTRAND *West-Vlaanderen* 533 E 14 *et* 716 C 1 – *voir à Knokke-Heist.*

ALLE *5550 Namur* C *Vresse-sur-Semois 2 847 h.* 534 O 23 *et* 716 H 6.
Bruxelles 163 – Bouillon 25 – Namur 104.

Host. Le Charme de la Semois, r. Liboichant 12, ✆ 0 61 50 80 70, *contact@charmedelasemois.be, Fax 0 61 50 80 75*, ←, ☂, ⛱ – TV P – 40. AE MC VISA
Repas *(fermé mardi et merc. sauf en juil.-août) Lunch 33* – 40/52, ♀ – **21 ch** ☕ 60/85 – ½ P 60/68.
◆ Une rénovation totale a propulsé cette hostellerie familiale du bord de Semois parmi les meilleurs lieux de séjour dans la région. Chambres spacieuses et de bon confort. Salle à manger affichant un petit air "cottage". Vue sur la rivière depuis votre table.
◆ Dankzij een grondige verbouwing is dit familiehotel aan de oevers van de Semois nu een van de beste van de streek. De kamers zijn ruim en comfortabel. De eetzaal kijkt uit op de rivier en ademt de sfeer van een Engelse cottage.

Aub. d'Alle, r. Liboichant 46, ✆ 0 61 50 03 57, *contact@aubergedalle.be, Fax 0 61 50 00 66*, ☂, ⛱, 🚲 – TV P – 25. AE ⓓ MC VISA. ✂
avril-déc. et week-end ; fermé janv. et dern. sem. de chaque mois sauf en juil.-août – **Repas** *Lunch 23* – 35/58, ♀ – **13 ch** ☕ 61/103 – ½ P 74/85.
◆ Auberge en pierres du pays où vous serez logés dans de menues chambres d'esprit ardennais ou dans l'un des studios répartis à l'annexe. Bar de style "stube". Goûteuses préparations servies dans un cadre bourgeois ou sur la terrasse d'été.
◆ Deze herberg beschikt over kleine kamers in Ardense sfeer en over een dependance met twee studio's. Bar in de stijl van een "stube". In de eetzaal met typisch bourgeoisdecor of 's zomers op het terras kunt u genieten van een smakelijke maaltijd.

Host. Fief de Liboichant, r. Liboichant 44, ✆ 0 61 50 80 30, *mail.to@lefiefdeliboichant.be, Fax 0 61 50 14 87*, ☂, ⛱ – ⇅ TV P – 30. AE MC VISA. ✂ rest
avril-5 janv. et week-end ; fermé 5 janv.-8 fév. – **Repas** *(fermé après 20 h 30) Lunch 25* – carte 31 à 42 – **25 ch** ☕ 60/85 – ½ P 68/72.
◆ En bord de Semois, adossée à une futaie, auberge de style régional dont la façade s'égaye d'une verrière. Chambres sans reproche et jardin tranquille sur l'arrière. Salle à manger de style classique-bourgeois révélateur du genre de cuisine que l'on y sert.
◆ Herberg met serre in regionale stijl aan de oever van de Semois, bij een woud met hoogstammige bomen. Onberispelijke kamers en rustige tuin aan de achterkant. Eetzaal in klassiek-traditionele stijl, die goed past bij de manier van koken.

ALOST *Oost-Vlaanderen – voir Aalst.*

ALSEMBERG *Vlaams-Brabant* 533 K 18 *et* 716 G 3 – *voir à Bruxelles, environs.*

AMAY *4540 Liège* 533 Q 19, 534 Q 19 *et* 716 I 4 – *13 065 h.*
Voir *Chasse★ et sarcophage mérovingien★ dans la Collégiale St-Georges.*
Bruxelles 95 – Liège 25 – Huy 8 – Namur 40.

XX **Jean-Claude Darquenne,** r. Trois Sœurs 14a (Nord : 3,5 km par N 614), ☎ 0 85 31 60 67, *Fax 0 85 31 36 96,* – P. VISA
fermé 18 août-18 sept., 22 déc.-2 janv., dim. soir, lundi et jeudi soir – **Repas** Lunch 40 – carte 58 à 78.
◆ Bungalow agrémenté d'une charmante terrasse-véranda de style Louisiane donnant sur un pimpant jardinet. Cuisine soignée voguant au gré de la marée.
◆ Bungalow met een mooi terras annex serre in Louisianastijl, dat uitkijkt op een goed onderhouden tuintje. Verzorgde keuken die meedeint met de golven van de zee.

AMBLÈVE (Vallée de l') ★★ *Liège* 533 U 20, 534 U 20 *et* 716 K 4 *G. Belgique-Luxembourg.*

AMEL (AMBLÈVE) *4770 Liège* 533 W 20, 534 W 20 *et* 716 L 4 – *5 119 h.*
Bruxelles 174 – Liège 78 – Malmédy 21 – Luxembourg 96.

XX **Kreusch** avec ch, Auf dem Kamp 179, ☎ 0 80 34 80 50, *hotel.kreusch@swing.be, Fax 0 80 34 03 69,* – TV P – 25 à 80. VISA.
fermé 2 prem. sem. juil., dim. soir hors saison et lundi – **Repas** Lunch 25 – 29/40 – 10 – **12 ch** 44/70 – ½ P 61/76.
◆ Au milieu du village, juste à côté de l'église, hostellerie traditionnelle fondée en 1854 par les aïeux des patrons actuels. Le gîte et le couvert dans un cadre bourgeois.
◆ Deze traditionele herberg midden in het dorp bij de kerk werd in 1854 gebouwd door de voorouders van de huidige eigenaren. Hier kunt u ouderwets goed eten en slapen.

ANDERLECHT *Région de Bruxelles-Capitale* 533 K 17 *et* 716 F 3 – *voir à Bruxelles.*

ANGLEUR *Liège* 533 S 19 *et* 534 S 19 – *voir à Liège, périphérie.*

ANHÉE *5537 Namur* 533 O 21, 534 O 21 *et* 716 H 5 – *6 798 h.*
Env. *à l'Ouest : Vallée de la Molignée★.*
Bruxelles 85 – Namur 24 – Charleroi 51 – Dinant 7.

Les Jardins de la Molignée, rte de la Molignée 1, ☎ 0 82 61 33 75, *reception@jardins.molignee.com, Fax 0 82 61 13 72,* – ch, TV P – 25 à 120. AE VISA
Repas *(fermé du 2 au 12 fév.)* (avec grillades) Lunch 14 – 25/35 bc – 9 – **28 ch** 62/68, – 2 suites – ½ P 63.
◆ Hôtel au confort moderne adossé à une forge du 17e s. bâtie en pierres du pays. Six salles de séminaires. L'ensemble borde un parc où s'écoule la Molignée. Ample salle à manger actuelle garnie d'un mobilier en rotin.
◆ Dit hotel naast een 17e-eeuwse smederij is heel geriefelijk en beschikt over zes congreszalen. Het restaurant is eigentijds ingericht met rotanmeubelen. Het complex kijkt uit op een grote tuin, waar de Molignée doorheen stroomt.

XXX **Host. Henrotte - Au Vachter** avec ch, chaussée de Namur 140, ☎ 0 82 61 13 14, *hotelvachter@skynet.be, Fax 0 82 61 28 58,* – TV P – 25. AE VISA. ch
fermé 15 déc.-13 fév. – **Repas** *(fermé dim. soir et lundi)* Lunch 36 – 44 bc/50, – **8 ch** 84/100 – ½ P 80.
◆ Cette belle auberge dont le jardin dévale vers la Meuse est estimée pour son hospitalité autant que pour la qualité de ses menus. Vue fluviale en terrasse. Sobres chambres.
◆ Mooie herberg met een tuin die zich tot aan de Maas uitstrekt. Gastvrij onthaal en eersteklas menu's. Terras met uitzicht op de rivier. Sobere kamers.

ANS *Liège* 533 S 19, 534 S 19 *et* 716 J 4 – *voir à Liège, environs.*

ANSEREMME *Namur* 533 O 21, 534 O 21 *et* 716 H 5 – *voir à Dinant.*

ANTWERPEN – ANVERS

2000 **P** 533 L 15 *et* 716 G 2 – *448 709 h.*

Bruxelles 48 ⑩ – Amsterdam 159 ④ – Luxembourg 261 ⑨ – Rotterdam 103 ④.

OFFICES DE TOURISME

Grote Markt 13 ☎ 0 3 232 01 03, visit@antwerpen.be, Fax 0 3 231 19 37 – Fédération provinciale de tourisme, Koningin Elisabethlei 16 ✉ 2018 ☎ 0 3 240 63 73, info@tpa.be, Fax 0 3 240 63 83.

RENSEIGNEMENTS PRATIQUES

18 9 *par ② : 15,5 km à Kapellen, G. Capiaulei 2 ☎ 0 3 666 84 56, Fax 0 3 666 44 37*

18 *par ⑩ : 10 km à Aartselaar, Kasteel Cleydael, Cleydaellaan 36 ☎ 0 3 887 00 79, Fax 0 3 887 00 15*

18 9 *par ⑥ : 10 km à Wommelgem, Uilenbaan 15 ☎ 0 3 355 14 30, Fax 0 3 355 14 35*

18 9 *par ⑥ : 13 km par N 116 à Broechem, Kasteel Bossenstein, Moor 16 ☎ 0 3 485 64 46, Fax 0 3 425 78 41*

9 *par ② et ③ : 11 km à Brasschaat, Miksebaan 248 ☎ 0 3 653 10 84, Fax 0 3 651 37 20*

9 *par ⑨ : 9 km à Edegem, Drie Eikenstraat 510 ☎ 0 3 228 51 10, Fax 03 288 51 07*

18 9 *par ⑤ : 13 km à 's Gravenwezel, St-Jobsteenweg 120 ☎ 0 3 380 12 80, Fax 0 3 384 29 33*

CURIOSITÉS

Voir *Autour de la Grand-Place et de la Cathédrale★★★ : Grand-Place★ (Grote Markt)* FY, *Vlaaikensgang★* FY, *Cathédrale★★★ et sa tour★★★* FY, *Maison des Bouchers★ (Vleeshuis) : instruments de musique★* FY **D** – *Maison de Rubens★★ (Rubenshuis)* GZ – *Intérieur★ de l'église St-Jacques* GY – *Place Hendrik Conscience★* GY – *Église St-Charles-Borromée★ (St-Carolus Borromeuskerk)* GY – *Intérieur★★ de l'Église St-Paul (St-Pauluskerk)* FY – *Jardin zoologique★★ (Dierentuin)* DEU – *Quartier Zurenborg★★* EV – *Le port (Haven)* ⛴ FY.

Musées : *de la Marine « Steen »★ (Nationaal Scheepvaartmuseum)* FY – *d'Etnographie★★ (Etnografisch museum)* FY **M¹** – *Plantin-Moretus★★★* FZ – *Mayer van den Bergh★★ : Margot l'enragée★★ (De Dulle Griet)* GZ – *Maison Rockox★ (Rockoxhuis)* GY **M⁴** – *Royal des Beaux-Arts★★★ (Koninklijk Museum voor Schone Kunsten)* CV **M⁵** – *de la Photographie★ (Museum voor Fotografie)* CV **M⁶** – *de la Sculpture en plein air Middelheim★ (Openluchtmuseum voor Beeldhouwkunst)* BS – *Provinciaal Museum Sterckshof - Zilvercentrum★* BR **M¹⁰** – *de la Mode★★ (Modemuseum)* FZ – *du Diamant★ (Diamantmuseum)* DEU **M⁸**.

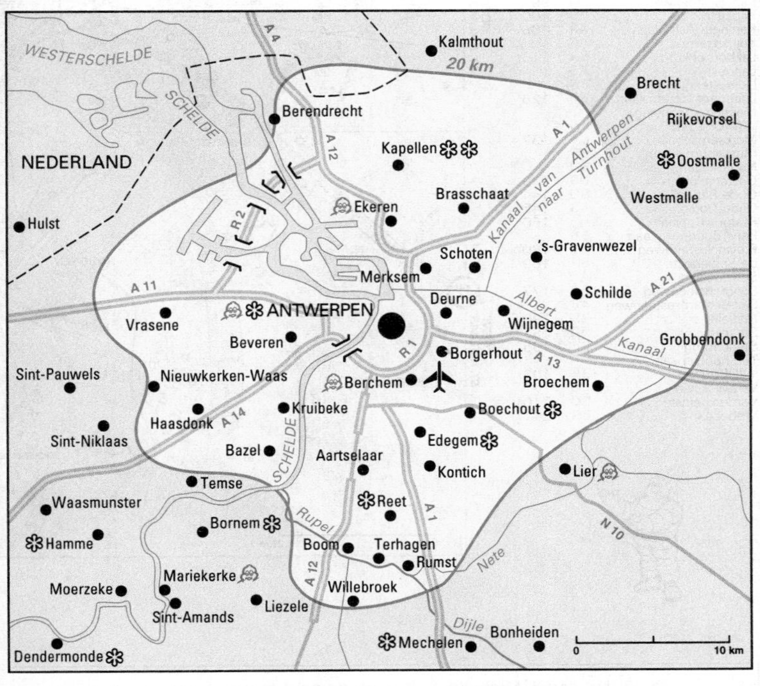

BELGIQUE

ANTWERPEN

Street	Grid	No.
Antwerpsesteenweg	AS	
Antwerpsestr.	BS	7
Aug. van de Wielelei	BR	9
Autolei	BR	10
Beatrijslaan	BR	
Berkenlaan	BS	13
Bisschoppenhoflaan	BR	
Blancefloerlaan	AR	
Boomsesteenweg	BS	
Borsbeeksesteenweg	BS	
Bosuilbaan	BQ	18
Bredabaan	BQ	
de Bruynlaan	BS	28
Calesbergdreef	BQ	30
Charles de Costerlaan	ABR	
Churchilllaan	BQ	34
Delbekelaan	BQ	40
Deurnestr.	BS	42
Doornstraat	BS	
Drakenhoflaan	BS	45
Edegemsestr.	BS	46
Eethuisstr.	BQ	48
Elisabethlaan	BS	49
Frans Beirenslaan	BS	
Gallifortlei	BR	61
Gitschotellei	BS	
Groenenborgerlaan	BS	73
Groenendaallaan	BQ	75
Groot Hagelkruis	BQ	76
Grotesteenweg	BS	
Guido Gezellelaan	BS	78
Herentalsebaan	BR	
Horstebaan	BQ	
Hovestr.	BS	85
Ijzerlaan	BQ	87
Ing. Menneslaan	BQ	88
Jan van Rijswijcklaan	BS	93
Jeurissensstr.	BQ	94
Juul Moretuslei	BS	
Kapelsesteenweg	BQ	99
Kapelstr.	AS	100
Koningin Astridlaan	AR	108
Krijgsbaan	AR	
Lakborslei	BR	115
Langestr.	AS	
Liersesteenweg	BS	
Luitenant Lippenslaan	BR	126
Mechelsesteenweg (MORTSEL)	BS	
Merksemsebaan	BR	132
Mussenhœvelaan	BS	
Noorderlaan	BQ	
Oosterveldlaan	BS	139
Oude Barreellei	BQ	144
Oude Godstr.	BS	145
Pastoor Coplaan	AR	150
Prins Boudewijnlaan	BS	
Provinciesteenweg	BS	160
de Robianostr.	BS	169
Scheldelaan	AQ	
Schotensteenweg	BR	177
Sint-Bernardsesteenweg	ABS	
Statielei	BS	190
Statiestr.	AR	192
Stenenbrug	BR	195
Turnhoutsebaan (DEURNE)	BR	198
Veltwijcklaan	BQ	
Vordensteinstr.	BQ	210
Vredebaan	BS	211

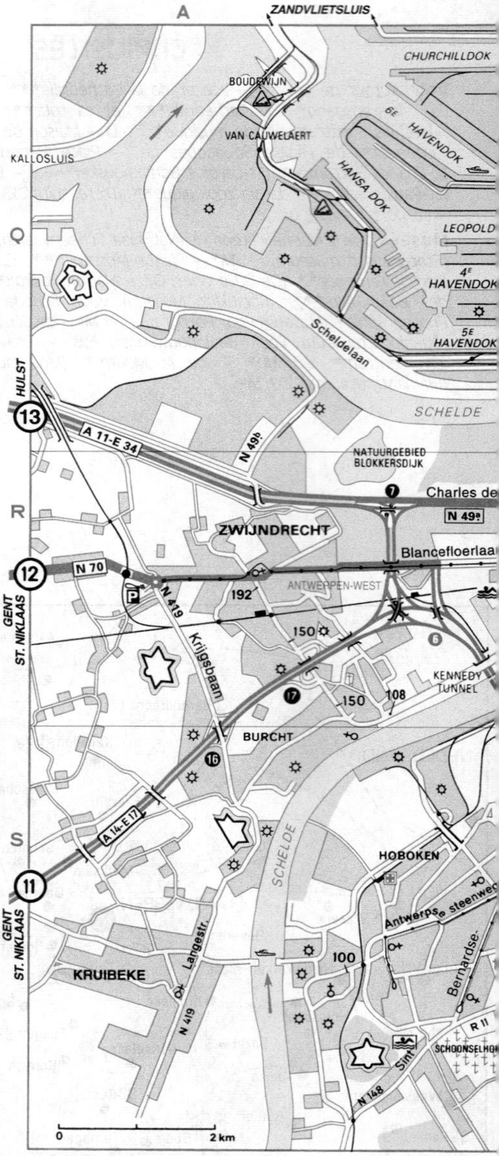

A
ZANDVLIETSLUIS
CHURCHILLDOK
BOUDEWIJN
VAN CAUWELAERT
6E HAVENDOK
HANSA DOK
KALLOSLUIS
LEOPOLD
4E HAVENDOK
5E HAVENDOK
Scheldelaan
Q
HULST
13
A 11-E 34
N 49b
SCHELDE
NATUURGEBIED BLOKKERSDIJK
7
Charles de
R
ZWIJNDRECHT
N 49a
Blancefloerlaa
12
N 70
N 419
ANTWERPEN-WEST
192
150
6
GENT ST. NIKLAAS
Krijgsbaan
17
150
108
KENNEDY TUNNEL
BURCHT
16
S
A 14-E 17
SCHELDE
HOBOKEN
11
Antwerpse steenweg
100
GENT ST. NIKLAAS
KRUIBEKE
Langestr.
N 419
Bernardse-
R 11
SCHOONSELHOF
Sint
N 148
0
2 km
A

Les **cartes Michelin** sont constamment tenues à jour.

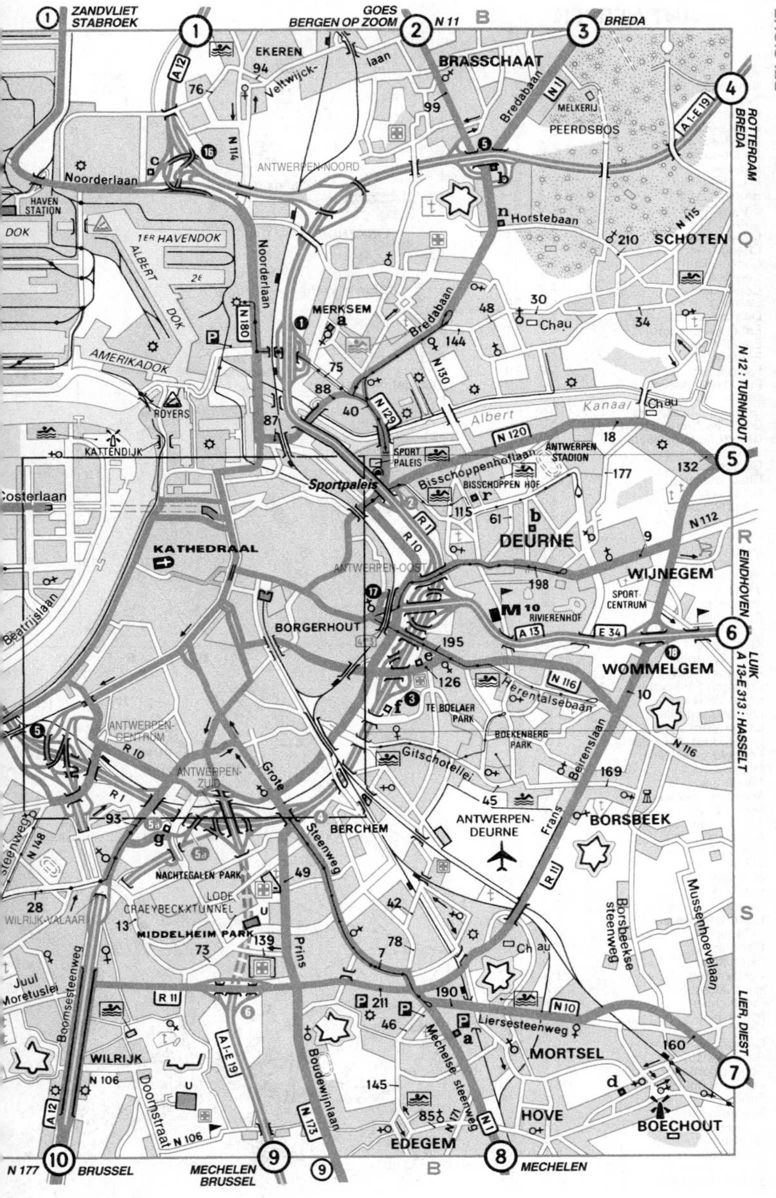
ZANDVLIET
STABROEK
GOES
BERGEN OP ZOOM
N 11
BREDA
ROTTERDAM
BREDA
EKEREN
BRASSCHAAT
Veltwijcklaan
Bredabaan
MELKERIJ
PEERDSBOS
Noorderlaan
ANTWERPEN-NOORD
HAVEN STATION
DOK
1ER HAVENDOK
ALBERT
DOK
Horstebaan
SCHOTEN
Noorderlaan
MERKSEM
Bredabaan
Chau
AMERIKADOK
ROYERS
Albert
Kanaal
Chau
N 12 : TURNHOUT
KATTENDIJK
SPORT PALEIS
ANTWERPEN STADION
Sportpaleis
Bisschoppenhoflaan
BISSCHOPPEN HOF
Oosterlaan
KATHEDRAAL
DEURNE
N 112
EINDHOVEN
WIJNEGEM
ANTWERPEN-OOST
SPORT-CENTRUM
RIVIERENHOF
BORGERHOUT
Beatrijslaan
WOMMELGEM
LUIK
A 13-E 313 : HASSELT
Herentalsebaan
TE BOELAER PARK
ANTWERPEN-CENTRUM
BOEKENBERG PARK
Gitschotellei
Beirenslaan
ANTWERPEN-ZUID
Grote Steenweg
BERCHEM
ANTWERPEN-DEURNE
Frans
BORSBEEK
NACHTEGALEN PARK
LODE
CRAEYBECKXTUNNEL
WILRIJK-VALAAR
MIDDELHEIM PARK
Prins
Borsbeekse steenweg
Mussenhoevelaan
Chau
Juul Moretuslei
Boomsesteenweg
Liersesteenweg
LIER, DIEST
Mechelse steenweg
MORTSEL
WILRIJK
Doornstraat
Boudewijnlaan
HOVE
BOECHOUT
EDEGEM
N 177
BRUSSEL
MECHELEN
BRUSSEL
MECHELEN

ANTWERPEN

Street	Grid	No.
van Aerdtstr.	DT	3
Amsterdamstr.	DT	4
Ankerrui	DT	6
Ballaerstr.	DV	12
Borsbeekbrug	EX	16
van Breestr.	DV	19
Brialmontlei	DV	21
Britselei	DV	22
Broederminstr.	CV	24
Brouwersvliet	DT	25
Brusselstr.	CV	27
Carnotstr.	EU	
Cassiersstr.	DT	31
Charlottalei	DV	33
Cockerillkaai	CV	36
Cogels-Osylei	EV	37
Cuperusstr.	EV	38
Dambruggestr.	ETU	39
Diksmuidelaan	EX	43
Emiel Banningstr.	CV	51
Emiel Vloorsstr.	CX	52
Erwtenstr.	ET	55
Falconplein	DT	58
Franklin Rooseveltpl.	DU	60
Gemeentestr.	DU	63
Gen. Armstrongweg	CX	64
Gen. van Merlenstraat	EV	65
Gerard Le Grellelaan	DX	66
de Gerlachekaai	CV	67
Gillisplaats	CV	69
Gitschotellei	EX	70
Graaf van Egmontstr.	CV	72
Haantjeslei	CDV	79
Halenstr.	ET	81
Hessenplein	DT	84
Jan de Voslei	CX	90
Jan van Gentstr.	CV	91
Jezusstr.	DU	96
Justitiestr.	DV	97
Kasteelpleinstr.	DV	102
de Keyserlei	DU	103
Kloosterstr.	CU	105
Kol. Silvertopstr.	CX	106
Koningin Astridplein	DEU	109
Koningin Elisabethlei	DX	110
Korte Winkelstr.	DTU	114
Lambermontplaats	CV	116
Lange Winkelstr.	DT	118
Leopold de Waelplein	CV	120
Leopold de Waelstr.	CV	121
Leysstr.	DU	123
Londenstr.	DT	124
Maria-Henriettalei	DV	125
Marnixplaats	CV	129
Mercatorstr.	DEV	130
Namenstr.	CV	133
van den Nestlei	EV	135
Offerandestr.	EU	136
Ommeganckstr.	EU	138
Orteliuskaai	DT	141
Osystr.	DU	142
Oude Leeuwenrui	DT	148
Pelikaanstr.	DU	151
Plantinkaai	CU	153
Ploegstr.	EU	154
Posthofbrug	EX	157
Prins Albertlei	DX	159
Provinciestr.	EUV	162
Pyckestr.	CX	163
Quellinstr.	DU	165
Quinten Matsijslei	DUV	166
Rolwagenstr.	EV	171
Schijnpoortweg	ET	174
van Schoonhovestr.	DEU	175
Simonsstr.	DEV	178
Sint-Bernardse steenweg	CX	180
Sint-Gummarusstr.	DT	181
Sint-Jansplein	DT	183
Sint-Jozefsstr.	DV	186
Sint-Michielskaai	CU	187
Turnhoutsebaan (BORGERHOUT)	EU	
Viaduct Dam	ET	202
Viséstraat	ET	204
Volksstraat	CV	207
Vondelstr.	DT	208
Waterloostraat	EV	210

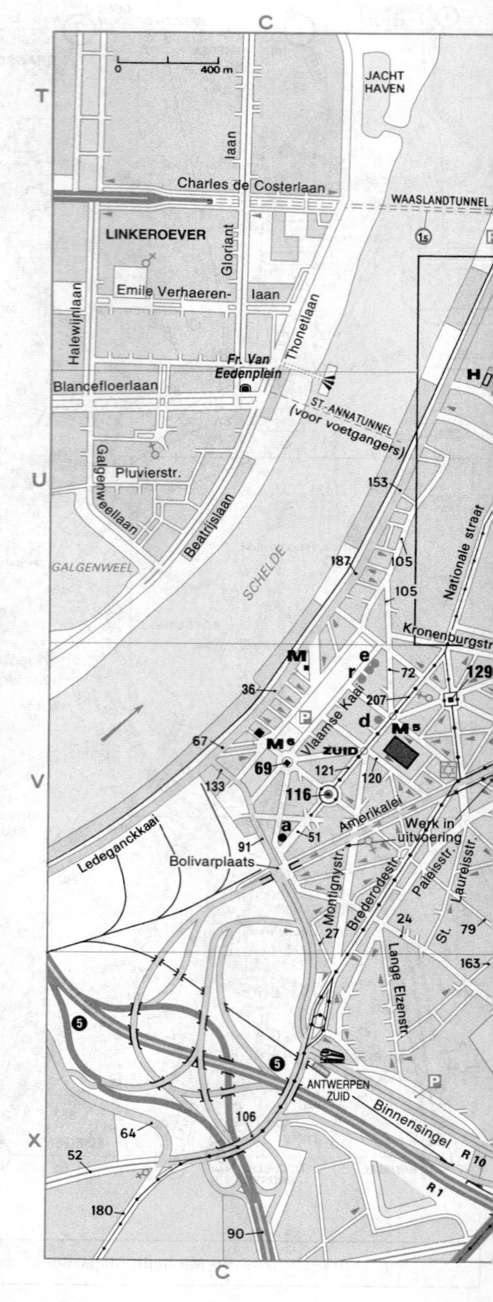

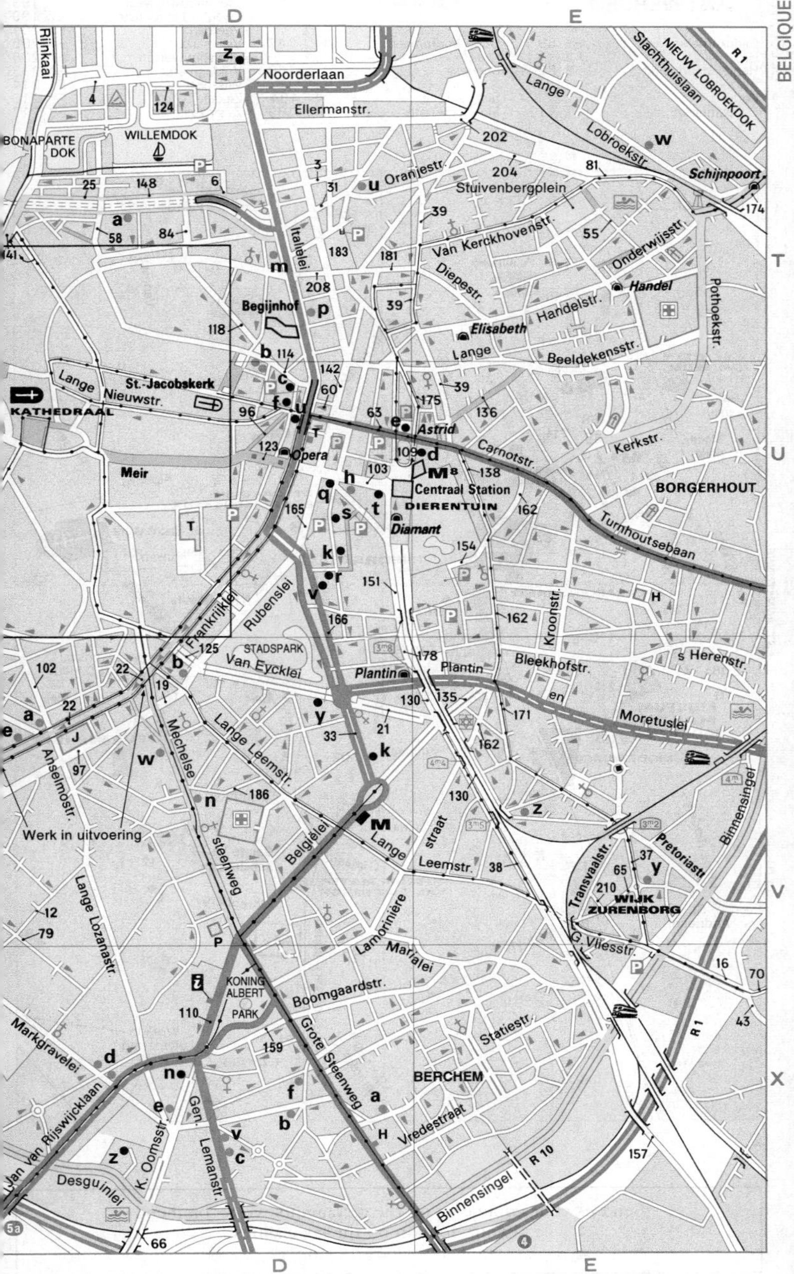

D
E
Rijnkaai
Noorderlaan
Ellermanstr.
WILLEMDOK
BONAPARTE DOK
NIEUW LOBROEKDOK
Slachthuislaan
Lange
Lobroekstr.
Schijnpoort
Oranjestr.
Stuivenbergplein
Van Kerckhovenstr.
Onderwijsstr.
Diepestr.
Handel
Handelstr.
Elisabeth
Lange
Beeldekensstr.
Pothoekstr.
Italiëlei
Begijnhof
St.-Jacobskerk
Lange Nieuwstr.
KATHEDRAAL
Meir
Opera
Astrid
Carnotstr.
Kerkstr.
BORGERHOUT
Centraal Station
DIERENTUIN
Diamant
Turnhoutsebaan
Rubenslei
Frankrijklei
STADSPARK
Van Eycklei
Plantin
Bleekhofstr.
s Herenstr.
Kroonstr.
Plantin en Moretuslei
Lange Leemstr.
Mechelse steenweg
Anselmostr.
Werk in uitvoering
Belgiëlei
Lange Leemstr.
straat
Lamorinière
Transvaalstr.
Pretoriastr.
WIJK ZURENBORG
Binnensingel
G. Vliesstr.
Lange Lozanastr.
Markgravelei
Marialei
KONING ALBERT PARK
Boomgaardstr.
Grote Steenweg
Statiestr.
BERCHEM
Vredestraat
Jan van Rijswijcklaan
K. Oomsstr.
Gen. Lemanstr.
Desguinlei
Binnensingel
R 10
R 1
T
U
V
X

ANTWERPEN

Gildekamerstr. .... FY 68
Groenplaats .... FZ
Handschoenmarkt ...... FY 82
Klapdorp .... GY
Korte Gasthuisstr. .... GZ 112
Maria Pijpelinckxstr. ...... GZ 127
Meir .... GZ
Nationalestr. .... FZ
Oude Koornmarkt ...... FYZ 147
Paardenmarkt .... GY
Repenstr. .... FY 168
Schoenmarkt .... FZ
Sint-Jansvliet .... FZ 184
Sint-Rochusstr. .... FZ 189
Steenhouwersvest ...... FZ 193
Twaalf Maandenstr. ...... GZ 199
Veemarkt .... FY 201
Vlasmarkt .... FYZ 205
Vleeshouwersstr. .... FY 206
Vrijdagmarkt .... FZ 213
Wisselstr. .... FY 214
Zirkstr. .... FY 216
Zwartzusterstr. .... FY 217

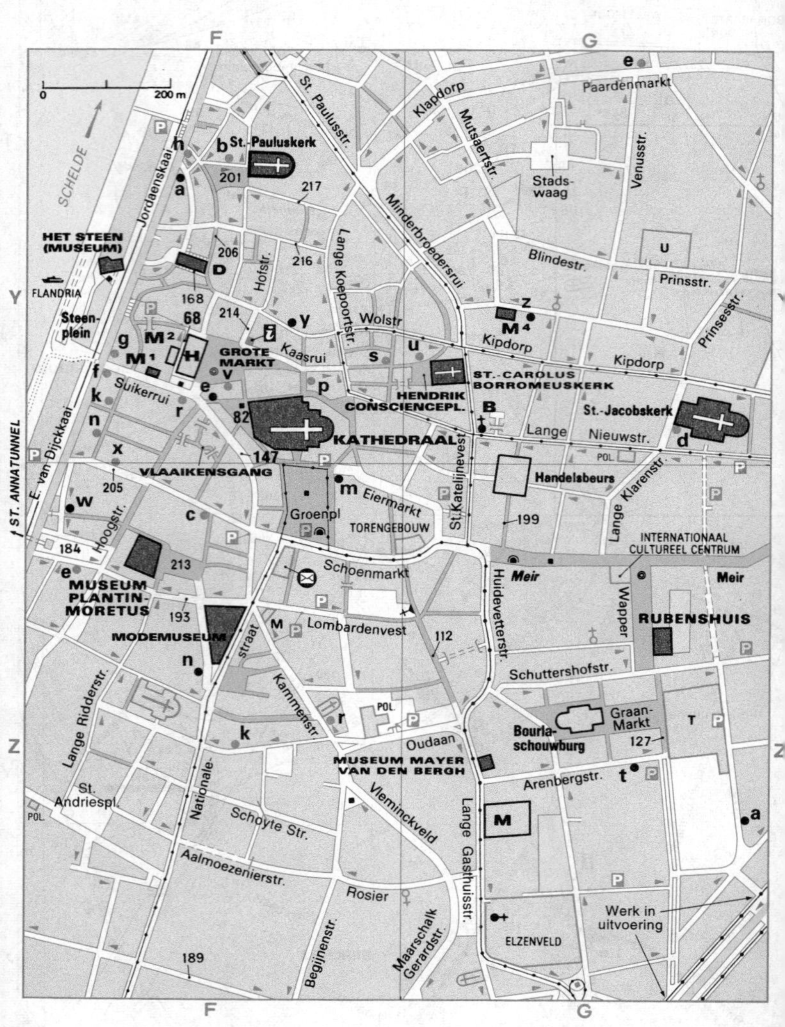

Send us your comments on the restaurants we recommend
and your opinion on the specialities
and local wines they offer.

Liste alphabétique des hôtels et restaurants
Alfabetische lijst van hotels en restaurants
Alphabetisches Hotel- und Restaurantverzeichnis
Alphabetical list of hotels and restaurants

RESTAURANT
HOTEL

Quartier Ancien - *plan p. 8 sauf indication spéciale :*

Hilton, Groenplaats, ✆ 0 3 204 12 12, *marc.depunt@hilton.com, Fax 0 3 204 12 13,* – |ǂ| – 30 à 1000. AE VISA JCB FZ m
Repas voir rest ***Het Vijfde Seizoen*** ci-après – 25 – **199 ch** 300/375, – 12 suites – ½ P 290.
• Hôtel de luxe dans un très bel immeuble début 20ᵉ s. : l'ancien Grand Bazar du Bon Marché. Vastes chambres très bien équipées. Agréables lounge et terrasse-véranda.
• Luxehotel in een prachtig gebouw uit het begin van de 20e eeuw : de voormalige Grand Bazar du Bon Marché. Zeer comfortabele, ruime kamers. Aangename lounge en overdekt terras.

De Witte Lelie sans rest, Keizerstraat 16, ✆ 0 3 226 19 66, *hotel@dewittelelie.be, Fax 0 3 234 00 19* – |ǂ|. AE VISA JCB GY z
fermé 28 déc.-10 janv. – **7 ch** 180/320, – 3 suites.
• Paisible et plein de charme, ce petit "grand hôtel" occupe un ensemble de maisons du 17ᵉ s. Chambres douillettes, décorées avec raffinement. Le patio invite à la détente.
• Dit kleine "grand hotel" is rustig en sfeervol en beslaat een aantal huizen uit de 17e eeuw. De kamers zijn behaaglijk en fraai gedecoreerd. De patio nodigt uit tot luieren.

Theater, Arenbergstraat 30, ✆ 0 3 203 54 10, *info@theater-hotel.be, Fax 0 3 233 88 58,* – |ǂ| – 25 à 50. AE VISA. GZ t
Repas *(fermé 19 juil.-17 août, sam. midi, dim. et jours fériés)* Lunch 16 – carte 32 à 42 – 20 – **122 ch** 130/235, – 5 suites – ½ P 89/142.
• Hôtel confortable et moderne, idéalement situé au cœur de la vieille ville, à deux pas du théâtre Bourla et de la maison Rubens. Chambres spacieuses aux tons chaleureux. À table, carte franco-méditerranéenne.
• Comfortabel en modern hotel, ideaal gelegen in het hart van de oude binnenstad, vlak bij de Bourla-schouwburg en het Rubenshuis. De kamers zijn ruim van formaat en in warme kleuren gehouden. Franse keuken met mediterrane invloeden.

't Sandt, Het Zand 17, ✆ 0 3 232 93 90, *info@hotel-sandt.be, Fax 0 3 232 56 13* – |ǂ| – 25 à 150. AE VISA JCB. FZ w
Repas *de kleine Zavel* Lunch 20 – carte 29 à 50, ♀ – **29 ch** 130/235, – 1 suite.
• Demeure du 19ᵉ s. dont la belle façade rococo contraste avec le décor intérieur, sobre et contemporain. Adorable jardin d'hiver à l'italienne. Chambres amples et élégantes. Bonne cuisine de bistrot à l'heure du repas.
• Mooi 19e-eeuws pand met een weelderig versierde rococogevel die contrasteert met het sobere, eigentijdse interieur. Prachtige wintertuin in Italiaanse stijl. Ruime, elegante kamers. Goede bistrokeuken.

Rubens sans rest, Oude Beurs 29, ✆ 0 3 222 48 48, *hotel.rubens@glo.be, Fax 0 3 225 19 40* – |ǂ|. AE VISA JCB. FY y
35 ch 170/230, – 1 suite.
• Tranquille et accueillante maison patricienne rénovée, toute proche de la Grand-Place et de la cathédrale. Certaines chambres donnent sur une cour intérieure fleurie en été.
• Rustig patriciërshuis dat pas is gerenoveerd, vlak bij de Grote Markt en de kathedraal. Sommige kamers kijken uit op een binnenplaats die 's zomers met bloemen is begroeid.

Villa Mozart, Handschoenmarkt 3, ✆ 0 3 231 30 31, *villa.mozart@wanadoo.be, Fax 0 3 231 56 85,* – |ǂ|. AE VISA JCB FY e
Repas (taverne-rest, ouvert jusqu'à 23 h) Lunch 19 – carte 25 à 42 – 13 – **25 ch** 99/148 – ½ P 64/89.
• Bien situé dans le centre animé, entre la Grand-Place et la cathédrale - visible depuis certaines chambres -, ce petit établissement est aussi pratique qu'agréable. Brasserie décorée à la mode d'aujourd'hui.
• Klein en aangenaam hotel, uitstekend gelegen in het centrum, tussen de Grote Markt en de kathedraal, waarop vanuit sommige kamers een blik te werpen is. De bijbehorende brasserie is eigentijds ingericht.

Antigone sans rest, Jordaenskaai 11, ✆ 0 3 231 66 77, *info@antigonehotel.be, Fax 0 3 231 37 74* – |ǂ| – 30. AE VISA JCB FY a
18 ch 75/95.
• Hôtel de confort simple mais très correct, dans une maison bourgeoise située sur les quais de l'Escaut, à deux pas du Steen Museum. Chambres personnalisées.
• Eenvoudig, maar prima hotel in een herenhuis op de kade langs de Schelde, een paar minuten lopen van het museum Het Steen. Alle kamers zijn verschillend.

Ibis sans rest, Meistraat 39 (Theaterplein), ✆ 0 3 231 88 30, *H1453@accor-hotels.com, Fax 0 3 234 29 21* – |ǂ| – 25 à 60. AE VISA GZ a
9 – **150 ch** 77/89.
• Proche de la maison Rubens et du Meir, axe commerçant, cet hôtel de chaîne où toutes les chambres sont identiques a été relooké dans le style actuel de l'enseigne Ibis.
• Ketenhotel met standaardkamers, die onlangs aan de nieuwe Ibis-look zijn aangepast. Gunstige ligging in de buurt van het Rubenshuis et de Meir, de belangrijkste winkelstraat.

BELGIQUE

Cammerpoorte sans rest, Nationalestraat 40, ✆ 0 3 231 97 36, *cammerpoorte@net4all.be*, *Fax 0 3 226 29 68* – AE ① ⓂⒸ VISA FZ n
– **39 ch** ☕ 75/90.

• Hôtel modeste mais fonctionnel, de fréquentation surtout touristique et familiale, situé à 200 m du musée Plantin-Moretus. Chambres sans fioriture et assez sombres.

• Eenvoudig, maar praktisch hotel, waar voornamelijk toeristen en gezinnen komen, op 200 m van het Museum Plantin-Moretus. Kamers zonder opsmuk en vrij somber.

XXX ✿ **'t Fornuis** (Segers), Reyndersstraat 24, ✆ 0 3 233 62 70, *Fax 0 3 233 99 03* – AE ① ⓂⒸ VISA. FZ c
fermé août, sam. et dim. – **Repas** (nombre de couverts limité - prévenir) carte 64 à 85, ♀.

• Dans une belle demeure du 17e s., table ambitieuse dont la carte, personnalisée, vous sera déclamée de façon théâtrale par un chef truculent. Intérieur rustico-bourgeois.

• Ambitieus restaurant in een mooi 17e-eeuws herenhuis met een rustiek interieur. De persoonlijke menukaart wordt door de kleurrijke chef-kok theatraal aan u voorgedragen.

Spéc. Aile de raie croustillante au beurre de moutarde en grains. Salade de poulet aux truffes. Sabayon au Champagne

XXX **Huis De Colvenier,** Sint-Antoniusstraat 8, ✆ 0 3 226 65 73, *info@colvenier.be*, *Fax 0 3 227 13 14*, – AE ① ⓂⒸ VISA FZ k
fermé sem. carnaval, août, sam. midi, dim. et lundi – **Repas** Lunch 50 – carte 65 à 80.

• Hôtel particulier fin 19e s. agrémenté de fresques murales et d'un jardin d'hiver. La cave à vins vous accueille à l'apéritif. Service prévenant.

• Patriciërshuis uit de late 19e eeuw met muurschilderingen en een wintertuin. Het aperitief wordt in de wijnkelder geschonken. Voorkomende bediening.

XXX **Het Vijfde Seizoen** - H. Hilton, Groenplaats, ✆ 0 3 204 12 12, *fb_antwerp@hilton.com*, *Fax 0 3 204 12 13* – AE ① ⓂⒸ VISA JCB FZ m
fermé 25 juil.-15 août, dim. et lundi – **Repas** Lunch 39 – 69, ♀.

• Ouvert sur l'animation du centre-ville grâce à une élégante verrière, ce restaurant de chaîne hôtelière est le point de rencontre idéal pour la clientèle d'affaires.

• Dit restaurant in het Hilton biedt dankzij de grote glaspui een kijkje op het levendige stadscentrum en is een geliefd trefpunt voor zakenmensen.

XXX **La Rade** 1er étage, E. Van Dijckkaai 8, ✆ 0 3 233 37 37, *larade@skynet.be*, *Fax 0 3 233 49 63* – AE ① ⓂⒸ VISA FY g
fermé du 12 au 17 avril, du 5 au 25 juil., sam. midi, dim. et jours fériés – **Repas** carte 34 à 47.

• Curieux restaurant établi dans une maison de notable du 19e s. On y découvre notamment un salon oriental, une coupole en mosaïque et un trône d'initiation maçonnique.

• Origineel restaurant in een 19e-eeuws herenhuis, met een Oosterse salon, mozaïekkoepel en inwijdingszetel voor de vrijmetselaarsloge.

XXX ✿ **De Kerselaar** (Michiels), Grote Pieter Potstraat 22, ✆ 0 3 233 59 69, *dekerselaar@pandora.be*, *Fax 0 3 233 11 49* – AE ① ⓂⒸ VISA JCB FY n
fermé 3 sem. en juil., sam. midi, dim., lundi midi et merc. midi – **Repas** Lunch 40 – carte 57 à 80.

• Les gourmets seront choyés dans cette maison familiale soigneusement décorée : cuisine française créative, carte bien conçue, captivant livre de cave et service stylé.

• Fijnproevers worden op hun wenken bediend in dit verzorgde restaurant : creatieve Franse keuken, evenwichtige menukaart, interessante wijnkelder en stijlvolle bediening.

Spéc. Tartare de thon et crevettes à la tomate confite. Marbré au foie d'oie, patta negra et canard. La corne de glace au chocolat blanc et fruits rouges

XX **'t Silveren Claverblat,** Grote Pieter Potstraat 16, ✆ 0 3 231 33 88, *Fax 0 3 231 31 46* – AE ① ⓂⒸ VISA. FY k
fermé mardi, merc. et sam. midi – **Repas** 35/70 bc.

• Jolie petite demeure dans le quartier ancien. Son enseigne, un trèfle à quatre feuilles en argent, vous portera bonheur. Carte classique, menu plébiscité et suggestions.

• Eetgelegenheid in een fraai pandje in de oude wijk. Het uithangbord, een zilveren klavertjevier, brengt geluk. Klassieke kaart met een aantrekkelijk menu.

XX **De Gulden Beer,** Grote Markt 14, ✆ 0 3 226 08 41, *Fax 0 3 232 52 09*, €, , Avec cuisine italienne – AE ① ⓂⒸ VISA. FY v
Repas Lunch 25 – 37/75.

• Cette vieille maison au beau pignon à redans se dresse sur la Grand-Place. Répertoire culinaire franco-italien mis en valeur par une cave prometteuse. Vue intéressante.

• Dit oude pand met zijn mooie trapgevel staat aan de Grote Markt. De wijnkelder is veelbelovend en een eerbewijs aan de Frans-Italiaanse keuken. Boeiend uitzicht.

XX **Het Nieuwe Palinghuis,** Sint-Jansvliet 14, ☎ 0 3 231 74 45, *hetnieuwepalinghuis@resto.be, Fax 0 3 231 50 53,* Produits de la mer – ▤. AE ⓓ ⓜ VISA. ✈ FZ e
fermé du 2 au 29 juin, 24 déc.-13 janv., lundi et mardi – **Repas** carte 39 à 75.
◆ L'anguille est chez elle dans cet établissement orienté "produits de la mer". Murs habillés de clichés nostalgiques du vieil Anvers. Bon choix de vins abordables.
◆ De paling voelt zich als een vis in het water in dit restaurant, waarvan de muren zijn behangen met oude foto's van Antwerpen. Ruime keuze aan goede en betaalbare wijnen.

XX **P. Preud'Homme,** Suikerrui 28, ☎ 0 3 233 42 00, *Fax 0 3 226 08 96,* ☂, Ouvert jusqu'à 23 h – ▤. AE ⓓ ⓜ VISA JCB. ✈ FY r
fermé 5 janv.-4 fév. – **Repas** Lunch 24 – carte 40 à 75, ♀.
◆ Demeure bourgeoise au décor contemporain, sobre mais plaisant, où se retrouve une clientèle touristique et locale. Carte complexe et variée. Moules à l'honneur en saison.
◆ Dit restaurant in een herenhuis is sober en modern ingericht en trekt zowel toeristen als Antwerpenaren. Op de zeer gevarieerde kaart staan onder meer mosselen.

XX **Neuze Neuze** 1er étage, Wijngaardstraat 19, ☎ 0 3 232 27 97, *neuzeneuze@pandora.be, Fax 0 3 225 27 38* – AE ⓓ ⓜ VISA JCB FY s
fermé du 5 au 25 août, du 25 au 29 déc., prem. sem. janv., sam. midi et dim. – **Repas** Lunch 25 – 50/76 bc.
◆ Adresse intime et accueillante où la clientèle d'affaires côtoie des couples romantiques. Salles séparées pour les banquets. L'assiette est généreuse et le service, stylé.
◆ In dit restaurant hangt een intieme sfeer die zowel geschikt is voor een zakenlunch als een romantisch diner. Aparte zalen voor partijen. Royale porties en correcte bediening.

XX **P'tit Vatelli,** Kammenstraat 75., ☎ 0 3 226 96 46, *Fax 0 3 226 96 46,* Ouvert jusqu'à 23 h – ▤. AE ⓓ ⓜ VISA FZ r
fermé dim. et lundi – **Repas** Lunch 22 – 45/62 bc.
◆ Derrière une menue façade de 1577, salle à manger actuelle plaisamment agencée, où habitués et visiteurs se retrouvent dans une ambiance cordiale. Cuisine d'aujourd'hui.
◆ Leuk opgezette eetzaal, achter een kleine gevel uit 1577, waar zowel de vaste als de bezoekende gast zich thuisvoelt. Vatelli zou de huidige receptuur wel waarderen !

X **Chez Raoul,** Vlasmarkt 21, ☎ 0 3 213 09 77, ☂ – ⓜ VISA. ✈ FYZ x
fermé Noël, Nouvel An, mardi et merc. – **Repas** Lunch 24 – carte 43 à 59.
◆ Trois jolies pièces où assouvir sa faim : salle ouverte sur la cuisine en rez-de-chaussée, petit boudoir au 1er étage et galerie d'art COBRA au 3e, pour plus d'intimité.
◆ Drie mooie vertrekken om fijn te tafelen : beneden een eetzaal met open keuken, op de eerste verdieping een kleinere ruimte en op de derde een kunstgalerij met intieme sfeer.

X **p. Zinc,** Veemarkt 9, ☎ 0 3 213 19 08, *philippe.grootaert@pandora.be, Fax 0 3 213 19 08,* ☂ – AE ⓜ VISA FY b
fermé 2e sem. vacances Pâques, 2e quinz. août, sam., dim. et jours fériés – **Repas** Lunch 22 – carte 45 à 75.
◆ Bistrot très convivial, avec ses petites tables serrées. Idéal pour les myopes : la carte est présentée sur ardoises géantes ! Cuisine simple mais savoureuse. Service avenant.
◆ Gezellige bistro met de tafeltjes dicht op elkaar. Ideaal voor bijzienden, want de kaart bestaat uit een reusachtig schoolbord ! Eenvoudig, maar lekker. Vriendelijke bediening.

X **Dock's Café,** Jordaenskaai 7, ☎ 0 3 226 63 30, *info@docks.be, Fax 0 3 226 65 72,* Brasserie-écailler, ouvert jusqu'à 23 h – ▤. AE ⓜ VISA. ✈ FY h
fermé sam. midi – **Repas** 28, ♀.
◆ Une vraie invitation au voyage que cette brasserie-écailler au décor futuriste d'esprit "paquebot". Salle à manger avec mezzanine et escalier néo-baroque. Réservation utile.
◆ Deze brasserie annex oesterbar heeft een futuristisch decor in de stijl van een passagiersschip. Eetzaal met tussenverdieping en neobaroktrap. Reserveren aanbevolen.

X **De Manie,** H. Conscienceplein 3, ☎ 0 3 232 64 38, *restaurant.demanie@pi.be, Fax 0 3 232 64 38* – AE ⓓ ⓜ VISA JCB GY u
fermé 15 août-2 sept., merc. et dim. soir – **Repas** Lunch 25 – carte 42 à 60, ♀.
◆ Sur une jolie placette jouxtant l'église St-Charles-Borromée, façade ancienne devancée d'une terrasse estivale. Salle à manger rustico-actuellle. Recettes de notre temps.
◆ Aan een mooi pleintje naast de St.-Carolus Borromeuskerk staat een oude gevel met daarvoor een zomers terras. Moderne eetzaal met rustieke accenten. Eigentijdse gerechten.

X **De Reddende Engel,** Torfbrug 3, ☎ 0 3 233 66 30, *Fax 0 3 233 73 79,* ☂ – AE ⓓ ⓜ VISA FY p
fermé 22 fév.-4 mars, 16 août-16 sept., mardi, merc. et sam. midi – **Repas** 24/31.
◆ Ambiance rustique dans une maison du 17e s. voisine de la cathédrale. Si le temps s'y prête, attablez-vous en terrasse. Accueil jovial et cuisine des régions de France.
◆ Rustieke ambiance in een 17e-eeuws pand bij de kathedraal. Franse streekgerechten en prima wijnkeuze voor een zacht prijsje.

BELGIQUE

Maritime, Suikerrui 4, ✆ 0 3 233 07 58, *restaurant.maritime@pandora.be, Fax 0 3 233 18 87,* – AE ⓓ ⓜ VISA JCB FY f
fermé juin, merc. et jeudi – **Repas** carte 35 à 78.
◆ Comme le suggère l'enseigne, les préparations sont gorgées d'iode. En saison, moules et anguilles, parmi les meilleures du coin. Beau choix en Bourgognes. Service prévenant.
◆ In dit visrestaurant worden lekkere mosselen en paling geserveerd. Mooie wijnkaart met bourgognes. Zeer voorkomende bediening.

Bernardin, Sint-Jacobsstraat 17, ✆ 0 3 213 07 00, *Fax 0 3 232 49 96,* – ⓜ VISA. GY d
fermé 1 sem. Pâques, 2 dern. sem. sept., fin déc., sam. midi, dim. et lundi – **Repas** Lunch 25 – carte 34 à 61.
◆ Sobre et contemporaine, la salle à manger contraste un peu d'avec la demeure du 17e s. qui l'abrite. L'été, repas en terrasse, à l'ombre du clocher de la St.-Jacobskerk.
◆ 17e-eeuws pand met een moderne, sobere eetzaal als contrast. 's Zomers worden de maaltijden op het terras geserveerd, in de schaduw van de klokkentoren van de St.-Jacobskerk.

Quartiers du Centre, Gare et Docks - *plans p. 6 et 7 sauf indication spéciale :*

Radisson SAS Park Lane, Van Eycklei 34, ✉ 2018, ✆ 0 3 285 85 85, *guest.antwerp@radissonsas.com, Fax 0 3 285 85 86,* – 25 à 600. AE ⓓ ⓜ VISA JCB. rest DV y
Repas *Longchamps* *(fermé dim.)* Lunch 30 – carte 38 à 55 – 23 – **163 ch** 176/220, – 14 suites – ½ P 96/141.
◆ Hôtel de luxe récent et bien situé sur un grand axe, à l'écart du centre-ville, en face d'un parc public. Clientèle d'affaires. Équipements et services très complets. Brasserie conjuguant cuisine internationale et saveurs du moment.
◆ Recentelijk gebouwd luxehotel, gunstig gelegen aan een grote verkeersader, tegenover een park. Clientèle van zakenmensen. Uitstekende voorzieningen en topservice. Restaurant met een internationale keuken die geheel voldoet aan de smaak van dit moment.

Astrid Park Plaza, Koningin Astridplein 7, ✉ 2018, ✆ 0 3 203 12 34, *appres@parkplazahotels.be, Fax 0 3 203 12 51,* – 25 à 500. AE ⓓ ⓜ VISA JCB. rest DEU e
Repas *(fermé dim.)* carte 28 à 43 – 20 – **225 ch** 220/285, – 3 suites.
◆ Bordant une place animée, à proximité de la gare centrale, ce nouvel hôtel-palace aux formes audacieuses occupe un site idéal. Belles chambres spacieuses et bien équipées. Recettes de notre temps servies dans une salle à manger lumineuse.
◆ Dit nieuwe luxehotel heeft een gewaagd ontwerp en is ideaal gelegen aan een druk plein, in de buurt van het Centraal Station. Mooie ruime kamers die modern zijn ingericht. In de lichte eetzaal worden eigentijdse gerechten geserveerd.

Carlton, Quinten Matsijslei 25, ✉ 2018, ✆ 0 3 231 15 15, *info@carltonhotel-antwerp.com, Fax 0 3 225 30 90* – – 25 à 100. AE ⓓ ⓜ VISA. rest DU v
Repas *(fermé 3 sem. en août et dim. soir)* (dîner seult) 42 – **127 ch** 189/320, – 1 suite.
◆ Confortable hôtel proche du centre diamantaire et d'un parc municipal. La plupart des chambres ont été rafraîchies. Belle vue aux étages supérieurs. Business center. Au restaurant, cuisine française et quelques plats d'inspiration flamande.
◆ Comfortabel hotel dicht bij de diamanthandelswijk en het Stadspark. De meeste kamers zijn onlangs opgeknapt. Mooi uitzicht vanaf de bovenste verdiepingen. Business center. In het restaurant worden Franse en Vlaamse gerechten geserveerd.

Alfa De Keyser sans rest, De Keyserlei 66, ✉ 2018, ✆ 0 3 206 74 60, *Fax 0 3 232 39 70,* – – 25 à 160. AE ⓓ ⓜ VISA DU t
20 – **120 ch** 130/180, – 3 suites.
◆ Avantageusement situé dans le centre animé, cet établissement d'accès aisé dispose de grandes chambres insonorisées, avec un bon équipement. Fréquentation d'affaires.
◆ Dit gunstig gelegen hotel in het centrum is gemakkelijk te bereiken. Grote, comfortabele kamers met goede geluidsisolatie. Veel mensen uit de zakenwereld.

Hyllit sans rest, De Keyserlei 28 (accès par Appelmansstraat), ✉ 2018, ✆ 0 3 202 68 00, *info@hyllithotel.be, Fax 0 3 202 68 90,* – – 25 à 120. AE ⓓ ⓜ VISA JCB. DU q
17 – **117 ch** 171/196, – 5 suites.
◆ Construction actuelle de type "flat-hôtel", judicieusement placée dans le centre-ville. Chambres et junior suites où l'on a vraiment ses aises. Clientèle d'affaires.
◆ Nieuwbouw van het type "flathotel", handig gelegen in het centrum. De kamers en junior suites zijn buitengewoon gerieflijk. Vooral populair bij zakenlieden.

Plaza sans rest, Charlottalei 49, ✉ 2018, ☎ 0 3 287 28 70, *book@plaza.be, Fax 0 3 287 28 71* – |‡| ⇆ ▤ TV ⇔ – 🎪 25. AE ◑ ◎ VISA. ✗ DV k
80 ch ☕ 150/175.
◆ Chaleur et cordialité pour cet hôtel de style à l'écart du centre. Vastes chambres cossues et personnalisées. Grand "lobby" à l'anglaise et bar victorien. Service bagages.
◆ Dit stijlvolle hotel even buiten het centrum heeft een warme sfeer. Ruime, luxueuze kamers met een persoonlijke toets. Grote lobby en bar in Victoriaanse stijl. Bagageservice.

Astoria sans rest, Korte Herentalsestraat 5, ✉ 2018, ☎ 0 3 227 31 30, *info@carltonhotel-antwerp.com, Fax 0 3 227 31 39,* ⚒ – |‡| ⇆ ▤ TV. AE ◑ ◎ VISA DU r
fermé 2 sem. en août et 2 sem. en déc. – **66 ch** ☕ 140/175.
◆ Hôtel avoisinant un parc municipal, un peu à l'écart de l'animation, non loin du quartier diamantaire. Façade et "lobby" en granit. Bonnes chambres avec équipement de base.
◆ Dit hotel ligt even buiten de drukte bij het Stadspark, niet ver van de diamanthandelswijk. Façade et lobby van graniet. Kamers met goede basisvoorzieningen.

Antverpia sans rest, Sint-Jacobsmarkt 85, ☎ 0 3 231 80 80, *antverpia@skynet.be, Fax 0 3 232 43 43* – |‡| TV ⇔. AE ◑ ◎ VISA. ✗ DU f
fermé 20 déc.-10 janv. – **18 ch** ☕ 97/175.
◆ Agréable petit hôtel du centre aménagé dans un immeuble étroit, près d'un grand carrefour. Belles chambres spacieuses et mobilier de qualité. Entretien et tenue impeccables.
◆ Prettig hotelletje in het centrum in een klein pand bij een groot kruispunt. Mooie, ruime kamers met meubilair van goede kwaliteit. Perfect onderhouden.

Alfa Empire sans rest, Appelmansstraat 31, ✉ 2018, ☎ 0 3 203 54 00, *info@empirehotel.be, Fax 0 3 233 40 60* – |‡| ⇆ ▤ TV. AE ◑ ◎ VISA DU s
☕ 15 – **70 ch** 135/155.
◆ Cet hôtel niché au cœur du quartier diamantaire dispose de grandes chambres dont les plus fringantes viennent d'être refaites de neuf. Garage fermé et surveillé.
◆ Dit hotel in het hart van de diamanthandelswijk beschikt over grote kamers, waarvan de mooiste onlangs geheel zijn verbouwd. Bewaakte parkeergarage.

NH Docklands Antwerp sans rest, Kempisch Dok Westkaai 84, ☎ 0 3 231 07 26, *nhdocklandsantwerp@nh-hotels.be, Fax 0 3 231 57 49* – |‡| ⇆ TV – 🎪 25. AE ◑ ◎ VISA. ✗ DT z
☕ 15 – **32 ch** 110/125.
◆ Façade en verre et aluminium, hall design et confortables chambres d'équipement standard avec mobilier moderne pour ce nouvel hôtel excentré construit devant le Kempisch Dok.
◆ Nieuw hotel buiten het centrum, bij het Kempisch Dok. Voorgevel van glas en aluminium, designhal en comfortabele kamers met standaardvoorzieningen en modern meubilair.

Colombus sans rest, Frankrijklei 4, ☎ 0 3 233 03 90, *colombushotel@skynet.be, Fax 0 3 226 09 46,* ⚒, ▢ – |‡| TV ⇔. AE ◑ ◎ VISA. ✗ DU u
32 ch ☕ 90.
◆ Cet hôtel du centre-ville occupe un immeuble à façade classique situé juste en face de l'Opéra. Chambres très bien insonorisées et communs de qualité avec décor recherché.
◆ Dit hotel in het centrum is gehuisvest in een gebouw met een klassieke gevel, tegenover de Opera. De kamers hebben mooie badkamers en een goede geluidsisolatie.

Eden sans rest, Lange Herentalsestraat 25, ✉ 2018, ☎ 0 3 233 06 08, *hotel.eden@skynet.be, Fax 0 3 233 12 28,* 🚲 – |‡| TV ⇔. AE ◑ ◎ VISA JCB DU k
66 ch ☕ 100/110.
◆ Hôtel simple mais bien tenu, bénéficiant d'une situation privilégiée en plein quartier diamantaire, tout près de la gare. Chambres progressivement rafraîchies.
◆ Eenvoudig, maar goed onderhouden hotel in het hart van de diamanthandelswijk, vlak bij het Centraal Station. De kamers worden stuk voor stuk gerenoveerd.

De Barbarie, Van Breestraat 4, ✉ 2018, ☎ 0 3 232 81 98, *Fax 0 3 231 26 78,* 🏠 – ▤. AE ◑ ◎ VISA JCB DV b
fermé vacances Pâques, 2 prem. sem. sept., vacances Noël, sam. midi, dim. et lundi – **Repas** Lunch 40 – carte 59 à 120.
◆ Une carte classico-créative avec spécialités de canard et un beau choix de vins vous attendent à cette adresse. Admirez la collection de pièces d'argenterie de table.
◆ Klassieke keuken die een creatieve geest verraadt, met eendspecialiteiten en een evenwichtige wijnkaart. Prachtige collectie tafelzilver.

La Luna, Italiëlei 177, ☎ 0 3 232 23 44, *info@laluna.be, Fax 0 3 232 24 41,* Cuisine de différentes nationalités, ouvert jusqu'à 23 h – ▤. AE ◑ ◎ VISA DT p
fermé du 13 au 19 avril, du 3 au 24 août, Noël-Nouvel An, sam. midi, dim. et lundi – **Repas** 29, ♀.
◆ L'ambiance brasserie américaine et l'inspiration cosmopolite de la carte attirent ici une jeune clientèle BCBG. Menu soigné à bon prix. Belle sélection vineuse.
◆ De Amerikaanse sfeer en kosmopolitische kaart van deze trendy stek trekken een chic publiek. Aantrekkelijk en vriendelijk geprijsd menu. Uitgelezen wijnkaart.

XX **de nieuwe HARMONY,** Mechelsesteenweg 169, ✉ 2018, ✆ 0 3 239 70 05, *acs.acs @tiscali.be, Fax 0 3 239 63 61* – ▤ P. AE ◑ MC VISA DV n
fermé du 1er au 16 mars, 19 juil.-10 août, lundi et sam. midi – **Repas** *Lunch 24* – 45/63 bc, ♀.
◆ Cet établissement installé dans une ancienne taverne rénovée fonctionne avec une carte au goût du jour. Menu business en semaine. Quelques vitraux ornent le plafond.
◆ Dit restaurant in een oude gerenoveerde taverne serveert eigentijdse gerechten. Business menu door de week. Mooi plafond met glas-in-loodramen.

XX **De Lepeleer,** Lange St-Annastraat 10, ✆ 0 3 225 19 31, *info@lepeleer.be, Fax 0 3 231 31 24,* 🏠 – ▤ P – 25 à 50. AE ◑ MC VISA DU b
fermé 21 juil.-18 août, sam. midi, dim. et jours fériés – **Repas** *Lunch 25* – 65/81 bc.
◆ Bel ensemble de petites maisonnettes situé le long d'une impasse pavée datant du 16e s. Cuisine classique servie dans une confortable salle à manger aux accents rustiques.
◆ Dit etablissement is gevestigd in een aantal huisjes in een geplaveid 16e-eeuws steegje. Comfortabele eetzaal met rustieke accenten. Klassieke keuken.

XX **'t Peerd,** Paardenmarkt 53, ✆ 0 3 231 98 25, *resto_t_peerd@yahoo.com, Fax 0 3 231 59 40,* 🏠 – ▤. AE ◑ MC VISA JCB plan p. 8 GY e
fermé 2 sem. Pâques, 2 sem. en oct., mardi et merc. – **Repas** *Lunch 35* – carte 40 à 71.
◆ À mi-chemin entre les docks et la cathédrale, agréable petit restaurant de caractère misant sur un registre culinaire traditionnel de bon aloi. Intéressante carte des vins.
◆ Dit sfeervolle restaurantje tussen de haven en de kathedraal serveert traditionele gerechten van goede kwaliteit. Interessante wijnkaart.

XX **De Zeste,** Lange Dijkstraat 36, ✉ 2060, ✆ 0 3 233 45 49, *dezeste@xs4all.be, Fax 0 3 232 34 18* – ▤. AE ◑ MC VISA DT u
fermé 2 sem. en juil., merc. soir et dim. – **Repas** *Lunch 60 bc* – carte 54 à 86.
◆ Table accueillante à dénicher hors du centre animé. Le chef y manie un répertoire classique assaisonné d'un zeste de nouveauté. Bon choix de vins. Réservation utile.
◆ Een prima adresje buiten de drukte van het centrum. De chef-kok mikt op het klassieke repertoire, maar wel met een vleugje vernieuwing. Goede wijnkaart. Reserveren aanbevolen.

XX **Dôme,** Grote Hondstraat 2, ✉ 2018, ✆ 0 3 239 90 03, *Fax 0 3 239 93 90* – ▤. AE ◑ MC VISA EV z
fermé 23 déc.-2 janv., lundi, mardi midi et sam. midi – **Repas** *Lunch 28* – carte 49 à 66, ♀.
◆ Maison du 19e s. qui abrita jadis un café. On s'attable dans une salle à manger de notre temps, sous une belle coupole baroque. Cuisine bien en phase avec l'époque.
◆ In dit 19e-eeuwse pand, dat vroeger een café was, wordt getafeld onder de mooie barokkoepel van de eetzaal, die verder eigentijds is. De keuken is eveneens van deze tijd.

X **Greens,** Mechelsesteenweg 76, ✉ 2018, ✆ 0 3 238 51 51, *Fax 0 3 238 58 18,* 🏠, Brasserie – AE ◑ MC VISA JCB DV w
fermé 2 prem. sem. mars, sam. midi et dim. – **Repas** *Lunch 21* – carte 30 à 59.
◆ Cette brasserie-écailler située entre le parc municipal et le parc Roi-Albert travaille avec une brève carte et un écriteau à suggestions. Terrasse ombragée à l'arrière.
◆ Deze brasserie annex oesterbar tussen het Stadspark en het Koning Albertpark heeft een vrij beknopte kaart. Lommerrijk terras aan de achterkant.

X **Casa Julián,** Italiëlei 32, ✆ 0 3 232 07 29, *Fax 0 3 233 09 53,* Cuisine espagnole – ▤. AE ◑ MC VISA. ✂ DT m
fermé mi-juil.-mi-août, lundi, mardi et sam. midi – **Repas** *Lunch 22 bc* – carte 28 à 36.
◆ Restaurant espagnol posté à mi-chemin entre la cathédrale et le quartier des docks. Carte fournie, avec quelques suggestions et d'authentiques spécialités ibériques.
◆ Spaans restaurant halverwege de kathedraal en de haven. Uitgebreide kaart met daarnaast enkele suggesties en authentieke Spaanse specialiteiten.

X **Pazzo,** Oude Leeuwenrui 12, ✆ 0 3 232 86 82, *pazzo@skynet.be, Fax 0 3 232 79 34,* Ouvert jusqu'à 23 h – ▤. AE ◑ MC VISA DT a
fermé 3 sem. en août, Noël, Nouvel An, sam., dim. et jours fériés – **Repas** *Lunch 19* – carte 30 à 46, ♀ 🍇.
◆ Installé près des docks dans un ancien entrepôt converti en brasserie contemporaine, ce restaurant animé propose une cuisine au goût du jour et de bons accords mets-vins.
◆ Deze drukke brasserie is ondergebracht in een oud pakhuis bij de haven. Eigentijdse gerechten, waarbij de geselecteerde wijnen perfect gezelschap zijn.

X **De Veehandel,** Lange Lobroekstraat 61 (face abattoirs), ✉ 2060, ✆ 0 3 271 06 06, *Fax 0 3 322 25 69,* 🏠 – ▤. AE ◑ MC VISA ET w
fermé sam. midi, dim. et jours fériés – **Repas** 30.
◆ Emplacement stratégique, face aux abattoirs, décor intérieur très "vache", atmosphère de bistrot de quartier et carte pour carnivores, comportant un menu deux couverts.
◆ Deze bistro is geknipt voor vleesliefhebbers, zoals blijkt uit de naam, de inrichting en de ligging tegenover het slachthuis. À la carte en een menu voor twee.

Rimini, Vestingstraat 5, ✉ 2018, ☎ 0 3 226 06 08, *Fax 0 3 232 49 89*, Avec cuisine italienne – ▤. AE MC VISA – *fermé 25 juil.-22 août et merc.* – **Repas** carte 23 à 49. DU h
◆ Proche de la gare et du quartier diamantaire, cette petite affaire familiale interprète un répertoire culinaire franco-transalpin. Choix à la carte et suggestions du jour.
◆ Klein familierestaurant in de buurt van het Centraal Station en de diamanthandelswijk Buiten de Frans-Italiaanse kaart zijn er dagelijks wisselende gerechten te verkrijgen.

Kuala Lumpur, Statiestraat 10, ✉ 2018, ☎ 0 3 225 14 33, *Fax 0 3 225 14 34*, Cuisine asiatique, ouvert jusqu'à minuit – ▤. AE D MC VISA JCB. DU d
fermé août et jeudi – **Repas** *Lunch 12* – carte 22 à 33.
◆ Table malaise du secteur animé de la gare. Carte alléchante annonçant une ribambelle de menus. Service avenant. Décor exotique. Les lumières brillent tard en soirée.
◆ Aziatisch eten in de buurt van het station. Aantrekkelijke kaart met een hele reeks menu's. Vriendelijke bediening en exotisch decor, waar de lichten pas 's avonds laat doven.

Yamayu Santatsu, Ossenmarkt 19, ☎ 0 3 234 09 49, *Fax 0 3 234 09 49*, Cuisine japonaise avec Sushi-bar – ▤. AE D MC VISA JCB DTU b
fermé 2 sem. en août, 25 déc.-5 janv., dim. midi et lundi – **Repas** *Lunch 12* – carte 36 à 47.
◆ Dans une maison ancienne postée à mi-distance de la cathédrale et de la gare centrale, agréable établissement japonais avec comptoir à sushis. Décor d'esprit nippon.
◆ Druk bezochte sushibar in een oud pand met een typisch Japanse inrichting, gunstig gelegen tussen de kathedraal en het Centraal Station.

Quartier Sud - *plans p. 6 et 7 sauf indication spéciale :*

Crowne Plaza, G. Legrellelaan 10, ✉ 2020, ☎ 0 3 259 75 00, *cpantwerp@ichotelsgroup.com, Fax 0 3 216 02 96*, – – ▤ TV P – 25 à 600. AE D MC VISA JCB plan p. 5 BS g
Repas ***Plaza One for two*** *Lunch 30* – carte 35 à 51 – 21 – **256 ch** 245/280, – 6 suites – ½ P 138/289.
◆ Hôtel international proche d'un échangeur autoroutier. Agréables chambres bien équipées, au décor actuel. Bonne infrastructure pour conférences et service à toute heure. Formule buffets au déjeuner.
◆ Internationaal hotel dat ideaal is gelegen langs de snelweg en veel zakenmensen trekt. Prettige kamers die aan de moderne eisen voldoen. Ook geschikt voor congressen. Doorlopende service en lunchbuffet.

Corinthia, Desguinlei 94, ✉ 2018, ☎ 0 3 244 82 11, *antwerp@corinthia.be, Fax 0 3 216 47 12*, – ▤ TV P – 25 à 590. AE D MC VISA. rest
Repas *(fermé sam. midi et dim.) Lunch 27* – carte 35 à 44, – 18 – **210 ch** 189/209, – 5 suites – ½ P 192/232.
◆ Cet hôtel de chaîne voisin du ring, de l'autoroute et de la gare du Midi dispose de chambres récemment rafraîchies. Sa façade en verre évoque un diamant.
◆ Dit ketenhotel nabij de Ring, de snelweg en station Zuid beschikt over kamers die onlangs zijn opgeknapt. De glazen voorgevel doet aan een diamant denken. DX z

Firean , Karel Oomsstraat 6, ✉ 2018, ☎ 0 3 237 02 60, *info@hotelfirean.com, Fax 0 3 238 11 68*, – ▤ TV . AE D MC VISA JCB DX n
fermé 27 juil.-20 août – **Repas** voir rest ***Minerva*** ci-après – **15 ch** 131/205.
◆ Paisible hôtel de charme avec jardin intérieur dans une construction Art déco jouxtant le parc Roi-Albert. Chambres au mobilier ancien et luxueux. Service non somnolent.
◆ Rustig en sfeervol hotel met binnentuin in een art-decogebouw bij het Koning Albertpark. Luxe kamers met antieke meubelen. Attent personeel dat dag en nacht voor u klaarstaat.

Industrie sans rest, Emiel Banningstraat 52, ☎ 0 3 238 66 00, *hotelindustrie@pandora.be, Fax 0 3 238 86 88* – TV . AE D MC VISA. CV a
13 ch 75/87.
◆ Ce petit établissement coquet occupe deux maisons de maître situées à proximité de deux beaux musées. Menues chambres bien équipées et légèrement personnalisées.
◆ Dit mooie hotel beslaat twee herenhuizen in de buurt van twee interessante musea. Kleine, maar praktische kamers met een persoonlijk karakter.

Loncin, Markgravelei 127, ✉ 2018, ☎ 0 3 248 29 89, *info@loncinrestaurant.be, Fax 0 3 248 38 66*, – ▤ P. AE D MC VISA DX d
fermé sam. midi et dim. – **Repas** *Lunch 35* – carte 46 à 155.
◆ Non loin du parc Roi-Albert, habitation bourgeoise au cadre élégant et discret. Choix classique avec menus et suggestions. Gibier en saison. Réservation nécessaire.
◆ Elegant restaurant in de buurt van het Koning Albertpark. Klassieke kaart met menu's en dagelijks wisselende gerechten. Wildschotels in het seizoen. Reserveren noodzakelijk.

Liang's Garden, Markgravelei 141, ✉ 2018, ☎ 0 3 237 22 22, *Fax 0 3 248 38 34*, Cuisine chinoise – ▤. AE D MC VISA DX d
fermé mi-juil.-mi-août et dim. – **Repas** *Lunch 24* – carte 29 à 54.
◆ L'un des plus vieux restaurants chinois d'Anvers, au décor immuable et typique, se cache près du parc Roi-Albert. Carte assez simple. Clientèle d'affaires et d'habitués.
◆ Een van de oudste Chinese restaurants van Antwerpen, met een typisch Aziatische inrichting, bij het Koning Albertpark. Vrij eenvoudige keuken, die veel vaste klanten trekt.

BELGIQUE

XX **Minerva** - H. Firean, Karel Oomsstraat 36, ✉ 2018, ℘ 0 3 216 00 55, *restaurantminerva@skynet.be, Fax 0 3 216 00 55* – ▤. AE ⓓ ⓜ VISA DX e
fermé fin juil.-20 août, 23 déc.-6 janv., dim. et lundi – **Repas** carte 44 à 75.
◆ Cette table au cadre actuel élégant s'est substituée à un garage dont la fosse reste intacte. Recettes classiques attrayantes et suggestions de saison. Parking aisé le soir.
◆ Dit actuele restaurant staat op de plaats van een garage, waarvan de werkkuil nog intact is. Klassieke, seizoengebonden keuken. 's Avonds ruim parkeergelegenheid.

XX **Kommilfoo,** Vlaamse Kaai 17, ℘ 0 3 237 30 00, *Fax 0 3 237 30 00* – ▤. AE ⓓ ⓜ VISA. ✻ CV e
fermé 2 prem. sem. juil., sam. midi, dim. et lundi – **Repas** *Lunch 30* – 45/70 bc.
◆ À deux pas de trois musées, devant un grand parking gratuit, ex-entrepôt devenu un restaurant "kommilfoo", au décor intérieur sobre et actuel. Carte bien dans l'air du temps.
◆ Dit voormalige pakhuis is nu een trendy restaurant op loopafstand van drie musea, tegenover een groot parkeerterrein (gratis). Sober, modern interieur en actuele menukaart.

XX **Het Gerecht,** Amerikalei 20, ℘ 0 3 248 79 28, *restaurant@hetgerecht.be, Fax 0 3 248 79 28,* 余 – AE ⓓ ⓜ VISA. ✻ DV e
fermé 2 sem. en sept., sam. midi, dim. et lundi – **Repas** *Lunch 21* – 40.
◆ Restaurant très honnête, comme le proclame son enseigne ("Le Tribunal"), en écho au palais de justice situé juste en face. Cuisine au goût du jour, assez soignée.
◆ De (dubbelzinnige) naam van dit restaurant verwijst naar het nabije Paleis van Justitie. Eerlijke keuken, hoe kan het ook anders met de rechterlijke macht aan de overkant !

X **Hippodroom,** Leopold de Waelplaats 10, ℘ 0 3 248 52 52, *resto@hippodroom.be, Fax 0 3 238 71 67,* 余, Ouvert jusqu'à 23 h 30 – AE ⓓ ⓜ VISA CV d
fermé dim. – **Repas** *Lunch 19* – carte 34 à 70.
◆ Le cadre d'une belle maison de maître, de savoureuses préparations, une petite cave intéressante : voici, dans l'ordre, le tiercé gagnant de ce restaurant "trendy".
◆ Het fraaie pand, de smakelijke gerechten en de kleine, maar interessante wijnkelder verklaren de razendsnelle opkomst van dit trendy restaurant.

X **River Kwai,** Vlaamse Kaai 14, ℘ 0 3 237 46 51, *kwai@pandora.be,* Cuisine thaïlandaise, ouvert jusqu'à 23 h – ▤. AE ⓜ VISA. ✻ CV r
fermé Noël-Nouvel An et merc. – **Repas** carte 28 à 51.
◆ Un salon colonial et d'authentiques saveurs thaïlandaises vous attendent ici. Belle carte avec suggestions. Attablez-vous en façade à l'étage pour profiter du panorama.
◆ Eetzaal in koloniale stijl, waar authentieke Thaise gerechten worden opgediend. Weids uitzicht vanaf de tafeltjes op de bovenverdieping, bij het raam aan de voorkant.

X **Bizzie-Lizzie,** Vlaamse Kaai 16, ℘ 0 3 238 61 97, *bizzielizzie@popmail.com, Fax 0 3 248 30 64,* Ouvert jusqu'à 23 h – 🛋 25. AE ⓓ ⓜ VISA CV e
fermé sam. midi et dim. – **Repas** *Lunch 22* – carte 24 à 43, ♀.
◆ Brasserie au décor moderne semé de touches rustiques : sol en damier, murs jaune toscan, fines poutres, brique nue, chaises campagnardes et peintures d'animaux de la ferme.
◆ Moderne bistro met rustieke accenten, zoals de tegelvloer, okergele muren, balken, ruwe bakstenen, landelijke stoelen en afbeeldingen van dieren op de boerderij.

X **Panna Cotta,** Kasteelpleinstraat 64, ℘ 0 3 237 07 86, *pannacotta@skynet.be, Fax 0 3 237 36 73,* Cuisine italienne – ⓜ VISA. ✻ DV a
fermé 2 dern. sem. juil., dim. et lundi – **Repas** *Lunch 19* – carte 30 à 47, ♀.
◆ Restaurant italien aménagé dans une ancienne boulangerie. Salle à manger design, blanche comme de la panna cotta. Recettes authentiques et cave transalpine bien montée.
◆ Italiaans restaurant in een oude bakkerij, waarvan de muren zo wit zijn als panna cotta. Authentieke recepten en lekkere Italiaanse wijnen.

Périphérie - *plans p. 4 et 5 sauf indication spéciale :*

au Nord – ✉ *2030 :*

🏨 **Novotel,** Luithagen-haven 6 (Haven 200), ℘ 0 3 542 03 20, *H0465@accor-hotels.com, Fax 0 3 541 70 93,* 余, ⛱, ✻, 🚲 – |♦| ⇆ ▤ 📺 🅿 – 🛋 25 à 180. AE ⓓ ⓜ VISA BQ c
Repas *Lunch 13* – carte 26 à 45 – ☕ 14 – **120 ch** 107 – ½ P 125/137.
◆ Cet hôtel de chaîne rénové situé au Nord-Est de la zone portuaire, à proximité d'une bretelle d'autoroute, borde un axe important le reliant directement au centre-ville.
◆ Dit onlangs gerenoveerde hotel ligt ten noordoosten van het havengebied, niet ver van de snelweg, aan een verkeersader die rechtstreeks naar de binnenstad loopt.

à Berchem C Antwerpen – ✉ 2600 Berchem :

Campanile, Potvlietlaan 2, ☎ 0 3 236 43 55, *antwerpen@campanile.be, Fax 0 3 236 56 53,* – 🛗 ⇔ TV ♿ P – 🏛 25 à 80. AE ⓓ MC VISA BR f
Repas (avec buffets) *Lunch 19* – 22 – ☕ 10 – **126 ch** 74 – ½ P 93.
◆ La plus grande unité Campanile du Benelux se trouve hors agglomération, au Sud-Est du centre-ville, près du ring et de l'aéroport d'Anvers-Deurne. Chambres insonorisées.
◆ Dit grootste hotel van de Campanile-groep in de Benelux ligt even buiten de stad, ten zuidoosten van het centrum, bij de Ring en de luchthaven van Antwerpen-Deurne. Kamers met goede geluidsisolatie.

De Tafeljoncker, Frederik de Merodestraat 13, ☎ 0 3 281 20 34, *restaurant.de-tafeljoncker@pandora.be, Fax 0 3 281 20 34,* – ▤. AE ⓓ MC VISA plan p. 7 DX f
fermé sem. carnaval, 2 prem. sem. sept., dim. soir, lundi et mardi – **Repas** *Lunch 50* – 62/90 bc.
◆ Dans une maison de maître agrémentée d'un jardinet où l'on dresse la terrasse en été, agréable restaurant proposant une brève et attrayante carte au goût du jour.
◆ Dit restaurant in een herenhuis met mooie tuin en terras, waar 's zomers de tafeltjes worden gedekt, biedt een beperkte, maar aantrekkelijke kaart met eigentijdse gerechten.

Brasserie Marly, Generaal Lemanstraat 64, ☎ 0 3 281 23 23, *info@marly.be, Fax 0 3 281 33 10* – AE ⓓ MC VISA. ✻ plan p. 7 DX c
fermé 19 juil.-16 août, sam. midi et dim. – **Repas** 25 bc/43, ♀.
◆ Accueillante brasserie équipée de viviers installée aux portes de la ville. Choix bien étudié où poissons, huîtres et homards sont à l'honneur. Service voiturier.
◆ Gemoedelijke brasserie aan de rand van de stad, met homarium. Op de kaart nemen vis en schaaldieren dan ook een grote plaats in. Valetservice.

Euterpia, Generaal Capiaumontstraat 2, ☎ 0 3 235 02 02, *Fax 0 3 235 58 64,* – AE MC VISA plan p. 7 EV y
fermé Pâques, 1re quinz. août, Noël, Nouvel An, lundi et mardi – **Repas** (dîner seult jusqu'à 23 h) carte 43 à 80.
◆ Au cœur du beau quartier Wijk Zurenborg, ce rendez-vous des artistes s'annonce par une intéressante façade éclectique 1900. Petite carte au goût du jour et ardoise.
◆ Dit kunstenaarstrefpunt in het hart van de mooie wijk Zurenborg gaat schuil achter een gevel in verschillende stijlen uit 1900. Kleine kaart en dagschotels op een schoolbord.

De Troubadour, Driekoningenstraat 72, ☎ 0 3 239 39 16, *info@detroubadour.be, Fax 0 3 230 82 71* – ▤ P. AE ⓓ MC VISA plan p. 7 DX a
fermé vacances Pâques, 2 prem. sem. août, dim. et lundi – **Repas** *Lunch 25* – 33, ♀.
◆ Intelligent répertoire culinaire dans le tempo actuel, pour ce restaurant chaleureux au cadre contemporain, apprécié par une belle clientèle d'affaires et d'habitués.
◆ Gezellig restaurant met een eigentijdse uitstraling en een culinair repertoire dat behalve zakenmensen ook veel vaste gasten trekt.

Willy, Generaal Lemanstraat 54, ☎ 0 3 218 88 07 – ▤. AE ⓓ MC VISA. ✻
fermé sam. et dim. – **Repas** *Lunch 12* – carte 23 à 43.
◆ À l'entrée de la ville, petite adresse plaisante et soignée, fonctionnant avec une carte classique assez concise mais diversifiée. Willy a plus de 25 ans d'expérience.
◆ Prima adresje aan de rand van de stad. De klassieke kaart is klein maar fijn en behoorlijk gevarieerd. Willy kan bogen op een ervaring van ruim 25 jaar. plan p. 7 DX v

à Berendrecht *par ① : 23 km au Nord* C *Antwerpen* – ✉ *2040 Berendrecht* :

Reigershof, Reigersbosdreef 2, ☎ 0 3 568 96 91, *reigershof@p.i.be, Fax 0 3 568 71 63* – 🏛 50. AE ⓓ MC VISA
Repas *Lunch 29* – 36/68 bc, ♀.
◆ Agréable maison de coin postée au bout du port marchand. Carte séduisante à deux volets : l'un classique et l'autre inventif. Cave globe-trotter et grands vins français.
◆ Aangenaam hoekhuis aan het eind van de koopvaardijhaven. Aanlokkelijke kaart die zowel klassiek als vernieuwend is. Internationale wijnkelder met grote Franse namen.

à Borgerhout C *Antwerpen* – ✉ *2140 Borgerhout* :

Scandic, Luitenant Lippenslaan 66, ☎ 0 3 235 91 91, *info-antwerp@scandic-hotels.com, Fax 0 3 235 08 96,* – 🛗 ⇔ ▤ TV ♿ P – 🏛 25 à 230. AE ⓓ MC VISA JCB. ✻ BR e
Repas *Lunch 25* – carte 37 à 63, ♀ – ☕ 17 – **201 ch** 185/236, – 3 suites.
◆ Hôtel de chaîne rénové et bien situé le long du ring, à proximité de la gare de Borgerhout, du musée Sterchshof (Zilvercentrum) et d'un terrain de golf. Centre d'affaires. Brasserie de style actuel avec une carte internationale.
◆ Dit gerenoveerde hotel maakt deel uit van een keten en staat langs de Ring, dicht bij station Borgerhout, het Sterchshof (museum voor kunstambachten) en een golfbaan. Business center. Modern restaurant met een internationale kaart.

à **Deurne** C *Antwerpen* – ✉ *2100 Deurne* :

XX **De Violin,** Bosuil 1, ☎ 0 3 324 34 04, *Fax 0 3 326 33 20*, – P. AE ① MC VISA.
fermé dim. et lundi soir – **Repas** *Lunch 41 bc* – carte 48 à 64.
◆ Ce restaurant de charme occupe une fermette aux volets peints. Cuisine classique et suggestions du marché annoncées oralement. En été, terrasse exquise évoquant l'Asie.
◆ Sfeervol restaurant in een boerderijtje met geverfde luiken. Klassieke kaart en suggesties die mondeling worden aangekondigd. Het terras doet in de zomer exotisch aan. BR r

X **Harvest,** Ter Rivierenlaan 100, ☎ 0 3 325 66 99, *Fax 0 3 326 69 82*, Cuisine asiatique, ouvert jusqu'à 23 h – ▤. AE ① MC VISA BR b
fermé lundis non fériés – **Repas** *Lunch 9* – carte 22 à 36.
◆ Harvest vous reçoit dans une sobre salle à manger au décor japonisant. La carte des plats se partage entre la Chine et l'Empire du Soleil levant. Formule "table de riz".
◆ Harvest ontvangt zijn gasten in een sober gedecoreerde eetzaal in Japanse stijl. Op de kaart staan gerechten uit China en het land van de rijzende zon. Ook rijsttafels.

à **Ekeren** C *Antwerpen* – ✉ *2180 Ekeren* :

X **De Mangerie,** Kapelsesteenweg 471 (par ②), ☎ 0 3 605 26 26, *Fax 0 3 605 24 16*, – P. AE ① MC VISA BQ
fermé sam. midi – **Repas** 29, ♀.
◆ Intérieur d'esprit marin et choix de mets classiques avec plats du marché pour cet établissement que signale une engageante façade "Louisiane". Mezzanine et terrasses.
◆ Vrolijke gevel in Louisiana-stijl en een interieur dat een ode brengt aan de zee. Klassieke kaart en dagelijks wisselende gerechten. Mezzanine en terrassen.

à **Merksem** C *Antwerpen* – ✉ *2170 Merksem* :

XX **Culinaria,** Ryenlanddreef 18, ☎ 0 3 645 77 72, *culinaria@pandora.be*, *Fax 0 3 290 01 25*, – P. AE ① MC VISA. BQ a
fermé 1 sem. carnaval, 1 sem. Pâques, 2 sem. en juil., lundi, merc. et sam. midi – **Repas** *Lunch 25* – carte 38 à 61.
◆ Ce restaurant de quartier a récemment bénéficié d'une importante rénovation intérieure. Cuisine à la fois classique et actuelle, basée sur de bons produits du marché.
◆ Dit buurtrestaurant is van binnen onlangs grondig verbouwd. Klassieke, eigentijdse keuken op basis van kwaliteitsproducten van de markt.

Environs

à **Aartselaar** *par ⑩ : 10 km – 14 378 h* – ✉ *2630 Aartselaar* :

Kasteel Solhof sans rest, Baron Van Ertbornstraat 116, ☎ 0 3 877 30 00, *info@solhof.be*, *Fax 0 3 877 31 31*, – | TV P. – 25 à 50. AE MC VISA.
fermé Noël-Nouvel An – ☕ 20 – **24 ch** 149/225.
◆ Au Sud d'Antwerpen, belle demeure patricienne cernée de douves et de chlorophylle, avec dépendances et terrasse ouverte sur un parc public. Chambres paisibles bien équipées.
◆ Prachtig kasteeltje omringd door een slotgracht en veel groen ten zuiden van Antwerpen, met bijgebouwen en een terras dat uitkijkt op een park. Rustige en comfortabele kamers.

X **De Cocotte,** Kleistraat 175, ☎ 0 3 887 56 85, *info@decocotte.be*, *Fax 0 3 887 22 56*, ←, – P. AE ① MC VISA. – *fermé sam. midi* – **Repas** *Lunch 25* – carte 26 à 50.
◆ Si le temps s'y prête, prenez place sur la délicieuse terrasse estivale, parmi la verdure dont s'environne cette accueillante villa. Recettes dans le tempo actuel.
◆ Op zomerse dagen is het heerlijk toeven op het terras tussen de weelderige begroeiing van deze charmante villa. Uitstekende eigentijdse keuken.

X **Hana,** Antwerpsesteenweg 116, ☎ 0 3 877 08 95, *Fax 0 3 877 08 95*, Cuisine japonaise avec Teppan-Yaki – ▤. AE MC VISA.
fermé mardi soir, sam. midi et dim. midi – **Repas** *Lunch 14* – carte 55 à 92.
◆ Une façace discrète au bord de l'autoroute A12 abrite ce sobre petit établissement traditionnel japonais équipé de trois Teppan-Yaki (tables de cuisson). Banzaï !
◆ Achter een onopvallende gevel langs de A12 schuilt dit sobere Japanse restaurant, waar de gasten rondom drie Teppan-Yaki kookplaten zitten. Banzaï !

à **Boechout** *- plan p. 5 – 11 886 h* – ✉ *2530 Boechout* :

XXX ✿ **De Schone van Boskoop** (Keersmaekers), Appelkantstraat 10, ☎ 0 3 454 19 31, *deschonevanboskoop@skynet.be*, *Fax 0 3 454 02 10*, – ▤ P. AE ① MC VISA. BS d
fermé sem. Pâques, 3 dern. sem. août, Noël-Nouvel An, dim. et lundi – **Repas** *Lunch 45* – carte 70 à 132, ♀.
◆ Bonne table au cadre contemporain franchement artistique. Carte personnalisée, assortie de suggestions. Pièce d'eau et statues en terrasse. Réservation impérative.
◆ Goed restaurant met een modern artistiek interieur. De originele kaart wordt aangevuld met suggesties. Terras met waterpartij en standbeelden. Reserveren noodzakelijk.
Spéc. Trois préparations de thon (printemps-été). Tête de veau tiède et sauce tartare. Ris de veau et son boudin truffé, sauce aux truffes

à Brasschaat - *plan p. 5* - *37 249 h* - ✉ *2930 Brasschaat :*

Afspanning De Kroon, Bredabaan 409 (par ③ : 1,5 km), ✆ 0 3 652 09 88, *info@dekroon.be, Fax 0 3 653 25 92* - , rest, . AE MC VISA. ch
Repas carte 28 à 49 - **13 ch** 115/165, - 2 suites.
✦ Au centre du bourg, petit hôtel assez cossu aménagé dans un relais du 18e s. au "look" d'auberge anglaise, agrandi d'une aile récente. Diverses catégories de chambres. Restaurant installé dans une ancienne grange avec mezzanine.
✦ Klein en vrij luxueus hotel in het centrum van Brasschaat in een 18e-eeuws poststation dat doet denken aan een Engelse herberg. Onlangs is er een nieuwe vleugel aangebouwd. Diverse categorieën kamers. Restaurant in een oude schuur met mezzanine.

à Edegem - *plan p. 5* - *22 024 h* - ✉ *2650 Edegem :*

Ter Elst, Terelststraat 310 (par Prins Boudewijnlaan), ✆ 0 3 450 90 00, *info@terelst.be, Fax 0 3 450 90 90*, , , , , - - 25 à 500. AE MC VISA. BS
Repas ***Couvert Classique*** *(fermé juil.-14 août, 24, 25 et 31 déc. et 1er janv.)* Lunch 35 - carte 45 à 56 - 17 - **53 ch** *(fermé 24, 25 et 31 déc. et 1er janv.)* 120/135.
✦ Hôtel récent situé au Sud d'Anvers et couplé à un centre sportif installé légèrement à l'écart. Bel auditorium moderne et grandes chambres avec équipement de base. Table aménagée dans la note néo-rustique. Cuisine classique revisitée. Choix de vins attirant.
✦ Nieuw hotel bij een sportcentrum ten zuiden van Antwerpen. Moderne hal en grote kamers met basisvoorzieningen. Restaurant in neorustieke stijl, waar klassieke gerechten in een eigentijds jasje worden geserveerd. Aantrekkelijke wijnkaart.

La Cabane (Vandersteen), Mechelsesteenweg 11, ✆ 0 3 454 58 98, *restaurantlacabane@skynet.be, Fax 0 3 455 34 26* - AE MC VISA. - *fermé 1 sem. Pâques, 19 juil.-8 août, 24 déc.-5 janv., sam. midi, dim. et lundi* - **Repas** Lunch 35 - 42/80 bc, carte 46 à 70, ♀.
✦ Décor intérieur moderne, assiettes soignées, flirtant avec les modes d'aujourd'hui, formule lunch avec choix et bon livre de cave. Une "cabane" de luxe, en fin de compte !
✦ Modern interieur en verzorgde keuken met een knipoog naar de laatste mode. Lunchformule met ruime keuze en lekkere wijnen. In deze "cabane" (hut) is het goed toeven !
Spéc. Tempura d'anguille fumée, vinaigrette tiède verdurette (été). Ris de veau et concombre à l'aigre-doux, sauce au Madère. Baba au rhum, glace à la noix de coco BS a

à 's Gravenwezel *par ⑤ : 13 km* *Schilde 19 595 h.* - ✉ *2970 's Gravenwezel :*

De Vogelenzang, Wijnegemsteenweg 193, ✆ 0 3 353 62 40, *devogelenzang@pandora.be, Fax 0 3 353 33 83*, , Taverne-rest - . AE MC VISA
fermé merc. - **Repas** carte 28 à 43.
✦ Plaisante taverne-restaurant appréciée pour sa cuisine simple avec plats bourgeois et du marché. Les huîtres de Zélande comptent parmi les suggestions de saison.
✦ Plezierige taverne met restaurant dat wordt gewaardeerd vanwege zijn smakelijke burgerpot op basis van verse producten. In het seizoen zijn er Zeeuwse oesters verkrijgbaar.

à Kapellen *par ② : 15,5 km* - *25 612 h* - ✉ *2950 Kapellen :*

De Bellefleur (Buytaert), Antwerpsesteenweg 253, ✆ 0 3 664 67 19, *Fax 0 3 665 02 01*, - . AE MC VISA
fermé juil., sam. midi et dim. - **Repas** Lunch 55 bc - 90/110 bc, carte 107 à 210, ♀.
✦ Ce restaurant de qualité interprète un répertoire classique actualisé. L'été venu, réservez votre table dans la jolie véranda avec pergola entourée d'un jardin fleuri.
✦ Kwaliteitsrestaurant met een eigentijdse keuken op klassieke basis. In de zomer kunt u een tafel reserveren onder de mooie pergola die door een bloementuin wordt omringd.
Spéc. Navarin de sole aux chanterelles et truffes d'été (avril-oct.). Cabillaud aux asperges et caviar. Grouse d'Ecosse et gratin de figues, son jus au pur malt

à Kontich *par ⑧ : 12 km* - *20 059 h* - ✉ *2550 Kontich :*

Afspanning De Jachthoorn, Doornstraat 11 (Ouest : 3 km, direction Wilrijk), ✆ 0 3 458 21 21, *info@restevent.be, Fax 0 3 457 93 77*, , Taverne-rest - - 25 à 350. AE MC VISA - *fermé lundi* - **Repas** Lunch 17 - 30.
✦ Cette ancienne ferme en pleine campagne, avec annexes aménagées, propose une cuisine traditionnelle soignée dans un cadre rustique. Séminaires et banquets possibles.
✦ In deze oude boerderij met bijgebouwen op het platteland worden met zorg bereide, traditionele maaltijden geserveerd in een rustiek kader. Ook geschikt voor partijen.

à Schilde *par ⑤ : 13 km* - *19 595 h* - ✉ *2970 Schilde :*

Euryanthe, Turnhoutsebaan 177, ✆ 0 3 383 30 30, *info@euryanthe.be, Fax 0 3 383 30 30*, - AE MC VISA
fermé 1 sem. carnaval, 2 prem. sem. août, sam. midi, dim. et lundi - **Repas** carte 37 à 58.
✦ Restaurant au décor sobre et stylé dans une imposante demeure du centre de Schilde. Choix classique modérément actualisé et suggestions faites oralement. Terrasse tranquille.
✦ Stijlvol restaurant in een imposant pand in het centrum van Schilde. Klassieke kaart die voorzichtig aan de huidige trend wordt aangepast. Ook dagsuggesties. Rustig terras.

à Schoten - *plan p. 5* - *32 777 h* - ✉ *2900 Schoten* :

XXX **Kleine Barreel,** Bredabaan 1147, ☎ 0 3 645 85 84, *info@kleine-barreel.be, Fax 0 3 645 85 03* - ▤ P - 25 à 60. AE ⓓ MC VISA JCB BQ n
Repas *Lunch 32* - 45/62 bc, ♀.
◆ Connu du tout-Anvers, ce confortable restaurant attire la clientèle d'affaires nombreuse. Choix classico-traditionnel renouvelé chaque mois et plats du marché.
◆ Dit comfortabele restaurant is in heel Antwerpen bekend en trekt veel zakenmensen. Klassiek-traditionele kaart die maandelijks verandert, en smakelijke dagsuggesties.

XX **De Linde,** Alice Nahonlei 92 (Est : 3 km, angle N 113), ☎ 0 3 658 47 43, *de.linde.bvba@skynet.be, Fax 0 3 658 11 84*, - P. AE ⓓ MC VISA
fermé 2 sem. carnaval, 3 sem. en juil., mardi et merc. - **Repas** *Lunch 36 bc* - carte 37 à 72.
◆ Villa des années1930 située sur un carrefour dans un quartier résidentiel boisé. Intérieur spacieux et moderne, aux accents Art déco. Cuisine mi-classique, mi-actuelle.
◆ Villa uit de jaren dertig op een kruispunt in een chique woonwijk met veel bomen. Ruim, modern interieur met art-deco-accenten. De keuken is zowel klassiek als eigentijds.

XX **Villa Doria,** Bredabaan 1293, ☎ 0 3 644 40 10, *info@villadoria.be*, Avec cuisine italienne - ▤ P. AE ⓓ MC VISA. BQ b
fermé 3 sem. en juil., Noël, Nouvel An et merc. - **Repas** *Lunch 25 bc* - carte 37 à 56, ♀.
◆ Une réputation flatteuse entoure ce restaurant au cadre à la fois rustique et moderne. Recettes franco-italiennes et cave majoritairement transalpine. Service voiturier.
◆ Dit restaurant in modern rustieke stijl geniet een goede reputatie. Frans-Italiaanse keuken met veel Italiaanse wijnen op de kaart. Valetservice.

XX **Uilenspiegel,** Brechtsebaan 277 (Nord-Ouest : 3 km sur N 115), ☎ 0 3 651 61 45, *Fax 0 3 652 08 08*, - P - 25. AE MC VISA.
fermé 16 fév.-4 mars, du 12 au 29 juil., mardi et merc. - **Repas** *Lunch 20* - 29/66 bc, ♀.
◆ Dans une belle villa coiffée d'un toit de chaume, avec jardin et terrasse, établissement bien tenu, fonctionnant avec une carte classique assortie d'un lunch et de menus.
◆ Klassiek restaurant in een mooie villa met rieten dak, tuin en terras. À la carte en verschillende keuzemenu's, waaronder een uitstekend lunchmenu.

à Wijnegem *par ⑤ : 2 km* - *8 717 h* - ✉ *2110 Wijnegem* :

XXX **Ter Vennen,** Merksemsebaan 278, ☎ 0 3 326 20 60, *tervennen@skynet.be, Fax 0 3 326 38 47*, - P - 50. AE ⓓ MC VISA JCB.
fermé du 13 au 18 avril, 26 juil.-8 août, du 2 au 7 nov., dim. soir et lundi - **Repas** *Lunch 44 bc* - 35/45 bc.
◆ Une jolie ferme cachée sous les frondaisons, avec terrasse et jardin aménagé, sert d'écrin à ce charmant restaurant. L'assiette est au goût du jour et la cave, bien montée.
◆ Prettig restaurant in een fraaie boerderij tussen het loof, met terras en tuin. Het eten past bij de hedendaagse smaak en de wijnkelder is goed opgezet.

XX **'t Heerenhuys,** Turnhoutsebaan 313, ☎ 0 3 353 41 61, *heerenhuys@skynet.be, Fax 0 3 354 03 35* - AE ⓓ MC VISA.
fermé août, mardi soir, merc. et sam. midi - **Repas** *Lunch 28* - carte 43 à 60, ♀.
◆ Cette chaleureuse petite maison de maître décorée de jardinières en façade possède ses habitués, fidélisés par une cuisine vivant gentiment avec son temps.
◆ Dit restaurant in een charmant herenhuis met fleurige bloembakken aan de gevel heeft een vaste klantenkring, bij wie de eigentijdse keuken zeer in de smaak valt.

ARBRE *Namur* 533 N 20, 534 N 20 *et* 716 H 4 - *voir à Profondeville.*

ARCHENNES (EERKEN) *1390 Brabant Wallon* C *Grez-Doiceau 12 053 h.* 533 N 18 *et* 716 H 3.
Bruxelles 35 - Charleroi 52 - Leuven 17 - Namur 39.

X **l'Ecrin des Gourmets,** chaussée de Wavre 153, ☎ 0 10 84 49 69, - P. AE ⓓ MC VISA.
fermé sem. carnaval, dern. sem. juil.-prem. sem. août et merc. - **Repas** *Lunch 20* - 30/40, ♀.
◆ Sur l'axe Wavre à Louvain, sympathique restaurant tenu en famille depuis une quinzaine d'années. Cuisine du moment composée à partir de bons produits des terroirs belges.
◆ Leuk restaurant aan de weg tussen Waver en Leuven, dat al ruim 15 jaar door dezelfde familie wordt gerund. Eigentijdse keuken met goede producten van Belgische bodem.

ARLON (AARLEN) *6700* P *Luxembourg belge* 534 T 24 *et* 716 K 6 - *25 261 h.*
Musée : *Luxembourgeois★ : section lapidaire gallo-romaine★★* Y.
🅱 *r. Faubourgs 2* ☎ *0 63 21 63 60, tourisme@swing.be*, Fax 0 63 21 63 60.
Bruxelles 187 ① - Luxembourg 31 ③ - Namur 126 ① - Ettelbrück 34 ②

ARLON

Rue	Carré	N°
Bastion (R. du)	Y	2
Capucins (R. des)	Y	3
Carmes (R. des)	Z	4
Chasseurs-Ardennais (Pl. des)	Y	6
Didier (Pl.)	Y	8
Diekirch (R. de)	Y	
Dr. Hollenfeltz (Pl.)	Y	9
Etienne-Lenoir (R.)	Z	10
Faubourgs (R. des)	Y	12
Frassem (R. de)	Y	13
Grand'Place	YZ	15
Grand'Rue	Z	16
Léopold (Pl.)	Z	19
Marché-au-Beurre (R. du)	Z	20
Marché-aux-Légumes	YZ	22
Marquisat (R. du)	Y	23
Michel-Hamelius (R.)	Z	25
Palais-de-Justice	Z	26
Paul-Reuter (R.)	Z	27
Porte-Neuve (R. de la)	Y	29
Remparts (R. des)	Y	30
Saint-Jean (R.)	YZ	32
Seymerich (R. de)	Y	34
Synagogue (R. de la)	Z	35
25-Août (R. du)	Z	40

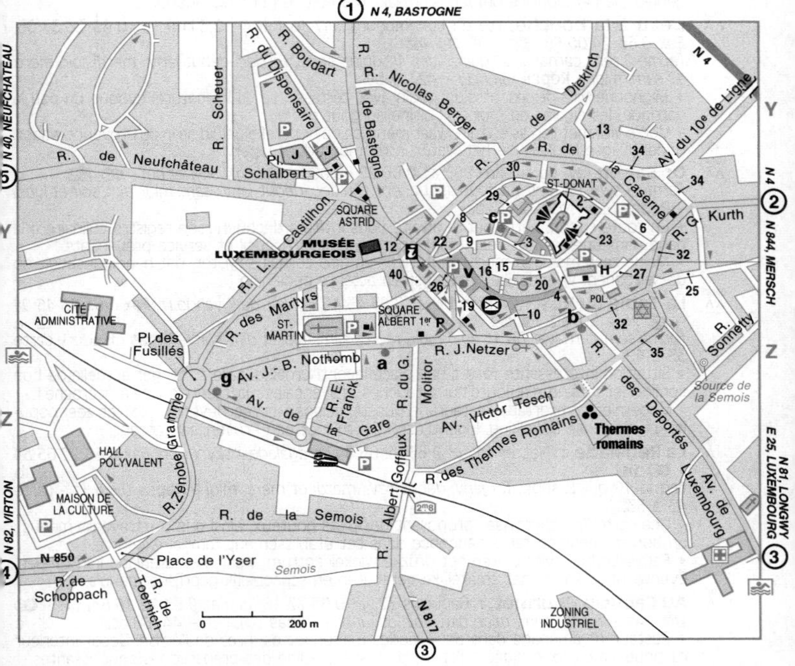

AC Arlux Ardennes, r. Lorraine (par E 411 - E 25, sortie ㉛, puis 1re rue à droite), ☎ 0 63 23 22 11, *hotel.arlux@autogrill.net, Fax 0 63 23 22 48,* – TV P – 25 à 200. AE Ⓓ Ⓜ VISA
Repas *(fermé sam. midi)* 31 bc – **78 ch** ☕ 71/92 – ½ P 88/109.
◆ Construction proche de l'autoroute, déployant quatre ailes contemporaines où sont aménagées des chambres assez spacieuses, pratiques et bien insonorisées. Un grand hall avec salon-bar donne accès à la salle à manger.
◆ Hotel in de buurt van de snelweg, bestaande uit vier moderne vleugels met vrij ruime, praktisch ingerichte kamers met goede geluidsisolatie. Een grote hal met zitjes en bar geeft toegang tot de eetzaal.

Host. du Peiffeschof, Chemin du Peiffeschof 111 (par ② : 800 m, puis à gauche), ☎ 0 63 41 00 50, *info@peiffeschof.be, Fax 0 63 22 44 05,* – TV P – 25. AE Ⓜ VISA. rest
fermé du 12 au 19 avril, 2 prem. sem. août et 2 sem. en nov. – **Repas** *(fermé mardi soir, merc. et sam. midi)* 38/73 bc, ♀ – **9 ch** ☕ 75/150 – ½ P 75/100.
◆ Cette hostellerie de la campagne arlonaise s'est offert un convaincant "lifting" intégral : façade et communs modernisés, jardin embelli et ajout de trois junior suites. À l'heure des repas, alternative restaurant gastronomique ou brasserie.
◆ Dit plattelandshotel heeft een complete facelift gehad : de gevel en gemeenschappelijke ruimten zijn gemoderniseerd, de tuin is verfraaid en er zijn drie junior suites bij gekomen. Brasserie en gastronomisch restaurant.

XXX **L'Arlequin** 1er étage, pl. Léopold 6, ☎ 0 63 22 28 30, *Fax 0 63 22 28 30* – AE MC VISA
fermé 1 sem. Pâques, prem. sem. sept., prem. sem. janv., lundi et jeudi soir – **Repas** *Lunch 45 bc* – carte env. 58. Z v
◆ Près d'un secteur piétonnier, au 1er étage d'une maison de ville. Accueil personnalisé, sens prononcé de l'hospitalité, plaisant décor intérieur : une bonne impression !
◆ Mooi ingericht restaurant op de eerste verdieping van een pand bij een voetgangersgebied. De persoonlijke ontvangst maakt meteen een prettige indruk.

XX **L'eau à la bouche,** rte de Luxembourg 317 (par N 4 : 2,5 km), ☎ 0 63 23 37 05, *Fax 0 63 24 00 56,* – P. MC VISA
fermé 2 sem. carnaval, 2e quinz. juin, 1re quinz. sept., fin déc.-début janv., mardi soir, merc. et sam. midi – **Repas** *Lunch 19* – 42/77 bc.
◆ Mignonne villa disposant d'un jardin avec terrasse. Le cadre naturel évoque un peu la garrigue, les cigales en moins... Cuisine au goût du jour.
◆ Mooie villa met terras en tuin, waar men zich op het krekelgeluid na in de Provence waant. Hedendaagse keuken die het water in de mond doet lopen...

XX **Or Saison,** av. de la Gare 85, ☎ 0 63 22 98 00, *orsaison@skynet.be* – MC VISA Z g
fermé 1 sem. Pâques, fin août-début sept., fin déc.-début janv., sam. midi, dim. soir et lundi – **Repas** *Lunch 22* – 42/67 bc.
◆ En toute saison, cette petite affaire vous invite à découvrir son registre culinaire à la page dans une salle de restaurant contemporaine. Accueil et service prévenants.
◆ Kleine zaak met een modern interieur en dito culinair register, dat handig inspeelt op de seizoenen. Vriendelijke ontvangst en attente bediening.

XX **La Table du Roy,** r. Netzer 11, ☎ 0 63 43 46 00, *ler_da@yahoo.fr, Fax 0 63 43 46 01* – 25 à 50. AE MC VISA Z a
fermé sem. carnaval, du 15 au 31 juil., merc., sam. midi et dim. soir – **Repas** *Lunch 13* – carte 33 à 49.
◆ Situation intéressante face à une place incontournable, salle à manger actuelle de bon confort et cuisine d'aujourd'hui à touches provençales : la clientèle locale accroche !
◆ Modern en comfortabel restaurant, gunstig gelegen aan een levendig plein en zeer populair bij de lokale bevolking. Eigentijdse keuken met een Provençaals accent.

X **La Régalade,** r. Netzer 41, ☎ 0 63 22 65 54, *laregalade@skynet.be, Fax 0 63 22 65 54* – MC VISA. Z b
fermé 1re quinz. sept., fin janv.-début fév., mardi et merc. midi – **Repas** *Lunch 15* – carte 43 à 53.
◆ Une carte "parcheminée" proposant des plats goûteux, ainsi que d'attrayants menus : un bon moment de table s'annonce dans cet établissement familial excentré.
◆ Familiebedrijf even buiten het drukke winkelcentrum, waar men urenlang kan tafelen. Evenwichtige kaart met smakelijke gerechten en schappelijk geprijsde menu's.

X **Au Capucin Gourmet,** r. Capucins 22, ☎ 0 63 22 16 63, *Fax 0 63 22 16 63,* – MC VISA. – *fermé sam. midi, dim. soir et lundi* – **Repas** *Lunch 18* – 44/68 bc. Y c
◆ Restaurant aménagé dans deux vieilles maisonnettes, près de l'église. Décor intérieur rustique. La carte, rédigée à l'encre de Chine, décline des préparations appétissantes.
◆ Dit restaurant is gevestigd in twee oude huisjes bij de kerk. Het interieur is in rustieke stijl gehouden. De gekalligrafeerde menukaart zal fijnproevers doen watertanden.

AS *3665 Limburg* 533 S 16 *et* 716 J 2 – *7 279 h.*
Bruxelles 99 – Maastricht 30 – Hasselt 25 – Antwerpen 95 – Eindhoven 58.

XXX **Host. Mardaga** avec ch, Stationsstraat 121, ☎ 0 89 65 62 65, *mardaga.hotel@skynet.be, Fax 0 89 65 62 66,* , , – , rest, TV P. – 25 à 50. AE MC VISA.
fermé du 12 au 29 juil. – **Repas** *(fermé sam. midi, dim. soir et lundi) Lunch 38* – 54 – **18 ch** 89/131.
◆ Fringante hostellerie où l'on vient faire des repas en accord avec l'époque dans un cadre élégant. Terrasse donnant sur un parc aux arbres centenaires. Chambres raffinées.
◆ Aantrekkelijk hotel-restaurant, waar u in een stijlvolle omlijsting kunt genieten van eigentijdse gerechten. Het terras kijkt uit op een park met eeuwenoude bomen. De kamers zijn geraffineerd ingericht.

ASSE *1730 Vlaams-Brabant* 533 K 17 *et* 716 F 3 – *28 310 h.*
Bruxelles 16 – Aalst 12 – Dendermonde 17.

XXX **De Pauw,** Lindendries 3, ☎ 0 2 452 72 45, *de-pauw-restaurant@hotmail.com, Fax 0 2 452 72 45,* – P. AE MC VISA
fermé du 16 au 26 fév., du 2 au 26 août, mardi soir, merc. et dim. soir – **Repas** *Lunch 29* – 40/75 bc.
◆ Villa entourée d'un jardin et devancée d'une terrasse équipée d'un mobilier neuf. Recettes classiques mises au goût du jour. Vins du monde.
◆ Villa met rondom een tuin en aan de voorkant een terras met nieuw meubilair. Klassieke keuken die aan de smaak van nu is aangepast. Wijnen uit diverse landen.

XX **Hof ten Eenhoorn,** Keierberg 80 (direction Enghien, puis rte à droite), ☎ 0 2 452 95 15, *hof.ten.eenhoorn@edp.be, Fax 0 2 452 95 05,* – P – 25 à 85. AE ⓓ MC VISA.
fermé 1 sem. carnaval, 3 sem. en juil., dim. soir, lundi et mardi – **Repas** Lunch 25 – 47/65 bc.
◆ Cette vieille ferme-brasserie brabançonne s'inscrit dans un site agreste très pittoresque. Chaleureuse salle à manger néo-rustique et espaces annexes réservées aux banquets.
◆ Oud-Brabantse boerderij annex bierbrouwerij in een pittoreske, landelijke omgeving. Gezellige eetzaal in neorustieke stijl en aparte zalen voor banketten.

ASSENEDE *9960 Oost-Vlaanderen* 533 H 15 *et* 716 E 2 – *13 519 h.*
Bruxelles 88 – Gent 22 – Brugge 41 – Sint-Niklaas 38.

X **Den Hoed,** Kloosterstraat 3, ☎ 0 9 344 57 03, *Fax 0 9 344 57 03* – AE ⓓ MC VISA
fermé sem. carnaval, 14 juin-3 juil., lundi soir et mardi – **Repas** 30/37 bc.
◆ Restaurant familial établi dans un ancien estaminet où l'on jouait naguère à la "boule plate" (krulbol). Cuisine bourgeoise. Portions copieuses mais présentations soignées.
◆ Familierestaurant in een oud café, waar vroeger "krulbol" werd gespeeld. Traditionele keuken. Royale porties en goed verzorgde presentatie.

ASTENE *Oost-Vlaanderen* 533 G 17 – *voir à Deinze.*

ATH (AAT) *7800 Hainaut* 533 H 19, 534 H 19 *et* 716 E 4 – *25 993 h.*
Voir *Ducasse★★ (Cortège des géants).*
Env. *au Sud-Ouest : 6 km à Moulbaix : Moulin de la Marquise★ – au Sud-Est : 5 km à Attre★ : Château★.* – *r. Pintamont 18* ☎ *0 68 26 51 70, centre.de.tourisme@ath.be,* Fax 0 68 26 51 79. – *Bruxelles 57 – Mons 25 – Tournai 29.*

Du Parc, r. Esplanade 13, ☎ 0 68 28 69 77 et 0 68 28 54 85 (rest), *motel.parc@skynet.be, Fax 0 68 28 57 63,* – TV – 25 à 70. AE ⓓ MC VISA. ch
Repas *(fermé vend. soirs, sam. midis et dim. soirs non fériés)* carte 24 à 52 – **11 ch** 65/100 – ½ P 64/110.
◆ Cet établissement tranquille exploité en famille renferme de menues chambres convenablement équipées et très bien insonorisées. Petite infrastructure pour conférences. Salle de restaurant au décor embourgeoisé.
◆ Rustig hotel dat door een familie wordt geleid, met kleine maar praktisch ingedeelde kamers met goede geluidsisolatie. Beperkte mogelijkheden voor congressen. Restaurant met een vrij klassieke inrichting.

X **Le Saint-Pierre,** Marché aux Toiles 18, ☎ 0 68 28 51 74 – AE ⓓ MC VISA
fermé 2e quinz. juil. et lundi – **Repas** 27.
◆ À 50 m de la Grand-Place, derrière une façade étroite, petit bistrot servant une cuisine classique assez simple, mais bien tournée. Parking aisé aux alentours.
◆ Op 50 m van de Grote Markt, achter een smalle gevel bevindt zich deze bistro, waar simpele maar goed klaargemaakte gerechten worden geserveerd. Voldoende parkeergelegenheid.

à Ghislenghien (Gellingen) *Nord-Est : 8 km* C *Ath* – ✉ *7822 Ghislenghien :*

XX **Aux Mets Encore,** chaussée de Bruxelles 431 (N 7), ☎ 0 68 55 16 07, *Fax 0 68 55 16 07,* – P. AE ⓓ MC VISA
fermé 2 sem. en août, mardi soir, merc. et dim. soir – **Repas** Lunch 17 – 23/54.
◆ Jeu de mots assez audacieux pour l'enseigne de cette table installée dans un ancien prieuré dont le cadre évoque une auberge de campagne. Cuisine classique actualisée.
◆ Restaurant in een oude priorij, waarvan de inrichting aan een herberg op het platteland doet denken. Klassieke keuken die aan de moderne tijd is aangepast.

AUBEL *4880 Liège* 533 U 18 *et* 716 K 3 – *3 931 h.*
Env. *au Sud-Est : 6 km à Henri-Chapelle, cimetière américain : de la terrasse ★.*
18 9 *au Sud-Est : 6 km à Henri-Chapelle, r. Vivier 3* ☎ *0 87 88 19 91, Fax 0 87 88 36 55* – 18 *au Nord-Est : 10 km à Gemmenich, r. Terstraeten 254* ☎ *0 87 78 92 80, Fax 0 87 78 75 55.*
Bruxelles 125 – Maastricht 27 – Liège 34 – Verviers 18 – Aachen 20.

L'Aub. Aubépine sans rest, Bushaye 279 (Sud-Ouest par N 642), ☎ 0 87 68 04 10, *aubepine@t-online.de, Fax 0 87 68 04 11,* – TV P. MC VISA.
fermé du 23 au 27 déc. – **7 ch** 67/115.
◆ Idéale pour une mise au vert, cette auberge créée à partir d'une ferme restaurée s'entoure de vallons bucoliques. Hébergement dans de coquettes chambres au décor personnalisé.
◆ Deze herberg in een gerestaureerde boerderij ligt in een prachtig natuurgebied en is dan ook ideaal voor wie behoefte heeft aan groen. Mooie kamers met een persoonlijke toets.

XX **Le Moulin du Val Dieu** 2e étage, Val Dieu 298, ✆ 0 87 68 01 70, *info@moulinduvaldieu.be, Fax 0 87 68 01 79* – ▤ P. AE ⓓ ⓜ VISA. ⚘
fermé du 1er au 6 janv., lundi et mardi – **Repas** 27/67 bc, ♀.
◆ Devant l'abbaye, pittoresque ensemble abritant un ancien moulin à eau. Table gastronomique dans l'ex-grenier et repas du terroir dans la véranda. Terrasse côté jardin.
◆ Pittoresk complex met een oude watermolen, tegenover de abdij. Gastronomische keuken op de voormalige graanzolder en streekgerechten in de serre. Tuin met terras.

AUDENARDE *Oost-Vlaanderen – voir Oudenaarde.*

AUDERGHEM (OUDERGEM) *Région de Bruxelles-Capitale* 533 L 18 *et* 716 G 3 – *voir à Bruxelles.*

AVE ET AUFFE *5580 Namur* Ⓒ *Rochefort 11 818 h.* 534 P 22 *et* 716 I 5.
Bruxelles 114 – Bouillon 49 – Namur 55 – Dinant 29 – Rochefort 10.

Host. Le Ry d'Ave, Sourd d'Ave 5, ✆ 0 84 38 82 20, *ry.d.ave@skynet.be, Fax 0 84 38 93 88*, ←, 斋, 🏊, 🐎, 🚲 – TV P. AE ⓓ ⓜ VISA
fermé du 15 au 18 mars, 29 juin-1er juil., du 7 au 16 sept., du 10 au 20 janv., merc. et jeudi hors saison – **Repas** (avec taverne-rest) carte 32 à 54, ♀ – **12 ch** ☕ 50/98 – ½ P 76/84.
◆ Cette hostellerie rose enchâssée sous les frondaisons dans un cadre champêtre tient son nom de l'affluent de la Lesse qui traverse le domaine. Chambres personnalisées. La carte du restaurant conjuge saveurs du terroir et mets gastronomiques.
◆ Dit landelijke hotelletje te midden van het groen ontleent zijn naam aan de zijrivier van de Lesse die door het terrein stroomt. De kamers hebben een persoonlijke uitstraling. Op de menukaart staan gastronomische gerechten met regionale invloeden.

AVELGEM *8580 West-Vlaanderen* 533 F 18 *et* 716 D 3 – *9 193 h.*
Bruxelles 72 – Kortrijk 16 – Tournai 23.

X **Karekietenhof,** Scheldelaan 20 (derrière l'église), ✆ 0 56 64 44 11, *Fax 0 56 64 44 11*, ←, 斋, Anguilles – P. ⓜ VISA
fermé du 16 au 31 août, mardi soir et merc. – **Repas** Lunch 12 – 31/45 bc.
◆ La "Cour des Fauvettes" mijote une cuisine bourgeoise dans un intérieur un brin suranné. Les mordus d'anguille y trouveront leur bonheur. Vue sur un bras de l'Escaut.
◆ Smakelijke burgerkost in een tikkeltje ouderwets interieur. Liefhebbers van paling komen hier beslist aan hun trekken ! Mooi uitzicht op een zijrivier van de Schelde.

AWENNE *Luxembourg belge* 534 Q 22 *et* 716 I 5 – *voir à St-Hubert.*

AYWAILLE *4920 Liège* 533 T 20, 534 T 20 *et* 716 K 4 – *10 386 h.*
ℹ *pl. J. Thiry 9a* ✆ *0 4 384 84 84.*
Bruxelles 123 – Liège 29 – Spa 16.

XXX **Host. Villa des Roses** avec ch, av. de la Libération 4, ✆ 0 4 384 42 36, *reservation.villadesroses@swing.be, Fax 0 4 384 74 40*, 斋 – ⇔ TV 🚗 P. AE ⓓ ⓜ VISA. ⚘ ch
fermé 16 fév.-4 mars, du 13 au 30 sept.-15 oct., merc. et jeudis midis non fériés de sept. à mai et lundis et mardis non fériés – **Repas** *(fermé après 20 h 30)* Lunch 25 – 50 bc – **8 ch** ☕ 65/75 – ½ P 62/86.
◆ Vénérable auberge familiale adossée à un coteau, aux portes d'Aywaille. Repas classique sagement actualisé, livre de cave bien renseigné et bonnes chambres côté rue.
◆ Deftig hotel-restaurant tegen een heuvel aan de rand van Aywaille. Klassiek eten, goed gevulde wijnkelder en ruime kamers aan de straatkant.

BALÂTRE *5190 Namur* Ⓒ *Jemeppe-sur-Sambre 17 679 h.* 533 M 20 *et* 534 M 20.
Bruxelles 55 – Namur 20 – Charleroi 23 – Mons 57.

L'escapade, pl. de Balâtre 123, ✆ 0 81 55 97 80, *Fax 0 81 55 97 81*, 斋 – TV P. – 🏛 25 à 250. AE ⓜ VISA
Repas *(fermé lundi et mardi)* Lunch 20 – 26/42 – **10 ch** ☕ 56/75 – ½ P 58/76.
◆ L'ancien presbytère - maison du 19e s. située au cœur du petit village - s'est trouvé une nouvelle vocation. Chambres toutes récentes, dont une junior suite. À table, préparations au goût du jour.
◆ Deze oude pastorie, een 19e-eeuws pand in het hart van het dorp, heeft een nieuwe bestemming gevonden als hotel. De kamers, waaronder een junior suite, zijn onlangs verbouwd. In het restaurant worden eigentijdse gerechten op tafel gezet.

BALEGEM *9860 Oost-Vlaanderen* ◻ *Oosterzele 13 287 h.* 533 H 17 *et* 716 E 3.
Bruxelles 49 – Gent 23 – Aalst 27 – Oudenaarde 20.

XXX **'t Parksken,** Geraardsbergsesteenweg 233 (à l'Est sur N 42), ☎ 0 9 362 52 20, *Fax 0 9 362 64 17*, – ▤ P – 30. AE ◑ ⊕ VISA.
fermé du 9 au 31 juil., du 1er au 13 janv., dim. soir, lundi et mardi – **Repas** Lunch 34 – 62.
• Accueillante auberge centenaire s'agrémentant d'un jardin. Spacieuses salles à manger classiquement agencées, où les gourmets du coin ont leur rond de serviette.
• Uitnodigende, honderd jaar oude herberg met tuin. Klassiek ingerichte eetzalen, waar de lekkerbekken uit de buurt hun eigen servetring hebben.

BALEN *2490 Antwerpen* 533 *Q 15 et* 716 *I 2 – 19 581 h.*
Bruxelles 87 – Antwerpen 58 – Hasselt 37 – Turnhout 29.

X **Theater,** Steegstraat 8, ☎ 0 14 81 19 06, *anne.stefandeboeck@planetinternet.be, Fax 0 14 81 19 07*, – ◑ ⊕ VISA
fermé 2 dern. sem. fév., 2 dern. sem. août, mardi soir et merc. – **Repas** Lunch 28 – carte 23 à 44.
• Ce restaurant exploité en famille doit son nom à la salle de spectacle qu'il abrita naguère, aujourd'hui disparue. Bon choix de préparations traditionnelles. Accueil avenant.
• Dit familierestaurant dankt zijn naam aan het thans verdwenen theatertje dat hier vroeger was gevestigd. Traditionele kaart met ruime keuze. Voorkomende bediening.

BALMORAL *Liège* 533 U 19, 534 U 19 *et* 716 K 4 – *voir à Spa.*

BARBENÇON *Hainaut* 533 K 21, 534 K 21 *et* 716 F 5 – *voir à Beaumont.*

BARVAUX *6940 Luxembourg belge* ◻ *Durbuy 10 014 h.* 533 R 20, 534 R 20 *et* 716 J 4.
18 *rte d'Oppagne 34* ☎ *0 86 21 44 54, Fax 0 86 21 44 49.*
Parc Julienas 1 ☎ *0 86 21 11 65, Fax 0 86 21 19 78.*
Bruxelles 121 – Arlon 99 – Liège 47 – Marche-en-Famenne 19.

XX **Le Cor de Chasse** avec ch, r. Petit Barvaux 97 (Nord : 1,5 km), ☎ 0 86 21 14 98, *Fax 0 86 21 35 85*, – TV P – 25. ⊕ VISA
fermé prem. sem. juil., 1re quinz. janv., jeudi sauf en juil.-août et merc. – **Repas** Lunch 18 – 29/59 bc – **9 ch** ☐ 50/56 – ½ P 57.
• Sympathique refuge gourmand embusqué aux abords d'un village touristique de l'agreste vallée de l'Ourthe. Savoureuse cuisine actuelle, ambiance familiale, nouvelle terrasse.
• Lekker restaurant voor smulpapen, aan de rand van een toeristisch dorp in het groene Ourthedal. Eigentijdse keuken, gemoedelijke ambiance en een spiksplinternieuw terras.

X **Au Petit Chef,** r. Basse-Sauvenière 8, ☎ 0 86 21 26 14, *Fax 0 86 21 26 14*, – ⊕ VISA
fermé janv., lundi et mardi – **Repas** 22/36.
• Cette petite maison au décor intérieur d'esprit bourgeois jouxte la place communale. Aux beaux jours, une terrasse est dressée en façade. Plats traditionnels.
• Dit pandje aan het dorpsplein ademt vanbinnen een typische bourgeoissfeer. Bij mooi weer worden de tafeltjes gedekt op het terras langs de voorgevel. Traditionele schotels.

à Bohon *Nord-Ouest : 3 km* ◻ *Durbuy* – ✉ *6940 Barvaux :*

Le Relais de Bohon, pl. de Bohon 50, ☎ 0 86 21 30 49, *info@lerelaisdebohon.com, Fax 0 86 21 35 95*, , – TV P. AE ⊕ VISA
fermé mars, début sept., fin nov et lundis soirs et mardis non fériés – **Repas** (taverne-rest) 22/40, ♀ – **16 ch** ☐ 70/80 – ½ P 53/77.
• Chaleureuse auberge ardennaise située dans un tranquille hameau voisin de la "plus petite ville du monde". Chambres fonctionnelles assez coquettes. Accueil familial. Agréable restaurant donnant sur le jardin et taverne où l'on petit-déjeune également.
• Gezellige Ardense herberg in een rustig dorpje vlak bij de "kleinste stad ter wereld". Keurige en praktische kamers. Vriendelijk onthaal. Aangenaam restaurant dat op de tuin uitkijkt en een café waar ook het ontbijt wordt geserveerd.

Dans ce guide
un même symbole, un même mot,
*imprimé en rouge ou en **noir**, en maigre ou en **gras**,*
n'ont pas tout à fait la même signification.
Lisez attentivement les pages explicatives.

BASTOGNE (BASTENAKEN) *6600 Luxembourg belge* 534 T 22 *et* 716 K 5 – *13 739 h.*

Voir Intérieur★ de l'église St-Pierre★ – Bastogne Historical Center★ – à l'Est : 3 km, Le Mardasson★.

Env. au Nord : 17 km à Houffalize : Site★.

pl. Mac Auliffe 24 ☎ *0 61 21 27 11, info@bastogne-tourisme.be,* Fax 0 61 21 27 25.

Bruxelles 148 – Bouillon 67 – Arlon 40 – Liège 88 – Namur 87.

Melba, av. Mathieu 49, ☎ 0 61 21 77 78, *info@hotel-melba.com, Fax 0 61 21 55 68,* – 25 à 80. AE VISA.

fermé du 1er au 20 janv. – **Repas** (dîner pour résidents seult) – **34 ch** 62/85 – ½ P 55/72.

◆ Hôtel de chaîne à taille humaine bordant une rue calme qui relie le centre à l'ancienne gare où débute le RAVEL (piste cyclable). Confort moderne dans les chambres.

◆ Dit hotel met modern comfort behoort tot een keten, maar is niet zo groot. Het staat aan een rustige straat tussen het centrum en het oude station, waar het fietspad begint.

Collin sans rest, pl. Mac Auliffe 8, ☎ 0 61 21 48 88, *Fax 0 61 21 80 83* – . AE VISA

fermé 3 prem. sem. avril – **16 ch** 70/85.

◆ Établissement encore flambant neuf, installé sur la "place to be" de Bastogne, où trône un char américain. Amples chambres correctement équipées, pour des nuits sans histoire.

◆ Nog spiksplinternieuw hotel aan een plein dat het kloppend hart is van Bastenaken. Ruime kamers met goede voorzieningen die garant staan voor een ongestoorde nachtrust.

Le Caprice sans rest, pl. Mac Auliffe 25, ☎ 0 61 21 81 40, *stjames.caprice@skynet.be, Fax 0 61 21 82 01,* – . AE VISA

13 ch 66/74.

◆ Treize chambres - au diable, les superstitions ! - dans cet hôtel pratique veillé par la statue du général McAuliffe, auteur de la fameuse réplique "Nuts" en décembre 1944.

◆ Dertien kamers - weg met het bijgeloof ! - telt dit hotel, waarover het beeld van generaal McAuliffe waakt, die in 1944 het Duitse ultimatum tot overgave afwees met "Nuts".

Au Coin Fleuri, chaussée d'Houffalize 5, ☎ 0 61 21 39 13, *francis.balaine@swing.be, Fax 0 61 21 10 11,* – P. VISA

fermé 16 fév.-4 mars, 10 et 11 juil., 1 sem. en sept., lundi et mardi – **Repas** 24/55.

◆ Aux portes de la ville, direction Houffalize, petite adresse familiale au cadre néo-rustique. Carte bourgeoise annonçant une spécialité de viande de bison de Recogne.

◆ Familierestaurantje in neorustieke stijl aan de rand van de stad, richting Houffalize. Traditionele kaart met als specialiteit bizonvlees uit Rocagne.

Léo, r. Vivier 16, ☎ 0 61 21 14 41, *restaurant@wagon-leo.com, Fax 0 61 21 65 08,* – P. VISA

fermé 20 juin-1er juil., 22 déc.-22 janv., lundi et mardi – Repas Lunch 20 – 31.

◆ Un wagon forme la façade de cette brasserie proposant une cuisine traditionnelle simple mais variée. Suggestions du marché, menus et plats enfants. Additions sages.

◆ Een wagon vormt de façade van deze brasserie, die eenvoudige, maar gevarieerde traditionele gerechten biedt. Dagsuggesties en menu's (ook voor kinderen). Niet duur.

BATTICE *4651 Liège* C *Herve 16 584 h.* 533 T 19, 534 T 19 *et* 716 K 4.

Bruxelles 117 – Maastricht 28 – Liège 27 – Verviers 9 – Aachen 31.

Aux étangs de la Vieille Ferme, Maison du Bois 66 (Sud-Ouest : 7 km, lieu-dit Bruyères), ✉ 4650, ☎ 0 87 67 49 19, *Fax 0 87 67 98 65,* – P. AE VISA

fermé 25 oct.-4 nov., du 1er au 13 janv., lundi, mardi, merc. soir et jeudi soir – **Repas** Lunch 28 – 42/75.

◆ Cette ferme rénovée vous reçoit dans un décor alliant modernisme et rusticité. Mets classiques sobrement actualisés. La terrasse s'ouvre sur un parc verdoyant et son étang.

◆ Gerenoveerde boerderij met een mix van modern en rustiek. Klassieke gerechten die voorzichtig worden gemoderniseerd. Terras met uitzicht op een weelderige tuin en vijver.

Au Vieux Logis, pl. du Marché 25, ☎ 0 87 67 42 53, *elisabethcrahay@hotmail.com* – VISA.

fermé 2 dern. sem. juil., prem. sem. janv., dim., lundi soir et mardi soir – **Repas** 43/58 bc.

◆ Une carte actuelle assez inventive est présentée dans ce "vieux logis" venant de retrouver l'éclat du neuf. Tables bien espacées, mise en place soignée et service avenant.

◆ Dit oude pand, dat onlangs in een nieuw jasje is gestoken, biedt een vrij inventieve, eigentijdse keuken. Tafeltjes op ruime afstand, verzorgde presentatie en attente service.

à Bolland *Nord-Ouest : 2 km* Ⓒ *Herve – ✉ 4653 Bolland :*

XX **Vincent cuisinier de campagne,** Saremont 10, ✆ 0 87 66 06 07, *Fax 0 87 66 14 68,* 席 – P – 🛆 40. AE ⓓ MC VISA

fermé prem. sem. fév., 2 sem. en juil., Noël-Nouvel An, dim. soir, lundi soir et merc. – **Repas** *Lunch 27* – 38/54 bc, ♀ 🍇.

◆ Bâtisse contemporaine dominant la campagne vallonnée. Cuisine actuelle attachée au terroir local, bel assortiment de vins français et terrasse donnant sur un jardin-potager.

◆ Modern pand dat over het heuvellandschap uitkijkt. Eigentijdse keuken op basis van lokale producten en mooie Franse wijnen. Terras met uitzicht op de moestuin.

BAUDOUR *Hainaut* 533 I 20, 534 I 20 *et* 716 E 4 – *voir à Mons.*

BAZEL *9150 Oost-Vlaanderen* Ⓒ *Kruibeke 14 684 h.* 533 K 16 *et* 716 F 2.

Bruxelles 45 – Antwerpen 17 – Gent 49 – Sint-Niklaas 15.

XX **'t Hofke van Bazel,** Koningin Astridplein 11, ✆ 0 3 744 11 40, *info@hofkevanbazel.be, Fax 0 3 744 24 00,* 席 – ▤. AE MC VISA

fermé 2 prem. sem. sept., lundi et sam. midi – **Repas** *Lunch 35* – 40/81 bc, ♀.

◆ Jolie maison ancienne postée sur la placette de l'église. Mets élaborés, servis dans un décor d'esprit vénitien où l'on joue du piano le jeudi soir : romantisme assuré !

◆ Mooi oud huis aan het kerkpleintje. Goed verzorgde maaltijd in een Venetiaans interieur, waar donderdagavond piano wordt gespeeld. Heel romantisch !

BEAUMONT *6500 Hainaut* 533 K 21, 534 K 21 *et* 716 F 5 – *6 630 h.*

ℹ *Grand'Place 10* ✆ *0 71 58 81 91, ot.beaumont@swing.be,* Fax 0 71 58 81 91.

Bruxelles 80 – Mons 32 – Charleroi 26 – Maubeuge 25.

XX **Le Maleguemme,** chaussée F. Deliège 48 (rte de Philippeville), ✆ 0 71 58 90 95, *Fax 0 71 58 94 83,* 席 – ▤ P. AE ⓓ MC VISA

fermé 3 prem. sem. sept., 2 sem. en janv., mardi, merc. soir et dim. soir – **Repas** 25/35.

◆ Aux portes de Beaumont, restaurant à l'ambiance familiale occupant une villa en bord de route. Préparations classiques de saison rassemblées en plusieurs menus multi-choix.

◆ Gemoedelijk restaurant in een villa langs de weg, aan de rand van Beaumont. Verschillende keuzemenu's met klassieke, seizoengebonden gerechten.

à Barbençon *Sud-Est : 4 km* Ⓒ *Beaumont – ✉ 6500 Barbençon :*

XX **Le Barbençon,** r. Couvent 11, ✆ 0 71 58 99 27, *Fax 0 71 58 99 27* – P. MC VISA

fermé merc. midis non fériés, mardi soir, merc. soir et dim. soir – **Repas** *Lunch 23* – 44/49.

◆ Accueil tout sourire, salon apéritif, mise en place soignée, choix classico-bourgeois avec plats du marché, assiettes bien présentées : au total, un restaurant plaisant.

◆ Vriendelijke ontvangst, salon voor het aperitief, prachtig gedekte tafel, klassieke kaart en dagschotels die fraai worden opgediend. Kortom, een heel plezierig restaurant.

à Grandrieu *Sud-Ouest : 7 km* Ⓒ *Sivry-Rance 4 529 h. – ✉ 6470 Grandrieu :*

XX **Le Grand Ryeu,** r. Goëtte 1, ✆ 0 60 45 52 10, *alain.boschman@legrand-ryeu.be, Fax 0 60 45 62 25,* 席 – P. AE ⓓ MC VISA

fermé du 15 au 31 août, du 2 au 20 janv., mardi, merc., jeudi et après 20 h 30 – **Repas** *Lunch 25* – 40/70 bc.

◆ Jolie ferme du 18e s. bâtie au centre d'un village voisin de la frontière française. Salle des repas redécorée avec goût. Recettes bien en phase avec l'époque.

◆ Mooie 18e-eeuwse boerderij in het hart van een dorp bij de Franse grens. De eetzaal is onlangs met smaak opnieuw ingericht. Eigentijdse gerechten.

à Solre-St-Géry *Sud : 4 km* Ⓒ *Beaumont – ✉ 6500 Solre-St-Géry :*

XXX ✿ **Host. Le Prieuré Saint-Géry** (Gardinal) 🐌 avec ch, r. Lambot 9, ✆ 0 71 58 97 00, *Fax 0 71 58 96 98,* 席 – TV P. AE ⓓ MC VISA

fermé du 6 au 21 sept. et du 10 au 25 janv. – **Repas** *(fermé dim. soir, lundi et mardi midi) Lunch 25* – 54/99 bc, carte 48 à 85, ♀ – **5 ch** *(fermé dim. soir et lundi)* ☕ 65/95, – 1 suite – ½ P 99.

◆ Cuisine inventive, servie dans un ancien prieuré au charme rustico-bourgeois. Terrasse dressée dans la cour intérieure fleurie à la belle saison. Chambres douillettes.

◆ Inventieve keuken in een oude priorij met een rustiek-klassieke charme. Bij mooi weer kan er op het terras van de fleurige patio worden gegeten. Behaaglijke kamers.

Spéc. Tartelette aux dés de thon et tomate confite (sept.-janv.). Foie d'oie fondu au witlof caramelisé, gingembre et Porto (nov.-mars). Parmentier de joue de bœuf braisée et ris de veau au chou vert et lentilles

BEAURAING *5570 Namur* 534 O 22 *et* 716 H 5 – *8 128 h.*

Voir *Lieu de pèlerinage*★.

Bruxelles 111 – Bouillon 46 – Namur 48 – Dinant 20 – Givet 10.

L'Aubépine, r. Rochefort 27, ✆ 0 82 71 11 59, *Fax 0 82 71 33 54*, – , rest, – 25 à 180. AE VISA

avril-2 janv. – **Repas** *Lunch 18* – 26/35 – **66 ch** 50/70 – ½ P 55.

◆ Cet établissement familial œuvrant depuis plus de 70 ans au centre du village renferme de sobres chambres rajeunies depuis peu. Espaces de réunions et séminaires. Préparations traditionnelles assez simples, mais variées.

◆ Dit familiehotel midden in het dorp bestaat al ruim 70 jaar. De kamers zijn sober, maar hebben onlangs een opknapbeurt gehad. Het hotel beschikt over congres- en vergaderzalen. De kaart is traditioneel en vrij eenvoudig, maar biedt een ruime keuze.

BEAUVOORDE *West-Vlaanderen* 533 A 16 – *voir à Veurne.*

BEERNEM *8730 West-Vlaanderen* 533 F 16 *et* 716 D 2 – *14 551 h.*

Bruxelles 81 – Brugge 20 – Gent 36 – Oostende 37.

di Coylde, St-Jorisstraat 82 (direction Knesselare), ✆ 0 50 78 18 18, *Fax 0 50 78 17 25*, – – 40. AE VISA.

fermé sem. carnaval, 19 juil.-12 août, sam. midi, dim. soir et lundi – **Repas** *Lunch 32* – 49/79 bc.

◆ Ravissant manoir du 18e s. décoré d'œuvres d'art moderne, protégé de douves et entouré de jardins soignés. Cuisine au goût du jour recherchée et cave de prestige.

◆ Schitterend 18e-eeuws kasteeltje met een slotgracht en een verzorgde tuin. Binnen zijn talrijke kunstwerken te bewonderen. Verfijnde eigentijdse keuken en prestigieuze wijnen.

à Oedelem *Nord : 4 km* C *Beernem* – ✉ *8730 Oedelem :*

Alain Meessen, Bruggestraat 259 (Ouest : 4 km sur N 337), ✆ 0 50 36 37 84, *Fax 0 50 36 01 94*, – . AE VISA

fermé 2 sem. Pâques, sam. midi, dim., lundi midi et après 20 h 30 – **Repas** *Lunch 40* – 55/75 bc, ♀.

◆ Un choix de mets classiques et une carte des vins bien remplie vous attendent dans cette villa flamande bâtie aux portes d'Oedelem. Jardin soigné. Réservation utile.

◆ Een keur van klassieke gerechten en een rijk gevulde wijnkelder staan u te wachten in deze Vlaamse villa met een mooie tuin aan de rand van Oedelem. Reserveren aanbevolen.

BEERSEL *Vlaams-Brabant* 533 K 18 *et* 716 F 3 – *voir à Bruxelles, environs.*

BELLEGEM *West-Vlaanderen* 533 E 18 *et* 716 C 3 – *voir à Kortrijk.*

BELLEVAUX-LIGNEUVILLE *4960 Liège* C *Malmédy 11 394 h.* 533 V 20, 534 V 20 *et* 716 L 4.

Bruxelles 165 – Liège 65 – Malmédy 8,5 – Spa 27.

St-Hubert, Grand'Rue 43 (Ligneuville), ✆ 0 80 57 08 92, *Fax 0 80 57 08 94*, , – – 25 à 60. VISA. ch

fermé merc. – **Repas** *Lunch 16* – carte 26 à 50 – **18 ch** 65/75 – ½ P 53/55.

◆ Au centre de Ligneuville, sage petit hôtel où règne une atmosphère provinciale. Les deux types de chambres - modernes ou à l'ancienne - offrent la tranquillité aux voyageurs. Restaurant maniant un registre classique avec spécialités régionales.

◆ Klein hotel met een provinciale sfeer, in het centrum van Ligneuville. De twee soorten kamers, modern of in oude stijl, bieden rust en kalmte. Het restaurant voert een klassiek register met regionale specialiteiten.

du Moulin avec ch, Grand'Rue 28 (Ligneuville), ✆ 0 80 57 00 81, *moulin.ligneuville@skynet.be, Fax 0 80 57 07 88*, , – . AE VISA

fermé du 2 au 6 fév., 29 mars-8 avril, 29 août-10 sept. et merc. et jeudis midis non fériés – Repas 30/100 bc, ♀ – **14 ch** 62/86 – ½ P 62/75.

◆ Charmante auberge concoctant une fine cuisine d'aujourd'hui magnifiée par une cave germanophile. Décor intérieur cossu, élégantes chambres et restaurant d'été à l'arrière.

◆ Sfeervolle herberg met een eigentijdse, gastronomische keuken en een uitstekende Duitse wijnkelder. Weelderig interieur, elegante kamers en terras aan de achterkant.

BELŒIL *7970 Hainaut* 533 H 19, 534 H 19 *et* 716 E 4 – *13 391 h.*

Voir *Château*★★ *: collections*★★★, *parc*★★, *bibliothèque*★.

Bruxelles 70 – Mons 22 – Tournai 28.

Hôtels et restaurants voir : Mons *Sud-Est : 22 km*

BELVAUX *Namur* 534 Q 22 *et* 716 I 5 *– voir à Rochefort.*

BERCHEM *Antwerpen* 533 L 15 *et* 716 G 2 *– voir à Antwerpen, périphérie.*

BERCHEM-STE-AGATHE (SINT-AGATHA-BERCHEM) *Région de Bruxelles-Capitale* 533 K 17 *et* 716 F 3 *– voir à Bruxelles.*

BERENDRECHT *Antwerpen* 533 K 14 *et* 716 F 1 *– voir à Antwerpen, périphérie.*

BERGEN P *Hainaut – voir Mons.*

BERLARE *9290 Oost-Vlaanderen* 533 J 16 *et* 716 F 2 *– 13 808 h.*
Bruxelles 38 – Gent 26 – Antwerpen 43 – Sint-Niklaas 24.

XXX ✿ **'t Laurierblad** (Van Cauteren) avec ch, Dorp 4, ✆ 0 52 42 48 01, *guy.vancauteren@pi.be, Fax 0 52 42 59 97,* ☂, ⚲ – |$|, ≡ ch, TV – 🔔 25 à 40. AE ⓓ ⓞ VISA JCB
fermé 18 août-1er sept., 26 janv.-2 fév., dim. soir, lundi et mardi midi – **Repas** *Lunch 35* – 74/89 bc, carte 68 à 98 ⚘ – **5 ch** ☕ 81/121.
◆ Devant l'église de Berlare, étape gastronomique honorant le terroir local. Intérieur douillet, terrasse embellie d'une pièce d'eau, cave bien fournie et chambres au diapason.
◆ Deze gastronomische pleisterplaats brengt een eerbetoon aan de streekkeuken. Gezellig, comfortabel interieur en dito kamers. Terras met waterpartij, goed gevulde wijnkelder.
Spéc. Filets d'anguilles habillés de verdure. Carré de cabillaud et morue en croûte briochée et persillée. Fondant de ris et tête de veau truffé aux champignons

aux étangs de Donkmeer *Nord-Ouest : 3,5 km :*

XXX ✿ **Lijsterbes** (Van Der Bruggen), Donklaan 155, ✉ 9290 Uitbergen, ✆ 0 9 367 82 29, *wendy@lijsterbes.be, Fax 0 9 367 85 50,* ☂ – P. AE ⓓ ⓞ VISA. ✂
fermé du 12 au 18 avril, 16 août-5 sept., du 2 au 10 janv., sam. midi, dim. soir et lundi – **Repas** *Lunch 36* – 54/100 bc, carte 68 à 89, ♀ ⚘.
◆ Le Sorbier (Lijsterbes) vous reçoit dans sa salle à manger contemporaine à touche rustique, ou en terrasse, bordée d'un jardin d'herbes aromatiques. Recettes au goût du jour.
◆ De Lijsterbes ontvangt u in een hedendaagse eetzaal met rustieke accenten of op het terras dat wordt omzoomd door een kruidentuin. De recepten zijn eveneens van deze tijd.
Spéc. Carpaccio de langoustines au caviar. Bar en croûte de sel. Beignets au chocolat coulant, glace au thé

XX **Elvira,** Donklaan 255, ✉ 9290 Overmere, ✆ 0 9 367 06 82, *elvira_donkmeer@yahoo.com, Fax 0 9 367 06 83,* ≤, ☂ – P. ⓓ ⓞ VISA. ✂
fermé 2 dern. sem. fév., 2 prem. sem. nov., lundi et mardi – **Repas** *Lunch 33 bc* – carte env. 46.
◆ Belle maison des années 1920 surveillant les étangs de Donkmeer. Salle de restaurant dont le décor rétro produit son effet. Carte recomposée au fil des saisons.
◆ Mooi pand uit de jaren twintig met uitzicht op het Donkmeer. Eetzaal met een prachtig interieur uit dezelfde periode. De menukaart wisselt met de seizoenen.

BERNEAU *4607 Liège* C *Dalhem 6 292 h.* 533 T 18 *et* 716 K 3.
Bruxelles 110 – Maastricht 14 – Liège 19 – Verviers 26 – Aachen 46.

XX **Le Vercoquin,** r. Warsage 2, ✆ 0 4 379 33 63, *vercoquin2001@hotmail.com, Fax 0 4 379 75 88,* ☂ – P. AE ⓓ ⓞ VISA
fermé 2 sem. en juil., dim. soir et lundi – **Repas** *Lunch 30* – 48/70 bc.
◆ Estimable adresse que vous débusquerez à un carrefour, sur la route reliant Battice à Maastricht. Plusieurs menus tentateurs composés dans un registre classique actualisé.
◆ Verdienstelijk restaurant op een kruispunt, aan de weg van Battice naar Maastricht. Verscheidene menu's in een klassiek register, dat aan de hedendaagse tijd is aangepast.

BERTRIX *6880 Luxembourg belge* 534 Q 23 *et* 716 I 6 *– 8 077 h.*
Bruxelles 149 – Bouillon 24 – Arlon 54 – Dinant 73.

XX **Le Péché Mignon,** r. Burhaimont 69 (lieu-dit Burhémont), ✆ 0 61 41 47 17, *Fax 0 61 41 47 17,* ☂ – P. ⓓ ⓞ VISA
fermé prem. sem. mars, du 1er au 20 juil., lundi soir et merc. – **Repas** *Lunch 25* – carte 40 à 51.
◆ Table mignonne misant sur une carte classique assortie de plusieurs propositions de menus, dont une alternative "dégustation" ou "terroir". L'assiette y est plutôt généreuse.
◆ Hier kan men zich bezondigen aan een overvloedige maaltijd. Klassieke kaart en verscheidene menu's, waaronder een menu "dégustation" en een menu "terroir".

X **Four et Fourchette,** r. Gare 103, ✆ 0 61 41 66 90, 🏠 - AE ⓓ ⓜ VISA
fermé 16 juil.-22 août et mardi – **Repas** *Lunch 12* – 31/41.
◆ Adorable restaurant établi au centre de Bertrix, dans une rue commerçante proche de la gare. Carte bien dans le coup et bons menus repensés chaque mois.
◆ Leuk restaurant in het centrum van Bertrix, in een winkelstraat dicht bij het station. Eigentijdse kaart en maandelijks wisselende menu's van uitstekende kwaliteit.

BÉVERCÉ *Liège* 533 *V 20,* 534 *V 20 et* 716 *L 4 – voir à Malmédy.*

BEVEREN (-Leie) *8791 West-Vlaanderen* C *Waregem 35 954 h.* 533 *F 17 et* 716 *C 3.*
Bruxelles 89 – Kortrijk 7 – Brugge 49 – Gent 44.

XX **De Grand Cru,** Kortrijkseweg 290, ✆ 0 56 70 11 10, *Fax 0 56 70 60 88* – ▤ P. AE ⓓ ⓜ VISA
fermé 21 juil.-15 août, dim. et lundi – **Repas** *Lunch 35 bc* – carte 38 à 89.
◆ Salle à manger contemporaine dont les baies vitrées procurent une vue sur un petit jardin agrémenté de pièces d'eau. Carte classique accompagnée de grands crus du Bordelais.
◆ De moderne eetzaal biedt goed zicht op de kleine tuin met waterpartijen. Bij de klassieke gerechten wordt een "Grand Cru" uit de streek rond Bordeaux geschonken.

BEVEREN (-Waas) *9120 Oost-Vlaanderen* 533 *K 15 et* 716 *F 2 – 45 168 h.*
Bruxelles 52 – Antwerpen 15 – Gent 49 – Sint-Niklaas 11 – Middelburg 86.

XX **Salsifis,** Gentseweg 536, ✆ 0 3 755 49 37, *Fax 0 3 755 49 37* – P. ⓜ VISA. ✂
fermé lundi, mardi et sam. midi – **Repas** *Lunch 28* – 37/62 bc.
◆ Restaurant d'un genre assez cossu implanté au bord de la route nationale reliant Beveren à St.-Niklaas. Alléchantes préparations actuelles. Bonne palette de menus.
◆ Rijke uitstraling voor dit restaurant aan de rijksweg tussen Beveren en Sint-Niklaas. Smakelijke, eigentijdse gerechten en verscheidene menu's.

BIÈVRE *5555 Namur* 534 *P 23 et* 716 *I 6 – 3 142 h.*
Bruxelles 134 – Bouillon 20 – Namur 78 – Arlon 80 – Charleville-Mézières 63.

X **Le Saint-Hubert,** r. Bouillon 45, ✆ 0 61 51 10 11, *Fax 0 61 32 13 18*, 🏠 – P. ⓜ VISA
fermé mardi soir et merc. – **Repas** 25/70 bc, ♀.
◆ Ancienne maison ardennaise rénovée où l'on vient faire des repas traditionnels soignés dans un cadre mi-rustique, mi-actuel. Restaurant d'été surplombant le jardin.
◆ Gerestaureerd pand in Ardense stijl, met een mix van rustiek en modern. Goed verzorgde, traditionele keuken. 's Zomers wordt het terras boven de tuin opgedekt.

BILZEN *3740 Limburg* 533 *S 17 et* 716 *J 3 – 29 475 h.*
Bruxelles 97 – Maastricht 16 – Hasselt 17 – Liège 29.

XX **'t Vlierhof,** Hasseltsestraat 57a, ✆ 0 89 41 44 18, *restaurant.vlierhof@belgacom.net, Fax 0 89 41 44 18*, 🏠 – ▤. AE ⓜ VISA. ✂
fermé fin juil.-début août, lundi soir, merc. et sam. midi – **Repas** *Lunch 26* – 38/65 bc.
◆ Le Clos du Sureau (Vlierhof), discret restaurant officiant à l'entrée du village, sert une cuisine au goût du jour renouvelée à chaque saison. Carte des vins fournie.
◆ Vrij discreet restaurant bij binnenkomst in het dorp, met een eigentijdse keuken die het ritme der seizoenen volgt. Mooie wijnkaart.

BINCHE *7130 Hainaut* 533 *J 20,* 534 *J 20 et* 716 *F 4 – 32 344 h.*
Voir *Carnaval★★★ (Mardi gras) – Vieille ville★ Z.*
Musée : *International du Carnaval et du Masque★ : masques★★* Z **M.**
Env. *au Nord-Est, 10 km par ① : Domaine de Mariemont★★ : parc★, musée★★.*
ℹ *Caves Bette, Parc communal, r. Promenades 2* ✆ *0 64 33 67 27, tourisme@binche.be, Fax 0 64 33 95 37.*
Bruxelles 62 ① – Mons 19 ⑤ – Charleroi 20 ② – Maubeuge 24 ④

Plan page suivante

XX **L'Aubade,** r. Bruxelles 37, ✆ 0 64 34 22 73, *laurence.motte@skynet.be, Fax 0 64 33 37 75* – ▤ P. AE ⓓ ⓜ VISA Y d
fermé 1 sem. après carnaval, 2 sem. en août, prem. sem. janv., mardi soir, merc. et dim. soir – **Repas** *Lunch 20* – 32/93 bc.
◆ Aux portes de la cité des Gilles, table classique aménagée dans une ancienne maison de notable donnant sur un grand jardin. Menus, plat du jour, suggestions et carte enfant.
◆ Klassiek restaurant in een herenhuis met een grote tuin, aan de rand van de stad van de Gilles. Menu's, dagschotel, suggesties en kindermenu.

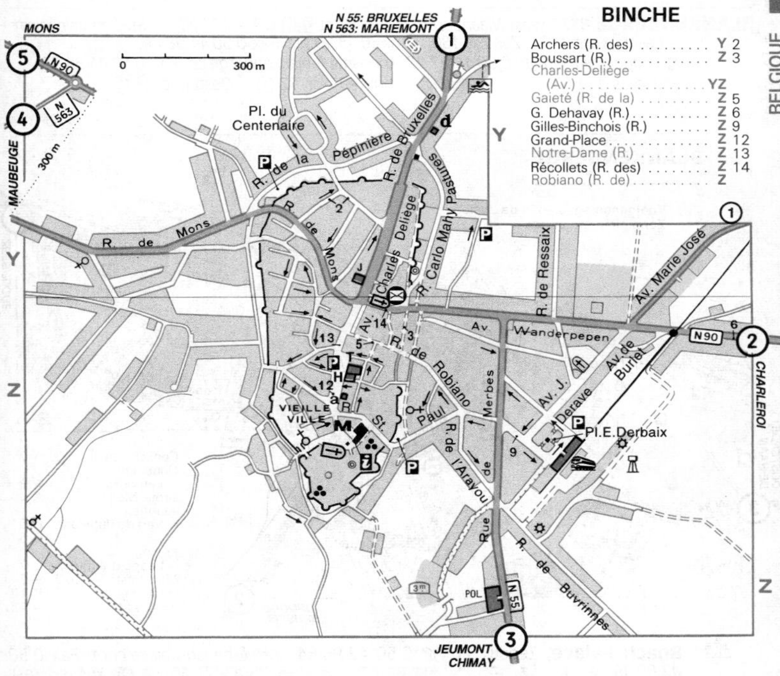

China Town, Grand'Place 12, ☎ 0 64 33 72 22, Cuisine chinoise, ouvert jusqu'à 23 h 30 – ▤. AE ⓞ ⓜ VISA Z a
fermé 2 sem. en août et merc. – **Repas** 22/31.
◆ Posté sur la Grand-Place, au cœur de la vieille ville, le China Town binchois vous reçoit dans une salle à manger au sobre décor exotique. Cuisine de l'Empire du Milieu.
◆ Deze Belgische China Town bevindt zich aan de Grote Markt, in het hart van de oude stad. Eetzaal met een exotisch decor zonder overdaad. Keuken uit het Rijk van het Midden.

à Bray *Ouest : 4 km* 🄲 *Binche* – ✉ *7130 Bray :*

Le Bercha, rte de Mons 763, ☎ 0 64 36 91 07, *Fax 0 64 36 91 07* – 🅿 – 100. AE ⓜ VISA
fermé prem. sem. janv., lundi et mardi – **Repas** Lunch 8 – 23/58 bc.
◆ Classique, la cuisine du Bercha fait aussi honneur aux produits du terroir, à travers quelques-unes des recettes figurant à la carte. La clientèle locale est conquise.
◆ Le Bercha presenteert een klassieke kaart, waarvan enkele gerechten een eerbetoon zijn aan de streekkeuken. Zeer tot genoegen van de plaatselijke bevolking !

à Buvrinnes *Sud-Est : 3 km* 🄲 *Binche* – ✉ *7133 Buvrinnes :*

La Fermette des Pins, r. Lustre 39 (par ③ : 3,5 km), ☎ 0 64 34 17 18, *Fax 0 64 34 17 18,* – 🅿. AE ⓞ ⓜ VISA
fermé 25 août-15 sept., du 2 au 15 janv., lundi soir, mardi et merc. – **Repas** Lunch 35 bc – 35/65 bc.
◆ Plats goûteux servis dans un décor champêtre, à l'image des abords de cette jolie fermette blanche. Agréable terrasse estivale dressée à la lisière des champs.
◆ Lekker eten in een schilderachtig boerderijtje in een landelijke omgeving. 's Zomers worden de tafels buiten gedekt op het terras aan de rand van de akkers.

BLANDEN *Vlaams-Brabant* 533 N 18 – *voir à Leuven.*

Si vous êtes retardé sur la route, dès 18 h, confirmez votre réservation par téléphone, c'est plus sûr... et c'est l'usage.

BLANKENBERGE *8370 West-Vlaanderen* 533 *D 15 et* 716 *C 2 – 17 726 h – Station balnéaire*★ *– Casino Kursaal A , Zeedijk 150, ✆ 0 50 43 20 20, Fax 0 50 41 98 40.*
i *Leopold III-plein ✆ 0 50 41 22 27, toerisme@blankenberge.be,* Fax 0 50 41 61 39.
Bruxelles 111 ② – Brugge 15 ② – Knokke-Heist 12 ① – Oostende 21 ③

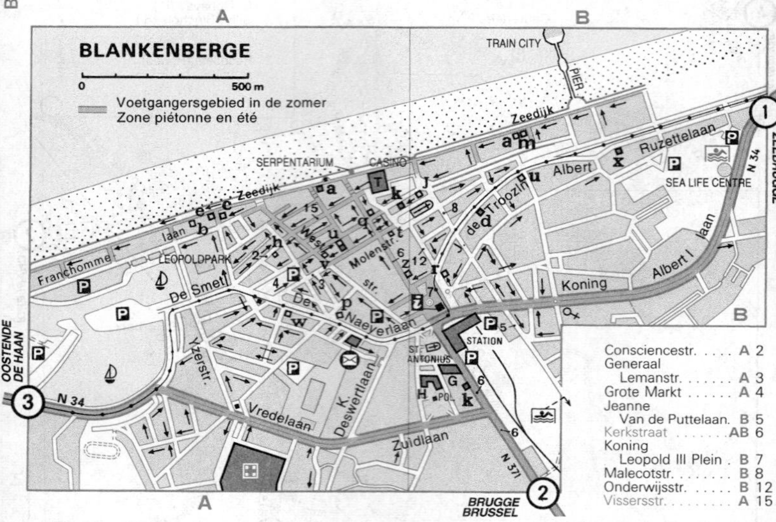

Beach Palace, Zeedijk 77, ✆ 0 50 42 96 64, *info@beach-palace.com, Fax 0 50 42 60 49,* ≤, – – 25 à 250. AE VISA. rest
Repas 39/97 bc – **97 ch** 123/166, – 3 suites – ½ P 72/105.
◆ Ce building récent dominant la plage renferme d'amples chambres pourvues d'un équipement moderne. La salle des petits-déjeuners offre la vue sur la digue. Piscine couverte. À table, carte classique et bonne sélection de vins.
◆ Dit nieuwe gebouw aan het strand beschikt over ruime kamers met moderne voorzieningen. De ontbijtzaal biedt uitzicht op de pier. Overdekt zwembad. Aan tafel klassieke gerechten, vergezeld van een goed glas wijn. A b

Azaert (annexe Aazaert - 21 ch), Molenstraat 31, ✆ 0 50 41 15 99, *info@azaert.be, Fax 0 50 42 91 46,* – rest, – – 25 à 70. VISA.
14 fév.-oct. – **Repas** *(fermé merc.)* (dîner seult jusqu'à 20 h 30) 29, ♀ – **51 ch** 85/107 – ½ P 64/78. A t
◆ Ensemble hôtelier comprenant plusieurs immeubles. Chambres de bon confort, salles de réunion, salons, piscine abritée, terrasse solarium et espaces de remise en forme. Restaurant chaleureux et cossu, restituant une atmosphère nostalgique.
◆ Dit hotelcomplex bestaat uit meerdere gebouwen. Comfortabele kamers, vergaderzalen, lounge, overdekt zwembad, zonneterras en fitnessruimte. Warm en rijk aandoend restaurant met een nostalgisch tintje.

Helios, Zeedijk 92, ✆ 0 50 42 90 20, *info@hotelhelios.be, Fax 0 50 42 86 66,* ≤, – rest, – 25 à 100. AE VISA JCB. A c
29 janv.-15 nov. – **Repas** ***Triton*** *(fermé mardi d'oct. à avril et merc.)* Lunch 15 – 30/55 bc – **34 ch** 120/150 – ½ P 70/100.
◆ Aménagement résolument design dans cet immeuble moderne surplombant l'animation de la digue. Chambres pimpantes, le plus souvent tournées vers la mer. Salle à manger contemporaine aux lignes épurées. Recettes classiques.
◆ Modern gebouw met een designinterieur, vlak bij de levendige pier. De kamers zien er piekfijn uit en bieden veelal uitzicht op zee. Eigentijdse en zeer gestileerde eetzaal, waar klassieke gerechten worden geserveerd.

Saint Sauveur, Langestraat 50, ✆ 0 50 42 70 00, *hotel@saintsauveur.be, Fax 0 50 42 97 38,* – rest, – 35. VISA JCB. A q
Repas (dîner pour résidents seult) – **49 ch** 100/150, – 3 suites – ½ P 65/85.
◆ Établissement engageant situé à un coup d'aile (de mouette) de la plage. Communs modernes, confortables chambres garnies d'un mobilier en bois stratifié. Piscine couverte.
◆ Uitnodigend etablissement op een steenworp afstand van het strand. Moderne, comfortabele kamers met meubilair van multiplex. Overdekt zwembad.

Riant Séjour, Zeedijk 188, ✆ 0 50 43 27 00, *wauters.jean@skynet.be, Fax 0 50 42 75 54*, ≤, ⛹, ⇔ - |♦|, ✈, TV ⇔. AE ◑ ◎ VISA. ✻ B a
fermé du 6 au 25 oct. et mardi, merc. et jeudi de Pâques à sept. – **Repas** *(fermé après 20 h)* Lunch 18 – carte 26 à 41 – **30 ch** ☕ 125, – 1 suite.
◆ Claires et spacieuses, toutes les chambres de cet hôtel dominant la plage offrent une vue dégagée sur la jetée et le large. Petite installation de remise en forme. Table classico-bourgeoise.
◆ Alle lichte en ruime kamers van dit hotel aan het strand bieden een onbelemmerd uitzicht op de pier en het ruime sop. Kleine fitnessruimte. Eenvoudige, klassieke keuken. Dit hotel staat garant voor een riant verblijf !

de la Providence sans rest, Zeedijk 191, ✆ 0 50 41 11 98, *karel.maes@skynet.be, Fax 0 50 41 80 79*, ≤, ⛹, ⇔ - |♦|, ▤ rest, TV. ◎ VISA. ✻ B m
14 fév.-7 nov. ; fermé 26 sept.-15 oct. – **24 ch** ☕ 77/115.
◆ Hôtel "providentiel" pour qui recherche la proximité immédiate du front de mer et de l'estacade. Avenantes chambres de différentes tailles. Fitness, sauna et solarium.
◆ Dit hotel is ideaal voor wie graag dicht bij zee en de pier verblijft. Prettige kamers van verschillende grootte. Fitnessruimte, sauna en solarium.

Malecot (annexe Avenue - 33 ch), Langestraat 91, ✆ 0 50 41 12 07, *Fax 0 50 42 80 42*, ⛹ - |♦| TV ⇔. ◎ VISA B j
avril-sept. – **Repas** (résidents seult) – **32 ch** ☕ 51/80 – ½ P 50/60.
◆ Ses façades couleur saumon signalent cet hôtel familial proche du casino et du rivage. Chambres pratiques, refaites de neuf. Quelques-unes se répartissent à l'annexe.
◆ Dit familiehotel bij het casino en het strand valt op door zijn zalmkleurige muren. De kamers zijn praktisch en volledig gerenoveerd ; sommige bevinden zich in de dependance.

Manitoba sans rest, Manitobaplein 11, ✆ 0 50 41 12 20, *manitoba@belgacom.net, Fax 0 50 42 98 08* – |♦|. ◎ VISA. ✻ A u
Pâques-début oct. – **20 ch** ☕ 80.
◆ Des chambres de bon confort vous attendent derrière l'élégante façade de cette demeure située dans la zone piétonnière. Petit-déjeuner soigné. Accueil familial.
◆ Achter de sierlijke gevel van dit pand in het voetgangersgebied wachten u kamers met een goed comfort. Hartelijk onthaal en verzorgd ontbijt.

Richmond Thonnon, Van Maerlantstraat 79, ✆ 0 50 42 96 92, *info@hotel-richmond.com, Fax 0 50 42 98 72*, ⇔, 🚲 - |♦| ✈, ▤ rest, TV ⇔ - 🏫 25. AE ◑ ◎ VISA. ✻ A p
Repas (résidents seult) – **38 ch** ☕ 115/124 – ½ P 79/88.
◆ Non loin du port de plaisance, de la plage et de la gare, petit immeuble d'angle renfermant une quarantaine de chambres standard convenablement équipées.
◆ Klein hoekpand, niet ver van de jachthaven, het strand en het station, met een veertigtal standaardkamers die goed zijn uitgerust.

Vivaldi, Koning Leopold III-plein 8, ✆ 0 50 42 84 37, *Fax 0 50 42 64 33* – |♦| TV ⇔. ◎ VISA. ✻ ch B r
fermé merc. – **Repas** *(fermé après 20 h)* Lunch 9 – carte env. 22 – **30 ch** ☕ 45/72 – ½ P 46/49.
◆ Pratique pour les usagers du rail, cet hôtel "quatre saisons" donne sur une place animée. Mobilier stratifié dans les chambres, parfois dotées d'un balconnet. Taverne-restaurant de mise simple.
◆ Dit hotel aan een druk plein is bijzonder handig voor treinreizigers, want het ligt vlak bij het station. Sommige kamers zijn voorzien van een balkonnetje. Eenvoudig café-restaurant, waar men snel een hapje kan eten alvorens weer op de trein te springen.

Moeder Lambic, J. de Troozlaan 93, ✆ 0 50 41 27 54, *info@moederlambic.be, Fax 0 50 41 09 44*, ☂ - |♦| TV ⇔. AE ◑ ◎ VISA. ✻ ch B u
fermé 8 janv.-8 fév. – **Repas** *(fermé merc. en hiver et jeudi)* Lunch 13 – 20/39 bc – **15 ch** ☕ 67/82 – ½ P 53/65.
◆ À 200 m de la plage, au coin d'une avenue desservie par le tram, établissement dont les coquettes chambres offrent un confort très correct, sans pour cela grever votre budget. Salle à manger agrémentée d'une grande véranda. Carte classique, menus à prix sages.
◆ Hotel op 200 m van het strand, nabij de tramhalte. Keurige, comfortabele kamers die geen aanslag zijn op uw budget. De eetzaal wordt opgeluisterd door een grote serre. Klassieke kaart en menu's voor een zacht prijsje.

Albatros sans rest, Consciencestraat 45, ✆ 0 50 41 13 49, *Fax 0 50 42 86 55*, ⇔ - |♦| TV P. ◎ VISA. ✻ A h
21 ch ☕ 60/95, – 4 suites.
◆ Petite affaire familiale située à quelques pas de la plage, disposant de chambres sobrement meublées et de quatre appartements avec salon séparé et kitchenette.
◆ Klein familiebedrijf, een paar minuten lopen van het strand. Naast de spaarzaam gemeubileerde kamers zijn er vier appartementen beschikbaar met zitkamer en kitchenette.

Claridge sans rest, de Smet de Naeyerlaan 81, ☎ 0 50 42 66 88, *Fax 0 50 42 77 04* – VISA. A w
fermé mardi, merc. et jeudi d'oct. à avril – **17 ch** 52/75.
◆ À deux pas de la Grand-Place, établissement de poche dont les chambres, agréables, sont décorées dans le style "Laura Ashley". Salon cossu. Service personnalisé.
◆ Klein hotel met prettige kamers in Laura Ashley-stijl, centraal gelegen bij de Grote Markt. Weelderige lounge. Persoonlijke service.

Alfa Inn sans rest, Kerkstraat 92, ☎ 0 50 41 81 72, *info@alfa-inn.com, Fax 0 50 42 93 24*, – VISA. AB z
13 fév.-15 nov. – **65 ch** 53/80.
◆ Rénovations progressives dans cet ancien couvent converti en hôtel. Chambres fonctionnelles sans grande ampleur, mais l'accueil est avenant.
◆ Oud klooster dat tot hotel is verbouwd en langzamerhand wordt opgeknapt. Kleine, maar handig ingedeelde kamers en vriendelijk personeel.

Du Commerce sans rest, Weststraat 64, ☎ 0 50 42 95 35, *info@hotel-du-commerce.be, Fax 0 50 42 94 40*, – AE VISA. A v
15 fév.-11 nov. – **29 ch** 50/76.
◆ Accueil plein de gentillesse et de bonne humeur dans cet hôtel créé en 1923 par les aïeux des patrons actuels. Chambres sobres, mais convenables. Clientèle touristique.
◆ Vriendelijke ontvangst in dit hotel dat in 1923 werd opgericht door de voorouders van de huidige eigenaren. Sobere, maar fatsoenlijke kamers. Veel toeristen.

Strand, Zeedijk 86, ☎ 0 50 41 16 71, *Fax 0 50 42 58 67* – AE VISA A e
fermé janv. – **Repas** (résidents seult) – **17 ch** 75/87 – ½ P 65/102.
◆ Établissement du front de mer renfermant de menues chambres aménagées avec simplicité. Six d'entre elles offrent une échappée vers la plage. Salon et tea-room.
◆ Hotel aan de boulevard met kleine kamers die eenvoudig zijn ingericht. Zes daarvan bieden een doorkijkje naar het strand. Lounge en tearoom.

Escapade J. de Troozlaan 39, ☎ 0 50 41 15 97, *Fax 0 50 42 88 64*, – AE VISA B d
fermé dern. sem. sept.-prem. sem. oct., dern. sem. janv., merc. du 15 oct. à Pâques et jeudi – **Repas** 25/45 bc.
◆ Copieux menus bien ficelés, honorable cave, décor intérieur témoignant d'une certaine recherche et terrasse d'été sur l'arrière font l'agrément de cette maison bourgeoise.
◆ De copieuze menu's, de lekkere wijnen, de verzorgde inrichting en het zomerterras aan de achterkant staan garant voor een prettige escapade.

St-Hubert, Manitobaplein 15, ☎ 0 50 41 22 42, *Fax 0 50 41 22 42*, – AE VISA JCB A u
fermé lundi et mardi – **Repas** carte 32 à 60.
◆ Cet établissement du centre piétonnier vous mitonne une ribambelle de plats classiques à dominante iodée. Menu "quatre services". Terrasse estivale dressée en façade.
◆ Restaurant in het voetgangersgebied met veel visspecialiteiten en een viergangenmenu. Klassieke keuken. Terras aan de voorkant, waar 's zomers buiten kan worden gegeten.

La Tempête avec ch, A. Ruzettelaan 37, ☎ 0 50 42 94 28, *hotel-la-tempete@hotmail.com, Fax 0 50 42 79 17* – VISA. ch B x
Repas *(fermé du 1er au 26 janv., lundi et merc. en hiver et mardi)* Lunch 18 – 29/60 bc – **9 ch** *(fermé du 2 au 26 janv. et lundi, mardi et merc. en hiver)* 70 – ½ P 45/49.
◆ Enseigne agitée à forte pour cette table offrant un bel éventail de plats traditionnels issus de la marée. Menus option "boissons comprises". Chambres pratiques.
◆ Hotel-restaurant, waar vis hoog in het vaandel staat en op traditionele wijze wordt bereid. Bij de menu's is de drank inbegrepen. De hotelkamers zijn praktisch en keurig.

Griffioen, Kerkstraat 163, ☎ 0 50 41 34 05, Produits de la mer, ouvert jusqu'à minuit – AE VISA B k
fermé du 1er au 30 janv., lundis non fériés hors saison et mardis non fériés – **Repas** Lunch 20 – carte 33 à 50.
◆ Aux abords de la gare, restaurant de quartier où l'on a plaisir à se retrouver entre amis autour de copieuses préparations dialoguant en direct avec le grand large.
◆ Buurtrestaurant bij het station, waar men gezellig met vrienden kan tafelen, onder het genot van een glas wijn. De copieuze schotels zijn een eerbetoon aan Neptunus.

't Fregat, Zeedijk 108, ☎ 0 50 41 34 86, *Fax 0 50 42 75 42*, ≤, , Taverne-rest. AE VISA A a
fermé du 1er au 15 déc., du 15 au 30 janv. et mardi – **Repas** Lunch 22 – carte 25 à 52.
◆ Une nouvelle frégate a échoué sur la digue. Deux formules s'y côtoient : taverne-bistrot au rez-de-chaussée et carte plus étoffée à l'étage. Terrasse d'été avec vue marine.
◆ Een nieuw fregat is op de kust geworpen. Twee formules : eenvoudige gerechten op de benedenverdieping en uitgebreide kaart op de bovenverdieping. Terras met uitzicht op zee.

La Lampara, Langestraat 69, ☎ 0 50 41 37 27, *minodimarco@freegates.be*, Cuisine italienne – MC VISA A k
fermé 2 prem. sem. juil., lundi sauf en été et mardi – **Repas** (dîner seult) carte 22 à 31.
• Dans une rue animée du centre, entre le casino et l'église St-Roch, restaurant au décor intérieur sobre. Cuisine simple tournée vers l'Italie. Cave bien fournie.
• Sober ingericht restaurant in een levendige straat in het centrum, tussen het casino en de St.-Rochuskerk. Sobere keuken die op Italië is gericht. Ruime keuze aan wijnen.

à Zuienkerke *par ② : 6 km – 2 779 h – ✉ 8377 Zuienkerke :*

Butler sans rest, Blankenbergsesteenweg 13a, ☎ 0 50 42 60 72, *Fax 0 50 42 61 35* – TV P – 25. AE ① MC VISA.
15 ch ☕ 55/75.
• Ce petit hôtel occupant un immeuble récent à l'architecture massive vous réserve un accueil personnalisé. Chambres agréables ; la moitié sont mansardées.
• Klein hotel in een nieuw gebouw met een wat zware architectuur. Persoonlijk onthaal en aangename kamers, waarvan de helft op de zolderverdieping ligt.

Hoeve Ten Doele, Nieuwesteenweg 1, ☎ 0 50 41 31 04, *Fax 0 50 42 63 11*, – P. MC VISA.
fermé du 8 au 26 mars, du 14 au 18 juin, 27 sept.-15 oct., du 27 au 31 déc. midi et lundis et mardis non fériés – **Repas** 38 bc/50 bc.
• Ferme du 19e s. dans un typique paysage de polders. Décor intérieur néo-rustique, salle de banquets séparée. Cuisine classique sensible au rythme des marées et des saisons.
• Boerderij uit de 19e eeuw in een typisch polderlandschap. Neorustiek interieur met aparte zaal voor partijen. Klassieke keuken die rekening houdt met het marktaanbod.

De Grote Stove, Nieuwesteenweg 140, ☎ 0 50 42 65 64, *info@degrotestove.be*, *Fax 0 50 42 65 64*, , Taverne-rest – P. MC VISA
fermé 12 nov.-6 déc., merc. sauf en juil.-août et mardi – **Repas** carte 25 à 46, ♀.
• Une exploitation agricole prête ses murs à cette taverne-restaurant. Salle à manger aménagée dans les anciennes étables. L'été, le couvert est aussi dressé en plein air.
• Taverne-restaurant in een boerderij, waarvan de oude stallen tot eetzaal zijn omgetoverd. 's Zomers kan er ook buiten worden gegeten.

BLAREGNIES *7040 Hainaut* C *Quévy 7 663 h.* 533 I 20, 534 I 20 *et* 716 E 4.

Bruxelles 80 – Mons 15 – Bavay 11.

Les Gourmands (Bernard), r. Sars 15, ☎ 0 65 56 86 32, *Fax 0 65 56 74 40* – P. MC VISA
fermé dim. soir, lundi et après 20 h 30 – **Repas** Lunch 60 bc – 49/110 bc, carte 52 à 89.
• Les gourmets ne s'y trompent pas : l'originalité de cette table tient nettement moins à son décor qu'au contenu des assiettes, personnalisé avec talent. Cave impressionnante.
• De originaliteit van dit restaurant zit hem niet zozeer in de inrichting als wel in de geheel eigen kookstijl van de talentvolle chef-kok. Indrukwekkende wijnkelder.
Spéc. Homard au four, jus au basilic. Foie d'oie poêlé aux fèves de cacao. Pintade et petits gris, crème à l'ail doux

---

BLÉGNY *4671 Liège* 533 T 18, 534 T 18 *et* 716 K 3 – *12 506 h.*

Bruxelles 105 – Maastricht 26 – Liège 12 – Verviers 22 – Aachen 33.

Barbothez , r. Entre deux Bois 55, ☎ 0 4 387 52 67, *restaurant@la-source.be*, *Fax 0 4 387 69 35*, , , – TV P – 25 à 100. AE ① MC VISA.
fermé du 2 au 16 janv. – **Repas *La Source*** Lunch 26 – 34/64 bc – ☕ 12 – **18 ch** 70/80 – ½ P 70/90.
• Dans une vallée bucolique, à la lisière d'un bois, ancien moulin à eau devenu un petit hôtel bien charmant. Chambres de bon confort, dont un tiers sont des suites. Restaurant d'été bercé par le chant de la rivière, avec les prairies pour toile de fond.
• Deze oude watermolen in een landelijk dal aan de rand van een bos is nu een sfeervol hotelletje. De kamers, waarvan een derde uit suites bestaat, zijn comfortabel. 's Zomers wordt het terras aan het water opgedekt, met uitzicht op de groene weiden.

à Housse *Ouest : 3 km* C *Blégny – ✉ 4671 Housse :*

Le Jardin de Caroline, r. Saivelette 8, ☎ 0 4 387 42 11, *lejardindecaroline@belgacom.net*, *Fax 0 4 387 42 11*, – P. AE ① MC VISA
fermé mardi et merc. – **Repas** Lunch 44 bc – carte 40 à 54.
• Villa contemporaine bâtie dans un quartier résidentiel. Mise en place soignée, registre culinaire en phase avec l'époque, véranda et jardinet rafraîchi par une pièce d'eau.
• Moderne villa in een rustige woonwijk. Verzorgde presentatie en een eigentijds culinair register. Serre en tuintje met waterpartij.

BOCHOLT *3950 Limburg* 533 S 15 *et* 716 J 2 – *11 981 h.*
Bruxelles 106 – Hasselt 42 – Antwerpen 91 – Eindhoven 38.

XXX **Kristoffel,** Dorpsstraat 28, ✆ 0 89 47 15 91, *restaurant.kristoffel@yucom.be, Fax 0 89 47 15 92* – ▤. AE ⓓ ⓜ VISA. ✈
fermé 12 juil.-3 août, du 1er au 12 janv., lundi et mardi – **Repas** Lunch 27 – 38/54.
◆ Confortable restaurant dont la cuisine, dans le tempo actuel, honore volontiers l'asperge en saison. Salon-bar moderne, salle à manger classique. Grand choix de vins.
◆ Comfortabel restaurant waarvan de eigentijdse keuken in het seizoen een eerbetoon brengt aan de asperge. Modern salon met bar en klassieke eetzaal. Uitgebreide wijnkaart.

BOECHOUT *Antwerpen* 533 L 16 *et* 716 G 2 – *voir à Antwerpen, environs.*

BOHON *Luxembourg belge* 534 R 20 – *voir à Barvaux.*

BOIS-DE-VILLERS *5170 Namur* Ⓒ *Profondeville 10 907 h.* 533 O 20, 534 O 20 *et* 716 H 4.
Bruxelles 74 – Namur 13 – Dinant 23.

X **Au Plaisir du Gourmet,** r. Elie Bertrand 75, ✆ 0 81 43 44 12, *Fax 0 81 43 44 12,* ☂ – P. ⓜ VISA
fermé fin août et mardis et merc. non fériés – **Repas** Lunch 31 – carte 23 à 33.
◆ Accueil cordial dans cette charmante fermette en pierres du pays qu'agrémente d'un jardin planté de rosiers. Préparations classico-traditionnelles, sans chichi.
◆ Joviale ontvangst in dit mooie boerderijtje van steen uit de streek, dat wordt opgevrolijkt door een tuin met rozenstruiken. Klassiek-traditionele keuken zonder poespas.

BOKRIJK *Limburg* 533 R 17 *et* 716 J 3 – *voir à Genk.*

BOLDERBERG *Limburg* 533 Q 17 *et* 716 I 3 – *voir à Zolder.*

BOLLAND *Liège* 533 T 19 *et* 534 T 19 – *voir à Battice.*

BONCELLES *Liège* 533 S 19, 534 S 19 *et* 716 J 4 – *voir à Liège, environs.*

BONHEIDEN *Antwerpen* 533 M 16 *et* 716 G 2 – *voir à Mechelen.*

BONLEZ *1325 Brabant Wallon* Ⓒ *Chaumont-Gistoux 10 476 h.* 533 N 18, 534 N 18 *et* 716 H 3.
Bruxelles 34 – Namur 31 – Charleroi 51 – Leuven 24 – Tienen 34.

X **32 Chemin de l'herbe,** Chemin de l'herbe 32, ✆ 0 10 68 89 61, *chemindelherbe@skynet.be, Fax 0 10 68 89 61,* ☂ – AE ⓜ VISA
fermé dim. soir et lundi – **Repas** Lunch 9 – carte 29 à 40.
◆ À l'entrée du village, dans un tournant, jolie fermette aux volets bleus et aux murs tapissés de lierre. Décor intérieur campagnard. Plats classiques et grillades.
◆ Aardig boerderijtje met blauwe luiken en met klimop begroeide muren in een bocht aan de rand van het dorp. Landelijk interieur. Klassieke keuken en grillspecialiteiten.

BOOM *2850 Antwerpen* 533 L 16 *et* 716 G 2 – *15 089 h.*
Bruxelles 30 – Antwerpen 18 – Gent 57 – Mechelen 16.

XX **Cheng's Garden,** Col. Silvertopstraat 5, ✆ 0 3 844 21 84, *kaho.cheng@chengsgarden.com, Fax 0 3 844 54 46,* Avec cuisine chinoise – ▤ P. AE ⓓ ⓜ VISA. ✈
fermé merc., jeudi midi et sam. midi – **Repas** carte 24 à 41.
◆ Si les délicatesses cantonaises vous tentent, attablez-vous dans cet agréable restaurant au cadre moderne européanisé. Cave bien fournie pour ce type d'adresse.
◆ Liefhebbers van de Kantonese keuken kunnen aanschuiven in dit aangename restaurant met een moderne inrichting in Europese stijl. Voor Chinese begrippen een goede wijnkelder.

à Terhagen *Sud-Est : 3 km* Ⓒ *Rumst 14 470 h* – ✉ *2840 Terhagen :*

XX **Epicurus,** Kardinaal Cardijnstraat 46, ✆ 0 3 888 33 11, *epicurus@skynet.be, Fax 0 3 888 33 11,* ☂ – ⓜ VISA. ✈
fermé juil., lundi, mardi et merc. – **Repas** Lunch 33 bc – carte env. 46.
◆ L'épicurien appréciera les recettes classiques actualisées que cette table du centre de la localité mitonne avec soin. Belle présentation sur l'assiette. Accueil souriant.
◆ Epicuristen zullen de modern-klassieke gerechten waarderen die hier met liefde worden bereid. Fraai opgemaakte borden en vriendelijke bediening.

BORGERHOUT *Antwerpen* 533 L 15 *et* 716 G 2 – *voir à Antwerpen, périphérie.*

BORGLOON (LOOZ) 3840 Limburg 533 R 18 et 716 J 3 – 10 056 h.

Bruxelles 74 – Maastricht 29 – Hasselt 28 – Liège 29.

Kasteel van Rullingen, Rullingen 1 (Ouest : 3 km à Kuttekoven), 0 12 74 31 46, *info@rullingen.com, Fax 0 12 74 54 86*, – 25 à 100. AE VISA.
Repas *(fermé sam. midi) Lunch 40* – 70, ♀ – 11 – **15 ch** 87/124 – ½ P 69/136.
♦ Des chambres personnalisées trouvent place dans ce ravissant petit château d'esprit Renaissance mosane. Installations pour séminaires. Parc entouré de douves et de vergers. D'allure aristocratique, le restaurant mise sur une carte d'orientation classique.
♦ Schitterend renaissancekasteeltje met mooie kamers en faciliteiten voor congressen. De kasteeltuin wordt omringd door greppels en boomgaarden. Het restaurant heeft beslist aristocratische allure en hanteert een klassiek georiënteerde kaart.

Pracha, Kogelstraat 3, 0 12 74 20 74, *info@pracha.be, Fax 0 12 74 57 04*, – VISA
Repas (résidents seult) – **7 ch** 87 – ½ P 64/75.
♦ Villa moderne où vous passerez un séjour "cocooning" dans une ambiance relax. Centre de remise en forme, salons douillets, sémillante véranda et jardin avec pièce d'eau.
♦ Moderne villa om in een relaxte sfeer te "cocoonen". Fitnesscentrum, behaaglijke zitkamers, aangename serre en tuin met waterpartij.

De Moerbei sans rest, Tongersesteenweg 26, 0 12 74 72 82, *Fax 0 12 74 51 42*, – VISA.
6 ch 92.
♦ Ancienne ferme (1845) devenue hôtel. Salon, jardin d'hiver, cour intérieure et verger où la vigne a aussi pris racine. Pimpantes chambres parquetées. Accueil personnalisé.
♦ Hotel in een boerderij uit 1845, met lounge, wintertuin, binnenhof en boomgaard. De kamers met parket zien er tiptop uit en de gasten krijgen nog echt persoonlijke aandacht.

Ambrozijn, Tongersesteenweg 30, 0 12 74 72 31, *info@restaurantambrozijn.be, Fax 0 12 74 72 31* – . VISA.
fermé 28 fév.-10 mars, 16 août-2 sept., lundi soir, mardi et sam. midi – **Repas** *Lunch 25* – 30/63 bc, ♀.
♦ Savoureuse cuisine au goût du jour - l'Ambroisie (Ambrozijn) n'est elle pas la nourriture des dieux ? - servie dans un intérieur au style actuel. Cave bien montée.
♦ Goddelijk eten - ambrozijn is tenslotte een godenspijs - in een eigentijds interieur dat goed bij de kookstijl past. Mooie wijnkaart.

Het Klaphuis avec ch, Kortestraat 2, 0 12 74 73 25, *sarto@portina.be, Fax 0 14 36 99 38*, – – 25 à 40. AE VISA JCB.
fermé 2 dern. sem. août – **Repas** *(fermé merc.) Lunch 19* – 32/67 bc, ♀ – **8 ch** 48/70 – ½ P 52/54.
♦ Une cuisine d'aujourd'hui se conçoit dans la stabilité derrière les fourneaux de ce restaurant jouxtant la maison communale. Apaisante salle à manger sans tape-à-l'œil.
♦ In dit restaurant naast het gemeentehuis wordt evenwichtig gekookt in hedendaagse stijl. Rustgevende eetzaal zonder overbodige franje.

BORGWORM *Liège – voir Waremme.*

BORNEM 2880 Antwerpen 533 K 16 et 716 F 2 – 19 906 h.

Bruxelles 36 – Antwerpen 28 – Gent 46 – Mechelen 21.

Bornem sans rest, Rijksweg 58, 0 3 889 03 40, *hotel.bornem@skynet.be, Fax 0 3 899 00 42*, – – 25 à 50. AE VISA.
fermé Noël et Nouvel An – **17 ch** 90.
♦ Au bord d'une route nationale et au voisinage des autoroutes E 17 et A 12, petit hôtel récent abritant des chambres standard correctement équipées. Salle de réunions.
♦ Moderne accommodatie aan de rijksweg, vlak bij de E17 en de A12. Standaardkamers met goede voorzieningen. Het hotel beschikt ook over een vergaderzaal.

Eyckerhof (Debecker), Spuistraat 21 (Eikevliet), 0 3 889 07 18, *eyckerhof@busmail.net, Fax 0 3 889 94 05*, – AE VISA.
fermé sem. carnaval, du 5 au 27 juil., du 1er au 4 janv., sam. midi, dim. soir et lundi – **Repas** (nombre de couverts limité - prévenir) *Lunch 39* – 52/90 bc, carte 68 à 89.
♦ Mignonne auberge dont le cadre champêtre et l'intérieur "cosy" se prêtent idéalement à l'interprétation d'un répertoire culinaire actuel, personnalisé avec délicatesse.
♦ Lieflijke herberg, waarvan de landelijke omgeving en het knusse interieur zich uitstekend lenen voor een hedendaags culinair repertoire met een licht persoonlijke toets.
Spéc. Poêlée de langoustines et carpaccio tiède de langue de bœuf (avril-juil.). Tronçon de turbot et carottes Vichy. Pigeon de Bresse farci au pied de porc et foie d'oie

BELGIQUE

De Notelaer avec ch, Stationsplein 2, ☎ 0 3 889 13 67, *info@denotelaer.be, Fax 0 3 899 13 36,* ☂, 🚲 – |♦|, ▤ rest, TV – 🏛 25 à 80. AE ◉ ◎ VISA JCB. ✂
fermé du 23 au 29 déc. – **Repas** *(fermé jeudi et sam. midi)* Lunch 28 – carte 41 à 75 – **12 ch** ☕ 75/95 – ½ P 86.
◆ Promue restaurant, naguère café de gare, la maison dispose aussi de chambres plaisantes. Déco contemporaine de bon ton et menu-carte bien dans le coup.
◆ Dit oude stationscafé is nu een restaurant met prettige kamers. Hedendaagse inrichting, met smaak gedaan. De kaart is vrij modern en er wordt ook een menu geserveerd.

Den Heerd, Sint-Amandsesteenweg 31, ☎ 0 3 899 21 22, *info@denheerd.com, Fax 0 3 889 59 12,* ☂ – ◎ VISA. ✂
fermé du 7 au 14 mars, Noël-Nouvel An, lundi et mardi – **Repas** carte 32 à 42.
◆ Ce restaurant tenu en famille depuis plus de dix ans met une ancienne grange à profit. Rustique salle à manger où flotte une atmosphère conviviale. Terrasse d'été.
◆ Dit restaurant in een oude graanschuur wordt al ruim 10 jaar door dezelfde familie geleid. Rustieke eetzaal met een gemoedelijke atmosfeer. Terras in de zomer.

à Mariekerke *Sud-Ouest : 4,5 km* C *Bornem* – ✉ *2880 Mariekerke :*

De Ster, Jan Hammeneckerstraat 141, ☎ 0 52 33 22 89, *restaurant.dester@busmail.net, Fax 0 52 34 24 89,* ☂ – P. AE ◉ ◎ VISA. ✂
fermé 2 dern. sem. mars, 2 dern. sem. août, mardi et merc. – **Repas** 29/64 bc, ♀.
◆ Autrefois relais de poste, cet établissement au sobre décor d'aujourd'hui vous réserve un accueil chaleureux. Cuisine mariant tradition et goût du jour. Menus attrayants.
◆ In dit zonder luxe ingerichte restaurant in een voormalig poststation wordt u gastvrij ontvangen. De keuken is een mix van traditioneel en actueel. Aantrekkelijke menu's.

Une réservation confirmée par écrit ou par fax est toujours plus sûre.

BOUGE *Namur* 533 O 20, 534 O 20 *et* 716 H 4 – *voir à Namur.*

BOUILLON *6830 Luxembourg belge* 534 P 24 *et* 716 I 6 – *5 393 h.*

Voir *Château*★★ Z *: Tour d'Autriche* ≤★★.
Musée : *Ducal*★ Y **M.**
Env. *par* ③ *: 8 km à Corbion : Chaire à prêcher* ≤★.
ℹ *au Château fort, Esplanade Godefroy de Bouillon* ☎ 0 61 46 62 57, *info@bouillon-sedan.org,* Fax 0 61 46 42 12 – (en saison) Pavillon, Porte de France ☎ 0 61 46 42 02.
Bruxelles 161 ① – *Arlon 64* ② – *Dinant 63* ① – *Sedan 18* ②

BOUILLON

Ange-Gardien (R. de l') . . . Y 2
Augustins (R. des) . . . . . Y 3
Brutz (R. du) . . . . Y 4
Collège (R. du) . . . . YZ
Ducale (Pl.) . . . . Y 5
Écoles (R. des) . . . . Y 6
Faubourg de France . . . Z 7
France (Pt de) . . . . Z 8
France (Pte de) . . . . Z 9
Godefroi-de Bouillon (Espl.) . . . . . Y 10
Hautes-Voies (R. des) . . . Y 11
Laitte (R. de) . . . . Z 12
Liège (Pt de) . . . . Y 13
Maladrerie (Q. de la) . . . Y 14
Maladrerie (R. de la) . . . Y 15
Moulin (R. du) . . . . Z 16
Nord (R. du) . . . . Y 18
Paroisse (All. de la) . . . . Z 19
Petit (R. du) . . . . Y 20
Poste (R. de la) . . . . Z 22
Poulie (Pt de la) . . . . . . Y 23
Poulie (R. de la) . . . . . . Y 24
Prison (R. de la) . . . . . . Y 26
Rempart (Q. du) . . . . . . YZ
St-Arnould (Pl.) . . . . Y 27
Saulx (Q. des) . . . . Y 28

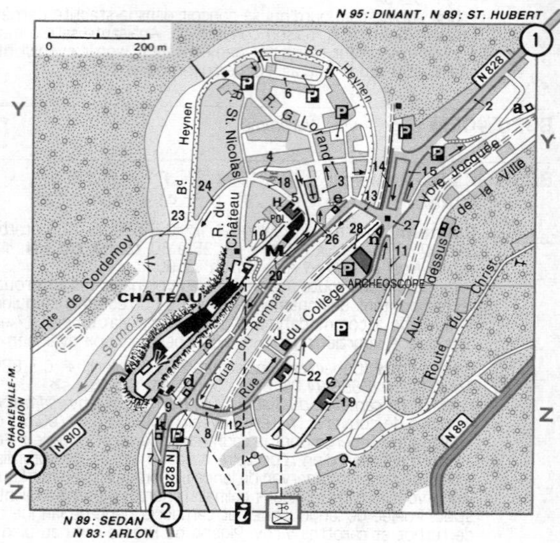

Les plans de villes sont disposés le Nord en haut.

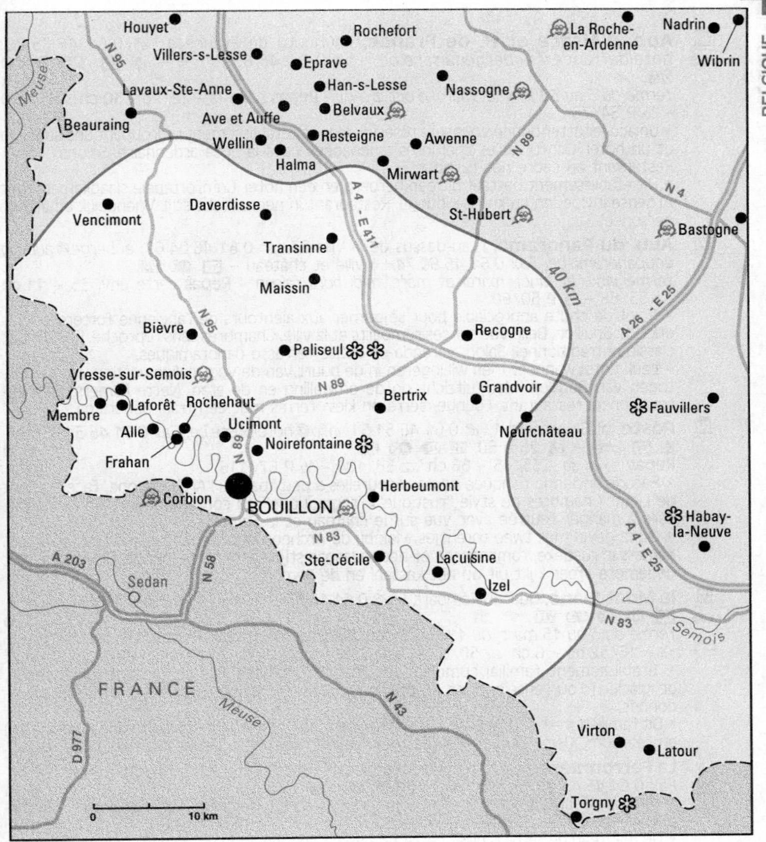

Panorama, r. au-dessus de la Ville 25, 0 61 46 61 38, *panorama@panoramahotels.be, Fax 0 61 46 81 22,* vallée et château, ch, rest Y c
fermé 25 juin-10 juil. et janv. – **Repas** *(fermé merc. et jeudi hors saison)* carte env. 43 – **24 ch** 73/90 – ½ P 62/70.
◆ Immeuble "panoramique" dominant la ville. Chambres bien agencées, salon douillet avec cheminée et terrasse procurant un coup d'œil intéressant sur le puissant château. Confortable restaurant au goût du jour, perché tel un belvédère.
◆ Dit hooggelegen gebouw biedt een weids uitzicht op de stad en zijn imposante burcht. Goed ingerichte kamers, gezellige lounge met open haard en terras. In het restaurant kunt u niet alleen genieten van de eigentijdse keuken, maar ook van het fraaie panorama.

La Porte de France, Porte de France 1, 0 61 46 62 66, *laportedefrance@hotmail.com, Fax 0 61 46 89 15,* 25. VISA. rest Z d
Repas Lunch 18 – 25/65 – **25 ch** 60/98 – ½ P 70/82.
◆ Posté au pied du rempart, cet agréable établissement d'aspect régional jouxte aussi le pont de France. Quatre catégories de chambres, pourvues d'un mobilier en merisier. Sobre salle des repas aux accents Art nouveau.
◆ Aangenaam hotel-restaurant in regionale stijl aan de voet van de stadsmuur, vlak bij de Pont de France. Er zijn vier categorieën kamers, die allemaal met kersenhouten meubelen zijn ingericht. Sobere eetzaal met art-nouveau-accenten.

BELGIQUE

Aub. d'Alsace et H. de France, Faubourg de France 1, ✆ 0 61 46 65 88, *hoteldefrance@aubergedalsace.be, Fax 0 61 46 83 21,* ≤ - |‡| TV. AE ⓓ ⓜⓒ VISA. ✂ Z k
fermé du 3 au 30 janv. et mardi d'oct. à avril – **Repas** *Lunch 15* – 22/26 – **30 ch** ☕ 54/79 – ½ P 54/76.
♦ Un accueil attentionné vous sera réservé dans cet établissement regroupant une auberge et un hôtel. Confortables chambres aménagées dans la note ardennaise. Salons "cosy". Restaurant au cadre néo-rustique.
♦ Dit etablissement bestaat uit een herberg en een hotel. Comfortabele slaapkamers met Ardense invloeden en knusse lounge. Restaurant in neorustieke stijl. Vriendelijk en attent personeel.

Aub. du Panorama, r. au-dessus de la Ville 23, ✆ 0 61 46 04 62, *auberge@aubergedupanorama.be, Fax 0 61 46 80 74,* ≤ ville et château – TV. ⓜⓒ VISA Y c
fermé janv. et lundi, mardi et merc. midi hors saison – **Repas** carte env. 35 – **11 ch** ☕ 55/68 – ½ P 50/60.
♦ Point de chute appréciable pour séjourner aux alentours de l'ancienne forteresse des ducs de Bouillon. Belle vue sur ses remparts et la ville. Chambres sans reproche. Restaurant classique-traditionnel. Salon, véranda et petite terrasse panoramiques.
♦ Leuk hotel wanneer men wil logeren in de buurt van de voormalige vesting van de hertogen van Bouillon. Mooi uitzicht op de omwalling en de stad. Nette kamers. Klassiek-traditioneel restaurant. Lounge, serre en klein terras met een fraai panorama.

Poste, pl. St-Arnould 1, ✆ 0 61 46 51 51, *info@hotelposte.be, Fax 0 61 46 51 65,* ≤ – |‡| TV 🚗 – 🎓 25 à 50. AE ⓓ ⓜⓒ VISA Y n
Repas *Lunch 30* – 35/45 – **66 ch** ☕ 56/104 – ½ P 67/116.
♦ Façade ancienne flanquée de deux tourelles à deux pas de l'Archéoscope, face au pont de Liège. Chambres de style "rustique", "romantique" ou contemporain. Salon agréable. Salle à manger feutrée avec vue sur le château et la Semois.
♦ Oude gevel met twee torentjes, vlak bij de Archeoscoop, tegenover de brug van Luik. Kamers in rustieke, romantische of hedendaagse stijl. Aangename lounge. De eetzaal met gedempte sfeer kijkt uit op het kasteel en de Semois.

le Mont Blanc, Quai du Rempart 3, ✆ 0 61 46 63 31, *Fax 0 61 46 82 74,* 🌂 – ▤ rest, TV. AE ⓓ ⓜⓒ VISA. ✂ ch Y e
fermé du 3 au 15 mars, du 1er au 15 oct., lundi soir et mardi – **Repas** (taverne-rest) *Lunch 13* – 16/32 bc – **6 ch** ☕ 50/65 – ½ P 53.
♦ Établissement familial cumulant les fonctions d'hôtel, de restaurant, de taverne, de glacier (d'où l'enseigne) et de tea-room. Menues chambres habillées de tissus coordonnés.
♦ Dit familiehotel heeft heel wat te bieden : een café, restaurant, ijssalon (vandaar de naam) en tearoom. Kleine kamers die met gevoel voor harmonie zijn gestoffeerd.

La Ferronnière 🐌 avec ch, Voie Jocquée 44, ✆ 0 61 23 07 50, *info@laferronniere.be, Fax 0 61 46 43 18,* ≤, 🌂, 🌳 – TV P. ⓜⓒ VISA Y a
fermé du 15 au 25 mars, 21 juin-9 juil., du 10 au 25 janv., lundi et mardi midi – **Repas** *(fermé après 20 h 30) Lunch 25* – 29/60 – **7 ch** ☕ 75/105 – ½ P 69/87.
♦ Un manteau de lierre tapisse cette jolie villa surplombant la vallée de la Semois. Élégante salle à manger d'esprit Art déco, chambres personnalisées et reposant jardinet.
♦ Mooie, met klimop begroeide villa boven het dal van de Semois. Elegante eetzaal geïnspireerd op de art-decostijl, kamers met een persoonlijk karakter en een rustige tuin.

à Corbion *par ③ : 7 km* © *Bouillon* – ✉ *6838 Corbion :*

Ardennes 🐌, r. Hate 1, ✆ 0 61 25 01 00, *contact@hoteldesardennes.be, Fax 0 61 46 77 30,* ≤, 🌳, ✂, 🚲 – |‡|, ▤ rest, TV P – 🎓 25. AE ⓓ ⓜⓒ VISA
mi-mars-début janv. – **Repas** *Lunch 25* – 30/55 – **29 ch** ☕ 90/110 – ½ P 70/85.
♦ Hostellerie ardennaise centenaire postée aux portes de Corbion. Chambres classiques personnalisées. Jardin ombragé offrant une vue dépaysante sur les collines boisées. Derrière les fourneaux, le chef valorise la tradition. Assiettes généreuses et goûteuses.
♦ Honderd jaar oude herberg in Ardense stijl aan de rand van Corbion. Klassieke kamers met een persoonlijke sfeer. De schaduwrijke tuin biedt een fraai uitzicht op de beboste heuvels. Achter het fornuis houdt de chef-kok de traditie in ere. Genereuze porties.

Le Relais, r. Abattis 5, ✆ 0 61 46 66 13, *info@hotellerelais.be, Fax 0 61 46 89 50,* 🌂 –
Repas *(fermé après 20 h 30)* 22/30 – **11 ch** ☕ 70 – ½ P 53.
♦ Au centre du village frontalier où séjourna Paul Verlaine, typique petite affaire familiale proposant des chambres fonctionnelles à prix "sympa". Terrasse d'été en façade. Restaurant "couleur locale" précédé d'un coin salon.
♦ Typisch familiehotel in het centrum van het grensplaatsje waar Paul Verlaine ooit verbleef. De kamers zijn functioneel en niet duur. 's Zomers terras aan de voorkant. Restaurant met veel "couleur locale" en een aparte zithoek.

à Ucimont *par ① : 8,5 km* ◻ *Bouillon* – ✉ *6833 Ucimont :*

du Saule , r. Fontinelle 9, ☏ 0 61 46 64 42, *hoteldusaule@bouillon.net, Fax 0 61 46 85 78,* , , – ◻ . AE MC VISA.
Repas *(fermé mardi midi et merc. midi) Lunch 27* – 30/60 bc – **11 ch** ☐ 67/95 – ½ P 71/75.
◆ Cette avenante hostellerie animant une bourgade tranquille renferme des chambres coquettes et correctement équipées. Le grand jardin invite au repos. Classique, la carte du restaurant annonce notamment un menu "homard". Terrasse d'été ombragée.
◆ Aangenaam hotel dat wat leven in de brouwerij brengt in dit rustige dorpje. De kamers zien er keurig uit en hebben goede voorzieningen. In de tuin is het heerlijk luieren. Klassieke kaart met een speciaal kreeftmenu. Lommerrijk terras in de zomer.

BOURG-LÉOPOLD *Limburg* – *voir Leopoldsburg.*

BOUSSU-EN-FAGNE *Namur* 534 L 22 *et* 716 G 5 – *voir à Couvin.*

BOVIGNY *Luxembourg belge* 534 U 21 *et* 716 K 5 – *voir à Vielsalm.*

BRAINE-L'ALLEUD (EIGENBRAKEL) *1420 Brabant Wallon* 533 L 18, 534 L 18 *et* 716 G 3 – *35 897 h.*
(2 parcours) *chaussée d'Alsemberg 1021* ☏ *0 2 353 02 46, Fax 0 2 354 68 75.*
Bruxelles 18 – Charleroi 37 – Nivelles 15 – Waterloo 4.

Jacques Marit, chaussée de Nivelles 336 (sur N 27, près R0, sortie ㉔), ☏ 0 2 384 15 01, *Fax 0 2 384 10 42,* – AE MC VISA
fermé 1 sem. après Pâques, août, prem. sem. janv., lundi et mardi – **Repas** *Lunch 35* – 48/82 bc, carte 52 à 74.
◆ Une soigneuse cuisine escoffière sobrement actualisée, que magnifient d'excellents vins, vous attend dans cette fermette cossue. La terrasse surplombe jardin et verger.
◆ Verzorgde keuken à la Escoffier met een vleugje vernieuwing en uitstekende wijnen in een weelderig ingericht boerderijtje. Het terras kijkt uit op de tuin en de boomgaard.
Spéc. Croquant de foie gras d'oie au Granny Smith. Agneau de notre élevage (mars-août). Fine feuille à l'huile de noisettes et praslin

à Ophain-Bois-Seigneur-Isaac *Sud : 2 km* ◻ *Braine-l'Alleud* – ✉ *1421 Ophain-Bois-Seigneur-Isaac*

Le Chabichou, r. Église 2, ☏ 0 2 385 07 76, *Fax 0 2 387 03 20,* – AE MC VISA
fermé Pâques, 21 juil.-15 août, Noël-Nouvel An, mardi soir, merc. et sam. midi – **Repas** *Lunch 14* – 28/40.
◆ À l'ombre du clocher, charmante fermette brabançonne du 16e s. interprétant un répertoire culinaire classique. Menus et choix de vins bien ficelés. Lunch à bon prix.
◆ Charmant Brabants boerderijtje uit de 16e eeuw met een klassiek culinair repertoire. Mooie menu's en een hecht doortimmerde wijnkaart. Voordelig lunchmenu.

BRAINE-LE-COMTE ('s-GRAVENBRAKEL) *7090 Hainaut* 533 J 19, 534 J 19 *et* 716 F 4 – *19 458 h.*
Bruxelles 34 – Mons 28.

Au Gastronome, r. Mons 1, ☏ 0 67 55 26 47, *Fax 0 67 55 26 47* – AE MC VISA
fermé 28 juin-20 juil. et dim. soirs et lundis non fériés – **Repas** *Lunch 16* – 22/45 bc.
◆ Lambris, poutres, lustres et appliques à l'ancienne donnent une touche chaleureuse à cette petite adresse mitonnant une cuisine classique sans fioriture. Plusieurs menus.
◆ De lambrisering, hanenbalken en antieke lampen geven dit restaurantje een warme uitstraling. Klassieke keuken zonder frutsels en fratsels. Verscheidene menu's.

BRASSCHAAT *Antwerpen* 533 L 15 *et* 716 G 2 – *voir à Antwerpen, environs.*

BRAY *Hainaut* 533 J 20, 534 J 20 *et* 716 F 4 – *voir à Binche.*

BRECHT *2960 Antwerpen* 533 M 14 *et* 716 G 1 – *25 451 h.*
Bruxelles 73 – Antwerpen 25 – Turnhout 25.

Torsk, Bethovenstraat 61 (près E 19 - sortie ③), ☏ 0 3 313 70 72, *info@torsk.be, Fax 0 3 313 44 80,* – AE MC VISA.
fermé mardi et merc. – **Repas** *Lunch 17* – 25/76 bc, ♀.
◆ Un jardin arboré borde cette villa proche d'une sortie d'autoroute. Intéressante carte de plats actuels, un rien personnalisés. Terrasse d'été garnie de meubles en teck.
◆ Deze villa bij de snelweg heeft een tuin met veel bomen. Kaart met eigentijdse gerechten, waaraan de kok een persoonlijke noot weet te geven. Terras met teakhouten meubelen.

XX **Cuvee Hoeve,** Vaartdijk 4 (Sud : 2,5 km par rte de Westmalle), ☎ 0 3 313 96 60, *Fax 0 3 313 73 96,* ☂, Avec taverne, ouvert jusqu'à 23 h – ▤ P. AE ⓓ ⓂⒸ VISA JCB
fermé 3 sem. en fév., 2 sem. en juil., lundi et mardi – **Repas** 26/40 bc.
◆ Ferme en briques isolée au bord d'un petit canal. Intérieur néo-rustique. Cuisine classico-traditionnelle déclinée en plusieurs menus. Jardin soigné. Affluence d'habitués.
◆ Afgelegen boerderij van baksteen langs een kanaal. Neorustiek interieur en klassiek-traditionele keuken met verscheidene menu's. Goed onderhouden tuin. Veel stamgasten.

X **E 10 Hoeve,** Kapelstraat 8a (Sud-Ouest : 2 km sur N 115), ☎ 0 3 313 82 85, *e10@groepvaneyck.be, Fax 0 3 313 73 12,* ☂, Avec grillades – P. – 🏛 35 à 500. AE ⓓ ⓂⒸ VISA JCB. ✂
Repas *Lunch 25* – carte 26 à 50.
◆ À proximité de l'autoroute, grande ferme aménagée en restaurant rustique ayant pour spécialité les grillades en salle. Cave fournie. Colossale infrastructure pour séminaires.
◆ Grote boerderij bij de snelweg, die rustiek is ingericht en bekendstaat om zijn vlees van de grill. Goed gevulde wijnkelder. Zeer geschikt voor grote groepen.

BREDENE *8450 West-Vlaanderen* 533 C 15 *et* 716 B 2 – *14 473 h.*

ℹ *Kapellestraat 70* ☎ *0 59 32 09 98, toerisme@bredene.be,* Fax 0 59 33 19 80.
Bruxelles 112 – Brugge 23 – Oostende 6.

à Bredene-aan-Zee *Nord : 2 km* C *Bredene* – ✉ *8450 Bredene :*

🏠 **Lusthof** 🔇, Zegelaan 18, ☎ 0 59 33 00 34, *info@hotel-lusthof.be, Fax 0 59 32 59 59,* 🏊, 🌳, 🚲 – TV P. VISA. ✂ ch
fermé 2 sem. en fév. et 2 sem. en oct. – **Repas** (résidents seult) – **13 ch** ☕ 43/71 – ½ P 38/41.
◆ Imposante villa située dans un quartier résidentiel paisible, proche de la plage. Chambres confortables à prix sages. La piscine est installée dans le jardin ombragé.
◆ Imposante villa in een rustige woonwijk dicht bij zee. Comfortabele kamers voor een zacht prijsje. Schaduwrijke tuin met zwembad. Een echt lusthof dus !

🏠 **de Golf** sans rest, Kapellestraat 73, ☎ 0 59 32 18 22, *info@hoteldegolf.be, Fax 0 59 32 48 28* – 🛗 TV P. ⓂⒸ VISA. ✂
fermé vacances Noël – **16 ch** ☕ 33.
◆ À deux pas du front de mer, construction récente renfermant des petites chambres fonctionnelles munies du double vitrage. Tea-room au rez-de-chaussée.
◆ Modern gebouw op twee minuten lopen van het strand. De kamers zijn klein, maar functioneel en voorzien van dubbele beglazing. Tearoom op de benedenverdieping.

BREE *3960 Limburg* 533 S 16 *et* 716 J 2 – *14 150 h.*

Env. au Sud-Est : 4,5 km à Tongerlo : Musée Léonard de Vinci★.
ℹ *Oud Stadhuis 13* ☎ *0 89 46 94 18, toerisme@bree.be,* Fax 0 89 47 39 79.
Bruxelles 100 – Hasselt 33 – Antwerpen 86 – Eindhoven 41.

XX **d'Itterpoort,** Opitterstraat 32, ☎ 0 89 46 80 17, *Fax 0 89 46 80 17* – ▤. AE ⓓ ⓂⒸ VISA. ✂
fermé sem. carnaval, dern. sem. juil.-2 prem. sem. août, mardi soir, merc. soir et sam. midi – **Repas** *Lunch 30* – carte 46 à 60.
◆ Officiant à l'entrée d'une rue piétonne, ce petit restaurant succède à une ancienne boucherie. Carte classique et menu annoncé oralement. Parking public juste en face.
◆ Dit restaurantje aan het begin van een voetgangersstraat was vroeger een slagerij. Klassieke kaart en mondeling aangekondigd menu. Parkeerruimte aan de overkant.

BROECHEM *Antwerpen* 533 M 15 *et* 716 G 2 – *voir à Lier.*

BRUGGE – BRUGES

8000 **P** *West-Vlaanderen* 533 E 15 *et* 716 C 2 – *116 836 h.*

Bruxelles 96 ③ *– Gent 45* ③ *– Lille 72* ④ *– Oostende 28* ⑤.

OFFICES DE TOURISME

Burg 11 ℘ 0 50 44 86 86, toerisme@brugge.be, Fax 0 50 44 86 00 et dans la gare, Stationsplein – Fédération provinciale de tourisme, Koning Albert I-laan 120, ℘ 0 50 30 55 00, info@westtoer.be, Fax 0 50 30 55 90.

RENSEIGNEMENTS PRATIQUES

18 *au Nord-Est : 7 km à Sijsele, Doornstraat 16 ℘ 0 50 35 35 72, Fax 0 50 35 89 25.*

CURIOSITÉS

Voir *La Procession du Saint-Sang★★★ (De Heilig Bloedprocessie) – Centre historique et canaux★★★ (Historisch centrum en grachten) : Grand-Place★★ (Markt)* AU, *Beffroi et Halles★★★ (Belfort en Hallen) ⩽★★ du sommet* AU, *Place du Bourg★★ (Burg)* AU, *Basilique du Saint-Sang★ (Basiliek van het Heilig Bloed) : chapelle basse★ ou chapelle St-Basile (beneden-of Basiliuskapel)* AU **B**, *Cheminée du Franc de Bruges★ (schouw van het Brugse Vrije) dans le Palais du Franc de Bruges (Paleis van het Brugse Vrije)* AU **S**, *Quai du Rosaire (Rozenhoedkaai) ⩽★★* AU 63, *Dijver ⩽★★* AU, *Pont St-Boniface (Bonifatiusbrug) : cadre★★* AU, *Béguinage★★ (Begijnhof)* AV *– Promenade en barque★★★ (Boottocht)* AU *– Église Notre-Dame★ (O.-L.-Vrouwekerk) : tour★★, statue de la Vierge et l'Enfant★★, tombeau★★ de Marie de Bourgogne★★* AV **N**.

Musées : *Groeninge★★★ (Stedelijk Museum voor Schone Kunsten)* AU *– Memling★★★ (St-Janshospitaal)* AV *– Gruuthuse★ : buste de Charles Quint★ (borstbeeld van Karel V)* AU **M¹** *– Arentshuis★* AU **M⁴** *– du Folklore★ (Museum voor Volkskunde)* DY **M²**.

Env. *par* ⑥ *: 10,5 km à Zedelgem : fonts baptismaux★ dans l'église St-Laurent (St-Laurentiuskerk) – au Nord-Est : 7 km : Damme★.*

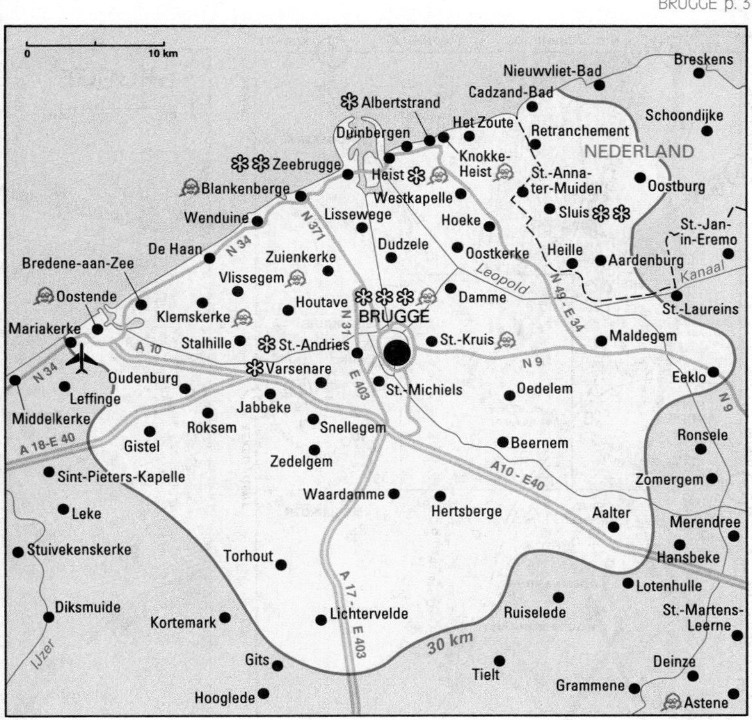

Les Bonnes Tables

Gourmets...

Nous distinguons à votre intention
certains hôtels (...) et restaurants (...)
par **Repas** @, ✿, ✿✿ ou ✿✿✿.

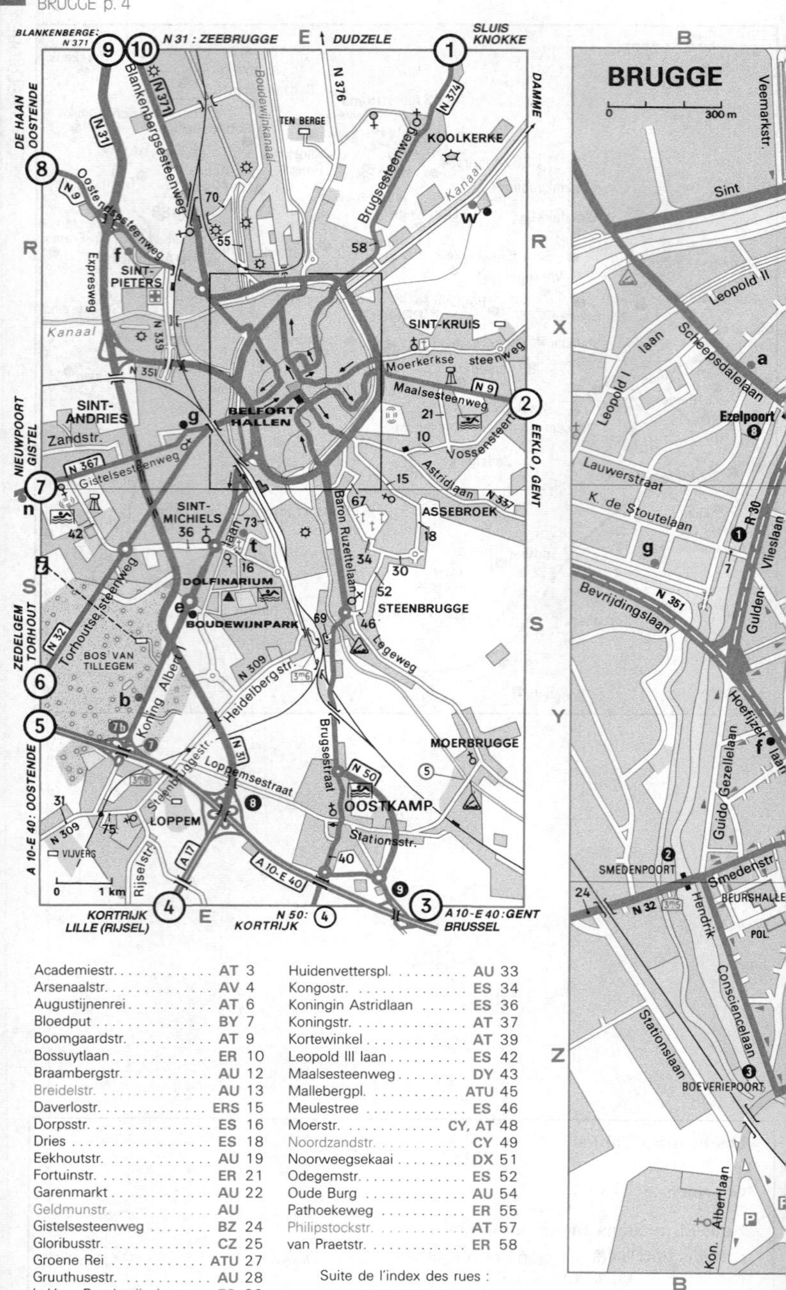

Suite de l'index des rues : Brugge p. 6

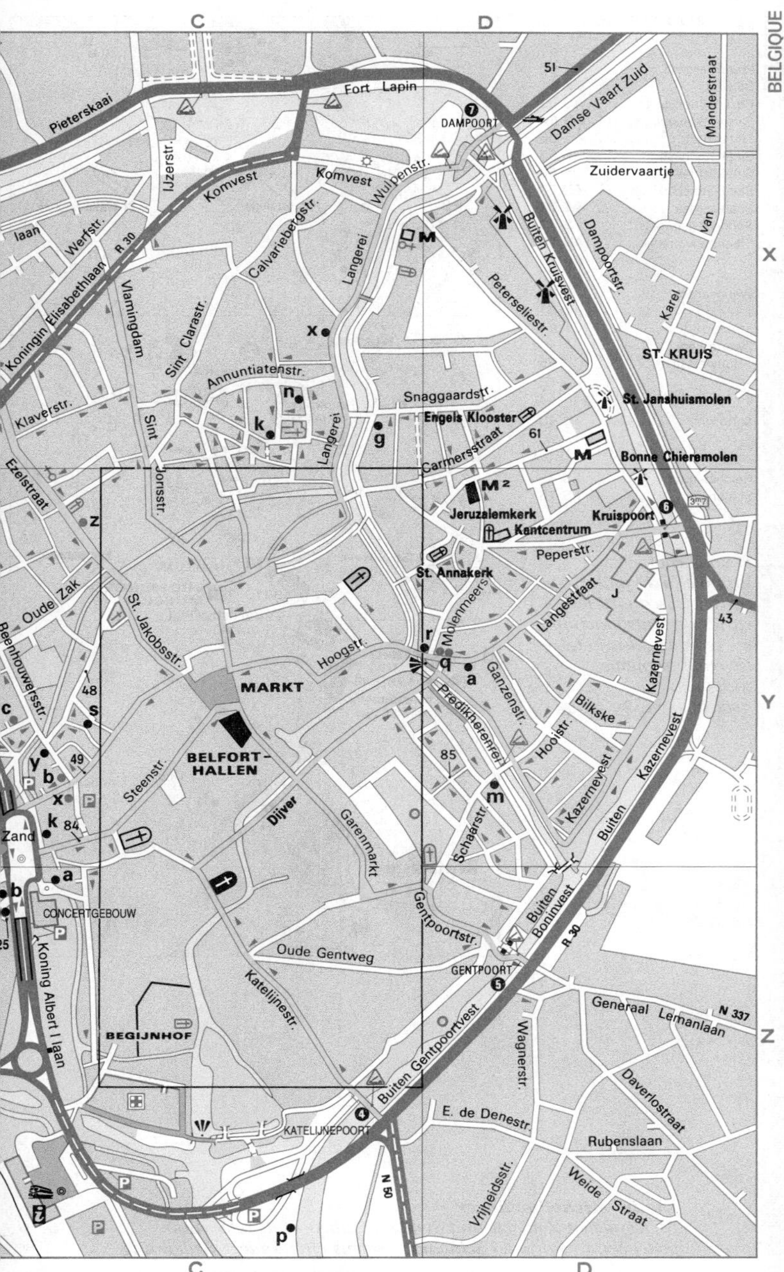
C
D
Pieterskaai
Fort Lapin
DAMPOORT
Damse Vaart Zuid
Manderstraat
Zuidervaartje
Komvest
Komvest
Wulpenstr.
IJzerstr.
Werfstr.
laan
R 30
Koningin Elisabethlaan
Vlamingdam
Calvariebergstr.
Langerei
Buiten Kruisvest
Dampoortstr.
Van
Karel
Peterseliestr.
Sint Clarastr.
Annuntiatenstr.
ST. KRUIS
Snaggaardstr.
St. Janshuismolen
Klaverstr.
Sint
Engels Klooster
Langerei
Carmersstraat
Bonne Chieremolen
Jorisstr.
Ezelstraat
Jeruzalemkerk
Kruispoort
Kantcentrum
Peperstr.
Oude Zak
St. Annakerk
Langestraat
St. Jakobsstr.
Molenmeers
Kazernevest
Reenhouwersstr.
Hoogstr.
MARKT
Ganzenstr.
Bilkske
Predikherenrei
Kazernevest
BELFORT-HALLEN
Hooistr.
Steenstr.
Dijver
Kazernevest
Buiten
Zand
Garenmarkt
Schaarstr.
Buiten Boninvest
CONCERTGEBOUW
Gentpoortstr.
R 30
Koning Albert I laan
Oude Gentweg
GENTPOORT
Katelijnestr.
Generaal Lemanlaan
N 337
BEGIJNHOF
Buiten Gentpoortvest
Wagnerstr.
Daverlostraat
E. de Denestr.
KATELIJNEPOORT
Rubenslaan
N 50
Vrijheidsstr.
Weide Straat
X
Y
Z

INDEX DES RUES
(fin)

Si vous cherchez un hôtel tranquille, consultez d'abord les cartes de l'introduction ou repérez dans le texte les établissements indiqués avec le signe ou

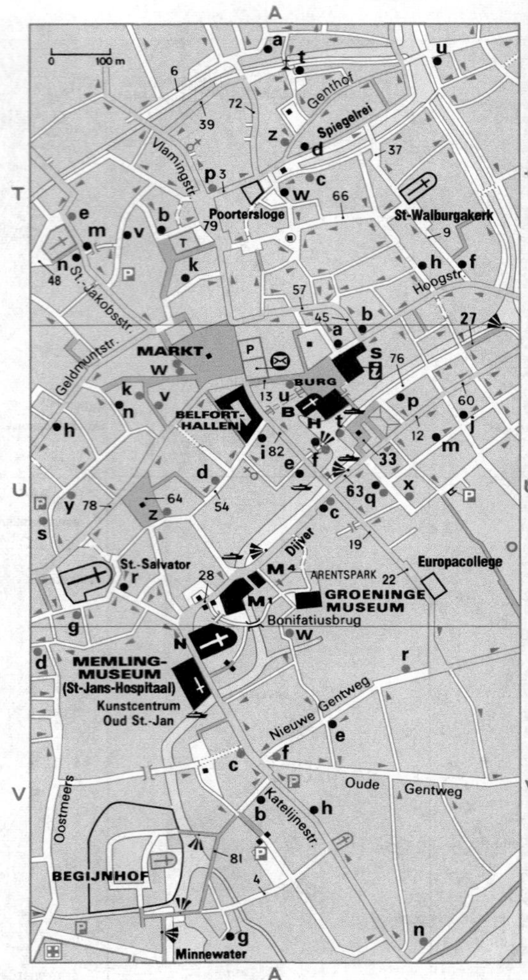

Die im Michelin-Führer *verwendeten Zeichen und Symbole haben -* ***fett*** *oder dünn gedruckt, in Rot oder* ***Schwarz*** *- jeweils eine andere Bedeutung.*

Lesen Sie daher die Erklärungen aufmerksam durch.

Liste alphabétique des hôtels et restaurants
Alfabetische lijst van hotels en restaurants
Alphabetisches Hotel- und Restaurantverzeichnis
Alphabetical list of hotels and restaurants

Quartiers du Centre :

Crowne Plaza, Burg 10, 0 50 44 68 44, *hotel@crowne-plaza-brugge.com, Fax 0 50 44 68 68*, – 25 à 400. AU a
Repas *Het Kapittel* *(fermé merc. soir, sam. midi et dim.)* Lunch 20 – 31/67 bc – ***De Linde*** Lunch 9 – 22/32 bc – 19 – **93 ch** 226/270, – 3 suites.
◆ Cet hôtel assez tranquille et de grand confort s'élève sur la place du Bourg. Les sous-sols recèlent d'importants vestiges et objets médiévaux. Repas gastronomique au Het Kapittel. Tea-room et restauration sous forme de buffets au De Linde.
◆ Vrij rustig en zeer comfortabel hotel aan de Burg. In de kelderverdieping zijn nog talloze overblijfselen uit de Middeleeuwen te zien. Gastronomische maaltijd in Het Kapittel. Tea-room en buffetten in De Linde.

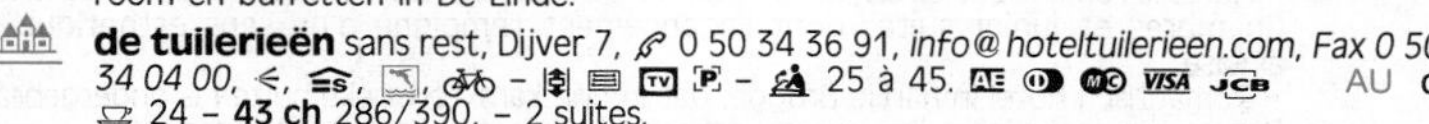

de tuilerieën sans rest, Dijver 7, 0 50 34 36 91, *info@hoteltuilerieen.com, Fax 0 50 34 04 00*, – 25 à 45. AU c
24 – **43 ch** 286/390, – 2 suites.
◆ Une élégante demeure bourgeoise du 17e s. bordant l'un des canaux pittoresques du centre abrite cet hôtel à l'intérieur cossu. Pimpantes chambres bien équipées.
◆ Mooi hotel in een sierlijke patriciërswoning uit de 17e eeuw, aan een van de schilderachtige grachten in het centrum. De kamers zijn comfortabel en zien er picobello uit.

Relais Oud Huis Amsterdam sans rest, Spiegelrei 3, 0 50 34 18 10, *info@oha.be, Fax 0 50 33 88 91*, – 25. AT d
20 – **32 ch** 198/238, – 2 suites.
◆ Le long d'un canal, ancien comptoir commercial hollandais du 17e s. converti en établissement de charme proposant des chambres avec vue très agréable. Garage fermé à 300 m.
◆ Oud-Hollands grachtenpand uit de 17e eeuw, dat van handelsbank tot sfeervol hotel is verbouwd. Kamers met zeer fraai uitzicht. Parkeergarage op 300 m.

de orangerie sans rest, Kartuizerinnenstraat 10, 0 50 34 16 49, *info@hotelorangerie.com, Fax 0 50 33 30 16*, AU e
24 – **19 ch** 233/312, – 1 suite.
◆ Tranquille hôtel dans une maison ancienne au bord d'un magnifique canal dont la vue profite à quatre chambres. Mobilier de style. Ravissant patio et terrasse à fleur d'eau.
◆ Rustig hotel in een oud grachtenpand met stijlmeubilair. Vier kamers bieden een prachtig uitzicht op de gracht. Mooie patio en terras aan het water.

Die Swaene, Steenhouwersdijk 1, 0 50 34 27 98, *info@dieswaene-hotel.com, Fax 0 50 33 66 74*, ch, – 30.
Repas *(fermé 2 sem. en juil., 2 sem. en janv., merc. et jeudi midi)* Lunch 40 – 54/99 bc – 18 – **30 ch** 185/295, – 2 suites. AU p
◆ Ce paisible hôtel de caractère offrant la vue sur un canal réjouira les amateurs d'ameublement de style. Les chambres, romantiques à souhait, sont habilement individualisées. Restaurant gastronomique intime et chaleureux. Service irréprochable.
◆ Dit rustige, karaktervolle hotel met uitzicht op de gracht zal in de smaak vallen bij liefhebbers van stijlmeubelen. De kamers, waarvan er geen twee hetzelfde zijn, zijn superromantisch. Gastronomisch restaurant met een intieme sfeer. Onberispelijke bediening.

Sofitel, Boeveriestraat 2, 0 50 44 97 11, *H1278@accor-hotels.com, Fax 0 50 44 97 99*, – 25 à 150. CZ b
Repas *Ter Boeverie* Lunch 30 bc – 40 bc/57 bc – 19 – **151 ch** 218.
◆ Bel hôtel de chaîne du centre-ville donnant sur une vaste place. Amples chambres garnies de meubles de divers styles, plus agréables à vivre depuis leur rénovation. Restaurant misant sur une cuisine classique, des plats traditionnels et un choix végétarien.
◆ Mooi ketenhotel, dat uitkijkt op een groot plein. De pas gerenoveerde kamers zijn ruim en met meubelen in verschillende stijlen ingericht. Restaurant dat het accent legt op de klassieke keuken, met traditionele gerechten en vegetarische schotels.

Acacia sans rest, Korte Zilverstraat 3a, 0 50 34 44 11, *info@hotel-acacia.com, Fax 0 50 33 88 17*, – 25 à 40.
fermé du 4 au 22 janv. – **46 ch** 130/190, – 2 suites. AU n
◆ Près de la Grand-Place, ressource hôtelière se distinguant par son entretien impeccable et son aménagement assez recherché. Chambres spacieuses, souvent duplex.
◆ Hotel in de buurt van de Markt, dat opvalt door zijn perfecte onderhoud en verzorgde inrichting. De kamers zijn ruim en vaak duplex.

de' Medici, Potterierei 15, 0 50 33 98 33, *reservation@hoteldemedici.com, Fax 0 50 33 07 64*, – 25 à 180. CX g
Repas voir rest ***Koto*** ci-après – **81 ch** 174/209.
◆ Établissement récent bâti à l'écart du centre, en face d'un canal. Intérieur contemporain. Grandes chambres très correctement équipées. Petit jardin japonais.
◆ Recent gebouw aan een gracht, even buiten het centrum. Modern interieur. Grote kamers met uitstekende voorzieningen. Kleine Japanse tuin.

BELGIQUE

Jan Brito sans rest, Freren Fonteinstraat 1, ☎ 0 50 33 06 01, *info@janbrito.com, Fax 0 50 33 06 52*, – 25 à 40. AU j
19 ch 109/220, – 3 suites.
◆ Typique façade à redans abritant des chambres amples et luxueuses au 1er étage, moins spacieuses, actuelles et mansardées au 2e. Décor intérieur des 16e, 17e et 18e s.
◆ Pand met trapgevel, dat in 16e-, 17e- en 18e-eeuwse stijl is ingericht. De kamers op de eerste verdieping zijn ruim en luxueus ; die op de tweede zijn kleiner en moderner.

Pandhotel sans rest, Pandreitje 16, ☎ 0 50 34 06 66, *info@pandhotel.com, Fax 0 50 34 05 56* – AU q
20 – **24 ch** 135/230.
◆ Adresse romantique et élégante : trois maisons de caractère nichées au cœur de Brugge. Chambres et junior suites dont l'agencement témoigne d'un sens esthétique très aiguisé.
◆ Romantisch hotel in hartje Brugge, dat in drie karakteristieke huizen is ondergebracht. De kamers en junior suites zijn op esthetisch verantwoorde wijze ingericht.

Heritage sans rest, N. Desparsstraat 11, ☎ 0 50 44 44 44, *info@hotel-heritage.com, Fax 0 50 44 44 40*, AT k
24 ch 125/218.
◆ Entre la Grand-Place et le théâtre, majestueuse demeure bourgeoise (19e s.) convertie en hôtel tranquille et confortable. Jolie cave avec coin fitness. Atmosphère feutrée.
◆ Tussen de Markt en de schouwburg staat dit majestueuze 19e-eeuwse herenhuis, dat nu een rustig en comfortabel hotel is. Mooie kelder met fitnessruimte. Vrij knus.

Walburg sans rest, Boomgaardstraat 13, ☎ 0 50 34 94 14, *hotelwalburg@skynet.be, Fax 0 50 33 68 84* – 30. AT f
fermé 5 janv.-5 fév. – **12 ch** 130/200, – 1 suite.
◆ Fière architecture néo-classique dont l'entrée cochère dessert un hall monumental où s'étagent deux hautes galeries animées de colonnes et balustrades. Chambres "king size".
◆ Fier neoclassicistisch bouwwerk, waarvan de oude koetspoort naar een monumentale hal leidt met twee bovengalerijen, gesierd door zuilen en balustrades. King-size kamers.

Novotel Centrum, Katelijnestraat 65b, ☎ 0 50 33 75 33, *H1033@accor-hotels.com, Fax 0 50 33 65 56*, – 50 à 400. AV h
Repas (dîner seult) carte 27 à 36, – 14 – **126 ch** 122/139.
◆ Cet hôtel de chaîne bâti à proximité du béguinage et du musée Memling propose des chambres refaites de neuf et bien tenues. Agréable lobby-bar. Le restaurant assure un service complet en soirée, mais plus restreint au déjeuner.
◆ Dit hotel, dat tot een keten behoort, ligt niet ver van de Begijnhof en het Memling-museum. De kamers zijn pas opgeknapt en worden goed onderhouden. Aangename lobby met bar. In het restaurant kan men snel lunchen, maar ook uitgebreid dineren.

Prinsenhof sans rest, Ontvangersstraat 9, ☎ 0 50 34 26 90, *info@prinsenhof.com, Fax 0 50 34 23 21* – CY s
16 ch 128/278.
◆ Petit hôtel accueillant et cossu dans une maison de maître rénovée, à l'écart de l'animation du centre. Toutes les chambres sont différentes et offrent un confort actuel.
◆ Klein hotel in een gerenoveerd herenhuis met een weelderige inrichting, waar u prinselijk wordt ontvangen. Alle kamers zijn verschillend en bieden modern comfort.

De Castillion (annexe Het Gheestelic Hof - 14 ch), Heilige Geeststraat 1, ☎ 0 50 34 30 01, *info@castillion.be, Fax 0 50 33 94 75*, – ch, – 25 à 50. rest AU r
Repas *le Manoir Quatre Saisons* *(fermé 25 juil.-13 août et dim. soirs, lundis midis et mardis midis non fériés)* Lunch 35 – 45/87 bc – **20 ch** 150/325 – ½ P 125/150.
◆ L'ancien palais épiscopal (1743) prête ses murs à cet hôtel mignon comme tout. Enfilade de pignons à redans, chambres personnalisées, salon Art déco et jolie cour intérieure. Salle à manger de notre temps, mais meublée dans la note Louis XVI.
◆ Magnifiek hotel in het voormalige bisschoppelijk paleis, dat uit 1743 dateert. Talrijke trapgevels, kamers met een persoonlijke sfeer, lounge in art-decostijl en mooie binnenplaats. De eetzaal is van onze tijd, maar in Louis XVI-stijl gemeubileerd.

Montanus sans rest, Nieuwe Gentweg 78, ☎ 0 50 33 11 76, *info@montanus.be, Fax 0 50 34 09 38*, – 40. AV e
24 ch 120/235.
◆ Charmant hôtel récemment créé dans une maison de maître à l'écart de l'animation. La moitié des coquettes chambres donnent sur le jardin et son pavillon anglais.
◆ Charmant hotel dat onlangs is geopend in een herenhuis buiten de drukte van het centrum. De helft van de fleurige kamers kijkt uit op de tuin en het Engelse paviljoen.

Aragon sans rest, Naaldenstraat 22, ✆ 0 50 33 35 33, *info@aragon.be, Fax 0 50 34 28 05* – 🛗 ▤ TV P – 🧑‍🏫 25. AE ⓓ MC VISA JCB. 🚫 AT v
42 ch ☕ 120/172.
◆ Hôtel chaleureux occupant deux maisons bourgeoises entièrement rénovées. Confort moderne dans les chambres, avenantes et bien isolées du bruit. Agréables lounge et bar.
◆ Gezellig hotel in twee herenhuizen die volledig zijn gerenoveerd. Prettige kamers met modern comfort en goede geluidsisolatie. Aangename lounge en bar.

Adornes sans rest, St-Annarei 26, ✆ 0 50 34 13 36, *hotel.adornes@proximedia.be, Fax 0 50 34 20 85*, ≤, 🚲 – 🛗 TV 🚗. AE ⓓ MC VISA AT u
fermé janv.-12 fév. – **20 ch** ☕ 90/120.
◆ Quatre jolies maisons mitoyennes avec vue sur le canal forment ce petit hôtel tranquille et soigné. Bonnes chambres, chaleureuse salle de breakfast et vieilles caves voûtées.
◆ Vier mooie belendende grachtenpanden vormen dit rustige, goed verzorgde hotel. Prima kamers, gezellige ontbijtzaal en oude gewelfde kelders.

Azalea sans rest, Wulfhagestraat 43, ✆ 0 50 33 14 78, *info@azaleahotel.be, Fax 0 50 33 97 00*, 🚲 – 🛗 🚭 TV 🚗 P. AE ⓓ MC VISA JCB CY y
fermé du 20 au 27 déc. – **25 ch** ☕ 122/160.
◆ Cette maison ancienne, naguère brasserie, s'agrémente d'un jardin-terrasse revigorant alangui au bord du canal. Pimpantes chambres, salon-bibliothèque et ambiance familiale.
◆ Hotel in een oude bierbrouwerij, met een mooie tuin en een terras langs de gracht. Frisse kamers, lounge met bibliotheek en huiselijke sfeer.

Portinari sans rest, 't Zand 15, ✆ 0 50 34 10 34, *info@portinari.be, Fax 0 50 34 41 80* – 🛗 🚭 ▤ TV 🚗 – 🧑‍🏫 25 à 80. AE ⓓ MC VISA JCB CY k
fermé du 4 au 30 janv. – **40 ch** ☕ 120/150.
◆ Établissement dont les chambres, fonctionnelles, ont été rajeunies ; celles situées à l'arrière procurent plus de quiétude. Une grande terrasse abritée s'ouvre sur le 't Zand.
◆ De praktische kamers van dit hotel hebben een verjongingskuur ondergaan ; die aan de achterkant zijn het rustigst. Een groot beschut terras kijkt uit op 't Zand.

Navarra sans rest, St-Jakobsstraat 41, ✆ 0 50 34 05 61, *reservations@hotelnavarra.com, Fax 0 50 33 67 90*, 🏋, ≘s, 🏊, 🌳 – 🛗 🚭 ▤ TV P – 🧑‍🏫 25 à 110. AE ⓓ MC VISA JCB. 🚫 AT n
87 ch ☕ 130/156.
◆ L'esprit du consul de Navarre - qui repose dans l'église à côté - hante encore les lieux. Sobres chambres, jazz bar, terrasse et jardin. On nage sous les voûtes de la cave.
◆ Hier waart nog de geest van de consul van Navarra, die in de kerk ernaast ligt begraven. Sobere kamers, jazzbar, terras en tuin. Onder de keldergewelven kan worden gezwommen.

Parkhotel sans rest, Vrijdagmarkt 5, ✆ 0 50 33 33 64, *info@parkhotel-brugge.be, Fax 0 50 33 47 63* – 🛗 ▤ TV 🚗 – 🧑‍🏫 25 à 250. AE ⓓ MC VISA CY j
86 ch ☕ 125/150.
◆ Cet hôtel adapté pour l'accueil des groupes comporte trois sortes de chambres presque toutes rafraîchies. Salle des petits-déjeuners coiffée d'une verrière pyramidale.
◆ Dit hotel is zeer geschikt voor groepen en beschikt over drie soorten kamers die vrijwel allemaal zijn gemoderniseerd. Ontbijtzaal met een piramidevormig glazen dak.

Karos sans rest, Hoefijzerlaan 37, ✆ 0 50 34 14 48, *hotel.karos@compaqnet.be, Fax 0 50 34 00 91*, 🏊, 🚲 – 🛗 TV P. AE ⓓ MC VISA BY f
fermé 2 janv.-1er janv. – **54 ch** ☕ 65/125.
◆ Façade à colombages bordant le ring. Plaisant salon décoré de vieilles cages aux oiseaux, jolie piscine couverte et sobres chambres. La plus avenante est mansardée.
◆ Hotel met een vakwerkgevel aan de Ring. Prettige lounge met oude vogelkooien, mooi overdekt zwembad en sobere kamers ; de gezelligste is op de zolderverdieping.

Ter Duinen 🐦 sans rest, Langerei 52, ✆ 0 50 33 04 37, *info@terduinenhotel.be, Fax 0 50 34 42 16*, ≤ – 🛗 ▤ TV 🚗. AE ⓓ MC VISA JCB. 🚫 CX x
20 ch ☕ 98/149.
◆ Paisible hôtel excentré se mirant dans les eaux du Langerei. Accueil souriant, chambres avec vue dégagée côté canal ou jardin, véranda et patio. Petits-déjeuners soignés.
◆ Rustig hotel buiten het centrum, dat wordt weerspiegeld in de Langerei. De kamers kijken uit op het water of de tuin, serre en patio. Vriendelijk onthaal en verzorgd ontbijt.

Flanders sans rest, Langestraat 38, ✆ 0 50 33 88 89, *info@flandershotel.be, Fax 0 50 33 93 45*, 🏊, 🚲 – 🛗 🚭 ▤ TV. AE ⓓ MC VISA. 🚫 DY a
fermé du 5 au 29 janv. – **39 ch** ☕ 115/175.
◆ Une façade verte signale cette maison bourgeoise des années 1910. Menues chambres rajeunies, aménagées à l'arrière pour plus de calme. Courette intérieure avec pièce d'eau.
◆ Dit herenhuis uit de vroege 20e eeuw valt op door zijn groene gevel. Kleine gerenoveerde kamers, rustig gelegen aan de achterkant. Binnenplaatsje met waterpartij.

BELGIQUE

Gd H. Oude Burg sans rest, Oude Burg 5, ✆ 0 50 44 51 11, *grandhotel.oudeburg@skynet.be, Fax 0 50 44 51 00,* – |♦| TV – 25 à 160. AE ⓓ MC VISA. AU i
138 ch ☕ 150/170.
◆ À l'ombre du beffroi, immeuble contemporain où vous trouverez des chambres actuelles sans reproche. Des boutiques et divers petits restaurants occupent la cour intérieure.
◆ Modern gebouw aan de voet van het belfort, met eigentijdse kamers waarop niets aan te merken valt. Rond de binnenplaats bevinden zich winkeltjes en diverse kleine restaurants.

Dante sans rest, Coupure 30, ✆ 0 50 34 01 94, *info@hoteldante.be, Fax 0 50 34 35 39,* ≤ – |♦| TV. AE ⓓ MC VISA. DY m
30 ch ☕ 116/131.
◆ Postée en bordure d'un canal, surveillant une écluse, demeure récente renfermant des chambres fonctionnelles toutes semblables, assez grandes et bien insonorisées.
◆ Vrij nieuw gebouw aan een gracht, bij een sluis. De kamers zijn functioneel en zien er allemaal hetzelfde uit, maar ze zijn vrij groot en hebben een goede geluidsisolatie.

Academie sans rest, Wijngaardstraat 7, ✆ 0 50 33 22 66, *info@hotelacademie.be, Fax 0 50 33 21 66* – |♦| TV. AE ⓓ MC VISA AV b
74 ch ☕ 140/160.
◆ Hôtel pratique installé près du lac d'Amour et du béguinage. Agréable patio, nouvelles chambres au mobilier actuel et salon mariant les styles classique et contemporain.
◆ Praktisch hotel bij het Minnewater en de Begijnhof. Aangename patio, nieuwe kamers met hedendaags meubilair en een lounge die een mengeling is van klassiek en modern.

Hans Memling sans rest, Kuipersstraat 18, ✆ 0 50 47 12 12, *hotel.memling@grouptorus.com, Fax 0 50 47 12 10* – |♦| TV – 25. AE ⓓ MC VISA JCB. AT b
36 ch ☕ 161/173.
◆ Maison de maître proche de la Grand-Place et du théâtre. Chambres aux tons radieux, d'ampleur variable mais d'un confort uniforme. Bar-lounge et terrasse close de murs.
◆ Herenhuis in de buurt van de Markt en de schouwburg. De kamers hebben heldere kleuren en verschillen in grootte, maar niet in comfort. Bar-lounge en ommuurd terras.

Ter Brughe sans rest, Oost-Gistelhof 2, ✆ 0 50 34 03 24, *info@hotelterbrughe.com, Fax 0 50 33 88 73* – TV. AE ⓓ MC VISA AT a
46 ch ☕ 100/175.
◆ Demeure de style gothique tardif se dressant à deux pas du canal Speelmansrei. Sobres chambres personnalisées. Petit-déjeuner servi dans les caves voûtées d'époque.
◆ Gebouw in laat-gotische stijl, vlak bij de Speelmansrei. Sobere kamers met een persoonlijk accent. Het ontbijt wordt genuttigd in de gewelfde kelderverdieping.

Bryghia sans rest, Oosterlingenplein 4, ✆ 0 50 33 80 59, *info@bryghiahotel.be, Fax 0 50 34 14 30* – |♦| TV. AE ⓓ MC VISA JCB. AT t
fermé 19 déc.-17 fév. – **18 ch** ☕ 67/135.
◆ Sur une place tranquille proche d'un canal qu'enjambe un petit pont, jolie façade du 15e s. abritant des chambres d'ampleur moyenne dotées du confort actuel.
◆ Achter een fraaie 15e-eeuwse gevel bij een bruggetje over de gracht gaan middelgrote hotelkamers schuil, die aan de huidige normen voldoen.

Botaniek sans rest, Waalsestraat 23, ✆ 0 50 34 14 24, *hotel.botaniek@pi.be, Fax 0 50 34 59 39* – |♦| TV P. MC VISA AU m
9 ch ☕ 85/96.
◆ Entre la place des Tanneurs et le parc Reine-Astrid, hôtel familial aménagé dans une maison bourgeoise à l'écart de l'animation. Menues chambres uniformément équipées.
◆ Rustig gelegen familiehotel in een herenhuis tussen het Huidenvettersplein en het Koningin Astridpark. Kleine kamers die standaard zijn ingericht.

Anselmus sans rest, Ridderstraat 15, ✆ 0 50 34 13 74, *info@anselmus.be, Fax 0 50 34 19 16* – TV. AE MC VISA. AT h
fermé janv. – **7 ch** ☕ 76/101.
◆ Pas loin du Markt et de la place du Bourg, maison dont la porte cochère s'ouvre sur un salon mignon comme tout. On séjourne dans des chambres classiquement aménagées.
◆ Niet ver van de Markt en de Burg staat dit pand, waarvan de oude koetspoort naar een prachtige hal leidt. De gasten verblijven in klassiek ingerichte kamers.

Relais Bourgondisch Cruyce sans rest, Wollestraat 41, ✆ 0 50 33 79 26, *bour.cruyce@ssi.be, Fax 0 50 34 19 68,* ≤ canaux et vieilles maisons flamandes – |♦| TV. AE ⓓ MC VISA AU f
16 ch ☕ 118/128.
◆ Jolie devanture à pans de bois procurant une vue unique sur les canaux bordés de vieilles maisons flamandes. Chambres agréables à vivre.
◆ Dit fraaie vakwerkhuis biedt een uniek uitzicht op de grachten die worden omzoomd door oude Vlaamse panden. Aangename kamers.

Maraboe sans rest, Hoefijzerlaan 9, ✆ 0 50 33 81 55, *hotel@maraboe.be, Fax 0 50 33 29 28* – ‹ *fermé 5 janv.-5 fév.* – **14 ch** 80/99.
• Confort simple mais très correct pour cet hôtel proche du 't Zand, dont les chambres aux tons frais et d'ampleur respectable sont équipées à l'identique. Accueil personnalisé.
• Eenvoudig, maar correct hotel in de buurt van 't Zand, met vrij ruime standaardkamers die in frisse kleuren zijn geschilderd. Persoonlijke service. CY f

Egmond sans rest, Minnewater 15 (par Katelijnestraat), ✆ 0 50 34 14 45, *info@egmond.be, Fax 0 50 34 29 40*, ≤, – AV g
fermé 4 janv.-15 fév. – **8 ch** 112/120.
• Un notaire scellait naguère les actes dans cette charmante résidence élevée au voisinage du lac d'Amour. Les chambres donnent sur un jardin reposant. Accès peu aisé.
• In dit charmante pand bij het Minnewater zetelde vroeger een notaris. De kamers kijken uit op een rustgevende tuin. Vrij lastig te bereiken.

Albert I sans rest, Koning Albert I-laan 2, ✆ 0 50 34 09 30, *hotel@albert1.com, Fax 0 50 33 84 18* – CZ e
fermé du 24 au 26 déc. – **10 ch** 85/95.
• Petit hôtel exploité en famille situé dans le quartier du 't Zand, juste en face d'une nouvelle salle de spectacles. Proprettes chambres classiquement agencées.
• Klein familiehotel in de wijk 't Zand, vlak tegenover een nieuwe theaterzaal. Keurige kamers die in klassieke stijl zijn ingericht.

Biskajer sans rest, Biskajersplein 4, ✆ 0 50 34 15 06, *info@hotelbiskajer.com, Fax 0 50 34 39 11* – AT w
17 ch 101/118.
• Petit hôtel soigneusement tenu, situé dans un quartier assez calme, aux abords du canal Spiegelrei et à seulement 5 mn du centre. Chambres basiques mais très convenables.
• Zorgvuldig onderhouden hotelletje in een vrij rustige wijk aan het water van de Spiegelrei, vijf minuten lopen van het centrum. Basic kamers die echter prima voldoen.

't Putje (annexe - 13 ch), 't Zand 31, ✆ 0 50 33 28 47, *hotelputje@pandora.be, Fax 0 50 34 14 23*, – CZ a
Repas (taverne-rest, ouvert jusqu'à 23 h) *Lunch 10* – 30/42 bc, ♀ – **25 ch** 80/105 – ½ P 100/125.
• À l'entrée de la ville, jouxtant le 't Zand, ressource hôtelière proposant des chambres accueillantes mais inégalement insonorisées. Service limité. Parking public. Taverne au cadre actuel épuré et restaurant plus intime. Terrasse en façade.
• Hotel aan de rand van de stad, niet ver van 't Zand. Prettige kamers met geluidsisolatie van wisselende kwaliteit. Beperkte faciliteiten. Parkeergarage. Modern café en restaurant met een wat intiemere sfeer. Terras aan de voorkant.

ter Reien sans rest, Langestraat 1, ✆ 0 50 34 91 00, *hotel.ter.reien@online.be, Fax 0 50 34 40 48* – DY r
fermé janv. – **23 ch** 70/85.
• Un hôtel "les pieds dans l'eau". Chambres sans ampleur - hormis la suite nuptiale -, souvent avec module sanitaire. Une dizaine d'entre-elles offre la vue sur le canal.
• Hotel pal aan het water. Op de bruidssuite na zijn de kamers klein en voorzien van standaardsanitair. Een tiental kamers biedt uitzicht op de gracht.

Bourgoensch Hof, Wollestraat 39, ✆ 0 50 33 16 45, *info@bourgoensch-hof.be, Fax 0 50 34 63 78*, ≤ canaux et vieilles maisons flamandes, – ch AU f
fermé 6 janv.-15 fév. – **Repas** *(fermé jeudi) Lunch 25* – carte 28 à 36 – **23 ch** 117 – ½ P 109/159.
• Au fond d'une impasse, vieille maison flamande dominant l'un des plus beaux canaux brugeois, visible depuis quelques chambres. Confort satisfaisant. Restaurant d'esprit "bistrot". Spécialités régionales et terrasse courtisée à la belle saison.
• Oud Vlaams pand aan het eind van een doodlopende steeg, met in sommige kamers uitzicht op een van de mooiste grachten van Brugge. Redelijk comfort. In de bistro worden regionale specialiteiten geserveerd. Bij mooi weer is het terras favoriet.

Gd H. du Sablon, Noordzandstraat 21, ✆ 0 50 33 39 02, *info@sablon.be, Fax 0 50 33 39 08* – 25 à 100. rest AU h
Repas (résidents seult) – **36 ch** 89/110 – ½ P 73.
• Ancienne hostellerie située à mi-chemin entre la cathédrale St-Sauveur et la Grand-Place. Hall 1900 coiffé d'une coupole Art déco. Chambres insonorisées et rajeunies.
• Oude herberg tussen de St.-Salvator en de Markt. De hal uit rond 1900 is overdekt met een art-decokoepel. Rustige kamers die onlangs een facelift hebben gehad.

Jacobs sans rest, Baliestraat 1, ✆ 0 50 33 98 31, *hoteljacobs@glo.be, Fax 0 50 33 56 94*, – *fermé 6 janv.-6 fév.* – **23 ch** 70/82. CX k
• Belle demeure sur angle avec pignon à redans au milieu du paisible quartier St-Gilles, à un petit kilomètre de la Grand-Place. Chambres assez spacieuses remises à neuf.
• Mooi hoekpand met een trapgevel in de rustige wijk Sint-Gillis, op nog geen kilometer afstand van de Markt. Vrij ruime kamers die in een nieuw jasje zijn gestoken.

De Barge, Bargeweg 15, ✆ 0 50 38 51 50, *info@debargehotel.com, Fax 0 50 38 21 25,* – TV P. AE ◑ MC VISA. ✂ ch CZ p
Repas *(fermé 19 déc.-10 fév., du 4 au 19 juil., dim. et lundi)* (dîner seult) carte 32 à 80 – **22 ch** *(fermé 19 déc.-10 fév.)* ☕ 92/140.
◆ Cette ancienne péniche amarrée le long du canal reliant Brugge à Gand est devenue un petit hôtel flottant où vous serez hébergés dans des "cabines" au pimpant décor nautique. Cuisine littorale à la table du capitaine.
◆ Deze oude aak, die in het kanaal tussen Brugge en Gent voor anker ligt, is een drijvend hotelletje. De hutten in nautische stijl zien er picobello uit. Lekker eten aan de "captain's table", met een keur van vis en schaal- en schelpdieren.

Boterhuis, St-Jakobsstraat 38, ✆ 0 50 34 15 11, *boterhuis@pandora.be, Fax 0 50 34 70 89* – TV. AE ◑ MC VISA JCB AT m
Repas *(fermé dim. soir de Toussaint à Pâques)* (ouvert jusqu'à 23 h) Lunch 14 – carte 24 à 35, ♀ – **8 ch** ☕ 65/93.
◆ Une tourelle garde cette construction ancienne postée à un tour de ronde du Markt. Elle abrite les deux meilleures chambres de la maison, desservies par un escalier tournant.
◆ Dit oude pand bij de wachttoren op de Markt heeft zelf ook een torentje, waarin zich de twee beste kamers van het hotel bevinden, te bereiken via een wenteltrap.

Fevery sans rest, Collaert Mansionstraat 3, ✆ 0 50 33 12 69, *paul@hotelfevery.be, Fax 0 50 33 17 91* – |♦| TV. AE MC VISA JCB. ✂ CX n
fermé 1 sem. en juin, dern. sem. nov., Nouvel An et 2e quinz. janv. – **10 ch** ☕ 70/80.
◆ Situation calme et tenue irréprochable pour ce point de chute familial du quartier St-Gilles. Chambres souvent rafraîchies, et toutes dotées de nouvelles salles de bains.
◆ Dit rustig gelegen, perfect onderhouden hotel in de wijk Sint-Gillis is zeer geschikt voor gezinnen. De kamers, waarvan de meeste zijn gerenoveerd, hebben nieuwe badkamers.

Malleberg sans rest, Hoogstraat 7, ✆ 0 50 34 41 11, *hotel@malleberg.be, Fax 0 50 34 67 69* – TV. AE MC VISA. ✂ ATU b
8 ch ☕ 70/94.
◆ Les chambres de ce petit hôtel voisin de la place du Bourg sont pourvues d'un mobilier actuel simple. La cave voûtée a été convertie en salle des petits-déjeuners.
◆ De kamers van dit kleine hotel bij de Burg zijn eenvoudig en modern gemeubileerd. Het ontbijt wordt genuttigd in de gewelfde kelderverdieping.

De Karmeliet (Van Hecke), Langestraat 19, ✆ 0 50 33 82 59, *Fax 0 50 33 10 11,* – P. AE ◑ MC VISA JCB. ✂ DY q
fermé 27 juin-15 juil., du 3 au 14 oct., 2 prem. sem. janv., mardi midi et dim. soir d'oct. à mai, dim. midi de juin à sept. et lundi – **Repas** Lunch 50 – 95/220 bc, carte 97 à 160, ♀.
◆ Décoré d'œuvres d'art modernes et agrémenté d'une terrasse intérieure, ce temple de la gastronomie décline un répertoire aussi respectueux des produits que de vos papilles.
◆ In deze tempel van de gastronomie kunt u genieten van tongstrelende gerechten op basis van eersteklas producten. Interieur met moderne kunstwerken en een binnenterras.
Spéc. Tuile sucrée-salée aux grosses langoustines rôties. Dos de gros turbot piqué au jambon, sabayon de pommes de terre aux crevettes deZeebrugge (avril-oct.). Ravioli à la vanille et pommes caramélisées en chaud-froid

De Snippe avec ch, Nieuwe Gentweg 53, ✆ 0 50 33 70 70, *desnippe@pandora.be, Fax 0 50 33 76 62,* – |♦|, ch, TV P. AE ◑ MC VISA AV r
Repas *(fermé 18 janv.-12 fév., dim. et lundi midi)* Lunch 38 – carte 51 à 104, ♀ – **9 ch** *(fermé 18 janv.-12 fév. et dim. de nov. à avril)* ☕ 145/275.
◆ Refuge gourmand établi dans une jolie maison du 18e s. Beau décor mural en salle, mets classiques innovants, bonne cave et chambres à thèmes. Ombre et jeux d'eau en terrasse.
◆ Een uitstekend adres voor fijnproevers. Fraaie eetzaal met een lommerrijk terras, klassieke maar spannende gerechten en heerlijke wijnen. De kamers hebben elk een eigen thema.

Den Braamberg, Pandreitje 11, ✆ 0 50 33 73 70, *Fax 0 50 33 99 73* – AE ◑ MC VISA
fermé du 13 au 31 juil., du 1er au 10 janv., jeudi et dim. – **Repas** Lunch 31 – 45/89 bc.
◆ Ce restaurant misant sur une appétissante carte classico-traditionnelle vous réserve un accueil familial chaleureux. Un vieux lit malinois à baldaquin sert de "table montre".
◆ Dit restaurant serveert lekkere, klassiek-traditionele gerechten in een gemoedelijke ambiance. Een oud Mechels hemelbed dient als uitstaltafel. AU q

Den Gouden Harynck (Serruys), Groeninge 25, ✆ 0 50 33 76 37, *goud.harynck@pandora.be, Fax 0 50 34 42 70* – P. AE ◑ MC VISA AUV w
fermé 1 sem. Pâques, 2 dern. sem. juil.-prem. sem. août, dern. sem. déc.-prem. sem. janv., sam. midi, dim. et lundi – **Repas** Lunch 50 – carte 67 à 91.
◆ Une belle carte inventive vous attend à cette enseigne proche des grands musées. Salle à manger bourgeoise où règne une ambiance feutrée. Mignonne cour fleurie en été.
◆ Dit restaurant nabij de grote musea biedt een mooie inventieve kaart. Eetzaal in bourgeoisstijl met een gedempte sfeer. Charmante binnentuin die 's zomers vol bloemen staat.
Spéc. Langoustines braisées au Vin Jaune et primeurs. Bar en croûte de sel parfumé de romarin. Pigeonneau à la fondue d'oignons et jus de truffes

XXX **'t Pandreitje,** Pandreitje 6, ✆ 0 50 33 11 90, *info@pandreitje.be, Fax 0 50 34 00 70* – AE Ⓓ MC VISA JCB AU x
fermé du 1er au 11 avril, du 4 au 21 juil., du 1er au 7 nov., merc. et dim. – **Repas** Lunch 40 – 55/110 bc, ♀.
◆ Orientée "produits de luxe", cette petite table assez créative offre style et confort dans une maison bourgeoise proche du centre touristique. Belle cave.
◆ Klein, maar stijlvol restaurant in een herenhuis dicht bij het centrum. De chef-kok is creatief en maakt bij voorkeur gebruik van luxeproducten. Mooie wijnkelder.

XXX **Duc de Bourgogne** avec ch, Huidenvettersplein 12, ✆ 0 50 33 20 38, *duc@ssi.be, Fax 0 50 34 40 37,* ≤ canaux et maisons typiques – rest, TV. AE Ⓓ MC VISA JCB AU t
fermé 3 sem. en juil. et janv. – **Repas** *(fermé lundi et mardi midi)* Lunch 36 – 58, ♀ – **10 ch** 110/150.
◆ À dénicher au bord d'un croisement de canaux des plus pittoresques, relais de bouche au décor rustique rehaussé de peintures murales style fin Moyen Âge. Mets classiques.
◆ Gastronomisch restaurant bij een plek waar twee pittoreske grachten elkaar kruisen. Rustiek interieur met muurschilderingen in laat-middeleeuwse stijl. Klassieke keuken.

XX **De Lotteburg,** Goezeputstraat 43, ✆ 0 50 33 75 35, *lotteburg@pi.be, Fax 0 50 33 04 04,* terrasse, Produits de la mer – . AE Ⓓ MC VISA JCB. AV d
fermé 28 juil.-12 août, du 6 au 28 janv., lundi, mardi et sam. midi – **Repas** Lunch 30 – 45/87 bc, ♀.
◆ Une délicieuse terrasse ombragée dotée de meubles en teck se cache derrière cette façade blanche égayée de volets bleus. Aux fourneaux, le chef verse volontiers dans la marée.
◆ Achter de witte gevel met blauwe luiken bevindt zich een heerlijk lommerrijk terras met teakhouten meubelen. In de keuken ligt het accent op vis.

XX **Patrick Devos,** Zilverstraat 41, ✆ 0 50 33 55 66, *info@patrickdevos.be, Fax 0 50 33 58 67,* terrasse – P. AE Ⓓ MC VISA JCB AU y
fermé 18 juil.-9 août, du 26 au 30 déc., sam. midi, dim. et jours fériés – **Repas** Lunch 37 – 55/66, ♀.
◆ Restaurant aménagé dans une ancienne demeure patricienne restaurée. Salon Louis XVI, éléments décoratifs Art nouveau en salle, joli patio et cuisine d'aujourd'hui.
◆ Restaurant in een oude gerestaureerde patriciërswoning. Louis XVI-salon, eetzaal met art-deco-elementen, mooie patio en eigentijdse keuken.

XX **'t Stil Ende,** Scheepsdalelaan 12, ✆ 0 50 33 92 03, *stilende@skynet.be, Fax 0 50 33 26 22,* terrasse – . MC VISA BX a
fermé sem. carnaval, 2e quinz. juil., Toussaint, sam. midi, dim. et lundi – **Repas** 30/80 bc.
◆ Attrayante adresse à débusquer hors des circuits touristiques. Agencement intérieur contemporain, étonnant système de réfrigération du vin, savoureux menus et terrasse d'été.
◆ Aanlokkelijk restaurant voor wie graag buiten de toeristische circuits blijft. Moderne inrichting, verbazingwekkend wijnkoelsysteem, lekkere menu's en terras in de zomer.

XX **Hermitage,** Ezelstraat 18, ✆ 0 50 34 41 73, *restaurant-hermitage@planetinternet.be, Fax 0 50 34 14 75* – AE Ⓓ MC VISA JCB CY z
fermé 1 sem. en juin, 1 sem. en oct., 1 sem. en janv., dim. soir et lundi – **Repas** Lunch 23 – carte 47 à 61.
◆ "1620", déchiffre-t-on sur le fier pignon à redans de cet établissement aussi pimpant que cossu. Choix classique mis au goût du jour. De-ci, delà, quelques jolies antiquités.
◆ "1620" staat gegrift in de trapgevel van dit restaurant, dat er weelderig uitziet en met antiek is verfraaid. Klassieke kaart die aan de huidige smaak is aangepast.

XX **De Florentijnen,** Academiestraat 1, ✆ 0 50 67 75 33, *info@deflorentijnen.be, Fax 0 50 67 75 33* – 25 à 60. AE MC VISA AT p
fermé 18 juil.-4 août, du 14 au 24 nov., du 1er au 15 janv., dim. non fériés et lundi – **Repas** Lunch 30 – 45/65 bc.
◆ Spacieux restaurant implanté dans un ancien comptoir commercial florentin, d'où l'enseigne. Cuisine du moment et décoration intérieure d'esprit contemporain.
◆ Groot restaurant in een voormalige Florentijnse factorij, vandaar de naam. Modern interieur, waarbij de kookstijl goed aansluit.

XX **Kardinaalshof,** St-Salvatorskerkhof 14, ✆ 0 50 34 16 91, *Fax 0 50 34 20 62* – AE Ⓓ MC VISA AUV g
fermé 2 prem. sem. juil., merc. et jeudi midi – **Repas** 35/83 bc.
◆ Près de la cathédrale, derrière une façade d'esprit baroque, table classique-actuelle présentant une carte assez poissonneuse. Confort douillet.
◆ Achter een fraaie barokgevel bij de kathedraal gaat dit behaaglijke en comfortabele restaurant schuil. De modern-klassieke kaart bevat veel visspecialiteiten.

BELGIQUE

XX **Den Dyver,** Dijver 5, ☎ 0 50 33 60 69, *dijver@busmail.net, Fax 0 50 34 10 64,* 🏞, Cuisine à la bière – AE MC VISA AU c
fermé merc. et jeudi midi – **Repas** *Lunch 30* – 39/67 bc.
• Cette maison animée au cadre chaleureux attire les amateurs de cuisine à la bière comme les curieux. Un beau col de mousse adéquat accompagne naturellement chaque préparation.
• Gezellig restaurant waar veel met bier wordt gekookt, wat typisch Vlaams is en de moeite waard om te proberen. Natuurlijk wordt bij het eten een schuimend biertje gedronken.

XX **Hemelrycke,** Dweersstraat 12, ☎ 0 50 34 83 43, *Fax 0 50 67 69 04* – AE D MC VISA JCB CY x
fermé 1 sem. en mars, 1 sem. en juil., mardi et merc. – **Repas** 22/56 bc, 𝕐.
• Intime petit établissement situé à proximité du 't Zand. Carte classique assortie de menus à bon prix. Possibilités de stationnement dans deux parkings publics voisins.
• Intiem restaurantje in de buurt van 't Zand, waar men zich in het hemelrijk waant. Klassieke kaart en aantrekkelijk geprijsde menu's. Twee parkeergarages vlakbij.

XX **Tanuki,** Oude Gentweg 1, ☎ 0 50 34 75 12, *Fax 0 50 33 82 42,* Cuisine japonaise avec Teppan-Yaki et Sushi-bar – ▤. AE MC VISA JCB AV f
fermé 1 sem. carnaval, 2 sem. en juil., 1 sem. Toussaint, lundi et mardi – **Repas** *Lunch 15* – 59.
• L'une des rares tables japonaises brugeoises. Authentique cuisine nippone, avec la spectaculaire formule Teppan-Yaki (table de cuisson) et un sushi bar. Décor de circonstance.
• Een van de weinige Japanse restaurants in Brugge. Authentieke keuken uit het Land van de Rijzende Zon, met de spectaculaire Teppan-Yaki-formule en een sushibar.

XX **Aneth,** Maria van Bourgondiëlaan 1 (derrière le parc Graaf Visart), ☎ 0 50 31 11 89, *info@aneth.be, Fax 0 50 32 36 46,* Produits de la mer – AE D MC VISA JCB BY g
fermé 2 prem. sem. janv., sam. midi, dim. et lundi – **Repas** *Lunch 40* – 60/95 bc, 𝕐.
• Ce restaurant installé dans une villa début 20e s., en face d'un canal et d'un parc public, fait des produits de la mer son répertoire privilégié. Parking aisé.
• Goed visrestaurant in een villa uit het begin van de 20e eeuw, met uitzicht op een gracht en een park. Voldoende parkeergelegenheid.

XX **Spinola,** Spinolarei 1, ☎ 0 50 34 17 85, *spinola@pandora.be, Fax 0 50 34 13 71,* 🏞 – ▤. D MC VISA AT c
fermé dern. sem. janv.-prem. sem. fév., dern. sem. juin-prem. sem. juil., dim. et lundi midi – **Repas** *Lunch 38* – 46.
• Plaisant établissement rustique proche du canal Spiegelrei et de la statue de Jan Van Eyck. Choix de préparations alléchantes que complète un très bel éventail de vins.
• Plezierig rustiek etablissement in de buurt van de Spiegelrei en het standbeeld van Jan van Eyck. Tongstrelende gerechten, waarbij een goed glas wijn wordt geschonken.

XX **'t Voermanshuys,** Oude Burg 14, ☎ 0 50 33 71 72, *johan.nelissen@pandora.be, Fax 0 50 34 09 91* – MC VISA AU d
fermé fin janv.-début fév., lundi et mardi – **Repas** *Lunch 20* – carte 38 à 65.
• Une superbe cave voûtée (16e s.) sert de cadre à ce restaurant jouxtant le beffroi. Registre culinaire mi-classique, mi-actuel, ambiance feutrée et romantisme assuré.
• Restaurant naast de Belforthallen met een gewelfde kelderverdieping uit de 16e eeuw, waar kan worden genoten van de half klassieke, half eigentijdse keuken. Superromantisch !

XX **'t Zwaantje,** Gentpoortvest 70, ☎ 0 50 34 38 85, *hetzwaantje@skynet.be, Fax 0 50 34 97 10,* 🏞 – MC VISA AV n
fermé merc., jeudi, vend. midi et sam. midi – **Repas** 38 𝕐.
• Trois petits cygnes (zwaantjes) égaient la devanture de cet adorable restaurant où flotte une atmosphère romantique. Recettes du moment. Véranda et terrasse arrière.
• Drie zwaantjes sieren de voorgevel van dit prachtige restaurant, waar een romantische sfeer hangt. Hedendaagse recepten. Serre en terras aan de achterkant.

X **Bhavani,** Simon Stevinplein 5, ☎ 0 50 33 90 25, *info@bhavani.be, Fax 0 50 34 89 52,* 🏞, Cuisine indienne – AE D MC VISA. ✂ AU z
Repas *Lunch 16* – carte 35 à 46.
• Tenté par un périple culinaire au pays des maharadjas, sans quitter Brugge ? Embarquement immédiat place S.-Stevin ! Cuisine indienne typique avec plats végétariens.
• Zin in een culinair uitstapje naar het land van de maharadja's ? Onmiddellijk instappen dan op het Simon Stevinplein ! Typisch Indiase keuken met vegetarische schotels.

X **Kurt's Pan,** St-Jakobsstraat 58, ☎ 0 50 34 12 24, *kurt.vandaele@planetinternet.be, Fax 0 50 49 11 97* – ▤. AE MC VISA AT e
fermé prem. sem. juil., 1 sem. en janv. et lundi et mardi midi sauf en juil.-août – **Repas** *Lunch 14* – 45 bc/60 bc.
• Petite adresse familiale au cadre sagement campagnard et au confort simple, dans une maisonnette flamande voisine de l'église St-Jacob. Choix classique et varié.
• Eenvoudig, maar lekker adres in een Vlaams pandje bij de St.-Jakobskerk. Rustiek interieur. Traditionele kaart met veel variatie.

X **De Stove,** Kleine Sint-Amandstraat 4, ✆ 0 50 33 78 35, *restaurant.de.stove@pandora.be, Fax 0 50 33 78 35* – AE ⓓ ⓜ VISA AU k
fermé 2 dern. sem. août, 2 sem. en janv., merc., jeudi et vend. midi – **Repas** 44.
◆ Une copieuse cuisine assez conventionnelle mais basée sur des produits soigneusement choisis vous attend dans cette maison sympathique proche du Markt et du beffroi.
◆ In dit sympathieke restaurant vlak bij de Markt en de Belforthallen worden vrij conventionele, copieuze maaltijden geserveerd op basis van zorgvuldig uitgekozen producten.

X **'T bezemtje,** Kleine Sint-Amandstraat 1, ✆ 0 50 33 91 68, *Fax 0 50 33 04 98* – AE ⓓ ⓜ VISA AU v
fermé du 1er au 15 janv., dim. soir et lundi – **Repas** *Lunch 31* – carte 31 à 47.
◆ Dans une rue piétonne, à mi-chemin entre le Markt et le beffroi, table déclinant un bon petit choix classique gentiment actualisé. Plats teintés d'influences méditerranéennes.
◆ Eethuisje in een voetgangersstraat, halverwege de Markt en de Belforthallen. Op de kleine kaart staan klassieke gerechten met een mediterraan accent.

X **Guillaume,** Korte Lane 20, ✆ 0 50 34 46 05, *guillaume2000@wol.be, Fax 0 50 34 46 05,* 㭊 – ⓜ VISA CY c
fermé 2 sem. en fév., 2 sem. en août, 2 sem. en nov., lundi et mardi – **Repas** (dîner seult jusqu'à minuit) carte 41 à 52.
◆ Un "p'tit resto d'amis" dont l'ambiance doit beaucoup au caractère jovial du patron, ainsi qu'à la musique pop que l'on y passe. Choix de plats recomposé chaque mois.
◆ Oergezellig tentje om met vrienden te eten, waar het joviale karakter van de baas en de swingende popmuziek de sfeer er goed inbrengen. De kaart verandert maandelijks.

X **Koto** - H. de' Medici, Potterierei 15, ✆ 0 50 44 31 31, *koto@hoteldemedici.com, Fax 0 50 33 07 64,* Cuisine japonaise avec Teppan-Yaki – P. AE ⓓ ⓜ VISA JCB. ✂ CX g
fermé du 3 au 18 janv., lundi, mardi midi et merc. midi – **Repas** *Lunch 24* – 42/77 bc, ♀.
◆ Le restaurant japonais du de' Medici attire les inconditionnels de la formule Teppan-Yaki (table de cuisson). Sushis et sashimis à gogo. Cadre actuel à touches nippones.
◆ Het Japanse restaurant van Hotel de' Medici is een must voor liefhebbers van sushi, sashimi en de Teppan-Yaki-formule. Eigentijds interieur met een Japanse toets.

X **Cafedraal,** Zilverstraat 38, ✆ 0 50 34 08 45, *Fax 0 50 33 52 41,* 㭊 – AE ⓓ ⓜ VISA JCB AU s
fermé dim. et lundi – **Repas** *Lunch 10* – carte 35 à 88.
◆ Une carte engageante s'emploie à apaiser votre faim dans cette brasserie animée mettant à profit une charmante demeure historique. Bar "cubain". Jolie terrasse intérieure.
◆ Levendige brasserie in een historisch pand, met een kaart waar ongetwijfeld iets bij zit om uw honger te stillen. Cubaanse bar en een mooi binnenterras.

X **den Amand,** Sint-Amandstraat 4, ✆ 0 50 34 01 22, *Fax 0 50 34 01 22,* 㭊, Bistrot – ⓜ VISA JCB AU w
fermé du 4 au 24 juin, du 12 au 25 nov., du 24 au 26 déc., 14 janv.-3 fév., merc. soir du 10 nov. au 27 avril et lundi – **Repas** 28.
◆ Bistrot familial posté à vingt mètres de l'incontournable Markt. Cuisine à vue. Recettes traditionnelles sans chichi. Pâtes, salades et quelques plats végétariens.
◆ Gezellige bistro op 20 m van de Markt. Open keuken, waar traditionele gerechten zonder franje worden bereid. Pasta's, salades en enkele vegetarische schotels.

X **'t Zonneke,** Genthof 5, ✆ 0 50 33 07 81, *Fax 0 50 34 52 13* – ⓜ VISA AT z
fermé fin janv.-début fév., dim. midi en juil.-août, dim. soir et lundi – **Repas** *Lunch 11* – carte 29 à 46.
◆ Établissement familial aussi convivial que décontracté, situé hors animation, dans une maisonnette rustique avec mezzanine. Cuisine bourgeoise simple mais correcte.
◆ Gemoedelijk familierestaurantje, even buiten de drukte, in een rustiek pandje met tussenverdieping. Eenvoudige burgerkost van goede kwaliteit.

X **Breydel - De Coninc,** Breidelstraat 24, ✆ 0 50 33 97 46, *Fax 0 50 34 61 74,* Homards, anguilles et moules – ⓜ VISA AU u
fermé du 24 au 26 déc., 31 déc.-2 janv., jeudi de déc. à juin et merc. sauf en juil.-août – **Repas** carte 26 à 68.
◆ Homards, mais aussi moules et anguilles en saison, sont à l'honneur dans cet établissement idéalement situé entre le Markt et le Burg. Service super gentil.
◆ Kreeft, mosselen en paling zijn in hun element in dit etablissement, dat centraal is gelegen tussen de Markt en de Burg. Zeer vriendelijke bediening.

X **Huyze Die Maene,** Markt 17, ✆ 0 50 33 39 59, *huyzediemaene@pandora.be, Fax 0 50 33 44 60,* 㭊, Taverne-rest – ▤. AE ⓓ ⓜ VISA AU w
fermé fév. – **Repas** *Lunch 13* – 22/31.
◆ Emplacement idéal sur le Markt, façade avenante, ambiance brasserie, carte avec suggestions du marché, telles sont les clés du succès de cette taverne-restaurant.
◆ De ideale ligging aan de Markt, de uitnodigende gevel, de brasserie-ambiance en de kaart met dagelijks wisselende gerechten verklaren het succes van dit bedrijf.

BELGIQUE

X **L'Intermède,** Wulfhagestraat 3, ✆ 0 50 33 16 74, 🏞 – MC VISA CY b
fermé 2 prem. sem. fév., 2 dern. sem. sept., dim. et lundi – **Repas** carte env. 46.
• Salle à manger ancienne avec escalier tournant et, en guise de papier-peint, des partitions (celles d'un intermède ?). Choix de préparations concis, mais de qualité constante.
• Oude eetzaal met wenteltrap en partituren als behang voor een culinair intermezzo. Beperkte keuze, maar kwalitatief gezien zonder enige valse noot.

X **Rock Fort,** Langestraat 15, ✆ 0 50 33 41 13, *peter.laloo@pandora.be, Fax 0 50 33 41 13,* Ouvert jusqu'à 23 h – MC VISA – *fermé 3 dern. sem. juil., dern. sem. déc.-2 prem. sem. janv., merc. et dim. midi* – **Repas** *Lunch 10* – carte 29 à 56. DY q
• Étroite salle aux tables cérusées et chaises design où l'on prend place devant une assiette actuelle, sinon innovante. Une adresse ne manquant pas de personnalité !
• Smalle eetzaal met geceruseerde tafels en designstoelen. De keuken is zeer eigentijds en zelfs vernieuwend. Een adresje met karakter !

Périphérie :

au Nord-Ouest – ✉ *8000* :

XXX **De gouden Korenhalm,** Oude Oostendsesteenweg 79a (Sint-Pieters), ✆ 0 50 31 33 93, *info@degoudenkorenhalm.be, Fax 0 50 31 18 96,* 🏞 – P. AE ⓓ MC VISA ER f
fermé fin fév.-début mars, fin août-début sept., lundi et mardi – **Repas** *Lunch 31* – 40/71 bc.
• Aux portes de Brugge. Une réputation flatteuse entoure cette construction récente de style flamand. Bon choix au goût du jour, plats de saison et cave française de qualité.
• Gerenommeerd restaurant in een nieuw gebouw in Vlaamse stijl aan de rand van Brugge. Mooie eigentijdse kaart met seizoengebonden gerechten en Franse wijnen als tafelpartner.

à Dudzele *au Nord par N 376 : 9 km* Ⓒ *Brugge* – ✉ *8380 Dudzele* :

🏠 **het Bloemenhof** 🐌, Damsesteenweg 96, ✆ 0 50 59 81 34, *hetbloemenhof@pi.be, Fax 0 50 59 84 28,* 🏊, 🏞, 🚲 – TV P
Repas (dîner pour résidents seult) – **7 ch** ☕ 50/72 – ½ P 87/97.
• Paisible et sympathique villa de type fermette, sur la route secondaire reliant Dudzele à Damme. Chambres coquettes, petit-déjeuner soigné et terrasse sur jardin.
• Rustig en vriendelijk boerderijtje aan de secundaire weg van Dudzele naar Damme. Keurige kamers, verzorgd ontbijt en terras aan de tuinzijde.

XX **De Zilverberk,** Westkapelsesteenweg 92, ✆ 0 50 59 90 80, *dezilverberk@skynet.be,* 🏞 – P. AE ⓓ MC VISA. ✗
fermé dim. soir, lundi et après 20 h 30 – **Repas** *Lunch 24* – 28/70 bc.
• Estimée pour sa carte au goût du jour et ses menus à prix raisonnable, cette villa de style flamand s'embellit d'un jardin bichonné. Coin salon avec cheminée ancienne.
• Dit restaurant in een typisch Vlaams pand wordt gewaardeerd om zijn eigentijdse kaart en vriendelijk geprijsde menu's. Salon met oude schouw. Mooi aangelegde tuin.

à Sint-Andries Ⓒ *Brugge* – ✉ *8200 Sint-Andries* :

🏠 **Host. Pannenhuis** 🐌, Zandstraat 2, ✆ 0 50 31 19 07, *hostellerie@pannenhuis.be, Fax 0 50 31 77 66,* 🏞, 🏞, 🚲 – TV ♿ P – 🧑‍🏫 25. AE MC VISA ER g
Repas *(fermé du 1er au 22 juil., 15 janv.-2 fév., mardi soir et merc.)* *Lunch 33* – 44/69 bc, 🍷 – **19 ch** *(fermé 15 janv.-2 fév.)* ☕ 95/125 – ½ P 95/120.
• Mignonne hostellerie créée dans les années 1930 et tout récemment rajeunie. Paisibles chambres bien dimensionnées. Terrasse d'été alanguie en surplomb d'un ravissant jardin. À table, carte très classique incluant quelques spécialités de poisson et de homard.
• Charmant hotel uit de jaren dertig dat pas is gerenoveerd, met rustige en ruime kamers. 's Zomers is het heerlijk toeven op het terras in de prachtige tuin. Aan tafel worden klassieke gerechten geserveerd, waaronder kreeft en andere visspecialiteiten.

XX ✿ **Herborist** (Hanbuckers) 🐌 avec ch, De Watermolen 15 (par ⑥ : 6 km puis à droite après E 40 - A 10), ✆ 0 50 38 76 00, *a.hanbuckers@aubergedeherborist.be, Fax 0 50 39 31 06,* 🏞, 🏞, 🚲 – ▤ rest, TV P. AE MC VISA. ✗
fermé 22 mars-2 avril, 21 juin-2 juil., 19 sept.-5 oct., du 19 au 31 déc., dim. soir, lundi et jeudi soir – **Repas** (menu unique) *Lunch 49* – 68/107 bc – **4 ch** ☕ 93/140.
• Cette auberge isolée dans un environnement champêtre a été aménagée avec beaucoup de goût. Menu unique proposé oralement, mis en valeur par une cave de prestige.
• Deze smaakvol ingerichte herberg ligt vrij afgelegen in een landelijke omgeving. Eén menu, dat mondeling wordt aangekondigd en waarbij prestigieuze wijnen worden geschonken.
Spéc. Foie de canard chaud et confit d'agrumes aux 7 poivres. Homard et salade de fines herbes maison (juin-août). Turbot et mousseline aux crevettes bouquets et persil

à Sint-Kruis Ⓒ *Brugge* – ✉ *8310 Sint-Kruis :*

Wilgenhof sans rest, Polderstraat 151, ☏ 0 50 36 27 44, *info@hotel-wilgenhof.be, Fax 0 50 36 28 21,* ←, – P. AE ⓓ ⓜ VISA. ER w
fermé 3 prem. sem. janv. – **6 ch** 75/145.
◆ Au bord du Damse Vaart, dans un paysage de campagne et polders, adorable fermette disposant de chambres sans reproche. Un feu de bûches ronfle au salon quand le froid sévit.
◆ Lieflijk boerderijtje aan de Damse Vaart, in een typisch polderlandschap. De kamers zijn onberispelijk en als het buiten koud is, knappert het haardvuur in de lounge.

XXX **Ronnie Jonkman,** Maalsesteenweg 438 (Est : 2 km), ☏ 0 50 36 07 67, *Fax 0 50 35 76 96,* – P. AE ⓓ ⓜ VISA JCB
fermé 2 sem. en mai, 2 sem. en oct., Noël-Nouvel An, dim. et lundi – **Repas** 33/63 bc.
◆ Une cuisine orientée "produits" vous sera servie dans cette jolie villa flamande. Carte actuelle et concise. Bons accords mets-vins. Agréables terrasses au mobilier en teck.
◆ Hier wordt uitsluitend met eersteklas producten gekookt. Kleine, eigentijdse kaart en wijnen die uitstekend bij de gerechten passen. Mooie terrassen met teakhouten meubelen.

X **'t Apertje,** Damse Vaart Zuid 223, ☏ 0 50 35 00 12, *Fax 0 50 37 58 48,* ←, , Bistrot – P. AE ⓓ ⓜ VISA ER w
fermé dern. sem. juin-prem. sem. juil., vacances Noël, dim. d'oct. à avril et lundi – **Repas** carte 28 à 37, ♀.
◆ Carte bistrot avec plats d'anguilles, décor intérieur dans l'air du temps et vue sur un canal se perdant dans les polders, telle est la recette du succès de cette auberge.
◆ Een smakelijke bistrokeuken, een eigentijds interieur en een mooi uitzicht op een kanaal in de polder, dat is het recept van deze herberg. De paling is werkelijk boterzacht.

à Sint-Michiels Ⓒ *Brugge* – ✉ *8200 Sint-Michiels :*

Campanile, Jagersstraat 20, ☏ 0 50 38 13 60, *brugge@campanile.be, Fax 0 50 38 45 42,* , – ⇌ ▣ ♿ P. – 25. AE ⓜ VISA ES e
Repas (avec buffets) *Lunch 7* – 22 – 10 – **56 ch** 80 – ½ P 105/113.
◆ À 3 km du centre-ville, près d'un parc d'attractions, hôtel dont les chambres, conformes aux standards de la chaîne, sont bien tenues et suffisamment insonorisées.
◆ Hotel op 3 km van het centrum, vlak bij een pretpark. De kamers voldoen aan de standaard van deze hotelketen ; ze zijn goed onderhouden en naar behoren geïsoleerd tegen geluid.

XXX **Weinebrugge,** Koning Albertlaan 242, ☏ 0 50 38 44 40, *weine-brugge@pi.be, Fax 0 50 39 35 63,* – P. AE ⓓ ⓜ VISA. ES b
fermé 2 dern. sem. juil. et mardi – **Repas** *Lunch 30* – 43.
◆ Ce restaurant très confortable, avec salon et bar séparés, occupe une villa flamande en lisière du bois de Tillegem. Cuisine classique actualisée. Accès aisé depuis Brugge.
◆ Luxueus restaurant met salon en bar in een landhuis bij het bos van Tillegem. Klassieke keuken die is aangepast aan de huidige tijd. Vanuit Brugge gemakkelijk te bereiken.

XX **Casserole** (Établissement d'application hôtelière), Groene-Poortdreef 17, ☏ 0 50 40 30 30, *casserole@tergroenepoorte.be, Fax 0 50 40 30 35,* – P. – 35. AE ⓓ ⓜ VISA ES t
fermé vacances scolaires, sam. et dim. – **Repas** (déjeuner seult, menu unique) 29/42 bc.
◆ Établissement d'application hôtelière installé dans une fermette entourée de verdure. Fringante salle à manger campagnarde, menu souvent recomposé et bons vins à prix d'ami.
◆ Restaurant van de hotelschool in een boerderijtje tussen het groen. Vrolijke eetzaal in landelijke stijl, regelmatig wisselende menu's en goede wijnen voor een zacht prijsje.

Environs

à Hertsberge *au Sud par N 50 : 12,5 km* Ⓒ *Oostkamp 21 230 h.* – ✉ *8020 Hertsberge :*

XXX **Manderley,** Kruisstraat 13, ☏ 0 50 27 80 51, *manderley@pandora.be, Fax 0 50 27 80 51,* – P. AE ⓓ ⓜ VISA
fermé 2 prem. sem. oct., 3 sem. en janv., mardi d'oct. à avril, dim. soir et lundi – **Repas** *Lunch 36* – 49/89 bc, ♀.
◆ Ancienne ferme agrémentée d'une belle terrasse d'été sur jardin. Choix de recettes au goût du jour, cave importante et, l'hiver venu, réconfortantes flambées en salle.
◆ Oude boerderij met 's zomers een fijn terras dat uitkijkt op de tuin. Eigentijdse keuken, goed gevulde wijnkelder en 'sãwinters een behaaglijk vuur in de eetzaal.

BELGIQUE

à Varsenare Jabbeke 13 692 h. – ✉ 8490 Varsenare :

XXX ✿ **Manoir Stuivenberg** (Scherrens frères) avec ch, Gistelsteenweg 27, ✆ 0 50 38 15 02, *info@manoirstuivenberg.be, Fax 0 50 38 28 92*, , – , rest, – 25 à 300. AE MC VISA.
fermé 19 juil.-5 août et du 1er au 26 janv. – **Repas** *(fermé sam. midi, dim. soir, lundi et mardi)* Lunch 42 – 108 bc, carte 76 à 102 – **8 ch** *(fermé dim. soir et lundi)* 124/162, – 1 suite – ½ P 130/158.
• Une carte classique revisitée à petits pas et une superbe cave n'attendent que votre visite dans ce manoir chic décoré avec le souci du détail. Service personnalisé.
• Dit landhuis is met veel oog voor detail ingericht. De klassieke spijskaart is gematigd eigentijds en in de kelder liggen geweldige wijnen. Attente bediening.
Spéc. Turbot braisé au citron et marmelade de tomates. Poitrine de pigeon en crapaudine. Gibier (en saison)

à Waardamme *au Sud par N 50 : 11 km* Oostkamp 21 230 h. – ✉ 8020 Waardamme :

XX **Ter Talinge,** Rooiveldstraat 46, ✆ 0 50 27 90 61, *Fax 0 50 28 00 52*, – . AE MC VISA
fermé 20 fév.-16 mars, dern. sem. août-prem. sem. sept., lundi soir, mardi soir, merc. et jeudi – **Repas** Lunch 28 – carte 28 à 67, ♀.
• La sarcelle (taling) a fait son nid dans une villa moderne à l'intérieur néo-rustique. Cuisine classico-traditionnelle et clientèle d'habitués. Jolie terrasse.
• De taling heeft zijn nest gemaakt in deze moderne villa met een neorustieke inrichting. De klassiek-traditionele keuken trekt veel vaste gasten. Mooi terras.

à Zedelgem *par ⑥ : 10,5 km – 21 918 h* – ✉ 8210 Zedelgem :

Zuidwege, Torhoutsesteenweg 128, ✆ 0 50 20 13 39, *angelo@zuidwege.be, Fax 0 50 20 17 39*, , – , ch, – 25. AE MC VISA. ch
Repas *(fermé prem. sem. juil., vacances Noël et sam.)* (taverne-rest) Lunch 10 – carte 22 à 41 – **20 ch** *(fermé vacances Noël)* 60/85 – ½ P 58.
• Hôtel voisin d'un carrefour. Fonctionnelles, les chambres sont munies du double vitrage. Ensemble bien tenu mais n'offrant qu'un service minimal. Petit-déjeuner buffet. Cadre actuel et ambiance détendue au restaurant.
• Hotel bij een kruispunt met functionele kamers die van dubbele beglazing zijn voorzien. Alles is goed onderhouden, maar de faciliteiten zijn minimaal. Ontbijtbuffet. Restaurant met een modern interieur, waar een ontspannen sfeer heerst.

XX **Ter Leepe,** Torhoutsesteenweg 168, ✆ 0 50 20 01 97, *Fax 0 50 20 88 54* – – 220. AE MC VISA
fermé 20 juil.-4 août, du 15 au 25 janv., dim. soir, lundi et merc. soir – **Repas** Lunch 38 bc – 46/59 bc.
• Dans une imposante villa. Sage carte de base classique, incluant un menu tout compris, très demandé. Choix de vieux millésimes. Salle réservée aux banquets à l'arrière.
• Restaurant in een imposante villa, met een klassieke kaart en een zeer gewild menu, waarbij alles is inbegrepen. Mooie oude wijnflessen. Feestzaal aan de achterkant.

BRUXELLES – BRUSSEL

1000 🅿 *Région de Bruxelles-Capitale – Brussels Hoofdstedelijk Gewest* 533 L 17 *et* 716 G 3 *– 978 384 h.*

Paris 308 ⑥ – Amsterdam 204 ⑪ – Düsseldorf 222 ② – Lille 116 ⑨ – Luxembourg 219 ④.

OFFICES DE TOURISME

TIB Hôtel de Ville, Grand'Place ✉ 1000, ☎ 0 2 513 89 40, tourism.brussels@tib.be, Fax 0 2 514 45 38.
Office de Promotion du Tourisme (OPT), r. Marché-aux-Herbes 63, ✉ 1000, ☎ 0 2 504 02 00, info@opt.le, Fax 0 2 513 69 50.
TIB, Gare du Midi, ✉ 1000.
Toerisme Vlaanderen, Grasmarkt 63, ✉ 1000, ☎ 0 2 504 03 90, info@toerismevlaanderen.be, Fax 0 2 504 02 70.

Pour approfondir votre visite touristique, consultez le Guide Vert Bruxelles *et le Plan de Bruxelles n° 44.*

RENSEIGNEMENTS PRATIQUES

BUREAUX DE CHANGE

– Principales banques : ferment à 16 h 30 et sam., dim.
– Près des centres touristiques il y a des guichets de change non-officiels.

TRANSPORTS

Principales compagnies de Taxis :
Taxis Verts ☎ 0 2 349 49 49, Fax 0 2 349 49 00
Taxis Oranges ☎ 0 2 349 43 43, Fax 0 2 349 43 00
En outre, il existe les Taxis Tours faisant des visites guidées au tarif du taximètre. Se renseigner directement auprès des compagnies.

Métro :
STIB ☎ 0 2 515 20 00 pour toute information.
Le métro dessert principalement le centre-ville, ainsi que certains quartiers de l'agglomération (Heysel, Anderlecht, Auderghem, Woluwé-St-Pierre). Aucune ligne de métro ne desservant l'aéroport, empruntez le train (SNCB) qui fait halte aux gares du Nord, Central et du Midi.
SNCB ☎ 0 2 555 25 25, Fax 0 2 525 93 13.

Trams et Bus :
En plus des nombreux réseaux quadrillant toute la ville, le tram 94 propose un intéressant trajet visite guidée avec baladeur (3 h). Pour tout renseignement et réservation, s'adresser au TIB (voir plus haut).

🚗 *☎ 0 2 555 25 25 et 555 25 55, Fax 0 2 525 93 13.*

CAPITALE VERTE

Parcs : de Bruxelles, Wolvendael, Woluwé, Laeken, Cinquantenaire, Duden. Bois de la Cambre. La Forêt de Soignes.

QUELQUES GOLFS

18 9 *par Tervurenlaan* (DN) *: 14 km à Tervuren, Château de Ravenstein ☎ 0 2 767 58 01, Fax 0 2 767 28 41 – 18 au Nord-Est : 14 km à Melsbroek, Steenwagenstraat 11 ☎ 0 2 751 82 05, Fax 0 2 751 84 25 – 18 à Anderlecht, Zone Sportive de la Pede* (AN)*, r. Scholle 1 ☎ 0 2 521 16 87, Fax 0 2 521 51 56 – 9 à Watermael-Boitsfort* (CN)*, chaussée de la Hulpe 53a ☎ 0 2 672 22 22, Fax 0 2 675 34 81 – 9 par ④ : 16 km à Overijse, Gemslaan 55 ☎ 0 2 687 50 30, Fax 0 2 687 37 68 – 9 par ⑧ : 8 km à Itterbeek, J.M. Van Lierdelaan 24 ☎ 0 2 569 00 38, Fax 0 2 567 00 38 – 18 au Nord-Est : 20 km à Kampenhout, Wildersedreef 56 ☎ 0 16 65 12 16, Fax 0 16 65 16 80 – 9 à l'Est : 18 km à Duisburg, Hertswegenstraat 59 ☎ 0 2 769 45 82, Fax 0 2 767 97 52.*

CURIOSITÉS

BRUXELLES VU D'EN HAUT

Atomium★ BK *– Basilique du Sacré Cœur★* ABL *– Arcades du Musée royal de l'Armée et d'Histoire militaire★* HS **M25**.

PERSPECTIVES CÉLÈBRES DE BRUXELLES

Palais de Justice ES**J** *– Cité administrative* KY *– Place Royale★* KZ.

QUELQUES MONUMENTS HISTORIQUES

Grand-Place★★★ JY *– Théâtre de la Monnaie★* JY *– Galeries St-Hubert★★* JKY *– Maison d'Erasme (Anderlecht)★★* AM *– Château et parc de Gaasbeek (Gaasbeek)★★ (Sud-Ouest : 12 km par N 282* AN*) – Serres royales (Laeken)★★* BK **R**.

ÉGLISES

Sts-Michel-et-Gudule★★ KY *– Église N.-D. de la Chapelle★* JZ *– Église N.-D. du Sablon★* KZ *– Abbaye de la Cambre (Ixelles)★★* FGV *– Sts-Pierre-et-Guidon (Anderlecht)★* AM **D**.

QUELQUES MUSÉES

Musée d'Art ancien★★★ KZ – *Musée du Cinquantenaire*★★★ HS **M**[11] – *Musée d'Art moderne*★★ KZ **M**[2] – *Centre Belge de la BD*★★ KY **M**[8] – *Autoworld*★★ HS **M**[3] – *Muséum des Sciences Naturelles*★★ GS **M**[29] – *Musée des instruments de Musique*★★★ KZ **M**[21] – *Musée Constantin Meunier (Ixelles)*★ FV **M**[13] – *Musée communal d'Ixelles (Ixelles)*★★ GT **M**[12] – *Musée Charlier*★ FR **M**[9] – *Bibliotheca Wittockiana (Woluwé-St-Pierre)*★ CM **C** – *Musée royal de l'Afrique centrale (Tervuren)*★★ *(par ③)* – *Musée Horta (St-Gilles)*★★ EFU **M**[20] – *Maison Van Buuren (Uccle)*★ EFV **M**[6] – *Musées Bellevue*★ KZ **M**[28].

ARCHITECTURE MODERNE

Atomium★ BK – *Centre Berlaymont* GR – *Parlement européen* GS – *Palais des Beaux Arts* KZ **Q**[1] – *La Cité administrative* KY – *Les cités-jardins Le Logis et Floréal (Watermael-Boitsfort)* DN – *Les Cités-jardins Kapelleveld (Woluwé-St-Lambert)* DM – *Campus de l'UCL (Woluwé-St-Lambert)* DL – *Palais Stoclet (Tervuren/Environs)*★ CM **Q**[4] – *Swift (La Hulpe/Environs)* – *Vitrine P. Hankar*★ KY **W** – *Maison Communale d'Ixelles* FS **K**[2] – *Hôtel Van Eetvelde*★ GR *187* – *Maison Cauchie (Etterbeek)*★ HS **K**[1] – *Old England*★ KZ **N.**

QUARTIERS PITTORESQUES

La Grand-Place★★★ JY – *Le Grand et le Petit Sablon*★★ JZ – *Les Galeries St-Hubert*★★ JKY – *La place du Musée* KZ – *La place Ste-Catherine* JY – *Le vieux centre (Halles St-Géry – voûtement de la Senne – Église des Riches Claires)* ER – *Rue des Bouchers*★ JY – *Manneken Pis*★★ JZ – *Les Marolles* JZ – *La Galerie Bortier* JY.

LE SHOPPING

Grands Magasins : *Rue Neuve* JKY.

Commerces de luxe : *Avenue Louise* BMN, *Avenue de la Toison d'Or* KZ, *Boulevard de Waterloo* KZ, *rue de Namur* KZ.

Antiquités : *Le Sablon et alentours* JKZ.

Marché aux puces : *Place du Jeu de Balles* ES.

Galeries commerçantes : *Basilix, Westland Shopping Center, Woluwé Shopping Center, City 2, Galerie Louise.*

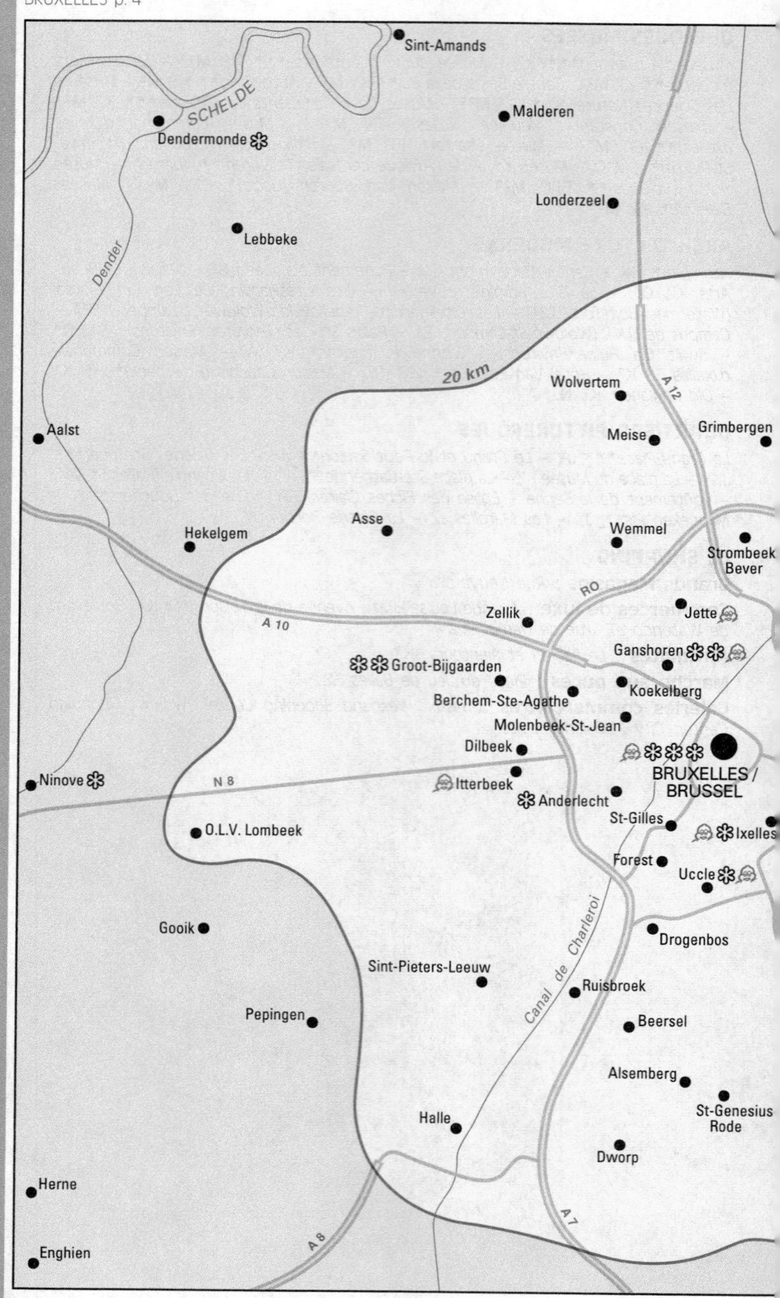
Sint-Amands
SCHELDE
Malderen
Dendermonde
Londerzeel
Lebbeke
Dender
20 km
Wolvertem
A 12
Aalst
Meise
Grimbergen
Asse
Hekelgem
Wemmel
Strombeek Bever
RO
Zellik
Jette
A 10
Ganshoren
Groot-Bijgaarden
Koekelberg
Berchem-Ste-Agathe
Molenbeek-St-Jean
Dilbeek
BRUXELLES / BRUSSEL
Ninove
N 8
Itterbeek
Anderlecht
St-Gilles
O.L.V. Lombeek
Ixelles
Forest
Uccle
Gooik
Drogenbos
Sint-Pieters-Leeuw
Canal de Charleroi
Ruisbroek
Pepingen
Beersel
Alsemberg
St-Genesius Rode
Halle
Dworp
Herne
A 7
A 8
Enghien

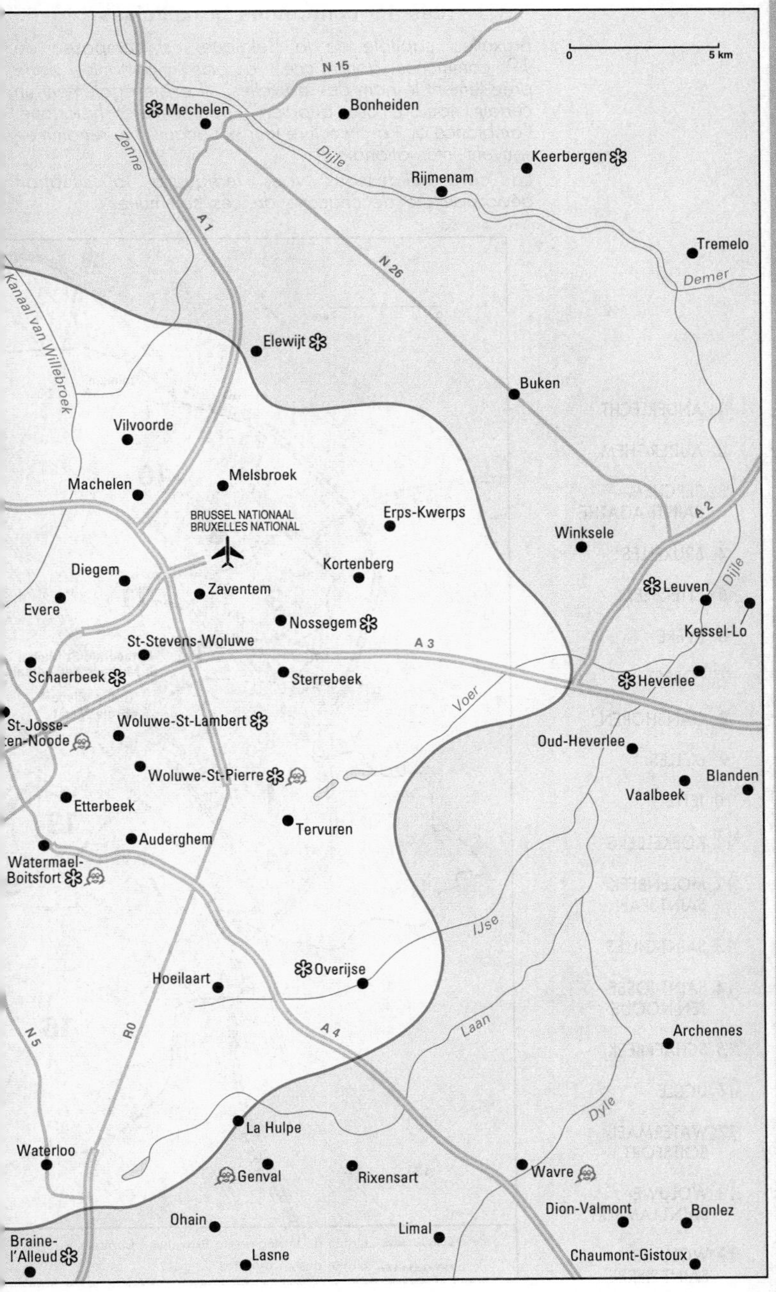
0
5 km
N 15
Mechelen
Bonheiden
Zenne
Dijle
Keerbergen
Rijmenam
A 1
N 26
Tremelo
Demer
Kanaal van Willebroek
Elewijt
Buken
Vilvoorde
Melsbroek
Machelen
BRUSSEL NATIONAAL
BRUXELLES NATIONAL
Erps-Kwerps
A 2
Winksele
Diegem
Kortenberg
Zaventem
Leuven
Dijle
Evere
Nossegem
Kessel-Lo
St-Stevens-Woluwe
A 3
Schaerbeek
Sterrebeek
Heverlee
Voer
St-Josse-ten-Noode
Woluwe-St-Lambert
Oud-Heverlee
Woluwe-St-Pierre
Blanden
Vaalbeek
Etterbeek
Tervuren
Auderghem
Watermael-Boitsfort
IJse
Overijse
Hoeilaart
R0
A 4
Laan
N 5
Archennes
Dyle
La Hulpe
Waterloo
Genval
Rixensart
Wavre
Dion-Valmont
Bonlez
Ohain
Limal
Braine-l'Alleud
Lasne
Chaumont-Gistoux

Les 19 communes bruxelloises

Bruxelles, capitale de la Belgique, est composée de 19 communes dont l'une, la plus importante, porte précisément le nom de "Bruxelles". Il existe également un certain nombre de "quartiers" dont l'intérêt historique, l'ambiance ou l'architecture leur ont acquis une renommée souvent internationale.

La carte ci-dessous vous indiquera la situation géographique de chacune de ces communes.

1 ANDERLECHT
2 AUDERGHEM
3 BERCHEM-SAINTE-AGATHE
4 BRUXELLES
5 ETTERBEEK
6 EVERE
7 FOREST
8 GANSHOREN
9 IXELLES
10 JETTE
11 KOEKELBERG
12 MOLENBEEK-SAINT-JEAN
13 SAINT-GILLES
14 SAINT-JOSSE-TEN-NOODE
15 SCHAERBEEK
16 UCCLE
17 WATERMAEL-BOITSFORT
18 WOLUWE-SAINT-LAMBERT
19 WOLUWE-SAINT-PIERRE

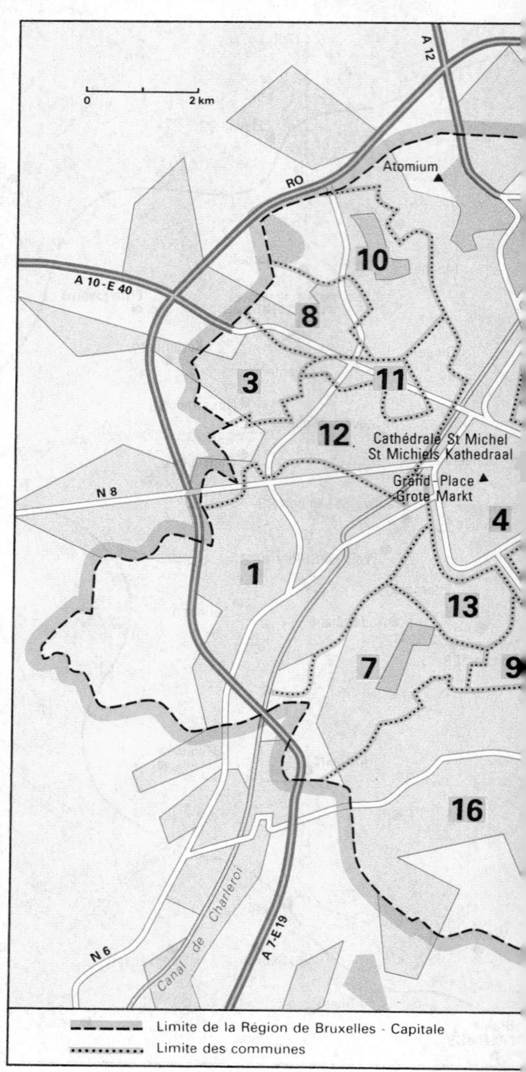

De 19 Brusselse gemeenten

Brussel, hoofdstad van België, bestaat uit 19 gemeenten, waarvan de meest belangrijke de naam "Brussel" draagt. Daar zijn een aantal wijken, waar de geschiedenis, de sfeer en de architectuur gezorgd hebben voor de, vaak internationaal, verworven faam.

Onderstaande kaart geeft U een overzicht van de geografische ligging van elk van deze gemeenten.

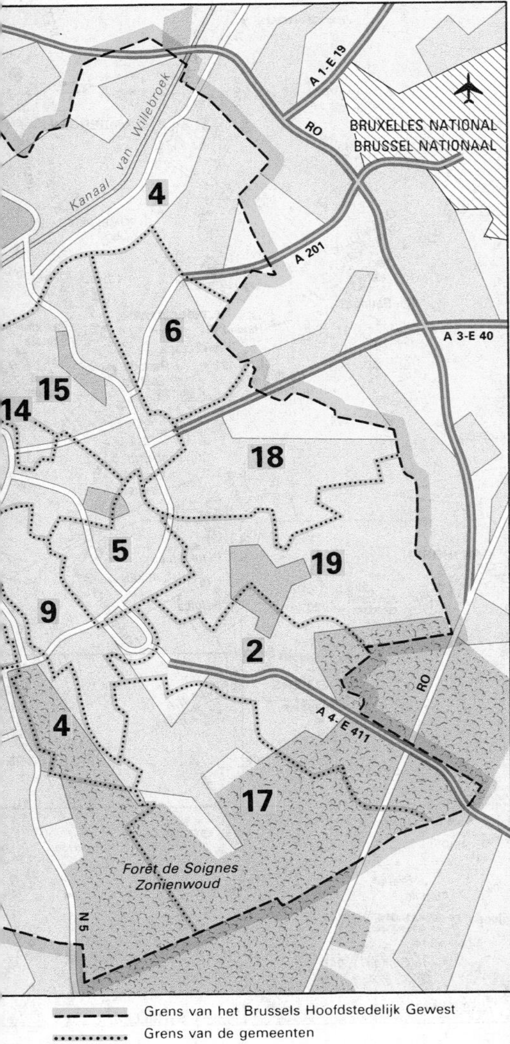

ANDERLECHT	1
OUDERGEM	2
SINT-AGATHA-BERCHEM	3
BRUSSEL	4
ETTERBEEK	5
EVERE	6
VORST	7
GANSHOREN	8
ELSENE	9
JETTE	10
KOEKELBERG	11
SINT-JANS-MOLENBEEK	12
SINT-GILLIS	13
SINT-JOOST-TEN-NODE	14
SCHAARBEEK	15
UKKEL	16
WATERMAAL-BOSVOORDE	17
SINT-LAMBRECHTS-WOLUWE	18
SINT-PIETERS-WOLUWE	19

BRUXELLES
BRUSSEL

Street	Grid	No.
Broqueville (Av. de)	CM	30
Charleroi (Chée de)	BM	34
Croix-du-Feu (Av. des)	BCK	54
Démosthène Poplimont (Av.)	BL	58
Edmond-Parmentier (Av.)	DM	69
Emile-Bockstael (Bd)	BL	75
Emile-Bossaert (Av.)	ABL	76
Emile-Vandervelde (Av.)	DM	82
France (R. de)	BM	100
Houba de Strooper (Av.)	BK	121
Jacques-Sermon (Av.)	BL	130
Jean-Sobiesky (Av.)	BKL	136
Jules-van-Praet (Av.)	BKL	144
Madrid (Av. de)	BK	166
Meysse (Av. de)	BK	175
Port (Av. du)	BL	198
Prince-de-Liège (Bd)	AM	202
Robiniers (Av. des)	BL	211
Stockel (Chée de)	DM	232
Veeweyde (R. de)	AM	244
Vétérinaires (R. des)	BM	247

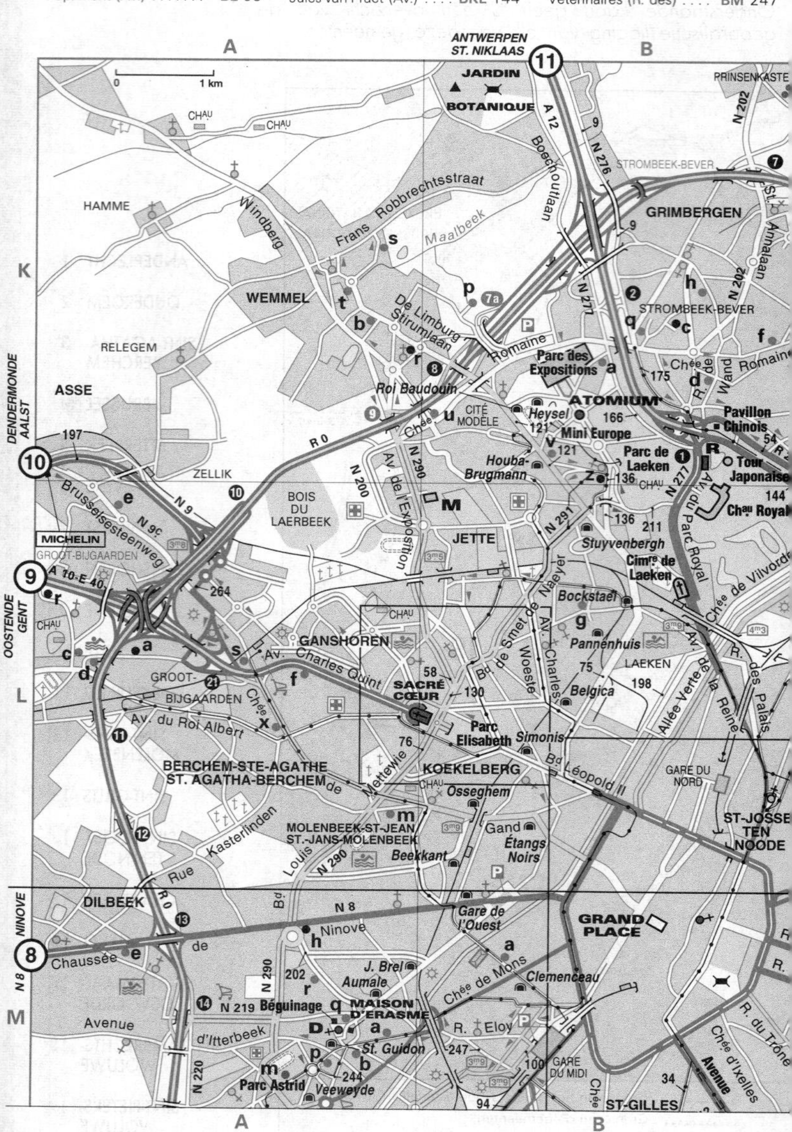

ENVIRONS

Michelin n'accroche pas de panonceau aux hôtels et restaurants qu'il signale.

BRUXELLES
BRUSSEL

Street	Grid	No.
Alfred-Madoux (Av.)	DM	6
Altitude 100 (Pl. de l')	BN	7
Broqueville (Av. de)	CM	30
Charleroi (Chée de)	BM	34
Charroi (R. du)	ABN	36
Delleur (Av.)	CN	57
Échevinage (Av. de l')	BN	67
Edith-Cavell (R.)	BN	68
Edmond-Parmentier (Av.)	DM	69
Emile-Vandervelde (Av.)	DM	82
Eugène-Flagey (Pl.)	BN	88
Fonsny (Av.)	BN	94
Foresterie (Av. de la)	CN	96
France (R. de)	BM	100
Frans van Kalken (Av.)	AN	103
Gén. Jacques (Bd)	CN	109
Houzeau (Av.)	BN	123
Louis-Schmidt (Bd)	CN	161
Mérode (R. de)	BN	174
Paepsem (Bd)	AN	186
Parc (Av. du)	BN	190
Plaine (Bd de la)	CN	196
Prince-de-Liège (Bd)	AM	202
Stockel (Chée de)	DM	232
Tervuren (Chée de)	DN	235
Th. Verhaegen (R.)	BN	237
Triomphe (Bd du)	CN	240
Veeweyde (R. de)	AM	244
Vétérinaires (R. des)	BM	247

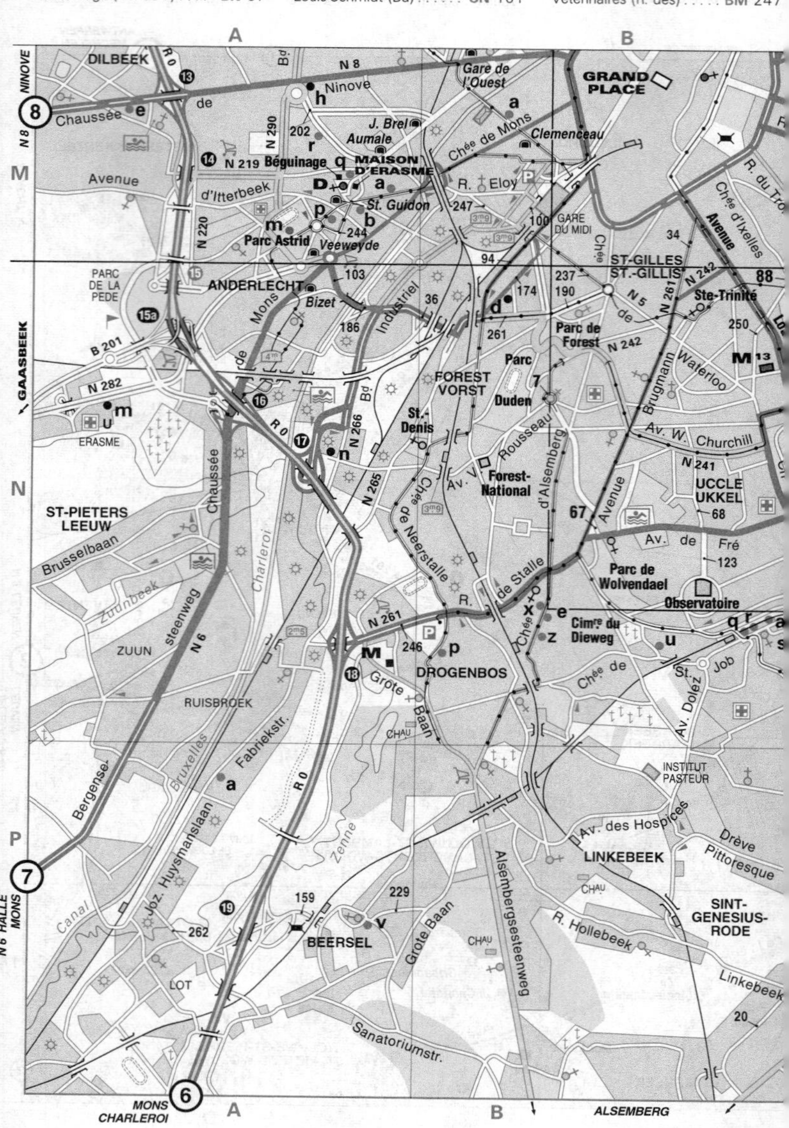

Vleurgat (Chée de) . . . . . . BN 250
Wielemans Ceuppens (Av.) . . . . BN 261
2e Rég.-de-Lanciers (Av. du) . . . . CN 265

ENVIRONS

BEERSEL

Lotsestr. . . . . AP 159

Schoolstraat . . . . AP 229
Zennestraat (Lot) . . . . AP 262

DROGENBOS

Verlengde Stallestraat . . . . AN 246

KRAAINEM

Wezembeek (Av. de) . . . . DM 259

ST-GENESIUS-RODE

Bevrijdingslaan . . . . BP 20
Zonienwoudlaan . . . . CP 263

Le Guide change, changez de guide tous les ans.

BRUXELLES
BRUSSEL

Street	Square	No.
Baudouin (Bd)	EQ	16
Bienfaiteurs (Pl. des)	GQ	21
Brabançonne (Av. de la)	GR	28
Edouard-de-Thibault (Av.)	HS	72
Europe (Bd de l')	ES	89
Frans Courtens (Av.)	HQ	102
Frère-Orban (Sq.)	FR	104
Froissart (R.)	GS	106
Gén. Eisenhower (Av.)	GQ	108
Hal (Porte de)	ES	114
Henri-Jaspar (Av.)	ES	117
Herbert-Hoover (Av.)	HR	118
Industrie (Quai de l')	ER	126
Jan-Stobbaerts (Av.)	GQ	133
Jardin Botanique (Bd du)	FQ	134
Jean-Jacobs (Pl.)	ES	135
Jean-Volders (Av.)	ET	138

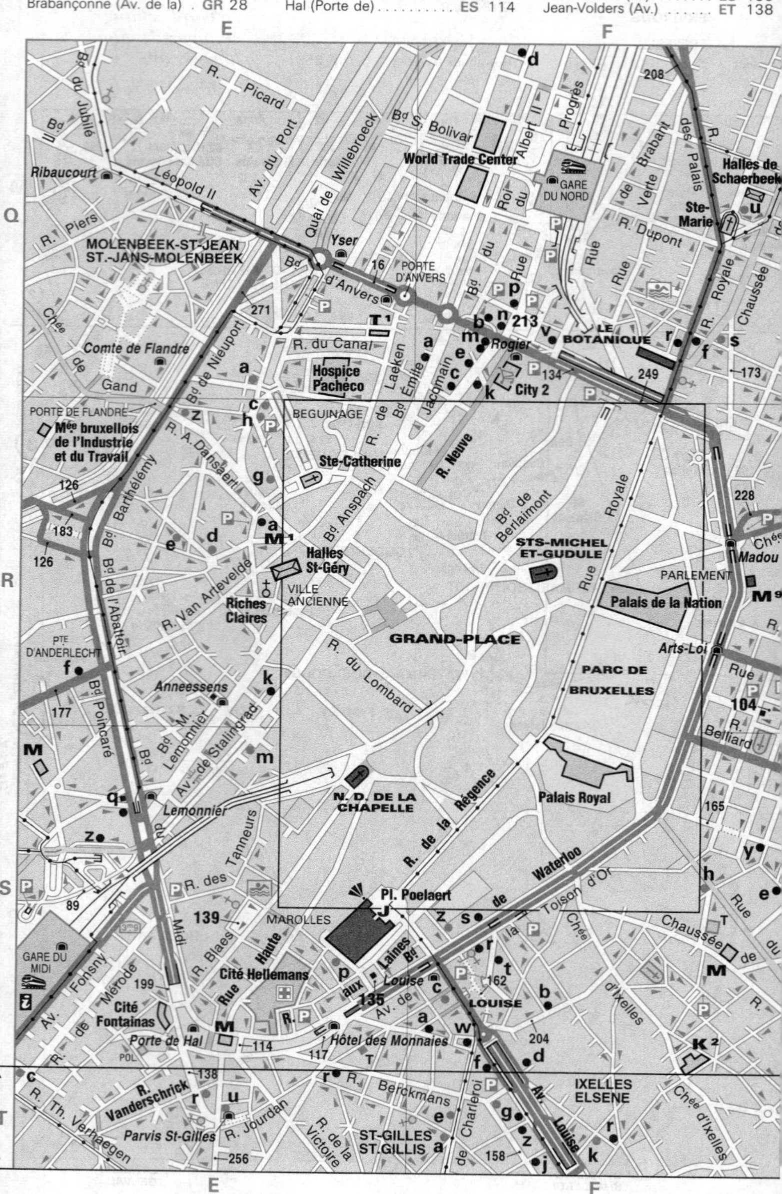

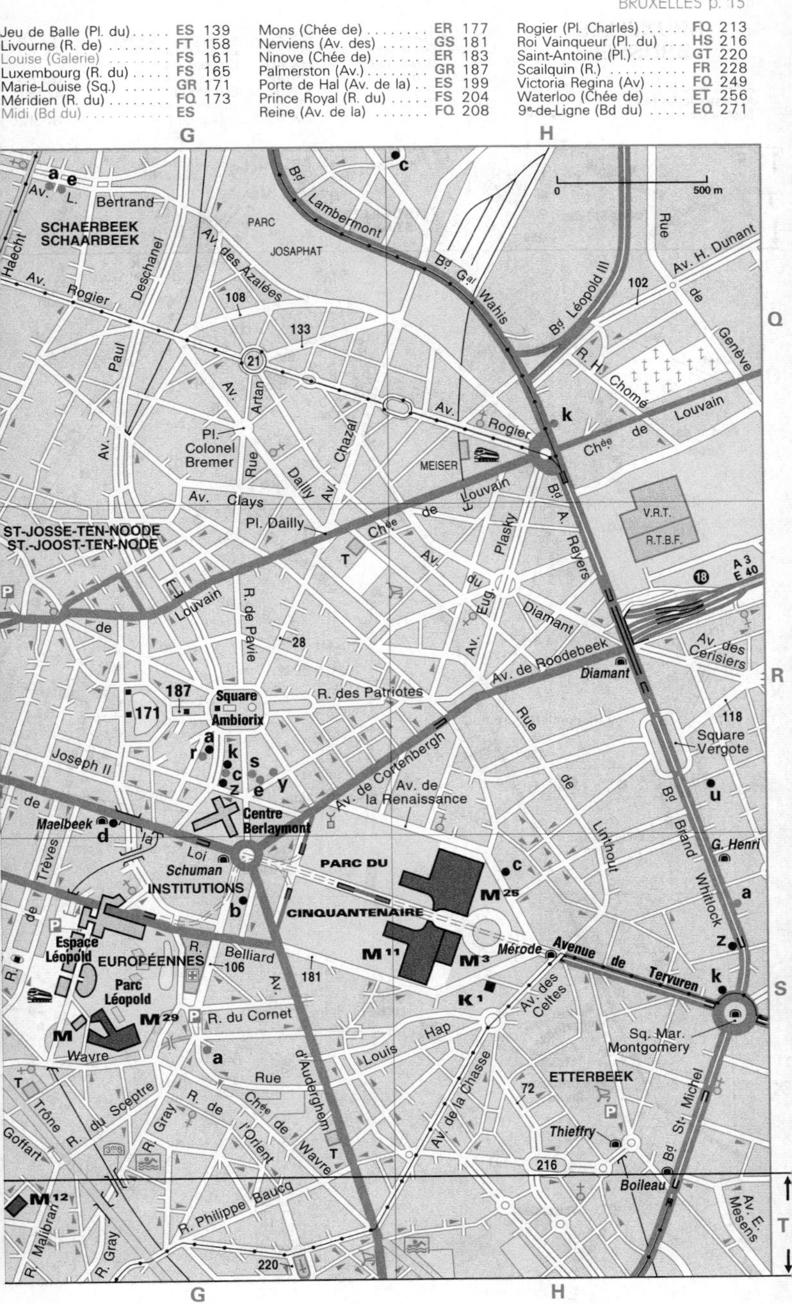

G
H
Q
R
S
T
0
500 m
SCHAERBEEK
SCHAARBEEK
PARC
JOSAPHAT
Av. L. Bertrand
Av. Rogier
Haecht
Deschanel
Av. des Azalées
Bd Lambermont
Bd Gal Wahis
Bd Léopold III
Rue de Genève
Av. H. Dunant
R. H. Chomé
Chée de Louvain
Av. Paul
Av. Artan
Rue Chazal
Av. Dailly
Pl. Colonel Bremer
Av. Clays
Pl. Dailly
MEISER
Rogier
Bd A. Reyers
Av. Plasky
V.R.T.
R.T.B.F.
A 3
E 40
18
ST-JOSSE-TEN-NOODE
ST.-JOOST-TEN-NODE
R. de Pavie
Av. Eug. Plasky
Av. du Diamant
Av. des Cerisiers
Av. de Roodebeek
Diamant
Square Ambiorix
R. des Patriotes
Rue de Linthout
Square Vergote
Joseph II
Av. de Cortenbergh
Av. de la Renaissance
Bd Brand Whitlock
G. Henri
Maelbeek
Centre Berlaymont
Rue de la Loi
Schuman
Trèves
INSTITUTIONS
EUROPÉENNES
PARC DU
CINQUANTENAIRE
Espace Léopold
Parc Léopold
R. Belliard
Av. d'Auderghem
Mérode
Avenue de Tervuren
Av. des Celtes
Sq. Mar. Montgomery
R. du Cornet
Wavre
Rue Louis Hap
ETTERBEEK
Av. de la Chasse
Bd St. Michel
Thieffry
Boileau
Trône
R. du Sceptre
R. Gray
R. de l'Orient
Chée de Wavre
Goffart
R. Philippe Baucq
R. Malibran
Av. E. Mesens
102
108
133
21
28
187
171
118
106
181
72
216
220
M 25
M 11
M 3
M 29
M 12
K 1

BRUXELLES BRUSSEL

Américaine (R.) . . . . FU 8
Auguste-Rodin (Av.) . . . . . . GU 12
Besme (Av.) . . . . EV 18
Boendael (Drève de) . . . . . . GX 22
Cambre (Bd de la) . . . . GV 33
Coccinelles (Av. des) . . . . . HX 40
Congo (Av. du) . . . . GV 48
Copernic (R.) . . . . FX 51
Doronée (R.) . . . . FV 61
Dries . . . . HX 63
Emile-de-Beco (Av.) . . . . . . GU 79
Emile-De-Mot (Av.) . . . . GV 81
Eperons d'Or (Av. des) . . . . GU 85
Everard (av.) . . . . EV 91
Hippodrome (Av. de l') . . . . GU 120

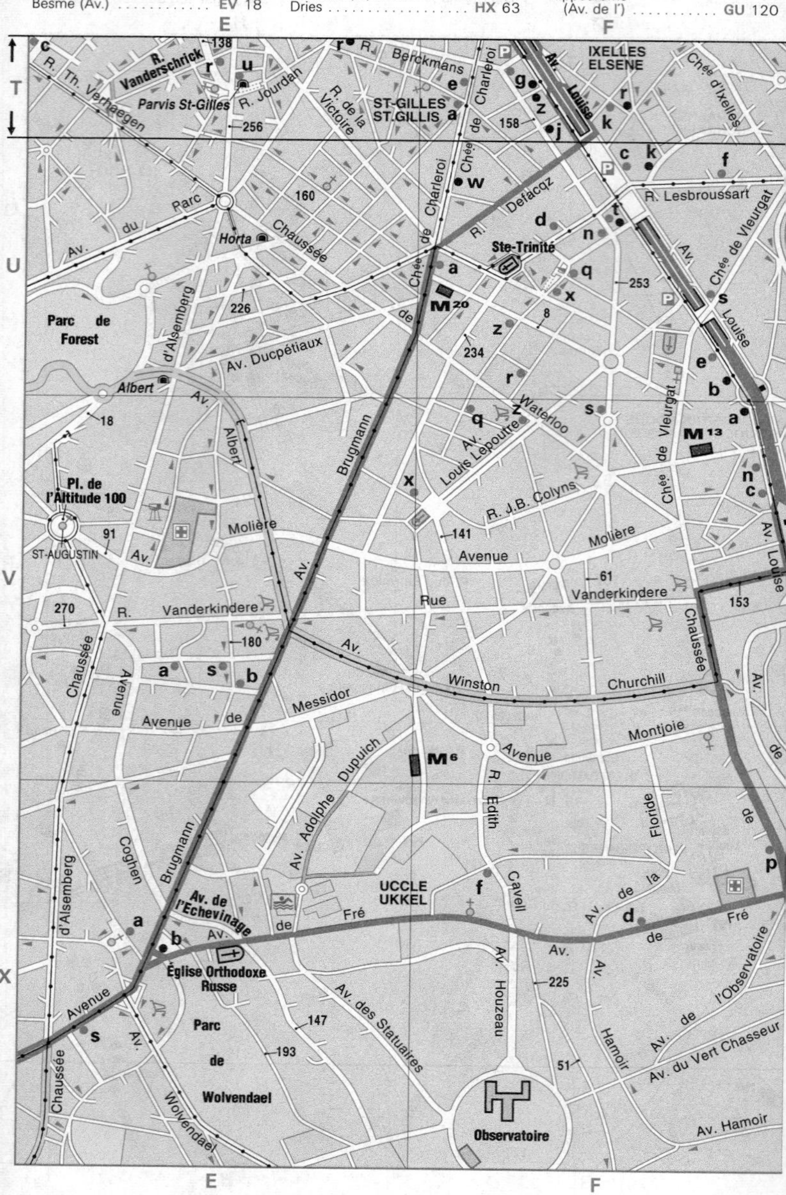

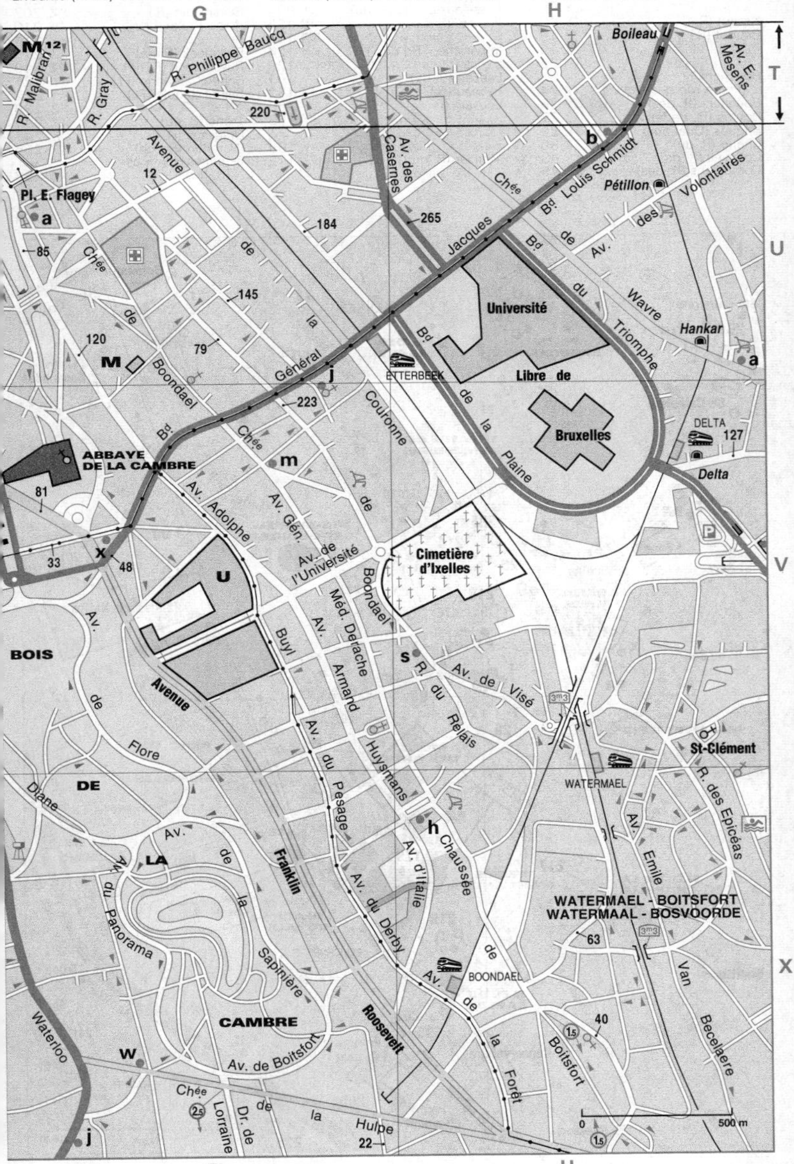

G
H
T
U
V
X
M12
R. Malibran
R. Gray
R. Philippe Baucq
220
Boileau
Av. E. Mesens
b
Avenue
Av. des Casernes
Chée
Bd Louis Schmidt
Pétillon
Av. des Volontaires
12
Pl. E. Flagey
a
265
184
Jacques
Bd de Wavre
85
Chée de Boondael
de la Couronne
145
Université
Bd du Triomphe
Hankar
120
M
79
Général
j
ETTERBEEK
Bd de la Plaine
Libre de
Bruxelles
223
DELTA
127
Delta
ABBAYE DE LA CAMBRE
m
81
Av. Adolphe Buyl
Av. Gén.
Av. de l'Université
Cimetière d'Ixelles
33
X
48
U
Boondael
Méd. Derache
Av. Armand Huysmans
BOIS
s
R. du Relais
Av. de Visé
Avenue Franklin Roosevelt
St-Clément
Av. du Pesage
Flore
WATERMAEL
R. des Epicéas
DE
Diane
h
Av. de la Sapinière
LA
Av. du Panorama
Av. d'Italie
Chaussée de Boitsfort
Av. Emile Van Becelaere
Av. du Derby
WATERMAEL - BOITSFORT
WATERMAAL - BOSVOORDE
63
BOONDAEL
Waterloo
CAMBRE
Av. de la Forêt
40
W
Av. de Boitsfort
Chée de la Hulpe
Lorraine
Dr. de
22
0
500 m

BRUXELLES BRUSSEL

Adolphe-Max (Bd) . . . . . . JY 3
Albertine (Pl. de l') . . . . . KZ 4
Anspach (Bd) . . . . JY
Assaut (R. d') . . . . KY 10
Baudet (R.) . . . . KZ 15
Beurre (Rue au) . . . . JY 19
Bortier (Galerie) . . . . JKZ 23
Bouchers (Petite rue des) . . . . . . JY 24
Bouchers (R. des) . . . . . . JY 25
Bourse (Pl. de la) . . . . . . JY 27
Briques (Quai aux) . . . . . JY 29
Chêne (R. du) . . . . JZ 39
Colonies (R. des) . . . . . . KY 43
Comédiens (R. des) . . . . KY 45
Commerce (R. du) . . . . . . KZ 46
Croix-de-Fer (R. de la) . . . . KY 52
Duquesnoy (Rue) . . . . JYZ 66
Ernest-Allard (R.) . . . . JZ 86
Étuve (R. de l') . . . . JZ 87
Europe (Carr. de l') . . . . . KY 90
Fossé-aux-Loups (R. du) . . JKY 99
Fripiers (R. des) . . . . JY 105
Grand-Sablon (Pl. du) . . . . KZ 112
Impératrice (Bd de l') . . . . KY 124
Ixelles (Chée d') . . . . KZ 129
Laeken (R. de) . . . . JY 151
Lebeau (R.) . . . . JZ 152
Louvain (R. de) . . . . KY 163
Marché-aux-Herbes (R. du) JY 168
Marché-aux-Poulets (R. du) . . . . JY 169
Mercier (R. du Card.) . . . . KY 172
Midi (R. du) . . . . JYZ
Montagne (Rue de la) . . . KY 178
Musée (Pl. du) . . . . KZ 179
Neuve (Rue) . . . . JY
Nord (Passage du) . . . . . . JY 182
Petit-Sablon (Pl. du) . . . . . KZ 195
Presse (R. de la) . . . . KY 201
Princes (Galeries des) . . . . JY 205
Ravenstein (R.) . . . . KZ 207
Reine (Galerie de la) . . . . . JY 210
Roi (Galerie du) . . . . KY 214
Rollebeek (R. de) . . . . JZ 217
Ruysbroeck (R. de) . . . . . . KZ 219
Sainte-Catherine (Pl.) . . . . JY 221
Sainte-Gudule (Pl.) . . . . . . KY 222
Toison d'Or (Av. de la) . . . . KZ 238
Trône (R. du) . . . . KZ 241
Ursulines (R. des) . . . . JZ 243
Waterloo (Bd de) . . . . KZ 255
6-Jeunes-Hommes (R. des) . . . . KZ 268

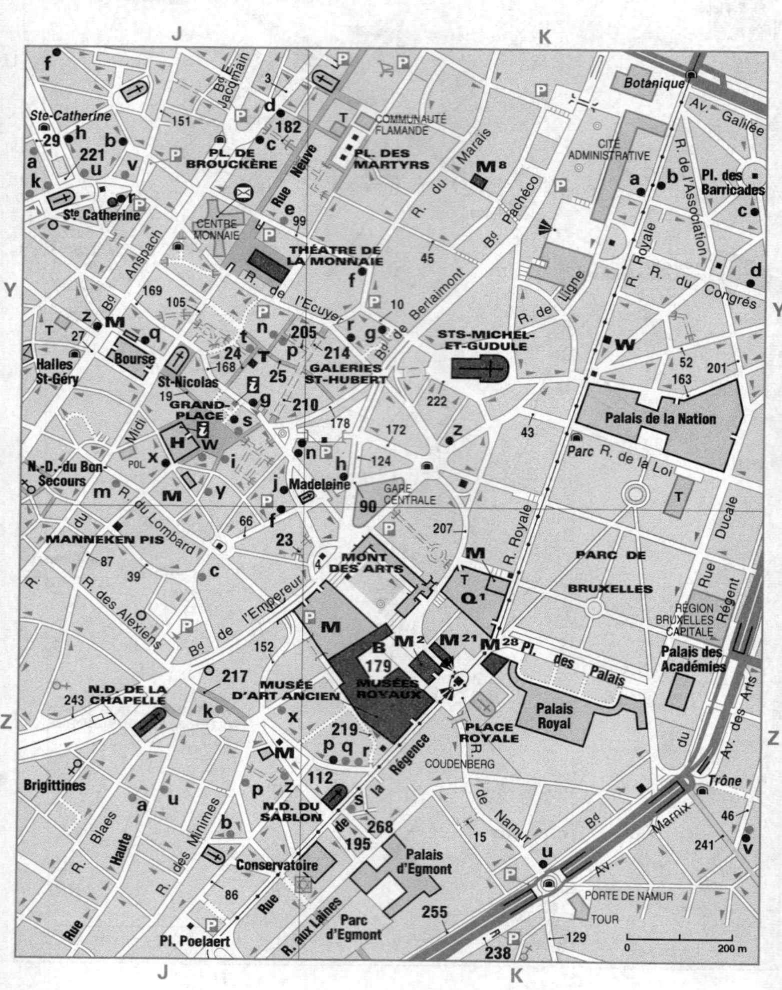

GANSHOREN JETTE KOEKELBERG

Basilique (Av. de la) . W 13
Château (Av. du) . . . . W 37
Constitution (Av. de la) W 49
Démosthène
Poplimont (Av.) . . . W 58
Duc Jean (Av. du) . . . W 64
Edouard Bénes (Av.) . W 70
Eglise St-Martin (R. de l') W 73
Emile-Bossaert (Av.) . W 76
Firmin-Lecharlier (Av.) W 92
Gloires Nationales
(Av. des) . . . . W 110
Jacques-Sermon (Av.) W 130
Laeken (Av. de) . . . . . W 150
Léon-Théodore (R.) . . W 154
Levis-Mirepoix (Av. de) W 156
Panthéon (Av. du) . . . W 189
Wemmel (Chée de) . . W 258

RÉPERTOIRE DES RUES DU PLAN DE BRUXELLES

Abattoir (Bd de l') . . p.12 ER
Adolphe-Buyl (Av.) . . p.15 GV
Adolphe-Dupuich (Av.) . p.14 EVX
Adolphe-Max (Bd) . . p.16 JY 3
Albert (Av.) . . . . p.14 EV
Albertine (Pl. de l') . p.16 KZ 4
Alexiens (R. des) . . . p.16 JZ
Alfred-Madoux (Av.) . p.11 DN 6
Alsemberg
(Chée d') . . . . p.10 BNP
Altitude 100
(Pl. de l') . . . . p.10 BN 7
Ambiorix (Square) . . p.13 GR
Américaine (R.) . . . . p.14 FU 8
Anspach (Bd) . . . . . p.16 JY
Antoine-Dansaert (R.) . p.12 ER
Anvers (Bd d') . . . . . p.12 EQ
Armand-Huymans
(Av.) . . . . p.15 GV
Artan (R.) . . . . p.13 GQ
van Artevelde (R.) . . p.12 ER
Arts (Av. des) . . . . . p.16 KZ
Assaut (R. d') . . . . . p.16 KY 10
Association (R. de l') . p.16 KY
Audergem (Av. d') . . p.13 GS
Auguste-Reyers (Bd) . p.13 HR
Auguste-Rodin (Av.) . p.15 GU 12
Azalées (Av. des) . . . p.13 GQ
Baron-Albert-d'Huart
(Av.) . . . . p. 9 DM
Barthélemy (Bd) . . . p.12 ER
Basilique (Av. de la) . p.17 W 13
Baudet (R.) . . . . p.16 KZ 15
Baudouin (Bd) . . . . . p.12 EQ 16
Belliard (R.) . . . . p.13 GS
Berckmans (R.) . . . . p.12 EFT
Berlaymont (Bd de) . p.16 KY
Besme (Av.) . . . . p.14 EV 18
Beurre (Rue au) . . . . p.16 JY 19
Bienfaiteurs (Pl. des) . p.13 GQ 21
Blaes (R.) . . . . p.12 ES
Boitsfort (Av. de) . . . p.15 GX
Boitsfort (Chée de) . p.15 HX
Bolivar (Bd Simon) . p.12 EFQ
Boondael (Chée de) . p.15 GUV
Boondael (Drève de) . p.15 GX 22
Bortier (Galerie) . . . . p.16 JKZ 23
Bouchers
(Petite rue des) . . p.16 JY 24
Bouchers (R. des) . . p.16 JY 25
Bourse (Pl. de la) . . . p.16 JY 27
Brabançonne
(Av. de la) . . . . . . p.13 GR 28
Brabant (R. de) . . . . p.12 FQ
Brand-Whitlock (Bd) . p.13 HRS
Briques (Quai aux) . p.16 JY 29
Broqueville (Av. de) . p. 9 CM 30
Brouckère (Pl. de) . . p.16 JY
Broustin (Av.) . . . . . . p.17 W
Brugmann (Av.) . . . . p.14 EVX
Cambre (Bd de la) . . p.15 GV 33
Canal (R. du) . . . . . . p.12 EQ
Carton de Wiart (Av.) . p.17 W
Casernes (Av. des) . p.15 GHU
Celtes (Av. des) . . . . p.13 HS
Cerisiers (Av. des) . . p.13 HR
Charleroi (Chée de) . p.12 EFU
Charles-Quint (Av.) . p. 8 AL
Charles-Woeste (Av.) . p. 8 BL
Charroi (R. du) . . . . . p.10 ABN 36
Chasse (Av. de la) . . p.13 HS
Château (Av. du) . . . p.17 W 37
Chazal (Av.) . . . . p.13 GQ
Chêne (R. du) . . . . . p.16 JZ 39
Clays (Av.) . . . . p.13 GQ
Coccinelles (Av. des) . p.15 HX 40
Coghen (Av.) . . . . . . p.14 EVX
Colonel-Bremer (Pl.) . p.13 GQ
Colonies (R. des) . . . p.16 KY 43
Comédiens (R. des) . p.16 KY 45
Commerce (R. du) . . p.16 KZ 46
Congo (Av. du) . . . . p.15 GV 48
Congrès (R. du) . . . . p.16 KY
Constitution
(Av. de la) . . . . . . p.17 W 49
Copernic (R.) . . . . . . p.14 FX 51
Cortenbergh (Av. de) . p.13 GR
Couronne (Av. de la) . p.15 GUV
Croix-de-Fer (R. de la) . p.16 KY 52
Croix-du-Feu (Av. des) . p. 8 BCK 54
Dailly (Av.) . . . . p.13 GQ
Dailly (Pl.) . . . . p.13 GR
Defacqz (R.) . . . . p.14 FU
Delleur (Av.) . . . . p.11 CN 57
Démosthène
Poplimont (Av.) . . p.17 W 58
Derby (Av. du) . . . . . p.15 GX
Diamant (Av. du) . . . p.13 HR
Diane (Av. de) . . . . . p.15 FGX
Dolez (Av.) . . . . p.10 BN
Dodonée (R.) . . . . . . p.14 FV 61
Dries . . . . p.15 HX 63
Duc Jean (Av. du) . . p.17 W 64
Ducale (Rue) . . . . . . p.16 KZ
Ducpétiaux (Av.) . . . p.14 EU
Duquesnoy (Rue) . . p.16 JYZ 66
Echevinage (av. de l') . p.14 EX
Ecuyer (R. de l') . . . . p.16 JKY
Edith-Cavell (R.) . . . . p.14 FX
Edmond
Parmentier (Av.) . p. 9 DM 69
Edmond-Mesens
(Av.) . . . . p.13 HT
Edouard-Bénes (Av.) . p.17 W 70
Edouard-de-Thibault
(Av.) . . . . p.13 HS 72
Eglise St-Martin
(R. de l') . . . . p.17 W 73
Eloy (Rue) . . . . p. 8 BM
Emile-Bockstael (Bd) . p. 8 BL 75
Emile-Bossaert (Av.) . p.17 W 76
Emile-de-Beco (Av.) . p.15 GU 79
Emile-De-Mot (Av.) . p.15 GV 81
Emile-Jacqmain (Bd) . p.12 FQ
Emile van Becelaere
(Av.) . . . . p.15 HX
Emile-Vandervelde
(Av.) . . . . p. 9 DM 82
Empereur (Bd de l') . p.16 JZ
Eperons d'Or
(Av. des) . . . . p.15 GU 85
Epicéas (R. des) . . . . p.15 HX
Ernest-Allard (R.) . . . p.16 JZ 86
Étuve (R. de l') . . . . . p.16 JZ 87
Eugène-Flagey (Pl.) . p.10 BN 88
Eugène-Plasky (Av.) . p.13 HR
Europe (Bd de l') . . . p.12 ES 89
Europe (Carr. de l') . p.16 KY 90
Everard (av.) . . . . . . p.14 EV 91
Exposition (Av. de l') . p. 8 AKL
Exposition Universelle
(Av. de l') . . . . p.17 W
Firmin-Lecharlier
(Av.) . . . . p.17 W 92
Flore (Av. de) . . . . . . p.15 GV
Floride (Av. de la) . . p.14 FX
Fonsny (Av.) . . . . . . p.10 BN 94

Foresterie (Av. de la) p.11 **CN** 96
Forêt (Av. de la) p.15 **HX**
Fossé-aux-Loups (R. du) p.16 **JKY** 99
France (R. de) p. 8 **BM** 100
Franklin-Roosevelt (Av.) p.15 **GVX**
Frans-Courtens (Av.) p.13 **HQ** 102
Frans van Kalken (Av.) p.10 **AN** 103
Fré (Av. de) p.12 **EFX**
Frère-Orban (Sq.) p.12 **FR** 104
Fripiers (R. des) p.16 **JY** 105
Froissart (R.) p.13 **GS** 106
Galilée (Av.) p.16 **KY**
Gand (Chée de) p. 8 **ABL**
Gén. Eisenhower (Av.) p.13 **GQ** 108
Gén. Jacques (Bd) p.15 **GHU**
Gén. Médecin Derache (Av.) p.15 **GV**
Gén. Wahis (Bd) p.13 **HQ**
Genève (R. de) p.13 **HQ**
Gloires Nationales (Av. des) p.17 **W** 110
Goffart (R.) p.13 **FGS**
Grand Place p.16 **JY**
Grand-Sablon (Pl. du) p.16 **KZ** 112
Gray (R.) p.13 **GST**
Haecht (Chée de) p. 9 **CL**
Hal (Porte de) p.12 **ES** 114
Hamoir (Av.) p.14 **FX**
Haute (R.) p.12 **ES**
Henri-Chomé (R.) p.13 **HQ**
Henri-Dunant (Av.) p.13 **HQ**
Henri-Jaspar (Av.) p.12 **ES** 117
Herbert-Hoover (Av.) p.13 **HR** 118
Hippodrome (Av. de l') p.15 **GU** 120
Hospices (Av. des) p.10 **BP**
Houba de Strooper (Av.) p. 8 **BK** 121
Houzeau (Av.) p.14 **FX**
la Hulpe (Chée de) p.11 **CN**
Impératrice (Bd de l') p.16 **KY** 124
Industrie (Quai de l') p.12 **ER** 126
Industriel (Bd) p.10 **AN**
Invalides (Bd des) p.15 **HV** 127
Italie (Av. d') p.15 **GHX**
Itterbeck (Av. d') p. 8 **AM**
Ixelles (Chée d') p.12 **FST**
Jacques-Sermon (Av.) p.17 **W** 130
Jan Stobbaerts (Av.) p.13 **GQ** 133
Jardin Botanique (Bd du) p.12 **FQ** 135
Jean-Baptiste-Colyns (R.) p.14 **FV**
Jean-Sobiesky (Av.) p. 8 **BK** 136
Jean-Volders (Av.) p.12 **ET** 138
Jette (Av. de) p.17 **W**
Jette (Chée de) p.17 **W**
Jeu de Balle (Pl. du) p.12 **ES** 139
Joseph-II (R.) p.13 **GR**
Joseph-Stallaert (R.) p.14 **FV** 141
Jourdan (R.) p.12 **ET**
Jubilé (Bd du) p.12 **EQ**
Jules-van-Praet (Av.) p. 8 **BKL** 144
Juliette-Wytsman (R.) p.15 **GU** 145
Kamerdelle (Av.) p.14 **EX** 147
Kasterlinden (R.) p. 8 **AL**
Laeken (Av. de) p.17 **W** 150
Laeken (R. de) p.12 **EQ**
Laines (R. aux) p.16 **JKZ**
Lambermont (Bd) p. 9 **CL**
Lebeau (R.) p.16 **JZ** 152
Legrand (Av.) p.14 **FV** 153
Léon-Théodore (R.) p.17 **W** 154
Léopold-II (Bd) p.12 **EQ**
Léopold-III (Bd) p. 9 **CL**
Lesbroussart (R.) p.14 **FU**
Levis Mirepoix (Av. de) p.17 **W** 156
Liberté (Av. de la) p.17 **W**
Ligne (R. de) p.16 **KY**
Linthout (R. de) p.13 **HRS**
Livourne (R. de) p.12 **FT** 158
Loi (R. de la) p.13 **GRS**
Lombard (R. du) p.16 **JYZ**
Lorraine (Drève de) p.11 **CN**
Louis-Bertrand (Av.) p.13 **GQ**
Louis-Hap (R.) p.13 **GHS**
Louis-Lepoutre (Av.) p.14 **FV**
Louis-Mettewie (Bd) p. 8 **ALM**
Louis-Morichar (Pl.) p.14 **EU** 160
Louis-Schmidt (Bd) p.15 **HU**
Louise (Av.) p.10 **BMN**
Louise (Galerie) p.12 **FS** 161
Louvain (Chée de) p.13 **GHQ**
Louvain (R. de) p.16 **KY** 163
Luxembourg (R. du) p.12 **FS** 165
Madrid (Av. de) p. 8 **BK** 166
Mai (Av. de) p. 9 **CM**
Malibran (R.) p.13 **GT**
Marais (R. du) p.16 **KY**
Marché-aux-Herbes (R. du) p.16 **JY** 168
Marché-aux-Poulets (R. du) p.16 **JY** 169
Marie-Louise (Sq.) p.13 **GR** 171
Marnix (Av.) p.16 **KZ**
Martyrs (Pl. des) p.16 **KY**
Maurice-Lemonnier (Bd) p.12 **ERS**
Mercier (R. du Card.) p.16 **KY** 172
Méridien (R. du) p.12 **FQ** 173
Mérode (R. de) p.10 **BN** 174
Messidor (Av. de) p.14 **EV**
Meysse (Av. de) p. 8 **BK** 175
Midi (Bd du) p.12 **ES**
Midi (R. du) p.16 **JYZ**
Minimes (R. des) p.16 **JZ**
Molière (Av.) p.12 **EFV**
Mons (Chée de) p. 8 **AMN**
Mont Saint-Jean (Route de) p.11 **DN**
Montagne (Rue de la) p.16 **KY** 178
Montgoméry (Square Maréchal) p.13 **HS**
Montjoie (Av.) p.14 **FV**
Musée (Pl. du) p.16 **KZ** 179
Mutualité (R. de la) p.14 **EV** 180
Namur (R. de) p.16 **KZ**
Neerstalle (Chée de) p.10 **AN**
Nerviens (Av. des) p.13 **GS** 181
Neuve (Rue) p.16 **JY**
Nieuport (Bd de) p.12 **EQ**
Ninove (Chée de) p. 8 **AM**
Nord (Passage du) p.16 **JY** 182
Nouvelle (Av.) p.15 **GU** 184
Observatoire (Av. de l') p.14 **FX**
Orient (R. de l') p.13 **GS**
van Overbeke (Av.) p.17 **W**
Pachéco (Bd) p.16 **KY**
Paepsem (Bd) p.10 **AN** 186
Paix (Av. de la) p.17 **W**
Palais (Pl. des) p.16 **KZ**
Palais (R. des) p.12 **FQ**
Palmerston (Av.) p.13 **GR** 187
Panorama (Av. du) p.15 **GX**
Panthéon (Av. du) p.17 **W** 189
Parc (Av. du) p.14 **EU**
Parc Royal (Av. du) p. 8 **BL**
Patriotes (R. des) p.13 **GR**
Paul-Deschanel (Av.) p.13 **GQ**
Paul-Hymans (Av.) p. 9 **CDM**
Paul-Stroobant (Av.) p.14 **EX** 193
Pavie (R. de) p.13 **GR**
Pesage (Av. du) p.15 **GVX**
Petit-Sablon (Pl. du) p.16 **KZ** 195
Philippe Baucq (R.) p.13 **GT**
Picard (R.) p.12 **EQ**
Piers (R.) p.12 **EQ**
Pittoresque (Drève) p.10 **BP**
Plaine (Bd de la) p.15 **HV**
Poelaert (Pl.) p.16 **JZ**
Poincaré (Bd) p.12 **ERS**
Port (Av. du) p.12 **EQ**
Porte de Hal (Av. de la) p.12 **ES** 199
Presse (R. de la) p.16 **KY** 201
Prince-de-Liège (Bd) p. 8 **AM** 202
Prince Royal (R. du) p.12 **FS** 204
Princes (Galeries des) p.16 **JY** 205
Progrès (R. du) p.12 **FQ**
Ravenstein (R.) p.16 **KZ** 207
Réforme (Av. de la) p.17 **W**
Régence (R. de la) p.16 **JKZ**
Régent (Bd du) p.16 **KZ**
Reine (Av. de la) p. 8 **BL**
Reine (Galerie de la) p.16 **JY** 210
Relais (R. du) p.15 **HV**
Renaissance (Av. de la) p.13 **HR**
Robiniers (Av. des) p. 8 **BL** 211
Rogier (Av.) p.13 **GHQ**
Rogier (Pl. Charles) p.12 **FQ** 213
Roi (Galerie du) p.16 **KY** 214
Roi Albert (Av. du) p. 8 **AL**
Roi Vainqueur (Pl. du) p.13 **HS** 216
Rollebeek (R. de) p.16 **JZ** 217
Roodebeek (Av. de) p.13 **HR**
Royale (R.) p.12 **FQR**
Ruysbroeck (R. de) p.16 **KZ** 219
Saint-Antoine (Pl.) p.13 **GT** 220
Saint-Hubert (Drève de) p.11 **CP**
Saint-Hubert (Galeries) p.16 **JKY**
Saint-Job (Chée de) p.10 **BN**
Saint-Michel (Bd) p.13 **HS**
Sainte-Catherine (Pl.) p.16 **JY** 221
Sainte-Gudule (Pl.) p.16 **KY** 222
Saisons (Av. des) p.15 **GV** 223
Sapinière (Av. de la) p.15 **GX**
Saturne (Av. de) p.14 **FX** 225
Savoie (R. de) p.14 **EU** 226
Scailquin (R.) p.12 **FR** 228
Sceptre (R. du) p.13 **GS**
de Smet de Naeyer (Bd) p. 8 **BL**
Stalingrad (Av. de) p.12 **ERS**
Stalle (R. de) p.10 **BN**
Statuaires (Av. des) p.14 **EX**
Stockel (Chée de) p. 9 **DM** 232
Tabellion (R. du) p.14 **FU** 234
Tanneurs (R. des) p.12 **ES**
Tervuren (Av. de) p.11 **DMN**
Tervuren (Chée de) p.11 **DN** 235
Théodore-Verhaegen (R.) p.12 **ET**
Toison d'Or (Av. de la) p.16 **KZ** 238
Trêves (R. de) p.13 **GS**
Triomphe (Bd du) p.15 **HU**
Trône (R. du) p.13 **FGS**
Université (Av. de l') p.15 **GV**
Ursulines (R. des) p.16 **JZ** 243
Vanderkindere (R.) p.14 **EFV**
Veeweyde (R. de) p. 8 **AM** 244
Verdun (Rue de) p. 9 **CL**
Vergote (Square) p.13 **HR**
Vert Chasseur (Av. du) p.14 **FX**
Verte (Allée) p. 8 **BL**
Verte (R.) p.12 **FQ**
Vétérinaires (R. des) p. 8 **BM** 247
Victoire (R. de la) p.12 **ET**
Victor Rousseau (Av.) p.10 **BN**
Victoria Regina (Av.) p.12 **FQ** 249
Vilvorde (Av. de) p. 9 **CK**
Vilvorde (Chée de) p. 9 **BCL**
Visé (Av. de) p.15 **HV**
Vleurgat (Chée de) p.14 **FUV**
Volontaires (Av. des) p.15 **HU**
Wand (R. de) p. 8 **BK**
Washington (R.) p.14 **FU** 253
Waterloo (Bd de) p.12 **FS**
Waterloo (Chée de) p.11 **BCN**
Wavre (Chée de) p.11 **CDN**
Wemmel (Chée de) p.17 **W** 258
Wielemans Ceuppens (Av.) p.10 **BN** 261
Willebroeck (Quai de) p.12 **EQ**
Winston-Churchill (Av.) p.14 **FV**
Woluwe (Bd de la) p. 9 **DLM**
Wolwendael (Av.) p.14 **EX**
2e Rég.-de-Lanciers (Av. du) p.15 **GHU** 265
6-Jeunes-Hommes (R. des) p.16 **KZ** 268
7-Bonniers (Av. des) p.14 **EV** 270
9e de-Ligne (Bd du) p.12 **EQ** 271

ENVIRONS

ASSE

Brusselse Steenweg (Zellik) p. 8 **AL**
Pontbeeklaan (Zellik) p. 8 **AK** 197
Zuiderlaan (Zellik) p. 8 **AL** 264

Liste alphabétique des hôtels et restaurants
Alfabetische lijst van hotels en restaurants
Alphabetisches Hotel- und Restaurantverzeichnis
Alphabetical list of hotels and restaurants

S

T

U – V

W – Y – Z

Les établissements à étoiles
Sterrenbedrijven
Die Stern-Restaurants
Starred establishments

✿✿✿

29	XXX	Comme Chez Soi

✿✿

58	XXXXX	Bijgaarden (De)
43	XXXX	Bruneau
29	XXXX	Sea Grill (H. Radisson SAS)
43	XXX	Claude Dupont

✿

60	XXXX	Barbizon
35	XXXX	Maison du Bœuf (H. Hilton)
37	XXXX	Villa Lorraine
53	XXX	Vieux Boitsfort (Au)
33	XXX	Écailler du Palais Royal (L')
58	XXX	Michel
60	XXX	Orangerie Roland Debuyst (L')
41	XXX	Saint Guidon
44	XXX	San Daniele
37	XXX	Truffe Noire (La)
41	XX	Brouette (La)
55	XX	Deux Maisons (Les)
54	XX	Maurice à Olivier (de)
51	X	Bon-Bon
44	X	Marie
53	X	Passage (Le)
50	X	Senza Nome

La cuisine que vous recherchez...
Het soort keuken dat u zoekt
Welche Küche, welcher Nation suchen Sie
That special cuisine

A la bière et régionale

Anguilles

Buffets

Grillades

Produits de la mer – Crustacés

Taverne – Brasserie – Bistrot

Chinoise

53 Le Dragon *Watermael-Boitsfort*
43 Le Jaspe *Etterbeek, Q. Cinquantenaire*
51 Le Lion *Uccle*
40 Lychee *Q. Atomium*
40 Maison du Dragon *Q. Botanique, Gare du Nord*
40 Ming Dynasty *Q. Atomium*
42 New Asia *Auderghem*

Créole

49 Couleurs et Saveurs *St-Gilles Q. Louise*

Espagnole

62 La Hacienda *Env. à Vilvoorde*
48 El Madrileño *St-Gilles*
48 Turon *St-Gilles*

Grecque

47 Notos *Ixelles Q. Louise*
33 Strofilia *Q. Ste-Catherine*

Indienne

37 Au Palais des Indes *Q. Louise*

Italienne

51 A'mbriana *Uccle*
50 Amici miei *Schaerbeek, Q. Meiser*
30 Amigo *Q. Grand'Place*
44 L'Ancienne Poissonnerie *Ixelles*
61 l'Arlecchino *H. Aub. de Waterloo Env. à Sint-Genesius-Rode*
37 L'Atelier de la Truffe Noire *Q. Louise*
50 La Buca di Bacco *Schaerbeek*
34 Castello Banfi *Q. des Sablons*
55 Le Coq en Pâte *Woluwe-St-Lambert*
54 Da Mimmo *Woluwe-St-Lambert*
29 Da Piero
45 Le Fellini *Ixelles Q. Bascule*
63 Il Brunello *Env. à Wemmel*
49 I Trulli *St-Gilles, Q. Louise*
33 Jolly du Grand Sablon *Q. Sablons*
38 Pappa e Citti *Q. de l'Europe*
53 Pasta Commedia *Uccle*
29 Piazza Navona
53 Au Repos des Chasseurs *Watermael-Boitsfort*
44 San Daniele *Ganshoren*
50 Senza Nome *Schaerbeek*
50 Le Stelle *Schaerbeek*
46 Tutto Pepe *Ixelles, Q. Louise*

Japonaise

34 L'Herbe Rouge *Q. Sablons*
29 Samourai
37 Tagawa *Q. Louise*
38 Take Sushi *Q. de l'Europe*

Marocaine

42 La Khaïma *Auderghem*

Portugaise

48 Coimbra *St-Gilles*
48 Le Forcado *St-Gilles*

Régionale française

54 Aux Portes du Béarn *Watermael-Boitsfort*
34 Orphyse Chaussette *Q. Ste-Catherine*

Thaïlandaise

51 Blue Elephant *Uccle*
35 Les Larmes du Tigre *Q. Palais de Justice*
45 Les Perles de Pluie *Ixelles, Q. Louise*

Vietnamienne

42 La Citronnelle *Auderghem*
47 Le Liseron d'Eau *Koekelberg*
54 Le Nénuphar *Woluwe-St-Lambert*
44 La Pagode d'Or *Ixelles, Q. Bonndael*
56 La Tour d'Argent *Woluwe-St-Pierre*
44 Le Yen *Ixelles*

BRUXELLES (BRUSSEL) - *plan p. 16 sauf indication spéciale :*

Radisson SAS, r. Fossé-aux-Loups 47, ✉ 1000, ☎ 0 2 219 28 28, *restaurant.brussels@radissonsas.com, Fax 0 2 219 62 62,* – 25 à 450. AE VISA. rest KY f
Repas voir rest ***Sea Grill*** ci-après – ***Atrium*** *Lunch 26* – carte 40 à 51, ♀ – 25 – **271 ch** 235, – 10 suites.
◆ Luxueux hôtel de chaîne dont l'atrium recèle des vestiges des fortifications de la ville (12e s.). Chambres "high-tech" différemment agencées. Bar "bédéphile". Ample restaurant coiffé d'une haute coupole. Semaines à thème culinaire. Pianiste.
◆ Luxehotel met in het atrium overblijfselen van de 12e-eeuwse vestingwerken van de stad. Hightechkamers die verschillend zijn ingedeeld. Bar voor stripliefhebbers. Groot restaurant met een hoge koepel. Culinaire themaweken. Pianist.

Astoria, r. Royale 103, ✉ 1000, ☎ 0 2 227 05 05, *H1154@accor-hotels.com, Fax 0 2 217 11 50,* – 25 à 210. AE VISA JCB. rest KY b
Repas ***Le Palais Royal*** *(fermé 15 juil.-15 août et week-end) Lunch 40* – 35/55 – 25 – **104 ch** 180/335, – 14 suites.
◆ Hiro Hito, Churchill, Dali et Gainsbourg furent les hôtes de cet élégant palace Belle Époque. Fastueux salons et chambres garnies de meubles de style. Restaurant opulent : profonds miroirs, cheminée de marbre, fresques et moulures.
◆ Hiro Hito, Churchill, Dalí et Gainsbourg logeerden in dit chique belle-époquehotel. Weelderige lounge en kamers met stijlmeubelen. Het restaurant is een lust voor de tong en het oog : grote spiegels, marmeren schouw, fresco's en sierlijsten.

Le Plaza, bd A. Max 118, ✉ 1000, ☎ 0 2 278 01 00, *reservations@leplaza-brussels.be, Fax 0 2 278 01 01* – – 25 à 800. AE VISA JCB
Repas *(fermé sam. midi et dim. soir) Lunch 29* – carte 39 à 52 – 25 – **187 ch** 350/450, – 6 suites – ½ P 105/160. plan p. 12 FQ e
◆ Chambres aménagées avec goût et salon-théâtre classé monument historique, dans un immeuble 1930 dont les plans s'inspirent de l'hôtel Georges V à Paris. Une coupole ornée d'une fresque céleste donne un air aérien au bar-restaurant.
◆ Luxehotel met smaakvol gedecoreerde kamers in een gebouw uit 1930, naar het ontwerp van het Georges V in Parijs. De feestzaal met podium staat op de monumentenlijst. Barrestaurant waarvan de koepel is versierd met een sterrenhemel.

Marriott, r. A. Orts 7 (face à la bourse), ✉ 1000, ☎ 0 2 516 90 90 et 516 91 00 (rest), *mhrs.brudt.ays.mgr@marriotthotels.com, Fax 0 2 516 90 00,* – 25 à 450. AE VISA JY z
Repas *(fermé dim. soir) Lunch 12* – carte 22 à 36, ♀ – 24 – **212 ch** 210/230, – 6 suites.
◆ Hôtel tout confort établi devant la Bourse. L'imposante façade 1900, les chambres et communs ont retrouvé l'éclat du neuf. Brasserie moderne où une cuisine internationale se conçoit sous vos yeux. Rôtissoire en salle.
◆ Zeer comfortabel hotel bij de Beurs in een hoekpand waarvan de imposante gevel uit 1900, de kamers en de gemeenschappelijke ruimten er weer als nieuw uitzien. Moderne brasserie met een open keuken en een internationale kaart. Vlees aan het spit.

Métropole, pl. de Brouckère 31, ✉ 1000, ☎ 0 2 217 23 00, *info@metropolehotel.be, Fax 0 2 218 02 20,* – 25 à 500. AE VISA JCB
Repas voir rest ***L'Alban Chambon*** ci-après – **291 ch** 279/429, – 14 suites – ½ P 318/418. JY c
◆ Palace fin 19e s. s'étirant sur la place de Brouckère, si bien chantée par Brel. Hall impressionnant et somptueux salons d'époque. Chambres agréables, de divers styles.
◆ Chic hotel uit de late 19e-eeuw aan het Brouckereplein, dat Brel zo mooi heeft bezongen. Indrukwekkende hal, luisterrijke lounge. Zeer comfortabele kamers in diverse stijlen.

NH Atlanta, bd A. Max 7, ✉ 1000, ☎ 0 2 217 01 20, *nhatlanta@nh-hotels.be, Fax 0 2 217 37 58,* – 25 à 160. AE VISA JY d
Repas *Lunch 10 bc* – carte env. 38 – 21 – **228 ch** 325/450, – 13 suites.
◆ D'importantes rénovations ont donné une seconde vie à ce bel hôtel élevé dans les années 1930 à deux pas du nostalgique passage du Nord et de la place de Brouckère. Luxueuse brasserie moderne avec carte franco-transalpine.
◆ Dit mooie hotel uit 1930, vlak bij een nostalgische winkelgalerij en het Brouckèreplein, heeft onlangs een verjongingskuur ondergaan. De bijbehorende brasserie is luxueus en modern en hanteert een Frans-Italiaanse kaart.

Bedford, r. Midi 135, ✉ 1000, ☎ 0 2 507 00 00, *info@hotelbedford.be, Fax 0 2 507 00 10,* – 25 à 550. AE VISA JCB.
Repas carte env. 44 – **318 ch** 230/320, – 8 suites. plan p. 12 ER k
◆ À deux pas du Manneken Pis et 500 m de la Grand-Place, établissement renfermant une douzaine d'appartements et des chambres correctement équipées. Restaurant dédiant à la France ses préparations et sa sélection de vins.
◆ Hotel op een steenworp afstand van Manneken Pis en de Grote Markt, met goed geëquipeerde kamers en een twaalftal appartementen. Het restaurant is sterk op Frankrijk gericht, zowel qua eten als drinken.

President Centre sans rest, r. Royale 160, ✉ 1000, ☎ 0 2 219 00 65, *thierry.sluys@presidentcentre.be*, *Fax 0 2 218 09 10* – |‡| ⇌ TV. AE ⓓ ⓜ VISA JCB. ✈ KY a
73 ch ☕ 170/245.
◆ Morphée vous tend les bras dans les confortables chambres insonorisées de l'hôtel President Centre. Précieux voiturier, service avenant et personnalisé, bar "cosy".
◆ In de rustige en comfortabele kamers van het President Centre valt u zo in de armen van Morpheus. Valetparking, uitstekende service en cosy bar.

Hesperia Grand'Place sans rest, r. Colonies 10, ✉ 1000, ☎ 0 2 504 99 10, *regency.palace@skynet.be*, *Fax 0 2 503 14 51* – |‡| ⇌ ▤ TV – 🏛 25. AE ⓓ ⓜ VISA KY z
47 ch ☕ 150/240.
◆ Nouvelle enseigne idéalement située entre la gare centrale et la cathédrale des Sts-Michel-et-Gudule. Chambres actuelles de bon confort. Lumineuse salle des petits-déjeuners.
◆ Dit hotel tussen het Centraal Station en de St.-Michielskathedraal bestaat nog maar kort. De moderne kamers zijn comfortabel en de ontbijtzaal baadt in het licht.

Scandic Grand'Place, r. Arenberg 18, ✉ 1000, ☎ 0 2 548 18 11, *grand.place@scandic-hotels.com*, *Fax 0 2 548 18 20*, ≘s – |‡| ⇌ ▤ TV ♿ – 🏛 25 à 80. AE ⓓ ⓜ VISA JCB
Repas (dîner seult le week-end, jours fériés et vacances scolaires) *Lunch 16* – carte 22 à 34 – **100 ch** ☕ 229/289. KY r
◆ À 250 m de la Grand-Place, accessible par les galeries St-Hubert, demeures de maître fin 19e s. renfermant de coquettes petites chambres, pour des nuits sans histoire. Brasserie au cadre actuel, sobre et chaleureux.
◆ Herenhuis uit de 19e eeuw, op 250 m van de Grote Markt, te bereiken via de St.-Hubertusgalerijen. De kamers zijn klein, maar rustig en zien er picobello uit. Brasserie met een hedendaagse, sobere inrichting die toch warm aandoet.

NH Grand Place Arenberg, r. Assaut 15, ✉ 1000, ☎ 0 2 501 16 16, *nhgrandplace@nh-hotels.com*, *Fax 0 2 501 18 18* – |‡| ⇌ ▤ TV – 🏛 25 à 85. AE ⓓ ⓜ VISA. ✈
Repas *(fermé sam.midi, dim. midi et jours fériés midis)* (taverne-rest) *Lunch 8* – 25 – ☕ 21 – **155 ch** 220/250. KY g
◆ Hôtel de chaîne bien positionné pour partir à la découverte de l'Îlot sacré et du "ventre" de la ville. Équipement standard dans les chambres, modernes et fonctionnelles.
◆ Ideaal gelegen hotel voor een ontdekkingstocht door de "buik van Brussel". De kamers zijn conform de standaard van deze hotelketen : modern en praktisch.

Agenda Midi sans rest, bd Jamar 11, ✉ 1060, ☎ 0 2 520 00 10, *midi@hotel-agenda.com*, *Fax 0 2 520 00 20* – |‡| ⇌ TV. AE ⓓ ⓜ VISA JCB. ✈ plan p. 12 ES z
35 ch ☕ 62/97.
◆ Immeuble rénové dominant la place Jamar, à un saut de la gare du Midi (TGV). Agréables chambres et salle des petits-déjeuners aux couleurs ensoleillées.
◆ Gerenoveerd gebouw aan het Jamarplein, vlak bij het station Brussel-Zuid (HST). Prettige kamers en ontbijtzaal in zonnige kleuren.

Chambord sans rest, r. Namur 82, ✉ 1000, ☎ 0 2 548 99 10, *hotel-chambord@hotel-chambord.be*, *Fax 0 2 514 08 47* – |‡| TV. AE ⓓ ⓜ VISA JCB. ✈ KZ u
69 ch ☕ 132/169.
◆ Construction des années 1960 jouxtant la porte de Namur. Les chambres, spacieuses et convenablement équipées, offrent plus de calme sur l'arrière. Parking public à 50 m.
◆ Gebouw uit de jaren zestig, naast de Naamse poort. De kamers zijn ruim en goed uitgerust ; die aan de achterkant zijn het rustigst. Openbare parkeergarage op 50 m afstand.

du Congrès sans rest, r. Congrès 42, ✉ 1000, ☎ 0 2 217 18 90, *info@hotelducongres.be*, *Fax 0 2 217 18 97* – |‡| TV – 🏛 25. AE ⓓ ⓜ VISA KY d
60 ch ☕ 105/120.
◆ Rénovations importantes dans ces quatre maisons bourgeoises voisines de la colonne du Congrès. Chambres standardisées de différentes tailles. Plusieurs salons.
◆ Dit hotel is gevestigd in vier grondig gerestaureerde herenhuizen, niet ver van de Congreszuil. Standaardkamers van verschillende grootte. Verscheidene lounges.

Queen Anne sans rest, bd E. Jacqmain 110, ✉ 1000, ☎ 0 2 217 16 00, *Fax 0 2 217 18 38* – |‡| ⇌ TV. AE ⓓ ⓜ VISA. ✈ plan p. 12 EFQ a
60 ch ☕ 110/130.
◆ Immeuble situé sur une grande artère reliant le quartier du World Trade Center à la vieille ville. Sobres et menues chambres soigneusement tenues et munies du double vitrage.
◆ Hotel aan een grote verkeersader die de wijk van het World Trade Center met het oude centrum verbindt. De sobere, kleine kamers zijn goed onderhouden en hebben dubbele ramen.

Sabina sans rest, r. Nord 78, ✉ 1000, ☎ 0 2 218 26 37, *info@hotelsabina.be*, *Fax 0 2 219 32 39* – |‡| TV. AE ⓓ ⓜ VISA. ✈ KY c
24 ch ☕ 75/90.
◆ Entre la colonne du Congrès et la place des Barricades, sage hôtel aux chambres simples et tranquilles, peu à peu rafraîchies. Petit-déjeuner dans un cadre bourgeois.
◆ Eenvoudig, maar rustig hotel tussen de Congreszuil en het Barricadenplein, waarvan de kamers stuk voor stuk worden opgeknapt. Ontbijtzaal met een typisch bourgeoisdecor.

XXXX ✿✿ **Sea Grill** - H. Radisson SAS, r. Fossé-aux-Loups 47, ✉ 1000, ☎ 0 2 227 31 20, *annick .colmant@radissonsas.com, Fax 0 2 227 31 05,* Produits de la mer - ▤ P. AE ⓓ MC VISA. ✈ KY f
fermé du 3 au 12 avril, 21 juil.-15 août, sam., dim. et jours fériés - **Repas** 49/110 bc, carte 83 à 140, ♀.
◆ Ambiance scandinave aux chaudes tonalités, ambitieuse carte à dominante marine et très belle cave. Salon avec comptoir à cigares. Accueil et service irréprochables.
◆ Scandinavische sfeer in warme tinten. Ambitieuze kaart met veel vis en heerlijke wijnen. Rooksalon met uitgelezen sigarenkeuze. Onberispelijke bediening.
Spéc. Tartare de thon rouge préparé à table. Bar entier cuit en croûte de sel. Manchons de crabe de la mer de Barents tiédis au beurre de persil plat

XXXX **L'Alban Chambon** - H. Métropole, pl. de Brouckère 31, ✉ 1000, ☎ 0 2 217 23 00, *info@metropolehotel.be, Fax 0 2 218 02 20* - ▤ P. AE ⓓ MC VISA JCB JY c
fermé 19 juil.-15 août, sam., dim. et jours fériés - **Repas** Lunch 35 - 55/90 bc.
◆ L'enseigne du restaurant du Métropole honore l'architecte des lieux. Cuisine classique légère servie dans une ancienne salle de bal garnie d'un mobilier de style.
◆ Dit restaurant van het Métropole is genoemd naar de architect van het hotel. Klassieke, lichte gerechten die worden opgediend in een oude balzaal met stijlmeubilair.

XXX ✿✿✿ **Comme Chez Soi** (Wynants), pl. Rouppe 23, ✉ 1000, ☎ 0 2 512 29 21, *info@comme chezsoi.be, Fax 0 2 511 80 52* - ▤ P. AE ⓓ MC VISA plan p. 12 ES m
fermé 1er mai, 4 juil.-2 août, Noël-Nouvel An, dim. et lundi - **Repas** (nombre de couverts limité - prévenir) Lunch 64 - 112/152, carte 64 à 214, ♀.
◆ Atmosphère Belle Époque restituée dans un décor Horta, talentueux répertoire culinaire honorant les saveurs du terroir, cave d'exception. Salle à manger hélas un rien exiguë.
◆ Belle-epoque interieur in Hortastijl, waar men wat krap, zij aan zij, kan genieten van de kookkunst op hoog niveau. Aandacht voor streek producten en uitgelezen wijnen.
Spéc. Filets de sole, mousseline au Riesling et aux crevettes grises. Émincé de bœuf et pommes de terre charlottes grillées aux herbes de Provence, sauté d'asperges et pimientos. Damier de fraises des bois glacé de frangipane et mousse de fraises

X **La Manufacture,** r. Notre-Dame du Sommeil 12, ✉ 1000, ☎ 0 2 502 25 25, *info@manufacture.be, Fax 0 2 502 27 15,* 🍴, Ouvert jusqu'à 23 h - AE ⓓ MC VISA plan p. 12 ER e
fermé sam. midi et dim. - **Repas** Lunch 13 - carte 30 à 50.
◆ Métaux, bois, cuir et granit président au décor "loft" de cette brasserie "trendy" aménagée dans l'ancien atelier d'une célèbre maroquinerie. Cuisine au goût du jour.
◆ Metaal, hout, leer en graniet hebben de overhand in deze hippe brasserie, die als een loft is ingericht in een voormalig lederwarenfabriekje. Trendy menukaart.

X **Piazza Navona,** Vieille Halle aux Blés 39, ✉ 1000, ☎ 0 2 503 00 68, *Fax 0 2 503 00 68,* 🍴, Cuisine italienne - AE MC VISA. ✈ JZ c
fermé sam. midi et dim. - **Repas** Lunch 14 - carte 23 à 55.
◆ Ça marche fort pour ce restaurant italien baptisé du nom d'une célèbre place romaine. Clichés dédiés à la "Ville éternelle" en salle. Recettes appétissantes. Cave transalpine.
◆ De zaken gaan goed in dit Italiaanse eettentje, dat naar een beroemd plein in Rome is genoemd. In de eetzaal hangen foto's van de "Eeuwige Stad". Italiaanse wijnen.

X **Samourai,** r. Fossé-aux-Loups 28, ✉ 1000, ☎ 0 2 217 56 39, *Fax 0 2 771 97 61,* Cuisine japonaise - ▤. AE ⓓ MC VISA JCB. ✈ JY e
fermé 15 juil.-16 août, mardi et dim. midi - **Repas** Lunch 22 - carte 40 à 84.
◆ Près du théâtre de la Monnaie, restaurant nippon dont la carte, explicite, offre un choix assez complet. Bel assortiment de crus bordelais.
◆ Deze Japanner bij de Muntschouwburg neemt u mee naar het land van de samoerai. De menukaart is vrij uitgebreid en er is een fraai assortiment bordeauxwijnen.

X **Da Piero,** r. Antoine Dansaert 181, ✉ 1000, ☎ 0 2 219 23 48, *da.piero@hotmail.com, Fax 0 2 219 23 48,* Cuisine italienne, ouvert jusqu'à 23 h - ▤. MC VISA plan p. 12 ER z
fermé du 8 au 23 août, 24 déc.-5 janv. et dim. - **Repas** Lunch 14 - 22/30.
◆ Sympathique établissement de quartier tenu en famille : goûteux mets transalpins, buffet d'antipasti, intéressante formule lunch et cave tournée vers l'Italie.
◆ Leuk buurtrestaurant dat door een Italiaanse familie wordt gerund, wat garant staat voor lekker eten en drinken. Het lunchmenu en het antipasti-buffet zijn een succesformule.

X **In 't Spinnekopke,** pl. du Jardin aux Fleurs 1, ✉ 1000, ☎ 0 2 511 86 95, *info@spinnekopke.be, Fax 0 2 513 24 97,* 🍴, Avec cuisine régionale - ▤. AE ⓓ MC VISA. ✈ plan p. 12 ER d
fermé sam. midi et dim. - **Repas** Lunch 9 - carte 22 à 42.
◆ Ce charmant estaminet bruxellois mitonne une cuisine régionale "bistrotière" escortée, selon votre inclination, de crus bourgeois ou de bières locales. Accueil souriant.
◆ Oud Brussels Estaminet dat bistrogerechten met regionale invloeden op tafel zet, vergezeld van een goed glas wijn of lokaal gebrouwen biertje. Vriendelijke bediening.

Quartier Grand'Place (Ilot Sacré) - *plan p. 16* :

Royal Windsor, r. Duquesnoy 5, ✉ 1000, ☎ 0 2 505 55 55, *sales.royalwindsor@warwickhotels.com, Fax 0 2 505 55 00,* – 25 à 350. AE VISA. JYZ f
Repas *Lunch 13* – carte 30 à 43 – ☐ 21 – **248 ch** 400/525, – 17 suites.
◆ Luxe, confort et raffinement caractérisent ce grand hôtel du centre historique. Paisibles chambres garnies de mobilier de style. Service "royal" et nombreuses facilités.
◆ Luxe, comfort en verfijning kenmerken dit schitterende hotel in het historische centrum. Rustige kamers met stijlmeubelen. "Vorstelijke" service en talloze faciliteiten.

Le Méridien, Carrefour de l'Europe 3, ✉ 1000, ☎ 0 2 548 42 11, *info@meridien.be, Fax 0 2 548 40 80,* – 25 à 200. AE VISA JCB. KY h
Repas ***L'Épicerie*** *(fermé 20 juil.-20 août et sam. midi) Lunch 49* – carte 53 à 62 – ☐ 25 – **216 ch** 440/600, – 8 suites.
◆ Majestueuse façade néo-classique postée juste en face de la gare centrale. Décor intérieur rutilant et cossu. Coquettes chambres dotées d'équipements dernier cri. Restaurant proposant une carte actuelle et une formule "brunch dominical".
◆ Majestueus neoclassicistisch gebouw met een luisterrijk interieur, tegenover het Centraal Station. Prima kamers met ultramoderne voorzieningen. Het restaurant biedt een eigentijdse menukaart en een uitgebreide brunch op zondag.

Amigo, r. Amigo 1, ✉ 1000, ☎ 0 2 547 47 47, *sales@hotelamigo.com, Fax 0 2 513 52 77,* – 25 à 200. AE VISA JCB. JY x
Repas (cuisine italienne) carte 38 à 56, ♀ – ☐ 25 – **152 ch** 450/540, – 7 suites.
◆ Situation privilégiée pour cette imposante demeure de 1958 aux accents "Renaissance espagnole". Chambres classiques diversement aménagées. Collection d'œuvres d'art. Confortable brasserie contemporaine d'orientation culinaire transalpine.
◆ Imposant pand uit 1958 met Spaanse renaissance-elementen en veel kunst. Gunstige ligging. Klassieke kamers die verschillend zijn ingedeeld. Lichte, moderne brasserie met Italiaanse kaart.

Le Dixseptième sans rest, r. Madeleine 25, ✉ 1000, ☎ 0 2 517 17 17, *info@ledixseptieme.be, Fax 0 2 502 64 24* – 25. AE VISA. JY j
18 ch ☐ 200/250, – 6 suites.
◆ Comme son nom l'indique, cet ancien hôtel particulier date du 17e s. Salons cossus et vastes chambres au confort "cosy", pourvues de meubles de styles de différentes époques.
◆ Zoals de naam al aangeeft, dateert dit grote herenhuis uit de 17e eeuw. Weelderige lounge en ruime, comfortabele kamers met meubelen uit verschillende perioden.

Carrefour de l'Europe sans rest, r. Marché-aux-Herbes 110, ✉ 1000, ☎ 0 2 504 94 00, *info@carrefoureurope.net, Fax 0 2 504 95 00* – 25 à 200. AE VISA JKY n
☐ 21 – **58 ch** 260/340, – 5 suites.
◆ Adossée à la place d'Espagne où trône Don Quichotte, construction récente en harmonie avec l'architecture de l'Îlot sacré. Chambres un peu ternes mais d'un bon calibre.
◆ Nieuw gebouw op een steenworp afstand van de Grote Markt. Centraal gelegen aan het Spanjeplein, waar Don Quichot zijn standbeeld heeft. Ruime, tikje saaie kamers.

Novotel off Grand'Place, r. Marché-aux-Herbes 120, ✉ 1000, ☎ 0 2 514 33 33, *H1030@accor-hotels.com, Fax 0 2 511 77 23,* – 25. AE VISA JCB. rest JKY n
Repas carte 26 à 44 – ☐ 15 – **136 ch** 179/199.
◆ Toutes les chambres de cet établissement idéalement situé à 200 m de la gare centrale et de la Grand-Place se conforment aux nouveaux standards de la chaîne.
◆ Ideaal gelegen hotel, op 200 m van het Centraal Station en de Grote Markt. De standaardkamers voldoen aan de nieuwe eisen van deze bekende hotelketen.

Aris sans rest, r. Marché-aux-Herbes 78, ✉ 1000, ☎ 0 2 514 43 00, *info@arishotel.be, Fax 0 2 514 01 19* – VISA JCB JY g
55 ch ☐ 210/235.
◆ Ce pratique petit hôtel occupant une maison bourgeoise en bordure de l'Îlot sacré jouxte aussi les verrières des galeries St-Hubert. Confort actuel dans les chambres.
◆ Praktisch hotel in een mooi pand aan de rand van de "buik van Brussel", naast de St.-Hubertusgalerijen met hun glazen overkapping. De kamers bieden hedendaags comfort.

Matignon, r. Bourse 10, ✉ 1000, ☎ 0 2 511 08 88, *Fax 0 2 513 69 27,* AE VISA JCB. rest JY q
Repas *(fermé janv.-fév. et lundi)* (taverne-rest) *Lunch 15* – carte 22 à 34 – **37 ch** ☐ 75/110 – ½ P 95/145.
◆ La moitié des douillettes chambres à double vitrage de ce plaisant établissement offrent un joli coup d'œil sur la Bourse. Clientèle essentiellement touristique. Taverne-restaurant servant une cuisine internationale. L'été, terrasse sur rue.
◆ Aangenaam hotel dat beschikt over gerieflijke kamers met dubbele ramen, waarvan de helft een fraai uitzicht biedt op de Beurs. De clientèle bestaat overwegend uit toeristen. Café-restaurant met internationale keuken en een zomers terras aan de straatkant.

Floris sans rest, r. Harengs 6, ✉ 1000, ☎ 0 2 514 07 60, *floris.grandplace@grouptorus.com, Fax 0 2 548 90 39* – |‡| TV. AE ⓓ ⓜ VISA JY s
12 ch ☕ 140/160.
◆ À 50 m de la Grand-Place, hôtel "de poche" dont les chambres, suffisamment spacieuses et pourvues de moquette ou de parquet, viennent d'être complètement rénovées.
◆ In dit kleine hotel op 50 m van de Grote Markt zijn de ruime kamers onlangs volledig gerenoveerd ; overal ligt vloerbedekking of parket.

XXXX **La Maison du Cygne,** r. Charles Buls 2, ✉ 1000, ☎ 0 2 511 82 44, *lecygne@skynet.be, Fax 0 2 514 31 48,* Avec L'Ommegang au rez-de-chaussée – ▤ P. AE ⓓ ⓜ VISA. ✈ JY w
fermé 31 juil.-30 août, du 24 au 30 déc., sam. midi, dim. et jours fériés – **Repas** *Lunch 40* – carte 65 à 192, ♀.
◆ Cette maison postée depuis le 17ᵉ s. sur la Grand-Place abrita la corporation des Bouchers. Intérieur lambrissé et salons à thèmes. Cuisine classique actualisée à petits pas.
◆ In dit 17e-eeuwse pand aan de Grote Markt zat vroeger het Slagersgilde. Binnen veel hout en salons met een bepaald thema. Klassieke keuken met een vleugje vernieuwing.

XX **Aux Armes de Bruxelles,** r. Bouchers 13, ✉ 1000, ☎ 0 2 511 55 98, *arbrux@beon.be, Fax 0 2 514 33 81,* Ouvert jusqu'à 23 h – ▤. AE ⓓ ⓜ VISA JY t
fermé mi-juin-mi-juil. et lundi – **Repas** *Lunch 23 bc* – 30/45 bc, ♀.
◆ Une véritable institution bruxelloise en plein Îlot sacré, que cette table vouée aux terroirs belges. Trois salles de styles classique, actuel et brasserie. Choix touffu.
◆ Een begrip in Brussel, in hartje oude centrum. Drie zalen, klassiek, actueel en brasseriestijl, waar de gasten worden onthaald op een keur van Belgische specialiteiten.

XX **Le Cerf,** Grand'Place 20, ✉ 1000, ☎ 0 2 511 47 91, *Fax 0 2 546 09 59,* Ouvert jusqu'à 23 h 30 – ▤. AE ⓓ ⓜ VISA JY s
fermé 18 juil.-16 août, sam. et dim. – **Repas** *Lunch 22 bc* – 46 bc/54 bc, ♀.
◆ Boiseries, vitraux et chaudes étoffes président au décor de ces maisons du début du 18ᵉ s. Deux tables, côté façade, embrassent la Grand-Place. Carte au goût du jour.
◆ Lambrisering, glas-in-loodramen en warme stoffen voeren de boventoon in deze panden uit de vroege 18e eeuw. Twee tafels hebben uitzicht op de Grote Markt. Eigentijdse kaart.

X **de l'Ogenblik,** Galerie des Princes 1, ✉ 1000, ☎ 0 2 511 61 51, *ogenblik@tiscalinet.be, Fax 0 2 513 41 58,* ☂, Ouvert jusqu'à minuit – AE ⓓ ⓜ VISA JY p
fermé dim. – **Repas** carte 47 à 64, ♀.
◆ Table tonitruante évoquant un ancien café, L'Ogenblik ("L'Instant") concocte une belle cuisine classique. Suggestions et plat du jour. Clientèle d'affaires locale.
◆ Druk restaurant met de uitstraling van een oud café, waar mooie klassieke gerechten worden geserveerd. Veel dagsuggesties voor zakenmensen uit de omgeving.

X **La Roue d'Or,** r. Chapeliers 26, ✉ 1000, ☎ 0 2 514 25 54, *Fax 0 2 512 30 81,* Ouvert jusqu'à minuit – AE ⓓ ⓜ VISA JY y
fermé 18 juil.-16 août – **Repas** *Lunch 10* – carte 26 à 45, ♀.
◆ Cet ancien café typique de la ville vous mitonne de bons petits plats de brasserie belge. Peintures murales surréalistes, façon Magritte. Superbe montre. Ambiance conviviale.
◆ Typisch Brussels café-restaurant met Belgische specialiteiten. Surrealistische muurschilderingen in de stijl van Magritte en een prachtige uitstalkast. Gemoedelijke ambiance.

X **Vincent,** r. Dominicains 8, ✉ 1000, ☎ 0 2 511 26 07, *info@restaurantvincent.com, Fax 0 2 502 36 93,* ☂, Ouvert jusqu'à 23 h 30 – ▤. AE ⓓ ⓜ VISA JCB JY n
fermé 1ʳᵉ quinz. août et du 2 au 12 janv. – **Repas** *Lunch 18* – carte 27 à 63.
◆ Savourez l'atmosphère bruxelloise de cette nostalgique rôtisserie ornée de fresques en carreaux de céramique peinte. Cuisine d'ici, avec spécialités carnivores et de moules.
◆ Proef de Brusselse sfeer van deze nostalgische rotisserie met muurschilderingen en beschilderde tegels. Belgische keuken met vleesschotels en mosselen in het seizoen.

X **À la Recherche du Temps Perdu,** r. Lombard 25, ✉ 1000, ☎ 0 2 513 78 84, *info@alarecherche.be, Fax 0 2 513 59 61* – ▤. AE ⓜ VISA JCB JY m
fermé dern. sem. juil.-2 prem. sem. août, sam. midi, dim. et lundi soir – **Repas** *Lunch 15* – 39.
◆ Murs lambrissés, cheminée d'époque et lustres anciens : une ambiance très proustienne règne dans ce restaurant se signalant par une belle devanture de style Art nouveau.
◆ Gelambriseerde muren, grote schouw en antieke kroonluchters zorgen voor een Proustiaanse sfeer in dit restaurant met zijn mooie art-nouveaugevel.

X **'t Kelderke,** Grand'Place 15, ✉ 1000, ☎ 0 2 513 73 44, *Fax 0 2 512 30 81,* Cuisine régionale, ouvert jusqu'à 2 h du matin – AE ⓓ ⓜ VISA JY i
fermé du 1ᵉʳ au 14 juil. – **Repas** *Lunch 8* – carte 22 à 40.
◆ Ce sympathique estaminet-restaurant vous accueille dans la cave voûtée d'une maison de la Grand-Place. Copieuses assiettes très "couleur locale", comme l'ambiance.
◆ Gezellige eetgelegenheid in de gewelfde kelderverdieping van een pand aan de Grote Markt. Copieuze maaltijden met veel "couleur locale", net als de ambiance.

Quartier Ste-Catherine (Marché-aux-Poissons) - *plan p. 16 sauf indication spéciale :*

Novotel Centre-Tour Noire, r. Vierge Noire 32, ✉ 1000, ☎ 0 2 505 50 50, *H2122@accor-hotels.com, Fax 0 2 505 50 00,* – 25 à 350. AE VISA JY r
Repas carte 24 à 41 – 15 – **217 ch** 165/180.
• Alliant élégance discrète et modernité fonctionnelle, l'hôtel doit son nom à l'un des vestiges de la première enceinte bruxelloise, restaurée dans l'esprit de Viollet-le-Duc.
• De naam van dit hotel herinnert aan een toren van de stadsmuur, die is gerestaureerd in de geest van Viollet-le-Duc. Geslaagde combinatie van functionaliteit en elegantie.

Welcome, r. Peuplier 1, ✉ 1000, ☎ 0 2 219 95 46, *info@hotelwelcome.com, Fax 0 2 217 18 87,* – rest, VISA JY h
Repas ***La Truite d'Argent*** *(fermé 1re quinz. août, 1re quinz. janv., sam. midi et dim.)* (produits de la mer, ouvert jusqu'à 23 h 30) 42/72 bc – 10 – **15 ch** 80/130.
• Hôtel abrité dans une belle maison d'angle où vous serez toujours "welcome". Le nouveau décor de chaque chambre évoque un pays différent. Lambris, banquettes et chandeliers donnent un petit air "cosy" au restaurant. Carte tournée vers le grand large.
• Hotel in een mooi hoekpand, waar u van harte welkom bent. Elke kamer roept de atmosfeer op van een ander land. De lambrisering, banken et kandelaars geven het restaurant iets gezelligs. Veel visspecialiteiten op de kaart.

Atlas sans rest, r. Vieux Marché-aux-Grains 30, ✉ 1000, ☎ 0 2 502 60 06, *info@atlas.be, Fax 0 2 502 69 35* – – 30. AE VISA.
88 ch 115/135. plan p. 12 ER a
• Sur une placette d'un quartier en plein essor où foisonnent les boutiques de mode, hôtel de maître du 18e s. dont la plupart des chambres donnent sur une cour intérieure.
• Hotel in een 18e-eeuws herenhuis aan een pleintje in een wijk die sterk in opkomst is en waar veel modewinkels te vinden zijn. De meeste kamers kijken uit op de binnenplaats.

Astrid Center sans rest, pl. du Samedi 11, ✉ 1000, ☎ 0 2 219 31 19, *info@astridhotel.be, Fax 0 2 219 31 70* – – 25 à 80. VISA JCB JY b
100 ch 175/200.
• Cette construction récente érigée entre les places Ste-Catherine et De Brouckère renferme de sobres chambres standard. Bar, coins salons et salles pour conférences.
• Nieuw gebouw tussen het St.-Katelijneplein en het Brouckereplein, met sobere standaardkamers. Bar, verscheidene lounges en congreszalen.

Noga sans rest, r. Béguinage 38, ✉ 1000, ☎ 0 2 218 67 63, *info@nogahotel.com, Fax 0 2 218 16 03,* – . AE VISA JCB JY f
19 ch 85/99.
• Petit hôtel occupant une maison bourgeoise dans un quartier calme. Les chambres, coquettement personnalisées, offrent un confort très convenable.
• Dit kleine hotel is gevestigd in een herenhuis in een rustige wijk. De kamers hebben een persoonlijk karakter en bieden een heel redelijk comfort.

Bistro M'Alain de la Mer, pl. Ste-Catherine 15, ✉ 1000, ☎ 0 2 217 90 12, *alain.troubat@skynet.be, Fax 0 2 219 07 38,* , Produits de la mer – AE VISA JY u
fermé dim. et lundi – **Repas** Lunch 25 – 38/53 bc.
• Comme son nom l'indique, ce nouvel établissement installé près de l'église conjugue ambiance "bistrot" et recettes au parfum d'embruns. Agréable terrasse estivale.
• Zoals de naam al doet vermoeden, speelt de zee en alles wat daarbij hoort een belangrijke rol in dit restaurant bij de kerk. Aangenaam terras in de zomer.

Le Jardin de Catherine, pl. Ste-Catherine 5, ✉ 1000, ☎ 0 2 513 19 92, *info@jardindecatherine.be, Fax 0 2 513 71 09,* – . AE VISA JY k
fermé sam. midi – **Repas** 30/50 bc.
• La place dédiée à sainte Catherine a désormais son jardin. Salle à manger habillée de tableaux aux couleurs chatoyantes. À l'arrière, grande terrasse d'été close de murs.
• Restaurant aan het St.-Katelijneplein met kleurrijke schilderijen. Aan de achterkant bevindt zich een groot ommuurd terras, waar 's zomers de tafeltjes worden gedekt.

François, quai aux Briques 2, ✉ 1000, ☎ 0 2 511 60 89, , Écailler, produits de la mer – AE VISA JCB JY k
fermé dim. et lundi – **Repas** Lunch 25 – 32/37, ♀.
• Une savoureuse cuisine iodée, arrosée de grands blancs, vous attend à cette table accueillante qui a le vent en poupe. Intérieur marin égayé de clichés nostalgiques.
• Heerlijke visgerechten en een goed glas witte wijn staan voor u klaar bij François, wiens liefde voor de zee ook tot uitdrukking komt in het interieur.

La Belle Maraîchère, pl. Ste-Catherine 11, ✉ 1000, ☎ 0 2 512 97 59, *Fax 0 2 513 76 91,* Produits de la mer – AE VISA JY k
fermé 2 sem. carnaval, 3 sem. en juil., merc. et jeudi – **Repas** 31/65 bc.
• Deux frères œuvrent au "piano" de ce restaurant sympathique. Choix constant et étoffé, dédié aux produits de la mer. Cave attrayante. Clientèle d'affaires et d'habitués.
• Leuk restaurant waar twee broers de scepter zwaaien. Ruime keuze aan visspecialiteiten en een aanlokkelijke wijnkelder. Er komen veel zakenmensen en stamgasten.

XX **Le Loup-Galant,** quai aux Barques 4, ✉ 1000, ☎ 0 2 219 99 98, *loupgalant@swing.be, Fax 0 2 219 99 98* – AE ⓓ MC VISA plan p. 12 EQ a
fermé 1 sem. Pâques, 1re quinz. août, 1 sem. Noël, dim. et lundi – **Repas** *Lunch 19* – 24/50 bc.
◆ Faites-vous conter la légende entourant cette vieille maison assise au bout du Vismet. Choix vaste et pluriel, de mets comme de vins. Cheminée et poutres apparentes en salle.
◆ Rond dit oude huis aan het eind van de Vismet hangt een legende, die men u graag vertelt. Uitgebreide kaart en goed gevulde wijnkelder. Eetzaal met schouw en balkenplafond.

X **L'Huîtrière,** quai aux Briques 20, ✉ 1000, ☎ 0 2 512 08 66, *Fax 0 2 512 12 81*, Produits de la mer – AE ⓓ MC VISA JY a
Repas *Lunch 15* – 25/40.
◆ Cuisine de la mer servie dans un cadre de boiseries, vitraux et fresques bruegeliennes, évocateur des charmes du vieux Bruxelles. Lunch-menu intéressant. Service aimable.
◆ Visrestaurant met een interessant lunchmenu. Fraai interieur met veel hout, glas-in-loodramen en Breugeliaanse muurschilderingen. Vriendelijke bediening.

X **Bistro M'Alain Tradition,** r. Flandre 6, ✉ 1000, ☎ 0 2 503 14 80, *alain.troubat@skynet.be, Fax 0 2 503 14 80* – AE ⓓ MC VISA ER g
fermé 1 sem. en août, 1 sem. en déc., dim. et lundi – **Repas** *Lunch 23* – 30/45 bc.
◆ Intéressante et bien équilibrée, la carte de ce nouveau venu dans le quartier annonce de savoureuses préparations à la fois bistrotières et régionales. Accueil très charmant.
◆ De interessante en evenwichtige kaart van deze nieuwkomer in de wijk belooft een smakelijke combinatie van bistro- en streekkeuken. Alleraardigste ontvangst.

X **Vismet,** pl. Ste-Catherine 23, ✉ 1000, ☎ 0 2 218 85 45, *Fax 0 2 218 85 46*, Produits de la mer, ouvert jusqu'à 23 h 30 – AE MC VISA JY v
fermé mi-juil.-mi-août, dim. et lundi – **Repas** *Lunch 15* – carte 34 à 47.
◆ En face de la tour Noire, enseigne au décor intérieur de style brasserie. Éventail de préparations poissonneuses sans complications. Les beaux jours, on mange en terrasse.
◆ Brasserie tegenover de Zwarte Toren met een keur van goed klaargemaakte visgerechten zonder fratsen. Bij mooi weer kan er buiten worden gegeten.

X **La Marée,** r. Flandre 99, ✉ 1000, ☎ 0 2 511 00 40, *Fax 0 2 511 86 19*, Produits de la mer – ▤. AE ⓓ MC VISA JCB ER h
fermé 15 juin-15 juil., 23 déc.-2 janv., lundi et mardi – **Repas** carte 22 à 49.
◆ Une façade du 17e s., fleurie aux beaux jours, dissimule ce resto convivial affichant un petit air d'ancien café. Cuisine à vue et recettes gorgées d'iode, "marée" oblige.
◆ Gemoedelijk 17e-eeuws pand met bloembakken, dat de sfeer heeft van een oud Brussels café. Open keuken en veel vis, want het heet niet voor niets La Marée (het tij).

X **Strofilia,** r. Marché-aux-Porcs 11, ✉ 1000, ☎ 0 2 512 32 93, *strofilia@pi.be, Fax 0 2 512 09 94*, Cuisine grecque, ouvert jusqu'à minuit – AE MC VISA. ✻
fermé 24 déc.-3 janv. et dim. – **Repas** *Lunch 11* – carte 24 à 35. plan p. 12 ER c
◆ "Ouzerie" améliorée dont l'enseigne se réfère à une presse à raisin. Grandes salles façon "loft" à touches byzantines. Préparations cent pour cent hellènes et cave assortie.
◆ Verbeterde ouzo-bar waarvan het uithangbord een druivenpers voorstelt. Loft-stijl zalen met een Byzantijnse noot. De keuken en de wijnkelder zijn honderd procent Grieks.

Quartier des Sablons - *plan p. 16* :

Jolly du Grand Sablon, r. Bodenbroek 2, ✉ 1000, ☎ 0 2 518 11 00, *jollyhotelsablon@jollyhotels.be, Fax 0 2 512 67 66* – |‡| ⇆ ▤ TV ♿ 🚗 – 🏛 25 à 150. AE ⓓ MC VISA. ✻ rest KZ p
Repas *(fermé du 1er au 25 août et 20 déc.-5 janv.)* (cuisine italienne) *Lunch 18* – 22, ♀ – **192 ch** ☕ 315/375, – 1 suite.
◆ La tradition hôtelière italienne à deux pas des prestigieux musées royaux. Équipement complet dans les chambres. Centre de congrès proposant de nombreux services sur mesure. Restaurant transalpin avec formule buffets et plat du jour.
◆ Dit hotel bij de prestigieuze Koninklijke Musea voor Schone Kunsten is in Italiaanse handen. De kamers zijn van alle faciliteiten voorzien. Talrijke faciliteiten voor congressen en service op maat. Italiaans restaurant met buffetten en dagschotels.

XXX **L'Écailler du Palais Royal** (Hahn), r. Bodenbroek 18, ✉ 1000, ☎ 0 2 512 87 51, *Fax 0 2 511 99 50*, Produits de la mer – ▤. AE ⓓ MC VISA. ✻ KZ r
fermé août, Noël-Nouvel An, dim. et jours fériés – **Repas** carte 58 à 107.
◆ Les assiettes marient ici les saveurs de la mer à l'esthétique de la présentation. Élégant camaïeu de bleu et choix du confort en salle : banquettes, chaises ou comptoir.
◆ Fraai opgemaakte borden met verrukkelijke visspecialiteiten in een elegant interieur in verschillende blauwe tinten. De gasten zitten op bankjes, stoelen of barkrukken.
Spéc. Moelleux de tourteau et croustillant de homard. Bouillabaise de poissons de la mer du Nord. Mariage de turbot et sauté de homard, les deux sauces à l'estragon

Trente rue de la Paille, r. Paille 30, ✉ 1000, ☎ 0 2 512 07 15, *info@resto-trenteruedelapaille.com, Fax 0 2 514 23 33* – ▤. AE ⓓ ⓜ VISA JZ x
fermé mi-juil.-mi-août, Noël-Nouvel An, sam. et dim. – **Repas** *Lunch 31* – carte 58 à 67.
◆ Poutres apparentes, briques, draperies, bouquets fleuris et vaisselle assortie composent le cadre chaleureux de cette table du quartier des antiquaires.
◆ Balken, bakstenen, draperieën, grote boeketten en het bloemetjesservies zorgen voor een warme ambiance in dit restaurant in de wijk van de antiquairs.

Castello Banfi, r. Bodenbroek 12, ✉ 1000, ☎ 0 2 512 87 94, *Fax 0 2 512 87 94*, Avec cuisine italienne – ▤. AE ⓓ ⓜ VISA KZ q
fermé prem. sem. Pâques, 3 dern. sem. août, fin déc., dim. soir et lundi – **Repas** *Lunch 27* – carte 37 à 79.
◆ Derrière une façade de 1729, restaurant gastronomique dont l'enseigne se réfère à un grand domaine viticole toscan et dont l'assiette se partage entre la Botte et l'Hexagone.
◆ Gastronomisch restaurant in een pand uit 1729, waarvan de naam verwijst naar een groot Toscaans wijndomein. Frans-Italiaanse keuken.

"Chez Marius" En Provence, pl. du Petit Sablon 1, ✉ 1000, ☎ 0 2 511 12 08, *chez.marius@skynet.be, Fax 0 2 512 27 89*, ☂ – AE ⓓ ⓜ VISA KZ s
fermé 20 juil.-20 août, sam., dim. et jours fériés – **Repas** *Lunch 22* – 39/71 bc.
◆ Cuisine aux accents provençaux, donc ensoleillée, servie dans un cadre rustico-bourgeois. L'été venu, savourez l'anisette en terrasse. Oh peuchère ! Pas fada, le Marius !
◆ Keuken met een Provençaals accent, geserveerd in een rustiek-klassiek interieur. Bij de eerste zonnestralen kunt u genieten van een pastis op het terras.

La Clef des Champs, r. Rollebeek 23, ✉ 1000, ☎ 0 2 512 11 93, *laclefdeschamps@resto.be, Fax 0 2 502 42 32*, ☂ – AE ⓓ ⓜ VISA JZ k
fermé sam. midi, dim. soir et lundi – **Repas** *Lunch 15* – 30/48 bc.
◆ Envie de prendre la clé des champs sans quitter le Sablon ? Cette sympathique adresse au décor frais et léger vous réserve un accueil enjoué. Mets des régions de France.
◆ Wie zin heeft om eens lekker Franse streekgerechten te eten, heeft hier een prima adres. Het interieur is fris en licht gehouden en het personeel is ongedwongen en opgeruimd.

Lola, pl. du Grand Sablon 33, ✉ 1000, ☎ 0 2 514 24 60, *restaurant.lola@skynet.be, Fax 0 2 514 26 53*, Brasserie, ouvert jusqu'à 23 h 30 – ▤. AE ⓜ VISA. ✂ JZ z
Repas carte 28 à 52, ♀.
◆ Brasserie conviviale au décor contemporain proposant une cuisine tournée vers les saveurs du moment. Alternative chaises ou banquettes. On mange également au comptoir.
◆ Gezellige brasserie met een hedendaagse inrichting en een keuken die ook aan de smaak van tegenwoordig voldoet. Er kan op een stoel, een bankje of een barkruk worden gegeten.

L'Herbe Rouge, r. Minimes 34, ✉ 1000, ☎ 0 2 512 48 34, *Fax 0 2 511 62 88*, Cuisine japonaise, ouvert jusqu'à 23 h – AE ⓜ VISA JZ p
fermé lundi – **Repas** *Lunch 15* – carte 26 à 48.
◆ Une carte nippone assez authentique et bien ficelée vous attend à cette enseigne. Sobre intérieur contemporain orné de coquines estampes japonaises.
◆ Authentiek Japans restaurant met een mooie kaart. Het sobere, eigentijdse interieur wordt door ondeugende Japanse prenten opgevrolijkt.

Orphyse Chaussette, r. Charles Hanssens 5, ✉ 100, ☎ 0 2 502 75 81, *Fax 0 2 513 52 04*, ☂, Bistrot avec cuisine du Sud-Ouest, ouvert jusqu'à 23 h – AE ⓜ VISA. ✂ JZ b
fermé du 5 au 12 avril, 24 juil.-juil.-16 août, 24 déc.-1er janv., dim., lundi et jours fériés – **Repas** *Lunch 14* – carte 30 à 45 ♣.
◆ Recommandable petit "bistrot-gastro" dont la cuisine vous promène dans le Sud-Ouest de la France, au même titre que la cave. Confort assez sommaire mais atmosphère vivante.
◆ Een goed adresje deze kleine bistro, waar zowel Zuid-Franse gerechten als wijnen worden geserveerd. Vrij eenvoudig comfort, maar een gezellige sfeer.

Quartier Palais de Justice - *plan p. 12 sauf indication spéciale :*

Hilton, bd de Waterloo 38, ✉ 1000, ☎ 0 2 504 11 11 et 0 2 504 13 33 (rest), *bruhitwrm@hilton.com, Fax 0 2 504 21 11*, ≤ ville, ₺, ≘s – |‡| ⇔ ▤ TV ⇔ – 🔺 45 à 650. AE ⓓ ⓜ VISA JCB. ✂ FS s
Repas voir rest ***Maison du Bœuf*** ci-après – ***Café d'Egmont*** *(avec buffets, ouvert jusqu'à minuit) Lunch 35* – carte 39 à 58, ♀ – ☕ 32 – **420 ch** 450/480, – 13 suites.
◆ La clientèle d'affaires internationale sera choyée dans cette imposante tour à l'enseigne prestigieuse, érigée à la charnière de deux mondes : ville haute et ville basse. Buffets et semaines à thème culinaire sous la verrière Art déco du Café d'Egmont.
◆ De internationale zakenwereld wordt in de watten gelegd in deze wolkenkrabber van het beroemde Hilton-hotel, op de scheidslijn tussen de boven- en de benedenstad. Rijke buffetten en themaweken onder de art-décokoepel van het Café d'Egmont.

Maison du Bœuf - H. Hilton, 1er étage, bd de Waterloo 38, ✉ 1000, ✆ 0 2 504 13 34, *bruhitwrm@hilton.com, Fax 0 2 504 21 11,* ≤ - ▤ P. AE ⓓ ⓜ VISA JCB. ✻ FS s
Repas *Lunch 55* – 58/98 bc, carte 53 à 186, ♀.
◆ Une belle carte rigoureusement classique, à l'image de l'opulent décor, vous sera soumise au restaurant gastronomique du Hilton. Cave très complète. Vue sur le parc d'Egmont.
◆ Dit gastronomische restaurant van het Hilton biedt een mooie kaart, die net als het weelderige interieur zeer klassiek is. Grote wijnkelder. Uitzicht op het Egmontpark.
Spéc. Côte de bœuf rôtie en croûte de sel. Bar rôti au thym frais, crème d'échalotes. Tartare maison au caviar

JB, r. Grand Cerf 24, ✉ 1000, ✆ 0 2 512 04 84, *restaurantjb@vt4.net, Fax 0 2 511 79 30,* ⛱ - ▤. AE ⓓ ⓜ VISA FS z
fermé sam. midi, dim. et jours fériés – **Repas** 20/40 bc.
◆ Nouvelle adresse et même affluence d'habitués pour cette table sympathique sise juste derrière le sélect boulevard de Waterloo. Avantageux menu-carte au goût du jour.
◆ Jong restaurant dat al snel een vaste klantenkring heeft opgebouwd, vlak achter de chique Waterloo boulevard. Trendy kaart en een voordelig menu.

L'Idiot du village, r. Notre Seigneur 19, ✉ 1000, ✆ 0 2 502 55 82, Ouvert jusqu'à 23 h – AE ⓓ ⓜ VISA JZ a
fermé 20 juil.-20 août, 23 déc.-2 janv., sam. et dim. – **Repas** *Lunch 15* – carte 39 à 49.
◆ Chaleureuse ambiance "bistrot", cuisine originalement actualisée, sage choix de vins, accueil tout sourire. Bref, une intelligente maison, quoi qu'en dise l'enseigne !
◆ Gemoedelijke bistrosfeer, originele keuken, mooie wijnkaart en vriendelijke bediening. Kortom, een zeer slim opgezette zaak, wat de naam ook moge suggereren !

Le Gourmandin, r. Haute 152, ✉ 1000, ✆ 0 2 512 98 92, *legourmandin@hotmail.com, Fax 0 2 512 98 92* – AE ⓓ ⓜ VISA plan p. 16 JZ u
fermé 1re quinz. juil., sam. midi, dim. soir et lundi – **Repas** *Lunch 15* – 25/45.
◆ Ce petit établissement familial du quartier des Marolles décline un répertoire bien à la page. Carte concise, comprenant menus et suggestions. Le chef s'active à vue.
◆ Familierestaurantje in de Marollenwijk met een culinair repertoire dat goed bij de tijd is. Kleine kaart met daarnaast menu's en dagsuggesties. Open keuken.

Les Larmes du Tigre, r. Wynants 21, ✉ 1000, ✆ 0 2 512 18 77, *Fax 0 2 502 10 03,* ⛱, Cuisine thaïlandaise – AE ⓓ ⓜ VISA ES p
fermé mardi et sam. midi – **Repas** *Lunch 11* – carte 24 à 35.
◆ Cap sur la Thaïlande dans cette maison de maître jouxtant le palais de Justice. Riche éventail de mets traditionnels et décor de circonstance. Formule buffets le dimanche.
◆ Thaise gastvrijheid in dit herenhuis naast het Paleis van Justitie. Keur van traditionele gerechten in een exotisch interieur. Lopend buffet op zondag.

Quartier Léopold *(voir aussi Ixelles) - plan p. 13 :*

Stanhope, r. Commerce 9, ✉ 1000, ✆ 0 2 506 91 11, *reservations@stanhope.be, Fax 0 2 512 17 08,* Lδ, ≘s - |‡| ▤ TV ⇔. AE ⓓ ⓜ VISA. ✻ KZ v
Repas voir rest **Brighton** ci-après – ☕ 25 – **80 ch** 255/425, – 15 suites – ½ P 292/314.
◆ Superbes chambres - parfois duplex - avec équipement informatique dans cet hôtel particulier où le voyageur épris de classicisme trouvera son bonheur. Terrasse close de murs.
◆ Prachtige kamers, soms duplex, met computervoorzieningen in dit patriciërshuis, waar liefhebbers van het classicisme niet teleurgesteld zullen worden. Ommuurd terras.

Brighton - H. Stanhope, r. Commerce 9, ✉ 1000, ✆ 0 2 506 95 55, *reservations@stanhope.be, Fax 0 2 512 17 08,* ⛱ - ▤ P. AE ⓓ ⓜ VISA. ✻ KZ v
fermé Noël, Nouvel An, sam., dim. et jours fériés – **Repas** *Lunch 37* – carte 52 à 90.
◆ Meubles de style, fresques délicates, chandeliers, colonnes orientales et parquet reluisant composent le cadre élégant de la table du Stanhope. Carte "tendance".
◆ Stijlmeubelen, muurschilderingen, kandelaars, Oosterse zuilen en een glanzend parket vormen de elegante omlijsting van dit restaurant van het Stanhope-hotel. Trendy kaart.

Quartier Louise *(voir aussi Ixelles et St-Gilles) - plans p. 12 et 14 :*

Conrad, av. Louise 71, ✉ 1050, ✆ 0 2 542 42 42, *brusselsinfo@conradhotels.com, Fax 0 2 542 42 00,* ⛱, ⑦, Lδ, ≘s, ▣ - |‡| ⇆ ▤ TV ⇔ - 🔬 25 à 450. AE ⓓ ⓜ VISA JCB FS f
Repas voir rest ***La Maison de Maître*** ci-après – ***Café Wiltcher's*** *Lunch 34* – carte 42 à 73 – ☕ 30 – **254 ch** 595/620, – 15 suites.
◆ Complexe hôtelier haut de gamme brillamment agrégé à une demeure de maître 1900. Vastes chambres dotées de mobilier classique. Équipement complet pour séminaires et loisirs. Café chic coiffé d'une verrière. Lunch-buffets et vue plongeante en terrasse.
◆ Luxe hotelcomplex dat knap is geïntegreerd in een herenhuis uit 1900. Ruime kamers met klassiek meubilair. Talrijke faciliteiten voor congresgangers en toeristen. Chic café met een glaskoepel. Lunchbuffetten en een fraai uitzicht vanaf het terras.

Bristol Stephanie, av. Louise 91, ✉ 1050, ℘ 0 2 543 33 11, *hotel_bristol@bristol.be, Fax 0 2 538 03 07*, - 25 à 400. AE VISA JCB. FT g

Repas *(fermé 17 juil.-22 août, 18 déc.-3 janv., sam. midi et dim. midi)* (avec buffets) carte 35 à 55, - 25 - **139 ch** 325/400, - 3 suites.

◆ Établissement de luxe dont les chambres, aussi spacieuses que gracieuses, se répartissent entre deux immeubles communiquants. Typique mobilier norvégien dans les suites. Cuisine au goût du jour à savourer dans un cadre scandinave. Formule buffets.

◆ Luxehotel waarvan de ruime, elegante kamers zijn verdeeld over twee panden die met elkaar in verbinding staan. Typisch Noors meubilair in de suites. Eigentijdse keuken in een Scandinavisch interieur. Buffetformule.

Le Châtelain, r. Châtelain 17, ✉ 1000, ℘ 0 2 646 00 55, *info@le-chatelain.net, Fax 0 2 646 00 88*, - - 25 à 280. AE VISA. FU t

Repas Lunch 17 - carte 39 à 48 - 25 - **106 ch** 310/430, - 2 suites.

◆ Cet hôtel récent renferme de coquettes et confortables chambres actuelles munies d'un équipement tout dernier cri. Vous y passerez des nuits sans histoire.

◆ Dit nieuwe hotel beschikt over frisse en comfortabele kamers die ultramodern zijn ingericht. Hier zult u weer helemaal fit en uitgerust uit de veren komen !

Hyatt Regency, av. Louise 381, ✉ 1050, ℘ 0 2 649 98 00, *brussels@hyattintl.com, Fax 0 2 640 17 64* - - 25 à 50. AE VISA JCB. FV a

Repas *Barsey* *(fermé dim.)* (ouvert jusqu'à minuit) Lunch 19 - carte 37 à 50 - 22 - **96 ch** 345/380, - 3 suites.

◆ Près du bois de la Cambre, hôtel de caractère adroitement relooké dans l'esprit Second Empire. Communs très soignés. Chambres cossues où rien ne manque. Service personnalisé. "Restaurant-lounge" au décor néo-classique griffé Jacques Garcia. Ambiance "trendy".

◆ Sfeervol hotel in second-empirestijl bij het Ter Kamerenbos. Fraaie gemeenschappelijke ruimten. Weelderige kamers waar werkelijk niets ontbreekt. Persoonlijke service. "Loungerestaurant" met een neoklassiek interieur van Jacques Garcia. Trendy ambiance.

Meliá Avenue Louise, r. Blanche 4, ✉ 1000, ℘ 0 2 535 95 00, *melia.avenue.louise@solmelia.com, Fax 0 2 535 96 00* - - 35. AE VISA. FT z

Repas (résidents seult) - 22 - **80 ch** 230/320.

◆ À deux pas de la place Stéphanie, vous serez hébergés dans des chambres très "cosy", personnalisées par un mobilier choisi avec soin. Beau salon agrémenté d'une cheminée.

◆ Vlak bij het Stefaniaplein kunt u de nacht doorbrengen in een knusse kamer met een persoonlijke, smaakvolle inrichting. Mooie lounge met open haard.

Floris Louise sans rest, r. Concorde 59, ✉ 1000, ℘ 0 2 515 00 60, *florislouise@busmail.net, Fax 0 2 503 35 19* - . AE VISA FS d

36 ch 140/160.

◆ Établissement installé dans deux maisons bourgeoises, légèrement en retrait de l'avenue Louise. Chambres actuelles bien équipées. Agréable salle des petits-déjeuners.

◆ Dit hotel is ondergebracht in twee herenhuizen, even achter de Louizalaan. Moderne kamers die van alle faciliteiten zijn voorzien. Aangename ontbijtzaal.

Brussels sans rest, av. Louise 315, ✉ 1050, ℘ 0 2 640 24 15, *brussels-hotel@skynet.be, Fax 0 2 647 34 63* - - 30. AE VISA JCB FU b

68 ch 195, - 1 suite.

◆ Immeuble de type "flat-hôtel" proposant deux sortes de spacieuses chambres standard - normales ou duplex avec kitchenette -, rafraîchies et convenablement insonorisées.

◆ Appartementenhotel met twee soorten ruime standaardkamers, normaal of duplex met kitchenette, die pas zijn opgeknapt en goed tegen geluid zijn geïsoleerd.

Agenda Louise sans rest, r. Florence 6, ✉ 1000, ℘ 0 2 539 00 31, *louise@hotel-agenda.com, Fax 0 2 539 00 63* - . AE VISA JCB FT j

37 ch 104/116.

◆ Posté à 50 m de l'élégante avenue Louise, cet hôtel entièrement rénové vous réserve un accueil avenant. Les chambres, assez grandes, offrent un équipement très correct.

◆ In dit volledig gerenoveerde hotel, op 50 m van de elegante Louizalaan, wacht u een vriendelijk onthaal. De kamers zijn redelijk groot en hebben goede voorzieningen.

La Maison de Maître - H. Conrad, av. Louise 77, ✉ 1050, ℘ 0 2 542 47 16, *brusselsinfo@conradhotels.com, Fax 0 2 542 42 00* - P. AE VISA JCB FS f

fermé août, sam. midi, dim., lundi et jours fériés - **Repas** Lunch 49 bc - carte 52 à 95.

◆ Restaurant gastronomique au décor cossu et raffiné, partageant ses murs avec l'hôtel Conrad. Classique et délicieusement personnalisée, la cuisine évolue au gré des saisons.

◆ Gastronomisch restaurant met een weelderige inrichting, ondergebracht in hotel Conrad. De seizoengebonden keuken is klassiek, maar getuigt van grote creativiteit.

XX **La Porte des Indes,** av. Louise 455, ✉ 1050, ☎ 0 2 647 86 51, *brussels@laporte desindes, Fax 0 2 640 30 59,* Cuisine indienne – ▤. AE ⓓ ⓜⓒ VISA. ⚹ FV c
fermé dim. midi – **Repas** Lunch 20 – carte 23 à 59.
◆ Envie de vous dépayser les papilles ? Franchissez donc la Porte des Indes, où vous attend une cuisine aussi chamarrée que parfumée. Intérieur décoré d'antiquités du pays.
◆ Wie door de Poort van India naar binnen gaat, betreedt een wereld die met zijn exotische smaken, geuren en kleuren alle zintuigen prikkelt.

XX **Tagawa,** av. Louise 279, ✉ 1050, ☎ 0 2 640 50 95, *Fax 0 2 648 41 36,* Cuisine japonaise – ▤ P. AE ⓓ ⓜⓒ VISA JCB. ⚹ FU e
fermé 2 et 3 janv., sam. midi, dim. et jours fériés – **Repas** Lunch 11 – carte 22 à 80.
◆ Ce sobre établissement à débusquer au fond d'une galerie commerçante vous entraîne au pays des samouraïs. Confort occidental ou nippon (tatamis). Bar à sushis.
◆ Sober ingericht Japans restaurant achter in een winkelgalerij. De gasten kunnen kiezen tussen Westers comfort of Japanse traditie (tatamis). De sushibar is bij velen favoriet.

X **L'Atelier de la Truffe Noire,** av. Louise 300, ✉ 1050, ☎ 0 2 640 54 55, *luigi.cici riello@truffenoire.com, Fax 0 2 648 11 44,* Avec cuisine italienne, ouvert jusqu'à 23 h – ▤. AE ⓓ ⓜⓒ VISA FU s
fermé 3 prem. sem. août, prem. sem. janv., dim. et lundi midi – **Repas** carte 40 à 57, ♀.
◆ Brasserie "hype" dont l'originalité et le succès tiennent à la rapidité de sa formule gastronomique où règne la truffe. Bien conçue, la carte est italianisante et variée.
◆ Deze brasserie is een "hype", dankzij de snelle gastronomische formule waarin de truffel centraal staat. De Italiaans getinte kaart is evenwichtig en gevarieerd.

X **Rouge Tomate,** av. Louise 190, ✉ 1050, ☎ 0 2 647 70 44, *rougetomate@skynet.be, Fax 0 2 646 63 10,* 🏠, Ouvert jusqu'à 23 h 30 – AE ⓓ ⓜⓒ VISA. ⚹ FU c
Repas carte env. 39.
◆ Derrière la façade d'une maison de maître du 19e s., lumineuse salle à manger design où s'attable une clientèle huppée. Préparations au goût du jour. Terrasse à l'arrière.
◆ Restaurant in een 19e-eeuws herenhuis, dat vooral wordt bezocht door yuppies. Trendy keuken en designinterieur. Bij mooi weer is het terras aan de achterkant zeer gewild.

Quartier Bois de la Cambre - *plan p. 15* :

XXXX ✿ **Villa Lorraine** (Vandecasserie), av. du Vivier d'Oie 75, ✉ 1000, ☎ 0 2 374 31 63, *inf o@villalorraine.be, Fax 0 2 372 01 95,* 🏠 – P. AE ⓓ ⓜⓒ VISA JCB GX w
fermé 3 dern. sem. juil. et dim. – **Repas** Lunch 50 – 120 bc, carte 68 à 172, ♀.
◆ Père et fils s'activent aux fourneaux de ce grand restaurant posté en lisière d'un bois. Cuisine classique, assortie au décor, et cave de prestige. Agréable terrasse ombragée.
◆ Vader en zoon staan achter het fornuis van dit chique restaurant aan de rand van het bos. De klassieke keuken past bij de inrichting. Prestigieuze wijnen. Lommerrijk terras.
Spéc. Salade de crevettes géantes et copeaux de foie gras à l'huile de truffes. Sole à la normande. Tartare de bœuf aux truffes d'été

XXX ✿ **La Truffe Noire,** bd de la Cambre 12, ✉ 1000, ☎ 0 2 640 44 22, *luigi.ciciriello@tr uffenoire.com, Fax 0 2 647 97 04* – ▤. AE ⓓ ⓜⓒ VISA GV x
fermé 3 prem. sem. août, Noël-Nouvel An, sam. midi et dim. – **Repas** Lunch 40 – 60/130 bc, carte 79 à 175, ♀.
◆ Entre le bois de la Cambre et l'abbaye du même nom, table soignée où l'amateur de truffes trouvera son bonheur. Décor intérieur élégant et patio-terrasse reposant. Belle cave.
◆ Verzorgd restaurant tussen het bos en de abdij van Ter Kameren, waar liefhebbers van truffels hun hart kunnen ophalen. Elegant interieur en patio met terras. Mooie wijnkelder.
Spéc. Carpaccio à la truffe. Saint-Pierre aux poireaux et truffes. Soufflé chaud aux noisettes grillées

Quartier de l'Europe - *plan p. 13* :

🏨 **Dorint,** bd Charlemagne 11, ✉ 1000, ☎ 0 2 231 09 09, *info@dorintbru.be, Fax 0 2 230 33 71,* 🏋, ♨, 🚲 – 🛗 ⚹ ▤ 📺 ♿ 🚗 – 🎤 25 à 150. AE ⓓ ⓜⓒ VISA. ⚹ rest GR c
Repas *L'Objectif* *(fermé sam. midi, dim. midi et jours fériés midis)* Lunch 24 – carte 45 à 54, ♀ – ☕ 24 – **210 ch** 260/290, – 2 suites.
◆ Récent hôtel de chaîne au "look" design, composé de deux immeubles communiquants. Spacieuses et fringantes chambres standard. Exposition de photographies contemporaines. Salle à manger bien dans l'air du temps, assortie au contenu des jolies assiettes.
◆ Nieuw designhotel van een keten, dat bestaat uit twee gebouwen die met elkaar zijn verbonden. De standaardkamers zijn ruim en vrolijk. Expositie van hedendaagse fotografie. De eetzaal is zeer eigentijds, net als de inhoud van het mooie servies.

Crowne Plaza Europa, r. Loi 107, ✉ 1040, ☎ 0 2 230 13 33, *brussels@ichotelsgroup.com, Fax 0 2 230 36 82,* – – 25 à 350. AE VISA JCB. GR d

Repas *(fermé août)* (ouvert jusqu'à 23 h) *Lunch 19* – carte 32 à 51 – **238 ch** 240/465, – 2 suites.

◆ Rénovations importantes dans cet immeuble des années 1970 situé à deux pas du cœur institutionnel européen. Équipement pour conférences et business center. Confortable salle de restaurant. Formule lunch-buffets et grande carte éclectique. Bonne cave.

◆ Dit gebouw uit de jaren 1970, op loopafstand van de Europese instellingen, is ingrijpend gerenoveerd. Faciliteiten voor congressen en business center. Comfortabel restaurant met een lunchformule, buffetten en een gevarieerde kaart. Goede wijnkelder.

Eurovillage, bd Charlemagne 80, ✉ 1000, ☎ 0 2 230 85 55, *Fax 0 2 230 56 35,* – – 25 à 130. AE VISA JCB GR a

Repas *(fermé du 1er au 25 août, sam. et dim. midi) Lunch 22* – carte 27 à 44 – 16 – **103 ch** 200/250.

◆ Cette construction moderne jouxtant un parc verdoyant renferme de menues chambres coquettes et de bonnes installations pour séminaires et affaires. Communs spacieux. Menus multi-choix et buffets dressés à l'heure du lunch.

◆ Modern gebouw bij een weelderig begroeid park. De kamers zijn klein, maar keurig en het hotel biedt veel faciliteiten voor congressen en zakenlieden. Grote gemeenschappelijke ruimten. Keuzemenu's en buffetten rond het middaguur.

Holiday Inn Schuman, r. Breydel 20, ✉ 1040, ☎ 0 2 280 40 00, *hotel@holiday-inn-brussels-schuman.com, Fax 0 2 282 10 70,* – – 45. AE VISA JCB. GS b

Repas (résidents seult) – 20 – **53 ch** 225/245 – ½ P 294/365.

◆ Nouvelle enseigne où "œuvre européenne" rime avec Schuman. Les chambres et les suites sont de bon confort. Petit-déjeuner en plein air aux beaux jours.

◆ Onlangs geopend hotel, dat hulde brengt aan de "vader van Europa". De kamers zijn heel gerieflijk, vooral de suites. Bij mooi weer kan er buiten worden ontbeten.

New Hotel Charlemagne, bd Charlemagne 25, ✉ 1000, ☎ 0 2 230 21 35, *brusselscharlemagne@new-hotel.be, Fax 0 2 230 25 10,* – – 30 à 50. AE VISA JCB. rest GR k

Repas (résidents seult) – 18 – **66 ch** 210/230.

◆ Entre le square Ambiorix et le centre Berlaymont, pratique petit hôtel où loge surtout la clientèle "UE". Réception, bar-salon et salle des petits-déjeuners en enfilade.

◆ Praktisch hotel tussen het Ambiorixsquare en het Europees Centrum Berlaymont, dat het vooral moet hebben van de "EU-klandizie". Receptie, bar-lounge en ontbijtzaal en suite.

Pappa e Citti, r. Franklin 18, ✉ 1000, ☎ 0 2 732 61 10, *pappaecitti@skynet.be, Fax 0 2 732 57 40,* , Cuisine italienne – AE VISA. GR e

fermé août, 20 déc.-6 janv., sam., dim. et jours fériés – **Repas** *Lunch 27* – carte 34 à 89.

◆ Les euro-fonctionnaires aiment à se retrouver dans ce sympathique petit restaurant italien. Spécialités sardes et vins de là-bas. Menu-lunch deux services. Véranda.

◆ Eurofunctionarissen komen graag bijeen in dit sympathieke Italiaanse eethuis. Sardinische specialiteiten en bijpassende wijnen. Lunchmenu met twee gangen. Aangename serre.

L'Atelier, r. Franklin 28, ✉ 1000, ☎ 0 2 734 91 40, *info@atelier-euro.be, Fax 0 2 735 35 98,* , Avec buffets – AE VISA GR y

fermé août, week-end et jours fériés – **Repas** *Lunch 18* – 22/28 bc.

◆ Restaurant avenant dont la carte combine menus et généreux buffets. Cave de bon aloi, rappelant la vocation initiale de cet ancien entrepôt. Collection d'étoffes khmers.

◆ Leuk restaurant met menu's en uitgebreide buffetten. Goede wijnkelder, die herinnert aan de oorspronkelijke bestemming van dit voormalige magazijn. Collectie Khmerstoffen.

Le Stevin, r. St-Quentin 29, ✉ 1000, ☎ 0 2 230 98 47, *Fax 0 2 230 04 94,* – AE VISA. GR r

fermé 30 juil.-22 août, 23 déc.-2 janv., sam., dim. et jours fériés – **Repas** *Lunch 20* – carte 33 à 49.

◆ Vingt ans de bons et loyaux services pour cette table sympathique déclinant un sage choix culinaire classique. "Zinc" Art déco d'époque, verrière et terrasse ombragée.

◆ Dit vriendelijke restaurant bewijst al 20 jaar trouwe diensten. Klassieke keuken, tapkast in art-decostijl, glazen dak en lommerrijk terras.

Take Sushi, bd Charlemagne 21, ✉ 1000, ☎ 0 2 230 56 27, *Fax 0 2 231 10 44,* , Cuisine japonaise avec Sushi-bar – AE VISA JCB GR z

fermé sam. et dim. midi – **Repas** *Lunch 28* – carte 27 à 72.

◆ Une touche nippone au cœur des institutions européennes. Décor, fond musical et jardinet assortis. Formules plateaux-menus. Le sushi-bar a ses fervents. Service en kimono.

◆ Een stukje Japan in het hart van Europa, met bijpassende inrichting, achtergrondmuziek en tuin. Lunchboxes en populaire sushibar. Bediening in kimono.

Balthazar, r. Archimède 63, ✉ 1000, ☎ 0 2 742 06 00, *Fax 0 2 735 70 07*, – AE MC VISA GR s
fermé 24 déc.-3 janv., sam. midi et dim. – **Repas** *Lunch 10* – carte 29 à 46.
◆ Ambiance "brasserie moderne", saveurs méridionales franco-italianisantes, vins du monde et service polyglotte dans cette maison de maître agrémentée d'un jardinet.
◆ In dit herenhuis met een tuintje heerst de ambiance van een moderne brasserie. Frans-Italiaanse keuken, wijnen uit de hele wereld en polyglot personeel.

Quartier Botanique, Gare du Nord *(voir aussi St-Josse-ten-Noode) - plan p. 12 :*

Sheraton Towers, pl. Rogier 3, ✉ 1210, ☎ 0 2 224 31 11, *reservations.brussels@sheraton.com, Fax 0 2 224 34 56*, – 25 à 600. AE MC VISA. rest FQ n
Repas (avec buffets) *Lunch 31* – carte 41 à 50, ♀ – 25 – **467 ch** 335/410, – 44 suites.
◆ Imposante tour super-équipée, dévolue à la clientèle d'affaires internationale. Vastes chambres "high tech". Les "Smart rooms" combinent ambiance de travail et relaxation. Au restaurant, plats ensoleillés, buffets et semaines à thèmes.
◆ Uitstekend geëquipeerd hotel in een torenflat, dat op de internationale zakenwereld mikt. De kamers zijn ruim en hightech. Wie werk en ontspanning wil combineren, kan terecht in de smart rooms. Restaurant met mediterrane gerechten, buffetten en themaweken.

President World Trade Center, bd du Roi Albert II 44, ✉ 1000, ☎ 0 2 203 20 20, *wtc.info@presidenthotels.be, Fax 0 2 203 24 40*, – 25 à 350. AE MC VISA JCB. rest FQ d
Repas *Lunch 27* – carte 45 à 66 – 19 – **286 ch** 248/348, – 16 suites.
◆ Immeuble-bloc s'élevant à l'extrémité du "Manhattan" bruxellois, non loin de la gare du Nord et des tours du World Trade Center. Bon confort dans les chambres. Classique, la carte du restaurant comporte menus et suggestions.
◆ Imposant gebouw aan de rand van het "Manhattan" van de Belgische hoofdstad, niet ver van het station Brussel-Noord en het World Trade Center. Comfortabele kamers. De klassieke kaart van het restaurant bevat tevens menu's en dagschotels.

Tulip Inn Boulevard, av. du Boulevard 17, ✉ 1210, ☎ 0 2 205 15 11, *info.hotel@tulipinnbb.be, Fax 0 2 201 15 15*, – 25 à 450. AE MC VISA JCB. FQ b
Repas (résidents seult) – **450 ch** 192/202, – 4 suites – ½ P 71/126.
◆ Second hôtel bruxellois par sa capacité, cet établissement flambant neuf propose de pimpantes petites chambres correctement équipées, pourvues de moquette ou de parquet.
◆ Dit spiksplinternieuwe hotel is qua capaciteit het op één na grootste van Brussel. Kleine, maar comfortabele kamers die er tiptop uitzien, met tapijt of parket.

Le Dome (annexe Le Dome II), bd du Jardin Botanique 12, ✉ 1000, ☎ 0 2 218 06 80, *dome@skypro.be, Fax 0 2 218 41 12*, – ch, – 25 à 80. AE MC VISA. FQ m
Repas *Lunch 17* – carte 29 à 40 – **125 ch** 112/124 – ½ P 132/154.
◆ Coiffé d'un globe terrestre, le dôme de cette façade 1900 contemple l'effervescence de la place Rogier. Communs Art nouveau. Chambres amples et agréables. Brasserie moderne avec mezzanine. Mets travaillés et plats simples.
◆ Een aardbol prijkt op de koepel van dit gebouw uit 1900, met een mooi uitzicht op het bruisende Rogierplein. Gemeenschappelijke ruimten in art-nouveaustijl. Prettige, ruime kamers. Moderne brasserie met mezzanine voor een eenvoudige hap of verfijnde maaltijd.

Vendôme, bd A. Max 98, ✉ 1000, ☎ 0 2 227 03 00, *brasserie@hotel-vendome.be, Fax 0 2 218 06 83* – – 25 à 80. AE MC VISA JCB FQ c
Repas *(fermé fin déc.-début janv., sam. midi et dim.)* (déjeuner seult pendant vacances scolaires) *Lunch 15* – carte 24 à 52, ♀ – **106 ch** 160/220 – ½ P 114/169.
◆ Entre les places Rogier et De Brouckère, hôtel refait de neuf et doté d'une petite infrastructure pour séminaires. Les chambres sont coquettes et confortables. Brasserie lambrissée misant sur une carte actuelle avec menus et suggestions.
◆ Gerenoveerd hotel tussen het Rogierplein en het Brouckereplein, dat zeer geschikt is voor congressen. De kamers zijn tiptop en comfortabel. Brasserie met veel hout, waar u behalve eigentijdse gerechten à la carte ook menu's kunt bestellen.

President Nord sans rest, bd A. Max 107, ✉ 1000, ☎ 0 2 219 00 60, *thierry.sluys@presidentnord.be, Fax 0 2 218 12 69* – . AE MC VISA JCB. FQ k
63 ch 145/195.
◆ Immeuble d'angle se dressant à un saut de puce de la très commerçante rue Neuve. Avenantes, les chambres standard ont récemment bénéficié d'un "lifting" intégral.
◆ Hoekpand op een steenworp afstand van de Nieuwstraat met zijn talloze winkels. De standaardkamers zijn prettig en hebben onlangs een facelift ondergaan.

Maison du Dragon, bd A. Max 146, ✉ 1000, ☎ 0 2 250 10 20, *hotel.maisondudragon.bru@skynet.be, Fax 0 2 218 18 25,* – ‖, ▤ ch, TV P – 25 à 80. AE ⓓ ⓜ VISA
FQ m

Repas (avec cuisine chinoise, ouvert jusqu'à 23 h 30) *Lunch 10* – 23/45 bc – **48 ch** ☕ 105/165.

• Établissement à management asiatique, comme le suggère l'enseigne. Chambres garnies d'un mobilier stratifié. Affluence touristique en période estivale. Cuisines chinoise et internationale servies dans une salle à manger étagée en mezzanine.

• Hotel met een Aziatisch management, zoals de naam al doet vermoeden. Kamers met meubelen van multiplex. Veel toeristen in de zomer. In de eetzaal met mezzanine kunnen de gasten kiezen tussen de Chinese en de internationale keuken.

Quartier Atomium (Centenaire - Trade Mart - Laeken - Neder-over-Heembeek) - *plan p. 8* :

Le Centenaire, av. Jean Sobieski 84, ✉ 1020, ☎ 0 2 479 56 00, *Fax 0 2 479 56 00* – TV. AE ⓓ ⓜ VISA
BK z

Repas *(fermé 21 juil.-15 août, sam. midi, dim. soir et lundi) Lunch 14* – 20/24 – **5 ch** ☕ 80.

• Seules quelques centaines de protons et d'électrons séparent cet hôtel de l'Atomium. Chambres décorées suivant un thème (africaine, asiatique, etc.) et dotées de kitchenettes. Deux belles fresques animent les murs de la salle de restaurant.

• Dit hotel is slechts een paar honderd protonen en elektronen verwijderd van het Atomium. Kamers met thema, bijvoorbeeld Afrikaans of Aziatisch, en kitchenette. Twee schilderingen sieren de muren van het restaurant.

Ming Dynasty, Parc des Expositions - av. de l'Esplanade BP 9, ✉ 1020, ☎ 0 2 475 23 45, *info@mingdynasty.be, Fax 0 2 475 23 50,* Cuisine chinoise, ouvert jusqu'à 23 h – ▤ P. AE ⓓ ⓜ VISA
BK a

Repas *Lunch 18* – carte 22 à 51.

• Escale asiatique face au parc des Expositions : carte chinoise explicite comprenant de nombreux menus, décor moderne et fond musical adaptés à la table. Honorable cave.

• Aziatische pleisterplaats tegenover het Tentoonstellingspark. Modern interieur, Chinese kaart met diverse menu's en bijpassende achtergrondmuziek. Goede wijnkelder.

Lychee, r. De Wand 118, ✉ 1020, ☎ 0 2 268 19 14, Cuisine chinoise, ouvert jusqu'à 23 h – ▤. AE ⓓ ⓜ VISA JCB
BK d

fermé du 15 au 30 juil. – **Repas** *Lunch 8* – 22/33.

• Un large éventail de mets chinois et un lunch très démocratique vous attendent à cette enseigne connue de longue date. Salle à manger étagée, avec véranda.

• Restaurant dat zijn sporen ruimschoots heeft verdiend, met een keur van Chinese specialiteiten en een zeer schappelijk lunchmenu. Trapsgewijze eetzaal met serre.

La Balade Gourmande, av. Houba de Strooper 95, ✉ 1020, ☎ 0 2 478 94 34, *Fax 0 2 479 89 52,* – ⓓ ⓜ VISA
BK v

fermé 2 sem. carnaval, 15 août-début sept., merc. midi, sam. midi et dim. – **Repas** *Lunch 15* – 30.

• Le menu-carte de cet établissement de quartier vous promène gentiment à travers un répertoire culinaire bourgeois accordé au goût du moment. Cadre actuel et mignon.

• Dit buurtrestaurant biedt een eenvoudige, eerlijke keuken die aan de huidige smaak is aangepast. Het interieur is eigentijds en charmant.

ANDERLECHT - *plans p. 8 et 10 sauf indication spéciale* :

Le Prince de Liège, chaussée de Ninove 664, ✉ 1070, ☎ 0 2 522 16 00, *reception.princedeliege@coditel.be, Fax 0 2 520 81 85* – ‖, ▤ ch, TV – 25. AE ⓓ ⓜ VISA JCB
AM h

Repas (taverne-rest) *Lunch 14* – 22/38 – **32 ch** ☕ 59/93 – ½ P 73/113.

• Hôtel familial situé aux abords d'un carrefour important. Les chambres, fonctionnelles et munies du double vitrage, ont récemment été rafraîchies. Taverne-restaurant où se mitonne une sage cuisine classique. Menus et suggestions du marché.

• Familiehotel bij een druk kruispunt. De functioneel ingerichte kamers hebben dubbele ramen en zijn onlangs opgeknapt. Taverne-restaurant met een licht klassieke kaart. Er zijn ook menu's en dagelijks wisselende gerechten te verkrijgen.

Ustel, Square de l'Aviation 6, ✉ 1070, ☎ 0 2 520 60 53 et 0 2 522 30 25 (rest), *grand.ecluse@grouptorus, Fax 0 2 520 33 28,* – ‖ ▤ TV – 25 à 100. AE ⓓ ⓜ VISA.
plan p. 12 ES q

Repas *(fermé mi-juil.-mi-aout, sam. et dim.)* (brasserie) (déjeuner seult) *Lunch 12* – carte 35 à 44 – **114 ch** ☕ 110/130.

• Au bord de la petite ceinture, hôtel particulier et ses dépendances renfermant de sobres chambres de diverses tailles, dont une vingtaine d'"appart's" avec kitchenette. La machinerie d'une ancienne écluse sert de cadre - insolite s'il en est - à la brasserie.

• Groot herenhuis met bijgebouwen langs de Kleine Ring. Sobere kamers van verschillend formaat, waaronder een twintigtal appartementen met kitchenette. In het bijbehorende restaurant is - bijzonder origineel - de machinerie van een oude sluis te zien.

Erasme, rte de Lennik 790, ✉ 1070, ℘ 0 2 523 62 82, *comfort@skynet.be, Fax 0 2 523 62 83,* ☂, – |♦|, ▤ ch, TV ♿ P – 25 à 80. AE ⓓ MC VISA JCB AN m
Repas *(fermé 24 déc.-2 janv.)* (taverne-rest) 17 – **73 ch** ☕ 75/129, – 1 suite.
◆ Aux portes de la ville, à 1 km du ring, établissement de chaîne proposant de menues chambres chaleureuses et convenablement insonorisées. Trois salles pour séminaires. À table, carte internationale variée.
◆ Ketenhotel aan de rand van de stad, op 1 km van de Ring. Kleine, maar warm ingerichte kamers die goed tegen geluid zijn geïsoleerd. Drie congreszalen. Aan tafel kunnen de gasten kiezen uit een gevarieerde, internationaal georiënteerde kaart.

Van Belle, chaussée de Mons 39, ✉ 1070, ℘ 0 2 521 35 16, *reservation@hotelvanbelle.be, Fax 0 2 527 00 02* – |♦| TV P – 25 à 100. AE ⓓ MC VISA. rest
Repas (dîner pour résidents seult) – **100 ch** ☕ 85/154. plan p. 12 ER f
◆ Hôtel familial bientôt centenaire occupant un ensemble de maisons d'époques différentes. Chambres pratiques et bien tenues. Le service navette vers le centre est offert.
◆ Bijna honderdjarig familiehotel in een aantal huizen uit verschillende perioden. Praktische, goed onderhouden kamers. Gratis pendeldienst naar het centrum.

Saint Guidon 2e étage du stade de football du R.S.C. d'Anderlecht, av. Théo Verbeeck 2, ✉ 1070, ℘ 0 2 520 55 36, *saint-guidon@skynet.be, Fax 0 2 523 38 27* – ▤ P – 25 à 500. ⓓ MC VISA. AM m
fermé 20 juin-21 juil., sam., dim. et jours de match du club – **Repas** (déjeuner seult) 55 bc, carte 55 à 75.
◆ Cette table hébergée dans le stade de football est la "cantine" des amis du prestigieux R.S.C. Anderlecht. Cuisine actuelle soignée évoluant au gré des saisons.
◆ Dit restaurant in het voetbalstadion is de "kantine" van de fans van R.S.C. Anderlecht. De verzorgde eigentijdse keuken is seizoengevoelig.
Spéc. Ravioles de homard aux truffes. Foie de veau poêlé au vinaigre balsanique et câpres. Côte à l'os Blanc Bleu Belge au gros sel

Alain Cornelis, av. Paul Janson 82, ✉ 1070, ℘ 0 2 523 20 83, *alaincornelis@skynet.be, Fax 0 2 523 20 83,* ☂ – AE ⓓ MC VISA AM p
fermé sem. avant Pâques, 1re quinz. août, Noël-Nouvel An, merc. soir, sam. midi, dim. et jours fériés – **Repas** 29/59 bc.
◆ Un restaurant classico-bourgeois, de sa cuisine jusqu'à son cellier. Terrasse à l'arrière, agrémentée d'un jardinet et d'une pièce d'eau. Menu-carte et plats du mois.
◆ Restaurant dat van keuken tot wijnkelder klassiek is. Het terras achter kijkt uit op een mooi tuintje met een waterpartij. Keuzemenu en schotels van de maand.

La Brouette, bd Prince de Liège 61, ✉ 1070, ℘ 0 2 522 51 69, *info@labrouette.be, Fax 0 2 522 51 69* – AE ⓓ MC VISA AM r
fermé du 15 au 21 mars, du 1er au 22 août, sam. midi, dim. soir et lundi – **Repas** *Lunch 20* – 33/65 bc, ♀.
◆ La clientèle d'habitués apprécie autant le soin apporté à la cuisine que l'harmonie des accords mets-vins dont ce confortable petit établissement de quartier a le secret.
◆ De vaste klanten waarderen zowel de verzorgde keuken als de harmonieuze spijs-wijncombinaties, waarvan dit comfortabele buurtrestaurant het patent heeft.
Spéc. Petits-gris en raviolis à la nage de céleri. Tonnelet fumé au foie gras, légumes en tartare et jus de truffes. Blanc de cabillaud étuvé aux champignons, à la flamande

Le Croûton, r. Aumale 22 (près pl. de la Vaillance), ✉ 1070, ℘ 0 2 520 79 36, *rudy.vandenbranden@skynet.be,* ☂ – AE ⓓ MC VISA JCB AM q
fermé 15 août-1er sept., 25 janv.-10 fév., dim. et lundi – **Repas** *Lunch 26* – 34/59 bc.
◆ Érasme, le "prince des humanistes", vécut cinq mois dans l'intéressante maison-musée qui porte son nom, en face de ce restaurant grand comme... un "croûton" ! Saveurs d'ici.
◆ De geleerdste humanist van zijn tijd woonde vijf maanden in het interessante Erasmusmuseum tegenover dit restaurant, dat werkelijk piepklein is. Belgische specialiteiten.

La Paix, r. Ropsy-Chaudron 49 (face abattoirs), ✉ 1070, ℘ 0 2 523 09 58, *Fax 0 2 520 10 39,* Taverne-rest – AE ⓓ MC VISA BM a
fermé 3 dern. sem. juil., sam. et dim. – **Repas** (déjeuner seult sauf vend.) carte 25 à 43.
◆ Un choix bourgeois "tendance carnivore" vous attend dans cette brasserie conviviale postée en face des abattoirs d'Anderlecht. Le steak tartare prend forme sous vos yeux.
◆ Eenvoudige, maar goed klaargemaakte vleesgerechten in dit gemoedelijke eethuis tegenover het abattoir van Anderlecht. De steak tartare is een aanrader.

Le Chapeau Blanc, r. Wayez 200, ✉ 1070, ℘ 0 2 520 02 02, *lechapeaublanc@proximedia.be, Fax 0 2 520 90 08,* ☂, Brasserie avec écailler, ouvert jusqu'à minuit – ▤. AE ⓓ MC VISA AM b
Repas *Lunch 9* – 20.
◆ À deux pas de la place de la Vaillance, venez vous attabler dans un décor de brasserie typique avec banc d'écailler. Terrasse à l'avant. Accueil et service avenants.
◆ Vlak bij het Dapperheidsplein kunt u aanschuiven in deze karakteristieke brasserie annex oesterbar. Terras aan de voorkant. Attente bediening.

X **René,** pl. de la Résistance 14, ✉ 1070, ✆ 0 2 523 28 76, 🏠, Moules en saison AM a
fermé dern. sem. juil.-3 prem. sem. août, lundi soir et mardi – **Repas** carte 22 à 35.
◆ Ancienne friterie populaire judicieusement transformée en restaurant pour le plus grand plaisir des bonnes fourchettes. Clientèle de quartier et d'affaires. Terrasse d'été.
◆ Deze oude "frituur" is omgetoverd tot een restaurantje voor smulpapen. Er komen veel buurtbewoners en zakenmensen. Terras in de zomer.

AUDERGHEM (OUDERGEM) - *plan p. 11 sauf indication spéciale :*

XX **La Grignotière,** chaussée de Wavre 2041, ✉ 1160, ✆ 0 2 672 81 85, *Fax 0 2 672 81 85* – AE MC VISA DN t
fermé du 1er au 20 août, dim. et lundi – **Repas** Lunch 35 – 46.
◆ À un saut d'écureuil de la forêt de Soignes. Côté salle : un cadre sobrement actuel ; côté "piano" : un classicisme mesuré. Menu multi-choix. Petit salon séparé.
◆ Restaurant in de buurt van het Zoniënwoud, met in de eetzaal een sober, eigentijds interieur en in de keuken een gematigd classicisme. Menu met veel keuze. Aparte salon.

XX **Le Pousse-Rapière,** chaussée de Wavre 1699, ✉ 1160, ✆ 0 2 672 76 20, *Fax 0 2 672 76 20,* 🏠 – ▤. AE ⓓ MC VISA CN v
fermé 15 juil.-15 août, dim. et lundi – **Repas** 28.
◆ Formules menu-carte et suggestions sur écriteau pour ce restaurant dont la clientèle, essentiellement composée d'habitués, n'a rien à voir avec des "traîneurs de rapière".
◆ Dit restaurant presenteert een kaart met menu's en dagsuggesties op een leitje. De clientèle bestaat hoofdzakelijk uit habitués, wat altijd een goed teken is.

X **New Asia,** chaussée de Wavre 1240, ✉ 1160, ✆ 0 2 660 62 06, *Fax 0 2 675 67 28,* 🏠, Cuisine chinoise – ▤. AE ⓓ MC VISA. ✻ plan p. 15 HU a
fermé 3 dern. sem. août et lundis non fériés – **Repas** Lunch 8 – 12/24.
◆ Une ambiance détendue règne dans cette maison fondée voici plus de 20 ans. Cuisine chinoise déclinée en abondants menus et cadre typique d'un restaurant asiatique de quartier.
◆ In deze zaak, die al ruim 20 jaar bestaat, heerst een ongedwongen sfeer. Chinese keuken met diverse menu's en de typische inrichting van een Aziatisch buurtrestaurant.

X **La Khaïma,** chaussée de Wavre 1390, ✉ 1160, ✆ 0 2 675 00 04, *Fax 0 2 675 00 04,* Cuisine marocaine – ▤. AE MC VISA. ✻ CN k
fermé août – **Repas** 27.
◆ Connue des amateurs de pastillas, tagines et couscous, cette petite adresse vous accueille sous une tente berbère (khaïma). Tout y est : tapis, poufs, cuivres martelés.
◆ Dit adresje is bekend bij liefhebbers van pastilla, tajine en couscous. Er wordt gegeten in een echte Berbertent (khaïma), compleet met tapijten, poefs en koperen tafeltjes.

X **La Citronnelle,** chaussée de Wavre 1377, ✉ 1160, ✆ 0 2 672 98 43, 🏠, Cuisine vietnamienne – AE ⓓ MC VISA CN f
fermé 2e quinz. août, lundi et sam. midi – **Repas** Lunch 11 – carte env. 33.
◆ Cap sur le golfe du Tonkin avec cette honorable enseigne dont la cuisine vietnamienne délicatement parfumée concède fort peu de choses à l'Occident. Fond musical adapté.
◆ Hijs met gerust gemoed de zeilen voor de Golf van Tonkin. In dit Vietnamees restaurant met bijpassende muziek, doet de keuken weinig concessies aan de Westerse smaak.

BERCHEM-STE-AGATHE (SINT-AGATHA-BERCHEM) - *plan p. 8 :*

X **La Brasserie de la Gare,** chaussée de Gand 1430, ✉ 1082, ✆ 0 2 469 10 09, *Fax 0 2 469 10 09* – ▤ P. AE ⓓ MC VISA AL s
fermé sam. midi et dim. – **Repas** Lunch 12 – 26, ♀.
◆ À portée de sifflet de la gare, brasserie lambrissée où règne une ambiance animée. Fresque naïve sur le thème ferroviaire. Plats traditionnels et cave aguichante.
◆ In deze brasserie, waar het fluitje van de stationschef haast te horen is, is het altijd druk. Primitief fresco met het spoor als thema. Traditioneel eten en goede wijnen.

ETTERBEEK - *plan p. 13 :*

XX **Stirwen,** chaussée St-Pierre 15, ✉ 1040, ✆ 0 2 640 85 41, *Fax 0 2 648 43 08* – AE ⓓ MC VISA GS a
fermé 2 sem. en août, sam. et dim. – **Repas** Lunch 25 – carte 37 à 55.
◆ L'enseigne de cette confortable brasserie aux légères touches Belle Époque signifie en breton "Étoile blanche". Recettes classico-bourgeoises à l'écoute des régions de France.
◆ Comfortabele brasserie in een ingetogen belle-époquestijl, waarvan de naam verwijst naar het Bretonse woord voor witte ster. Klassieke Franse streekgerechten.

Quartier Cinquantenaire (Montgomery) - *plan p. 13 sauf indication spéciale :*

Park sans rest, av. de l'Yser 21, ✉ 1040, ☎ 0 2 735 74 00, *info@parkhotelbrussels.be, Fax 0 2 735 19 67,* , , -   - 25 à 65. AE ⓓ ⓜⓒ VISA JCB HS c
51 ch 250/350.
◆ Juste en face du parc du Cinquantenaire, deux maisons de maître renfermant de confortables chambres, dont 25 singles. La salle des petits-déjeuners donne sur un jardinet.
◆ Twee herenhuizen tegenover het Jubelpark met gerieflijke kamers, waarvan 25 éénpersoons. De ontbijtzaal kijkt uit op een kleine tuin.

Le Jaspe, bd Louis Schmidt 30, ✉ 1040, ☎ 0 2 734 22 30, *Fax 0 2 734 22 30*, Cuisine chinoise - . AE ⓓ ⓜⓒ VISA plan p. 15 HU b
fermé 15 juil.-5 août et lundis non fériés - **Repas** Lunch 9 - 22/28.
◆ La façade de ce restaurant chinois au sobre décor extrême-oriental "en impose". Pour conventionnels qu'ils soient, les plats n'en sont pas moins goûteux.
◆ De façade van dit Chinese restaurant met zijn sobere, typisch Aziatische decor boezemt ontzag in. Het eten is weliswaar conventioneel, maar daarom niet minder smakelijk.

EVERE - *plan p. 9 :*

Belson sans rest, chaussée de Louvain 805, ✉ 1140, ☎ 0 2 708 31 00, *resa@gresham-belsonhotel.com, Fax 0 2 708 31 66,* -   - 25. AE ⓓ ⓜⓒ VISA. CL z
 20 - **132 ch** 260/310, - 3 suites.
◆ Vous aurez aussi facilement accès au centre-ville qu'à l'aéroport (Zaventem) depuis cet hôtel de chaîne renfermant deux catégories de chambres. Espace de remise en forme.
◆ Vanuit dit ketenhotel is zowel het centrum als de luchthaven Zaventem heel gemakkelijk te bereiken. Het Belson telt twee categorieën kamers en een fitnessruimte.

Mercure, av. Jules Bordet 74, ✉ 1140, ☎ 0 2 726 73 35, *H0958@accor-hotels.com, Fax 0 2 726 82 95* - , rest,   - 25 à 120. AE ⓓ ⓜⓒ VISA JCB. rest CL a
Repas *(fermé mi-juil.-mi-août, vend. soir, sam. et dim. midi)* Lunch 20 bc - carte 27 à 47, - 17 - **113 ch** 175/200, - 7 suites.
◆ À deux pas de l'OTAN et 5 mn des pistes de Zaventem, un "classique" du groupe Accor : chambres conformes aux standards de l'enseigne hôtelière et salles pour séminaires. Restaurant au sobre décor égayé de planches de B.D.
◆ Deze klassieker van de hotel-groep ligt vlakbij de NAVO en de luchthaven Zaventem. De kamers voldoen aan de standaard van de hotelketen en er zijn congreszalen. Het sober ingerichte restaurant wordt opgevrolijkt door striptekeningen.

FOREST (VORST) - *plan p. 10 sauf indication spéciale :*

De Fierlant sans rest, r. De Fierlant 67, ✉ 1190, ☎ 0 2 538 60 70, *de_fierlant@skynet.be, Fax 0 2 538 91 99* - . AE ⓓ ⓜⓒ VISA. BN d
40 ch 70/80.
◆ Entre la gare du Midi et la salle de concerts Forest-National, hôtel aussi pratique que convenable, occupant un petit immeuble récent. Chambres standard insonorisées.
◆ Praktisch en keurig hotel in een nieuw gebouw tussen het station Brussel-Zuid en de concertzaal Vorst-Nationaal. Standaardkamers met een goede geluidsisolatie.

GANSHOREN - *plan p. 17 sauf indication spéciale :*

Bruneau, av. Broustin 75, ✉ 1083, ☎ 0 2 421 70 70, *Fax 0 2 425 97 26,* - . AE ⓓ ⓜⓒ VISA W a
fermé du 1er au 10 fév., août, mardi, merc. et jeudis fériés - **Repas** Lunch 65 bc - 175 bc, carte 73 à 227.
◆ Une table de renom, qui atteint l'équilibre parfait entre classicisme et créativité, tout en valorisant les produits régionaux. Cave prestigieuse. L'été, on mange en terrasse.
◆ Gerenommeerd restaurant met een volmaakt evenwicht tussen classicisme en creativiteit, met het accent op regionale producten. Prestigieuze wijnkelder. Terras in de zomer.
Spéc. Rosace de homard à la truffe. Epigramme de bar aux girolles, beurre blanc au curry (juil.-oct.). Galette de pigeon de Vendée et ses cuisses caramélisées au soja

Claude Dupont, av. Vital Riethuisen 46, ✉ 1083, ☎ 0 2 426 00 00, *claudedupont@resto.be, Fax 0 2 426 65 40* - AE ⓓ ⓜⓒ VISA W b
fermé juil., lundi et mardi - **Repas** Lunch 45 - 65/130 bc, carte 66 à 121, .
◆ Travail de maître dans une maison de maître. Aucun doute : les diplômes et distinctions gastronomiques qui ornent le hall d'entrée ne sont pas usurpés. Somptueux cellier.
◆ De oorkonden en gastronomische onderscheidingen in de hal van dit herenhuis kondigen al aan dat hier met meesterschap wordt gekookt. Indrukwekkende wijnkelder.
Spéc. Aiglefin rôti à l'émulsion de truffes d'été (juin-sept.). Timbale de homard en mousseline de jeunes poireaux. Gibier en saison (sept.-fév.)

XXX **San Daniele** (Spinelli), av. Charles-Quint 6, ✉ 1083, ✆ 0 2 426 79 23, *Fax 0 2 426 92 14*, Avec cuisine italienne – ▤. AE ⓓ ⓜⓒ VISA W c
fermé 15 juil.-15 août, 1 sem. en avril, dim. et lundi – **Repas** 50, carte 37 à 54 ♧.
◆ L'accueil familial et gentil, autant que l'ampleur de la carte italianisante, escortée d'une affriolante sélection de crus transalpins, attire ici une clientèle assidue.
◆ De vriendelijke ontvangst, de ruime keuze van de Italiaans georiënteerde kaart en de aanlokkelijke selectie Italiaanse wijnen trekken veel vaste klanten.
Spéc. Calamaretti, gamberetti et scampis en friture. Ris de veau en crépinette de chou-vert aux truffes. Soufflé d'ananas glacé à l'orange sanguine

XX **Cambrils** 1er étage, av. Charles-Quint 365, ✉ 1083, ✆ 0 2 465 50 70, *restaurant.cambrils@skynet.be, Fax 0 2 465 76 63*, 余 – ▤. AE ⓜⓒ VISA plan p. 8 AL f
fermé 12 juil.-2 août, dim., lundi soir et jeudi soir – **Repas** Lunch 22 – 30/55 bc.
◆ Les cuisines de ce restaurant plaisant s'ouvrent sur la salle, et celle-ci, sur l'avenue Charles-Quint. Choix classique. Bar au rez-de-chaussée. Terrasse pour les beaux jours.
◆ De keukens van dit prettige restaurant komen uit op de eetzaal, die op zijn beurt uitkijkt op de Keizer Karellaan. Klassieke kaart. Bar op de benedenverdieping. Zonnig terras.

IXELLES (ELSENE) - *plan p. 14 sauf indication spéciale :*

XX **Le Yen,** r. Lesbroussart 49, ✉ 1050, ✆ 0 2 649 07 47, 余, Cuisine vietnamienne – AE ⓓ ⓜⓒ VISA. ✻ FU f
fermé sam. midi et dim. – **Repas** Lunch 9 – 18/23.
◆ Rien à voir avec la devise nippone ! "L'Hirondelle" (Yen) vous reçoit dans un cadre asiatique aussi moderne que dépouillé. Préparations vietnamiennes aux noms poétiques.
◆ Deze Yen heeft niets te maken met de Japanse munt, maar betekent zwaluw. In een even modern als sober interieur wordt u onthaald op Vietnamese schotels met poëtische namen.

X **L'Ancienne Poissonnerie,** r. Trône 65, ✉ 1050, ✆ 0 2 502 75 05, Cuisine italienne. AE ⓓ ⓜⓒ VISA plan p. 12 FS h
fermé 3 dern. sem. août, sam. midi, dim., lundi soir, mardi soir et merc. soir – **Repas** carte 30 à 48.
◆ Ancienne poissonnerie Art nouveau récemment transformée en table italienne au goût du jour. Accueil et service charmants, ambiance sympathique et comptoir pour gens pressés.
◆ Vroegere art nouveau viswinkel, waarin een hedendaags Italiaanse eetgelegenheid is gevestigd. Charmant onthaal en bediening, sympathieke sfeer en eettoog voor de gehaasten.

Quartier Boondael (Université) - *plan p. 15 :*

XX **L'Aub. de Boendael,** square du Vieux Tilleul 12, ✉ 1050, ✆ 0 2 672 70 55, *auberge-de-boendael@resto.be, Fax 0 2 660 75 82*, 余, Grillades – P. AE ⓓ ⓜⓒ VISA HX h
fermé 19 juil.-15 août, 24 déc.-1er janv., sam., dim. et jours fériés – **Repas** 45 bc.
◆ Intérieur dans la note rustique, âtre crépitant et carte bourgeoise orientée "grillades", pour ce restaurant installé dans une maison du 17e s. Banquets les week-ends.
◆ Restaurant in een 17e-eeuws pand met een rustiek interieur, knapperend houtvuur en traditionele kaart met veel geroosterd vlees. Feestzaal beschikbaar in het weekend.

X **Les Foudres,** r. Eugène Cattoir 14, ✉ 1050, ✆ 0 2 647 36 36, *foudres@skynet.be, Fax 0 2 649 09 86*, 余 – P. AE ⓓ ⓜⓒ VISA GUV j
fermé sam. midi et dim. – **Repas** 30.
◆ On s'attable ici dans un ancien chai voûté, dont les énormes "foudres" de chêne élèvent encore le vin. Répertoire culinaire classico-traditionnel. Parking privé gratuit.
◆ Restaurant in een oude gewelfde wijnkelder met reusachtige eikenhouten vaten, waarin de wijn nog ligt na te rijpen. Klassiek-traditionele keuken. Gratis parkeren.

X **La Pagode d'Or,** chaussée de Boondael 332, ✉ 1050, ✆ 0 2 649 06 56, *Fax 0 2 649 09 00*, 余, Cuisine vietnamienne, ouvert jusqu'à 23 h – AE ⓓ ⓜⓒ VISA. ✻ GV m
fermé lundi – **Repas** Lunch 9 – 23/35.
◆ Un honorable petit ambassadeur du Vietnam à Ixelles : carte explicite et consistante, avec menus et "table de riz" ; intime salle à manger aux discrètes touches exotiques.
◆ Dit restaurantje is een uitstekende ambassadeur van Vietnam in Elsene. Mooie kaart met menu's en rijsttafels. De eetzaal is vrij intiem en heeft een licht exotische toets.

X **Marie,** r. Alphonse De Witte 40, ✉ 1050, ✆ 0 2 644 30 31, *Fax 0 2 644 27 37* – ▤. AE ⓜⓒ VISA. ✻ GU a
fermé 18 juil.-17 août, 24 déc.-4 janv., sam. midi, dim. et lundi – **Repas** Lunch 16 – carte 46 à 60, ♀ ♧.
◆ Cuisine traditionnelle, assaisonnée de notes méridionales et rehaussée d'une attrayante sélection de vins, dans ce sympathique bistrot gourmand au format de poche.
◆ In deze kleine, sympathieke bistro kan men verrukkelijk eten. De traditionele keuken krijgt pit door zijn mediterrane noot ; een regionale wijnkaart speelt hier goed op in.
Spéc. Brandade de morue à l'huile d'olives, concassée de tomates et coulis de poivrons. Tian d'épaule d'agneau braisée et aubergines rôties. Filet de daurade royale grillé au fenouil, jus de bouillabaisse au pistou

X **Le Doux Wazoo,** r. Relais 21, ✉ 1050, ☎ 0 2 649 58 52, Bistrot, ouvert jusqu'à 23 h – AE ⓓ ⓜⓒ VISA HV s
fermé 18 juil.-16 août, fin déc.-début janv., sam. midi, dim. et lundi soir – **Repas** *Lunch 12* – 25, ♀.
◆ Un tantinet embourgeoisée, la carte de ce restaurant-bistrot s'autorise toutefois quelques plats "canaille". Collection d'objets, affiches et clichés empreints de nostalgie.
◆ De kaart van deze bistro is een tikkeltje burgerlijk, maar bevat ook een paar spannende gerechten. De collector's items, affiches en foto's zijn doordrenkt van nostalgie.

Quartier Bascule, Châtelain, Ma Campagne *- plan p. 14 :*

XX **Maison Félix** 1er étage, r. Washington 149, ✉ 1050, ☎ 0 2 345 66 93, *Fax 0 2 344 92 85* – AE ⓓ ⓜⓒ VISA. ✂ FV s
fermé du 1er au 23 août, du 3 au 12 janv., dim. et lundi – **Repas** *Lunch 35* – 38/60 bc, ♀ 🍇.
◆ On traverse la boutique traiteur de Monsieur Félix - astuce pour aiguiser l'appétit des hôtes ? - avant de s'attabler à l'étage. Cuisine "produits". Superbe livre de cave.
◆ De gasten moeten eerst door de delicatessenwinkel - een truc om de eetlust op te wekken - alvorens boven aan tafel te gaan. Keuken met eersteklas producten en goede wijnen.

XX **O' comme 3 Pommes,** pl. du Châtelain 40, ✉ 1050, ☎ 0 2 644 03 23, *resto@oc3pommes.be, Fax 0 2 644 03 23,* ☂ – AE ⓓ ⓜⓒ VISA FU q
fermé sam. midi, dim. et lundi midi – **Repas** *Lunch 12* – 28/47.
◆ Salle à manger fraîche et actuelle où l'on prend plaisir à "tomber dans les pommes" ! Menu-carte sur ardoise, bien à la page et rehaussé par-ci, par-là de notes asiatiques.
◆ Frisse, moderne eetzaal, waar u kunt genieten van tongstrelende spijzen. Eigentijdse keuken met een vleugje Aziatisch. Zeer schappelijk geprijsde lunch.

XX **Aux Beaumes de Venise,** r. Darwin 62, ✉ 1050, ☎ 0 2 343 82 93, *Fax 0 2 346 08 96,* ☂ – ▤. AE ⓜⓒ VISA. ✂ EFV x
fermé 21 juil.-15 août, Noël-Nouvel An, dim. et lundi – **Repas** *Lunch 18* – 35.
◆ Restaurant dont la cave, très peu "Côtes du Rhône", désavoue donc l'enseigne. Fresques et peintures en salle. Menus et suggestions. Véranda donnant sur une terrasse d'été.
◆ Restaurant waarvan de wijnkelder niet biedt wat zijn naam belooft. Fresco's en schilderijen in de eetzaal. Menu's en dagsuggesties. De serre kijkt uit op een zomerterras.

X **La Quincaillerie,** r. Page 45, ✉ 1050, ☎ 0 2 533 98 33, *info@quincaillerie.be, Fax 0 2 539 40 95,* Brasserie avec écailler, ouvert jusqu'à minuit – ▤ P. AE ⓓ ⓜⓒ VISA JCB
fermé sam. midi, dim. midi et jours fériés midis – **Repas** *Lunch 13* – carte 36 à 73, ♀.
◆ Brasserie rutilante et majestueuse aménagée dans ancienne quincaillerie de style Art déco. Plat du jour et banc d'écailler. Accueil et service très "pro". Voiturier. FU z
◆ Majestueuze, fonkelende brasserie in een oude ijzerwinkel in art-decostijl. Oesterbar en dagschotels. Zeer professionele bediening. Valetparking.

X **Toucan,** av. Louis Lepoutre 1, ✉ 1050, ☎ 0 2 345 30 17, *toucanbrasserie@hotmail.com, Fax 0 2 345 64 78,* Taverne-rest, ouvert jusqu'à 23 h – AE ⓓ ⓜⓒ VISA FV z
fermé 24 déc. soir, 25 déc., 31 déc. soir et 1er janv. – **Repas** carte 29 à 46, ♀.
◆ Taverne-restaurant au look "trendy" : petites tables serrées revêtues d'émail coloré, lustres modernes et imposante œuvre d'art contemporaine. Préparations "bistrotières".
◆ Café-restaurant met een trendy "look" : tafeltjes van gekleurd email, moderne kroonluchters en een indrukwekkend hedendaags kunstwerk. Het eten is in bistrostijl.

X **Les Perles de Pluie,** r. Châtelain 25, ✉ 1050, ☎ 0 2 649 67 23, *info@lesperlesdepluie.be, Fax 0 2 644 07 60,* ☂, Cuisine thaïlandaise, ouvert jusqu'à 23 h – AE ⓜⓒ VISA
fermé lundi et sam. midi – **Repas** *Lunch 15* – carte 24 à 52. FU n
◆ Table thaïlandaise dont le nom lance un clin d'œil au "grand Jacques". Recettes et décor typiques. Deux salles reproduisent un intérieur traditionnel orné de boiseries.
◆ Authentiek Thais restaurant, waarvan de naam een knipoog is naar Jacques Brel. Twee eetzalen met een traditioneel interieur en fraai houtwerk.

X **Bistrot Du Mail,** r. Mail 81, ✉ 1050, ☎ 0 2 539 06 97, *Fax 0 2 539 06 97,* Ouvert jusqu'à 23 h – ▤. AE ⓓ ⓜⓒ VISA FU r
fermé sam. midi, dim. et lundi – **Repas** *Lunch 17* – carte 32 à 53, ♀.
◆ Bistrot amélioré où l'on vient faire des repas au goût du jour dans une atmosphère cordiale et chaleureuse. Petite carte et ardoise à suggestions. Salle à manger rajeunie.
◆ Verbeterde bistro, waar in een gezellige sfeer actuele gerechten worden geserveerd. Kleine kaart en suggesties op een leienbord. De eetzaal heeft een opknapbeurt gehad.

X **Le Fellini,** pl. du Châtelain 32, ✉ 1050, ☎ 0 2 534 47 49, *fellini@belgacom.net,* ☂, Avec cuisine italienne, ouvert jusqu'à 23 h – ▤. ⓓ ⓜⓒ VISA. ✂ FU x
fermé merc. midi – **Repas** – carte 30 à 49.
◆ Préparations majoritairement tournées vers l'Italie, servies dans une salle à manger d'esprit Art nouveau. L'été, agréable terrasse sur la place. En résumé : "La Dolce Vita".
◆ Een kaart met overwegend Italiaanse gerechten, een fraai interieur in art-nouveaustijl en 's zomers een prettig terras aan het plein. Kortom "La Dolce Vita" !

La Canne en Ville, r. Réforme 22, ✉ 1050, ☎ 0 2 347 29 26, *canneenville@skynet.be, Fax 0 2 347 69 89,* – AE ① MC VISA. – *fermé Noël, Nouvel An, sam. soir en juil.-août, sam. midi et dim.* – **Repas** Lunch 11 – carte 32 à 45. FV q

◆ Bientôt vingt ans de présence pour ce bistrot paisible et accueillant qui succède à une boucherie, comme l'attestent des pans de carrelage préservés. Cuisine du marché.

◆ Deze bistro, die al bijna 20 jaar bestaat, was vroeger een slagerij, zoals de bewaard gebleven tegels bewijzen. De kok maakt uitsluitend gebruik van dagverse marktproducten.

Tutto Pepe, r. Faider 123, ✉ 1050, ☎ 0 2 534 96 19, *tuttopepe@skynet.be, Fax 0 2 538 65 68,* Cuisine italienne – . AE ① MC VISA. FU d *fermé août, sam., dim. et jours fériés* – **Repas** carte 40 à 125.

◆ Microscopique et dépaysant, ce restaurant enjoué vous réserve un accueil cent pour cent italien, donc assez théâtral. Choix culinaire transalpin annoncé sur écriteaux.

◆ Piepklein Italiaans eettentje, waar de patron u met veel gevoel voor theater bedient, zoals nu eenmaal bij zijn volksaard hoort. Het menu staat op een bord geschreven.

Quartier Léopold *(voir aussi Bruxelles) - plan p. 12 :*

Renaissance, r. Parnasse 19, ✉ 1050, ☎ 0 2 505 29 29, *renaissance.brussels@renaissancehotels.com, Fax 0 2 505 22 76,* , , , – – 25 à 360. AE ① MC VISA JCB. FS e

Repas ***Symphony*** *(fermé sam. midi, dim. midi et jours fériés midis)* Lunch 19 – carte 42 à 65, – 23 – **256 ch** 269, – 6 suites.

◆ Hôtel jouxtant le quartier institutionnel européen. Équipement moderne dans les chambres. Bonnes installations pour affaires, conférences et délassement. Service complet. Restaurant misant sur une carte au goût du jour et une formule lunch.

◆ Hotel dat grenst aan de wijk van de Europese instellingen. Moderne voorzieningen in de kamers. Veel faciliteiten voor zaken, congressen en ontspanning. Uitstekende service. Restaurant met een eigentijdse keuken en een aantrekkelijk lunchmenu.

Leopold, r. Luxembourg 35, ✉ 1050, ☎ 0 2 511 18 28, *reservations@hotel-leopold.be, Fax 0 2 514 19 39,* – – 25 à 80. AE ① MC VISA. rest FS y

Repas ***Salon Les Anges*** *(fermé sam. midi et dim.)* (en août déjeuner seult) Lunch 35 – carte 47 à 65 – 18 – **86 ch** 174/248 – ½ P 106/200.

◆ Établissement qui ne cesse de s'agrandir en s'améliorant : chambres coquettes et confortables, communs fignolés, jardin d'hiver sur cour intérieure ombragée, tranquillité. Angélique restaurant feutré. Carte classico-bourgeoise et intéressante cave.

◆ Dit bedrijf wordt steeds groter en beter : comfortabele kamers, mooie lounges, een wintertuin die uitkijkt op een schaduwrijke binnenplaats, en rust. Hemels restaurant met klassieke kaart en interessante wijnkelder.

Quartier Louise *(voir aussi Bruxelles et St-Gilles) - plans p. 12 et 14 :*

Sofitel sans rest, av. de la Toison d'Or 40, ✉ 1050, ☎ 0 2 514 22 00, *H1071@accor-hotels.com, Fax 0 2 514 57 44,* – – 25 à 120. AE ① MC VISA JCB. 23 – **166 ch** 330, – 4 suites. FS r

◆ Luxe discret et confort douillet dans cet hôtel rénové pour mieux satisfaire les attentes de la clientèle d'affaires internationale. Terrasse sur jardin suspendu.

◆ Bescheiden luxe en behaaglijk comfort kenmerken dit gerenoveerde hotel, waar veel gasten uit de internationale zakenwereld verblijven. Hangende tuin en terras.

Four Points Sheraton, r. Paul Spaak 15, ✉ 1000, ☎ 0 2 645 61 11, *reservations.brussels@sheraton.com, Fax 0 2 646 63 44,* , – – 25 à 40. AE ① MC VISA JCB FU k

Repas (ouvert jusqu'à 23 h) Lunch 16 – carte env. 37, – 19 – **128 ch** 230.

◆ Établissement de chaîne jouxtant l'avenue Louise. Amples chambres un rien surannées, mais bien équipées. Sauna, jacuzzi et jardin de repos pour "décompresser". Salle de restaurant célébrant la "gent" bovine et carte avec spécialités suisses. Meuh !

◆ Ketenhotel aan de Louizalaan. Ruime kamers, ietwat ouderwets, maar met goede voorzieningen. Sauna, jacuzzi en tuin om tot rust te komen. In het restaurant kan men de inwendige mens versterken met vleesschotels en Zwitserse specialiteiten.

Argus sans rest, r. Capitaine Crespel 6, ✉ 1050, ☎ 0 2 514 07 70, *reception@hotel-argus.be, Fax 0 2 514 12 22* – . AE ① MC VISA FS t **42 ch** 100/120.

◆ Cette façade de la ville haute abrite de sobres chambres standard insonorisées. Breakfast illuminé d'une verrière d'esprit Art déco. L'affaire reste bien côtée à l'Argus !

◆ Adres in de bovenstad met sobere kamers die goed tegen geluid zijn geïsoleerd. Ontbijt onder een mooie art-decokoepel. Het attente personeel lijkt wel argusogen te hebben...

Beau-Site sans rest, r. Longue Haie 76, ✉ 1000, ☎ 0 2 640 88 89, *beausite@coditel.net, Fax 0 2 640 16 11* – . AE ① MC VISA JCB FT r **38 ch** 97/157.

◆ Installé dans un petit immeuble de coin, à 100 m de l'artère la plus sélecte de Bruxelles, cet hôtel aussi fonctionnel que mignon vous réserve un accueil familial.

◆ In dit praktische en vriendelijke hotel in een hoekpand, op slechts 100 m van de chicste avenue van Brussel, wacht u een gastvrij onthaal.

Beverly Hills sans rest, r. Prince Royal 71, ✉ 1050, ☎ 0 2 513 22 22, *beverlyhills@infonie.be, Fax 0 2 513 87 77,* - AE MC VISA FS b
5 - **40 ch** 95/125.
◆ Hôtel proche de l'avenue de la Toison d'Or où, à défaut de rencontrer la bande à Brandon et Kelly, vous dormirez dans des chambres de bon confort. Fitness et sauna.
◆ Hotel bij de Gulden Vlieslaan, waar u de kliek van Brandon en Kelly niet zult aantreffen, maar wel kunt slapen in een kamer met goed comfort. Fitnessruimte en sauna.

Notos, r. Livourne 154, ✉ 1000, ☎ 0 2 513 29 59, *info@notos.be, Fax 0 2 644 07 20,* Cuisine grecque - AE MC VISA. FU t
fermé août et lundi - **Repas** (dîner seult jusqu'à 23 h) carte 34 à 45.
◆ Dans un ancien garage, restaurant grec "branché" dont le décor intérieur, harmonieusement épuré, évite de verser dans l'amphore. Saveurs hellènes sortant des sentiers battus.
◆ Dit Griekse restaurant in een oude garage is helemaal in. Gestileerde, harmonieuze inrichting en Griekse specialiteiten die nu eens buiten de platgetreden paden gaan.

De la Vigne... à l'Assiette, r. Longue Haie 51, ✉ 1000, ☎ 0 2 647 68 03, *Fax 0 2 647 68 03,* Bistrot - AE MC VISA FT k
fermé 26 juil.-26 août, sam. midi, dim. et lundi - **Repas** Lunch 13 - 20/32, ♀.
◆ Les disciples de Bacchus seront aux anges à cette enseigne animée, et les novices se fieront aux conseils avisés d'un grand sommelier. Cadre simple. Sage carte "bistrot".
◆ De volgelingen van Bacchus zijn in de wolken in dit restaurant, waar men gerust kan vertrouwen op het kundig advies van de sommelier. Simpele inrichting en lekker bistro-eten.

JETTE - *plan p. 17 sauf indication spéciale :*

Rôtiss. Le Vieux Pannenhuis, r. Léopold Ier 317, ✉ 1090, ☎ 0 2 425 83 73, *levieuxpannenhuis@belgacom.net, Fax 0 2 420 21 20,* , Avec grillades - . AE MC VISA plan p. 8 BL g
fermé juil., sam. midi et dim. - **Repas** Lunch 21 - 30/44 bc.
◆ Ancien relais de poste au charme rustique agréablement préservé. Choix conséquent, de type classico-bourgeois, avec d'appétissantes grillades exécutées en salle.
◆ Dit voormalige poststation heeft zijn rustieke charme weten te behouden. Evenwichtige kaart met klassieke gerechten, waaronder vlees dat in de eetzaal wordt geroosterd.

French Kiss, r. Léopold Ier 470, ✉ 1090, ☎ 0 2 425 22 93, *Fax 0 2 428 68 24,* Avec grillades - . AE MC VISA W f
fermé 19 juil.-16 août et lundi - **Repas** Lunch 17 - 27 .
◆ Sympathique restaurant-grill tout de briques revêtu, émaillé de sobres touches modernes. Grande carte diversifiée et sélection de vins bien vue. Affluence d'habitués.
◆ Sympathiek grillrestaurant met bakstenen muren en een paar moderne accenten. Zeer gevarieerde kaart en een goede selectie wijnen. Veel vaste bezoekers.

Chez Soje, av. de Jette 85, ✉ 1090, ☎ 0 2 426 77 54 - . MC VISA W y
fermé lundi et mardi - **Repas** Lunch 14 - carte 22 à 40.
◆ Cuisine "bistrot" façon grand-mère servie dans un café bruxellois de 1903. Lambris, comptoir, miroirs et banquettes vibrent au passage du tram ! Coude-à-coude jovial.
◆ Bistrokeuken uit grootmoeders tijd in een Brussels café uit 1903, met een joviale atmosfeer. Lambrisering, toog, spiegels en bankjes staan te trillen als de tram langskomt !

KOEKELBERG - *plan p. 17 :*

Le Liseron d'eau, av. Seghers 105, ✉ 1081, ☎ 0 2 414 68 61, *Fax 0 2 414 68 61,* Cuisine vietnamienne - AE MC VISA W k
fermé août, merc. et sam. midi - **Repas** Lunch 12 - 18/33.
◆ Restaurant vietnamien jouxtant la basilique du Sacré-Cœur. Intérieur contemporain d'un exotisme mesuré et ambiance musicale en rapport. Choix aussi explicite qu'étoffé.
◆ Vietnamees restaurant naast de Basiliek van het H. Hart. Hedendaags interieur met een licht exotisch accent en bijpassende achtergrondmuziek. Ruime keuze.

MOLENBEEK-ST-JEAN (SINT-JANS-MOLENBEEK) - *plan p. 8 :*

Béguine des Béguines, r. Béguines 168, ✉ 1080, ☎ 0 2 414 77 70, *Fax 0 2 414 77 70,* Avec cuisine à la bière - AE MC VISA AL m
fermé 21 juil.-15 août, sam. midi, dim. soir et lundi - **Repas** Lunch 14 - 27/36.
◆ Rares sont les béguines à cette accueillante table de style néo-rustique qui demeure toutefois, depuis plus de vingt ans, le béguin des amateurs de cuisine à la bière belge.
◆ Restaurant in neorustieke stijl dat al ruim 20 jaar Belgische specialiteiten serveert. Een belangrijk ingrediënt is bier, wat de gerechten een heel speciaal aroma geeft.

ST-GILLES (SINT-GILLIS) - *plans p. 12 et 14 :*

Cascade sans rest, r. Berckmans 128, ✉ 1060, ☎ 0 2 538 88 30, *info@cascadehotel.be, Fax 0 2 538 92 79* – 25. AE VISA JCB. ES r
80 ch 215/280.
◆ Bâti autour d'une grande cour intérieure, cet immeuble récent et moderne abrite de coquettes chambres standard correctement équipées, avec moquette et double vitrage.
◆ Hotel in een nieuw en modern gebouw rondom een grote binnenplaats. Keurige en comfortabele standaardkamers die van vaste vloerbedekking en dubbele beglazing zijn voorzien.

Le Forcado, chaussée de Charleroi 192, ✉ 1060, ☎ 0 2 537 92 20, *Fax 0 2 537 92 20,* Cuisine portugaise – AE VISA FU a
fermé sem. carnaval, août, dim., lundi et jours fériés – **Repas** (dîner seult) carte env. 35.
◆ Un petit coin de Portugal : salle à manger feutrée ornée de vieilles lanternes et rehaussée d'azulejos, lumineuse véranda, carte lusitanienne avec menu "vin compris".
◆ Een stukje Portugal in Brussel : eetzaal met azulejo's en oude lantaarns, zonnige serre en Lusitaanse kaart met een menu waarbij de wijn inclusief is.

Khnopff, r. St-Bernard 1, ✉ 1060, ☎ 0 2 534 20 04, *info@khnopff.be, Fax 0 2 534 34 95* – AE VISA FT a
fermé sam. midi et dim. – **Repas** *Lunch 13* – 26/40, ♀.
◆ Le peintre symboliste belge Fernand Khnopff brossa quelques toiles en ces lieux, d'où l'enseigne du restaurant. Accueil charmant, cuisine du moment et ambiance "trendy".
◆ De Belgische symbolistische schilder Fernand Khnopff had hier zijn atelier, vandaar de naam van het restaurant. Vriendelijke ontvangst, actuele keuken en trendy sfeer.

Coimbra, av. Jean Volders 54, ✉ 1060, ☎ 0 2 538 65 35, *info@restaurant-coimbra.be, Fax 0 2 538 65 35,* Avec cuisine portugaise – AE VISA. ET r
fermé août et merc. – **Repas** 29/35.
◆ Les standards de la cuisine portugaise, révélés dans un intérieur chargé, mais des plus typiques, revêtu de carreaux de faïence. Quelques plats bourgeois. Vins de là-bas.
◆ Hier kunt u kennismaken met de toppers van de Portugese keuken. Drukke inrichting, typisch Portugees, met tegels van aardewerk. Uiteraard komt de wijn ook uit het land zelf.

Turon arrière-salle, r. Danemark 29, ✉ 1060, ☎ 0 2 534 01 74, Taverne-rest, cuisine espagnole – AE VISA. EST c
fermé 20 juil.-20 août et mardi – **Repas** *Lunch 10* – carte 22 à 37, ♀.
◆ À deux pas de la gare du Midi, sympathique café-restaurant espagnol tenu en famille. Mets, cave, atmosphère et clientèle en accord, "muy tipico" !
◆ Dit gezellige café-restaurant bij het station Brussel-Zuid is in handen van een Spaanse familie. Het eten, het drinken en de ambiance zijn "muy tipico español" !

El Madrileño, chaussée de Waterloo 50, ✉ 1060, ☎ 0 2 537 69 82, Café espagnol, ouvert jusqu'à 23 h ET u
fermé août, merc. soir et jeudi – **Repas** *Lunch 13* – carte 22 à 51.
◆ Authentiques spécialités ibériques servies dans un petit bar-restaurant très "couleur locale" avec sa rangée de jambons suspendus au-dessus du comptoir. Musique du pays.
◆ Authentieke Spaanse schotels in een Madrileens café-restaurant met dikke hammen boven de bar en veel "couleur locale". Opzwepende Spaanse muziek.

Quartier Louise *(voir aussi Bruxelles et Ixelles) - plans p. 12 et 14 :*

Manos Premier (annexe Manos Stéphanie 50 ch - 5 suites), chaussée de Charleroi 102, ✉ 1060, ☎ 0 2 537 96 82 et 0 2 533 18 30 (rest), *manos@manoshotel.com, Fax 0 2 539 36 55,* – ch, – 25 à 100. AE VISA JCB. ch FU w
Repas ***Kolya*** *(fermé 2 prem. sem. août, 2 dern. sem. déc., sam. midi et dim.)* (ouvert jusqu'à 23 h) *Lunch 15* – 35 – **44 ch** 285/310, – 5 suites.
◆ La grâce d'un hôtel particulier fin 19e s. doté d'un riche mobilier Louis XV et Louis XVI. Breakfast sous véranda, jardin d'agrément et espaces fitness. Restaurant chic avec "lounge" feutré et jolie terrasse dressée sur un patio rafraîchissant.
◆ Elegant hotel in een herenhuis uit de late 19e eeuw, prachtig ingericht met Louis XV- en Louis XVI-meubilair. Fitnessruimte, siertuin en ontbijtserre voor een goed begin van de dag. Chic restaurant met lounge en mooi terras op een heerlijk koele patio.

NH Brussels City Centre, chaussée de Charleroi 17, ✉ 1060, ☎ 0 2 539 01 60, *nhbrussels.city.centre@nh-hotels.com, Fax 0 2 537 90 11* – – 25 à 75. AE VISA FS w
Repas *(fermé sam. midi et dim. midi)* carte 22 à 35 – 19 – **246 ch** 175/215.
◆ Cet immeuble trapu perché sur les hauteurs de la ville met diverses catégories de chambres - dont une dizaine d'"executives" - à votre disposition. Accueil dynamique. Nouvelle brasserie où l'on trouvera son bonheur au déjeuner comme au dîner.
◆ Dit massieve gebouw staat in de bovenstad. Het beschikt over verschillende categorieën kamers, waarvan een tiental "executives". Dynamische ontvangst. Nieuwe brasserie, waar zowel gerechten voor de lunch als het diner worden geserveerd.

NH Stéphanie sans rest, r. Jean Stas 32, ✉ 1060, ☎ 0 2 537 42 50, *nhstephanie@nh-hotels.be, Fax 0 2 539 33 79* – 🛗 ⇔ 📺 🚗 – 🏛 30. AE ⓓ ⓜ VISA FS a
68 ch ☕ 190/210.
◆ Hôtel de chaîne implanté en léger retrait du tumulte occasionné par la très grouillante place Stéphanie. Chambres claires et actuelles. Parking public tout à côté.
◆ Dit hotel is onderdeel van een keten en ligt even buiten het lawaai van het drukke Stefaniaplein. Moderne, lichte kamers. Openbare parkeergarage ernaast.

I Trulli, r. Jourdan 18, ✉ 1060, ☎ 0 2 537 79 30, *Fax 0 2 538 98 20*, 🏡, Cuisine italienne, ouvert jusqu'à 23 h – ▤. AE ⓓ ⓜ VISA JCB FS c
fermé du 11 au 31 juil., 21 déc.-5 janv. et dim. – **Repas** Lunch 17 – carte 37 à 70.
◆ Recettes italianisantes dont les saveurs "pugliese" trouvent un écho dans les peintures murales montrant des trulli, maisons typiques des Pouilles. Buffet d'antipasti.
◆ Mediterrane gerechten met Zuid-Italiaanse invloeden die ook zijn terug te vinden in de muurschilderingen van "trulli", de voor Apulië zo kenmerkende huizen. Antipasti-buffet.

Couleurs et Saveurs, chaussée de Charleroi 73, ✉ 1060, ☎ 0 2 539 19 75, *micheldebauw@skynet.be, Fax 0 2 539 45 93*, 🏡, Avec cuisine créole, ouvert jusqu'à 23 h – ▤. AE ⓓ ⓜ VISA FT e
fermé du 15 au 30 juil., sam. midi et dim. – **Repas** Lunch 19 – carte 33 à 44, ♀.
◆ Derrière la façade d'une maison bourgeoise, salle à manger où règne une ambiance gentiment "doudou". Appétissante carte aux accents créoles. Agréable terrasse estivale.
◆ In dit restaurant in een herenhuis hangt een vrolijke Antilliaanse sfeer. Appetijtelijke kaart met Creoolse accenten. Aangenaam terras in de zomer.

La Faribole, r. Bonté 6, ✉ 1060, ☎ 0 2 537 82 23, *Fax 0 2 537 82 23* – ▤. AE ⓓ ⓜ VISA FT g
fermé 21 juil.-18 août, sam. midi, dim. et lundi soir – **Repas** Lunch 13 – 25/35 bc.
◆ Cuisine mi-classique, mi-"bistrot" servie dans un décor méditerranéen mignon comme tout. Menu du marché, ardoise à suggestions, et point de fariboles !
◆ Klassieke spijzen en bistrogerechten geserveerd in een sfeervol mediterraan decor. Menu van de markt en dagsuggesties op een schoolbord. Het leven kan zo simpel zijn !

ST-JOSSE-TEN-NOODE (SINT-JOOST-TEN-NODE) - *plan p. 12* :

Quartier Botanique *(voir aussi Bruxelles) : - plan p. 12* :

Gd H. Mercure Royal Crown, r. Royale 250, ✉ 1210, ☎ 0 2 220 66 11, *H1728@accor-hotels.com, Fax 0 2 217 84 44*, 🏋, 🛁 – 🛗 ⇔ ▤ 📺 🚗 – 🏛 50 à 550. AE ⓓ ⓜ VISA JCB. ✻ rest FQ r
Repas voir rest ***Rue Royale*** ci-après – ☕ 20 – **310 ch** 235, – 4 suites.
◆ Confortable hôtel de chaîne avoisinant le Botanique (Centre culturel) et ses jardins en terrasse. Nombreuses salles de conférences, voiturier, bagagiste et room-service.
◆ Comfortabel ketenhotel naast de Botanique (Waals cultureel centrum) met zijn tuinen en terras. Verscheidene congreszalen, valetparking, kruier en roomservice.

Crowne Plaza, r. Gineste 3, ✉ 1210, ☎ 0 2 203 62 00, *sales@crowneplaza.gth.be, Fax 0 2 203 55 55*, 🏡, 🏋 – 🛗 ⇔ ▤ 📺 – 🏛 25 à 500. AE ⓓ ⓜ VISA. ✻ FQ v
Repas *(fermé sam. et dim. midi)* Lunch 15 – 35 – ☕ 24 – **356 ch** 150/300, – 1 suite.
◆ Palace Belle Époque dont quelques chambres sont encore animées de l'esprit "1900". Communs agrémentés de meubles de style, centre de séminaires et d'affaires. Grande brasserie Art déco attirant une clientèle assez huppée.
◆ Luxehotel uit de belle époque met enkele kamers uit dezelfde stijlperiode. Stijlmeubelen in de lounge en andere gemeenschappelijke gedeelten. Congreszaal en business center. Grote brasserie in art-decostijl, waar een vrij chic publiek komt.

Comfort Art H. Siru, pl. Rogier 1, ✉ 1210, ☎ 0 2 203 35 80, *art.hotel.siru@skynet.be, Fax 0 2 203 33 03* – 🛗 ⇔ 📺 – 🏛 25 à 80. AE ⓓ ⓜ VISA JCB. ✻ rest FQ p
Repas *Le Saint-Germain* *(fermé 15 juil.-15 août, sam., dim. et jours fériés)* (brasserie) Lunch 14 – carte 30 à 46, ♀ – **101 ch** ☕ 130 – ½ P 150/170.
◆ Le décor de chacune des chambres de cet immeuble "années folles" a été confié à un artiste belge contemporain différent. Les lieux accueillirent jadis Verlaine et Rimbaud. Table jouant la carte "brasserie parisienne", assortie au décor. Ambiance décontractée.
◆ Elke kamer van dit hotel uit de "roerige jaren twintig", waar Verlaine en Rimbaud ooit verbleven, is gedecoreerd door een hedendaagse Belgische kunstenaar. Het restaurant ademt de sfeer van een Parijse brasserie met dito kaart.

Villa Royale, r. Royale 195, ✉ 1210, ☎ 0 2 226 04 60, *Fax 0 2 226 04 80*, 🛁 – 🛗 ⇔, ▤ ch, 📺. AE ⓓ ⓜ VISA. ✻ ch FQ f
fermé juil. – **Repas** *(fermé sam. midi et dim. soir)* Lunch 7 – 24 – **45 ch** ☕ 110/125.
◆ Cet immeuble élevé au bord d'une artère passante constitue un bon point de chute pour découvrir la capitale de l'Europe. Chambres actuelles munies du double vitrage. Préparations sagement bourgeoises servies dans une salle des repas de notre temps.
◆ Deze locatie aan een doorgaande weg vormt een goede uitvalsbasis om de hoofdstad van Europa te verkennen. Moderne kamers met dubbele ramen. Eigentijdse eetzaal, waar de gasten traditionele gerechten krijgen voorgeschoteld.

XXX **Rue Royale** - Gd H. Mercure Royal Crown, r. Royale 250, ✉ 1210, ☎ 0 2 220 66 11, *H1728@accor-hotels.com, Fax 0 2 217 84 44* - AE VISA JCB. FQ r
fermé 18 juil.-15 août, sam., dim. et jours fériés – **Repas** *Lunch 25* – carte 35 à 55.
• Cadre "seventies" et cuisine actuelle, avec un lunch-menu bien ficelé, valorisée par l'aguichante sélection "grands vins Mercure". Au total, un agréable restaurant d'hôtel.
• Dit restaurant hoort bij het Mercure-hotel. Jaren zeventig interieur en eigentijdse keuken met een aantrekkelijk lunchmenu, waarbij de selectie Mercure-wijnen perfect past.

X **Les Dames Tartine,** chaussée de Haecht 58, ✉ 1210, ☎ 0 2 218 45 49, *Fax 0 2 218 45 49* - VISA FQ s
fermé 3 prem. sem. août, sam. midi, dim. et lundi – **Repas** *Lunch 19* – 30/39.
• Deux "Dames Tartine" sont aux commandes de cette intime petite maison fidèle à son passé. On s'attable sur des socles de machines à coudre, parmi les portraits des aïeux.
• Twee "Dames Tartine" zwaaien de scepter in dit eettentje, dat het verleden in ere houdt. Er wordt gegeten aan oude naaimachinetafels, onder het wakend oog van de voorvaderen.

SCHAERBEEK (SCHAARBEEK) - *plans p. 12 et 13* :

XX **Le Stelle,** av. Louis Bertrand 53, ✉ 1030, ☎ 0 2 245 03 59, *lestelle53@hotmail.com, Fax 0 2 245 03 59*, Cuisine italienne avec trattoria Osteria – 25 à 70. AE VISA GQ a
Repas *Lunch 11* – carte 35 à 59.
• Restaurant italien "classico", dans ses recettes comme dans son confort, complété d'une trattoria-osteria au cachet Belle Époque, où la formule buffets a ses inconditionnels.
• Italiaans restaurant dat heel "classico" is, zowel qua receptuur als comfort, aangevuld met een trattoria in belle-époquestijl, waar de buffetformule een groot succes is.

X **Senza Nome** (Bruno), r. Royale Ste-Marie 22, ✉ 1030, ☎ 0 2 223 16 17, *senzanome@skynet.be, Fax 0 2 223 16 17*, Cuisine italienne – VISA. FQ u
fermé août, 23 déc.-1er janv., sam. midi et dim. – **Repas** carte 38 à 47, ♀.
• Malgré dix ans de présence, ce très bon petit "ristorante" demeure "Sans Nom". Alléchantes suggestions transalpines à l'écriteau. Vins de là-bas. Ambiance familiale assortie.
• Ondanks zijn tienjarig bestaan blijft dit familierestaurantje "zonder naam". Uitstekende Italiaanse suggesties op een leien bord en wijnen van daarginder. Gemoedelijke sfeer.
Spéc. Vitello de Tonnato. Linguine Vongole. Panna Cotta

X **La Buca di Bacco,** av. Louis Bertrand 65, ✉ 1030, ☎ 0 2 242 42 30, *Fax 0 2 242 42 30*, Cuisine italienne avec buffet, ouvert jusqu'à 23 h – AE VISA GQ e
fermé lundi – **Repas** *Lunch 15* – carte 28 à 52, ♀.
• "Enoteca" à façade Art nouveau. Buffet d'antipasti, carte italienne, suggestions orales et très beau choix de vins mûris dans la "Botte". Zinc parisien de 1870 en salle.
• "Enoteca" met art-nouveaugevel. Antipasti tafel, Italiaanse kaart, suggesties en bijzonder fraai assortiment wijnen uit heel Italië. Parijse tapkast uit 1870 in de eetzaal.

Quartier Meiser : - *plan p. 13* :

Lambermont sans rest (annexes 61 chs -), bd Lambermont 322, ✉ 1030, ☎ 0 2 242 55 95, *info@lambermont-hotel.com, Fax 0 2 215 36 13* – AE VISA JCB GHQ c
45 ch 110/120.
• Sur un grand boulevard dont il emprunte le nom, immeuble hôtelier de bon confort, excentré mais profitant d'un accès aisé au centre et du calme d'un quartier bourgeois.
• Gerieflijk en rustig gelegen hotel buiten het centrum, dat gemakkelijk te bereiken is via de grote boulevard waaraan het Lambermont zijn naam ontleent.

X **Amici miei,** bd Général Wahis 248, ✉ 1030, ☎ 0 2 705 49 80, *Fax 0 2 705 29 65*, Cuisine italienne – AE VISA HQ k
fermé sam. midi et dim. – carte 23 à 47.
• L'Amici miei (mes Amis), c'est aussi l'ami des vedettes du "showbiz" et du sport, à en juger par le décor. Et comme les amis de "mes Amis" sont nos amis... Cuisine italienne.
• "Amici miei" is ook de vriend van sterren en sportcoryfeeën, getuige de fotocollectie van deze Italiaan. En aangezien de vrienden van "mijn vrienden" onze vrienden zijn...

UCCLE (UKKEL) - *plans p. 14 et 15 sauf indication spéciale* :

County House, square des Héros 2, ✉ 1180, ☎ 0 2 375 44 20, *countyhouse@skynet.be, Fax 0 2 375 31 22* – rest, – 25 à 150. AE VISA. EX b
Repas carte 34 à 45 – **86 ch** 175, – 16 suites.
• Nombreuses plus-values récentes dans ce building jouxtant le parc Wolvendael. Toutes les chambres, correctement équipées, s'agrémentent d'une terrasse séparée. Ample salle de restaurant. Cuisine d'aujourd'hui avec formule quatre services en semaine.
• Dit hotel bij het Wolvendaelpark is de laatste tijd sterk verbeterd. De kamers zijn van alle comfort voorzien en hebben een privé-terras. Groot restaurant met een eigentijdse kaart en een viergangenmenu door de week.

XXXX **Le Chalet de la Forêt,** Drêve de Lorraine 43, ✉ 1180, ✆ 0 2 374 54 16, *chaletdelaforet@skynet.be, Fax 0 2 374 35 71,* 余 - P - 30. AE ① MC VISA
fermé sam. et dim. – **Repas** *Lunch 24* – carte 59 à 82, ♀.
◆ Ancienne laiterie nichée en lisière de la forêt de Soignes. Belles salles au décor contemporain très "léché", cuisine au goût du jour et sélection vineuse bien balancée.
◆ Oude melkerij aan de rand van het Zoniënwoud. Mooie eetzalen met een zeer gelikt modern decor, eigentijdse keuken en evenwichtige wijnkaart. plan p. 11 CN c

XXX **Les Frères Romano,** av. de Fré 182, ✉ 1180, ✆ 0 2 374 70 98, *Fax 0 2 374 04 18* – P. AE ① MC VISA FX d
fermé 1 sem. Pâques, 2 dern. sem. août et dim. – **Repas** *Lunch 35* – carte 40 à 64.
◆ Trois frères président au destin de cette élégante villa 1900 interprétant sans fausses notes un répertoire culinaire traditionnel, quelquefois sobrement actualisé.
◆ Drie broers dirigeren dit restaurant in een villa uit 1900, waar zonder wanklank een traditioneel culinair repertoire wordt vertolkt, soms met een licht vernieuwende noot.

XXX **Villa d'Este,** r. Etoile 142, ✉ 1180, ✆ 0 2 376 48 48, *Fax 0 2 376 48 48,* 余 – P. AE ① MC VISA plan p. 10 BN p
fermé juil., fin déc., dim. soir et lundi – **Repas** 30/50.
◆ Deux beaux menus multi-choix ("tradition" ou "prestige") et deux cartes des vins - la vigne ne pousse-t-elle pas en terrasse ? - s'offrent à vous dans cette villa bourgeoise.
◆ Twee mooie keuzemenu's ("traditie" of "prestige") en twee verschillende wijnkaarten - de druiven zijn immers zo te plukken op het terras - bieden zich aan in deze villa.

XX **Blue Elephant,** chaussée de Waterloo 1120, ✉ 1180, ✆ 0 2 374 49 62, *brussels@blueelephant.com, Fax 0 2 375 44 68,* Cuisine thaïlandaise – P. AE ① MC VISA.
fermé sam. midi – **Repas** *Lunch 12* – 45. GX j
◆ Antiquités du pays, confort "rotin", compositions florales et mise en place très "couleur locale" entretiennent l'ambiance exotique de cette table thaïlandaise.
◆ Authentiek Thais restaurant met veel Aziatisch antiek, comfortabele rotanmeubelen, prachtige bloemstukken en een exotische ambiance. Een aanrader !

XX **Le Pain et le Vin,** chaussée d'Alsemberg 812a, ✉ 1180, ✆ 0 2 332 37 74, *info@painvin.be, Fax 0 2 332 17 40,* 余 – AE MC VISA plan p. 10 BN z
fermé Pâques, prem. sem. sept., Noël, Nouvel An, sam. midi, dim. et lundi – **Repas** *Lunch 19* – carte 42 à 69, ♀.
◆ Salle à manger moderne et épurée laissant entrevoir le "piano" où mijotent sagement les produits de saison. Côté cave, l'embarras du choix... et de précieux conseils.
◆ De moderne, gestileerde eetzaal heeft een halfopen keuken, waar seizoengebonden gerechten worden bereid. Keus te over op de wijnkaart, maar gelukkig krijgt u vakkundig advies.

XX **A'mbriana,** r. Edith Cavell 151, ✉ 1180, ✆ 0 2 375 01 56, *Fax 0 2 375 84 96,* Avec cuisine italienne – AE ① MC VISA FX f
fermé août, lundi soir, mardi et sam. midi – **Repas** *Lunch 18* – 32/42 bc.
◆ Cuisine traditionnelle transalpine concoctée à la minute par la "Fée du logis" (A'mbriana) et assortie, comme il se doit, de vins du cru. Carte avec lunch et menus.
◆ Traditionele Italiaanse gerechten "al dente", waarvan de smaak goed tot zijn recht komt bij een lekkere wijn uit het land. Kaart met lunchformule en menu's.

X **Bon-Bon** (Hardiquest), r. Carmélites 93, ✉ 1180, ✆ 0 2 346 66 15, *Fax 0 2 346 66 15* – AE ① MC VISA. EV a
fermé 21 juil.-15 août, du 1er= au 7 janv., sam. midi, dim. et lundi – **Repas** *Lunch 25* – carte 49 à 71.
◆ Comptoir, lambris, parquet, jeux de miroirs, chaises en fer forgé et lustre en cristal : voilà pour le décor. Bonne cuisine d'aujourd'hui ; ingrédients d'origines certifiées.
◆ Een toog, lambrisering, parketvloer, spiegels, smeedijzeren stoelen en kristallen kroonluchter : het décor is gezet ! Smakelijke, actuele keuken ; produkten van goede herkomst.
Spéc. Brochette de ris de veau citronné aux langoustines. Volaille de l'Aisne et barigoule de violets. Gratin de fraises des bois

X **Le Lion,** chaussée de Waterloo 889, ✉ 1180, ✆ 0 2 374 48 43, *Fax 0 2 374 41 97,* Cuisine chinoise – AE ① MC VISA FX p
Repas *Lunch 9* – 24/27.
◆ Deux lions gardent l'entrée de cet établissement chinois offrant un choix abondant et bien commenté. Cadre soigné, avec pièces d'eau intérieures où batifolent des carpes.
◆ Twee leeuwen bewaken de ingang van dit Chinese restaurant, dat een keur van heerlijke gerechten biedt. Verzorgd interieur met vijvertjes waarin karpers spartelen.

X **Le Petit Prince,** av. du Prince de Ligne 16, ✉ 1180, ✆ 0 2 374 73 03, *lepetitprince@skynet.be, Fax 0 2 381 26 50* – AE ① MC VISA plan p. 10 BCN s
fermé dim. soir et lundi – **Repas** *Lunch 13* – 25/45 bc.
◆ Dessine-moi un mouton, ou plutôt, un gigotin d'agneau colorié au miel et tacheté de thym ! Sagement bourgeoise, la cuisine du Petit Prince propose d'avantageux menus.
◆ Deze Kleine Prins biedt voordelige menu's met traditionele gerechten als lamsrug met honing en tijm. Om de vingers bij af te likken !

X **Brasseries Georges,** av. Winston Churchill 259, ✉ 1180, ☎ 0 2 347 21 00, *info@brasseriesgeorges.be, Fax 0 2 344 02 45,* ⛱, Ecailler, ouvert jusqu'à minuit – ▤ P. AE ⓓ ⓜ VISA FV n
Repas *Lunch 20* – carte 26 à 46, ♀.
◆ L'une des plus grandes brasseries-écailler bruxelloises aménagées "à la parisienne". Petit "menu zinc" au déjeuner. Ambiance et service aimables. Voiturier bien pratique.
◆ Deze grootste brasserie en oesterbar van Brussel ademt een typisch Parijse sfeer. Het "menu zinc" is ideaal als snelle lunch. Vriendelijke bediening en valetparking.

X **L'Eau Bénite,** av. Brugmann 518, ✉ 1180, ☎ 0 2 347 05 89, *Fax 0 2 347 08 18,* ⛱ – AE ⓜ VISA EX s
fermé sam. midi et dim. – **Repas** *Lunch 13* – 25/34 bc, ♀.
◆ Dans une villa au décor chaleureux. Assiettes au goût du jour et bon choix de vins, avec l'option "surprise" qui consiste en une dégustation à l'aveugle.
◆ Villa met een warm aandoend interieur. Eigentijdse keuken en mooie wijnkaart met een verrassing van het huis, die bestaat uit een blinde proeverij.

X **Les Deux Frères,** av. Vanderaey 2 (hauteur 810 de la chaussée d'Alsemberg), ✉ 1180, ☎ 0 2 376 76 06, *info@les2freres.be, Fax 0 2 332 38 08,* Ouvert jusqu'à 23 h – AE ⓓ ⓜ VISA. ✈ plan p. 10 BN e
fermé 28 juil.-15 août, 24 déc.-1er janv., sam. midi et dim. – **Repas** *Lunch 12* – 25/40.
◆ Refuge gourmand où flotte une atmosphère romantique rappelant un peu les années d'entre-deux-guerres. Carte pourtant bien dans le coup. Démocratique formule lunch.
◆ Lekker restaurant met een romantische sfeer die een beetje aan de jaren dertig doet denken. De kaart voldoet echter aan de huidige smaak en biedt een schappelijk lunchmenu.

X **Le Petit Pont,** r. Doyenné 114, ✉ 1180, ☎ 0 2 346 49 49, *lepetitpont@tiscalinet.be, Fax 0 2 346 44 38,* ⛱, Ouvert jusqu'à minuit – ▤. AE ⓓ ⓜ VISA EX a
Repas *Lunch 11* – 24.
◆ Bistrot-restaurant au décor empreint de nostalgie : vieux cadres et plaques émaillées, collection d'anciens postes de radio. Saveurs "brasserie" et spécialités régionales.
◆ Deze bistro straalt een en al nostalgie uit : vergeelde foto's, geëmailleerde reclameborden en een verzameling oude radio's. Regionale specialiteiten.

X **Les Petits Pères,** r. Carmélites 149, ✉ 1180, ☎ 0 2 345 66 71, *Fax 0 2 345 66 71,* ⛱, Ouvert jusqu'à 23 h – ▤. AE ⓓ ⓜ VISA EV s
fermé du 1er au 15 août, dim. et lundi – **Repas** *Lunch 10* – carte 22 à 34.
◆ On doit traverser la cuisine pour s'attabler dans ce sympathique petit restaurant de quartier occupant deux maisons ouvrières. Recettes embourgeoisées et accueil avenant.
◆ Via de keuken komt u bij uw tafeltje in dit vriendelijke buurtrestaurant, dat in twee arbeidershuisjes is gevestigd. Traditionele keuken en voorkomende bediening.

X **Le Coq au Vin,** chaussée d'Alsemberg 897, ✉ 1180, ☎ 0 2 376 43 13, *Fax 0 2 376 43 13* – AE ⓜ VISA. ✈ plan p. 10 BN x
fermé sam. midi et dim. – **Repas** 30/45.
◆ La volaille bressane et les délicatesses bourguignonnes sont à l'honneur à cette enseigne pour le moins... "cocorico" ! Appétissante carte "tradition". Lunch et menus-choix.
◆ Kip uit Bresse en wijn uit de Bourgogne vormen een perfect koppel in dit restaurant, waar de haan koning kraait ! Aanlokkelijke kaart met traditionele schotels en menu's.

X **Le Petit Cottage,** r. Cottages 150, ✉ 1180, ☎ 0 2 343 88 09, ⛱ – AE ⓜ VISA EV b
fermé 3 sem. en juil., sam. midi, dim., lundi et mardi soir – **Repas** *Lunch 21* – 30/65 bc, ♀.
◆ Décor intérieur cossu façon "cottage", cuisine bien à la page, produits choisis avec soin et présentations esthétiques sur l'assiette. Un bon moment de table s'annonce !
◆ Het fraaie interieur doet denken aan een cottage. Hedendaagse keuken met uitgekozen ingredienten. Oogstrelende opmaak van de borden. Hier staat tafelgenot op het menu !

Quartier St-Job *- plan p. 10 :*

XX **Les Menus Plaisirs,** r. Basse 7, ✉ 1180, ☎ 0 2 374 69 36, *lesmenusplaisirs@belgacom.net, Fax 0 2 331 38 13,* ⛱ – AE ⓓ ⓜ VISA BN u
fermé 1 sem. carnaval, 1 sem. Pâques, prem. sem. sept., Noël-Nouvel An, sam. midi, dim. et lundi soir – **Repas** *Lunch 13* – 30.
◆ Coquette petite adresse bien assise dans le quartier, grâce à un registre culinaire actuel gentiment personnalisé. L'été, les "menus plaisirs" s'apprécient au jardin.
◆ Prima adresje met een goede naam in de buurt. Moderne recepten met een persoonlijke inbreng. 's Zomers kan in de tuin van de "kleine pleziertjes" van het leven worden genoten.

XX **le pré en bulle,** av. J. et P. Carsoel 5, ✉ 1180, ☎ 0 2 374 08 80, *Fax 0 2 372 93 67,* ⛱ – P. AE ⓜ VISA BN r
fermé lundi soir et mardi – **Repas** *Lunch 13* – 28/44 bc, ♀.
◆ Fermette du 17e s. au décor simple mais mignon, où vous attend une carte classico-créative assortie de plusieurs menus tentateurs. Agréable terrasse pour les beaux jours.
◆ 17e-eeuws boerderijtje, simpel maar smaakvol ingericht, waar de chef-kok creatief aan de slag gaat met klassieke recepten. Aantrekkelijke menu's. Fijn terras voor mooie dagen.

Le Passage, av. J. et P. Carsoel 13, ✉ 1180, ☎ 0 2 374 66 94, *restaurant@lepassage.be, Fax 0 2 374 69 26,* – P. AE ⓓ MC VISA BN q
fermé 3 sem. en juil., prem. sem. janv., sam. midi, dim. et jours fériés – **Repas** Lunch 19 – 36/46, carte 40 à 68.
◆ L'imagination est aux fourneaux de ce restaurant de poche jouant paisiblement dans la cour des grands. Salle à manger rehaussée de discrètes touches méridionales.
◆ Dit piepkleine restaurantje, waar een fantasievolle chef-kok de scepter zwaait, doet niet onder voor zijn grote broers. De eetzaal heeft hier en daar een Zuid-Franse toets.
Spéc. Carpaccio de bœuf et foie d'oie aux brisures de truffes. Escalopines de ris de veau croustillantes, épinards et beurre au citron. Blanc de turbotin cuit au lait épicé, mousseline de crevettes grises

Pasta Commedia, av. J. et P. Carsoel 3, ✉ 1180, ☎ 0 2 372 06 07, , Cuisine italienne, ouvert jusqu'à minuit – P. AE ⓓ MC VISA BN a
Repas Lunch 13 – carte 31 à 41, ♀.
◆ Préparations transalpines légères - dont les incontournables pâtes maison - servies dans un cadre inattendu, tenant du théâtre et de la trattoria. Cave italo-française.
◆ Licht Italiaans eten, zoals de onvermijdelijke verse pasta, in een origineel interieur, dat het midden houdt tussen een theater en een trattoria. Frans-Italiaanse wijnkaart.

WATERMAEL-BOITSFORT (WATERMAAL-BOSVOORDE)

- plan p. 11 sauf indication spéciale :

Au Repos des Chasseurs, av. Charle Albert 11, ✉ 1170, ☎ 0 2 660 46 72, *info@aureposdeschasseurs.be, Fax 0 2 672 12 84,* – TV – 25 à 80. AE MC VISA DN m
Repas (avec cuisine italienne, ouvert jusqu'à 23 h) Lunch 21 – carte 22 à 69 – **11 ch** 109/139.
◆ Les "chasseurs de repos" n'hésiteront pas à poser leurs besaces dans cette ancienne laiterie postée à l'orée du bois. Chambres confortablement aménagées. À table, choix de recettes classiques franco-italiennes. Vaste terrasse estivale.
◆ In deze oude herberg aan de rand van het bos kunnen jagers zich te ruste leggen in een van de comfortabel ingerichte kamers, na te hebben getafeld in klassieke Frans-Italiaanse stijl. Op zomerse dagen is het grote terras favoriet.

Au Vieux Boitsfort (Gillet), pl. Bischoffsheim 9, ✉ 1170, ☎ 0 2 672 23 32, *Fax 0 2 660 22 94,* – AE ⓓ MC VISA CN z
fermé 3 prem. sem. août, sam. midi et dim. – **Repas** (nombre de couverts limité - prévenir) 40/85 bc, carte 57 à 70, ♀.
◆ La façade d'une maison d'angle dissimule cette table ayant troqué ses atours d'antan contre un décor intérieur de notre temps. Cuisine classique soignée et cave bien montée.
◆ Dit restaurant is ondergebracht in een hoekpand dat zijn oude praal heeft verruild voor een eigentijds interieur. Verzorgde klassieke keuken en een goed opgezette wijnkelder.
Spéc. Escalope de foie d'oie poêlée et céleri confit. Risotto de Saint-Jacques au cresson et vieux parmesan. Noix de ris de veau à la crème d'artichauts en persillade d'échalotes

Le Grill, r. Trois Tilleuls 1, ✉ 1170, ☎ 0 2 672 95 13, *Fax 0 2 660 22 94,* – AE ⓓ MC VISA JCB CN r
fermé 2 prem. sem. juil., sam. midi et dim. – Repas 25.
◆ Maison officiant à un saut de chevreuil de la forêt de Soignes. Salle à manger joliment relookée dans l'esprit contemporain, carte classico-bourgeoise et bonnes grillades.
◆ Restaurant op een steenworp afstand van het Zoniënwoud. Eetzaal met een eigentijdse "look", klassiek-traditionele kaart en sappig vlees van de grill.

le Coriandre, r. Middelbourg 21, ✉ 1170, ☎ 0 2 672 45 65, *Fax 0 2 672 47 68* – AE ⓓ MC VISA CN n
fermé du 1er au 18 août, 1 sem. en janv., dim. et lundi – **Repas** Lunch 20 – 28/60 bc.
◆ Derrière une devanture aux vitres fumées, restaurant au goût du jour misant sur une carte avec menus multi-choix. Livre de cave intéressant. Glaces turbinées à la minute.
◆ Achter een pui met ramen van rookglas kan worden genoten van eigentijdse gerechten à la carte en verschillende keuzemenu's. Interessante wijnkelder. Zelfgemaakt ijs.

Le Dragon, pl. Léopold Wiener 11, ✉ 1170, ☎ 0 2 675 80 89, Cuisine chinoise – AE ⓓ MC VISA JCB CN a
fermé lundis non fériés – **Repas** Lunch 8 – 15/27 bc.
◆ Par la gentillesse de son accueil et la sagesse de sa carte, ce petit "chinois" de quartier a tôt fait de s'imposer sur la place, fidélisant une clientèle surtout locale.
◆ Dankzij de vriendelijke ontvangst en de aanlokkelijke kaart heeft deze Chinees snel een plaats in de buurt veroverd. Zeer populair bij de lokale bevolking.

X **Aux Portes du Béarn,** r. Philippe Dewolfs 7, ✉ 1170, ☎ 0 2 672 87 20, *Fax 0 2 672 87 20*, , Cuisine du Sud-Ouest – AE MC VISA CN b
fermé fin avril-début mai, 2 sem. en août, sam. midi, dim. soir et lundi – **Repas** *Lunch 14* – carte 34 à 48.
• Cet établissement vous ouvre les portes du Béarn. Chaises rhabillées, chemins de table et toiles modernes participent au décor de la salle à manger. Cuisine du Sud-Ouest.
• Dit etablissement opent voor u de poorten van de Béarn. Beklede stoelen, tafellopers en moderne doeken dragen bij aan de sfeer van de zaal. Keuken uit Zuidwest-Frankrijk.

WOLUWE-ST-LAMBERT (SINT-LAMBRECHTS-WOLUWE)

- plans p. 9 et 10 sauf indication spéciale :

Sodehotel La Woluwe, av. E. Mounier 5, ✉ 1200, ☎ 0 2 775 21 11, *sodehotel@sodehotel.be, Fax 0 2 770 47 80*, – – 25 à 200. AE MC VISA. rest DL e
Repas ***Leonard*** *Lunch 23* – carte 37 à 61 – 21 – **120 ch** 275/315, – 6 suites.
• Excentré, mais d'accès assez aisé, cet hôtel de chaîne aux chambres spacieuses conjugue tranquillité et confort moderne. Patio lumineux. Centre d'affaires et de congrès. Salle de restaurant contemporaine aux lignes épurées. Cuisine dans le tempo actuel.
• Dit ketenhotel bevindt zich buiten het centrum, dat echter goed bereikbaar is. De kamers zijn ruim, rustig en comfortabel. Lichte patio. Congreszalen en business center. Restaurant met een modern, gestileerd interieur. Kookstijl die past bij de huidige trend.

Monty sans rest, bd Brand Whitlock 101, ✉ 1200, ☎ 0 2 734 56 36, *info@monty-hotel.be, Fax 0 2 734 50 05* – . AE MC VISA plan p. 13 HS z
18 ch 100.
• Ancien hôtel particulier habilement rénové dans l'esprit contemporain. Le sens de l'accueil et l'aménagement design des parties communes et des chambres sont ses deux atouts.
• Dit oude herenhuis is fraai gerestaureerd in moderne stijl. Pluspunten zijn het gastvrije onthaal en het designinterieur van de kamers.

Lambeau sans rest, av. Lambeau 150, ✉ 1200, ☎ 0 2 732 51 70, *info@hotellambeau.com, Fax 0 2 732 54 90* – . AE MC VISA. plan p. 13 HR u
16 ch 77/93.
• Dans un quartier résidentiel, juste en face d'une sortie de métro, petit établissement familial renfermant de menues chambres sobres et actuelles, équipées à l'identique.
• Familiehotel in een rustige woonwijk, vlak tegenover het metrostation. De kleine kamers zijn sober en modern ingericht en hebben allemaal dezelfde voorzieningen.

XX **Da Mimmo,** av. du Roi Chevalier 24, ✉ 1200, ☎ 0 2 771 58 60, *mimmo1961@yahoo.it, Fax 0 2 771 58 60*, , Cuisine italienne – . AE MC VISA. CM b
fermé du 1er au 30 août, fin déc.-début janv., sam. midi et dim. – **Repas** *Lunch 25* – carte 43 à 67, ♀.
• Cuisine transalpine sans concessions aux habitudes alimentaires belges, servie dans une plaisante salle à manger actuelle. Bons vins reçus en direct de la "Botte".
• Italiaanse gerechten zonder concessies aan de Belgische eetgewoonten, geserveerd in een prettige, moderne eetzaal. Goede wijnen die uit Italië worden geïmporteerd.

XX ✿ **de Maurice à Olivier** (Detombe) dans l'arrière-salle d'une librairie, chaussée de Roodebeek 246, ✉ 1200, ☎ 0 2 771 33 98 – . AE MC VISA CM r
fermé du 15 au 31 juil., dim. et lundi soir – **Repas** *Lunch 20* – 40/50, carte 44 à 61 .
• Père et fils sont aux commandes de ce petit restaurant curieusement situé à l'arrière de la librairie paternelle. Saveurs "tradition" et ambiance "Bernard Pivot" !
• Vader en zoon zwaaien de scepter in dit traditionele restaurantje, dat merkwaardig genoeg achter in de boekhandel van papa is gevestigd. Gerechten met leesvoer dus !
Spéc. Foie gras d'oie et canard en terrine. Noix de cochon de lait rôtie et jus aigre-doux au poivre Sichuan. Faux mille-feuille de chocolat noir amer et café blanc, crème d'œuf au Costa Rica

X **le Nénuphar,** chaussée de Roodebeek 76, ✉ 1200, ☎ 0 2 770 08 88, *Fax 0 2 770 08 88*, , Cuisine vietnamienne – . AE MC VISA. plan p. 11 DM v
fermé août et sam. midi – **Repas** *Lunch 13* – 23/25 bc.
• Vietnamien de quartier niché dans une petite rue à sens unique. Choix typique bien présenté, intérieur fleuri et service avenant. L'été venu, attablez-vous au jardin.
• Vietnamees restaurant in een straatje met eenrichtingsverkeer. Authentieke keuken, bloemrijk interieur en attente bediening. Bij mooi weer kan in de tuin worden gegeten.

X **Le Brasero,** av. des Cerisiers 166, ✉ 1200, ☎ 0 2 772 63 94, *Fax 0 2 762 57 17*, – AE MC VISA. plan p. 11 CM e
fermé 23 déc.-2 janv., lundi et sam. midi – **Repas** *Lunch 17* – carte 27 à 43.
• Préparations variées, avec spécialité de grillades au feu de bois, dans cette agréable brasserie au cadre actuel. Plat du jour, lunch trois services et menu dominical.
• Prettig restaurant met een gevarieerde kaart in een hedendaags interieur. Op houtskool geroosterd vlees, dagschotel, lunchmenu met drie gangen en op zondag een speciaal menu.

X **La table de Mamy,** av. des Cerisiers 212, ✉ 1200, ☎ 0 2 779 00 96, 🍽 - AE ⓓ MC VISA CM d
fermé 3 sem. en août, sam. et dim. – **Repas** 25.
◆ Retrouvez, dans une atmosphère sympathique, les bon p'tits plats tels que nous les mitonnaient nos aïeux. Décor intérieur à la fois nostalgique et bien dans l'air du temps.
◆ In een gezellige ambiance vindt u hier de keuken uit grootmoeders tijd terug. De decoratie is nostalgisch, maar past ook wel goed bij de huidige mode.

X **Les Amis du Cep,** r. Th. Decuyper 136, ✉ 1200, ☎ 0 2 762 62 95, *Fax 0 2 771 20 32,* 🍽 - AE MC VISA JCB DL d
fermé 21 juil.-4 août, fin déc., dim. et lundi – **Repas** *Lunch 16* – carte env. 46, ♀.
◆ "Bistrot gourmand", précise l'enseigne de cette petite villa estimée pour sa cuisine au goût du jour arrosée d'une sélection vineuse "de derrière les fagots".
◆ "Bistrot gourmand" staat op het uithangbord van deze kleine villa. Wie eenmaal het eten en de wijn heeft geproefd, zal volmondig toegeven dat dit niets te veel is gezegd !

X **Le Coq en Pâte,** Tomberg 259, ✉ 1200, ☎ 0 2 762 19 71, *Fax 0 2 762 19 71,* 🍽, Avec cuisine italienne – AE ⓓ MC VISA CM b
fermé 1 sem. en sept., lundi et jeudi soir – **Repas** *Lunch 13* – 20/35 bc, ♀.
◆ Vous vous sentirez comme des coqs en pâte à cette adresse : recettes italianisantes dans l'air du temps, service souriant et efficace, terrasse estivale dressée sur le devant.
◆ Dit adresje valt zeer in de smaak vanwege de eigentijdse, Italiaans getinte gerechten, de vriendelijke en efficiënte bediening, en het zomerse terras langs de voorgevel.

WOLUWE-ST-PIERRE (SINT-PIETERS-WOLUWE)

- plans p. 9 et 11 sauf indication spéciale :

Montgomery ⛰, av. de Tervuren 134, ✉ 1150, ☎ 0 2 741 85 11, *banqueting@montgomery.be, Fax 0 2 741 85 00,* Ⅎ, ≘ - |♦| ⅍ ▤ TV 🚗 - 🏛 35. AE ⓓ MC VISA. ⅍ plan p. 13 HS k
Repas *(fermé du 17 au 25 juil., 18 déc.-2 janv., sam. et dim.)* 25, ♀ – ☕ 20 – **61 ch** 360/380, – 2 suites.
◆ Petit hôtel de luxe dont les chambres, personnalisées avec goût, s'inspirent de styles divers : colonial, anglais et "Ralph Lauren". Salon-bibliothèque, fitness et sauna. Restaurant assez "cosy". Cuisine bien dans le coup.
◆ Luxehotel waarvan de kamers smaakvol en met een persoonlijke toets in diverse stijlen zijn ingericht : koloniaal, Engels en "Ralph Lauren". Lounge met bibliotheek, fitnessruimte en sauna. Sfeervol restaurant met een trendy keuken.

XXX **Des 3 Couleurs,** av. de Tervuren 453, ✉ 1150, ☎ 0 2 770 33 21, *Fax 0 2 770 80 45,* 🍽 - AE MC VISA DN q
fermé 2 sem. Pâques, 2e quinz. août, sam. midi, dim. soir et lundi – **Repas** *Lunch 57 bc* – 52/99.
◆ Poutres et mobilier cérusés, assortis à la pierre de Bourgogne, donnent un certain cachet au décor intérieur de cette villa cossue. Carte classique. Jolie terrasse.
◆ Balken en meubelen van geceruseerd hout, die goed bij de Bourgondische steensoort passen, geven deze fraaie villa een zeker cachet. Klassieke menukaart. Prettig terras.

XXX **Le Vignoble de Margot,** av. de Tervuren 368, ✉ 1150, ☎ 0 2 779 23 23, *Fax 0 2 779 05 45,* �, 🍽, Avec écailler – ▤ P. AE ⓓ MC VISA. ⅍ DM r
fermé sam. midi, dim. et jours fériés – **Repas** carte 44 à 74.
◆ Près d'une passerelle design, dominant parcs et étangs, ancien buffet de gare entouré de son "vignoble". Choix classique élaboré, avec banc d'écailler. Salle de banquets.
◆ Voormalig stationnetje, omringd door zijn "wijngaard", vlak bij een mooie loopbrug naar het park en de vijvers. Klassieke menukaart met oesters. Aparte feestzaal.

XX ✿ **Les Deux Maisons** (Demartin), Val des Seigneurs 81, ✉ 1150, ☎ 0 2 771 14 47, *lesdeuxmaisons@skynet.be, Fax 0 2 771 14 47,* 🍽 - ▤. AE ⓓ MC VISA DM e
fermé prem. sem. Pâques, 3 prem. sem. août, Noël-Nouvel An, dim. et lundi – **Repas** 33/82 bc, carte 45 à 93.
◆ Sobre salle à manger au visage contemporain. Soigneuse cuisine classique actualisée que sublime une riche sélection de vins. Menus "Dégustation" et "Tradition".
◆ Sobere eetzaal in eigentijdse stijl. De goed verzorgde, modern-klassieke keuken komt subliem tot zijn recht bij de wijnen. Menu "dégustation" en menu "tradition".
Spéc. Bar en croûte de sel. Carpaccio de bonite au vinaigre d'abricot et gingembre confit. Blanquette de langues d'agneau à l'huile d'amandes

XX **Medicis,** av. de l'Escrime 124, ✉ 1150, ☎ 0 2 779 07 00, *Fax 0 2 779 19 24,* 🍽 - AE ⓓ MC VISA. ⅍ DM w
fermé Pâques, sam. midi et dim. – **Repas** *Lunch 15* – 30/55.
◆ Une villa de style anglo-normand abrite ce restaurant où une carte actuelle bien vue s'emploie à vous aiguiser l'appétit. Cave franco-italienne et bel assortiment de desserts.
◆ Villa in Anglo-Normandische stijl met een restaurant waarvan de eigentijdse menukaart een heerlijke maaltijd belooft. Keur van desserts en een Frans-Italiaanse wijnkelder.

XX **l'auberg'in,** r. au Bois 198, ✉ 1150, ☎ 0 2 770 68 85, *Fax 0 2 770 68 85*, 斎, Grillades – P. AE ① MC VISA DM s

fermé sam. midi, dim. et jours fériés – **Repas** 30.

◆ Fermette brabançonne du 19e s. convertie en restaurant convivial au décor néo-rustique, où grésille un âtre réconfortant. Spécialité de grillades exécutées en salle.

◆ Brabants boerderijtje dat is verbouwd tot een gezellig restaurant in neorustieke stijl met een knapperend haardvuur. De grillspecialiteiten worden in de eetzaal bereid.

X **La Tour d'Argent,** av. Salomé 1, ✉ 1150, ☎ 0 2 762 99 80, Cuisine vietnamienne – MC VISA DM b

fermé merc., jeudi midi et sam. midi – **Repas** Lunch 11 – 24.

◆ Glorieuse enseigne pour ce modeste établissement vietnamien tenu en famille. Dépaysantes recettes vagabondant entre Hanoï et Ho Chi Minh Ville. Accueil sympathique.

◆ Vietnamees eettentje dat niets te maken heeft met het beroemde gelijknamige restaurant in Parijs. Uitheemse recepten van Hanoi tot Ho Tsji Minhstad. Sympathieke ontvangst.

X **Le Train,** r. François Gay 152, ✉ 1150, ☎ 0 2 779 46 92, *restaurant@letrain.be, Fax 0 2 772 32 91* – 35. AE MC VISA. ✻

fermé 21 juil.-15 août, dim. et lundi – **Repas** Lunch 14 – 25/65 bc.

◆ Il flotte une atmosphère ferroviaire dans ce restaurant de quartier établi en angle de rue, pas loin de la petite ceinture. Cuisine du moment. Formule table d'hôte à l'avant.

◆ Dit buurtrestaurant op een hoek, niet ver van de ringweg, is als een trein ingericht. Moderne keuken met aantrekkelijke table d'hôte-formule.

ENVIRONS DE BRUXELLES

à Alsemberg *par chaussée d'Alsemberg* BP *: 12 km - plan p. 10 - C Beersel 23 043 h. – ✉ 1652 Alsemberg :*

XX **'t Hoogveld,** Alsembergsesteenweg 1057, ☎ 0 2 380 30 30, *Fax 0 2 381 06 07*, 斎 – P. AE ① MC VISA

fermé lundi soir, merc. soir et jeudi – **Repas** Lunch 16 – 28/73 bc.

◆ Cuisine classique de saison servie dans une fermette ancienne s'ouvrant sur un grand jardin à l'arrière. Salle à manger actuelle. Sage choix de vins français.

◆ Oud boerderijtje met een grote tuin aan de achterkant. In de hedendaagse eetzaal worden klassieke, seizoengebonden gerechten geserveerd. Fraai assortiment Franse wijnen.

à Beersel *- plan p. 10 – 23 043 h – ✉ 1650 Beersel :*

X **3 Fonteinen,** Herman Teirlinckplein 3, ☎ 0 2 331 06 52, *guido.debelder@pandora.be, Fax 0 2 331 07 03*, 斎, Taverne-rest, avec spécialités à la bière régionale – AE ① MC VISA AP v

fermé fin déc.-début janv., mardi et merc. – **Repas** carte 21 à 38.

◆ Taverne-restaurant dont la carte bourgeoise réjouira les amateurs de plats à la bière. Kriek et gueuze maison sortent de la micro-brasserie familiale, ouverte à la visite.

◆ In deze typisch Belgische taverne wordt veel met bier gekookt. De kriek en geuze komen uit de huisbrouwerij, die ook te bezichtigen is.

à Diegem *par A 201, sortie Diegem - plan p. 9 - C Machelen 11 972 h. – ✉ 1831 Diegem :*

Crowne Plaza Airport, Da Vincilaan 4, ☎ 0 2 416 33 33, *cpbrusselsairport@ichotelsgroup.com, Fax 0 2 416 33 44*, 斎, Fö, ≘s, – |‡| ⇔ ▤ TV ♿ P – 25 à 400. AE ① MC VISA. ✻ rest DK c

Repas carte env. 22 – ☐ 21 – **312 ch** 355/430, – 3 suites.

◆ Cette nouvelle unité de la chaîne Crowne Plaza s'intègre à un parc d'affaires côtoyant l'aéroport. Grandes chambres tout confort. Bonnes installations conférencières. Choix de préparations actuelles et formule "lunch-buffet" au restaurant.

◆ Nieuw hotel van de keten Crowne Plaza aan een business park dichtbij de luchthaven. Ruime kamers met alle comfort. Goede vergaderzalen. Keuze uit actuele bereidingen en formule lunch-buffet in het restaurant.

Sofitel Airport, Bessenveldstraat 15, ☎ 0 2 713 66 66, *H0548@accor-hotels.com, Fax 0 2 721 43 45*, Fö, ⛱ – ⇔ ▤ TV P – 25 à 300. AE ① MC VISA JCB. ✻ rest DL x

Repas ***La Pléiade*** *(fermé sam. midi et dim. midi)* Lunch 25 – carte 28 à 56, ♀ – ☐ 21 – **125 ch** 265/295.

◆ Hôtel de chaîne haut de gamme érigé au bord de l'autoroute, à 4 km des pistes de Zaventem. Équipement complet pour loisirs et conférences. Silencieuses chambres rénovées. Restaurant agréable concoctant d'appétissantes préparations goût du jour.

◆ Ketenhotel uit de betere klasse langs de snelweg, op 4 km van de luchthaven Zaventem. Talrijke faciliteiten voor congressen en ontspanning. Gerenoveerde kamers met uitstekende geluidsisolatie. Aangenaam restaurant met smakelijke, eigentijdse gerechten.

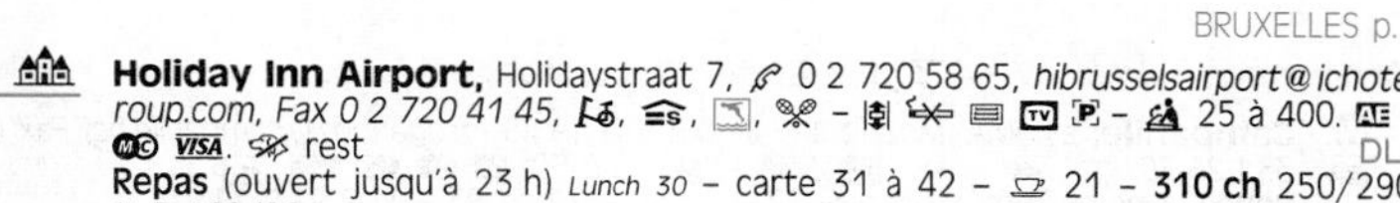

Holiday Inn Airport, Holidaystraat 7, ☎ 0 2 720 58 65, *hibrusselsairport@ichotelsgroup.com, Fax 0 2 720 41 45*, - rest - 25 à 400. rest DL w

Repas (ouvert jusqu'à 23 h) Lunch 30 – carte 31 à 42 – 21 – **310 ch** 250/290 – ½ P 169/294.

◆ La proximité du tarmac, des chambres reposantes, plus tout ce qu'il faut pour se réunir et se divertir : espaces congrès, fitness, sauna, hammam, solarium, piscine, tennis. Formule de restauration un peu "touche à tout", avec quelques plats "Tex-Mex".

◆ Hotel vlak bij de ringweg, met rustige kamers en werkelijk alles om werk en plezier te combineren : congreszalen, fitnessruimte, sauna, hamam, solarium, zwembad en tennisbaan. De restaurantformule is een beetje "van alles wat", met enkele Tex-Mex-schotels.

NH Brussels Airport, De Kleetlaan 14, ☎ 0 2 203 92 52, *nhbrusselsairport@nh-hotels.be, Fax 0 2 203 92 53*, - - 25 à 80. DKL z

Repas *(fermé vend. soir, sam. et dim.)* (avec buffets) Lunch 30 – carte 29 à 50 – 21 – **234 ch** 275/300.

◆ Construction moderne élevée au voisinage des installations aéroportuaires. Chambres actuelles et confortables, fidèles aux normes de la chaîne. Bonne isolation phonique. Au restaurant, carte déclinant les saveurs du moment.

◆ Eigentijds gebouw bij de luchthaven. De kamers zijn conform de normen van deze hotelketen : modern, comfortabel en goed tegen geluid geïsoleerd. Ook het restaurant voldoet qua eten en inrichting aan de smaak van dit moment.

Novotel Airport, Da Vinci laan 25, ☎ 0 2 725 30 50, *H0467@accor-hotels.com, Fax 0 2 721 39 58*, - rest, - 25 à 100. DK y

Repas Lunch 35 bc – carte 27 à 44, ♀ – 15 – **207 ch** 165/200.

◆ Hôtel pratique lorsqu'on a un avion à prendre, et conforme en tous points aux standards Novotel. Chambres toutes semblables, salles de séminaires et piscine en plein air.

◆ Praktisch hotel voor luchtreizigers, dat in alle opzichten voldoet aan de normen van de keten. Identieke kamers, congreszalen en een openluchtzwembad.

Rainbow Airport, Berkenlaan 4, ☎ 0 2 721 77 77, *info@rainbowhotel.be, Fax 0 2 721 55 96*, - , rest, - 25 à 100. DL a

Repas *(fermé sam. midi et dim. midi)* carte env. 38, ♀ – 16 – **76 ch** 189 – ½ P 122/225.

◆ Fringantes petites chambres d'une tenue irréprochable, dans un établissement où la clientèle d'aéroport compensera tranquillement l'éventuel décalage horaire. Salle à manger au décor actuel. Cuisine à consonnance bourgeoise.

◆ Hotel waar luchtreizigers in alle rust kunnen bijkomen van een eventuele jet lag. De kamers zijn klein, maar zien er tiptop uit. Het restaurant heeft een eigentijds interieur en biedt zijn gasten een eenvoudige, traditionele keuken.

à Dilbeek *par ⑧ : 7 km - plans p. 8 et 10 – 38 326 h – ✉ 1700 Dilbeek :*

Relais Delbeccha ⌂, Bodegemstraat 158, ☎ 0 2 569 44 30, *relais.delbeccha@skynet.be, Fax 0 2 569 75 30*, - - 25 à 100.

fermé 3 dern. sem. juil. – **Repas** *(fermé dim. soir)* Lunch 25 – 31/64 bc – **12 ch** 93/120.

◆ Paisible villa vous réservant un accueil familial. Intérieur bourgeois, salon "cosy", chambres douillettes au mobilier classique, salles de réunions et jardin de repos. Restaurant assez stylé, où les repas peuvent se prendre en plein air par beau temps.

◆ Rustige villa, waar u door de familie gastvrij wordt ontvangen. Bourgeoisinterieur, gezellige lounge, behaaglijke kamers met klassiek meubilair, vergaderzalen en tuin om te relaxen. Stijlvol restaurant, dat bij mooi weer zijn tafeltjes buiten zet.

🍴🍴 **Host. d'Arconati** ⌂ avec ch, d'Arconatistraat 77, ☎ 0 2 569 35 00, *arconati@hotmail.com, Fax 0 2 569 35 04*, - - 40.

fermé fév. et dern. sem. juil. – **Repas** *(fermé dim. soir, lundi et mardi)* carte 43 à 52 – **4 ch** 87.

◆ Le charme de cette villa Art déco tient surtout à son environnement : le jardin arboré, richement fleuri en été, est une invitation à la détente. Chambres croquignolettes.

◆ Deze art-decovilla dankt zijn charme vooral aan de weelderige tuin, die 's zomers prachtig in bloei staat en uitnodigt tot "far niente". De kamers zijn ronduit beeldig.

🍴🍴 **De Kapblok,** Ninoofsesteenweg 220, ☎ 0 2 569 31 23, *reservatie@dekapblok.be, Fax 0 2 569 67 23* – . AM e

fermé 2 sem. Pâques, fin juil.-début août, fin déc.-début janv., dim. et lundi – **Repas** Lunch 33 – 45/75 bc.

◆ Au rez-de-chaussée d'un immeuble, petit restaurant de quartier dont l'enseigne signifie "billot de boucher". Cuisine classique de bon aloi, menus appétissants et vins choisis.

◆ Klein buurtrestaurant op een benedenverdieping van een flatgebouw. Klassieke keuken van goede kwaliteit, aantrekkelijke menu's en uitgelezen wijnen.

à Drogenbos - *plan p. 10* - *4 731 h* - *1620 Drogenbos* :

Campanile, av. W.A. Mozart 11, 0 2 331 19 45, *drogenbos@campanile.be, Fax 0 2 331 25 30*, - - 25 à 50. AN n
Repas (avec buffets) *Lunch 10* - 22 - 10 - **77 ch** 83 - ½ P 97/117.
◆ Proximité du ring, parking à vue, petites chambres basiques égayées de tissus fleuris, prix "plancher". Voici donc un "clone" parfait de la grande famille des Campanile !
◆ Goedkoop ketenhotel bij de Ring met parkeergelegenheid in het zicht. Kleine, basale kamers met bloemetjesstoffen. Een perfecte kloon van de grote Campanile-familie !

à Dworp *(Tourneppe) par ⑥ : 16 km* - *plan p. 10* - *Beersel 23 043 h.* - *1653 Dworp* :

Kasteel Gravenhof, Alsembergsesteenweg 676, 0 2 380 44 99, *info@gravenhof.be, Fax 0 2 380 40 60*, - , ch, - 25 à 120.
Repas (taverne-rest) *Lunch 17* - carte 25 à 43 - 15 - **26 ch** 100/155 - ½ P 132.
◆ Tenté par la vie de château ? Cette "folie" du 17e s. vous ravira : bibelots anciens, meubles de style et spacieuses chambres offrant la vue sur un parc agrémenté d'étangs. Sympathique taverne-restaurant retranchée dans les caves voûtées séculaires.
◆ Spreekt het kasteelleven u aan ? Aan is dit 17e-eeuwse lustslot echt iets voor u ! Oude snuisterijen, stijlmeubelen en ruime kamers die uitkijken op een park met vijvers. Het sfeervolle restaurant is in de oude overwelfde kelder ondergebracht.

à Grimbergen *au Nord par N 202 BK : 11 km* - *plan p. 8* - *33 072 h* - *1850 Grimbergen* :

Abbey, Kerkeblokstraat 5, 0 2 270 08 88, *info@hotelabbey.be, Fax 0 2 270 81 88*, - , rest, - 30 à 200. ch
fermé juil. - **Repas 't Wit Paard** *(fermé sam. et dim.) Lunch 32* - carte 48 à 64 - 15 - **28 ch** 125/150.
◆ Architecture massive rappelant une ferme flamande. Les chambres sont paisibles et spacieuses. Salles de réunions, bar, espace de remise en forme et sauna. Au restaurant, cuisine de base classique, feu de bûches en hiver et terrasse dressée en été.
◆ Zwaar bouwwerk dat aan een Vlaamse boerderij doet denken. De kamers zijn ruim en rustig. Vergaderzalen, bar, fitnessruimte en sauna. In het restaurant worden klassieke gerechten geserveerd, 's winters bij het haardvuur en 's zomers op het terras.

à Groot-Bijgaarden - *plan p. 8* - *Dilbeek 38 326 h.* - *1702 Groot-Bijgaarden* :

Waerboom, Jozef Mertensstraat 140, 0 2 463 15 00, *info@waerboom.com, Fax 0 2 463 10 30*, , - - 25 à 270. ch AL r
fermé mi-juil.-mi-août - **Repas** (résidents seult) - **35 ch** 97/165.
◆ Une grande ferme flamande joliment rénovée sert de cadre à cet hôtel familial. Chambres classiques, piscine intérieure, sauna et jardin soigné. Banquets et séminaires.
◆ Een grote Vlaamse boerderij, fraai gerenoveerd, is de setting van dit familiehotel. Traditionele kamers, binnenbad, sauna en verzorgde tuin. Zeer geschikt voor seminaries.

Gosset, Gossetlaan 52, 0 2 466 21 30, *info@gosset.be, Fax 0 2 466 18 50*, - - 25 à 200. AL a
fermé 20 déc.-5 janv. - **Repas** *Lunch 10* - carte 22 à 48 - **48 ch** 100/125 - ½ P 125.
◆ Hôtel de confort moderne occupant un petit immeuble récent dans une zone industrielle proche du ring. Chambres convenablement insonorisées. Navette vers le centre-ville. Ample salle à manger contemporaine coiffée d'une fresque céleste.
◆ Hotel met modern comfort in een klein en nieuw gebouw op een industrieterrein bij de Ring. De kamers hebben een goede geluidsisolatie. Pendeldienst naar het centrum. Grote, hedendaagse eetzaal met een prachtig fresco aan het plafond.

De Bijgaarden, I. Van Beverenstraat 20, 0 2 466 44 85, *debijgaarden@skynet.be, Fax 0 2 463 08 11*, , - AL c
fermé du 5 au 12 avril, du 9 au 30 août, du 2 au 5 janv., sam. midi et dim. - **Repas** *Lunch 50* - 65/225 bc, carte 95 à 169.
◆ Une demeure enchanteresse : environnement bucolique, intérieur cossu, fine cuisine classique, cellier "grand seigneur" et, en toile de fond, le château de Groot-Bijgaarden.
◆ Een betoverend plekje : schilderachtige omgeving, weelderig interieur, fijne klassieke keuken, prestigieuze wijnkelder en op de achtergrond het kasteel van Groot-Bijgaarden.
Spéc. Beignet de foie gras d'oie caramelisé au Porto. Homard norvégien rôti à la vanille. Ris de veau de lait au beurre truffé, champignons des bois en civet

Michel (Van Landeghem), Gossetlaan 31, 0 2 466 65 91, *restaurant.michel@belgacom.net, Fax 0 2 466 90 07*, - AL d
fermé du 10 au 28 août, 18 déc.-1er janv., dim. et lundi - **Repas** 46/80 bc.
◆ Le décor de cette table gastronomique ne crée pas la surprise, à l'inverse des assiettes, très soignées et d'un classicisme rigoureux. Bonne cave. L'été, repas en plein air.
◆ De inrichting van dit gastronomische restaurant is niet erg verrassend, in tegenstelling tot de zeer verzorgde klassieke keuken. Goede wijnkelder. Buiten eten in de zomer.
Spéc. œuf poché aux jets de houblon (mi-fév.-mi avril). Perdreau rôti à la feuille de vigne (oct.-nov). Mijoté de homard aux champignons des bois et grenailles

à Hoeilaart - *plan p. 11 - 9 939 h - ✉ 1560 Hoeilaart :*

XX **Aloyse Kloos,** Terhulpsesteenweg 2 (à Groenendaal), ☎ 0 2 657 37 37, *Fax 0 2 657 37 37,* - P. VISA DP f
fermé août, sam. midi, dim. soir et lundi - **Repas** Lunch 25 - 47/70 bc.
• Cuisine classique et crus d'exception honorant le vignoble luxembourgeois, dans cette villa postée en lisière du massif de Soignes. Spécialité de champignons, dont la truffe.
• Deze villa bij het Zoniënwoud heeft klassieke gerechten en uitstekende wijnen van Luxemburgse bodem te bieden. De specialiteit van het huis is champignons, waaronder truffels.

X **Tissens,** Groenendaalsesteenweg 105 (à Groenendaal), ☎ 0 2 657 04 09, *tissens@tiscali.be,* , Grillades et anguilles - P. AE VISA DP k
fermé juil., fin déc.-début janv., merc. et jeudi - **Repas** carte 33 à 41.
• Déjà 40 ans de présence pour cette affaire familiale assise à l'orée de la forêt. Carte bourgeoise où l'anguille concurrence les viandes grillées. L'été, repas en plein air.
• Familiebedrijf aan de rand van het Zoniënwoud, dat al 40 jaar bestaat. Traditionele kaart, waarop paling wedijvert met gegrild vlees. In de zomer kan buiten worden gegeten.

à Itterbeek *par ⑧ : 8 km - plans p. 8 et 10* C *Dilbeek 38 326 h. - ✉ 1701 Itterbeek :*

X **De Ster,** Herdebeekstraat 169 (lieu-dit Sint-Anna-Pede), ☎ 0 2 569 78 08, *Fax 0 2 569 37 97,* , Estaminet - P. VISA
fermé 2 sem. en août, sam. midi, dim. midi, lundi et mardi - **Repas** Lunch 16 - 35/45.
• Une belle façade à colombages signale cette ancienne auberge surveillant un carrefour. Salles de restaurant aménagées sur plusieurs niveaux. Agréable terrasse estivale.
• Deze oude herberg in de schaduw van het kerkje valt op door zijn mooie vakwerkgevel. De intieme zaaltjes bevinden zich op verschillende niveaus. Aangenaam terras in de zomer.

à Kortenberg *par ② : 15 km - plan p. 9 - 17 631 h - ✉ 3070 Kortenberg :*

XX **Hof te Linderghem,** Leuvensesteenweg 346, ☎ 0 2 759 72 64, *info@33masters.com, Fax 0 2 759 66 10* - P. AE VISA
fermé juil., lundi soir et mardi - **Repas** Lunch 28 - carte 39 à 72.
• Ce restaurant familial officie depuis plus de trente ans dans une ferme du 19e s. La salle à manger, récemment rafraîchie, diffuse une ambiance "cosy".
• Dit familierestaurant is ruim 30 jaar geleden geopend in een 19e-eeuwse boerderij. De eetzaal is onlangs opgeknapt en heeft een knusse ambiance.

à Machelen - *plan p. 9 - 11 972 h - ✉ 1830 Machelen :*

XXX **Pyramid,** Heirbaan 210, ☎ 0 2 253 54 56, *rest.pyramid@skynet.be, Fax 0 2 253 47 65,* - P. AE VISA JCB DK m
fermé 18 juil.-9 août, sam. et dim. - **Repas** Lunch 36 - 70, ♀.
• Vous aurez les fourneaux en point de mire. Le coup de feu n'est pas exclu ! Cadre moderne, jardin anglais, terrasse et pièce d'eau : la sérénité. Cuisine d'aujourd'hui.
• Modern interieur met een eigentijdse keuken, waar u de koks in het oog kunt houden. Het terras en de Engelse tuin met waterpartij stralen iets sereens uit.

à Meise *par ⑪ : 14 km - plan p. 8 - 18 471 h - ✉ 1860 Meise :*

XXX **Aub. Napoléon,** Bouchoutlaan 1, ☎ 0 2 269 30 78, *Fax 0 2 269 79 98,* Grillades - P. AE VISA
fermé août - **Repas** Lunch 36 - 56/74 bc, ♀.
• À l'entrée de Meise, petite auberge chaleureuse évoquant une fermette. Décoration intérieure dans la note rustique, sur le thème de Napoléon. Grillades exécutées en salle.
• Gezellige herberg in een boerderijtje aan de rand van Meise. De decoratie van het rustieke interieur is een eerbetoon aan Napoleon. In de eetzaal wordt het vlees geroosterd.

XX **Koen Van Loven,** Brusselsesteenweg 11, ☎ 0 2 270 05 77, *koen.van.loven@proximedia.be, Fax 0 2 270 05 46,* - 25 à 150. AE VISA.
fermé sem. carnaval, vacances bâtiment, lundi et mardi - **Repas** 30/73 bc.
• Cette demeure bourgeoise du début du 20e s. abrite un restaurant de style contemporain. Cave bien montée. Grande salle pour banquets et séminaires.
• In dit herenhuis uit de vroege 20e eeuw is een hedendaags restaurant gevestigd. De wijnkelder is uitstekend opgezet. Grote zaal voor partijen.

à Melsbroek - *plan p. 9 -* C *Steenokkerzeel 10 534 h. - ✉ 1820 Melsbroek :*

XXX **Boetfort,** Sellaerstraat 42, ☎ 0 2 751 64 00, *boetfort@proximedia.be, Fax 0 2 751 62 00,* - P - 25 à 50. AE VISA. DK p
fermé sem. carnaval, merc. soir, sam. midi et dim. - **Repas** Lunch 34 - 38/53.
• Manoir du 17e s. agrémenté d'un parc, cette "folie" accueillit le Roi Soleil en personne. Sans nul doute, le cachet de l'ensemble revêt une forte connotation historique.
• Op dit 17e-eeuwse landgoed met een prachtig park heeft de Zonnekoning nog in hoogsteigen persoon gelogeerd. U kunt er vorstelijk eten in een historische omgeving.

à Nossegem *par ② : 13 km - plan p. 9 - Ⓒ Zaventem 27 537 h. – ✉ 1930 Nossegem :*

XXX ✿ **L'Orangeraie Roland Debuyst,** Leuvensesteenweg 614, ✆ 0 2 757 05 59, *roland .debuyst@wanadoo.be, Fax 0 2 759 50 08,* ☂ – 🅿 – 🏛 35. AE ⓓ ⓜ VISA. ✗
fermé 1 sem. Pâques, 2 prem. sem. août, sam. midi, dim. et lundi – **Repas** Lunch 41 – 60/96 bc, carte 64 à 92, ♀.

♦ Concerto culinaire pour "piano", dans le tempo actuel. La gamme des tons du restaurant est apaisante. Terrasse d'été sous pergola, avec son écrin de verdure.

♦ Laat u zich eens culinair verrassen in dit eigentijdse restaurant met rustgevende kleuren. Buiten eten onder de pergola in het groen. Zakelijke clientèle.

Spéc. Tarte fine aux pommes, boudin noir, foie d'oie rôti, tranche de lard paysan et éclats de truffes. Papillote de turbot aux asperges, morilles et jambon cru. Pigeonneau fumé et désossé à la rhubarbe et poivre vert

à Overijse *par ④ : 16 km - plan p. 11 – 23 864 h – ✉ 3090 Overijse :*

ℹ *Justus Lipsiusplein 9, ✆ 0 2 785 33 73, informatie@overijse.be,* Fax 0 2 687 77 22

Soret ⛷, Kapucijnendreef 1 (à Jezus-Eik), ✆ 0 2 657 37 82, *hotel.soret.bvba@pandora.be, Fax 0 2 657 72 66,* 🏋, ≘, 🏊, 🚲 – |♦| 📺 🅿 – 🏛 40. AE ⓓ ⓜ VISA. ✗ DN s
Repas voir rest ***Istas*** ci-après – **38 ch** ☕ 82, – 1 suite.

♦ Hôtel moderne et flambant neuf, installé en lisière de la forêt de Soignes. Pimpantes chambres à géométrie variable mais toujours assez spacieuses. Tranquillité assurée.

♦ Modern en spiksplinternieuw hotel aan de rand van het Zoniënwoud. Kraakheldere kamers die verschillend zijn ingedeeld, maar altijd vrij ruim zijn. Rust gegarandeerd !

XXXX ✿ **Barbizon** (Deluc), Welriekendedreef 95 (à Jezus-Eik), ✆ 0 2 657 04 62, *barbizon@euronet.be, Fax 0 2 657 40 66,* ☂ – 🅿. AE ⓜ VISA DN n
fermé 13 juil.-4 août, du 6 au 28 janv., mardi et merc. – **Repas** Lunch 36 – 46/100 bc, carte 78 à 108 🍇.

♦ À l'orée de la forêt, charmante villa dont le style "normand" s'harmonise au cadre bucolique. Cuisine classique recherchée. Terrasse et jardin délicieux aux beaux jours.

♦ Charmante villa, waarvan de Normandische bouwstijl harmonieert met de bosrijke omgeving. Verfijnde klassieke keuken. Tuin met terras, waar het 's zomers heerlijk toeven is.

Spéc. Tournedos de langoustines juste raidi, compotée de tomates douces et roquette, crème au cresson. Barbue aux échalotes confites, coulis de Côtes du Rhône à la carotte. Gibier (sept.-janv.)

XX **Lipsius,** Brusselsesteenweg 671 (à Jezus-Eik), ✆ 0 2 657 34 32, *Fax 0 2 657 31 47* – 🅿. AE ⓓ ⓜ VISA DN r
fermé vacances Pâques, 25 juil.-30 août, 20 déc.-3 janv., dim. midi sauf 15 oct.-15 fév., sam. midi, dim. soir et lundi – **Repas** Lunch 35 – carte 44 à 70.

♦ Poutres, briques apparentes, murs "terracotta" et chaises chasubles président au décor de cette table. Menus option boissons comprises et belle sélection de vins.

♦ Hanenbalken, ruwe bakstenen, terracottamuren en stoelen met overtrek bepalen het interieur van dit restaurant. Keuzemenu's inclusief drank en een mooie selectie wijnen.

X **Istas** - H. Soret, Brusselsesteenweg 652 (à Jezus-Eik), ✆ 0 2 657 05 11, ☂, Taverne-rest – 🅿. ⓜ VISA DN s
fermé du 1er au 30 août, du 24 au 31 déc., merc. et jeudi – **Repas** carte 22 à 43.

♦ Taverne-restaurant centenaire située à un saut de biche de la forêt de Soignes. Plats traditionnels et en-cas "couleur locale", servis dans une ambiance cordiale.

♦ Honderdjarig taverne-restaurant aan de rand van het Zoniënwoud. Traditionele schotels en hapjes met veel "couleur locale", opgediend in een vriendelijke ambiance.

à Ruisbroek *- plan p. 10 - Ⓒ Sint-Pieters-Leeuw 30 186 h. – ✉ 1601 Ruisbroek :*

X **De Mayeur,** Fabriekstraat 339, ✆ 0 2 331 52 61, *Fax 0 2 331 52 63,* ☂ – AE ⓜ VISA AP a
fermé 3 sem. en août, mardi, merc. et sam. midi – **Repas** Lunch 20 – carte 26 à 62.

♦ Bonne table traditionnelle, dans une jolie maison ancienne dont la devanture contraste fort d'avec l'extension arrière, résolument moderne, où se déploie la terrasse d'été.

♦ Goed, traditioneel restaurant in een mooi oud pand, waarvan de voorgevel sterk contrasteert met de ultramoderne aanbouw aan de achterkant, waar zich ook een terras bevindt.

à Sint-Genesius-Rode *(Rhode-St-Genèse) par ⑤ : 13 km - plan p. 11 – 17 830 h – ✉ 1640 Sint-Genesius-Rode :*

Aub. de Waterloo, chaussée de Waterloo 212, ✆ 0 2 358 35 80, *aubergedewaterloo@skynet.be, Fax 0 2 358 38 06,* 🏋, ≘ – |♦| ✗ ▤ 📺 – 🏛 25 à 70. AE ⓓ ⓜ VISA
fermé 1re quinz. août et fin déc. – **Repas** voir rest ***l'Arlecchino*** ci-après – **87 ch** ☕ 129/191.

♦ Cet hôtel récent dispose de "Bonaparte" : deux sortes de chambres, plus des studios au décor chinois ou syrien. Proximité du site historique. Clientèle d'affaires.

♦ Nieuw zakenhotel dat zijn Waterloo niet zal vinden, ondanks de nabijheid van deze historische plek. Twee soorten kamers, plus studio's met een Chinees of Syrisch decor.

XX **l'Arlecchino** - H. Aub. de Waterloo, chaussée de Waterloo 212, ☎ 0 2 358 34 16, *Fax 0 2 358 28 96*, , Cuisine italienne, avec trattoria – AE VISA
fermé août, lundi et mardi midi – **Repas** 33/41 bc.
• Ristorante dont la carte ravira les amateurs de cuisine transalpine, associé à une trattoria pour les fervents de pizza. Vins franco-italiens choisis. Buon appetito !
• Ristorante dat de liefhebbers van de echte Italiaanse keuken zal verrukken, met daarnaast een eenvoudige pizzeria. Exclusieve wijnen uit Frankrijk en Italië. Buon appetito !

XX **Michel D,** r. Station 182, ☎ 0 2 381 20 66, *Fax 0 2 380 45 80*, – AE VISA
fermé 2 dern. sem. juil.-prem. sem. août, sam. midi, dim. et lundi – **Repas** *Lunch 20* – 40/110 bc, ♀.
• Loin du "système D" : la stabilité. Cette maison garnie d'un mobilier "rotin" vous installe dans un cadre actuel assez confortable. Choix étoffé.
• In dit restaurant met rotanmeubelen kunt u in een eigentijdse en vrij comfortabele omgeving genieten van de kookkunsten van de kok. De kaart biedt een ruime keuze.

X **L'Alter Ego,** Parvis Notre-Dame 15, ☎ 0 2 358 29 15, *Fax 0 2 358 29 15*, – AE VISA JCB
fermé août, dim. et lundi – **Repas** (déjeuner seult sauf vend. et sam.) *Lunch 11* – carte 27 à 43.
• Cette mignonne affaire familiale installée dans une maison de coin accueille le client sur un air classique. Les plats se déclinent à l'ardoise au gré du marché.
• Plezierig familierestaurant in een hoekpand. De klassieke gerechten op het uithangbord wisselen volgens het aanbod op de markt.

X **Dominique De Neve,** Termeulenstraat 44, ☎ 0 2 380 34 85, *Fax 0 2 380 34 85*, – AE VISA
fermé 15 juil.-15 août, fin déc., sam. midi, dim., lundi et jours fériés – **Repas** *Lunch 16* – 26/70 bc.
• Estimable restaurant au goût du jour créé à partir d'un estaminet. Atmosphère coloniale en salle, confortée par quelques touches décoratives exotiques. Terrasse à l'arrière.
• Dit oude kroegje is nu een eigentijdse eetgelegenheid die goed aangeschreven staat. De koloniale sfeer wordt versterkt door de exotische accenten. Terras aan de achterkant.

à Sint-Pieters-Leeuw *Sud-Ouest : 13 km par Brusselbaan* AN - *plan p. 10* – *30 186 h* – ✉ *1600 Sint-Pieters-Leeuw* :

Green Park , V. Nonnemanstraat 15, ☎ 0 2 331 19 70, *greenparkhotel@belgacom.be, Fax 0 2 331 03 11*, , , , – – 25 à 100. AE VISA
fermé juil. – **Repas** (résidents seult) – **18 ch** 74/88 – ½ P 148.
• Conçu voici quelques années dans un environnement paisible et verdoyant, l'hôtel se rafraîchit au bord d'un étang. Petit centre de remise en forme. Affluence d'affaires.
• Dit hotel heeft enkele jaren geleden zijn deuren geopend in een rustige, groene omgeving bij een vijver. Het beschikt over een kleine fitnessruimte. Zakelijke clientèle.

à Sint-Stevens-Woluwe (*Woluwe-St-Étienne*) - *plan p. 9* C *Zaventem 27 537 h.* – ✉ *1932 Sint-Stevens-Woluwe* :

Hobbit sans rest, Jozef Van Damstraat 85, ☎ 0 2 709 78 00, *hobbit.bxl@pandora.be, Fax 0 2 709 78 01* – AE VISA DL f
7 – **26 ch** 52.
• À proximité du boulevard de la Woluwe, hôtel de chaîne récent prisé par la clientèle d'affaires. Chambres actuelles de bon confort. Parking privé.
• Dit nieuwe hotel behoort tot een keten en ligt niet ver van de boulevard Woluwedal. Het is vooral populair bij zakenlui. Moderne en comfortabele kamers. Eigen parkeergarage.

à Sterrebeek *par ② : 13 km* - *plan p. 9* C *Zaventem 27 537 h.* – ✉ *1933 Sterrebeek* :

X **la chasse des princes,** Hypodroomlaan 141, ☎ 0 2 731 19 64, *paul.emile.saute@skynet.be, Fax 0 2 731 09 68*, – AE VISA
fermé lundi et mardi midi – **Repas** *Lunch 13* – 23/45.
• Sympathique, l'adresse présente un cadre épuré ne manquant pas d'élégance. Le chef, en "bon prince", vous concocte un menu raisonné. Au lunch, point de coup de fusil !
• Plezierig restaurant met een sobere, maar smaakvolle inrichting. De chef-kok weet een prinselijk menu op tafel te zetten voor een schappelijke prijs.

à Strombeek-Bever - *plan p. 8* - C *Grimbergen 33 072 h.* – ✉ *1853 Strombeek-Bever* :

Rijckendael , J. Van Elewijckstraat 35, ☎ 0 2 267 41 24, *rijckendael@alfarijckendael.gth.be, Fax 0 2 267 94 01*, , – – 25 à 40. AE VISA
Repas *Lunch 23* – 35/65 bc – 16 – **49 ch** 150 – ½ P 114/186. BK c
• Cet hôtel de conception moderne a élu domicile à une portion d'asphalte de l'Atomium et du Heysel. Chambres à l'identique bien équipées. Parking privé. Restaurant au cachet rustique aménagé dans une ancienne fermette.
• Hotel met een modern concept, dat op de Heizel bij het Atomium domicilie heeft gekozen. De kamers zijn allemaal eender en van alle comfort voorzien. Eigen parkeergarage. Het restaurant is ondergebracht in een oud boerderijtje en heeft een rustiek karakter.

XX **'t Stoveke,** Jetsestraat 52, ✆ 0 2 267 67 25, 🏠, Produits de la mer – AE ⓓ MC VISA. ✂ BK q
fermé 3 sem. en juin, Noël-Nouvel An, dim., lundi et jours fériés – **Repas** *Lunch 31* – carte 56 à 71.
◆ Un "foyer" familial mitonnant les classiques du grand large. Salle à manger de poche offrant la vue sur les fourneaux. Petite terrasse bordée de chlorophylle.
◆ Goed visrestaurant met echte klassiekers op de kaart en in de kelder. Kleine eetzaal met zicht op het fornuis en een terras omringd met groene planten.

XX **Val Joli,** Leestbeekstraat 16, ✆ 0 2 460 65 43, *info@valjoli.be, Fax 0 2 460 04 00,* 🏠 – P – 🏛 25 à 40. MC VISA BK p
fermé 2 sem. en juin, fin oct.-début nov., lundi, mardi et merc. midi – **Repas** *Lunch 10* – 28.
◆ Villa avec jardin et terrasses. De votre table, vous ne perdrez pas une miette des canards batifolant sur la pièce d'eau. Cuisine variée.
◆ Villa met tuin en terrassen. Vanaf uw tafel hoeft u geen kruimel te missen van het grappige schouwspel van de eendjes in het water. De keuken is bijzonder gevarieerd.

X **Blink,** Sint-Amandsstraat 52, ✆ 0 2 267 37 67, *info@restaurantblink.be, Fax 0 2 267 99 68,* 🏠 – MC VISA BK h
fermé du 1er au 18 août, 20 déc.-2 janv., dim. soir et lundi – **Repas** *Lunch 20* – 34.
◆ Longue brasserie contemporaine aux tonalités bleutées. Cuisine française du moment, joliment présentée et semée de pointes d'exotisme. Une terrasse d'été se cache à l'arrière.
◆ Langgerekt, eigentijds restaurant in blauwe tinten. Actuele Franse gerechten met hier een daar een exotische noot ; fraaie presentatie. Zomerterras aan de achterzijde.

à Tervuren *par ③ : 14 km - plan p. 11 – 20 167 h – ✉ 3080 Tervuren :*

XX **De Linde,** Kerkstraat 8, ✆ 0 2 767 87 42, *Fax 0 2 767 87 42,* 🏠 – MC VISA. ✂
fermé 3 sem. en juil., 2 sem. en janv., lundi, mardi et sam. midi – **Repas** *Lunch 13* – 48/66 bc.
◆ À côté de l'église, menue façade ancienne au charme typiquement villageois. Carte classico-bourgeoise bien ficelée et sage cave française. Jolie terrasse d'été.
◆ Oud pandje met een typisch dorpse charme naast de kerk. Evenwichtige klassiek-traditionele kaart en mooie Franse wijnen. Aangenaam terras in de zomer.

à Vilvoorde *(Vilvorde) - plans p. 8 et 9 – 35 567 h – ✉ 1800 Vilvoorde :*

🏨 **Campanile,** Luchthavenlaan 2, ✆ 0 2 253 97 67, *vilvoorde@campanile.be, Fax 0 2 253 97 69,* 🏠 – 🛗 ⇔ 📺 ♿ P – 🏛 25 à 160. AE ⓓ MC VISA JCB. ✂ rest DK a
Repas (avec buffets) *Lunch 10* – 22, ♀ – ☕ 10 – **85 ch** 81 – ½ P 89/99.
◆ Sobres chambres convenablement insonorisées dans ce petit hôtel "budget" voisin de la gare et proche du ring par lequel vous gagnerez l'aéroport en moins de 5 mn.
◆ Klein budgethotel in de buurt van het station en de Ring, die u binnen vijf minuten naar de luchthaven voert. De sobere kamers zijn van geluidsisolatie voorzien.

XXX **La Hacienda,** Koningslosteenweg 34, ✆ 0 2 649 26 85, *lahacienda@lahacienda.be, Fax 0 2 647 43 50,* 🏠, Cuisine espagnole – P – 🏛 25. AE ⓓ MC VISA. ✂ CK h
fermé mi-juil.-mi-août, dim. et lundi – **Repas** *Lunch 24* – 39.
◆ Lumineuse hacienda embusquée dans une impasse proche du canal. On y goûte une vraie cuisine ibérique avec menus régionaux et grillades en salle. Vaste choix de vins espagnols.
◆ Deze haciënda ligt verscholen in een doodlopende straat bij het kanaal. Authentieke Spaanse keuken met streekmenu's en vlees aan het spit. Groot assortiment Spaanse wijnen.

XX **de Rembrandt,** Lange Molensstraat 60, ✆ 0 2 251 04 72, *vandaelejoris@hotmail.com* – AE ⓓ MC VISA CK c
fermé mi-juil.-mi-août, sam. et dim. – **Repas** (dîner sur réservation) *Lunch 41* – carte 41 à 61.
◆ Une tour de guet du 15e s. domine ce restaurant familial d'orientation classique. Cellier conséquent, fourneaux à vue, mezzanine et collection de tableaux hétéroclites.
◆ Een 15e-eeuwse wachttoren steekt boven dit familiebedrijf uit, dat qua eten en drinken klassiek is georiënteerd. Open keuken, mezzanine en een bonte verzameling schilderijen.

XX **Rouge Glamour,** Fr. Rooseveltlaan 18, ✆ 0 2 253 68 39, *rouge.glamour@advalvas.be, Fax 0 2 253 68 39* – MC VISA CDK s
fermé 2e quinz. sept., sam. midi, dim. midi, lundi et sam. midi – **Repas** *Lunch 20* – 30/69 bc.
◆ Table au goût du jour où l'on prend place dans un décor recréant habilement l'ambiance d'un cabaret. À l'arrière, verdoyante terrasse d'été dotée de meubles en bois exotique.
◆ Restaurant met een eigentijdse keuken en een inrichting die de sfeer van een cabaret oproept. Weelderig zomerterras aan de achterkant met meubelen van tropisch hout.

X **Spectrum,** Romeinsesteenweg 220 (Koningslo), ✆ 0 2 267 00 45, *Fax 0 2 267 00 46,* 🏠 – AE ⓓ MC VISA BK
fermé 1 sem. Pâques, sam. midi et dim. – **Repas** 28.
◆ Restaurant contemporain - lustres halogènes, banquettes et chaises design rhabillées de cuir - fréquenté par une clientèle d'habitués et d'affaires. Plats de brasserie.
◆ Trendy restaurant met halogeenlampen en designbanken en -stoelen van leer, waar veel zakenmensen en vaste klanten komen. Keuken in brasseriestijl.

à Wemmel - *plan p. 8* - *14 256 h* - ✉ *1780 Wemmel* :

La Roseraie, Limburg Stirumlaan 213, ☎ 0 2 456 99 10 et 0 2 460 51 34 (rest), *hotel@laroseraie.be, Fax 0 2 460 83 20,* – AE MC VISA AK r
Repas *(fermé sam. midi, dim. soir et lundi)* Lunch 22 – carte 35 à 52 – **8 ch** 125/150.
◆ Jolie villa abritant un hôtel à taille humaine. Chambres assez confortables au décor personnalisé : africain, japonais, romain, etc. Accueil familial. Salle de restaurant classiquement aménagée et préparations actualisée à petits pas.
◆ Mooie villa waarin een prettig klein hotel is gehuisvest. Vrij comfortabele kamers in verschillende stijlen : Afrikaans, Japans, Romeins, enz. Hartelijke ontvangst. Klassiek ingerichte eetzaal en gerechten die geleidelijk worden gemoderniseerd.

Le Gril aux herbes d'Evan, Brusselsesteenweg 21, ☎ 0 2 460 52 39, *Fax 0 2 461 19 12,* – AE MC VISA AK t
fermé du 1er au 21 juil., du 24 au 31 déc., sam. midi et dim. – **Repas** Lunch 30 – 55/80 bc.
◆ Cette petite villa profite de l'agrément d'un grand jardin. Cuisine à base de produits choisis et cellier honorant la réputation du vignoble français.
◆ Deze kleine villa profiteert van de charme van een grote tuin. Keuken op basis van eersteklas producten en een wijnkelder die een eerbetoon is aan de Franse wijnboeren.

L'Aub. de l'Isard, Romeinsesteenweg 964, ☎ 0 2 479 85 64, *isard@wanadoo.be, Fax 0 2 479 16 49,* – – 25. AE MC VISA BK u
fermé 1 sem. Pâques, 20 juil.-12 août, dim. soir, lundi et jeudi soir – **Repas** Lunch 15 – 38/62 bc.
◆ Agencé avec soin et récemment rafraîchi, l'intérieur donne dans des tonalités douces. Les mets au goût du jour dominent la carte. Lunch et menus.
◆ Pas opgeknapt en zorgvuldig ingericht restaurant, dat in pasteltinten is gehouden. Overwegend moderne gerechten op de kaart en verschillende menu's, ook voor de lunch.

Parkhof, Parklaan 7, ☎ 0 2 460 42 89, *Fax 0 2 460 25 10,* – AE MC VISA AK s
fermé dim. soir et lundi – **Repas** Lunch 19 – 35/60 bc.
◆ À quelques foulées de la réserve naturelle du Beverbos, vous trouverez cette ancienne villa alanguie dans un parc public. Elle vous reçoit aussi agréablement en terrasse.
◆ Deze oude villa is rustig gelegen in een mooi park, een paar minuten lopen van het natuurreservaat Het Beverbos. Bij mooi weer worden de tafeltjes op het terras gedekt.

Il Brunello, Vijverslaan 1, ☎ 0 2 460 55 64, *Fax 0 2 460 13 92,* , Cuisine italienne, ouvert jusqu'à 23 h – AE MC VISA AK b
Repas Lunch 13 – carte 27 à 43.
◆ Une carte majoritairement transalpine et plutôt bien fournie est présentée à cette adresse. Déco intérieure contemporaine à l'italienne. Coin trattoria et restaurant d'été.
◆ Uitgebreide kaart met een duidelijk Italiaans accent. Hedendaagse inrichting in Italiaanse stijl. Trattoria-gedeelte en 's zomers gelegenheid om buiten te eten.

à Wolvertem par ⑪ : *15 km* - *plan p. 8* C *Meise 18 471 h.* – ✉ *1861 Wolvertem* :

Falko sans rest, Stationsstraat 54a, ☎ 0 2 263 04 50, *info@falkohotel.be, Fax 0 2 263 04 79,* – AE MC VISA.
19 ch 134/157.
◆ Hôtel œuvrant au cœur de Wolvertem. Amples chambres bien équipées, bar "trendy" et fringant espace breakfast sous véranda. Communs égayés de toiles d'une vive polychromie.
◆ Hotel in het hart van Wolvertem. Ruime, goed ingerichte kamers, trendy bar en fraaie ontbijtruimte in veranda. Gemeenschappelijke ruimtes met schilderijen in vrolijke kleuren.

à Zaventem - *plan p. 9* - *27 537 h* - ✉ *1930 Zaventem* :

Sheraton Airport, à l'aéroport (Nord-Est par A 201), ☎ 0 2 710 80 00, *reservations.brussels@sheraton.com, Fax 0 2 710 80 80,* – – 25 à 600. AE MC VISA JCB DK b
Repas ***Concorde*** *(fermé sam. midi)* Lunch 25 – carte 30 à 61 – 25 – **292 ch** 395/470, – 2 suites.
◆ À un tour de piste à la ronde, le plus "airport" des hôtels de luxe bruxellois. Apte à gérer même les cas d'urgence, l'enseigne attire la clientèle d'affaires tous azimuts. Carte internationale et lunch-buffets, idéal pour businessmen "supersoniques".
◆ Vanuit de lucht landt u bijna rechtstreeks in een van de gerieflijke kamers van dit luxehotel. Het personeel is bijzonder flexibel en kan omgaan met noodsituaties. De internationale kaart en de lunchbuffetten zijn een uitkomst voor "supersonische" zakenlui.

Stockmansmolen 1er étage, H. Henneaulaan 164, ☎ 0 2 725 34 34, *info@stockmansmolen.be, Fax 0 2 725 75 05,* Avec taverne-rest – AE MC VISA DL c
fermé 2 dern. sem. juil.-prem. sem. août, Noël, Nouvel An, sam. et dim. – **Repas** Lunch 48 – 58/93 bc.
◆ La brasserie et le restaurant - situé à l'étage - se partagent les deux ailes de ce moulin à eau du 13e s. Environnement alliant des matières nobles : le bois et la pierre.
◆ De brasserie en het restaurant - op de bovenverdieping - delen de twee vleugels van deze watermolen uit de 13e eeuw, die is gebouwd van edele materialen : hout en steen.

à Zellik *par ⑩ : 8 km - plan p. 8 - Asse 28 310 h. – ✉ 1731 Zellik :*

XX **Angelus,** Brusselsesteenweg 433, ☎ 0 2 466 97 26, *restoangelus@skynet.be, Fax 0 2 466 83 84,* – P. AE ⓓ ⓜ VISA AL e
fermé du 1er au 8 mars, 15 juil.-8 août, sam. midi, dim. midi, lundi et jeudi soir – **Repas** *Lunch 18* – 25/50 bc.
◆ Villa surélevée, que devance un parking pratique. Cuisine à consonances bourgeoises concoctée par la patronne. Angélus en cave, mais l'addition reste angélique !
◆ Verhoogde villa met een parkeerterrein. Traditionele gerechten die door de bazin zelf worden bereid. De wijn behoeft geen krans en ook de rekening blijft engelachtig !

S.A. MICHELIN BELUX, Brusselsesteenweg 494, bus 1 AL – ✉ 1731 ZELLIK (Asse), ☎ 0 2 274 43 53/55, Fax 0 2 274 45 16

BUKEN *1910 Vlaams-Brabant Kampenhout 10 809 h.* 533 M 17 *et* 716 G 3.
Bruxelles 28 – Antwerpen 42 – Leuven 10 – Liège 68 – Namur 64 – Turnhout 74.

XX **de notelaar,** Bukenstraat 142, ☎ 0 16 60 52 69, *denotelaar@online.be, Fax 0 16 60 69 09,* – ▤ P. AE ⓓ ⓜ VISA.
fermé 16 fév.-4 mars, 12 juil.-12 août, mardi, merc. et jeudi – **Repas** *Lunch 25* – 29/63 bc.
◆ Au bord d'une route de campagne, fermette flamande restaurée donnant sur un jardin soigné. Salle à manger néo-rustique. Derrière ses fourneaux, le chef mise sur la tradition.
◆ Gerestaureerd Vlaams boerderijtje met een goed onderhouden tuin aan een landweggetje. De eetzaal is neorustiek. Achter het fornuis houdt de chef-kok de traditie hoog.

BÜLLINGEN (BULLANGE) *4760 Liège* 533 W 20, 534 W 20 *et* 716 L 4 – *5 360 h.*
Bruxelles 169 – Liège 77 – Aachen 57.

Haus Tiefenbach - Grüner Baum, Triererstr. 21, ☎ 0 80 64 73 06, *tommy.lux@swing.be, Fax 0 80 64 26 58,* , , – , ▤ rest, P – 25 à 190. ⓜ VISA.
fermé 20 mars-8 avril et 25 juin-10 juil. – **Repas** *(fermé lundi et mardi) Lunch 14* – 22 – **27 ch** 57/86, – 2 suites – ½ P 54/64.
◆ Agréable hôtel fagnard dont les deux gros pavillons entourés d'un parc se reflètent à la surface d'un étang. Plusieurs catégories de chambres correctement équipées. Ample salle à manger classiquement aménagée et carte assez étoffée.
◆ Aangenaam hotel, waarvan de twee grote paviljoens in het park zich weerspiegelen in de vijver. Er zijn verschillende categorieën kamers, allemaal met goede voorzieningen. Ruime eetzaal in klassieke stijl en een vrij uitgebreide menukaart.

X **Kreutz,** Hauptstr. 55e, ☎ 0 80 64 79 03 – ▤ P. VISA
fermé 22 juil.-5 août, 27 sept.-5 oct., lundi soir, mardi soir et merc. soir – **Repas** *Lunch 25* – carte 29 à 45.
◆ Sympathique petite adresse familiale où la clientèle locale, fidélisée par une cuisine traditionnelle simple mais très honnête, a ses habitudes depuis plus de vingt ans.
◆ Sympathiek familierestaurantje dat al ruim 20 jaar een vaste clientèle trekt, die trouw blijft aan de simpele, maar eerlijke traditionele keuken.

BURG-REULAND *4790 Liège* 533 V 21, 534 V 21 *et* 716 L 5 – *3 825 h.*
Voir *Donjon* ≤★.
Bruxelles 184 – Liège 95.

Paquet , Lascheid 43 (Sud-Ouest : 1 km, lieu-dit Lascheid), ☎ 0 80 32 96 24, *Fax 0 80 32 98 22,* ≤ campagne vallonnée – P. ⓜ VISA.
fermé 26 juin-9 juil. et dim. soir et lundi hors saison – **Repas** (résidents seult) – **19 ch** 45/82 – ½ P 53/58.
◆ Bientôt vingt-cinq ans de bons et loyaux services pour cet hôtel dominant la campagne vallonnée. Sommeils réparateurs dans de spacieuses chambres d'une tenue irréprochable.
◆ Dit hotel, dat weldra zijn 25-jarig jubileum zal vieren, kijkt uit over het heuvellandschap. De ruime en perfect onderhouden kamers staan garant voor een goede nachtrust.

Val de l'Our , Dorfstr. 150, ☎ 0 80 32 90 09, *val.de.lour@skynet.be, Fax 0 80 32 97 00,* , , , , , – , ▤ rest, P – 25. ⓜ VISA.
fermé du 1er au 10 juin, du 10 au 28 janv. et lundis hors saison – **Repas** (dîner seult jusqu'à 20 h) carte 34 à 59 – **15 ch** 75/90 – ½ P 75/95.
◆ À l'entrée du village, au creux d'un vallon boisé, auberge riche en distractions : piscine chauffée, tennis, billard, fitness, sauna, pêche, vélo, karting... Bonnes chambres. Au restaurant, duo de menus et vue sur le jardin.
◆ Deze herberg aan de rand van het dorp, in een bebost dal, biedt tal van activiteiten : zwemmen (verwarmd), vissen, tennissen, biljarten, fietsen, skelteren, fitness en sauna. Prettige kamers. In het restaurant met tuinzicht zijn twee menu's verkrijgbaar.

à Ouren *Sud : 9 km* *Burg-Reuland – 4790 Burg-Reuland :*

Dreiländerblick, Dorfstr. 29, 0 80 32 90 71, *hotel.dreilaenderblick@swing.be, Fax 0 80 32 93 88,* ←, – P – 25. VISA.
fermé mi-sept.-début oct., 3 sem. en janv. et mardi – **Repas** *(fermé après 20 h 30)* Lunch 18 – carte env. 39 – **13 ch** 57/76, – 1 suite – ½ P 58/66.
• Accueillante hostellerie officiant au cœur d'un petit village de l'agreste vallée de l'Our. Chambres garnies de meubles de style. Grande terrasse ombragée. Sobre salle à manger où un choix de recettes traditionnelles entend apaiser votre appétit.
• Vriendelijke herberg in het hart van een dorpje in het landelijke dal van de Our. De kamers zijn met stijlmeubilair ingericht. Het grote terras biedt veel schaduw. In de sobere eetzaal worden traditionele gerechten op tafel gezet.

Rittersprung, Dorfstr. 19, 0 80 32 91 35, *Fax 0 80 32 96 31,* ←, – P. VISA.
fermé 13 déc.-15 janv. – **Repas** *(fermé lundis non fériés et après 20 h)* Lunch 19 – carte 22 à 40 – **16 ch** 65/82 – ½ P 53/57.
• Aux portes d'Ouren, dans un cadre bucolique, double chalet renfermant de tranquilles chambres procurant souvent une jolie vue sur le cours de l'Our qui murmure en contrebas. Restaurant avec formules "week-end gastronomique" pour la clientèle résidente.
• Dubbel chalet aan de rand van Ouren, in een zeer landelijke omgeving. Rustige kamers, de meeste met uitzicht op de Our, die iets lager kabbelt. In het restaurant worden voor de hotelgasten gastronomische weekends georganiseerd.

BÜTGENBACH *4750 Liège* 533 W 20, 534 W 20 *et* 716 L 4 – *5 513 h.*
Centre Worriken 1 (au lac) 0 80 44 63 58, Fax 0 80 44 70 89.
Bruxelles 164 – Liège 72 – Aachen 52.

Bütgenbacher Hof, Marktplatz 8, 0 80 44 42 12, *info@hotelbutgenbacherhof.com, Fax 0 80 44 48 77,* – P – 40. AE VISA.
fermé 2 sem. avant Pâques et 2 prem. sem. juil. – **Repas** *(fermé lundi, mardi et après 20 h 30)* Lunch 15 – carte 33 à 56 – **21 ch** 60/95, – 2 suites – ½ P 75/93.
• Hostellerie d'esprit ardennais avec chambres modernes ou de style régional Eifel, chaleureuse salle de petits-déjeuners et bel équipement de relaxation. Terrasse sur jardin. Salle à manger bourgeoise semée de touches rustiques. L'assiette est généreuse.
• Typisch Ardense herberg met kamers in moderne of regionale stijl. De ontbijtzaal doet gezellig aan en het hotel beschikt over talloze faciliteiten voor ontspanning. Terras aan de tuinzijde. Klassieke eetzaal met rustieke accenten. Royale porties.

Lindenhof, Neuerweg 1 (Ouest : 3 km, lieu-dit Weywertz), 0 80 44 50 86, *Fax 0 80 44 48 26,* – P. rest
fermé du 1er au 15 juil. – **Repas** *(fermé lundi)* Lunch 24 – 28/52 bc, ♀ – **15 ch** 55/70 – ½ P 75/80.
• Hébergement propice au repos, ce petit ensemble hôtelier donnant vie au hameau de Weywertz comprend trois maisons mitoyennes en pierres du pays et deux annexes. Restaurant bien installé, dans la villa blanche jouxtant le bâtiment principal.
• Dit kleine hotelcomplex in het gehuchtje Weywertz is ideaal voor wie op zoek is naar rust. Het bestaat uit drie belendende stenen huizen en twee bijgebouwen. In de witte villa naast het hoofdgebouw bevindt zich het restaurant.

du Lac, Seestr. 53, 0 80 44 64 13, *hoteldulac@skynet.be, Fax 0 80 44 44 55,* – . VISA.
fermé mardi, merc. et jeudi d'oct. à mars sauf vacances scolaires – **Repas** (résidents seult) – **26 ch** 55/67 – ½ P 49/64.
• Immeuble-chalet pourvu de chambres sans fioriture mais d'un niveau de confort très acceptable. Grande terrasse estivale. Patron un peu "tour operator" à ses heures !
• Groot chalet met kamers zonder tierelantijnen, die echter een zeer redelijk comfort bieden. Groot terras in de zomer. De eigenaar fungeert op zijn tijd ook als tour operator !

Seeblick, Zum Konnenbusch 24 (Nord-Est : 3 km, lieu-dit Berg), 0 80 44 53 86, *Fax 0 80 44 80 05,* ← lac, –
fermé 25 juin-8 juil. – **Repas** (dîner pour résidents seult) – **12 ch** 33/50 – ½ P 40/45.
• Paisible petit hôtel occupant deux bâtiments distincts reliés par une verrière. Chambres pratiques dotées de terrasses privatives offrant une vue plongeante sur le plan d'eau.
• Rustig hotel in twee gebouwen die door een glazen dak met elkaar zijn verbonden. Praktische kamers met een eigen terras en mooi uitzicht op het water beneden.

La Belle Époque, Bahnhofstr. 85 (Ouest : 3 km, lieu-dit Weywertz), 0 80 44 55 43 – P. AE VISA
fermé 2 sem. en mars, 2 sem. en sept. et merc. – **Repas** Lunch 15 – 28/45.
• Ce restaurant familial où l'on se sent un peu comme chez soi a des allures de bonbonnière avec son décor d'inspiration Belle Époque. Choix de recettes classiques.
• Dit familierestaurant, waar men zich onmiddellijk thuis voelt, heeft wel iets weg van een bonbonnière door zijn belle-époquedecor. De keuken is op klassieke leest geschoeid.

BELGIQUE

Vier Jahreszeiten avec ch, Bermicht 8 (Nord : 3 km, lieu-dit Nidrum), 0 80 44 56 04, *Fax 0 80 44 49 30*, – P.
fermé 1re quinz. juil., 1re quinz. janv. et mardi soir et merc. sauf vacances scolaires – **Repas** (taverne-rest) carte 30 à 47 – **15 ch** 40/75 – ½ P 58/70.
◆ Auberge de campagne récente curieusement aménagée à l'autrichienne. Cuisine très classique, superbe cave et chambres reposantes. Au total : une halte originale et dépaysante !
◆ Nieuwe plattelandsherberg, die merkwaardigerwijs in Oostenrijkse stijl is ingericht. Klassieke keuken, fantastische wijnen en rustige kamers. Om er even helemaal uit te zijn !

BUVRINNES *Hainaut* 533 K 20, 534 K 20 *et* 716 F 4 – *voir à Binche*.

CASTEAU *Hainaut* 533 J 19, 534 J 19 *et* 716 F 4 – *voir à Soignies*.

CELLES *Namur* 533 P 21, 534 P 21 *et* 716 I 5 – *voir à Houyet*.

CERFONTAINE *5630 Namur* 534 L 21 *et* 716 G 5 – *4 409 h.*
Bruxelles 100 – Charleroi 38 – Dinant 45 – Maubeuge 44.

à Soumoy *Nord-Est : 3 km* C *Cerfontaine* – ✉ *5630 Soumoy* :

Relais du Surmoy, r. Bironfosse 38, 0 71 64 32 13, *relais.surmoy@belgacom.net, Fax 0 71 64 47 09*, – TV P – 25 à 80. AE VISA
15 mars-15 oct. et week-end – **Repas** *Lunch 10* – 22/24 – **24 ch** 51/60 – ½ P 44/48.
◆ Légèrement à l'écart du village, dans un site tranquille, ferme ancienne bâtie en pierres du pays et devenue un agréable hôtel familial. Chambres sans reproche. Salle de restaurant rustique. Choix de préparations classiques à prix "tout doux".
◆ Familiehotel in een oude boerderij die uit de plaatselijke steensoort is opgetrokken, even buiten het dorp, in een rustige omgeving. De kamers zijn onberispelijk. Rustieke eetzaal, waar u voor een zacht prijsje kunt genieten van klassieke gerechten.

CHARLEROI

6000 Hainaut 533 L 20, 534 L 20 *et* 716 G 4 - *200 578 h.*

Bruxelles 61 ① - *Liège 92* ③ - *Lille 123* ① - *Namur 38* ③.

RENSEIGNEMENTS PRATIQUES

🅸 *par* ⑤ *à Marcinelle, Maison communale annexe, av. Mascaux 100 ☎ 0 71 86 61 52, office.tourisme@charleroi.be, Fax 0 71 86 61 57 – Pavillon, Square de la Gare du Sud ☎ 0 71 31 82 18, Fax 0 71 31 82 18.*

⛳18 *au Nord : 13 km à Frasnes-lez-Gosselies (Les-Bons-Villers), Chemin du Grand Pierpont 1 ☎ 0 71 85 17 75, Fax 0 71 85 15 43.*

CURIOSITÉS

Musées : *du verre★* BYZ **M** – *par* ⑤ *à Mont-sur-Marchienne : de la Photographie★.*
Env. *par* ⑤ *: 13 km à l'Abbaye d'Aulne★ : chevet et transept★★ de l'église abbatiale – par* ⑤ *à Marcinelle : l'Espace du 8 août 1956★★ au Bois du Cazier★.*

RÉPERTOIRE DES RUES DU PLAN DE CHARLEROI

Rue	Carré	N°
Albert-1er (Pl.)	ABZ	
Alliés (Av. des)	AZ	
Arthur-Decoux (R.)	AY	
Audent (Bd)	ABZ	
Baudouin (Pont)	AZ	3
Brabant (Quai du)	ABZ	
Brigade-Piron (R.)	BZ	
Broucheterre (R. de la)	ABY	6
Bruxelles (Chée de)	AY	
Charleroi (Chée de)	BZ	
Charles-II (Pl.)	BZ	10
Defontaine (Bd)	BYZ	
Digue (Pl. de la)	AZ	
Écluse (R. de l')	BZ	21
Émile-Buisset (Pl.)	AZ	23
Émile-Devreux (Bd)	BZ	24
Émile-Tumelaire (R.)	BZ	
Europe (Av. de l')	AYZ	
Flandre (Quai de)	AZ	25
Fort (R. du)	ABY	
Fr.-Dewandre (Bd)	BY	30
Gare du Sud (Quai de la)	AZ	
Général-Michel (Av.)	BZ	
Grand-Central (R. du)	AZ	
Grand'Rue	BY	
G.-Roullier (Bd)	BY	
Heigne (R. de)	AY	
Isaac (R.)	BY	
Jacques-Bertrand (Bd)	ABY	
Jean-Monnet (R.)	AZ	35
Joseph-Hénin (Bd)	BY	37
Joseph-Tirou (Bd)	ABZ	
Joseph-Wauters (R.)	AY	
Joseph-II (Bd)	BY	
Jules-Destrée (R.)	BY	
Lebeau (R.)	BY	38
Léon-Bernus (R.)	BY	
Mambourg (R. du)	BY	
Manège (Pl. du)	BY	41
Marcinelle (R. de)	BZ	43
Mayence (Bd P.)	BZ	44
Mons (Route de)	AZ	
Montagne (R. de la)	ABZ	45
Montigny (R. de)	BZ	
Neuve (R.)	BY	48
Olof-Palme (Pont)	AZ	49
Orléans (R. d')	BZ	50
Paix (R. de la)	BZ	
Paul-Janson (Bd)	BY	
Paul-Pastur (Av.)	AZ	
P.-J.-Lecomte (R.)	AY	
Pont-Neuf (R. du)	BZ	
Régence (R. de la)	BY	58
Roton (R. du)	ABY	
Saint-Charles (R.)	BZ	
Science (R. de la)	BYZ	
Solvay (Bd)	BY	61
Spinois (R.)	BY	
Turenne (R.)	AZ	
Villette (R. de la)	AZ	
Waterloo (Av. de)	BY	69
Willy-Ernst (R.)	BZ	
Yser (Bd de l')	AZ	
Zenobe-Gramme (R.)	BY	73
Zoé-Dryon (Bd)	BY	

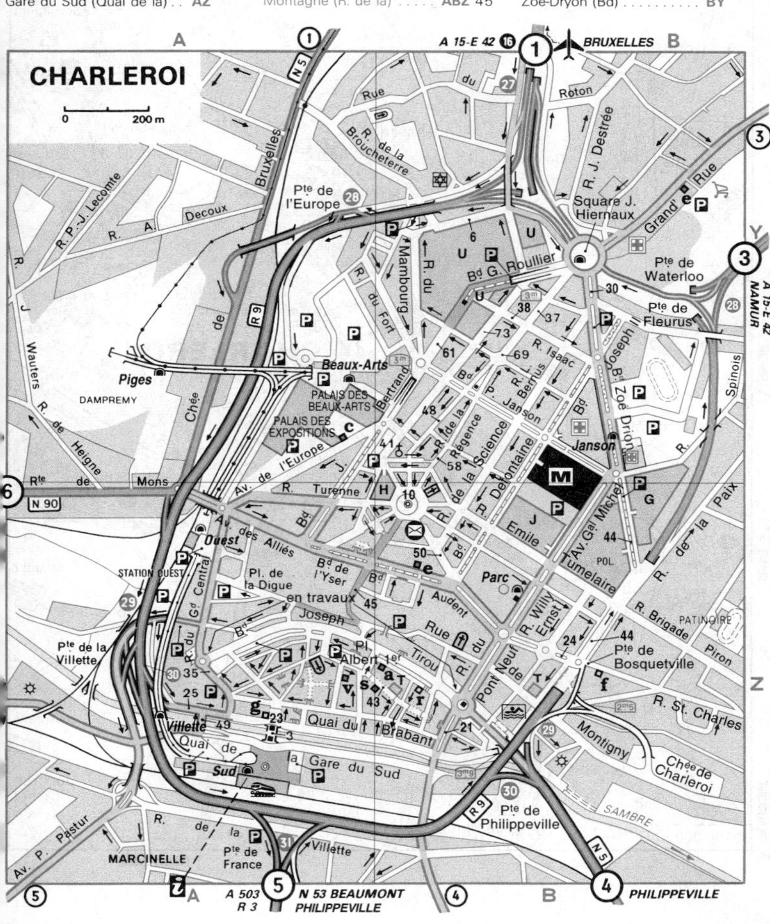

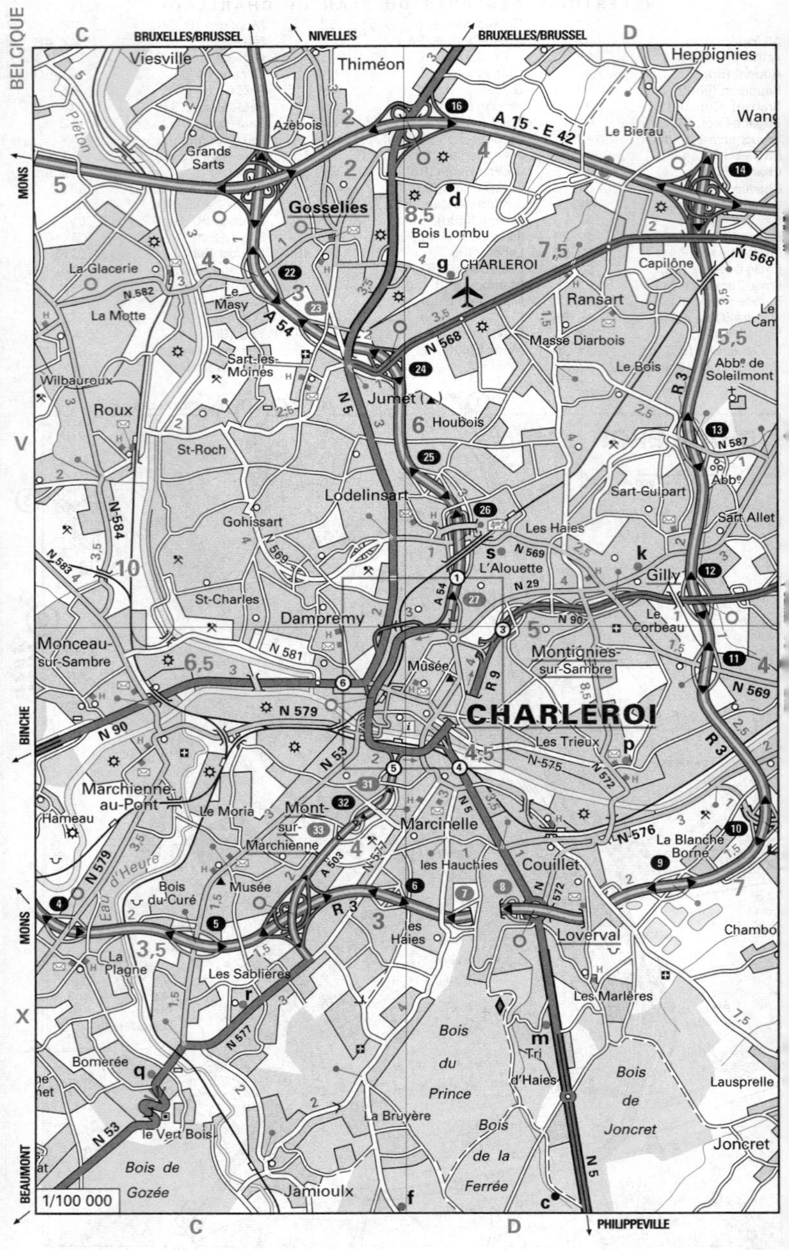
BRUXELLES/BRUSSEL
NIVELLES
BRUXELLES/BRUSSEL
C
D
Viesville
Thiméon
Heppignies
Wang
Azèbois
A 15 - E 42
Le Bierau
Piéton
Grands Sarts
MONS
Gosselies
8,5
Bois Lombu
CHARLEROI
7,5
Capilône
N 568
La Glacerie
N 582
Le Masy
Ransart
La Motte
A 54
3,5
Masse Diarbois
5,5
Abbe de Soleilmont
Sart-les-Moines
Le Bois
R 3
Wilbauroux
N 5
Jumet
Roux
Houbois
N 587
V
St-Roch
Abbe
Sart-Culpart
Lodelinsart
Sart Allet
Gohissart
N-584
N 569
Les Haies
L'Alouette
Gilly
N 583
10
St-Charles
N 29
Dampremy
N 90
Le Corbeau
Monceau-sur-Sambre
6,5
N 581
Montignies-sur-Sambre
Musée
N 579
R 9
CHARLEROI
BINCHE
N 90
Les Trieux
4,5
N-575
N 572
N 53
Marchienne-au-Pont
Hameau
Le Moria
Mont-sur-Marchienne
Marcinelle
N-576
La Blanche Borne
N 579
Eau d'Heure
A 503
N 577
les Hauchies
Couillet
Bois du Curé
Musée
R 3
N 572
MONS
3,5
les Haies
Loverval
Chambo
La Plagne
Les Sablières
Les Marlères
X
N 577
Bois du Prince
Tri d'Haies
Bomerée
Bois de Joncret
Lausprelle
La Bruyère
N 53
le Vert Bois
Bois de la Ferrée
Joncret
BEAUMONT
Bois de Gozée
Jamioulx
N 5
1/100 000
PHILIPPEVILLE

Socatel, bd Tirou 96, ☎ 0 71 31 98 11, *sotel@skynet.be, Fax 0 71 30 15 96* – AE VISA BZ r

Repas *Lunch 8* – carte 22 à 38 – 9 – **69 ch** 85/115, – 1 suite – ½ P 99/199.

• Architecture moderne bordant l'artère principale de la capitale du Pays noir. Chambres personnalisées de différentes tailles, propices à des sommeils réparateurs. Confortable brasserie-restaurant.

• Modern gebouw aan de hoofdweg van de belangrijkste stad van het Zwarte Land. Kamers van verschillende grootte met een persoonlijk karakter, die een ongestoorde nachtrust in petto hebben. Gerieflijk taverne-restaurant.

Business, bd Mayence 1a, ☎ 0 71 30 24 24, *info@businesshotel.be, Fax 0 71 30 49 49*, – 25 à 180. AE VISA. BZ f

Repas *Lunch 13* – carte env. 37 – 9 – **57 ch** 80 – ½ P 95/100.

• Cet immeuble récent dont les façades semblent percées de meurtrières renferme des chambres actuelles bien isolées du bruit, proximité du ring oblige ! Des buffets sont dressés à l'heure des repas.

• Nieuw gebouw, waarvan de gevels met schietgaten lijken te zijn doorboord. Moderne kamers met een goede geluidsisolatie, wat zo vlak bij de Ring geen overbodige luxe is ! 's Middags en 's avonds kunnen de gasten zich te goed doen aan de buffetten.

Ibis sans rest, quai de Flandre 12, ☎ 0 71 20 60 60, *h2088@accor-hotels.com, Fax 0 71 70 21 91* – AE VISA AZ g

9 – **72 ch** 75.

• Un oiseau exotique s'est posé au bord de la Sambre, près de la gare et du pont Baudouin. Chambres modernes toutes identiques, conformes à l'esprit de la chaîne.

• Deze vreemde ibisvogel nestelt aan de oever van de Samber, vlak bij het station en de Boudewijnbrug. Moderne standaardkamers, geheel in de geest van deze bekende hotelketen.

Le D'Agnelli, bd Audent 23a, ☎ 0 71 30 90 96, *Fax 0 71 30 90 96*, , Cuisine italienne – . AE VISA BZ e

fermé sem. carnaval, Ascension, 27 juil.-16 août, sam. midi, dim. soir et lundi – **Repas** *Lunch 40* – carte 49 à 77.

• Attablez-vous en confiance sur la terrasse d'été abritée ou à l'intérieur de cet élégant restaurant italien. Fine cuisine transalpine, assez iodée, et vins du pays, "certo" !

• Deze verleidelijke Italiaan biedt u een spannend culinair avondje. Smakelijke mediterrane keuken met veel vis, waarbij de wijnen een sprankelende tafeldame zijn.

La Mirabelle 1er étage, r. Marcinelle 7, ☎ 0 71 33 39 88 – . AE VISA ABZ s

fermé 1 sem. carnaval, du 15 au 30 août, dim., lundi soir, merc. soir et jeudi soir – **Repas** *Lunch 25* – 35/43 bc.

• Un escalier étroit conduit à ce restaurant au cadre résolument contemporain mitonnant des plats classiques. La carte est renouvelée à chaque saison, ou presque.

• Een smalle trap leidt naar dit restaurant met zijn eigentijdse interieur, waar klassieke gerechten worden geserveerd. De menukaart wordt vrijwel elk seizoen vernieuwd.

Le Square Sud, bd Tirou 70, ☎ 0 71 32 16 06, *Fax 0 71 30 44 05* – . AE VISA BZ a

fermé du 23 au 29 fév., du 10 au 18 avril, 17 juil.-8 août, sam. midi et dim. – **Repas** *Lunch 23* – 43/78 bc.

• Tables et chaises rustiques meublent plaisamment ces authentiques caves voûtées du 17e s. abritant une "œnothèque" riche de quelque 500 appellations.

• Rustieke tafels en stoelen bepalen de sfeer in deze gewelfde kelderverdieping uit de 17e eeuw, die beschikt over een "vinotheek" met maar liefst 500 verschillende wijnen.

Au Provençal, r. Puissant 10, ☎ 0 71 31 28 37, *jcbarral@skynet.be, Fax 0 71 31 28 37* – . AE VISA AZ v

fermé 15 juil.-15 août et dim. – **Repas** *Lunch 33* – carte 34 à 52.

• Maison familiale étageant sa salle à manger fleurie sur deux niveaux. Registre culinaire classico-traditionnel. En cave, "fiasques" et "topettes" font bon ménage.

• Familierestaurant met een fleurige eetzaal op twee niveaus. Klassiek-traditionele menukaart. In de wijnkelder vormen de dikke ronde flessen en de dunne lange een perfect duo.

A la Tête de Bœuf, pl. de l'Abattoir 5, ☎ 0 71 48 77 64, *Fax 0 71 42 27 04*, Taverne-rest – AE VISA JCB. DV s

fermé 1 sem. Pâques, 1 sem. en juil., fin déc., sam. midi, dim., lundi soir, mardi soir et jeudi soir – **Repas** *Lunch 11* – 20.

• Place de l'abattoir, le chef et les tripes sont copains comme cochons. L'aménagement des lieux donne dans le campagnard, sans vraiment faire un "effet bœuf".

• In dit landelijk ingerichte restaurant zijn de chef-kok en ingewanden twee handen op één buik. Hoe kan het ook anders aan het slachthuisplein !

BELGIQUE

Piccolo Mondo, Grand'Rue 87, ☎ 0 71 42 00 17, *Fax 0 71 42 00 17*, Trattoria, Cuisine italienne – MC VISA BY e
fermé du 15 au 31 juil. et dim. – **Repas** (déjeuner seult sauf vend. et sam.) carte 23 à 35.
◆ Le "Petit Monde" (de Don Camillo ?) accueille simplement les amateurs de "cucina come a casa" autour de tables et chaises de style bistrot. Hé, Gino, c'est "Cervi" !
◆ Gezellig restaurantje met tafels en stoelen in bistrostijl en eenvoudig, maar lekker Italiaans eten "à la mamma". Hé Gino, schenk nog eens een glaasje vino...

L'Amusoir, av. de l'Europe 7, ☎ 0 71 31 61 64, *y-leroy61@bhotmail.com, Fax 0 71 31 61 64*, Ouvert jusqu'à 23 h – AE D MC VISA AY c
Repas *Lunch 17* – 24/48 bc, ♀.
◆ Cette petite adresse feutrée jouxtant le palais des Beaux-Arts et celui des Expositions vous concocte des préparations classico-traditionnelles. Prix "sympa", sinon amusants.
◆ Leuk adresje naast het Paleis voor Schone Kunsten en het Paleis der Tentoonstellingen, waar u kunt smullen van klassiek-traditionele schotels. En de prijs ? Die blijft amusant !

à Gerpinnes *par ④ : Sud Est 13 km – 12 054 h – ✉ 6280 Gerpinnes :*

Le Délice du Jour, chaussée de Philippeville 195, ☎ 0 71 21 93 43 – P. MC VISA.
fermé prem. sem. janv., mardi, merc. et après 20 h 30 – **Repas** *Lunch 20* – 30/57 bc.
◆ Dans la cité emblématique des "marches" d'Entre-Sambre-et-Meuse, restaurant familial dont la salle des repas procure la vue sur un jardinet. Mets en phase avec l'époque.
◆ In dit dorp in het land van Samber en Maas worden "soldatenprocessies" gehouden. De eetzaal van dit familierestaurant kijkt uit op een tuintje. Eigentijdse keuken.

à Gilly C *Charleroi – ✉ 6060 Gilly :*

Il Pane Vino, chaussée de Fleurus 125, ☎ 0 71 41 53 36, *Fax 0 71 41 53 36*, Avec cuisine italienne – ▤. AE D MC VISA. DV k
fermé juil., merc. et dim. soir – **Repas** *Lunch 20* – carte 22 à 42.
◆ Derrière une façade discrète, trattoria "simpatica" dont la fourchette s'étend d'Aoste à Palerme. On y mange au coude-à-coude dans une ambiance familiale.
◆ Achter een onopvallende gevel gaat deze trattoria schuil, met recepten van Aosta tot Palermo. Men tafelt er gebroederlijk naast elkaar in een huiselijke ambiance. "Simpatica" !

à Gosselies C *Charleroi – ✉ 6041 Gosselies :*

Le Piersoulx, r. Grand Piersoulx 8 (Gosselies I - douane), ☎ 0 71 91 91 00, *le-piersoulx@swing.be, Fax 0 71 35 70 03* – ▤ rest, TV P – 40. AE D MC VISA DV d
Repas 22/34 – ☕ 9 – **14 ch** 80/100.
◆ Petit immeuble récent situé près de l'aéroport, au cœur de la zone industrielle de Gosselies. Les chambres, actuelles, offrent au businessman un confort correct. Salle de restaurant actuelle. Choix de recettes régulièrement renouvelé et vins du Bordelais.
◆ Klein en nieuw gebouw vlak bij de luchthaven, midden op het industrieterrein van Gosselies. De moderne kamers bieden zakenmensen een goed comfort. Eigentijds restaurant met regelmatig wisselende gerechten op de kaart en uitstekende bordeauxwijnen.

Le Saint-Exupéry, chaussée de Fleurus 181 (près Aéropole), ☎ 0 71 35 59 62, *Fax 0 71 37 35 96*, ←, – P – 25. AE D MC VISA DV g
fermé 23 fév.-1er mars, du 1er au 10 avril, 26 juil.-9 août, du 2 au 4 janv. et sam. midi – **Repas** (déjeuner seult sauf vend. et sam.) 39/66 bc.
◆ Par beau temps, pourquoi ne pas "se poser" en terrasse de ce restaurant servant une cuisine classico-traditionnelle composée selon les arrivages du marché. Vue sur les pistes.
◆ Bij mooi weer kunt u neerstrijken op het terras van dit restaurant, met uitzicht op het vliegveld. Klassiek-traditionele gerechten, afhankelijk van het aanbod op de markt.

à Loverval C *Gerpinnes 12 054 h. – ✉ 6280 Loverval :*

Le Saint Germain des Prés (Durieux), rte de Philippeville 62, ☎ 0 71 43 58 12, – P. AE D MC VISA DX m
fermé du 16 au 23 mai, du 6 au 16 sept., 22 déc.-11 janv., sam. midi, dim. soir et lundi – **Repas** 49/80, carte 58 à 75.
◆ Les fines fourchettes fréquentent assidûment cette imposante villa perchée sur un coteau à la périphérie de Charleroi. Salle à manger feutrée, cuisine traditionnelle soignée.
◆ Deze imposante villa op een heuvel aan de rand van Charleroi is zeer in trek bij fijnproevers. In de cosy eetzaal worden verzorgde traditionele schotels geserveerd.
Spéc. Raviole de foie gras au coulis de pois gourmands et truffes. Cabillaud, risotto à la truffe et bouillon de parmesan. Bar rôti en croûte de sel et beurre blanc

à Montignies-sur-Sambre C *Charleroi – ✉ 6061 Montignies-sur-Sambre :*

Au Petit Gastronome, pl. Albert Ier 43, ☎ 0 71 32 10 20, *Fax 0 71 32 10 20* – ▤. MC VISA DX p
fermé lundi – **Repas** *Lunch 15* – 23/36 bc.
◆ Sur la place centrale du village, adresse au cadre assez intime dont l'intéressant choix de recettes varie en fonction des disponibilités du marché. Salle de banquets.
◆ Restaurant aan het dorpsplein met een vrij intieme sfeer. De kok kookt op basis van wat er op de markt te verkrijgen is, wat altijd voor verrassingen zorgt. Feestzaal.

BELGIQUE

à Montigny-le-Tilleul – *10 273 h – ✉ 6110 Montigny-le-Tilleul :*

XX **L'éveil des Sens** (Zioui), r. Station 105 (lieu-dit Bomerée), ☎ 0 71 31 96 92, *eveildessens@skynet.be, Fax 0 71 31 96 92* – ▤ P. AE MC VISA CX q
✿ *fermé 1 sem. en avril, 15 juil.-prem.sem. août, 24 déc. soir, 25 et 31 déc. soir, 1er janv., 1 sem. fin janv., sam. midi, dim. soir et lundis non fériés* – **Repas** *Lunch 26* – 45/115 bc, carte 62 à 76, ♀.
◆ Une nouvelle enseigne qui a déjà le vent en poupe, et pour cause : décor intérieur des plus fringants, cuisine savoureusement inventive et sélection de vins bien montée.
◆ Deze nieuwkomer heeft in een mum van tijd een goede naam opgebouwd en terecht : vrolijk interieur, inventieve keuken en heerlijke wijnen. Een genot voor alle zintuigen !
Spéc. Homard et ris de veau caramelisés, bouillon mousseux aux sucs de crustacés et Porto blanc. Pigeonneau d'Anjou en 2 services. Soufflé chaud aux fruits de la passion et banane

à Mont-sur-Marchienne C *Charleroi* – ✉ *6032 Mont-sur-Marchienne :*

XXX **La Dacquoise,** r. Marcinelle 181, ☎ 0 71 43 63 90, *ladacquoise@belgacom.net, Fax 0 71 47 45 01,* 余 – ▤ P. AE ⓓ MC VISA CX r
fermé début juil.-début août, fin déc.-début janv., mardi soir, merc. et dim. soir – **Repas** *Lunch 34* – 40/80 bc, ♀.
◆ La plaisante salle à manger, garnie d'un mobilier cérusé, donne sur une accueillante terrasse d'été. Mets mariant tradition et goût du jour. Belle gamme de crus bordelais.
◆ Prettig restaurant met meubelen van geceruseerd hout en een zomers terras. Het eten is een geslaagde mix van traditioneel en modern. Fraai assortiment bordeauxwijnen.

à Nalinnes C *Ham-sur-Heure-Nalinnes 13 263 h.* – ✉ *6120 Nalinnes :*

Laudanel sans rest, r. Vallée 117 (lieu-dit Le Bultia), ☎ 0 71 21 93 40, *laudanel@swing.be, Fax 0 71 21 93 37,* ▣, 余 – TV. AE MC VISA. ✗ DX c
fermé du 21 au 31 juil. et du 16 au 31 janv. – ☕ 11 – **6 ch** 98/105.
◆ Villa de notre temps postée à l'orée de la forêt. Paisibles chambres contemporaines aménagées à l'identique, où descendent volontiers les businessmen. Piscine couverte.
◆ Hedendaagse villa aan de rand van het bos. Rustige, eigentijdse kamers die allemaal hetzelfde zijn ingericht en waar voornamelijk zakenmensen logeren. Overdekt zwembad.

XX **Guy De Wilde,** r. Marcinelle 119, ☎ 0 71 21 68 06, *Fax 0 71 21 68 41* – ▤ P. MC VISA. ✗ CX f
fermé 2 prem. sem. avril, 2 prem. sem. oct., 2 prem. sem. janv, dim. soir, lundi et jeudi – **Repas** *Lunch 19* – 33/66 bc.
◆ Guy de Wilde vous reçoit désormais chez lui, dans une salle à manger ample et confortable, décorée à la mode d'aujourd'hui. Choix classique annonçant plusieurs menus.
◆ Guy de Wilde ontvangt u voortaan in zijn eigen restaurant. De eetzaal is ruim en comfortabel en naar de laatste mode ingericht. Klassieke kaart en verscheidene menu's.

CHAUDFONTAINE

4050 Liège 533 S 19, 534 S 19 *et* 716 J 4 – *20 665 h* – *Casino, Esplanade 1* ☎ *0 4 365 07 41, Fax 0 4 365 37 62.*
i *Maison Sauveur, Parc des Sources* ☎ *0 4 361 56 30, commune@chaudfontaine.be,* Fax 0 4 361 56 40.
Bruxelles 104 – Liège 10 – Verviers 22.

Il Castellino, av. des Thermes 147, ☎ 0 4 365 75 08, *Fax 0 4 367 41 53,* 余 – TV P – 🏛 25 à 400. AE ⓓ MC VISA. ✗ ch
Repas *(fermé mardis non fériés)* (avec cuisine italienne) *Lunch 16* – carte 22 à 37 – **8 ch** ☕ 55/70 – ½ P 86.
◆ Cette massive construction ardennaise élevée au bord de la route abrite un petit nombre de chambres bénéficiant toutes d'une bonne isolation phonique. Carte franco-italienne proposée dans une salle des repas rustique.
◆ Dit hotel met zijn solide, typisch Ardense architectuur ligt aan de kant van de weg. Het beschikt over een klein aantal kamers die allemaal van goede geluidsisolatie zijn voorzien. In de rustiek ingerichte eetzaal worden Frans-Italiaanse gerechten geserveerd.

CHAUMONT-GISTOUX

1325 Brabant Wallon 533 N 18, 534 N 18 *et* 716 H 3 – *10 476 h.*
Bruxelles 37 – Namur 32 – Wavre 10.

X **Le Moulin du Bloquia,** r. Manypré 96, ☎ 0 10 68 04 31, *Fax 0 10 68 04 91,* 余 – ▤ P. AE MC VISA
fermé 2e quinz. sept., dern.sem. janv.-prem. sem. fév., sam. midi, dim. soir et lundi – **Repas** 26/34.
◆ Table de style rustique-moderne intégrée à un ensemble où se sont succédé, depuis 1194, un moulin à grain, puis à papier, une cartonnerie et une villégiature. Belle terrasse.
◆ Etablissement in modern-rustieke stijl in een complex, waar zich sinds 1194 successievelijk een graanmolen, papiermolen, kartonfabriek en vakantieoord bevonden. Mooi terras.

à Dion-Valmont *Nord-Ouest : 7 km* [C] *Chaumont-Gistoux – ✉ 1325 Dion-Valmont :*

XX **L'Or Ange Bleu,** chaussée de Huy 71, ✆ 0 10 68 96 86, *olivier@lorangebleu.com, Fax 0 10 88 09 30,* – P. AE MC VISA
fermé sem. Pâques, 2e quinz. août, Noël-Nouvel An, lundi et sam. midi – **Repas** *Lunch 25* – 49, ♀.
◆ Pimpante fermette convertie en refuge gourmand. Harmonie de bleu, d'orange et d'ivoire dans une lumineuse salle à manger-véranda au parquet blond. Accueil et service avenants.
◆ In dit frisse en vrolijke boerderijtje kunt u culinair genieten. Lichte eetzaal met serre in een harmonieuze kleurcombinatie van blauw, oranje en ivoor. Voorkomende bediening.

CHÊNÉE *Liège* 533 S 19 *et* 534 S 19 – *voir à Liège, périphérie.*

CHEVETOGNE *5590 Namur* [C] *Ciney 14 689 h.* 533 P 21, 534 P 21 *et* 716 I 5.
Voir *Domaine provincial Valéry Cousin*★.
Bruxelles 90 – Namur 43 – Dinant 29 – Liège 73.

Les Rhodos, dans le Domaine provincial, ✆ 0 83 68 89 00, *lesrhodos@tiscali.be, Fax 0 83 68 90 75,* – TV P – 30. MC VISA. ch
fermé janv. et mardi sauf en juil.-août – **Repas** 25/58 bc – **15 ch** 59 – ½ P 46/70.
◆ Un paisible parc provincial de 500 ha borde cet ancien pavillon de chasse aux abords fleuris de rhododendrons. Confort correct dans les chambres-bungalows. Restaurant au décor intérieur soigné. Plats classiques axés "terroir", accompagnés de bons bordeaux.
◆ Dit oude jachtpaviljoen tussen de rododendrons grenst aan een rustig park van 500 ha. Kamers en bungalows met goede voorzieningen. Het restaurant heeft een verzorgd interieur. Klassieke schotels op basis van streekproducten, met daarbij een goede bordeaux.

Ecrivez-nous...
Vos louanges comme vos critiques seront examinées avec le plus grand soin. Nous reverrons sur place les informations que vous nous signalez. Par avance merci !

CHIMAY *6460 Hainaut* 534 K 22 *et* 716 F 5 – *9 867 h.*
Env. *au Nord-Est : 3 km, Étang*★ *de Virelles.*
Bruxelles 110 – Charleroi 50 – Dinant 61 – Mons 56 – Hirson 25.

X **Le Froissart,** pl. Froissart 8, ✆ 0 60 21 26 19, *Fax 0 60 21 42 45,* – MC VISA
fermé sem. carnaval, 2 dern. sem. août, merc. et jeudi – **Repas** carte 25 à 43.
◆ Outre son registre culinaire classique, la maison propose une carte "brasserie" qui séduira les amateurs du genre. Côté addition, pas de quoi "froisser" une grosse coupure !
◆ Dit restaurant biedt behalve klassieke gerechten ook lekkere schotels in typische brasseriestijl. Uitstekende prijs-kwaliteitverhouding.

X **Xi Wou,** pl. Froissart 25, ✆ 0 60 21 17 27, Cuisine chinoise – MC VISA
fermé merc. midi – **Repas** *Lunch 11* – 16/43.
◆ Tenté par un périple culinaire dans l'Empire du Milieu sans quitter le pays des moines trappistes ? Xi Wou est alors une halte toute indiquée. Authentique et goûteux !
◆ Xi Wou is de ideale gelegenheid voor een culinair uitstapje naar het Chinese Rijk zonder het land van de trappisten te hoeven verlaten. Authentiek en smakelijk !

à l'étang de Virelles *Nord-Est : 3 km* [C] *Chimay – ✉ 6461 Virelles :*

XX **Chez Edgard et Madeleine,** r. Lac 35, ✆ 0 60 21 10 71, *Fax 0 60 21 52 47,* – MC VISA
fermé 2 sem. en juil., 2 sem. en janv. et lundis soirs et mardis non fériés – **Repas** 43/55 bc.
◆ Cette adresse perpétue un savoir-faire familial vieux de quatre générations. Edgard et Madeleine dressent pour vous, selon votre choix, une table bourgeoise ou régionale.
◆ Hier wordt de culinaire traditie al vier generaties lang doorgegeven. Edgard en Madeleine zetten u, naar keuze, klassieke of regionale gerechten voor.

à Lompret *Nord-Est : 7 km sur N 99* [C] *Chimay – ✉ 6463 Lompret :*

Franc Bois sans rest, r. courtil aux Martias 18, ✆ 0 60 21 44 75, *francbois@swing.be, Fax 0 60 21 51 40* – TV. AE MC VISA.
8 ch 70/75.
◆ Près de l'église, maison de pays en pierre calcaire disposant d'un petit nombre de chambres gaies et actuelles. Équipement fonctionnel sans reproche.
◆ Dit karakteristieke kalkstenen huis bij de kerk beschikt over enkele frisse en vrolijke kamers. Functionele voorzieningen waar niets op aan te merken valt.

à **Momignies** *Ouest : 12 km – 5 117 h – ✉ 6590 Momignies :*

Host. du Gahy ⛰, r. Gahy 2, ✆ 0 60 51 10 93, *Fax 0 60 51 30 05*, ≤, 🍽, 🌳 – 📺 🅿 – 🏛 30. AE ⓓ ⓞ VISA. ✂
Repas *Lunch 16* – 25/50 – **6 ch** ☕ 75/85.
• Cadre bucolique et quiétude font le charme de cette demeure ancienne abritant quelques chambres assez spacieuses et correctement équipées. Salle à manger intime où vous dégusterez une cuisine de saison bien tournée.
• De landelijke omgeving en de rust vormen de charme van deze oude hostellerie. De kamers zijn vrij ruim en hebben goede voorzieningen. Eetzaal met een intieme sfeer, waar seizoengebonden gerechten van uitstekende kwaliteit worden geserveerd.

CINEY *5590 Namur* 533 P 21, 534 P 21 *et* 716 I 5 – *14 689 h.*
Bruxelles 86 – Namur 30 – Dinant 16 – Huy 31.

Surlemont ⛰ sans rest, r. Surlemont 9, ✆ 0 83 23 08 68, *hotel.surlemont@skynet.be, Fax 0 83 23 08 69*, ≤, 🏊, 🌳, 🚲 – ⇆ 📺 🅿 – 🏛 80 à 200. ⓓ ⓞ VISA. ✂
fermé du 1er au 15 janv. et dim. – **13 ch** ☕ 55/90.
• Ancienne ferme seigneuriale jouissant du calme de la campagne environnante. Mignonnes chambres actuelles et coquette salle des petits-déjeuners.
• Oude herenboerderij, rustig gelegen op het platteland. De eigentijdse kamers zijn spic en span en ook de ontbijtzaal ziet er piekfijn uit.

L'Alexandrin, r. Commerce 121, ✆ 0 83 21 75 95, *restaurant.alexandrin@belgacom.net, Fax 0 83 21 75 95*, 🍽 – 🅿. AE ⓓ ⓞ VISA
fermé sem. carnaval, 1 sem. en juil., sem. Toussaint, jeudi, sam. midi et dim. soir – **Repas** *Lunch 20* – 33/90 bc.
• Ami poète, entre deux emplettes dans cette rue plutôt chouette, pourquoi ne pas envisager une césure à l'Alexandrin ? Intérieur contemporain feutré et accueillante terrasse.
• In dit restaurant in een gezellige winkelstraat kunt u na het shoppen de inwendige mens versterken. Sfeervol hedendaags interieur en een zeer uitnodigend terras.

CLERMONT *Liège* 533 U 19, 534 U 19 *et* 716 J 4 – *voir à Thimister.*

COMBLAIN-LA-TOUR *4180 Liège* Ⓒ *Hamoir 3 558 h.* 533 S 20, 534 S 20 *et* 716 J 4.
Env. *au Nord à Comblain-au-Pont, grottes★.*
Bruxelles 122 – Liège 32 – Spa 29.

Host. St-Roch, r. Parc 1, ✆ 0 4 369 13 33, *saintroch@relaischateaux.com, Fax 0 4 369 31 31*, ≤, 🍽, 🌳, 🚲 – 📺 🅿 – 🏛 25. AE ⓓ ⓞ VISA
Repas *(15 mars-1er janv. ; fermé lundi et merc. midi sauf en juil.-août et mardi) Lunch 32* – 48/65 – **10 ch** *(15 mars-1er janv. ; fermé lundi et mardi sauf en juil.-août)* ☕ 150/170, – 5 suites – ½ P 124/144.
• Demeure centenaire élevée au bord de l'Ourthe. Élégantes chambres garnies d'un mobilier de style et plaisant jardin-terrasse fleuri. Salle à manger cossue. Recettes alliant classicisme et modernité. Agréable restaurant d'été rafraîchi par la rivière.
• Eeuwenoud pand aan de oever van de Ourthe. Elegante kamers met stijlmeubilair en aangenaam terras in een weelderige tuin. De eetzaal doet luxueus aan. De recepten zijn een spannende combinatie van klassiek en modern. Bij mooi weer kunt u aan de waterkant eten.

COO *Liège* 533 U 20, 534 U 20 *et* 716 K 4 – *voir à Stavelot.*

CORBION *Luxembourg belge* 534 P 24 *et* 716 I 6 – *voir à Bouillon.*

CORROY-LE-GRAND *1325 Brabant Wallon* Ⓒ *Chaumont-Gistoux 10 476 h.* 533 N 19, 534 N 19 *et* 716 H 4.
Bruxelles 35 – Namur 35 – Charleroi 38 – Tienen 29.

Le Grand Corroy avec ch, r. Eglise 13, ✆ 0 10 68 98 98, *legrandcorroy@wanadoo.be, Fax 0 10 68 94 78*, 🍽 – 📺. AE ⓓ ⓞ VISA
fermé du 12 au 20 avril, du 13 au 21 sept., 20 déc.-4 janv., sam. midi, dim. soir et lundi – **Repas** *Lunch 24* – 36/87 bc – **4 ch** ☕ 100.
• Poussez la grille du jardin clos et attablez-vous dans l'un des caveaux voûtés de cette ancienne ferme brabançonne. Chambres spacieuses agencées avec goût.
• Wie het hek van de omheinde tuin openduwt, kan aan tafel schuiven in een van de gewelfde kelders van deze oude Brabantse boerderij. Ruime kamers die smaakvol zijn ingericht.

COURTRAI *West-Vlaanderen – voir Kortrijk.*

COURT-SAINT-ETIENNE *1490 Brabant Wallon* 533 M 19, 534 M 19 *et* 716 G 4 – *8 866 h.*
Bruxelles 33 – Namur 38 – Charleroi 34.

XX **Les Ailes,** av. des Prisonniers de Guerre 3, ✆ 0 10 61 61 61, *lesailes@skynet.be, Fax 0 10 61 46 32* – P. AE MC VISA JCB
fermé 18 fév.-4 mars, 18 août-9 sept., dim. soir, lundi et mardi – **Repas** Lunch 20 – 33/73 bc.
◆ Jolie salle à manger rythmée de poutres et éclairée par de grandes baies vitrées. Les menus sont composés avec des produits du terroir : cochon de lait, volaille, truite, etc.
◆ Mooie eetzaal met balkenzoldering en grote glaspuien. De menu's zijn samengesteld uit streekproducten, waaronder speenvarken, gevogelte en forel.

COUVIN *5660 Namur* 534 L 22 *et* 716 G 5 – *13 313 h.*
Voir *Grottes de Neptune★.*
r. Falaise 3 ✆ 0 60 34 01 40, *info.tourisme@couvin.be, Fax 0 60 34 01 43.*
Bruxelles 104 – Namur 64 – Charleroi 44 – Dinant 47 – Charleville-Mézières 46.

X **Nulle Part Ailleurs** avec ch, r. Gare 10, ✆ 0 60 34 52 84, *fred.corman@skynet.be, Fax 0 60 34 52 84*
Repas *(fermé lundi)* Lunch 27 – 28/46 bc – ☕ 5 – **5 ch** 45/50.
◆ Une carte "tradition" ponctuée de spécialités belges vous sera présentée à cette enseigne. Sémillantes salles à manger actuelles évoquant la campagne. Chambres mignonnes.
◆ Traditionele kaart met Belgische specialiteiten. De vrolijke eetzalen in hedendaagse stijl roepen een landelijke sfeer op. Beeldige kamers.

X **Le Jardin de Jade,** r. Gare 53, ✆ 0 60 34 66 32, *Fax 0 60 34 66 32,* Cuisine chinoise, ouvert jusqu'à 23 h – AE MC VISA
fermé fin juil.-début août et mardi – **Repas** Lunch 8 – 15/33.
◆ Dans la rue principale, près de la gare, agréable restaurant asiatique au décor intérieur "made in China". Menus bien ficelés et belle cave pour le genre de la maison.
◆ Aangenaam Aziatisch restaurant in de hoofdstraat, met een "made in China" interieur. Mooie menu's en voor Chinese begrippen een goede wijnkelder.

à Boussu-en-Fagne *Nord-Ouest : 4,5 km* C *Couvin* – ✉ *5660 Boussu-en-Fagne :*

Manoir de la Motte, r. Motte 21, ✆ 0 60 34 40 13, *Fax 0 60 34 67 17,* ←, – AE MC VISA.
fermé du 1er au 15 sept., Noël, Nouvel An, janv., dim. soir et lundi – **Repas** Lunch 25 – 28 – **7 ch** ☕ 65/80 – ½ P 65/75.
◆ Gentilhommière du 14e s. postée à l'écart du village, dans un environnement calme. Chambres personnalisées, équipées simplement mais meublées avec recherche. Agréable salle de restaurant au cadre bourgeois. Choix de mets classico-traditionnels.
◆ Kasteeltje uit de 14e eeuw, even buiten het dorp, in een rustige omgeving. Eenvoudige kamers met een persoonlijke uitstraling en smaakvolle meubilering. In de eetzaal voelt u zich een "grand seigneur". Klassiek-traditionele menukaart.

à Frasnes *Nord : 5,5 km par N 5* C *Couvin* – ✉ *5660 Frasnes :*

Le Tromcourt, lieu-dit Géronsart 15, ✆ 0 60 31 18 70, *eric.patigny@pi.be, Fax 0 60 31 32 02,* – TV P – 30. AE MC VISA. rest
fermé 22 fév.-20 mars, 17 août-3 sept., du 1er au 10 janv., mardi et merc. – **Repas** *(fermé après 20 h 30)* Lunch 28 – carte 44 à 66 – **10 ch** ☕ 66/114 – ½ P 82/94.
◆ Retirée en pleine campagne, cette paisible ferme-château du 17e s. renferme des chambres sans fioriture, égayées par la présence de quelques meubles rustiques. À table, répertoire culinaire d'inclination classique.
◆ Vredige kasteelboerderij uit de 17e eeuw, midden op het platteland. De kamers zijn zonder veel opsmuk, maar hebben een paar mooie rustieke meubelen. Aan tafel krijgen de gasten klassieke gerechten voorgeschoteld.

CRUPET *5332 Namur* C *Assesse 6 086 h.* 533 O 20, 534 O 20 *et* 716 H 4.
Bruxelles 79 – Namur 27 – Dinant 16.

Le Moulin des Ramiers, r. Basse 31, ✆ 0 83 69 90 70, *info@moulins.ramiers.com, Fax 0 83 69 98 68,* – TV P. AE MC VISA
fermé du 8 au 26 mars, 15 déc.-15 janv., lundi et mardi – **Repas** voir rest ***Les Ramiers*** ci-après – ☕ 12 – **6 ch** 113/135 – ½ P 120/130.
◆ Cet ancien moulin à eau du 18e s. aux abords verdoyants abrite d'assez amples chambres garnies d'un mobilier de style. Rafraîchissant jardin baigné par le ruisseau.
◆ Deze voormalige watermolen uit de 18e eeuw ligt midden in het groen. De vrij ruime kamers zijn met stijlmeubilair verfraaid. Door de tuin stroomt een verfrissend beekje.

XX **Les Ramiers** - H. Le Moulin des Ramiers, r. Basse 32, ☎ 0 83 69 90 70, *info@moulins.ramiers.com, Fax 0 83 69 98 68,* ≤, 🏖 - 🅿. AE ⓓ ⓜ VISA
fermé du 8 au 26 mars, prem. sem. juil., 15 déc.-15 janv., lundi midi sauf en juil.-août, lundi soir et mardi - **Repas** *Lunch 28* - 36/100 bc.
◆ Salle à manger bourgeoisement décorée et plaisante terrasse estivale dressée en bordure du Crupet offrent une bucolique échappée sur les collines namuroises.
◆ Klassiek ingerichte eetzaal. In de zomer kan worden gegeten op het aangename terras aan de rand van het riviertje, waar men een fraai uitzicht heeft op de vallei.

X **A l'abri des Etoiles,** r. Haute 14, ☎ 0 83 69 05 41, *Fax 0 83 69 92 68,* 🏖 - ▤ 🅿. AE ⓓ ⓜ VISA.
fermé du 15 au 30 déc., du 10 au 17 janv., dim. soir, lundi et merc. soir - **Repas** *Lunch 25* - 32/65 bc, ♀.
◆ Sympathique petite maison de bouche ardennaise œuvrant à côté de l'église de Crupet. Produits régionaux travaillés d'une façon très naturelle. Intéressante sélection vineuse.
◆ Leuk Ardens restaurantje naast de kerk van Crupet. De regionale producten worden zo veel mogelijk in hun waarde gelaten. Interessante wijnkaart.

CUSTINNE *Namur* 533 P 21, 534 P 21 *et* 716 I 5 - *voir à Houyet.*

DADIZELE *8890 West-Vlaanderen* ⓒ *Moorslede 10 710 h.* 533 D 17 *et* 716 C 3.
Bruxelles 111 - Kortrijk 18 - Brugge 41.

Host. Daiseldaele, Meensesteenweg 201, ☎ 0 56 50 94 90, *info@daiseldaele.be, Fax 0 56 50 99 36,* 🏖, - TV 🅿. AE ⓓ ⓜ VISA.
Repas *(fermé 15 juil.-12 août, lundi soir, mardi et après 20 h 30) Lunch 12* - 22/38 - **12 ch** 46/73.
◆ Petite hostellerie familiale bâtie en retrait de la route. Chambres au confort simple réparties entre le bâtiment principal et l'annexe flanquant le jardin. La carte du restaurant propose des recettes classico-bourgeoises. Addition sans rondeurs.
◆ Klein familiehotel dat even van de weg af ligt. Kamers met eenvoudig comfort die zijn verdeeld over het hoofdgebouw en het bijgebouw naast de tuin. In het restaurant worden simpele gerechten op klassieke basis geserveerd. De rekening blijft laag.

DALHEM *4608 Liège* 533 T 18 *et* 716 K 3 - *6 292 h.*
Bruxelles 108 - Maastricht 18 - Liège 17 - Namur 77 - Eijsden 9.

X **La Chaume,** r. Vicinal 17, ☎ 0 4 376 65 64, *info@lachaume.be, Fax 0 4 376 60 66,* 🏖 - 🅿 - 25 à 100. AE ⓜ VISA
Repas *(fermé lundi)* (déjeuner seult sauf vend. et sam.) *Lunch 34* - carte 40 à 48, ♀.
◆ Ancienne grange à colombages (1637) surplombant une route agreste. Adorable salle à manger d'esprit rustique, cuisine classique et bon accueil familial depuis 30 ans.
◆ Deze voormalige vakwerkschuur uit 1637 staat boven aan een landweggetje. Mooie rustieke eetzaal, klassieke keuken en al 30 jaar een gastvrij onthaal door dezelfde familie.

DAMME *8340 West-Vlaanderen* 533 E 15 *et* 716 C 2 - *11 038 h.*
Voir *Hôtel de Ville★ (Stadhuis) - Tour★ de l'église Notre-Dame (O.L. Vrouwekerk).*
18 *au Sud-Est : 7 km à Sijsele, Doornstraat 16* ☎ *0 50 35 35 72, Fax 0 50 35 89 25.*
🅸 *Jacob van Maerlantstraat 3* ☎ *0 50 28 86 10, toerismedamme@village.uunet.be, Fax 0 50 37 00 21.*
Bruxelles 103 - Brugge 7 - Knokke-Heist 12.

De Speye, Damse Vaart Zuid 5, ☎ 0 50 54 85 42, *de.speye@belgacom.net, Fax 0 50 37 28 09,* 🏖, - TV. ⓜ VISA. ch
fermé 3 prem. sem. déc. et lundi - **Repas** (taverne-rest) 26 bc - **5 ch** 55/78 - ½ P 50/56.
◆ Ce modeste hôtel situé en face du Damse Vaart et près d'un moulin vous ouvre les portes de ses chambres pourvues d'un mobilier actuel et de sanitaires complets. Taverne-restaurant dans la note néo-campagnarde. Tea-room l'après-midi. Terrasse d'été.
◆ Dit bescheiden hotel bij een molen aan de Damse Vaart beschikt over kamers met modern meubilair en alle sanitaire voorzieningen. Café-restaurant in neorustieke stijl. Theesalon in de namiddag. Op zomerse dagen is het heerlijk toeven op het terras.

XX **Pallieter,** Kerkstraat 12 (Markt), ☎ 0 50 35 46 75, *Fax 0 50 37 28 71,* 🏖 - ▤. ⓜ VISA
fermé fév. et lundi - **Repas** carte 28 à 50.
◆ Auberge centenaire au cœur de la localité. Salle à manger rénovée où dominent des tons rouges et gris-bleus. Sage cuisine classique. Les beaux jours, repas en plein air.
◆ Oude herberg in het hart van Damme. In de pas gerenoveerde eetzaal overheersen de kleuren rood en grijs-blauw. Licht klassieke keuken. Bij mooi weer kan buiten worden gegeten.

XX **De Lieve,** Jacob van Maerlantstraat 10, ✆ 0 50 35 66 30, *Fax 0 50 35 21 69,* – VISA.
fermé janv. et lundis soirs et mardis non fériés – **Repas** *Lunch 50 bc* – 28/90.
◆ Établissement officiant depuis plus de vingt-cinq ans au centre de cette mélancolique petite ville que borde le canal Brugge-Sluis. Immuable décor néo-rustique en salle.
◆ Al ruim 25 jaar staat dit etablissement in het centrum van dit historische stadje langs het kanaal Brugge-Sluis. Eetzaal met een onveranderlijk neorustiek interieur.

XX **De Maerlant,** Kerkstraat 21 (Markt), ✆ 0 50 35 29 52, *Fax 0 50 37 11 86,* – P. AE VISA
fermé fin nov.-début déc., mardi et merc. – **Repas** *Lunch 30* – carte 29 à 47.
◆ Une vraie histoire de famille : la plus longue lignée de restaurateurs dammois tient toujours le haut du pavé, Kerkstraat 21. Allez-y, vous serez entre de bonnes mains !
◆ Een echte familiekroniek, dit restaurant dat al generaties lang bestaat en nog steeds de toon aangeeft in Damme. En dat zonder enige valse noot !

X **De Bonheur,** Kerkstraat 26 (transfert prévu Blankenbergsesteenweg 1 à Brugge), ✆ 0 50 37 49 23, *Fax 0 50 37 49 23,* , Ouvert jusqu'à 23 h – VISA
fermé mardi – **Repas** *Lunch 25* – carte 36 à 47.
◆ Un pignon à pas de moineaux veille sur cette petite affaire optant pour une cuisine au goût du jour. Menu-carte proposé sur ardoise et attrayante sélection de vins.
◆ Leuk eettentje dat zijn geluk beproeft met een kookstijl die bij de huidige trend aansluit. Gerechten à la carte en menu op een schoolbord. Aantrekkelijke selectie wijnen.

X **de Zuidkant,** Jacob van Maerlantstraat 6, ✆ 0 50 37 16 76, – VISA
fermé dern. sem. juin-prem. sem. juil., fin déc., merc., jeudi et vend. midi – **Repas** carte 40 à 53.
◆ Adresse aussi "sympa" que "riquiqui", égayée d'un souriant décor rustico-provençal. Plats classiques et cuisine du marché se partagent la carte, courte mais engageante.
◆ Sfeervol restaurantje met een vrolijk interieur in rustieke Provençaalse stijl. Beperkte, maar aantrekkelijke kaart met klassieke gerechten en verse producten van de markt.

X **Napoleon,** Damse Vaart Zuid 4, ✆ 0 50 35 32 99, *restaurant.napoleon@belgacom.net, Fax 0 50 35 32 99,* – VISA JCB
fermé du 8 au 19 mars, 20 sept.-14 oct., mardi soir et merc. – **Repas** *Lunch 28* – 43/62 bc.
◆ Surveillant le canal, petite affaire dédiée à l'empereur français. Préparations en phase avec l'époque, salle de restaurant décorée avec soin et terrasse d'été à l'avant.
◆ Dit restaurantje aan het kanaal is opgedragen aan de grote Franse keizer. De eetzaal is met zorg ingericht en de keuken is eigentijds. Zonnig terras aan de voorkant.

X **Den Heerd,** Jacob van Maerlantstraat 7, ✆ 0 50 35 44 00, *info@denheerd.be, Fax 0 50 36 25 37,* , Grillades – . AE VISA
fermé 2 prem. sem. juil., merc. et jeudi – **Repas** *Lunch 15* – 38 bc.
◆ Table familiale affable où l'on prend place dans une salle à manger façon "brasserie moderne". Les beaux jours, le couvert est également dressé sur deux mini-terrasses.
◆ Dit vriendelijke familierestaurant heeft een eetzaal in de stijl van een moderne brasserie. Op zomerse dagen worden de twee miniterrasjes opgedekt.

à Hoeke *Nord-Est : 6 km par rive du canal* Ⓒ *Damme* – ✉ *8340 Hoeke :*

Welkom sans rest, Damse Vaart Noord 34 (près N 49), ✆ 0 50 60 24 92, *info@hotelwelkom.be, Fax 0 50 62 30 31,* , – TV P. AE VISA.
fermé du 11 au 22 oct. – **8 ch** ☕ 60/70.
◆ "Bienvenue" : enseigne révélatrice de l'accueil qu'on vous réserve dans cette bâtisse élevée le long du canal. Chambres simples, toutes aménagées dans le même esprit.
◆ In dit kleine hotel langs het kanaal bent u een welkome gast. De kamers zijn eenvoudig en allemaal in dezelfde stijl ingericht.

à Oostkerke *Nord-Est : 5 km par rive du canal* Ⓒ *Damme* – ✉ *8340 Oostkerke :*

Vierschare , Processieweg 1, ✆ 0 50 60 60 10, *terdycken@planetinternet.be,* , , – TV P. AE VISA
Repas *(fermé mardi et merc.)* 33 – **8 ch** ☕ 95/115.
◆ Auberge blottie au cœur d'un village typique des polders. Chambres récemment refaites de neuf ; certaines sont accessibles par la cour intérieure. Jardin-verger à l'arrière. Cuisine traditionnelle et ambiance "bistrot" au restaurant.
◆ Deze herberg staat midden in een typisch polderdorp. De kamers zijn nieuw en sommige zijn toegankelijk via de binnenplaats. Mooie tuin met boomgaard aan de achterkant. Restaurant met een traditionele keuken en bistrosfeer.

XX **Bruegel,** Damse Vaart Zuid 26, ✆ 0 50 50 18 66, *Fax 0 50 50 18 66,* – P. VISA
fermé 16 sept.-1er oct., mardi soir et merc. – **Repas** *Lunch 25* – 45/65 bc.
◆ Bruegel n'aurait certainement pas dédaigné la cuisine concoctée dans cette belle villa flamande paressant au milieu des polders. On mange dehors par météo clémente.
◆ Bruegel zou de gerechten in deze mooie Vlaamse villa in de polder vast niet hebben versmaad. Als het weer geen roet in het eten gooit, worden de tafeltjes buiten gedekt.

X **Siphon,** Damse Vaart Oost 1 (Sud : 2 km), ☎ 0 50 62 02 02, ≤, terrasse, Anguilles et grillades – P. ✻
fermé du 1er au 21 fév., du 1er au 15 oct., jeudi et vend. – **Repas** carte 22 à 31 ✻.
◆ On vient ici en nombre se délecter d'anguilles et autres grillades, instruments du succès de cette affaire établie à la croisée de deux canaux bordés de peupliers.
◆ Op het kruispunt van twee met populieren omzoomde kanalen ligt dit drukbezochte restaurant, waar paling en grillspecialiteiten succes oogsten.

X **de Krinkeldijk,** Monnikenredestraat 6, ☎ 0 50 62 51 52, *Fax 0 50 61 12 11*, terrasse – P. ⓓ ⓜⓒ VISA
fermé 1 sem. en fév., déc., merc. et jeudi – **Repas** 28/45.
◆ Établissement posté aux abords du village, dans un environnement champêtre. Salle à manger moderne agrandie d'une véranda. Plaisantes terrasse et pièce d'eau.
◆ Restaurant aan de rand van het dorp, in een landelijke omgeving. De moderne eetzaal is uitgebreid met een serre. Prettig terras met een fraaie waterpartij.

DAVERDISSE *6929 Luxembourg belge* 534 P 22 *et* 716 I 5 – *1 355 h.*
Bruxelles 122 – Bouillon 37 – Arlon 72 – Dinant 41 – Marche-en-Famenne 35 – Neufchâteau 36.

Le Moulin ✻, r. Lesse 61, ☎ 0 84 38 81 83, *info@daverdisse.com, Fax 0 84 38 97 20*, terrasse, jardin, vélo – |♦| TV P – 25. AE ⓓ ⓜⓒ VISA. ✻ rest
fermé 23 août-3 sept., du 13 au 22 déc., janv. et merc. hors saison sauf vacances scolaires de déc. à Pâques – **Repas** Lunch 29 – carte 39 à 54 – **18 ch** ☐ 68/104 – ½ P 76/81.
◆ Ce vieux moulin converti en hôtel est entouré de bois propices aux balades. Fringantes chambres meublées avec goût et jardin au bord de la rivière... Relax ! Cuisine de notre temps à savourer dans une salle à manger aux couleurs du Sud.
◆ Hotel in een oude molen in een bosrijke omgeving. Vrolijke en smaakvol gemeubileerde kamers. De tuin aan de oever van het riviertje geeft optimale ontspanning. In de eetzaal, die met zijn zuidelijke kleuren warm aandoet, kunt u genieten van actuele gerechten.

XX **Le Trou du Loup,** Chemin du Corray 2, ☎ 0 84 38 90 84, *info@trouduloup.be, Fax 0 84 36 88 65*, terrasse – P. ⓜⓒ VISA
fermé du 10 au 25 juin, 23 sept.-8 oct., du 5 au 30 janv., mardi et merc. – **Repas** Lunch 24 – 36/70 bc, ♀.
◆ Un condensé d'Ardenne se déploie autour de ce chalet dont le cadre intérieur cossu s'agrémente de trophées de chasse. Terrasse dressée face au jardin.
◆ Chalet in een typisch Ardense omgeving, met jachttrofeeën in de comfortabele eetzaal. Terras aan de tuinzijde, waar bij mooi weer kan worden gegeten.

De – *voir au nom propre.*

DEERLIJK *8540 West-Vlaanderen* 533 F 17 *et* 716 D 3 – *11 365 h.*
Bruxelles 83 – Kortrijk 8 – Brugge 49 – Gent 38 – Lille 39.

XX **Severinus,** Hoogstraat 137, ☎ 0 56 70 41 11, *severinus@resto.be, Fax 0 56 72 20 15*, terrasse – AE ⓓ ⓜⓒ VISA
fermé dern. sem. juil.-1re quinz. août, dim. soir et lundi – **Repas** (dîner sur réservation) Lunch 31 – 35/61 bc, ♀.
◆ Lustres en cristal et reproductions d'œuvres de Toulouse-Lautrec président au décor de ce restaurant cossu doté d'une terrasse et d'un jardin d'hiver. Appétissants menus.
◆ Kristallen kroonluchters en reproducties van Toulouse-Lautrec kenmerken de weelderige decoratie van dit restaurant. Mooi terras en wintertuin. Aanlokkelijke menu's.

DEINZE *9800 Oost-Vlaanderen* 533 G 17 *et* 716 D 3 – *27 682 h.*
Bruxelles 67 – Brugge 41 – Gent 21 – Kortrijk 26.

XXX **D'Hulhaege - Kasteel Ten Bosse** avec ch, Karel Picquélaan 140, ☎ 0 9 386 56 16, *info@dhulhaege.be, Fax 0 9 380 05 06*, terrasse, jardin – |♦| TV P – 25 à 250. AE ⓓ ⓜⓒ VISA JCB
Repas *(fermé 2e quinz. juil., dim. soir et lundi)* Lunch 28 bc – 38/65 bc – **7 ch** ☐ 73/80.
◆ Côté cadre : décor d'un genre assez classique. Côté bouche : préparations assorties, produits de choix et, surtout : cave "de derrière les fagots". Chambres au diapason.
◆ Vrij klassiek interieur, wat goed bij de kookstijl past. Alleen de allerbeste producten komen op tafel, natuurlijk vergezeld van een mooie wijn. Ook de kamers zijn prima.

à Astene *sur N 43 : 2,5 km* 🄲 *Deinze* – ✉ *9800 Astene :*

XX **Au Bain Marie,** Emiel Clauslaan 141, ✆ 0 9 222 48 65, *aubainmarie@skynet.be, Fax 0 9 222 76 58,* ≤, Ouvert jusqu'à 23 h, – AE ⓓ ⓜ VISA
fermé vacances Pâques, 2e quinz. août et merc. – **Repas** *Lunch 12* – 33/57 bc.
◆ Belle villa Art Nouveau conçue en 1895 par l'architecte belge van de Velde, qui y vécut. Vue sur les rives bucoliques de la Leie (Lys) en terrasse. Mets classiques actualisés.
◆ Art-Nouveau villa uit 1895 waarin de Belgische architekt van de Velde zelf woonde. Terras met weids zicht op de landelijke oevers van de Leie. Klassiek-eigentijdse gerechten.

XX **Savarin,** Emiel Clauslaan 77, ✆ 0 9 386 19 33, *Fax 0 9 380 29 43* – P. AE ⓓ ⓜ VISA
fermé sem. carnaval, du 2 au 22 juil., merc. et jeudi – **Repas** *Lunch 35 bc* – 45 bc/75 bc.
◆ Ce restaurant où vous serez reçu dans une sobre salle à manger compte de nombreux adeptes conquis par sa cuisine variée. Le jardin est aménagé pour accueillir des banquets.
◆ Dit sober ingerichte restaurant trekt veel vaste gasten, bij wie de gevarieerde keuken zeer in de smaak valt. De tuin is geschikt voor feesten en partijen.

X **Gasthof Halifax,** Emiel Clauslaan 143, ✆ 0 9 282 31 02, *gasthof.halifax@pandora.be, Fax 0 9 282 91 35,* ≤, , Grillades, ouvert jusqu'à minuit, – P. AE ⓓ ⓜ VISA
fermé 20 juil.-1er août, 24 déc.-2 janv., sam. midi, dim. et jours fériés – **Repas** *Lunch 12* – 28/47 bc.
◆ Fermette ancienne disposant d'une terrasse dressée au bord de la Leie (Lys). Carte de spécialités belgo-belges qu'on peut accompagner de bons vins. Grill au feu de bois.
◆ Oud boerderijtje met een terras aan de Leie. Kaart met typisch Belgische specialiteiten, waarbij een goede fles wijn wordt opengetrokken. Op houtskool geroosterd vlees.

à Grammene *Ouest : 3,5 km par N 440, puis à gauche* 🄲 *Deinze* – ✉ *9800 Grammene :*

X **Westaarde,** Westaarde 40, ✆ 0 9 386 99 59, *Fax 0 9 386 99 59,* – P. AE ⓜ VISA
fermé vacances Pâques, 2e quinz. déc., sam. et dim. – **Repas** carte 38 à 86.
◆ Au bord de la Leie (Lys), perdue au milieu des champs, fermette du 19e s. dont la carte, agrémentée de spécialités de grillades, se complète d'une ardoise de suggestions.
◆ Boerderijtje uit de 19e eeuw, aan de oever van de Leie, midden tussen de akkers. De kaart wordt aangevuld met suggesties. Grillspecialiteiten.

à Sint-Martens-Leerne *Nord-Est : 6,5 km* 🄲 *Deinze* – ✉ *9800 Sint-Martens-Leerne :*

XXX **D'Hoeve,** Leernsesteenweg 218, ✆ 0 9 282 48 89, *Fax 0 9 282 24 31,* – P – 30. AE ⓓ ⓜ VISA
fermé lundi soir et mardi – **Repas** *Lunch 30* – 44/70 bc.
◆ Rustique, l'intérieur de cette jolie maison : âtre, poutres, carrelage ancien, etc. La carte offre un vaste choix de recettes et la cave renferme de nombreux crus.
◆ Mooie hoeve met een rustiek interieur : open haard, balken, plavuizen, enz. De kaart biedt een keur van heerlijke gerechten en in de kelder liggen vele goede wijnen te wachten.

DENDERMONDE (TERMONDE) *9200 Oost-Vlaanderen* 533 J 16 *et* 716 F 2 – *43 168 h.*

Voir *Oeuvres d'art★ dans l'église Notre-Dame★★ (O.L. Vrouwekerk).*

🄱 *Stadhuis, Grote Markt* ✆ *0 52 21 39 56, dendermonde@toerismevlaanderen.be, Fax 0 52 22 19 40.*

Bruxelles 32 – Antwerpen 41 – Gent 34.

City sans rest, Oude Vest 121, ✆ 0 52 20 35 40, *Fax 0 52 20 35 50* – TV. AE ⓓ ⓜ VISA.
fermé 25 déc.-2 janv. – **12 ch** 50/75.
◆ Le City dispose de chambres simples, mais assez confortables, équipées du double vitrage pour offrir des nuitées plus tranquilles... Et hop, sous la couette !
◆ Het City-hotel beschikt over eenvoudige, maar vrij comfortabele kamers met dubbele ramen. Goede nachtrust gegarandeerd, dus allez hop, snel onder het dons !

XX ✿ **'t Truffeltje** (Mariën), Bogaerdstraat 20, ✆ 0 52 22 45 90, *truffeltje@compaqnet.be, Fax 0 52 21 93 35,* – AE ⓓ ⓜ VISA.
fermé 1 sem. après Pâques, 21 juil.-15 août, sam. midi, dim. soir et lundi – **Repas** *Lunch 33* – 48/90 bc, carte 58 à 79.
◆ Derrière une façade aussi discrète qu'élégante, salle à manger moderne et spacieuse offrant la vue sur les fourneaux où se conçoit une talentueuse cuisine personnalisée.
◆ Achter een gevel die even bescheiden als sierlijk is, schuilt een modern en ruim restaurant met een open keuken, waar de chef-kok zijn talent en vakmanschap laat zien.
Spéc. Dim Sum aux langoustines et poireaux, vinaigrette à la truffe. Ris de veau lardé de sa langue et pomme de terre à la truffe. Thé de fruits exotiques à la glace vanille bourbon

X **Arte Shock,** St-Gillislaan 24, ✆ 0 52 22 34 47, *info@arteshock.be, Fax 0 52 25 61 08,* - VISA.
fermé dern. sem. juin, dern. sem. déc., lundi, mardi et sam. midi – **Repas** Lunch 18 – carte 39 à 49.
◆ Maison de notable devenue un sympathique restaurant d'esprit "trendy", dont l'enseigne se réfère à l'artichaut. Cuisine d'aujourd'hui. Repas en plein air à la belle saison.
◆ Trendy restaurant in een herenhuis, waarvan de naam naar de artisjok verwijst. Eigentijdse keuken. Bij mooi weer kan buiten worden gegeten.

DESSEL *2480 Antwerpen* 533 P 15 *et* 716 I 2 – *8 555 h.*
Bruxelles 86 – Eindhoven 43 – Antwerpen 58 – Hasselt 45 – Turnhout 19.

Alauda, Turnhoutsebaan 28, ✆ 0 14 37 50 71, *Fax 0 14 38 92 99,* - P. AE VISA.
Repas *(fermé 1 sem. Noël)* carte 30 à 46 – **16 ch** 62/89.
◆ Au centre d'une petite localité campinoise, hôtel dont les chambres, actuelles et de bon confort, se répartissent entre une ancienne villa et une aile plus récente. Repas gentiment classique. L'été, il s'apprécie aussi en terrasse, dans un écrin verdoyant.
◆ Een dorpje in de Belgische Kempen. Centraal gelegen hotel waarvan de moderne en comfortabele kamers zijn verdeeld over een oude villa en een nieuwe vleugel. De maaltijd is klassiek en kan bij mooi weer ook worden gebruikt op het terras tussen het groen.

DEURLE *Oost-Vlaanderen* 533 G 16 *et* 716 D 2 – *voir à Sint-Martens-Latem.*

DEURNE *Antwerpen* 533 L 15 *et* 716 G 2 – *voir à Antwerpen, périphérie.*

DIEGEM *Vlaams-Brabant* 533 L 17 *et* 716 G 3 – *voir à Bruxelles, environs.*

DIEST *3290 Vlaams-Brabant* 533 P 17 *et* 716 I 3 – *22 312 h.*
Voir *Oeuvres d'art★ dans l'église St-Sulpice (St-Sulpitiuskerk)* AZ – *Béguinage★★ (Begijnhof)* BY.
Musée : *Communal★ (Stedelijk Museum)* AZ **H.**
Env. *par ④ : 8 km, Abbaye d'Averbode★ : église★.*
Stadhuis, Grote Markt 1 ✆ *0 13 35 32 73, diest@toerismevlaanderen.be, Fax 0 13 32 23 06.*
Bruxelles 59 ③ – Antwerpen 60 ① – Hasselt 25 ②

Plan page suivante

De Fransche Croon, Leuvensestraat 26, ✆ 0 13 31 45 40, *info@defranschecroon.be, Fax 0 13 33 31 59,* - , ch, - 40. AE VISA JCB. AZ e
fermé fin déc. – **Repas** (dîner pour résidents seult) – **22 ch** 75/95 – ½ P 75.
◆ Une extension récente, coiffée d'un puits de lumière central, héberge les nouvelles chambres de cet établissement familial situé à proximité du centre-ville.
◆ Familiehotel in de buurt van het stadscentrum. In het onlangs aangebouwde stuk met centrale lichtkoker zijn de nieuwe kamers te vinden. In de keuken worden gerechten bereid op basis van dagverse producten van de markt.

XXX **De Proosdij,** Cleynaertstraat 14, ✆ 0 13 31 20 10, *proosdij@skynet.be, Fax 0 13 31 23 82,* - P. AE VISA JCB AZ c
fermé du 12 au 30 juil., sam. midi, dim. soir et lundi – **Repas** Lunch 33 – 42/98 bc.
◆ Une allée étroite bordée d'un verdoyant jardin clos de murs mène à cette maison bourgeoise du 17e s. abritant une salle à manger au cadre soigné. Produits faits "maison".
◆ Een smal pad langs een weelderige ommuurde tuin voert naar dit 17e-eeuwse herenhuis. Verzorgde eetzaal en maaltijd van verse producten, allemaal "home made".

X **Dyosta,** Michel Theysstraat 5, ✆ 0 13 32 68 84, *veerle@dyosta.com, Fax 0 13 32 68 85* - VISA AY a
fermé mardi – **Repas** Lunch 30 – 37/67 bc.
◆ En face de la clinique, l'une des adresses les plus courtisées de la ville : cadre "méridional" aussi original que la cuisine, service prévenant et vins à prix d'amis.
◆ Een van de populairste eettentjes van de stad, tegenover de kliniek. Het mediterrane decor is even origineel als de keuken. Attente bediening en wijnen voor een zacht prijsje.

DIEST

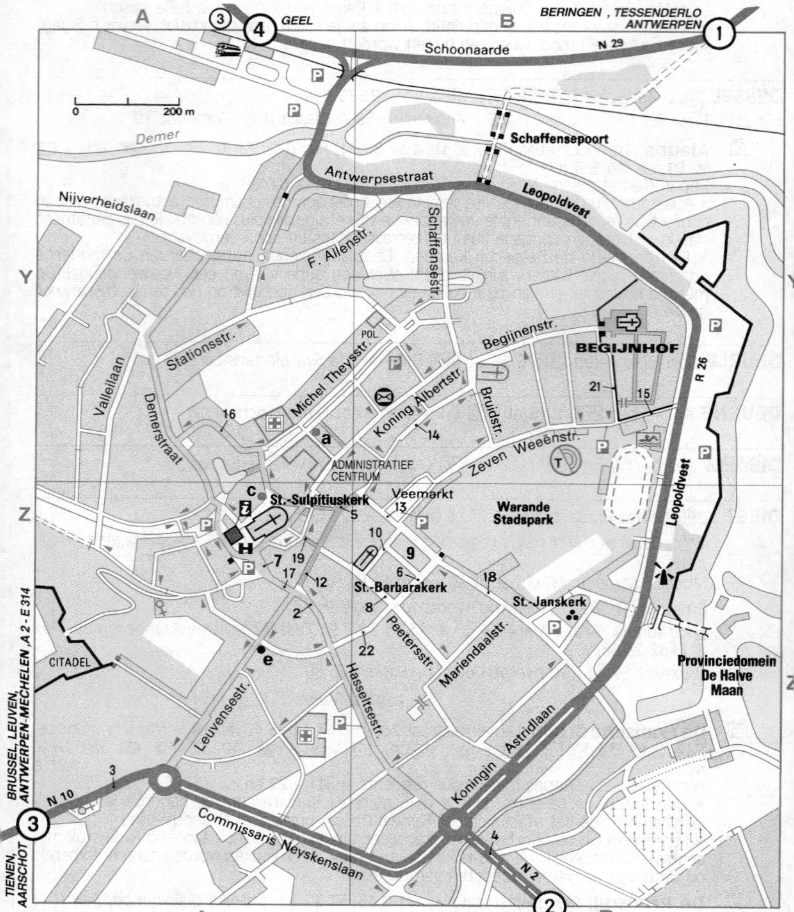

DIKSMUIDE (DIXMUDE) *8600 West-Vlaanderen* 533 C 16 *et* 716 B 2 – *15 480 h.*

Voir *Tour de l'Yser (IJzertoren)* ✱★.

Beerstblotestraat 1 ✆ *0 51 51 94 19, toerisme@diksmuide.be, Fax 0 51 51 00 21.*
Bruxelles 118 – Brugge 44 – Gent 72 – Ieper 23 – Oostende 27 – Veurne 19.

Pax sans rest, Heilig Hartplein 2, ✆ 0 51 50 00 34, *pax.hotel@skynet.be*, *Fax 0 51 50 00 35* – 30. AE VISA.
fermé du 1er au 15 déc. – **37 ch** 70/95.

◆ Le dernier né des hôtels de Diksmuide : édifice encore flambant neuf, abritant des chambres de taille correcte sobrement décorées dans un style actuel.

◆ Pax is de meest recente aanwinst van Diksmuide : een spiksplinternieuw gebouw met vrij ruime kamers, sober gedecoreerd in eigentijdse stijl.

De Vrede, Grote Markt 35, ✆ 0 51 50 00 38, *devrede@skynet.be, Fax 0 51 51 06 21,* – TV – 25 à 70. AE VISA.
fermé du 1er au 15 déc. – **Repas** *(fermé dim. soir sauf en juil.-août et merc.)* carte 24 à 38 – **17 ch** 45/80.
◆ Une aile récente, déployée sur l'arrière du bâtiment, concentre la majorité des chambres - souvent vastes - de cette affaire tournée vers le Grote Markt. Parking aisé. Des poutres apparentes et une cheminée participent au décor de la salle des repas.
◆ Hotel aan de Grote Markt met een nieuwe vleugel aan de achterkant, waar het merendeel van de veelal ruime kamers te vinden is. Voldoende parkeergelegenheid. De eetzaal heeft houten balken aan het plafond en een grote schouw.

Polderbloem, Grote Markt 8, ✆ 0 51 50 29 05, *polderbloem@pi.be, Fax 0 51 50 29 06,* – TV. AE VISA JCB
fermé 2 sem. carnaval et 2 sem. Toussaint – **Repas** *(fermé mardi)* (anguilles) Lunch 8 – carte 28 à 49 – **9 ch** 30/52 – ½ P 39/45.
◆ Position stratégique à l'angle de la place du marché pour cette demeure répondant au doux nom de "Fleur de polder". Le touriste y trouvera des chambres convenables. Taverne-restaurant misant sur une carte assez copieuse et quelques suggestions.
◆ Dit hotel in een herenhuis met poëtische naam heeft een strategische ligging op de hoek van het marktplein en is echt iets voor toeristen. Taverne-restaurant met vrij copieuze gerechten à la carte en enkele dagschotels.

à Leke *Nord : 8 km* C *Diksmuide* – ✉ *8600 Leke :*

De Lekebek, Schorestraat 39, ✆ 0 51 50 24 27, *Fax 0 51 51 06 29,* ≤ – P.
VISA
fermé 26 janv.-12 mars, 13 sept.-15 oct., lundi, mardi, merc., jeudi midi et vend. midi – **Repas** (menu unique) 60 bc.
◆ Belle fermette dont la lumineuse salle à manger procure, à chacune des tables, une échappée sur les polders. Cuisine actuelle sous forme d'un menu unique.
◆ Mooi boerderijtje waar elk tafeltje in de lichte eetzaal uitzicht biedt op de polder. Er is maar één menu verkrijgbaar, dat uit eigentijdse gerechten is samengesteld.

à Stuivekenskerke *Nord-Ouest : 7 km* C *Diksmuide* – ✉ *8600 Stuivekenskerke :*

Kasteelhoeve Viconia, Kasteelhoevestraat 2, ✆ 0 51 55 52 30, *viconia@skynet.be, Fax 0 51 55 55 06,* – TV P – 25. VISA.
fermé du 1er au 15 sept., janv. et dim. soir – **Repas** (dîner pour résidents seult) – **23 ch** 45/75 – ½ P 42/50.
◆ Une route étroite et sinueuse conduit à cette ancienne ferme-château d'un ordre religieux isolée dans les polders. Chambres garnies de meubles de style. Alentours verdoyants.
◆ Een smalle kronkelweg leidt naar deze afgelegen kasteelboerderij in de polder, die vroeger aan een kloosterorde toebehoorde. Landelijke omgeving.

DILBEEK *Vlaams-Brabant* 533 K 17 *et* 716 F 3 – *voir à Bruxelles, environs.*

DILSEN *3650 Limburg* C *Dilsen-Stokkem 18 486 h.* 533 T 16 *et* 716 K 2.
Bruxelles 110 – Maastricht 33 – Hasselt 44 – Roermond 31.

Host. Vivendum avec ch., Vissersstraat 2, ✆ 0 89 57 28 60, *alex.clevers@proximedia.be, Fax 0 89 57 28 60,* – P. AE VISA.
Repas *(fermé merc.)* Lunch 30 – carte 49 à 75, ♀ – **4 ch** 75/100 – ½ P 105/140.
◆ Belle reconversion pour cette ancienne demeure paroissiale (1736) côtoyant un parc public et abritant désormais un restaurant au goût du jour ainsi que quelques chambres.
◆ In deze fraai gerestaureerde pastorie uit 1736, die aan een park grenst, is nu een eigentijds restaurant gehuisvest, waar de gasten ook kunnen blijven slapen.

à Lanklaar *Sud : 2 km* C *Dilsen-Stokkem* – ✉ *3650 Lanklaar :*

Host. La Feuille d'Or avec ch, Hoeveweg 145 (Est : 5,5 km par N 75), ✆ 0 89 65 97 12, *lafeuilledor@skynet.be, Fax 0 89 65 97 22,* – TV P. AE VISA
fermé 2 dern. sem. juil.-2 prem. sem. août et du 1er au 14 janv. – **Repas** *(fermé lundi, mardi et sam. midi)* Lunch 35 bc – 60, ♀ – **6 ch** 75/100 – ½ P 110/118.
◆ Ancienne ferme-château esseulée dans les bois. Au programme : calme, chlorophylle et restaurant d'été au jardin, embelli d'une pièce d'eau et de sculptures. Bonnes chambres.
◆ Deze oude kasteelhoeve in de bossen biedt rust, groen en frisse lucht. 's Zomers wordt in de tuin gegeten, die met beelden en een waterpartij is verfraaid. Goede kamers.

DINANT *5500 Namur 533 O 21, 534 O 21 et 716 H 5 – 12 763 h – Casino, bd des Souverains 6 ✆ 0 82 69 84 84, Fax 0 82 69 99 95.*

Voir *Site★★ – Citadelle★ ≤★★* **M** *– Grotte la Merveilleuse★* **B** *– par ② : Rocher Bayard★ – par ⑤ : 2 km à Bouvignes : Château de Crèvecœur ≤★★ – par ② : 3 km à Anseremme : site★.*

Env. *Cadre★★ du domaine de Freyr (château★, parc★) – par ② : 6 km, Rochers de Freyr★ – par ① : 8,5 km à Foy-Notre-Dame : plafond★ de l'église – par ② : 10 km à Furfooz : ≤★ sur Anseremme, Parc naturel de Furfooz★ – par ② : 12 km à Vêves : château★ – par ② : 10 km à Celles : dalle funéraire★ dans l'église romane St-Hadelin.*

Exc. *Descente de la Lesse★ en kayak ou en barque : ≤★ et ✻★.*

18 par ② : 18,5 km à Houyet, Tour Léopold-Ardenne 6 ✆ 0 82 66 62 28, Fax 0 82 66 74 53.

av. Cadoux 8, ✆ 0 82 22 28 70, info@dinant-tourisme.be, Fax 0 82 22 77 88.

Bruxelles 93 ⑤ – Namur 29 ⑤ – Liège 75 ① – Charleville-Mézières 78 ③

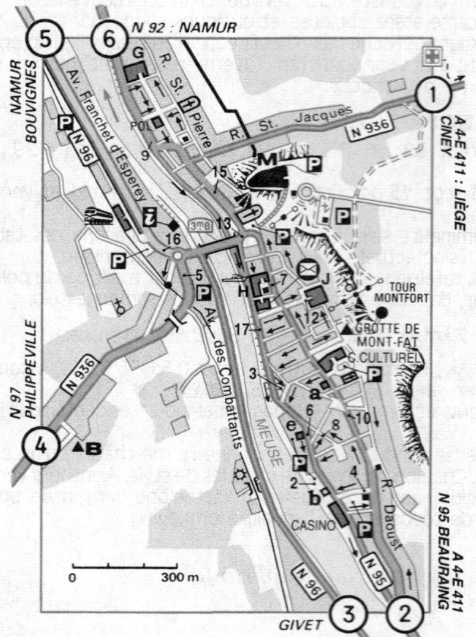

DINANT

Adolphe-Sax (R.)	
Albeau (Pl. d')	2
Albert-Ier (Pl.)	3
Armes (Pl. d')	4
Bribosia (R.)	5
Cousot (R.)	6
Grande (R.)	7
Huybrechts (R.)	8
J.-B.-Culot (Quai)	9
Léopold (R.)	10
Palais (Pl. du)	12
Reine-Astrid (Pl.)	13
Sax (R.A.)	15
Station (R. de la)	16
Winston-Churchill (Av.)	17

Ibis sans rest, Rempart d'Albeau 16, ✆ 0 82 21 15 00, *hotelibis.dinant@belgacom.net, Fax 0 82 21 15 79,* ≤ – 30. AE VISA b
9 – **59 ch** 69/74.

◆ Retrouvez, en bord de Meuse, aux pieds d'un coteau boisé, l'éventail des prestations hôtelières propres à la chaîne Ibis. La moitié des chambres jouit d'une vue fluviale.
◆ De nieuwe aanwinst van deze hotelketen ligt aan de oever van de Maas en aan de voet van een beboste heuvel. De helft van de kamers kijkt uit op de rivier.

Le Jardin de Fiorine, r. Cousot 3, ✆ 0 82 22 74 74, *jardindefiorine@belgacom.net, Fax 0 82 22 74 74,* – AE VISA e
fermé 2 sem. carnaval, 3 prem. sem. juil., merc. et dim. soir – **Repas** *Lunch 20* – 30/57 bc, ♀.

◆ Enseigne horticole pour cette maison de bouche proposant un choix de mets classiques actualisés avec sobriété. Terrasse dressée dès l'arrivée des beaux jours.
◆ Dit restaurant biedt een keur van klassieke gerechten, die voorzichtig aan de huidige trend worden aangepast. Zodra het mooi weer is, worden de tafeltjes op het terras gedekt.

Le Grill, r. Rivages 88 (par ② : près du Rocher Bayard), ✆ 0 82 22 69 35, *Fax 0 82 22 54 36,* Grillades – VISA
fermé dern. sem. juin, mi-sept.-début oct., fin janv.-début fév., lundi soir et mardi – **Repas** 25/44 bc.

◆ À l'ombre du Rocher Bayard, agréable rôtisserie comprenant plusieurs petites salles où les vrais carnivores aiment à se repaître de plantureuses grillades au feu de bois.
◆ Aangename rotisserie met verscheidene zaaltjes, waar de echte carnivoor nog een hele kluif heeft aan de grote stukken vlees die op houtskool worden geroosterd.

X **La Broche,** r. Grande 22, ✆ 0 82 22 82 81 – ▤. MC VISA a
fermé 1 sem. en mars, du 1er au 15 juil., prem. sem. janv., mardi et merc. midi – **Repas** 21/35.
◆ Estimable restaurant implanté dans la grande rue commerçante dinantaise, face au centre culturel. Décoration intérieure actuelle et carte traditionnelle à prix muselés.
◆ Uitstekend restaurant in de voornaamste winkelstraat van Dinant, tegenover het cultureel centrum. Modern interieur en traditionele kaart met scherp geprijsde gerechten.

à Anseremme *par ② : 3 km* C *Dinant* – ✉ *5500 Anseremme :*

Mercure ⛰, rte de Walzin 36, ✆ 0 82 22 28 44, *H0512@accor-hotels.com, Fax 0 82 21 63 03*, – 25 à 170. AE MC VISA. rest
Repas *Lunch 29* – 25/72 bc – **79 ch** 89/150, – 1 suite – ½ P 111/125.
◆ Cet établissement de la vallée de la Lesse niché au milieu d'un parc arboré, à proximité de l'aurotoute E 411, renferme des chambres conformes aux standards "mercuriens".
◆ Dit hotel ligt midden in een boomrijk park in het dal van de Lesse, niet ver van de E411. De kamers zijn geheel conform de normen van de hotelketen.

XX **Host. Le Freyr** ⛰ avec ch, chaussée des Alpinistes 22 (au Sud : 2 km sur N 95, direction Beauraing), ✆ 0 82 22 25 75, *lefreyr@belgacom.net, Fax 0 82 22 70 42*, – 30. MC VISA
avril-déc. et week-end ; fermé mardi et merc. – **Repas** *(fermé après 20 h 30)* 32/50 – **6 ch** 70/77 – ½ P 75/85.
◆ Cette hostellerie perchée au sommet des célèbres rochers vous accueille dans une salle intime garnie de meubles de style. Préparations de saison. Petit motel en annexe.
◆ Deze hostellerie op de top van de beroemde rotsen ontvangt zijn gasten in een intieme zaal met stijlmeubilair. Seizoengebonden keuken. Klein motel ernaast.

X **Le Mosan,** r. Joseph Dufrenne 2, ✆ 0 82 22 24 50, *Fax 0 82 22 24 50*, ≤ – P. MC VISA
fermé mi-déc.-mi-janv., mardi et merc. – **Repas** *Lunch 20* – 30.
◆ Dans un cul-de-sac, restaurant du rivage mosan où officie un chef intraitable sur la qualité des produits. Salle à manger-véranda et terrasse au bord du chemin de halage.
◆ In dit restaurant in een doodlopende steeg aan de Maas neemt de chef-kok alleen met het allerbeste genoegen. Eetzaal met serre en terras langs het oude jaagpad.

à Falmignoul *par ② : 9 km* C *Dinant* – ✉ *5500 Falmignoul :*

XX **Les Crétias** ⛰ avec ch, r. Crétias 99, ✆ 0 82 74 42 11, *Fax 0 82 74 40 56*, – P. AE MC VISA.
fermé janv.-début fév., 2 dern. sem. juin, 2 dern. sem. sept., lundi et mardi – **Repas** 32/80 bc – **11 ch** 50/70 – ½ P 60.
◆ Vieille ferme en pierre située à l'écart du village. Cuisine très classique et cordiale ambiance. Terrasse estivale donnant sur un jardin paysager bichonné.
◆ Oude boerderij van steen, even buiten het dorp. Klassieke keuken en een gemoedelijke ambiance. Het zomerse terras kijkt uit op een met zorg aangelegde en onderhouden tuin.

à Furfooz *par ② : 8 km* C *Dinant* – ✉ *5500 Furfooz :*

La Ferme des Belles Gourmandes ⛰, r. Camp Romain 20, ✆ 0 82 22 55 25, *Fax 0 82 22 55 25*, – P. AE MC VISA
Repas *(fermé mardi en janv.-fév., dim. soir, lundi et après 20 h 30) Lunch 19* – 29 – **7 ch** 44/50 – ½ P 40/53.
◆ Près de l'église, donc facile à trouver, jolie ferme du 17e s. adroitement restaurée, hébergeant quelques paisibles chambres assez amples et d'un confort satisfaisant. Belles et gourmandes recettes servies dans une salle de restaurant actuelle.
◆ Deze fraaie 17e-eeuwse boerderij, die vakkundig is gerestaureerd, staat vlak bij de kerk en is dus gemakkelijk te vinden. De kamers zijn rustig, ruim en gerieflijk. In de eigentijdse eetzaal worden tongstrelende gerechten geserveerd.

à Lisogne *par ⑥ : 7 km* C *Dinant* – ✉ *5501 Lisogne :*

XXX **Moulin de Lisogne** ⛰ avec ch, r. Lisonnette 60, ✆ 0 82 22 63 80, *info@moulindelisogne.be, Fax 0 82 22 21 47*, – P. AE MC VISA
fermé 15 déc.-10 fév., dim. soir, lundi et mardi – **Repas** *Lunch 30* – 40/82 bc – **10 ch** 70/100 – ½ P 105.
◆ Ensemble de caractère en pierres du pays, niché dans un vallon boisé de la Leffe et entouré d'un vaste parc. Chaleureuse salle à manger bourgeoise. Chambres "king size".
◆ Karakteristiek pand van steen uit de streek, midden in een groot park in het beboste dal van de Leffe. Sfeervolle eetzaal, vrij klassiek. De kamers zijn kingsize.

à Sorinnes *par ① : 10 km* Ⓒ *Dinant* – ✉ *5503 Sorinnes :*

XXX ✿ **Host. Gilain** avec ch, r. Aiguigeois 1 (près E 411 - A 4, sortie ⑳, lieu-dit Liroux), ☎ 0 83 21 57 42, *hostelleriegilain@belgacom.net, Fax 0 83 21 12 38*, ≤, – TV P. AE ⓓ ⓜⓒ VISA
fermé 18 fév.-4 mars, 18 août-2 sept., 3 et 4 nov., lundi et mardi – **Repas** *Lunch 27* – 41/84 bc, carte 54 à 63 – **6 ch** ☕ 86/96 – ½ P 80/106.
• Cadre agreste, salle à manger décorée avec goût, verrière, terrasse, sans oublier les spacieuses chambres : une hôtellerie bien charmante ! Fine cuisine classique revisitée.
• Met zijn landelijke omgeving, smaakvol ingerichte eetzaal, glaskoepel, terras en ruime kamers is dit een zeer charmant hotel. Fijne klassieke keuken in een eigentijds jasje.
Spéc. Gratin de petits-gris aux scaroles et copeaux de parmesan. Homard "demoiselle" rôti à l'huile d'amandes (mi-avril-juil.). Duo de mousses au chocolat belge et beurre de ferme

---

DION-VALMONT *Brabant Wallon* 533 M 18, 534 M 18 *et* 716 G 3 – *voir à Chaumont-Gistoux.*

DIXMUDE *West-Vlaanderen – voir Diksmuide.*

DONKMEER *Oost-Vlaanderen* 533 I 16 *et* 716 E 2 – *voir à Berlare.*

DOORNIK *Hainaut – voir Tournai.*

DORINNE *Namur* 533 O 21, 534 O 21 *et* 716 H 5 – *voir à Spontin.*

DROGENBOS *Vlaams-Brabant* 533 K 18 – *voir à Bruxelles, environs.*

DUDZELE *West-Vlaanderen* 533 E 15 *et* 716 C 2 – *voir à Brugge, périphérie.*

DUINBERGEN *West-Vlaanderen* 533 E 14 *et* 716 C 1 – *voir à Knokke-Heist.*

DURBUY *6940 Luxembourg belge* 533 R 20, 534 R 20 *et* 716 J 4 – *10 014 h.*

Voir *Site★.*
🏌18 *à l'Est : 5 km à Barvaux, rte d'Oppagne 34* ☎ *0 86 21 44 54, Fax 0 86 21 44 49.*
ℹ *pl. aux Foires 25* ☎ *0 86 21 24 28, info@durbuyinfo.be, Fax 0 86 21 36 81.*
Bruxelles 119 – Arlon 99 – Huy 34 – Liège 51 – Marche-en-Famenne 19.

Au Vieux Durbuy, r. Jean de Bohême 6, ☎ 0 86 21 32 62, *reservation@sanglier-des-ardennes.be, Fax 0 86 21 24 65* – |$| TV ♿ – 🏛 25. AE ⓓ ⓜⓒ VISA JCB
fermé prem. sem. janv. – **Repas** voir rest ***Le Sanglier des Ardennes*** ci-après – ☕ 12 – **12 ch** 105/140 – ½ P 95.
• Un intérieur de caractère fait l'attrait de cette maison de pays bâtie au centre du vieux Durbuy. Chambres douillettes, de confort moderne mais d'esprit rustique.
• Het karakteristieke interieur is de grootste aantrekkingskracht van dit hotel in het oude centrum van Durbuy. Knusse kamers met modern comfort, maar een rustieke uitstraling.

Jean de Bohême, pl. aux Foires 2, ☎ 0 86 21 28 82, *reservation@jean-de-boheme.be, Fax 0 86 21 11 68*, – |$| TV P – 🏛 25 à 330. AE ⓓ ⓜⓒ VISA JCB
Repas *Lunch 34* – 45 – ☕ 12 – **26 ch** 87/112 – ½ P 85/97.
• Jean de Bohême vous accueille sur la place principale de "la plus petite ville du monde". Grandes chambres équipées d'un mobilier pratique. Salles de conférences. Alternative brasserie ou restaurant.
• Jan van Bohemen ontvangt u aan het hoofdplein van "de kleinste stad ter wereld". Het hotel beschikt over grote kamers die heel praktisch zijn ingericht. Congres- en vergaderzaal. Voor het eten heeft u de keuze uit de brasserie of het restaurant.

La Prévôté, r. Récollectines 4, ☎ 0 86 21 28 68, *info@prevote.be, Fax 0 86 21 27 84*, – TV 🚗 – 🏛 25. AE ⓓ ⓜⓒ VISA. ✻ ch
Repas *(fermé 15 fév.-8 mars et merc.)* (grillades) carte 26 à 39 – ☕ 12 – **10 ch** *(fermé 15 fév.-8 mars et merc. de nov. à juin)* 62/77 – ½ P 72/78.
• Une ambiance nostalgique façon "retour d'Afrique" flotte dans cet hôtel intimiste mettant à profit une maison typique du cœur de Durbuy. Chambres bien agencées. Gril-restaurant au "look" tribal : toile de Khorogo, masques d'ancêtres, bronzes du Bénin, etc.
• Dit vrij intieme hotel in een karakteristiek pand, hartje Durbuy, is vervuld van heimwee naar Afrika. De kamers zijn goed ingericht. Grillrestaurant met een etnische look : doek van Khorogo, Afrikaanse maskers, bronzen beelden uit Benin, enz.

Le Vieux Pont, pl. aux Foires 26, ✆ 0 86 21 28 08, *contact@levieuxpont.be, Fax 0 86 21 82 73,* – . VISA. ch
fermé 3 janv.-4 fév. – **Repas** *(fermé merc. sauf vacances scolaires)* (taverne-rest) Lunch 17 – carte 23 à 39 – **13 ch** 57/74 – ½ P 50/55.
◆ Cet hôtel bordant la Place aux Foires dispose de chambres fonctionnelles dotées d'un mobilier en pin. Pour dormir comme une bûche, préférez celles sur l'arrière. Taverne-restaurant néo-rustique complétée d'une terrasse.
◆ Dit hotel aan de Place aux Foires biedt functionele kamers met grenen meubelen. Wie heerlijk wil slapen, kan het beste een van de kamers aan de achterkant nemen. Het hotel beschikt verder over een neorustiek café-restaurant met terras.

Le Sanglier des Ardennes avec ch, (annexe Château Cardinal –), r. Comte Th. d'Ursel 14, ✆ 0 86 21 32 62, *rerservation@sanglier-des-ardennes.be, Fax 0 86 21 24 65,* <, – – 25 à 140. AE VISA JCB
Repas *(fermé janv. et jeudis non fériés)* Lunch 46 bc – 50/65 – 12 – **15 ch** *(fermé prem. sem. janv.)* 140, – 2 suites – ½ P 95/150.
◆ Terrasse Belle Époque, salon "cosy", intérieur cossu s'ouvrant sur l'Ourthe, fine cuisine classique, remarquable cave à vins et "armagnacothèque". Chambres sans reproche.
◆ Belle-époqueterras, gezellige lounge, weelderige eetzaal met zicht op de Ourthe, fijne klassieke keuken, goede wijnkelder met een rijke verzameling armagnacs en prima kamers.

Clos des Récollets avec ch, r. Prévôté 9, ✆ 0 86 21 29 69, *info@closdesrecollets.be, Fax 0 86 21 36 85,* – . VISA
fermé 29 août-16 sept. et 2 sem. en janv. – **Repas** *(fermé mardi et merc.)* Lunch 22 – 46/77 bc, ♀ – **8 ch** 65/82 – ½ P 73/96.
◆ Une rue aux pavés joufflus mène à ce restaurant installé dans une maison ancienne. Plaisant décor de vieilles poutres et pierres apparentes. Chambres très convenables.
◆ Een met kinderkopjes geplaveide straat leidt naar dit restaurant in een oud pand. Plezierig interieur met oude balken en stenen. De kamers voldoen uitstekend.

Le Moulin, pl. aux Foires 17, ✆ 0 86 21 29 70, *Fax 0 86 21 00 84,* – AE VISA
fermé 1 sem. en mars, prem. sem. sept., prem. sem. janv. et mardi hors saison – **Repas** Lunch 20 – 31/56 bc.
◆ Terrasse dallée et intérieur méridional chaleureux, à l'image de l'ambiance. L'agrément est encore plus prononcé à l'étage, sous la jolie charpente. Goûteuse cuisine actuelle.
◆ Betegeld terras en een mediterraan interieur, dat net als de ambiance warm aandoet. Vooral de bovenverdieping met zijn hanenbalken is knus. Smakelijke eigentijdse gerechten.

Le Saint Amour, pl. aux Foires 18, ✆ 0 86 21 25 92, *Fax 0 86 21 46 80,* – AE VISA
fermé du 10 au 31 janv. et merc. hors saison – **Repas** Lunch 20 – 23/50 bc.
◆ Cette enseigne romantique du cœur de Durbuy vous reçoit gentiment dans sa coquette salle à manger ou son agréable véranda. Registre culinaire classique.
◆ Dit restaurant staat in het hart van Durbuy. De gasten zitten aan tafel in de mooie eetzaal of de serre. Het culinaire register is klassiek.

le fou du Roy, r. Comte Th. d'Ursel 4, ✆ 0 86 21 08 68, *Fax 0 86 21 08 55,* – VISA
fermé lundis et mardis non fériés sauf en juil.-août – **Repas** Lunch 21 – 33, ♀.
◆ Maisonnette proche du pont, au pied du château dont elle était la conciergerie. Bonne cuisine d'aujourd'hui, collection d'objets d'hier en salles et terrasse très charmante.
◆ Dit restaurant bij de brug was vroeger de portierswoning van het kasteel. Goede eigentijdse keuken, eetzalen met verzameling oude voorwerpen en 's zomers een heerlijk terras.

à Grandhan *Sud-Ouest : 6 km C Durbuy – ✉ 6940 Grandhan :*

La Passerelle, r. Chêne à Han 1, ✆ 0 86 32 21 21, *info@la-passerelle.be, Fax 0 86 32 36 20,* , , – – 30. ch
fermé janv. – **Repas** *(fermé lundi sauf vacances scolaires)* 23 – **23 ch** 55/70 – ½ P 55.
◆ Bâtisse en pierre postée au bord de l'Ourthe. Des escaliers étroits desservent les spacieuses chambres plaisamment aménagées. Quelques-unes se trouvent dans l'annexe, en face. Salle de restaurant agrandie d'une véranda.
◆ In dit stenen gebouw aan de oever van de Ourthe leiden smalle trappen naar de ruime, prettig ingerichte kamers. In het bijgebouw ertegenover bevinden zich ook nog enkele kamers. Het restaurant is uitgebreid met een serre.

DWORP (TOURNEPPE) *Vlaams-Brabant* 533 K 18, 534 K 18 *et* 716 F 3 – *voir à Bruxelles, environs.*

ÉCAUSSINNES-LALAING *7191 Hainaut* Ⓒ *Écaussinnes 9 810 h.* 533 K 19, 534 K 19 *et* 716 F 4.
Bruxelles 42 – Mons 29.

XX **Le Pilori,** r. Pilori 10, ☎ 0 67 44 23 18, *Fax 0 67 44 26 03,* – AE ⓓ ⓜ VISA
fermé vacances Pâques, 3 prem. sem. août, vacances Noël, sam. midi, dim., lundi soir, mardi soir et merc. soir – **Repas** *Lunch 23* – 27/103 bc, ♀.
◆ Au centre de la localité, maison de pays dont la cuisine à base classique est mâtinée d'un zeste de nouveauté. Cave fournie.
◆ Dit pand midden in het dorp is kenmerkend voor de lokale architectuur. De keuken is klassiek, maar met een vleugje vernieuwing. Goed gevulde wijnkelder.

EDEGEM *Antwerpen* 533 L 16 *et* 716 G 2 – *voir à Antwerpen, environs.*

EDINGEN *Hainaut* – *voir Enghien.*

EEKLO *9900 Oost-Vlaanderen* 533 G 15 *et* 716 D 2 – *19 029 h.*
Bruxelles 89 – Brugge 29 – Gent 21 – Antwerpen 66.

Shamon sans rest, Gentsesteenweg 28, ☎ 0 9 378 09 50, *hotel.shamon@pi.be, Fax 0 9 378 12 77,* – TV P – 25. ⓜ VISA
8 ch ☐ 87.
◆ Un accueil familial vous sera réservé dans cette villa Belle Époque proche de la gare, dont le rez-de-chaussée de style Art nouveau mérite le coup d'oeil. Chambres "cosy".
◆ Vriendelijk onthaal in deze villa uit de belle époque, bij het station. De benedenverdieping is geheel in art-nouveaustijl en beslist een kijkje waard. Sfeervolle kamers.

XX **Hof ter Vrombaut,** Vrombautstraat 139, ☎ 0 9 377 25 77, *Fax 0 9 327 07 27,* – P – 30. AE ⓓ ⓜ VISA.
fermé du 1er au 14 juil., merc., sam. midi et dim. soir – **Repas** *Lunch 23* – 38.
◆ Une tour d'angle signale aux passants cette maison bourgeoise postée aux portes de la ville. Côté cave, la Marianne et l'Oncle Sam font bon ménage.
◆ Aan de rand van Eeklo staat dit restaurant, dat is gevestigd in een herenhuis met een goed herkenbare hoektoren. In de wijnkelder vormen Marianne en Uncle Sam een mooi paar.

Si le coût de la vie subit des variations importantes,
les prix que nous indiquons peuvent être majorés.
Lors de votre réservation à l'hôtel, faites-vous préciser le prix définitif.

EERKEN *Brabant Wallon* – *voir Archennes.*

ÉGHEZÉE *5310 Namur* 533 O 19, 534 O 19 *et* 716 H 4 – *13 699 h.*
Bruxelles 55 – Namur 16 – Charleroi 55 – Hasselt 62 – Liège 53 – Tienen 30.

à Noville-sur-Mehaigne *Nord-Ouest : 2 km* Ⓒ *Éghezée* – ✉ *5310 Noville-sur-Mehaigne :*

XXX ✿ **L'Air du Temps** (Degeimbre), chaussée de Louvain 181 (N 91), ☎ 0 81 81 30 48, *info@airdutemps.be, Fax 0 81 81 28 76* – ⓜ VISA
fermé 2 sem. Pâques, 3 sem. en août, fin déc.-début janv., merc. et jeudi – **Repas** *Lunch 25* – 45/100 bc, carte 53 à 70, ♀.
◆ Étape gourmande sur la route de Louvain. Décor intérieur "dans l'air du temps", aux tons gris chocolat et rouge cardinal. Cuisine novatrice et grands vins du monde. Véranda.
◆ Gastronomische halte langs de baan naar Leuven. Recente renovatie "dans l'air du temps" in gedurfde kleuren. Vernieuwende keuken en grootse wereldwijnen. Veranda.
Spéc. Pigeonneau et consommé à la fève de Tonka. Bouillon d'orge perlé au foie gras fumé et langoustines aux pousses d'épinards (printemps-été). Fromages affinés du moment en dégustation, préparations modernes (printemps-été)

EIGENBRAKEL *Brabant Wallon* – *voir Braine-l'Alleud.*

EISDEN *Limburg* 533 T 17 *et* 716 K 3 – *voir à Maasmechelen.*

EKEREN *Antwerpen* 533 L 15 *et* 716 G 2 – *voir à Antwerpen, périphérie.*

ELENE *Oost-Vlaanderen* 533 H 17 – *voir à Zottegem.*

ELEWIJT *1982 Vlaams-Brabant* Ⓒ *Zemst 20 910 h.* 533 M 17 *et* 716 G 3.

au Sud-Est : 6 km à Kampenhout, Wildersedreef 56 ☎ 0 16 65 12 16, Fax 0 16 65 16 80.

Bruxelles 23 – Antwerpen 32 – Leuven 26.

Kasteel Diependael (Neckebroeck), Tervuursesteenweg 511, ☎ 0 15 61 17 71, *kasteeldiependael@online.be, Fax 0 15 61 68 97,* ≤, – P – 30. AE MC VISA.
fermé carnaval, 2 dern. sem. juil.-2 prem. sem. août, fin déc.-début janv., sam. midi, dim. soir et lundi – **Repas** Lunch 37 – 56/92 bc, carte 86 à 115.
• Au travers de ses verrières, la salle à manger intime et raffinée de cette opulente villa donne à contempler un parc-jardin à la française. Savoureuse cuisine au goût du jour.
• Deze luisterrijke villa heeft een intieme en geraffineerde eetzaal met grote glaspuien die goed zicht bieden op de mooie Franse tuin. Heerlijke eigentijdse keuken.
Spéc. Langoustines aux asperges et curry vert. Lasagne de homard, épinards et foie d'oie au coulis. Turbot et risotto à la tomate

ELLEZELLES (ELZELE) *7890 Hainaut* 533 H 18, 534 H 18 *et* 716 E 3 – *5 616 h.*

Bruxelles 55 – Gent 44 – Kortrijk 39.

Au Couvent des Collines ⛰, Ruelle des Écoles 25, ☎ 0 68 65 94 94, *hotel.c.collines@skynet.be, Fax 0 68 26 61 81,* – TV P – 25 à 80. AE MC VISA.
Repas Lunch 25 – 32/50 bc – 9 – **40 ch** 116/125 – ½ P 136/145.
• Dans un village de campagne, tranquille hôtel de caractère créé à partir d'un pensionnat (1830) de jeunes filles. Chambres sans reproche. Plaine de jeux pour les enfants. Restaurant servant des repas classiques.
• Rustig hotel in een meisjesinternaat uit 1830 in een landelijk dorpje. Onberispelijke kamers. Speelveldje voor kinderen. Restaurant met klassieke maaltijden.

Château du Mylord (Thomaes frères), r. St-Mortier 35, ☎ 0 68 54 26 02, *chateaudumylord@pi.be, Fax 0 68 54 29 33,* – P. AE MC VISA
fermé du 13 au 21 avril, du 16 au 30 août, 23 déc.-10 janv., dim. soir, lundis midis non fériés, lundi soir et merc. soir – **Repas** Lunch 40 – 60/133 bc, carte 68 à 111, ♀.
• Splendide gentilhommière du 19e s. nichée dans un parc bichonné. Décor élégant, superbe terrasse, mets flirtant avec les saveurs d'aujourd'hui, crus millésimés : exquis !
• Schitterend 19e-eeuws kasteel in een fraai aangelegd park. Elegant interieur, prachtig terras, spijzen die flirten met de smaken van nu en grote wijnen, in één woord geweldig !
Spéc. Ravioli ouvert de foie gras et anguilles laquées. Morue confite, calmars fumés et jus de viande. Pavé de bar aux asperges de Malines et épinards aux coquillages (mai-juin)

ELLIKOM *Limburg* 533 S 16 – *voir à Meeuwen.*

ELSENE *Brussels Hoofdstedelijk Gewest – voir Ixelles à Bruxelles.*

ELVERDINGE *West-Vlaanderen* 533 B 17 *et* 716 B 3 – *voir à Ieper.*

ELZELE *Hainaut – voir Ellezelles.*

EMBOURG *Liège* 533 S 19, 534 S 19 *et* 716 J 4 – *voir à Liège, environs.*

ENGHIEN (EDINGEN) *7850 Hainaut* 533 J 18, 534 J 18 *et* 716 F 3 – *11 190 h.*

Voir *Parc★.*

Bruxelles 38 – Mons 32 – Aalst 30 – Tournai 50.

Aub. du Vieux Cèdre ⛰ avec ch, av. Elisabeth 1, ☎ 0 2 397 13 00, *info@aubergeduvieuxcedre.com, Fax 0 2 397 13 19,* ≤, – TV P – 25. AE MC VISA.
Repas *(fermé 20 fév.-2 mars, 16 juil.-9 août, 26 déc.-5 janv., vend. et sam. midis non fériés et dim. soir)* Lunch 21 – 32/51, ♀ – **13 ch** 85/100, – 1 suite – ½ P 40/85.
• Cette imposante villa agrémentée d'une pièce d'eau trône au centre d'Enghien. Chambres tranquilles et coup d'œil sur le parc communal, dont l'origine remonte au 15e s.
• Deze imposante villa in het centrum van Edingen wordt opgeluisterd door een waterpartij. Rustige kamers met uitzicht op het stadspark, dat in de 15e eeuw werd aangelegd.

Les Délices du Parc, pl. P. Delannoy 32, ☎ 0 2 395 47 89, *Fax 0 2 395 47 89* – AE MC VISA
fermé 1 sem. en fév., 2e quinz. sept., mardi soir et merc. – **Repas** 27/58 bc.
• Aux abords du noble parc, restaurant "sympa" occupant les anciennes écuries (18e s.) du château. Cadre d'esprit rustique. Recettes classiques escortées de suggestions.
• Dit restaurant, dat in de 18e-eeuwse stallen van het kasteel is ondergebracht, ligt bij het park. Rustiek interieur. Klassieke gerechten à la carte en suggesties.

EPRAVE *Namur* 534 Q 22 *et* 716 I 5 – *voir à Rochefort.*

EREZÉE *6997 Luxembourg belge* 533 S 21, 534 S 21 *et* 716 J 5 – *2 813 h.*
Bruxelles 127 – Liège 60 – Namur 66.

XX **L'Affenage** avec ch, r. Croix Henquin 7 (Sud : 1 km, lieu-dit Blier), 0 86 47 08 80, *affenage@ibelgique.com, Fax 0 86 47 08 99* – TV P. AE MC VISA
fermé du 2 au 17 fév., 28 juin-21 juil., dim., lundi et mardi midi – **Repas** Lunch 30 – 45/64 – **9 ch** 72/80 – ½ P 72/104.
• Halte gastronomique paisible, mettant à profit une ancienne dépendance de la ferme-château de Blier. Fringante salle à manger contemporaine, cuisine de même. Bonnes chambres.
• Gastronomische pleisterplaats, rustig gelegen in een oud bijgebouw van de kasteelhoeve van Blier. Zwierige, moderne eetzaal en eigentijdse keuken. Goede kamers.

à Fanzel *Nord : 6 km* C *Erezée* – ✉ *6997 Erezée* :

XX **Aub. du Val d'Aisne** avec ch, r. Aisne 15, 0 86 49 92 08, *Fax 0 86 49 98 73*, ←, , – TV. MC VISA. rest
fermé 20 juin-18 juil., 24 déc.-janv., mardi, merc. et jeudi – **Repas** Lunch 25 – 35/62 bc – **8 ch** 85 – ½ P 65.
• Charmante ferme du 17e s. et sa grange postées sur l'une des berges champêtres de l'Aisne. Très belle terrasse surplombant le cours de la rivière. Petites chambres.
• Charmante boerderij met schuur uit de 17e eeuw, landelijk gelegen aan de oever van de Aisne. Het prachtige terras steekt boven de rivier uit. Kleine kamers.

ERMETON-SUR-BIERT *5564 Namur* C *Mettet 11 500 h.* 533 N 21, 534 N 21 *et* 716 H 5.
Bruxelles 84 – Namur 32 – Dinant 20.

XX **Le Molign'Art,** r. Maredret 11, 0 71 72 57 89, *Fax 0 71 72 60 00*, – P. AE MC VISA
fermé mi-fév.-prem. sem. mars, mardi midi en hiver, mardi soir et merc. – **Repas** Lunch 22 – 45/70 bc, ♀.
• À l'écart du village, ancien moulin à eau converti en restaurant jouissant de la quiétude des bois environnants. Jardin et étang complètent ce tableau éminemment bucolique.
• Deze oude watermolen, even buiten het dorp, is tot restaurant verbouwd. De omringende bossen, tuin en vijver maken het tot een idyllisch geheel.

ERONDEGEM *Oost-Vlaanderen* 533 I 17 – *voir à Aalst.*

ERPE *Oost-Vlaanderen* 533 I 17 *et* 716 E 3 – *voir à Aalst.*

ERPS-KWERPS *3071 Vlaams-Brabant* C *Kortenberg 17 631 h.* 533 M 17 *et* 716 G 3.
Bruxelles 19 – Leuven 6 – Mechelen 19.

XX **Rooden Scilt,** Dorpsplein 7, 0 2 759 94 44, *Fax 0 2 759 74 45*, – P. AE MC VISA
fermé 16 fév.-4 mars, du 16 au 30 août, dim. soir, lundi et merc. soir – **Repas** Lunch 28 – 43/69 bc.
• Près de l'église, vénérable auberge où ripaillaient naguère les notables du coin, aujourd'hui remplacés par les pilotes de ligne. Salon, véranda et restaurant d'été.
• Vanouds bekende herberg waar vroeger de lokale notabelen hun stek hadden ; tegenwoordig bestaat de clientèle uit piloten. Salon, veranda, zomerrestaurant en tuinterras.

ERTVELDE *9940 Oost-Vlaanderen* C *Evergem 31 307 h.* 533 H 15 *et* 716 E 2.
Bruxelles 86 – Gent 15 – Brugge 38 – Sint-Niklaas 36.

XX **Paddenhouck,** Holstraat 24, 0 9 344 55 56, *Fax 0 9 344 55 56* – P. AE MC VISA
fermé 31 août-13 sept., 24 déc.-3 janv., dim. et lundi – **Repas** Lunch 28 – 34/56 bc.
• Villa excentrée, le "Coin des Crapauds" (Paddenhouck) renferme une riche collection d'eaux-de-vie dégustatives. En cave, grands vins du Bordelais et de la Bourgogne.
• Deze villa buiten het centrum heeft een rijke collectie brandewijnen die kunnen worden geproefd. In de kelder liggen grote wijnen uit de streek rond Bordeaux en de Bourgogne.

ESTAIMBOURG *7730 Hainaut* C *Estaimpuis 9 650 h.* 533 E 18, 534 E 18 *et* 716 D 3.
Bruxelles 100 – Kortrijk 20 – Mons 62 – Tournai 12 – Lille 34.

XXX **La Ferme du Château,** pl. de Bourgogne 2, 0 69 55 72 13, *Fax 0 69 55 98 29*, – 25 à 80. MC VISA.
fermé 2 sem. carnaval, 3 sem. en août et merc. – **Repas** (déjeuner seult sauf vend. et sam.) Lunch 35 – 44/67 bc.
• Table plaisante aménagée dans l'ancienne auberge du village. Cuisine et décor intérieur sensibles aux saisons. Terrasse d'été dotée de meubles en teck. Beau jardin.
• Plezierig restaurant in de voormalige dorpsherberg. Zowel de keuken als de inrichting zijn gevoelig voor de seizoenen. Terras met teakhouten meubelen in de zomer. Mooie tuin.

ETTERBEEK *Région de Bruxelles-Capitale – voir à Bruxelles.*

EUPEN *4700 Liège* 533 *V 19,* 534 *V 19 et* 716 *L 4 – 17 606 h.*

Voir *Carnaval★★ (défilé : veille du Mardi gras) – par ② : 5 km, Barrage de la Vesdre★ (Talsperre).*

Env. *par ③ : Hautes Fagnes★★, Signal de Botrange ⩽★, Sentier de découverte nature★ – Les Trois Bornes★ (Drielandenpunt) : de la tour Baudouin ✳★, rte de Vaals (Pays-Bas) ⩽★.*

Marktplatz 7 ✆ 0 87 55 34 50, tourist.info.eupen@swing.be, Fax 0 87 55 66 39.
Bruxelles 131 ⑥ – Maastricht 46 ⑥ – Liège 40 ⑥ – Verviers 15 ⑤ – Aachen 17 ①

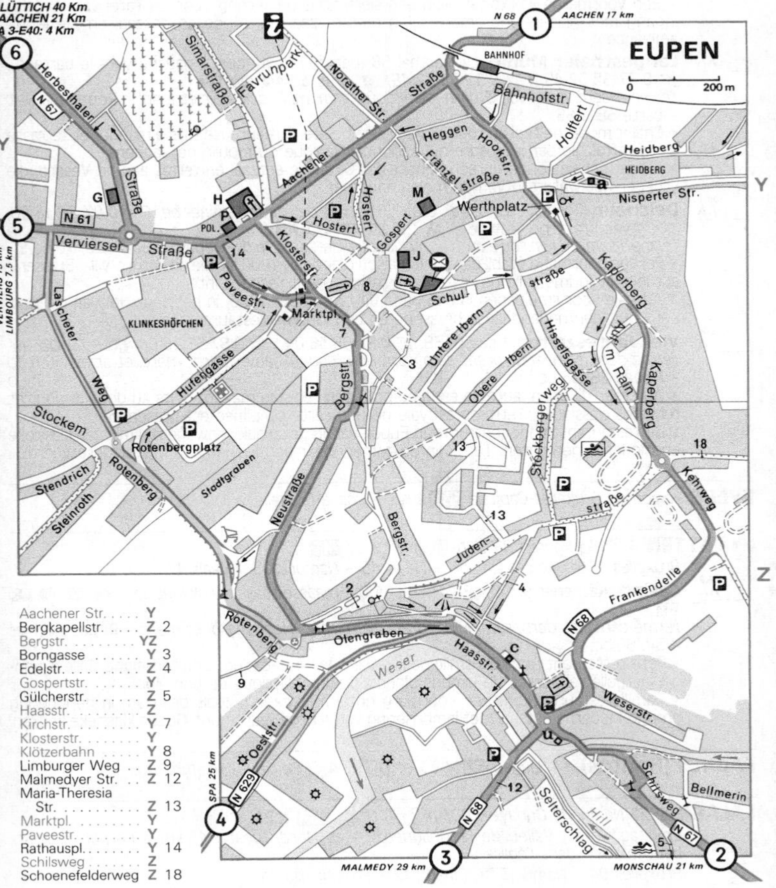

Ambassador, Haasstr. 81, ✆ 0 87 74 08 00, *ambassador.bosten@skynet.be, Fax 0 87 74 48 41* – 25 à 300. AE VISA. Z u
Repas voir rest ***Le Gourmet*** ci-après – **28 ch** 90/140 – ½ P 70/140.
◆ Établissement familial rénové surplombant la Weser. Bonnes chambres bien agencées, vieux café traditionnel et ancien théâtre. Parmi les classiques hôteliers de la région.
◆ Gerenoveerd familiehotel dat boven de Weser ligt. Goed ingerichte kamers, een ouderwets, traditioneel café en een oud theater. Een van de klassieke adressen van deze streek.

XX **Le Gourmet** - H. Ambassador, Haasstr. 81, ✆ 0 87 74 08 00, *ambassador.bosten@skynet.be, Fax 0 87 74 48 41* – ▤. AE ⓓ MC VISA. ✈ Z u
Repas *Lunch 25* – 35/85 bc.
• Restaurant de bonne renommée locale partageant ses murs avec l'hôtel Ambassador. Cuisine classique goûtée des gourmets de cette région germanophone.
• Dit restaurant grenst aan het hotel Ambassador en staat goed bekend bij de bevolking van deze Duitstalige streek. Klassieke keuken voor fijnproevers.

XX **La Table de Vincent,** Hütte 64 (par ② : 3 km, sortie Park Hütte), ✆ 0 87 56 14 31, *vincentcools@swing.be, Fax 0 87 56 14 31,* 🏖 – P – 🏔 25 à 200. MC VISA. ✈
fermé 2 dern. sem. juil., sam., dim. soir et lundi – **Repas** *Lunch 26* – carte 43 à 62.
• Un ancien atelier de ferronnerie sert de cadre à la Table de Vincent. Entrée ornée de vitraux, salon-mezzanine, salle à manger bien de notre temps et ambiance plaisante.
• Een voormalige werkplaats van een siersmid is de setting voor de Tafel van Vincent. Ingang met glas-in-loodramen, salon met mezzanine, moderne eetzaal en plezierige ambiance.

XX **Langesthaler Mühle,** Langesthal 58 (par ② : 2 km, puis à gauche vers le barrage), ✆ 0 87 55 32 45, *Fax 0 87 55 32 45,* 🏖 – P. AE ⓓ MC VISA
fermé 1 sem. carnaval, 3 dern. sem. août, sam. midi, dim. soir et lundi – **Repas** *Lunch 30* – carte 38 à 68.
• Chalet moderne tapi au fond d'une vallée boisée. Chaleureuse salle à manger et terrasse d'été rafraîchie par la Vesdre qui actionnait la roue du moulin de naguère.
• Modern chalet onder in een bebost dal. Gezellige eetzaal en terras aan de Vesdre, die vroeger het waterrad van de molen aandreef.

XX **Delcoeur,** Gospertstr. 22, ✆ 0 87 56 16 66, *delcoeur@skynet.be, Fax 0 87 56 16 96,* 🏖, Avec brasserie – ▤ P – 🏔 25. AE ⓓ MC VISA Y a
fermé 1 sem. en juin., du 2 au 10 janv., jeudi midi et sam. midi – **Repas** *Lunch 22* – 30/70 bc, ♀.
• Refuge gourmand établi dans une maison d'époque 1900 située en centre-ville. Brasserie actuelle et intime salle de restaurant se partagent l'espace intérieur.
• Adresje voor smulpapen in een pand uit omstreeks 1900, in het centrum van de stad. Keuze uit een hedendaagse brasserie en een intieme restaurantzaal.

X **Vier Jahreszeiten,** Haasstr. 38, ✆ 0 87 55 36 04, *Fax 0 87 55 36 04,* 🏖 – AE MC VISA
fermé dern. sem. août-prem. sem. sept., du 5 au 14 janv., mardi, merc. et après 20 h 30 – **Repas** 28/55 bc. Z c
• Au cœur d'Eupen, adresse estimée pour son registre mariant plats au goût du jour et recettes classiques. Terrasse estivale où une carte simplifiée est présentée.
• Dit restaurant in het centrum van Eupen valt in de smaak vanwege zijn mix van klassieke en moderne gerechten. Terras in de zomer, waar een kleine kaart wordt geserveerd.

EVERE *Région de Bruxelles-Capitale* 533 L 17 – *voir à Bruxelles.*

EYNATTEN *4731* Ⓒ *Raeren 9 717 h.* 533 V 18 *et* 716 L 3.
Bruxelles 136 – Maastricht 56 – Liège 45 – Namur 105 – Vaals 12.

XX **Casino,** Aachener Str. 9, ✆ 0 87 86 61 00, *maassen.casino@skynet.be* – ▤. AE ⓓ MC VISA
fermé carnaval, dern. sem. juil.-2 prem. sem. août, Noël, mardi et merc. – **Repas** *Lunch 25* – 34/66 bc.
• Petit restaurant familial installé dans un ancien hôtel-casino, d'où l'enseigne. Salle à manger actuelle rehaussée de lambris blonds. Cuisine classique de bon aloi.
• Familierestaurantje in een voormalig hotel met casino, zoals de naam in herinnering brengt. Moderne eetzaal met lambrisering van lichtgekleurd hout. Goede klassieke keuken.

FAGNES (Hautes) ★★ *Liège* 533 V 20 *et* 716 L 4 *G. Belgique-Luxembourg.*

FALAËN *5522 Namur* Ⓒ *Onhaye 3 083 h.* 533 N 21, 534 N 21 *et* 716 H 5.
Env. *au Nord : Vallée de la Molignée★ – au Nord-Ouest : 15 km à Furnaux : fonts baptismaux★ dans l'église.*
Bruxelles 94 – Namur 37 – Dinant 12 – Philippeville 21.

🏠 **Gd H. de la Molignée** 🐌, r. Gare 87, ✆ 0 82 69 91 73, *info@hotel-molignée.be, Fax 0 82 69 96 13,* 🏖 – TV P – 🏔 40. AE ⓓ MC VISA JCB
fermé merc. – **Repas** ***Condroz*** *Lunch 18* – 24/62 bc – **24 ch** ☕ 50/89 – ½ P 67.
• Vallée forestière, murs en pierres du pays, terrasse abritée... Cet établissement ne manque décidément pas d'atouts. Chambres offrant un confort simple, mais suffisant. Mets classiques et régionaux, dont on se repaît dans un cadre bourgeois.
• Dit etablissement heeft heel wat te bieden : bosrijke vallei, muren van steen uit de streek en beschut terras. De kamers bieden eenvoudig comfort. In de traditioneel ingerichte eetzaal worden klassieke en regionale gerechten geserveerd.

FALLAIS *4260 Liège* ⓒ *Braives 5 458 h.* 533 Q 19 *et* 534 Q 19.
Bruxelles 73 – Namur 26 – Liège 30 – Hasselt 50.

XX **Le Chardon,** r. Chardon 10, ✆ 0 19 69 94 12, *info@lechardon.be, Fax 0 19 69 94 12,* – P – 25 à 120. AE MC VISA
fermé 1 sem. en nov., janv., dim. soir, lundi, mardi, merc. et après 20 h 30 – **Repas** 34/49.
◆ Les origines de cette ancienne ferme hesbignonne remontent au 17e s. Une porte charretière donne accès à la grande cour intérieure où se trouve l'entrée du restaurant.
◆ Deze Haspengouwse boerderij dateert uit de 17e eeuw. Een koetspoort geeft toegang tot de grote binnenplaats, waar zich de ingang van het restaurant bevindt.

FALMIGNOUL *Namur* 533 O 21, 534 O 21 *et* 716 H 5 – *voir à Dinant.*

FANZEL *Luxembourg belge* 533 S 21, 534 S 21 *et* 716 J 5 – *voir à Erezée.*

FAUVILLERS *6637 Luxembourg belge* 534 S 23 *et* 716 K 6 – *1 880 h.*
Bruxelles 172 – Bouillon 61 – Arlon 28 – Bastogne 23.

Le martin pêcheur, r. Bodange 28 (Est : 3 km, lieu-dit Bodange), ✆ 0 63 60 00 66, *Fax 0 63 60 08 06,* , – TV P. AE MC VISA
fermé fév. sauf carnaval, lundi soir du 15 nov. à mars et mardi – **Repas** *(fermé après 20 h 30)* carte 35 à 48 – **6 ch** ☕ 47/83 – ½ P 53/70.
◆ Maison familiale paressant au bord de la Sûre, dans un environnement calme et boisé. Authentique décor intérieur des années 50. Chambres promettant un séjour agréable. Foi de martin pêcheur : les "becs fins" apprécieront les truites que mitonne le restaurant.
◆ Dit familiehotel ligt aan de oever van de Sauer in een bosrijke omgeving. Authentiek interieur uit het midden van de 20e eeuw. De kamers beloven een prettig verblijf. In het restaurant zullen fijnproevers de forel waarderen, de specialiteit van het huis.

XXX ✿ **Le Château de Strainchamps** (Vandeputte) avec ch, Strainchamps 12 (Nord : 6 km, lieu-dit Strainchamps), ✆ 0 63 60 08 12, *info@chateaudestrainchamps.com, Fax 0 63 60 12 28,* , – TV P. AE MC VISA
fermé 2 prem. sem. juil., fin déc.-début janv., merc. et jeudi – **Repas** Lunch 30 – 50/95 bc, carte 41 à 80, ♀ – **7 ch** ☕ 65/110 – ½ P 70/90.
◆ Un village ardennais typique sert de cadre à cette fière demeure ancienne et son parc. Salon confortable, restaurant classiquement agencé et mets goûtés des gastronomes.
◆ Een typisch Ardens dorp vormt de setting van deze herenboerderij met het park. Gerieflijke salon en klassiek ingerichte eetzaal met een gastronomische keuken.
Spéc. Parmentier de queue de bœuf au céleri-rave. Croustillant de langoustines, sauce au curry. Poularde de Bresse en croûte de sel, ragoût de légumes

FAYMONVILLE *Liège* 533 V 20, 534 V 20 *et* 716 L 4 – *voir à Waimes.*

FELUY *7181 Hainaut* ⓒ *Seneffe 10 597 h.* 533 K 19, 534 K 19 *et* 716 F 4.
Bruxelles 39 – Mons 28 – Charleroi 31.

XX **Les Peupliers,** Chemin de la Claire Haie 109 (Sud : E 19 - A 7, sortie ⑳), ✆ 0 67 87 82 05, – P. AE MC VISA
fermé 15 août-15 sept, Noël, Nouvel An et lundi – **Repas** (déjeuner seult sauf vend. et sam.) Lunch 28 – carte 33 à 51.
◆ Cette jolie fermette isolée dans la campagne vous réserve un accueil familial. Nombre de couverts limité : il est donc prudent de réserver. Clientèle d'habitués et d'affaires.
◆ Mooi boerderijtje op het platteland, waar u vriendelijk wordt onthaald. Gezien het beperkte aantal couverts is het verstandig te reserveren. Veel vaste klanten en zakenmensen.

FLEMALLE-HAUTE *Liège* 533 R 19, 534 R 19 *et* 716 J 4 – *voir à Liège, environs.*

FLEURUS *6220 Hainaut* 533 M 20, 534 M 20 *et* 716 G 4 – *22 324 h.*
Bruxelles 62 – Namur 26 – Mons 48 – Charleroi 12.

Ibis Charleroi Aéroport sans rest, chaussée de Charleroi 590, ✆ 0 71 81 01 30, *Fax 0 71 81 23 44* – TV P – 30. AE MC VISA
☕ 9 – **64 ch** 70.
◆ Hôtel de chaîne situé à quelques minutes de l'aéroport de Gosselies, près de l'autoroute E 42. Chambres fonctionnelles toutes identiques, munies du double vitrage.
◆ Ketenhotel op een paar minuten van de luchthaven van Gosselies, vlak bij de E42. Functionele, identieke kamers met dubbele ramen.

XX **Les Tilleuls,** rte du Vieux Campinaire 85 (Sud : 3 km par N 29 puis N 568), ☎ 0 71 81 18 10, *Fax 0 71 81 37 52*, 🏞 – P. AE ① MC VISA
fermé 2e quinz. juil., sam. midi, dim. soir et lundi – **Repas** *Lunch 55 bc* – 36.
• Un choix de plats au goût du jour variant avec les saisons vous attend dans cette maison située à l'extérieur de la ville. La cave renferme quelques prestigieuses bouteilles.
• In dit restaurant buiten de stad worden eigentijdse, seizoengebonden gerechten geserveerd. In de kelder liggen prestigieuze wijnen op een feestelijke gelegenheid te wachten.

X **Clos Bernardin,** r. Emile Vandervelde 9, ☎ 0 71 81 46 82, *Fax 0 71 81 46 82* – ▤. ① MC VISA
fermé sam. midi, dim. soir et lundi soir – **Repas** *Lunch 17* – carte 32 à 40.
• Dans une rue étroite du centre-ville, restaurant familial où une carte importante et variée se donne pour mission de combler votre appétit. Parking aisé juste en face.
• Familierestaurant in een smal straatje in het centrum van de stad. Uitgebreide en gevarieerde kaart. Voldoende parkeergelegenheid aan de overkant.

X **Le Relais du Moulin,** chaussée de Charleroi 199, ☎ 0 71 81 34 50
fermé 23 fév.-3 mars, 16 août-8 sept., mardi soir et merc. – **Repas** carte 26 à 39.
• Déjà 25 ans de présence pour ce petit restaurant bordant la rue principale de Fleurus. Clientèle fidélisée de longue date par de sages préparations classiques.
• Dit restaurantje aan de hoofdstraat van Fleurus kan bogen op 25 jaar ervaring en vakmanschap. De licht klassieke gerechten vallen zeer in de smaak bij de vaste clientèle.

FLOREFFE *5150 Namur 533 N 20, 534 N 20 et 716 H 4 – 7 187 h.*

Bruxelles 63 – Namur 10 – Charleroi 28 – Dinant 30 – Leuven 59 – Wavre 39.

XX **Le Relais Gourmand,** r. Émile Lessive 1 (N 90), ☎ 0 81 44 64 34, *Fax 0 81 44 64 34*, 🏞 – P. AE ① MC VISA
fermé dern. sem. janv.-prem. sem. fév., Ascension, prem. sem. sept., lundi soir, mardi soir et merc. – **Repas** *Lunch 20* – 38.
• Aux portes de Floreffe, maison traditionnelle vous réservant un accueil enjoué. Deux salles des repas, dont une véranda installée au-dessus de la rivière. Menu-carte actuel.
• Traditioneel gebouw aan de rand van Floreffe, waar u een vriendelijk onthaal wacht. Twee eetzalen met een serre boven de rivier. Eigentijdse keuken. Menu's en à la carte.

à Floriffoux *Nord : 2,5 km* C *Floreffe* – ✉ *5150 Floriffoux :*

XX **Le Mas des Cigales,** r. Moncia 9, ☎ 0 81 44 48 47, *lemasdescigales@hotmail.com, Fax 0 81 44 48 47*, 🏞 – P. AE ① MC VISA
fermé mardi soir, merc., jeudi soir et après 20 h 30 – **Repas** *Lunch 23* – 35/50 bc, ♀.
• Belle évocation de la Provence dans cette petite villa de campagne s'adossant, tel un mas, à une butte verdoyante. Menus intelligemment composés. Terrasse entourée d'une haie.
• De Provençaalse sfeer is goed getroffen in deze kleine villa die als een Zuidfranse boerderij tegen een groene heuvel ligt. Zorgvuldig samengestelde menu's. Omhaagd terras.

FLORIFFOUX *Namur 533 N 20, 534 N 20 et 716 H 4 – voir à Floreffe.*

FLORENVILLE *6820 Luxembourg belge 534 Q 24 et 716 I 6 – 5 504 h.*

Env. *au Nord : 6,5 km et 10 mn à pied, Route de Neufchâteau ≤★ sur le défilé de la Semois – à l'Ouest : 5 km, Route de Bouillon ≤★ sur Chassepierre.*

Exc. *au Nord : 5 km, parcours de 8 km, Descente en barque★ de Chiny à Lacuisine.*

ℹ *Pavillon, pl. Albert Ier* ☎ *0 61 31 12 29, touristinfo.florenville@attglobal.net, Fax 0 61 31 32 12.*

Bruxelles 183 – Bouillon 25 – Arlon 39 – Sedan 38.

à Izel *Est : 5 km* C *Chiny 4 866 h.* – ✉ *6810 Izel :*

🏠 **Le Nid d'Izel** 🐎, av. Germain Gilson 97, ☎ 0 61 32 10 24, *info@lenid.be, Fax 0 61 32 09 65*, 🏞, ⑩, ≘s, ▭, 🚗 – |‡| TV 🚗 P. MC VISA. ✂
fermé 28 juin-5 juil., 30 août-2 sept., dim. soir et lundi – **Repas** *Lunch 25* – 30/45 – **22 ch** ☐ 75/90 – ½ P 73/78.
• Petite auberge villageoise dont la façade proprette s'anime de fenêtres à châssis jaunes. Chambres parquetées, garnies d'un mobilier actuel en bois clair. Beau jardin. Pimpante salle à manger aux tables bien espacées.
• Kleine dorpsherberg met geel geschilderde vensters aan de kraakheldere voorgevel. De kamers zijn voorzien van parket en modern meubilair van licht hout. De eetzaal ziet er piekfijn uit en biedt voldoende ruimte tussen de tafels. Mooie tuin.

à Lacuisine *Nord : 3 km* 🄲 *Florenville - ✉ 6821 Lacuisine :*

La Roseraie, rte de Chiny 2, ☎ 0 61 31 10 39, *laroseraie.lc@skynet.be, Fax 0 61 31 49 58,* ... - ... rest
fermé du 8 au 21 mars et 20 sept.-7 oct. – **Repas** *(fermé mardi et merc.) Lunch 33* – 20/87 bc – **14 ch** ☐ 91/104 – ½ P 85.
◆ Charmant établissement entouré de grands arbres et agrémenté d'un plaisant jardin bordé par la Semois. Chambres tout confort, pourvues d'un mobilier de style. À table, recettes aux notes actuelles, jouées par un chef qui connaît ses classiques.
◆ Charmant hotel met grote bomen en een mooie tuin aan de oever van de Semois. De kamers zijn heel comfortabel en van stijlmeubelen voorzien. In het restaurant worden eigentijdse gerechten geserveerd, bereid door een kok die zijn klassieken kent.

FOREST (VORST) *Région de Bruxelles-Capitale* 533 K 18 – *voir à Bruxelles.*

FOSSES-LA-VILLE *5070 Namur* 533 N 20, 534 N 20 *et* 716 H 4 – *8 937 h.*
Bruxelles 78 – Namur 19 – Charleroi 22 – Dinant 30.

Le Castel ..., r. Chapitre 10, ☎ 0 71 71 18 12, *lecastel@lecastel.be, Fax 0 71 71 23 96,* ... – ...
fermé sam. midi, dim. soir et lundi – **Repas** *Lunch 30* – 39/69 bc – **10 ch** ☐ 85/122 – ½ P 78/87.
◆ De plaisantes chambres bien préservées du bruit ont été aménagées dans cette demeure du 19e s. bâtie à flanc de colline, près de l'église. Élégante salle à manger donnant sur une terrasse d'été meublée en teck. Goûteux repas actuel à connotations régionales.
◆ Hotel in een 19e-eeuws pand op de flank van een heuvel, vlak bij de kerk. Prettige kamers die goed tegen geluid zijn geïsoleerd. Stijlvolle eetzaal en terras met teakhouten meubelen. Eigentijdse keuken met regionale invloeden.

FOURON-LE-COMTE *Limburg – voir 's Gravenvoeren.*

FRAHAN *Luxembourg belge* 534 P 23 *et* 716 I 6 – *voir à Poupehan.*

FRAMERIES *Hainaut* 533 I 20, 534 I 20 *et* 716 E 4 – *voir à Mons.*

FRANCORCHAMPS *4970 Liège* 🄲 *Stavelot 6 631 h.* 533 U 20, 534 U 20 *et* 716 K 4.
Exc. *au Sud : parcours★ de Francorchamps à Stavelot.*
Bruxelles 146 – Liège 47 – Spa 9.

XXX **Host. Le Roannay** avec ch (annexe ... - 8 ch), rte de Spa 155, ☎ 0 87 27 53 11, *info@roannay.com, Fax 0 87 27 55 47,* ... – ..., ... rest, ... – ... 25. ...
fermé 5 janv.-4 fév., 29 nov.-16 déc. et mardi – **Repas** *Lunch 42* – 70/95 bc ... – **12 ch** ☐ 122/195 – ½ P 110/130.
◆ Hostellerie traditionnelle se prévalant de 75 années de bons et loyaux services. Salle à manger cossue, cuisine classique et pas moins de 600 crus en cave. Sobres chambres.
◆ Traditionele hostellerie die kan terugblikken op 75 jaar trouwe diensten. Luxueuze eetzaal. Klassieke keuken en een wijnkelder met maar liefst 600 flessen. Sobere kamers.

FRASNES *Namur* 534 M 22 *et* 716 G 5 – *voir à Couvin.*

FROYENNES *Hainaut* 533 F 19, 534 F 19 *et* 716 D 4 – *voir à Tournai.*

FURFOOZ *Namur* 533 O 21, 534 O 21 *et* 716 H 5 – *voir à Dinant.*

FURNES *West-Vlaanderen – voir Veurne.*

GAND *Oost-Vlaanderen – voir Gent.*

GANSHOREN *Région de Bruxelles-Capitale* 533 K 17 *et* 716 F 3 – *voir à Bruxelles.*

GEEL *2440 Antwerpen* 533 O 15 *et* 716 H 2 – *34 169 h.*

Voir *Mausolée★ dans l'église Ste-Dymphne (St-Dimfnakerk).*

Markt 33 ℘ 0 14 57 09 50, toerisme@geel.be, Fax 0 14 59 15 57.

Bruxelles 66 – Antwerpen 43 – Hasselt 38 – Turnhout 18.

XX **De Cuylhoeve,** Hollandsebaan 7 (Sud : 3 km, lieu-dit Winkelomheide), ℘ 0 14 58 57 35, *cuylhoeve@innet.be, Fax 0 14 58 24 08,* – P. AE MC VISA
fermé 1 sem. en mars, mi-juil.-mi-août, Noël-Nouvel An, merc., sam. midi et dim. – **Repas** *Lunch 31* – 55.

◆ Cette fermette postée à l'orée d'un bois dispose d'une terrasse très agréable par beau temps. Menus thématiques revisités au fil des semaines. Cave "châtelaine".

◆ Op het terras van deze hoeve naast het bos is het bij goed weer heerlijk toeven. Themamenu's die om de paar weken worden vernieuwd. De wijnkelder is een kasteelheer waardig.

GELDENAKEN *Brabant Wallon – voir Jodoigne.*

GELLINGEN *Hainaut – voir Ghislenghien à Ath.*

GELUWE *8940 West-Vlaanderen* C *Wervik 17 617 h.* 533 D 18 *et* 716 C 3.

Bruxelles 109 – Kortrijk 19 – Ieper 20 – Lille 27.

XX **Oud Stadhuis,** St-Denijsplaats 7, ℘ 0 56 51 66 49, *Fax 0 56 51 79 12* – AE ⓘ MC VISA
fermé du 2 au 11 avril, 21 juil.-15 août, mardi soir, merc. et dim. soir – **Repas** *Lunch 30* – 75 bc, ♀.

◆ L'enseigne révèle l'ancienne destination de ce bâtiment situé face à l'église : une maison communale (stadhuis). Intérieur actuel, sobre et plaisant.

◆ Het uithangbord herinnert aan de voormalige bestemming van dit pand recht tegenover de kerk. Het interieur is modern, sober en aangenaam.

Les pages explicatives de l'introduction vous aideront à mieux profiter de votre Guide Michelin.

GEMBLOUX *5030 Namur* 533 N 19, 534 N 19 *et* 716 H 4 – *20 899 h.*

Env. *au Sud : 4 km à Corroy-le-Château : château féodal★.*

18 *au Sud : 8 km à Mazy, Ferme-château de Falnuée, r. Emile Pirson 55 ℘ 0 81 63 30 90, Fax 0 81 63 37 64.*

r. Sigebert 1 ℘ 0 81 62 69 60, otgembloux@hotmail.com, Fax 0 81 62 69 64.

Bruxelles 44 – Namur 18 – Charleroi 26 – Tienen 34.

Les 3 Clés, chaussée de Namur 17 (N 4), ℘ 0 81 61 16 17, *hotel@3cles.be, Fax 0 81 61 41 13,* – rest, TV P – 25 à 220. AE ⓘ MC VISA
Repas *Lunch 18* – 32/37, ♀ – **45 ch** 72/108.

◆ Depuis trois générations, la même famille est aux commandes de cet établissement. Chambres sobrement équipées, mais néanmoins fonctionnelles. Salle de restaurant aménagée dans la note contemporaine. Préparations classiques et traditionnelles.

◆ Dit hotel wordt al drie generaties lang door een en dezelfde familie gerund. De (3) sleutelwoorden van het bedrijf : sober uitgeruste, functionele kamers en een modern restaurant, waar de gasten klassiek-traditionele gerechten krijgen voorgeschoteld.

La Gloriette, chaussée de Charleroi 206 (Est : 2 km), ℘ 0 81 62 54 60, *Fax 0 81 60 14 79,* – TV P – 25 à 80. AE ⓘ MC VISA
Repas *Lunch 13* – carte 31 à 43 – 8 – **16 ch** 50/80 – ½ P 65.

◆ Pas loin de Gembloux, grosse villa où vous passerez des nuits sans remous après quelques moments de détente : centre de relaxation, fitness, mini-golf, tennis et pétanque. Ample et lumineux restaurant-vérada.

◆ In deze grote villa bij Gembloux slaapt u als een roos na de talloze in- en ontspanningsmogelijkheden, zoals een ontspanningscenter, fitness, midgetgolf, tennis en pétanque. Ruim en licht restaurant met serre.

X **Piccoline et Romarin,** r. Théo Toussaint 10, ℘ 0 81 61 46 58, *piccoline@skynet.be, Fax 0 81 61 46 58* – MC VISA.
fermé 2 prem. sem. mars, 2 prem. sem. août, lundi et mardi – **Repas** *Lunch 19* – carte 38 à 53.

◆ Bonne petite adresse à dénicher en centre-ville. Jolie salle aux tons chauds, mise en place raffinée sur les tables et curieux bar créé à partir d'une chaloupe. Choix actuel.

◆ Leuk adresje in het centrum. Mooie eetzaal met warme kleuren, geraffineerd gedekte tafels en een opmerkelijke bar in de vorm van een sloep. Moderne keuken.

GENAPPE (GENEPIËN) *1470 Brabant Wallon 533 L 19 et 716 G 4 – 13 959 h.*

à l'Est : 1,5 km à Ways, r. E. François 9 ☎ 0 67 77 15 71, Fax 0 67 77 18 33.
Bruxelles 35 – Charleroi 24 – Nivelles 12.

à Ways *Est : 1,5 km* *Genappe – ✉ 1474 Ways :*

Le Relais du Lothier, r. Emile Marcq 3 (N 5), ☎ 0 67 77 37 98, *relais.du.lothier@wanadoo.be, Fax 0 67 77 37 98,* – AE MC VISA
fermé du 1er au 15 mars, du 1er au 15 oct., mardi soir, merc. et dim. soir – **Repas** *Lunch 15* – 30/58 bc.
• Cette petite affaire sympathique située à un carrefour courtise les produits locaux. Menus et suggestions régalent les habitués. En cave, vins des régions de France.
• Klein restaurant op een kruispunt, waar veel stamgasten komen. Menu's en dagaanbod op basis van lokale producten, die worden weggespoeld met een lekkere Franse wijn.

GENEPIËN *Brabant Wallon – voir Genappe.*

GENK *3600 Limburg 533 S 17 et 716 J 3 – 62 949 h.*

Voir *à l'Ouest : 5 km, Domaine provincial de Bokrijk★ : Musée de plein air★★ (Openluchtmuseum), Domaine récréatif★ : arboretum★.*

Wiemesmeerstraat 109 ☎ 0 89 35 96 16, Fax 0 89 36 41 84.

Gemeentehuis, Dieplaan 2 ☎ 0 89 30 95 62, toerisme@genk.be, Fax 0 89 30 51 68.

Bruxelles 97 ⑤ – Maastricht 24 ③ – Hasselt 21 ④

Plan page suivante

NH Genk, Albert Remansstraat 1, ☎ 0 89 36 41 50, *nhgenk@nh-hotels.be, Fax 0 89 36 41 51,* ≤, – – 25 à 210. AE MC VISA. rest X e
Repas *(fermé sam. midi et dim. soir) Lunch 30* – carte 31 à 51 – **81 ch** 135/150, – 2 suites – ½ P 160/200.
• Entre le Molenvijver - beau parc public de 15 ha agrémenté d'un vaste étang - et un centre commercial, hôtel de chaîne bénéficiant d'un équipement moderne complet. Restaurant agrémenté d'une terrasse d'été.
• Dit hotel behoort tot een keten en ligt tussen het winkelcentrum en de Molenvijver, een mooi park van 15 ha met een grote vijver. De kamers zijn vrij comfortabel. Het restaurant heeft een terras, waar 's zomers de tafeltjes worden gedekt.

Golfhotel La Résidence , Wiemesmeerstraat 105 (Spiegelven), ☎ 0 89 35 58 28, *info@golfhotel-la-residence.com, Fax 0 89 35 58 03,* ≤, – – 25 à 400. AE MC VISA Z d
Repas *Lunch 29* – 33/79 bc, ♀ – 12 – **70 ch** 72/82 – ½ P 70/83.
• Construction façon "cottage" aux abords verdoyants malgré le voisinage de l'autoroute. Avenantes chambres toutes rafraîchies. Bonne infrastructure pour la tenue de réunions. Businessmen et golfeurs s'attablent dans un cadre rénové. Cuisine au goût du jour.
• Dit hotel in de "cottage-stijl" ligt tussen het groen, maar het is wel goed bereikbaar. Prettige, gerenoveerde kamers. Faciliteiten voor vergaderingen. Zakenlieden en golfers schuiven graag aan in het moderne restaurant om van de trendy keuken te genieten.

Atlantis sans rest, Fletersdel 1, ☎ 0 89 35 65 51, *info@hotelatlantis.be, Fax 0 89 35 35 29,* – – 35. AE MC VISA. Z a
fermé 24 déc.-7 janv. – **24 ch** 70/130.
• Petit hôtel d'une tenue irréprochable, implanté à distance respectable du centre-ville. Chambres correctes et, surtout, calme d'un quartier résidentiel.
• Perfect onderhouden hotelletje op enige afstand van het centrum van de stad. De kamers zijn correct en hebben als voordeel de rust van een chique woonwijk.

Ecu sans rest, Europalaan 46, ☎ 0 89 36 42 44, *mail@hotelecu.com, Fax 0 89 36 42 50,* – – 25. AE MC VISA. X r
40 ch 75/115.
• Immeuble moderne proche de la gare, sur l'artère principale de Genk. Décoration intérieure design. Trois catégories chambres, dont une quinzaine de junior suites.
• Deze moderne flat staat aan de hoofdweg van Genk, vlak bij het station. Designinterieur. Er zijn drie categorieën kamers, waaronder vijftien junior suites.

Europa, Sledderloweg 85, ☎ 0 89 35 42 74, *info@europa-horecaservice.com, Fax 0 89 35 75 79,* – – 25 à 100. AE MC VISA. Z b
Repas *(fermé dim.)* carte 27 à 40 – **18 ch** 45/80.
• Engageante affaire familiale avoisinant une zone industrielle de Genk. Ses sobres chambres retrouvent progressivement l'éclat du neuf.
• Uitnodigend familiebedrijf naast het industrieterrein van Genk. De sobere kamers worden stuk voor stuk in een nieuw jasje gestoken.

GENK

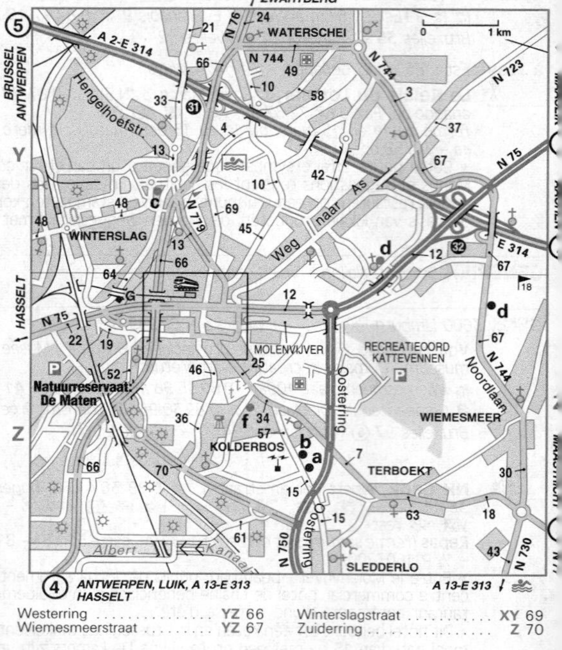

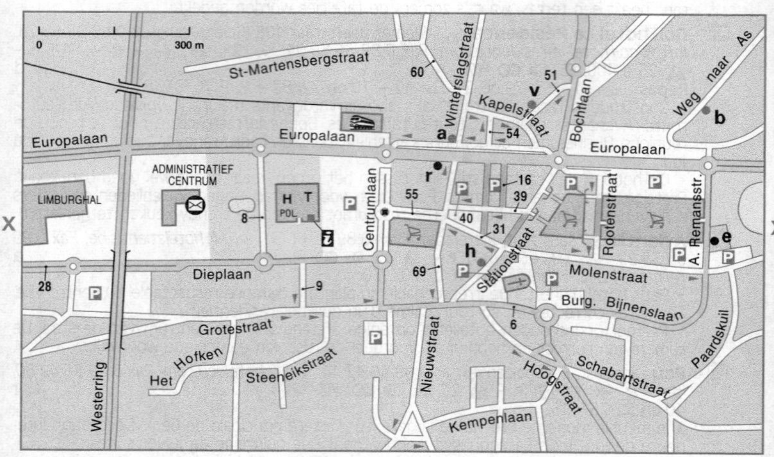

Ne confondez pas :

Confort des hôtels : 🏨🏨🏨🏨🏨 ... 🏨
Confort des restaurants : XXXXX ... X
Qualité de la table : ✿✿✿, ✿✿, ✿, **Repas**

XXX **Da Vinci,** Pastoor Raeymaekersstraat 3, ✆ 0 89 30 60 59, *info@davinci.be, Fax 0 89 30 60 56* – ▤ P. AE ⓓ ⓜ VISA. ✂ X v
fermé 21 juil.-5 août, prem. sem. janv., sam. midi, dim. et lundi – **Repas** Lunch 35 – 39/67 bc, ♀.
◆ Restaurant entièrement modernisé : spacieuses salles bien agencées, vaisselle design et carte actuelle succincte mais comportant tout de même sept préparations de homard.
◆ Volledig gemoderniseerd restaurant met ruime en mooi ingerichte eetzalen, design-servies en een beknopte eigentijdse kaart met kreeft op zeven verschillende manieren bereid.

XX **De Boote,** Neerzijstraat 41, ✆ 0 89 30 59 00, *info@deboote.com, Fax 0 89 30 39 39*, 🍴 – P. AE ⓓ ⓜ VISA Y d
fermé du 11 au 25 juil., du 12 au 19 sept., prem. sem. janv., merc. soir, sam. midi et dim. – **Repas** Lunch 30 – carte 46 à 72, ♀.
◆ Intérieur moderne rehaussé de notes indiennes et nipponnes, assiettes actuelles assez imaginatives, avec de discrètes notes exotiques, menus bien vus et beau restaurant d'été.
◆ Modern interieur met Indiase en Japanse accenten, fantasierijke keuken met een exotische toets, evenwichtige menu's en 's zomers lekker buiten eten.

XX **En Chanté,** Weg naar As 28, ✆ 0 89 30 86 40, *elvire.neyens@enchante.be*, 🍴 – P. AE ⓓ ⓜ VISA X a
fermé 2 sem. en sept., lundi et sam. midi – **Repas** Lunch 25 – 30/60 bc.
◆ Une carte classique assortie de deux menus actualisés est présentée dans cette petite villa des hauteurs de Genk. Salle feutrée donnant sur une véranda et sa terrasse.
◆ In deze kleine villa in de heuvels van Genk kunt u kiezen uit een klassieke kaart en twee eigentijdse menu's. Eetzaal met serre en terras. Binnen hangt een gedempte sfeer.

XX **Mélange,** Hooiweg 51, ✆ 0 89 36 72 02, *Fax 0 89 36 72 02*, 🍴 – P. AE ⓓ ⓜ VISA. ✂ Z f
fermé dern. sem. juil.-prem. sem. août, dern. sem. janv., merc. et sam. midi – **Repas** Lunch 25 – 50/80 bc, ♀.
◆ Restaurant établi dans un quartier résidentiel excentré. Mise en place soignée sur les table, cuisine féminine de bonne facture et terrasse arrière devancée d'un coin salon.
◆ Restaurant met aparte zithoek en terras aan de achterkant, in een rustige woonwijk buiten het centrum. Fraai gedekte tafels en goed verzorgde keuken met een vrouwelijke toets.

XX **St. Maarten,** Stationsstraat 13, ✆ 0 89 35 26 57, *paul.vanormelingen@proximedia.be, Fax 0 89 30 31 87*, 🍴 – P. AE ⓓ ⓜ VISA. ✂ X h
fermé 2 sem. en mars, 2 prem. sem. août, lundi et sam. midi – **Repas** Lunch 28 – carte env. 48.
◆ Devant l'église, ancienne maison de notable où l'on vient faire des repas classiques actualisés. Parking public à côté (carte de sortie fournie en quittant l'établissement).
◆ Oud herenhuis tegenover de kerk, waar u van modern-klassieke gerechten kunt genieten. Parkeergarage ernaast (als u het restaurant verlaat, krijgt u een uitrijkaart).

XX ⓑ **'t Konijntje,** Vennestraat 74 (Winterslag), ✆ 0 89 35 26 45, *Fax 0 89 30 53 18*, 🍴, Moules en saison – P. AE ⓓ ⓜ VISA. ✂ Y c
fermé 23 juin-15 juil., mardi soir et merc. – **Repas** 16/40 bc.
◆ Le P'tit Lapin ('t Konijntje) vous reçoit dans son nouveau "terrier" au confort accru. Recettes bourgeoises et menus choyés par la clientèle. Grandes terrasses à l'arrière.
◆ Dit konijntje ontvangt u in zijn nieuwe hol, dat nu nog gerieflijker is. Traditionele gerechten en menu's die zeer in de smaak vallen bij de clientèle. Groot terras achter.

XX **Double Dragons,** Hasseltweg 214 (Ouest : 2 km sur N 75), ✆ 0 89 35 96 90, *Fax 0 89 36 44 28*, Cuisine asiatique, ouvert jusqu'à minuit – ▤ P. AE ⓓ ⓜ VISA. ✂
Repas 30/63, ♀.
◆ Imposant restaurant dont les toits en pagode affichent ouvertement la vocation exotique. Saveurs dépaysantes ponctuées de quelques spécialités indonésiennes.
◆ Indrukwekkend restaurant, waarvan het pagodedak al van verre wijst op zijn exotische bestemming. Aziatische gerechten, waaronder enkele Indonesische specialiteiten.

X **Peper en Zout,** Europalaan 81, ✆ 0 89 35 74 67, *dirk.appeltans@proximedia.be, Fax 0 89 30 78 05* – AE ⓓ ⓜ VISA. ✂ X b
fermé prem. sem. sept., prem. sem. nov., 1 sem. en janv., dim. et lundi – **Repas** Lunch 24 – 30/64 bc.
◆ Bon petit restaurant central dont le jeune chef anime aussi une émission culinaire sur une radio locale. Cuisine du moment, à base de produits soigneusement choisis.
◆ Goed en centraal gelegen zaakje. De jonge chef brengt zijn culinair programma op een lokale radio. De uitgekozen ingrediënten dansen op een aktueel ritme.

GENT – GAND

9000 **P** *Oost-Vlaanderen* 533 H 16 *et* 716 E 2 – *226 220 h.*

Bruxelles 55 ③ – *Antwerpen 60* ② – *Lille 71* ⑤.

RENSEIGNEMENTS PRATIQUES

Raadskelder Belfort, Botermarkt 17 a ☎ 0 9 266 52 32, toerisme@gent.be, Fax 0 9 225 62 88 – Fédération provinciale de tourisme, Woodrow Wilsonplein 3 ☎ 0 9 267 70 20, toerisme@oost-vlaanderen.be, Fax 0 9 267 71 99.

18 *au Sud-Ouest : 9 km à Sint-Martens-Latem, Latemstraat 120 ☎ 0 9 282 54 11, latem@golf.be, Fax 0 9 282 90 19.*

CURIOSITÉS

Voir *Vieille ville★★★ (Oude Stad) – Cathédrale St-Bavon★★ (St-Baafskathedraal)* FZ *: Polyptyque★★★ de l'Adoration de l'Agneau mystique par Van Eyck (Veelluik de Aanbidding van Het Lam Gods), Crypte★ : triptyque du Calvaire★ par Juste de Gand (Calvarietriptiek van Justus van Gent)* FZ *– Beffroi et Halle aux Draps★★★ (Belfort en Lakenhalle)* FY *– Pont St-Michel (St-Michielsbrug) ⋞★★★* EY *– Quai aux Herbes★★★ (Graslei)* EY *– Château des Comtes de Flandre★★ (Gravensteen) : ⋞★ du sommet du donjon* EY *– St-Niklaaskerk★* EY *– Petit béguinage★ (Klein Begijnhof)* DX *– Réfectoire★ des ruines de l'abbaye St-Bavon (Ruïnes van de St-Baafsabdij)* DV **M5**.

Musées *: du Folklore★ (Huis van Alijn) : cour★ intérieure de l'hospice des Enfants Alyn (Alijnsgodshuis)* EY **M1** *– des Beaux-Arts★★ (Museum voor Schone Kunsten)* CX **M2** *– de la Byloke★★ (Oudheidkundig Museum van de Bijloke)* CX **M3** *– des Arts décoratifs et du Design★ (Museum voor Sierkunst en Vormgeving)* EY **M4** *– d'Art contemporain★★ (S.M.A.K.) (Stedelijk Museum voor Actuele Kunst)* CX *– d'Archéologie Industrielle et du Textile★ (MIAT) (Museum voor Industriële Archeologie en Textiel)* DV **X**.

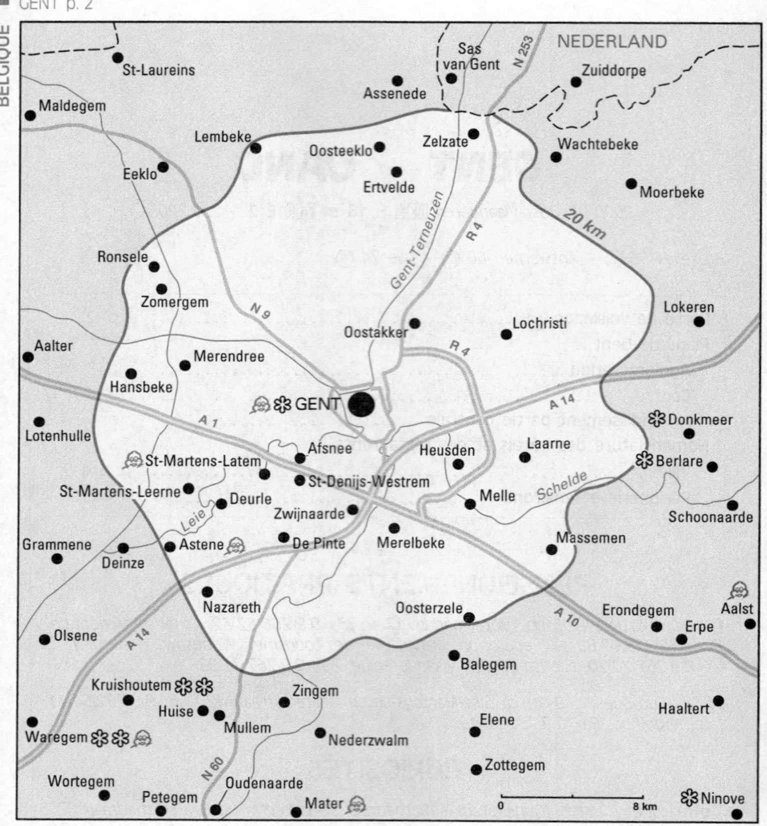

Les Bonnes Tables

Gourmets...

Nous distinguons à votre intention
certains hôtels (⌂ ... ⌂⌂⌂⌂⌂) et restaurants (✗ ... ✗✗✗✗✗)
par Repas ☺, ✿, ✿✿ ou ✿✿✿.

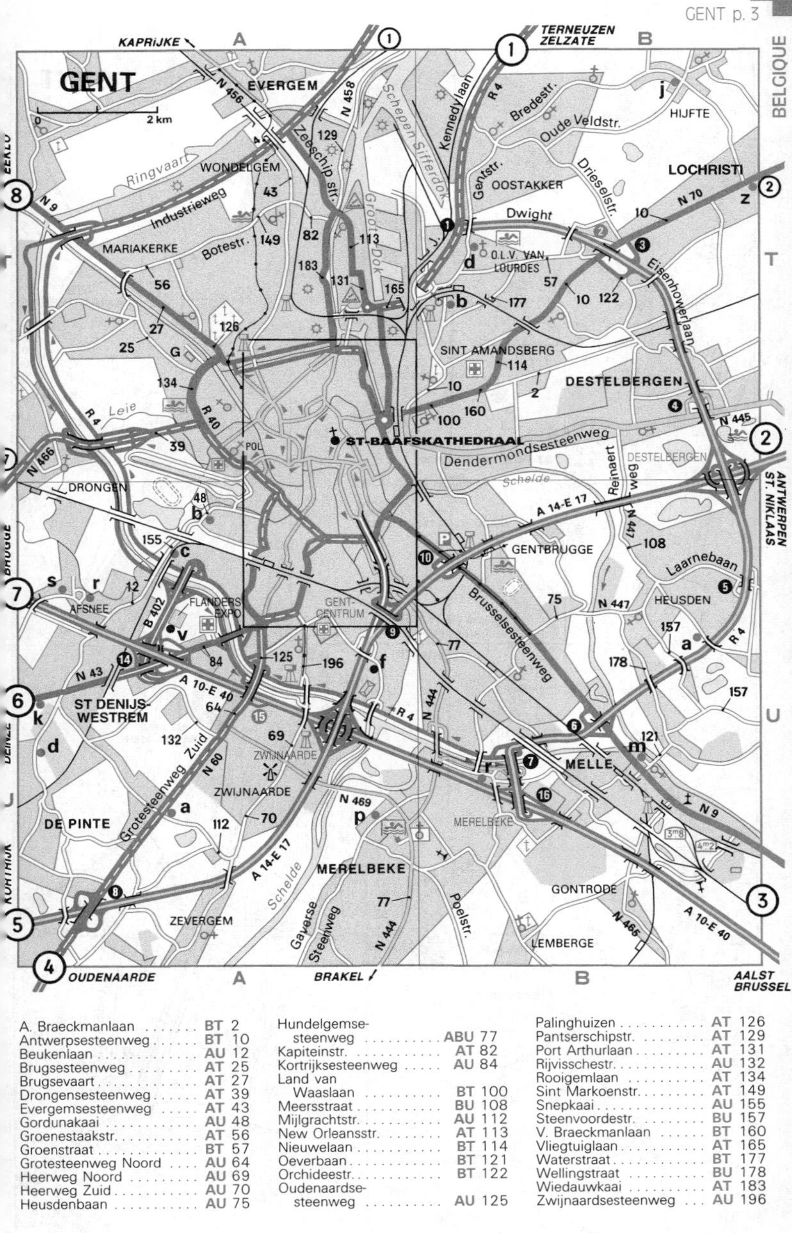

A. Braeckmanlaan	BT	2
Antwerpsesteenweg	BT	10
Beukenlaan	AU	12
Brugsesteenweg	AT	25
Brugsevaart	AT	27
Drongensesteenweg	AT	39
Evergemsesteenweg	AT	43
Gordunakaai	AU	48
Groenestaakstr.	AT	56
Groenstraat	BT	57
Grotesteenweg Noord	AU	64
Heerweg Noord	AU	69
Heerweg Zuid	AU	70
Heusdenbaan	AU	75
Hundelgemsesteenweg	ABU	77
Kapiteinstr.	AT	82
Kortrijksesteenweg	AU	84
Land van Waaslaan	BT	100
Meersstraat	BU	108
Mijlgrachtstr.	AU	112
New Orleansstr.	AT	113
Nieuwelaan	BT	114
Oeverbaan	BT	121
Orchideestr.	BT	122
Oudenaardsesteenweg	AU	125
Palinghuizen	AT	126
Pantserschipstr.	AT	129
Port Arthurlaan	AT	131
Rijvisschestr.	AU	132
Rooigemlaan	AT	134
Sint Markoenstr.	AT	149
Snepkaai	AU	155
Steenvoordestr.	BU	157
V. Braeckmanlaan	BT	160
Vliegtuiglaan	AT	165
Waterstraat	BT	177
Wellingstraat	BU	178
Wiedauwkaai	AT	183
Zwijnaardsesteenweg	AU	196

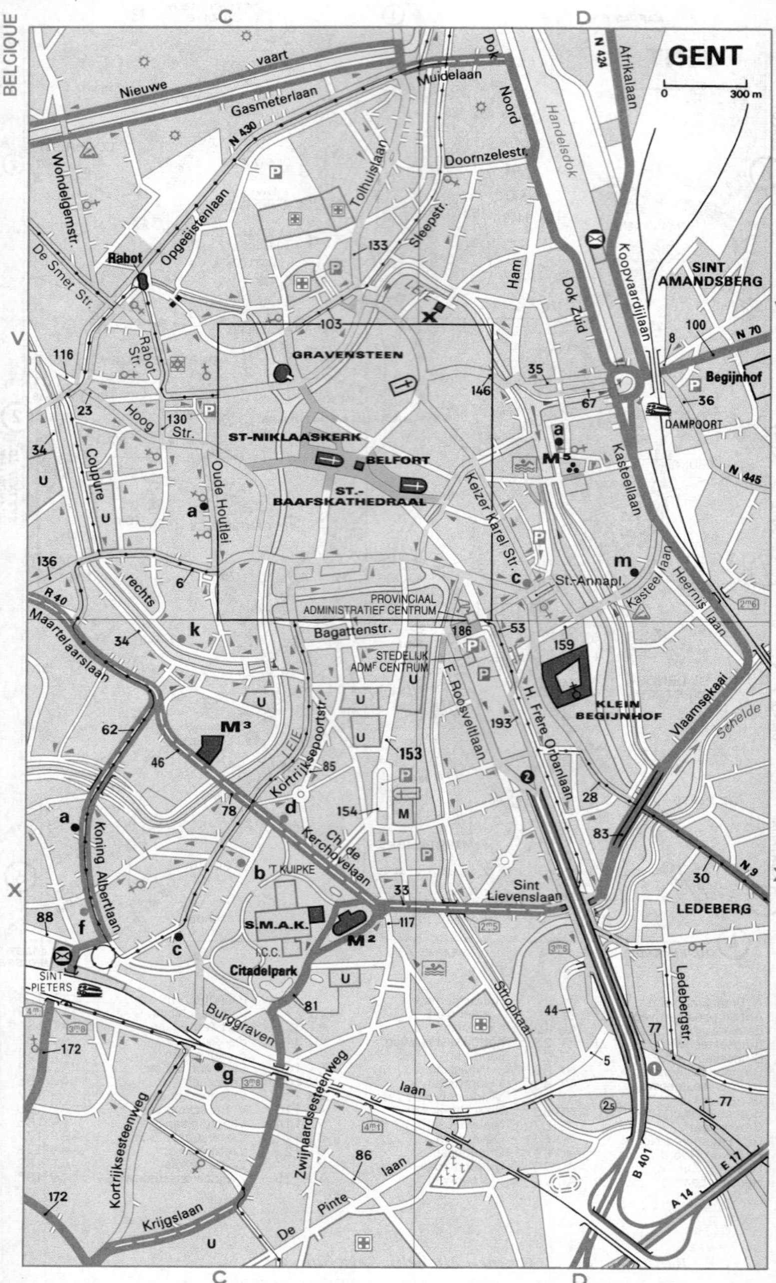
GENT
0
300 m
Nieuwe vaart
Gasmeterlaan
Muidelaan
Dok Noord
Handelsdok
Afrikalaan
N 424
N 430
Wondelgemstr.
Opgeëistenlaan
Tolhuislaan
Sleepstr.
Doornzelestr.
De Smet Str.
Rabot
Rabot Str.
133
Ham
Dok Zuid
Koopvaardijlaan
SINT AMANDSBERG
LEIE
103
GRAVENSTEEN
116
23
Hoog Str.
130
35
146
67
100
8
N 70
Begijnhof
36
DAMPOORT
34
ST-NIKLAASKERK
BELFORT
ST.-BAAFSKATHEDRAAL
M5
Kasteellaan
N 445
Coupure
Oude Houtlei
Keizer Karel Str.
136
R 40
rechts
6
St.-Annapl.
Kasteellaan
Heernislaan
PROVINCIAAL ADMINISTRATIEF CENTRUM
Maartelaarslaan
34
k
Bagattenstr.
186
53
159
STEDELIJK ADMF CENTRUM
F. Rooseveltlaan
H. Frère Orbanlaan
KLEIN BEGIJNHOF
Vlaamsekaai
Schelde
62
M3
193
46
Kortrijksepoortstr.
85
153
78
d
154
28
Koning Albertlaan
Ch. de Kerchovelaan
83
30
N 9
b
'T KUIPKE
33
Sint Lievenslaan
LEDEBERG
88
f
S.M.A.K.
117
M2
I.C.C.
Citadelpark
SINT PIETERS
Stropkaai
44
Ledebergstr.
172
Burggraven
81
77
g
Zwijnaardsesteenweg
laan
5
77
Kortrijksesteenweg
86
B 401
laan
172
Krijgslaan
De Pinte
A 14
E 17
C
D
V
X

GENT

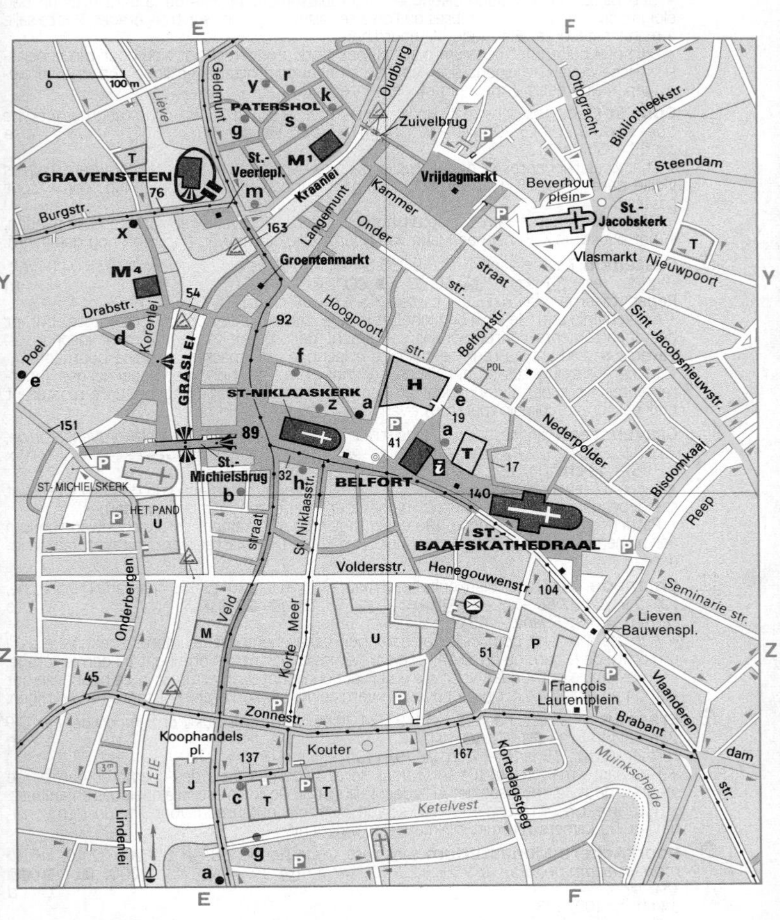

Si vous cherchez un hôtel tranquille ou isolé,
consultez d'abord les cartes de l'introduction
ou repérez dans le texte les établissements indiqués avec le signe ou

BELGIQUE

Quartiers du Centre - *plans p. 4 et 5 sauf indication spéciale :*

Novotel Centrum, Gouden Leeuwplein 5, ☎ 0 9 224 22 30, *H0840@accor-hotels.com, Fax 0 9 224 32 95,* – 25 à 150. AE VISA EY a
Repas carte 28 à 41 – 15 – **110 ch** 144, – 4 suites.
◆ Ce Novotel porte bien son nom ! Derrière sa façade contemporaine, on trouve un grand lobby sous verrière ainsi que d'amples chambres agencées selon les standards de la chaîne. Restaurant au goût du jour. Banquets dans une cave voûtée du 14e s.
◆ Dit Novotel past precies bij zijn naam : moderne voorgevel, grote lobby met glazen dak en ruime kamers die geheel aan de standaard van de keten voldoen. Restaurant met een eigentijdse keuken. Feestzaal in een overwelfde kelder uit de 14e eeuw.

NH Gent, Koning Albertlaan 121, ☎ 0 9 222 60 65, *dirnhgest@nh-hotels.be, Fax 0 9 220 16 05* – – 25 à 80. AE VISA. rest CX a
Repas *(fermé dim.)* (dîner seult) carte env. 35 – 17 – **47 ch** 140/160, – 2 suites.
◆ Une façade néoclassique distingue cet établissement proche de la gare mais un peu éloigné du centre-ville. Chambres où l'on a ses aises, réparties sur trois étages. Petite salle à manger décorée à la mode d'aujourd'hui.
◆ Dit hotel buiten het centrum maar bij het station onderscheidt zich door zijn neoclassicistische gevel. De eigentijdse kamers zijn heel comfortabel en liggen op drie verdiepingen. Kleine eetzaal met een modern interieur.

Cour St-Georges sans rest, Hoogpoort 75, ☎ 0 9 224 24 24, *courstgeorges@skynet.be, Fax 0 9 224 26 40,* – . AE VISA FY e
13 – **31 ch** 115/145.
◆ Chambres fringantes et douillettes dispersées dans deux maisons de caractère. La plus vieille date de 1228. Marie de Bourgogne, Charles Quint et même Napoléon y sont passés.
◆ De vrolijke, knusse kamers van dit hotel zijn verdeeld over twee karaktervolle panden. In het oudste (1228) hebben Maria van Bourgondië, Karel V en Napoleon nog gelogeerd.

Castelnou, Kasteellaan 51, ☎ 0 9 235 04 11, *info@castelnou.be, Fax 0 9 235 04 04,* – , rest, – 30. AE VISA DV m
Repas (taverne-rest) *Lunch 9* – carte 22 à 37 – **36 ch** 84/97 – ½ P 57.
◆ À mi-chemin entre le Klein Begijnhof et la gare, immeuble de conception récente abritant des appartements contemporains sobrement décorés et convenablement insonorisés. Taverne-restaurant au registre culinaire éclectique : du snack à la cuisine bourgeoise.
◆ Modern gebouw tussen het Klein Begijnhof en het station, met hedendaagse appartementen die sober zijn ingericht en een goede geluidsisolatie hebben. Café-restaurant met een breed culinair spectrum : van snack tot uitgebreid diner.

Gravensteen sans rest, Jan Breydelstraat 35, ☎ 0 9 225 11 50, *hotel@gravensteen.be, Fax 0 9 225 18 50,* – – 30. AE VISA JCB EY x
15 – **49 ch** 104/154.
◆ Face au Gravensteen (château des Comtes), demeure patricienne du début du 19e s. et ses dépendances réparties autour d'une cour intérieure. Chambres modernes.
◆ Patriciërshuis uit de vroege 19e eeuw met moderne kamers en bijgebouwen rondom een binnenplaats. Ertegenover staat het Gravensteen, het kasteel van de graven van Vlaanderen.

Chamade sans rest, Blankenbergestraat 2, ☎ 0 9 220 15 15, *chamade@unicall.be, Fax 0 9 221 97 66* – – 25. AE VISA CX c
fermé 24 déc.-5 janv. – **45 ch** 105/125.
◆ Adresse à retenir pour celles et ceux qui recherchent des chambres fonctionnelles à proximité de la gare ou du S.M.A.K. Le café et les croissants se prennent au dernier étage.
◆ Adres om te onthouden voor wie een functionele hotelkamer zoekt in de buurt van het station en het S.M.A.K. Op de bovenste verdieping zijn koffie en croissants te verkrijgen.

Erasmus sans rest, Poel 25, ☎ 0 9 224 21 95, *hotel.erasmus@proximedia.be, Fax 0 9 233 42 41,* – . AE VISA. EY e
fermé 20 déc.-15 janv. – **7 ch** 79/110.
◆ Ravissante maison du 16e s. où vous serez hébergés dans des chambres garnies de meubles de style. Le Musée des Arts décoratifs et du Design n'est qu'à quelques enjambées.
◆ Hotel in een schitterend 16e-eeuws pand, dicht bij het Museum voor Sierkunst en Vormgeving. De kamers zijn met stijlmeubelen ingericht.

PoortAckere Monasterium sans rest, Oude Houtlei 58, ☎ 0 9 269 22 10, *info@monasterium.be, Fax 0 9 269 22 30,* – – 25 à 200. AE VISA. CV a
34 ch 100/125.
◆ Hôtel original aménagé dans un ancien couvent. Chambres quelquefois munies d'une kitchenette, distribuées autour d'une cour intérieure. Église convertie en salle de réunion.
◆ Origineel hotel in een oud klooster. De kamers liggen rondom een binnenplaats en sommige zijn voorzien van een kitchenette. De vroegere kerk is tot vergaderzaal verbouwd.

Ibis Opera sans rest, Nederkouter 24, ✆ 0 9 225 07 07, *H1455@accor-hotels.com, Fax 0 9 223 59 07* – ▯ ⇔ ▯ ▯. AE ⓓ ⓜⓒ VISA EZ a
☕ 9 – **134 ch** 82.
◆ Cet hôtel au "look" contemporain surplombe une voie passante. Confort convenable dans des chambres bien isolées du bruit et mises aux dernières normes Ibis.
◆ Dit hotel met zijn eigentijdse "look" bevindt zich aan een drukke weg. Comfortabele kamers met goede geluidsisolatie.

The Boatel sans rest, Voorhoutkaai 44, ✆ 0 9 267 10 30, *info@theboatel.com, Fax 0 9 267 10 39* – ▯. AE ⓓ ⓜⓒ VISA DV a
fermé fin déc.-début janv. – **7 ch** ☕ 105/130.
◆ Alternative aux formules d'hébergement classiques, cette péniche amarrée met à votre disposition de jolies cabines personnalisées dans l'esprit actuel. Vue sur l'eau.
◆ Wie op een originele manier wil overnachten, kan terecht in deze aak met mooie hutten die in eigentijdse stijl zijn ingericht en een persoonlijk karakter hebben.

Jan Van den Bon, Koning Leopold II laan 43, ✆ 0 9 221 90 85, *Fax 0 9 245 08 92*, ▯ – AE ⓓ ⓜⓒ VISA. ▯ CX b
fermé 1 sem. Pâques, 18 juil.-19 août, fin déc.-début janv., sam. midi, dim. et jours fériés – **Repas** *Lunch 40* – 55/68, carte 58 à 87.
◆ Maison bourgeoise voisine du musée d'Art contemporain. La salle à manger, égayée de toiles modernes, s'ouvre sur un jardin d'herbes potagères. Fine cuisine à touche créative.
◆ Dit herenhuis bevindt zich bij het museum van hedendaagse kunst. De eetzaal, die met moderne schilderijen is gesierd, kijkt uit op een moestuin. Verfijnde, creatieve keuken.
Spéc. Persillade d'écrevisses sur fricassée d'artichauts (mai-sept.). Lièvre en poivrade et croustillants de chou rouge (mi-oct.-fin déc.). Foie d'oie aux witlof et jus de raisins macérés (janv.-avril)

De Gouden Klok, Koning Albertlaan 31, ✆ 0 9 222 99 00, *Fax 0 9 222 10 92*, ▯ – ▯ P. AE ⓜⓒ VISA. ▯ CX f
fermé sem. carnaval, 3 dern. sem. juil., sem. Toussaint, merc. et dim. – **Repas** *Lunch 41* – carte 48 à 69.
◆ Boiseries et carreaux de faïence président au décor intérieur de cet hôtel de maître élevé à l'aube du 20e s. Le caneton est le péché mignon du chef. Cave prestigieuse.
◆ Hout en tegeltjes voeren de boventoon in dit hotel, dat in een herenhuis uit de vroege 20e eeuw is gevestigd. Eend is de specialiteit van het huis. Prestigieuze wijnkelder.

Agora, Klein Turkije 14, ✆ 0 9 225 25 58, *Fax 0 9 224 17 88*, Ouvert jusqu'à 23 h – ▯. AE ⓓ ⓜⓒ VISA. ▯ EY z
fermé 15 juil.-15 août, dim. et lundi – **Repas** *Lunch 15* – 32/62 bc.
◆ Table classique œuvrant depuis bientôt 30 ans au pied de la St.-Niklaaskerk. La salle de restaurant marie briques nues, étançons d'acier, cheminée inox et touches végétales.
◆ Dit klassieke restaurant bij de St.-Niklaaskerk bestaat al bijna 30 jaar. Eetzaal met kale bakstenen, ijzeren balken, een haard van roestvrij staal en her en der wat planten.

Georges, Donkersteeg 23, ✆ 0 9 225 19 18, *Fax 0 9 225 68 71*, Produits de la mer – ▯. AE ⓓ ⓜⓒ VISA EY f
fermé 27 mai-20 juin, du 7 au 15 janv., lundi et mardi – **Repas** *Lunch 18* – carte 33 à 83.
◆ Faites donc escale chez Georges ! Cette affaire familiale bien arrimée à une rue piétonne met le cap sur le grand large : recettes à base de poissons et fruits de mer.
◆ Zet eens voet aan wal bij Georges ! Dit familierestaurant ligt voor anker in een voetgangersstraat, maar de kok kiest het ruime sop met zijn visschotels en zeebanket.

Central-Au Paris, Botermarkt 10, ✆ 0 9 223 97 75, *cardon@centralauparis.be, Fax 0 9 233 69 30*, ▯ – AE ⓓ ⓜⓒ VISA. ▯ FY a
fermé 2e quinz. août, merc. et dim. soir – **Repas** 25/55 bc, ▯.
◆ Ce petit établissement présent depuis plus d'un quart de siècle entre le beffroi et l'hôtel de ville présente une carte traditionnelle vivant avec son époque. Âtre en salle.
◆ Dit kleine restaurant tussen het belfort en het stadhuis heeft ruim 25 jaar geleden zijn deuren geopend. Traditionele kaart die aan de huidige tijd is aangepast. Open haard.

Grade, Charles de Kerchovelaan 81, ✆ 0 9 224 43 85, *info@grade.be, Fax 0 9 233 11 29*, ▯ – AE ⓓ ⓜⓒ VISA CX d
fermé 2 dern. sem. août, dim. et lundi – **Repas** carte 30 à 43.
◆ Brasserie moderne avec véranda, équidistante du S.M.A.K. et du Musée de la Bijloke. Chaque plats est disponible en portion réduite. Artiste à ses heures, la patronne expose.
◆ Moderne brasserie met serre, halverwege het S.M.A.K. en het Museum van de Bijloke. Alle schotels zijn ook in kleinere porties verkrijgbaar. De kunst is van de eigenares zelf.

Le Homard Rouge, Ketelvest 9, ✆ 0 9 233 87 03, *homard.rouge@pandora.be, Fax 0 9 330 89 94*, ▯, Homards, ▯ – AE ⓓ ⓜⓒ VISA EZ g
fermé du 26 au 29 juil., 3 sem. en sept. et jeudi – **Repas** (dîner seult) 60.
◆ Les amateurs de homard trouveront leur bonheur à cette enseigne. On prend place dans une chaleureuse cave voûtée ou sur la terrasse estivale dressée au bord du canal.
◆ Liefhebbers van kreeft komen hier beslist aan hun trekken. Er kan worden gegeten in de sfeervolle gewelfde kelder of bij mooi weer op het terras aan de gracht.

Patyntje, Gordunakaai 91, ✆ 0 9 222 32 73, *info@patyntje.be, Fax 0 9 244 51 15,* ≤, ☂, Brasserie, ouvert jusqu'à 23 h – P. AE ◑ MC VISA plan p. 3 AU b
Repas *Lunch 15* – carte 27 à 50, ♀.
◆ Une jolie villa d'esprit colonial sert de cadre à ce restaurant posté au bord de la Leie (Lys). Choix attrayant, service charmant et ambiance "brasserie dans l'air du temps".
◆ Een mooie villa in koloniale stijl is de setting van dit restaurant aan de Leie. Aantrekkelijke menukaart, charmante bediening en de ambiance van een moderne brasserie.

Basile, Coupure Rechts 70, ✆ 0 9 233 26 12, *basile@plat-du-jour.be, Fax 0 9 233 55 74,* ☂ – AE MC VISA. ⊘ CX k
fermé 1 sem. Pâques, 2 dern. sem. août et dim. – **Repas** *(déjeuner seult sauf vend. en sam.) Lunch 12* – carte 29 à 45.
◆ Adresse discrète paressant en bordure du canal, à l'écart du centre-ville. Carte concise complétée d'une suggestion de menu et d'une formule lunch.
◆ Discreet adresje aan de gracht, even buiten het centrum. De kaart is vrij beperkt, maar wordt aangevuld met een menusuggestie en een lunchformule.

Italia-Grill, St-Annaplein 16, ✆ 0 9 224 30 42, *Fax 0 9 224 30 42,* Avec cuisine italienne, ouvert jusqu'à 23 h – ▤. AE ◑ MC VISA. ⊘ DV c
fermé 15 juil.-15 août et lundi – **Repas** *Lunch 15* – carte 27 à 66.
◆ Estimé des appétits carnivores comme des friands de "cucina italiana", ce resto affiche un "look" un rien mûrissant mais ses préparations sont bien dans leurs assiettes.
◆ Dit restaurant is echt iets voor vleeseters die bovendien van de "cucina italiana" houden. Het interieur is een tikkeltje ouderwets, maar de gerechten zijn goed bij de tijd.

Pakhuis, Schuurkenstraat 4, ✆ 0 9 223 55 55, *info@pakhuis.be, Fax 0 9 225 71 05,* Brasserie-écailler, ouvert jusqu'à minuit – ▤. AE ◑ MC VISA EYZ b
fermé 27 juil.-2 août et dim. – **Repas** *Lunch 11* – 23/29, ♀.
◆ Près du St.-Michielsbrug (panorama intéressant), entrepôt de la fin du 19e s. reconverti en une brasserie-écailler à la mode, étagée sur plusieurs niveaux. Additions légères.
◆ Trendy brasserie met oesterbank in een pakhuis uit de late 19e eeuw. De rekening is licht verteerbaar. Vanaf de nabije St.-Michielsbrug ontvouwt zich een interessant panorama.

Het Blauwe Huis, Drabstraat 17, ✆ 0 9 233 10 05, *Fax 0 9 233 51 81,* ☂, Brasserie, ouvert jusqu'à 23 h – AE ◑ MC VISA. ⊘ EY d
fermé août et lundi – **Repas** *Lunch 28* – carte 30 à 40.
◆ La couleur de la façade ne contredit pas l'enseigne de cette brasserie moderne : Het Blauwe Huis (La Maison Bleue). À l'intérieur, ça ne désemplit pas.
◆ De kleur van de voorgevel past perfect bij de naam van deze eigentijdse brasserie, waar het altijd stampvol zit. Lekker eten in een levendige ambiance.

Café Théâtre, Schouwburgstraat 5, ✆ 0 9 265 05 50, *cafe.theatre@pi.be, Fax 0 9 265 05 59,* Brasserie, ouvert jusqu'à 23 h – ▤. AE ◑ MC VISA EZ c
fermé mi-juil.-mi-août et sam. midi – **Repas** *Lunch 14* – carte 31 à 42, ♀.
◆ Brasserie contemporaine fort courtisée, où l'on s'installe dans une salle à manger avec mezzanine, coiffée d'une coupole. Carte importante. Serveuses jeunes et mignonnes.
◆ Populaire brasserie, waarvan de eetzaal een tussenverdieping heeft met een glazen koepel. Zeer uitgebreide kaart. Jonge en knappe serveersters.

Othello, Ketelvest 8, ✆ 0 9 233 00 09, *Fax 0 9 233 00 09,* ☂ – AE ◑ MC VISA EZ g
fermé 1 sem. en juil., lundi midi de juin à août, sam. midi, dim. et lundi soir – **Repas** carte env. 62, ♀.
◆ Une ruelle conduit à cette maison familiale au cadre d'inspiration "bistrot", courue pour sa gigantesque cave rendant un vibrant hommage au nectar du divin Bacchus.
◆ Een steegje leidt naar deze bistro, waar u in een gemoedelijke atmosfeer van een smakelijke maaltijd kunt genieten. De reusachtige wijnkelder is een hommage aan Bacchus.

C-Jean, Cataloniëstraat 3, ✆ 0 9 223 30 40, *Fax 0 9 330 00 01,* ☂ – MC VISA EY h
fermé dim. et lundi – **Repas** *Lunch 15* – carte 35 à 49.
◆ Affaire placée sous la protection de la St.-Niklaaskerk (église St.-Nicolas). Petite restauration, préparations "tendance" et spécialités régionales notées à l'écriteau.
◆ Dit restaurant heeft vast de zegen van de St.-Niklaaskerk. De menukaart bestaat uit kleine schotels, trendy gerechten en regionale specialiteiten op een leitje.

Le Grand Bleu, Snepkaai 15, ✆ 0 9 220 50 25, *info@legrandbleu.be, Fax 0 9 329 50 25,* ☂, Produits de la mer – ▤. AE ◑ MC VISA plan p. 3 AU c
fermé sam. midi, dim. midi et lundi – **Repas** *Lunch 10* – carte 29 à 66.
◆ Le homard dessiné sur la façade du restaurant laisse aisément deviner l'orientation de la carte, où ce noble crustacé tient toujours la vedette. Atmosphère vivante.
◆ De kreeft die op de voorgevel prijkt geeft vast een voorproefje van de kaart, waarop dit edele schaaldier de boventoon voert. Levendige ambiance.

Quartier Ancien (Patershol) - *plan p. 5 :*

XX **De Blauwe Zalm,** Vrouwebroersstraat 2, ✆ 0 9 224 08 52, *Fax 0 9 234 18 98*, 🍽, Produits de la mer – AE ◑ MC VISA. ✈ EY r
fermé 19 juil.-15 août, 25 déc.-1er janv., sam. midi, dim. et lundi midi – **Repas** *Lunch 28* – 51.
◆ Au cœur du Patershol, l'un des plus anciens quartiers de la ville, saveurs de la mer déclinées sur un mode créatif. Décor plutôt léché et service tout sourire.
◆ Visrestaurant met een creatieve chef-kok achter het fornuis, in het hart van het Patershol, een van de oudste wijken van de stad. Smaakvol interieur en elegante bediening.

XX **De 3 Biggetjes,** Zeugsteeg 7, ✆ 0 9 224 46 48, *Fax 0 9 224 46 48*, 🍽 – ▤. AE ◑ MC VISA. ✈ EY g
fermé 2 sem. Pâques, 2 sem. en août, Noël-Nouvel An, mardi, sam. midi et dim. soir – **Repas** *Lunch 16* – 27/50 bc.
◆ Une bonne réputation entoure ce restaurant occupant une maison du 16e s. La salle à manger, avec véranda, marie le moderne et l'ancien. Terrasse d'été sur cour intérieure.
◆ Dit restaurant in een 16e-eeuws pand geniet een uitstekende reputatie. De eetzaal met serre is een geslaagde combinatie van oud en modern. Zomerterras op de patio.

X **Le Baan Thaï,** Corduwaniersstraat 57, ✆ 0 9 233 21 41, *Fax 0 9 233 20 09*, Cuisine thaïlandaise – ▤. AE ◑ MC VISA. ✈ EY s
fermé fin juil.-début août, dern. sem. déc. et lundi – **Repas** (dîner seult sauf dim.) carte 22 à 33.
◆ Envie de dépayser vos papilles ? Voici un resto thaïlandais, dissimulé dans la cour intérieure d'une demeure patricienne. Ambiance "zen" et bibelots siamois... ou presque.
◆ Zin om uw gehemelte met exotische smaken te prikkelen ? Dat kan in dit Thaise restaurant op de binnenplaats van een patriciërshuis. Serene sfeer en Siamese snuisterijen.

X **'t Buikske Vol,** Kraanlei 17, ✆ 0 9 225 18 80, *info@buikskevol.com, Fax 0 9 223 04 31* – AE ◑ MC VISA. ✈ EY m
fermé 27 juil.-12 août, merc., sam. midi et dim. – **Repas** *Lunch 26* – carte 25 à 45.
◆ Brasserie moderne installée dans une maison de ville du 17e s. : un authentique compromis historique ! Pour manger à l'étage, il suffit d'emprunter le vieil escalier.
◆ Deze moderne brasserie in een 17e-eeuws herenhuis is een goed voorbeeld van een historisch compromis. Een oude trap leidt naar boven, waar men het buikje vol kan eten...

X **Karel de Stoute,** Vrouwebroersstraat 5, ✆ 0 9 224 17 35, *Fax 0 9 224 17 65*, 🍽 – AE ◑ MC VISA. ✈ EY y
fermé 2e quinz. fév., 2e quinz. sept., merc. et sam. midi – **Repas** *Lunch 25* – 40/65 bc.
◆ L'an 1516 a vu naître cette demeure patricienne abritant aujourd'hui un sympathique petit restaurant. Cour intérieure. Agréable terrasse d'été. Carte des vins franco-ibérique.
◆ Dit gezellige etablissement is gevestigd in een patriciërshuis uit 1516 met een binnenplaats en een zomers terras. De wijnkaart is een Frans-Spaanse alliantie.

X **'t Klokhuys,** Corduwaniersstraat 65, ✆ 0 9 223 42 41, *info@buikskevol.com, Fax 0 9 223 04 31*, Ouvert jusqu'à 23 h – AE ◑ MC VISA EY k
fermé du 27 au 29 juil. – **Repas** *Lunch 24* – carte 22 à 39.
◆ Ce bistrot du Patershol, agencé sur deux niveaux, renferme une belle collection de pendules murales... Mais grâce à l'enseigne (La Maison de l'Horloge), vous le saviez déjà !
◆ Deze twee verdiepingen tellende bistro in het Patershol bezit een fraaie collectie hangklokken, maar dat wist u vermoedelijk al toen u het uithangbord zag.

Périphérie - *plan p. 3 sauf indication spéciale :*

au Nord-Est - ✉ *9000 :*

XX **Ter Toren,** St-Bernadettestraat 626, ✆ 0 9 251 11 29, *Fax 0 9 251 11 29*, 🍽 – P. AE ◑ MC VISA. ✈ BT b
fermé sept., dim. soir, lundi, mardi soir et merc. soir – **Repas** *Lunch 25* – carte 33 à 54.
◆ Villa bourgeoise, parc ombragé sur l'arrière, lustres et fresque décorant le plafond de l'une des salles à manger... En somme, un établissement à visage humain.
◆ Mooie villa met een schaduwrijk park aan de achterkant. Kroonluchters en fresco's sieren het plafond van een van de eetzalen. Uitstekende keuken en attente bediening.

au Sud - ✉ *9000 :*

Holiday Inn, Akkerhage 2, ✆ 0 9 222 58 85, *hotel@holiday-inn-gentuz.com, Fax 0 9 220 12 22*, 🏊 – |‡| ✈ ▤ 📺 ♿ P – 🏛 25 à 360. AE ◑ MC VISA. ✈ rest AU f
Repas (dîner seult le week-end et en juil.-août) *Lunch 20* – carte env. 38 – ☕ 17 – **139 ch** 168/206, – 1 suite.
◆ Le nœud autoroutier E 17-E 40 et le centre-ville ne sont qu'à quelques kilomètres de cet hôtel de chaîne disposant de grandes chambres où rien ne manque. Au restaurant, cuisine franco-belge à dominante classique.
◆ Het knooppunt van de E17-E40 en de binnenstad zijn slechts enkele kilometers verwijderd van dit ketenhotel, dat over grote kamers beschikt waarin het aan niets ontbreekt. In het restaurant worden klassieke Frans-Belgische gerechten geserveerd.

Astoria sans rest, Achilles Musschestraat 39, ✆ 0 9 222 84 13, *info@astoria.be, Fax 0 9 220 47 87* – ⇕ TV P – 25. AE ⓓ MC VISA plan p. 4 CX g
18 ch ☕ 65/99.
♦ Pas loin de la gare, hôtel d'une tenue irréprochable, abritant de bonnes chambres habillées de tissus coordonnés. Reposant jardinet et jolie salle de breakfast avec véranda.
♦ Perfect onderhouden hotel in de buurt van het station. Mooie kamers met goed bij elkaar passende stoffen. Rustig tuintje en fraaie ontbijtzaal met serre.

à Afsnee C *Gent* – ✉ *9051 Afsnee :*

Nenuphar, Afsneedorp 28, ✆ 0 9 222 45 86, *de.waterlelie@pandora.be, Fax 0 9 221 22 32*, ≤, 余, ⚓ – ▤ – 40. AE ⓓ MC VISA AU r
fermé 2e quinz. août, 2 dern. sem. déc., merc., jeudi et dim. soir – **Repas** Lunch 25 – 30/85 bc, ♀.
♦ La même famille se relaie depuis trois générations à la barre de cette maison de tradition jouissant d'une situation digne d'une carte postale. Joli coup d'œil sur la Leie.
♦ Al drie generaties lang staat dezelfde familie aan het roer van dit traditionele restaurant, dat door zijn ligging zo op een ansichtkaart kan. Mooi uitzicht op de Leie.

de Fontein Kerse, Broekkantstraat 52, ✆ 0 9 221 53 02, *Fax 0 9 221 53 02*, 余 – P. AE ⓓ MC VISA. ✻ AU s
fermé 2 dern. sem. juil., 2 dern. sem. janv., mardi, merc. et dim. soir – **Repas** Lunch 28 – 42/69 bc.
♦ Plus de dix ans de bons et loyaux services pour cette adresse. Salle à manger contemporaine agrémentée d'une petite fontaine centrale. Cuisine créative, produits de qualité.
♦ Dit restaurant bewijst al 10 jaar trouwe diensten. Midden in de hedendaagse eetzaal prijkt een fonteintje. Creatieve kookkunst op basis van kwaliteitsproducten.

à Oostakker C *Gent* – ✉ *9041 Oostakker :*

't Boerenhof, Gentstraat 2, ✆ 0 9 251 03 14, *info@boerenhof.be, Fax 0 9 251 07 72*, 余 – ▤ P – 25 à 500. AE ⓓ MC VISA JCB BT d
fermé 25 oct.-9 nov., du 27 au 30 déc., lundi soir, mardi soir et merc. – **Repas** Lunch 21 bc – 35 bc/65 bc.
♦ Les produits venus en direct de Normandie tiennent le haut du pavé (de bœuf !) à cette vénérable enseigne. Grillades saisies à la braise de la cheminée. Restaurant d'été.
♦ Hier wordt gekookt met producten die rechtstreeks uit Normandië komen. Boven het vuur in de eetzaal worden grote stukken vlees geroosterd. 's Zomers kan men buiten eten.

à Sint-Denijs-Westrem C *Gent* – ✉ *9051 Sint-Denijs-Westrem :*

Holiday Inn Expo, Maaltekouter 3, ✆ 0 9 220 24 24, *hotel@holiday-inn-gentexpo.com, Fax 0 9 222 66 22*, ⚲, ≘, ⊡ – ⇕ ✻ ▤ TV ♿ P – 25 à 200. AE ⓓ MC VISA JCB. ✻ rest AU v
Repas Lunch 16 – carte env. 39 – ☕ 17 – **134 ch** 180/195, – 1 suite.
♦ À proximité immédiate de l'autoroute et des halles du Flanders Expo, immeuble hôtelier dont les chambres tout confort accueillent le businessman à bras ouverts. Le restaurant, propice aux repas d'affaires, se déploie sous les verrières de l'atrium.
♦ Hotelcomplex bij de snelweg en de hallen van Flanders Expo, waar de zakenwereld met open armen wordt ontvangen. Goed voorziene kamers. Het restaurant onder het glazen dak van het atrium is ideaal voor een businesslunch met een van uw relaties.

Oranjehof, Kortrijksesteenweg 1177, ✆ 0 9 222 79 07, *rest.oranjehof@skynet.be, Fax 0 9 222 74 06*, 余 – P. AE ⓓ MC VISA. ✻ AU k
fermé 2e quinz. août, sam. midi et dim. – **Repas** (déjeuner seult sauf vend. et sam.) Lunch 25 – 38/52 bc.
♦ Maison de maître soigneusement réaménagée dans la note Art nouveau. Par beau temps, on dresse le couvert au jardin, à côté d'un verger. Choix classico-traditionnel.
♦ Fraai gerestaureerd herenhuis in art-nouveaustijl. Op zonnige dagen worden de tafeltjes in de tuin naast de boomgaard gedekt. Klassiek-traditionele keuken.

à Zwijnaarde C *Gent* – ✉ *9052 Zwijnaarde :*

De Klosse, Grotesteenweg Zuid 49 (sur N 60), ✆ 0 9 222 21 74, *Fax 0 9 371 49 69* – P. AE ⓓ MC VISA. ✻ AU a
fermé 2 sem. carnaval, 15 juil.-8 août, sam. midi, dim. et lundi – **Repas** Lunch 24 – 45.
♦ Aux abords d'un carrefour, auberge d'époque 1800 dont l'intérieur a été réaménagé dans l'esprit du moment. Une cuisine classique de bon aloi se conçoit derrière les fourneaux.
♦ Deze herberg bij een kruispunt dateert uit 1800, maar heeft net een nieuw interieur, dat geheel bij de huidige tijdgeest past. Klassieke keuken van goede kwaliteit.

Environs

à Heusden - *plan p. 3* - Destelbergen *17 164 h.* – *9070 Heusden* :

Rooselaer, Berenbosdreef 18 (par R4, sortie ⑤), 0 9 231 55 13, *info@rooselaer.be, Fax 0 9 231 07 32,* , Avec grillades – P. AE VISA BU a
fermé prem. sem. mars, 2 prem. sem. sept., mardi soir et merc. – **Repas** Lunch 25 – 38/75 bc.
◆ Près de l'autoroute, bâtisse de l'entre-deux-guerres s'agrémentant d'un jardin fleuri. Accueil et service familial, menus bien composés, vins de France et du monde.
◆ Gebouw uit het interbellum met een mooie bloementuin, niet ver van de snelweg. Gemoedelijke ontvangst, goed samengestelde menu's en wijnen uit Frankrijk en andere landen.

à Lochristi - *plan p. 3* – *19 280 h* – *9080 Lochristi* :

Leys, Dorp West 89 (N 70), 0 9 355 86 20, *info@restaurantleys.be, Fax 0 9 356 86 26,* – P. AE VISA JCB. BT z
fermé sem. carnaval, 2 sem. en juil., dim. soir, lundi soir et merc. – **Repas** Lunch 26 – 54/72 bc, ♀.
◆ La décoration de cette imposante villa Belle Époque est soignée : meubles de style, tableaux, lustres en cristal. Mets classico-traditionnels sobrement actualisés.
◆ Imposante belle-époquevilla met een gesoigneerd interieur : stijlmeubelen, schilderijen en kroonluchters. Klassiek-traditionele gerechten die geleidelijk worden geactualiseerd.

't Wethuis, Hijfte-Center 1 (Nord : 3 km), 0 9 355 28 02, *info.twethuis@pandora.be,* – P. VISA. BT j
fermé fin déc.-début janv., sam. midi, dim. soir, lundi et mardi – **Repas** Lunch 30 – 41/70 bc.
◆ Cet édifice du 16e s. a occupé diverses fonctions : justice de paix, mairie, etc. avant d'abriter un restaurant d'esprit néo-rustique. Terrasse d'été sur jardin à l'arrière.
◆ Dit 16e-eeuwse gebouw deed onder andere dienst als rechtbank en gemeentehuis, voordat het een neorustiek restaurant werd. Zomerterras in de tuin aan de achterkant.

à Melle - *plan p. 3* – *10 509 h* – *9090 Melle* :

Prado sans rest, Brusselsesteenweg 100 (sur N 9), 0 9 231 14 10, *contact@hotel_prado.be, Fax 0 9 231 68 08,* – TV P. AE VISA BU
fermé 24 déc.-1er janv. – **19 ch** 75/85.
◆ Hôtel implanté dans une villa au voisinage de l'autoroute reliant le littoral à la capitale. Intérieur classiquement agencé. Chambres sans reproche, dont quatre junior-suites.
◆ Hotel in een villa, vlak bij de snelweg die van de kust naar de Belgische hoofdstad loopt. Klassiek interieur en zeer goed onderhouden kamers, waaronder vier junior suites.

De Branderij, Wezenstraat 34, 0 9 252 41 66, *debranderij@compaqnet.be,* – AE VISA. BU m
fermé 23 fév.-5 mars, 16 août-2 sept., sam. midi, dim. soir, lundi et après 20 h 30 – **Repas** Lunch 26 – 34/54 bc.
◆ L'enseigne évoque l'ancienne destination - une brûlerie de café - de cette charmante maisonnette bâtie pendant les années trente. Restaurant d'été et salle des repas rénovée.
◆ De naam van dit charmante pandje uit omstreeks 1930 herinnert aan het feit dat hier vroeger een koffiebranderij zat. Gerenoveerde eetzaal en 's zomers buiten eten.

à Merelbeke - *plan p. 3* – *21 976 h* – *9820 Merelbeke* :

De Blauwe Artisjok, Gaversesteenweg 182, 0 9 231 79 28, *de.blauwe.artisjok@pandora.be, Fax 0 9 230 12 54,* – P. AE VISA AU p
fermé dern. sem. juil.-2 prem. sem. août, lundi, mardi soir et merc. soir – **Repas** Lunch 25 – 38/92 bc.
◆ Beau jardin, terrasse plaisante, tables bien espacées et décoration intérieure classique-actuelle produisant tout son effet. Choix de préparations en phase avec l'époque.
◆ Een mooie tuin, prettig terras en modern-klassiek interieur met veel ruimte tussen de tafels kenmerken deze Blauwe Artisjok. De gerechten zijn ook goed bij de tijd.

Torenhove, Fraterstraat 214, 0 9 231 61 61, *Fax 0 9 231 69 89,* – P. AE VISA
fermé mardis et sam. midis non fériés – **Repas** Lunch 29 – 31/46. BU r
◆ Un petit parc arboré environne cet établissement installé dans les dépendances d'un "castel" flanqué de tours en poivrière... Passez à table, et vous verrez la salière !
◆ Dit etablissement is ondergebracht in de bijgebouwen van een kasteeltje, waar aan weerszijden een peperbustoren staat. Het zoutvaatje staat gelukkig op tafel !

à De Pinte - *plan p. 3* – *10 101 h* – *9840 De Pinte* :

Te Lande, Baron de Gieylaan 112, 0 9 282 42 00, *Fax 0 9 282 42 00* – P. AE VISA AU d
fermé 16 fév.-3 mars, 8 août-1er sept., mardi, merc. et sam. midi – **Repas** Lunch 15 – 34/70 bc.
◆ Cette maison de campagne évoquant une fermette abrite plusieurs petites salles à manger classiquement aménagées. Terrasse champêtre où l'on sert l'apéritif en été.
◆ Dit buitenhuis lijkt op een boerderijtje en telt meerdere eetzalen die klassiek zijn ingericht. In de zomer kan worden geborreld op het terras, met uitzicht op het platteland.

GENVAL *1332 Brabant Wallon* C *Rixensart 21 446 h.* 533 L 18, 534 L 18 *et* 716 G 3.
Bruxelles 22 – Charleroi 42 – Namur 52.

Château du Lac , av. du Lac 87, ☎ 0 2 655 71 11, *cdl@martins-hotels.com, Fax 0 2 655 74 44,* ≤ lac et vallon boisé, , , , , – – 30 à 1000. AE VISA. rest
Repas *Genval les Bains* (ouvert jusqu'à minuit) Lunch 15 – 38, ♀ – **120 ch** 330/410, – 1 suite.
◆ Au creux d'un vallon boisé, magnifique hôtel dont les chambres offrent tout le confort moderne. Perspective imprenable sur le lac. Spécialité "maison" : les séminaires. La salle de restaurant a été habilement relookée dans le genre "brasserie design".
◆ Schitterend hotel in een beboste vallei, met een adembenemend uitzicht op het meer. De kamers bieden modern comfort. Deze zaak is bij uitstek geschikt voor congressen. Het restaurant heeft onlangs een nieuw design gekregen.

Le Manoir du Lac sans rest, av. Hoover 4, ☎ 0 2 655 63 11, *mdl@martins-hotels.com, Fax 0 2 655 64 55,* ≤, , – – 25 à 60. AE VISA
13 ch 200/250.
◆ Demeure victorienne entourée d'un parc verdoyant. Quelques beaux meubles de divers styles personnalisent les élégantes chambres "full options". Quiétude et romantisme.
◆ Victoriaans pand in een weelderig park. Meubelen uit diverse stijlperioden geven een persoonlijke toets aan de elegante kamers met "full options". Rust en romantiek.

L'Amandier, r. Limalsart 9 (près du lac), ☎ 0 2 653 06 71, *Fax 0 2 652 43 83,* – AE VISA
fermé du 15 au 30 août, du 1er au 10 janv., merc., sam. midi et dim. soir – **Repas** Lunch 20 – 40 bc/65 bc.
◆ Halte gourmande à 200 m du lac de Genval, dans une jolie villa bordée d'arbres. Fringant décor intérieur à touche féminine, carte appétissante et vins servis au verre.
◆ Gastronomische pleisterplaats op 200 m van het meer van Genval, in een mooie villa tussen de bomen. Smaakvol interieur, aanlokkelijke menukaart en wijn per glas.

l'Echalote, av. Albert Ier 24, ☎ 0 2 653 31 57, *Fax 0 2 653 31 57,* Cuisine du Sud-Ouest – AE VISA
fermé du 1er au 24 juil., lundi soir et mardi – **Repas** 28.
◆ L'Echalote propose un choix de recettes venues en droite ligne du Sud-Ouest de la France. Des vins de même origine et des principaux vignobles de l'Hexagone les accompagnent.
◆ De recepten van deze "sjalot" komen linea recta uit Zuidwest-Frankrijk. Ook de wijnen zijn afkomstig uit die streek, aangevuld met de oogst van andere Franse wijngaarden.

à Rixensart *Est : 4 km – 21 446 h – ✉ 1330 Rixensart :*

Le Lido sans rest, r. Limalsart 20 (près du lac de Genval), ☎ 0 2 634 34 34, *lelido@martins-hotels.com, Fax 0 2 634 34 44,* ≤, , – – 25 à 80. AE VISA
fermé 20 déc.-5 janv. – **27 ch** 120/140.
◆ Lieu de séjour estimé des congressistes, cette maison à colombages et son étang forment un petit havre de paix à quelques ricochets du lac de Genval. Chambres rénovées.
◆ Dit vakwerkhuis met vijver ligt op een steenworp afstand van het meer van Genval en is een oase van rust. De kamers zijn onlangs gerenoveerd. Zeer populair bij congresgangers.

Le Brocéliande, av. de Mérode 114, ☎ 0 2 652 13 07, *Fax 0 2 652 13 07,* – VISA.
fermé carnaval, 1re quinz. juil., merc., sam. midi et dim. – **Repas** Lunch 13 – 23/27.
◆ La forêt du légendaire Merlin l'Enchanteur prête son nom à cet établissement format de poche décoré avec goût. Répertoire culinaire proportionnel à la taille du restaurant.
◆ Dit kleine, smaakvolle restaurant is genoemd naar het bos van de legendarische Merlijn de Tovenaar. Het culinaire repertoire is evenredig aan het formaat van de eetzaal.

GERAARDSBERGEN (GRAMMONT) *9500 Oost-Vlaanderen* 533 I 18 *et* 716 E 3 – *30 879 h.*
Voir *Site*★.
Markt 1, ☎ 0 54 43 72 89, toerismegeraardsbergen@skynet.be, Fax 0 54 43 72 80.
Bruxelles 43 – Gent 44 – Aalst 29 – Mons 42 – Oudenaarde 25.

't Grof Zout, Gasthuisstraat 20, ☎ 0 54 42 35 46, *grof.zout@wanadoo.be, Fax 0 54 42 35 47,* – VISA
fermé sam. midi, dim. soir et lundi – **Repas** Lunch 26 – carte 44 à 51.
◆ Bon p'tit relais de bouche installé dans une ancienne miroiterie. En salle, aménagement contemporain pour le moins astucieux : des cuillers à soupe en guise d'appliques !
◆ Eettentje in een oude spiegelfabriek, waar u kunt genieten van een verzorgde maaltijd. De moderne inrichting is vindingrijk : soeplepels als wandlampjes !

GERPINNES *Hainaut* 533 M 20, 534 M 20 *et* 716 G 4 – *voir à Charleroi.*

GESVES *5340 Namur* 533 P 20, 534 P 20 *et* 716 I 4 – *5 905 h.*
Bruxelles 81 – Namur 29 – Dinant 30 – Liège 53 – Marche-en-Famenne 31.

XX **L'Aubergesves** avec ch, Pourrain 4, ☎ 0 83 67 74 17, *Fax 0 83 67 81 57*, – TV P. AE ① MO VISA
fermé lundi et mardi – **Repas** Lunch 23 – 34/71 bc, ♀ – 13 – **6 ch** 90/105 – ½ P 88/98.
◆ Abords verdoyants, façade où grimpe le lierre, cadre rustique, terrasse plaisante à la belle saison : une idée de repas à la campagne. Cave très complète. Chambres charmantes.
◆ Weelderig groene omgeving, rustiek interieur, goede wijnkelder, zonnig terras... kortom, alle ingrediënten voor een heerlijke maaltijd op het platteland. Sfeervolle kamers.

X **La Pineraie,** r. Pineraie 2, ☎ 0 83 67 73 46, *Fax 0 83 67 73 46*, – P. AE MO VISA.
fermé sem. carnaval, 2 dern. sem. août-début sept., lundi et mardi – **Repas** Lunch 25 bc – 37/62 bc.
◆ Voici un peu plus d'une décennie que cette fermette en pierres du pays, dépendance du château de Gesves, est devenue un restaurant familial attentif à la qualité des produits.
◆ Dit karakteristieke boerderijtje hoort bij het kasteel van Gesves en veranderde ruim 10 jaar geleden in een familierestaurant, waar de kwaliteit van de producten voorop staat.

GHISLENGHIEN (GELLINGEN) *Hainaut* 533 I 19, 534 I 19 *et* 716 E 4 – *voir à Ath.*

GILLY *Hainaut* 533 L 20, 534 L 20 *et* 716 G 4 – *voir à Charleroi.*

GISTEL *West-Vlaanderen* 533 C 16 *et* 716 B 2 – *voir à Oostende.*

GITS *West-Vlaanderen* 533 D 17 *et* 716 C 3 – *voir à Roeselare.*

GOETSENHOVEN (GOSSENCOURT) *Vlaams-Brabant* 533 O 18 – *voir à Tienen.*

GOOIK *1755 Vlaams-Brabant* 533 J 18 *et* 716 F 3 – *8 877 h.*
Bruxelles 24 – Aalst 22 – Mons 45 – Tournai 66.

XX **'t Krekelhof,** Drie Egyptenbaan 11 (par N 285, puis direction Neigem), ☎ 0 54 33 48 57, *info@krekelhof.be, Fax 0 54 33 41 96*, – P – 40. AE ① MO VISA
fermé 2e quinz. juil., dern. sem. oct., mardi et merc. – **Repas** Lunch 28 – 40/68 bc.
◆ Ah, la campagne du Pajottenland ! Côté véranda, on goûte à des plats moins recherchés que ceux servis au restaurant. Cave de dégustation pour œnophiles. Terrasse bucolique.
◆ Ach, dat mooie Pajottenland ! In de serre wordt eenvoudiger gegeten dan in het restaurant. Wijnkenners kunnen heerlijk proeven in de kelder. Idyllisch terras.

GOSSELIES *Hainaut* 533 L 20, 534 L 20 *et* 716 G 4 – *voir à Charleroi.*

GOSSENCOURT *Vlaams-Brabant – voir Goetsenhoven.*

GRAMMENE *Oost-Vlaanderen* 533 F 17 – *voir à Deinze.*

GRAMMONT *Oost-Vlaanderen – voir Geraardsbergen.*

GRAND-HALLEUX *Luxembourg belge* 533 U 21, 534 U 21 *et* 716 K 5 – *voir à Vielsalm.*

GRANDHAN *Luxembourg belge* 533 R 21, 534 R 21 *et* 716 J 5 – *voir à Durbuy.*

GRAND-LEEZ *5031 Namur* C *Gembloux 20 899 h.* 533 N 19 *et* 716 H 4.
Bruxelles 46 – Namur 22 – Charleroi 36 – Tienen 33.

XXX **Luc Bellings,** r. Petit-Leez 129 (au château de Petit-Leez), ☎ 0 81 65 60 00, *info@lucbellings.be, Fax 0 81 65 90 00*, <, – P – 25 à 50. AE MO VISA
fermé 1 sem. après Pâques, du 1er au 15 sept., du 1er au 15 janv., dim. soir, lundi et mardi – **Repas** Lunch 33 – carte env. 67, ♀.
◆ Dans les dépendances du château, sculptures et objets contemporains ornent une confortable salle à manger voûtée. En terrasse, vue sur des statues équestres "au galop".
◆ In een bijgebouw van het kasteel bevindt zich een gerieflijke, gewelfde eetzaal met beeldhouwwerken en moderne objecten. Terras met uitzicht op beelden van paarden in galop.

GRANDRIEU *Hainaut* 534 K 21 *et* 716 F 5 – *voir à Beaumont.*

GRANDVOIR *Luxembourg belge* 534 R 23 *et* 716 J 6 – *voir à Neufchâteau.*

's GRAVENBRAKEL *Hainaut – voir Braine-le-Comte.*

's GRAVENVOEREN (FOURON-LE-COMTE) *3798 Limburg* C *Voeren 4 328 h.* 533 T 18 *et* 716 K 3.

Kerkplein 216, 0 4 381 07 36, toerismevoeren@toerismelimburg.be, Fax 0 4 381 21 59.

Bruxelles 102 – Maastricht 15 – Liège 23.

De Kommel, Kerkhofstraat 117d, 0 4 381 01 85, *info@dekommel.be, Fax 0 4 381 23 30,* – – 30. rest

fermé du 2 au 23 janv. – **Repas** *(fermé lundi midi, jeudi et sam. midi)* Lunch 30 – 37/62 bc, – **11 ch** 60/80 – ½ P 65/70.

• Cette construction récente juchée sur une colline profite du coup d'œil sur la vallée et le village. Chambres convenablement équipées, garnies de meubles en rotin. Restaurant doté d'une belle terrasse panoramique. Cuisine d'aujourd'hui.

• Recentelijk gebouwd hotel op een heuvel, vanwaar zich een weids uitzicht op het dal en het dorp ontvouwt. De kamers hebben goede voorzieningen en zijn met rotanmeubelen ingericht. Het restaurant heeft een mooi panoramaterras. Eigentijdse keuken.

The Golden Horse, Hoogstraat 242, 0 4 381 02 29, *Fax 0 4 381 20 44,* – .

fermé 2 sem. en sept., jeudi, vend. midi et sam. midi – **Repas** Lunch 26 – 35/71 bc.

• Poutres cérusées, murs éclatants et nappages dorés : voilà pour le décor de la salle. Côté bouche : produits nobles, grands vins et millésimes. Agréable terrasse close.

• Interieur met geceruseerde balken, muren in felle kleuren en goudkleurig tafelgoed. Eersteklas producten, grote wijnen uit topjaren en een aangenaam ommuurd terras.

's GRAVENWEZEL *Antwerpen* 533 M 15 *et* 716 G 2 – *voir à Antwerpen, environs.*

GRIMBERGEN *Vlaams-Brabant* 533 L 17 *et* 716 G 3 – *voir à Bruxelles, environs.*

GROBBENDONK *Antwerpen* 533 N 15 *et* 716 H 2 – *voir à Herentals.*

GROOT-BIJGAARDEN *Vlaams-Brabant* 533 K 17 *et* 716 F 3 – *voir à Bruxelles, environs.*

GULLEGEM *West-Vlaanderen* 533 E 17 *et* 716 C 3 – *voir à Wevelgem.*

HAALTERT *9450 Oost-Vlaanderen* 533 J 17 *et* 716 F 3 – *17 178 h.*

Bruxelles 29 – Aalst 6 – Gent 36 – Mons 59.

Apriori, Sint-Goriksplein 19, 0 53 83 89 54, *info@a-priori.be,* – .

fermé 3 sem. en août, 1 sem. en janv., mardi soir, merc. et sam. midi – **Repas** Lunch 30 – 45/75 bc.

• Derrière l'église, maison familiale dont le registre culinaire s'oriente résolument vers les saveurs actuelles. Belle salle à manger rénovée procurant une vue sur le parc.

• Familiebedrijf achter de kerk, waarvan het culinaire register sterk op het heden is gericht. Mooie gerenoveerde eetzaal met uitzicht op het park.

De HAAN *8420 West-Vlaanderen* 533 D 15 *et* 716 C 2 – *11 580 h – Station balnéaire.*

Koninklijke baan 2 0 59 23 32 83, Fax 0 59 23 37 49.

Gemeentehuis, Leopoldlaan 24 0 59 24 21 34, tourism.de.haan@pophost.cevi.be, Fax 0 59 24 21 36 – (Pâques-sept. et vacances scolaires) Tramstation 0 59 24 21 35.

Bruxelles 113 – Brugge 21 – Oostende 12.

Manoir Carpe Diem sans rest, Prins Karellaan 12, 0 59 23 32 20, *manoircarpediem@hotmail.com, Fax 0 59 23 33 96,* – – 25.

fermé janv. et lundi, mardi et merc. du 12 nov. à fév. sauf vacances scolaires – **12 ch** 110/140, – 3 suites.

• La célèbre maxime latine inspire l'enseigne de cette villa bâtie à proximité du littoral. Les chambres, spacieuses et pimpantes, sont rehaussées d'une "british touch".

• In deze mooie villa vlak bij de kust is het niet moeilijk de dag te plukken ! De kamers zijn ruim en goed onderhouden, met een onmiskenbare "British touch".

Aub. des Rois-Beach H., Zeedijk 1, ☎ 0 59 23 30 18, *Fax 0 59 23 60 78*, ≤, - ||| TV P. MC VISA.
fermé 3 janv.-19 fév., 24 fév.-2 avril et 17 oct.-21 déc. – **Repas** *(fermé merc.)* 38/80 bc – **16 ch** 93/136, – 6 suites – ½ P 81/102.
• Hôtel 1900 ancré sur la digue, à quelques pas de la plage. Chambres agréables ; certaines profitent un peu plus que d'autres du panorama maritime. Lumineuses salles des repas au décor soigné.
• Hotel uit 1900 aan de dijk, op loopafstand van het strand. Aangename kamers, waarvan sommige meer van het zeezicht profiteren dan andere. Het restaurant telt verscheidene eetzalen met een verzorgd interieur en veel licht.

Les Dunes sans rest, Leopoldplein 5, ☎ 0 59 23 31 46, *Fax 0 59 23 31 46*, - ||| TV P. MC VISA.
mars-oct. – **20 ch** 113.
• Cette résidence de l'entre-deux-guerres borde un petit square aménagé à 50 m des premiers pâtés de sable. Chambres amples et insonorisées, réparties sur quatre étages.
• Dit pand uit het interbellum ligt aan een klein plantsoen, op 50 m van het strand. Grote kamers met goede geluidsisolatie, die over vier verdiepingen zijn verdeeld.

Arcato sans rest, Nieuwe Steenweg 210, ☎ 0 59 23 57 77, *Fax 0 59 23 88 66*, - ||| TV P. MC VISA
14 ch 50/74.
• Hôtel moderne bien pensé, adjoignant une kitchenette à la plupart de ses chambres. Calmes et ensoleillées, toutes donnent sur l'arrière et disposent d'un balcon meublé.
• Modern en comfortabel hotel met rustige, zonnige kamers die allemaal aan de achterkant liggen en voorzien zijn van een mooi balkon. Vele zijn uitgerust met een kitchenette.

Rubens sans rest, Rubenslaan 3, ☎ 0 59 24 22 00, *info@hotel-rubens.be, Fax 0 59 23 72 98*, - TV. MC VISA.
fermé 15 nov.-15 déc. et du 10 au 20 janv. – **11 ch** 72/80.
• Élevée dans un secteur résidentiel, cette jolie villa transformée en hôtel familial propose des chambres coquettes. Salle des petits-déjeuners assez mignonne, elle aussi.
• Mooie villa in een rustige woonwijk, die tot familiehotel is verbouwd. De kamers zien er piekfijn uit, net als de ontbijtzaal overigens.

Belle Epoque, Leopoldlaan 5, ☎ 0 59 23 34 65, *Fax 0 59 23 38 14*, - ||| TV. MC VISA
Repas *(fermé du 2 au 26 déc., 5 janv.-12 fév. et lundi)* (taverne-rest) 18/26 – **14 ch** *(fermé du 5 au 31 janv.)* 60/74, – 3 suites – ½ P 55/62.
• La nostalgie de la Belle Époque imprègne l'architecture de cette élégante résidence bordant une des avenues de la station. Amples chambres sobrement actuelles. À table, recettes aux saveurs marines. L'été, on mange sous les stores de la terrasse.
• De architectuur van dit sierlijke gebouw aan een van de lanen van de badplaats druipt van heimwee naar de belle époque. De ruime, moderne kamers zijn sober ingericht. Restaurant met veel vis. 's Zomers kan onder de markies op het terras worden gegeten.

Internos sans rest, Leopoldlaan 12, ☎ 0 59 23 35 79, *Fax 0 59 23 54 43*, - TV P. AE MC VISA
19 ch 65/78.
• Grosse villa postée sur une route fréquentée, dans le centre de la station. Ses chambres refaites disposent souvent d'un coin salon, voire d'une kitchenette.
• Grote villa aan een drukke weg in het centrum van het vakantieoord. De kamers zijn kort geleden opgeknapt en hebben meestal een zithoek, sommige zelfs een kitchenette.

Gd H. Belle Vue, Koninklijk Plein 5, ☎ 0 59 23 34 39, *Fax 0 59 23 75 22*, - ||| TV P. MC VISA
15 mars-15 oct. – **Repas** Lunch 17 – 34 – **40 ch** 65/100 – ½ P 63/67.
• Ce charmant édifice d'esprit normand datant du début du 20e s. abrite des chambres simples de différentes tailles, au cadre agréablement suranné. Vaste salle à manger complétée d'une terrasse estivale.
• Charmant gebouw in Normandische stijl uit het begin van de 20e eeuw. Eenvoudige kamers van verschillende grootte, met een heerlijk ouderwetse inrichting. De grote eetzaal wordt in het hoogseizoen uitgebreid met een zonnig terras.

De Gouden Haan sans rest, B. Murillolaan 1, ☎ 0 59 23 32 32, *Fax 0 59 23 74 92* – TV P.
9 ch 55/82.
• Belle villa du début du 20e s. convertie en hôtel de poche. Les quelques chambres, spacieuses et claires, sont garnies d'un mobilier choisi avec goût.
• Mooie villa uit het begin van de 20e eeuw, die tot een aangenaam hotel is verbouwd. Er zijn slechts een paar kamers, maar die zijn wel ruim, licht en smaakvol gemeubileerd.

Duinhof sans rest, Ringlaan Noord 40, ☎ 0 59 24 20 20, *duinhof@skynet.be, Fax 0 59 24 20 39,* ... 25 à 60. MC VISA
10 ch ☐ 90.
◆ Cet immeuble contemporain jouxtant une ferme du 18e s. abrite des chambres personnalisées qui profitent de la paix d'un quartier résidentiel exempt de chambard.
◆ Dit hotel is gevestigd in een hedendaags gebouw naast een 18e-eeuwse boerderij. De kamers hebben een persoonlijk karakter en profiteren van de rust van een chique woonwijk.

Bon Accueil sans rest, Montaignelaan 2, ☎ 0 59 23 31 14, *lebonaccueil@pi.be, Fax 0 59 23 91 15,* ... MC VISA.
fermé déc.-janv. et merc. – **13 ch** ☐ 55/66.
◆ Hôtel "post années folles" agrémenté d'un jardin verdoyant, au cœur d'un tranquille quartier résidentiel. Chambres assez amples et confortables.
◆ Hotel van vlak na de roaring twenties, met een weelderige tuin in het hart van een rustige woonwijk. De kamers zijn vrij ruim en comfortabel.

des Familles, Koninklijke Baan 30, ☎ 0 59 23 33 86, *hotel.des.familles@pandora.be, Fax 0 59 23 70 41* – ... AE MC VISA. rest
fermé 15 nov.-15 déc. – **Repas** (dîner pour résidents seult) – **24 ch** ☐ 60/86 – ½ P 68.
◆ L'enseigne le dit : les familles se sentent ici un peu "comme chez elles". La réception, malgré les apparences, ne les mène pas en bateau, et les chambres sont convenables.
◆ Zoals de naam al doet vermoeden, voelen gezinnen zich hier snel thuis. Meldt u aan bij de receptie in de vorm van een sloep ; de "kajuiten" zijn geriefelijk.

Bilderdijk sans rest, Bilderdijklaan 4, ☎ 0 59 23 62 00, *info@hotelbilderdijk.be, Fax 0 59 23 95 37,* ... MC VISA
fermé du 17 au 26 déc. – **8 ch** ☐ 55/70.
◆ Un établissement à taille humaine et encore dans sa prime jeunesse, où certaines chambres sont plus spacieuses que d'autres. Ambiance et accueil familiaux.
◆ Een hotel van menselijk formaat, dat nog in zijn prille jeugdjaren is. De kamers zijn verschillend van grootte. Gemoedelijke ambiance en hartelijke ontvangst.

XX **Cocagne,** Stationsstraat 9, ☎ 0 59 23 93 28, *restaurant.cocagne@pandora.be* – MC VISA
fermé du 1er au 12 juil., 2 sem. en déc., merc. midi d'oct. à mars, merc. soir et jeudi – **Repas** Lunch 20 – 32/80 bc.
◆ Cette petite affaire montée depuis peu a pris ses quartiers sur la voie commerçante de la station balnéaire. Suggestions quotidiennes et appétissant menu mensuel.
◆ Klein restaurant dat sinds kort zijn kwartier heeft betrokken in de voornaamste winkelstraat van deze badplaats. Dagelijks suggesties en een appetijtelijk menu van de maand.

X **L'Espérance,** Driftweg 1, ☎ 0 59 32 69 00, *Fax 0 59 32 69 01* – MC VISA
fermé dern. sem. sept., 1 sem. en janv., mardi et merc. – **Repas** Lunch 25 – carte 43 à 53.
◆ En face d'un bel arrêt de tram 1900, minuscule restaurant dont l'élégante salle à manger accueille la clientèle d'affaires et touristique. Carte au goût du jour.
◆ Tegenover de geklasseerde tramhalte uit 1900 ligt dit kleine restaurantje, waar zowel zakenlieden als toeristen komen. De kookstijl is helemaal van nu.

X **Casanova,** Zeedijk 15, ☎ 0 59 23 45 55, ≤, – MC VISA
fermé mi-déc.-mi-janv. et jeudi – **Repas** Lunch 13 – 32/35.
◆ Aucune garantie de manger ici en compagnie du légendaire séducteur ! Pour vous consoler, mesdames et mesdemoiselles : échappée maritime, saveurs transalpines et menus à thème.
◆ Aangenaam restaurant, waar de visspecialiteiten, Italiaanse gerechten en themamenu's even verleidelijk zijn als de legendarische Casanova.

à Klemskerke *Sud : 5,5 km* C *De Haan* – ✉ *8420 Klemskerke :*

X **de Kruidenmolen,** Dorpsstraat 1, ☎ 0 59 23 51 78, – P
fermé 2 sem. en avril, 2 sem. en nov., merc. et jeudi – **Repas** 35.
◆ La haute silhouette d'un moulin à vent en bois du 18e s. veille sur ce logis du meunier réaménagé en bistrot moderne. Plats régionaux et suggestions du marché.
◆ Het hoge silhouet van een houten windmolen uit de 18e eeuw waakt over deze molenaarswoning, die tot moderne bistro is verbouwd. Regionale gerechten en dagschotels.

à Vlissegem *Sud-Est : 6,5 km* C *De Haan* – ✉ *8421 Vlissegem :*

XX **Vijfwege,** Brugsebaan 12 (N 9), ☎ 0 59 23 31 96, , Anguilles – P
fermé 15 fév.-15 mars, 15 sept.-15 oct., mardi et merc. – **Repas** 25.
◆ L'anguille et la côte à l'os figurent parmi les "must" du Vijfwege. Mieux vaut prendre les devants et réserver sa table, car ça ne désemplit pas !
◆ Paling en ribstuk behoren tot de toppers van de Vijfwege. Het is verstandig het zekere voor het onzekere te nemen en een tafel te reserveren, want het is er altijd bomvol !

XX **Lepelem,** Brugsebaan 16 (N 9), ☎ 0 59 23 57 49, – P. AE MC VISA.
fermé 3 sem. en fév., 3 sem. en sept., lundi soir, merc. et jeudi – **Repas** 27/90 bc.
◆ Grosse auberge isolée dans les polders, au bord de la "route de l'anguille", sur le tronçon Brugge-Oostende. Salle de restaurant confortable. Cuisine classique du marché.
◆ Afgelegen herberg in de polder, langs de "palingroute" tussen Brugge en Oostende. Comfortabel restaurant met een klassieke keuken, afhankelijk van het aanbod op de markt.

HAASDONK *9120 Oost-Vlaanderen* C *Beveren 45 168 h.* 533 K 15 et 716 F 2.

Bruxelles 51 – Antwerpen 19 – Gent 44 – Sint-Niklaas 11 – Middelburg 90.

X **Willem Van Doornick,** Willem Van Doornyckstraat 2, ☎ 0 3 755 85 89, *willem.vandoornick@skynet.be, Fax 0 3 755 84 89* – AE MC VISA

fermé 1 sem. carnaval, 2 sem. en juil., 1 sem. Toussaint, lundi, mardi midi et sam. midi – **Repas** carte 33 à 48.

♦ Belle brasserie où l'on se repaît dans un cadre contemporain semé de touches nostalgiques, comme cette cuisinière d'un autre âge exposée en salle. Ambiance "trendy".

♦ Fraaie brasserie met een hedendaags interieur en hier en daar een nostalgische noot, zoals het antieke fornuis in de eetzaal. Trendy ambiance.

HABAY-LA-NEUVE *6720 Luxembourg belge* C *Habay 7 313 h.* 534 S 24 et 716 J 6.

Bruxelles 185 – Bouillon 55 – Arlon 14 – Bastogne 37 – Neufchâteau 22 – Luxembourg 40.

X **Tante Laure,** r. Emile Baudrux 6, ☎ 0 63 42 23 63, *Fax 0 63 42 35 91,* – MC VISA

fermé 20 janv.-10 fév., 20 sept.-10 oct., merc. soir et jeudi – **Repas** Lunch 12 – 22/32 bc.

♦ Au centre, devant un parking, maison familiale dont la "cartounette" de préparations traditionnelles met volontiers le terroir à l'honneur. Salle à manger néo-rustique.

♦ Familierestaurant in het centrum, bij een parkeerplaats. In de neorustieke eetzaal kunt u genieten van traditionele gerechten op basis van producten uit de streek.

à l'Est : *2 km par N 87, lieu-dit Pont d'Oye :*

Les Ardillières, r. Pont d'Oye 6, ☎ 0 63 42 22 43, *info@lesforges.be, Fax 0 63 42 28 52,* <, – TV P MC VISA

fermé du 1er au 22 janv. – **Repas** voir rest ***Les Forges*** ci-après – **9 ch** 185, – 1 suite.

♦ Charmant hôtel en pierres du pays blotti au creux d'un vallon boisé. La moitié des chambres, douillettes et "full equipment", profitent de l'environnement verdoyant.

♦ Charmant hotel gelegen in een bosrijk dal en opgetrokken uit de lokale steensoort. Behaaglijke kamers met volledige accomodatie en waarvan de helft uitkijkt op het groen.

Château, r. Pont d'Oye 1, ☎ 0 63 42 01 30, *info@chateaudupontdoye.be, Fax 0 63 42 01 36,* <, – P – 25 à 100. AE MC VISA. rest

Repas *(fermé dim. soir et lundi)* Lunch 26 – 38/78 bc – **16 ch** 53/130, – 2 suites – ½ P 65/78.

♦ Un parc d'environ 15 ha parsemé d'étangs agrémente cette folie du 18e s. adossée à l'épaisse forêt d'Anlier. Chambres personnalisées par de coquets décors. Salle de restaurant où règne une atmosphère mi-aristocratique, mi-guillerette.

♦ Dit 18e-eeuwse lustslot in een park van circa 15 ha met vijvers ligt tegen het dichte bos van Anlier. De kamers zijn mooi ingericht en hebben een persoonlijk karakter. In het restaurant heerst een aristocratische sfeer, die echter niet stijf is.

XXXX **Les Forges** (Thiry frères) - H. Les Ardillières, r. Pont d'Oye 6, ☎ 0 63 42 22 43, *info@lesforges.be, Fax 0 63 42 28 52,* <, – P MC VISA

fermé 28 juin-15 juil., du 1er au 22 janv., mardi, merc. et sam. midi – **Repas** Lunch 36 – 72/119 bc, carte 71 à 99.

♦ Vallée forestière, cascades bruissantes, salle actuelle épurée, terrasse sur jardin fleuri, cave élaborée et "armagnacothèque" de prestige... Le coup de foudre, ça existe !

♦ Bosrijk dal, klaterende watervallen, moderne eetzaal, terras aan een bloementuin, prestigieuze wijnkelder met veel armagnacs... Bij ons was het liefde op het eerste gezicht !

Spéc. Ormeaux et berniques rôtis meunière, souris de jambon et sauce diable. Effiloché de pommes de terre Roswald, crème mousseuse au jus de canard gavé. Filet de veau de lait rôti, jus simple de coriandre

X **Les Plats Canailles de la Bleue Maison,** r. Pont d'Oye 7, ☎ 0 63 42 42 70, *Fax 0 63 42 43 17,* <, – P VISA

fermé 30 août-16 sept., du 1er au 22 janv., dim. soir, lundi et mardi midi – **Repas** Lunch 25 – carte env. 41.

♦ Qui connaît Hansel et Gretel sera d'autant plus séduit par cette petite auberge. Salle des repas colorée, égayée d'une cheminée. Véranda côté ruisseau. Soirées à thème.

♦ Deze herberg doet aan het huisje van Hans en Grietje denken. In vrolijke kleurtjes geschilderde eetzaal met schouw. Serre aan de kant van een klaterend beekje. Themaavonden.

Si vous cherchez un hôtel tranquille,
consultez d'abord les cartes de l'introduction
ou repérez dans le texte les établissements indiqués avec le signe

HALLE (HAL) *1500 Vlaams-Brabant* 533 K 18, 534 K 18 *et* 716 F 3 – *33 939 h.*

Voir *Basilique*★★ *(Basiliek)* X.

Historisch Stadhuis, Grote Markt 1 ✆ *0 2 356 42 59, pajottenland-zennevallei@toerismevlaanderen.be, Fax 0 2 361 33 50.*

Bruxelles 17 ① – *Charleroi 47* ② – *Mons 41* ④ – *Tournai 67* ⑤

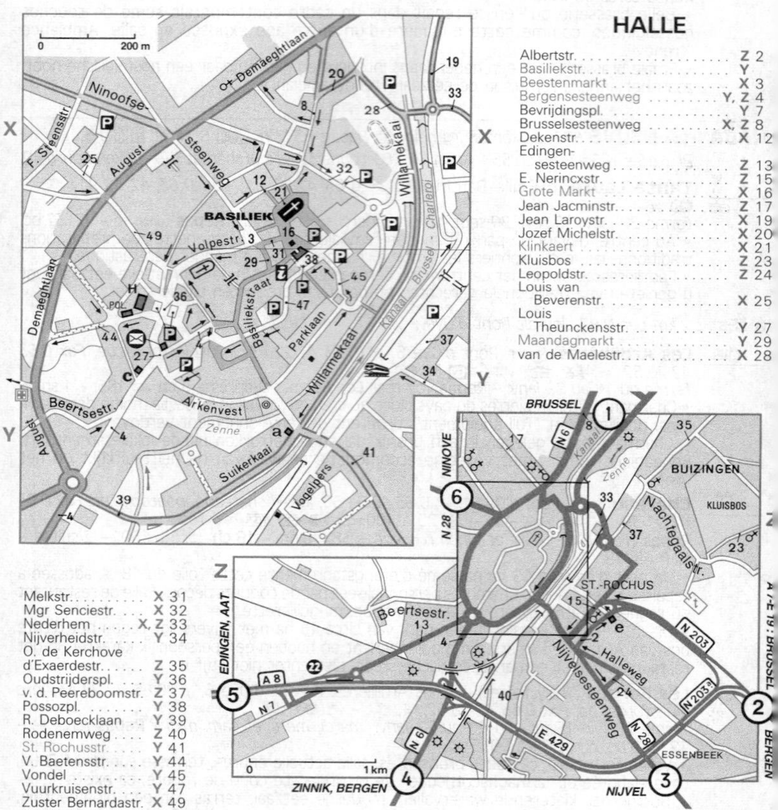

Les Eleveurs avec ch, Basiliekstraat 136, ✆ 0 2 361 13 40, *les.eleveurs@tijd.com, Fax 0 2 361 24 62,* – – 25. AE VISA — Y a

fermé vend., sam. midi, dim. soir, lundis fériés et jours fériés soirs – **Repas** *Lunch 39* – 55/65, – **14 ch** 92/120 – ½ P 81/125.

◆ Cet établissement doit son nom aux rendez-vous que s'y donnaient, autrefois, les éleveurs de chevaux brabançons. Menu-carte, cave d'exception. Chambres avenantes.

◆ Dit etablissement was vroeger een trefpunt van Brabantse paardenfokkers, zoals de naam doet vermoeden. Menu of à la carte en een uitstekende wijnkelder. Prettige kamers.

Kinoo, Albertstraat 70, ✆ 0 2 356 04 89, *bkinoo@yahoo.fr, Fax 0 2 361 53 50* – AE VISA — Z e

fermé 22 juil.-18 août, du 26 au 31 déc., dim. soir, lundi et merc. soir – **Repas** *Lunch 38* – 44/68 bc.

◆ À dénicher dans la périphérie de Halle, menue table - le nombre de couverts est limité - concoctant des recettes attrayantes et diversifiées. Terrasse apéritive.

◆ Adresje aan de rand van Halle, met beperkt aantal couverts. Smakelijke en gevarieerde keuken. Het aperitief kan op het terras worden gebruikt.

X **Peking Garden,** Bergensesteenweg 50, ☎ 0 2 360 31 20, *Fax 0 2 360 31 20*, Cuisine chinoise – ▤ P. MC VISA. ✈ Y c
fermé 2 dern. sem. juil. et merc. – **Repas** *Lunch 28* – carte 22 à 58.
◆ Le cœur de Halle ne pourrait être confondu avec la Cité Interdite, quoique... Deux lions dorés gardent l'entrée du Peking Garden, au cadre intérieur "chinois contemporain".
◆ Soms wordt het centrum van Halle voor de Verboden Stad aangezien... Twee vergulde leeuwen bewaken de ingang van dit restaurant met een hedendaags Chinees interieur.

HALMA *Luxembourg belge* 534 P 22 *et* 716 I 5 – *voir à Wellin.*

HAM *3945 Limburg* 533 P 16 *et* 716 I 2 – *9 387 h.*
Bruxelles 78 – Hasselt 25 – Antwerpen 50.

XX **Host. The Fox** avec ch, Genendijkerveld 5 (Sud-Est : 4 km, lieu-dit Genendijk), ☎ 0 13 66 48 50, *foxsmolders@compaqnet.be, Fax 0 13 67 28 33*, , , , – TV P. AE MC VISA. ✈
Repas *(fermé du 1er au 24 mars, du 1er au 24 sept., lundi et mardi)* carte 23 à 39 – **8 ch** 62/85 – ½ P 55/98.
◆ Hostellerie familiale entourée d'arbres, au voisinage d'un héliport. Salle à manger néo-rustique prolongée d'une véranda. Formule menu-carte. Chambres aménagées sous le toit.
◆ Dit familiehotel ligt tussen de bomen ; het bezit een helihaven. Neorustieke eetzaal met serre. À la carte en menu. Op de zolderverdieping zijn kamers ingericht.

HAMME *9220 Oost-Vlaanderen* 533 N 18 *et* 716 F 2 – *22 749 h.*
Bruxelles 38 – Antwerpen 29 – Gent 36.

Het Zoete Water, Damstraat 64, ☎ 0 52 47 00 92, *info@hetzoetewater.be, Fax 0 52 47 00 93* – ▤ TV P. AE MC VISA. ✈
Repas (résidents seult) – 8 – **8 ch** 90/105.
◆ Ce petit établissement à façade Art déco a profité d'une rénovation intérieure intégrale. Belles chambres modernes ; parties communes de même. Accueil personnalisé.
◆ Dit hotelletje met art-decogevel is vanbinnen volledig gerenoveerd. Fraaie moderne kamers en gemeenschappelijke ruimten in dezelfde stijl. Persoonlijk getint onthaal.

XXX ✿ **De Plezanten Hof** (Putteman), Driegoten 97 (près de l'Escaut-Schelde), ☎ 0 52 47 38 50, *plezantenhof.hamme@skynet.be, Fax 0 52 47 86 56*, – P. AE MC VISA
fermé 2 sem. en sept., fin déc.-début janv., mardi de mai à août, dim. soir et lundi – **Repas** 58/90 bc, carte 84 à 109.
◆ Qu'il est plaisant, ce jardin fleuri et agrémenté d'une pièce d'eau, au bord duquel paresse la terrasse d'été ! Cuisine joliment personnalisée et beaux flacons en cave.
◆ De naam van dit restaurant is goed gekozen, want wat is het plezierig tafelen op het terras aan de fraaie bloementuin met waterpartij ! Persoonlijke kookstijl en mooie wijnen.
Spéc. Turbot cuit à l'huile d'olive aux petits gris, champignons et artichauts. Sole meunière à la mousseline de pommes de terre, sauce au caviar. Trois façons de manger l'agneau

XX **Ter Schroeven,** Dendermondse Steenweg 15 (Sud : 2 km sur N 470), ☎ 0 52 47 61 31, *Fax 0 52 47 61 31*, – P. MC VISA. ✈
fermé début sept., lundi, mardi et merc. – **Repas** *Lunch 30* – 38/63 bc.
◆ Se tenant en retrait de la chaussée, grosse villa blanche aux abords soignés, dont la décoration intérieure s'inspire du style provençal. Menus "all-in".
◆ Grote witte villa die even van de weg af staat. De directe omgeving maakt meteen al een verzorgde indruk en het interieur is geïnspireerd op de Provence. All-in menu's.

à Moerzeke *Sud-Est : 4 km* C *Hamme* – ✉ *9220 Moerzeke :*

XX **Wilgenhof,** Bootdijkstraat 90, ☎ 0 52 47 05 95, *wilgenhof@skynet.be, Fax 0 52 48 03 92* – ▤ P. AE MC VISA
fermé 23 fév.-2 mars, du 1er au 21 sept., lundi et mardi – **Repas** *Lunch 30* – 55 bc.
◆ Cette gentille auberge familiale bordant une petite route de campagne distille une atmosphère "bon enfant". À table, répertoire culinaire d'un classicisme immuable.
◆ Deze vriendelijke herberg ligt aan een landweggetje en ademt een gemoedelijke sfeer. In de eetzaal genieten de gasten van de onveranderlijk klassieke keuken.

X **'t Jachthuis,** Bootdijkstraat 88, ☎ 0 52 48 02 91, *Fax 0 52 48 11 91*, – AE MC VISA
fermé 2 prem. sem. juil., sem. Toussaint, merc., jeudi et sam. midi – **Repas** *Lunch 22* – 30/55 bc.
◆ Mets classiques et préparations plus contemporaines servis dans une ancienne ferme au joli décor intérieur rustico-actuel. Tables dressées dans l'esprit "Marie-Claire".
◆ Deze oude boerderij heeft een modern-rustieke inrichting. De fleurig gedekte tafeltjes verraden een vrouwelijke hand. Klassieke spijzen, maar ook meer eigentijdse gerechten.

BELGIQUE

HAMOIR *4180 Liège* 533 *S 20,* 534 *S 20 et* 716 *J 4 – 3 558 h.*
Bruxelles 111 – Liège 44 – Huy 28.

XX **La Bonne Auberge,** pl. Delcour 10, ☎ 0 86 38 82 08, *labonneaubergehamoir@skynet.be, Fax 0 86 38 82 08,* – MC VISA.
fermé 2 prem. sem. juil., 2 prem. sem. janv., dim. soir, lundi midi et merc. – **Repas** 26/39.
♦ Une allée "garden" mène au seuil de cette sympathique petite maison où l'on mitonne des plats traditionnels. Si la météo est clémente, les parasols fleurissent au jardin.
♦ Een kunstig aangelegde laan leidt naar dit aardige restaurant, waar traditionele gerechten worden geserveerd. Als het weer meewerkt, "ontluiken" kleurige parasols in de tuin.

HAMONT-ACHEL *3930 Limburg* 533 *S 15 et* 716 *J 2 – 13 653 h.*
Bruxelles 107 – Eindhoven 28 – Hasselt 43.

à Achel *Ouest : 4 km* C *Hamont-Achel – ✉ 3930 Achel :*

Koeckhofs, Michielsplein 4, ☎ 0 11 64 31 81, *info@koeckhofs.be, Fax 0 11 66 24 42,* – TV – 25 à 55. AE MC VISA JCB. rest
Repas *(fermé 1 sem. en juil., 26 déc.-10 janv., dim. et lundi) Lunch 34* – carte 49 à 69 – **16 ch** *(fermé 1 sem. en juil., 26 déc.-10 janv. et dim.)* 70/90 – ½ P 72.
♦ Le voyageur en quête d'un hôtel familial dans les parages de la frontière hollandaise pourra compter ici avec des chambres vastes et douillettes. Salles de séminaires. Au restaurant, choix de recettes classiques actualisées pas à pas.
♦ Reizigers die op zoek zijn naar een familiehotel bij de Nederlandse grens, kunnen hier rekenen op behaaglijke kamers. Er zijn ook vergaderzalen. Restaurant met een klassieke keuken, aan de huidige tijd aangepast.

HAM-SUR-HEURE *6120 Hainaut* C *Ham-sur-Heure-Nalinnes 13 263 h.* 533 *L 21,* 534 *L 21 et* 716 *G 5.*
Bruxelles 75 – Mons 49 – Beaumont 17 – Charleroi 16.

XX **Le Pré Vert,** r. Folie 24, ☎ 0 71 21 56 09, *Fax 0 71 21 50 15,* – P. MC VISA
fermé 18 août-12 sept., lundi et mardi – **Repas** 28/61 bc, ♀.
♦ Belle résidence postée aux abords du village. Salle à manger rustique au sol parqueté. Contenu de l'assiette sensible au rythme des saisons. Quelques crus prestigieux.
♦ Mooie villa aan de rand van het dorp. Rustieke eetzaal met parket. De samenstelling van de maaltijden volgt het ritme van de seizoenen. Enkele prestigieuze wijnen.

HANNUT (HANNUIT) *4280 Liège* 533 *P 18,* 534 *P 18 et* 716 *I 3 – 13 447 h.*
rte de Grand Hallet 19a ☎ 0 19 51 30 66, Fax 0 19 51 53 43.
Bruxelles 60 – Namur 32 – Liège 43 – Hasselt 38.

XX **Les Comtes de Champagne,** chaussée de Huy 23, ☎ 0 19 51 24 28, *Fax 0 19 51 31 10,* – P – 25 à 200. AE MC VISA
fermé du 5 au 25 août et merc. – **Repas** (déjeuner seult sauf vend. et sam.) *Lunch 25* – 40.
♦ Ancienne maison de notable recluse derrière les grilles d'un petit parc. Salle de restaurant où l'on propose le meilleur accord entre vins et mets bourgeois.
♦ Oud herenhuis met een klein park dat door een hek wordt omsloten. In de eetzaal worden uitstekende wijn-spijscombinaties op tafel gezet.

HANSBEKE *9850 Oost-Vlaanderen* C *Nevele 10 894 h.* 533 *G 16 et* 716 *D 2.*
Bruxelles 75 – Brugge 37 – Gent 18.

XX **'t Oud Gemeentehuis,** Vaartstraat 2, ☎ 0 9 371 47 10, *gastro-guest@pandora.be, Fax 0 9 371 88 51,* – P. AE MC VISA
fermé vacances Pâques, 1 sem. en août, vacances Noël, merc. soir, sam. midi, dim. et jours fériés – **Repas** *Lunch 13* – 36.
♦ Charmante maisonnette disposant d'une terrasse ombragée, bien agréable quand perce le soleil. Choix de plats classiques, dont quelques grillades préparées en salle.
♦ Charmant restaurant met een lommerrijk terras, wat wel fijn is als de zon hoog aan de hemel staat. Klassieke kaart met enkele grillspecialiteiten die in de zaal worden bereid.

HAN-SUR-LESSE *Namur* 534 *Q 22 et* 716 *I 5* – *voir à Rochefort.*

HARELBEKE *8530 West-Vlaanderen* 533 E 17 *et* 716 C 3 *– 26 099 h.*
Bruxelles 86 – Kortrijk 4 – Brugge 46 – Gent 42.

Shamrock, Gentsesteenweg 99, ✆ 0 56 70 21 16, *shamrock@belgacom.net, Fax 0 56 70 46 24,* – P. AE VISA.
fermé du 1er au 15 août – **Repas** *(fermé sam. midi et dim. soir)* Lunch 38 bc – carte 39 à 52 – **8 ch** 60/80 – ½ P 70.
• On se sent ici un peu comme chez soi. En raison de la proximité d'un important nœud routier, les chambres, bien que donnant sur le jardin, sont équipées du double vitrage. Plats classico-bourgeois à l'heure du repas. Terrasse d'été dressée sur la pelouse.
• In dit hotel voelt u zich meteen thuis. Hoewel de kamers aan de achterkant liggen, hebben ze dubbele ramen vanwege de nabijheid van een druk verkeersknooppunt. In het restaurant worden eenvoudige, klassieke maaltijden opgediend. Zomerterras op het gazon.

HASSELT *3500* P *Limburg* 533 Q 17 *et* 716 I 3 *– 68 771 h.*
Musée : *national du genièvre★ (Nationaal Jenevermuseum)* Y **M¹**.
Env. *par ⑦ : Domaine provincial de Bokrijk★.*
18 Vissenbroekstraat 15 ✆ 0 11 26 34 82, Fax 0 11 26 34 83 - 9 par ⑤ : 9 km à Lummen, Golfweg 1b ✆ 0 13 52 16 64, Fax 0 13 52 17 69 - 18 par ① : 12,5 km à Houthalen, Golfstraat 1 ✆ 0 89 38 35 43, Fax 0 89 84 12 08.
Stadhuis, Lombaardstraat 3 ✆ 0 11 23 95 44, toerisme@hasselt.be, Fax 0 11 22 50 23 – Fédération provinciale de tourisme, Willekensmolenstraat 140 ✆ 0 11 23 74 50, info@toerismelimburg.be, Fax 0 11 23 74 66.
Bruxelles 82 ⑥ – Maastricht 33 ④ – Antwerpen 77 ⑧ – Liège 42 ④ – Eindhoven 59 ①

Plan page suivante

Holiday Inn, Kattegatstraat 1, ✆ 0 11 24 22 00, *hotel@holiday-inn-hasselt.com, Fax 0 11 22 39 35,* – – 25 à 240. AE VISA JCB. rest Y a
Repas (avec buffets) Lunch 20 – 25 – 16 – **107 ch** 184/214 – ½ P 119/254.
• Cet hôtel moderne bordant le ring est situé à seulement 300 m du musée national du Genièvre, "la" spécialité hasseltoise appelée ici "witteke". Chambres spacieuses. Salle à manger contemporaine agencée sur plusieurs niveaux. Buffets et menu-carte.
• Dit moderne hotel ligt aan de Ring, op slechts 300 m van het Nationaal Jenevermuseum. Deze drank is een Hasseltse specialiteit die hier "witteke" wordt genoemd. Ruime kamers en een eigentijdse eetzaal. À la carte, menu en buffet.

Hassotel, St-Jozefstraat 10, ✆ 0 11 23 06 55, *info@hassotel.be, Fax 0 11 22 94 77,* – , rest, – 25 à 200. AE VISA. Z d
Repas Lunch 10 – carte 29 à 43 – **36 ch** 93/130 – ½ P 59/95.
• Immeuble des années 1980 posté en léger retrait du ring enserrant le cœur de la capitale du Limbourg belge. Chambres avant tout fonctionnelles, plus calmes à l'arrière.
• Dit hotel uit 1980 staat even buiten de Ring die om het centrum van de hoofdplaats van Belgisch Limburg loopt. De kamers zijn vooral functioneel en achter wat rustiger.

Portmans, Minderbroederstraat 12 (Walputsteeg), ✆ 0 11 26 32 80, *hotel.portmans@wolputsteeg.com, Fax 0 11 26 32 81,* – , ch, P – 25 à 40. AE VISA. Y r
Repas (avec cuisine italienne) Lunch 17 – carte 26 à 36 – **14 ch** 85.
• Bel hôtel dont l'entrée se cache dans un passage reliant la grand-place à une rue commerçante. De l'atrium, un ascenseur panoramique dessert des chambres sans reproche. Plusieurs possibilités pour se restaurer simplement : pâtes, grillades, snacks, etc.
• De ingang van dit mooie hotel bevindt zich in een winkelgalerij aan de Grote Markt. Vanuit het atrium brengt een glazen lift u naar een van de onberispelijke kamers. Mogelijkheid om eenvoudig te eten, zoals pastaschotels, grillspecialiteiten en diverse snacks.

Express by Holiday Inn sans rest, Thonissenlaan 37, ✆ 0 11 37 93 00, *Fax 0 11 37 93 01* – – 25 à 45. AE VISA JCB Y d
89 ch 92.
• Cet établissement de chaîne implanté au bord du ring ceinturant la ville renferme de pimpantes chambres aux tons frais. Les plus calmes se distribuent à l'arrière du bâtiment.
• Dit Holiday Inn-hotel bij de ringweg biedt kamers in frisse kleuren die er tiptop uitzien ; die aan de achterkant zijn het rustigst.

Figaro, Mombeekdreef 38, ✆ 0 11 27 25 56, *figaro@figaro.be, Fax 0 11 27 31 77,* ←, – P – 25. AE VISA X a
fermé du 1er au 20 août, lundi et merc. – **Repas** Lunch 35 – carte 60 à 75.
• Élégant décor en camaïeu, beaux jardins, patio évocant une hacienda, terrasse estivale dressée au bord de la pièce d'eau : des lieux conçus pour le plaisir des yeux.
• Deze villa is werkelijk een lust voor het oog : een elegant decor in ton sur ton, een weelderige tuin, een patio zoals op een haciënda en een zonnig terras met een waterpartij.

HASSELT

Badderijstr.	Y 2
Banneuxstr.	V 3
Boerenkrijgsingel	X 6
Botermarkt	Y 7
Demerstr.	Y
Diesterstr.	YZ 8
Dorpstraat	Y 10
Genkersteenweg	V 12
Gouverneur Roppesingel	X 15
Gouverneur Verwilghensingel	V 16
Grote Markt	Z
Havermarkt	Z 18
Hendrik van Veldekesingel	V 19
Herkenrodesingel	V 21
Hoogstr.	Y 22
Kapelstr.	Z 23
Kempische Steenweg	VY 24
Kolonel Dusartpl.	Y 26
Koning Albertstr.	Z 27
Koning Boudewijnlaan	VY 28
Koningin Astridlaan	VY 30
Kuringersteenweg	V 31
Kunstlaan	Z 32
Lombaardstr.	Y 34
Maastrichtersteenweg	VY 35
Maastrichterstr.	YZ 36
Prins Bisschopsingel	X 38
Ridder Portmanstr.	Z 39
Runkstersteenweg	V 40
Salvatorstr.	X 42
de Schiervellaan	Z 43
St. Jozefstr.	Z 44
St. Lambrechts Herkstraat	X 46
St. Truidersteenweg	X 47
Universiteitslaan	V 49
Windmolenstraat	Z 50
Zuivelmarkt	Y 51

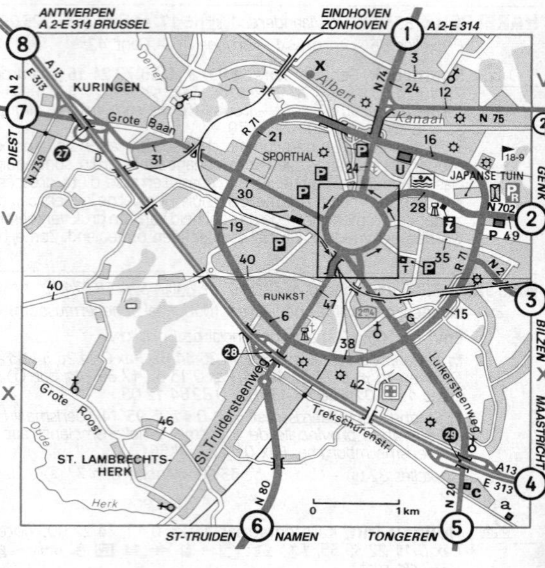

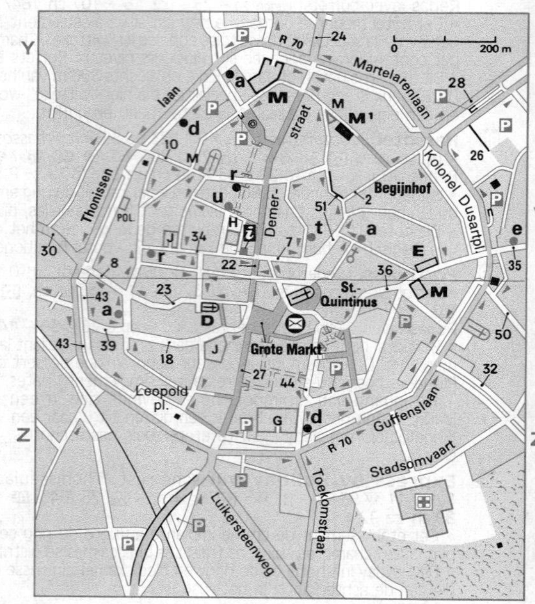

Pour visiter
la **Belgique**
utilisez
le **guide vert**
Michelin
Belgique
Grand-Duché de
Luxembourg

Send us your comments on the restaurants we recommend
and your opinion on the specialities
and local wines they offer.

XXX **'t Claeverblat,** Lombaardstraat 34, ✆ 0 11 22 24 04, *info@claeverblat.be, Fax 0 11 23 33 31* – ▤. AE ⓓ ⓂⒸ VISA. ✻ Y r
fermé jeudi, sam. midi et dim. – **Repas** carte 54 à 94.
◆ Maison de bouche connue de très longue date. Intérieur cossu, un peu "protocolaire", vite réchauffé par un accueil cordial. Menus plébiscités et vins à bons prix.
◆ Dit restaurant staat al jaren goed bekend. Rijk aandoend interieur, een beetje stijf, maar vriendelijke bediening. De menu's zijn zeer in trek en de wijnen redelijk geprijsd.

XX **JER,** Persoonstraat 16, ✆ 0 11 26 26 47, *Fax 0 11 26 26 48*, 🏠 – ▤. AE ⓂⒸ VISA. ✻ Y a
fermé lundi, mardi et sam. midi – **Repas** *Lunch 26* – carte 49 à 82, ♀.
◆ Préparations traditionnelles, mais également au goût du jour, dont on se délecte dans une salle à manger garnie de meubles de style. Sélection de vins assez bien balancée.
◆ In dit restaurant, dat met stijlmeubelen is ingericht, kunt u genieten van traditionele gerechten die toch aan de huidige smaak voldoen. Uitgebalanceerde wijnkaart.

XX **l'Aubergine,** Luikersteenweg 358, ✆ 0 11 27 17 77, *Fax 0 11 27 17 77* – P. AE ⓓ ⓂⒸ VISA X c
fermé 2 prem. sem. janv., mardi et sam. midi – **Repas** *Lunch 24* – carte 41 à 66.
◆ Belle villa résidentielle désormais vouée aux plaisirs de la table. Une adresse familiale à débusquer au Sud-Est de la ville, direction Tongeren, près de l'autoroute.
◆ Mooie villa met een huiselijke sfeer ten zuidoosten van de stad, richting Tongeren, bij de snelweg. Hier kunt u zich de geneugten des levens laten smaken.

XX **'t Kleine Genoegen,** Raamstraat 3, ✆ 0 11 22 57 03, *kleinegenoegen@pandora.be, Fax 0 11 22 57 03* – ▤. AE ⓓ ⓂⒸ VISA. ✻ Y t
fermé juil., dim. et lundi – **Repas** *Lunch 16* – 35/56 bc.
◆ Ce restaurant du centre de Hasselt tire parti d'un bâtiment séculaire, jadis hôpital de femmes. L'intérieur, avec mezzanine, produit une agréable impression d'espace ouvert.
◆ Dit restaurant in het centrum zit in een eeuwenoud pand, dat vroeger een vrouwenhospitaal was. Het interieur met mezzanine geeft de aangename indruk van een open ruimte.

X **Da Chico,** Maastrichtersteenweg 20, ✆ 0 11 22 67 37, *info@dachico.be, Fax 0 11 23 62 80*, 🏠 – AE ⓂⒸ VISA. ✻ Y e
fermé du 1er au 16 sept., lundi et sam. midi – **Repas** carte 38 à 51.
◆ Restaurant familial estimé pour sa goûteuse cuisine hispano-transalpine et sa plaisante atmosphère "Sud" confortée par une véranda et une terrasse estivale entourée de vigne.
◆ Dit familierestaurant met serre staat bekend om zijn lekkere mediterrane keuken en plezierige zuidelijke atmosfeer. Het zomerse terras wordt door wijnranken omringd.

X **De Egge,** Walputstraat 23, ✆ 0 11 22 49 51, *Fax 0 11 22 49 51* – AE ⓓ ⓂⒸ VISA
fermé 2 prem. sem. août, sam. midi et dim. – **Repas** *Lunch 24* – 32/50 bc. Y u
◆ Sage petit établissement dont l'enseigne (La Herse) évoque les travaux aux champs. Cuisine simple et savoureuse mais accueil et service parfois un rien distants.
◆ Goed restaurantje, waarvan de naam herinnert aan het werk op het land. Eenvoudige, smakelijke keuken, maar ietwat afgemeten bediening.

X **Jürgen,** Diesterstraat 18, ✆ 0 11 21 03 70 – AE ⓂⒸ VISA. ✻ Z a
fermé merc. et sam. midi – **Repas** (menu unique) *Lunch 19* – 32/65 bc.
◆ Adresse familiale où se conçoit une bonne cuisine du marché. Enfilade de salles à manger sobres et apaisantes. Pas de carte ; seulement deux menus déclamés par le chef.
◆ Gemoedelijk restaurant met verschillende zaaltjes die sober zijn ingericht. Geen kaart, maar twee mondeling doorgegeven menu's met dagverse producten van de markt.

à Herk-de-Stad *(Herck-la-Ville) par ⑦ : 12 km – 11 629 h – ✉ 3540 Herk-de-Stad :*

XX **Rôtiss. De Blenk,** Endepoelstraat 50 (Sud : 1 km par rte de St-Truiden, puis rte de Rummen), ✆ 0 13 55 46 64, *de.blenk@pi.be*, 🏠 – ▤ P. AE ⓂⒸ VISA. ✻
fermé 14 août-4 sept., jeudi, sam. midi et dim. – **Repas** *Lunch 34* – carte 49 à 66.
◆ Fermette à colombages bâtie dans un quartier résidentiel. Côté agrément, c'est le jardin d'hiver qui l'emporte d'une courte tête devant la terrasse réservée aux beaux jours.
◆ Mooi vakwerkboerderijtje in een rustige woonwijk. Wat charme betreft wint de wintertuin het nog net van het terras dat voor zomerse dagen is bestemd.

à Kortessem *par ⑤ : 8 km – 8 060 h – ✉ 3720 Kortessem :*

XX **Het Jachthuis,** Reeweg 96, ✆ 0 11 37 60 64, *jachthuis@skynet.be, Fax 0 11 37 60 64*, 🏠 – P. ⓂⒸ VISA
fermé 1 sem. en sept., mardi et merc. – **Repas** *Lunch 25* – carte 34 à 49.
◆ Ancienne ferme à dénicher en pleine campagne. Repas actuel dans une accueillante salle à touche rustique ou sur la belle terrasse environnée de champs et de prairies.
◆ Landelijk gelegen boerderij. Eigentijdse keuken in een aangename eetzaal met een rustiek karakter. Bij mooi weer is het terras met uitzicht op de akkers en weilanden een must.

à Kuringen *C Hasselt – ✉ 3511 Kuringen :*

XX **Orangerie 't Krekelhof,** Rechterstraat 6, ✆ 0 11 22 28 12, *info@orangerie-krekelhof.be, Fax 0 11 26 12 42,* – ▤ P – 25 à 350. AE MC VISA. V x
fermé sem. carnaval, sam. midi, dim. midi, lundi, mardi et merc. – **Repas** *Lunch 40 bc* – carte 47 à 61.
◆ À l'étage d'une grande villa alanguie sur les rives du canal Albert, ample et apaisante salle à manger couleur ivoire, rehaussée de toiles modernes. Petite terrasse perchée.
◆ Restaurant op de bovenverdieping van een grote villa aan het Albertkanaal. Ruime, rustige eetzaal in ivoorkleur, opgevrolijkt met moderne doeken. Hooggelegen terrasje.

à Lummen *par ⑧ : 9 km – 13 569 h – ✉ 3560 Lummen :*

XXX ✿ **Hoeve St. Paul** (Robyns), Rekhovenstraat 20 (près de l'échangeur E 314 - A 2 / E 313 - A 13), ✆ 0 13 52 14 15, *info@hoeve_st_paul.be, Fax 0 13 52 14 20,* – P. AE ① MC VISA JCB.
fermé 2e quinz. juil., prem. quinz. janv., lundi, mardi, jeudi soir et sam. midi – **Repas** *Lunch 48* – 75/135 bc, carte 62 à 112.
◆ Table gastronomique aménagée dans une ravissante ferme à colombages. Décor intérieur, terrasse et jardin du plus bel effet. Menu-choix recomposé toutes les six semaines.
◆ Gastronomisch restaurant in een schitterende vakwerkboerderij. Het interieur, het terras en de tuin zijn allemaal even prachtig. Keuzemenu dat om de zes weken wordt veranderd.
Spéc. Tarte fondante au foie d'oie, homard et artichaut. Goujonnettes de soles croquantes, cappuccino au Noilly et oseille. Filet de bar sur sa peau et tapenade d'olives vertes

à Romershoven *Sud-Est : 10 km C Hoeselt 9 212 h. – ✉ 3730 Romershoven :*

XXX **Ter Beuke,** Romershovenstraat 148, ✆ 0 89 51 18 81, *terbeuke@skynet.be, Fax 0 89 51 11 06,* ←, – P – 25. AE ① MC VISA.
fermé 24 juil.-18 août, merc. et sam. midi – **Repas** 35/74 bc.
◆ De la jolie terrasse dressée dans le jardin à la belle saison, la vue porte sur les alentours agrestes. Large choix de recettes actualisées et de crus bourguignons.
◆ Vanaf het terras in de tuin, waar bij mooi weer kan worden gegeten, ontvouwt zich een prachtig uitzicht op de landelijke omgeving. Eigentijdse keuken en goede bourgognewijnen.

HASTIÈRE-LAVAUX *5540 Namur C Hastière 5 131 h.* 533 N 21, 534 N 21 *et* 716 H 5.
Bruxelles 100 – Namur 42 – Dinant 10 – Philippeville 25 – Givet 9.

XX **Le Chalet des Grottes,** r. Anthée 52, ✆ 0 82 64 41 86, *Fax 0 82 64 57 55,* – P. AE ① MC VISA
fermé merc. et jeudi de janv. à mars sauf sem. carnaval, lundi et mardi – **Repas** *Lunch 25* – 44/93 bc.
◆ L'un des "incontournables" de la région : environnement boisé, voisinage des grottes, décor intérieur néo-rustique, plats de saison et du terroir, et cave bien fournie.
◆ Een must in deze streek : bosrijke omgeving, nabijgelegen grotten, neorustiek interieur, seizoengebonden keuken met regionale invloeden en een rijk gevulde wijnkelder.

XX **La Meunerie,** r. Larifosse 17, ✆ 0 82 64 51 33, *Fax 0 82 64 51 33,* – 25. AE ① MC VISA.
fermé janv.-12 fév., 16 août-16 sept., merc. sauf en juil.-août et mardi – **Repas** *Lunch 24* – 30/70 bc, ♀.
◆ Restaurant établi dans un moulin à eau de la vallée du Féron. Menus bien vus et cave riche en vins d'Alsace et de Bourgogne. La machinerie tient lieu de salle à manger.
◆ Deze watermolen in het dal van de Féron is nu een restaurant, waarvan de eetzaal in de machinekamer is ondergebracht. Lekkere menu's en wijnen uit de Elzas en de Bourgogne.

à Hastière-par-Delà *Sud : 2 km C Hastière – ✉ 5541 Hastière-par-Delà :*

Le Val des Colverts, rte de Blaimont 8, ✆ 0 82 64 45 48, *Fax 0 82 64 57 84,* – TV P. AE ① MC VISA
Repas *(fermé janv.-mi-fév. sauf week-end, lundi et mardi)* (taverne-rest) *Lunch 20* – carte 22 à 31 – **7 ch** *(fermé mardi de sept. à mars)* 67/105.
◆ Auberge dont la façade blanche animée de marquises rouges capte volontiers le regard. Chambres parées de tissus coordonnés aux tons frais. Typique petit café villageois. Taverne-restaurant toute indiquée pour un repas sans prise de tête.
◆ Deze herberg springt in het oog door de rode markiezen op de witte gevel. Kamers met frisse kleuren en bijpassende stoffen. Typisch dorpscafeetje en een restaurant dat garant staat voor een smakelijke maaltijd zonder poespas.

HASTIÈRE-PAR-DELÀ *Namur* 533 O 21, 534 O 21 *et* 716 H 5 – *voir à Hastière-Lavaux.*

HAUTE-BODEUX *Liège* 533 T 20, 534 T 20 *et* 716 K 4 – *voir à Trois-Ponts.*

HAVELANGE *5370 Namur* 533 Q 20, 534 Q 20 *et* 716 I 4 – *4 708 h.*

à l'Est : 9 km à Méan, Ferme du Grand Scley ☎ 0 86 32 00 35, Fax 0 86 32 00 45.

Bruxelles 98 – Namur 39 – Dinant 30 – Liège 40.

Le Petit Criel, Malihoux 1, ☎ 0 83 63 36 60, *jfluzin@swing.be, Fax 0 83 63 36 60,* – P. AE ⓓ ⓜⓒ VISA

fermé mi-juin-mi-juil., mardi et merc. – **Repas** 22/30.

◆ Cette maison aux abords fleuris a su tirer le meilleur parti de sa situation champêtre. Voûtes et cheminée en salle. Repas en plein air par beau temps. Additions digestes !

◆ Dit door bloemen omringde huis is heel landelijk gelegen. Gewelfde eetzaal met open haard. Bij mooi weer kan buiten worden gegeten. De rekening ligt niet zwaar op de maag !

HÉBRONVAL *Luxembourg belge* 533 T 21 *et* 534 T 21 – *voir à Vielsalm.*

HEIST *West-Vlaanderen* 533 E 14 *et* 716 C 1 – *voir à Knokke-Heist.*

Les prix

Pour toutes précisions sur les prix indiqués dans ce guide, reportez-vous aux pages explicatives.

HEKELGEM *1790 Vlaams-Brabant* C *Affligem 11 744 h.* 533 J 17 *et* 716 F 3.

Bruxelles 23 – Aalst 6 – Charleroi 75 – Mons 79.

Anobesia, Brusselbaan 216 (sur N 9), ☎ 0 53 68 07 69, *g.gheysels@belgacom.net, Fax 0 53 66 59 25,* – P. AE ⓓ ⓜⓒ VISA JCB.

fermé 2 dern. sem. fév., 2 dern. sem. août, lundi soir, mardi et sam. midi – **Repas** Lunch 34 – 49/90 bc, ♀.

◆ L'enseigne paraît évoquer une fleur exotique, mais il n'en est rien ! Cette villa d'époque Art déco nichée dans un jardin ombragé sert une cuisine au goût du jour. Terrasse.

◆ De naam van deze art-decovilla zou naar een exotische bloem kunnen verwijzen. In dit restaurant wordt een eigentijdse keuken geserveerd. Terras en lommerrijke tuin.

HERBEUMONT *6887 Luxembourg belge* 534 Q 24 *et* 716 I 6 – *1 503 h.*

Voir Château : du sommet ≤★★.

Env. à l'Ouest : 11 km, Roches de Dampiry ≤★ – au Nord-Ouest : 12 km, Variante par Auby : au mont Zatron ≤★.

Bruxelles 170 – Bouillon 24 – Arlon 55 – Dinant 78.

Host. du Prieuré de Conques , r. Conques 2 (Sud : 2,5 km), ✉ 6820 Florenville, ☎ 0 61 41 14 17, *info@conques.be, Fax 0 61 41 27 03,* ≤, , , – TV P – 25. AE ⓓ ⓜⓒ VISA JCB. rest

fermé janv.-fév. et 30 août-10 sept. – **Repas** *(fermé merc. de nov. à avril, mardi et après 20 h 30)* Lunch 29 – 42/58, ♀ – **18 ch** 110/136 – ½ P 90/110.

◆ Ancien prieuré et son agréable parc inscrits dans un paysage de collines et d'épaisses forêts. Vue sur le cours paresseux de la Semois. Chambres en annexe. Préparations classiques sobrement mises à la page, servies sous les voûtes de la salle à manger.

◆ Deze oude priorij met zijn mooie park ligt temidden van heuvels en dichte bossen, met uitzicht op de rustig kabbelende Semois. Kamers in de dependance. Onder de gewelven van de eetzaal worden klassieke gerechten met een snufje modern geserveerd.

La Châtelaine - Aux Chevaliers, Grand-Place 8, ☎ 0 61 41 14 22, *contact@chatelaine.be, Fax 0 61 41 22 04,* , , – TV P – 25. AE ⓓ ⓜⓒ VISA. rest

12 mars-déc. ; fermé 28 juin-9 juil. et 23 août-3 sept. – **Repas** *(fermé merc., dim. soir et après 20 h 30)* Lunch 27 – carte 22 à 45, ♀ – **18 ch** 50/85 – ½ P 60/85.

◆ Hôtel du centre de la localité regroupant deux bâtiments. Les chambres, un brin surannées, sont parfois équipées de kitchenettes. Piscine au jardin. La carte du restaurant panache saveurs régionales et traditionnelles.

◆ Dit hotel bestaat uit twee gebouwen in het centrum van het dorp. De kamers zijn een tikkeltje ouderwets en soms voorzien van een kitchenette. Zwembad in de tuin. In het restaurant kunnen regionale en traditionele spijzen worden besteld.

HERENTALS *2200 Antwerpen* 533 O 15 *et* 716 H 2 – *25 572 h.*

Voir *Retable★ de l'église Ste-Waudru (St-Waldetrudiskerk).*

au Nord : 8 km à Lille, Haarlebeek 3 ☎ 0 14 55 19 30, Fax 0 14 55 19 31 - au Sud : 5 km à Noorderwijk, Witbos ☎ 0 14 26 21 71, Fax 0 14 26 60 48.

Grote Markt 41, ☎ 0 14 21 90 88, herentals@toerismevlaanderen.be, Fax 0 14 22 28 56.

Bruxelles 70 – Antwerpen 30 – Hasselt 48 – Turnhout 24.

de Zalm, Grote Markt 21, ☎ 0 14 28 60 00, *hotel@dezalm.be, Fax 0 14 28 60 10,* – 25. AE VISA.
Repas *(fermé 1 sem. avant Pâques, 2 dern. sem. juil., merc. soir, sam. midi et dim.)* (taverne-rest) *Lunch 26* – 45, ♀ – **24 ch** 75/90 – ½ P 88/101.

◆ Rénové dans l'esprit contemporain, cet hôtel officiant sur le Grote Markt se complète de deux salles de cinéma. Plaisant espace de breakfast doté d'une belle terrasse d'été. Chaleureuse taverne-restaurant à l'ancienne. Carte traditionnelle.

◆ Dit hotel aan de Grote Markt is in hedendaagse stijl gerenoveerd en beschikt over twee bioscoopzalen. Prettige ontbijtruimte met een mooi zomerterras. Sfeervol café-restaurant vol nostalgie. Traditionele kaart.

't Ganzennest, Watervoort 68 (direction Lille : 1 km, puis à droite), ☎ 0 14 21 64 56, *Fax 0 14 21 82 36,* – P. VISA
fermé lundi et mardi – **Repas** *Lunch 23* – 29.

◆ Une ambiance chaleureuse et cossue flotte dans ce restaurant procurant l'agrément d'une fermette à la campagne. Carte un peu "touche à tout". Appétissant menu multi-choix.

◆ In dit luxueuze restaurant met de charme van een plattelandsboerderijtje heerst een warme sfeer. De kaart is een beetje "van alles wat". Aanlokkelijk menu met veel keus.

à Grobbendonk *Ouest : 4 km – 10 534 h – ✉ 2280 Grobbendonk :*

Aldhem, Jagersdreef 1 (près E 313 - A 13, sortie ⑳), ☎ 0 14 50 10 01, *info@aldhem.be, Fax 0 14 50 10 13,* – rest, P – 25 à 640. AE VISA.
Repas (cuisine italienne) *Lunch 24* – carte 36 à 49 – **65 ch** 113/129 – ½ P 75/89.

◆ Chambres toutes identiques réparties sur les trois étages de cette construction moderne qui abrite un des centres de congrès les mieux équipés de la province. Élégante salle de restaurant. Recettes et cave franco-italiennes.

◆ Modern gebouw met identieke kamers op drie verdiepingen en een congrescentrum dat tot de best geoutilleerde van de hele provincie behoort. Elegant restaurant, waar Frans-Italiaanse gerechten en bijpassende wijnen worden geserveerd.

HERK-DE-STAD (HERCK-LA-VILLE) *Limburg* 533 Q 17 *et* 716 I 3 – *voir à Hasselt.*

HERNE *1540 Vlaams-Brabant* 533 J 18, 534 J 18 *et* 716 F 3 – *6 327 h.*

Bruxelles 42 – Aalst 27 – Mons 31 – Tournai 52.

Kokejane, Van Cauwenberghelaan 3, ☎ 0 2 396 16 28, *restaurant@kokejane.be, Fax 0 2 396 02 40,* – P – 25 à 40. AE VISA
fermé 19 juil.-7 août, 26 déc.-15 janv., dim. soir, lundi et mardi – **Repas** *Lunch 50 bc* – 58/98 bc.

◆ Salle à manger rénovée. Détail intéressant : à la belle saison, on se prélasse sur une relaxante terrasse dressée au bord de la piscine. Fine cuisine classique.

◆ Gerenoveerde eetzaal met een fijne klassieke keuken. Interessant detail : bij mooi weer kunt u ontspannen eten op het fraai gedekte terras aan de rand van het zwembad.

HERSEAUX *Hainaut* 533 E 18 *et* 716 C 3 – *voir à Mouscron.*

HERSTAL *Liège* 533 S 18, 534 S 18 *et* 716 J 3 – *voir à Liège, environs.*

HERTSBERGE *West-Vlaanderen* 533 E 16 *et* 716 C 2 – *voir à Brugge, environs.*

Het – *voir au nom propre.*

Nos guides hôteliers, nos guides touristiques et nos cartes routières sont complémentaires. Utilisez-les ensemble.

HEURE *5377 Namur* ☐ *Somme-Leuze 4 276 h.* 533 Q 21, 534 Q 21 *et* 716 I 5.
Bruxelles 102 – Namur 41 – Dinant 35 – Liège 54.

XX **Le Fou est belge** (Van Lint), rte de Givet 24, ✆ 0 86 32 28 12, *Fax 0 86 32 39 02,* ☂ – P. MC VISA
✿ *fermé 20 juin-13 juil., 5 oct.-12 déc., 19 déc.-19 janv., dim., lundi et jeudi soir* – **Repas** *Lunch 20* – 30/57 bc, carte 34 à 59, ♀.
• Intérieur rustique, terrasse estivale, jardin fleuri en saison, mets savoureux, vins de France et d'ailleurs... La table la plus abordable du gratin culinaire belge !
• Rustiek interieur, zomers terras, weelderige tuin, tongstrelende gerechten, wijnen uit Frankrijk en andere landen... Belgische topgastronomie voor een betaalbare prijs !
Spéc. Croquettes fondantes aux crevettes grises. Boudin noir rôti "en baudruche", pommes caramélisées. Homard rôti aux nouilles fraîches

HEUSDEN *Limburg* 533 Q 16 *et* 716 I 2 – *voir à Zolder.*

HEUSDEN *Oost-Vlaanderen* 533 H 16 *et* 716 E 2 – *voir à Gent, environs.*

HEUSY *Liège* 533 U 19, 534 U 19 *et* 716 K 4 – *voir à Verviers.*

HEVERLEE *Vlaams-Brabant* 533 N 17 *et* 716 H 3 – *voir à Leuven.*

HOEI *Liège – voir Huy.*

HOEILAART *Vlaams-Brabant* 533 L 18 *et* 716 G 3 – *voir à Bruxelles, environs.*

HOEKE *West-Vlaanderen* 533 F 15 – *voir à Damme.*

HOLLAIN *Hainaut* 533 F 19, 534 F 19 *et* 716 D 4 – *voir à Tournai.*

HOOGLEDE *West-Vlaanderen* 533 D 17 *et* 716 C 3 – *voir à Roeselare.*

HOOGSTRATEN *2320 Antwerpen* 533 N 14 *et* 716 H 1 – *18 036 h.*
☐ *Stadhuis, Vrijheid 149* ✆ *0 3 340 19 55, hoogstraten@toerismevlaanderen.be, Fax 0 3 340 19 66.*
Bruxelles 88 – Antwerpen 37 – Turnhout 18.

XXX **Noordland,** Lodewijk De Konincklaan 276, ✆ 0 3 314 53 40, *dk@noordland.be, Fax 0 3 314 83 32,* ☂ – ☐ P. AE ⓓ MC VISA. ✂
fermé 2 sem. en fév., 16 juil.-5 août, merc. et jeudi – **Repas** 62.
• Demeure entourée d'arbres, abritant un salon apéritif et une lumineuse salle à manger garnie de meubles de style. Jolie terrasse estivale côté jardin, très soigné, lui aussi.
• Fraai restaurant tussen de bomen, met een aparte salon voor het aperitief en een heerlijk lichte eetzaal met stijlmeubilair. Mooi zomerterras aan de tuinzijde.

XX **Host. De Tram** avec ch, Vrijheid 192, ✆ 0 3 314 65 65, *info@de.tram.be, Fax 0 3 314 70 06,* ☂ – TV P. AE MC VISA
fermé 2ᵉ quinz. août – **Repas** *(fermé dim. et lundi)* 32/65 bc – **5 ch** ☐ 98/105.
• Hôtellerie familiale établie à l'ombre de la vertigineuse tour-porche - 105 m de haut ! - de l'église Ste-Catherine. Mets classiques, terrasse d'été et chambres coquettes.
• Familiehotel bij de indrukwekkende portaaltoren van de St.-Catharinakerk, die maar liefst 105 m hoog is. Klassieke keuken, zomers terras en kraakheldere kamers.

XX **Begijnhof,** Vrijheid 108, ✆ 0 3 314 66 25, *Fax 0 3 314 88 13* – ☐. AE MC VISA. ✂
fermé mardi et merc. – **Repas** *Lunch 23* – 31/65 bc.
• Face au béguinage et son église baroque (17ᵉ s.), établissement dont la façade ancienne dissimule un intérieur moderne et confortable. Recettes classiques.
• Achter de oude gevel van dit restaurant tegenover het Begijnhof met zijn 17e-eeuwse barokkerk gaat een verrassend modern en comfortabel interieur schuil. Klassieke kookstijl.

BELGIQUE

HOTTON *6990 Luxembourg belge* 533 R 21, 534 R21 *et* 716 J 5 – *5 024 h.*

Voir *Grottes★★.*

r. Simon 14 ✆ 0 84 46 61 22, contact@hotton.be, Fax 0 86 46 76 98.

Bruxelles 116 – Liège 60 – Namur 55.

La Besace r. Monts 9 (Est : 4,5 km, lieu-dit Werpin), ✆ 0 84 46 62 35, *info@labesace.be, Fax 0 84 46 70 54,* – TV P – 25. MC VISA.
Repas (dîner pour résidents seult) – **8 ch** 56/74 – ½ P 59.
◆ Franchissez le pont : vous voici devant une sympathique auberge de poche noyée dans la chlorophylle. Chambres fonctionnelles où l'on peut poser sa besace pour la nuit.
◆ Als u de brug oversteekt, komt u bij deze kleine sympathieke herberg, die tussen het groen ligt verscholen. De kamers zijn functioneel en voldoen prima voor een nachtje.

HOUDENG-AIMERIES *Hainaut* 533 J 20, 534 J 20 *et* 716 F 4 – *voir à La Louvière.*

HOUDENG-GOEGNIES *Hainaut* 533 J 20 *et* 534 J 20 – *voir à La Louvière.*

HOUFFALIZE *6660 Luxembourg belge* 534 T 22 *et* 716 K 5 – *4 565 h.*

pl. Janvier 45 ✆ 0 61 28 81 16, info@houffalize.be, Fax 0 61 28 95 59.

Bruxelles 164 – Luxembourg 95 – Arlon 63 – Liège 71 – Namur 97.

à Achouffe *Nord-Ouest : 6 km* C *Houffalize* – ✉ *6666 Houffalize :*

L'Espine , Achouffe 19, ✆ 0 61 28 81 82, *espine@caramail.com, Fax 0 61 28 90 82,* – TV P. MC VISA
fermé début juil. et début janv. – **Repas** (dîner pour résidents seult) – **11 ch** 65/138 – ½ P 69/74.
◆ Une villa qui ne manque pas d'atouts, avec sa verte campagne environnante, le silence ambiant, et ses chambres offrant le coup d'œil sur la vallée de l'Ourthe.
◆ Deze villa heeft heel wat te bieden : landelijke omgeving, weldadige stilte en kamers met uitzicht op het groene dal van de Ourthe.

à Wibrin *Nord-Ouest : 9 km* C *Houffalize* – ✉ *6666 Wibrin :*

Le Cœur de l'Ardenne sans rest, r. Tilleul 7, ✆ 0 61 28 93 15, *lecœurdelardenne@belgacom.net, Fax 0 61 28 91 67* – TV P.
5 ch 60/85.
◆ Maison de pays convertie en hôtel familial dont la poignée de chambres offre au voyageur calme et confort. Terrasse et jardinet sur l'arrière.
◆ Dit huis met zijn typische streekarchitectuur is verbouwd tot familiehotel met een paar rustige en comfortabele kamers. Terras en kleine tuin aan de achterzijde.

HOUSSE *Liège* 533 T 18 *et* 534 T 18 – *voir à Blégny.*

HOUTAIN-LE-VAL *1476 Brabant Wallon* C *Genappe 13 959 h.* 533 L 19, 534 L 19 *et* 716 G 4.

Bruxelles 41 – Charleroi 33 – Mons 46 – Nivelles 11.

XX **La Meunerie,** r. Patronage 1a, ✆ 0 67 77 28 16, *la_meunerie@swing.be, Fax 0 67 77 33 37,* – P. AE MC VISA
fermé sam. midi, dim. soir, lundi et après 20 h 30 – **Repas** Lunch 22 – 31/58 bc, ♀.
◆ Dans les murs d'une ancienne meunerie, restaurant de campagne où les produits du terroir forment la base d'une cuisine qui se goûte aussi en terrasse, l'été venu.
◆ Plattelandsrestaurant in een oude maalderij. De kok werkt uitsluitend met producten uit de streek en dat proef je ! Bij mooi weer kan op het terras worden gegeten.

HOUTAVE *8377 West-Vlaanderen* C *Zuienkerke 2 779 h.* 533 D 15 *et* 716 C 2.

Bruxelles 109 – Brugge 31 – Oostende 16.

XX **De Roeschaert,** Kerkhofstraat 12, ✆ 0 50 31 95 63, *Fax 0 50 31 95 63* – AE MC VISA
fermé 17 août-7 sept., 21 déc.-3 janv., dim. soir, lundi et mardi – **Repas** Lunch 24 – 38/70 bc, ♀.
◆ Établissement familial adossé à l'église d'un petit village des polders. Belle salle à manger rustique ornée de deux cheminées. Attrayant choix de mets en phase avec l'époque.
◆ Burgerhuis naast de kerk van een polderdorpje. Mooie rustieke eetzaal met twee schouwen. Aantrekkelijke menukaart met gerechten die bij de huidige kookstijl passen.

HOUTHALEN *3530 Limburg* Ⓒ *Houthalen-Helchteren 29 438 h.* 533 R 16 *et* 716 J 2.

Golfstraat 1 ☎ 0 89 38 35 43, Fax 0 89 84 12 08.

Grote Baan 112a ☎ 0 11 60 05 40, toerisme@houthalen-helchteren.be, Fax 0 11 60 05 03.

Bruxelles 83 – Maastricht 40 – Hasselt 12 – Diest 28.

XXXX ✿ **De Barrier** (Vandersanden) avec ch, Grote Baan 9 (près E 314 - A 2, sortie ㉙), ☎ 0 11 52 55 25, *info@debarrier.be, Fax 0 11 52 55 45,* – P. AE ① MC VISA. ch

fermé du 23 au 29 fév., 18 juil.-2 août, dim. midi d'oct. à fév., dim. soir et lundi – **Repas** *Lunch 42* – 65/120 bc, carte 82 à 107 – ☐ 15 – **8 ch** 150/200, – 2 suites.

◆ Un jardin paysager à l'anglaise rayonne sur un patio italianisant dont la galerie est rythmée de colonnades. Belle salle de restaurant actuelle ; cuisine de même.

◆ De Engelse tuin omringt een patio in Italiaanse stijl, compleet met zuilengalerij. De mooie eetzaal is echt van deze tijd, net als het culinaire register.

Spéc. Parmentière de tartare d'huîtres et Saint-Jacques (oct.-avril). Double côte de veau de lait à l'ail et aux champignons. Suprêmes de pigeon au foie d'oie, girolles et oignons glacés

XX **ter Laecke,** Daalstraat 19 (Nord : 2 km par N 74 à Laak), ☎ 0 11 52 67 44, *Fax 0 11 52 59 15,* – P. AE ① MC VISA.

fermé lundi soir, mardi et merc. – **Repas** *Lunch 25* – 33/69 bc, ♀.

◆ On passe, en quelques pas, de la jolie véranda au jardin soigné de cette maison construite dans un quartier résidentiel. La cave sillonne les régions de France.

◆ In een paar stappen bent u van de mooie serre in de goed verzorgde tuin van dit huis in een rustige woonwijk. De wijnkelder doorkruist verschillende Franse streken.

X **De Postkoets,** Weg naar Zwartberg 96 (Houthalen-Oost), ☎ 0 89 38 20 79, *Fax 0 89 38 36 58,* – P – 25 à 70. ① MC VISA.

fermé du 5 au 18 fév., du 16 au 30 sept., lundi, mardi et merc. – **Repas** *Lunch 12* – 24.

◆ Connue de longue date pour ses bons p'tits plats classico-traditionnels à prix "sympa", La Malle-poste (De Postkoets) présente une carte assortie d'un trio de menus.

◆ De Postkoets staat sinds jaar en dag bekend om zijn uitstekende prijs-kwaliteitverhouding. De klassiek-traditionele menukaart wordt aangevuld met een drietal menu's.

HOUYET *5560 Namur* 534 P 21 *et* 716 I 5 – *4 411 h.*

Env. au Nord : 10 km à Celles : dalle funéraire★ dans l'église romane St-Hadelin.

Tour Léopold-Ardenne 6 ☎ 0 82 66 62 28, Fax 0 82 66 74 53.

Bruxelles 110 – Bouillon 66 – Namur 54 – Dinant 34 – Rochefort 23.

à Celles *Nord : 10 km* Ⓒ *Houyet* – ✉ *5561 Celles :*

Aub. de la Lesse, Gare de Gendron 1 (N 910, lieu-dit Gendron), ☎ 0 82 66 73 02, *aubergelesse@skynet.be, Fax 0 82 66 76 15,* – TV P. MC VISA JCB

Repas *(fermé lundi soir et mardi sauf vacances scolaires)* (taverne-rest) carte 22 à 31 – **14 ch** ☐ 57/64 – ½ P 54/57.

◆ Dans un site bucolique, à 200 m d'une rivière propice à la pratique du kayak, bâtiment récent hébergeant de grandes chambres auxquelles on accède directement par l'extérieur. Taverne-restaurant au cadre néo-rustique. Préparations bourgeoises sans chichi.

◆ Nieuw gebouw in een schitterende omgeving, op 200 m van een riviertje waar men kan kajakken. De grote kamers zijn van buitenaf rechtstreeks toegankelijk. Café-restaurant in neorustieke stijl, waar een smakelijke burgerpot wordt geserveerd.

XX **La Clochette** avec ch, r. Vêves 1, ☎ 0 82 66 65 35, *Fax 0 82 66 77 91,* – TV P. AE MC VISA

fermé 16 fév.-10 mars, 21 juin-8 juil. et lundis midis et merc. sauf en juil.-août – **Repas** *Lunch 25* – 33/45 – **7 ch** ☐ 55/70 – ½ P 57/62.

◆ Charmante auberge ardennaise où l'on fait des repas classico-traditionnels dans une salle dont les lambris s'égayent d'une collection de clochettes. Chambres proprettes.

◆ Charmante, typisch Ardense herberg, waarvan de gelambriseerde eetzaal door een verzameling bellen wordt opgevrolijkt. Klassiek-traditionele keuken en keurige kamers.

à Custinne *Nord-Est : 7 km* Ⓒ *Houyet* – ✉ *5562 Custinne :*

XX **Host. "Les Grisons"** avec ch, rte de Neufchâteau 23, ☎ 0 82 66 79 84, *Fax 0 82 66 79 85,* – rest, TV P. AE ① MC VISA

fermé fin mai, début sept. et début janv. – **Repas** *(fermé lundi et mardi)* 40/50 – **4 ch** ☐ 78/87, – 2 suites – ½ P 80/90.

◆ Hostellerie composée d'une belle demeure en pierres du pays abritant le restaurant et, au fond du jardin, d'un chalet "suisse" où vous dormirez comme une bûche. Bon accueil.

◆ Hotel-restaurant met een mooi natuurstenen huis om lekker te kunnen eten en achter in de tuin een Zwitsers chalet om lekker te kunnen slapen. Goede ontvangst.

HUISE *Oost-Vlaanderen* 533 G 17 *et* 716 D 3 – *voir à Zingem.*

La HULPE (TERHULPEN) *1310 Brabant Wallon* 533 L 18, 534 L 18 *et* 716 G 3 – *6 950 h.*

Voir *Parc★ du domaine Solvay.*

Bruxelles 20 – Charleroi 44 – Namur 54.

XXX **La Salicorne,** r. P. Broodcoorens 41, ☎ 0 2 654 01 71, *la.salicorne@yucom.be, Fax 0 2 653 71 23,* – 🅿. AE ⓓ MC VISA – *fermé 2 sem. carnaval, dern. sem. juin-2 prem. sem. juil., 2 sem. Toussaint, dim. et lundi* – **Repas** *Lunch 25* – 42/84 bc, ♀.

◆ À la périphérie de La Hulpe, villa agrandie et transformée, avec salon, riantes salles à manger et plaisante terrasse estivale face à une pièce d'eau où se jette une cascade.

◆ Deze "zeekraal" is te vinden in een verbouwde villa aan de rand van Terhulpen. Aparte zithoek, vrolijke eetzalen en zonnig terras met uitzicht op een waterval.

X **Le Gris Moulin,** r. Combattants 110, ☎ 0 2 653 10 61, *grismoulin@yahoo.fr* – AE ⓓ MC VISA

fermé 2 dern. sem. juil., dim. et lundi – **Repas** *Lunch 9* – 20/45 bc.

◆ Cette affaire gentiment tenue en famille affiche un petit air de taverne-restaurant : banquettes revêtues de velours, comptoir avec pompes à bière et mise en place simple.

◆ Gezellig eettentje dat door een familie wordt gerund. Het eenvoudige interieur wordt opgeluisterd met fluwelen bankjes. Aan de bar kan tapbier worden besteld.

HULSHOUT *2235 Antwerpen* 533 N 16 *et* 716 H 2 – *8 813 h.*

Bruxelles 51 – Antwerpen 40 – Mechelen 27 – Turnhout 37.

XX ✿ **Hof Ter Hulst** (Schroven), Kerkstraat 19, ☎ 0 15 25 34 40, *hofterhulst@skynet.be, Fax 0 15 25 34 36* – 🅿 – 25. AE ⓓ MC VISA – *fermé fin août-début sept., 2 sem. en janv., mardi et sam. midi* – **Repas** *Lunch 26* – 40/73 bc, carte 56 à 73.

◆ Estimée pour sa fine cuisine vivant avec son temps, cette ravissante villa de style fermette vous attable dans un cadre rustico-actuel des plus avenants.

◆ Deze prachtige villa in boerderijstijl nodigt uit om aan tafel te gaan in een modern interieur met rustieke accenten. De fijne eigentijdse keuken is veelbelovend.

Spéc. Tarte au thon, avocat, tomate et mozzarella (été). Rognons de veau et pommes de terre sarladaises. Ravioles de foie gras au chou vert, cappuccino de champignons (automme-hiver)

HUY (HOEI) *4500 Liège* 533 O 19, 534 O 19 *et* 716 I 4 – *19 297 h.*

Voir *Collégiale Notre-Dame★ : trésor★* Z – *Fort★ : ≤★★* Z.

Musée : *communal★* Z **M.**

Env. par N 617 : 7,5 km à Amay : chasse★ et sarcophage mérovingien★ dans la Collégiale St-Georges – par N 617 : 10 km à Jehay-Bodegnée : collections★ dans le château★ de Jehay.

⛳ *par ④ : 11 km à Andenne, Ferme du Moulin, Stud 52 ☎ 0 85 84 34 04, Fax 0 85 84 34 04.*

ℹ *Quai de Namur 1 ☎ 0 85 21 29 15, tourisme@huy.be, Fax 0 85 23 29 44.*

Bruxelles 83 ⑤ – Namur 35 ④ – Liège 33 ①

Plan page ci-contre

Sirius sans rest, quai de Compiègne 47 (par ① : 1,5 km), ☎ 0 85 21 24 00, *info@hotelsirius.be, Fax 0 85 21 24 01* – 🅿 – 25 à 50. AE ⓓ MC VISA.

fermé 28 juin-11 juil. et 20 déc.-2 janv. – **24 ch** ☕ 72/113, – 2 suites.

◆ Hôtel de bon confort établi aux portes de la ville. Actuelles et lumineuses, les chambres sont toutes identiques mais celles situées en façade offrent la vue sur la Meuse.

◆ Comfortabel hotel aan de rand van de stad. De moderne, lichte kamers zijn allemaal eender, maar die aan de voorkant kijken uit op de Maas.

X **Le Sorgho Rouge** 1er étage, quai d'Autrebande 1/01, ☎ 0 85 21 41 88, ≤, Cuisine chinoise – AE ⓓ MC VISA Z n

fermé 3 sem. en juil. et mardi – **Repas** *Lunch 12* – 18/39, ♀.

◆ Restaurant chinois très fiable dominant le pont Roi Baudouin qui enjambe la Meuse. Meubles et objets d'art de l'Empire du Milieu égayent sobrement la salle au "look eighties".

◆ Goede Chinees boven de Koning Boudewijnbrug over de Maas. Meubelen en kunstvoorwerpen uit het Rijk van het Midden sieren bescheiden de eetzaal met zijn "eighties look".

X **Li Cwerneu,** Grand'Place 2, ☎ 0 85 25 55 55, *flypiet@swing.be, Fax 0 85 25 55 55,* – MC VISA Z a

fermé 2 sem. en mars, 2 sem. en nov., 2 sem. en juin, lundi et mardi – **Repas** *Lunch 25* – carte 31 à 42, ♀.

◆ Vénérable petite maison hutoise blottie contre l'hôtel de ville. Salle mignonne et chaleureuse où l'on se repaît d'une cuisine féminine bien montée, volontiers inventive.

◆ Goed restaurant in een karakteristiek oud pand naast het stadhuis. Gezellige eetzaal, waar inventieve gerechten worden opgediend die een vrouwelijke hand verraden.

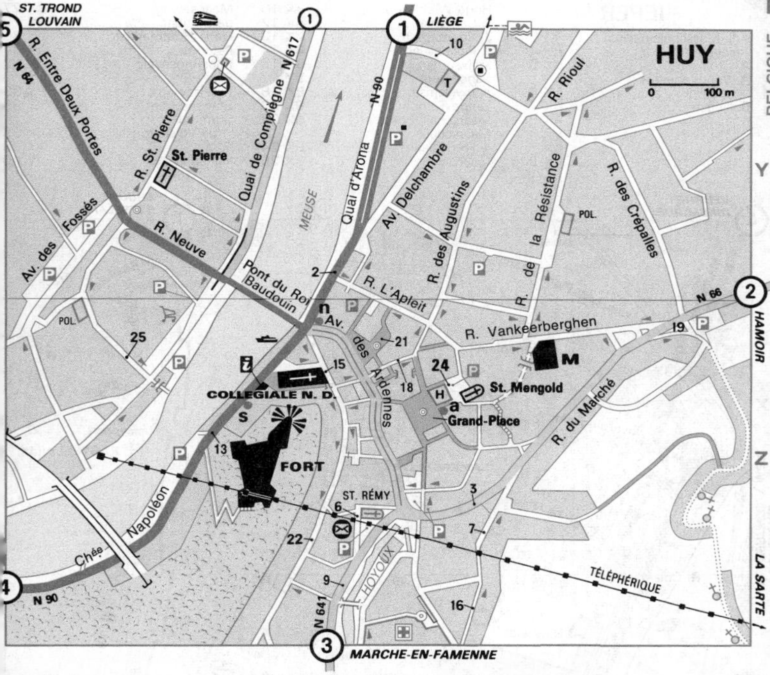

Autrebande (Quai d')	Y 2	Joseph-Lebeau (Av.)	Y 10	St-Denis (Pl.)	Z 19
Condroz (Av. du)	Z 3	Namur (Quai de)	Z 13	St-Pierre (R.)	Y
Foulons (R. des)	Z 6	Neuve (R.)	Y	St-Séverin (Pl.)	Z 21
Haut-Chêne (R. du)	Z 7	Pont (R. du)	Z 15	Sous-le-Château (R.)	Z 22
Hoyoux (Av. du)	Z 9	Reine (R. de la)	Z 16	Verte (Place)	Z 24
		Rôtisseurs (R. des)	Z 18	Vieux Pont (R. du)	Z 25

Le Guide change, changez de guide tous les ans.

IEPER (YPRES) *8900 West-Vlaanderen* 533 C 17 *et* 716 B 3 – *35 081 h.*

Voir *Halles aux draps★ (Lakenhalle)* ABX.

Musée : *In Flanders Fields Museum★★* ABX **M**[4].

18 au Sud-Est : 7 km à Hollebeke, Eekhofstraat 14 ☎ 0 57 20 04 36, Fax 0 57 21 89 58 - 9 Industrielaan 24 ☎ 0 57 21 66 88, Fax 0 57 21 82 10.

Grote Markt 34 ☎ 0 57 22 85 84, toerisme@ieper.be, Fax 0 57 22 85 89.

Bruxelles 125 ② – Brugge 52 ① – Kortrijk 32 ② – Dunkerque 48 ⑥

Plan page suivante

Novotel Sint-Jacobsstraat 15, ☎ 0 57 42 96 00, *H3172@accor-hotels.com, Fax 0 57 42 96 01*, – – 25 à 120. AE VISA. rest
Repas *Lunch 13 bc* – 25/35 – 14 – **122 ch** 110/125 – ½ P 89/118. BX b
◆ Hôtel implanté sur le site d'un ancien couvent dont certains éléments ont été maintenus en façade. Les chambres sont bien tenues et conformes aux standards de la chaîne.
◆ Novotel op de plek van een oud klooster, waarvan enkele overblijfselen in de gevel zijn opgenomen. De kamers zijn goed onderhouden en conform de standaard van deze hotelketen.

Ariane, Slachthuisstraat 58, ☎ 0 57 21 82 18, *info@ariane.be, Fax 0 57 21 87 99*, , , , – – 25 à 90. AE VISA. rest AX e
Repas *(fermé sam. midi) Lunch 10* – carte 23 à 44 – **51 ch** 100 – ½ P 68/93.
◆ Immeuble récent devancé d'une pelouse égayée de massifs de fleurs. Paisibles chambres sobrement équipées et agrément d'une pièce d'eau. Table misant sur une carte traditionnelle. Terrasse estivale s'ouvrant sur le jardin.
◆ Nieuw gebouw met een gazon dat door bloemperken wordt opgefleurd. Rustige kamers met eenvoudige voorzieningen en een mooi uitzicht op de waterpartij. Het restaurant mikt op traditie. Aangenaam terras in de zomer, aan de tuinzijde.

IEPER

Adj. Masscheleinlaan. . . . . BX 2
Arsenaalstr. . . . . AY 4
A. Stoffelstr. . . . . BX 5
A. Vandenpeere-
boompl. . . . . AX 6
Bollingstr. . . . . BX 7
Boterstraat . . . . AX 8
Diksmuidestr. . . . . BX
G. de Stuersstr. . . . . AX
Grote Markt . . . . BX 9
Hoge Wieltjesgracht . . . . . BX 10
J. Capronstr. . . . . AX 12
J. Coomansstr. . . . . AX 13
J. Picanollaan . . . . BY 14
Kalfvaartstr. . . . . BX 15
Kanonweg . . . . BY 17
Kauwekijnstr. . . . . BX 18
Lange Torhoutstr. . . . . BX 22
Maarschalk Fochlaan . . . . . AX 23
Maarschalk
Frenchlaan . . . . BX 24
Meensestr. . . . . BX 26
Meenseweg . . . . BX 27
de Montstr. . . . . AY 29
Oude Houtmarktstr. . . . . . . BX 30
Patersstr. . . . . AX 31
Poperingseweg . . . . AX 32
Rijselsestr. . . . . BXY
Rijselseweg . . . . BY 33
Stationsstraat . . . . AXY 35
Surmont
de Volsbergestr. . . . . . . ABX 36
Tempelstr. . . . . AX 38
Wateringsstr. . . . . BY 40

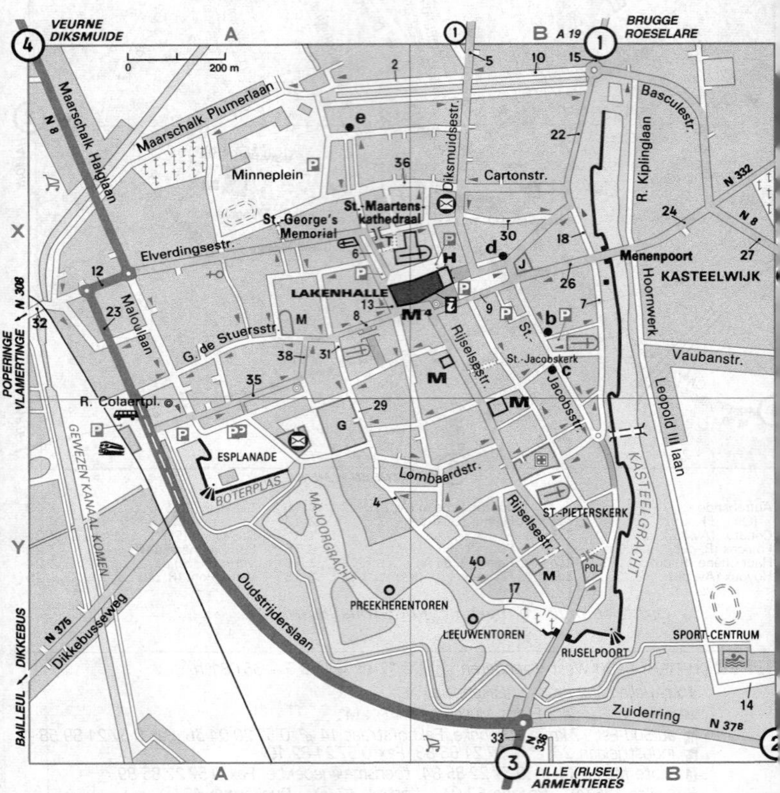

Flanders Lodge, Industrielaan 19 (par ① : 2,5 km), ✆ 0 57 21 70 00, *bw-ieper@skynet.be, Fax 0 57 21 94 74*, – rest, – 25 à 120. AE VISA – *fermé 24 déc.-2 janv. et dim.* – **Repas Tybaert** Lunch 14 – 22/38 bc – **39 ch** 69/89 – ½ P 29/49.

• Dans une zone industrielle, grand bâtiment tout de bois vêtu dont les chambres, bien insonorisées, sont rassemblées dans une aile sur l'arrière. Espaces pour séminaires. Salle des repas confortable et chaleureuse, agencée sur deux niveaux.

• Groot houten gebouw op een industrieterrein. De kamers zijn afdoende voorzien van geluidsisolatie en liggen gegroepeerd in een vleugel aan de achterzijde. Faciliteiten voor congressen. De eetzaal telt twee verdiepingen en is warm en comfortabel.

Albion sans rest, Sint-Jacobsstraat 28, ✆ 0 57 20 02 20, *info@albionhotel.be, Fax 0 57 20 02 15* – AE VISA. BX c
18 ch 78/96.

• Belle demeure ayant naguère abrité des services administratifs. Communs spacieux aménagés dans la note Art déco. Chambres à l'identique. Accueil familial.

• In dit mooie gebouw waren vroeger overheidsdiensten gehuisvest. Royale gemeenschappelijke ruimten in art-decostijl. De kamers zijn identiek. Vriendelijke ontvangst.

Gasthof 't Zweerd, Grote Markt 2, ☎ 0 57 20 04 75, *zweerd@pandora.be*, *Fax 0 57 21 78 96* – |‡| TV – 🏔 100. AE ⓓ MC VISA. ⚘ rest BX d
Repas *(fermé mardi)* Lunch 12 – 22/52 bc – **17 ch** ☕ 70 – ½ P 47.
◆ Sur le Grote Markt, petite affaire tenue en famille depuis une vingtaine d'années. Les chambres, d'un confort moderne, viennent d'être rafraîchies. Salle à manger classiquement aménagée.
◆ Dit hotelletje, centraal gelegen aan de Grote Markt, bestaat al zo'n 20 jaar en wordt door een familie gerund. De kamers bieden modern comfort en hebben niet lang geleden een facelift gehad. De eetzaal is in klassieke stijl ingericht.

à Elverdinge *Nord-Ouest : 5 km* C *Ieper* – ✉ *9606 Elverdinge :*

XXX **Host. St-Nicolas** (Vanderhaeghe), Veurnseweg 532 (sur N 8), ☎ 0 57 20 06 22, *st.nicolas@pi.be*, *Fax 0 57 46 98 99*, 余 – ▤ P. AE MC VISA. ⚘
fermé 18 juil.-10 août, sam. midi, dim. soir et lundi – **Repas** Lunch 39 – 54/95 bc, carte 49 à 84, 𝕐.
◆ Élégante villa moderne agrémentée d'une belle terrasse d'été dressée côté jardin, près d'une pièce d'eau. Fine cuisine au goût du jour, cave bien montée et service stylé.
◆ Deze sierlijke moderne villa heeft een mooi terras aan de tuinzijde en een waterpartij. Fijne eigentijdse keuken, goede wijnkelder en stijlvolle bediening.
Spéc. Gravlax. Pommes de terre écrasées à l'œuf poché et crevettes grises, sauce mousseline. Turbotin grillé, croquette de crabe, sauce mousseline aux fines herbes et Nantua

à Zillebeke *par ③ : 3 km* C *Ieper* – ✉ *8902 Zillebeke :*

XX **De Steenen Haene,** Komenseweg 21, ☎ 0 57 20 54 86, *info@desteenenhaene.be*, *Fax 0 57 21 50 42*, 余 – P. AE MC VISA
fermé 16 fév.-3 mars, 2 dern. sem. août, mardi soir et merc. – **Repas** Lunch 30 bc – 29/64 bc.
◆ Une fermette familiale à la campagne, où poutres apparentes, parements de briques et mobilier rustique président à un décor empreint d'authenticité. Terrasse ensoleillée.
◆ Plattelandsboerderijtje, waar de hanenbalken, het bakstenen parementwerk en het rustieke meubilair voor een authentieke uitstraling zorgen. Zonovergoten terras.

ITTERBEEK *Vlaams-Brabant* 533 K 18 – *voir à Bruxelles, environs.*

ITTRE (ITTER) *1460 Brabant Wallon* 533 K 19, 534 K 19 *et* 716 F 4 – *5 729 h.*
Bruxelles 32 – Nivelles 10 – Soignies 21.

XX **L'estaminet de la Couronne,** Grand'Place 3, ☎ 0 67 64 63 85, *estaminet@skynet.be*, *Fax 0 67 64 89 18*, 余 – ▤. AE MC VISA
fermé 1 sem. en fév., 2 sem. en août, dim. soir, lundi et mardi – **Repas** Lunch 22 – 38.
◆ Ce charmant petit restaurant côtoyant l'église a succédé à un ancien estaminet. Salle à manger de notre temps et carte actuelle lorgnant vers le Sud-Ouest de la France.
◆ Dit charmant restaurantje tegenover de kerk was vroeger een oude kroeg. De eetzaal is van deze tijd. Menukaart met invloeden uit Zuid-West Frankrijk.

IVOZ-RAMET *Liège* 533 R 19, 534 R 19 *et* 716 J 4 – *voir à Liège, environs.*

IXELLES (ELSENE) *Région de Bruxelles-Capitale – voir à Bruxelles.*

IZEGEM *8870 West-Vlaanderen* 533 E 17 *et* 716 C 3 – *26 551 h.*
Bruxelles 103 – Kortrijk 13 – Brugge 36 – Roeselare 7.

XX **Ter Weyngaerd,** Burg. Vandenbogaerdelaan 32, ☎ 0 51 30 95 41, *info@terweyngaerd.be*, *Fax 0 51 31 96 52*, 余 – AE ⓓ MC VISA
fermé 1 sem. Pâques, 21 juil.-11 août, mardi soir, merc. et dim. soir – **Repas** Lunch 16 – 26/60 bc.
◆ Demeure bourgeoise avec jardin et terrasse ensoleillée, conviant à sa table habitués et hommes d'affaires. Salle de restaurant d'esprit classique, comme la cuisine.
◆ Herenhuis met tuin en zonnig terras, waar voornamelijk zakenlieden en vaste gasten komen. De eetzaal is zowel qua inrichting als qua keuken in klassieke stijl.

XX **Retro,** Meensestraat 159, ☎ 0 51 30 03 06, *Fax 0 51 30 03 06*, 余 – ▤. AE MC VISA
fermé 1 sem. en fév., 3 sem. en août, sam. midi, dim. soir et lundi – **Repas** 28/66 bc.
◆ Adresse avoisinant le centre, Retro a su se faire une place dans le concert de fourchettes izegemoises. Véranda "no smoking" et restaurant d'été. Recettes au goût du jour.
◆ Deze eetgelegenheid nabij het centrum neemt een geheel eigen plaats in tussen de restaurants van Izegem. Serre voor niet-rokers en buiten eten in de zomer. Eigentijdse keuken.

De Dischhoeve, Meenseteenweg 72, ✆ 0 51 31 07 01, *de.dischhoeve@skynet.be Fax 0 51 31 72 42,* – P. AE MC VISA
fermé sam. midi, dim. midi, lundi soir et mardi – **Repas** Lunch 16 – carte 42 à 55.
◆ Petit refuge gourmand dans une ancienne ferme protégée de fossés. Cadre agreste et atmosphère rustique en salle. Cuisinier-sommelier suivant le tempo culinaire du moment.
◆ In deze oude hoeve met slotgracht komen fijnproevers aan hun trekken. Rustieke eetzaal waar de chef-kok annex sommelier eigentijdse culinaire hoogstandjes vertoont.

Bistro d'Halve Maan, Melkmarkt 12, ✆ 0 51 31 84 22, *Fax 0 51 31 84 22,* – MC VISA
fermé 5 juil.-3 août, lundi et mardi – **Repas** carte 24 à 32.
◆ Au bord d'une placette, maison localement appréciée pour ses plats traditionnels énoncés sur ardoise, son service aimable et sa sage politique de prix.
◆ Dit restaurant aan een plein valt bij de bevolking zeer in de smaak vanwege de traditionele schotels, de vriendelijke service en de schappelijke prijzen.

IZEL *Luxembourg belge* 534 R 24 – *voir à Florenville.*

JABBEKE *8490 West-Vlaanderen* 533 D 15 *et* 716 C 2 – *13 692 h.*
Musée : *Permeke★ (Provinciaal Museum Constant Permeke).*
Bruxelles 102 – Brugge 13 – Kortrijk 57 – Oostende 17.

Haeneveld, Krauwerstraat 1, ✆ 0 50 81 27 00, *info@haeneveld.be, Fax 0 50 81 12 77,* – 25 à 140. MC VISA
Repas *(fermé 23 fév.-9 mars, 27 sept.-11 oct., mardi et merc. soir)* Lunch 35 – 50 – **8 ch** 69/92 – ½ P 96/120.
◆ Cette ferme flamande proche de l'autoroute s'entoure d'un écrin verdoyant. Les chambres, vastes et confortables, sont aménagées dans une aile récente. Au restaurant, répertoire culinaire classico-créatif. On mange en terrasse les beaux jours.
◆ Deze Vlaamse boerderij bij de snelweg wordt door een tuin omgeven. De kamers in de onlangs aangebouwde vleugel zijn ruim en comfortabel. In het restaurant worden creatieve en klassieke gerechten geserveerd. Bij mooi weer wordt het terras opgedekt.

à Snellegem *Sud-Est : 3 km* C *Jabbeke* – ✉ *8490 Snellegem :*

't Oosthof, Oostmoerstraat 1, ✆ 0 50 81 16 53, *mail@oosthof.be, Fax 0 50 81 46 56,* – P. AE MC VISA
fermé 16 fév.-4 mars, du 12 au 28 juil., du 6 au 10 déc., lundi soir, mardi soir et merc. – **Repas** Lunch 20 – 38/68 bc.
◆ La ferme fortifiée d'autrefois, recluse derrière ses douves, a mis bas les armes et s'est donnée une nouvelle mission : régaler ses hôtes d'une cuisine classico-bourgeoise.
◆ Deze versterkte hoeve van weleer, die zich achter zijn gracht had verschanst, heeft zich overgegeven aan een nieuwe taak : de gasten onthalen op klassiek-traditionele spijzen.

à Stalhille *Nord : 3 km* C *Jabbeke* – ✉ *8490 Stalhille :*

Hove Ter Hille sans rest, Nachtegaalstraat 46 (sur N 377), ✆ 0 50 81 11 97, *Fax 050 81 45 17,* –
14 ch 50/60.
◆ Une mise au vert à la ferme, ça vous tente ? Entre Brugge et Oostende, chambres agréables et studios pourvus de kitchenettes pour permettre des séjours prolongés.
◆ Behoefte aan groen ? Dat biedt deze boerderij tussen Brugge en Oostende volop. Aangename kamers en studio's met kitchenette voor een langer verblijf.

JALHAY *4845 Liège* 533 U 19, 534 U 19 *et* 716 K 4 – *7 712 h.*
Bruxelles 130 – Liège 40 – Eupen 12 – Spa 13 – Verviers 8.

La Crémaillère, r. Fagne 17, ✆ 0 87 64 73 14, *info@la-cremaillere.be, Fax 0 87 64 70 20,* – P – 30. AE MC VISA. rest
fermé 1re quinz. juil. et 2e quinz. déc. – **Repas** *(fermé mardi, merc. et après 20 h 30)* Lunch 20 – 29/36 – **8 ch** 45/79 – ½ P 55/65.
◆ Auberge familiale disposant de chambres en nombre limité, amples et bien équipées, toutes aménagées dans l'annexe située à deux pas du bâtiment principal. Oiseaux naturalisés, assiettes et bibelots décorent la salle de restaurant bourgeoise.
◆ Familieherberg met in de nabijgelegen dependance een beperkt aantal kamers, die ruim en goed geëquipeerd zijn. Opgezette vogels, borden en snuisterijen decoreren de eetzaal die in typische bourgeoisstijl is ingericht.

XX **Au Vieux Hêtre** avec ch, rte de la Fagne 18, ☎ 0 87 64 70 92, *vieuxhetre@skynet.be, Fax 0 87 64 78 54*, ☂, ☂, 🚲 – TV P. MC VISA
fermé lundi, mardi et merc. sauf en juil.-août – **Repas** Lunch 25 – 22/30 – **12 ch** ☐ 65/90 – ½ P 55/75.
◆ Une fresque, œuvre d'un célèbre auteur de BD, égaye la salle à manger de cette maison ancienne. Terrasse d'été, jardin avec volière et pièce d'eau. Chambres rénovées.
◆ Een muurschildering van een beroemde striptekenaar sieren de eetzaal van dit oude pand. Terras in de zomer, tuin met volière en waterpartij. De kamers zijn gerenoveerd.

JETTE *Région de Bruxelles-Capitale* 533 K 17 – *voir à Bruxelles.*

JODOIGNE (GELDENAKEN) *1370 Brabant Wallon* 533 O 18 *et* 716 H 3 – *11 754 h.*
Bruxelles 50 – Namur 36 – Charleroi 52 – Hasselt 50 – Liège 61 – Tienen 12.

à Mélin *(Malen) Nord-Ouest : 5 km* C *Jodoigne* – ✉ *1370 Mélin :*

XX **La Villa du Hautsart,** r. Hussompont 29, ☎ 0 10 81 40 10, *villa.hausart@lavilladuhausart.com, Fax 0 10 81 44 34*, ☂ – P. AE ⓓ MC VISA
fermé janv., dim. soir, lundi et mardi – **Repas** Lunch 20 – 30/65 bc.
◆ La Villa du Hautsart a choisi pour vous mettre à table un village pittoresque. Menus attrayants, et terroir à la fête dans les assiettes. Vins des régions de France.
◆ Mélin is een pittoresk dorp waar u heerlijk kunt tafelen. Aantrekkelijke menu's met streekgerechten. De wijn komt uit verschillende Franse regio's.

JUPILLE *Luxembourg belge* 534 S 21 – *voir à La Roche-en-Ardenne.*

JUPILLE-SUR-MEUSE *Liège* 533 S 19, 534 S 19 *et* 716 J 4 – *voir à Liège, périphérie.*

KALMTHOUT *2920 Antwerpen* 533 L 14 *et* 716 G 1 – *17 369 h.*
Bruxelles 76 – Antwerpen 22 – Roosendaal 20 – Turnhout 42.

XX **Keienhof,** Putsesteenweg 133 (Sud-Ouest : 2 km sur N 111, De Kalmthoutse Heide), ☎ 0 3 666 25 50, *info@keienhof.be, Fax 0 3 666 25 56*, ☂ – P. AE ⓓ MC VISA
fermé 3 et 4 fév., du 13 au 17 avril, du 3 au 25 août, dim. et lundi – **Repas** 28/80 bc, ♀.
◆ En été, les terrasses de cette gentilhommière d'inspiration coloniale sont dressées tout contre la forêt. Plats de saison et suggestions orales. Vins du monde.
◆ De terrassen van dit kasteeltje in koloniale stijl liggen in een lommerrijk bos. Seizoengebonden gerechten en mondeling aangekondigde dagsuggesties. Wereldwijnen.

KANNE *3770 Limburg* C *Riemst 15 755 h.* 533 T 18 *et* 716 K 3.
Bruxelles 118 – Maastricht 6 – Hasselt 37 – Liège 30.

 **Limburgia,** Op 't Broek 4, ☎ 0 12 45 46 00, *hotellimburgia@pandora.be, Fax 0 12 45 66 28*, ☂ – TV P – 🏠 25 à 75. AE MC VISA. ✂
fermé du 22 au 31 déc. – **Repas** *(fermé merc.)* (dîner seult sauf dim.) carte 25 à 35 – **19 ch** ☐ 60/100.
◆ L'hôtel, situé à la frontière belgo-néerlandaise, a dû en voir défiler du monde depuis 1936, année de sa création... Une aile récente regroupe des chambres sans reproche.
◆ Dit hotel aan de Belgisch-Nederlandse grens heeft sinds 1936, het jaar van zijn oprichting, al heel wat gasten ontvangen. De onberispelijke kamers liggen in de nieuwe vleugel.

KAPELLEN *Antwerpen* 533 L 15 *et* 716 G 2 – *voir à Antwerpen, environs.*

KASTERLEE *2460 Antwerpen* 533 O 15 *et* 716 H 2 – *17 664 h.*
☐ *Gemeentehuis* ☎ *0 14 85 99 15, toerisme@kasterlee.be, Fax 0 14 85 07 77.*
Bruxelles 77 – Antwerpen 49 – Hasselt 47 – Turnhout 9.

 **De Watermolen** ⑤, Houtum 61 (par Geelsebaan), ☎ 0 14 85 23 74, *info@watermolen.be, Fax 0 14 85 23 70*, ←, ☂, ☂, 🚲 – TV P – 🏠 25. AE MC VISA. ✂ rest
fermé 16 août-4 sept. et du 3 au 21 janv. – **Repas** Lunch 35 – 46/89 bc, ♀ – ***Brasserie De Brustele*** 25, ♀ – ☐ 10 – **18 ch** 84/106 – ½ P 84/105.
◆ L'enseigne ne raconte pas d'histoire : vous dormirez dans un ancien moulin à eau qui tirait sa force de la Kleine Nete, charmante rivière visible depuis les calmes chambres. Au Brustele, repas de qualité à savourer dans une lumineuse salle de type brasserie.
◆ Hier logeert u in een oude watermolen die zijn kracht uit de Kleine Nete haalde, het riviertje dat vanuit de rustige kamers te zien is. In een prettige, lichte eetzaal van brasserie Brustele kunt u lekker eten.

Den en Heuvel, Geelsebaan 72, ✆ 0 14 85 04 97, *info@denenheuvel.be, Fax 0 14 85 04 96*, 🍽, 🚲 – 📺 🅿 – 🎭 25 à 100. AE MC VISA
fermé du 17 au 31 juil. et du 1er au 15 janv. – **Repas** 35/85 bc, 🍷 – ☕ 10 – **24 ch** 60/95 – ½ P 73/78.
◆ Immeuble moderne où touristes et clientèle d'affaires séjournent dans des chambres rénovées de diverses tailles. Salles de séminaires judicieusement équipées. À table, préparations classico-traditionnelles avec une préférence marquée pour le homard.
◆ Modern gebouw met gerenoveerde kamers van verschillende grootte, waar vooral toeristen en zakenmensen komen. Vergaderzalen met tal van faciliteiten. Restaurant met een klassiek-traditionele keuken en veel kreeft op de kaart.

Kastelhof, Lichtaartsebaan 33 (Sud-Ouest sur N 123), ✆ 0 14 85 18 43, *Fax 0 14 85 31 25*, 🍽 – 🅿. AE ⓓ MC VISA
fermé du 10 au 25 juil., mardi, merc., sam. midi et après 20 h 30 – **Repas** *Lunch 38* – 47/77 bc, 🍷.
◆ Villa dodue dont le jardin a été complètement redessiné il y a quelques temps. La terrasse est plaisante quand le soleil brille. Choix de vins exceptionnel.
◆ Fraaie villa, waarvan de tuin onlangs volledig nieuw is aangelegd. Als de zon schijnt, is het terras favoriet. Uitstekende wijnkelder.

Potiron, Geelsebaan 73, ✆ 0 14 85 04 25, *d.verheyen@proximedia.be, Fax 0 14 85 04 26*, 🍽 – ▤ 🅿. AE MC VISA. ✈
fermé 23 fév.-11 mars, 2 prem. sem. sept., merc. et sam. midi – **Repas** 25/41 bc.
◆ La grosse courge, excellente en soupe, a prêté son nom à cette jeune affaire familiale. Carte au goût du jour complétée en saison d'une ardoise de suggestions.
◆ De pompoen, die zo heerlijk is als soep, heeft zijn naam verbonden aan dit jonge familiebedrijf. De eigentijdse menukaart wordt in het hoogseizoen aangevuld met suggesties.

à Lichtaart *Sud-Ouest : 6 km* 🄲 *Kasterlee* – ✉ *2460 Lichtaart :*

De Residentie, Steenfortstraat 5, ✆ 0 14 55 18 34, *info@residentie.be, Fax 0 14 55 18 35*, 🍽, 🏋, ♨, 🏊 – 🛗 📺 🅿 – 🎭 25 à 300. AE ⓓ MC VISA. ✈
Repas *Lunch 29* – carte 33 à 62 – **36 ch** ☕ 79/104 – ½ P 81/109.
◆ Pelotonnée dans un paisible environnement boisé, grande villa des années 1970 renfermant des chambres de bon séjour. Piscine couverte, salle de remise en forme et sauna.
◆ Grote villa uit de jaren 1970 in een rustige en bosrijke omgeving, met kamers die garant staan voor een prettig verblijf. Overdekt zwembad, fitnessruimte en sauna.

De Pastorie, Plaats 2, ✆ 0 14 55 77 86, *depastorie@belgacom.net, Fax 0 14 55 77 94*, 🍽 – 🅿. AE ⓓ MC VISA. ✈
fermé 16 août-6 sept., lundi et mardi – **Repas** *Lunch 33* – 50/80 bc, 🍷.
◆ Au cœur de Lichtaart, ancien presbytère du 17e s. agrémenté d'un jardin soigné et d'une agréable terrasse. En cave, des crus qui ont de la bouteille.
◆ Deze 17e-eeuwse pastorie in het hart van Lichtaart heeft een goed verzorgde tuin en een aangenaam terras. Eerbiedwaardige oude wijnen in de kelder.

Keravic avec ch, Herentalsesteenweg 72, ✆ 0 14 55 78 01, *info@keravic.be, Fax 0 14 55 78 16*, 🍽, 🌳, 🚲 – 📺 🅿 – 🎭 25. AE ⓓ MC VISA. ✈ ch
Repas *(fermé 13 juil.-4 août, 25 déc.-2 janv., sam. midi, dim. et lundi midi) Lunch 32* – 44/77 bc – **11 ch** ☕ 79/104 – ½ P 105/133.
◆ Typique hostellerie flamande dans son écrin verdoyant. Classiquement agencée, l'agréable salle à manger à touche rustique entretient une ambiance feutrée.
◆ Typisch Vlaamse hostellerie in een groene omgeving. Prettige klassieke eetzaal met een rustieke noot, waar een gedempte sfeer hangt.

KEERBERGEN *3140 Vlaams-Brabant* 533 M 16 *et* 716 G 2 – *12 110 h.*
🏌18 *Vlieghavenlaan 50* ✆ *0 15 23 49 61, Fax 0 15 23 57 37.*
Bruxelles 34 – Antwerpen 36 – Leuven 20.

The Paddock, R. Lambertslaan 4, ✆ 0 15 51 19 34, *the.paddock@skynet.be, Fax 0 15 52 90 08*, 🍽 – 🅿. AE ⓓ MC VISA
fermé 9 fév.-3 mars, 16 août-9 sept., mardi et merc. – **Repas** *Lunch 37* – 90 bc, carte 52 à 92.
◆ Céder aux plaisirs de la table dans une superbe villa nichée au beau milieu d'un véritable havre de verdure ? C'est ce qui va vous arriver au Paddock ! Terrasse ombragée.
◆ In deze schitterende villa verscholen tussen het groen zult u geen weerstand kunnen bieden aan het genot van een gastronomische maaltijd. Lommerrijk terras.
Spéc. Asperges régionales, sauce au Champagne (avril-23 juin). Côte de veau de lait au poivre et genièvre. Mille-feuille de framboises, glace au yoghourt

XX **Hof van Craynbergh,** Mechelsebaan 113, ✆ 0 15 51 65 94, *info@hofvancraynbergh.be, Fax 0 15 51 65 94,* 🏡 - P. AE ① MC VISA. ✈
fermé 1 sem. Pâques, 19 juil.-6 août, 26 déc.-6 janv., sam. midi, dim. soir, lundi et merc. midi – **Repas** Lunch 30 – 45/80 bc.
◆ Aux abords du village, sur une butte, villa entourée d'un parc boisé et fleuri. En saison, l'asperge y est mise à bon nombre de sauces. Choix de bordeaux.
◆ Villa op een heuvel aan de rand van het dorp. In de tuin groeien veel bomen en bloemen. In het seizoen allerlei gerechten met asperges. Goede keuze bordeaux.

XX **Ming Dynasty,** Haachtsebaan 20, ✆ 0 15 52 03 79, *info@mingdynasty.be, Fax 0 15 52 27 22,* 🏡, Cuisine chinoise, ouvert jusqu'à 23 h – ▤. AE ① MC VISA
fermé mardi – **Repas** Lunch 19 – carte 22 à 51.
◆ Salle à manger plaisamment décorée et confortable terrasse estivale s'offrent de guider votre gourmandise à travers les provinces chinoises. Multitude de menus et de vins.
◆ In de fraai gedecoreerde eetzaal en op het gerieflijke terras kunt u een culinaire ontdekkingsreis maken door de Chinese provincies. Ruime keuze aan menu's en wijnen.

XX **Postelein,** Tremelobaan 136a, ✆ 0 16 53 86 89, *postelein@busmail.net, Fax 0 16 53 97 56,* 🏡 – P. AE ① MC VISA
fermé 2e quinz. mars, 2e quinz. sept., lundi et mardi – **Repas** 31/94 bc, ♀.
◆ Fringante villa ouverte sur un jardin boisé. Grand salon aux sièges en cuir clair, salle de restaurant garnie de meubles en rotin, façon "colonies", et tables bien espacées.
◆ Vrolijke villa met een tuin vol bomen. Grote salon met leren fauteuils, eetzaal met rotanmeubelen in koloniale stijl en veel ruimte tussen de tafels.

KEMMEL *8956 West-Vlaanderen* C *Heuvelland 8 332 h.* 533 B 18 *et* 716 B 3.

ℹ *Reningelststraat 11 ✆ 0 57 45 04 55, heuvelland@toerismevlaanderen.be, Fax 0 57 44 89 99.*

Bruxelles 133 – Brugge 63 – Ieper 11 – Lille 33.

XXX **Host. Kemmelberg** 🐎 avec ch, Kemmelbergweg 34, ✆ 0 57 44 41 45, *info@kemmelberg.be, Fax 0 57 44 40 89,* ≤ plaine des Flandres, 🏡 – TV P – 🏃 25. AE ① MC VISA
fermé 12 janv.-13 fév., du 12 au 29 juil., dim. soir et lundi – **Repas** Lunch 40 bc – 10/75 bc – **16 ch** ☕ 62/110 – ½ P 74/92.
◆ "Le plat pays qui est le mien... " : panorama saisissant sur la plaine des Flandres ponctuée à l'horizon de terrils fossiles. Chambres dotées de balcons.
◆ Magnifiek panorama van Vlaanderen, "mijn vlakke Vlaanderenland...", met zwarte slakkenbergen die zich tegen de horizon aftekenen. Alle kamers hebben een balkon.

KESSEL-LO *Vlaams-Brabant* 533 N 17 *et* 716 H 3 – *voir à Leuven.*

KLEMSKERKE *West-Vlaanderen* 533 D 15 *et* 716 C 2 – *voir à De Haan.*

KLUISBERGEN *9690 Oost-Vlaanderen* 533 G 18 *et* 716 D 3 – *6 054 h.*

Bruxelles 67 – Kortrijk 24 – Gent 39 – Valenciennes 75.

XXX **Te Winde,** Parklaan 17 (Berchem), ✆ 0 55 38 92 74, *Fax 0 55 38 62 92,* 🏡 – AE ① MC VISA. ✈
fermé sem. carnaval, du 12 au 30 juil., dim. soir, lundi et mardi soir – **Repas** Lunch 50 – carte 44 à 66.
◆ Imposante villa bordée d'un luxuriant jardin arboré et agrémenté d'une pièce d'eau. Salle de restaurant cossue, véranda, belle terrasse, spécialités belges et bons millésimes.
◆ Imposante villa en een weelderige tuin met bomen en een waterpartij. Rijk aandoende eetzaal, serre, mooi terras, Belgische specialiteiten en wijnen van goede jaargangen.

sur le Kluisberg *(Mont de l'Enclus) Sud : 4 km* C *Kluisbergen* – ✉ *9690 Kluisbergen :*

🏨 **La Sablière,** Bergstraat 40, ✆ 0 55 38 95 64, *Fax 0 55 38 78 11,* 🏡 – |‡| TV P. AE MC VISA. ✈ ch
fermé sem. carnaval, dern. sem. août et déc. – **Repas** *(fermé vend.)* Lunch 14 – 55/79 bc – **10 ch** ☕ 80/90 – ½ P 70/120.
◆ Beaux rêves en perspective : le marchand de sable passe forcément au sommet du Kluisberg ! Quelques chambres rénovées bénéficient d'une décoration soignée. Carte traditionnelle proposée dans un cadre élégant. En cave, la France pavoise.
◆ Mooie dromen in het vooruitzicht, want het zandmannetje komt beslist langs de top van de Kluisberg ! Enkele gerenoveerde kamers met zeer verzorgde inrichting. Traditioneel eten in een sierlijk interieur. In de wijnkelder wappert de Franse vlag.

KNOKKE-HEIST *8300 West-Vlaanderen* 533 *E 14 et* 716 *C 1 – 33 451 h – Station balnéaire*★★ *– Casino AY , Zeedijk-Albertstrand 509 ℘ 0 50 63 05 00, Fax 0 50 61 20 49.*

Voir *le Zwin*★ *: réserve naturelle (flore et faune) EZ.*

(2 parcours) à Het Zoute, Caddiespad 14 ℘ 0 50 60 12 27, Fax 0 50 62 30 29.

Zeedijk 660 (Lichttorenplein) à Knokke ℘ 0 50 63 03 80, toerisme@knokke-heist.be, Fax 0 50 63 03 90 – (avril-sept., vacances scolaires et week-end) Tramhalte, Heldenplein à Heist ℘ 0 50 63 03 80, Fax 0 50 63 03 90.

Bruxelles 108 ① – Brugge 18 ① – Gent 49 ① – Oostende 33 ③

à Knokke – ✉ *8300 Knokke-Heist :*

des Nations sans rest, Zeedijk 704, ℘ 0 50 61 99 11, *Fax 0 50 61 99 99*, ≤, – |‡|, rest, – 25. AE VISA. BY f
fermé fin janv.-début fév. et fin nov.-début déc. – **36 ch** 200/220, – 4 suites.
◆ Immeuble moderne dominant l'animation de la digue. Soixante pour cent des chambres ont vue sur le front de mer. Centre de remise en forme. Soins esthétiques sur rendez-vous.
◆ Modern flatgebouw dat boven de levendige dijk uittorent. Zestig procent van de kamers biedt uitzicht op zee. Fitnesscentrum. Schoonheidsbehandelingen op afspraak.

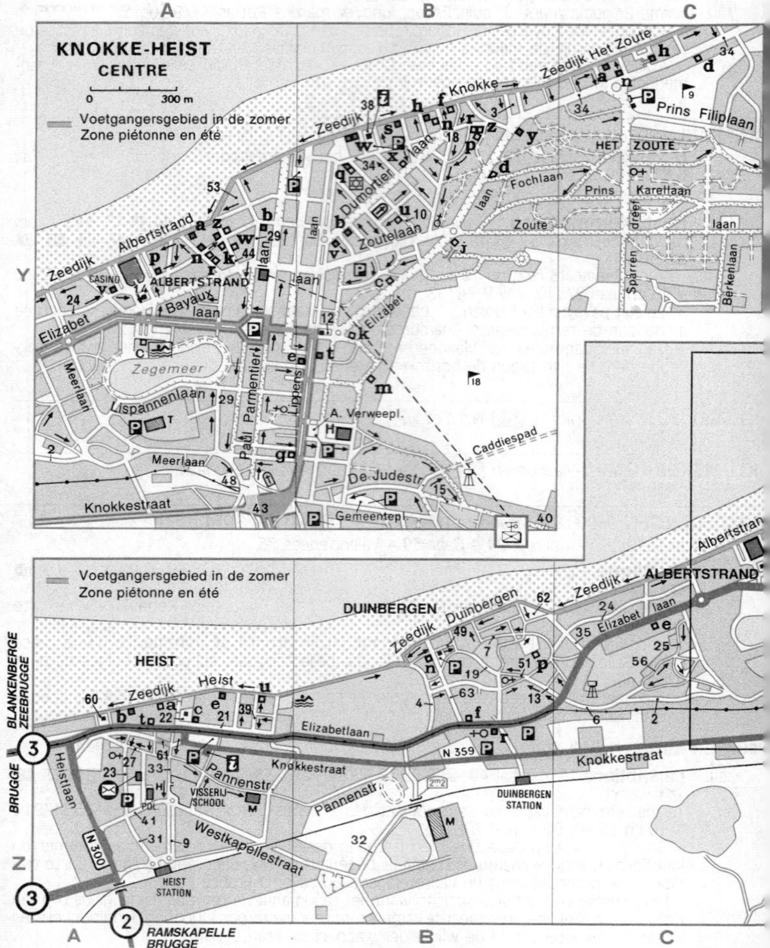

Figaro sans rest, Dumortierlaan 127, ✆ 0 50 62 00 62, *info@hotelfigaro.be, Fax 0 50 62 53 28* – |‡| 📺. MC VISA. ✈ BY x
fermé 3 dern. sem. janv.-prem. sem. fév. et 2 dern. sem. nov.-3 prem. sem. déc. – **18 ch** ☕ 90/120.

◆ Dans une rue commerçante du centre, construction récente renfermant de menues chambres actuelles. Accueil et service avenants. Agréable salle des petits-déjeuners.

◆ Modern gebouw met kleine, eigentijdse kamers in een gezellige winkelstraat in het centrum. Attente service. Aangename ontbijtzaal voor een goed begin van de dag.

Adagio sans rest, Van Bunnenlaan 12, ✆ 0 50 62 48 44, *hotel.adagio@planetinternet.be, Fax 0 50 62 59 36*, ≘ – |‡| 📺 🚗 – 🎓 25. MC VISA. ✈ BY q
20 ch ☕ 115.

◆ Hôtel de bon confort situé en léger retrait du centre animé. Chambres revêtues de moquette et munies du double vitrage. Salon sous verrière, solarium, sauna et bain turc.

◆ Comfortabel hotel even buiten de drukte van het centrum. Kamers met vaste vloerbedekking en dubbele ramen. Lounge met glaskoepel. Solarium, sauna en Turks bad.

KNOKKE-HEIST DUINBERGEN ALBERTSTRAND HET ZOUTE

Street	Grid	No.
cacialaan	CZ	2
lbertplein	BY	3
nemonenlaan	BZ	4
'kadenlaan	CZ	6
ergdreef	BZ	7
ondgenotenlaan	AZ	9
an Bunnenlaan	BY	10
urgemeester Frans Desmidtplein	BY	12
an Cailliedreef	BZ	13
anada Square	AY	14
harles de Costerlaan	BY	15
riehoeksplein	BY	18
uinbergenlaan	BZ	19
umortierlaan	BY	
Graaf Leon Lippensdreef	EZ	20
Graaf d'Ursellaan	AZ	21
Heldenplein	AZ	22
Hermans-Lybaertstr.	AZ	23
Jozef Nellenslaan	CZ	24
Kapellaan	CZ	25
Kerkstraat	AZ	27
Konijnendreef	EZ	28
Koningslaan	AY	29
Koudekerkelaan	AZ	31
Krommedijk	BZ	32
Kursaalstraat	AZ	33
Kustlaan	BCY	34
Leeuwerikenlaan	CZ	35
Lekkerbekhelling	EZ	36
Lichttorenplein	BY	38
Lippenslaan	ABY	
Louis Parentstr.	AZ	39
Magere Schorre	DZ	40
Marktstraat	AZ	41
Maurice Lippensplein	AY	43
Meerminlaan	AY	44
Oosthoekplein	EZ	47
Pastoor Opdedrinckplein	AY	48
Patriottenstraat	BZ	49
Poststraat	BZ	51
Rubensplein	AY	53
Theresialaan	CZ	56
Vissershuldeplein	AZ	60
Vlamingstraat	AZ	61
De Wandelaar	BZ	62
Zeegrasstraat	BZ	63

BELGIQUE

Van Bunnen sans rest, Van Bunnenlaan 50, ✆ 0 50 62 93 63, *info@hotelvanbunnen.be, Fax 0 50 62 29 66* – |♦| TV P. AE MC VISA BY u
18 ch ☕ 97/113.
◆ Affaire familiale installée dans une demeure de style Art déco. Les chambres, de taille satisfaisante, ont été rénovées. L'espace breakfast donne sur une jolie terrasse.
◆ Familiehotel in een art-decogebouw. De kamers zijn redelijk groot en onlangs gerenoveerd. De ontbijtruimte kijkt uit op een mooi terras.

Eden sans rest, Zandstraat 18, ✆ 0 50 61 13 89, *info@edenhotel.be, Fax 0 50 61 07 62* – |♦| TV BY n
19 ch ☕ 52/87.
◆ À quelques pas de la plage, petit immeuble-bloc dont les chambres aux tons frais ont récemment fait peau neuve. Accueil et service personnalisés.
◆ Klein flatgebouw op loopafstand van het strand. De kamers zijn onlangs in een nieuw jasje gestoken en in frisse kleuren geschilderd. Persoonlijke aandacht voor de gasten.

Prins Boudewijn sans rest, Lippenslaan 35, ✆ 0 50 60 10 16, *hotel.prins.boudewijn@proximedia.be, Fax 0 50 62 35 46* – |♦| TV – 25 à 40. MC VISA JCB ABY g
44 ch ☕ 85.
◆ Chambres fonctionnelles bien insonorisées et de dimensions correctes, dans un hôtel surplombant la principale artère commerçante de Knokke. La gare est toute proche.
◆ Functionele kamers met behoorlijke afmetingen en een goede geluidsisolatie in een hotel aan de belangrijkste winkelstraat van Knokke. Het station ligt vlakbij.

La Croisette, Van Bunnenplein 24, ✆ 0 50 61 28 39, *restaurantlacroisette@hotmail.com, Fax 0 50 61 63 47* – ▤. AE ⓓ MC VISA BY q
fermé mardi sauf en juil.-août et merc. – **Repas** *Lunch 19* – 30/55 bc.
◆ Non loin de l'estran, enseigne évocant le soleil, les stars et les paillettes. Cuisine à la page, trio de menus joliment ficelés et plaisants accords mets-vins.
◆ De naam van dit restaurant nabij het strand doet denken aan zon, glamour en filmsterren. Eigentijdse keuken, drie hecht doortimmerde menu's en goede wijn-spijscombinaties.

Panier d'Or, Zeedijk 659, ✆ 0 50 60 31 89, *Fax 0 50 60 31 89*, ≤, 🏖 – ▤. AE ⓓ MC VISA BY w
fermé mi-nov.-mi-déc., lundi soir, merc. et jeudi soir d'oct. à mars et mardi sauf vacances scolaires – **Repas** 24/45 bc.
◆ Ambiance "brasserie maritime" à cette table de la promenade. Terrasse d'été dressée côté digue, camaïeu de bleu en salle, menus pleins de sagesse, donc très demandés.
◆ Restaurant aan de boulevard met de ambiance van een "maritieme brasserie". Eetzaal in verschillende tinten blauw, terras in de zomer en goedkope menu's die zeer in trek zijn.

Le P'tit Bedon, Zeedijk 672, ✆ 0 50 60 06 64, *pucci@pandora.be, Fax 0 50 60 06 64*, 🏖, Avec grillades – ▤. AE ⓓ MC VISA BY s
fermé fin nov.-mi-déc. et merc. – **Repas** 23/39.
◆ Clairement présentée, la liste des mets du P'tit Bedon comporte un volet grillades - préparées en salle - et plusieurs menus-carte avantageux. Terrasse sur front de mer.
◆ De overzichtelijke spijskaart van le P'tit Bedon bevat onder meer voordelige menu's en grillspecialiteiten die in de eetzaal worden bereid. Terras met uitzicht op zee.

Le Chardonnay, Swolfsstraat 7, ✆ 0 50 62 04 39, *restaurant@chardonnay.be, Fax 0 50 62 58 52*, Produits de la mer – ▤. AE MC VISA BY h
fermé jeudi d'oct. à Pâques et merc. – **Repas** *Lunch 17* – 26/59 bc.
◆ Une valeur montante à Knokke-Heist : savoureuses recettes honorant la marée, cave dédiée au chardonnay, coquette décoration intérieure, accueil et service irréprochables.
◆ Dit restaurant is een vaste waarde in Knokke-Heist : smakelijke visgerechten, verrukkelijke chardonnays, mooie inrichting en onberispelijke bediening.

Hippocampus, Kragendijk 188, ✆ 0 50 60 45 70, *hippocampus@proximedia.be, Fax 0 50 62 02 73*, 🏖 – ▤ P. AE ⓓ MC VISA JCB DZ k
fermé 3 sem. carnaval, 2 prem. sem. oct., mardi soir en hiver, merc. et sam. midi – **Repas** *Lunch 25* – 39/66 bc, ♀.
◆ Fermette misant sur un choix de préparations au goût du jour pour combler votre appétit. Salle de restaurant dont les murs de briques nues s'égayent de quelques marines.
◆ In dit boerderijtje kunt u de honger stillen met gerechten die aan de huidige smaak voldoen. Eetzaal met enkele zeegezichten aan de ruwe bakstenen muren.

Open Fire, Zeedijk 658, ✆ 0 50 60 17 26, *Fax 0 50 60 17 26*, ≤, 🏖 – ▤. AE ⓓ MC VISA BY a
fermé merc. sauf en juil.-août – **Repas** 25/32 bc.
◆ Engageante affaire familiale devancée d'une terrasse. Salle à manger vivant avec son temps et choix classique où poissons crabes et homards se taillent la part du lion.
◆ Dit uitnodigende restaurant met terras is een familiebedrijf. Eigentijdse eetzaal met een klassieke keuken, waar krab en kreeft zich als een vis in het water voelen.

De Savoye, Dumortierlaan 18, ✆ 0 50 62 23 61, *Fax 0 50 62 60 30*, Produits de la mer – ▤. ⓓ ⓜ VISA BY v
fermé 2 dern. sem. juin, 3 dern. sem. nov.-prem. sem. déc., merc. soir hors saison et jeudi – **Repas** *Lunch 22* – 35/62 bc, ♀.
◆ Ce restaurant orienté "poisson et fruits de mer" vous reçoit dans un cadre actuel garni de meubles cérusés. Lunch intéressant, cave fournie, accueil et service aimables.
◆ Dit huis is gespecialiseerd in vis en zeevruchten. Eigentijds interieur met geceruseerde meubelen. Interessant lunchmenu, goed gevulde wijnkelder en vriendelijk personeel.

l'Orchidée, Lippenslaan 130, ✆ 0 50 62 38 84, *orchidee.thai@belgacom.net, Fax 0 50 62 51 88*, Cuisine thaïlandaise, ouvert jusqu'à 1 h du matin – ▤. AE ⓓ ⓜ VISA. ✂ AY t
fermé du 2 au 24 mars, 16 nov.-14 déc. et merc. – **Repas** (dîner seult sauf dim. et jours fériés) 36/47 bc.
◆ L'un des rares restaurants thaïlandais de Knokke-Heist : tables fleuries d'orchidées, décor "bambou", confort "rotin" et statuaire bouddhiste. Saveurs du Triangle d'or.
◆ Dit is een van de weinige Thaise restaurants in Knokke-Heist. Orchideeën op tafel, bamboe aan de muren, rotanmeubelen en boeddhabeeldjes. Recepten uit de Gouden Driehoek.

't Kantientje, Lippenslaan 103, ✆ 0 50 60 54 11, *Fax 0 50 61 63 76*, ☂, Moules en saison – ▤. ⓜ VISA ABY e
fermé dern. sem. juin-prem. sem. juil., 15 nov.-15 déc., lundi soir sauf en juil.-août et mardi – **Repas** 19/23.
◆ La p'tite Cantine ('t Kantientje) vous reçoit dans une ambiance qu'on peut qualifier de décontractée. Goûteuse cuisine bourgeoise et moules à gogo les mois en "r".
◆ 't Kantientje ontvangt zijn gasten in een sfeer die als relaxed kan worden bestempeld. Eenvoudige, maar smakelijke gerechten en volop mosselen als de "r" in de maand zit.

Ciccio, Dumortierlaan 64, ✆ 0 50 60 96 61, *Fax 0 50 34 46 50*, ☂, Avec cuisine italienne – ⓜ VISA BY b
fermé merc. et jeudi – **Repas** (dîner seult sauf week-end) carte 39 à 64.
◆ Cet agréable établissement du centre animé vous installe dans un intérieur italianisant orné de fresques murales. Carte franco-transalpine avec suggestions. Cave bien montée.
◆ Dit aangename etablissement in het centrum ontvangt u in een Italiaans aandoend interieur met muurschilderingen. Frans-Italiaanse menukaart en suggesties. Goede wijnkelder.

à Het Zoute – ✉ *8300 Knokke-Heist* :

Manoir du Dragon sans rest, Albertlaan 73, ✆ 0 50 63 05 80, *manoirdudragon@pandora.be, Fax 0 50 63 05 90*, ≤ golf, ☂, 🚲 – |♦| ▤ TV P. AE ⓓ ⓜ VISA. ✂ BY m
fermé du 1er au 22 déc. – **11 ch** ☐ 190/250, – 4 suites.
◆ Élégant manoir dont la plupart des chambres jouissent d'une terrasse avec vue sur le golf. Accueil et service personnalisés, atmosphère romantique et cadre verdoyant.
◆ Elegant landhuis, waarvan de meeste kamers een eigen terras hebben met uitzicht op de golfbaan. Een romantisch adresje met veel groen en persoonlijke aandacht voor de gast.

Lugano, Villapad 14, ✆ 0 50 63 05 30, *lugano@hotelvanhollebeke.com, Fax 0 50 63 05 20*, ☂, ☂ – |♦|, ▤ ch, TV P – 🔑 25. AE ⓓ ⓜ VISA. ✂ BY p
fermé janv. – **Repas** (dîner pour résidents seult) – **27 ch** ☐ 120/190, – 2 suites – ½ P 148/218.
◆ Résidence façon "villa normande" profitant de la proximité immédiate de la plage. Chambres agréables ; quelques-unes s'ouvrent sur un jardin ravissant aux beaux jours. Restaurant avec formules "week-end gastronomique" à l'attention de la clientèle résidente.
◆ Hotel in de stijl van een Normandische villa, gunstig gelegen bij het strand. Prettige kamers, waarvan sommige toegang geven tot de tuin die 's zomers prachtig in bloei staat. Restaurant met gastronomische weekendformules voor hotelgasten.

Approach (annexe 5 ch), Kustlaan 172, ✆ 0 50 61 11 30, *Fax 0 50 61 16 28*, ☂ – |♦| ✂, ▤ ch, TV ⇔ – 🔑 25 à 50. AE ⓓ ⓜ VISA CY d
Repas carte 47 à 100 – ☐ 30 – **25 ch** 350.
◆ Hôtel planté à un jet de frisbee du sable fin. On séjourne dans des chambres de bon confort ; cinq d'entre elles sont regroupées à l'annexe. Salles d'eau avec "bain-bulles".
◆ Hotel op een frisbeeworp afstand van het fijne zand. De gasten verblijven in kamers met goed comfort, waarvan vijf in de dependance liggen. Badkamers met bubbelbad.

Britannia sans rest, Elizabetlaan 85, ✆ 0 50 62 10 62, *britannia@pandora.be, Fax 0 50 62 00 63*, 🚲 – |♦| TV P – 🔑 25. AE ⓓ ⓜ VISA BY c
18 fév.-18 nov. et vacances Noël – **30 ch** ☐ 80/145.
◆ Imposante résidence balnéaire évoquant à la fois les styles normand et "Louisiane". Communs cossus, grand salon "cosy", chambres amples et douillettes. Accueil familial.
◆ Imposant badhotel in Normandische en Louisianastijl. Weelderige gemeenschappelijke ruimten, grote en sfeervolle lounge, ruime en behaaglijke kamers. Vriendelijke ontvangst.

BELGIQUE

Rose de Chopin sans rest, Elizabetlaan 94, ✆ 0 50 62 08 88, *rosedechopin@hotelsvanhollebeke.com, Fax 0 50 62 04 13,* – BY k
fermé 15 nov.-15 déc. – **11 ch** 150/250.
◆ Entre le golf et la principale artère commerçante de Knokke, jolie villa abritant onze chambres spacieuses de bon goût. Jardin croquignolet. Service avenant.
◆ Mooie villa tussen de golfbaan en de belangrijkste winkelstraat van Knokke. Elf ruime kamers die smaakvol zijn ingericht. Beeldige tuin. Aardig personeel.

Duc de Bourgogne - Golf, Zoutelaan 175, ✆ 0 50 61 16 14, *golfhotelzoute@skynet.be, Fax 0 50 62 15 90,* – 25. EZ n
fermé 15 janv.-15 fév. – **Repas** *(fermé merc.)* (taverne-rest) Lunch 24 – 32/42 bc – **26 ch** 120/175 – ½ P 92/120.
◆ Demeure engageante bordant une longue avenue qui traverse le cœur du Zoute. Chambres paisibles et confortables. Clientèle essentiellement "senior".
◆ Hotel in een uitnodigend pand aan een lange laan dwars door het centrum van Het Zoute. Rustige en comfortabele kamers. De clientèle bestaat overwegend uit senioren.

Andrews sans rest, Kustlaan 72, ✆ 0 50 61 08 47 – BY r
fermé 3 janv.3 fév. – **10 ch** 115/160.
◆ Massive villa moderne distante de 150 m de la digue. Chambres standard avec balcon, bien insonorisées et équipées d'un mobilier actuel de série.
◆ Eigentijdse solide villa, op 150 m van de dijk. Standaardkamers met balkon, goede geluidsisolatie en modern meubilair.

Locarno sans rest, Generaal Lemanpad 5, ✆ 0 50 63 05 60, *locarno@hotelsvanhollebeke.com, Fax 0 50 63 05 70* – BY p
fermé du 10 au 31 janv. – **15 ch** 110/155.
◆ À deux pas de la plage, corpulente résidence balnéaire dont les chambres, assez amples et récemment renouvelées, conviennent au repos de la clientèle en villégiature.
◆ Het Locarno is een middelgroot hotel voor badgasten, vlak bij het strand. De vrij ruime kamers, die onlangs zijn gerenoveerd, bieden de vakantiegangers alle rust.

The Tudor sans rest, Elizabetlaan 22, ✆ 0 50 62 59 69, *Fax 0 50 62 59 99,* – BY d
14 ch 137/162.
◆ Comme le suggère son enseigne, cet agréable hôtel adopte le "look" Tudor jusque dans ses coquettes chambres. Petit "pub" et coin salon-bibliothèque : so british !
◆ Zoals de naam al doet vermoeden, heeft dit mooie hotel de Tudorstijl tot in de kleinste details doorgevoerd. Prettige kamers, gezellige pub en lounge met leeshoek. So British !

Les Arcades sans rest, Elizabetlaan 50, ✆ 0 50 60 10 73, *hotel.les.arcades@pandora.be, Fax 0 50 60 49 98* – BY j
fermé fév.-mars, du 15 au 30 nov. et du 15 au 30 janv. – **11 ch** 115.
◆ Le rivage et le golf sont à 5mn de cette villa balnéaire tranquille jouxtant un carrefour. Équipement convenable dans les chambres. Clientèle d'habitués.
◆ De kust en de golfbaan liggen op 5 minuten afstand van deze rustige villa aan een kruispunt. De kamers hebben goede voorzieningen en trekken regelmatig terugkerende gasten.

Aquilon, Elizabetlaan 6, ✆ 0 50 60 12 74, *aquilon@resto.be, Fax 0 50 62 09 72,* – BY y
fermé 15 janv.-7 fév., 1re quinz. déc., merc. sauf en juil.-août et mardi – **Repas** Lunch 23 bc – 75 bc.
◆ L'enseigne de cette table désigne le fameux vent du Nord, "qu'a fait craquer la terre entre Zeebrugge et l'Angleterre". Mets classiques sobrement actualisés. Lunch et menus.
◆ Aquilon is de beruchte noordenwind "waardoor de aarde tussen Zeebrugge en Engeland is opengebarsten". Klassieke gerechten met een vleugje vernieuwing. Lunchformule en menu's.

De Oosthoek, Oosthoekplein 25, ✆ 0 50 62 23 33, *deoosthoek@tiscali.be, Fax 0 50 62 25 13,* – EZ k
fermé sem. carnaval, dern. sem. juin, 1re quinz. déc., mardi midi en hiver, mardi soir sauf en juil.-août et merc. – **Repas** Lunch 23 – 55/80 bc, ♀.
◆ Répertoire culinaire assez ambitieux et personnalisé, interprété dans un intérieur plutôt élégant. Service "classe". Une bonne adresse pour clôturer la visite du Zwin.
◆ Vrij ambitieus culinair repertoire dat de hand van de meester verraadt. Elegant interieur en stijlvolle bediening. Een genot om hier een bezoek aan Het Zwin af te sluiten !

Le Bistro de la Mer, Oosthoekplein 2, ✆ 0 50 62 86 98 – EZ a
ferme dern. sem. juin, 3 dern. sem. nov., lundi et mardi – **Repas** carte 43 à 73.
◆ Le Bistro de la Mer vous reçoit dans une salle à manger au décor nautique, aussi chaleureuse que cossue. Plats bourgeois et spécialités de la côte belge. "Sympa" !
◆ Deze bistro ontvangt u in een sfeervolle eetzaal die in nautische stijl is gedecoreerd. Lekkere burgerkeuken en specialiteiten van de Belgische kust. Uiterst plezant !

XX **L'Echiquier** 1er étage, De Wielingen 8, ☎ 0 50 60 88 82, *Fax 0 50 60 88 82* – ▤. AE ⓓ ⓜⓒ VISA. ✻ CY h
fermé du 5 au 21 janv., lundi soir, mardi et merc. – **Repas** 47 bc/52 bc.
◆ À un jet de pierre de la digue, discrète table au cadre contemporain installée à l'étage d'une résidence balnéaire. Carte dans le tempo actuel. Sage petite cave.
◆ Eigentijds restaurant, verstopt in een klein straatje bij de dijk ; op de eerste verdieping. De menukaart sluit aan bij de huidige trend. De wijnkelder is klein maar fijn.

XX **Si Versailles** avec ch, Zeedijk 795, ☎ 0 50 60 28 50, *Fax 0 50 62 58 65*, ≤, 🏖 – |‡|, ▤ rest, TV. AE ⓓ ⓜⓒ VISA. ✻ ch CY a
fermé 12 nov.-13 déc. – **Repas** *(fermé merc.)* (moules en saison) carte 32 à 79 – **6 ch** ☕ 120.
◆ Posté sur le front de mer, ce restaurant style brasserie cossue opte pour une carte variée avec spécialité de moules en saison. Grandes chambres de bon confort.
◆ Dit restaurant in brasseriestijl aan de dijk hanteert een gevarieerde kaart met mosselen in het seizoen. Grote en comfortabele kamers voor wie wil blijven slapen.

X **Marie Siska** avec ch, Zoutelaan 177, ☎ 0 50 60 17 64, *Fax 0 50 62 32 00*, 🏖, 🌳 – TV P. AE ⓓ ⓜⓒ VISA. ✻ ch EZ g
avril-6 oct. et week-end – **Repas** (taverne-rest) *Lunch 13* – carte 30 à 42 – **7 ch** ☕ 77/105.
◆ Un paradis de la gaufre que cette adresse très touristique où les enfants sont rois. Repas classique, tea-room, terrasse, jardin ludique avec minigolf. Chambres coquettes.
◆ Dit toeristische adres, waar de kinderen koning zijn, is een heus wafelparadijs. Klassieke keuken, tearoom, terras en speeltuin met midgetgolf. De kamers zien er piekfijn uit.

X **Lady Ann,** Kustlaan 301, ☎ 0 50 60 96 77, 🏖, Taverne-rest – ▤. AE ⓓ ⓜⓒ VISA CY n
fermé 3 sem. en mars, 3 sem. en déc., jeudi hors saison et merc. – **Repas** *Lunch 23* – carte 22 à 52.
◆ Petite taverne-restaurant assez "cosy" où vous sera soumise une carte simple annonçant un menu de la mer. Les lieux se muent en salon de thé durant l'après-midi.
◆ Gezellig klein café-restaurant, waar u uit een eenvoudige kaart en een "menu van de zee" kunt kiezen. 's Middags verandert de ruimte in een theesalon.

à Albertstrand – ✉ *8300 Knokke-Heist* :

La Réserve, Elizabetlaan 160, ☎ 0 50 61 06 06, *info@la-reserve.be, Fax 0 50 60 37 06*, ≤, 🏖, ⊕, 🏋, ≘, 🏊, ⚓, 🎾 – |‡| ⇔ TV P – 🏛 25 à 350. AE ⓓ ⓜⓒ VISA. ✻ rest
Repas ***La Sirène*** *Lunch 44* – 82 – **110 ch** ☕ 184/365 – ½ P 193. AY c
◆ Au bord du Zegemeer, imposante construction renfermant des chambres cossues de diverses catégories et quatorze salles de séminaires. Centre de thalassothérapie. Salle de restaurant aménagée dans la note classique. Registre culinaire assorti.
◆ Imposant gebouw aan de oever van het Zegemeer. Weelderige kamers in verschillende prijsklassen en veertien vergaderzalen. Thalassocentrum. Het restaurant is in klassieke stijl ingericht en biedt een bijpassend culinair register.

Binnenhof sans rest, Jozef Nellenslaan 156, ☎ 0 50 62 55 51, *info@binnenhof.be, Fax 0 50 62 55 50* – |‡| TV ♿ 🚗 P – 🏛 25. AE ⓜⓒ VISA AY n
25 ch ☕ 97/135.
◆ Résidence balnéaire moderne proche de la plage. Coquettes et douillettes, la plupart des chambres s'agrémentent d'un balcon. Petit-déjeuner soigné. Accueil personnalisé.
◆ Modern hotel bij het strand. Mooie en behaaglijke kamers, waarvan het merendeel een balkon heeft. Goed verzorgd ontbijt. Persoonlijke ontvangst.

Parkhotel, Elizabetlaan 204, ✉ 8301, ☎ 0 50 60 09 01, *Fax 0 50 62 36 08*, 🏖 – |‡|, ▤ rest, TV 🚗. ⓜⓒ VISA. ✻ CZ e
Repas *(avril-5 janv. dim. soir et lundi)* 52 bc/69 bc – **14 ch** *(fermé 5 janv.-12 fév., mardi, merc. et jeudi en fév. et du 15 nov. au 19 déc.)* ☕ 106/128 – ½ P 67/89.
◆ Grosse maison bâtie en léger retrait d'une avenue passante, à faible distance de la digue. Confort convenable dans les chambres ; préférez celles donnant sur l'arrière. Restaurant devancé par une terrasse. Choix de préparations classiques.
◆ Statig pand aan de vrij drukke kustweg, maar slechts op een steenworp afstand van de dijk. Redelijk comfortabele kamers, waarvan die aan de achterkant de voorkeur verdienen. Restaurant met terras aan de voorzijde. Klassieke menukaart.

Atlanta, Jozef Nellenslaan 162, ☎ 0 50 60 55 00, *info@atlantaknokke.be, Fax 0 50 62 28 66*, 🏖, 🚲 – |‡| TV P. ⓜⓒ VISA. ✻ rest AY k
fermé du 1er au 14 fév., mardis, merc. et jeudis non fériés d'oct. à Pâques sauf vacances scolaires – **Repas** *Lunch 15* – 35/55 – **33 ch** ☕ 100/110 – ½ P 66/81.
◆ Près de l'estran, lieu recommandable pour séjourner en demi-pension. Les chambres du 1er étage possèdent un balcon et toutes les salles d'eau ont été rhabillées de marbre. Goûteuse cuisine classique servie à l'heure du dîner.
◆ Dit hotel aan de kust is bij uitstek geschikt voor logies op basis van halfpension. De kamers op de eerste verdieping hebben een balkon en alle badkamers zijn met marmer bekleed. Tijdens het diner krijgen de gasten smakelijke klassieke gerechten voorgezet.

BELGIQUE

Lido, Zwaluwenlaan 18, ✆ 0 50 60 19 25, *info@lido-hotel.be, Fax 0 50 60 04 57*, – |‡|, TV, P – 30. MC VISA. rest AY r
Repas (résidents seult) – **40 ch** 95/124 – ½ P 62/72.
• Petite adresse familiale récemment rénovée, bénéficiant de la proximité immédiate de la plage. Chambres fonctionnelles de taille satisfaisante. Affluence d'habitués.
• Klein familiehotel dat onlangs is gerenoveerd. Gunstige ligging in de buurt van het strand. De kamers zijn functioneel en goed van formaat. Er komen veel stamgasten.

Nelson's, Meerminlaan 36, ✆ 0 50 60 68 10, *admin@nelsonshotel.com, Fax 0 50 61 18 38*, – |‡|, rest, TV – 25. AE MC VISA. rest AY z
avril-sept., week-end et vacances scolaires – **Repas** (résidents seult) – **48 ch** 105/115 – ½ P 65/75.
• Immeuble-bloc dominant un petit carrefour à quelques pas du front de mer. Chambres aux murs crépis, garnies d'un mobilier de série. Salon au premier étage.
• Flatgebouw bij een klein kruispunt, op een paar minuten lopen van zee. Kamers met bepleisterde muren en standaardmeubilair. Lounge op de eerste verdieping.

Albert Plage sans rest, Meerminlaan 22, ✆ 0 50 60 59 64, *admin@nelsonshotel.com, Fax 0 50 61 18 38*, – |‡| TV. AE MC VISA AY w
fermé 29 nov.-23 déc. – **16 ch** 80/85.
• Établissement de poche dont les chambres, de mise simple mais convenables, se répartissent sur cinq niveaux. Pratique pour les inconditionnels d'Albert-Plage.
• Klein hotel met eenvoudige, maar keurige kamers op vijf verdiepingen. Een ideaal adresje voor wie graag zijn vakantie doorbrengt in Albertstrand.

XXX **Esmeralda** (Verhasselt), Jozef Nellenslaan 161, ✆ 0 50 60 33 66, *Fax 0 50 60 33 66* – AE MC VISA AY p
fermé du 15 au 25 juin, du 15 au 30 nov., du 10 au 31 janv., lundi et mardi – **Repas** Lunch 30 – 100 bc, carte 56 à 102.
• Face au casino, table élégante mais détendue où l'on vient savourer une cuisine intraitable sur la qualité des produits. Presque toute la famille met la main à la pâte.
• Elegant restaurant tegenover het casino, waar men ontspannen geniet van een maaltijd op basis van eersteklas producten. Bijna de hele familie steekt de handen uit de mouwen.
Spéc. Carpaccio de thon et tempura de légumes. Saint-Pierre braisé à l'aigre-doux. Bar en croûte de sel, émulsion de cresson

XX **Jardin Tropical** (Van den Berghe), Zwaluwenlaan 12, ✆ 0 50 61 07 98, *info@jardintropical.be, Fax 0 50 61 61 03* – AE MC VISA AY n
fermé 2 sem. en mars, dern. sem. juin, 2 sem. en oct., 1 sem. en déc., merc. soir et jeudi soir sauf en juil.-août, merc. midi et jeudi midi – **Repas** Lunch 35 – 52/93 bc, carte 57 à 97.
• Ce sympathique restaurant accueille ses hôtes dans un décor des plus fringants, à la fois moderne et romantique. Choix de recettes au goût du jour, appétissant menu-carte.
• Dit sympathieke restaurant ontvangt zijn gasten in een heel vrolijk decor, dat zowel modern als romantisch is. Eigentijdse keuken en een aanlokkelijk keuze-menu.
Spéc. Langoustines de deux façons. Cabillaud au beurre blanc. Dessert du jour.

XX **Lispanne,** Jozef Nellenslaan 201, ✆ 0 50 60 05 93, *Fax 0 50 62 64 92* – AE MC VISA
fermé 16 janv.-4 fév., du 3 au 21 oct., mardi soir sauf vacances scolaires et merc. – **Repas** Lunch 16 – 19/57 bc, ♀. AY z
• Un florilège de mets classiques ficelés en plusieurs menus vous sera soumis à cette enseigne toute proche de la digue. Accueil et service avenants. Additions digestes.
• Dit restaurant bij de dijk biedt een keur van klassieke gerechten die in verschillende menu's zijn samengebracht. Vriendelijke bediening. Licht verteerbare rekening.

XX **Olivier,** Jozef Nellenslaan 159, ✆ 0 50 60 55 70, *Fax 0 50 60 55 70* – AE MC VISA
fermé merc. sauf vacances scolaires – **Repas** Lunch 22 – 35/58 bc. AY v
• Fermement enraciné, l'Olivier déploie sa ramure à un tour de roulette du casino. Salle à manger fraîche et radieuse, menus multi-choix avec option vin compris, bonne cave.
• Deze olijfboom heeft wortel geschoten bij het casino. Frisse en vrolijke eetzaal, keuzemenu's waarbij ook de drank inclusief kan zijn. Goede wijnkelder.

XX **Les Flots Bleus,** Zeedijk 538, ✆ 0 50 60 27 10, *restaurant@lesflotsbleus.be, Fax 0 50 60 63 83*, <, – AE MC VISA AY a
fermé mi-nov.-début déc., mi-janv.-début fév., merc. soir sauf en juil.-août, mardi soir et merc. midi – **Repas** Lunch 19 – 37/49.
• Relais de bouche officiant sur la digue. La carte se recompose régulièrement et le homard qu'elle annonce est puisé au vivier. Terrasse et vue sur les "flots", pas si bleus !
• Leuk restaurant op de dijk. De kaart verandert regelmatig en de kreeft komt uit het eigen homarium. Terras met uitzicht op de golven, die hier alleen niet blauw zijn !

X **Cédric,** Koningslaan 230a, ✆ 0 50 60 77 95, – AE MC VISA AY b
fermé 1 sem. carnaval, prem. sem. juil., 2 sem. en nov., lundi soir sauf vacances scolaires et mardi – **Repas** Lunch 23 – 35/75 bc.
• Adresse estimable pour s'offrir un bon repas classique à Albertstrand. Lumineuse salle de restaurant et terrasse abritée garnie de meubles en teck. Formule lunch bien cotée.
• Respectabel etablissement voor een goede klassieke maaltijd in Albertstrand. Lichte eetzaal en beschut terras met teakhouten meubelen. De lunchformule is zeer populair.

à Duinbergen C *Knokke-Heist – ✉ 8301 Heist :*

Monterey sans rest, Bocheldreef 4, ✆ 0 50 51 58 65, *info@monterey.be, Fax 0 50 51 01 65,* ←, , – TV P. MC VISA JCB. BZ p
fermé 15 nov.-23 déc. – **8 ch** ☕ 93/115.
◆ Cette villa paisible "perchée" sur une hauteur de Heist met à votre disposition de coquettes chambres agencées dans la note romantique. Salon, véranda et terrasse.
◆ Deze villa is rustig gelegen op de top van een heuvel in Heist. De kamers zijn in romantische stijl ingericht en zien er zeer verzorgd uit. Lounge, serre en terras.

Du Soleil, Patriottenstraat 15, ✆ 0 50 51 11 37, *hotel.du.soleil@compaqnet.be, Fax 0 50 51 69 14,* , – TV . AE MC VISA. rest BZ n
fermé 15 nov.-15 déc. – **Repas** Lunch 15 – 22/46 bc – **27 ch** ☕ 87/99 – ½ P 45/65.
◆ À quelques mètres de la plage, une enseigne qui semble vouloir exorciser les sombres augures de Monsieur météo. Menues chambres fonctionnelles. Jeune clientèle familiale. Cuisine classico-traditionnelle au restaurant. Formules lunch et demi-pension.
◆ Dit hotel staat op een paar meter van het strand en probeert met zijn naam slechte weerberichten te bezweren. Kleine, functionele kamers, waar voornamelijk jonge gezinnen komen. Klassiek-traditionele keuken in het restaurant, met lunchmenu's en halfpension.

Pauls sans rest, Elizabetlaan 305, ✆ 0 50 51 39 32, *paulshotel@skynet.be, Fax 0 50 51 67 40,* – TV P. MC VISA. rest BZ f
Repas (dîner pour résidents seult) – **14 ch** ☕ 65/90 – ½ P 58/79.
◆ Affaire familiale occupant une villa résidentielle postée en bordure d'une avenue assez fréquentée. Confortables chambres récemment rajeunies. Affluence d'habitués.
◆ Dit familiehotel is ondergebracht in een mooie villa aan een vrij drukke straat. De kamers zijn comfortabel en hebben onlangs een verjongingskuur ondergaan. Veel vaste gasten.

Den Baigneur, Elizabetlaan 288, ✆ 0 50 51 16 81 – AE MC VISA JCB BZ r
fermé dim. soir et lundi – **Repas** (dîner seult sauf dim.) 100 bc, ♀.
◆ Un répertoire culinaire classique, et très respectueux des produits, est au programme de cette minuscule salle à manger de style Art déco que devance un jardin bichonné.
◆ Een klassiek culinair repertoire met groot respect voor de producten staat op het programma van dit kleine restaurant in art-decostijl met zijn fraaie voortuintje.

à Heist C *Knokke-Heist – ✉ 8301 Heist :*

Bristol, Zeedijk 291, ✆ 0 50 51 12 20, *info@bristolaanzee.be, Fax 0 50 51 15 54,* ← – , ▤ rest, TV P. MC VISA. AZ u
3 avril-27 sept. – **Repas** *(fermé après 20 h 30)* 25/37 – **27 ch** ☕ 110/125 – ½ P 75/79.
◆ Voici bientôt trois quarts de siècle que cet hôtel de tradition scrute le large. Presque toutes les chambres, sobrement équipées et rajeunies, dominent la digue. Salle de restaurant contemporaine procurant une vue marine. Bel éventail de recettes bourgeoises.
◆ Al bijna driekwart eeuw gaat dit traditionele hotel geen golf te hoog. De gerenoveerde kamers hebben sobere voorzieningen en kijken vrijwel allemaal uit op zee. Ook vanuit de eigentijdse eetzaal is het ruime sop te zien. Ruime keuze aan traditionele gerechten.

Beau Séjour-Ter Duinen, Duinenstraat 9, ✆ 0 50 51 19 71, *Fax 0 50 51 08 40,* – TV. AE MC VISA AZ t
Repas *(fermé lundi et mardi soir sauf en juil.-août)* (dîner seult sauf dim.) 25/56 bc – **32 ch** ☕ 65/115 – ½ P 58/83.
◆ Vraiment près de la digue, deux immeubles récents renfermant des chambres douillettes de diverses tailles. Neuf d'entre elles possèdent une kitchenette. Ample salle des repas au décor assez cossu. Carte classique proposant de sages menus.
◆ Dit hotel ligt achter de dijk en bestaat uit twee moderne flats. Prettige kamers, waarvan negen over een kitchenette beschikken. De eetzaal is ruim en vrij weelderig ingericht. Klassieke kaart en goed doordachte menu's.

St. Yves, Zeedijk 204, ✆ 0 50 51 10 29, *Fax 0 50 51 63 87,* ←, – , ▤ rest, TV. MC VISA. AZ a
Repas *(fermé 1 sem. en déc., 2 sem. en janv., lundi sauf en juil.-août, mardi et après 20 h 30)* Lunch 20 – 25/42 – **8 ch** *(fermé 2 sem. en janv.)* ☕ 118/146 – ½ P 60/73.
◆ Plaisante échappée balnéaire depuis la moitié des chambres de ce petit hôtel familial refait de neuf ; toutes bénéficient d'un confort relativement moderne. À table, choix de plats classico-traditionnels. Lunch et menus.
◆ Klein familiehotel dat onlangs in een nieuw jasje is gestoken. De kamers, waarvan de helft op zee uitkijkt, bieden redelijk modern comfort. Aan tafel kunt u kiezen uit klassiek-traditionele gerechten à la carte en aantrekkelijke menu's.

BELGIQUE

Bartholomeus (Desmidt), Zeedijk 267, ✆ 0 50 51 75 76, *rest.bartholomeus@pandora.be, Fax 0 50 51 75 76*, ≤ - ▤. AE MC VISA. ✈ - *fermé du 16 au 26 juin, 19 sept.-2 oct., merc. et jeudi* - **Repas** Lunch 29 - 50/115 bc, carte 82 à 137. AZ e
• Fauteuils "alcantara" et toiles de petits maîtres président au décor de cette bonne table de la digue. Cuisine personnalisée avec doigté. Accueil souriant de la patronne.
• "Alcántara" fauteuils en doeken van kleine meesters sieren dit uitstekende restaurant aan zee. Karaktervolle en persoonlijke keuken. Hartelijke ontvangst door de gastvrouw.
Spéc. Crabe royal à l'aigre-doux et gingembre. Poularde de Bresse au foie d'oie, chou vert et pommes gaufrettes. Turbot au caviar, poireaux et pommes de terre à l'huile d'olives

Old Fisher, Heldenplein 33, ✆ 0 50 51 11 14, *Fax 0 50 51 71 51*, ☂ - ▤. AE ⓓ MC VISA - *fermé dern. sem. juin-début juil., 2 prem. sem. oct., mardi soir sauf en juil.-août et merc.* - **Repas** Lunch 19 - 30/60 bc. AZ c
• Le "Vieux Pêcheur" vous reçoit dans sa nouvelle salle à manger ornée d'un grand vitrail représentant un rouget, ce qui n'est pas sans rapport avec le contenu de la carte.
• De "Oude Visser" ontvangt u in zijn nieuwe eetzaal met een groot glas-in-loodraam, waarvan de voorstelling, een rode poon, niet zonder verband is met de inhoud van de kaart.

De Waterlijn, Zeedijk 173, ✆ 0 50 51 35 28, *gerritdegroote@yahoo.com, Fax 0 50 51 15 16*, ☂ - MC VISA AZ b
fermé 2 sem. en mars, 2 sem. en oct., mardi et merc. - **Repas** Lunch 18 - 37.
• Affaire familiale décontractée postée à l'extrémité de la digue de Heist. Cuisine classique, avec ambiance musicale les lundis soirs. Demandez l'agenda des dîners à thème.
• Familiebedrijfje met een ontspannen sfeer, aan het uiteinde van de dijk van Heist. Klassieke keuken met live-muziek op maandagavond. Vraag naar de agenda van de themadiners.

à **Westkapelle** *par ① : 3 km* Ⓒ *Knokke-Heist* - ✉ *8300 Westkapelle* :

Ter Dycken, Kalvekeetdijk 137, ✆ 0 50 60 80 23, *terdycken@planetinternet.be, Fax 0 50 61 40 55*, ☂ - ▤ Ⓟ. AE ⓓ MC VISA
fermé 16 fév.-5 mars, 2 sem. en nov., mardi sauf 15 juil.-15-août et lundi - **Repas** Lunch 45 - 68/139 bc.
• Villa flamande agrémentée d'un jardin soigné. Concertos culinaires pour fins gourmets, dans le tempo actuel. Aménagement cossu, véranda et terrasse adorables.
• In deze typisch Vlaamse villa genieten fijnproevers van een culinair concert. Weelderig interieur, mooie serre, zonnig terras en goed verzorgde tuin.

KOEKELBERG *Brabant* - *voir à Bruxelles*.

KOKSIJDE *8670 West-Vlaanderen* 533 *A 16 et* 716 *A 2* - *20 230 h* - *Station balnéaire*.
Bruxelles 135 ① - Brugge 50 ① - Oostende 31 ① - Veurne 7 ② - Dunkerque 27 ③

Plan page ci-contre

à **Koksijde-Bad** *Nord : 1 km* Ⓒ *Koksijde* - ✉ *8670 Koksijde*.
ℹ *Zeelaan 24 (Casino)* ✆ *0 58 53 30 55, toerisme@koksijde.be*, Fax 0 58 52 25 77 :

Terlinck, Terlinckplaats 17, ✆ 0 58 52 00 00, *hotel.terlinck@skynet.be, Fax 0 58 51 76 15*, ≤, Ꮇ - ⎅, ▤ rest, TV ⇔ Ⓟ - 🏛 25 à 40. AE ⓓ MC VISA C a
fermé 15 nov.-janv. - **Repas** *(fermé mardi soir d'oct. à mars et merc.)* Lunch 12 - 25/50 bc - **37 ch** ☕ 62/90 - ½ P 61/85.
• Trois sortes de chambres bien agencées dans cet agréable établissement posé sur la digue. Les plus vastes, à l'angle du bâtiment, jouissent d'une vue quasi-panoramique. Salle des repas soutenue par des colonnes et coiffée de verrières. Cuisine classique.
• Aangenaam hotel op de dijk met drie soorten kamers die goed zijn uitgerust. De grootste kamers, op de hoek van het gebouw, bieden een haast panoramisch uitzicht. Eetzaal met zuilen en een glazen koepel, waar klassieke gerechten worden geserveerd.

Apostroff ⛵ (annexe 🏠 - 15 ch) sans rest, Lejeunelaan 38, ✆ 0 58 52 06 09, *info@apostroff.be, Fax 0 58 52 07 09*, Ꮇ, ≘, ▣, ⛱, ✂, 🚲 - ⎅ TV ⇔ Ⓟ - 🏛 35. AE ⓓ MC VISA JCB C c
40 ch ☕ 77/124.
• Cette construction récente de type résidence et son annexe - qui occupe une villa distante d'un petit kilomètre - renferment des chambres actuelles correctement équipées.
• Dit hotel is gevestigd in een nieuw gebouw met een dependance in een villa, een kilometer verderop. De kamers zijn modern en hebben goede voorzieningen.

Carnac, Koninklijke Baan 62, ✆ 0 58 51 27 63, *carnac@pi.be, Fax 0 58 52 04 59*, ☂ - ⎅ TV Ⓟ. AE MC VISA C d
fermé 12 nov.-14 déc. et 2 dern. sem. janv. - **Repas** *(fermé mardi d'oct. à mars et merc.)* 35 - **9 ch** ☕ 80 - ½ P 58/65.
• Adresse n'ayant de mégalithique que le nom. Chambres spacieuses et claires. Salle des petits-déjeuners garnie d'une collection de mini-bouteilles de liqueurs.
• Behalve zijn naam is er niets prehistorisch aan dit hotel. Ruime, lichte kamers. In de ontbijtzaal is een collectie likeuren in miniatuurflesjes te bewonderen.

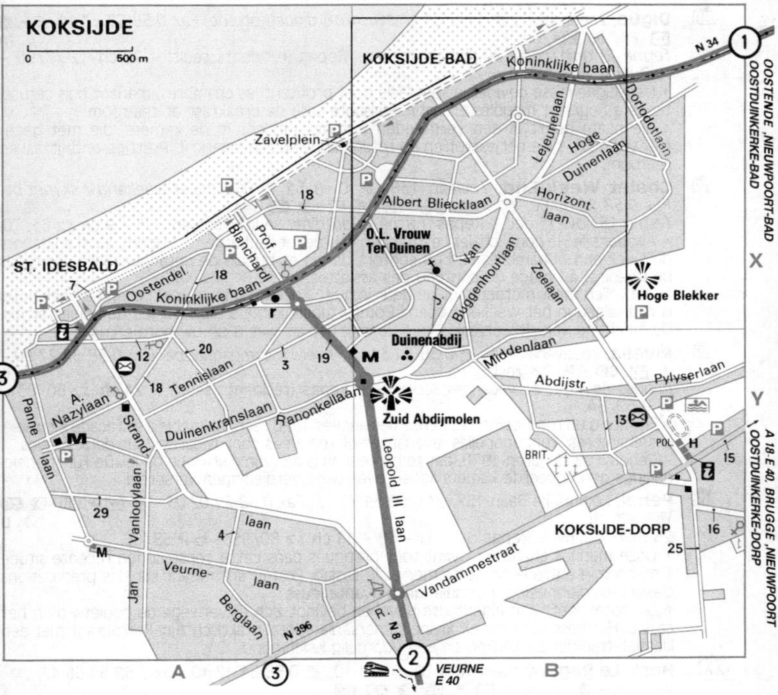

KOKSIJDE

0 500 m

A B

KOKSIJDE-BAD
Koninklijke baan
N 34
1
OOSTENDE, NIEUWPOORT-BAD
OOSTDUINKERKE-BAD
Zavelplein
Lejeunelaan
Hoge Duinenlaan
Dorlodotlaan
Albert Bliecklaan
Horizontlaan
O.L. Vrouw Ter Duinen
J. Van Buggenhoutlaan
Zeelaan
Hoge Blekker
ST. IDESBALD
Oostendel.
Blanchardl
Prof.
Koninklijke baan
Duinenabdij
Middenlaan
Abdijstr.
Pylyserlaan
Zuid Abdijmolen
Ranonkellaan
Tennislaan
A. Nazylaan
Strand
Duinenkranslaan
Pannelaan
Vanlooylaan
Leopold III laan
BRIT.
POL.
KOKSIJDE-DORP
A 18-E 40, BRUGGE, NIEUWPOORT
OOSTDUINKERKE-DORP
Veurnelaan
Jan Berglaan
Vandammestraat
R. N 8
N 396
2
3
VEURNE E 40

X Y

A B

C

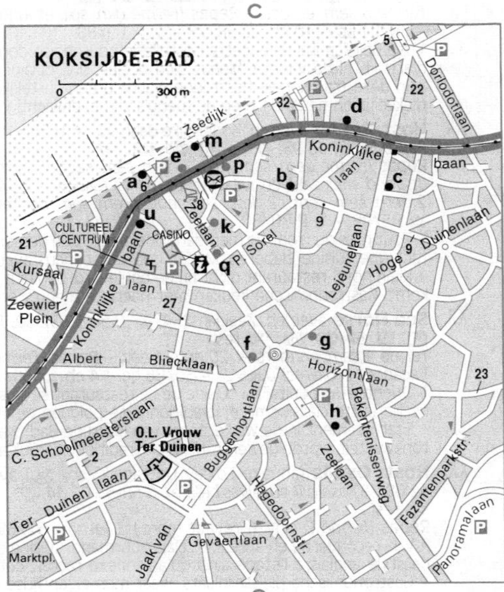

C

Digue, Zeedijk 331, ✆ 0 58 51 14 15, *info@digue-hotel.be, Fax 0 58 52 27 44,* ← – C m
fermé 2e quinz. nov.-20 déc. et merc. – **Repas** (résidents seult) – **20 ch** 77/90 – ½ P 115/130.
◆ L'enseigne laisse deviner le spectacle dont profitent les chambres, mariant bois cérusé, tissus à fleurs et meubles en rotin. Plaisante salle de breakfast et tea-room.
◆ De naam geeft al een vermoeden van het uitzicht in de kamers, die met geceruseerd hout, bloemetjesstoffen en rotanmeubelen zijn ingericht. Prettige ontbijtzaal en tearoom.

Chalet Week-End, Zeelaan 136, ✆ 0 58 51 12 06, *chalet.weekend@skynet.be, Fax 0 58 52 09 00,* – AE VISA C h
fermé 15 nov.-15 déc. – **Repas** *(fermé jeudi)* (dîner seult) carte env. 25 – **9 ch** 63/70.
◆ Avouons-le : le nom "chalet" est un rien usurpé, et l'auberge fonctionne aussi en dehors du week-end... Chambres de bon confort. Jardin et terrain de pétanque. Salle des repas bourgeoise, à l'image du contenu des assiettes.
◆ We vallen maar meteen met de deur in huis : chalet is iets te veel gezegd en het hotel is niet alleen in het weekend open ! Comfortabele kamers. Tuin en jeu-de-boulesterrein. De inrichting van de eetzaal is traditioneel, net als wat u op uw bordje krijgt.

Rivella, Zouavenlaan 1, ✆ 0 58 51 31 67, *rivella@compaqnet.be, Fax 0 58 52 27 90* – VISA. rest C b
Pâques-fin sept. et vacances scolaires – **Repas** (résidents seult) – **24 ch** 60/83 – ½ P 59/64.
◆ En face d'un rond-point, résidence des années 1970 reconnaissable à sa façade incurvée. Les chambres, fonctionnelles, avenantes et rénovées sont réparties sur deux étages.
◆ Gebouw uit de jaren 1970, dat te herkennen is aan zijn halfronde gevel. De functionele, onlangs gerenoveerde kamers liggen over twee verdiepingen verspreid.

Penel, Koninklijke Baan 157, ✆ 0 58 51 73 23, *Fax 0 58 51 02 03* – AE VISA. ch C u
25 mars-6 janv. – **Repas** Lunch 13 – 30 – **11 ch** 80/95 – ½ P 58/66.
◆ Onze menues chambres avant tout pratiques dans cette construction récente située à mi-chemin entre le front de mer et le casino. Restaurant misant sur des préparations classico-traditionnelles. Formule lunch avantageuse.
◆ Dit hotel heeft een eigentijdse gevel en bevindt zich halverwege de boulevard en het casino. Het beschikt over elf kleine kamers, die vooral praktisch zijn. Restaurant met een klassiek-traditionele keuken en een voordelig lunchmenu.

Host. Le Régent avec ch, A. Bliecklaan 10, ✆ 0 58 51 12 10, *Fax 0 58 51 66 47,* – rest, AE VISA C f
fermé 3 sem. en oct. – **Repas** *(fermé dim. soir et lundi sauf vacances scolaires)* Lunch 30 – 36/91 bc – **10 ch** 58/78 – ½ P 69/88.
◆ Accueil familial dans cette hostellerie bourgeoise dont la carte des mets ne manque ni d'attrait, ni de variété. Menus bien ficelés. Une dizaine de chambres confortables.
◆ In deze traditionele hostellerie wacht u een hartelijke ontvangst. De spijskaart is aantrekkelijk en gevarieerd en de menu's zijn evenwichtig. Een tiental comfortabele kamers.

Host. Bel-Air avec ch, Koninklijke Baan 95, ✆ 0 58 51 77 05, *bel-air.koksijde@skynet.be, Fax 0 58 51 16 93,* – VISA. C p
Repas *(fermé dern. sem. juin, 2 dern. sem. sept., 2 dern. sem. nov.-prem. sem. déc., jeudi et vend. midi sauf en juil.-août et merc.)* Lunch 25 – 30/50 – **4 ch** *(fermé dern. sem. juin, 2 dern. sem. sept., 2 dern. sem. nov.-prem. sem. déc. et merc. et jeudi sauf en juil.-août)* 85/99 – ½ P 70/80.
◆ Tout près du front de mer, dans une artère que dessert le tram, petite enseigne concoctant une cuisine élaborée. Menus goûteux conçus avec des produits choisis.
◆ Klein hotel-restaurant dicht bij de boulevard, aan een verkeersader waar de tram langskomt. Gastronomische keuken met heerlijke menu's op basis van eersteklas producten.

Sea Horse avec ch, Zeelaan 254, ✆ 0 58 52 32 80, *Fax 0 58 52 32 75,* – rest, AE VISA. rest C q
fermé 1 sem. en mars et 20 nov.-4 déc. – **Repas** *(fermé mardi soir en oct. et merc. sauf vacances scolaires)* Lunch 20 – 30/66 bc – **4 ch** 55/70 – ½ P 80.
◆ Orientée "produits", la cuisine de ce restaurant situé sur l'axe commerçant de la station oscille entre classicisme et tradition. Une poignée de chambres fonctionnelles.
◆ Etablissement in de winkelstraat van Koksijde-Bad, waar uitsluitend met producten van topkwaliteit wordt gewerkt. Klassiek-traditionele keuken. Een paar functionele kamers.

Host. Oxalis (annexe Loxley Cottage -3 ch) avec ch, Lejeunelaan 12, ✆ 0 58 52 08 79, *oxalis@advalvas.be, Fax 0 58 51 06 34,* – AE VISA. rest C g
Repas *(fermé 6 janv.-6 fév. et merc.)* Lunch 20 – 52/65 bc – **4 ch** 69/99 – ½ P 93.
◆ Villa reconvertie en agréable relais gourmand. Cuisine de notre temps et jolies chambres de style anglais à l'étage ainsi qu'à l'annexe façon "cottage" (dont un appartement).
◆ Gastronomische pleisterplaats, waar men eigentijdse gerechten bereidt. Mooie kamers in Engelse stijl op de bovenverdieping en in de bijbehorende cottage ; 1 appartement.

De Huifkar, Koninklijke Baan 142, 0 58 51 16 68, *restaurant.dehuifkar@pi.be*, *Fax 0 58 52 45 71* – AE VISA C e
fermé prem. sem. juil., 2 sem. en janv., merc. soir de nov. à avril et jeudi – **Repas** *Lunch 9* – 30/50 bc.
• Une "roulotte" (huifkar) qui va son petit bonhomme de chemin. Décor intérieur à la mode d'aujourd'hui et éventail de recettes bourgeoises rythmées par les marées.
• Deze huifkar gaat kalm zijn eigen weg. Het interieur is eigentijds en de kok volgt de beweging van de getijden, dus lekkere visschotels op het menu.

Bistro Pinot Blanc, Mariastraat 2, 0 58 51 53 10, *Fax 0 58 51 53 10*, – VISA. C k
fermé 1 sem. en juin, 27 nov.-5 déc., mardi et merc. – **Repas** *Lunch 33* – carte 46 à 58.
• Villa balnéaire 1930 aménagée dans l'esprit "mer du Nord". Cuisine du marché énoncée sur ardoise, cave diversifiée, jardin fleuri et terrasse. Ambiance décontractée.
• Villa uit 1930, zoals men die in veel badplaatsen aan de Noordzee ziet. Dagsuggesties op een schoolbord, gevarieerde wijnkelder, fleurige tuin en terras. Ontspannen sfeer.

à Sint-Idesbald C *Koksijde* – *8670 Koksijde.*
(Pâques-sept. et vacances scolaires) Koninklijke Baan 330, 0 58 51 39 99 :

Soll Cress, Koninklijke Baan 225, 0 58 51 23 32, *hotel@sollcress.info*, *Fax 0 58 51 91 32*, – rest, TV P – 25 à 65. VISA. ch AX r
fermé du 4 au 27 oct., 30 nov.-8 déc. et du 11 au 20 janv. – **Repas** *(fermé lundi soir et mardi sauf vacances scolaires) Lunch 10* – 25/33 – **38 ch** 50/75 – ½ P 55/60.
• À 500 m de la plage, auberge tenue en famille renfermant des chambres de mise sobre, mais assez amples et actuelles. Grande piscine couverte et espace fitness. Divers menus très sages, dont un lunch à prix d'ami, vous attendent à l'heure du repas.
• Dit hotel-restaurant bevindt zich op 500 m van het strand en wordt gerund door een familie. De kamers zijn sober, maar vrij ruim en actueel. Groot overdekt zwembad en fitnessruimte. Diverse menu's voor een zacht prijsje, waaronder een heerlijk lunchmenu.

KONTICH *Antwerpen* 533 L 16 et 716 G 2 – *voir à Antwerpen, environs.*

KORTEMARK *8610 West-Vlaanderen* 533 D 16 et 716 C 2 – *12 149 h.*

Bruxelles 103 – Brugge 33 – Kortrijk 38 – Oostende 34 – Lille 52.

't Fermetje, Staatsbaan 3, 0 51 57 01 94, *Fax 0 51 57 01 94*, Bistrot – P. VISA
fermé 21 juil.-14 août, mardi soir, merc. soir, jeudi soir et sam. midi – **Repas** 50 bc.
• Une accueillante "fermette" sert de cadre à ce petit restaurant sympathique mitonnant un éventail de recettes gentiment classiques. Intérieur dans la note néo-rustique.
• Een uitnodigend boerderijtje is de setting van dit sympathieke restaurant, waar licht klassieke gerechten worden geserveerd. Het interieur is in neorustieke stijl gehouden.

KORTENBERG *Vlaams-Brabant* 533 M 17 et 716 G 3 – *voir à Bruxelles, environs.*

KORTESSEM *Limburg* 533 R 17 et 716 J 3 – *voir à Hasselt.*

KORTRIJK (COURTRAI) *8500 West-Vlaanderen* 533 E 18 et 716 C 3 – *74 558 h.*

Voir *Hôtel de Ville (Stadhuis) : salle des Échevins★ (Schepenzaal), salle du Conseil★ (Oude Raadzaal)* CZ **H** – *Église Notre-Dame★ (O.L. Vrouwekerk) : statue de Ste-Catherine★, Élévation de la Croix★* DY – *Béguinage★ (Begijnhof)* DZ.
Musée : *National du Lin et de la Dentelle★ (Nationaal Vlas-, Kant- en Linnenmuseum)* BX **M.**
St-Michielsplein 5 0 56 23 93 71, kortrijk@toerismevlaanderen.be, Fax 0 56 23 93 72.
Bruxelles 90 ② – Brugge 51 ⑥ – Gent 45 ② – Oostende 70 ⑥ – Lille 28 ⑤

Plans pages suivantes

Broel, Broelkaai 8, 0 56 21 83 51, *infobroel@hotelbroel.be*, *Fax 0 56 20 03 02*, – TV – 25 à 450. AE VISA DY e
fermé 19 juil.-8 août – **Repas *Castel*** *(fermé sam. et dim. non fériés) Lunch 25* – 40/50 bc – ***Bistro*** *(ouvert jusqu'à 23 h) Lunch 13* – 38 – **70 ch** 129/145.
• Un hôtel plaisant : intérieur au cachet ancien, spacieux et cossu, chambres de bon séjour, installations pour séminaires, piscine, sauna et fitness flambant neuf. Salle à manger de style classique, à l'image des préparations figurant à la carte.
• Prettig hotel door zijn ruime en luxe interieur met een Bourgondisch cachet, gerieflijke kamers, faciliteiten voor congressen, zwembad, sauna en spiksplinternieuwe fitnessruimte. De eetzaal is in klassieke stijl en past uitstekend bij de gerechten.

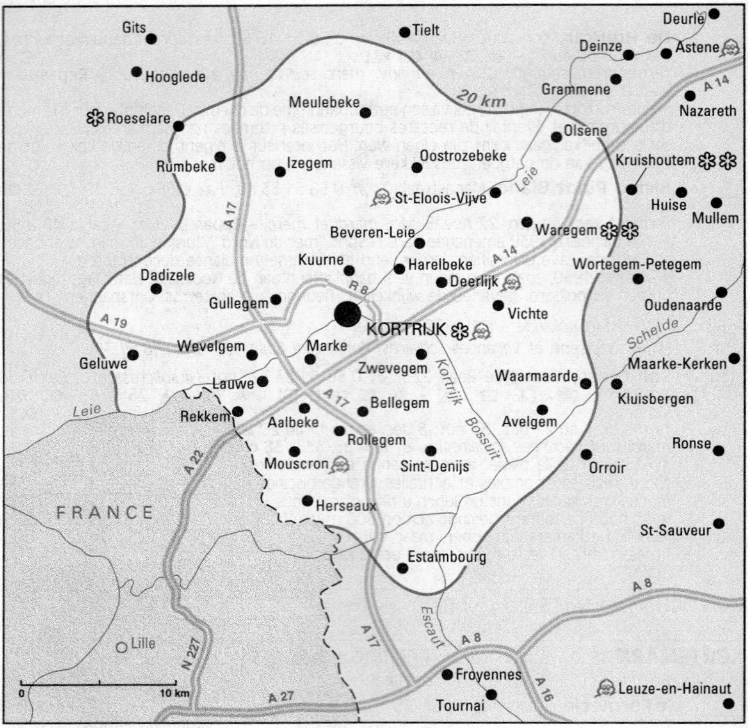

 **Damier** sans rest, Grote Markt 41, ✆ 0 56 22 15 47, *info@hoteldamier.be*, *Fax 0 56 22 86 31*, – 25 à 120. AE VISA JCB. CZ a
48 ch 99/139, – 1 suite.
◆ Une façade rococo surmontée de deux lions des Flandres dorés signale cet agréable établissement de la Grand-Place. Vastes chambres personnalisées, dans la note "british".
◆ Een rococogevel met twee Vlaamse leeuwen kenmerkt dit gezellige etablissement op de Grote Markt. Ruime, gepersonaliseerde, Brits aandoende kamers.

Messeyne, Groeningestraat 17, ✆ 0 56 21 21 66, *hotel@messeyne.com*, *Fax 0 56 45 68 22*, – 25. AE VISA. DY t
fermé dern. sem. déc.-prem. sem. janv. – **Repas** *(fermé sam. et dim.)* carte 35 à 46 – **28 ch** 115/140.
◆ Ce nouvel établissement a élu domicile dans une belle demeure patricienne rénovée. Décor intérieur mi-classique, mi-moderne. Salon exquis. Parc avec pièce d'eau à l'arrière. Salle de restaurant dans l'air du temps. Âtre réconfortant et quiétude assurée.
◆ Deze nieuwkomer heeft zich gevestigd in een mooie gerenoveerde patriciërswoning. Het interieur is zowel klassiek als modern. Schitterende lounge. Park met waterpartij aan de achterkant. Eigentijds restaurant met een behaaglijk haardvuur. Rust gegarandeerd.

Parkhotel, Stationsplein 2, ✆ 0 56 22 03 03, *info.parkhotel@parkhotel.be*, *Fax 0 56 22 14 02*, – 25 à 80. AE VISA CZ r
fermé 26 juil.-13 août – **Repas** ***Four Seasons*** *(fermé dim. soir)* 35/45 bc – **98 ch** 95/120.
◆ À deux pas de la gare, hôtel confortable et pratique pour l'homme d'affaires usager du rail. Chambres relativement amples et bien équipées, réparties sur trois étages. Cuisine classico-bourgeoise servie dans un cadre actuel.
◆ Comfortabel hotel bij het station, ideaal voor zakenmensen die van het spoor gebruik maken. Relatief ruime kamers met goede voorzieningen die over drie verdiepingen zijn verspreid. Klassiek-traditionele keuken in een eigentijds interieur.

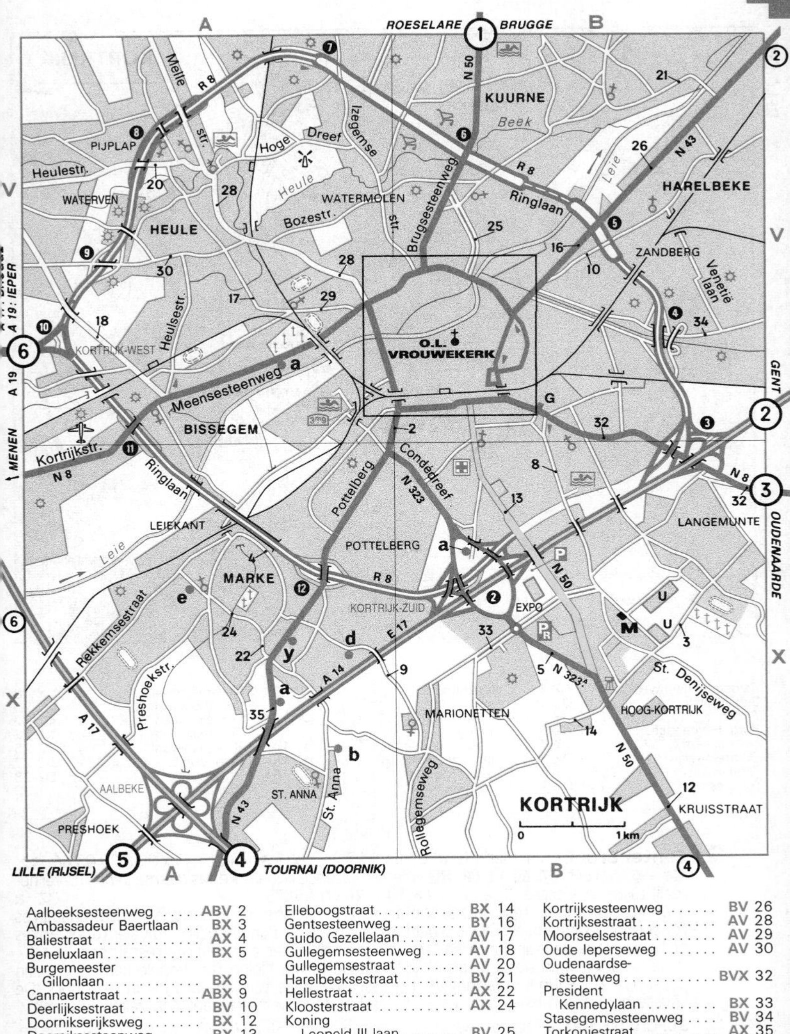

Aalbeeksesteenweg ..... ABV 2
Ambassadeur Baertlaan .. BX 3
Baliestraat .... AX 4
Beneluxlaan .... BX 5
Burgemeester Gillonlaan .... BX 8
Cannaertstraat .... ABX 9
Deerlijksestraat .... BV 10
Doornikserijksweg .... BX 12
Doorniksesteenweg ...... BX 13
Elleboogstraat .... BX 14
Gentsesteenweg .... BY 16
Guido Gezellelaan .... AV 17
Gullegemsesteenweg ..... AV 18
Gullegemsestraat .... AV 20
Harelbeeksestraat .... BV 21
Hellestraat .... AX 22
Kloosterstraat .... AX 24
Koning Leopold III laan .... BV 25
Kortrijksesteenweg ...... BV 26
Kortrijksestraat .... AV 28
Moorseelsestraat .... AV 29
Oude Ieperseweg .... AV 30
Oudenaardsesteenweg .... BVX 32
President Kennedylaan .... BX 33
Stasegemsesteenweg .... BV 34
Torkonjestraat .... AX 35

Belfort, Grote Markt 52, ✆ 0 56 22 22 20, *info@belforthotel.be, Fax 0 56 20 13 06,* – |‡|, ▤ ch, TV. AE ⓓ ⓜⓒ VISA CZ c

Repas (taverne-rest) *Lunch 13* – carte 28 à 48 – **29 ch** ☕ 85/97 – ½ P 90/100.

◆ Dans le sillage du beffroi, construction d'esprit baroque flamand renfermant des chambres de différentes tailles. Agréable salle des petits-déjeuners lambrissée. Des fresques de notre temps ornent la salle à manger.

◆ Dit gebouw is opgetrokken in Vlaamse barokstijl en staat aan de voet van het belfort. De kamers zijn van verschillende grootte. Aangename ontbijtzaal met lambrisering en eetzaal met moderne muurschilderingen.

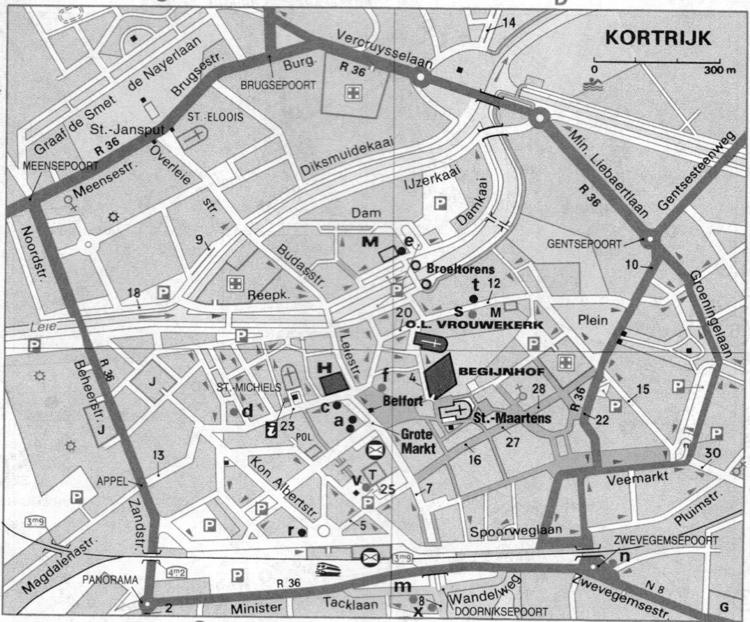

KORTRIJK

Aalbeeksesteenweg	CZ 2		Groeningestr.	DY 12		Nijverheidskaai	CY 18
Begijnhofstr.	DZ 4		Grote Markt	CDZ		O.L. Vrouwestr.	DY 20
Budastr.	CY		H. Consciencestr.	CY 13		Romeinselaan	DZ 22
Burg. Reynaertstr.	CZ 5		Koning Leopold III laan	DY 14		Rijselsestr.	CZ 23
Doorniksestr.	DZ 7		Lange Meersstr.	DZ 15		Schouwburgpl.	CDZ 25
Doorniksewijk	DZ 8		Lange Steenstr.	DZ 16		Steenpoort	DZ 27
Fabriekskaai	CY 9		Leiestr.	CYZ		Voorstr.	DZ 28
Gentsestr.	DY 10					Wandelingstr.	DZ 30

Center Broel, Graanmarkt 6, ✆ 0 56 21 97 21, *cbh@skynet.be, Fax 0 56 20 03 66,* – rest, AE VISA – *fermé vacances Noël* – **Repas** *(fermé vend.)* (taverne-rest) *Lunch 30* – carte 28 à 46 – 10 – **26 ch** 55/75. CZ a

◆ Un établissement très central, comme le laisse deviner son enseigne. Petites chambres fonctionnelles rajeunies. Sauna, solarium et fitness. Parkings publics aux alentours. Boxes et banquettes de cuir confèrent un charme particulier à la taverne-restaurant.

◆ Centraal gelegen hotel, zoals al blijkt uit de naam. Kleine functionele kamers die zijn gerenoveerd. Sauna, solarium en fitness. Openbare parkeergarages in de buurt. De knusse hoekjes en leren bankjes verlenen het taverne-restaurant een zekere charme.

XXX ✿ **St.-Christophe** (Pélissier), Minister Tacklaan 5, ✆ 0 56 20 03 37, *info@stchristophe.be, Fax 0 56 20 01 95,* – AE VISA. – *fermé 2 sem. avant Pâques, 27 juil.-13 août, 6 et 7 janv., dim. soir, lundi et mardi soir* – **Repas** *Lunch 49* – 73/139 bc, carte 70 à 87.

◆ Ancienne maison de maître dont l'intérieur conjugue avec harmonie classicisme et bon goût contemporain. Cuisine soignée magnifiée par une cave de prestige. Terrasse ombragée.

◆ Oud herenhuis met een interieur dat een geslaagde combinatie is van klassiek en modern. Verzorgde keuken die volledig tot ontplooiing komt bij de wijnen. Schaduwrijk terras.

Spéc. Soupe de truffes aux tronçons de homard. Queues de langoustines en gelée de crustacés. Ris de veau braisé et jus d'Arabica DZ m

XX **Boerenhof,** Walle 184, ✆ 0 56 21 31 72, *boerenhof@tijd.com, Fax 0 56 22 87 01* – P. AE VISA – *fermé 2 sem. en fév., 21 juil.-19 août, lundi et mardi* – **Repas** *(déjeuner seult sauf vend. et sam.) Lunch 40 bc* – carte env. 53. BX a

◆ Au Sud de la ville, près du ring et de l'autoroute, fermette de la fin du 19e s. concoctant des plats du marché dans un cadre rustique. Très belle carte des vins.

◆ Rustiek boerderijtje uit de late 19e eeuw in het zuiden van de stad, makkelijk te bereiken. De kok kookt met verse producten van de markt. Uitstekende wijnkelder.

XX **Akkerwinde,** Doorniksewijk 12, ✆ 0 56 22 82 33, *restaurant.akkerwinde@pandora.be*, – AE MC VISA JCB DZ x
fermé 2 sem. avant Pâques, 22 juil.-22 août, dern. sem. nov.-prem. sem. déc., merc., jeudi soir, sam. midi et dim. soir – **Repas** *Lunch 38 bc* – 50/71 bc.
◆ Plafonds ouvragés, riches lambris et vieux tableaux évoquant la culture du lin président au décor "couleur locale" de cette maison bourgeoise. Menus plébiscités.
◆ Fraai bewerkte plafonds, lambrisering en oude schilderijen kenmerken het interieur van dit restaurant vol "couleur locale". De menu's zijn een groot succes.

XX **Langue d'oc,** Meensesteenweg 155, ✆ 0 56 34 44 85, *barttaillieu@hotmail.com*, *Fax 0 56 37 29 33*, . AE D MC VISA AV a
fermé mardi soir, merc., jeudi soir et dim. soir Lunch 25 – 38.
◆ Belle salle à manger bourgeoise, mets au goût du jour, sélection de vins du Languedoc, table romantique pour deux dans la cave, accueillant salon d'attente et jolie terrasse.
◆ Traditionele eetzaal, eigentijdse keuken, wijnen uit de Languedoc, romantische tafel voor twee in de kelder, sfeervolle salon voor het aperitief en mooi terras.

X **Brasserie César,** Grote Markt 2, ✆ 0 56 22 22 60, , Taverne-rest – . AE D MC VISA
fermé 21 juil.-15 août et mardi – **Repas** *Lunch 14* – carte 27 à 48. CZ f
◆ Ambiance "brasserie contemporaine" dans cette taverne-restaurant assez courue où l'on s'attable en toute confiance. Choix à la carte. Service jeune et avenant.
◆ In dit druk bezochte etablissement hangt de sfeer van een hedendaagse brasserie en kunt u alle vertrouwen hebben in de kookkunsten van de kok. Jong en vriendelijk personeel.

X **De Open Haard,** Zwevegemsestraat 65, ✆ 0 56 21 19 33, *Fax 0 56 25 93 82*, Grillades – . AE D MC VISA DZ n
fermé 21 juil.-15 août, mardi et sam. midi – **Repas** *Lunch 29 bc* – 34 bc/41 bc.
◆ Le Feu Ouvert (Open Haard) vous installe dans un décor intérieur réactualisé où les pièces de viande rôtissent sous vos yeux. Petit choix bourgeois avec menus et suggestions.
◆ In dit eigentijdse restaurant worden grote stukken vlees voor iedereen zichtbaar geroosterd. Kleine kaart met eenvoudige gerechten, maar ook menu's en dagsuggesties.

X **Bistro Aubergine,** Groeningestraat 16, ✆ 0 56 25 79 80, *aubergine@pandora.be*, *Fax 0 56 20 18 97*, – MC VISA DY s
fermé du 1er au 15 août, sam. midi, dim. soir et lundi – **Repas** *Lunch 13 bc* – 35 bc.
◆ Sympathique enseigne pour cette brasserie dans l'air du temps où vous seront présentés une grande carte "bistrotière" et un sage menu sur écriteau. Cave "globe-trotter".
◆ Sympathieke bistro in eigentijdse stijl met een uitgebreide kaart en een aantrekkelijk menu op een schoolbord. Kosmopolitische wijnkelder.

X **Bistro Botero,** Schouwburgplein 12, ✆ 0 56 21 11 24, *info@botero.be*, *Fax 0 56 21 33 67*, – . MC VISA CZ v
fermé du 11 au 18 avril, 26 juil.-15 août, dim. et jours fériés – **Repas** *Lunch 12* – carte 30 à 69, ♀.
◆ Une pimpante façade 1900 abrite ce bistrot animé servant un éventail de préparations simples dont une ribambelle de salades. Aux murs, des reproductions de toiles de Botero.
◆ Bistro met een mooie gevel uit 1900. Ruime keuze aan eenvoudige gerechten, waaronder een hele reeks salades. Aan de muren hangen reproducties van Botero.

X **Huyze Decock,** Louis Verweestraat 1, ✆ 0 56 25 28 54, *restaurant@huyzedecock.be*, *Fax 0 56 25 61 16* – . MC VISA CZ d
fermé 2 sem. en fév., fin juil.-début août, dim. midi, lundi et mardi – **Repas** *Lunch 15* – 35/43 bc.
◆ Lithographies, peintures et madrigaux encadrés donnent une certaine poésie à cette affaire familiale. Plats mijotés, lunch et intéressant menu mensuel "boissons comprises".
◆ Litho's, schilderijen en ingelijste madrigalen geven dit familierestaurant iets poëtisch. Stoofschotels, lunchformule en een interessant maandmenu inclusief wijn.

au Sud :

XXX **Gastronomisch Dorp "Eddy Vandekerckhove"** avec ch, St-Anna 9, ✆ 0 56 22 47 56, *Fax 0 56 22 71 70*, , – – 25. AE D MC VISA AX b
fermé 1 sem. avant Pâques et 2 sem. en août – **Repas** *(fermé dim. soir et lundi) Lunch 42* – carte 81 à 89 – **7 ch** 112/118.
◆ Un beau repas en perspective : cuisine escoffière que rehausse un cadre raffiné. Une verrière moderne coiffe le jardin exotique et sa pièce d'eau. Chambres douillettes.
◆ Hier staat u een gastronomische maaltijd à la Escoffier te wachten in een verfijnd interieur. Exotische tuin en waterpartij met moderne glazen overkapping. Knusse kamers.

XXX **Host. Klokhof** avec ch, St-Anna 2, ✆ 0 56 22 97 04, *info@klokhof.be*, *Fax 0 56 25 73 25*, , – – 25 à 320. AE D MC VISA. ch AX a
fermé du 21 au 28 fév. et 24 juil.-13 août – **Repas** *(fermé dim. soir et lundi) Lunch 40 bc* – carte 52 à 66 – **9 ch** 93/103.
◆ Jolie ferme aménagée pour recevoir banquets et séminaires. Registre culinaire classique. Carte avec menus, suggestions et lunch-choix. Confort moderne dans les chambres.
◆ Deze mooie boerderij is zeer geschikt voor partijen en congressen. Klassiek culinair register. Kaart met menu's, dagsuggesties en lunchformule. Modern comfort in de kamers.

à Aalbeke *par ⑤ : 7 km* C *Kortrijk – ✉ 8511 Aalbeke :*

St-Cornil, Plaats 15, ✆ 0 56 41 35 23, *Fax 0 56 40 29 09,* Grillades – *fermé août, sam. et dim.* – **Repas** 30 bc.

◆ Auberge au cadre bourgeois proposant une belle brochette de grillades où la côte à l'os - issue de la boucherie familiale - a ses fervents. Une valeur sûre.

◆ Traditioneel restaurant, waar de gegrilde vleesspies en ribstuk uit de eigen slagerij van de familie tot de favorieten behoren. Een betrouwbaar adresje !

à Bellegem *par ④ : 5 km* C *Kortrijk – ✉ 8510 Bellegem :*

Troopeird, Doornikserijksweg 74, ✆ 0 56 22 26 85, *info@hotel-troopeird.be, Fax 0 56 22 33 63,* – P. VISA *fermé 20 déc.-5 janv.* – **Repas** (dîner pour résidents seult) – **14 ch** 70/90 – ½ P 65/90.

◆ Cette jolie villa flamande accordée au cachet rural de Bellegem renferme de grandes chambres correctement équipées. Véranda et petit centre de relaxation en annexe.

◆ Deze mooie Vlaamse villa past uitstekend in de landelijke omgeving van Bellegem. Grote kamers met goede voorzieningen. Serre en kleine fitnessruimte in het bijgebouw.

à Kuurne *par ① : 3,5 km – 12 650 h – ✉ 8520 Kuurne :*

Bourgondisch Kruis, Brugsesteenweg 400, ✆ 0 56 70 24 55, *info@het-bourgondisch-kruis.be, Fax 0 56 70 56 65,* – P. AE VISA *fermé 1 sem. en mars, 16 août-5 sept., mardi soir, merc. et dim. soir* – **Repas** Lunch 42 bc – carte 47 à 99.

◆ Mets classiques personnalisés servis dans un cadre lumineux et cossu où règne la pierre de Bourgogne. Carte avec lunch et menu. Terrasse délicieuse et cave-salon.

◆ Licht en weelderig interieur, waarin steen uit Bourgondië domineert. Klassieke keuken met een persoonlijke noot. Lunchformule en menu. Prachtig terras en salon in de kelder.

à Marke C *Kortrijk – ✉ 8510 Marke :*

Marquette avec ch, Kannaertstraat 45, ✆ 0 56 20 18 16, *marquette@online.be, Fax 0 56 20 14 37,* – rest, P. – 25 à 200. AE VISA AX d *fermé 18 juil.-17 août* – **Repas** *(fermé dim. et lundi)* Lunch 56 bc – carte 58 à 70 – 9 – **9 ch** 86/112.

◆ Luxueuse hostellerie spécialisée dans les banquets et soirées à thème. Cuisines que l'on visite, riche collection de vins en caveau. Chambres agréables.

◆ Luxueus hotel-restaurant dat zich toelegt op feestmaaltijden en thema-avonden en waar de gasten een kijkje in de keuken mogen nemen. Rijke wijnkelder en aangename kamers.

Ten Beukel, Markekerkstraat 19, ✆ 0 56 21 54 69, *tenbeukel@pandora.be, Fax 0 56 32 89 65* – AE VISA AX e *fermé 23 fév.-2 mars, 16 août-8 sept., sam. midi, dim. soir, lundi et merc. soir* – **Repas** Lunch 38 bc – 45/86 bc.

◆ Une "Lady chef" officie aux fourneaux de ce petit restaurant familial où un choix de préparations classiques tout doucettement adaptées au goût du jour vous sera proposé.

◆ Klein familiebedrijf, waar een vrouwelijke chef de leiding heeft over de keukenbrigade. Klassieke gerechten die voorzichtig aan de huidige smaak worden aangepast.

Het Vliegend Tapijt, Pottelberg 189, ✆ 0 56 22 27 45, *st.francois@skynet.be, Fax 0 56 22 27 45* – P. VISA – *fermé sem. carnaval, dern. sem. juil.-2 prem. sem. août, dim. et lundi* – **Repas** carte 33 à 41. AX y

◆ Un sympathique bistrot contemporain baptisé Le Tapis Volant (Vliegend Tapijt) s'est posé dans cette villa au bord de la route. Salle à manger habillée de lambris modernes.

◆ Deze sympathieke en eigentijdse bistro is gevestigd in een villa langs de weg. De eetzaal is modern en van lambrisering voorzien.

à Rollegem *par ⑤ : 9 km* C *Kortrijk – ✉ 8510 Rollegem :*

Scalini, Lampestraat 89, ✆ 0 56 40 35 00, *scalini@tijd.com,* – P. *fermé 21 juil.-15 août, dern. sem. janv., lundi et sam. midi* – **Repas** Lunch 30 – 40.

◆ Cette plaisante petite table décline un registre culinaire classico-bourgeois dans une salle de restaurant croquignolette parée de belles fresques.

◆ Leuk eettentje met mooie muurschilderingen, waar u kunt smullen van simpele, maar lekkere schotels die op klassieke leest zijn geschoeid.

KRUIBEKE *9150 Oost-Vlaanderen* 533 K 15 *et* 716 F 2 – *14 684 h.*

Bruxelles 49 – Antwerpen 12 – Gent 53 – Sint-Niklaas 19.

De Ceder, Molenstraat 1, ✆ 0 3 774 30 52, *restaurant.deceder@pandora.be, Fax 0 3 774 30 52,* – P. AE VISA. *fermé dim. soir et lundi* – **Repas** Lunch 29 – 38/64 bc, ♀.

◆ Enraciné de longue date à Kruibeke, Le Cèdre déploie une frondaison de mets classiques. Agréable jardin d'hiver et repas à l'extérieur une fois la sève bien montée.

◆ Deze ceder is stevig geworteld in Kruibeke en zit vol klassieke knoppen. Aangename wintertuin en heerlijk buiten eten zodra de boom begint uit te botten.

KRUISHOUTEM *9770 Oost-Vlaanderen 533 G 17 et 716 D 3 – 7 927 h.*
Bruxelles 73 – Gent 29 – Kortrijk 25 – Oudenaarde 9.

XXX ✿✿ **Hof van Cleve** (Goossens), Riemegemstraat 1 (près N 459, autoroute E 17 - A 14, sortie ⑥), ☎ 0 9 383 58 48, *vancleve@relaischateaux.com, Fax 0 9 383 77 25*, ≤, 余 – P. AE ⊙ ⊙ VISA. ✂
fermé 1 sem. Pâques, 25 juil.-16 août, fin déc.-début janv., dim. et lundi – **Repas** Lunch 60 – 95/185 bc, carte 96 à 189, ♀ ☸.
◆ L'un des "must" de la gastronomie belge : cuisine inventive servie dans une fermette au cadre raffiné avec, en toile de fond, l'échappée en plongée sur une vallée bucolique.
◆ Dit is een van de toppers van de Belgische gastronomie : sfeervol boerderijtje, inventieve keuken en een magnifiek uitzicht op het dal.
Spéc. Sot-l'y-laisse caramélisés et crevettes grises à la fondue de poireaux au gingembre et coulis de crustacés. Pigeonneau au lard croustillant, parmentière aux truffes et Banyuls. Crabe royal, caviar et mousseline de pommes de terre

KURINGEN *Limburg 533 Q 17 et 716 I 3 – voir à Hasselt.*

KUURNE *West-Vlaanderen 533 E 17 et 716 C 3 – voir à Kortrijk.*

La *– voir au nom propre.*

LAARNE *9270 Oost-Vlaanderen 533 I 16 716 E 2 – 11 569 h.*
Voir *Château★ : collection d'argenterie★.*
Bruxelles 51 – Gent 14 – Aalst 29.

XX **Kasteel van Laarne,** Eekhoekstraat 7 (dans les dépendances du château), ☎ 0 9 230 71 78, *info@kasteelvanlaarne-rest.be, Fax 0 9 230 33 05*, ≤, 余 – P – 🏛 25 à 50. AE ⊙ ⊙ VISA
fermé 3 dern. sem. juil., du 2 au 9 janv., lundi et mardi – **Repas** Lunch 25 – 35/65 bc, ♀.
◆ Restaurant occupant les dépendances du château, sur lequel la terrasse dressée au bord des douves offre une jolie vue. Élégante salle à manger au décor classique actualisé.
◆ Restaurant in de bijgebouwen van het kasteel, dat goed te zien is vanaf het terras aan de rand van de slotgracht. Elegante eetzaal met een modern-klassiek interieur.

XX **Dennenhof,** Eekhoekstraat 62, ☎ 0 9 230 09 56, *info@dennenhof.com, Fax 0 9 231 23 96* – ▤ P. AE ⊙ VISA
fermé du 8 au 18 mars, 19 juil.-10 août, dim. soir, lundi et jeudi soir – **Repas** Lunch 30 – 35/83 bc, ♀.
◆ À portée de mousquet du château, table classique dans sa cuisine et son décor. Nombreuses préparations de homard et cave honorant le vignoble californien. Terrasse apéritive.
◆ Dit restaurant bij het kasteel van Laarne kent zijn klassieken ! Kreeftspecialiteiten en Californische wijnen. Op het terras kan het aperitief worden genuttigd.

LACUISINE *Luxembourg belge 534 Q 24 et 716 I 6 – voir à Florenville.*

LAETHEM-ST-MARTIN *Oost-Vlaanderen 533 G 16 et 716 D 2 – voir Sint-Martens-Latem.*

LAFORET *Namur 534 O 23 – voir à Vresse-sur-Semois.*

LANAKEN *3620 Limburg 533 S 17 et 716 J 3 – 24 033 h.*
ℹ *Koning Albertlaan 110 ☎ 0 89 72 24 67, info@vvvlanaken.be, Fax 0 89 72 25 30.*
Bruxelles 108 – Maastricht 8 – Hasselt 29 – Liège 34.

🏨 **Eurotel,** Koning Albertlaan 264 (Nord : 2 km sur N 78), ☎ 0 89 72 28 22, *eurotel@skynet.be, Fax 0 89 72 28 24*, 余, ⚒, ≘s, ▣, 🚲 – ⫼ ▣ P – 🏛 25 à 140. AE ⊙ ⊙ VISA. ✂
Repas ***Arte*** *(fermé sam. midi)* Lunch 22 – 40 – **82 ch** ☕ 71/135 – ½ P 93/122.
◆ Établissement récent construit aux portes de la ville. Chambres fonctionnelles de diverses tailles, fraîchement rénovées. Salles de réunions et centre de remise en forme. À table, répertoire culinaire classico-traditionnel diversifié. Cave franco-transalpine.
◆ Vrij nieuw hotel aan de rand van de stad, met functionele, moderne kamers van verschillend formaat. Vergaderzalen en fitnessruimte. Op tafel een zeer gevarieerd klassiek-traditioneel repertoire, begeleid door een mooie Franse of Italiaanse wijn.

Slot Pietersheim ⚘, Waterstraat 54, ✆ 0 89 71 03 60, *reservaties@slotpietersheim.be, Fax 0 89 71 40 94,* ←, ☂, ⚲ – |♦| TV P – 🎓 25 à 40. AE ⓓ ⓜ VISA. ✈
Repas *Lunch 36* – carte 42 à 62 – **10 ch** ☐ 80/109 – ½ P 72/77.

◆ Ce paisible châtelet s'ouvrant sur un parc public héberge des chambres plutôt pratiques, mais de bon ton, réparties sur deux étages, ainsi que plusieurs salons. Salle à manger profitant d'une vue sur le parc. Cuisine au goût du jour.

◆ Dit vredige kasteeltje grenst aan een openbaar park. De kamers zijn praktisch, maar smaakvol en over twee verdiepingen verdeeld. Ook zijn er verscheidene lounges. Vanuit de eetzaal ontvouwt zich een fraai uitzicht op het park. Eigentijdse keuken.

à Neerharen *Nord : 3 km sur N 78* C *Lanaken* – ✉ *3620 Neerharen :*

Host. La Butte aux Bois ⚘, Paalsteenlaan 90, ✆ 0 89 73 97 70, *info@labutteauxbois.be, Fax 0 89 72 16 47,* ☂, ⚲, ≘s, ⊡, ⚲, ⚲ – |♦| TV P – 🎓 25 à 350. AE ⓓ ⓜ VISA
Repas *Lunch 30* – 37/84 bc, ♀ – ☐ 15 – **38 ch** 99/215, – 2 suites – ½ P 110/160.

◆ Tranquillité assurée dans cette imposante gentilhommière émergeant de la verdure. Grandes chambres douillettes et bonnes installations pour se réunir ou "décompresser".

◆ Rust verzekerd in dit imposante landhuis tussen het groen. Grote behaaglijke kamers en uitstekende voorzieningen om te vergaderen of te relaxen.

à Rekem *Nord : 6 km sur N 78* C *Lanaken* – ✉ *3621 Rekem :*

Vogelsanck, Steenweg 282, ✆ 0 89 71 72 50, *Fax 0 89 71 87 69* – ▤ P. AE ⓜ VISA
fermé prem. sem. juil., prem. sem. sept., prem. sem. janv., lundi, mardi et sam. midi – **Repas** *Lunch 22* – carte 35 à 46.

◆ Petite affaire familiale occupant un chalet-villa, le Chant d'Oiseau (Vogelsanck) mitonne un éventail de recettes classico-bourgeoises. Plat du jour, suggestions et menus.

◆ Klein familiebedrijf in een chaletachtige villa, waar klassiek-traditionele schotels op het vuur staan te pruttelen. Dagschotels, wisselende gerechten en menu's.

LANGDORP *Vlaams-Brabant* 533 O 17 *et* 716 H 3 – *voir à Aarschot.*

LANKLAAR *Limburg* 533 T 16 – *voir à Dilsen.*

LASNE *1380 Brabant Wallon* 533 L 18, 534 L 18 *et* 716 G 3 – *13 641 h.*

⛳18 *(2 parcours)* ⛳9 *au Nord : 1 km à Ohain, Vieux Chemin de Wavre 50* ✆ *0 2 633 18 50, Fax 0 2 633 28 66.*
Bruxelles 27 – Charleroi 41 – Mons 54 – Nivelles 20.

Le Caprice des Deux, r. Genleau 8, ✆ 0 2 633 65 65, *Fax 0 2 652 39 00* – AE ⓓ ⓜ VISA
fermé Pâques, 2 prem. sem. sept., dim. et lundi – **Repas** *Lunch 23* – 40/66 bc.

◆ À deux pas de la gare de Lasne, restaurant au format "poche" servant une cuisine bien en phase avec l'époque dans un intérieur guilleret aux tonalités jaune-ocre et fuchsia.

◆ Restaurantje in "zakformaat", vlak bij het station van Lasne. Vrolijk interieur in okergeel en fuchsia, waar eigentijdse gerechten worden geserveerd.

à Plancenoit *Sud-Ouest : 5 km* C *Lasne* – ✉ *1380 Plancenoit :*

Le Vert d'Eau, r. Bachée 131, ✆ 0 2 633 54 52, *vertd'eau@pi.be, Fax 0 2 633 54 52,* ☂ – AE ⓜ VISA
fermé 2 sem. carnaval, 2 sem. en sept., lundi soir, mardi et sam. midi – **Repas** *Lunch 14* – 26/45.

◆ Adresse sympathique et dans l'air du temps, connue pour son répertoire culinaire classico-traditionnel soigné et son choix de savoureux menus. Réservation conseillée.

◆ Dit sympathieke restaurant is een kind van zijn tijd. Het staat bekend om zijn goed verzorgde klassiek-traditionele keuken en zijn heerlijke menu's. Reserveren aanbevolen.

LATOUR *Luxembourg belge* 534 S 25 *et* 716 J 7 – *voir à Virton.*

LAUWE *8930 West-Vlaanderen* C *Menen 32 156 h.* 533 E 18 *et* 716 C 3.

Bruxelles 100 – Kortrijk 10 – Lille 22.

't Hoveke ⚘ avec ch, Larstraat 206, ✆ 0 56 41 35 84, *Fax 0 56 41 55 11,* ☂, ⚲, ⚲ – ▤ TV P – 🎓 25 à 150. AE ⓓ ⓜ VISA
fermé 20 juil.-10 août, du 5 au 15 janv., dim. soir, lundi soir et mardi – **Repas** *Lunch 42 bc* – carte 48 à 85 – **4 ch** ☐ 92/104 – ½ P 140.

◆ Cette jolie ferme du 18e s. cernée de douves vous installe dans une salle à manger cossue coiffée de robustes poutres. Cuisine classique et cave fournie.

◆ Mooie 18e-eeuwse hoeve met een slotgracht, waar u aan tafel gaat in een rijk aandoende eetzaal met robuuste balken. Klassieke keuken en een goed gevulde wijnkelder.

XXX **Ter Biest,** Lauwbergstraat 237, ✆ 0 56 41 47 49, *Fax 0 56 42 13 86*, – P – 25 à 70. AE VISA
fermé du 1er au 14 août, mardi soir, merc. et dim. soir – **Repas** *Lunch 40 bc* – carte 41 à 65.
◆ Ferme ancienne dont l'environnement champêtre et le cadre rustico-bourgeois s'harmonisent bien avec l'orientation culinaire classico-traditionnelle du chef.
◆ Oude boerderij, waarvan de landelijke omgeving en het rustieke interieur in harmonie zijn met de klassiek-traditionele stijl van de chef-kok.

XX **de Mangerie,** Wevelgemstraat 37, ✆ 0 56 42 00 75, *info@demangerie.be, Fax 0 56 42 42 62*, – VISA.
fermé fin fév.-début mars, 2e quinz. août-début sept., sam. midi, dim. soir et lundi – **Repas** *Lunch 28 bc* – 37/65 bc.
◆ Une petite carte engageante, avec son menu vedette, vous sera soumise dans cette maison bourgeoise proche de la place du marché. Réservez votre table dans le jardin d'hiver.
◆ In dit herenhuis bij het marktplein krijgt u een kleine, maar aanlokkelijke kaart gepresenteerd. Het menu is bij menigeen favoriet. Reserveer een tafel in de wintertuin.

XX **Culinair,** Dronckaertstraat 508, ✆ 0 56 42 67 33, *info@restaurantculinair.be, Fax 0 56 42 67 34*, – P. AE VISA.
fermé 23 fév.-1er mars, 23 août-6 sept., dim. soir et lundi – **Repas** *Lunch 29* – 39/71 bc.
◆ Grosse villa transformée en restaurant maniant un registre culinaire au goût du jour. Intérieur sémillant, avec véranda. L'été, on dresse quelques tables au jardin.
◆ Deze grote villa is nu een restaurant met een culinair register dat goed bij deze tijd past. Vrolijke eetzaal met serre. 's Zomers worden enkele tafeltjes in de tuin gedekt.

LAVAUX-SAINTE-ANNE *5580 Namur* C *Rochefort 11 818 h.* 534 P 22 *et* 716 I 5.
Bruxelles 112 – Bouillon 64 – Namur 50 – Dinant 34 – Rochefort 16.

Maison Lemonnier, r. Baronne Lemonnier 82, ✆ 0 84 38 88 83, *restolavaux@swing.be, Fax 0 84 38 88 95*, – TV P. AE VISA JCB
fermé 23 juin-8 juil., 20 déc.-29 janv., lundi et mardi – **Repas** voir rest ***du Château*** ci-après – 9 – **8 ch** 87/112 – ½ P 90.
◆ Au centre du village, imposante demeure famenoise bâtie en pierres du pays. Grandes chambres paisibles, aussi charmantes que douillettes. Coin salon et jardin de repos.
◆ Dit indrukwekkende gebouw is opgetrokken van steen uit de Famenne en staat midden in het dorp. Grote rustige kamers die knus aandoen. Zithoek en tuin om lekker te luieren.

XXX **du Château** - H. Maison Lemonnier, r. Château 10, ✆ 0 84 38 88 83, *restolavaux@swing.be, Fax 0 84 38 88 95*, – P – 50. AE VISA JCB
fermé 23 juin-8 juil., 20 déc.-29 janv., lundi et mardi – **Repas** *Lunch 25* – 45/90 bc.
◆ Table toute d'élégance et de sobriété, installée dans les dépendances (17e s.) du château. Carte actuelle et recherchée, variant avec les saisons. Cave de grand seigneur.
◆ Sober en elegant restaurant in de 17e-eeuwse bijgebouwen van het kasteel. Eigentijdse kaart die met de seizoenen verandert. De wijnkelder hoort bij een grand seigneur.

Le – *voir au nom propre.*

LEBBEKE *9280 Oost-Vlaanderen* 533 J 16 *et* 716 F 3 – *17 305 h.*
Bruxelles 27 – Antwerpen 41 – Gent 37.

XX **Rembrandt,** Laurierstraat 6, ✆ 0 52 41 04 09, *Fax 0 52 41 45 75*, Avec taverne – P. AE VISA
fermé 2 dern. sem. juil.-prem. sem. août, lundi soir et mardi – **Repas** *Lunch 20* – 45.
◆ Occupant plusieurs maisons mitoyennes, ce restaurant niché au cœur du bourg présente un intérieur rustique à touches modernes. Recettes classiques. Partie taverne.
◆ Dit café-restaurant in het hart van het dorp beslaat een aantal belendende panden. Het interieur is rustiek met een moderne toets. Klassieke recepten.

LEFFINGE *West-Vlaanderen* 533 C 15 *et* 716 B 2 – *voir à Oostende.*

LEISELE *8691 West-Vlaanderen* C *Alveringem 4 865 h.* 533 A 17 *et* 716 A 3.
Bruxelles 143 – Brugge 67 – Ieper 27 – Oostende 45 – Veurne 20.

De Zoeten Inval, Lostraat 7, ✆ 0 58 29 99 64, *info@hotelzoeteninval.be, Fax 0 58 29 80 55*, , , – , ch, TV P. AE VISA.
fermé janv. – **Repas** (dîner pour résidents seult) – **6 ch** 100 – ½ P 70/100.
◆ Petite auberge familiale isolée en pleine campagne et profitant d'un grand jardin. Menues chambres personnalisées, parfois munies d'un jacuzzi.
◆ Kleine plattelandsherberg met een grote tuin. De kamers zijn klein, maar hebben een persoonlijk karakter en sommige zijn voorzien van een jacuzzi.

LEKE *West-Vlaanderen* 533 C 16 *et* 716 B 2 – *voir à Diksmuide.*

LEMBEKE *9971 Oost-Vlaanderen* © *Kaprijke 6 111 h.* 533 G 15 *et* 716 D 2.
Bruxelles 75 – Gent 19 – Antwerpen 63 – Brugge 35.

Host. Ter Heide, Tragelstraat 2, ☎ 0 9 377 19 23, *Fax 0 9 377 51 34*, – TV P – 25 à 100. AE ① MC VISA
fermé du 24 au 31 déc. – **Repas** Lunch 23 – carte 38 à 75 – ☐ 13 – **8 ch** 87 – ½ P 93.
• À proximité du bois de Lembeke, dans un quartier résidentiel chic, hostellerie cossue dont les chambres, coquettes, ne manquent ni de sérénité, ni d'espace. Jardin soigné. Opulente brasserie habillée de marbre. Choix de préparations bourgeoises.
• Luxueus hotel in een chique woonwijk bij het bos van Lembeke. In de kamers, die er tiptop uitzien, ontbreekt het noch aan rust noch aan ruimte. Verzorgde tuin. Luxueuze brasserie met veel marmer, waar traditionele gerechten worden geserveerd.

LENS *7870 Hainaut* 533 I 19, 534 I 19 *et* 716 E 4 – *3 823 h.*
Bruxelles 55 – Mons 13 – Ath 13.

XX **Aub. de Lens** avec ch, r. Calvaire 142 (Nord-Ouest : 1,5 km sur N 56), ☎ 0 65 22 90 41, – TV P. MC VISA.
fermé mi-déc.-mi-janv. – **Repas** *(fermé dim. soir et lundi)* Lunch 25 – carte 22 à 46 – ☐ 6 – **6 ch** 40/60 – ½ P 45/50.
• Villa postée aux portes de Lens, à quelques battements d'ailes du parc Paradisio. Mets classiques, salle à manger un brin désuète - comme les chambres -, terrasse et jardin.
• Villa met terras en tuin aan de rand van Lens, op een steenworp afstand van het Paradisiopark. De kamers zijn net als de eetzaal ietwat ouderwets. Klassieke spijzen.

LEOPOLDSBURG (BOURG-LÉOPOLD) *3970 Limburg* 533 Q 16 *et* 716 I 2 – *13 966 h.*
Seringenstraat 7 ☎ 0 11 39 17 80, Fax 0 11 39 11 70.
Bruxelles 83 – Antwerpen 64 – Liège 71 – Eindhoven 44 – Maastricht 59

XXX **'t Pannehuis,** Leopoldsburgsesteenweg 99 (Heppen), ☎ 0 11 34 55 93, *Fax 0 11 34 55 93*, – P. AE MC VISA.
fermé 2e quinz. août, merc. et jeudi – **Repas** Lunch 45 – carte 42 à 58.
• Ravissante "fermette" d'esprit rustique, dont les murs s'animent de colombages. À l'arrière, une terrasse d'été s'ouvre sur un jardin délicieux. Repas au goût du jour.
• Prachtig rustiek vakwerkboerderijtje. Aan de achterkant bevindt zich een tuin met terras, waar het 's zomers heerlijk toeven is. Het eten voldoet aan de huidige smaak.

LESSINES (LESSEN) *7860 Hainaut* 533 I 18, 534 I 18 *et* 716 E 3 – *17 340 h.*
Voir *N.-D.-à la Rose*★.
r. Grammont 2 ☎ 0 68 33 36 90, info@notredamealarose.com, Fax 0 68 33 36 90.
Bruxelles 57 – Mons 35 – Aalst 35 – Gent 49 – Tournai 45.

X **Le Napoléon,** r. Lenoir Scaillet 25, ☎ 0 68 33 39 39 – AE ① MC VISA
fermé 22 janv.-10 fév., 23 août-15 sept. et merc. – **Repas** (déjeuner seult sauf sam.) Lunch 8 – 24.
• Gentiment classiques, les menus-carte composés par cet établissement familial excentré ne vous fâcheront pas avec votre banquier. Clientèle locale fidélisée de longue date.
• Een etentje in dit familierestaurant even buiten het centrum doet geen pijn in uw portemonnee. Licht klassieke kaart en menu's. Veel trouwe klanten die er al jarenlang komen.

Dans ce guide
un même symbole, un même mot,
imprimé en rouge ou en ***noir****, en maigre ou en* ***gras****,*
n'ont pas tout à fait la même signification.
Lisez attentivement les pages explicatives.

LEUVEN (LOUVAIN) *3000* P *Vlaams-Brabant* 533 N 17 et 716 H 3 – *89 152 h.*

Voir *Hôtel de Ville*** (Stadhuis)* BYZ **H** – *Collégiale St-Pierre* (St-Pieterskerk) : musée d'Art religieux**, Cène**, Tabernacle*, Tête de Christ*, Jubé** BY **A** – *Grand béguinage** (Groot Begijnhof)* BZ – *Plafonds* de l'Abbaye du Parc (Abdij van't Park)* DZ **B** – *Façade* de l'église St-Michel (St-Michielskerk)* BZ **C**.

Musée : *communal Vander Kelen - Mertens* (Stedelijk Museum)* BY **M**.

Env. *Korbeek-Dijle : retable* de l'église St-Barthélemy (St-Batholomeüskerk) par N 253 : 7 km* DZ.

au Sud-Ouest : 15 km à Duisburg, Hertswegenstraat 59 ☎ 0 2 769 45 85, Fax 0 2 767 97 52 - par ② : 13 km à Sint-Joris-Winge par ② : 13 km, Leuvensesteenweg 252, ☎ 0 16 63 40 53, Fax 0 16 63 21 40.

Grote Markt 9 ☎ 0 16 21 15 39, toerisme@leuven.be, Fax 0 16 21 15 49 – Fédération provinciale de tourisme, Diestsesteenweg 52, ✉ 3010 Kessel-Lo, ☎ 0 16 26 76 20, toerisme@vl-brabant.be, Fax 0 16 26 76 76.

Bruxelles 27 ⑥ – *Antwerpen 48* ⑨ – *Liège 74* ④ – *Namur 53* ⑤ – *Turnhout 60* ①

Plans pages suivantes

Begijnhof sans rest, Tervuursevest 70, ☎ 0 16 29 10 10, *info@begijnhofcongreshotel.be, Fax 0 16 29 10 22*, – AE VISA BZ g
64 ch 180/200, – 5 suites.
◆ Ensemble récent dont le style s'harmonise à l'architecture du grand béguinage qu'il jouxte. Communs cossus, chambres douillettes et ravissant jardin d'agrément.
◆ Vrij nieuw hotel dat qua bouw goed bij de architectuur van het naburige Groot Begijnhof past. Weelderige gemeenschappelijke ruimten, gezellige kamers en een schitterende tuin.

Novotel, Vuurkruisenlaan 4, ☎ 0 16 21 32 00, *H3153@accor-hotels.com, Fax 0 16 21 32 01*, – 25 à 180. AE VISA
Repas Lunch 15 – carte 22 à 40 – 14 – **139 ch** 125/130. CY z
◆ Nouvel hôtel situé aux abords de la gare et des célèbres brasseries. L'aménagement des chambres est en tout fidèle à l'enseigne Novotel. Parking souterrain commode.
◆ Nieuw hotel in de buurt van het station en de bekende bierbrouwerijen. De kamers zijn in alle opzichten trouw aan de Novotelformule. Handige ondergrondse parkeergarage.

Binnenhof sans rest, Maria-Theresiastraat 65, ☎ 0 16 20 55 92, *info@hotelbinnenhof.be, Fax 0 16 23 69 26* – – 25 à 50. AE VISA. CY a
60 ch 110/122.
◆ Bien pratique pour les usagers du rail, cet ensemble hôtelier abrite une soixantaine de chambres convenablement équipées. Salle des petits-déjeuners et bar plaisants.
◆ Dit hotelcomplex is ideaal voor treinreizigers. Het beschikt over een zestigtal kamers met goede voorzieningen. Prettige ontbijtzaal en bar.

New Damshire sans rest, Pater Damiaanplein-Schapenstraat 1, ☎ 0 16 23 21 15, *reservations@newdamshire.com, Fax 0 16 23 32 08* – AE VISA.
fermé 23 déc.-4 janv. – **34 ch** 120/136, – 1 suite. BZ m
◆ La consonance anglo-saxonne de l'enseigne est trompeuse : l'établissement n'a en effet pas grand chose de "british". Bonnes chambres agencées d'une façon avenante.
◆ De Engels klinkende naam zet u op het verkeerde been, want het New Damshire is niet zo "British". De hotelkamers zijn prima en op een aantrekkelijke manier ingericht.

Theater sans rest, Bondgenotenlaan 20, ☎ 0 16 22 28 19, *reservations@theaterhotel.be, Fax 0 16 28 49 39* – AE VISA. BY v
fermé fin déc.-3 janv. – **21 ch** 112/135.
◆ Cet hôtel jouxtant le théâtre met quelques chambres duplex à votre disposition. Une galerie d'art moderne tient lieu de salle de breakfast. Taverne avec petite restauration.
◆ Dit hotel tegenover de schouwburg beschikt over enkele duplexkamers. Het ontbijt wordt genuttigd in een moderne kunstgalerie. In de taverne kunt u een klein hapje eten.

Ibis sans rest, Brusselsestraat 52, ☎ 0 16 29 31 11, *H1457@accor-hotels.com, Fax 0 16 23 87 92* – AE VISA BY b
9 – **72 ch** 88.
◆ Construction du début des années 1990 distribuant ses chambres standard sur cinq étages. Une cure de rajeunissement vient de les accorder aux nouvelles normes Ibis.
◆ Hotel uit het begin van de jaren 1990 met vijf etages. De standaardkamers hebben onlangs een verjongingskuur ondergaan om ze aan de nieuwe normen van de keten aan te passen.

XXX **Sire Pynnock,** Hogeschoolplein 10, ☎ 0 16 20 25 32, *sirepynnock@frankfol.be, Fax 0 16 20 11 26* – – 30. AE VISA. BZ n
fermé du 8 au 30 août, 26 déc.-3 janv., sam. midi, dim. soir et lundi – **Repas** Lunch 36 – 54/85.
◆ Sur une placette de la vieille ville, maison de maître déclinant un répertoire culinaire assez élaboré, où les légumes sont à l'honneur. Vins du monde. Intérieur cossu.
◆ Restaurant met een weelderig interieur in een herenhuis aan een pleintje in de oude stad. Vrij verfijnde keuken, met het accent op groenten. Wijnen uit allerlei landen.

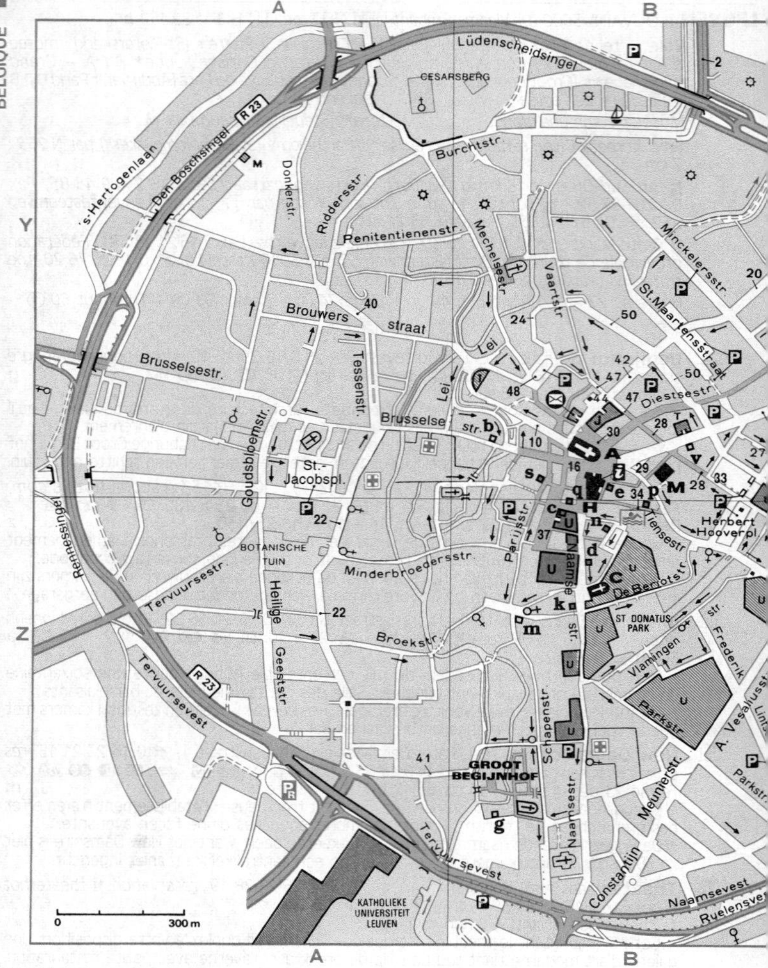

XXX ✿ **Belle Epoque** (Tubee), Bondgenotenlaan 94, ✆ 0 16 22 33 89, *Fax 0 16 22 37 42*, ⛱ – ▤. AE ⓓ ⓜ VISA – *fermé 2 sem. carnaval, 22 juil.-15 août, dim. et lundi* – **Repas** *Lunch 30* – 53/79 bc, carte 53 à 86. CY d

◆ L'enseigne fêtait ses 20 ans en l'an 2000. Cuisine classico-traditionnelle soignée servie dans le cadre raffiné d'une jolie demeure bourgeoise. Cave prestigieuse.

◆ Dit restaurant in een geraffineerd ingericht herenhuis heeft in 2000 zijn twintigjarige jubileum gevierd. Verzorgde klassiek-traditionele keuken en prestigieuze wijnkelder.

Spéc. Tournedos de langoustines rôtis à la "mozzarella di Bufala". Filet de barbue aux nouilles et girolles. Pigeon de Bresse à l'essence de truffes

XX **Ming Dynasty,** Oude Markt 9, ✆ 0 16 29 20 20, *info@mingdynasty.be, Fax 0 16 29 44 04*, ⛱, Cuisine chinoise, ouvert jusqu'à 23 h – ▤. AE ⓓ ⓜ VISA BYZ c
fermé mardi sauf en été – **Repas** *Lunch 18* – 24/88 bc.

◆ Manger chinois sans chinoiseries ? La carte de cette table asiatique au décor européanisé vous promène entre le Sichuan, Canton, Shanghai et Pékin. Ribambelle de menus.

◆ Chinees eten zonder chinoiserieën ? De kaart van dit Aziatische restaurant met zijn Europese decor voert u naar Sichuan, Kanton, Shanghai en Peking. Ruime keuze menu's.

LEUVEN

Aarschotsesteenweg . . BY 2
Bierbeekpleindreef . . . . DZ 3
Bondgenotenlaan . . . BCY 5
Borstelstr. . . . . DZ 6
Boudewijnlaan . . . . DZ 7
Brusselsestr. . . . . AY
Celestijnenlaan . . . . . . DZ 8
Diestsesteenweg . . . . . DZ 9
Dirk Boutslaan . . . . BY 10
Eenmeilaan . . . . DZ 11
Fonteinstraat . . . . DZ 12
Geldenaaksebaan . . . . DZ 15
Grote Markt . . . . BY 16
Grote Molenweg . . . . . . DZ 18
Holsbeek-sesteenweg . . . . DZ 19
Jean Baptiste van Monsstr. . . BCY 20
Kapeldreef . . . . DZ 21
Kapucijnenvoer . . . . . . AZ 22
Kard. Mercierlaan . . . . DZ 23
Karel v. Lotharingenstr . . BY 24
Leopoldstr. I . . . . BY 27
Leopold Vanderkelenstr. . BY 28
Maarschalk Fochpl. . . . . BY 29
Margarethapl. . . . . BY 30
Martelarenpl. . . . . CY 31
Mgr Ladeuzepl . . . . BY 33
Muntstr. . . . . BY 34
Naamsesteenweg . . . . . DZ 35
Naamsestr. . . . . BZ
Nieuwe Mechelsesteenweg . . DZ 36
Oude Markt . . . . BZ 37
Pakenstr. . . . . DZ 39
Petermannenstr. . . . . AY 40
Redingenstr. . . . . ABZ 41
Rijschoolstr. . . . . BY 42
Smolderspl. . . . . BY 44
Tiensesteenweg . . . . DZ 45
Tiensestr. . . . . BCY
Vaartstr. . . . . BY 47
Vismarkt . . . . BY 48
Vital Decosterstr. . . . . . . BY 50
Waversebaan . . . . DZ 51

Si vous cherchez un hôtel tranquille ou isolé, consultez d'abord les cartes de l'introduction ou repérez dans le texte les établissements indiqués avec le signe ⚲ *ou* ⚲

XX **Ramberg Hof,** Naamsestraat 60, ✆ 0 16 29 32 72, *reservatie@ramberghof.be, Fax 0 16 20 10 90,* ☂, Ouvert jusqu'à 23 h – AE ◑ MC VISA. ✈ BZ k
fermé dern. sem. août-2 prem. sem. sept., fin déc., dim. soir et lundi – **Repas** Lunch 22 – 36/56 bc.
• Au cœur du quartier universitaire, restaurant-véranda que dessert une porte cochère. Mets classico-bourgeois et suggestions de saison. L'été venu, on mange au jardin.
• Een koetspoort leidt naar dit restaurant met serre in de universiteitswijk. Klassiek-burgerlijke keuken en seizoengebonden schotels. Bij mooi weer wordt in de tuin gegeten.

XX **Beluga,** Krakenstraat 12, ✆ 0 16 23 43 93, *beluga@proximedia.be, Fax 0 16 20 51 76,* Avec produits de la mer – ▤. AE MC VISA. ✈ BYZ q
fermé sam. midi, dim. et lundi midi – **Repas** Lunch 30 – carte 50 à 74, ♀.
• Amateurs de cuisine de la mer, votre bonheur se trouve à cette petite adresse située dans une rue piétonne du centre animé. Salle à manger agrémentée de lambris et vitraux.
• Visliefhebbers komen beslist aan hun trekken in dit restaurantje aan een voetgangersstraat in het levendige centrum. De eetzaal is verfraaid met houtwerk en glas-in-loodramen.

X **Oesterbar,** Muntstraat 23, ✆ 0 16 20 28 38, *info@oesterbar.be, Fax 0 16 20 54 84*, Produits de la mer – AE MC VISA. BYZ p
fermé 1 sem. en avril, 2 prem. sem. sept., prem. sem. janv., dim. et lundi – **Repas** Lunch 24 – 42.
◆ Une faim de loup (de mer) ? Laissez-vous donc dériver vers ce bar à huîtres au cadre actuel et avenant. Superbe cave franco-italienne à écumer. Coude à coude sympathique.
◆ Honger als een (zee)wolf ? Laat u zich dan afdrijven naar deze moderne oesterbar, waar u knus schouder aan schouder zit. Geweldige Frans-Italiaanse wijnkelder.

X **'t Zwart Schaap,** Boekhandelstraat 1, ✆ 0 16 23 24 16, *Fax 0 16 23 24 16* – AE MC VISA BY e
fermé 15 juil.-15 août, dim., lundi et jours fériés – **Repas** Lunch 17 – carte 31 à 51.
◆ Au coin d'une ruelle piétonne jouxtant l'hôtel de ville, restaurant familial dont le décor lambrissé évoque un bistrot ancien. Préparations franco-belges de bon aloi.
◆ Familiebedrijf op de hoek van een voetgangerssteeg naast het stadhuis, dat door zijn lambrisering aan een oude bistro doet denken. Frans-Belgische keuken van goede kwaliteit.

X **De Vlaamsche Reus,** Naamsestraat 53, ✆ 0 16 23 41 21, *Fax 0 16 23 13 91*, – AE MC VISA. BZ d
fermé 1 sem. Pâques, 22 juil.-21 août, sam. midi, dim. midi et lundi – **Repas** Lunch 20 – 40/65 bc.
◆ Il règne une atmosphère cordiale dans ce petit resto de quartier concoctant un choix de recettes au goût du jour. Salle à manger façon "bistrot". Service prévenant.
◆ Buurtrestaurantje met een gemoedelijke sfeer, waar u kunt smullen van eigentijdse gerechten. De eetzaal is als bistro ingericht. Voorkomende bediening.

X **Y-Sing,** Parijsstraat 18, ✆ 0 16 22 80 52, *Fax 0 16 23 40 47*, Cuisine asiatique – . AE MC VISA. BY s
fermé 29 janv.-11 fév., du 17 au 30 juin et merc. – **Repas** 15/20.
◆ Plus de quarante ans de bons et loyaux services pour ce doyen de la restauration asiatique louvaniste ! Grande carte sino-thaïlandaise assez authentique, incluant des menus.
◆ Y-Sing bestaat al ruim 40 jaar en is daarmee het oudste Aziatische restaurant van Leuven. Uitgebreide kaart met vrij authentieke Chinees-Thaise specialiteiten en menu's.

X **De Rijsttafel,** Tiensestraat 181, ✆ 0 16 22 50 46, Cuisine asiatique – MC VISA. CZ e
fermé mi-juil.-mi-août et lundi – **Repas** Lunch 7 – 17/31.
◆ Le large éventail de mets, menus et suggestions que déploie La Table de riz (De Rijsttafel) vous invite à zigzaguer entre la Chine et le Vietnam. Savoureux et dépaysant !
◆ Aan deze rijsttafel pendelt u tussen China en Vietnam, dankzij de ruime keuze aan gerechten à la carte en smakelijke menu's. Wat men ver haalt, is lekker !

à Blanden *par ⑤ : 7 km* C *Oud-Heverlee 10 640 h.* – ✉ *3052 Blanden :*

XX **Meerdael,** Naamsesteenweg 90 (sur N 25), ✆ 0 16 40 24 02, *meerdael@tijd.com, Fax 0 16 40 81 37*, – P. AE MC VISA.
fermé du 7 au 15 mars, 8 août-1er sept., 26 déc.-10 janv., sam. midi, dim. et lundi – **Repas** Lunch 25 – 45/65 bc.
◆ Jolie fermette transformée en auberge familiale. Cuisine sagement classique, salle à manger égayée de notes rustiques, verdoyante terrasse d'été ombragée et jardin.
◆ Mooi boerderijtje dat tot familierestaurant is verbouwd. Klassieke keuken, eetzaal met rustieke accenten, lommerrijk terras en uitnodigende tuin.

à Heverlee C *Leuven* – ✉ *3001 Heverlee :*

XXX **Arenberg** (Demeestere), Kapeldreef 46, ✆ 0 16 22 47 75, *restaurant.arenberg@pandora.be, Fax 0 16 29 40 64*, ←, – P – 25 à 125. AE MC VISA. DZ r
✿ *fermé 22 fév.-1er mars, 25 juil.-19 août, 31 oct.-8 nov., dim. et lundi* – **Repas** 35/72 bc.
◆ L'élégance contemporaine du décor s'harmonise aux saveurs de notre temps. Réservez votre table dans l'orangerie, adossée aux dépendances du château. Banquets et séminaires.
◆ De elegante, eigentijdse inrichting harmonieert perfect met de kookstijl. Reserveer een tafel in de oranjerie, die tegen de bijgebouwen van het kasteel aan ligt. Ook partijen.
Spéc. Gorge de porc braisée au foie d'oie. Langue de veau et son ris croquant, sabayon de champignons. Tarte tatin au foie d'oie poêlé et sirop de vinaigre de cidre

XX **Couvert couvert,** St-Jansbergsesteenweg 171, ✆ 0 16 29 69 79, *Fax 0 16 29 59 15*, ←, – P. AE MC VISA DZ n
fermé 2 sem. Pâques, 2 prem. sem. sept., sam. midi, dim. et lundi midi – **Repas** Lunch 30 – 45/77 bc, ♀.
◆ Mets au goût du jour servis dans un intérieur design. Belle cave visible par une coupole. Accès par la terrasse arrière où l'on dresse le couvert en saison. Jardin d'aromates.
◆ Trendy keuken en designinterieur. Mooie wijnkelder die door de glaskoepel zichtbaar is. Toegang via het terras aan de achterkant, waar 's zomers wordt gegeten. Kruidentuin.

XX **Boardroom** avec ch, J. Vandenbemptlaan 6, ✆ 0 16 31 44 55, *info@boardroom.be, Fax 0 16 31 44 56,* 🏞, 🚲 - ▤ ch, 📺 - 🏋 40. AE ⓓ Ⓜ VISA. ✈ DZ a
Repas *(fermé sam. midi) Lunch 31* - carte 35 à 61, ♀ - ☕ 11 - **9 ch** 100.
◆ Luxueuse brasserie étendant ses tables dans deux salles à manger ; l'une d'elles s'ouvre sur une agréable terrasse d'été. Chambres confortables, le plus souvent avec balcon.
◆ Luxueuze brasserie met twee eetzalen, waarvan één uitkomt op een terras dat in de zomer bijzonder aangenaam is. Comfortabele kamers, veelal met balkon.

X **Het land aan de Overkant,** L. Scheursvest 87, ✆ 0 16 22 61 81, *info@hetlandaandeoverkant.be, Fax 0 16 22 59 69,* 🏞 - ▤. AE Ⓜ VISA. ✈ CZ b
fermé sam. midi, dim. et lundi midi - **Repas** *Lunch 26* - 37/79 bc, ♀.
◆ Cette façade discrète dissimule une ample salle dont les lignes, modernes et épurées, évoquent la structure d'un navire. Plats aux accents méditerranéens, délicatement iodés.
◆ Onopvallend gebouw met een grote eetzaal, die door zijn moderne en gestileerde belijning aan een schip doet denken. Visschotels met een mediterraan sausje.

X **Den Bistro,** Hertogstraat 160, ✆ 0 16 40 54 88, *den.bistro@skynet.be, Fax 0 16 40 80 91,* 🏞 - AE ⓓ Ⓜ VISA. ✈ DZ t
fermé dern. sem. avril, 24 août-15 sept., 28 déc.-12 janv., mardi, merc. et sam. midi - **Repas** 28.
◆ Aménagé dans la note néo-rustique, ce bistrot aussi mignon que "sympa" opte pour une carte "brasserie" : préparations traditionnelles présentées avec soin.
◆ Gezellige bistro met een neorustiek interieur, waar een typische "brasseriekaart" wordt gehanteerd. Traditionele gerechten die met zorg zijn klaargemaakt.

à Kessel-Lo Ⓒ *Leuven* - ✉ *3010 Kessel-Lo :*

XX **In Den Mol,** Tiensesteenweg 347, ✆ 0 16 25 11 82, *indenmol@wanadoo.be, Fax 0 16 26 22 65,* 🏞 - Ⓟ. AE ⓓ Ⓜ VISA. ✈ DZ f
fermé dim. soir, lundi et mardi - **Repas** *Lunch 24* - 40.
◆ Au charme intérieur de ce relais rustique du 18e s. s'ajoute l'agrément d'une jolie terrasse et d'un jardin avec volière. Mets classiques et cave bien montée.
◆ Rustiek restaurant in een 18e-eeuws pand met een sfeervol interieur. Mooi terras en tuin met volière. Klassieke keuken en een wijnkelder om met volle teugen van te genieten.

à Oud-Heverlee *par* ⑤ *: 7,5 km - 10 640 h -* ✉ *3050 Oud-Heverlee :*

XX **Spaans Dak,** Maurits Noëstraat 2 (Zoet Water), ✆ 0 16 47 33 33, *info@spaansdak.be, Fax 0 16 47 38 12,* 🏞 - Ⓟ. AE ⓓ Ⓜ VISA
fermé du 12 au 30 juil., lundi et mardi - **Repas** *Lunch 30* - 42/67 bc, ♀.
◆ Les vestiges d'un manoir du 16e s. dominant un étang accueillent cette salle de restaurant moderne, douillette et feutrée. L'assiette, elle aussi, vit avec son temps.
◆ De overblijfselen van een 16e-eeuws kasteeltje aan een vijver vormen de setting van dit moderne restaurant, dat warm en behaaglijk aandoet. De keuken is eveneens eigentijds.

à Vaalbeek *par* ⑤ *: 6,5 km* Ⓒ *Oud-Heverlee 10 640 h. -* ✉ *3054 Vaalbeek :*

XX **De Bibliotheek,** Gemeentestraat 12, ✆ 0 16 40 05 58, *info@debibliotheek.be, Fax 0 16 40 20 69,* 🏞 - Ⓟ - 🏋 25 à 70. AE ⓓ Ⓜ VISA JCB - *fermé 1 sem. carnaval, 2 dern. sem. juil., mardi, merc. et sam. midi* - **Repas** *Lunch 28* - 40/67 bc, ♀.
◆ Table élégante et "cosy" dont l'ambiance, autant que le décor, tout récemment rénové, évoque un "british club". Registre culinaire au goût du jour, avec lunch et menus.
◆ Stijlvol restaurant, waarvan het pas gerenoveerde interieur en de ambiance aan een Engelse herensociëteit doen denken. Eigentijdse kaart met een lunchformule en menu's.

à Winksele *par* ⑧ *: 5 km* Ⓒ *Herent 19 040 h. -* ✉ *3020 Winksele :*

X **De Pachtenhoef,** Dorpsstraat 29b, ✆ 0 16 48 85 41, *Fax 0 16 48 85 41* - ▤ Ⓟ. AE ⓓ Ⓜ VISA. ✈
fermé 2e quinz. juin, lundi, mardi et merc. - **Repas** 30/45.
◆ Au cœur de Winksele, restaurant champêtre proposant un petit choix de recettes classico-traditionnelles. Le sage menu-carte est plébiscité.
◆ Rustiek restaurant in het hart van Winksele. Kleine kaart met klassiek-traditionele gerechten en een schappelijk geprijsd menu dat zeer gewild is.

LEUZE-EN-HAINAUT *7900 Hainaut* 533 G 19, 534 G 19 *et* 716 D 4 - *13 116 h.*

Bruxelles 70 - Mons 15 - Gent 56 - Tournai 16.

🏠 **La Cour Carrée,** chaussée de Tournai 5, ✆ 0 69 66 48 25, *Fax 0 69 66 18 82,* 🏋, 🏞 - 📺 Ⓟ - 🏋 25 à 40. AE ⓓ Ⓜ VISA. ✈
fermé vend. soir, sam. midi et dim. - **Repas** *Lunch 15* - 22/48 bc - **9 ch** ☕ 45/59 - ½ P 60.
◆ Ferme-auberge agrandie d'une aile récente renfermant quelques chambres fonctionnelles. Le regard de certaines embrasse la campagne, les autres donnent côté "cour carrée". Salle à manger au charme suranné. Carte classico-régionale actualisée.
◆ Herberg in een boerenhoeve, waar onlangs een vleugel is aangebouwd. De kamers zijn functioneel en bieden uitzicht op het platteland of de vierkante binnenplaats. De eetzaal straalt een ouderwetse charme uit. Klassieke en regionale gerechten.

BELGIQUE

XX **Le Châlet de la Bourgogne,** chaussée de Tournai 1, ✆ 0 69 66 19 78, *Fax 0 69 66 19 78* – ▤ P. AE ① ⓔ VISA
fermé du 1er au 12 mars, du 12 au 30 juil., du 15 au 26 nov. et merc. – **Repas** (déjeuner seult sauf week-end) 30/55 bc.
◆ Au bord de la grand-route, agréable restaurant orienté vers une cuisine au goût du jour. Les menus, plus classiques, changent avec les saisons. Service tout sourire.
◆ Aangenaam restaurant langs de grote weg, dat zich op een eigentijdse kookstijl toelegt. De menu's zijn wat klassieker en veranderen met de seizoenen. Vriendelijke bediening.

LIBRAMONT *6800 Luxembourg belge* C *Libramont-Chevigny 9 412 h.* 534 R 23 *et* 716 J 6.
Bruxelles 143 – Bouillon 33 – Arlon 52 – Dinant 68 – La Roche-en-Ardenne 43.

à Recogne *Sud-Ouest : 1 km* C *Libramont-Chevigny* – ✉ *6800 Recogne :*

L'Amandier, av. de Bouillon 70, ✆ 0 61 22 53 73, *hotel.l.amandier@skynet.be, Fax 0 61 22 57 10,* Fδ, ≘s, ♂ – |‡| TV P – 🔬 25 à 200. AE ① ⓔ VISA. ✗ rest
Repas *(fermé dim. soir et lundi) Lunch 23* – 35/56 bc – **24 ch** ☐ 60/78 – ½ P 82.
◆ Chambres fonctionnelles, fitness, sauna, solarium, salles de réunions et restaurant se partagent l'intérieur de cette construction récente située en léger retrait de la route.
◆ Hotel in een nieuw gebouw, even van de weg af, dat plaats biedt aan functionele kamers, vergaderzalen, een fitnessruimte, een sauna, een solarium en een restaurant.

LICHTAART *Antwerpen* 533 O 15 *et* 716 H 2 – *voir à Kasterlee.*

LICHTERVELDE *West-Vlaanderen* 533 D 16 *et* 716 C 2 – *voir à Torhout.*

LIÈGE – LUIK

4000 **P** 533 S 19, 534 S 19 *et* 716 J 4 – *185 131 h.*

Bruxelles 97 ⑨ – Amsterdam 242 ① – Antwerpen 119 ⑫ – Köln 122 ② – Luxembourg 159 ⑤ – Maastricht 32 ①.

OFFICES DE TOURISME

En Féronstrée 92 ☎ 0 4 221 92 21, office.tourisme@liege.be, Fax 0 4 221 92 22 et Gare des Guillemins ☎ 0 4 252 44 19 – Fédération provinciale de tourisme, bd de la Sauvenière 77 ☎ 0 4 232 65 10, ftpl@ftpl.be, Fax 0 4 232 65 11.

RENSEIGNEMENTS PRATIQUES

9 r. Bernalmont 2 (BT) ☎ 0 4 227 44 66, Fax 0 4 227 91 92 – 18 par ⑥ : 8 km à Angleur, rte du Condroz 541 ☎ 0 4 336 20 21, Fax 0 4 337 20 26 – 18 par ⑤ : 18 km à Gomzé-Andoumont, Sur Counachamps, r. Gomzé 30 ☎ 0 4 360 92 07, Fax 0 4 360 92 06.

☎ 0 4 342 52 14, Fax 0 4 229 27 33.

CURIOSITÉS

Voir *Citadelle* <** DW, *Parc de Cointe* <* CX – *Vieille ville*** : *Palais des Princes-Évêques** : *grande cour*** EY, *Le perron** EY **A**, *Cuve baptismale**** *dans l'église St-Barthélemy* FY, *Trésor*** *de la Cathédrale St-Paul : reliquaire de Charles le Téméraire*** EZ – *Église St-Jacques*** : *voûtes de la nef*** EZ – *Retable** *dans l'église St-Denis* EY – *Statues** *en bois du calvaire et Sedes Sapientiae** *de l'église St-Jean* EY – *Aquarium** FZ **D**.

Musées : *d'Art Moderne et d'Art Contemporain** DX **M**[7] – *de la Vie wallonne*** EY – *d'Art religieux et d'Art mosan** FY **M**[5] – *Curtius et musée du Verre** *(Musées d'Archéologie et d'Arts décoratifs) : Évangéliaire de Notger****, *collection d'objets de verre** FY **M**[1] – *d'Armes** FY **M**[3] – *d'Ansembourg** FY **M**[2].

Env. *par ① : 20 km : Blégny-Trembleur*** – *par ⑥ : 27 km : Fonts baptismaux** *dans l'église** *de St-Séverin – par ① : 17 km à Visé : Châsse de St-Hadelin** *dans l'église collégiale.*

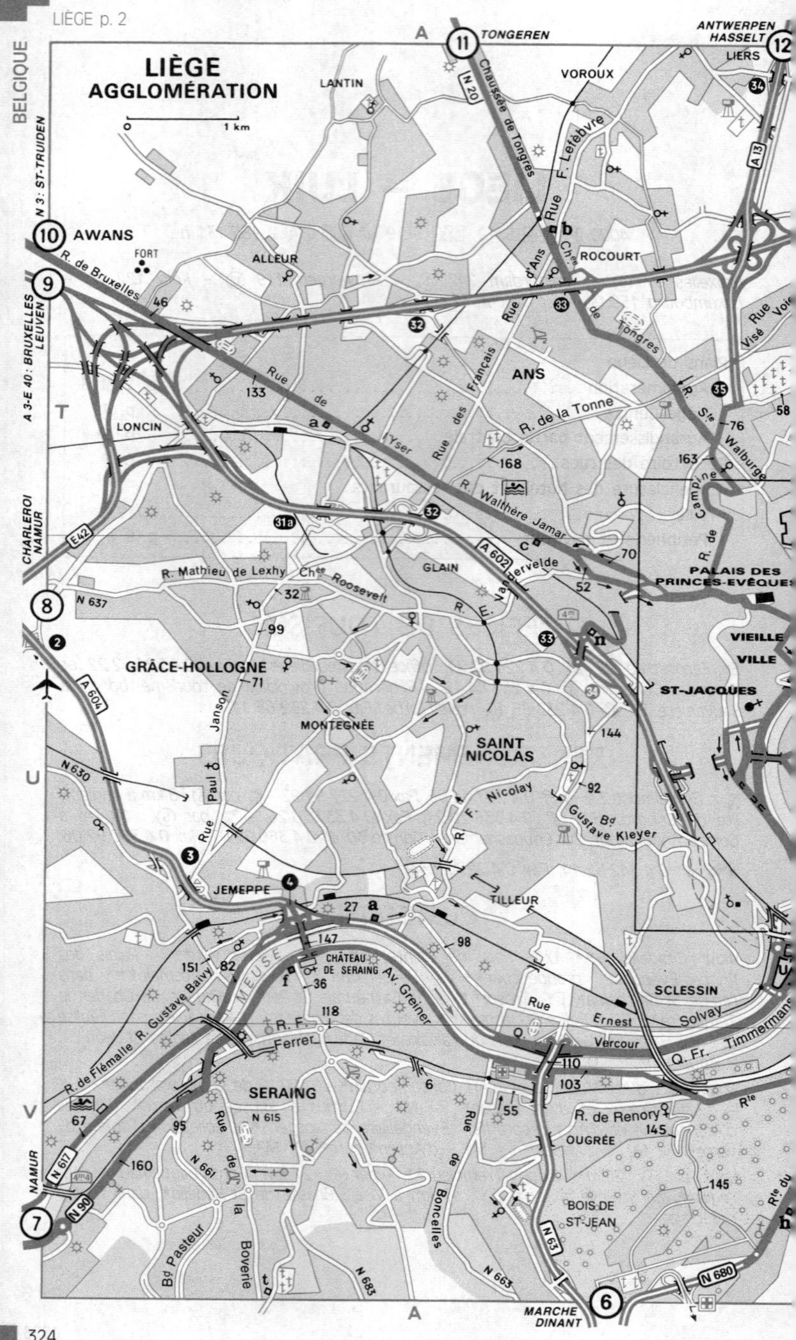
LIÈGE
AGGLOMÉRATION
0
1 km
TONGEREN
ANTWERPEN
HASSELT
LANTIN
VOROUX
LIERS
AWANS
FORT
ALLEUR
ROCOURT
ANS
LONCIN
GLAIN
GRÂCE-HOLLOGNE
MONTEGNÉE
SAINT NICOLAS
JEMEPPE
TILLEUR
SCLESSIN
SERAING
OUGRÉE
BOIS DE ST-JEAN
PALAIS DES PRINCES-ÉVÊQUES
VIEILLE VILLE
ST-JACQUES
CHÂTEAU DE SERAING
MEUSE
N 3: ST-TRUIDEN
A 3-E 40: BRUXELLES LEUVEN
CHARLEROI NAMUR
NAMUR
MARCHE DINANT
R. de Bruxelles
Rue de l'Yser
Chaussée de Tongres
Rue F. Lefèbvre
Rue d'Ans
Rue des Français
R. de la Tonne
R. Walthère Jamar
R. Ste Walburge
R. de Campine
R. Mathieu de Lexhy
Chée Roosevelt
R. m. Vandervelde
Rue Paul Janson
R. F. Nicolay
Bd Gustave Kleyer
R. Gustave Baivy
R. de Flémalle
Av. Greiner
R. F. Ferrer
Rue Ernest Solvay
Q. Vercour
Q. Fr. Timmermans
R. de Renory
Rue de Boncelles
Rue de la Boverie
Bd Pasteur
Rue Visé Voie
N 20
A 13
E 42
A 602
A 604
N 637
N 630
N 615
N 661
N 683
N 663
N 63
N 617
N 90
N 680

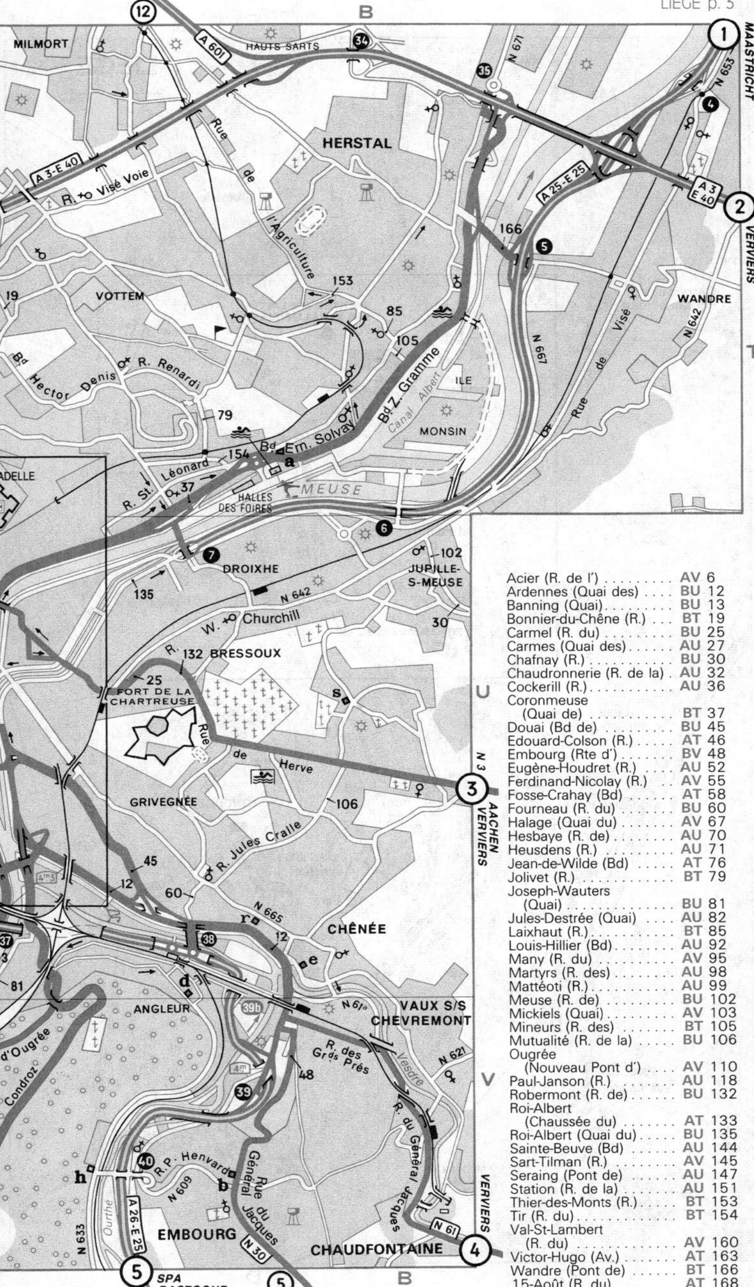
BELGIQUE
B
MILMORT
HAUTS SARTS
A 601
A 3-E 40
HERSTAL
MAASTRICHT
N 653
N 671
A 25-E 25
A 3
E 40
AACHEN
VERVIERS
R. Visé Voie
Rue de l'Agriculture
VOTTEM
WANDRE
N 642
N 667
Rue de Visé
Bd Hector Denis
R. Renardi
Bd Z. Gramme
Canal Albert
ILE
MONSIN
Bd Em. Solvay
R. St Léonard
MEUSE
HALLES DES FOIRES
TADELLE
DROIXHE
JUPILLE-S-MEUSE
N 642
W. Churchill
R. BRESSOUX
FORT DE LA CHARTREUSE
Rue de Herve
N 3
AACHEN
VERVIERS
GRIVEGNÉE
R. Jules Cralle
N 665
CHÊNÉE
ANGLEUR
VAUX S/S CHEVREMONT
R. des Grds Prés
Vesdre
N 621
R. du Général Jacques
Rue du Général Jacques
d'Ougrée
Condroz
R. P. Henvard
N 609
Ourthe
N 633
A 26-E 25
EMBOURG
N 30
CHAUDFONTAINE
N 61
VERVIERS
SPA
BASTOGNE
T
U
V

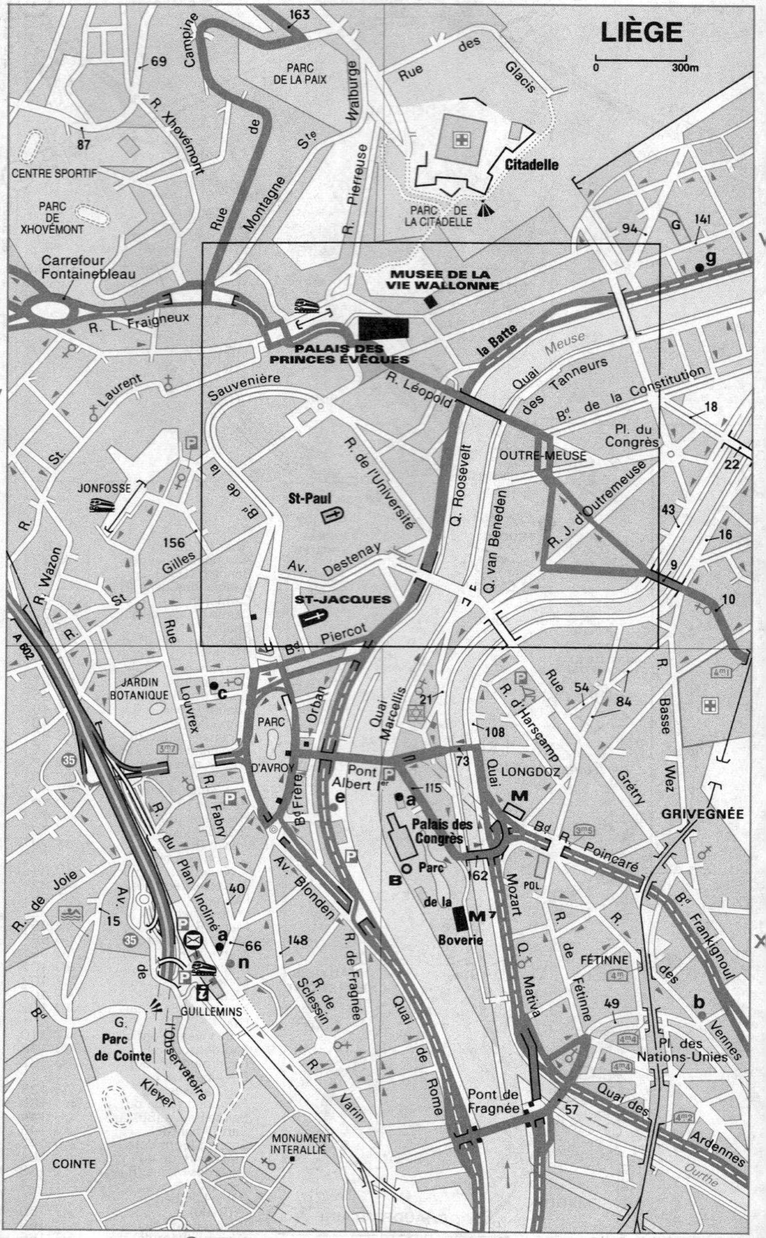

BELGIQUE

LIÈGE

0 300m

C D

Rue des Glacis
PARC DE LA PAIX
Campine
Rue de Montagne Ste Walburge
R. Pierreuse
R. Xhovémont
Citadelle
PARC DE LA CITADELLE
CENTRE SPORTIF
PARC DE XHOVÉMONT
Carrefour Fontainebleau
MUSEE DE LA VIE WALLONNE
R. L. Fraigneux
PALAIS DES PRINCES ÉVÊQUES
la Batte
Meuse
Quai des Tanneurs
Bd de la Constitution
R. Léopold
Sauvenière
St. Laurent
Pl. du Congrès
OUTRE-MEUSE
JONFOSSE
Bd de la Sauvenière
St-Paul
R. de l'Université
Q. Roosevelt
Q. van Beneden
R. J. d'Outremeuse
R. Wazon
St Gilles
Av. Destenay
ST-JACQUES
Bd Piercot
A 602
Rue Louvrex
JARDIN BOTANIQUE
PARC D'AVROY
Orban
Quai Marcellis
Rue d'Harscamp
Rue Basse Wez
Grétry
LONGDOZ
Quai
Pont Albert Ier
Bd Frère
Palais des Congrès
Parc de la Boverie
R. Fabry
R. du Plan Incliné
Av. Blonden
R. de Fragnée
Bd R. Poincaré
GRIVEGNÉE
R. de Joie
Av.
Mozart
Q. Mativa
POL.
R. de Fétinne
FÉTINNE
Bd Frankignoul
R. des Vennes
R. de Sclessin
Quai de Rome
Pl. des Nations-Unies
GUILLEMINS
Bd de l'Observatoire
G. Parc de Cointe
Kleyer
R. Varin
Pont de Fragnée
Quai des Ardennes
Ourthe
MONUMENT INTERALLIÉ
COINTE

163 69 87 94 141 g 18 22 43 16 9 10 156 c 21 54 84 108 73 115 e a M 162 B M7 40 66 148 15 n 49 b 57 35

W X

C D

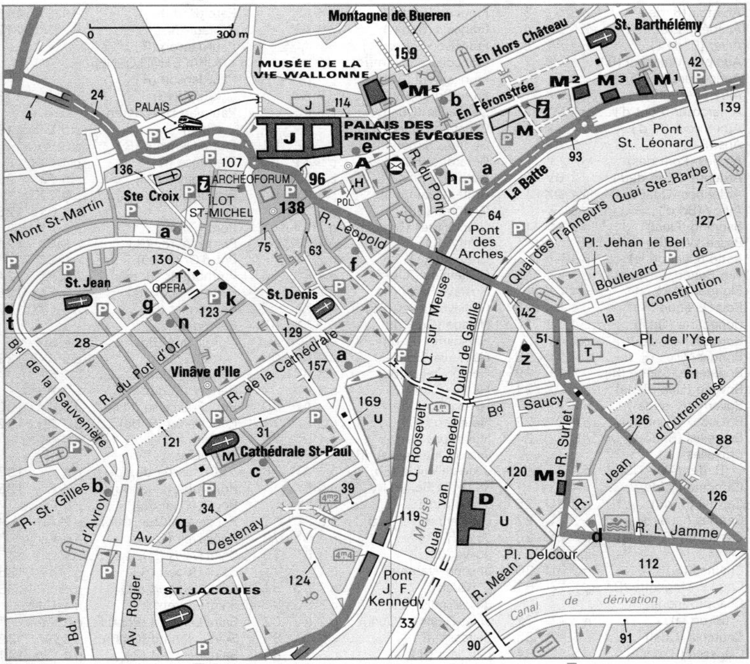

Académie (R. de l') . . . . . . EY 4
Adolphe-Maréchal (R.) . . . . FY 7
Amercoeur (Pont d') . . . . . DW 9
Amercoeur (R. d') . . . . DW 10
Bois-l'Evêque (R.) . . . . CX 15
Bonaparte (Quai) . . . . DW 16
Bonnes-Villes (R. des) . . . DW 18
Boverie (Quai de la) . . . . . DX 21
Bressoux (Pont de) . . . . . . DW 22
Bruxelles (R. de) . . . . EY 24
Casquette (R. de la) . . . . . EYZ 28
Cathédrale (R. de la) . . . . . EZ
Charles-Magnette (R.) . . . . EZ 31
Churchill (Quai) . . . . FZ 33
Clarisses (R. des) . . . . EZ 34
Croisiers (R. des) . . . . EZ 39
Dartois (R.) . . . . CX 40
Déportés (Pl. des) . . . . . . FY 42
Dérivation (Quai de la) . . . DW 43
Emile de Laveleye (Bd) . . . DX 49
En Féronstrée . . . . FY
Est (Bd de l') . . . . FYZ 51
Fer (R. du) . . . . DX 54
Fétinne (Pont de) . . . . DX 57
Georges-Simenon (R.) . . . . FZ 61
Gérardrie (R.) . . . . EY 63
Goffe (Quai de la) . . . . FY 64
Guillemins (R. des) . . . . . . CX 66
Hauteurs (Bd des) . . . . . . CW 69
Huy (Pont de) . . . . DX 73
Joffre (R.) . . . . EY 75
Lairesse (R.) . . . . DX 84
Léon-Philippet (Bd) . . . . . CW 87
Léopold (R.) . . . . EFY
Liberté (R. de la) . . . . FZ 88
Longdoz (Pont de) . . . . . . FZ 90
Longdoz (Quai de) . . . . . . FZ 91
Maastricht
(Quai de) . . . . FY 93
Maghin (R.) . . . . DW 94
Marché (Pl. du) . . . . EY 96
Notger (Square) . . . . EY 107
Orban (Quai) . . . . DX 108
Ourthe (Quai de l') . . . . . . FZ 112
Palais (R. du) . . . . EY 114
Parc (R. du) . . . . DX 115
Paul van Hoegaerden (Quai) . EFZ 119
Pitteurs (R. des) . . . . FZ 120
Pont d'Avroy (R.) . . . . EZ 121
Pont d'Ile . . . . EY 123
Prémontrés (R. des) . . . . . EZ 124
Puits-en-Sock (R.) . . . . . . FZ 126
Ransonnet (R.) . . . . FY 127
Régence (R. de la) . . . . . . EYZ 129
Rép. Française (Pl.) . . . . . EY 130
Saint-Gilles (R.) . . . . EZ
Saint-Hubert (R.) . . . . EY 136
Saint-Lambert (Pl.) . . . . . . EY 138
Saint-Léonard (Quai) . . . . FY 139
Saint-Léonard (R.) . . . . . . DW 141
Saint-Pholien (R. et Pl.) . . FY 142
Serbie (R. de) . . . . CX 148
Trappé (R.) . . . . CW 156
Université (R. de l') . . . . . EYZ 157
Ursulines (Imp. des) . . . . . FY 159
Vennes (Pont des) . . . . . . DX 162
Victor-Hugo (Av.) . . . . CW 163
Vinâve d'Ile (R.) . . . . EZ
20-Août (Pl. du) . . . . EZ 169

Sur la route :
la signalisation routière est rédigée
dans la langue de la zone linguistique traversée.
Dans ce guide,
les localités sont classées selon leur nom officiel :
Antwerpen pour Anvers, **Mechelen** por Malines.

RÉPERTOIRE DES RUES DE LIÈGE

Rue	Page	Carré	N°
Abattoir (R. de l')	p.3	BT	3
Académie (R. de l')	p.5	EY	4
Acier (R. de l')	p.2	AV	6
Adolphe-Maréchal (R.)		FY	7
Agriculture (R. de l')	p.3	BT	
Albert-Ier (Pont)	p.4	CX	
Amercœur (Pont d')	p.4	DW	9
Amercœur (R. d')	p.4	DW	10
Ans (R. d')	p.2	AT	
Arches (Pont des)	p.5	FY	
Ardenne (Voie de l')	p.3	BV	
Ardennes (Quai des)	p.4	DX	
Avroy (Bd d')	p.5	EZ	
Banning (Quai)	p.3	BU	13
Basse Wez (R.)	p.4	DX	
Batte (Quai de la)	p.5	FY	
van Beneden (Quai)	p.5	FZ	
Blonden (Av.)	p.4	CX	
Bois-l'Evêque (R.)	p.4	CX	15
Bonaparte (Quai)	p.4	DW	16
Boncelles (R. de)	p.2	AV	
Bonnes-Villes (R. des)	p.4	DW	18
Bonnier-du-Chêne (R.)	p.3	BT	19
Boverie (Quai de la)	p.4	DX	21
Boverie (R. de la)	p.2	AV	
Bressoux (Pont de)	p.4	DW	22
Bruxelles (R. de)	p.5	EY	24
Bruxelles (R. de) (AWANS)	p.2	AT	
Campine (R. de)	p.4	CW	
Carmel (R. du)	p.3	BU	25
Carmes (Quai des)	p.2	AU	27
Casquette (R. de la)	p.5	EYZ	28
Cathédrale (R. de la)	p.5	EZ	
Chafnay (R.)	p.3	BU	30
Charles-Magnette (R.)	p.5	EZ	31
Chaudronnerie (R. de la)	p.2	AU	32
Churchill (Quai)	p.5	FZ	33
Clarisses (R. des)	p.5	EZ	34
Cockerill (R.)	p.2	AU	36
Condroz (Rte du)	p.3	BV	
Congrès (Pl. du)	p.4	DW	
Constitution (Bd de la)	p.5	FY	
Coronmeuse (Quai de)	p.3	BT	37
Croisiers (R. des)	p.5	EZ	39
Dartois (R.)	p.4	CX	40
Delcourt (Pl.)	p.5	FZ	
Déportés (Pl. des)	p.5	FY	42
Dérivation (Quai de la)	p.4	DW	43
Destenay (Av.)	p.5	EZ	
Douai (Bd de)	p.3	BU	45
Edouard-Colson (R.)	p.2	AT	46
Embourg (Rte d')	p.3	BV	48
Emile de Laveleye (Bd)	p.4	DX	49
Emile-Vandervelde (R.)	p.2	AU	
Emile-Zola (Quai)	p.2	AV	
En Féronstrée	p.5	FY	
En Hors Château	p.5	FY	
Ernest-Solvay (Bd)	p.3	BT	
Ernest-Solvay (R.)	p.2	AU	
Est (Bd de l')	p.5	FYZ	51
Eugène-Houdret (R.)	p.2	AU	52
Fabry (R.)	p.4	CX	
Fer (R. du)	p.4	DX	54
Ferdinand-Nicolay (R.) (SERAING)	p.2	AV	55
Ferdinand-Nicolay (R.) (ST-NICOLAS)	p.2	AU	
Fétinne (Pont de)	p.4	DX	57
Fétinne (R. de)	p.4	DX	
Flémalle (R. de)	p.2	AV	
Fontainebleau (Carrefour)	p.4	CW	
Fosse-Crahay (Bd)	p.2	AT	58
Fourneau (R. du)	p.3	BU	60
Fragnée (Pont de)	p.4	DX	
Fragnée (R. de)	p.4	CX	
Français (R. des)	p.2	AT	
Francisco-Ferrer (R.)	p.2	AUV	
François-Lefebvre (R.)	p.2	AT	
Frankignoul (Bd)	p.4	DX	
Frère-Orban (Bd)	p.4	CX	
De Gaulle (Quai)	p.5	FZ	
Général-Jacques (R. du)	p.3	BV	
Georges-Simenon (R.)	p.5	FZ	61
Gérardrie (R.)	p.5	EY	63
Glacis (R. des)	p.4	DW	
Goffe (Quai de la)	p.5	FY	64
Gramme (Bd)	p.3	BT	
Grands-Prés (R. des)	p.3	BV	
Grétry (R.)	p.4	DX	
Greiner (Av.)	p.2	AU	
Guillemins (R. des)	p.4	CX	66
Gustave-Baivy (R.)	p.2	AU	
Gustave-Kleyer (Bd)	p.2	AU	
Halage (Quai du)	p.2	AV	67
Harscamp (R. d')	p.4	DX	
Hauteurs (Bd des)	p.4	CW	69
Hector-Denis (Bd)	p.3	BT	
Herve (R. de)	p.3	BU	
Hesbaye (R. de)	p.2	AU	70
Heusdens (R.)	p.2	AU	71
Huy (Pont de)	p.4	DX	73
Jean-d'Outremeuse (R.)	p.5	FZ	
Jean-de-Wilde (Bd)	p.2	AT	76
Jehan le Bel (Pl.)	p.5	FY	
Joffre (R.)	p.5	EY	
J.F.-Kennedy (Pont)	p.5	FZ	
Joie (R. de)	p.4	CX	78
Jolivet (R.)	p.3	BT	79
Joseph-Wauters (Quai)	p.3	BU	81
Jules-Cralle (R.)	p.3	BU	
Jules-Destrée (Quai)	p.2	AU	82
Lairesse (R.)	p.4	DX	84
Laixhaut (R.)	p.3	BT	85
Léon-Philippet (Bd)	p.4	CW	87
Léopold (R.)	p.5	EFY	
Liberté (R. de la)	p.5	FZ	88
Longdoz (Pont de)	p.5	FZ	90
Longdoz (Quai de)	p.5	FZ	91
Louis-Fraigneux (R.)	p.4	CW	
Louis-Hillier (Bd)	p.2	AU	92
Louis-Jamme (R.)	p.5	FZ	
Louvrex (R.)	p.4	CX	
Maastricht (Quai de)	p.5	FY	93
Maghin (R.)	p.4	DW	94
Many (R. du)	p.2	AV	95
Marcellis (Quai)	p.4	DX	
Marché (Pl. du)	p.5	EY	96
Martyrs (R. des)	p.2	AU	98
Mathieu-de-Lexhy (R.)	p.2	AU	
Mativa (Quai)	p.4	DX	
Mattéoti (R.)	p.2	AU	99
Méan (R.)	p.5	FZ	100
Meuse (Quai sur)	p.5	FZ	
Meuse (R. de)	p.3	BU	102
Mickiels (Quai)	p.2	AV	103
Mineurs (R. des)	p.3	BT	105
Mont Saint-Martin	p.5	EY	
Montagne Ste-Walburge	p.4	CW	
Mozart (Quai)	p.4	DX	
Mutualité (R. de la)	p.3	BU	106
Nations Unies (Pl. des)	p.4	DX	
Notger (Square)	p.5	EY	107
Observatoire (Av. de l')	p.4	CX	
Orban (Quai)	p.4	DX	108
Ougrée (Nouveau Pont d')	p.2	AV	110
Ougrée (R.)	p.3	BV	
Ourthe (Quai de l')	p.5	FZ	112
Palais (R. du)	p.5	EY	114
Parc (R. du)	p.4	DX	115
Pasteur (R.)	p.2	AU	117
Paul-Janson (R.) (GRACE-HOLLOGNE)	p.2	AU	
Paul-Janson (R.) (SERAING)	p.2	AU	118
Paul van Hoegaeren (Quai)	p.5	EFZ	119
Pierre-Henvard (R.)	p.3	BV	
Pierreuse (R.)	p.4	CW	
Pitteurs (R. des)	p.5	FZ	120
Plan Incliné (R. du)	p.4	CX	
Pont d'Ile	p.5	EY	123
Pont (R. du)	p.5	FY	
Pont d'Avroy (R.)	p.5	EZ	121
Pot d'Or (R. du)	p.5	EZ	
Prémontrés (R. des)	p.5	EZ	124
Puits-en-Sock (R.)	p.5	FZ	126
Ransonnet (R.)	p.5	FY	127
Raymond-Poincaré (Bd)	p.4	DX	
Régence (R. de la)	p.5	EYZ	129
Rénardi (R.)	p.3	BT	
Renory (R. de)	p.2	AV	
Rép. Française (Pl.)	p.5	EY	130
Robermont (R. de)	p.3	BU	132
Rogier (Av.)	p.5	EZ	
Roi-Albert (Chaussée du)	p.2	AT	133
Roi-Albert (Quai du)	p.3	BU	135
Rome (Quai de)	p.4	DX	
Roosevelt (Chaussée)	p.2	AU	
Roosevelt (Quai)	p.5	FZ	
Saint-Gilles (R.)	p.4	CW	
Saint-Hubert (R.)	p.5	EY	136
Saint-Lambert (Pl.)	p.5	EY	138
Saint-Laurent (R.)	p.4	CW	
Saint-Léonard (Pont)	p.5	FY	
Saint-Léonard (Quai)	p.5	FY	139
Saint-Léonard (R.)	p.4	DW	141
Saint-Pholien (R. et Pl.)	p.5	FY	142
Sainte-Barbe (Quai)	p.5	FY	
Sainte-Beuve (Bd)	p.2	AU	144
Sainte-Walburge (R.)	p.2	AT	
Sart-Tilman (R.)	p.2	AV	145
Saucy (Bd)	p.5	FZ	
Sauvenière (Bd de la)	p.5	EZ	
Sclessin (R. de)	p.4	CX	
Seraing (Pont de)	p.2	AU	147
Serbie (R. de)	p.4	CX	148
Station (R. de la)	p.2	AU	151
Surlet (R.)	p.5	FZ	
Tanneurs (Quai des)	p.5	FY	
Thier-des-Monts (R.)	p.3	BT	153
Timmermans (Quai)	p.2	AU	
Tir (R. du)	p.3	BT	154
Tongres (Chée de)	p.2	AT	
Tonne (R. de la)	p.2	AT	
Trappé (R.)	p.4	CW	156
Université (R. de l')	p.5	EYZ	157
Ursulines (Imp. des)	p.5	FY	159
Val-St-Lambert (R. du)	p.2	AV	160
Varin (R.)	p.4	CX	
Vennes (Pont des)	p.4	DX	162
Vennes (R. des)	p.4	DX	
Vercour (Quai)	p.2	AV	
Victor-Hugo (Av.)	p.4	CW	163
Vinâve d'Ile (R.)	p.5	EZ	
Visé (R. de)	p.3	BT	
Walthère-Jamar (R.)	p.2	AT	
Wandre (Pont de)	p.3	BT	166
Wason (R.)	p.4	CW	
Winston-Churchill (R.)	p.3	BU	
Yser (Pl. de l')	p.5	FZ	
Yser (R. de l')	p.2	AT	
15-Août (R. du)	p.2	AT	168
20-Août (Pl. du)	p.5	EZ	169

plan p. 4 sauf indication spéciale :

Bedford, quai St-Léonard 36, 0 4 228 81 11, *hotelbedfordlg@pophost.eunet.be, Fax 0 4 227 45 75,* , , - ch, - 25 à 240. AE VISA. DW g
Repas *Lunch 25* – carte 23 à 39 – **147 ch** 210/235, – 2 suites – ½ P 78/180.
◆ Cet immeuble hôtelier où vous serez hébergé dans de bonnes chambres bien insonorisées a remplacé un couvent sur ce quai mosan au trafic soutenu. Jardin-terrasse intérieur. Salle à manger aménagée sous des voûtes du 17e s. Carte de type brasserie.
◆ Dit hotelcomplex staat op de plek van een klooster aan een kade langs de Maas, waar veel verkeer langskomt. De kamers zijn prima en van goede geluidsisolatie voorzien. Binnentuin met terras. Eetzaal in brasseriestijl, met 17e-eeuwse gewelven.

Le Cygne d'Argent sans rest, r. Beeckman 49, 0 4 223 70 01, *info@cygnedargent.be, Fax 0 4 222 49 66* – . AE VISA CX c
8 – **20 ch** 62/78.
◆ Demeure située à l'écart de l'animation, entre le jardin botanique et le parc d'Avroy. Chambres sans reproche pour l'étape liégeoise, peu à peu modernisées.
◆ Deze "Zilveren Zwaan" ligt rustig tussen de botanische tuin en het park van Avroy. Keurige kamers die een voor een worden gemoderniseerd. Ideaal voor wie op doorreis is.

Campanile, r. Jules de Laminne 18 (par A 602, sortie Burenville), 0 4 224 02 72, *Fax 0 4 224 03 80* – , rest, – 35. AE VISA. ch plan p. 2 AU n
Repas (avec buffets) 22 – 10 – **50 ch** 80 – ½ P 90/100.
◆ Hôtel de chaîne implanté à proximité de l'autoroute, aux portes de la "Cité ardente". Les petites chambres, dotées du double vitrage, sont fonctionnelles et bien tenues.
◆ Dit ketenhotel staat bij de snelweg, aan de rand van de "Vurige Stad". De kleine kamers met dubbele ramen zijn functioneel en goed onderhouden.

Jean-Marie Bouille, bd Frère Orban (bord de Meuse), 0 4 252 13 21, *heliport_liege@msn.com, Fax 0 4 252 57 50,* , – – 25 à 50. AE VISA CX e
fermé du 1er au 10 nov., du 1er au 12 janv., merc. soir, sam. midi et dim. – **Repas** *Lunch 35* – carte 50 à 74, ♀.
◆ Restaurant gastronomique situé le long du fleuve, près du pont Albert-1er. Cadre nautique et carte ambitieuse, surtout vouée à la marée. Terrasse abritée. Parking aisé.
◆ Gastronomisch restaurant aan de rivier, vlak bij de Albertbrug. Maritieme sfeer en veel visspecialiteiten op de kaart. Beschut terras. Voldoende parkeergelegenheid.

Vieille Ville *- plan p. 5 :*

Mercure, bd de la Sauvenière 100, 0 4 221 77 11, *mercureliege@alliance-hospitality.com, Fax 0 4 221 77 01* – – 25 à 100. AE VISA EY t
Repas *(fermé sam. midi et dim.)* carte 22 à 31 – **105 ch** 164/208.
◆ Situation centrale, sur un grand boulevard, pour cet hôtel de chaîne récemment rafraîchi. Les chambres promettent des nuitées récupératrices à deux pas du trépidant "Carré". Rebaptisée Bar à Thym, la brasserie mise sur une cuisine valorisant les épices.
◆ Dit ketenhotel, dat net een opknapbeurt heeft gehad, is centraal gelegen aan een grote boulevard, vlak bij de bruisende "Carré". De kamers beloven een weldadige nachtrust. De brasserie, die niet voor niets "Tijmbar" heet, mikt op een keuken met kruiden.

Ibis Opera sans rest, pl. de la République Française 41, 0 4 230 33 33, *H0864-gm@accor-hotels.com, Fax 0 4 223 04 81* – – 25 à 40. AE VISA EY k
9 – **78 ch** 69.
◆ Établissement intégré au centre commercial Opéra, proche de tout et commode pour la découverte de la "Cité ardente". Chambres fonctionnelles, bonne isolation phonique.
◆ Dit zeer centraal gelegen hotel bevindt zich in het winkelcentrum Opera en is een ideale uitvalsbasis om Luik te verkennen. Functionele kamers met een goede geluidsisolatie.

Au Vieux Liège, quai Goffe 41, 0 4 223 77 48, *Fax 0 4 223 78 60* – . AE VISA FY a
fermé mi-juil.-mi-août, merc. soir, dim. et jours fériés – **Repas** *Lunch 29* – 40/59 bc.
◆ Cette jolie demeure du 16e s. au cadre rustique abrite l'une des plus vieilles tables de Liège. Recettes classico-bourgeoises quelquefois sagement actualisées.
◆ In dit rustieke 16e-eeuwse pand is een van de oudste restaurants van Luik gevestigd. Eenvoudige klassieke recepten, af en toe met moderne invloeden.

Max, pl. Verte 2, 0 4 222 08 59, *Fax 0 4 222 90 02,* , Produits de la mer et écailler, ouvert jusqu'à 23 h – – 25. AE VISA EY a
Repas *Lunch 30* – carte 46 à 70.
◆ En plein centre animé, brasserie cossue au décor griffé Luc Genot. Réputation fermement ancrée en matière de produits de la mer. Banc d'écailler et terrasse chauffée.
◆ Deze weelderige brasserie in hartje Luik is verfraaid door Luc Genot. Max heeft een goede reputatie opgebouwd met zijn superverse oesters en visschotels. Verwarmd terras.

XX **La Parmentière,** pl. Cockerill 10, ✆ 0 4 222 43 59, *erieklamarre@skynet.be, Fax 0 4 222 43 59* – ▤. AE ⓓ ⓜ VISA EZ a
fermé 21 juil.-15 août, dim. et lundi – **Repas** *Lunch 25* – 40/51 bc.
◆ Restaurant tranquille dont la façade discrète contemple l'université. Cadre actuel assez réussi, formule menu-carte avantageuse et vins des régions de France.
◆ Rustig restaurant met een onopvallende gevel die uitkijkt op de universiteit. Het moderne interieur is geslaagd te noemen. Gerechten à la carte, voordelig menu en Franse wijn.

XX **Folies Gourmandes,** r. Clarisses 48, ✆ 0 4 223 16 44, 余 – AE ⓓ ⓜ VISA EZ q
fermé 2e quinz. avril, dim. soir et lundi – **Repas** 31/50 bc, ♀.
◆ Bon petit restaurant familial établi dans une maison de maître 1900. Menu-choix appétissant et plats minceur. Par beau temps, profitez de la terrasse arrière.
◆ Uitstekend familierestaurantje dat in een herenhuis uit 1900 is gevestigd. Aanlokkelijk keuzemenu en lichte gerechten. Bij mooi weer is het terras aan de achterkant favoriet.

XX **Septime,** r. St-Paul 12, ✆ 0 4 221 03 06, *Fax 0 4 221 02 04*, Rôtisserie – ▤. AE ⓓ ⓜ VISA EZ c
Repas carte 24 à 45.
◆ Dans une rue piétonne animée, surplombée par la cathédrale. Intérieur "béton brut et velours gris souris", ambiance décontractée et carte pour carnivores.
◆ Restaurant voor vleesliefhebbers in een levendige voetgangersstraat in de schaduw van de kathedraal. Interieur van ruw beton en grijs velours. Ontspannen sfeer.

XX **Asti,** r. Madeleine 22, ✆ 0 4 223 29 89, *Fax 0 4 221 20 50*, Avec cuisine italienne – AE ⓓ ⓜ VISA EY f
fermé 1 sem. carnaval, août et merc. – **Repas** carte 22 à 41.
◆ Près de la place St-Lambert et d'un quartier chaud bordant le quai Sur-Meuse, restaurant au décor un peu mûrissant, servant une cuisine d'esprit transalpin.
◆ Dit Italiaanse restaurant, waarvan de inrichting wat gedateerd aandoet, is te vinden bij de Place St.-Lambert en de rosse buurt langs de Maaskade, de Quai Sur-Meuse.

XX **L'Écailler,** r. Dominicains 26, ✆ 0 4 222 17 49, *info@ecailler.be, Fax 0 4 387 63 74*, 余, Produits de la mer – ▤. AE ⓓ ⓜ VISA EY n
Repas *Lunch 35* – carte 33 à 46.
◆ L'enseigne de cette brasserie à dénicher aux abords du "Carré" est explicite : les produits de la mer sont ici chez eux. Ambiance nostalgique, façon bistrot parisien.
◆ Deze brasserie met zijn nostalgische ambiance in de buurt van de "Carré" heet De Oesterverkoper, een voorbode van wat u hier krijgt voorgeschoteld.

X **La Maison Blanche** 1er étage, bd d'Avroy 18, ✆ 0 4 222 42 02, *Fax 0 4 221 48 88* – ▤. ⓜ VISA EZ b
fermé sam. midi et dim. – **Repas** *Lunch 24* – carte 46 à 58, ♀.
◆ Table hautement recommandable établie à l'étage d'une ancienne maison de notable. Clin d'œil aux présidents des États-Unis en salle. Fine cuisine dans le goût du moment.
◆ Dit restaurant op de bovenverdieping van een oud herenhuis is een aanrader. Knipoog naar de presidenten van Amerika in de eetzaal. Fijne keuken die geheel van deze tijd is.

X **Enoteca,** r. Casquette 5, ✆ 0 4 222 24 64, *Fax 0 4 222 24 64* – ▤. ⓜ VISA EY g
fermé sam. midi et dim. – **Repas** 18/48 bc.
◆ Halte sympathique estimée pour ses goûteuses préparations et sa cave privilégiant l'Italie. Intérieur contemporain avec cuisine à vue. Le lunch : une bonne affaire !
◆ Leuk restaurant dat geliefd is vanwege het lekkere eten en de goede wijnen, die veelal uit Italië komen. Hedendaags interieur met een open keuken. Het lunchmenu is een koopje !

X **Le Danieli,** r. Hors-Château 46, ✆ 0 4 223 30 91, *Fax 0 4 223 30 91*, 余, Avec cuisine italienne – VISA FY b
fermé juil., dim. et lundi – **Repas** (menu unique) 22.
◆ Près de plusieurs musées, à deux pas des plus hauts lieux de la "Cité ardente", maison de bouche émergeant de la mêlée des tables italiennes. Le tout-Liège s'y presse.
◆ Danieli is gunstig gelegen bij de voornaamste bezienswaardigheden van de stad en steekt bovendien met kop en schouders boven het gros van de Italiaanse restaurants uit.

X **Le Bistrot d'en face,** r. Goffe 8, ✆ 0 4 223 15 84, *Fax 0 4 223 15 86*, 余 – AE ⓜ VISA FY h
fermé lundi et sam. midi – **Repas** carte 31 à 39.
◆ Un adorable bouchon lyonnais "made in Liège" se dissimule derrière cette belle devanture en bois postée à l'arrière des anciennes halles aux viandes. Chaleur et convivialité.
◆ Deze karakteristieke bistro met een mooie houten voorgevel bevindt zich achter de oude vleesmarkt. Hier kunt u heerlijk eten in een gezellige ambiance.

X **As Ouhès,** pl. du Marché 19, ✆ 0 4 223 32 25, *as.ouhes@skynet.be, Fax 0 4 237 03 77*, 余, Brasserie, ouvert jusqu'à 23 h – AE ⓓ ⓜ VISA EY e
Repas carte 23 à 36.
◆ Comprenez "Les Oiseaux". Carte classique et brasserie, assortie de suggestions et plats du terroir. Une institution liégeoise avoisinant le fier perron, symbole de la ville.
◆ As Ouhès, dat "De Vogels" betekent, is een begrip in Luik en staat vlak bij Le Perron, het fiere symbool van de stad. Klassieke kaart met dagschotels en streekgerechten.

Guillemins - *plan p. 4 :*

Comfort Inn sans rest, r. Guillemins 116, ☎ 0 4 254 55 55, *comfort.inn.liege@skynet.be, Fax 0 4 254 55 00* – |♦| ⇔ TV 🚗 – 🏛 25 à 60. AE ① ⓜ VISA CX a
51 ch ☐ 64/99.
◆ Anxieux de rater votre TGV ? Cet hôtel de chaîne avoisine la gare des Guillemins, dormez donc sur vos deux oreilles ! Chambres insonorisées et bien tenues.
◆ Voor wie bang is de HST te missen, is dit ketenhotel bij het station de oplossing. Hier kunt u met een gerust hart gaan slapen ! Goed onderhouden kamers met geluidsisolatie.

Le Duc d'Anjou, r. Guillemins 127, ☎ 0 4 252 28 58, Moules en saison, ouvert jusqu'à 23 h 30 – ▤. AE ① ⓜ VISA CX n
Repas 21/31.
◆ Une carte aussi variée qu'étendue, avec cuisine belge et un intéressant menu-choix, draine ici clients de passage et habitués. Vins à prix sages. Moules à gogo en saison.
◆ Uitgebreide en gevarieerde kaart met Belgische specialiteiten en een interessant keuzemenu. Volop mosselen in het seizoen. Schappelijk geprijsde wijnen. Veel stamgasten.

Rive droite (Outremeuse - Palais des Congrès) - *plans p. 4 et 5 sauf indication spéciale :*

Holiday Inn sans rest, Esplanade de l'Europe 2, ✉ 4020, ☎ 0 4 349 20 00, *hiliege@alliance-hospitality.com, Fax 0 4 343 48 10,* ≤, 🏋, ≘s, 🏊 – |♦| ⇔ ▤ TV ♿ 🚗 🅿 – 🏛 40 à 70. AE ① ⓜ VISA DX a
214 ch ☐ 184/214, – 5 suites.
◆ Hôtel des bords de Meuse dominant le palais des congrès et un grand parc public où se tient le musée d'Art moderne. Confort actuel dans les chambres. Clientèle d'affaires.
◆ Dit hotel aan de Maas torent boven het congrescentrum en een groot park uit, waar het Museum van Moderne Kunst te vinden is. Modern comfort in de kamers. Zakelijke clientèle.

Passerelle sans rest, chaussée des Prés 24, ✉ 4020, ☎ 0 4 341 20 20, *Fax 0 4 344 36 43* – |♦| TV 🚗. AE ① ⓜ VISA. ⚘ FZ z
☐ 8 – **15 ch** 62.
◆ Aux abords de la passerelle dont il emprunte le nom, hôtel sans chichis occupant une maison de coin du quartier St-Pholien en Outremeuse. Chambres munies du double vitrage.
◆ Hotel zonder kapsones in een hoekpand van de wijk St.-Pholien en Outremeuse, bij de voetgangersbrug ("passerelle") waaraan het zijn naam ontleent. Kamers met dubbele ramen.

Michel Germeau, r. Vennes 151, ✉ 4020, ☎ 0 4 343 72 42, *michelgermeau@hotmail.com, Fax 0 4 344 03 86,* 🍽 – AE ① ⓜ VISA DX b
fermé du 17 au 21 fév., 23 août-10 sept., du 13 au 18 déc., dim. soir et lundi – **Repas** 25/82 bc.
◆ Cette maison bourgeoise du faubourg de Fétinne abrita le consulat de Suède. Une fresque angélique anime le haut plafond mouluré de la salle à manger. Fine cuisine française.
◆ In dit herenhuis in de buitenwijk Fétinne zetelde vroeger het Zweedse consulaat. Een fresco met engelen siert het hoge plafond van de eetzaal. Fijne Franse keuken.

Les Cyclades, r. Ourthe 4, ✉ 4020, ☎ 0 4 342 25 86 – ▤. AE ① ⓜ VISA. ⚘ FZ d
fermé mi-août-début sept., merc. et jeudi – **Repas** Lunch 22 – 29/49 bc.
◆ Non loin du musée Tchantchès et de la petite rue Roture, très festive les soirs de week-end, restaurant coquet servant une cuisine bourgeoise avec menus-choix.
◆ Mooi restaurant, niet ver van het Musée Tchantchès en de kleine Rue Roture, die in het weekend een echte uitgaansstraat is. Eenvoudige, maar smakelijke keuken met keuzemenu's.

Périphérie - *plans p. 2 et 3 :*

à Angleur ⓒ *Liège –* ✉ *4031 Angleur :*

Le Val d'Ourthe sans rest, rte de Tilff 412, ☎ 0 4 365 91 71, *Fax 0 4 365 62 89* – ⇔ ▤ TV 🚗 🅿. AE ① ⓜ VISA. ⚘ rest BV h
☐ 9 – **12 ch** 82.
◆ Perché dans la verdure près d'une sortie d'autoroute, ce petit hôtel correctement tenu domine la vallée de l'Ourthe entre Angleur et Tilff. Grandes chambres actuelles.
◆ Dit kleine, goed onderhouden hotel ligt tussen het groen, niet ver van de snelweg, hoog in het Ourthedal tussen Angleur en Tilff. Grote moderne kamers.

L'Orchidée Blanche, rte du Condroz 457 (N 680), ☎ 0 4 365 11 48, *Fax 0 4 367 09 16,* 🍽 – 🅿. AE ① ⓜ VISA AV h
fermé 14 juil.-4 août, dern. sem. janv., mardi soir et merc. – **Repas** Lunch 27 – 39/57 bc.
◆ Grosse villa coiffée d'un toit de chaume, au sommet de la côte du Sart-Tilman. Choix étoffé, d'orientation classique. Musée en plein air à proximité (campus universitaire).
◆ Grote villa met rieten dak boven aan de helling naar Sart-Tilman, dichtbij het openluchtmuseum van de campus. Uitgebreide, klassiek getinte kaart.

X **La Devinière,** r. Tiff 39, ✆ 0 4 365 00 32, *Fax 0 4 365 00 32* – AE ⓓ ⓜⓒ VISA BU d
fermé 14 juil.-6 août, jeudi soir, sam. midi et dim. – **Repas** *Lunch 35* – carte 38 à 48.
• "Devinez" ce qui se cache derrière cette façade un rien austère : un agréable petit restaurant familial travaillant sérieusement avec une carte classique attrayante.
• Achter een ietwat strenge voorgevel gaat dit plezierige familierestaurantje schuil, waar met veel liefde wordt gekookt. Aantrekkelijke klassieke menukaart.

à Chênée C *Liège* – ✉ *4032 Chênée* :

XXX **Le Gourmet,** r. Large 91, ✆ 0 4 365 87 97, *info@legourmet.be, Fax 0 4 365 38 12*, – P. AE ⓓ ⓜⓒ VISA BU r
fermé 2 sem. en juil., 2 prem. sem. janv., mardi et merc. – **Repas** *Lunch 25* – 30/64 bc.
• Une carte saisonnière bien balancée s'emploie à vous flatter les papilles dans ce restaurant entièrement rajeuni. Décor intérieur sobre et actuel. Accueillante véranda.
• De seizoengebonden spijzen van de uitgebalanceerde kaart strelen de tong in dit volledig opgefriste restaurant. Sober, eigentijds interieur met een uitnodigende serre.

XX **Le Vieux Chênée,** r. Gravier 45, ✆ 0 4 367 00 92, *Fax 0 4 367 59 15*, Moules en saison – AE ⓓ ⓜⓒ VISA BU e
fermé jeudi – **Repas** *Lunch 22 bc* – 25/43 bc.
• Maison ancienne au cadre ardennais où défile une clientèle d'affaires fidèle et d'habitués. Cuisine bourgeoise, vivier à homards et moules en saison.
• Oud huis met een interieur in Ardense stijl, waar voornamelijk zakenmensen en vaste gasten komen. Traditionele keuken met kreeft en mosselen in het seizoen.

à Jupille-sur-Meuse C *Liège* – ✉ *4020 Jupille-sur-Meuse* :

XX **Donati,** r. Bois de Breux 264, ✆ 0 4 365 03 49, *Fax 0 4 365 03 49*, Cuisine italienne – ⓓ ⓜⓒ VISA. BU s
fermé 8 août-2 sept., sam. midi, dim. et lundi – **Repas** *Lunch 28* – carte 26 à 48.
• Sa carte italienne ambitieuse et son large choix de vins transalpins font de cette maison juchée sur les coteaux de Jupille une petite adresse hautement recommandable.
• Dankzij de ambitieuze Italiaanse kaart en zijn keur van bijpassende wijnen is dit restaurant op een van de heuvels van Jupille absoluut een aanrader.

à Rocourt C *Liège* – ✉ *4000 Rocourt* :

X ✿ **La Petite Table** (Gillard), pl. Reine Astrid 3, ✆ 0 4 239 19 00, *Fax 0 4 239 19 77* – ⓜⓒ VISA AT b
fermé 28 mars-16 avril, du 1er au 20 août, 27 déc.-18 janv., lundi, mardi et sam. midi – **Repas** (nombre de couverts limité - prévenir) *Lunch 30* – carte 55 à 75.
• Sur une place passante, charmant petit restaurant familial jouant tranquillement dans la cour des grands. Fourneaux à vue et répertoire culinaire au goût du jour.
• Eenvoudig huiselijk restaurantje aan een plein, dat zich ondanks zijn kleine formaat met de groten kan meten. Open keuken met een eigentijds culinair repertoire.
Spéc. Marbré de foie d'oie et jambon de Parme aux pommes. Ravioles de Saint-Jacques au salpicon de homard. Homard braisé au four, poireaux et jus crème

Environs

à Ans - *plan p. 2* – *27 587 h* – ✉ *4430 Ans* :

XX **Le Marguerite,** r. Walthère Jamar 171, ✆ 0 4 226 43 46, *Fax 0 4 226 38 35*, – AE ⓓ ⓜⓒ VISA AU c
fermé sam. midi, dim. et lundi soir – **Repas** *Lunch 28* – 35/62 bc.
• Cuisine de saison avec menu du marché et menu de fête mensuel dans cette maison avenante qui s'est offert une cure de jouvence pour célébrer ses 25 ans.
• Dit restaurant, dat al 25 jaar bestaat, is na een opknapbeurt weer een jonge blom ! Seizoengebonden keuken met een menu van de markt en een maandelijks wisselend feestmenu.

XX **La Fontaine de Jade,** r. Yser 321, ✆ 0 4 246 49 72, *la_fontaine@skynet.be, Fax 0 4 263 69 53*, Cuisine chinoise, ouvert jusqu'à 23 h – ▤. AE ⓓ ⓜⓒ VISA. AT a
fermé mi-juil.-mi-août et mardi – **Repas** *Lunch 13* – 22/36, ♀.
• Les restaurants chinois ne manquent pas le long de cette chaussée très empruntée. Celui-ci se distingue par son cadre exotique assez cossu et par l'ampleur de sa carte.
• Het wemelt van de Chinese restaurants aan deze drukke weg. De "Fontein van Jade" springt eruit vanwege zijn weelderige exotische interieur en uitgebreide menukaart.

à Boncelles *par* ⑥ : *10 km* C *Seraing 60 407 h.* – ✉ *4100 Boncelles* :

Ibis sans rest, rte du Condroz 15b, ✆ 0 4 338 53 97, *ibis.boncelles@belgacom.net, Fax 0 4 338 45 11* – ▤ TV P. AE ⓓ ⓜⓒ VISA
☕ 9 – **66 ch** 69.
• Cette nouvelle unité de la chaîne Ibis est couplée à un centre commercial et récréatif (grandes surfaces, restos, bowling, fitness, discothèques, etc.). Confort fonctionnel.
• De benjamin van deze hotelketen is gekoppeld aan een winkelcentrum met talloze faciliteiten (o.a. restaurants, bowling, fitness en discotheken). Functionele kamers.

à Embourg - *plan p. 3* 🄲 *Chaudfontaine 20 665 h.* – ✉ *4038 Embourg :*

X **Robertissimo,** (Ferme des Croisiers), voie de l'Ardenne 58, ✆ 0 4 365 72 12, *robertissimo@wanadoo.be, Fax 0 4 365 77 14,* , Cuisine italienne – P. AE MC VISA BV b
fermé 24 déc. – **Repas** Lunch 20 – 26/39 bc, ♀.
◆ Restaurant bien dans le coup, mettant habilement à profit un vieil édifice de pierre. Intérieur design et cuisine au goût du jour d'inspiration transalpine. "Correctissimo" !
◆ Dit restaurant in een oud stenen pand is momenteel helemaal in. Designinterieur en Italiaans georiënteerde trendy keuken. Correctissimo !

à Flémalle *par ⑦ : 16 km – 25 501 h –* ✉ *4400 Flémalle :*

XXX **la Ciboulette,** chaussée de Chokier 96, ✆ 0 4 275 19 65, *la-ciboulette@teledisnet.be, Fax 0 4 275 05 81,* – . AE MC VISA
fermé du 11 au 20 avril, 25 juil.-8 août, du 3 au 12 janv., sam. midi, dim. soir, lundi et merc. soir – **Repas** Lunch 50 bc – 24/100 bc.
◆ Un bel ensemble de maisons mosanes abrite cette table au cadre soigné. Carte de saison aussi engageante que celle des vins. Patio avec vue sur la terrasse.
◆ Dit verzorgde restaurant is ondergebracht in een aantal huizen in de stijl van het Maasland. Seizoengebonden keuken en aanlokkelijke wijnkaart. Patio en terras.

XX **Le Gourmet Gourmand,** Grand-Route 411, ✆ 0 4 233 07 56, *Fax 0 4 233 19 21,* – . AE D MC VISA
fermé lundi, mardi soir, merc. soir et jeudi soir – **Repas** Lunch 30 – 40/60 bc.
◆ Petit établissement d'un genre assez classique mitonnant une cuisine de saison, à la fois régionale et au goût du jour. Bonne cave. Clientèle d'affaires.
◆ Klein etablissement uit het klassieke genre, dat veel zakenmensen trekt. De keuken is zowel regionaal als eigentijds en houdt rekening met de seizoenen. Goede wijnkelder.

XX **Jacques Koulic,** chaussée de Chockier 82, ✆ 0 4 275 53 15, *jacques.koulic@cybernet.be,* – AE D MC VISA JCB.
fermé du 1er au 15 mars, du 1er au 15 sept., mardi et merc. – **Repas** 31/90 bc, ♀.
◆ Demeure ancienne des bords de Meuse. Cuisine sagement actualisée dans un accueillant intérieur rustique. Cave variée et vins au verre. Jardin clos et terrasse.
◆ Oud pand aan de oever van de Maas. Vrij moderne keuken in een aangenaam rustiek interieur. Gevarieerde wijnen die ook per glas kunnen worden besteld. Ommuurde tuin en terras.

à Herstal - *plan p. 3* – *36 359 h* – ✉ *4040 Herstal :*

XX **La Bergamote,** bd Ernest Solvay 72 (lieu-dit Coronmeuse), ✆ 0 4 342 29 47, *bergamote@sky.be, Fax 0 4 248 17 61,* – MC VISA BT a
fermé prem. sem. vacances Pâques, 17 juil.-2 août, prem. sem. janv., dim., lundi et jours fériés – **Repas** 29/37.
◆ Estimable enseigne à débusquer dans le quartier de Coronmeuse. Choix de menus en phase avec l'époque, dont une intelligente formule multi-choix. Plus d'intimité à l'étage.
◆ Respectabel restaurant met een eigentijdse keuken in de wijk Coronmeuse. Fraai à la carte-menu met ruime keuze. De bovenverdieping is wat intiemer.

à Ivoz-Ramet *par ⑦ : 16 km* 🄲 *Flémalle 25 501 h.* – ✉ *4400 Ivoz-Ramet :*

X **Chez Cha-Cha,** pl. François Gérard 10, ✆ 0 4 337 18 43, *Fax 0 4 385 07 59,* , Grillades – P. AE D MC VISA
fermé du 15 au 31 août, du 15 au 31 janv., sam. midi, dim., lundi soir et mardi soir – **Repas** carte 27 à 39.
◆ Le tout-Liège et sa région défilent dans cette maison à l'ambiance animée, connue pour ses savoureuses grillades au feu de bois. Petite carte bourgeoise.
◆ De inwoners van Luik en omstreken komen massaal af op dit gezellige restaurant, dat bekendstaat om zijn sappige vlees van de grill. Kleine kaart met eenvoudige gerechten.

à Liers *par ⑫ : 8 km* 🄲 *Herstal 36 359 h.* – ✉ *4042 Liers :*

X **La Bartavelle,** r. Provinciale 138, ✆ 0 4 278 51 55, *info@labartavelle.be, Fax 0 4 278 51 57,* – P – 25 à 50. AE D MC VISA
fermé carnaval, du 15 au 30 juil. et sam. midi – **Repas** (déjeuner seult sauf week-end) 28/50 bc.
◆ Adresse conviviale de type bistrot-brasserie avec feu ouvert. Cuisine d'inspiration provençale, comme le suggère ce volatile sympathique sur l'enseigne. Jolie terrasse.
◆ In deze gemoedelijke bistro annex brasserie brandt 's winters een behaaglijk vuur. De chef-kok haalt zijn inspiratie uit de Provence. Mooi terras.

à Neuville-en-Condroz *par ⑥ : 18 km* C *Neupré 9 696 h. – ✉ 4121 Neuville-en-Condroz :*

XXXX ✿ **Le Chêne Madame** (Mme Tilkin), av. de la Chevauchée 70 (Sud-Est : 2 km sur N 62, dans le bois de Rognac), ✆ 0 4 371 41 27, *Fax 0 4 371 29 43,* – P. AE ① MC VISA
fermé août, dim. soir, lundi et jeudi soir – **Repas** 43/75, carte 55 à 75.
• Un haut lieu de la gastronomie liégeoise que ce relais de campagne élégant dans un parc boisé. Beau choix classique de saison orienté "produits nobles". Cave de prestige.
• Dit restaurant behoort tot de crème de la crème van de Luikse gastronomie. Keur van klassieke seizoengebonden gerechten op basis van "edele producten". Prestigieuze wijnen.
Spéc. Foie gras de canard poêlé aux pommes caramélisées, sauce au jus de truffes. Sandre farci en croûte et beurre blanc (juin-fév.). Gibier (sept.-janv.)

à Seraing - *plan p. 2 – 60 407 h – ✉ 4100 Seraing :*

XX **Le Moulin à Poivre,** r. Plainevaux 30, ✆ 0 4 336 06 13, *Fax 0 4 338 28 95,* – AE ① MC VISA AV t
fermé 1 sem. en mars, 2 dern. sem. août, dim. soir, lundi et mardi – **Repas** *Lunch 23* – carte 39 à 66.
• Restaurant jouxtant un petit parc sur les hauteurs de Seraing. Goûteuse cuisine classique actualisée servie dans un décor intérieur stylé, à la fois baroque et romantique.
• Dit restaurant grenst aan een parkje op de heuvels van Seraing. Smakelijke klassieke keuken in een vrij gestileerd modern interieur, dat zowel barok als romantisch aandoet.

XX **La Table d'Hôte,** quai Sadoine 7, ✆ 0 4 337 00 66, *info@tabledhote.be, Fax 0 4 336 98 27,* – AE ① MC VISA AU f
fermé juin-juil., 23 déc.-4 janv., sam. midi, dim. soir et lundi – **Repas** *Lunch 29* – 36/59 bc, ♀.
• À deux minutes du Val-St-Lambert, le long d'un quai mosan au trafic dense, maison de maître 1900 où la clientèle d'affaires locale a ses habitudes. Recettes bourgeoises.
• Herenhuis uit 1900 bij Val-St-Lambert, aan een kade langs de Maas waar veel verkeer langskomt. Traditionele keuken die veel lof oogst bij het plaatselijke zakenleven.

à Tilleur - *plan p. 2* C *St-Nicolas 22 959 h. – ✉ 4420 Tilleur :*

X **Chez Massimo,** quai du Halage 78, ✆ 0 4 233 69 27, *Fax 0 4 234 00 31,* , Cuisine italienne – MC VISA AU a
fermé sam. midi, dim. et lundi – **Repas** 28/37.
• Cette étape gourmande des quais de Meuse est connue depuis belle lurette pour son registre italien associant spécialités régionales et préparations plus conventionnelles.
• Dit adresje aan de Maas staat al jaren bekend om zijn Italiaanse kookkunst, waarbij regionale specialiteiten en meer klassieke gerechten goed met elkaar worden gecombineerd.

LIER (LIERRE) *2500 Antwerpen* 533 M 16 *et* 716 G 2 – *32 456 h.*

Voir Église St-Gommaire★★ (St-Gummaruskerk) : jubé★★, verrière★ Z – Béguinage★ (Begijnhof) Z – Horloge astronomique★ de la tour Zimmer (Zimmertoren) Z **A**.

au Nord : 10 km à Broechem, Kasteel Bossenstein, Moor 16 ✆ 0 3 485 64 46, Fax 0 3 425 78 41.

Stadhuis, Grote Markt 57 ✆ 0 3 491 13 93, toerisme@lier.be, Fax 0 3 488 12 76.

Bruxelles 45 ④ – Antwerpen 22 ⑤ – Mechelen 15 ④

Plan page ci-contre

XX **De Werf,** Werf 17, ✆ 0 3 480 71 90, *Fax 0 3 488 74 73* – AE MC VISA. Z e
fermé 15 juil.-14 août, dim. et lundi – **Repas** *Lunch 30* – 49.
• Petite table familiale au cadre moderne, derrière une pimpante façade voisine de la tour Zimmer (horloge astronomique). Recettes classiques actualisées.
• Familierestaurantje met een mooie gevel en een modern interieur naast de Zimmertoren met zijn astronomische klok. Klassieke recepten die naar de huidige tijd zijn vertaald.

XX **Numerus Clausus,** Keldermansstraat 2, ✆ 0 3 480 51 62, *Fax 0 3 480 51 62,* – AE MC VISA. Z c
fermé 1 sem. en juin, 2 sem. en sept., sam. midi, dim. et lundi – **Repas** *Lunch 27* – 29.
• Adresse sympathique dont le décor, sobre mais assez mode, se rapproche du style "Marie-Claire". Cuisine traditionnelle de saison. Menus courtisés. Intime petite terrasse.
• Leuk restaurant met een sobere en vrij modieuze inrichting in "Marie-Clairestijl". Traditionele seizoengebonden kaart met een bijzonder populair menu. Intiem terrasje.

XX **Cuistot,** Antwerpsestraat 146, ✆ 0 3 488 46 56, *info@restaurantcuistot.be, Fax 0 3 488 46 56,* – AE ① MC VISA JCB Y a
fermé 14 juil.-1er août, mardi et merc. – **Repas** (dîner seult) 39/68 bc.
• Salle à manger d'esprit contemporain, carte de préparations vivant, elle aussi, avec son temps, menus bien conçus, vins de France à bon prix et ambiance décontractée.
• Dit restaurant is zowel qua inrichting als eten up-to-date. Ontspannen ambiance, evenwichtig samengestelde menu's en Franse wijnen voor een zacht prijsje.

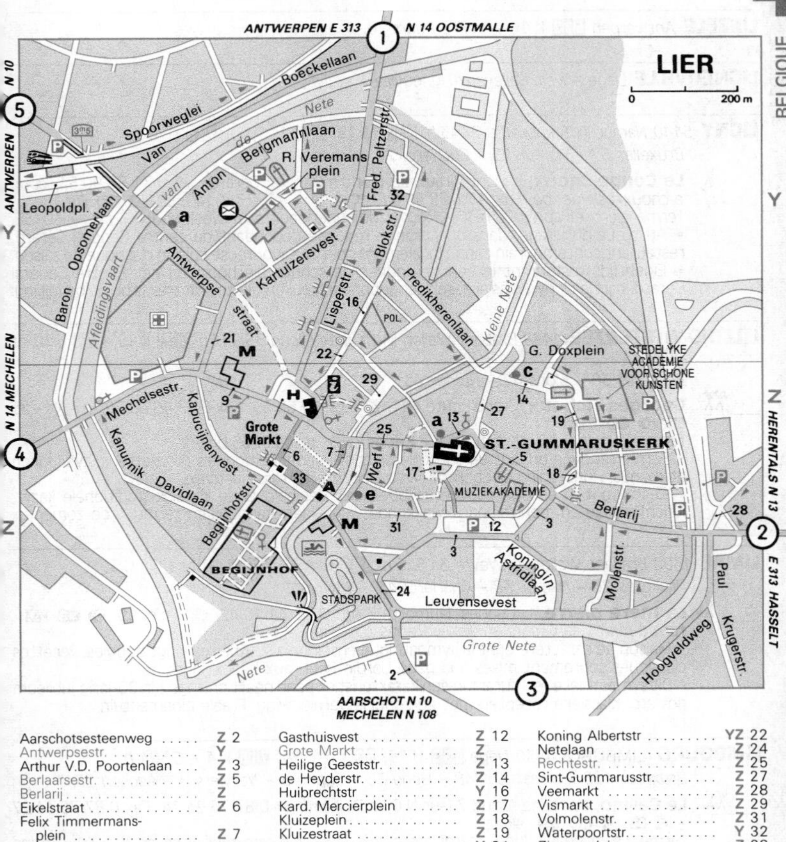

Aarschotsesteenweg . . . . . Z 2
Antwerpsestr. . . . . Y
Arthur V.D. Poortenlaan . . . Z 3
Berlaarsestr. . . . . Z 5
Berlarij . . . . Z
Eikelstraat . . . . Z 6
Felix Timmermans-plein . . . . Z 7
Fl. Van Cauwenberghstr. . . Z 9
Gasthuisvest . . . . Z 12
Grote Markt . . . . Z
Heilige Geeststr. . . . . Z 13
de Heyderstr. . . . . Z 14
Huibrechtstr . . . . Y 16
Kard. Mercierplein . . . . . . Z 17
Kluizeplein . . . . Z 18
Kluizestraat . . . . Z 19
Kolveniersvest . . . . Y 21
Koning Albertstr . . . . YZ 22
Netelaan . . . . Z 24
Rechtestr. . . . . Z 25
Sint-Gummarusstr. . . . . . . Z 27
Veemarkt . . . . Z 28
Vismarkt . . . . Z 29
Volmolenstr. . . . . Z 31
Waterpoortstr. . . . . Y 32
Zimmerplein . . . . Z 33

't Cleyn Paradijs, Heilige Geeststraat 2, 0 3 480 78 57, *smekens.karel@pandora.be, Fax 0 3 480 78 57* – VISA Z a
fermé 2 prem. sem. août, fin déc.-début janv., mardi, merc. et sam. midi – **Repas** 27/47 bc.
◆ Une courte carte au goût du jour, incluant des menus, vous sera soumise dans cette discrète maison du 17e s. Juste en face, la St.-Gummaruskerk mérite aussi la visite.
◆ Klein paradijsje in een bescheiden 17e-eeuws pand tegenover de St.-Gummaruskerk, die beslist een bezoekje waard is. De vrij beperkte kaart wordt aangevuld met menu's.

à Broechem *Nord : 10 km* C *Ranst 17 639 h.* – *2520 Broechem :*

Bossenstein, Moor 16 (Nord : 2 km, direction Oelegem), 0 3 485 64 46, *Fax 0 3 485 78 41*, – TV P – 35. VISA.
fermé 23 déc.-fin janv. – **Repas** *(fermé lundis non fériés) Lunch 26* – 34 – **16 ch** 135/175 – ½ P 160/225.
◆ Face à un parc avec golf entourant un château médiéval, établissement dont les chambres, bien conçues, sont aussi amples que confortables. Accueil et service avenants. Cuisine de notre temps servie dans le cadre agréable du "club house" du golf.
◆ Dit hotel ligt tegenover een middeleeuws kasteel in een park met golfbaan. De kamers zijn goed ontworpen en zowel ruim als comfortabel. Vriendelijke ontvangst en service. In het club house van de golf worden eigentijdse gerechten geserveerd.

LIERS *4042 Liège* 533 S 18 *et* 534 S 18 – *voir à Liège, environs.*

LIEZELE *Antwerpen* 533 K 16 – *voir à Puurs.*

LIGNEUVILLE *Liège – voir Bellevaux-Ligneuville.*

LIGNY *5140 Namur* C *Sombreffe 7443 h.* 533 M 19, 534 M 19 *et* 716 G 4.

Bruxelles 57 – Namur 25 – Charleroi 22 – Mons 51.

Le Coupe-Choux, r. Pont Piraux 23 (centre Général Gérard), ☎ 0 71 88 90 51, *coupe-choux@skynet.be, Fax 0 71 88 90 51,* – P – 25 à 140. AE VISA

fermé merc. et après 20 h 30 – **Repas** (déjeuner seult sauf week-end) *Lunch 20* – 30/38.

◆ Au cœur du village, dans une grange rénovée dépendant du centre Général Gérard, restaurant contemporain connu localement pour sa savoureuse cuisine classique de saison.

◆ Eigentijds restaurant in een gerenoveerde schuur die hoort bij het Centre Général Gérard, hartje Ligny. Klassieke, seizoengebonden keuken die zeer in trek is bij de bevolking.

LILLOIS-WITTERZÉE *1428 Brabant Wallon* C *Braine-l'Alleud 35897 h.* 533 L 19, 534 L 19 *et* 716 G 4.

Bruxelles 30 – Mons 47 – Namur 43.

Georges Tichoux, Grand'Route 491, ☎ 0 67 21 65 33, *Fax 0 67 49 08 79,* ≤, – P. AE VISA

fermé 2e quinz. juil. et sam. midi – **Repas** *Lunch 15* – 29/65 bc.

◆ Ferme rénovée offrant un choix de plats classico-traditionnels prometteur, avec lunch et menus. Honorable sélection de vins. Plaisante terrasse estivale.

◆ Restaurant in een gerenoveerde boerderij. Veelbelovende klassiek-traditionele kaart, lunchformule en menu's. Indrukwekkende wijnkelder. Aangenaam terras in de zomer.

LIMAL *1300 Brabant Wallon* C *Wavre 31526 h.* 533 M 18, 534 M 18 *et* 716 G 3.

Bruxelles 26 – Namur 39 – Charleroi 43 – Wavre 4.

La mère pierre, r. Charles Jaumotte 3, ☎ 0 10 41 16 42, – P. AE VISA

fermé mardi, sam. midi et dim. – **Repas** *Lunch 17* – 28/42.

◆ Maison de caractère dont la sympathique enseigne a soufflé ses vingt bougies. Recettes classiques sobrement mises à la page. Jardin fleuri aux beaux jours.

◆ Dit sympathieke restaurant in een karakteristiek pand heeft onlangs zijn 20-jarig jubileum gevierd. Klassieke recepten met een snufje vernieuwing. Fraaie bloementuin.

LIMBOURG (LIMBURG) *4830 Liège* 533 U 19, 534 U 19 *et* 716 K 4 – *5504 h.*

Bruxelles 126 – Maastricht 48 – Liège 36 – Eupen 8 – Verviers 8 – Aachen 23.

Le Casino, av. Reine Astrid 7 (sur N 61 à Dolhain), ☎ 0 87 76 23 74, *Fax 0 87 76 44 27* – P. AE VISA.

fermé 2 sem. en juil., lundi, mardi, merc. soir, jeudi soir, sam. midi et après 20 h 30 – **Repas** *Lunch 20* – 29/53 bc, ♀.

◆ Un petit assortiment de plats bourgeois, complété d'un lunch et de plusieurs menus bien ficelés, vous sera présenté à cette table. Faites vos jeux, tout va pour le mieux !

◆ Klein assortiment traditionele gerechten, aangevuld met een lunchformule en een aantal evenwichtige menu's. Alles is tiptop voor elkaar, alleen uw inzet nog !

LIMELETTE *1342 Brabant Wallon* C *Ottignies-Louvain-la-Neuve 28372 h.* 533 M 18, 534 M 18 *et* 716 G 3.

18 *à l'Est : 1 km à Louvain-la-Neuve, r. A. Hardy 68* ☎ *0 10 45 05 15, Fax 0 10 45 44 17.*

Bruxelles 29 – Namur 40 – Charleroi 41.

Château de Limelette , r. Ch. Dubois 87, ☎ 0 10 42 19 99, *chateau-de-limelette@chateau-de-limelette.be, Fax 0 10 41 57 59,* , , , , , , , – TV P – 25 à 600. AE VISA.

Repas ***Saint-Jean-des-Bois*** *(fermé 24 déc. soir) Lunch 25* – 55/60, ♀ – **88 ch** 87/257 – ½ P 127/340.

◆ Élégant manoir anglo-normand ressuscité dans les années 1980. Chambres de bon ton, installations pour séminaires, centre de remise en forme, terrasses, jardins et cascades. Salle de restaurant en rotonde agrandie d'une terrasse couverte. Carte classique.

◆ Kasteeltje in Anglo-Normandische stijl, dat in de jaren 1980 in zijn oorspronkelijke luister is hersteld. Smaakvolle kamers, faciliteiten voor congressen, fitnessruimte, terrassen, tuinen en watervallen. Ronde eetzaal met een overdekt terras. Klassieke kaart.

LISOGNE *Namur* 533 O 21, 534 O 21 *et* 716 H 5 – *voir à Dinant.*

LISSEWEGE *8380 West-Vlaanderen* © *Brugge 116 836 h.* 533 E 15 *et* 716 C 2.

Voir *Grange abbatiale★ de l'ancienne abbaye de Ter Doest.*

Bruxelles 107 – Brugge 11 – Knokke-Heist 12.

XXX **De Goedendag,** Lisseweegsvaartje 2, ☎ 0 50 54 53 35, *luc.goedendag@yucom.be, Fax 0 50 54 57 68* – ▤ P. AE ⓓ ⓜⓒ VISA
fermé merc. – **Repas** Lunch 22 – carte 48 à 72.
◆ Décor rustique soigné pour la salle à manger de cette jolie auberge-relais. Côté fourneaux, on fait montre d'un certain classicisme. Menus et suggestions. Vins choisis.
◆ Deze mooie herberg heeft een verzorgd interieur in rustieke stijl. De keuken geeft blijk van een zeker classicisme. Menu's en dagsuggesties. Uitgelezen wijnen.

X **Hof Ter Doest,** Ter Doeststraat 4 (Sud : 2 km, à l'ancienne abbaye), ☎ 0 50 54 40 82, *info@terdoest.be, Fax 0 50 54 40 82,* ≤, 𝄞, Grillades – P. – 25 à 60. AE ⓓ ⓜⓒ VISA
Repas carte 24 à 54, ♀.
◆ Une ferme monastique à tourelle (16e s.), flanquée d'une belle grange dîmière du 13e s., sert d'écrin à cette table champêtre. Grillades en salle. Cave de doyen de chapitre.
◆ Een kloosterboerderij met een 16e-eeuws torentje en een tiendschuur uit de 13e eeuw vormt de fraaie setting van dit landelijke restaurant. Grillspecialiteiten en goede wijnen.

LIVES-SUR-MEUSE *Namur* 533 O 20 *et* 534 O 20 – *voir à Namur.*

LO *8647 West-Vlaanderen* © *Lo-Reninge 3 281 h.* 533 B 17 *et* 716 B 3.

Bruxelles 142 – Brugge 66 – Kortrijk 51 – Veurne 13.

XX **Huize Cocagne,** Ooststraat 94, ☎ 0 58 28 94 24, *Fax 0 58 28 95 93* – P. AE ⓜⓒ VISA
fermé 2 prem. sem. sept., dim. soir et lundi – **Repas** Lunch 30 – carte env. 38.
◆ En retrait de la route, belle villa s'entourant d'un jardin. De la salle à manger, comme de la terrasse, profitez de l'échappée sur les polders. Choix de recettes actuelles.
◆ Mooie villa met een tuin rondom, even van de weg af. Zowel de eetzaal als het terras bieden een fraai uitzicht op het polderlandschap. Eigentijdse keuken.

X **De Hooipiete,** Fintele 7, ☎ 0 58 28 89 09, *hooipiete@skynet.be, Fax 0 58 28 99 85,* Taverne-rest, anguilles, ⚓ – P. VISA
fermé 2 sem. en sept., 2 sem. en janv., mardi et merc. – **Repas** carte 26 à 40.
◆ La carte de cette taverne-restaurant alanguie dans un paysage agreste, entre le canal et l'Yser, est axée "produits de la mer". Spécialités d'anguilles en saison.
◆ Dit café-restaurant ligt in een landelijke omgeving tussen het kanaal en de IJzer. Wie van vis houdt, is hier aan het goede adres. Palingspecialiteiten in het seizoen.

LOBBES *6540 Hainaut* 533 K 20, 534 K 20 *et* 716 F 4 – *5 499 h.*

Env. *au Nord-Ouest : 3 km à Thuin : site★.*

Bruxelles 60 – Mons 29 – Charleroi 22 – Maubeuge 35.

Le Relais de la Haute Sambre, r. Fontaine Pépin 12 (au site Avigroup), ☎ 0 71 59 79 69, *rhs@skynet.be, Fax 0 71 59 79 80,* 𝄞, – ▤ rest, TV P. – 40. AE ⓓ ⓜⓒ VISA. ✂ ch
Repas *(fermé janv.-15 fév. et lundi)* Lunch 10 – 22/42 bc – **15 ch** *(fermé 4 janv.-15 fév.)* ☕ 73 – ½ P 83/108.
◆ Sur un domaine touristique offrant de nombreux loisirs, petit hôtel dont les chambres, au confort convenable, sont proposées à prix sages. Environnement verdoyant. Salle de restaurant avec vue sur le manège et le plan d'eau. Ambiance détendue.
◆ Dit kleine hotel bevindt zich op een recreatieterrein met talloze activiteiten voor toeristen. De kamers zijn redelijk comfortabel en niet duur. Eetzaal met uitzicht op de manege en het water. Ontspannen ambiance. Veel groen.

LOCHRISTI *Oost-Vlaanderen* 533 I 16 *et* 716 E 2 – *voir à Gent, environs.*

LOKEREN *9160 Oost-Vlaanderen* 533 J 16 *et* 716 E 2 – *36 772 h.*

Markt 2 ☎ 0 9 340 94 74, lokeren@toerismevlaanderen.be, Fax 0 9 340 94 77.

Bruxelles 41 – Gent 28 – Aalst 25 – Antwerpen 38.

La Barakka, Kerkplein 1, ☎ 0 9 340 56 86, *info@labarakka.com, Fax 0 9 340 56 80,* 𝄞 – ▤ rest, TV. AE ⓜⓒ VISA. ✂ ch
Repas *(fermé jeudi)* (taverne-rest) 21/45 bc – ☕ 6 – **13 ch** 56/69.
◆ À l'ombre du clocher de la Kerkplein, hostellerie familiale engageante, dont les chambres, munies du double vitrage, offrent un confort tout à fait convenable. Alternative brasserie ou restaurant.
◆ Dit vriendelijke familiehotel staat aan de voet van de klokkentoren op het Kerkplein. De kamers zijn voorzien van dubbele ramen en bieden een heel redelijk comfort. Voor het eten hebben de gasten de keuze uit de brasserie of het restaurant.

XXX **'t Vier Emmershof,** Krommestraat 1 (par Karrestraat 3 km), ☎ 0 9 348 63 98, *info@vieremmershof.be, Fax 0 9 348 00 02*, – P. AE ① MC VISA
fermé 2 sem. en sept., dim. soir, lundi et mardi – **Repas** Lunch 30 – 50/73 bc, ♀.
◆ À quelques minutes du centre-ville, dans un quartier résidentiel verdoyant, villa moderne qu'agrémente une terrasse sur jardin. Cuisine classique sobrement actualisée.
◆ Moderne villa in een woonwijk met veel groen, op een paar minuten van het centrum. Fijn terras aan de tuinzijde. Klassieke gerechten met een eigentijds tintje.

X **Vienna,** Stationsplein 6, ☎ 0 9 349 03 02, *Fax 0 9 349 30 28*, , Brasserie – MC VISA
fermé fin fév.-début mars, 3 sem. en sept., lundi et mardi – **Repas** Lunch 20 – 30/40.
◆ Une agréable brasserie a élu domicile dans cette maison de maître jouxtant la gare. Menus de saison, suggestions et beau choix de desserts, également servis l'après-midi.
◆ Aangename brasserie gevestigd in een herenhuis tegenover het station. Seizoengebonden menu's en suggesties. Verrukkelijke desserts die u ook in de namiddag kunt proeven.

LOMMEL *3920 Limburg* 533 Q 15 *et* 716 I 2 – *30 947 h.*

Dorp 56 ☎ 0 11 54 02 21, info@toerismelommel.be, Fax 0 11 55 22 66.
Bruxelles 93 – Eindhoven 30 – Hasselt 37.

die Prince sans rest, Mezenstraat 1, ☎ 0 11 54 44 61, *Fax 0 11 54 64 12* – TV P. AE ① MC VISA.
4 – **26 ch** 60/78.
◆ Immeuble des années 1970 dont les chambres, assez tranquilles et convenablement équipées, se répartissent sur deux étages. Bar et salons "cosy". Accueil familial gentil.
◆ Hotel in een gebouw uit de jaren 1970. De vrij rustige, goed geëquipeerde kamers zijn over twee verdiepingen verdeeld. Gezellige bar en lounge. Vriendelijk onthaal.

Carré, Dorperheide 31 (Ouest : 3 km sur N 712), ☎ 0 11 54 60 23, *hotelcarre@skynet.be, Fax 0 11 55 42 42*, , , – rest, TV – 25 à 120. MC VISA. rest
Repas *(fermé lundi)* Lunch 15 – carte 24 à 39 – **12 ch** 52/66.
◆ À 2 mn du centre, petit hôtel familial renfermant une douzaine de chambres rafraîchies, munies chacune d'un grand bureau. Les plus paisibles occupent l'arrière du bâtiment. Un éventail de mets classico-bourgeois vous attend au restaurant. Terrasse d'été.
◆ Klein familiehotel op twee minuten van het centrum, met een twaalftal kamers die zijn opgeknapt en allemaal een groot bureau hebben ; de rustigste liggen aan de achterkant. Het restaurant biedt een keur van klassiek-traditionele gerechten. Terras in de zomer.

Lommel Broek, Kanaalstraat 91 (Sud : 9 km, lieu-dit Kerkhoven), ☎ 0 11 39 10 34, *lommelbroek@pandora.be, Fax 0 11 39 10 74*, – TV P. MC VISA
fermé nov. et merc. – **Repas** (taverne-rest) Lunch 7 – carte 22 à 39 – **7 ch** 53/70 – ½ P 42/50.
◆ Sept chambres actuelles "king size" dont cinq familiales - avec salon et lit-sofa supplémentaire - dans cette construction récente proche du Kattenbos (réserve naturelle).
◆ Hotel in een modern gebouw bij het natuurreservaat het Kattenbos. Zeven kingsize kamers met zithoek en extra bedbank, geschikt voor gezinnen.

XXX **St Jan,** Koning Leopoldlaan 94, ☎ 0 11 54 10 34, *info@restaruant-st-jan.be, Fax 0 11 54 62 22* – P. AE ① MC VISA.
fermé 25 juil.-12 août et jeudis soirs et dim. non fériés – **Repas** Lunch 30 – 34/70 bc, ♀.
◆ Cuisine classico-traditionnelle servie dans une confortable salle à manger d'esprit Art nouveau. Mise en place soignée sur les tables. Livre de cave bien fourni.
◆ Comfortabele eetzaal in art-nouveaustijl, waar klassiek-traditionele gerechten worden geserveerd. Verzorgde mise en place en rijk gevulde wijnkelder.

XX **den Bonten Oss,** Dorp 33, ☎ 0 11 54 15 97, *smakelijk@skynet.be, Fax 0 11 54 47 47* – P. AE ① MC VISA
fermé carnaval, lundi et sam. midi – **Repas** Lunch 25 – 28.
◆ Cet ancien relais de la malle-poste converti en restaurant bourgeois décline un sage registre culinaire oscillant entre classicisme et tradition.
◆ Dit voormalige poststation is tot een geriefelijk restaurant verbouwd. Het culinaire register schommelt tussen klassiek en traditioneel.

XX **Le Soleil,** Luikersteenweg 443 (Kolonie), ☎ 0 11 64 87 83 – P. AE ① MC VISA.
fermé du 13 au 23 avril, du 6 au 17 sept., merc. et jeudi – **Repas** (dîner seult) 33/80 bc, ♀.
◆ Petite villa bichonnée où l'on se sent directement entre de bonnes mains. Accueil cordial, expo d'objets d'art et préparations bien dans le coup, à base de produits choisis.
◆ In deze vriendelijk ogende villa bent u in goede handen. Hartelijke ontvangst, tentoonstelling van kunstvoorwerpen en eigentijdse gerechten met ingrediënten van topkwaliteit.

XX **De Tafel van Adrian,** Kerkstraat 3, ☎ 0 11 55 20 65, *Fax 0 11 55 18 35*, – ▤ – 25. AE ⓓ ⓜ VISA
fermé 2 sem. en juin, 2 sem. en oct., mardi et sam. midi – **Repas** *Lunch 13* – 23/43.
◆ Une adresse chaleureuse et très sympathique, située à l'angle d'une rue commerçante du cœur de Lommel. Carte classique annonçant plusieurs menus. Mobilier de bistrot.
◆ Heel gezellig restaurant met meubilair in bistrostijl, op de hoek van een winkelstraat in het centrum van Lommel. Klassieke kaart met verscheidene menu's.

LOMPRET *Hainaut* 534 L 22 *et* 716 G 5 – *voir à Chimay.*

LONDERZEEL *1840 Vlaams-Brabant* 533 K 16 *et* 716 F 2 – *17 137 h.*
Bruxelles 22 – Antwerpen 28 – Gent 60 – Mechelen 20.

XX **'t Notenhof,** Meerstraat 113, ☎ 0 52 31 15 00, *notenhof@freegates.be*, *Fax 0 52 31 14 44*, – AE ⓓ ⓜ VISA
fermé 19 fév.-1er mars, 26 juil.-13 août, mardi, merc. et sam. midi – **Repas** *Lunch 20* – 30/80 bc.
◆ À l'entrée de la ville, près de la voie ferrée, villa sur jardin proposant une sobre cuisine classique. Accueil et service avenants. Terrasse délicieuse par beau temps.
◆ Villa met tuin bij de ingang van de stad, bij de spoorbaan. Sobere klassieke keuken. Vriendelijke ontvangst en service. Mooi terras voor zomerse dagen.

à Malderen *Nord-Ouest : 6 km* C *Londerzeel* – ✉ *1840 Malderen :*

XX **'t Vensterke,** Leopold Van Hoeymissenstraat 29, ☎ 0 52 34 57 67, *info@vensterke.be*, – P. AE ⓓ ⓜ VISA.
fermé dim. soir, lundi et mardi – **Repas** *Lunch 30* – 39/77 bc, ♀.
◆ Table engageante et bien dans l'air du temps, La P'tite Fenêtre ('t Vensterke) interprète en famille un solide répertoire de recettes classiques renouvelé au fil des saisons.
◆ Uitnodigend restaurant met een hedendaags interieur, waar de hele familie de handen uit de mouwen steekt. Solide repertoire van klassieke gerechten die wisselen per seizoen.

LOOZ *Limburg – voir Borgloon.*

LOTENHULLE *Oost-Vlaanderen* 533 F 16 *et* 716 D 2 – *voir à Aalter.*

LOUVAIN *Vlaams-Brabant – voir Leuven.*

LOUVAIN-LA-NEUVE *Brabant Wallon* 533 M 18, 534 M 18 *et* 716 G 3 – *voir à Ottignies.*

La LOUVIÈRE *7100 Hainaut* 533 K 20, 534 K 20 *et* 716 F 4 – *76 535 h.*
Env. *à l'Ouest : 6 km à Strépy-Thieu, Canal du Centre : les Ascenseurs hydrauliques★.*
pl. Mansart 17 ☎ *0 64 26 15 00, Fax 0 64 21 51 25.*
Bruxelles 52 – Mons 28 – Binche 10 – Charleroi 26.

XXX **Aub. de la Louve,** r. Bouvy 86, ☎ 0 64 22 87 87, *Fax 0 64 28 20 53* – P – 25 à 200. AE ⓓ ⓜ VISA.
fermé août, sam. midi, dim. soir, lundi et merc. soir – **Repas** *Lunch 20* – 40/67 bc, ♀.
◆ Auberge ancienne dont le décor intérieur, chaleureux et cossu, s'accorde pleinement avec le contenu des assiettes, goûteux et sobrement actualisé. Menus plébiscités.
◆ Oude herberg met een warm en rijk aandoend interieur, dat uitstekend bij de gastronomische maaltijd past. De menu's zijn erg in trek. Redelijk moderne keuken.

à Houdeng-Aimeries *Ouest : 3 km* C *La Louvière* – ✉ *7110 Houdeng-Aimeries :*

XX **Le Damier,** r. Hospice 59, ☎ 0 64 22 28 70, *ledamier@tiscalinet.be*, *Fax 0 64 22 28 70*, – P. AE ⓓ ⓜ VISA.
fermé mi-juil.-mi-août, dim. soir, lundi et merc. soir – **Repas** *Lunch 29* – 45/62.
◆ Pas loin du canal du Centre et de ses ascenseurs hydrauliques, corpulente maison de notable où se conçoit un choix de mets classiques revisités en douceur. Terrasse abritée.
◆ Groot herenhuis niet ver van het Canal du Centre met zijn hydraulische liften. Binnen wacht u een keur van klassieke gerechten met een vleugje modern. Beschut terras.

BELGIQUE

à Houdeng-Goegnies *Ouest : 2 km* C *La Louvière* – ✉ *7110 Houdeng-Goegnies :*

X **La Maison du Garde-Barrière,** r. Cimetière 121 (sortie 20 sur E 42 - A 15), ☎ 0 64 84 99 25, *gaetanpelletti@skynet.be, Fax 0 64 28 45 22* – P. AE ⓓ MC VISA
fermé 1re quinz. août, 2e quinz. fév., sam. midi, dim. soir et lundi soir – **Repas** *Lunch 24* – 50/85 bc.
◆ Le garde-barrière a cédé la place à un cuisinier plutôt bien avisé. Pour un repas sortant un peu des sentiers battus dans ce petit coin du Hainaut. Nombre de couverts limité.
◆ Dit huis midden in het dorp bewaakte vroeger een spoorwegovergang. De keuken verlaat de gebaande paden in dit stukje Henegouwen. Beperkt aantal couverts.

LOVERVAL *Hainaut* 533 L 20, 534 L 20 *et* 716 G 4 – *voir à Charleroi.*

LUBBEEK *3210 Vlaams-Brabant* 533 O 17 *et* 716 H 3 – *13 620 h.*
Bruxelles 32 – Antwerpen 57 – Liège 71 – Namur 59.

XX **Maelendries,** Hertbosweg 5 (Sud : 3 km), ☎ 0 16 73 48 60, *Fax 0 16 73 48 60*, ≤,
– P. AE ⓓ MC VISA. ✂
fermé 3 prem. sem. août, 26 déc.-2 janv., merc., sam. midi et dim. soir – **Repas** *Lunch 32* – carte 32 à 48.
◆ Isolée sur une agreste colline, charmante fermette abritant une salle à manger néo-rustique à l'ambiance familiale. Carte classique avec menus et suggestions.
◆ Dit lieflijke boerderijtje staat eenzaam op een groene heuvel. De neorustieke eetzaal ademt een huiselijke sfeer. Klassieke kaart met dagschotels.

LUIK *Liège – voir Liège.*

LUMMEN *Limburg* 533 Q 17 *et* 716 I 3 – *voir à Hasselt.*

MAARKE-KERKEM *Oost-Vlaanderen* 533 G 18 – *voir à Oudenaarde.*

MAASEIK *3680 Limburg* 533 T 16 *et* 716 K 2 – *23 193 h.*
Stadhuis, Markt 1 ☎ 0 89 81 92 90, toerisme.maaseik@maaseik.be, Fax 0 89 81 92 99.
Bruxelles 118 – Hasselt 41 – Maastricht 33 – Roermond 20.

Kasteel Wurfeld ✈, Kapelweg 60, ☎ 0 89 56 81 36, *info@kasteelwurfeld.be, Fax 0 89 56 87 89*, , , – TV P – 25 à 100. AE MC VISA. ✂
Repas *(fermé lundi midi, mardi midi et sam. midi) Lunch 33* – 41/55 – **16 ch** ☐ 75 – ½ P 82/87.
◆ Aux portes de Maaseik, imposante demeure ouverte sur un beau parc arboré invitant au repos. Les chambres, tranquilles et personnalisées, jouissent d'un confort douillet. Une véranda verdoyante sert de cadre au restaurant. Cuisine dans le tempo actuel.
◆ Imposant gebouw aan de rand van Maaseik, met een boomrijk park waar u volledig kunt ontspannen. De comfortabele kamers zijn rustig en hebben een persoonlijk karakter. In de weelderige serre kunt u genieten van de eigentijdse kookkunst van de kok.

Aldeneikerhof ✈, Hamontweg 103 (Est : 2 km, lieu-dit Aldeneik), ☎ 0 89 56 67 77, *aldeneikerhof@pi.be, Fax 0 89 56 67 78*, , , – TV P – 25 à 70. MC VISA. ✂
fermé fév. – **Repas** (dîner pour résidents seult) **8 ch** ☐ 65/88 – ½ P 77/98.
◆ Ancienne maison de notable jouxtant l'église romano-gothique d'un hameau proche de Maaseik. Chambres aussi paisibles que confortables. Accueil familial gentil.
◆ Vriendelijk onthaal in dit 19e-eeuwse herenhuis naast de romaans-gotische kerk in een dorpje dicht bij Maaseik. De kamers zijn zowel rustig als comfortabel.

XX **La Cloche,** Markt 35, ☎ 0 89 86 54 05, *info@lacloche.be, Fax 0 89 86 13 89*, , Produits de la mer – . AE ⓓ MC VISA. ✂
fermé sem. carnaval, sem. Toussaint et merc. – **Repas** *Lunch 29* – 63.
◆ Table au "look" nautique où les friands de produits de la mer seront comme des poissons dans l'eau. L'été, on se tape aussi la cloche en terrasse, sous les tilleuls du Markt.
◆ Liefhebbers van zeeproducten zullen zich als een vis in het water voelen in dit restaurant. In de zomer worden de tafeltjes op het terras aan de Grote Markt gedekt.

XX **de Loteling,** Willibrordusweg 5 (Est : 2 km, lieu-dit Aldeneik), ☎ 0 89 56 35 89, *Fax 0 89 56 35 89*, – P. ✂
fermé mardi soir, merc. et après 20 h 30 – **Repas** *Lunch 30* – 45, ♀.
◆ Au beau milieu du site pittoresque d'Aldeneik, près de la frontière hollandaise, villa récente estimée pour sa cuisine au goût du jour. L'été venu, on mange en terrasse.
◆ Moderne villa in het schilderachtige Aldeneik, vlak bij de Nederlandse grens. Tongstrelende eigentijdse gerechten, die bij mooi weer op het terras worden geserveerd.

Tiffany's, Markt 19, 0 89 56 40 89, – AE MC VISA.
fermé lundi et sam. midi – **Repas** (menu unique) 31.
◆ Agréable restaurant posté sur la Grand-Place où trônent les statues des frères Van Eyck, deux célèbres enfants du pays. Menu unique au goût du jour, élaboré selon le marché.
◆ Aangenaam restaurant aan de Markt met de standbeelden van de gebroeders Van Eyck, die in Maaseik zijn geboren. Slechts één dagmenu, afhankelijk van het aanbod op de markt.

à Opoeteren *Sud-Ouest : 12 km par N 778 C Maaseik – 3680 Opoeteren :*

Oeterdal, Neeroeterenstraat 41, 0 89 51 82 70, *info@hoteloeterdal.be, Fax 0 89 51 82 71,* – TV P – 25 à 60. AE D MC VISA
fermé 24 déc.-2 janv. – **Repas** (dîner pour résidents seult) – **25 ch** 65/95 – ½ P 70/80.
◆ Aux abords du hameau, en léger retrait de la route nationale, petit hôtel de construction récente dont les menues chambres fonctionnelles viennent d'être rajeunies.
◆ Klein hotel in een nieuw gebouw aan de rand van het dorp, even van de rijksweg af. De kamers zijn niet ruim, maar functioneel en kort geleden opgeknapt.

MAASMECHELEN *3630 Limburg 533 T 17 et 716 K 3 – 35 751 h.*

Bruxelles 106 – Maastricht 15 – Hasselt 30 – Aachen 42.

Da Lidia, Rijksweg 215, 0 89 76 41 34, *res.dalidia@worldonline.be, Fax 0 89 77 42 10,* , Cuisine italienne – AE MC VISA.
fermé sem. carnaval, 24 et 31 déc. soir, lundi et mardi – **Repas** carte 28 à 43, ♀.
◆ Enseigne transalpine auréolée d'une certaine reconnaissance locale, depuis 30 ans. Salle actuelle et bonne ambiance très familiale. Restaurant d'été sur la pelouse du jardin.
◆ Deze Italiaan geniet al 30 jaar een goede reputatie bij de bevolking. Moderne eetzaal en zeer gemoedelijke sfeer. Bij mooi weer wordt in de tuin op het gras gegeten.

à Eisden *Nord : 3 km C Maasmechelen – 3630 Eisden :*

Lika sans rest, Pauwengraaf 2, 0 89 76 01 26, *hotel.lika@pi.be, Fax 0 89 76 55 72,* , , , – TV – 25 à 150. AE MC VISA
42 ch 77/107.
◆ Cet établissement d'allure moderne niché au centre du village renferme des chambres pratiques garnies d'un mobilier de série. Piscine couverte, sauna et salles de réunion.
◆ Modern hotel in het centrum van het dorp, met praktische kamers die van standaard-meubilair zijn voorzien. Overdekt zwembad, sauna en vergaderzalen.

à Opgrimbie *Sud : 5 km C Maasmechelen – 3630 Opgrimbie :*

La Strada, Rijksweg 634 (N 78), 0 89 76 69 12, *lastrada@skynet.be, Fax 0 89 76 69 12,* , Cuisine italienne – P. AE D MC VISA – *fermé sem. carnaval, 2 dern. sem. juil., merc., jeudi et sam. midi* – **Repas** Lunch 25 – carte 30 à 54.
◆ Bonne cuisine italienne concoctée dans la stabilité : ce n'est pas par hasard que La Strada compte quelques grands cuisiniers limbourgeois parmi sa fidèle clientèle.
◆ Goede Italiaanse keuken, die al jaren dezelfde kwaliteit weet hoog te houden. Niet verwonderlijk dus dat een aantal Limburgse topkoks tot de vaste cliëntèle behoort.

MACHELEN *Vlaams-Brabant 533 L 17 et 716 G 3 – voir à Bruxelles, environs.*

MAISSIN *6852 Luxembourg belge C Paliseul 5 024 h. 534 Q 23 et 716 I 6.*

Bruxelles 135 – Bouillon 26 – Arlon 65 – Dinant 49 – St-Hubert 19.

Chalet-sur-Lesse, av. Bâtonnier Braun 1, 0 61 65 53 91, *info@chalet-sur-lesse.be, Fax 0 61 65 56 88,* , , , – P. D MC VISA. rest
Pâques-oct., week-end et vacances scolaires ; fermé du 1er au 8 juil. et du 1er au 30 janv.
– **Repas** carte 29 à 47 – **25 ch** 65/119, – 1 suite – ½ P 63/99.
◆ Grand chalet aménagé avec goût en confortable hostellerie. Chambres actuelles bien agencées mais dépourvues de TV, salon "cosy", bar anglais et agréable terrasse sur jardin. Petite restauration au déjeuner et repas classique au dîner.
◆ Comfortabel hotel in een groot en smaakvol chalet. Moderne kamers zonder tv, "cosy" lounge, Engelse pub en prettig terras in de tuin. Kleine lunchkaart en klassieke diners.

MALDEGEM *9990 Oost-Vlaanderen 533 F 15 et 716 D 2 – 22 081 h.*

Bruxelles 89 – Brugge 23 – Gent 29 – Antwerpen 73.

Beukenhof, Brugse Steenweg 200, 0 50 71 55 95, *Fax 0 50 71 55 95,* – AE MC VISA
fermé 2 sem. carnaval, 2 dern. sem. juil., merc. et jeudi – **Repas** 33/45 bc.
◆ Gentille petite affaire familiale installée dans une fermette aux portes de Maldegem. Registre culinaire classique sagement actualisé. Salon-bar, terrasse sur l'arrière.
◆ Aardig familiebedrijfje in een boerderijtje aan de rand van Maldegem. Klassieke keuken met een vleugje vernieuwing. Salon met bar en terras aan de achterzijde.

MALDEREN *Vlaams-Brabant* 533 K 16 *et* 716 F 2 – *voir à Londerzeel.*

MALEN *Brabant Wallon – voir Mélin.*

MALINES *Antwerpen – voir Mechelen.*

MALLE *2390 Antwerpen* 533 N 15 *et* 716 H 2 – *14 070 h.*
Bruxelles 75 – Antwerpen 30 – Turnhout 18.

à Oostmalle *Est : 2 km* C *Malle – ✉ 2390 Oostmalle :*

XX **De Eiken** (Smets), Lierselei 173 (Sud : 2 km sur N 14), ☎ 0 3 311 52 22, *info@de-eiken.be, Fax 0 3 311 69 45,* <, 🌂 – P. AE ① ⊙ VISA JCB. ✂
✿ *fermé 24 fév.-4 mars, 20 juil.-12 août, sam. midi, dim. et lundi* – **Repas** *Lunch 45* – 66/101 bc, carte 80 à 97, ♀.
◆ Une bonne table campinoise : cuisine actuelle brillamment personnalisée, servie par beau temps au grand air dans un environnement boisé agrémenté d'une pièce d'eau.
◆ Een uitstekend adres in de Kempen, waar u kunt genieten van een eigentijdse keuken met een persoonlijk karakter. Bij mooi weer wordt er tussen de bomen aan het water gegeten.
Spéc. Asperges du terroir et homard, tomates séchées et pesto (mai-juil.). Pigeonneau au carpaccio de pommes de terre et jus de truffes. Tarte aux noisettes, parfait glacé et amaretto

à Westmalle *Ouest : 2 km* C *Malle – ✉ 2390 Westmalle :*

🏠 **De Witte Lelie,** Antwerpsesteenweg 333, ☎ 0 3 309 09 61, *Fax 0 3 309 01 55,* 🌂 – ▤ rest, TV P. AE ① ⊙ VISA
Repas *(fermé sam. midi et dim.)* (taverne-rest) *Lunch 25* – carte 26 à 45 – ☕ 8 – **14 ch** 50/70 – ½ P 72.
◆ Au centre du village, hôtel familial de petit format proposant des chambres fonctionnelles assez menues ; quatre d'entre elles sont des singles. Taverne-restaurant misant sur une carte aux saveurs "bistrotières".
◆ Dit kleine familiehotel bevindt zich in het centrum van het dorp. Het beschikt over vrij kleine, maar functionele kamers, waarvan vier eenpersoons. In het café-restaurant kunnen de gasten kiezen uit smakelijke bistrogerechten van de kaart.

MALMÉDY *4960 Liège* 533 V 20, 534 V 20 *et* 716 L 4 – *11 394 h.*
Voir *Site★ – Carnaval★ (dimanche avant Mardi-gras).*
Env. *au Nord : Hautes Fagnes★★, Signal de Botrange <★, Sentier de découverte nature★ – au Sud-Ouest : 6 km, Rocher de Falize★ – au Nord-Est : 6 km, Château de Reinhardstein★.*
ℹ *pl. Albert Ier 29a* ☎ *0 80 33 02 50, Fax 0 80 77 05 88.*
Bruxelles 156 – Liège 57 – Eupen 29 – Clervaux 57.

🏠 **Le Chambertin,** Chemin-rue 46, ☎ 0 80 33 03 14, *chambertin@skynet.be, Fax 0 80 77 03 38* – |‡| TV. ⊙ VISA. ✂ ch
fermé début sept. et lundi – **Repas** *Lunch 12* – carte env. 32 – **8 ch** ☕ 65 – ½ P 55/60.
◆ Au cœur de Malmédy, à l'angle de la principale rue commerçante, petit établissement dont les chambres offrent un confort correct. Salle des repas sobrement décorée. Assortiment de plats traditionnels. Tea-room l'après-midi pendant les week-ends.
◆ Dit hotelletje staat op de hoek van de belangrijkste winkelstraat van Malmédy. De kamers zijn redelijk comfortabel. In de sober gedecoreerde eetzaal worden traditionele schotels geserveerd. Theesalon op zaterdag- en zondagmiddag.

XX **Plein Vent** avec ch, rte de Spa 44 (Ouest : 7 km, lieu-dit Burnenville), ☎ 0 80 33 05 54, *pleinvent@busmail.net, Fax 0 80 33 70 60,* < vallées, 🌂 – ▤ rest, TV P. AE ① ⊙ VISA. ✂
fermé fin juil.-début août, fin déc.-début janv., lundi soir et mardi – **Repas** *(fermé après 20 h 30)* 28/65 – **6 ch** ☕ 82/100 – ½ P 60/69.
◆ Cette villa "nez au vent" entourée de verdure embrasse la vallée du regard. Cuisine classique de bon aloi. Chambres lambrissées. Proximité du circuit national de vitesse.
◆ In deze villa met uitzicht op het groene dal waait een frisse wind ! Gelambriseerde kamers. Eerlijke, klassieke keuken. Vlak bij het Nationale Autocircuit van Francorchamps.

XX **Albert Ier** avec ch, pl. Albert Ier 40, ☎ 0 80 33 04 52, *info@hotel-albertpremier.be, Fax 0 80 33 06 16,* 🌂 – ▤ ch, TV. AE ① ⊙ VISA. ✂
fermé carnaval, du 1er au 15 juil., merc. soir, jeudi et dim. soir – **Repas** *Lunch 32* – 42/49 – **6 ch** ☕ 55/85 – ½ P 75.
◆ Alléchantes recettes actuelles aux accents transalpins et belle carte de vins italiens à cette enseigne de la place la plus animée de Malmédy. Chambres correctes.
◆ Dit etablissement is te vinden aan het meest levendige plein van Malmédy. Smakelijke eigentijdse gerechten met een Italiaans accent en bijpassende wijnen. Keurige kamers.

Au Petit Louvain, Chemin-rue 47, ☎ 0 80 33 04 15, *Fax 0 80 44 86 53* – AE ⓓ ⓜ VISA – *fermé lundi soir et merc.* – **Repas** *Lunch 10* – 18/30.
◆ Aimable petite affaire familiale localement appréciée pour ses copieuses préparations traditionnelles. Le gibier s'y arroge la part du lion en saison de chasse.
◆ Vriendelijk familiebedrijfje dat plaatselijk wordt gewaardeerd om zijn copieuze traditionele schotels. Wild neemt het leeuwendeel voor zijn rekening in het jachtseizoen.

à Bévercé *Nord : 3 km* C *Malmédy* – ✉ *4960 Bévercé :*

Host. Trôs Marets, rte des Trôs Marets 2 (N 68), ☎ 0 80 33 79 17, *info@trosmarets.be, Fax 0 80 33 79 10,* ≤ vallées, – TV P. AE ⓓ ⓜ VISA. rest
fermé du 1er au 26 mars et du 6 au 23 déc. – **Repas** *(fermé dim. soirs et lundis non fériés)* *Lunch 43* – 68 – **7 ch** 102/206, – 4 suites – ½ P 95/147.
◆ Au pied des Hautes Fagnes, en contrebas d'une route sinueuse, charmante hostellerie procurant une vue bucolique sur la vallée. Jardin soigné. Chambres confortables. Restaurant garni de meubles de style. Registre culinaire classique actualisé. Belle terrasse.
◆ Aan de voet van de Hoge Venen, onder aan een kronkelweg, staat dit charmante hotel met prachtig uitzicht op het dal. Comfortabele kamers. Restaurant met stijlmeubelen. Het culinaire register is modern-klassiek. Mooi terras en verzorgde tuin.

Maison Géron (annexe Géronprés - 4 ch) sans rest, rte de la Ferme Libert 4, ☎ 0 80 33 00 06, *geron@busmail.net, Fax 0 80 77 03 17,* – TV P. AE ⓜ VISA.
10 ch 55/100.
◆ Cette villa engageante construite au 18e s. s'agrémente d'une véranda, d'une terrasse et d'un jardin croquignolet. Chambres personnalisées, à l'image de l'accueil.
◆ De aantrekkingskracht van deze 18e-eeuwse villa wordt nog versterkt door zijn serre, terras en mooie tuin. De kamers hebben een persoonlijke uitstraling, net als de ontvangst.

Ferme Libert - Le Grand Champs, Bévercé-Village 26, ☎ 0 80 33 02 47, *Fax 0 80 33 98 85,* ≤ vallées, – TV – 25 à 80. AE ⓜ VISA. ch
Repas *(fermé après 20 h)* (taverne-rest) *Lunch 20* – 25/53 bc – **45 ch** 48/71 – ½ P 62.
◆ Bâtisse à colombage voisine d'un domaine skiable. Petites chambres avec douche ou installations sanitaires plus complètes à l'annexe Le Grand Champs. Vue sur la vallée. À table, ambiance ardennaise et solide cuisine traditionnelle régionale.
◆ Vakwerkhuis in een skigebied, met uitzicht op het dal. Kleine kamers met douche of compleet sanitair in de dependance Le Grand Champs. Typisch Ardens restaurant met traditionele gerechten uit de streek.

MALONNE *Namur* 533 N 20, 534 N 20 *et* 716 H 4 – *voir à Namur.*

MANAGE *7170 Hainaut* 533 K 19, 534 K 19 *et* 716 F 4 – *22 022 h.*
Bruxelles 47 – Mons 25 – Charleroi 24.

Le Petit Cellier, Grand'rue 88, ☎ 0 64 55 59 69, *lepetitcellier@skynet.be, Fax 0 64 55 56 07,* – P. AE ⓓ ⓜ VISA – *fermé dim. soir et lundi* – **Repas** *Lunch 29* – 39/72 bc.
◆ Cette vénérable enseigne du centre de Manage signale une maison de caractère appréciée pour ses recettes au goût du jour que valorise un bon "petit cellier".
◆ Karakteristiek pand in het centrum van Manage. Het restaurant valt zeer in de smaak vanwege de eigentijdse gerechten, waarvoor een goede wijn uit de kast wordt gehaald.

MARCHE-EN-FAMENNE *6900 Luxembourg belge* 533 R 21, 534 R 21 *et* 716 J 5 – *16 622 h.*
r. Brasseurs 7 ☎ *0 84 31 21 35, marche.en.famenne@belgique.com, Fax 0 84 32 31 09.*
Bruxelles 107 – Arlon 80 – Liège 56 – Namur 46.

Quartier Latin, r. Brasseurs 2, ☎ 0 84 32 17 13, *contact@quartier-latin.be, Fax 0 84 32 17 12,* – TV P – 25 à 120. AE ⓓ ⓜ VISA
Repas (brasserie) *Lunch 15* – 25/41, ♀ – 12 – **45 ch** 80/110, – 6 suites.
◆ Au centre de Marche, hôtel intégrant un ancien lieu de culte des Pères jésuites. Chambres assez avenantes et bonne infrastructure pour... séminaires ! Accueil aimable. Confortable salle à manger actuelle. Cuisine de type brasserie et mets plus élaborés.
◆ Centraal gelegen hotel op een plek waar de jezuïeten hun eredienst hielden. De kamers zien er uitnodigend uit en er zijn faciliteiten voor... seminars ! Vriendelijk onthaal. Comfortabel, eigentijds restaurant met eenvoudige of uitgebreide kaart.

Château d'Hassonville, rte d'Hassonville 105 (Sud-Ouest : 4 km par N 836), ☎ 0 84 31 10 25, *info@hassonville.be, Fax 0 84 31 60 27,* ≤, – P – 30. AE ⓓ ⓜ VISA.
fermé 2 sem. en janv. et mardi – **Repas** voir rest ***le Grand Pavillon*** ci-après – 15 – **20 ch** 100/150 – ½ P 265/315.
◆ Superbe château du 17e s. s'entourant d'un vaste parc agrémenté d'un étang. Belles chambres romantiques (sans TV) aménagées dans le corps de logis et ses dépendances.
◆ Prachtig 17e-eeuws kasteel, omringd door een groot park met een vijver. Mooie romantische kamers zonder tv in het hoofdgebouw en de bijgebouwen.

XXX **le Grand Pavillon** - H. Château d'Hassonville, rte d'Hassonville 105 (Sud-Ouest : 4 km par N 836), ☎ 0 84 31 10 25, *info@hassonville.be, Fax 0 84 31 60 27*, ≤, 余 - ▤ P. AE ⓓ MC VISA. ✻
fermé 2 sem. en janv., mardi et merc. midi – **Repas** *Lunch 35* – 55/130 bc.
◆ Le restaurant du Château d'Hassonville vous reçoit avec style dans une élégante orangerie recelant une cave à vins "grand seigneur". Savoureuses recettes au goût du jour.
◆ Het restaurant van het Château d'Hassonville ontvangt u met stijl in de elegante oranjerie. Fijne eigentijdse keuken en een wijnkelder die een "grand seigneur" waardig is.

XX **Aux Menus Plaisirs** avec ch, r. Manoir 2, ☎ 0 84 31 38 71, *info@manoir.be, Fax 0 84 31 52 81*, 余 - ▤ rest, TV P. MC VISA. ✻ ch
fermé 1re quinz. juil., prem. sem. oct., dern. sem. janv., dim. soir et lundi – **Repas** *Lunch 20* – 35/40 – ☕ 8 – **6 ch** 97 – ½ P 62.
◆ Agréable moment de table en perspective dans ce petit manoir du 17e s. s'ouvrant sur un jardin d'hiver cossu où l'on prend place sous une large coupole.
◆ In dit 17e-eeuwse kasteeltje met een weelderige overkoepelde wintertuin, kunt u van de kleine pleziertjes van het leven genieten.

XX **Les 4 Saisons,** rte de Bastogne 108 (Sud-Est : 2 km, lieu-dit Hollogne), ☎ 0 84 32 18 10, *Fax 0 84 32 18 81*, 余 - P. MC VISA
fermé 1re quinz. juil. et mardis soirs, merc. et dim. soirs non fériés – **Repas** *Lunch 22* – 28/58 bc.
◆ Postée aux portes de la ville, cette fermette pimpante et guillerette bâtie en pierre du pays interprète un répertoire culinaire attrayant, au léger accent méridional.
◆ Dit karakteristieke stenen boerderijtje aan de rand van de stad ziet er fris en vrolijk uit. Aantrekkelijk culinair register met een licht zuidelijke tongval.

X **des Arts** 1er étage, pl. du Roi Albert Ier 21, ☎ 0 84 31 61 81, *Fax 0 84 31 61 81* – AE MC VISA. ✻
fermé 1 sem. en juil., prem. sem. janv., lundis midis non fériés, dim. soir et lundi soir – **Repas** 30/77 bc.
◆ Salle de restaurant contemporaine, chaleureuse et colorée, aménagée à l'étage d'une maison jouxtant l'église, sur la place principale. Menus saisonniers et du marché.
◆ Hedendaags restaurant in warme kleuren op de bovenverdieping van een pand naast de kerk, aan het hoofdplein van Marche. Menu van het seizoen en menu van de markt.

X **Le Yang-Tsé,** r. Neuve 3, ☎ 0 84 31 26 88, *sunying71@hotmail.com, Fax 0 84 32 31 88*, Cuisine chinoise – AE ⓓ MC VISA
Repas *Lunch 7* – 22/55 bc.
◆ L'une des rares enseignes asiatiques de Marche. Cuisine chinoise servie dans une longue salle à manger garnie de meubles laqués, comme le canard. Carte assez étoffée.
◆ Een van de weinige Aziatische restaurants van Marche. Lange eetzaal met gelakte meubelen, waar u kunt kiezen uit een uitgebreide kaart met Chinese lekkernijen als pekingeend.

MARCOURT *6987 Luxembourg belge* C *Rendeux 2 212 h.* 533 S 21, 534 S 21 *et* 716 J 5.
Bruxelles 126 – Arlon 84 – Marche-en-Famenne 19 – La Roche-en-Ardenne 9.

XX **Le Marcourt** avec ch, Pont de Marcourt 7, ☎ 0 84 47 70 88, *Fax 0 84 47 70 88*, 余, 余 - P. MC VISA. ✻
fermé 21 juin-3 juil., sept.-2 oct., 30 déc.-janv., merc. et jeudi – **Repas** *(fermé après 20 h 30)* 32/52 – **6 ch** ☕ 71 – ½ P 70/75.
◆ Sympathique petite adresse que cette maison de briques voisine du pont de Marcourt ! Menus traditionnels bien balancés. Terrasse d'appoint et grand jardin arboré.
◆ Dit restaurant in een bakstenen huis bij de brug van Marcourt is een goed adresje. Evenwichtige, traditionele menu's. Zomerterras en een grote tuin met veel bomen.

MARENNE *6990 Luxembourg belge* C *Hotton 5 024 h.* 533 R 21, 534 R 21 *et* 716 J 5.
Bruxelles 109 – Dinant 44 – Liège 55 – Namur 53 – La Roche-en-Ardenne 22.

XX **Les Pieds dans le Plat,** r. Centre 3, ☎ 0 84 32 17 92, *jmd@lespiedsdansleplat.be, Fax 0 84 32 36 92*, 余 - P
fermé du 20 au 30 déc., lundi, mardi, merc. soir et jeudi soir – **Repas** *Lunch 23* – 25/65 bc, ♀.
◆ Quoi qu'en dise l'enseigne de cet établissement champêtre, le chef évite vraiment de mettre "les pieds dans le plat" ! Cuisine ambitieuse et livre de cave bien fourni.
◆ In dit landelijke etablissement staat ook de chef-kok met beide benen op de grond ! Ambitieuze kookstijl, waarbij de wijnen een uitstekende tafelpartner zijn.

MARIAKERKE *West-Vlaanderen* 533 C 15 *et* 716 B 2 – *voir à Oostende.*

MARIEKERKE *Antwerpen* 533 K 16 *et* 716 F 2 – *voir à Bornem.*

MARILLES *1350 Brabant Wallon* Ⓒ *Orp-Jauche 7 509 h.* 533 O 18, 534 O 18 *et* 716 H 3.
Bruxelles 57 – Namur 43 – Liège 50 – Tienen 19.

La Bergerie, Grand-Route 1 (sur N 240), ☎ 0 19 63 32 41, *Fax 0 19 63 23 07* – P. AE ① MC VISA
fermé août, lundi et mardi – **Repas** Lunch 17 – carte 34 à 51.
◆ Au bord de la route, dans un environnement agreste, mignonne auberge rustique localement réputée pour sa carte dédiée aux carnivores, mais ne boudant toutefois pas la marée.
◆ Lieflijke en rustieke herberg langs de weg, in een landelijke omgeving. De menukaart is echt iets voor vleesliefhebbers, hoewel de kok ook heel goed raad weet met vis.

MARKE *West-Vlaanderen* 533 E 18 *et* 716 C 3 – *voir à Kortrijk.*

MARTELANGE *6630 Luxembourg belge* 534 T 24 *et* 716 K 6 – *1 464 h.*
Bruxelles 168 – Luxembourg 53 – Arlon 18 – Bastogne 21 – Diekirch 40 – Ettelbrück 36.

Host. An der Stuff avec ch (annexe), r. Roche Percée 1 (Nord : 2 km sur N 4), ☎ 0 63 60 04 28, *Fax 0 63 60 13 92*, ←, – TV P. AE MC VISA. ch
fermé janv. – **Repas** *(fermé dim. soirs et lundis non fériés)* Lunch 33 – carte 48 à 56 – **12 ch** ☕ 66/74 – ½ P 57/82.
◆ Cordiale table au décor ardennais où ronronne, par temps de froidure, un âtre réconfortant. Recettes d'orientation classique relevées de touches régionales. Abords verdoyants.
◆ Behaaglijk restaurant met een Ardens interieur, waar het haardvuur knappert als het buiten koud en guur is. Klassieke recepten met regionale invloeden. Bosrijke omgeving.

MASSEMEN *9230 Oost-Vlaanderen* Ⓒ *Wetteren 22 818 h.* 533 I 17 *et* 716 E 3.
Bruxelles 45 – Gent 19 – Antwerpen 65.

Geuzenhof, Lambroekstraat 90, ☎ 0 9 369 80 34, *info@geuzenhof.be, Fax 0 9 368 20 68*, – P – 25 à 80. AE ① MC VISA.
fermé vacances Pâques, dim. soir, lundi et mardi – **Repas** Lunch 30 – 47/69 bc, ♀.
◆ Ancienne ferme promue maison de bouche, le Geuzenhof décline un registre culinaire actuel dans un élégant décor bourgeois semé, de-ci de-là, de notes modernes.
◆ Deze oude boerderij is tot restaurant verbouwd. Elegant bourgeoisinterieur met hier en daar een modern accent. Culinair gezien is de Geuzenhof goed bij de tijd.

MATER *Oost-Vlaanderen* 533 H 17 – *voir à Oudenaarde.*

MECHELEN (MALINES) *2800 Antwerpen* 533 L 16 *et* 716 G 2 – *75 946 h.*
Voir *Tour*** de la cathédrale St-Rombaut** (St. Romboutskathedraal)* AY – *Grand-Place* (Grote Markt)* ABY **26** – *Hôtel de Ville* (Stadhuis)* BY **H** – *Pont du Wollemarkt (Marché aux laines)* ←* AY **F**.
Musée : *Manufacture Royale de Tapisseries Gaspard De Wit* (Koninklijke Manufactuur van Wandtapijten Gaspard De Wit)* AY **M¹**.
Env. par ③ : *3 km à Muizen : Parc zoologique de Plankendael**.*
Stadhuis, Grote Markt 21 ☎ *0 15 29 76 55, toerisme@mechelen.be, Fax 0 15 29 76 53.*
Bruxelles 30 ④ – *Antwerpen 26* ⑥ – *Leuven 24* ③

Plans pages suivantes

Novotel, Van Beethovenstraat 1, ☎ 0 15 40 49 50, *h3154@accor-hotels.com, Fax 0 15 40 49 51*, – TV – 25 à 110. AE ① MC VISA JCB
Repas Lunch 25 bc – carte 22 à 39 – ☕ 14 – **121 ch** 124/144, – 1 suite – ½ P 106/170.
◆ Novotel "nouvelle génération" installé dans un immeuble moderne bâti en centre-ville. Espaces communs et chambres dont l'agencement "colle" bien à l'époque. Brasserie au cadre contemporain. Carte diversifiée, apte à satisfaire la plupart des appétits. AZ b
◆ Een Novotel "nieuwe stijl" in een modern gebouw in het centrum. De kamers en andere ruimten passen geheel in de huidige tijdgeest. Brasserie met een hedendaagse inrichting en een gevarieerde kaart met voor elk wat wils.

Gulden Anker, Brusselsesteenweg 2, ☎ 0 15 42 25 35, *info@guldenanker.be, Fax 0 15 42 34 99*, – rest, TV P – 25 à 120. AE ① MC VISA AZ u
Repas *(fermé 3 dern. sem. juil., sam. midi et dim. soir)* Lunch 24 – 35/70 bc – **24 ch** ☕ 94/119 – ½ P 82/117.
◆ "Jetée" aux portes de la ville, en face d'un canal, L'Ancre d'Or (Gulden Anker) propose des chambres refaites de neuf offrant un bon niveau de confort. Salle des repas actuelle. Préparations classiques égayées de notes régionales.
◆ Dit hotel ligt voor anker bij een gracht aan de rand van de stad. Het beschikt over kamers die volledig zijn gerenoveerd en goed comfort bieden. In de moderne eetzaal worden klassieke gerechten met regionale invloeden geserveerd.

MECHELEN

Antwerpsesteenweg	C 2
Battelsesteenweg	C 4
Brusselsesteenweg	C 12
Colomalaan	C 14
Eikestraat	C 20
Europalaan	C 23
Hanswijkvaart	C 30
Hombeeksesteenweg	C 32
Liersesteenweg	C 47
Postzegellaan	C 57
Steppeke	C 66
Stuivenbergbaan	C 67
Tervuursesteenweg	C 69

NH Mechelen sans rest, Korenmarkt 24, ☎ 0 15 42 03 03, *nhmechelen@nh-hotels.be, Fax 0 15 42 37 88* – ⎮‡⎮ ✕ TV 🚗 – 🏛 25. AE ⓓ ⓜⓒ VISA AZ s
☕ 17 – **43 ch** 120.

• Cette imposante façade de briques située au centre-ville abrite des chambres amples et douillettes, agencées dans l'esprit "british". Bar rutilant et salon "cosy".

• Centraal gelegen hotel met een imposante bakstenen gevel. De ruime, behaaglijke kamers zijn in Engelse stijl ingericht. Fonkelende bar, sfeervolle lounge.

Hobbit sans rest, Battelsesteenweg 455 F, ☎ 0 15 27 20 27, *hobbithotel@yucom.be, Fax 0 15 27 20 28* – ✕ TV ♿ P. AE ⓓ ⓜⓒ VISA. ✕ C t
☕ 7 – **21 ch** 48.

• Entre la Dijle et le canal, à portée d'autoroute, petit établissement d'allure moderne renfermant des chambres standard insonorisées, avant tout fonctionnelles.

• Klein en modern etablissement tussen de Dijle et het kanaal, vlak bij de snelweg. Standaardkamers die in de eerste plaats functioneel zijn en een goede geluidsisolatie hebben.

Egmont sans rest, Oude Brusselstraat 50, ☎ 0 15 42 13 99, *hotel_egmont@hotmail.com, Fax 0 15 41 34 98* – ⎮‡⎮ TV 🚗. AE ⓓ ⓜⓒ VISA BZ e
19 ch ☕ 68/94.

• Accueil familial dans cet immeuble jouxtant le ring de Mechelen. Les chambres, un tantinet désuètes, mais munies du double vitrage, se répartissent sur quatre étages.

• In dit vier verdiepingen tellende gebouw langs de Ring van Mechelen wacht u een vriendelijk onthaal. De kamers zijn ietwat sleets, maar hebben wel dubbele ramen.

Carolus, Guido Gezellelaan 49, ☎ 0 15 28 71 41, *hotel@hetanker.be, Fax 0 15 21 71 42,* 🏠 – ✕ TV P. 🏛 30. AE ⓓ ⓜⓒ VISA AY a
Repas *(fermé 3 prem. sem. juil. et merc.)* 36/47 bc – **22 ch** *(fermé dern. sem. déc.)* ☕ 73/93 – ½ P 93.

• À deux pas du béguinage, hôtel implanté sur le site de la célèbre brasserie malinoise Het Anker, dans un ancien entrepôt. Chambres de notre temps. Ample taverne-restaurant proposant des plats traditionnels accompagnés d'un col de mousse approprié.

• Dit hotel is gevestigd in het pakhuis van een oude brouwerij bij het begijnhof. Eigentijdse kamers. Groot café-restaurant met traditionele gerechten, waarbij natuurlijk een biertje wordt gedronken.

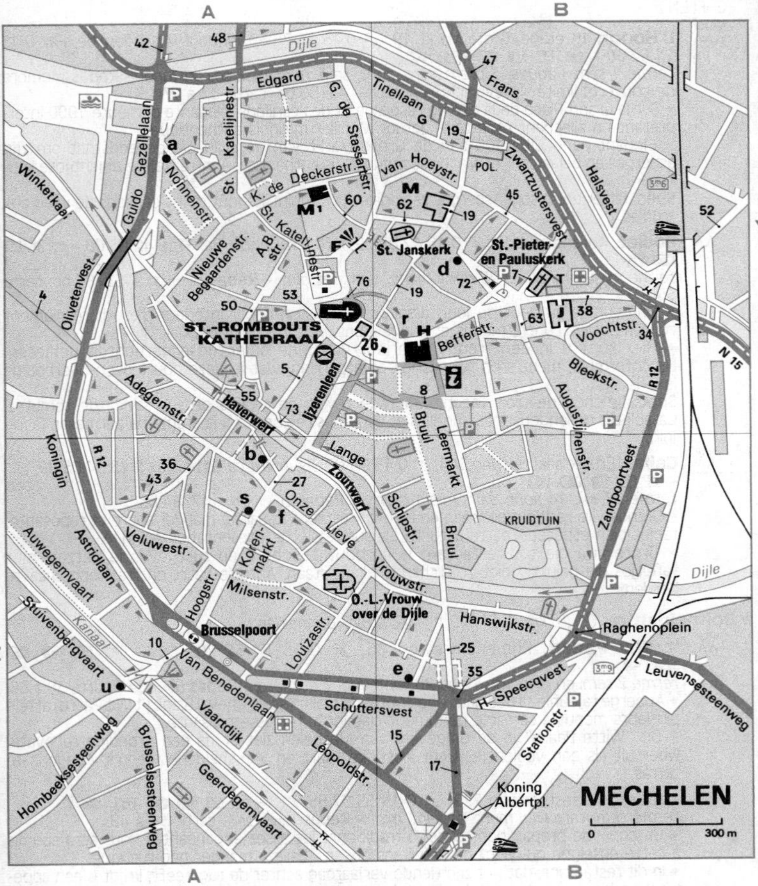

Battelsesteenweg	AY 4	Guldenstr.	AZ 27	Liersesteenweg	BY 47
Begijnenstr.	AY 5	Hoogstr.	AZ	Maurits Sabbestr.	AY 48
Blokstr.	BY 7	Hoogstratenplein	BY 34	Melaan	AY 50
Botermarkt	BY 8	Kardinaal Mercierplein	BZ 35	Nekkerspoelstr.	BY 52
Brusselsepoortstr.	AZ 10	Karmelietenstr.	AZ 36	Onder den Toren	AY 53
Bruul	BYZ	Keizerstr.	BY 38	Persoonshoek	AY 55
Colomastr.	BZ 15	Korenmarkt	AZ	Schoutetstr.	AY 60
Consciencestr.	BZ 17	IJzerenleen	AY	St.-Janstr.	BY 62
Frederik de Merodestr.	BY 19	O.L. Vrouwstr.	ABZ	St.-Pietersberg	BY 63
Gr. van Egmontstr.	BZ 25	O. Van Kesbeeckstr.	AY 42	Veemarkt	BY 72
Grote Markt	ABY 26	Korte Pennincstr.	AZ 43	Vismarkt	AY 73
		Lange Heergracht	BY 45	Wollemarkt	AY 76

Express by Holiday Inn sans rest, Veemarkt 3, ✆ 0 15 44 84 20, *hotel@express-himechelen.com, Fax 0 15 44 84 21* – 25. AE VISA JCB BY d

69 ch ☕ 110.

◆ Hôtel récent, stratégiquement situé dans le centre-ville, en bordure du Marché aux bestiaux (Veemarkt). Chambres sans reproche, équipées à l'identique. Parking privé.

◆ Dit nieuwe hotel is strategisch gelegen in de binnenstad, aan de Veemarkt. Onberispelijke kamers die identiek zijn ingericht. Eigen parkeergarage.

XXX ✿ **D'Hoogh** 1er étage, Grote Markt 19, ✆ 0 15 21 75 53, *dhoogh@pandora.be, Fax 0 15 21 67 30* – ▤. AE ⓓ ⓜ VISA. ✻ BY r
fermé 1 sem. Pâques, 3 prem. sem. août, sam. midi, dim. soir et lundi – **Repas** (nombre de couverts limité - prévenir) Lunch 48 bc – 45/80 bc, carte 52 à 73.
◆ Sur la Grand-Place de la cité de l'asperge et des carillons, élégante demeure 1900 interprétant un alléchant répertoire actuel. Mobilier malinois authentique.
◆ Elegant pand uit 1900 aan de Grote Markt van de stad die bekendstaat om zijn asperges en beiaards. Het Mechelse meubilair is authentiek. Aantrekkelijke eigentijdse keuken.
Spéc. Gibier en saison. Asperges régionales (avril-juin). Ragoût de ris et pieds de veau aux truffes

XX ✿ **Folliez,** Korenmarkt 19, ✆ 0 15 42 03 02, *info@folliez.be, Fax 0 15 42 03 08* – ▤ P. AE ⓜ VISA AZ f
fermé mi-juil.-mi-août, 25 déc.-9 janv., sam., et dim. – **Repas** Lunch 34 – 52/85 bc, carte 55 à 74, ♀ ✻.
◆ Fine cuisine au goût du jour, à savourer dans un décor intérieur d'esprit résolument contemporain. Lunch, menus et suggestions. Voiturier providentiel.
◆ Hier kunt u in een trendy interieur van fijne eigentijdse gerechten genieten. Lunchformule, menu's en suggesties. Valetparking, wat in deze buurt geen overbodige luxe is.
Spéc. Le thon de trois façons. Daurade royale en croûte de sel, ravioli de tomates. Cassolette de langoustines, morilles et asperges régionales à la crème de parmesan (avril-juin)

XX **Callas,** Brusselsesteenweg 544, ✆ 0 15 34 03 88, *info@callas.be, Fax 0 15 34 03 89*, ☂ – P. AE ⓓ ⓜ VISA C a
fermé 27 juil.-14 août, sam. midi et dim. – **Repas** Lunch 29 – 47/84 bc.
◆ Grande villa résidentielle réaménagée en restaurant. Salle à manger sobre et reposante, tables bien espacées, carte actuelle et, sur l'assiette, présentation soignée.
◆ Grote villa die tot restaurant is verbouwd. Sobere en rustgevende eetzaal met tafeltjes die gelukkig niet zo dicht op elkaar staan. Actuele kaart en fraai opgemaakte borden.

à Bonheiden *par ② : 6 km – 14 229 h – ✉ 2820 Bonheiden :*

XX **'t Wit Paard,** Rijmenamseweg 85, ✆ 0 15 51 32 20, ☂ – P. AE ⓓ ⓜ VISA. ✻
fermé 2 sem. en mars, du 1er au 20 sept., mardi et merc. – **Repas** Lunch 29 – carte 38 à 66.
◆ Auberge rajeunie située dans une bourgade malinoise, le Cheval Blanc ('t Wit Paard) attèle plusieurs menus à sa carte gentiment classique. Terrasse plaisante.
◆ Dit "Witte Paard" in de omgeving van Mechelen ziet er na een grondige renovatie weer uit als een veulentje ! Licht klassieke kaart en verscheidene menu's. Aangenaam terras.

X **Zellaer,** Putsesteenweg 229, ✆ 0 15 55 07 55, ☂ – P. AE ⓓ ⓜ VISA. ✻
fermé sem. carnaval, merc. et sam. midi – **Repas** Lunch 29 – carte 38 à 48.
◆ Un choix de préparations classico-traditionnelles assez engageantes vous sera soumis à cette enseigne qui vient de fêter ses dix ans. Salle à manger néo-rustique.
◆ In dit restaurant, dat net zijn tiende verjaardag achter de rug heeft, krijgt u een appetijtelijke kaart met klassiek-traditionele gerechten aangereikt. Neorustieke eetzaal.

à Rijmenam *par ② : 8 km* C *Bonheiden 14 229 h. – ✉ 2820 Rijmenam :*

Host. In den Bonten Os, Rijmenamseweg 214, ✆ 0 15 52 04 50, *info@bontenos.be, Fax 0 15 52 07 19*, ☂, ⛱, ✻ – TV P – ✻ 25 à 40. AE ⓓ ⓜ VISA
Repas *(fermé 31 déc.-6 janv. et dim. soir)* (dîner seult sauf dim.) 22 bc/75 bc – **24 ch** ☕ 110/140.
◆ Élégante hostellerie nichée dans la verdure. Communs chaleureux, chambres coquettes et espace breakfast baigné de lumière. Clientèle d'affaires et de séminaires. Table à la fois classique et régionale. Brunch au champagne le premier dimanche du mois.
◆ Elegant hotel met sfeervolle gemeenschappelijke ruimten, mooie kamers en een ontbijtzaal waar veel licht naar binnen valt. Clientèle van zakenmensen en congresgangers. De keuken is zowel klassiek als regionaal. Asperges in het seizoen.

à Rumst *par ⑥ : 8 km – 14 470 h – ✉ 2840 Rumst :*

XXX **La Salade Folle,** Antwerpsesteenweg 84, ✆ 0 15 31 53 41, *info@saladefolle.be, Fax 0 15 31 08 28*, ☂ – ▤ P – ✻ 25 à 70. AE ⓓ ⓜ VISA JCB. ✻
fermé 19 juil.-8 août, du 2 au 12 janv., sam. midi et dim. soir – **Repas** Lunch 32 – 57/82 bc, ♀.
◆ Cet agréable restaurant installé dans une villa en retrait de la route déploie un éventail de recettes traditionnelles actualisées. Cave globe-trotter bien balancée.
◆ Aangenaam restaurant in een villa die even van de weg af staat. De traditionele recepten zijn aan de huidige tijd aangepast. Wijnkelder met ambassadeurs uit diverse landen.

MEERHOUT *2450 Antwerpen* 533 P 16 *et* 716 I 2 – *9 239 h.*
Bruxelles 79 – Antwerpen 47 – Hasselt 39 – Turnhout 28.

XX **Rembrandt,** Meiberg 10, ☎ 0 14 30 81 03, *rest-rembrandt@planetinternet.be, Fax 0 14 30 81 03,* – P. AE ⓓ MC VISA
fermé 2 sem. en juil., 1 sem. en août, sam. midi, dim. soir, lundi, mardi soir et après 20 h – **Repas** *Lunch 27* – 33/62 bc.
◆ Cette longue bâtisse en lisière du village est une ancienne ferme-relais où Rembrandt aurait aimé poser son chevalet. Menus au goût du jour. Salle à manger bourgeoise.
◆ Deze langwerpige boerderij aan de rand van het dorp is een oud relais, waar Rembrandt graag zijn ezel zou hebben neergezet. Eetzaal in bourgeoisstijl en eigentijdse menu's.

MEEUWEN *3670 Limburg* C *Meeuwen-Gruitrode 12 543 h.* 533 S 16 *et* 716 J 2.
Bruxelles 105 – Hasselt 26 – Maastricht 42 – Roermond 42.

à Ellikom *Nord : 3 km* C *Meeuwen-Gruitrode –* ✉ *3670 Ellikom :*

Ellekenhuys, Weg naar Ellikom 286, ☎ 0 11 61 06 80, *info@ellekenhuys.be, Fax 0 11 63 61 80,* – TV – 25 à 80. MC VISA.
Repas *Lunch 34* – carte 44 à 59 – **12 ch** ☐ 55/85 – ½ P 48/58.
◆ Une pimpante façade de briques signale ce petit hôtel "perdu" dans un village limbourgeois. Confort convenable dans les chambres. Les plus paisibles ouvrent sur l'arrière. Salle des repas avec verrière en demi-rotonde. Recettes classiques sagement actualisées.
◆ Dit kleine hotel met een mooie bakstenen gevel staat wat verloren in een Limburgs dorp. Redelijk comfortabele kamers, waarvan die aan de achterkant het rustigste zijn. Eetzaal met halfronde glaskoepel. Klassieke recepten die voorzichtig worden gemoderniseerd.

MEISE *Vlaams-Brabant* 533 K 17 *et* 716 F 3 – *voir à Bruxelles, environs.*

MÉLIN *Brabant Wallon* 533 O 18 *et* 716 H 3 – *voir à Jodoigne.*

MELLE *Oost-Vlaanderen* 533 H 17 *et* 716 E 2 – *voir à Gent, environs.*

MELSBROEK *Vlaams-Brabant* 533 L 17 – *voir à Bruxelles, environs.*

MEMBRE *Namur* 534 O 23 *et* 716 H 6 – *voir à Vresse-sur-Semois.*

MENEN (MENIN) *8930 West-Vlaanderen* 533 D 18 *et* 716 C 3 – *32 156 h.*
Bruxelles 105 – Kortrijk 13 – Ieper 24 – Lille 23.

Ambassador sans rest, Wahisstraat 34, ☎ 0 56 31 32 72, *ambassador@ambassadorhotel.be, Fax 0 56 31 55 28,* – TV P. AE ⓓ MC VISA
30 ch ☐ 75/90.
◆ Hôtel dont on apprécie le calme, autant que l'ampleur des chambres, actuelles, égayées de tissus coordonnés aux tons chauds. Petite terrasse sur cour, salon de lecture et bar.
◆ Dit hotel wordt gewaardeerd om zijn rust en de ruime, moderne kamers, waarvan de stoffering bij de warme kleuren past. Klein terras op de binnenplaats, leeszaal en bar.

XX **Royale Axkit,** Bruggestraat 260, ☎ 0 56 53 06 07, *Fax 0 56 53 06 07,* – P. AE MC VISA
fermé mardi soir et merc. – **Repas** *Lunch 25 bc* – 37/45 bc.
◆ Salle de restaurant actuelle jouissant d'une échappée sur une prairie où s'ébattent des chevaux. Clientèle d'affaires et d'habitués. Les beaux jours, on mange à l'extérieur.
◆ Vanuit dit eigentijdse restaurant ziet u de paarden rondrennen in de wei. Naast zakenlieden komen er ook veel vaste gasten. Op zomerse dagen kan buiten worden gegeten.

à Rekkem *Est : 4 km* C *Menen –* ✉ *8930 Rekkem :*

XXX **La Cravache,** Gentstraat 215 (Sud-Est : 4 km sur N 43), ☎ 0 56 42 67 87, *info@lacravache.com, Fax 0 56 42 67 97,* – P – 30. AE ⓓ MC VISA
fermé 2 prem. sem. avril, 2 prem. sem. sept., sam. midi, dim. soir et lundi – **Repas** *Lunch 28* – 46/80 bc.
◆ Villa cossue aux abords verdoyants, La Cravache vous dorlotera dans un décor classique assorti à son style de cuisine, où la truffe règne en maître. Terrasse agréable.
◆ In deze weelderige villa wordt u gastronomisch verwend. De klassieke inrichting past perfect bij de stijl van de keuken, waar de truffel heer en meester is. Prettig terras.

MERELBEKE *Oost-Vlaanderen* 533 H 17 *et* 716 E 3 – *voir à Gent, environs.*

MERENDREE *9850 Oost-Vlaanderen* © *Nevele 10 894 h.* 533 G 16 *et* 716 D 2.
Bruxelles 71 – Brugge 42 – Gent 13.

XXX **De Waterhoeve,** Durmenstraat 6, ☎ 0 9 371 59 42, *info@dewaterhoeve.be, Fax 0 9 371 94 46,* ≤, 🏞 – ▤ P. AE ⓓ ⓜ VISA
fermé 19 juil.-15 août, merc., sam. midi et dim. soir – **Repas** *Lunch 25* – carte 37 à 54 🍇.
◆ Ce restaurant environné de prairies et de champs évoque quelque peu une ferme-château. Élégantes salles, salon en mezzanine et jardin pomponné s'égayant d'une pièce d'eau.
◆ Dit restaurant te midden van weiden en akkers doet aan een kasteelhoeve denken. Elegante eetzalen, salon en mezzanine. De mooie tuin wordt opgeluisterd door een waterpartij.

MERKSEM *Antwerpen* 533 L 15 *et* 716 G 2 – *voir à Antwerpen, périphérie.*

MEULEBEKE *8760 West-Vlaanderen* 533 E 17 *et* 716 C 3 – *10 991 h.*
Bruxelles 84 – Kortrijk 15 – Brugge 36 – Gent 39.

XX **'t Gisthuis,** Baronielaan 28, ☎ 0 51 48 76 02, *marleen.d.hulster@pandora.be, Fax 0 51 48 76 02,* 🏞 – P. AE ⓓ ⓜ VISA
fermé dim. soir et lundi – **Repas** *Lunch 30* – 45/80 bc.
◆ Beau moment de table en perspective dans cette grosse villa dont la terrasse estivale en hémicycle s'entoure de haies soignées. Salle à manger cossue. Cave intéressante.
◆ Deze grote villa met een weelderige eetzaal en halfrond zomerterras dat door een haag wordt omzoomd, heeft mooie culinaire momenten voor u in petto. Interessante wijnkelder.

MEUSE NAMUROISE (Vallée de la) ★★ *Namur* 533 O 21 - Q 19, 534 O 21 - Q 19 *et* 716 H 5 - K 3 *G. Belgique-Luxembourg.*

MIDDELKERKE *8430 West-Vlaanderen* 533 B 15 *et* 716 B 2 – *16 930 h – Station balnéaire – Casino Kursaal, Zeedijk* ☎ *0 59 31 95 95, Fax 0 59 30 52 84.*
ℹ *Dr J. Casselaan 4* ☎ *0 59 30 03 68, toerisme@middelkerke.be, Fax 0 59 31 11 95.*
Bruxelles 124 – Brugge 37 – Oostende 8 – Dunkerque 43.

🏨 **Were-Di,** P. de Smet de Naeyerstraat 19, ☎ 0 59 30 11 88, *info@hotelweredi.be, Fax 0 59 31 02 41,* ≘ – |‡| TV. ⓓ ⓜ VISA. ✗ ch
fermé du 2 au 19 mars et du 12 au 29 oct. – **Repas** *(fermé lundi d'oct. à Pâques et merc.)* 37/65 bc – **18 ch** ☐ 65/84 – ½ P 65.
◆ Dans l'artère commerçante de Middelkerke, à quelques enjambées de la digue, immeuble dont les menues chambres fonctionnelles, avec mini-bar, se distribuent sur trois étages. À l'heure du repas : carte classico-bourgeoise incluant menus et suggestions.
◆ Dit hotel staat in de winkelstraat van Middelkerke, vlak bij de dijk. Kleine, functionele kamers met minibar die over drie verdiepingen zijn verspreid. Het restaurant presenteert een eenvoudige klassieke kaart met verschillende menu's en suggesties.

🏨 **Excelsior** sans rest, A. Degreefplein 9a, ☎ 0 59 30 18 31, *Fax 0 59 31 27 02,* ≤, ≘, 🚲 – |‡| TV. AE ⓜ VISA
fermé en sem. hors saison – **Repas** – **32 ch** ☐ 50/75.
◆ Avantagé par sa proximité du front de mer - visible depuis la salle de breakfast -, ce building érigé à l'entrée de la station dispose de petites chambres sans fioriture.
◆ Bij binnenkomst in deze badplaats staat dit hotel, gunstig gelegen in de buurt van de kustlijn, die vanaf de eetzaal goed te zien is. Kleine kamers zonder veel opsmuk.

🏨 **Isaura,** Koninginnelaan 86, ☎ 0 59 30 38 13, *Fax 0 59 31 04 11* – TV P. AE ⓓ ⓜ VISA. ✗ ch
fermé 2 dern. sem. nov. et 2 dern. sem. janv. – **Repas** *(fermé lundi soir et mardi)* carte env. 26 – **10 ch** ☐ 52/67 – ½ P 52/70.
◆ Résidence hôtelière bâtie au bord d'une route à circulation dense. Chambres de mise simple, mais pratiques et munies du double vitrage. Accueil familial.
◆ Dit hotel ligt aan een drukke weg. De kamers zijn eenvoudig, maar praktisch en voorzien van dubbele beglazing. De ontvangst is vriendelijk.

XX **La Tulipe,** Leopoldlaan 81, ☎ 0 59 30 53 40, *la_tulipe_middelkerke@hotmail.com, Fax 0 59 30 61 39* – AE ⓓ ⓜ VISA
fermé sem. carnaval, 2 prem. sem. oct., lundi et mardi – **Repas** 20/70 bc.
◆ Aussi classique dans ses recettes que dans son décor, cet établissement voisin de la promenade balnéaire accompagne sa carte saisonnière de plusieurs menus. Service stylé.
◆ Dit etablissement staat bij de boulevard en is in zijn inrichting even klassiek als in zijn manier van koken. Seizoengebonden kaart met diverse menu's. Stijlvolle bediening.

XX **De Vlaschaard,** Leopoldlaan 246, ☎ 0 59 30 18 37, *Fax 0 59 31 40 40* – ▤. AE ⓓ ⓜ VISA
fermé merc. – **Repas** 25/58 bc.
◆ Pas loin de la plage, restaurant dont le nom et certains éléments du décor intérieur se réfèrent à un célèbre roman de l'écrivain flamand Stijn Streuvels. Portions copieuses.
◆ Eethuis dicht bij het strand. De naam en sommige elementen van het interieur herinneren aan een beroemde roman van de Vlaamse schrijver Stijn Streuvels. Flinke porties.

XX **Renty,** L. Logierlaan 51 (près du château d'eau Krokodil), ☎ 0 59 31 20 77, *Fax 0 59 30 07 54*, 余 – P. ⓜ VISA. ✻ – *fermé merc. soir et jeudi sauf vacances scolaires* – **Repas** (de fin nov. à avril déjeuner seult sauf week-end) Lunch 15 – 20/37 bc.
◆ Villa "mer du Nord" postée au bord de la route menant à Westende. Cuisine littorale que valorise une intéressante sélection de vins. Terrasse et véranda. Addition digeste.
◆ Villa aan de Noordzee, langs de weg naar Westende. Visgerechten waarvan de smaak uitstekend tot zijn recht komt bij de wijnen. Serre en terras. Licht verteerbare rekening.

à Sint-Pieters-Kapelle *Sud-Est : 9 km* Ⓒ *Middelkerke* – ✉ *8433 Sint-Pieters-Kapelle :*

X **Kapelle,** Diksmuidsestraat 68, ☎ 0 59 27 84 34, *Fax 0 59 27 84 34*, 余 – ⓜ VISA
fermé du 21 au 25 juin, 18 oct.-4 nov., mardi sauf en juil.-août et lundi – **Repas** Lunch 18 – 25/47 bc.
◆ Bâtisse aux murs blanchis, dans un petit village de l'arrière-pays de Middelkerke. Salle à manger néo-rustique. Lorsque la météo le permet, le couvert est dressé en terrasse.
◆ Neorustieke eetzaal in een pand met witgekalkte muren in een dorpje in het achterland van Middelkerke. Als het weer het toelaat, worden de tafeltjes op het terras gedekt.

MILLEN *Limburg* 533 *S 18 et* 716 *J 3 – voir à Riemst.*

MIRWART *6870 Luxembourg belge* Ⓒ *St-Hubert 5 646 h.* 534 *Q 22 et* 716 *I 5.*
Bruxelles 129 – Bouillon 55 – Arlon 71 – Marche-en-Famenne 26 – Namur 68 – St-Hubert 11.

Beau Site ⛰ sans rest, pl. Communale 5, ☎ 0 84 36 62 27, *Fax 0 84 36 71 18*, ≤ – TV P. ⓜ VISA – *fermé mardi* – **9 ch** ☕ 52/64.
◆ Assez spacieuses et aménagées en annexe dans l'esprit campagnard, toutes les chambres de cette paisible petite auberge rustique profitent d'une échappée forestière.
◆ Deze rustig gelegen herberg beschikt over vrij ruime kamers in de dependance, die in rustieke stijl zijn ingericht en allemaal uitkijken op de bosrijke omgeving.

XX **Aub. du Grandgousier** ⛰ avec ch, r. Staplisse 6, ☎ 0 84 36 62 93, *grandgousier @belgacom.net, Fax 0 84 36 65 77*, 余, 🛏, 🚲 – TV P. ⓜ
fermé 21 juin-7 juil., 23 août-9 sept., 2 janv.-3 fév., mardi et merc. sauf vacances scolaires et après 20 h 30 – **Repas** 29/55 – **9 ch** ☕ 55/70 – ½ P 60/67.
◆ Charmante auberge traditionnelle dont la façade est animée de colombages. Les menus saisonniers s'effeuillent dans une salle à manger à poutres apparentes. Chambres pratiques.
◆ Traditionele herberg met een mooie vakwerkgevel en praktische kamers. Onder de hanenbalken van de robuuste eetzaal worden seizoengebonden menu's geserveerd.

MODAVE *4577 Liège* 533 *Q 20,* 534 *Q 20 et* 716 *I 4 – 3 664 h.*
Voir *Château★ : ≤★ de la terrasse de la chambre du Duc de Montmorency.*
Env. *au Sud : 6 km à Bois-et-Borsu, fresques★ dans l'église romane.*
Bruxelles 97 – Liège 38 – Marche-en-Famenne 25 – Namur 46.

X **Le Pavillon du Vieux Château,** Vallée du Houyoux 9 (Sud-Ouest : 2 km, lieu-dit Pont de Vyle), ☎ 0 85 41 13 43, *Fax 0 85 41 13 43*, 余 – P. ⓓ ⓜ VISA
fermé 2 sem. en sept., lundi et mardi en juil.-août et jeudi soir – **Repas** Lunch 19 – carte 22 à 38.
◆ Ce café converti en restaurant traditionnel profite du voisinage rafraîchissant du Hoyoux. Sa carte bourgeoise comblera les amateurs de truites et d'écrevisses.
◆ Dit traditionele eethuis, dat vroeger een café was, ligt vlak bij de rivier de Hoyaux. De kaart zal vooral bij liefhebbers van forel en rivierkreeft in de smaak vallen.

MOERBEKE *9180 Oost-Vlaanderen* 533 *I 15 et* 716 *E 2 – 5 762 h.*
Bruxelles 54 – Gent 26 – Antwerpen 38.

XX **'t Molenhof,** Heirweg 25, ☎ 0 9 346 71 22, *molenhof@proximedia.be, Fax 0 9 346 71 22*, 余 – P. ⓜ VISA
fermé sept., Noël-Nouvel An, sam. midi, dim. soir, lundi et mardi – **Repas** Lunch 45 – carte 36 à 57, ♀.
◆ Cuisine d'esprit classique servie dans le cadre néo-rustique d'une fermette flamande entourée de champs. Accueil familial prévenant. Clientèle d'habitués.
◆ Vlaams boerderijtje met een neorustiek interieur, temidden van landerijen. De keuken is op klassieke leest geschoeid. Vriendelijke en attente bediening. Veel stamgasten.

MOERZEKE *Oost-Vlaanderen* 533 *J 16 et* 716 *F 2 – voir à Hamme.*

MOESKROEN *Hainaut – voir Mouscron.*

MOL *2400 Antwerpen* 533 *P 15 et* 716 *I 2 – 31 919 h.*

Kiezelweg 78 (Rauw) ☎ 0 14 81 62 34, Fax 0 14 81 62 78 – Steenovens 89 (Postel) ☎ 0 14 37 36 61, Fax 0 14 37 36 62.

Markt 1a ☎ 0 14 33 07 85, mol@toerismevlaanderen.be, Fax 0 14 33 07 87.

Bruxelles 78 – Antwerpen 54 – Hasselt 42 – Turnhout 23.

XXX **Hippocampus,** St-Jozeflaan 79 (Est : 7 km à Wezel), ☎ 0 14 81 08 08, *chef@hippocampus.be, Fax 0 14 81 45 90,* – AE VISA
fermé fin août, dim. soir et lundi – **Repas** *Lunch 30* – 55/82 bc.
• Demeure ancienne ouverte sur un parc soigné, se mirant à la surface d'une vaste pièce d'eau. Salle à manger aménagée avec harmonie et recettes assez élaborées.
• Oud landhuis met een goed onderhouden park, dat wordt weerspiegeld in een grote vijver. De eetzaal is harmonieus ingericht en de keuken is vrij verfijnd.

XXX ✿ **'t Zilte** (Geunes), Martelarenstraat 74, ☎ 0 14 32 24 33, *tzilte@pandora.be, Fax 0 14 32 13 27,* – P. AE VISA. – *fermé 2 sem. en août, lundi soir, mardi et sam. midi* – **Repas** *Lunch 30* – 56/85 bc, carte 58 à 94.
• Le nom de celle confortable villa au goût du jour officiant à la périphérie de Mol est sur toutes les (fines) bouches de la région. Terrasse d'été cossue dressée au jardin.
• De naam van deze moderne, comfortabele villa aan de rand van Mol ligt op de lippen van alle fijnproevers in de streek. Tuin met prachtig terras, waar 's zomers wordt gegeten.
Spéc. Thon et crabe aux artichauts. Homard bleu poêlé et son risotto. Petites gaufres minute tout vanille

XX **De Partituur,** Corbiestraat 62, ☎ 0 14 31 94 82, *contact@partituur.be, Fax 0 14 32 36 05,* – AE VISA.
fermé sam. midi, dim. et lundi midi – **Repas** *Lunch 30* – 35/75 bc, ♀.
• Au "piano" de cet établissement actuel et engageant, le chef interprète une partition culinaire sur un mode classico-traditionnel. Cave bien orchestrée. Ambiance "jazzy".
• In dit vriendelijke, eigentijdse restaurant vertolkt de chef-kok een klassiek-traditioneel repertoire, waarbij de wijn in harmonie is. De ambiance heeft een "jazzy" ondertoon.

MOLENBEEK-ST-JEAN (SINT-JANS-MOLENBEEK) *Région de Bruxelles-Capitale – voir à Bruxelles.*

MOMIGNIES *Hainaut* 534 *J 22 et* 716 *F 5 – voir à Chimay.*

MONS (BERGEN) *7000* P *Hainaut* 533 *I 20,* 534 *I 20 et* 716 *E 4 – 90 955 h.*

Voir *Collégiale Ste-Waudru★★* CY – *Beffroi★* CY **D.**

Musées : *de la Vie montoise★ (Maison Jean Lescarts)* DY **M**[1] – *Collection de pendules★★ dans le Musée François Duesberg★* CY **M**[5].

Env. *par ① : 15 km à Strépy-Thieu, Canal du Centre : les Ascenseurs hydrauliques★ – par ④ : 9,5 km à Hornu : Le Grand-Hornu★★.*

par ① : 6 km à Erbisoeul, Chemin de la Verrerie 2 ☎ 0 65 22 02 00, Fax 0 65 22 02 09 – par ⑥ : 6 km à Baudour, r. Mont Garni 3 ☎ 0 65 62 27 19, Fax 0 65 62 34 10. – Grand'Place 22 ☎ 0 65 33 55 80, ot1@mons.be, Fax 0 65 35 63 36 – Fédération provinciale de tourisme, r. Clercs 31 ☎ 0 65 36 04 64, *federation.tourisme@hainaut.be, Fax 0 65 33 57 32.*

Bruxelles 67 ① – Charleroi 36 ② – Namur 72 ① – Tournai 48 ⑤ – Maubeuge 20 ③

Plans pages suivantes

Lido sans rest, r. Arbalestriers 112, ☎ 0 65 32 78 00, *info@lido.be, Fax 0 65 84 37 22,* – AE VISA JCB DY b
73 ch ☐ 85/137.
• Immeuble résolument contemporain jouxtant la Porte de Nimy, le Lido renferme des chambres standard aménagées dans la note actuelle. Banquets et séminaires assez fréquents.
• Hotel in een modern flatgebouw bij de Porte de Nimy, met standaardkamers die in eigentijdse stijl zijn ingericht. Het Lido leent zich bij uitstek voor partijen en congressen.

ST JAMES sans rest, pl. de Flandre 8, ☎ 0 65 72 48 24, *Fax 0 65 72 48 11* – P. AE VISA. DY c
21 ch ☐ 77/93.
• Ancienne maison de notable dont l'intérieur a été entièrement redessiné dans un style contemporain non dénué de cachet. Chambres plus tranquilles à l'arrière et dans l'annexe.
• Dit oude herenhuis is vanbinnen volledig gemoderniseerd, zonder zijn cachet te hebben verloren. De kamers aan de achterkant en in de dependance zijn het rustigst.

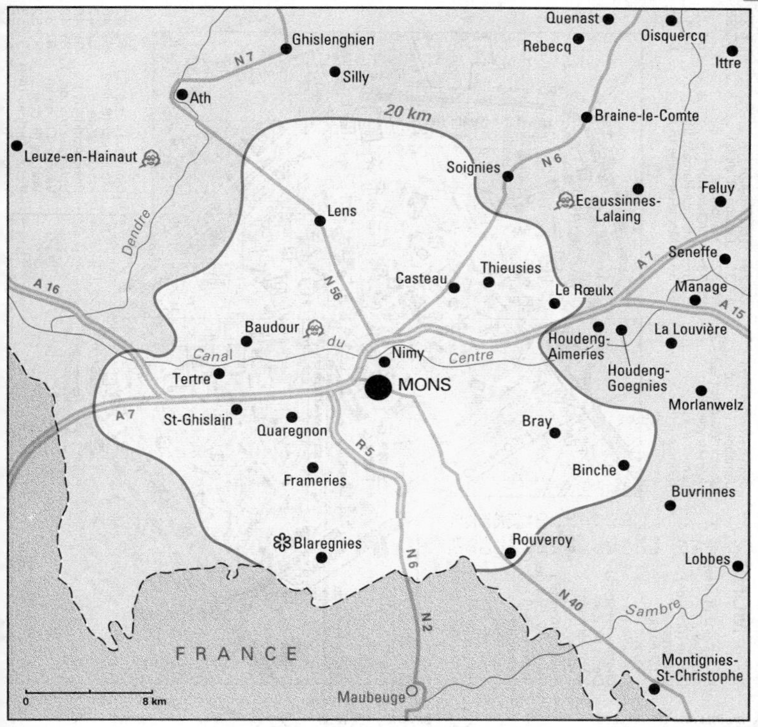

Infotel sans rest, r. Havré 32, ☎ 0 65 40 18 30, *info@infonie.be, Fax 0 65 35 62 24* – 🛗 TV P. AE ⓓ MC VISA DY s
20 ch ☕ 71/90.
◆ En plein centre, dans un secteur piétonnier voisin de la Grand-Place, hôtel récent et pratique dont les chambres insonorisées se répartissent sur trois étages.
◆ Modern en praktisch hotel, zeer centraal gelegen in een voetgangersgebied bij de Grote Markt. De kamers zijn goed tegen geluid geïsoleerd en over drie verdiepingen verdeeld.

XXX **Devos,** r. Coupe 7, ☎ 0 65 35 13 35, *Fax 0 65 35 37 71* – ▤. AE MC VISA. ✗ DY r
fermé du 5 au 18 août, merc. soir et dim. soir – **Repas** *Lunch 30* – 50/70, ♀.
◆ Ancien relais de poste ordonné autour d'une cour intérieure. Mets traditionnels servis dans une salle lambrissée agrémentée de meubles de style et d'une maquette du beffroi.
◆ Voormalig poststation rond een binnenplaats. Traditionele gerechten, opgediend in een gelambriseerde eetzaal met stijlmeubelen en een maquette van het belfort.

XXX **Le Vannes,** chaussée de Binche 177 (par ②), ☎ 0 65 35 14 43, *Fax 0 65 35 57 58,* ☂ – ▤ – 40. AE ⓓ MC VISA JCB
fermé du 1er au 20 juil., dim. soir et merc. – **Repas** *Lunch 23* – carte 39 à 50.
◆ Restaurant situé à l'Est de Mons, sur la route de Binche. Carte classique avec lunch et menus renouvelés quatre fois l'an. L'été, on hésite entre la terrasse et le jardin.
◆ Restaurant ten oosten van Bergen, aan de weg naar Binche. Klassieke kaart met een lunchformule en elk seizoen een ander menu. Fijn terras en mooie tuin voor zomerse dagen.

XX **Chez John,** av. de l'Hôpital 10, ☎ 0 65 33 51 21, *john@proximedia.be, Fax 0 65 33 76 87* – 25. AE MC VISA DY e
fermé fin août-début sept. et dim. et lundis non fériés – **Repas** *Lunch 63 bc* – 59/112 bc.
◆ Cette affaire familiale établie aux portes de la Cité du Doudou concocte une goûteuse cuisine du marché que rehausse un choix de vins exceptionnel.
◆ Dit familiebedrijf aan de rand van de Cité du Doudou bereidt smakelijke gerechten op basis van verse producten van de markt, waarbij een lekker wijntje wordt geschonken.

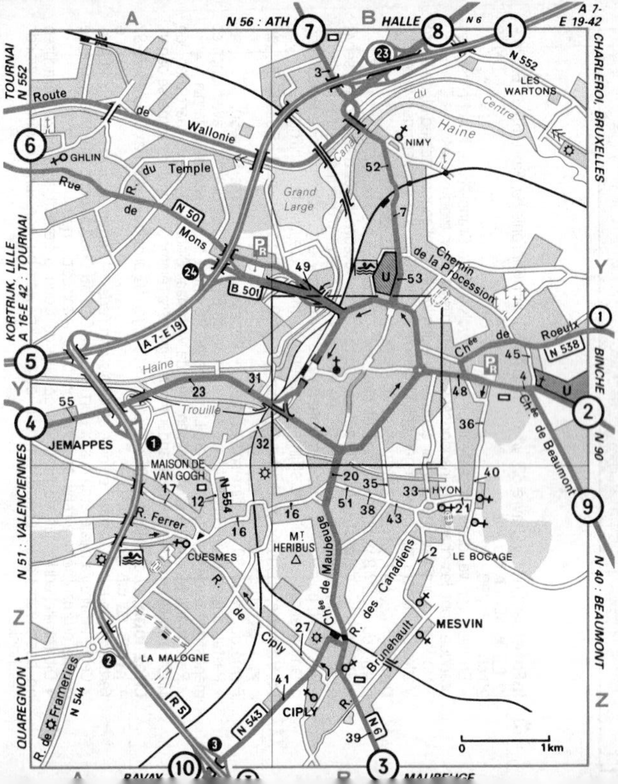

MONS

Street	Ref.
Américains (R. des)	BZ 2
Ath (Rte d')	BY 3
Binche (Chée de)	BY 4
Bruxelles (Chée de)	BY 7
Capucins (R. des)	CZ 8
Chaussée (R. de la)	CY 10
Chemin-de-Fer (R.)	AZ 12
Clercs (R. des)	CY 13
E.-Vandervelde (R.)	ABZ 16
Etang-Derbaix (R.)	AZ 17
Gaulle (Av. Gén.-de)	BZ 20
Genièvrerie (R.)	BZ 21
Grand-Route	AY 23
Grand-Rue	CZ 24
Havré (R. d')	DY 25
Héribus (R. de l')	BZ 27
Houssière (R. de la)	CY 28
Jean-d'Avesnes (Av.)	CZ 29
Jemappes (Av. de)	AY 31
Joseph-Wauters (Av.)	AY 32
Jules-Hoyois (R.)	BZ 33
Lemiez (Av.)	BZ 35
Léon-Savé (R.)	BY 36
Léopold-II (R.)	CY 37
Licorne (R. de la)	BZ 38
Maubeuge (Chée de)	BZ 39
Maurice-Flament (R.)	BZ 40
Monte-en-Peine (R.)	BZ 41
Montreuil-s-Bois (R.)	BZ 43
Mourdreux (R. des)	BY 45
Pte-Guirlande (R.)	CZ 47
Reine-Astrid (Av.)	BY 48
Université (Av. de l')	BY 49
Vallière (Ch. de la)	BZ 51
Viaducs (R. des)	BY 52
Victor-Maistriau (Av.)	BY 53
Wilson (Av.)	AY 55

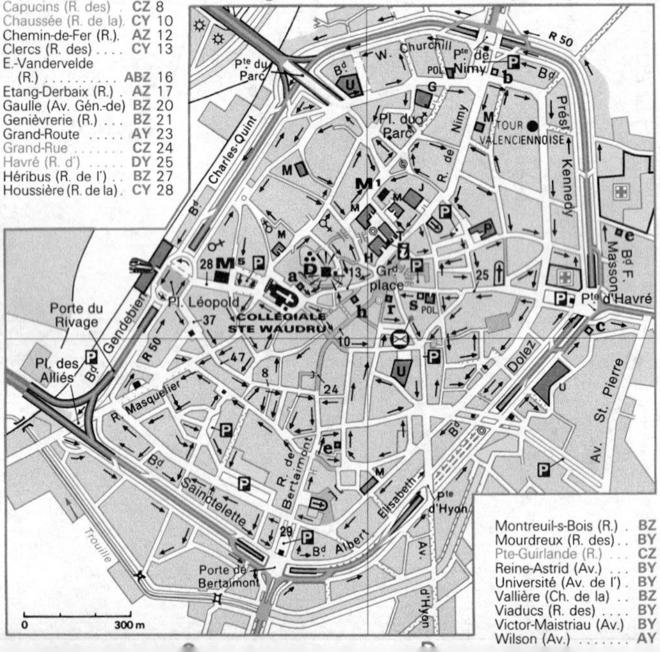

XX **Marchal,** Rampe Ste-Waudru 4, ✆ 0 65 31 24 02, *contact@marchal.be, Fax 0 65 36 24 69,* – 45. AE ⓓ MC VISA JCB CY a
fermé 26 juil.-16 août, prem. sem. janv., dim. soir, lundi et mardi – **Repas** *Lunch 20* – 26/64 bc, ♀.
◆ Agréable moment de table en perspective dans cette maison bourgeoise sise au pied de la collégiale. Recettes partagées entre classicisme, terroir et goût du jour.
◆ In dit herenhuis aan de voet van de collegiale kerk kunt u zich culinair laten verrassen. De gerechten zijn een spannende combinatie van klassiek, regionaal en modern.

X **La Table des Matières,** r. Grand Trou Oudart 16, ✆ 0 65 84 17 06, *Fax 0 65 84 91 45,* , Cuisine italienne – AE MC VISA. CZ e
fermé 21 juil.-20 août, 24 déc.-5 janv., merc., sam. midi et dim. soir – **Repas** *Lunch 24* – 40/57 bc.
◆ Demeure de maître du 18e s. que signale une enseigne sympathique, la Table des Matières décline un registre culinaire transalpin. Cave de circonstance. Ambiance cordiale.
◆ Sympathiek restaurant in een 18e-eeuws herenhuis. De "inhoudstafel" : Italiaanse keuken, bijpassende wijnen en een gezellige ambiance.

X **La Coquille St-Jacques,** r. Poterie 27, ✆ 065 84 36 53, *piejac@busmail.net, Fax 0 65 84 36 53* – MC VISA CY h
fermé 21 juil.-15 août, dim. soir, lundi et après 20 h 30 – **Repas** 21.
◆ Proche de toutes les curiosités du centre de Mons, ce restaurant familial au décor sagement rustique sert une cuisine traditionnelle du marché. Additions "sympa".
◆ Rustiek familierestaurant nabij de bezienswaardigheden van Bergen. Traditionele keuken, afhankelijk van het aanbod op de markt. De prijzen rijzen in elk geval niet de pan uit !

à Baudour *par ⑥ : 12 km* C *Saint-Ghislain 22 014 h.* – ✉ *7331 Baudour :*

XX **Chez Fernez,** pl. de la Résistance 1, ✆ 0 65 64 44 67, *chezfernez@fernez.com, Fax 0 65 52 18 28* – 40. AE ⓓ MC VISA.
fermé 21 juil.-15 août et lundi – **Repas** (déjeuner seult sauf vend. et sam.) *Lunch 35* – 40/76 bc, ♀.
◆ Au cœur de Baudour, table accueillante connue pour sa ribambelle de menus et sa sélection de vins très portée sur la vallée du Rhône. Salle à manger un rien surannée.
◆ Uitnodigend restaurant, hartje Baudour, dat bekendstaat om zijn talrijke menu's en goede selectie wijnen, voornamelijk uit het Rhônedal. De eetzaal is een tikkeltje ouderwets.

X **Le Faitout,** av. Louis Goblet 161, ✆ 0 65 64 48 57, *faitout@fernez.com, Fax 0 65 60 07 74,* , Grillades – 30. AE ⓓ MC VISA
fermé mardi soir – **Repas** 26.
◆ Les carnivores friands de plantureuses grillades au feu de bois - exécutées en salle - trouveront leur bonheur à cette enseigne. Recettes traditionnelles de bon aloi.
◆ Vleesliefhebbers kunnen hun tanden zetten in de grote sappige stukken vlees die in de eetzaal op houtskool worden geroosterd. Eerlijke, traditionele keuken.

à Frameries *par ⑩ : 6 km – 20 667 h* – ✉ *7080 Frameries :*

XXX **l'assiette au beurre,** r. Industrie 278, ✆ 0 65 67 76 73, *jeanlouis.simonet@skynet.be, Fax 0 65 66 43 87* – P – 30. AE ⓓ MC VISA
fermé 2e quinz. août, dim. soir, lundi et merc. soir – **Repas** *Lunch 25* – 40/77 bc, ♀.
◆ Imposante maison de style régional située aux avant-postes de Frameries-centre. Cuisine traditionnelle personnalisée à petits pas. Salle à manger intime et coquette.
◆ Imposant huis in regionale stijl even buiten het centrum van Frameries. Mooie en intieme eetzaal. Traditionele keuken met een persoonlijke noot.

à Nimy *par ⑦ : 6 km* C *Mons* – ✉ *7020 Nimy :*

La Forêt sans rest, r. Fusillés 12, ✆ 0 65 72 36 85, *Fax 0 65 72 41 44,* – TV P – 25 à 80. AE ⓓ MC VISA
52 ch ☕ 95/115 – ½ P 90/109.
◆ Émergeant d'un site paisible imprégné de chlorophylle, cet immeuble de briques récent renferme des chambres de bon confort, garnies d'un mobilier de style.
◆ Dit hotel is gehuisvest in een nieuw bakstenen gebouw in een rustige, bosrijke omgeving. De comfortabele kamers zijn met stijlmeubelen ingericht.

MONTAIGU *Vlaams-Brabant* – *voir Scherpenheuvel.*

Si le coût de la vie subit des variations importantes,
les prix que nous indiquons peuvent être majorés.
Lors de votre réservation à l'hôtel, faites-vous préciser le prix définitif.

MONTIGNIES-ST-CHRISTOPHE *6560 Hainaut* Ⓒ *Erquelinnes 9 622 h.* 533 K 21, 534 K 21 et 716 F 5.
Bruxelles 70 – Mons 25 – Charleroi 30 – Maubeuge 20.

XX **La Villa Romaine,** chaussée de Mons 52, ✆ 0 71 55 56 22, *Fax 0 71 55 62 03* – ▤ P. AE ⓓ ⓜⓒ VISA
fermé du 23 au 27 fév., 25 août-16 sept., du 2 au 6 janv., merc., jeudi et jours fériés midis – **Repas** Lunch 25 – 48, ♀.
◆ À quelques pas seulement du pont "romain" enjambant la Hantes, institution de bouche dont le décor intérieur et le contenu des assiettes affichent un classicisme mesuré.
◆ Dit restaurant staat vlak bij de "Romeinse" brug over de Hantes en is een begrip in Montignies. Zowel het interieur als de keuken geven blijk van een gematigd classicisme.

MONTIGNIES-SUR-SAMBRE *Hainaut* 533 L 20, 534 L 20 *et* 716 G 4 – *voir à Charleroi.*

MONTIGNY-LE-TILLEUL *Hainaut* 533 L 20, 534 L 20 *et* 716 G 4 – *voir à Charleroi.*

MONT-SUR-MARCHIENNE *Hainaut* 533 L 20, 534 L 20 *et* 716 G 4 – *voir à Charleroi.*

MORLANWELZ *7140 Hainaut* 533 K 20, 534 K 20 *et* 716 F 4 – *18 505 h.*
Bruxelles 56 – Mons 31 – Charleroi 24 – Maubeuge 35.

XX **Le Mairesse** avec ch, chaussée de Mariemont 77, ✆ 0 64 44 23 77, *lemairesse@msn.com, Fax 0 64 44 27 70* – P. ⓓ ⓜⓒ VISA
fermé 3 sem. en juil., dim. soir, lundi et mardi soir – **Repas** Lunch 20 – 25/62 bc – **6 ch** ☕ 50 – ½ P 57.
◆ Cette grosse villa des années 1900 - où l'on peut désormais séjourner - vous reçoit dans une salle à manger spacieuse, au décor rafraîchi. Formule menu-carte.
◆ Deze grote villa uit de vroege 20e eeuw ontvangt zijn gasten in een ruime eetzaal, die onlangs opnieuw is gedecoreerd. Keuzemenu. Mogelijkheid om te overnachten.

MOUSCRON (MOESKROEN) *7700 Hainaut* 533 E 18, 534 E 18 *et* 716 C 3 – *52 293 h.*
🅘 *pl. Gérard Kasiers 15* ✆ *0 56 86 03 70, mouscron.tourisme@mouscron.be, Fax 0 56 86 03 71.*
Bruxelles 101 ③ *– Kortrijk 13* ④ *– Mons 71* ⑤ *– Tournai 23* ⑤ *– Lille 23* ③

Plan page ci-contre

XX **Au Petit Château,** bd des Alliés 243 (par ⑤ : 2 km sur N 58), ✉ 7700 Luingne, ✆ 0 56 33 22 07, *Fax 0 56 84 02 11* – ▤ P. AE ⓓ ⓜⓒ VISA
fermé 27 juil.-12 août, dim. soir, lundi soir, mardi soir et merc. – **Repas** Lunch 27 – 35/70 bc, ♀.
◆ Nuançons l'enseigne : la construction tient davantage de la villa corpulente que du "Petit Château". Choix classique de saison, avec des menus bien montés. Accueil familial.
◆ Dit restaurant lijkt qua bouw meer op een grote villa dan op een klein kasteel, maar ach... Klassieke seizoengebonden kaart met evenwichtige menu's. Vriendelijke ontvangst.

XX **Le Petit Boclé,** r. Boclé 56 (par ⑤ : 1 km sur N 58), ✉ 7700 Luingne, ✆ 0 56 33 21 00, *Fax 0 56 33 21 00,* 余 – P. ⓜⓒ VISA
fermé 15 août-début sept., merc., sam. midi et dim. soir – **Repas** Lunch 18 – 25/65 bc.
◆ Une table qui rencontre un certain succès dans la région. Salon agencé sous une très jolie véranda donnant sur un jardin soigné. Plats variés et intéressante formule menu.
◆ Het succesrecept van dit restaurant ? Een prachtige serre, een verzorgde tuin, een gevarieerde kaart, een interessant menu en wijnen om met volle teugen van te genieten !

XX **l'Escapade,** Grand'Place 34, ✆ 0 56 84 13 13, *info@moresto.be, Fax 0 56 84 36 46,* 余 – ▤. AE ⓓ ⓜⓒ VISA B a
fermé 2e quinz. juil. – **Repas** (déjeuner seult sauf vend. et sam.) 32/46 bc.
◆ Escapade gourmande sur la Grand'Place. Ample salle à manger agencée dans un style contemporain et cuisine un peu moins poissonneuse qu'auparavant, mais de qualité inchangée.
◆ Zin in een culinaire escapade ? Dat kan in dit eigentijdse restaurant op de Grote Markt. Wat minder vis dan vroeger, maar nog altijd even lekker.

XX **Madame,** r. Roi Chevalier 17, ✆ 0 56 34 43 53, *Fax 0 56 34 43 53,* 余 – ⓓ ⓜⓒ VISA A c
fermé 21 juil.-14 août, lundis midis et mardis midis non fériés, dim. soir, lundi soir et mardi soir – **Repas** Lunch 20 bc – 26/58 bc, ♀.
◆ Affable et sympathique, Madame vous installe dans un plaisant cadre actuel. Recettes bourgeoises de bonne facture. En face, le parc de Mons offre une promenade digestive.
◆ Madame ontvangt u gastvrij in een prettig eigentijds interieur. De gerechten zijn eenvoudig, maar goed klaargemaakt. Na het eten kunt een wandelingetje in het park maken.

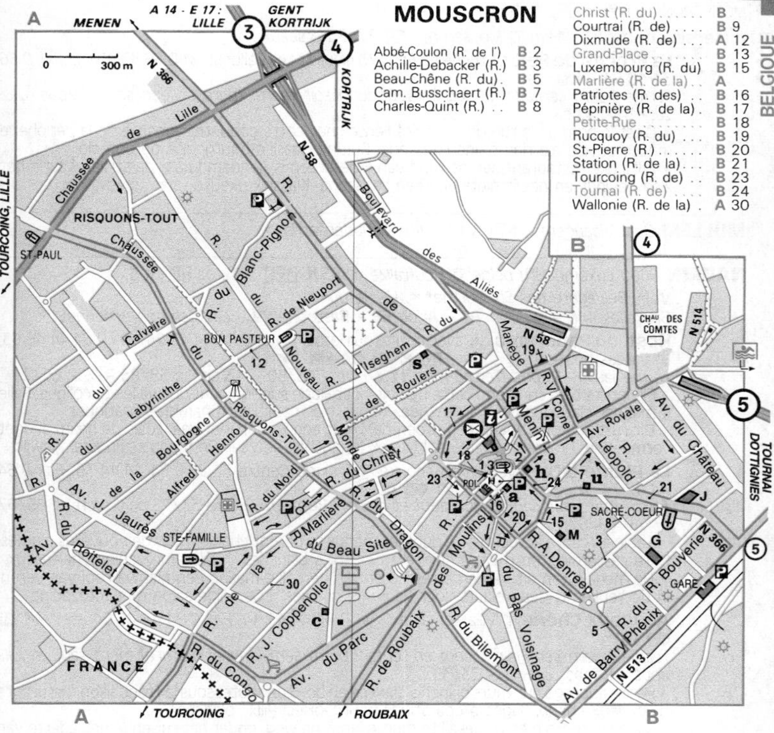

X **Au Jardin de Pékin,** r. Station 9, ✆ 0 56 33 72 88, *Fax 0 56 33 77 88*, Cuisine chinoise, ouvert jusqu'à 23 h – ▤. AE DC MC VISA. B u
fermé lundis non fériés – **Repas** Lunch 8 – carte 22 à 33.
◆ Tout l'éventail des saveurs de l'Empire du Milieu, avec une faveur spéciale pour les régions de Canton et Pékin, se déploie à cette enseigne. Décor intérieur "made in China".
◆ Heel de waaier van smaken uit het Rijk van het Midden ontvouwt zich hier, met een speciale voorkeur voor Kanton en Peking. Het interieur is "made in China".

X **l'Aquarelle,** r. Menin 185, ✆ 0 56 34 55 36, *Fax 0 56 34 55 36* – ▤. MC VISA B s
fermé 2 sem. en mars, 3 sem. en sept., mardi soir et merc. – **Repas** 29/48 bc.
◆ Ce petit restaurant vous reçoit dans une salle à manger croquignolette. La carte, traditionnelle et relativement étoffée, comprend plusieurs menus assez courtisés.
◆ De eetzaal van dit kleine restaurant ziet er bijzonder appetijtelijk uit. De vrij uitgebreide kaart omvat traditionele gerechten en een aantal menu's die zeer in trek zijn.

X **La Cloche,** r. Tournai 9, ✆ 0 56 85 50 30, *info@moresto.be, Fax 0 56 85 50 33*, Brasserie, ouvert jusqu'à 23 h – ▤. AE DC MC VISA B h
fermé 24 déc. soir – **Repas** Lunch 11 – 18/28.
◆ Grande brasserie de quartier à l'ambiance bon enfant, La Cloche résonne de convivialité. Lambris et poutres habillent la salle de restaurant. Menus "canaille" à prix sages.
◆ In deze grote buurtbrasserie is het een al gezelligheid wat de klok slaat. Eetzaal met lambrisering en balkenzoldering. Menu's met een ondeugend tikje voor een brave prijs.

X **le bistro des anges,** r. Tombrouck 6 (par ⑤ : 2 km sur N 58), ✉ 7700 Luingne, ✆ 0 56 33 00 55, *Fax 0 56 33 00 55*, Ouvert jusqu'à 23 h – ▤ P. AE DC MC VISA
fermé août, merc. soir et jeudi – **Repas** Lunch 30 bc – carte 25 à 39.
◆ Cette sympathique auberge familiale décline des préparations bistrotières diversifiées, pour toutes les bourses. Ambiance décontractée.
◆ In deze sympathieke bistro kunt u genieten van een eenvoudige, doch voedzame maaltijd die voor iedereen betaalbaar is. Gevarieerde kaart en ongedwongen ambiance.

BELGIQUE

à Herseaux *par ⑤ : 4 km* 🄲 *Mouscron* – ✉ *7712 Herseaux :*

✗ **La Broche de Fer,** r. Broche de Fer 273 (lieu-dit Les Ballons), ✆ 0 56 33 15 16, *Fax 0 56 34 10 54* – VISA

fermé 1 sem. carnaval, 20 juil.-14 août, lundi soir, mardi, merc. et jeudi soir – **Repas** *Lunch 20* – 37/54 bc.

◆ C'est le nom de la rue qui a inspiré l'enseigne : cette coquette auberge de la périphérie mouscronoise n'a rien d'une rôtisserie. Cuisine classico-bourgeoise de bon aloi.

◆ Dit leuke restaurant aan de rand van Moeskroen is genoemd naar de straat waarin het zich bevindt en heeft niets van een rotisserie. Klassieke keuken van goed allooi.

MULLEM *Oost-Vlaanderen* 533 G 17 – *voir à Oudenaarde.*

NADRIN *6660 Luxembourg belge* 🄲 *Houffalize 4 565 h.* 534 T 22 *et* 716 K 5.

Voir *Belvédère des Six Ourthe★★, Le Hérou★★.*

Bruxelles 140 – Bouillon 82 – Arlon 68 – Bastogne 29 – La Roche-en-Ardenne 13.

✗✗ **Host. du Panorama** avec ch, rte du Hérou 41, ✆ 0 84 44 43 24, *Fax 0 84 44 46 63,* ≤ vallées boisées, – TV P. AE MC VISA. ch

fermé janv. – **Repas** *(fermé merc.) Lunch 30* – 40/50 – **13 ch** 58/85 – ½ P 65/74.

◆ Elle porte bien son nom, cette paisible hostellerie surplombant une vallée bucolique. Salle à manger classiquement aménagée. Menus très courtisés. Chambres pratiques.

◆ Dit rustige hotel boven een groen dal biedt een fraai panorama, zoals de naam al doet vermoeden. Praktische kamers. Klassiek ingerichte eetzaal. De menu's zijn zeer gewild.

✗✗ **La Plume d'Oie** avec ch en annexe, pl. du Centre 3, ✆ 0 84 44 44 36, *Fax 0 84 44 47 74,* ≤, , – TV. AE MC VISA

fermé mardi soir sauf en juil.-août et merc. – **Repas** *Lunch 25* – 33/75 bc – **4 ch** 65/67 – ½ P 69/87.

◆ Table au cadre actuel cossu, dont les menus se parent chaque mois de nouvelles plumes. Côté casseroles, on n'a pas affaire à des "oies blanches" ! Salon-mezzanine chaleureux.

◆ De menu's van dit moderne restaurant krijgen elke maand een nieuwe tooi van veren. In de keuken is geen plaats voor "domme gansjes" ! Gezellige salon met mezzanine.

✗ **Au Vieux Chêne,** r. Villa Romaine 4, ✆ 0 84 44 41 14, *Fax 0 84 44 46 04,* – P. AE MC VISA

fermé 2 dern. sem. juin, 2 sem. en sept., 2 prem. sem. janv. et mardi et merc. sauf en juil.-août – **Repas** *Lunch 18* – 23/33.

◆ Petite auberge aux murs blanchis plantée en bord de route, sous la frondaison rassurante d'un vieux chêne. Sages préparations bourgeoises. Prix "plancher".

◆ Kleine herberg met witgekalkte muren langs de weg, onder het ruisende gebladerte van een oude eik. Eenvoudige burgerkeuken voor een zacht prijsje.

NALINNES *Hainaut* 533 L 21, 534 L 21 *et* 716 G 5 – *voir à Charleroi.*

NAMUR – NAMEN

5000 🅿 533 O 20, 534 O 20 *et* 716 H 4 – *105 393 h.*

Bruxelles 64 ① *– Charleroi 38* ⑥ *– Liège 61* ① *– Luxembourg 158* ③.

RENSEIGNEMENTS PRATIQUES

Casino BZ, *av. Baron de Moreau 1* ☏ *0 81 22 30 21, Fax 0 81 22 90 22.*

ℹ *Square de l'Europe Unie* ☏ *0 81 24 64 49, tourisme@ville.namur.be, Fax 0 81 26 23 60 et (en saison) Chalet, pl. du Grognon* ☏ *0 81 24 64 48, Fax 0 81 24 71 28 – Fédération provinciale de tourisme, av. Reine Astrid 22,* ☏ *0 81 74 99 00, tourisme@ftpn.be, Fax 0 81 74 99 29.*

⛳9 *à l'Est : 22 km à Andenne, Ferme du Moulin, Stud 52* ☏ *0 85 84 34 04, Fax 0 85 84 34 04.*

CURIOSITÉS

Voir *Citadelle★* ☀★★ BZ – *Trésor★★ du prieuré d'Oignies aux sœurs de Notre-Dame* BCZ **K** – *Église St-Loup★* BZ – *Le Centre★*.

Musées : *Archéologique★* BZ **M²** – *des Arts Anciens du Namurois★* BY **M³** – *Diocésain et trésor de la cathédrale★* BYZ **M⁴** – *de Groesbeek de Croix★* BZ **M⁵**.

Env. *par* ⑤ *: 11 km à Floreffe : stalles★ de l'église abbatiale .*

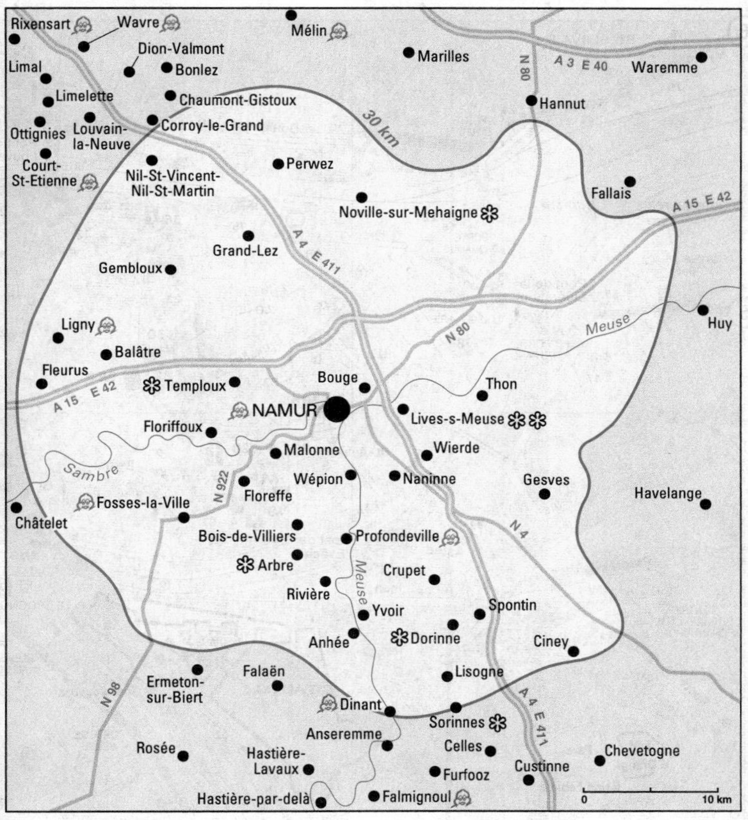

Quartiers du Centre :

Les Tanneurs, r. Tanneries 13, ✆ 0 81 24 00 24, *info@tanneurs.com, Fax 0 81 24 00 25,* – ch, – 25 à 80. AE VISA. ch CZ x
Repas voir rest ***L'Espièglerie*** ci-après – ***Le Grill des Tanneurs*** *Lunch 8* – 25/37 bc – 8 – **29 ch** 38/210 – ½ P 70/300.

◆ Chambres de bon confort distribuées dans une vieille tannerie promue hostellerie au terme d'une rénovation complète. Le "Visiteur" Jean Reno y a dormi comme une bûche. À l'étage, restaurant-grill au cadre rustique. Intéressant menu-choix. Terrasse perchée.

◆ Deze oude leerlooierij is na een ingrijpende verbouwing een aantrekkelijk hotel geworden. De comfortabele kamers staan garant voor een goede nachtrust. Rustiek restaurant annex grillroom met een interessant keuzemenu op de bovenverdieping. Hooggelegen terras.

Ibis sans rest, r. Premier Lanciers 10, ✆ 0 81 25 75 40, *h3151@accor-hotels.com, Fax 0 81 25 75 50* – AE VISA CY a
9 – **92 ch** 59.

◆ Les fidèles habitués de l'enseigne trouveront ici des chambres un rien moins austères qu'à l'accoutumée. Bar d'esprit nautique où l'on prend aussi le café et les croissants.

◆ Trouwe gasten van de Ibisketen zullen de kamers hier iets minder sober vinden dan normaal. Bar in nautische stijl, waar ook koffie en croissants kunnen worden genuttigd.

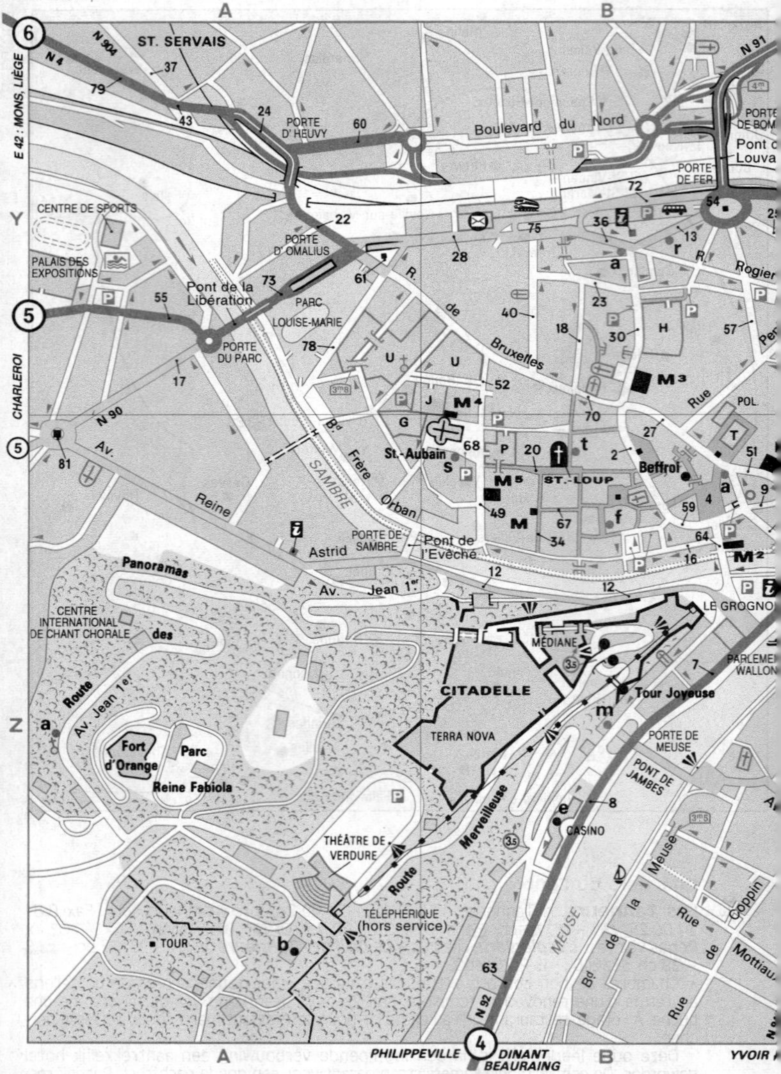

XX **L'Espièglerie** - H. Les Tanneurs, r. Tanneries 13, ✆ 0 81 24 00 24, *info@tanneurs.com*, *Fax 0 81 24 00 25* – P. AE ⓓ ⓜ VISA. ✂ CZ x
fermé sam. midi et dim. soir – **Repas** *Lunch 26* – carte 53 à 70 ♀.
◆ Beau restaurant agrégé à l'hôtel Les Tanneurs. Salles à manger en enfilade séparées par des arcades de pierre. Mets goûtés des fines fourchettes. Excellent choix de bordeaux.
◆ Mooi restaurant in hotel Les Tanneurs. De eetzalen worden door stenen bogen van elkaar afgescheiden. Gastronomische keuken en uitstekende selectie bordeauxwijnen.

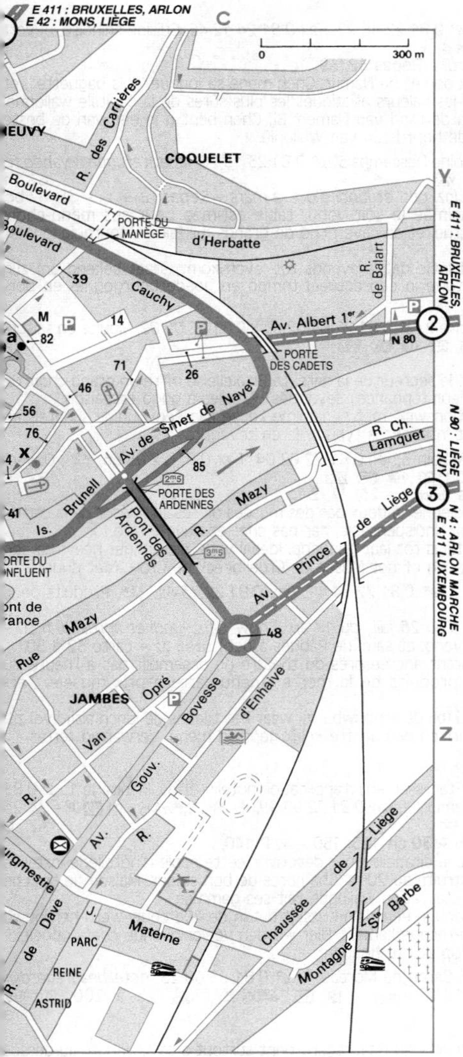

NAMUR

Ange (R.de l')	BZ 2
Armes (Pl. d')	BZ 4
Baron-L.-Huart (Bd.)	BZ 7
Baron-de-Moreau (Av.)	BZ 8
Bas-de-la-Place (R.)	BZ 9
Bord-de-l'Eau (R. du)	ABZ 12
Borgnet (R.)	BY 13
Bourgeois (R. des)	CY 14
Brasseurs (R des)	BZ 16
Cardinal-Mercier (Av.)	AY 17
Carmes (R. des)	BY 18
Célestines (Pl. des)	CY 19
Collège (R. du)	BZ 20
Combattants (Av. des)	AY 22
Croisiers (R. des)	BY 23
Croix-du-Feu (Av. des)	AY 24
Dewez (R.)	BCY 25
École des Cadets (Pl. de l')	CY 26
Emile-Cuvelier (R.)	BYZ 27
Ernest-Mélot (Bd.)	BY 28
Fernand-Golenvaux (Av.)	BZ 31
Fer (R. de)	BY 30
Fumal (R.)	BZ 34
Gare (Av. de la)	BY 36
Gembloux (R. de)	AY 37
Général-Michel (R.)	CY 39
Godefroid (R.)	BY 40
Gravière (R. de)	CZ 41
Hastedon (Pl. d')	AY 43
Ilon (Pl. l')	CZ 44
J.-B.-Brabant (R.)	CY 46
Joséphine-Charlotte (Pl.)	CZ 48
Joseph-Saintraint (R.)	BZ 49
Julie-Billiard (R)	BZ 51
Lelièvre (R.)	BY 52
Léopold (Pl.)	BY 54
Léopold-II (Av.)	AY 55
Lombard (R. du)	CYZ 56
Lucien-Namèche (R.)	BY 57
Marchovelette (R. de)	BZ 59
Merckem (Bd de)	AY 60
Omalius (Pl. d')	AY 61
Plante (Av. de la)	BZ 63
Pont (R. du)	BZ 64
Rupplémont (R.)	BZ 67
St-Aubain (Pl.)	BZ 68
St-Jacques (R)	BY 70
St-Nicolas (R.)	CY 71
Square-Léopold (Av. du)	BY 72
Stassart (Av. de)	AY 73
Station (Pl. de la)	BY 75
Tanneries (R. des)	CYZ 76
Vierge (Rempart de la)	AY 78
Waterloo (chaussée de)	AY 79
Wiertz (Pl.)	AZ 81
1er-Lanciers (R. du)	BY 82
4-Fils-Aymon (R. des)	CZ 85

Blaise 1er étage, r. Saint-Loup 4, ✆ 0 81 26 25 25, *restaurant.blaise@busmail.net*, *Fax 0 81 26 25 26*, – AE ① ⓒ VISA. BZ t

fermé dim. soir et lundi – **Repas** *Lunch 25* – 31/87 bc.

◆ Maison de notable où l'on se repaît en toute confiance dans un cadre design très léché. Bar, lounge-tea-room, salon privé et terrasse sur cour intérieure. À l'aise... Blaise !

◆ Herenhuis met een strak designinterieur. Bar, lounge, theesalon en terras op de binnenplaats. Hier zult u zich beslist op uw gemak voelen !

BELGIQUE

XX **Chez Chen,** r. Borgnet 8, ☎ 0 81 22 48 22, *Fax 0 81 24 12 46*, Cuisine chinoise, ouvert jusqu'à 23 h – ▤. MC VISA. ⋈ BY r
fermé 3 sem. en juil. et mardi – **Repas** 18/39.
◆ Un petit coin de Chine aux portes de Namur. Chen mène sa jonque "à la baguette", et son enseigne compte parmi les valeurs asiatiques les plus sûres de la capitale wallonne.
◆ Een klein stukje China aan de rand van Namen. Bij Chen bent u in een van de beste Aziatische restaurants van de hoofdstad van Wallonië.

XX **La Petite Fugue,** pl. Chanoine Descamps 5, ☎ 0 81 23 13 20, *lapetitefugue@yahoo.fr, Fax 0 81 23 13 20*, ☂. MC VISA BZ f
fermé 2 sem. Pâques, 1re quinz. oct. et lundi d'oct. à mars – **Repas** *Lunch 21* – 35/57 bc.
◆ Sur une placette très animée le soir venu, table estimée pour ses menu-choix composés dans le tempo actuel et sa cave riche de grands millésimes bourguignons et bordelais.
◆ Dit restaurant aan een pleintje dat 's avonds tot leven komt, staat bekend om zijn keuzemenu's. Culinair repertoire in een actueel tempo en goede bourgogne- en bordeauxwijnen.

X **La Bruxelloise,** av. de la Gare 2, ☎ 0 81 22 09 02, *Fax 0 81 22 09 02*, Moules en saison, ouvert jusqu'à 23 h 30 – ▤. AE ① MC VISA BY a
Repas carte 25 à 34.
◆ Adresse assez courue dans le secteur de la gare, La Bruxelloise offre un grand choix de plats bourgeois. Décor intérieur tendance "seventies". Moules à gogo en saison.
◆ Populair adresje in de stationswijk, met een ruime keuze aan eenvoudige schotels en mosselen in het seizoen. Het interieur is typisch jaren zeventig.

X **Brasserie Henry,** pl. St-Aubain 3, ☎ 0 81 22 02 04, *Fax 0 81 22 05 66*, ☂, Ouvert jusqu'à minuit – 🏛 25 à 200. AE ① MC VISA BZ s
fermé 2e quinz. juil. – **Repas** *Lunch 8* – 23/27, ♀.
◆ La tradition "brasserie parisienne" à deux pas des musées diocésain (trésor de la cathédrale) et Groesbeeck de Croix. Indispensable, car pas cher et ouvert tard.
◆ Deze brasserie in Parijse stijl is tot laat geopend. Ideaal voor wie honger heeft na een bezoek aan het Musée Diocésain of het Musée de Groesbeeck de Croix. Niet duur !

X **Les Embruns,** r. La Tour 2, ☎ 0 81 22 74 41, *Fax 0 81 22 73 41*, ☂, Produits de la mer – MC VISA. ⋈ BZ a
fermé du 1er au 7 mars, du 5 au 26 juil., du 1er au 7 nov., dim., lundi et après 20 h 30 – **Repas** (déjeuner seult sauf vend. et sam. de Pâques à oct.) *Lunch 22* – carte 32 à 50.
◆ Cette poissonnerie-restaurant ancrée près du théâtre ne désemplit pas à l'heure du déjeuner. Grand choix de produits de la mer et menu-carte à prix muselé. Terrasse chauffée.
◆ Restaurant annex viswinkel (bij de schouwburg), waar het tijdens de lunch altijd vol zit. Natuurlijk veel vis op de kaart en een aantrekkelijk geprijsd menu. Verwarmd terras.

direction Citadelle :

Château de Namur ⛭ (Établissement d'application hôtelière), av. Ermitage 1, ☎ 0 81 72 99 00, *info@chateaudenamur.be, Fax 0 81 72 99 99*, ≤, ☂, ⚔, 🚲 – |‡| TV P – 🏛 25 à 150. AE ① MC VISA JCB. ⋈ AZ b
Repas *Lunch 29* – 45 – ☕ 13 – **30 ch** 125/150 – ½ P 140.
◆ Hissez-vous au sommet de la citadelle pour découvrir cette école d'hôtellerie installée dans une petite folie reconstruite au 20e s. Chambres de bon séjour. Maison de bouche où le futur "gratin" de la restauration wallonne fait ses gammes.
◆ Deze hotelschool is gevestigd in een klein lustslot dat in de 20e eeuw werd herbouwd op de top van de Citadelle. Prettige kamers. Hier worden veelbelovende chefs opgeleid, om de Waalse gastronomie op peil te houden.

Beauregard sans rest, av. Baron de Moreau 1, ☎ 0 81 23 00 28, *hotel.beauregard@skynet.be, Fax 0 81 24 12 09*, 🚲 – |‡| TV 🚗 P – 🏛 25 à 200. AE ① MC VISA BZ e
47 ch ☕ 60/110.
◆ Avis aux flambeurs : l'originalité du Beauregard tient surtout à sa situation, au-dessus du Casino. Équipement correct dans les chambres, dont la moitié contemple la Meuse.
◆ Door de ligging, boven het casino, is dit hotel een goed adres voor wie graag een gokje waagt. Correcte voorzieningen in de kamers, waarvan de helft op de Maas uitkijkt.

XXX **Biétrumé Picar,** Tienne Maquet 16 (par ④ : 3 km sur N 92, La Plante), ☎ 0 81 23 07 39, *bietrume.picar@proximedia.be, Fax 0 81 23 10 32*, ☂ – P – 🏛 40. AE ① MC VISA
fermé dim. soir et lundi – **Repas** *Lunch 28* – 45/60 bc.
◆ L'enseigne évoque une figure locale du 18e s. : un gamin sympathique et frondeur, sorte de "Fanfan la Tulipe". Recettes au goût du jour servies dans un cadre cosy.
◆ De naam slaat op een lokale figuur uit de 18e eeuw, een soort Pietje Bell. Binnen is echter weinig weerspannigheid te ontwaren : eigentijdse keuken in een sfeervol interieur.

XX **L'Olivier,** av. Jean Ier 5 (rte des panoramas), ✆ 0 81 74 41 41, *Fax 0 81 73 98 44*, – P. AE ① MC VISA AZ a
fermé du 6 au 19 avril, 21 déc.-3 janv., dim. et lundi – **Repas** Lunch 25 – 44/85 bc, ♀.
◆ L'Olivier s'est enraciné au bord de la route serpentant du centre-ville à la citadelle, près du fort d'Orange et du parc d'attractions Reine Fabiola. Cuisine d'aujourd'hui.
◆ Deze olijfboom is stevig geworteld langs de weg die naar de Citadelle omhoog kronkelt, vlak bij het Fort d'Orange en het Parc Fabiola (recreatiepark). Eigentijdse keuken.

X **Au Trois Petits Cochons,** av. de la Plante 4, ✆ 0 81 22 70 10, *Fax 0 81 22 70 10*, – AE ① MC VISA BZ m
fermé 3 dern. sem. mars, 3 dern. sem. août, sam. midi, dim. et lundi – **Repas** Lunch 19 – 33.
◆ Au pied de la citadelle, coquette adresse appréciée pour son ambiance et son registre culinaire bien dans le coup. Un "bouchon lyonnais à la namuroise", pourrait-on dire !
◆ Leuk adresje aan de voet van de Citadelle, dat zeer in de smaak valt vanwege zijn gezellige ambiance en eigentijdse culinaire register.

à Bouge *par ② : 3 km* C *Namur* – ✉ *5004 Bouge :*

La Ferme du Quartier , pl. Ste Marguerite 4, ✆ 0 81 21 11 05, *Fax 0 81 21 59 18*, , – P – 25 à 160. AE ① MC VISA.
fermé juil., du 22 au 31 déc., dim. soir et jours fériés soirs – **Repas** Lunch 25 – carte 27 à 41 – **14 ch** 25/40.
◆ Une ferme imposante et paisible, dont l'origine remonte au 16e s., procure un cadre plaisant à cet établissement familial renfermant de menues chambres de mise simple. Restaurant agrémenté d'une terrasse. Choix de préparations classico-bourgeoises varié.
◆ Dit aangename en rustige familiehotel is gevestigd in een imposante boerderij, waarvan de oorsprong tot de 16e eeuw teruggaat. De kamers zijn klein en eenvoudig. Restaurant met terras. Gevarieerde kaart met eenvoudige gerechten in klassieke stijl.

à Lives-sur-Meuse *par ③ : 9 km* C *Namur* – ✉ *5101 Lives-sur-Meuse :*

New Hotel de Lives, chaussée de Liège 1178, ✆ 0 81 58 05 13, *info@newhotelde lives.com, Fax 0 81 58 15 77*, , , – TV P – 25 à 50. AE ① MC VISA JCB. rest
Repas (résidents seult) – **20 ch** 59/115 – ½ P 74/145.
◆ Entre Namur et Andenne, le long de la chaussée de Liège, grande auberge en pierres du pays vous réservant un accueil familial. Chambres convenables où l'on a ses aises.
◆ In deze grote herberg van steen uit de streek, tussen Namen en Andenne, langs de weg naar Luik, wacht u een vriendelijke ontvangst. Keurige kamers waar u volop ruimte heeft.

XXXX ✿✿ **La Bergerie** (Lefevere) (hôtel prévu), r. Mosanville 100, ✆ 0 81 58 06 13, *marc@ber gerielives.be, Fax 0 81 58 19 39* – P. AE ① MC VISA
fermé 2e quinz. fév.-début mars, 2e quinz. août-début sept., dim. soir, lundi et mardi – **Repas** Lunch 40 – 55/108 bc, carte 67 à 80, ♀.
◆ Un cadre de verdure luxuriant ajoute au charme de cette élégante maison de bouche namuroise bordée de pièces d'eau. Cuisine délicieusement classique et cave au diapason.
◆ De weelderig groene omgeving draagt zeker bij tot de charme van dit elegante Naamse restaurant met zijn mooie waterpartij. Zowel de kok als de sommelier kennen hun klassieken !
Spéc. Truites de notre vivier. Agneau rôti "Bergerie". Gâteau de crêpes soufflées

à Malonne *par ⑤ : 8 km* C *Namur* – ✉ *5020 Malonne :*

XX **Alain Peters,** Trieux des Scieurs 22, ✆ 0 81 44 03 32, *Fax 0 81 44 60 20*, – P. MC VISA
fermé 2 sem. carnaval, dern. sem. juil., 2 prem. sem. sept., lundi soir, mardi et merc. – **Repas** Lunch 26 – 43/69 bc.
◆ Accueil chaleureux et service avenant dans cette villa moderne dont la terrasse estivale s'agrémente d'une pièce d'eau. Appétissant menu-carte avec l'option "vins compris".
◆ Warm onthaal en voorkomende bediening in deze moderne villa, waarvan het zomerterras met een waterpartij wordt opgeluisterd. Aantrekkelijk wijnarrangement.

à Temploux *par ⑥ : 7 km* C *Namur* – ✉ *5020 Temploux :*

XXX ✿ **l'essentiel** (Gersdorff), r. Roger Clément 32 (2,5 km par Chemin du Moustier), ✆ 0 81 56 86 16, *info@lessentiel.net, Fax 0 81 56 86 36*, – P – 25 à 40. AE ① MC VISA
fermé dern. sem. juil.-prem. sem. août, dern. sem. déc.-prem. sem. janv., dim. et lundi – **Repas** Lunch 30 – 52/100 bc, ♀.
◆ Enseigne "essentielle" pour se mettre au vert en s'émoustillant les papilles. Recettes au goût du jour, remarquable choix de vins, terrasse agrémentée d'une pièce d'eau.
◆ Wat een feest om een dagje op het platteland te besluiten met een etentje in dit restaurant ! Eigentijdse keuken, uitgelezen wijnen en een prettig terras met waterpartij.
Spéc. Cannelloni de foie gras confit aux pommes et witlof. Filet de thon mi-cuit en habit d'herbes. Filet d'agneau farci aux anchois et à l'hysope

BELGIQUE

à Thon *par ③ : 11 km* ▢ *Andenne 23 854 h. – ✉ 5300 Thon :*

XX **Les Jardins du Luxembourg,** rte de Liège 2 (N 90), ✆ 0 81 58 86 51, *jardins.luxembourg@skynet.be, Fax 0 81 58 07 62,* ≤, ☂ – P – 🔑 40. ⓓ ⓜ VISA
fermé sem. carnaval, 22 juil.-6 août, lundi soir, mardi soir et merc. – **Repas** Lunch 21 – 27/74 bc, ♀.
◆ Une carte assez engageante et soucieuse de valoriser les produits de saison vous sera soumise dans cette demeure imposante que prolonge un jardin en bord de Meuse.
◆ Léon is gehuisvest in een mooi pand met een uitgestrekte tuin aan de oever van de Maas. Aanlokkelijke spijskaart met veel aandacht voor de producten van het seizoen.

à Wépion *par ④ : 4,5 km* ▢ *Namur – ✉ 5100 Wépion :*

Villa Gracia ⛺ sans rest, chaussée de Dinant 1455, ✆ 0 81 41 43 43, *hotel@villagracia.com, Fax 0 81 41 12 25,* ≤, ⛱, 🚲, ⚓ – |‡| TV P – 🔑 30. AE ⓓ ⓜ VISA JCB
☕ 9 – **8 ch** 95/173.
◆ Paisible demeure mosane de 1923, la Villa Gracia renferme une poignée de chambres amples et douillettes. Certaines s'agrémentent d'une terrasse-balcon avec vue fluviale.
◆ Rustig hotel in een pand dat in 1923 in de stijl van het Maasland is gebouwd. Ruime en behaaglijke kamers, waarvan sommige een terras hebben met uitzicht op de rivier.

Novotel, chaussée de Dinant 1149, ✆ 0 81 46 08 11, *H0594@accor-hotels.com, Fax 0 81 46 19 90,* ≤, 🏊, 🏊, ⛱, 🚲, ⚓ – ✈ ▤ TV P – 🔑 25 à 300. AE ⓓ ⓜ VISA. ✂ rest
Repas Lunch 27 bc – carte 24 à 37, ♀ – ☕ 14 – **110 ch** 89/99 – ½ P 96/134.
◆ Au bord du fleuve, construction récente dont les chambres, conformes aux standards de la chaîne hôtelière, se répartissent sur deux étages. Jolie piscine couverte.
◆ Nieuw gebouw aan de oever van de rivier, met kamers op twee verdiepingen die aan de standaard van deze hotelketen voldoen. Mooi overdekt zwembad.

XX **La Petite Marmite,** chaussée de Dinant 683, ✆ 0 81 46 09 06, *pmarmite@pi.be, Fax 0 81 46 02 06,* ≤ Meuse (Maas), ⚓ – P. AE ⓓ ⓜ VISA
fermé vacances Pâques, 3 prem. sem. oct., mardi soir et merc. soir de mi-nov. à mars, jeudi soir sauf en juil.-août, dim. soir et lundi – **Repas** Lunch 35 bc – 53 bc/64 bc.
◆ Une clientèle fidélisée fréquente cette maison mosane à colombages surveillant l'ex-chemin de halage. La salle à manger en demi-rotonde offre une vue agréable sur la Meuse.
◆ Vakwerkhuis dat op het vroegere trekpad uitkijkt en in de bouwstijl van het Maasland is opgetrokken. De halfronde eetzaal biedt een fraai uitzicht op de Maas. Vaste clientèle.

à Wierde *par ③ : 9 km* ▢ *Namur – ✉ 5100 Wierde :*

XX **Le Petit Marais** ⛺ avec ch, r. Lambaitienne 7, ✆ 0 81 40 25 65, *lepetitmarais@tiscali.be, Fax 0 81 40 20 72,* ≤, ☂, ⛱, 🚲 – TV P. AE ⓜ VISA
fermé 2 sem. en sept., mardi et merc. – **Repas** Lunch 24 – 45/82 bc, ♀ – ☕ 10 – **4 ch** 90 – ½ P 124/158.
◆ L'adresse, à l'écart du village, profite du cadre agreste de la vallée du Tronquoy. L'imagination est aux fourneaux et toutes les régions de France, en cave. Accueil aimable.
◆ Dit restaurant staat even buiten het dorp in het prachtige dal van de Tronquoy. Fantasievolle keuken en een wijnkelder waarin alle Franse streken zijn vertegenwoordigd.

NANINNE *5100 Namur* ▢ *Namur 105 393 h.* 533 O 20, 534 O 20 *et* 716 H 4.
Bruxelles 70 – Namur 13 – Marche-en-Famenne 38.

XX **Clos St-Lambert,** r. Haie Lorrain 2, ✆ 0 81 40 06 30, *Fax 0 81 40 14 61,* ☂, Avec grillades – ⓜ VISA
fermé 1re quinz. fév., 2e quinz. août, mardi et merc. – **Repas** 28/53 bc.
◆ Près de l'église, dans les anciennes dépendances du château, affaire familiale appréciée pour sa cuisine classico-traditionnelle orientée "grillades". On rôtit sous vos yeux !
◆ Familierestaurant bij de kerk, in de voormalige bijgebouwen van het kasteel. Klassiek-traditionele menukaart met veel vlees dat voor uw neus aan het spit wordt geroosterd.

NASSOGNE *6950 Luxembourg belge* 534 R 22 *et* 716 J 5 – *4 816 h.*
Bruxelles 121 – Bouillon 56 – Dinant 45 – Liège 71 – Namur 62.

Beau Séjour ⛺, r. Masbourg 30, ✆ 0 84 21 06 96, *hotel.beausejour.nassogne@wanadoo.be, Fax 0 84 21 40 62,* ☂, 🏊, 🏊, ⛱ – TV ♿ P – 🔑 25. ⓜ VISA. ✂ rest
fermé 1 sem. en avril, 1 sem. en juin, 2 dern. sem. sept., 1 sem. en déc. et 1 sem. en janv.
– **Repas** *(fermé merc. et jeudi midi hors saison)* Lunch 20 – carte 43 à 57 – **23 ch** ☕ 65/95 – ½ P 60/95.
◆ Devenue hôtel, l'ancienne école du village se prête en effet à un "beau séjour" : accueil gentil, chambres tranquilles, salon coquet, piscine couverte et jardin reposant. Lumineuse salle des repas contemporaine garnie de meubles d'allure plus traditionnelle.
◆ Deze voormalige dorpsschool is verbouwd tot hotel, waar u een prettig verblijf zult hebben. Aardig personeel, rustige kamers, mooie lounge, overdekt zwembad en verkwikkende tuin. In de eigentijdse eetzaal met traditioneel meubilair valt veel licht naar binnen.

XX **la gourmandine** avec ch, r. Masbourg 2, ✆ 0 84 21 09 28, *lagourmandine@proximedia.be, Fax 0 84 21 09 23*, – TV P. AE MC VISA.
fermé lundi soir en juil.-août, merc. sauf en juil.-août et mardi – **Repas** 25/42 – **6 ch** 72/80 – ½ P 80.
◆ Maison de pays transformée en lieu de bouche d'esprit actuel. Salon cossu et fringante salle à manger. Recettes bien dans l'air du temps, parsemées de connotations régionales.
◆ Dit karakteristieke pand is omgebouwd tot een modern restaurant. Sfeervolle eetzaal met aparte zithoek. De recepten zijn geheel van deze tijd en tonen regionale invloeden.

Ecrivez-nous...
Vos louanges comme vos critiques seront examinées avec le plus grand soin.
Nous reverrons sur place les informations que vous nous signalez.
Par avance merci !

NAZARETH *9810 Oost-Vlaanderen 533 G 17 et 716 D 3 – 10 918 h.*

Bruxelles 65 – Gent 18 – Kortrijk 34 – Oudenaarde 16.

Nazareth, Autostrade E 17 -A 14, ✆ 0 9 385 60 83, *info@hotelnazareth.be, Fax 0 9 385 70 43*, – TV P – 25 à 250. AE MC VISA
Repas (ouvert jusqu'à minuit) *Lunch 17* – carte 23 à 45 – **80 ch** 80/90 – ½ P 65/75.
◆ Au bord de l'autoroute, entre Gent et Kortrijk, établissement bien pratique pour l'étape, doté de grandes chambres actuelles et confortables.
◆ Dit hotel aan de snelweg tussen Gent en Kortrijk is ideaal voor wie op doorreis is. De kamers zijn groot en comfortabel, zodat u de volgende dag weer fit in de auto stapt.

NEDERZWALM *9636 Oost-Vlaanderen C Zwalm 7 686 h. 533 H 17 et 716 E 3.*

Bruxelles 51 – Gent 26 – Oudenaarde 9.

XX **'t Kapelleke,** Neerstraat 39, ✆ 0 55 49 85 29, *Fax 0 55 49 66 97*, – P. AE MC VISA
fermé dern. sem. juil., 2 sem. en août, 2 sem. en janv., dim. soir, lundi et jeudi soir – **Repas** *Lunch 32 bc* – 55 bc/63 bc.
◆ L'enseigne est déroutante : le restaurant occupe une fermette, et non une "petite chapelle" (kapelleke). Préparations à la page et vins prestigieux. Charmante terrasse d'été.
◆ De naam van dit restaurant is wat misleidend, want het kapelletje blijkt een boerderijtje te zijn. Moderne keuken en prestigieuze wijnen. Charmant terras in de zomer.

NEERHAREN *Limburg 533 T 17 et 716 K 3 – voir à Lanaken.*

NEERPELT *3910 Limburg 533 R 15 et 716 J 2 – 15 681 h.*

Bruxelles 108 – Eindhoven 24 – Hasselt 40 – Antwerpen 86.

X **De Landerije,** Broeseinderdijk 32 (Nord : 1 km direction Grote Heide), ✆ 0 11 66 45 16, *delanderije@skynet.be*, – P. AE MC VISA.
fermé 2 sem. en août, lundi et mardi – **Repas** (déjeuner sur réservation) 34/50, ♀.
◆ Une petite villa à la campagne sert de cadre à cet adorable refuge gourmand. Accueil personnalisé, salle à manger actuelle aux tables bien espacées et vue agreste en terrasse.
◆ Dit buitenhuis vormt een stijlvolle omlijsting voor een avondje culinair genieten. Moderne eetzaal met veel ruimte tussen de tafels en terras met uitzicht op het platteland.

X **Au Bain Marie,** Heerstraat 34, ✆ 0 11 66 31 17, *bertsmeets@pandora.be, Fax 0 11 80 25 61* – AE MC VISA.
fermé vacances Pâques, 2 dern. sem. août, mardi soir et merc. – **Repas** *Lunch 25* – 43/50.
◆ Rassurez-vous : le "bain-marie" n'est pas le seul mode de cuisson adopté par ce sympathique restaurant du centre associé à une boutique de traiteur. Carte selon le marché.
◆ In dit sympathieke restaurant dat bij een delicatessenwinkel hoort, wordt meer dan alleen "au bain-marie" gekookt. De kok maakt gebruik van verse producten van de markt.

NEUFCHÂTEAU *6840 Luxembourg belge 534 R 23 et 716 J 6 – 6 322 h.*

Bruxelles 153 – Bouillon 41 – Arlon 36 – Dinant 71.

X **Au Coin Du Feu,** r. Lucien Burnotte 13, ✆ 0 61 27 81 32, *Fax 0 61 27 91 71*, – AE MC VISA
fermé fin juin, fin sept., début janv., merc. et sam. midi – **Repas** *Lunch 25* – 31/55 bc.
◆ Restaurant officiant sur la place centrale de Neufchâteau. Salle à manger façon "Art déco" où l'on vient faire des repas classiques-traditionnels.
◆ Restaurant aan het centrale plein van Neufchâteau. De eetzaal is in art-decostijl ingericht. Klassiek-traditionele keuken.

à Grandvoir *Nord-Ouest : 7 km* *Neufchâteau – ✉ 6840 Grandvoir :*

Cap au Vert Chemin du Moulin de la Roche 24, ☎ 0 61 27 97 67, *geers@capauvert.be, Fax 0 61 27 97 57,* ← – 🅿 – 25. AE VISA.
fermé 2 janv.12 fév., 30 août-17 sept., du 2 au 17 janv. et dim. soirs et lundis non fériés sauf en juil.-août – **Repas *Les Claytones du Cap*** (dîner seult jusqu'à 20 h 30) – 46/104 bc – **12 ch** 107/146 – ½ P 112/117.
• Embusqué au creux d'un vallon, entre étang et sapinière, cet hôtel promet un séjour revigorant. Grandes chambres et salle de breakfast sous verrière "tropicale". À table, répertoire culinaire classique-actuel sagement personnalisé. Restaurant d'été.
• Dit hotel in een dal, tussen een meertje en een dennenbos, garandeert een verkwikkend verblijf. Grote kamers en ontbijtzaal met glaskoepel en tropische sfeer. Modern-klassieke keuken met een persoonlijke toets. 's Zomers kan er buiten worden gegeten.

NEUVILLE-EN-CONDROZ *Liège* 533 R 19, 534 R 19 *et* 716 J 4 – *voir à Liège, environs.*

NIEUWERKERKEN *Limburg* 533 Q 17 *et* 716 I 3 – *voir à Sint-Truiden.*

NIEUWKERKEN-WAAS *Oost-Vlaanderen* 533 K 15 *et* 716 F 2 – *voir à Sint-Niklaas.*

NIEUWPOORT *8620 West-Vlaanderen* 533 B 16 *et* 716 B 2 – *10 468 h – Station balnéaire.*
Stadhuis, Marktplein 7 ☎ 0 58 22 44 44, nieuwpoort@toerismevlaanderen.be, Fax 0 58 22 44 28.
Bruxelles 131 – Brugge 44 – Oostende 19 – Veurne 13 – Dunkerque 31.

Clarenhof , Hoogstraat 4, ☎ 0 58 22 48 00, *ph.blanchart@skynet.be, Fax 0 58 22 48 01,* – 🅿 – 25 à 70. AE VISA.
Repas *(fermé lundi, mardi et merc.)* (buffets, dîner seult jusqu'à 23 h) 29 bc – 10 – **26 ch** 60/80.
• Ancien couvent malicieusement converti en une charmante hostellerie, le Clarenhof renferme désormais des chambres bien calibrées et fort coquettes. Jardin claustral. Ambiance "nef de pirates" au restaurant. Buffets à écumer !
• Oud klooster dat knap is verbouwd tot een sfeervol hotel met een kloostertuin. De kamers zijn goed van formaat en zien er tiptop uit. Het restaurant is ingericht als piratenschip, waar de buffetten leeggeplunderd mogen worden !

Martinique, Brugse Steenweg 7 (à l'écluse), ☎ 0 58 24 04 08, *info@hotelmartinique.be, Fax 0 58 24 04 07,* – 🅿. VISA. ch
21 mars-21 déc. et week-end ; fermé 2 sem. en janv. – **Repas** *(fermé mardi en été)* 25/58 bc, – **6 ch** 55/80 – ½ P 55/60.
• Enseigne "doudou" pour cette villa érigée aux portes de Nieuwpoort. Chambres avenantes, d'ampleur correcte. L'été venu, le ti' punch se sirote sur la terrasse ombragée. Table mitonnant des recettes aux saveurs créoles et une cuisine française au goût du jour.
• Antilliaanse sferen in deze villa aan de rand van Nieuwpoort. Aantrekkelijke en ruime kamers. Bij de eerste zonnestralen wordt de ti' punch op het lommerrijke terras geserveerd. De kaart bestaat uit een mix van eigentijdse Creoolse en Franse gerechten.

De Vierboete, Halve Maanstraat 2a (Nord-Est : 2 km, au port de plaisance), ☎ 0 58 23 34 33, *devierboete@skynet.be, Fax 0 58 23 81 61,* ←, – 🅿 – 25 à 80. VISA.
fermé du 1er au 15 fév. et merc. hors saison – **Repas** carte 23 à 49.
• Au bord du bassin des yachts, agréable restaurant dont le panorama portuaire, en phase avec le décor intérieur récemment rajeuni, ajoute au plaisir de l'assiette et du verre.
• Aangenaam restaurant bij de jachthaven. Het pas opgeknapte interieur is een afspiegeling van wat u ziet als u naar buiten kijkt. Uitstekende keuken en wijnen.

't Vlaemsch Galjoen 1er étage, Watersportlaan 11 (Nord-Est : 1 km, au port de plaisance), ☎ 0 58 23 54 95, *galjoen@pi.be,* ← port de plaisance, – AE VISA
fermé 15 janv.-15 fév. – **Repas** (d'oct. à Pâques déjeuner seult sauf vend. et sam.) 18/40 bc.
• Sage carte bourgeoise à découvrir dans ce Galion Flamand (Vlaemsch Galjoen) d'aujourd'hui embrassant du regard tout le port de plaisance. Additions sans sel.
• Galjoen in een moderne versie, van waaruit in één blik de hele jachthaven te zien is. Hier kunt u smullen van eenvoudige gerechten zonder gepeperde rekening.

Café de Paris, Kaai 16, ☎ 0 58 24 04 80, *Fax 0 58 24 03 90,* Taverne-rest avec produits de la mer, ouvert jusqu'à 23 h – . AE VISA
Repas carte 31 à 60.
• La flottille de pêche locale accoste juste en face de cet établissement aménagé dans l'esprit "brasserie parisienne". Spécialité de poissons et fruits de mer, donc.
• De plaatselijke vissersvloot ligt precies tegenover dit etablissement, dat aan een Parijse brasserie doet denken. Visspecialiteiten en zeevruchten, hoe kan het ook anders !

à Nieuwpoort-Bad : *(Nieuport-les-Bains) N : 1 km* C *Nieuwpoort* – ✉ *8620 Nieuwpoort* :

Cosmopolite, Albert I-laan 141, ✆ 0 58 23 33 66, *info@cosmopolite.be, Fax 0 58 23 81 35* – |♦|, ▤ rest, TV – 25 à 150. AE ⓓ MC VISA
Repas *Lunch 15* – 27/38 – **52 ch** ☕ 52/107 – ½ P 60/75.
◆ À un jet d'ancre de la jetée, établissement où descend volontiers la clientèle touristique "cosmopolite", comme semble le proclamer son enseigne. Chambres confortables. La carte du restaurant est axée sur les trésors de la marée et ceux du plancher des vaches.
◆ Dit hotel met comfortabele kamers vlak bij de pier trekt een kosmopolitisch publiek van toeristen als men het uithangbord moet geloven. De spijskaart van het restaurant is gericht op de schatten van de zee, maar ook van de vaste wal.

Duinhotel Carlton, Albert I-laan 101, ✆ 0 58 23 31 54, *info@cosmopolite.be, Fax 0 58 24 27 55,* ☂, ≘s, ▣, ☂ – |♦|, ▤ rest, TV P – 25 à 150. AE ⓓ MC VISA
avril-sept., vacances scolaires et week-end – **Repas** (ouvert jusqu'à 23 h) 22/29 – **38 ch** ☕ 52/107 – ½ P 60/75.
◆ Demeure située à 700 m de la plage, au bord d'une longue avenue passante que dessert la ligne côtière du tramway. Chambres fonctionnelles. Terrasse dressée côté jardin. Salle des repas actuelle. Formules buffets associées à un choix de grillades. Prix sages.
◆ Hotel op 700 m van het strand, gelegen aan de kustlaan waar de tram langs rijdt. Functionele kamers. Terras aan de tuinzijde. Eigentijdse eetzaal met buffetten en vlees van de grill. De prijzen blijven bescheiden.

XX **Gérard,** Albert I-laan 253, ✆ 0 58 23 90 33, *lucgerard@hotmail.com, Fax 0 58 23 07 17* – ▤. AE ⓓ MC VISA
fermé 1 sem. en oct., janv., merc. sauf vacances scolaires et mardi – **Repas** 25/87 bc, ♀.
◆ Il sait y faire, Monsieur Gérard : goûteuses préparations traditionnelles de saison servies dans une salle à manger de notre temps. Un bon moment de table en perspective.
◆ Monsieur Gérard weet van wanten : traditionele seizoengebonden gerechten opgediend in een eetzaal van deze tijd. Puur gastronomisch genieten...

X **De Tuin,** Zeedijk 6, ✆ 0 58 23 91 00, *Fax 0 58 24 09 80,* ☂ – MC VISA
fermé 12 nov.-5 déc., lundi et jeudi soir en hiver, mardi soir sauf en juil.-août et merc. – **Repas** *Lunch 11* – 23/47 bc.
◆ L'un de ces restaurants typiques de la côte belge. Cuisine à la fois bistrotière et bourgeoise, façon "mer du Nord". Clientèle balnéaire. Additions sans sel.
◆ Dit is een van die restaurants die zo kenmerkend zijn voor de Belgische kust. Eenvoudige bistrokeuken met een flinke scheut "Noordzee". De rekening geeft geen bittere nasmaak.

X **Brasserie Casino,** Zeedijk 29, ✆ 0 58 23 33 10, *Fax 0 58 23 11 07,* ☂ – MC VISA
fermé du 16 au 30 nov., du 16 au 30 janv. et lundi – **Repas** carte 36 à 63.
◆ Cette belle brasserie moderne surveillant la digue propose une carte classique-actuelle affichant un petit faible pour le homard. Terrasse d'été avec vue marine.
◆ Deze mooie eigentijdse brasserie aan de kust biedt een modern-klassieke menukaart, waaruit een voorliefde voor kreeft blijkt. Het terras in de zomer kijkt op zee uit.

NIJVEL *Brabant Wallon – voir Nivelles.*

NIL-ST-VINCENT-ST-MARTIN *1457 Brabant Wallon* C *Walhain 5 688 h.* 533 N 19, 534 N 19 *et* 716 H 4.
Bruxelles 39 – Namur 30.

XX **Le Provençal,** rte de Namur 11 (sur N 4), ✆ 0 10 65 51 84, *Fax 0 10 65 51 75* – P. ⓓ MC VISA
fermé 27 janv.-7 fév., 29 juil.-8 août, dim. soir et lundi – **Repas** 27/40.
◆ Déjà plus de 40 ans de présence pour ce restaurant familial installé dans un ancien relais de poste. Salle à manger bourgeoise. Menus-cartes raisonnés et cave bien fournie.
◆ Dit familierestaurant, dat in bourgeoisstijl is ingericht, is al ruim 40 jaar gevestigd in een oud poststation. Evenwichtige kaart met menu's en een goed gevulde wijnkelder.

NIMY *Hainaut* 533 I 20, 534 I 20 *et* 716 E 4 *– voir à Mons.*

Si vous êtes retardé sur la route, dès 18 h, confirmez votre réservation par téléphone, c'est plus sûr... et c'est l'usage.

NINOVE *9400 Oost-Vlaanderen* 533 J 17 *et* 716 F 3 – *34 744 h.*

Voir *Boiseries★ dans l'église abbatiale.*

Geraardsbergsestraat 80, ✆ 0 54 33 78 57, ninove@toerismevlaanderen.be, Fax 0 54 31 38 49.

Bruxelles 24 – Gent 46 – Aalst 15 – Mons 47 – Tournai 58.

De Croone, Geraardsbergsestraat 49, ✆ 0 54 33 30 03, *decroone@wanadoo.be, Fax 0 54 33 30 03,* – – 25 à 200. AE VISA JCB. rest
Repas *(fermé 15 juil.-15 août, lundi midi et sam. midi)* Lunch 9 – 28/43 bc – **21 ch** 65/85 – ½ P 54/96.

◆ À proximité du centre, ressource hôtelière utile pour la clientèle d'affaires. Elle y trouvera des chambres pratiques pourvues d'un mobilier de série et du double vitrage. Salle de restaurant sobrement lambrissée. Cuisine classico-traditionnelle de saison.

◆ Dit hotel ligt vlak bij het centrum en is geknipt voor zakenlieden. Praktische kamers met dubbele ramen en standaardmeubilair. In het sober gelambriseerde restaurant worden klassiek-traditionele gerechten geserveerd die zijn afgestemd op de seizoenen.

Hof ter Eycken (Vanheule), Aalstersesteenweg 298 (Nord-Est : 2 km par N 405, 2e feu à droite), ✆ 0 54 33 70 81, *Fax 0 54 32 81 74,* – AE VISA JCB
fermé sem. carnaval, 2 dern. sem juil. – prem. sem. août, mardi soir, merc. et sam. midi – **Repas** Lunch 37 – 65/105 bc, carte 69 à 98.

◆ Les dépendances d'un ancien haras abritent une table aussi inventive dans ses recettes que dans son décor mêlant fer forgé et merisier. Cave d'exception. Terrasse sur jardin.

◆ Origineel restaurant in een voormalige stoeterij. De keuken is al even inventief als het decor van smeedijzer en kersenhout. Uitstekende wijnkelder. Tuin en terras.

Spéc. Salade de homard et foie d'oie à la vinaigrette de basilic. Coquilles Saint-Jacques et salsifis à la truffe (oct.-fév.). Huîtres au Champagne et caviar (sept.-mars)

Brasserie Paulus, Burchtstraat 27, ✆ 0 54 32 33 51, *info@brasseriepaulus.be, Fax 0 54 32 79 48,* – AE VISA JCB
fermé lundi et mardi – **Repas** Lunch 17 – carte 32 à 54.

◆ Maison bourgeoise située dans une rue commerciale, au cœur de Ninove. Intérieur richement garni d'antiquités. Beau jardin clos de murs. Plats d'inspiration méditerranéenne.

◆ Herenhuis in een winkelstraat in het hart van Ninove. Prachtig interieur met veel antiek. Mooie ommuurde tuin. Mediterrane keuken.

De Lavendel, Lavendelstraat 11, ✆ 0 54 33 32 03, *Fax 0 54 33 32 03* – . VISA
fermé mi-août-mi-sept., dim. soir et lundi – **Repas** Lunch 25 – 36.

◆ En centre-ville, petit restaurant localement estimé pour ses préparations ne lésinant ni sur la qualité des produits, ni sur le soin dans la présentations des assiettes.

◆ Klein restaurant in het centrum dat bij de inwoners van Ninove een goede reputatie geniet, dankzij de kwaliteit van de producten en de fraaie opmaak van de borden.

NISMES *5670 Namur* C *Viroinval 5 647 h.* 534 M 22 *et* 716 G 5.

Bruxelles 113 – Charleroi 51 – Couvin 6 – Dinant 42 – Charleville-Mézières 50.

Le Melrose , r. Albert Grégoire 33, ✆ 0 60 31 23 39, *Fax 0 60 31 10 13,* , – – 40. AE VISA – *fermé sem. carnaval* – **Repas** *(fermé dim. soir, lundi, mardi soir et après 20 h 30)* Lunch 21 – carte 23 à 33 – **8 ch** 39/48 – ½ P 54/93.

◆ Paisible demeure patricienne dont le parc, reposant, s'est récemment vu loti d'une annexe nantie de quelques chambres pratiques et assez mignonnes. Salle à manger aménagée dans le style bourgeois où se décline un registre culinaire assez traditionnel.

◆ Dit patriciërshuis staat in een rustgevend park, waar onlangs een dependance is gebouwd met enkele praktische kamers die er ook nog aantrekkelijk uitzien. In de eetzaal, die in bourgeoisstijl is ingericht, worden vrij traditionele gerechten geserveerd.

NIVELLES (NIJVEL) *1400 Brabant Wallon* 533 L 19, 534 L 19 *et* 716 G 4 – *23 944 h.*

Voir *Collégiale Ste-Gertrude★★.*

Env. *Plan incliné de Ronquières★ O : 9 km.*

(2 parcours) Chemin de Baudemont 23 ✆ 0 67 89 42 66, Fax 0 67 21 95 17 - au Nord-Est : 10 km à Vieux-Genappe, Bruyère d'Hulencourt 15 ✆ 0 67 79 40 40, Fax 0 67 79 40 48.

Waux-Hall, pl. Albert Ier ✆ 0 67 21 54 13, Fax 0 67 21 57 13.

Bruxelles 34 – Charleroi 28 – Mons 35.

Nivelles-Sud, chaussée de Mons 22 (E 19 - A 7, sortie ⑲), ✆ 0 67 21 87 21, *nivelles sud@valk.com, Fax 0 67 22 10 88,* , – – 25 à 450. AE VISA
Repas Lunch 9 – carte 22 à 42 – 9 – **115 ch** 71/92 – ½ P 100.

◆ Aux portes de Nivelles, près d'une bretelle d'autoroute, motel de chaîne entièrement rénové renfermant des chambres insonorisées, disponibles en cinq tailles.

◆ Volledig gerenoveerd ketenmotel aan de rand van Nijvel, vlak bij de snelweg. De kamers hebben een goede geluidsisolatie en zijn in vijf verschillende afmetingen beschikbaar.

Ferme de Grambais, chaussée de Braine-le-Comte 102 (Ouest : 3 km sur N 533), ☎ 0 67 22 01 18, *ferme.de.grambais@proximedia.be, Fax 0 67 84 13 07*, – – 35. AE VISA – *fermé du 1er au 15 janv.* – **Repas** *(fermé dim. soir et lundi)* (taverne-rest) *Lunch 13* – 27/44 bc – **10 ch** 50/55.
◆ Accueil familial dans cette ancienne exploitation agricole devenue une auberge tranquille. Pimpantes chambres sobrement équipées. Cour intérieure, abords campagnards. Au restaurant, plats bourgeois et ambiance rustique.
◆ Vriendelijk onthaal in deze oude boerderij die nu een rustige herberg is. De kamers hebben sobere voorzieningen, maar zien er piekfijn uit. Grote binnenplaats en landelijke omgeving. In het rustieke restaurant worden traditionele gerechten geserveerd.

Le Clocheton, r. Namur 124, ☎ 0 67 84 01 20, *leclocheton.be, Fax 0 67 84 01 20* – AE VISA. – *fermé 10 août-2 sept., sam. midi, dim. soir et lundi* – **Repas** *Lunch 20* – 40.
◆ Coquettement décoré dans la note Laura Ashley, Le Clocheton tinte de gaieté. Registre culinaire au goût du moment. Lunch renouvelé chaque jour et menu prometteur.
◆ Dit restaurant is vrolijk gedecoreerd in Laura Ashleystijl. Het culinaire register past geheel in de huidige trend. Dagelijks wisselende lunchformule en veelbelovend menu.

Le Champenois, r. Brasseurs 14, ☎ 0 67 21 35 00, *Fax 0 67 21 35 00* – VISA
fermé du 11 au 28 août, du 14 au 22 janv., merc., sam. midi et dim. soir – **Repas** *Lunch 17* – 32.
◆ Une carte concise, mais engageante et bien en phase avec son temps vous sera soumise dans cette maisonnette proche de la Grand-Place. Assiettes joliment mises en scène.
◆ In dit pandje in de buurt van de Grote Markt kunt u kiezen uit een beperkte, maar aanlokkelijke kaart die goed bij de tijd is. Prachtig opgemaakte borden.

à Petit-Rœulx-lez-Nivelles *Sud : 7 km* C *Seneffe 10 597 h.* – ✉ *7181 Petit-Rœulx-lez-Nivelles :*

L'Aub. Saint-Martin, r. Grinfaux 44, ☎ 0 67 87 73 80, *Fax 0 67 87 73 80* – AE VISA. – *fermé sem. carnaval, 15 juil.-15 août, mardi soir, merc., sam. midi et dim. soir* – **Repas** *Lunch 28* – 36/70 bc.
◆ À l'extrémité du village, petite auberge aux accents rustiques occupant l'ancienne étable d'une ferme. Recettes classiques sobrement actualisées. Service aimable.
◆ Kleine herberg met rustieke accenten in de oude stal van een boerderij aan de rand van het dorp. Klassieke recepten die langzamerhand wat moderner worden. Aardige bediening.

NOIREFONTAINE

6831 Luxembourg belge C *Bouillon 5 393 h.* 534 P 24 *et* 716 I 6.
Env. *à l'Ouest : 7 km, Belvédère de Botassart* ≤★★.
Bruxelles 154 – Bouillon 8 – Arlon 67 – Dinant 59.

Aub. du Moulin Hideux, rte de Dohan 1 (Sud-Est : 2,5 km par N 865), ☎ 0 61 46 70 15, *info@moulinhideux.be, Fax 0 61 46 72 81*, ≤, – AE VISA. rest
15 mars-nov. – **Repas** *(fermé merc. soir et jeudi midi de mars à juil. et merc. midi)* 60/100 bc, carte 70 à 108 – **10 ch** 200/240, – 2 suites – ½ P 140/150.
◆ N'ayez crainte : le nom de cet ancien moulin réaménagé dans un cadre bucolique dérive simplement du wallon "l'y deux molins". Chambres personnalisées. Terrasse exquise. Restaurant cossu servant une belle cuisine de base classique. Cave remarquable.
◆ Dit hotel-restaurant is ondergebracht in een oude molen in een schilderachtige omgeving. De kamers hebben een persoonlijk karakter. Prachtig terras. Weelderige eetzaal, waar fijne gerechten op klassieke basis worden geserveerd. Opmerkelijke wijnkelder.
Spéc. Couronne de Saint-Pierre au beurre rouge, mousseline de céleri truffée. Gibier en saison. Selle d'agneau en croûte de champignons

---

NOSSEGEM

Brabant 533 M 17 *et* 716 G 3 – *voir à Bruxelles, environs.*

NOVILLE-SUR-MEHAIGNE

Namur 533 O 19 *et* 534 O 19 – *voir à Éghezée.*

OCQUIER

4560 Liège C *Clavier 4 150 h.* 533 R 20, 534 R 20 *et* 716 J 4.
Bruxelles 107 – Liège 41 – Dinant 40 – Marche-en-Famenne 21.

Le Castel du Val d'Or, Grand'Rue 62, ☎ 0 86 34 41 03, *castel@castel-valdor.be, Fax 0 86 34 49 56*, – – 25 à 200. AE VISA. ch
fermé prem. sem. juil. et 2 sem. en janv. – **Repas** *(fermé sam. midi, dim. midi et mardi) Lunch 24* – 38/80 bc, ♀ – 12 – **14 ch** 76/101, – 1 suite – ½ P 69.
◆ Cet ancien relais de poste (17e s) conservant son charme délicieusement rustique est établi dans l'un des "plus beaux villages du Condroz". Chambres de bon séjour. Mets classico-créatifs dont on se régale dans une salle à manger pleine de cachet.
◆ Dit 17e-eeuwse relais heeft zijn rustieke charme bewaard en is gevestigd in een van de "mooiste dorpen van de Condroz". De kamers staan garant voor een prettig verblijf. Klassieke keuken die van creativiteit getuigt en een eetzaal met cachet.

BELGIQUE

OEDELEM *West-Vlaanderen* 533 F 15 *et* 716 D 2 – *voir à Beernem.*

OHAIN *1380 Brabant Wallon* C *Lasne 13 641 h.* 533 L 18, 534 L 18 *et* 716 G 3.
18 *(2 parcours)* 9 *Vieux Chemin de Wavre 50* ✆ *0 2 633 18 50, Fax 0 2 633 28 66.*
Bruxelles 23 – Charleroi 39 – Nivelles 17.

XX **Le Dernier Tri,** r. Try Bara 33, ✆ 0 2 633 34 20, *dernier.tri@skynet.be, Fax 0 2 633 57 41,* – AE ① MC VISA
fermé du 1er au 15 mars, du 1er au 15 oct., dim. soir et lundi – **Repas** *Lunch 11* – 25/40
◆ Au Sud de la capitale, mignonne auberge à l'ambiance provinciale, localement réputée pour ses savoureuses préparations du marché. Accueil et service aimables.
◆ Mooie herberg ten zuiden van de hoofdstad, die een goede reputatie geniet door zijn smakelijke gerechten op basis van verse producten van de markt. Vriendelijk personeel

X **Aub. de la Roseraie,** rte de la Marache 4, ✆ 0 2 633 13 74, *Fax 0 2 633 54 67,* – P – 25. AE ① MC VISA
fermé 15 août-4 sept., Noël-Nouvel An et merc. – **Repas** *Lunch 12* – 32/46, ♀.
◆ Cette fermette du 19e s. proche voisine de l'église possède sur l'arrière une jolie terrasse paysagère. Décor intérieur façon "estaminet rustique". Additions sans épines.
◆ Dit 19e-eeuwse boerderijtje bij de kerk beschikt over een weelderig terras aan de achterkant. Het interieur doet aan een oude dorpskroeg denken. Rooskleurige rekening !

OIGNIES-EN-THIÉRACHE *5670 Namur* C *Viroinval 5 647 h.* 534 M 22 *et* 716 G 5.
Bruxelles 120 – Namur 81 – Chimay 30 – Dinant 42 – Charleville-Mézières 40.

XX ✿ **Au Sanglier des Ardennes** (Buchet) avec ch, r. J.-B. Périquet 4, ✆ 0 60 39 90 89, *Fax 0 60 39 02 83* – rest, TV. AE MC VISA.
fermé 16 fév.-mi-mars, dim. soir en saison de chasse, lundi et mardi – **Repas** *Lunch 35* – 55/80 bc, carte 38 à 71 – 11 – **9 ch** 50/62 – ½ P 84.
◆ Petite auberge très couleur locale, nichée au cœur d'un village typiquement ardennais Menus à thèmes et gibier en saison de vénerie. Ambiance "chasse". Chambres avenantes
◆ Kleine herberg met veel "couleur locale" en jachttrofeeën aan de muren, in het hart van een typisch Ardens dorp. Wildmenu's in het jachtseizoen. Prettige kamers.
Spéc. Foie gras d'oie en terrine. Sanglier et chevreuil du pays (août et oct.-janv.). Nougat glacé, coulis de fruits rouges

OISQUERCQ *Brabant Wallon* 533 K 18 *et* 534 K 18 – *voir à Tubize.*

OLEN *2250 Antwerpen* 533 O 16 *et* 716 H 2 – *10 976 h.*
9 *à l'Ouest : 1,5 km à Noorderwijk, Witbos* ✆ *0 14 26 21 71, Fax 0 14 26 60 48.*
Bruxelles 67 – Antwerpen 33 – Hasselt 46 – Turnhout 27.

XXX **Doffenhof,** Geelseweg 28a (Nord-Est : 5 km sur N 13), ✆ 0 14 22 35 28, *Fax 0 14 23 29 12,* – P. AE MC VISA
fermé vacances bâtiment, vacances Noël, mardi, merc. et sam. midi – **Repas** *Lunch 32* – 61
◆ Cette ravissante maison à colombages habilement reconstituée vous attable dans un intérieur néo-rustique cossu. Assiettes au goût du jour. Terrasse invitante l'été venu.
◆ Prachtig gerestaureerd vakwerkhuis met een neorustiek interieur dat rijk aandoet. De kookstijl past in de huidige trend. Op zomerse dagen ziet het terras er uitnodigend uit

X **De Blauwe Regen,** Kanaalstraat 1 (Nord-Est : 4 km, près N 13), ✆ 0 14 21 55 34, *blauweregen@wanadoo.be, Fax 0 14 23 37 74,* – P. AE MC VISA.
fermé 2 sem. en juil., lundi, mardi et merc. soir – **Repas** *Lunch 40 bc* – 38/66 bc.
◆ Une façade couverte de plantes grimpantes signale cette fermette. Salle à manger affichant un petit air romantique. Mise en place soignée. Joli jardin aménagé sur l'arrière.
◆ Dit boerderijtje is te herkennen aan zijn gevel met blauweregen. De eetzaal heeft een licht romantische uitstraling. Verzorgde mise en place. Mooie tuin aan de achterkant.

X **Pot au feu,** Dorp 37, ✆ 0 14 27 70 56, *Fax 0 14 26 32 43,* – MC VISA.
fermé 29 mars-6 avril, du 6 au 17 sept., lundi et mardi – **Repas** *Lunch 24* – carte 33 à 42
◆ Brasserie familiale dont le succès tient à ses nombreuses suggestions du marché inscrites sur un écriteau et à son intéressante cave franco-espagnole.
◆ Gezellige brasserie die zijn succes niet alleen te danken heeft aan de talrijke suggesties, maar ook aan de interessante wijnkelder met flessen uit Frankrijk en Spanje.

OLSENE *9870 Oost-Vlaanderen* C *Zulte 14 584 h.* 533 F 17 *et* 716 D 3.
Bruxelles 73 – Gent 30 – Kortrijk 18.

XXX **Eikenhof,** Kasteelstraat 20, ✆ 0 9 388 95 46, *Fax 0 9 388 40 33,* – P. AE ① MC VISA
fermé dern. sem. janv.-prem. sem. fév., mardi soir, merc. et dim. soir – **Repas** 25/60
◆ Agréable moment de table en perspective dans cette villa flamande massive s'ouvrant sur un jardin. Mets classiques tout doucettement actualisés. Cave d'épicurien.
◆ In deze Vlaamse villa met tuin kunt u met volle teugen genieten van een heerlijke maaltijd Klassieke spijzen met een vleugje vernieuwing, in volmaakte harmonie met de wijnen.

O.L.V. LOMBEEK *Vlaams-Brabant* C *Roosdaal 10 623 h.* 533 J 18 *et* 716 F 3 – ✉ *1760 Roosdaal.*
Bruxelles 23 – Halle 16 – Ninove 8.

XX **De Kroon,** Koning Albertstraat 191, ☎ 0 54 33 23 81, *Fax 0 54 32 62 19* – P. VISA. ⚘
fermé 12 juil.-7 août, 2 dern. sem. janv., lundi, mardi et sam. midi – **Repas** 44.
◆ Au centre du village, juste en face de l'église, ancien relais de poste construit en 1760 et préservant son caractère rustique. Cuisine traditionnelle. Accueil familial.
◆ Dit voormalige poststation tegenover de dorpskerk in het centrum dateert uit 1760 en heeft zijn rustieke karakter behouden. Traditionele keuken. Vriendelijke ontvangst.

OOSTAKKER *Oost-Vlaanderen* 533 H 16 *et* 716 E 2 – *voir à Gent, périphérie.*

OOSTDUINKERKE *8670 West-Vlaanderen* C *Koksijde 20 230 h.* 533 B 16 *et* 716 B 2.
ℹ *Oud-Gemeentehuis, Leopold II-laan 2* ☎ *0 58 53 21 21, Fax 0 58 53 21 21.*
Bruxelles 133 – Brugge 48 – Oostende 24 – Veurne 8 – Dunkerque 34.

X **De Hoeve,** Polderstraat 148, ☎ 0 58 23 93 58, 🏖 – P. VISA
Pâques-15 nov. et week-end ; fermé merc. – **Repas** carte 24 à 45.
◆ Typique fermette des polders alanguie dans l'arrière-pays. Moules et anguilles en pagaille, savoureuses viandes, bonne humeur communicative et terrasse d'été côté jardin.
◆ Dit typische polderboerderijtje ligt loom en landelijk in het achterland. Mosselen en paling in overvloed, maar ook mals vlees. Zonnig terras aan de tuinzijde.

à Oostduinkerke-Bad *Nord : 1 km* C *Koksijde* – ✉ *8670 Oostduinkerke.*
ℹ *(Pâques-sept. et vacances scolaires) Albert I-laan 78a,* ☎ *0 58 51 13 89 :*

Hof ter Duinen, Albert I-laan 141, ☎ 0 58 51 32 41, *info@hofterduinen.be, Fax 0 58 52 04 21,* – P – 25. AE VISA JCB. ⚘ rest
fermé 20 sept.-7 oct. et 5 janv.-5 fév. – **Repas** voir rest ***Eglantier*** ci-après – **16 ch** 110/130 – ½ P 65/89.
◆ À quelques foulées de la plage, résidences récentes dont les chambres offrent deux visages : l'un, fringant et moderne, l'autre, plutôt convenu. Espace breakfast ra-di-eux !
◆ Hotel in een nieuw gebouw, vlak bij het strand. De kamers hebben twee gezichten : het ene modern en vrolijk, het andere nogal gewoon. In de ontbijtzaal begint de dag stralend !

Artan Beach sans rest, IJslandplein 12 (Zeedijk), ☎ 0 58 52 11 70, *artan.beach.hotel @advalvas.be, Fax 0 58 52 07 83,* ←, – P. VISA
fermé prem. sem. oct. et 12 nov.-début déc. – **16 ch** 71/101.
◆ La vue sur l'estran et les dunes ne sont pas les seuls atouts de cette enseigne littorale : chambres de belle ampleur, piscine, sauna, hammam, jacuzzi et solarium.
◆ Naast een mooi uitzicht op het strand en de duinen biedt dit badhotel ruime kamers, een zwembad, sauna, hamam, jacuzzi en solarium.

Britannia Beach, Zeedijk 435, ☎ 0 58 51 11 77, *Fax 0 58 52 15 77,* ←, – – 30. VISA. ⚘ ch
Repas *(fermé 4 janv.-14 fév., 15 nov.-15 déc., mardi sauf en juil.-août et après 20 h 30)* (taverne-rest) carte 23 à 41 – **29 ch** *(fermé 15 nov.-15 déc. et mardi)* 110 – ½ P 60/74.
◆ Confort douillet, insonorisation optimale et échappée balnéaire dans la plupart des chambres de cet immeuble étroit surveillant la digue. Service toutefois "minimaliste". Taverne-restaurant proposant snacks et plats de brasserie. Terrasse et véranda.
◆ Hotel in een smal en hoog gebouw dat de dijk bewaakt, met gerieflijke kamers die perfect tegen geluid zijn geïsoleerd en waarvan de meeste op zee uitkijken. De service is helaas minimaal. Café-restaurant met snacks en dagschotels. Serre en terras.

Argos , Rozenlaan 20, ☎ 0 58 52 11 00, *Fax 0 58 52 12 00,* – P. AE VISA. ⚘
Repas *(fermé merc., jeudi et après 20 h 30)* (déjeuner sur réservation) 35/55 bc – **6 ch** 51/74 – ½ P 55/63.
◆ Auberge avenante tenue en famille, située au cœur d'un quartier résidentiel paisible. Les chambres, assez coquettes et menues, sont aménagées à l'étage. Accueil aimable. Salle à manger animée d'une cheminée. Recettes traditionnelles d'esprit "mer du Nord".
◆ Deze vriendelijke herberg in een rustige woonwijk wordt door een familie gerund. De kleine kamers op de bovenverdieping zien er keurig uit. Hartelijke ontvangst. Eetzaal met schouw en een keuken waarin u de Noordzee proeft.

Albert I sans rest, Astridplein 11, ☎ 0 58 52 08 69, *Fax 0 58 52 09 04* – . VISA
22 ch 76/92.
◆ Immeuble étroit s'élevant à proximité du rivage. Chambres standard de mise assez simple, mais de taille respectable et convenablement équipées.
◆ Hotel in een smal en hoog gebouw, niet ver van de dijk. De standaardkamers zijn eenvoudig ingericht, maar hebben goede voorzieningen en zijn prettig van formaat.

Vanneuville, Albert I-laan 109, ✆ 0 58 51 26 20, *Fax 0 58 51 26 24* – TV. MO VISA. ✻ ch
Repas *(fermé 22 déc.-9 janv., dim. soir et après 20 h 30)* *Lunch 28* – 30/52 – **12 ch** ☕ 52/75 – ½ P 58.
◆ Sur l'axe principal de la station, affaire familiale que signale une façade fleurie aux beaux jours. Confort correct dans les chambres, calibrées au "format poche". Restaurant déployant un éventail de préparations locales, souvent gorgées d'iode.
◆ Dit familiehotel staat aan de hoofdstraat van de badplaats. De met bloemen versierde gevel is 's zomers een blikvanger. Vrij geriefelijke kamers in "zakformaat". Het restaurant biedt een keur van streekgerechten, die veelal zo uit het zilte nat komen.

Eglantier - H. Hof ter Duinen, Albert I-laan 141, ✆ 0 58 51 32 41, *info@hofterduinen.be, Fax 0 58 52 04 21,* – P. AE O MO VISA JCB. ✻
fermé 20 sept.-7 oct., 5 janv.-5 fév., lundi soir et mardi soir sauf vacances scolaires et après 20 h 30 – **Repas** 30/78 bc, ♀.
◆ Associée à l'hôtel Hof ter Duinen, cette table plaisante agrémentée d'une verrière propose plusieurs menus alléchants. Formules lunch et week-ends gastronomiques.
◆ Dit aangename restaurant met glazen dak hoort bij hotel Hof ter Duinen. Aantrekkelijke menu's, lunchformules en gastronomische weekends.

OOSTEEKLO *9968 Oost-Vlaanderen C Assenede 13 519 h.* 533 H 15 *et* 716 E 2.

Bruxelles 82 – Gent 20 – Middelburg 51 – Lille 97.

Torenhuyze, Rijkestraat 10, ✆ 0 9 373 43 63, *info@torenhuyze.be, Fax 0 9 373 43 63,* – P. – 30. MO VISA. ✻
fermé 1 sem. après carnaval, prem. sem. sept., sam. midi, dim. midi, lundi et mardi – **Repas** *Lunch 25* – carte 37 à 65, ♀.
◆ Restaurant œuvrant à la campagne, dans une bâtisse de caractère flanquée d'une tour et entourée de pelouses et de plantations soignées. Belle mise en place dans l'assiette.
◆ Restaurant op het platteland, in een karakteristiek pand met een toren, midden in het groen. Verzorgde presentatie van de gerechten.

OOSTENDE (OSTENDE) *8400 West-Vlaanderen* 533 C 15 *et* 716 B 2 – *67 574 h – Station balnéaire – Casino Kursaal* CYZ , *Oosthelling ✆ 0 59 70 51 11, Fax 0 59 70 85 86.*

18 par ① : 9 km à De Haan, Koninklijke baan 2 ✆ 0 59 23 32 83, Fax 0 59 23 37 49.

Liaison maritime Oostende-Dover : Hover Speed Fast Ferries, Natiënkaai 9, ✆ 0 59 55 99 11, Fax 0 59 55 99 17.

Monacoplein 2 ✆ 0 59 70 11 99, info@toerisme-oostende.be, Fax 0 59 70 34 77.

Bruxelles 115 ③ – Brugge 27 ③ – Gent 64 ③ – Dunkerque 55 ⑤ – Lille 81 ④

Plans pages suivantes

Andromeda, Kursaal Westhelling 5, ✆ 0 59 80 66 11, *reservation@andromedahotel.be, Fax 0 59 80 66 29,* ≤, – TV – 25 à 80. AE O MO VISA. ✻ rest CZ t
Repas 40/65 – ☕ 13 – **92 ch** 95/205.
◆ Immeuble dominant la digue et le casino. Chambres spacieuses dont près de la moitié scrute l'horizon marin. Exposition permanente d'œuvres d'art, piscine couverte et fitness. Une grande terrasse d'été devance le restaurant.
◆ Dit flatgebouw torent boven de dijk en het casino uit. Ruime kamers, waarvan bijna de helft uitkijkt op zee. Permanente expositie van kunstwerken, overdekt zwembad en fitnessruimte. Op het grote terras vóór het restaurant is het 's zomers heerlijk toeven.

Thermae Palace, Koningin Astridlaan 7, ✆ 0 59 80 66 44, *info@thermaepalace.be, Fax 0 59 80 52 74,* ≤, – TV P – 25 à 650. AE O MO VISA. ✻ rest A
Repas *(fermé dim. soir et lundi soir)* *Lunch 28* – 46/55 bc – ☕ 13 – **156 ch** 165/215.
◆ Palace rénové s'étirant sur le front de mer, juste devant l'hippodrome. Chambres de standing, aussi spacieuses que paisibles. Colossale infrastructure pour séminaires. Salle de restaurant aménagée dans la note "Art déco". Brunch dominical.
◆ Gerenoveerd luxehotel op de dijk, vlak voor de renbaan. Ruime en rustige kamers met standing. Grote congreszalen met talrijke faciliteiten. De eetzaal is in art-decostijl ingericht. Op zondag wordt er een uitgebreide brunch geserveerd.

Golden Tulip Bero sans rest, Hofstraat 1a, ✆ 0 59 70 23 35, *hotel.bero@oostendе.net, Fax 0 59 70 25 91,* – TV – 25 à 80. AE O MO VISA CY t
69 ch ☕ 85/125, – 3 suites.
◆ À une pirouette de cerf-volant du port des yachts et de la promenade Albert Ier, établissement de bon confort mettant à votre disposition des chambres agréables à vivre.
◆ Dit comfortabele hotel is gunstig gelegen op een steenworp afstand van de jachthaven en de Albert I-Promenade. Het beschikt over aangename kamers waarin het fijn logeren is.

OOSTENDE

Acces, Van Iseghemlaan 21, ☎ 0 59 80 40 82, *info@hotelacces.be, Fax 0 59 80 88 39,* – 25. AE VISA. CY a
Repas (dîner pour résidents seult) – **63 ch** ☐ 78/114 – ½ P 68/79.
• À une petite encablure de la digue, immeuble cubique renfermant des chambres toutes identiques, garnies d'un mobilier actuel. Sauna, solarium et salle de remise en forme.
• Dit hotel in een kubusvormig gebouw ligt op loopafstand van de zee. De kamers zien er allemaal eender uit en zijn modern gemeubileerd. Sauna, solarium en fitnessruimte.

NH Oostende, Hertstraat 15, ☎ 0 59 80 37 73, *nhoostende@nh-hotels.be, Fax 0 59 80 23 90,* – 25 à 80. AE VISA. rest CY d
Repas (dîner seult) 22/33 bc – **94 ch** ☐ 75/110 – ½ P 132/189.
• Building relooké dont les chambres, correctement équipées, sont réparties sur sept étages. L'estran n'est qu'à quelques pâtés de sable et le casino, à un tour de roulette.
• Gerenoveerd hotel waarvan de kamers goede voorzieningen hebben en over zeven verdiepingen zijn verspreid. Het nabijgelegen strand en casino zorgen voor het nodige vertier.

Holiday Inn Garden Court, Leopold II-laan 20, ☎ 0 59 70 76 63, *hotel@holiday-inn-oostende.com, Fax 0 59 80 84 06,* – 25. AE VISA JCB. CZ b
Repas (dîner seult) 22/35 bc – ☐ 15 – **90 ch** 110/125 – ½ P 80/195.
• Établissement formé par deux immeubles communicants. Le plus ancien jouxte un mini-square, en bordure d'une avenue passante. Chambres conformes aux standards de l'enseigne. Restaurant au cadre moderne. Additions sans sel.
• Hotelcomplex van twee gebouwen die met elkaar in verbinding staan ; het oudste bevindt zich naast een plantsoentje aan een drukke weg. De kamers zijn conform de standaard van deze hotelketen. Modern restaurant, waar u voor een prikje kunt eten.

OOSTENDE

Adolf Buylstr. . . . . CY 2
Alfons Pieterslaan . . . . CZ
Edith Cavellstr. . . . . CZ 4
Ernest Feyspl. . . . . CZ 6
Filip Van Maestrichtpl. . . . . CZ 8
Graaf de Smet de Naeyerlaan . . . . . CZ 9
Groentemarkt . . . . CY 10
Hendrik Serruyslaan . . . . CZ 13
Kanunnik Dr. Louis Colensstr. . . . . CZ 14
Kapellestr. . . . . CZ
Koninginnelaan . . . . CZ 18
Nieuwpoortsesteenweg . . . . CZ 22
Oesterbankstr. . . . . CZ 24
Sir Winston Churchill Kaai . . . . . . CY 27
Stockholmstr. . . . . CZ 28
Vlaanderenstr. . . . . CY 30
Wapenpl. . . . . CY 32
Warschaustr. . . . . CZ 33
Wellingtonstr. . . . . CZ 35
Wittenonnenstr. . . . . CZ 36

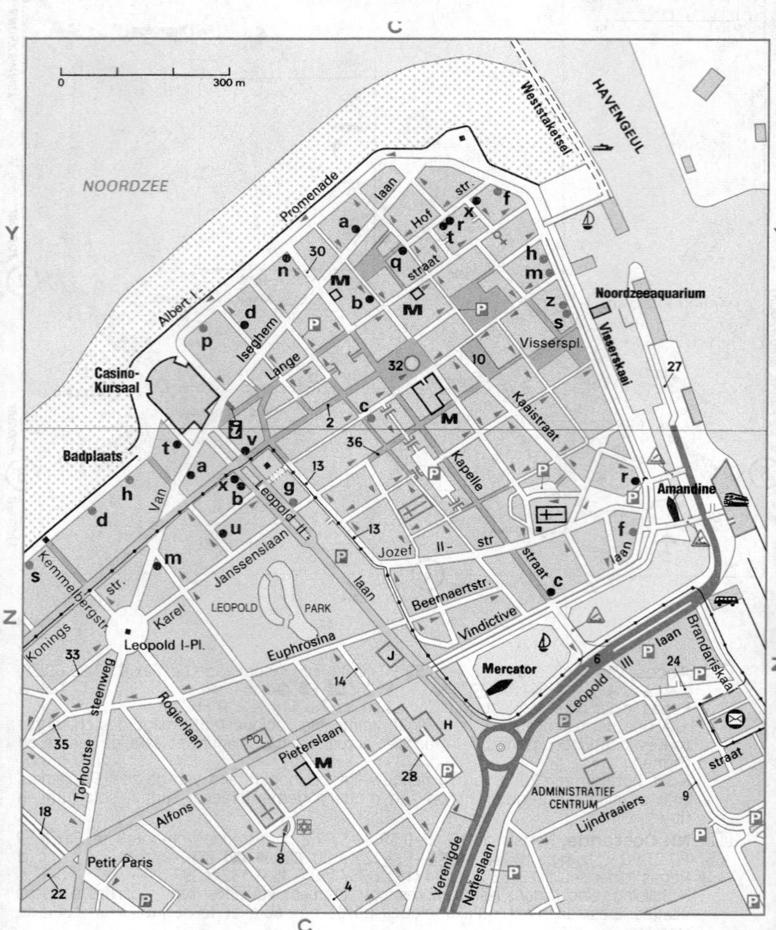

Strand, Visserskaai 1, ✆ 0 59 70 33 83, *strandhotel@busmail.net, Fax 0 59 80 36 78,* ≤, – |‡|, ≡ rest, TV. AE MC VISA. ch CZ r
fermé 30 nov.-12 janv. – **Repas** *(fermé merc.)* (produits de la mer) *Lunch 19* – 30/49 – **21 ch** ☐ 68/120 – ½ P 66/82.

◆ Cette auberge surveillant le chenal et l'Amandine - dernier bateau flamand ayant pêché en mer d'Islande - vous réserve un accueil familial. Amples chambres. Salle à manger procurant une vue sur le quai des Pêcheurs. Cuisine de la mer. Terrasse abritée.

◆ In deze herberg bij de havengeul en de Amandine, de laatste Vlaamse IJslandvaarder, wordt u gastvrij ontvangen in ruime kamers. In de eetzaal, die een fraai uitzicht op de Visserskaai biedt, worden visgerechten geserveerd. Beschut terras.

Burlington sans rest, Kapellestraat 90, ☎ 0 59 55 00 30, *info@hotelburlington.be*, *Fax 0 59 70 81 93*, – 25 à 90. CZ c
42 ch 61/100.
◆ Immeuble-bloc se dressant en surplomb du bassin des yachts où stationne le navire-école Mercator. Chambres sobres, mais relativement amples.
◆ Dit flatgebouw steekt boven de jachthaven uit, waar het opleidingszeilschip Mercator ligt aangemeerd. De kamers zijn sober ingericht, maar relatief groot.

Glenmore, Hofstraat 25, ☎ 0 59 70 20 22, *info@hotelglenmore.be*, *Fax 0 59 70 47 08*, rest, – 25. rest CY x
fermé 2 janv.-19 fév. – **Repas** (dîner pour résidents seult) – **39 ch** 65/95 – ½ P 56/64.
◆ À mi-chemin entre la digue et le port de plaisance, construction récente n'ayant de "british" que le nom. Chambres actuelles, correctement équipées. Centre "thalasso".
◆ Halverwege de boulevard en de jachthaven staat dit hotel in een nieuw gebouw, waarvan alleen de naam Engels is. Moderne kamers met goede voorzieningen. Thalassotherapie.

Pacific, Hofstraat 11, ☎ 0 59 70 15 07, *info@pacifichotel.com*, *Fax 0 59 80 35 66*, CY r
Repas (dîner pour résidents seult) – **50 ch** 80/100 – ½ P 70/85.
◆ Établissement familial du centre animé où vous poserez vos valises dans des chambres sans reproche. Une poignée d'entre elles s'offre même une vue balnéaire.
◆ In dit familiehotel in het levendige centrum van de badplaats logeert u in onberispelijke kamers, waarvan een aantal een doorkijkje biedt op het ruime sop.

Prado sans rest, Leopold II-laan 22, ☎ 0 59 70 53 06, *info@hotelprado.be*, *Fax 0 59 80 87 35* – CZ x
fermé 4 janv.-13 fév. – **28 ch** 70/90.
◆ Proximité de la digue pour prendre le vent, d'une ligne de tramway pour bouger et du centre animé pour faire du shopping. Chambres fonctionnelles munies du double vitrage.
◆ De nabijheid van de dijk om een frisse neus te halen, de tram om een ritje langs de kust te maken en het centrum om te shoppen. Functionele kamers met dubbele ramen.

die Prince sans rest, Albert I Promenade 41, ☎ 0 59 70 65 07, *info@hotel-dieprince.be*, *Fax 0 59 80 78 51*, – 25. CY n
60 ch 65/107.
◆ Cet immeuble-bloc avantageusement situé sur la promenade, juste en face de l'estacade, dispose de chambres standard convenablement équipées et peu à peu rajeunies.
◆ Dit hotel in een flatgebouw is gunstig gelegen aan de boulevard, recht tegenover de dijk. Standaardkamers met redelijke voorzieningen, die geleidelijk worden opgeknapt.

Danielle sans rest, IJzerstraat 5, ☎ 0 59 70 63 49, *hoteldanielle@skynet.be*, *Fax 0 59 24 23 90*, – CZ u
24 ch 60/80.
◆ Adresse familiale voisine d'un parc public. Menues chambres de mise simple, mais correctement tenues. Un copieux petit-déjeuner vous aidera à bien commencer la journée.
◆ Dit familiehotel ligt vlak bij een park. De kleine kamers zijn eenvoudig, maar goed onderhouden. Het copieuze ontbijt is een stevig begin van de dag.

Europe, Kapucijnenstraat 52, ☎ 0 59 70 10 12, *info@europehotel.be*, *Fax 0 59 80 99 79*, – – 25. CY q
Repas (dîner pour résidents seult) – **62 ch** 76/100 – ½ P 52/78.
◆ Hôtel où le passage à l'euro fut sans doute couronné de succès, comme le laisse supposer son enseigne. Confort satisfaisant dans les chambres. Sauna et salle de fitness.
◆ De overgang naar de euro was in hotel Europe vast een klinkend succes. De kamers bieden redelijk comfort. In de fitnessruimte en sauna kunt u zich in- en ontspannen.

Royal Astrid, Wellingtonstraat 1, ☎ 0 59 33 96 96, *info@royalastrid.com*, *Fax 0 59 51 51 56*, – – 25 à 380. rest AB x
Repas (résidents seult) – **92 ch** 79/97.
◆ Centre de revalidation promu hôtel, le Royal Astrid vous accueille dans des chambres standard avec ou sans kitchenette. Voisinage d'un arrêt de tram et de l'hippodrome.
◆ Het Royal Astrid, dat vroeger een revalidatiecentrum was, beschikt over standaardkamers met of zonder kitchenette. De tramhalte en de renbaan zijn vlakbij.

Cardiff, St-Sebastiaanstraat 4, ☎ 0 59 70 28 98, *Fax 0 59 51 46 27* – . ch CY c
fermé mi-nov.-mi-déc. et mardi hors saison – **Repas** *(fermé après 20 h 30)* 16/26 – **16 ch** 61/68 – ½ P 51.
◆ Dans une rue piétonne proche de la Wapenplein, sympathique hôtel familial dont les chambres - récemment rénovées - présentent les caractéristiques du confort moderne. Restaurant mitonnant une cuisine classico-bourgeoise.
◆ Dit sympathieke familiehotel bevindt zich in een voetgangersstraat bij het Wapenplein. De comfortabele kamers zijn onlangs gemoderniseerd. In het restaurant worden eenvoudige klassieke gerechten op tafel gezet.

Impérial sans rest, Van Iseghemlaan 76, ✆ 0 59 80 67 67, *info@hotel-imperial.be, Fax 0 59 80 78 38* – |‡| 📺. AE ⓓ ⓜⓒ VISA CZ a
60 ch ☕ 90/120.
◆ Pratiques avant tout, les chambres de cet hôtel proche de la promenade balnéaire conviennent au repos du touriste soucieux à la fois de son petit confort et de ses finances.
◆ De kamers van dit hotel bij de boulevard zijn vooral praktisch en bieden rust aan toeristen die gesteld zijn op comfort, maar niet al te veel geld willen neertellen.

Du Parc sans rest, Marie-Joséplein 3, ✆ 0 59 70 16 80, *hotel@duparcoostende.com, Fax 0 59 80 08 79*, – |‡| 📺. AE ⓓ ⓜⓒ VISA JCB. CZ v
fermé du 15 au 31 janv. – **51 ch** ☕ 57/87.
◆ Une immuable ressource hôtelière ostendaise que cette construction des années 1930 se donnant des airs de petit palace. Chambres fonctionnelles. Belle taverne Art déco.
◆ Dit hotel is niet meer weg te denken uit Oostende en is gevestigd in een pand uit de jaren 1930 dat beslist allure heeft. Functionele kamers. Taverne in art-decostijl.

Lido 2000 sans rest, L. Spilliaertstraat 1, ✆ 0 59 70 08 06, *lido2000.oostende@skynet.be, Fax 0 59 80 40 07* – |‡| 📺 . AE ⓓ ⓜⓒ VISA CZ m
5 mars-3 janv. – **62 ch** ☕ 50/82.
◆ Non loin de la digue, immeuble ancien dont les chambres, sobrement équipées et quelquefois pourvues d'une kitchenette, sont réparties sur sept étages.
◆ Dit hotel is gevestigd in een oude flat, niet ver van de kust. De kamers zijn over zeven verdiepingen verspreid en hebben sobere voorzieningen, waaronder soms een kitchenette.

Louisa sans rest, Louisastraat 8b, ✆ 0 59 50 96 77, *hotellouisa@pi.be, Fax 0 59 51 37 55* – |‡| 📺. AE ⓓ ⓜⓒ VISA. CY b
fermé janv.-fév. – **15 ch** ☕ 48/79.
◆ Le peintre ostendais James Ensor - l'un des annonciateurs du mouvement surréaliste - vécut à deux pas de cette demeure bourgeoise 1900 abritant des chambres convenables.
◆ De in Oostende geboren schilder James Ensor, een van de voorlopers van het surrealisme, woonde vlak bij dit herenhuis uit 1900, dat keurige kamers ter beschikking heeft.

XXX **Villa Maritza,** Albert I Promenade 76, ✆ 0 59 50 88 08, *villa-maritza@freegates.be, Fax 0 59 70 08 40*, ← – P. AE ⓓ ⓜⓒ VISA CZ s
fermé mardi et dim. soir d'oct. à mai et lundi – **Repas** Lunch 30 – 55/100 bc.
◆ Élégante demeure bourgeoise du 19e s., la Villa Maritza entretient pieusement son décor d'époque : vitraux délicats, riches lambris et tapisseries. Mets au goût du jour.
◆ Elegant herenhuis uit de 19e eeuw dat zijn oorspronkelijke interieur heeft bewaard : sierlijke glas-in-loodramen, rijke lambrisering en mooie tapisserieën. Eigentijdse keuken.

XX **Auteuil,** Albert I Promenade 54, ✆ 0 59 70 00 41, *Fax 0 59 70 00 41*, ← – AE ⓓ ⓜⓒ VISA JCB CY p
fermé merc. et jeudi – **Repas** Lunch 28 – 46/70 bc.
◆ Au rez-de-chaussée d'un immeuble sur digue, confortable maison de bouche où une cuisinière interprète un répertoire culinaire dans le tempo du moment. Cadre chic.
◆ Comfortabel en chic restaurant op de benedenverdieping van een flatgebouw aan de kust, waar een kokkin een culinair repertoire uitvoert in een zeer eigentijds tempo !

XX **'t Vistrapje** avec ch, Visserskaai 37, ✆ 0 59 80 23 82, *Fax 0 59 80 95 68*, – ▤ rest, 📺. ⓜⓒ VISA CY m
Repas *(fermé lundi soir d'oct. à mai sauf vacances scolaires)* 28/70 bc – **6 ch** ☕ 70/100 – ½ P 65.
◆ Une valeur sûre parmi la ribambelle de restaurants qui s'étire le long du quai des Pêcheurs. Carte alléchante assortie de menus bien balancés. Mobilier de style.
◆ Een betrouwbaar adresje tussen de hele rits restaurants langs de Visserskaai. Aantrekkelijke kaart met uitgebalanceerde menu's. Stijlmeubilair.

XX **Le Grillon,** Visserskaai 31, ✆ 0 59 70 60 63, *Fax 0 59 51 52 51* – ▤. AE ⓓ ⓜⓒ VISA JCB
fermé oct. et jeudi – **Repas** 27/38.
◆ Le sympathique "cricri" sur l'enseigne annonce une table plaisante et de plus en plus courtisée pour sa cuisine classico-traditionnelle de bon aloi. Menu avec choix.
◆ De sympathieke krekel op het uithangbord belooft een aangename maaltijd in dit restaurant dat stevig aan de weg timmert met zijn klassiek-traditionele keuken. Mooi keuzemenu. CY s

XX **Petit Nice,** Albert I Promenade 62b, ✆ 0 59 80 39 28, *Fax 0 59 80 96 44*, ←, – ▤. AE ⓜⓒ VISA. CZ h
fermé 10 janv.-10 fév., du 11 au 21 oct., mardi hors saison, merc. et après 20 h 30 – **Repas** 28/60 bc.
◆ Une méchante fringale vous tenaille après la bronzette ? Le Petit Nice, sur la digue, peut y remédier : beaux menus plébiscités, en phase avec l'époque, et service gentil.
◆ Wie na het bruinbakken rammelt van de honger, kan terecht in dit restaurant op de dijk. Smakelijke menu's die in de huidige trend passen. Aardige bediening.

XX **David Dewaele,** Visserskaai 39, ✆ 0 59 70 42 26, *Fax 0 59 70 42 26,* – ▤. AE ◑ ⊙ VISA CY h
fermé du 15 au 22 juin, du 10 au 31 janv. et lundi sauf en juil.-août – **Repas** 28/72 bc.
◆ Côté salle, une ambiance maritime contemporaine, contrepoint du voisinage de l'avant-port. Côté "piano", une partition culinaire actuelle. Côté cave, un peu de tout.
◆ In de zaal een moderne maritieme sfeer, nog versterkt door de nabijheid van de voorhaven. In de keuken een eigentijdse manier van koken. Gevarieerde wijnkaart.

XX **Bistro Chez Freddy,** Albert I Promenade 67f, ✆ 0 59 70 49 47, *Fax 0 59 51 57 31,* ≤, , Produits de la mer – AE ◑ ⊙ VISA CZ d
fermé 1re quinz. oct., 1re quinz. janv., lundi soir en hiver et mardi – **Repas** Lunch 14 – 25/30.
◆ Une carte classique tout doucettement rajeunie vous sera soumise chez Freddy. Situation privilégiée, avec perspective balnéaire. Intérieur moderne. Personnel prévenant.
◆ Bij Freddy krijgt u een klassieke kaart die voorzichtig aan de huidige tijd is aangepast. Schitterend uitzicht op zee. Modern interieur. Voorkomende bediening.

XX **Marina,** Albert I Promenade 9, ✆ 0 59 70 35 56, *restomarina@skynet.be, Fax 0 59 51 85 92,* ≤, Cuisine italienne – ▤ P. AE ⊙ VISA CY f
Repas Lunch 22 – carte 38 à 53, ♀.
◆ Ce resto italien, posté en face de l'estacade, offre une vue maritime depuis la salle à manger au décor soigné. Choix condensé de plats savoureux. Cave bien fournie.
◆ Dit Italiaanse restaurant tegenover de pier biedt vanuit de verzorgde eetzaal een mooi uitzicht op zee. Beperkte kaart met smakelijke gerechten en een goed gevulde wijnkelder.

X **L'Hermitage,** Vindictivelaan 25c, ✆ 0 59 80 50 98, *info@lhermitage.be, Fax 0 59 80 50 98,* – AE ◑ ⊙ VISA CZ f
fermé prem. sem. juil., 2 sem. en janv., mardi soir et merc. – **Repas** Lunch 15 – 27/50.
◆ Table plaisante installée aux abords de la gare, près du chenal et du bateau-musée l'Amandine. La carte, avec menus, mise sur un choix traditionnel. Terrasse d'été.
◆ Plezierig restaurant in de buurt van het station, bij de havengeul en de IJslandvaarder Amandine. De kaart met een aantal menu's mikt op traditie. Terras in de zomer.

X **Au Vieux Port** Visserskaai 32, ✆ 0 59 70 31 28, *au.vieux.port@skynet.be, Fax 0 59 80 12 57* – ▤. AE ◑ ⊙ VISA JCB CY z
fermé 17 nov.-4 déc. et lundi – **Repas** 25/50.
◆ Au voisinage du port de pêche et de l'Aquarium de la mer du Nord, établissement familial proposant une palette de mets savoureux dans une salle de restaurant bourgeoise.
◆ Dit familierestaurant staat niet ver van de vissershaven en het Noordzeeaquarium. De eetzaal is in bourgeoisstijl ingericht en biedt een fraai palet van heerlijke gerechten.

X **Bistro Mathilda,** Leopold II-laan 1, ✆ 0 59 51 06 70, *Fax 0 59 51 06 70,* Ouvert jusqu'à 23 h – AE ◑ ⊙ VISA. ✂ CZ g
fermé 2 sem. en fév., 2 sem. en juin, 2 sem. en oct., lundi soir et mardi – **Repas** carte 29 à 48, ♀.
◆ Une statue de femme bien en chair - la Grosse Mathilda (Dikke Matille) - a susurré son nom à cette taverne-bistrot très prisée les midis. Réservation conseillée.
◆ Het standbeeld van een goed gevulde dame, de Dikke Matille, was de inspiratiebron voor de naam van deze bistro. Reserveren aanbevolen, want vooral 's middags zit het bomvol.

à Gistel *par ④ : 12 km – 11 199 h – ✉ 8470 Gistel :*

X **Malbec,** Hoogstraat 5, ✆ 0 59 27 84 54, *resto@malbec.be, Fax 0 59 27 97 14* – 25 à 120. ⊙ VISA. ✂
fermé du 15 au 31 juil., mardi et merc. – **Repas** Lunch 22 – 31/54 bc, ♀.
◆ Petite affaire au centre d'une localité vouant un culte particulier à sainte Godelieve. Cuisine au goût du jour avec menu-choix et suggestions. Belle sélection de vins.
◆ Dit restaurantje staat midden in het dorp dat een bijzondere verering heeft voor de heilige Godelieve. Eigentijdse keuken met keuzemenu en suggesties. Mooie selectie wijnen.

à Leffinge *par ④ : 7,5 km* C *Middelkerke 16 930 h. – ✉ 8432 Leffinge :*

X **Het Molenhuis,** Torhoutsesteenweg 3, ✆ 0 59 27 78 03, *Fax 0 59 27 78 03,* , Grillades – ▤ P. ⊙ VISA
fermé 21 fév.-1er mars, du 16 au 30 août, lundi et mardi midi – **Repas** 30/50 bc.
◆ Ancienne maison de meunier habilement mise à profit. Salle à manger rustique garnie de poutres apparentes et d'une grande cheminée en briques. Grillades au feu de bois.
◆ Deze oude molenaarswoning is knap verbouwd tot restaurant. De eetzaal doet rustiek aan met zijn hanenbalken en grote bakstenen schouw. Het vlees wordt op houtskool geroosterd.

BELGIQUE

à Mariakerke C Oostende – ✉ 8400 Oostende :

Royal Albert, Zeedijk 167, ☎ 0 59 70 42 36, *royal.albert.oostende@flanderscoast.be, Fax 0 59 80 61 09,* ≤, – |‡|, ▤ rest, TV – 25. AE ⓓ ⓜ VISA JCB. ✗ rest
6 avril-2 nov. – **Repas** (dîner seult jusqu'à 20 h) carte 28 à 40 – **22 ch** ☐ 60/90 – ½ P 78/108. A e

◆ Cet établissement familial borde la digue. Chambres un rien désuètes, mais correctement insonorisées et offrant pour la plupart le spectacle des bains de mer. Belle salle des repas où s'attable une clientèle d'habitués et de touristes. Sage cuisine classique.

◆ Dit familiehotel staat op de dijk. De kamers zijn een tikkeltje ouderwets, maar hebben een goede geluidsisolatie en kijken voor het merendeel uit op zee. In de mooie eetzaal doen de vaste gasten en toeristen zich te goed aan klassieke gerechten.

Glenn, Aartshertogstraat 78, ☎ 0 59 70 26 72, *info@hotelglenn.be, Fax 0 59 70 50 26,* , – |‡| TV. AE ⓓ ⓜ VISA A r
fermé 21 sept.-15 oct. et du 1er au 15 janv. – **Repas** (résidents seult) – **22 ch** ☐ 37/74 – ½ P 59.

◆ Ce petit point de chute où l'on se sent un peu comme chez soi abrite d'assez coquettes chambres personnalisées. Salon pourvu d'un mobilier de style. Patio fleuri.

◆ In dit hotelletje zult u zich vast thuis voelen. De kamers zien er aardig uit en hebben een persoonlijke toets. De lounge is met stijlmeubelen ingericht. Fleurige patio.

XX **Au Grenache,** Aartshertogstraat 80, ☎ 0 59 70 76 85, *au.grenache@skynet.be* – AE ⓓ ⓜ VISA A r
fermé lundi – **Repas** 87.

◆ Doucement actualisée, la brève carte que déploie cette maison bourgeoise n'en reste pas moins classique, avec un penchant pour les produits nobles. Service prévenant.

◆ De beknopte kaart van dit restaurant in een herenhuis blijft ondanks enkele nieuwigheden toch zeer klassiek, met een voorliefde voor "edele" producten. Attente service.

OOSTERZELE *9860 Oost-Vlaanderen* 533 H 17 *et* 716 E 3 – *13 287 h.*

Bruxelles 57 – Gent 19 – Aalst 28.

XX **De Bareel,** Geraardsbergsesteenweg 54, ☎ 0 9 362 82 28, *Fax 0 9 363 01 95,* – P. ⓜ VISA
fermé 2 dern. sem. août-prem. sem. sept., mardi soir, merc. et dim. soir – **Repas** 38/68 bc.

◆ Ancien relais de poste désormais connu pour ses recettes au goût du jour, sans sophistication inutile. Terrasse sur l'arrière, agréable lorsque le soleil est de la partie.

◆ Dit voormalige poststation wordt tegenwoordig druk bezocht vanwege zijn eigentijdse keuken zonder overbodige franje. Terras aan de achterkant voor zonnige dagen.

OOSTKERKE *West-Vlaanderen* 533 E 15 *et* 716 C 2 – *voir à Damme.*

OOSTMALLE *Antwerpen* 533 N 15 *et* 716 H 2 – *voir à Malle.*

OOSTROZEBEKE *8780 West-Vlaanderen* 533 F 17 *et* 716 D 3 – *7 319 h.*

Bruxelles 85 – Kortrijk 15 – Brugge 41 – Gent 41.

XX **Swaenenburg** avec ch, Ingelmunstersteenweg 173, ☎ 0 56 66 33 44, *swaenenburg@skynet.be, Fax 0 56 66 33 55,* , – TV P. AE ⓜ VISA
fermé sem. carnaval, 12 juil.-7 août, merc. et dim. soir – **Repas** Lunch 30 – 45 bc/65 bc, ♀ – **6 ch** ☐ 55/68 – ½ P 72/80.

◆ Un agréable restaurant d'été borde le jardin de cette imposante villa. Cuisine d'aujourd'hui servie dans un cadre actuel. Chambres bien équipées, peu à peu rafraîchies.

◆ Imposante villa met een aangenaam zomerterras aan de tuinzijde. Hedendaags interieur en dito keuken. De kamers hebben goede voorzieningen en worden een voor een opgeknapt.

OPGLABBEEK *3660 Limburg* 533 S 16 *et* 716 J 2 – *9 228 h.*

Bruxelles 94 – Maastricht 36 – Hasselt 25 – Antwerpen 79 – Eindhoven 53.

XXX ✿ **Slagmolen** (Meewis), Molenweg 177 (Nord-Est : 3 km, direction Opoeteren, puis 1re rue à droite), ☎ 0 89 85 48 88, *info@slagmolen.be, Fax 0 89 81 27 82,* – ▤ P. ⓜ VISA
fermé 2 sem. carnaval, 2e quinz. août, mardi, merc. et sam. midi – **Repas** Lunch 38 – 110 bc, carte 62 à 100.

◆ Aux avant-postes du village, presque à la campagne, ex-moulin au cachet rustique préservé. Mets classiques élaborés avec dextérité. Engrenage en salle. Terrasse délicieuse.

◆ Deze oude rustieke molen staat aan de rand van het dorp, bijna op het platteland. De klassieke gerechten worden met vakmanschap bereid. Prachtig terras voor zomerse dagen.

Spéc. Salade de homard aux pommes. Turbot grillé, sauce dijonnaise. Dame blanche

OPGRIMBIE *Limburg* 533 T 17 *et* 716 K 3 – *voir à Maasmechelen.*

OPHAIN-BOIS-SEIGNEUR-ISAAC *Brabant Wallon* 533 L 19 *et* 716 G 3 – *voir à Braine-l'Alleud.*

OPOETEREN *Limburg* 533 S 16 *et* 716 J 2 – *voir à Maaseik.*

OPZULLIK *Hainaut – voir Silly.*

ORROIR *7750 Hainaut* C *Mont-de-l'Enclus 3 255 h.* 533 F 18 *et* 716 D 3.
Bruxelles 73 – Kortrijk 22 – Gent 48 – Valenciennes 45.

XXX **Le Bouquet,** Enclus du Haut 5 (au Mont-de-l'Enclus), ☎ 0 69 45 45 86, *Fax 0 69 45 41 58,* – P – 25 à 100. AE ① MC VISA
fermé lundi soir et mardi – **Repas** Lunch 35 – 46/76 bc.
◆ Grosse hostellerie dont la pimpante façade s'égaye de volets rouges. Confortable salle à manger au décor assez opulent. Terrasse d'été donnant sur un jardin romantique.
◆ Grote villa met vrolijke rode luiken. De comfortabele eetzaal is vrij weelderig ingericht. Het zomerterras komt uit op een romantische tuin.

ORVAL (Abbaye d') ★★ *Luxembourg belge* 534 R 25 *et* 716 J 7 *G. Belgique-Luxembourg.*

OTTIGNIES *1340 Brabant Wallon* C *Ottignies-Louvain-la-Neuve 28 372 h.* 533 M 18, 534 M 18 *et* 716 G 3.
Env. *à l'Est : 8 km à Louvain-la-Neuve*★, *dans le musée : legs Charles Delsemme*★.
18 *à l'Est : 8 km à Louvain-la-Neuve, r. A. Hardy 68* ☎ *0 10 45 05 15, Fax 0 10 45 44 17.*
Bruxelles 31 – Namur 39 – Charleroi 36.

XX **Le Chavignol,** r. Invasion 99, ☎ 0 10 45 10 40, *ciuro@lechavignol.com, Fax 0 10 45 54 19,* – AE MC VISA
fermé mardi, merc. et dim. soir – **Repas** 25/65 bc, ♀.
◆ Meubles façon "colonies", plafond luisant et marbre du Portugal composent un intérieur de bon goût, en parfaite osmose avec le contenu des assiettes. Menus aguichants.
◆ Meubelen in koloniale stijl, een glanzend plafond en Portugees marmer kenmerken het smaakvolle interieur. In volmaakte harmonie met het eten. Verleidelijke menu's.

à Louvain-la-Neuve *Est : 8 km* C *Ottignies-Louvain-la-Neuve* – ✉ *1348 Louvain-la-Neuve :*

Mercure, bd de Lauzelle 61, ☎ 0 10 45 07 51, *H2200@accor-hotels.com, Fax 0 10 45 09 11,* – TV P – 25 à 220. AE ① MC VISA. rest
Repas (taverne-rest) carte 22 à 32 – **77 ch** 92/103.
◆ Hôtel et centre de séminaires tout à la fois, l'établissement vient d'être rajeuni pour mieux satisfaire aux normes de l'enseigne Mercure. Menues chambres munies d'un balcon.
◆ Dit hotel annex congrescentrum heeft onlangs een verjongingskuur gehad om nog beter te voldoen aan de normen van de hotelketen. Kleine kamers met balkon.

X **Il Doge,** Agora 22, ☎ 0 10 45 30 63, *info@ildoge-vea.be, Fax 0 10 45 30 86,* Avec cuisine italienne, ouvert jusqu'à minuit – AE ① MC VISA
Repas carte 22 à 44.
◆ Registre culinaire franco-transalpin sans fioriture et vins élevés dans la Botte, voilà le programme de ce restaurant dont la salle à manger s'habille de masques vénitiens.
◆ Eerlijke Frans-Italiaanse gerechten en wijnen uit de laars van Italië staan op het culinaire programma van dit Belgische dogenpaleis. Venetiaanse maskers aan de muren.

OUDENAARDE (AUDENARDE) *9700 Oost-Vlaanderen* 533 G 17 *et* 716 D 3 – *28 089 h.*
Voir *Hôtel de Ville*★★★ *(Stadhuis)* Z – *Église N.-D. de Pamele*★ *(O.L. Vrouwekerk van Pamele)* Z.
18 9 *par* ④ : *5 km à Wortegem-Petegem, Kortrijkstraat 52* ☎ *0 55 31 41 61, Fax 0 55 31 98 49.*
Stadhuis, Markt 1 ☎ *0 55 31 72 51, toerisme@oudenaarde.be, Fax 0 55 30 92 48.*
Bruxelles 61 ② – *Gent 29* ⑥ – *Kortrijk 28* ④ – *Valenciennes 61* ③

Plan page suivante

de Rantere (annexe - 8 ch), Jan Zonder Vreeslaan 8, ☎ 0 55 31 89 88, *info@derantere.be, Fax 0 55 33 01 11,* – TV – 25 à 40. AE ① MC VISA Z e
Repas *(fermé 17 juil.-8 août, dim. et jours fériés)* Lunch 24 – 30/72 bc – **19 ch** 75/105.
◆ Au voisinage des quais et du béguinage, construction récente distribuant ses chambres de bon confort sur trois étages et dans une annexe aussi paisible que moderne. Salle des repas égayée de toiles abstraites. Importante carte classique-actuelle.
◆ Hotel in een modern gebouw in de buurt van de kaden en het begijnhof. Comfortabele kamers op drie verdiepingen en in het bijgebouw, waar het heerlijk rustig is. Abstracte schilderijen sieren de eetzaal. Uitgebreide kaart met modern-klassieke gerechten.

OUDENAARDE

Aalststraat	Z	
Achterburg	Z	2
Achter de Wacht	Y	3
Baarstraat	Z	
Bekstraat	Y	
Bergstraat	Z	
Beverestraat	Y	4
Bourgondiëstraat	Z	7
Broodstraat	Z	9
Burg	Z	10
Burgschelde	Z	14
Dijkstraat	Y	
Doornikstraat	Z	
Fortstraat	Y	
Gevaertsdreef	Y	
Grote Markt	Z	
Hoogstraat	YZ	17
Jezuïetenplein	Z	18
Kasteelstraat	Z	21
Kattestraat	Y	
Krekelput	Z	23
Louise-Mariekaai	Z	26
Margaretha van Parmastr.	Z	32
Marlboroughlaan	YZ	
Matthijs Casteleinstr.	Z	
Meerspoortplein	Z	33
Minderbroedersstr.	Z	34
Nederstraat	YZ	35
Parkstraat	Y	
Prins Leopoldstraat	Y	
Remparden	Z	
Simon de Paepestraat	Y	37
Stationsstraat	Y	
Tacambaroplein	Y	38
Tussenbruggen	Z	40
Tussenmuren	Z	
Voorburg	Z	42
Wijngaardstraat	Y	46
Woeker	Y	

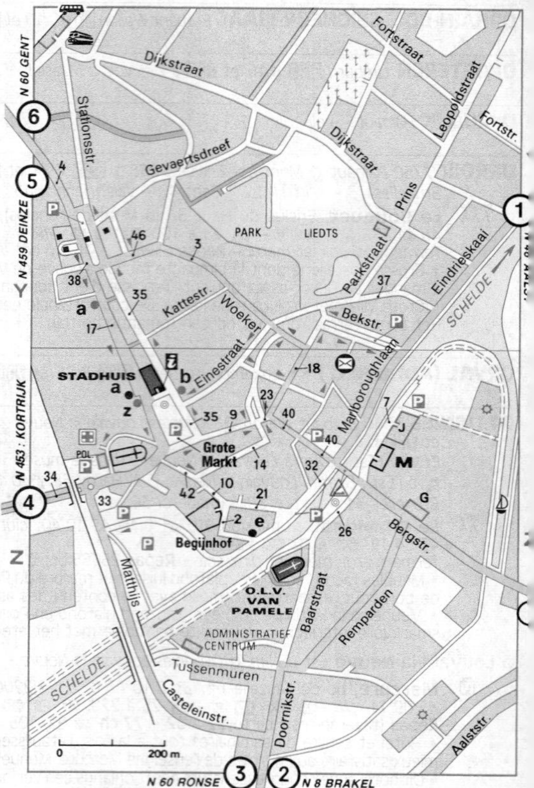

🏨 **CESAR,** Markt 6, ✆ 0 55 30 13 81, *info@hotel-cesar.be, Fax 0 55 33 02 36,* – 🛗 ▤ 📺 – 🅰 40. AE ⓓ ⓜ VISA – *fermé dern. sem. nov.* – **Repas** *(fermé dim. et lundi)* (taverne-rest) *Lunch 11* – carte 25 à 37 – **9 ch** ☕ 70/85 – ½ P 55. Z b

◆ Sur la place du marché, ancienne maison de notable dont l'élégante façade capte volontiers le regard. Vous y serez hébergés dans de grandes chambres bien équipées. Taverne-restaurant servant des salades, des plats de brasserie et des pâtes.

◆ De sierlijke gevel van dit oude herenhuis aan de Grote Markt is een echte blikvanger. U logeert er in grote kamers met goede voorzieningen. In het café-restaurant worden salades, eenvoudige schotels en pasta's geserveerd.

🏨 **de Zalm,** Hoogstraat 4, ✆ 0 55 31 13 14, *de.zalm@vt4.net, Fax 0 55 31 84 40,* 🚲 – 🛗, ▤ rest, 📺 🚗 – 🅰 25 à 150. AE ⓓ ⓜ VISA. ✂ Z a

fermé 13 juil.-4 août et 24 janv.-1er fév. – **Repas** *(fermé dim. soir et lundi) Lunch 13* – carte 27 à 37 – **7 ch** ☕ 70/90 – ½ P 87.

◆ Affaire familiale jouxtant l'hôtel de ville, remarquable édifice public de style flamboyant achevé en 1530. Chambres avant tout pratiques. Poutres, lambris, lustres à bougies et cheminée réchauffent l'atmosphère de la salle à manger. Cuisine bourgeoise.

◆ Familiehotel naast het stadhuis, een schitterend bouwwerk in laatgotische stijl dat in 1530 werd voltooid. De kamers zijn in de eerste plaats praktisch. Balken, lambrisering, kroonluchters met kaarsen en de open haard geven de eetzaal sfeer. Burgerkeuken.

🏨 **Da Vinci** sans rest, Gentstraat 58 (par ⑥), ✆ 0 55 31 13 05, *Fax 0 55 31 15 03,* 🚲 – 📺. AE ⓓ ⓜ VISA

fermé fin déc. – **5 ch** ☕ 67/87, – 1 suite.

◆ Derrière la gare, demeure de caractère imprégnée d'un charme provincial désuet. Chambres individualisées, douillettes et cossues. Terrasse sur cour. Service personnalisé.

◆ Karakteristiek pand met een ouderwetse provinciale charme achter het station. Mooie kamers met een persoonlijke uitstraling. Terras op de binnenplaats. Service op maat.

Wijnendael, Berchemweg 13 (par ②, sur N 8), ☎ 0 55 30 49 90, *info@wijnendael.com, Fax 0 55 31 84 95,* ☂, ≘, ⚲ – TV P. AE MC VISA. ✗ rest
fermé juil. et 20 déc.-2 janv. – **Repas** (dîner pour résidents seult) – **8 ch** ☐ 65/87 – ½ P 44/76.
◆ Petit établissement excentré, le Wijnendael abrite une poignée de chambres correctement équipées, toutes situées en rez-de-chaussée.
◆ Dit kleine hotel ligt even buiten het centrum. Wijnendael beschikt over enkele kamers met goede voorzieningen, die allemaal gelijkvloers zijn.

Host. La Pomme d'Or avec ch, Markt 62, ☎ 0 55 31 19 00, *info@lapommedor.be, Fax 0 55 30 08 44,* ☂, ⛵, ⚲ – |‡| TV – 🏛 25 à 80. AE ⓓ MC VISA Z z
Repas *(fermé lundi en hiver)* Lunch 14 – 34/52 – **10 ch** ☐ 72/97.
◆ Belle reconversion pour ce relais postal du 15e s. devenu une plaisante maison de bouche. Mobilier Empire en salle. Menus alléchants et bons bordeaux. Chambres élégantes.
◆ Dit 15e-eeuwse relais heeft een smaakvolle nieuwe bestemming gekregen. Eetzaal met empiremeubilair. Aantrekkelijke menu's en goede bordeauxwijnen. Elegante kamers.

wine and dine CAFé, Hoogstraat 34, ☎ 0 55 23 96 97, *info@derantere.be, Fax 0 55 33 01 11,* Ouvert jusqu'à 23 h – ▤. AE ⓓ MC VISA Y a
fermé 19 juil.-8 août – **Repas** carte 28 à 38, ♀.
◆ Le succès de cet établissement tient à ses recettes bistrotières simples mais composées de bons produits et soigneusement mises en scène sur l'assiette. Vins du monde.
◆ Dit etablissement dankt zijn succes aan het eenvoudige bistro-eten, dat van uitstekende kwaliteit is en met zorg op de borden wordt gepresenteerd. Kosmopolitische wijnkaart.

à Maarke-Kerkem *Sud-Est : 4 km sur N 60, puis N 457* C *Maarkedal 6 434 h.* – ✉ *9680 Maarke-Kerkem :*

Het genot op den Berg, Bovenstraat 4 (Kerkem), ☎ 0 55 30 35 56, *info@genotopdenberg.be, Fax 0 55 30 40 24,* ≤, ☂ – P. AE MC VISA
fermé 16 fév.-17 mars, du 4 au 20 oct., lundi, mardi et merc. – **Repas** 30/43.
◆ Esseulée sur une butte en pleine campagne, cette ancienne ferme à colombages se coiffe d'un joli toit de chaume et de tuiles. Salle rustique, véranda et terrasse panoramique.
◆ Deze oude vakwerkboerderij met een mooi dak van riet en pannen staat afgelegen op een heuvel midden op het platteland. Rustieke eetzaal met serre en panoramaterras.

à Mater *par ② : 4 km sur N 8* C *Oudenaarde* – ✉ *9700 Mater :*

Zwadderkotmolen, Zwadderkotstraat 2 (par Kerkgatestraat : 1 km, puis à gauche), ☎ 0 55 49 84 95, *Fax 0 55 49 84 95,* ☂ – P. AE MC
fermé 3 prem. sem. sept., Noël, Nouvel An, mardi et merc. – **Repas** Lunch 38 bc – 40 bc/54 bc, ♀.
◆ En pleine campagne, vieux moulin à eau transformé en restaurant de charme dont l'intérieur rustique, étagé en mezzanine, conserve une partie de la machinerie originale.
◆ Deze oude watermolen op het platteland is nu een sfeervol restaurant. In het rustieke interieur met tussenverdieping is nog een deel van de oorspronkelijke machinerie te zien.

à Mullem *par ⑥ : 7,5 km sur N 60* C *Oudenaarde* – ✉ *9700 Mullem :*

Moriaanshoofd avec ch, Moriaanshoofd 27, ☎ 0 9 384 37 87, *Fax 0 9 384 67 25,* ☂, ⛱ – TV P. ⓓ MC VISA. ✗
Repas Lunch 13 – carte 26 à 60 – **12 ch** ☐ 40/65 – ½ P 45/53.
◆ Mignonne auberge tenue en famille, le Moriaanshoofd propose une sage carte bourgeoise assortie d'un lunch et de menus. Chambres standard à l'arrière. Jardin reposant.
◆ Lieflijke herberg die door een familie wordt gerund. Standaardkamers aan de achterkant. Rustgevende tuin. Eenvoudige kaart met een lunchformule en menu's.

OUDENBURG *8460 West-Vlaanderen* 533 *D 15 et* 716 *C 2 – 8 794 h.*

Bruxelles 109 – Brugge 19 – Oostende 8.

Abdijhoeve, Marktstraat 1, ☎ 0 59 26 51 67, *info@abdijhoeve.com, Fax 0 59 26 53 10,* ☂, ⊘, ⚑, ≘, ⛱, ⛱, ⚲ – TV P – 🏛 25 à 250. AE ⓓ MC VISA. ✗ rest
fermé 1 sem. en nov. – **Repas** *(fermé lundi sauf en juil.-août)* (taverne-rest) Lunch 10 – 23/53 bc – **24 ch** ☐ 78/116 – ½ P 80/85.
◆ Nouvelle vocation pour cette grosse ferme abbatiale du 17e s. : chambres pratiques, piscine couverte, espaces de remise en forme et de réunions. Environnement de polders. L'ancienne grange tient lieu de salle à manger, classiquement agencée.
◆ Deze grote 17e-eeuwse kloosterboerderij in een prachtig polderlandschap heeft nu een nieuwe roeping : praktische kamers, overdekt zwembad, fitnessruimte en vergaderzalen. De oude schuur is in een eetzaal met een klassiek interieur omgetoverd.

à Roksem *Sud-Est : 4 km* 🄲 *Oudenburg – ✉ 8460 Roksem :*

De Stokerij , Hoge dijken 2, ☎ 0 59 26 83 80, *hotel@hoteldestokerij.be, Fax 0 59 26 89 35*, , , – ▤ TV ♿ P. MC VISA
fermé 2 sem. en nov. – **Repas** voir rest ***Jan Breydel*** ci-après – **9 ch** ☕ 62/160 – ½ P 70/100.
◆ Cette paisible auberge rurale aménagée dans une ancienne distillerie dispose de chambres personnalisées avec un goût sûr ; cinq d'entre elles offrent l'agrément d'un jacuzzi.
◆ Deze rustige plattelandsherberg is ondergebracht in een oude stokerij. De kamers zijn smaakvol en persoonlijk ingericht ; vijf ervan zijn voorzien van een jacuzzi.

XX **Ten Daele,** Brugsesteenweg 65, ☎ 0 59 26 80 35, *Fax 0 59 26 80 35*, – P. MC VISA
fermé 21 juin-8 juil., 22 déc.-1er janv., lundi soir et jeudi soir de nov. à mars, mardi soir, merc., dim. soir et après 20 h – **Repas** Lunch 30 bc – carte env. 71.
◆ Tranquille fermette promue restaurant : préparations assez classiques, intérieur bourgeois, terrasse estivale dressée au jardin, et, en prime, l'air pur de la campagne.
◆ Restaurant in een rustig boerderijtje, met een vrij klassieke keuken, bourgeoisinterieur en zomerterras in de tuin. De schone lucht op het platteland krijgt u er gratis bij !

X **Jan Breydel** - H. De Stokerij, Brugsesteenweg 108, ☎ 0 59 26 82 97, *restaurant@janbreydel.be, Fax 0 59 26 89 35*, , Produits de la mer – ▤ P. AE MC VISA
fermé 20 fév.-3 mars, 15 nov.-3 déc., mardi et merc. – **Repas** Lunch 12 – carte 31 à 61, ♀.
◆ Le décor, très "nostalgie", fait son effet : collections de vieux pots de chambre, de téléphones d'antan et autres objets hétéroclites chers à nos aïeux. Produits de la mer.
◆ Dit restaurant druipt van de nostalgie : oude pispotten, telefoontoestellen en andere voorwerpen uit grootmoeders tijd. De menukaart is echt iets voor visliefhebbers.

OUDERGEM *Brussels Hoofdstedelijk Gewest – voir Auderghem à Bruxelles.*

OUD-HEVERLEE *Vlaams-Brabant* 533 N 17 *et* 716 H 3 *– voir à Leuven.*

OUD-TURNHOUT *Antwerpen* 533 O 15 *et* 716 H 2 *– voir à Turnhout.*

OUREN *Liège* 533 V 22, 534 V 22 *et* 716 L 5 *– voir à Burg-Reuland.*

OVERIJSE *Vlaams-Brabant* 533 M 18 *et* 716 G 3 *– voir à Bruxelles, environs.*

PALISEUL *6850 Luxembourg belge* 534 P 23 *et* 716 I 6 *– 5 024 h.*
Bruxelles 146 – Bouillon 18 – Arlon 65 – Dinant 55.

XXX ✿✿ **Au Gastronome** (Libotte) avec ch, r. Bouillon 2 (Paliseul-Gare), ☎ 0 61 53 30 64, *Fax 0 61 53 38 91*, , – ▤ TV P. MC VISA
fermé 29 juin-9 juil., 1er janv.-6 fév., dim. soir, lundi et mardi – **Repas** Lunch 52 bc – 62/100, carte 59 à 95 – ☕ 10 – **8 ch** 90/175 – ½ P 95/130.
◆ Hostellerie ardennaise cossue où une fine cuisine classique délicieusement revisitée s'élabore dans la stabilité. Élégante salle feutrée, belles chambres et piscine au jardin.
◆ Luxueus Ardens hotel-restaurant met een fijne keuken in klassieke stijl, waaraan een vleugje eigentijds niet ontbreekt. Sierlijke eetzaal, mooie kamers en zwembad in de tuin.
Spéc. Cuisses de grenouilles au jus de persil, raviole frite de fromage de chèvre aux radis. Pigeonneau en crapaudine cuit à la broche, taboulé à l'orientale. Carré de cochon de lait caramélisé, cuisse fumée en boudin, épaule farcie de poivre et pieds en Tatin

XX **à la hutte Lurette** avec ch, r. Station 64, ☎ 0 61 53 33 09, *lahuttelurette@skynet.be, Fax 0 61 53 52 79*, , , – TV P. AE MC VISA
Repas *(fermé 16 fév.-mars, mardi soir et merc.)* Lunch 17 – 30/56 bc – **7 ch** *(fermé 16 fév.-mars et merc. soir hors saison)* ☕ 50/64 – ½ P 52/55.
◆ Auberge néo-rustique connue depuis "belle lurette" à Paliseul. Préparations classiques et traditionnelles, grande terrasse côté jardin et chambres fonctionnelles proprettes.
◆ Deze neorustieke herberg geniet plaatselijk een goede reputatie. Keurige, functionele kamers. Klassieke en traditionele gerechten. Groot terras aan de kant van de tuin.

De PANNE (LA PANNE) *8660 West-Vlaanderen* 533 A 16 *et* 716 A 2 *– 9 877 h – Station balnéaire.*
Voir *Plage*★.
🅸 *Gemeentehuis, Zeelaan 21, ☎ 0 58 42 18 18, toerisme@depanne.be, Fax 0 58 42 16 17.*
Bruxelles 143 ① *– Brugge 55* ① *– Oostende 31* ① *– Veurne 6* ② *– Dunkerque 20* ③

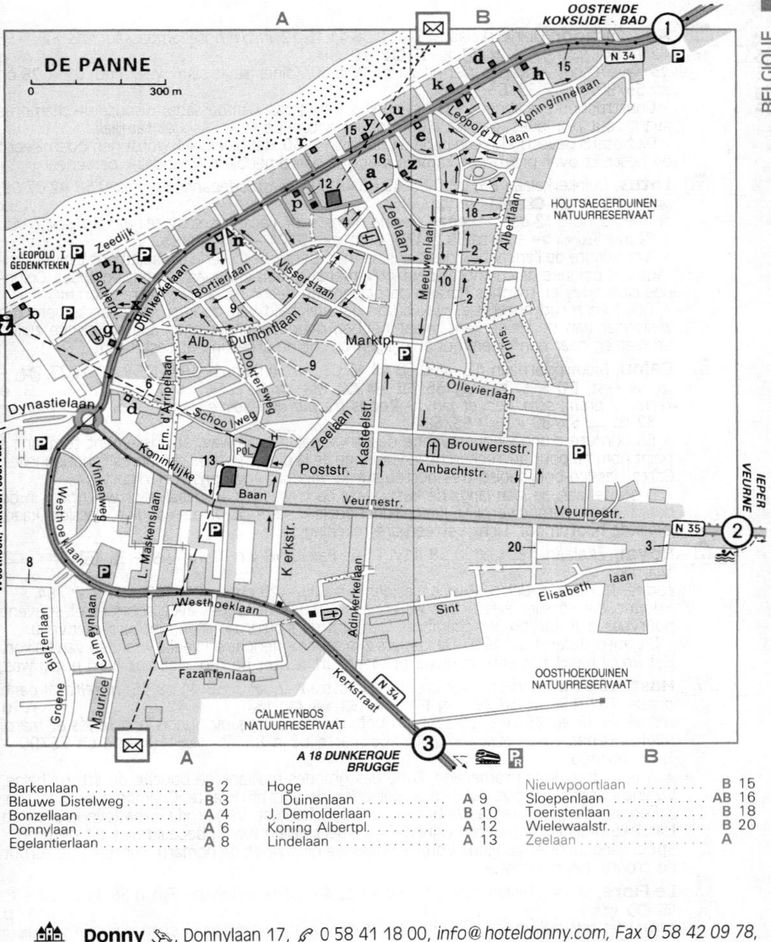

DE PANNE

Barkenlaan	B 2	Hoge Duinenlaan	A 9	Nieuwpoortlaan	B 15
Blauwe Distelweg	B 3	J. Demolderlaan	B 10	Sloepenlaan	AB 16
Bonzellaan	A 4	Koning Albertpl.	A 12	Toeristenlaan	B 18
Donnylaan	A 6	Lindelaan	A 13	Wielewaalstr.	B 20
Egelantierlaan	A 8			Zeelaan	A

Donny [quiet], Donnylaan 17, [phone] 0 58 41 18 00, *info@hoteldonny.com, Fax 0 58 42 09 78*, [view], [terrace], [spa], [fitness], [pool], [garden], [park], [bicycles] – [lift] [TV] [P] – [meeting] 25 à 80. AE MC VISA. [no dogs] rest — A d

fermé du 17 au 27 déc. et 1re quinz. janv. – **Repas** *(fermé dim.) Lunch 20* – 25/59 bc – **45 ch** [breakfast] 80/95 – ½ P 63/88.

◆ À 300 m de la plage, chambres de bon séjour distribuées sur trois étages. Équipements complets, aussi bien pour se réunir que pour se laisser vivre et prendre soin de soi. Restaurant prolongé d'une terrasse invitante quand le soleil est au rendez-vous.

◆ Dit hotel ligt op 300 m van het strand en beschikt over aangename kamers op drie verdiepingen. Talrijke faciliteiten voor werk, ontspanning en lichaamsverzorging. Het restaurant heeft een terras dat lokt als de zon van de partij is.

Iris, Duinkerkelaan 41, [phone] 0 58 41 51 41, *info@hotel-iris.be, Fax 0 58 42 11 77*, [terrace], [fitness], [spa], [garden] – [lift], [no smoking] ch, [TV] [garage] [P] – [meeting] 35. MC VISA. [no dogs] ch — A n

Repas *(fermé mardi et merc.) Lunch 15* – carte env. 44 – **23 ch** [breakfast] 84/117.

◆ Cet hôtel bordant l'axe principal de la station se partage entre deux unités dont un bloc d'architecture contemporaine abritant les meilleures chambres, avec bain-bulles. Salle à manger de notre temps. Recettes classico-bourgeoises.

◆ Dit hotel aan de hoofdweg van de badplaats bestaat uit twee gebouwen. De beste kamers bevinden zich in het nieuwe gebouw en hebben een bubbelbad. In de eigentijdse eetzaal worden de gasten onthaald op eenvoudige klassieke gerechten.

BELGIQUE

Ambassador, Duinkerkelaan 43, ✆ 0 58 41 16 12, *info@hotel-ambassador.be, Fax 0 58 42 18 84,* ... A q
15 fév.-10 nov. – **Repas** *(fermé après 20 h 30)* (dîner seult sauf week-end) 22 – **28 ch** ⊒ 56/80 – ½ P 53/63.
◆ Construction des années 1930 rajeunie à petits pas, l'Ambassador dispose de chambres avant tout pratiques, garnies d'un mobilier actuel de série. Accueil familial.
◆ Dit hotel is gevestigd in een pand uit de jaren 1930, dat geleidelijk wordt gemoderniseerd en beschikt over praktische kamers met standaardmeubilair. Vriendelijk personeel.

Lotus, Duinkerkelaan 83, ✆ 0 58 42 06 44, *info@lotusdepanne.be, Fax 0 58 42 07 09,* ... ch A x
fermé 12 nov.-12 déc. – **Repas** *(fermé merc. sauf vacances scolaires et dim. soir d'oct. à Pâques)* Lunch 25 – carte 39 à 47 – **8 ch** ⊒ 55/74 – ½ P 79/83.
◆ À proximité de l'animation des bains de mer, petite hostellerie aimablement tenue, abritant une poignée de chambres peut-être menues, mais convenablement équipées. Colonnes classiques et touches florales participent au décor de la salle de restaurant.
◆ Goed verzorgd hotelletje, vlak bij de bedrijvigheid van de kust. De paar kamers zijn weliswaar aan de kleine kant, maar hebben goede voorzieningen. Classicistische zuilen en hier en daar een bloemmotief dragen bij tot de sfeer in het restaurant.

Cajou, Nieuwpoortlaan 42, ✆ 0 58 41 13 03, *info@cajou.be, Fax 0 58 42 01 23,* ... rest, ... 35. ... B e
fermé 2 prem. sem. déc. et janv. – **Repas** *(fermé dim. soir et lundi)* Lunch 12 – 24/60 bc – **32 ch** ⊒ 55/80 – ½ P 53/59.
◆ En bordure d'une longue avenue desservie par le tramway, établissement tombant à point nommé pour qui recherche le voisinage de la digue. Petites chambres fonctionnelles. Carte classico-bourgeoise très portée sur le poisson. Additions fort digestes.
◆ Dit hotel aan de laan langs de kust, waar de tram rijdt, is ideaal voor wie graag in de buurt van het strand verblijft. Kleine functionele kamers. Op de eenvoudige, klassieke kaart is vis de hoofdmoot. Licht verteerbare rekening.

Royal, Zeelaan 180, ✆ 0 58 41 11 16, *Fax 0 58 41 10 16,* ... A a
fermé 15 nov.-26 déc. – **Repas** (résidents seult) – **20 ch** ⊒ 66/108 – ½ P 71/84.
◆ Immeuble hôtelier élevé dans les années 1930. Aménagées avec sobriété et souvent pourvues d'un balcon, les chambres viennent de s'offrir un lifting intégral bienvenu.
◆ Dit hotel dateert uit 1930. De kamers zijn sober ingericht en veelal voorzien van balkon. Het Royal heeft net een grondige opknapbeurt achter de rug, wat ook hard nodig was.

Host. Le Fox (Buyens) avec ch, Walckiersstraat 2, ✆ 0 58 41 28 55, *hotelfox@pandora.be, Fax 0 58 41 58 79* – ... A u
fermé du 18 au 23 avril, 26 sept.-14 oct., du 10 au 21 janv., lundis non fériés et mardi midi – **Repas** Lunch 45 bc – 70/100 bc, carte 65 à 85, ♀ – ⊒ 10 – **13 ch** 75/90 – ½ P 100/105.
◆ À deux pas de la promenade, l'une des grandes maisons de bouche du littoral belge. Cuisine classico-créative soignée et sélection de vins affriolante. Chambres au diapason.
◆ Een van de grote restaurants aan de Belgische kust. Verzorgde, creatieve keuken op klassieke basis en uitgelezen wijnen. De kamers vallen hierbij bepaald niet uit de toon.
Spéc. Langoustines au vieux Comté. Fricassée de sole et de homard. Suprême de turbot en croûte, beurre nantais

Le Flore, Duinkerkelaan 19b, ✆ 0 58 41 22 48, *info@leflore.be, Fax 0 58 41 53 36* – ... A p
fermé fin fév.-début fév., fin nov.-debut déc., merc. hors saison et mardi – **Repas** Lunch 27 – 33/83 bc.
◆ Salle à manger contemporaine façon Art déco et registre culinaire classique concédant juste ce qu'il faut aux modes d'aujourd'hui : un bon moment de table en perspective.
◆ Hedendaagse eetzaal in art-decostijl en een klassiek culinair register dat in de juiste proporties toegeeft aan de huidige mode. Verrassend lekker !

Trio's, Nieuwpoortlaan 75, ✆ 0 58 41 13 78, *trio's@vt4.net, Fax 0 58 42 04 16* – ... B k
fermé 1 sem. après carnaval, prem. sem. nov., mardi soir, merc. et dim. soir – **Repas** 27/54 bc.
◆ Aimable petit restaurant presque aussi classique dans son décor que dans ses assiettes, tout doucettement mises à la page. Accueil familial gentil.
◆ Dit vriendelijke restaurantje vormt een mooi klassiek trio van eten, inrichting en service. Hier kunt u heerlijk tafelen in een ongedwongen ambiance.

Host. Avenue, Nieuwpoortlaan 56, ✆ 0 58 41 13 70, *Fax 0 58 41 35 40* – ... B v
fermé 17 nov.-5 déc. et merc. – **Repas** Lunch 33 – carte 39 à 54.
◆ Ici, toque et tablier se transmettent en famille depuis quatre générations. Les menus, quant à eux, tanguent entre tradition et goût du jour, au gré des marées et des saisons.
◆ Hier worden de koksmuts en de voorschoot van generatie op generatie overgedragen. De menu's deinen op de half moderne, half traditionele golven van de (jaar)getijden.

La Coupole, Nieuwpoortlaan 9, ✆ 0 58 41 54 54, *Fax 0 58 42 05 49,* – AE MC VISA A y
fermé 3 dern. sem. janv., merc. de nov. à fév., jeudi et vend. midi – **Repas** Lunch 15 – 40/50.
◆ Établissement sympathique et assez animé, La Coupole entretient une ambiance brasserie. Choix de plats appétissant, service affable et additions sans rondeurs.
◆ In deze leuke brasserie is het altijd druk. Niet verwonderlijk als men de aanlokkelijke kaart, de hoffelijke bediening en de schappelijke prijzen in aanmerking neemt.

@ **De Braise,** Bortierplein 1, ✆ 0 58 42 23 09, *hotelfox@pandora.be,* – AE MC VISA
fermé du 15 au 30 mars, du 15 au 30 nov., merc. soir et vend. midi sauf du 15 sept. au 15 juin et jeudi – **Repas** 33. A g
◆ Estimé pour ses savoureux menus, son livre de cave planétaire et sa belle terrasse estivale dotée de meubles en teck, De Braise a les faveurs d'une clientèle plutôt sélecte.
◆ Hier komt een vrij select publiek, aangetrokken door de smakelijke menu's, de kosmopolitische wijnkelder en het mooie zomerterras met teakhouten meubelen.

Bistrot Merlot, Nieuwpoortlaan 70, ✆ 0 58 41 40 61, *Fax 0 58 41 51 92,* , Ouvert jusqu'à 23 h – MC VISA B h
fermé 14 mars-1er avril, 27 juin-4 juil., jeudi et vend. midi – **Repas** carte 32 à 42, ♀.
◆ Aux portes de la ville, petite affaire familiale qui a le vent en poupe. Recettes "bistrotières", assorties au décor intérieur. Atmosphère décontractée. Ample terrasse d'été.
◆ Dit familiebedrijf aan de rand van de Panne heeft de wind in de zeilen ! De bistrokeuken past uitstekend bij het interieur. Gemoedelijke sfeer. Groot terras in de zomer.

Baan Thai, Sloepenplaats 22, ✆ 0 58 41 49 76, *baanthai@yucom.be, Fax 0 58 41 04 26,* , Cuisine thaïlandaise, ouvert jusqu'à 23 h – AE MC VISA AB z
fermé 16 nov.-16 déc. et mardi et merc. d'oct. à juin sauf vacances scolaires – **Repas** Lunch 14 – carte 25 à 62.
◆ Une valeur sûre parmi les tables asiatiques de La Panne : saveurs thaïlandaises déclinées dans une salle à manger plaisante et choix de vins inhabituel à ce genre de maison.
◆ Van de Aziatische restaurants in De Panne is dit een betrouwbaar adres. Prettige eetzaal, Thaise keuken en voor Oosterse begrippen een goede wijnkaart.

La Bonne Auberge, Zeedijk 3, ✆ 0 58 41 13 98 – AE MC VISA A r
21 mars-21 déc. et week-end ; fermé jeudi – **Repas** carte env. 39.
◆ Typique restaurant aménagé au rez-de-chaussée d'un immeuble du front de mer, La Bonne Auberge vous concocte sans effets de manches de sages menus bien calibrés.
◆ Typisch Belgisch restaurant op een benedenverdieping van een gebouw op de dijk. Hier kunt u genieten van eenvoudige, maar lekkere menu's die bovendien zeer royaal zijn.

Pauillac, Nieuwpoortlaan 55, ✆ 0 58 42 25 86, *pauillac@pandora.be, Fax 0 58 42 25 87,* – AE MC VISA B d
fermé fin nov.-début déc., merc. hors saison et mardi – **Repas** 25/49 bc.
◆ Adresse où touristes et habitués se coudoient en toute convivialité. Salle des repas aux tons guillerets, terrasse d'été fleurie, plats traditionnels et menu à bon prix.
◆ In dit restaurant zitten toeristen en stamgasten gezellig schouder aan schouder. Eetzaal in vrolijke kleuren, fleurig zomerterras, traditionele schotels en goedkope menu's.

Imperial, Leopold I Esplanade 9, ✆ 0 58 41 42 28, *imperial@skynet.be, Fax 0 58 41 33 61,* ≤, , Taverne-rest – 25. AE MC VISA A b
fermé 2 sem. en janv. et merc. – **Repas** 35/65 bc.
◆ Taverne-restaurant "trendy", devant le monument au roi Léopold Ier. Expos d'œuvres d'art en salle, terrasse invitante, vue balnéaire, salles de réunions et "business center".
◆ Trendy taverne tegenover het koning Leopold I-monument. Expositie van kunstwerken in de zaal. Uitnodigend terras met uitzicht op zee. Vergaderzalen met business center.

Parnassia, Zeedijk 103, ✆ 0 58 42 05 20, , Taverne-rest – MC VISA A h
fermé mardi sauf en juil.-août et merc. – **Repas** carte 30 à 48.
◆ À l'extrémité de la digue, grande taverne-bistrot devancée aux beaux jours d'une petite terrasse. On y mange simplement, mais convenablement.
◆ Grote taverne annex bistro aan het eind van de Zeedijk. Op zomerse dagen moet men vechten om een plaatsje op het kleine terras. Eenvoudig, maar goed eten.

PARIKE

9661 Oost-Vlaanderen C *Brakel 13 669 h.* 533 H 18 *et* 716 E 3.
Bruxelles 48 – Gent 47 – Mons 55 – Tournai 42.

Molenwiek , Molenstraat 1, ✆ 0 55 42 26 15, *info@molenwiek.be, Fax 0 55 42 77 29,* , – TV P. VISA
fermé vacances Noël – **Repas** *(fermé dim. soirs non fériés sauf vacances scolaires)* 22/48 – **10 ch** 50/69 – ½ P 50/66.
◆ Villa à fière allure nichée dans un cadre champêtre. Accueil familial avenant, intérieur bourgeois semé de touches rustiques, et chambres classiquement agencées. Derrière ses fourneaux, le chef favorise volontiers les produits régionaux.
◆ Landelijk gelegen villa met allure, waar u gastvrij wordt ontvangen. Traditioneel interieur met rustieke accenten en klassiek ingerichte kamers. Achter het fornuis maakt de chef-kok bij voorkeur streekgerechten klaar.

PEER *3990 Limburg* 533 R 16 *et* 716 J 2 – *15 521 h.*
Bruxelles 99 – Hasselt 30 – Antwerpen 78 – Eindhoven 33.

XX **Fleurie,** Baan naar Bree 27, ☎ 0 11 63 26 33, *fleurie@attglobal.net, Fax 0 11 66 26 33* – AE VISA.
fermé 2 sem. en juil., mardi soir et merc. – **Repas** *Lunch 28* – 36/67 bc, ♀.
◆ Une façade "fleurie" durant tout l'été signale ce petit restaurant sympathique posté à l'entrée du village. Menus attrayants, renouvelés au fil des saisons.
◆ Sympathiek restaurantje dat bij binnenkomst in het dorp 's zomers goed te herkennen is aan zijn fleurige voorgevel. Aantrekkelijke menu's die elk seizoen worden veranderd.

PEPINGEN *1670 Vlaams-Brabant* 533 J 18, 534 J 18 *et* 716 F 3 – *4 289 h.*
Bruxelles 21 – Leuven 55 – Gent 54 – Mons 61.

X **Artmosfeer,** Ninoofsesteenweg 93, ☎ 0 2 361 37 62, *Fax 0 2 361 31 44,* – VISA.
fermé 21 août-12 sept., lundi, mardi, merc. et jeudi midi – **Repas** 36.
◆ Cette affaire familiale a pris ses quartiers dans une ancienne ferme du début du 20e s. Petite salle à manger campagnarde. Cour intérieure où l'on s'attable par beau temps.
◆ Dit familiebedrijfje heeft zijn intrek genomen in een oude boerderij uit de vroege 20e eeuw. Kleine eetzaal in rustieke stijl. Bij mooi weer worden de tafeltjes buiten gedekt.

PEPINSTER *4860 Liège* 533 T 19, 534 T 19 *et* 716 K 4 – *9 325 h.*
Env. *au Sud-Ouest : Tancrémont, Statue★ du Christ dans la chapelle.*
Bruxelles 126 – Liège 26 – Verviers 6.

XXX ✿ **Host. Lafarque** avec ch, Chemin des Douys 20 (Ouest : 4 km par N 61, lieu-dit Goffontaine), ☎ 0 87 46 06 51, *Fax 0 87 46 97 28,* ←, – AE VISA. ch
fermé 3 sem. en mars, 3 sem. en sept., lundi et mardi – **Repas** *(fermé après 20 h 30) Lunch 65 bc* – 70/75, carte 73 à 85 – 13 – **11 ch** 95/150.
◆ Sur les hauteurs, au milieu d'un parc arboré, élégante construction à colombages rappelant les manoirs normands. Les fines fourchettes y sont choyées. Chambres douillettes.
◆ Dit sierlijke vakwerkhuis in Normandische stijl op een heuvel met boomrijk park beschikt over gerieflijke kamers. De keuken zal zelfs het meest verwende gehemelte bevallen.
Spéc. Tartare de tourteaux et caviar osciètre. Turbot, sauce au Vin Jaune. Gibier en saison

X **Au Pot de Beurre,** r. Neuve 116, ☎ 0 87 46 06 43, *aupotbeurre@hotmail.com, Fax 0 87 46 06 43* – AE VISA
fermé du 19 au 28 avril, 16 août-2 sept., du 3 au 12 janv., mardi soir et merc. – **Repas** 25/73 bc.
◆ Un choix de préparations bourgeoises discrètement actualisées entend combler votre appétit à cette adresse du centre de Pepinster. Accueil et service attentionnés, en famille.
◆ Op dit adresje in het centrum kunt u de honger stillen met eenvoudige gerechten die voorzichtig aan de huidige tijd worden aangepast. Attente bediening door een familie.

à Wegnez *Nord : 2 km* C *Pepinster* – ✉ *4860 Wegnez :*

XX **Host. du Postay** avec ch, r. Laurent Mairlot 22, ☎ 0 87 46 14 77, *hostellerie.postay@skynet.be, Fax 0 87 46 00 80,* ←, – AE VISA.
Repas *(fermé du 1er au 10 août, sam. midi, dim. soir et lundi) Lunch 27* – 55/78 bc – **8 ch** 65/75 – ½ P 92.
◆ Ancienne ferme réaménagée en relais de bouche, à débusquer au faîte du village. Ambitieuse carte bien dans le coup. Véranda et restaurant d'été procurant une vue agreste.
◆ Deze oude boerderij, hoog in het dorp, is nu een uitstekend restaurant. Ambitieuze kaart met de nieuwste culinaire trends. Serre en terras met uitzicht op het platteland.

PERWEZ (PERWIJS) *1360 Brabant Wallon* 533 N 19, 534 N 19 *et* 716 H 4 – *7 192 h.*
Bruxelles 46 – Namur 27 – Charleroi 42 – Leuven 35 – Tienen 27.

XX **La Frairie,** av. de la Roseraie 9, ☎ 0 81 65 87 30, *frairie@swing.be, Fax 0 81 65 87 30,* – AE VISA JCB
fermé 2 sem. en mars, fin juil.-début août, fin déc., dim. soir, lundi et mardi – **Repas** *Lunch 24* – 30/70 bc.
◆ L'enseigne n'évoque-t-elle pas une joyeuse partie de plaisir et de bonne chère ? Agréable moment de table en perspective, donc. Mets au goût du jour et menus alléchants.
◆ La Frairie, dat in dialect "het dorpsfeest" betekent, staat garant voor een genoeglijk avondje uit. Kaart met eigentijdse gerechten en verleidelijke menu's.

PETIT-RECHAIN *Liège* 533 U 19, 534 U 19 *et* 716 K 4 – *voir à Verviers.*

PETIT-ROEULX-LEZ-NIVELLES *Hainaut* 533 K 19, 534 K 19 *et* 716 F 4 – *voir à Nivelles.*

PETIT-THIER *Luxembourg belge* 534 U 21 *et* 716 K 5 *- voir à Vielsalm.*

PHILIPPEVILLE *5600 Namur* 534 M 21 *et* 716 G 5 *- 8 042 h.*

au Nord-Est : 10 km à Florennes, r. Henri de Rohan Chabot 120 ☎ 0 71 68 15 40, Fax 0 71 68 88 48.

r. Religieuses 2 ☎ 0 71 66 89 85, tourisme.philippeville@swing.be, Fax 0 71 66 89 85.
Bruxelles 88 - Namur 44 - Charleroi 26 - Dinant 29.

XXX **La Côte d'Or** avec ch, r. Gendarmerie 1, ☎ 0 71 66 81 45, *info@lacotedor.com, Fax 0 71 66 67 97,* - TV P - 25 à 80. AE VISA
Repas *(fermé carnaval, dim. soir, lundi et merc. soir)* Lunch 25 - 35/62 bc, - **8 ch** 48/80 - ½ P 52/97.
◆ Fière villa entourée d'un beau jardin. Salon "cosy", salle à manger classique-actuelle, cave d'exception, espaces de réunions et de banquets et chambres sans reproche.
◆ Fiere villa met een mooie tuin, gezellige lounge, modern-klassieke eetzaal, uitstekende wijnkelder, vergaderruimten, feestzalen en onberispelijke kamers.

X **Aub. des 4 Bras,** r. France 49, ☎ 0 71 66 72 38, *collardfab@swing.be, Fax 0 71 66 93 59,* - P. AE VISA
fermé 2e quinz. fév., 1re quinz. sept., du 24 au 31 déc., dim. soir sauf en juil.-août et lundi - **Repas** Lunch 12 - 22/40.
◆ Auberge postée au croisement de "4 Bras", comme le proclame sa devanture. Les menus, eux aussi, sont à la croisée des chemins : classico-bourgeois et régionaux.
◆ De naam van deze herberg verwijst naar de viersprong waaraan hij is gelegen. De menu's staan op een tweesprong tussen klassiek en regionaal.

De PINTE *Oost-Vlaanderen* 533 G 17 *et* 716 D 3 *- voir à Gent, environs.*

PLANCENOIT *Brabant Wallon* 533 L 19, 534 L 19 *et* 716 G 4 *- voir à Lasne.*

POLLEUR *4910 Liège* C *Theux 11 464 h.* 533 U 19, 534 U 19 *et* 716 K 4.
Bruxelles 129 - Liège 38 - Namur 98 - Maastricht 52 - Vaals 38

Host. le Val de Hoëgne, av. Félix Deblon 1, ☎ 0 87 22 44 26, *val_de_hoegne@hotmail.com, Fax 0 87 22 55 91,* - TV P - 25. VISA.
fermé du 1er au 10 sept. et du 3 au 25 janv. - **Repas** *(fermé mardi et merc. hors saison)* Lunch 25 - carte 26 à 55 - **11 ch** 50/80 - ½ P 46/52.
◆ Petite hostellerie traditionnelle établie sur les rives de la Hoëgne, à l'entrée du village, près du "Vieux Pont". Chambres bien tenues, véranda, terrasse et jeux d'enfants. Chaleureux restaurant au décor néo-rustique. Cuisine actuelle.
◆ Klein traditioneel hotel-restaurant aan de oevers van de Hoëgne, bij de ingang van het dorp, vlak bij de "Oude Brug". Goed onderhouden kamers, serre, terras en speeltuintje. Gezellig restaurant in neorustieke stijl. Eigentijdse keuken.

POPERINGE *8970 West-Vlaanderen* 533 B 17 *et* 716 B 3 *- 19 376 h.*

Grote Markt 1 ☎ 0 57 34 66 76, poperinge@toerismevlaanderen.be, Fax 0 57 33 57 03.
Bruxelles 134 - Brugge 64 - Kortrijk 41 - Oostende 54 - Lille 45.

Manoir Ogygia , Veurnestraat 108, ☎ 0 57 33 88 38, *info@ogygia.be, Fax 0 57 33 88 77,* - TV P. AE VISA JCB.
fermé du 1er au 10 avril et 15 déc.-5 janv. - **Repas** voir rest ***Amfora*** ci-après - **6 ch** 100/110, - 3 suites - ½ P 125/135.
◆ Cet hôtel très charmant met à profit une gentilhommière alanguie dans un parc centenaire. Décor intérieur élégant, belles chambres personnalisées et espace de relaxation.
◆ Dit bijzonder charmante hotel is gevestigd in een kasteeltje met 19e-eeuws park. Fraai interieur, mooie kamers met een persoonlijk tintje ; fitness- en verwenruimte.

Belfort, Grote Markt 29, ☎ 0 57 33 88 88, *hotelbelfort@pandora.be, Fax 0 57 33 74 75,* - TV P - 200. VISA
Repas *(fermé 17 nov.-8 déc., dim. et lundi)* (taverne-rest) Lunch 9 - 22/36 bc - **12 ch** *(fermé 17 nov.-8 déc. et lundi en hiver)* 50/70 - ½ P 55.
◆ Ce petit hôtel du cœur de Poperinge abrite une douzaine de chambres fonctionnelles dont cinq se complètent d'une kitchenette. Accueil familial, affable et souriant. Taverne-restaurant classiquement aménagée.
◆ Dit hotelletje ligt in het hart van Poperinge. Het beschikt over een twaalftal functionele kamers, waarvan vijf zijn uitgerust met een kitchenette. Alleraardigste ontvangst. Het bijbehorende taverne-restaurant is klassiek ingericht.

BELGIQUE

XXX **Pegasus et H. Recour** avec ch, Guido Gezellestraat 7, ☎ 0 57 33 57 25, *info@pegasusrecour.be, Fax 0 57 33 54 25,* – 30. AE VISA JCB.
Repas *(fermé du 12 au 20 avril, du 23 au 31 août, 20 déc.-4 janv., dim. soir et lundi)* Lunch 28 – 43/75 bc – 14 – **8 ch** *(fermé 25 déc.-1er janv.)* 75/225 – ½ P 140/200.
• Table créative officiant dans une belle maison de notable. Élégant décor intérieur alliant classicisme et goût du jour, avenante terrasse et superbes chambres tout confort.
• Restaurant in een mooi herenhuis dat vanbinnen een stijlvolle mix van klassiek en modern vormt. Creatieve chef-kok. Uitnodigend terras en geweldige kamers met alle comfort.

XXX **D'Hommelkeete,** Hoge Noenweg 3 (Sud : 3 km par Zuidlaan), ☎ 0 57 33 43 65, *hommelkeete@yahoo.com, Fax 0 57 33 65 74,* – AE VISA
fermé 20 juil.-20 août, Noël, Nouvel An, dim soir, lundi et merc. soir – **Repas** Lunch 34 – 47/79 bc.
• Jolie fermette agrémentée d'un jardin exquis, avec pièce d'eau. Salle à manger aux accents rustiques. Les jets de houblon sont, en saison, la grande spécialité de la maison.
• Mooi boerderijtje met een schitterende tuin en waterpartij. Eetzaal met rustieke accenten. Hopscheuten of "jets de houblon" zijn in het voorjaar de specialiteit van het huis.

XX **Amfora** - H. Manoir Ogygia, avec ch, Grote Markt 36, ☎ 0 57 33 88 66, *info@amfora.be, Fax 0 57 33 88 77,* – . AE VISA
fermé du 1er au 10 avril et 15 déc.-7 janv. – **Repas** *(fermé merc.)* Lunch 8 – 38/54 bc – **7 ch** 75/80 – ½ P 65.
• Sur la Grand-Place, demeure ancienne dont la typique façade flamande s'anime de pignons à redans. Salle de restaurant cossue, jolies terrasse, véranda et chambres de bon ton.
• Oud pand met een typisch Vlaamse trapgevel aan de Grote Markt. Fraaie eetzaal, aardig terras, veranda en smaakvolle kamers.

XX **'t Hoppeblad en Gasthof De Kring** avec ch, Burg. Bertenplein 7, ☎ 0 57 33 38 61, *info@dekring.be, Fax 0 57 33 92 20,* – – 25 à 200. AE VISA JCB. ch
fermé 16 fév.-4 mars et 26 juil.-12 août – **Repas** *(fermé dim. soir et lundi)* Lunch 9 – 30/49 bc, – **7 ch** 50/70 – ½ P 55/58.
• À l'ombre de St-Bertin, aimable hostellerie où l'on se plie en quatre pour vos banquets et séminaires. Jets de houblon à gogo de février à avril. Chambres pratiques.
• Hotel bij de St-Bertinuskerk, waar het personeel zich uitsloofl om uw feesten en partijen tot een succes te maken. Volop hopscheuten tussen februari en april. Praktische kamers.

XX **Quadrille,** Ieperstraat 21, ☎ 0 57 33 77 41, *appetito@yucom.be, Fax 0 57 33 77 49* – VISA.
fermé août et lundi – **Repas** Lunch 20 – 30/52 bc.
• Un ancien magasin de confection sert de cadre à cet établissement du centre-ville dont le nom vous invite à entrer dans la danse. Choix de préparations au goût du jour.
• Een oud confectiemagazijn is de setting van dit eigentijdse restaurant in het centrum van de stad. Wie weet wordt er na het eten nog de quadrille gedanst...

X **Palace** avec ch, Ieperstraat 34, ☎ 0 57 33 30 93, *palace.hotel@planetinternet.be, Fax 0 57 33 35 35,* – – 25 à 200. AE VISA. rest
fermé 15 juil.-15 août – **Repas** *(fermé merc. et dim. soir)* Lunch 9 – carte 27 à 47 – **11 ch** 50/70 – ½ P 55.
• Accueil familial, ambiance provinciale et repas régional singularisent cet établissement du centre. Salle à manger relookée. Menues chambres de mise simple, mais convenables.
• Vriendelijke ontvangst, provinciale sfeer en goede streekkeuken. De eetzaal heeft onlangs een nieuwe "look" gekregen. De kamers zijn klein en eenvoudig, maar keurig.

POUPEHAN *6830 Luxembourg belge* C *Bouillon 5 393 h.* 534 P 24 *et* 716 I 6.
Bruxelles 165 – Bouillon 12 – Arlon 82 – Dinant 69 – Sedan 23.

à Frahan *Nord : 5 km* C *Bouillon – ✉ 6830 Poupehan :*

Aux Roches Fleuries , r. Crêtes 32, ☎ 0 61 46 65 14, *info@auxrochesfleuries.be, Fax 0 61 46 72 09,* – VISA
fermé mars, 11 nov.-20 déc. sauf week-end et 2 janv.-4 fév. – **Repas** Lunch 20 – 26/52 – 10 – **14 ch** 76/81 – ½ P 65/75.
• Tranquille hostellerie nichée dans un vallon boisé où se glisse la Semois. Les meilleures chambres, avec balcon, se trouvent à l'arrière. Terrasse d'été et jardin délicieux. Salle à manger panoramique. Bons menus à prix raisonnables, servis par table entière.
• Rustig hotel in een bebost dal, waar de Semois zich een weg baant. De beste kamers, met balkon, liggen aan de achterkant. Panoramarestaurant, zomerterras en mooie tuin. Goede menu's voor een zacht prijsje, mits het hele tafelgezelschap hetzelfde menu neemt.

Beau Séjour, r. Tabac 7, 0 61 46 65 21, *info@hotel-beausejour.be, Fax 0 61 46 78 80,* – *fermé 21 juin-9 juil. et 15 déc.-30 janv.* – **Repas** *(fermé mardi soir, merc. et après 20 h 30)* Lunch 19 – 22/39 – **14 ch** 56/75 – ½ P 56/67.

◆ La Semois dessine l'un de ses plus gracieux méandres autour du village au bout duquel s'élève cette mignonne auberge familiale. Chambres de "Beau Séjour". Jardin reposant. Repas classico-bourgeois servi dans un cadre "provincial". Vue sur la vallée.

◆ De Semois meandert sierlijk om Frahan, waar aan het eind deze mooie herberg te vinden is. De kamers bieden een aangenaam verblijf. Rustgevende tuin. In de provinciaal aandoende eetzaal worden klassiek-traditionele maaltijden geserveerd. Uitzicht op het dal.

PROFONDEVILLE *5170 Namur 533 O 20, 534 O 20 et 716 H 4 – 10 907 h.*

Voir Site★.

Env. au Sud-Ouest : 5 km à Annevoie-Rouillon : Parc★★ du Domaine et intérieur★ du château – à l'Est : 5 km à Lustin : Rocher de Frênes★, ≤★.

Chemin du Beau Vallon 45 0 81 41 14 18, Fax 0 81 41 21 42.

Bruxelles 74 – Namur 14 – Dinant 17.

La Sauvenière, chaussée de Namur 57, 0 81 41 33 03, *Fax 0 81 57 02 43,* –
fermé prem. sem. sept. et lundi – **Repas** 20/83 bc.

◆ Table mosane ne manquant pas d'atouts pour séduire : accueil gentil, salle à manger chaleureuse, terrasse d'été invitante... Plats traditionnels et au goût du jour.

◆ Restaurant in de bouwstijl van het Maasland, met een vriendelijke bediening, sfeervolle eetzaal en uitnodigend terras. Traditionele schotels die bij de huidige smaak passen.

La Source Fleurie, av. Général Gracia 11, 0 81 41 22 28, *Fax 0 81 41 21 86,* –
fermé 2e quinz. juin et merc. – **Repas** (déjeuner seult sauf vend. et sam.) Lunch 22 – 40/57 bc.

◆ On découvre bel et bien une source fleurie dans le ravissant jardin de cette villa blanche. La cuisine est classique et la cave "en pince" pour le vignoble autrichien.

◆ De schitterende tuin van deze witte villa staat vol bloemen. De spijzen zijn met een klassiek sausje overgoten en in de kelder liggen tal van Oostenrijkse wijnen.

à Arbre *Sud-Ouest : 5 km par N 928 C Profondeville – ✉ 5170 Arbre :*

L'Eau Vive (Résimont), rte de Floreffe 37, 0 81 41 11 51, *eauvive@netcourrier.com, Fax 0 81 41 40 16,* ≤, –
fermé fin juin, 2 prem. sem. sept., Noël, Nouvel An, dern. sem. janv., mardi et merc. – **Repas** Lunch 30 – 45/90 bc, carte 64 à 80.

◆ Ancienne chaudronnerie blottie au creux d'un vallon boisé. Rafraîchissante terrasse estivale dressée devant la cascade. Côté cuisine, on panache tradition et modernité.

◆ Oude koperslagerij onder in een bebost dal. In de zomer is het terras bij de waterval heerlijk verfrissend. De kookstijl is een combinatie van traditioneel en modern.

Spéc. Truite du vivier au bleu. Foie poêlé à la rhubarbe. Pigeonneau rôti au foin et romarin

PUURS *2870 Antwerpen 533 K 16 et 716 F 2 – 15 813 h.*

Bruxelles 32 – Antwerpen 29 – Gent 50 – Mechelen 18.

à Liezele *Sud : 1,5 km C Puurs – ✉ 2870 Liezele :*

Hof ten Broeck, Liezeledorp 3, 0 3 899 28 00, *Fax 0 3 899 38 10,* ≤ –
fermé 16 août-10 sept., dim. soir, lundi et mardi – **Repas** Lunch 30 – carte env. 60.

◆ Demeure ancienne assez cossue avec sa ceinture de douves et son jardin soigné où dialoguent sculptures et pièce d'eau. L'assiette, dans le tempo actuel, est convaincante.

◆ Weelderig gebouw met een slotgracht en een verzorgde tuin, die wordt opgeluisterd met beeldhouwwerken en een waterpartij. De eigentijdse kookstijl is overtuigend.

QUAREGNON *7390 Hainaut 533 I 20, 534 I 20 et 716 E 4 – 19 006 h.*

Bruxelles 77 – Mons 11 – Tournai 37 – Valenciennes 30.

Dimitri, pl. du Sud 27 (Lourdes), 0 65 66 69 69, *Fax 0 65 66 69 69* –
fermé 3 sem. en août, prem. sem. janv., dim. soir et lundi – **Repas** Lunch 40 bc – 42/80 bc.

◆ Au Nord de Quaregnon, adresse familiale où marbres, fresques et boiseries renvoient aux origines grecques du patron. Menus intéressants. Cave bien montée.

◆ Familierestaurant ten noorden van Quaregnon, waar marmer, fresco's en houtwerk herinneren aan de Griekse afkomst van de baas. Interessante menu's en goede wijnen.

QUENAST *1430 Brabant Wallon* C *Rebecq 9 866 h.* 533 J 18, 534 J 18 *et* 716 F 3.
Bruxelles 28 – Charleroi 51 – Mons 40.

XX **La Ferme du Faubourg,** r. Faubourg 2, ☎ 0 67 63 69 03, *Fax 0 67 63 69 03,* – P. AE ⓓ ⓜ VISA
fermé du 1er au 10 sept., du 3 au 27 janv.-5 fév., lundi et mardi – **Repas** *Lunch 34 bc* – 28/49.
• Les murs de cette grosse ferme brabançonne de plan carré dissimulent une cour avec jardin, où la terrasse est dressée aux beaux jours. Carte assortie de menus et suggestions.
• Grote Brabantse boerderij met een vierkant grondplan, binnenplaats en tuin, waar bij mooi weer op het terras kan worden gegeten. Spijskaart met menu's en suggesties.

RANCE *6470 Hainaut* C *Sivry-Rance 4 529 h.* 534 K 22 *et* 716 F 5.
Bruxelles 92 – Mons 44 – Charleroi 39 – Chimay 12.

XX **La Braisière,** rte de Chimay 13, ☎ 0 60 41 10 83, *Fax 0 60 41 10 83,* – P. AE ⓓ ⓜ VISA
fermé du 15 au 26 mars, du 21 au 30 juin, 23 août-17 sept., mardis et merc. non fériés et après 20 h 30 – **Repas** (déjeuner seult sauf vend. et sam.) *Lunch 36* – 45/69 bc.
• Au bord d'une grand-route, confortable établissement dont la salle à manger feutrée, garnie de meubles de style, se complète d'une orangerie. Cuisine du marché.
• Comfortabel etablissement aan een grote weg. De eetzaal, die met stijlmeubelen is ingericht, is uitgebreid met een oranjerie. Keuken met dagverse producten van de markt.

à Sautin *Nord-Ouest : 4 km* C *Sivry-Rance* – ✉ *6470 Sautin :*

Le Domaine de la Carrauterie sans rest, r. Station 11, ☎ 0 60 45 53 52, *carrauterie@skynet.be, Fax 0 60 45 66 96,* – TV P. AE ⓓ ⓜ VISA.
fermé 24 et 25 déc., 31 déc.-2 janv. et dim. – **5 ch** 72/99.
• Chaleureuse maison de pays où vous serez hébergés dans de tranquilles chambres coquettement personnalisées, façon "cottage". Espace beauté-relaxation. Accueil avenant.
• Dit sfeervolle pand in de steen van de streek biedt rustige kamers in cottagestijl, die er allemaal anders uitzien. Schoonheidssalon en ontspanningscentrum. Attente service.

REBECQ *1430 Brabant Wallon* 533 J 18, 534 J 18 *et* 716 F 4 – *9 866 h.*
Bruxelles 33 – Charleroi 50 – Mons 40.

XX **Nouveau Relais d'Arenberg,** pl. de Wisbecq 30 (par E 429 - A 8, sortie ㉔, lieu-dit Wisbecq), ☎ 0 67 63 60 82, *relais.arenberg@belgacom.net, Fax 0 67 63 72 03,* – P – 25. AE ⓓ ⓜ VISA.
fermé carnaval, 2e quinz. août, lundis midis non fériés, dim. soir et lundi soir – **Repas** *Lunch 16* – 25/55 bc.
• Près de l'église, restaurant dont la terrasse surplombe un jardin plaisant. Lunch avantageux et menu-carte épatant. Intéressant choix de bordeaux rouges.
• Dit restaurant bij de kerk heeft een terras en een mooie tuin. Voordelige lunchformule en een verbluffend goed menu. Interessante selectie rode bordeauxwijnen.

RECOGNE *Luxembourg belge* 534 R 23 *et* 716 J 6 – *voir à Libramont.*

REET *2840 Antwerpen* C *Rumst 14 470 h.* 533 L 16 *et* 716 G 2.
Bruxelles 32 – Antwerpen 17 – Gent 56 – Mechelen 11.

XXX **Pastorale** (De Pooter), Laarstraat 22, ☎ 0 3 844 65 26, *pastorale@belgacom.net, Fax 0 3 844 73 47,* ←, – P – 45. AE ⓓ ⓜ VISA
✿ *fermé du 12 au 22 juil., du 5 au 29 juil., 27 déc.-6 janv., merc. et sam. midi* – **Repas** *Lunch 36* – 50/85 bc, carte 64 à 86.
• Presbytère (19e s.) veillant sur un parc public. Beau jardin, élégante salle à manger bénie des muses (poèmes, œuvres d'art), mets d'aujourd'hui et somptueux livre de cave.
• Deze 19e-eeuwse pastorie kijkt uit op een park. Mooie tuin, elegante eetzaal met beeldende kunst en poëzie aan de muur. Eigentijdse gerechten en prestigieuze wijnen.
Spéc. Farandole aux asperges (mai). Lièvre grillé et compotes hivernales (15 oct.-déc.). Framboises et mousse de chocolat blanc

La REID *Liège* 533 T 20, 534 T 20 *et* 716 K 4 – *voir à Spa.*

REKEM *Limburg* 533 T 17 *et* 716 K 3 – *voir à Lanaken.*

REKKEM *West-Vlaanderen* 533 D 18 *et* 716 C 3 – *voir à Menen.*

REMOUCHAMPS *Liège – voir Sougné-Remouchamps.*

RENAIX *Oost-Vlaanderen – voir Ronse.*

RENDEUX *6987 Luxembourg belge* 533 S 21, 534 S 21 *et* 716 J 5 – *2 212 h.*
Bruxelles 119 – Arlon 83 – Marche-en-Famenne 15 – La Roche-en-Ardenne 11.

XX **Au Moulin de Hamoul,** r. Hotton 86 (lieu-dit Rendeux-Bas), ✆ 0 84 47 81 81, *moulin.de.hamoul@proximedia.be, Fax 0 84 47 81 85,* ← – P – 25. AE MC VISA
fermé fin août, dim. soir, lundi et après 20 h 30 – **Repas** *Lunch 20* – 35/61 bc.
◆ Sur les rives de l'Ourthe, belle maison de pays où l'on vient goûter de sages menus oscillant entre tradition et goût du jour. Salle à manger rajeunie, jardin et terrasse.
◆ Fraai pand in de bouwstijl van de streek, aan de oever van de Ourthe. Mooie menu's die tussen traditioneel en modern schommelen. Gerenoveerde eetzaal, tuin en terras.

RENINGE *8647 West-Vlaanderen* C *Lo-Reninge 3 281 h.* 533 B 17 *et* 716 B 3.
Bruxelles 131 – Brugge 54 – Ieper 22 – Oostende 53 – Veurne 21.

XXXX ✿ **'t Convent** (De Volder) avec ch, Halve Reningestraat 1 (Ouest : 3 km, direction Oostvleteren), ✆ 0 57 40 07 71, *convent@itinera.be, Fax 0 57 40 11 27,* ←, – ch, TV P – 25. AE MC VISA
fermé 18 fév.-11 mars et 23 août-2 sept. – **Repas** *(fermé merc.)* 50/115, carte 83 à 121 – 18 – **10 ch** 110/200, – 4 suites – ½ P 180/275.
◆ Délicieuse hostellerie pleine de caractère : au dehors, truffière, vigne, jardin fleuri, et les polders pour toile de fond ; au dedans, cadre raffiné, chambres de même.
◆ Sfeervol hotel met karakter en een verfijnde inrichting, ook in de kamers. Op het landgoed liggen een truffelveld, wijngaard en bloementuin en dat midden in de polders !
Spéc. Homard norvégien, salade de légumes croquants. Filet de turbot aux pâtes fraîches et truffe. La truffe dans toute sa splendeur

RESTEIGNE *6927 Luxembourg belge* C *Tellin 2 282 h.* 534 Q 22 *et* 716 I 5.
Bruxelles 116 – Bouillon 49 – Dinant 35 – Namur 57.

Host. de la Lesse , Grand'rue 25, ✆ 0 84 38 81 29, *info@lesse.com, Fax 0 84 38 83 82,* – TV P – 25. AE MC VISA
fermé lundis, mardis et merc. non fériés sauf en juil.-août – **Repas** *Lunch 33* – 37/70 bc – **9 ch** 65/85 – ½ P 65/75.
◆ Au centre d'un village ardennais, vénérable enseigne tenue par la même famille depuis quatre générations. L'intérieur bénéficie d'une décoration soignée. Chambres paisibles. Restaurant avec véranda donnant sur le grand jardin. Recettes traditionnelles.
◆ Dit eerbiedwaardige hotel is al vier generaties in handen van dezelfde familie en staat in het centrum van een dorp in de Ardennen. Verzorgd interieur en rustige kamers. Restaurant met serre die uitkijkt op een grote tuin. Traditionele keuken.

RETIE *2470 Antwerpen* 533 P 15 *et* 716 I 2 – *9 899 h.*
Bruxelles 89 – Eindhoven 38 – Antwerpen 51 – Turnhout 12.

XXX **De Pas,** Passtraat 11, ✆ 0 14 37 80 35, *depas@pandora.be, Fax 0 14 37 33 36,* – AE MC VISA.
fermé lundi, mardi et sam. midi – **Repas** *Lunch 30* – 45/78, ♀.
◆ La salle à manger de cette demeure du 17e s. renferme une collection d'antiquités, dont quelques jolies toiles et des pièces en bronze. Registre culinaire assez ambitieux.
◆ De eetzaal van dit mooie 17e-eeuwse pand bevat een antiekverzameling, waaronder enkele fraaie schilderijen en bronzen beelden. Het culinaire register is tamelijk ambitieus.

RHODE-ST-GENÈSE *Région de Bruxelles-Capitale – voir Sint-Genesius-Rode à Bruxelles, environs.*

RIEMST *3770 Limburg* 533 S 18 *et* 716 J 3 – *15 755 h.*
Bruxelles 111 – Maastricht 9 – Hasselt 30 – Liège 24.

à Millen *Sud : 3 km* C *Riemst* – ✉ *3770 Millen :*

XX **Hoeve Dewalleff,** Tikkelsteeg 13, ✆ 0 12 23 70 89, *info@hoeve-dewalleff.be, Fax 0 12 26 25 30,* – P – 25 à 450. AE MC VISA
fermé mardi, merc. et dim. soir – **Repas** *Lunch 29* – 32/55 bc.
◆ Ferme limbourgeoise du 17e s. dissimulant une cour intérieure fleurie. Un restaurant assez charmant et plusieurs salles de banquets se partagent les ailes du bâtiment.
◆ Limburgse hoeve uit de 17e eeuw met een binnenplaats vol bloemen. In de vleugels zijn een sfeervol restaurant en een aantal feestzalen ondergebracht.

RIJKEVORSEL *2310 Antwerpen* 533 N 14 *et* 716 H 1 – *10 464 h.*
Bruxelles 80 – Antwerpen 34 – Turnhout 16 – Breda 41.

XX **Waterschoot,** Bochtenstraat 11, ☎ 0 3 314 78 78, *info@restaurant-waterschoot.be, Fax 0 3 314 78 78,* – VISA.
fermé 22 fév.-1er mars, 16 août-6 sept., dim. et lundi – **Repas** Lunch 29 – 25/71 bc, ♀.
◆ Au cœur du village, adresse familiale où, par beau temps, les parasols envahissent le jardin situé sur l'arrière. Carte saisonnière comportant menus et suggestions.
◆ Familierestaurant in het midden van het dorp. In de tuin aan de achterkant worden bij mooi weer de parasols opengeklapt. Seizoengebonden kaart met menu's en suggesties.

RIJMENAM *Antwerpen* 533 M 16 *et* 716 G 2 – *voir à Mechelen.*

RIVIÈRE *5170 Namur* C *Profondeville 10 907 h.* 533 O 20, 534 O 20 *et* 716 H 4.
Bruxelles 78 – Namur 16 – Charleroi 38 – Dinant 15 – Liège 77 – Wavre 54.

Les 7 meuses, r. Sarte à Soilles 27, ☎ 0 81 25 75 75, *Fax 0 81 25 75 70,* vallée de la Meuse (Maas), – P. VISA.
fermé janv.-fév., lundi et mardi en nov.-déc., sam. midi et dim. midi – **Repas** (taverne-rest) Lunch 15 – carte 29 à 45 – **6 ch** 50/80.
◆ Perché tel un nid d'aigle sur un coteau mosan, cet hôtel de style contemporain offre, depuis chaque chambre, une vue inoubliable sur la vallée et les méandres du fleuve. Ample taverne-restaurant panoramique au "look" design. Superbe échappée en terrasse.
◆ Dit moderne hotel ligt als een adelaarsnest hoog op een heuvel langs de Maas. Elke kamer biedt een adembenemend uitzicht op het dal en de meanders van de rivier. Groot panoramarestaurant met designmeubelen. Ook het terras biedt een schitterend uitzicht.

RIXENSART *Brabant Wallon* 533 M 18, 534 M 18 *et* 716 G 3 – *voir à Genval.*

ROBERTVILLE *4950 Liège* C *Waimes 6 559 h.* 533 V 20, 534 V 20 *et* 716 L 4.
Voir *Lac*★, ≤★.
r. Centrale 53 ☎ *0 80 44 64 75, robertville@ com,* Fax 0 80 44 66 64.
Bruxelles 154 – Liège 58 – Malmédy 14 – Aachen 40.

Domaine des Hautes Fagnes, r. Charmilles 67 (lieu-dit Ovifat), ☎ 0 80 44 69 87, *info@hotel2.be, Fax 0 80 44 69 19,* – P – 25 à 130. AE VISA.
Repas (résidents seult) – **70 ch** 97/148, – 1 suite – ½ P 99/122.
◆ Parc et forêt encadrent cet hôtel contemporain dont les chambres, réparties sur deux étages, sont garnies d'un mobilier actuel. Infrastructures pour se réunir et se divertir. À table, répertoire culinaire de base classique, actualisé à petits pas.
◆ Dit eigentijdse hotel wordt omgeven door een park en een bos. De kamers zijn modern gemeubileerd en liggen op twee verdiepingen. Talrijke faciliteiten om werk en plezier te combineren. Klassieke keuken die voorzichtig aan de huidige tijd wordt aangepast.

La Chaumière du Lac, r. Barrage 23 (lieu-dit Ovifat), ☎ 0 80 44 63 39, *ch-lac@sky net.be, Fax 0 80 44 46 01,* – P. VISA. rest
fermé 2 prem. sem. juil. – **Repas** *(fermé lundi et mardi hors saison et après 20 h 30)* 22/40 – **10 ch** 57/84 – ½ P 59/75.
◆ Imposante villa dont le toit de chaume bien peigné encapuchonne quelques chambres tant fonctionnelles que plaisantes. Le jardin invite à "décompresser". Salle de restaurant en accord avec son temps. Accueil chaleureux.
◆ Deze imposante villa met rieten dak bezit kamers die zowel functioneel als aangenaam zijn. De tuin nodigt uit tot relaxen. De eetzaal is in eigentijdse stijl ingericht. Hartelijke ontvangst.

Host. du Chêneux, Chemin du Chêneux 32 (lieu-dit Ovifat), ☎ 0 80 44 04 00, *info@cheneux.be, Fax 0 80 44 04 10,* – P. VISA
Repas (dîner pour résidents seult) – **8 ch** 57/84 – ½ P 59/67.
◆ Une rue en cul-de-sac conduit à ce nouvel établissement familial s'entourant d'un jardin avec pièce d'eau. Chambres équipées d'un mobilier récent.
◆ Een doodlopende straat leidt naar dit nieuwe familiehotel, dat wordt omringd door een tuin met een waterpartij. De kamers zijn geriefelijk.

Aub. du Lac, r. Lac 24, ☎ 0 80 44 41 59, *Fax 0 80 44 58 20,* – P. VISA. ch
Repas *(fermé lundi et mardi)* (taverne-rest) carte 22 à 30 – **6 ch** 38/55.
◆ En traversant Robertville, l'automobiliste fatigué comme le randonneur fourbu trouveront le repos dans cette maison familiale jouxtant l'église. Chambres de bon confort. Grande salle à manger dont la décoration recrée quelque peu l'atmosphère d'une ferme.
◆ Vermoeide automobilisten en wandelaars kunnen heerlijk uitrusten in de comfortabele kamers van dit familiehotel naast de kerk. De grote eetzaal is onlangs opnieuw gedecoreerd en ademt een beetje de sfeer van een oude boerderij.

International, r. Lac 41, ✆ 0 80 44 62 58, *hotelinternational@belgique.com, Fax 0 80 44 76 93,* ☂ – 25. AE ⓓ MC VISA. ✂ rest
fermé 21 juin-2 juil., 20 sept.-8 oct., du 5 au 30 janv., mardi et merc. – **Repas** *(fermé après 20 h 30)* 25/45 – **11 ch** ☕ 43/67 – ½ P 54/63.
◆ Au cœur de la localité, derrière une façade blanche, affaire tenue en famille disposant de chambres assez simples mais nettes, auxquelles s'ajoute une salle de réunion.
◆ Dit hotel met witte gevel staat in het centrum van Robertville en is eigendom van een familie. De kamers zijn vrij eenvoudig, maar netjes en er is ook een vergaderzaal.

du Barrage, r. Barrage 46, ✆ 0 80 44 62 61, *Fax 0 80 44 88 47,* ≤ lac, ☂ – MC VISA
fermé 2 sem. en mars, 2 dern. sem. août, 2 dern. sem. nov., lundi soir et mardi – **Repas** Lunch 14 – 26/44 bc.
◆ Cet établissement familial surveillant la route jouit d'un panorama enviable sur le barrage et son lac de retenue. Par beau temps, le repas peut se prendre en terrasse.
◆ Dit familierestaurant dat boven de weg uitsteekt, biedt een schitterend panorama van de dam en het stuwmeer. Op zonnige dagen kan op het terras worden gegeten.

Si vous cherchez un hôtel tranquille,
consultez d'abord les cartes de l'introduction
ou repérez dans le texte les établissements indiqués avec le signe ♘

La ROCHE-EN-ARDENNE *6980 Luxembourg belge* 534 *S 21 et* 716 *J 5 – 4 117 h.*

Voir *Site*★★ – *Chapelle Ste-Marguerite* ✳★★ A B.

Env. *par* ② : *14,5 km, Belvédère des Six Ourthe*★★, *le Hérou*★★ – *Point de vue des Crestelles*★.

pl. du Marché 15 ✆ *0 84 41 13 42, infolr@skynet.be,* Fax 0 84 41 23 43 – Fédération provinciale de tourisme, Quai de l'Ourthe 9 ✆ 0 84 41 10 11, *info@ftlb.be, Fax 0 84 41 24 39.*

Bruxelles 127 ⑤ – *Bouillon 69* ④ – *Arlon 75* ④ – *Liège 77* ① – *Namur 66* ⑤

LA ROCHE-EN-ARDENNE

Bastogne (Rte de) .... A 2
Beausaint (R. de) ..... B 3
Beausaint (Vlle Rte de) . A 4
Bon-Dieu-de-Maka (R.) . B 7
Châlet (R. du) .... B 8
Chamont (R.) .... B 10
Champlon (Rte de) .... A 12
Chanteraine (Pl.) ..... B 13
Chanteraine (R. de) ... B 14
Chats (R. des) .... B 15
Cielle (Rte de) .... A 16
Église (R. de l') ...... B 17
Faubourg (Pont du) .. B 18
Gare (R. de la) .... B 20
Gravier (Pt du) .... B 21
Gravier (Q. du) .... B 22
Hospice (R. de l') ..... B 24
Hotton (Rte de) .... A 25
Marché (Pl. du) .... B 27
Moulin (R. du) .... B 28
Nulay (R.) .... B 30
Ourthe (Q. de l') ..... B 32
Pafy (Ch. du) .... A 33
Presbytère (R. du) .... B 35
Purnalet (R. du) ...... B 36
Rompré (R.) .... B 37
Val-du-Pierreux ...... A 39

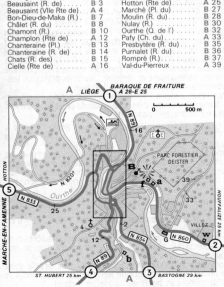

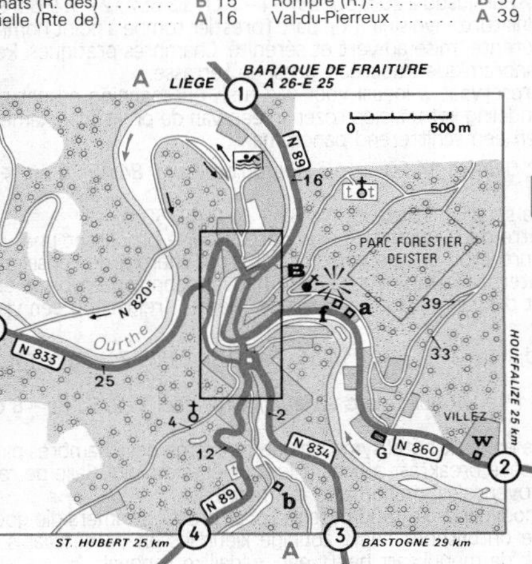

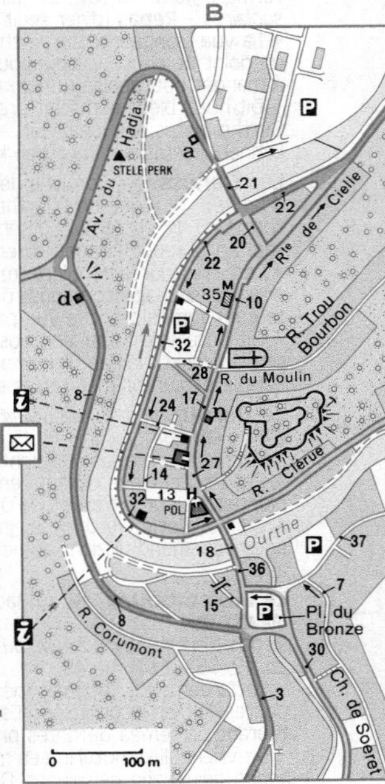

BELGIQUE

Host. Linchet, rte de Houffalize 11, ☎ 0 84 41 13 27, *hostellerie.linchet@skynet.be, Fax 0 84 41 24 10*, <, – TV P. AE MC VISA. ch A w
fermé 15 mars-2 avril, 22 juin-16 juil., du 3 au 21 janv., mardi et merc. – **Repas** *(fermé après 20 h)* (déjeuner seult sauf week-end et en juil.-août) 33/77 bc – 8 – **11 ch** 87/104 – ½ P 75/88.
◆ Une atmosphère cossue flotte dans cette grosse villa bâtie au pied d'un coteau verdoyant. Décor et mobilier personnalisés dans chaque chambre. Restaurant bien installé, dont les grandes baies vitrées et la terrasse procurent une jolie vue sur la vallée.
◆ Deze grote villa aan de voet van een groene heuvel straalt een en al luxe uit. De kamers hebben een persoonlijk karakter. Gunstig gelegen restaurant, waarvan de grote glaspuien en het terras een fraai uitzicht bieden op het dal.

La Claire Fontaine, rte de Hotton 64 (par ⑤ : 2 km), ☎ 0 84 41 24 70, *logis@clairefontaine.be, Fax 0 84 41 21 11*, <, – TV P. – 25 à 80. AE MC VISA
Repas Lunch 19 – 25/84 bc – **28 ch** 65/113 – ½ P 73/106.
◆ Cette bâtisse massive bordant une route "carte postale" abrite des chambres spacieuses ; la plupart d'entre elles donnent sur un plaisant jardin ombragé baigné par l'Ourthe. Salle à manger garnie de meubles de style. Véranda apéritive.
◆ Massief gebouw aan een weg die zo op een ansichtkaart kan. Ruime kamers, waarvan de meeste uitkijken op een mooie schaduwrijke tuin, waar de Ourthe langsloopt. De eetzaal is met stijlmeubelen ingericht. Het aperitief wordt in de serre gebruikt.

Moulin de la Strument , Petite Strument 62, ☎ 0 84 41 15 07, *strument@skynet.be, Fax 0 84 41 10 80*, – TV P. MC VISA. A b
fermé janv. – **Repas** *(fermé lundis, mardis et merc. non fériés sauf en juil.-août)* Lunch 22 – carte 30 à 44 – **8 ch** 69/76 – ½ P 62/93.
◆ Hôtel tranquille aménagé dans les dépendances d'un moulin à eau auquel se consacre un petit musée. Fringantes chambres habillées de tissus coordonnés. Restaurant au "look" rustique-contemporain, devancé d'une brasserie. Répertoire culinaire traditionnel.
◆ Rustig hotel in de bijgebouwen van een watermolen, waaraan een klein museum is gewijd. De kamers zien er met hun bijpassende stoffen tiptop uit. De modern-rustieke eetzaal ligt achter een brasserie. Traditioneel culinair repertoire.

Le Chalet, r. Chalet 61, ☎ 0 84 41 24 13, *lechalet@skynet.be, Fax 0 84 41 13 38*, < – TV P. AE MC VISA. B d
fermé 2 jjanv.-13 fév., 22 juin-6 juil., du 1er au 20 déc. et lundi et mardi sauf vacances scolaires – **Repas** (dîner seult jusqu'à 20 h 30) 33/48 – **17 ch** 62/77 – ½ P 72/96.
◆ La vue plongeante sur le château, la ville et le méandre de l'Ourthe font de cet hôtel un point de chute valable pour découvrir les richesses de ce petit coin d'Ardenne. Salle à manger bourgeoise où l'on goûte des plats classiques et traditionnels.
◆ Dit hotel biedt een schitterend uitzicht op het kasteel, de stad en de meander van de Ourthe. Het is een ideale uitvalsbasis om de rijkdommen van dit stukje Ardennen te verkennen. Restaurant met een klassiek-traditionele inrichting en dito keuken.

Les Genêts , Corniche de Deister 2, ☎ 0 84 41 18 77, *info@lesgenets.be, Fax 0 84 41 18 93*, < vallée de l'Ourthe et ville, – TV P. AE MC VISA. A f
fermé du 1er au 15 juil., 1 sem. en sept., 3 sem. en janv., merc. de nov. à mars et jeudi sauf en juil.-août – **Repas** (dîner seult jusqu'à 20 h 30) 25/34 – **7 ch** 65/72 – ½ P 64/90.
◆ Cette ressource hôtelière "miniature" avoisinant un parc forestier tombe à point nommé pour qui souhaite conjuguer détente, mise au vert et sérénité. Chambres pratiques. Restaurant familial dont la vue panoramique s'apprécie aussi en terrasse.
◆ Dit hotelletje naast een bosreservaat is ideaal voor wie rust, ontspanning en natuurschoon zoekt. Na een flinke wandeling ligt u als op rozen in een van de praktische kamers. Familierestaurant met terras en een schitterend panorama.

Le Hérou, av. de Villez 53, ☎ 0 84 41 14 20, *info@leherou.be, Fax 0 84 45 72 20*, < – TV P. MC VISA A a
fermé janv. – **Repas** (résidents seult) – **10 ch** 44/81 – ½ P 49/58.
◆ Petit hôtel élevé durant l'entre-deux-guerres sur un coteau boisé procurant une vue plongeante sur la vallée de l'Ourthe où chasse parfois le "Hérou" (héron) de l'enseigne.
◆ Dit hotelletje werd in het interbellum op een beboste heuvel gebouwd en biedt een adembenemend uitzicht op het dal van de Ourthe, waar de "Hérou" (reiger) op een visje aast.

Le Luxembourg, av. du Hadja 1a, ☎ 0 84 41 14 15, *Fax 0 84 41 19 71*, – TV P. AE MC VISA B a
Repas *(fermé janv.-12 fév., du 1er au 10 juil., merc. et jeudi)* (dîner seult) 22/51 bc – **8 ch** 42/55 – ½ P 44/49.
◆ Cette demeure 1900 recyclée en petit hôtel sympathique renferme des chambres pimpantes et bien insonorisées. Espace breakfast affichant les couleurs du Midi. Salle de restaurant parsemée de notes provençales, menu-carte de même.
◆ Dit vriendelijke hotel in een mooi pand uit 1900 beschikt over prettige kamers die goed tegen geluid zijn geïsoleerd. De ontbijthoek heeft zonnige kleurtjes en de eetzaal is in Provençaalse stijl ingericht. Ook de menukaart heeft een zuidelijke tongval.

XX **La Huchette,** r. Église 6, ☎ 0 84 41 13 33, *Fax 0 84 41 13 33*, – AE MC VISA
fermé prem. sem. juil., 2 sem. en janv., lundis soirs, mardis soirs et merc. non fériés sauf en saison – **Repas** 23/50. B n
◆ À l'intérieur règnent le bois et la brique, tandis qu'à l'extérieur la terrasse d'été vit au rythme d'une rue commerçante. Cuisine classique. Gibier en saison de chasse.
◆ Rustgevend interieur met hout en steen en een rumoerig terras in de drukke winkelstraat. Klassieke keuken en wildgerechten in het seizoen, maar de rekening is niet gepeperd!

à Jupille *par ⑤ : 6 km* C *Rendeux 2 212 h.* – ✉ *6987 Hodister :*

Host. Relais de l'Ourthe, r. Moulin 3, ☎ 0 84 47 76 88, *relais@pi.be, Fax 0 84 47 70 85*, , , – ch, TV P. MC VISA.
fermé 28 juin-8 juil., 25 août-2 sept. et du 1er au 25 janv. – **Repas** *(fermé mardi et merc.)* Lunch 21 – 37/75 bc, ♀ – **9 ch** 70 – ½ P 57/87.
◆ Cette ancienne ferme du 17e s. bâtie en léger contrebas de la route possède un adorable jardin. Pour un maximum d'agrément, offrez-vous la junior-suite aménagée sous le toit. Restaurant au décor intérieur soigné. L'été, repas-plaisir au jardin.
◆ Deze 17e-eeuwse boerderij ligt iets lager dan de weg en heeft een prachtige tuin. De junior suite op de zolderverdieping is het mooist. Het restaurant heeft een verzorgd interieur. 's Zomers mag u zich het genoegen van een maaltijd in de tuin niet ontzeggen!

XX **Les Tilleuls** avec ch, Clos Champs 11, ☎ 0 84 47 71 31, *info@les-tilleuls.be, Fax 0 84 47 79 55*, ≤ vallée de l'Ourthe, , , – TV P – 25. AE MC VISA
fermé janv. et dim. soir, lundi et mardi hors saison – **Repas** *(fermé après 20 h 30)* Lunch 25 – 42/70 bc – **8 ch** 64/76 – ½ P 63/89.
◆ Villa tranquille dont le délicieux jardin embrasse du regard l'agreste vallée de l'Ourthe. On ripaille en plein air dès l'arrivée des beaux jours. Chambres pratiques.
◆ Rustige villa met een weelderige tuin, die een weids uitzicht biedt op het Ourthedal. Bij de eerste zonnestralen worden de tafeltjes buiten gedekt. Praktische kamers.

ROCHEFORT *5580 Namur* 534 *Q 22 et* 716 *I 5 – 11 818 h.*
Voir *Grotte★.*
Env. *au Sud-Ouest : 6 km à Han-sur-Lesse, Grotte★★★ - Safari★ - Fragment de diplôme★ (d'un vétéran romain) dans le Musée du Monde souterrain – au Nord-Ouest : 15 km à Chevetogne, Domaine provincial Valéry Cousin★.*
r. Behogne 5 ☎ 0 84 21 25 37, rochefort.tourisme@skynet.be, Fax 0 84 22 13 74.
Bruxelles 117 – Bouillon 52 – Namur 58 – Dinant 32 – Liège 71.

Le Vieux Logis sans rest, r. Jacquet 71, ☎ 0 84 21 10 24, *Fax 0 84 22 12 30*, – TV. AE MC VISA
fermé 15 sept.-1er oct. et dim. – **10 ch** 52/64.
◆ Hôtel familial occupant un logis charmant élevé au soir du 17e s. L'intérieur conserve de beaux vestiges du passé : portes, poutres, planchers... Chambres assez mignonnes.
◆ Dit familiehotel is ondergebracht in een sfeervol pand uit de late 17e eeuw, waarvan de deuren, balken en vloeren nog origineel zijn. De kamers zien er aantrekkelijk uit.

XX **Les Falizes** avec ch, r. France 90, ☎ 0 84 21 12 82, *Fax 0 84 22 10 86*, , – TV P. AE MC VISA
fermé fin janv.-début mars, lundi soir etmardi – **Repas** Lunch 23 – 48/50 – 8 – **6 ch** 53/60 – ½ P 75/80.
◆ Auberge typique où l'on se sent tout de suite entre de bonnes mains. Salon feutré, salle à manger bourgeoise, belle carte classique et cave unique. Terrasse et jardin soignés.
◆ In deze Ardense herberg bent u in goede handen. Mooie salon, eetzaal in bourgeoisstijl, klassieke kaart en goede wijnen. Terras en verzorgde tuin.

XX **Le Limbourg** avec ch, pl. Albert Ier 21, ☎ 0 84 21 10 36, *info@hotellimbourg.com, Fax 0 84 21 44 23* – TV. AE MC VISA
fermé du 15 au 31 janv. – **Repas** *(fermé merc.)* Lunch 16 – 22/44 – **6 ch** 44/56 – ½ P 52.
◆ Enseigne du centre de Rochefort qui vous paraîtra pour le moins atypique dans ce contexte bas-ardennais. Les chambres, plus ou moins spacieuses, se trouvent à l'étage.
◆ De naam van dit restaurant in het hart van Rochefort ligt niet bepaald voor de hand in de Lage Ardennen. De kamers zijn van verschillende grootte.

X **Trou Maulin,** rte de Marche 19, ☎ 0 84 21 32 40, *troumaulin@tiscali.be, Fax 0 84 21 32 40*, – P. AE MC VISA.
fermé mardi et merc. – **Repas** Lunch 17 – 25/47 bc.
◆ Cette auberge familiale bordant la Lomme a récemment fait peau neuve et est aisément repérable par l'automobiliste. L'été, les repas se prennent aussi sous la pergola.
◆ Deze herberg aan de Lomme is pas gerenoveerd en makkelijk te vinden voor automobilisten. Als het weer geen roet in het eten gooit, wordt de maaltijd onder de pergola gebruikt.

BELGIQUE

Le Relais du Château, r. Jacquet 22, 0 84 21 09 81, *michelalbert@tiscali.be, Fax 0 84 21 09 81,* – . AE VISA
fermé 21 fév.-2 mars et merc. soir et jeudi hors saison – **Repas** Lunch 18 – 24/33.
◆ Aux portes de la petite cité qui hébergea Lafayette, adresse bien appréciée de la clientèle locale. Salle à manger d'esprit néo-rustique. Moules à gogo en saison.
◆ Dit restaurant aan de rand van het stadje waar La Fayette heeft gelogeerd, valt zeer in de smaak bij de bevolking. Neorustieke eetzaal met volop mosselen in het seizoen.

à Belvaux *Sud-Ouest : 9 km* *Rochefort* – *5580 Belvaux :*

Aub. des Pérées avec ch, r. Pairées 37, 0 84 36 62 77, *aubergeperees@skynet.be, Fax 0 84 36 72 05,* , – VISA
fermé dern. sem. sept.-prem. sem. oct., dern. sem. janv.-prem. sem. fév., mardi soir et merc. sauf en juil.-août et mardi midi – Repas *(fermé après 20 h 30)* 25/60 bc, – **6 ch** 60 – ½ P 62.
◆ Auberge sympathique réservant un bon accueil. En été, le couvert est dressé sur la terrasse fleurie, face au jardin. Repas goûteux. Chambres paisibles, à l'image du patelin.
◆ Deze sympathieke herberg bereidt u een hartelijke ontvangst. Rustige kamers en lekker eten. In de zomer worden de tafeltjes gedekt op het bloemrijke terras aan de tuinzijde.

à Eprave *Sud-Ouest : 7 km* *Rochefort* – *5580 Eprave :*

Aub. du Vieux Moulin avec ch en annexe , r. Aujoule 51, 0 84 37 73 18, *auberge@eprave.com, Fax 0 84 37 84 60,* , , – – 25. AE VISA
fermé 5 janv.-9 fév., 30 août-8 sept. et dim. soir, lundi et mardi soir sauf vacances scolaires – **Repas** Lunch 22 – 33/50 bc, – **14 ch** 90/125 – ½ P 88.
◆ Ancienne maison paroissiale côtoyant l'église et l'une des rives de la Lomme. Chambres design à l'annexe. En terrasse, vue sur le mouvement des roues à aubes du vieux moulin.
◆ Herberg in de voormalige pastorie naast de kerk, aan de Lomme. Designkamers in het bijgebouw. Het terras biedt uitzicht op het schoepenrad van de oude molen.

à Han-sur-Lesse *Sud-Ouest : 6 km* *Rochefort* – *5580 Han-sur-Lesse :*

des Ardennes (annexe Ardennes 2 -), r. Grottes 2, 0 84 37 72 20, *Fax 0 84 37 80 62,* , – – 30. AE VISA
Repas *(fermé du 3 au 31 janv. et merc.)* Lunch 19 – 22/35 – **27 ch** 68/78 – ½ P 74.
◆ Agréable hostellerie familiale toute proche de la sortie des grottes de Han. Chambres ayant récemment retrouvé l'éclat du neuf. L'annexe, côté jardin, abrite les meilleures. Bonne table classique-bourgeoise devancée d'une terrasse couverte.
◆ Aangenaam familiehotel bij de beroemde grotten van Han. De kamers hebben pas een verjongingskuur ondergaan ; die in het bijgebouw, aan de tuinzijde, zijn het rustigst. Goed restaurant met een klassiek-traditionele keuken en overdekt terras.

ROCHEHAUT *6830 Luxembourg belge* *Bouillon 5 393 h.* 534 P 23 *et* 716 I 6.
Voir ★★. – *r. Palis 7* *0 61 46 40 60, Fax 0 61 46 83 82.*
Bruxelles 159 – Bouillon 20 – Arlon 76 – Dinant 63 – Sedan 26.

L'Aub. de la Ferme (annexes), r. Cense 12, 0 61 46 10 00, *Fax 0 61 46 10 01,* , , , – – 50. AE VISA. rest
fermé du 5 au 16 janv. – **Repas** *(fermé après 20 h 30)* 30/60 – **60 ch** 56/74, – 1 suite – ½ P 65/139.
◆ Ambiances ardennaises, maisons de pays et chambres douillettes réparties aux quatre coins du village : une auberge rustique tient lieu de case-départ à ce "jeu de l'oie". Cuisine actuelle connotée "terroir" et caveau où bonifient quelque 50 000 bouteilles.
◆ Deze rustieke Ardense herberg lijkt wel het eerste hokje van een ganzenbordspel, want de behaaglijke kamers zijn verspreid in huizen door het hele dorp. Eigentijdse keuken met regionale invloeden en een wijnkelder met zo'n 50 000 flessen.

Les Tonnelles, pl. Marie Howet 5, 0 61 46 40 18, *info@tonnelles.com, Fax 0 61 46 40 12,* – . VISA. rest
fermé 20 juin-4 juil. et du 4 au 29 janv. – **Repas** carte 22 à 36 – **17 ch** 58/68 – ½ P 53.
◆ Adresse opportune pour s'offrir un repas classico-traditionnel sans ronds de jambes ou une bonne nuit de sommeil après une épuisante balade en forêt.
◆ Dit adres is geschikt voor een klassiek-traditionele maaltijd zonder franje of een goede nachtrust na een stevige wandeling in het bos.

L'An 1600 avec ch, r. Palis 7, 0 61 46 40 60, *an1600@an1600.be, Fax 0 61 46 83 82,* , , – . AE VISA
avril-20 nov., 20 déc.-2 janv. et week-end ; fermé 22 juin-14 juil. – **Repas** *(fermé après 20 h 30)* Lunch 20 – 22/50 – **9 ch** 90 – ½ P 70.
◆ Ancienne ferme avoisinant l'église. Ambiance familiale, restaurant au cadre rustique ardennais, mignonne cave convertie en salon, amples chambres bien agencées.
◆ Oude boerderij naast de kerk. Huiselijke sfeer, restaurant in rustieke Ardense stijl, sfeervolle kelder die tot lounge is verbouwd en ruime, goed ingerichte kamers.

ROCOURT *Liège* 533 S 18, 534 S 18 *et* 716 J 3 – *voir à Liège, périphérie.*

ROESELARE (ROULERS) *8800 West-Vlaanderen* 533 *D 17 et* 716 *C 3 – 54 688 h.*

Zuidstraat 3 ☎ 0 51 26 24 50, infowinkel@roeselare.be, Fax 0 51 26 24 60.

Bruxelles 111 ③ – Kortrijk 20 ③ – Brugge 34 ① – Lille 45 ③

Parkhotel (annexe Flanders Inn - 16 ch), Vlamingstraat 8, ☎ 0 51 26 31 31, *info@parkhotel-roeselare.be, Fax 0 51 26 31 13,* – – 25 à 50. AE VISA JCB BY a

Repas *(fermé du 1er au 23 août, dim. et lundi midi)* Lunch 12 – 22/50 bc – **42 ch** 75/105, – 4 suites.

◆ Cet établissement familial de conception moderne et sa nouvelle annexe, le Flanders Inn, se partagent des chambres d'ampleur identique, correctement insonorisées.

◆ Dit moderne familiehotel en zijn nieuwe dependance, de Flanders Inn, beschikken over kamers van dezelfde grootte met een goede geluidsisolatie.

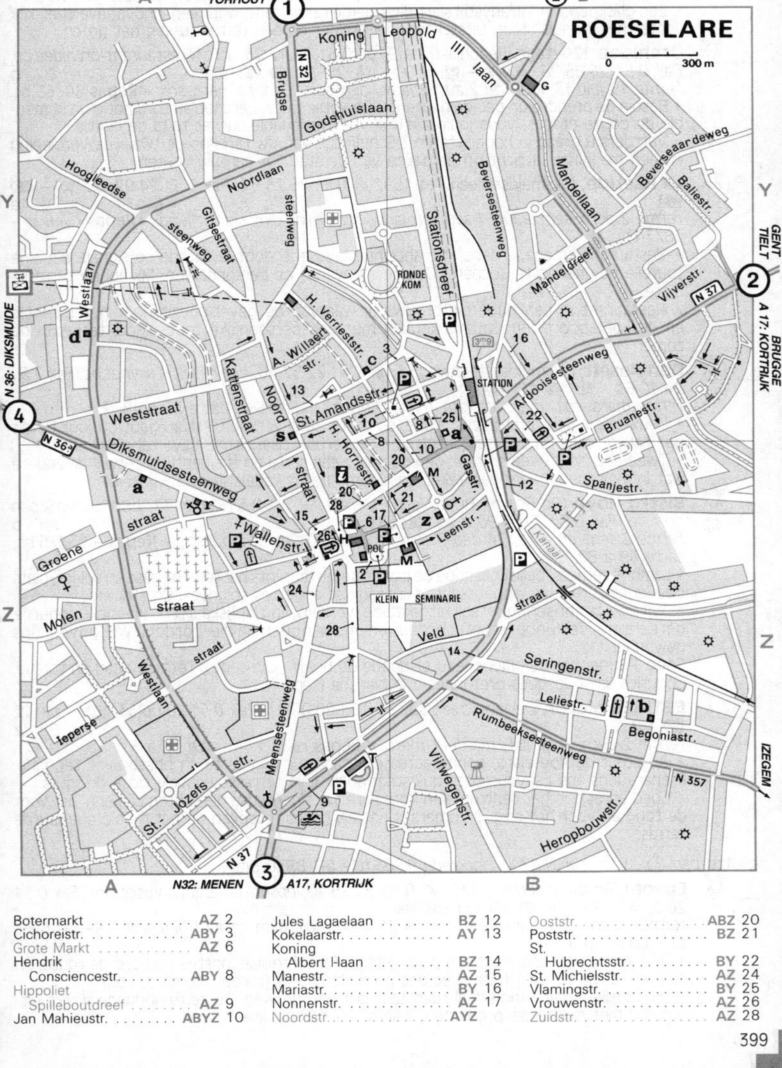

Botermarkt .... AZ 2	Jules Lagaelaan .... BZ 12	Ooststr. .... ABZ 20
Cichoreistr. .... ABY 3	Kokelaarstr. .... AY 13	Poststr. .... BZ 21
Grote Markt .... AZ 6	Koning Albert Haan .... BZ 14	St. Hubrechtsstr. .... BY 22
Hendrik Consciencestr. .... ABY 8	Manestr. .... AZ 15	St. Michielsstr. .... AZ 24
Hippoliet Spilleboutdreef .... AZ 9	Mariastr. .... BY 16	Vlamingstr. .... BY 25
Jan Mahieustr. .... ABYZ 10	Nonnenstr. .... AZ 17	Vrouwenstr. .... AZ 26
	Noordstr. .... AYZ	Zuidstr. .... AZ 28

BELGIQUE

XXX **Savarin** avec ch, Westlaan 359, ☎ 0 51 22 59 16, *jansavarin@hotmail.com, Fax 0 51 22 07 99,* ⛱, ⛱, 🚲 – TV P – 25 à 60. AE ⓓ MC VISA AY d
Repas *(fermé dim. soir et lundi)* Lunch 35 – 55/83 bc, ♀ – **10 ch** 61/86 – ½ P 86.
◆ Parmi les meilleures maisons de Roeselare : décor intérieur élégant, mets classiques relevés d'une touche créative et vins prestigieux. Nouvelles chambres côté jardin.
◆ Savarin behoort tot de toprestaurants van Roeselare : elegant interieur, klassieke gerechten met een creatieve noot en prestigieuze wijnen. Nieuwe kamers aan de tuinzijde.

XXX **De Ooievaar,** Noordstraat 91, ☎ 0 51 20 54 86, *restaurantdeooievaar@pi.be, Fax 0 51 24 46 76,* ⛱ – P. AE ⓓ MC VISA. ✻ AY s
fermé fin fév.-début mars, mi-juil.-mi-août, dim. soir et lundi – **Repas** Lunch 33 – 45/70 bc, ♀.
◆ Des verrières de style Tiffany égayent le plafond de ce restaurant intime où l'on sert des plats agrémentés d'un zeste d'innovation. Cave bien montée. Terrasse "au vert".
◆ Een glaskoepel in Tiffanystijl siert dit intieme restaurant, waar een innovatieve chef-kok achter het fornuis staat. Uitstekende wijnkelder en een terras tussen het groen.

XX **Orchidee** 12e étage, Begoniastraat 9, ☎ 0 51 21 17 23, *info@restaurant-orchidee.be, Fax 0 51 26 85 28,* ≤ ville – P – 25. AE ⓓ MC VISA BZ b
fermé 19 juil.-13 août, du 2 au 12 janv., dim. soir, lundi et merc. soir – **Repas** 30/65 bc.
◆ Besoin de prendre un peu de hauteur ? De votre table, perchée au sommet d'un immeuble de douze étages, vous jouirez d'une vue imprenable sur les toits de la ville !
◆ Vertoeft u graag in hoger sferen ? Schuif dan aan uw tafel op de twaalfde verdieping en een magnifiek uitzicht op de daken van de stad ligt aan uw voeten !

XX **La Bastide,** Diksmuidsesteenweg 159, ☎ 0 51 25 23 64, *Fax 0 51 24 97 47,* ⛱ – MC VISA AZ a
fermé 2 dern. sem. août, 1 sem. en janv., sam. midi, dim. soir et lundi – **Repas** Lunch 30 – 38/74 bc, ♀.
◆ Restaurant aménagé dans une ancienne brasserie dont la façade se signale par une tourelle et une porte cochère. Cuisine innovante et personnalisée. Mignonne terrasse d'été.
◆ Restaurant in een oude bierbrouwerij, waarvan de gevel opvalt door het torentje en de koetspoort. Innovatieve keuken met een persoonlijke toets. Mooi terras in de zomer.

XX **Den Haselt,** Diksmuidsesteenweg 53, ☎ 0 51 22 52 40, *den.haselt@skynet.be, Fax 0 51 24 10 64* – AE ⓓ MC VISA AZ r
fermé mardi soir, merc. et sam. midi – **Repas** Lunch 40 bc – carte 33 à 48, ♀.
◆ Deux salles, deux ambiances : l'une, en partie sous véranda, est au goût du jour tandis que l'autre, plus "cosy", se conforme à un certain classicisme. Cave rabelaisienne.
◆ Twee eetzalen, twee sferen : de ene heeft een serre en is eigentijds, terwijl de andere wat intiemer is en naar een zeker classicisme neigt. Rabelaisiaanse wijnkelder.

XX ✿ **Bistro Novo** (De Bruyn), Hugo Verrieststraat 12, ☎ 0 51 24 14 77, *bistro.novo@pandora.be, Fax 0 51 20 09 90* – . MC VISA AY c
fermé 2 sem. en août, 24 déc.-3 janv., sam. midi, dim. et lundi soir – **Repas** – 25/75 bc, carte 39 à 80, ♀.
◆ Lambris cérusés, belle collection de cartes de restaurants habilement mise en valeur, plats classiques actualisés, appétissants écriteaux et assiettes soignées. On s'incline !
◆ Wittige lambrisering, fraai uitgestalde verzameling spijskaarten, klassiek-moderne gerechten, verfijnde stoofschotels en mooi opgemaakte borden. Wij geven ons gewonnen !
Spéc. Parmentier de pigeonneau et queue de bœuf (juin-sept.). Tête de veau en tortue. Coquilles Saint-Jacques bretonnes à la plancha (sept.-fév.)

X **EETHUIS pieter,** Delaerestraat 32, ☎ 0 51 20 00 07, *Fax 0 51 20 06 53,* ⛱ – . AE MC VISA BZ z
fermé 2 dern. sem. juil., mardi et merc. – **Repas** Lunch 22 – carte 33 à 51.
◆ Au cœur de Roeselare, bonne adresse misant sur une carte en phase avec l'époque. Préparations aussi savoureuses qu'esthétiques. Jolie terrasse estivale close de murs.
◆ Goed adresje in het centrum van Roeselare. De eigentijdse gerechten zijn een lust voor de tong én voor het oog. 's Zomers is het aangenaam toeven op het mooie ommuurde terras.

à Gits *par ① : 5 km sur N 32 C Hooglede 9 803 h. – ✉ 8830 Gits :*

XX **Epsom,** Bruggesteenweg 175, ☎ 0 51 20 25 10, *epsom.dujardin@yucom.be, Fax 0 51 20 52 43,* ⛱ – P. AE ⓓ MC VISA. ✻
fermé 2 dern. sem. juil.-prem. sem. août, merc. soir, sam. midi et dim. soir – **Repas** Lunch 37 – carte 38 à 51.
◆ Déjà plus de dix ans d'activité pour cette affaire familiale postée en bord de route. En cuisine, l'envie de bien faire avec des produits choisis (turbot, homard, etc.).
◆ Dit familiebedrijf timmert al ruim tien jaar aan de weg. De keukenbrigade werkt uitsluitend met eersteklas producten, waaronder tarbot, kreeft, enz.

à Hooglede *par Hoogleedsesteenweg Nord-Est : 7 km - AY – 9 803 h – ✉ 8830 Hooglede :*

De Vossenberg sans rest, Hogestraat 194, ☎ 0 51 70 25 83, *info@passim.be, Fax 0 51 70 18 10*, ≤, ✂, 🚲 – TV P – 25 à 800. VISA
☕ 15 – **15 ch** 72/105.
◆ Établissement moderne regroupant, de part et d'autre d'une cour intérieure, une colossale infrastructure conférencière et des chambres actuelles avec vue sur un étang.
◆ Dit hotelcomplex bestaat uit moderne gebouwen aan weerszijden van een binnenplaats. Reusachtige congreszalen en eigentijdse kamers die uitkijken op een vijver.

à Rumbeke *Sud-Est : 3 km* C *Roeselare – ✉ 8800 Rumbeke :*

Host. Vijfwegen, Groene Herderstraat 171 (au domaine Sterrebos), ☎ 0 51 24 34 72, *hotel-vijfwegen@mdr.be, Fax 0 51 24 16 74*, 🏖, 🚲 – |‡|, ▤ ch, TV P. AE ⓓ ⓜⓒ VISA
Repas ***Bistro Frogs*** Lunch 17 – carte 28 à 52 – **30 ch** ☕ 59/89 – ½ P 95/105.
◆ Juste en face du domaine provincial "Sterrebos", hostellerie familiale bien en phase avec l'époque, renfermant de bonnes chambres parfaitement insonorisées. Bistrot "hype" estimé pour ses cuisses de grenouilles et son "filet américain" (steak tartare).
◆ Dit familiehotel, dat goed met zijn tijd meegaat, ligt recht tegenover het Sterrebos en beschikt over prettige kamers met een uitstekende geluidsisolatie. Trendy bistro met kikkerbilletjes en filet américain als specialiteiten.

Cá d'Oro, Hoogstraat 97, ☎ 0 51 24 71 81, *Fax 0 51 24 56 27*, 🏖, Cuisine italienne – AE ⓓ ⓜⓒ VISA
fermé 31 août-24 sept., mardi et merc. – **Repas** Lunch 37 – carte 29 à 59.
◆ Côté décor : miroirs et lambris. Côté fourneaux : recettes oscillant entre la France et l'Italie. Cave dans le même esprit, plutôt bien fournie. Terrasse estivale ombragée.
◆ Interieur met spiegels en houtwerk. Spijzen die uit Frankrijk en Italië komen. Goed gevulde wijnkelder die volgens hetzelfde recept is opgezet. Schaduwrijk terras in de zomer.

Le RŒULX *7070 Hainaut* 533 J 19, 534 J 19 *et* 716 F 4 – *8 007 h.*
Bruxelles 55 – Mons 19 – Binche 12 – Charleroi 27.

Aub. Saint-Feuillien, chaussée de Mons 1, ☎ 0 64 66 22 85, *Fax 0 64 66 22 85* – ⓓ ⓜⓒ VISA
fermé mi-juil.-mi-août, mardi soir, merc. soir et dim. – **Repas** Lunch 24 – 55.
◆ Au centre du village, auberge ancienne gentiment reconvertie en restaurant familial aimant son petit confort. La cuisine du chef fait l'objet d'une certaine recherche.
◆ Deze oude herberg midden in het dorp is nu een prettig familierestaurant dat op zijn comfort is gesteld. De kookstijl van de chef-kok getuigt van verfijning.

ROKSEM *West-Vlaanderen* 533 D 15 *et* 716 C 2 – *voir à Oudenburg.*

ROLLEGEM *West-Vlaanderen* 533 E 18 – *voir à Kortrijk.*

ROMERSHOVEN *Limburg* 533 R 17 – *voir à Hasselt.*

RONSE (RENAIX) *9600 Oost-Vlaanderen* 533 G 18 *et* 716 D 3 – *23 697 h.*
Voir *Crypte★ de la Collégiale St-Hermès.*
🅸 *Hoge Mote, De Biesestraat 2,* ☎ *0 55 23 28 16, ronse@toerismevlaanderen.be* Fax 0 55 23 28 19. – *Bruxelles 57 – Kortrijk 34 – Gent 38 – Valenciennes 49.*

Host. Lou Pahou, Zuidstraat 25, ☎ 0 55 21 91 11, *loupahou@online.be, Fax 0 55 20 91 04*, 🚲 – TV. AE ⓓ ⓜⓒ VISA. ✖
fermé 15 juil.-5 août. – **Repas** *(fermé mardi, merc. midi et dim. midi)* Lunch 15 – 30 bc/60 bc – **6 ch** ☕ 46/62 – ½ P 46/61.
◆ Charmante demeure 1900 installée en plein centre-ville, près de l'église St-Martens et non loin de la grand-place. Chambres correctement équipées. Jardin reposant. Salle de restaurant au décor bourgeois : cheminée de marbre, lustre en cristal, chandeliers.
◆ Charmant pand uit 1900 in het centrum van de stad, bij de St-Maartenskerk, niet ver van de Grote Markt. De kamers bieden goede voorzieningen. Rustgevende tuin. De kroonluchter, marmeren schouw en kandelaren kenmerken het bourgeoisinterieur van het restaurant.

Host. Shamrock avec ch, Ommegangstraat 148 (Louise-Marie, Nord-Est : 7 km par N 60), ✉ 9681 Maarkedal, ☎ 0 55 21 55 29, *shamrock@edpnet.be, Fax 0 55 21 56 83*, ≤, 🏖, 🌳 – TV P. AE ⓓ ⓜⓒ VISA. ✖
fermé 2 dern. sem. juil., 2 prem. sem. janv., lundi, mardi et après 20 h 30 – **Repas** Lunch 40 – 71/128 bc – **4 ch** ☕ 150/200, – 1 suite.
◆ Beau manoir à l'anglaise. De la terrasse sur "garden" aux chambres "cosy", une seule réflexion vient à l'esprit : "it's so quiet ! " Fine cuisine actuelle. Cave prestigieuse.
◆ Fraai landhuis in Engelse stijl. Van het terras in de garden tot de cosy kamers komt er maar één gedachte bij ons op : "it's so quiet ! " Fijne keuken en prestigieuze wijnkelder.

XX **Beau Séjour,** Viermaartlaan 109, ✆ 0 55 21 33 65, *dominique.vangrembergen@pi.be, Fax 0 55 21 92 65,* – P. AE MC VISA
fermé fin juil.-début août, fin janv-début fév., dim. soir, lundi et merc. soir – **Repas** *Lunch 23* – 34/58 bc.
◆ Père et fils ont longtemps œuvré côte à côte dans cette maison, avant que les aînés ne passent la main. Carte classique assortie de suggestions et d'un trio de menus.
◆ Vader en zoon stonden lang zij aan zij in dit restaurant, totdat de oudere generatie het voor gezien hield. Klassieke kaart met suggesties en een drietal menu's.

X **Bois Joly,** Hogerlucht 7, ✆ 0 55 21 10 17, *bois-joly@skynet.be, Fax 0 55 21 10 17,* – P. AE MC VISA
fermé 1 sem. carnaval, 2 sem. en août, mardi soir et merc. – **Repas** *Lunch 9* – 35.
◆ Restaurant familial dont l'assiette évolue dans un registre classique. À épingler : une dizaine de préparations de homard et de copieuses fondues. Véranda et terrasse d'été.
◆ Gemoedelijk restaurant met een klassieke keuken. Aanraders zijn de kopieuze fondues en de kreeft, die op wel tien verschillende manieren wordt bereid. Serre en zomerterras.

RONSELE *Oost-Vlaanderen* 533 G 16 – *voir à Zomergem.*

ROSÉE *5620 Namur* C *Florennes 10 706 h.* 533 N 21, 534 N 21 *et* 716 H 5.
Bruxelles 91 – Namur 36 – Charleroi 37 – Dinant 18.

X **La Clairière,** rte Charlemagne 189, ✆ 0 82 68 84 68, *agnesmathieu@wanadoo.be, Fax 0 82 68 80 30,* – AE MC VISA
fermé lundi soir et merc. d'oct. à avril – **Repas** *Lunch 23* – 37/70 bc, ♀.
◆ Ancienne auberge montant la garde aux portes de la base militaire de Florennes. Deux formules sous le même toit : café-brasserie et restaurant misant sur carte "à rallonge".
◆ Dit nieuwe restaurant houdt de wacht bij de poort van de militaire basis van Florennes. Twee formules onder één dak : café-brasserie en restaurant met een uitgebreidere kaart.

ROULERS *West-Vlaanderen* – *voir Roeselare.*

ROUVEROY *7120 Hainaut* C *Estinnes 7 499 h.* 533 J 20, 534 J 20 *et* 716 F 4.
Bruxelles 74 – Mons 17 – Charleroi 33 – Maubeuge 21.

Les Ramiers sans rest, Barrière d'Aubreux 2 (rte de Mons), ✆ 0 64 77 12 61, *hotelramiers@tiscali.be, Fax 0 64 55 43 53* – P. AE MC VISA.
fermé dim. et jours fériés – 9 – **6 ch** 57/75.
◆ Bordant un axe transfrontalier fréquenté, petit établissement dont les quelques chambres, très bien insonorisées, sont toutes de plain-pied, à la façon d'un motel.
◆ Klein hotel aan een drukke weg naar de grens. De kamers hebben een uitstekende geluidsisolatie en zijn allemaal gelijkvloers, net als in een motel.

X **La Brouette,** Barrière d'Aubreux 4 (rte de Mons), ✆ 0 64 77 13 42, *Fax 0 64 77 13 42,* – P. AE MC VISA JCB.
fermé du 1er au 10 fév., mardi soir, merc. et après 20 h 30 – **Repas** *Lunch 25* – carte 28 à 46.
◆ Auberge-relais postée sur la grand-route. Préparations assez simples, mise en place soignée et terrasse d'été dressée à l'arrière.
◆ Dit voormalige relais staat aan de grote weg. In de verzorgde eetzaal worden vrij eenvoudige gerechten opgediend. s' Zomers wordt het terras achter opgedekt.

RUISBROEK *Vlaams-Brabant* 533 K 18 *et* 716 F 3 – *voir à Bruxelles, environs.*

RUISELEDE *8755 West-Vlaanderen* 533 F 16 *et* 716 D 2 – *5 030 h.*
Bruxelles 79 – Brugge 31 – Gent 29.

XX **Lindenhof,** Tieltstraat 29, ✆ 0 51 68 75 39, *info@lindenhof.be, Fax 0 51 68 62 15,* – P. AE MC VISA JCB.
fermé 2e quinz. juil., mardi soir et merc. – **Repas** *Lunch 25* – 40/70 bc.
◆ Derrière les façades jaunes de cette construction récente vous attend un choix de plats à la carte et de menus classico-bourgeois. Service aimable.
◆ Achter de vrolijke gele gevels van dit vrij recente gebouw wacht u een keur van smakelijke gerechten à la carte en eenvoudige klassieke menu's. Vriendelijke bediening.

RUMBEKE *West-Vlaanderen* 533 D 17 *et* 716 C 3 – *voir à Roeselare.*

RUMST *Antwerpen* 533 L 16 *et* 716 G 2 – *voir à Mechelen.*

SAINTE-CÉCILE *6820 Luxembourg belge* C *Florenville 5 504 h.* 534 Q 24 *et* 716 I 6.
Bruxelles 171 – Bouillon 18 – Arlon 46 – Neufchâteau 30.

Host. Sainte-Cécile, r. Neuve 1, 0 61 31 31 67, *info@hotel-ste-cecile.com, Fax 0 61 31 50 04*, – TV P. AE VISA. rest
fermé 16 fév.-18 mars, 30 août-9 sept. et du 5 au 29 janv. – **Repas** *(fermé dim. soirs et lundis non fériés sauf en juil.-août)* Lunch 22 – 31/54 – 8 – **14 ch** 57/98 – ½ P 142/184.
• Charmante demeure de pays agrémentée sur l'arrière, au bord du ruisseau, d'un adorable jardin. Silencieuses chambres personnalisées. Salle à manger au décor chaleureux et pimpant, semé de-ci de-là de pointes de raffinement.
• Dit sfeervolle pand is karakteristiek voor de streek en heeft een beeldige tuin met een beekje. Rustige kamers met een persoonlijke toets. De eetzaal ziet er warm en aantrekkelijk uit, met hier en daar een vleugje raffinement.

ST-GEORGES-SUR-MEUSE *4470 Liège* 533 R 19, 534 R 19 *et* 716 J 4 – *6 539 h.*
Bruxelles 87 – Liège 20 – Marche-en-Famenne 60 – Namur 43.

Philippe Fauchet, r. Warfée 62, 0 4 259 59 39, *philippe.fauchet@skynet.be, Fax 0 4 259 59 39*, – P. VISA.
fermé prem. sem. janv., lundi, mardi et sam. midi – **Repas** Lunch 24 – carte 42 à 95.
• Ancienne fermette dans un environnement champêtre. Confortable salle des repas surmontée d'une mezzanine et beau jardin servant de restaurant d'été. Cuisine du moment.
• Restaurant in een oud boerderijtje op het platteland. Comfortabele eetzaal met mezzanine en een mooie tuin, waar 's zomers de tafeltjes worden gedekt. Eigentijdse keuken.

ST-GHISLAIN *7330 Hainaut* 533 H 20, 534 H 20 *et* 716 E 4 – *22 014 h.*
Bruxelles 78 – Mons 11 – Tournai 41 – Valenciennes 30.

Chez Romano, r. Ath 17, 0 65 79 29 79, *Fax 0 65 79 29 79*, Avec cuisine italienne – AE VISA
fermé du 6 au 25 août, merc. et dim. soir – **Repas** Lunch 35 – carte 22 à 34.
• La bonne humeur de Romano, l'ambiance conviviale de son restaurant, ainsi que ses préparations franco-italiennes ont séduit bon nombre de clients du secteur. Et vous ?
• Het goede humeur van Romano, de gezellige ambiance in het restaurant en het lekkere Frans-Italiaanse eten hebben al menigeen verleid. Bent u de volgende ?

ST-GILLES (SINT-GILLIS) *Région de Bruxelles-Capitale – voir à Bruxelles.*

ST-HUBERT *6870 Luxembourg belge* 534 R 22 *et* 716 J 5 – *5 646 h.*
Voir *Intérieur★★ de la Basilique St-Hubert★.*
Env. *au Nord : 7 km à Fourneau-St-Michel★★ : Musée du Fer et de la Métallurgie ancienne★ – Musée de la Vie rurale en Wallonie★★.*
r. St-Gilles 12 *0 61 61 30 10, info@saint-hubert-tourisme.be, Fax 0 61 61 51 44.*
Bruxelles 137 – Bouillon 44 – Arlon 60 – La Roche-en-Ardenne 25 – Sedan 59.

Le Cor de Chasse avec ch, av. Nestor Martin 3, 0 61 61 16 44, *Fax 0 61 61 33 15*, – TV. VISA
fermé 1re quinz. mars, 2e quinz. juin et 2e quinz. sept. – **Repas** *(fermé lundi, mardi et après 20 h 30)* Lunch 12 – 26/38 – **10 ch** 58/62 – ½ P 46/51.
• Enseigne de circonstance pour cette sympathique adresse au centre d'une bourgade ardennaise placée sous la bannière du patron des chasseurs. Bons menus bien conçus.
• Deze "jachthoorn" is een sympathiek adresje in het hart van het Ardenner dorp dat naar de schutspatroon van de jagers is genoemd. Lekkere, goed doordachte menu's.

à Awenne *Nord-Ouest : 9 km* C *St-Hubert* – *6870 Awenne :*

L'Aub. du Sabotier et Les 7 Fontaines, Grand'rue 21, 0 84 36 65 04, *aubergedusabotier@skynet.be, Fax 0 84 36 63 68*, – TV P. AE VISA. rest
Repas *(fermé carnaval et 2 sem. avant Pâques)* Lunch 22 – 32/76 bc, – **20 ch** 63/90 – ½ P 88/122.
• Halte rustique à souhait, idéale pour un séjour calme au cœur d'un village forestier. Chambres proprettes. Jardin invitant à décompresser. Chaleureuse salle à manger d'un caractère ardennais bien trempé. Carte actuelle flirtant avec les produits du terroir.
• Dit landelijke hotel garandeert een rustig verblijf in een door bossen omringd dorpje. Mooie kamers en een fijne tuin om optimaal tot ontspanning te komen. Sfeervolle eetzaal met een typisch Ardens karakter. Eigentijdse keuken met een regionaal accent.

ST-JOSSE-TEN-NOODE (SINT-JOOST-TEN-NODE) *Région de Bruxelles-Capitale – voir à Bruxelles.*

ST-NICOLAS *Oost-Vlaanderen – voir Sint-Niklaas.*

ST-SAUVEUR *7912 Hainaut C Frasnes-lez-Anvaing 10 597 h.* 533 G 18, 534 G 18 *et* 716 D 3.
Bruxelles 73 – Kortrijk 40 – Gent 48 – Tournai 20 – Valenciennes 45.

XX **Les Marronniers,** r. Vertes Feuilles 7, ✆ 0 69 76 99 58, *restaurant_les_marronniers@hotmail.com, Fax 0 69 76 99 58,* ≤, – P. AE ① MC VISA
fermé 2 sem. en mars, 2 sem. en sept., lundi, mardi et merc. – **Repas** 30/48 bc.
◆ Vue plongeante sur une vallée verdoyante, tant depuis la salle à manger rénovée que de la terrasse d'été. Menus et suggestions saisonnières.
◆ Weids uitzicht op de groene vallei, zowel vanuit de gerenoveerde eetzaal als vanaf het zomerterras. Menu's en seizoengebonden suggesties.

X **les prés bossus,** r. Bruyère-Seutine 18 (direction Les Hauts), ✆ 0 69 76 95 06, *pres.bossus@swing.be, Fax 0 69 76 95 06,* – P. ① MC VISA.
fermé 2 prem. sem. sept., prem. sem. janv., lundi soir, mardi, merc. et jeudi – **Repas** 25/40, ♀.
◆ Cette avenante fermette blanche domine un paysage de "prés bossus" : les Ardennes flamandes. Cuisine du terroir, simple mais attrayante. L'été, repas au jardin.
◆ Dit vriendelijke witte boerderijtje ontleent zijn naam aan het landschap van "gebochelde weiden" : de Vlaamse Ardennen. Eerlijke streekkeuken en lekker buiten eten in de zomer.

ST-TROND *Limburg – voir Sint-Truiden.*

ST-VITH *Liège – voir Sankt-Vith.*

SANKT-VITH (ST-VITH) *4780 Liège* 533 V 21, 534 V 21 *et* 716 L 5 – *9 023 h.*
Mühlenbachstr. 2 ✆ 0 80 22 76 64, info@eastbelgium.com, Fax 0 80 22 65 39.
Bruxelles 180 – Liège 78 – La Roche-en-Ardenne 51 – Clervaux 36.

Pip-Margraff, Hauptstr. 7, ✆ 0 80 22 86 63, *info@pip.be, Fax 0 80 22 87 61,* – TV – 25 à 80. AE MC VISA JCB.
fermé 29 mars-8 avril et 28 juin-9 juil. – **Repas** *(fermé dim. soirs et lundis non fériés) Lunch 20* – 30/40 – **20 ch** 70/115, – 3 suites – ½ P 70/105.
◆ Après un plongeon dans la piscine et un peu de relaxation au "bain-bulles", vous regagnerez tranquillement votre chambre. Sommeils plus réparateurs à l'arrière du bâtiment. Salon sous verrière, salle à manger actuelle, généreuses préparations traditionnelles.
◆ Na een duik in het zwembad en een zit in het "bubbelbad" gaat u voor een verkwikkend slaapje naar een van de hotelkamers, die aan de achterkant het rustigst zijn. Onder het glazen dak van de moderne eetzaal worden overvloedige, traditionele schotels opgediend.

Am Steineweiher, Rodter Str. 32, ✆ 0 80 22 72 70, *Fax 0 80 22 91 53,* – TV P. MC VISA
Repas *(fermé après 20 h 30) Lunch 22* – 24/49 – **14 ch** 47/68 – ½ P 48/53.
◆ Près d'un étang, adresse paisible, entourée de sapins et d'un parc de 3 ha, dont la desserte est assurée par une allée privée. Chambres aménagées à l'ancienne. Par météo clémente, il fait bon s'attabler sur la terrasse estivale au bord de l'eau.
◆ Een mooie laan leidt naar dit rustige hotel in een park van 3 ha met veel sparren en een vijver. De kamers zijn in grootmoeders stijl ingericht. Als het weer het toelaat, kunt u uitgebreid tafelen op het terras aan de rand van het water.

XXX ✿ **Zur Post** (Pankert) avec ch, Hauptstr. 39, ✆ 0 80 22 80 27, *zurpost@swing.be, Fax 0 80 22 93 10* – TV. AE MC VISA
fermé du 1er au 17 juin, du 6 au 13 sept., du 2 au 20 janv., dim. soir, lundi et mardi midi – **Repas** *Lunch 39* – 65/89, carte 64 à 86, ♀ – **8 ch** 78/109 – ½ P 95/110.
◆ Hostellerie gourmande et typique de cette région frontalière. Façade fleurie en été, salle des repas complètement relookée et agréable jardin d'hiver. Une valeur sûre !
◆ Dit hotel is typerend voor de grensstreek. Gevel die 's zomers vol bloemen is, volledig gerenoveerde eetzaal en prettige wintertuin. Een betrouwbaar adresje voor fijnproevers !
Spéc. Homard tiède à la vinaigrette de framboises. Gigue de chevreuil aux baies de sureau (sept.-déc.). Carré d'agneau en croûte d'herbes

XX **Le Luxembourg** arrière-salle, Hauptstr. 71, ✆ 0 80 22 80 22 – MC VISA.
fermé 2 sem. après carnaval, dern. sem. juin-2 prem. sem. juil., merc. soir et jeudi – **Repas** *Lunch 40* – carte env. 60.
◆ Un petit bistrot devance l'accueillante salle à manger lambrissée du Luxembourg. Belle mise en place des tables. Recettes actuelles composées à partir de bons produits.
◆ Achter een cafeetje bevindt zich de uitnodigende eetzaal met lambrisering van Le Luxembourg. Eigentijdse gerechten op basis van kwaliteitsproducten en prachtig gedekte tafels.

SART *Liège* 533 U 19, 534 U 19 *et* 716 K 5 – *voir à Spa.*

SAUTIN *Hainaut* 534 K 22 *et* 716 F 5 – *voir à Rance.*

SCHAERBEEK (SCHAARBEEK) *Région de Bruxelles-Capitale* 533 L 17 – *voir à Bruxelles.*

SCHERPENHEUVEL (MONTAIGU) *3270 Vlaams-Brabant* C *Scherpenheuvel-Zichem 21 671 h.* 533 O 17 *et* 716 H 3.
Bruxelles 52 – Antwerpen 52 – Hasselt 31.

XX **De Zwaan** avec ch, Albertusplein 12, ☎ 0 13 77 13 69, *Fax 0 13 78 17 77* –, rest, TV P – 25. AE MC VISA.
Repas *(fermé sam. de sept. à avril et après 20 h 30)* Lunch 24 – 39/69 bc – **9 ch** 46/79 – ½ P 71.
◆ Une véritable institution locale, sur laquelle le temps a peu d'emprise. Ample salle de restaurant aux tables accolées qu'agrémente une belle argenterie. Chambres correctes.
◆ De Zwaan is echt een begrip, waarop de tand des tijds weinig invloed heeft gehad. Grote eetzaal met prachtig zilver op de tafels, die dicht naast elkaar staan. Prima kamers.

SCHILDE *Antwerpen* 533 M 15 *et* 716 G 2 – *voir à Antwerpen, environs.*

SCHOONAARDE *9200 Oost-Vlaanderen* C *Dendermonde 43 168 h.* 533 J 17 *et* 716 F 2.
Bruxelles 39 – Gent 26 – Aalst 11 – Dendermonde 7.

X **het Palinghuis,** Oude Brugstraat 16, ☎ 0 52 42 32 46, *Fax 0 52 42 57 69*, <, Anguilles – P. AE MC VISA.
fermé 15 déc.-4 janv., vend. et sam. midi – **Repas** carte 23 à 40.
◆ À la grande satisfaction d'une clientèle d'assidus, l'anguille reste ici "la" spécialité d'une tradition culinaire transmise de génération en génération. Avis aux amateurs !
◆ Tot groot plezier van de vaste clientèle blijft paling hier dé specialiteit ; een culinaire traditie die van generatie op generatie wordt doorgegeven. Dat u het maar weet !

SCHOTEN *Antwerpen* 533 L 15 *et* 716 G 2 – *voir à Antwerpen, environs.*

SEMOIS (Vallée de la) ★★ *Luxembourg belge et Namur* 534 P 24 - T 24 716 J 7 - H 6 *G. Belgique-Luxembourg.*

SENEFFE *7180 Hainaut* 533 K 19, 534 K 19 *et* 716 F 4 – *10 597 h.*
Bruxelles 43 – Mons 27 – Charleroi 28 – Maubeuge 54.

L'Aquarelle sans rest, r. Scrawelle 64, ☎ 0 64 23 96 23, *direction@hotelaquarelle.be, Fax 0 64 23 96 20*, <, – TV P – 25. AE MC VISA.
10 – **27 ch** 94/104.
◆ Tout nouvel hôtel construit dans un quartier résidentiel. Chambres actuelles et bien équipées, dont quatre familiales. Vue sur les champs et le petit bois avoisinants.
◆ Spiksplinternieuw hotel in een rustige woonwijk. Moderne en comfortabele kamers, waarvan vier geschikt zijn voor gezinnen. Uitzicht op de velden en een klein bos.

SERAING *Liège* 533 S 19, 534 S 19 *et* 716 J 4 – *voir à Liège, environs.*

SILLY (OPZULLIK) *7830 Hainaut* 533 I 19, 534 I 19 *et* 716 E 4 – *7 711 h.*
Bruxelles 49 – Mons 26 – Gent 61 – Tournai 45.

X **Aux 9 Tilleuls,** pl. Communale 24, ☎ 0 68 56 85 27, *Fax 0 68 56 85 27*, – P. MC VISA
fermé lundi soir et mardi – **Repas** Lunch 8 – 18/43.
◆ Ce resto familial posté derrière l'église doit son enseigne à la place arborée qu'il jouxte. Choix varié de plats gentiment bourgeois et vins pour toutes les bourses.
◆ Dit familierestaurant achter de kerk dankt zijn naam aan het aangrenzende plein met linden. Gevarieerde kaart met eenvoudige, smakelijke gerechten en wijnen voor elke beurs.

SINT-AGATHA-BERCHEM *Brussels Hoofdstedelijk Gewest – voir Berchem-Ste-Agathe à Bruxelles.*

SINT-AMANDS *2890 Antwerpen* 533 K 16 *et* 716 F 2 – *7 578 h.*
Bruxelles 40 – Antwerpen 32 – Mechelen 23.

X **De Veerman,** Kaai 26, ☎ 0 52 33 32 75, *Fax 0 52 33 25 70*, <, –. AE MC VISA
fermé lundi et mardi – **Repas** Lunch 50 bc – 59/70 bc.
◆ Le rêve inavoué de toute anguille qui se respecte : terminer sa carrière dans les casseroles de ce restaurant insensible aux modes. Perspective fluviale.
◆ De heimelijke wens van iedere zichzelf respecterende paling is zijn carrière te beëindigen in de pan van dit restaurant, dat ongevoelig is voor modes. Uitzicht op de rivier.

BELGIQUE

't ebdiep, Emile Verhaerenstraat 14a, ☎ 0 52 34 14 16, *ebdiep@skynet.be, Fax 0 52 34 10 50*, ≤, 余 – P. MO VISA
fermé 2 sem. carnaval, 2 sem. Toussaint, lundi et mardi – **Repas** 34/56 bc.
◆ Joli coup d'œil vers l'Escaut (Schelde) depuis l'ample salle à manger de ce restaurant. L'été, il s'apprécie encore mieux en s'attablant sur la terrasse. Mets assez élaborés.
◆ De grote eetzaal biedt een mooi uitzicht op de Schelde, die 's zomers vanaf het terras nog beter te zien is. Hier kunt u genieten van redelijk verfijnde gerechten.

SINT-ANDRIES *West-Vlaanderen* 533 *E 14 et* 716 *C 2 – voir à Brugge, périphérie.*

SINT-DENIJS *West-Vlaanderen* 533 *F 18 et* 716 *D 3 – voir à Zwevegem.*

SINT-DENIJS-WESTREM *Oost-Vlaanderen* 533 *H 16 et* 716 *D 2 – voir à Gent, périphérie.*

SINT-ELOOIS-VIJVE *West-Vlaanderen* 533 *F 17 et* 716 *D 3 – voir à Waregem.*

SINT-GENESIUS-RODE *Vlaams-Brabant* 533 *L 18 et* 716 *G 3 – voir à Bruxelles, environs.*

SINT-GILLIS *Brussels Hoofdstedelijk Gewest – voir St-Gilles à Bruxelles.*

SINT-HUIBRECHTS-LILLE *3910 Limburg* C *Neerpelt 15 681 h.* 533 *R 15 et* 716 *J 2.*
Bruxelles 113 – Eindhoven 23 – Antwerpen 84.

Sint-Hubertushof, Broekkant 23, ☎ 0 11 66 27 71, *sinthubertushof@pandora.be, Fax 0 11 66 28 83*, 余 – P. AE MO VISA.
fermé 22 fév.-10 mars, 15 août-1er sept., lundi, mardi et sam. midi – **Repas** Lunch 40 – 50/80 bc, ♀.
◆ Jadis, les lieux résonnaient du pas des bateliers et des chevaux de halage. C'est désormais votre tour d'être les hôtes de ce relais "1900" reconverti avec goût. Grands crus.
◆ Vroeger klonken hier de stappen van schippers en hun jaagpaarden, maar nu is het uw beurt om dit oude relais binnen te stappen, dat smaakvol is verbouwd. Prestigieuze wijnen.

SINT-IDESBALD *West-Vlaanderen* 533 *A 16 et* 716 *A 2 – voir à Koksijde-Bad.*

SINT-JAN-IN-EREMO *Oost-Vlaanderen* 533 *G 15 et* 716 *D 2 – voir à Sint-Laureins.*

SINT-JANS-MOLENBEEK *Brussels Hoofdstedelijk Gewest – voir Molenbeek-St-Jean à Bruxelles.*

SINT-JOOST-TEN-NODE *Brussels Hoofdstedelijk Gewest – voir St-Josse-Ten-Noode à Bruxelles.*

SINT-KRUIS *West-Vlaanderen* 533 *E 15 et* 716 *C 2 – voir à Brugge, périphérie.*

SINT-LAMBRECHTS-WOLUWE *Brussels Hoofdstedelijk Gewest – voir Woluwe-St-Lambert à Bruxelles.*

SINT-LAUREINS *9980 Oost-Vlaanderen* 533 *G 15 et* 716 *D 2 – 6 504 h.*
Bruxelles 98 – Brugge 31 – Gent 30 – Antwerpen 70.

Slependamme, Lege Moerstraat 26 (Sud-Est : 5,5 km sur N 434), ☎ 0 9 377 78 31, *info@slependamme.be, Fax 0 9 377 78 31*, 余 – ▤ P. AE MO VISA
fermé 17 août-3 sept., merc. et jeudi midi – **Repas** Lunch 30 – 44.
◆ Maison de tradition où se mitonne, depuis près d'un quart de siècle, un solide répertoire de plats classiques, aujourd'hui sobrement actualisé. Terrasse estivale et jardin.
◆ Traditioneel restaurant dat al ruim 25 jaar bekendstaat om zijn solide repertoire van klassieke gerechten, die nu voorzichtig worden geactualiseerd. Tuin en zomerterras.

à Sint-Jan-in-Eremo *Nord-Est : 5,5 km* C *Sint-Laureins – ✉ 9982 Sint-Jan-in-Eremo :*

De Warande, Warande 10 (Bentille), ☎ 0 9 379 00 51, *warande@de-warande.be, Fax 0 9 379 03 77*, ≤, 余 – P. AE O MO VISA
fermé 17 fév.-5 mars, du 5 au 17 sept., mardi et merc. – **Repas** Lunch 32 – 48/67 bc.
◆ Ample restaurant dont la confortable salle à manger s'ouvre sur une terrasse estivale devançant un grand jardin agrémenté de haies basses et d'une pièce d'eau.
◆ Dit ruim opgezette restaurant beschikt over een gerieflijke eetzaal met terras. De grote tuin wordt opgevrolijkt door lage hagen en een waterpartij.

SINT-MARTENS-LATEM (LAETHEM-ST-MARTIN) *9830 Oost-Vlaanderen* 533 G 16 *et* 716 D 2 – *8 372 h.*

Latemstraat 120 ℘ 0 9 282 54 11, Fax 0 9 282 90 19.
Bruxelles 65 – Gent 13 – Antwerpen 70.

XX **Sabatini,** Kortrijksesteenweg 114, ℘ 0 9 282 80 35, *Fax 0 9 282 80 35*, Avec cuisine italienne – AE VISA
fermé 15 juil.-15 août, 24 déc.-1er janv., merc. et sam. midi – **Repas** Lunch 32 bc – 31/41.
◆ Rien à voir avec le tennis : de goûteuses préparations typiquement transalpines tiennent ici la vedette, devant quelques classiques français. Cave dans le même esprit.
◆ Ver buiten het tennisveld wedijveren typisch Italiaanse gerechten hier met Franse klassiekers. In de wijnkelder wordt dezelfde competitie gevoerd.

XX **Meersschaut,** Kortrijksesteenweg 134, ℘ 0 9 282 38 56, *Fax 0 9 282 02 14*, Produits de la mer – AE VISA
fermé 15 août-13 sept., dim. et lundi – **Repas** Lunch 25 – 38/72 bc.
◆ Table plaisante tenue par une famille de poissonniers, ce qui laisse deviner l'orientation culinaire, comme du reste le décor intérieur. Véranda où l'on s'abstient de fumer.
◆ Dit plezierige restaurant is in handen van een familie van vishandelaars, dus het laat zich raden wat u op uw bordje krijgt. In de serre mag niet worden gerookt.

XX **De Klokkeput,** Dorp 8, ℘ 0 9 282 47 75, *rene@klokkeput.com, Fax 0 9 282 47 75*, Avec grillades, ouvert jusqu'à 23 h – AE VISA.
fermé 2 dern. sem. sept. – **Repas** Lunch 12 – carte 32 à 83, ♀.
◆ Sur la place de l'église, au cœur du village, auberge dont les préparations sortent un peu du lot dans ce petit coin de Flandre. Vins des régions de France. Service "relax".
◆ Deze herberg aan het kerkplein, in het hart van het dorp, serveert Franse streekgerechten met een persoonlijk accent. Franse wijnen en "relaxte" service.

XX **d'Oude Schuur,** Baarle Frankrijkstraat 1, ℘ 0 9 282 33 65, *oudeschuur@hotmail.com, Fax 0 9 282 89 21*, – AE VISA.
fermé vacances Pâques, du 15 au 30 sept., merc. et jeudi – **Repas** Lunch 27 bc – 30/66 bc.
◆ Dans un quartier résidentiel assez cossu, typique fermette devancée d'une terrasse où l'on s'attable par beau temps. Clientèle d'habitués, fidélisée de longue date.
◆ Karakteristiek boerderijtje in een vrij chique woonwijk, dat al jarenlang een vaste klantenkring heeft. Op zomerse dagen kan op het terras aan de voorkant worden gegeten.

X **brasserie Latem,** Kortrijksesteenweg 9, ℘ 0 9 282 36 17, *petervandenbossche@brasserielatem.be, Fax 0 9 281 06 23*, Ouvert jusqu'à minuit – VISA.
fermé vacances Pâques, 2 dern. sem. août, vacances Noël et dim. – **Repas** carte 42 à 62, ♀.
◆ Villa des années 1930 surveillant la grand-route. Ambiance brasserie, assortie aux assiettes. Liste des vins à rallonge, classée par cépages. Une affaire qui tourne bien.
◆ Deze goed lopende brasserie is te vinden in een villa uit 1930 aan de grote weg. Typische brasseriekaart en een lange lijst van wijnen, die naar druivenras zijn ingedeeld.

à Deurle *Est : 2 km* C *Sint-Martens-Latem – ✉ 9831 Deurle :*

Aub. du Pêcheur, Pontstraat 41, ℘ 0 9 282 31 44, *info@auberge-du-pecheur.be, Fax 0 9 282 90 58*, – rest, – 25 à 120. AE VISA
Repas *Orangerie* *(fermé 2e quinz. déc., sam. midi, dim. soir et lundi)* Lunch 28 – 46/60 – ***The Green*** (taverne-rest) Lunch 11 – 22/46 bc – 12 – **32 ch** *(fermé du 24 au 30 déc.)* 85/123, – 1 suite.
◆ Au pays des peintres, villa néo-classique cossue que rafraîchit le cours de la Leie (Lys). Chambres rénovées, assez menues mais confortables. Terrasse et jardin délicieux. Restaurant sous orangerie, avec vue sur la rivière. Carte appétissante et belle cave.
◆ Weelderige neoklassieke villa met terras en tuin aan de Leie, in de streek van de schilders van de Latemse school. Gerenoveerde kamers, vrij klein maar comfortabel. Restaurant in de oranjerie, met uitzicht op de rivier. Aanlokkelijke kaart en mooie wijnkelder.

XX **de Meander,** Pontstraat 96, ℘ 0 9 282 20 11, *demeander@skynet.be, Fax 0 9 281 04 67*, – VISA
fermé mardi soir, merc. et sam. midi – **Repas** Lunch 25 – 30/61 bc.
◆ Cette jolie villa paressant au bord d'un langoureux méandre comblera les fines fourchettes portées sur la cuisine classique actualisée. Salle de restaurant bourgeoise.
◆ Deze mooie villa ligt loom aan een meander van de rivier. De eetzaal is in bourgeoisstijl ingericht. Gasstronomische keuken in het modern-klassieke register.

X **Brasserie Vinois,** Ph. de Denterghemlaan 31, ℘ 0 9 282 70 18, *info@brasserie-vinois.com, Fax 0 9 282 68 04*, – AE VISA
fermé 15 août-5 sept., lundi, mardi et sam. midi – **Repas** Lunch 16 – 33 bc, ♀.
◆ Affaire familiale aménagée dans une belle villa "balnéaire" des années 1930. Banquettes en cuir, chaises bistrot et tables en marbre garnissent plaisamment la salle à manger.
◆ Familiebedrijf in een mooie villa uit de jaren 1930, die men eerder in een badplaats zou verwachten. In de eetzaal staan leren bankjes, bistrostoelen en marmeren tafels.

SINT-MARTENS-LEERNE *Oost-Vlaanderen* 533 G 16 – *voir à Deinze.*

SINT-MICHIELS *West-Vlaanderen* 533 E 14 *et* 716 C 2 – *voir à Brugge, périphérie.*

SINT-NIKLAAS (ST-NICOLAS) *9100 Oost-Vlaanderen* 533 J 15 *et* 716 F 2 – *68 473 h.*

Grote Markt 45 ☎ 0 3 777 26 81, land-van-waas@toerismevlaanderen.be, Fax 0 3 776 27 48.

Bruxelles 47 ② – Antwerpen 25 ② – Gent 39 ③ – Mechelen 32 ②

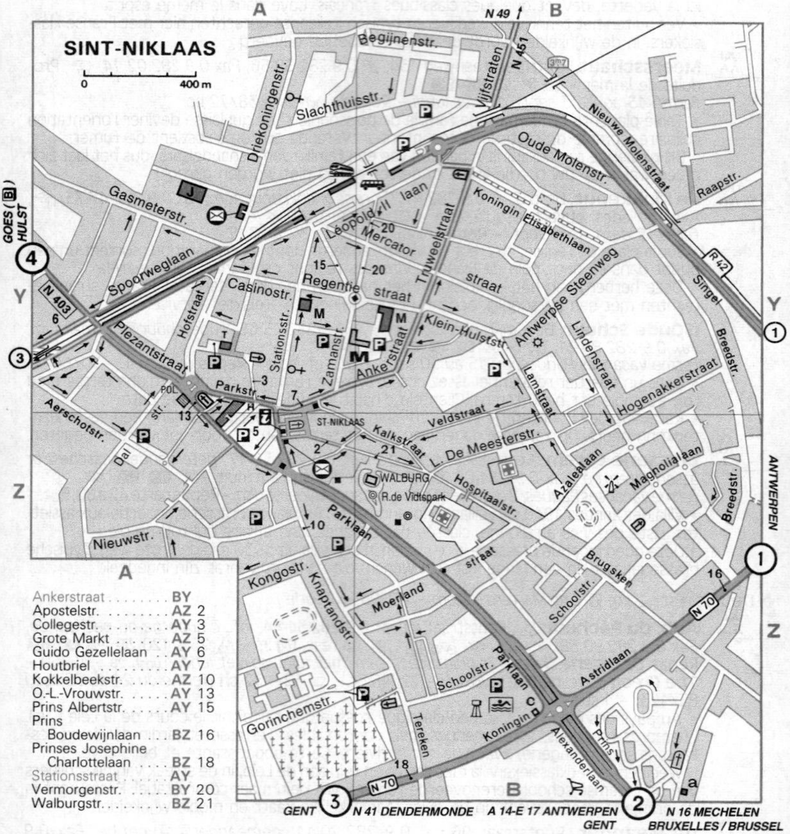

SINT-NIKLAAS

Ankerstraat	BY
Apostelstr.	AZ 2
Collegestr.	AY 3
Grote Markt	AZ 5
Guido Gezellelaan	AY 6
Houtbriel	AY 7
Kokkelbeekstr.	AZ 10
O.-L.-Vrouwstr.	AY 13
Prins Albertstr.	AY 15
Prins Boudewijnlaan	BZ 16
Prinses Josephine Charlottelaan	BZ 18
Stationsstraat	AY
Vermorgenstr.	BY 20
Walburgstr.	BZ 21

Serwir, Koningin Astridlaan 57, ☎ 0 3 778 05 11, *info@serwir.be, Fax 0 3 778 13 73,* – 25 à 500. AE ① ⓞ VISA. BZ c

Repas ***Renardeau*** *(fermé 4 juil.-9 août, Noël-Nouvel An, sam. midi, dim. et lundi)* Lunch 30 – 47, ♀ – ***The Balloon*** *(fermé 24 et 25 déc.)* (brasserie) Lunch 15 – 35 – **42 ch** ☕ 80/140 – ½ P 95/125.

◆ Confort accru et efforts tangibles de rénovation dans cet immeuble excentré. Chambres standard d'ampleur respectable, réparties sur trois étages. Onze salles de réunions. Restaurant au "look" contemporain plutôt léché. Préparations dans le tempo actuel.

◆ Het comfort in dit hotel even buiten het centrum is na een renovatie een stuk verbeterd. Ruime standaardkamers op drie verdiepingen, plus elf vergaderzalen. Restaurant met een hedendaagse "look", waar eigentijdse gerechten worden geserveerd.

XXX **Den Silveren Harynck,** Grote Baan 51 (par ① : 5 km sur N 70), ☎ 0 3 777 50 62, *Fax 0 3 766 67 61*, – P. AE MC VISA
fermé 3 dern. sem. juil., 26 déc.-3 janv., sam. midi, dim. soir et lundi – **Repas** Lunch 29 – 45/66 bc, ♀.
◆ L'enseigne - un hareng d'argent - reflète les préférences du chef, qui ne dédaigne toutefois pas les produits "terrestres". Nouveau décor chaleureux. Découpes en salle.
◆ De naam is een duidelijke aanwijzing voor de culinaire voorkeur van de chef-kok, maar ook zijn aan tafel gesneden vleesgerechten zijn niet te versmaden. Nieuw, warm interieur.

XX **Bistro De Eetkamer,** De Meulenaerstraat 2, ☎ 0 3 776 28 73, *bistro.de.eetkamer@skynet.be, Fax 0 3 766 24 61*, – P. AE ① MC VISA BZ a
fermé du 15 au 24 mars, du 5 au 27 juil., du 24 au 31 déc., lundi et mardi – **Repas** Lunch 20 – 35.
◆ Villa sur jardin à l'entrée d'un quartier résidentiel. Décor intérieur bourgeois égayé de lambris clairs, et terrasse dressée à la belle saison. Lunch et menus très demandés.
◆ Villa met tuin in een rustige woonwijk. Bourgeoisinterieur met licht houtwerk. Bij mooi weer wordt het terras opgedekt. De lunchformule en menu's zijn zeer in trek.

X **Gasthof Malpertus,** Beeldstraat 10 (par ① : 5 km, près du parc récréatif), ☎ 0 3 776 73 44, *malpertus@pi.be, Fax 0 3 766 50 18*, , Taverne-rest – P – 25 à 150. AE ① MC VISA
fermé du 15 au 28 fév., 3 dern. sem. juil., mardi et merc. – **Repas** Lunch 21 – 34/50 bc.
◆ Taverne-restaurant établie dans un cadre forestier. Recettes où pointe parfois le soleil de la Méditerranée. Tous les menus ont une option "vins compris". Terrasse ombragée.
◆ Café-restaurant in een bosrijke omgeving. In de recepten breekt af en toe de Zuid-Franse zon door. Alle menu's bieden een interessant wijnarrangement. Schaduwrijk terras.

à Nieuwkerken-Waas *Nord-Est : 4,5 km par N 451* C *Sint-Niklaas* – ✉ *9100 Nieuwkerken-Waas :*

XX **'t Korennaer,** Nieuwkerkenstraat 4, ☎ 0 3 778 08 45, *info@korennaer.be, Fax 0 3 778 08 43*, – . AE MC VISA
fermé 2 sem. avant Pâques, 2 dern. sem. août, mardi, merc. et sam. midi – **Repas** Lunch 30 – 37/66 bc, ♀.
◆ Salon confortable, fringantes salles de restaurant semées de légères touches contemporaines, belle terrasse et grand jardin. Mets actuels ou résolument innovants.
◆ Gerieflijke salon, zwierige eetzalen met een licht contemporain accent, mooi terras en grote tuin. Eigentijdse en zelfs vernieuwende keuken.

à Sint-Pauwels *par ④ : 7 km* C *Sint-Gillis-Waas 17 328 h.* – ✉ *9170 Sint-Pauwels :*

XX **De Rietgaard,** Zandstraat 221 (sur N 403), ☎ 0 3 779 55 48, *derietgaard@compaqnet.be, Fax 0 3 779 55 85*, – P. AE MC VISA.
fermé du 13 au 16 avril, 2 sem. en juil., lundi soir et mardi – **Repas** Lunch 28 – 36/60 bc.
◆ Jolie villa bourgeoise encapuchonnée sous un toit de chaume bien peigné. Registre culinaire classique actualisé. Salle à manger rajeunie. Restaurant d'été au jardin.
◆ Mooie villa met rieten dak. Klassiek culinair register dat aan de huidige smaak is aangepast. De eetzaal is onlangs vernieuwd. 's Zomers kan in de tuin worden gegeten.

SINT-PAUWELS *Oost-Vlaanderen* 533 J 15 *et* 716 F 2 – *voir à Sint-Niklaas.*

SINT-PIETERS-KAPELLE *West-Vlaanderen* 533 C 16 *et* 716 B 2 – *voir à Middelkerke.*

SINT-PIETERS-LEEUW *Vlaams-Brabant* 533 K 18 *et* 716 F 3 – *voir à Bruxelles, environs.*

SINT-PIETERS-WOLUWE *Brussels Hoofdstedelijk Gewest – voir Woluwe-St-Pierre à Bruxelles.*

SINT-STEVENS-WOLUWE (WOLUWE-ST-ÉTIENNE) *Vlaams-Brabant* 533 L 17 – *voir à Bruxelles, environs.*

SINT-TRUIDEN (ST-TROND) *3800 Limburg* 533 Q 17 *et* 716 I 3 – *37 314 h.*

Stadhuis, Grote Markt ☎ *0 11 70 18 18, info.toerisme@sint-truiden.be, Fax 0 11 70 18 20.*
Bruxelles 63 ⑥ – *Hasselt 17* ② – *Liège 35* ④ – *Namur 50* ⑤ – *Maastricht 39* ③

Plan page suivante

Cicindria sans rest, Abdijstraat 6, ☎ 0 11 68 13 44, *hotel.cicindria.nv@pandora.be, Fax 0 11 67 41 38* – TV P. AE ① MC VISA JCB. A s
fermé 19 déc.-5 janv. – **25 ch** 65/95.
◆ Établissement familial de conception récente jouxtant un centre commercial et l'ancienne abbaye fondée par saint Trond. Deux catégories de chambres : "de luxe" et "standard".
◆ Nieuw familiehotel naast een winkelcentrum en de voormalige abdij van de H. Trond. Twee categorieën kamers : luxe en standaard.

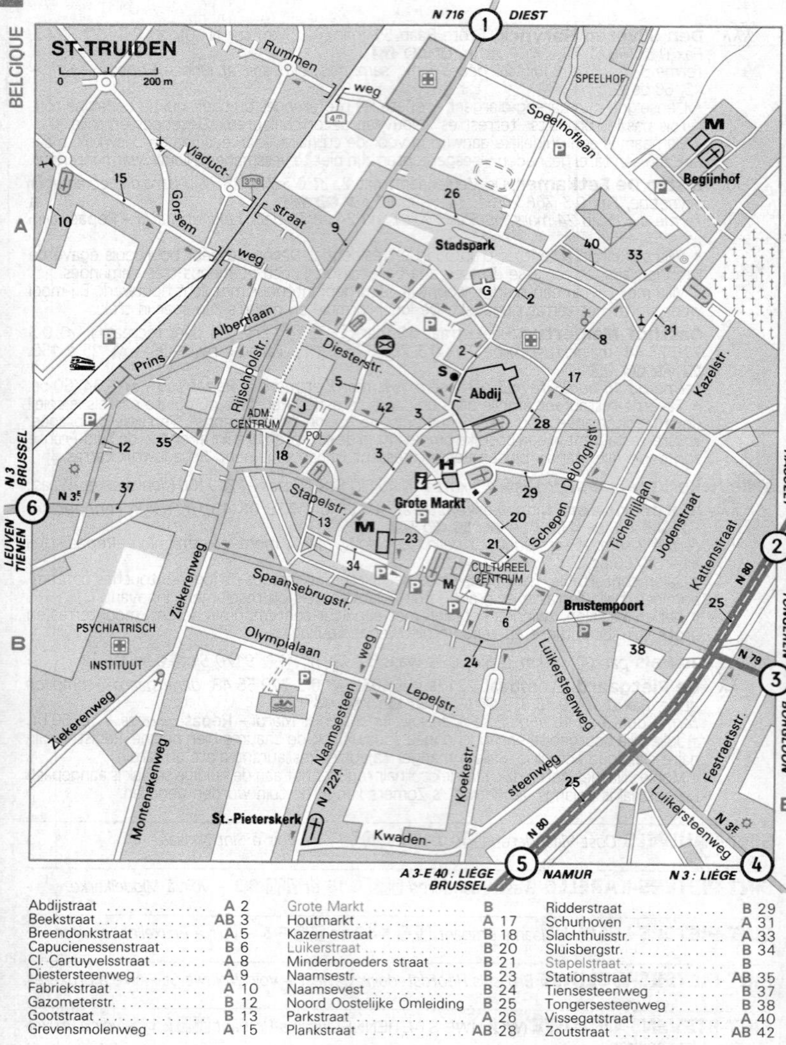

Abdijstraat	A 2	Grote Markt	B	Ridderstraat	B 29
Beekstraat	AB 3	Houtmarkt	A 17	Schurhoven	A 31
Breendonkstraat	A 5	Kazernestraat	B 18	Slachthuisstr.	A 33
Capucienessenstraat	B 6	Luikerstraat	B 20	Sluisbergstr.	B 34
Cl. Cartuyvelsstraat	A 8	Minderbroeders straat	B 21	Stapelstraat	B
Diestersteenweg	A 9	Naamsestr.	B 23	Stationsstraat	AB 35
Fabriekstraat	A 10	Naamsevest	B 24	Tiensesteenweg	B 37
Gazometerstr.	B 12	Noord Oostelijke Omleiding	B 25	Tongersesteenweg	B 38
Gootstraat	B 13	Parkstraat	A 26	Vissegatstraat	A 40
Grevensmolenweg	A 15	Plankstraat	AB 28	Zoutstraat	AB 42

Four Seasons sans rest, Tiensesteenweg 264 (par ⑥ sur N 3), ✆ 0 11 69 42 28, *hotelfourseasons@tiscalinet.be*, *Fax 0 11 69 16 78* – TV P. AE VISA
15 ch ☕ 56/62.

◆ Grand pavillon bâti de plain-pied, à une distance respectable du centre. Hébergement décent dans des chambres fonctionnelles. Service navette vers les restaurants de la ville.

◆ Hotel in een groot vrijstaand gebouw zonder verdiepingen, vrij ver van het centrum. Prettig verblijf in functionele kamers. Pendeldienst naar restaurants in de stad.

XXX **De Fakkels,** Hasseltsesteenweg 61 (Nord-Est : 2 km sur N 722, lieu-dit Melveren), ☎ 0 11 68 76 34, *info@defakkels.be, Fax 0 11 68 67 63,* – P – 25 à 40. AE MC VISA.
fermé 1 sem. Pâques, 3 dern. sem. août, dim. soir et lundi – **Repas** Lunch 31 – 47/79 bc.
◆ Maison bourgeoise 1900 précédée, côté jardin, d'une mignonne terrasse estivale. Sage décor intérieur mi-classique, mi-actuel. Recettes de notre temps.
◆ Herenhuis uit het begin van de 20e eeuw, met een tuin en een mooi terras voor zomerse dagen. Het interieur is half klassiek, half modern. De gerechten zijn eigentijds.

XXX **Aen de Kerck van Melveren,** St-Godfriedstraat 15 (Nord-Est : 3 km par N 722, lieu-dit Melveren), ☎ 0 11 68 39 65, *info@aendekerck.be, Fax 0 11 69 13 05,* ≤ – AE MC VISA.
fermé 22 fév.-2 mars, 21 juil.-10 août, sam. midi, dim. soir, lundi et mardi soir – **Repas** Lunch 32 – 60/85 bc.
◆ Jolie reconversion pour ce presbytère caché derrière l'église et à présent dévolu aux plaisirs de la table. Salle à manger-véranda donnant sur l'ancien jardin de curé.
◆ Deze fraai verbouwde pastorie achter de kerk wijdt zich nu aan het versterken van de inwendige mens. De eetzaal met serre kijkt uit op de voormalige kloostertuin.

à Nieuwerkerken *Nord : 6 km – 6 486 h – ✉ 3850 Nieuwerkerken :*

XX **Kelsbekerhof,** Kerkstraat 2, ☎ 0 11 69 13 87, *geert.boonen@pandora.be, Fax 0 11 69 13 87,* – P. AE MC VISA.
fermé prem. sem. sept., prem. sem. janv., mardi, merc. et sam. midi – **Repas** Lunch 34 – 40/70 bc.
◆ Un choix de mets classiques actualisés entend combler votre appétit dans cette ancienne ferme totalement remaniée. Belle terrasse avec un magnifique jardin pour toile de fond.
◆ In deze oude, van top tot teen verbouwde boerderij kunt u de honger stillen met een keur van modern-klassieke gerechten. Mooi terras met een prachtig uitzicht op de tuin.

SNELLEGEM *West-Vlaanderen* 533 D 16 *et* 716 C 2 – *voir à Jabbeke.*

SOHEIT-TINLOT *4557 Liège* C *Tinlot 2 204 h.* 533 R 20, 534 R 20 *et* 716 J 4.

Bruxelles 96 – Liège 29 – Huy 13.

XX **Le Coq aux Champs,** r. Montys 33, ☎ 0 85 51 20 14, *Fax 0 85 51 20 14,* – P. AE MC VISA
fermé du 23 au 31 mars, du 1er au 9 juin, du 7 au 15 sept., 24 et 25 déc., 2 prem. sem. janv., mardi et merc. – **Repas** Lunch 23 – 30/68 bc.
◆ Adorable auberge en pierres du pays, au bord d'une route se glissant à travers la campagne condruzienne. Nouvelle équipe en place, décidée à maintenir le cap gastronomique.
◆ Charmante herberg van steen uit de streek, aan een kronkelig landweggetje. Er staat een nieuw team aan het roer, dat van plan is de juiste gastronomische koers te houden !

SOIGNIES (ZINNIK) *7060 Hainaut* 533 J 19, 534 J 19 *et* 716 F 4 – *24 750 h.*

Voir *Collégiale St-Vincent★★.*

Bruxelles 41 – Mons 21 – Charleroi 40.

XX **La Fontaine St-Vincent,** r. Léon Hachez 7, ☎ 0 67 33 95 95, *pierre.leonard@skynet.be* – MC VISA
fermé 1 sem. carnaval, mi-juil.-mi-août, dim. soir, lundi soir et mardi – **Repas** Lunch 30 – 38/71 bc.
◆ Au centre-ville, maison du 16e s. connue pour ses préparations saisonnières "tendance" et pour sa cave digne de St-Vincent, patron des vignerons.
◆ Restaurant in een 16e-eeuws pand in het centrum, met een seizoengebonden trendy keuken. De wijnkelder brengt een ode aan de H. Vincentius, de schutspatroon van de wijnboeren.

XX **L'Embellie,** r. Station 115, ☎ 0 67 33 31 48, *Fax 0 67 33 31 48,* – AE MC VISA
fermé 20 juil.-13 août, du 2 au 8 janv., sam. midi, dim. soir et lundi – **Repas** Lunch 25 – 35/45.
◆ Petite adresse de notre temps située au voisinage de la gare. Salon apéritif cossu et terrasse dressée si le soleil luit. On ne badine pas avec la qualité des produits.
◆ Eigentijds restaurant bij het station, met een weelderige salon voor het aperitief en een mooi terras voor zomerse dagen. De kok neemt alleen genoegen met topkwaliteit.

X **Le Bouchon et l'Assiette,** Chemin du Saussois 5a (par N 6 : 2 km direction Mons, puis 2e rue à gauche), ☎ 0 67 33 18 14, *info@bouchonetlassiette.com, Fax 0 67 33 68 64,* ≤, – P. MC VISA
fermé lundi soir, mardi soir et merc. – **Repas** Lunch 17 – carte 27 à 41.
◆ Bien recevoir et faire plaisir : telle est la philosophie du patron. Vue agreste depuis votre table, en salle ou en terrasse. Plats traditionnels. Vins des régions de France.
◆ De baas maakt het zijn gasten graag naar de zin. Zowel vanuit de eetzaal als het terras ontvouwt zich een landelijk uitzicht. Traditionele schotels en Franse wijnen.

à Casteau *Sud : 7 km par N 6 C Soignies – ✉ 7061 Casteau :*

Casteau Resort, chaussée de Bruxelles 38, ☎ 0 65 32 04 00, *info@casteauresort.be, Fax 0 65 72 87 44,* – 25 à 250. AE VISA JCB
Repas *(fermé lundi midi)* (dîner seult) carte 22 à 42 – **74 ch** 80/99 – ½ P 98/130.
◆ En retrait de la route nationale qui relie Soignies à Maisières, construction de la fin des années 1960 renfermant des chambres actuelles, coquettes et douillettes. Salle à manger garnie d'un confortable mobilier en rotin et agrémentée d'une véranda.
◆ Dit hotel in een gebouw uit het eind van de jaren 1960 staat even van de rijksweg af die Zinnik met Maisières verbindt. De kamers zijn modern, behaaglijk en aantrekkelijk. De eetzaal heeft een serre en is ingericht met comfortabele rotanmeubelen.

à Thieusies *Sud : 6 km par N 6 C Soignies – ✉ 7061 Thieusies :*

La Saisinne, r. Saisinne 133, ☎ 0 65 72 86 63, *b.delaunois@easynet.be, Fax 0 65 73 02 61* – P. AE VISA.
fermé 1 sem. Pâques, juil., dim. et lundi – **Repas** 36/63 bc.
◆ Fermette rénovée au beau milieu des prés, La Saisinne vous fait bénéficier de son atmosphère sagement rustique. Vue bucolique depuis la terrasse apéritive.
◆ Dit gerenoveerde boerderijtje midden in de weilanden laat u graag meegenieten van zijn rustieke atmosfeer. Wie op het terras een borreltje drinkt, heeft een prachtig uitzicht.

La Maison d'Odile, r. Sirieu 303, ☎ 0 65 73 00 72, – VISA
fermé 12 et 13 avril, 11 août-2 sept., 24 déc.-1er janv., mardi soir, merc., dim. soir et jours fériés soir – **Repas** 37/79 bc.
◆ Une ancienne forge abrite cette table plaisante aménagée dans l'esprit campagnard. Salon mignon comme tout, où un feu ouvert réconfortant crépite pendant tout l'hiver.
◆ Deze oude smederij is nu een plezierig plattelandsrestaurant. In de sfeervolle salon brandt 's winters een behaaglijk vuur.

SOLRE-ST-GÉRY *Hainaut* 534 K 21 *et* 716 F 5 – *voir à Beaumont.*

SORINNES *Namur* 533 O 21, 534 O 21 *et* 716 H 5 – *voir à Dinant.*

SOUGNÉ-REMOUCHAMPS *4920 Liège C Aywaille 10 386 h.* 533 T 20, 534 T 20 *et* 716 K 4.
Voir *Grottes*★★.
r. Broux 18 ☎ 0 4 384 52 42.
Bruxelles 122 – Liège 28 – Spa 13.

Bonhomme avec ch, r. Reffe 26, ☎ 0 4 384 40 06, *info@hotelbonhomme.be, Fax 0 4 384 37 19,* – AE VISA. ch
fermé sem. carnaval, dern. sem. mars, dern. sem. juin, dern. sem. sept.-prem. sem. oct., 25 nov.-10 déc., jeudi hors saison et merc. – **Repas** 32/50 – **11 ch** 60/87 – ½ P 68/72.
◆ Auberge ardennaise tenue en famille depuis 1768. Décor intérieur préservé. Repas "tradition" et chambres où Mistinguett, Fernandel et têtes couronnées firent de beaux rêves.
◆ Ardense herberg met oorspronkelijk interieur die al sinds 1768 eigendom is van dezelfde familie. Traditionele keuken en kamers waar vorsten en filmsterren hebben gelogeerd.

SOUMOY *Namur* 534 L 21 *et* 716 G 5 – *voir à Cerfontaine.*

SPA *4900 Liège* 533 U 20, 534 U 20 *et* 716 K 4 – *10 394 h – Station thermale*★★ *– Casino AY, r. Royale 4 ☎ 0 87 77 20 52, Fax 0 87 77 02 06.*
Voir *par ② : Promenade des Artistes*★.
Musée : *de la Ville d'eaux : collection*★ *de "jolités"* AY **M.**
Env. *par ③ : 9 km, Circuit autour de Spa*★ *- Parc à gibier de la Reid*★.
18 par ① : 2,5 km à Balmoral, av. de l'Hippodrome 1 ☎ 0 87 79 30 30, Fax 0 87 79 30 39.
Pavillon des Petits Jeux, pl. Royale 41 ☎ 0 87 79 53 53, officetoerisme@skynet.be, Fax 0 87 79 53 54.
Bruxelles 139 ③ – Liège 38 ③ – Verviers 16 ③

Plan page ci-contre

La Villa des Fleurs sans rest, r. Albin Body 31, ☎ 0 87 79 50 50, *info@villadesfleurs.be, Fax 0 87 79 50 60,* – AE VISA JCB. AY e
fermé 2 janv.-1er fév. – **12 ch** 74/127.
◆ Élégante demeure patricienne du 19e s. s'ouvrant, à l'arrière, sur un jardin clos de murs où donnent la plupart des chambres, assez spacieuses. Aménagement cossu.
◆ Sierlijk patriciërshuis uit de 19e eeuw met een ommuurde tuin aan de achterkant. Weelderig interieur. De kamers zijn vrij ruim en kijken vrijwel allemaal op de tuin uit.

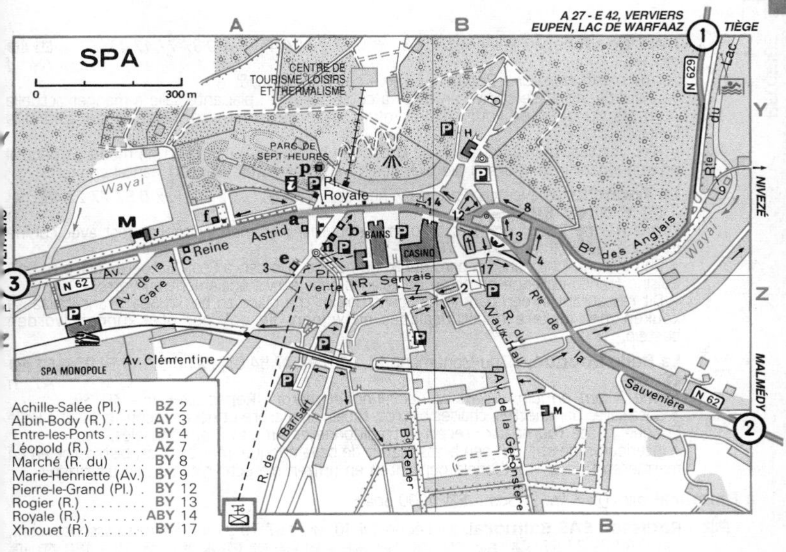

La Heid des Pairs sans rest, av. Prof. Henrijean 143 (Sud-Ouest : 1,5 km), 0 87 77 43 46, *info@heiddespairs.be*, *Fax 0 87 77 06 44*, – . *VISA*. par av. Clémentine AZ
8 ch 99/139.
◆ Dans un quartier résidentiel excentré, confortable villa agrémentée d'un vaste jardin reposant et d'une piscine. Bonnes chambres personnalisées. Salon "cosy".
◆ Comfortabele villa met grote tuin en zwembad in een rustige woonwijk buiten het centrum. Goede kamers met een persoonlijk karakter. Sfeervolle lounge.

L'Auberge, pl. du Monument 3, 0 87 77 44 10, *info@hotel-thermes.be*, *Fax 0 87 77 48 40*, – , rest, – 25. *VISA*. rest AY a
Repas *(fermé prem. sem. déc. et 2 prem. sem. janv.)* *Lunch 22* – 25/45 bc – **18 ch** *(fermé 2 prem. sem. janv.)* 98/102, – 12 suites – ½ P 82/127.
◆ Établissement très central dont la jolie façade, fleurie en été, s'anime de colombages. Chambres fonctionnelles et suites avec kitchenette à l'annexe. Miroirs, cuivres, banquettes en cuir et lustres graciles président au décor du restaurant.
◆ Zeer centraal gelegen hotel in een vakwerkhuis, waarvan de gevel 's zomers één bloemenpracht is. Functionele kamers en suites met kitchenette in de dependance. Spiegels, koperwerk, leren bankjes en kroonluchters sieren het restaurant.

Le Pierre , av. Reine Astrid 86, 0 87 77 52 10, *hotellepierre@lepierre.be*, *Fax 0 87 77 52 20*, – . *VISA* AY c
fermé 1re quinz. janv. – **Repas** (dîner pour résidents seult) – **14 ch** 100 – ½ P 70/82.
◆ Cette façade bourgeoise du centre de la ville d'eau dissimule une extension récente accueillant des chambres de plain-pied, autour d'une petite pelouse. Tranquillité assurée.
◆ Dit centraal gelegen herenhuis in een kuuroord is uitgebreid. De nieuwe kamers op de gelijkvloers liggen rond een klein gazon. Rust verzekerd !

Le Relais, pl. du Monument 22, 0 87 77 11 08, *info@hotelrelais-spa.be*, *Fax 0 87 77 25 93*, – . *VISA* AY b
Repas *(fermé 21 nov.-17 déc., dim. soir de janv. à avril et lundi midi)* 22/47 bc – **11 ch** *(fermé 28 nov.-17 déc.)* 60/75 – ½ P 68/77.
◆ Ce petit hôtel tenu en famille se partage entre deux maisons mitoyennes situées à un jet d'eau des bains et à un tour de roulette du casino. Chambres correctement équipées. Repas traditionnel. Terrasse d'été dressée en façade.
◆ Dit hotel wordt door een familie gerund en beslaat twee belendende panden. Van hieruit kunt u gemakkelijk een bad in de bronnen nemen of uw geluk beproeven in het casino. De kamers bieden goede voorzieningen. Traditionele keuken en zomerterras aan de voorkant.

BELGIQUE

XX **L'art de vivre,** av. Reine Astrid 53, ☎ 0 87 77 04 44, *Fax 0 87 77 17 43*, – AE MC VISA AY f
fermé merc. et jeudi – **Repas** Lunch 30 – carte 48 à 66, ♀.
• "L'art de vivre" se cultive en effet à cette adresse : plaisante salle à manger actuelle et mets au goût du jour relevés d'un zeste de créativité. Nombre de couverts limité.
• Hier verstaat men inderdaad "de kunst van het leven" : een prettige moderne eetzaal en een eigentijdse kookstijl die blijk geeft van creativiteit. Beperkt aantal couverts.

X **La Tonnellerie** avec ch, Parc de 7 heures, ☎ 0 87 77 22 84, *Fax 0 87 77 22 48*, – TV P AE MC VISA JCB AY p
Repas *(fermé 2 sem. en mars, 2e quinz. sept., mardi et merc.)* (taverne-rest avec cuisine italienne) 23, ♀ – **7 ch** 70/80 – ½ P 60.
• Ce pavillon niché dans un parc public du centre-ville est, à Spa, l'actuelle "place to be". Cuisine franco-italienne escortée de salades. Vins servis également au verre.
• Dit restaurant in een park in het centrum is "the place to be" in Spa. Frans-Italiaanse keuken met lekkere maaltijdsalades en wijnen die ook per glas kunnen worden besteld.

X **La Belle Epoque,** pl. du Monument 15, ☎ 0 87 77 54 03, *Fax 0 87 77 54 03* – AE MC VISA AY n
fermé 2 sem. en juin, 2 sem. en déc., lundi et mardi – **Repas** Lunch 19 – 30/39.
• Côté salle : banquettes, chaises bistrot, tables en marbre et décor façon "brasserie Belle Époque". Côté fourneaux : recettes traditionnelles simples à prix muselés.
• Interieur in de stijl van een brasserie uit de belle époque, met bankjes, bistrostoelen en marmeren tafels. Traditionele gerechten en prijzen die echt niet de pan uit rijzen !

à Balmoral *par ① : 3 km* C *Spa –* ✉ *4900 Spa :*

Radisson SAS Balmoral, av. Léopold II 40, ☎ 0 87 79 21 41, *info@radissonsas.com, Fax 0 87 79 21 51*, – TV P – 25 à 180. AE MC VISA JCB.
Repas ***Entre Terre et Mer*** (rôtissoire en salle) Lunch 25 – carte 38 à 78 – **51 ch** 155/180, – 38 suites – ½ P 108/135.
• Sur les hauteurs, en lisière de forêt, petit palace 1900 récemment rénové, mais conservant son "look" anglo-normand. Chambres dernier cri, disponibles en quatre tailles. Ambitieux restaurant au goût du jour. Brunch en musique les dimanches et fêtes.
• Luxehotel uit 1900 op een heuvel bij het bos. Ondanks de verbouwing heeft het zijn Anglo-Normandische karakter bewaard. Ultramoderne kamers in vier verschillende maten. Ambitieus restaurant in eigentijdse stijl. Op zon- en feestdagen brunch met livemuziek.

Dorint, rte de Balmoral 33, ☎ 0 87 79 32 50, *dorintspa@dorintspa.be, Fax 0 87 77 41 74*, ← vallée boisée, – , rest, TV P – 25 à 200. AE MC VISA. rest
Repas Lunch 30 – 35/70 bc – **98 ch** 130/195 – ½ P 102/209.
• Immeuble émergeant de la colline boisée qui domine le lac de Warfaaz. Chambres rafraîchies, aussi confortables que pimpantes, et munies d'un balcon. Espace de remise en forme.
• Dit hotel staat op een beboste heuvel hoog boven het meer van Warfaaz. De gerenoveerde kamers met balkon zijn comfortabel en zien er piekfijn uit. Fitnessruimte.

à la Reid *par ③ : 9 km* C *Theux 11 464 h. –* ✉ *4910 La Reid :*

Le Menobu, rte de Menobu 546, ☎ 0 87 37 60 42, *Fax 0 87 37 69 35*, – TV P MC VISA
fermé du 10 au 25 janv. – **Repas** *(fermé mardi et merc.)* Lunch 35 – carte 30 à 45 – **6 ch** 58 – ½ P 47.
• Paisible petite auberge familiale surveillant une route de campagne. Préférez les chambres situées à l'arrière : elles offrent la vue sur le jardin et les champs. Restaurant-tea-room. L'été, quelques tables sont dressées sur la pelouse.
• Rustig familiehotelletje bij een landweg. De kamers aan de achterkant verdienen de voorkeur, omdat ze uitkijken op de tuin en de velden. Restaurant annex theesalon. In de zomer worden enkele tafeltjes op het grasveld gedekt.

à Sart *par ① : 7 km* C *Jalhay 7 712 h. –* ✉ *4845 Sart :*

L'Aub. du Wayai sans rest, rte du Stockay 2, ☎ 0 87 47 53 93, *wayai@hotel-du-wayai.be, Fax 0 87 47 53 95*, – TV P AE MC VISA
18 ch 65/100.
• Aux avant-postes du village, dans un vallon agreste, ensemble de maisonnettes disposées en carré autour d'une cour agrémentée de pelouses et d'une piscine.
• Deze auberge aan de rand van het dorp, in een landelijk dal, bestaat uit huisjes die in een vierkant om de met gras begroeide binnenplaats staan, waar ook een zwembad is.

XX **Aub. les Santons** avec ch, Cokaifagne 47 (rte de Francorchamps), ☎ 0 87 47 43 15, *info@aubergelessantons.be, Fax 0 87 47 43 16,* – TV P. MC VISA. ch
15 avril-15 nov., week-end et jours fériés ; fermé 22 nov.-23 déc., mardi soir et merc. – **Repas** *(fermé après 20 h 30)* Lunch 26 – 38/50 – **6 ch** 75/100 – ½ P 65/75.
◆ Une auberge qui n'a de provençal que l'enseigne. Agréable salle à manger au décor bourgeois. Terrasse estivale invitante dressée au jardin.
◆ In deze herberg is alleen het uithangbord Provençaals. Aangename eetzaal in de stijl van de gegoede burgerij. 's Zomers is het heerlijk toeven op het terras in de tuin.

XX **Le Petit Normand,** r. Roquez 47 (Sud-Est : 3 km, direction Francorchamps), ☎ 0 87 47 49 04, *lepetitnormand@hotmail.com, Fax 0 87 47 49 04,* – P. MC VISA
fermé 1re quinz. sept., 1re quinz. janv., merc. et jeudi – **Repas** Lunch 22 – 30/48.
◆ Confort accru pour cette villa de campagne profitant d'alentours boisés. Le cœur du chef, bardé de distinctions gastronomiques, balance entre tradition et tempo actuel.
◆ Comfortabele villa in een bosrijke omgeving. De chef-kok, die met talloze gastronomische onderscheidingen is geëerd, houdt zowel van traditioneel als van modern.

SPONTIN *5530 Namur* C *Yvoir 8 061 h.* 533 P 21, 534 P 21 *et* 716 I 5.
Voir *Château★.*
Bruxelles 83 – Namur 24 – Dinant 11 – Huy 31.

à Dorinne *Sud-Ouest : 2,5 km* C *Yvoir* – ✉ *5530 Dorinne :*

XXX **Le Vivier d'Oies** (Godelet), r. État 7, ☎ 0 83 69 95 71, *Fax 0 83 69 90 36,* – P. AE ✿ ⓓ MC VISA
fermé du 12 au 18 mars, 18 juin-8 juil., 22 sept.-7 oct., merc. et jeudis non fériés – **Repas** Lunch 27 – 43/86 bc, carte 55 à 69, ♀.
◆ Demeure ancienne en pierres du pays. Les spécialités de la maison en témoignent : aux fourneaux, on n'a pas affaire à des "oies blanches" ! Repas en terrasse par beau temps.
◆ Mooi oud pand van steen uit de streek, dat een culinaire maaltijd van hoog niveau voor u in petto heeft. Op zomerse dagen worden de tafeltjes op het terras gedekt.
Spéc. Fond d'artichaut aux queues d'écrevisses, coulis à l'estragon (mai-nov.). Tête de veau, vinaigrette aux herbes(déc.-mars). Pigeonneau royal d'Anjou rôti à la sauge, gaufre de pommes de terre au lard et oignons

---

SPRIMONT *4140 Liège* 533 T 19, 534 T 19 *et* 716 JK 4 – *12 570 h.*
Bruxelles 112 – Liège 19 – Spa 12.

XXX **La Maison des Saveurs,** r. Grand Bru 27 (sur N 30, direction Liège), ☎ 0 4 382 35 60, *Fax 0 4 382 35 63,* – P. AE ⓓ MC VISA.
fermé 1re quinz. sept., lundi et mardi – **Repas** Lunch 27 – carte 46 à 59.
◆ Beau restaurant d'esprit contemporain, confortablement installé dans une villa du hameau de Ognée. Repas savoureux, confirmant ainsi ce que proclame l'enseigne.
◆ Mooi eigentijds restaurant in een comfortabele villa in het gehuchtje Ognée. De maaltijd is bijzonder smakelijk, zoals het uithangbord ook belooft.

STALHILLE *West-Vlaanderen* 533 D 15 *et* 716 C 2 – *voir à Jabbeke.*

STAVELOT *4970 Liège* 533 U 20, 534 U 20 *et* 716 K 4 – *6 631 h.*
Voir *Carnaval du Laetare★★ (3e dim. avant Pâques) – Châsse de St-Remacle★★ dans l'église St-Sébastien.*
Musées : *religieux régional dans l'Ancienne Abbaye : section des Tanneries★ – Ancienne abbaye★.*
Env. *à l'Ouest : Vallée de l'Amblève★★ de Stavelot à Comblain-au-Pont – à l'Ouest : 8,5 km : Cascade★ de Coo, Montagne de Lancre ★.*
ℹ *Musée de l'Ancienne Abbaye, Cour de l'Hôtel de Ville* ☎ *0 80 86 27 06, etc@abbayedestavelot.be, Fax 0 80 86 27 06.*
Bruxelles 158 – Liège 59 – Bastogne 64 – Malmédy 9 – Spa 18.

d'Orange, Devant les Capucins 8, ☎ 0 80 86 20 05, *logis@hotel-orange.be, Fax 0 80 86 42 92,* – TV P – 30. AE ⓓ MC VISA
mai-nov., vacances scolaires et week-end – **Repas** *(fermé mardi soir, merc. et après 20 h 30)* Lunch 18 – 26/61 bc – **17 ch** 90 – ½ P 61/86.
◆ Auberge affable occupant l'un de ces anciens relais de la malle-poste édifiés voici plus de deux cents ans. L'affaire se transmet de génération en génération depuis 1789.
◆ Vriendelijke herberg in een van de vele oude poststations die deze streek telt. Al sinds 1789 wordt de traditie hier van generatie op generatie overgedragen.

BELGIQUE

XXX **Le Val d'Amblève** avec ch, rte de Malmédy 7, ✆ 0 80 28 14 40, *info@levaldamble ve.com, Fax 0 80 28 14 59,* ⛱, 🚗 - ▤ rest, TV P - 🏋 35. AE ⓓ MC VISA
fermé janv. – **Repas** *(fermé lundis non fériés)* Lunch 34 – 48/81 bc – **20 ch** ☕ 76/115.
◆ Aux portes de Stavelot, élégante résidence des années 1930 blottie dans son parc, sous les frondaisons d'arbres centenaires. Cuisine maîtrisée. Chambres au diapason.
◆ Dit sierlijke gebouw uit de jaren 1930 staat aan de rand van Stavelot in een prachtige grote tuin met eeuwenoude bomen. De keuken getuigt van vakmanschap. Prima kamers.

STERREBEEK *Vlaams-Brabant* 533 L 17 *et* 716 G 3 – *voir à Bruxelles, environs.*

STOUMONT *4987 Liège* 533 T 20, 534 T 20 *et* 716 K 4 – *2 957 h.*
Env. à l'Ouest : Belvédère "Le Congo" ≤★ – Site★ du Fonds de Quareux.
Bruxelles 139 – Liège 45 – Malmédy 24.

X **Zabonprés,** Zabonprés 3 (Ouest : 4,5 km sur N 633, puis route à gauche), ✆ 0 80 78 56 72, *zabonpres@swing.be, Fax 0 80 78 61 41,* ⛱ – P. ⓓ MC VISA
21 mars-21 sept. et week-end ; fermé sem. carnaval, sem. Toussaint, Noël-Nouvel An, lundi et mardi – **Repas** Lunch 25 – 30/47 bc.
◆ Préparations au goût du jour servies dans l'atmosphère sympathique d'une fermette à pans de bois surveillant le cours de l'Amblève. Accueil et service gentils. Menus bien vus.
◆ Vakwerkboerderijtje met een gezellige sfeer aan de oever van de Amblève, waar u van eigentijdse gerechten kunt genieten. Vriendelijke ontvangst en bediening. Mooie menu's.

Ecrivez-nous...
Vos louanges comme vos critiques seront examinées avec le plus grand soin. Nous reverrons sur place les informations que vous nous signalez. Par avance merci !

STROMBEEK-BEVER *Vlaams-Brabant* 533 L 17 *et* 716 G 3 – *voir à Bruxelles, environs.*

STUIVEKENSKERKE *West-Vlaanderen* 533 C 16 – *voir à Diksmuide.*

TAMISE *Oost-Vlaanderen – voir Temse.*

TEMPLOUX *Namur* 533 N 20, 534 N 20 *et* 716 H 4 – *voir à Namur.*

TEMSE (TAMISE) *9140 Oost-Vlaanderen* 533 K 16 *et* 716 F 2 – *25 937 h.*
🅘 *De Watermolen, Wilfordkaai 23* ✆ *0 3 771 51 31, temse@toerismevlaanderen.be, Fax 0 3 711 94 34.*
Bruxelles 40 – Gent 41 – Antwerpen 26 – Mechelen 25 – Sint-Niklaas 7,5.

XX **La Provence,** Doornstraat 252 (Nord : 2 km, lieu-dit Velle), ✆ 0 3 711 07 63, *info@ restaurantlaprovence.be, Fax 0 3 771 69 03,* ⛱ – P. AE MC VISA
fermé mardi et merc. – **Repas** (dîner seult sauf dim.) 39/60 bc.
◆ Ancienne ferme et sa terrasse estivale dressée face au jardin agrémenté d'une pièce d'eau. Salle de restaurant cossue évoquant la Provence ; carte et menus de même.
◆ Deze boerderij heeft een terras dat 's zomers wordt opgedekt en uitkijkt op de tuin met vijver. De luxe eetzaal doet aan de Provence denken, net als de kaart en de menu's.

XX **de Sonne,** Markt 10, ✆ 0 3 771 37 73, *desonne@pandora.beet, Fax 0 3 771 37 73,* ⛱ – AE ⓓ MC VISA
fermé 14 juil.-1er août, merc. et jeudi – **Repas** Lunch 28 – 40/71 bc.
◆ Maison de notable postée depuis 1870 sur la place du marché. Derrière son "piano", le chef adapte sagement ses recettes au goût du moment. Salle à manger aux douces tonalités.
◆ Dit herenhuis staat al sinds 1870 aan het marktplein. De chef-kok past zijn recepten voorzichtig aan de huidige tijd aan. De eetzaal is in zachte tinten gehouden.

TERHAGEN *Antwerpen* 533 L 16 – *voir à Boom.*

TERHULPEN *Brabant Wallon – voir La Hulpe.*

TERMONDE *Oost-Vlaanderen – voir Dendermonde.*

TERTRE *7333 Hainaut* [C] *St-Ghislain 22 014 h.* 533 H 20, 534 H 20 *et* 716 E 4.

18 *au Nord-Est : 4 km à Baudour, r. Mont Garni 3* ☎ *0 65 62 27 19, Fax 0 65 62 34 10.*

Bruxelles 77 – Mons 12 – Tournai 37 – Valenciennes 30.

XX **Le Vieux Colmar,** rte de Tournai 197 (N 50), ☎ 0 65 62 26 79, *Fax 0 65 62 36 14,* – P. AE ① ⓜ VISA

fermé 2 sem. carnaval, 19 juil.-10 août et mardi – **Repas** (déjeuner seult sauf vend. et sam.) *Lunch 27* – 42/76 bc.

• Auberge-villa à la campagne, servant une cuisine aux références classiques, sensible au cycle des saisons. Par beau temps, on mange au jardin, fleuri tout l'été. Bon accueil.

• Plattelandsvilla met een klassieke keuken die gevoelig is voor de seizoenen. Bij mooi weer wordt in de tuin gegeten, die de hele zomer in bloei staat.

XX **La Cense de Lalouette,** rte de Tournai 188 (N 547), ☎ 0 65 62 08 70, *jeanne.van derlinden@pi.be,* – P. AE ① ⓜ VISA

fermé 14 août-10 sept., du 1er au 15 janv. et lundi – **Repas** (déjeuner seult sauf sam.) 25/85 bc.

• L'une de ces anciennes fermes hennuyères construites pour durer... Celle-ci, coquette et rustique à souhait, date de 1704. Terrasse dans la cour intérieure aux pavés joufflus.

• Een van die oude Henegouwse boerderijen die zo stevig zijn gebouwd dat ze nooit vergaan. Deze is mooi en rustiek en dateert uit 1704. Terras op de binnenplaats met kasseien.

TERVUREN *Vlaams-Brabant* 533 M 18 *et* 716 G 3 – *voir à Bruxelles, environs.*

TESSENDERLO *3980 Limburg* 533 P 16 *et* 716 I 2 – *16 206 h.*

Voir *Jubé★ de l'église St-Martin (St-Martinuskerk).*

Gemeentehuis, Markt ☎ *0 13 66 17 15, vvv@tessenderlo.be, Fax 0 13 67 36 93.*

Bruxelles 66 – Antwerpen 57 – Liège 70.

XX **La Forchetta,** Stationsstraat 69, ☎ 0 13 66 40 14, *Fax 0 13 66 40 14,* – P. AE ⓜ VISA

fermé 1 sem. après carnaval, dern. sem. juil.-2 prem. sem. août, dim. soir et lundi – **Repas** *Lunch 34* – carte 37 à 52.

• Accueil affable, intimes salle à manger, terrasse exquise, jardin pomponné, mets classiques et cave franco-transalpine : les bonnes fourchettes du coin sont conquises !

• Gastvrije ontvangst, intieme eetzaal, heerlijk terras, mooie tuin, klassieke keuken en Frans-Italiaanse wijnen, dat is de succesformule van dit restaurant !

TEUVEN *3793 Limburg* [C] *Voeren 4 328 h.* 533 U 18 *et* 716 K 3.

Bruxelles 134 – Maastricht 22 – Liège 43 – Verviers 26 – Aachen 22.

XXX **Hof de Draeck** avec ch, Hoofstraat 6, ☎ 0 4 381 10 17, *info@hof-de-draeck.be, Fax 0 4 381 11 88,* – TV P. AE ① ⓜ VISA.

fermé du 16 au 28 fév., du 16 au 30 août, lundi et mardi – **Repas** *Lunch 41 bc* – 39/65 bc, – **11 ch** 86.

• Jolie ferme-château isolée dans la campagne limbourgeoise. Salle de restaurant "grand seigneur" et bonne cuisine traditionnelle actualisée. Grand parc et chambres spacieuses.

• Mooie kasteelhoeve op het Limburgse platteland. In de chique eetzaal worden goede traditionele gerechten met een vleugje vernieuwing geserveerd. Groot park en ruime kamers.

THEUX *4910 Liège* 533 T 19, 534 T 19 *et* 716 K 4 – *11 464 h.*

Bruxelles 131 – Liège 31 – Spa 7 – Verviers 12.

XX **L'Aubergine,** chaussée de Spa 87, ☎ 0 87 53 02 59, *aubergine.theux@belgacom.net, Fax 0 87 53 02 59* – P. ⓜ VISA

fermé fin juin-début juil., 1 sem. en janv., mardi soir et merc. – **Repas** *Lunch 25* – 37/52 bc.

• Une belle carte mise au goût du jour, avec lunch et menus prometteurs, vous sera soumise dans cette villa récente située aux avant-postes de Theux. Nombre de couverts limité.

• In deze nieuwe villa even buiten Theux kunt u kiezen uit een mooie kaart met eigentijdse gerechten, een lunchformule en veelbelovende menu's. Beperkt aantal couverts.

THIEUSIES *Hainaut* 533 J 19, 534 J 19 *et* 716 F 4 – *voir à Soignies.*

THIMISTER *4890 Liège* ⒸThimister-Clermont *5 268 h.* 533 U 19, 534 U 19 *et* 716 K 4.
Bruxelles 121 – Maastricht 34 – Liège 29 – Verviers 12 – Aachen 22.

à Clermont *Est : 2 km* Ⓒ *Thimister-Clermont* – ✉ *4890 Clermont :*

XXX **Le Charmes-Chambertin,** Crawhez 40, ☎ 0 87 44 50 37, *lecharmeschambertin@skynet.be, Fax 0 87 44 71 61,* – P – 25 à 60. AE ⓓ MC VISA
fermé mi-juil.-mi-août, mardi soir, merc. et dim. soir – **Repas** *Lunch 30* – 43/80 bc.
◆ Sur le plateau bucolique du pays de Herve, ancienne ferme restaurée qui séduit par sa cuisine classique actualisée et sa cave d'épicurien. Décor intérieur néo-rustique.
◆ Deze gerestaureerde boerderij met een neorustiek interieur is schilderachtig gelegen in het Land van Herve. De klassiek-moderne keuken en wijnkelder zijn beide uitmuntend.

THON *Namur* 533 P 20, 534 P 20 *et* 716 I 4 – *voir à Namur.*

TIELT *8700 West-Vlaanderen* 533 F 17 *et* 716 D 2 – *19 177 h.*
Bruxelles 85 – Brugge 34 – Kortrijk 21 – Gent 32.

Shamrock, Euromarktlaan 24 (près rte de ceinture), ☎ 0 51 40 15 31, *info@shamrock.be, Fax 0 51 40 40 92,* , – |‡|, ▤ rest, TV P – 25 à 250. AE ⓓ MC VISA
fermé 2 dern. sem. juil.-prem. sem. août – **Repas** *(fermé dim. et lundi)* carte 39 à 48 – **29 ch** *(fermé dim.)* ☐ 65/95.
◆ Imposante villa des années 1970 installée aux portes de Tielt. Chambres fonctionnelles de taille satisfaisante, munies du double vitrage. Jardin paisible. Salle à manger dans l'air du temps, où règne une atmosphère feutrée.
◆ Deze imposante villa is in de jaren 1970 aan de rand van Tielt gebouwd. De functionele kamers zijn goed van formaat en hebben dubbele ramen. Rustige tuin. In de eetzaal, die naar de laatste mode is ingericht, heerst een gedempte atmosfeer.

XX **De Meersbloem,** Polderstraat 3 (Nord-Est : 4,5 km, direction Ruiselede, puis rte à gauche), ☎ 0 51 40 25 01, *Fax 0 51 40 77 52,* ≤, – ▤ P. MC VISA
fermé du 15 au 31 août, Noël-Nouvel An, mardi soir, merc. et dim. soir – **Repas** *Lunch 30* – 50/75 bc.
◆ Adorable fermette perdue dans la campagne. L'assiette y est généreuse, la salle de restaurant, "classico-moderne", et la cave, assez bien balancée. Jardin soigné.
◆ Dit lieflijke boerderijtje staat afgelegen op het platteland. Het interieur is modern-klassiek, het eten verfijnd en de wijnkelder evenwichtig. Goed onderhouden tuin.

TIENEN (TIRLEMONT) *3300 Vlaams-Brabant* 533 O 18 *et* 716 H 3 – *31 423 h.*
Voir *Église N.-D.-au Lac★ (O.L. Vrouw-ten-Poelkerk) : portails★* ABY **D.**
Env. *par ② : 3 km à Hakendover, retable★ de l'église St-Sauveur (Kerk van de Goddelijke Zaligmaker) – à l'Est : 15 km à Zoutleeuw, Église St-Léonard★★ (St-Leonarduskerk) : intérieur★★ (musée d'art religieux, tabernacle★★).*
Grote Markt 4 ☎ 0 16 80 56 86, tienen@toerismevlaanderen.be, Fax 0 16 82 27 04.
Bruxelles 46 ④ – Charleroi 60 ④ – Hasselt 35 ② – Liège 57 ④ – Namur 47 ④

Plan page ci-contre

Alpha, Leuvensestraat 95, ☎ 0 16 82 28 00, *info@alphahotel.be, Fax 0 16 82 24 54,* , – |‡| TV P – 25 à 90. AE MC VISA AY a
Repas *(fermé 1re quinz. août, sam. et dim.) Lunch 15* – 22/40 bc – ☐ 10 – **18 ch** 75/95 – ½ P 73/100.
◆ Pratique avant tout, et aussi proche de la gare que de la place du marché, cet établissement familial met à votre disposition trois étages de petites chambres insonorisées.
◆ Praktisch familiehotel, centraal gelegen bij het station en de Grote Markt. De kleine kamers hebben een goede geluidsisolatie en zijn over drie verdiepingen verspreid.

XXX **De Fidalgo,** Outgaardenstraat 23 (Bost), ☎ 0 16 81 73 58, *info@defidalgo.be, Fax 0 16 82 28 17,* – P. AE ⓓ MC VISA. AZ e
fermé 2 dern. sem. juil.-prem. sem. août, vacances Noël, lundi et sam. midi – **Repas** *Lunch 25* – 30/70 bc.
◆ Dans un quartier résidentiel, ancienne ferme promue relais de bouche inventif. Cadre rustico-actuel élégant, orangerie et terrasse d'été côté jardin, embelli d'un étang.
◆ Deze oude boerderij in een rustige woonwijk is nu een restaurant met een inventieve kookstijl. Elegant rustiek-modern interieur, oranjerie, terras en tuin met vijver.

XX **Vigiliae,** Grote Markt 10, ☎ 0 16 81 77 03, , Ouvert jusqu'à 23 h – ▤. AE ⓓ MC VISA. AY n
fermé vacances bâtiment et lundis non fériés – **Repas** 35.
◆ Ce "ristorante" de la Grand-Place opte pour une carte franco-transalpine assez diversifiée, annonçant suggestions et menu. Vins de l'Hexagone et de la Botte.
◆ Dit Frans-Italiaanse restaurant aan de Grote Markt biedt een vrij gevarieerde kaart met suggesties en menu. De wijnen komen uit Frankrijk en Italië.

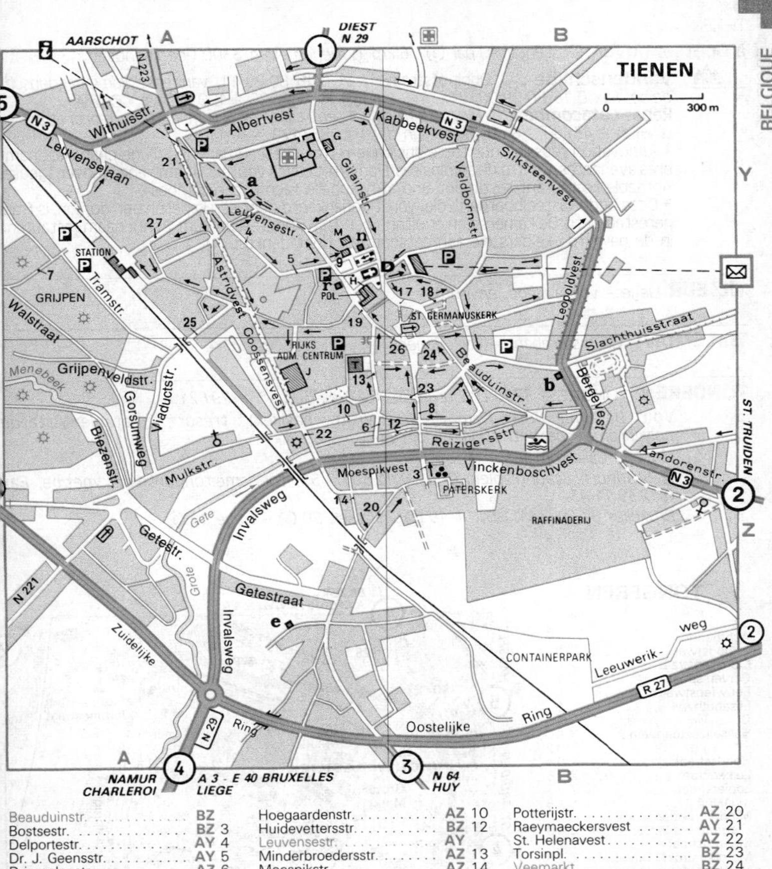

Beauduinstr.	BZ	Hoegaardenstr.	AZ 10	Potterijstr.	AZ 20
Bostsestr.	BZ 3	Huidevettersstr.	BZ 12	Raeymaeckersvest	AY 21
Delportestr.	AY 4	Leuvensestr.	AY	St. Helenavest	AZ 22
Dr. J. Geensstr.	AY 5	Minderbroedersstr.	AZ 13	Torsinpl.	BZ 23
Driemolenstr.	AZ 6	Moespikstr.	AZ 14	Veemarkt	BZ 24
Grijpenlaan	AY 7	Nieuwstr.	BY 17	Viaductstr.	AY 25
Grote Bergstr.	BZ 8	O. L. V. Broedersstr.	BY 18	Wolmarkt	BZ 26
Grote Markt	AY 9	Peperstr.	AY 19	4de Lansierslaan	AY 27

X **Casa Al Parma,** Grote Markt 40, ☎ 0 16 81 68 55, terrasse, Avec cuisine italienne, ouvert jusqu'à 23 h 30 – ▤. AE ⓓ ⓜⓒ VISA JCB. ✂ — AY r
fermé 3 prem. sem. sept. et merc. – **Repas** carte 31 à 47.
◆ Une adresse qui marche fort et dont l'orientation culinaire, comme la teneur de la cave, se devine aisément à la lecture de l'enseigne. Accueil et service à l'italienne.
◆ Goed lopend eethuisje, waarvan het uithangbord wel laat raden uit welke hoek de wind draait. Ontvangst en bediening op zijn Italiaans.

X **De Refugie,** Kapucijnenstraat 75, ☎ 0 16 82 45 32, *derefugie@proximedia.be, Fax 0 16 82 45 32,* terrasse – AE ⓓ ⓜⓒ VISA — BZ b
fermé dern. sem. juil.-prem. sem. août, prem. sem. janv., mardi soir, merc. et sam. midi – **Repas** *Lunch 20* – 27/56 bc.
◆ Au bord du ring, dans le voisinage du centre industriel sucrier, affaire familiale assez mignonne, où il est agréable de trouver "refuge". Préparations de saison.
◆ Dit leuke familierestaurant is te vinden aan de Ring, in de buurt van de suikerraffinaderij. De keuken is gevoelig voor het ritme van de seizoenen.

à Goetsenhoven *(Gossencourt) par ③ : 6 km* Ⓒ *Tienen* – ✉ *3300 Goetsenhoven :*

Vandenschilde ⛔, Doolhofstraat 1, ☎ 0 16 80 29 11, *vandenschilde@vandenschilde.be, Fax 0 16 80 29 00,* 🍽, 🚲 – 🛗 📺 🅿 – 🏫 25 à 120. AE ⓓ ⓜⓒ VISA
Repas ***Catacomben de Merode*** *(fermé 1 sem. carnaval, 2 sem. en août, mardi et merc.)* *Lunch 32* – 43/60 – **8 ch** *(fermé fin déc.)* ☕ 86/129, – 1 suite.
◆ Rénovation réussie pour cette ancienne ferme-château flanquée d'une chapelle. Chambres avenantes. Centre de séminaires. Donjon et caves voûtées à l'ambiance moyenâgeuse. Agréable restaurant restituant une atmosphère façon "catacombes".
◆ Deze oude kasteelboerderij, die wordt geflankeerd door een kapel en een donjon, is fraai gerestaureerd. De kamers zien er uitnodigend uit. Congrescentrum. Aangenaam restaurant in de gewelfde kelders die aan catacomben doet denken.

TILLEUR *Liège – voir à Liège, environs.*

TIRLEMONT *Vlaams-Brabant – voir Tienen.*

TONGEREN (TONGRES) *3700 Limburg* 533 *R 18 et* 716 *J 3 – 29 621 h.*

Voir *Basilique Notre-Dame★★ (O.L. Vrouwebasiliek) : trésor★★, retable★, statue polychrome★ de Notre-Dame, cloître★* Y.
Musée : *Gallo-romain★* Y **M¹**.
🅘 *Stadhuis, Stadhuisplein 9* ☎ *0 12 39 02 55, toerisme.tongeren@skynet.be, Fax 0 12 39 11 43.*
Bruxelles 87 ④ – Maastricht 19 ② – Hasselt 20 ⑤ – Liège 19 ③

TONGEREN

Achttiende-Oogstwal Y 2
Clarissenstraat Y 4
Corversstraat YZ 5
Eeuwfeestwal Y 6
Elisabethwal Z 9
Grote Markt Y
Hasseltsesteenweg Y 10
Hemelingenstraat Y 12
Hondsstraat Y 14
Luikerstraat Z 15
Looierstraat Z 17
Maastrichterstraat Y 18
Minderbroederstraat Z 19
Moerenstraat Y 20
Momberstraat Z 23
Muntstraat Z 24
Nevenstraat Y 25
Piepelpoel Y 27
Plein Y 28
Pliniuswal Y 30
Predikherenstraat Y 31
Regulierenplein Z 34
Riddersstraat Y 35
de Schiervelstraat Y 37
St. Catharinastraat Y 38
St. Jansstraat Z 39
St. Maternuswal Y 41
St. Truidenstraat Y 42
Stationslaan Y 44
Vermeulenstraat Y 46
11 Novemberwal Y 47

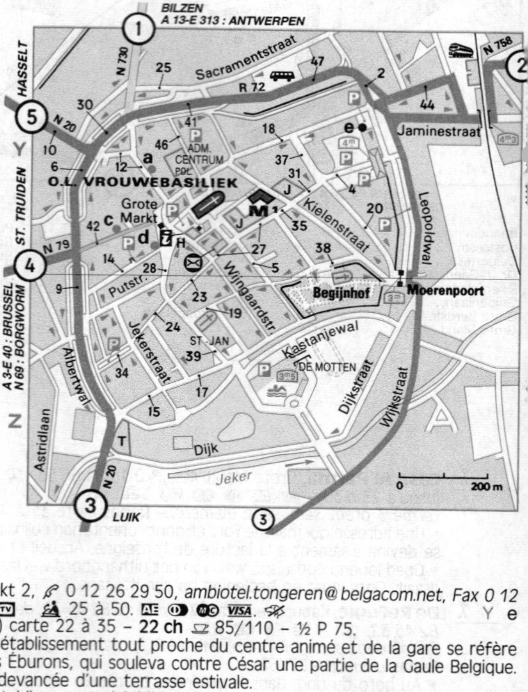

Ambiotel, Veemarkt 2, ☎ 0 12 26 29 50, *ambiotel.tongeren@belgacom.net, Fax 0 12 26 15 42,* 🍽 – 🛗 📺 – 🏫 25 à 50. AE ⓓ ⓜⓒ VISA. ✂ Y e
Repas (taverne-rest) carte 22 à 35 – **22 ch** ☕ 85/110 – ½ P 75.
◆ L'enseigne de cet établissement tout proche du centre animé et de la gare se réfère à Ambiorix, chef des Éburons, qui souleva contre César une partie de la Gaule Belgique. Taverne-restaurant devancée d'une terrasse estivale.
◆ De naam van dit etablissement vlak bij het levendige centrum en het station verwijst naar Ambiorix, koning van de Eburones, die een opstand tegen Caesar uitlokte in een deel van Belgisch Gallië. Taverne-restaurant met terras aan de voorkant voor mooie dagen.

XXX **Biessenhuys,** Hemelingenstraat 23, ✆ 0 12 23 47 09, *info@biessenhuys.com, Fax 0 12 23 83 76,* – – 25. AE VISA Y a
fermé 22 fév.-3 mars, 19 juil.-12 août et mardis soirs, merc. et sam. midis non fériés – **Repas** Lunch 27 – 40/76 bc, ♀.
◆ Ancienne maison de convalescence des Templiers ouvrant sur un jardin où l'on s'attable à la belle saison. Carte au goût du jour, avec plats à la bière. Cave rabelaisienne.
◆ Voormalig herstellingsoord van de tempeliers met een tuin waarin wordt gegeten. Eigentijdse menukaart met enkele in bier gestoofde gerechten. Rabelaisiaanse wijnkelder.

XXX **De Mijlpaal,** Sint-Truiderstraat 25, ✆ 0 12 26 42 77, *Fax 0 12 26 43 77,* – VISA Y c
fermé 1 sem. en fév., 2 sem. en juil. et jeudi – **Repas** Lunch 29 – carte 40 à 49.
◆ Dans une rue piétonne, restaurant dont l'intérieur affiche un "look" moderne épuré. L'été, on dresse aussi le couvert sur le gravier de l'arrière-cour close de vieux murs.
◆ Restaurant in een voetgangersstraat, met een supermodern interieur. In de zomer worden de tafeltjes op de ommuurde binnenplaats aan de achterkant opgedekt.

X **De Brasserie,** Grote Markt 31, ✆ 0 12 23 85 51, *Fax 0 12 23 85 51,* – VISA. Y d
fermé mi-oct.-mi-nov., merc., jeudi midi et sam. midi – **Repas** 25/35, ♀.
◆ Sobre et lumineuse salle à manger de type bistrot contemporain, musique "lounge", carte classique-actuelle, menu annoncé de vive voix et mini-terrasse urbaine sur le trottoir.
◆ Sobere en lichte eetzaal in de stijl van een hedendaagse bistro, loungemuziek, modern-klassieke kaart, mondeling aangekondigd menu en piepklein terrasje op de stoep.

à Vliermaal *par ⑤ : 5 km* C *Kortessem 8 060 h.* – ✉ *3724 Vliermaal :*

XXXXX ✿✿ **Clos St. Denis** (Denis), Grimmertingenstraat 24, ✆ 0 12 23 60 96, *info@closstdenis.be, Fax 0 12 26 32 07* – P. AE VISA.
fermé du 12 au 19 avril, du 13 au 28 juil., du 1er au 8 nov., 28 déc.-10 janv., mardi et merc. – **Repas** Lunch 55 – 99/185 bc, carte 82 à 155.
◆ Cuisine escoffière délicieusement revisitée, servie dans une fastueuse ferme-château du 17e s. regorgeant d'objets d'art. Jolie terrasse et adorable jardin. Cave de haut vol.
◆ Prachtige 17e-eeuwse kasteelhoeve met talloze kunstschatten. De kookstijl is een eigentijdse versie van de keuken van Escoffier. Fijn terras en beeldige tuin. Grote wijnen.
Spéc. Gourmandise de homard, saumon mariné et raifort. Blanc de turbot, bintjes écrasées à l'huile d'olive citron et câpres. Le grand dessert

---

TORGNY *Luxembourg belge* 534 R 25 *et* 716 J 7 – *voir à Virton.*

TORHOUT *8820 West-Vlaanderen* 533 D 16 *et* 716 C 2 – *18 790 h.*
Kasteel Ravenhof ✆ 0 50 22 07 70, torhout@toerismevlaanderen.be, Fax 0 50 22 15 04.
Bruxelles 107 – Brugge 23 – Oostende 25 – Roeselare 13.

Host. 't Gravenhof, Oostendestraat 343 (Nord-Ouest : 3 km à Wijnendale), ✆ 0 50 21 23 14, *tgravenhof@online.be, Fax 0 50 21 69 36,* , , – TV P – 25 à 320. AE VISA
Repas *(fermé 1 sem. Toussaint, mardi et merc.)* Lunch 24 – carte 40 à 63 – **10 ch** 65/90 – ½ P 70/75.
◆ Voisine du château de Wijnendale, cette ancienne laiterie récemment agrandie d'une annexe a troqué cuves et cruches contre quelques chambres assez confortables. Salle de restaurant à la flamande. Plats traditionnels de saison.
◆ Dit oude zuivelfabriekje bij het Slot Wijnendale is onlangs uitgebreid met een bijgebouw. De melkbussen zijn verruild voor enkele kamers die vrij comfortabel zijn. In de Vlaamse eetzaal worden traditionele, seizoengebonden gerechten geserveerd.

XX **Forum,** Rijksweg 42 (Sud-Ouest : 7 km sur N 35 à Sint-Henricus), ✆ 0 51 72 54 85, *info@restaurantforum.be, Fax 0 51 72 63 57* – P. AE VISA
fermé du 3 au 17 août, dim. soir et lundi – **Repas** Lunch 23 – 50/65 bc.
◆ Petite adresse engageante, connue pour la variété de ses recettes où l'on percevra de légers accents du Sud. Lunch et menus bien ficelés. Décoration intérieure actuelle.
◆ Dit populaire adresje staat bekend om zijn gevarieerde keuken, waarin een licht zuidelijk accent te herkennen is. Aantrekkelijke lunchformule en menu's. Eigentijds interieur.

X **Dining Villa Maciek,** Aartrijkestraat 265, ✆ 0 50 22 26 96, *Fax 0 50 22 26 96,* – P. AE VISA
fermé lundi soir et mardi – **Repas** Lunch 25 – 42/55 bc.
◆ Une villa sur jardin abrite cette affaire familiale dont la carte énonce un bon menu "all in" que le chef repense entièrement chaque mois. Repas en plein air aux beaux jours.
◆ Familiebedrijf in een villa met tuin. De chef-kok bedenkt elke maand weer een ander lekker menu, waarbij alles is inbegrepen. Bij mooi weer kan buiten worden gegeten.

à Lichtervelde *Sud : 7 km – 8 250 h – ✉ 8810 Lichtervelde :*

De Voerman, Koolskampstraat 105 (par E 403 - A 17, sortie ⑨), ☎ 0 51 74 67 67, *Fax 0 51 74 80 80,* – rest, – 25. VISA.
fermé 1re quinz. nov. et du 24 au 31 déc. – **Repas** *(fermé sam., dim. et jours fériés)* (taverne-rest) *Lunch 7* – carte env. 27 – **10 ch** 37/55.
◆ Établissement fonctionnel dont les chambres, fraîches et munies du double vitrage, sont toutes de plain-pied, à la façon d'un motel. Accueil familial.
◆ Dit functionele hotel beschikt over frisse kamers met dubbele ramen die, net als in een motel, allemaal gelijkvloers zijn. Gastvrije ontvangst.

De Bietemolen, Hogelaanstraat 3 (direction Ruddervoorde : 3 km à Groenhove), ☎ 0 50 21 38 34, *Fax 0 50 22 07 60,* ≤, – AE VISA
fermé 3 sem. en août, 2 sem. en janv., sam. midi, dim. soir, lundi et jeudi soir – **Repas** *Lunch 45* – 55/85 bc.
◆ En plein Houtland, dans un paysage agreste, ancienne ferme joliment convertie en restaurant. Carte au goût du jour. Cave d'épicurien. Terrasse estivale fleurie et jardin.
◆ Dit restaurant is gehuisvest in een oude boerderij in de schilderachtige omgeving van het Houtland. Eigentijdse menukaart en uitstekende wijnkelder. Fleurig terras en tuin.

TOURNAI (DOORNIK) *7500 Hainaut* 533 F 19, 534 F 19 *et* 716 D 4 – *67 232 h.*

Voir *Cathédrale Notre-Dame*★★★ : *trésor*★★ C – *Pont des Trous*★ : ≤★ AY – *Beffroi*★ C.
Musées : *des Beaux-Arts*★ *(avec peintures anciennes*★*)* C **M²** – *d'histoire et d'archéologie : sarcophage en plomb gallo-romain*★ C **M³**.

Env. *au Nord : 6 km à Mont-St-Aubert* ★ AY.

Vieux Marché-aux-Poteries 14 (au pied du Beffroi) ☎ *0 69 22 20 45, tourisme@tournai.be, Fax 0 69 21 62 21.*

Bruxelles 86 ② – Kortrijk 29 ⑥ – Mons 48 ② – Charleroi 93 ② – Gent 70 ⑥ – Lille 28 ⑥

Plan page ci-contre

d'Alcantara sans rest, r. Bouchers St-Jacques 2, ☎ 0 69 21 26 48, *hotelalcantara@hotmail.com, Fax 0 69 21 28 24* – – 25 à 40. AE VISA.
fermé du 24 au 30 déc. – **17 ch** 73/105. C d
◆ Brillamment restaurée, cette maison patricienne élevée au siècle des Lumières renferme des chambres modernes et paisibles, disponibles en trois tailles. Communs soignés.
◆ Dit oude patriciërshuis uit de Verlichting (18e eeuw) is prachtig verbouwd. Moderne, rustige kamers van drie verschillende afmetingen. Verzorgde gemeenschappelijke ruimten.

Cathédrale, pl. St-Pierre 2, ☎ 0 69 21 50 77, *hotelcathedrale@belgacom.net, Fax 0 69 21 50 78,* – , ch, – 25 à 180. AE VISA. C b
Repas *(fermé dim.)* (dîner seult) 17/31 bc – 11 – **59 ch** 94/105 – ½ P 121/124.
◆ Nouvelle enseigne pour cet hôtel de chaîne avantagé par sa proximité de la cathédrale. Chambres de notre temps, bien calibrées, assez tranquilles et correctement équipées.
◆ Nieuw ketenhotel, gunstig gelegen bij de kathedraal. Eigentijdse, rustige kamers van prettig formaat en met redelijk goede voorzieningen.

Le Carillon, Grand'Place 64, ☎ 0 69 21 18 48, *Fax 0 69 21 33 79* – . AE VISA JCB C r
fermé 17 août-9 sept., sam. midi, dim. soir et lundi – **Repas** 30/60 bc, ♀.
◆ Haut plafond-miroir, mobilier d'aujourd'hui et grande fresque évoquant des scènes médiévales tournaisiennes composent le décor de cette demeure de la Grand-Place.
◆ Een hoog spiegelplafond, eigentijds meubilair en een grote muurschildering met middeleeuwse taferelen uit Doornik kenmerken het interieur van dit pand aan de Grote Markt.

Charles-Quint, Grand'Place 3, ☎ 0 69 22 14 41, *prandinimarie@hotmail.com, Fax 0 69 22 14 41* – . AE VISA C a
fermé du 17 au 24 mars, 12 juil.-7 août, merc. soir, jeudi et dim. soir – **Repas** *Lunch 28* – 39.
◆ Au pied du plus vieux beffroi belge, table plaisante dont la façade s'agrémente d'un pignon à redans. Salle de restaurant dans la note Art déco. Large choix de vins.
◆ Plezierige eetgelegenheid in een pand met een trapgevel, aan de voet van het oudste belfort van België. Eetzaal in art-decostijl. Groot assortiment wijnen.

Le Pressoir, Vieux Marché aux Poteries 2, ☎ 0 69 22 35 13, *Fax 0 69 22 35 13,* ≤ – 25 à 70. AE VISA C u
fermé sem. carnaval, 3 dern. sem. août, dim. soir, lundi soir et mardi – **Repas** *Lunch 29* – 35/65 bc.
◆ Belle maison du 17e s. dont la devanture fleurie jouxte la cathédrale. Salle à manger cossue, pleine de caractère. Alléchant menu-carte à prix d'ami. Cave de grand seigneur.
◆ Dit mooie 17e-eeuwse huis met een fleurige gevel staat naast de kathedraal. Weelderige eetzaal met karakter. Smakelijk à la carte-menu voor een zacht prijsje. Goede wijnen.

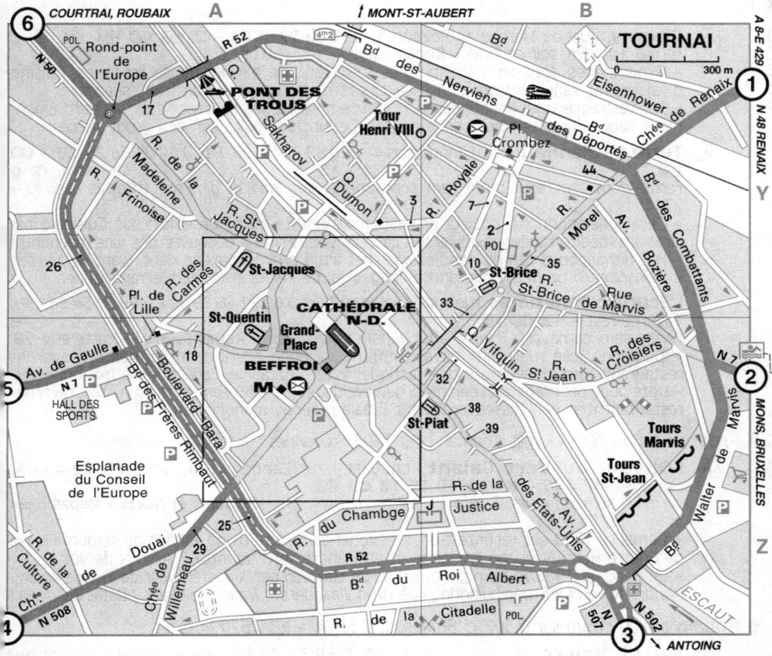

TOURNAI

COURTRAI, ROUBAIX
MONT-ST-AUBERT
A 8-E 429
N 48 RENAIX
A 16-E 42
MONS, BRUXELLES
ANTOING
0 300 m
PONT DES TROUS
Tour Henri VIII
Pl. Crombez
St-Brice
St-Jacques
St-Quentin
CATHÉDRALE N.-D.
Grand-Place
BEFFROI
St-Piat
Tours Marvis
Tours St-Jean
HALL DES SPORTS
Esplanade du Conseil de l'Europe
Rond-point de l'Europe
Bd des Nerviens
Bd Eisenhower
Chée de Renaix
Bd des Déportés
Bd des Combattants
Av. Bozière
Rue de Marvis
R. des Croisiers
R. St Jean
Q. Vifquin
R. St-Brice
R. Morel
R. Royale
Q. Dumon
Q. Sakharov
R. St-Jacques
R. de la Madeleine
R. Frinoise
R. des Carmes
Pl. de Lille
Av. de Gaulle
Bd des Frères Rimbaut
Boulevard Bara
R. de la Justice
R. du Chambge
Av. des États-Unis
Bd Walter de Marvis
Bd du Roi Albert
R. de la Citadelle
Chée de Willemeau
Chée de Douai
R. de la Culture
ESCAUT

- Athénée (R. de l') . . . . BY 2
- Becquerelle (R. du) . . . . . . AY 3
- Bourdon-St-Jacques (R. du) . . . . C 4
- Chapeliers (R. des) . . . . . . C 6
- Childeric (R.) . . . . BY 7
- Clairisses (R. des) . . . . C 8
- Clovis (Pl.) . . . . BY 10
- Cordonnerie (R. de la) . . . . C 14
- Curé-N.-Dame (R. du) . . . . C 15
- Delwart (Bd) . . . . AY 17
- Dorez (R.) . . . . AZ 18
- Gallait (R.) . . . . C 20
- Grand-Place C
- Hôpital-Notre-Dame (R. de l') . . . . C 23
- Lalaing (Bd) . . . . AZ 25
- Léopold (Bd) . . . . AY 26
- Marché-au-Poisson (Quai du) . . . . C 27
- Montgomery (Av.) . . . . . . AZ 29
- Notre-Dame (Quai) . . . . . . C 30
- Paul-E.-Janson (Pl.) . . . . . C 31
- Poissonsceaux (Quai des) . . . . BZ 32
- Pont (R. de) . . . . BYZ 33
- Puits-d'Eau (R. des) . . . . C 34
- Quesnoy (R. du) . . . . BY 35
- Royale (R.) . . . . BY
- Saint-Piat (R.) . . . . BZ 38
- Sainte-Catherine (R.) . . . . . BZ 39
- Tête-d'Argent (R.) . . . . C 42
- Volontaires (R. des) . . . . BY 44
- Wallonie (R. de la) . . . . C 45

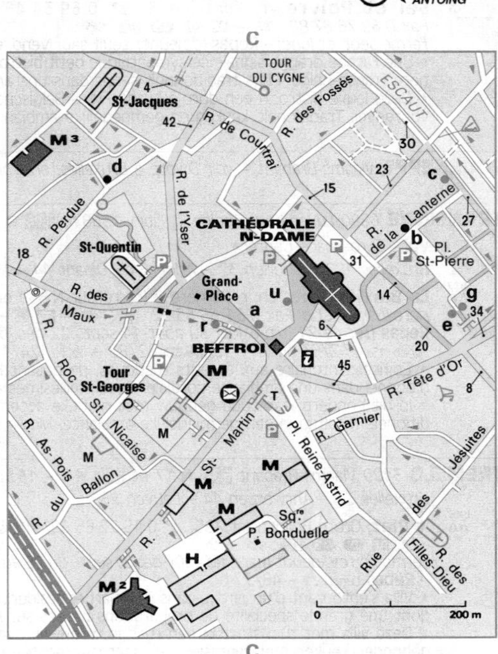

XX **Giverny,** quai du Marché au Poisson 6, ✆ 0 69 22 44 64 – AE ⓓ ⓜ VISA. C c
fermé juil., dim. soir et lundi – **Repas** *Lunch 20* – 35/90 bc, ♀.
◆ Trois pièces dont les murs patinés s'égayent de miroirs et de fresques. Cuisine d'aujourd'hui sagement personnalisée. Les formules lunch ont un franc succès.
◆ Drie vertrekken met gepatineerde muren die met spiegels en fresco's zijn versierd. Eigentijdse keuken met een persoonlijke toets. De lunchformules zijn een groot succes.

X **Terre de Sienne,** ruelle d'Ennetières 4, ✆ 0 69 21 56 26, *Fax 0 69 21 56 26,* – ⓜ VISA C g
fermé dern. sem. août-prem. sem. sept., merc., sam. midi et dim. soir – **Repas** *Lunch 22* – 27/45 bc, ♀.
◆ L'enseigne annonce la couleur de cette maisonnette qui ne désemplit pas. Cuisine d'inspirations méditerranéennes diverses. La cave vous invite à découvrir des vins méconnus.
◆ Het uithangbord van dit pandje, waar het altijd druk is, bekent kleur, want de keuken is geïnspireerd op het Middellandse-Zeegebied. De kelder met mediterrane wijnen.

X **L'Écurie d'Ennetières,** ruelle d'Ennetières 7, ✆ 0 69 21 56 89, *Fax 0 69 21 56 96,* , Taverne-rest – ⓓ ⓜ VISA C e
fermé sem. carnaval, 15 juil.-5 août, lundi et mardi soir – **Repas** *Lunch 21* – carte env. 28.
◆ Dans une jolie ruelle aux pavés joufflus, ancienne écurie transformée en taverne-restaurant aussi chaleureuse que rustique, avec mezzanine. Collection de marionnettes.
◆ Deze oude paardenstal in een mooi geplaveid steegje is nu een warm en rustiek taverne-restaurant met een tussenverdieping. Fraaie collectie marionetten.

à Froyennes *par ⑥ : 4 km* Ⓒ *Tournai* – ✉ *7503 Froyennes :*

XX **l'Oustau du Vert Galant,** chaussée de Lannoy 106, ✆ 0 69 22 44 84, *Fax 0 69 23 54 46* – P – 60. AE ⓓ ⓜ VISA
fermé 1 sem. en mars, 3 sem. en juil., sam. midi, dim. soir, lundi et mardi – **Repas** *Lunch 21 bc* – 33/54 bc.
◆ Demeure 1900 qui, raconte-t-on, s'élèverait sur le site d'une abbaye où séjourna le roi de France Henri IV quand il guerroyait en Flandre. Info ou intox ? À vous de voir !
◆ Dit pand uit 1900 zou zijn gebouwd op de plek van een klooster waar de Franse koning Hendrik IV verbleef toen hij oorlog voerde in Vlaanderen. Waar of onwaar ? Dat is de vraag !

à Hollain *par ③ : 8 km sur N 507* Ⓒ *Brunehaut 7 539 h.* – ✉ *7620 Hollain :*

X **Sel et Poivre,** r. Fontaine 3, ✆ 0 69 34 46 67, *seletpoivre@skynet.be, Fax 0 69 76 67 80,* – AE ⓓ ⓜ VISA.
fermé sept. et lundi – **Repas** (déjeuner seult sauf vend. et sam.) *Lunch 10* – carte 22 à 45.
◆ Une façade orange signale ce sympathique petit bistrot villageois situé près de la frontière franco-belge. Plats traditionnels servis dans une ambiance décontractée.
◆ Deze leuke bistro in een dorpje bij de Frans-Belgische grens valt op door zijn oranje voorgevel. Traditionele keuken en gemoedelijke ambiance.

TOURNEPPE *Vlaams-Brabant – voir Dworp à Bruxelles, environs.*

TRANSINNE *6890 Luxembourg belge* Ⓒ *Libin 4 368 h.* 534 Q 23 *et* 716 I 6.

Voir *Euro Space Center*★.

Bruxelles 129 – Bouillon 32 – Arlon 64 – Dinant 44 – Namur 73.

XX **La Barrière** avec ch, r. Barrière 2 (carrefour N 899 et N 40), ✆ 0 61 65 50 37, *labarriere@skynet.be, Fax 0 61 65 55 32,* , – TV P – 25. AE ⓓ ⓜ VISA
Repas *(fermé 21 juin-6 juil., 30 août-14 sept., 22 déc.-6 janv., lundi, mardi et sam. midi) Lunch 15* – 32/63 bc – **13 ch** 62/82 – ½ P 124/187.
◆ Édifice centenaire aux accents rustiques, proposant le gîte et le couvert. Repas traditionnel dans une ambiance cordiale. Beaux millésimes en cave. Terrasse et jardin.
◆ In dit honderd jaar oude gebouw met rustieke accenten kunt u eten en slapen. Traditionele maaltijd in een gemoedelijke ambiance. Mooie wijnkelder. Terras en tuin.

TREMELO *3120 Vlaams-Brabant* 533 N 17 *et* 716 H 3 – *13 538 h.*

Bruxelles 37 – Antwerpen 44 – Leuven 25.

XX **'t Riet,** Grote Bollostraat 195, ✆ 0 15 22 65 60, *info@riet.be, Fax 0 15 22 65 61,* – P. AE ⓓ ⓜ VISA.
fermé fin fév.-début mars, fin août-début sept., du 25 au 30 déc., lundi, mardi et sam. midi – **Repas** *Lunch 32* – 48/77 bc.
◆ Villa s'entourant d'un jardin, dans un quartier résidentiel excentré. Recettes de saison, dont une grande spécialité de préparations basées sur l'asperge, d'avril à juin.
◆ Deze villa met tuin staat in een rustige woonwijk even buiten het centrum. Seizoengebonden keuken met fantasievolle aspergegerechten van april tot en met juni.

TROIS-PONTS *4980 Liège* 533 U 20, 534 U 20 *et* 716 K 4 – *2 389 h.*
Exc. *Circuit des panoramas*★.
ℹ *pl. Communale 1* ✆ *0 80 68 40 45, Fax 0 80 68 52 68.*
Bruxelles 152 – Liège 54 – Stavelot 6.

Le Beau Site ⛰, r. Villas 45, ✆ 0 80 68 49 44, *beausite@skynet.be, Fax 0 80 68 49 60,* ← vallée et confluent du Salm et de l'Amblève, 🚲 – TV P. AE ① MC VISA. ✻ rest
fermé du 20 au 25 juin, 29 août-3 sept. et 19 déc.-23 janv. – **Repas** *(fermé merc.)* (dîner seult sauf week-end et jours fériés) carte 34 à 49 – **16 ch** ☕ 54/75 – ½ P 65.
◆ Perché tel un belvédère, ce petit hôtel à l'ambiance familiale procure une jolie vue sur le site de Trois-Ponts où confluent la Salm et l'Amblève. Accès par un chemin privé. Cuisine actuelle à touche régionale servie dans une salle à manger panoramique.
◆ Een eigen weg leidt naar dit hooggelegen familiehotel, dat een prachtig uitzicht biedt op de samenloop van de Salm en de Amblève. In het panoramarestaurant kunt u genieten van de eigentijdse keuken met een regionaal accent.

à Haute-Bodeux *Sud-Ouest : 7 km* C *Trois-Ponts* – ✉ *4983 Haute-Bodeux :*

Host. Doux Repos ⛰ Haute-Bodeux 34, ✆ 0 80 68 42 07, *hoteldouxrepos@skynet.be, Fax 0 80 68 42 82,* ←, 🌳, 🏖, 🚲 – ✈ TV P – 🏋 25. AE ① MC VISA
avril-22 nov. et du 17 au 31 déc. ; fermé du 3 au 9 juil., lundi et mardi – **Repas** 40 bc – **14 ch** ☕ 65/90, – 1 suite – ½ P 60/79.
◆ Hostellerie familiale dont les chambres, correctement équipées et d'une tenue irréprochable, se prêtent effectivement à un "doux repos". Restaurant au décor ardennais, avec terrasse d'été panoramique dominant la vallée.
◆ Deze hostellerie wordt door een familie gerund. De perfect onderhouden kamers bieden goede voorzieningen en staan inderdaad garant voor een "zachte nachtrust". Restaurant in Ardense stijl met terras, dat een weids uitzicht biedt op het dal.

à Wanne *Sud-Est : 6 km* C *Trois-Ponts* – ✉ *4980 Wanne :*

La Métairie, Wanne 4, ✆ 0 80 86 40 89, *lametairie@skynet.be, Fax 0 80 88 08 37,* 🌳, Avec taverne-rest – AE ① MC VISA
fermé 1 sem. Pâques, fin juin-début juil., 1 sem. Noël, merc. de déc. à fév., lundi et mardi – **Repas** Lunch 25 – 32/60 bc, 🍷.
◆ Sur les hauteurs, dans un hameau équidistant de Stavelot et de Trois-Ponts, coquette maison typique combinant deux formules : cuisine d'aujourd'hui et petite restauration.
◆ Mooi karakteristiek pand op een heuvel in een gehuchtje precies halverwege Stavelot en Trois-Ponts. Het restaurant biedt zowel een kleine als grote kaart. Eigentijdse keuken.

TROOZ *4870 Liège* 533 T 19, 534 T 19 *et* 716 K 4 – *7 657 h.*
Bruxelles 110 – Liège 16 – Verviers 18.

Château Bleu, r. Rys-de-Mosbeux 52, ✆ 0 4 351 74 57, *indo@chateaubleu.be, Fax 0 4 351 73 43,* 🌳, ≋s, 🏖 – 🛗 TV P – 🏋 25. MC VISA. ✻
fermé 2 sem. en juil. – **Repas** *(fermé jeudis non fériés)* (dîner seult) 25, 🍷 – ☕ 10 – **12 ch** 80/111.
◆ Tenté par la vie de château ? Cette belle demeure du 19e s. nichée au creux d'une vallée boisée n'attend alors que vous ! Grandes chambres garnies de meubles de style. Dîner aux chandelles. Carte partagée entre classicisme, tradition et tempo actuel.
◆ Oefent het kasteelleven een onweerstaanbare aantrekkingskracht op u uit ? Dan is dit mooie 19e-eeuwse gebouw in een bebost dal wat voor u ! Grote kamers met stijlmeubelen. Dineren bij kaarslicht. De kaart is een mengeling van klassiek, traditioneel en modern.

TUBIZE (TUBEKE) *1480 Brabant Wallon* 533 K 18, 534 K 18 *et* 716 F 3 – *21 429 h.*
Bruxelles 24 – Charleroi 47 – Mons 36.

Le Pivert, r. Mons 183, ✆ 0 2 355 29 02, *Fax 0 2 355 29 02* – AE ① MC VISA
fermé 1 sem. Pâques, 22 juil.-13 août, mardi soir, merc. et dim. soir – **Repas** Lunch 16 – 22/58 bc, 🍷.
◆ Un sympathique volatile préside au destin de cette plaisante adresse sise à quelques battements d'ailes du centre. La carte, abordable, déploie une ribambelle de menus.
◆ Deze "groene specht" heeft een prettig nest op een paar vleugelslagen van het centrum. De spijskaart bevat een hele zwerm menu's tegen prijzen die gelukkig niet omhoogvliegen !

à Oisquercq *Sud-Est : 4 km* C *Tubize* – ✉ *1480 Oisquercq :*

La Petite Gayolle, r. Bon Voisin 79, ✆ 0 67 64 84 44, *info@lapetitegayolle.be, Fax 0 67 64 84 44,* 🌳 – P. AE MC VISA
fermé 20 août-10 sept., dim. soir, lundi et jeudi soir – **Repas** Lunch 20 – 35/55 bc.
◆ Fermette mignonne comme tout, dont l'enseigne désigne une cage à oiseaux en wallon. Registre culinaire dans le coup et cave assez bien montée. Terrasse estivale fleurie.
◆ Schattig boerderijtje, waarvan de naam verwijst naar een vogelkooi. Modern culinair register en goede wijnkelder. Mooi terras in de zomer met veel bloemen.

BELGIQUE

TURNHOUT *2300 Antwerpen* 533 *O 15 et* 716 *H 2 – 39 017 h.*

Grote Markt 44 ☎ 0 14 44 33 55, toerisme@turnhout.be, Fax 0 14 44 33 54.
Bruxelles 84 ⑤ – Antwerpen 45 ⑤ – Liège 99 ④ – Breda 37 ① – Eindhoven 44 ③ – Tilburg 28 ②

TURNHOUT

Street	Square	No.
Baron Fr. Du Fourstr.	Y	2
Beekstr.	Y	3
Deken Adamsstr.	Z	5
Druivenstr.	Z	6
Gasthuisstr.	Z	7
Guldensporenlei	Y	9
Hannuitstr.	Y	12
Hofpoort	Z	13
Kasteelstr.	Y	14
Koningin Elisabethlei	Y	16
Korte Gasthuisstr.	Z	17
Kwakkelstr	Z	18
Mermansstr.	Z	19
Otterstr	Z	21
Oude Vaartstr	Y	22
Renier Sniedersstr.	Z	23
Sint Antoniusstr.	Z	25
Spoorwegstr	Z	26
Veldstr.	Z	28
Victoriestr.	Z	29
Wezenstr.	Y	31

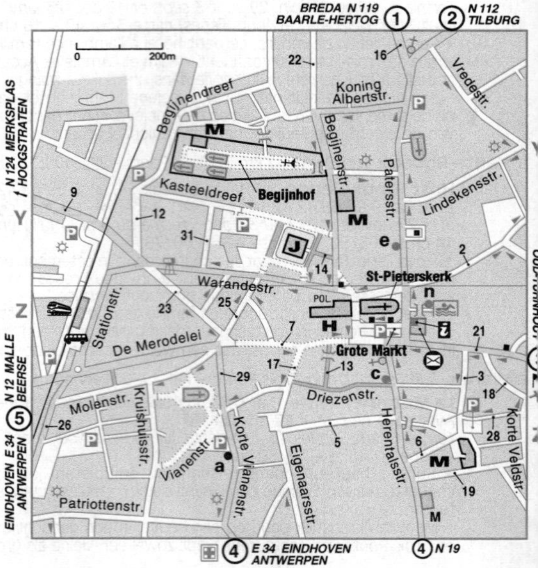

Corsendonk Viane, Korte Vianenstraat 2, ☎ 0 14 88 96 00, *info@corsendonkviane.be, Fax 0 14 88 96 99,* – – – 25 à 580. AE VISA. Z a
Repas *(fermé sam., dim. et jours fériés)* (dîner seult) 22 – **84 ch** 100/127 – ½ P 122/149.
◆ À mi-chemin entre la gare et la Grand-Place, immeuble récent distribuant ses chambres standardisées sur quatre étages. Neuf salles de séminaires correctement équipées.
◆ Oude abdij bij een openbaar park. De paters hebben hun cellen verlaten, maar de seminaries zijn er talrijker dan ooit.

Ter Driezen sans rest, Herentalsstraat 18, ☎ 0 14 41 87 57, *terdriezen@yahoo.com, Fax 0 14 42 03 10* – . AE VISA Z c
fermé 22 déc.-3 janv. – **13 ch** 90/135.
◆ Charmant hôtel dont les chambres et parties communes offrent un bon niveau de confort. Au rayon farniente, salons "cosy" et belle terrasse ouverte sur un jardinet soigné.
◆ Charmant en comfortabel hotel met aangename kamers. De sfeervolle lounges, het mooie terras en het goed onderhouden tuintje nodigen uit tot het dolce far niente.

Cucinamarangon, Patersstraat 9, ☎ 0 14 42 43 81, *cucinamarangon@pandora.be, Fax 0 14 43 87 00,* , Cuisine italienne – AE VISA Y e
fermé dim. et lundi – **Repas** Lunch 32 – 50/63, ♀.
◆ L'enseigne annonce la couleur de l'assiette : goûteuse cuisine transalpine aux accents vénitiens, et décor intérieur évoquant la cité des Doges. Vins élevés dans la "Botte".
◆ Smakelijke Italiaanse keuken met Venetiaanse invloeden en een interieur dat een ode brengt aan de dogenstad. Ook de wijnen komen rechtstreeks uit Italië.

Boeket, Klein Engeland 67 (par ① : 5 km, direction Breda), ☎ 0 14 42 70 28, *boeket@compaqnet.be, Fax 0 14 42 70 28,* – . AE VISA
fermé prem. sem. sept., prem. sem. janv., merc., jeudi midi et sam. midi – **Repas** Lunch 26 – 45/71 bc.
◆ Non loin des étangs de la 't Kleine Engeland, villa coquette où se conçoit une cuisine actuelle de saison. Fourneaux visibles de la salle. Terrasse au cadre reposant.
◆ Mooie villa bij de vijvers van 't Kleine Engeland, met een eigentijdse, seizoengebonden keuken. Het fornuis is vanuit de eetzaal te zien. Terras in een rustgevende omgeving.

X **d'Achterkeuken,** Baron Fr. du Fourstraat 4 (Bloemekensgang), ✆ 0 14 43 86 42, *dachterkeuken@proximedia.be, Fax 0 14 43 86 42,* ☂ – MC VISA Z n
fermé dim. et lundi – **Repas** *Lunch 25* – carte 28 à 44.
◆ Petite affaire tenue entre femmes, dans une ruelle animée du cœur de Turnhout. Savoureuses préparations au goût du jour. Ambiance sympathique.
◆ Vrouwen zwaaien de scepter in dit kleine restaurant in een levendig straatje in het centrum van Turnhout. Smakelijke eigentijdse keuken en een gezellige ambiance.

à Oud-Turnhout *par ③ : 4 km – 12 456 h – ✉ 2360 Oud-Turnhout :*

Priorij Corsendonk sans rest, Corsendonk 5 (près E 34 - A 21, sortie ㉕), ✆ 0 14 46 28 00, *info@corsendonk.be, Fax 0 14 46 28 99,* ⛱, ⚘, ✂, 🚲 – TV P – 🎓 25 à 250. AE MC VISA
☕ 12 – **71 ch** 74/110.
◆ Un ancien prieuré s'ouvrant sur un parc public sert de cadre à cet hôtel. Les cellules de naguère ont fait place aux chambres mais de nombreux séminaires ont toujours lieu !
◆ Dit hotel bij het park is gevestigd in een oude priorij, waar nog steeds seminars worden gehouden ! De gasten logeren in de vroegere kloostercellen.

XX **'t Vrouwenhuys,** Corsendonk 5a (près E 34 - A 21, sortie ㉕), ✆ 0 14 46 28 97, *info@vrouwenhuys.be, Fax 0 14 45 03 96,* ☂ – P. MC VISA. ✂
fermé lundi, mardi et sam. midi – **Repas** *Lunch 35* – 45/87 bc.
◆ Adroite reconversion pour ces dépendances d'un monastère du 17ᵉ s. devenues une élégante maison de bouche. En été, repas au jardin, joliment aménagé et orné de haies basses.
◆ De bijgebouwen van een 17e-eeuws klooster hebben een nieuwe roeping als elegante eetgelegenheid gevonden. 's Zomers worden de tafeltjes gedekt in de mooie tuin met lage hagen.

UCCLE (UKKEL) *Région de Bruxelles-Capitale* 533 L 18 *et* 716 G 3 – *voir à Bruxelles.*

UCIMONT *Luxembourg belge* 534 P 24 *et* 716 I 6 – *voir à Bouillon.*

VAALBEEK *Vlaams-Brabant* 533 N 18 – *voir à Leuven.*

VARSENARE *West-Vlaanderen* 533 D 15 *et* 716 C 2 – *voir à Brugge, environs.*

VENCIMONT *5575 Namur* C *Gedinne 4 337 h.* 534 O 22 *et* 716 H 5.
Bruxelles 129 – Bouillon 38 – Dinant 35.

XX **Le Barbouillon** avec ch, r. Grande 25, ✆ 0 61 58 82 60, *Fax 0 61 58 82 60,* ☂ – TV P – 🎓 70. MC VISA
fermé 25 juin-15 juil., du 23 au 26 août, du 4 au 15 janv. et merc. non fériés – **Repas** 25/57 – **6 ch** ☕ 52/60 – ½ P 50/55.
◆ Au centre d'un village ardennais, petite auberge typique où l'on vient autant pour l'assiette, classico-régionale et plutôt généreuse, que pour l'ambiance "couleur locale".
◆ In deze karakteristieke dorpsherberg in de Ardennen komt men zowel voor de keuken, die klassiek-regionaal en overvloedig is, als voor de ambiance met veel "couleur locale".

VERVIERS *4800 Liège* 533 U 19, 534 U 19 *et* 716 K 4 – *53 020 h.*
Musées : *des Beaux-Arts et de la Céramique*★ D **M¹** – *d'Archéologie et de Folklore : dentelles*★ D **M²**.
Env. *par ③ : 14 km, Barrage de la Gileppe*★★, ≤★★.
⛳18 *par ③ : 16 km à Gomzé-Andoumont, Sur Counachamps, r. Gomzé 30* ✆ *0 4 360 92 07, Fax 0 4 360 92 06.*
🅘 *r. Chapelle 24* ✆ *0 87 30 79 26, info@verviersima.be, Fax 0 87 31 20 95.*
Bruxelles 122 ④ – Liège 32 ④ – Aachen 36 ④

Plan page suivante

Amigo ⛱, r. Herla 1, ✆ 0 87 22 11 21, *hotelamigov@skynet.be, Fax 0 87 23 03 69,* ☂, ≘s, ⛱, ⚘ – 🛗 TV P – 🎓 25 à 100. AE ⓓ MC VISA B a
Repas (résidents seult) – **49 ch** ☕ 85/115, – 1 suite – ½ P 75/110.
◆ Immeuble des années 1960 s'élevant dans un paisible quartier résidentiel excentré. Spacieuses chambres peu à peu rénovées. Piscine couverte, sauna et jardin reposant.
◆ Dit gebouw uit de jaren 1960 staat buiten het centrum in een rustige woonwijk. De ruime kamers worden geleidelijk gerenoveerd. Overdekt zwembad, sauna en tuin om te relaxen.

VERVIERS

Anne-de-Molina (R.)	B	3
Brou (R. du)	C	4
Carmes (R. des)	D	6
Chapelle (R. de la)	B	7
Chêne (Pont du)	C	8
Clément XIV (R.)	B	9
Coronmeuse (R.)	D	10
Crapaurue	D	
Déportés (R. des)	B	12
Fabriques (R. des)	B	15
Franchimont (R. de)	B	16
Franchimontois (R. des)	B	17
Grandjean (R.)	C	18
Grappe (R. de la)	B	19
Grétry (R.)	B	20
Harmonie (Av. de l')	C	22
Heid des Fawes	B	24
Lions (Pont aux)	D	25
Maçons (Quai des)	D	27
Martyr (Pl. du)	C	28
Namur (R. de)	C	29
Ortmans-Hauzeur (R.)	D	30
Palais de Justice (Pl. du)	D	31
Paroisse (R. de la)	D	33
Raines (R. des)	D	34
Récollets (Pont des)	C	36
Saint-Laurent (Pont)	C	37
Sommeleville (Pl.)	D	39
Sommeleville (Pont)	D	40
Spintay (R.)	C	
Théâtre (R. du)	C	42
Thier-Mère-Dieu (R.)	D	43
Tribunal (R. du)	D	45
Verte (Pl.)	C	
Verviers (R. de)	B	46

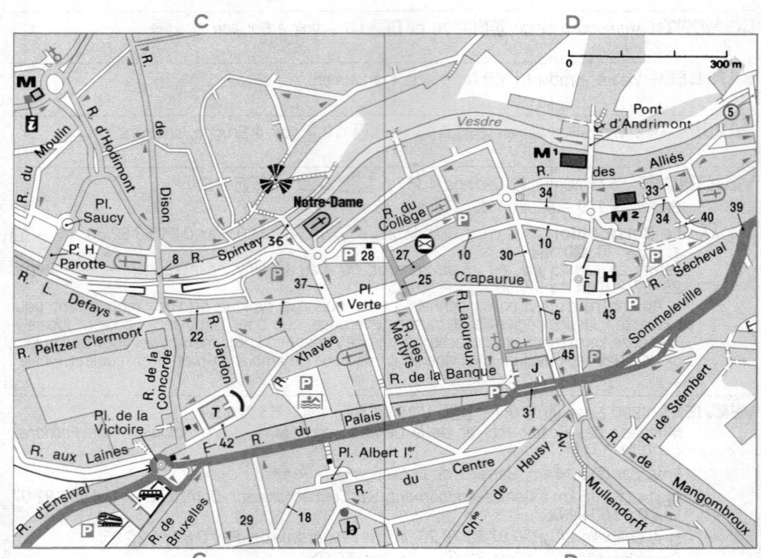

Château Peltzer, r. Grétry 1, ☎ 0 87 23 09 70, *nicolas.thomas@chateau-peltzer.com, Fax 0 87 23 08 71,* – P. AE ① MC VISA. B d

fermé 16 fév.-4 mars, 30 août-5 sept., dim. soir, lundi et mardi – **Repas** 38/124 bc.

◆ Splendide petit château néo-gothique s'entourant d'un parc centenaire. Aménagements intérieurs classiques du plus bel effet. Repas soigné. Accueil et service en rapport.

◆ Schitterend neogotisch kasteeltje in een park met eeuwenoude bomen. De klassieke inrichting is bijzonder geslaagd. Verzorgde maaltijden en uitstekende service.

XXX **Chez Paul** avec ch, pl. Albert Ier 5, ☎ 0 87 23 22 21, *info@chezpaul.be, Fax 0 87 22 76 87,* ⛱, – TV P. AE ① MC VISA C b
Repas *(fermé 1 sem. en mars, 2 sem. en août, 1 sem. en janv., dim. soir et lundi)* 34 bc/52 – **4 ch** ☕ 75/100.
◆ Ce ravissant manoir néo-classique abritait naguère un cercle littéraire verviétois. Élégante salle à manger, chambres actuelles de bon confort et jardin soigné avec terrasse.
◆ Prachtig neoklassiek landhuis waarin het plaatselijke literaire genootschap was ondergebracht. Elegante eetzaal, moderne kamers met goed comfort en verzorgde tuin met terras.

à Heusy C *Verviers* – ✉ *4802 Heusy* :

XXX **La Croustade,** r. Hodiamont 13 (par N 657), ☎ 0 87 22 68 39, *croustade@belgacom.net, Fax 0 87 22 79 21,* ⛱ – P – 30. AE ① MC VISA B
fermé du 20 au 29 fév., du 10 au 31 août, 24 déc.-2 janv., sam. midi, dim. soir et lundi – **Repas** Lunch 28 – 31/82 bc.
◆ Sur les hauteurs, dans un quartier plutôt chic, maison 1900 que signale une façade égayée de colombages. Mets au goût du jour. Terrasse d'été invitante dressée au jardin.
◆ Dit vakwerkhuis uit 1900 staat op een heuvel in een vrij chique woonwijk. De gerechten passen bij de huidige smaak. Op zomerse dagen wordt het terras in de tuin opgedekt.

XX **La Toque d'Or,** av. Nicolaû 43, ☎ 0 87 22 11 11, *fernand.laschet@skynet.be, Fax 0 87 22 94 59,* ⛱ – P. AE ① MC VISA B u
fermé dim. soir, lundi soir et merc. soir – **Repas** Lunch 25 – carte 30 à 56.
◆ Grosse villa où la même famille officie depuis plus de 20 ans, en salle comme aux fourneaux. Recettes classico-traditionnelles. Beau jardin accueillant un restaurant d'été.
◆ Grote villa die al ruim 20 jaar door dezelfde familie wordt bemand, zowel in de zaal als in de keuken. Klassiek-traditionele gerechten. Mooie tuin om 's zomers buiten te eten.

à Petit-Rechain *Nord-Ouest : 2 km* C *Verviers* – ✉ *4800 Petit-Rechain* :

XX **La Chapellerie,** chaussée de la Seigneurie 13, ☎ 0 87 31 57 41, *lachapellerie@skynet.be, Fax 0 87 31 57 41,* ⛱ – P – 40. AE MC VISA
fermé 1 sem. Pâques, 2 sem. en juil., 1 sem. Toussaint, prem. sem. janv., lundi soir d'oct. à mars, mardi midi en juil.-août, mardi soir, merc. et sam. midi – **Repas** Lunch 23 – 31/58 bc.
◆ Agréable restaurant contemporain confortablement installé dans l'ancienne chapellerie familiale, massive maison de pays proche de l'église. Aguichante terrasse sur cour.
◆ Aangenaam en comfortabel restaurant in hedendaagse stijl, in een robuust pand bij de kerk ; vroeger had de familie hier een hoedenzaak. Plezierig terras op de binnenplaats.

VEURNE (FURNES) *8630 West-Vlaanderen* 533 *B 16 et* 716 *B 2 – 11 794 h.*

Voir *Grand-Place★★ (Grote Markt) – Procession des Pénitents★★ (Boetprocessie) – Cuirs★ à l'intérieur de l'Hôtel de Ville (Stadhuis).*

Env. *à l'Est : 10 km à Diksmuide, Tour de l'Yser (IJzertoren) ※★.*

ℹ *Grote Markt 29* ☎ *0 58 33 05 31, veurne@toerismevlaanderen.be, Fax 0 58 33 05 96.*

Bruxelles 134 – Brugge 47 – Oostende 26 – Dunkerque 21.

Host. Croonhof, Noordstraat 9, ☎ 0 58 31 31 28, *info@croonhof.be, Fax 0 58 31 56 81* – |‡| TV. AE ① MC VISA
fermé du 3 au 12 fév. et du 13 au 26 sept. – **Repas** voir rest ***Orangerie*** ci-après – **14 ch** ☕ 60/105 – ½ P 75/83.
◆ Maison de maître rénovée, toute proche de la pittoresque Grand-Place. Chambres d'ampleur satisfaisante, bénéficiant du confort moderne. Atmosphère d'hostellerie familiale.
◆ Dit gemoedelijke familiehotel is ondergebracht in een gerenoveerd herenhuis vlak bij de pittoreske Grote Markt. De kamers zijn groot genoeg en bieden modern comfort.

't Kasteel en 't Koetshuys sans rest, Lindendreef 7, ☎ 0 58 31 53 72, *Fax 0 58 31 53 72,* ⛱, 🚲 – ⟷. MC VISA.
fermé prem. sem. fév. et 2 sem. en oct. – **6 ch** ☕ 70/90.
◆ Belle demeure 1900 misant sur une formule d'hébergement de type "bed and breakfast". Les chambres sont paisibles mais parfois dépourvues de salle d'eau. Tea-room côté jardin.
◆ In dit schitterende pand uit 1900 kunt u terecht voor "bed and breakfast". De kamers zijn rustig, maar hebben niet altijd een eigen badkamer. Theesalon in de tuin.

de Loft sans rest, Oude Vestingstraat 36, ☎ 0 58 31 59 49, *deloft@pi.be, Fax 0 58 31 68 12* – TV – 25. MC VISA
8 ch ☕ 52/62.
◆ Au centre, mais à l'écart du circuit touristique, ancien atelier de forgeron converti en "loft"-hôtel accueillant. Les chambres, assez sobres, sont toutefois très convenables.
◆ Deze oude smederij is omgetoverd tot een "lofthotel" in het centrum, even buiten het toeristische circuit. De kamers zijn vrij sober, maar voldoen uitstekend.

XX **Orangerie** H. Host. Croonhof, Noordstraat 9, ☎ 0 58 31 31 28, *info@croonhof.be, Fax 0 58 31 56 81* – ▤. AE ⓓ ⓜⓒ VISA
fermé du 3 au 12 fév., du 13 au 26 sept., dim. soir et lundi – **Repas** Lunch 23 – 35/81 bc.
◆ Restaurant d'hôtel sortant du lot, où l'on prend place dans une salle à manger agencée avec goût. Cuisine actuelle assortie de vins français et italiens. Service "pro".
◆ Dit restaurant met zijn smaakvolle interieur hoort bij een hotel, maar onderscheidt zich gunstig. Eigentijdse keuken en Frans-Italiaanse wijnen. Professionele service.

X **Olijfboom,** Noordstraat 3, ☎ 0 58 31 70 77, *olijfboom@pandora.be, Fax 0 58 31 42 08* – ⓜⓒ VISA
fermé 1 sem. en sept., 2 sem. en janv., dim. et lundi – **Repas** Lunch 21 – 42 ♀.
◆ Bonne petite adresse à débusquer près du Grote Markt. Décor intérieur contemporain, fourneaux à vue où s'active un chef "new style", assiettes soignées et beau livre de cave.
◆ Goed adresje bij de Grote Markt. Hedendaags interieur, open keuken waarin een chef-kok "nieuwe stijl" aan het werk is, mooi opgemaakte borden en lekkere wijnen.

à Beauvoorde *Sud-Ouest : 8 km* Ⓒ *Veurne* – ✉ *8630 Veurne :*

XX **Driekoningen** avec ch, Wulveringemstraat 40, ☎ 0 58 29 90 12, *info@driekoningen.be, Fax 0 58 29 80 22,* ☂ – TV P – 25 à 120. AE ⓓ ⓜⓒ VISA
fermé 17 janv.-4 fév., 22 sept.-1er oct., lundi soir et mardi midi d'oct. à mars, mardi soir et merc. – **Repas** 34/57 bc – **7 ch** ☕ 55/67 – ½ P 64.
◆ Un village charmant sert de cadre à cette auberge du 17e s. où les touristes de passage trouveront le gîte et le couvert, aussi corrects l'un que l'autre. Accueil familial.
◆ Deze 17e-eeuwse herberg in een charmant dorp is een prima slaap- en eetgelegenheid voor toeristen, die er gastvrij worden ontvangen.

VICHTE *8570 West-Vlaanderen* Ⓒ *Anzegem 13 879 h.* 533 F 18 *et* 716 D 3.

Bruxelles 83 – Kortrijk 13 – Brugge 49 – Gent 38 – Lille 37.

🏨 **Rembrandt,** Oudenaardestraat 22, ☎ 0 56 77 73 55, *rembrandt.bvba@pandora.be, Fax 0 56 77 57 04,* – ▤ rest, TV P – 25 à 280. AE ⓓ ⓜⓒ VISA. ✻
fermé 21 juil.-15 août – **Repas** *(fermé dim. soir)* Lunch 30 – carte 32 à 51 – **17 ch** ☕ 50/80.
◆ Aux portes de Vichte et pas loin de l'autoroute, ancien relais converti en auberge renfermant des chambres de mise simple, mais convenables. Petit-déjeuner copieux. Agréable restaurant au décor "composite". Cour intérieure sous verrière. Plats traditionnels.
◆ Herberg aan de rand van Vichte, bij de snelweg. De kamers zijn eenvoudig, maar keurig. Aangenaam restaurant dat in verschillende stijlen is ingericht. De binnenplaats is met een glaskoepel overdekt. Traditionele keuken.

VIELSALM *6690 Luxembourg belge* 533 U 21, 534 U 21 *et* 716 K 5 – *7 254 h.*

ℹ *r. Chasseurs Ardennais 1* ☎ *0 80 21 50 52, infosalm@wanadoo.be, Fax 0 80 21 74 62.*
Bruxelles 171 – Arlon 86 – Malmédy 28 – Clervaux 40.

🏨 **Belle Vue,** r. Jean Bertholet 5, ☎ 0 80 21 62 61, *Fax 0 80 21 62 01,* ≤ lac, ☂, – TV. ⓜⓒ VISA. ✻
fermé 30 juin-12 juil., 31 août-12 sept., du 1er au 12 janv., dim. soir et lundi – **Repas** Lunch 19 – 24/60 bc – **14 ch** ☕ 54/71.
◆ L'enseigne dit vrai : une "belle vue" plongeante se dévoile sur le lac depuis chacune des chambres tournées vers l'arrière de cet hôtel de tradition édifié au début du 20e s. Salle à manger panoramique aménagée à l'ardennaise.
◆ Het uithangbord van dit traditionele hotel uit de vroege 20e eeuw zegt niets te veel, want vanuit elke kamer aan de achterzijde ontvouwt zich een mooi uitzicht op het meer. De eetzaal is in Ardense stijl ingericht en biedt eveneens een panoramisch uitzicht.

à Bovigny *Sud : 7 km* Ⓒ *Gouvy 4 719 h.* – ✉ *6671 Bovigny :*

🏨 **St-Martin,** Courtil 5, ☎ 0 80 21 55 42, *hotelsaintmartin@skynet.be, Fax 0 80 21 77 46,* – TV P. ⓜⓒ VISA. ✻ rest
fermé 31 mars-9 avril et 30 déc.-15 janv. – **Repas** *(fermé dim. soir et après 20 h)* Lunch 18 – 28/55 bc – ☕ 8 – **12 ch** 53 – ½ P 45/55.
◆ Maison ardennaise en pierres du pays, au bord de la route traversant le hameau. Chambres fonctionnelles, dont la plupart ont été remises à neuf. Réel sens de l'hospitalité. Salle de restaurant au décor assez typé, assorti au tempérament régional du menu.
◆ Dit pand is in typisch Ardense stijl uit steen opgetrokken langs de weg die door het dorpje loopt. Functionele kamers, waarvan de meeste zijn gerenoveerd. Gastvrij onthaal. De karakteristieke eetzaal past uitstekend bij het regionale karakter van het menu.

à Grand-Halleux *Nord : 5 km* C *Vielsalm –* ✉ *6698 Grand-Halleux :*

Host. Les Linaigrettes, Rocher de Hourt 60, ☎ 0 80 21 59 68, *Fax 0 80 21 46 64,* – TV P. AE ① MC VISA.
fermé du 1er au 15 sept., merc. et jeudi – **Repas** (dîner seult) 32 – **10 ch** ☐ 50/80 – ½ P 110.

◆ Auberge discrète le long d'une jolie route suivant la vallée. Situées à l'arrière, les menues chambres offrent un petit confort, mais aussi le chant de la rivière. La Salm méandre au pied de la terrasse où l'on s'attable dès l'arrivée des beaux jours.

◆ Deze herberg staat onopvallend aan een mooie weg door het dal. Aan de achterkant liggen kleine kamers met beperkt comfort, maar wel met uitzicht op de rivier. De Salm kronkelt aan de voet van het terras, waar bij goed weer de tafeltjes worden gedekt.

L'Ecurie, av. de la Résistance 30, ☎ 0 80 21 59 54, *restaurant.ecurie@swing.be, Fax 0 80 21 76 43,* ≤, , Avec cuisine italienne, ouvert jusqu'à 23 h – P. AE ① MC VISA
fermé prem. sem. sept. et lundis et mardis non fériés sauf vacances scolaires – **Repas** carte 22 à 44.

◆ Cuisine franco-transalpine servie dans les anciennes dépendances d'un pensionnat de jeunes filles. La plupart des tables embrassent du regard une vallée bucolique.

◆ In de voormalige bijgebouwen van een meisjesinternaat genieten de gasten van Frans-Italiaanse gerechten. Het merendeel van de tafels kijkt uit op het schilderachtige dal.

à Hébronval *Ouest : 10 km* C *Vielsalm –* ✉ *6690 Vielsalm :*

Le Val d'Hébron, Hébronval 10, ☎ 0 80 41 88 73, *Fax 0 80 41 80 73,* , – TV – 25. AE ① MC VISA. rest
fermé 1 sem. en mars et 18 août-3 sept. – **Repas** *(fermé mardi)* (avec taverne) *Lunch 19* – 25/45 – ☐ 7 – **12 ch** 32/48 – ½ P 52.

◆ Accueil familial affable dans cette petite auberge érigée au bord de la route. Les meilleures chambres sont à l'annexe, au bout du jardin, près de l'église. Restaurant rénové où ronfle une cheminée. Menus bien conçus, service prévenant et vue sur la campagne.

◆ In deze herberg wordt u vriendelijk ontvangen. De beste kamers bevinden zich in de dependance achter in de tuin, bij de kerk. In de gerenoveerde eetzaal knappert 's winters het haardvuur. Mooie menu's, voorkomende bediening en uitzicht op het platteland.

à Petit-Thier *Nord-Est : 5 km* C *Vielsalm –* ✉ *6692 Petit-Thier :*

Au Moulin Minguet, Moulin 128 (La Ferme de la Reine des Prés), ☎ 0 80 21 58 01, *jphenquet@yucom.be, Fax 0 80 21 79 66,* – P. MC VISA
fermé sem. carnaval, sem. Toussaint, mardi soir et merc. – **Repas** *Lunch 24* – carte 22 à 45.

◆ Dans un ancien moulin, table idéale pour un repas exempt de prise de tête. Préparations simples mais soignées. Truites puisées directement au vivier. Additions sans arêtes !

◆ Deze oude molen is ideaal voor een ongedwongen maaltijd. Eenvoudige, maar verzorgde schotels. De forel komt zo uit de vijver en in de rekening hoeft u zich niet te verslikken !

VIEUXVILLE *4190 Liège* C *Ferrières 4 307 h.* 533 S 20, 534 S 20 *et* 716 J 4.

r. Principale 34 ☎ *0 86 21 30 88, Fax 0 86 38 82 09.*
Bruxelles 120 – Liège 42 – Marche-en-Famenne 27 – Spa 30.

Château de Palogne sans rest, rte du Palogne 3, ☎ 0 86 21 38 74, *chateau.de.palogne@swing.be, Fax 0 86 21 38 76,* – TV P. MC VISA
☐ 15 – **11 ch** 74/148.

◆ Le château de Palogne, paisible gentilhommière datant de 1890, s'agrémente d'un parc soigné. Chambres et communs cossus. Service personnalisé. Petit-déjeuner de grand style.

◆ Het kasteel van Palogne uit 1890 is rustig gelegen in een mooi park. Weelderige kamers en gemeenschappelijke ruimten. Service met persoonlijke aandacht. Vorstelijk ontbijt.

Au Vieux Logis, rte de Logne 1, ☎ 0 86 21 14 60, *Fax 0 86 21 86 74* – P. AE ① MC VISA
fermé fin août-début sept. et lundis, mardis, merc. et jeudis non fériés – **Repas** *Lunch 31* – 54/80 bc.

◆ Cuisine classique tout doucettement actualisée et renouvelée au fil des saisons, servie dans une ancienne auberge au charme agreste joliment préservé. Cave bien tenue.

◆ Oude herberg met een goed bewaard gebleven landelijke charme. Klassieke, seizoengebonden keuken die voorzichtig aan de huidige tijd wordt aangepast. Uitstekende wijnkelder.

VILLERS-LA-VILLE *1495 Brabant Wallon* 533 M 19, 534 M 19 *et* 716 G 4 – *9 166 h.*

Voir *Ruines de l'abbaye★★.*

r. Châtelet 62 ☎ 0 71 87 77 65, Fax 0 71 87 77 83 - *au Sud-Ouest : 3 km à Sart-Dames-Avelines, r. Jumerée 1* ☎ 0 71 87 72 67, Fax 0 71 87 43 38.

r. Abbaye 53 ☎ 0 71 87 98 98, Fax 0 71 87 98 98.

Bruxelles 36 – Charleroi 28 – Namur 33.

le Cigalon, av. Arsène Tournay 40, ☎ 0 71 87 85 54, *cigalon@cigalon.be, Fax 0 71 87 53 63,* – P. AE O MC VISA
fermé dim. soir et lundi – **Repas** Lunch 18 – 32/65 bc, ♀.
• Une carte bourgeoise assortie d'un lunch et de menus vous sera soumise à cette table décorée dans la note provençale. Côté cave, les régions de France sont à l'honneur.
• Dit restaurant met een Provençaals interieur biedt een vrij eenvoudige kaart met een lunchformule en menu's. In de wijnkelder strijken de Franse regio's met de eer.

VILLERS-LE-BOUILLET *4530 Liège* 533 Q 19, 534 Q 19 *et* 716 I 4 – *5 716 h.*

Bruxelles 86 – Namur 37 – Liège 25 – Huy 8.

Un temps pour Soi, r. Résistance 7, ☎ 0 85 25 58 55, *tempspoursoi@belgacom.net, Fax 0 85 21 31 84,* – P. MC VISA
fermé prem. sem. sept., prem. sem. janv., lundis non fériés et sam. midi – **Repas** 41/46.
• Maison de pays dans la campagne résidentielle hesbignonne. Cuisine actuelle bien faite. Décor du restaurant et mise en place sur les tables de mêmes. Terrasse et jardin.
• Mooi ingericht restaurant met een uitstekende, eigentijdse keuken in een karakteristiek pand op het Haspengouwse platteland. Terras en tuin.

VILLERS-SUR-LESSE *5580 Namur* C *Rochefort 11 818 h.* 534 P 22 *et* 716 I 5.

Bruxelles 115 – Bouillon 55 – Namur 54 – Dinant 25 – Rochefort 9.

Château de Vignée, r. Montainpré 27 (Ouest : 3,5 km près E 411 - A 4, sortie ㉒, lieu-dit Vignée), ☎ 0 84 37 84 05, *chateaudevignee@skynet.be, Fax 0 84 37 84 26,* <, , , – TV P – 25 à 180. AE MC VISA
fermé lundi soir et mardi – **Repas** Lunch 30 – carte 51 à 64 – 9 – **6 ch** 90/114, – 3 suites – ½ P 100/127.
• Ferme-château du 18ᵉ s. s'entourant d'un parc dont les terrasses offrent une vue plongeante sur la Lesse et la campagne. Chambres personnalisées, garnies de meubles anciens. Élégante salle à manger d'esprit Art déco. Mets classiques revisités pas à pas.
• Deze 18e-eeuwse kasteelboerderij heeft een park en terrassen met uitzicht op de Lesse en het platteland. De kamers hebben antieke meubelen en een persoonlijk karakter. Elegante eetzaal in art-decostijl. Klassieke gerechten met een vleugje vernieuwing.

Beau Séjour, r. Platanes 16, ☎ 0 84 37 71 15, *contact@beausejour.be, Fax 0 84 37 81 34,* <, , , , – TV P – 25. AE MC VISA. ch
fermé 1 sem. en mars, 2 prem. sem. juil., 3 sem. en janv. et mardi – **Repas** ***Du four à la Table*** *(fermé lundi midi, mardi, merc. midi et après 20 h 30)* Lunch 25 – 45/70 bc – **12 ch** 81/120 – ½ P 88/95.
• Au cœur du village, auberge s'ouvrant sur un jardin généreusement fleuri à la belle saison. Chambres de "beau séjour" et piscine extérieure chauffée de mai à septembre. Repas dans le tempo actuel, cave bien fournie, belle terrasse d'été et service avenant.
• Deze dorpsherberg heeft een tuin die 's zomers prachtig in bloei staat. De kamers staan garant voor een prettig verblijf en het buitenzwembad wordt van mei tot eind september verwarmd. Eigentijdse keuken, goede wijnen, mooi zomerterras en hoffelijke bediening.

Aub. du bief de la Lesse, r. Bief 1, ☎ 0 84 37 84 21, <, – P
fermé lundi et mardi – **Repas** carte env. 28.
• Cette ancienne ferme (18ᵉ s.) à la façade fleurie en été vous reçoit dans un agréable décor rustique. Âtre au salon. Plats goûteux soigneusement présentés. Vue sur jardin.
• In deze 18e-eeuwse boerderij met een fleurige gevel en rustiek interieur wordt u gastvrij ontvangen. Lounge met open haard. Verzorgde keuken. Uitzicht op de tuin.

VILVOORDE (VILVORDE) *Vlaams-Brabant* 533 L 17 *et* 716 G 3 – *voir à Bruxelles, environs.*

VIRELLES *Hainaut* 534 K 22 *et* 716 F 5 – *voir à Chimay.*

Dans ce guide
un même symbole, un même mot,
imprimé en rouge ou en ***noir,*** *en maigre ou en* ***gras,***
n'ont pas tout à fait la même signification.
Lisez attentivement les pages explicatives.

VIRTON *6760 Luxembourg belge* 534 S 25 *et* 716 J 7 *– 10 935 h.*

Pavillon, r. Grasses Oies 2b ✆ 0 63 57 89 04, si.virton@skynet.be, Fax 0 63 57 71 14.
Bruxelles 221 – Bouillon 53 – Arlon 29 – Longwy 32 – Montmédy 15.

XX **Le Franc Gourmet,** r. Roche 13, ✆ 0 63 57 01 36, *Fax 0 63 58 17 19*, – AE VISA.
fermé sem. carnaval, sam. midi, dim. soir et lundi – **Repas** 25/35.
◆ Adresse en phase avec son temps, faisant face à la Maison du Tourisme de Gaume. Salle de restaurant contemporaine et plaisante cuisine au goût du jour. Jardin et terrasse.
◆ Dit adresje tegenover het Maison du Tourisme is goed bij de tijd, getuige de moderne eetzaal en de lekkere keuken die voldoet aan de huidige smaak. Tuin en terras.

X **Au Fil des Saisons,** Faubourg d'Arival 40b, ✆ 0 63 58 22 02, *Fax 0 63 58 22 02*, – P. VISA.
fermé dern. sem. janv.-prem. sem. fév., dim. soir et lundi – **Repas** *Lunch 10* – 35/67 bc.
◆ Au cœur de Virton, dans une vieille forge en pierre du pays, ample salle à manger où s'étagent plusieurs mezzanines. Carte actuelle, menus et plat du jour. Terrasse sur cour.
◆ Deze smederij van steen uit de streek, hartje Virton, is nu een groot restaurant met meerdere tussenverdiepingen. Actuele kaart, menu's en dagschotel. Binnenplaats met terras.

à Latour *Est : 4 km* C *Virton – ✉ 6761 Latour :*

Le Château de Latour, r. 24 Août 1, ✆ 0 63 57 83 52, *Fax 0 63 60 82 12*, ←, , – TV P. – 30. AE VISA. rest
fermé 23 août-3 sept. et du 1er au 22 janv. – **Repas** *(fermé dim. soir et lundi) Lunch 20* – carte 37 à 45 – 8 – **14 ch** 60/70 – ½ P 88.
◆ Au calme, dans une demeure ancienne adroitement restaurée, hôtel assez original renfermant des chambres classiquement aménagées et souvent flambant neuves. Salle à manger bourgeoise au bel appareil de pierres nues. Recettes personnalisées.
◆ Vrij origineel hotel in een fraai gerestaureerd pand, rustig gelegen. Klassiek ingerichte kamers, voor het merendeel spiksplinternieuw. Eetzaal in bourgeoisstijl met fraai metselwerk. De kookstijl heeft iets heel eigens.

à Torgny *Sud : 6 km* C *Rouvroy 1 950 h. – ✉ 6767 Torgny :*

L'Empreinte du Temps, r. Escofiette 12, ✆ 0 63 60 81 80, *lempreinte@skynet.be, Fax 0 63 57 18 63* – TV P. AE VISA. rest
fermé dern. sem. janv.-2 prem. sem. fév., dern. sem. août-2 prem. sem. sept., dim. soir, lundi et mardi midi – **Repas** carte env. 23 – **11 ch** 70/110.
◆ Petit hôtel plein de charme établi dans l'ancienne école de Torgny. Sa belle façade en pierres du pays, millésimée "1803", contraste fort avec l'intérieur, très contemporain.
◆ Bijzonder charmant hotelletje in de oude school van Torgny. De mooie voorgevel (1803) van plaatselijke steen contrasteert met het uitgesproken hedendaagse interieur.

XX **Aub. de la Grappe d'Or** (Boulanger) avec ch et annexe, r. Ermitage 18, ✆ 0 63 57 70 56, *la.grappe.dor@skynet.be, Fax 0 63 57 03 44*, – TV P. AE VISA. rest
fermé dern. sem. janv.-mi-fév., dern. sem. août-mi-sept., dim. soir, lundi et mardi midi – **Repas** *Lunch 32* – 49/125 bc, carte 49 à 84 – **10 ch** 94/120 – ½ P 105.
◆ Un joli village sert de cadre à cette maison du 19e s. transformée en relais de bouche savoureux et charmant. Chambres rustiques à l'étage, actuelles en rez-de-jardin.
◆ Dit 19e-eeuwse pand in een mooi dorp is nu een sfeervol en lekker restaurant. Rustieke kamers op de bovenverdieping en moderne op de begane grond.
Spéc. Homard en salade gourmande aux tomates confites. Poêlée de sot-l'y-laisse aux crêtes et rognons de coq. Consommé d'abricots au lait de vanille mousseux, sorbet aux fraises

VLIERMAAL *Limburg* 533 R 17 *et* 716 J 3 *– voir à Tongeren.*

VLISSEGEM *West-Vlaanderen* 533 D 15 *et* 716 C 2 *– voir à De Haan.*

VORST *Brussels Hoofdstedelijk Gewest – voir Forest à Bruxelles.*

VRASENE *9120 Oost-Vlaanderen* C *Beveren 45 168 h.* 533 K 15 *et* 716 F 2.
Bruxelles 55 – Antwerpen 13 – Gent 49 – Sint-Niklaas 8.

XXX **Herbert Robbrecht,** Hogenakker 1 (sur N 451), ✆ 0 3 755 17 75, *info@herbertrobbrecht.be, Fax 0 3 755 17 36*, – P. VISA.
fermé 29 mars-8 avril, 19 juil.-5 août, mardi soir, jeudi et sam. midi – **Repas** *Lunch 31* – 45/81 bc.
◆ Aux portes de Vrasene, villa récente s'ouvrant sur un jardin agrémenté d'une terrasse estivale et d'une pièce d'eau. Registre culinaire au goût du jour, orienté "produits".
◆ Hedendaagse villa aan de rand van Vrasene met een tuin, zomerterras en waterpartij. Eigentijdse keuken, waarbij de kwaliteit van de producten hoog in het vaandel staat.

VRESSE-SUR-SEMOIS *5550 Namur* 534 *O 23 et* 716 *H 6 – 2 847 h.*

Env. *au Nord-Est : Gorges du Petit Fays* ★ *– Route de Membre à Gedinne* ≤★★ *sur "Jambon de la Semois" : 6,5 km.* – *r. Albert Raty 83* ✆ *0 61 29 28 27, tourisme.vresse@belgacom.net Fax 0 61 29 28 32.* – *Bruxelles 154 – Bouillon 29 – Namur 95 – Charleville-Mézières 30.*

Le Relais, r. Albert Raty 72, ✆ 0 61 50 00 46, *le.relais.vresse@skynet.be, Fax 0 61 50 02 26,* – rest, TV. AE ① MC VISA
10 avril-1er janv. ; fermé merc. et jeudi sauf juil.-20 sept. – **Repas** *(fermé après 20 h 30)* *Lunch 18* – 25 – **14 ch** 56/71 – ½ P 80/115.

◆ Devancée d'une terrasse estivale animée, cette auberge accueillante nichée au cœur d'un village touristique propose deux catégories de chambres correctement équipées. Ambiance ardennaise, menus bien vus et prix muselés : trois raisons de s'attabler ici.

◆ Deze vriendelijke herberg in een toeristisch dorp heeft een populair zomerterras aan de voorkant en twee categorieën kamers met prima voorzieningen. Ardense sfeer, aantrekkelijke menu's en schappelijke prijzen : drie goede redenen om hier aan tafel te gaan.

Pont St. Lambert avec ch, r. Ruisseau 8, ✆ 0 61 50 04 49, *pontstlambert@skynet.be, Fax 0 61 50 16 93,* ≤, – AE ① MC VISA
fermé 22 mars-8 avril, 21 juin-8 juil., 20 sept.-1er oct. et mardi soir et merc. sauf en juil.-août – **Repas** *(fermé après 20 h 30)* 16/35 – **7 ch** 43/55 – ½ P 39/45.

◆ Un petit choix régional actualisé, proposant plusieurs menus, vous attend à cette enseigne. La terrasse offre la vue sur un vieux pont enjambant la Semois. Chambres pratiques.

◆ Terras met uitzicht op de oude brug over de Semois. De eigentijdse kaart met regionale invloeden is beknopt, maar wordt uitgebreid met een aantal menu's. Praktische kamers.

à Laforêt *Sud : 2 km* C *Vresse-sur-Semois* – ✉ *5550 Laforêt :*

Aub. du Moulin Simonis, rte de Charleville 42 (sur N 935), ✆ 0 61 50 00 81, *courrier@moulinsimonis.com, Fax 0 61 50 17 41,* , – TV – 40. MC VISA. rest
fermé janv.-carnaval, prem. sem. juil. et dim. soir et lundi hors saison – **Repas** *(fermé après 20 h 30)* 20/68 bc, – **11 ch** 55/70 – ½ P 47/50.

◆ Ancien moulin à eau isolé dans une clairière, sur un site imprégné de chlorophylle. Petites chambres de mise simple, mais d'une grande tranquillité. Accueil familial. Plats traditionnels et régionaux, menus tentateurs, choix de bourgognes et additions sages.

◆ Deze oude watermolen staat afgelegen op een open plek in het groen. Kleine, eenvoudige kamers, die echter veel rust bieden. Vriendelijke ontvangst. Traditionele en regionale gerechten, aanlokkelijke menu's, lekkere bourgognewijnen en billijke prijzen.

à Membre *Sud : 3 km* C *Vresse-sur-Semois* – ✉ *5550 Membre :*

des Roches, rte de Vresse 93, ✆ 0 61 50 00 51, *hoteldesroches@hotmail.com, Fax 0 61 50 20 67* – P. MC VISA.
fermé janv.-carnaval, dern. sem. sept. et merc. hors saison – **Repas** *(fermé après 20 h 30)* 22/42 – **14 ch** 45/50 – ½ P 44/46.

◆ Au bord de la route de Vresse, engageante petite auberge ardennaise tenue en famille depuis quatre générations. Chambres convenables. Clientèle surtout touristique. Table chaleureuse misant sur une carte classique-bourgeoise.

◆ Deze kleine Ardense herberg aan de weg naar Vresse ziet er uitnodigend uit en wordt al vier generaties lang door dezelfde familie geleid. Keurige kamers, waar overwegend toeristen komen. Gezellig restaurant met een traditionele klassieke kaart.

VROENHOVEN *3770 Limburg* C *Riemst 15 755 h.* 533 *S 18 et* 716 *J 3.*

Bruxelles 106 – Maastricht 6 – Hasselt 37 – Liège 26 – Aachen 42.

Mary Wong, Maastrichtersteenweg 242, ✆ 0 12 45 57 57, *info@marywong.be, Fax 0 12 45 72 90,* , Cuisine chinoise – P. AE ① MC VISA
fermé 19 juil.-6 août et merc. – **Repas** (dîner seult sauf dim.) 30/49.

◆ Agréable restaurant asiatique voisin de la frontière belgo-hollandaise, Mary Wong décline toutes les saveurs de l'Empire du Milieu. Présentations soignées. Service aimable.

◆ Aangenaam Aziatisch restaurant bij de Belgisch-Nederlandse grens, waar alle smaken van de Chinese keuken aan bod komen. Verzorgde presentatie en vriendelijke bediening.

WAARDAMME *West-Vlaanderen* 533 *E 16 et* 716 *C 2 – voir à Brugge, environs.*

WAARMAARDE *8581 West-Vlaanderen* C *Avelgem 9 193 h.* 533 *F 18 et* 716 *D 3.*

Bruxelles 64 – Kortrijk 20 – Gent 42 – Tournai 26.

De Gouden Klokke, Trappelstraat 25, ✆ 0 55 38 85 60, *info@goudenklokke.be, Fax 0 55 38 79 29,* – P. AE ① MC VISA.
fermé 1 sem. carnaval, 16 août-8 sept., dim. soir, lundi, mardi soir et merc. soir – **Repas** *Lunch 33* – 50/85 bc, .

◆ Ferme flamande à la campagne. Cuisine très "tendance", servie dans un décor alliant rusticité, touches classiques et notes modernes. Terrasse invitante par beau temps.

◆ Vlaamse boerderij op het platteland met een trendy keuken. Het interieur is een mengeling van rustiek, klassiek en modern. Het terras ziet er 's zomers zeer aanlokkelijk uit.

WAASMUNSTER 9250 Oost-Vlaanderen 533 J 16 et 716 F 2 – 10 411 h.

Bruxelles 39 – Antwerpen 29 – Gent 31.

XXX **La Cucina,** Belselestraat 4 (sur E 17 - A 14, sortie ⑬), ✆ 0 52 46 00 29, *info@restaurant-lacucina.be, Fax 0 52 46 34 59,* – AE ⓘ ⓜ VISA. ✻
fermé sem. carnaval, 3 sem. en juil., sem. Toussaint, mardi soir, merc. et sam. midi – **Repas** Lunch 25 – 50/70 bc.
◆ Construction récente évoquant un mas provençal, la Cucina vous attable dans un intérieur coquet. Cuisine d'aujourd'hui teintée d'un léger accent du Midi. Cave bien montée.
◆ Vrij nieuw gebouw in de stijl van een Provençaalse herenboerderij. In de mooie eetzaal kunt u genieten van de eigentijdse keuken met een licht Zuid-Frans accent. Goede wijnen.

XX **De Snip,** Schrijberg 122 (carrefour N 446 et N 70), ✆ 0 3 772 20 81, *info@desnip.be, Fax 0 3 722 06 95,* – P. AE ⓘ ⓜ VISA
fermé 2 sem. Pâques, 3 dern. sem. juil., 21 déc.-7 janv., dim. et lundi – **Repas** Lunch 38 – 60/90 bc.
◆ Une villa d'esprit néo-classique sert de nid à la bécasse (snip). Recettes dans l'air du temps et décor intérieur assez raffiné. Terrasse d'été rafraîchie par une pièce d'eau.
◆ Een neoklassieke villa is het nest van deze snip. De gerechten passen bij de huidige smaak en het interieur is vrij geraffineerd. Zomerterras met een verkoelende waterpartij.

WACHTEBEKE 9185 Oost-Vlaanderen 533 I 15 et 716 E 2 – 6 836 h.

Bruxelles 73 – Gent 18 – Middelburg 55 – Sas van Gent 10.

X **L'olivette,** Meersstraat 33, ✆ 0 9 342 04 17, *Fax 0 9 342 05 19,* – ⓘ ⓜ VISA JCB
fermé du 15 au 30 juin, dim. et lundi – **Repas** Lunch 27 – carte 39 à 51.
◆ Petit restaurant charmant au bord d'un chemin de halage longeant un canal. Attrayante carte inspirée par la Provence et ardoise de suggestions saisonnières.
◆ Leuk restaurantje aan het oude jaagpad langs het kanaal. Aantrekkelijke kaart met Provençaalse gerechten en suggesties afhankelijk van het seizoen.

WAIMES (WEISMES) 4950 Liège 533 V 20, 534 V 20 et 716 L 4 – 6 559 h.

Bruxelles 164 – Liège 65 – Malmédy 8 – Spa 27.

Hotleu, r. Hottleux 106 (Ouest : 2 km), ✆ 0 80 67 97 05, *info@hotleu.be, Fax 0 80 67 84 62,* – TV P – 25 à 90. AE ⓘ ⓜ VISA. ✻ rest
fermé 2 sem. Pâques, 2 sem. en janv. et merc. – **Repas** Lunch 25 – carte 38 à 46 – **15 ch** 66/84.
◆ Sur les hauteurs de Waimes, confortable hôtel familial offrant plusieurs possibilités de distractions ou détente : piscine et court de tennis au jardin, hammam flambant neuf. L'été, une délicieuse terrasse dominant la vallée vous invite à un repas panoramique.
◆ Dit comfortabele familiehotel in de heuvels van Weismes biedt talloze mogelijkheden voor ontspanning : zwembad en tennisbaan in de tuin en een gloednieuwe hamam. In de zomer nodigt het prachtige terras boven het dal tot een panoramische maaltijd.

Cyrano, r. Chanteraine 11, ✆ 0 80 67 99 89, *info@cyrano.be, Fax 0 80 67 83 85,* – TV P – 25 à 120. AE ⓜ VISA. ✻
Repas *(fermé 1 sem. en janv., merc. et sam. midi)* Lunch 31 – 3248/60 – **14 ch** 55/90 – ½ P 65/98.
◆ Juste "un peu de nez" suffit pour découvrir cet établissement sympathique. Toutefois, le héros de la pièce de Rostand n'aurait pu que s'y plaire, avec la belle Roxane ! Actuelle et inventive, la carte du restaurant trouve sa rime dans le vignoble de Bergerac.
◆ Wie een fijne neus heeft, vindt moeiteloos de weg naar dit sympathieke etablissement, dat is opgedragen aan de beroemde held uit het stuk van Rostand. De eigentijdse en inventieve keuken komt goed tot zijn recht bij de wijnen uit... Bergerac !

X **Aub. de la Warchenne** avec ch, r. Centre 20, ✆ 0 80 67 93 63, *Fax 0 80 67 84 59,* – TV P. AE ⓘ ⓜ VISA
fermé merc. et après 20 h 30 – **Repas** 19/35 – **7 ch** 44/72 – ½ P 48.
◆ Cette petite auberge familiale aménagée à la manière d'un chalet vient de souffler ses vingt-cinq bougies. Aux fourneaux, on mise sur la tradition. Chambres insonorisées.
◆ Deze kleine herberg die aan een chalet doet denken, heeft onlangs zijn 25-jarig bestaan gevierd. In de keuken wordt de traditie in ere gehouden. Kamers met geluidsisolatie.

à Faymonville Est : 2 km C Waimes – ✉ 4950 Faymonville :

XXX **Au Vieux Sultan** avec ch, r. Wemmel 12, ✆ 0 80 67 91 97, *auvieuxsultan@mail.com, Fax 0 80 67 81 28,* – rest, TV P – 25 à 80. AE ⓘ ⓜ VISA. ✻
fermé fin juin-mi-juil., dim. soir et lundi – **Repas** Lunch 20 – 29/48 – **10 ch** 48/75 – ½ P 53/68.
◆ Au centre d'un village tranquille, hostellerie connue pour ses mets classiques de saison, revisités en douceur. Salle à manger actuelle. Chambres pratiques, assez agréables.
◆ Deze herberg in een rustig dorp staat bekend om zijn klassieke, seizoengebonden gerechten met een vleugje vernieuwing. Eigentijdse eetzaal. Praktische, vrij aangename kamers.

WALCOURT *5650 Namur* 533 L 21, 534 L 21 *et* 716 G 5 – *16 927 h.*

Voir *Basilique St-Materne★ : jubé★, trésor★.*

Env. *au Sud : 6 km, Barrage de l'Eau d'Heure★, Barrage de la Plate Taille★.*

Grand'Place 25 ☎ 0 71 61 25 26.

Bruxelles 81 – Namur 57 – Charleroi 21 – Dinant 43 – Maubeuge 44.

Host. Dispa avec ch, r. Jardinet 7, ☎ 0 71 61 14 23, *Fax 0 71 61 11 04,* – P. AE VISA. ch
fermé 15 fév.-15 mars, dern. sem. juin, 2 sem. en sept., jeudi soir sauf en juil.-août, mardi soir et merc. – Repas *Lunch 22* – 32/78 bc – **6 ch** 62/87 – ½ P 72.

◆ Deux ambiances contrastées dans cette ancienne maison de notable où il fait bon s'attabler : salle feutrée au décor bourgeois ou véranda. Mets classiques soignés.

◆ Twee verschillende sferen in dit herenhuis, waar u goed kunt tafelen : eetzaal in bourgeoisstijl of serre. Verzorgde klassieke keuken.

WANNE *Liège* 533 U 20, 534 U 20 *et* 716 K 4 – *voir à Trois-Ponts.*

WAREGEM *8790 West-Vlaanderen* 533 F 17 *et* 716 D 3 – *35 954 h.*

Bergstraat 41 ☎ 0 56 60 88 08, Fax 0 56 62 18 23.

Bruxelles 79 – Kortrijk 16 – Brugge 47 – Gent 34.

St-Jan, Anzegemseweg 26 (Sud : 3 km, près E 17 - A 14, sortie ⑤), ☎ 0 56 61 08 88, *sint_janshof@pi.be, Fax 0 56 60 34 45* – P – 25 à 40. AE VISA.
fermé 20 déc.-4 janv. – **Repas** (dîner pour résidents seult) – **21 ch** 60/80 – ½ P 72/114.

◆ À portée d'autoroute, imposante villa érigée au bord d'une chaussée passante traversant une zone industrielle. Chambres standard de bon format, munies du double vitrage.

◆ Imposante villa aan een doorgaande weg op een industrieterrein langs de snelweg. De standaardkamers zijn van goed formaat en hebben dubbele ramen.

de peracker, Caseelstraat 45 (Ouest : 3 km sur rte de Desselgem, puis rte à gauche), ☎ 0 56 60 03 31, *deperacker@pandora.be, Fax 0 56 60 03 25,* ←, , – P – 40 à 100. AE VISA.
fermé 24 déc.-2 janv. et vend. et dim. soir de sept. à Pâques – **Repas** (dîner seult sauf dim.) carte 23 à 53, ♀ – **14 ch** 75/85.

◆ Cet hôtel familial excentré voisinant un étang que l'on peut sillonner en barque l'été venu, est spécialisé dans la tenue de banquets et séminaires. Chambres fonctionnelles.

◆ Dit familiehotel ligt even buiten Waregem bij een meertje, waar 's zomers bootjes te huur zijn. Het is gespecialiseerd in congressen en feesten. Functionele kamers.

't Oud Konijntje (Mmes Desmedt), Bosstraat 53 (Sud : 2 km près E 17 - A 14), ☎ 0 56 60 19 37, *info@oudkonijntje.be, Fax 0 56 60 92 12,* – P. AE VISA
fermé 1 sem. Pâques, fin juil.-début août, Noël-Nouvel An, jeudi soir, vend. et dim. soir – **Repas** 75/145 bc, carte 79 à 140, ♀.

◆ Décor intérieur joliment dédié au lapin, exquise terrasse rafraîchie d'une fontaine, jardin délicieusement fleuri en été : pareil écrin méritait bien la félicité culinaire !

◆ Culinair genieten in een interieur dat geheel in het teken staat van dit sympathieke knaagdier. Mooi terras met fontein en een tuin die 's zomers prachtig in bloei staat.

Spéc. Bouillon aux langoustines et morilles parfumé au basilic. Tronçon de turbot aux noisettes grillées et truffe (déc.-fév.). Pigeonneau rôti au romarin et mousseline de pommes de terre surprise

Hobo's, Wortegemseweg 51 (près E 17 - A 14, sortie ⑤), ☎ 0 56 61 69 54, *info@hoboswaregem, Fax 0 56 60 90 56,* – P. AE VISA JCB
fermé du 18 au 29 fév., 22 juil.-13 août, dim. soir et lundi – **Repas** *Lunch 25* – 38/55 bc.

◆ Accueillant restaurant style "bistrot bien dans le coup". Ample et lumineuse salle où domine le bois blond, grande terrasse d'été et quelques spécialités nippones à la carte.

◆ Gezellig restaurant in de stijl van een moderne bistro. Ruime en lichte eetzaal, waarin hout de boventoon voert. Groot terras en enkele Japanse specialiteiten op de kaart.

à Sint-Eloois-Vijve *Nord-Ouest : 3 km* C *Waregem* – *8793 Sint-Eloois-Vijve :*

De Houtsnip, Posterijstraat 56, ☎ 0 56 61 13 77, *info@houtsnip.be, Fax 0 56 61 28 10,* – P. AE VISA
fermé 30 juil.-16 août, du 2 au 10 janv., mardi soir, merc. et dim. soir – **Repas** 28/54 bc, ♀.

◆ Un volatile sympathique s'est posé sur l'enseigne de ce plaisant restaurant. Salle à manger d'un style classique actualisé, tout comme les préparations, assez ambitieuses.

◆ Deze sympathieke vogel is neergestreken op het uithangbord van dit plezierige restaurant. Eetzaal in modern-klassieke stijl, evenals de gerechten, die vrij ambitieus zijn.

X **bistro desanto,** Gentseweg 558, ✆ 0 56 60 24 13, *bistro.desanto@pandora.be, Fax 0 56 61 17 84*, ☂, Ouvert jusqu'à 23 h – P. AE ① MC VISA
fermé du 1er au 20 août, 24 déc.-4 janv., sam. midi, dim. et lundi – **Repas** Lunch 16 – carte 25 à 45.
◆ Atmosphère conviviale, service avenant, saveurs "bistrotières" et suggestions plus travaillées font le succès de cette maison bourgeoise au décor intérieur contemporain.
◆ De gemoedelijke sfeer, attente bediening, bistrogerechten en ook verfijndere schotels zijn het succesrecept van dit restaurant in een herenhuis met een eigentijds interieur.

X **Anna's Place** avec ch, Gentseweg 606, ✆ 0 56 60 11 72, *info@annas-place.be, Fax 0 56 61 45 86*, ☂ – TV P. MC VISA
fermé du 26 au 31 déc. – **Repas** *(fermé lundi midi, merc. et sam. midi)* Lunch 38 – carte env. 45 – **11 ch** ☕ 61/104.
◆ L'affaire, qui a fêté ses dix ans, surveille un carrefour au trafic soutenu. Petite adresse de cuisine traditionnelle prisée pour son menu vedette. Chambres insonorisées.
◆ Dit etablissement, dat pas zijn tienjarig bestaan heeft gevierd, staat aan een druk kruispunt. Eenvoudige, traditionele kaart met een gewild menu. Kamers met geluidsisolatie.

WAREMME (BORGWORM) *4300 Liège* 533 Q 18, 534 Q 18 *et* 716 I 3 – *13 456 h.*

Bruxelles 76 – Namur 47 – Liège 28 – Sint-Truiden 19.

XX **Le Petit Axhe,** r. Petit-Axhe 12 (Sud-Ouest : 2 km, lieu-dit Petit Axhe), ✆ 0 19 32 37 22, *Fax 0 19 32 88 92*, ☂ – P. AE ① MC VISA
fermé 1 sem en mars, 2 sem. en juil., 1 sem. en oct., lundi, mardi, merc. soir et sam. midi – **Repas** Lunch 30 – 43/72 bc.
◆ Maison appréciée pour son répertoire culinaire assez inventif, le confort de ses salles à manger et le soin apporté à la mise en place sur les tables. L'été, repas au jardin.
◆ Dit restaurant valt in de smaak vanwege zijn vrij inventieve culinaire repertoire, comfortabele eetzalen en fraai gedekte tafels. Bij goed weer kan in de tuin worden gegeten.

WATERLOO *1410 Brabant Wallon* 533 L 18, 534 L 18 *et* 716 G 3 – *28 898 h.*

18 (2 parcours) 9 à l'Est : 5 km à Ohain, Vieux Chemin de Wavre 50 ✆ 0 2 633 18 50, Fax 0 2 633 28 66 - 18 (2 parcours) 9 au Sud-Ouest : 5 km à Braine-l'Alleud, chaussée d'Alsemberg 1021 ✆ 0 2 353 02 46, Fax 0 2 354 68 75.

chaussée de Bruxelles 149 ✆ 0 2 354 99 10, tourisme.waterloo@advalvas.be, Fax 0 2 354 22 23 – Fédération provinciale de tourisme, chaussée de Bruxelles 218 ✆ 0 2 351 12 00, brabant.wallon.tourisme@skynet.be, Fax 0 2 351 13 00.

Bruxelles 17 – Charleroi 37 – Nivelles 15.

Grand H., chaussée de Tervuren 198, ✆ 0 2 352 18 15, *ghw@martins-hotels.com, Fax 0 2 352 18 88*, ☂, Fø – |‡| ⇸, ▤ rest, TV – 🔬 25 à 85. AE ① MC VISA
Repas *(fermé sam. midi et dim. midi)* Lunch 12 – 22/55 bc – **79 ch** ☕ 250/320 – ½ P 100/175.
◆ Cet hôtel cossu aménagé dans un ensemble industriel du 19e s. renferme des chambres spacieuses de bon ton, offrant tout le confort moderne. Room service. Ample salle de restaurant voûtée, mise en place simple et recettes orientées "épices".
◆ Dit luxueuze hotel is gevestigd in een industriecomplex uit de 19e eeuw. De mooie en ruime kamers zijn van alle moderne gemakken voorzien. Roomservice. Grote gewelfde eetzaal met bistrotafels. Keuken waarin veel met kruiden wordt gewerkt.

Le Côté Vert ⛬, chaussée de Bruxelles 200g, ✆ 0 2 354 01 05, *info@cotevert.be, Fax 0 2 354 08 60* – |‡| ⇸ TV P – 🔬 40. AE ① MC VISA
fermé Nouvel An – **Repas** voir rest ***La Cuisine "au Vert"*** ci-après – **29 ch** ☕ 131/146.
◆ Près du centre-ville, mais au calme, immeuble récent dont les chambres, munies d'un mobilier de série, donnent côté arrière sur un jardin et un paysage de prairies.
◆ Nieuw gebouw, rustig gelegen bij het centrum van de stad. De kamers zijn met standaardmeubilair ingericht en kijken aan de achterkant uit op de tuin en de weilanden.

Le Joli-Bois ⛬ sans rest, r. Ste-Anne 59 (Sud : 2 km à Joli-Bois), ✆ 0 2 353 18 18, *info@waterloohotel.be, Fax 0 2 353 05 16*, ⛱ – |‡| TV P. AE ① MC VISA
14 ch ☕ 80/106.
◆ Établissement à taille humaine situé dans un quartier résidentiel paisible, proche du ring. Chambres confortables. Petit-déjeuner dans la véranda ouvrant sur le jardin.
◆ Dit hotel in een rustige woonwijk, niet ver van de Ring, heet u graag welkom. De kamers zijn gerieflijk. Het ontbijt wordt gebruikt in de serre, die uitkijkt op de tuin.

BELGIQUE

XX **La Cuisine "au Vert"** - H. Le Côté Vert, chaussée de Bruxelles 200g, ✆ 0 2 357 34 94, *info@cotevert.be, Fax 0 2 354 08 60,* ☂ - P. AE ⓓ MC VISA
fermé dern. sem. juil.-2 prem. sem. août, dern. sem. déc.-prem. sem. janv., sam. et dim. – **Repas** Lunch 18 – carte 35 à 47.
◆ Cuisine au goût du jour servie dans un cadre actuel plaisant. Terrasse estivale dressée au jardin, offrant la vue sur les champs où paissent des vaches.
◆ Eigentijdse keuken en dito interieur. Op zomerse dagen worden de tafeltjes gedekt op het terras in de tuin, dat een mooi uitzicht biedt op de weilanden met grazende koeien.

XX **Le Jardin des Délices,** chaussée de Bruxelles 253, ✆ 0 2 354 80 33, *jardin_des_delices@hotmail.com, Fax 0 2 354 80 33,* ☂ - AE ⓓ MC VISA
fermé 29 août-15 sept., dim. soir, lundi et mardi – **Repas** Lunch 11 – 25/33 bc.
◆ Lambris blonds, murs écarlates, colonnes blanches, tableaux modernes, chaises et banquettes zébrées : un décor qui a du punch ! Formule menu-carte à composer soi-même.
◆ Lichtgele lambrisering, scharlakenrode muren, witte zuilen, moderne schilderijen en stoelen en bankjes in zebraprint : een interieur met schwung ! Aantrekkelijk à la carte-menu.

XX **Rêve Richelle,** Drêve Richelle 96, ✆ 0 2 354 82 24, *Fax 0 2 354 82 24,* ☂ - P. AE MC VISA
fermé 1 sem. Pâques, 3 sem. en août, 1 sem. Toussaint, dim. et lundi – **Repas** Lunch 17 – carte 36 à 50.
◆ Le nom de la rue a inspiré cette onirique enseigne. Registre culinaire classique. Bons vins à prix "sympa". Une terrasse devance le jardin, à l'arrière de la villa.
◆ Dromen zijn niet altijd bedrog : hier vindt men een goede klassieke keuken en lekkere wijnen voor een zeer schappelijk prijsje. Tuin met terras aan de achterkant van de villa.

X **Yves Lemercier,** chaussée de Charleroi 72 (N 5, direction butte du lion), ✆ 0 2 387 17 78, *Fax 0 2 387 17 78,* ☂, Rôtissoire à vue – P. AE ⓓ MC VISA
fermé 1 sem. carnaval, 1re quinz. juil., 1 sem. Toussaint, Noël-Nouvel An et mardi et merc. en juil.-août – **Repas** (déjeuner seult sauf en juil.-août et week-end) carte 30 à 60.
◆ Restaurant simple et convivial, au bord d'un axe passant, pas loin de la butte du lion. Mets traditionnels à base de bons produits des terroirs belges. Rôtissoire en salle.
◆ Gemoedelijk restaurant aan een drukke verkeersader, vlak bij de Leeuwenheuvel. Traditionele gerechten op basis van goede producten van het Belgische land. Grill in de eetzaal.

WATERMAEL-BOITSFORT (WATERMAAL-BOSVOORDE) *Région de Bruxelles-Capitale* 533 L 18 – *voir à Bruxelles.*

WATOU *8978 West-Vlaanderen* C *Poperinge 19 376 h.* 533 A 17 *et* 716 A 3.
Bruxelles 146 – Brugge 81 – Kortrijk 55 – Lille 49.

X **Gasthof 't Hommelhof,** Watouplein 17, ✆ 0 57 38 80 24, *info@hommelhof.be, Fax 0 57 38 85 90,* ☂, Avec cuisine à la bière – 150. AE ⓓ MC VISA
fermé 1 sem. en juin, 1 sem. en oct., 24 déc.-6 janv. et merc. sauf en juil.-août – **Repas** (déjeuner seult sauf week-end et en juil.-août) 24/43.
◆ Table blottie au centre d'un village brassicole proche de la frontière française. Du houblon séché orne les murs des deux coquettes salles. Savoureuse cuisine traditionnelle.
◆ Restaurant in een brouwersdorp, vlak bij de Franse grens. De muren van de twee eetzalen zijn versierd met gedroogde hop. Smakelijke traditionele keuken.

WAVRE (WAVER) *1300* P *Brabant Wallon* 533 M 18, 534 M 18 *et* 716 G 3 – *31 526 h.*
18 9 *chaussée du Château de la Bawette 5 ✆ 0 10 22 33 32, Fax 0 10 22 90 04* - 18 *au Nord-Est : 10 km à Grez-Doiceau, Les Gottes 1 ✆ 0 10 84 15 01, Fax 0 10 84 55 95.*
Hôtel de Ville, r. Nivelles 1 ✆ 0 10 23 03 52, Fax 0 10 23 03 56.
Bruxelles 27 – Namur 37 – Charleroi 45 – Liège 87.

Plans pages suivantes

Novotel, r. Wastinne 45, ✉ 1301, ✆ 0 10 41 13 63, *H1645@accor-hotels.com, Fax 0 10 41 19 22,* ☂, – 25 à 170. AE ⓓ MC VISA B a
Repas *(fermé sam. midi)* Lunch 15 – carte 27 à 40 – 14 – **102 ch** 107.
◆ Retrouvez, aux portes de Wavre, près de l'autoroute et d'un grand parc d'attractions, toutes les prestations habituelles de l'enseigne Novotel. Chambres refaites de neuf.
◆ Dit hotel aan de rand van Waver, vlak bij de snelweg en een groot pretpark, biedt alle voorzieningen die gebruikelijk zijn voor deze keten. De kamers zijn pas gerenoveerd.

AC Hotel Wavre-Nord, av. Lavoisier 12, ✆ 0 10 22 60 50, *hotel.wavre@autogrill.net, Fax 0 10 22 57 01,* ☂ – 25 à 60. AE ⓓ MC VISA. rest A b
Repas *(fermé sam. midi et dim.)* carte env. 29 – **64 ch** 64/72.
◆ Hôtel de chaîne dont la façade style "Louisiane" introduit un brin de fantaisie dans ce quartier à vocation industrielle. Chambres menues mais pratiques et rénovées.
◆ Ketenhotel waarvan de gevel in Louisianastijl voor enige fantasie zorgt in dit industriegebied. De kamers zijn klein, maar praktisch en onlangs gerenoveerd.

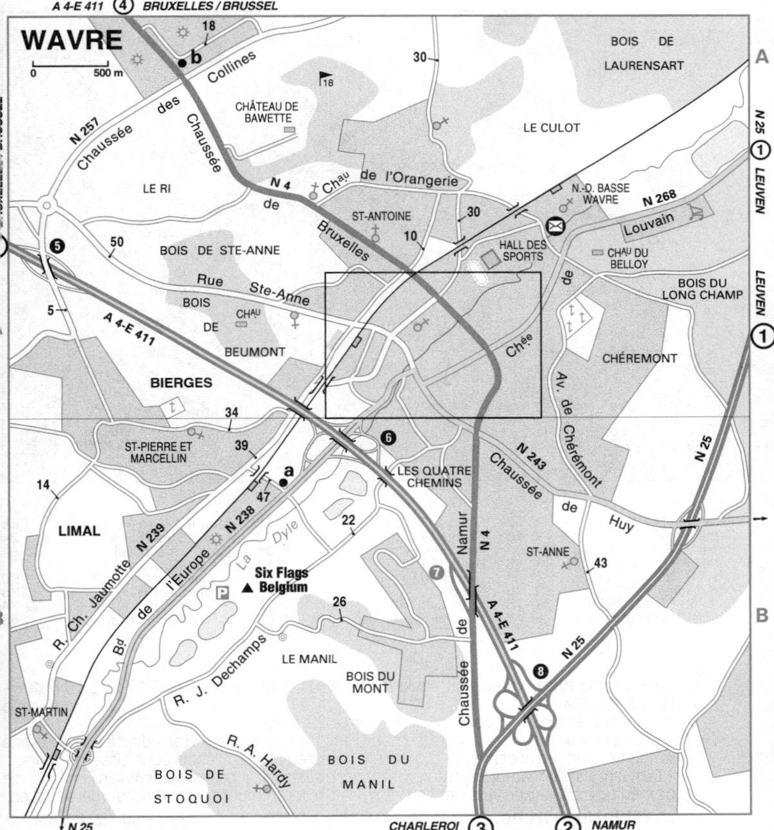

Champles (R. de)	A 5	Manil (R. du)	B 22	Provinciale (R.)	B 39
Gaulois (Chaussée des)	A 10	Maréchaux (Chemin des)	B 26	Vieusart (Chemin de)	B 43
Haie (R. de la)	B 14	Ottenbourg (Chaussée d')	A 30	Wastinne (R. de la)	B 47
Lavoisier (Av.)	A 18	Poilu (R. du)	AB 34	Wavre (R. de)	A 50

at home sans rest, pl. Bosch 33, 0 10 22 83 83, *melinda.bacq@skynet.be*, *Fax 0 10 81 69 39* – – 25. AE MC VISA C f
19 ch 60/75.
◆ Étape idéale au cœur de la capitale du Brabant wallon : accueil familial, chambres et communs fringants, semés de touches provençales ou exotiques, et salles d'eau "nickel".
◆ Hotel in het centrum van de hoofdstad van Waals-Brabant. Piekfijne kamers en gemeenschappelijke ruimten met een Provençaalse of exotische noot. De badkamers zijn spic en span.

Carte Blanche, av. Reine Astrid 8, 0 10 24 23 63, *Fax 0 10 81 67 09*, – MC VISA D c
fermé 21 juil.-15 août, du 1er au 15 janv., sam. midi, dim. soir, lundi et après 20 h 30 – **Repas** Lunch 17 – 25/37.
◆ Affaire familiale avoisinant un carrefour dit du "Fin bec". Le chef y a carte blanche pour concocter ses menus entre classicisme et tradition. Décor intérieur chaleureux.
◆ Dit familiebedrijf staat bij een kruispunt dat ook wel de lekkerbek wordt genoemd. De chef-kok heeft "carte blanche" voor zijn klassiek-traditionele menu's. Warm interieur.

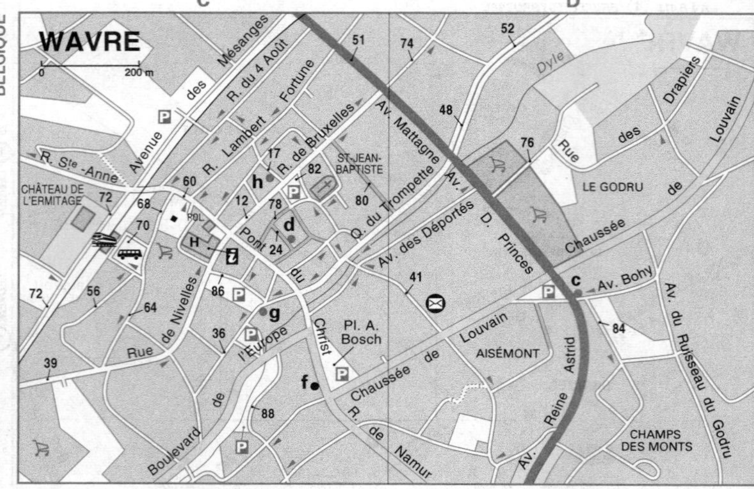

Belle Voie (Av.) . . . . D 52
Berger (Pl. Henri) . . . . C 70
Bruxelles (Chée de) . . . . . . C 51
Carabinier (R. des) . . . . . . C 86
Clos (Av. du) . . . . D 84
Commerce (R. du) . . . . C 78
Croix du Feu (R. des) . . . . . D 76
Désiré Yemaux (Av.) . . . . . . D 48
Ermitage (R. de l') . . . . C 72
Flandre (R.) . . . . C 17
Fontaines (R.) . . . . C 36
Haute (R.) . . . . C 12
Letroye (R.F.) . . . . CD 41
Mercier (Pl. Cardinal) . . . . C 82
Meunier (R. du) . . . . C 88
Moulin à Vent (R. du) . . . . . C 56
Nuit et Jour (Ruelle) . . . . . . C 24
Piat (R. Théophile) . . . . C 64
Pré de Wildre (Ruelle du) . . . . CD 80
Provinciale (R.) . . . . C 39
Saint-Roch (R.) . . . . CD 74
Volontaires (R. des) . . . . . . C 68

XX **Le Bateau Ivre,** Ruelle Nuit et Jour 19, ☏ 0 10 24 37 64, *Fax 0 10 24 37 64*, – AE D MC VISA. C d
fermé dim. et lundi – **Repas** Lunch 15 – carte 29 à 40.
• Dans une ruelle piétonne, adresse dont l'ami Rimbaud n'aurait sans doute pas dédaigné la cuisine méditerranéenne, ni d'ailleurs la jolie terrasse d'été sur cour close de murs.
• De naam van dit restaurant in een voetgangersstraat slaat op een gedicht van Rimbaud, die de mediterrane keuken vast niet had versmaad. Mooi ommuurd terras voor zomerse dagen.

X **La table du marché,** r. Flandre 11, ☏ 0 10 88 13 50, *Fax 0 10 88 13 50* – AE MC VISA. C h
fermé 15 août-6 sept., dim. et lundi – **Repas** Lunch 16 – 30.
• Au voisinage de la place dominée par l'église St-Jean-Baptiste, table dont les savoureux mets au goût du jour connaissent un succès grandissant auprès des habitants de Wavre.
• Dit restaurant bevindt zich in de buurt van het plein met de kerk St.-Jean-Baptiste. De smakelijke, eigentijdse gerechten oogsten steeds meer succes bij de inwoners van Waver.

X **Rotissimus,** r. Fontaines 60, ☏ 0 10 24 54 54, *rotissimus@restowavre.be*, , Grillades – AE D MC VISA. C g
fermé 21 juil.-15 août, merc. soir, sam. midi et dim. – **Repas** Lunch 15 – carte 29 à 42.
• Une façade bordeaux signale cette maisonnette du centre-ville accueillant ses hôtes dans un cadre actuel. Rôtissoire en salle et choix de recettes classico-bourgeoises.
• Rotisserie in een pandje in het centrum met een bordeauxrode gevel en een eigentijds interieur, waar u eenvoudig klassiek kunt eten. Het vlees wordt in de eetzaal geroosterd.

WAYS *Brabant Wallon* 533 L 19 – *voir à Genappe.*

WEELDE *2381 Antwerpen* C *Ravels 13 238 h.* 533 O 14 *et* 716 H 1.
Bruxelles 94 – Antwerpen 44 – Turnhout 11 – Breda 38 – Eindhoven 47 – Tilburg 20.

XX **de Groes,** Meir 1, ☏ 0 14 65 64 84, *de.groes@proximedia.be, Fax 0 14 65 64 84*, – P. AE D MC VISA
fermé du 2 au 11 janv., mardi soir, merc. et sam. midi – **Repas** Lunch 24 – carte 41 à 52.
• À proximité de la frontière batave, ancienne ferme convertie en restaurant au cadre rustique dont un éclairage tamisé renforce l'intimité. Carte classique avec lunch et menus.
• Deze oude boerderij bij de Nederlandse grens is verbouwd tot rustiek restaurant, waar het gedempte licht een intieme sfeer geeft. Klassieke kaart met lunchformule en menu's.

WEGNEZ *Liège* 533 T 19 *et* 534 T 19 *– voir à Pepinster.*

WEISMES *Liège – voir Waimes.*

WELLIN *6920 Luxembourg belge* 534 P 22 *et* 716 I 5 *– 2 884 h.*
Bruxelles 110 – Bouillon 44 – Dinant 34 – Namur 53 – Rochefort 14.

La Papillote, r. Station 55, ✆ 0 84 38 88 16, *Fax 0 84 38 70 46* – MC VISA
fermé 15 juil.-7 août, 1 sem. en janv., sam. midi sauf en été, mardi soir, merc. et dim. soir – **Repas** 42/67 bc.
• Maison bourgeoise nichée au cœur du village. Menu au goût du jour reprenant des plats de la carte, homards pêchés dans le vivier et suggestions quotidiennes sur écriteau.
• Herenhuis in het hart van het dorp. Het eigentijdse menu bestaat uit gerechten van de kaart, maar u kunt ook kiezen voor kreeft uit het homarium of suggesties op een leitje.

à Halma *Sud-Est : 3 km* C *Wellin* – ✉ *6922 Halma :*

Host. Le Père Finet avec ch, r. Libin 75 (lieu-dit Neupont), ✆ 0 84 38 81 35, *Fax 0 84 38 82 12*, – P. AE MC VISA
fermé 1 sem. en mars, 1 sem. en sept., 1 sem. en janv., dim. soir et lundi midi hors saison, lundi soir, mardi et après 20 h 30 – **Repas** Lunch 24 – carte 38 à 48, ♀ – **10 ch** 59/72 – ½ P 65/72.
• Auberge concoctant une cuisine actuelle souvent composée de produits régionaux. Terrasse estivale dressée au jardin, près d'un étang. Confort simple dans les chambres.
• Herberg met een eigentijdse keuken op basis van streekproducten. In de zomer wordt het terras opgedekt in de tuin, bij de vijver. Eenvoudig comfort in de kamers.

WEMMEL *Vlaams-Brabant* 533 K 17 *et* 716 F 3 *– voir à Bruxelles, environs.*

WENDUINE *8420 West-Vlaanderen* C *De Haan 11 580 h.* 533 D 15 *et* 716 C 2.
Bruxelles 111 – Brugge 17 – Oostende 16.

Host. Tennis, Astridplein 2, ✆ 0 50 41 21 37, *hostellerie.tennis@pandora.be, Fax 0 50 42 36 26*, – TV. MC VISA. rest
Repas *(fermé mardi soir, merc. et jeudi midi)* Lunch 30 – 50/70 bc – **10 ch** 50/80 – ½ P 60/65.
• La façade blanche de cette villa tranche avec la terre battue des terrains de tennis voisins. Bonne isolation phonique dans les chambres, assez confortables. Petit jardin. Salle à manger agencée avec soin. Carte actuelle.
• De witte gevel van deze villa steekt fel af tegen het gravel van de tennisbanen ernaast. De kamers zijn vrij comfortabel en hebben een goede geluidsisolatie. Kleine tuin. De eetzaal is met zorg gedecoreerd. Eigentijdse keuken.

Georges sans rest, De Smet de Naeyerlaan 19, ✆ 0 50 41 90 17, *hotel.georges@pandora.be, Fax 0 50 41 21 99*, – TV – 30. AE MC VISA
fermé 15 nov.-2 déc. et mardi sauf vacances scolaires – **18 ch** 55/80.
• Cet hôtel de confort simple mais correct met à profit un monument du début du 20e s. Architecture Art nouveau, au même titre que certains détails décoratifs des chambres.
• Hotel in een gebouw uit het begin van de 20e eeuw ; eenvoudig maar correct comfort. Architectuur en een aantal decoratieve elementen van de kamers in art nouveau-stijl.

Odette, Kerkstraat 34, ✆ 0 50 41 36 90, *Fax 0 50 42 81 34* – AE MC VISA
fermé du 1er au 15 oct., mardi et merc. – **Repas** Lunch 25 – 36/60 bc.
• L'une des valeurs sûres du centre de Wenduine : que de chemin parcouru depuis les années 1960, lorsque cette affaire familiale n'était encore qu'une simple friterie !
• Een betrouwbaar adresje in het hart van Wenduine. Wat een lange weg heeft dit familiebedrijf niet afgelegd sinds de jaren 1960, toen het nog een eenvoudige frituur was !

Rita, Kerkstraat 6, ✆ 0 50 41 19 09, *Fax 0 50 41 19 09*, – VISA
fermé mi-nov.-mi-déc. et lundi – **Repas** 22/38.
• Dans la grande rue commerçante de la station, restaurant dont la carte se partage entre terroir et marée. On y mange simplement, mais correctement. Terrasse d'été en façade.
• In dit restaurant in de drukke winkelstraat van deze badplaats eet men eenvoudig, maar goed. De menukaart bevat zowel vis als streekgerechten. Druk terras aan de voorkant.

WÉPION *Namur* 533 O 20, 534 O 20 *et* 716 H 4 *– voir à Namur.*

WESTENDE *8434 West-Vlaanderen* [C] *Middelkerke 16 930 h.* 533 B 16 *et* 716 B 2 *– Station balnéaire.*

Bruxelles 127 – Brugge 40 – Oostende 11 – Veurne 14 – Dunkerque 40.

à Westende-Bad *Nord : 2 km* [C] *Middelkerke –* ✉ *8434 Westende :*

Roi Soleil, Charles de Broquevillelaan 17, ✆ 0 59 30 08 08, *Fax 0 59 31 50 74,* – TV P. VISA

Repas *(12 fév.-12 nov. ; fermé mardi et merc.)* 45/65 bc – **6 ch** 70/95.

◆ Villa devancée d'une terrasse d'été meublée en teck, où l'on petit-déjeune quand brille le Roi Soleil. Chambres douillettes nommées d'après les courtisanes de Louis XIV. Confortable restaurant aux tons chamarrés. Repas servi en plein air par temps clément.

◆ Als de Zonnekoning straalt, wordt er ontbeten op het terras met teakhouten meubelen aan de voorkant van deze villa. De behaaglijke kamers zijn genoemd naar de maîtresses van Lodewijk XIV. Gerieflijke eetzaal in een originele kleurstelling.

Host. Melrose, Henri Jasparlaan 127, ✆ 0 59 30 18 67, *hotel@melrose.be, Fax 0 59 31 02 35,* – TV P. AE VISA

Repas *(fermé du 15 au 30 oct. et merc. et dim. soir du 15 sept. au 15 juin)* Lunch 30 – 46/68 bc – **10 ch** 55/82 – ½ P 66.

◆ Cette grande demeure implantée à proximité de la plage met à votre disposition des chambres actuelles spacieuses et de bon confort. L'accueil est familial. Carte classique au restaurant.

◆ Dit grote pand ligt op een steenworp afstand van het strand en beschikt over ruime en moderne kamers met goed comfort. De ontvangst is vriendelijk. Het restaurant presenteert een klassiek georiënteerde menukaart.

St-Laureins , Strandlaan 12 (Ouest : 1 km, Sint-Laureinsstrand), ✆ 0 58 23 39 58, *info@st-laureins.be, Fax 0 58 23 08 99,* ≤ plage et dunes, – rest, TV. VISA

fermé 15 nov.-15 déc. – **Repas** *(fermé merc. hors saison et après 20 h 30)* (taverne-rest) Lunch 21 – 24/30 bc – **9 ch** 55/80 – ½ P 65.

◆ Plaisante échappée littorale depuis chacune des chambres - personnalisées - de ce petit immeuble niché parmi les dunes, juste au bord de la plage. Bonjour les embruns ! Taverne-restaurant avec vue côtière.

◆ Dit hotel ligt geïsoleerd in de duinen, vlak bij het strand. Alle kamers hebben een persoonlijk karakter en kijken op zee uit. Ook vanuit het café-restaurant hebben de gasten een mooi uitzicht op het ruime sop.

Splendid, Meeuwenlaan 20, ✆ 0 59 30 00 32, *Fax 0 59 31 09 17* – TV. AE VISA. ch

avril-sept. et week-end jusqu'au 15 nov. – **Repas** (résidents seult) – **18 ch** 60/80 – ½ P 60/65.

◆ À une encablure du front de mer, construction 1900 que signale une pimpante façade récemment ravalée. Sobres et pratiques, les chambres se répartissent sur quatre étages. Table jouant la carte tradition, avec spécialités de la côte belge. Prix doux.

◆ Op een paar bootlengtes van de zeeboulevard onderscheidt deze 1900 constructie zich door een elegante, onlangs opgeknapte gevel. De sobere en praktische kamers bevinden zich op vier verdiepingen. Specialiteiten van de kust in het restaurant. Zachte prijzen.

Isba, Henri Jasparlaan 148, ✆ 0 59 30 23 64, *Fax 0 59 31 06 26,* – TV. AE VISA

fermé 27 janv.-11 fév., du 4 au 14 mars, 28 nov.-27 déc. et mardi et merc. d'oct. à Pâques – **Repas** (dîner pour résidents seult) – **6 ch** 45/75 – ½ P 53/58.

◆ Imposante villa balnéaire des années 1920 postée en léger retrait d'une avenue passante. Chambres insonorisées, de tailles différentes. Le jardin invite au repos.

◆ Deze imposante villa uit de jaren 1920 staat even van een drukke weg af. De kamers met geluidsisolatie zijn verschillend van formaat. In de tuin kunt u heerlijk luieren.

Nelson, Priorijlaan 30, ✆ 0 59 30 23 07, *Fax 0 59 30 25 22* – AE VISA

fermé 23 sept.-3 oct., 1er déc.-2 janv. et mardi soir et merc. d'avril au 20 sept. sauf vacances scolaires – **Repas** Lunch 20 – carte 29 à 51, ♀.

◆ Sur la place centrale de la station, petite adresse dont l'amiral Nelson aurait peut-être bien fait l'éloge. Carte à dominante iodée, avec lunch et menus. Vins choisis.

◆ Admiraal Nelson zou vast de loftrompet hebben gestoken over dit adresje aan het hoofdplein van deze badplaats. Veel vis op de kaart. Lunchformule en menu's. Uitgelezen wijnen.

La Plage, Meeuwenlaan 4, ✆ 0 59 30 11 90, *Fax 0 59 30 11 90* – . AE

fermé 5 janv.-13 fév., 15 nov.-20 déc. et jeudi sauf vacances scolaires – **Repas** carte 22 à 40.

◆ À un jet de frisbee de la plage, restaurant drainant une clientèle essentiellement touristique. Éventail habituel des préparations du littoral belge.

◆ Dit restaurant op een frisbeeworp afstand van het strand trekt voornamelijk toeristen. Op de kaart staan de voor de Belgische kust gebruikelijke gerechten.

WESTERLO *2260 Antwerpen* 533 O 16 *et* 716 H 2 – *22 202 h.*

Env. *au Nord : 2 km à Tongerlo, Musée Léonard de Vinci★.*

Boerenkrijglaan 25 ☎ 0 14 54 54 28, westerlo@toerismevlaanderen.be, Fax 0 14 54 76 56. – *Bruxelles 57 – Antwerpen 46 – Diest 20 – Turnhout 30.*

XXX **Geerts** avec ch, Grote Markt 50, ☎ 0 14 54 40 17, *info@hotel-geerts.be, Fax 0 14 54 18 80,* – rest, – 25. AE VISA. ch
fermé 18 fév.-3 mars et 16 août-6 sept. – **Repas** *(fermé merc. et dim. soir)* Lunch 30 – 50/90 bc – **18 ch** 82/106 – ½ P 65/95.
◆ Hostellerie familiale et traditionnelle où l'on se sent en de bonnes mains. Mets classiques pour fines fourchettes. Chambres amples et douillettes. Jardin exquis à l'arrière.
◆ Traditionele hostellerie, waar u in goede handen bent. Klassieke gerechten voor fijnproevers. Ruime, behaaglijke kamers. Prachtige tuin aan de achterkant.

XX **'t Kempisch Pallet,** Bergveld 120 (Ouest : 4 km sur N 15), ☎ 0 14 54 70 97, *info@kempischpallet.be, Fax 0 14 54 70 57,* – AE VISA.
fermé dim. soir et lundi – **Repas** Lunch 35 – 50.
◆ Dans un site verdoyant, jolie villa flamande interprétant un répertoire culinaire classique actualisé. Accueil gentil, salle à manger refaite de neuf et service prévenant.
◆ Mooie Vlaamse villa in een schilderachtige omgeving met een culinair palet in modern-klassieke stijl. Vriendelijke ontvangst, gerenoveerde eetzaal en voorkomende bediening.

WESTKAPELLE *West-Vlaanderen* 533 E 15 *et* 716 C 2 – *voir à Knokke-Heist.*

WESTMALLE *Antwerpen* 533 N 15 *et* 716 H 2 – *voir à Malle.*

WESTOUTER *8954 West-Vlaanderen* *Heuvelland 8 332 h.* 533 B 18 *et* 716 B 3.

Bruxelles 136 – Brugge 66 – Ieper 14 – Lille 39.

Reverie, Rodebergstraat 26, ☎ 0 57 44 48 19, *hotel.reverie@attglobal.net, Fax 0 57 44 87 40,* – 25. VISA.
fermé début juil. – **Repas** (dîner pour résidents seult) – **8 ch** 65/95 – ½ P 60/75.
◆ Construction de style "cottage" s'entourant d'un paysage agreste. Confortables, les chambres jouissent d'une vue sur le mont Kemmel et vous invitent à la rêverie.
◆ Dit landelijk gelegen hotel is opgetrokken in de stijl van een cottage. De comfortabele kamers kijken uit op de Kemmelberg en nodigen uit tot rêverieën...

XXX ✿ **Picasso** (Van Kerckhove), Rodebergstraat 69, ☎ 0 57 44 69 08, *Fax 0 57 44 69 08,* plaine des Flandres, – AE VISA.
fermé du 13 au 21 avril, 2 sem. en juil., vacances Noël, mardi et merc. – **Repas** Lunch 35 – 88 bc, carte 59 à 79.
◆ Une valeur montante de la chaîne des Monts de Flandre. Cuisine soignée servie dans une fermette dont la salle à manger embrasse du regard la plaine flamande, jusqu'à la côte.
◆ Picasso is een rijzende ster in het Vlaamse Heuvelland. Verzorgde keuken in een boerderijtje met een weids uitzicht van de Vlaamse laagvlakte tot aan de kust.
Spéc. Foie gras de canard de la région au vin rouge. Turbot grillé au coulis d'oseille, stoemp de crevettes grises. Tarte mazarine aux abricots confits (juin-août)

WEVELGEM *8560 West-Vlaanderen* 533 E 18 *et* 716 C 3 – *31 276 h.*

Bruxelles 99 – Kortrijk 8 – Brugge 54 – Lille 23.

Cortina, Lauwestraat 59, ☎ 0 56 41 25 22, *Fax 0 56 41 45 67* – – 25 à 600. AE VISA
fermé 21 juil.-15 août – **Repas** voir rest ***Pinogri*** ci-après – **26 ch** 74/98.
◆ Établissement bien organisé pour la tenue de banquets et séminaires. On séjourne dans des chambres actuelles, d'une tenue irréprochable. Accueil et service "pro".
◆ Dit etablissement leent zich bij uitstek voor banketten en congressen. De gasten overnachten in perfect onderhouden, moderne kamers. Zeer professioneel personeel.

Bell-X sans rest, Kortrijkstraat 351 (direction Bissegem, près de l'aérodrome), ☎ 0 56 37 17 71, *info@hotel-bell-x.com, Fax 0 56 35 92 82* – AE VISA
13 ch 62/79.
◆ Près de l'aéroport et du ring de Kortrijk, demeure bourgeoise adroitement rénovée dont l'enseigne n'a, en dépit des apparences, rien de grivois. Chambres insonorisées.
◆ Dit hotel is gevestigd in een fraai gerenoveerd herenhuis, dicht bij de luchthaven en de Ring van Kortrijk. De kamers zijn goed tegen het geluid geïsoleerd.

X **Pinogri** - H. Cortina, Lauwestraat 59, ☎ 0 56 42 41 41, *bistro@pinogri.be, Fax 0 56 42 23 31,* – AE VISA
fermé 21 juil.-15 août – **Repas** Lunch 24 – carte 25 à 54.
◆ Salle à manger façon bistrot moderne, ambiance plaisante et choix de mets diversifié assorti d'un lunch : autant de raisons de ne pas bouder ce restaurant d'hôtel.
◆ Dit restaurant hoort bij een hotel en is niet te versmaden vanwege het moderne bistro-interieur, de plezierige ambiance, de gevarieerde kaart en het aantrekkelijke lunchmenu.

Biggles 1er étage, Luchthavenstraat 1 (dans l'aérodrome), 0 56 37 33 00, *Fax 0 56 36 05 36*, – *fermé mi-juil.-mi-août, vacances Noël, mardi soir et merc.* – **Repas** *Lunch 13* – 36.

◆ Au premier étage d'un bâtiment de l'aérodrome régional, salle de restaurant en demi-rotonde dont la baie vitrée offre un regard sur l'activité des pistes. Carte actuelle.

◆ Halfronde eetzaal op de eerste verdieping van een gebouw op het regionale vliegveld. De grote glaspui biedt een goed uitzicht op de startbaan. Eigentijdse menukaart.

à Gullegem *Nord : 5 km* *Wevelgem* – *8560 Gullegem :*

Gouden Kroon, Koningin Fabiolastraat 41, 0 56 40 04 76, *Fax 0 56 42 83 66*, – – 25. *fermé 26 juil.-12 août, sam. midi, dim. soir, lundi et merc. soir* – **Repas** *Lunch 52 bc* – 48/80 bc.

◆ Maison de maître 1900 située au centre de Gullegem. Le chef, qui a fait ses armes auprès de la famille royale à Laeken, propose une cuisine classique de bon aloi.

◆ Herenhuis uit 1900 in het centrum van Gullegem, met een goede klassieke keuken. De chef-kok heeft zijn proeve van bekwaamheid afgelegd bij de koninklijke familie in Laken.

WIBRIN *Luxembourg belge* 534 T 22 *et* 716 K 5 – *voir à Houffalize.*

WIERDE *Namur* 533 O 20, 534 O 20 *et* 716 H 4 – *voir à Namur.*

WIJNEGEM *Antwerpen* 533 M 15 *et* 716 G 2 – *voir à Antwerpen, environs.*

WILLEBROEK *2830 Antwerpen* 533 L 16 *et* 716 G 2 – *22 622 h.*

Bruxelles 29 – Antwerpen 22 – Mechelen 10 – Sint-Niklaas 22.

Fevaca Inn, Victor Dumonlaan 6 (Klein-Willebroek, au bord du port de plaisance), 0 3 844 20 00, *Fax 0 3 844 69 00*, – 60. ch *fermé du 20 au 30 déc.* – **Repas** 27/50 – **15 ch** 85/118.

◆ Vous passerez des nuits sans remous dans cet hôtel amarré au bord du port de plaisance. Amples chambres actuelles profitant d'une vue sur les bateaux ou le jardin. Cuisine traditionnelle au restaurant. Lorsque la météo le permet, on mange en terrasse.

◆ Dit hotel dat bij de jachthaven voor anker ligt, belooft een rustig nachtje zonder turbulentie. Grote, moderne kamers met uitzicht op de boten of de tuin. Restaurant met een traditionele keuken. Als het weer het toelaat, wordt op het terras gegeten.

Breendonck, Dendermondsesteenweg 309 (près du fort), 0 3 886 61 63, *breendonck@planetinternet.be, Fax 0 3 886 25 40*, – *fermé 2 dern. sem. juil., vend. soir et sam. midi* – **Repas** *Lunch 11* – 34/65 bc.

◆ Affaire familiale postée face au fort de Breendonck, mémorial national complété d'un petit musée. L'assiette est traditionnelle et la salle à manger, chaleureuse.

◆ Familiebedrijfje tegenover het fort van Breendonck, een nationaal gedenkteken met een klein museum. De eetzaal doet warm aan en de kookstijl is traditioneel.

WINKSELE *Vlaams-Brabant* 533 M 17 *et* 716 H 3 – *voir à Leuven.*

WOLUWE-ST-ÉTIENNE *Vlaams-Brabant – voir Sint-Stevens-Woluwe à Bruxelles, environs.*

WOLUWE-ST-LAMBERT (SINT-LAMBRECHTS-WOLUWE) *Région de Bruxelles-Capitale* 533 L 17 *et* 716 G 3 – *voir à Bruxelles.*

WOLUWE-ST-PIERRE (SINT-PIETERS-WOLUWE) *Région de Bruxelles-Capitale* 533 L 18 *et* 716 G 3 – *voir à Bruxelles.*

WOLVERTEM *Vlaams-Brabant* 533 K 17 *et* 716 F 3 – *voir à Bruxelles, environs.*

WORTEGEM-PETEGEM *9790 Oost-Vlaanderen* 533 G 17 *et* 716 D 3 – *6 009 h.*

18 9 *Kortrijkstraat 52* *0 55 33 41 61, Fax 0 55 31 98 49.*

Bruxelles 81 – Kortrijk 21 – Gent 36 – Oudenaarde 8.

Bistronoom, Waregemseweg 155 (Wortegem), 0 56 61 11 22, *bistronoom@easyresto.be, Fax 0 56 60 38 18*, – *fermé vacances Pâques, 2 sem. en sept., merc. soir, jeudi et sam. midi* – **Repas** *Lunch 25* – carte 30 à 84.

◆ Fière villa donnant sur un jardin où l'on dresse le couvert en été. Salles de restaurant étagées, carte actuelle-bourgeoise un peu bistrotière, accueil et service dynamiques.

◆ Fiere villa met tuin, waar u 's zomers heerlijk buiten kunt eten. Eetzalen op meerdere verdiepingen, actuele kaart met bistrogerechten. Accurate bediening.

YPRES *West-Vlaanderen – voir Ieper.*

YVOIR *5530 Namur* 533 *O 21,* 534 *O 21 et* 716 *H 5 – 8 061 h.*

Env. *à l'Ouest : Vallée de la Molignée★.*

18 au Nord : 10 km à Profondeville, Chemin du Beau Vallon 45 ℘ 0 81 41 14 18, Fax 0 81 41 21 42.

Bruxelles 92 – Namur 22 – Dinant 8.

X **La Tonnelle,** r. Fenderie 41, ℘ 0 82 61 13 94, *Fax 0 82 61 13 94,* – P. AE ① MC VISA

fermé sem. carnaval, 2 prem. sem. juil., dern. sem. nov., mardi et merc. – **Repas** *Lunch 21 – 36/61 bc.*

◆ Accueil familial tout sourire dans cette maisonnette postée à l'entrée du village. Recettes de saison. Par beau temps, repas au jardin, sous la tonnelle. Lunch et menus.

◆ Bij binnenkomst in het dorp wacht u in dit pandje een alleraardigste ontvangst. Seizoengebonden kaart met lunchformule en menu's. Bij mooi weer wordt in het prieeltje gegeten.

ZAVENTEM *Vlaams-Brabant* 533 *L 17 et* 716 *G 3 – voir à Bruxelles, environs.*

ZEEBRUGGE *West-Vlaanderen* C *Brugge 116 836 h.* 533 *E 14 et* 716 *C 1 – ✉ 8380 Zeebrugge (Brugge).*

Liaison maritime Zeebrugge-Hull : P and O North Sea Ferries, Leopold II Dam 13 (Kaaien 106-108) ℘ 0 50 54 34 30, Fax 0 50 54 71 12.

Bruxelles 111 ② – Brugge 15 ② – Knokke-Heist 8 ① – Oostende 25 ③

ZEDELGEM *West-Vlaanderen* 533 *D 16 et* 716 *C 2 – voir à Brugge, environs.*

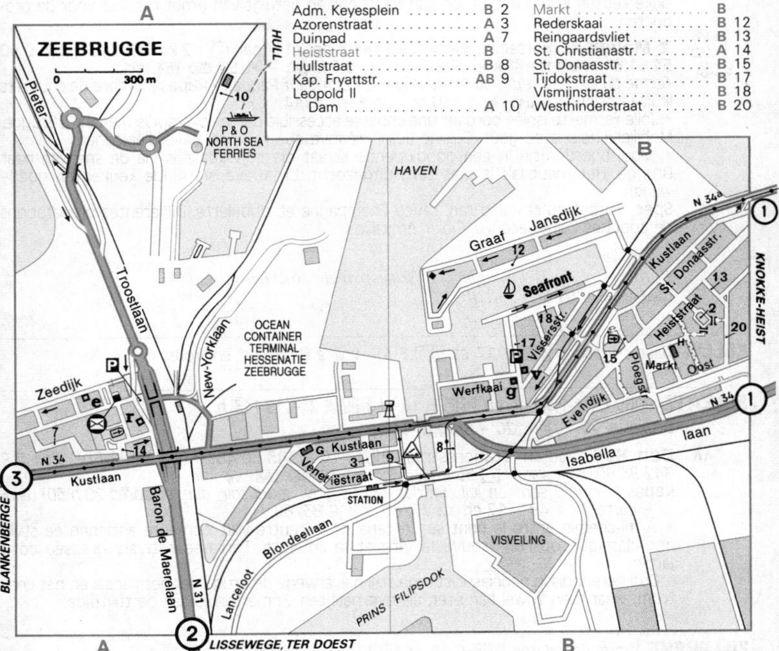

Monaco, Baron de Maerelaan 26, ✆ 0 50 54 44 37, *Fax 0 50 54 44 85*, – 25. *Repas* (*fermé vend.*) carte 27 à 36 – **15 ch** 70/85 – ½ P 87/95. A r

◆ Pratique lorsque l'on a un ferry à prendre, ce petit hôtel bénéficie aussi de la proximité de la digue. Bon confort dans les chambres, bien calibrées, claires et actuelles. Repas simple, mais généreusement iodé. Choix uniquement à la carte.

◆ Dit kleine hotel ligt vlak bij de kust en is ideaal voor wie de ferry neemt. Goed comfort in de kamers, die ruim en licht zijn. De spijskaart is eenvoudig, maar bevat veel visspecialiteiten. Uitsluitend à la carte.

Maritime sans rest, Zeedijk 6, ✆ 0 50 54 40 66, *hotelmaritime@skynet.be*, *Fax 0 50 54 66 08*, ≤ – A e

12 ch 72/90.

◆ Immeuble du front de mer dont les deux étages renferment des chambres correctement équipées. La moitié d'entre elles donne sur la plage et l'entrée du port.

◆ Dit hotel in een twee verdiepingen tellend gebouw aan de boulevard beschikt over goede kamers, waarvan de helft uitkijkt op het strand en de toegang tot de haven.

Maison Vandamme, Tijdokstraat 7 (transfert prévu), ✆ 0 50 55 13 51, *maisonvandamme@resto.be*, *Fax 0 50 55 01 79*, ≤, Produits de la mer – . B g

fermé 2 prem. sem. juil., 2 prem. sem. oct., 2 prem. sem. janv., mardi et merc. – **Repas** Lunch 40 – 70/125 bc, carte 77 à 194.

◆ Talentueuse cuisine de la mer servie dans un cadre moderne. Plusieurs menus tentateurs, dont un "branché" caviar. Cave de prestige. Vue sur les docks.

◆ Uitstekend visrestaurant met een modern interieur dat uitkijkt op de haven. Aantrekkelijke menu's, waaronder een trendy kaviaarmenu. Prestigieuze wijnkelder.

Spéc. Langoustines poêlées, crème de chou-fleur et caviar Sevruga. Turbot grillé, sauce dijonaise. Pigeonneau de Bresse rôti au thym

De Barcadère, Tijdokstraat 8, ✆ 0 50 54 49 69, *Fax 0 50 54 40 05*, , Produits de la mer – . B v

fermé 21 mars-4 avril, dim. et lundi – **Repas** Lunch 38 – 50/83 bc.

◆ Agréable restaurant habillé de boiseries patinées, en cèdre du Canada, s'il vous plaît ! Plats classiques honorant la marée, exécutés avec un grand respect des produits.

◆ Aangenaam restaurant met gepatineerde lambrisering van Canadees cederhout. De klassieke keuken is een eerbetoon aan Neptunus en getuigt van groot respect voor de producten.

't Molentje (Horseele), Baron de Maerelaan 211 (par ② : 2 km sur N 31), ✆ 0 50 54 61 64, *molentje@pi.be*, *Fax 0 50 54 79 94*, –

fermé du 6 au 30 sept., du 1er au 9 janv. et dim. sauf Pâques – **Repas** (nombre de couverts limité - prévenir) Lunch 42 – 130 bc, carte 90 à 114.

◆ Jolie fermette isolée bordant une impasse accessible par la voie rapide menant à Brugge. Mobilier choisi avec goût. Cuisine aussi créative que raffinée. Cave d'épicurien.

◆ Mooi boerderijtje in een doodlopende straat die bereikbaar is via de snelweg naar Brugge. Het meubilair is met zorg uitgezocht. Creatieve, verfijnde keuken en goede wijnen.

Spéc. Turbot au caviar d'Iran, sauce Champagne et ciboulette. Différentes préparations de coquilles Saint-Jacques. Gibier en saison

ZELLIK *Vlaams-Brabant* 533 K 17 *et* 716 F 3 – *voir à Bruxelles, environs.*

ZELZATE *9060 Oost-Vlaanderen* 533 H 15 *et* 716 E 2 – *12 113 h.*

Bruxelles 76 – Gent 20 – Brugge 44.

Den Hof avec ch, Stationsstraat 22, ✆ 0 9 345 60 48, *info@denhof.be*, *Fax 0 9 342 93 60*, – – 25 à 50. ch

Repas (*fermé 3 sem. en juil., fin déc.-début janv., jeudi soir, dim. et après 20 h 30*) Lunch 12 – carte 32 à 49 – **17 ch** 75/85 – ½ P 83/88.

◆ À mi-chemin entre le pont sur le canal et le centre-ville, demeure ancienne de style néo-classique où l'on trouve le gîte et le couvert. Terrasse estivale dressée côté jardin.

◆ Oud herenhuis in neoclassicistische stijl halverwege de brug over het kanaal en het centrum, waar men zowel kan eten als overnachten. Zomerterras aan de tuinzijde.

ZILLEBEKE *West-Vlaanderen* 533 C 18 *et* 716 B 3 – *voir à Ieper.*

ZINGEM *9750 Oost-Vlaanderen 533 G 17 et 716 D 3 – 6 579 h.*
Bruxelles 57 – Gent 23 – Kortrijk 35 – Oudenaarde 9.

à Huise *Ouest : 2,5 km C Zingem – ✉ 9750 Huise :*

Gasthof 't Peerdeke, Gentsesteenweg 45 (N 60), ☎ 0 9 384 55 11, *motel@peerdeke.be, Fax 0 9 384 26 16,* – TV P – 25 à 50. AE MO VISA.
Repas *(fermé 2 dern. sem. juil.-prem. sem. août, 24, 25 et 31 déc., 1er janv., sam. midi et dim.)* (ouvert jusqu'à 23 h) *Lunch 35* – carte 35 à 57 – **15 ch** 65/85 – ½ P 90/100.
◆ Sur l'axe Gent-Oudenaarde, petit motel installé dans une construction en briques rappelant une ferme régionale. Chambres fonctionnelles desservies par une cour intérieure. Salle des repas décorée dans la note néo-campagnarde.
◆ Klein motel aan de as Gent-Oudenaarde, in een bakstenen gebouw dat aan een boerderij uit de streek doet denken. De functionele kamers zijn toegankelijk via de binnenplaats. De eetzaal is in neorustieke stijl ingericht.

ZINNIK *Hainaut – voir Soignies.*

ZOLDER *3550 Limburg C Heusden-Zolder 30 269 h. 533 Q 16 et 716 I 2.*
18 au Nord-Est : 10 km à Houthalen, Golfstraat 1 ☎ 0 89 38 35 43, Fax 0 89 84 12 08.
Bruxelles 77 – Maastricht 46 – Hasselt 12 – Diest 22.

au Sud-Ouest *: 7 km par N 729, sur Omloop (circuit) Terlamen – ✉ 3550 Zolder :*

XXX **De Gulden Schalmei,** Sterrenwacht 153, ☎ 0 11 25 17 50, *deguldenschalmei@skynet.be, Fax 0 11 25 38 75* – P. AE MO VISA
fermé dern. sem. juin-prem. sem. juil., 2 dern. sem. sept., merc., jeudi midi, sam. midi et dim. soir – **Repas** *Lunch 33* – 64.
◆ Belle villa établie dans une impasse du quartier résidentiel verdoyant qui domine le circuit de vitesse. Gros efforts de modernisation, derrière les fourneaux comme en salle.
◆ Mooie villa in een doodlopende straat in een woonwijk bij het autocircuit. Er heeft een grootscheepse modernisatie plaatsgevonden, zowel in de eetzaal als achter het fornuis.

à Bolderberg *Sud-Ouest : 8 km sur N 729 C Heusden-Zolder – ✉ 3550 Zolder :*

Soete Wey, Kluisstraat 48, ☎ 0 11 25 20 66, *info@soete-wey.be, Fax 0 11 87 10 59,* – TV P – 25 à 60. AE MO VISA. rest
Repas *(fermé 23 juil.-4 août et dim.)* (dîner seult) carte 61 à 82, ♀ – **21 ch** 60/80 – ½ P 91/111.
◆ Ressource hôtelière nichée à l'ombre des frondaisons, dans un secteur résidentiel éminemment bucolique. Calmes chambres entièrement rajeunies et jardin reposant. Parements de briques, feu ouvert et poutres apparentes donnent un air rustique au restaurant.
◆ Dit hotel staat verscholen tussen het groen, in een rustige woonwijk die landelijk aandoet. Stille, gerenoveerde kamers en een rustgevende tuin. De bakstenen parementen, open haard en hanenbalken geven het restaurant iets rustieks.

XX **'t Wit Huys,** St-Jobstraat 83, ☎ 0 11 25 33 66, *bosnv@vt4.net, Fax 0 11 25 33 92,* – P. MO VISA
fermé du 16 au 30 août, 26 déc.-6 janv., sam. midi, dim. soir et lundi – **Repas** *Lunch 30* – 48.
◆ Auberge-relais centenaire venant tout juste de retrouver l'éclat du neuf. Décoration intérieure contemporaine d'esprit "zen" et restaurant d'été pourvu de meubles en teck.
◆ Deze oude herberg, waar vroeger de paarden werden ververst, is pas helemaal opgeknapt. Rustgevend, eigentijds interieur en terras met teakhouten meubelen om buiten te eten.

à Heusden *Nord-Ouest : 6 km C Heusden-Zolder – ✉ 3550 Heusden :*
Terlaemenlaan 1 ☎ 0 11 53 02 30, heusden-zolder@toerismevlaanderen.be, Fax 0 11 53 02 31

XX **Convivium,** Guido Gezellelaan 140, ☎ 0 11 42 55 58, *convivium@skynet.be, Fax 0 11 45 55 17,* , Avec cuisine italienne – P. MO VISA.
fermé 2 dern. sem. juil., lundi et sam. midi – **Repas** *Lunch 25* – carte 46 à 59.
◆ Confortable restaurant établi dans une villa moderne flanquée d'une terrasse d'été. Salle à manger agencée à la mode d'aujourd'hui. Cuisine franco-italienne et cave de même.
◆ Comfortabel restaurant in een moderne villa met terras. De eetzaal is volgens de huidige mode ingericht. Frans-Italiaanse keuken en wijnkelder.

XX **De Wijnrank,** Kooidries 10, ☎ 0 11 42 55 57, *restaurant.de.wijnrank@pandora.be, Fax 0 11 43 29 73,* – AE MO VISA
fermé 3 sem. en sept., mardi et sam. midi – **Repas** 33/61 bc.
◆ Cette villa à toit de chaume recèle une vieille charrette de glacier convertie en bar pour isoler la partie bistrot du restaurant. Plats bourgeois. Livre de cave calligraphié.
◆ Deze villa met rieten dak heeft nog een oude ijscowagen, die nu als bar dienstdoet en het bistrogedeelte van het restaurant afscheidt. Lekkere burgerkeuken met mooie wijnen.

ZOMERGEM *9930 Oost-Vlaanderen* 533 G 16 *et* 716 D 2 *– 8 170 h.*
Bruxelles 77 – Gent 21 – Brugge 38 – Roeselare 53.

à Ronsele *Nord-Est : 3,5 km* C *Zomergem – ✉ 9932 Ronsele :*

XX **Landgoed Den Oker,** Stoktevijver 36, ✆ 0 9 372 40 76, – P – 25. MC VISA
fermé du 1er au 20 mars, du 1er au 20 sept., dim. soir et lundi – **Repas** *Lunch 35* – 59.
◆ Ancienne ferme proche du canal. Salle à manger foisonnante d'antiquités. Produits choisis, accommodés en préparations classiques, généreuses et maîtrisées. Jardin charmant.
◆ Oude boerderij bij het kanaal met veel antiek in de eetzaal. Het eten is klassiek, smakelijk, overvloedig en met eersteklas ingrediënten. Charmante tuin.

ZOTTEGEM *9620 Oost-Vlaanderen* 533 H 17 *et* 716 E 3 *– 24 507 h.*
Bruxelles 46 – Gent 29 – Aalst 24 – Oudenaarde 18.

XX **New Century 2000,** Buke 4, ✆ 0 9 360 99 50, *Fax 0 9 360 93 03,* Cuisine chinoise, ouvert jusqu'à 23 h – P. MC VISA.
fermé lundi – **Repas** *Lunch 10* – carte 22 à 51.
◆ Important choix de recettes représentant toutes les régions de Chine, menus nombreux et suggestions : de quoi mettre l'eau à la bouche aux amateurs du genre !
◆ Uitgebreide kaart met gerechten die alle Chinese regio's bestrijken, talrijke menu's en dagsuggesties. Liefhebbers van de Aziatische keuken komen hier beslist aan hun trekken !

à Elene *Nord : 2 km* C *Zottegem – ✉ 9620 Elene :*

XX **Bistro Alain,** Leopold III straat 1 (angle Elenestraat), ✆ 0 9 360 12 94, *Fax 0 9 361 08 03,* – P. AE MC VISA
fermé dern. sem. janv.-prem. sem. fév., 2e quinz. août-début sept., merc. et jeudi – **Repas** *Lunch 30* – 45/79 bc.
◆ Dans un ancien moulin à eau, bistrot "design" jouant sur le contraste du rouge et du blanc. Arrière-salle plus "gastro" et vivifiante terrasse d'été dotée de meubles en teck.
◆ Deze designbistro in een oude watermolen speelt met het contrast tussen rood en wit. In de achterste zaal kan gastronomisch worden getafeld. Terras met teakhouten meubelen.

HET ZOUTE *West-Vlaanderen* C *Knokke-Heist* 533 E 14 *et* 716 C 1 *– voir à Knokke-Heist.*

ZUIENKERKE *West-Vlaanderen* 533 D 15 *et* 716 C 2 *– voir à Blankenberge.*

ZUTENDAAL *3690 Limburg* 533 S 17 *et* 716 J 3 *– 6 809 h.*
Oosterzonneplein 1, ✆ 0 89 62 94 51, toerisme@zutendaal.be, Fax 0 89 62 94 30.
Bruxelles 104 – Maastricht 16 – Hasselt 20 – Liège 38.

XX **De Klok** avec ch, Daalstraat 9, ✆ 0 89 61 11 31, *Fax 0 89 61 24 70,* – TV. AE MC VISA.
Repas *(fermé merc. et sam. midi) Lunch 35* – carte 45 à 83 – **11 ch** 60/100 – ½ P 70.
◆ Auberge de bonne renommée dans un petit coin du Limbourg. Lumineuse et confortable salle de restaurant, carte classique, vinothèque à vue et chambres sans reproche.
◆ Deze herberg geniet een goede reputatie in dit stukje Limburg. Lichte en comfortabele eetzaal met een klassieke kaart en uitstekende wijnen. Onberispelijke kamers.

ZWEVEGEM *8550 West-Vlaanderen* 533 F 18 *et* 716 D 3 *– 23 404 h.*
Bruxelles 91 – Kortrijk 6 – Brugge 48 – Gent 46 – Lille 31.

Sachsen, Avelgemstraat 23, ✆ 0 56 75 94 75, *hotel.sachsen@proximedia.be, Fax 0 56 75 50 66,* – TV P – 60. AE MC VISA
Repas (taverne-rest) *Lunch 9* – carte env. 31 – **21 ch** 62/82.
◆ Au milieu du village, entre l'église et le moulin, récente construction en briques dont les chambres, amples et bien équipées, se répartissent sur trois étages. Chaleureuse ambiance tyrolienne dans la taverne-restaurant.
◆ Dit nieuwe bakstenen gebouw staat midden in het dorp, tussen de kerk en de molen. De ruime, goed geëquipeerde kamers liggen over drie verdiepingen verspreid. Gezellige Tiroler sfeer in het café-restaurant.

XX **Molenberg,** Kwadepoelstraat 51, ✆ 0 56 75 93 97, *Fax 0 56 75 93 97,* – P. AE MC VISA JCB
fermé mi-juil.-mi-août, merc, sam. midi et dim. soir – **Repas** *Lunch 40* – 58/85 bc.
◆ Maison de meunier dans un cadre champêtre. Briques, vieux carrelage et poutres font l'attrait de la salle à manger. À table, produits nobles et classicisme revisité.
◆ Deze oude molenaarswoning is landelijk gelegen. Bakstenen, plavuizen en balken vormen de aantrekkingskracht van de eetzaal. Edele producten op tafel in modern-klassieke stijl.

à Sint-Denijs *Sud : 6 km* C *Zwevegem 23 451 h.* – ✉ *8554 Sint-Denijs :*

X **De Muishond,** Zandbeekstraat 15 (par N 50, puis prendre Beerbosstraat), ☎ 0 56 45 51 11, 余, Grillades – P. AE.
fermé 25 juil.-16 août, lundi soir, mardi et sam. midi – **Repas** carte 31 à 52.
◆ Affaire tenue en famille depuis trente ans, à dénicher derrière la façade d'une fermette aux murs blanchis. Grillades sur feu de bois en salle. Jolie terrasse d'été.
◆ Dit restaurant in een witgekalkt boerderijtje wordt al 30 jaar door dezelfde familie gerund. Het vlees wordt in de eetzaal op houtskool geroosterd. Mooi terras in de zomer.

ZWIJNAARDE *Oost-Vlaanderen* 533 H 17 *et* 716 E 2 – *voir à Gent, périphérie.*

Grand-Duché de Luxembourg

Lëtzebuerg

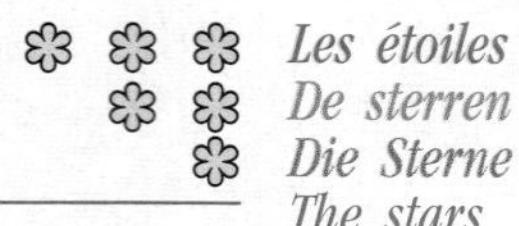

Les étoiles
De sterren
Die Sterne
The stars

"Bib Gourmand"

Repas 33 *Repas soignés à prix modérés*
Verzorgde maaltijden voor een schappelijke prijs
Sorgfältig zubereitete preiswerte Mahlzeiten
Good food at moderate prices

...

L'agrément
Aangenaam verblijf
Annehmlichkeit
Peaceful atmosphere and setting

Carte de voisinage : voir à la ville choisie
Kaart van de omgeving in de buurt van grote steden
Stadt mit Umgebungskarte
Town with a local map

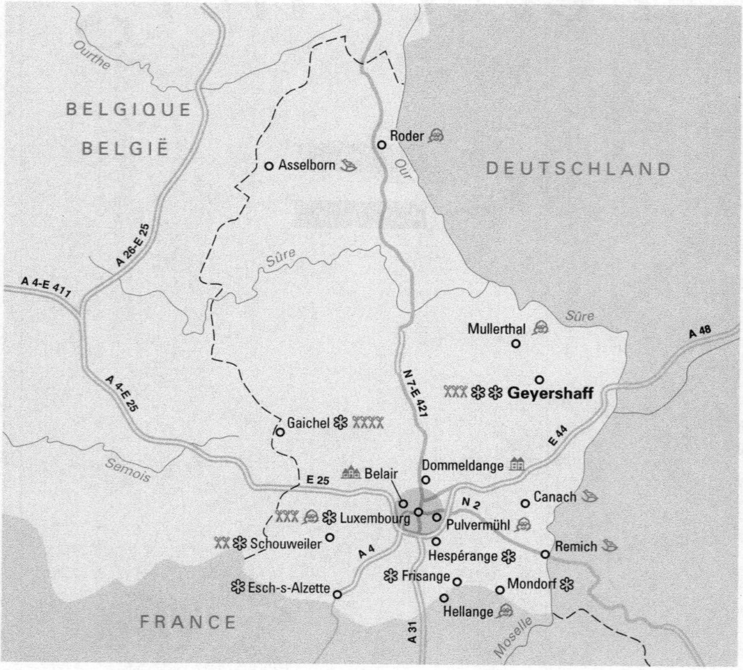

AHN (OHN) C *Wormeldange 2 306 h.* 717 X 25 *et* 716 M 7.
Luxembourg 36 – Ettelbrück 51 – Remich 15 – Trier 27.

XX **Mathes,** rte du Vin 37, ✉ 5401, ☎ 76 01 06, *mathesah@cmdnet.lu, Fax 76 06 45,* ≤, 🏞, 🚢 – P. MC VISA
fermé 23 fév.-5 mars, du 1er au 12 nov., 27 déc.-14 janv., lundi et mardi – **Repas** Lunch 31 – 49/65, 🍷.
◆ Ce restaurant qui existe depuis près de 30 ans domine la Moselle. Mise en place soignée. Terrasse estivale abritée et jardin avec pièce d'eau. Service aimable.
◆ Dit restaurant bestaat al bijna 30 jaar en kijkt uit over de Moezel. Verzorgde inrichting. Schaduwrijk zomerterras en tuin met waterpartij. Vriendelijke bediening.

ALZINGEN (ALZÉNG) 717 V 25 – *voir à Luxembourg, environs.*

ASSELBORN (AASSELBUR) C *Wincrange 3 403 h.* 717 U 22 *et* 716 K 5.
Luxembourg 75 – Clervaux 13 – Ettelbrück 47 – Bastogne 26.

🏠 **Domaine du Moulin** 🔇, Maison 158, ✉ 9940, ☎ 99 86 16, *moulinas@pt.lu, Fax 99 86 17,* 🏞, 🌳 – TV P – 🏛 25. AE MC VISA
fermé du 5 au 31 janv. – **Repas** 44/55, 🍷 – **15 ch** ☕ 55/88 – ½ P 79/84.
◆ Au creux d'une vallée verdoyante, hôtel tranquille aménagé dans un ancien moulin dont un musée retrace l'histoire. Chambres assez petites, un rien surannées. Salle à manger rustique.
◆ In de kom van een groen dal heeft dit rustige hotel een oude molen betrokken, waarvan de geschiedenis in een museum in beeld wordt gebracht. Tamelijk kleine en ietwat sleetse kamers. Rustieke eetzaal.

BASCHARAGE (NIDDERKÄERJHÉNG) 717 U 25 *et* 716 K 7 – *6 713 h.*
Luxembourg 19 – Esch-sur-Alzette 14 – Arlon 21 – Longwy 17.

🏠 **Beierhaascht,** av. de Luxembourg 240, ✉ 4940, ☎ 26 50 85 50, *info@beierhaascht.lu, Fax 26 50 85 99,* 🏞, 🚲 – 🛗 TV ♿ 🚗 P. AE ① MC VISA
fermé 24 déc. soir et 25 déc. midi – **Repas** (ouvert jusqu'à 23 h) Lunch 10 – carte 23 à 38 – **28 ch** ☕ 65/75 – ½ P 75/84.
◆ Cet hôtel contemporain est curieusement agrégé à une brasserie artisanale et à une boucherie-charcuterie spécialisée dans les salaisons ! Bonnes chambres parquetées. Deux grandes cuves de brassage trônent dans la spacieuse taverne-restaurant.
◆ Dit eigentijdse hotel bevindt zich onder één dak met een ambachtelijke brouwerij en een slagerij gespecialiseerd in ham en worstsoorten. Goede kamers met parketvloer. In het grote café-restaurant accentueren twee brouwkuipen de ambachtelijke entourage.

XX **Le Pigeonnier,** av. de Luxembourg 211, ✉ 4940, ☎ 50 25 65, *Fax 50 53 30,* 🏞 – AE ① MC VISA. 🚭
fermé mi-août-mi-sept., sam. midi, dim. soir, lundi et mardi – **Repas** Lunch 323 – carte 46 à 54.
◆ Une ancienne grange restaurée - murs de pierre, épaisses poutres, etc. - sert de cadre à ce restaurant bien placé à l'entrée du bourg. Les banquets se tiennent à l'étage.
◆ Een oude, gerestaureerde schuur - stenen muren, dikke balken - vormt het decor van dit restaurant aan de rand van het dorp. Boven zijn faciliteiten voor banketten.

XX **Digne des Gourmets,** r. Continentale 1, ✉ 4917, ☎ 50 72 86, *Fax 50 72 50,* 🏞 – AE ① MC VISA
fermé 3 sem. en sept., 1 sem. en janv., lundi soir et mardi – **Repas** Lunch 12 – 39, 🍷.
◆ Auberge traditionnelle transformée en table au goût du jour sous l'impulsion d'un couple avisé. Recettes quelquefois surprenantes. Desserts tentateurs. L'été, repas au jardin.
◆ Deze oude herberg is door het echtpaar Digne verbouwd tot een modern restaurant. Verrassende gerechten en verleidelijke desserts. 's Zomers wordt in de tuin geserveerd.

BEAUFORT (BEFORT) 717 W 23 *et* 716 L 6 – *1 615 h.*
Voir *Ruines du château★ – au Sud-Est : 4 km et 30 mn AR à pied, Gorges du Hallerbach★.*
🅱 *Grand-Rue 87,* ✉ *6310,* ☎ *83 60 99, beaufort@pt.lu, Fax 86 91 08.*
Luxembourg 38 – Diekirch 15 – Echternach 15 – Ettelbrück 25.

🏨 **Meyer** 🔇, Grand-Rue 120, ✉ 6310, ☎ 83 62 62, *homeyer@pt.lu, Fax 86 90 85,* 🏞, 🏋, 🧖, 🏊, 🌳, 🚲 – 🛗, 🍽 rest, TV 🚗 P – 🏛 30. AE ① MC VISA. 🚭 rest
2 avril-2 janv. – **Repas** *(fermé après 20 h 30)* carte 38 à 50 – **33 ch** ☕ 63/123 – ½ P 70/87.
◆ Imposante hostellerie postée à l'entrée d'un village connu pour sa liqueur de cassis : le Cassero. Bonnes chambres garnies de meubles en bois cérusé. Ambiance familiale. Cuisine classique servie, l'été venu, sur une terrasse côté jardin.
◆ Imposant hotel aan de rand van een dorp dat bekend is om zijn zwartebessenlikeur : de Cassero. Goede kamers met meubilair van geceruseerd hout. Gezellige ambiance en klassieke keuken. In de zomer wordt op een terras aan de tuinkant geserveerd.

Aub. Rustique, r. Château 55, 6313, 83 60 86, *info@aubergerustique.lu, Fax 86 92 22,* – rest, .
15 fév.-12 nov. – **Repas** *(fermé après 20 h 30) Lunch 15* – 32 – **8 ch** 45/65 – ½ P 42.
• Auberge miniature construite près des ruines romantiques du château de Beaufort, auquel Victor Hugo en personne a dédié quelques lignes. Chambres assez confortables. Restaurant misant sur un éventail de préparations régionales sans complications.
• Herberg in "zakformaat", gebouwd bij de romantische ruïne van het kasteel van Beaufort, waaraan de Franse schrijver Victor Hugo enkele regels heeft gewijd. Vrij gerieflijke kamers. Restaurant met op de menukaart eerlijke streekgerechten.

BELAIR – *voir à Luxembourg, périphérie.*

BERDORF (BÄERDREF) 717 X 24 *et* 716 M 6 – *1 345 h.*

Voir *au Nord-Ouest : Île du Diable★★ – au Nord : Plateau des Sept Gorges★ (Sieweschluff), Kasselt★ – au Sud : 2 km, Werschrumschluff★.*
Exc. *Promenade à pied★★ : Perekop.*
r. Laach 7, 6550, 79 06 43, berdorf@gmx.net, Fax 79 91 82.
Luxembourg 38 – Diekirch 24 – Echternach 6 – Ettelbrück 31.

Bisdorff , r. Heisbich 39, 6551, 79 02 08, *hotelbisdorff@pt.lu, Fax 79 06 29,* – 25. rest
Pâques-14 nov. – **Repas** *(fermé lundi, mardi et après 20 h 30)* 30/40 – **25 ch** 58/115 – ½ P 74/94.
• Du repos et des loisirs : voici ce à quoi vous pouvez vous attendre à cette enseigne familiale nichée dans la verdure. Chambres bien équipées et insonorisées. Salle des repas classiquement aménagée, avec vue champêtre.
• Rust en ontspanning is wat u kunt verwachten op dit adresje midden in het groen. Kamers met goed comfort en voorzien van geluidsisolatie. Klassiek ingerichte eetzaal die uitzicht biedt op een landelijke omgeving.

Kinnen, rte d'Echternach 2, 6550, 79 01 83, *hotelkinneng@pt.lu, Fax 790 18 35 00,* – .
2 avril-12 nov. – **Repas** *(fermé après 20 h 30) Lunch 20* – 25/33 – **25 ch** 50/85 – ½ P 53/58.
• Cette hostellerie du centre de Berdorf fêtera prochainement son cent cinquantième anniversaire. Terrasse abritée de la pluie. Un tiers des chambres ont été rénovées. À table, plats classico-traditionnels parsemés de touches luxembourgeoises.
• Dit hotel in het centrum van Berdorf viert binnenkort zijn honderdvijftigste verjaardag. Overdekt terras. Een derde van de kamers is gerenoveerd. In het restaurant worden klassiek-traditionele gerechten met een Luxemburgs accent geserveerd.

BOLLENDORF-PONT (BOLLENDORFER BRÉCK) C *Berdorf 1 345 h* 717 X 23 *et* 716 M 6.
Luxembourg 40 – Diekirch 21 – Echternach 7 – Ettelbrück 27.

André, rte de Diekirch 23, 6555, 72 03 93, *info@hotel-andre.com, Fax 72 87 70,* – .
fermé 20 déc.-4 fév. – **Repas** (dîner seult jusqu'à 20 h sauf dim. et du 15 juil. au 31 août) 35 – **21 ch** 60/90 – ½ P 55/63.
• Une route pittoresque conduit à cet établissement alangui au creux d'une verte vallée, en plein cœur de la Petite Suisse luxembourgeoise. Chambres spacieuses. Restaurant proposant des mets inspirés par la région. En été, le couvert est dressé en terrasse.
• Een schilderachtige weg voert naar dit etablissement, dat in een groen dal ligt in het hart van het Luxemburgse Klein Zwitserland. Ruime kamers. Restaurant met op de streek georiënteerde menukaart. In de zomer wordt er op het terras geserveerd.

BOULAIDE (BAUSCHELT) 717 T 23 *et* 716 K 6 – *756 h.*
Luxembourg 65 – Ettelbrück 35 – Arlon 30 – Bastogne 27.

Hames, r. Curé 2, 9640, 99 30 07, *laboulle@pt.lu, Fax 99 36 49,* – . rest
fermé 21 juin-2 juil., 30 août-17 sept., janv., mardi soir et merc. – **Repas** *Lunch 12* – carte 27 à 44 – **10 ch** 39/67 – ½ P 42/47.
• Cette petite affaire est installée dans un village qu'un bref trajet en voiture sépare de la frontière belge. Chambres un rien désuètes, aménagées à l'identique. Cuisine familiale servie dans un intérieur bourgeois.
• Dit kleine hotel is gevestigd in een dorp vanwaar het maar een stukje rijden is naar de Belgische grens. Enigszins sleetse kamers die identiek zijn ingericht. In een bourgeois decor wordt een familiekeuken bereidt.

BOUR (BUR) C *Tuntange 1 034 h.* 717 V 24 *et* 716 L 6.
Env. *au Nord-Est : 4 km, Hunnebour : cadre*★.
Luxembourg 16 – Ettelbrück 27 – Mersch 12 – Arlon 18.

Gwendy, rte de Luxembourg 3, ✉ 7412, ☎ 308 88 81, *hotelgwendy@online.lu, Fax 30 79 99,* – TV P. AE ① MC VISA
Repas *(fermé jeudi soir et dim. soir)* Lunch 9 – carte 22 à 40 – **12 ch** *(fermé dim. soir)* ☕ 58/70 – ½ P 70/80.
◆ Hôtel récent renfermant des chambres assez grandes et bien insonorisées, ainsi que deux appartements équipés d'une kitchenette pour des séjours prolongés. Salle de restaurant contemporaine au décor chaleureux et soigné.
◆ Dit vrij nieuwe hotel heeft tamelijk grote kamers met goede geluidsisolatie en twee appartementen met kitchenette voor een langer verblijf. Eigentijdse restaurantzaal met een verzorgde inrichting en een gezellige ambiance.

XXX **Janin,** r. Arlon 2, ✉ 7412, ☎ 30 03 78, *Fax 30 79 02,* – P. MC VISA
fermé fin août-début sept., lundi et mardi – **Repas** carte 51 à 78.
◆ La génération montante a repris les commandes de cette maison de bouche. Confortable salle à manger au "look" agréablement suranné. Plats classiques appétissants.
◆ De jongere generatie heeft in dit restaurant het roer overgenomen. Comfortabele eetzaal met een gezellig ouderwetse look. Smakelijke klassieke gerechten.

BOURGLINSTER (BUERGLËNSTER) C *Junglinster 5 813 h.* 717 W 24 *et* 716 L 6.
Luxembourg 20 – Echternach 25 – Ettelbruck 29.

XX **La Distillerie,** r. Château 8, ✉ 6162, ☎ 787 87 81, *mail@bourglinster.lu, Fax 78 78 78 52,* ≤ – P – 25 à 100. AE ① MC VISA.
fermé 9 fév.-3 mars, dim. soir, lundi et mardi – **Repas** Lunch 27 – 57/70.
◆ Envie de s'offrir un bon moment de table dans un château fort dominant la ville ? La Distillerie est alors l'adresse indiquée ! Vue plongeante sur les toits de Bourglinster.
◆ Zin om lekker uit eten te gaan in een slot dat boven de stad uittorent ? Dan is de Distillerie het aangewezen adres ! Mooi uitzicht op de daken van Bourglinster.

BOURSCHEID (BUURSCHENT) 717 V 23 *et* 716 L 6 – *1 230 h.*
Voir *Route du château* ≤★★ *– Ruines*★ *du château*★, ≤★.
Luxembourg 47 – Diekirch 14 – Ettelbrück 18 – Wiltz 22.

St-Fiacre, Groussgaass 4, ✉ 9140, ☎ 99 00 23, *stfiacre@pt.lu, Fax 99 06 66,* ≤, – TV P. AE ① MC VISA.
15 mars-déc. – **Repas** *(fermé mardi soir, merc. et après 20 h 30)* Lunch 12 – 35 – **19 ch** ☕ 63/87 – ½ P 58/64.
◆ Grosse maison accueillante dont les chambres, assez amples et pourvues d'un mobilier de série, offrent une échappée sur les collines alentour. Tout en mangeant, profitez du coup d'œil sur le paysage agreste.
◆ Een gastvrij hotel in een robuust pand. De vrij ruime kamers zijn met standaardmeubilair ingericht en kijken uit op de omringende heuvels. Ook aan tafel kunt u genieten van deze landelijke omgeving.

à Bourscheid-Moulin *(Buurschenter-millen) Est : 4 km :*

du Moulin , Maison 1, ✉ 9164, ☎ 99 00 15, *dumoulin@pt.lu, Fax 99 07 40,* ≤, , , – TV P. ① MC VISA
14 fév.-24 nov. – **Repas** *(fermé lundi, mardi et après 20 h 30)* Lunch 22 – 25/30 – **14 ch** ☕ 70/100 – ½ P 69/85.
◆ Établissement tranquille situé dans la bucolique vallée de la Sûre. Chambres spacieuses. Ambiance vacances confortée par la nouvelle piscine à vagues couverte. De la salle à manger, vue plaisante sur la rivière.
◆ Dit rustige etablissement ligt in het idyllische landschap van het Sûre-dal. Ruime kamers. Het nieuwe, overdekte golfslagbad zorgt voor nog meer vakantiepret. De eetzaal biedt een fraai uitzicht op de rivier.

à Bourscheid-Plage *Est : 5 km :*

Theis , ✉ 9164, ☎ 99 00 20, *info@hotel-theis.com, Fax 99 07 34,* ≤, , , , – , rest, TV P – 30. ① MC VISA.
13 mars-15 nov. – **Repas** *(fermé merc. et jeudi)* 28/35 – **14 ch** ☕ 58/97 – ½ P 60/68.
◆ Tenté par une mise au vert ? Cet hôtel familial installé au bord de la Sûre et cerné par la forêt fera l'affaire. Bon confort dans les chambres. Au restaurant, cuisine traditionnelle, cave franco-luxembourgeoise et terrasse d'été.
◆ Voor natuurliefhebbers is dit familiehotel midden in het bos, aan de oever van de Sûre, de uitgelezen verblijfplaats. Goed comfort in de kamers. Restaurant met traditionele keuken en Frans-Luxemburgse wijnkaart. Zomerterras.

BRIDEL (BRIDDEL) 717 V 25 – *voir à Luxembourg, environs.*

CANACH (KANECH) Ⓒ *Lenningen 1 203 h.* 717 W 25 *et* 716 L 7.
Scheierhaff, ✉ 5412, ☎ 35 61 35, Fax 35 74 50.
Luxembourg 16 – Mondorf-les-Bains 19 – Saarbrücken 88.

Mercure, Scheierhaff (Sud : 2,5km), ✉ 5412, ☎ 26 35 41, *H2898@accor-hotels.com, Fax 26 35 44 44*, – 40 à 220. AE VISA. rest
Repas carte 26 à 50, – 14 – **72 ch** 129/149, – 2 suites – ½ P 105/150.
• Hôtel de chaîne moderne niché dans un vallon champêtre, au milieu d'un terrain de golf. Pimpantes chambres bien calibrées, garnies de meubles en bois clair. Ouverte sur le "green", salle de restaurant entretenant une ambiance "club house".
• Dit moderne hotel ligt midden op een golfcourse die in een landelijk dal is aangelegd. De ruime, elegante kamers zijn met licht houten meubilair ingericht. Gezellige clubhuis-ambiance in het restaurant, dat uitkijkt op de green.

CAPELLEN (KAPELLEN) Ⓒ *Mamer 6 767 h.* 717 U 25 *et* 716 K 7.
Luxembourg 15 – Ettelbrück 37 – Mondorf-les-Bains 37 – Arlon 18 – Longwy 30.

Drive-In sans rest, rte d'Arlon 1, ✉ 8310, ☎ 30 91 53, *Fax 30 73 53* – AE VISA
fermé 20 déc.-7 janv. – 7 – **22 ch** 55/90.
• L'enseigne le laisse deviner : nous avons affaire à un motel. Chambres de plain-pied ou situées à l'étage, assez spacieuses, accessibles par l'extérieur. Parking à vue.
• De naam zegt het al : het gaat hier om een motel. De vrij ruime kamers op de begane grond en de verdieping zijn van buitenaf toegankelijk. Parkeerterrein in het zicht.

CLAUSEN (KLAUSEN) – *voir à Luxembourg, périphérie.*

CLERVAUX (KLIERF) 717 V 22 *et* 716 L 5 – *1 h.*
Voir *Site★★ – Château★ : exposition de maquettes★ – au Sud : route de Luxembourg ≤★★.*
au Nord-Ouest : 3 km à Eselborn, Mecherwee, ✉ 9748, ☎ 92 93 95, Fax 92 94 51.
(avril-oct.) Château, ✉ 9712, ☎ 92 00 72, Fax 92 93 12.
Luxembourg 62 – Diekirch 30 – Ettelbrück 34 – Bastogne 28.

International, Grand-rue 10, ✉ 9710, ☎ 92 93 91, *mail@interclervaux.lu, Fax 92 04 92*, – rest, – 25 à 80. AE VISA. rest
fermé 24 et 25 déc. – **Repas** Lunch 18 – carte 32 à 47 – **50 ch** 95/180, – 2 suites – ½ P 67/126.
• Bon point de chute au centre d'une localité touristique dont l'agrément tient surtout au site qu'elle occupe et à la présence d'un château féodal. Chambres confortables. Salle à manger de mise actuelle. Par beau temps, on mange en terrasse.
• Een goede pleisterplaats in het centrum van een toeristisch stadje, dat een middeleeuws slot heeft en in een prachtige omgeving ligt. Comfortabele kamers en eigentijds ingerichte eetzaal. Bij mooi weer wordt op het terras geserveerd.

Koener, Grand-rue 14, ✉ 9710, ☎ 92 10 02, *mail@koenerclervaux.lu, Fax 92 08 26*, – AE VISA
fermé 19 janv.-11 fév. – **Repas** *(fermé après 20 h 30)* Lunch 10 – 22/32 – **38 ch** 83/140 – ½ P 56/75.
• Au cœur de Clervaux, sur une place piétonne, établissement familial renfermant des chambres standard de taille satisfaisante, distribuées sur trois étages. À table, préparations classiques. Additions sans rondeurs.
• Aan een pleintje in het autovrije centrum van Clervaux herbergt dit familiehotel standaardkamers die redelijk van afmeting zijn en verspreid liggen over drie verdiepingen. In het restaurant worden klassieke gerechten geserveerd. Schappelijke prijzen.

du Commerce, r. Marnach 2, ✉ 9709, ☎ 92 10 32, *hotelcom@pt.lu, Fax 92 91 08*, – – 60. AE VISA JCB. rest
18 mars-nov. – **Repas** *(fermé mardi midi, merc. midi et après 20 h)* Lunch 10 – 22/25 – **54 ch** 57/102 – ½ P 56/84.
• Près du château, hôtel disposant de chambres souvent menues, mais convenables. Jolie piscine intérieure, espace de remise en forme et terrasse d'été perchée sur le toit.
• Hotel vlak bij het kasteel, met enigszins krappe maar vrij gerieflijke kamers. Mooi binnenzwembad, fitnessruimte en in de zomer terras op het dak.

Le Claravallis, r. Gare 3, ✉ 9707, ☎ 92 10 34, *info@claravallis.lu, Fax 92 90 89*, – AE VISA
mi-mars-mi-déc. – **Repas** *(fermé jeudi hors saison)* 15/31 – **28 ch** 60/90 – ½ P 62/77.
• Immeuble un peu excentré construit au cours des années 1970 en lisière des bois, dans la rue rejoignant la gare. Chambres fonctionnelles souvent munies d'un balcon. Salle des repas classiquement aménagée.
• Dit hotel uit de jaren zeventig van de vorige eeuw ligt wat buiten het centrum aan de bosrand, in de straat die naar het station voert. Functionele kamers, de meeste met balkon. Klassiek ingerichte eetzaal.

du Parc , r. Parc 2, ✉ 9708, ☎ 92 06 50, *hduparc@pt.lu, Fax 92 10 68,* ←, – TV P. MC VISA
fermé janv.-fév. – **Repas** *(fermé lundi et mardi)* carte 27 à 38 – **7 ch** ☕ 47/75 – ½ P 62.
◆ Demeure bourgeoise centenaire entourée d'un parc reposant. Sobrement personnalisées, les petites chambres sont agencées à l'ancienne, au même titre que les communs.
◆ Een 100 jaar oud herenhuis in een rustig park. De kleine kamers hebben elk een persoonlijk tintje en ademen de sfeer van grootmoeders tijd, net als de overige ruimten.

du Vieux Château 1er étage, Montée du Château 4, ✉ 9712, ☎ 92 00 12, *pshancke@pt.lu, Fax 92 05 52,* , Taverne-rest – AE ① MC VISA
15 fév.-20 nov. ; fermé mardi et merc. midi – **Repas** 25/33, ♀.
◆ Taverne-restaurant miniature retranchée dans la tour de garde du château fort. Ambiance sagement rustique. Terrasse estivale sur cour. Affluence touristique en saison.
◆ Klein café-restaurant dat zich heeft verschanst in de wachttoren van het slot. Rustieke ambiance. Zomerterras op de binnenplaats. Veel toeristen in het seizoen.

à Reuler *(Reiler) Est : 1 km par N 18* C *Clervaux :*

St-Hubert, ✉ 9768, ☎ 92 04 32, *Fax 92 93 04,* ←, , , – TV P. AE ① MC VISA.
mi-mars-mi-nov. ; fermé mardi – **Repas** *(fermé après 20 h 30)* carte 22 à 35 – **19 ch** ☕ 60/80 – ½ P 56.
◆ Une façade fleurie aux beaux jours signale ce gros chalet situé aux avant-postes de Clervaux. Certaines chambres, dotées d'un balcon, ont vue sur la campagne. Table dédiée à saint Hubert, patron des chasseurs. Le gibier foisonne en saison de vénerie.
◆ Dit grote chalet aan de rand van Clervaux is 's zomers herkenbaar aan de bloemrijke façade. Enkele kamers met balkon kijken uit op het platteland. De keuken staat in het teken van de H. Hubertus, schutspatroon van de jagers. In het jachtseizoen dus volop wild.

à Roder *(Roeder) Est : 4,5 km* C *Munshausen 832 h :*

Manoir Kasselslay avec ch, Maison 21, ✉ 9769, ☎ 95 84 71, *contact@kasselslay.lu, Fax 26 95 02 72,* , – TV P. MC VISA.
fermé 16 fév.-2 mars, 13 et 14 avril, 1 et 2 juin, 30 août-17 sept. et 27 déc.-7 janv. – **Repas** *(fermé lundi et mardi)* *Lunch 30* – 33/79 bc, ♀ – **6 ch** ☕ 60/125.
◆ Auberge familiale providentielle pour une halte gastronomique dans ce joli village proche de la station touristique de Clervaux. Recettes d'aujourd'hui. Belle terrasse étagée.
◆ Zin in een culinaire stop ? Dan komt deze herberg in een charmant dorp dicht bij het toeristenoord Clervaux vast als geroepen. Eigentijdse keuken. Mooi, trapsgewijs terras.

DIEKIRCH (DIKRECH) 717 V 23 et 716 L 6 – *6 167 h.*

Env. *au Nord : 8 km et 15 mn AR à pied, Falaise de Grenglay* ←★★.
ℹ *pl. de la Libération 3,* ✉ *9201,* ☎ *80 30 23, tourisme@diekirch.lu, Fax 80 27 86.*
Luxembourg 33 – Clervaux 30 – Echternach 28 – Ettelbrück 5 – Bastogne 46.

du Parc, av. de la Gare 28, ✉ 9233, ☎ 803 47 21, *info@hotel-du-parc.lu, Fax 80 98 61* – TV P. MC VISA
fermé 15 déc.-15 fév. et mardi – **Repas** carte 29 à 41 – **40 ch** ☕ 65/82 – ½ P 63/67.
◆ Près de la gare, au cœur d'une petite localité "brassicole", hôtel familial renfermant des chambres assez confortables ; une poignée d'entre elles se trouvent dans l'annexe. Salle de restaurant agréablement désuète.
◆ Dit familiehotel bevindt zich in het hart van een brouwersplaatsje, dicht bij het station. Het beschikt over vrij gerieflijke kamers, waarvan sommige in de dependance zijn ingericht. Gezellig ouderwetse eetzaal.

Hiertz avec ch, r. Clairefontaine 1, ✉ 9220, ☎ 80 35 62, *Fax 80 88 69,* , – rest, TV. AE ① MC VISA JCB
fermé 2 dern. sem. août., fin déc.-mi-janv., sam. midi, dim. soir et lundi – **Repas** *Lunch 36* – 74 – **8 ch** ☕ 60/75 – ½ P 85.
◆ Adresse de tradition où, en été, des fleurs colorent le jardin suspendu et la belle terrasse où sont servis les repas. L'Italie inspire certains mets. Chambres correctes.
◆ Traditioneel adresje met een hangende tuin die 's zomers in bloei staat en een mooi terras waar enkele Italiaans getinte gerechten te verkrijgen zijn. Keurige kamers.

DOMMELDANGE (DUMMELDÉNG) 717 V 25 – *voir à Luxembourg, périphérie.*

DUDELANGE (DIDDELENG) 717 V 26 *et* 716 L 7 – *17 411 h.*
Luxembourg 16 – Esch-sur-Alzette 13 – Thionville 17.

1900, r. Commerce 10, ✉ 3450, ☎ 51 28 48, *hotelrestaurant1900@yahoo.com, Fax 51 28 48 41,* – 🛗 📺. AE ⓓ ⓜⓒ VISA.
Repas *(fermé lundi)* carte 23 à 44, 🍷 – ☕ 6 – **15 ch** 48.
◆ Enseigne de circonstance : la façade de cet immeuble s'élevant au centre de Dudelange, ville frontalière, est de style Art nouveau. Chambres fonctionnelles et junior suites. Boiseries, lustres et verrières président au décor du restaurant.
◆ Hotel-restaurant met een gelegenheidsnaam : de façade van dit pand in het centrum van de grensplaats Dudelange is in art-nouveaustijl opgetrokken. Functionele kamers en junior suites. Lambrisering, kroonluchters en glas bepalen het decor van het restaurant.

Parc Le'h, r. Parc (par A 3, sortie ③, puis au 1er rond-point prendre à droite), ✉ 3542, ☎ 51 99 90, *parcleh@pt.lu, Fax 51 16 90,* – 🅿. AE ⓓ ⓜⓒ VISA
fermé 2e quinz. août, du 1er au 7 janv., lundi soir et mardi – **Repas** Lunch 11 – 29/67 bc, 🍷.
◆ Pavillon érigé au beau milieu d'un parc verdoyant. Salle à manger claire et contemporaine, aux tables bien espacées offrant une vue "plein cadre" sur les fourneaux.
◆ Dit paviljoen is gebouwd midden in een park. Lichte en eigentijdse eetzaal met grote ruimte tussen de tafels, waarvan sommige zicht hebben op de fornuizen.

ECHTERNACH (IECHTERNACH) 717 X 24 *et* 716 M 6 – *4 555 h.*
Voir *Place du Marché★* Y **10** - *Abbaye★* X – *à l'Ouest : Gorge du Loup★★ (Wolfschlucht), ≤★ du belvédère de Troosknepchen* Z.
ℹ *Porte St-Willibrord, Parvis de la Basilique,* ✉ *6401,* ☎ *72 02 30, Fax 72 75 24.*
Luxembourg 36 ② – Diekirch 28 ③ – Ettelbrück 30 ③ – Bitburg 21 ①

ECHTERNACH

Bénédictins (R. des) . . . Y 2
Bons Malades (R. des) . . . Y 3
Breilekes (R.) . . . Y
Duchscher (R. André) . . . Y
Ermesinde (R.) . . . X 5
Gare (R. de la) . . . X
Gibraltar (R.) . . . Y
Haut-Ruisseau (R.) . . . X 6
Hoovelek . . . Y
Hôpital (R. de l') . . . Y
Luxembourg (R. de) . . . Y 9
Marché (Pl. du) . . . Y 10
Maximilien (R.) . . . XY
Merciers (R. des) . . . X 12
Montagne (R. de la) . . . Y 13
Pont (R. du) . . . XY
Remparts (R. des) . . . Y
Sigefroi (R. Comte) . . . Y 15
Sûre (R. de la) . . . Y
Val des Roses . . . X
Wasserbillig (R. de) . . . Y 17

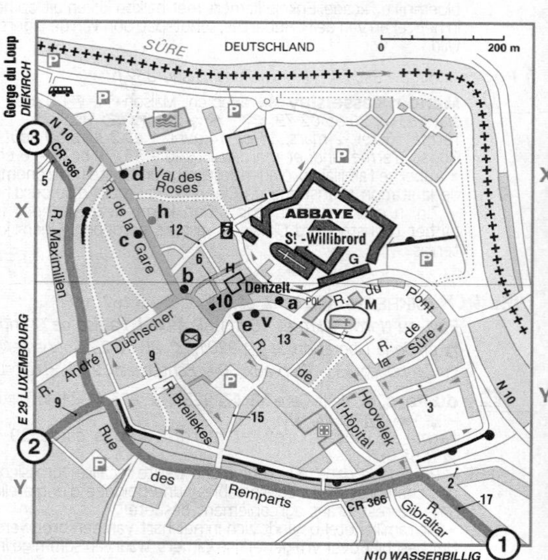

Eden au Lac 🌿, Oam Nonnesees (au-dessus du lac), ✉ 6474, ☎ 72 82 83, *hotel@edenaulac.lu, Fax 72 81 44,* ≤ ville et vallée boisée, – 🛗, rest, 📺 🅿 – 🏛 25 à 45. AE ⓜⓒ VISA.
15 mars-15 nov. – **Repas** ***Le Jardin d'Épices*** *(fermé merc. et sam.)* (dîner seult sauf dim. et jours fériés) 90 – **60 ch** ☕ 87/178, – 2 suites – ½ P 80/114.
◆ En pleine nature, dominant le lac et la villa romaine, bonnes chambres avec balcon panoramique aménagées dans trois unités communicantes, dont deux chalets. Repos et loisirs. De la salle à manger comme de la terrasse, vue sur les toits d'Echternach.
◆ Dit hotel midden in de natuur kijkt uit op het meer en de Romeinse villa. Het heeft goede kamers met balkon, die zijn ondergebracht in drie geschakelde panden, waaronder twee chalets. Eetzaal en terras bieden uitzicht op Echternach.

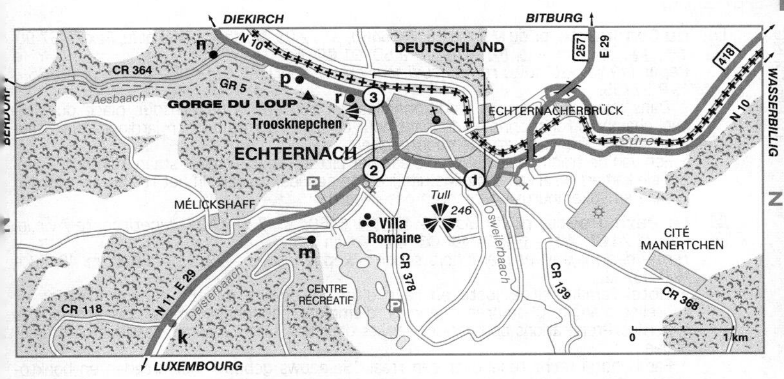

Grand H., rte de Diekirch 27, 6430, 72 96 72, *grandhot@pt.lu, Fax 72 90 62*, , , , - TV P. AE VISA JCB. Z p
20 mars-15 nov. – **Repas** *(fermé après 20 h)* (dîner seult sauf week-end et jours fériés) 40 – **32 ch** 95/160, – 8 suites – ½ P 70/110.
◆ Ensemble hôtelier proche de la fameuse Gorge du Loup. Chambres sans reproche, salon garni de meubles de style, jolie piscine intérieure et espace de remise en forme. La plupart des tables du restaurant offre une plaisante échappée sur la vallée boisée.
◆ Hotelcomplex dicht bij de fameuze Gorge du Loup. Onberispelijke kamers, met stijlmeubilair ingerichte lounge, fraai binnenzwembad en fitnessruimte. De meeste tafels in het restaurant kijken uit op het beboste dal.

Bel Air , rte de Berdorf 1, 6409, 72 93 83, *belair@pt.lu, Fax 72 86 94*, , , , , , , - TV P - 25 à 80. AE VISA. Z n
fermé du 2 au 15 janv. – **Repas** *Lunch 41* – 52/65 – **31 ch** 85/136, – 8 suites – ½ P 87/120.
◆ Ce confortable établissement lové au creux d'une vallée verdoyante s'entoure d'un parc propice au ressourcement. Salon cossu et reposantes chambres. Salle à manger procurant un coup d'œil plaisant sur les pelouses, parterres et pièce d'eau.
◆ Dit comfortabele hotel bevindt zich in een groen dal en wordt omringd door een park waar u nieuwe inspiratie kunt opdoen. Weelderige lounge en rustige kamers. De eetzaal kijkt uit op de gazons, de bloemperken en een waterpartij.

Welcome, rte de Diekirch 9, 6430, 72 03 54, *info@hotelwelcome.lu, Fax 72 85 81*, , , - TV P. VISA. Z r
mars-nov. – **Repas** *(fermé merc. et après 20 h 30)* 25/43 – **26 ch** 77/88 – ½ P 51/67.
◆ À deux pas d'un belvédère qui mérite - hautement ! - l'ascension, construction allongée bordant la grand-route et le lit de la Sûre. Chambres douillettes, souvent avec balcon.
◆ Nabij een belvédère die een prachtig uitzicht biedt, strekt zich langs de weg en de rivier het langgerekte pand van dit hotel uit. Behaaglijke kamers, de meeste met balkon.

Host. de la Basilique, pl. du Marché 7, 6460, 72 94 83, *info@hotel-basilique.lu, Fax 72 88 90*, , , - TV . AE VISA. Y a
25 mars-16 nov. – **Repas** (dîner seult sauf week-end et jours fériés) 35/45 – **14 ch** 91/108 – ½ P 66/104.
◆ Accueil familial chaleureux dans cette grosse maison postée sur une place aux pavés joufflus. Chambres fonctionnelles bien calibrées. Proximité immédiate de l'abbaye. Alternative brasserie ou restaurant.
◆ Vriendelijk en gastvrij onthaal in dit robuuste huis aan een plein dat met kinderhoofdjes is geplaveid en in de directe nabijheid van de abdij ligt. Functionele kamers van goede afmetingen. Keuze tussen brasserie en restaurant.

Le Pavillon, r. Gare 2, 6440, 72 98 09, *diedling@pt.lu, Fax 72 86 23*, - TV . AE VISA XY b
Repas *Lunch 10* – 23/49 bc, – **10 ch** 62/72 – ½ P 55/75.
◆ Étape idéale pour découvrir la capitale de la Petite Suisse luxembourgeoise, cet établissement du centre piétonnier renferme des chambres au décor bourgeois.
◆ Een ideaal rustpunt om de hoofdstad van Luxemburgs Klein Zwitserland te verkennen. Dit etablissement in het autovrije centrum beschikt over kamers met een bourgeois decor.

du Commerce, pl. du Marché 16, ✉ 6460, ☎ 72 03 01, *chactour@pt.lu, Fax 72 87 90,* – ⇕ TV – 25 à 50. AE MC VISA Y e
Repas *(19 fév.-20 nov. ; fermé jeudi sauf en juil.-août)* 12/42 bc, ♀ – **44 ch** ☐ 48/75 – ½ P 52/55.
◆ Dans l'une des maisons traditionnelles qui bordent la pittoresque place du Marché, chambres fonctionnelles donnant pour certaines sur un mignon jardinet. Au restaurant, cuisine française et luxembourgeoise.
◆ Een van de traditionele huizen die aan het pittoreske marktplein staan, herbergt functionele kamers waarvan sommige uitkijken op een leuk tuintje. In het restaurant worden Franse en Luxemburgse gerechten geserveerd.

Le Petit Poète, pl. du Marché 13, ✉ 6460, ☎ 720 07 21, *lepetitpoete@vip.lu, Fax 72 74 83,* – TV. AE MC VISA. ch Y v
fermé déc.-mi-janv. et mardi hors saison – **Repas** Lunch 9 – 22/33 – **12 ch** ☐ 40/58 – ½ P 45/52.
◆ Hôtel familial situé juste en face d'un bel édifice du 15e s. avec arcades et tourelles d'angle. Chambres rajeunies, d'ampleur convenable, mais sans accessoires superflus. Préparations bourgeoises servies dans une salle à manger classiquement aménagée.
◆ Familiehotel recht tegenover een fraai 15e-eeuws gebouw met arcaden en hoektorentjes. Gerenoveerde kamers van redelijke afmetingen, maar zonder overbodige accessoires. De eenvoudige maaltijden worden geserveerd in een klassiek ingerichte eetzaal.

St-Hubert, r. Gare 21, ✉ 6440, ☎ 72 03 06, *Fax 72 87 72,* – ⇕ TV P. AE MC VISA X c
fermé lundis et mardis non fériés d'oct. à mars – **Repas** carte 22 à 46, ♀ – **18 ch** ☐ 65/80 – ½ P 52/68.
◆ Cet établissement bordant la longue rue piétonne, très animée, abrite des chambres de mise simple, mais bien tenues. Quatre d'entre elles sont équipées d'une kitchenette. À table, recettes traditionnelles.
◆ Dit etablissement in de lange en zeer levendige voetgangersstraat heeft eenvoudig ingerichte, maar goed onderhouden kamers, waarvan er vier zijn uitgerust met een kitchenette. Menukaart met traditionele gerechten.

des Ardennes, r. Gare 38, ✉ 6440, ☎ 72 01 08, *ardennes@pt.lu, Fax 72 94 80,* – ⇕ TV – 25. AE MC VISA. X d
Repas *(fermé mi-janv.-fin fév., jeudi et dim. soir)* 23/36 – **30 ch** ☐ 65/80 – ½ P 63.
◆ Petite adresse dont l'entrée se donne des airs d'hostellerie "cotée". Sobres chambres réparties sur trois étages, bar, espace de remise en forme et jardin croquignolet.
◆ Dit adresje heeft wel een heel chique entree ! Eenvoudige kamers op drie verdiepingen, bar, fitnessruimte en een schattig tuintje.

La Coppa, r. Gare 22, ✉ 6440, ☎ 72 73 24, *Fax 26 72 05 57,* – AE MC VISA X h
fermé 3 dern. sem. juin, lundi soir et mardi – **Repas** Lunch 10 – carte 35 à 49.
◆ Parmi les valeurs sûres du centre, lorsqu'il s'agit de passer à table. Plaisante salle à manger décorée dans la note provençale, convivialité et mets aux accents du Sud.
◆ Dit is een van de betere eetgelegenheden in het centrum. Charmante, gezellige eetzaal met een Provençaalse noot en gerechten met een zuidelijk accent.

à Geyershaff *(Geieschhaff)* *par ② : 6,5 km par E 29 C Bech 943 h :*

La Bergerie (Phal), ✉ 6251, ☎ 79 04 64, *Fax 79 07 71,* <, – P. AE MC VISA
fermé 2 janv.-12 fév., dim. soir et lundi – **Repas** (dîner seult de sept. à mai) – 99, carte 84 à 121.
◆ Entre forêt et champs, coquette maison de bouche concoctant une cuisine délicieusement inventive. Cave franco-luxembourgeoise. Ravissant jardin et véranda.
◆ Aantrekkelijk restaurant tussen bos en akkers, met een heerlijk inventieve keuken. De wijnen komen uit Frankrijk en Luxemburg. Serre en een prachtige tuin.
Spéc. Foie gras aux cinq saveurs. Carré d'agneau de Sisteron grillé. Suprême de turbot, sauce au Champagne. **Vins** Pinot gris, Gewurztraminer

à Lauterborn *(Lauterbur)* *C Echternach :*

Au Vieux Moulin avec ch, Maison 6, ✉ 6562, ☎ 720 06 81, *avmoulin@pt.lu, Fax 72 71 25,* – TV P. AE MC VISA. Z k
fermé janv. et lundi – **Repas** *(fermé après 20 h 30)* carte 38 à 46 – **8 ch** ☐ 72, – 1 suite – ½ P 57/61.
◆ Hostellerie de caractère installée dans un vieux moulin, comme le confirme son enseigne. La carte, au goût du jour, comporte plusieurs menus. Chambres de bon confort.
◆ Karaktervolle hostellerie in een oude molen, zoals de naam al aangeeft. Op de eigentijdse kaart staan verschillende menu's. Kamers met een goed comfort.

à Steinheim (Stenem) *par ① : 4 km* 🄲 *Rosport 1 885 h :*

Gruber, rte d'Echternach 36, ✉ 6585, ☎ 72 04 33, *info@hotelgruber.com,* *Fax 72 87 56*, ☂, ☀, ✂, 🚲 – 📺 P. ⓓ ⓜ VISA. ✗ rest
18 mars-13 déc. – **Repas** *(fermé après 20 h 30)* carte 22 à 37 – **18 ch** ☕ 54/83 – ½ P 53/62.
◆ Auberge familiale bordant la route d'Echternach. Plus récentes et plus amples, les chambres réparties dans l'aile arrière sont aussi les plus tranquilles. La salle à manger procure une vue séduisante sur le parc clos de haies.
◆ Deze herberg is te vinden aan de weg naar Echternach. De kamers in de achterste vleugel, die van latere datum zijn en ruimer, liggen het rustigst. De eetzaal biedt een fraai uitzicht op een met heggen omheind park.

EHNEN (ÉINEN) 🄲 *Wormeldange 2 306 h.* 717 X 25 *et* 716 M 7.
Luxembourg 31 – Ettelbrück 55 – Remich 10 – Trier 32.

Bamberg's, rte du Vin 131, ✉ 5416, ☎ 76 00 22, *Fax 76 00 56*, ← – |‡| 📺. AE ⓓ ⓜ VISA. ✗
fermé déc.-15 janv. et mardi – **Repas** carte 43 à 76 – **12 ch** ☕ 65/90 – ½ P 68.
◆ Cet hôtel tenu en famille depuis 1911 paresse au bord de la Moselle, au pied d'un coteau planté de vignes : route du vin oblige ! Certaines chambres ont un balcon panoramique. Au restaurant, plats classiques et sélection de crus du vignoble luxembourgeois.
◆ Dit hotel wordt sinds 1911 door dezelfde familie gerund en staat in alle rust langs de Moezel, aan de voet van een helling met wijnstokken. Sommige kamers hebben een balkon met panoramisch uitzicht. Restaurant met klassieke keuken en Luxemburgse wijnen.

XX **Simmer** avec ch, rte du Vin 117, ✉ 5416, ☎ 76 00 30, *info@hotel-simmer.lu,* *Fax 76 03 06*, ←, ☂, 🚲 – P. AE ⓓ ⓜ VISA. ✗
fermé 5 janv.-7 fév., lundi soir et mardi – **Repas** Lunch 25 – 45, ♀ – **12 ch** ☕ 42/72 – ½ P 74/79.
◆ Hostellerie élevée à la fin du 19e s. sur les berges de la Moselle. Mets traditionnels et bonne cave régionale. Terrasse dressée aux beaux jours. Chambres un rien désuètes.
◆ Hostellerie die aan het einde van de 19e eeuw aan de Moezel is gebouwd. Traditionele gerechten en goede regionale wijnkaart. Terras bij mooi weer. Ietwat sleetse kamers.

EICH (EECH) – *voir à Luxembourg, périphérie.*

ELLANGE (ELLÉNG) 717 W 25 – *voir à Mondorf-les-Bains.*

ERNZ NOIRE (Vallée de l') (MULLERTHAL-MËLLERDALL) ★★★ 717 W 24 *et* 716 L 6 *G. Belgique-Luxembourg.*

ERPELDANGE (IERPELDÉNG) 717 V 23 *et* 716 L 6 – *voir à Ettelbruck.*

ESCHDORF (ESCHDUERF) 🄲 *Heiderscheid 1 175 h.* 717 U 23 *et* 716 K 6.
Env. *au Sud : 4,5 km à Rindschleiden : Église paroissiale★.*
Luxembourg 46 – Diekirch 22 – Ettelbrück 17 – Bastogne 17.

Braas, an Haesbich 1, ✉ 9150, ☎ 83 92 13, *info@hotel-braas.lu, Fax 83 95 78* – |‡| 📺 P. ⓜ VISA JCB. ✗ rest
fermé janv.-15 fév. – **Repas** *(fermé lundi soir, mardi et après 20 h 30)* Lunch 10 – carte 22 à 48 – **11 ch** ☕ 50/70 – ½ P 43/55.
◆ La vallée de la Sûre décrit ses plus beaux méandres à quelques minutes de cette auberge familiale restée insensible aux modes depuis sa naissance dans les années 1970. Le restaurant propose une formule lunch à prix "plancher".
◆ De Sûre beschrijft zijn mooiste meanders in het stukje dal in de buurt van deze herberg, die sinds de bouw rond 1970 ongevoelig is gebleven voor trends. Het restaurant biedt een lunchformule tegen "bodemprijs".

ESCH-SUR-ALZETTE (ESCH-UELZECHT) 717 U 26 *et* 716 K 7 – *27 244 h.*
🅱 *Hôtel de Ville,* ✉ *4004,* ☎ *54 16 37, touristinfo@esch-city.lu, Fax 54 73 86.*
Luxembourg 18 ① – Longwy 26 ① – Thionville 32 ③

Plan page suivante

Mercure Renaissance ⛔, pl. Boltgen 2, ✉ 4044, ☎ 54 19 91, *h2017@accor-hotels.com, Fax 54 19 90*, ☂ – |‡|, ≡ rest, 📺 🚗 – 🎤 25. AE ⓓ ⓜ VISA BZ t
Repas Lunch 12 – carte 29 à 38, ♀ – ☕ 11 – **41 ch** 80/89 – ½ P 121/139.
◆ Cet établissement de chaîne déploie tout l'éventail des prestations hôtelières propres à l'enseigne Mercure. Chambres fonctionnelles où l'on ne manque pas d'espace.
◆ Dit etablissement spreidt alle hotelprestaties tentoon die de Mercure-keten eigen zijn. Functionele kamers waar het beslist niet aan ruimte ontbreekt.

ESCH-SUR-ALZETTE

Alzette (R. de l') . . . . ABZ
Boltgen (Pl.) . . . . BZ 8
Commerce (R. du) . . . . . . BZ 12
Charbons (R. des) . . . . AZ 13
Dellheicht (R.) . . . . BY 14
Gare (Av. de la) . . . . BZ 15
Grand-Rue . . . . BZ 16
Hôtel-de-Ville (Pl. de l') . . . BZ 18
Joseph-Wester (R.) . . . . AY 20
Léon-Jouhaux (R.) . . . . AY 21
Léon-Weirich (R.) . . . . AYZ 23
Libération (R. de la) . . . . . BZ 24
Mathias-Koener (R.) . . . . BY 25
Norbert-Metz (Pl.) . . . . BZ 26
Remparts (Pl. des) . . . . BZ 29
Remparts (R. des) . . . . BZ 30
Résistance (Pl. de la) . . . . . AZ 32
Sacrifiés 1940-45 (Pl. des) AY 33
St.-Michel (Pl.) . . . . BZ 34
St.-Vincent (R.) . . . . BZ 36
Sidney-Thomas (R.) . . . . . . AYZ 37
Stalingrad (R. de) . . . . AZ 39
Synagogue (Pl. de la) . . . . BZ 40
Wurth-Paquet (R.) . . . . BY 42
Xavier-Brasseur (R.) . . . . . . BZ 43
Zénon-Bernard (R.) . . . . . . ABZ 44
10-Septembre (R. du) . . . . ABZ 45

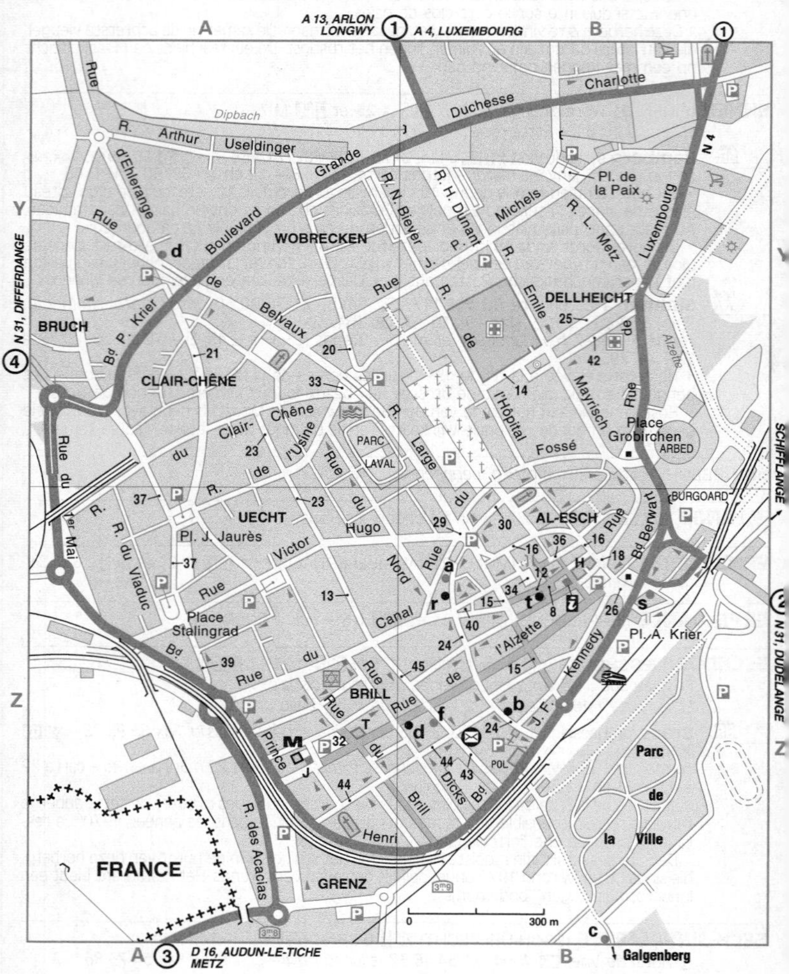

For Gourmets

We distinguish for your use certain hotels (🏨🏨🏨🏨🏨 ... 🏠) and restaurants (XXXXX ...X) by awarding them « ✿✿✿ », « ✿✿ », « ✿ » or « Ⓡ ».

Topaz sans rest, r. Remparts 5, ✉ 4303, ☎ 531 44 11, *Fax 53 14 54* – |♦| TV. AE ⓓ MC VISA. ✈ BZ r
22 ch ☐ 65/87.
◆ Hôtel récent installé dans une paisible petite rue du centre. Chambres équipées d'un mobilier en bois clair. Salle de breakfast s'ouvrant sur une terrasse fleurie en été.
◆ Hotel van recente datum in een rustig straatje van het centrum. Kamers met licht houten meubilair. De ontbijtzaal kijkt uit op een terras dat 's zomers vol bloemen staat.

de la Poste sans rest, r. Alzette 107, ✉ 4011, ☎ 265 45 41, *contact@hotel-de-la-poste.lu, Fax 265 45 48 00* – |♦| TV. MC VISA BZ d
20 ch ☐ 95/125.
◆ Cet immeuble bâti en 1919 a tout récemment retrouvé l'éclat du neuf. Façade bourgeoise modernisée, cage d'escalier à touche Art déco et chambres bien équipées.
◆ Dit pand uit 1919 is onlangs geheel gerenoveerd. Gemoderniseerde statige voorgevel, trappenhuis met accenten in art deco en kamers met een goed comfort.

Acacia, r. Libération 10, ✉ 4210, ☎ 54 10 61, *hacacia@pt.lu, Fax 54 35 02* – |♦|, ▤ rest, TV. AE ⓓ MC VISA BZ b
fermé du 24 au 31 déc. – **Repas** *(fermé dim. et jours fériés)* Lunch 35 – 25/65 bc, ♀ – **23 ch** ☐ 63/88 – ½ P 65/77.
◆ Adresse familiale dont la situation s'avère bien commode pour les usagers du rail. Les chambres, un peu menues et décorées avec sobriété, offrent toutefois un confort correct. Salle de restaurant où le feu ronfle dans la cheminée quand le froid sévit.
◆ Familiehotel dat voor treinreizigers praktisch is gelegen. De kamers zijn wat aan de krappe kant en eenvoudig ingericht, maar correct. Restaurantzaal met open haard waarin bij koud weer een behaaglijk vuurtje knappert.

Aub. Royale (Favaro), r. Remparts 19, ✉ 4303, ☎ 542 72 31, *auberge.royale@mail.lu, Fax 54 27 23 20,* Avec cuisine italienne – ▤ – 🏛 40. AE ⓓ MC VISA. ✈ BZ a
fermé dern. sem. mai, fin août-début sept., fin janv.-début fév., sam. midi, dim. soir et lundi – **Repas** Lunch 50 bc – 65/90, carte 61 à 83, ♀ ❀.
◆ Repaire gourmand rénové dans un souci d'esthétique et de confort. Trois petites salles actuelles et intimes. Carte au goût du jour où se distingue l'Italie. Bonne cave.
◆ Met smaak gerenoveerd, comfortabel adres met een goede keuken en wijnkelder. Drie actuele, intieme zaaltjes. Eigentijdse kaart waarin Italië de boventoon voert.
Spéc. Faux cannelloni de tartare de saumon. Agnolotti au Castelmagne, beurre à la sauge. Truffes blanches d'Alba (oct.-nov.). **Vins** Pinot gris, Riesling

Fridrici, rte de Belvaux 116, ✉ 4026, ☎ 55 80 94, *restaurantfridrici@internet.lu, Fax 57 33 35* – ▤ P. AE ⓓ MC VISA AY d
fermé sem. carnaval, du 2 au 24 août, mardi, jeudi soir et sam. midi – **Repas** Lunch 45 – 55/77, carte 56 à 68, ♀.
◆ Deux grosses maisons de notable abritent cette talentueuse table classique régalant les fines fourchettes depuis une décennie. Beaux produits travaillés avec soin.
◆ Twee grote patriciërshuizen bieden onderdak aan dit klassieke restaurant, waar fijnproevers sinds 10 jaar hun hart kunnen ophalen. Mooie gerechten die met zorg worden bereid.
Spéc. Navarin de homard et caviar en croustade. Bar de ligne poêlé, crème aux fines herbes. Noisettes de chevreuil à la gueuze framboisée (21 déc.-21 mars). **Vins** Riesling, Pinot gris

Postkutsch, r. Xavier Brasseur 8, ✉ 4040, ☎ 54 51 69, *magninclaude@hotmail.com, Fax 54 82 35* – ▤. AE ⓓ MC VISA BZ f
fermé lundi et sam. midi – **Repas** Lunch 19 – 33/98 bc.
◆ Une longue carte assortie de menus hebdomadaires vous sera présentée au Postkutsch. Mémorable chariot de fromages affinés. Fresques évoquant l'ère des diligences.
◆ Deze "postkoets" heeft een uitgebreide kaart met wekelijkse menu's. Mis vooral de verzorgde kaaswagen niet. Fresco's herinneren aan de tijd van de diligences.

Le Pavillon, Parc Galgebierg (au-dessus du stade Emile Mayrisch), ✉ 4142, ☎ 54 02 28, *daniel2@pt.lu, Fax 54 74 28,* 🏠 – P. MC VISA BZ c
fermé du 17 au 25 août, 26 déc.-1er janv., sam. midi, dim. soir et lundi – **Repas** Lunch 12 – carte 33 à 49.
◆ Agréable restaurant aménagé dans un grand parc boisé, aux portes de la ville. Lunch et menus bien ficelés, salle à manger d'esprit 1900 et terrasse estivale invitante.
◆ Aangenaam restaurant in een groot park met bomen, aan de rand van de stad. Goed samengestelde lunch en menu's, eetzaal met decor van omstreeks 1900 en uitnodigend zomerterras.

Bec Fin, pl. Norbert Metz 15, ✉ 4239, ☎ 54 33 22, *Fax 54 00 99* – AE ⓓ MC VISA BZ s
fermé 1 sem. carnaval, prem. sem. sept., dim. soir et lundi – **Repas** Lunch 14 – carte 22 à 36.
◆ Sur une placette jouxtant le ring, sympathique petite table familiale où les "fins becs" du coin ont leurs habitudes. Nombre de couverts limité : mieux vaut donc réserver.
◆ Op een pleintje vlak bij de ringweg bevindt zich dit sympathieke eethuis waar de lekkerbekken uit de buurt graag vertoeven. Beperkt aantal couverts : reserveren dus aanbevolen.

à Foetz (Féitz) par ① : 5 km C Mondercange 6 099 h :

De Foetz, r. Avenir 1 (dans zoning commercial), ✉ 3895, ☎ 57 25 45, *hfoetz@pt.lu, Fax 57 25 65* – TV P. AE ① MC VISA. ✗
Repas *(fermé dim.)* Lunch 8 – 22 – **40 ch** *(fermé 19 déc.-4 janv.)* ☐ 44/64 – ½ P 45/65.
◆ Établissement récent s'ouvrant sur une rue en cul-de-sac. Chambres standard pratiques pour la clientèle d'affaires, foisonnante dans le zoning commercial de Foetz.
◆ Vrij nieuw hotel in een doodlopend straatje. Praktisch ingerichte standaardkamers voor een zakelijke clientèle. Aan gasten geen gebrek dankzij het bedrijvenpark van Foetz.

ESCH-SUR-SÛRE (ESCH SAUER) 717 U 23 et 716 K 6 – *331 h.*

Voir *Site★ – Tour de Guet ←★.*

Env. *à l'Ouest : rte de Kaundorf ←★ – à l'Ouest : Lac de la Haute-Sûre★, ←★ – au Sud-Ouest : Hochfels★.*

ℹ *Maison du Parc Naturel de la Haute-Sûre, rte de Lultzhausen 15,* ✉ *9650,* ☎ *899 33 11, Fax 89 95 20.*

Luxembourg 48 – Diekirch 24 – Ettelbrück 19 – Bastogne 27.

de la Sûre ⛰ (annexe - 14 ch), r. Pont 1, ✉ 9650, ☎ 83 91 10, *info@hotel-de-la-sure.lu, Fax 89 91 01,* ←, 🏞, ⛵, ≘, 🚲 – TV. AE MC VISA. ✗ rest
fermé 16 déc.-30 janv. – **Repas** ***Comte de Godefroy*** *(fermé lundi et mardi)* Lunch 15 – 28/50 bc, ♀ – **9 ch** ☐ 87/174 – ½ P 43/94.
◆ Dans un patelin mignon comme tout, massive construction régionale abritant diverses catégories de chambres, également aménagées dans l'annexe voisine. Accueil familial. Salle à manger bourgeoise dotée d'une mezzanine.
◆ Dit robuuste pand in regionale stijl beschikt over diverse categorieën kamers, waarvan er ook enkele in de ernaast gelegen dependance zijn ingericht. Vriendelijke ontvangst. Eetzaal met mezzanine.

Le Postillon, r. Eglise 1, ✉ 9650, ☎ 89 90 33, *conrad@lepostillon.lu, Fax 89 90 34,* 🏞 – |‡| TV. MC VISA. ✗
fermé janv. – **Repas** *(fermé après 20 h 30)* 22/35 – **24 ch** ☐ 54/80 – ½ P 65.
◆ Une tour de guet médiévale domine l'escarpement rocheux au pied duquel se dresse cette imposante auberge traditionnelle. La Sûre méandre en contrebas de l'hôtel. On mange sur la terrasse par météo clémente.
◆ Een middeleeuwse wachttoren beheerst de steile rotshelling, waar aan de voet deze imposante, traditionele herberg staat. Nog iets lager meandert de rivier de Sûre. Bij mooi weer wordt op het terras geserveerd.

ETTELBRÜCK (ETTELBRÉCK) 717 V 23 et 716 L 6 – *7 340 h.*

Env. *au Nord-Est : 2,5 km à Erpeldange : cadre★.*

ℹ *pl. de la Gare 1,* ✉ *9044,* ☎ *81 20 68, site@pt.lu,* Fax 81 98 39.

Luxembourg 28 – Clervaux 34 – Bastogne 41.

Central, r. Bastogne 25, ✉ 9010, ☎ 81 21 16, *info@hotelcentral.lu, Fax 81 21 38,* 🏞 – |‡| TV. AE ① MC VISA. ✗
fermé 2 dern. sem. août – **Repas** voir rest ***Le Châteaubriand*** ci-après – **13 ch** ☐ 52/82 – ½ P 62/67.
◆ Cet hôtel officiant de longue date au centre d'Ettelbrück constitue un bon petit point de chute pour rayonner dans la basse vallée de la Sûre. Ambiance familiale.
◆ Dit hotel in het centrum van Ettelbrück is al sinds lang een goed vertrekpunt voor excursies in het benedendal van de Sûre. Huiselijke sfeer.

Lanners, r. Gare 1, ✉ 9044, ☎ 812 12 71, *Fax 81 62 77,* 🏞 – |‡| TV. ① MC VISA. ✗
Repas *(fermé 23 déc.-8 janv. et sam.)* Lunch 13 – carte 32 à 44 – **11 ch** *(fermé 16 août-6 sept.)* ☐ 57/70 – ½ P 52/54.
◆ À un jet de vapeur de la gare, sur une avenue passante, auberge disposant de chambres fonctionnelles inégalement insonorisées, mais convenables pour l'étape.
◆ Deze herberg nabij het station, aan een doorgaande weg, heeft functionele kamers die niet allemaal een even beste geluidsisolatie hebben, maar voor een etappe prima voldoen.

Le Châteaubriand - H. Central, 1er étage, r. Bastogne 25, ✉ 9010, ☎ 81 21 16, *info@hotelcentral.lu, Fax 81 21 38* – AE ① MC VISA. ✗
fermé 2 dern. sem. août, dim. soir et lundi – **Repas** 39/65 bc.
◆ Bénéficiant d'une reconnaissance locale non négligeable, ce restaurant installé dans l'hôtel Central sert dans sa salle à manger cossue une cuisine assez ambitieuse.
◆ Dit restaurant van Hôtel Central staat bij de lokale bevolking behoorlijk goed aangeschreven. Weelderig ingerichte eetzaal en vrij ambitieuze keuken.

Le Navarin, r. Prince Henri 15, ✉ 9047, ☎ 81 80 82, *navarin@pt.lu, Fax 81 13 12* – AE ① MC VISA JCB
fermé 2e quinz. fév., 2e quinz. août, lundi soir et mardi – **Repas** Lunch 10 – 25/68 bc.
◆ Salle de restaurant miniature aménagée dans un ancien café. Plats bourgeois à prix d'ami et choix de vins intéressant témoignent bien de la passion qui anime le patron.
◆ Zeer klein restaurant in een voormalig café. Eenvoudige maaltijden voor een vriendenprijsje, een interessante wijnkaart en een patron met veel liefde voor het vak !

à Erpeldange (Ierpeldéng) *Nord-Est : 2,5 km par N 27 – 2023 h*

Dahm, Porte des Ardennes 57, ✉ 9145, ☎ 816 25 51, *dahm@pt.lu, Fax 816 25 52 10,* – 25 à 120. AE ① MC VISA. rest
fermé 20 déc.-21 janv. – **Repas** *(fermé lundi, jeudi soir et après 20 h 30)* Lunch 10 – carte 22 à 63 – **25 ch** 57/95 – ½ P 78/92.
◆ Maison imposante dont la façade s'agrémente de colombages et d'arcades. Chambres spacieuses ; une dizaine d'entre elles offrent un confort plus moderne. Jardin fleuri en été. Repas traditionnel servi dans un décor intérieur rustique. Terrasse estivale.
◆ Een imposant vakwerkhuis met arcaden. Ruime kamers waarvan een tiental is voorzien van moderner comfort. Tuin vol bloemen in de zomer. In een rustiek interieur wordt een traditionele maaltijd geserveerd. Zomerterras.

FOETZ (FÉITZ) 717 V 25 – *voir à Esch-sur-Alzette.*

FRISANGE (FRÉISENG) 717 W 25 *et* 716 L 7 – *2919 h.*
Luxembourg 12 – Thionville 20.

de la Frontière, r. Robert Schuman 52 (au poste frontière), ✉ 5751, ☎ 23 61 51, *hotfront@pt.lu, Fax 23 66 17 53,* – AE MC VISA
fermé 2 dern. sem. fév., fin déc., lundi et mardi midi – **Repas** carte 22 à 33 – **18 ch** 45/70 – ½ P 46/56.
◆ Enseigne pertinente, puisque le poste de douane se trouve juste en face de cet hôtel tenu en famille. Chambres bien calibrées, garnies d'un mobilier robuste. Le couvert est dressé dans une salle à manger de style bourgeois actualisé.
◆ Een relevante naam, want de douanepost bevindt zich recht tegenover dit hotel in familiebeheer. De ruime kamers zijn met robuust meubilair ingericht. De maaltijd wordt geserveerd in een gemoderniseerde eetzaal.

Lea Linster, rte de Luxembourg 17, ✉ 5752, ☎ 23 66 84 11, *léalin@pt.lu, Fax 23 67 64 47,* – AE ① MC VISA.
fermé 16 août-2 sept., 20 déc.-6 janv., lundi et mardi – **Repas** 80, carte 73 à 105.
◆ Refuge gourmand dont la façade végétale dissimule une apaisante salle à manger élégamment agencée. Belle terrasse procurant une vue agreste. Patronne-cuisinière aux fourneaux.
◆ Achter de begroeide voorgevel van dit restaurant gaat een stijlvol ingerichte eetzaal schuil. Mooi terras met landelijk uitzicht. De eigenaresse is tevens de chef-kok.
Spéc. Salade tiède de homard cuit au moment. Selle d'agneau en croûte de pomme de terre. Bar de ligne en croûte de sel. **Vins** Riesling, Pinot gris

à Hellange (Helléng) *Ouest : 3 km* C *Frisange :*

Lëtzebuerger Kaschthaus, r. Bettembourg 4 (face à l'église), ✉ 3333, ☎ 51 65 73, *Fax 51 65 73,* – AE MC VISA
fermé du 4 au 26 août, 22 déc.-3 janv., mardi et merc. midi – **Repas** carte 30 à 39, ♀.
◆ Charmante auberge où l'on vient goûter une cuisine féminine soignée dans une ambiance décontractée. L'arrière-cour, close de murs, accueille un adorable restaurant d'été.
◆ Charmante herberg met ongedwongen ambiance en een verzorgde keuken die door een vrouwelijke chef-kok wordt bereid. 's Zomers wordt op de gezellige binnenplaats geserveerd.

GAICHEL (GÄICHEL) C *Hobscheid 2579 h.* 717 U 24 *et* 716 K 6.
☎ 39 71 08, Fax 39 00 75.
Luxembourg 35 – Diekirch 35 – Arlon 5.

La Gaichel avec ch, rte de Mersch 5, ✉ 8469 Eischen, ☎ 39 01 29, *gaichel@relaischateaux.com, Fax 39 00 37,* – 30. AE MC VISA.
fermé 22 août-2 sept., 9 janv.-10 fév., dim. soir et lundi – **Repas** (fermé dim. soir, lundi et mardi midi) Lunch 40 – 55/150 bc, carte 60 à 84, ♀ – **13 ch** 115/145 – ½ P 137/147.
◆ Un splendide parc ombragé entoure cette prestigieuse auberge traditionnelle. Mets soignés. Chambres personnalisées avec bon goût et dotées d'un balcon. Parcours de golf.
◆ Prestigieuze traditionele herberg in een prachtig park met veel bomen. Verzorgde keuken. De kamers zijn persoonlijk en smaakvol ingericht en hebben een balkon. Golfbaan.
Spéc. Queues de langoustines royales rôties en carapace. Tartare de saumon. Canard nantais, parmentier dauphinois au foie gras. **Vins** Pinot blanc, Riesling

XXX **Host. La Bonne Auberge** avec ch, Maison 7, ✉ 8469 Eischen, ☎ 39 01 40, *gaichel2@pt.lu, Fax 39 71 13,* ≤, – TV P. AE O MC VISA
fermé 1 sem. en mars et 1 sem. en août – **Repas** *(fermé mardi et sam. midi)* Lunch 17 – 29/74 bc, ♀ – **17 ch** 60/92 – ½ P 70/80.
◆ La salle à manger classiquement aménagée, la terrasse estivale et les chambres d'ampleur variable profitent toutes du coup d'œil sur le parc d'en face et sa pièce d'eau.
◆ De klassiek ingerichte eetzaal, het zomerterras en de in grootte variërende kamers kijken alle uit op het park met waterpartij aan de overkant.

GEYERSHAFF (GEIESCHHAFF) – *voir à Echternach.*

GONDERANGE (GONNERÉNG) C *Junglinster 5 813 h.* 717 W 24 *et* 716 L 6.

au Nord : 3 km à Junglinster, Domaine de Behlenhaff, ✉ 6141, ☎ 78 00 68, Fax 78 71 28.

Luxembourg 16 – *Echternach* 22 – *Ettelbrück* 30.

Euro, rte de Luxembourg 11, ✉ 6182, ☎ 78 85 51, *eurohotel@vo.lu, Fax 78 85 50,* – rest, TV P. – 25 à 100. AE O MC VISA
Repas Lunch 9 – carte 22 à 51, ♀ – **50 ch** 69/86 – ½ P 51/60.
◆ Cet hôtel fonctionnel aux communs assez vastes dispose de chambres récentes et bien équipées. Clientèle de groupes et d'hommes d'affaires. Salle de restaurant actuelle, à l'image de la carte.
◆ Dit functionele hotel met vrij grote gemeenschappelijke ruimten beschikt over moderne, goed uitgeruste kamers. De clientèle bestaat uit groepen en zakelijke gasten. Eigentijdse restaurantzaal, net als de menukaart.

Dans ce guide
un même symbole, un même mot,
imprimé en rouge ou en noir, en maigre ou en gras,
n'ont pas tout à fait la même signification.
Lisez attentivement les pages explicatives.

GORGE DU LOUP (WOLLEFSSCHLUCHT) ★★ 717 X 24 *et* 716 M 6 *G. Belgique-Luxembourg.*

GRUNDHOF (GRONDHAFF) C *Beaufort 1 615 h.* 717 W 23 *et* 716 L 6.
Luxembourg 37 – *Diekirch* 18 – *Echternach* 10 – *Ettelbrück* 24.

Brimer, rte de Beaufort 1, ✉ 6360, ☎ 268 78 71, *info@hotel-brimer.lu, Fax 26 87 63 13,* – TV P. AE O MC VISA.
mars-15 nov. – **Repas** *(fermé après 20 h 30)* Lunch 25 – 30/42 – **25 ch** 88/140 – ½ P 85/95.
◆ La route pittoresque reliant Diekirch à Echternach mène à cette adresse blottie au creux de la verte vallée de la Sûre. Des chambres de luxe viennent tout juste d'être créées. Table classique agencée dans la note néo-rustique.
◆ Dit hotel in het groene dal van de Sûre staat aan de schilderachtige weg van Diekirch naar Echternach. De luxekamers zijn nog maar sinds kort ingericht. Eetzaal met neorustiek decor, klassieke keuken.

Ferring sans rest, rte de Beaufort 4, ✉ 6360, ☎ 83 60 15, *Fax 86 91 40* – TV. AE O MC VISA.
5 avril-5 nov. – **25 ch** 45/70.
◆ Une gentille affaire familiale au voisinage de la rivière, abritant sur trois étages des chambres au confort correct, équipées d'un mobilier un brin suranné.
◆ Dit vriendelijke familiehotel vlak bij de rivier heeft vrij gerieflijke kamers die over drie verdiepingen verspreid liggen en zijn ingericht met ietwat sleets meubilair.

XXX **L'Ernz Noire** avec ch, rte de Beaufort 2, ✉ 6360, ☎ 83 60 40, *lernznoire@pt.lu, Fax 86 91 51,* – TV P. AE MC VISA.
fermé janv.-fév. et prem. sem. déc. – **Repas** *(fermé mardi)* Lunch 36 – 61/67 – **11 ch** 64/97 – ½ P 62/74.
◆ Sur un carrefour, établissement dont l'enseigne reprend le nom du cours d'eau local. Spécialité de la maison : les plats à base de champignons. Chambres pratiques.
◆ Dit etablissement aan een kruispunt is genoemd naar de rivier die in de omgeving stroomt. Specialiteit van het huis : gerechten op basis van paddestoelen. Praktische kamers.

HALLER (HALER) C *Waldbillig 1 220 h.* 717 W 24 *et* 716 L 6.

Voir *Gorges du Hallerbach★ : 30 mn AR à pied.*

Luxembourg 35 – Echternach 20 – Ettelbrück 20 – Mersch 19.

Hallerbach r. Romains 2, ✉ 6370, ☎ 83 65 26, *info@hotel-hallerbach.lu, Fax 83 61 51,* – ▮ TV P – 25. AE ① MC VISA. rest *15 fév.-nov.* – **Repas** *(fermé lundi midi et mardi midi)* 32/56, ♀ – **16 ch** ☐ 65/110 – ½ P 67/81.

◆ Au centre d'un village de la Petite Suisse, affaire exploitée en famille depuis quatre générations. Chambres personnalisées. Côté détente : jardin, piscine, sauna et fitness. À table, cuisine traditionnelle.

◆ Dit hotel, in het hart van een dorp in Klein Zwitserland, wordt al vier generaties lang door dezelfde familie gerund. De kamers hebben een persoonlijke toets. Tal van faciliteiten voor ontspanning : tuin, zwembad, sauna et fitnessruimte. Traditionele keuken.

HAUT-MARTELANGE (UEWER-MAARTEL) C *Rambrouch 3 397 h.* 717 T 24 *et* 716 K 6.

Luxembourg 53 – Diekirch 38 – Ettelbrück 38 – Bastogne 22.

à Rombach-Martelange *(Rombech-Maarteléng) Nord : 1,5 km* C *Rambrouch :*

Maison Rouge, rte d'Arlon 5, ✉ 8832, ☎ 23 64 00 06, *Fax 23 64 90 14,* – ▤ P. AE ① MC VISA.

fermé mi-fév.-mi-mars, fin août-début sept., lundi soir, merc. soir et jeudi. – **Repas** Lunch 25 – 42.

◆ Grosse maison rouge construite juste à la frontière belge. Mise en place soignée sur les tables. Agréable jardin d'hiver.

◆ Restaurant in een groot rood huis dat precies bij de Belgische grens is gebouwd. Met zorg gedekte tafels. Aangename wintertuin.

HELLANGE (HELLÉNG) 717 V 25 – *voir à Frisange.*

HESPERANGE (HESPER) 717 V 25 *et* 716 L 7 – *voir à Luxembourg, environs.*

HOSCHEID (HOUSCHENT) 717 V 23 *et* 716 L 6 – *424 h.*

Luxembourg 42 – Clervaux 19 – Ettelbrück 15 – Vianden 14.

Des Ardennes, Haaptstr. 33, ✉ 9376, ☎ 99 00 77, *info@hotel-des-ardennes.lu, Fax 99 07 19* – TV P. ① MC VISA

fermé 16 déc.-30 janv. – **Repas** Lunch 8 – carte 26 à 41, ♀ – **24 ch** ☐ 76 – ½ P 47/55.

◆ Les habitués ont sans doute déjà fait leur compte : plus de vingt ans ont passé depuis l'apparition de cette enseigne au cœur du village. Chambres fonctionnelles. La salle des repas tient à l'écart des modes son immuable décor rustique.

◆ De vaste gasten weten het ongetwijfeld : al meer dan twintig jaren zijn verstreken sinds dit hotelletje zijn entree maakte midden in het dorp. Functionele kamers. Het duurzame rustieke decor van de eetzaal is door de jaren heen zichzelf gebleven.

HOSTERT (HUESCHERT) 717 W 25 – *voir à Luxembourg, environs.*

HULDANGE (HULDANG) C *Troisvierges 2 520 h.* 717 V 22 *et* 716 L 5.

Luxembourg 75 – Clervaux 22 – Ettelbrück 47.

Knauf avec ch, r. Stavelot 67 (Est : sur N 7), ✉ 9964, ☎ 97 90 56, *Fax 99 75 16,* – ▤ rest, TV P. AE ① MC VISA

fermé lundis non fériés – **Repas** *(fermé après 20 h 30)* (grillades) 22/38 bc – **4 ch** ☐ 30/47.

◆ Chez Knauf, sur le toit du Luxembourg, on peut manger soit au restaurant, soit dans la taverne avec gril bénéficiant d'un décor plus pittoresque. Chambres sobres.

◆ Bij Knauf in het uiterste noorden van Luxemburg kunt u in het restaurant eten of in de taverne met grill, waar het decor wat pittoresker is. Eenvoudige kamers.

JUNGLINSTER (JONGLËNSTER) 717 W 24 *et* 716 L 6 – *5 813 h.*

18 *Domaine de Behlenhaff, 6141,* ☎ *78 00 68, Fax 78 71 28.*

Luxembourg 17 – Echternach 19 – Ettelbrück 27.

Parmentier avec ch, r. Gare 7, ✉ 6117, ☎ 78 71 68, *Fax 78 71 70,* – ▤ rest, TV. MC VISA **Repas** *(fermé 2 sem. en fév., 3 sem. en août, mardi et merc.)* Lunch 9 – 29/49 – **10 ch** *(fermé 3 sem. en août)* ☐ 60/70 – ½ P 60/74.

◆ Maison discrète située au centre de la localité. Des fresques égayent les deux salles de restaurant, claires et amples. Plats variés et alléchants. Chambres rénovées.

◆ Een bescheiden huis in het centrum van het dorp. Fresco's verfraaien de twee restaurantzalen, die licht zijn en ruim. Smakelijke en gevarieerde gerechten. Gerenoveerde kamers.

KAUTENBACH (KAUTEBAACH) 717 V 23 *et* 716 L 6 – *257 h.*

Luxembourg 56 – Clervaux 24 – Ettelbrück 28 – Wiltz 11.

Hatz Maison 24, ✉ 9663, ☎ 95 85 61, *contact@hotel-hatz.lu, Fax 95 81 31,* – rest
13 mars-15 déc. ; fermé merc. et jeudi midi – **Repas** 22/35 – **16 ch** 58/89, – 1 suite – ½ P 58/69.
◆ Au beau milieu d'un minuscule village entouré de forêts, grosse maison à la façade avenante abritant des chambres dont le confort a été récemment amélioré. Les repas sont servis dans une salle de restaurant au charme suranné.
◆ Midden in een gehucht dat wordt omringd door bossen staat dit grote huis met vriendelijk ogende gevel. Het beschikt over kamers waarvan het comfort onlangs is verbeterd. De maaltijden worden geserveerd in een restaurantzaal met ouderwetse charme.

KOPSTAL (KOPLESCHT) 717 V 24 *et* 716 L 7 – *voir à Luxembourg, environs.*

LAROCHETTE (an der FIELS) 717 W 24 *et* 716 L 6 – *1 791 h.*

Voir *à l'Ouest : 5 km, Nommerlayen★.*

Hôtel de Ville, ✉ *7619,* ☎ *83 76 76, info@larochette.lu,* Fax 87 96 46.

Luxembourg 27 – Diekirch 12 – Echternach 20 – Ettelbrück 17 – Arlon 35.

du Château, r. Medernach 1, ✉ 7619, ☎ 83 75 98, *hotelduchateau@msn.com, Fax 87 96 36,* – – 40. AE VISA
Repas *(fermé jeudi en hiver)* (ouvert jusqu'à 23 h) *Lunch 13* – carte 22 à 36, ♀ – **38 ch** 57/69 – ½ P 70/95.
◆ Les ruines du palais des Créhange se dressent derrière cette hostellerie. Chambres claires et assez spacieuses ; les plus récentes se trouvent dans l'annexe.
◆ De ruïne van het kasteel van het geslacht Créhange verrijst achter dit hotel. Lichte kamers die vrij ruim zijn. De nieuwste kamers bevinden zich in de dependance.

Résidence, r. Medernach 14, ✉ 7619, ☎ 83 73 91, *visser@hotels.lu, Fax 87 94 42,* – AE VISA. rest
mars-nov. – **Repas** (dîner seult) carte 25 à 46, ♀ – **20 ch** 63/80 – ½ P 61/65.
◆ Aimable adresse familiale nichée au cœur de Larochette, centre de villégiature de la vallée de l'Ernz Blanche. Les chambres, bien tenues, sont de mise assez simple. Salle des repas au décor néo-rustique un rien mûrissant.
◆ Leuk familiehotel in het hartje van Larochette, een vakantieoord in het dal van de Ernz Blanche. De goed onderhouden kamers zijn tamelijk eenvoudig ingericht. Eetzaal met ietwat overjarig neorustiek decor.

Aub. Op der Bleech avec ch, pl. Bleech 4, ✉ 7610, ☎ 87 80 58, *bleech@pt.lu, Fax 87 97 25,* – VISA
fermé 1er au 17 sept. et 24 déc.-5 janv. – **Repas** *(fermé mardi et merc. hors saison)* carte 22 à 39 – **9 ch** 55/75.
◆ Cette affaire vient de souffler ses dix bougies. Un bar flanque le petit restaurant aux tables dressées avec soin. Grande terrasse d'été. Chambres pratiques.
◆ Deze herberg heeft inmiddels tien kaarsjes uitgeblazen. In het restaurantje zijn de tafels met zorg gedekt. Ernaast bevindt zich een bar. Groot zomerterras. Praktische kamers.

LAUTERBORN (LAUTERBUR) 717 X 24 – *voir à Echternach.*

LIPPERSCHEID (LËPSCHT) C *Bourscheid 1 230 h.* 717 V 23 *et* 716 L 6.

Voir *à l'Est : 2 km et 15 mn AR à pied, Falaise de Grenglay* ≤★★.

Luxembourg 45 – Clervaux 24 – Diekirch 10 – Ettelbrück 18.

Leweck, contrebas E 421, ✉ 9378, ☎ 99 00 22, *cleweck@pt.lu, Fax 99 06 77,* ≤, – 25 à 100. AE VISA
fermé du 1er au 21 mars et du 5 au 18 juil. – **Repas** *(fermé mardi midi)* carte 32 à 49, ♀ – **47 ch** 85/125 – ½ P 75/97.
◆ Chambres personnalisées, soins esthétiques, espace fitness, vue sur la revigorante vallée depuis le jardin arboré et embelli d'une pièce d'eau : un sacré "capital séduction". Salle à manger d'inspiration tyrolienne, revêtue de jolies boiseries.
◆ Hier vindt u karaktervolle kamers, een welness-center met fitness en een park dat uitzicht heeft op het dal. Eetzaal in Tiroler stijl.

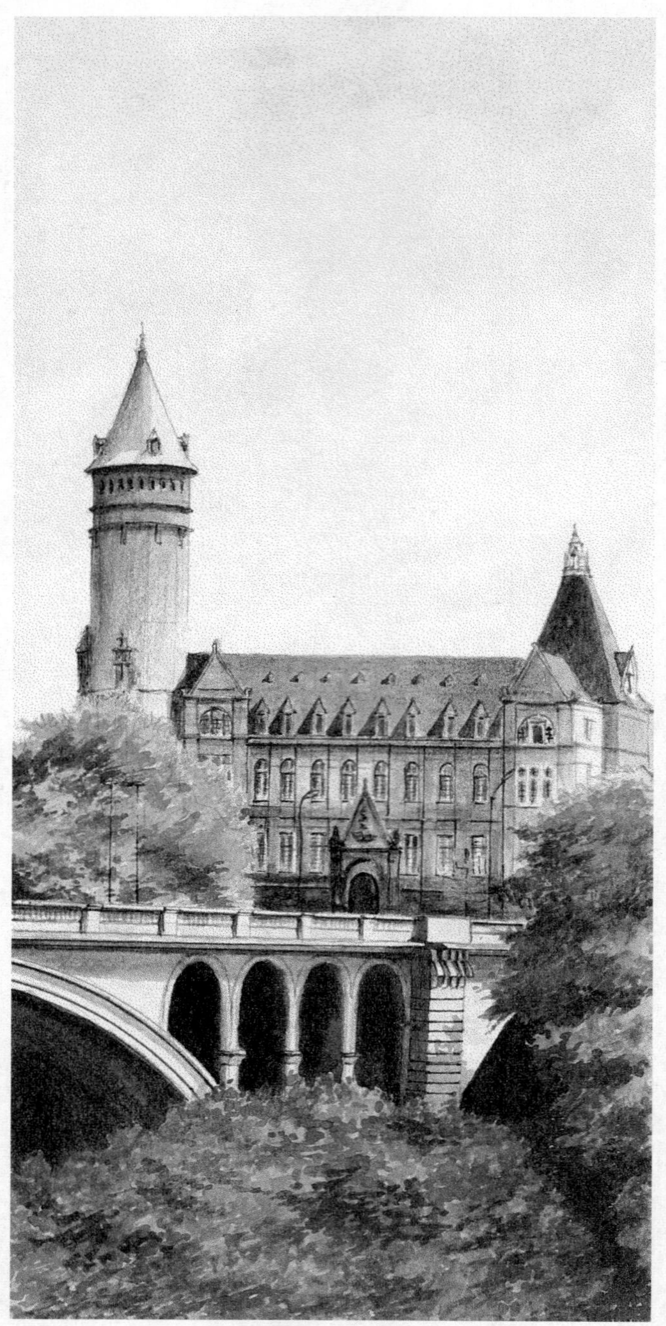

LUXEMBOURG – LËTZEBUERG

717 V 25 et 716 L 7 – *77 965 h.*

Amsterdam 391 ⑧ – Bonn 190 ③ – Bruxelles 219 ⑧.

OFFICES DE TOURISME

pl. d'Armes, ✉ 2011, ☎ 22 28 09, touristinfo@luxembourg-city.lu, Fax 46 70 70
Air Terminus, gare centrale, ✉ 1010, ☎ 42 82 82 20, info@ont.lu. Fax 42 82 82 30.
Aérogare à Findel ☎ 42 82 82 21 info@ont.lu. Fax 42 82 82 30

RENSEIGNEMENTS PRATIQUES

BUREAUX DE CHANGE

La ville de Luxembourg est connue pour la multitude de banques qui y sont représentées, et vous n'aurez donc aucune difficulté à changer de l'argent.

TRANSPORTS

Il est préférable d'emprunter les bus (fréquents) qui desservent quelques parkings périphériques.
Principale compagnie de Taxi : Taxi Colux ☎ 48 22 33, Fax 40 26 80 16.
Transports en commun : Pour toute information ☎ 47 96 29 75, Fax 29 68 08.

COMPAGNIES DE TRANSPORT AÉRIEN

Renseignements départs-arrivées ☎ 47 98 50 50 et 47 98 50 51. Findel par E 44 : 6 km ☎ 42 82 82 21 – Aérogare : pl. de la Gare ☎ 48 11 99.

GOLF

18 *Hoehenhof (Senningerberg) près de l'Aéroport, rte de Trèves 1, ✉ 2633, ☎ 340 00 90, Fax 34 83 91.*

LE SHOPPING

Grand'Rue et rues piétonnières autour de la Place d'Armes F *– Quartier de la Gare* CDZ.

CURIOSITÉS

POINTS DE VUE

Place de la Constitution★★ F *– Plateau St-Esprit*★★ G *– Chemin de la Corniche*★★ G *– Le Bock*★★ G *– Boulevard Victor Thorn*★ G 121 *– Les Trois Glands*★ DY.

MUSÉE

Musée national d'Histoire et d'Art★ *: section gallo-romaine*★ *et section Vie luxembourgeoise (arts décoratifs, arts et traditions populaires)*★★ G **M¹** *– Musée d'Histoire de la Ville de Luxembourg*★ G **M³**.

AUTRES CURIOSITÉS

Les Casemates du Bock★★ G *– Palais Grand-Ducal*★ G *– Cathédrale Notre-Dame*★ F *– Pont Grande-Duchesse Charlotte*★ DY.

ARCHITECTURE MODERNE

Sur le plateau de Kirchberg : Centre Européen DEY.

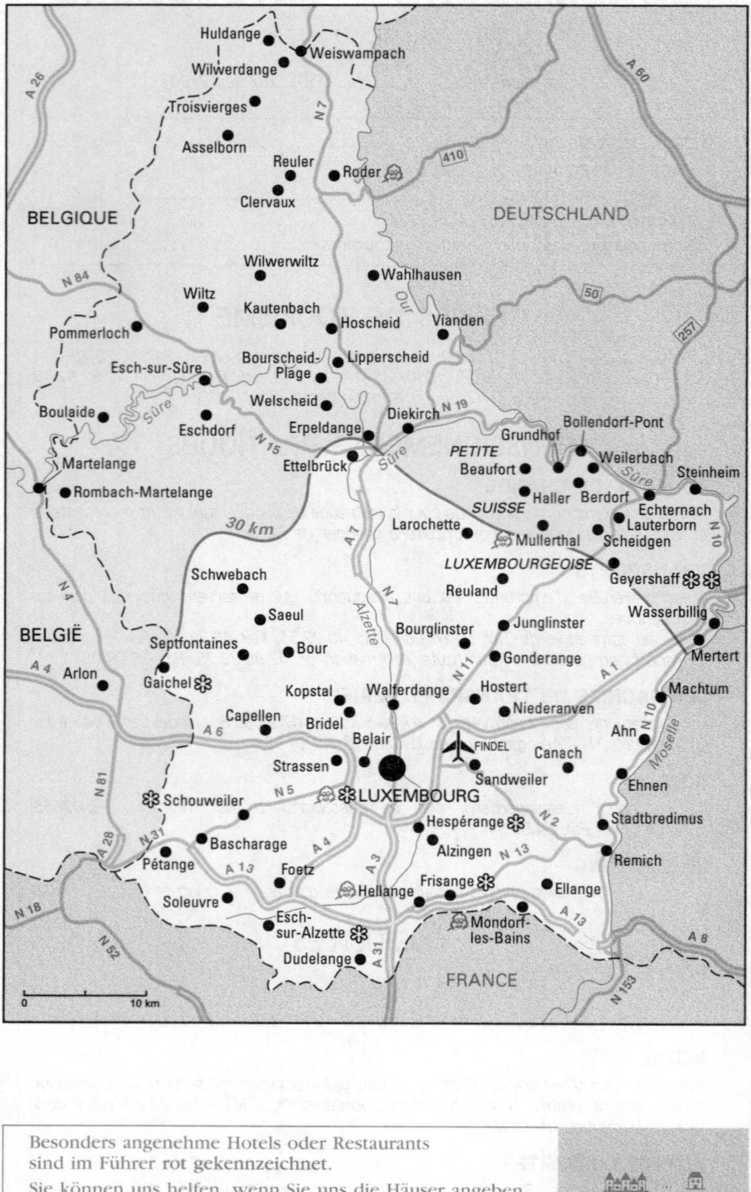

Huldange
Weiswampach
Wilwerdange
A 26
A 60
Troisvierges
N 7
Asselborn
410
Reuler
Roder
Clervaux
BELGIQUE
DEUTSCHLAND
Wilwerwiltz
Wahlhausen
N 84
Our
50
Wiltz
Kautenbach
257
Pommerloch
Hoscheid
Vianden
Bourscheid-Plage
Lipperscheid
Esch-sur-Sûre
Welscheid
Sûre
Boulaide
Eschdorf
Diekirch
N 19
Erpeldange
Bollendorf-Pont
N 15
Grundhof
PETITE
Weilerbach
Ettelbrück
Sûre
Beaufort
Steinheim
Martelange
Sûre
Rombach-Martelange
Haller
Berdorf
SUISSE
Echternach
30 km
A 7
Larochette
Lauterborn
N 10
Mullerthal
Scheidgen
LUXEMBOURGEOISE
Schwebach
Geyershaff
Reuland
N 4
N 7
Wasserbillig
Saeul
Alzette
Junglinster
BELGIË
Bourglinster
Septfontaines
Bour
Mertert
Gonderange
A 4
N 11
A 1
Arlon
Gaichel
Hostert
Machtum
Kopstal
Walferdange
Niederanven
Capellen
N 10
Bridel
Ahn
A 6
Belair
FINDEL
Moselle
Canach
Strassen
Sandweiler
N 81
Ehnen
N 5
LUXEMBOURG
Schouweiler
N 2
Stadtbredimus
Hespérange
A 28
N 31
Bascharage
Alzingen
N 13
A 4
Remich
Pétange
A 13
Foetz
A 3
Frisange
Ellange
N 18
Hellange
Soleuvre
A 13
Esch-sur-Alzette
Mondorf-les-Bains
A 8
N 52
Dudelange
A 31
FRANCE
N 153
0
10 km

Besonders angenehme Hotels oder Restaurants sind im Führer rot gekennzeichnet.

Sie können uns helfen, wenn Sie uns die Häuser angeben, in denen Sie sich besonders wohl gefühlt haben.

Jährlich erscheint eine komplett überarbeitete Ausgabe aller Roten **Michelin-Führer**.

LUXEMBOURG

Rue	Carroyage	N°
Arlon (Rte d')	AV	
Auguste-Charles (R.)	BX	10
Beggen (R. de)	ABV	
Carrefours (R. des)	AV	18
Cents (R.)	BV	19
Cimetière (R. du)	BX	25
Echternach (Rte d')	BV	
Eich (R. d')	BV	36
Guillaume (Av.)	AV	55
Hamm (R. de)	BVX	
Hamm (Val de)	BV	
Hespérange (R. d')	BX	61
Itzig (R. d')	BX	
Kohlenberg	AX	
Kopstal (Rte de)	AV	
Longwy (Rte de)	AVX	
Merl (R. de)	AX	76
Mulhenbach (R. de)	AV	79
Neudorf (R. de)	BV	
Patton (Bd du Général)	BV	86
Rollingergrund (R. de)	AV	102
Strassen (R. de)	AV	112
Thionville (Rte de)	BX	
10-Septembre (Av. du)	AV	127

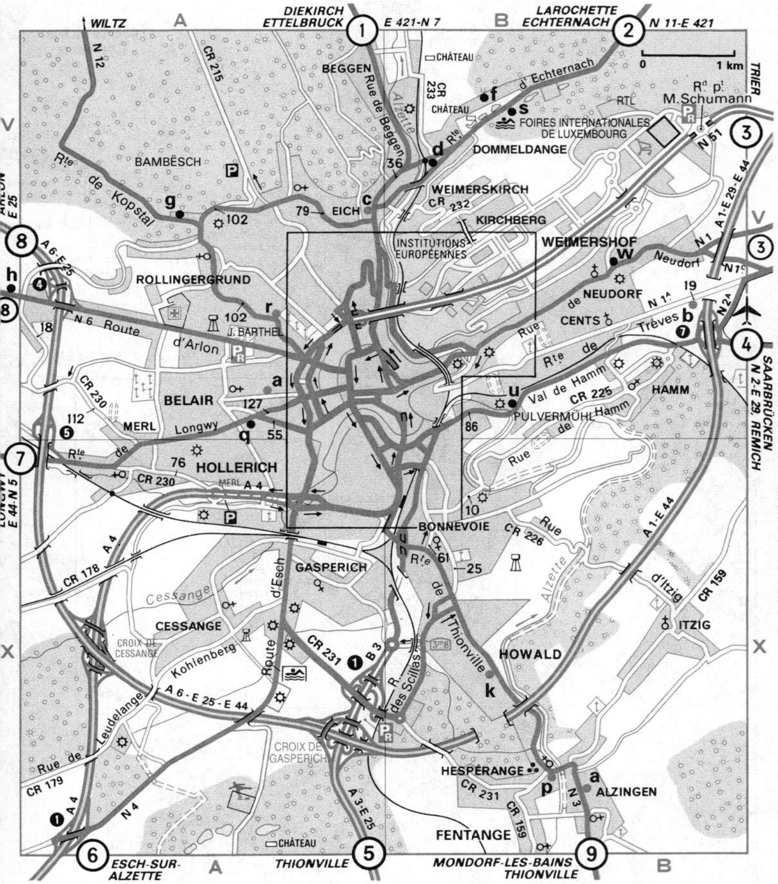

Sur la route :
la signalisation routière est rédigée
dans la langue de la zone linguistique traversée.
Dans ce guide,
les localités sont classées selon leur nom officiel :
Antwerpen pour Anvers, **Mechelen** pour Malines.

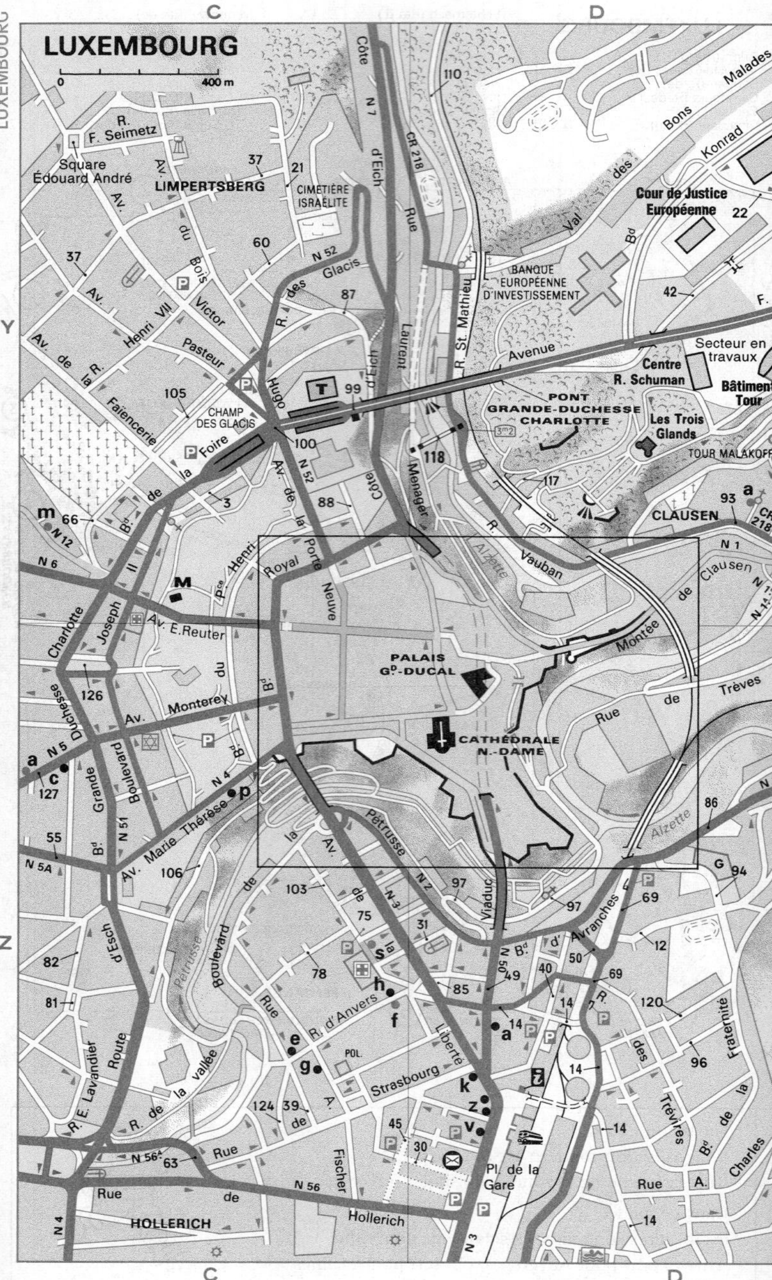
LUXEMBOURG
0
400 m
C
D
Y
Z
R. F. Seimetz
Square Édouard André
LIMPERTSBERG
CIMETIÈRE ISRAÉLITE
Av. du Bois
Av. Victor
Av. Henri VII
Av. Pasteur
Av. de la Faïencerie
R. des Glacis
CHAMP DES GLACIS
Av. de la Porte Neuve
R. Hugo
Côte d'Eich
Rue Laurent Menager
R. St. Mathieu
Val des Bons Malades
Bd Konrad
Cour de Justice Européenne
BANQUE EUROPÉENNE D'INVESTISSEMENT
Avenue
Secteur en travaux
Centre R. Schuman
Bâtiment Tour
PONT GRANDE-DUCHESSE CHARLOTTE
Les Trois Glands
TOUR MALAKOFF
CLAUSEN
Bd de la Foire
Bd Royal
Pce Henri
Av. E.Reuter
R. Vauban
Alzette
Montée de Clausen
PALAIS Gd-DUCAL
CATHÉDRALE N.-DAME
Rue de Trèves
Bd Joseph II
Bd Charlotte
Av. Monterey
Bd du Prince Henri
Bd Grande Duchesse Charlotte
Boulevard
Av. Marie Thérèse
Bd de la Pétrusse
Av. de la Liberté
Bd d'Avranches
Viaduc
Pétrusse
Boulevard de la Pétrusse
Route d'Esch
R. E. Lavandier
R. de la vallée
Rue de Strasbourg
R. d'Anvers
Rue de Hollerich
HOLLERICH
Rue Fischer
R. des Trèvires
Bd de la Charles
Pl. de la Gare
Rue A.
POL.
N 7
N 52
CR 218
N 12
N 6
N 1
N 5
N 4
N 51
N 5A
N 2
N 3
N 56
N 564
N 50
T
M
G
F.
3m2
110 37 21 60 87 99 105 100 118 117 88 3 66 93 22 42 126 127 55 106 103 97 75 31 78 85 49 40 50 69 12 120 96 14 86 94 82 81 124 39 45 30 63
a c m p s h f e g k z v

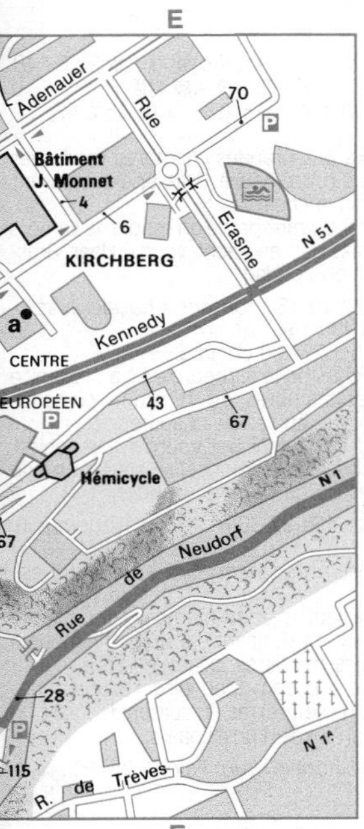

Adames (R.) .... CY 3
Albert-Wehrer (R.) ...... EY 4
Alcide-de-Gasperi (R.) ... EY 6
Aldringen (R.) .... F 7
Athénée (R. de l'Ancien). F 9
Auguste-Lumière (R.) .... DZ 12
Bains (R. des) .... F 13
Bonnevoie (R. de) ...... DZ 14
Boucherie (R. de la) .... G 15
Bruxelles (Pl. de) .... F 16
Capucins (R. des) ...... F
Cerisiers (R. des) .... CY 21
Charles-Léon-Hammes (R.) .... DY 22
Chimay (R.) .... F 24
Clairefontaine (Pl.) ...... FG 27
Clausen (R. de) .... EY 28
Commerce (R. du) ..... CDZ 30
Curé (R. du) .... F
Dicks (R.) .... CDZ 31
Eau (R. de l') .... G 33
Ermesinde (R.) .... CY 37
Etats-Unis (R. des) ..... CZ 39
Fort Neipperg (R. du) ... DZ 40
Fort Niedergrünewald (R. du) .... DY 42
Fort Thüngen (R. du) .... EY 43
Fort Wedell (R. du) ..... CDZ 45
Fossé (R. du) .... F 46
Franklin-Roosevelt (Bd) .. F 48
Gare (Av. de la) .... DZ 49
Gaulle (Av. du Gén.-de) . DZ 50
Grand-Rue .... F
Guillaume (Av.) .... CZ 55
Guillaume-Schneider (R.) .... CY 60
Jean-Baptiste-Merkels (R.) .... CZ 63
Jean-Ulveling (Bd) ...... FG 64
J.P.-Probst (R.) .... CY 66
Jules-Wilhem (R.) .... EY 67
Laboratoire (R. du) ..... DZ 69
Léon-Hengen (R.) .... EY 70
Liberté (Av. de la) ...... CDZ
Marché (Pl. du) .... G 72
Marché-aux-Herbes (R. du) .... FG 73
Martyrs (Pl. des) .... CZ 75
Michel-Rodange (R.) .... CZ 78
Münster (R.) .... G 79
Nancy (Pl. de) .... CZ 81
Nassau (R. de) .... CZ 82
Notre-Dame (R.) .... F 84
Paris (Pl. de) .... DZ 85
Patton (Bd du Général) ..... DZ 86
Paul-Eyschen (R.) ...... CY 87
Pescatore (Av.) .... CY 88
Pfaffenthal (Montée de) .... FG 90
Philippe-II (R.) .... F 91
Pierre-de-Mansfeld (Allée) .... DY 93
Pierre-et-Marie-Curie (R.) .... DZ 94
Pierre-Hentges (R.) ..... DZ 96
Porte-Neuve (Av. de la) .... CY
Prague (R. de) .... DZ 97
Robert-Schuman (Bd) .. CY 99
Robert-Schuman (Rond-Point) .... CY 100
Sainte-Zithe (R.) .... CZ 103
Scheffer (Allée) .... CY 105
Semois (R. de la) ...... CZ 106
Sigefroi (R.) .... G 108
Sosthène Weis (R.) .... G 109
Stavelot (R. de) .... DY 110
Strasbourg (R. de) .... CDZ
Théâtre (Pl. du) .... F 114
Tour Jacob (Av. de la) .... EY 115
Trois-Glands (R. des) ... DY 117
Vauban (Pont) .... DY 118
Verger (R. du) .... DZ 120
Victor-Thorn (Bd) ...... G 121
Willy-Georgen (R.) ..... F 123
Wilson (R.) .... CZ 124
Winston-Churchill (Pl.) .. CZ 126
10-Septembre (Av. du) . CZ 127

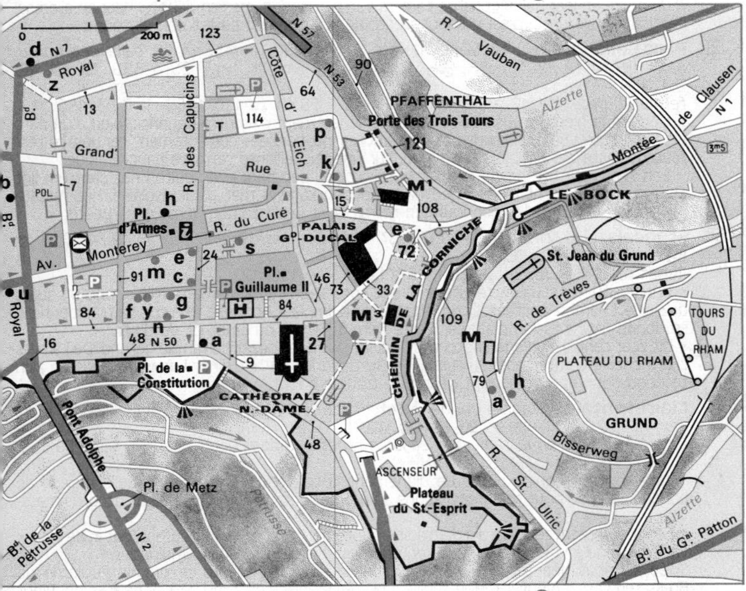

LUXEMBOURG

Luxembourg-Centre - *plan p. 5 sauf indication spéciale :*

Le Royal, bd Royal 12, ✉ 2449, ☎ 241 61 61, *reservations@hotelroyal.lu, Fax 22 59 48,* – 25 à 350. AE ⓓ ⓜⓒ VISA F d
Repas voir rest ***La Pomme Cannelle*** ci-après – ***Le Jardin*** *Lunch 25* – carte 36 à 47, ♀ – ☕ 24 – **185 ch** 330/460, – 20 suites.
◆ En plein "Wall Street" luxembourgeois, hôtel de luxe aux grandes chambres modernes royalement équipées. Service complet et personnalisé à toute heure. Brasserie-restaurant au cadre méditerranéen. Formule lunch-buffets les dimanches.
◆ Luxehotel in het hart van het Luxemburgse "Wall Street", met grote en moderne kamers die van alle gemakken zijn voorzien. Het personeel staat dag en nacht voor u klaar. Brasserie-restaurant met mediterrane sfeer. Lunchbuffet op zondag.

Gd H. Cravat, bd Roosevelt 29, ✉ 2450, ☎ 22 19 75, *contact@hotelcravat.lu, Fax 22 67 11* – rest, – 25. AE ⓓ ⓜⓒ VISA. ch F a
Repas *(fermé août)* (taverne-rest) *Lunch 12* – 35/65 bc, ♀ – **60 ch** ☕ 235/275.
◆ Petit palace classique installé à l'ombre des fines flèches de la cathédrale et à proximité de la zone piétonne. Ameublement bourgeois dans les chambres. Au 1er étage, plaisante table classico-traditionnelle et taverne-restaurant cossue au rez-de-chaussée.
◆ Klein en klassiek luxehotel aan de voet van de kathedraal, vlak bij het voetgangersgebied. Kamers met ameublement in bourgeoisstijl. Plezierig klassiek-traditioneel restaurant op de eerste verdieping en een schitterend café-restaurant op de begane grond.

Domus, av. Monterey 37, ✉ 2163, ☎ 467 87 81 et 467 87 88 (rest), *info@domus.lu, Fax 46 78 79,* –. AE ⓜⓒ VISA. F u
Repas *le sot l'y laisse* *(fermé 3 sem. en août, 2 dern. sem. déc., sam., dim. et jours fériés),* ♀ – ☕ 11 – **38 ch** 115/131.
◆ "Flat-hôtel" contemporain dont les chambres, spacieuses et modernes, sont toutes munies d'une kitchenette bien équipée. Brasserie-restaurant donnant sur un jardin meublé et sa terrasse. Carte traditionnelle. Exposition de toiles d'artistes locaux en salle.
◆ Modern flathotel met ruime, moderne kamers die alle een goed uitgeruste kitchenette hebben. Het café-restaurant kijkt uit op de tuin met terras. Traditionele kaart. In de eetzaal is een expositie te zien van schilderijen van lokale kunstenaars.

Rix sans rest, bd Royal 20, ✉ 2449, ☎ 47 16 66, *rixhotel@vo.lu, Fax 22 75 35,* – ⓜⓒ VISA. F b
fermé 19 déc.-3 janv. – **21 ch** ☕ 152/175.
◆ Coquettes et identiques, toutes les chambres de ce plaisant établissement familial ont leur propre balcon. La salle des petits-déjeuners "en impose". Précieux parking privé.
◆ De nette en identiek ingerichte kamers van dit aangename familiehotel hebben allemaal een balkon. De ontbijtzaal is imponerend, de privéparking beslist een pluspunt.

Parc-Belle-Vue, av. Marie-Thérèse 5, ✉ 2132, ☎ 456 14 11, *bellevue@hpb.lu, Fax 456 14 12 22,* – – 25 à 350. AE ⓓ ⓜⓒ VISA JCB plan p. 4 CZ p
fermé 20 déc.-1er janv. – **Repas** 30/38 bc, ♀ – **58 ch** ☕ 110/125 – ½ P 83/155.
◆ L'enseigne n'est pas usurpée : cet hôtel légèrement excentré bénéficie bien d'un parc et d'une belle vue, mais surtout de chambres insonorisées correctement tenues. Le restaurant invite à s'attabler, l'été venu, sur une accueillante terrasse panoramique.
◆ Een zeer terechte naam voor dit hotel, dat bij een park even buiten het centrum ligt en een mooi uitzicht biedt. Goed onderhouden kamers met geluidsisolatie. Het restaurant heeft een gezellig, panoramisch terras waar in de zomer wordt geserveerd.

Français, pl. d'Armes 14, ✉ 1136, ☎ 47 45 34, *hfinfo@pt.lu, Fax 46 42 74,* – – 30. AE ⓓ ⓜⓒ VISA F h
Repas *Lunch 11* – 26, ♀ – **21 ch** ☕ 97/125 – ½ P 116/122.
◆ Bonne situation au centre-ville pour cet hôtel tenu par la même famille depuis un quart de siècle. Chambres actuelles confortables et d'ampleur honnête. Une cuisine traditionnelle se donne pour mission d'apaiser votre faim à l'heure du lunch et du dîner.
◆ Dit zeer centraal gelegen hotel wordt al 25 jaar door dezelfde familie gerund. De kamers zijn modern, comfortabel en ruim. Tijdens de lunch en het diner kunnen de gasten zich te goed doen aan gerechten waarin de traditie hoogtij viert.

XXXX ✿ **Clairefontaine** (Magnier), pl. de Clairefontaine 9, ✉ 1341, ☎ 46 22 11, *clairefo@pt.lu, Fax 47 08 21,* – AE ⓓ ⓜⓒ VISA G v
fermé 3 sem. en août, sam., dim. et jours fériés – **Repas** *Lunch 60 bc* – 67, carte 59 à 92.
◆ Une nouvelle équipe perpétue dignement la tradition de cette très belle maison de bouche estimée pour ses préparations au goût du jour et ses harmonieux accords mets-vins.
◆ Een nieuw team zet waardig de traditie voort in dit prachtige restaurant, dat in de smaak valt vanwege zijn eigentijdse keuken en harmonieuze wijn-spijscombinaties.
Spéc. Gambas géantes croustillantes au chou-fleur et crème citronnée. Poularde de Bresse en vessie Albufera. Mille-feuille à la crème anisée et céleri vert. **Vins** Riesling, Pinot blanc

XXX **Le Bouquet Garni Salon Saint Michel** (Duhr), r. Eau 32, ✉ 1449, ☎ 26 20 06 20, *Fax 26 20 09 11* – AE ⓓ ⓜⓒ VISA G e
✿ *fermé sem. Toussaint, 23 déc.-7 janv., sam. midi, dim. et lundi midi* – **Repas** *Lunch 38 bc* – 50/70, carte 54 à 78, ♀.
◆ Table au cadre rustique élégant, dans une rue longeant le palais Grand-Ducal. Plats classiques revisités par petites touches, menu dégustation et desserts affriolants.
◆ Elegant rustiek restaurant in een straat waar ook het Groothertogelijk paleis staat. Klassieke gerechten met een snufje modern, degustatiemenu en verrukkelijke desserts.
Spéc. Salade tiède de pommes de terre de Noirmoutier et homard rôti. Gibier en saison. Pêche rôtie au basilic et caramel, glace à la vanille (juil.-sept.). **Vins** Vin de la Barrique, Riesling

XXX **Speltz,** r. Chimay 8, ✉ 1333, ☎ 47 49 50, *info@restaurant-speltz.lu, Fax 47 46 77*, 🏠 – AE ⓓ ⓜⓒ VISA F c
✿ *fermé 23 fév., du 3 au 12 avril, du 20 au 23 mai, du 14 au 30 août, 24 déc.-2 janv., sam. midi, dim. et jours fériés* – **Repas** *Lunch 40* – 49/99 bc, carte 51 à 70, ♀.
◆ Dans une salle à manger non dénuée de raffinement, savoureuse cuisine d'aujourd'hui magnifiée par une cave représentative du vignoble luxembourgeois.
◆ In een verfijnde eetzaal worden smakelijke eigentijdse gerechten geserveerd en opgeluisterd door een representatieve selectie van Luxemburgse wijnen.
Spéc. Carpaccio de homard et aïoli froid de courgettes. Gibier en saison. Croquant de fraises au poivre noir et sorbet à la menthe (juin-sept.). **Vins** Pinot gris, Riesling Koeppchen

XXX **La Pomme Cannelle** - H. Le Royal, bd Royal 12, ✉ 2449, ☎ 241 61 67 36, *reservations@hotelroyal.lu, Fax 22 59 48* – ▤ P. AE ⓓ ⓜⓒ VISA. ✂ F d
fermé sam. midi, dim. et jours fériés – **Repas** *Lunch 45* – 65/120 bc, ♀ 🍇.
◆ Le restaurant du Royal interprète un registre original où les épices du Nouveau Monde sont à l'honneur. Intérieur à la fois chic et chaleureux, évoquant l'Empire des Indes.
◆ Dit restaurant biedt origineel culinair genot met het geurige accent van specerijen uit nieuwe werelden. Het chique en warme interieur ademt de sfeer van het Indische Rijk.

XXX **Jan Schneidewind,** r. Curé 20, ✉ 1368, ☎ 22 26 18, *info@schneidewind.lu, Fax 46 24 40*, 🏠 – AE ⓓ ⓜⓒ VISA F s
fermé sam. midi, dim. midi et lundi – **Repas** *Lunch 40* – 85, ♀.
◆ Une appétissante carte de saison vous sera soumise dans ce restaurant coincé entre les places d'Armes et Guillaume II. Les murs bruts de la salle s'égayent de toiles modernes.
◆ In dit restaurant tussen de Place d'Armes en de Place Guillaume II wacht u een heerlijke seizoenkaart. Aan de ruwe muren van de eetzaal hangen moderne schilderijen.

XX **La Lorraine** 1er étage, pl. d'Armes 7, ✉ 1136, ☎ 47 14 36, *lorraine@pt.lu, Fax 47 09 64*, 🏠, Avec écailler et produits de la mer – ▤. AE ⓓ ⓜⓒ VISA F e
fermé dim. – **Repas** carte 58 à 66, ♀.
◆ Belle maison sur la place d'Armes. Cuisine du terroir et banc d'écailler en saison au rez-de-chaussée ; repas gastronomique au goût du jour dans une salle Art déco à l'étage.
◆ Mooi pand aan de Place d'Armes. Beneden : streekgerechten en oesterbar in het seizoen. Boven : actuele gastronomische gerechten in een art deco-zaal.

XX **L'Océan,** r. Louvigny 7, ✉ 1946, ☎ 22 88 66, *braunpatrick@hotmail.com, Fax 22 88 67*, 🏠, Écailler et produits de la mer – ▤. AE ⓓ ⓜⓒ VISA F f
fermé du 5 au 25 juil., 26 déc.-11 janv., dim. soir et lundi – **Repas** 39, ♀.
◆ L'enseigne, comme le banc d'écailler installé à l'entrée, sont explicites : on choisit cette table pour son bel éventail de produits de la mer accompagné de vins blancs.
◆ De naam en de oesterbank bij de ingang zeggen genoeg : hier treedt u een wereld binnen waar heerlijke producten van de zee worden vergezeld van passende witte wijnen.

X **Caves Gourmandes,** r. Eau 32, ✉ 1449, ☎ 46 11 24, *lescaves@pt.lu, Fax 46 11 24*, 🏠 – ▤. AE ⓜⓒ VISA G e
fermé sam. midi et dim. – **Repas** *Lunch 20* – carte 35 à 52, ♀.
◆ Dans une ruelle pittoresque de la vieille ville, restaurant de terroir vouant la plupart de ses recettes à l'Aquitaine. Ancienne cave voûtée convertie en salle à manger.
◆ Dit eethuis in een pittoresk straatje in de oude stad staat in het teken van de streekgerechten, de meeste uit Aquitanië. Eetruimte in een oude, gewelfde kelder.

X **la fourchette à droite,** av. Monterey 5, ✉ 2163, ☎ 22 13 60, *Fax 22 24 95*, 🏠 – AE ⓓ ⓜⓒ VISA F m
fermé sam. midi et dim. – **Repas** *Lunch 19* – 26/46 bc, ♀.
◆ Une clientèle variée se presse à cette avenante adresse située au cœur de l'animation. La carte annonce un sage petit lunch. Salle façon "brasserie", parée de bois blond.
◆ Een zeer gemêleerde klantenkring verdringt zich in dit gezellige eethuis midden in het drukke centrum. Op de kaart een degelijke kleine lunch. Eetzaal in brasseriestijl.

X **Wengé,** r. Louvigny 15, ✉ 1946, ☎ 26 20 10 58, *wenge@vo.lu, Fax 26 20 12 59,* – AE MC VISA F y
fermé du 12 au 19 avril, du 15 au 31 août, du 1er au 11 janv. et dim. – **Repas** *Lunch 28* – 35/75 bc, ♀.
◆ L'essence de wengé - un précieux bois exotique - prête son nom à cette table bien dans l'air du temps. Intime salle à manger où dominent des tons pourpres. Mets à la page.
◆ Dit moderne restaurant is genoemd naar het kostbare tropisch hardhout wengé. In de intieme eetzaal voeren purpertinten de boventoon. De kookstijl is up-to-date.

X **Roma,** r. Louvigny 5, ✉ 1946, ☎ 22 36 92, *Fax 22 04 96,* , Cuisine italienne – . AE MC VISA F g
fermé dim. soir et lundi – **Repas** carte 29 à 53.
◆ Établissement italien où deux cartes distinctes - suggestions et recettes plus conventionnelles - s'emploient à satisfaire votre faim. Pâtes faites "maison". Vins de là-bas.
◆ Italiaans eethuis met twee aparte kaarten - menusuggesties en meer conventionele gerechten - om uw honger te stillen. Pasta's van het huis, wijnen van daarginds.

X **Chiggeri,** 1er étage, r. Nord 15, ✉ 2229, ☎ 22 99 36, *chiggeri@pt.lu, Fax 22 81 35,* – AE MC VISA F p
Repas *Lunch 25* – 65/100 bc, ♀.
◆ Surprenant décor "néo-baroque" dans cette imposante maison du 19e s. Carte de saison aux influences méditerranéennes et plats végétariens. Ambiance détendue. Jardin d'hiver.
◆ Verrassend neobarok decor in dit imposante 19e-eeuwse huis. Seizoenkaart met mediterrane invloeden en vegetarische schotels. Ontspannen ambiance. Wintertuin.

X **Thai Céladon,** r. Nord 1, ✉ 2229, ☎ 47 49 34, *Fax 47 49 34,* Cuisine thaïlandaise – AE MC VISA. FG k
fermé sam. midi et dim. – **Repas** *Lunch 18* – 46.
◆ Ce restaurant exotique du centre tient son nom d'un vernis précieux utilisé par les potiers thaïs. Salle élégante et épurée. Cuisine thaïlandaise avec plats végétariens.
◆ Dit exotische restaurant is genoemd naar een glazuur dat door Thaise pottenbakkers wordt gebruikt. Smaakvol ingerichte eetzaal. Thaise keuken met vegetarische gerechten.

X **La Table de François,** bd Royal 25, ✉ 2449, ☎ 46 58 88, – MC VISA F z
fermé 21 août-5 sept., 24 déc.-3 janv., mardi soir, sam. midi, dim. et jours fériés – **Repas** *Lunch 13* – carte 33 à 59, ♀.
◆ Établissement d'esprit "bistrot actuel" où François vous concocte une cuisine du marché, aussi simple que naturelle. Choix à l'écriteau et formule lunch.
◆ Eethuis in moderne bistrostijl, waar François eenvoudige maar eerlijke gerechten bereidt met dagverse producten van de markt. Suggesties op een schoolbord en lunchformule.

X **Yamayu Santatsu,** r. Notre-Dame 26, ✉ 2240, ☎ 46 12 49, *Fax 46 05 71,* Cuisine japonaise avec Sushi-bar – AE MC VISA F n
fermé 3 prem. sem. août, Noël-prem. sem. janv., dim. midi, lundi et jours fériés midis – **Repas** *Lunch 14* – 28/39.
◆ Les délicatesses du pays des samouraïs vous tentent ? Ce restaurant japonais au décor épuré vous attend à 200 m de la cathédrale. Sushi bar et choix typique varié. Banzaï !
◆ Houdt u van gerechten uit het land van de samoerai ? Probeer dan dit verfijnde Japanse restaurant vlak bij de kathedraal. Sushibar en gevarieerde menukaart. Banzai !

Luxembourg-Grund - *plan p. 5 :*

XXXX ✿ **Mosconi,** r. Münster 13, ✉ 2160, ☎ 54 69 94, *Fax 54 00 43,* , Cuisine italienne – AE MC VISA G a
fermé 1 sem. Pâques, du 9 au 30 août, 24 déc.-3 janv., dim., lundi et jours fériés – **Repas** *Lunch 34* – 40, carte 60 à 76.
◆ Ancienne maison de notable en bord d'Alzette. Salon accueillant et ristorante au luxe discret où l'on goûte une fine cuisine italienne. Jolie terrasse près de l'eau.
◆ Voormalig patriciërshuis aan de oever van de Alzette. Sfeervolle salon, luxueus restaurant met ingetogen ambiance en terras bij het water. Fijne Italiaanse keuken.
Spéc. Pâté de foie de poulet à la crème de truffes blanches. Risotto aux truffes blanches (oct.-déc.). Arista au Chianti (côte de porc)

X **Kamakura,** r. Münster 4, ✉ 2160, ☎ 47 06 04, *kamakura@pe.lu, Fax 46 73 30,* Cuisine japonaise – AE MC VISA. G h
fermé 3 sem. en août, jours fériés midis, sam. midi et dim. – **Repas** *Lunch 10* – 25/63 bc.
◆ Ambiance "zen" et cadre design pour cette table japonaise sans concessions à l'Occident. Bon sushi bar et menus fidèles aux coutumes nippones. Une valeur sûre.
◆ Ambiance "zen" en designdecor voor dit concessieloze Japanse restaurant. Goede sushibar en menu's die de Japanse tradities trouw blijven. Een prima optie !

Luxembourg-Gare - *plan p. 4* :

Gd H. Mercure Alfa, pl. de la Gare 16, ✉ 1616, ☎ 490 01 11, *H2058@accor-hotels.com, Fax 49 00 09* - |‡| ⇹ ▤ TV - 🏛 25 à 80. AE ⓓ MC VISA. ⚘ rest DZ z
Repas (brasserie) *Lunch 18* - carte 26 à 50 - ☕ 18 - **140 ch** 170/215, - 1 suite.
◆ Commode pour l'usager du rail, cet hôtel de chaîne réaménagé abrite des chambres agréables où vous trouverez le sommeil du juste. Une ambiance de brasserie parisienne flotte dans le restaurant Art déco. Carte "touche-à-tout". Banc d'écailler.
◆ Dit gerenoveerde hotel is ideaal voor treinreizigers en beschikt over aangename kamers die garant staan voor een ongestoorde nachtrust. Het art-decorestaurant ademt de sfeer van een Parijse brasserie. De menukaart is een beetje "van alles wat". Oesterbar.

President sans rest, pl. de la Gare 32, ✉ 1024, ☎ 48 61 61, *president@pt.lu, Fax 48 61 80* - |‡| ⇹ ▤ TV P - 🏛 30. AE ⓓ MC VISA DZ v
42 ch ☕ 130/160.
◆ Ce bel hôtel au luxe discret situé juste devant la gare renferme de confortables chambres rénovées et meublées avec goût.
◆ Dit mooie hotel met zijn nonchalante luxe bij het station beschikt over gerenoveerde comfortabele kamers die smaakvol zijn ingericht.

City sans rest, r. Strasbourg 1, ✉ 2561, ☎ 291 12 21, *mail@cityhotel.lu, Fax 29 11 33* - |‡| TV 🚗 - 🏛 25 à 80. AE ⓓ MC VISA DZ k
35 ch ☕ 110/154.
◆ Immeuble ancien bénéficiant d'installations intérieures modernes. Vastes chambres où rien ne manque, au décor sagement personnalisé. Accueil et service attentionnés.
◆ Een oud pand met moderne voorzieningen. Grote kamers met een eigen karakter en waar het aan niets ontbreekt. Attente ontvangst en service.

Christophe Colomb (annexe Marco Polo - 18 ch) sans rest, r. Anvers 10, ✉ 1130, ☎ 408 41 41, *mail@christophe-colomb.lu, Fax 40 84 08* - |‡| TV - 🏛 25. AE ⓓ MC VISA CZ h
24 ch ☕ 144/154.
◆ À 500 m de la gare, petit hôtel idéal pour les voyageurs du rail, n'en déplaise aux "grands navigateurs". Chambres standard assez spacieuses, garnies d'un mobilier actuel.
◆ Met alle respect voor de "grote zeevaarders" is dit een ideaal hotelletje voor treingebruikers, op 500 m van het station. Vrij ruime standaardkamers met modern meubilair.

International, pl. de la Gare 20, ✉ 1616, ☎ 48 59 11, *info@hotelinter.lu, Fax 49 32 27* - |‡| ⇹, ▤ rest, TV - 🏛 25 à 50. AE ⓓ MC VISA DZ z
Repas *(fermé 23 déc.-9 janv. et sam. midi) Lunch 18* - 26/40 bc - **67 ch** ☕ 112/137, - 1 suite - ½ P 107/130.
◆ Immeuble récemment rénové faisant face à la gare. Les chambres, avenantes et confortables, disposent des connexions pour modem et fax. Salon Internet. Intime salle de restaurant revêtue de boiseries. Menu à prix plancher.
◆ Recentelijk gerenoveerd pand tegenover het station. De vriendelijke en comfortabele kamers hebben een modem- en faxaansluiting. Internetruimte. Intieme restaurantzaal die met lambrisering is bekleed. Menu tegen een bodemprijs.

Le Châtelet (annexe 🏠 - 9 ch) sans rest, bd de la Pétrusse 2, ✉ 2320, ☎ 40 21 01, *contact@chatelet.lu, Fax 40 36 66* - |‡| TV. AE ⓓ MC VISA CZ e
36 ch ☕ 89/120.
◆ Cet hôtel surveillant la vallée de la Pétrusse regroupe plusieurs maisons dont l'une est flanquée une fine tourelle. Mobilier en sapin dans les chambres, bien insonorisées.
◆ Dit hotel kijkt uit over het Pétrusse-dal en omvat diverse huizen waarvan één met een rank torentje. Kamers met goede geluidsisolatie en ingericht met sparrenhouten meubilair.

Nobilis, av. de la Gare 47, ✉ 1611, ☎ 49 49 71, *info@hotel-nobilis.com, Fax 40 31 01* - |‡| ▤ TV - 🏛 50. AE ⓓ MC VISA DZ a
Repas *Lunch 17* - carte env. 22 - ☕ 15 - **46 ch** 115.
◆ Nombreuses rénovations dans ce building situé à mi-chemin entre la gare et le viaduc qui vous conduit à la vieille ville. Chambres fonctionnelles munies du double vitrage.
◆ Er zijn veel renovatiewerkzaamheden uitgevoerd in dit gebouw halverwege het station en het viaduct naar de oude stad. Functionele kamers met dubbele beglazing.

Delta, r. Ad. Fischer 74, ✉ 1521, ☎ 493 09 61, *info@hoteldelta.lu, Fax 40 43 20,* ☂, ⇌s - |‡| TV P - 🏛 25. AE ⓓ MC VISA CZ g
fermé 14 août-6 sept. et 24 déc.-3 janv. - **Repas** *(fermé sam., dim., lundi soir et jours fériés) Lunch 14* - 35, 𝕐 - **16 ch** ☕ 82/135, - 3 suites - ½ P 102/125.
◆ Trois petites maisons mitoyennes à l'écart de l'animation forment cet établissement familial engageant. Chambres mignonnes garnies d'un mobilier de qualité. Aux beaux jours, repas en plein air sur la terrasse ombragée.
◆ Drie aangrenzende, kleine huizen weg van de drukte vormen dit aantrekkelijke familiehotel. Genoeglijke kamers die met kwaliteitsmeubilair zijn ingericht. Bij mooi weer kan er buiten op het lommerrijke terras worden gegeten.

Arpège, r. Sainte Zithe 29, ✉ 2763, ☎ 48 88 08, *restaurantlarpege@msm.com, Fax 48 88 20*, – ▤. AE ⓓ MC VISA CZ s
fermé 2e quinz. août, fin déc.-prem. sem. janv. et dim. – **Repas** *Lunch 20* – carte 29 à 44, ♀.
◆ Dans une rue piétonne du plateau Bourbon. Choix classique, incluant un menu simple et un autre plus élaboré. Salle à manger ornée de toiles contemporaines. Confort "rotin".
◆ In een voetgangersstraat op het Plateau Bourbon. Klassieke kaart en een eenvoudig plus een verfijnd menu. Eetzaal met hedendaagse schilderijen en rotanmeubelen.

Italia avec ch, r. Anvers 15, ✉ 1130, ☎ 486 62 61, *italia@euro.lu, Fax 48 08 07*, , Avec cuisine italienne – TV. AE ⓓ MC VISA CZ f
Repas carte 32 à 46 – **20 ch** ☕ 68/88.
◆ Table transalpine misant sur une longue carte avec suggestions. Cave italo-française et vins de Moselle. Dîner aux chandelles en musique les vendredis de septembre à juin.
◆ Italiaans restaurant met een uitgebreide kaart en menusuggesties. Frans-Italiaanse wijnselectie en Moezelwijnen. September-juni diner bij kaarslicht en vrijdagavond muziek.

Périphérie - *plan p. 3 sauf indication spéciale :*

à l'Aéroport *par ③ : 8 km :*

Sheraton Aérogolf , rte de Trèves 1, ✉ 1019, ☎ 34 05 71, *Fax 34 02 17* – ▤ TV P – 25 à 120. AE ⓓ MC VISA
Repas ***Le Montgolfier*** (ouvert jusqu'à minuit) *Lunch 35* – carte 40 à 63, ♀ – ☕ 20 – **147 ch** 209/340, – 1 suite.
◆ Chambres tout confort, luxe sans tape-à-l'œil, insonorisation optimale et service "nickel", comme il se doit dans un hôtel haut de gamme. En prime : la vue sur les pistes. Salle de restaurant actuelle pourvue d'un mobilier inspiré des siècles passés.
◆ Comfortabele kamers, nonchalante luxe, uitstekende geluidsisolatie en optimale service ; echt een tophotel. Het uitzicht op de landingsbaan krijgt u er gratis bij. Het meubilair in de eigentijdse eetzaal is op vroegere eeuwen geïnspireerd.

Ibis, rte de Trèves, ✉ 2632, ☎ 43 88 01, *H0974@accor-hotels.com, Fax 43 88 02*, , – ▤ TV P – 25 à 80. AE ⓓ MC VISA
Repas *Lunch 10* – carte 22 à 41 – ☕ 10 – **120 ch** 80/90.
◆ Établissement de chaîne aux communs assez avenants pour la catégorie. Les chambres, d'ampleur limitée, offrent le niveau de confort habituel à l'enseigne. Annexe "low-budget". Une rotonde vitrée abrite le restaurant.
◆ Dit hotel heeft voor zijn klasse vrij aangename gemeenschappelijke ruimten. De kamers zijn niet al te groot, maar bieden het comfort dat voor deze hotelketen gebruikelijk is. Dependance low budget. Een ronde zaal met glazen wand herbergt het restaurant.

Campanile, rte de Trèves 22, ✉ 2633, ☎ 34 95 95, *luxembourg@campanile.com, Fax 34 94 95*, – TV P – 25 à 90. AE ⓓ MC VISA
Repas (avec buffets) *Lunch 14* – 22 – ☕ 10 – **108 ch** 77 – ½ P 88/114.
◆ Hôtel occupant un immeuble récent. On accède par l'intérieur aux petites chambres avec double vitrage, garnies d'un mobilier assez simple. Accueil à toute heure.
◆ Hotel in een nieuw gebouw. De kleine kamers met dubbele ramen zijn vrij eenvoudig gemeubileerd en binnendoor toegankelijk. De receptie is dag en nacht open.

Trust Inn sans rest, r. Neudorf 679 (par rte de Trèves), ✉ 2220, ☎ 423 05 11, *trustinn@pt.lu, Fax 42 30 56*, – ▤ TV P. AE ⓓ MC VISA
7 ch ☕ 62/72.
◆ Hôtel format "pocket" renfermant de coquettes chambres correctement équipées, où le petit-déjeuner - seul service offert - vous sera "livré", faute de salle à manger.
◆ Klein hotel met aantrekkelijke, correct geëquipeerde kamers. Het ontbijt is de enige service die het hotel biedt en wordt, bij gebrek aan een eetzaal, op de kamer gebracht.

Le Grimpereau, r. Cents 140, ✉ 1319, ☎ 43 67 87, *bridard@pt.lu, Fax 42 60 26*, – P. AE ⓓ MC VISA JCB BV b
fermé Pâques, 3 prem. sem. août, sam. midi, dim. soir et lundi – **Repas** 30/39.
◆ Dans une villa nichée sous les frondaisons où chantent les grimpereaux, restaurant néo-rustique proposant une belle variété de plats. Clientèle d'habitués et d'aéroport.
◆ Neorustiek restaurant in een villa verscholen tussen het loof, waar voornamelijk vaste gasten en luchtreizigers komen. De menukaart biedt een mooie variatie.

à Belair C *Luxembourg :*

Albert Premier sans rest, r. Albert Ier 2a, ✉ 1117, ☎ 442 44 21, *hotel-albert-premier@resto.lu, Fax 44 74 41*, – TV . AE ⓓ MC VISA
☕ 13 – **14 ch** 220/240. plan p. 4 CZ c
◆ Hôtel "chic" situé aux portes de la ville. Décor anglais cossu réalisé avec le souci du détail, exquises chambres bien équipées, accueil et service prévenants.
◆ Chic hotel aan de rand van de stad. Het weelderige interieur in Engelse stijl getuigt van oog voor detail. Schitterende en uiterst gerieflijke kamers. Uitstekende service.

Parc Belair, av. du X Septembre 111, ✉ 2551, ☎ 442 32 31, *paribel@hpb.lu, Fax 44 44 84,* ≤, ⛱, 🏋, ≘s, 🚲 - |‡| ⇆, ▤ rest, TV 🚗 - 🏛 25 à 260. AE ⓓ MC VISA AV q
Repas ***Le Bistrot*** *(fermé sam. midi, dim. midi et jours fériés)* (ouvert jusqu'à 23 h) carte 24 à 36 - **52 ch** ☕ 210/251 - ½ P 135/308.
◆ En lisière d'un parc, luxueux hôtel dont on appréciera le caractère "cosy". Chambres modernes et excellentes installations pour séminaires. Une carte assez conséquente s'emploie à combler votre appétit dans le petit bistrot d'en face.
◆ Luxueus hotel met een "cosy" karakter aan de rand van een park. Moderne kamers en uitstekende faciliteiten voor congressen. In de kleine bistro aan de overkant kan de inwendige mens worden versterkt. Vrij uitgebreide kaart.

XX **Astoria,** av. du X Septembre 44, ✉ 2550, ☎ 44 62 23, *Fax 45 82 96* - ▤. AE ⓓ MC plan p. 4 CZ a
fermé du 21 au 28 fév., sam., dim. soir et lundi soir - **Repas** Lunch 23 - carte 28 à 58.
◆ Restaurant officiant à l'entrée de la capitale, dans une demeure bourgeoise avenante dont la façade dévoile des touches Art déco. Carte classico-traditionnelle concise.
◆ Wie de Luxemburgse hoofdstad binnenrijdt, ziet vrijwel meteen dit restaurant in een mooi herenhuis met een art-decogevel. Beknopte klassiek-traditionele kaart.

X **Thailand,** av. Gaston Diderich 72, ✉ 1420, ☎ 44 27 66, Cuisine thaïlandaise - AE ⓓ MC VISA. ✂ AV a
fermé 15 août-15 sept., lundi et sam. midi - **Repas** carte 36 à 54.
◆ Au cœur de Belair, table exotique se distinguant par sa ribambelle de recettes thaïlandaises et son décor typique sans surcharge. Des parasols ornent le plafond.
◆ Deze Thai in het hart van Belair onderscheidt zich door de veelheid van gerechten. Typisch Aziatisch interieur zonder overdaad en een plafond dat met parasols is versierd.

à Clausen (Klausen) Ⓒ *Luxembourg* :

XX **les jardins du President** ⛰ avec ch pl. Ste-Cunégonde 2, ✉ 1367, ☎ 260 90 71, *jardins@president.lu, Fax 26 09 07 73,* ⛱, ☀ - |‡|, ▤ ch, TV P. AE ⓓ MC VISA
Repas *(fermé sam. midi et dim.)* Lunch 24 - carte 40 à 55, ♀ - **7 ch** ☕ 150/180 - ½ P 220/280. DY a
◆ Élégant et intime relais gourmand niché dans un écrin de verdure. Terrasse s'agrémentant d'un jardin où bruisse une cascade. Cuisine du moment. Belles chambres personnalisées.
◆ Elegante, intieme pleisterplaats voor lekkerbekken midden in het groen. Terras en een tuin met waterval. Seizoengebonden keuken. De mooie kamers hebben elk een eigen karakter.

à Dommeldange (Dummeldéng) Ⓒ *Luxembourg* :

Hilton ⛰, r. Jean Engling 12, ✉ 1466, ☎ 4 37 81, *hilton_luxembourg@hilton.com, Fax 43 60 95,* ≤, 🏋, ≘s, 🏊, 🚲 - |‡| ⇆ ▤ TV 🚗 P - 🏛 25 à 360. AE ⓓ MC VISA JCB BV f
Repas voir rest ***Les Continents*** ci-après - ***Café Stiffchen*** Lunch 30 - carte 34 à 55, ♀ - **298 ch** ☕ 298/358, - 39 suites.
◆ À l'orée de la forêt, hôtel de luxe dont les lignes épousent celles de la vallée. Chambres tout confort, service avenant et infrastructure pour conférences très complète. Restauration de type brasserie et lunch-buffets en semaine au Café Stiffchen.
◆ Dit luxehotel, waarvan de belijning harmonieert met de glooiingen van het dal, staat aan de rand van het bos. Gerieflijke kamers, goede service en talrijke faciliteiten voor congressen. Brasserieschotels en door de week een lunchbuffet in het Café Stiffchen.

Parc, rte d'Echternach 120, ✉ 1453, ☎ 435 64 30, *info@parc-hotel.lu, Fax 43 69 03,* ⛱, 🏋, ≘s, 🏊, ☀, 🎾 - |‡|, ▤ rest, TV P - 🏛 25 à 1500. AE ⓓ MC VISA BV s
Repas *(fermé 24, 26 et 27 déc.)* carte 26 à 49 - **217 ch** ☕ 115/140, - 3 suites.
◆ Dans un parc entouré de bois, établissement familial rappelant un hôtel de chaîne. Les communs, comme les chambres rénovées, ne manquent ni d'ampleur, ni d'agrément. Restaurant-véranda surplombant la piscine. Choix de grillades.
◆ Dit familiehotel in een park met bossen rondom doet denken aan een ketenhotel. De gemeenschappelijke ruimten en de gerenoveerde kamers zijn ruim en aantrekkelijk. Restaurant met een serre die boven het zwembad uitsteekt. Grillspecialiteiten.

Host. du Grünewald, rte d'Echternach 10, ✉ 1453, ☎ 43 18 82, *hostgrun@pt.lu, Fax 42 06 46,* ☀, 🚲 - |‡|, ▤ rest, TV P - 🏛 25 à 40. AE ⓓ MC VISA. ✂ rest
Repas *(fermé du 1er au 17 juil., du 1er au 20 janv., sam. midi, dim. et lundi midi)* 49/85 - **26 ch** ☕ 120/145, - 2 suites - ½ P 100/120. BV d
◆ Adorable hostellerie traditionnelle au charme désuet. Chambres de divers gabarits, mignonnes comme tout. Assez cossu, l'ensemble produit une atmosphère romantique. Une belle carte classique et une cave d'épicurien vous attendent au restaurant.
◆ Een bekoorlijke, traditionele hostellerie met een ouderwetse charme. De kamers variëren in grootte, maar zijn alle even vriendelijk. Overal hangt een sfeer van luxe en romantiek. Restaurant met een mooie klassieke kaart en verfijnde wijnselectie.

XXXX **Les Continents** - H. Hilton, 1er étage, r. Jean Engling 12, ✉ 1466, ☎ 43 78 81 03, *hilton_luxembourg@hilton.com, Fax 43 60 95,* ≤, ☂ – ▤ P. AE ① MC VISA JCB
fermé août, sam. midi, dim. et lundi – **Repas** *Lunch 39* – carte 64 à 81, ♀. BV f
◆ Le succès de ce restaurant d'hôtel tient à sa belle carte de saison, ses menus tentateurs et ses harmonieux accords mets-vins, le tout, dans un cadre classique opulent.
◆ Het succesrecept van dit restaurant van het Hilton ? Weelderig klassiek interieur, mooie seizoengebonden kaart, aanlokkelijke menu's en harmonieuze wijn-spijscombinaties.

à Eich *(Eech)* C *Luxembourg :*

XX **La Mirabelle,** pl. d'Argent 9, ✉ 1413, ☎ 42 22 69, *calaianni@email.lu, Fax 42 22 69,* ☂, Ouvert jusqu'à 23 h – ▤. AE ① MC VISA JCB AV c
fermé sam. midi et dim. – **Repas** *Lunch 24* – carte 30 à 59, ♀.
◆ La carte classico-bourgeoise de cet établissement façon "brasserie" comprend des plats lorrains, des suggestions et un menu quotidiens, plus un menu dégustation.
◆ De klassiek-traditionele kaart van dit etablissement in brasseriestijl bevat Lotharingse gerechten, dagsuggesties, een menu van de dag en een degustatiemenu.

au plateau de Kirchberg *(Kiirchbierg) :*

Sofitel ⛵, r. Fort Niedergrünewald 6 (Centre Européen), ✉ 2015, ☎ 43 77 61, *H1314@accor-hotels.com, Fax 42 50 91* – |♦| ⇔ ▤ TV ♿ 🚗 P – 🏂 25 à 75. AE ① MC VISA plan p. 5 EY a
Repas *Oro e Argento* *(fermé août et sam.)* carte env. 50 – ☕ 20 – **100 ch** 295, – 4 suites.
◆ En plein quartier institutionnel européen, hôtel au plan ovale audacieux, avec atrium central. Chambres spacieuses très confortables. Accueil et service en rapport. Intime ristorante "d'or et d'argent", teinté de notes vénitiennes. Cuisine transalpine.
◆ Hotel met een gedurfd ovaal grondplan en een atrium in het midden, in de wijk van de Europese instellingen. Ruime en zeer comfortabele kamers. Uitstekende service. Sfeervol Italiaans restaurant met veel goud en zilver en hier en daar een Venetiaanse noot.

Novotel ⛵, r. Fort Niedergrünewald 6 (Centre Européen), ✉ 2226, ☎ 429 84 81, *H1930@accor-hotels.com, Fax 43 86 58,* ☂ – |♦| ⇔ ▤ TV ♿ P – 🏂 25 à 300. AE ① MC VISA plan p. 5 EY a
Repas (ouvert jusqu'à 23 h) *Lunch 22* – carte 19 à 38 – ☕ 15 – **206 ch** 155.
◆ Voisin de son grand frère, cet établissement géré par le même groupe dispose d'une infrastructure pour séminaires très complète et d'agréables chambres de belle ampleur.
◆ Dit Novotel staat naast zijn grote broer en wordt door dezelfde groep geleid. Aangename kamers van goed formaat en talrijke faciliteiten voor congressen.

à Neudorf *(Neiduerf)* C *Luxembourg :*

Ponte Vecchio sans rest, r. Neudorf 271, ✉ 2221, ☎ 424 72 01, *vecchio@pt.lu, Fax 424 72 08 88* – |♦| ▤ TV P. AE ① MC VISA BV w
46 ch ☕ 89/107.
◆ Ancien site brassicole adroitement réaffecté : fringantes chambres avec ou sans kitchenette - dont 9 duplex - et communs ornés de romantiques fresques italianisantes.
◆ Hotel in een oude bierbrouwerij. Mooie kamers met of zonder kitchenette, waaronder 9 split-level, en gemeenschappelijke ruimten met romantische Italiaanse fresco's.

à Rollingergrund *(Rolléngergronn)* C *Luxembourg :*

Sieweburen, r. Septfontaines 36, ✉ 2534, ☎ 44 23 56, *Fax 44 23 53,* ≤, ☂, 🛋 – TV P. MC VISA AV g
Repas *(fermé 24 déc.-8 janv. et merc.)* (taverne-rest) *Lunch 11* – carte 26 à 45, ♀ – **14 ch** ☕ 88/115 – ½ P 95/110.
◆ Sur un site inondé de chlorophylle, maison à colombage offrant le choix entre plusieurs tailles de chambres au confort standard. Certaines d'entre elles sont mansardées.
◆ Dit vakwerkhuis wordt door veel groen omringd. Kamers met standaardcomfort van verschillende grootte, waarvan sommige op de zolderverdieping liggen.

X **Théâtre de l'Opéra,** r. Rollingergrund 100, ✉ 2440, ☎ 25 10 33, *opera@tp.lu, Fax 25 10 29,* ☂ – AE ① MC VISA JCB AV r
fermé sam. midi et dim. – **Repas** *Lunch 12* – carte 36 à 50.
◆ Engageante demeure rénovée dissimulant une salle de restaurant étagée et agencée dans l'esprit "bistrot". Cuisine actuelle avec menu du jour et choix à la carte au dîner.
◆ Fraai gerenoveerd pand met een eetzaal op verschillende niveaus, die in bistrostijl is ingericht. Eigentijdse keuken met een menu van de dag en à la carte bij het diner.

X **Himalaya,** r. Rollingergrund 8 (pl. de l'Étoile), ✉ 2440, ☎ 25 23 85, *Fax 45 61 19,* Cuisine indienne – AE ① MC VISA plan p. 4 CY m
fermé dim. – **Repas** *Lunch 9* – carte env. 28.
◆ Une table indienne attrayante se cache derrière cette façade ornée de moulures. Choix assez étoffé, avec plats népalais et végétariens. Fond musical en rapport.
◆ Achter deze gevel met sierlijsten gaat een leuk Indiaas eettentje schuil. Vrij uitgebreide kaart met Nepalese en vegetarische schotels. Bijpassende achtergrondmuziek.

Environs

à Alzingen *(Alzéng) - plan p. 4* C *Hesperange 10 519 h :*

X **Opium,** rte de Thionville 427, ✉ 5887, ☎ 26 36 01 60, *info@opiumrestaurant.com, Fax 26 36 16 06,* 🏠, Avec cuisine asiatique, ouvert jusqu'à minuit – ▤ P. AE ⓘ MC VISA BX a
fermé sam. midi, dim. midi et lundi midi – **Repas** *Lunch 10* – carte 40 à 57.
◆ Une véranda reliant deux immeubles d'appartements abrite ce restaurant asiatique original où règne une ambiance à la fois "zen" et "lounge". Service très prévenant.
◆ Dit originele Aziatische restaurant in een overdekte galerij tussen twee flatgebouwen ademt een sfeer die zowel "zen" als "lounge" is. Zeer voorkomende bediening.

à Bridel *(Briddel) par N 12 : 7 km - AV -* C *Kopstal 3 001 h :*

XX **Le Rondeau,** r. Luxembourg 82, ✉ 8140, ☎ 33 94 73, *Fax 33 37 46,* 🏠 – P. AE ⓘ MC VISA
fermé 2 sem. en mars, 3 sem. en août, lundi et mardi – **Repas** *Lunch 28* – 54/95 bc.
◆ Carte classico-traditionnelle, généreux menus et choix de vins prometteur dans ce sympathique restaurant familial. D'intéressantes toiles contemporaines égaient les murs.
◆ Klassiek-traditionele kaart, royale menu's en veelbelovende wijnkeuze in dit sympathieke familierestaurant. De muren worden opgevrolijkt door interessante hedendaagse doeken.

XX **Brideler Stuff,** r. Lucien Wercollier 1, ✉ 8156, ☎ 33 87 34, *bridstuf@pt.lu, Fax 33 90 64,* 🏠 – P. AE ⓘ MC VISA
fermé fin déc.-début janv. et lundi – **Repas** *Lunch 12* – carte 33 à 49, ♀.
◆ Cette auberge fondée au 19e s. doit son affluence à un éventail de copieux plats bourgeois et de spécialités régionales roboratives. Décor de style "stubbe" en salle.
◆ Deze 19e-eeuwse herberg dankt zijn populariteit aan de keur van eenvoudige schotels en regionale specialiteiten, die allemaal even copieus zijn. De eetzaal is rustiek.

à Hesperange *(Hesper) - plan p. 4* – *10 519 h*

XXX ✿ **L'Agath** (Steichen), rte de Thionville 274 (Howald), ✉ 5884, ☎ 48 86 87, *restaurant@agath.lu, Fax 48 55 05,* 🏠 – P – 🚣 60. AE ⓘ MC VISA BX k
fermé du 12 au 19 avril, 31 mai-7 juin, du 1er au 16 août, du 1er au 9 janv., sam. midi, dim. et lundi – **Repas** *Lunch 58* – carte 62 à 75, ♀ 🍇.
◆ Une cuisine au goût du jour soignée vous sera servie dans cette villa massive postée en retrait de la route. Un trompe-l'œil orne la coupole de l'opulente salle à manger.
◆ In deze massieve villa, die even van de weg af staat, kunt u genieten van een verzorgde eigentijdse keuken. Een trompe-l'oeil siert de koepel van de weelderige eetzaal.
Spéc. Carpaccio de bœuf à l'huile de truffes, copeaux de parmesan et foie gras. Daurade royale, légumes confits et coulis de poivrons doux. Carré d'agneau persillé et pommes Darphin aux herbes. **Vins** Riesling, Pinot gris

XX **Le Jardin Gourmand,** rte de Thionville 432, ✉ 5886, ☎ 36 08 42, *Fax 36 08 43,* 🏠 – AE MC VISA BX p
fermé 25 août-8 sept., sam. midi, dim. soir et lundi – **Repas** *Lunch 11* – 28, ♀.
◆ Établissement implanté au centre du bourg. L'été, une terrasse est dressée côté jardin, au bord de l'Alzette ; quant aux gourmandises, elles défilent dans vos assiettes.
◆ Dit etablissement is midden in het dorp te vinden. Op zomerse dagen kan worden gegeten op het terras aan de tuinzijde, aan de oever van de Alzette.

à Hostert *(Hueschert) par* ③ *: 12 km* C *Niederanven 5 446 h :*

XX **Chez Pascal-Le Gastronome,** r. Andethana 90, ✉ 6970, ☎ 34 00 39, *belnoup@pt.lu, Fax 26 34 01 06,* 🏠 – P. AE ⓘ MC VISA
fermé du 8 au 23 août, sam. midi, dim. soir et jours fériés – **Repas** (dîner sur réservation) *Lunch 31* – 49.
◆ Le nouvel intérieur de ce restaurant niché au cœur du patelin contraste avec la simplicité de sa façade. Cuisine très classique et amusant décor naïf en trompe-l'œil.
◆ Het nieuwe interieur van dit restaurant midden in Hostert contrasteert met de sobere gevel en heeft een grappige trompe-l'oeil in naïeve stijl. De kok kent zijn klassieken !

à Kopstal *(Koplescht) par N 12 : 9 km - AV* – *3 001 h*

XX **Weidendall** avec ch, r. Mersch 5, ✉ 8181, ☎ 30 74 66, *weidenda@pt.lu, Fax 30 74 67* – TV. AE ⓘ MC VISA JCB
Repas *(fermé 2 sem. carnaval, 2 prem. sem. sept. et mardi) Lunch 11* – 26/36 – **9 ch** ☕ 46/70 – ½ P 54/65.
◆ Près de l'église, engageante auberge-restaurant tenue en famille. Côté fourneaux et salle à manger, on fait preuve du même classicisme. Chambres commodes pour l'étape.
◆ Deze aardige herberg bij de kerk wordt door een familie gerund. Zowel de inrichting als de keuken van het restaurant zijn klassiek. De kamers voldoen prima voor een nachtje.

à Sandweiler *par ④ : 7 km – 2 665 h*

XX **Hoffmann,** r. Principale 21, ✉ 5240, ☎ 35 01 80, *hoffmann@resto.lu, Fax 35 79 36,* – P. AE MC VISA.
fermé 2 sem. carnval, mi-août-mi-sept., dim. soir, lundi et mardi soir – **Repas** 42, ♀.
• Faim de homard ou d'une pièce de viande rôtie à la broche ? Cette table au cadre "cosy" peut assouvir vos désirs. Carte de saison dans le tempo actuel et bonne petite cave.
• Zin in kreeft of vlees aan het spit ? In dit gezellige restaurant wordt u op uw wenken bediend ! Eigentijdse, seizoengebonden kaart en kleine, maar fijne wijnkelder.

à Strassen *(Stroossen) - plan p. 4 – 5 869 h*

L'Olivier avec appartements, rte d'Arlon 140, ✉ 8008, ☎ 31 36 66, *olivier@mail.lu, Fax 31 36 27* – TV P – 25 à 50. AE MC VISA JCB AV h
Repas voir rest ***La Cime*** ci-après – **38 ch** 139/187, – 4 suites – ½ P 97/159.
• Immeuble récent situé à 400 m de l'autoroute. Confort actuel et double vitrage dans les chambres, souvent des duplex avec kitchenette. Vue champêtre à l'arrière.
• Hotel in een nieuw gebouw, op 400 m van de snelweg. Modern comfort en dubbele ramen in de kamers, veelal split-level met kitchenette. Landelijk uitzicht aan de achterkant.

Mon Plaisir sans rest, rte d'Arlon 218 (par ⑧ : 4 km), ✉ 8010, ☎ 31 15 41, *mplaisir@pt.lu, Fax 31 61 44* – TV P. AE MC VISA
fermé 23 déc.-1er janv. – **26 ch** 65/76.
• Hôtel d'un bon petit confort dont la façade jaune ne passe pas inaperçue sur cet axe fréquenté rejoignant Luxembourg. Chambres sobrement équipées, mais bien tenues.
• Redelijk geriefelijk hotel met een opvallende gele gevel aan een drukke weg naar de Luxemburgse hoofdstad. De kamers zijn sober, maar goed onderhouden.

XX **La Cime** - H. L'Olivier, rte d'Arlon 140a, ✉ 8008, ☎ 31 88 13, *olivier@mail.lu, Fax 31 36 27,* – P. AE MC VISA JCB AV h
fermé sam. – **Repas** Lunch 15 – 36/63 bc, ♀.
• Ce restaurant d'hôtel propose une carte classique variée, avec plusieurs menus incluant une formule végétarienne et un menu-choix. Salle à manger ample et moderne.
• Dit restaurant, dat bij een hotel hoort, biedt een gevarieerde klassieke kaart met meerdere menu's, waaronder een vegetarisch menu en een keuzemenu. Ruime, moderne eetzaal.

XX **Le Nouveau Riquewihr,** rte d'Arlon 373 (par ⑧ : 5 km), ✉ 8011, ☎ 31 99 80, *leriquewihr@email.lu, Fax 31 97 05,* – P. AE MC VISA
fermé 24 déc.-1er janv. et dim. – **Repas** Lunch 34 – carte 40 à 49.
• La nouveauté du Riquewihr concerne davantage le décor - recomposé avec des notes Renaissance italienne - que la carte, toujours aussi sagement classique et étoffée.
• De nieuwigheid zit hem meer in het interieur, dat onlangs in Italiaanse renaissancestijl is gedecoreerd, dan in de kaart, die nog altijd licht klassiek en zeer uitgebreid is.

à Walferdange *(Walfer) par ① : 5 km – 6 451 h*

Moris, pl. des Martyrs, ✉ 7201, ☎ 330 10 51, *contact@morishotel.lu, Fax 33 30 70,* – rest, TV P – 50. AE MC VISA
Repas *(fermé du 2 au 22 août et 24 déc.-2 janv.)* Lunch 35 – carte 34 à 49, ♀ – **24 ch** *(fermé 24 déc.-2 janv.)* 85/110.
• Hôtel octogonal se dressant près de l'église du village, devant un carrefour. Chambres fonctionnelles assez amples mais inégalement insonorisées. Parking. Table au cadre harmonieux et accueillant. Carte classico-bourgeoise avec plats régionaux.
• Achthoekig hotel bij een kruispunt in de buurt van de dorpskerk. De functionele kamers zijn vrij ruim, maar niet altijd even goed tegen geluid geïsoleerd. Parkeerruimte. Restaurant met een harmonieus interieur. Eenvoudige klassieke kaart met streekgerechten.

XX **l'Etiquette,** rte de Diekirch 50, ✉ 7220, ☎ 33 51 68, *Fax 33 51 69,* – P. AE MC VISA
fermé 25 août-5 sept., 27 déc.-5 janv., mardi et dim. soir – **Repas** Lunch 17 – 22/42, ♀.
• Registre culinaire classico-traditionnel et exceptionnel choix de vins régionaux dans cette maison où tout débuta par une "vinothèque", qui existe d'ailleurs toujours.
• Dit restaurant is begonnen als "vinotheek", die overigens nog steeds bestaat. Klassiek-traditionele keuken en een keur van goede wijnen uit verschillende streken.

MACHTUM (MIECHTEM) C *Wormeldange 2 306 h.* 717 X 25 *et* 716 M 7.
Luxembourg 31 – Ettelbrück 46 – Grevenmacher 4 – Mondorf-les-Bains 29.

XX **Chalet de la Moselle,** rte du Vin 35, ✉ 6841, ☎ 75 91 91, *maryde@pt.lu, Fax 26 74 55 91,* – MC VISA
fermé merc. – **Repas** Lunch 20 – 30/46.
• Sur la route du vin, dominant la rivière, bel établissement au décor intérieur sobre, mais de bon goût. Mise en place soignée. Formule menu-carte. Nombreux crus locaux.
• Dit mooie etablissement ligt aan de wijnroute en kijkt uit op de rivier. Eenvoudig maar smaakvol decor. Verzorgde inrichting. À la carte en menu. Veel lokale wijnen.

X **Aub. du Lac,** rte du Vin 77, ✉ 6841, ☎ 75 02 53, *Fax 75 88 87*, ←, ☂ – P. AE ⓓ ⓜⓒ VISA – *fermé 15 déc.-15 janv. et mardi* – **Repas** Lunch 30 – 35/55 bc, ♀.
◆ L'été en terrasse, ou toute l'année depuis les grandes fenêtres de la salle à manger, cette auberge familiale vous offre la vue sur la Moselle. Très important choix de plats.
◆ Deze herberg biedt in de zomer vanaf het terras en het hele jaar door via de grote ramen uitzicht op de Moezel. Zeer uitgebreide kaart.

MERTERT (MÄERTERT) 717 X 24 *et* 716 M 6 – *3 324 h.*
Luxembourg 32 – Ettelbrück 46 – Thionville 56 – Trier 15.

XXX **Goedert** avec ch, pl. de la Gare 4, ✉ 6674, ☎ 74 00 21, *Fax 74 84 71*, ☂ – ▤ rest, TV P. AE ⓜⓒ VISA – *fermé 16 août-3 sept., 28 déc.-15 janv., dim. soir et lundi* – **Repas** Lunch 27 – 42/57 – **8 ch** ☐ 57/83 – ½ P 75.
◆ Choix de recettes appétissantes et menus alléchants : la carte du Goedert ne manque pas d'intérêt. Salle à manger contemporaine. Chambres récentes et assez sobres.
◆ Een scala van smakelijke gerechten en aanlokkelijke menu's : de kaart van Goedert heeft heel wat bijzonders te bieden. Eigentijdse eetzaal. Vrij eenvoudige kamers.

XX **Paulus,** r. Haute 1, ✉ 6680, ☎ 74 00 70, *restpaulus@euro.lu, Fax 74 84 02* – AE ⓓ ⓜⓒ VISA JCB
fermé sem. carnaval, août, lundi et mardi – **Repas** Lunch 10 – 34/49, ♀.
◆ Au cœur de l'actif port fluvial, établissement familial dont l'enseigne porte le nom du chef-patron. Longue terrasse couverte. Portions généreuses.
◆ In het hart van de bedrijvige rivierhaven staat dit familiehotel, dat naar de patron is genoemd. Langgerekt overdekt terras. Royale porties.

MONDORF-LES-BAINS (MUNNERËF) 717 W 25 *et* 716 L 7 – *3 690 h – Station thermale –*
Casino 2000, r. Flammang, ✉ 5618, ☎ 23 61 11, Fax 23 61 12 29.
Voir *Parc★ – Mobilier★ de l'église St-Michel.*
Env. *à l'Est : Vallée de la Moselle Luxembourgeoise★ de Schengen à Wasserbillig.*
ℹ *av. des Bains 26, ✉ 5610, ☎ 66 75 75, Fax 66 16 17.*
Luxembourg 19 – Remich 11 – Thionville 22.

Parc ⛰ Domaine thermal, av. Dr E. Feltgen, ✉ 5601, ☎ 23 66 60, *domaine@mondorf.lu, Fax 23 66 10 93*, ☂, Ⓢ, ₣₅, ≘s, ⛶, ⛲, ⛱, ⛳ – |‡| ⛔ TV ♿ 🚗 P – 🏛 25 à 350. AE ⓓ ⓜⓒ VISA. ⛒ rest
Repas *De Jangeli* *(fermé 27 déc.-14 janv., sam. midi, dim. soir et lundi)* Lunch 26 – 42/70 bc – **114 ch** *(fermé du 26 au 30 déc.)* ☐ 171/188, – 20 suites – ½ P 121/302.
◆ Bonne adresse pour les curistes, nichée dans le parc de la source Kind. Communs spacieux. Mobilier actuel dans les chambres, réparties entre le bâtiment principal et l'annexe. À table, mets classiques discrètement mis à la page. Belle sélection de crus locaux.
◆ Goed adres voor kuurgasten, in het park van de Kind-bron. Grote gemeenschappelijke ruimten. Modern meubilair in de kamers, die over het hoofdgebouw en de annexe verspreid liggen. Klassieke gerechten met een licht modern accent. Goede selectie lokale wijnen.

Grand Chef ⛰, av. des Bains 36, ✉ 5610, ☎ 23 66 80 12, *granchef@pt.lu, Fax 23 66 15 10*, ⛲, ⛱, 🚲 – |‡| TV 🚗 P – 🏛 30. AE ⓓ ⓜⓒ VISA. ⛒ rest
14 mars-21 nov. – **Repas** *(fermé merc. midis non fériés)* Lunch 23 – 31/37 – **35 ch** ☐ 65/98, – 2 suites – ½ P 66/76.
◆ Vous rêviez depuis toujours de séjourner dans un ancien hôtel particulier ? C'est fait, vous y êtes ! Beaux salons du temps passé, bar opulent et chambres spacieuses. Au restaurant, cuisine classique peu à peu remise en phase avec l'époque.
◆ Altijd al gedroomd van een verblijf in zo'n oud en voornaam herenhuis ? Dan is dit uw kans ! Mooie salons van weleer, weelderige bar en grote kamers. Restaurant met klassieke keuken die mondjesmaat wat meer eigentijdse accenten krijgt.

Casino 2000, r. Flammang, ✉ 5618, ☎ 23 61 11, *info@casino2000.lu, Fax 23 61 12 29* – |‡| ▤ TV P – 🏛 25 à 600. AE ⓓ ⓜⓒ VISA. ⛒ rest
fermé 24 déc. – **Repas** voir rest ***Les Roses*** ci-après – **27 ch** ☐ 109/133, – 3 suites.
◆ Que vous soyez flambeur ou pas, la chance voudra vous sourire dès que vous aurez posé votre valise... Chambres amples et bien équipées. Importante infrastructure de réunions.
◆ Zware gokker of niet, het geluk lacht u toe zodra hier de koffers zijn neergezet. De ruime kamers zijn van alle gemakken voorzien. Grote infrastructuur voor bijeenkomsten.

Beau Séjour, av. Dr Klein 3, ✉ 5630, ☎ 236 10, *info@beau-sejour.lu, Fax 23 66 08 89* – TV. AE ⓜⓒ VISA. ⛒
fermé 15 déc.-15 janv. – **Repas** Lunch 20 – carte 37 à 48 – **10 ch** ☐ 65/88 – ½ P 67/72.
◆ Petite affaire familiale située à proximité des thermes. Les chambres, de taille correcte sans plus, et munies du double vitrage, se répartissent sur deux étages. Salle des repas aux murs et plafond lambrissés.
◆ Familiehotelletje dat vlak bij het thermale centrum ligt. De kamers, die redelijk van afmetingen zijn, hebben dubbele beglazing en zijn verdeeld over twee verdiepingen. Eetzaal met gelambriseerde wanden en plafond.

XXX **Les Roses** - H. Casino 2000, r. Flammang, ✉ 5618, ☎ 23 61 11, *info@casino2000.lu, Fax 23 61 11* – P. AE ① MC VISA.
fermé août, 24 déc., 1 sem. en janv., lundi et mardi sauf jours fériés – **Repas** *Lunch 20* – 59, carte 60 à 87, ♀.
◆ Le thème de la rose inspire l'élégante décoration de cette salle de restaurant en rotonde coiffée d'une plaisante verrière. Cuisine aussi innovante qu'élaborée.
◆ De roos was een bron van inspiratie bij de elegante inrichting van dit restaurant met zijn ronde eetzaal en mooie glaskoepel. De keuken is even verfijnd als vernieuwend.
Spéc. Faux mille-feuille de grosse langoustine, légumes étuvés au gingembre. Tronçon de turbot cloutée aux truffes noires et rôtie sur l'arête, sauce Noilly Prat. Filet de bœuf Charolais, foie gras matignon à la Riche. **Vins** Pinot gris, Riesling

à Ellange-gare *(Elléng) Nord-Ouest : 2,5 km* C *Mondorf-les-Bains* :

XXX **La Rameaudière,** r. Gare 10, ✉ 5690, ☎ 23 66 10 63, *la_rameaudiere@internet.lu, Fax 23 66 10 64,* – P. AE ① MC VISA
fermé dern. sem. juin, dern. sem. août-prem. sem. sept., janv. et lundis et mardis non fériés – **Repas** 45/70.
◆ Cette maison accueillante était autrefois la gare du village. Salle à manger contemporaine. En été, on mange sur la terrasse fleurie, à l'ombre des arbres fruitiers.
◆ Dit gezellige restaurant was vroeger het dorpsstation. Eigentijdse eetzaal. In de zomer wordt op het fleurige terras gegeten, in de schaduw van de fruitbomen.

MULLERTHAL (MËLLERDALL) C *Waldbillig 1 220 h.* 717 W 24 *et* 716 L 6.

Voir *Vallée des Meuniers*** (Vallée de l'Ernz Noire).*

18 9 *au Sud-Ouest : 2 km à Christnach,* ✉ *7641,* ☎ *87 83 83, Fax 87 95 64.*

Luxembourg 30 – Echternach 14 – Ettelbrück 31.

XXX **Le Cigalon** avec ch, r. Ernz Noire 1, ✉ 6245, ☎ 79 94 95, *le_cigalon@internet.lu, Fax 79 93 83,* – TV P. MC VISA. rest
fermé janv.-fév. – **Repas** *(fermé lundi en hiver et mardi)* 31/75, ♀ – **11 ch** 75/94, – 3 suites – ½ P 72/78.
◆ Un concentré de Provence au Luxembourg, avec sa crèche et ses santons ! Le chef fait une cuisine appétissante inspirée de son Midi d'origine. Terrasse. Chambres bien équipées.
◆ Een stukje Provence in Luxembourg, met kribbe en santons ! De chef-kok bereidt een heerlijke keuken die is geïnspireerd op zijn geboortestreek. Terras. Kamers met goed comfort.

NEUDORF (NEIDUERF) – *voir à Luxembourg, périphérie.*

NIEDERANVEN (NIDDERANWEN) 717 W 25 *et* 716 L 7 – *5 446 h.*

Luxembourg 13 – Ettelbrück 36 – Grevenmacher 16 – Remich 19.

XX **Host. de Niederanven,** r. Munsbach 2, ✉ 6941, ☎ 34 00 61, *Fax 34 93 92* – AE MC VISA.
fermé 2e quinz. août et lundi – **Repas** *Lunch 15* – 24/50, ♀.
◆ Cette hostellerie engageante, tenue en famille depuis plus de vingt-cinq ans et reconnaissable à ses façades roses, dispose d'une belle salle à manger actuelle.
◆ Deze uitnodigende hostellerie wordt al meer dan 25 jaar door de familie gerund. Het pand is te herkennen aan de roze gevel. Mooie, eigentijdse eetzaal.

OUR (Vallée de l') (URDALL) ★★ 717 V 22 *et* 716 L 5 - L 6 *G. Belgique-Luxembourg.*

PÉTANGE (PÉITÉNG) 717 U 25 *et* 716 K 7 – *13 986 h.*

Luxembourg 22 – Esch-sur-Alzette 15 – Arlon 18 – Longwy 14.

Threeland, r. Pierre Hamer 50, ✉ 4737, ☎ 265 08 00, *threelan@pt.lu, Fax 26 50 28 20,* – TV P – 25 à 150. AE ① MC VISA.
Repas *Lunch 25* – carte 34 à 55 – **57 ch** 57/79, – 2 suites.
◆ Hôtel récent construit à proximité des frontières belge et française. Communs spacieux. Banquets et congrès ont lieu au 1er étage. Certaines chambres sont mansardées. Salle à manger moderne en forme de rotonde.
◆ Dit recentelijk gebouwde hotel ligt vlak bij de Belgisch-Franse grens. Grote gemeenschappelijke ruimten. Feesten en congressen op de eerste verdieping. Sommige kamers hebben een schuine dakwand. Moderne eetzaal in de vorm van een rotonde.

POMMERLOCH (POMMERLACH) Ⓒ *Winseler 869 h.* 717 U 23 *et* 716 K 6.

Luxembourg 56 – Diekirch 37 – Ettelbrück 7 – Wiltz 7 – Bastogne 12.

Pommerloch, Wohlber 2, ✉ 9638, ☎ 269 51 51, *Fax 26 95 06 20,* – TV P. AE VISA
Repas *Lunch 10* – carte 26 à 39 – **8 ch** 55/75.
◆ Établissement familial encore flambant neuf dominant un rond-point fréquenté. Bonne insonorisation des chambres, spacieuses et fonctionnelles.
◆ Spiksplinternieuw familiehotel dat aan een drukke rotonde staat. De ruime, functionele kamers zijn van goede geluidsisolatie voorzien.

Motel Bereler Stuff sans rest, rte de Bastogne 6, ✉ 9638, ☎ 95 79 09, *Fax 95 79 08* – TV P. VISA
18 ch 29/47.
◆ Ce motel est un point de chute pratique pour les usagers de la route. Les chambres, de belle ampleur et toutes identiques, baignent dans une atmosphère un peu surannée.
◆ Dit motel is een praktische pleisterplaats voor weggebruikers. De sfeer is een beetje vergane glorie, maar de identiek ingerichte kamers zijn ruim.

REMICH (RÉIMECH) 717 X 25 *et* 716 M 7 – *2 885 h.*

Voir *Vallée de la Moselle Luxembourgeoise★ de Schengen à Wasserbillig.*

18 *au Nord-Ouest : 12 km à Canach, Scheierhaff,* ✉ *5412,* ☎ *35 61 35, Fax 35 74 50.*

(juil.-août) Esplanade (gare routière), ✉ *5533,* ☎ *23 69 84 88, Fax 23 69 72 95.*

Luxembourg 22 – Mondorf-les-Bains 11 – Saarbrücken 77.

Saint Nicolas, Esplanade 31, ✉ 5533, ☎ 26 66 30, *hotel@saint-nicolas.lu, Fax 26 66 36 66,* ←, – TV – 40. AE VISA JCB. ch
Repas *Lohengrin* *Lunch 26 bc* – 29/49, ♀ – **40 ch** 77/122 – ½ P 74/86.
◆ Ancien relais de bateliers et son tranquille jardin clos de murs postés au bord de la Moselle. Seize chambres ont déjà été modernisées et dotées d'un mobilier en bois clair. Vue sur la rivière depuis la salle à manger habillée de belles boiseries.
◆ Voormalige schippersherberg met rustige, ommuurde tuin, aan de oever van de Moezel. Er zijn inmiddels zestien kamers gemoderniseerd en ingericht met lichtkleurig houten meubilair. Vanuit de mooi gelambriseerde eetzaal uitzicht op de rivier.

des Vignes , rte de Mondorf 29, ✉ 5552, ☎ 23 69 91 49, *info@hotel-vignes.lu, Fax 23 69 84 63,* ← vignobles et vallée de la Moselle, – , rest, TV P – 25. AE VISA – *fermé 20 déc.-20 janv.* – **Repas** 33/65 bc, ♀ – **24 ch** 74/93 – ½ P 68/101.
◆ Au sommet d'un coteau, établissement dont les chambres, munies d'un balcon ou d'une terrasse, offrent un panorama grandiose sur les vignes et la vallée de la Moselle. Un vieux pressoir à vin trône dans la salle de restaurant agrandie d'une véranda.
◆ Dit etablissement boven op een heuvel heeft kamers die zijn voorzien van terras of balkon en die een schitterend panorama bieden van de wijngaarden en het Moezel-dal. In de eetzaal met serre staat een oude druivenpers.

de l'Esplanade, Esplanade 5, ✉ 5533, ☎ 23 66 91 71, *esplanade@pt.lu, Fax 23 69 89 24,* ←, – TV. VISA. rest – *fermé 2 janv.-8 fév. et merc. sauf 15 juin-15 sept.* – **Repas** *Lunch 18* – 25/35, ♀ – **18 ch** 57/78 – ½ P 50/55.
◆ La rivière et l'embarcadère sont à deux pas de cette adresse située dans le centre animé de Remich. Petites chambres sobrement décorées. L'été, on peut prendre son repas sous les stores de la terrasse. Profitez alors de la vue sur la Moselle.
◆ De rivier en de aanlegsteiger liggen op loopafstand van dit adres in het levendige centrum van Remich. Kleine kamers met eenvoudig decor. In de zomer kan de maaltijd worden genuttigd onder de markies op het terras, dat uitkijkt op de Moezel.

Domaine la Forêt avec ch, rte de l'Europe 36, ✉ 5531, ☎ 23 69 99 99, *laforet@pt.lu, Fax 23 69 98 98,* ←, – TV P. AE VISA. rest
Repas *(fermé du 15 au 31 juil., 2 sem. en janv., mardis midis non fériés d'oct. à mars et lundis non fériés)* 34/65 bc, ♀ – **14 ch** *(fermé du 15 au 31 juil.)* 70/95 – ½ P 65.
◆ Élégante salle à manger en demi-rotonde dominant du regard la vallée de la Moselle. Grandes chambres et junior suites assez cossues.
◆ Halfcirkelvormige restaurantzaal die smaakvol is ingericht en uitkijkt op de Moezelvallei. Grote, vrij luxueus ingerichte kamers en junior suites.

REULAND Ⓒ *Heffingen 850 h.* 717 W 24 *et* 716 L 6.

Luxembourg 24 – Diekirch 18 – Echternach 19 – Ettelbrück 24.

Reilander Millen, Est : 2 km sur rte Junglinster-Müllerthal, ✉ 7639, ☎ 83 72 52, *Fax 87 97 43,* – P. VISA. – *fermé 3 sem. carnaval, fin août-début sept., lundi et sam. midi* – **Repas** *Lunch 13* – carte 26 à 53, ♀.
◆ Charme agreste d'un ancien moulin du 18e s. isolé en pleine forêt. Carte assez succincte mais alléchante, renouvelée au fil des saisons. Le vin est la marotte du patron.
◆ Rustieke charme van een 18e-eeuwse afgelegen molen midden in het bos. Vrij beperkte, maar aanlokkelijke en seizoengebonden menukaart. Wijn is het stokpaardje van de patron.

REULER (REILER) 717 V 22 – *voir à Clervaux.*

RODER (ROEDER) 717 V 22 – *voir à Clervaux.*

ROLLINGERGRUND (ROLLÉNGERGRONN) – *voir à Luxembourg, périphérie.*

ROMBACH-MARTELANGE (ROMBECH-MAARTELÉNG) 717 T 24 – *voir à Haut-Martelange.*

SAEUL (SËLL) 717 U 24 *et* 716 K 6 – *468 h.*

Luxembourg 21 – Ettelbrück 22 – Mersch 11 – Arlon 14.

XX **Maison Rouge,** r. Principale 10, ✉ 7470, ☎ 23 63 02 21, *Fax 23 63 07 58,* – MC VISA

fermé 3 sem. en fév., 3 sem. en août, lundi, mardi et jeudi soir – **Repas** 45/50.

◆ L'enseigne dit vrai : une façade rouge signale cette grosse auberge familiale - autrefois relais de poste - érigée au cœur du village. Terrasse sur pelouse avec vue agreste.

◆ De naam spreekt de waarheid : een rode gevel markeert deze robuuste herberg - vroeger een uitspanning - midden in het dorp. Terras met landelijk uitzicht.

SANDWEILER 717 W 25 *et* 716 L 7 – *voir à Luxembourg, environs.*

SCHEIDGEN (SCHEEDGEN) C *Consdorf 1 779 h.* 717 X 24 *et* 716 M 6.

Luxembourg 35 – Echternach 8 – Ettelbrück 36.

de la Station, rte d'Echternach 10, ✉ 6250, ☎ 79 08 91, *info@hoteldelastation.lu, Fax 79 91 64,* ←, , , – | TV – 25 à 40. MC VISA. rest

avril-15 nov. – **Repas** *(fermé lundi et mardi)* (dîner seult jusqu'à 20 h 30) carte 34 à 42 – **25 ch** 45/70 – ½ P 50/57.

◆ Établissement tranquille entre les mains de la même famille depuis un siècle. La plupart des chambres ont vue sur la campagne. Accueil gentil et jardin revigorant. Table dressée dans un intérieur affichant un petit air typiquement luxembourgeois.

◆ Rustig etablissement dat al ruim een eeuw in handen is van dezelfde familie. De meeste kamers kijken uit op het platteland. Vriendelijke ontvangst en koele tuin. Bescheiden Luxemburgse ambiance in de eetzaal.

SCHOUWEILER (SCHULLER) C *Dippach 3 233 h.* 717 U 25 *et* 716 K 7.

Luxembourg 14 – Mondorf-les-Bains 29 – Arlon 20 – Longwy 18.

XX **La Table des Guilloux,** r. Résistance 17, ✉ 4996, ☎ 37 00 08, *Fax 37 11 61,* – P

fermé du 3 au 11 mai, du 2 au 24 août, fin déc.-début janv., lundi, mardi et sam. midi – **Repas** carte 50 à 72.

◆ Au centre du village, ferme-auberge fleurie aux beaux jours, abritant d'intimes petites salles garnies de meubles d'hier. Terrasse ombragée et jardin avec étang. Mets soignés.

◆ Gerenoveerde boerderij in het dorpscentrum. De intieme kleine eetzalen hebben meubelen uit grootmoeders tijd. Schaduwrijk terras en tuin met vijver. Uitstekende keuken.

Spéc. Fleurs de courgettes farcies (été). Blanc de turbot en marinière. Côte de veau élevé sous la mère au jus de cuisson. **Vins** Pinot gris, Riesling

X **Toit pour toi,** r. IX Septembre 2, ✉ 4996, ☎ 26 37 02 32 – P. VISA

fermé du 3 au 13 mai, du 2 au 26 août, 22 déc.-8 janv. et jeudi – **Repas** (dîner seult jusqu'à 23 h) carte 32 à 47.

◆ Une grange restaurée avec une certaine originalité donne son "toit" à cette affaire. Mise en place simple. Salades et viandes rôties, portions copieuses. Service aimable.

◆ Dit eethuis heeft onderdak gevonden in een fraai gerestaureerde korenschuur. Eenvoudige inrichting. Salades en gebraden vlees, royale porties. Vriendelijke bediening.

SCHWEBACH (SCHWIEBECH) C *Saeul 468 h.* 717 U 24.

Luxembourg 23 – Ettelbrück 22 – Mersch 13 – Arlon 16.

XX **Reimen,** Maison 1 (Schwebach-Pont), ✉ 8561, ☎ 23 63 03 81, *reimen@pt.lu, Fax 23 63 95 96* – P. AE MC VISA.

fermé 18 août-10 sept., 27 déc.-23 janv., lundi, mardi et après 20 h 30 – **Repas** carte 33 à 50.

◆ L'affaire, familiale, rencontre un certain succès auprès de la clientèle locale. Les plats appétissants suggérés par la carte y sont sûrement pour quelque chose !

◆ Dit restaurantje staat bij de lokale bevolking vrij goed aangeschreven. De kaart met aantrekkelijke gerechten liegt er in ieder geval niet om !

SEPTFONTAINES (SIMMER) 717 U 24 *et* 716 K 6 – *790 h.*

Voir *Vallée de l'Eisch★ de Koerich à Mersch.*

Luxembourg 24 – Diekirch 32 – Ettelbrück 28 – Arlon 13.

XX **Host. du Vieux Moulin,** Léisbech (Est : 1 km), ✉ 8363, ✆ 30 50 27, ≤, 🏡 – ▤ P. MC VISA

fermé 5 janv.-11 fév. et lundis et mardis non fériés – **Repas** 56.

◆ Vue agreste depuis la salle à manger rustique de cette imposante hostellerie blottie au creux d'un vallon boisé, dans une région pittoresque traversée par l'Eisch.

◆ Deze imposante hostellerie ligt in een bebost dal, in een pittoreske streek waar de Eisch doorheen stroomt. De rustieke eetzaal biedt een idyllisch uitzicht.

SOLEUVRE (ZOLWER) C *Sanem 13 276 h.* 717 U 25 *et* 716 K 7.

Luxembourg 22 – Esch-sur-Alzette 8 – Arlon 27 – Longwy 22.

XX **La Petite Auberge,** r. Aessen 1 (CR 110 - rte de Sanem), ✉ 4411, ✆ 59 44 80, *Fax 59 53 51* – P. AE ① MC VISA. ✗

fermé sem. Pentecôte, 2 dern. sem. août, fin déc.-début janv., dim. et lundi – **Repas** Lunch 14 – carte 40 à 58, ♀.

◆ Ancienne ferme transformée en une confortable auberge. Préparations classiques et traditionnelles. La passion du vin anime le patron ; résultat : une cave bien montée.

◆ Voormalige boerderij die is verbouwd tot een comfortabele herberg. Klassieke en traditionele gerechten. De patron heeft een passie voor wijnen. Resultaat : een prima wijnkaart !

STADTBREDIMUS (STADBRIEDEMES) 717 X 25 *et* 716 M 7 – *1 236 h.*

Env. *au Nord : rte de Greiveldange* ≤★.

Luxembourg 25 – Mondorf-les-Bains 14 – Saarbrücken 80.

🏠 **l'Écluse,** rte du Vin 29, ✉ 5450, ✆ 236 19 11, *info@hotel-ecluse.com, Fax 23 69 76 12,* 🏡, 🛋 – TV 🚗 P. AE MC VISA. ✗ rest

Repas *(fermé 2 sem. Noël-Nouvel An, 2 sem. en juin, merc. midi et jeudi)* (taverne-rest) carte 22 à 39, ♀ – **16 ch** ☕ 47/62 – ½ P 48.

◆ Comme son nom l'indique, cet hôtel récent fait face à une écluse sur la Moselle. Chambres sobrement décorées, garnies d'un mobilier robuste. Une jolie véranda abrite la taverne-restaurant. L'assiette y est généreuse.

◆ Zoals de naam al aangeeft, staat dit moderne hotelgebouw tegenover een sluis in de Moezel. De eenvoudig gedecoreerde kamers zijn met robuust meubilair ingericht. Het taverne-restaurant is ingericht in een leuke serre. Copieuze maaltijden.

STEINHEIM (STENEM) 717 X 24 – *voir à Echternach.*

STRASSEN (STROOSSEN) 717 V 25 *et* 716 L 7 – *voir à Luxembourg, environs.*

SUISSE LUXEMBOURGEOISE (Petite) ★★★ 717 W 24 - X 24 *et* 716 L 6 - M 6 *G. Belgique-Luxembourg.*

SÛRE (Vallée de la) (SAUERDALL) ★★ 717 T 23 - Y 24 *et* 716 K 6 *G. Belgique-Luxembourg.*

TROISVIERGES (ELWEN) 717 U 22 *et* 716 L 5 – *2 520 h.*

Luxembourg 75 – Clervaux 19 – Bastogne 28.

XX **Aub. Lamy** avec ch, r. Asselborn 51, ✉ 9907, ✆ 99 80 41, *Fax 97 80 72,* ≤, 🏡 – |‡| TV P. AE ① MC VISA

fermé mardis non fériés – **Repas** Lunch 20 – 39 bc/42 – **5 ch** ☕ 30/47.

◆ Une auberge qui "ratisse large" : grande carte classique-bourgeoise, restaurant d'été, pub à bières, coin pizzeria et chambres convenables. Coup d'œil sur la nature.

◆ Deze herberg in het groen weet van wanten : grote klassieke kaart, bierpub, kleine pizzeria en vrij geriefelijke kamers.

Dans ce guide
un même symbole, un même mot,
imprimé en rouge ou en ***noir,*** *en maigre ou en* ***gras,***
n'ont pas tout à fait la même signification.
Lisez attentivement les pages explicatives.

VIANDEN (VEIANEN) 717 W 23 *et* 716 L 6 – *1 457 h.*

Voir *Site★★, ≤★★, ✻★★ par le télésiège – Château★★ : chemin de ronde ≤★.*

Env. *au Nord-Ouest : 4 km, Bassins supérieurs du Mont St-Nicolas (route ≤★★ et ≤★) – au Nord : 3,5 km à Bivels : site★ – au Nord : Vallée de l'Our★★.*

r. Vieux Marché 1, ✉ 9417, ☎ 834 25 71, viasi@pt.lu, Fax 84 90 81.

Luxembourg 44 – Clervaux 31 – Diekirch 11 – Ettelbrück 16.

Belvédère, rte de Diekirch 4 (Nord : 1 km), ✉ 9409, ☎ 26 87 42 44, *belveder@pt.lu, Fax 26 87 42 43,* ≤, 🏠, 🏊 – 🛗 📺 ♿ 🅿 – 🏋 25. AE ⓓ ⓜ VISA. ✂ rest
fermé 15 nov.-2 déc. et 9 janv.-2 fév. – **Repas** *Lunch 25* – carte 46 à 56, ♀ – **16 ch** ☐ 97/115 – ½ P 85/95.
◆ Une rénovation totale a donné un second souffle à cet accueillant hôtel familial. Nouveau mobilier dans des chambres bien calibrées, certaines offrant la vue sur le château. Cuisine classique actualisée servie dans une salle à manger contemporaine.
◆ Een volledige renovatie heeft dit gezellige familiehotel nieuw leven ingeblazen. Nieuw meubilair in de kamers, die redelijk van afmeting zijn en waarvan sommige uitzicht bieden op het kasteel. Klassiek-moderne keuken in een eigentijdse eetzaal.

Oranienburg, Grand-Rue 126, ✉ 9411, ☎ 834 15 31, *oranienburg@hotmail.com, Fax 83 43 33,* 🏞 – 🛗 📺 – 🏋 25 à 40. AE ⓓ ⓜ VISA
avril-15 nov. – **Repas** voir rest ***Le Châtelain*** ci-après – **10 ch** ☐ 53/106, – 2 suites – ½ P 59/72.
◆ Établissement familial dont la flatteuse réputation est faite depuis longtemps dans cette charmante petite ville. Bonnes chambres et belle terrasse d'été au pied du château.
◆ Familiehotel dat al lange tijd een complimenteuze reputatie geniet in dit charmante stadje. Goede kamers en mooi zomerterras aan de voet van het kasteel.

Heintz, Grand-Rue 55, ✉ 9410, ☎ 83 41 55, *hoheintz@pt.lu, Fax 83 45 59,* 🏠, 🏞 – 🛗 📺 🅿. AE ⓜ VISA
8 avril-12 nov. – **Repas** *(fermé merc. midi et jeudi midi sauf en juil.-août) Lunch 12* – 22/35 – **30 ch** ☐ 59/78 – ½ P 48/57.
◆ La même famille vous accueille depuis plusieurs générations dans cette hôtellerie établie aux abords de l'église. Chambres avec ou sans balcon. Terrasse et jardin de repos.
◆ Al sinds diverse generaties ontvangt de familie de gasten in dit hotel, dat in de nabijheid van de kerk ligt. Kamers met en zonder balkon. Terras en tuin om te relaxen.

Aub. du Château, Grand-Rue 74, ✉ 9401, ☎ 83 45 74, *chateau@pt.lu, Fax 83 47 20,* 🏠, 🏞 – ✂ 📺. ⓜ VISA. ✂ rest
fermé 15 déc.-20 janv. – **Repas** *(fermé merc. sauf 15 juil.-25 août)* 30/49 – **26 ch** ☐ 53/74 – ½ P 48/52.
◆ Point de chute enviable pour le touriste, cette belle auberge située au centre de Vianden dispose de petites chambres fonctionnelles aménagées à l'identique.
◆ Een begerenswaardige pleisterplaats voor de toerist, deze mooie herberg in het centrum van Vianden. De kleine, functionele kamers zijn identiek ingericht.

Le Châtelain - H. Oranienburg, Grand-Rue 126, ✉ 9411, ☎ 834 15 31, *oranienburg@hotmail.com, Fax 83 43 33,* 🏠 – ▤. AE ⓓ ⓜ VISA
avril-15 nov. ; fermé lundi midi et mardi sauf en juil.-août – **Repas** *Lunch 29* – 51/68.
◆ Le Châtelain vous installe très confortablement dans un décor plaisant. Mise en place soignée. Courte carte d'appétissantes préparations. Important choix de vins.
◆ De "Kasteelheer" installeert zijn gasten bijzonder comfortabel in een charmant decor. Verzorgde inrichting. Kleine kaart met smakelijke gerechten. Uitgebreide wijnkaart.

Aub. Aal Veinen "Beim Hunn" avec ch, Grand-Rue 114, ✉ 9411, ☎ 83 43 68, *ahahn@pt.lu, Fax 83 40 84,* 🏠 – 📺. AE ⓓ ⓜ VISA
fermé fin nov.-début déc. et lundi et mardi sauf juil.-sept. – **Repas** (grillades) *Lunch 9* – carte 22 à 34, ♀ – **8 ch** ☐ 60/70 – ½ P 54.
◆ Maison de caractère bâtie en contrebas du château. Décoration intérieure rustique. Cuisine sans chichi, axée sur les grillades au feu de bois. Chambres sobres.
◆ Karakteristiek pand aan de voet van het kasteel. Rustiek interieur. Eerlijke keuken met gerechten die boven houtskoolvuur worden geroosterd. Eenvoudige kamers.

WAHLHAUSEN (WUELËSSEN) C *Hosingen 1 512 h.* 717 V 23.

Luxembourg 51 – Clervaux 17 – Ettelbrück 24 – Vianden 12.

E'slecker Stuff, Am Duerf 37, ✉ 9841, ☎ 92 16 21, *ahahn@pt.lu, Fax 92 05 10,* 🏠, Grillades – ⓜ VISA
fermé 23 déc.-23 janv. – **Repas** *Lunch 9* – carte 22 à 33, ♀.
◆ Un petit restaurant de village dont les viandes grillées à la braise de la cheminée feront le bonheur des carnivores. Salle à manger rustique non dénuée de caractère.
◆ Een klein dorpsrestaurant waar het vlees in de open haard wordt geroosterd. Een walhalla voor carnivoren. Rustieke eetzaal met karakter.

WALFERDANGE (WALFER) 717 V 25 *et* 716 L 7 – *voir à Luxembourg, environs.*

WASSERBILLIG (WAASSERBËLLEG) *Mertert 3 324 h.* 717 X 24 *et* 716 M 6.
Luxembourg 33 – Ettelbrück 48 – Thionville 58 – Trier 18.

XX **Kinnen** avec ch, rte de Luxembourg 32, ✉ 6633, ☎ 74 00 88, *Fax 74 01 08*, – – P. AE MC VISA.
fermé prem. sem. fév., du 1er au 15 juil., merc. et jeudi soir – **Repas** *Lunch 35* – carte 39 à 59 – **10 ch** 45/65.
◆ Adresse familiale postée aux abords de la localité. Ample salle à manger. L'été, repas en terrasse. Pour les hébergés, réception au bar et chambres d'un bon calibre.
◆ Restaurant aan de rand van het plaatsje. Ruime eetzaal. 's Zomers wordt er op het terras geserveerd. Voor de overnachters, receptie aan de bar en kamers van een goed kaliber.

WEILERBACH (WEILERBAACH) *Berdorf 1 345 h.* 717 X 23 *et* 716 M 6.
Luxembourg 39 – Diekirch 24 – Echternach 5 – Ettelbrück 29.

Schumacher, rte de Diekirch 1, ✉ 6590, ☎ 720 13 31, *hotschum@pt.lu, Fax 72 87 13*, <, , , – P. MC VISA.
15 mars-nov. – **Repas** *(fermé merc. et après 20 h 30)* 39 – **25 ch** 65/82 – ½ P 54.
◆ La Sûre - qui matérialise la frontière avec l'Allemagne - coule devant cette hostellerie. Chambres bien équipées. Terrasse sur le toit, offrant un panorama sur la vallée.
◆ De Sûre - die de grens vormt met Duitsland - stroomt langs dit hotel. De kamers zijn van alle gemakken voorzien. Vanaf het dakterras uitzicht op het dal.

WEISWAMPACH (WÄISWAMPECH) 717 V 22 *et* 716 L 5 – *1 159 h.*
Luxembourg 69 – Clervaux 16 – Diekirch 36 – Ettelbrück 41.

Keup, rte de Stavelot 143 (sur N 7), ✉ 9991, ☎ 997 59 93 00, *hotel@keup.lu, Fax 997 59 94 40* – , rest, P – 40. AE MC VISA
Repas *(fermé merc.) Lunch 9* – 22/32, – **25 ch** *(fermé merc. hors saison)* 41/104 – ½ P 52.
◆ Cet hôtel récent est une halte bienvenue pour les usagers de la route. Les chambres, assez vastes et convenablement insonorisées, se répartissent sur deux étages. Grande salle à manger classiquement aménagée.
◆ Dit vrij nieuwe hotel is een welkome etappeplaats voor weggebruikers. De vrij grote kamers zijn voorzien van geluidsisolatie en liggen verspreid over twee verdiepingen. Grote, klassiek ingerichte eetzaal.

XX **Host. du Nord** avec ch, rte de Stavelot 113, ✉ 9991, ☎ 99 83 19, *Fax 99 74 61*, , – P. AE MC VISA
Repas *Lunch 8* – 25/45 bc – **8 ch** 37/55 – ½ P 50/66.
◆ Une nouvelle équipe a repris les rênes de cette hostellerie dont la véranda s'ouvre sur un jardin où les parasols fleurissent en été. Chambres de mise simple.
◆ Een nieuw team heeft de teugels overgenomen van deze hostellerie, waarvan de serre aan een tuin grenst die 's zomers vol fleurige parasols staat. Eenvoudige kamers.

WELSCHEID (WELSCHENT) *Bourscheid 1 230 h.* 717 V 23 *et* 716 L 6.
Luxembourg 38 – Diekirch 13 – Ettelbrück 8.

XX **Reuter** avec ch, Waarkstrooss 2 (centre village), ✉ 9191, ☎ 81 29 17, *infos@hotel-reuter.lu, Fax 81 73 09*, , – , rest, P. MC VISA.
fermé 8 fév.-12 mars, 12 nov.-17 déc., lundi soir et mardi – **Repas** *Lunch 30* – 29/60 bc – **17 ch** 65/74 – ½ P 56/69.
◆ Établissement tenu en famille depuis 1875. Recettes variées et alléchantes. Belle sélection de vins locaux. Certaines chambres offrent plus d'espace que d'autres.
◆ Etablissement dat al sinds 1875 door de familie wordt gerund. Gevarieerde en aanlokkelijke gerechten. Mooie selectie lokale wijnen. Sommige kamers zijn ruimer dan andere.

WILTZ (WOLZ) 717 U 23 *et* 716 K 6 – *4 507 h.*
Château, ✉ *9516*, ☎ *95 74 44, siwiltz@pt.lu*, Fax 95 75 56.
Luxembourg 55 – Clervaux 21 – Ettelbrück 26 – Bastogne 21.

Aux Anciennes Tanneries , r. Jos Simon 42a, ✉ 9550, ☎ 95 75 99, *tannerie@pt.lu, Fax 95 75 95*, , – P – 25 à 80. MC VISA
fermé 23 août-12 sept. et du 12 au 27 déc. – **Repas** *(fermé merc. et jeudi)* carte 24 à 55 – **12 ch** 63/133 – ½ P 68/91.
◆ L'enseigne rappelle l'ancienne destination des lieux et, plus largement, l'activité qui valut à Wiltz une certaine notoriété. Coquettes chambres de notre temps. Salle de restaurant voûtée. Confortable terrasse estivale dressée au bord de la rivière.
◆ De naam herinnert aan de oude leerlooierijen die hier vroeger waren gevestigd en Wiltz zekere faam hebben bezorgd. Nette, eigentijdse kamers. Gewelfde restaurantzaal. Comfortabel zomerterras aan de rivier.

XXX **du Vieux Château** avec ch, Grand-Rue 1, ✉ 9530, ☎ 958 01 81, *vchateau@pt.lu, Fax 95 77 55*, , , – TV P. AE ⓓ MC VISA. ch
fermé 3 prem. sem. août et 2 prem. sem. janv. – **Repas** *(fermé dim. soirs et lundis non fériés)* Lunch 25 – 45/82 bc, ♀ – **7 ch** ☕ 81/87, – 1 suite – ½ P 84.
◆ Belle demeure construite dans un quartier pittoresque, non loin du vieux château comtal de Wiltz. Terrasse ombragée. Cuisine sagement personnalisée. Chambres calmes.
◆ Mooi pand in een schilderachtige wijk niet ver van het oude grafelijke kasteel van Wiltz. Beschaduwd terras. Keuken met een persoonlijk accent. Rustige kamers.

XX **Host. des Ardennes,** Grand-Rue 61, ✉ 9530, ☎ 95 81 52, *Fax 95 94 47*, ← – AE ⓓ MC VISA.
fermé 15 fév.-7 mars, du 1er au 22 août, sam. et après 20 h 30 – **Repas** carte 28 à 45.
◆ Au centre-ville, affaire familiale dont le café - où l'on sert des plats du jour - flanque une jolie salle de restaurant offrant la vue sur la vallée boisée.
◆ Deze hostellerie bevindt zich in het centrum. Naast het café - waar dagschotels worden geserveerd - is een leuke restaurantzaal ingericht met uitzicht op het beboste dal.

WILWERDANGE (WILWERDANG) C *Troisvierges 2 520 h.* 717 V 22 *et* 716 L 5.
Luxembourg 71 – Diekirch 41 – Ettelbrück 43 – Bastogne 31.

XX **L'Ecuelle,** r. Principale 15, ✉ 9980, ☎ 99 89 56, *ecuellew@pt.lu, Fax 97 93 44*, – P. AE ⓓ MC VISA.
fermé dern. sem. juil., janv., lundi soir, mardi soir et merc. – **Repas** 31/65.
◆ Un bref trajet en voiture sépare la frontière belge de cette auberge villageoise. La maison fume elle-même certains produits : truite, saumon, etc. Formule menu-carte.
◆ Vanuit deze dorpsherberg is het maar even rijden naar de Belgische grens. Het "huis" rookt zelf enkele producten, waaronder zalm en forel. À la carte en menu.

WILWERWILTZ (WËLWERWOLZ) 717 V 23 *et* 716 L 6 – *602 h.*
Luxembourg 64 – Clervaux 11 – Ettelbrück 11 – Wiltz 11 – Bastogne 32.

Host. La Bascule, Op der Gare 13, ✉ 9776, ☎ 92 14 15, *info@baschle.lu, Fax 92 10 88* – TV P. AE MC VISA.
fermé 19 déc.-15 janv. – **Repas** 22 – **12 ch** ☕ 48/76 – ½ P 60/65.
◆ La route pittoresque reliant Wiltz à Clervaux conduit à cette hostellerie familiale postée en face d'une minuscule gare. Chambres fonctionnelles. L'addition d'un repas pris à "La Bascule" ne vous fera certainement pas tomber à la renverse !
◆ De pittoreske weg die Wiltz met Clervaux verbindt, voert naar deze hostellerie, die tegenover een piepklein stationnetje staat. Functionele kamers. Van de rekening voor een maaltijd in de Bascule zult u zeker niet uit balans raken !

Nederland
Pays-Bas

Het is gebruikelijk, dat bepaalde restaurants in Nederland pas geopend zijn vanaf 16 uur, vooral in het weekend. Reserveert u daarom uit voorzorg.

L'usage veut que certains restaurants aux Pays-Bas n'ouvrent qu'à partir de 16 heures, en week-end particulièrement. Prenez donc la précaution de réserver en conséquence.

Les étoiles
De sterren
Die Sterne
The stars
"Bib Gourmand"
Repas 33
Repas soignés à prix modérés
Verzorgde maaltijden voor een schappelijke prijs
Sorgfältig zubereitete preiswerte Mahlzeiten
Good food at moderate prices
L'agrément
Aangenaam verblijf
Annehmlichkeit
Peaceful atmosphere and setting
Carte de voisinage : voir à la ville choisie
Kaart van de omgeving in de buurt van grote steden
Stadt mit Umgebungskarte
Town with a local map
Schoorl
Alkmaar
Castricum
Wijk aan Zee
Beverwij
Zaandar
Bloemendaal
XXXX Overveen
Heemstede
XXX
Amstelvee
Ouderkerk aan de Amstel
Warmond
A 4-E 19
Noorden
XXX Oegstgeest
Leiden
Den Haag
Voorburg XXXX
A 12-E 25
Wateringen
Rijswijk
Delft XXX
Hoek van Holland
Schiedam
Rijsoord
ROTTERDAM
A 16-E 19
Middelharnis
Schuddebeurs
Breda
Etten-Leur
XXX Wolphaartsdijk
Goes
Yerseke
N 62
A 58-E 312
Kruiningen
XXXX
A 4
A 12
Breskens
Sluis XXX
A 1-E 19
A 14-E 17
BELGIQUE
Leie
A 18-E 40
A 10-E 40
Schelde
IJzer
A 17
A 10-E 40
A1-E19
A 14-E 17
Bruxelles
Brussel
A3-E40

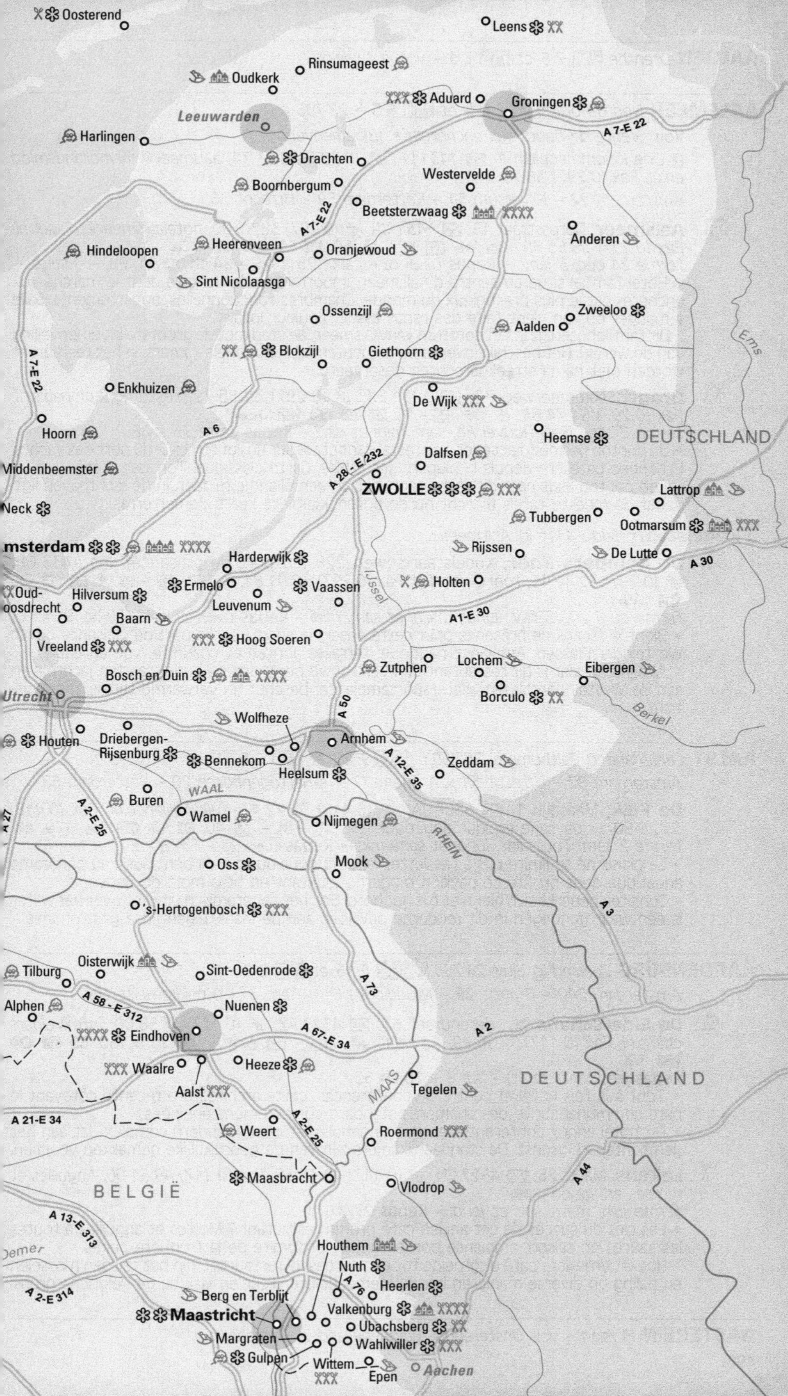

Oosterend
Leens
Rinsumageest
Oudkerk
Aduard
Groningen
Leeuwarden
Harlingen
A 7-E 22
Drachten
Westervelde
Boornbergum
Beetsterzwaag
A 7-E 22
Anderen
Hindeloopen
Heerenveen
Oranjewoud
Sint Nicolaasga
Ossenzijl
Zweeloo
Aalden
Blokzijl
Giethoorn
Ems
A 7-E 22
Enkhuizen
De Wijk
A 6
Hoorn
Heemse
DEUTSCHLAND
Dalfsen
Middenbeemster
A 28 - E 232
ZWOLLE
Lattrop
Neck
Tubbergen
Ootmarsum
msterdam
Rijssen
De Lutte
Harderwijk
A 30
Ermelo
Vaassen
IJssel
Holten
Oud-
oosdrecht
Hilversum
Leuvenum
Baarn
A1-E 30
Vreeland
Hoog Soeren
Zutphen
Lochem
Eibergen
Bosch en Duin
Borculo
Utrecht
A 50
Wolfheze
Berkel
Houten
Driebergen-
Rijsenburg
Arnhem
Bennekom
Heelsum
A 12-E 35
Zeddam
WAAL
Buren
A 27
A 2-E 25
Wamel
Nijmegen
RHEIN
Oss
Mook
A 3
's-Hertogenbosch
Oisterwijk
Tilburg
Sint-Oedenrode
A 73
A 58 - E 312
Alphen
Nuenen
A 67-E 34
A 2
Eindhoven
Waalre
Heeze
Aalst
MAAS
Tegelen
DEUTSCHLAND
A 21-E 34
Weert
A 2-E 25
Roermond
A 44
Maasbracht
BELGIË
Vlodrop
A 13-E 313
Demer
Houthem
Nuth
A 76
Heerlen
A 2-E 314
Berg en Terblijt
Valkenburg
Maastricht
Ubachsberg
Margraten
Wahlwiller
Gulpen
Wittem
Epen
Aachen

AALDEN *Drenthe* 531 Z 6 *et* 715 L 3 – *voir à Zweeloo.*

AALSMEER *Noord-Holland* 532 N 9 *et* 715 F 5 – *22 705 h.*

Voir *Vente de fleurs aux enchères★★ (Bloemenveiling).*

Drie Kolommenplein 1, ✉ 1431 LA, ☎ (0 297) 32 53 74, aalsmeer@vvvhollandsmidden.nl, Fax (0 297) 38 75 54.

Amsterdam 22 – Hilversum 31 – Rotterdam 59 – Utrecht 36.

Aalsmeer, Dorpsstraat 15, ✉ 1431 CA, ☎ (0 297) 38 55 00, *hotelaalsmeer@planet.nl, Fax (0 297) 38 55 38* – 50. AE VISA JCB
fermé 24 déc.-3 janv. – **Repas** *Lunch 18* – carte 25 à 45 – **54 ch** 71/92, – 1 suite.
◆ Hôtel familial situé au centre d'Aalsmeer, importante ville floricole dont le marché aux enchères est le plus prestigieux du monde. Chambres fonctionnelles, appartements. Salle à manger où l'on vient faire des repas assez "couleur locale".
◆ Dit familiehotel ligt in het centrum van Aalsmeer, de stad met de grootste bloemenveiling van de wereld. Het beschikt over appartementen en functionele kamers. In het restaurant worden met name streekgerechten geserveerd.

Dragt, Stommeerweg 72, ✉ 1431 EX, ☎ (0 297) 32 55 79, *restdrag@globalxs.nl, Fax (0 297) 34 74 63,* ←, – AE VISA JCB
fermé 2 sem. Noël-Nouvel An, sam. midi et dim. – **Repas** carte 35 à 68.
◆ Un ponton permet d'accéder à ce restaurant établi sur un îlot au cœur du port des yachts. Échappée batelière depuis la plupart des tables. Carte classique. Terrasse d'été.
◆ Een ponton leidt naar dit restaurant, dat op een eilandje midden in de jachthaven ligt. Vanaf de meeste tafels uitzicht op de boten. Klassieke kaart. Zomerterras.

à Kudelstaart *Sud : 4 km* C *Aalsmeer :*

De Kempers Roef, Kudelstaartseweg 228 (au port de plaisance), ✉ 1433 GR, ☎ (0 297) 32 41 45, *roef@xskall.nl, Fax (0 297) 36 01 81,* ←, – AE VISA JCB
fermé du 4 au 15 fév., lundi, mardi et sam. midi – **Repas** *Lunch 29* – 43/79 bc, ♀.
◆ Bientôt 30 ans de présence pour cette enseigne ancrée sur le port de plaisance du lac Westeinder Plassen. Ambiance nautique, terrasse abritée et chauffée, vue agréable.
◆ Al bijna 30 jaar is dit restaurant een vertrouwd beeld aan de Kudelstaartse jachthaven aan de Westeinderplassen. Watersportambiance, beschut en verwarmd terras, mooi uitzicht.

AALST *Gelderland* C *Zaltbommel 25 759 h.* 532 P 12 *et* 715 G 6.

Amsterdam 82 – Utrecht 51 – Arnhem 77 – 's-Hertogenbosch 20 – Rotterdam 68.

De Fuik, Maasdijk 1, ✉ 5308 JA, ☎ (0 418) 55 22 47, *fuik@alliance.nl, Fax (0 418) 55 29 80,* ← paysage typique aquatique, – 40. AE VISA JCB.
fermé 2 sem. Toussaint, lundi et sam. midi – **Repas** *Lunch 45* – 63/80, ♀.
◆ Le plaisir ne se limite pas à l'assiette, mise au goût du jour : il tient aussi au panorama aquatique dont profite ce pavillon moderne jouxtant un bras mort du fleuve.
◆ Genieten beperkt zich hier niet tot het bord. Ook het panoramisch uitzicht over het water is een waar genoegen in dit moderne paviljoen aan de Maas. Eigentijdse gastronomie.

AARDENBURG *Zeeland* C *Sluis 24 753 h.* 532 F 15 *et* 715 B 8.

Amsterdam 240 – Brugge 26 – Middelburg 61 – Gent 37 – Knokke-Heist 16.

De Elderschans , Herendreef 67, ✉ 4527 AZ, ☎ (0 117) 37 58 00, *info@elderschans.nl, Fax (0 117) 37 58 99,* – 25 à 150. AE VISA.
Repas (résidents seult) – 8 – **70 ch** 55.
◆ Tout à la fois hôtel et centre de conférences, cette architecture récente côtoyant le parc communal abrite des chambres standard correctement équipées.
◆ Dit hotel annex conferentiecentrum is gehuisvest in een modern complex dat aan het gemeentepark grenst. De standaardkamers zijn van de gebruikelijke gemakken voorzien.

Lekens, Markt 25, ✉ 4527 CN, ☎ (0 117) 49 14 35, *Fax (0 117) 49 31 00,* Anguilles et moules en saison –
fermé juin, merc. soir et jeudi – **Repas** 27/46 bc.
◆ Les clés du succès de cet ancien café promu restaurant ? Moules et anguilles à toutes les sauces en saison, ambiance bon enfant et proximité de la frontière belge.
◆ Hoe dit vroegere café uitgroeide tot een succesvol restaurant ? In het seizoen mosselen en paling op diverse manieren bereid, gemoedelijke sfeer en vlak bij de Belgische grens.

AASTEREIN *Fryslân – voir Oosterend à Waddeneilanden (Terschelling).*

PAYS-BAS

ABCOUDE *Utrecht* 531 O 9, 532 O 9 et 715 F 5 – *8 524 h.*
Amsterdam 15 – Utrecht 25 – Hilversum 20.

Abcoude, Kerkplein 7, ✉ 1391 GJ, ☎ (0 294) 28 12 71, *info@hotelabcoude.nl, Fax (0 294) 28 56 21* – |♦|, TV P – 50. AE ① MC VISA JCB. rest
Repas *De Wakende Haan* *(fermé 18 juil.-9 août, 19 déc.-3 janv., dim. et lundi)* (dîner seult) carte env. 36 – ☕ 9 – **19 ch** 73/89.
• Au centre de la localité, juste devant l'église, petite ressource hôtelière dont les chambres, d'un confort convenable, se partagent entre deux maisons voisines. Le Coq Veilleur (Wakende Haan) vous plonge le temps d'un repas dans une atmosphère "cocorico" !
• Een klein hotel in het centrum van Abcoude, recht tegenover de kerk. De comfortabel ingerichte kamers liggen verspreid over twee aangrenzende panden. In het sfeervolle restaurant De Wakende Haan zult u niet gemakkelijk boven uw bord in slaap vallen.

ADUARD *Groningen* 531 X 3 et 715 K 2 – *voir à Groningen.*

AFFERDEN *Limburg* C *Bergen 13 539 h.* 532 V 13 et 715 J 7.
Amsterdam 142 – Eindhoven 61 – Nijmegen 30 – Venlo 32.

XXX **Aub. De Papenberg** avec ch, Hengeland 1a (Nord : 1 km sur N 271), ✉ 5851 EA, ☎ (0 485) 53 17 44, *info@papenberg.nl, Fax (0 485) 53 22 64,* TV P – 30. AE MC VISA.
fermé 23 juil.-12 août et 27 déc.-10 janv. – **Repas** *(fermé dim.)* (dîner seult) 38/72 bc – **21 ch** ☕ 70/93 – ½ P 70/88.
• Auberge moderne bâtie en léger retrait de la route. Une accueillante terrasse estivale sépare le restaurant des chambres. Jardin avec pièce d'eau. Service personnalisé.
• Deze moderne herberg ligt iets van de weg af. Tussen het restaurant en de kamers is een gezellig zomerterras ingericht. Tuin met waterpartij. Persoonlijke service.

AFSLUITDIJK (DIGUE DU NORD) ★★ *Fryslân et Noord-Holland* 531 Q 4 et 715 G 3 *G. Hollande.*

AKERSLOOT *Noord-Holland* C *Castricum 23 330 h.* 531 N 7 et 715 F 4.
Amsterdam 30 – Haarlem 23 – Alkmaar 13.

Akersloot, Geesterweg 1a (près A 9), ✉ 1921 NV, ☎ (0 251) 36 18 88, *info@ajersloot.valk.nl, Fax (0 251) 31 45 08,* – |♦|, rest, TV P – 25 à 600. AE ① MC VISA JCB
Repas (ouvert jusqu'à 23 h) Lunch 13 – carte 22 à 44, ♀ – **212 ch** ☕ 95.
• Proche de l'autoroute, motel de chaîne contemporain dont les chambres, de plain-pied ou en étage, assez amples et "cosy", sont dotées de bureaux et correctement insonorisées.
• Eigentijds ketenmotel vlak bij de snelweg. De ruime en knusse kamers, die op de begane grond en de eerste verdieping liggen, zijn voorzien van geluidsisolatie en een bureau.

XX **The Flying Dragon,** De Crimpen 2, ✉ 1921 BW, ☎ (0 251) 31 09 49, *Fax (0 251) 31 56 05,* Cuisine chinoise – P. AE ① MC VISA
fermé 18 fév.-4 nov. et lundis non fériés – **Repas** (dîner seult) carte 30 à 44, ♀.
• Tenté par un "trip" culinaire en Chine ? Embarquement immédiat au Dragon Volant. Plats typiques de l'Empire du Milieu, servis dans une salle à manger actuelle.
• Zin in een culinaire trip naar China ? Ga dan direct aan boord van De Vliegende Draak. Specialiteiten uit het Rijk van het Midden worden geserveerd in een eigentijdse eetzaal.

AKKRUM *Fryslân* C *Boarnsterhim 18 738 h.* 531 U 4 et 715 I 2.
Amsterdam 137 – Leeuwarden 23 – Groningen 60 – Zwolle 74.

De Oude Schouw, Oude Schouw 6 (Nord-Ouest : 3 km), ✉ 8491 MP, ☎ (0 566) 65 21 25, *postbus@oudeschouw.nl, Fax (0 566) 65 21 02,* ←, – TV P. AE ① MC VISA
Repas 44 – **16 ch** ☕ 89/99 – ½ P 88.
• À un croisement de canaux, ancien relais de halage peut-être plusieurs fois centenaire, devancé d'une grande terrasse estivale dressée à fleur d'eau. Chambres fonctionnelles. Chaleureuse salle de restaurant profitant d'un coup d'œil "batelier".
• Dit eeuwenoude veerhuis annex uitspanning ligt aan de kruising van twee waterwegen. Langs het water aan de voorkant is een groot zomerterras ingericht. Functionele kamers. Restaurant met een warme ambiance en uitzicht op de voorbijvarende boten.

ALBERGEN *Overijssel* 531 Z 8 et 715 L 4 – *voir à Tubbergen.*

ALDTSJERK (OUDKERK) *Fryslân* 531 T 3 et 715 I 2 – *voir à Leeuwarden.*

ALKMAAR *Noord-Holland* 531 N 7 et 715 F 4 – *92 992 h.*

Voir *Marché au fromage*★★ *(Kaasmarkt) sur la place du Poids public (Waagplein)* Y 34 – *Grandes orgues*★, *petit orgue*★ *dans la Grande église ou église St-Laurent (Grote of St. Laurenskerk)* Y **A**.

18 *Sluispolderweg 7,* ✉ *1817 BM,* ☎ *(0 72) 515 68 07, Fax (0 72) 520 99 18.*

Waagplein 3, ✉ *1811 JP,* ☎ *(0 72) 511 42 84, info@vvvalkmaar.nl, Fax (0 72) 511 75 13.*

Amsterdam *39* ③ *– Haarlem 31* ③ *– Leeuwarden 109* ②

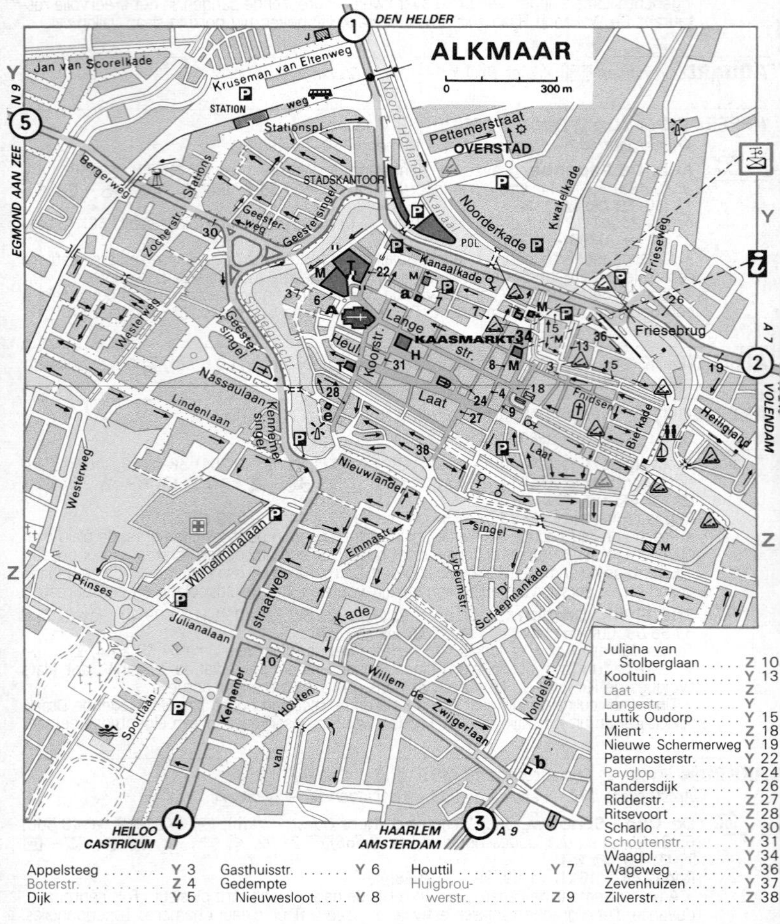

Golden Tulip sans rest, Arcadialaan 7, ✉ 1813 KN, ☎ (0 72) 540 14 14, *info@gtalkmaar.nl, Fax (0 72) 547 01 41,* – – 25 à 120. AE MC VISA. Z b

76 ch 115/140.

◆ Hôtel posté sur une esplanade. Bonne isolation phonique dans les chambres, conformes aux standards de la chaîne. Des peintures d'artistes locaux ornent les murs des couloirs.

◆ Hotel op een esplanade. Kamers met goede geluidsisolatie en ingericht conform de normen van de keten. In de gangen hangen schilderijen van lokale kunstenaars.

XX **Bios,** Gedempte Nieuwesloot 54a, ✉ 1811 KT, ☎ (0 72) 512 44 22, *ditmar.kookt@planet.nl, Fax (0 72) 512 44 99, Ouvert jusqu'à minuit* – ▤. AE ⓓ MC VISA JCB. ✂ Y a
fermé 2 dern. sem. août, dim. midi et lundi – **Repas** Lunch 30 – 32/68 bc, ♀.
◆ Cette demeure du 17e s. abrita un cinéma (bios) avant de devenir une brasserie. Salle à manger moderne, toujours un peu branchée 7e Art. Cuisine et cave globe-trotter.
◆ Voordat het tot brasserie werd verbouwd, huisvestte dit 17e-eeuwse pand een bioscoop. Eigentijdse eetzaal met glamourdesign. Keuken en wijnkaart zijn reislustig van aard.

XX **'t Stokpaardje,** Vrouwenstraat 1, ✉ 1811 GA, ☎ (0 72) 512 88 70, *info@stokpaardjealkmaar.nl, Fax (0 72) 511 28 58* – ▤. AE ⓓ MC VISA JCB. ✂ Z e
fermé mardi et merc. – **Repas** (dîner seult) carte 40 à 51, ♀.
◆ Bistrot cossu à débusquer dans une ruelle du centre, le "Cheval de bataille" (Stokpaardje) a pris un sacré coup de jeune, des mors aux sabots. Appétissante carte actuelle.
◆ Dit culinaire rasdier staat op stal in een steegje in het centrum en heeft een volledige facelift ondergaan. Luxueuze bistro met eigentijdse menukaart.

à **Noord-Scharwoude** *Nord : 8 km* C *Langedijk 24 724 h :*

De Buizerd, Spoorstraat 124, ✉ 1723 NG, ☎ (0 226) 31 23 88, *Fax (0 226) 31 76 27*, – ▤ rest, TV P – 80. MC VISA JCB. ✂
fermé 24 déc.-1er janv. – **Repas** carte 27 à 49, ♀ – **12 ch** 44/89 – ½ P 64/81.
◆ Au bord d'un canal, tranquille petit hôtel familial composé de quatre maisonnettes communicantes, coiffées de toits pentus. Chambres fonctionnelles. Restaurant misant sur un choix de préparations simples mais assez généreuses.
◆ Een rustig familiehotelletje langs het kanaal. Het omvat vier huizen met puntdak die met elkaar in verbinding staan en functionele kamers herbergen. In het restaurant worden eenvoudige maar vrij royale maaltijden geserveerd.

ALMELO *Overijssel* 531 Z 8, 532 Z 8 *et* 715 K 4 – *71 026 h.*

à l'Ouest : 4 km à Wierden, Rijssensestraat 142a, ✉ 7642 NN, ☎ (0 546) 57 61 50, Fax (0 546) 57 81 09.

Centrumplein 2, ✉ 7607 SB, ☎ (0 546) 81 87 65, info@vvvalmelo.nl, Fax (0 546) 82 30 12.

Amsterdam 146 – Zwolle 48 – Enschede 23.

Theater, Schouwburgplein 1, ✉ 7607 AE, ☎ (0 546) 80 30 00, *info@theaterhotel.nl, Fax (0 546) 82 16 65*, – TV – 25 à 750. AE ⓓ MC VISA JCB
Repas carte 23 à 40, ♀ – 9 – **112 ch** 60/75 – ½ P 85/165.
◆ Ancien théâtre municipal récemment agrandi d'une annexe moderne accueillant des chambres amples et actuelles. Colossale infrastructure conférencière. Une atmosphère un rien nostalgique flotte dans la salle de restaurant.
◆ Voormalig stadstheater dat onlangs is uitgebreid met een moderne annexe waarin ruime, eigentijdse kamers zijn ingericht. Het beschikt over een kolossale infrastructuur voor congressen en vergaderingen. In de restaurantzaal hangt een ietwat nostalgische sfeer.

ALMEN *Gelderland* C *Gorssel 13 375 h.* 532 W 10 *et* 715 J 5.
Amsterdam 119 – Apeldoorn 32 – Arnhem 42 – Enschede 52.

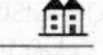

De Hoofdige Boer, Dorpsstraat 38, ✉ 7218 AH, ☎ (0 575) 43 17 44, *hoofdigeboer@tref.nl, Fax (0 575) 43 15 67*, – TV P – 25 à 150. AE ⓓ MC VISA. ✂
fermé 31 déc.-6 janv. – **Repas** *(fermé après 20 h 30)* 30/40 – **23 ch** 95 – ½ P 145.
◆ Sage petite auberge tenue en famille, à dénicher au cœur d'Almen, juste à côté de l'église. Chambres tout doucettement rajeunies et jardin adorable à la belle saison. Avec la complicité du soleil, le couvert est dressé sur une délicieuse terrasse estivale.
◆ Degelijk hotelletje in familiebeheer, direct naast de kerk midden in Almen. Kamers die stukje bij beetje zijn gemoderniseerd en 's zomers een prachtige tuin. Als de zon meewerkt, worden de tafels gedekt op een heerlijk zomerterras.

Si le coût de la vie subit des variations importantes,
les prix que nous indiquons peuvent être majorés.
Lors de votre réservation à l'hôtel, faites-vous préciser le prix définitif.

ALMERE *Flevoland* 531 Q 8, 532 Q 8 *et* 715 G 4 – *158 902 h.*

Watersnipweg 21, ✉ 1341 AA, ☎ (0 36) 521 91 32, Fax (0 36) 521 91 31.

Spoordreef 20 (Almere-Stad), ✉ 1315 GP, ☎ (0 36) 533 46 00, almere@vvvflevoland.nl, Fax (0 36) 534 36 65.

Amsterdam 30 – Lelystad 34 – Apeldoorn 86 – Utrecht 46.

à Almere-Haven C *Almere :*

Brasserie Bakboord, Veerkade 10, ✉ 1357 PK, ☎ (0 36) 540 40 40, *bakboord@uwnet.nl, Fax (0 36) 540 40 41,* ≤, Avec taverne, – P. MC VISA
fermé 27 déc.-3 janv. – **Repas** *Lunch 24* – 31/50 bc, ♀.
• Taverne-restaurant embrassant du regard le port de plaisance. Cuisine du moment, formule menu-choix et vins servis en bouteille ou au verre. Terrasses d'été au ras de l'eau.
• Brasserie aan de jachthaven. Seizoengebonden keuken, keuzemenu en wijn per fles of glas. In de zomer is het heerlijk toeven op een van de terrassen aan het water.

Bestevaer, Sluiskade 16, ✉ 1357 NX, ☎ (0 36) 531 15 57, – AE ⓓ MC VISA.
fermé lundi d'oct. à mars et mardi – **Repas** (déjeuner sur réservation) 28.
• Une terrasse estivale précède cette plaisante petite table ancrée devant le port des yachts. Registre culinaire classique actualisé. Menu mensuel courtisé.
• Dit charmante restaurantje ligt verankerd bij de jachthaven en heeft aan de voorzijde een zomerterras. Klassiek culinair register in een modern jasje en favoriet maandmenu.

à Almere-Stad C *Almere :*

Bastion, Audioweg 1 (près A 6, sortie ③, Almere-West), ✉ 1322 AT, ☎ (0 36) 536 77 55, *bastion@bastionhotel.nl, Fax (0 36) 536 70 09* – TV P. AE ⓓ MC VISA.
Repas (grillades, ouvert jusqu'à 23 h) carte env. 30, ♀ – ☕ 10 – **100 ch** 78/100.
• Proximité de l'autoroute, parking à vue, chambres pratiques de taille convenable, petit-déjeuner buffet... Bref, une copie conforme de tous les hôtels de la chaîne batave.
• Nabij de snelweg, parking in het zicht, praktische kamers van redelijk formaat, ontbijtbuffet... Kortom, een exacte kopie van de hotels die tot deze Nederlandse keten behoren.

ALPHEN *Noord-Brabant* C *Alphen-Chaam 9 447 h.* 532 O 14 *et* 715 H 6.

Amsterdam 122 – 's-Hertogenbosch 37 – Breda 25 – Tilburg 14.

Bunga Melati, Oude Rielseweg 2 (Nord-Est : 2 km), ✉ 5131 NR, ☎ (0 13) 508 17 28, *bungamelati@hotmail.com, Fax (0 13) 508 19 63,* Cuisine indonésienne – P. AE ⓓ MC VISA JCB
Repas (dîner seult sauf week-end) 24/28.
• Un bel éventail de "rijsttafels" (tables de riz) est déployé à cette enseigne indonésienne. Décor intérieur à la hollandaise, terrasse champêtre et jardin soigné.
• Dit Indonesische restaurant heeft een mooi scala aan rijsttafels op de menukaart staan. Interieur met Hollands decor, landelijk terras en verzorgde tuin.

ALPHEN AAN DEN RIJN *Zuid-Holland* 532 M 10 *et* 715 F 5 – *70 649 h.*

Kromme Aarweg 5, ✉ 2403 NB, ☎ (0 172) 47 45 67, Fax (0 172) 49 46 60.

Wilhelminalaan 1, ✉ 2405 EB, ☎ (0 172) 49 56 00, info@vvvalphenaandenrijn.nl, Fax (0 172) 47 33 53.

Amsterdam 36 – Rotterdam 41 – Den Haag 32 – Utrecht 38.

Avifauna, Hoorn 65, ✉ 2404 HG, ☎ (0 172) 48 75 75, *reservations@avifauna.valk.nl, Fax (0 172) 48 75 06,* – rest, TV P – 25 à 400. AE ⓓ MC VISA
Repas (ouvert jusqu'à 23 h) carte 22 à 41, ♀ – ☕ 9 – **94 ch** 70/80 – ½ P 67/97.
• Vieille auberge désormais englobée dans un parc ornithologique. Les chambres, assez spacieuses, sont aménagées dans une annexe récente. Nombreuses possibilités de loisirs.
• Deze oude herberg maakt tegenwoordig deel uit van het gelijknamige vogelpark. De vrij ruime kamers zijn in een moderne dependance ingericht. Tal van recreatieve mogelijkheden.

Golden Tulip, Stationsplein 2, ✉ 2405 BK, ☎ (0 172) 49 01 00, *info@gtalphenadrijn.nl, Fax (0 172) 49 37 81,* – rest, TV P – 25 à 125. AE ⓓ MC VISA
Repas *Lunch 19* – carte 27 à 39, ♀ – ☕ 13 – **53 ch** 118/128 – ½ P 130/160.
• Immeuble contemporain élevé à deux pas de la gare. Chambres fonctionnelles rajeunies depuis peu et convenablement insonorisées. Huit salles de séminaires. À table, choix de recettes bourgeoises.
• Dit eigentijdse pand bij het station beschikt over functionele kamers die onlangs zijn gerenoveerd en voorzien van goede geluidsisolatie. Acht zalen voor seminars. In het restaurant worden eenvoudige gerechten geserveerd.

AMELAND (Ile de) *Fryslân* 531 T 2 *et* 715 I 1 – *voir à Waddeneilanden.*

AMERONGEN *Utrecht* 532 R 10 *et* 715 H 5 – *7 220 h.*

Amsterdam 71 – Utrecht 29 – Arnhem 38.

Herberg Den Rooden Leeuw, Drostestraat 35, ✉ 3958 BK, ☎ (0 343) 45 40 55, *info@denroodenleeuw.nl, Fax (0 343) 45 77 65* – P. AE ◑ MC VISA JCB
fermé mi-juil.-mi-août, mardi et merc. – **Repas** (déjeuner sur réservation) carte 32 à 44.
◆ À l'entrée du village, vénérable auberge champêtre que signale une belle enseigne en fer forgé. L'ancienne écurie sert aussi de halte repas aux promeneurs du dimanche.
◆ Een smeedijzeren uithangbord signaleert deze oude, landelijke herberg aan de rand van het dorp. De voormalige stalhouderij is op zondag ook een pleisterplaats voor wandelaars.

AMERSFOORT *Utrecht* 532 R 10 *et* 715 H 5 – *129 720 h.*

Voir *Vieille Cité★ : Maisons de rempart★ (muurhuizen)* BYZ – *Tour Notre-Dame★ (O.-L.-Vrouwetoren)* AZ **S** – *Koppelpoort★* AY.

Env. *au Sud : 14 km à Doorn : Collection d'objets d'art★ dans le château (Huis Doorn).*

Stationsplein 9, ✉ 3818 LE, ☎ 0 900-112 23 64, info@vvvamersfoort.nl, Fax (0 33) 465 01 08.

Amsterdam 51 ① – Utrecht 21 ④ – Apeldoorn 46 ① – Arnhem 51 ③

Plan page suivante

Berghotel, Utrechtseweg 225, ✉ 3818 EG, ☎ (0 33) 422 42 22, *info@berghotel.nl, Fax (0 33) 465 05 05,* – – 25 à 160. AE ◑ MC VISA JCB AX a
Repas Lunch 28 – 35/51 bc, ♀ – ☕ 15 – **90 ch** 124/153 – ½ P 174/203.
◆ Aux avant-postes de la ville natale du peintre Mondrian, auberge centenaire entourée d'espaces verts et mettant à votre disposition des chambres sans reproche.
◆ Dit honderd jaar oude hotel aan de rand van de geboortestad van Piet Mondriaan staat in een prachtige omgeving met veel natuurschoon en beschikt over onberispelijke kamers.

Campanile, De Brand 50 (Nord-Est : 4 km près A 1, sortie ⑬), ✉ 3823 LM, ☎ (0 33) 455 87 57, *amersfoort@campanile.com, Fax (0 33) 456 26 20,* – – 25 à 150. AE ◑ MC VISA. ✗ rest
Repas (avec buffets) Lunch 13 – 22 – ☕ 10 – **75 ch** 82 – ½ P 50/60.
◆ Officiant depuis plus de dix ans, établissement de chaîne dont le succès tient autant à l'aspect pratique de sa formule d'hébergement qu'à sa politique de prix "sympa".
◆ Praktisch ingerichte kamers en een sympathiek prijsbeleid kenmerken dit ketenhotel, dat al ruim tien jaar klaarstaat om het zijn gasten naar de zin te maken en... met succes.

Het Bergpaviljoen, Utrechtseweg 180, ✉ 3818 ES, ☎ (0 33) 461 50 00, *info@bergpaviljoen.nl, Fax (0 33) 461 89 45,* – P. AE MC VISA AX k
fermé fin déc., sam. midi et dim. – **Repas** Lunch 25 – carte 45 à 70, ♀.
◆ Une luxueuse brasserie a pris place dans ce pavillon Art déco établi en lisière d'un parc public. Cuisine du moment, beaux plateaux de fruits de mer et plaisante terrasse.
◆ Dit art-decopaviljoen aan de rand van een openbaar park biedt onderdak aan een luxueus restaurant. Seizoengebonden keuken, mooie plateaus met fruits de mer, aangenaam terras.

Tollius, Utrechtseweg 42, ✉ 3818 EM, ☎ (0 33) 465 17 93, *info@tollius.nl, Fax (0 33) 463 87 96,* – AE MC VISA ABX d
fermé dern. sem. juil.-prem. sem. août, 31 déc.-1er janv., sam. midi, dim. et lundi – **Repas** Lunch 28 – 33/43, ♀.
◆ Aux portes d'Amersfoort, petite maison de bouche dont la salle à manger classico-moderne s'harmonise au contenu des assiettes. Cave à vue, avec salon de dégustation.
◆ Een restaurantje aan de rand van de stad, waar de klassiek-moderne eetzaal in prima harmonie is met de menukaart. De wijnkelder staat open voor proeverijen.

Dorloté, Bloemendalsestraat 24, ✉ 3811 ES, ☎ (0 33) 472 04 44, *restaurant@dorlote.nl, Fax (0 33) 475 35 18,* – P. AE MC VISA. ✗ BY n
fermé 26 déc.-4 janv., sam. midi, dim. et lundi – **Repas** Lunch 30 – carte 44 à 56.
◆ L'enseigne le laisse supposer : on sera effectivement un peu dorloté à cette adresse. Préparations aux légers accents cosmopolites, travaillées à la mode d'aujourd'hui.
◆ De naam zegt het al : hier wordt de gast inderdaad een beetje vertroeteld. Gerechten met lichte kosmopolitische accenten en op eigentijdse wijze bereid.

't Bloemendaeltje, Bloemendalsestraat 3, ✉ 3811 EP, ☎ (0 33) 475 00 01, *info@bloemendaeltje.com, Fax (0 33) 475 88 01* – AE ◑ MC VISA. ✗ BY f
fermé 2 sem. carnaval, mi-juil.-prem. sem. août, sam. midi et dim. – **Repas** Lunch 32 – 35/60 bc.
◆ Table plaisante située à proximité des Muurhuizen, à mi-chemin de la Koppelpoort et du centre animé. Recettes au goût du jour servies dans un intérieur chaleureux.
◆ Aangenaam restaurant in de buurt van de Muurhuizen, halverwege de Koppelpoort en het levendige centrum. In een gezellige ambiance worden eigentijdse gerechten geserveerd.

AMERSFOORT

Arnhemsestr.	AZ	4
Arnhemseweg	BX	3
Bergstraat	BX	5
Bloemendalse Binnenpoort	ABY	6
van Campenstr.	AX	8
Everard Meysterweg	BX	9
Gasthuislaan	BX	10
Groenmarkt	BY	12
Grote Spui	AY	14
Herenstr.	BZ	15
Kersenbaan	ABX	16
Kleine Spui	AY	17
Krankeledenstr.	AZ	18
Krommestr.	AY	20
Kwekersweg	AX	21
Langestr.	ABZ	
Lieve Vrouwekerkhof	AZ	23
Lieve Vrouwestr.	AZ	24
Utrechtsestr.	AZ	26
Varkensmarkt	AZ	27
Vondellaan	AX	29
Windsteeg	BY	30
Windsteeg	BY	30
Zielhorsterweg	BX	32

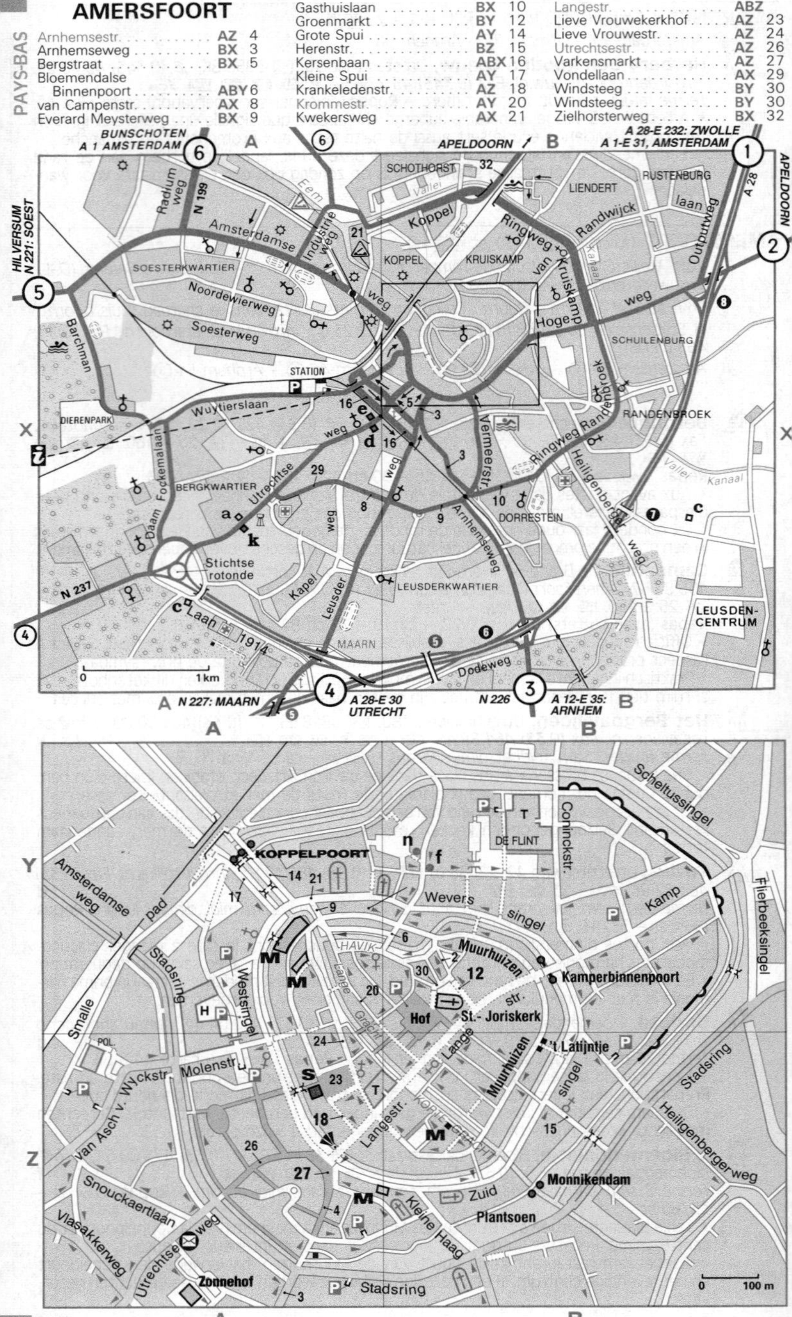

PAYS-BAS

X **tottweeduizendzeven,** Utrechtseweg 29, ✉ 3811 NA, ✆ (0 33) 448 04 68, *info @tot2007.nl*, – P. MC VISA AX e
fermé 31 déc., sam. midi, dim. midi et lundi – **Repas** 25/38.
◆ Agencé un peu comme un "loft", ce "lounge"-restaurant doté d'un mobilier design squatte la salle d'exposition d'un ancien garage. Carte actuelle variée et service avenant.
◆ Dit restaurant in een verbouwde autoshowroom heeft wel iets weg van een loft en is ingericht met designmeubilair. Gevarieerde, eigentijdse kaart en vriendelijke bediening.

à Leusden *Sud-Est : 4 km – 29 038 h*

Leusden, Philipsstraat 18, ✉ 3833 LC, ✆ (0 33) 434 53 45, *leusden@vdvalk.com, Fax (0 33) 434 53 00*, – TV P – 25 à 350. AE MC VISA BX c
Repas *Lunch 14* – 22/27 bc – **152 ch** 95/105, – 7 suites – ½ P 84/113.
◆ Entre Amersfoort et Leusden, au voisinage de l'autoroute, immeuble récent renfermant quatre catégories de chambres de bonne taille, douillettes et pimpantes. Salle de restaurant italianisante. Formule lunch à prix raboté.
◆ Modern gebouw tussen Amersfoort en Leusden, dicht bij de snelweg. Het hotel beschikt over vier categorieën ruime kamers met een zeer verzorgd en behaaglijk interieur. Restaurantzaal met een Italiaans decor. Lunchformule voor een redelijke prijs.

XX **Ros Beyaart,** Hamersveldseweg 55, ✉ 3833 GL, ✆ (0 33) 494 31 27, *info@rosbeyaart.nl, Fax (0 33) 432 12 48*, – P – 25 à 100. AE MC VISA JCB.
fermé 2 dern. sem. juil. – **Repas** *Lunch 29* – 35, ♀.
◆ Imposante villa blanche associant un centre de séminaires à une brasserie moderne. Carte dans le tempo actuel, où les plats de résistance peuvent aussi être servis en entrées.
◆ Deze imposante witte villa herbergt zowel een zalencentrum als een modern restaurant. Eigentijdse menukaart met hoofdgerechten die ook als entree kunnen worden geserveerd.

AMMERZODEN *Gelderland* C *Maasdriel 23 576 h.* 532 Q 12 *et* 715 G 6.
Amsterdam 81 – Utrecht 49 – 's-Hertogenbosch 8.

X **'t Oude Veerhuis,** Molendijk 1, ✉ 5324 BC, ✆ (0 73) 599 13 42, *oudeveerhuis@cs.com, Fax (0 73) 599 44 02*, ≤, – P. AE MC VISA JCB
fermé 27 déc.-20 janv. et lundi – **Repas** *Lunch 30* – carte 36 à 51, ♀.
◆ Restaurant des rives mosanes où la même famille se relaie aux fourneaux depuis six générations. Accueil souriant, véranda, terrasse, anguilles à gogo et vue sur les pontons.
◆ Restaurant aan de Maas, waar inmiddels de zesde generatie achter het fornuis staat. Vriendelijke ontvangst, serre, terras, uitzicht op de steigers en... volop paling.

AMSTELVEEN *Noord-Holland* 531 O 9, 532 O 9 *et* 715 F 5 – *voir à Amsterdam, environs.*

AMSTERDAM

Noord-Holland 531 O 8, 532 O 8 *et* 715 G 4 – *735 526 h.*

Bruxelles 204 ③ – *Düsseldorf 227* ③ – *Den Haag 60* ④ – *Luxembourg 419* ③ – *Rotterdam 76* ④.

OFFICE DE TOURISME

V.V.V. Amsterdam, Stationsplein 10. ✉ *1012 AB* ✆ *(020) 201 88 00, info@amsterdam tourist.nl, Fax (020) 625 28 69.*
Pour approfondir votre visite touristique, consultez le Guide Vert Amsterdam *et le Plan d'Amsterdam nº 36.*

RENSEIGNEMENTS PRATIQUES

TRANSPORTS

Un réseau étendu de transports publics (tram, bus et métro) dessert toute la ville, et le "canalbus" couvre toute la ceinture des canaux grâce à une série d'embarcadères. Les taxis sur l'eau ou "Water Taxi" sont également très rapides.
Le soir, il est préférable et conseillé de se déplacer en taxi.

AÉROPORT

*À Schiphol (*p. 6 AQR*) : 9,5 km* ✆ *0900 72 44 74 65.*

QUELQUES GOLFS

18 *par* ⑥ *à Halfweg, Machineweg 1b,* ✉ *1165 NB,* ✆ *(023) 513 29 39, Fax (023) 513 29 35 –* 9 *à Duivendrecht* (CQ)*, Zwarte Laantje 4,* ✉ *1099 CE,* ✆ *(020) 694 36 50, Fax (020) 663 46 21 –* 18 *par* ① *, Buikslotermeerdijk 141,* ✉ *1027 AC,* ✆ *(020) 632 56 50, Fax (020) 634 35 06 –* 18 *à Holendrecht* (DR)*, Abcouderstraatweg 46,* ✉ *1105 AA,* ✆ *(0294) 28 12 41, Fax (0294) 28 63 47.*

LE SHOPPING

Grands Magasins :
Centre piétonnier, Shopping Center et Magna Plaza.

Commerces de luxe :
Beethovenstraat FU – *P.C. Hooftstraat* JKZ – *Van Baerlestraat.*

Marché aux fleurs★ *(Bloemenmarkt)* KY.

Marché aux puces *(Vlooienmarkt) :*
Waterlooplein LXY.

Antiquités et Objets d'Art :
Autour du Rijksmuseum et du Spiegelgracht.

CASINO

Holland Casino KY, *Max Euweplein 62,* ✉ *1017 MB (près Leidseplein)* ☎ *(020) 521 11 11, Fax (020) 521 11 10.*

CURIOSITÉS

POINTS DE VUE

Keizersgracht★★ KVY – *du Pont-écluse Oudezijds Kolk-Oudezijds Voorburgwal★* LX.

QUELQUES MONUMENTS HISTORIQUES

Dam : Palais Royal★ (Koninklijk Paleis) KX – *Béguinage★★ (Begijnhof)* KX – *Maisons Cromhout★ (Cromhouthuizen)* KY **A⁴** – *Westerkerk★* KX – *Nieuwe Kerk★★* KX – *Oude Kerk★* LX.

MUSÉES HISTORIQUES

Musée Historique d'Amsterdam★★ (Amsterdams Historisch Museum) KX – *Musée Historique Juif★ (Joods Historisch Museum)* LY – *Musée Allard Pierson★ : collections archéologiques* LXY – *Maison d'Anne Frank★★* KX – *Musée d'Histoire maritime des Pays-Bas★★ (Nederlands Scheepvaart Museum)* MX – *Musée des Tropiques★ (Tropenmuseum)* HT – *Musée Van Loon★* LY – *Musée Willet-Holthuysen★* LY.

COLLECTIONS CÉLÈBRES

Rijksmuseum★★★ KZ – *Museum Van Gogh★★★* JZ – *Musée Municipal★★★ (Stedelijk Museum) : art moderne* JZ – *Amstelkring "Le Bon Dieu au Grenier"★ (Museum Amstelkring Ons' Lieve Heer op Solder) : ancienne chapelle clandestine* LX – *Maison de Rembrandt★ (Rembrandthuis) : oeuvres graphiques du maître* LX – *Cobra★ (art moderne)* BR **M⁵**.

ARCHITECTURE MODERNE

Logements sociaux dans le quartier Jordaan et autour du Nieuwmarkt – Créations contemporaines à Amsterdam Zuid-Oost (banque ING).

QUARTIERS PITTORESQUES ET PARCS

Vieil Amsterdam★★★ – Herengracht★★★ KVY – *Les canaux★★★ (Grachten) avec bateaux-logements (Amstel) – Le Jordaan (Prinsengracht★★, Brouwersgracht★, Lijnbaansgracht, Looiersgracht, Egelantiersgracht★, Bloemgracht★)* KX-JKY – *Reguliersgracht★* LY – *Westerdok* BN – *Dam★* KX – *Pont Maigre★ (Magere Brug)* LY – *De Walletjes★★ (Quartier chaud)* LX – *Sarphatipark* GU – *Oosterpark* HT – *Vondelpark* JZ – *Artis (jardin zoologique)★* MY – *Singel★★* KY.

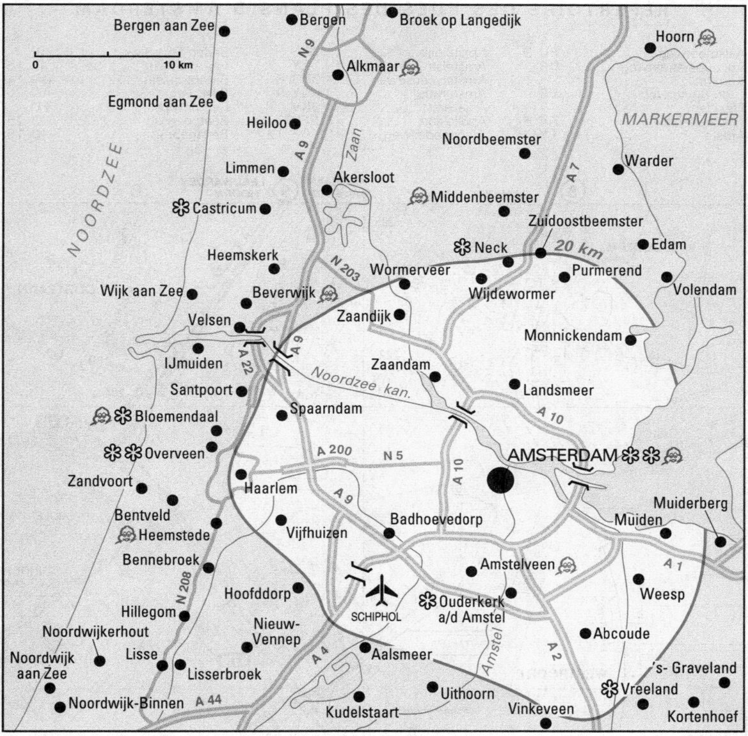

Bergen aan Zee
Bergen
Broek op Langedijk
Hoorn
0 10 km
Alkmaar
N 9
Egmond aan Zee
MARKERMEER
Heiloo
A 9
Zaan
Noordbeemster
NOORDZEE
Limmen
A 7
Warder
Akersloot
Middenbeemster
Castricum
Zuidoostbeemster
Edam
Neck
20 km
Heemskerk
N 203
Wormerveer
Purmerend
Wijk aan Zee
Wijdewormer
Volendam
Beverwijk
Zaandijk
Velsen
Monnickendam
A 9
IJmuiden
A 22
Zaandam
Noordzee kan.
Santpoort
Landsmeer
Spaarndam
Bloemendaal
A 10
Overveen
A 200
N 5
AMSTERDAM
Zandvoort
A 10
Haarlem
A 9
Muiderberg
Bentveld
Muiden
Badhoevedorp
Heemstede
Vijfhuizen
Bennebroek
Amstelveen
A 1
N 208
Weesp
Hoofddorp
Ouderkerk a/d Amstel
Hillegom
SCHIPHOL
Nieuw-Vennep
Noordwijkerhout
Abcoude
Amstel
Noordwijk aan Zee
Lisse
A 4
Aalsmeer
A 2
's- Graveland
Lisserbroek
Vreeland
Noordwijk-Binnen
A 44
Uithoorn
Kudelstaart
Vinkeveen
Kortenhoef

RÉPERTOIRE DES RUES DES PLANS D'AMSTERDAM

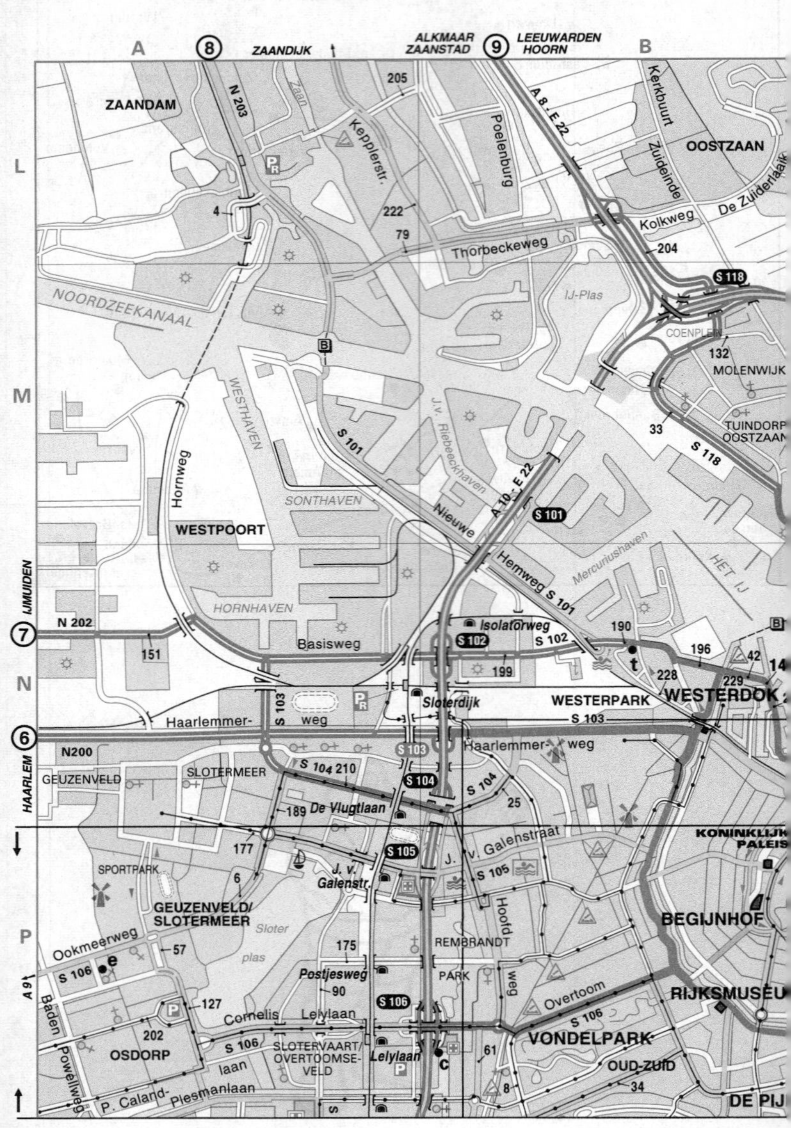

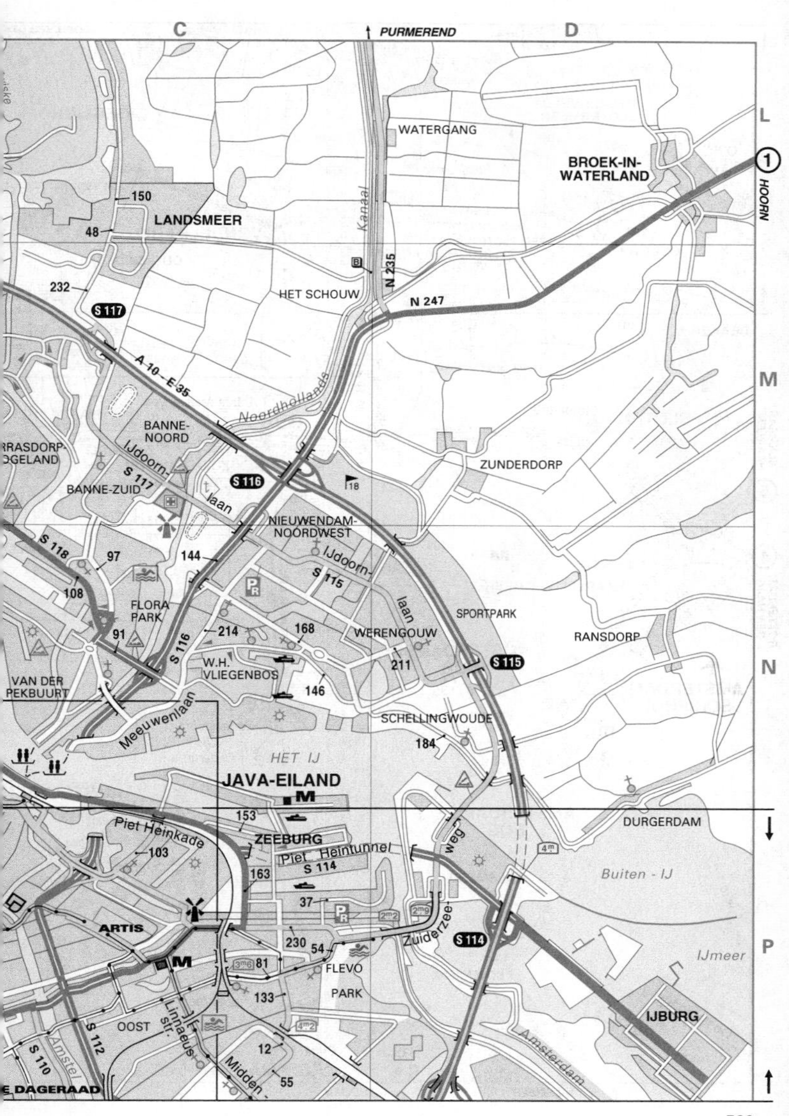

C
D
PURMEREND
L
M
N
P
WATERGANG
BROEK-IN-WATERLAND
HOORN
1
LANDSMEER
150
48
Kanaal
N 235
HET SCHOUW
N 247
232
S 117
A 10 - E 35
Noordhollands
BANNE-NOORD
IJdoorn-laan
S 117
BANNE-ZUID
S 116
18
ZUNDERDORP
NIEUWENDAM-NOORDWEST
S 118
97
144
108
FLORA PARK
S 115
168
WERENGOUW
SPORTPARK
RANSDORP
91
214
S 116
W.H. VLIEGENBOS
211
S 115
146
VAN DER PEKBUURT
Meeuwenlaan
SCHELLINGWOUDE
184
HET IJ
JAVA-EILAND
153
Piet Heinkade
103
ZEEBURG
Piet Heintunnel
S 114
163
DURGERDAM
Buiten - IJ
weg
37
ARTIS
230
54
Zuiderzee-
S 114
81
FLEVO
PARK
133
IJmeer
OOST
Linnaeus-str.
S 112
S 110
Amstel
12
55
Midden
IJBURG
Amsterdam
DAGERAAD

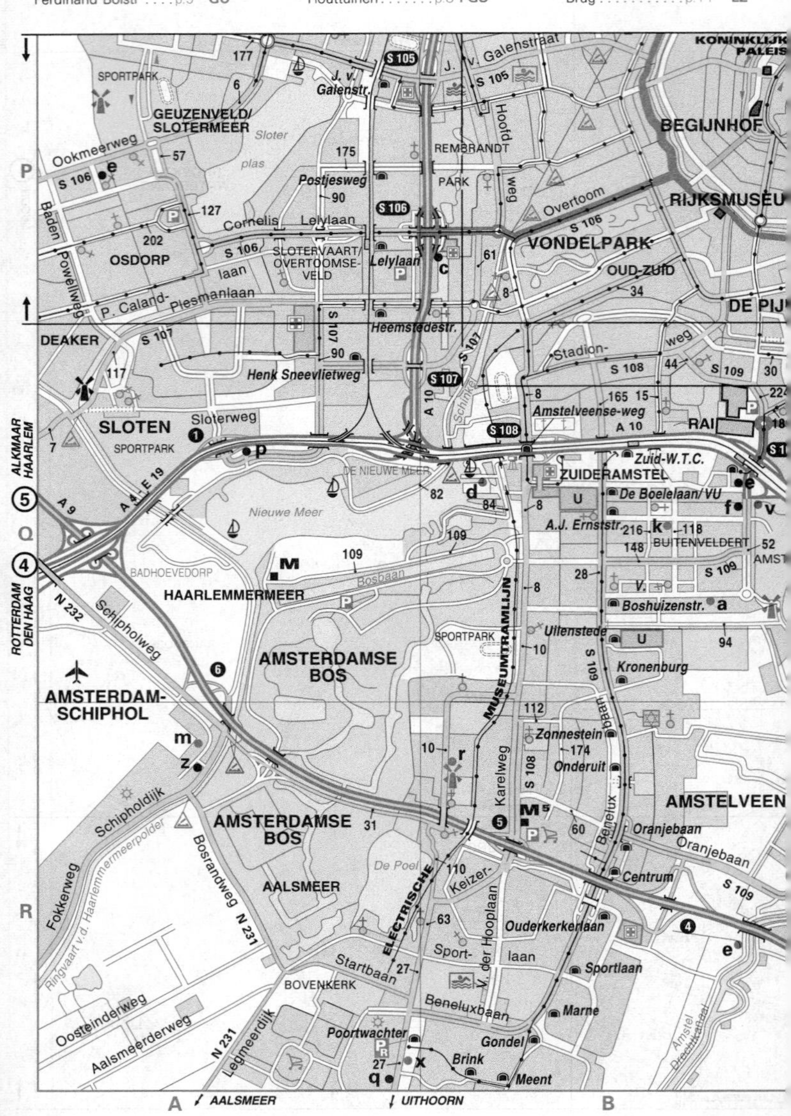
KONINKLIJK PALEIS
BEGIJNHOF
RIJKSMUSEU
VONDELPARK
OUD-ZUID
DE PIJ
J. v. Galenstraat
J. v. Galenstr.
SPORTPARK
GEUZENVELD/ SLOTERMEER
Sloter plas
Ookmeerweg
REMBRANDT PARK
Hoofd weg
Overtoom
Postjesweg
Cornelis Lelylaan
OSDORP
SLOTERVAART/ OVERTOOMSE-VELD
Lelylaan
Baden Powellweg
P. Calandlaan
Plesmanlaan
Heemstedestr.
DEAKER
Henk Sneevlietweg
Stadionweg
Amstelveense-weg
RAI
Zuid-W.T.C.
SLOTEN
Sloterweg
ZUIDERAMSTEL
De Boelelaan/VU
A.J. Ernststr.
BUITENVELDERT
DE NIEUWE MEER
Nieuwe Meer
BADHOEVEDORP
HAARLEMMERMEER
Bosbaan
Boshuizenstr.
Uilenstede
Kronenburg
AMSTERDAMSE BOS
MUSEUMTRAMLIJN
AMSTERDAM-SCHIPHOL
Schipholweg
Schipholdijk
Zonnestein
Onderuit
Karelweg
AMSTELVEEN
Oranjebaan
Centrum
Beneluxbaan
De Poel
Keizer-
ELECTRISCHE
AALSMEER
Bosrandweg
Fokkerweg
Ringvaart v.d. Haarlemmermeerpolder
Ouderkerkerlaan
Sportlaan
V. der Hooplaan
Startbaan
BOVENKERK
Marne
Oosteinderweg
Aalsmeerderweg
Legmeerdijk
Poortwachter
Gondel
Brink
Meent
Amstel Drechtkanaal
ALKMAAR HAARLEM
ROTTERDAM DEN HAAG
A ↙ AALSMEER
↓ UITHOORN
B

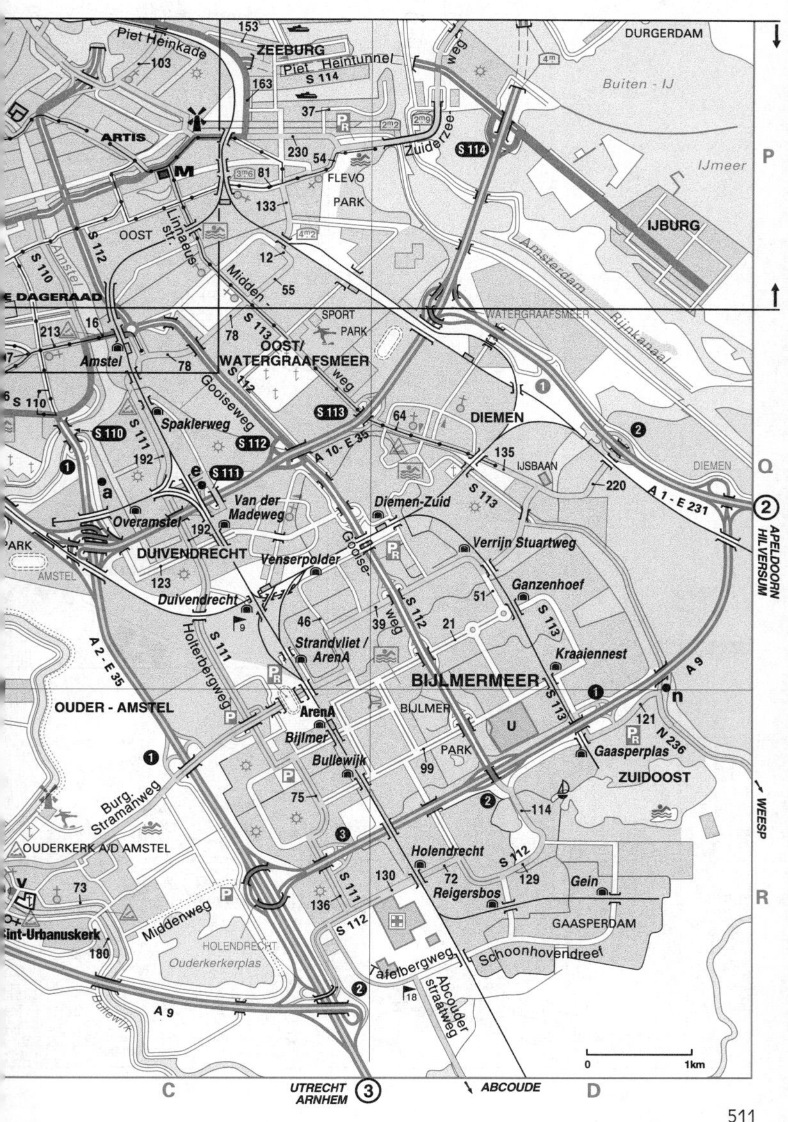
Piet Heinkade
ZEEBURG
Piet Heintunnel
S 114
DURGERDAM
Buiten - IJ
IJmeer
ARTIS
Zuiderzeeweg
FLEVO PARK
IJBURG
OOST
Linnaeusstr.
Amstel
Midden -
Amsterdam - Rijnkanaal
E DAGERAAD
SPORT PARK
WATERGRAAFSMEER
OOST/ WATERGRAAFSMEER
Amstel
Gooiseweg
DIEMEN
Spaklerweg
A 10 - E 35
IJSBAAN
DIEMEN
A 1 - E 231
Overamstel
Van der Madeweg
Diemen-Zuid
Verrijn Stuartweg
APELDOORN HILVERSUM
DUIVENDRECHT
Venserpolder
AMSTEL
Ganzenhoef
Duivendrecht
Holterbergweg
Strandvliet / ArenA
Kraaiennest
A 2 - E 35
BIJLMERMEER
OUDER - AMSTEL
ArenA
Bijlmer
BIJLMER PARK
Gaasperplas
N 236
Bullewijk
ZUIDOOST
Burg. Stramanweg
WEESP
OUDERKERK A/D AMSTEL
Holendrecht
Gein
Reigersbos
Sint-Urbanuskerk
Middenweg
GAASPERDAM
HOLENDRECHT
Ouderkerkerplas
Tafelbergweg
Schoonhovendreef
Abcouder straatweg
A 9
0 1km
UTRECHT ARNHEM
ABCOUDE
C
D
P
Q
R

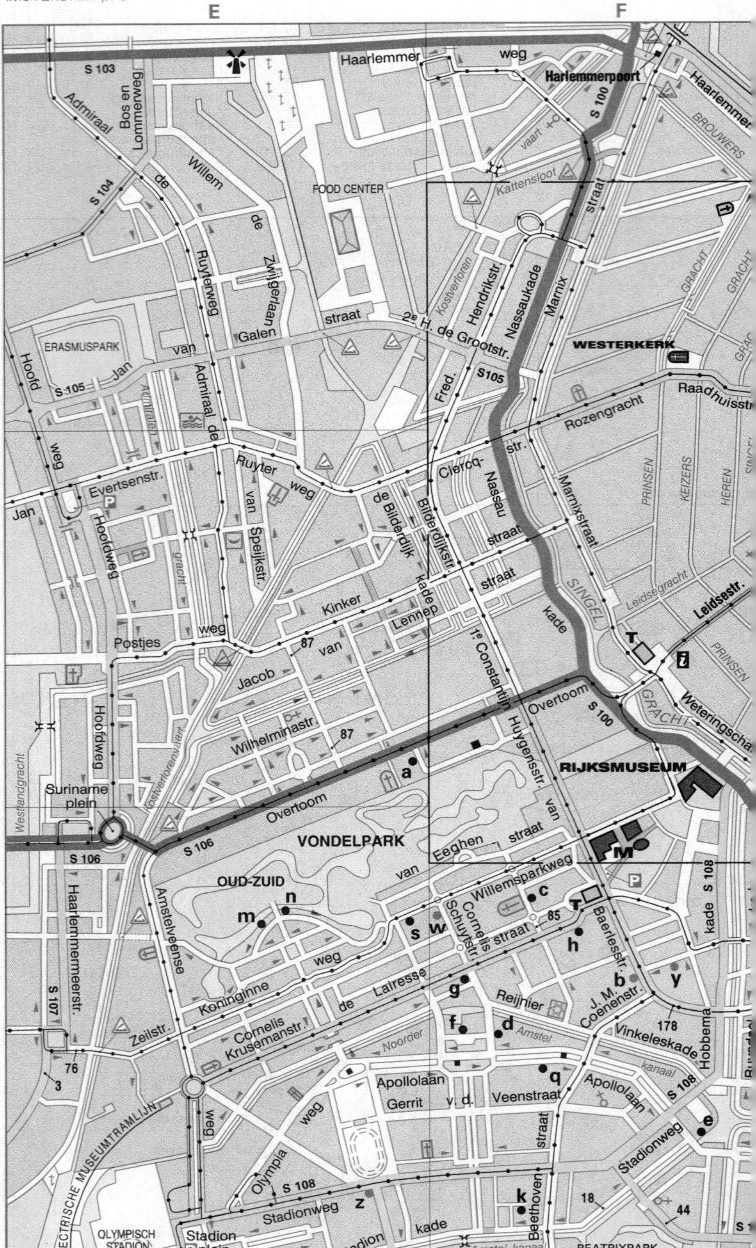

E F

S 103
Haarlemmer weg
Harlemmerpoort
Haarlemmer
BROUWERS
Bos en Lommerweg
Admiraal de Ruyterweg
Willem de Zwijgerlaan
S 100
vaart
S 104
FOOD CENTER
Kattensloot
straat
Marnix
S
GRACHT
Kostverloren
Hendrikstr.
Nassaukade
2e H. de Grootstr.
Galen straat
Jan van
ERASMUSPARK
WESTERKERK
Hoofd weg
S 105
Admiralen gracht
Fred.
Raadhuisstr
Rozengracht
Clercq-str.
Ruyter weg
Evertsenstr.
Jan
Hoofdweg
de Bilderdijk kade
Bilderdijkstr.
Nassau straat
Marnixstraat
PRINSEN
KEIZERS
HEREN
van Speijkstr.
straat
T
Kinker
Lennep
SINGEL
Leidsegracht
Leidsestr.
kade
Postjes weg
87
van
Jacob
1e Constantijn Huygensstr.
T
PRINSEN
GRACHT
Weteringschans
Overtoom
S 100
Hoofdweg
Wilhelminastr.
87
RIJKSMUSEUM
a
Westlandgracht
Suriname plein
Kostverlorenvaart
Overtoom
S 106
VONDELPARK
van Eeghen straat
M
S 106
OUD-ZUID
van
Willemsparkweg
c
T
P
kade
S 108
Haarlemmermeerstr.
Amstelveense weg
n
m
s
w
Cornelis Schuytstr.
85
straat
Baerlesstr.
h
weg
S 107
Koninginne weg
Lairesse
de
g
Reijnier
b
y
J. M. Coenenstr.
U
Zeilstr.
Cornelis Krusemanstr.
Noorder
f
d
Amstel
178
Vinkeleskade
Hobbema
76
3
kanaal
Apollolaan
q
Apollolaan
S 108
ELECTRISCHE MUSEUMTRAMLIJN
weg
Gerrit v. d. Veenstraat
e
Olympia weg
straat
Stadionweg
S 108
z
k
18
Beethoven
44
OLYMPISCH STADION
Stadion plein
P
Stadionweg
Stadion kade
Zuider Amstel kanaal
BEATRIXPARK
RAI
S 1

E F

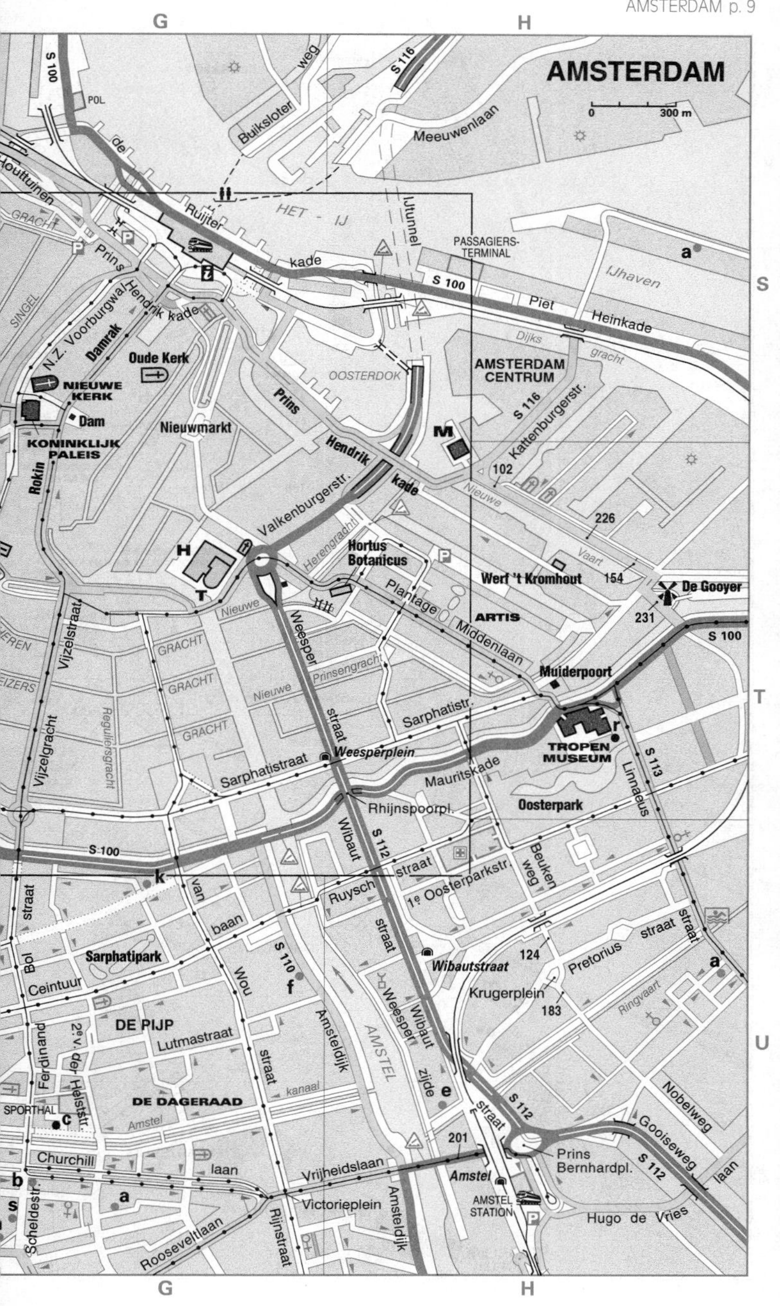
AMSTERDAM
0
300 m
HET - IJ
IJtunnel
PASSAGIERS-TERMINAL
IJhaven
Piet Heinkade
De Ruijter kade
Prins Hendrik kade
N.Z. Voorburgwal
Damrak
Oude Kerk
NIEUWE KERK
Dam
KONINKLIJK PALEIS
Rokin
Nieuwmarkt
OOSTERDOK
AMSTERDAM CENTRUM
Kattenburgerstr.
Valkenburgerstr.
Hortus Botanicus
Plantage Middenlaan
Werf 't Kromhout
ARTIS
De Gooyer
Muiderpoort
TROPEN MUSEUM
Weesperplein
Sarphatistraat
Mauritskade
Oosterpark
Rhijnspoorpl.
Wibautstraat
Linnaeusstraat
1e Oosterparkstr.
Ruyschstraat
Beukenweg
Pretoriusstraat
Krugerplein
Ringvaart
Sarphatipark
Ceintuur baan
DE PIJP
Lutmastraat
DE DAGERAAD
Amsteldijk
AMSTEL
Weesperzijde
Nobelweg
Gooiseweg
Prins Bernhardpl.
Amstel
AMSTEL STATION
Hugo de Vrieslaan
Vrijheidslaan
Victorieplein
Churchilllaan
Rooseveltlaan
Rijnstraat
Scheldestr.
SPORTHAL
Ferdinand Bolstraat
2e v. der Helststr.
Vijzelstraat
Vijzelgracht
Reguliersgracht
Van Woustraat
Nieuwe Herengracht
Nieuwe Prinsengracht
Nieuwe Vaart
Dijksgracht
Meeuwenlaan
Buiksloterweg
Houttuinen
SINGEL
POL
S 100
S 116
S 112
S 113
S 110
102
226
154
231
124
183
201
G
H
S
T
U

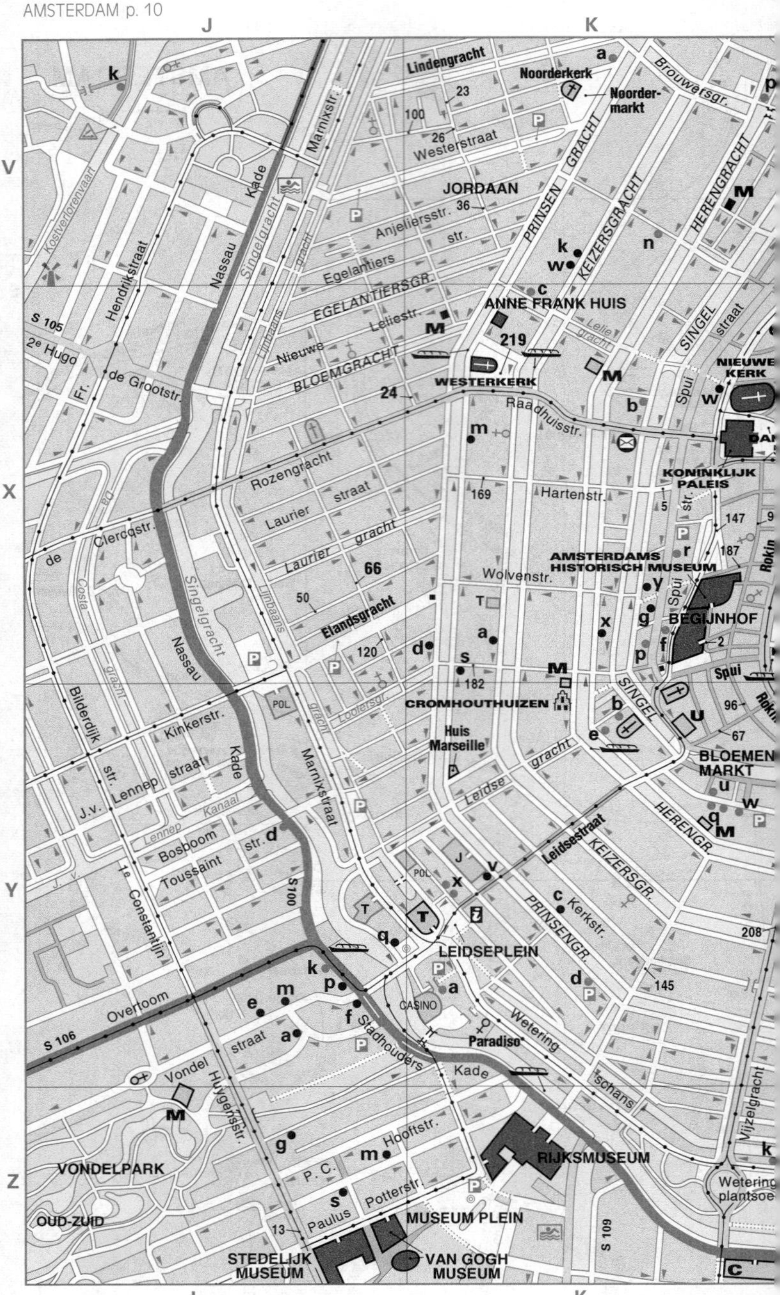

J K

V

X

Y

Z

J K

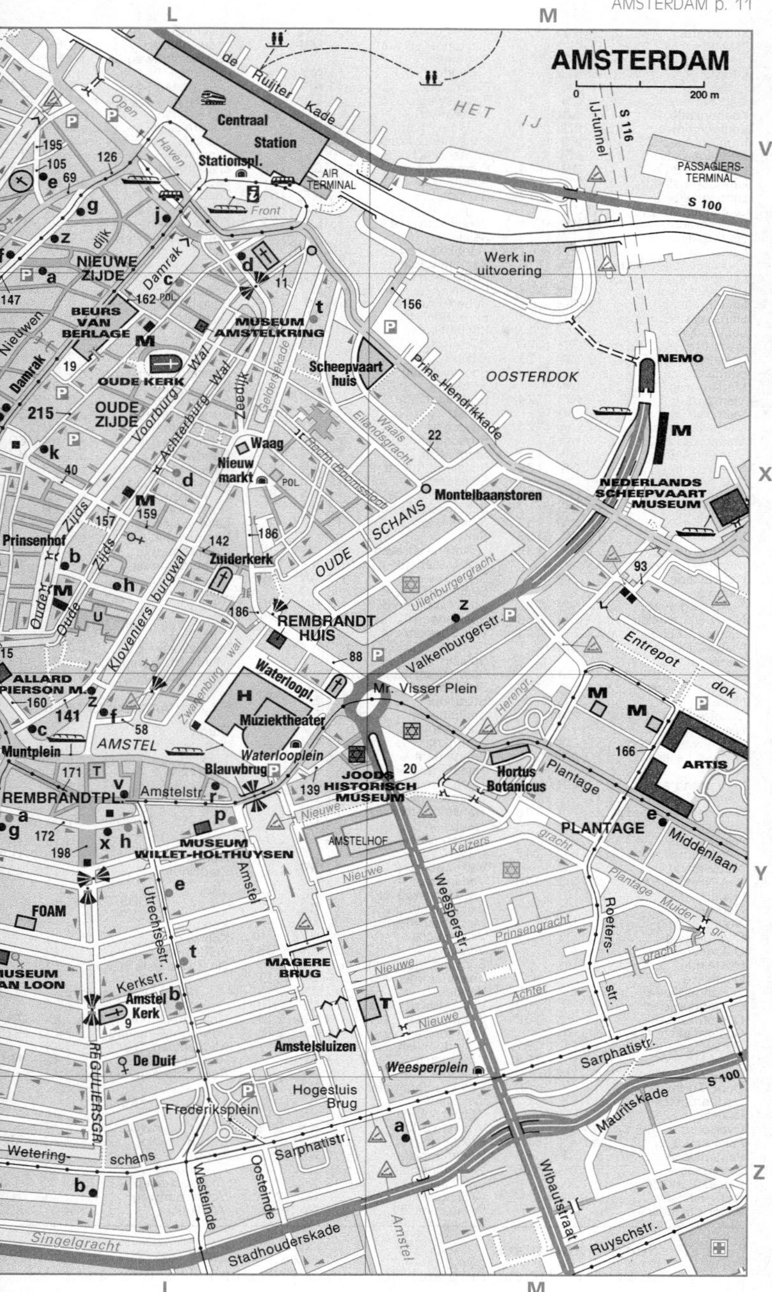

AMSTERDAM
0
200 m
L
M
V
X
Y
Z
HET IJ
IJ-tunnel
S 116
S 100
PASSAGIERS-TERMINAL
de Ruijter Kade
Centraal Station
Stationspl.
AIR TERMINAL
Open Haven Front
Werk in uitvoering
NIEUWE ZIJDE
Damrak
BEURS VAN BERLAGE
Nieuwen
MUSEUM AMSTELKRING
OUDE KERK
OUDE ZIJDE
Scheepvaart huis
Prins Hendrikkade
OOSTERDOK
NEMO
NEDERLANDS SCHEEPVAART MUSEUM
Voorburg Wal
Achterburg Wal
Zeedijk
Geldersekade
Waals Eilandsgracht
Recht Boomssloot
Waag
Nieuw markt
POL
Montelbaanstoren
OUDE SCHANS
Prinsenhof
Zijds
Oude
Kloveniers burgwal
Zuiderkerk
Uilenburgergracht
Valkenburgerstr.
Entrepot dok
REMBRANDT HUIS
Waterloopl.
Muziektheater
Zwanenburg wal
Mr. Visser Plein
Herengr.
ALLARD PIERSON M.
Muntplein
AMSTEL
Waterlooplein
Blauwbrug
JOODS HISTORISCH MUSEUM
Hortus Botanicus
Plantage
PLANTAGE
ARTIS
Middenlaan
REMBRANDTPL.
Amstelstr.
MUSEUM WILLET-HOLTHUYSEN
AMSTELHOF
Nieuwe
Keizers gracht
Plantage Muider gr.
Roeters-str.
FOAM
Utrechtsestr.
Amstel
Weesperstr.
Prinsengracht
MAGERE BRUG
Achter
USEUM AN LOON
Kerkstr.
Amstel Kerk
REGULIERSGR.
De Duif
Amstelsluizen
Weesperplein
Sarphatistr.
Mauritskade
Hogesluis Brug
Frederiksplein
Wetering-schans
Westeinde
Oosteinde
Wilbautstraat
Ruyschstr.
Singelgracht
Stadhouderskade

Keizersgracht p.10 KVY
President Kennedylaan p.7 CQ 106
Kerkstr p.10 KLY
Kinkerstr p.10 JY
Klaprozenweg p.5 CN 108
Koenenkade p.6 ABQ 109
Koninginneweg p.8 EU
Krugerpl p.9 HU
De Lairessestr p.8 EFU
Langbroekdreef p.7 DR 114
Langebrugsteeg p.11 LX 115
Langsomlaan p.6 AQ 117
Laurierstr p.10 JX
Leidsegracht p.10 KY
Leidseplein p.10 KY
Leidsestr p.10 KY
Van Leijenberghlaan p.6 BQ 118
Leliegracht p.10 KX
Lijnbaansgracht p.10 JVX
Lindengracht p.10 JKV
Linnaeusstr p.9 HTU
Looiersdwarsstr. (1e) p.10 JX 120
Loosdrechtdreef p.7 DR 121
Lutmastr p.9 GU
Magerebrug p.11 LY
Maritzsrtr p.9 HU 124
Marnixstr p.10 JVY
Martelaarsgracht p.11 LV 126
Mauritskade p.11 MYZ
Meer en Vaart p.4 AP 127
Meerkerkdreef p.7 DR 129
Meeuwenlaan p.5 CN
Meibergdreef p.7 DR 130
Middenweg p.5 CPQ
Molenaarsweg p.4 BM 132
Molukkenstr p.5 CP 133
Muntbergweg p.7 CR 136
Muntplein p.11 LY
Nassaukade p.10 JVY
Nieuwe Achtergracht p.11 MY
Nieuwe Amstelstr p.11 LY 139
Nieuwe Doelenstr p.11 LY 141
Nieuwe Hemweg p.4 BMN
Nieuwe Herengracht p.11 LMY
Nieuwe Hoogstr p.11 LX 142
Nieuwe Keizersgracht p.11 LMY
Nieuwe Leeuwarderweg p.5 CN 144
Nieuwe Leliestr p.10 JKX
Nieuwe Prinsengracht p.11 LMY
Nieuwe Spiegelstr p.10 KY 145
Nieuwendammerdijk p.5 CN 146
Nieuwendijk p.11 LVX
Nieuwezijds Voorburgwal p.10 KLX 147
Nieuwmarkt p.11 LX
Van Nijenrodeweg p.6 BQ 148
Nobelweg p.9 HU
Noordermarkt p.10 KV
Noordzeeweg p.4 AN 151
Olympiaweg p.8 EU
Ookmeerweg p.4 AP
Oosteinde p.11 LY
Oostelijke Handelskade p.5 CP 153
Oostenburgerstr p.9 HT 154
Oosterdokskade p.11 MX 156
Oosterparkstr. (1e) p.9 HU
Oude Doelenstr p.11 LX 157
Oude Hoogstr p.11 LX 159
Oude Schans p.11 LMX
Oude Turfmarkt p.11 LY 160
Oudebrugsteeg p.11 LX 162
Oudezijds Kolk p.11 LVX 11
Overtoom p.10 JY
Paleisstraat p.10 KX 5
Panamalaan p.5 CP 163
Parnassusweg p.6 BQ 165
Paulus Potterstr p.10 JKZ
Piet Heinkade p.5 CNP
Pieter Calandlaan p.4 AP
Pieter Com Hooftstr p.10 JKZ
Plantage Kerklaan p.11 MY 166
Plantage Middenlaan p.11 MY
Plesmanlaan p.4 AP
Postjesweg p.8 ET
Pretoriusstr p.9 HU
Prins Bernhardpl p.9 HU
Prins Hendrikkade p.11 MX
Prinsengracht p.10 KVY
Purmerweg p.5 CN 168
Raadhuisstr p.10 KX
Reestraat p.10 KX 169
Reguliersbreestr p.11 LY 171
Reguliersdwarsstr p.11 LY 172
Reijnier Vinkeleskade p.8 FU
Rembrandtplein p.11 LY
Rhijnspoorpl p.9 HT
Rijnstr p.9 GU
Robert Fruinlaan p.4 AP 175
Burg. Röellstr p.4 AP 177
Roelof Hartstr p.8 FU 178
Roetersstr p.11 MY
Rokin p.11 LY
Rooseveltlaan p.6 BQ 181
Rozengracht p.10 JX
De Ruijterkade p.11 LV
Runstr p.10 KX 182
Ruyschstr p.11 MZ
Ruysdaelkade p.8 FU
Sarphatistr p.11 LMZ
Schalk Burgerstr p.9 HU 183
Scheldestr p.9 GU
Schellingwouderdijk p.5 DN 184
Schoonhovendreef p.7 DR
Singel p.10 KXY
Sint Antoniesbreestr p.11 LX 186
Sint Luciënsteeg p.10 KX 187
Slotermeerlaan p.4 AN 189
Sloterweg p.6 AQ
Spaarndammerdijk p.4 BN 190
Spaklerweg p.7 CQ 192
Van Speijkstr p.8 ET
Spui p.10 KXY
Spuistr p.10 KX
Stadhouderskade p.10 JKY
Stadionkade p.8 EFU
Stadionpl p.8 EU
Stadionweg p.8 EU
Stationsplein p.11 LV
Stromarkt p.11 LV 195
Surinamepl p.8 ET
Tafelbergweg p.7 CDR
Tasmanstr p.4 BN 196
Thorbeckeplein p.11 LY 198
Transformatorweg p.4 BN 199
Treublaan p.9 HU 201
Tussen Meer p.4 AP 202
Utrechtsestr p.11 LY
Valkenburgerstr p.11 MX
Verlengde Stellingweg p.4 BL 204
Victorieplein p.7 CQ 207
Mr. Visser Plein p.11 MY
Vijzelgracht p.10 KYZ
Vijzelstr p.10 KY 208
Burg. de Vlugtlaan p.4 AN 210
Volendammerweg p.5 DN 211
Vondelstr p.10 JY
Vrijheidslaan p.7 CQ 213
Waddenweg p.5 CN 214
Warmoesstr p.11 LX 215
Waterlooplein p.11 LXY
Weesperstr p.11 MY
Weesperzijde p.9 HU
Van Weldammelaan p.6 BQ 216
Westeinde p.11 LZ
Westerdoksdijk p.4 BN 217
Westermarkt p.10 KX 219
Westerstr p.10 KV
Weteringplantsoen p.10 KZ
Weteringschans p.10 KYZ
Wibautstr p.11 MZ
Wielingenstr p.8 FU 224
Wilhelminastr p.8 ET
Willem de Zwijgerlaan p.8 ES
Willemsparkweg p.8 FU
Wittenburgergracht p.9 HT 226
Wolvenstr p.10 KX
Van Woustr p.9 GU
IJdoornlaan p.5 CMN
Zaanstr p.4 BN 228
Zandhoek p.4 BN 229
Zeeburgerdijk p.5 CP 230
Zeeburgerstr p.9 HT 231
Zeedijk p.11 LX
Zeilstr p.8 EU
Zuiderzeeweg p.5 DP
Zwanenburgwal p.11 LXY

AALSMEER

Aalsmeerderweg p.6 AR
Bosrandweg p.6 AR
Oosteinderweg p.6 AR

AMSTELVEEN

Amsterdamseweg p.6 BQR 10
Beneluxlaan p.6 BQR
Bovenkerkerweg p.6 ABR 27
Burg. Colijnweg p.6 AR 31
Mr. G. Groen v. Prinstererlaan p.6 BR 60
Handweg p.6 BR 63
Van der Hooplaan p.6 BR
Keizer Karelweg p.6 BR
Laan Nieuwer Amstel p.6 BR 110
Laan Walcheren p.6 BQR 112
Legmeerdijk p.6 AR
Oranjebaan p.6 BR
Rembrandtweg p.6 BR 174
Sportlaan p.6 BR
Startbaan p.6 AR

DIEMEN

Hartveldseweg p.7 DQ 64
Muiderstraatweg p.7 DQ 135
Weteringweg p.7 DQ 220

HAARLEMMERMEER

Burg. Amersfoortdlaan p.6 AQ 7
Fokkerweg p.6 AR
Schipholdijk p.6 AR
Schipholweg p.6 AQ

LANDSMEER

Dorpsstr p.5 CL 48
Noordeinde p.5 CL 150
Zuideinde p.5 CM 232

OOSTZAAN

Kerkbuurt p.4 BL
Kolkweg p.4 BL
Zuideinde p.4 BL
De Zuiderlaaik p.4 BL

OUDER AMSTEL

Holendrechterweg p.7 CR 73
Van der Madeweg p.7 CQ 123
Middenweg p.7 CR
Rondehoep-Oost p.7 CR 180
Burg. Stramanweg p.7 CR

ZAANSTAD

Albert Heijnweg p.4 AL 4
Den Huylweg p.4 AL 79
Kepplerstr p.4 AL
Poelenburg p.4 BL
Thorbeckeweg p.4 BL
Vermiljoenweg p.4 AL 205
Wibautstr p.4 AL 222

Service and taxes

In Belgium, Luxembourg and Netherlands prices include service and taxes.

Liste alphabétique des hôtels et restaurants
Alfabetische lijst van hotels en restaurants
Alphabetisches Hotel- und Restaurantverzeichnis
Alphabetical list of hotels and restaurants

La cuisine que vous recherchez...
Het soort keuken dat u zoekt
Welche Küche, welcher Nation suchen Sie
That special cuisine

Buffets

34 Greenhouse *H. Hilton Schiphol, Env. à Schiphol*

Grillades

33 Bastion Airport *à Hoofddorp*
31 Bastion Amstel *Q. Est et Sud-Est*
32 Bastion Noord *Q. Nord*
33 Bastion Schiphol, *Env. à Schiphol*
29 Bastion Zuid-West *Q. Sud et Ouest*

Produits de la mer

24 Lucius *Q. Centre*
28 La Sirène *H. Le Méridien Apollo Q. Sud et Ouest*
24 Oesterbar *Q. Centre*
24 Le Pêcheur *Q. Centre*
29 Visaandeschelde *Q. Sud et Ouest*

Taverne – Brasserie – Bistrot

18 Crowne Plaza American *Q. Centre*
17 The Amstel Bar and Brasserie *H. Amstel Q. Centre*
28 Brasserie Le Camelia *H. Okura, Q. Sud et Ouest*
17 Brasserie De Palmboom *H. Radisson SAS, Q. Centre*
31 Brasserie Richard *Q. Sud et Ouest*
28 Brasserie van Baerle *Q. Rijksmuseum*
22 Café Roux *H. The Grand, Sofitel Demeure Q. Centre*
19 Eden *Q. Centre*
21 Ibis Stropera *Q. Centre*
20 NH City Centre *Q. Centre*
31 Novotel *Est et Sud-Est*
20 Die Port van Cleve *Q. Centre*
29 Quartier Sud Chez Denise *Q. Sud et Ouest*
32 Ravel *Q. Buitenveldert*
20 NH Schiller *Q. Centre*
31 VandeMarkt *Q. Sud et Ouest*
25 Vooges *Q. Centre*

Américaine

31 *H. Holiday Inn, Q. Buitenveldert*

Asiatique

34 East West *H. Hilton Schiphol, Env. à Schiphol*
18 Blakes *Q. Centre*

Chinoise

23 Sichuan Food *Q. Centre*

Hollandaise régionale

18 Dorrius *Crowne Plaza City Centre, Q. Centre*
20 De Roode Leeuw *H. Amsterdam, Q. Centre*

Indienne

26 **Memories of India** ***Q. Centre***

30 **Pakistan** ***Q. Sud et Ouest***

Indonésienne

25 **Bleu pepper** ***Q. Centre***

23 **Indrapura** ***Q. Centre***

28 **Radèn Mas** ***Q. Rijksmuseum***

25 **Tempo doeloe** ***Q. Centre***

Italienne

26 **Bice** ***H. NH Amsterdam Centre Q. Rijksmuseum***

18 **Caruso** ***H. Jolly Carlton, Q. Centre***

20 **NH City Centre** ***Q. Centre***

35 **Radisson SAS Airport** ***Env. à Schiphol***

28 **Roberto's** ***H. Hilton, Q. Sud et Ouest***

24 **Segugio** ***Q. Centre***

19 **Swissôtel** ***Q. Centre***

Japonaise

23 **Hosokawa** ***Q. Centre***

30 **Kaiko** ***Q. Sud et Ouest***

28 **Sazanka** ***H. Okura, Q. Sud et Ouest***

29 **Yamazato** ***H. Okura, Q. Sud et Ouest***

Orientale

22 **Dynasty** ***Q. Centre***

23 **Manchurian** ***Q. Centre***

Vietnamienne

25 **L'Indochine** ***Q. Centre***

Quartiers du Centre - *plans p. 10 et 11 sauf indication spéciale :*

Amstel, Prof. Tulpplein 1, ✉ 1018 GX, ☎ (0 20) 622 60 60, *Fax (0 20) 622 58 08*, ←, ⛲, 🏋, ≋, 🏊, 🚲, ⚓ - |♦| ⇋ ▤ 📺 🅿 - 🏛 25 à 180. AE ⓓ MC VISA JCB. ✂
Repas voir rest ***La Rive*** ci-après - ***The Amstel Bar and Brasserie*** (ouvert jusqu'à 23 h 30) carte env. 56, ♀ - ☕ 29 - **64 ch** 530/570, - 15 suites. MZ a
◆ Un vrai havre de luxe et de bon goût que ce palace au bord de l'Amstel. Vastes chambres décorées avec le souci du détail, mobilier de style, services efficaces et complets. Bar-bibliothèque "cosy" misant sur une appétissante carte aux influences cosmopolites.
◆ Een bastion van stijl en luxe, dit paleis aan de Amstel. Grote kamers die met zorg voor details zijn ingericht, stijlmeubilair, efficiënte service en alle denkbare faciliteiten. De behaaglijke bar-brasserie heeft een smakelijke, kosmopolitische kaart.

The Grand Sofitel Demeure, O.Z. Voorburgwal 197, ✉ 1012 EX, ☎ (0 20) 555 31 11, *h2783@accor-hotels.com, Fax (0 20) 555 32 22*, 🏋, ≋, 🏊, 🌳, ⚓ - |♦| ⇋ ▤ 📺 🚗 🅿 - 🏛 25 à 300. AE ⓓ MC VISA JCB. ✂ LX b
Repas voir rest ***Café Roux*** ci-après - ☕ 25 - **270 ch** 380/465, - 12 suites.
◆ D'authentiques salons Art nouveau, des chambres exquises et un jardin intérieur vous attendent derrière cette superbe façade historique où séjourna Marie de Médicis.
◆ Authentieke salons in art nouveau, voortreffelijke kamers en een binnenhof met tuin gaan schuil achter deze prachtige historische gevel, waar Maria de' Medici ooit verbleef.

NH Gd H. Krasnapolsky, Dam 9, ✉ 1012 JS, ☎ (0 20) 554 91 11, *reflet@nhkrasnapolsky.nh-hotels.nl, Fax (0 20) 622 86 07*, 🏋, ⚓ - |♦| ⇋ ▤ 📺 🚗 - 🏛 25 à 750. AE ⓓ MC VISA JCB LX k
Repas ***Reflet*** *(fermé dim.)* (dîner seult) 33, ♀ - ☕ 21 - **461 ch** 230/375, - 7 suites.
◆ Sur le Dam, grand hôtel aux chambres "business" ou "executives" et appartements au mobilier moderne ou traditionnel. Jardin d'hiver 19ᵉ s. Né en 1883, le Reflet conserve son éclat et entretient une atmosphère cossue.
◆ Grand Hôtel aan de Dam, met business en executive rooms, evenals appartementen met modern of traditioneel meubilair. 19e-eeuwse wintertuin. Restaurant Reflet (1883) weerspiegelt nog altijd de sfeer van de belle époque. Japans restaurant met teppan yaki.

de l'Europe, Nieuwe Doelenstraat 2, ✉ 1012 CP, ☎ (0 20) 531 17 77, *hotel@leurope.nl, Fax (0 20) 531 17 78*, ←, 🏋, ≋, 🏊, 🚲, ⚓ - |♦| ▤ 📺 🅿 - 🏛 25 à 80. AE ⓓ MC VISA JCB LY c
Repas voir rest ***Excelsior*** et ***Le Relais*** ci-après - ☕ 25 - **94 ch** 285/495, - 6 suites.
◆ Hôtel-palace de la fin du 19ᵉ s. alliant le charme à la tradition. Chambres décorées avec un goût sûr. Collection de tableaux de paysagistes néerlandais. Belle vue sur l'eau.
◆ Luxehotel (eind 19e eeuw) dat charme en traditie combineert. Zeer smaakvol ingerichte kamers. Collectie doeken van Nederlandse landschapschilders. Mooi zicht op het water.

NH Barbizon Palace, Prins Hendrikkade 59, ✉ 1012 AD, ☎ (0 20) 556 45 64, *info@nhbarbizon-palace.nh-hotels.nl, Fax (0 20) 624 33 53*, 🏋, ≋, ⚓ - |♦| ⇋ ▤ 📺 ♿ 🚗 - 🏛 25 à 300. AE ⓓ MC VISA JCB. ✂ LV d
Repas voir rest ***Vermeer*** ci-après - ***Hudson's Terrace and Restaurant*** (ouvert jusqu'à 23 h) Lunch 30 - carte env. 47, ♀ - ☕ 20 - **272 ch** 240/390, - 3 suites.
◆ Cet hôtel jouxtant la gare a bénéficié d'importantes rénovations. Les chambres mansardées sont les plus chaleureuses, mais toutes ont été refaites avec soin. Estimable restaurant au goût du jour entretenant une ambiance maritime.
◆ Dit hotel tegenover het station is grondig gerenoveerd. Alle kamers zijn met zorg opnieuw ingericht, maar die op de dakverdieping zijn wel heel sfeervol. Respectabel, eigentijds restaurant met maritieme ambiance.

Radisson SAS, Rusland 17, ✉ 1012 CK, ☎ (0 20) 623 12 31, *reservations.amsterdam@radissonsas.com, Fax (0 20) 520 82 00*, 🏋, ≋, ⚓ - |♦| ⇋ ▤ 📺 ♿ 🚗 - 🏛 25 à 180. AE ⓓ MC VISA JCB. ✂ rest LX h
Repas ***Brasserie De Palmboom*** Lunch 29 - carte 35 à 45, ♀ - ☕ 19 - **242 ch** 295, - 1 suite.
◆ Hôtel de chaîne moderne dont l'atrium intègre un presbytère du 18ᵉ s. Bonnes chambres standard et business, de styles scandinave, hollandais, oriental ou Art déco. Brasserie actuelle décontractée servant une cuisine hollandaise et internationale.
◆ Modern hotel waar in het atrium een 18e-eeuwse pastorie is geïntegreerd. Kamers in diverse stijlen : Scandinavisch, Hollands, oriëntaals of art deco. Moderne brasserie met ongedwongen sfeer en een culinair repertoire van Nederlandse en internationale gerechten.

Renaissance, Kattengat 1, ✉ 1012 SZ, ☎ (0 20) 621 22 23, *renaissance.amsterdam@renaissancehotels.com, Fax (0 20) 627 52 45*, 🏋, ≋, 🚲, ⚓ - |♦| ⇋ ▤ 📺 ♿ 🚗 - 🏛 25 à 400. AE ⓓ MC VISA JCB. ✂ LV e
Repas (dîner seult) carte 37 à 46, ♀ - ☕ 21 - **382 ch** 249/299, - 6 suites.
◆ Hôtel remis à neuf et doté de remarquables installations pour conférences sous le dôme d'une ancienne église. Confort actuel dans les chambres, suites et junior suites. Brasserie-restaurant jouant la carte internationale.
◆ Volledig gerenoveerd hotel dat onder de koepel van een voormalige kerk over een unieke accommodatie beschikt voor vergaderingen en evenementen. Actueel comfort in de kamers, suites en junior suites. Brasserie-restaurant met internationale kaart.

Crowne Plaza City Centre, N.Z. Voorburgwal 5, ✉ 1012 RC, ☎ (0 20) 620 05 00, *info@crownplaza.nl, Fax (0 20) 620 11 73,* – 25 à 270. AE VISA JCB. LV g
Repas *Dorrius* *(fermé dim.)* (avec cuisine hollandaise, dîner seult jusqu'à 23 h) carte 32 à 57 – 22 – **268 ch** 310/340, – 2 suites.
◆ Immeuble voisin de la gare. Bonnes chambres bénéficiant d'équipements complets. Vue sur les toits de la ville depuis le "lounge club" perché au dernier étage. Restaurant lambrissé et authentique café du 19e s. Choix classique panaché de plats locaux.
◆ De kamers in dit hotel vlak bij het station bieden alle comfort. Vanuit de club lounge uitzicht over de daken van de stad. Restaurant met lambrisering en een authentiek 19e-eeuws bruin café. Mix van klassieke keuken en lokale gerechten.

Pulitzer, Prinsengracht 323, ✉ 1016 GZ, ☎ (0 20) 523 52 35, *sales.amsterdam@starwoodhotels.com, Fax (0 20) 627 67 53,* – 25 à 150. AE VISA JCB KX m
Repas *Pulitzers* Lunch 45 – carte env. 53, – 25 – **227 ch** 450/515, – 3 suites.
◆ Ensemble de caractère composé de 24 maisons des 17e et 18e s. admirablement réhabilitées. Les nouvelles chambres vous raviront, comme le reste de l'établissement. Café-restaurant original et moderne, avec un clin d'œil plein d'humour au peintre Frans Hals.
◆ Karaktervol complex van 24 gerenoveerde grachtenpanden uit de 17e en 18e eeuw. De nieuwe kamers zullen zeker in de smaak vallen, net als de rest van het hotel. Modern en origineel café-restaurant, met een humoristische knipoog naar Frans Hals.

Crowne Plaza American, Leidsekade 97, ✉ 1017 PN, ☎ (0 20) 556 30 00, *american@ichotelsgroup.com, Fax (0 20) 556 30 01,* ch, – 25 à 150. AE VISA. JY q
Repas (taverne-rest Art déco, ouvert jusqu'à 23 h 30) Lunch 28 – carte 32 à 42, – 22 – **172 ch** 285/385, – 2 suites.
◆ Cette imposante façade historique abrite un hôtel avenant dont les chambres, meublées à l'identique, sont d'ampleur différente. Clientèle internationale. Taverne-restaurant aux accents Art déco, immuable et sélecte.
◆ Achter de imposante, historische façade gaat een aangenaam hotel schuil. De kamers variëren in grootte, maar zijn identiek gemeubileerd. Internationale clientèle. Beneden bevindt zich een chic café-restaurant met ambiance in de tijdeloze art deco.

Victoria, Damrak 1, ✉ 1012 LG, ☎ (0 20) 623 42 55, *vicres@parkplazahotels.nl, Fax (0 20) 625 29 97,* – 30 à 150. AE VISA JCB. LV j
Repas Lunch 27 – carte 32 à 44 – 20 – **295 ch** 280/330, – 10 suites – ½ P 310/360.
◆ Ce palace classique et son aile récente bénéficient d'une situation privilégiée pour les utilisateurs du rail. Quatre sortes de chambres. Hall coiffé d'une jolie verrière. Repas au goût du jour.
◆ Dit klassieke luxehotel met recentelijk aangebouwde vleugel is voor treinreizigers zeer gunstig gelegen. Het hotel beschikt over vier typen kamers. De lobby is bekroond met een fraaie glaskoepel. Eigentijdse keuken.

Blakes, Keizersgracht 384, ✉ 1016 GB, ☎ (0 20) 530 20 10, *hotel@blakes.nl, Fax (0 20) 530 20 30,* ch, – 30. AE VISA. KX a
Repas *(fermé sam. midi et dim.)* (avec cuisine asiatique) Lunch 28 – carte 59 à 74 – 18 – **38 ch** 390/990, – 3 suites.
◆ "Ordre et beauté ; luxe, calme et volupté..." Découvrez l'harmonie secrète de cette demeure au surprenant décor design d'inspiration orientale. Chambres personnalisées. Table actuelle au "look zen", avec un penchant pour les saveurs du levant.
◆ "Stijl, schoonheid, luxe, rust en exotiek." Ontdek de geheime harmonie van dit verrassende hotel met oosters geïnspireerd designdecor. Kamers met elk een bijzondere ambiance. Eigentijds restaurant met harmonieuze zen-look. Accent op de oriëntaalse keuken.

Jolly Carlton, Vijzelstraat 4, ✉ 1017 HK, ☎ (0 20) 622 22 66 et 623 83 20 (rest), *reservations@jollycarlton.nl, Fax (0 20) 626 61 83* – – 25 à 150. AE VISA. LY n
Repas *Caruso* *(fermé 25 déc.)* (cuisine italienne, dîner seult jusqu'à 23 h) carte 50 à 71 – **218 ch** 255/455.
◆ Hôtel de chaîne installé dans un immeuble 1900, à deux pas du marché aux fleurs et de la place Rembrandt. Chambres standard insonorisées, garnies d'un mobilier italien. Élégante table transalpine. Carte et menus bien balancés.
◆ Ketenhotel in een pand uit 1928, op een steenworp afstand van de bloemenmarkt en het Rembrandtplein. Standaardkamers met geluidsisolatie en Italiaans interieur. Verfijnde Italiaanse keuken. Evenwichtige kaart en menu's.

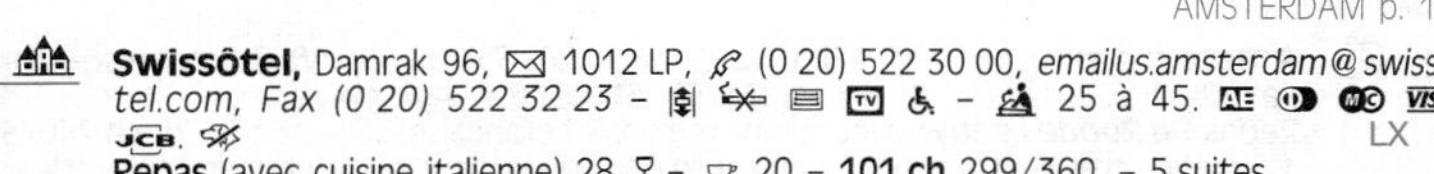

Swissôtel, Damrak 96, ✉ 1012 LP, ☎ (0 20) 522 30 00, *emailus.amsterdam@swissotel.com, Fax (0 20) 522 32 23* – 25 à 45. LX s

Repas (avec cuisine italienne) 28, – 20 – **101 ch** 299/360, – 5 suites.

◆ Tout récemment rajeunies, les chambres et junior suites de cet établissement proche du Dam disposent d'un équipement aussi complet qu'actuel. Business center. Brasserie-restaurant à la page. Registre culinaire d'inspiration "Sud", où se distingue l'Italie.

◆ De kamers en junior suites van dit etablissement vlak bij de Dam hebben onlangs een facelift gehad en zijn van alle moderne comfort voorzien. Business center. Eigentijds restaurant. Mediterrane keuken met duidelijk Italiaanse invloeden.

Sofitel, N.Z. Voorburgwal 67, ✉ 1012 RE, ☎ (0 20) 627 59 00, *h1159@accor-hotels.com, Fax (0 20) 623 89 32,* – 25 à 55. KX q

Repas carte 31 à 72 – 20 – **148 ch** 305 – ½ P 310/360.

◆ A 500 m de la gare centrale, hôtel de chaîne occupant une demeure ancienne et un édifice récent mitoyens. Façade et chambres viennent d'être rafraîchies. Atmosphère "Orient express" au restaurant. Carte traditionnelle.

◆ Dit ketenhotel op 500 m van het Centraal Station is gehuisvest in een karakteristiek oud pand en een aangrenzend modern gebouw. Voorgevel en kamers zijn onlangs opgeknapt. Restaurant met ambiance "Orient Express". Traditionele menukaart.

Toren sans rest, Keizersgracht 164, ✉ 1015 CZ, ☎ (0 20) 622 63 52, *info@hoteltoren.nl, Fax (0 20) 626 97 05,* – KV w

12 – **39 ch** 130/215, – 1 suite.

◆ La maison d'Anne Frank se dresse à 200 m de cet hôtel familial aux pimpantes chambres de dimensions variées, toutes neuves, bien équipées et isolées du bruit.

◆ Het huis van Anne Frank ligt op 200 m van dit geheel gerenoveerde familiehotel. Elegante kamers met geluidsisolatie, verschillend van grootte en goed uitgerust.

NH Doelen sans rest, Nieuwe Doelenstraat 24, ✉ 1012 CP, ☎ (0 20) 554 06 00, *nhdoelen@nh-hotels.nl, Fax (0 20) 622 94 10,* – – 25 à 100. LY z

16 – **85 ch** 190/230.

◆ Cet établissement érigé en 1856 au bord de l'Amstel compte parmi les plus anciens hôtels de la ville. Chambres de style anglais inégalement insonorisées.

◆ Het hotel in dit pand (1856) aan de Amstel behoort tot de oudste van de stad. De in Engelse stijl ingerichte kamers hebben geluidsisolatie, maar van ongelijke kwaliteit.

Seven One Seven sans rest, Prinsengracht 717, ✉ 1017 JW, ☎ (0 20) 427 07 17, *info@717hotel.nl, Fax (0 20) 423 07 17,* – KY c

8 ch 390/640.

◆ En quête d'un petit hôtel intime ? Aménagée avec recherche, cette maison du 18e s. a de quoi vous combler. Les chambres, amples et individualisées, sont de vrais bijoux.

◆ Op zoek naar een intiem hotelletje ? Dan is dit echt iets voor U ! De ruime, smaakvol ingerichte kamers in dit 18e-eeuwse pand zijn stuk voor stuk juweeltjes.

Ambassade sans rest, Herengracht 341, ✉ 1016 AZ, ☎ (0 20) 555 02 22, *info@ambassade-hotel.nl, Fax (0 20) 555 02 77,* – KX x

16 – **51 ch** 165/195, – 8 suites.

◆ Un ensemble de maisons typiques du 17e s. sert de cadre à ce charmant hôtel bordé de canaux. Chambres et suites coquettement personnalisées. Intéressante bibliothèque.

◆ Een aantal 17e-eeuwse grachtenhuizen vormt het decor van dit charmante hotel. De kamers en suites hebben allemaal een eigen karakter. Interessante bibliotheek.

Estheréa sans rest, Singel 305, ✉ 1012 WJ, ☎ (0 20) 624 51 46, *estherea@xs4all.nl, Fax (0 20) 623 90 01* – KX y

14 – **71 ch** 237/280.

◆ Cet hôtel à dénicher hors de l'animation du centre, entre le musée historique et le Singel, comprend plusieurs petites habitations mitoyennes. Chambres agréables à vivre.

◆ Dit hotel buiten het drukke centrum, tussen het Historisch Museum en de Singel, omvat enkele kleinere aangrenzende grachtenhuizen. Gerieflijke kamers.

Eden, Amstel 144, ✉ 1017 AE, ☎ (0 20) 530 78 78, *info.eden@edenhotelgroup.com, Fax (0 20) 623 32 67* – ch, LY r

Repas (taverne-rest, ouvert jusqu'à 23 h) Lunch 13 – 22/37 bc – 14 – **327 ch** 190/200.

◆ Présumerait-on que ces deux étroites façades au bord de l'Amstel dissimulent un établissement comptant plus de 300 chambres ? Touristes individuels et groupes. Taverne-restaurant avec vue sur la rivière.

◆ Wie zou ook maar kunnen vermoeden dat er achter deze twee smalle gevels aan de oever van de Amstel een hotel schuilgaat met meer dan 300 kamers ? Zowel voor individuele toeristen als voor groepen. Het café-restaurant biedt uitzicht op het water.

Amsterdam, Damrak 93, ✉ 1012 LP, ☎ (0 20) 555 06 66, *info@hotelamsterdam.nl, Fax (0 20) 620 47 16* – 🛗 ⇔ ≡ TV. AE ⓓ ⓜ VISA JCB. ✱ rest LX s
Repas ***De Roode Leeuw*** (avec cuisine régionale hollandaise) 30 – ☕ 17 – **79 ch** 240/310.
◆ Situation très centrale, sur la populeuse Damstraat, pour ce vétéran de l'hôtellerie amstellodamoise. Chambres sans reproche. Parkings publics aux alentours. Brasserie misant sur un choix de préparations traditionnelles typiquement hollandaises.
◆ Een veteraan in de Amsterdamse horeca en uiterst centraal gelegen aan het drukke Damrak. Onberispelijke kamers. Openbare parkings in de buurt. De menukaart van het restaurant bestaat uit traditionele, Nederlandse gerechten.

NH Schiller, Rembrandtsplein 26, ✉ 1017 CV, ☎ (0 20) 554 07 00, *info@nhschiller.nh-hotels.nl, Fax (0 20) 626 68 31,* 🍽 – 🛗 ⇔ TV. AE ⓓ ⓜ VISA JCB. ✱ ch LY x
Repas (brasserie) *Lunch 20* – 30 – ☕ 16 – **91 ch** 190/230, – 1 suite – ½ P 161.
◆ Édifice 1900 élevé sur une place effervescente veillée par la statue de Rembrandt. Chambres convenablement équipées, garnies d'un mobilier de qualité. Agréable "lobby". Brasserie Art déco où vous pourrez vous mesurer à la Frisse Frits, brassée "maison".
◆ Dit pand uit 1912 staat aan een bruisend plein waar het standbeeld van Rembrandt de wacht houdt. Kwaliteitsmeubilair in de kamers. Aangename lobby. In de art-decobrasserie wacht u een uitdaging : Frisse Frits, het huisbier.

Albus Gd H. sans rest, Vijzelstraat 49, ✉ 1017 HE, ☎ (0 20) 530 62 00, *sales@albusgrandhotel.com, Fax (0 20) 530 62 99* – 🛗 ⇔ TV. AE ⓜ VISA. ✱ LY g
☕ 13 – **74 ch** 160/205.
◆ Établissement flambant neuf, tout proche du marché aux fleurs. Les chambres, bien insonorisées, sont fonctionnelles et d'ampleur différente, mais meublées à l'identique.
◆ Spiksplinternieuw etablissement vlak bij de bloemenmarkt. De functionele kamers zijn van goede geluidsisolatie voorzien, variëren in grootte, maar zijn identiek gemeubileerd.

NH Caransa sans rest, Rembrandtsplein 19, ✉ 1017 CT, ☎ (0 20) 554 08 00, *info@nhcaransa.nh-hotels.nl, Fax (0 20) 626 68 31* – 🛗 ⇔ TV – 🎤 25 à 100. AE ⓓ ⓜ VISA. ✱ LY v
☕ 16 – **66 ch** 190/230.
◆ Hôtel abritant des chambres fonctionnelles, d'ampleur très satisfaisante et bien tenues, aménagées dans le style "British". Quatre salles accueillent les séminaires.
◆ Het hotel beschikt over functionele, goed onderhouden kamers die behoorlijk ruim zijn en in Britse stijl zijn ingericht. Vier zalen voor seminars.

die Port van Cleve, N.Z. Voorburgwal 178, ✉ 1012 SJ, ☎ (0 20) 624 48 60, *salesmarketing@dieportvancleve.com, Fax (0 20) 622 02 40* – 🛗 ⇔, ≡ rest, TV – 🎤 40. AE ⓓ ⓜ VISA JCB. ✱ KX w
Repas (brasserie) *Lunch 20* – carte 24 à 53, 🍷 – ☕ 18 – **119 ch** 199/295, – 1 suite.
◆ Le premier groupe brassicole batave naquit au 19e s. derrière cette imposante façade jouxtant le palais royal. À épingler : six junior-suites et un charmant bar à genièvres. Restaurant à grillades où le steak tient le haut du pavé !
◆ Achter deze imposante façade vlak bij het Koninklijk Paleis op de Dam begon Heineken in de 19e eeuw zijn eerste brouwerij. Het hotel heeft zes junior suites en een sfeervolle jeneverbar. In het grillrestaurant kunt u uw tanden zetten in een sappige steak.

Dikker en Thijs Fenice sans rest, Prinsengracht 444, ✉ 1017 KE, ☎ (0 20) 620 12 12, *info@dtfh.nl, Fax (0 20) 625 89 86,* ⚓ – 🛗 ⇔ TV. AE ⓓ ⓜ VISA JCB KY v
42 ch ☕ 145/345.
◆ Édifice classique érigé à 100 m de la Leidseplein, juste en face d'un petit pont enjambant le canal des Princes, qu'on aperçoit depuis quelques-unes des chambres.
◆ Een klassiek hotelpand vlak bij het Leidseplein, gebouwd op een hoek recht tegenover een bruggetje over de Prinsengracht ; enkele kamers kijken hierop uit.

NH City Centre, Spuistraat 288, ✉ 1012 VX, ☎ (0 20) 420 45 45, *nhcitycentre@nh-hotels.nl, Fax (0 20) 420 43 00,* ≤, ⚓ – 🛗 ⇔ TV ♿ 🚗. AE ⓓ ⓜ VISA JCB. ✱ KX g
Repas (taverne-rest avec cuisine italienne) *Lunch 16* – carte 22 à 32, 🍷 – ☕ 16 – **186 ch** 175 – ½ P 196/211.
◆ Coincé entre le quai du Singel et le béguinage, cet hôtel de chaîne aux chambres standard sobrement équipées offre de vastes communs mais un service "minimaliste".
◆ Dit ketenhotel tussen de Singel en het Begijnhof beschikt over standaardkamers met eenvoudig comfort. Grote gemeenschappelijke ruimten, maar een weinig service.

Mercure Arthur Frommer sans rest, Noorderstraat 46, ✉ 1017 TV, ☎ (0 20) 622 03 28, *h1032@accor-hotels.com, Fax (0 20) 620 32 08* – 🛗 ⇔ ≡ TV 🚗 P. AE ⓓ ⓜ VISA JCB LYZ j
☕ 14 – **90 ch** 145/165.
◆ Ensemble de maisons situé dans une rue calme, à un saut du Rijksmuseum et deux pas du musée Van Loon. Chambres standard. Service assez sommaire, mais utile parking.
◆ Het hotel omvat een aantal huizen in een rustige straat, vlak bij het Rijksmuseum en het Museum van Loon. Standaardkamers. Vrij beperkt servicepakket, wel parkeergelegenheid.

Canal House sans rest, Keizersgracht 148, ✉ 1015 CX, ☎ (0 20) 622 51 82, *info@canalhouse.nl, Fax (0 20) 624 13 17* – ⛓. AE ⊕ ⊕ VISA JCB. ✻ KV k
26 ch ☕ 150/190.
◆ Le long d'un canal, demeure du 17e s. au cachet préservé. Chambres personnalisées, plus panoramiques sur le devant, mais plus calmes à l'arrière. Mobilier de divers styles.
◆ Hotel in een karaktervol 17e-eeuws grachtenpand. De kamers, die elk een eigen sfeer hebben, bieden aan de voorkant meer uitzicht, aan de achterkant meer rust. Stijlmeubilair.

Inntel sans rest, Nieuwezijdskolk 19, ✉ 1012 PV, ☎ (0 20) 530 18 18, *infoamsterdam@hotelinntel.com, Fax (0 20) 422 19 19* – ⛓ ✻ ▤ TV ♿. AE ⊕ ⊕ VISA JCB LVX a
☕ 16 – **236 ch** 199/325.
◆ Établissement moderne situé au cœur du trépidant Nieuwe Zijde, quartier commerçant jouxtant la gare. Chambres à double vitrage, isolées du couloir par un sas.
◆ Modern hotel in het bruisende Nieuwe Zijde-kwartier, een buurt met winkels en warenhuizen dicht bij het station. Kamers met dubbele beglazing en een dubbele deur naar de gang.

City Center sans rest, N.Z. Voorburgwal 50, ✉ 1012 SC, ☎ (0 20) 422 00 11, *info@ams.nl, Fax (0 20) 420 03 57* – ⛓ ✻ TV ♿. AE ⊕ ⊕ VISA JCB. ✻ LV f
☕ 12 – **101 ch** 189.
◆ Immeuble contemporain posté en bordure du Nieuwe Zijde, à 400 m de la gare centrale. Chambres pratiques bien tenues. Un atout précieux : le parking public souterrain.
◆ Modern pand aan de rand van het kwartier Nieuwe Zijde, op 400 m van het station. Praktische, goed onderhouden kamers. Belangrijk pluspunt : de openbare ondergrondse parking.

Avenue sans rest, N.Z. Voorburgwal 33, ✉ 1012 RD, ☎ (0 20) 530 95 30, *info@avenue-hotel.nl, Fax (0 20) 530 95 99*, 🚲 – ⛓ TV. AE ⊕ ⊕ VISA JCB. ✻ LV z
77 ch ☕ 110/155.
◆ Cette affaire du Nieuwe Zijde occupe un petit immeuble et une maison attenante. La réception a pris la place de la cave et les chambres font peu à peu peau neuve.
◆ Dit hotel in het kwartier Nieuwe Zijde is gevestigd in een voormalig pakhuis en een pand ernaast. De kelder fungeert nu als receptie, de kamers worden geleidelijk opgeknapt.

Nicolaas Witsen sans rest, Nicolaas Witsenstraat 4, ✉ 1017 ZH, ☎ (0 20) 626 65 46, *info@hotelnicolaaswitsen.nl, Fax (0 20) 620 51 13* – ⛓ TV. AE ⊕ VISA. ✻ LZ b
29 ch ☕ 75/110.
◆ Cette maison soigneusement tenue offre le choix entre plusieurs sortes de chambres sobrement équipées. Courrez admirer la Ronde de nuit au Rijksmuseum.
◆ Dit keurig onderhouden pand beschikt over verschillende typen kamers die eenvoudig zijn ingericht. Het Rijksmuseum met de beroemde Nachtwacht bevindt zich op loopafstand.

Wiechmann sans rest, Prinsengracht 328, ✉ 1016 HX, ☎ (0 20) 626 33 21, *info@hotelwiechmann.nl, Fax (0 20) 626 89 62* – TV. ⊕ VISA. ✻ KX d
37 ch ☕ 75/140.
◆ Établissement occupant trois maisonnettes se mirant dans le canal des Princes. Bon à savoir : les meilleures chambres, sagement rustiques, occupent les angles.
◆ Dit etablissement omvat drie huizen, die zich spiegelen in het water van de Prinsengracht. Een tip : de beste kamers, die rustiek zijn ingericht, liggen op de hoeken.

Nes sans rest, Kloveniersburgwal 137, ✉ 1011 KE, ☎ (0 20) 624 47 73, *info@hotelnes.nl, Fax (0 20) 620 98 42* – ⛓ TV. AE ⊕ ⊕ VISA JCB LY f
38 ch ☕ 110/130.
◆ Au bord de l'Amstel, près de la place Rembrandt et de deux pontons d'embarquement, typique demeure bourgeoise aux chambres assez avenantes, propres et nettes.
◆ Dit karakteristieke patriciërshuis ligt aan de Amstel, vlak bij het Rembrandtplein en twee aanlegsteigers. De vrij comfortabele kamers zijn erg netjes.

Lancaster sans rest, Plantage Middenlaan 48, ✉ 1018 DH, ☎ (0 20) 535 68 88, *Fax (0 20) 535 68 89* – ⛓ TV. AE ⊕ ⊕ VISA JCB. ✻ MY e
☕ 14 – **92 ch** 130/172.
◆ Imposante demeure ancienne entièrement rénovée, située en face du zoo dans un quartier résidentiel légèrement excentré. Chambres très convenables d'ampleur différente.
◆ Imposant oud pand dat volledig is gerenoveerd. Het ligt in een woonwijk iets buiten het centrum, tegenover de dierentuin. Vrij gerieflijke kamers, variërend in grootte.

Ibis Stopera, Valkenburgerstraat 68, ✉ 1011 LZ, ☎ (0 20) 531 91 35, *h3044-re@accor-hotels.com, Fax (0 20) 531 91 45* – ⛓ ✻ ▤ TV ♿. AE ⊕ ⊕ VISA JCB MX z
Repas (taverne-rest, dîner seult) carte env. 28 – ☕ 13 – **207 ch** ☕ 135/160.
◆ Cet hôtel de chaîne flambant neuf dispose de chambres fonctionnelles distribuées sur sept étages. Petits-déjeuners servis sur la terrasse intérieure aux beaux jours.
◆ Dit gloednieuwe ketenhotel heeft functionele kamers die over zeven verdiepingen verspreid liggen. Bij mooi weer wordt het ontbijt op het terras in de binnentuin geserveerd.

XXXX ✿✿ **La Rive** - H. Amstel, Prof. Tulpplein 1, ✉ 1018 GX, ☎ (0 20) 520 32 64, *evert_groot@inter conti.com, Fax (0 20) 520 32 66*, ≤, ⚓ – ▤ P. AE ⦿ MC VISA JCB. ✗ MZ a
fermé du 1er au 23 août, 31 déc.-12 janv., sam. midi et dim. – **Repas** *Lunch 48 bc* – 85/98, carte 69 à 94, ♀ ⛀.
• Ambiance feutrée, décor raffiné et confort incomparable caractérisent le restaurant gastronomique de l'Amstel. Attablé en façade, vous admirerez à loisir la fameuse "rive".
• Stemmige ambiance, geraffineerd decor en een subliem comfort kenmerken het gastronomische restaurant van het Amstel Hotel. Aan de raamzijde kijkt u prachtig op het water.
Spéc. Turbot et truffe enrobés de pommes de terre, blettes et jus de veau. Pigeonneau grillé et poivron rouge, sauce au maïs. Feuilleté aux pommes, cannelle, glace vanille et caramel au beurre salé

XXXX **Excelsior** - H. de l'Europe, Nieuwe Doelenstraat 2, ✉ 1012 CP, ☎ (0 20) 531 17 05, *hotel@leurope.nl, Fax (0 20) 531 17 78*, ≤, ⛱, Ouvert jusqu'à 23 h, ⚓ – ▤ P. AE ⦿ MC VISA JCB LY c
fermé du 1er au 10 janv., sam. midi et dim. midi – **Repas** *Lunch 45* – 65/95 bc, ♀.
• Ce palace centenaire vous accueille dans son restaurant plaisamment redécoré. Côté terrasse, vue sur la Munttoren et le va-et-vient des embarcations sur l'Amstel.
• In dit restaurant van het 100 jaar oude Hotel de l'Europe wacht u een stijlvolle ontvangst in een fraai, vernieuwd decor. Het terras kijkt uit op de Munttoren en de Amstel.

XXX ✿✿ **Vermeer** - NH Barbizon Palace, Prins Hendrikkade 59, ✉ 1012 AD, ☎ (0 20) 556 48 85, *vermeer@nh-hotels.nl, Fax (0 20) 556 48 58*, ⚓ – ▤ P. AE ⦿ MC VISA JCB. ✗ LV d
fermé 19 juil.-22 août, 24 déc.-9 janv., sam. midi, dim. et jours fériés – **Repas** *Lunch 35* – 40/125, carte 72 à 82, ♀.
• Détrompez-vous : Vermeer n'a jamais posé son chevalet à cette adresse proposant une belle cuisine de base classique, relevée de notes assez inventives.
• Nee hoor, Vermeer heeft hier met zijn schildersezel nooit een voet binnengezet ! Verfijnde keuken op klassieke basis, die met vrij inventieve accenten wordt opgeluisterd.
Spéc. Foie de canard fumé, confit d'oignons blancs. Ris de veau sauté et rognon rissolé, crème de chou-fleur mousseuse. Cinq petits desserts au chocolat

XXX ✿ **Christophe** (Royer), Leliegracht 46, ✉ 1015 DH, ☎ (0 20) 625 08 07, *info@christophe.nl, Fax (0 20) 638 91 32* – ▤. AE MC VISA KVX c
fermé 27 déc.-5 janv., dim. et lundi – **Repas** (dîner seult) 51/65, carte 61 à 86, ♀.
• Le long du canal des Lys. Cuisine ambitieuse semée de touches méditerranéennes, servie dans un cadre luxueux. À deux pas : la maison d'Anne Frank et le quartier Jordaan.
• Dit restaurant vlak bij het Anne Frank Huis en de Jordaan bereidt een ambitieuze keuken die is doorspekt met mediterrane accenten en wordt geserveerd in een luxueus decor.
Spéc. Lapin de 4 heures au foie gras et jus de cassis. Filet de bar poêlé et fenouil mariné, jus à l'ail fumé. Brochette d'agneau aux dattes fraîches, purée d'aubergine au curry

XXX **Dynasty,** Reguliersdwarsstraat 30, ✉ 1017 BM, ☎ (0 20) 626 84 00, *Fax (0 20) 622 30 38*, ⛱, Cuisine orientale – ▤. AE ⦿ MC VISA. ✗ KY q
fermé 27 déc.-27 janv. et mardi – **Repas** (dîner seult) carte 32 à 50.
• Papillonnez sur le marché aux fleurs avant de vous attabler dans cet agréable restaurant oriental au décor multicolore et rafraîchissant. Spécialités du Sud-Est asiatique.
• Na een bezoek aan de bloemenmarkt is het een plezier om aan te schuiven in het bonte, verfrissende decor van dit oriëntaalse restaurant. Specialiteiten uit Zuidoost-Azië.

XX **d'Vijff Vlieghen,** Spuistraat 294 (par Vlieghendesteeg 1), ✉ 1012 VX, ☎ (0 20) 530 40 60, *restaurant@vijffvlieghen.nl, Fax (0 20) 623 64 04*, ⛱, ⚓ – AE ⦿ MC VISA JCB. ✗ KX p
Repas (dîner seult) 33, ♀.
• "Cinq mouches" (Vijff Vlieghen) se sont posées sur ces maisonnettes du 17e s. renfermant un dédale de salles mignonnes et rustiques. Choix classique avec menus.
• De "vliegen" zijn neergestreken in deze vijf 17e-eeuwse pandjes, die diverse charmante en rustieke eetkamers herbergen. Keuze uit klassieke gerechten en menu's.

XX ☺ **Café Roux** - H. The Grand Sofitel Demeure, O.Z. Voorburgwal 197, ✉ 1012 EX, ☎ (0 20) 555 35 60, *h2783-fb@accor-hotels.com, Fax (0 20) 555 32 90*, ⛱ – ▤ P. AE ⦿ MC VISA JCB. ✗ LX b
Repas *Lunch 29* – 34/48 bc, ♀.
• Belle brasserie Art déco agrégée à un hôtel de luxe. Cuisine dans le tempo actuel. Une peinture murale de K. Appel's, artiste du groupe COBRA, est visible près de l'entrée.
• Een prachtige brasserie in art deco, verbonden aan een luxueus hotel. De keuken sluit aan bij de huidige trend. Bij de ingang is een muurschildering te zien van Karel Appel.

XX **Het Tuynhuys,** Reguliersdwarsstraat 28, ✉ 1017 BM, ☎ (0 20) 627 66 03, *Fax (0 20) 423 59 99*, ⛱ – ▤. AE ⦿ MC VISA JCB KY q
fermé 31 déc.-1er janv., sam. midi et dim. midi – **Repas** *Lunch 30* – carte 41 à 87.
• Une carte au goût du jour vous sera soumise dans cette "Maison de jardin" (Tuynhuys) profitant d'une jolie terrasse intérieure. Salle à manger contemporaine ornée d'azulejos.
• Het Tuynhuys heeft aan de achterzijde een leuk terras en presenteert een menukaart met eigentijdse gerechten. De moderne eetzaal is met azulejo's gedecoreerd.

XX **Indrapura,** Rembrandtplein 42, ✉ 1017 CV, ☎ (0 20) 623 73 29, *info@indrapura.nl, Fax (0 20) 624 90 78,* Cuisine indonésienne – ▤. AE ⓓ ⓜ VISA LY h
fermé 31 déc. – **Repas** (dîner seult) 25/39.
◆ Sur une place populaire et animée. Bon choix de plats indonésiens, avec l'incontournable formule "rijsttafel" (table de riz). Clientèle touristique, habitués et groupes.
◆ Indonesisch restaurant aan een populair en levendig plein. Ruime keuze aan authentieke gerechten, met natuurlijk de fameuze rijsttafel. Toeristen, vaste gasten en groepen.

XX ✿ **Sichuan Food,** Reguliersdwarsstraat 35, ✉ 1017 BK, ☎ (0 20) 626 93 27, *Fax (0 20) 627 72 81,* Cuisine chinoise – ▤. AE ⓓ ⓜ VISA. ✂ KY u
fermé 31 déc. – **Repas** (dîner seult, nombre de couverts limité - prévenir) 31/43, carte 35 à 63.
◆ Cette façade banale abrite un vrai temple de la gastronomie asiatique où les saveurs du Sichuan sont à l'honneur. Décor typique d'un restaurant chinois de quartier.
◆ Achter deze alledaagse gevel gaat een tempel van Aziatische gastronomie schuil waar de keuken van Sichuan wordt aanbeden. Karakteristiek decor van een Chinees buurtrestaurant.
Spéc. Dim Sum. Canard laqué à la pékinoise. Huîtres sautées maison

XX **Hosokawa,** Max Euweplein 22, ✉ 1017 MB, ☎ (0 20) 638 80 86, *info@hosokawa.nl, Fax (0 20) 638 22 19,* Cuisine japonaise avec Teppan-Yaki – AE ⓓ ⓜ VISA JCB. ✂ KY a
fermé dern. sem. juil.-2 prem. sem. août – **Repas** (dîner seult) carte 24 à 77.
◆ Sobre et moderne restaurant japonais équipé de huit Teppan-Yaki (tables de cuisson). Le spectacle des produits virevoltant sous vos yeux mérite le détour. Parking public.
◆ Eenvoudig en modern Japans restaurant met acht teppan-yaki's. Het is fantastisch om te zien hoe de gerechten met veel zwier op de bakplaat worden bereid. Openbare parking.

XX ✿ **Van Vlaanderen** (Philippart), Weteringschans 175, ✉ 1017 XD, ☎ (0 20) 622 82 92, 🏠, ⚓ – ▤. AE ⓜ VISA KZ k
fermé mi-juil.-prem. sem. août, dern. sem. déc., dim. et lundi – **Repas** (dîner seult, nombre de couverts limité - prévenir) 40, carte 56 à 63, ♀.
◆ Une fine cuisine française au goût du jour et quelques recettes d'inspiration belge vous attendent à cette bonne enseigne proche du musée Van Loon et du Rijksmuseum.
◆ Een verfijnde, eigentijdse Franse keuken en enkele Belgische gerechten zijn de smaakmakers in dit goede restaurant vlak bij het Museum Van Loon en het Rijksmuseum.
Spéc. Emincé de cabillaud, homard et pommes de terre au coulis de crevettes. Caneton rôti, tarte tatin de figues et pommes sautées. Profiterolles au caramel de beurre salé et compote de coings

XX **Breitner,** Amstel 212, ✉ 1017 AH, ☎ (0 20) 627 78 79, *Fax (0 20) 330 29 98* – AE ⓓ ⓜ VISA JCB. ✂ LY p
fermé 2 dern. sem. juil.-début août, 25 déc.-1er janv. et dim. – **Repas** (dîner seult) carte 47 à 72, ♀.
◆ Restaurant moderne empruntant son nom à un impressionniste local. Cuisine actuelle aux nuances méditerranéennes et internationales. Vins du monde. Vue sur l'Amstel.
◆ Modern restaurant dat zijn naam ontleent aan de lokale impressionist. Hedendaagse keuken met mediterrane en internationale nuances. Wereldwijnen. Uitzicht op de Amstel.

XX **Takens,** Runstraat 17d, ✉ 1016 GJ, ☎ (0 20) 627 06 18, *Fax (0 20) 624 28 61,* Ouvert jusqu'à 23 h – AE ⓓ ⓜ VISA KX s
fermé Noël-5 janv. – **Repas** (déjeuner sur réservation) carte 39 à 51, ♀.
◆ Table accueillante située à un saut des maisons Cromhout. Registre culinaire classique sagement revisité et cave bien montée. Ambiance de restaurant de quartier.
◆ Gastvrij restaurant met de knusse ambiance van een buurteethuis, op een steenworp afstand van de Cromhout-huizen. Klassieke keuken in een modern jasje. Uitgebreide wijnkaart.

XX **Manchurian,** Leidseplein 10a, ✉ 1017 PT, ☎ (0 20) 623 13 30, *info@manchurian.nl, Fax (0 20) 626 21 05,* Cuisine orientale – ▤. AE ⓓ ⓜ VISA. ✂ KY x
fermé 30 avril et 31 déc. – **Repas** 22/44, ♀.
◆ Aux abords de la passagère Leidseplein, restaurant asiatique dont la carte sino-thaïlandaise traverse les régions de Canton, de Shanghai et du Sichuan.
◆ De Chinees-Thaise menukaart van dit Aziatische restaurant vlak bij het drukke Leidseplein is net een culinaire reis door de regio's Canton, Shanghai en Sichuan.

XX **blauw aan de wal** O.Z. Achterburgwal 99,, ✉ 1012 DD, ☎ (0 20) 330 22 57, *Fax (0 20) 330 20 06,* 🏠 – ▤. AE ⓜ VISA. ✂ LX d
fermé du 25 au 31 déc. et dim. – **Repas** (dîner seult jusqu'à 23 h 30) carte env. 52, ♀.
◆ Une oasis de tranquillité, au fond d'un cul-de-sac de l'effervescent quartier des Walletjes. Préparations en phase avec l'époque et cave franco-transalpine assez bien montée.
◆ Een oase van rust midden in het bruisende kwartier van de Walletjes, achter in een steegje. Trendy gerechten. Vrij goede selectie Franse en Italiaanse wijnen.

XX **Segugio,** Utrechtsestraat 96, ✉ 1017 VS, ☎ (0 20) 330 15 03, *adriano@scgugio.nl, Fax (0 20) 330 15 16,* Cuisine italienne – ▤. AE ⓓ ⓜ VISA. ⚡ LY b
fermé 24 déc.-2 janv. et dim. – **Repas** (dîner seult jusqu'à 23 h) carte 45 à 58, ♀.
◆ Un peu de flair suffit pour dénicher ce "ristorante" tirant son nom d'une race de chien de chasse ; un toutou également utilisé comme truffier ! Bon choix de vins du pays.
◆ Een beetje flair is genoeg om dit Italiaanse restaurant op te sporen. Het is genoemd naar een jachthondenras dat ook als truffelhond wordt gebruikt. Goede selectie landwijnen.

XX **Le Pêcheur,** Reguliersdwarsstraat 32, ✉ 1017 BM, ☎ (0 20) 624 31 21, *Fax (0 20) 624 31 21,* ☂, Produits de la mer – AE ⓓ ⓜ VISA JCB. ⚡ KY w
fermé dim. – **Repas** *Lunch 33* – carte 42 à 63.
◆ Ancré dans une petite "rue de bouche" longeant le marché aux fleurs, Le Pêcheur voue sa cuisine à l'océan. Terrasse à l'arrière et parking public à proximité immédiate.
◆ De "Visser" ligt voor anker in de "grootste eetstraat" van de stad, waar zijn kookkunst in het teken van de oceaan staat. Terras aan de achterkant, openbare parking vlakbij.

XX **d' theeboom,** Singel 210, ✉ 1016 AB, ☎ (0 20) 623 84 20, *info@theeboom.nl, Fax (0 20) 421 25 12,* ☂ – AE ⓓ ⓜ VISA JCB KX b
fermé 24 déc.-6 janv. et dim. – **Repas** (dîner seult) 33/43.
◆ Enraciné au bord du Singel, à 200 m du Dam, "Le théier" n'a rien d'un tea-room : c'est un restaurant préparant une cuisine à la page, avec un menu intéressant.
◆ Deze theeboom, die langs de Singel wortel heeft geschoten, heeft niets weg van een tearoom, maar is een restaurant waar een eigentijdse keuken wordt bereid. Interessant menu.

XX **Le Relais** - H. de l'Europe, Nieuwe Doelenstraat 2, ✉ 1012 CP, ☎ (0 20) 531 17 77, *hotel@leurope.nl, Fax (0 20) 531 17 78,* Ouvert jusqu'à 23 h, ⚓ – ▤. AE ⓓ ⓜ VISA JCB LY c
Repas *Lunch 24* – 29, ♀.
◆ Dans un grand hôtel, petit restaurant cossu où l'on se sent directement entre de bonnes mains. Choix classique et carte déclinant un thème culinaire particulier.
◆ Een klein, weelderig restaurant in een grand hôtel. U voelt hier onmiddellijk dat u in goede handen bent. Klassieke gerechten en een kaart met een speciaal culinair thema.

XX **Oesterbar,** Leidseplein 10, ✉ 1017 PT, ☎ (0 20) 623 29 88, *Fax (0 20) 623 21 99,* Produits de la mer – ▤. AE ⓓ ⓜ VISA. ⚡ KY x
fermé 25, 26 et 31 déc. – **Repas** (dîner seult jusqu'à minuit) carte 44 à 158.
◆ Une carte classique résolument iodée vous attend dans ce "bar à huîtres" occupant les trois étages d'un édifice voisin du théâtre de la Leidseplein. Mieux vaut réserver.
◆ Een klassieke viskaart dient als "aas" om de klanten uit het nabij gelegen theater te lokken. Reserveren aanbevolen.

X **Bordewijk,** Noordermarkt 7, ✉ 1015 MV, ☎ (0 20) 624 38 99, *Fax (0 20) 420 66 03* – ▤. AE ⓓ ⓜ VISA. ⚡ KV a
fermé dern sem. juil.-2 prem. sem. août et lundi – **Repas** (dîner seult) carte 52 à 60.
◆ L'une des adresses les plus courues du quartier Jordaan. Sobre et moderne salle à manger où règne une ambiance animée. Appétissante carte actuelle et bon livre de cave.
◆ Een van de populairste adressen in de Jordaan. Moderne, eenvoudig ingerichte eetzaal met een gezellige ambiance. Smaakvolle, eigentijdse menukaart en een mooie wijnkelder.

X **De Compagnon,** Guldehandsteeg 17, ✉ 1012 RA, ☎ (0 20) 620 42 25, *info@decompagnon.nl, Fax (0 20) 421 15 56,* ☂, ⚓ – AE ⓓ ⓜ VISA LX c
Repas *Lunch 30* – carte 49 à 64, ♀.
◆ Face au Damrak, dans une impasse proche du quartier rouge et de la bourse. Salles étroites étagées sur quatre niveaux. Choix varié et assez bien fourni. Cave prometteuse.
◆ In een doodlopend steegje achter het Damrak, vlak bij de Walletjes en de Beurs. Smalle zalen verdeeld over vier niveaus. Ruime, gevarieerde keuze. Veelbelovende wijnkaart.

X **Zuid Zeeland,** Herengracht 413, ✉ 1017 BP, ☎ (0 20) 624 31 54, *Fax (0 20) 428 31 71,* ☂, Ouvert jusqu'à 23 h – AE ⓜ VISA KY e
fermé sam. midi et dim. midi – **Repas** 30/35, ♀.
◆ Repaire gourmand à débusquer au bord du canal des Seigneurs, pas très loin du marché aux fleurs. Fine cuisine d'aujourd'hui. Bon menu multi-choix servi à l'heure du dîner.
◆ Een culinaire pleisterplaats dicht bij de pittoreske bloemenmarkt. Verfijnde, hedendaagse keuken. 's Avonds wordt u ook een prima keuzemenu voorgelegd.

X **Lucius,** Spuistraat 247, ✉ 1012 VP, ☎ (0 20) 624 18 31, *seafood@lucius.nl, Fax (0 20) 627 61 53,* Produits de la mer – AE ⓓ ⓜ VISA JCB KX r
Repas (dîner seult jusqu'à minuit) 25/35.
◆ Cuisine de la mer du Nord valorisant les produits locaux : hareng, huître de Zélande, anguille... Collection d'anémones des mers du Sud et poissons tropicaux en aquarium.
◆ Noordzeekeuken met Hollandse specialiteiten als haring, Zeeuwse oesters en paling. Collectie anemonen uit de zuidelijke zeeën en tropische vissen in een aquarium.

Chez Georges et Betsie, Herenstraat 3, ✉ 1015 BX, ☎ (0 20) 626 33 32 – ▤. AE MC VISA KV n
fermé du 11 au 18 avril, 18 juil.-8 août, 26 déc.-5 janv., merc. et dim. – **Repas** (dîner seult jusuq'à 23 h) 30/40.
◆ Entre le Jordaan et le Nieuwe Zijde. Assez exigu, donc souvent complet, ce restaurant classique de style bonbonnière fonctionne majoritairement avec son cercle d'habitués.
◆ Dit smaakvol ingerichte restaurantje tussen de Jordaan en het historische stadshart is vrij klein en dus vaak vol. Het draait voornamelijk op een vaste klantenkring.

Haesje Claes, Spuistraat 275, ✉ 1012 VR, ☎ (0 20) 624 99 98, *info@haesjeclaes.nl, Fax (0 20) 627 48 17,* – ▤. AE D MC VISA JCB. KX f
fermé 30 avril et 25, 26 et 31 déc. – **Repas** 19/29, ♀.
◆ Une clientèle nombreuse défile à cette adresse reflétant l'ambiance de la ville. Cuisine batave simple et copieuse servie dans un cadre chaleureux. Musée historique à 100 m.
◆ Het is een komen en gaan op dit adres, dat de sfeer van de stad weerspiegelt. Eenvoudige maar overvloedige "Hollandse pot". Gemoedelijke ambiance. Historisch Museum op 100 m.

Entresol, Geldersekade 29, ✉ 1011 EJ, ☎ (0 20) 623 79 12, *entresol@chello.nl* – ▤. MC VISA LX t
fermé 3 sem. en juil., lundi et mardi – **Repas** (dîner seult) carte env. 40.
◆ Cette charmante petite affaire familiale proche du "Chinatown" amstellodamois occupe une maison du 17e s. Salles à manger au décor hollandais étagées sur deux niveaux.
◆ Dit kleine, charmante restaurant vlak bij het Amsterdamse Chinatown is gevestigd in een 17e-eeuws pand. Eetzalen met Hollands decor, verdeeld over twee niveaus.

Van de Kaart, Prinsengracht 512, ✉ 1017 KH, ☎ (0 20) 625 92 32, *info@vandekaart.com* – AE D MC VISA. KY d
fermé dim. – **Repas** (déjeuner sur réservation) carte 34 à 64.
◆ Restaurant établi à l'entresol d'une maison de canal. Accueil et service charmants, ambiance amstellodamoise quelquefois survoltée et choix actuel avec menus "surprise".
◆ Restaurant op de entresol van een grachtenpand. Typisch Amsterdamse en soms wat opgewonden sfeer. Charmante ontvangst en bediening. Eigentijdse keuken met verrassingsmenu's.

Tempo doeloe, Utrechtsestraat 75, ✉ 1017 VJ, ☎ (0 20) 625 67 18, *Fax (0 20) 639 23 42,* Cuisine indonésienne – ▤. AE D MC VISA. LY t
fermé 25, 26 et 31 déc., 1er janv. et dim. – **Repas** (dîner seult jusqu'à 23 h 30) 29/64 bc.
◆ Puisque les bonne petites tables indonésiennes ne manquent pas à Amsterdam, autant en profiter ! Celle-ci se cache à 200 m du Pont-Maigre, derrière une façade discrète.
◆ Aan Indonesische restaurantjes geen gebrek in Amsterdam. Profiteer er dus van ! Dit adresje is te vinden op 200 m van de Magere Brug, achter een onopvallende gevel.

blue pepper, Nassaukade 366h, ✉ 1054 AB, ☎ (0 20) 489 70 39, *info@restaurantbluepepper.com,* Cuisine indonésienne – AE D MC VISA JCB. JY d
fermé dim. – **Repas** (dîner seult) carte 33 à 43.
◆ Lumière tamisée, camaïeu de bleus et touches florales délicates composent l'apaisant décor du blue pepper. Préparations "javanaises" raffinées, dans de jolies assiettes.
◆ Indonesisch restaurant met rustige ambiance, gedempt licht, verschillende tinten blauw en subtiele bloemaccenten. Verfijnde gerechten die op mooie borden worden geserveerd.

De Belhamel, Brouwersgracht 60, ✉ 1013 GX, ☎ (0 20) 622 10 95, *info@belhamel.nl, Fax (0 20) 623 88 40,* ⩤, – ▤. AE MC VISA. KV p
Repas (dîner seult) 32.
◆ Brasserie de quartier postée au confluent de ravissants canaux. Petit choix de base classique et menu sur écriteau. Salle à manger de style Belle Époque, avec mezzanine.
◆ Buurtrestaurant op een prachtige lokatie, aan de kruising van twee grachten. Kleine kaart op klassieke basis, menu op een lei. Eetzaal in art nouveau, met tussenverdieping.

L'Indochine, Beulingstraat 9, ✉ 1017 BA, ☎ (0 20) 627 57 55, *kietle@wxs.nl,* Cuisine vietnamienne – ▤. AE D MC VISA JCB. KY b
fermé lundi – **Repas** (dîner seult) carte 34 à 47.
◆ C'est à une savoureuse escapade entre les golfes du Siam et du Tonkin que vous convie ce petit restaurant au cadre dépouillé et à l'enseigne "coloniale". Vins de la Métropole.
◆ In dit kleine restaurant met sober decor wordt u meegenomen op een culinair avontuur tussen de Golf van Thailand en de Golf van Tonkin. Wijnkaart met accent op Franse wijnen.

Vooges, Utrechtsestraat 51, ✉ 1017 VJ, ☎ (0 20) 330 56 70, *vooges40@zonnet.nl, Fax (0 20) 330 29 88,* Taverne-rest – AE D MC VISA JCB LY e
Repas (dîner seult) carte env. 28.
◆ Ancien "bruin café" promu taverne-restaurant grâce à quelques embellissements de-ci de-là. Carte fréquemment recomposée, ambiance sympathique et clientèle d'habitués.
◆ Een voormalige bruin café, maar na wat aanpassingen in het interieur nu een restaurant. Regelmatig wisselende menukaart, sympathieke ambiance en een vaste klantenkring.

Memories of India, Reguliersdwarsstraat 88, ✉ 1017 BN, ☎ (0 20) 623 57 10, *Fax (0 20) 638 75 84*, Cuisine indienne – ▤. AE ⓓ ⓜ VISA JCB. ✂ LY a
Repas (dîner seult jusqu'à 23 h 30) carte 22 à 37, ♀.
◆ Des spécialités du Nord et du centre du sous-continent, un décor des mille et une nuits modernisé, et voici recréée près d'une place animée l'ambiance "Empire des Indes".
◆ Specialiteiten uit Noord- en Midden-India en een decor uit de sprookjes van duizend-en-een-nacht in moderne versie. Kortom, een stukje India vlak bij een gezellig plein.

Quartier Rijksmuseum (Vondelpark) - *plans p. 8 et 10* :

Marriott, Stadhouderskade 12, ✉ 1054 ES, ☎ (0 20) 607 55 55, *amsterdam@mariotthotels.com, Fax (0 20) 607 55 11*, ⛹, ≘, 🚲 – |‡| ✈ ▤ ⊡ ♿, 🚗 – 👥 25 à 450. AE ⓓ ⓜ VISA JCB. ✂ JY f
Repas (dîner seult jusqu'à minuit) carte 34 à 44, ♀ – ☕ 20 – **387 ch** 215, – 5 suites.
◆ Hôtel haut de gamme conçu à l'américaine au bord d'un axe important. Vastes chambres dotées d'équipements complets. Bonne infrastructure pour séminaires et centre d'affaires.
◆ Eersteklas hotel op Amerikaanse leest geschoeid, aan een belangrijke verkeersader. Grote, volledig uitgeruste kamers. Business center, goede faciliteiten voor seminars.

NH Amsterdam Centre, Stadhouderskade 7, ✉ 1054 ES, ☎ (0 20) 685 13 51, *nhamsterdamcentre@nh-hotels.nl, Fax (0 20) 685 16 11*, ⛹, ≘ – |‡| ✈ ▤ ⊡ ♿ – 👥 25 à 200. AE ⓓ ⓜ VISA JCB. ✂ JY p
Repas carte 31 à 41 – ***Bice*** *(fermé dim.)* (cuisine italienne, dîner seult) carte env. 46 – ☕ 19 – **227 ch** 230/320, – 2 suites.
◆ Le long du Singelgracht, établissement de chaîne entièrement rénové et dont l'accès ne pose aucune difficulté. Amples chambres très confortables, garnies de meubles de style. Brasserie dont les lumières brillent assez tard. Table transalpine bien dans le coup.
◆ Dit volledig gerenoveerde hotel staat aan de Singel in hartje Amsterdam, maar is desondanks goed bereikbaar. Ruime, zeer comfortabele kamers, ingericht met stijlmeubilair. De brasserie is tot vrij laat in de avond geopend. Zeer eigentijdse Italiaanse keuken.

The Gresham Memphis sans rest, De Lairessestraat 87, ✉ 1071 NX, ☎ (0 20) 673 31 41, *info@gresham-memphishotel.nl, Fax (0 20) 673 73 12*, ⛹ – |‡| ✈ ⊡ – 👥 40. AE ⓓ ⓜ VISA JCB. ✂ FU g
☕ 18 – **74 ch** 108/250.
◆ Bonnes chambres au look "british", insonorisées et progressivement rafraîchies. Service attentionné. La ligne 16 du tramway, desservant le centre, passe devant l'hôtel.
◆ Goede kamers met een Engelse look en met geluidsisolatie, die geleidelijk worden opgeknapt. Attente service. Tramlijn 16 stopt bij het hotel.

Jan Luyken sans rest, Jan Luykenstraat 58, ✉ 1071 CS, ☎ (0 20) 573 07 30, *jan-luyken@bilderberg.nl, Fax (0 20) 676 38 41* – |‡| ✈ ▤ ⊡. AE ⓓ ⓜ VISA JCB JZ m
☕ 16 – **62 ch** 200/258.
◆ Trois belles demeures 1900 composent cet hôtel aux grandes chambres bien équipées. Décor intérieur d'esprit contemporain. Situation pratique en plein quartier des musées.
◆ Een hotel in drie fraaie herenhuizen uit rond 1900, met grote kamers die zeer comfortabel zijn. Eigentijds interieur. Praktisch gelegen, op een steenworp afstand van de musea.

Toro 🐌 sans rest, Koningslaan 64, ✉ 1075 AG, ☎ (0 20) 673 72 23, *toro@ams.nl, Fax (0 20) 675 00 31* – |‡| ⊡. AE ⓓ ⓜ VISA JCB. ✂ EU m
☕ 15 – **22 ch** 199/235.
◆ Aux portes du Vondelpark. Villa tranquille dont l'intérieur, aménagé avec goût, ne manque ni de charme, ni de chaleur. Chambres personnalisées. Terrasse donnant sur un étang.
◆ Rustig gelegen en smaakvol ingerichte villa aan de rand van het Vondelpark. Sfeervolle, vriendelijke ambiance. Kamers met een persoonlijke noot. Tuin met terras aan het water.

Vondel (annexes) sans rest, Vondelstraat 28, ✉ 1054 GE, ☎ (0 20) 612 01 20, *info@hotelvondel.nl, Fax (0 20) 685 43 21*, 🚗 – |‡| ⊡. AE ⓓ ⓜ VISA JCB JY m
70 ch ☕ 120/140.
◆ L'établissement occupe cinq maisons de la fin du 19ᵉ s. Le bâtiment accueillant la réception abrite les meilleures chambres, de style très soigné. Salons cossus.
◆ Het hotel beslaat vijf herenhuizen uit het einde van de 19e eeuw. Het pand met de receptie beschikt over de beste kamers, die zeer verzorgd zijn ingericht. Luxueuze salons.

Piet Hein sans rest, Vossiusstraat 53, ✉ 1071 AK, ☎ (0 20) 662 72 05, *info@hotelpiethein.nl, Fax (0 20) 662 15 26* – |‡| ✈ ▤ ⊡. AE ⓓ ⓜ VISA JCB. ✂ JZ g
61 ch ☕ 90/140.
◆ Ancienne maison de notable renfermant des chambres modernes. À deux pas : la chlorophylle du Vondelpark, l'animation de la Leidseplein et plusieurs beaux musées.
◆ Hotel met moderne kamers, gevestigd in een prachtig herenhuis. Op loopafstand liggen het groene Vondelpark, het gezellige Leidseplein en diverse interessante musea.

Lairesse sans rest, De Lairessestraat 7, ✉ 1071 NR, ✆ (0 20) 671 95 96, *Fax (0 20) 671 17 56* – 🛗 ⇋ 📺. AE ⓓ MC VISA JCB. ✗ FU h
☕ 15 – **29 ch** 235.
◆ Une façade assez banale abrite cet hôtel bien tenu bénéficiant de la proximité de trois musées prestigieux. Chambres spacieuses garnies d'un mobilier actuel.
◆ Achter een vrij alledaagse gevel gaat dit goed onderhouden hotel schuil, dicht bij drie prestigieuze musea. De ruime kamers zijn met geriefelijk meubilair ingericht.

Terdam sans rest, Tesselschadestraat 23, ✉ 1054 ET, ✆ (0 20) 612 68 76, *info@ams.nl, Fax (0 20) 683 83 13* – 🛗 ⇋ ▤ 📺. AE ⓓ MC VISA JCB. ✗ JY a
☕ 12 – **89 ch** 179/189.
◆ Chambres de taille respectable et de bon confort, distribuées entre deux bâtiments mitoyens dont l'un a profité d'un rajeunissement intérieur complet.
◆ De comfortabele, ruime kamers liggen verspreid over twee aangrenzende panden. Het interieur van een van de twee is onlangs volledig vernieuwd.

Fita sans rest, Jan Luykenstraat 37, ✉ 1071 CL, ✆ (0 20) 679 09 76, *info@fita.nl, Fax (0 20) 664 39 69* – 🛗 ⇋ 📺. AE ⓓ MC VISA. ✗ JZ s
fermé 13 déc.-14 janv. – **16 ch** ☕ 110/140.
◆ Idéal pour le tourisme individuel, ce petit hôtel aux chambres fonctionnelles, de trois calibres différents, bénéficie de la proximité des plus grands musées d'Amsterdam.
◆ Dit kleine hotel is ideaal voor de individuele toerist. Het heeft functionele kamers in drie verschillende prijsklassen en ligt vlak bij de grote musea van de stad.

De Filosoof ⛆ sans rest, Anna van den Vondelstraat 6, ✉ 1054 GZ, ✆ (0 20) 683 30 13, *reservations@hotelfilosoof.nl, Fax (0 20) 685 37 50* – 🛗 📺 – 🎓 25. AE MC VISA. ✗ ET a
38 ch ☕ 108/122.
◆ L'originalité de cet hôtel donnant sur une rue à sens unique qui longe le Vondelpark tient au décor des chambres, inspiré de thèmes culturels ou philosophiques.
◆ Het decor van de kamers, dat is geïnspireerd op culturele en filosofische thema's, maakt dit hotel in een eenrichtingstraat bij het Vondelpark tot een origineel adres.

Villa Borgmann ⛆ sans rest, Koningslaan 48, ✉ 1075 AE, ✆ (0 20) 673 52 52, *info@hotel-borgmann.nl, Fax (0 20) 676 25 80*, 🚲 – 🛗 📺. AE ⓓ MC VISA. ✗ EU n
11 ch ☕ 98/155.
◆ Paisible adresse familiale voisine du rafraîchissant Vondelpark, cette jolie villa 1900 bâtie en briques rouges met à votre disposition des chambres amples et actuelles.
◆ Dit rustige familiehotel vlak bij het Vondelpark is gehuisvest in een fraaie, rode bakstenen villa uit omstreeks 1900. De kamers zijn ruim en actueel.

Prinsen sans rest, Vondelstraat 36, ✉ 1054 GE, ✆ (0 20) 616 23 23, *manager@prinsenhotel.demon.nl, Fax (0 20) 616 61 12*, 🌳 – 🛗 📺. AE ⓓ MC VISA JCB JY e
45 ch ☕ 120/135.
◆ Des chambres sobres et menues, mais pimpantes et lumineuses, se cachent derrière cette sombre façade 1900. La salle des petits-déjeuners donne sur un jardinet.
◆ Achter de donkere façade van dit pand uit circa 1900 gaan kamers schuil die klein en eenvoudig zijn, maar wel zeer verzorgd en licht. De ontbijtzaal kijkt uit op een tuintje.

Zandbergen sans rest, Willemsparkweg 205, ✉ 1071 HB, ✆ (0 20) 676 93 21, *info@hotel-zandbergen.com, Fax (0 20) 676 18 61* – ⇋ 📺. AE ⓓ MC VISA. ✗ EU s
fermé du 15 au 26 déc. et du 4 au 16 janv. – **18 ch** ☕ 93/143.
◆ À 100 m du Vondelpark, dans une rue à tramway, petit hôtel dont les compactes chambres ont été rénovées. Un double vitrage efficace les prémunit des bruits de la circulation.
◆ Hotelletje in een herenhuis nabij het Vondelpark. Door de straat rijdt een tram, maar dankzij de dubbele beglazing hebben de kleine, gerenoveerde kamers geen geluidsoverlast.

Radèn Mas, Stadhouderskade 6, ✉ 1054 ES, ✆ (0 20) 685 40 41, *Fax (0 20) 685 39 81*, Cuisine indonésienne, ouvert jusqu'à 23 h – ▤. AE ⓓ MC VISA JCB. ✗ JY k
Repas *Lunch 30* – carte 34 à 64.
◆ Une réputation flatteuse entoure ce restaurant indonésien qui ranime dignement l'héritage culinaire de l'ancienne colonie hollandaise. Piano tous les soirs, sauf le mardi.
◆ Een gerenommeerd Indonesisch restaurant dat het culinaire erfgoed van de voormalige Hollandse kolonie alle eer aandoet. 's Avonds speelt er een pianist, behalve op dinsdag.

Le Garage, Ruysdaelstraat 54, ✉ 1071 XE, ✆ (0 20) 679 71 76, *info@rest-legarage.nl, Fax (0 20) 662 22 49*, Avec bar à tapas Le Garage en Pluche, ouvert jusqu'à 23 h – ▤. AE ⓓ MC VISA FU y
fermé Pâques, Pentecôte, 2 dern. sem. juil., Noël, Nouvel An, sam. midi et dim. midi – **Repas** *Lunch 30* – 33/49, 🍸.
◆ Ambiance artistique et effervescence cosmopolite dans cette brasserie moderne dont la carte décline un bon petit choix bien ficelé. Tapas bar-restaurant très "sympa" à côté.
◆ Moderne brasserie met artistiek decor en bruisende kosmopolitische ambiance. Vrij kleine, maar goed doortimmerde menukaart. De buurman heeft een sympathieke, tapasachtige bar.

Spring, Willemsparkweg 177, ✉ 1071 GZ, ☎ (0 20) 675 44 21, *info@restaurantspring.nl, Fax (0 20) 676 94 14,* – . AE ⓓ ⓜ VISA FU w
fermé sam. midi, dim. et jours fériés – **Repas** *Lunch 30* – carte env. 52, ♀.
◆ Très "trendy" : la devanture n'exhibe ni enseigne ni menu, mais seulement deux stèles. Une longue banquette centrale traverse la salle. Bons produits travaillés avec soin.
◆ Heel trendy : buiten geen naambord en geen menu, maar alleen twee zuiltjes. Een lange, dubbele bank deelt de eetzaal in tweeën. Kwaliteitsproducten worden hier met zorg bereid.

Brasserie van Baerle, Van Baerlestraat 158, ✉ 1071 BG, ☎ (0 20) 679 15 32, *brasserie@hetnet.nl, Fax (0 20) 671 71 96,* , Ouvert jusqu'à 23 h – AE ⓓ ⓜ VISA. FU b
fermé 25 déc.-1er janv. et sam. midi – **Repas** *Lunch 33* – 34, ♀.
◆ Agréable restaurant où afflue une clientèle surtout amstellodamoise, fidélisée par un attrayant menu-carte suggérant aussi d'harmonieux accords mets-vins. Brunch dominical.
◆ Aangename brasserie die vooral bij Amsterdammers populair is. Aantrekkelijke kaart met menu, waarbij de geserveerde wijnen harmonieus gezelschap zijn. Brunch op zondag.

Quartiers Sud et Ouest - *plans p. 8 et 9 sauf indication spéciale :*

Okura , Ferdinand Bolstraat 333, ✉ 1072 LH, ☎ (0 20) 678 71 11, *sales@okura.nl, Fax (0 20) 671 23 44,* , , , – – 25 à 1200. AE ⓓ ⓜ VISA JCB. GU c
Repas voir rest ***Ciel Bleu*** et ***Yamazato*** ci-après – ***Sazanka*** (cuisine japonaise avec Teppan-Yaki) (dîner seult) 49/67, ♀ – ***Brasserie Le Camelia*** (ouvert jusqu'à 23 h) carte env. 44, ♀ – 25 – **358 ch** 340/410, – 12 suites.
◆ Un vrai "village japonais" que ce luxueux hôtel international dominant le canal Noorder Amstel. Superbe health center et colossale infrastructure pour séminaires. Restaurant nippon doté de tables de cuisson. Cuisine française variée à la brasserie Le Camelia.
◆ Net Japan in 't klein, dit internationale luxehotel aan de Noorder Amstel, dat bij uitstek geschikt is voor feestelijke en zakelijke bijeenkomsten. Prachtig health center. Japans restaurant met teppan yaki. Gevarieerde Franse keuken in brasserie Le Camelia.

Hilton, Apollolaan 138, ✉ 1077 BG, ☎ (0 20) 710 60 00, *info_amsterdam@hilton.com, Fax (0 20) 710 60 80,* ≤, , , , – – 25 à 550. AE ⓓ ⓜ VISA. rest FU f
Repas ***Roberto's*** (cuisine italienne avec buffet) *Lunch 24* – carte 35 à 62 – 25 – **267 ch** 360/440, – 4 suites.
◆ L'établissement a bénéficié d'une rénovation intégrale. Pimpantes chambres design et - invitation au farniente - jardin et terrasses en bordure de canal. Plaisante salle à manger méditerranéenne battant pavillon italien. Menu-choix et buffets d'anti-pasti.
◆ Het volledig gerenoveerde hotel heeft elegante kamers in design. De tuin en de terrassen aan het water nodigen uit tot een dolce far niente. De mediterrane restaurantzaal is een prima setting voor de Italiaanse gerechten. Keuzemenu en buffetten met antipasti.

Bilderberg Garden, Dijsselhofplantsoen 7, ✉ 1077 BJ, ☎ (0 20) 570 56 00, *garden@bilderberg.nl, Fax (0 20) 570 56 54* – – 25 à 150. AE ⓓ ⓜ VISA JCB FU d
Repas voir rest ***Mangerie de Kersentuin*** ci-après – 20 – **120 ch** 165/350, – 2 suites.
◆ Ce tout petit "grand hôtel" à l'ambiance très personnalisée combine luxe et charme discrets. Chambres fort bien équipées, décorées avec goût et sens du détail.
◆ Bescheiden luxe en charme karakteriseren de persoonlijke ambiance van dit kleine Grand Hotel. De kamers zijn zeer goed uitgerust en smaakvol ingericht met gevoel voor details.

Le Meridien Apollo, Apollolaan 2, ✉ 1077 BA, ☎ (0 20) 673 59 22, *info@apollo.com, Fax (0 20) 570 57 44,* ≤, , , – – 25 à 200. AE ⓓ ⓜ VISA JCB FU e
Repas ***La Sirène*** (produits de la mer) *Lunch 33* – carte 39 à 78 – 21 – **217 ch** 290/390, – 2 suites – ½ P 353.
◆ Hôtel de chaîne international situé à l'écart de l'animation, au croisement de cinq canaux. Chambres de bon confort, récemment rajeunies. Service assez complet. Ample restaurant au goût du jour complété d'une terrasse d'été au bord de l'eau. Cuisine littorale.
◆ Dit internationale hotel behoort tot een keten en ligt buiten het drukke centrum, bij de kruising van vijf grachten. De comfortabele kamers zijn onlangs gemoderniseerd. Vrij compleet servicepakket. Eigentijds visrestaurant met terras aan het water.

Tulip Inn City West, Reimerswaalstraat 5, ✉ 1069 AE, ☎ (0 20) 410 80 00, *info@tiamsterdamcw.nl, Fax (0 20) 410 80 30* – – 25 à 70. AE ⓓ ⓜ VISA plan p. 6 AP a
Repas (dîner seult) carte 22 à 34 – 14 – **162 ch** 135/175.
◆ Dans un quartier assez tranquille, récent hôtel de chaîne dont les atouts sont l'ampleur des chambres et des espaces communs ainsi que les facilités de parking aux alentours. Une carte classique actualisée est présentée au restaurant.
◆ Pluspunten van deze nieuwkomer in een vrij rustige wijk zijn de ruime kamers, de grote gemeenschappelijke ruimten en de parkeerfaciliteiten in de omgeving. Het restaurant voert een klassieke kaart die in een modern jasje is gestoken.

Tulip Inn Art (annexe Golden Tulip Art - 60 ch), Spaarndammerdijk 302 (Westerpark), ✉ 1013 ZX, ℘ (0 20) 410 96 70, *art@westlordhotels.nl, Fax (0 20) 681 08 02,* - 25. AE VISA. plan p. 4 BN t
Repas *Lunch 18* – 25 – 15 – **130 ch** 170 – ½ P 210.
◆ Près d'une bretelle du ring, hôtel de notre temps renfermant des chambres adaptées aux besoins de la clientèle d'affaires. Exposition de toiles d'artistes contemporains. Taverne-restaurant façon "brasserie branchée".
◆ Dit eigentijdse hotel vlak bij een afrit van de rondweg beschikt over kamers die geheel op de zakelijke gast zijn afgestemd. Expositie van doeken van hedendaagse kunstenaars. Café-restaurant in trendy brasseriestijl.

Delphi sans rest, Apollolaan 105, ✉ 1077 AN, ℘ (0 20) 679 51 52, *delphi-hotel@tref.nl, Fax (0 20) 675 29 41* – AE VISA JCB. FU q
50 ch 100/160.
◆ À deux pas de la commerçante Beethovenstraat, petit hôtel proposant des chambres confortables, garnies d'un mobilier anglais. Ambiance feutrée et tranquillité assurée.
◆ Dit kleine hotel ligt nabij de Beethovenstraat met zijn vele winkels. De comfortabele kamers zijn met Engels meubilair ingericht. Stemmige sfeer, rust verzekerd.

La Richelle sans rest, Holbeinstraat 41, ✉ 1077 VC, ℘ (0 20) 671 79 71, *Fax (0 20) 671 05 41* – AE VISA FU k
15 – **12 ch** 120/180.
◆ Modeste, mais aussi sympathique qu'accueillant, cet établissement comporte quelques bonnes chambres assez amples. Certaines offrent la vue sur un ravissant petit patio.
◆ Dit bescheiden hotel is even sympathiek als gastvrij en beschikt over enkele goede en vrij ruime kamers, waarvan sommige uitzicht bieden op een leuke, kleine patio.

Bastion Zuid-West, Nachtwachtlaan 11, ✉ 1058 EV, ℘ (0 20) 669 16 21, *bastion@bastionhotel.nl, Fax (0 20) 669 16 31,* – P. AE VISA. plan p. 6 BP c
Repas (grillades, ouvert jusqu'à 23 h) carte env. 30 – 10 – **80 ch** 86.
◆ Cet hôtel de chaîne excentré se dresse aux abords du parc Rembrandt, près d'une sortie d'autoroute (A 10). Les chambres, fonctionnelles et insonorisées, ont été rajeunies.
◆ Dit ketenhotel ligt buiten het centrum, aan de rand van het Rembrandtpark en bij een afrit van de A10. Functionele, gemoderniseerde kamers met geluidsisolatie.

Ciel Bleu - H. Okura, 23e étage, Ferdinand Bolstraat 333, ✉ 1072 LH, ℘ (0 20) 678 71 11, *sales@okura.nl, Fax (0 20) 671 23 44,* ≤ ville, – P. AE VISA JCB. GU c
fermé mi-juil.-mi-août et 28 déc.-4 janv. – **Repas** (dîner seult) 73, ♀.
◆ Au sommet d'un palace à gestion nippone, table de haute voltige culinaire, procurant une vue splendide sur les toits de la ville. Carte aussi appétissante qu'inventive.
◆ Dit uitgelezen restaurant op de bovenste verdieping van een hotel dat in Japanse handen is, biedt een schitterend uitzicht op de stad. Aantrekkelijke en inventieve menukaart.

Yamazato - H. Okura, Ferdinand Bolstraat 333, ✉ 1072 LH, ℘ (0 20) 678 83 51, *sales@okura.nl, Fax (0 20) 678 77 88,* Cuisine japonaise, – P. AE VISA JCB. GU c
Repas *Lunch 39* – 50/90, carte 39 à 68, ♀.
◆ Ambiance et décor "zen" dans ce restaurant nippon où l'on déguste, sous l'œil prévenant des geishas, toute la gamme des préparations traditionnelles. Petit salon séparé.
◆ Zendecor en dito ambiance in dit Japanse restaurant, waar onder het wakende oog van de geisha's het hele scala van traditionele gerechten wordt geserveerd. Kleine salon.
Spéc. Gyu Tohban-Yaki (bœuf). Kamakura (thon, loup) (oct.-mars). Ishikari-nabe (saumon)

visaandeschelde, Scheldeplein 4, ✉ 1078 GR, ℘ (0 20) 675 15 83, *info@visaandeschelde.nl, Fax (0 20) 471 46 53,* , Produits de la mer, ouvert jusqu'à 23 h – AE VISA JCB. GU m
fermé 24 déc.-5 janv., sam. midi et dim. midi – **Repas** *Lunch 29* – carte 42 à 65, ♀.
◆ En vitrine, une maquette de bateau annonce l'orientation culinaire de la maison. Recettes gorgées d'iode. Salle à manger claire et dépouillée, dans les tons bleu et blanc.
◆ De maquette van een boot achter het raam verraadt de culinaire ambitie van dit huis. Het is bijna alles vis wat de klok slaat. Lichte, sobere eetzaal in blauw-witte tinten.

Quartier Sud Chez Denise, Olympiaplein 176, ✉ 1076 AM, ℘ (0 20) 675 39 90, *Fax (0 20) 675 42 60* – AE VISA EU z
fermé Noël, 31 déc.-1er janv., jours fériés, sam. midi et dim. midi – **Repas** carte 38 à 59, ♀.
◆ Enseigne en vogue où règne une atmosphère détendue de brasserie de quartier. La médiatique Denise y compose une belle carte un rien bourgeoise et bien de son temps.
◆ Een populair restaurant met de ontspannen ambiance van een buurteethuis. De mediagenieke Denise heeft een mooi, eigentijds repertoire met een klassieke basis.

XX **Het Bosch,** Jollenpad 10, ✉ 1081 KC, ✆ (0 20) 644 58 00, *restaurant@hetbosch.com, Fax (0 20) 644 19 64*, ≤, 斧, ⚓ - P. AE ⓓ ⓜ VISA. ✂ plan p. 6 BQ d
fermé fin déc., sam. et dim. – **Repas** *Lunch 39* – carte 41 à 66.
◆ Pavillon caché sur le port de plaisance, à l'entrée du Nieuwe Meer. Goûteuse cuisine classique-actuelle et sélection de vins recherchée. Terrasse panoramique au bord du lac.
◆ Deze culinaire stek ligt aan de jachthaven bij het Nieuwe Meer. Smakelijke, klassiek-eigentijdse keuken en goed samengestelde wijnkaart. Panoramisch terras aan het water.

XX **Mangerie de Kersentuin** - H. Bilderberg Garden, Dijsselhofplantsoen 7, ✉ 1077 BJ, ✆ (0 20) 570 56 00, *garden@bilderberg.nl, Fax (0 20) 570 56 54*, 斧 - ▤ P. AE ⓓ ⓜ VISA JCB. ✂ rest FU d
fermé 31 déc.-1er janv., sam. midi et dim. – **Repas** *Lunch 28* – 32 bc/50, ♀.
◆ Une mangerie plagiant franchement le "look" d'une brasserie, avec ses cuivres rutilants et ses banquettes rouges rebondies. Engageante carte actuelle. Belle terrasse estivale.
◆ Glimmend koperwerk en rode banken geven dit restaurant de uitgesproken look van een brasserie. Uitnodigende, eigentijdse menukaart. Mooi zomerterras.

X **Blender,** Van der Palmkade 16, ✉ 1051 RE, ✆ (0 20) 486 98 60, *info@blender2004.com, Fax (0 20) 486 98 51*, 斧 - AE ⓓ ⓜ VISA JV k
Repas (dîner seult jusqu'à 23 h) carte 37 à 45, ♀.
◆ Restaurant d'esprit jeune occupant le rez-de-chaussée d'un immeuble en rotonde. Ambiance "trendy" autour d'un comptoir en hémicycle. Service charmant.
◆ Jong restaurant dat is gevestigd op de benedenverdieping van een rond gebouw. De halfcirkelvormige bar is het kloppende hart van deze trendy ambiance. Charmante bediening.

X **Le Hollandais,** Amsteldijk 41, ✉ 1074 HV, ✆ (0 20) 679 12 48, *lehollandais@planet.nl* – ▤. AE ⓜ VISA JCB – *fermé dim.* – **Repas** (dîner seult) carte env. 46, ♀. GU f
◆ Attachante petite adresse attirant une clientèle un peu "bourgeois-bohème", ce bistrot de quartier promu restaurant sert une cuisine de notre temps dans un cadre dépouillé.
◆ Een charmant adresje met een wat yuppieachtige clientèle. Dit voormalige buurtcafé is uitgegroeid tot een restaurant dat een eigentijdse keuken serveert in een sober decor.

X **Brasserie Richard,** Scheldestraat 23, ✉ 1078 GD, ✆ (0 20) 675 78 08, *diri@wanadoo.nl, Fax (0 20) 662 33 85* – AE ⓜ VISA – *fermé dern. sem. juil.-prem. sem. août, prem. sem. janv. et dim.* – **Repas** (dîner seult jusqu'à 23 h) carte env. 36. GU b
◆ Un choix de préparations classiques françaises s'emploie à combler votre appétit dans cette brasserie avoisinant le RAI. Décor intérieur actuel, d'inspiration méditerranéenne.
◆ In deze brasserie in de buurt van de RAI krijgt u een menukaart voorgelegd met klassieke Franse gerechten. Modern interieur in mediterrane sfeer.

X **Pakistan,** Scheldestraat 100, ✉ 1078 GP, ✆ (0 20) 675 39 76, *Fax (0 20) 675 39 76*, Cuisine indienne – AE ⓓ ⓜ VISA GU s
Repas (dîner seult jusqu'à 23 h) 25/45.
◆ Pas loin du RAI, authentique restaurant pakistanais dont la dépaysante carte, assortie de généreux menus, exclut logiquement le porc de ses recettes, au profit du bœuf.
◆ Authentiek Pakistaans restaurant vlak bij de RAI. Op de uitheemse kaart staan ook uitgebreide menu's, maar gerechten met varkensvlees zijn uiteraard de grote afwezigen.

X **AlaFerme,** Govert Flinckstraat 251, ✉ 1073 BX, ✆ (0 20) 679 82 40, *alaferme@xs4all.nl, Fax (0 20) 679 30 92*, 斧 GU k
fermé du 17 au 31 juil., 24 déc.-1er janv., dim. et lundi – **Repas** (dîner seult) 29, ♀.
◆ "À la Ferme", ni cruches ni bottes de foin, mais une sage petite carte recomposée tous les 15 jours pour éviter toute lassitude. Grande table d'hôtes dressée côté véranda.
◆ Geen wijnkruiken en hooibalen "bij de boer", maar een kleine kaart die voor de broodnodige variatie elke twee weken wordt vervangen. Grote gastentafel in de serre.

X **Kaiko,** Jekerstraat 114 (angle Maasstraat), ✉ 1078 MJ, ✆ (0 20) 662 56 41, *Fax (0 20) 676 54 66*, Cuisine japonaise avec Sushi-bar – ▤. AE ⓜ VISA JCB. ✂ GU a
fermé dern. sem. juil.-2 prem. sem. août, dern. sem. déc., jeudi et dim. – **Repas** (dîner seult) 35/60.
◆ Sympathique sushi-bar apprécié pour l'authenticité de sa cuisine japonaise et son service prévenant. Salle aux discrètes touches nippones.
◆ Sympathieke sushibar die in trek is vanwege de authentieke Japanse keuken en voorkomende service. Eetzaal met bescheiden Japanse accenten.

Quartiers Est et Sud-Est - *plan p. 7 sauf indication spéciale* :

Mercure a/d Amstel, Joan Muyskenweg 10, ✉ 1096 CJ, ✆ (0 20) 665 81 81, *h1244@accor-hotels.com, Fax (0 20) 694 87 35*, Fō, ≘, ⚓ - |‡| ⇆ ▤ TV ♿ P - 🏛 25 à 450. AE ⓓ ⓜ VISA. ✂ CQ a
Repas *Lunch 21* – carte 37 à 48, ♀ – ☕ 17 – **368 ch** 210/250.
◆ Cet hôtel posté juste à l'entrée de la ville dispose d'une importante infrastructure pour séminaires et de bonnes chambres aménagées selon les standards de l'enseigne Mercure. À table, carte internationale et sélection de vins de la chaîne.
◆ Dit hotel aan de rand van de stad heeft een royale infrastructuur voor seminars en goede kamers die zijn ingericht naar de normen van de keten. Het restaurant presenteert een internationale kaart met wijnen uit de Mercure-selectie.

AC Hotel, Provincialeweg 38 (sur A 9, sortie S 113), ✉ 1108 AB, ☎ (0 20) 312 14 16, *amsterdam@autogrill.net, Fax (0 20) 312 14 65,* ←, ✂, - 🛗 ⇌ 📺 ♿ 🅿 - 🏛 25 à 220. AE ⓓ ⓜⓒ VISA DQR n
Repas carte env. 35 - **192 ch** ⊐ 122/172 - ½ P 117/168.
◆ Hôtel de chaîne excentré, proche de l'autoroute, d'un lac et d'une rivière. Bonnes chambres à l'identique - certaines avec vue sur la Gaasp. Terrasse sur ponton d'amarrage.
◆ Hotel buiten het centrum, dicht bij de snelweg, een meer en een rivier. Goede, identiek ingerichte kamers, sommige met uitzicht op de Gaasperplas. Terras op aanlegsteiger.

NH Tropen, Linnaeusstraat 2c, ✉ 1092 CK, ☎ (0 20) 692 51 11, ← - 🛗 ⇌ 📺 🅿 - 🏛 80. AE ⓓ ⓜⓒ VISA JCB. ✂ plan p. 9 HT r
Repas *(fermé vend., sam. et dim.)* carte 22 à 30 - ⊐ 13 - **80 ch** 189.
◆ À côté du musée des Tropiques. Immeuble récent dont les chambres, bien insonorisées, ont été rénovées selon les standards de la chaîne. Vue sur l'Oosterpark et son étang.
◆ Een modern pand naast het Tropenmuseum. De kamers zijn voorzien van geluidsisolatie en gerenoveerd naar de normen van de keten. Uitzicht op het Oosterpark met vijver.

Bastion Amstel, Verlengde van Marwijk Kooystraat 30 (sur A 10, sortie S 111), ✉ 1096 BX, ☎ (0 20) 663 45 67, *bastion@bastionhotel.nl, Fax (0 20) 663 31 16* - 🛗 ⇌ 📺 🅿. AE ⓓ ⓜⓒ VISA. ✂ CQ e
Repas (grillades, ouvert jusqu'à 23 h) carte env. 30, ♀ - ⊐ 10 - **152 ch** 86/91.
◆ La plus jeune des quatre enseignes Bastion d'Amsterdam. Chambres basiques mais de taille correcte, bien tenues et isolées des bruits du ring et du chemin de fer.
◆ Het jongste van de vier Bastions in Amsterdam. Eenvoudige, goed onderhouden kamers van redelijk formaat. Geluidsisolatie beschermt tegen overlast van de ringweg en het spoor.

Voorbij het Einde, Sumatrakade 613, ✉ 1019 PS, ☎ (0 20) 419 11 43, *aperlot@wxs.nl, Fax (0 33) 479 31 92,* - ⓓ ⓜⓒ VISA. ✂ plan p. 9 HS a
fermé 12 juil.-2 août, 26 déc.-11 janv., dim., lundi et mardi - **Repas** (déjeuner sur réservation) carte 42 à 50, ♀.
◆ Surprenante table retranchée derrière une rangée d'immeubles austères. Mobilier design, cloisons luminescentes, cuisine à vue et verrière moderne s'ouvrant sur un mini-parc.
◆ Een verrassend restaurant achter een rij streng uitziende gebouwen. Designmeubilair, lichtgevende kolommen, halfopen keuken en moderne glaswand die uitkijkt op een parkje.

De Kas, Kamerlingh Onneslaan 3, ✉ 1097 DE, ☎ (0 20) 462 45 62, *info@restaurantdekas.nl, Fax (0 20) 462 45 63,* ←, - ▤. AE ⓓ ⓜⓒ VISA. ✂ plan p. 9 HU a
fermé 24 déc.-3 janv., sam. midi et dim. - **Repas** (menu unique) Lunch 31 - 42.
◆ Une curiosité locale. Restaurant établi dans une énorme serre où l'on produit un ensemble de cultures maraîchères. Menu unique renouvelé quotidiennement, en direct du potager.
◆ Een lokale curiositeit ! Restaurant in een reusachtige kas waar groenten worden gekweekt. Elke dag een nieuw, supervers menu zo vanuit de kas op tafel.

VandeMarkt, Schollenbrugstraat 8, ✉ 1091 EZ, ☎ (0 20) 468 69 58, *bos.catering@wxs.nl, Fax (0 20) 463 04 54,* - AE ⓓ ⓜⓒ VISA. ✂ HU e
fermé 2 sem. vacances bâtiment, 29 déc.-4 janv., dim. et jours fériés - **Repas** (dîner seult) 36/45, ♀.
◆ Brasserie résolument contemporaine à débusquer dans une rangée de façades un peu austères. La terrasse d'été, au bord du canal, contemple la caserne des pompiers.
◆ Een zeer eigentijds restaurant dat zich heeft verschanst tussen een rij gevels die er enigszins streng uitzien. Het terras aan het water kijkt uit op de brandweerkazerne.

Quartier Buitenveldert (RAI) - *plan p. 6 :*

Holiday Inn, De Boelelaan 2, ✉ 1083 HJ, ☎ (0 20) 646 23 00, *reservations.amsnt@ichotelsgroup.nl, Fax (0 20) 517 27 64,* - 🛗 ⇌ ▤ 📺 ♿ 🅿 - 🏛 25 à 350. AE ⓓ ⓜⓒ VISA BQ e
Repas (cuisine américaine) carte 31 à 48, ♀ - ⊐ 20 - **254 ch** 295/425, - 2 suites.
◆ Situé à 800 m du RAI, cet hôtel de chaîne entièrement rajeuni dispose d'un équipement complet et de bonnes chambres amples et avenantes. Accueil et service attentionnés. Restauration à la mode "yankee" ; cave au diapason.
◆ Dit ketenhotel op 800 m van de RAI biedt een volledig pakket faciliteiten. De ruime, vriendelijke kamers zijn van alle gemakken voorzien. Attente ontvangst en service. Keuken op Amerikaanse leest geschoeid, dito wijnkaart.

Novotel, Europaboulevard 10, ✉ 1083 AD, ☎ (0 20) 541 11 23, *h0515@accor-hotels.com, Fax (0 20) 646 82 23,* - 🛗 ⇌ ▤ 📺 ♿ 🅿 - 🏛 25 à 225. AE ⓓ ⓜⓒ VISA BQ f
Repas (taverne-rest, ouvert jusqu'à minuit) Lunch 20 - 22, ♀ - ⊐ 17 - **611 ch** 195/260.
◆ Immeuble hôtelier imposant, dont l'infrastructure s'adapte aussi bien aux groupes qu'à l'homme d'affaires isolé. Chambres aménagées selon les standards de la chaîne.
◆ Imposant hotelcomplex met faciliteiten die zowel op groepen als op de individuele zakelijke gast zijn afgestemd. De kamers zijn ingericht naar de normen van de keten.

Rosarium, Amstelpark 1, ✉ 1083 HZ, ☎ (0 20) 644 40 85, *info@rosarium.net, Fax (0 20) 646 60 04,* ←, – P – 25 à 250. AE VISA JCB BQ v
fermé sam. et dim. – **Repas** *Lunch 30* – carte 44 à 52, ♀.
◆ Cette architecture moderne émergeant de l'Amstelpark abrite un spacieux restaurant au goût du jour, un bar à vins et huit salles de réunions. Décor design assez léché.
◆ Deze moderne architectuur in het Amstelpark herbergt een ruim opgezet en eigentijds restaurant, een wijnbar en acht vergaderzalen. Vrij gelikt designdecor.

Ravel, Gelderlandplein 233 (dans centre commercial), ✉ 1082 LX, ☎ (0 20) 644 16 43, *info@ravelrestaurant.nl, Fax (0 20) 642 86 84,* Taverne-rest – P. AE VISA BQ k
fermé 30 avril, 25 déc., 1er janv. et dim. midi – **Repas** 33, ♀.
◆ Grande taverne-restaurant officiant depuis plus de vingt ans au rez-de-chaussée d'un centre commercial. Carte classico-traditionnelle et, derrière les fourneaux, la stabilité.
◆ Dit grote café-restaurant speelt al 20 jaar een klassiek-traditioneel culinair repertoire op de begane grond van een winkelcentrum. Standvastigheid troef achter het fornuis !

par autoroute de Den Haag (A 4 – E 19) *- plan p. 6 :*

Mercure Airport, Oude Haagseweg 20 (sortie ① Sloten), ✉ 1066 BW, ☎ (0 20) 617 90 05, *h1315-re@accor-hotels.com, Fax (0 20) 615 90 27* – TV P – 25 à 300. AE VISA JCB. AQ p
Repas *Lunch 20* – 30 bc, ♀ – 17 – **152 ch** 190/210 – ½ P 232/252.
◆ Hôtel situé en bordure de l'autoroute, à 3 km de l'aéroport (service navette). Conformes aux normes de la chaîne, ses grandes chambres conviennent au repos du voyageur.
◆ Hotel langs de snelweg, op 3 km van Schiphol (shuttleservice). De grote kamers zijn ingericht naar de normen van de hotelketen en bieden de reiziger de nodige rust.

Environs

à Amstelveen *- plans p. 4 et 6 – 77 337 h.*

Thomas Cookstraat 1, ✉ *1181 ZS,* ☎ *(0 20) 441 55 45, info@vvvhollandsmidden.nl,* Fax (0 20) 647 19 66

Grand Hotel, Bovenkerkerweg 81 (Sud : 2,5 km, direction Uithoorn), ✉ 1187 XC, ☎ (0 20) 645 55 58, *info@grandhotelamstelveen.nl, Fax (0 20) 641 21 21,* – TV P. AE VISA JCB. AR q
Repas voir rest ***Résidence Fontaine Royale*** ci-après, par navette – **97 ch** 153/173, – 2 suites.
◆ Sur un axe important, à cinq minutes de l'aéroport, ressource hôtelière proposant des des chambres spacieuses et actuelles, assez bien isolées du bruit.
◆ Dit hotel ligt aan een belangrijke verkeersader, op 5 min. van Schiphol. Het beschikt over ruime, eigentijdse kamers, alle met vrij goede geluidsisolatie.

De Jonge Dikkert, Amsterdamseweg 104a, ✉ 1182 HG, ☎ (0 20) 643 33 33, *Fax (0 20) 645 91 62,* – P. AE VISA BR r
fermé sam. midi et dim. midi – **Repas** *Lunch 31* – 32/45, ♀.
◆ Cuisine d'aujourd'hui servie dans un cadre pittoresque : derrière sa pimpante façade, la salle à manger rustique intègre la base d'un moulin à vent du 17e s. Original !
◆ Hedendaagse keuken in een schilderachtig decor : achter de elegante voorgevel is in de rustieke eetzaal het voetstuk van een 17e-eeuwse windmolen geïntegreerd. Origineel idee !

Résidence Fontaine Royale - H. Grand Hotel, Dr Willem Dreesweg 1 (Sud : 2 km, direction Uithoorn), ✉ 1185 VA, ☎ (0 20) 640 15 01, *reservering@fontaineroyale.nl, Fax (0 20) 640 16 61,* – P – 25 à 225. AE VISA JCB ABR x
fermé sam. midi, dim. et lundi soir – **Repas** *Lunch 24* – carte 38 à 52, ♀.
◆ La table du Grand Hotel occupe un pavillon séparé, à 150 m, de l'autre côté de la route. Recettes dans le tempo actuel. Espaces réservés aux banquets et séminaires.
◆ Restaurant van het Grand Hotel, 150 m verderop, aan de overkant van de weg. Actuele gerechten. Aparte ruimten voor partijen en seminars.

à Badhoevedorp *par Schipholweg* AQ - C *Haarlemmermeer 118 553 h :*

Dorint, Sloterweg 299, ✉ 1171 VB, ☎ (0 20) 658 81 11, *Fax (0 20) 658 81 00,* , , – , ch, TV P – 25 à 150. AE VISA JCB. rest
Repas *Lunch 22* – carte 30 à 45, ♀ – 19 – **211 ch** 100, – 9 suites.
◆ Au Sud-Ouest d'Amsterdam, non loin de l'aéroport (service navette) et de l'autoroute, hôtel de chaîne récent aux grandes chambres insonorisées, disposant du confort moderne.
◆ Aan de zuidwestkant van Amsterdam, niet ver van de luchthaven (shuttleservice) en de snelweg. Een ketenhotel met grote kamers, voorzien van geluidsisolatie en modern comfort.

De Herbergh avec ch, Sloterweg 259, ✉ 1171 CP, ☎ (0 20) 659 26 00, *info@herbergh.nl, Fax (0 20) 659 83 90*, – ▤ rest, TV P – 35. AE ⊙ MC VISA. ✂ ch
Repas *(fermé sam. midi)* Lunch 23 – carte 37 à 51, ♀ – ☕ 11 – **24 ch** 111/120 – ½ P 140/160.
◆ Auberge centenaire où l'on vient faire des repas au goût du jour. Bonnes installations pour la tenue de petits séminaires "executives". Chambres fonctionnelles sans reproche.
◆ Honderdjarige herberg met "up to date" - kaart en goede infrastruktuur voor het houden van "executives" seminars. Onberispelijke en praktische kamers.

à Hoofddorp *par autoroute A 4-E 19 ④ - C Haarlemmermeer 118 553 h. – voir aussi à Schiphol.*
Binnenweg 20, ✉ 2132 CT, ☎ (0 23) 563 33 90, hoofddorp@vvvhollandsmidden.nl, Fax (0 23) 562 77 59

Crowne Plaza Amsterdam-Schiphol, Planeetbaan 2, ✉ 2132 HZ, ☎ (0 23) 565 00 00, *sales.amsap@ichotelsgroup.com, Fax (0 23) 565 05 21*, – ▤ TV P – 25 à 350. AE ⊙ MC VISA
Repas Lunch 26 – carte 36 à 44, ♀ – ☕ 20 – **230 ch** 240/345, – 12 suites.
◆ Établissement haut de gamme situé entre le centre de Hoofddorp et l'autoroute menant à l'aéroport Amsterdam-Schiphol. Chambres et suites tout confort. Service diligent. Salle à manger "classico-contemporaine". Préparations dans le tempo actuel.
◆ Dit eersteklas hotel ligt tussen het centrum van Hoofddorp en de snelweg naar Amsterdam-Schiphol. Kamers en suites zijn van alle comfort voorzien. Toegewijde service. In de klassiek-moderne eetzaal worden eigentijdse gerechten geserveerd.

Courtyard by Marriott - Amsterdam Airport, Kruisweg 1401, ✉ 2131 MD, ☎ (0 23) 556 90 00, *courtyard@claus.nl, Fax (0 23) 556 90 09*, – ▤ TV ♿ P – 25 à 160. AE ⊙ MC VISA JCB. ✂
Repas Lunch 20 – 25, ♀ – ☕ 18 – **148 ch** 120/165.
◆ Entre Haarlem et l'aéroport, hôtel récent implanté en bordure d'un vaste parc. Spacieuses chambres actuelles où les businessmen rechargeront leurs accus. Sauna et fitness.
◆ Nieuw hotel tussen Haarlem en de luchthaven, aan de rand van een park. Grote, eigentijdse kamers waarin zakelijke gasten de accu weer kunnen opladen. Sauna en fitness.

Schiphol A 4, Rijksweg A 4 nr 3 (Sud : 4 km, Den Ruygen Hoek), ✉ 2132 MA, ☎ (0 252) 67 53 35, *info@schiphol.valk.nl, Fax (0 252) 62 92 45*, – TV ♿ P – 25 à 1500. AE ⊙ MC VISA JCB
Repas (ouvert jusqu'à 23 h) Lunch 15 – carte 28 à 56, ♀ – ☕ 15 – **430 ch** 85/100, – 2 suites.
◆ Le toucan Van der Valk s'est posé sur cet établissement pratique lorsqu'on a un avion à prendre. Nombreuses catégories de chambres. Colossale infrastructure conférencière.
◆ De Van der Valk toekant heeft zich hier gesetteld in een hotel dat praktisch is gelegen voor wie per vliegtuig reist. Veel categorieën kamers. Kolossale congresinfrastructuur.

Bastion Airport, Vuursteen 1 (près A 4, De Hoek), ✉ 2132 LZ, ☎ (0 20) 653 26 11, *bastion@bastionhotel.nl, Fax (0 20) 653 34 78* – TV P. AE ⊙ MC VISA. ✂
Repas (grillades, ouvert jusqu'à 23 h) carte env. 30, ♀ – **80 ch** ☕ 86/91.
◆ Établissement de la chaîne Bastion montant la garde aux avant-postes de l'aéroport, près d'une bretelle de l'autoroute A 4. Chambres de mise simple, mais correctes.
◆ Dit Bastion heeft een voorpost van Schiphol betrokken, direct bij een afrit van de A4. Eenvoudige maar keurige kamers.

Bastion Schiphol, Adrianahoeve 8 (Ouest : 5 km près N 201), ✉ 2131 MN, ☎ (0 23) 562 36 32, *bastion@bastionhotel.nl, Fax (0 23) 562 28 48* – TV P. AE ⊙ MC VISA. ✂
Repas (grillades, ouvert jusqu'à 23 h) carte env. 30 – ☕ 10 – **80 ch** 76.
◆ Une "copie conforme" de tous les hôtels arborant l'étendard Bastion. L'avantage de celui-ci tient surtout à sa facilité d'accès, depuis Amsterdam, Schiphol ou Haarlem.
◆ Een exacte kopie van alle hotels onder het vaandel van Bastion. Hier geldt als belangrijkste troef : gemakkelijk te bereiken vanaf Amsterdam, Schiphol en Haarlem.

Marktzicht, Marktplein 31, ✉ 2132 DA, ☎ (0 23) 561 24 11, *info@restaurant-marktzicht.nl, Fax (0 23) 563 72 91*, – AE ⊙ MC VISA. ✂
Repas Lunch 30 – carte env. 44.
◆ Sur le Markt, vénérable auberge (1860) élevée lors de la création du polder où s'étend l'aéroport de Schiphol. La carte tourne autour des plats traditionnels hollandais.
◆ Een eerbiedwaardig restaurant (1860) op de Markt, gebouwd toen de Schipholpolder werd ingericht. Er worden traditionele Hollandse gerechten geserveerd.

à Ouderkerk aan de Amstel *- plans p. 6 et 7 - C Amstelveen 77 337 h :*

't Jagershuis, Amstelzijde 2, ✉ 1184 VA, ☎ (0 20) 496 20 20, *info@jagershuis.com, Fax (0 20) 496 45 41*, <, – ▤ TV P – 30. AE ⊙ MC VISA JCB. ✂
BCR u
fermé 29 déc.-2 janv. – **Repas** *(fermé sam. midi)* Lunch 38 – carte 45 à 59, ♀ – **11 ch** ☕ 195.
◆ Auberge-restaurant dont la terrasse d'été et la salle à manger chaleureuse offrent un beau panorama sur l'Amstel. Menu-carte étoffé. Chambres garnies de meubles de style.
◆ Hotel-restaurant dat een terras en een gezellige eetzaal heeft met een mooi uitzicht op de Amstel. À la carte en menu, ruime keuze. Met stijlmeubilair ingerichte kamers.

XX **Ron Blaauw,** Kerkstraat 56, ✉ 1191 JE, ☎ (0 20) 496 19 43, *info@ronblaauw.nl, Fax (0 20) 496 57 01,* – AE MC VISA CR v
fermé dern. sem. juil.-prem. sem. août, sam. midi, dim. et lundi – **Repas** *Lunch 38* – carte 49 à 58, ♀.
• Sur la place du village, devant l'église. Cuisine à la page présentée dans un cadre moderne, aux légers accents nippons. Carte ambitieuse régulièrement recomposée.
• Op het dorpsplein tegenover de kerk. Eigentijdse keuken in een modern decor met een licht Japans accent. Ambitieuze kaart die regelmatig wordt vervangen.
Spéc. Filet de bar aux couteaux. Crevettes rouges au chutney. Cocktail d'orange et mandarines, glace au pain perdu

XX **Klein Paardenburg,** Amstelzijde 59, ✉ 1184 TZ, ☎ (0 20) 496 13 35, *info@kleinpaardenburg.nl, Fax (0 20) 472 32 57,* – P. AE MC VISA JCB BCR t
fermé sam. midi – **Repas** *Lunch 35* – 45/60 bc, ♀.
• Petit refuge gourmand établi sur une rive de l'Amstel convoitée par le secteur de la restauration. Fringante salle à manger-véranda où dominent la brique, le cuir et le bois.
• Dit kleine restaurant met warme ambiance staat aan de oever van de Amstel, samen met andere soortgenoten. In de fleurige eetzaal met serre overheersen baksteen, leer en hout.

XX **Lute,** De Oude Molen 5, ✉ 1184 VW, ☎ (0 20) 472 24 62, *info@luterestaurant.nl, Fax (0 20) 472 24 63,* – P. AE MC VISA BR e
fermé 26 juil.-7 août, 27 déc.-9 janv., sam. midi et dim. – **Repas** *Lunch 30* – carte 50 à 61, ♀.
• Restaurant contemporain assez surprenant implanté dans le site réaffecté d'une ancienne poudrière. Architecture post-industrielle façon "loft". Belle verrière ombragée.
• Een vrij verrassend, eigentijds restaurant op het terrein van een voormalige kruitfabriek. Postindustriële architectuur type loft. Schaduwrijk terras met glazen overkapping.

X **De Voetangel,** Ronde Hoep Oost 3 (Sud-Est : 3 km), ✉ 1191 KA, ☎ (0 20) 496 13 73, *voetang@euronet.nl, Fax (0 294) 28 49 39,* ←, – P. AE MC VISA.
fermé 25 juil.-8 août, 23 déc janv., sam. midi, dim. et lundi – **Repas** *Lunch 23* – carte 34 à 46.
• Sur un polder sillonné de canaux, établissement de longue tradition familiale mettant à profit un relais de batellerie plusieurs fois centenaire. Plats classico-régionaux.
• Restaurant in een eeuwenoude schippersherberg, waar al enkele generaties lang dezelfde familie aan het roer staat. Klassieke keuken en streekgerechten.

à Schiphol *(Aéroport international) - par A 4-E 19 ④ - Haarlemmermeer 118 553 h. – voir aussi à Hoofddorp – Casino AQR , Luchthaven Schiphol, Terminal Centraal, ☎ (0 23) 574 05 74, Fax (0 23) 574 05 77*

Sheraton Airport, Schiphol bd 101, ✉ 1118 BG, ☎ (0 20) 316 43 00, *sales.amsterdam@starwoodhotels.com, Fax (0 20) 316 43 99,* – 25 à 500. AE MC VISA JCB.
Repas ***Voyager*** *Lunch 45* – carte 51 à 59, ♀ – 25 – **400 ch** 420/515, – 8 suites.
• A l'entrée de l'aéroport, ensemble hôtelier conçu pour la clientèle d'affaires. Chambres offrant un équipement "dernier cri". Bel atrium. Service très complet. Brasserie moderne dont la coupole bleutée suggère le zénith. Buffets en soirée.
• Hotelcomplex op de luchthaven, afgestemd op de zakelijke clientèle. De kamers zijn van de allerlaatste snufjes voorzien. Mooi atrium. Zeer volledige service. Moderne brasserie met blauwachtige koepel die het zenit voorstelt. 's Avonds buffetten.

Hilton Schiphol, Schiphol Bd 701, ✉ 1118 ZK, ☎ (0 20) 710 40 00, *fb_ap7-schiphil@hilton.nl, Fax (0 20) 710 40 80,* – P. – 25 à 60. AE MC VISA JCB. rest
Repas ***East West*** *(fermé juil., sam. et dim.)* (avec cuisine asiatique, dîner seult) carte 44 à 64env. 58, ♀ – ***Greenhouse*** *(ouvert jusqu'à 23 h)* (buffets) carte 35 à 68, ♀ – 25 – **278 ch** 169/349, – 2 suites.
• Hôtel de chaîne haut de gamme, proche des pistes d'atterrissage. Chambres rafraîchies, tout confort. Service "nickel', business center et infrastructure pour séminaires. Au dîner, métissage de saveurs occidentales et asiatiques.
• Eersteklas hotel, vlak bij de landingsbanen. Gemoderniseerde kamers met optimaal comfort. Perfecte service, business center en faciliteiten voor seminars. De keuken vormt een mix van westerse en Aziatische gerechten.

Dorint Schiphol Airport, Stationsplein Zuid-West 951 (Schiphol-Oost), ✉ 1117 CE, ☎ (0 20) 540 07 77, *info@dsaa.dorint.nl, Fax (0 20) 540 08 88,* – 25 à 640. AE MC VISA JCB AR z
Repas ***Nadar*** (déjeuner seult) carte 26 à 39 – 19 – **393 ch** 325/470, – 4 suites.
• Entre l'aéroport et le bois d'Amsterdam, hôtel-centre de congrès moderne disposé autour d'un patio. Nombreuses chambres "executives". Bar façon pub anglais ouvert en continu. Un pilote d'aérostat prête son nom au restaurant.
• Dit hotel annex congrescentrum tussen Schiphol en het Amsterdamse Bos is gebouwd rond een patio. Veel kamers in de categorie "executive". De bar heeft een pubambiance en is 24 uur per dag geopend. Het restaurant is genoemd naar een zeppelinvaarder.

Radisson SAS Airport, Boeing Avenue 2 (Sud : 4 km par N 201 à Rijk), ✉ 1119 PB, ☎ (0 20) 655 31 31, *reservations.amsterdam.airport@radissonsas.com, Fax (0 20) 655 31 00*, – 25 à 600. AE VISA JCB.
Repas *Lunch 20* – carte 27 à 42, ♀ – ☕ 19 – **277 ch** 255, – 2 suites.
◆ Proximité du tarmac et de l'autoroute, ampleur et convivialité des lieux, chambres au luxe discret, hyper-équipées. Au total : un hôtel idéal pour le "trip" d'affaires. Vouée à la Méditerranée, la carte du restaurant manifeste un penchant pour l'Italie.
◆ Vlak bij het luchthavenplatform en de snelweg. Ruim opgezet en gastvrij hotel, kamers met bescheiden luxe en alle denkbare voorzieningen. Kortom, een ideaal hotel voor een zakenreis. Mediterrane menukaart met het accent op de Italiaanse keuken.

XX **De Oude Toren,** 3e étage, Stationsplein Zuid-West 602 (Schiphol-Oost), ✉ 1117 CN, ☎ (0 20) 405 96 10, *info@deoudetoren-schiphol.nl, Fax (0 20) 405 96 11*, ←, Avec brasserie au rez-de-chaussée – 55. AE VISA. AR m
fermé sam. midi, dim. et jours fériés – **Repas** *Lunch 30* – carte 44 à 72, ♀.
◆ Brasserie au rez-de-chaussée, restaurant stylé au 3e étage et "lounge-bar" au 4e, l'ancienne tour de contrôle a trouvé sa nouvelle vocation. Vue privilégiée sur les pistes.
◆ Brasserie beneden, stijlvol restaurant op de derde verdieping, lounge met bar daarboven : de oude verkeerstoren volgt een nieuwe koers ! Uitzicht op de start- en landingsbanen.

ANDEREN *Drenthe* C *Aa en Hunze 25 552 h.* 531 Z 4 *et* 715 L 2.
Amsterdam 196 – Groningen 30 – Assen 11 – Zwolle 84.

't Heinen-Hoes, 't Loeg 4, ✉ 9465 TM, ☎ (0 592) 24 87 77, *heinenhoes@hetnet.nl, Fax (0 592) 24 86 66*, – AE VISA.
Repas (dîner pour résidents seult) – **8 ch** ☕ 70 – ½ P 63/66.
◆ Au pays des "hunebedden" (alignements de dolmens), dans un site verdoyant, ancienne ferme saxonne emmitouflée sous son typique toit de chaume. Chambres de bon séjour.
◆ In het land van de hunebedden gaat deze voormalige Saksische boerderij schuil onder een karakteristiek rieten dak. Prettige kamers. Omgeving met veel groen.

ANNA PAULOWNA *Noord-Holland* 531 N 5 *et* 715 F 3 – *13 981 h.*
Amsterdam 71 – Alkmaar 32 – Den Helder 15 – Hoorn 43.

XX **La Première,** Smidsweg 4, ✉ 1761 BJ, ☎ (0 223) 53 19 66, *info@lapremiere.nl, Fax (0 223) 53 41 65*, – AE VISA
fermé 2e quinz. juil., 2e quinz. janv., mardi et merc. – **Repas** (déjeuner sur réservation) 43/55, ♀.
◆ Agréable petit restaurant familial aménagé dans un esprit romantique et devancé d'une terrasse estivale. Carte assortie de menus. Accueil tout sourire de la patronne.
◆ Aangenaam restaurantje met een romantische ambiance en een vrouw des huizes die een en al vriendelijkheid is. Aan de voorkant is een zomerterras ingericht.

APELDOORN *Gelderland* 532 U 9 *et* 715 I 5 – *154 859 h.*
Voir *Musée-Palais (Nationaal Museum Paleis) Het Loo★★★ : appartements★★★, porte★★★ vers la terrasse, jardins★★* X.
à l'Ouest : 6 km à Hoog Soeren, Hoog Soeren 57, ✉ 7346 AC, ☎ (0 55) 519 12 75, Fax (0 55) 519 11 26 - au Sud : 4 km à Lieren, Albaweg 43, ✉ 7364 CB, ☎ (0 55) 505 12 62, Fax (0 55) 505 23 88 - par ④ : 10 km au Domaine de Bussloo, Bussloselaan 6, ✉ 7383 RP, ☎ (0 571) 26 19 55, Fax (0 571) 26 20 89.
Stationsstraat 72, ✉ 7311 MH, ☎ 0 900 168 16 36, info@vvvapeldoorn.nl, Fax (0 55) 521 12 90.
Amsterdam 90 ⑦ – Arnhem 33 ⑥ – Enschede 73 ④ – Groningen 145 ② – Utrecht 72 ⑦

Plan page suivante

De Keizerskroon, Koningstraat 7, ✉ 7315 HR, ☎ (0 55) 521 77 44, *info@keizerskroon.nl, Fax (0 55) 521 47 37*, ch, – 25 à 220. AE VISA. rest X a
Repas *(fermé sam. midi et dim.) Lunch 31* – 37/64 bc, ♀ – ☕ 19 – **92 ch** 111/207, – 2 suites – ½ P 94/124.
◆ Hôtel haut de gamme situé aux portes d'Apeldoorn, juste à côté du musée-palais (Het Loo) et ses jardins fastueux. Chambres complètement équipées, spacieuses et pimpantes. Chaleureuse salle à manger décorée sans faute de goût.
◆ Zeer comfortabel hotel aan de rand van de stad, vlak naast paleis Het Loo en het weelderige paleispark. De ruime kamers zien er piekfijn uit en zijn van alle comfort voorzien. Smaakvol ingerichte eetzaal met een warme ambiance.

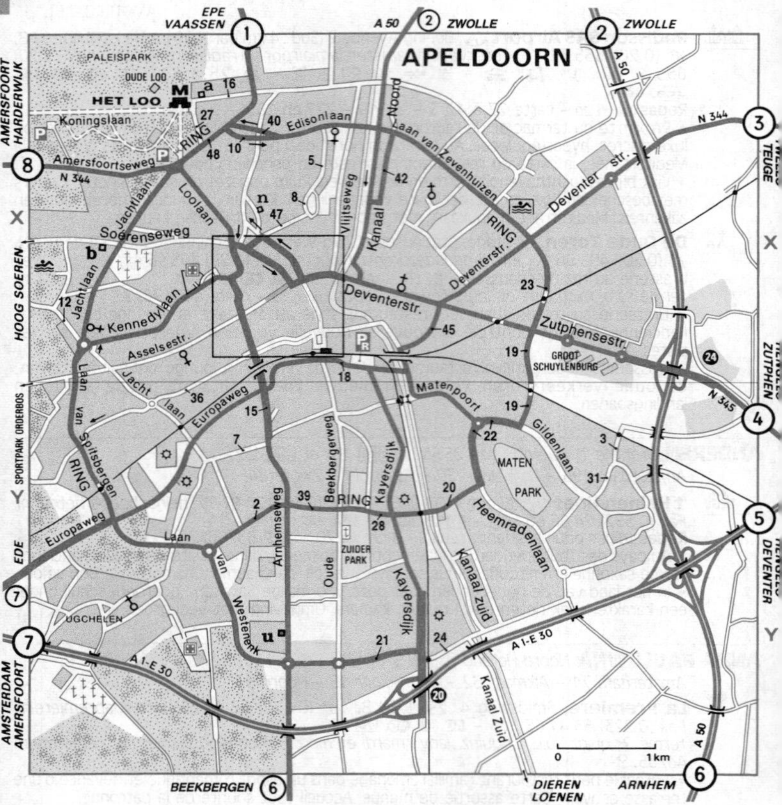

APELDOORN

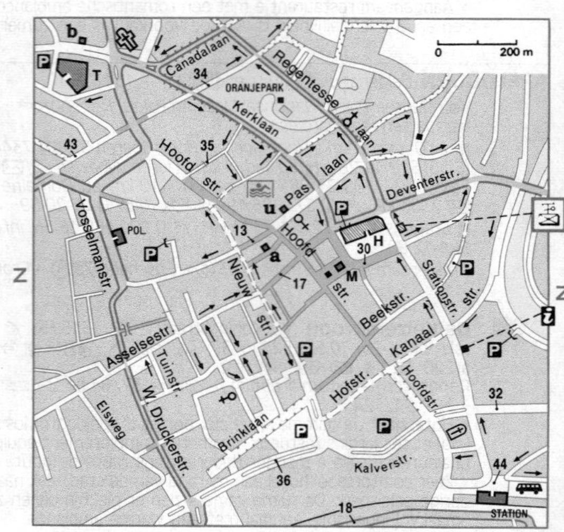

0
200 m
b
T
Canadalaan
34
ORANJEPARK
Regentesse laan
Kerklaan
43
Hoofd str.
35
Pas laan
Deventerstr.
Vosselmanstr.
POL.
13
a
Hoofd str.
30
H
M
17
Nieuw str.
Beekstr.
Stationsstr.
Kanaal
Asselsestr.
Tuinstr.
Hofstr.
Hoofdstr.
32
Elsweg
W. Druckerstr.
Brinklaan
36
Kalverstr.
44
18
STATION
Z

De Cantharel, Van Golsteinlaan 20 à Ugchelen (Sud-Ouest : par Europaweg, près A 1), ✉ 7339 GT, ☎ (0 55) 541 44 55, *cantharel@valk.com, Fax (0 55) 533 41 07,* – rest, – 25 à 450. Y
Repas (ouvert jusqu'à 23 h) *Lunch 15* – carte 22 à 30, – 8 – **90 ch** 65 – ½ P 61/122.
◆ Comode pour les usagers de l'autoroute, cet établissement excentré, membre de la chaîne Van der Valk, renferme des chambres de bon confort. Les meilleures sont sur l'arrière.
◆ Een praktisch hotel voor weggebruikers, dat wat buitenaf ligt nabij de snelweg. Het is aangesloten bij Van der Valk en heeft comfortabele kamers, de beste aan de achterkant.

Apeldoorn, Soerenseweg 73, ✉ 7313 EH, ☎ (0 55) 355 45 55, *info@hotelapeldoorn.nl, Fax (0 55) 355 73 61,* – rest, – 25 à 300. X b
Repas (buffets) *Lunch 13* – carte env. 29 – **61 ch** 80/90 – ½ P 63.
◆ Construction 1900 située dans un quartier résidentiel verdoyant au voisinage du ring. Chambres fonctionnelles aux tons frais. Nouvelles salles de bains. Restaurant agencé dans la note bourgeoise. Formules buffets.
◆ Dit pand uit omstreeks 1900 ligt in een groene woonwijk op een steenworp afstand van de rondweg. Functionele kamers in frisse tinten. Nieuwe badkamers. Mooi ingericht restaurant, buffetformules.

Astra, Bas Backerlaan 14, ✉ 7316 DZ, ☎ (0 55) 522 30 22, *info@hotelastra.nl, Fax (0 55) 522 30 21,* – X n
fermé 17 déc.-3 janv. – **Repas** (dîner pour résidents seult) – **26 ch** 68/95.
◆ Gentil accueil familial dans ces deux maisons de maître communicantes récemment flanquées d'une annexe. Chambres standard un peu menues, mais convenables.
◆ Vriendelijk, gastvrij onthaal in deze twee doorgebroken herenhuizen waarnaast onlangs een annexe is gebouwd. De standaardkamers zijn wat aan de kleine kant, maar comfortabel.

Aub. Navet, Arnhemseweg 350, ✉ 7334 AC, ☎ (0 55) 541 86 64, *aubergenavet@planet.nl, Fax (0 55) 533 60 93,* – Y u
fermé sam. midi et dim. – **Repas** *Lunch 27* – 31/53 bc.
◆ L'auberge, quoi qu'en dise l'enseigne, n'a rien d'un "navet" : salle à manger d'esprit provençal, cuisine de notre temps, aussi généreuse que goûteuse, et service avenant.
◆ Deze herberg mag dan Knol heten, het oog ziet iets verfijnders : eetzaal in Provençaalse stijl, eigentijdse keuken die even smaakvol als royaal is, vriendelijke bediening.

Peter'sburgh, Van Kinsbergenstraat 4, ✉ 7311 BM, ☎ (0 55) 579 18 74, *info@petersburgh.nl, Fax (0 55) 579 18 91* – Z a
fermé du 1er au 16 août, 24 déc.-3 janv., sam. midi, dim. et lundi – **Repas** *Lunch 33* – 43/65.
◆ Restaurant officiant dans une rue de bouche du centre. Décoration intérieure contemporaine, cuisine de même. Carte des vins proposant également toutes ses références au verre.
◆ Restaurant in een eetstraat in het centrum van de stad. Het interieur is goed bij de tijd, net als de keuken. De wijnen op de kaart worden ook per glas geschonken.

Poppe, Paslaan 7, ✉ 7311 AH, ☎ (0 55) 522 32 86, *informatie@poppe-apeldoorn.nl, Fax (0 55) 578 51 73,* Ouvert jusqu'à minuit – Z u
fermé lundi – **Repas** *Lunch 22* – 28/46 bc.
◆ Cette table sympathique que dissimule une façade bourgeoise assez coquette compte parmi les valeurs sûres du centre animé. Recettes d'aujourd'hui. Clientèle d'habitués.
◆ Dit sympathieke restaurant achter een keurige, klassieke gevel behoort tot de gevestigde adressen in het levendige centrum. Eigentijdse keuken. Vaste klantenkring.

La Palette, Soerenseweg 4, ✉ 7314 CC, ☎ (0 55) 577 71 46, *info@lapalette.nl, Fax (0 55) 577 71 47,* – Z b
fermé sam. midi et dim. midi – **Repas** *Lunch 23* – carte 36 à 61.
◆ Face au théâtre, anciennes maisons de notable où l'on fait des repas bien dans l'air du temps. Fringante salle traversée par un escalier et colorée de grande toiles modernes.
◆ In deze herenhuizen tegenover het theater worden trendy gerechten geserveerd. Fleurige eetzaal met trap en grote moderne schilderijen die voor een kleurrijke noot zorgen.

à Beekbergen *par ⑥ : 5 km* *Apeldoorn :*

Landgoed de Wipselberg, Wipselbergweg 30 (Sud-Est : 3 km), ✉ 7361 TK, ☎ (0 55) 506 26 26, *info@gtwipselberg.nl, Fax (0 55) 506 31 49,* – – 25 à 80.
Repas 27 – **90 ch** 130/150 – ½ P 125.
◆ Providentiel pour un séjour "au vert", l'établissement se compose de huit petits chapelets de bungalows assez confortables, disséminés dans un domaine boisé. Avec la complicité du soleil, on ripaille en terrasse.
◆ Dit verrassende etablissement voor een verblijf in het groen bestaat uit acht kleine, vrij comfortabele bungalowgroepen die verspreid liggen over een bebost landgoed. Als de zon een beetje meewerkt, kan er buiten op het terras worden gegeten.

Engelanderhof, Arnhemseweg 484, ✉ 7361 CM, ☎ (0 55) 506 33 18, *hr.engelanderhof@chello.nl, Fax (0 55) 506 32 20,* – 25 à 40. AE VISA JCB.
fermé 27 déc.-13 janv. – **Repas** 22/25 bc – **28 ch** 55/85 – ½ P 51/97.
• Cette petite ressource hôtelière entourée de verdure vous offre de séjourner dans des chambres fonctionnelles de plain-pied. Service familial personnalisé. Jardin reposant. L'été, repas en plein air. Carte de préparations franco-bataves à prix muselés.
• Dit kleine hotel midden in het groen beschikt over functionele kamers op de begane grond. Vriendelijke en persoonlijke service. Rustige tuin. 's Zomers wordt de maaltijd buiten geserveerd. Menukaart met Frans-Nederlandse gerechten voor schappelijke prijzen.

à Hoog Soeren *Ouest : 6 km par Soerenseweg* X *Apeldoorn :*

De Echoput (de Kok) hôtel prévu, Amersfoortseweg 86 (par ⑧ : 5 km), ✉ 7346 AA, ☎ (0 55) 519 12 48, *info@echoput.nl, Fax (0 55) 519 14 09,* – AE VISA JCB
fermé 27 déc.-9 janv., lundi et sam. midi – **Repas** Lunch 43 – 45/63, carte 53 à 74, ♀.
• Agréable maison de bouche fondée voici près de 50 ans. Cuisine classique franchement revisitée, servie dans une salle à manger rénovée. Terrasse et jardin avec pièce d'eau.
• Dit aangename restaurant, dat bijna 50 jaar geleden is gestart, heeft zijn klassieke keuken in een nieuw jasje gestoken. Gerenoveerde eetzaal. Terras en tuin met waterpartij.
Spéc. Quatre préparations de foie d'oie. Lasagne de sole grillée aux œufs brouillés, crabe et tomates séchées. Selle de chevreuil rôtie aux champignons et sauce vin rouge (janv.-mi-mars et juin-août)

Het Jachthuis, Hoog Soeren 55, ✉ 7346 AC, ☎ (0 55) 519 13 97, *Fax (0 55) 519 18 06,* – AE VISA
fermé 19 juil.-9 août et lundi – **Repas** Lunch 43 – 50, ♀.
• Au milieu des bois, ancienne ferme traditionnelle coiffée d'un toit de chaume et égayée de volets blancs. Carte classique, collection de peintures naïves et terrasse d'été.
• Restaurant in een oude, traditionele boerderij met rieten dak en witte luiken, midden in de bossen. Klassieke menukaart, schilderijen van naïeven en zomerterras.

APPELSCHA (APPELSKEA) *Fryslân* ⓒ *Ooststellingwerf 26 726 h.* 531 W 5 *et* 715 K 3.
Amsterdam 190 – Groningen 49 – Leeuwarden 55 – Assen 19.

Appelscha, Boerestreek 2, ✉ 8426 BP, ☎ (0 516) 43 15 93, *info@hotelappelscha.nl, Fax (0 516) 43 26 63* – – 50. AE VISA.
fermé janv. – **Repas** *(fermé après 20 h)* carte 25 à 35, ♀ – **34 ch** 38 – ½ P 50.
• Avantagé par la proximité de plusieurs structures récréatives et d'itinéraires de promenades, cet établissement renferme des chambres au confort simple mais convenable. Un choix de recettes traditionnelles hollandaises est proposé au dîner.
• Dit hotel bevindt zich in de nabijheid van diverse recreatieve faciliteiten en wandelroutes. Het beschikt over kamers met eenvoudig maar voldoende comfort. Voor het diner heeft u de keuze uit een aantal traditionele gerechten van Hollandse bodem.

APPINGEDAM *Groningen* 531 AA 3 *et* 715 L 2 – *12 443 h.*

Voir ≤★ *de la passerelle (Smalle brug).*

Env. *au Nord-Ouest : 20 km à Uithuizen★ : Château Menkemaborg★.*

Professor Cleveringaplein 1a, ✉ *9901 AZ,* ☎ *(0 596) 62 03 00, vvv-anwb.appingedam@wanadoo.nl,* Fax (0 596) 62 82 51.

Amsterdam 208 – Groningen 26.

Landgoed Ekenstein , Alberdaweg 70 (Ouest : 3 km), ✉ 9901 TA, ☎ (0 596) 62 85 28, *info@ekenstein.com, Fax (0 596) 62 06 21,* – 25 à 200. AE VISA. rest
fermé 31 déc.-1er janv. – **Repas** Lunch 27 – carte env. 34 – **25 ch** 85 – ½ P 112.
• L'origine de ce petit château-manoir remonterait au 17e s. L'ensemble est agrandi d'une aile récente accueillant les chambres, sobrement actuelles. Salon néo-gothique. Cuisine au goût du jour servie dans une salle de restaurant classiquement aménagée.
• De oorsprong van dit landhuis zou in de 17e eeuw liggen. In de moderne nieuwbouwvleugel zijn eenvoudige, eigentijdse kamers ingericht. Neogotische lounge. In de klassiek ingerichte eetzaal worden gerechten uit de hedendaagse keuken geserveerd.

Het Wapen van Leiden, Wijkstraat 44, ✉ 9901 AJ, ☎ (0 596) 62 29 63, *wvl@appingedam.nl, Fax (0 596) 62 48 53,* – . AE VISA. rest
Repas carte 22 à 41 – **26 ch** 58/75 – ½ P 55.
• Au centre d'un bourg renommé pour ses marchés agricoles, vieille auberge rénovée renfermant de petites chambres fonctionnelles réparties sur deux étages. Accueil familial.
• Oude gerenoveerde herberg in het centrum van een stadje dat bekend is om zijn agrarische markten. Kleine functionele kamers op twee verdiepingen. Gastvrij onthaal.

ARCEN *Limburg* C *Arcen en Velden 8 962 h.* 532 W 14 *et* 715 J 7.

Wal 26, ✉ 5944 AW, ☎ (0 77) 473 12 47, arcen@regiovvv.nl, Fax (0 77) 473 30 19.

Amsterdam 167 – Maastricht 88 – Nijmegen 53 – Venlo 13.

Rooland, Roobeekweg 1 (Nord : 3 km sur N 271), ✉ 5944 EZ, ☎ (0 77) 473 66 66, *info@rooland.nl, Fax (0 77) 473 66 67,* – 25 à 250. AE VISA JCB

Repas Lunch 18 – carte 25 à 34 – **54 ch** 75/98 – ½ P 56/62.

◆ Construction moderne bordant une route passante. Pour plus de tranquillité, préférez les chambres situées à l'arrière. Breakfast avec buffets. Accueil gentil.

◆ Dit moderne gebouw staat aan een doorgaande weg. Voor wat meer rust kunt u beter naar een kamer aan de achterzijde vragen. Ontbijtbuffet. Vriendelijke ontvangst.

De Maasparel, Schans 3, ✉ 5944 AE, ☎ (0 77) 473 12 96, *maasparel@hetnet.nl, Fax (0 77) 473 13 35,* – VISA. ch

fermé du 17 au 27 fév. – **Repas** (déjeuner sur réservation) carte 28 à 40 – **16 ch** 80 – ½ P 58/68.

◆ Ces deux jolies maisons du 19e s. situées au cœur du village touristique assurent le gîte et le couvert. Chambres avenantes, petit jardin bichonné et jeux d'enfants. L'une des deux salles à manger s'agrémente d'une pergola chauffée durant l'arrière-saison.

◆ In het hart van dit toeristische dorp bieden deze twee fraaie 19e-eeuwse huizen zowel tafel als bed. Aangename kamers en mooi aangelegde tuin met speelhoek voor de kinderen. Een van de twee eetzalen heeft in het naseizoen een overdekt, verwarmd terras.

ARNHEM P *Gelderland* 532 U 11 *et* 715 I 6 – *140 736 h.*

Voir *Parc de Sonsbeek★ (Sonsbeek Park)* CY – *Burgers' Zoo★★.*

Musées : *Néerlandais de plein air★★ (Het Nederlands Openluchtmuseum)* AV – *Musée d'art moderne★ (Museum voor Moderne Kunst)* AVX **M²** – *Historique Het Burgerweeshuis★* DZ **M¹**.

Env. *au Nord-Est : Parc National (Nationaal Park) Veluwezoom★, route de Posbank ※★ par ②.*

Papendallaan 22, ✉ 6816 VD, ☎ (0 26) 482 12 82, Fax (0 26) 482 13 48 - au Sud-Ouest : 8 km à Elst, Grote Molenstraat 173, ✉ 6661 NH, ☎ (0 481) 37 65 91, Fax (0 481) 37 70 55.

Willemsplein 8, ✉ 6811 KL, ☎ 0 900-202 40 75, info@vvvarnhemplus.nl, Fax (0 26) 442 26 44.

Amsterdam 100 ⑥ – Apeldoorn 27 ① – Nijmegen 19 ④ – Utrecht 64 ⑥ – Essen 110 ③

Plans pages suivantes

Landgoed Groot Warnsborn , Bakenbergseweg 277, ✉ 6816 VP, ☎ (0 26) 445 57 51, *info@grootwarnsborn.nl, Fax (0 26) 443 10 10,* ←, – 25 à 175. AE VISA JCB. AV e

fermé 27 déc.-16 janv. – **Repas** *(fermé dim. midi)* Lunch 32 – carte 48 à 62, – 13 – **30 ch** 90/175 – ½ P 100/140.

◆ Charmant manoir enrobé de chlorophylle et embelli d'un parc en terrasses. Bonnes chambres classiques dans le corps de logis et contemporaines dans les dépendances. Salle à manger dotée d'une véranda, salon cossu et restaurant d'été. Cuisine de notre temps.

◆ Dit charmante landhuis ligt midden in een bos en wordt omringd door fraaie, terrasvormige tuinen. Goede, klassieke kamers in het hoofdgebouw en moderne kamers in de dependances. Eetzaal met serre, weelderige lounge en zomerterras. Eigentijdse keuken.

NH Rijnhotel, Onderlangs 10, ✉ 6812 CG, ☎ (0 26) 443 46 42, *nhrijnhotel@nh-hotels.nl, Fax (0 26) 445 48 47,* ←, – 25 à 80. AE VISA JCB. AX a

Repas *Le Saumon* *(fermé sam. midi et dim. midi)* Lunch 29 – carte 35 à 52 – 15 – **67 ch** 120/130, – 1 suite – ½ P 108.

◆ Immeuble moderne dominant les rives du Rhin. Chambres conformes aux exigences de la clientèle d'affaires, parfois équipées d'un balcon tourné vers le fleuve. Le restaurant et sa terrasse d'été procurent également une vue aquatique plongeante.

◆ Modern hotelpand aan de oever van de Rijn. De kamers zijn afgestemd op de wensen van de zakelijke cliëntèle. Aan de rivierkant zijn sommige kamers voorzien van een balkon. Ook het restaurant en het zomerterras bieden uitzicht op het water.

Molendal sans rest, Cronjéstraat 15, ✉ 6814 AG, ☎ (0 26) 442 48 58, *info@hotelmolendal.nl, Fax (0 26) 443 66 14* – . AE VISA CY p

17 ch 90/110.

◆ Cette demeure imposante élevée à l'aube du 20e s. ravira sans doute les amateurs du Jugendstil, tendance germanique de l'Art nouveau. Mobilier de style dans les chambres.

◆ Dit imposante pand uit het begin van de 20e eeuw zal zeker in de smaak vallen bij de liefhebbers van Jugendstil. Kamers met stijlmeubilair.

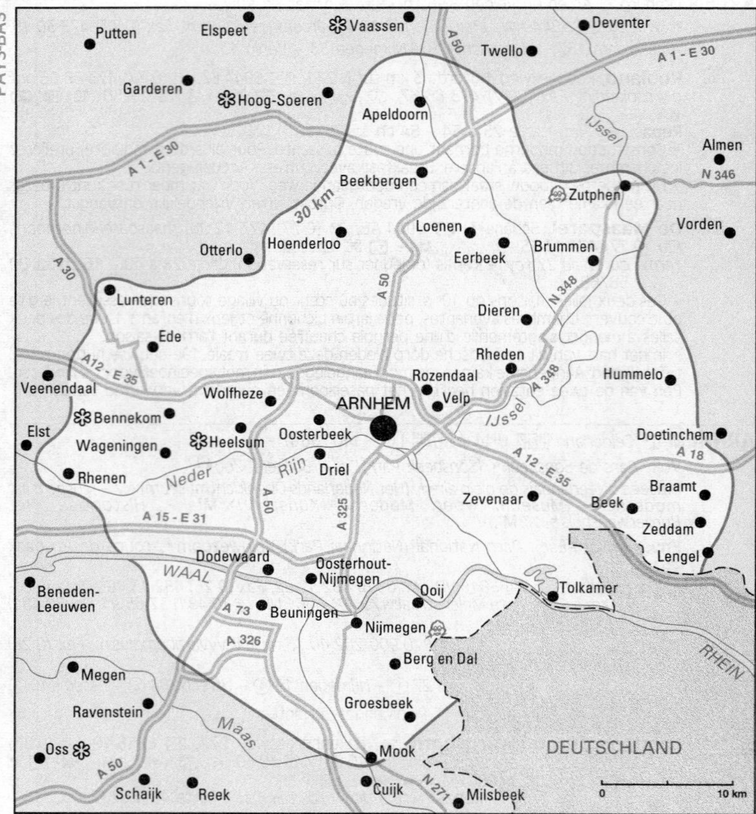

Mercure, Europaweg 25 (près A 12), ✉ 6816 SL, ☎ (0 26) 357 33 33, *h2105@accor-hotels.com, Fax (0 26) 357 33 61,* ⛱, 🚲 - |‡| ⇹ 📺 ♿ 🅿 - 🏛 25 à 400. AE ⓓ ⓜⓒ VISA JCB. ✂ ABV d
Repas *Lunch 13* - carte 35 à 46, ♀ - ☕ 14 - **83 ch** 94/106 - ½ P 62.
◆ Hôtel de chaîne excentré, proche à la fois de l'autoroute, d'un beau musée de plein air et d'un terrain de golf. Chambres pratiques, adaptées aux standards "mercuriens".
◆ Hotel buiten het centrum, dicht bij de snelweg, een mooi openluchtmuseum en een golfterrein. De praktische kamers voldoen aan de standaardnormen van de Mercure-keten.

Haarhuis, Stationsplein 1, ✉ 6811 KG, ☎ (0 26) 442 74 41, *info@hotelhaarhuis.nl, Fax (0 26) 442 74 49* - |‡| ⇹, ▤ rest, 📺 🅿 - 🏛 25 à 500. AE ⓓ ⓜⓒ VISA CZ f
Repas *Lunch 14* - 22 - **84 ch** ☕ 98/156 - ½ P 72/107.
◆ En face de la gare et à deux pas du centre, établissement cumulant les fonctions d'hôtel et de centre de séminaires. Chambres de différentes tailles, peu à peu rénovées. Une grande carte classique franco-hollandaise est présentée au restaurant.
◆ Dit hotel tegenover het station en op loopafstand van het centrum is tevens een zalencentrum. De in grootte variërende kamers worden geleidelijk gerenoveerd. Het restaurant heeft een grote, klassieke menukaart die een Frans-Nederlandse alliantie vormt.

Old Dutch sans rest, Stationsplein 8, ✉ 6811 KG, ☎ (0 26) 442 07 92, *info@old-dutch.nl, Fax (0 26) 445 78 30* - |‡| 📺. AE ⓓ ⓜⓒ VISA. ✂ CZ k
21 ch ☕ 73/120.
◆ Petit hôtel familial bien positionné pour rendre service aux usagers du rail, avec ses chambres fonctionnelles insonorisées. Salle de breakfast sous véranda.
◆ Klein familiehotel dat voor treinreizigers bijzonder gunstig ligt en beschikt over functionele kamers die zijn voorzien van geluidsisolatie. Ontbijt in de serre.

ARNHEM

Arnhemsestraatweg . . . . . . BV 4
Beekhuizenseweg . . . . BV 6
Beukenweg . . . . BV 7
Bronbeeklaan . . . . BV 10
Burg Matsersingel . . . . AX 12
Cattepoelseweg . . . . AV 13
van Heemstralaan . . . . AV 18
Heijenoordseweg . . . . AV 19
Hulkesteinseweg . . . . AX 22
Huygenslaan . . . . BV 24
Jacob Marislaan . . . . AV 27
Johan de Wittlaan . . . . AX 33
Koppelstraat . . . . AX 36
Lerensteinselaan . . . . BV 37
Nijmeegseweg . . . . AX 42
Nordlaan . . . . BV 43
van Oldenbarneveldstr. . . . . AX 45
Onderlangs . . . . AX 46
Parkweg . . . . AV 49
President Kennedylaan . . . BV 52
Ringallee . . . . BV 54
Rosendaalseweg . . . . BV 57
Thomas a Kempislaan . . . . AV 58
Voetiuslaan . . . . ABX 64
Weg achter het Bos . . . . . AV 67
Zijpendaalseweg . . . . AV 69
Zutphensestraatweg . . . . . BV 70

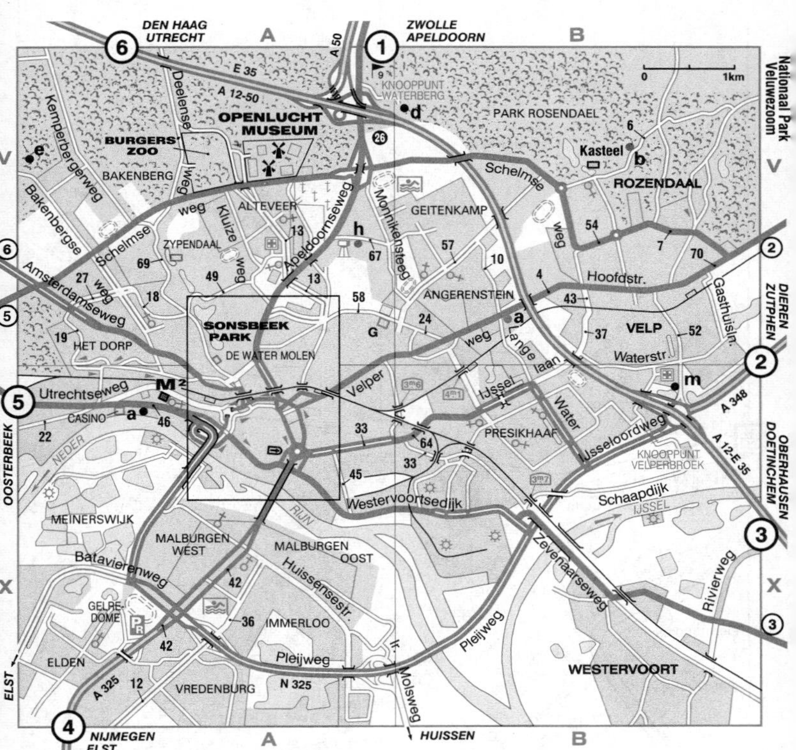

XXX **Artamis** Velperweg 168, ✉ 6824 MD, ℰ (0 26) 376 40 00, *info@artamis.nl, Fax (0 26) 376 40 64*, 🍽 – P. AE ① MC VISA. ⚔ BV a
fermé 19 juil.-2 août, 27 déc.-3 janv., sam. midi et dim. – **Repas** *Lunch 43* – carte 65 à 85, ♀.
◆ Demeure néoclassique cossue où défilent les fines fourchettes amatrices d'aménagement contemporain. Cuisine du moment, beaux flacons en cave et galerie d'art à l'étage.
◆ Dit weelderige, neoklassieke pand is in trek bij liefhebbers van lekker eten in een moderne setting. Seizoengebonden keuken, mooie wijnen en een kunstgalerie op de verdieping.

XX **De Steenen Tafel,** Weg achter het Bosch 1, ✉ 6822 LV, ℰ (0 26) 443 53 13, *Fax (0 26) 442 16 59*, 🍽 – P. AE ① MC VISA. ⚔ AV h
fermé 16 fév.-2 mars, du 2 au 24 août, sam. midi, dim. et lundi – **Repas** *Lunch 33* – 66, ♀.
◆ Un château d'eau émergeant d'une colline boisée abrite cette table - "de pierre", dit l'enseigne - aussi intime que discrète. Mets classiques-actuels présentés avec soin.
◆ Een watertoren op een beboste heuvel biedt onderdak aan dit restaurant. Ingetogen, intieme ambiance. De klassieke-eigentijdse gerechten worden met zorg opgediend.

X **La Rusticana,** Bakkerstraat 58, ✉ 6811 EJ, ℰ (0 26) 351 56 07, *info@rusticana.nl, Fax (0 26) 351 56 07*, 🍽, Cuisine italienne – AE ① MC VISA CZ m
fermé mardi – **Repas** (dîner seult) carte 27 à 37.
◆ Cuisine italienne classique puisant l'essentiel de son inspiration dans le Nord de la "Botte". Vins de là-bas. Terrasse estivale sur cour intérieure. Service non somnolent.
◆ Klassieke Italiaanse keuken die zijn inspiraties vooral put uit het noordelijke deel van de Laars. Wijnen van daarginds. Zomerterras op de binnenplaats. Attente bediening.

ARNHEM

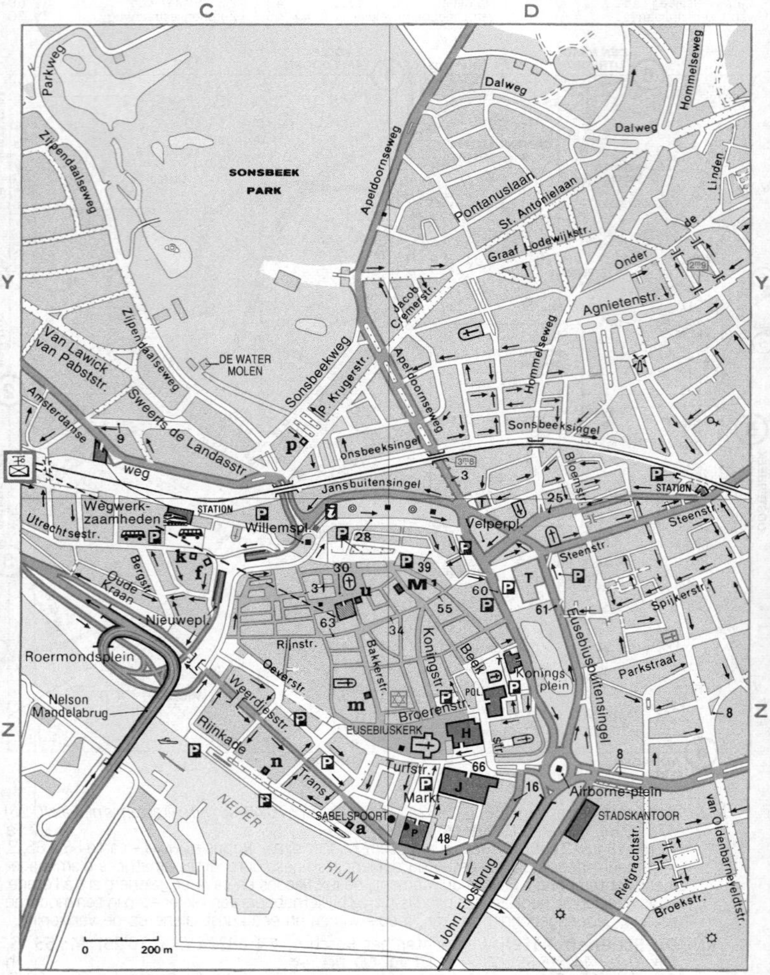

Bijzonder aangename hotels of restaurants worden in de gids in het rood aangeduid.

U kunt helpen door ons attent te maken op bedrijven, waarvan u uit ervaring weet dat zij aangenaam zijn.

Uw **Michelingids** zal dan nog beter zijn.

X **Smaak,** Rijnkade 39, ✉ 6811 HA, ☎ (0 26) 442 66 64, *info@smaak.org, Fax (0 26) 442 32 63,* ☂ - ▤. AE ⊙ MC VISA JCB CZ n
Repas (dîner seult en hiver) *Lunch 18* - 28/57 bc, ♀.
◆ Agréable restaurant au goût du jour officiant sur les quais du Rhin. Accueil tout sourire, ambiance "relax", terrasse fluviale, saveurs et décor intérieur de notre temps.
◆ Plezierig restaurant aan de kade langs de Rijn. Zeer vriendelijke ontvangst, relaxte ambiance, terras aan het water, eigentijds interieur en dito keuken.

X **Zilli en Zilli,** Mariënburgstraat 1, ✉ 6811 CS, ☎ (0 26) 442 02 88, *info@zillizilli.nl, Fax (0 26) 442 48 95,* ☂, Cuisine italienne - MC VISA. ✂ CZ u
fermé dim. midi et lundi - **Repas** *Lunch 7* - 28/33.
◆ Au bord d'une place animée, sympathique trattoria actuelle dont l'alléchant menu-carte ne vous fera pas froisser une grosse coupure. Livre de cave transalpin bien expliqué.
◆ Sympathieke, eigentijdse trattoria aan een gezellig plein. Aanlokkelijke kaart met menu waarmee u zich zeker niet in de vinger zult snijden. Prima Italiaanse wijnkaart.

X **Salathai,** Rijnkade 65, ✉ 6811 HC, ☎ (0 26) 446 08 48, *salathai@xs4all.nl, Fax (0 26) 325 61 60,* ☂, Cuisine thaïlandaise - AE ⊙ MC VISA. ✂ CZ a
Repas (dîner seult) 29.
◆ Table thaïlandaise établie face au Rhin. Accueil et service féminins en tenue traditionnelle, carte bien balancée et jolie terrasse arrière où bruisse une mini-cascade.
◆ Thais restaurant met uitzicht op de Rijn. Bediening door dames in traditionele Thaise kledij, uitgebalanceerde menukaart en aan de achterkant een mooi terras met miniwaterval.

à Driel *5 km par Batavierenweg* AX C *Overbetuwe 40 284 h :*

XX **Ambacht,** Drielse Rijndijk 87, ✉ 6665 LR, ☎ (0 26) 472 17 43, *Fax (0 26) 472 14 59,* ≤, ☂ - ▤ P. AE MC VISA. ✂
fermé sam. midi, dim. et lundi midi - **Repas** *Lunch 33* - carte 47 à 56, ♀.
◆ Devant le Rhin, auberge ancienne entièrement rajeunie sous l'impulsion d'un chef bien avisé. Lumineuse salle à manger design. Bonne cuisine d'aujourd'hui. Produits de choix.
◆ Deze oude herberg heeft dankzij een welberaden chef een complete facelift ondergaan. Schitterende eetzaal in design. Goede, eigentijdse keuken van eersteklas producten.

à Rozendaal - *1 529 h*

XX **Residence Roosendael,** Beekhuizenseweg 1, ✉ 6891 CZ, ☎ (0 26) 361 15 97, *info@residenceroosendael.nl, Fax (0 26) 364 70 63,* ≤, ☂ - P - 🏛 25 à 40. AE ⊙ MC VISA BV b
Repas *Lunch 27* - carte 37 à 63, ♀ 🍇.
◆ Ce chalet surplombant un parc vallonné monte la garde aux abords du château de Rozendaal, que vous admirerez de la terrasse. Salle à manger actuelle originalement éclairée.
◆ Dit chalet kijkt uit op een heuvelachtig park en ligt dicht bij kasteel Rosendael, dat vanaf het terras te zien is. Eigentijdse eetzaal met originele verlichting.

à Velp C *Rheden 44 831 h :*

🏨 **Velp,** Pres. Kennedylaan 102, ✉ 6883 AX, ☎ (0 26) 364 98 49, *arnhem-velp@bilderberg.nl, Fax (0 26) 364 24 27,* ≘s, 🚲 - ⇆ TV P - 🏛 25 à 150. AE ⊙ MC VISA JCB. ✂ rest BVX m
fermé 19 déc.-4 janv. - **Repas** carte 24 à 39, ♀ - ☕ 15 - **74 ch** 130/170 - ½ P 75/85.
◆ Facilité d'accès, proximité de l'autoroute et des portes d'Arnhem, chambres actuelles bien agencées, salles de réunion... Bref, un hôtel taillé pour la clientèle d'affaires ! Le restaurant s'agrémente d'une belle terrasse d'été alanguie au bord d'un étang.
◆ Gemakkelijk te bereiken, vlak bij de snelweg en de rand van Arnhem, eigentijdse en goed ingedeelde kamers, vergaderzalen... Kortom, een hotel op maat voor de zakelijke clientèle. Het restaurant heeft een fraai zomerterras aan een vijver.

ARUM *Fryslân* 531 R 4 *et* 715 H 2 - *voir à Harlingen.*

ASSEN P *Drenthe* 531 Y 5 *et* 715 K 3 - *60 230 h.*

Voir *Musée de la Drenthe★ (Drents Museum) : section archéologique★ - Ontvangershuis★* Y **M¹**.

Env. *au Nord-Ouest à Midwolde, monument funéraire★ dans l'église - à l'Est à Eexterhalte, hunebed★ (dolmen).*

ℹ *Marktstraat 8,* ✉ *9401 JH,* ☎ *0 900-202 23 93, vvv-assen@home.nl, Fax (0 592) 24 18 52.*

Amsterdam 187 ③ - Groningen 27 ① - Zwolle 76 ③

ASSEN

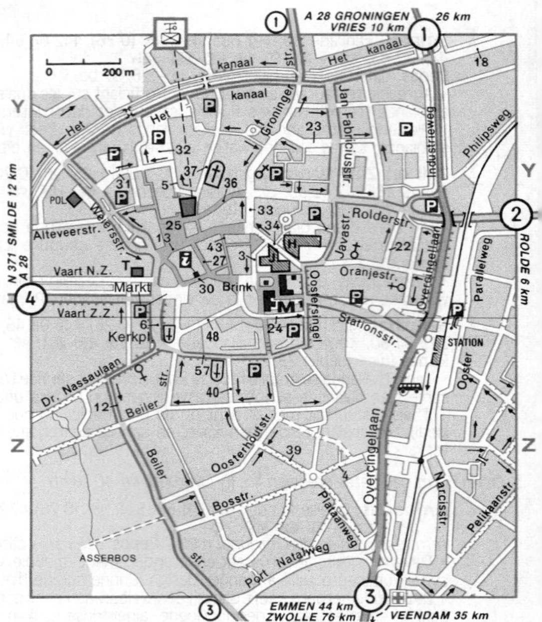

Assen, Balkenweg 1 (par ④ : 2 km), ✉ 9405 CC, ℘ (0 592) 85 15 15, *info@assen.valk.nl*, *Fax (0 592) 85 15 16*, – rest, – 25 à 400. AE MC VISA JCB. ch

Repas carte 22 à 38 – 8 – **137 ch** 70/75 – ½ P 89.

◆ Non loin de l'autoroute et à distance respectable du chef-lieu de la Drenthe, confortable hôtel de chaîne distribuant ses chambres insonorisées sur trois étages.

◆ Dit comfortabele ketenhotel dicht bij de snelweg en op 2 km van de Drentse hoofdstad beschikt over drie verdiepingen met kamers die voorzien zijn van geluidsisolatie.

ASTEN *Noord-Brabant* 532 T 14 *et* 715 I 7 – *15 936 h.*

Musée : *National du Carillon★ (Nationaal Beiaardmuseum).*

Env. *au Sud-Est : De Groote Peel★ (réserve naturelle d'oiseaux).*

Amsterdam 152 – Eindhoven 26 – 's-Hertogenbosch 63 – Helmond 14 – Venlo 33.

Nobis, Nobisweg 1 (près A 67), ✉ 5721 VA, ℘ (0 493) 68 13 00, *receptie@nobis.nl*, *Fax (0 493) 69 10 58*, – – 25 à 450. AE MC VISA. ch

Repas (taverne-rest) *Lunch 13* – carte 22 à 40, – 11 – **56 ch** 78/83 – ½ P 71/108.

◆ Architecture contemporaine avoisinant l'autoroute. Les chambres, de mise assez simple mais d'ampleur convenable, se répartissent au rez-de-chaussée et à l'étage.

◆ Modern gebouw aan de snelweg. De vrij eenvoudige kamers zijn redelijk van formaat en liggen verspreid over de begane grond en de verdieping.

In 't Eeuwig Leven, Pr. Bernhardstraat 22, ✉ 5721 GC, ℘ (0 493) 69 35 62, *restaurant@eeuwigleven.nl*, *Fax (0 493) 69 53 17* – 30. AE MC VISA.

fermé 2 dern. sem. vacances bâtiment, merc., sam. midi et dim. midi – **Repas** *Lunch 19* – carte 38 à 48.

◆ Accueil familial dans cette ancienne auberge nichée au cœur d'un bourg connu pour son musée du Carillon. Recettes traditionnelles valorisant les produits de saison.

◆ Voormalige herberg in een plaatsje dat bekend is om zijn Beiaardmuseum. Vriendelijk onthaal. Seizoenproducten vormen de hoofdingrediënten van de traditionele keuken.

AXEL *Zeeland* ◻C *Terneuzen 46 888 h.* 532 I 15 *et* 715 C 8.

Justaasweg 4, ✉ 4571 NB, ☎ (0 115) 56 44 67, Fax (0 115) 56 48 51.

Amsterdam 206 – Middelburg 44 – Antwerpen 42 – Gent 29.

XXX **Zomerlust,** Boslaan 1, ✉ 4571 SW, ☎ (0 115) 56 16 93, *restaurantzomerlust@planet.nl, Fax (0 115) 56 36 45,* – P. AE ◑ MC VISA JCB.
fermé 22 juil.-5 août, lundi et sam. midi – **Repas** Lunch 33 bc – 43/82 bc.
• Un agréable restaurant a pris place sous le toit de chaume de cette imposante villa agrémentée d'une terrasse d'été et d'un jardin au bord de l'eau. Assiettes au goût du jour.
• Onder het rieten dak van deze imposante villa gaat een aangenaam restaurant schuil. Zomerterras en tuin aan het water. Eigentijdse gerechten.

X **in d'Ouwe Baencke,** Kerkstraat 10, ✉ 4571 BC, ☎ (0 115) 56 33 73, *baecke@zeelandnet.nl, Fax (0 115) 56 33 73,* – AE MC VISA JCB.
fermé dern. sem. juil.-prem. sem. août, 29 déc.-7 janv., mardi et merc. – **Repas** Lunch 29 – carte 30 à 46.
• Dans une rue piétonne menant à l'église, adresse plaisante où l'on se sent un peu comme chez soi. Salle à manger "format poche", cuisine d'aujourd'hui et cave blindée !
• In dit prettige restaurantje in een voetgangersstraat naar de kerk voelt men zich echt een beetje thuis. Eetzaal in "zakformaat", eigentijdse keuken, wijnkelder in de brandkast.

BAARN *Utrecht* 532 Q 9 *et* 715 G 5 – *24 469 h.*

Stationsplein 7, ✉ 3743 KK, ☎ (0 35) 541 32 26, vvvbaarn@worldonline.nl, Fax (0 35) 543 08 28.

Amsterdam 38 – Utrecht 26 – Apeldoorn 53.

Kasteel De Hooge Vuursche, Hilversumsestraatweg 14 (Ouest : 2 km), ✉ 3744 KC, ☎ (0 35) 541 25 41, *h2114@accor-hotels.com, Fax (0 35) 542 32 88,* – TV P – 25 à 100. AE ◑ MC VISA JCB
Repas *(fermé 20 déc.-4 janv.)* (dîner seult) carte 31 à 48 – 14 – **25 ch** *(fermé 27 déc.-2 janv.)* 161/240.
• Tenté par la vie de château ? Celui-ci date des années 1910 et s'ouvre sur un parc délicieux, dont les terrasses s'agrémentent de fontaines. Chambres de bon séjour. Dans la chaumière voisine, salle à manger plaisante et confortable, garnie de meubles anciens.
• Voelt u zich aangetrokken tot de romantiek van het kasteelleven ? Deze buitenplaats uit 1910 staat in een prachtig park met terrassen en fonteinen. Zeer comfortabele kamers. Aangenaam restaurant met antiek meubilair in het bijbehorende huis met rieten dak.

La Promenade, Amalialaan 1, ✉ 3743 KE, ☎ (0 35) 541 29 13, *info@hotelpromenade.nl, Fax (0 35) 541 57 75,* – TV. AE MC VISA.
Repas carte env. 35, ♀ – 11 – **21 ch** 75/88.
• Auberge œuvrant depuis 1875 au centre de Baarn. Chaleureuses chambres dotées d'une literie propice à des sommeils réparateurs. Salle des repas lambrissée, pourvue d'un mobilier de style et égayée de peintures naïves. Joli caveau pour ripailler en groupe.
• Al in 1875 werd deze herberg in het centrum geopend. Kamers met een warme ambiance en bedden die garant staan voor een verkwikkende nachtrust. Gelambriseerde eetzaal met stijlmeubilair en schilderijen van naïeven. De fraaie kelder is bestemd voor groepen.

à Lage-Vuursche *Sud-Ouest : 7 km* ◻C *Baarn :*

XXX **De Kastanjehof** avec ch, Kloosterlaan 1, ✉ 3749 AJ, ☎ (0 35) 666 82 48, *info@dekastanjehof.nl, Fax (0 35) 666 84 44,* – TV P – 30. AE ◑ MC VISA
fermé 25, 26 et 31 déc, 1er janv. et sam. midi – **Repas** Lunch 34 – 39/60, ♀ – 13 – **10 ch** 86/129.
• Délicieux moment de table en perspective dans cette auberge aux accents romantiques. L'été venu, terrasses invitantes et adorable jardin fleuri. Chambres coquettes.
• In de romantische ambiance van dit etablissement heeft u een genoeglijk uurtje tafelen in het vooruitzicht. Heerlijk zomerterras en prachtige bloementuin. Verzorgde kamers.

BADHOEVEDORP *Noord-Holland* 531 N 8, 532 N 8 *et* 715 F 4 – *voir à Amsterdam, environs.*

BALK *Fryslân* ◻C *Gaasterlân-Sleat 10 259 h.* 531 S 5 *et* 715 H 3.

Voir *à l'Est : 6 km à Sloten (Sleat)★ (ville fortifiée).*

Amsterdam 119 – Leeuwarden 50 – Groningen 84 – Zwolle 63.

à Harich *Nord-Ouest : 1 km* ◻C *Gaasterlân-Sleat :*

Welgelegen, Welgelegen 15, ✉ 8571 RG, ☎ (0 514) 60 50 50, *Fax (0 514) 60 51 99,* – TV P – 25 à 200. AE ◑ MC VISA JCB. rest
Repas (dîner pour résidents seult) – **22 ch** 65 – ½ P 75/83.
• Ancienne ferme seigneuriale devenue hôtel. Chambres pratiques. Celles de plain-pied s'ouvrent parfois sur une terrasse. Les meilleures, à l'étage, sont dotées d'un balcon.
• Voormalige herenboerderij die tot hotel is verbouwd. Praktische kamers. Beneden hebben sommige een terras. De beste kamers liggen op de bovenverdieping en hebben een balkon.

BALLUM *Fryslân* 531 T 2 *et* 715 I 1 – *voir à Waddeneilanden (Ameland).*

BARCHEM *Gelderland* 532 X 10 *et* 715 K 5 – *voir à Lochem.*

BARENDRECHT *Zuid-Holland* 532 M 11 *et* 715 E 6 – *voir à Rotterdam, environs.*

BAVEL *Noord-Brabant* 532 O 13 – *voir à Breda.*

BEEK *Gelderland* 532 W 11 *et* 715 J 6 – *voir à Zeddam.*

BEEK *Limburg* 532 T 17 *et* 715 I 9 – *voir à Maastricht.*

BEEKBERGEN *Gelderland* 532 U 10 *et* 715 I 5 – *voir à Apeldoorn.*

BEEK EN DONK *Noord-Brabant* C *Laarbeek 21 543 h.* 532 S 13 *et* 715 H 7.
Amsterdam 116 – Eindhoven 20 – Nijmegen 54.

X **Woo Ping,** Piet van Thielplein 10 (Donk), ✉ 5741 CP, ☎ (0 492) 46 22 13, *Fax (0 492) 46 57 98,* Cuisine asiatique – AE ⓓ ⓜ VISA.
fermé lundis non fériés – **Repas** (dîner seult sauf sam. et dim.) carte 22 à 33.
◆ Au rez-de-chaussée d'un immeuble bordant la place de Donk, restaurant asiatique dont le registre culinaire jongle entre Chine et Indonésie.
◆ Dit Aziatische restaurant op de benedenverdieping van een pand aan het plein in Donk jongleert met Chinese en Indonesische culinaire tradities.

BEETSTERZWAAG (BEETSTERSWEACH) *Fryslân* C *Opsterland 28 828 h.* 531 V 4 *et* 715 J 2.
18 *van Harinxmaweg 8a,* ✉ *9244 CJ,* ☎ *(0 512) 38 35 90, Fax (0 512) 38 37 39.*
Amsterdam 143 – Groningen 41 – Leeuwarden 34.

Lauswolt (annexe), Van Harinxmaweg 10, ✉ 9244 CJ, ☎ (0 512) 38 12 45, *lauswolt@bilderberg.nl, Fax (0 512) 38 14 96,* – TV P – 25 à 80. AE ⓓ ⓜ VISA JCB
Repas voir rest ***De Heeren van Harinxma*** ci-après – 19 – **63 ch** 225/260, – 2 suites – ½ P 145/195.
◆ Fastueuse demeure du 19e s. nichée dans un parc arboré, véritable paradis des golfeurs. Chambres et communs aménagés avec un goût sûr. Centre esthétique. Service complet.
◆ Luisterrijk 19e-eeuws landhuis in een boomrijk park, een paradijs voor golfers. Zeer smaakvolle kamers en gemeenschappelijke ruimten. Beautycenter. Uitstekende service.

XXXX ✿ **De Heeren van Harinxma** - H. Lauswolt, Van Harinxmaweg 10, ✉ 9244 CJ, ☎ (0 512) 38 12 45, *lauswolt@bilderberg.nl, Fax (0 512) 38 14 96,* – P. AE ⓓ ⓜ VISA JCB.
fermé sam. midi et dim. midi – **Repas** *Lunch 45* – 63/75, carte env. 74, ♀.
◆ Le restaurant gastronomique du Lauswolt vous reçoit en grand seigneur dans une salle à manger confortable. Cuisine d'orientation escoffière, sagement actualisée.
◆ In het gastronomisch restaurant van het Lauswolt wordt u stijlvol ontvangen in een comfortabele eetzaal. Klassieke Franse keuken in een bescheiden eigentijds jasje.
Spéc. Queue de bœuf braisée et son carpaccio aux truffes. Saint-Jacques et homard de quatre façons (mai-sept.). Crumble d'ananas à la cardamome et son sorbet (automne-hiver)

XX **Prins Heerlijck,** Hoofdstraat 23, ✉ 9244 CL, ☎ (0 512) 38 24 55, *info@prinsheerlijck.nl, Fax (0 512) 38 33 71,* – P. AE ⓓ ⓜ VISA JCB
fermé du 16 au 26 fév. et 27 déc.-2 janv. – **Repas** 31/43 bc, ♀.
◆ Dans la rue principale, maison de maître où l'on s'attable pour un repas au goût du jour. Ambiance décontractée. Agréable terrasse estivale dressée sur l'arrière.
◆ In de hoofdstraat gaat u in dit herenhuis aan tafel voor een eigentijdse maaltijd. Ongedwongen ambiance. Aangenaam zomerterras aan de achterkant.

à Olterterp *Nord-Est : 2 km* C *Opsterland :*

XX **Het Witte Huis** avec ch, van Harinxmaweg 20, ✉ 9246 TL, ☎ (0 512) 38 22 22, *witte-huis@planet.nl, Fax (0 512) 38 23 07,* ≤, – rest, TV P – 25 à 75. AE ⓓ ⓜ VISA
fermé 31 déc.-1er janv. – **Repas** *(fermé lundi midi)* 25/41 bc – **8 ch** 48/80 – ½ P 65/73.
◆ George "W" n'a jamais mis les pieds dans cette Maison Blanche (Witte Huis) coiffée d'un toit de chaume : tant pis pour lui ! Jardin avec pièce d'eau. Chambres bien tenues.
◆ George "W" heeft in dit Witte Huis met rieten dak nog nooit een voet gezet. Dat is dan jammer voor hem ! Tuin met waterpartij. Goed onderhouden kamers.

BEILEN *Drenthe* C *Midden-Drenthe 32 691 h.* 531 Y 5 *et* 715 K 3.
Amsterdam 169 – Assen 17 – Groningen 44 – Leeuwarden 70 – Zwolle 59.

à Spier *Sud-Ouest : 5 km* C *Midden-Drenthe :*

De Woudzoom, Oude Postweg 2, ✉ 9417 TG, ✆ (0 593) 56 26 45, *woudzoom@bestwestern.nl, Fax (0 593) 56 25 50,* – 25 à 200. AE MC VISA.
fermé 27 déc.-12 janv. – **Repas** carte 26 à 45 – 12 – **37 ch** 70/90 – ½ P 93/113.
◆ Construction basse située près de l'autoroute, dans un village de la Drenthe. Chambres de bonnes proportions, salle de breakfast aux accents toscans et grande terrasse. Ample restaurant agrémenté de verrières modernes. L'été, repas en plein air.
◆ Dit lage hotelpand heeft zijn stek gevonden in een Drents dorp, vlak bij de snelweg. Kamers van goed formaat, ontbijtzaal met Toscaanse accenten en groot terras. Ruim restaurant met moderne ramen. In de zomer kunt u er heerlijk buiten eten.

BELFELD *Limburg* C *Venlo 91 400 h.* 532 V 15 *et* 715 J 8.
Amsterdam 172 – Maastricht 67 – Eindhoven 61 – Roermond 17.

De Krekelberg, Parallelweg 11 (Sud-Ouest : 2 km sur N 271), ✉ 5951 AP, ✆ (0 77) 475 12 66, *Fax (0 77) 475 35 05* – – 100. AE MC VISA
Repas (dîner pour résidents seult) – **14 ch** 54/68 – ½ P 67/93.
◆ En bord de route, face au fleuve, auberge agrandie d'annexes où les chambres, spacieuses et bien insonorisées, sont toutes de plain-pied, à la façon d'un motel.
◆ Etablissement langs de weg, tegenover een rivier, met annexen waarvan de ruime kamers met goede geluidsisolatie alle op de begane grond liggen, net als in een motel.

BENEDEN-LEEUWEN *Gelderland* C *West Maas en Waal 18 241 h.* 532 S 11 *et* 715 H 6.
Amsterdam 90 – Arnhem 42 – 's-Hertogenbosch 34 – Nijmegen 30.

De Twee Linden, Zandstraat 100, ✉ 6658 CX, ✆ (0 487) 59 12 34, *info@detweelinden.nl, Fax (0 487) 59 42 24,* – rest, – 25 à 350. AE MC VISA JCB.
fermé 24 déc.-5 janv. – **Repas** ***De Gelagkamer*** 26 – **14 ch** 69/89 – ½ P 64/83.
◆ Cette auberge villageoise rénovée, dont l'origine remonte à 1871, se complète d'une aile récente renfermant les meilleures chambres. Agréable café devancé d'une véranda. Nouveau restaurant au goût du jour aménagé à la façon d'une brasserie cossue.
◆ Dit hotel in een gerenoveerde dorpsherberg uit 1871 is uitgebreid met een moderne vleugel waarin de beste kamers liggen. Aangenaam café met serre aan de voorkant. Het nieuwe, eigentijdse restaurant heeft de ambiance van een weelderige brasserie.

BENNEBROEK *Noord-Holland* 531 M 9, 532 M 9 *et* 715 E 5 – *5 329 h.*
Voir *à l'Ouest : 1,5 km à Vogelenzang* ≤★ *: Tulipshow*★.
Amsterdam 27 – Haarlem 8 – Den Haag 37 – Rotterdam 62.

De Geleerde Man, Rijksstraatweg 51, ✉ 2121 AB, ✆ (0 23) 584 87 32, *info@degeleerdeman.nl, Fax (0 23) 584 87 33,* – AE MC VISA
fermé 18 juil.-1er août, 27 déc.-10 janv., sam. midi, dim. midi et lundi – **Repas** Lunch 24 – 30, ♀.
◆ L'Érudit (De Geleerde Man) vous attable dans un décor contemporain du genre "brasserie hype". Dédiées à la tulipe, de grandes toiles d'une vive polychromie animent les murs.
◆ Deze "wijze" laat zijn gasten plaats nemen in het hedendaags decor van een trendy brasserie. De tulp vormt het centrale thema van de grote bontgekleurde doeken aan de wanden.

Les Jumeaux, Bennebroekerlaan 19b, ✉ 2121 GP, ✆ (0 23) 584 63 34, *info@lesjumeaux.nl, Fax (0 23) 584 96 83,* – AE MC VISA
fermé mardi, sam. midi et dim. midi – **Repas** 29/59 bc, ♀.
◆ Aux portes de Bennebroek, devant un typique petit canal, maison patricienne maniant un répertoire culinaire dans le tempo actuel. Peintures modernes en salle. Patio couvert.
◆ Dit patriciërshuis aan de rand van Bennebroek, tegenover een karakteristieke vaart, heeft een eigentijds culinair repertoire. Decor met moderne schilderijen. Overdekte patio.

à Vogelenzang *Ouest : 1,5 km* C *Bloemendaal 17 097 h :*

La Tulipe Noire, Bekslaan 35 (à l'ancienne gare), ✉ 2114 CB, ✆ (0 23) 584 91 55, *restaurant@latulipenoire.nl, Fax (0 23) 584 28 01,* – AE MC VISA
fermé mardi et merc. – **Repas** (déjeuner sur réservation) carte env. 45.
◆ Logis de garde-barrière promu restaurant. Détail amusant : murs et tables vibrent au passage des trains. Carte dans le vent. L'addition ne vous fera pas dérailler !
◆ Restaurant in een oud seinwachtershuis. Amusant detail : de muren en tafels trillen als de trein langskomt. Trendy menukaart. Van de rekening zult u hier echt niet ontsporen !

BENNEKOM Gelderland C Ede 103 708 h. 532 T 10 et 715 I 5.

Amsterdam 83 – Arnhem 21 – Apeldoorn 45 – Utrecht 45.

XXX ✿ **Het Koetshuis** (Löhr), Panoramaweg 23a (Est : 3 km), ✉ 6721 MK, ☎ (0 318) 41 73 70, *koetshuis@tref.nl, Fax (0 318) 42 01 16,* – P. AE D MC VISA JCB
fermé 31 déc.-4 janv., dim. et lundi – **Repas** Lunch 29 – 45/91 bc, carte 59 à 73, ₸.
• À l'orée des bois, chaumière rustique à souhait où se conçoit une talentueuse cuisine d'aujourd'hui. Terrasses exquises dressées aux beaux jours. Belle cave planétaire.
• Rustiek pand met rieten dak aan de rand van het bos, waar met veel talent een eigentijdse keuken wordt bereid. Prima terrassen voor zomerse dagen. Internationale wijnkaart.
Spéc. Salade de homard et foie gras à la truffe. Queues de langoustines au poireau et ciboulette en sauce. Cannelloni de canard et foie d'oie, sauce aux raisins secs

BENTVELD Noord-Holland 531 M 8 et 532 M 8 – *voir à Zandvoort.*

BERGAMBACHT Zuid-Holland 532 N 11 et 715 F 6 – 9 225 h.

Amsterdam 64 – Rotterdam 25 – Gouda 11 – Utrecht 34.

De Arendshoeve, Molenlaan 14 (Ouest : par N 207), ✉ 2861 LB, ☎ (0 182) 35 10 00, *Fax (0 182) 35 11 55,* – TV P. – 25 à 150. AE D MC VISA JCB
fermé 27 déc.-3 janv. – **Repas *Onder de Molen*** Lunch 30 – carte 32 à 52 – **24 ch** ☕ 145, – 3 suites.
• Un fier moulin signale cette ancienne ferme flanquée d'une villa récente. Intérieur cossu, chambres tout confort, jardin soigné, centre esthétique et jolie piscine romaine. Restaurant aménagé "sous le moulin" (onder de molen), dans une maison pittoresque.
• Een trotse molen markeert deze voormalige boerderij waarnaast een moderne villa is gebouwd. Luxueus interieur, kamers met alle comfort, verzorgde tuin, beautycenter en een fraai Romeins zwembad. Het pittoreske huis onder de molen herbergt een brasserie.

BERGEN Noord-Holland 531 N 6 et 715 F 3 – 31 926 h.

Plein 1, ✉ 1861 JX, ☎ (0 72) 581 31 00, info@vvvbergen.com, Fax (0 72) 581 38 90.
Amsterdam 43 – Haarlem 38 – Alkmaar 6.

Parkhotel, Breelaan 19, ✉ 1861 GC, ☎ (0 72) 589 78 67, *info@parkhotelbergen.nl, Fax (0 72) 589 74 35,* – TV – 30 à 70. AE D MC VISA JCB
Repas Lunch 15 – carte 22 à 36, ₸ – **26 ch** ☕ 65/104 – ½ P 59/84.
• Ces deux résidences modernes élevées au centre de Bergen proposent des chambres standard correctement équipées. Chaleureux salon agrémenté d'une cheminée. À l'heure du repas, cuisine classique hollandaise ou petite restauration. Terrasse populaire.
• Deze twee moderne gebouwen in het centrum van Bergen hebben standaardkamers die van het nodige comfort zijn voorzien. Lounge met warme ambiance en een schouw. Er worden klassieke, Hollandse maaltijden geserveerd, maar ook kleinere gerechten. Populair terras.

Duinpost sans rest, Kerkelaan 5, ✉ 1861 EA, ☎ (0 72) 581 21 50, *hotelduinpost@hotmail.com, Fax (0 72) 589 96 96,* – TV P.
14 ch ☕ 34/67.
• Dans une allée paisible et verdoyante, construction massive renfermant des chambres assez mignonnes, quelquefois munies d'un balcon. Terrasses et jardinet.
• Dit massieve pand staat aan een rustige, groene laan en herbergt vrij gerieflijke kamers, waarvan er enkele een balkon hebben. Terrassen en tuintje.

X **Onder de Linde,** Prinsesselaan 22, ✉ 1861 EN, ☎ (0 72) 581 21 08, *ch.van.diest@zonnet.nl, Fax (0 72) 581 56 78,* – AE MC VISA
fermé lundi sauf en juil.-août, sam. midi et dim. midi – **Repas** Lunch 28 – carte env. 37.
• Jolie petite table à dénicher au fin fond d'une ruelle : carte au goût du jour, agréable terrasse dressée à l'ombre des tilleuls et chauffée en hiver, service tout sourire.
• Leuk restaurantje achter in een steegje. Eigentijdse menukaart, aangenaam terras in de schaduw van de lindebomen ('s winters verwarmd) en zeer vriendelijke bediening.

X **De Kleine Prins,** Oude Prinsweg 29, ✉ 1861 CS, ☎ (0 72) 589 69 69 – AE MC VISA
fermé lundi et mardi – **Repas** (dîner seult jusqu'à 1 h du matin) carte 39 à 47, ₸.
• Au cœur du village, face aux vestiges de l'église, ancienne fermette assez charmante dont le décor intérieur évoque les typiques "bruine cafés" (cafés bruns).
• Dit oude, vrij pittoreske boerderijtje staat midden in het dorp, recht tegenover de overblijfselen van de kerk. Het interieur ademt de sfeer van een typisch bruin café.

à Bergen aan Zee *Ouest : 5 km* **C** *Bergen – Station balnéaire.*

Van der Wijckplein 8, ✉ 1865 AP, ☎ (0 72) 581 31 00, info@vvvbergenaanzee.nl, Fax (0 72) 581 61 41

Nassau Bergen, Van der Wijckplein 4, ✉ 1865 AP, ☎ (0 72) 589 75 41, *info@hotel-nassau.nl, Fax (0 72) 589 70 44*, ≤, ⚬, ⚬, ⚬ – TV P – ⚬ 25 à 60. MC VISA. ⚬ rest *fermé 25 déc.* – **Repas** (dîner pour résidents seult) – **40 ch** ⚬ 65/125 – ½ P 50/98.
◆ Construction des années 1950 surveillant le littoral et les dunes. Équipement correct dans les chambres, récemment rafraîchies. Piscine extérieure et fitness au sous-sol.
◆ Dit gebouw uit het midden van de vorige eeuw waakt over de kust en de duinen. De comfortabele kamers zijn onlangs opgeknapt. Buitenzwembad, fitnessruimte in het souterrain.

Victoria, Zeeweg 33, ✉ 1865 AB, ☎ (0 72) 581 23 58, *Fax (0 72) 589 60 01*, ⚬, ⚬ – ⚬ rest, TV – ⚬ 25 à 40. AE ⚬ MC VISA
Repas Lunch 18 – carte 22 à 45 – **32 ch** ⚬ 57/120 – ½ P 48/83.
◆ À une encablure de la plage et deux pas de l'aquarium, petit établissement approprié pour quelques jours de villégiature balnéaire en famille. Nouvelles chambres lumineuses. Restaurant avec véranda où vous vous mesurerez aux classiques culinaires bataves.
◆ Dit kleine etablissement dicht bij het strand en het zeeaquarium is heel geschikt voor een paar daagjes aan zee met het gezin. Nieuwe, lichte kamers. Restaurant met serre, waar u zich te goed kunt doen aan Hollandse culinaire klassiekers.

Prins Maurits, Van Hasseltweg 7, ✉ 1865 AL, ☎ (0 72) 581 23 64, *hotel@prins-maurits.nl, Fax (0 72) 581 82 98*, ⚬ – TV ⚬ P. ⚬
fév.-oct. – **Repas** (dîner pour résidents seult) – **23 ch** ⚬ 65/90 – ½ P 57/62.
◆ Seulement quelques-unes de vos amples foulées séparent le front de mer de cet immeuble trapu à débusquer en bordure de Bergen. Chambres actuelles dotées d'un balconnet.
◆ Slechts enkele flinke passen scheiden de zee van dit massief ogende hotelpand aan de rand van Bergen. De moderne kamers hebben alle een balkonnetje.

BERG EN DAL *Gelderland* 532 U 12 *et* 715 I 6 – *voir à Nijmegen.*

BERG EN TERBLIJT *Limburg* 532 T 16 *et* 715 I 9 – *voir à Valkenburg.*

BERGEN OP ZOOM *Noord-Brabant* 532 K 14 *et* 715 D 7 – *65 793 h.*

Voir *Markiezenhof*★ AY **M¹**.

⛳18 par ③ : 5 km, Zoomvlietweg 66, ✉ 4624 RP, ☎ (0 165) 37 71 00, Fax (0 165) 37 71 01.
Amsterdam 143 ② – 's-Hertogenbosch 90 ② – Breda 40 ② – Rotterdam 70 ② – Antwerpen 39 ③

Plan page suivante

Mercure De Draak, Grote Markt 36, ✉ 4611 NT, ☎ (0 164) 25 20 50, *info@hoteldedraak.com, Fax (0 164) 25 70 01*, ⚬ – ⚬ ⚬, ⚬ ch, TV P – ⚬ 40. AE ⚬ MC VISA JCB. ⚬ AY a
Repas *(fermé 26 déc.-2 janv., sam. midi et dim. midi)* Lunch 24 – carte 40 à 54 – **55 ch** *(fermé 24 déc.-2 janv.)* ⚬ 118/203, – 3 suites.
◆ Cet hôtel de tradition officiant depuis plus de 600 ans est entré en 1996 dans le giron de la chaîne internationale Mercure. Façades, chambres et communs soignés. Élégante table franco-transalpine.
◆ Dit traditionele hotel bestaat al ruim 600 jaar en heeft zich in 1996 aangesloten bij de internationale hotelketen Mercure. De buitenkant, de kamers en de gemeenschappelijke ruimten zien er verzorgd uit. Fijne Frans-Italiaanse keuken.

Parkhotel, Gertrudisboulevard 200, ✉ 4615 MA, ☎ (0 164) 26 02 02, *reserveringen@gtparkhotel.nl, Fax (0 164) 26 03 03*, ⚬, ⚬ – ⚬ ⚬ TV ⚬ P – ⚬ 25 à 200. AE ⚬ MC VISA JCB AZ d
Repas Lunch 24 – carte 30 à 44, ♀ – ⚬ 15 – **51 ch** 133/189.
◆ Aux portes de la ville, immeuble récent dominant un plan d'eau récréatif et une voie de chemin de fer. Chambres fonctionnelles insonorisées. Style de restauration digne de Pancho Villa et l'Oncle Sam réunis.
◆ Dit moderne hotelgebouw aan de rand van de stad kijkt uit over een recreatieplas en een spoorlijn. De functionele kamers zijn voorzien van geluidsisolatie. De keuken kan behagen aan zowel Pancho Villa en Uncle Sam !

Tulip Inn De Schelde sans rest, Antwerpsestraat 56, ✉ 4611 AK, ☎ (0 164) 26 52 65, *info@tulipinndeschelde.nl, Fax (0 164) 26 65 24* – ⚬ ⚬ TV ⚬. AE ⚬ MC VISA. ⚬
⚬ 11 – **68 ch** 88/110. BZ e
◆ Établissement un peu excentré, voisin d'un centre commercial. Chambres actuelles où l'on a ses aises, réparties entre le bâtiment principal et plusieurs proches annexes.
◆ Dit hotel ligt wat uit het centrum, vlak bij een complex met winkels. De moderne, comfortabele kamers zijn verdeeld over het hoofdgebouw en enkele nabijgelegen annexen.

BERGEN OP ZOOM

Antwerpsestraatweg . . . . . . BZ 3
Arn. Asselbergsstr. . . . . BY 4
Auvergnestr. . . . . AZ 6
Blauwehandstr. . . . . BY 7
Boutershemstr. . . . . AZ 8
Burg. Stulemeijerlaan . . . . . AY 9
Burg. van Hasseltstr. . . . . . . BZ 10
De Boulevard Noord . . . . . . AZ 12
Fortuinstr. . . . . AY 13
Glymesstr. . . . . AZ 14
Grote Markt . . . . AY 15
Halsterseweg . . . . AY 16
Kerkstr. . . . . BZ 20
Kloosterstr. . . . . BZ 22
Kortemeestr. . . . . AY 23
Kremerstr. . . . . AY 24
Lange Parkstr. . . . . BY 25
Lieve Vrouwestr. . . . . AY 26
Minderbroedersstr. . . . . . . ABY 28
van Overstratenlaan . . . . . . AY 30
van der Rijtstr. . . . . BY 32
St. Josephstr. . . . . BYZ 34
Stationsstr. . . . . BY 36
Steenbergsestr. . . . . AY 37
Rooseveltlaan . . . . BZ 39
Wouwsestraatweg . . . . BY 41
Zuivelstr. . . . . BY 43

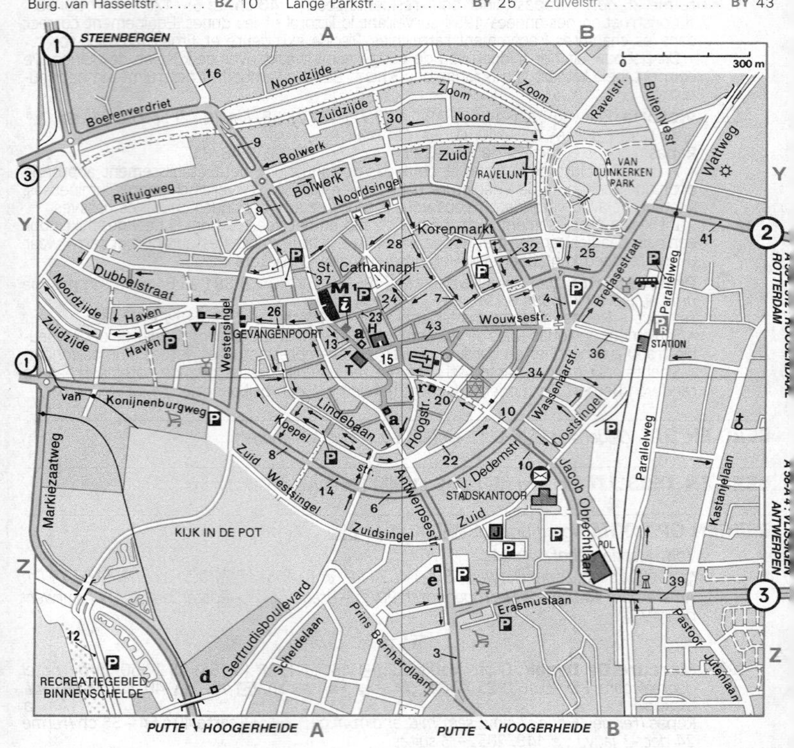

XXX **Moerstede,** Vogelenzang 5 (Moerstraatsebaan, Nord : 2 km), ✉ 4614 PP, ☎ (0 164) 25 88 00, *moerstede@planet.nl, Fax (0 164) 25 99 21,* – P – 25 à 120. AE ⓓ ⓜⓒ VISA JCB. – *fermé 27 déc.-2 janv., sam. midi, dim. midi et lundi* – **Repas** *Lunch 30* – 43.
◆ Plaisante maison de bouche "perdue" dans les bois. Recettes classiques gentiment actualisées, à l'image de la décoration intérieure. Terrasse dressée à la belle saison.
◆ Aangenaam restaurant midden in de bossen. Klassieke gerechten met een modern accent, net als de inrichting van de eetzaal. Terras in de zomer. par Ravelstraat BY

XX **'t Spuihuis,** Spui 1, ✉ 4611 GX, ☎ (0 164) 23 31 96, *info@spuihuis.nl, Fax (0 164) 29 91 31,* – AE ⓓ ⓜⓒ VISA. AY v
fermé 1 sem. carnaval, sam. midi et dim. midi – **Repas** 25/30, ♀.
◆ Cette monumentale construction néo-classique est ancrée depuis 1839 à l'extrémité des quais de l'ancien port. Intérieur traité en mezzanine et grande terrasse d'été.
◆ Dit monumentale neoklassieke pand ligt sinds 1839 verankerd achter aan de kaden van de oude haven. Interieur met tussenverdieping, groot terras in de zomer.

X **De Boschpoort,** Bosstraat 9, ✉ 4611 NA, ☎ (0 164) 23 03 04, *boschpoort@house.nl, Fax (0 164) 23 01 86,* – . AE ⓜⓒ VISA AZ a
fermé dern. sem. juil.-2 prem. sem. août, lundi et mardi – **Repas** (dîner seult) 28/43.
◆ Sur une placette du centre, maison réaménagée en agréable petit restaurant bien dans le coup, du décor de la salle à manger jusqu'au contenu de la carte. La saveur y est !
◆ Dit huis aan een pleintje in het centrum is verbouwd tot een prettig restaurantje waar hedendaags het sleutelwoord is, van het decor van de eetzaal tot de inhoud van de kaart.

X **De Bloemkool,** Wouwsestraatweg 146 (par ②), ✉ 4623 AS, ☎ (0 164) 23 30 45, *debloemkool@nl.proximedia.com, Fax (0 164) 21 01 22,* 🏞 - P. AE MC VISA
fermé fin déc.-3 janv., sam. midi et dim. midi – **Repas** 24/27 bc, ♀.
◆ Ancien relais de poste situé à l'Est de Bergen op Zoom, au voisinage de l'autoroute. Plats traditionnels attentifs à la qualité des produits. Ambiance "auberge brabançonne".
◆ Voormalig uitspanning aan de oostkant van Bergen op Zoom, vlak bij de snelweg. Traditionele gerechten op basis van kwaliteitsproducten. Ambiance van een Brabantse herberg.

X **Napoli,** Kerkstraat 10, ✉ 4611 NV, ☎ (0 164) 24 37 04, Cuisine italienne, ouvert jusqu'à 23 h – AE ⓓ MC VISA. ✂ BZ r
fermé sem. carnaval, 24 et 31 déc. et 1er janv. – **Repas** 29/50.
◆ L'enseigne de cette maison jouxtant l'emblématique Peperbus annonce sans détour la couleur de l'assiette : cuisine italienne honorable, toutefois un rien convenue.
◆ Dit restaurant is gevestigd in een herenhuis naast de Peperbus. De naam bekent ronduit kleur : vrij goede Italiaanse keuken, maar een tikje alledaags.

BERKEL-ENSCHOT *Noord-Brabant* 532 P 13 *et* 715 G 7 – *voir à Tilburg.*

BEST *Noord-Brabant* 532 R 13 *et* 715 H 7 – *27 450 h.*

Golflaan 1, ✉ 5683 RZ, ☎ (0 499) 39 14 43, Fax (0 499) 39 32 21.
Amsterdam 111 – Eindhoven 11 – 's-Hertogenbosch 22 – Breda 53.

NH Best, De Maas 2 (Sud : 2 km par A 58, sortie ⑦), ✉ 5684 PL, ☎ (0 499) 39 01 00, *info@nhbest.nh-hotels.nl, Fax (0 499) 39 16 50,* 🏞, 🏊, 🚲 - 🛗 ✂ TV ♿ P - 🎤 25 à 160. AE ⓓ MC VISA
Repas 28 – **68 ch** ☕ 121 – ½ P 80/135.
◆ Hôtel de chaîne contemporain, bien pratique pour qui choisit de poser ses valises en périphérie de Eindhoven. Chambres un peu menues, mais récemment rénovées. Restaurant complété d'une terrasse d'été.
◆ Modern ketenhotel dat praktisch is gelegen voor wie dicht bij Eindhoven een slaapplaats zoekt. De kamers zijn wat klein, maar onlangs gerenoveerd. Restaurant met zomerterras.

X **Qu4tre Bras,** Nieuwstraat 79, ✉ 5683 KB, ☎ (0 499) 37 14 50, *info@quatrebras.nl, Fax (0 499) 39 05 20,* 🏞, Avec taverne – P – 🎤 25 à 100. AE ⓓ MC VISA. ✂
Repas *Lunch 19* – carte 35 à 46, ♀.
◆ Ces "Qu4tre Bras" vous tendent "d2ux possibilités" pour assouvir votre appétit : brasserie et restaurant avec cuisine d'aujourd'hui. Formule lunch à bon compte.
◆ Deze vier armen reiken twee mogelijkheden aan voor de inwendige mens : een brasserie en een restaurant met eigentijdse keuken. Goedkope lunchformule.

BEUNINGEN *Gelderland* 532 T 11 *et* 715 I 6 – *voir à Nijmegen.*

BEUNINGEN *Overijssel* 531 AB 8 – *voir à Denekamp.*

BEVERWIJK *Noord-Holland* 531 M 8 *et* 715 E 4 – *35 780 h.*

Amsterdam 28 – Haarlem 13 – Alkmaar 22.

XX **'t Gildehuys,** Baanstraat 32, ✉ 1942 CJ, ☎ (0 251) 22 15 15, *info@gildehuys.nl, Fax (0 251) 21 38 66,* 🏞 – VISA
fermé du 9 au 16 août et lundi – **Repas** (dîner seult) 25/56 bc.
◆ Au centre de Beverwijk, bonne adresse où défilent les fines fourchettes du secteur. Produits choisis, travaillés avec soin. Menu hebdomadaire courtisé. Terrasse ombragée.
◆ Goed adres in het centrum, waar fijnproevers uit de stad af en aan lopen. Kwaliteitsproducten worden met zorg bereid. Het weekmenu is favoriet. Lommerrijk terras.

XX **De Hoge Heren,** Baanstraat 26, ✉ 1942 CJ, ☎ (0 251) 21 18 77, *info@hogeheren.nl, Fax (0 251) 21 44 67* – ▤. AE MC VISA JCB
fermé merc., sam. midi et dim. midi – **Repas** *Lunch 30* – carte 43 à 51, ♀.
◆ Les Grands Seigneurs (De Hoge Heren) vous concoctent sans effets de manches inutiles un choix de recettes au goût du jour.
◆ Deze notabelen bereiden hier een eigentijdse keuken met eerlijke gerechten zonder frutsels en fratsels.

X **de Jonge Halewijn,** Duinwijklaan 46, ✉ 1942 GC, ☎ (0 251) 22 08 59, *info@halewijn.nl,* 🏞 – AE MC VISA JCB
fermé sam. midi et dim. midi – **Repas** *Lunch 25* – 23/42 bc.
◆ Restaurant refait de neuf, misant sur une carte bien dans le coup. À l'arrière, terrasse d'été plaisante et intime dressée sous les frondaisons d'un vieux châtaignier.
◆ Restaurant dat in een nieuw jasje is gestoken en trendy gerechten serveert. Aangenaam en intiem zomerterras aan de achterzijde, onder het bladerdak van een oude kastanje.

BIDDINGHUIZEN *Flevoland* Ⓒ *Dronten 36 369 h.* 531 T 8 *et* 715 I 4.
Amsterdam 70 – Apeldoorn 58 – Utrecht 74 – Zwolle 41.

Dorhout Mees, Strandgaperweg 30 (Sud : 6 km, direction Veluwemeer), ✉ 8256 PZ, ☎ (0 321) 33 11 38, *info@dorhoutmees.nl, Fax (0 321) 33 10 57*, – 25 à 600. VISA
fermé 25, 26 et 31 déc. et 1er janv. – **Repas** Lunch 9 – carte env. 32 – **42 ch** 88/115.
• Établissement isolé dans la campagne et encadré de deux terrains de golf. Chambres de bon séjour, stands de tir aux clays et équipement complet pour la tenue de séminaires. À table, ambiance "pavillon de chasse".
• Afgelegen etablissement midden in de natuur en omgeven door twee golfterreinen. Comfortabele kamers. Kleiduivenbanen en uitstekende faciliteiten voor bijeenkomsten en seminars. De eetzaal heeft de ambiance van een jachtpaviljoen.

De BILT *Utrecht* 532 P 10 *et* 715 G 5 – *42 309 h.*
Amsterdam 49 – Utrecht 7 – Apeldoorn 65.

De Biltsche Hoek, De Holle Bilt 1 (sur N 225), ✉ 3732 HM, ☎ (0 30) 220 58 11, *reservations@biltschehoek.valk.nl, Fax (0 30) 220 28 12*, – – 25 à 200. AE VISA. ch
Repas Lunch 15 – carte 22 à 38 – 9 – **102 ch** 70/75.
• Ce motel de chaîne proche de l'autoroute et d'Utrecht abrite une centaine de chambres spacieuses réparties entre plusieurs ailes disposées autour d'une ancienne auberge.
• Dit ketenmotel vlak bij de snelweg en de stad Utrecht telt een honderdtal ruime kamers, verspreid over diverse vleugels die rond een voormalige herberg zijn gebouwd.

BILTHOVEN *Utrecht* Ⓒ *De Bilt 42 309 h.* 532 Q 10 *et* 715 G 5.
Amsterdam 48 – Utrecht 10 – Apeldoorn 65.

Heidepark, Jan Steenlaan 22, ✉ 3723 VB, ☎ (0 30) 228 24 77, *info@heidepark.nl, Fax (0 30) 229 21 84*, – – 25 à 150. AE VISA. ch
Repas *(fermé dim.)* Lunch 30 – carte 27 à 41 – 12 – **21 ch** 99/129.
• Ancien cinéma devenu un paisible hôtel où vous séjournerez dans des chambres refaites de neuf ou dans l'une des trois junior suites dotées d'une kitchenette et d'un balcon.
• Een rustig hotel in een voormalige bioscoop, waar u uw keus kunt laten vallen op een gerenoveerde kamer of op een van de drie junior suites met kitchenette en balkon.

De Kuuk, Soestdijkseweg-Noord 492 (Nord : 2 km), ✉ 3723 HM, ☎ (0 30) 225 00 52, *info@dekuuk.nl, Fax (0 30) 225 00 35*, – AE VISA.
fermé 2 dern. sem. juil. et sam. midi – **Repas** Lunch 34 – carte 38 à 48, ♀.
• Aux portes de Bilthoven, ancienne ferme profitant d'alentours boisés et d'une plaisante terrasse d'été. Côté fourneaux, le souci de faire bon avec des produits simples.
• Deze voormalige boerderij aan de rand van Bilthoven ligt in een bosrijke omgeving en heeft een prettig zomerterras. Met zorg wordt van eenvoudige producten iets goeds bereid.

BLADEL *Noord-Brabant* 532 Q 14 *et* 715 G 7 – *19 046 h.*
Markt 21a, ✉ 5531 BC, ☎ (0 497) 38 33 00, vvv@iae.nl, Fax (0 497) 38 59 22.
Amsterdam 141 – Eindhoven 26 – 's-Hertogenbosch 52 – Antwerpen 67.

Bladel, Europalaan 77, ✉ 5531 BE, ☎ (0 497) 38 33 19, *info@hotel-bladel.nl, Fax (0 497) 38 36 30*, – – 25. AE VISA JCB. ch
Repas Lunch 18 – 26/31 – **14 ch** 53/83 – ½ P 64/69.
• Ce petit immeuble des années 1980 avoisinant le centre de Bladel dispose de chambres fonctionnelles munies du double vitrage. Accueil familial. Repas à la carte ; formules lunch et menu de qualité constante.
• Klein hotelpand uit circa 1980, nabij het centrum. Functionele kamers met dubbele beglazing. Vriendelijk onthaal. À la carte, lunchformules en menu van constante kwaliteit.

Aub. Central, Europalaan 28a, ✉ 5531 BH, ☎ (0 497) 38 69 28, *lroijmans2102@hotmail.com, Fax (0 497) 38 57 83*, – AE VISA JCB.
fermé 1 sem. en juil. – **Repas** (dîner pour résidents seult) – **5 ch** 45/64 – ½ P 48/61.
• Elles se comptent sur les doigts d'une seule main, les chambres de ce minuscule hôtel situé à proximité du centre-ville. Jardin avec pièce d'eau.
• De kamers in dit minuscule hotel vlak bij het centrum zijn op één hand te tellen. Tuin met waterpartij.

De Hofstee, Sniederslaan 121, ✉ 5531 EK, ☎ (0 497) 38 15 00, *Fax (0 497) 38 80 93*, – VISA – *fermé dern. sem. juil.-prem. sem. août, merc., sam. midi et dim. midi* – **Repas** Lunch 28 – 37/48, ♀.
• Un adorable jardin et une exquise terrasse dressée aux beaux jours agrémentent cette jolie fermette rustique coiffée d'un toit de chaume. Menus affriolants. Cave bien montée.
• Een bekoorlijke tuin en een verrukkelijk zomerterras geven dit mooie, rustieke boerderijtje met rieten dak extra charme. Aanlokkelijke menu's. Goed voorziene wijnkelder.

BLARICUM *Noord-Holland* 531 *Q 9,* 532 *Q 9 et* 715 *G 5 - 9 343 h.*

Amsterdam 34 - Apeldoorn 63 - Hilversum 9 - Utrecht 24.

XX **Rust Wat,** Schapendrift 79, ✉ 1261 HP, ☎ (0 35) 538 32 86, *info@restaurantrustwat.nl, Fax (0 35) 533 44 93,* – AE ⓓ ⓜ VISA.
fermé lundi – **Repas** *Lunch 23* – carte 47 à 57.
◆ En bordure d'une réserve naturelle boisée, près d'un étang tapissé de nénuphars, auberge typique où se mitonne une cuisine dans le tempo actuel. Terrasse très agréable.
◆ Deze karakteristieke herberg aan de rand van een bosrijk natuurgebied kijkt uit op een vijver met waterlelies. Verzorgde eigentijdse keuken. Zeer aangenaam terras.

XX **De Goede Gooier,** Crailoseweg 151 (près A 1 - E 231, sortie ⑧ direction Huizen), ✉ 1261 AA, ☎ (0 35) 691 93 04, *rogier@degoedegooier.nl, Fax (0 35) 692 05 91,* ←, – P. AE ⓓ ⓜ VISA
fermé 25, 26 et 31 déc.-1er janv. – **Repas** *Lunch 33* – 34/43.
◆ Ancienne auberge postée à la lisière du Blaricum heide, vaste étendue de landes appréciée des promeneurs. Carte avec menus-choix. Terrasse d'été garnie de meubles en osier.
◆ Oude herberg aan de rand van de uitgestrekte Blaricumse heide, een favoriet wandelgebied. Kaart met keuzemenu's. Zomerterras met rieten meubels.

BLERICK *Limburg* 532 *V 14 et* 715 *J 7 – voir à Venlo.*

BLOEMENDAAL *Noord-Holland* 531 *M 8,* 532 *M 8 et* 715 *E 4 – voir à Haarlem.*

BLOKZIJL *Overijssel* C *Steenwijkerland 41 870 h.* 531 *U 6 et* 715 *I 3.*

Voir *Grande Église (Grote Kerk) : intérieur★.*
Amsterdam 102 - Zwolle 33 - Assen 66 - Leeuwarden 65.

XX ✿ **Kaatje bij de Sluis** avec ch, Brouwerstraat 20, ✉ 8356 DV, ☎ (0 527) 29 18 33, *kaatje@planet.nl, Fax (0 527) 29 18 36,* ←, – ▤. AE ⓓ ⓜ VISA
fermé fév., 1 sem. après Noël, lundi, mardi et sam. midi – **Repas** *Lunch 45* – 63/128 bc, carte 75 à 112, ♀ – ☕ 18 – **8 ch** 150 – ½ P 165/180.
◆ Le long d'un canal, entre une écluse et un typique pont à bascule, restaurant-bonbonnière estimé pour sa cuisine d'aujourd'hui. Intéressantes fresques animalières en salle.
◆ Smaakvol ingericht restaurant aan een kanaal, tussen een sluis en een ophaalbrug. De eigentijdse keuken staat goed aangeschreven. Fraaie wandschilderingen van dieren.
Spéc. Tartare de Saint-Jacques à la crème de laitue, sauce aux huîtres. Saumon tiède aux asperges, sauce au café. Medaillons de chevreuil au jus (15 janv.-1er oct.)

XX **Hof van Sonoy** avec ch, Kerkstraat 9, ✉ 8356 DN, ☎ (0 527) 29 17 08, *info@hofvansonoy.nl, Fax (0 527) 29 17 09,* – TV. AE ⓓ ⓜ VISA JCB.
fermé 2 sem. en mars, 1 sem. en oct., dim. non fériés sauf en juil.-août, lundi et sam. midi – **Repas** 33/70 bc, ♀ – **4 ch** ☕ 93 – ½ P 74/100.
◆ Un ancien établissement scolaire du 19e s. sert de cadre à ce vaste restaurant étagé en mezzanine. Choix concis, avec de bons menus. Chambres conçues comme des studios.
◆ Een 19e-eeuwse school vormt het decor van dit grote restaurant met vide. Kaart met beperkte keuze en goede menu's. Er zijn ook enkele eenkamerappartementen met keukenhoek.

à Muggenbeet *Nord-Est : 3 km* C *Steenwijkerland 41 870 h :*

Geertien Muggenbeet 3, ✉ 8356 VK, ☎ (0 527) 29 12 45, *info@geertien.nl, Fax (0 527) 29 15 16,* – ▤ rest, TV P – 25 à 40. AE ⓓ ⓜ VISA JCB. ch
fermé 31 déc.-1er janv. – **Repas** *(fermé merc. de sept. à mai) Lunch 31* – carte 34 à 49 – **12 ch** ☕ 78/98, – 2 suites – ½ P 77.
◆ Ce sympathique petit hôtel champêtre et familial dispose de chambres actuelles de taille convenable, équipées d'un mobilier de série. Café "couleur locale" et terrasse d'été. À table, carte traditionnelle incluant plusieurs menus.
◆ Dit landelijk gelegen, sympathieke hotelletje beschikt over eigentijdse, comfortabele kamers die met standaardmeubilair zijn ingericht. Authentiek bruin café en zomerterras aan het water. Op de traditionele kaart staan ook enkele menu's.

BODEGRAVEN *Zuid-Holland* 532 *N 10 et* 715 *F 5 - 19 605 h.*

Amsterdam 48 - Rotterdam 36 - Den Haag 45 - Utrecht 30.

AC Hotel, Goudseweg 32 (près A 12, sortie ⑫), ✉ 2411 HL, ☎ (0 172) 65 00 03, *bodegraven@autogrill.net, Fax (0 172) 61 81 01* – TV P – 25 à 90. AE ⓓ ⓜ VISA
Repas (avec buffets) carte env. 25 – ☕ 10 – **64 ch** 71/81.
◆ Près de l'autoroute reliant Den Haag à Utrecht, hôtel de chaîne aussi bien équipé pour la clientèle d'affaires que pour les familles et la tenue de séminaires.
◆ Dit ketenhotel dicht bij de snelweg Den Haag-Utrecht is geschikt voor een zakelijk verblijf, maar ook voor een tussenstop. Faciliteiten voor seminars.

BOEKELO *Overijssel* 532 Z 9 *et* 715 L 5 – *voir à Enschede.*

BOLLENVELDEN (CHAMPS DE FLEURS) ★★★ *Zuid-Holland* 531 L 9 *à* N 5, 532 J 10 *à* M 8 *et* 715 E 5 *à* G 3 *G. Hollande.*

BOLSWARD (BOALSERT) *Fryslân* 531 S 4 *et* 715 H 2 – *9 378 h.*

Voir *Hôtel de ville★ (Stadhuis) – Stalles★ et chaire★ de l'église St-Martin (Martinikerk).*

Env. *au Sud-Ouest : Digue du Nord★★ (Afsluitdijk).*

Amsterdam 114 – Leeuwarden 29 – Zwolle 85.

Hid Hero Hiem, Kerkstraat 51, ✉ 8701 HR, ✆ (0 515) 57 52 99, *Fax (0 515) 57 30 52*, – TV – 30. MC VISA JCB.
Repas (dîner seult) carte env. 27 – **14 ch** 68/94.
◆ Une ruelle étroite dessert ce paisible hôtel aménagé dans un ancien orphelinat. Studios avec kitchenette. Cour intérieure agrémentée d'un jardin et d'une terrasse d'été.
◆ Een smal straatje voert naar dit rustige hotel, dat onderdak heeft gevonden in een voormalig weeshuis. Eenkamerflat met kitchenette. Binnenhof met tuin en terras.

De Lavendelhof, Nieuwmarkt 24, ✉ 8701 KL, ✆ (0 515) 57 79 88, *info@lavendelhof.nl, Fax (0 515) 57 34 45* – – 25 à 200. AE MC VISA JCB.
fermé sam. midi, dim. et lundi midi – **Repas** *Lunch 25* – 23/33, ♀.
◆ Les saveurs de la Provence sont à l'honneur dans cette vénérable auberge du centre de Bolsward. Choix diversifié s'articulant sur plusieurs menus bien ficelés. Service jovial.
◆ De smaak van de Provence zult u zeker aantreffen in dit eerbiedwaardige pand in hartje Bolsward. Gevarieerde keuze met diverse uitgebalanceerde menu's. Vriendelijke bediening.

BOORNBERGUM (BOARNBURGUM) *Fryslân* 531 V 4 *et* 715 J 2 – *voir à Drachten.*

BORCULO *Gelderland* 532 Y 10 *et* 715 K 5 – *10 502 h.*

Hofstraat 5, ✉ 7271 AP, ✆ (0 545) 27 19 66, info@vvvborculo.nl, Fax (0 545) 27 19 66.

Amsterdam 134 – Arnhem 61 – Apeldoorn 48 – Enschede 34.

De Stenen Tafel (Prinsen), Het Eiland 1, ✉ 7271 BK, ✆ (0 545) 27 20 30, *mail@destenentafel.nl, Fax (0 545) 27 33 36*, – AE MC VISA
fermé 3 sem. en fév., fin août-début sept., lundi et mardi – **Repas** (déjeuner sur réservation) 55/110 bc, carte 57 à 77, ♀.
◆ L'une des meilleures tables du Gelderland, rustique et pittoresque, installée dans un double moulin à eau du 17e s. dont le mécanisme anime la salle. Terrasse ombragée.
◆ Een van de beste restaurants in Gelderland, rustiek en pittoresk, in een dubbele 17e-eeuwse watermolen, waarvan het raderwerk in de eetzaal is geïntegreerd. Lommerrijk terras.
Spéc. Saint-Jacques grillées et rémoulade de céleri-rave aux truffes. Chevreuil régional aux baies de genièvre et cèpes séchées (en saison). Crème brûlée à la vanille

BORN *Limburg* C *Sittard-Geleen 97 953 h.* 532 T 16 *et* 715 I 8.

Amsterdam 190 – Maastricht 28 – Eindhoven 62 – Roermond 23 – Aachen 43.

Amrâth, Langereweg 21 (Est : 2 km près A 2 - E 9), ✉ 6121 SB, ✆ (0 46) 485 16 66, *info@hotel-born.nl, Fax (0 46) 485 12 23*, – TV – 25 à 200. AE MC VISA JCB. rest
Repas *(fermé sam. midi et dim. midi)* 22/33 – 14 – **59 ch** 95/109 – ½ P 89/104.
◆ Cet hôtel de chaîne contemporain, un peu excentré, renferme des chambres rénovées où l'on ne manque pas d'espace. La clientèle d'affaires y a ses habitudes. Double formule au restaurant : plats de brasserie ou repas d'esprit méditerranéen à la carte.
◆ Deze moderne telg van een hotelketen ligt wat buiten het centrum en blijkt voor de zakelijke gast een prima uitvalsbasis te zijn. Ruime, gerenoveerde kamers. Het restaurant biedt twee opties : brasserieschotels en mediterraan geörienteerde gerechten à la carte.

BORNE *Overijssel* 531 Z 9, 532 Z 9 *et* 715 L 5 – *20 729 h.*

Nieuwe Markt 7, ✉ 7622 DD, ✆ 0 900 202 19 81, info@vvvborne.nl, Fax (0 74) 266 93 01.

Amsterdam 145 – Apeldoorn 61 – Arnhem 83 – Groningen 135 – Munster 77.

Dorset Mansion House, Grotestraat 167, ✉ 7622 GE, ✆ (0 74) 266 19 25, *info@dorset.nl, Fax (0 74) 267 05 53*, – 40. AE MC VISA.
fermé vacances bâtiment, sam. midi, dim. midi, lundi et mardi – **Repas** *Lunch 29* – 40/89, ♀.
◆ Beau moment de table en perspective dans cette opulente demeure patricienne élevée au soir du 19e s. pour un baron du textile. Atmosphère "british", très "cosy".
◆ Dat wordt echt genieten in het weelderige decor van dit herenhuis. Het werd eind 19e eeuw voor een textielbaron gebouwd en heeft een zeer behaaglijke, Engelse ambiance.

Den BOSCH 🅿 *Noord-Brabant – voir 's-Hertogenbosch.*

BOSCH EN DUIN *Utrecht* 532 Q 10 *et* 715 G 5 *– voir à Zeist.*

BOSSCHENHOOFD *Noord-Brabant* 532 M 13 *et* 715 E 7 *– voir à Roosendaal.*

BOXMEER *Noord-Brabant* 532 U 13 *et* 715 I 7 *– 29 282 h.*

Amsterdam 139 – 's-Hertogenbosch 57 – Eindhoven 46 – Nijmegen 31.

van Diepen, Spoorstraat 74, ✉ 5831 CM, ✆ (0 485) 57 13 45, *info@hotelvandiepen.nl, Fax (0 485) 57 62 13,* – – 25 à 125. AE VISA
fermé 24 déc.-1er janv. – **Repas** *(fermé sam.)* carte 22 à 34 – **21 ch** 68/85.
◆ On apprécie le confort fonctionnel de ce petit hôtel situé à l'angle d'une rue passante, près d'une voie ferrée. Chambres d'ampleur respectable, munies du double vitrage. Salle à manger bourgeoise, carte classico-traditionnelle et terrasse dressée en été.
◆ Het functionele comfort in dit kleine hotel valt goed in de smaak. Het pand staat op de hoek van een doorgaande straat, nabij een spoorweg. Kamers van respectabel formaat en met dubbele beglazing. Klassieke eetzaal, klassiek-traditionele kaart en zomerterras.

BOXTEL *Noord-Brabant* 532 Q 13 *et* 715 G 7 *– 29 371 h.*

Amsterdam 101 – Eindhoven 21 – 's-Hertogenbosch 12 – Breda 48.

XX **De Ceulse Kaar,** Eindhovenseweg 41 (Sud-Est : 2 km), ✉ 5283 RA, ✆ (0 411) 67 62 82, *Fax (0 411) 68 52 12,* – 🅿. AE VISA JCB
fermé 28 déc.-début janv., sam. midi, dim. midi, lundi et mardi – **Repas** 26/35.
◆ Aux avant-postes de la localité, ancienne ferme-auberge brabançonne du 18e s. où l'on mange au coude à coude dans une salle de restaurant rustique. Terrasse dressée en été.
◆ Deze oude Brabantse boerderij uit de 18e eeuw staat aan de rand van Boxtel. In de rustieke eetzaal zitten de gasten dicht bij elkaar rond de dis. Zomerterras.

XX **De Negenmannen,** Fellenoord 8, ✉ 5281 CB, ✆ (0 411) 67 85 64, *info@negenmannen.nl, Fax (0 411) 67 62 76* – . AE VISA JCB.
fermé carnaval, 31 déc., sam. midi, dim. midi et lundi – **Repas** Lunch 25 – carte 38 à 56, ♀.
◆ La clientèle du secteur paraît avoir adopté cette agréable adresse du centre-ville. Menus fricotant un peu avec les saveurs d'aujourd'hui.
◆ Dit aangename negental in het centrum van de stad lijkt door de plaatselijke clientèle geadopteerd te zijn. De menu's flirten wat met eigentijdse smaken.

X **Aub. van Boxtel** avec ch, Stationsplein 2, ✉ 5281 GH, ✆ (0 411) 67 22 37, *info@auberge.nl, Fax (0 411) 67 41 24,* – 30. AE VISA JCB. ch
fermé du 2 au 17 août et 23 déc.-4 janv. – **Repas** *(fermé mardi)* (dîner seult) carte 35 à 48 – **10 ch** 75/100 – ½ P 71/100.
◆ Petite affaire familiale bordant une placette voisine de la gare de Boxtel. Registre culinaire dans le tempo actuel et sélection de vins assez cosmopolite. Chambres pratiques.
◆ Klein restaurant aan een pleintje naast het station van Boxtel. Eigentijds culinair register en een vrij kosmopolitische selectie wijnen. Praktische kamers.

BRAAMT *Gelderland* 532 W 11 *– voir à Zeddam.*

BREDA *Noord-Brabant* 532 N 13 *et* 715 F 7 *– 163 427 h – Casino B , Bijster 30, ✉ 4817 HX, ✆ (0 76) 525 11 00, Fax (0 76) 522 50 29.*

Voir *Carnaval★ – Grande église ou Église Notre-Dame★ (Grote of O.-L.-Vrouwekerk) : clocher★, tombeau★ d'Englebert II de Nassau* C **R** *– Valkenberg★* D.

Env. *au Nord par ①, Parc national De Biesbosch★ : promenade en bateau★ – par ① : 15 km à Raamsdonksveer, Musée national de l'Automobile★.*

18 *par ② : 4 km à Molenschot, Veenstraat 89, ✉ 5124 NC, ✆ (0 161) 41 12 00, Fax (0 161) 41 17 15 et* 18 *Bavelseweg 153, ✉ 5124 PX, ✆ (0 161) 43 18 11, Fax (0 161) 45 35 54 -* 9 *au Nord-Ouest : 4 km à Prinsenbeek, Wiemersedreef 19, ✉ 4841 KG, ✆ (0 76) 541 94 49, Fax (0 76) 541 91 16.*

Willemstraat 17, ✉ 4811 AJ, ✆ 0 900 522 24 44, info@vvvbreda.nl, Fax (0 76) 521 85 30.

Amsterdam 103 ① – Rotterdam 52 ⑦ – Tilburg 22 ② – Utrecht 72 ① – Antwerpen 56 ⑤

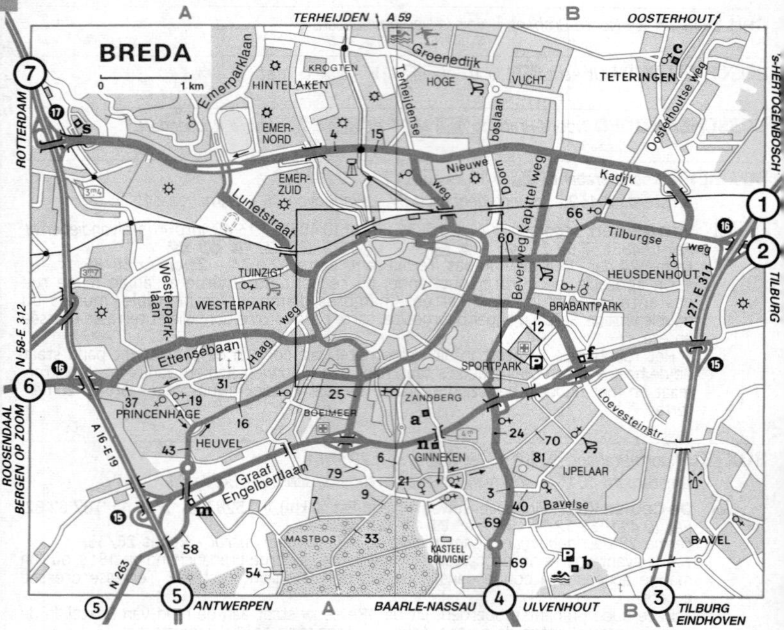

BREDA

Rue	Carré	N°
Allerheiligenweg	B	3
Backer en Ruebweg	A	4
Baronielaan	AB	6
Burg. de Manlaan	A	7
Burg. Kerstenlaan	A	9
Claudius Prinsenlaan	B	12
Crogtdijk	A	15
Dr. Struyckenstr.	A	16
Dreef	A	19
Duivelsbruglaan	B	21
Fatimastraat	B	24
Graaf Hendrik III laan	A	25
Heuvelstraat	A	31
Huisdreef	A	33
Liesboslaan	A	37
Marialaan	B	40
Mastbosstraat	A	43
Overaseweg	A	54
Rijsbergseweg	A	58
Sint Ignatiusstr.	B	60
Teteringsedijk	B	66
Ulvenhoutselaan	B	69
Valkenierslaan	B	70
Willem van Oranjelaan	A	79
Zwijnsbergenstr.	B	81

Mercure, Stationsplein 14, ✉ 4811 BB, ✆ (0 76) 522 02 00, *h1316@accor-hotels.com, Fax (0 76) 521 49 67,* , - - 25 à 150. AE VISA JCB CD b

Repas *(fermé sam. midi et dim. midi) Lunch 17* – carte 27 à 44, – 14 – **40 ch** 120/131 – ½ P 115/165.

◆ Confort et qualité d'accueil propres à l'enseigne Mercure, s'ajoutant à une situation idéale : en face de la gare, près d'un beau parc ombragé et à 700 m du centre animé. Carte avec lunch et menu. Sélection de vins "maison".

◆ Comfort en een gastvrij onthaal, zoals gebruikelijk bij Mercure, zijn hier gecombineerd met een ideale lokatie : tegenover het station, vlak bij een mooi lommerrijk park en 700 m van het levendige centrum. Kaart met lunch en menu. Wijnselectie "van het huis".

Keyser, Keizerstraat 5, ✉ 4811 HL, ✆ (0 76) 520 51 73, *info@hotel-keyser.nl, Fax (0 76) 520 52 25,* , - - 25 à 60. AE VISA. D h

Repas *(fermé 11 et 12 avril, 30 et 31 mai, 25, 26 et 31 déc., 1er janv., sam. midi et dim.) Lunch 19* – carte env. 38, – 14 – **78 ch** 112/135 – ½ P 149/164.

◆ Halte recommandable au centre de l'ancien fief des Nassau, dont vous connaîtrez l'histoire en visitant le musée voisin. Les chambres ont récemment retrouvé d'éclat du neuf.

◆ Aan te bevelen adres in het centrum van de vroegere residentie van de Nassau's, met het museum ernaast voor een stukje lokale geschiedenis. De kamers zijn onlangs gerenoveerd.

Brabant, Heerbaan 4, ✉ 4817 NL, ✆ (0 76) 522 46 66, *info@hotelbrabant.nl, Fax (0 76) 521 95 92,* , , , - - 25 à 300. AE VISA. rest B f

Repas *Lunch 20* – 22/40 – 11 – **71 ch** 112/128 – ½ P 115/137.

◆ Aux portes de Breda et à portée d'autoroute, établissement fonctionnel aussi bien équipé pour les séjours en famille que pour l'homme d'affaires ou la tenue de séminaires.

◆ Dit functionele etablissement aan de rand van Breda, dicht bij de snelweg, is zowel geschikt voor een familieuitstapje als voor een business trip of het houden van seminars.

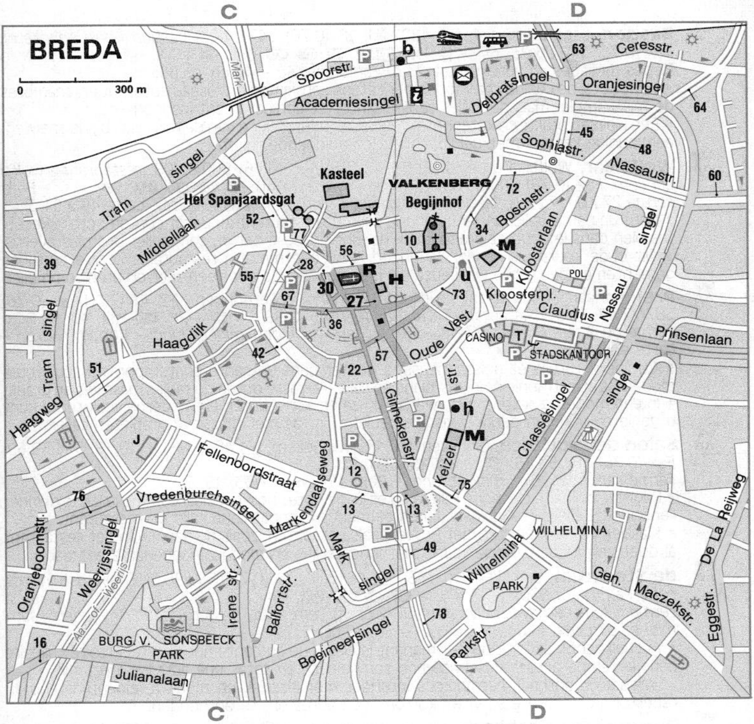

BREDA

0 — 300 m

Street	Grid	No.
Catharinastraat	CD	10
Concordiastr.	C	12
van Coothplein	CD	13
Dr. Struyckenstr.	C	16
Eindstraat	C	22
Ginnekenstraat	C	
Grote Markt	C	27
Haven	C	28
Havermarkt	C	30
J. F. Kennedylaan	D	34
Lange Brugstraat	C	36
Lunetstraat	C	39
Markendaalseweg	C	42
Mauritsstraat	D	45
Nieuwe Boschstraat	D	48
Nieuwe Ginnekenstraat	CD	49
Nieuwe Haagdijk	C	51
Nieuwe Prinsenkade	C	52
Prinsenkade	C	55
Reigerstr.	C	56
Ridderstraat	C	57
Sint Ignatiusstraat	D	60
Terheijdenstraat	D	63
Teteringenstraat	D	64
Tolbrugstraat	C	67
Valkenstraat	D	72
Veemarktstraat	D	73
Vierwindenstraat	D	75
Vincent van Goghstr.	C	76
Wihlelminastraat	D	78

Novotel, Dr. Batenburglaan 74, ✉ 4837 BR, ☎ (0 76) 565 92 20, *h0516@accor-hotels.com, Fax (0 76) 565 87 58,* – ▮ – 25 à 150. AE ① MC VISA JCB
A m

Repas *(fermé 25 et 31 déc.)* Lunch 15 – carte 22 à 45 – ☕ 15 – **106 ch** 115/125 – ½ P 75/95.

◆ Retrouvez, aux avant-postes de la ville et à un saut de puce du tronçon d'autoroute Antwerpen-Rotterdam, l'éventail habituel des prestations de la chaîne Novotel.

◆ Aan de zuidrand van de stad, vlak bij de snelweg Antwerpen-Rotterdam, wordt het gebruikelijke scala geboden van hotellerieprestaties die de Novotel-keten eigen zijn.

Campanile, Minervum 7090 (par ②), ✉ 4817 ZK, ☎ (0 76) 578 77 00, *breda@campanile.nl, Fax (0 76) 578 77 01,* – 25 à 180. AE ① MC VISA.
rest

Repas *(fermé sam. midi et dim. midi)* Lunch 9 – 22 – ☕ 10 – **83 ch** 70 – ½ P 96/98.

◆ Hôtel excentré profitant néanmoins d'une situation bien pratique aux abords de l'autoroute A27. Chambres aménagées en conformité avec les tout nouveaux standards Campanile.

◆ Dit hotel buiten de stad ligt op een heel praktische lokatie bij de A27. De kamers zijn naar de nieuwste normen van de Campanile-keten ingericht.

PAYS-BAS

Bastion, Lage Mosten 4, ✉ 4822 NJ, ☎ (0 76) 542 04 03, *bastion@bastionhotel.nl, Fax (0 76) 542 06 03,* – P. AE VISA. A s
Repas (grillades, ouvert jusqu'à 23 h) carte env. 30 – **40 ch** 69.
◆ Petit hôtel de chaîne commode pour l'étape : proximité du réseau autoroutier, chambres de mise simple, mais de tailles satisfaisantes et correctement insonorisées.
◆ Een klein en praktisch ketenhotel voor een onderbreking van de reis : vlak bij de snelweg, eenvoudige kamers met geluidsisolatie en voldoende ruimte.

XX **Wolfslaar,** Wolfslaardreef 100, ✉ 4803 EV, ☎ (0 76) 560 80 08, *restaurant@wolfslaar.com, Fax (0 76) 560 80 09,* – P. – 25 à 40. AE VISA. B b
fermé 27 juil.-17 août, 26 déc.-6 janv., dim. et lundi – **Repas** *Lunch 28* – carte 49 à 61, ♀.
◆ Dans un parc public, ancienne écurie promue restaurant au décor contemporain. Recettes bien dans le coup et grand choix de vins proposé par un sommelier des plus avertis.
◆ Dit oude koetshuis op een landgoed is nu een modern restaurant. Zeer eigentijdse gerechten en een grote wijnkeuze die is samengesteld door een zeer ervaren sommelier.

XX **Prei,** Adriaan Oomenstraat 1a (Nord-Est : 2 km à Teteringen), ✉ 4847 DH, ☎ (0 76) 587 77 17, *info@restaurantprei.nl, Fax (0 76) 572 98 37,* – P. VISA. B c
fermé du 2 au 16 août, 27 déc.-3 janv., sam. midi, dim. midi et lundi – **Repas** *Lunch 30* – carte env. 57.
◆ Cuisine naturelle et poissonneuse, à goûter dans un cadre contemporain : sculptures modernes et harmonie noir-gris-blanc en salle. Terrasse dotée de tables massives en granit.
◆ In een moderne setting van zwarte, grijze en witte tinten en moderne sculpturen kunt u genieten van een eerlijke, visrijke keuken. Terras met massieve granieten tafels.

XX **Salon de Provence,** Ginnekenweg 172 (Ginneken), ✉ 4835 NH, ☎ (0 76) 561 59 69, *Fax (0 76) 561 59 65,* – . VISA. B n
fermé sam. midi, dim. midi et lundi – **Repas** *Lunch 23* – 33/45, ♀.
◆ Registre culinaire classique relevé, ici et là, de notes provençales, comme le laisse deviner l'enseigne. Belle carte incluant lunch et menus. Sympathique salle de restaurant.
◆ Klassiek culinair register met Provençaalse accenten, zoals de naam van het restaurant al doet vermoeden. Mooie kaart, met lunchopties en menu's. Aangename eetzaal.

XX **de Stadstuin,** Ginnekenweg 138, ✉ 4818 JK, ☎ (0 76) 530 96 36, *destadstuin@cs.com, Fax (0 76) 530 97 77,* – AE VISA. B a
fermé 1 sem. carnaval, dern. sem. juil.-2 prem. sem. août, fin déc.-début janv., merc., sam. midi et dim. midi – **Repas** *Lunch 25* – 30/79 bc, ♀.
◆ Accueil gentil, décor intérieur mariant le classique au contemporain, répertoire culinaire dans le tempo actuel et service non somnolent : au total, une adresse à retenir.
◆ Vriendelijk onthaal, harmonieus interieur met klassiek en modern, eigentijds culinair repertoire en attente service : kortom, een adres om te onthouden.

XX **Boswachter Liesbosch,** Nieuwe Dreef 4 (par ⑥ : 8 km), ✉ 4839 AJ, ☎ (0 76) 521 27 36, *Fax (0 76) 520 06 34,* – P. – 25. AE VISA.
fermé lundi – **Repas** *Lunch 25* – 36/53 bc.
◆ Au milieu des bois, coquette auberge littéralement nichée sous les frondaisons de chênes et châtaigniers magnifiques. Terrasses aguichantes lorsque le soleil est là.
◆ Deze charmante herberg midden in de bossen ligt letterlijk verscholen onder het bladerdak van prachtige eiken en kastanjebomen. Verleidelijke terrassen voor zonnige dagen.

X **Boschlust,** Oosterhoutseweg 139 (Nord-Est : 2,5 km à Teteringen), ✉ 4847 DB, ☎ (0 76) 571 33 83, *info@boschlust.nl, Fax (0 76) 571 33 83,* – P. – 30. AE VISA JCB.
fermé 2 prem. sem. août, sam. midi, dim. midi et lundi – **Repas** 29/45, ♀.
◆ Grande brasserie aux abords verdoyants située en périphérie immédiate de la ville, sur la route d'Oosterhout. Lunch, menus et suggestions sur écriteau.
◆ Grote brasserie in de bosrijke omgeving net buiten de stad, aan de weg naar Oosterhout. Lunch, menu's en dagsuggesties die op een bord staan aangekondigd.

X **da Nino,** Vlaszak 2, ✉ 4811 GR, ☎ (0 76) 522 79 55, *Fax (0 76) 520 31 97,* , Cuisine italienne – VISA D u
fermé carnaval, mi-juil.-mi-août, Noël, lundi et mardi – **Repas** (dîner seult) carte 34 à 47.
◆ Définitivement terminé, le temps des pizzas ! Da Nino tourne la page et se concentre désormais sur sa cuisine toscane, sans concession aux habitudes alimentaires bataves.
◆ De tijd van de pizza's is voorbij ! Da Nino heeft zijn koers gewijzigd en richt zich nu helemaal op de Toscaanse keuken, zonder enige concessie aan de Nederlandse eetgewoonten.

à Bavel *par ③ : 5 km* C *Breda :*

XX **Vanouds de Brouwers,** Gilzeweg 24, ✉ 4854 SG, ☎ (0 161) 43 22 72, *Fax (0 161) 43 39 67,* – P. AE VISA.
fermé 2 sem. en mars, lundis et mardis non fériés, sam. midi et dim. midi – **Repas** *Lunch 25* – 40/44, ♀.
◆ Auberge traditionnelle œuvrant en face d'un petit carrefour tranquille. Repas au goût du jour. Deux terrasses estivales, dont la plus jolie est installée à l'arrière.
◆ Traditionele herberg bij een rustig klein kruispunt. Actuele keuken. Twee zomerterrassen, waarvan het mooiste aan de achterkant ligt.

à **Ulvenhout** *par ④ : 7 km* 🄲 *Alphen-Chaam 9 447 h :*

't Jagthuijs, Dorpstraat 3, ✉ 4851 CJ, ☎ (0 76) 565 69 56, *jagthuijs@zonnet.nl, Fax (0 76) 565 48 21,* – P. AE MC VISA
fermé lundi – **Repas** 30/53, ♀.
◆ Plats de saison servis dans une ancienne auberge aménagée à la façon d'un bistrot hollandais cossu. Repas à l'extérieur avec la complicité du soleil.
◆ Seizoengerechten worden hier geserveerd in een oude herberg die als een gezellige Hollandse bistro is ingericht. Bij mooi weer wordt buiten geserveerd.

BRESKENS *Zeeland* 🄲 *Sluis 24 753 h.* 532 G 14 *et* 715 B 7.

vers Vlissingen : Prov. Stoombootdiensten Zeeland ☎ (0 118) 46 09 00, Fax (0 118) 46 80 96 (Pas de voitures !). Durée de la traversée : 20 min.

Kaai 1, ✉ *4511 RC, ☎ (0 117) 38 18 88, breskens@vvvzvl.nl,* Fax (0 117) 38 38 67.
Amsterdam 213 – Middelburg 53 – Antwerpen 87 – Brugge 41.

de Milliano sans rest, Promenade 4, ✉ 4511 RB, ☎ (0 117) 38 18 55, *info@milliano.nl, Fax (0 117) 38 35 92,* ≤ embouchure de l'Escaut (Schelde), – TV P. AE ⓓ MC VISA
23 ch ☕ 120.
◆ La plupart des chambres de cet immeuble érigé à l'embouchure de l'Escaut disposent d'une kitchenette, d'un balcon et d'une jolie vue littorale. Proximité immédiate du bac.
◆ De meeste kamers in dit hotel aan de monding van de Schelde hebben een kitchenette, een balkon en een mooi uitzicht op de kust. De veerpont is vlakbij.

Scaldis, Langeweg 3, ✉ 4511 GA, ☎ (0 117) 38 24 20, *hotelscaldis@zeelandnet.nl, Fax (0 117) 38 60 21,* – TV P – 30. AE ⓓ MC VISA
fermé oct. – **Repas** (grillades) carte 22 à 36, ♀ – **10 ch** ☕ 40/66 – ½ P 51/58.
◆ Dans une rue calme du centre-ville, pavillon des années 1970 renfermant des chambres fonctionnelles, d'un format convenable et fort bien insonorisées. Accueil familial.
◆ Dit moderne pand uit de jaren zeventig staat in een rustige straat in het centrum. Functionele kamers van redelijk formaat en met goede geluidsisolatie. Gastvrije ontvangst.

de Milliano, Scheldekade 27, ✉ 4511 AW, ☎ (0 117) 38 18 12, *info@milliano.nl,* *Fax (0 117) 38 35 92,* Produits de la mer – P. AE ⓓ MC VISA
fermé janv., lundi, jeudi et après 20 h 30 – **Repas** Lunch 25 – 48/61.
◆ Petit restaurant chaleureusement habillé de lambris, ancré de longue date au bord de ce quai jouxtant la jetée et le port de pêche. Cuisine classique et de la mer.
◆ Dit restaurantje ligt al jarenlang verankerd aan de kade bij de pier en de vissershaven. Gelambriseerde eetzaal met een warme ambiance. Klassieke keuken en visgerechten.

BREUGEL *Noord-Brabant* 🄲 *Son en Breugel 14 805 h.* 532 S 13 *et* 715 H 7.

Amsterdam 114 – Eindhoven 13 – 's-Hertogenbosch 27.

de Gertruda Hoeve, Van den Elsenstraat 23, ✉ 5694 ND, ☎ (0 499) 47 10 37, *info@gertrudahoeve.nl, Fax (0 499) 47 68 84,* – P. AE ⓓ MC VISA JCB.
fermé du 20 au 25 fév., du 5 au 26 juil. et lundi – **Repas** Lunch 27 – 38/50, ♀.
◆ L'origine de cette ancienne ferme typiquement brabançonne encapuchonnée sous son toit de chaume bien peigné remonte à 1670. Ambiance intime et rustique.
◆ De oorsprong van deze voormalige, typisch Brabantse boerderij, die weggedoken ligt onder een rieten kap, gaat terug tot 1670. Intieme en rustieke ambiance.

BREUKELEN *Utrecht* 532 P 9 *et* 715 G 5 – *14 256 h.*

Env. *au Sud : route* ≤★.
Amsterdam 27 – Utrecht 12.

Breukelen, Stationsweg 91 (près A 2), ✉ 3621 LK, ☎ (0 346) 26 58 88, *info@breukelen.valk.nl, Fax (0 346) 26 28 94,* – TV P – 25 à 180. AE ⓓ MC VISA JCB
Repas (ouvert jusqu'à minuit) carte 22 à 32, ♀ – ☕ 11 – **141 ch** 83 – ½ P 73/93.
◆ Un pavillon chinois, ouvert sur un jardin conçu dans le même esprit, sert de cadre à cet établissement de la chaîne Van der Valk. Proximité de l'autoroute et de la gare. Restaurant et bar avec "lounge-library".
◆ Een Chinees paleis met tuin die in dezelfde stijl is aangelegd, vormt het originele decor van dit Van der Valk-hotel. Het ligt dicht bij de snelweg en het station. Restaurant en bar met lounge-bibliotheek.

BREUKELEVEEN *Noord-Holland* 532 P 9 *et* 715 G 5 – *voir à Oud-Loosdrecht.*

PAYS-BAS

BRIELLE *Zuid-Holland* 532 J 11 *et* 715 D 6 – *16 001 h.*

Krabbeweg 9, 3231 NB, (0 181) 41 78 09, Fax (0 181) 41 00 26.
Amsterdam 100 – Rotterdam 29 – Den Haag (bac) 37 – Breda 75.

De Zalm, Voorstraat 6, 3231 BJ, (0 181) 41 33 88, *Fax (0 181) 41 77 12* – ch, TV P. AE VISA. – *fermé Noël et Nouvel An* – **Repas** *(fermé dim. et après 20 h 30)* carte 34 à 43 – **35 ch** 75/120.
◆ Établissement central où descend volontiers la clientèle d'affaires en visite à l'Europoort. Chambres de différentes tailles réparties entre plusieurs maisons anciennes. Salle à manger bourgeoise. Registre culinaire classico-traditionnel.
◆ Centraal gelegen etablissement waar zakelijke Europoortgangers graag te gast zijn. De kamers variëren in grootte en liggen verspreid over enkele oude panden. Klassieke eetzaal. Klassiek-traditioneel culinair register.

Bastion, Amer 1, 3232 HA, (0 181) 41 65 88, *bastion@bastionhotel.nl, Fax (0 181) 41 01 15* – TV P. AE VISA.
Repas (grillades, ouvert jusqu'à 23 h) carte env. 30 – 10 – **66 ch** 72.
◆ Aux portes de la ville, copie conforme de toutes les structures hôtelières arborant l'enseigne aux trois lunes. Chambres fonctionnelles récemment rafraîchies.
◆ Aan de rand van de stad staat een exacte kopie van de hotels die onder de Nederlandse keten met de drie manen vallen. De functionele kamers zijn onlangs opgeknapt.

Pablo, Voorstraat 89, 3231 BG, (0 181) 41 29 60, *ind.rest.pablo@planet.nl, Fax (0 181) 41 02 06*, Cuisine indonésienne – . AE VISA
fermé 20 sept.-20 oct. et lundis non fériés – **Repas** carte 22 à 35.
◆ Bientôt trente ans de présence pour cette bonne table indonésienne au décor présidé par poutres, arcades en briques, collection de vieux pistolets et récipients en étain.
◆ Al bijna dertig jaar geeft dit goede Indonesische restaurant acte de présence in een decor van balken, bogen en bakstenen. Collectie oude pistolen en tinnen schalen.

BROEKHUIZEN *Limburg* C *Horst aan de Maas 28 476 h.* 532 V 14 *et* 715 J 7.

Amsterdam 167 – Eindhoven 60 – Nijmegen 60 – Venlo 28.

't Veerhuis avec ch, Veerweg 11, 5872 AE, (0 77) 463 21 14, *het.veerhuis@wxs.nl, Fax (0 77) 463 28 67*, <, , – TV P. AE VISA JCB.
fermé carnaval – **Repas** Lunch 32 – 45/80 bc – **10 ch** 75/125, – 2 suites – ½ P 85/115.
◆ Ancien café de passeurs d'eau agrandi d'une construction neuve abritant de grandes et quiètes chambres dont les balcons contemplent la Meuse. Cuisine actuelle.
◆ Dit voormalige veerhuis is uitgebreid met een nieuwe aanbouw waarin grote, rustige kamers zijn ingericht. De balkons kijken uit op de Maas. Eigentijdse keuken.

BROEK OP LANGEDIJK *Noord-Holland* C *Langedijk 24 724 h.* 531 N 6 *et* 715 F 3.

Amsterdam 48 – Alkmaar 11 – Den Helder 38 – Hoorn 25.

Akkers, Stationsweg 3, 1721 CD, (0 226) 32 03 28, *mail@restaurantakkers.nl, Fax (0 226) 34 04 64*, – P. – 25. VISA JCB.
fermé lundi et mardi – **Repas** (déjeuner sur réservation) carte 38 à 49.
◆ Chaises drapées, parquet reluisant, murs orangés et plafond paré de tissu blanc concourent à l'élégance contemporaine de cette salle à manger officiant depuis les années 1930.
◆ Gedrapeerde stoelen, glimmend parket, oranje getinte muren, wit bekleed plafond... Kortom, eigentijdse elegantie voor een restaurant dat sinds 1930 de deuren heeft openstaan.

BROUWERSHAVEN *Zeeland* C *Schouwen-Duiveland 34 503 h.* 532 I 12 *et* 715 C 6.

Amsterdam 143 – Middelburg 57 – Rotterdam 79.

De Brouwerie, Molenstraat 31, 4318 BS, (0 111) 69 18 80, *Fax (0 111) 69 25 51*, – P. AE VISA JCB
fermé mars, du 7 au 14 juin, du 15 au 24 nov., du 10 au 26 janv., merc. de nov. à mars, lundi sauf en juil.-août et mardi – **Repas** (déjeuner sur réservation) 25/48.
◆ Cette maisonnette de pêcheurs reconvertie borde une rue calme entre le centre-ville et le port de plaisance. Ambiance rustique, plats bourgeois et choix de vins intéressant.
◆ Dit verbouwde vissershuis staat aan een rustige straat tussen het centrum en de jachthaven. Rustieke ambiance, eenvoudige maar goede keuken en interessante wijnen.

BRUINISSE *Zeeland* C *Schouwen-Duiveland 34 503 h.* 532 J 13 *et* 715 D 7.

Amsterdam 156 – Middelburg 56 – Breda 95 – Rotterdam 81.

De Vluchthaven, Zijpe 1 (par Rijksstraatweg), 4311 RK, (0 111) 48 12 28, <, , Produits de la mer, – P. VISA
fermé 1 sem. en juin, lundi et mardi – **Repas** 27/33.
◆ Jolie vue sur la sortie d'une écluse de l'Oosterschelde, depuis la terrasse estivale et la rotonde de ce petit restaurant servant une cuisine d'inspiration méditerranéenne.
◆ Geen nood, in dit restaurantje bent u veilig ! Het zomerterras en de ronde eetzaal bieden mooi uitzicht op een sluis in de Oosterschelde. Mediterraan georiënteerde keuken.

BRUMMEN *Gelderland* 532 V 10 *et* 715 J 5 – *21 613 h.*
Amsterdam 113 – Arnhem 22 – Apeldoorn 25 – Enschede 63.

Kasteel Landgoed Engelenburg ⑤, Eerbeekseweg 6, ✉ 6971 LB, ☎ (0 575) 56 99 99, *info@engelenburg.com, Fax (0 575) 56 99 92*, ←, ☂, ☂, ✂, ☆ – |‡|, ▤ ch, TV P – ♣ 25 à 80. AE ① ⓪ VISA. ✂
fermé 24 déc.-4 janv. – **Repas** *(fermé sam. midi et dim. midi) Lunch 35* – carte 36 à 47, ♀ – ☐ 17 – **30 ch** 135 – ½ P 115/185.
• Un beau parc où les golfeurs s'en donnent à cœur joie borde cette fastueuse demeure ceinturée de douves. Chambres "king size" décorées avec goût, parfois en style colonial. Repas classique dans la véranda. Cave sud-africaine et collection de whiskies.
• Weelderig buitenverblijf met een slotgracht en een park waar golfers naar hartenlust aan de slag kunnen. Vorstelijke en smaakvolle kamers, sommige in koloniale stijl. Klassieke maaltijden in de serre. Zuid-Afrikaanse wijnkelder en collectie whisky's.

BUNNIK *Utrecht* 532 Q 10 *et* 715 G 5 – *13 845 h.*
Amsterdam 49 – Utrecht 9 – Arnhem 52.

Mercure, Kosterijland 8 (sur A 12), ✉ 3981 AJ, ☎ (0 30) 656 92 22, *h2113@accor-hotels.com, Fax (0 30) 656 40 74*, ☆ – |‡| ✂, ▤ rest, TV ♿ P – ♣ 25 à 300. AE ① ⓪ VISA
Repas *(fermé sam. midi et dim. midi)* carte 31 à 39, ♀ – ☐ 14 – **80 ch** 112/142 – ½ P 74/163.
• Hôtel de chaîne fonctionnel posté à la sortie de l'autoroute A 12 qui dessert Bunnik. Chambres de plain-pied et à l'étage. Nombreuses salles de réunions.
• Functioneel ketenhotel bij de afslag Bunnik van de A12. De kamers liggen op de begane grond en de verdieping. Grote hoeveelheid vergaderzalen.

BUNSCHOTEN *Utrecht* 532 R 9 *et* 715 H 5 – *19 327 h.*
Voir *Costumes traditionnels*★.
ℹ *Oude Schans 90 à Spakenburg, ✉ 3752 AH, ☎ (0 33) 298 21 56, info@vvvspakenburg.nl, Fax (0 33) 299 62 35.*
Amsterdam 46 – Utrecht 32 – Amersfoort 12 – Apeldoorn 52.

à Spakenburg *Nord : 2,5 km* Ⓒ *Bunschoten :*

✗✗ **de Mandemaaker,** Kerkstraat 103, ✉ 3751 AT, ☎ (0 33) 298 02 55, *info@demandemaaker.nl, Fax (0 33) 298 03 55*, ☂ – AE ① ⓪ VISA JCB
fermé dim. – **Repas** *Lunch 27* – carte 34 à 57, ♀.
• Affluence touristique à cette enseigne de Spakenburg, petite cité célèbre pour son mode de vie resté traditionnel, bâtie au bord d'un lac où l'on taquine l'anguille.
• Een toeristische trekpleister, dit restaurantje. Het stadje met zijn nog bestaande traditionele leefgewoonten ligt aan een meer waar paling wordt gevangen.

BUREN (BUEREN) *Fryslân* 531 T 2 *et* 715 I 1 – *voir à Waddeneilanden (Ameland).*

BUREN *Gelderland* 532 R 11 *et* 715 H 6 – *25 609 h.*
18 9 *à l'Est : 4 km à Zoelen, Oost Kanaalweg 1, ✉ 4011 LA, ☎ (0 344) 62 43 70, Fax (0 344) 61 30 96.*
Amsterdam 74 – Utrecht 37 – 's-Hertogenbosch 29 – Nijmegen 48.

✗✗✗ **Gravin van Buren,** Kerkstraat 4, ✉ 4116 BL, ☎ (0 344) 57 16 63, *gravin@alliance.nl, Fax (0 344) 57 21 81*, ☂ – AE ① ⓪ VISA
fermé 30 avril, 20 juil.-9 août, 5 déc., 21 déc.-3 janv., sam. midi, dim. et lundi – **Repas** *Lunch 43* – 63/75, ♀.
• À l'ombre du clocher, petite demeure paroissiale convertie en agréable maison de bouche. Mets classico-créatifs et beau choix de vins du monde. Jolie terrasse d'été.
• Het kleine parochiehuis in de schaduw van de klokkentoren is tot een aangenaam eethuis verbouwd. Creatieve, klassieke keuken en mooie selectie wereldwijnen. Fraai zomerterras.

✗ **Brasserie Floris,** Kerkstraat 5, ✉ 4116 BL, ☎ (0 344) 57 27 70, *Fax (0 344) 57 21 81*, ☂ – AE ① ⓪ VISA
fermé 30 avril, 20 juil.-9 août, 21 déc.-3 janv., dim. et lundi – **Repas** (dîner seult) 28, ♀.
• Brasserie décontractée occupant l'une des anciennes habitations ouvrières de la ruelle qui contourne l'église. La salle à manger, assez coquette, s'étage sur deux niveaux.
• Brasserie met een ongedwongen ambiance, die te vinden is in een van de oude arbeiderswoningen in het straatje rond de kerk. Vrij verzorgde eetzaal met twee niveaus.

Den BURG *Noord-Holland* 531 N 4 *et* 715 F 2 – *voir à Waddeneilanden (Texel).*

BURGH-HAAMSTEDE *Zeeland* C *Schouwen-Duiveland 34 503 h.* 532 H 12 *et* 715 C 6.
Amsterdam 142 – Middelburg 37 – Rotterdam 69.

Duinhotel, Torenweg 1 (Nieuw-Haamstede), ✉ 4328 JC, ☎ (0 111) 88 77 66, *info@duinhotel.nl, Fax (0 111) 88 77 55,* ≤, , , , – , ▣ ℗ – 25 à 250. AE ⓓ ⓜ VISA.
Repas 26/36 – **41 ch** ☐ 90/140 – ½ P 89.
◆ Hôtel récent élevé devant une piste de vol à voile, à la lisière les dunes et d'un parc national. Chambres de belle ampleur, espaces de réunions et grande terrasse d'été. Restaurant où vous serez au premières loges pour profiter du spectacle des planeurs.
◆ Dit nieuwe hotelcomplex ligt aan de rand van de duinen en een natuurgebied en kijkt uit op een zweefvliegveld. Ruime kamers, vergaderzalen en groot zomerterras. In het restaurant kunt u in stijl genieten van de capriolen van de zweefvliegers.

BUSSUM *Noord-Holland* 531 P 9, 532 P 9 *et* 715 G 5 – *31 014 h.*
Amsterdam 21 – Apeldoorn 66 – Utrecht 30.

NH Jan Tabak, Amersfoortsestraatweg 27, ✉ 1401 CV, ☎ (0 35) 695 99 11, *nhjantabak@nh-hotels.nl, Fax (0 35) 695 94 16,* , – , ▣ , ℗ – 25 à 350. AE ⓓ ⓜ VISA. ch
Repas *The Garden* *(fermé 19 juil.-15 août, 27 déc.-4 janv., sam. et dim.)* Lunch 35 – carte 42 à 56, ♀ – ☐ 15 – **86 ch** 180, – 1 suite – ½ P 175/235.
◆ Établissement haut de gamme, récemment entré dans le giron de la chaîne espagnole NH. Chambres décorées sans faute de goût, salon "cosy" et bonne infrastructure conférencière. Brasserie cossue s'ouvrant sur un jardin où l'on dresse quelques tables en été.
◆ Dit eersteklas etablissement is onlangs toegetreden tot de Spaanse hotelketen NH. Zeer smaakvolle kamers, behaaglijke lounge, goede infrastructuur voor bijeenkomsten en seminars. Luxueuze brasserie en een tuin waar 's zomers enkele tafels worden gedekt.

CADZAND *Zeeland* C *Sluis 24 755 h.* 532 F 14 *et* 715 B 7.
ℹ *Boulevard de Wielingen 44d à Cadzand-Bad,* ✉ *4506 JK,* ☎ *(0 117) 39 12 98, cadzand@vvvzvl.nl, Fax (0 117) 39 25 60.*
Amsterdam 224 – Brugge 29 – Middelburg 64 – Gent 53 – Knokke-Heist 12.

à Cadzand-Bad *Nord-Ouest : 3 km* C *Sluis :*

De Blanke Top, Boulevard de Wielingen 1, ✉ 4506 JH, ☎ (0 117) 39 20 40, *info@blanketop.nl, Fax (0 117) 39 14 27,* ≤ mer et dunes, , , , – , rest, ▣ ℗ – 25 à 45. AE ⓓ ⓜ VISA JCB
fermé 5 janv.-12 fév. – **Repas** 36/60 – **48 ch** ☐ 91/216 – ½ P 89/145.
◆ Réparties sur trois étages, la plupart des chambres de ce confortable hôtel isolé dans les dunes disposent d'un balcon d'où l'on embrasse du regard toute la plage. Recettes classiques servies dans la salle à manger panoramique ou sous la coupole de la taverne.
◆ Dit afgelegen, comfortabele hotel in de duinen telt drie verdiepingen met kamers, waarvan de meeste een balkon hebben met uitzicht over het strand. Klassieke gerechten, die worden geserveerd in de panoramische eetzaal of onder de koepel van het restaurant.

Strandhotel, Boulevard de Wielingen 49, ✉ 4506 JK, ☎ (0 117) 39 21 10, *info@strandhotel-cadzand.nl, Fax (0 117) 39 15 35,* ≤, , , , – , rest, ▣ ℗ – 25 à 50. AE ⓓ ⓜ VISA. rest
fermé 21 nov.-17 déc. – **Repas** *(fermé après 20 h 30)* 38 – **43 ch** ☐ 83/130.
◆ Résidence hôtelière récente postée à flanc de dune, en léger retrait du boulevard. La majorité des chambres, réactualisées, s'agrémentent d'un balcon ou d'une terrasse. Table procurant une jolie perspective littorale. Terasse d'été.
◆ Dit moderne hotelgebouw staat iets van de boulevard af, tegen de duin. De kamers zijn in een nieuw jasje gestoken en de meeste zijn voorzien van balkon of terras. Het restaurant biedt een mooi uitzicht op de kust. Zomerterras.

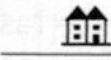

Noordzee, Noordzeestraat 2, ✉ 4506 KM, ☎ (0 117) 39 18 10, *info@hotelnoordzee.com, Fax (0 117) 39 14 16,* ≤, , , – , rest, ▣ ℗ – 30. AE ⓓ ⓜ VISA
fermé 7 janv.-7 fév. – **Repas** *(fermé après 20 h 30)* Lunch 25 – carte 35 à 52 – **24 ch** ☐ 99/142, – 10 suites – ½ P 70/93.
◆ Exposées aux embruns, tranquilles chambres et suites garnies de meubles en bois exotique et dotées d'une terrasse ou d'un balcon et, parfois, d'une kitchenette. Salle à manger agrémentée d'une véranda. Recettes de la mer et plats plus "terre à terre".
◆ Dit hotel ligt op een duin direct aan zee. De kamers en suites zijn ingericht met meubels van exotisch hout en voorzien van terras of balkon, sommige van een kitchenette. Eetzaal met serre. Visgerechten en traditionele schotels.

De Wielingen, Kanaalweg 1, ✉ 4506 KN, ℘ (0 117) 39 15 11, *wieling@xs4all.nl*, *Fax (0 117) 39 16 30*, ≤, – ♿, ▤ rest, TV ♿ P – 25 à 40. AE MC VISA
Repas *(fermé après 20 h 30)* Lunch 13 – carte 32 à 62 – **31 ch** ☐ 60/140.
◆ Ambiances familiales, jeux d'enfants, proximité immédiate de l'estran, chambres bien calibrées et appartements avec kitchenette. Un bon petit hôtel de plage, en somme. Repas sagement classiques, et sans mondanités.
◆ Gezellige sfeer, speelfaciliteiten voor kinderen, direct aan het strand, ruime kamers en appartementen met kitchenette. Kortom, een goed en niet al te groot strandhotel. Eerlijke keuken met degelijke, klassieke gerechten.

De Schelde, Scheldestraat 1, ✉ 4506 KL, ℘ (0 117) 39 17 20, *info@hoteldeschelde.nl*, *Fax (0 117) 39 22 24*, – TV P – 30. AE ① MC VISA JCB.
Repas *(fermé mardi et merc.)* Lunch 29 – carte 36 à 61, ♀ – **29 ch** ☐ 100/121 – ½ P 59/75.
◆ Petit établissement familial situé à l'entrée de la station. Chambres de mise simple mais assez coquettes, peu à peu rafraîchies et correctement insonorisées. Intime salle de restaurant d'esprit néo-rustique.
◆ Dit kleine familiehotel ligt aan de rand van de badplaats en beschikt over eenvoudige, maar vrij nette kamers die geleidelijk worden opgeknapt en zijn voorzien van geluidsisolatie. Intieme restaurantzaal met neorustiek decor.

CALLANTSOOG *Noord-Holland* C *Zijpe 11 316 h.* 531 N 5 *et* 715 F 3.

Jewelweg 8, ✉ 1759 HA, ℘ (0 224) 58 40 40, callantsoog@vvv-knh.nl, Fax (0 224) 58 15 40.

Amsterdam 67 – Alkmaar 27 – Den Helder 22.

Strandhotel Landgoed de Horn sans rest, Previnaireweg 4a, ✉ 1759 GX, ℘ (0 224) 58 12 42, *info@strandhoteldehorn.nl*, *Fax (0 224) 58 25 18*, ≤, – TV P – 30. MC VISA.
avril-oct. – **30 ch** ☐ 67/95.
◆ Un écran de verdure protège les deux ailes de cet hôtel dont le jardin s'agrémente d'un étang. Chambres fonctionnelles et confortables. Les meilleures sont à l'arrière.
◆ Een groenstrook beschermt de twee vleugels van dit hotel, waarvan de tuin is opgeluisterd met een vijver. Functionele, comfortabele kamers. De beste liggen aan de achterkant.

CAMPERDUIN *Noord-Holland* 531 M 6 *et* 715 E 3 – *voir à Schoorl.*

CAPELLE AAN DEN IJSSEL *Zuid-Holland* 532 M 11 *et* 715 E 6 – *voir à Rotterdam, environs.*

CASTRICUM *Noord-Holland* 531 M 7 *et* 715 E 4 – *23 330 h.*

Amsterdam 33 – Haarlem 20 – Alkmaar 11.

Apicius (de Winter), Van der Mijleweg 16 (Nord-Ouest : 2 km, lieu-dit Bakkum), ✉ 1901 KD, ℘ (0 251) 67 67 60, *info@restaurantapicius.com*, *Fax (0 251) 67 64 04*, – ▤. AE ① MC VISA
fermé 2 prem. sem. juil., 2e sem. oct., lundi et mardi – **Repas** Lunch 44 bc – 35/50, carte 44 à 62, ♀.
◆ Bonne table œuvrant au centre d'un hameau. Salon doté de fauteuils en cuir et salle au cadre actuel soigné. Cuisine créative escortée de grands crus du Bordelais et du monde.
◆ Een fijne keuken in het hartje van dit gehucht. Salon met lederen zetels. Verzorgd interieur. Creatieve kaart. Uitstekende bordeaux- en wereldwijnen.
Spéc. Suprême de turbot braisé à la truffe et betteraves rouges (automne-hiver). Risotto de homard et ris de veau croustillant. Crème brûlée à l'advocaat et glace vanille

Le Moulin, Dorpsstraat 96, ✉ 1901 EN, ℘ (0 251) 65 15 00, – AE ① MC VISA.
fermé lundi et mardi – **Repas** (déjeuner sur réservation) carte env. 47, ♀.
◆ Repas classico-traditionnel servi non pas dans un moulin - quoi qu'en dise l'enseigne -, mais dans une maison ancienne. Salle à manger rustique patiemment entretenue.
◆ De klassiek-traditionele gerechten worden niet geserveerd in een molen - ook al wekt de naam wel die indruk - maar in een oud huis. Met zorg onderhouden, rustieke eetzaal.

CHAMPS DE FLEURS – *voir Bollenvelden.*

De COCKSDORP *Noord-Holland* 531 O 4 *et* 715 F 2 – *voir à Waddeneilanden (Texel).*

COEVORDEN *Drenthe* 531 Z 7 *et* 715 L 4 – *35 756 h.*

Haven 2, ✉ 7741 JV, ☎ (0 524) 52 51 50, vvvcoevorden@vvvzuidoostdrenthe.nl, Fax (0 524) 51 19 23.

Amsterdam 163 – Assen 54 – Enschede 72 – Groningen 75 – Zwolle 53.

XX **Gasterie Het Kasteel,** Kasteel 29, ✉ 7741 GC, ☎ (0 524) 51 21 70, *gasterie-hetkasteel@wanadoo.nl, Fax (0 524) 51 57 80,* – P. AE ⓓ MC VISA
fermé fin juil.-mi-août, 28 déc.-8 janv., sam. midi, dim. et lundi – **Repas** Lunch 24 – 28/47 bc, ♀.
• La cave voûtée d'un castel plusieurs fois remanié abrite ce restaurant proposant un choix de mets classiques présentés à la mode d'aujourd'hui. Jolie terrasse estivale.
• De gewelfde kelder van een meermaals verbouwd kasteel herbergt dit restaurant, waar klassieke gerechten in een eigentijds jasje worden geserveerd. Mooi zomerterras.

CROMVOIRT *Noord-Brabant* C *Vught 25 610 h.* 532 Q 13 *et* 715 G 7.

Amsterdam 93 – Eindhoven 36 – 's-Hertogenbosch 9.

XX **Busio,** Sint Lambertusstraat 59, ✉ 5266 AD, ☎ (0 411) 64 38 88, *info@restaurant-busio.nl, Fax (0 411) 64 48 99* – AE ⓓ MC VISA
fermé carnaval, sam. midi, dim. midi, lundi et mardi – **Repas** Lunch 33 – 43.
• À quelques minutes de 's-Hertogenbosch, ferme du 19e s. entièrement rénovée, prêtant ses murs à une spacieuse salle de restaurant contemporaine. Cuisine au goût du jour.
• Op enkele minuten van Den Bosch is in deze 19e-eeuwse, volledig gerenoveerde boerderij een ruime, eigentijdse eetzaal ingericht. De keuken volgt de smaak van het moment.

CUIJK *Noord-Brabant* 532 U 12 *et* 715 I 6 – *24 415 h.*

Amsterdam 130 – Arnhem 41 – 's-Hertogenbosch 46 – Eindhoven 58 – Nijmegen 22.

Cuijk, Raamweg 10, ✉ 5431 NH, ☎ (0 485) 33 51 23, *sales@cuijk.valk.nl, Fax (0 485) 33 51 24,* – TV P – 25 à 400. AE ⓓ MC VISA JCB
Repas (ouvert jusqu'à 23 h) Lunch 13 – carte 22 à 53, ♀ – **76 ch** 62 – ½ P 45.
• Confortable hôtel de chaîne proche de l'autoroute Nijmegen-Keulen (Cologne) et de la frontière germano-batave. Chambres avenantes et bien tenues. Centre de conférences.
• Comfortabel ketenhotel vlak bij de snelweg Nijmegen-Keulen en de Duits-Nederlandse grens. Aangename, goed onderhouden kamers. Congrescentrum.

XX **Carpe Diem,** Kerkstraat 1, ✉ 5431 DS, ☎ (0 485) 31 88 90, *restaurantcarpediem@hotmail.com, Fax (0 485) 31 55 53,* – MC VISA
fermé 1 sem. carnaval, 3 dern. sem. juin, sam. midi, dim. midi, lundi et mardi – **Repas** Lunch 25 – 34/52 bc, ♀.
• Une adresse appréciée des bons vivants, comme son enseigne le laisse deviner. S'il s'agit d'expier un éventuel péché de gourmandise, l'église se trouve juste en face !
• Pluk de dag ! Rasechte bon-vivants zullen zich hier prima thuis voelen. En wie zijn boekje te buiten is gegaan, kan aan de overkant zijn zonde opbiechten !

DALFSEN *Overijssel* 531 W 7 *et* 715 J 4 – *26 061 h.*

Prinsenstraat 18, ✉ 7721 AJ, ☎ (0 529) 43 37 11, info.dalfsen@vechtdalvvv.nl, Fax (0 529) 43 46 27.

Amsterdam 130 – Zwolle 20 – Assen 64 – Enschede 64.

Hof van Dalfsen, Haersolteweg 3, ✉ 7722 SE, ☎ (0 529) 43 18 18, *info@hofvandalfsen.nl, Fax (0 529) 43 48 92,* – TV P – 25 à 300. AE ⓓ MC VISA
fermé 1er janv. – **Repas** Lunch 19 – 23 – **17 ch** 50/82 – ½ P 54/69.
• Cet établissement entouré de verdure renferme des chambres fonctionnelles réparties sur deux étages et plusieurs salles équipées pour la tenue de séminaires. À table, plats classico-traditionnels et menu à prix doux.
• Dit etablissement midden in het groen heeft functionele kamers die over twee verdiepingen verspreid liggen en diverse zalen voor seminars. In het restaurant worden klassiek-traditionele gerechten à la carte geserveerd en een menu voor een zacht prijsje.

X **De Witte Gans,** Heinoseweg 30 (Sud : 4 km direction Heino), ✉ 7722 JP, ☎ (0 529) 43 05 15, *Fax (0 529) 43 59 75,* – P. MC VISA
fermé mardi – **Repas** (dîner seult sauf dim.) 27/52 bc, ♀.
• La carte, au goût du jour, pourrait faire un jeu de l'oie... Côté fourneaux, toutefois, on n'a pas affaire à une "oie blanche" (witte gans) ! Cadre champêtre en terrasse.
• De eigentijdse kaart zou misschien als ganzenbord kunnen dienen... Achter het fornuis weet deze gans in elk geval wel raad met de pionnen ! Terras in een landelijk decor.

De – *voir au nom propre.*

DEIL *Gelderland* C *Geldermalsen 25 055 h.* 532 Q 11 et 715 G 6.

Amsterdam 63 – Utrecht 33 – Arnhem 56 – Gorinchem 28 – 's-Hertogenbosch 25.

X **de Os en het Paard** avec ch, Deilsedijk 73, ✉ 4158 EG, ☎ (0 345) 65 16 13, *info@osenpaard.nl, Fax (0 345) 65 22 87,* – TV P. AE ① MC VISA JCB. ch

fermé 19 juil.-9 août et 27 déc.-2 fév. – **Repas** *(fermé sam. midi, dim. et lundi)* Lunch 25 – 32/45 – **4 ch** 87/115 – ½ P 88.

◆ Auberge engageante dont l'enseigne - un bœuf (os) et un cheval (paard) - se réfère aux armes de la localité. Préparations classiques bataves. Chambres personnalisées.

◆ De naam van deze gasterij verwijst naar het wapen van het stadje. Klassieke, Nederlandse keuken. De kamers hebben elk een geheel eigen ambiance.

DELDEN *Overijssel* C *Hof van Twente 35 041 h.* 531 Z 9, 532 Z 9 et 715 L 5.

Langestraat 29, ✉ 7491 AA, ☎ (0 74) 376 63 63, info@vvvdelden.nl, Fax (0 74) 376 63 64.

Amsterdam 144 – Zwolle 60 – Apeldoorn 59 – Enschede 17.

Carelshaven, Hengelosestraat 30, ✉ 7491 BR, ☎ (0 74) 376 13 05, *info@carelshaven.nl, Fax (0 74) 376 12 91,* – TV P – 40. AE ① MC VISA JCB

fermé 27 déc.-9 janv. – **Repas** Lunch 32 – 42, ♀ – 10 – **20 ch** 70/90 – ½ P 95/105.

◆ Aux portes de Delden, hôtellerie de tradition tenue par la même famille depuis 1837. Chambres de bon confort, jardin bichonné et terrasse royale. L'été, on peut s'attabler au grand air, et en hiver, dans la nostalgique Gelagkamer. Carte actuelle. Belle cave.

◆ Dit traditionele hotel aan de rand van Delden wordt sinds 1837 door dezelfde familie gerund. Comfortabele kamers, verzorgde tuin, royaal terras. 's Zomers kan er buiten worden getafeld, 's winters in de nostalgische Gelagkamer. Eigentijdse kaart, mooie wijnen.

Aparthotel, Sportlaan 7, ✉ 7490 AA, ☎ (0 74) 377 76 66, *info@aparthoteldelden.nl, Fax (0 74) 377 76 77,* – rest, TV P – 25 à 125. AE ① MC VISA.

Repas Lunch 13 – 22/39, ♀ – **63 ch** 69/88 – ½ P 61/99.

◆ Les chambres et junior suites de cet hôtel sont en fait des studios équipés d'une kitchenette. Activités sportives et distractions en rapport avec la nature environnante.

◆ De kamers en junior suites in dit hotel zijn in feite appartementen met een kitchenette. Sportfaciliteiten. Tal van recreatieve mogelijkheden in een prachtige natuur.

XX **In den Drost van Twenthe** avec ch, Hengelosestraat 8, ✉ 7491 BR, ☎ (0 74) 376 40 55, *Fax (0 74) 376 54 12,* – TV P – 40. AE ① MC VISA JCB. rest

Repas *(fermé 1 sem. carnaval, dim. et lundi)* (dîner seult) 33/43, ♀ – **6 ch** 66/105.

◆ Ferme-auberge élevée au 19e s. à proximité du château Twickel et aujourd'hui convertie en restaurant. Registre culinaire bien dans le coup. Grandes chambres en rez-de-jardin.

◆ Deze 19e-eeuwse herenboerderij nabij het kasteel van Twickel herbergt nu een restaurant. Eigentijds culinair register. Grote kamers op de begane grond, aan de tuinzijde.

X **in den Weijenborg,** Spoorstraat 16, ✉ 7491 CK, ☎ (0 74) 376 30 79, *info@restaurant-weijenborg.nl, Fax (0 74) 376 13 27,* – AE ① MC VISA

fermé 29 fév.-5 mars, mardi et merc. – **Repas** (dîner seult jusqu'à 23 h) 25.

◆ Déjà plus de vingt ans d'activité pour ce restaurant sympathique installé dans ce qui fut jadis une écurie. Décor intérieur rustique et préparations sagement actualisées.

◆ Al ruim 20 jaar wordt door dit sympathieke restaurant gekokereld in wat vroeger een paardenstal was. Rustiek decor. Gerechten die met zorg aan de moderne smaak zijn aangepast.

DELFT *Zuid-Holland* 532 L 10 et 715 E 5 – *96 936 h.*

Voir *Nouvelle Église★ (Nieuwe Kerk) : mausolée de Guillaume le Taciturne★, de la tour ≤★ CDY – Vieux canal★ (Oude Delft) CYZ – Pont de Nieuwstraat ≤★ CY – Porte de l'Est★ (Oostpoort) DZ – Promenade sur les canaux★ CZ – Centre historique et canaux★★.*

Musées : *Prinsenhof★ CY – Museum Lambert van Meerten★ : collection de carreaux de faïence★ CY* **M²** *– Royal de l'Armée des Pays-Bas★ (Koninklijk Nederlands Legermuseum) CZ* **M¹**.

18 *à l'Est : 12 km à Bergschenhoek, Rottebandreef 40, ✉ 2661 JK, ☎ (0 10) 522 07 03, Fax (0 10) 521 93 50.*

Hippolytusbuurt 4, ✉ 2611 HN, ☎ (0 15) 215 40 51, info@tipdelft.nl, Fax (0 15) 215 40 55.

Amsterdam 58 ④ – Rotterdam 16 ① – Den Haag 13 ④ – Utrecht 62 ④

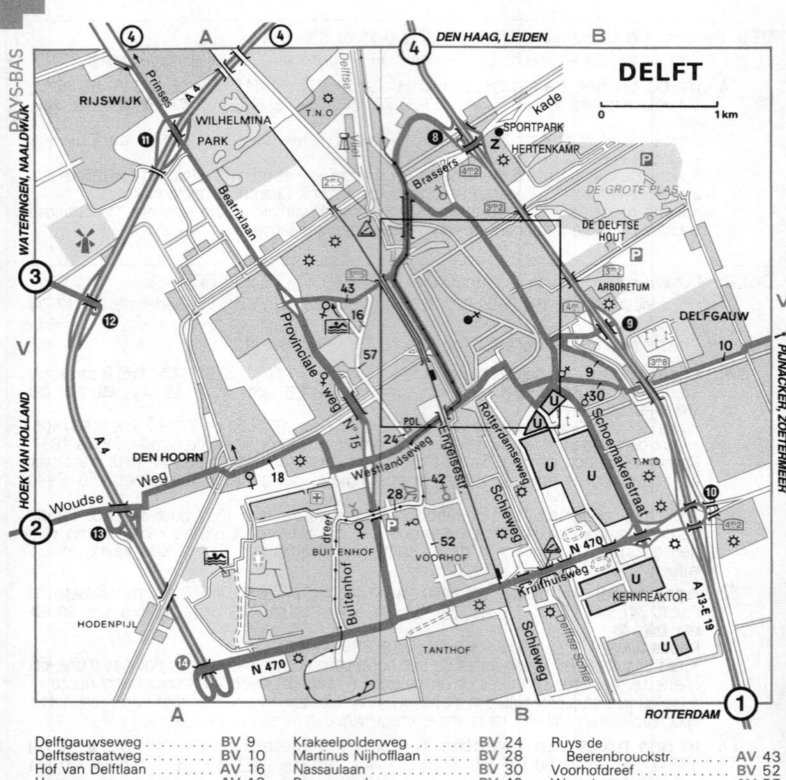

Delftgauwseweg	BV 9	Krakeelpolderweg	BV 24	Ruys de Beerenbrouckstr.	AV 43
Delftsestraatweg	BV 10	Martinus Nijhofflaan	BV 28	Voorhofdreef	BV 52
Hof van Delftlaan	AV 16	Nassaulaan	BV 30	Westplantsoen	AV 57
Hoornseweg	AV 18	Papsouwselaan	BV 42		

Museumhotel (annexe Residence - 21 ch et 2 suites) sans rest, Oude Delft 189, 2611 HD, (0 15) 215 30 70, *info@museumhotel.nl, Fax (0 15) 215 30 79* – AE VISA JCB CY a
fermé 23 déc.-2 janv. – 15 – **30 ch** 115/170.
• Un point de chute tenant un peu du musée, idéalement situé pour découvrir le vieux Delft. L'annexe, décorée de céramiques modernes, renferme les meilleures chambres.
• Pleisterplaats en museum tegelijk, op een ideale lokatie voor een ontdekkingstocht door het oude Delft. De annexe is met modern keramiek gedecoreerd en heeft de beste kamers.

Johannes Vermeer sans rest, Molslaan 18, 2611 RM, (0 15) 212 64 66, *info@hotelvermeer.nl, Fax (0 15) 213 48 35* – – 25. AE VISA JCB. DY t
25 ch 112/125.
• Un ensemble de copies de toiles de Vermeer - l'enfant du pays - agrémente l'intérieur de cet hôtel rénové regroupant plusieurs maisons patriciennes. Chambres plaisantes.
• Kopieën van doeken van Vermeer sieren het interieur van dit gerenoveerde hotel, dat zijn intrek heeft genomen in enkele patriciërshuizen. Gerieflijke kamers.

Bridges House sans rest, Oude Delft 74, 2611 CD, (0 15) 212 40 36, *info@bridges-house.com, Fax (0 15) 213 36 00* – VISA. CZ k
8 ch 113/245.
• Proche de la gare et du cœur historique, cette maison où vécut le peintre Jan Steen - célèbre pour ses scènes de genre - abrite des junior suites aménagées avec goût.
• Dit pand vlak bij het station en het historische centrum was het woonhuis van Jan Steen, die beroemd werd om zijn genreschilderijen. Smaakvol ingerichte junior suites.

DELFT

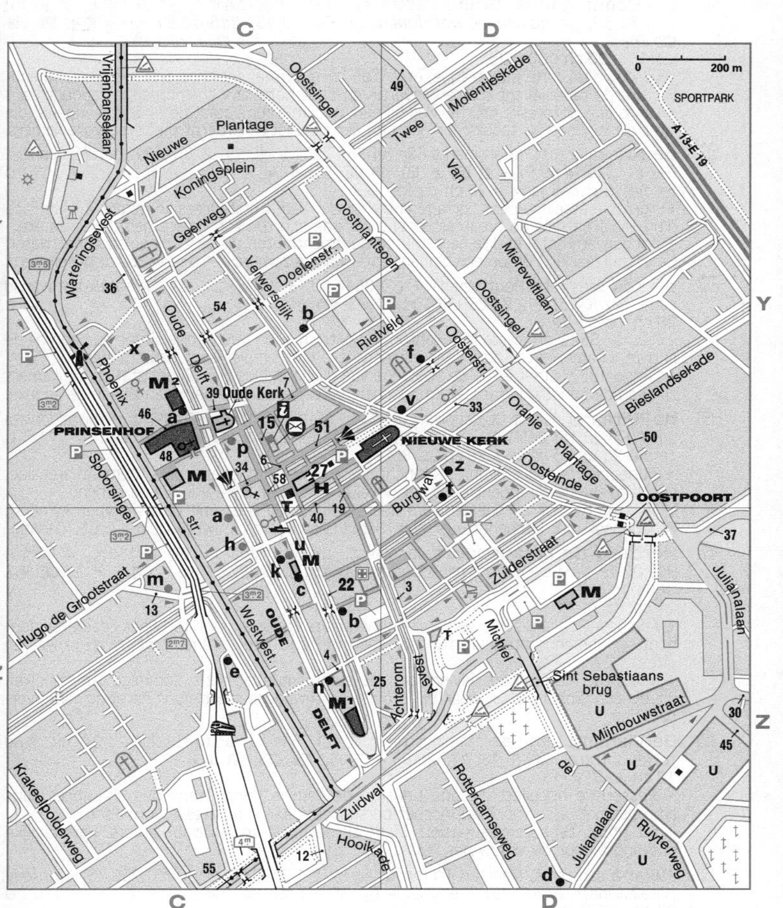

De Koophandel sans rest, Beestenmarkt 30, Code postal 2611 GC, Tel. (0 15) 214 23 02, *hotel@hoteldekoophandel.nl*, *Fax (0 15) 212 06 74* – DY z
24 ch 75/90.

◆ Agréable établissement bordant une placette animée où, en été, s'alignent les terrasses de restaurants. Chambres de bonne taille, munies du double vitrage.

◆ Comfortabel hotel aan een levendig pleintje waar 's zomers restaurantterrasjes worden uitgezet. De ruime kamers zijn voorzien van dubbele beglazing.

Leeuwenbrug sans rest, Koornmarkt 16, ✉ 2611 EE, ☎ (0 15) 214 77 41, *Fax (0 15) 215 97 59* – TV. AE MC VISA JCB. CZ b
fermé 20 déc.-3 janv. – **36 ch** ☕ 75/104.
◆ Adresse utile pour séjourner au centre de Delft. Chambres de différents formats, mais d'un confort uniforme et toutes non-fumeur, aménagées dans deux hôtels particuliers.
◆ Een praktisch adres in het centrum van Delft. De kamers, alle niet-roken, zijn ondergebracht in twee patriciërshuizen en variëren in grootte, maar hebben hetzelfde comfort.

Les Compagnons "Grand Canal" sans rest, Breestraat 1, ✉ 2611 CB, ☎ (0 15) 215 71 33, *grand.canal@worldonline.nl, Fax (0 15) 215 44 91* – TV. AE MC VISA CZ n
☕ 13 – **20 ch** 100/125.
◆ Le long d'un canal pittoresque, près d'un beau musée, ancienne prison devenue manufacture de tabac avant d'être convertie en petit hôtel aux chambres très coquettes.
◆ Langs een pittoreske gracht, vlak bij een mooi museum, staat de oude gevangenis, die later dienst deed als tabaksfabriek en nu een hotelletje herbergt met sfeervolle kamers.

de Ark sans rest, Koornmarkt 65, ✉ 2611 EC, ☎ (0 15) 215 79 99, *hotel@deark.nl, Fax (0 15) 214 49 97* – TV P. AE MC VISA JCB CZ c
fermé 19 déc.-5 janv. – **28 ch** ☕ 99/128.
◆ Agréable établissement partagé entre trois maisons restaurées se mirant à la surface d'un canal. La salle de breakfast donne sur une cour où l'on dresse des tables en été.
◆ Aangenaam hotel in drie gerestaureerde grachthuizen die zich spiegelen in het water. De ontbijtzaal kijkt uit op een binnenplaats, waar 's zomers het ontbijt wordt geserveerd.

de Kok sans rest, Houttuinen 14, ✉ 2611 AJ, ☎ (0 15) 212 21 25, *hotelkok@wanadoo.nl, Fax (0 15) 212 21 25* – TV P. AE MC VISA. CZ e
28 ch ☕ 80/90.
◆ "Anno 1852", proclame la devanture de cette maison bourgeoise située aux abords de la gare. Chambres correctement équipées. Les plus simples sont dans l'annexe.
◆ "Anno 1852" staat er op de voorzijde van dit herenhuis vlak bij het station. De kamers zijn van de benodigde faciliteiten voorzien, de eenvoudigste bevinden zich in de annexe.

de Plataan sans rest, Doelenplein 10, ✉ 2611 BP, ☎ (0 15) 212 60 46, *info@hoteldeplataan.nl, Fax (0 15) 215 73 27* – TV P – 35. AE MC VISA JCB. CY b
fermé 25 déc.-5 janv. – **28 ch** ☕ 83/93.
◆ Plusieurs types de chambres - fonctionnelles, avec kitchenette ou à thème (marocaine, nuptiale) - vous attendent dans cet hôtel proche du centre-ville. Vaste parking.
◆ In dit hotel vlak bij het centrum heeft de gast de keuze uit diverse typen kamers : functioneel, met kitchenette of een thema (Marokkaans, huwelijkssuite). Grote parking.

Herberg de Emauspoort sans rest, Vrouwenregt 11, ✉ 2611 KK, ☎ (0 15) 219 02 19, *emauspoort@emauspoort.nl, Fax (0 15) 214 82 51*, – TV P. AE MC VISA JCB. rest DY v
21 ch ☕ 78/88.
◆ Au chevet de la Nieuwe Kerk, mignonne affaire familiale dont certaines chambres donnent sur une cour intérieure où deux anciennes roulottes gitanes sont transformées en gîtes.
◆ Achter de Nieuwe Kerk bevindt zich dit leuke familiehotelletje. Sommige kamers kijken uit op een binnenplaats, waar twee oude woonwagens staan voor een originele overnachting.

De Vlaming sans rest, Vlamingstraat 52, ✉ 2611 KZ, ☎ (0 15) 213 21 27, *info@hoteldevlaming.nl, Fax (0 15) 212 20 06* – TV. AE MC VISA JCB DY f
12 ch ☕ 70/110.
◆ Ressource hôtelière façon "pension de famille" proposant des chambres sans ampleur mais assez paisibles. Accueil personnalisé par la maîtresse de maison.
◆ Dit hotel, type familiepension, biedt kleine maar vrij rustige kamers. Persoonlijke ontvangst door de vrouw des huizes.

Juliana sans rest, Maerten Trompstraat 33, ✉ 2628 RC, ☎ (0 15) 256 76 12, *info@hoteljuliana.nl, Fax (0 15) 256 57 07* – TV. AE MC VISA. DZ d
27 ch ☕ 78/96.
◆ Cette villa excentrée voisine des institutions universitaires et de la manufacture de bleu de Delft (De Porceleyne Fles) dispose de petites chambres correctement équipées.
◆ Deze villa ligt buiten het centrum, in de buurt van de universiteitsgebouwen en De Porceleyne Fles, de fabriek van Delfts blauw. Kleine, comfortabele kamers.

Campanile Kleveringweg 53 (près A 13, sortie ⑧), ✉ 2616 LZ, ☎ (0 15) 279 90 00, *delft@campanile.nl, Fax (0 15) 279 90 01*, – TV P – 25 à 140. AE MC VISA JCB BV z
Repas (avec buffets) *Lunch 14* – 19/22 bc – ☕ 10 – **94 ch** 79/87 – ½ P 50/70.
◆ Nouvel établissement implanté à proximité de l'autoroute A13, au Nord de Deflt. Le confort des chambres se conforme aux standards de la chaîne. Bonne isolation phonique.
◆ Nieuw hoteletablissement vlak bij de A13, aan de noordkant van Delft. Het comfort van de kamers voldoet aan de normen van de hotelketen. Goede geluidsisolatie.

XXX **De Zwethheul,** Rotterdamseweg 480 (Sud-Est : 6 km le long du canal), ✉ 2629 HJ, ✆ (0 10) 470 41 66, *info@zwethheul.nl, Fax (0 10) 470 65 22,* ≤, – P. AE VISA JCB BV
fermé 25 déc.-10 janv., sam. midi, dim. midi et lundi – **Repas** Lunch 68 bc – 63/80, carte 53 à 86, ♀.
◆ Repas-plaisir en perspective dans cette ancienne auberge rajeunie surveillant le trafic des péniches. Cuisine délicieusement inventive et belle terrasse estivale panoramique.
◆ De maaltijd is een waar genot in deze oude, gerenoveerde herberg die de passerende binnenvaartuigen in het oog houdt. Heerlijk inventieve keuken en mooi, panoramisch terras.
Spéc. Raviolis de poulet noir de Bresse aux langoustines sautées. Méli-mélo de ris de veau, escargots, langoustines et artichauts, crème légère à l'ail et persil. Selle de chevreuil au four aromatisée au Porto rouge (mai-sept.)

XX **L'Orage,** Oude Delft 111a, ✉ 2611 BE, ✆ (0 15) 212 36 29, *pim@euronet.nl, Fax (0 15) 214 19 34,* – AE VISA CZ h
fermé lundi – **Repas** (dîner seult) 33/55.
◆ Enseigne tumultueuse pour ce restaurant dans l'air du temps, où une cuisinière avertie s'active aux fourneaux. Salon-bibliothèque en trompe-l'œil et véranda à toit ouvrant.
◆ "Onweersachtige" naam voor dit eigentijdse restaurant, waar een echte keukenprinses de scepter zwaait. Leessalon in trompe l'oeil en serre met dak dat kan worden geopend.

XX **Le Vieux Jean,** Heilige Geestkerkhof 3, ✉ 2611 HP, ✆ (0 15) 213 04 33, *restaurant@levieuxjean.nl, Fax (0 15) 214 67 20* – AE VISA CY p
fermé 25 juil.-8 août, 25 déc.-1er janv., dim. et lundi – **Repas** 31/41, ♀.
◆ Bonne petite adresse offrant de s'attabler au coeur de Delft. Mets classiques et épais livre de cave. Le Vieux Jean c'est aussi le clocher penché, juste en face du restaurant.
◆ Een goed adresje om in hartje Delft aan tafel te gaan. Klassieke gerechten, dik wijnboek. Oude Jan is ook de naam van de toren aan de overkant, die ietwat uit het lood staat.

XX **l'Escalier,** Oude Delft 125, ✉ 2611 BE, ✆ (0 15) 212 46 21, *info@restaurantlescalier.nl, Fax (0 15) 215 80 48,* – AE VISA. CZ a
fermé 26 déc.-3 janv., sam. midi et dim. – **Repas** Lunch 28 – 33, ♀.
◆ Établissement de l'Oude Delft gravissant progressivement les marches de la notoriété. Cuisine à la page. Les beaux jours, le couvert est dressé en terrasse. Bonne affluence.
◆ Restaurant aan de Oude Delft, dat geleidelijk de trap naar de roem beklimt. Trendy keuken. Bij mooi weer worden de tafeltjes op het terras gedekt. Populaire eetgelegenheid.

XX **de Klikspaan,** Koornmarkt 85, ✉ 2611 ED, ✆ (0 15) 214 15 62, *klik@xs4all.nl, Fax (0 15) 214 74 30* – AE VISA CZ u
fermé dern. sem. avril, 2 prem. sem. sept., prem. sem. janv., lundi et mardi – **Repas** (dîner seult jusqu'à 23 h) 33, ♀.
◆ Sur le Koornmarkt, près de l'embarcadère, entrepôt transformé en restaurant au décor intérieur chargé. Un perroquet (Klikspaan), mascotte de la maison, trône en salle.
◆ Dit pakhuis aan de Koornmarkt, vlak bij de aanlegsteiger, is verbouwd tot een restaurant met een overladen interieur. De Klikspaan, de huismascotte, troont in de eetzaal.

X **Bastille,** Havenstraat 6, ✉ 2613 VK, ✆ (0 15) 213 23 90, *Fax (0 15) 214 65 31* – AE VISA CZ m
fermé 15 juil.-15 août, lundi et mardi – **Repas** (dîner seult) 28.
◆ Une carte traditionnelle incluant quelques spécialités bataves vous sera soumise à cette table du quartier de la gare. Salle à manger rustique. Ambiance décontractée.
◆ Dit restaurant in de stationswijk voert een traditionele kaart met enkele Hollandse specialiteiten. Rustieke eetzaal. Ontspannen ambiance.

X **Van der Dussen,** Bagijnhof 118, ✉ 2611 AS, ✆ (0 15) 214 72 12, *info@restaurantvanderdussen.nl, Fax (0 15) 215 91 37* – AE VISA CY x
fermé 26 déc.-3 janv. – **Repas** (dîner seult) 34/51 bc, ♀.
◆ Poutres basses, fresques patinées, carrelage et escalier du temps jadis font le charme de ce restaurant installé dans un béguinage remontant au 13e s. Repas aux chandelles.
◆ Laag balkenplafond, fresco's, plavuizen en een antieke trap behoren tot de charmante details van dit restaurant in een begijnhof uit de 13e eeuw. Diner bij kaarslicht.

DELFZIJL *Groningen 531 AA 3 et 715 L 1 – 29 018 h.*

J. v.d. Kornputplein 1a, ✉ 9934 EA, ✆ (0 596) 61 81 04, Fax (0 596) 61 65 50.
Amsterdam 213 – Groningen 30.

du Bastion, Waterstraat 78, ✉ 9934 AX, ✆ (0 596) 61 87 71, *info@dubastion.nl, Fax (0 596) 61 71 47* – . AE VISA JCB. rest
Repas *(fermé sam. midi et dim. midi)* Lunch 17 – carte 26 à 34 – **40 ch** 53/67 – ½ P 50/69.
◆ Dans le voisinage de la gare et à quelques encablures du port de plaisance, cet établissement gentiment tenu en famille propose des chambres équipées avec sobriété. Une carte traditionnelle batave s'emploie à combler votre appétit au restaurant.
◆ Dit vriendelijke etablissement in familiebeheer, in de stationbuurt en op loopafstand van de jachthaven, beschikt over eenvoudige kamers. In het restaurant wordt een traditionele Nederlandse kaart gehanteerd om aan uw eetlust tegemoet te komen.

X **De Kakebrug,** Waterstraat 8, ✉ 9934 AV, ☎ (0 596) 61 71 22, – AE MC
fermé 3 sem. vacances bâtiment, 2 sem. après Noël, dim. et lundi – **Repas** Lunch 28 – 30/35, ♀.

◆ Cette enseigne postée à l'entrée d'une rue piétonne signale l'une des valeurs sûres de la ville. Cuisine au goût du jour, à l'image du décor de la salle à manger.

◆ Dit restaurant aan het begin van een voetgangersstraat behoort tot de trefzekere adressen van de stad. Eigentijdse keuken, net als het decor van de restaurantzaal.

à Woldendorp *Sud-Est : 7 km par N 362* C *Delfzijl :*

Wilhelmina, A.E. Gorterweg 1, ✉ 9946 PA, ☎ (0 596) 60 16 41, *hotel.wilhelmina@worldonline.nl, Fax (0 596) 60 15 21,* – TV P. AE D MC VISA JCB. ch
Repas carte 22 à 31 – **9 ch** ☕ 49/70 – ½ P 60/76.

◆ Petit hôtel installé dans l'ancienne maison communale de Woldendorp. Les chambres, munies du double vitrage, offrent un confort fonctionnel. Accueil familial. À l'heure du dîner, préparations bourgeoises hollandaises.

◆ Klein hotel in het voormalige gemeentehuis van Woldendorp. De kamers zijn voorzien van dubbele beglazing en functioneel comfort. Gastvrije ontvangst. 's Avonds worden er eenvoudige maar goede Hollandse gerechten geserveerd.

Den – *voir au nom propre.*

DENEKAMP *Overijssel* C *Dinkelland 26 064 h.* 531 *AB 8 et* 715 *M 4.*

Kerkplein 2, ✉ 7591 DD, ☎ 0 900 202 19 81, info@vvvdenekamp.demon.nl, Fax (0 541) 35 57 42.

Amsterdam 169 – Zwolle 77 – Apeldoorn 85 – Enschede 19.

X **De Watermolen,** Schiphorstdijk 4 (près château Singraven), ✉ 7591 PS, ☎ (0 541) 35 13 72, *info@wateremolen-singraven.nl, Fax (0 541) 35 51 50,* ≤, – P. MC
fermé du 1er au 20 janv., lundi et après 20 h – **Repas** carte env. 35.

◆ Un vieux moulin à eau transformé en petit musée sert de cadre à cette plaisante taverne-restaurant de style rustique. Terrasse d'été sous les frondaisons.

◆ Een oude watermolen die tot een klein museum is verbouwd, vormt het decor van dit aangename restaurant met rustiek interieur. Zomerterras onder het bladerdak.

à Beuningen *Sud-Ouest : 2 km* C *Losser 22 703 h :*

Dinkeloord, Denekamperstraat 48, ✉ 7588 PW, ☎ (0 541) 35 13 87, *info@hotel-dinkeloord.nl, Fax (0 541) 35 38 75,* – TV P – 25 à 200. AE D MC VISA. rest
fermé fin déc.-2 prem. sem. janv. – **Repas** Lunch 13 – carte 22 à 39, ♀ – ☕ 9 – **45 ch** 55/100 – ½ P 75/100.

◆ Construction récente située aux avant-postes de Denekamp. Chambres avec terrasse ou balcon. Infrastructures pour se réunir, prendre soin de soi et se laisser vivre. Grande salle à manger agencée sous véranda.

◆ Deze moderne accommodatie vlak bij Denekamp beschikt over kamers met terras en balkon. Infrastructuur voor bijeenkomsten, schoonheidsverzorging en ontspanning. De eetzaal is ingericht in een grote serre.

DEURNE *Noord-Brabant* 532 *T 14 et* 715 *I 7 – 32 124 h.*

Amsterdam 136 – Eindhoven 25 – 's-Hertogenbosch 51 – Venlo 33.

XX **Hof van Deurne,** Haageind 29, ✉ 5751 BB, ☎ (0 493) 31 21 41, *info@hofvandeurne.nl,* – P – 40 à 125. MC VISA.
fermé carnaval, vacances bâtiment, sam. midi, dim. midi, lundi et mardi – **Repas** Lunch 26 – 33/61 bc, ♀.

◆ Ancienne ferme métamorphosée en restaurant actuel. On mange sous les regards de quelques figures locales immortalisées sur une curieuse fresque rappelant la Cène.

◆ In deze oude, tot eigentijds restaurant verbouwde boerderij eet u in gezelschap van enkele lokale figuren die op een curieus fresco van het Laatste Avondmaal zijn vereeuwigd.

DEVENTER *Overijssel* 531 *W 9,* 532 *W 9 et* 715 *J 5 – 86 072 h.*

Voir *Ville★ – Bergkwartier★★ (Vieux Quartier) Z – Poids public★ (Waag) Z.*

18 *au Nord : 5 km à Diepenveen, Golfweg 2, ✉ 7431 PR, ☎ (0 570) 59 32 69, Fax (0 570) 59 01 02.*

Keizerstraat 22, ✉ 7411 HH, ☎ (0 570) 64 99 59, vvvdeventer@anwb.nl, Fax (0 570) 64 33 38.

Amsterdam 106 ④ – Arnhem 44 ④ – Zwolle 38 ② – Apeldoorn 16 ⑤ – Enschede 59 ④

Plans pages suivantes

DEVENTER

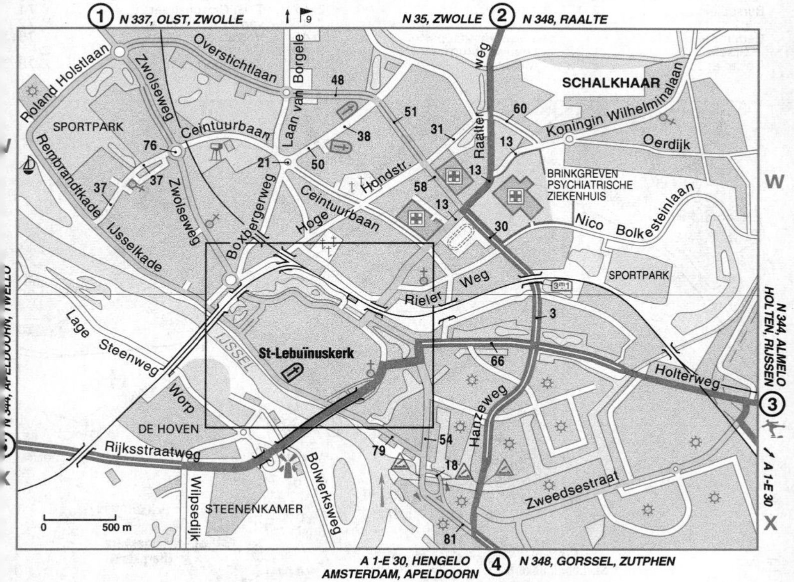

Mercure, Deventerweg 121 (par ④ : 2 km près A 1), ✉ 7418 DA, ✆ (0 570) 62 40 22, *H2110@accor-hotels.com, Fax (0 570) 62 53 46,* – 25 à 250. AE VISA
Repas *Lunch 15* – carte env. 33, ♀ – ☐ 14 – **99 ch** 103/118 – ½ P 60/69.
◆ Retrouvez, aux portes de Deventer, près de l'autoroute Amsterdam-Hengelo, l'éventail des facilités et prestations hôtelières portant la griffe Mercure. Chambres rénovées.
◆ Aan de rand van Deventer, vlak bij de snelweg Amsterdam-Hengelo, vindt u alle hotellerieprestaties en faciliteiten die Mercure eigen zijn. Gerenoveerde kamers.

Gilde sans rest, Nieuwstraat 41, ✉ 7411 LG, ✆ (0 570) 64 18 46, *receptie@gildehotel.nl, Fax (0 570) 64 18 19* – 25 à 45. AE VISA. YZ a
24 ch ☐ 85/130.
◆ Au cœur de l'ancienne ville hanséatique, cloître du 18e s. dont les cellules ont été opportunément converties en chambres douillettes et modernes. Hall orné de vitraux.
◆ In het hart van de oude hanzestad zijn de cellen van dit oude 18e-eeuwse klooster eind vorige eeuw verbouwd tot moderne, behaaglijke kamers. Lobby met gebrandschilderde ramen.

De Leeuw sans rest, Nieuwstraat 25, ✉ 7411 LG, ✆ (0 570) 61 02 90, *deleeuw@home.nl, Fax (0 570) 64 16 49* – AE VISA. Z r
fermé 25 déc.-15 janv. – **11 ch** ☐ 94/119.
◆ Une jolie façade couronnée d'un pignon à redans personnalise cette demeure du 17e s. où l'on trouvera des chambres très convenables, souvent équipées d'une kitchenette.
◆ Een fraaie trapgevel geeft dit 17e-eeuwse monumentale pand een eigen karakter. De kamers zijn vrij comfortabel, de meeste hebben een kitchenette.

le Bistro Navet, Golstraat 6, ✉ 7411 BP, ✆ (0 570) 61 95 08, *info@bistronavet.nl, Fax (0 570) 61 95 08,* – 25 à 60. AE VISA JCB Z c
fermé merc. – **Repas** (dîner seult) carte 29 à 38, ♀.
◆ Préparations au goût du jour servies dans un cadre rustique très soigné. Une charpente massive coiffe la plus charmante des salles, garnie de longues tables reluisantes.
◆ In een zeer verzorgd en rustiek decor worden eigentijdse gerechten geserveerd. Massief dakgebint bekroont de charmantste eetzaal, waar lange glimmende tafels staan opgesteld.

DEVENTER

Bagijnenstraat Y 3
Bergkerkplein Z 6
Binnensingel Y 9
Bokkingshang Z 10
Brink Z
Brinkpoortstr Y 15
Broederenstr Z 16
Burseplein Z 17
Engestraat Z 19
Gedempte Gracht Y 22
Golstraat Z 23
Graven Z 24
Grote Kerkhof Z 25
Grote Overstraat Z 27
Grote Poot Z 28
Hofstraat Z 33
Hoge Hondstraat Y 34
Industrieweg Z 36
Kapjeswelle Y 39
Kleine Overstr Z 40
Kleine Poot Z 42
Korte Bisschopsstr Z 45
Lange Bisschopsstr Z 46
Leeuwenbrug Y 49
Menstraat Z 52
Nieuwstraat YZ
Noordenbergstr Z 57
Ossenweerdstraat Y 61
Pontsteeg Z 63
Roggestraat Z 64
Sijzenbaanpl Y 65
Snipperlingsdijk Z 66
Spijkerboorsteeg Z 67
Stromarkt Z 69
T. G. Gibsonstraat Y 71
van Twickelostraat Y 72
Verzetslaan Y 75
Walstraat Z
Zandpoort Z 78

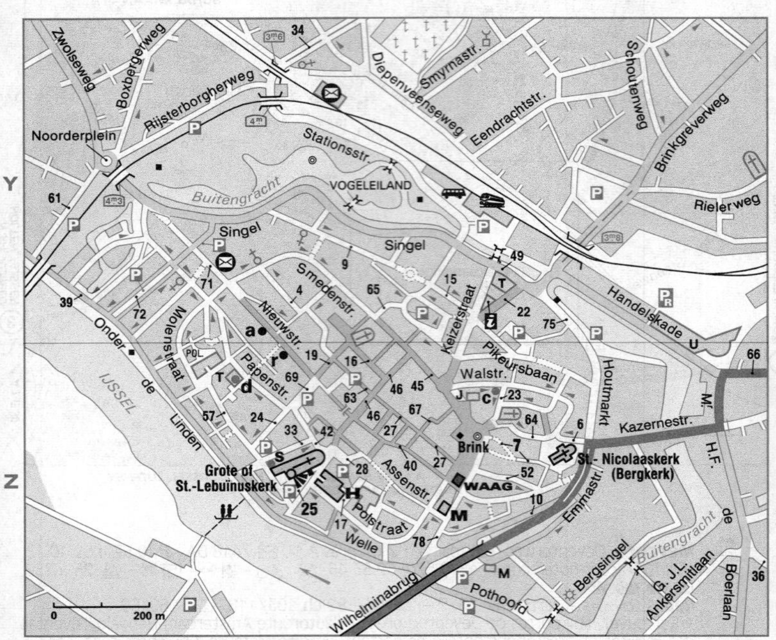

't Arsenaal, Nieuwe Markt 33, ✉ 7411 PC, ☏ (0 570) 61 64 95, *emausrob@cs.com, Fax (0 570) 61 57 52,* – AE Ⓓ MC VISA Z s
fermé sam. midi et dim. – **Repas** *Lunch 25* – carte 40 à 51, ♀.
◆ Cette vénérable maison réaménagée à la façon d'une brasserie jouxte le parvis de la Grote of St.-Lebuïnuskerk. Carte actuelle assortie de plusieurs menus. Vins du mois.
◆ Dit eerbiedwaardige, tot restaurant verbouwde huis staat aan het plein met de Grote of St.-Lebuïnuskerk. Actuele kaart met verschillende menu's. Maandelijks wisselende wijnen.

Theater bouwkunde, Klooster 2, ✉ 7411 NH, ☏ (0 570) 61 40 75, *info@theater bouwkunde.nl, Fax (0 570) 64 21 34,* – MC VISA Z d
fermé du 3 au 13 août, dim. et lundi – **Repas** (dîner seult) 22, ♀.
◆ Cet agréable restaurant situé dans un secteur résidentiel du centre-ville connaît un franc succès. Le 1er étage abrite un théâtre, d'où l'enseigne. Ambiance brasserie.
◆ Dit aangename restaurant in een woonwijk in het centrum oogst ronduit succes. Op de eerste verdieping bevindt zich een theater, vandaar de naam. Brasseriesfeer.

à Diepenveen *Nord : 5 km* Ⓒ *Deventer :*

De Roetertshof, Kerkplein 6, ✉ 7431 EE, ☏ (0 570) 59 25 28, *aroetert@roetertsh of.nl, Fax (0 570) 59 32 60,* – P. AE Ⓓ MC VISA JCB
fermé 11 juil.-2 août, 27 déc.-9 janv., mardi, merc. et sam. midi – **Repas** *Lunch 32* – 44/70 bc.
◆ Mignonne auberge rustique bordant une placette ombragée, à l'ombre du clocher. L'assiette, au goût du jour, flirte quelque peu avec les saveurs du terroir.
◆ Charmant, rustiek restaurant aan een lommerrijk pleintje, in de schaduw van de klokkentoren. De eigentijdse keuken heeft een romance met producten uit de streek.

DIEPENHEIM *Overijssel* [C] *Hof van Twente 35 041 h.* 532 *Y 9 et* 715 *K 5.*
Amsterdam 137 – Zwolle 53 – Apeldoorn 47 – Arnhem 72 – Enschede 31.

Den Haller, Watermolenweg 34, ✉ 7478 PW, ℘ (0 547) 35 12 87, *denhaller@wanadoo.nl, Fax (0 547) 35 24 34,* ≤, – P. VISA
fermé du 3 au 27 janv., mardi sauf en juil.-août et lundi – **Repas** 30/43 bc, ♀.
◆ Ancienne ferme saxonne précédée d'une adorable terrasse estivale offrant la vue sur un vieux moulin à eau. Cuisine inventive accompagnée de vins du monde. Service avenant.
◆ Oude Saksische boerderij met aan de voorzijde een heerlijk terras dat uitkijkt op een oude watermolen. Vindingrijke keuken en wereldwijnen. Vriendelijke service.

DIEPENVEEN *Overijssel* 531 *V 9 et* 715 *J 5 – voir à Deventer.*

DIEREN *Gelderland* [C] *Rheden 44 831 h.* 532 *V 10 et* 715 *J 5.*
Amsterdam 106 – Arnhem 17 – Lelystad 80 – Utrecht 83 – Zwolle 62.

De Pastorie, Wilhelminaweg 57, ✉ 6951 BN, ℘ (0 313) 45 00 55, *info@de-pastorie.nl, Fax (0 313) 41 98 78,* – P. AE VISA.
fermé 27 déc.-10 janv., sam. midi, dim. midi et lundi – **Repas** *Lunch 23* – carte env. 41.
◆ Restaurant établi dans une ancienne salle paroissiale rappelant une chapelle. De sobres vitraux diluent la lumière du jour en salle. Mignonne terrasse close à l'arrière.
◆ Het interieur van dit restaurant in een voormalige parochiezaal is net een kapel, waar sobere glas-in-loodramen het daglicht filteren. Omsloten terras aan de achterkant.

DIEVER *Drenthe* [C] *Westerveld 19 158 h.* 531 *W 5 et* 715 *J 3.*
Amsterdam 159 – Assen 27 – Groningen 52 – Leeuwarden 69 – Zwolle 49.

De Walhof ⚘, Hezenes 6, ✉ 7981 LC, ℘ (0 521) 59 17 93, *info@dewalhof.nl, Fax (0 521) 59 25 57,* – TV P – 25 à 60. AE VISA.
fermé 31 déc.-24 janv. – **Repas** *(fermé après 20 h)* carte env. 34 – **9 ch** 96 – ½ P 115/125.
◆ On trouvera le gîte et le couvert dans cette petite auberge familiale au charme bucolique nichée entre bois et pâturages. Salle à manger bourgeoise. Terrasse d'été.
◆ Dit kleine familiehotel met restaurant ligt verscholen tussen bos en weiden en ademt een idyllische charme. Klassieke eetzaal. Zomerterras.

DIFFELEN *Overijssel* 531 *Y 7 – voir à Hardenberg.*

DIGUE DU NORD *– voir Afsluitdijk.*

DODEWAARD *Gelderland* [C] *Neder-Betuwe 4 511 h.* 532 *S 11 et* 715 *H 6.*
Amsterdam 98 – Arnhem 29 – 's-Hertogenbosch 49 – Lelystad 109 – Utrecht 64.

Herberg De Engel, Waalbandijk 102, ✉ 6669 ME, ℘ (0 488) 41 12 80, *info@de-engel.nl, Fax (0 488) 41 23 95,* ≤, – P. VISA JCB
fermé du 19 au 23 juil. et 24 déc.-2 janv. – **Repas** *Lunch 27* – carte 32 à 51.
◆ Au bord d'un bras mort du Waal, charmante auberge traditionnelle qui serait la doyenne du pays. Carte classique, cave planétaire et trois vins du cru. Terrasse en teck.
◆ Zeer oude, traditionele herberg aan een dode arm van de Waal. Klassieke keuken en wijnen uit alle windstreken, ook van eigen wijngaard ! Terras met teakhouten meubels.

DOENRADE *Limburg* 532 *U 17 – voir à Sittard.*

DOETINCHEM *Gelderland* 532 *W 11 et* 715 *J 6 – 48 701 h.*
au Nord-Ouest : 8 km à Hoog-Keppel, Oude Zutphenseweg 15, ✉ *6997 CH,* ℘ *(0 314) 38 14 16, Fax (0 314) 36 65 23.*
IJsselkade 30, ✉ *7001 AP,* ℘ *(0 314) 32 33 55, info@vvvdoetinchem.nl, Fax (0 314) 34 50 27.*
Amsterdam 130 – Arnhem 33 – Apeldoorn 43 – Enschede 60.

de Graafschap sans rest, Simonsplein 12, ✉ 7001 BM, ℘ (0 314) 32 45 41, *stadsmotel-de-graafschap@hetnet.nl, Fax (0 314) 32 58 63* – TV P. AE VISA JCB
26 ch 59/94.
◆ Hôtel installé de longue date au centre de Doetinchem, cité moderne connue pour sa tradition artisanale du sabot. Chambres fonctionnelles réparties sur deux étages.
◆ Dit hotel is een vertrouwd beeld in het centrum van Doetichem, een moderne stad waar nog altijd klompen worden gemaakt. Functionele kamers op twee verdiepingen.

Den DOLDER *Utrecht* 532 *Q 10 et* 715 *G 5 – voir à Zeist.*

DOMBURG *Zeeland* C *Veere 21 985 h.* 532 F 13 *et* 715 B 7 – *Station balnéaire.*

Schuitvlotstraat 32, ✉ *4357 EB,* ☎ *0 900-202 02 80, info@vvvwnb.nl, Fax (0 118) 58 35 45.*

Amsterdam 190 – Middelburg 16 – Rotterdam 111.

Bommeljé, Herenstraat 24, ✉ 4357 AL, ☎ (0 118) 58 16 84, *bommelje@zeelandnet.nl, Fax (0 118) 58 22 18,* – 30.
Repas *(fermé mardi et merc. de nov. à fév.)* (dîner seult) carte 36 à 50, – **32 ch** 134, – 9 suites – ½ P 63/93.

◆ Dans une rue calme, près des dunes, hôtel flambant neuf que signale une pimpante façade à balcons. Intérieur moderne. Bonnes chambres et studios avec kitchenette. Salle à manger "mode" : tables nues, parquet luisant et chaises vêtues de cuir rouge.

◆ In een rustige straat vlak bij de duinen signaleert een fleurige gevel met balkons dit spiksplinternieuwe hotel. Modern interieur. Goede kamers en studio's met kitchenette. Trendy eetzaal met glimmend parket, rood leren stoelen en tafels zonder kleedjes.

The Wigwam, Herenstraat 12, ✉ 4357 AL, ☎ (0 118) 58 12 75, *info@wigwamhotel.nl, Fax (0 118) 58 25 25* –
13 fév.-28 nov. – **Repas** (dîner seult jusqu'à 20 h) 26/32 – **31 ch** 88/125.

◆ L'hôtel, quoi qu'en dise l'enseigne, n'a rien d'un tipi ni d'un village indien. Chambres insonorisées, d'ampleur et de confort respectables, souvent munies d'un balcon.

◆ U komt hier echt niet terecht in een tipi of indianendorp, al doet de naam wel zoiets vermoeden. Ruime, comfortabele kamers met geluidsisolatie en de meeste met balkon.

Wilhelmina sans rest, Noordstraat 20, ✉ 4357 AP, ☎ (0 118) 58 12 62, *info@wilduin.nl, Fax (0 118) 58 41 10,* –
fermé mi-nov.-26 déc. – **16 ch** 80/135, – 4 suites.

◆ À quelques encablures de la plage, dans une rue calme proche du centre, coquette hostellerie dont les chambres, actuelles et douillettes, s'ordonnent autour d'un petit patio.

◆ In een rustige straat dicht bij het centrum en op loopafstand van het strand biedt dit charmante hotel eigentijdse, behaaglijke kamers, die rond een kleine patio liggen.

Strandhotel Duinheuvel sans rest, Badhuisweg 2, ✉ 4357 AV, ☎ (0 118) 58 12 82, *info@wilduin.nl, Fax (0 118) 58 33 45* –
20 ch 70/125.

◆ Ambiance vacances à cette adresse dominant le chapelet de dunes qui précède l'estran. Chambres de différentes tailles. Galerie d'œuvres d'art où l'on petit-déjeune.

◆ Hotel met een echte vakantiesfeer, dat uitkijkt over de duinenrij langs het strand. De kamers variëren in grootte. Ontbijt in de kunstgalerie.

Mondriaan, Ooststraat 6, ✉ 4357 BE, ☎ (0 118) 58 44 34, *info@restaurant-mondriaan.nl, Fax (0 118) 58 39 23,* –
fermé du 1er au 11 fév., du 10 au 31 janv. et lundi de nov. à mars – **Repas** (dîner seult) 25.

◆ Sur l'artère touristique de Domburg, brasserie de notre temps possédant sur l'arrière une petite terrasse semi-abritée. Grand choix de plats au goût du jour.

◆ Dit moderne eethuis in een toeristische straat in Domburg heeft aan de achterzijde een deels beschut terras. Grote keuze aan eigentijdse gerechten.

DORDRECHT *Zuid-Holland* 532 N 12 *et* 715 F 6 – *120 222 h.*

Voir *La Vieille Ville★ – Grande Église ou église Notre-Dame★ (Grote of O.-L.-Vrouwekerk) : stalles★, de la tour* ≤★★ CV **R** – *Groothoofdspoort : du quai* ≤★ DV.

Musée : *Mr. Simon van Gijn★* CV **M**².

Baanhoekweg 50, ✉ *3313 LP,* ☎ *(0 78) 621 12 21, Fax (0 78) 616 10 36.*

au Nord-Ouest : 23 km par ④ à Rotterdam-Zestienhoven ☎ *(0 10) 446 34 44, Fax (0 10) 446 34 99.*

Stationsweg 1, ✉ *3311 JW,* ☎ *0 900 463 68 88, info@vvvzhz.nl, Fax (0 78) 613 17 83.*

Amsterdam 95 ① – Rotterdam 28 ④ – Den Haag 53 ④ – Arnhem 106 ① – Breda 29 ② – Utrecht 58 ①

Plans pages suivantes

Dordrecht, Achterhakkers 72, ✉ 3311 JA, ☎ (0 78) 613 60 11, *info@hoteldordrecht.nl, Fax (0 78) 613 74 70,* – ch, CX d
fermé 24 déc.-2 janv. – **Repas** *(fermé week-end)* (dîner seult) carte env. 32 – **21 ch** 87/130 – ½ P 110/140.

◆ Ancienne demeure bourgeoise postée face aux quais, au bord du ring intérieur. Chambres "king size" correctement équipées, plus menues dans l'annexe jouxtant le jardin. Cuisine classico-batave servie dans un décor marin.

◆ Oud herenhuis tegenover de kade, aan de rand van de binnenring. Comfortabele king size kamers in het oorspronkelijke pand, wat kleinere kamers in de dependance aan de tuin. Klassieke Nederlandse gerechten worden geserveerd in een scheepvaartdecor.

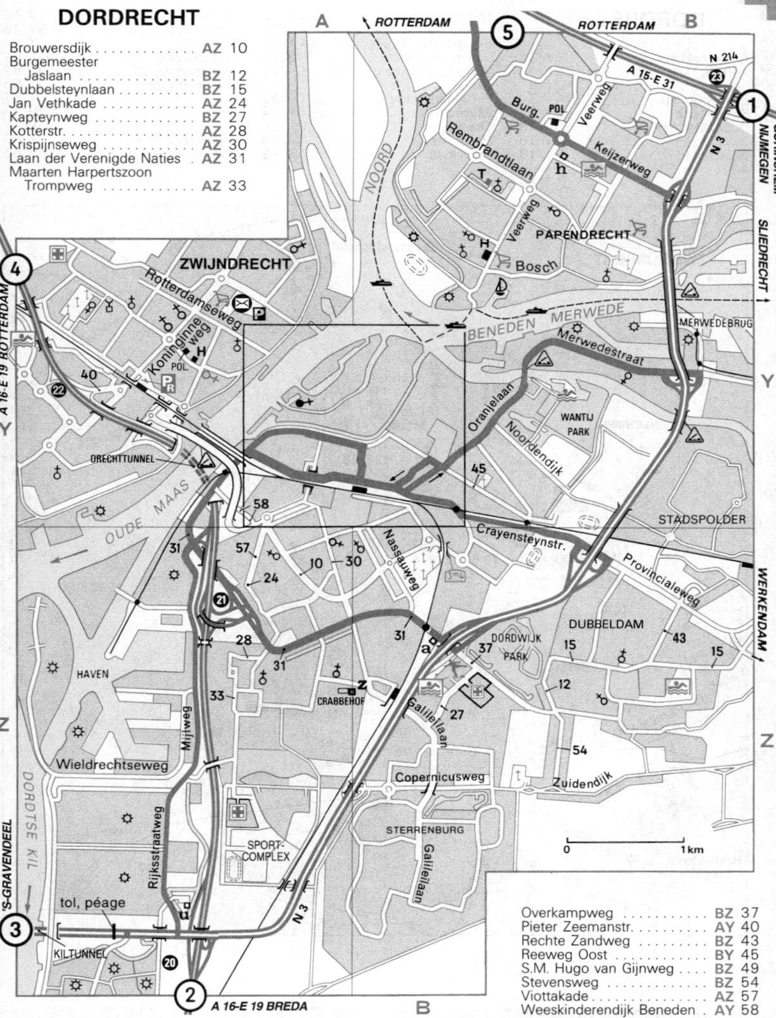

Mercure, Rijksstraatweg 30 (par A 16 - E 19, sortie ⑳), ✉ 3316 EH, ☎ (0 78) 618 44 44, *h2106@accor-hotels.com, Fax (0 78) 618 79 40,* – ▮ ⇌, ≡ rest, TV ♿ P – 🏛 25 à 500. AE ⓓ ⓜ VISA JCB AZ u

Repas *Lunch 14* – carte env. 35 – ☕ 14 – **96 ch** 105/142 – ½ P 128/135.

◆ Proximité de l'autoroute, confort standard dans les chambres, business-center et bonnes installations conférencières : bref, le concept hôtelier propre à la chaîne.

◆ Lokatie dicht bij de snelweg, standaardcomfort in de kamers, business center en goede faciliteiten voor bijeenkomsten en seminars. Kortom : het hotelconcept van de keten.

Bastion, Laan der Verenigde Naties 363, ✉ 3318 LA, ☎ (0 78) 651 15 33, *bastion@bastionhotel.nl, Fax (0 78) 617 81 63,* – ⇌ TV P. AE ⓓ ⓜ VISA. ✂ BZ a

Repas (grillades, ouvert jusqu'à 23 h) carte env. 30 – ☕ 10 – **40 ch** 72.

◆ Un petit hôtel identique à ses nombreux frères partageant la même enseigne : voisinage du réseau autoroutier et chambres fonctionnelles pourvues du double vitrage.

◆ Dit kleine hotel is identiek aan zijn soortgenoten van dezelfde keten : ligging in de buurt van de snelweg en functionele kamers met dubbele beglazing.

DORDRECHT

Achterhakkers . . . . CX 3
Aert de Gelderstr. . . . . CX 4
Bagijnhof . . . . DV 6
Blauwpoortspl. . . . . CV 7
Bleijenhoek . . . . DV 9
Dubbeldamseweg . . . . DX 13
Groenmarkt . . . . CV 16
Groothoofd . . . . DV 18
Grote Kerksbuurt . . . . CV 19
Grote Spuistr. . . . . CV 21
Hoogstratensingel . . . . DVX 22
Johan de Wittstr. . . . . DX 25
Korte Engelenburgerkade . . CV 26
Lange Geldersekade . . . . . . CV 32
Museumstr. . . . . DV 34
Oranjelaan . . . . DX 36
Papeterspad . . . . CX 39
Prinsenstr. . . . . CV 42
Riedijk . . . . DV 46
Scheffersp1. . . . . CDV 48
Spuiweg CX
Stationsweg . . . . DX 51
Steegoversloot . . . . DV 52
Twintighuizen . . . . CX 55
Visstr. . . . . CV 57
Voorstr. . . . . CDV
Vriesestr. . . . . DV
Wilgenbos . . . . CX 60
Wolwevershaven . . . . CV 61

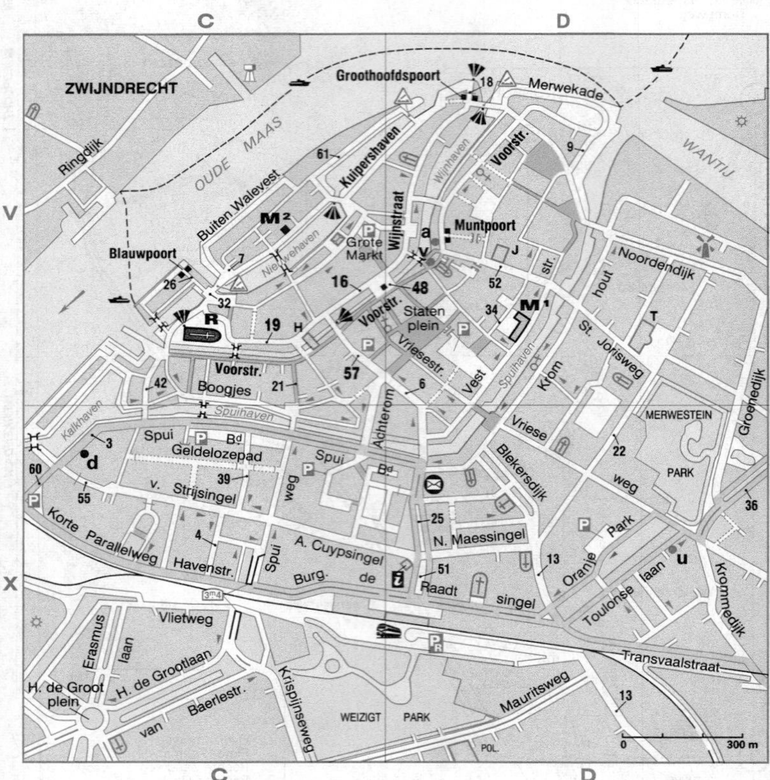

Hein en Hoogvliet, Toulonselaan 12, ✉ 3312 ET, ☎ (0 78) 613 50 09, *info@heinenhoogvliet.nl, Fax (0 78) 631 57 37,* – AE ⓓ ⓜⓒ VISA JCB — DX u
fermé 2 sem. vacances bâtiment, 2 sem. après Noël, lundi et mardi – **Repas** *Lunch 27* – carte 43 à 56, ♀.
◆ Ce restaurant un peu excentré s'est récemment offert une cure de rajeunissement ainsi qu'une nouvelle identité. Recettes bien dans l'air du temps. Terrasse estivale.
◆ Dit wat uit het centrum gelegen restaurant heeft onlangs een complete metamorfose ondergaan, zowel in uiterlijk als wat identiteit betreft. Eigentijdse gerechten. Zomerterras.

Da Moreno, Voorstraat 215, ✉ 3311 EP, ☎ (0 78) 614 99 04, *Fax (0 78) 614 65 65,* Cuisine italienne – ▤. AE ⓓ ⓜⓒ VISA JCB. ✻ — DV a
fermé 31 déc., jeudi et dim. midi – **Repas** 35, ♀.
◆ Table bordant l'artère commerçante la plus fréquentée de la ville. Salle de restaurant aménagée sur trois niveaux. Goûteuse cuisine italienne. Buffet d'antipasti.
◆ Restaurant aan de drukste winkelstraat van de stad. De restaurantzaal telt drie niveaus. Smaakvolle Italiaanse keuken. Antipastabuffet.

De Hoff'nar, Talmaweg 10, ✉ 3317 RB, ✆ (0 78) 618 04 66, *crabbehoff@dordt.nl, Fax (0 78) 618 45 54* – P – 25 à 125. AE ① MC VISA JCB ABZ z
fermé dern. sem. juil.-2 prem. sem. août, lundi et mardi – **Repas** (dîner seult) carte env. 54, ♀.
◆ Au Sud de la ville, dans une dépendance du château Crabbehof, affaire familiale assez mignonne avec sa salle à manger traitée en jardin d'hiver. Cuisine d'aujourd'hui.
◆ Dit charmante restaurant heeft zijn intrek genomen in het oude koetshuis van kasteel Crabbehof aan de zuidkant van de stad. Eetzaal in de serre. Eigentijdse keuken.

De Stroper, Wijnbrug 1, ✉ 3311 EV, ✆ (0 78) 613 00 94, *info@destroper.nl*, Produits de la mer – . AE MC VISA DV v
fermé sam. midi et dim. midi – **Repas** *Lunch 25* – 23/53 bc, ♀.
◆ Dressée aux beaux jours, la terrasse du Braconnier (Stroper) flotte au pied du Pont du Vin (Wijnbrug) : tout un programme ! Saveurs du grand large. Intérieur relooké.
◆ Bij mooi weer richt deze volhardende velddief zijn terras in aan de voet van de Wijnbrug. Visgerechten. Compleet nieuw interieur.

à Papendrecht *Nord-Est : 4 km – 30 276 h*

Mercure, Lange Tiendweg 2, ✉ 3353 CW, ✆ (0 78) 615 20 99, *info@hotelmercure.nl, Fax (0 78) 615 85 97*, , – , rest, P – 25 à 300. AE ① MC VISA
Repas *(fermé dim.)* (ouvert jusqu'à 23 h) *Lunch 21* – carte env. 40 – ☕ 14 – **76 ch** 112/135 – ½ P 147/222. BY h
◆ Confortable établissement de chaîne bâti aux avant-postes de Dordrecht, à deux tours de roue de l'autoroute Rotterdam-Groningen. Chambres et communs actuels, d'un bon gabarit.
◆ Comfortabel ketenhotel aan de rand van Dordrecht, vlak bij de snelweg Rotterdam-Groningen. De kamers en gemeenschappelijke ruimten zijn ruim opgezet.

DRACHTEN *Fryslân* C *Smallingerland 53 493 h.* 531 V 4 *et* 715 J 2.

Museumplein 4, ✉ 9203 DD, ✆ (0 512) 51 77 71, vvv.anwbdrachten@euronet.nl, Fax (0 512) 53 24 13.
Amsterdam 147 – Groningen 38 – Leeuwarden 27 – Zwolle 85.

Drachten, Zonnedauw 1, ✉ 9202 PE, ✆ (0 512) 52 07 05, *info@drachten.valk.nl, Fax (0 512) 52 32 32*, , , – P – 25 à 200. AE ① MC VISA JCB
Repas *Lunch 16* – carte 22 à 45 – ☕ 9 – **48 ch** 70 – ½ P 117/122.
◆ Le toucan de la chaîne Van der Valk préside au destin de cet hôtel dont la pyramide servira de point de repère aux automobilistes. Chambres fonctionnelles. Salle à manger en demi-rotonde, ouverte sur une terrasse d'été.
◆ De toekan van de Van der Valk-keten heeft het lot van dit hotel in handen en houdt zijn prooi goed in de gaten. De piramide vormt een herkenningspunt voor de automobilisten. Functionele kamers. Halfronde eetzaal met zomerterras.

Marathon, Eikesingel 64, ✉ 9203 PA, ✆ (0 512) 54 35 55, *info@marathonhotel.nl, Fax (0 512) 54 34 54*, , – P. AE ① MC VISA JCB. rest
Repas (résidents seult) – **39 ch** ☕ 55/75 – ½ P 57/75.
◆ Point de chute bien pratique pour poser ses valises à l'entrée de Drachten, centre commercial et industriel aux rues animées. Petites chambres actuelles de mise simple.
◆ Een praktische pleisterplaats aan de rand van Drachten, een bedrijvig stadje met levendige straten. Kleine, moderne kamers met eenvoudig comfort.

De Wilgenhoeve, De Warren 2, ✉ 9203 HT, ✆ (0 512) 51 25 10, *rest.dewilgenhoeve@planet.nl, Fax (0 512) 53 14 19*, – P. AE ① MC VISA
fermé dern. sem. juil.-prem. sem. août, 31 déc.-7 janv., sam. midi, dim. midi et lundi – **Repas** *Lunch 29* – 50/63 bc, ♀.
◆ Une jolie terrasse d'été est dressée à l'avant de cette ancienne ferme aux volets peints. Mets classiques flirtant avec les modes d'aujourd'hui. Salle à manger agréable.
◆ Aan de voorkant van deze voormalige boerderij met geschilderde luiken is een leuk terras ingericht. De klassieke gerechten flirten met nieuwe trends. Aangename eetzaal.

Koriander (Gaastra), Burgemeester Wuiteweg 18, ✉ 9203 KK, ✆ (0 512) 54 88 50, *info@dekoriander.nl, Fax (0 512) 54 81 24* – AE ① MC VISA
fermé 26 juil.-18 août, 27 déc.-11 janv., lundi et mardi – **Repas** (dîner seult) carte env. 52.
◆ Belle démonstration culinaire au goût du jour, inventive et pleine de panache, dans cette maison du centre. Briques, lambris et escalier en fer forgé participent au décor.
◆ In dit pand in het centrum wordt met verve en inventiviteit een fraai staaltje van eigentijdse kookkunst geleverd. Interieur met baksteen, lambrisering en smeedijzeren trap.
Spéc. Coquilles Saint-Jacques sautées et esprot fumé au sorbet de poivron doux. Risotto de lotte à la tomate et basilic. Turbot effeuillé au foie d'oie fondu et jus de volaille

à Boornbergum (Boarnburgum) *Sud-Ouest : 5 km* Ⓒ *Smallingerland :*

XX **Het Spijshuys,** Westerbuorren 2, ✉ 9212 PL, ✆ (0 512)38 30 47, *het.spijshuys@zonnet.nl, Fax (0 512) 38 17 80,* – AE ⓓ ⓜ VISA
fermé vacances bâtiment, 31 déc.-1er janv., sam. midi, dim. midi et lundi – **Repas** *Lunch 25* – 30/39.
◆ Au cœur du village, à l'angle de la Westerbuorren, sympathique petite affaire tenue en famille, où se mitonne une cuisine bien dans le coup. Vins du monde.
◆ Een sympathiek restaurantje midden in de dorpskern, dat in familiebeheer wordt gerund. In dit eethuis wordt een eigentijdse keuken bereid. Wereldwijnen.

à Rottevalle (Rottefalle) *Nord : 4 km* Ⓒ *Smallingerland :*

XX **De Herberg van Smallingerland,** Muldersplein 2, ✉ 9221 SP, ✆ (0 512) 34 20 64, *herberg@tijdrarelhaar.nl, Fax (0 512) 34 22 39,* – P – 25 à 40. ⓓ ⓜ VISA JCB
fermé 3 sem. vacances bâtiment et lundi – **Repas** (déjeuner sur réservation) 30/54 bc, ♀.
◆ Cette vénérable auberge entretient avec art la nostalgie du temps jadis : faïence de Makkum, lampes anciennes et lit à alcôve en salle. Le chef, lui, vit avec son temps.
◆ Deze herberg ademt de nostalgische sfeer naar vervlogen tijden : aardewerk uit Makkum, antieke lampen en bedstee in de eetzaal. De chef-kok staat met beide benen in het heden.

DRIEBERGEN-RIJSENBURG *Utrecht* 532 Q 10 *et* 715 G 5 – *18 438 h.*

ℹ *Hoofdstraat 12a, ✉ 3971 XE, ✆ (0 343) 51 31 62, vvvdriebergen-rijsenburg@wanadoo.nl, Fax (0 343) 53 24 11.*
Amsterdam 54 – Utrecht 15 – Amersfoort 22 – Arnhem 49.

XX ✿ **Lai Sin,** Arnhemse Bovenweg 46, ✉ 3971 MK, ✆ (0 343) 51 68 58, *Fax (0 343) 51 17 17,* , Cuisine chinoise – AE ⓓ ⓜ VISA JCB.
fermé sam. midi, dim. et lundi – **Repas** *Lunch 55 bc* – 63/88, carte 33 à 55, ♀.
◆ Un temple de la gastronomie chinoise. Les amateurs du genre s'y laisseront séduire par un éventail de recettes authentiques relevées d'un zeste de créativité. À vénérer !
◆ Een tempel van Chinese gastronomie. Liefhebbers van dit genre zullen zeker vallen voor het scala van authentieke gerechten met een creatieve touch. Goddelijk !
Spéc. Asperges vertes, crabe et œufs de cailles aux caviars terre et mer. Filet de cabillaud piquant et croustillant. Bœuf "Wagyu" braisé et chou chinois

XX **La Provence,** Hoofdstraat 109, ✉ 3971 KG, ✆ (0 343) 51 29 20, *la_provence@planet.nl, Fax (0 343) 52 08 33* – AE ⓓ ⓜ VISA JCB.
fermé dern. sem. juil.-2 prem. sem. août, sam. midi, dim. et lundi – **Repas** *Lunch 37* – carte 44 à 56.
◆ Petite affaire familiale dont le décor intérieur, rustico-contemporain, vous transporte en Provence. La cuisine, actuelle, adopte toutefois un tempérament hollandais.
◆ Klein familierestaurant waar u zich in het rustiek-eigentijdse decor in de Provence waant. De eigentijdse keuken heeft echter een onmiskenbaar Hollands temperament.

DRIEL *Gelderland* 532 T 11 *et* 715 I 6 – *voir à Arnhem.*

DRONRIJP (DRONRYP) *Fryslân* Ⓒ *Menaldumadeel 14 230 h.* 531 S 3 *et* 715 H 2.

Amsterdam 138 – Leeuwarden 11 – Sneek 23 – Zwolle 110.

X **Op Hatsum,** Hatsum 13 (Sud : 2 km), ✉ 9035 VK, ✆ (0 517) 23 16 88, *info@ophatsum.nl, Fax (0 517) 23 21 63,* , Anguilles – P. AE ⓓ ⓜ VISA JCB
fermé 25 déc.-1er janv., lundi et mardi – **Repas** (dîner seult) carte 34 à 52.
◆ Ancien café de la gare converti en restaurant convivial, dans l'esprit "bistrot français". Plats gorgés d'iode et spécialité d'anguille - fumée "maison", s'il vous plaît !
◆ Dit voormalige stationscafé is verbouwd tot een gastvrij restaurant met de ambiance van een Franse bistro. Visgerechten met als specialiteit huisgerookte paling.

DRONTEN *Flevoland* 531 T 7 *et* 715 I 4 – *36 369 h.*

Amsterdam 72 – Lelystad 23 – Apeldoorn 51 – Leeuwarden 94 – Zwolle 31.

Het Galjoen, De Rede 50, ✉ 8251 EW, ✆ (0 321) 31 70 30, *info@hotelhetgaljoen.nl, Fax (0 321) 31 58 22,* – P – 25 à 350. AE ⓓ ⓜ VISA
Repas carte 27 à 51, ♀ – 10 – **19 ch** 55/75 – ½ P 70/110.
◆ Sur la place centrale de Dronten, hôtel-restaurant familial dont les chambres, pas très grandes mais toutes entièrement refaites de neuf, se distribuent sur trois étages.
◆ Dit hotel-restaurant, een familiebedrijf in het centrum van Dronten, telt drie verdiepingen met kamers die niet al te groot zijn, maar wel volledig zijn gerenoveerd.

à Ketelhaven *Nord : 8 km* [C] *Dronten :*

X **Lands-End,** Vossemeerdijk 25, ✉ 8251 PM, ☎ (0 321) 31 33 18, *info@lands-end.nl, Fax (0 321) 31 42 49,* ≤, terrasse, ⚓ – P. AE MC VISA
fermé fin janv.-début fév. et lundi – **Repas** *Lunch 19* – carte 27 à 53.
◆ "La Fin des Terres" (Lands-End), avertit l'enseigne de cette table offrant une vue agréable sur le port de plaisance. Recettes traditionnelles hollandaises.
◆ "Pas op, straks heeft u geen vaste grond meer onder de voeten", waarschuwt de naam van dit restaurantje. Aangenaam uitzicht op de jachthaven. Traditionele Hollandse gerechten.

Ecrivez-nous...
Vos louanges comme vos critiques seront examinées avec le plus grand soin.
Nous reverrons sur place les informations que vous nous signalez.
Par avance merci !

DRUNEN *Noord-Brabant* [C] *Heusden 43 138 h.* 532 P 12 *et* 715 G 6.
Amsterdam 101 – 's-Hertogenbosch 15 – Breda 34 – Rotterdam 73.

Royal, Raadhuisplein 13, ✉ 5151 JH, ☎ (0 416) 37 23 81, *Fax (0 416) 37 88 63,* terrasse, vélos – TV. AE MC VISA JCB
fermé sem. carnaval et du 1er au 6 janv. – **Repas** *(fermé sam. midi et dim. midi) Lunch 10* – 25/48, ♀ – **14 ch** ☕ 60/80 – ½ P 80/100.
◆ Ambiance familiale dans cette petite auberge située au centre du village, juste en face de la place du marché. Chambres moyennement insonorisées, mais très convenables. Repas aux chandelles. Carte d'asperges en saison.
◆ Huiselijke sfeer in dit kleine hotel in het centrum van het dorp, recht tegenover het marktplein. Hoewel de geluidsisolatie matig is, zijn de kamers heel redelijk. Diner bij kaarslicht. Asperges in het seizoen.

MICHELIN NEDERLAND N.V., Bedrijvenpark Groenewoud II, Huub van Doorneweg 2 – ✉ 5151 DT, ☎ (0 416) 38 41 00, Fax (0 416) 38 41 26

DWINGELOO *Drenthe* [C] *Westerveld 19 158 h.* 531 X 5 *et* 715 K 3.
Brink 1, ✉ 7991 CG, ☎ (0 521) 59 13 31, vvvdwingeloo@hotmail.com, Fax (0 521) 59 37 11.
Amsterdam 158 – Assen 30 – Groningen 50 – Leeuwarden 70 – Zwolle 50.

Wesseling, Brink 26, ✉ 7991 CH, ☎ (0 521) 59 15 44, *info@hotelwesseling.nl, Fax (0 521) 59 25 87,* terrasse, vélos – ascenseur TV ♿ P – salle 35. AE ⓓ MC VISA
fermé 31 déc.-17 janv. – **Repas** *(fermé après 20 h 30) Lunch 23* – 25/38 bc, ♀ – **23 ch** ☕ 63/95.
◆ Quatre générations se sont relayé aux commandes de cette auberge bordant la placette ombragée d'un village pittoresque. Chambres actuelles de bonne ampleur. Grande salle à manger-véranda. Cuisine au goût du jour.
◆ De vierde generatie bestiert inmiddels dit familiehotel aan een lommerrijk pleintje in een schilderachtig dorp. De kamers zijn ruim en modern. In de grote serre is de eetzaal ingericht. Eigentijdse keuken.

De Brink, Brink 30, ✉ 7991 CH, ☎ (0 521) 59 13 19, *info@hoteldebrink.nl, Fax (0 521) 59 06 66,* terrasse – TV P – salle 25 à 250. MC VISA
fermé 2 sem. en janv. – **Repas** *(fermé après 20 h 30)* (taverne-rest) *Lunch 19* – 25/29 – **10 ch** ☕ 63/95.
◆ L'enseigne de cet établissement traditionnel évoque la place plantée d'arbres aérant le centre des villages de la Drenthe. Amélioration du confort des chambres. Repas sans prise de tête.
◆ De naam van dit traditionele hotel verwijst naar de typische Drentse dorpspleintjes met bomen. Het comfort van de kamers is verbeterd. Eenvoudige maaltijd zonder liflafjes.

à Lhee *Sud-Ouest : 1,5 km* [C] *Westerveld :*

De Börken ⛺, Lhee 76, ✉ 7991 PJ, ☎ (0 521) 59 72 00, *info@deborken.nl, Fax (0 521) 59 72 87,* terrasse, fitness, sauna, piscine, jardin, tennis, vélos – TV ♿ P – salle 25 à 100. AE ⓓ MC VISA. ✱ rest
Repas *Lunch 25* – carte env. 44, ♀ – **42 ch** ☕ 76/111 – ½ P 83.
◆ Une chaumière ancienne précède le bâtiment abritant les chambres, spacieuses et souvent pourvues d'une menue terrasse. Nombreuses distractions au programme. Restaurant habillé de lambris clairs, baignant dans une lumière tamisée.
◆ Achter een oud huisje met rieten dak ligt het gebouw met de kamers, die ruim zijn en waarvan de meeste een klein terras hebben. Tal van faciliteiten voor sport en ontspanning. Restaurant met lambrisering van licht hout en sfeervol gedempt licht.

EARNEWÂLD (EERNEWOUDE) *Fryslân* Ⓒ *Tytsjerksteradiel 31 413 h.* 531 U 4 *et* 715 I 2.
Amsterdam 148 – Leeuwarden 19 – Drachten 18 – Groningen 50.

Princenhof, P. Miedemaweg 15, ✉ 9264 TJ, ✆ (0 511) 53 92 06, *info@princenhof.nl, Fax (0 511) 53 93 19*, – 25 à 200. AE VISA. rest
fermé 31 déc.-1er janv. – **Repas** *Lunch 16* – carte 37 à 47 – **43 ch** 70/115 – ½ P 72/79.
◆ Construction déployant ses deux ailes au bord de l'eau. Les chambres, toutes rafraîchies, sont très souvent pourvues d'une terrasse ou d'un balcon avec vue aquatique. Salle de restaurant profitant d'une jolie perspective batelière.
◆ Dit hotel heeft zijn twee vleugels langs het water uitgespreid. De kamers zijn in een nieuw jasje gestoken en hebben bijna allemaal een terras of balkon met uitzicht over het Friese merengebied. Ook het restaurant kijkt uit op de voortglijdende boten.

ECHT *Limburg* Ⓒ *Echt-Susteren 32 187 h.* 532 U 16 *et* 715 I 8.
Amsterdam 180 – Maastricht 36 – Eindhoven 51 – Venlo 37.

à Peij *Est : 3 km* Ⓒ *Echt-Susteren :*

Hof van Herstal, Pepinusbrug 8, ✉ 6102 RJ, ✆ (0 475) 48 41 50, *bruggemangz@zonnet.nl, Fax (0 475) 48 85 63*, – AE VISA.
fermé du 16 au 27 fév., du 2 au 19 août, lundi et sam. midi – **Repas** 29/60 bc, ♀.
◆ Les murs de ce petit cloître d'un autre temps renferment désormais un confortable restaurant classiquement aménagé, dont l'enseigne a fêté ses dix ans à l'aube du 21e s.
◆ De muren van dit kleine klooster uit andere tijden omsluiten nu een klassiek ingericht, comfortabel restaurant dat inmiddels zijn tiende verjaardag heeft gevierd.

EDAM *Noord-Holland* Ⓒ *Edam-Volendam 27 833 h.* 531 P 7 *et* 715 G 4.
Damplein 1, ✉ 1135 BK, ✆ (0 299) 31 51 25, info@vvv-edam.nl, Fax (0 299) 37 42 36.
Amsterdam 22 – Alkmaar 28 – Leeuwarden 116.

De Fortuna, Spuistraat 3, ✉ 1135 AV, ✆ (0 299) 37 16 71, *fortuna@fortuna-edam.nl, Fax (0 299) 37 14 69*, – AE VISA JCB.
Repas (dîner seult) 33, ♀ – **24 ch** 73/100 – ½ P 95/104.
◆ Le charme de l'adresse tient dans ces quelques maisonnettes typiques ordonnées autour d'un jardin bichonné que longe un canal. Chambres bien tenues. Conçu à la façon d'une brasserie cossue, le restaurant s'agrémente de toiles anciennes hollandaises.
◆ Vrouwe Fortuna spreidt hier al haar charme tentoon in vijf karakteristieke herenhuizen die rond een tuin aan het water liggen. Goed onderhouden kamers. Het restaurant heeft de ambiance van een luxueuze brasserie en is verfraaid met oude Hollandse schilderijen.

EDE *Gelderland* 532 S 10 *et* 715 I 5 – *103 708 h.*
Env. *au Nord-Est : 13 km, Parc National de la Haute Veluwe★★★ (Nationaal Park De Hoge Veluwe) : Parc★★★, Musée national (Rijksmuseum) Kröller-Müller★★★ – Parc à sculptures★★ (Beeldenpark).*
De Manenberg, Molenstraat 80, ✉ 6711 AW, ✆ (0 318) 61 44 44, info@vvvede.nl, Fax (0 318) 65 03 35.
Amsterdam 81 – Arnhem 23 – Apeldoorn 32 – Utrecht 43.

De Reehorst, Bennekomseweg 24, ✉ 6717 LM, ✆ (0 318) 64 11 88, *info@reehorst.nl, Fax (0 318) 62 21 07*, – 25 à 580. AE VISA
Repas *Lunch 16* – carte 27 à 46, ♀ – 10 – **90 ch** 95/110 – ½ P 75/110.
◆ Hôtel récent, surtout spécialisé dans l'organisation d'événements. Espaces de réunions aussi nombreux que polyvalents : salles de cinéma, d'expositions, de spectacles, etc. Carte maniant un double registre culinaire : franco-hollandais.
◆ Modern hotel dat is gespecialiseerd in het organiseren van evenementen. Groot scala aan multifunctionele zalen : voor bioscoop, theater, exposities, congressen, feesten, enzovoort. Kaart met Frans-Nederlands culinair register.

La Façade, Notaris Fischerstraat 31, ✉ 6711 BB, ✆ (0 318) 61 62 54, *Fax (0 318) 65 19 80*, – AE VISA
fermé lundi et mardi – **Repas** (dîner seult) 28/45, ♀.
◆ Une enseigne appropriée, tant la façade à redans qui la supporte capte l'attention dans cette petite rue tranquille. Recettes d'aujourd'hui déclinées en menus du marché.
◆ Gepaste naam voor dit restaurant, waarvan de trapgevel onmiddellijk de aandacht trekt in het rustige straatje. Menu's met eigentijdse gerechten van dagverse producten.

EEMNES *Utrecht* 532 Q 9 *et* 715 G 5 – *8 609 h.*

Beukenlaan 1, ✉ 3755 MP, ☎ (0 35) 539 31 00, Fax (0 35) 539 31 25.

Amsterdam 34 – Utrecht 22 – Apeldoorn 61 – Hilversum 5.

De Witte Bergen, Rijksweg 2 (sur A 1), ✉ 3755 MV, ☎ (0 35) 539 58 00, *reservations@wittebergen.valk.nl, Fax (0 35) 531 38 48,* – 25 à 300. AE MC VISA. rest

Repas (ouvert jusqu'à 23 h) carte 22 à 41 – 7 – **150 ch** 78/96 – ½ P 63.

◆ Près de l'autoroute, établissement de la chaîne Van der Valk hébergeant des chambres de différentes catégories, en partie regroupées dans une aile plus récente.

◆ Dit ketenhotel dicht bij de snelweg valt onder Van der Valk en heeft kamers in verschillende categorieën, die deels in de nieuw aangebouwde vleugel zijn ondergebracht.

't Oude Raadhuys, Wakkerendijk 30, ✉ 3755 DC, ☎ (0 35) 538 92 56, *restaurant@ouderaadhuys.nl, Fax (0 35) 531 36 72,* ≤, – P. AE MC VISA

fermé mardi, sam. midi et dim. midi – **Repas** *Lunch 27* – carte 34 à 47.

◆ Restaurant implanté dans l'ex-mairie d'Eemnes. Décor intérieur classique-actuel, cuisine du moment et grand choix de vins servis au verre. Jolie vue sur le polder en terrasse.

◆ Restaurant met een klassiek-eigentijds interieur, seizoengebonden keuken en een grote selectie wijnen die per glas worden geschonken. Terras met mooi uitzicht op de polder.

EERBEEK *Gelderland* © *Brummen 21 613 h.* 532 V 10 *et* 715 J 5.

Amsterdam 107 – Apeldoorn 23 – Arnhem 26 – Enschede 71.

Landgoed Het Huis te Eerbeek , Prof. Weberlaan 1, ✉ 6961 LX, ☎ (0 313) 65 91 35, *info@hhte.com, Fax (0 313) 65 41 75,* – P – 25 à 100. AE MC VISA.

Repas (dîner seult) 35/40, – **46 ch** 83/111 – ½ P 78/95.

◆ Chambres réparties entre trois bâtiments élevés dans un beau parc où se pavanent des paons. Le manoir néoclassique et son ancienne remise (koetshuis) abritent les meilleures. Salle de restaurant aménagée dans l'ex-corps de logis. Plats aux accents du Sud.

◆ De kamers liggen verspreid over drie gebouwen in een mooi park waar pauwen lopen te pronken. Het neoklassieke landhuis en het koetshuis herbergen de beste kamers. Het restaurant is ondergebracht in het oude hoofdgebouw. Gerechten met een zuidelijk accent.

EERNEWOUDE *Fryslân – voir Earnewâld.*

EERSEL *Noord-Brabant* 532 Q 14 *et* 715 G 7 – *18 386 h.*

Markt 30a, ✉ 5521 AN, ☎ (0 497) 51 31 63, info@vvveersel.nl, Fax (0 497) 51 41 32.

Amsterdam 136 – Eindhoven 19 – 's-Hertogenbosch 47 – Antwerpen 72.

Promessa, Markt 3, ✉ 5521 AJ, ☎ (0 497) 53 05 10, *info@promessa.nl, Fax (0 497) 53 05 09* – AE MC VISA

fermé 22 fév.-2 mars, du 2 au 22 août et lundi – **Repas** (dîner seult) 28/33.

◆ Banquettes rouges, sièges club et rutilante cuisine moderne à vue donnent un "look" résolument "hype" à cette salle de restaurant où flotte une atmosphère de "lounge".

◆ Rode banken, clubfauteuils en een blinkende moderne keuken waarin u letterlijk een kijkje krijgt, geven deze restaurantzaal met loungeambiance een zeer trendy look.

EGMOND AAN ZEE *Noord-Holland* © *Bergen 31 926 h.* 531 M 7 *et* 715 E 4.

Voorstraat 82a, ✉ 1931 AN, ☎ (0 72) 581 31 00, info@vvvegmond.nl, Fax (0 72) 506 50 54.

Amsterdam 46 – Haarlem 34 – Alkmaar 10.

Zuiderduin, Zeeweg 52, ✉ 1931 VL, ☎ (0 72) 750 20 00, *info@zuiderduin.nl, Fax (0 72) 750 20 01,* – P – 25 à 800. AE MC VISA. rest

Repas (buffets) 25 – **365 ch** 110/235.

◆ Immense hôtel posté à deux pas du front de mer. Les chambres, fonctionnelles, sont bien tenues. Grande infrastructure pour séminaires, complexe de remise en forme et bar. Formule buffets au restaurant.

◆ Dit immense hotel ligt op loopafstand van het strand en beschikt over functionele kamers die goed worden onderhouden. Het heeft een grote infrastructuur voor bijeenkomsten en seminars, evenals een fitnesscentrum en bar. Buffetformule in het restaurant.

de Boei, Westeinde 2, ✉ 1931 AB, ☏ (0 72) 506 93 93, *deboei@deboei.nl, Fax (0 72) 506 24 54,* – – 25 à 40. VISA
Repas carte 23 à 39 – 9 – **26 ch** 46/76, – 12 suites – ½ P 99.
◆ Au centre de la station, près du phare, hôtel mettant à votre disposition des chambres pratiques ainsi qu'une douzaine d'appartements avec kitchenette. Cuisine hollandaise servie dans un cadre néo-rustique. Énorme terrasse chauffée durant l'arrière-saison.
◆ Dit hotel in het centrum van de badplaats, vlak bij de vuurtoren, beschikt over praktische kamers en een twaalftal appartementen met kitchenette. Gerechten uit de Nederlandse keuken worden in een neorustiek decor geserveerd. Verwarmd terras in het naseizoen.

de Vassy sans rest, Boulevard Ir. de Vassy 3, ✉ 1931 CN, ☏ (0 72) 506 15 73, *info@vassy.nl, Fax (0 72) 506 53 06,* – .
5 mars-3 nov. – **17 ch** 40/88.
◆ Les deux étages de ce petit hôtel bâti à une pirouette de cerf-volant de la plage renferment des chambres actuelles sans reproche. Fonctionnement familial.
◆ Dit kleine hotel ligt direct aan het strand, vlak bij het centrum, en telt twee verdiepingen met onberispelijke, eigentijdse kamers. Familiebedrijf.

Golfzang, Boulevard Ir. de Vassy 19, ✉ 1931 CN, ☏ (0 72) 506 15 16, *golfzang@planet.nl, Fax (0 72) 506 22 22* – . VISA.
fermé 15 déc.-15 janv. – **Repas** (dîner pour résidents seult) – **23 ch** 43/88 – ½ P 58/63.
◆ Immeuble de conception récente construit à l'arrière de la digue. Si l'on aime s'accouder au balcon, mieux vaut opter pour l'une des chambres disposées sur le devant.
◆ Dit modern opgezette pand is net achter de zeewering gebouwd. Wie graag over het balkon leunt, kan beter een kamer aan de voorkant vragen.

La Châtelaine, Smidstraat 7, ✉ 1931 EX, ☏ (0 72) 506 23 55, *restaurant@lachatelaine.nl, Fax (0 72) 506 69 26* – VISA
fermé janv. et merc. – **Repas** (dîner seult) 24/32.
◆ De vieux ustensiles de cuisine et de pâtisserie décorent une salle à manger rustique où un feu ouvert crépite hiver comme été. Atmosphère un peu "vieille forge".
◆ Oude bakvormen uit de keuken en de patisserie sieren een rustieke eetzaal waar zomer en winter een haardvuurtje knappert. De ambiance heeft wat weg van een oude smidse.

EIBERGEN *Gelderland* 532 Y 10 *et* 715 K 5 – *16 726 h.*

Amsterdam 146 – Arnhem 71 – Apeldoorn 60 – Enschede 24.

De Greune Weide , Lutterweg 1 (Sud : 2 km), ✉ 7152 CC, ☏ (0 545) 47 16 92, *info@degreuneweide.nl, Fax (0 545) 47 74 15,* , , – – 25. VISA.
fermé 30 déc.-30 janv. – **Repas** (dîner seult) 25/60 – **19 ch** 68/95 – ½ P 60.
◆ Le jardin soigné entourant cette villa s'harmonise au caractère champêtre du site. Chambres agréables, dont six duplex avec kitchenette, dans les deux annexes. Calme garanti ! Restaurant-véranda. Repas traditionnel également servi en plein air par beau temps.
◆ De verzorgde tuin rond deze villa is in harmonie met de landelijke omgeving. Aangename kamers - waarvan zes split-level met kitchenette - in de twee dependances. Rust verzekerd ! Restaurant met serre. Traditionele keuken. Bij mooi weer kunt u ook buiten eten.

Belle Fleur, J.W. Hagemanstraat 85, ✉ 7151 AE, ☏ (0 545) 47 21 49, *Fax (0 545) 47 59 53,* – VISA.
fermé 25 juil.-12 août, 27 déc.-13 janv. et lundi – **Repas** (dîner seult) carte 38 à 54.
◆ Près de la frontière allemande, ancienne ferme où transparaît un réel souci de coquetterie, des abords jusqu'à la mise en place des tables dans la jolie salle à manger.
◆ In deze voormalige boerderij vlak bij de Duitse grens is chic het sleutelwoord, vanaf de stoep tot aan de schikking van de tafels in de fraaie eetzaal.

The Green House, Haaksbergseweg 27, ✉ 7151 AR, ☏ (0 545) 47 29 23, *Fax (0 545) 47 50 25,* , Cuisine asiatique – VISA.
fermé mardi – **Repas** *Lunch 17* – carte 27 à 35, ♀.
◆ Les recettes concoctées dans cette grande villa vagabondent entre plusieurs contrées d'Asie et fusionnent même parfois avec des saveurs plus occidentales. Accueil gentil.
◆ De gerechten die in deze grote villa worden bereid, komen uit diverse Aziatische streken en mengen zich soms zelfs met wat westerser smaken. Vriendelijk onthaal.

EIJSDEN *Limburg* 532 T 18 *et* 715 I 9 – *12 029 h.*

Amsterdam 224 – Maastricht 9 – Heerlen 33 – 's-Hertogenbosch 135 – Liège 22.

De Kapoen, Diepstraat 1, ✉ 6245 BJ, ☏ (0 43) 409 35 54, *Fax (0 43) 409 09 37,* – VISA.
fermé du 15 au 26 fév., du 8 au 26 sept., lundi et mardi – **Repas** (dîner seult) 35/52, ♀.
◆ Refuge gourmand des plus coquets, où l'on fait de savoureux repas s'inspirant volontiers des grandes maisons de bouche du royaume. Le menu noté à l'écriteau : un bon choix !
◆ Een allercharmantst restaurant dat heerlijke gerechten bereidt en zich graag laat inspireren door de groten onder de nationale vakbroeders. Het menu op de lei is een aanrader !

EINDHOVEN *Noord-Brabant* 532 S 14 et 715 H 7 – *204 776 h – Casino* BY, *Heuvel Galerie 134,* ✉ *5611 DK,* ☎ *(0 40) 235 73 57, Fax (0 40) 235 73 60.*

Musée : *Van Abbe★ (Stedelijk Van Abbemuseum)* BZ **M¹**.

Ch. Roelslaan 15, ✉ *5644 HX,* ☎ *(0 40) 252 09 62, Fax (0 40) 293 22 38 -* *à l'Ouest : 5 km à Veldhoven, Locht 140,* ✉ *5504 RP,* ☎ *(0 40) 253 44 44, Fax (0 40) 254 97 47.*

✈ *5 km par Noord Brabantlaan* AV ☎ *(0 40) 291 98 18, Fax (0 40) 291 98 20.*

Stationsplein 17, ✉ *5611 AC,* ☎ *(0 40) 232 31 66, info@vvveindhoven.nl, Fax (0 40) 243 31 35.*

Amsterdam 122 ⑦ – 's-Hertogenbosch 35 ⑦ – Maastricht 86 ③ – Tilburg 36 ⑥ – Antwerpen 86 ④ – Duisburg 99 ③

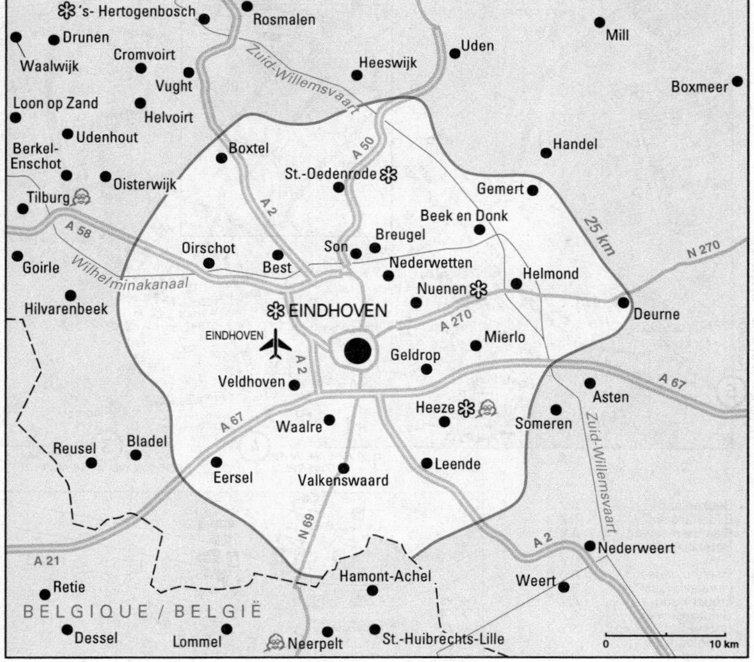

Dorint, Vestdijk 47, ✉ 5611 CA, ☎ (0 40) 232 61 11, *info@dhe.dorint.nl, Fax (0 40) 244 01 48*, – 25 à 1500. AE VISA JCB BY h

Repas *Lunch 18* – carte 34 à 53 – 22 – **256 ch** 185/275, – 4 suites.

◆ L'un des meilleurs hôtels de la cinquième ville batave. Espaces communs soignés, agencés dans l'esprit contemporain, chambres modernes, appartements et suites.

◆ Een van de beste hotels in de vijfde stad van Nederland. Verzorgde, gemeenschappelijke ruimten met eigentijdse inrichting, moderne kamers, appartementen en suites.

Holiday Inn, Veldm. Montgomerylaan 1, ✉ 5612 BA, ☎ (0 40) 235 82 35, *holidayinn.eindhoven@ichotelsgroup.com, Fax (0 40) 244 92 35*, – 40 à 200. AE VISA JCB BY t

Repas *(fermé vend. soir et dim.)* carte 38 à 48, – 22 – **199 ch** 210/251.

◆ Près de la gare et du campus, établissement mettant à votre disposition plusieurs catégories de chambres fidèles aux normes de la chaîne et aménagées selon divers styles.

◆ Hotel in de buurt van het station en de campus. De diverse typen kamers zijn in verschillende stijlen ingericht en bieden het comfort dat gebruikelijk is binnen de hotelketen.

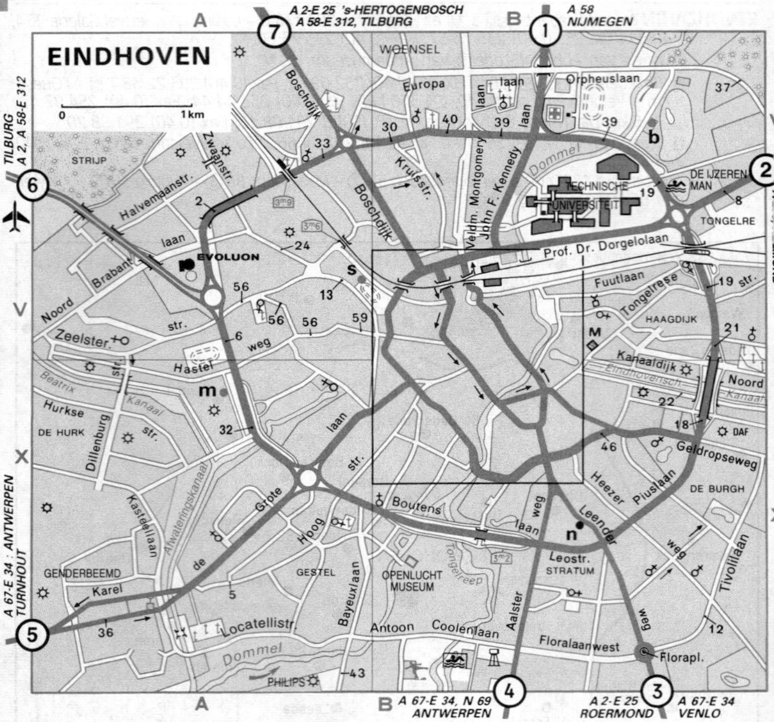

EINDHOVEN

A 2-E 25 's-HERTOGENBOSCH
A 58-E 312, TILBURG
A 58
NIJMEGEN
TILBURG A 2, A 58-E 312
A 67-E 34 : ANTWERPEN TURNHOUT
A 67-E 34, N 69 ANTWERPEN
A 2-E 25 ROERMOND
A 67-E 34 VENLO
WOENSEL
STRIJP
EVOLUON
TECHNISCHE UNIVERSITEIT
DE IJZEREN MAN
TONGELRE
HAAGDIJK
DE HURK
DAF
DE BURGH
GENDERBEEMD
GESTEL
OPENLUCHT MUSEUM
STRATUM
PHILIPS
Boschdijk
Kruisstr.
Europa
Veldm. Montgomery laan
John F. Kennedy laan
Orpheuslaan
Dommel
Zwaanstr.
Halvemaanstr.
Brabant laan
Noord Brabant laan
Zeelstr.
Hastel weg
Beatrix Kanaal
Hurkse str.
Dillenburg str.
Kastelenlaan
Afwateringskanaal
Karel de Grote laan
Hoog str.
Boutens laan
Locatellistr.
Bayeuxlaan
Antoon Coolenlaan
Tongelreep
Aalster weg
Leender weg
Heezer weg
Piuslaan
Tivolilaan
Leostr.
Floralaanwest
Florapl.
Prof. Dr. Dorgelolaan
Futlaan
Tongelrese str.
Kanaaldijk
Eindhovensch Kanaal
Geldropseweg

Beukenlaan .... AV 2
Bilderdijklaan .... BZ 3
Blaarthemseweg .... AX 5
Botenlaan .... AV 6
Demer .... BY
Eisenhowerlaan .... BV 8
Floralaan Oost .... BX 12
Frederiklaan .... AV 13
Geldropseweg .... BZ 15
Hermanus Boexstr. .... BY 16
Hugo van der Goeslaan .... BX 18
Insulindelaan .... BV 19
Jeroen Boschlaan .... BV 21
Kanaaldijk Zuid .... BX 22
Kastanjelaan .... AV 24
Keizersgracht .... BY 25
Kerkstr. .... BY 28
Kleine Berg .... BY 27
Kronehoefstr. .... BV 30
Lardinoisstr. .... BY 31
Limburglaan .... AX 32
Marconilaan .... AV 33
Mecklenburgstr. .... BZ 34
Meerveldhovenseweg .... AX 36
v. Oldenbarneveltlaan .... BV 37
Onze Lieve Vrouwstr. .... BV 39
Pastoriestr. .... BV 40
P. C. Hooftlaan .... BZ 42
Prof. Holstlaan .... AX 43
Rechtestr. .... BY 45
St. Jorislaan .... BZ 48
Stadhuispl. .... BZ 50
Stationspl. .... BY 51
Stationsweg .... BY 53
Stratumseind .... BY 54
Strijpsestr. .... AV 56
Ten Hagestr. .... BY 57
Vrijstr. .... BY
Willemstr. .... AV 59
18 Septemberpl. .... BY 60

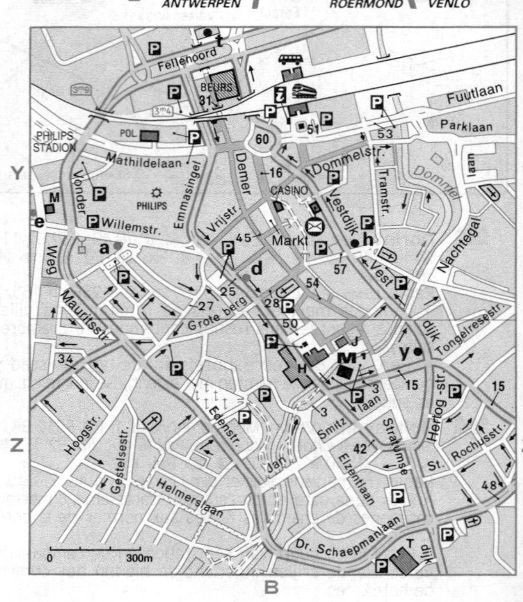

Mandarin Park Plaza, Geldropseweg 17, ✉ 5611 SC, ☎ (0 40) 212 50 55, *mppres @parkplazahotels.nl, Fax (0 40) 212 15 55,* - 30 à 60. AE MC VISA. BZ y
Repas ***Mandarin Garden*** (cuisine chinoise, dîner seult) carte 34 à 55, 𝕐 - 17 - **100 ch** 180/205, - 2 suites - ½ P 210/235.
◆ Cet immeuble de notre temps situé à l'entrée d'Eindhoven, au voisinage du ring, renferme plusieurs catégories de chambres "full equipment", arrangées sans faute de goût. Salles de restaurant exclusivement consacrées à la cuisine asiatique.
◆ Dit moderne pand aan de rand van Eindhoven, vlak bij de ringweg, beschikt over verschillende categorieën kamers met alle comfort, die bijzonder smaakvol zijn ingericht. De restaurants staan geheel in het teken van de Aziatische keuken.

Pierre, Leenderweg 80, ✉ 5615 AB, ☎ (0 40) 212 10 12, *info@hotelpierre.nl, Fax (0 40) 212 12 61,* - 25 à 150. AE MC VISA JCB. rest BX n
Repas *(fermé sam. midi et dim. midi)* Lunch 18 - carte 22 à 63 - 13 - **60 ch** 105/116 - ½ P 137.
◆ Hôtel fonctionnel bâti à l'écart du centre animé. Façade et réception ont récemment fait l'objet d'une rénovation. Chambres standard distribuées sur trois étages.
◆ Functioneel hotel buiten het drukke centrum. De gevel en de receptie zijn onlangs gerenoveerd. Standaardkamers die over drie verdiepingen verspreid liggen.

Campanile, Noord-Brabantlaan 309 (près A 2, sortie ㉛), ✉ 5657 GB, ☎ (0 40) 254 54 00, *eindhoven@campanile.com, Fax (0 40) 254 44 10,* - 40. AE MC VISA JCB
Repas (avec buffets) Lunch 12 - 22 - 10 - **84 ch** 78.
◆ L'une des plus grandes unités Campanile des Pays-Bas, à quelques kilomètres seulement du centre-ville et de l'aéroport. Chambres de mise simple, mais rafraîchies.
◆ Een van de grootste vestigingen van Campanile in Nederland, op slechts enkele kilometers van het stadscentrum en de luchthaven. Eenvoudige maar opgeknapte kamers.

De Karpendonkse Hoeve, Sumatralaan 3, ✉ 5631 AA, ☎ (0 40) 281 36 63, *info@karpendonksehoeve.nl, Fax (0 40) 281 11 45,* ≤, - AE MC VISA. BV b
fermé du 22 au 29 fév., 9 et 12 avril, 31 mai, 24 et 31 déc., sam. midi et dim. - **Repas** Lunch 47 bc - 63/80, carte 48 à 91, 𝕐.
◆ Une étoile brille depuis 25 ans dans l'élégante salle à manger de cette ancienne ferme. Jolie terrasse avec vue sur un parc et son lac. Mets classiques actualisés.
◆ Boven deze elegante hoeve fonkelt al 25 jaar een ster. Leuk zicht op een park met vijver vanop het mooie terras. Door een huidige bril gelezen klassieke receptuur.
Spéc. Terrine de foie gras gelée au Sauternes. Saint-Jacques laquées au soja, jets de soja et gingembre. Asperges régionales, thon mariné et grillé au sabayon de Xères

Avant-Garde (van Groeninge), Frederiklaan 10d (Philips stadion, entrée 7 - 3e étage), ✉ 5616 NH, ☎ (0 40) 250 56 40, *j.vangroeninge@avant-garde.nl, Fax (0 40) 250 56 43,* ≤, - AE MC VISA - *fermé 26 juil.-16 août, 25 déc.-4 janv., sam. midi, dim., lundi, jours fériés et jours de match du club* - **Repas** Lunch 35 - 52/125 bc, carte 54 à 79, 𝕐.
◆ Habilement intégrée au stade du PSV, cette nouvelle table gastronomique vous accueille dans un cadre contemporain où flotte une atmosphère "zen". Cuisine inventive. ABV s
◆ Dit nieuwe gastronomische restaurant is geïntegreerd in het voetbalstadion van PSV. U wordt er onthaald in een eigentijds decor met ietwat "Zen" ambiance. Inventieve keuken.
Spéc. Turbot grillé à la truffe d'été. Poussin en vessie, sauce aux morilles. Gratin de figues, sabayon au marc de Champagne

De Luytervelde, Jo Goudkuillaan 11 (Nord-Ouest : 7 km par ⑦ à Acht), ✉ 5626 GC, ☎ (0 40) 262 31 11, *info@deluytervelde.nl, Fax (0 40) 262 40 03,* - AE MC VISA. - *fermé fin déc., sem. carnaval, 3 sem. vacances bâtiment, sam. midi et dim.* - **Repas** Lunch 23 - 45/90 bc, 𝕐.
◆ Ancienne résidence profitant d'un beau domaine : jardin arboré, pièces d'eau et parterres fleuris en été. Cuisine du marché. Ravissantes terrasses estivales.
◆ Voormalige boerderij met bomentuin, waterpartijen en bloemperken. De gerechten worden bereid van vers verkrijgbare producten. Schitterend zomerterras.

Willem van Oranje, Willemstraat 43a, ✉ 5611 HC, ☎ (0 40) 296 38 19, *willem.van .oranje@planet.nl, Fax (0 40) 296 38 20* - AE MC VISA. BY a
fermé 28 juil.-18 août, 28 déc.-5 janv. et dim. - **Repas** Lunch 30 - 33/50, 𝕐.
◆ En peu de temps, cette adresse s'est hissée parmi les valeurs montantes du centre-ville. Savoureuse cuisine d'aujourd'hui, servie dans une salle à manger contemporaine.
◆ In korte tijd is dit adres tot de betere restaurants van de stad gaan behoren. Smakelijke hedendaagse gerechten, die in een moderne eetzaal worden geserveerd.

Bali, Keizersgracht 13, ✉ 5611 GC, ☎ (0 40) 244 56 49, *Fax (0 40) 246 01 90,* Cuisine indonésienne - AE MC VISA BY d
Repas Lunch 9 - 16/23.
◆ Restaurant indonésien tout en longueur. Au choix à la carte s'ajoute évidemment l'habituelle formule "rijsttafel" (table de riz). Décor intérieur d'un exotisme mesuré.
◆ Indonesisch restaurant in een lange ruimte. Op de kaart ontbreekt de gebruikelijke rijsttafel uiteraard niet. Het decor is bescheiden exotisch.

XX **De Blauwe Lotus,** Limburglaan 20, ✉ 5652 AA, ☎ (0 40) 251 48 76, *info@deblauwelotus.nl, Fax (0 40) 251 15 25,* Cuisine asiatique – ▤. AE ◑ MC VISA JCB. ✂ AX m
fermé sam. midi et dim. – **Repas** *Lunch 23* – 30/44.
◆ L'enseigne de cet établissement asiatique plaira aux bédéphiles, puisqu'elle emprunte le titre d'une aventure de Tintin. En salles, habillage oriental assez plaisant.
◆ De restaurantnaam zal bij stripliefhebbers zeker in de smaak vallen, want die is ontleend aan een avontuur van Kuifje. De eetzalen hebben een prettige, oriëntaalse ambiance.

X **The Old Valley,** Sint Antoniusstraat 18, ✉ 5616 RT, ☎ (0 40) 257 39 39, *info@theoldvalley.nl, Fax (0 40) 256 92 31* – ▤. AE MC VISA. ✂ BY e
fermé du 4 au 19 août, 27 déc.-3 janv. et lundi – **Repas** (déjeuner sur réservation) 25/60 bc.
◆ Seulement quelques foulées séparent cette affaire familiale du Philips Stadion, le stade de football du PSV. En saison, les asperges sont toujours de la partie.
◆ Dit restaurant ligt niet ver van het Philips Stadion, de thuisbasis van PSV. In het seizoen zijn de asperges altijd van de partij.

à l'aéroport *Ouest : 5 km :*

🏨 **Novotel,** Anthony Fokkerweg 101, ✉ 5657 EJ, ☎ (0 40) 252 65 75, *H1018@accor-hotels.com, Fax (0 40) 252 28 50,* ☂, ⛱, 🚲 – |♦| ✈, ▤ ch, TV ♿ P – 🏛 25 à 200. AE ◑ MC VISA
Repas *Lunch 25* – carte 26 à 39 – ☕ 14 – **92 ch** 122/128 – ½ P 111/199.
◆ Hôtel de chaîne occupant une position stratégique : proximité de l'aéroport et de l'autoroute. Chambres bien insonorisées. Espaces pour la tenue de conférences.
◆ Ketenhotel op een strategische lokatie : vlak bij de luchthaven en de autosnelweg. De kamers zijn van een goede geluidsisolatie voorzien. Conferentiezalen aanwezig.

ELSLOO *Limburg* C *Stein 26 520 h.* 532 T 17 *et* 715 I 9.
Amsterdam 205 – Maastricht 20 – Eindhoven 70.

XX **Kasteel Elsloo** avec ch, Maasberg 1, ✉ 6181 GV, ☎ (0 46) 437 76 66, *info@kasteelelsloo.nl, Fax (0 46) 437 75 70,* ☂, ⛱, 🎾, 🚲 – TV P – 🏛 25 à 90. AE ◑ MC VISA. ✂ rest
fermé 27 déc.-3 janv. – **Repas** *(fermé sam. midi et dim. midi) Lunch 30* – 34/47, ♀ – ☕ 11 – **24 ch** 60/80 – ½ P 75/85.
◆ En bord de Meuse, demeure pleine de cachet, avec sa puissante tour défensive, son vieux moulin à eau restauré et son parc reposant. Cuisine actuelle ; chambres de même.
◆ Dit buitenverblijf aan de Maas heeft met zijn imposante verdedigingstoren, gerestaureerde watermolen en rustgevende park ronduit cachet. Eigentijdse gerechten en dito kamers.

ELSPEET *Gelderland* C *Nunspeet 26 317 h.* 531 T 9, 532 T 9 *et* 715 I 5.
Amsterdam 82 – Arnhem 50 – Lelystad 44 – Utrecht 62 – Zwolle 39.

🏨 **Landgoed Stakenberg** ⛰, Stakenberg 86 (Nord-Est : 6 km), ✉ 8075 RH, ☎ (0 577) 49 12 71, *stakenberg@planet.nl, Fax (0 577) 49 11 00,* ☂, ⛱, 🎾, 🚲 – TV P – 🏛 25 à 80. AE MC VISA. ✂ ch
Repas (dîner seult jusqu'à 20 h sauf week-end) carte env. 34 – **35 ch** ☕ 42/60 – ½ P 52.
◆ Cet hôtel tranquille à débusquer dans les bois se compose d'une longue aile de chambres - sobres et proprettes - flanquant une demeure ancienne où l'on retirera sa clé. Appétissante carte actuelle au restaurant.
◆ Dit rustige hotel in de bossen heeft eenvoudige, nette kamers. Deze zijn ondergebracht in een lange vleugel die tegen het oude woonhuis is aangebouwd, waar de sleutel kan worden opgehaald. Restaurant met een smakelijke, actuele menukaart.

ELST *Utrecht* 532 R 11 *et* 715 H 6 – *voir à Rhenen.*

EMMELOORD *Flevoland* C *Noordoostpolder 44 252 h.* 531 T 6 *et* 715 I 3.
ℹ *De Deel 21a, ✉ 8302 EK, ☎ (0 527) 61 20 00, emmeloord@vvvflevoland.nl, Fax (0 527) 61 44 57.*
Amsterdam 89 – Groningen 94 – Leeuwarden 66 – Zwolle 36.

🏨 **Emmeloord,** Het Hooiveld 9 (sortie ⑮ sur A 6), ✉ 8302 AE, ☎ (0 527) 61 23 45, *info@emmeloord.valk.nl, Fax (0 527) 61 28 45,* ☂, 🏋, ≘s, 🚲, ⛽ – |♦| TV – 🏛 25 à 350. AE ◑ MC VISA JCB
Repas (ouvert jusqu'à 23 h) *Lunch 11* – carte 22 à 42, ♀ – ☕ 7 – **107 ch** 57/64 – ½ P 60.
◆ Un petit port de plaisance privé avoisine cette unité de la chaîne Van der Valk. Nouvelle aile de chambres confortables, bar à l'anglaise et health center flambant neuf.
◆ Een kleine privéjachthaven ligt naast dit hotel van de Van der Valk-keten. Nieuwe vleugel met comfortabele kamers, Engelse pub en een gloednieuw healthcenter.

't Voorhuys, De Deel 20, ✉ 8302 EK, ☎ (0 527) 61 28 70, *info@voorhuys.nl, Fax (0 527) 61 79 03,* 🏠, 🚲 – |‡|, ▤ rest, 📺 – 🏛 25 à 520. AE ◑ ◉ VISA JCB. ⚿ ch
fermé 31 déc. et 1er janv. – **Repas** (taverne-rest) *Lunch 26* – 29/40 bc, ♀ – **25 ch** ☕ 68/85 – ½ P 53/59.
◆ Établissement familial du centre-ville, totalement rénové et redécoré voici quelque temps. Chambres fraîches et actuelles, pourvues d'un équipement standard. Taverne-restaurant animée. Ambiance "grand café" aux accents Art déco.
◆ Dit familiehotel in het centrum is onlangs volledig gerenoveerd en opnieuw ingericht. De frisse, eigentijdse kamers zijn voorzien van standaardcomfort. Gezellig restaurant. Ambiance grand café met accenten in art-decostijl.

Le Mirage 2e étage, Beursstraat 2, ✉ 8302 CW, ☎ (0 527) 69 91 04, *info@lemirage.nl, Fax (0 527) 69 80 35* – ▤. AE ◑ ◉ VISA. ⚿
Repas (déjeuner sur réservation) *Lunch 28* – 32/54 bc, ♀.
◆ Adresse sympathique et bien dans l'air du temps située au cœur d'Emmeloord. Ample salle à manger avec sièges en rotin et tables nues. Mezzanine où l'on sert l'apéritif.
◆ Sympathiek, eigentijds eethuis in hartje Emmeloord. Ruime eetzaal met rotanstoelen en tafels zonder kleedjes. In de vide wordt het aperitief geserveerd.

EMMEN *Drenthe* 531 AA 6 *et* 715 L 3 – *108 367 h.*

Voir *Dolmen d'Emmer Dennen★ (hunebed) – Jardin zoologique★ (Noorder Dierenpark).*

Env. *à l'Ouest : 6,5 km à Noordsleen : Dolmen★ (hunebed) – au Nord-Ouest : 18 km à Orvelte★.*

⛳18 *à l'Ouest : 12 km à Aalden, Gebbeveenweg 1, ✉ 7854 TD, ☎ (0 591) 37 17 84, Fax (0 591) 37 24 22.*

ℹ *Hoofdstraat 22, ✉ 7811 EP, ☎ (0 591) 61 30 00, info@vvvemmen.nl, Fax (0 591) 64 41 06.*

Amsterdam 180 – Assen 44 – Groningen 57 – Leeuwarden 97 – Zwolle 70.

De Giraf, Van Schaikweg 55, ✉ 7811 HN, ☎ (0 591) 64 20 02, *giraf@bestwestern.nl, Fax (0 591) 64 96 54,* 🏋, 🎾, 🚲 – |‡| ⇌ 📺 ♿ 🅿 – 🏛 25 à 1100. AE ◑ ◉ VISA JCB. ⚿ rest
Repas carte 22 à 38, ♀ – ☕ 10 – **83 ch** 70/90 – ½ P 108/142.
◆ En retrait de l'animation du centre-ville, établissement couplé à un important centre de congrès. Diverses catégories de chambres et bonne infrastructure sportive.
◆ Dit hoteletablissement ligt wat buiten de drukte van het centrum en is gekoppeld aan een omvangrijk congrescentrum. Diverse categorieën kamers en goede sportfaciliteiten.

ENKHUIZEN *Noord-Holland* 531 Q 6 *et* 715 G 3 – *17 076 h.*

Voir *La vieille ville★ – Jubé★ dans l'église de l'Ouest ou de St-Gommaire (Wester of St-Gomaruskerk)* AB *– Drommedaris★ : du sommet ✳★, du quai ⇐★* B.

Musée : *du Zuiderzee★ (Zuiderzeemuseum) : Binnenmuseum★ en Buitenmuseum★★* B.

⛴ *vers Stavoren : Rederij V and O B.V., Oosterhavenstraat 13 ☎ (0 228) 32 60 06, Fax (0 228) 31 82 97. Durée de la traversée : 1 h 25. - vers Urk : Rederij FRO FFF à Urk ☎ (0 527) 68 34 07. Durée de la traversée : 1 h 30.*

ℹ *Tussen Twee Havens 1, ✉ 1601 EM, ☎ (0 228) 31 31 64, vvvenkhuizeneo@hetnet.nl, Fax (0 228) 31 55 31.*

Amsterdam 62 ① – Hoorn 19 ② – Leeuwarden 113 ①

Plan page suivante

De Koepoort, Westerstraat 294, ✉ 1601 AS, ☎ (0 228) 31 49 66, *info@dekoepoort.nl, Fax (0 228) 31 90 30* – ▤ 📺 🅿. AE ◑ ◉ VISA. ⚿ A a
Repas *Lunch 18* – carte 29 à 51 – **13 ch** ☕ 57/117 – ½ P 65/83.
◆ Une ancienne porte de la ville, la Koepoort, prête son nom à cet hôtel familial où vous passerez des nuits sans histoire dans des chambres correctement équipées. À l'heure du repas, mets classiques escortés de grands crus de Bourgogne et du Bordelais.
◆ Een oude stadspoort heeft zijn naam gegeven aan dit familiehotel, waar de comfortabele kamers garant staan voor een ongestoorde nachtrust. Aan tafel worden de klassieke gerechten vergezeld van grands crus uit de Bourgogne en de Bordelais.

Die Drie Haringhe, Dijk 28, ✉ 1601 GJ, ☎ (0 228) 31 86 10, *Fax (0 228) 32 11 35,* ⇐, 🏠 – AE ◑ ◉ VISA. ⚿ B b
fermé sam. midi, dim. midi, lundi de nov. à mars et mardi – **Repas** *Lunch 30* – 27/44.
◆ Les produits régionaux sont à l'honneur dans cet entrepôt du 17e s. habilement converti en restaurant. Vue sur le Drommedaris, tour massive surveillant l'entrée du port.
◆ In dit tot restaurant verbouwde pakhuis uit de 17e eeuw worden streekgerechten geserveerd. Uitzicht op de Drommedaris, de massieve toren die de ingang van de haven bewaakt.

ENKHUIZEN

Bocht	B 3		Melkmarkt	B 12		Venedie	B 25
Driebanen	B 4		Nieuwstraat	B 13		Vijzelstr.	B
Hoornseveer	A 6		Noorder Havendijk	B 15		Waagstraat	B 27
Kaasmarkt	B 7		Oosterhavenstr.	B 16		Wegje	B 28
Karnemelksluis	B 9		St. Janstraat	B 19		Westerstraat	AB
Klopperstraat	A 10		Spijtbroeksburgwal	A 21		Zuider Boerenvaart	A 30
			Staeleversgracht	B 22		Zuider Havendijk	B 31
			Sijbrandsplein	B 24		Zuiderspui	B 33
						Zwaanstraat	B 34

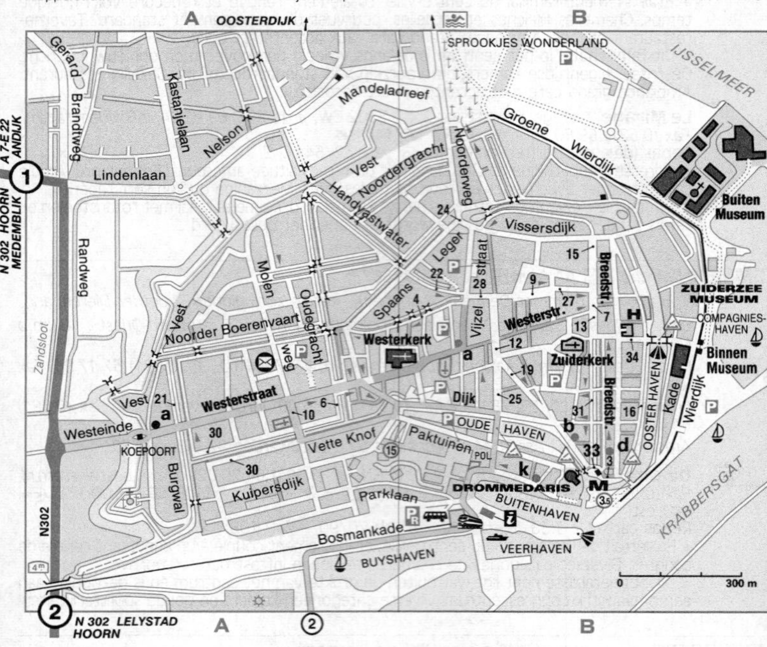

---

d'Alsace, Westerstraat 116, ✉ 1601 AM, ☎ (0 228) 31 52 25, *Fax (0 228) 31 52 25*, – AE MC VISA B a
fermé mardi d'oct. à mars et lundi – **Repas** (déjeuner sur réservation) 30.
◆ Une rue piétonne de la vieille ville mène à cette maison ancienne qui n'a d'alsacien que le nom. Salle à manger actuelle avec mezzanine. Terrasse d'été fleurie à l'arrière.
◆ Een voetgangersstraat in de oude stad leidt naar een oud huis, dat alleen in naam iets van de Elzas heeft. Moderne eetzaal met tussenverdieping. Zomerterras aan de achterkant.

De Smederij, Breedstraat 158, ✉ 1601 KG, ☎ (0 228) 31 46 04, *Fax (0 228) 32 30 79* – AE ⓓ MC VISA JCB B d
fermé jeudi de nov. à mars et merc. – **Repas** (déjeuner sur réservation) carte env. 39.
◆ Petit bistrot dont l'enseigne, La Forge (De Smederij), rappelle la destination première des lieux. Salle à manger rustique. Service convivial, tout comme l'ambiance.
◆ Kleine bistro waarvan de naam herinnert aan de vroegere bestemming van het pand. Rustieke eetzaal. Vriendelijke bediening en gezellige ambiance.

De Boei, Havenweg 5, ✉ 1601 GA, ☎ (0 228) 31 42 80, *info@restaurantdeboei.com, Fax (0 228) 32 30 48*, – AE ⓓ MC VISA B k
fermé du 1er au 7 mars, 25 et 26 déc. et lundi – **Repas** Lunch 25 – 29/38 bc.
◆ Maison bourgeoise se mirant dans les eaux du port de plaisance. Salle de restaurant façon bistrot avec vue batelière, agréable terrasse estivale et cuisine à la page.
◆ Restaurant in een herenhuis dat zich spiegelt in het water van de jachthaven. Eetzaal in bistrostijl, met uitzicht op de boten. Eigentijdse keuken en aangenaam zomerterras.

Les pages explicatives de l'introduction vous aideront à mieux profiter de votre Guide Michelin.

ENSCHEDE *Overijssel* 531 AA 9, 532 AA 9 *et* 715 L 5 – *151 346 h – Casino* Z , *Boulevard 1945 nr 105,* ✉ *7511 AM,* ☎ *(0 53) 750 27 50, Fax (0 53) 750 27 00.*

Musée : *de la Twente*★ *(Rijksmuseum Twenthe)* V.

⛳9 *Maatmanweg 27,* ✉ *7522 AN,* ☎ *(0 53) 433 79 92* - ⛳18 *par* ① : *Veendijk 100,* ✉ *7525 PZ,* ☎ *(0 541) 53 03 31, Fax (0 541) 53 16 90* - ⛳9 *par* ③ : *9 km à Hengelo, Enschedesestraat 381,* ✉ *7552 CV,* ☎ *(074) 250 84 66, Fax (0 74) 250 93 88.*

✈ *Twente* ☎ *(0 53) 486 22 22, Fax (0 53) 435 96 91.*

ℹ *Oude Markt 31,* ✉ *7511 GB,* ☎ *(0 53) 432 32 00, info@vvvenschede.nl, Fax (0 53) 430 41 62.*

Amsterdam 160 ⑤ *– Zwolle 73* ⑥ *– Groningen 148* ① *– Düsseldorf 141* ④ *– Münster 64* ②

Plan page suivante

De Broeierd, Hengelosestraat 725 (par ⑥ : 3 km), ✉ 7521 PA, ☎ (0 53) 850 65 00, *sales@broeierd.nl, Fax (0 53) 850 65 10,* – 25 à 70. AE ⓓ ⓜ VISA.

Repas *(fermé 2 sem. en juil., 27 déc.-4 janv., dim. et lundi)* (dîner seult) carte 35 à 50 – ☕ 14 – **61 ch** 115 – ½ P 100/154.

◆ Une ancienne ferme typique bordée d'arbres sert de cadre à cette ravissante auberge modernisée, agrandie d'une nouvelle annexe. Chambres et junior suites de bon séjour. Poutres vernies, sièges écarlates et piano décorent la salle de restaurant. Jolie terrasse.

◆ Een oude, karakteristieke boerderij vormt het decor van dit schitterende, gemoderniseerde hotel dat met een nieuwe annexe is uitgebreid. Comfortabele kamers en junior suites. Eetzaal met gelakte balken, scharlakenrode zittingen en piano. Leuk terras.

Het Koetshuis Schuttersveld, Hengelosestraat 111, ✉ 7514 AE, ☎ (0 53) 432 28 66, *koetshuis@alliance.nl, Fax (0 53) 433 39 57,* – P. AE ⓓ ⓜ VISA JCB. V r

fermé 18 juil.-4 août, 23 déc.-11 janv., sam. midi, dim. et lundi – **Repas** 40/70, ♀.

◆ Cuisine créative à savourer dans les dépendances d'une demeure avoisinante. Les asperges font l'objet d'un menu en saison. Salon avec cheminée. Accueil et service prévenants.

◆ In deze dependance van een aangrenzend woonverblijf worden originele gerechten geserveerd, met in het seizoen asperges. Salon met schouw. Voorkomende ontvangst en service.

La Petite Bouffe, Deurningerstraat 11, ✉ 7514 BC, ☎ (0 53) 430 30 40, *info@lapetitebouffe.nl, Fax (0 53) 436 23 72,* – AE ⓓ ⓜ VISA Y u

fermé du 1er au 9 mars, lundi et mardi – **Repas** (dîner seult) 34/50.

◆ Une enseigne tombant à point nommé pour se faire une bonne "petite bouffe" ! Salle à manger actuelle rénovée et terrasse croquignolette dressée les beaux jours d'été.

◆ Een naam die als geroepen komt wanneer u aan een lekkere maaltijd toe bent ! Eigentijdse, gerenoveerde eetzaal en bij mooi weer een snoeperig terras.

à Boekelo *par* ④ : *8 km* C *Enschede* :

Bad Boekelo, Oude Deldenerweg 203, ✉ 7548 PM, ☎ (0 53) 428 30 05, *info@belevingshotel.com, Fax (0 53) 428 30 35,* – 25 à 220. AE ⓓ ⓜ VISA JCB.

Repas Lunch 18 – carte env. 38 – **76 ch** ☕ 90/110, – 2 suites – ½ P 140/160.

◆ Amoureux de la petite reine et congressistes en quête d'une certaine tranquillité pourront compter sur cet établissement entouré de bois. Chambres rénovées.

◆ Fietsliefhebbers en congresgangers die op zoek zijn naar een beetje rust, komen geheel aan hun trekken in dit etablissement midden in de bossen. Gerenoveerde kamers.

à Usselo *par* ④ : *4 km* C *Enschede* :

Hanninkshof, Usselerhofweg 5, ✉ 7548 RZ, ☎ (0 53) 428 31 29, *Fax (0 53) 428 21 29,* – P. ⓓ ⓜ VISA.

fermé 29 déc.-2 janv. et sam. midi – **Repas** 25/50 bc, ♀.

◆ Ferme-auberge engageante située en léger retrait d'un carrefour. Décor intérieur rappelant un peu le style Laura Ashley. Préparations dans le tempo actuel. Prix sages.

◆ Restaurant in een boerderijwoning die iets van een kruispunt af ligt. Interieur in de stijl van Laura Ashley. Eigentijdse gerechten. Schappelijke prijzen.

PAYS-BAS

ENSCHEDE

Achter't Hofje	Z 3
Bisschopstr.	X 4
Blijdensteinlaan	V 6
Brammelerstr.	Y 7
Gronausestr.	X 9
Haverstraatpassage	Z 10
Hendrik Jan van Heekpl.	Z 12
Hofpassage	Z 13
Kalanderstr.	Z 16
Klokkenplas	YZ 18
Korte Haaksbergerstr.	YZ 19
Korte Hengelosestr.	Y 21
Langestr.	Z 22
van Lochemstr.	Y 24
van Loenshof	Z 25
Marktstr.	Y 27
Minkmaatstr.	V 28
Nijverheidstr.	Z 31
Piet Heinstr.	Y 33
Pijpenstr.	Z 34
Raadhuisstr.	Z 36
Schouwinkstr.	V 37
Stadsgravenstr.	Y 39
Visserijstr.	Y 40
Volksparksingel	X 42
Walstr.	YZ 43
Windbrugstr.	Z 46

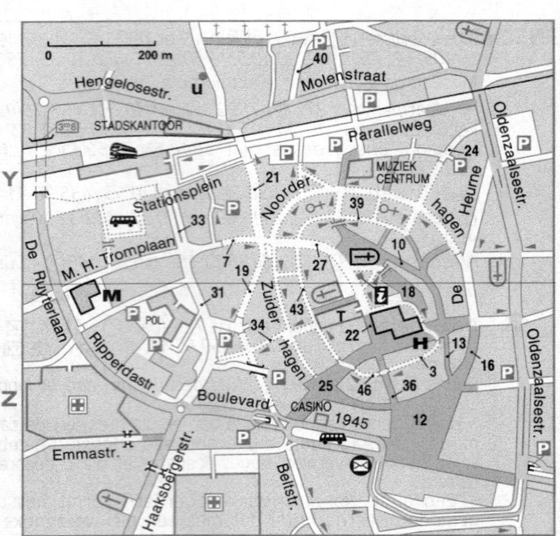

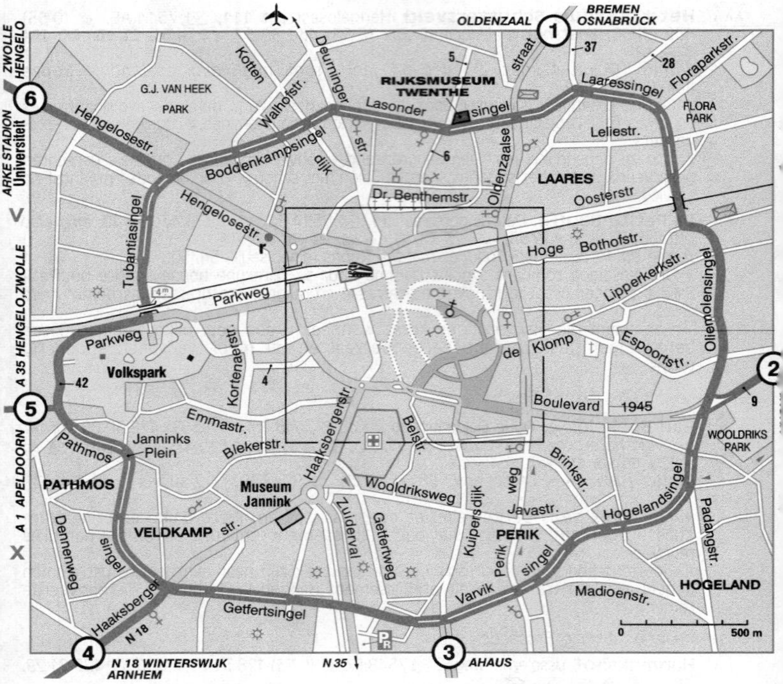

Bediening en belasting
In België, in Luxemburg en in Nederland zijn bediening en belasting bij de prijzen inbegrepen.

ENTER *Overijssel* *Ⓒ Wierden 23 429 h.* 531 Y 9, 532 Y 9 *et* 715 K 5.
Amsterdam 131 – Zwolle 45 – Apeldoorn 45 – Enchede 33.

X **bistro T-bone,** Dorpsstraat 154, ✉ 7468 CS, ☎ (0 547) 38 12 59, *bistrot-bone@wxs.nl, Fax (0 547) 38 27 67,* , Grillades – P. AE ⓓ ⓜ VISA JCB.
fermé du 4 au 26 août, mardi et merc. – **Repas** (dîner seult) carte 28 à 74.
◆ Le boeuf tient le haut du pavé dans cette maison aussi typique qu'animée. Grillades exécutées en salle et ambiance bistrotière. Plats de saison annoncés à l'écriteau.
◆ Rund voert de boventoon in dit karakteristieke, drukke restaurant. Grillades worden in de eetzaal bereid. Bistrosfeer. Seizoengerechten worden op een lei geschreven.

EPE *Gelderland* 531 U 8, 532 U 8 *et* 715 I 4 – *33 224 h.*
Pastoor Somstraat 6, ✉ 8162 AK, ☎ (0 578) 61 26 96, vvvepe@tref.nl, Fax (0 578) 61 55 81.
Amsterdam 97 – Arnhem 44 – Apeldoorn 21 – Zwolle 25.

Golden Tulip, Dellenweg 115, ✉ 8161 PW, ☎ (0 578) 61 28 14, *sales@gtepe.nl, Fax (0 578) 61 54 93,* , , , , – |‡|, rest, TV P – 25 à 275. AE ⓓ ⓜ VISA JCB.
Repas *Lunch 15* – 25 – **138 ch** 125/160 – ½ P 80.
◆ Hôtel de chaîne planté au milieu d'une forêt. Chambres progressivement rajeunies, sauna bien installé, bowling et bar agréable. Assez de calme, malgré les nombreux séminaires.
◆ Dit ketenhotel ligt midden in de bossen. De kamers worden geleidelijk gerenoveerd. Fraaie sauna, bowling en gezellige bar. Vrij rustig, ondanks de vele seminars.

Dennenheuvel, Heerderweg 27 (Nord : 2 km), ✉ 8161 BK, ☎ (0 578) 61 23 26, *dennenheuvel@dennenheuvel.nl, Fax (0 578) 67 76 99,* , , , – |‡|, rest, TV P – 25 à 50. AE ⓓ ⓜ VISA. rest
fermé 27 déc.-6 janv. – **Repas** carte env. 42 – **34 ch** 85/100 – ½ P 55/70.
◆ Une deuxième génération d'hôteliers est aux commandes de cette auberge postée en retrait de la route. Aile neuve avec chambres variant surface et type d'ameublement. Alternative restaurant ou brasserie.
◆ De tweede generatie staat nu aan het roer van dit hotel, dat van de weg af ligt. Nieuwe vleugel met kamers die qua grootte en inrichting variëren. Restaurant en brasserie.

XXX **'t Soerel,** Soerelseweg 22 (Ouest : 7 km, direction Nunspeet), ✉ 8162 PB, ☎ (0 578) 68 82 76, *info@soerel.nl, Fax (0 578) 68 82 86,* – P. AE ⓓ ⓜ VISA JCB
fermé du 17 au 29 fév., 28 sept.-10 oct., lundi et sam. midi – **Repas** *Lunch 30* – 35/60 bc, ♀.
◆ Dans un environnement boisé, jolie maison à toit de chaume devancée d'une terrasse où l'on dresse le couvert en été. La cuisine courtise un peu les produits régionaux.
◆ Restaurant in een mooi huis met rieten dak in een bosrijke omgeving. 's Zomers wordt op het terras aan de voorkant geserveerd. De keuken heeft een oogje op streekproducten.

EPEN *Limburg* *Ⓒ Gulpen-Wittem 15 435 h.* 532 U 18 *et* 715 I 9.
Voir *Route de Epen à Slenaken* ≤★.
Julianastraat 15, ✉ 6285 AG, ☎ 0 900 97 98, epen@vvvzuidlimburg.nl, Fax (0 43) 609 85 25.
Amsterdam 235 – Maastricht 24 – Aachen 15.

NH Zuid Limburg, Julianastraat 23a, ✉ 6285 AH, ☎ (0 43) 455 18 18, *Fax (0 43) 455 24 15,* ≤, , , , , – TV P – 25 à 140. AE ⓓ ⓜ VISA JCB.
Repas (résidents seult) – 13 – **77 ch** 108/145 – ½ P 86/108.
◆ Trente chambres supplémentaires : une capacité d'hébergement presque doublée pour cet établissement à peine distant de quelques kilomètres des frontières belge et allemande. La terrasse du restaurant offre un coup d'œil agreste.
◆ Maar liefst dertig extra kamers ! Dit hotel op slechts enkele kilometers van de Belgische en Duitse grens heeft zijn overnachtingscapaciteit bijna verdubbeld. Het terras van het restaurant biedt uitzicht op een landelijke omgeving.

Creusen, Wilhelminastraat 50, ✉ 6285 AW, ☎ (0 43) 455 12 15, *info@hotelcreusen.nl, Fax (0 43) 455 21 01,* ≤, – |‡|, rest, TV P – 25. AE ⓜ VISA JCB.
fermé 31 déc.-15 fév. – **Repas** (résidents seult) – **19 ch** 63/101 – ½ P 48.
◆ Grand salon confortable donnant sur un jardin avec pièce d'eau, chambres assez spacieuses, vue sur la campagne environnante : une hostellerie familiale tranquille.
◆ Een rustig familiehotel met een grote comfortabele lounge die uitkijkt op een tuin met waterpartij, vrij ruime kamers en uitzicht op het omringende platteland.

Ons Krijtland, Julianastraat 22, ✉ 6285 AJ, ℘ (0 43) 455 15 57, *info@krijtland.nl, Fax (0 43) 455 21 45,* ≤, – |‡| TV P – 30. VISA.
fermé du 5 au 19 janv. – **Repas** *(fermé après 20 h) Lunch 19* – carte 25 à 39 – **50 ch** ☐ 98.
• Aux abords du village, ressource hôtelière familiale active depuis 1931. Différentes catégories de chambres bénéficiant d'une reposante perspective champêtre. De la salle de restaurant, comme de la terrasse, panorama sur un vallon bucolique.
• Dit familiehotel aan de rand van het dorp maakt het zijn gasten al sinds 1931 naar de zin. Het beschikt over verschillende categorieën kamers met een rustgevend, landelijk uitzicht. Eetzaal en terras kijken uit op een idyllisch dal.

Os Heem, Wilhelminastraat 19, ✉ 6285 AS, ℘ (0 43) 455 16 23, *osheem@bestwestern.nl, Fax (0 43) 455 22 85,* – |‡| TV ♿. AE VISA JCB. rest
Repas (dîner pour résidents seult) – **24 ch** ☐ 82/105 – ½ P 70/140.
• Petite ressource hôtelière très valable pour séjourner au centre d'Epen. Chambres d'un calibre très convenable, et dont l'équipement est parmi les plus complets de la région.
• Een zeer acceptabel hotelletje voor wie in het centrum van Epen wil verblijven. De kamers zijn zeer redelijk van formaat en behoren tot de best uitgeruste van de streek.

Berg en Dal, Roodweg 18, ✉ 6285 AA, ℘ (0 43) 455 13 83, *Fax (0 43) 455 27 05,* – |‡| TV P. VISA JCB. rest
Repas *Lunch 18* – carte 22 à 47 – **33 ch** ☐ 60/83 – ½ P 44/50.
• Cet établissement tenu en famille depuis plusieurs générations dispose de trois sortes de chambres distribuées sur deux étages. Jardin ombragé pour le farniente. Salle à manger classiquement aménagée et restaurant d'été.
• Dit etablissement wordt al generaties lang in familiebeheer gerund. Het beschikt over drie soorten kamers die over twee verdiepingen verspreid liggen. De lommerrijke tuin nodigt uit tot lekker luieren. Klassiek ingerichte eetzaal en zomerrestaurant.

Inkelshoes, Terzieterweg 12, ✉ 6285 NE, ℘ (0 43) 455 17 42, *info@hotel-inkelshoes.nl, Fax (0 43) 455 24 53,* ≤, – |‡| TV ♿ P – 50.
10 mars-déc. – **Repas** (résidents seult) – **25 ch** ☐ 44/60, – 1 suite.
• En pleine campagne, point de chute familial taillé sur mesure pour les randonneurs cyclistes ou pédestres souhaitant découvrir ce charmant petit coin du Limbourg. Vue agreste.
• Dit familiehotel midden in de natuur is een ideale pleisterplaats voor wandelaars en fietsers die graag een pittoresk stukje Limburg willen ontdekken. Landelijk uitzicht.

Landgoed Schoutenhof, Molenweg 1, ✉ 6285 NJ, ℘ (0 43) 455 20 02, *info@schoutenhof.nl, Fax (0 43) 455 26 05,* ≤ campagne vallonnée, – TV P. AE VISA JCB.
Repas (dîner pour résidents seult) – **10 ch** ☐ 62/114 – ½ P 87/97.
• Paisible petit manoir où séjournèrent des membres de la famille royale hollandaise. À l'arrière, quelques chambres dévoilent une vue imprenable sur les prairies vallonnées.
• Klein, rustig buitenverblijf waar ook leden van het Nederlandse Koninklijk Huis te gast zijn geweest. Aan de achterkant prachtig uitzicht op het groene heuvellandschap.

Alkema, Kap. Houbenstraat 12, ✉ 6285 AB, ℘ (0 43) 455 13 35, *hotel.alkema@iae.nl, Fax (0 43) 455 27 44* – |‡| TV P. VISA. rest
Repas (dîner pour résidents seult) – **18 ch** ☐ 42/54 – ½ P 62.
• Qui souhaite passer un séjour en toute quiétude pourra compter sur cette adresse. Chambres fonctionnelles parfois dotées d'un balconnet. Accueil gentil.
• Wie een vakantie in alle rust wil doorbrengen, heeft hier een prima adres. Functionele kamers waarvan sommige met een balkonnetje. Vriendelijke ontvangst.

ERMELO *Gelderland* 531 S 9, 532 S 9 *et* 715 H 5 – *26 760 h.*

Amsterdam 75 – Arnhem 55 – Lelystad 33 – Utrecht 54 – Zwolle 46.

Heerlickheijd van Ermelo, Staringlaan 1, ✉ 3852 LA, ℘ (0 341) 56 85 85, *sales@heerlickheijd.nl, Fax (0 341) 56 85 00,* – |‡| TV P – 25 à 450. AE VISA
Repas *Lunch 23* – carte 23 à 64, ♀ – ☐ 18 – **127 ch** 148/275 – ½ P 70/143.
• Hôtel de standing entouré de bois. Pièces d'eau modernes au jardin, communs amples et luxueux, chambres tout confort et bons équipements pour se délasser ou se ressourcer. Sobre et spacieux bar-brasserie agrémenté d'une belle cheminée en bois de style "1900".
• Luxehotel in het bos. Tuin met moderne vijvers, grote en chique gemeenschappelijke ruimtes, zeer comfortabele kamers en goede faciliteiten voor ontspanning of om nieuwe energie op te doen. Sobere, ruime bar-brasserie met mooie houten schouw in 1900-stijl.

XXX **De Roggebot,** Staringlaan 1, ✉ 3852 LA, ☎ (0 341) 56 85 58, *info@deroggebot.nl, Fax (0 341) 56 85 57* – P. AE ① MC VISA – *fermé 25 juil.-9 août, 30 déc.-11 janv., sam. midi, dim. et lundi* – **Repas** Lunch 59 bc – 43/113 bc, carte 52 à 93, ♀.
✿
◆ Table gastronomique au cadre contemporain aménagée dans la véranda de l'hôtel Heerlickheijd van Ermelo. Cuisine actuelle innovante. Jolie cave visitable sur demande.
◆ Gastronomisch adres met een hedendaags decor in de veranda van het Hotel Heerlickheijd van Ermelo. Vindingrijke, actuele keuken. Op verzoek kan de mooie kelder worden bekeken.
Spéc. Foie de canard de 2 façons (juil.-sept.). Tournedos d'agneau au romarin (mai-juil.). Ris de veau croquant, mousseline de pommes de terre à l'huile d'olives et jus de morilles

ESCAUT ORIENTAL (Barrage de l'), Stormvloedkering – *voir Oosterscheldedam, Stormvloedkering.*

ETTEN-LEUR *Noord-Brabant* 532 M 13 *et* 715 E 7 – *38 613 h.*
Amsterdam 115 – 's-Hertogenbosch 63 – Breda 13 – Rotterdam 56 – Antwerpen 59.

Huis Ten Bosch sans rest, Oude Bredaseweg 2, ✉ 4872 AE, ☎ (0 76) 501 23 40, *info@huis_ten_bosch.nl, Fax (0 76) 503 81 22*, – TV. AE ① MC VISA
25 ch ☕ 80/90.
◆ Maison blanche postée en face d'une église. Grandes et confortables, les chambres vous permettront de passer des nuits agréables avant de reprendre votre chemin.
◆ In een wit pand tegenover de kerk biedt dit hotel grote, comfortabele kamers waar u goed uitgerust aan de volgende dag kunt beginnen.

XXX **De Zwaan,** Markt 7, ✉ 4875 CB, ☎ (0 76) 501 26 96, *info@restaurant-dezwaan.nl, Fax (0 76) 501 73 59* – AE ① MC VISA JCB – *fermé du 21 au 27 fév., 25 juil.-16 août, fin déc.-début janv., sam. midi, dim. et lundi* – **Repas** Lunch 45 – 63 bc/75 carte 52 à 76, ♀.
✿
◆ Belle cuisine au goût du jour servie dans une salle à manger élégante et intime, habillée d'une remarquable collection de tableaux impressionnistes et contemporains.
◆ Mooie, eigentijdse keuken die wordt geserveerd in een elegante eetzaal met intieme ambiance en een opmerkelijke collectie impressionistische en hedendaagse schilderijen.
Spéc. Cassolette de homard et ris de veau croquant aux lardons. Paupiette de filet de sole et foie d'oie au jus de veau. Crème caramel, Irish coffee et glace moka

XX **De Hooghe Neer,** Hoge Neerstraat 1 (par A 58 - E 312, sortie ⑱, direction Rijsbergen), ✉ 4873 LM, ☎ (0 76) 503 10 64, *info@dehoogheneer.nl, Fax (0 76) 504 02 88*, – P – 25 à 200. AE MC VISA
fermé lundi d'oct. à mars, mardi, sam. midi et dim. midi – **Repas** 31/42, ♀.
◆ Restaurant aménagé dans une ferme brabançonne du 19e s. dont le cachet rustique est sobrement mis en valeur à travers un décor intérieur bourgeois. Terrasse d'été.
◆ Restaurant in een 19e-eeuwse Brabantse boerderij, waarvan de rustieke sfeer wordt benadrukt door een traditioneel interieur. Zomerterras.

EXLOO *Drenthe* 531 AA 5 *et* 715 L 3 – *voir à Odoorn.*

FRANEKER (FRJENTSJER) *Fryslân* C *Franekeradeel 20 743 h.* 531 S 3 *et* 715 H 2.
Voir *Hôtel de Ville★ (Stadhuis) – Planetarium★. – Amsterdam 122 – Leeuwarden 19.*

Tulip Inn De Valk, Hertog van Saxenlaan 78, ✉ 8802 PP, ☎ (0 517) 39 80 00, *info@tulipinn-franeker.nl, Fax (0 517) 39 31 11*, – TV P – 25 à 350. AE ① MC VISA
Repas Lunch 23 – carte env. 34 – **42 ch** ☕ 62/110 – ½ P 59.
◆ Avant de partir pour Franeker, ville où Descartes fut inscrit à l'université, le businessman n'oubliera pas d'emporter cette adresse dans ses bagages. Trois types de chambres. Ample et lumineuse salle à manger sous verrière.
◆ Als u op zakenreis naar Franeker gaat, de stad waar Descartes zich aan de universiteit inschreef, vergeet dan niet dit adres in uw koffertje te stoppen. Drie typen kamers. Ruime en lichte eetzaal in de serre.

FREDERIKSOORD *Drenthe* C *Westerveld 19 158 h.* 531 W 5 *et* 715 J 3.
Amsterdam 154 – Assen 37 – Groningen 62 – Leeuwarden 62 – Zwolle 44.

Frederiksoord, Maj. van Swietenlaan 20, ✉ 8382 CG, ☎ (0 521) 38 55 55, *info@hotelfrederiksoord.nl, Fax (0 521) 38 15 24*, – TV P – 25 à 80. AE ① MC VISA – *fermé 27 déc.-3 janv.* – **Repas** *(fermé lundi d'oct. à mars et après 20 h 30)* carte env. 45 – **11 ch** ☕ 44/75 – ½ P 58/64.
◆ En deux cents ans d'existence, cette sympathique petite hostellerie provinciale exploitée en famille a rendu bien des services aux voyageurs. Chambres peu à peu rénovées. Possibilité de prendre son repas au jardin à la belle saison.
◆ Dit sympathieke provinciehotelletje wordt in familieverband geëxploiteerd en heeft in de tweehonderd jaar van zijn bestaan zijn gasten heel wat diensten bewezen. De kamers worden geleidelijk gerenoveerd. Bij mooi weer kan er in de tuin worden gegeten.

GARDEREN *Gelderland* C *Barneveld 48 958 h.* 532 T 9 *et* 715 I 5.

Oud Milligenseweg 5, 3886 MB, (0 577) 46 15 66, info@vvvgarderen.nl, Fax (0 577) 46 15 66.

Amsterdam 72 – Arnhem 47 – Apeldoorn 20 – Utrecht 54.

Résidence Groot Heideborgh, Hogesteeg 50 (Sud : 1,5 km), 3886 MA, (0 577) 46 27 00, *heideborgh@bilderberg.nl, Fax (0 577) 46 28 00,* – 25 à 300. rest
fermé 31 déc.-1er janv. – **Repas** *Lunch 28* – carte 38 à 48, – 17 – **84 ch** 154/200 – ½ P 80/150.

◆ Établissement moderne entouré de bois et landes de bruyères. Toutes les chambres sont des junior suites "full equipment". Centre esthétique et espaces de remise en forme. Au restaurant, cuisine classique française et recettes aux accents cosmopolites.

◆ Modern etablissement omringd door bos en heide. De kamers zijn allemaal junior suites die van alle faciliteiten zijn voorzien. Beautycenter en fitnessruimte. Het restaurant serveert een klassieke Franse keuken en gerechten met kosmopolitische accenten.

't Speulderbos, Speulderbosweg 54, 3886 AP, (0 577) 46 15 46, *speulderbos@bilderberg.nl, Fax (0 577) 46 11 24,* rest, – 25 à 250. rest
fermé 31 déc. et 1er janv. – **Repas** carte 45 à 61, – 16 – **100 ch** 130/151, – 2 suites – ½ P 106/119.

◆ Un séjour familial ou un congrès à organiser ? Cet hôtel retiré dans les bois n'attend alors que vous. Chambres de bon séjour. Trotteurs mis à la disposition des enfants. Salle de restaurant au décor actuel.

◆ Moet u een congres organiseren of gaat u eropuit met het gezin ? Dan is dit hotel midden in de bossen geknipt voor u. Comfortabele kamers. Voor de kinderen staan de trapautootjes klaar. De restaurantzaal heeft een eigentijds decor.

Overbosch, Hooiweg 23 (Sud : 1,5 km), 3886 PM, (0 577) 46 13 14, *info@overbosch-horeca.nl, Fax (0 577) 46 20 79,* – – 25 à 500.
fermé 27 déc.-3 janv. – **Repas** *Lunch 28* – carte 35 à 54 – **46 ch** 73/120 – ½ P 73/78.

◆ Sacré coup de jeune pour cette structure hôtelière située dans un quartier résidentiel parsemé de sapinières. Toutes les chambres viennent de retrouver l'éclat du neuf. À table, les plats s'accompagnent de vins mûris sous diverses latitudes.

◆ Wat een metamorfose heeft het hotel ondergaan ! De kamers in dit etablissement midden in de bossen, aan de rand van Garderen, zien er allemaal weer als nieuw uit. Aan tafel krijgen de gerechten gezelschap van wijnen uit diverse windstreken.

Richard's, Oud Milligenseweg 62, 3886 MJ, (0 577) 46 19 51, *garderen@richardshotels.nl, Fax (0 577) 46 23 58,* – – 25 à 200.
Repas *Lunch 14* – carte env. 28 – **64 ch** 73/93 – ½ P 60/80.

◆ Situation tranquille à distance respectable du village, pimpantes petites chambres très pratiques, salons et lounge-café agréables. Tenue générale et entretien exemplaires. Une brève carte traditionnelle est présentée au restaurant.

◆ Een rustig gelegen hotel op aanzienlijke afstand van het dorp, met kleine maar zeer praktische en verzorgde kamers, aangename zalen en een lounge-café. Alles ziet er prima onderhouden uit. Het restaurant heeft een kleine, traditionele menukaart.

Camposing, Oud Milligenseweg 7, 3886 MB, (0 577) 46 22 88, *manchung@hetnet.nl, Fax (0 577) 40 29 80,* Cuisine chinoise –
fermé du 8 au 28 janv. et lundi et mardi midi sauf en juil.-août – **Repas** *Lunch 17* – 27/32.

◆ Le vent actionne encore les ailes du vieux moulin avoisinant cette dépaysante affaire familiale. Grand choix de plats chinois. Belle terrasse estivale sur le devant.

◆ Een wat vreemde eend in de bijt, dit Chinese restaurant naast de oer-Hollandse molenwieken, maar dat niettemin een keur aan gerechten biedt. Mooi zomerterras aan de voorzijde.

GEERTRUIDENBERG *Noord-Brabant* 532 O 12 *et* 715 F 6 – *20 988 h.*

au Nord : 6 km à Hank, Kurenpolderweg 33, 4273 LA, (0 162) 40 28 20.

Amsterdam 90 – 's-Hertogenbosch 36 – Breda 20 – Rotterdam 55.

't Weeshuys, Markt 52, 4931 BT, (0 162) 51 36 98, *info@weeshuys.nl, Fax (0 162) 51 60 02,* –
fermé du 21 au 24 fév., du 12 au 25 juil., sam. midi et dim. midi – **Repas** *Lunch 35* – carte 46 à 65.

◆ Sur le Markt d'un petit bourg au passé de place forte, devant la fontaine baroque, agréable restaurant mettant à profit une chapelle élevée en 1310. Terrasse à l'arrière.

◆ Op de markt van dit oude vestingplaatsje bevindt zich tegenover de barokke fontein een prettig restaurant in een kapelletje uit 1310. Terras aan de achterzijde.

GEERVLIET *Zuid-Holland* Ⓒ *Bernisse 12 760 h.* 532 K 11 *et* 715 D 6.
Amsterdam 93 – Rotterdam 19 – Den Haag 41.

XXX **In de Bernisse Molen,** Spuikade 1, ✉ 3211 BG, ☎ (0 181) 66 12 92, *bernisse@publishnet.nl, Fax (0 181) 64 14 46,* – P. AE ⓓ MC VISA JCB
fermé 12 juil.-2 août, 27 déc.-5 janv., dim. et lundi – **Repas** *Lunch 30* – carte 38 à 53, ♀.
◆ Un fier moulin à vent du 19e s. donne un toit à cette chaleureuse salle à manger en demi-rotonde décorée dans l'esprit néo-rustique. Verger et étang.
◆ Een trotse 19e-eeuwse windmolen biedt onderdak aan dit restaurant. Halfronde eetzaal met warme ambiance en neorustiek decor. Boomgaard en vijver.

GELDROP *Noord-Brabant* Ⓒ *Geldrop-Mierlo 40 000 h.* 532 S 14 *et* 715 H 7.
Amsterdam 137 – Eindhoven 7 – 's-Hertogenbosch 49 – Venlo 48 – Aachen 106.

NH Geldrop, Bogardeind 219 (près A 67), ✉ 5664 EG, ☎ (0 40) 286 75 10, *nhgeldrop@nh-hotels.nl, Fax (0 40) 285 57 64,* , , , , , , – , , rest, TV ♿ P – 25 à 180. AE ⓓ MC VISA.
Repas *Lunch 13* – carte env. 33 – ☕ 13 – **131 ch** 185/195 – ½ P 121.
◆ Cet hôtel de chaîne situé dans une petite ville proche de Eindhoven renferme des chambres fonctionnelles assez spacieuses. La clientèle d'affaires y a ses habitudes.
◆ Dit ketenhotel in een stadje dicht bij Eindhoven beschikt over functionele, vrij grote kamers. Een zakelijke cliëntèle is er kind aan huis.

De Gouden Leeuw sans rest, Korte Kerkstraat 46, ✉ 5664 HH, ☎ (0 40) 286 23 93, *Fax (0 40) 285 69 41* – TV – 25 à 60. AE MC VISA.
(fermé dern. sem. déc.-prem. sem. janv. et dim.) – **15 ch** ☕ 58/78.
◆ Une rue piétonne à vocation commerçante longe cet immeuble trapu du centre de Geldrop. Menues chambres de mise simple, toutefois pratiques et insonorisées.
◆ Dit massief ogende hotelpand in het centrum staat aan een voetgangersstraat met winkels. Kleine eenvoudige kamers, maar functioneel en voorzien van geluidsisolatie.

GELEEN *Limburg* Ⓒ *Sittard-Geleen 97 953 h.* 532 U 17 *et* 715 I 9.
Amsterdam 202 – Eindhoven 74 – Maastricht 23 – Aachen 33.

Bastion, Rijksweg Zuid 301, ✉ 6161 BN, ☎ (0 46) 474 75 17, *bastion@bastionhotel.nl, Fax (0 46) 474 89 33* – TV P. AE ⓓ MC VISA.
Repas (grillades, ouvert jusqu'à 23 h) carte env. 30 – ☕ 10 – **40 ch** 55.
◆ Près de l'autoroute, hôtel de chaîne dont chacune des chambres a récemment fait l'objet d'un "lifting" intégral. Elles disposent à présent de la connexion pour modem.
◆ De kamers in dit ketenhotel vlak bij de snelweg hebben onlangs stuk voor stuk een complete facelift ondergaan en beschikken nu allemaal over een modemaansluiting.

XX **de lijster,** Rijksweg Zuid 172, ✉ 6161 BV, ☎ (0 46) 474 39 57, *i.sleypen@wxs.nl, Fax (0 46) 474 38 38,* – P. AE ⓓ MC VISA
fermé du 20 au 28 fév., mardi, sam. midi et dim. midi – **Repas** *Lunch 28* – carte 34 à 51.
◆ Ancienne maison de notable où l'on se restaure dans une salle de style composite : ornements muraux classiques, sièges Biedermeier et éclairage italien moderne.
◆ Restaurant in een prachtig herenhuis. De eetzaal is een geslaagde combinatie van stijlen : klassieke wandornamenten, biedermeier stoelen en moderne Italiaanse verlichting.

X **Angelique's,** Rijksweg Centrum 24, ✉ 6161 EE, ☎ (0 46) 474 22 63, *angeliquesrestaurant@hotmail.com, Fax (0 46) 474 22 63* – . MC VISA.
fermé 28 déc.-6 janv., lundi et mardi – **Repas** (dîner seult) carte 27 à 46.
◆ Cet angélique petit bistrot moderne officiant au cœur de la localité est, à l'heure du dîner, l'adresse toute indiquée pour un repas "sans prise de tête".
◆ Deze kleine, moderne bistro spreidt zijn kookkunst tentoon in het centrum van de stad en is rond etenstijd het aangewezen adres voor een lekkere maaltijd.

GEMERT *Noord-Brabant* Ⓒ *Gemert-Bakel 27 729 h.* 532 T 13 *et* 715 I 7.
Amsterdam 111 – Eindhoven 24 – Nijmegen 54.

XX **Kastanjehof,** Heuvel 4, ✉ 5421 CN, ☎ (0 492) 36 19 12, *info@kastanjehof.com, Fax (0 492) 36 81 00,* – P – 25. AE ⓓ MC VISA.
fermé du 21 au 25 fév., du 9 au 29 août, 31 déc.-1er janv. et merc. – **Repas** *Lunch 20* – carte 39 à 57, ♀.
◆ On traverse un jardinet bichonné où bruisse une fontaine pour s'attabler dans cette demeure patricienne convertie en restaurant. Recettes d'aujourd'hui. Salon agréable.
◆ Een verzorgde voortuin met fontein voert naar de entree van dit statige herenhuis dat tot restaurant is verbouwd. Eigentijdse keuken. Aangename salon.

à Handel *Nord-Est : 3,5 km* Ⓒ *Gemert-Bakel :*

Handelia, Past. Castelijnsstraat 1, ✉ 5423 SP, ☎ (0 492) 32 12 90, *hotel@handelia.nl, Fax (0 492) 32 38 41,* – TV. MC VISA.
fermé 24 déc.-2 janv. – **Repas** (résidents seult) – **12 ch** ☐ 80 – ½ P 55/70.
◆ Quelques-unes des chambres, donnant sur une grande pelouse bordée d'arbres, se complètent d'une terrasse estivale. La bonhomie d'un petit hôtel villageois tenu en famille.
◆ Enkele kamers, die uitkijken op een groot grasveld met bomen, hebben een zomerterras. Etablissement met de gemoedelijke sfeer van een klein dorpshotel in familiebeheer.

GEYSTEREN *Limburg* 532 V 13 *et* 715 J 7 – *voir à Wanssum.*

GIETEN *Drenthe* Ⓒ *Aa en Hunze 25 552 h.* 531 Z 4 *et* 715 L 2.
Amsterdam 200 – Groningen 30 – Assen 16 – Leeuwarden 92 – Zwolle 88.

De Biester, Asserstraat 85, ✉ 9461 TT, ☎ (0 592) 26 41 80, *hoteldebiester@planet.nl, Fax (0 592) 26 49 96,* – TV P – 25 à 40. AE MC
Repas (dîner seult jusqu'à 20 h) carte env. 32 – **13 ch** ☐ 66/84.
◆ Récent hôtel plagiant l'architecture traditionnelle des fermes de la Drenthe. Ambiance familiale, chambres spacieuses et actuelles, belle terrasse d'été au bord de l'eau. Repas servi en plein air aux beaux jours.
◆ Een nieuw hotel dat als een traditionele Drentse boerderij is gebouwd en beschikt over ruime, eigentijdse kamers. Gemoedelijke ambiance en een fraai terras aan het water. Bij mooi weer worden de maaltijden buiten geserveerd.

GIETHOORN *Overijssel* Ⓒ *Steenwijkerland 41 870 h.* 531 V 6 *et* 715 J 3.
Voir *Village lacustre★★.*
(bateau) Beulakerweg 114a, ✉ *8355 AL,* ☎ *(0 521) 36 12 48, giethoorn@kopvanoverijssel.nl, Fax (0 521) 36 22 81.*
Amsterdam 135 – Zwolle 28 – Assen 63 – Leeuwarden 63.

De Harmonie , Beulakerweg 55 (Nord : 2 km), ✉ 8355 AB, ☎ (0 521) 36 13 72, *info@harmonie-giethoorn.nl, Fax (0 521) 36 10 82,* – TV P – 25 à 100. AE MC VISA JCB.
Repas *Lunch 28* – 40/43 – **16 ch** ☐ 70/110 – ½ P 70/83.
◆ Près d'un beau village lacustre, hôtel familial dont huit chambres occupent une annexe. Embarcadère privé où vous pourrez amarrer votre canot. Au restaurant, les classiques bataves s'associent à des plats venus d'ailleurs.
◆ Familiehotel in het Venetië van het Noorden. Acht van de kamers zijn in een dependance ingericht. Het huis heeft een eigen steiger, waar u uw bootje kunt aanleggen. In het restaurant mengen culinaire Hollandse klassiekers zich met uitheemse gerechten.

De Kruumte sans rest, Kerkweg 48a (Est : 1,5 km), ✉ 8355 BJ, ☎ (0 521) 36 15 17, *info@dekruumte.com, Fax (0 521) 36 18 80,* – TV P.
7 ch ☐ 56/87.
◆ Ce calme petit hôtel familial aux chambres sans reproche organise des visites guidées en bateau et propose même la location de canots électriques pour sillonner les canaux.
◆ Rustig, klein familiehotel met kamers waar niets op aan te merken valt. Organisatie van rondleidingen per boot en verhuur van electrobootjes om de kanalen te verkennen.

De Pergola, Ds. T.O. Hylkemaweg 7, ✉ 8355 CD, ☎ (0 521) 36 13 21, *hotel-depergola@planet.nl, Fax (0 521) 36 13 21,* – TV P
avril-oct. – **Repas** *(fermé jeudi d'avril à juin et après 20 h 30)* (taverne-rest) 17/25 – **23 ch** ☐ 61.
◆ Établissement bâti un peu à l'écart du centre de Giethoorn. Chambres de tailles correctes, dont l'équipement standard répond aux besoins pratiques du voyageur. Taverne-restaurant au décor néo-rustique. Terrasse d'été qu'abrite une pergola.
◆ Dit etablissement ligt iets buiten het centrum van Giethoorn. De redelijk ruime kamers zijn voorzien van standaardcomfort dat tegemoet komt aan de praktische behoeften van de reiziger. Grand café met neorustiek decor. Zomerterras onder een pergola.

De Lindenhof (Kruithof), Beulakerweg 77 (Nord : 1,5 km), ✉ 8355 AC, ☎ (0 521) 36 14 44, *info@restaurantdelindenhof.nl, Fax (0 521) 36 05 95,* – P. AE MC VISA JCB.
fermé 1 sem. carnaval, 1 sem. Toussaint et jeudi – **Repas** *Lunch 59* – 79, carte 55 à 65.
◆ Cette adorable fermette typique entourée de tilleuls abrite sous son toit de chaume l'une des grandes tables de l'Overijssel. Belle cuisine travaillée dans le tempo actuel.
◆ Dit allercharmantste, karakteristieke boerderijtje tussen de linden herbergt onder zijn rieten dak een van de grote restaurants van Overijssel. Verfijnde, eigentijdse keuken.
Spéc. Langoustines en aigre-doux de miel. Truite légèrement fumée, salade de pommes de terre au céleri-rave et crème raifort. Cannellonis de queue de bœuf braisée aux morilles

à Wanneperveen *Sud : 6 km* 🄲 *Steenwijkerland :*

Prinsenije, Veneweg 294, ✉ 7946 LX, ☎ (0 522) 28 11 85, *mail@prinsenije.nl, Fax (0 522) 28 14 93,* ≤, 帝, ≘, ⛱, ✂, 🚲, ⚓ - 📺 🅿 - 🏫 25 à 200. AE MC VISA
fermé 27 déc.-7 janv. – **Repas** *(fermé lundi et mardi en janv.-fév. et après 20 h 30)* carte 27 à 42 – ☕ 9 – **15 ch** 89.
◆ Construction récente en forme de rotonde agréablement située au bord du lac. Chambres confortables avec vue sur les quais où accostent les embarcations des plaisanciers. Salle à manger décorée sur le thème du "village englouti" (légende locale).
◆ Dit vrij nieuwe, ronde hotel is prachtig gelegen aan een meer. De comfortabele kamers bieden uitzicht op de kaden waar plezierboten aanleggen. Het decor van de eetzaal ademt de sfeer van Het Verdronken Dorp (lokale legende).

GILZE *Noord-Brabant* 🄲 *Gilze en Rijen 24 737 h.* 532 O 13 *et* 715 F 7.
Amsterdam 105 – 's-Hertogenbosch 37 – Breda 15 – Tilburg 10.

Gilze-Rijen, Klein Zwitserland 8 (près A 58), ✉ 5126 TA, ☎ (0 161) 45 49 51, *recept ie@hotelgilzerijen.nl, Fax (0 161) 45 21 71,* 帝, 🏋, ≘, ⛱, ✂, 🚲 - 🛗 📺 ♿ 🅿 - 🏫 25 à 400. AE ⓓ MC VISA
Repas *Lunch 18* – carte 26 à 41, ♀ – ☕ 9 – **133 ch** 73, – 3 suites – ½ P 56.
◆ Entre Breda et Tilburg, l'une des "grandes pointures" de la chaîne hôtelière Van der Valk. Différentes catégories de chambres. Piscine, whirlpool et sauna.
◆ Een van de grotere hotels van de Van der Valk-keten, tussen Breda et Tilburg. Verschillende categorieën kamers. Zwembad, whirlpool en sauna.

GLIMMEN *Groningen* 531 Y 4 *et* 715 K 2 – *voir à Haren.*

GOEDEREEDE *Zuid-Holland* 532 I 12 *et* 715 C 6 – *11 363 h.*
Amsterdam 118 – Rotterdam 44 – Den Haag 66 – Middelburg 76.

De Gouden Leeuw, Markt 11, ✉ 3252 BC, ☎ (0 187) 49 13 71, *Fax (0 187) 49 15 31,* 帝 - AE ⓓ MC VISA
fermé janv. et lundi hors saison – **Repas** 22/49 bc, ♀.
◆ Vénérable auberge déjà présente au cœur du village en 1480. Ses préparations n'ont d'autres prétentions que celle de satisfaire simplement l'appétit des hôtes de passage.
◆ Eerbiedwaardige herberg die al sinds 1480 een vertrouwd beeld is in de dorpskern. Pretentieloze gerechten om de honger van passanten te stillen.

GOES *Zeeland* 532 I 13 *et* 715 C 7 – *36 047 h.*
Voir *Grande Église★ (Grote Kerk).*
18 9 Kurkweg 29, ✉ 4465 BH, ☎ (0 113) 22 95 56, Fax (0 113) 22 95 54.
ℹ Stationsplein 3, ✉ 4461 HP, ☎ 0 900-168 16 66, vvvgoes@planet.nl, Fax (0 113) 25 13 50.
Amsterdam 165 – Middelburg 22 – Breda 78 – Rotterdam 87 – Antwerpen 68.

Bolsjoi, Grote Markt 28, ✉ 4461 AJ, ☎ (0 113) 23 23 23, *bolsjoi@zeelandnet.nl, Fax (0 113) 25 17 55,* 帝 - 📺 🅿 - 🏫 25 à 40. AE ⓓ MC VISA JCB
Repas *(fermé 25 et 26 déc. et 1er janv.)* (taverne-rest) carte 22 à 31 – **12 ch** *(fermé 24, 25, 26 et 31 déc. et 1er janv.)* ☕ 67/79 – ½ P 82.
◆ Établissement familial s'annonçant par une façade ancienne où s'alignent des auvents. Réparties sur l'arrière, les chambres offrent espace et mobilier actuel. À la belle saison, la taverne-restaurant se complète d'une terrasse sur la place.
◆ Dit familiehotel is te herkennen aan een oude gevel met luifels. De ruime kamers liggen aan de achterkant en zijn met moderne meubels ingericht. Het café-restaurant heeft in het seizoen een terras op het plein.

De Stadsschuur, Schuttershof 32, ✉ 4461 DZ, ☎ (0 113) 21 23 32, *info@stadssc huur.nl, Fax (0 113) 25 02 29,* 帝 - AE ⓓ MC VISA
fermé 31 déc.-2 janv., sam. midi et dim. – **Repas** 32/43, ♀.
◆ Au centre-ville, vieille grange adroitement reconvertie en salle de restaurant. Portail élevé en 1645 et terrasse d'été ombragée. Carte recomposée d'une saison à l'autre.
◆ Deze oude schuur in het centrum is vakkundig tot restaurant verbouwd. De poort dateert uit 1645. Lommerrijk zomerterras. Met de seizoenen wisselende menukaart.

Het Binnenhof, De Bocht van Guinea 6 (accès par St-Jacobstraat), ✉ 4461 BC, ☎ (0 113) 22 74 05, *Fax (0 113) 22 25 52,* 帝 - AE ⓓ MC VISA
fermé 2 prem. sem. janv., merc. et jeudi – **Repas** (dîner seult) 30/50.
◆ Un passage étroit mène à cette sympathique affaire familiale retranchée dans une courette du vieux Goes. Recettes valorisant les produits du coin. Poisson fumé "maison".
◆ Een smal steegje leidt naar dit sympathieke eethuis dat verscholen ligt aan een hofje in het oude Goes. Gerechten op basis van streekproducten. Huisgerookte vis.

X **De Witte Lelie,** Opril Grote Markt 8, ✉ 4461 AK, ☎ (0 113) 22 02 76, *info@wittelelie.nl, Fax (0 113) 25 23 43* – AE ⓓ ⓜ VISA JCB
fermé du 1er au 14 août, lundi et mardi – **Repas** (dîner seult) 36/67 bc.
• Bon petit relais de bouche à débusquer dans une ruelle piétonne avoisinant la Grand-Place. Décoration intérieure soignée et savoureuse cuisine au goût du jour.
• Goed eethuisje in een voetgangersstraatje naast de Grote Markt. In het verzorgde interieur worden smaakvolle, eigentijdse gerechten geserveerd.

GOIRLE *Noord-Brabant* 532 *P 13 et* 715 *G 7 – voir à Tilburg.*

GORINCHEM *Zuid-Holland* 532 *O 11 et* 715 *F 6 – 34 324 h.*

au Nord : 3 km à Spijk, Haarweg 3, ✉ 4212 KJ, ☎ (0 183) 62 80 77.
Amsterdam 74 – Utrecht 37 – Den Haag 68 – Breda 41 – 's-Hertogenbosch 40 – Rotterdam 42.

't Spinnewiel, Eind 18, ✉ 4201 CR, ☎ (0 183) 63 10 57, *hetspinnewiel@zonnet.nl, Fax (0 183) 66 00 95* – ▤ rest, TV – 🏛 25. AE ⓓ ⓜ VISA. ✂
fermé 25 déc.-2 janv. – **Repas** *(fermé sam. midi, dim. midi et lundi)* 22/46 – **13 ch** ☕ 76/89 – ½ P 96/139.
• Mignonne auberge du quartier ancien se mirant dans les eaux de la Linge. Les chambres, sobrement équipées, sont refaites de neuf. Bonne ambiance familiale. Restaurant façon "brasserie actuelle".
• Dit charmante hotel-restaurant in de historische kern spiegelt zich in het water van de Linge. De gerenoveerde kamers zijn eenvoudig ingericht. Gezellige, intieme sfeer. Het restaurant heeft de ambiance van een eigentijdse brasserie.

XX **Solo,** Zusterhuis 1, ✉ 4201 EH, ☎ (0 183) 63 77 90, *Fax (0 183) 63 77 91* – ▤ – 🏛 25. AE ⓓ ⓜ VISA
fermé dern. sem. juil.-2 prem. sem. août, sam. midi, dim. midi et lundi – **Repas** Lunch 31 – carte 28 à 42.
• Il flotte une atmosphère "trendy" dans cette maison de la typique place du marché. Aménagement intérieur à la mode d'aujourd'hui. Carte actuelle assortie d'un lunch.
• In dit pand aan het karakteristieke marktplein hangt een trendy sfeer. Het interieur is naar hedendaagse smaak ingericht. Eigentijdse menukaart met lunch.

X **Bistro de Poort,** Eind 19, ✉ 4201 CP, ☎ (0 183) 66 05 22, *bistro-depoort@hetnet.nl, Fax (0 78) 699 01 78,* ≤ Merwede, 🏠 – ▤. ⓜ VISA. ✂
fermé dim. de sept. à mai – **Repas** carte env. 45.
• Pour agrémenter votre repas d'une plaisante échappée batelière, prenez place sur la véranda, orientée côté quais, ou, l'été venu, en terrasse, dressée sur l'écluse.
• Voor een gezellig uitzicht op de boten tijdens het eten kunt u plaatsnemen in de serre, die naar de kade is gericht, of 's zomers op het terras, dat uitkijkt op de sluis.

GOUDA *Zuid-Holland* 532 *N 10 et* 715 *F 5 – 71 688 h.*

Voir *Le Cœur de la ville★ – Hôtel de Ville★ (Stadhuis)* BY **H**¹ – *Vitraux★★★ de l'église St-Jean★ (St. Janskerk)* BY **A**.
Musée : *Het Catharina Gasthuis★* BY **M**¹.
Env. *par ① : Étangs de Reeuwijk★ (Reeuwijkse Plassen) – de Gouda à Oudewater route de digue ≤★ par Goejanverwelledijk* BZ.
Markt 27, ✉ 2801 JJ, ☎ 0 900 468 32 88, info@vvvgouda.nl, Fax (0 182) 58 47 08.
Amsterdam 53 ④ – Rotterdam 27 ③ – Den Haag 30 ④ – Utrecht 36 ④

Plan page ci-contre

XX **Rôtiss. l'Etoile,** Blekerssingel 1, ✉ 2806 AA, ☎ (0 182) 51 22 53, *info@letoile.nl, Fax (0 182) 55 11 07,* 🏠 – ▤ – 🏛 80. AE ⓓ ⓜ VISA. ✂ BY a
fermé dern. sem. juil.-prem. sem. août, sam. midi, dim. et lundi – **Repas** Lunch 30 – 33/70 bc, ♀.
• Plus de 25 ans de présence font de ce restaurant en rotonde l'une des valeurs sûres de la ville fromagère. Terrasse perchée sur le toit, courtisée les soirs d'été.
• Met zijn ruim 25-jarig bestaan behoort dit ronde restaurant tot de trefzekere adressen van de kaasstad. Het dakterras is op zomeravonden favoriet.

XX **Jean Marie,** Oude Brugweg 4, ✉ 2808 NP, ☎ (0 182) 51 62 62, *restjeanmarie@hetnet.nl,* 🏠 – ⓜ VISA BZ e
fermé 13 juil.-9 août, dim. et lundi – **Repas** (dîner seult) carte 27 à 44, ♀.
• Une intime petite table familiale se dissimule derrière cette pimpante façade en bois peint. Carte traditionnelle, avec un quatuor de menus. Accueil et service aimables.
• Een intiem restaurantje gaat schuil achter deze fleurige gevel van geschilderd hout. Traditionele kaart met een viertal menu's. Vriendelijke ontvangst en service.

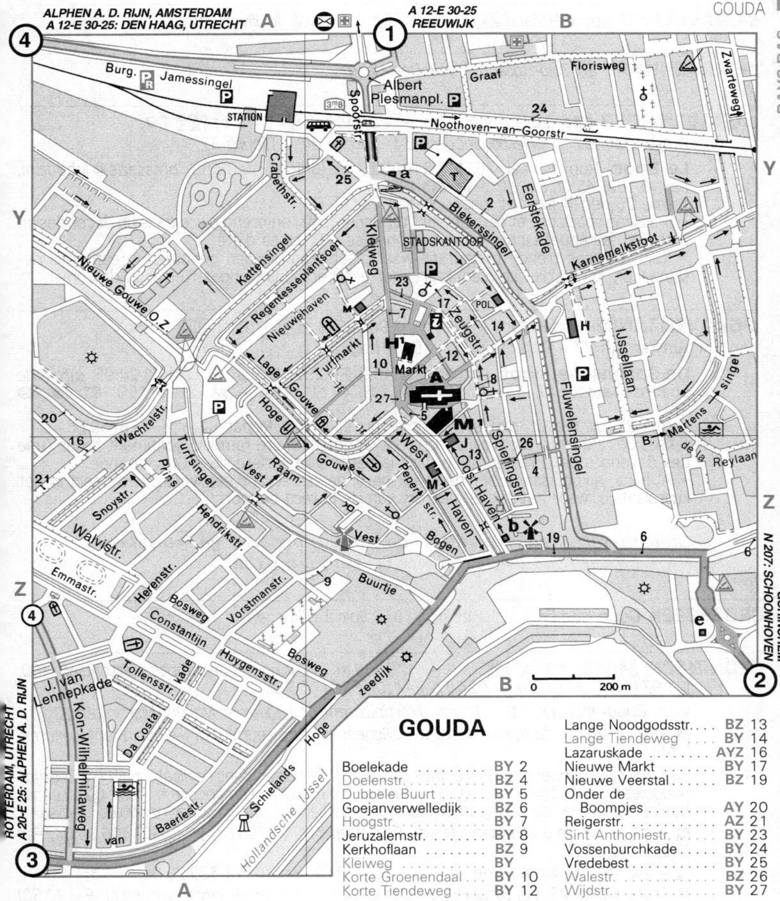

GOUDA

Rue	Carré	N°
Boelekade	BY	2
Doelenstr.	BZ	4
Dubbele Buurt	BY	5
Goejanverwelledijk	BZ	6
Hoogstr.	BY	7
Jeruzalemstr.	BY	8
Kerkhoflaan	BZ	9
Kleiweg	BY	
Korte Groenendaal	BY	10
Korte Tiendeweg	BY	12
Lange Noodgodsstr.	BZ	13
Lange Tiendeweg	BY	14
Lazaruskade	AYZ	16
Nieuwe Markt	BY	17
Nieuwe Veerstal	BZ	19
Onder de Boompjes	AY	20
Reigerstr.	AZ	21
Sint Anthoniestr.	BY	23
Vossenburchkade	BY	24
Vredebest	BY	25
Walestr.	BZ	26
Wijdstr.	BY	27

XX **De Mallemolen,** Oosthaven 72, ✉ 2801 PG, ☎ (0 182) 51 54 30, *p.wponsioen@freeler.nl, Fax (0 182) 51 54 30,* 🍴 – ▤. AE ⓓ MC VISA BZ b
fermé fin déc.-début janv., mardi en juil.-août, sam. midi, dim. midi et lundi – **Repas** (déjeuner sur réservation) carte 35 à 46.
◆ Restaurant aménagé au bord d'un quai, dans une jolie maison ancienne proche du parc public où se dresse le moulin de rempart. Peintures et fresques habillent les salles.
◆ Restaurant langs een kade, in een leuk oud huis vlak bij het park waar de walmolen staat. Aan de muren van de eetzalen prijken schilderijen en fresco's.

à Reeuwijk *par ① : 6 km – 12 898 h*

XX **Kaagjesland,** Kaagjesland 60 (par N 207, au pont-levis direction Reeuwijk), ✉ 2811 KL, ☎ (0 182) 39 64 21, *info@kaagjesland.nl, Fax (0 182) 39 66 19,* ≤, 🍴 – ▤ P. VISA.
fermé 19 juil.-10 août, 25 déc.-11 janv., lundi et mardi – **Repas** (dîner seult) 38/43, ♀.
◆ Situation pittoresque pour cet établissement design : un village typique de la région, avec ses villas fleuries aux beaux jours, ses passerelles, ses canaux et ses polders.
◆ Pittoreske omgeving voor dit designrestaurant : een karakteristiek dorp in een polderlandschap, met bruggetjes, grachten en villa's die er 's zomers fleurig bij staan.

's-GRAVELAND *Noord-Holland* 532 P 9 *et* 715 G 5 – *voir à Hilversum.*

's-GRAVENHAGE P *Zuid-Holland – voir Den Haag.*

's GRAVENMOER *Noord-Brabant* C *Dongen 25 143 h.* 532 O 13 *et* 715 F 7.
Amsterdam 97 – 's-Hertogenbosch 34 – Breda 24 – Tilburg 32.

XX **Le Bouc,** Hoofdstraat 75, ✉ 5109 AB, ☎ (0 162) 45 08 88, *brasserie@lebouc.nl, Fax (0 162) 45 08 88,* – P. MC VISA
fermé 26 déc.-4 janv. et lundi – **Repas** 28/34, ₸.
◆ Brasserie spacieuse et résolument "tendance", où l'on prend place dans un décor design assez réussi. Appétissante carte personnalisée. Terrasse d'été.
◆ Ruim en zeer trendy restaurant waar plaats kan worden genomen in een fraai designdecor. Aantrekkelijke menukaart met een persoonlijke noot. Terras in de zomer.

's-GRAVENZANDE *Zuid-Holland* C *Westland 96 000 h.* 532 J 10 *et* 715 D 5.
Amsterdam 77 – Rotterdam 32 – Den Haag 17.

X **De Spaansche Vloot,** Langestraat 137, ✉ 2691 BD, ☎ (0 174) 41 24 95, *info@despaanschevloot.nl, Fax (0 174) 41 71 24,* – P – 25 à 150. AE ① MC VISA JCB
fermé 21 juil.-4 août, dim. sauf en mai-juin et lundi – **Repas** Lunch 25 – 28/58 bc.
◆ Près de cinquante ans d'existence font de cette affaire familiale gentiment tenue l'une des doyennes de la restauration dans la petite ville côtière de 's-Gravenzande.
◆ Al bijna vijftig jaar is dit vriendelijk gerunde restaurant een vertrouwd beeld in het kustplaatsje, waar het tot de nestors van de horeca behoort.

Indien u opgehouden wordt op de baan, is het beter en gebruikelijk uw reser-veringen per telefoon te bevestigen na 18u.

GROESBEEK *Gelderland* 532 U 12 *et* 715 I 6 – *voir à Nijmegen.*

GRONINGEN P 531 Y 3 *et* 715 K 2 – *175 569 h – Casino* Z, *Gedempte Kattendiep 150,* ✉ *9711 PV,* ☎ *(0 50) 317 23 17, Fax (0 50) 317 23 00.*

Voir *Goudkantoor★* Z **B** – *Tour★ (Martinitoren) de l'église St-Martin (Martinikerk)* Z.
Musée : *maritime du Nord★ (Noordelijk Scheepvaartmuseum)* Z **M²** – *Groninger Museum★* Z **M¹**.

Env. *par ② à Loppersum : Les églises rurales★ (fresques★ dans l'église) – par ② à Zeerijp : coupoles★ dans l'église – par ⑦ à Uithuizen : château Menkemaborg★★ – par ⑥ à Leens : buffet d'orgues★ dans l'église St-Pierre (Petruskerk) – par ② à Garmerwolde : église★.*

18 *par ④ : 12 km à Glimmen (Haren), Pollselaan 5,* ✉ *9756 CJ,* ☎ *(0 50) 406 20 04, Fax (0 50) 406 19 22.*

✈ *par ④ : 12 km à Eelde* ☎ *(0 50) 309 70 70, Fax (0 50) 309 70 09.*

ℹ *Grote Markt 25,* ✉ *9712 HS,* ☎ *0 900-202 30 50, info@vvvgroningen.nl, Fax (0 50) 311 38 55.*

Amsterdam 181 ⑤ – Leeuwarden 59 ⑥ – Bremen 181 ③

Plans pages suivantes

Mercure, Expositielaan 7 (Sud : 2 km près N 7), ✉ 9727 KA, ☎ (0 50) 525 84 00, *H1241@accor-hotels.com, Fax (0 50) 527 18 28,* – – 30 à 60. AE ① MC VISA JCB. rest X v
Repas *(fermé sam. midi et dim. midi)* Lunch 15 – carte 27 à 37, ₸ – 14 – **156 ch** 93, – 2 suites.
◆ Établissement de chaîne construit à l'entrée de la ville, près d'une sortie d'autoroute et de l'hippodrome. Chambres fonctionnelles aménagées selon les standards Mercure.
◆ Ketenhotel aan de rand van de stad, vlak bij de renbaan en een afrit van de snelweg. Functionele kamers die naar de normen van Mercure zijn ingericht.

Hotel de Ville, Oude Boteringestraat 43, ✉ 9712 GD, ☎ (0 50) 318 12 22, *hotel@deville.nl, Fax (0 50) 318 17 77* – . AE ① MC VISA JCB Z r
Repas voir rest ***Bistro 't Gerecht*** ci-après – 13 – **45 ch** 115/215.
◆ Hôtel formé de deux maisons anciennes et d'une construction récente. Communs amples et cossus, chambres agréables à vivre, cour intérieure avec terrasse d'été.
◆ Dit hotel is gevestigd in twee oude huizen en een modern pand. Zeer comfortabele kamers en grote, luxueus ingerichte gemeenschappelijke ruimten. Binnenplaats met zomerterras.

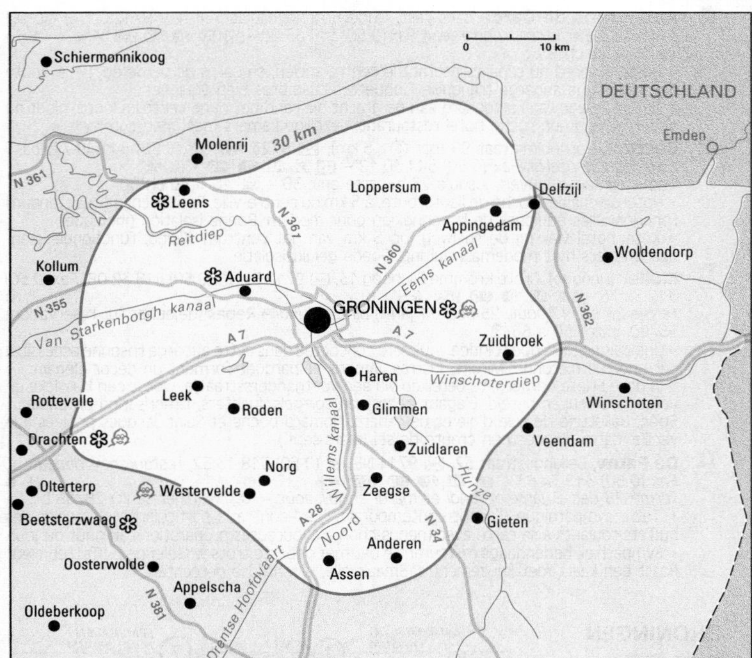

Schimmelpenninck Huys, Oosterstraat 53, ✉ 9711 NR, ✆ (0 50) 318 95 02 et 368 60 44 (rest), *info@schimmelpenninckhuys.nl, Fax (0 50) 318 31 64 et 318 31 64 (rest),* – – 25 à 70. AE VISA JCB Z h

Repas *de Parelvisser* *(fermé sam. midi, dim. et lundi)* (produits de la mer, ouvert jusqu'à 23 h) *Lunch 33* – 36/87 bc – 13 – **46 ch** 110/158 – ½ P 121/156.

• Six sortes de chambres dans cette charmante demeure du 18e s. Mobilier de différentes époques, ravissant patio et cave moyenâgeuse. Bistrot cossu dont la carte vogue au gré des marées. L'été, belle terrasse dressée dans la cour.

• Dit charmante patriciërshuis (18e eeuw) herbergt zes typen kamers. Stijlmeubilair uit diverse perioden, heerlijke patio en middeleeuwse kelder. Weelderige bistro waar de menukaart meedeint op de golven. Mooi zomerterras in de tuin.

Cityhotel sans rest, Gedempte Kattendiep 25, ✉ 9711 PM, ✆ (0 50) 588 65 65, *res.city@edenhotelgroup.com, Fax (0 50) 311 51 00,* – . AE VISA JCB. Z b

13 – **93 ch** 150.

• Hôtel pratique occupant un immeuble récent situé entre le casino et le port de plaisance. Chambres de dimensions correctes, bien tenues et munies du double vitrage.

• Praktisch hotel dat is gevestigd in een modern gebouw tussen het casino en de jachthaven. Goed onderhouden kamers van redelijke afmetingen en voorzien van dubbele beglazing.

NH Groningen, Hanzeplein 132, ✉ 9713 GW, ✆ (0 50) 584 81 81, *nhgroningen@nh-hotels.com, Fax (0 50) 584 81 80,* – – 25 à 70. AE VISA. rest YZ g

Repas (dîner seult) carte env. 32 – 13 – **104 ch** 90 – ½ P 80/125.

• Unité de la chaîne hôtelière espagnole NH établie à distance respectable du centre-ville. Spacieuses chambres bien équipées et d'une tenue irréprochable.

• Dit etablissement maakt deel uit van de Spaanse hotelketen NH en ligt op enige afstand van het centrum. De uitstekend onderhouden kamers zijn ruim en bieden alle comfort.

Aub. Corps de Garde sans rest, Oude Boteringestraat 74, ✉ 9712 GN, ☎ (0 50) 314 54 37, *info@corpsdegarde.nl, Fax (0 50) 313 63 20* – TV. AE ⓓ MC VISA JCB Y n
☕ 10 – **23 ch** 83.

◆ Posté au bord du canal ceinturant le centre ancien, ce corps de garde du 17e s. abrite désormais une auberge tranquille. Coquettes chambres bien équipées.

◆ Deze 17e-eeuwse kortegaard aan de gracht die rond het oude centrum loopt, biedt nu onderdak aan een rustig hotel-restaurant. Gezellige kamers met goed comfort.

Bastion, Bornholmstraat 99 (par ③ : 5 km), ✉ 9723 AW, ☎ (0 50) 541 49 77, *bastion@bastionhotel.nl, Fax (0 50) 541 30 12* – TV P. AE ⓓ MC VISA.
Repas (grillades, ouvert jusqu'à 23 h) carte env. 30 – ☕ 10 – **40 ch** 60.

◆ Hôtel de chaîne proche de l'autoroute, à 5 km du centre-ville. Petites chambres standard fonctionnelles équipées de la connexion pour modem. Bonne isolation phonique.

◆ Ketenhotel vlak bij de snelweg, op 5 km van het centrum. Kleine, functionele standaardkamers met modemaansluiting. Goede geluidsisolatie.

Muller (Hengge), Grote Kromme Elleboog 13, ✉ 9712 BJ, ☎ (0 50) 318 32 08, *Fax (0 50) 312 58 76* – ▤. AE ⓓ MC VISA JCB Z c
fermé 25 juil.-17 août, 25 déc.-11 janv., dim. et lundi – **Repas** (déjeuner sur réservation) 55/80, carte 50 à 66, ♀.

◆ Une cuisine classique soignée vous sera concoctée dans cette auberge frisonne accessible par une rue piétonne. Miroirs, lustres, lambris et parquet forment un décor élégant.

◆ In deze Friese herberg, te bereiken via een voetgangersstraatje, wordt een klassieke verzorgde keuken bereid. Elegant decor van spiegels, luchters, lambrisering en parket.

Spéc. Ballottine de foie d'oie et de canard. Homard poché et Saint-Jacques poêlées à la vanille. Carré d'agneau en croûte de sel (mars-sept.)

De Pauw, Gelkingestraat 52, ✉ 9711 NE, ☎ (0 50) 318 13 32, *restaurant@depauw.nl, Fax (0 50) 313 34 63* – ▤. AE ⓓ MC VISA JCB Z e
fermé 28 déc.-8 janv. et lundi et mardi en juil.-août – **Repas** (dîner seult) 28/58 bc, ♀.

◆ Table sympathique d'esprit contemporain, "Le Paon" a la particularité d'associer des buffets roulants à sa carte avec menus-choix. Savoureuses préparations au goût du jour.

◆ Sympathiek hedendaags restaurantje dat met gepaste trots wisselende buffetten biedt naast een kaart met keuzemenu's. Smaakvolle, eigentijdse gerechten.

GRONINGEN

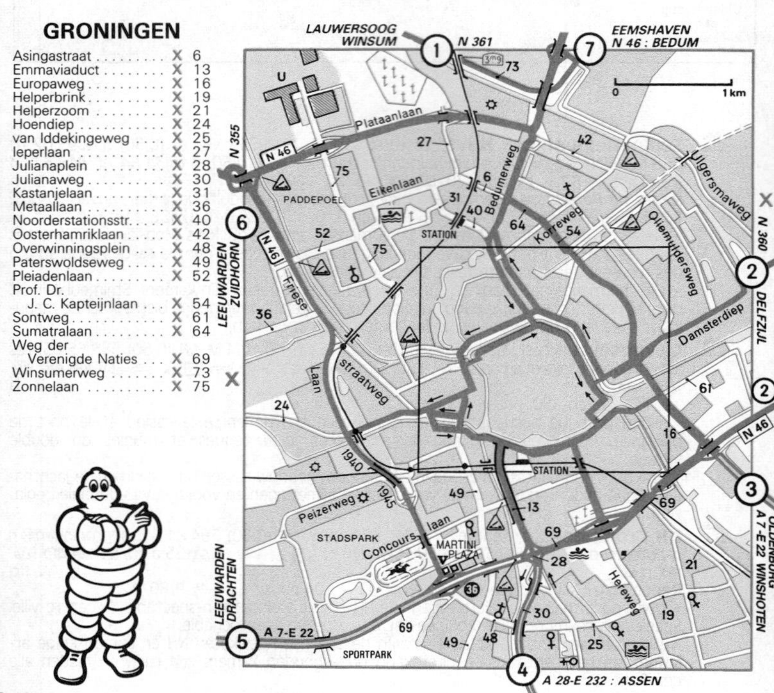

GRONINGEN

Street		
A-Kerkhof	Z	3
A-Straat	Z	4
de Brink	Z	7
Brugstraat	Z	9
Eeldersingel	Z	10
Eendrachtskade N.Z.	Z	11
Eendrachtskade Z.Z.	Z	12
Emmaviaduct	Z	13
Gedempte Zuiderdiep	Z	18
Grote Markt	Z	
Herestraat	Z	
Lopende Diep	Y	33
Martinikerkhof	Z	34
Noorderhaven N. Z.	Y	37
Noorderhaven Z. Z.	Z	39
Oosterstraat	Z	
Ossenmarkt	Y	43
Oude Boteringestr.	Z	45
Oude Ebbingestr.	Y	46
Paterswoldseweg	Z	49
Rademarkt	Z	55
Radesingel	Z	57
Schuitendiep	Z	58
St. Jansstraat	Z	60
Spilsluizen	Y	63
Verlengde Oosterstr.	Z	66
Vismarkt	Z	67
Westerhaven	Z	70
Westersingel	Z	72
Zuiderpark	Z	76

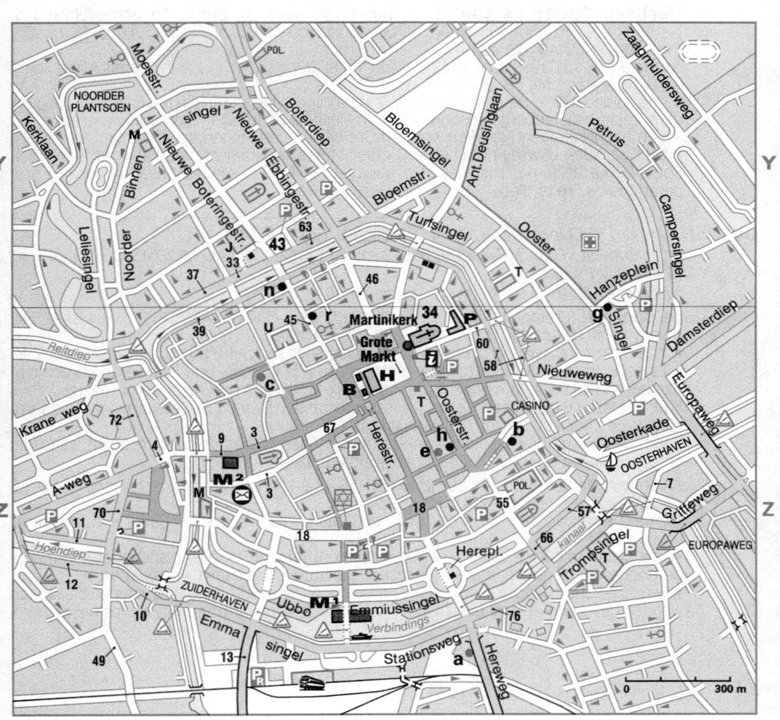

XX **Bistro't Gerecht** Hotel de Ville, Oude Boteringestraat 45, ✉ 9712 GD, ✆ (0 50) 589 18 59, *hotel@deville.nl, Fax (0 50) 318 17 77*, – AE ⓓ ⓜⓒ VISA JCB Z r

fermé 27 déc.-6 janv. et dim. et lundi en mi-juil-mi-août – **Repas** (dîner seult) carte 30 à 55, ♀.

• Recettes du moment à goûter dans l'ambiance animée d'un bistrot chic : banquettes rehaussées de velours rouges, lambris et grand comptoir rutilant. Service non somnolent.

• In een warme ambiance van met rood velours beklede banken, lambrisering en een grote, glimmende toog serveert deze chique bistro seizoengebonden gerechten. Attente service.

XX **Ni Hao,** Hereweg 1, ✉ 9726 AA, ✆ (0 50) 318 14 00, *info@nihaogroup.com, Fax (0 50) 313 11 37*, Cuisine chinoise – P. AE ⓓ ⓜⓒ VISA. Z a

Repas 21/45.

• Faim de chinoiseries ? Cet établissement asiatique situé aux portes de la ville, côté gare, déploie un large éventail de menus et une ribambelle de plats à la carte.

• Zin in Chinees ? Dit Aziatische restaurant aan de rand van de stad, aan de kant van het station, biedt een ruime keuze aan menu's en een hele reeks gerechten à la carte.

à Aduard *par ⑧ : 6 km* 🄲 *Zuidhorn 18 167 h :*

Aduard, Friesestraatweg 13 (sur N 355), ✉ 9831 TB, ☎ (0 50) 403 14 00, *mail@hoteladuard.nl, Fax (0 50) 403 12 16,* – ▣ P – 80. AE ⓓ ⓜⓒ VISA JCB. rest
Repas (ouvert jusqu'à 23 h) carte 22 à 32 – **22 ch** 48/80 – ½ P 47.
◆ Petit hôtel familial bien tenu, situé en léger retrait de la chaussée. Les chambres, fonctionnelles et de tailles correctes, offrent la vue sur la campagne environnante.
◆ Goed onderhouden familiehotelletje, dat iets van de weg af ligt. De functionele, redelijk ruime kamers kijken uit op het omringende platteland.

XXX **Herberg Onder de Linden** (Slenema) avec ch, Burg. van Barneveldweg 3, ✉ 9831 RD, ☎ (0 50) 403 14 06, *herberg-linden@slenema.nl, Fax (0 50) 403 18 14,* , – ▣ P. AE ⓓ ⓜⓒ VISA JCB
fermé du 1er au 6 fév., du 6 au 20 juil., du 19 au 26 oct., dim. et lundi – **Repas** (dîner seult) – 60/68, carte env. 68, ♀ – **5 ch** 98/113.
◆ Une cuisine délicieusement actualisée, et de grands vins, s'emploient à flatter vos papilles dans cette belle auberge frisonne (18e s.). Meubles bourgeois. Chambres feutrées.
◆ Een heerlijke eigentijdse keuken en grote wijnen verwennen de smaakpapillen in deze prachtige, 18e-eeuwse Friese herberg. Chique meubilair. Kamers met een ingetogen sfeer.
Spéc. Dégustation de crustacés et coquillages (21 juin-21 sept.). Agneau régional. 3 préparations de fruits d'été

GULPEN *Limburg* 🄲 *Gulpen-Wittem 15 435 h.* 532 U 18 *et* 715 I 9.

au Sud-Est : 6 km à Mechelen, Dalbissenweg 22, ✉ *6281 NC,* ☎ *(0 43) 455 13 97, Fax (0 43) 455 15 76.*

Amsterdam 229 – Maastricht 16 – Aachen 16.

XX **Le Sapiche** (Cremers), Rijksweg 12, ✉ 6271 AE, ☎ (0 43) 450 38 33, *lesapiche@introweb.nl, Fax (0 43) 450 20 97,* – AE ⓜⓒ VISA.
fermé sem. carnaval, mardi et merc. – **Repas** (dîner seult) 46/99 bc, carte 67 à 83, ♀.
◆ La seule lecture de la carte vous mettra l'eau à la bouche. Une jolie véranda recouvre partiellement la salle à manger d'où l'on aperçoit le chef œuvrer aux fourneaux.
◆ Bij het lezen van de kaart begint u al te watertanden ! Vanuit de eetzaal met fraaie serre kunt u de chef-kok achter het fornuis ziet kokkerellen.
Spéc. Déclinaison de foie d'oie. Saint-Jacques grillées et pied de porc croquant, sauce au citron confit au sel. Loup en papillote au jus de langoustines

XX **l'Atelier,** Markt 9, ✉ 6271 BD, ☎ (0 43) 450 44 90, *info@restaurantatelier.nl, Fax (0 43) 450 29 62,* – AE ⓜⓒ VISA.
fermé 2 sem. carnaval, fin sept.-début oct., merc. d'oct. à mars et jeudi – **Repas** (dîner seult) 33/64 bc.
◆ Une demeure du 15e s. abrite cet établissement familial. Poutres, plancher et parements de briques confèrent aux lieux un cachet rustique. L'été, repas en terrasse.
◆ Een 15e-eeuws pand herbergt dit gezellige restaurant. Balken, houten vloer en bakstenen wanden geven de eetzaal een rustiek cachet. 's Zomers wordt op het terras geserveerd.

DEN HAAG

P *Zuid-Holland* 532 K 10 *et* 715 D 5 *– 457 726 h.*

Amsterdam 55 ② – Bruxelles 182 ④ – Rotterdam 27 ④ – Delft 13 ④.

RENSEIGNEMENTS PRATIQUES

Kon. Julianaplein 30. ✉ 2595 AA. ☎ 0 900-340 35 05, info@denhaag.com, Fax (070) 347 21 02.

Amsterdam-Schiphol Nord-Est : 37 km ☎ (020) 601 91 11, Fax (020) 604 14 75 – Rotterdam-Zestienhoven Sud-Est : 17 km ☎ (010) 446 34 44, Fax (020) 446 34 99.

18 à Rijswijk (BR), Delftweg 58 ✉ 2289 AL ☎ (070) 319 24 24, Fax (070) 399 50 40 – 18 au Nord-Est : 11 km à Wassenaar, Groot Haesebroekseweg 22, ✉ 2243 EC, ☎ (070) 517 96 07, Fax (070) 514 01 71 et 18 Dr Mansveltkade 15, ✉ 2242 TZ, ☎ (070) 517 88 99, Fax (0 70) 551 93 02 – 18 à Leidschendam (CQ), Elzenlaan 31, ✉ 2495 AZ, ☎ (070) 399 10 96, Fax (070) 399 86 15 – 9 à Kijkduin, Wijndaelerduin 25, ✉ 2554 BX, ☎ (070) 368 66 39.

CURIOSITÉS

Voir *Binnenhof★ : salle des Chevaliers★ (Ridderzaal)* JY *– Étang de la Cour (Hofvijver)* ≤★ HJY *– Lange Voorhout★* HJX *– Madurodam★★* ET *– Scheveningen★★.*

Musées : *Mauritshuis★★★* JY *– Galerie de peintures Prince Guillaume V★ (Schilderijengalerij Prins Willem V)* HY **M²** *– Panorama Mesdag★* HX *– Musée Mesdag★* EU *– Municipal★★ (Gemeentemuseum)* DEU *– Bredius★* JY *– Museum Beelden aan Zee★★ (Musée de la sculpture) à Scheveningen* DS.

RÉPERTOIRE DES RUES DU PLAN DE DEN HAAG

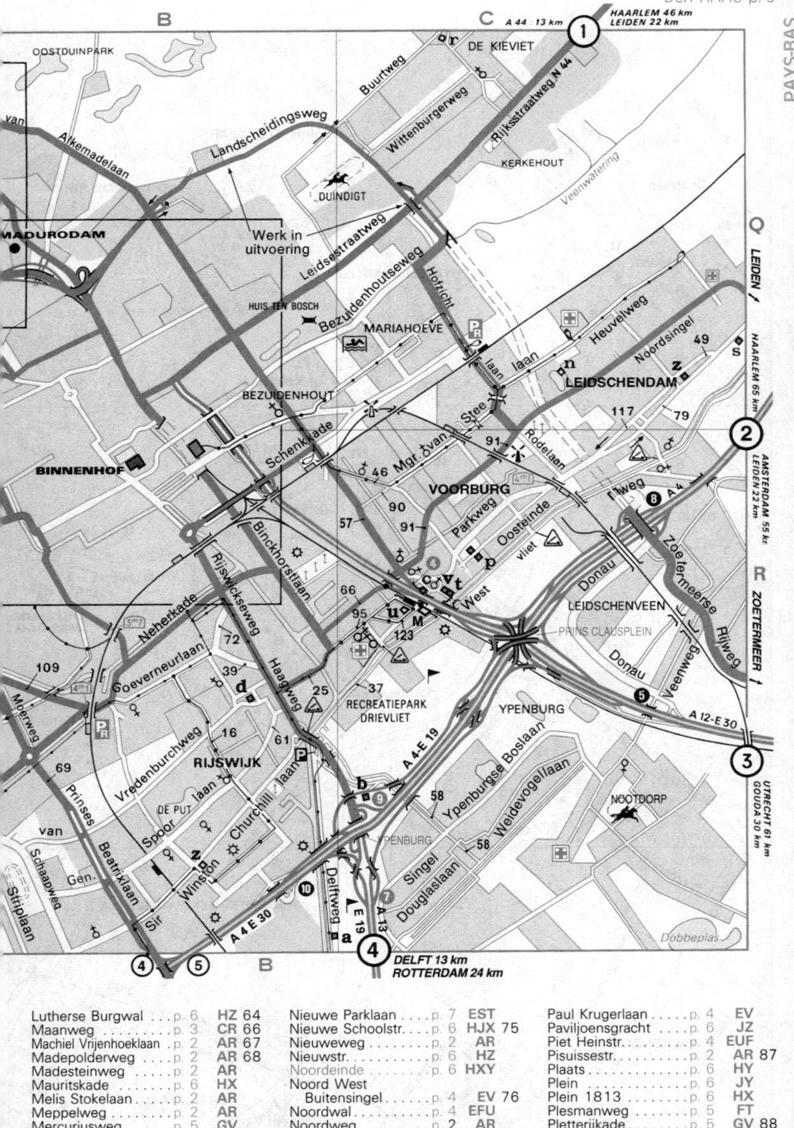
B
C
A 44 13 km
1
HAARLEM 46 km
LEIDEN 22 km
OOSTDUINPARK
DE KIEVIET
Buurtweg
Wittenburgerweg
Rijksstraatweg N 44
Landscheidingsweg
Alkemadelaan
KERKEHOUT
Veenwatering
DUINDIGT
MADURODAM
Werk in
uitvoering
Leidsestraatweg
Bezuidenhoutseweg
Hofzicht
Q
LEIDEN
HUIS TEN BOSCH
MARIAHOEVE
Heuvelweg
Noordsingel
49
HAARLEM 65 km
laan
laan
LEIDSCHENDAM
BEZUIDENHOUT
Stee
117
79
2
Schenkkade
91
Rodelaan
BINNENHOF
46
Mgr. van
AMSTERDAM 55 km
LEIDEN 22 km
VOORBURG
Rijweg
A 4
90
Parkweg
Oosteinde
57
91
vliet
Binckhorstlaan
Donau
R
Zoetermeerse
Rijswickseweg
West
66
LEIDSCHENVEEN
ZOETERMEER
Neherkade
95
123
PRINS CLAUSPLEIN
72
Rijweg
109
Goeverneurlaan
39
Haagweg
25
37
Donau
Veenweg
Moerweg
RECREATIEPARK
DRIEVLIET
YPENBURG
A 12-E 30
16
A 4-E 19
Ypenburgse Boslaan
61
RIJSWIJK
69
Vredenburchweg
laan
3
Prinses
58
Weidevogellaan
NOOTDORP
DE PUT
UTRECHT 61 km
GOUDA 30 km
van
Spoor
Churchill
YPENBURG
58
Schaapweg
Beatrixlaan
Gen.
Winston
Singel
Douglaslaan
Striplaan
Delftweg
E 19
A 13
Sir
A 4 E 30
Dobbeplas
4
5
B
4
DELFT 13 km
ROTTERDAM 24 km

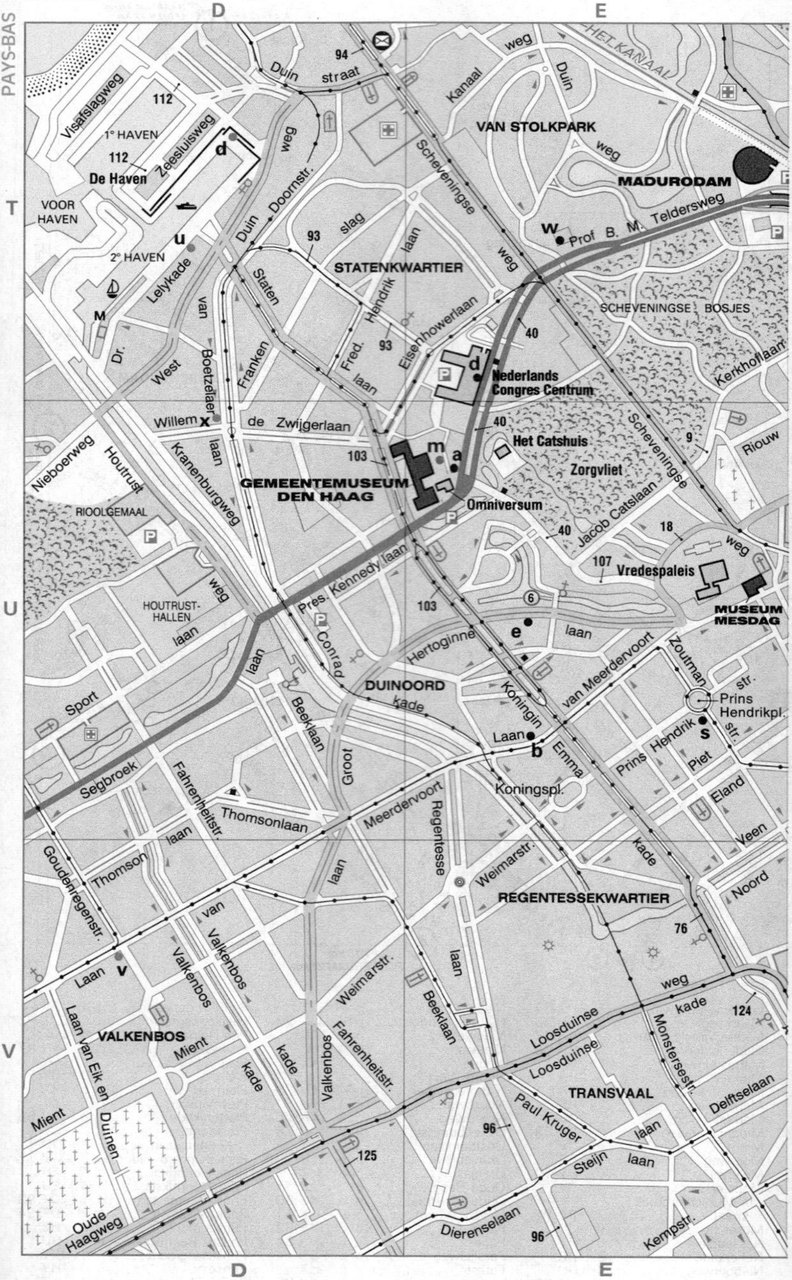

D
E
HET KANAAL
Visafslagweg
112
1° HAVEN
112
Zeesluisweg
d
De Haven
VOOR HAVEN
u
2° HAVEN
Lelykade
M
94
Duin straat
Kanaal weg
Duin weg
VAN STOLKPARK
MADURODAM
Duin Doornstr. weg
Scheveningse weg
93 slag
STATENKWARTIER
Hendrik laan
W
Prof B. M. Teldersweg
SCHEVENINGSE BOSJES
Staten
van Boetzelaer
Franken
Fred. laan
93
Eisenhowerlaan
40
d
Nederlands Congres Centrum
Kerkhoflaan
Dr. West
Willem x de Zwijgerlaan
40
Het Catshuis
Scheveningse
9
Riouw
Nieboerweg
Houtrust
Kranenburgweg laan
103
m
a
GEMEENTEMUSEUM DEN HAAG
Zorgvliet
Omniversum
RIOOLGEMAAL
40
Jacob Catslaan
18
weg
107
Vredespaleis
Pres. Kennedy laan
103
6
MUSEUM MESDAG
HOUTRUST-HALLEN laan
weg
e
laan
Conrad laan
Hertoginne
van Meerdervoort
Zoutman str.
DUINOORD
Prins Hendrikpl.
kade
Koningin
Sport
Beeklaan
Laan
b
s
Prins Hendrik
Piet
str.
Emma
Segbroek
Fahrenheitstr.
Groot
Koningspl.
Eland
Thomsonlaan
Meerdervoort
Regentesse
Veen
Thomson laan
laan
kade
Goudenregenstr.
Weimarstr.
REGENTESSEKWARTIER
Noord
van Valkenbos
laan
76
Laan v
Valkenbos
Weimarstr.
weg
Beeklaan
kade
124
Laan van Eik en Duinen
VALKENBOS
Mient
kade
kade
Fahrenheitstr.
Valkenbos
Loosduinse
Loosduinse
Monstersestr.
TRANSVAAL
Delftselaan
Mient
96
Paul Kruger laan
125
Steijn laan
Oude Haagweg
Dierenselaan
96
Kempstr.
T
U
V
D
E

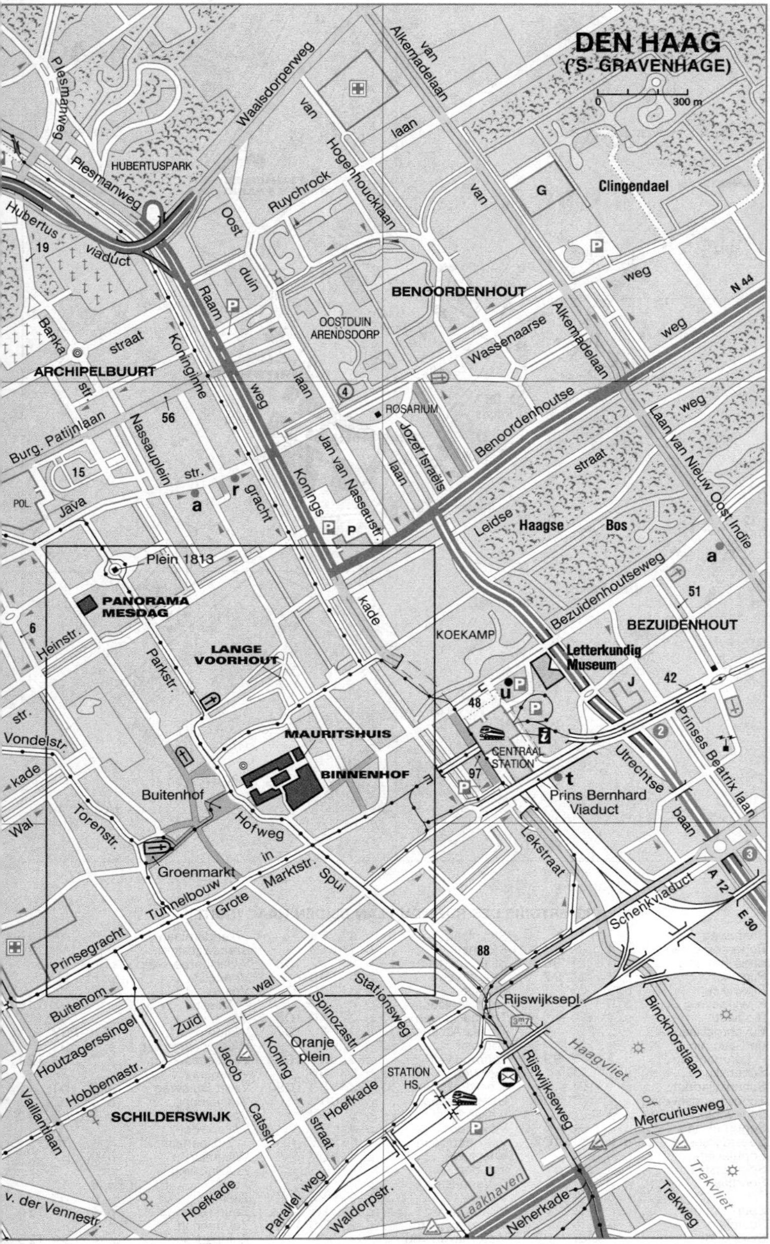

DEN HAAG
('S- GRAVENHAGE)

0 300 m

F G

T U V

Plesmanweg
Waalsdorperweg
van Alkemadelaan
van Hogenhoucklaan
HUBERTUSPARK
Plesmanweg
Hubertus viaduct
19
Ruychrock
Oost duin
Raam
Clingendael
G
P
weg
N 44
BENOORDENHOUT
OOSTDUIN ARENDSDORP
Banka straat
ARCHIPELBUURT
str.
Koninginne
weg
laan
4
RØSARIUM
Wassenaarse
Alkemadelaan
weg
56
Nassauplein
Burg. Patijnlaan
15
Jozef Israëls laan
Benoordenhoutse weg
Laan van Nieuw Oost Indië
POL.
Java str.
a
r
gracht
Konings
Jan van Nassaustr.
P
Leidse straat
Haagse Bos
a
Plein 1813
PANORAMA MESDAG
kade
Bezuidenhoutseweg
51
KOEKAMP
BEZUIDENHOUT
6
Heinstr.
Parkstr.
LANGE VOORHOUT
Letterkundig Museum
u
48
J
42
str.
Vondelstr.
MAURITSHUIS
CENTRAAL STATION
2
Prinses Beatrix laan
kade
BINNENHOF
97
t
Prins Bernhard Viaduct
Utrechtse baan
Buitenhof
Hofweg
Wal
Torenstr.
Groenmarkt
Lekstraat
3
in
Tunnelbouw
Grote Marktstr.
Spui
Schenkviaduct
A 12
E 30
Prinsegracht
88
wal
Stationsweg
Rijswijksepl.
Buitenom
Zuid
Houtzagerssingel
Jacob Catsstr.
Koning straat
Spinozastr.
Oranje plein
Binckhorstlaan
Haagvliet
Hobbemastr.
STATION HS.
Rijswijkseweg
Vaillantlaan
SCHILDERSWIJK
Hoefkade
of
Mercuriusweg
P
U
Trekvliet
Hoefkade
Laakhaven
Trekweg
v. der Vennestr.
Parallel weg
Waldorpstr.
Neherkade

F G

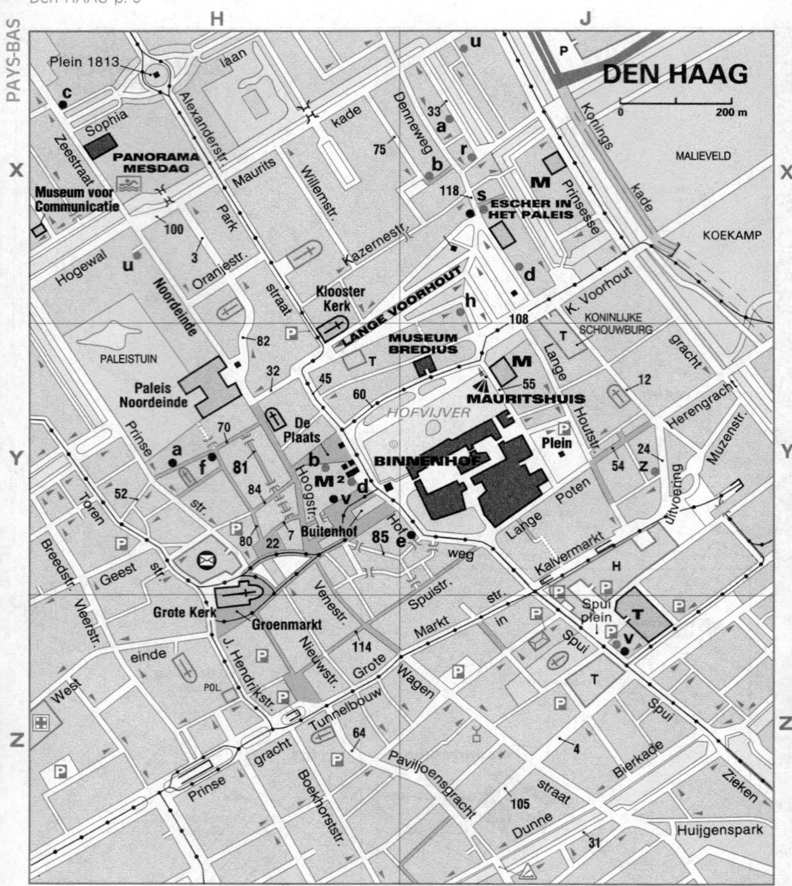

RÉPERTOIRE DES RUES DU PLAN DE DEN HAAG (SUITE)

Raamweg	p. 5	FTU	
Regentesselaan	p. 4	EUV	
de la Reyweg	p. 4	EV	96
Rijnstr.	p. 5	GU	97
Rijswijksepl.	p. 5	GV	
Rijwijkseweg	p. 5	GV	
Riouwstr.	p. 4	EUF	
Ruychrocklaan	p. 5	FGT	
de Savornin Lohmanlaan	p. 2	AR	99
Schenkkade	p. 3	BCR	
Schenkviaduct	p. 5	GV	
Scheveningseveer	p. 6	HX	100
Scheveningseweg	p. 4	ETU	
Segbroeklaan	p. 4	DU	
Soestdijksekade	p. 2	AR	102
Sophialaan	p. 6	HX	
Spinozastr.	p. 5	FV	
Sportlaan	p. 2	AR	
Spuistr.	p. 6	JYZ	
Spui	p. 6	JZ	
Spuiplein	p. 6	JZ	
Stadhouderslaan	p. 4	DEU	103
Statenlaan	p. 7	DT	
Stationsweg	p. 5	FGV	
Steijnlaan	p. 4	EV	
Stevinstr.	p. 7	ES	
Stille Veerkade	p. 6	JZ	105
Strandweg	p. 7	DS	
Striplaan	p. 3	BR	
Thomsonlaan	p. 4	DUV	
Thorbeckelaan	p. 2	AR	106
Tobias Asserlaan	p. 4	EU	107
Torenstr.	p. 6	HY	
Tournooiveld	p. 6	JXY	108
Trekweg	p. 5	GV	
Troelstrakade	p. 3	BR	109
Utrechtsebaan	p. 5	GUV	
Vaillantlaan	p. 5	FV	
Valkenboskade	p. 4	DV	
Valkenboslaan	p. 4	DV	
Veenkade	p. 4	EUV	
van der Vennestr.	p. 5	FV	
Venestr.	p. 6	HYZ	
Visafslagweg	p. 7	DT	
Visserhavenstr	p. 7	DS	110
Visserhavenweg	p. 7	DT	112
Vlamingstr.	p. 6	HZ	114
Vleerstr.	p. 6	HZ	
Volendamlaan	p. 2	AR	115
Vreeswijkstr.	p. 2	AR	120
Waalsdorperweg	p. 5	FT	
Vondelstr.	p. 5	FU	
Vos in Tuinstr.	p. 6	JX	118
Wagenstr.	p. 6	JZ	
Waldorpstr.	p. 5	FGV	
Wassenaarseweg	p. 5	GT	
Wassenaarsestr.	p. 7	DS	121
Weimarstr.	p. 4	DEV	
West Duinweg	p. 7	DT	
Westeinde	p. 6	HZ	
Westmadeweg	p. 2	AR	119
Willem de Zwijgerlaan	p. 4	DU	
Willemstr.	p. 6	HX	
Zeesluisweg	p. 7	DT	
Zeestr.	p. 6	HX	
Zieken	p. 6	JZ	
Zoutkeetsingel	p. 4	EV	124
Zoutmanstr.	p. 4	EU	
Zuidparklaan	p. 4	DV	125
Zuidwal	p. 5	FV	
Zwolsestr.	p. 7	ES	

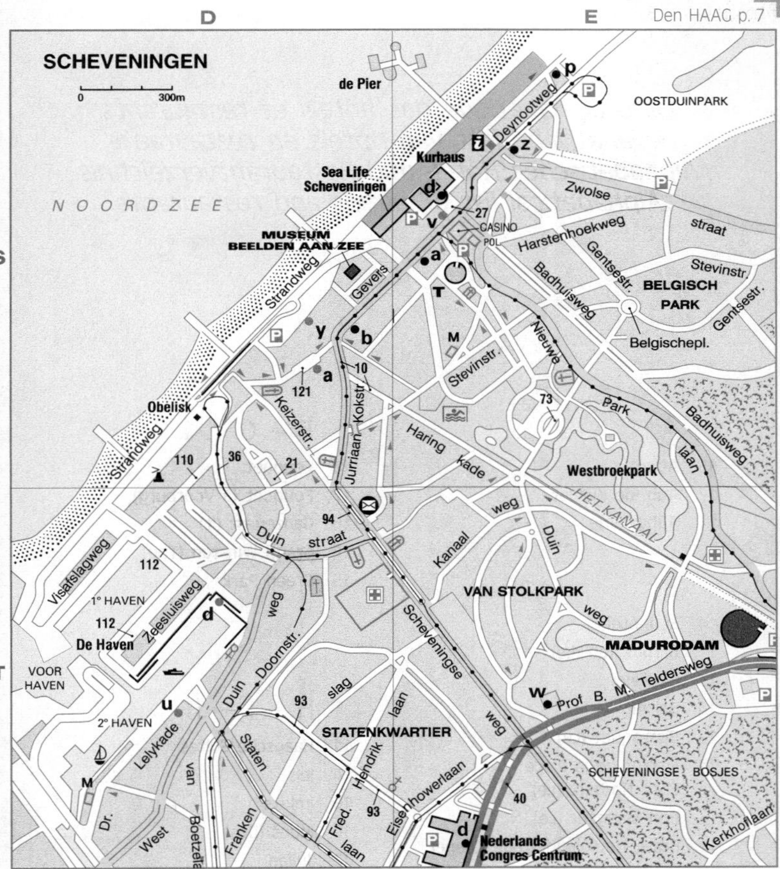

RÉPERTOIRE DES RUES DU PLAN DE DEN HAAG (FIN)

LEIDSCHENDAM

Donau	p. 3	CR	
Heuvelweg	p. 3	CQ	
Koningin Julianaweg	p. 3	CQ	49
Noordsingel	p. 3	CQ	
Oude Trambaan	p. 3	CQ	79
Veenweg	p. 3	CR	
Voorburgseweg	p. 3	CQ	117
Westvlietweg	p. 3	CR	
Zoetermeerse Rijweg	p. 3	CR	

RIJSWIJK

Burg. Elsenlaan	p. 3	BR	16
Delftweg	p. 3	BR	
Douglaslaan	p. 3	CR	
Geestbrugweg	p. 3	BR	25
Gen. Spoorlaan	p. 3	BR	
Haagweg	p. 3	BR	
Jan Thijssenweg	p. 3	CR	37
Laan van Hoornwijck	p. 3	CR	58
Lindelaan	p. 3	BR	61
Prinses Beatrixlaan	p. 3	BR	
Schaapweg	p. 3	BR	
Singel	p. 3	CR	
Sir Winston Churchilllaan	p. 3	BR	
Van Vredenburchweg	p. 3	BR	
Weidevogellaan	p. 3	CR	
Ypenburgse Boslaan	p. 3	CR	

VOORBURG

Koningin Julianalaan	p. 3	CR	46
Laan van Nieuw Oost Einde	p. 3	CR	57
Mgr. van Steelaan	p. 3	CQR	
Oosteinde	p. 3	CR	
Parkweg	p. 3	CR	
Potgieterlaan	p. 3	CR	90
Prins Bernhardlaan	p. 3	CR	91
Prinses Mariannelaan	p. 3	CR	95
Rodelaan	p. 3	CR	
Westeinde	p. 3	CR	123

Zoekt u een rustig of afgelegen hotel, raadpleeg dan de kaart in de inleiding of kijk in de tekst naar hotels met het teken 🐎

Liste alphabétique des hôtels et restaurants
Alfabetische lijst van hotels en restaurants
Alphabetisches Hotel- und Restaurantverzeichnis
Alphabetical list of hotels and restaurants

PAYS-BAS

Quartiers du Centre - *plans p. 5 et 6 sauf indication spéciale :*

Des Indes, Lange Voorhout 54, ✉ 2514 EG, ℘ (0 70) 361 23 45, *info@desindes.com, Fax (0 70) 361 23 50* – 🛗 TV P – 25 à 100. AE ⓞ MC VISA JCB. ✈ rest JX s
Repas ***Le Restaurant*** *(fermé sam. midi et dim.)* *Lunch 33* – 39/69 bc, ♀ – ☐ 23 – **71 ch** 300/370, – 6 suites.
◆ Maison de maître fin 19e s. jouxtant une place du quartier institutionnel. Élégant lounge classique, chambres avec mobilier de style, accueil et service avenants. Opulente salle de restaurant classique et cuisine continentale en phase avec l'époque.
◆ Stadspaleis uit het einde van de 19e eeuw, aan een lommerrijke laan vlak bij de regeringsgebouwen. Elegante lounge, kamers met stijlmeubilair, vriendelijke ontvangst en service. Klassieke, luxueus ingerichte restaurantzaal, eigentijdse continentale keuken.

Crowne Plaza Promenade, van Stolkweg 1, ✉ 2585 JL, ℘ (0 70) 352 51 61, *info@crowneplazadenhaag.nl, Fax (0 70) 354 10 46,* <, , , , – 🛗 TV ♿ P – 25 à 425. AE ⓞ MC VISA JCB plan p. 4 ET w
Repas ***Brasserie Promenade*** *Lunch 30* – 35/40, ♀ – ***Trattoria dell'Arte*** *(fermé sam. midi)* (cuisine italienne, ouvert jusqu'à minuit et dîner seult en juil.-août) *Lunch 29* – carte 40 à 49 – ☐ 23 – **93 ch** 295, – 1 suite – ½ P 357/366.
◆ Grand hôtel de chaîne bâti en bordure du ring intérieur, face à un vaste parc. Confort actuel dans les chambres, collection de tableaux modernes, service non somnolent. Brasserie décontractée pour un repas simple. Trattoria au cadre contemporain.
◆ Groot ketenhotel aan de binnenste ring, tegenover een groot park. Modern comfort in de kamers, collectie moderne schilderijen, attente service. Brasserie met ontspannen ambiance voor een eenvoudige maaltijd. Trattoria met eigentijds decor.

Dorint sans rest, Johan de Wittlaan 42, ✉ 2517 JR, ℘ (0 70) 416 91 11, *info@dhd.dorint.nl, Fax (0 70) 416 91 00,* , , – 🛗 TV ♿ – 25 à 2000. AE ⓞ MC VISA. ✈ rest plan p. 4 ET d
☐ 18 – **214 ch** 370, – 2 suites.
◆ L'une des perles du groupe Dorint : situation stratégique "sur" le palais des congrès, modernisme, chambres amples et pimpantes, colossale infrastructure pour séminaires.
◆ Een van de parels van de groep Dorint, op een strategisch punt bij het congrescentrum. Moderne setting, ruime en elegante kamers, kolossale infrastructuur voor seminars.

Carlton Ambassador , Sophialaan 2, ✉ 2514 JP, ℘ (0 70) 363 03 63, *info@ambassador.carlton.nl, Fax (0 70) 360 05 35,* – 🛗 TV P – 25 à 150. AE ⓞ MC VISA JCB. ✈ ch HX c
Repas ***Henricus*** (ouvert jusqu'à 23 h) *Lunch 29* – 33/51, ♀ – ☐ 21 – **77 ch** 290/330, – 1 suite – ½ P 295/330.
◆ Les chambres de ce petit palace du diplomatique quartier Mesdag sont de style hollandais ou anglais. Insonorisation inégale, mais ensemble de caractère. Apaisante salle à manger fleurie. Cuisine d'inspiration méditerranéenne.
◆ De kamers van dit kleine luxehotel dicht bij de ambassades en Panorama Mesdag zijn in Hollandse of Engelse stijl ingericht. De kwaliteit van de geluidsisolatie is niet overal gelijk. De eetzaal straalt rust uit. Mediterraan geïnspireerde keuken.

Bel Air, Johan de Wittlaan 30, ✉ 2517 JR, ℘ (0 70) 352 53 54, *info@goldentulipbelairhotel.nl, Fax (0 70) 352 53 53,* , – 🛗 TV P – 25 à 250. AE ⓞ MC VISA JCB plan p. 4 EU a
Repas *Lunch 20* – carte 30 à 55 – ☐ 16 – **348 ch** 195.
◆ Ressource hôtelière massive dont les chambres, d'un calibre honorable et convenablement équipées, se distribuent sur neuf étages. Espaces communs de bonne ampleur.
◆ Robuust hotelcomplex waarvan de vrij ruime en zeer comfortabele kamers over negen verdiepingen verspreid liggen. Royale gemeenschappelijke ruimten.

Sofitel, Koningin Julianaplein 35, ✉ 2595 AA, ℘ (0 70) 381 49 01, *h0755@accor-hotels.com, Fax (0 70) 382 59 27* – 🛗 TV ♿ P – 25 à 150. AE ⓞ MC VISA JCB GU u
Repas *(fermé sam. midi et dim. midi)* *Lunch 28* – 35 – ☐ 20 – **143 ch** 265/365, – 1 suite.
◆ Pratique pour les utilisateurs du rail, cet hôtel occupe un immeuble contemporain jouxtant la gare. Les chambres offrent le niveau de confort habituel à l'enseigne. Table actuelle recréant l'ambiance d'un atelier d' artiste.
◆ Dit hotel is gevestigd in een modern pand bij het station, dus praktisch voor treinreizigers. De kamers bieden het comfort dat gebruikelijk is binnen de keten. Eigentijds restaurant met de ambiance van een kunstenaarsatelier.

Mercure Central sans rest, Spui 180, ✉ 2511 BW, ℘ (0 70) 363 67 00, *h1317@accor-hotels.com, Fax (0 70) 363 93 98* – 🛗 TV ♿ P – 25 à 135. AE ⓞ MC VISA. ✈ JZ v
☐ 16 – **156 ch** 160/165, – 3 suites.
◆ Chambres fonctionnelles bien tenues et munies du double vitrage dans ce building très central édifié au cours des années 1980. Service "minimaliste". Clientèle d'affaires.
◆ Goed onderhouden, functionele kamers met dubbele beglazing in een centraal gelegen pand uit de jaren tachtig van de vorige eeuw. Beperkt servicepakket. Zakelijke clientèle.

Parkhotel sans rest, Molenstraat 53, ✉ 2513 BJ, ✆ (0 70) 362 43 71, *reserveringen@parkhoteldenhaag.nl, Fax (0 70) 361 45 25,* – |♦| TV – 25 à 200. AE ⓓ ⓜ VISA JCB. HY a
114 ch 140/240.
◆ Cet établissement créé en 1910 avoisine l'agréable parc arboré du Paleis Noordeinde. Atmosphère "cosy" dans les chambres ; un tiers d'entre elles sont des singles.
◆ Dit etablissement is gebouwd in 1910 en grenst aan de tuin van het Paleis Noordeinde. Behaaglijke ambiance in de kamers, waarvan een derde deel eenpersoons is.

Corona, Buitenhof 42, ✉ 2513 AH, ✆ (0 70) 363 79 30, *hotelcorona@planet.nl, Fax (0 70) 361 57 85* – |♦| TV – 25 à 100. AE ⓓ ⓜ VISA JCB HY v
Repas voir rest ***Marc Smeets*** ci-après – 15 – **35 ch** 155/175, – 1 suite.
◆ Sur la place du Buitenhof, petit hôtel occupant trois maisons de maître. Coquettes chambres bourgeoises de différentes tailles. Clientèle ministérielle et diplomatique.
◆ Klein hotelcomplex aan het Buitenhof, dat drie herenhuizen omvat. Keurige kamers die in grootte variëren. Clientèle van ministers en diplomaten.

Haagsche Suites sans rest, Laan van Meerdervoort 155, ✉ 2517 AX, ✆ (0 70) 364 78 79, *info@haagschesuites.nl, Fax (0 70) 345 65 33,* – |♦| TV P. AE ⓜ VISA
fermé janv. – **1 ch** 340/425, – 3 suites. plan p. 4 EU b
◆ Petit hébergement select et discret dont l'intérieur, intime, témoigne d'un sens esthétique des plus subtils. Jardin design. Entrée dérobée pour le parking privé : s'informer.
◆ Klein, bijzonder select hotel waarvan het interieur getuigt van een zeer verfijnde smaak. Designtuin. Informeer naar de afgesloten privé parkeerplaats.

Paleis sans rest, Molenstraat 26, ✉ 2513 BL, ✆ (0 70) 362 46 21, *info@paleishotel.nl, Fax (0 70) 361 45 33* – |♦| TV. AE ⓓ ⓜ VISA JCB HY f
20 ch 150/160.
◆ Une engageante façade bourgeoise rose saumon signale ce petit hôtel de luxe où vous séjournerez dans de sémillantes chambres richement décorées. Belles salles de bains rétro.
◆ Dit kleine luxehotel is gevestigd in een pand met een fraaie, zalmkleurige voorgevel. De kamers zijn gezellig en zeer luxueus ingericht. Fraaie badkamers in klassieke stijl.

Novotel, Hofweg 5, ✉ 2511 AA, ✆ (0 70) 364 88 46, *h1180@accor-hotels.com, Fax (0 70) 356 28 89* – |♦| TV – 25 à 100. AE ⓓ ⓜ VISA HJY e
Repas (ouvert jusqu'à 23 h) carte 22 à 33 – 15 – **106 ch** 155/160.
◆ Juste en face du Binnenhof, dans un immeuble ancien abritant un passage commercial, hôtel dont les chambres se conforment parfaitement aux standards de la chaîne.
◆ Dit hotel recht tegenover het Binnenhof is gehuisvest in een oud pand met een winkelpassage. De kamers beantwoorden geheel aan de normen van de keten.

Petit sans rest, Groot Hertoginnelaan 42, ✉ 2517 EH, ✆ (0 70) 346 55 00, *petit@worldonline.nl, Fax (0 70) 346 32 57* – |♦| TV P. AE ⓓ ⓜ VISA JCB plan p. 4 EU e
20 ch 83/110.
◆ Installé en léger retrait du centre, sur un grand boulevard résidentiel, ce brave "petit" hôtel familial renferme des chambres actuelles sobrement équipées.
◆ Dit kleine familiehotel ligt wat buiten het centrum aan een grote laan met woonhuizen en beschikt over moderne kamers met eenvoudig comfort.

Sebel sans rest, Zoutmanstraat 40, ✉ 2518 GR, ✆ (0 70) 345 92 00, *info@hotelsebel.nl, Fax (0 70) 345 58 55* – TV. AE ⓓ ⓜ VISA. plan p. 4 EU s
26 ch 95.
◆ Trois maisons mitoyennes alignées dans une rue passagère (tramway) forment cet hôtel de confort simple mais tout à fait convenable. Chambres avec double vitrage.
◆ Drie aangrenzende huizen in een doorgaande straat (tram) vormen dit eenvoudige maar vrij gerieflijke hotel. Kamers met dubbele beglazing.

Calla's (van der Kleijn), Laan van Roos en Doorn 51a, ✉ 2514 BC, ✆ (0 70) 345 58 66, *Fax (0 70) 345 57 10* – AE ⓓ ⓜ VISA. JX u
fermé 25 juil.-16 août, 25 déc.-3 janv., sam. midi, dim. et lundi – **Repas** Lunch 59 bc – 63/114 bc, carte 68 à 109.
◆ Ancien entrepôt relooké en restaurant moderne. Salle à manger design aux tons crème et corail, offrant la vue sur les cuisines. Mets classiques actualisés avec doigté.
◆ Dit pakhuis is verbouwd tot een modern restaurant. Designeetzaal in roomkleurige en koraalrode tinten met open keuken. Klassieke gerechten in een eigentijds jasje.
Spéc. Brochette de Saint-Jacques à la réglisse et witlof (oct.-avril). Turbot en soufflé de pommes de terre aillées (mai-déc.). Crêpes farcies glacées et glace vanille

Aubergerie, Nieuwe Schoolstraat 19, ✉ 2514 HT, ✆ (0 70) 364 80 70, *info@aubergerie.nl, Fax (0 70) 360 73 38,* – AE ⓓ ⓜ VISA JX b
fermé sam. midi, dim. et lundi – **Repas** Lunch 23 – 27/63 bc, ♀.
◆ Une appétissante carte française aux accents provençaux - à l'image du décor intérieur - vous sera soumise à cette adresse. Ambiance souriante. Une valeur sûre !
◆ In een mediterraan decor wordt een aantrekkelijke Franse kaart met Provençaalse accenten gepresenteerd. Vriendelijke ambiance. Een prima optie.

PAYS-BAS

XX **Le Bistroquet,** Lange Voorhout 98, ✉ 2514 EJ, ✆ (0 70) 360 11 70, *info@bistroqu et.nl, Fax (0 70) 360 55 30,* – ▤. AE ⓓ MC VISA JCB JX d
fermé 23 déc.-2 janv., sam. midi et dim. – **Repas** *Lunch 28* – carte 50 à 72, ♀.
◆ Atmosphère intime et nostalgie des années folles dans ce chaleureux "Bistroquet" du quartier diplomatico-parlementaire. Cuisine française escortée de vins du monde.
◆ Intieme ambiance en nostalgie naar de roaring twenties in deze gezellige bistro in de nabijheid van ambassades en regeringsgebouwen. Franse keuken en wereldwijnen.

XX **Saur,** Lange Voorhout 47, ✉ 2514 EC, ✆ (0 70) 346 25 65, *restaurant.saur@12move.nl, Fax (0 70) 362 13 13,* , Produits de la mer – ▤. AE ⓓ MC VISA JCB JX h
fermé sam. midi, dim. et jours fériés – **Repas** *Lunch 33* – carte 46 à 113, ♀.
◆ Poissons, crustacés et fruits de mer rêvent d'une seule chose : passer à la casserole dans cet établissement qui vient tout juste de faire "peau neuve". Bar à huîtres.
◆ Vis, schaaldieren en fruits de mer trappelen hier van ongeduld tot ze via de pan de eeuwige roem tegemoet gaan in dit pas gerenoveerde restaurant. Oesterbar.

XX **Rousseau,** Van Boetzelaerlaan 134, ✉ 2581 AX, ✆ (0 70) 355 47 43, – MC VISA plan p. 4 DU x
fermé du 21 au 29 fév., 25 juil.-23 août, 24 déc.-3 janv., dim. et lundi – **Repas** *Lunch 25* – 30/50, ♀.
◆ L'esprit du Douanier Rousseau - homonyme du patron - a investi les lieux. Une jolie fresque à sa façon orne la salle de restaurant. La carte affiche un menu "quinzaine".
◆ Hier waart de geest rond van Rousseau, homoniem van de patron. Een fresco in de stijl van deze Franse schilder siert de eetzaal. Op de kaart een tweewekelijks menu.

XX **Julien,** Vos in Tuinstraat 2a, ✉ 2514 BX, ✆ (0 70) 365 86 02, *info@julien.nl, Fax (0 70) 365 31 47* – AE ⓓ MC VISA JX s
fermé dim. – **Repas** carte 45 à 62.
◆ Cette table ravira les entichés d'Art nouveau. Salles à manger feutrées, mezzanine et bar rutilants respirent l'atmosphère 1900. Cuisine classico-traditionnelle de saison.
◆ Aangename eetzaal, mezzanine en blinkende bars : kortom, ambiance fin de siècle en art nouveau. Klassiek-traditionele keuken met seizoengebonden gerechten.

XX **The Raffles,** Javastraat 63, ✉ 2585 AG, ✆ (0 70) 345 85 87, *Fax (0 70) 356 00 84,* Cuisine indonésienne – ▤. AE ⓓ MC VISA JCB. ✂ FU r
fermé fin juil.-début août, 1 sem. en janv. et dim. – **Repas** (dîner seult) carte 31 à 52, ♀.
◆ Savoureuse et authentique cuisine indonésienne servie dans un cadre approprié. Est-ce un hasard, d'ailleurs, si cette "rue de bouche" porte le nom de Javastraat ?
◆ Hier wordt een smaakvolle en authentieke Indonesische keuken in een passend decor geserveerd. Is het toeval dat dit adres in de Javastraat te vinden is ?

XX **Marc Smeets** - H. Corona, Buitenhof 42, ✉ 2513 AH, ✆ (0 70) 363 79 30, *rest.marcsmeets@planet.nl, Fax (0 70) 361 57 85,* – ▤. AE ⓓ MC VISA JCB. ✂ HY v
fermé dim. soir – **Repas** *Lunch 30* – carte 45 à 72.
◆ Marc Smeets, le patron-cuisinier, a prêté son nom à ce restaurant installé au rez-de-chaussée de l'hôtel Corona. Nouveau décor intérieur. Lunch et menus au goût du jour.
◆ De patron en chef-kok heeft zijn eigen naam gegeven aan dit restaurant op de benedenverdieping van hotel Corona. Vernieuwd decor. Eigentijdse lunch en menu's.

XX **Sapphire** 25e étage, Jan van Riebeekstraat 571, ✉ 2595 TZ, ✆ (0 70) 383 67 67, *info@sapphire.nl, Fax (0 70) 347 50 54,* ✳ ville, Cuisine chinoise – ▤ P. AE MC VISA. ✂ GU t
fermé 2 sem. vacances bâtiment, sam. midi, dim. midi et jours fériés midi – **Repas** *Lunch 16* – 26/68.
◆ Perché au sommet d'une haute tour, ce restaurant panoramique offre un coup d'œil vertigineux sur la ville. Carte chinoise parcourant les régions de Canton et du Sichuan.
◆ Dit panoramische restaurant boven in een hoge toren biedt een duizelingwekkend uitzicht over de stad. Chinese kaart met gerechten uit Canton en Sichuan.

X **Shirasagi,** Spui 170 (transfert prévu), ✉ 2511 BW, ✆ (0 70) 346 47 00, *shirasagi@planet.nl, Fax (0 70) 346 26 01,* Cuisine japonaise avec Teppan-Yaki – ▤. AE ⓓ MC VISA JCB. ✂ JZ v
fermé 30 déc.-3 janv., sam. midi, dim. midi et lundi midi – **Repas** *Lunch 23* – 40/73.
◆ Décor intérieur et cuisine à l'emblème du soleil levant pour le Shirasagi, restaurant adossé à un hôtel de chaîne. Choix à la carte - avec menus - ou formule Teppan-Yaki.
◆ Decor en keuken uit het land van de rijzende zon in dit restaurant naast een kentenhotel. Keuze uit de kaart, waarop ook menu's staan, of formule teppan-yaki.

X **Koesveld,** Maziestraat 10, ✉ 2514 GT, ☎ (0 70) 360 27 23, *Fax (0 70) 360 27 23,* – AE ⓓ MC VISA HX u
fermé juil., dim. et lundi – **Repas** (dîner seult jusqu'à 23 h) carte env. 36, ♀.
◆ Entre le Panorama Mesdag et le Paleis Noordeinde, petite table interprétant un répertoire culinaire en phase avec l'époque. Menu-carte attrayant et assiettes bien présentées.
◆ Dit kleine restaurant tussen Panorama Mesdag en het Paleis Noordeinde draait een trendy culinair repertoire. Aantrekkelijke menukaart en prachtig opgemaakte borden.

X **ZouitdeZee,** Hooikade 14, ✉ 2514 BH, ☎ (0 70) 346 26 03, *Fax (0 70) 365 40 76,* – AE MC VISA. JX a
fermé 27 déc.-3 janv., dim. et lundi – **Repas** (dîner seult) carte 38 à 60, ♀.
◆ Ce restaurant établi dans un quartier de sorties est une adresse valable pour faire un repas à dominante littorale. Salle à manger mariant plaisamment le moderne et l'ancien.
◆ Dit restaurant staat in een uitgaansbuurt en is, zoals de naam aangeeft, gespecialiseerd in zeeproducten. Eetzaal waar oud en nieuw fraai gecombineerd zijn.

X **Le Strasbourg,** Laan van Nieuw Oost Indië 1f, ✉ 2593 BH, ☎ (0 70) 383 88 56, *info@lestrasbourg.nl, Fax (0 70) 335 15 80,* – AE ⓓ MC VISA JCB GU a
fermé fin avril-début mai, 2 sem. en août, fin-déc.-début janv., dim. et lundi – **Repas** (dîner seult) 40/60, ♀.
◆ L'enseigne de cette petite adresse donne le ton : mets et cave influencés par l'Alsace. L'arrière du restaurant s'ouvre sur une courette où l'on dresse le couvert en été.
◆ De naam van dit adresje zegt het al : u vindt hier gerechten en wijnen uit de Elzas. Aan de achterkant ligt een binnenplaatsje waar 's zomers wordt geserveerd.

X **Le Bistrot de la Place Chez Norbert,** Plaats 27, ✉ 2513 AD, ☎ (0 70) 364 33 27, *Fax (0 70) 364 33 27,* – AE ⓓ MC VISA HY b
fermé 24 déc.-4 janv., sam. et dim. – **Repas** *Lunch 30* – carte 40 à 52, ♀.
◆ Un bel éventail de préparations traditionnelles et bourgeoises vous attend chez Norbert, bistrot dont l'atmosphère, autant que le décor, rappelle les "bouchons lyonnais".
◆ Een mooi scala van traditionele en klassieke gerechten bij deze Norbert op de Plaats, een bistro met een eenvoudig decor en de "bouchon lyonnais" ambiance.

X **Les Ombrelles,** Hooistraat 4a, ✉ 2514 BM, ☎ (0 70) 365 87 89, *info@lesombrelles.nl,* , Produits de la mer – P. AE ⓓ MC VISA JCB JX r
fermé 24 déc.-4 janv., sam. midi et dim. – **Repas** *Lunch 28* – 32/37.
◆ Spécialisée dans les produits de la mer, la maison fait aussi dans l'ombrelle, comme en témoignent enseigne et décor. Salle à manger actuelle avec vue sur les cuisines.
◆ Dit in vis gespecialiseerde restaurant doet blijkbaar ook in parasols, als we tenminste afgaan op de naam en het decor. Eigentijdse eetzaal met zicht op de keuken.

X **Wox,** Buitenhof 36, ✉ 2513 AH, ☎ (0 70) 365 37 54, Avec cuisine asiatique – ▤ – 25. AE MC VISA JCB. HY d
fermé sam. midi, dim., lundi et mardi midi – **Repas** carte env. 40.
◆ Restaurant en vogue s'ouvrant sur le Buitenhof. La carte privilégie les saveurs du moment et comporte quelques mets aux accents asiatiques. Ambiance un rien "hype".
◆ Een populair restaurant dat uitkijkt op het Binnenhof. Trendy seizoenkeuken, maar ook enkele Aziatisch georiënteerde gerechten. Ambiance tikje hype.

X **Fouquet,** Javastraat 31a, ✉ 2585 AC, ☎ (0 70) 360 62 73, *denhaag@fouquet.nl, Fax (0 15) 361 34 55,* – AE ⓓ MC VISA JCB FU a
Repas (déjeuner sur réservation) carte env. 33.
◆ Brasserie accueillante formée de trois coquettes pièces en enfilade, plus une jolie terrasse à l'arrière. Recettes au goût du jour, formule menu-carte et sage cellier.
◆ Gezellig restaurant met drie keurige eetruimten en suite en een leuk terras aan de achterzijde. Eigentijdse keuken, keuzemenu en goede wijnkaart.

X **Zilt,** President Kennedylaan 1 (Statenkwartier), ✉ 2517 JK, ☎ (0 70) 338 76 22, *zilt@hetnet.nl, Fax (0 70) 338 77 28,* – P. MC VISA EU m
fermé lundi – **Repas** *Lunch 29* – carte 32 à 43, ♀.
◆ Établissement aménagé dans le complexe du musée municipal construit suivant les plans de Berlage. Salle à manger sobrement décorée. Terrasse estivale côté jardin.
◆ Dit restaurant bevindt zich in het complex van het Gemeentemuseum, dat is gebouwd naar een ontwerp van Berlage. Eenvoudig gedecoreerde eetzaal. Terras aan de tuinkant.

X **Basiliek,** Fluwelen Burgwal 11c, ✉ 2511 CH, ☎ (0 70) 360 61 44, *debasiliek@wanadoo.nl, Fax (0 70) 399 55 99,* – MC VISA. JY z
fermé fin juil.-début août, lundi et mardi – **Repas** (dîner seult) carte 32 à 43.
◆ En plein centre-ville, affaire familiale affichant un petit air "bistrot" et misant sur une carte actuelle. Lorsque la météo est clémente, le repas est servi en terrasse.
◆ Dit restaurant midden in het centrum heeft een bistroachtige ambiance en een eigentijds georiënteerde menukaart. Bij mooi weer kan buiten worden gegeten.

à Scheveningen - *plan p. 7* - *C 's-Gravenhage – Station balnéaire★★ – Casino* ES, *Kurhausweg 1, ✉ 2587 RT, ☎ (0 70) 306 77 77, Fax (0 70) 306 78 88.*

i Gevers Deynootweg 1134, ✉ 2586 BX, ☎ 0 900-340 35 05, vvvscheveningen@spd h.net, Fax (0 70) 352 04 26

Kurhaus, Gevers Deynootplein 30, ✉ 2586 CK, ☎ (0 70) 416 26 36, *info@kurhaus.nl, Fax (0 70) 416 26 46,* ←, ⓓ, Ⅎ₆ – |‡| ⇆, ▤ TV ♿ P – 🏛 35 à 600. AE ⓓ MC VISA JCB. ✂ rest — ES d
Repas ***Kandinsky*** *(fermé sam. midi et dim.)* (dîner seult en juil.-août) *Lunch 30* – 40/95 bc, ♀ – ***Kurzaal*** (avec écailler) *Lunch 23* – 34, ♀ – ☕ 20 – **247 ch** 265/285, – 8 suites – ½ P 95/115.
◆ Ce palace somptueux bordant la plage renferme une remarquable salle de concert fin 19e s. convertie en restaurant. Chambres raffinées, offrant tout le confort moderne. Belle carte classique actualisée au Kandinsky. Banc d'écailler sous la coupole du Kurzaal.
◆ Dit luxueuze hotel aan de boulevard heeft stijlvolle kamers met alle moderne comfort. Restaurant Kandinsky in de voormalige concertzaal (eind 19e eeuw) serveert een klassieke keuken met een eigentijds accent. Onder de koepel van de Kurzaal oesters en vis.

Europa, Zwolsestraat 2, ✉ 2587 VJ, ☎ (0 70) 416 95 95, *europa@bilderberg.nl, Fax (0 70) 416 95 55,* ⛱, ≘, ☐, 🚲 – |‡| ⇆, ▤ rest, TV 🚗 – 🏛 25 à 460. AE ⓓ MC VISA JCB. ✂ rest — ES z
Repas ***Oxo*** (dîner seult jusqu'à 23 h) 30/53 bc, ♀ – ☕ 17 – **174 ch** 177/216 – ½ P 82/104.
◆ Rénovations récentes pour cet hôtel jouxtant un carrefour proche de la digue. Chambres actuelles avec balcon, bien équipées et insonorisées. Certaines ont vue sur la mer. Restaurant au décor très "tendance", maniant un répertoire culinaire à la page.
◆ Dit hotel aan een kruispunt achter de Scheveningse boulevard is onlangs gerenoveerd. Moderne kamers met balkon, goed uitgerust en met geluidsisolatie. Sommige kijken uit op zee. Zeer trendy decor in het restaurant, dat een al even trendy menukaart heeft.

Carlton Beach, Gevers Deynootweg 201, ✉ 2586 HZ, ☎ (0 70) 354 14 14, *info@beachcarlton.nl, Fax (0 70) 352 00 20,* ←, Ⅎ₆, ≘, ☐, 🚲 – |‡| ⇆ TV P – 🏛 25 à 250. AE ⓓ MC VISA JCB — ES p
Repas 35 – ☕ 20 – **183 ch** 225/235.
◆ Building contemporain posté au bout de la digue. Chambres et appartements, rafraîchis, donnent côté plage ou parking. Bonne isolation phonique. Infrastructure sportive. Salle de restaurant coiffée d'une délicate verrière. Formule menu-choix.
◆ Modern gebouw aan het einde van de Scheveningse boulevard. De gemoderniseerde kamers en appartementen kijken uit op het strand of op de parking. Goede geluidsisolatie. Sportvoorzieningen. De restaurantzaal is bekroond met een glazen koepel. Keuzemenu.

Badhotel, Gevers Deynootweg 15, ✉ 2586 BB, ☎ (0 70) 351 22 21, *info@badhotelscheveningen.nl, Fax (0 70) 355 58 70* – |‡| ⇆ ▤ TV P – 🏛 25 à 100. AE ⓓ MC VISA JCB — DS b
Repas (dîner seult) carte 33 à 49 – ☕ 15 – **90 ch** 110/158.
◆ Entre le centre et le port, près de la promenade, immeuble remis à neuf dominant une artère passante. Équipement correct dans les chambres, plus calmes à l'arrière.
◆ Dit gerenoveerde hotel staat aan een doorgaande weg nabij de boulevard, tussen het centrum van Scheveningen en de haven. Comfortabele kamers, aan de achterkant wat rustiger.

Ibis, Gevers Deynootweg 63, ✉ 2586 BJ, ☎ (0 70) 354 33 00, *h1153@accor-hotels.com, Fax (0 70) 352 39 16* – |‡| ⇆ TV ♿ P – 🏛 25 à 40. AE ⓓ MC VISA — ES a
Repas (dîner seult) carte env. 23 – ☕ 10 – **88 ch** 66/90.
◆ Hôtel récent situé sur un boulevard important. Conformes aux normes de la chaîne, les deux types de chambres (economy et standard) se prêtent bien au repos du touriste.
◆ Modern hotel aan een doorgaande weg. De twee typen kamers, economy en standard, zijn naar de normen van de keten ingericht en bieden toeristen de nodige rust.

XXX **Seinpost,** Zeekant 60, ✉ 2586 AD, ☎ (0 70) 355 52 50, *mail@seinpost.nl, Fax (0 70) 355 50 93,* ←, Produits de la mer – ▤. AE ⓓ MC VISA JCB — DS y
fermé sam. midi, dim. et jours fériés – **Repas** *Lunch 38* – 48/93 bc, ♀ ⚘.
◆ Le dieu Neptune domine ce pavillon en rotonde où les produits marins règnent sur une carte attrayante. Vue balnéaire depuis la confortable salle à manger contemporaine.
◆ Neptunus kijkt uit over dit ronde paviljoen waar zeebanket de verleidelijke kaart beheerst. Vanuit de moderne, comfortabele eetzaal uitzicht op zee.

XX **Cap Ouest,** Schokkerweg 37, ✉ 2583 BH, ☎ (0 70) 306 09 35, *info@capouest.nl, Fax (0 70) 350 84 54,* ←, ⛱ – ▤. AE ⓓ MC VISA JCB — DT d
fermé sam. midi et dim. midi – **Repas** *Lunch 23* – 25, ♀.
◆ Une cuisine à dominante iodée vous attend dans ce pavillon en surplomb des quais, dont la salle à manger, moderne, offre une échappée sur les ports de pêche et de plaisance.
◆ Dit restaurant boven de kaden onthaalt zijn gasten op gerechten waarin vis de hoofdmoot is. De moderne eetzaal kijkt uit op de vissers- en jachthaven.

XX **Radèn Mas,** Gevers Deynootplein 125, ✉ 2586 CR, ✆ (0 70) 354 54 32, *Fax (0 70) 350 60 42*, Avec cuisine indonésienne, ouvert jusqu'à 23 h – ▤. AE ⓓ MC VISA JCB. ✈ ES v
Repas *Lunch 30* – carte 34 à 62, ♀.
◆ Étape extrême-orientale sur la place animée de Scheveningen. Au menu : spécialités indonésiennes - incluant des tables de riz - et plats chinois. Ambiance "javanaise".
◆ Een stukje Verre Oosten aan het levendige plein van Scheveningen. Op het menu : Indonesische specialiteiten, inclusief de rijsttafels, en Chinese gerechten. Javaanse ambiance.

XX **China Delight,** Dr Lelykade 116, ✉ 2583 CN, ✆ (0 70) 355 54 50, *info@chinadelight.nl, Fax (0 70) 354 66 52*, Cuisine chinoise, ouvert jusqu'à 23 h – ⓓ MC VISA JCB DT u
Repas (déjeuner sur réservation) carte env. 28.
◆ Ample restaurant chinois occupant un ancien entrepôt posté au bord d'un bassin. Son "honorable" carte vous emmène vers Pékin et le Sichuan. Décor laqué, comme le canard.
◆ Groot Chinees restaurant in een voormalig havenpakhuis. De respectabele kaart voert de gast naar Peking en Sichuan. Het interieur is net zo gelakt als de pekingeend.

X **Le Bon Mangeur,** Wassenaarsestraat 119, ✉ 2586 AM, ✆ (0 70) 355 92 13, *mangeur@worldonline.nl* – AE ⓓ MC VISA. ✈ DS a
fermé dern. sem. juil.-2 prem. sem. août, dern. sem. déc., dim. et lundi – **Repas** (dîner seult) 29/39.
◆ On mange au "coude à coude" à cette sympathique petite adresse familiale dont la carte de saison comprend un menu-choix. Cuisines à vue et clientèle d'habitués.
◆ In dit sympathieke restaurantje, gerund door een echtpaar, zitten de gasten gezellig dicht bij elkaar. Seizoenkaart met keuzemenu. Open keuken. Vaste klantenkring.

à Kijkduin *Ouest : 4 km - plan p. 2 - C 's-Gravenhage :*

Atlantic, Deltaplein 200, ✉ 2554 EJ, ✆ (0 70) 448 24 82, *info@atlantichotel.nl, Fax (0 70) 368 67 21*, ≤, ☂, ≘, ▣, ⚲ – |‡| ⋡ TV P – 🏛 25 à 300. AE ⓓ MC VISA JCB. ✈ AR e
Repas (buffet) carte env. 35 – **152 ch** ☐ 158/260 – ½ P 183/265.
◆ Vue sur la plage ou les dunes depuis la plupart des chambres et studios de cet hôtel surveillant la digue. Accueil et service avenants. Piscine et espace de relaxation. Salle à manger offrant une échappée en direction du large. Formules buffets.
◆ Uitzicht op het strand of de duinen vanuit de meeste kamers en studio's in dit hotel, dat boven de zeewering uittorent. Vriendelijke ontvangst en service. Zwembad en sauna. De eetzaal kijkt uit op de zee. Buffetformule.

Environs

à Leidschendam *- plan p. 3* C *Leidschendam-Voorburg 43 185 h :*

Green Park, Weigelia 22, ✉ 2262 AB, ✆ (0 70) 320 92 80, *info@greenpark.nl, Fax (0 70) 327 49 07*, ≤, ♿, ⚲ – |‡| TV P – 🏛 25 à 250. AE ⓓ MC VISA JCB CQ n
Repas voir rest ***Chiparus*** ci-après – **92 ch** ☐ 139/177, – 4 suites – ½ P 98/174.
◆ Grand hôtel de chaîne construit sur pilotis, au bord d'un étang. Confort actuel dans les chambres, réparties autour d'un lumineux atrium. Service prévenant.
◆ Dit grote ketenhotel is gebouwd op palen, aan de rand van een grote plas. Modern comfort in de kamers, die rond een licht atrium liggen. Attente service.

XXX **Villa Rozenrust,** Veursestraatweg 104, ✉ 2265 CG, ✆ (0 70) 327 74 60, *villarozenrust@planet.nl, Fax (0 70) 327 50 62*, ☂ – P. AE ⓓ MC VISA. ✈ CQ s
fermé dim. – **Repas** (dîner seult) carte 40 à 70.
◆ À l'Est de Den Haag, villa entièrement rénovée, dont la salle à manger ne manque pas d'attrait. Terrasse charmante que l'on dresse l'été venu. Recettes au goût du jour.
◆ Deze volledig gerenoveerde villa aan de oostkant van Den Haag heeft een zeer sfeervolle restaurantzaal en een charmante terrastuin voor in de zomer. Eigentijdse keuken.

XX **Chiparus** - H. Green PArk, Weigelia 22, ✉ 2262 AB, ✆ (0 70) 320 92 80, *info@greenpark.nl, Fax (0 70) 327 49 07*, ≤ – ▤ P. AE ⓓ MC VISA JCB CQ n
fermé dim. non fériés – **Repas** *Lunch 30* – carte 33 à 52, ♀.
◆ Chiparus, sculpteur roumain du début du 20e s., a donné son nom à cette table dont la salle à manger procure une vue sur l'eau. Carte actuelle tournée vers la Méditerranée.
◆ Dit restaurant is genoemd naar een Roemeense beeldhouwer uit het begin van de 20e eeuw. De eetzaal kijkt uit op het water. Eigentijdse, mediterraan georiënteerde kaart.

à Rijswijk - *plan p. 3* - *54 690 h*

The Grand Winston (ouverture prévue printemps) Generaal Eisenhowerplein 1, ✉ 2288 AE, ☎ (0 70) 327 93 92, *info@grandwinston.nl* - **Repas** voir rest ***Imko's*** ci-après - **252 ch.** BR z

◆ "Débarquement" réussi pour ce tout nouvel hôtel côtoyant la gare ! Sa réception est placée sous la protection de W. Churchill. Chambres distribuées dans deux tours modernes. Brasserie de style contemporain.

◆ Dit nieuwe hotel bij het station heeft een goede "landing" gemaakt. Een portret van W. Churchill siert de ingang. De kamers zijn verdeeld over twee moderne torengebouwen. Brasserie in eigentijdse stijl.

XXX **Savarin,** Laan van Hoornwijck 29, ✉ 2289 DG, ☎ (0 70) 307 20 50, *info@savarin.nl, Fax (0 70) 307 20 55,* - P - 25 à 120. AE VISA JCB CR b
fermé 27 déc.-5 janv., sam. midi et dim. midi - **Repas** *Lunch 30* - 35/45, ♀.

◆ Enseigne à la gloire du célèbre gastronome français. Cuisine d'aujourd'hui papillonnant entre la France, l'Italie, les Pays-Bas et le Nouveau Monde.

◆ Een restaurant ter meerdere eer en glorie van de beroemde Franse gastronoom. Eigentijdse keuken met invloeden uit Frankrijk, Italië, Nederland en de Nieuwe Wereld.

XX ✿ **Imko's** (Binnerts) (ouverture prévue printemps), Generaal Eisenhowerplein 1, ✉ 2288 AE, ☎ (0 70) 327 93 92, *info@grandwinston.nl,* Produits de la mer - P. AE VISA JCB. BR z
fermé lundi, mardi et sam. midi - **Repas** *Lunch 33* - 43/80 bc, carte 52 à 75, ♀.

◆ C'est en confiance que nous recommandons ce restaurant design bientôt incorporé à un palace moderne. Salle "suspendue", éclairage "high-tech" et cuisine littorale raffinée.

◆ Met vertrouwen bevelen we dit design restaurant aan dat weldra in een moderne palace zal huizen. "Hangende" eetzaal, high-tech lichtspel en fijne keuken uit de zee.

Spéc. Croquettes aux crevettes, mayonnaise au citron. Salade Niçoise maison. Turbot grillé et sa béarnaise

XX **'t Ganzenest,** Delftweg 58 (près A 13 - E 19, sortie ⑧ Rijswijk-Zuid), ✉ 2289 AL, ☎ (0 70) 414 06 42, *ganzenest@wxs.nl, Fax (0 70) 414 07 05,* ←, - P. AE VISA. BCR a
fermé 2 sem. vacances bâtiment fin déc.-début janv., sam. midi, dim., lundi et mardi midi - **Repas** *Lunch 34* - 40/65, ♀.

◆ Cet accueillant "Nid d'oie" (Ganzenest) squatte une fermette alanguie sur un terrain de golf. Décor intérieur fringant, affriolante carte au goût du jour et terrasse exquise.

◆ Dit vriendelijke restaurant heeft een boerderijtje betrokken aan de rand van een golfterrein. Zwierig interieur, aanlokkelijke eigentijdse menukaart en heerlijk terras.

X ✿ **Paul van Waarden,** Tollensstraat 10, ✉ 2282 BM, ☎ (0 70) 414 08 12, *info@paulvanwaarden.nl, Fax (0 70) 414 03 91,* - AE VISA JCB BR d
fermé sam. midi, dim. et jours fériés - **Repas** *Lunch 53 bc* - 32/59 bc, carte 49 à 75, ♀.

◆ Paul van Waarden vous reçoit dans l'une des pièces en enfilade qui composent son restaurant conçu à la façon d'une brasserie moderne. Mets inventifs. Terrasse close de murs.

◆ Paul van Waarden ontvangt u in een van de kamers "en suite" van het restaurant, dat als een moderne brasserie is opgezet. Inventieve gerechten, ommuurd terras.

Spéc. Quatre préparations de quatre foies différents. Cabillaud croquant au potage de pois cassés et anguille fumée (21 sept.-21 mars). Tatin à la rhubarbe (mars-août)

à Voorburg - *plan p. 3* C *Leidschendam-Voorburg 43 185 h :*

Mövenpick, Stationsplein 8, ✉ 2275 AZ, ☎ (0 70) 337 37 37, *hotel.den-haag@moevenpick.com, Fax (0 70) 337 37 00,* - 25 à 160. AE VISA JCB CR u
Repas *Lunch 16* - carte 22 à 41, ♀ - 14 - **125 ch** 114/149.

◆ Hôtel de chaîne aux lignes modernes renfermant des chambres fonctionnelles de bonnes dimensions, aussi correctement tenues qu'insonorisées. Accueil souriant. À l'heure des repas, l'embarras du choix : buffets, grillades, pâtes ou plats sautés au "wok".

◆ Ketenhotel met moderne vormgeving. De ruime en goed onderhouden kamers zijn functioneel en voorzien van een goede geluidsisolatie. Vriendelijke ontvangst. Aan tafel is er keuze in overvloed : buffetten, grillgerechten, pasta's en wokgerechten.

XXXX ✿ **Savelberg** avec ch, Oosteinde 14, ✉ 2271 EH, ☎ (0 70) 387 20 81, *info@restauranthotelsavelberg.nl, Fax (0 70) 387 77 15,* ←, - P - 35. AE VISA JCB CR p
Repas *(fermé sam. midi, dim. et lundi) Lunch 43* - 60/120 bc, carte 67 à 91, ♀ - 16 - **14 ch** 138/195 - ½ P 142.

◆ Un régal doublé d'un vrai plaisir des yeux, dans une fastueuse demeure du 17ᵉ s. Cuisine classique innovante. Terrasse d'été dominant un parc. Chambres personnalisées.

◆ Een waar festijn en een lust voor het oog ! In dit luisterrijke 17e-eeuwse pand wordt een innovatieve, klassieke keuken bereid. Kamers met een eigen stijl. Terras aan het park.

Spéc. Salade de homard maison. Turbot façon saisonnier. Pigeon de Bresse rôti au four, artichaut violette, tomates sechées et jus d'olives vertes

Brasserie Savelberg - De Koepel, Oosteinde 1, ✉ 2271 EA, ☎ (0 70) 369 35 72, *Fax (0 70) 360 32 14,* – AE ⊕ MC VISA JCB
Repas (dîner seult jusqu'à 23 h) 30, ♀.
◆ Brasserie cossue aménagée dans un bâtiment monumental en forme de rotonde, coiffé d'une jolie coupole. Terrasse estivale et parc agréable pour une promenade digestive.
◆ Restaurant in een monumentaal rond pand met een fraaie koepel. Terras in de zomer en aangenaam park voor een avondwandelingetje.

Fouquet, Kerkstraat 52, ✉ 2271 CT, ☎ (0 70) 386 29 00, *Fax (0 70) 386 29 00,* – ▤. MC VISA CR t
fermé lundi – **Repas** (dîner seult) 30/40, ♀.
◆ Ce chaleureux restaurant de style brasserie actuelle - banquettes rouges, murs jaunes, tables accoudées et jeux de miroirs - met à profit deux maisons classées du 19e s.
◆ Gastvrij restaurant in twee 19e-eeuwse panden die op de monumentenlijst staan. Moderne brasseriestijl met spiegels, rode banken, gele muren en tafeltjes dicht op elkaar.

Papermoon, Herenstraat 175, ✉ 2271 CE, ☎ (0 70) 387 31 61, *info@papermoon.nl, Fax (0 70) 387 75 20,* – ▤. MC VISA CR c
fermé 31 déc.-1er janv. et lundi – **Repas** (dîner seult) 28/51 bc, ♀.
◆ Une engageante carte actuelle annonçant plusieurs menus vous sera soumise à cette sympathique adresse dont la salle à manger entretient une atmosphère feutrée.
◆ Dit sympathieke adres heeft een uitnodigende, eigentijdse kaart met verschillende menu's. Eetzaal met ingetogen sfeer.

Le Barquichon, Kerkstraat 6, ✉ 2271 CS, ☎ (0 70) 387 11 81 – ▤. AE MC VISA JCB CR v
fermé 2 dern. sem. juil.-prem. sem. août, 25, 26 et 31 déc.1er janv. et merc. – **Repas** (dîner seult) carte 32 à 46.
◆ Ce gentil petit établissement familial du centre piétonnier tourne surtout avec sa clientèle d'assidus, fidélisée par une cuisine classique simple, mais convaincante.
◆ Dit vriendelijke restaurantje in het voetgangerscentrum draait vooral op een bestand van klanten die de eenvoudige, klassieke maar overtuigende keuken trouw blijven.

à Wassenaar *au Nord-Est : 11 km – 25 801 h*

Aub. de Kieviet 🐌, Stoeplaan 27, ✉ 2243 CX, ☎ (0 70) 511 92 32, *receptie@dekieviet.nl, Fax (0 70) 511 09 69,* – ▤ ▤ TV ♿ P – 🏛 25 à 90. AE ⊕ MC VISA plan p. 3 CQ r
Repas *(fermé sam. midi et dim. midi)* carte 36 à 54, ♀ – ☕ 15 – **23 ch** 110/190, – 1 suite.
◆ Auberge à dénicher dans un quartier résidentiel huppé. Les chambres, rafraîchies, offrent le confort actuel et, pour certaines, la vue sur la terrasse fleurie en été. Salle de restaurant coquette. Préparations dans l'air du temps, menus et suggestions.
◆ Deze herberg is gevestigd in een chique woonwijk. De gemoderniseerde kamers bieden een eigentijds comfort en sommige kijken uit op het fleurige zomerterras. Verzorgd restaurant. Seizoenkeuken, à la carte, menu's en dagelijks wisselende gerechten.

De Markiezen van Wassenaer, Langstraat 10, ✉ 2242 KM, ☎ (0 70) 514 34 18, *Fax (0 70) 514 34 04,* – AE ⊕ MC VISA JCB
fermé dern. sem. juil.-prem. sem. août, 24 déc.-4 janv., dim. et lundi – **Repas** Lunch 20 – 24/78, ♀.
◆ Savoureuse cuisine au goût du jour basée sur de beaux produits. Petite fantaisie : un train miniature parcourt la salle de restaurant. Menus multi-choix. Brasserie à l'avant.
◆ Smakelijke, eigentijdse gerechten, bereid met kwaliteitsproducten. Iets origineels : er rijdt een treintje door de eetzaal. Uitgebreid keuzemenu. Brasserie aan de voorzijde.

Duinoord, Wassenaarseslag 26 (Ouest : 3 km), ✉ 2242 PJ, ☎ (0 70) 511 93 32, *info@hotelduinoord.nl, Fax (0 70) 511 22 10,* – P – 🏛 25. AE MC VISA
fermé 31 déc.-1er janv. et lundi midi – **Repas** Lunch 20 – carte 33 à 53.
◆ Alanguie dans les dunes, affaire familiale aussi appréciable pour sa situation que pour son choix de mets classiques et le charme rustico-bourgeois de sa salle à manger.
◆ Dit restaurant in de duinen is een aangename optie, niet alleen vanwege de ligging, maar ook om de klassieke gerechten en de sfeervolle rustieke eetzaal.

In deze gids
heeft eenzelfde letter of teken,
zwart of rood, dun of dik gedrukt
niet helemaal dezelfde betekenis.
Lees aandachtig de bladzijden met verklarende tekst.

HAAKSBERGEN *Overijssel* 532 Z 10 *et* 715 L 5 – *24 193 h.*
Amsterdam 163 – Apeldoorn 78 – Arnhem 78 – Enschede 21.

Morssinkhof 't Hoogeland, Eibergsestraat 157 (N 18), ✉ 7481 HJ, ✆ (0 53) 573 10 20, *info@hotelmorssinkhof.nl, Fax (0 53) 573 10 25,* – 25 à 350. rest
fermé 27 déc.-5 janv. – **Repas** carte 28 à 42 – 9 – **36 ch** 63 – ½ P 55/70.
◆ Établissement familial disposant de chambres plaisantes et actuelles, habillées de tissus coordonnés. Les meilleures, à l'arrière, profitent du coup d'œil sur les champs. Terrasse ombragée où l'on dresse le couvert en été. Plats traditionnels.
◆ Dit familiehotel beschikt over prettige, eigentijdse kamers die smaakvol zijn gestoffeerd. De beste kamers liggen aan de achterkant en kijken uit op de velden. Op het lommerrijke terras worden in de zomer de tafels gedekt. Traditionele gerechten.

XXX **de Blanckenborgh,** Enschedesestraat 65, ✉ 7481 CL, ✆ (0 53) 574 11 55, *info@blanckenborgh.nl, Fax (0 53) 574 11 65,* , Avec brasserie – – 30.
fermé 2 sem. vacances bâtiment, dim. et lundi – **Repas** *Lunch 30* – carte env. 52, ♀.
◆ Belle villa 1900 donnant sur un parc public garni de sculptures modernes. Repas au goût du jour servi dans une salle à manger chaleureuse ou sur l'agréable terrasse d'été.
◆ Deze mooie villa uit rond 1900 staat in het stadspark, dat met moderne sculpturen is verfraaid. Eigentijdse gerechten. Sfeervolle eetzaal en aangenaam zomerterras.

XX **Bi'j de Watermölle** avec ch, Watermolenweg 3, ✉ 7481 VL, ✆ (0 53) 572 92 50, *info@watermolle.nl, Fax (0 53) 572 92 05,* –
fermé 27 déc.-12 janv. – **Repas** *(fermé sam. midi et dim. midi) Lunch 33* – 28/60 bc, ♀ – **5 ch** 105/165 – ½ P 125.
◆ Au milieu des bois, ferme regardant un moulin à eau centenaire. Salle de restaurant néo-campagnarde. Carte à la page, proposée en terrasse l'été venu. Chambres luxueuses.
◆ Deze boerderij in de bossen kijkt uit op een honderd jaar oude watermolen. Neorustieke restaurantzaal en eigentijdse menukaart. 's Zomers wordt op het terras geserveerd.

Onze hotelgidsen, toeristische gidsen en wegenkaarten vullen elkaar aan. Gebruik ze samen.

HAARLEM P *Noord-Holland* 531 M 8, 532 M 8 *et* 715 E 4 – *147 831 h.*
Voir *Grand-Place★ (Grote Markt)* BY – *Grande église ou église St-Bavon★★ (Grote of St-Bavokerk) : grille★ du chœur, grandes orgues★, tour-lanterne★* BCY – *Hôtel de Ville★ (Stadhuis)* BY **H** – *Halle aux viandes★ (Vleeshal)* BY.
Musées : *Frans Hals★★★* BZ – *Teylers★ : dessins★★* CY **M³**.
Env. *par ③ : 7,5 km, Champs de fleurs★★ – par ③ : 13 km, Parc de Keukenhof★★ (fin mars à mi-mai), passerelle du moulin ≤★★ – au Nord : 16 km par ⑦, Écluses★ d'IJmuiden.*
par ⑦ : 10 km à Velsen-Zuid, Recreatieoord Spaarnwoude, Het Hoge Land 2, ✉ 1981 LT, ✆ (0 23) 538 27 08, Fax (0 23) 538 72 74.
au Sud-Est : 14 km par ⑤ à Amsterdam-Schiphol ✆ (0 20) 601 91 11, Fax (0 20) 604 14 75.
Stationsplein 1, ✉ 2011 LR, ✆ 0 900-616 16 00, info@vvvzk.nl, Fax (0 23) 534 05 37.
Amsterdam 20 ⑥ – *Den Haag 59 ⑤ – Rotterdam 79 ⑤ – Utrecht 54 ⑤*

Plans pages suivantes

Lion d'Or, Kruisweg 34, ✉ 2011 LC, ✆ (0 23) 532 17 50, *reservations@hotelliondor.nl, Fax (0 23) 532 95 43* – ch, – 25 à 100. BCX d
Repas *(fermé fin déc.)* 22/28 – **34 ch** 165/185 – ½ P 105/115.
◆ Vénérable enseigne toute proche de la gare, le Lion d'Or héberge les voyageurs depuis plus de 150 ans. Chambres de notre temps, convenablement insonorisées. Une carte classique sans complications est là pour vous apaiser, si vous avez les "crocs".
◆ Eerbiedwaardig hotel vlak bij het station, dat het zijn gasten al ruim 150 jaar naar de zin maakt. De eigentijdse kamers zijn voorzien van geluidsisolatie. Een eerlijke klassieke kaart probeert knorrende magen in stijl te vullen.

Haarlem Zuid, Toekanweg 2, ✉ 2035 LC, ✆ (0 23) 536 75 00, *info@haarlemzuid.valk.nl, Fax (0 23) 536 79 80,* – – 25 à 500. AV b
Repas (ouvert jusqu'à 23 h 30) *Lunch 14* – carte 22 à 41 – 12 – **287 ch** 69/109, – 6 suites – ½ P 64/99.
◆ Un établissement excentré, membre de la chaîne hôtelière Van der Valk, dont le succès tient surtout à la proximité de l'autoroute et à l'ampleur des chambres.
◆ Dit Van der Valk kentenhotel is buiten het centrum gelegen. Gemakkelijk bereikbaar vanwege de ligging bij de snelweg en de ruime kamers.

XX **Peter Cuyper,** Kleine Houtstraat 70, ✉ 2011 DR, ☎ (0 23) 532 08 85, *Fax (0 23) 534 33 85,* 🏠 – AE ⓓ MC VISA BZ s
fermé 2 sem. en août, sam. midi, dim. et lundi – **Repas** 33/45 bc, ♀.
• Restaurant au goût du jour aménagé dans l'ancien mont-de-piété, un édifice monumental hérité du 17e s. L'arrière-cour abrite une mignonne terrasse d'été.
• Modern restaurant dat is gevestigd in een voormalig pandjeshuis, een monumentaal gebouw uit de 17e eeuw. Op de achterplaats wordt in de zomer een gezellig terras ingericht.

XX **dè Eetkamer van Haarlem,** Lange Veerstraat 45, ✉ 2011 DA, ☎ (0 23) 531 22 61, *eetkamervanhaarlem@hetnet.nl,* 🏠 – AE ⓓ MC VISA JCB CY h
fermé lundi et mardi – **Repas** (dîner seult jusqu'à 23 h) 25/32.
• Une rue piétonne du centre mène à cette adresse. Des toiles et clichés nostalgiques d'Haarlem égayent la salle de restaurant lambrissée. Cuisine du moment.
• Een voetgangersstraatje in het centrum leidt naar dit restaurant. Gelambriseerde eetzaal met schilderijen en nostalgische clichés van Haarlem. Eigentijdse keuken.

XX **De Gekroonde Hamer,** Breestraat 24, ✉ 2011 ZZ, ☎ (0 23) 531 22 43, *degekroondekamer@cs.com, Fax (0 23) 525 63 25,* 🏠 – AE ⓓ MC VISA. ✂ BZ h
fermé 1 sem. en juil., fin déc. et merc. – **Repas** (dîner seult) 30, ♀.
• Salle à manger disposée autour de la cuisine, carte déclinant un choix de préparations sans chichi et, à l'étage, mini-terrasse estivale rafraîchie par une tonnelle.
• De eetzaal is rond de keuken ingericht. Op de kaart staat een selectie eerlijke gerechten. Boven bevindt zich een miniterras met pergola voor zomerse dagen.

X **Bronkhorst en Bruyns,** Twijnderslaan 7, ✉ 2012 BG, ☎ (0 23) 531 07 17, *Fax (0 23) 531 87 96,* 🏠 – P. AE ⓓ MC VISA AU p
fermé mardi, vend. midi et sam. midi – **Repas** Lunch 25 – carte 28 à 44.
• Ça marche pas mal pour cette affaire familiale établie dans un quartier résidentiel, près du petit ring de Haarlem. Le soir venu, tendez vos clés et on parquera votre voiture.
• Een goed lopend restaurant in een woonwijk vlak bij de kleine ring van Haarlem. 's Avonds even de sleutel overhandigen en de auto wordt voor u geparkeerd.

X **Lambermon's,** Spaarne 96, ✉ 2011 CL, ☎ (0 23) 542 78 04, *info@lambermons.nl, Fax (0 23) 542 78 26* – ▤. AE MC VISA. ✂ CZ t
fermé fin août, 26 déc.-8 janv., dim. et lundi – **Repas** (dîner seult) 24/80, ♀.
• Une superbe façade de brique distingue ce restaurant moderne, naguère maison de brasseur. Fourneaux à vue. Un mets différent est proposé toutes les demi-heures dès 18h 30.
• Dit moderne restaurant in een voormalige brouwerij valt op door de prachtige bakstenen façade. Open keuken. Vanaf 18.30 uur wordt elk half uur een ander gerecht geserveerd.

X **Eetkamer Karmozijn,** Gierstraat 69, ✉ 2011 GC, ☎ (0 23) 542 10 95, *karmozijn@cs.com* – MC VISA JCB. ✂ BZ a
fermé lundi et mardi – **Repas** (dîner seult) 35.
• Cette petite table vous installe dans une salle à manger rustique garnie d'une cheminée en vieux carrelages de Delft. Menue carte misant sur les saveurs du moment.
• Dit aangename restaurantje ontvangt zijn gasten in een rustieke eetzaal waar een schouw staat met oude Delftse tegels. Kleine kaart met seizoengebonden gerechten.

X **Napoli,** Houtplein 1, ✉ 2012 DD, ☎ (0 23) 532 44 19, 🏠, Cuisine italienne, ouvert jusqu'à 23 h – AE ⓓ MC VISA. ✂ BZ e
fermé 24 et 31 déc., 1er janv., sam. midi et dim. midi – **Repas** 28/47.
• L'un des "ristoranti" bien connus en ville. Espace intérieur scindé en deux parties : l'une à vocation de pizzeria tandis que l'autre reçoit ses hôtes plus élégamment.
• Een van de bekendere ristoranti in de stad. De restaurantzaal is in tweeën gedeeld : het ene deel is meer een pizzeria, in het andere wordt de gast wat stijlvoller ontvangen.

à Bloemendaal *Nord-Ouest : 4 km – 17 097 h*

XX ✿ **Chapeau ! ,** Hartenlustlaan 2, ✉ 2061 HB, ☎ (0 23) 525 29 25, *restaruantchapeau@planet.nl, Fax (0 23) 525 53 19,* 🏠 – P. AE ⓓ MC VISA JCB AT r
fermé 2 dern. sem. août, 1 sem. après Noël, sam. midi, dim. et lundi – **Repas** Lunch 35 – 50/59, carte 55 à 63.
• Villa blanche devancée d'une terrasse. Salle des repas actuelle vêtue d'un camaïeu de gris, fourneaux à vue, exquise cuisine à la page et service dans les règles de l'art.
• "Petje af" voor dit restaurant in een witte villa : eigentijdse eetzaal in grijze tinten, open keuken, voortreffelijke trendy gerechten, bediening volgens het boekje en terras.
Spéc. Salade de Pata Negra, langoustines et crème de câpres salés (mai-sept.). Filet de plie au foie de canard et crème de chanterelles (juin-juil.). Mousse d'orange au Campari et sorbet au fromage blanc

HAARLEM

Street	Grid	No.
Amerikaweg	AV	3
Amsterdamse Vaart	AU	4
Anegang	BCY	
Bakenessergracht	CY	6
Barrevoetestr.	BY	7
Barteljorisstr.	BY	9
Binnenweg	AV	10
Bloemendaalseweg	ATU	12
Botermarkt	BYZ	13
Cesar Francklaan	AV	15
Cruquiusweg	AV	16
Damstr.	CY	18
Donkere Spaarne	CY	19
Duinlustweg	AU	21
Europaweg	AV	22
Fonteinlaan	AV	24
Frans Halsstr.	CX	25
Friese Varkenmarkt	CXY	27
Gasthuisvest	BZ	28
Ged. Voldersgracht	BY	30
Gierstr.	BZ	31
Groot Heiligland	BZ	33
Grote Houtstr.	BYZ	
Hagestr.	CZ	34
Hartenlustlaan	AT	36
Hoge Duin en Daalseweg	AT	37
Hoogstr.	CZ	39
Jacobstr.	BY	40
Julianapark	AT	42
Kamperlaan	AV	43
Keizerstr.	BY	45
Kennemerweg	AT	46
Klokhuispl.	CY	48
Koningstr.	BY	49
Kruisstr.	BY	
Lanckhorstlaan	AV	51
van Merlenlaan	AV	52
Nassaustr.	BY	54
Nieuwe Groenmarkt	BY	55
Ostadestr.	BX	57
Oude Groenmarkt	BCY	58
Paviljoenslaan	AV	60
Prins Bernhardlaan	AU	61
Raadhuisstr.	AV	63
Schoterweg	AU	64
Smedestr.	BY	66
Spaarndamseweg	CX	67
Spaarnwouderstr.	CZ	69
Spanjaardslaan	AV	70
Tuchthuisstr.	BZ	72
Verspronckweg	AU	73
Verwulft	BYZ	75
Westergracht	AU	76
Zandvoortselaan	AV	78
Zijlsingel	BY	79
Zijlstr.	BY	
Zijlweg	AU	81
Zomerzorgerlaan	AT	82
Zuiderhoutlaan	AV	84

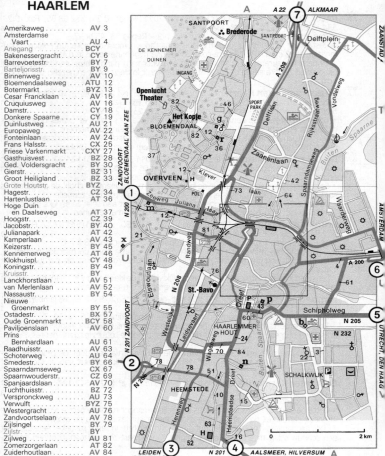

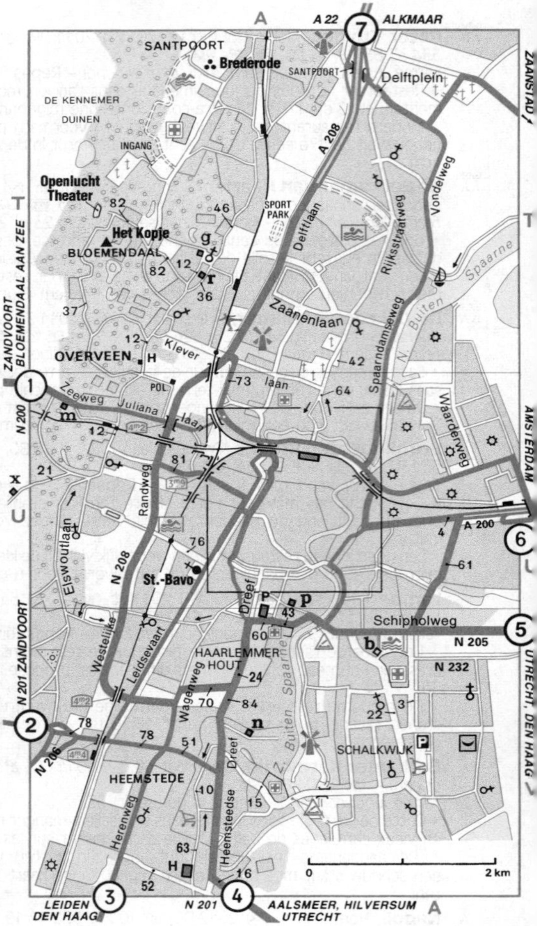

Terra Cotta, Kerkplein 16a, ✉ 2061 JD, ✆ (0 23) 527 79 11, *info@terra-cotta.nl, Fax (0 23) 525 89 97,* – AE VISA — AT g
fermé merc., sam. midi et dim. midi – **Repas** *Lunch 27* – 30/58 bc, ♀.
◆ À un petit kilomètre de la plus haute dune des Pays-Bas, ancienne maison bourgeoise avoisinant une église et son parc. Recettes aux accents du Sud. Menu bien vu.
◆ Op loopafstand van de hoogste duin van Nederland staat dit oude herenhuis naast een kerk met tuin. Gerechten met zuidelijke accenten en een menu dat bijzonder in trek is.

à Heemstede *Sud : 4 km – 25 898 h*

Cheval Blanc, Jan van Goyenstraat 29, ✉ 2102 CA, ✆ (0 23) 529 31 73, *info@cheval-blanc.nl, Fax (0 23) 529 61 73,* – AE MC VISA JCB. — AV n
fermé 30 avril, 25 déc., 31 déc.-7 janv. et lundi – **Repas** (dîner seult) 33/50, ♀.
◆ Le Cheval Blanc a subi une cure de jeunesse, de la crinière aux sabots. Pour combiner la diversité à un certain plaisir, la carte des plats est recomposée six fois par an.
◆ Dit Witte Paard heeft een facelift gehad, van zijn manen tot zijn hoeven. Ter verhoging van het eetplezier wordt zes keer per jaar een nieuwe menukaart samengesteld.

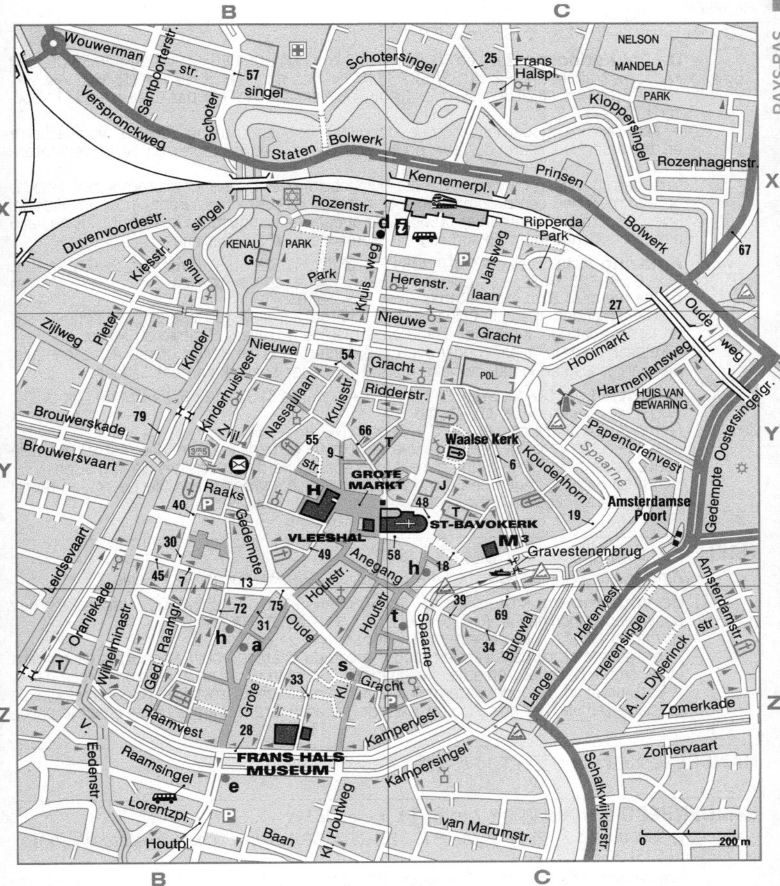

X **Landgoed Groenendaal,** Groenendaal 3 (1,5 km par Heemsteedse Dreef), ✉ 2104 WP, ☎ (0 23) 528 15 55, *info@landgoedgroenendaal.nl, Fax (0 23) 529 18 41,* - AE ⓓ MC VISA. *fermé lundi* – **Repas** 29, ♀.

◆ Hostellerie traditionnelle d'esprit néo-classique retirée parmi les bois. On s'y plie en quatre pour l'organisation de vos grandes agapes. Terrasse estivale ombragée.

◆ Traditioneel restaurant in neoklassieke stijl, dat verscholen ligt in de bossen. Hier wordt echt alles gedaan om van een feestmaal een succes te maken. Lommerrijk zomerterras.

X **Sari,** Valkenburgerlaan 48, ✉ 2103 AP, ☎ (0 23) 528 45 36, *restsari@hotmail.com, Fax (0 23) 528 14 16,* Cuisine indonésienne – ▤. AE ⓓ MC VISA. *fermé 25 et 31 déc.* – **Repas** (dîner seult) carte 22 à 32, ♀.

◆ Les amateurs de cuisine exotique pourront se dépayser les papilles dans ce sympathique petit restaurant indonésien aménagé au coeur de Heemstede. Formules "table de riz".

◆ Liefhebbers van de exotische keuken kunnen hun smaakpapillen weer eens flink verwennen in dit sympathieke Indonesische restaurantje in hartje Heemstede. Rijsttafels.

à Overveen *Ouest : 4 km* Ⓒ *Bloemendaal 17 097 h :*

XXXX ✿✿ **De Bokkedoorns,** Zeeweg 53 (par ① : 2 km), ✉ 2051 EB, ☎ (0 23) 526 36 00, *bokkedoorns@alliance.nl, Fax (0 23) 527 31 43,* ≤ lac, ☂ – ▤ P. AE ◑ MC VISA JCB. ✈
fermé 30 avril, 5 et 24 déc., 28 déc.-4 janv., lundi et sam. midi – **Repas** *Lunch 43* – 63/114 bc, carte 76 à 95, ♀ ✿.
◆ Architecture moderne entourée de dunes boisées, intérieur design, vue lacustre en terrasse : un cadre de rêve pour l'une des meilleures tables de Hollande-Septentrionale.
◆ Modern paviljoen midden in bebost duingebied, designinterieur en terras met uitzicht op een meertje : een droomdecor voor een van de beste restaurants in Noord-Holland.
Spéc. Risotto au Parmesan et brunoise de queues de langoustines (mai-sept.). Ris de veau aux petits pannequets de son rognon. Homard braisé à la badiane

XXX **Amazing Asia,** Zeeweg 3, ✉ 2051 EB, ☎ (0 23) 525 60 57, *amazing_asia@planet.nl, Fax (0 23) 525 34 32,* ☂, Cuisine chinoise – ▤ P. AE ◑ MC VISA. ✈ AU m
fermé merc. et dim. midi – **Repas** *Lunch 33* – 38/63.
◆ Salle à manger "made in China" sans surcharge, agréable terrasse estivale donnant sur un jardin asiatique, longue et savoureuse marche à travers l'Empire du Milieu.
◆ Eetzaal "made in China" zonder overdaad, zomerterras dat uitkijkt op een Aziatische tuin. De kaart is als een lange, culinaire mars dwars door het Rijk van het Midden.

XX **Kraantje Lek,** Duinlustweg 22, ✉ 2051 AB, ☎ (0 23) 524 12 66, *Fax (0 23) 524 82 54,* ☂, Avec crêperie – P. AE ◑ MC VISA AU x
fermé du 14 au 22 fév. et merc. – **Repas** *Lunch 30* – 43.
◆ Les pêcheurs venaient jadis boire une bière ou un verre de genièvre dans cette vénérable petite auberge adossée à une dune. Les crêpes : une des spécialités de la maison.
◆ In deze herberg tegen een duin kwamen de vissers vroeger een biertje of een borrel drinken. Pannenkoeken behoren tot de specialiteiten van het huis.

HAELEN *Limburg* 532 U 15 *et* 715 I 8 – *10 105 h.*
Amsterdam 176 – Maastricht 54 – Eindhoven 48 – Roermond 10 – Venlo 23.

XXX **de vogelmolen,** Kasteellaan 15, ✉ 6081 AN, ☎ (0 475) 59 42 00, *restaurant@devogelmolen.demon.nl, Fax (0 475) 59 52 00,* ☂ – P. AE ◑ MC VISA
fermé 26 juil.-11 août et sam. midi – **Repas** *Lunch 28* – 34/43, ♀.
◆ Restaurant établi dans l'ancien moulin à eau du château voisin. Spécialités de homard et de truite. Découpes en salle, sur guéridon. Terrasse verte embellie d'une pièce d'eau.
◆ Restaurant in de oude watermolen van het naburige kasteel. Kreeft en forel zijn de specialiteiten van het huis. Aan tafel wordt getrancheerd. Tuin met terras en waterpartij.

HANDEL *Noord-Brabant* 532 T 13 *et* 715 I 7 – *voir à Gemert.*

HARDENBERG *Overijssel* 531 Y 7 *et* 715 K 4 – *57 483 h.*
ℹ *Badhuisweg 2, ✉ 7772 XA, ☎ (0 523) 26 20 00, info.hardenberg@vechtdalvvv.nl, Fax (0 523) 26 65 95.*
Amsterdam 149 – Zwolle 39 – Assen 59 – Enschede 58.

à Diffelen *Sud-Ouest : 7 km* Ⓒ *Hardenberg :*

X **De Gloepe,** Rheezerweg 84a, ✉ 7795 DA, ☎ (0 523) 25 12 31, *info@degloepe.nl, Fax (0 523) 25 20 61,* ☂, Taverne-rest – P. MC VISA JCB
fermé 2 prem. sem. fév., lundi, mardi et sam. midi – **Repas** 30/35, ♀.
◆ Voici bien longtemps que le chant du coq ne rythme plus la vie de cette ferme typique, bâtie au crépuscule du 19e s. Une halte providentielle pour les randonneurs à vélo.
◆ Het is alweer een poosje geleden dat op deze karakteristieke boerderij uit circa 1900 de dag begon met het kraaien van de haan. Een welkome onderbreking voor fietsrecreanten.

à Heemse *Ouest : 1 km* Ⓒ *Hardenberg :*

XX ✿ **De Bokkepruik** (Istha) avec ch, Hessenweg 7, ✉ 7771 CH, ☎ (0 523) 26 15 04, *bokkepruik@planet.nl, Fax (0 523) 26 74 73,* ☂, ☂, ✿ – |‡| TV P – 🔺 25 à 150. AE ◑ MC VISA JCB. ✈
fermé 28 déc.-10 janv. – **Repas** *(fermé sam. midi, dim. et lundi midi) Lunch 43* – 55 bc, carte 48 à 70, ♀ – **23 ch** ☕ 75/100 – ½ P 68/88.
◆ Cuisine escoffière revisitée avec originalité, servie dans une confortable salle à manger d'inspiration "british". Jardin fleuri à la belle saison. Chambres pratiques.
◆ Een klassieke Franse keuken in een origineel nieuw jasje wordt geserveerd in een comfortabele eetzaal in Engelse stijl. Bloeiende zomertuin. Praktische kamers.
Spéc. Dégustation de Saint-Jacques. Crème de champignons des bois (juil.-nov.). Chevreuil régional (janv.-mars, mai-août)

HARDERWIJK *Gelderland* 531 S 8, 532 S 8 *et* 715 H 4 – *40 399 h.*

Voir *Dolfinarium★.*

18 9 à l'Ouest : à Zeewolde, Golflaan 1, ✉ 3896 LL, ☎ (0 36) 522 20 73, Fax (0 36) 522 41 00 et 9 Pluvierenweg 7, ✉ 3898 LL, ☎ (0 320) 28 81 16, Fax (0 320) 28 80 09.

Havendam 58, ✉ 3841 AA, ☎ (0 341) 42 66 66, info@vvvharderwijk.nl, Fax (0 341) 42 77 13.

Amsterdam 72 – Arnhem 71 – Apeldoorn 32 – Utrecht 54 – Zwolle 42.

Baars, Smeepoortstraat 52, ✉ 3841 EJ, ☎ (0 341) 41 20 07, *baars@bestwestern.nl, Fax (0 341) 41 87 22,* – – 25 à 150. AE VISA JCB
Repas *Lunch 15* – carte 22 à 37 – **45 ch** 101/109 – ½ P 87/128.
◆ Au centre-ville, hôtel familial où vous séjournerez dans des chambres aussi bien tenues qu'équipées. Cinq générations se sont relayé derrière le comptoir de la réception. Restaurant-véranda côtoyant l'église.
◆ De kamers in dit familiehotel in het centrum zijn goed onderhouden en comfortabel. Inmiddels staat de vijfde generatie achter de balie. Restaurant met serre naast de kerk.

Marktzicht - Klomp sans rest, Markt 8, ✉ 3841 CE, ☎ (0 341) 41 30 32, *Fax (0 341) 41 32 30* – . AE VISA
35 ch 55/87.
◆ Cet établissement situé en zone piétonne, sur le Markt, dispose de quelques places de parking à 100 m de là. Chambres fonctionnelles de tailles respectables.
◆ Dit hotel staat aan de autovrije markt, maar heeft 100 m verderop enkele parkeerplaatsen. Functionele kamers van respectabel formaat.

XX **Olivio** (Zwaart), Vischmarkt 57a, ✉ 3841 BE, ☎ (0 341) 41 52 90, *info@olivio.nl, Fax (0 341) 43 35 10,* – AE VISA
✿ *fermé 26 juil-11 août, 19 janv.-6 fév., dim. et lundi* – **Repas** (dîner seult) – 47/95 bc, carte 54 à 70, ♀.
◆ Bonne table occupant une chapelle gothique dont les vieux murs contrastent fort d'avec la décoration intérieure contemporaine. Plats d'inspiration méditerranéenne.
◆ Goed restaurant in een gotische kapel waarvan de oude muren in schril contrast staan met het eigentijdse interieur. Mediterraan georiënteerde gerechten.
Spéc. Risotto aux chanterelles, cèpes, truffe et Vieux Rijpenaer. Bar et brandade d'anguille fumée (mai-sept.). Ananas rôti et glace à l'infusion de clous de girofle (janv.-mars)

X **'t Nonnetje,** Vischmarkt 38, ✉ 3841 BG, ☎ (0 341) 41 58 48, *info@hetnonnetje.nl, Fax (0 341) 42 25 78,* – . AE VISA JCB
✿ *fermé du 3 au 18 fév., du 5 au 20 oct., mardi et merc.* – **Repas** (dîner seult) carte 46 à 67, ♀.
◆ Bon petit relais de bouche au goût du jour œuvrant sur une placette pittoresque. Intérieur contemporain aux tons chauds et à touches rustiques vaguement hispaniques.
◆ Kleine maar goed bij zijn tijdse gastronomische stek aan een pittoresk plaatsje. Warm hedendaags interieur met een Spaans rustiek tintje.
Spéc. L'asperge en trois préparations. Pigeon rôti et risotto aux champignons. Mangue marinée, tartare de fruits exotiques et sorbet

HARDINXVELD-GIESSENDAM *Zuid-Holland* 532 N 12 *et* 715 F 6 – *17 741 h.*

Amsterdam 78 – Utrecht 42 – Den Haag 58 – Arnhem 87 – Breda 45 – Rotterdam 32.

XX **Kampanje,** Troelstrastraat 5, ✉ 3371 VJ, ☎ (0 184) 61 26 13, *Fax (0 184) 61 19 53,* – – 25 à 300. AE VISA.
fermé 19 juil.-1er août, sam. midi, dim. et jours fériés – **Repas** *Lunch 33* – 38/59, ♀.
◆ Au cœur du bourg, confortable restaurant présentant un "look" rajeuni, tendance "design". Cuisine classique actualisée. Carte avec lunch et menus. Clientèle d'affaires.
◆ Dit comfortabele restaurant in het centrum heeft een jongere look gekregen in trendy design. Klassieke keuken in een modern jasje. Kaart met lunch en menu's. Zakelijke gasten.

HAREN *Groningen* 531 Y 3 *et* 715 K 2 – *18 644 h.*

18 au Sud : 2 km à Glimmen, Pollselaan 5, ✉ 9756 CJ, ☎ (0 50) 406 20 04, Fax (0 50) 406 19 22.

Amsterdam 207 – Groningen 8 – Zwolle 99.

Mercure, Emmalaan 33 (Sud-Ouest : 1 km sur A 28), ✉ 9752 KS, ☎ (0 50) 534 70 41, *h2107@accor-hotels.com, Fax (0 50) 534 01 75,* , – – 25 à 450. AE VISA JCB.
Repas *Lunch 18* – carte 30 à 39, ♀ – 14 – **97 ch** 79/121 – ½ P 76/143.
◆ Les infrastructures de l'hôtel ont été rénovées de fond en comble comme l'attestent les chambres fonctionnelles et les espaces de conférences bien équipés.
◆ De infrastructuur van het hotel is van top tot teen gerenoveerd. De functionele kamers en de goed uitgeruste conferentiezalen vormen het bewijs.

XX **Villa Sasso,** Meerweg 221 (Ouest : 2 km), ✉ 9752 XC, ✆ (0 50) 309 13 65, *info@villasasso.nl, Fax (0 50) 309 39 34,* ≤, Cuisine italienne, – P. AE MC VISA
fermé 28 déc.-3 janv., sam. midi et lundi – **Repas** 30/50 bc.
◆ Salle de restaurant moderne entretenant une plaisante ambiance Sud, belle terrasse d'été dressée le long du lac, accueil avenant et bonne cuisine italienne.
◆ Moderne restaurantzaal met een prettige zuidelijke ambiance, mooi zomerterras aan het meer, vriendelijk onthaal en goede, Italiaanse keuken.

à **Glimmen** *Sud : 2 km* C *Haren :*

XXX **Le Grillon,** Rijksstraatweg 10, ✉ 9756 AE, ✆ (0 50) 406 13 92, *legrillon@planet.nl, Fax (0 50) 406 31 69,* – P. AE D MC VISA JCB.
fermé 19 juil.-8 août, du 9 au 24 janv., sam. midi et dim. – **Repas** *Lunch 26* – 29/33, ♀.
◆ Élégante villa embellie, au jardin, d'une terrasse très courtisée à l'heure du repas, sous le soleil estival. Recettes de base classique interprétées dans le tempo actuel.
◆ Deze elegante villa heeft een tuinterras waar de gasten in de zomer graag aan tafel gaan. Aan de klassieke basis van de gerechten wordt een eigentijdse invulling gegeven.

HARICH *Fryslân* 531 S 5 – *voir à Balk.*

HARLINGEN (HARNS) *Fryslân* 531 R 3 *et* 715 H 2 – *15 533 h.*

Voir *Noorderhaven★ (bassin portuaire).*

vers Terschelling : Rederij Doeksen, Willem Barentszkade 21 à West-Terschelling ✆ 0 900 363 57 36, Fax (0 562) 44 32 41. Durée de la traversée : 1 h 45. Il existe aussi un service rapide (pour passagers uniquement). Durée de la traversée : 50 min.

vers Vlieland : Rederij Doeksen, Willem Barentszkade 21 à West-Terschelling ✆ 0 900 363 57 36, Fax (0 562) 44 32 41. Durée de la traversée : 1 h 45. Il existe aussi un service rapide. Durée de la traversée : 50 min.

Amsterdam 113 – Leeuwarden 27.

Zeezicht, Zuiderhaven 1, ✉ 8861 CJ, ✆ (0 517) 41 25 36, *receptie@hotelzeezicht.nl, Fax (0 517) 41 90 01,* ≤, – TV P – 35. AE D MC VISA
fermé mi-déc.-mi-janv. – **Repas** *Lunch 15* – carte 22 à 70 – **24 ch** 60/95 – ½ P 80/95.
◆ Auberge familiale avec vue sur les quais d'un vieux port d'où les marins-pêcheurs partaient traquer la baleine jusqu'au Groenland. Chambres pratiques. À table, cuisine hollandaise. Véranda donnant sur les docks et l'ancien poids public.
◆ Familiehotel met uitzicht op de kaden van een oude haven, vanwaar de vissersboten uitvoeren voor de walvisjacht bij Groenland. Praktische kamers. Hollandse keuken. De serre kijkt uit op de dokken en de oude waag.

Stadslogement "Almenum" sans rest, Kruisstraat 8 (accès par Heiligeweg), ✉ 8861 EB, ✆ (0 517) 41 77 06, *info@stadslogementharlingen.nl, Fax (0 517) 43 47 85,* – TV. MC VISA
9 – **12 ch** 60/76.
◆ Au cœur du bourg portuaire, dans une ruelle d'accès peu aisé, jolie maison ancienne disposant de petits studios avec kitchenette. Certains donnent sur une cour intérieure.
◆ Dit mooie, oude pand in een moeilijk toegankelijk steegje in het centrum van de havenplaats herbergt kleine studio's met kitchenette. Sommige kijken uit op een binnenplaats.

Anna Casparii, Noorderhaven 69, ✉ 8861 AL, ✆ (0 517) 41 20 65, *Fax (0 517) 41 45 40,* – TV – 40. AE D MC VISA. rest
Repas *Lunch 20* – carte env. 34 – **14 ch** 78 – ½ P 134.
◆ Trois maisons bourgeoises, trois façades anciennes toutes différentes pour un établissement situé à un coup de rame des premiers yachts de plaisance. Chambres convenables. Une verrière actuelle inonde de lumière la salle des repas.
◆ Drie herenhuizen en ook drie heel verschillende, oude voorgevels voor dit etablissement, dat op loopafstand van de eerste plezierjachten ligt. Vrij gerieflijke kamers. De eetzaal baadt in het licht dat door een eigentijds glasdak naar binnen valt.

XX **De Gastronoom,** Voorstraat 38, ✉ 8861 BM, ✆ (0 517) 41 21 72, *gastronoom@wxs.nl, Fax (0 517) 41 39 26,* – 60. AE D MC VISA JCB
fermé lundi d'oct. à avril – **Repas** (déjeuner sur réservation) 30/46, ♀.
◆ Affaire familiale sympathique nichée dans la commerçante Voorstraat. Recettes d'aujourd'hui travaillées à partir de produits d'ici. Une valeur sûre au centre de Harlingen.
◆ Sympathiek restaurant in een drukke winkelstraat. Eigentijdse gerechten worden met lokale producten bereid. Een trefzekere optie in het centrum van de stad.

à Arum *Sud-Est : 6 km* *Wûnseradiel 11 972 h :*

Eesterburen, Allengaweg 12, 8822 WJ, (0 517) 53 13 77, *eesterbuur@hetnet.nl, Fax (0 517) 53 20 80,* – VISA.
fermé nov.-2 prem. sem. déc. – **Repas** (dîner pour résidents seult) – **10 ch** 61/70 – ½ P 54.

◆ Cette ancienne ferme entourée de champs s'agrémente d'un jardin fleuri à la belle saison. Accueil familial chaleureux, grandes chambres et ambiance "bed and breakfast".

◆ Deze voormalige boerderij in een landelijke omgeving heeft 's zomers een prachtig bloeiende tuin. Gemoedelijke ontvangst, grote kamers en "bed and breakfast" ambiance.

HARMELEN *Utrecht* *Woerden 47 549 h.* 532 O 10 *et* 715 F 5.
Amsterdam 44 – Utrecht 13 – Den Haag 54 – Rotterdam 49.

Kloosterhoeve, Kloosterweg 2, 3481 XC, (0 348) 44 40 40, *info@kloosterhoeve.nl, Fax (0 348) 44 42 35,* – – 25 à 120. AE VISA.
fermé 24 juil.-8 août, 28 déc.-9 janv., sam. midi et dim. – **Repas** *Lunch 35* – 45/65, ♀.

◆ Dès les beaux jours, la terrasse de cette ancienne ferme du 18e s. reprend sa place sur une pelouse arborée, avec le clocher en toile de fond. Atmosphère chaleureuse.

◆ Zodra het warmer wordt, neemt het terras van deze oude, 18e-eeuwse boerderij weer zijn stekkie op het grasveld in, met de klokkentoren op de achtergrond. Gemoedelijke sfeer.

HASSELT *Overijssel* *Zwartewaterland 22 178 h.* 531 V 7 *et* 715 J 4.
Amsterdam 111 – Zwolle 20 – Meppel 20.

De Herderin, Hoogstraat 1, 8061 HA, (0 38) 477 33 00, *info@herderin.nl, Fax (0 38) 477 23 05,* – 25. AE VISA
fermé 27 déc.-11 janv., sam. midi, dim. et lundi – **Repas** *Lunch 27* – carte 27 à 37, ♀.

◆ De Herderin (La Bergère) a élu domicile au cœur du petit bourg, à environ 100 m d'un parking public. Plats goûteux. Terrasse estivale garnie d'un mobilier en teck.

◆ Deze herderin heeft in de dorpskern domicilie gekozen, op ongeveer 100 m van een openbaar parkeerterrein. Smaakvolle gerechten. Zomerterras met teakhouten meubilair.

HATTEM *Gelderland* 531 V 8 *et* 715 J 4 – *11 693 h.*
Amsterdam 116 – Assen 83 – Enschede 80 – Zwolle 7.

Herberg Molecaten, Molecaten 7, 8051 PN, (0 38) 444 69 59, *info@herbergmolecaten.nl, Fax (0 38) 444 68 49,* – VISA.
fermé janv., dim. et lundi – **Repas** *Lunch 20* – 35.

◆ Auberge de caractère (1858) profitant du calme des bois aux alentours. Vieux moulin à eau remis en état de marche. Jardin soigné où le chef fait provision d'aromates en été.

◆ Karakteristieke herberg (1858) in een rustige bosrijke omgeving. Oude watermolen die weer in gebruik is genomen. Goed onderhouden tuin met kruiden voor de chef-kok.

HAUTE VELUWE (Parc National de la) – *voir Hoge Veluwe.*

HEELSUM *Gelderland* *Renkum 32 250 h.* 532 T 11 *et* 715 I 6.
Amsterdam 90 – Arnhem 13 – Utrecht 52.

Klein Zwitserland, Klein Zwitserlandlaan 5, 6866 DS, (0 317) 31 91 04, *klein-zwitserland@bilderberg.nl, Fax (0 317) 31 39 43,* – – 25 à 200. AE VISA. rest
fermé 27 déc.-3 janv. – **Repas** voir rest ***De Kromme Dissel*** ci-après – ***De Kriekel*** 34/54 bc, ♀ – 19 – **68 ch** 100/150 – ½ P 100/113.

◆ Cet hôtel de standing installé dans un secteur résidentiel boisé déploie ses ailes autour d'une cour circulaire où se prélasse une terrasse d'été. Chambres avec balcon. Salle de restaurant habillée d'une charpente apparente et de murs de briques.

◆ Dit hotel van standing ligt in de bosrijke omgeving van Heelsum en heeft zijn vleugels uitgespreid rond een cirkelvormige binnenplaats waar 's zomers een heerlijk terras wordt ingericht. Kamers met balkon. Restaurantzaal met kapgebint en bakstenen muren.

De Kromme Dissel - H. Klein Zwitserland, Klein Zwitserlandlaan 5, 6866 DS, (0 317) 31 31 18, *klein-zwitserland@bilderberg.nl, Fax (0 317) 31 39 43,* – AE VISA.
fermé 27 déc.-3 janv., sam. midi, dim. midi et lundi midi – **Repas** *Lunch 51 bc* – 46/70, carte 50 à 70, ♀.

◆ Ancienne ferme saxonne où l'on prend place sous les poutres massives d'une charmante salle à manger rustique que réchauffe une flambée bienfaisante. Cuisine personnalisée.

◆ In deze oude Saksische boerderij wordt getafeld onder de massieve balken van een rustieke eetzaal, waar een behaaglijk vuurtje knappert. Keuken met een persoonlijke touch.

Spéc. Risotto et sandre au witlof (juin-mars). Carpaccio de langoustines à l'estragon, caviar et crème de limon. Beignets de ris de veau, salade de scaroles aux truffes

HEEMSE *Overijssel* 531 Y 7 *et* 715 K 4 *– voir à Hardenberg.*

HEEMSKERK *Noord-Holland* 531 N 7 *et* 715 F 4 *– 36 281 h.*

18 Communicatieweg 18, ✉ 1967 PR, ☎ (0 251) 25 00 88, Fax (0 251) 24 16 27.

Amsterdam 28 – Haarlem 18 – Alkmaar 18.

XX **de Vergulde Wagen,** Rijksstraatweg 161 (Nord : 1,5 km, direction Castricum), ✉ 1969 LE, ☎ (0 251) 23 24 17, *Fax (0 251) 25 35 94,* – AE ⓓ ⓜ VISA.
fermé sam. midi, dim. et lundi – **Repas** *Lunch 35* – carte 45 à 59, ♀.
◆ Une Lady-chef conduit ce "fiacre doré" (vergulde wagen) estimé pour sa cuisine joliment troussée. Sommelier averti. Chaque table est personnalisée par une sculpture.
◆ Een dame als chef-kok op de bok van deze wagen, die een smaakvol ritje voor u in petto heeft. Deskundige sommelier. Een sculptuur geeft elke tafel een eigen accent.

HEEMSTEDE *Noord-Holland* 531 M 8, 532 M 8 *et* 715 E 4 *– voir à Haarlem.*

HEERENVEEN (IT HEARRENFEAN) *Fryslân* 531 U 5 *et* 715 I 3 *– 41 784 h.*

9 Heidemeer 2, ✉ 8445 SB, ☎ (0 513) 63 65 19, Fax (0 513) 63 69 45.

Minckelersstraat 11, ✉ 8442 CE, ☎ (0 513) 62 55 55, vvv.heerenveen@12move.nl, Fax (0 513) 65 06 09.

Amsterdam 129 – Leeuwarden 30 – Groningen 58 – Zwolle 62.

XX **Sir Sèbastian,** Kûper 18 (sur A 7, sortie Heerenveen-West, Businesspark Friesland), ✉ 8447 GK, ☎ (0 513) 65 04 08, *info@sirsebastian.nl, Fax (0 513) 65 05 62,* – P. AE ⓓ ⓜ VISA
fermé 2 sem. vacances bâtiment, 1er janv., sam. midi et dim. et lundi – **Repas** 33/50.
◆ Déménagement réussi pour Sir Sèbastian qui vient de prendre ses quartiers dans la rue de Kuper. Salle à manger moderne, voire un peu "trendy". Lunch et menu.
◆ Geslaagde verhuizing voor Sir Sèbastian, die nu op een andere stek kwartier heeft gemaakt. Moderne, zelfs een beetje trendy eetzaal. Lunch en menu.

XX **perBacco,** Herenwal 186, ✉ 8441 BG, ☎ (0 513) 64 82 85, *perbacco@tiscali.nl, Fax (0 513) 64 82 85,* , Cuisine italienne – ▤. ⓓ ⓜ VISA.
fermé mardi en été, dim. en hiver et lundi – **Repas** (dîner seult) 33/36.
◆ Nouveau "ristorante" installé dans une maison de coin postée en face d'un petit canal. Décor intérieur actuel, carte transalpine au goût du jour.
◆ Deze nieuwe ristorante is gevestigd in een hoekhuis tegenover een klein kanaal. Actueel interieur, eigentijdse Italiaanse kaart.

à Oranjewoud *(Oranjewâld) Sud : 4 km* C *Heerenveen :*

Tjaarda, Koningin Julianaweg 98, ✉ 8453 WH, ☎ (0 513) 43 35 33, *info@tjaarda.nl, Fax (0 513) 43 35 99,* , , – |♦| ▭ & P – 25 à 450. AE ⓓ ⓜ VISA JCB
Repas ***De Oranjetuin*** *(fermé sam. midi et dim. midi) Lunch 33* – 30/45 – ***Grand Café Tjaarda*** 25, ♀ – ☐ 15 – **70 ch** 103/135 – ½ P 90.
◆ Tapis dans une touffe de verdure, cet établissement récent et très confortable abrite de bonnes chambres aménagées avec recherche. Communs spacieux, d'une élégance moderne. Salle de restaurant contemporaine et cossue. Saveurs en phase avec l'époque.
◆ Dit vrij nieuwe, zeer comfortabele etablissement midden in de bossen herbergt goede kamers die smaakvol zijn ingericht. De grote gemeenschappelijke ruimten stralen moderne elegantie uit. Moderne, luxueuze restaurantzaal. Eigentijdse gerechten.

HEERLEN *Limburg* 532 U 17 *et* 715 I 9 *– 95 004 h.*

18 (2 parcours) 9 au Nord : 7 km à Brunssum, Rimburgerweg 50, ✉ 6445 PA, ☎ (0 45) 527 09 68, Fax (0 45) 525 12 80 - 18 au Sud-Ouest : 5 km à Voerendaal, Hoensweg 17, ✉ 6367 GN, ☎ (0 45) 575 44 88, Fax (0 45) 575 09 00.

Bongerd 22, ✉ 6411 JM, ☎ 0 900-97 98, info@vvvzuidlimburg.nl, Fax (0 43) 609 85 25.

Amsterdam 214 – Maastricht 25 – Roermond 47 – Aachen 18.

Kasteel Ter Worm, Terworm 5 (direction Heerlen-Noord, sortie zoning In de Cramer), ✉ 6411 RV, ☎ (0 45) 400 11 11, *reception@terworm.valk.nl, Fax (0 45) 400 11 22,* , , – |♦|, ▤ rest, ▭ & P – 25. AE ⓓ ⓜ VISA.
Repas 33/63 bc – ☐ 14 – **36 ch** 100/115, – 4 suites – ½ P 97.
◆ Château néoclassique avec dépendances, bâti à la fin du 19e s. sur un îlot entouré de douves. Chambres aux notes rustiques, toutes personnalisées. Jardin rococo et orangerie. Aristocratique salle à manger où l'on vient savourer une cuisine actuelle.
◆ Dit neoklassieke kasteel met dependances is eind 19e eeuw gebouwd en wordt omringd door een slotgracht. Kamers met rustieke accenten en een eigen karakter. Rococotuin en oranjerie. In de aristocratische eetzaal kunt u genieten van een eigentijdse keuken.

Grand H., Groene Boord 23, 6411 GE, (0 45) 571 38 46, *info@grandhotel-heerlen.nl, Fax (0 45) 574 10 99,* , – , rest, – 25 à 180. rest
Repas *(fermé dim. soir) Lunch 18* – 22/35 bc, – 14 – **102 ch** 90/125, – 6 suites – ½ P 94/126.
• Une adresse bien échue pour les hommes d'affaires de passage à Heerlen, ancien centre minier mais aussi ville frontière avec l'Allemagne. Chambres bien équipées.
• Dit adres is prima geschikt voor de zakelijke clientèle op doorreis in Heerlen, een oude mijnstad aan de grens met Duitsland. De kamers zijn van alle gemakken voorzien.

Heerlen, Terworm 10 (direction Heerlen-Noord, sortie zoning In de Cramer), 6411 RV, (0 45) 571 94 50, *reservations@heerlen.valk.nl, Fax (0 45) 571 51 96,* , , , , – , rest, – 25 à 500. ch
Repas (ouvert jusqu'à 23 h) *Lunch 13* – carte 22 à 35 – 8 – **146 ch** 70.
• Importante unité de la chaîne hôtelière Van der Valk. Grandes chambres distribuées sur trois étages, salles de congrès et centre de loisirs.
• Groot hotel van de Van der Valk-keten. Ruime comfortabele kamers verspreid over drie verdiepingen, congreszalen en sportcentrum.

de Paris, Geleenstraat 1, 6411 HP, (0 45) 400 91 91, *info@hotelparis.nl, Fax (0 45) 400 91 92,* – .
Repas (taverne-rest) 23/29 – 8 – **20 ch** 65/89 – ½ P 65/86.
• Cet hôtel dont la devanture résume la vocation initiale - un grand magasin de l'entre-deux-guerres - est situé à l'entrée d'un secteur commerçant, devant l'église romane. Grande brasserie chaleureuse avec mezzanine et terrasse urbaine.
• De voorgevel van dit hotel herinnert aan de oorspronkelijke bestemming van het pand : een warenhuis tijdens het interbellum. Het ligt voor de romaanse kerk aan het begin van een winkelgebied. Grote brasserie met gemoedelijke sfeer, mezzanine en terras.

Bastion, In de Cramer 199 (direction Heerlen-Noord, sortie zoning In de Cramer), 6412 PM, (0 45) 575 45 40, *bastion@bastionhotel.nl, Fax (0 45) 575 45 44,* –
Repas (grillades, ouvert jusqu'à 23 h) carte env. 30 – 10 – **40 ch** 55.
• Hôtel de chaîne fonctionnel où chaque chambre possède désormais sa propre connexion pour modem : un petit détail technique qui plaira sans doute aux "accros du Web".
• Functioneel ketenhotel waar elke kamer nu zijn eigen modemaansluiting heeft. Een technisch detail dat cybernauten ongetwijfeld zullen toejuichen.

De Boterbloem (Winthaegen), Laanderstraat 27, 6411 VA, (0 45) 571 42 41, *boterbloem@wanadoo.nl, Fax (0 45) 574 37 73,* – .
fermé 1 sem. carnaval, 2 sem. en août, sam. midi, dim. et lundi – **Repas** *Lunch 58 bc* – 40/57, carte 49 à 61, .
• Vitraux, boiseries et lampes design en forme de spirales garnissent l'intime salle à manger. Les produits du terroir sont à la fête sur l'assiette. Cave accessible.
• Glas-in-loodramen, lambrisering en spiraalvormige designlampen sieren de intieme eetzaal. Lokale producten zijn hier op het bord volkomen in hun sas. Betaalbare wijnen.
Spéc. Salade riche de foie d'oie, crevette géante et huître. Méli-mélo de joue de veau, homard canadien et beurre monté à la truffe. Beignets au chocolat, ananas confit et glace à l'infusion de cloux de girofle

Geleenhof, Valkenburgerweg 54, 6419 AV, (0 45) 571 80 00, *info@geleenhof.nl, Fax (0 45) 571 80 86,* – .
fermé 1 sem. carnaval, 19 juil.-2 août, 29 déc.-5 janv., sam. midi, dim. midi et lundi – **Repas** 25/50, .
• Si l'endroit résonnait jadis du pas des chevaux, le décor de la salle de restaurant n'a rien conservé du cachet d'une ancienne ferme du 18e s. Tableaux contemporains.
• Klonk hier ooit het hoefgetrappel van de paarden, in het decor van het restaurant is niets terug te vinden van de sfeer van een 18e-eeuwse boerderij. Moderne schilderijen.

à Welten *Sud : 2 km* C *Heerlen :*

In Gen Thún, Weltertuynstraat 31, 6419 CS, (0 45) 571 16 16, *igt@cuci.nl, Fax (0 45) 571 09 74,* – – 25 à 50. .
fermé carnaval et 2 sem. vacances bâtiment – **Repas** (dîner seult sauf vend.) carte 41 à 52.
• Salle de restaurant moderne produisant tout son effet et espace bistrot baignant dans une atmosphère de "bruin café" si typique aux Pays-Bas. Cuisine du moment.
• Restaurant met een sterk contrast tussen de modern ingerichte eetzaal en de bistroruimte, die de typisch Nederlandse ambiance heeft van een bruin café. Seizoengebonden keuken.

HEESWIJK *Noord-Brabant* C *Bernheze 28 780 h.* 532 R 13 *et* 715 H 7.
Amsterdam 102 – Eindhoven 31 – 's-Hertogenbosch 16 – Breda 63 – Nijmegen 39.

De Leygraaf, Meerstraat 45a (Nord : 2 km), ✉ 5473 VX, ☎ (0 413) 29 30 16, *info@leygraaf.nl, Fax (0 413) 29 37 08,* – – 25 à 125. AE MC VISA.
fermé 31 déc.-1er janv. – **Repas** *Lunch 28* – carte 22 à 41 – **9 ch** 58/78 – ½ P 77/100.
• Cette ancienne ferme familiale renferme des chambres coquettes, convenant tant à l'amoureux de la petite reine qu'aux businessmen de passage dans la région.
• Deze voormalige boerderij herbergt keurige kamers, die zowel geschikt zijn voor fietsliefhebbers als voor de zakelijke clientèle die hier in de regio op doorreis is.

HEEZE *Noord-Brabant* C *Heeze-Leende 15 333 h.* 532 S 14 *et* 715 H 7.
Amsterdam 139 – Eindhoven 13 – 's-Hertogenbosch 50 – Roermond 42 – Venlo 50.

Boreas, Jan Deckersstraat 7, ✉ 5591 HN, ☎ (0 40) 226 32 32, *restaurant.boreas@planet.nl, Fax (0 40) 226 50 77,* – AE MC VISA
fermé 20 fév.-1er mars, 3 sem. vacances bâtiment, sam. midi, dim. et lundi – **Repas** *Lunch 28* – carte 48 à 58, ♀.
• Au cœur du bourg, grosse maison blanche où l'on mange agréablement dans un cadre contemporain. Cuisine de notre temps. Salon douillet avec cheminée. Service prévenant.
• In dit robuuste witte pand in het centrum is het aangenaam tafelen in een hedendaags decor. Eigentijdse keuken. Behaaglijke salon met schouw. Attente bediening.
Spéc. Barbue en croûte et homard à la mousseline de persil. Filets de sole grillés au foie gras et girolles. Orange vanillée et crêpe à la mousse de citron

Host. Van Gaalen avec ch, Kapelstraat 48, ✉ 5591 HE, ☎ (0 40) 226 35 15, *info@hostellerie.nl, Fax (0 40) 226 38 76,* – rest, AE MC VISA
fermé sem. carnaval et fin déc. – **Repas** *(fermé sam. midi, dim. et lundi midi) Lunch 29* – 34/42, ♀ – 10 – **13 ch** 78/88, – 1 suite – ½ P 80/110.
• Hostellerie dont le décor de la salle à manger, autant que l'assiette, vous entraînent dans une plaisante escapade méridionale. Terrasse d'été et jardin. Chambres et suite.
• Hostellerie waar het decor van de eetzaal en de inhoud van het bord u meenemen op een genoeglijk, mediterraan avontuur. Zomerterras en tuin. Kamers en suite.

HEIJEN *Limburg* C *Gennep 16 847 h.* 532 U 12 *et* 715 I 6.
Amsterdam 140 – Maastricht 115 – Eindhoven 67 – Nijmegen 26 – Venlo 38.

Mazenburg, Boxmeerseweg 61 (Sud-Ouest : 3 km, Zuidereiland), ✉ 6598 MX, ☎ (0 485) 51 71 71, *info@mazenburg.nl, Fax (0 485) 51 87 87,* ←, – AE MC VISA.
fermé carnaval, 1re quinz. nov., merc. de sept. à avril, sam. midi et dim. midi – **Repas** *Lunch 30* – 39/80 bc, ♀.
• Auberge charmante esseulée au bord d'un paisible méandre de la Meuse. Ample salle de restaurant panoramique. Spécialité d'asperges en saison. Ambiance familiale.
• Charmant restaurant dat eenzaam aan de oever van een rustige bocht in de Maas ligt. Ruime panoramische eetzaal. Specialiteit van asperges in het seizoen. Gemoedelijke sfeer.

HEILLE *Zeeland* 532 F 15 – *voir à Sluis.*

HEILOO *Noord-Holland* 531 N 7 *et* 715 F 4 – *21 976 h.*
Amsterdam 36 – Haarlem 27 – Alkmaar 5.

Golden Tulip, Kennemerstraatweg 425, ✉ 1851 PD, ☎ (0 72) 505 22 44, *info@gtheiloo.nl, Fax (0 72) 505 37 66,* – rest, – 40 à 800. AE MC VISA.
Repas *Lunch 18* – carte 29 à 49, ♀ – **41 ch** 80/108 – ½ P 55/65.
• L'été venu, des champs de tulipes fleurissent autour de cet hôtel de chaîne internationale. Chambres réparties dans une aile coiffée de toits en dents de scie.
• Zodra het zomer wordt, staan rond dit internationale ketenhotel de tulpenvelden in bloei. De kamers zijn ondergebracht in een vleugel met zaagdak.

de Loocatie, 't Loo 20 (dans centre commercial), ✉ 1851 HT, ☎ (0 72) 533 33 52, *info@loocatie.nl,* – MC VISA JCB
fermé lundi et mardi – **Repas** (déjeuner sur réservation) carte 33 à 48.
• Une adresse bienvenue pour toutes celles et ceux qui souhaitent conjuguer les joies du shopping à un certain plaisir de la table. Recettes au goût du jour.
• Een adres dat goed van pas komt voor wie de geneugten van het shoppen wil combineren met culinaire genoegens. Eigentijdse gerechten.

à Limmen *Sud : 2 km* ◻ *Castricum 23 330 h :*

XX **Gastronome,** Rijksweg 100, ✉ 1906 BK, ☎ (0 72) 505 12 96, *gastronome@planet.nl, Fax (0 72) 505 34 74,* – P. MC VISA
fermé dim. non fériés et sam. midi – **Repas** (déjeuner sur réservation) carte 35 à 52, ♀.
◆ Enseigne engageante à l'heure du repas pour cette villa bordant la route nationale. Coquette salle à manger d'inspiration méditerranéenne. Carte "journalistique".
◆ Aanlokkelijke naam voor deze villa langs de weg door het dorp, zeker als de maag begint te knorren. Charmante eetzaal met mediterraan decor. De kaart leest als een krant.

HELDEN *Limburg* 532 V 15 *et* 715 I 8 – *19 510 h.*
Amsterdam 174 – Maastricht 68 – Eindhoven 46 – Roermond 24 – Venlo 15.

Antiek, Mariaplein 1, ✉ 5988 CH, ☎ (0 77) 306 72 00, *info@antiek-helden.nl, Fax (0 77) 306 72 19,* – TV P – 30. AE MC VISA.
fermé 27 déc.-4 janv. – **Repas** *(fermé dim.)* Lunch 25 – 26/55 bc, ♀ – ☕ 9 – **12 ch** 51/69 – ½ P 57.
◆ Auberge familiale un peu mélancolique, mais toujours prête pour rendre service au voyageur. Sobres et pimpantes chambres quelquefois dotées de cadres de lits en cuivre. Brasserie et restaurant d'allure bourgeoise pourvu d'une cheminée en carreaux de Delft.
◆ Het hotel heeft een wat nostalgische sfeer en staat altijd klaar voor zijn gasten. Eenvoudig ingerichte maar piccobello kamers, sommige met een koperen ledikant. Restaurant met klassieke ambiance en een schouw met Delfts blauw. Brasserie.

Den HELDER *Noord-Holland* 531 N 5 *et* 715 F 3 – *60 083 h.*

au Sud : 7 km à Julianadorp, Van Foreestweg, ✉ 1787 PS, ☎ (0 223) 64 01 25, Fax (0 223) 64 01 26.

vers Texel : Rederij Teso, Pontweg 1 à Den Hoorn (Texel) ☎ (0 222) 36 96 00, Fax (0 222) 36 96 59. Durée de la traversée : 20 min.

Bernhardplein 18, ✉ 1781 HH, ☎ (0 223) 62 55 44, denhelder@vvv-knh.nl, Fax (0 223) 61 48 88.

Amsterdam 79 – Haarlem 72 – Alkmaar 40 – Leeuwarden 90.

Lands End, Havenplein 1, ✉ 1781 AB, ☎ (0 223) 62 15 70, *hotel@landsend.nl, Fax (0 223) 62 85 40,* ← – TV. AE MC VISA
Repas carte 22 à 36 – **24 ch** ☕ 65/85 – ½ P 63/85.
◆ Construction d'aujourd'hui élevée à portée de canon du ponton d'où l'on s'embarque pour l'île de Texel. Chambres fonctionnelles de bonnes dimensions.
◆ Eigentijds hotel binnen kanonbereik van de ponton waar men inscheept voor het eiland Texel. Functionele kamers van goede afmetingen.

à Huisduinen *Ouest : 2 km* ◻ *Den Helder :*

Beatrix , Badhuisstraat 2, ✉ 1783 AK, ☎ (0 223) 62 40 00, *gtbeaho@xs4all.nl, Fax (0 223) 62 73 24,* ←, , – rest, TV P – 25 à 100. AE MC VISA.
Repas *(fermé sam. midi et dim. midi)* (ouvert jusqu'à 23 h) Lunch 33 – carte env. 48 – **50 ch** ☕ 87/165 – ½ P 117/185.
◆ Hôtel tranquille à dénicher près de Den Helder, forteresse napoléonienne devenue port de guerre national. Bonnes chambres pour des nuits sans remous. Sports et farniente. Jolie salle à manger "scottish touch", avec vue littorale.
◆ Rustig gelegen hotel vlak bij Den Helder, waar Napoleon een fort liet bouwen en nu de marinehaven ligt. Goede kamers voor een ongestoorde nachtrust en faciliteiten voor sport en ontspanning. Leuke eetzaal met een Schots tintje en uitzicht op de kust.

HELLENDOORN *Overijssel* 531 X 8 *et* 715 K 4 – *36 011 h.*
Amsterdam 142 – Zwolle 35 – Enschede 42.

Tulip Inn, Johanna van Burenstraat 9, ✉ 7447 HB, ☎ (0 548) 65 54 25, *info@hotelhellendoorn.nl, Fax (0 548) 65 58 33,* , – TV – 25 à 80. AE MC VISA.
Repas (dîner pour résidents seult) – **28 ch** ☕ 63/93 – ½ P 53/70.
◆ Une tourelle d'angle attire le regard sur cet hôtel mettant à votre disposition des chambres sans reproche. Rafraîchissante pièce d'eau bordée de caillebotis.
◆ Een hoektorentje vestigt de aandacht op het hotel, dat over onberispelijke kamers beschikt. Verkoelende waterpartij met houten vlonders.

HELLEVOETSLUIS *Zuid-Holland* 532 *J 12 et* 715 *D 6 – 39 017 h.*

Env. *à l'Ouest : 10 km, Barrage du Haringvliet★★ (Haringvlietdam).*

Amsterdam 101 – Rotterdam 31 – Den Haag 51 – Breda 74.

XX **Hazelbag,** Rijksstraatweg 151, ✉ 3222 KC, ☎ (0 181) 31 22 10, *hazelbag@hetnet.nl, Fax (0 181) 31 26 77,* – P. AE ① MC VISA.
fermé fév., lundi et mardi – **Repas** (dîner seult) 25, ♀.
◆ La salle de restaurant vient de s'offrir un nouveau décor : fresques murales exécutées en trompe-l'œil, évoquant une architecture antique. Cuisine classique de bon aloi.
◆ De restaurantzaal heeft een geheel nieuw decor gekregen : fresco's in trompe-l'oeil met een voorstelling van een antieke architectuur. Smaakvolle, klassieke keuken.

HELMOND *Noord-Brabant* 532 *T 14 et* 715 *I 7 – 82 853 h.*

Voir *Château★ (Kasteel).*

Verliefd Laantje 3b, ☎ (0 492) 52 78 77, Fax (0 492) 47 59 23.

Amsterdam 124 – Eindhoven 15 – 's-Hertogenbosch 39 – Roermond 47.

West-Ende, Steenweg 1, ✉ 5707 CD, ☎ (0 492) 52 41 51, *info@westende.nl, Fax (0 492) 54 32 95,* – TV P. – 25 à 100. AE MC VISA JCB.
Repas *Lunch 18* – carte 32 à 56 – 12 – **28 ch** 87/11 – ½ P 59/90.
◆ Dans le centre-ville, près d'un viaduc au trafic soutenu, belle demeure patricienne de style néo-classique proposant diverses catégories de chambres dont deux junior suites. Restaurant contemporain, avec un "bar-lounge" pour l'apéritif ou le pousse-café.
◆ In het centrum, vlak bij een viaduct met aanhoudend verkeer, biedt deze mooie patriciërswoning in neoklassieke stijl diverse categorieën kamers (twee junior suites). Eigentijds restaurant met een bar-lounge voor het aperitief of een afzakkertje.

XXX **de Warande,** Warande 2 (Nord-Ouest : 1 km), ✉ 5707 GP, ☎ (0 492) 53 63 61, *Fax (0 492) 52 26 15,* ≤, – P. AE ① MC VISA.
fermé 2 dern. sem. juil., sam. midi et dim. – **Repas** *Lunch 32* – 40/55 bc, ♀.
◆ Cuisine classique actualisée servie dans une ambiance feutrée, assez romantique. Véranda et terrasse estivale procurent un plaisant coup d'œil sur un parc et son étang.
◆ In een stemmige, romantische ambiance worden klassieke gerechten met een modern accent geserveerd. Serre en zomerterras bieden een aangenaam uitzicht op een park met vijver.

XX **de Raymaert,** Mierloseweg 130, ✉ 5707 AR, ☎ (0 492) 54 18 18, *raymaert@tiscali.nl, Fax (0 492) 52 56 38,* – P. MC VISA.
fermé dern. sem. juil.-prem. sem. août et lundi – **Repas** (dîner seult) 26/55 bc.
◆ Une imposante maison de notable abrite cette affaire familiale très courtisée le week-end. Carte appétissante, intérieur classiquement aménagé et jolie terrasse d'été.
◆ Een statig herenhuis herbergt dit familiebedrijf, dat in het weekend erg in trek is. Smaakvolle kaart, klassiek interieur en leuk zomerterras.

X **de Steenoven,** Steenovenweg 21, ✉ 5708 HN, ☎ (0 492) 50 75 07, *info@restaurantdesteenoven.nl, Fax (0 492) 50 75 05,* – P. MC VISA.
fermé sam. midi et dim. – **Repas** *Lunch 24* – 26/46 bc, ♀.
◆ Restaurant installé dans les murs d'une ancienne briqueterie, comme le précise son enseigne (le Four à Briques). Salle des repas au décor néo-rustique.
◆ Zoals de naam al aangeeft, heeft dit restaurant zijn intrek genomen in een oude steenbakkerij. De eetzaal heeft een neorustiek decor.

HELVOIRT *Noord-Brabant* C *Haaren 14 137 h.* 532 *Q 13 et* 715 *G 7.*

Amsterdam 98 – Eindhoven 36 – 's-Hertogenbosch 9 – Tilburg 13.

XX **De Helvoirtse Hoeve,** Margrietweg 9 (Nord-Ouest : 5,5 km), ✉ 5268 LW, ☎ (0 411) 64 16 61, *info@dehelvoirtsehoeve.nl, Fax (0 411) 64 38 67,* – P. AE ① MC VISA JCB.
fermé lundi et mardi – **Repas** 30/60 bc, ♀.
◆ Les bois offrent un cadre apaisant à cette petite auberge familiale coiffée d'un toit de chaume. Une table opportune pour les promeneurs sillonnant les dunes de Drunen.
◆ De bossen vormen een rustgevend decor voor dit kleine restaurant met rieten dak. Een uitgelezen adres voor wandelaars in de Drunense Duinen.

XX **De Zwarte Leeuw,** Oude Rijksweg 20, ✉ 5268 BT, ☎ (0 411) 64 12 66, *info@dezwarteleeuw.nl, Fax (0 411) 64 22 51,* – P. AE ① MC VISA.
fermé 2e quinz. juil., dern. sem. déc., mardi, merc. et dim. midi – **Repas** *Lunch 25* – 34.
◆ Le temps a peu d'emprise sur ce vénérable Lion Noir (Zwarte Leeuw) "rugissant" depuis le 19e s. au bord de l'axe Tilburg-Den Bosch. La carte, classique, donne les crocs !
◆ De tijd heeft weinig vat op deze koning der dieren, die al sinds de 19e eeuw zijn prooi bespiedt langs de weg Tilburg-Den Bosch. De klassieke kaart is om in te bijten !

HENGELO *Overijssel* 531 Z 9, 532 Z 9 *et* 715 L 5 – *80 910 h – Ville industrielle.*

Enschedesestraat 381, ✉ 7552 CV, ☎ (0 74) 250 84 66, Fax (0 74) 250 93 88.

au Nord-Est : 6 km à Enschede-Twente ☎ (0 53) 486 22 22, Fax (0 53) 435 96 91.

Molenstraat 26, ✉ 7551 DC, ☎ (0 74) 242 11 20, info@vvvhengelo.nl, Fax (0 74) 242 17 80.

Amsterdam 149 – Zwolle 61 – Apeldoorn 62 – Enschede 9.

Hengelo, Bornsestraat 400 (près A 1, direction Borne), ✉ 7556 BN, ☎ (0 74) 255 50 55, *receptie@hengelo-valk.nl, Fax (0 74) 255 50 10,* – 25 à 1500.

Repas (ouvert jusqu'à 23 h) *Lunch 10* – 22 – 8 – **208 ch** 60/70, – 1 suite – ½ P 83.

◆ Établissement typique de la chaîne hôtelière hollandaise Van der Valk, symbolisée par un toucan. Aux grandes chambres s'ajoute une infrastructure de réunions colossale.

◆ Een typisch etablissement van de Nederlandse hotelketen Van der Valk, met de bekende toekan als logo. Grote kamers en kolossale infrastructuur voor bijeenkomsten.

't Lansink, C.T. Storkstraat 18, ✉ 7553 AR, ☎ (0 74) 291 00 66, *info@lansinkhotel.nl, Fax (0 74) 243 58 91,* – 25 à 80.

Repas *(fermé dim.) Lunch 33* – carte 30 à 63, – **16 ch** 65/90 – ½ P 79/104.

◆ Dans un quartier résidentiel tranquille, immeuble charmant construit à la fin du 19e s. Un rien désuètes, les chambres se distribuent sur deux étages. Salle à manger évoquant un peu le style "british cottage".

◆ Dit hotel in een charmant pand uit het einde van de 19e eeuw bevindt zich in een rustige woonwijk. De ietwat sleetse kamers liggen over twee verdiepingen verspreid. De ambiance in de eetzaal heeft iets weg van een Engelse cottage.

HENGEVELDE *Overijssel* C *Hof van Twente 35 041 h.* 532 Y 9 *et* 715 K 5.

Amsterdam 135 – Zwolle 63 – Apeldoorn 53 – Arnhem 32 – Enschede 18.

Pierik, Goorsestraat 25 (sur N 347), ✉ 7496 AB, ☎ (0 547) 33 30 00, *info@hotelpierik.nl, Fax (0 547) 33 36 56,* – 30. rest

fermé 23 déc.-2 janv. – **Repas** 22/33 – **40 ch** 59/83 – ½ P 52/56.

◆ Toute la famille veille à la bonne marche de l'établissement. Juste en face, une annexe regroupe un quart des chambres, qui sont également les plus récentes. Restaurant agencé dans la note néo-rustique. Additions sans rondeurs.

◆ De hele familie waakt over de goede gang van zaken in het etablissement. In een dependance aan de overkant is een kwart van de kamers ingericht, die ook het meest recent zijn. Restaurant met neorustieke inrichting. Redelijke prijzen.

HERKENBOSCH *Limburg* 532 V 16 *et* 715 J 8 – *voir à Roermond.*

's-HERTOGENBOSCH ou Den BOSCH P *Noord-Brabant* 532 Q 12 *et* 715 G 6 – *131 697 h.*

Voir *Cathédrale St-Jean★★ (St-Janskathedraal) : retable★* Z.

Musée : *du Brabant Septentrional★ (Noordbrabants Museum)* Z **M³**.

Env. *au Nord-Est : 3 km à Rosmalen, collection de véhicules★ dans le musée du transport Autotron – a l'Ouest : 25 km à Kaatsheuvel, De Efteling★★ (parc récréatif).*

Leunweg 40, ✉ 5221 BC, ☎ (0 73) 633 06 44, Fax (0 73) 633 06 45 - Meerendonkweg 2, ✉ 5216 TZ, ☎ (0 73) 613 66 30 - par ④ : 10 km à St-Michielsgestel, Zegenwerp 12, ✉ 5271 NC, ☎ (0 73) 551 23 16, Fax (0 73) 551 94 41 - au Nord : 8 km à Kerkdriel, Piekenwaardweg 3, ☎ (0 418) 63 48 03, Fax (0 418) 63 46 30.

par ④ : 32 km à Eindhoven-Welschap ☎ (0 40) 291 98 18, Fax (0 40) 291 98 20.

lignes directes France, Suisse, Italie, Autriche, Yougoslavie et Allemagne ☎ 0 900-92 96.

Markt 77, ✉ 5211 JX, ☎ (0 73) 614 99 86, Fax (0 73) 612 89 30.

Amsterdam 83 ⑦ – Eindhoven 33 ④ – Nijmegen 47 ② – Tilburg 23 ⑤ – Utrecht 51 ⑦

Plans pages suivantes

Central, Burg. Loeffplein 98, ✉ 5211 RX, ☎ (0 73) 692 69 26, *info@hotel-central.nl, Fax (0 73) 614 56 99* – rest, – 25 à 280. Z c

Repas *Leeuwenborgh* *(fermé dim. soir) Lunch 21* – 28 – 14 – **123 ch** 118/213, – 1 suite.

◆ Confortable hôtel situé à l'entrée du secteur piétonnier entourant le Markt, place effervescente où trône la statue d'un célèbre enfant du pays : le peintre Jérôme Bosch. Salle à manger agrémentée de fresques. Recettes goût du jour.

◆ Comfortabel hotel aan de rand van het voetgangersgebied rond de Markt, een bruisend plein waar het standbeeld troont van de schilder Jeroen Bosch, die hier werd geboren. Eetzaal verfraaid met fresco's. Eigentijdse recepten.

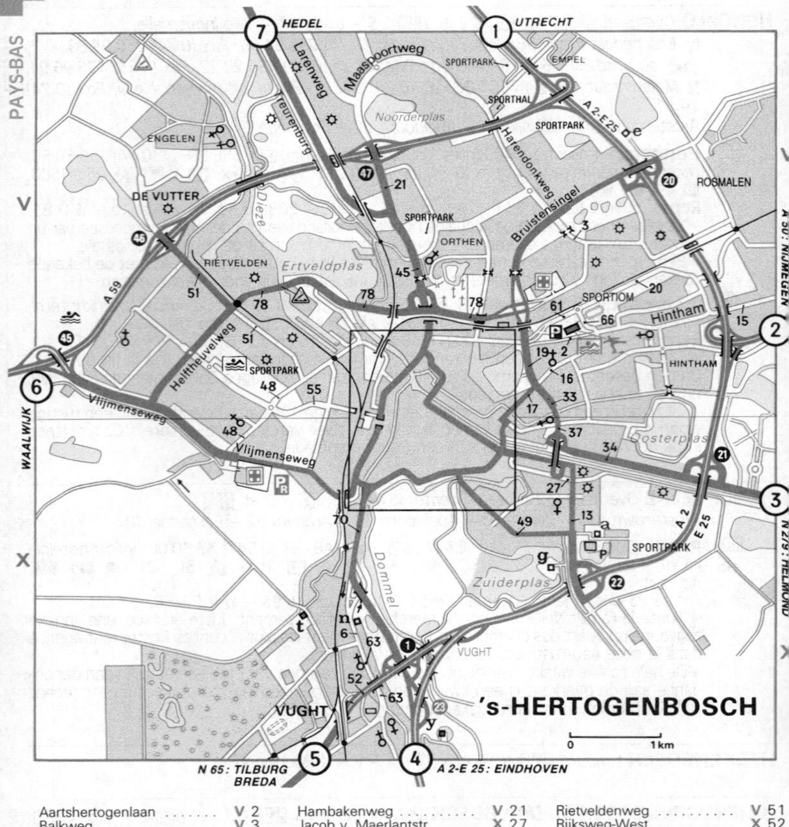

Aartshertogenlaan	V 2	Hambakenweg	V 21	Rietveldenweg	V 51
Balkweg	V 3	Jacob v. Maerlantstr.	X 27	Rijksweg-West	X 52
Bosscheweg	X 6	Lagelandstr.	V 33	Simon Stevinweg	V 55
Gestelseweg	X 13	Maastrichtseweg	X 34	Stadionlaan	V 61
Graafsebaan	V 15	Merwedelaan	X 37	Taalstr.	X 63
Graafseweg	V 16	Orthenseweg	V 45	Victorialaan	V 66
van Grobbendoncklaan	V 19	Oude Vlijmenseweg	VX 48	Vughterweg	X 70
Grote Elst	Y 20	Pettelaarseweg	X 49	Zandzuigerstr.	V 78

Mövenpick, Pettelaarpark 90, ✉ 5216 PH, ☎ (0 73) 687 46 74, *hotel.s-hertogenbosch@moevenpick.com, Fax (0 73) 687 46 35*, ≤, ch, 25 à 85. AE VISA JCB X a

Repas (taverne-rest) *Lunch 17* – carte 22 à 46 – ☕ 14 – **92 ch** 117/150 – ½ P 118/157.

◆ Architecture contemporaine un peu excentrée, se reflétant à la surface d'un étang. Espaces communs modernes, d'une belle ampleur. Chambres actuelles d'esprit scandinave. Taverne-restaurant complétée d'une terrasse d'été au bord de l'eau.

◆ De moderne architectuur van dit pand net buiten het centrum weerspiegelt zich in de vijver. Grote en moderne gemeenschappelijke ruimten. Eigentijdse kamers in Scandinavische sfeer. Grand café met zomerterras aan het water.

Eurohotel sans rest, Hinthamerstraat 63, ✉ 5211 MG, ☎ (0 73) 613 77 77, *eurohotel@xs4all.nl, Fax (0 73) 612 87 95* – – 25 à 150. AE VISA. Z d

fermé 24 déc.-2 janv. – ☕ 7 – **42 ch** 65/105.

◆ L'une des plus belles cathédrales des Pays-Bas - édifice de style gothique tardif, célèbre pour ses concerts de carillon - se dresse à deux pas de cet hôtel familial.

◆ Een van de mooiste kathedralen van Nederland - gebouwd in laat-gotische stijl en beroemd om de carillonconcerten - staat op een steenworp afstand van dit familiehotel.

's-HERTOGENBOSCH

Street	Grid	No.
Bethaniestr.	Z	4
de Bossche Pad	Z	7
Burg. Loeffpl.	YZ	9
Emmaplein	Y	10
Geert van Woustr.	Y	12
Graafseweg	Y	16
Havensingel	Y	22
Hinthamereinde	Z	24
Hinthamerstr.	Z	
Hoge Steenweg	Z	25
Jan Heinsstr.	Y	28
Kerkstr.	Z	30
Koninginnenlaan	Y	31
Maastrichtseweg	Z	34
Muntelbolwerk	Y	39
van Noremborghstr.	Y	40
Oostwal	Z	42
Oranje Nassaulaan	Z	43
Orthenstr.	Y	46
Schapenmarkt	Z	54
Sint-Jacobstr.	Z	57
Sint-Josephstr.	Z	58
Spinhuiswal	Z	60
Stationsweg	Z	62
Torenstr.	Z	65
Visstraat	Z	67
Vlijmenseweg	Z	69
Vughterstr.	Z	
Vughterweg	Z	70
van der Weeghensingel	Y	73
Wilhelminaplein	Z	75
Willemsplein	Z	76

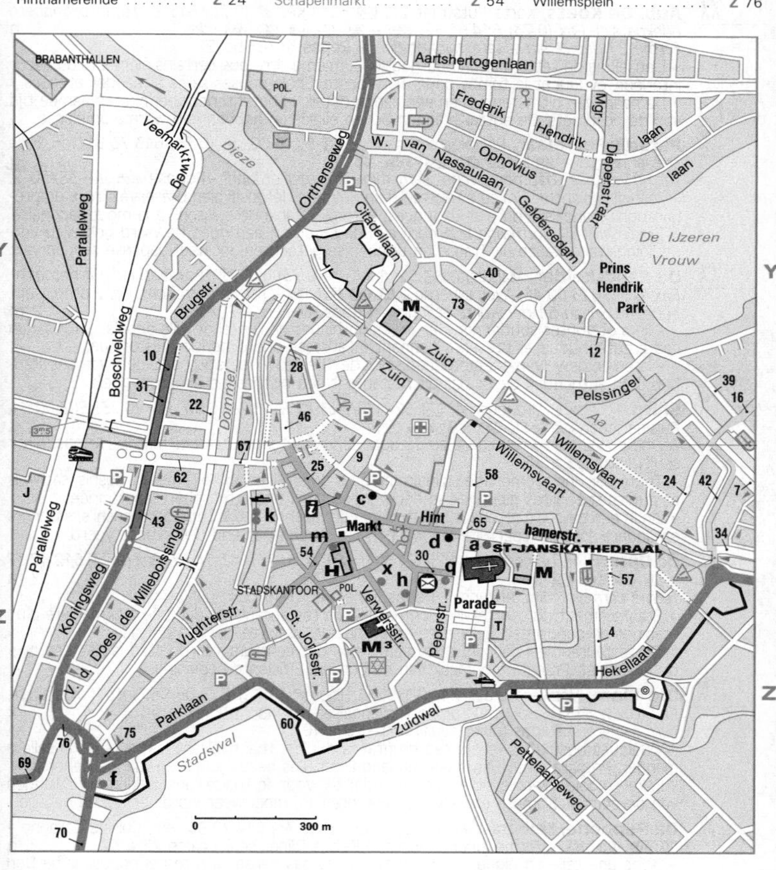

XXX **Chalet Royal** (Greveling), Wilhelminaplein 1, ⊠ 5211 CG, ☎ (0 73) 613 57 71, *chalet@alliance.nl, Fax (0 73) 614 77 82*, ←, 🍴 – 🅿 – 25. AE ⓓ ⓜ VISA Z f

fermé du 21 au 26 fév., 20 juil.-10 août, fin déc.-début janv., sam. midi, dim. et lundi – **Repas** *Lunch 44 bc* – 57/76, carte 55 à 65, 𝕐.

◆ Villa cossue agrémentée d'une terrasse estivale panoramique : vue sur les douves et la campagne en arrière-plan. Cuisine mariant avec bonheur classicisme et goût du jour.

◆ Luxueuze villa met panoramisch zomerterras : uitzicht op de oude vestinggracht en het achterliggende landschap. Klassiek en eigentijds vormen een prima paar in de keuken.

Spéc. Cannelloni de homard et épinards, sauce aux truffes. Râble de lièvre au foie d'oie (oct.-déc.). Langoustines tièdes dans leur jus à la cardamome (janv.-mai)

XX **de Veste,** Uilenburg 2, ✉ 5211 EV, ✆ (0 73) 614 46 44, *Fax (0 73) 612 49 34,* – AE ⓓ MC VISA Z k
fermé dern. sem. juil.-2 prem. sem. août, sam. et dim. – **Repas** *Lunch 32* – carte 39 à 48.
◆ Le long d'un canal tranquille, petite maison de bouche où vous serez gentiment reçu. L'été, une mini terrasse sous auvent est dressée au bord de l'eau. Repas classique.
◆ In dit kleine eethuis langs een rustig kanaal wacht de gast een vriendelijk onthaal. In de zomer is er een overdekt miniterras aan het water. Klassieke maaltijden.

XX **Aub. De Koets,** Korte Putstraat 23, ✉ 5211 KP, ✆ (0 73) 613 27 79, *info@aubergedekoets.nl, Fax (0 73) 614 62 52,* – . AE ⓓ MC VISA. Z h
fermé 27 déc.-2 janv., sam. midi et dim. – **Repas** 35/83 bc, ♀.
◆ L'enseigne de cette maison bourgeoise, au même titre que certains éléments du décor intérieur, évoquent le temps de la malle-poste. Chaleureuses salles à manger étagées.
◆ De naam van dit herenhuis en een aantal details in het interieur herinneren aan de tijd van de postkoets. De eetzalen liggen boven elkaar en hebben een warme ambiance.

XX **Paradis-Pettelaar,** Pettelaarseschans 1, ✉ 5216 CG, ✆ (0 73) 613 73 51, *info@pettelaar.nl,* – P. AE MC VISA JCB. X g
fermé vacances bâtiment, vend., sam. midi, dim. midi et lundi – **Repas** *Lunch 23* – 33/50, ♀.
◆ Jolie villa blanche élevée à l'entrée d'un ouvrage défensif bien préservé. Choix de préparations françaises ou plus exotiques. Formule "table de cuisson" à la mode japonaise.
◆ Fraaie witte, voormalige boerderij aan de rand van een goed bewaard gebleven verdedigingswerk. Keuze uit franse en uitheemse gerechten, inclusief Japanse teppan-yaki.

XX **De Raadskelder,** Markt 1a, ✉ 5211 JV, ✆ (0 73) 613 69 19, *raadskelder@hetnet.nl, Fax (0 73) 613 00 46,* Avec taverne – AE MC VISA. – *fermé dern. sem. juil.-2 prem. sem. août, du 21 au 31 déc., dim. et lundi* – **Repas** *Lunch 17* – 22/36. Z m
◆ Piliers et voûtes soutiennent les caves gothiques de l'hôtel de ville depuis le 16e s. : un cadre authentique et préservé donnant à l'adresse une dimension historique.
◆ Pilaren en gewelven ondersteunen sinds de 16e eeuw de gotische kelders van het stadhuis. Een authentiek decor dat dit restaurant een historische dimensie geeft.

X **Shiro** 1er étage, Uilenburg 4, ✉ 5211 EV, ✆ (0 73) 612 76 00, *Fax (0 73) 503 00 61,* Cuisine japonaise – AE MC VISA JCB Z k
fermé du 22 au 24 fév., du 2 au 18 août, 27 déc.-4 janv., lundi et mardi – **Repas** (dîner seult) carte 35 à 56.
◆ Tenté par une promenade culinaire au pays du soleil levant ? Tempura, sushis, sashimis et autres spécialités nippones se déclinent ici dans une atmosphère appropriée.
◆ Zin in een culinaire reis door het land van de rijzende zon ? Tempoera, sushi's, sashimi's en andere Japanse specialiteiten worden hier in een passend decor geserveerd.

X **de Opera,** Hinthamerstraat 115, ✉ 5211 MH, ✆ (0 73) 613 74 57, *Fax (0 73) 612 47 37* – AE ⓓ MC VISA JCB Z a
fermé carnaval, dim. et lundi – **Repas** (dîner seult) 48, ♀.
◆ Établissement du centre-ville dont la salle de restaurant est décorée à la manière d'un "cabinet de curiosités". Belle mise en scène sur l'assiette. Service efficace.
◆ De restaurantzaal van dit etablissement in het centrum van de stad is net een rariteitenkabinet. Prachtige opmaak van de borden. Efficiënte bediening.

X **Old Siam,** Verwersstraat 24, ✉ 5211 HW, ✆ (0 73) 613 06 86, *info@oldsiam.nl, Fax (0 73) 613 06 86,* , Cuisine thaïlandaise – . MC VISA. Z x
fermé mardi – **Repas** (dîner seult) carte 25 à 40.
◆ Quelques beaux bas-reliefs représentatifs de l'art thaï habillent les murs de la salle à manger. Préparations "siamoises" et japonaises. Les beaux jours, on mange dehors.
◆ Enkele mooie bas-reliëfs die representatief zijn voor de Thaise kunst bekleden de wanden van de eetzaal. Siamese en Japanse gerechten. Bij mooi weer wordt er buiten gegeten.

X **Da Peppone,** Kerkstraat 77, ✉ 5211 KE, ✆ (0 73) 614 78 94, , Cuisine italienne – AE ⓓ MC VISA – *fermé lundi et mardi* – **Repas** (dîner seult) carte 25 à 37. Z q
◆ Avec une telle enseigne, il est difficile de ne pas penser à l'éternel opposant de Don Camillo, un maire bouillonnant incarné au cinéma par Gino Cervi. Pâtes et pizzas.
◆ De naam doet direct denken aan de eeuwige tegenstander van Don Camillo, de onstuimige burgemeester die door Gino Cervi op het witte doek werd gezet. Pasta's en pizza's.

à Rosmalen *Est : 3 km* C *'s-Hertogenbosch :*

Mercure, Burg. Burgerslaan 50 (près A 2), ✉ 5245 NH, ✆ (0 73) 521 91 59, *H2112@accor-hotels.com, Fax (0 73) 521 62 15,* – TV P – 25 à 250. AE ⓓ MC VISA. rest V e
Repas *Lunch 20* – carte 22 à 40 – 14 – **82 ch** 99/119.
◆ Hôtel de chaîne construit près de l'autoroute, à 5 mn du cœur de Den Bosch. Chambres sans surprise, sinon la vue sur un étang que procurent celles situées à l'arrière. Salle des repas profitant, elle aussi, d'un coup d'œil reposant.
◆ Dit ketenhotel is vlak bij de snelweg gebouwd en ligt op 5 min. van hartje Den Bosch. De kamers hebben geen verrassing in petto, behalve misschien het uitzicht op een vijver aan de achterkant. Ook de eetzaal biedt een rustgevend uitzicht.

XXX **Die Heere Sewentien,** Sparrenburgstraat 9, ✉ 5244 JC, ☎ (0 73) 521 77 44, *Fax (0 73) 521 00 75,* – P. MC VISA
fermé du 1er au 23 août, 27 déc.-3 janv., sam. midi, dim. et lundi – **Repas** *Lunch 29* – 40/77 bc.
• Accueillante auberge entourée de verdure, dans un quartier résidentiel d'une localité consacrant un beau petit musée à l'histoire automobile. Terrasse et jardin exquis.
• Gezellig restaurant omgeven door groen, in een woonwijk van een stadje waar een museum is gewijd aan de geschiedenis van de auto. Terras en heerlijke tuin.

à Vught *Sud : 4 km – 25 610 h*

Vught, Bosscheweg 2, ✉ 5261 AA, ☎ (0 73) 658 77 77, *receptievught@vdvalk.com, Fax (0 73) 658 77 77,* , , , , – , rest, – 25 à 400. AE MC VISA. X n
Repas (ouvert jusqu'à 23 h) *Lunch 13* – 22 – 12 – **116 ch** 88, – 6 suites.
• Assez proche de l'autoroute et du centre-ville, hôtel Van der Valk dont l'aménagement des chambres n'étonnera pas les habitués de la chaîne. Sports et congrès.
• Nabij de snelweg en het centrum staat hotel Van der Valk, waar de kamers zijn ingericht zoals de vaste gasten van de keten dat gewend zijn. Sport- en congresfaciliteiten.

XXX **Ons Kabinet,** Kampdijklaan 80, ✉ 5263 CK, ☎ (0 73) 657 17 10, *info@onskabinet.nl, Fax (0 73) 657 25 62,* – P – 25 à 80. AE MC VISA JCB X t
fermé 1 sem. carnaval, 2 sem. vacances bâtiment, sam. midi et dim. – **Repas** *Lunch 28* – 30/66 bc, ♀.
• Pavillon bâti dans un secteur résidentiel, près d'un canal. Salle de restaurant de notre temps. Terrasse d'été garnie d'un mobilier en teck. Préparations bien balancées.
• Dit paviljoen staat in een woonwijk, vlak bij een kanaal, en heeft een modern ingerichte restaurantzaal. Teakhouten meubilair op het zomerterras. Goed uitgebalanceerde keuken.

XX **Kasteel Maurick,** Dijk van Maurick 3 (sur N 2), ✉ 5261 NA, ☎ (0 73) 657 91 08, *info@maurick.nl, Fax (0 73) 656 04 40,* – P – 25 à 170. AE MC VISA. X y
fermé du 22 au 29 fév., 25 juil.-8 août, 26 déc.-1er janv., sam. midi et dim. – **Repas** *Lunch 30* – carte 50 à 61.
• Un jardin bichonné agrémente cet adorable petit château protégé par un pont-levis. Terrasse estivale sur cour intérieure. L'endroit se prête bien à la tenue de banquets.
• Een verzorgd aangelegde tuin siert dit fraaie kasteeltje met ophaalbrug. In de zomer wordt op de binnenplaats een terras ingericht. De lokatie leent zich goed voor partijen.

X **De Heer Kocken,** Taalstraat 173, ✉ 5261 BD, ☎ (0 73) 656 94 94, *Fax (0 73) 657 69 80,* – P. AE MC VISA.
fermé 1 sem. carnaval, mi-juil.-mi-août, dim. et lundi – **Repas** (dîner seult) carte 40 à 53.
• Adresse un peu "mode", très courtisée à l'heure du dîner. Cuisine actuelle et cadre contemporain produisant son effet. On aperçoit De Heer Kocken œuvrer aux fourneaux.
• Succesvol avondrestaurant met trendy sfeer. De eigentijdse keuken en moderne setting werpen vrucht af. De heer Kocken zelf staat achter het fornuis.

HEUSDEN *Noord-Brabant 532 P 12 et 715 G 6 – 43 138 h.*

Amsterdam 96 – Utrecht 57 – 's-Hertogenbosch 19 – Breda 43 – Rotterdam 67.

XXX **In den Verdwaalde Koogel** avec ch, Vismarkt 1, ✉ 5256 BC, ☎ (0 416) 66 19 33, *info@indenverdwaaldekoogel.nl, Fax (0 416) 66 12 95,* – rest, – 30. MC VISA JCB
fermé 27 déc.-12 janv. – **Repas** *(fermé dim. du 7 nov. au 14 mars) Lunch 27* – 33/72 bc, ♀ – **12 ch** 78/86 – ½ P 70/85.
• Restaurant aménagé dans une jolie maison du 17e surveillant le Vismarkt (marché au poisson) d'un bourg fluvial au passé mouvementé de place forte. Chambres pratiques.
• Restaurant in een mooi 17e-eeuws pand in een garnizoenstadje aan de rivier, dat als vesting roerige tijden heeft gekend. Praktische kamers.

HILLEGOM *Zuid-Holland 531 M 9, 532 M 9 et 715 E 5 – 20 845 h.*

Amsterdam 36 – Den Haag 33 – Haarlem 12.

Flora, Hoofdstraat 55, ✉ 2181 EB, ☎ (0 252) 51 51 00, *Fax (0 252) 52 93 14,* – , , rest, – 25 à 200. AE MC VISA
Repas *(fermé 24, 25 et 30 déc.)* 25 – **27 ch** *(fermé 30 déc.)* 86 – ½ P 45/55.
• L'enseigne de cet hôtel en dit long sur la vocation de la région, à savoir la floriculture. Séjour sans histoire dans des chambres sommairement équipées, mais bien tenues. À table, florilège de recettes au goût du jour et bouquet de menus.
• De naam spreekt boekdelen over de roeping van de streek, de bollenteelt. Eenvoudige, maar goed onderhouden kamers voor een ongestoorde nachtrust. Aan tafel krijgt u een bloemlezing van eigentijdse gerechten en een boeket menu's aangeboden.

HILVARENBEEK *Noord-Brabant* 532 P 14 et 715 G 7 – *14 851 h.*
Amsterdam 120 – 's-Hertogenbosch 31 – Eindhoven 30 – Tilburg 12 – Turnhout 33.

Herberg St Petrus, Gelderstraat 1, ✉ 5081 AA, ☎ (0 13) 505 21 66, *Fax (0 13) 505 46 19,* – . ch
fermé 25 et 26 déc. et du 5 au 8 janv. – **Repas** carte 30 à 38, ♀ – **6 ch** 50/65.
• Cette petite auberge postée sur le Vrijthof, devant l'église, constitue un point de départ valable pour partir à la découverte d'un bourg touristique. Menues chambres. Salle à manger décorée de statues de saints.
• Deze kleine herberg aan het vrijthof, tegenover de kerk, is een goede uitvalsbasis voor verkenning van het toeristische plaatsje. Kleine kamers. De eetzaal is opgeluisterd met heiligenbeelden.

Aub. Het Kookhuys, Vrijthof 27, ✉ 5081 CB, ☎ (0 13) 505 14 33, *kookhuys@planet.nl, Fax (0 13) 505 49 23,* – . .
fermé du 9 au 23 août et lundi – **Repas** (dîner seult sauf dim.) 31/44.
• Restaurant dont la jolie terrasse verte où bruisse une fontaine fera des heureux, avec la complicité du soleil. Salle à manger moderne. Le soir, lumière tamisée.
• Dit restaurant heeft een mooi, groen terras met fontein, waar het bij warm weer werkelijk genieten is. Moderne eetzaal. 's Avonds gedempt licht.

Pieter Bruegel, Gelderstraat 7, ✉ 5081 AA, ☎ (0 13) 505 17 58 – .
fermé carnaval, vacances bâtiment, du 26 au 31 déc., mardi et merc. – **Repas** (dîner seult) carte 40 à 60, ♀.
• Pieter Bruegel, qui n'était pas le dernier des bons vivants, aurait pu se plaire à cette table du cœur de la localité. Plats classico-traditionnels. Atmosphère hollandaise.
• Pieter Bruegel, zelf een ware bon-vivant, zou het best naar zijn zin hebben gehad in dit restaurant in het centrum. Klassiek-traditionele keuken. Hollandse ambiance.

HILVERSUM *Noord-Holland* 532 Q 9 et 715 G 5 – *83 096 h.*
Voir *Hôtel de ville*★ *(Raadhuis)* Y **H** – *Le Gooi*★ *(Het Gooi).*
Env. *par* ④ : *7 km, Étangs de Loosdrecht*★★ *(Loosdrechtse Plassen).*
Noordse Bosje 1, ✉ *1211 BD,* ☎ *(0 35) 624 17 51, info@vvvhollandsmidden.nl, Fax (0 35) 623 74 60.*
Amsterdam 34 ⑤ – *Utrecht 20* ③ – *Apeldoorn 65* ① – *Zwolle 87* ①

Plan page ci-contre

Lapershoek, Utrechtseweg 16, ✉ 1213 TS, ☎ (0 35) 623 13 41, *info@lapershoek.nl, Fax (0 35) 628 43 60,* – – 25 à 300. . X e
Repas Lunch 35 – carte 37 à 57, ♀ – 15 – **80 ch** 145/175 – ½ P 75.
• Spécialisée dans la tenue de séminaires, cette villa donnant sur un rond-point dispose d'une douzaine de salles de réunions et de petites chambres sobrement équipées. Bon moment de table au restaurant Vivaldi ou repas simple dans la véranda.
• Dit hotel is geheel afgestemd op bijeenkomsten en seminars. De villa kijkt uit op een rotonde en beschikt over een twaalftal vergaderzalen en kleine, eenvoudige kamers. Culinair avontuur in restaurant Vivaldi of een eenvoudige maaltijd in de serre.

Richard's, Koninginneweg 30, ✉ 1217 LA, ☎ (0 35) 623 24 44, *hilversum@richardshotel.nl, Fax (0 35) 623 49 76,* . Y z
Repas *(fermé vend., sam. et dim.)* (dîner seult) 22 – **58 ch** 90/115 – ½ P 110/135.
• Proche du Media Park, imposante villa complétée, à l'arrière, d'une construction moderne où se répartissent des chambres spacieuses et paisibles.
• Deze imposante villa nabij het Media Park heeft aan de achterzijde een moderne aanbouw waarin ruime, rustige kamers liggen.

Ravel sans rest, Emmastraat 35, ✉ 1213 AJ, ☎ (0 35) 621 06 85, *info@ravel.nl, Fax (0 35) 624 37 77,* – . . Z d
19 ch 100/130.
• Villa résidentielle où l'on séjourne dans des chambres personnalisées avec recherche. Au petit-déj', vue ressourçante sur la terrasse et sa pièce d'eau tapissée de nénuphars.
• In deze villa verblijft u in smaakvol ingerichte kamers die alle een eigen karakter hebben. Aan het ontbijt, inspirerend uitzicht op het terras en de vijver met waterlelies.

Spandershoeve, Bussumergrintweg 46, ✉ 1217 BS, ☎ (0 35) 621 11 30, *Fax (0 35) 623 51 53,* , Cuisine indonésienne – . . V s
fermé dern. sem. déc., sam. midi et dim. midi – **Repas** Lunch 25 – 40, carte 29 à 40.
• Temple de la gastronomie orientale. Une fine cuisine indonésienne s'y conçoit depuis plus de vingt ans. Élégant cadre "javanais", accueil et service sans reproche. À vénérer !
• Tempel van oriëntaalse gastronomie. Al ruim 20 jaar wordt hier een fijne Indonesische keuken bereid. Elegant Javaans decor, onberispelijke ontvangst en bediening. Goddelijk !
Spéc. Oedang Boemboe Bali (crevettes). Ajam Pangang Djakarta (poulet). Deng-deng Belado (bœuf)

HILVERSUM

AGGLOMÉRATION

CENTRE

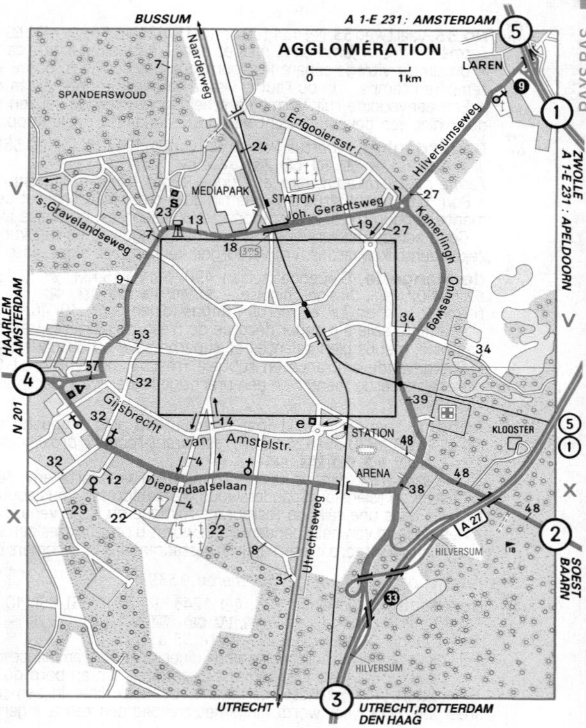

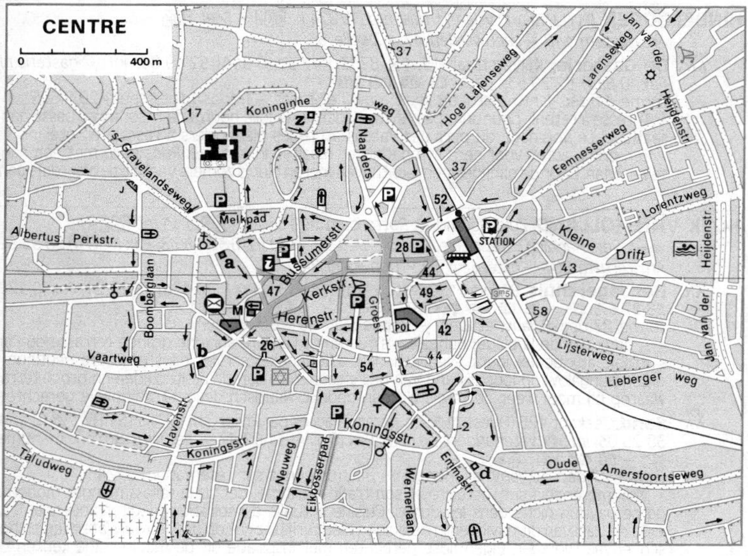

XX **No.33,** Vaartweg 33, ✉ 1211 JD, ☎ (0 35) 621 45 56, ☂ - P. AE ⓓ MC VISA. ✂ Z b
fermé 27 déc.-5 janv., sam. midi et dim. – **Repas** Lunch 28 – carte 32 à 47, ♀.
◆ Un simple vitrage sépare les fourneaux des convives, parmi lesquels on reconnaît, de temps en temps, l'un ou l'autre visage familier du petit écran hollandais.
◆ Een eenvoudige ruit vormt de scheidslijn tussen de keuken en de gasten. Af en toe duikt hier een bekend gezicht van de Nederlandse televisie op.

XX **De Uitdaging,** Albertus Perkstraat 3, ✉ 1217 NK, ☎ (0 35) 624 93 13, *deuitdaging @xs4all.nl* – ▤. AE ⓓ MC VISA JCB. ✂ Y a
fermé mi-juil.-mi-août, dim. et lundi – **Repas** (dîner seult jusqu'à 23 h) 33/80 bc, ♀.
◆ Bon "p'tit resto" situé à mi-chemin du secteur piétonnier et de la cubique Raadhuis, qui mérite le coup d'œil. Préparations assez élaborées, en phase avec l'époque.
◆ Goed adresje halverwege het voetgangersgebied en het kubusvormige Raadhuis, dat zeker een blik waard is. Vrij verzorgde keuken met eigentijdse gerechten.

XX **de Mangerie,** Diependaalselaan 490, ✉ 1215 KM, ☎ (0 35) 672 07 84, *Fax (0 35) 672 04 07,* ☂, Cuisine chinoise – ▤. AE ⓓ MC VISA. ✂ X v
fermé 2 sem. en juil. et mardi – **Repas** (dîner seult) 30/40.
◆ Apaisante salle à manger décorée de fresques délicates, recettes issues des provinces de Chine, menus bien balancés et superbe cave où Bacchus tend les bras au Bouddha.
◆ Rustgevende ambiance en subtiele fresco's, gerechten uit Chinese provincies, goed uitgebalanceerde menu's en een prachtige kelder waar Bacchus de armen naar Boeddha uitstrekt.

X **Robert,** Spanderslaan 1 (par Naarderweg puis à gauche par Bussumergrintweg), ✉ 1217 DB, ☎ (0 35) 624 56 95, *restaurant-robert@proximedia.nl, Fax (0 35) 672 05 40,* ☂ - P. AE ⓓ MC VISA. ✂ V
fermé sam. midi, dim. et lundi – **Repas** Lunch 33 – carte env. 38, ♀.
◆ Postée en lisière du Spanderswoud, cette adresse vous soumet son attrayante carte actuelle dans une salle de restaurant rustique ou, l'été venu, sur une agréable terrasse.
◆ Aan de rand van het Spanderswoud wordt u op dit adres een aantrekkelijke, eigentijdse kaart gepresenteerd in een rustieke restaurantzaal of 's zomers op een aangenaam terras.

à 's-Graveland *par ④ : 7 km* Ⓒ *Wijdemeren 9 339 h :*

XX **Berestein,** Zuidereinde 208, ✉ 1243 KR, ☎ (0 35) 656 10 30, *pc_peter@hetnet.nl, Fax (0 35) 656 98 44,* ☂ - ▤. AE MC VISA JCB
fermé lundi – **Repas** Lunch 28 – carte 33 à 47, ♀.
◆ Typique auberge hollandaise pour dîner dans une ambiance chaleureuse et détendue. Aux beaux jours, une jolie terrasse prend position au bord du chemin de halage.
◆ Karakteristiek Hollandse restaurant voor een diner in een gemoedelijke, ontspannen sfeer. Bij mooi weer wordt langs het trekpad een terras ingericht.

HINDELOOPEN (HYLPEN) *Fryslân* Ⓒ *Nijefurd 10 924 h.* 531 R 5 *et* 715 H 3.

Amsterdam 118 – Leeuwarden 47 – Zwolle 86.

XX **De Gasterie,** Kalverstraat 13, ✉ 8713 KV, ☎ (0 514) 52 19 86, *info@gasterie.nl, Fax (0 514) 52 20 53,* ☂ - AE ⓓ MC VISA
fermé 31 déc.-janv., mardi de sept. à avril et merc. – **Repas** (dîner seult) 29/45, ♀.
◆ Adresse à retenir pour un repas "sympa" dans une jolie bourgade frisonne au passé hanséatique. Le voisinage du port des yatchs attire les plaisanciers à l'escale en été.
◆ Een prima adres voor een "sympathieke" maaltijd in een leuk Fries dorp met een hanzeverleden. Door de nabijgelegen jachthaven meren hier 's zomers veel pleziervaarders aan.

HOEK VAN HOLLAND *Zuid-Holland* Ⓒ *Rotterdam 598 660 h.* 532 J 11 *et* 715 O 6.

vers Harwich : Stena Line, Stationsweg 10, ☎ (0 174) 38 93 33, Fax (0 174) 38 93 89.

Amsterdam 80 – Rotterdam 32 – Den Haag 24.

XX **Het Jagershuis,** Badweg 1 (Ouest : 1 km), ✉ 3151 HA, ☎ (0 174) 38 22 51, *Fax (0 174) 38 27 67,* ☂ - P. AE ⓓ MC VISA JCB
fermé 27 déc.-8 janv. et lundi. – **Repas** Lunch 18 – 30/60 bc.
◆ À deux pas de la plage, bungalow s'ouvrant à l'arrière sur une grande terrasse où l'on s'attable aux beaux jours. Préparations traditionnelles servies dans un cadre nautique.
◆ Een bungalow op loopafstand van het strand, met aan de achterzijde een groot terras waarop bij mooi weer de tafels worden gedekt. Nautisch decor. Traditionele gerechten.

XX **Sand,** Zeekant 125 (Ouest : 1,5 km, Strand - accès par Rivierkant), ✉ 3151 HW, ☎ (0 174) 38 25 03, *info@waterlandestate.com, Fax (0 174) 31 02 47,* ≤ estuaire et trafic maritime, ☂ - AE MC VISA JCB
fermé 27 déc.-10 janv. et merc. – **Repas** (déjeuner sur réservation) 31/43.
◆ Vue imprenable sur l'estuaire et son trafic maritime, depuis la salle à manger moderne de ce pavillon niché dans les dunes. Cuisine actuelle d'inspiration méditerranéenne.
◆ De eetzaal van dit paviljoen in de duinen biedt vrij uitzicht op de Nieuwe Waterweg en het scheepvaartverkeer. Eigentijdse gerechten met inspiratie uit de mediterrane keuken.

PAYS-BAS

HOENDERLOO *Gelderland* [C] *Apeldoorn 154 859 h.* 532 U 10 *et* 715 I 5.
Amsterdam 88 – Arnhem 21 – Apeldoorn 14.

Buitenlust, Apeldoornseweg 30, ✉ 7351 AB, ☎ (0 55) 378 13 62, *hotel-buitenlust@hetnet.nl, Fax (0 55) 378 17 29,* – TV P. MC VISA JCB. *fermé 21 déc.-janv.* – **Repas** *(fermé après 20 h 30) Lunch 20* – carte 27 à 39 – **14 ch** 70/75 – ½ P 58.
◆ Cette auberge familiale inondée de chlorophylle procure un toit idéal aux voyageurs souhaitant rayonner dans le parc national De Hoge Veluwe. Chambres fonctionnelles. Restaurant prolongé d'une véranda. Repas au jardin les jours ensoleillés.
◆ Dit familiehotel midden in een bosrijke omgeving biedt reizigers die het Nationaal Park De Hoge Veluwe willen bezoeken, een ideaal dak boven het hoofd. Functionele kamers. Restaurant met serre. Bij mooi weer wordt in de tuin geserveerd.

HOEVELAKEN *Gelderland* [C] *Nijkerk 37 327 h.* 532 R 9 *et* 715 H 5.
18 9 *à l'Est : 10 km à Voorthuizen, Hunnenweg 16,* ✉ *3781 NN,* ☎ *(0 342) 47 38 32, Fax (0 342) 47 10 37.*
Amsterdam 50 – Utrecht 28 – Arnhem 57 – Amersfoort 8 – Apeldoorn 42 – Zwolle 66.

De Klepperman, Oosterdorpsstraat 11, ✉ 3871 AA, ☎ (0 33) 253 41 20, *klepperman@bilderberg.nl, Fax (0 33) 253 74 34,* – rest, TV P – 25 à 225. AE MC VISA
Repas voir rest ***De Gasterie*** ci-après – ***Eethuys 't Backhuys*** (dîner seult) 30/49 bc, ♀ – 17 – **79 ch** 158/190 – ½ P 89/204.
◆ Ce confortable hôtel proche de l'autoroute se partage entre trois anciennes fermes traditionnelles du Sud de la Veluwe. Chambres garnies de meubles de style. Beauty center. Formule brasserie dans une atmosphère plaisante et décontractée.
◆ Dit zeer comfortabele hotel nabij de snelweg heeft zijn intrek genomen in drie traditionele, Zuid-Veluwse boerderijen. De kamers zijn met stijlmeubilair ingericht. Beautycenter. Brasserieformule in een prettige en ongedwongen sfeer.

XXX **De Gasterie** - H. De Klepperman, Oosterdorpsstraat 11, ✉ 3871 AA, ☎ (0 33) 253 41 20, *klepperman@bilderberg.nl, Fax (0 33) 253 74 34,* – P. AE MC VISA *fermé 18 juil.-29 août, sam. midi et dim.* – **Repas** *Lunch 30* – carte 49 à 58, ♀.
◆ Préparations d'aujourd'hui servies dans une ferme-fromagerie coquettement réaménagée. Grande salle à manger fleurie, avec cheminée centrale. Repas aux chandelles.
◆ Op dit adres worden eigentijdse gerechten geserveerd in een charmant verbouwde kaasboerderij. Grote, fleurige eetzaal met schouw in het midden. Diner bij kaarslicht.

De HOGE VELUWE (Nationaal Park) (Parc National de la HAUTE VELUWE) ★★★ : Musée *Kröller-Müller★★★ Gelderland* 532 U 10 *et* 715 I 5 *G. Hollande.*

HOLLANDSCHE RADING *Utrecht* 532 Q 9 *et* 715 G 5 – *voir à Maartensdijk.*

HOLLUM *Fryslân* 531 S 2 *et* 715 H 1 – *voir à Waddeneilanden (Ameland).*

HOLTEN *Overijssel* [C] *Rijssen-Holten 35 637 h.* 531 X 9, 532 X 9 *et* 715 K 5.
Voir *Natuurdiorama★ sur le Holterberg.*
Dorpsstraat 27, ✉ *7451 BR,* ☎ *(0 548) 36 15 33, info@vvvholten.nl, Fax (0 548) 36 69 54.*
Amsterdam 124 – Zwolle 40 – Apeldoorn 40 – Enschede 42.

AC Hotel, Langstraat 22 (sur A 1, sortie Struik), ✉ 7451 ND, ☎ (0 548) 36 26 80, *holten@autogrill.nl,* – TV P – 25 à 200. AE MC VISA
Repas (avec buffets) *Lunch 11* – carte 22 à 34 – 10 – **58 ch** 61/89, – 2 suites.
◆ Proximité immédiate de l'autoroute, grand parking à vue et chambres fonctionnelles correctement insonorisées ; au total, un AC Hotel "tout ce qu'il y a de plus classique".
◆ Directe nabijheid van de snelweg, grote parking in het zicht en functionele kamers die van goede geluidsisolatie zijn voorzien. Kortom : de klassieke formule van de keten.

sur le Holterberg :

XX **Hoog Holten** avec ch, Forthaarsweg 7, ✉ 7451 JS, ☎ (0 548) 36 13 06, *hoogholten@a1.nl, Fax (0 548) 36 30 75,* – TV P – 30. AE MC VISA JCB. rest
fermé 29 déc.-5 janv. – **Repas** *Lunch 30* – carte 38 à 51, ♀ – 13 – **22 ch** 75/110, – 2 suites – ½ P 85/115.
◆ Sur les hauteurs boisées, belle auberge où l'on trouve le gîte et le couvert. Décor intérieur soigné, salon-bibliothèque anglais, terrasse exquise et chambres douillettes.
◆ Dit mooie hotel-restaurant ligt midden in de bossen op de Holterberg. Verzorgd interieur, Engelse lounge-bibliotheek, verrukkelijk terras en behaaglijke kamers.

Bistro de Holterberg, Forthaarsweg 1, ✉ 7451 JS, ☎ (0 548) 36 38 49, *restaurant@bistrodeholterberg.nl, Fax (0 548) 36 51 12,* ←, ☂ - P. AE ⓓ ⓜⓒ VISA
fermé 2 prem. sem. janv. et lundi – **Repas** (dîner seult) 29/34.
• Plus d'un atout pour cette table perchée sur le Holterberg : belle cuisine au goût du jour, ambiance conviviale, service avenant et terrasse estivale dominant la vallée.
• Deze bistro op de Holterberg heeft zijn gasten heel wat te bieden : mooie eigentijdse keuken, gastvrije ambiance, vriendelijke bediening en zomerterras met uitzicht op het dal.

HOOFDDORP *Noord-Holland* 531 N 9, 532 N 9 *et* 715 F 5 – *voir à Amsterdam, environs.*

HOOFDPLAAT *Zeeland* Ⓒ *Sluis 24 755 h.* 532 G 14 *et* 715 C 7.
Amsterdam 205 – Middelburg 45 – Terneuzen 18 – Brugge 50.

De Kromme Watergang, Slijkplaat 6 (Ouest : 4 km, Slijkplaat), ✉ 4513 KK, ☎ (0 117) 34 86 96, *krommewatergang@zeelandnet.nl, Fax (0 117) 34 86 79,* ☂ - P. AE ⓜⓒ VISA
fermé 2 dern. sem. juin, début d'août, prem. sem. janv., lundi et mardi – **Repas** Lunch 40 – 64/107 bc, ♀.
• Bonne maison de bouche aménagée dans l'ancienne école du village. Par beau temps, repas-plaisir en terrasse, au bord d'un adorable jardin paysager. Produits régionaux.
• Goed restaurant in de voormalige dorpsschool. Bij mooi weer kan men de maaltijd genieten op het terras, dat uitkijkt op een bekoorlijke Engelse tuin. Regionale produkten.

HOOGEVEEN *Drenthe* 531 X 6 *et* 715 K 3 – *53 186 h.*
au Nord-Est : 7 km à Tiendeveen, Haarweg 22, ✉ *7936 TP,* ☎ *(0 528) 33 15 58, Fax (0 528) 33 14 77.*
Hoofdstraat 13, ✉ *7902 EA,* ☎ *(0 528) 26 83 73, vvvhoogeveen@planet.nl, Fax (0 528) 22 11 35.*
Amsterdam 155 – Assen 34 – Emmen 32 – Zwolle 45.

De Herberg, Hoogeveenseweg 27 (Nord : 2 km, Fluitenberg), ✉ 7931 TD, ☎ (0 528) 27 59 83, *Fax (0 528) 22 07 30,* ☂ - P. AE ⓜⓒ VISA
fermé vacances bâtiment, 29 déc.-6 janv., sam. midi, dim. et lundi – **Repas** Lunch 33 – 40/48, ♀.
• Accueil tout sourire, service avenant, décor intérieur coquet, registre culinaire actualisé, terrasse estivale dressée à l'arrière... Au total, une bonne petite adresse.
• Ontvangst met een glimlach, vriendelijke bediening, charmant interieur, eigentijds culinair register, zomerterras aan de achterkant... Wat wilt u nog meer ?

HOOG-SOEREN *Gelderland* 532 U 9 *et* 715 I 5 – *voir à Apeldoorn.*

HOORN *Noord-Holland* 531 P 7 *et* 715 G 4 – *66 458 h.*
Voir *Le vieux quartier*★ YZ – *Rode Steen*★ Z – *Façade*★ *du musée de la Frise Occidentale (Westfries Museum)* Z **M'** – *Veermanskade*★ Z.
au Nord-Est : 8 km à Westwoud, Zittend 19, ✉ *1617 KS,* ☎ *(0 228) 56 31 28, Fax (0 228) 56 27 40.*
Veemarkt 4, ✉ *1621 JC,* ☎ *(0 72) 511 42 84, info@vvvhoorn.nl, Fax (0 229) 21 50 23.*
Amsterdam *40 ② – Alkmaar 26 ② – Enkhuizen 19 ① – Den Helder 52 ③*

Plan page ci-contre

Petit Nord, Kleine Noord 53, ✉ 1621 JE, ☎ (0 229) 21 27 50, *hotelpetitnord@quicknet.nl, Fax (0 229) 21 57 45* – |♦| ⇆ ▤ TV – 🏃 25 à 80. AE ⓓ ⓜⓒ VISA. ✂ Y r
Repas ***New Jersey*** *(fermé 31 déc.)* (cuisine asiatique, déjeuner sur réservation) 28/38 bc, ♀ – **33 ch** ☐ 56/75 – ½ P 66/91.
• À défaut de "Grand Nord", offrez-vous donc le Petit Nord, hôtel format poche occupant deux maisons au voisinage de la gare et du lac. Chambres sans reproche. Restaurant au décor intérieur contemporain. Éventail de préparations tournées vers l'Asie.
• Aangezien Grand Nord verstek laat gaan, is zijn broertje een goede optie. Dit hotel in "zakformaat" beslaat twee panden in de buurt van het station en het meer. Keurige kamers. Restaurant met modern decor en Aziatisch georiënteerde gerechten.

L'Oasis de la Digue, De Hulk 16, ✉ 1622 DZ, ☎ (0 229) 55 33 44, *info@loasis.nl,* ←, ☂ - P. AE ⓜⓒ VISA par Westerdijk X
fermé du 1er au 14 août, sam. midi, dim. et lundi – **Repas** Lunch 27 – 43/60 bc.
• Agréable restaurant aménagé au bord de l'IJsselmeer, dans une ancienne station de pompage. Salle à manger et terrasse d'été surplombent le polder, la digue et le plan d'eau.
• Aangenaam restaurant aan het IJsselmeer, in een voormalig polderbemaling. Eetzaal en zomerterras kijken uit over het land, de dijk en het water.

HOORN

Achterstraat . . . . Y 2
Berkhouterweg . . . . X 3
Bierkade . . . . Z 5
Breed . . . . Y
Breestraat . . . . Z 6
van Dedemstraat . . . . X 8
Gedempte Turfhaven . . . . . Y 9
Gouw . . . . Y
Grote Noord . . . . YZ
Hoge Vest . . . . Y 10
Joh. Messchaerstr. . . . . . . Y 12
Joh. Poststraat . . . . X 14
Keern . . . . Y 15
Kerkplein . . . . Z 17
Kerkstraat . . . . Z 18
Koepoortsplein . . . . Y 20
Koepoortsweg . . . . X 21
Korenmarkt . . . . Z 23
Korte Achterstr. . . . . Y 24
Lange Kerkstraat . . . . Z 26
Liornestraat . . . . X 27
Muntstraat . . . . Y 29
Nieuwendam . . . . Z 30
Nieuwsteeg . . . . Y 32
Nieuwstraat . . . . YZ 33
Noorderstraat . . . . Y 35
Noorderveemarkt . . . . Y 36
Onder de Boompjes . . . . . Y 38
Oude Doelenkade . . . . Z 39
Scharloo . . . . Y 41
Slapershaven . . . . Z 42
Spoorsingel . . . . Y 44
Stationweg . . . . Y 45
Veermanskade . . . . Z 47
Westerdijk . . . . Z 48
Wijdebrugsteeg . . . . Z 50
Zon . . . . Z 51
Zwaagmergouw . . . . X 53

LEEUWARDEN DEN OEVER — 3 — E 22 — A 7 — AMSTERDAM ALKMAAR — 2 — NIEUWE STEEN — POL — KERSENBOOGERD — DE BLAUWE BERG — Keern — S 9 — Willemsweg — 1 — ENKHUIZEN — GROTE WAAL — Westerdijk — HOORNSCHE HOP — IJSSELMEER — 0 — 1 km — X

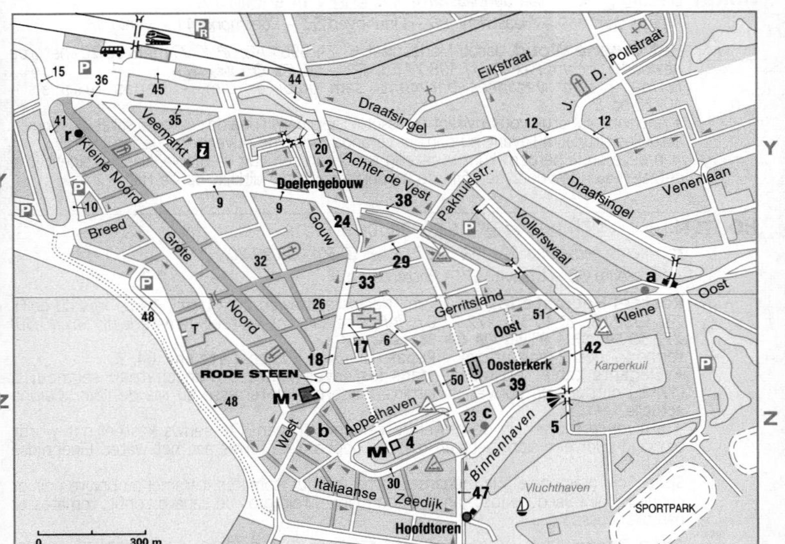

XX **La Porte de l'Est,** Kleine Oost 39, ✉ 1621 GR, ℘ (0 229) 21 31 15, *Fax (0 229) 21 31 15,* Z a
– ▤. MC VISA
fermé lundi – **Repas** (dîner seult) 35/40, ♀.
◆ Cet ancien bistrot promu maison de bouche jouxte la porte de l'Est et abrite sa plaisante terrasse estivale sous une tonnelle où grimpe la vigne vierge. Salon "club" douillet.
◆ Dit restaurantje vlak bij de Oosterpoort heeft een charmant terras ingericht onder een door wingerd overwoekerde pergola. Behaaglijke salon met clubfauteuils.

Hendrickje Stoffels, Oude Doelenkade 5, ✉ 1621 BH, ☎ (0 229) 21 04 17, *info@hendrickje-stoffels.nl, Fax (0 229) 21 04 17*, – AE ⓓ ⓜ VISA Z c
fermé prem. sem. juil., 2 dern. sem. janv., merc. et jeudi – **Repas** (dîner seult) 26/36, ♀.
◆ Jolie maisonnette où flotte une atmosphère de brasserie, face au port des yachts et près de la Hoofdtoren marquant l'entrée des bassins. Carte classique. Cave franco-ibérique.
◆ Leuk huisje met gezellige brasseriesfeer, tegenover de jachthaven bij de Hoofdtoren, bij de ingang van de bassins. Klassieke kaart. Frans-Spaanse wijnselectie.

De Zomertuin, West 52, ✉ 1621 AW, ☎ (0 229) 21 56 57, *de-zomertuin@wanadoo.nl, Fax (0 229) 27 90 74* – ⓜ VISA Z b
fermé lundi et mardi – **Repas** (dîner seult) 25, ♀.
◆ Établissement tout proche de la pittoresque Rode Steen (Poids public et musée d'histoire). Cuisine bourgeoise actualisée et salle de restaurant aux accents méditerranéens.
◆ Restaurant vlak bij het Rode Steen (Waag en historisch museum). Traditionele keuken met een modern accent en restaurantzaal in mediterrane sfeer.

Den HOORN *Noord-Holland* 531 N 4 *et* 715 F 2 – *voir à Waddeneilanden (Texel).*

HORN *Limburg* 532 U 15 *et* 715 I 8 – *voir à Roermond.*

HORST *Limburg* C *Horst aan de Maas 28 476 h.* 532 V 14 *et* 715 J 7.
Amsterdam 160 – Maastricht 86 – Eindhoven 53 – Roermond 41 – Venlo 13.

Het Groene Woud, Jacob Merlostraat 6, ✉ 5961 AB, ☎ (0 77) 398 38 20, *hetgroenewoud@cs.com, Fax (0 77) 398 77 55*, – AE ⓓ ⓜ VISA JCB
fermé 2 sem. vacances bâtiment, sam. midi et dim. – **Repas** Lunch 30 – 40/70 bc, ♀.
◆ Ancienne auberge vous invitant à passer à table dans l'une de ses jolies salles classiques-actuelles situées à l'avant ou dans la véranda moderne ouverte sur le jardin.
◆ In deze oude herberg kunt u gezellig tafelen in een van de mooie, klassiek-eigentijdse eetzalen aan de voorzijde of in de moderne serre die uitkijkt op de tuin.

HOUTEN *Utrecht* 532 P 10 *et* 715 G 5 – *38 106 h.*
Heemsteedseweg 32a, ✉ 3992 LS, ☎ (0 30) 636 99 20.
Amsterdam 38 – Utrecht 12 – Rotterdam 63.

Kasteel Heemstede (van Doorn), Heemsteedseweg 20 (Ouest : 4 km, près du golf), ✉ 3992 LS, ☎ (0 30) 272 22 07, *info@restaurant-kasteelheemstede.nl, Fax (0 30) 272 30 39*, – P. AE ⓓ ⓜ VISA JCB.
fermé 27 déc.-9 janv. et dim. – **Repas** Lunch 38 – 108 bc, carte env. 64, ♀.
◆ Élégante table retranchée dans les caves voûtées d'un château seigneurial (17e s.) entouré de douves et jardins. Passerelle et terrasse au ras de l'eau. Cuisine actuelle.
◆ Stijlvol restaurant in de gewelfde kelders van een 17e-eeuws kasteel dat wordt omringd door een slotgracht en tuinen. Loopbrug en terras aan het water. Eigentijdse keuken.
Spéc. Foie gras poêlé à la rhubarbe. Tarte Tatin de tomates, caramel au poivre noir et coquilles Saint-Jacques (oct.-janv.). Thon mariné, foie gras de canard confit, tomates et pamplemousse

Coco Pazzo, Plein 20 (Oude Dorp), ✉ 3991 DL, ☎ (0 30) 637 14 03, *Fax (0 30) 637 18 23*, , Avec cuisine italienne – AE ⓜ VISA.
fermé 19 juil.-9 août, 25 déc.-4 janv., sam. midi, dim. et lundi – **Repas** 28/50 bc, ♀.
◆ Ce restaurant sympathique concocte une cuisine méditerranéenne goûteuse, zigzaguant gaiement entre la Botte et l'Hexagone. Menus intéressants. Belle cave franco-transalpine.
◆ Sympathiek restaurant met een smakelijke mediterrane keuken die vrolijk heen en weer pendelt tussen de Laars en Frankrijk. Interessante menu's. Frans-Italiaanse wijnkaart.

HOUTHEM *Limburg* 532 T 17 – *voir à Valkenburg.*

HUISDUINEN *Noord-Holland* 531 N 5 – *voir à Den Helder.*

HUIZEN *Noord-Holland* 531 *Q 9,* 532 *Q 9 et* 715 *G 5 – 42 230 h.*
Amsterdam 31 – Apeldoorn 65 – Hilversum 10 – Utrecht 27.

Newport, Labradorstroom 75, ✉ 1271 DE, ☎ (0 35) 528 96 00, *info@hotelnewport.nl, Fax (0 35) 528 96 11,* ←, – – 25 à 250. AE VISA JCB.
Repas voir rest ***l'Escale*** ci-après – ☕ 15 – **14 ch** 222, – 47 suites.
• La vue imprenable sur le port de plaisance du Gooimeer profite à chacune des chambres de ce petit palace contemporain. Communs modernes, au luxe discret.
• Alle kamers in dit kleine, eigentijdse kwaliteitshotel hebben vrij uitzicht op de jachthaven van het Gooimeer. De moderne, gemeenschappelijke ruimten ademen bescheiden luxe.

l'Escale - H. Newport, Labradorstroom 75, ✉ 1271 DE, ☎ (0 35) 528 96 00, *info@hotelnewport.nl, Fax (0 35) 528 96 11,* ← marina, – . AE VISA JCB.
fermé dim. – **Repas** *Lunch 23* – 30/57 bc, ♀.
• L'escale idéale si vous posez vos valises au Newport : salle à manger en accord avec son temps, repas au goût du jour et terrasse d'été embrassant la marina du regard.
• Een ideale culinaire ankerplaats voor wie zijn bivak opslaat in het Newport : eetzaal met moderne ambiance, eigentijdse keuken en zomerterras met uitzicht op de jachthaven.

HULST *Zeeland* 532 *J 15 et* 715 *D 8 – 27 840 h.*
Grote Markt 19, ✉ 4561 EA, ☎ (0 114) 38 92 99, hulst@vvvzvl.nl, Fax (0 114) 38 91 35.
Amsterdam 196 – Antwerpen 32 – Middelburg 56 – Sint-Niklaas 16.

L'Aubergerie, van der Maelstedeweg 4a, ✉ 4561 GT, ☎ (0 114) 31 98 30, *laubergerie@zeelandnet.nl, Fax (0 114) 31 14 31* – – 30. AE VISA. rest
Repas *(fermé 20 déc.-6 janv.)* (dîner seult jusqu'à 20 h 30) carte 26 à 34 – **26 ch** ☕ 53/75 – ½ P 65.
• Hôtel familial situé en léger retrait du circuit touristique de Hulst, ancienne place forte et capitale de la région frontalière dite des Quatre-Métiers (Vier Ambachten).
• Dit familiehotel ligt wat buiten het toeristische circuit van Hulst, een oude vestingplaats en hoofdstad van de grensstreek die de Vier Ambachten wordt genoemd.

Napoleon, Stationsplein 10, ✉ 4561 GC, ☎ (0 114) 31 37 91, *info@restaurantnapoleon.nl, Fax (0 114) 31 67 82,* – AE VISA
fermé du 23 au 26 fév., du 12 au 29 juil., mardi soir et merc. – **Repas** carte 28 à 49.
• Déjà plus de 30 ans de présence pour cette table traditionnelle à l'enseigne impériale. Pas de Waterloo en vue depuis la reprise de l'affaire par la génération montante !
• Al ruim dertig jaar is dit traditionele restaurant met de keizerlijke naam een vertrouwd beeld in Hulst. Geen Waterloo in zicht sinds de jongere generatie de scepter zwaait !

HUMMELO *Gelderland* C *Hummelo en Keppel 4 516 h.* 532 *W 10 et* 715 *J 5.*
à l'Ouest : 3 km à Hoog-Keppel, Oude Zutphenseweg 15, ✉ 6997 CH, ☎ (0 314) 38 14 16, Fax (0 314) 36 65 23.
Amsterdam 126 – Arnhem 29 – Apeldoorn 37.

De Gouden Karper, Dorpsstraat 9, ✉ 6999 AA, ☎ (0 314) 38 12 14, *Fax (0 314) 38 22 38,* – – 25 à 250. AE VISA
Repas carte 29 à 41, ♀ – **12 ch** ☕ 41/78.
• Une Carpe d'Or (Gouden Karper) frétille sur la devanture de cette auberge rustique fondée en 1642, l'année précise où Rembrandt exécuta sa fameuse Ronde de nuit. Salle de restaurant restituant l'ambiance d'un vieux café de village.
• Een gouden karper spartelt aan de voorzijde van dit rustieke hotel-restaurant, dat dateert uit 1642, hèt jaar waarin Rembrandt zijn beroemde Nachtwacht schilderde. De restaurantzaal ademt de sfeer van een oud dorpscafé.

HYLPEN *Fryslân – voir Hindeloopen.*

Dans ce guide
un même symbole, un même mot,
imprimé en rouge ou en ***noir****, en maigre ou en* ***gras****,*
n'ont pas tout à fait la même signification.
Lisez attentivement les pages explicatives.

IJMUIDEN *Noord-Holland* C *Velsen 67 407 h.* 531 M 8 *et* 715 E 4.

Voir *Écluses★.*

à Velsen-Zuid, Het Hoge Land 2, ✉ 1981 LT, Recreatieoord Spaarnwoude ☎ (0 23) 538 27 08, Fax (0 23) 538 72 74.

vers Newcastle : DFDS Seaways, Felison Terminal, Sluisplein 33 ☎ (0 255) 54 66 66.

Zeeweg 189, ✉ 1971 HB, ☎ (0 255) 51 56 11, ijm@vvvzk.nl, Fax (0 255) 52 42 26.

Amsterdam 25 – Haarlem 14 – Alkmaar 26.

Holiday Inn Seaport Beach, Kennemerboulevard 250 (Strand), ✉ 1976 EG, ☎ (0 255) 56 69 99, *info@holidayinn-ijmuiden.nl, Fax (0 255) 56 69 00,* ←, – – 25 à 450. AE VISA JCB
Repas Lunch 31 – carte env. 37, ♀ – 18 – **146 ch** 195/229 – ½ P 163/277.
◆ Enseigne adéquate, vu la position stratégique qu'occupe ce bel hôtel de chaîne : on contemple le front de mer depuis le balcon de chaque chambre. Restaurant et terrasse procurent également une échappée sur les dunes et le port des yachts.
◆ Treffende naam gezien de strategische ligging van dit mooie ketenhotel : de kamers hebben allemaal een balkon met uitzicht op de zee. Het restaurant en het terras kijken ook uit op de duinen en de jachthaven.

Augusta, Oranjestraat 98 (direction Sluizen), ✉ 1975 DD, ☎ (0 255) 51 42 17, *info@augusta.nl, Fax (0 255) 53 47 03,* – rest, – 25 à 100. AE VISA JCB.
Repas *(fermé 19 juil.-2 août, sam. midi et dim. midi)* Lunch 25 – carte 41 à 51, ♀ – **25 ch** *(fermé 24 et 25 déc.)* 70/120.
◆ Ensemble de maisons bourgeoises "1900" aménagées dans le style Art déco. Les chambres ne manquent ni de cachet, ni d'ampleur, sauf les singles, nettement plus menues. À l'heure du repas, on s'attable dans une atmosphère nostalgique.
◆ Dit hotel-restaurant omvat enkele herenhuizen uit rond 1900 en is in art deco ingericht. Het ontbreekt de kamers zeker niet aan cachet of ruimte, behalve de eenpersoons, die beduidend kleiner zijn. Maaltijden in een nostalgische ambiance.

à Velsen-Zuid *sortie IJmuiden sur A 9* C *Velsen :*

Het Roode Hert, Zuiderdorpstraat 15, ✉ 1981 BG, ☎ (0 255) 51 57 97, *info@roodehert.nl, Fax (0 255) 52 31 55,* – . VISA JCB.
fermé 27 déc.-4 janv., sam. midi, dim. midi et lundi – **Repas** Lunch 35 – carte 45 à 61, ♀.
◆ Charmante auberge du 17e s. située dans un quartier pittoresque, avec ses nombreuses façades agrémentées de pignons à redans. Cadre rustique et cuisine au goût du jour.
◆ Restaurant in een charmante herberg uit de 17e eeuw, in een karakteristieke wijk waar tal van façades met trapgevels zijn bekroond. Rustieke ambiance en eigentijdse keuken.

Beeckestijn, Rijksweg 136, ✉ 1981 LD, ☎ (0 255) 51 44 69, *Fax (0 255) 51 12 66,* ←, – – 80. AE VISA
fermé lundi et mardi – **Repas** carte 30 à 44.
◆ Les grilles du portail s'ouvrent sur une petite "folie" du 18e s., au milieu d'un grand parc. On ripaille dans les dépendances, bien équipées pour la tenue de banquets.
◆ De hekken van de poort geven toegang tot een 18e-eeuwse buitenplaats in een groot park. Het restaurant bevindt zich in een koetshuis. Goede faciliteiten voor partijen.

IJSSELSTEIN *Utrecht* 532 P 10 *et* 715 G 5 – *32 401 h.*

Amsterdam 47 – Utrecht 14 – Breda 61 – 's-Hertogenbosch 45 – Rotterdam 60.

Les Arcades, Weidstraat 1, ✉ 3401 DL, ☎ (0 30) 688 39 01, *info@lesarcades.nl, Fax (0 30) 687 15 74* – 80. AE VISA JCB
fermé 19 juil.-9 août, sam. midi et dim. – **Repas** Lunch 30 – carte env. 46.
◆ Le couvert est dressé sous les jolies voûtes de la cave - plusieurs fois centenaire - de l'ancienne salle du Conseil communal. Cuisine classique revisitée.
◆ De fraaie gewelven van een eeuwenoude kelder vormen het decor van dit restaurant onder het voormalige stadhuis. Klassieke keuken in een eigentijds jasje.

JOURE (DE JOUWER) *Fryslân* C *Skarsterlân 27 239 h.* 531 T 5 *et* 715 I 3.

au Sud : 7,5 km à Sint Nicolaasga, Legemeersterweg 16, ✉ 8527 DS, ☎ (0 513) 49 94 66, Fax (0 513) 49 97 77.

Midstraat 99, ✉ 8501 AH, ☎ (0 513) 41 60 30, vvv@joure.nl, Fax (0 513) 41 52 82.

Amsterdam 122 – Leeuwarden 37 – Sneek 14 – Zwolle 67.

't Plein, Douwe Egbertsplein 1a, ✉ 8501 AB, ☎ (0 513) 41 70 70, *plein@euronet.nl, Fax (0 513) 41 72 21,* – . AE VISA
fermé du 10 au 20 oct., 31 déc.-12 janv., sam. midi et dim. – **Repas** 33/66 bc, ♀.
◆ Maison basse postée sur une placette du centre de Joure, ville natale d'un certain Douwe Egbert. Carte actuelle assortie de menus bien composés.
◆ Het lage restaurantpand staat aan een pleintje in het centrum van Joure, de geboortestad van Douwe Egbert. Actuele kaart met goed samengestelde menu's.

KAAG *Zuid-Holland* Ⓒ *Alkemade 14 409 h.* 532 M 9.

Amsterdam 42 – Rotterdam 60 – Den Haag 25 – Haarlem 22.

XX **Tante Kee,** Julianalaan 14 (par bac), ✉ 2159 LA, ☎ (0 252) 54 42 06, *Fax (0 252) 54 52 90*, ≤, 🏖, ⚓ – P. AE MC VISA. ✈
fermé du 2 au 16 janv. – **Repas** 25/32.
• Auberge à dénicher sur une île-polder quadrillée de petits canaux, près d'un village pittoresque. Terrasse estivale panoramique au bord du Kagerplassen. Ponton d'amarrage.
• Restaurant op een eiland dicht bij een pittoresk dorp, in een polder waar tal van kanaaltjes doorheen stromen. Panoramisch zomerterras aan de Kagerplassen. Aanlegsteiger.

KAART *Fryslân* 531 Q 2 – *voir à Waddeneilanden (Terschelling).*

KAATSHEUVEL *Noord-Brabant* Ⓒ *Loon op Zand 23 058 h.* 532 P 13 *et* 715 G 7.

Voir *De Efteling★★.*

⛳18 *Veldstraat 6, ✉ 5176 NB, ☎ (0 416) 28 83 99, Fax (0 416) 28 84 39.*

Amsterdam 107 – 's-Hertogenbosch 26 – Breda 25 – Tilburg 12.

Efteling, Horst 31, ✉ 5171 RA, ☎ (0 416) 28 71 11, *Fax (0 416) 28 71 99*, 🏖, 🚲 – 🛗 ⇔, ▤ ch, TV ♿ P – 🏛 25 à 275. MC VISA. ✈ rest
Repas carte 26 à 37 – ☕ 15 – **120 ch** 95.
• Aux portes d'Efteling (parc d'attractions), architecture moderne assez fantaisiste, évoquant ces châteaux forts des contes de fées. Junior suites avec décor à thème.
• Dit moderne, vrij fantasievolle bouwwerk aan de rand van het attractiepark de Efteling is net een sprookjeskasteel. Junior suites met themadecor.

XX **De Molen,** Vaartstraat 102, ✉ 5171 JG, ☎ (0 416) 53 02 30, *info@restaurantdemolen.nl, Fax (0 416) 53 00 31*, 🏖 – TV P. AE ⓓ MC VISA
fermé carnaval, dern. sem. juil.-prem. sem. août, sam. midi, dim. midi et lundi – **Repas** Lunch 33 – 44/79 bc, ♀.
• Moulin à vent - toujours en activité - promu restaurant dont la carte s'acoquine aux saveurs du moment. Petit détail : le pain est réalisé avec la farine obtenue sur place.
• Een nog altijd bedrijvige windmolen vormt het decor van dit restaurant, waar de kaart de smaak van het moment volgt. Detail : brood wordt gebakken van het hier gemalen meel.

XX **Rasa Senang,** Horst 1, ✉ 5171 RA, ☎ (0 416) 28 44 76, *Fax (0 416) 53 07 59*, 🏖, Cuisine indonésienne – P. AE ⓓ MC VISA JCB. ✈
fermé mardi – **Repas** (dîner seult) 25/45.
• Envie d'une escapade orientale ? Cette adresse tombe à point nommé : goûteuse cuisine indonésienne, formule "rijsttafel" (table de riz), beau livre de cave et service avenant.
• Zin in een oosters avontuur ? Dan komt dit adres als geroepen : smakelijke Indonesische keuken, rijsttafelformule, mooie wijnkaart en vriendelijke bediening.

KAMPEN *Overijssel* 531 U 7 *et* 715 I 4 – *48 394 h.*

Voir *Rive droite de l'IJssel* ≤★ Y – *Ancien hôtel de ville★ (Oude Raadhuis) : cheminée★ dans la salle des échevins★ (Schepenzaal)* Y **H** – *Hanap★ dans le musée municipal (Stedelijk Museum)* Y **M** – *Cellebroederspoort★* Z.

🅸 *Oudestraat 151, ✉ 8261 CL, ☎ (0 38) 331 35 00, info@vvvkampen.nl, Fax (0 38) 332 89 00.*

Amsterdam 115 ② – Zwolle 14 ① – Leeuwarden 86 ③

Plan page suivante

Van Dijk sans rest, IJsselkade 30, ✉ 8261 AC, ☎ (0 38) 331 49 25, *l.wessels@worldonline.nl, Fax (0 38) 331 65 08*, 🚲 – TV – 🏛 25 à 40. MC VISA JCB Y r
fermé du 19 au 31 déc. – **20 ch** ☕ 70.
• Ce petit hôtel familial de confort simple, mais très correct, est un point de chute appréciable pour découvrir les nombreuses curiosités de Kampen. Chambres proprettes.
• Dit eenvoudige, maar vrij gerieflijke familiehotel is een aangename pleisterplaats voor wie de bezienswaardigheden van de hanzestad wil bezoeken.

XX **De Bottermarck,** Broederstraat 23, ✉ 8261 GN, ☎ (0 38) 331 95 42, *bottermarck@worldmail.nl, Fax (0 38) 332 89 95* – AE ⓓ MC VISA JCB Y s
fermé 29 fév.-8 mars, 18 juil.-9 août, sam. midi, dim. et lundi – **Repas** Lunch 25 – 45, ♀.
• Adresse agréable à dénicher dans une ruelle du centre animé. Le tabac, plante qui valut son renom à Kampen, est ici l'ingrédient vedette. Cuisine assez inventive, donc.
• Aangenaam adres in een steegje in het levendige centrum. Ooit stond Kampen als sigarenstad bekend, nu is tabak als culinair ingrediënt de vedette. Vrij inventieve keuken dus.

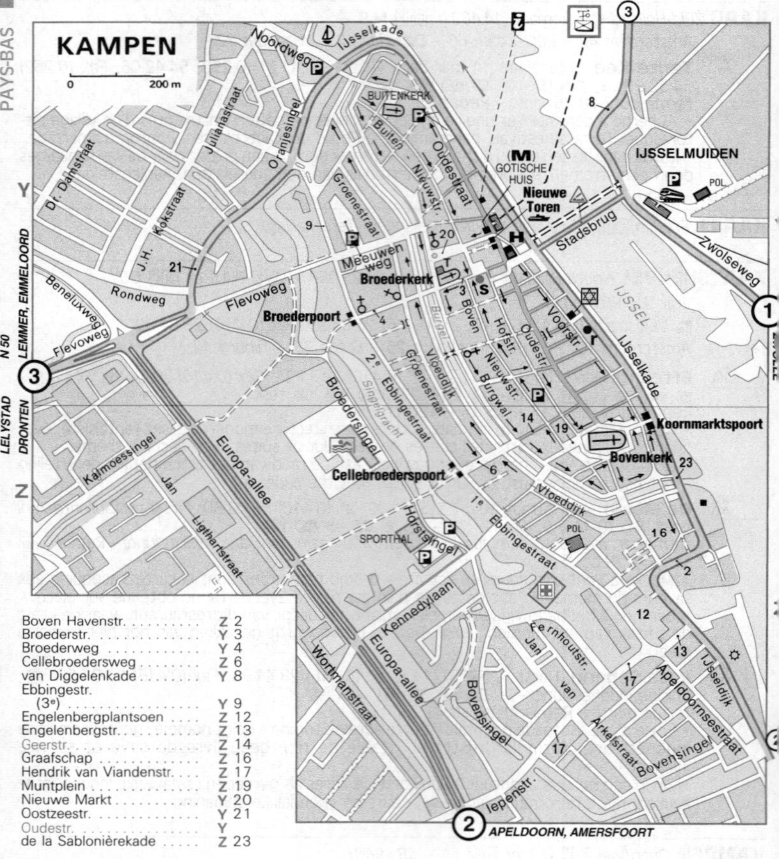

Les prix

Pour toutes précisions sur les prix indiqués dans ce guide, reportez-vous aux pages explicatives.

KATWIJK AAN ZEE *Zuid-Holland* C *Katwijk 41 254 h.* 532 L 9 *et* 715 E 5.

Vuurbaakplein 11, 2225 JB, 0 900-528 99 58, katwijk@hollandrijnland.nl, Fax (0 71) 407 63 42.

Amsterdam 44 – Rotterdam 43 – Den Haag 19 – Haarlem 34.

Noordzee, Boulevard 72, 2225 AC, (0 71) 401 57 42, *info@hotelnoordzee.nl, Fax (0 71) 407 51 65,* ←, – P – 40. AE VISA. ch *fermé 19 déc.-13 janv.* – **Repas** (dîner seult) (avec cuisine italienne) carte 22 à 55 – **47 ch** 75/140, – 2 suites – ½ P 58/88.

• Cet hôtel de la digue a inauguré une nouvelle aile de chambres modernes à l'arrière. Plus ordinaires, celles situées sur le devant ont l'avantage de la vue balnéaire. Bistrot-pizzeria avec terrasse d'été au rez-de-chaussée ; table franco-hollandaise à l'étage.

• Dit hotel aan de boulevard heeft aan de achterzijde een nieuwe vleugel met moderne kamers. De kamers aan de voorkant zijn eenvoudiger, maar bieden uitzicht op zee. Bistro-pizzeria met zomerterras op de begane grond ; Frans-Nederlandse keuken op de verdieping.

Zeezicht sans rest, Boulevard 50, ✉ 2225 AD, ☎ (0 71) 401 40 55, *parlevliet@hotel-zeezicht.nl, Fax (0 71) 407 58 52,* – **30 ch** 45/110.
◆ Le long de la promenade, établissement familial où vous poserez vos bagages dans des petites chambres sommairement équipées mais tout à fait convenables pour l'étape.
◆ Dit familiehotel aan de boulevard beschikt over kleine kamers met eenvoudig comfort, die voor een onderbreking van de reis echter prima voldoen.

Brittenburg, Boulevard 70, ✉ 2225 AG, ☎ (0 71) 407 76 24, *dik.haasnoot@12move.nl, Fax (0 71) 401 54 34,* , Produits de la mer – AE VISA.
fermé 20 déc.-12 janv., sam. midi et dim. – **Repas** carte 37 à 63.
◆ Agencé dans le style brasserie, ce restaurant avec banc d'écailler mitonne une savoureuse cuisine de la mer. L'été, on dresse une terrasse abritée en façade.
◆ Dit in brasseriestijl ingerichte restaurant met oesterbar bereidt smaakvolle visgerechten. In de zomer kan men aan de voorzijde plaatsnemen op een beschut terras.

De Zwaan, Boulevard 111, ✉ 2225 HC, ☎ (0 71) 401 20 64, *info@restaurantdezwaan.nl, Fax (0 71) 407 48 86,* ≤, – AE VISA JCB.
fermé 20 déc.-3 janv. et lundi – **Repas** Lunch 30 – 35/53 bc, ♀.
◆ Joli coup d'œil sur le littoral, que ce soit en terrasse aux beaux jours ou de derrière les baies d'une salle à manger ample et plaisante. Grande carte franco-hollandaise.
◆ Fraai uitzicht op de kust, zowel vanaf het zomerterras als vanachter de ramen van een ruime en plezierige eetzaal. Uitgebreide Frans-Nederlandse kaart.

KERKRADE *Limburg 532 V 17 et 715 J 9 – 50 680 h.*

Voir *Abbaye de Rolduc★ (Abdij Rolduc) : chapiteaux★ de la nef.*
Amsterdam 225 – Maastricht 33 – Heerlen 12 – Aachen 12.

Brughof , Oud Erensteinerweg 6, ✉ 6468 PC, ☎ (0 45) 546 13 33, *info@erenstein.chateauhotels.nl, Fax (0 45) 546 07 48,* – – 25 à 230. AE VISA JCB
Repas voir rest ***Kasteel Erenstein*** ci-après – 18 – **44 ch** 115/175 – ½ P 105/165.
◆ Hôtel aménagé dans une ravissante ferme du 18e s. Chambres, junior suites et senior suites toutes personnalisées, et aussi pimpantes que douillettes. Tea-room sous véranda.
◆ Hotel in een mooie 18e-eeuwse boerderij. De kamers, junior suites en senior suites hebben alle een eigen karakter en zijn even sfeervol als behaaglijk. Tearoom in de serre.

Winseler Hof , Tunnelweg 99 (Ouest : 2 km à Landgraaf), ✉ 6372 XH, ☎ (0 45) 546 43 43, *info@winselerhof.com, Fax (0 45) 535 27 11,* – – 25 à 120. AE VISA
Repas *Pirandello* (dîner seult) 50/90, ♀ – ***Luigi's Trattoria*** *(fermé dim.)* (déjeuner seult sauf vend. et sam.) 33, ♀ – 18 – **48 ch** 120/153, – 1 suite – ½ P 115/190.
◆ Ancienne ferme adroitement restaurée, blottie dans un vallon tranquille. Chambres meublées avec élégance et belle terrasse sur cour fleurie. Restaurant franco-italien au goût du jour, agrandi d'une orangerie. Avenante trattoria recluse dans une cave voûtée.
◆ Oude, vakkundig verbouwde boerderij in een rustig dal. Stijlvol ingerichte kamers en een mooi terras op een fleurige binnenplaats. Eigentijds Frans-Italiaans restaurant met oranjerie. Sfeervolle trattoria in de gewelfde kelder.

Kasteel Erenstein - H. Brughof, Oud Erensteinerweg 6, ✉ 6468 PC, ☎ (0 45) 546 13 33, *info@erenstein.chateauhotels.nl, Fax (0 45) 546 07 48,* – . AE VISA JCB.
fermé dim. – **Repas** (déjeuner sur réservation) 35, ♀.
◆ Table papillonnant à travers les régions de France, dans un château du 14e s. entouré de douves et d'un parc arboré. Atmosphère "bistrot de luxe", mais pas du tout guindée.
◆ Een 14e-eeuws kasteel, omringd door een slotgracht en een park met bomen. De kok bereidt Franse streekgerechten. De sfeer is die van een luxueuze bistro, maar zonder poespas.

KESSEL *Limburg 532 V 15 et 715 J 8 – 4 194 h.*

Amsterdam 178 – Maastricht 65 – Eindhoven 50 – Roermond 21 – Venlo 14.

Château De Neerhof avec ch, Kasteelhof 1, ✉ 5995 BX, ☎ (0 77) 462 84 62, *info@deneerhof.nl, Fax (0 77) 462 84 69,* ≤ Meuse (Maas), – – 30. AE VISA.
fermé carnaval et 31 déc.-1er janv. – **Repas** *(fermé lundi et mardi)* (déjeuner sur réservation) 38/92 bc, ♀ – **6 ch** 110 – ½ P 80/150.
◆ Voici des lunes que les vigies ne scrutent plus la Meuse du haut de ce puissant château médiéval : un cadre historique dont profite le restaurant. Belles chambres.
◆ Het is alweer even geleden dat wachters vanaf deze machtige middeleeuwse vesting de Maas afspeurden. Een historische decor voor dit restaurant. Mooie kamers.

KETELHAVEN *Flevoland 531 T 7 et 715 I 4 – voir à Dronten.*

KEUKENHOF ** *Zuid-Holland* 532 M 9 *et* 715 E 5 *G. Hollande.*

KIJKDUIN *Zuid-Holland* 532 K 10 *et* 715 D 5 – *voir à Den Haag.*

KINDERDIJK (Molens van) (Moulins de KINDERDIJK) ** *Zuid-Holland* 532 M 11 *et* 715 E 6 *G. Hollande.*

KOLLUM *Fryslân* C *Kollumerland en Nieuwkruisland 13 264 h.* 531 V 3 *et* 715 J 2.
Amsterdam 174 – Groningen 34 – Leeuwarden 30.

XX **De Kolibrie,** Voorstraat 63, ✉ 9291 CD, ✆ (0 511) 45 33 78, *info@dekolibrie.nl, Fax (0 511) 45 06 55* – AE MC VISA. ✂
fermé sam. midi, dim. et lundi – **Repas** (déjeuner sur réservation) carte env. 42, ♀.
◆ Au centre du bourg, demeure ancienne transformée en restaurant dont la carte, classique actualisée, fait la part belle aux produits frisons. Toiles modernes en salle.
◆ Dit oude pand in het centrum van Kollum is verbouwd tot een restaurant waarvan de klassiek-moderne kaart Friese producten het hof maakt. Moderne schilderijen in de eetzaal.

Si le coût de la vie subit des variations importantes, les prix que nous indiquons peuvent être majorés. Lors de votre réservation à l'hôtel, faites-vous préciser le prix définitif.

De KOOG *Noord-Holland* 531 N 4 *et* 715 F 2 – *voir à Waddeneilanden (Texel).*

KORTENHOEF *Noord-Holland* C *Wijdemeren 9 339 h.* 532 P 9 *et* 715 G 5.
Amsterdam 26 – Utrecht 23 – Hilversum 7.

XX **De Nieuwe Zuwe** 1er étage, Zuwe 20 (Ouest : 2 km sur N 201), ✉ 1241 NC, ✆ (0 35) 656 33 63, *info@nieuwe-zuwe.nl, Fax (0 35) 656 40 41,* ⋞, 🍴, ⚓ – P – 25 à 80. AE DC MC VISA
fermé 27 déc.-5 janv., dim. d'oct. à mars et lundi – **Repas** Lunch 29 – 38/45, ♀.
◆ Affaire familiale aménagée dans l'enceinte d'un port de plaisance des Kortenhoeftse Plassen, entre Hilversum et Vreeland. Terrasse panoramique dressée en été.
◆ Dit culinaire familiebedrijf ligt verankerd op het terrein van de jachthaven aan de Kortenhoeftse Plassen, tussen Hilversum en Vreeland. Panoramisch terras in de zomer.

KORTGENE *Zeeland* C *Noord-Beveland 7 052 h.* 532 H 13 *et* 715 C 7.
Amsterdam 165 – Middelburg 26 – Goes 11 – Rotterdam 82.

XX **De Korenbeurs** avec ch, Kaaistraat 12, ✉ 4484 CS, ✆ (0 113) 30 13 42, *info@korenbeurs-kortegene.nl, Fax (0 113) 30 23 94* – TV – 25 à 100. AE DC MC VISA
fermé 18 janv.-8 fév. et dim. du 16 nov. au 8 fév. – **Repas** *(fermé sam. midi et dim. midi)* 27/40 – **7 ch** ☕ 55/85 – ½ P 58/63.
◆ Changement de décor dans la salle à manger de cette auberge villageoise : c'est clair, abondamment fleuri et garni de fauteuils confortables. Crustacés en saison.
◆ Verandering van decor in de eetzaal van dit dorpsetablissement : licht interieur, comfortabele fauteuils en veel bloemen. Schaaldieren in het seizoen.

X **Overstag,** Hoofdstraat 36, ✉ 4484 CG, ✆ (0 113) 30 24 54, *r.vandebos@12move.nl, Fax (0 113) 30 10 20,* 🍴, Taverne-rest – VISA
fermé 2 sem. janv. et lundis non fériés – **Repas** *(dîner seult d'oct. à mars)* carte 26 à 47.
◆ Taverne-restaurant familiale œuvrant dans la rue principale. Salle dotée d'un mobilier massif en pin verni. Détails décoratifs évoquant vaguement l'univers des marins.
◆ Café-restaurant in familiebeheer. De eetzaal is ingericht met massief meubilair van gelakt grenen en heeft decoratieve details met een knipoog naar het zeemansleven.

X **Shangrila,** Kaaistraat 15, ✉ 4484 CS, ✆ (0 113) 30 16 68, Cuisine chinoise – ▤. AE MC VISA
fermé lundi de nov. à avril – **Repas** (dîner seult) carte 22 à 40, ♀.
◆ L'escale la plus exotique de ce petit coin de Zélande. Parmi les délicatesses de l'Empire du Milieu figurant à la carte, laissez-vous tenter par les spécialités du chef.
◆ De meest exotische ankerplaats in dit stukje Zeeland. Op de kaart staan tussen alle lekkernijen uit het Rijk van het Midden enkele verleidelijke specialiteiten van het huis.

KOUDEKERKE *Zeeland* 532 G 14 *et* 715 B 7 – *voir à Vlissingen.*

KOUDUM *Fryslân* C *Nijefurd 10 924 h.* 531 R 5 *et* 715 H 3.

Amsterdam 129 – Leeuwarden 50 – Bolsward 22 – Zwolle 76.

GalamaDammen, Galamadammen 1, ✉ 8723 CE, ☎ (0 514) 52 13 46, *info@galamadammen.nl, Fax (0 514) 52 24 01*, – 25 à 200. AE VISA

Repas *Lunch 23* – 30 – **48 ch** 87/110 – ½ P 110/133.

◆ Établissement privilégié par sa situation au bord du lac, devant le port des yachts. Chambres et duplex où l'on a ses aises, souvent avec cuisinette. Piscine sous verrière. Restaurant maniant un registre culinaire traditionnel.

◆ Dit hotel-restaurant ligt op een unieke lokatie aan het water, tussen twee jachthavens. Comfortabele kamers en split-level appartementen, de meeste met kitchenette. Zwembad onder glas. Het restaurant hanteert een traditioneel register.

KRAGGENBURG *Flevoland* C *Noordoostpolder 44 252 h.* 531 U 7 *et* 715 I 4.

Amsterdam 96 – Emmeloord 16 – Zwolle 32.

Van Saaze, Dam 16, ✉ 8317 AV, ☎ (0 527) 25 23 53, *Fax (0 527) 25 25 59*, – 40 à 200. AE VISA

Repas *Lunch 15* – 22/36 bc – **16 ch** 50/68 – ½ P 95/116.

◆ Petit hôtel très convenable, dont la capacité d'hébergement a presque doublé au tournant du 20e s. Accueil familial gentil et bon breakfast pour bien débuter la journée. Salle à manger au décor bourgeois. Préparations hollandaises.

◆ Vrij gerieflijk hotelletje dat rond de eeuwwisseling zijn overnachtingscapaciteit bijna heeft verdubbeld. Vriendelijk en gastvrij onthaal en een stevig ontbijt voor een goed begin van de dag. Eetzaal met klassiek decor. Hollandse keuken.

KRALINGEN *Zuid-Holland – voir à Rotterdam, périphérie.*

KRÖLLER-MÜLLER (Musée) ★★★ *Gelderland* 532 U 10 *et* 715 I 5 *G. Hollande.*

KRUININGEN *Zeeland* C *Reimerswaal 20 831 h.* 532 J 14 *et* 715 D 7.

au Sud-Est : 13 km à Rilland Bath, Grensweg 21, ✉ 4411 ST, ☎ (0 113) 55 12 65, Fax (0 113) 55 12 64.

Amsterdam 169 – Middelburg 34 – Breda 67 – Antwerpen 56.

Le Manoir, Zandweg 2 (Ouest : 1 km), ✉ 4416 NA, ☎ (0 113) 38 17 53, *info@interscaldes.nl, Fax (0 113) 38 17 63*, AE VISA JCB

fermé du 18 au 26 oct. et 2 prem. sem. janv. – **Repas** voir rest ***Inter Scaldes*** ci-après – 21 – **10 ch** 180/200, – 2 suites – ½ P 178/195.

◆ Sur un polder parsemé de vergers, gros manoir à toit de chaume agrémenté d'un jardin bichonné où alternent haies, roseraies et arbres fruitiers. Chambres de bon séjour.

◆ Dit grote landhuis met rieten dak staat in een polder met boomgaarden. In de verzorgde tuin wisselen heggen, rozenstruiken en fruitbomen elkaar af. Zeer comfortabele kamers.

Inter Scaldes (Brevet) - H. Le Manoir, Zandweg 2 (Ouest : 1 km), ✉ 4416 NA, ☎ (0 113) 38 17 53, *info@interscaldes.nl, Fax (0 113) 38 17 63*, – AE VISA JCB

fermé du 18 au 26 oct., 2 prem. sem. janv., lundi et mardi.

◆ Réouverture du restaurant prévue au printemps, après un sévère incendie.

◆ In de lente is de heropening voorzien van het door een brand geteisterde restaurant.

KUDELSTAART *Noord-Holland* 532 N 9 *– voir à Aalsmeer.*

LAGE-VUURSCHE *Utrecht* 532 Q 9 *et* 715 G 5 *– voir à Baarn.*

LANGWEER (LANGWAR) *Fryslân* C *Skarsterlân 27 239 h.* 531 T 5 *et* 715 I 3.

Amsterdam 122 – Leeuwarden 51 – Sneek 13 – Zwolle 68.

't Jagertje, Buorren 7, ✉ 8525 EB, ☎ (0 513) 49 92 97, *Fax (0 513) 49 95 26*, – AE VISA

fermé fév., lundi et mardi de nov. à mars et merc. – **Repas** (déjeuner sur réservation) carte env. 47, ♀.

◆ La salle à manger de cette maison bâtie au milieu d'un petit port pittoresque a récemment opté pour un style contemporain. Recettes dans le vent.

◆ De eetzaal van dit restaurant in het centrum van een pittoresk havenplaatsje heeft onlangs een nieuwe outfit in eigentijdse stijl gekregen. Trendy gerechten.

LAREN *Noord-Holland* 532 *Q 9 et* 715 *G 5 – 11 862 h.*
Env. *à l'Ouest : Le Gooi★ (Het Gooi).*
Amsterdam 29 – Utrecht 23 – Apeldoorn 61 – Hilversum 6.

XX **Stijl,** Naarderstraat 46, ✉ 1251 BD, ✆ (0 35) 538 68 58, *Fax (0 35) 538 95 88,* – P. AE MC VISA
Repas 30/55 bc.
◆ Restaurant aménagé dans une jolie chaumière sur jardin, face au musée Singer présentant l'école picturale dite de Laren. Cuisine classique actualisée. Grande terrasse.
◆ Klassieke kookkunst met moderne invulling in een huisje met rieten dak en tuin. Het Singer Museum aan de overkant exposeert doeken van de school van Laren. Groot terras.

XX **Le Mouton,** Krommepad 5, ✉ 1251 HP, ✆ (0 35) 531 04 27, *bonhoreca@zonnet.nl, Fax (0 35) 531 99 37* – AE MC VISA JCB.
fermé lundi – **Repas** (dîner seult) 33.
◆ Une ruelle mène à cette discrète adresse où vous dînerez dans une salle à manger aux murs de briques peintes décorés de toiles contemporaines. Plats au goût du jour.
◆ Een steegje voert naar dit bescheiden adres, waar u wordt ontvangen in een eetzaal met geschilderde bakstenen muren en moderne schilderijen. Eigentijdse gerechten.

X **Oesters aan de Brink,** Brink 10, ✉ 1251 KV, ✆ (0 35) 533 54 03, *info@oestersaandebrink.nl, Fax (0 35) 533 54 21,* Produits de la mer – AE MC VISA.
fermé sam. midi et dim. midi – **Repas** *Lunch 30* – carte 40 à 124, ♀.
◆ Le mariage du rouge et du noir confère une touche résolument design à la salle de restaurant de cette nouvelle "place to be" à Laren. Cuisine au parfum d'embruns.
◆ De restaurantzaal van deze nieuwe "place to be" heeft door de combinatie van rood en zwart een designdecor gekregen. Visspecialiteiten.

LATTROP *Overijssel* 531 *AA 8 et* 715 *L 4 – voir à Ootmarsum.*

LEEK *Groningen* 531 *X 3 et* 715 *K 2 – 19 349 h.*
Amsterdam 170 – Groningen 17 – Leeuwarden 52.

Leek, Euroweg 1, ✉ 9351 EM, ✆ (0 594) 51 88 00, *info@hotelleek.nl, Fax (0 594) 51 74 55,* – TV P – 25 à 200. AE MC VISA JCB.
Repas *(fermé sam. midi et dim. midi) Lunch 12* – carte 30 à 42, ♀ – ☕ 9 – **35 ch** 47 – ½ P 50/74.
◆ Établissement fonctionnel proposant des chambres insonorisées réparties au rez-de-chaussée et à l'étage. Préférez tout de même celles tournant le dos au carrefour.
◆ Functioneel hotel met kamers die zijn voorzien van geluidsisolatie, op de begane grond en de verdieping. U doet er goed aan een kamer te vragen die van het kruispunt af ligt.

LEENDE *Noord-Brabant* C *Heeze-Leende 15 333 h.* 532 *S 14 et* 715 *H 7.*
Maarheezerweg N. 11, ✉ 5595 ZC, ✆ (0 40) 206 18 18.
Amsterdam 139 – Eindhoven 15 – 's-Hertogenbosch 51 – Roermond 38 – Venlo 54.

XX **Jagershorst,** Valkenswaardseweg 44 (près A 2, sortie ㉞), ✉ 5595 XB, ✆ (0 40) 206 13 86, *jagershorst@hotmail.com, Fax (0 40) 206 27 55,* – P – 25 à 60. AE MC VISA. – *fermé sam. midi* – **Repas** *Lunch 33* – 44/72.
◆ Ce confortable établissement se compose d'une brasserie et d'un restaurant prolongé par deux jardins d'hiver. S'il fait soleil, service assuré dans un petit parc ombragé.
◆ Dit comfortabele etablissement heeft een brasserie en een restaurant met twee wintertuinen. Bij mooi weer wordt geserveerd in een lommerrijk parkje.

X **Kris,** Dorpstraat 42, ✉ 5595 CH, ✆ (0 40) 206 17 31, *info@muzerick.nl, Fax (0 40) 206 19 15,* – P. AE MC VISA JCB
fermé mardi et merc. – **Repas** (déjeuner sur réservation) 33/72 bc.
◆ Près du clocher, maison engageante où l'on s'attable dans une salle aux couleurs de la Toscane. Terrasse adorable l'été venu. Formule menu unique. Repas en musique.
◆ Restaurant in een charmant huis bij de klokkentoren, waar wordt getafeld in een Toscaans decor. Bekoorlijke terras voor zomerse dagen. Één enkel menu. Dinerconcerten.

LEENS *Groningen* C *De Marne 11 186 h.* 531 *X 2 et* 715 *K 1.*
Amsterdam 196 – Groningen 27 – Assen 51 – Leeuwarden 52.

XX ✿ **Schathoes Verhildersum** (Soek), Wierde 42, ✉ 9965 TB, ✆ (0 595) 57 22 04, *shathoes@inn.nl,* – P. AE MC VISA JCB
fermé 26 déc.-20 janv., lundi et mardi – **Repas** (déjeuner sur réservation) *Lunch 34* – 80 bc, carte env. 47, ♀.
◆ Table axée "terroir", dans les anciennes dépendances du manoir voisin, protégé de douves et entouré d'un domaine boisé. Décoration campagnarde. Expo de sculptures au jardin.
◆ Dit restaurant in een bijgebouw van de naburige borg (een versterkte boerderij) legt het accent op streekproducten. Rustiek interieur. Tuin met expositie van beeldhouwwerken.
Spéc. Sole au beurre blanc. Matelote de brochet aux morilles. Déclinaison de fraises

LEEUWARDEN (JOUWERT) **P** *Fryslân* **531** T 3 *et* **715** I 2 – *90 516 h.*
Musées : *Frison★★ (Fries Museum/Verzetsmuseum)* CY – *Het Princessehof, Musée néerlandais de la céramique★★ (Nederlands Keramiek Museum)* BY.
par ①, Woelwijk 101, ✉ 8926 XD, ☎ (0 511) 43 22 99, Fax (0 58) 257 33 67.
Sophialaan 4, ✉ 8911 AE, ☎ (0 58) 234 75 50, vvvleeuwarden@vvvleeuwarden.nl, Fax (0 58) 234 75 51.
Amsterdam 139 ④ – Groningen 59 ① – Sneek 24 ③

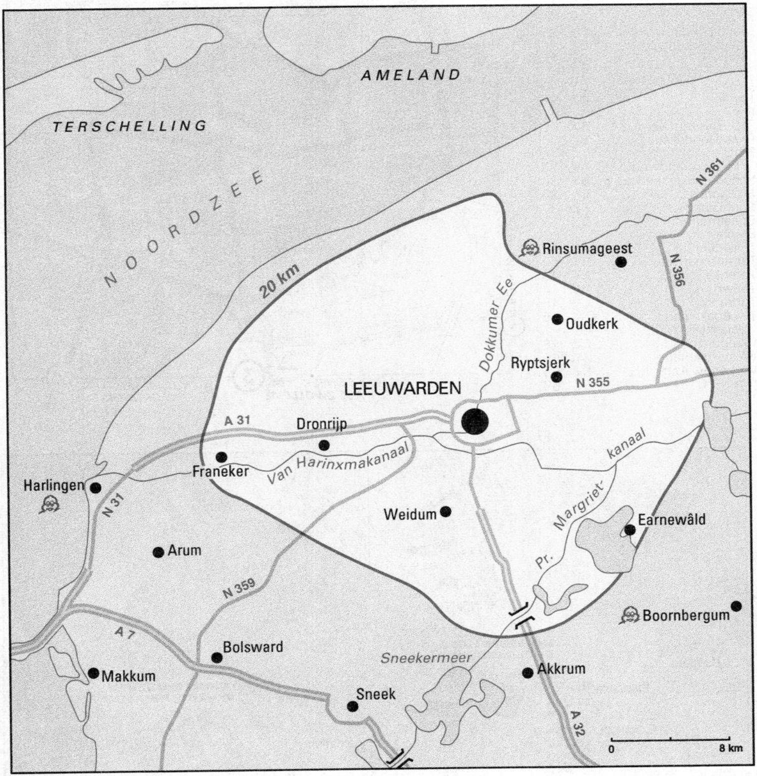

Oranje, Stationsweg 4, ✉ 8911 AG, ☎ (0 58) 212 62 41, *oranjehotel@bilderberg.nl, Fax (0 58) 212 14 41,* –, rest, – 25 à 350. AE VISA JCB. rest BZ a
Repas *(fermé 25 déc.-2 janv., sam. midi et dim. midi)* Lunch 25 – 40, – **78 ch** *(fermé 24 déc.-2 janv.)* 108/138 – ½ P 66/145.
◆ Hôtel posté devant la gare, situation rassurante pour ceux qui ne connaissent pas la ville. Le niveau d'équipement des chambres va crescendo avec la dépense consentie. Belle salle à manger lambrissée et bar à l'ambiance "pub".
◆ Dit hotel staat tegenover het station, een geruststellende lokatie voor wie de stad niet kent. Het comfort van de kamers is navenant met de prijs. Mooie, gelambriseerde eetzaal en bar met de ambiance van een Engelse pub.

Paleis het Stadhouderlijk Hof, Hofplein 29, ✉ 8911 HJ, ☎ (0 58) 216 21 80, *info@stadhouderlijkhof.nl, Fax (0 58) 216 38 90,* – P – 25 à 120. AE VISA JCB BY v
Repas (dîner seult) 25 – 13 – **28 ch** 90/120, – 4 suites – ½ P 78.
◆ Tour à tour résidence des gouverneurs frisons, puis de la famille royale jusqu'en 1970, ce palais élevé au cœur de Leeuwarden abrite de vastes chambres. Six sont "design".
◆ Dit hotel in het hart van de stad, voormalige residentie van de Friese stadhouders en koninklijk paleis tot 1970, herbergt vorstelijke kamers, waarvan zes in design-stijl.

LEEUWARDEN

Blokhuispl.	CZ	4
de Brol	CZ	6
Drachtsterweg	AX	7
Druifstreek	CZ	9
Europaplein	AV	10
Franklinstr.	AX	12
Groningerstraatweg	CY	13
Harlingersingel	BY	15
Harlingerstraatweg	BY	16
Hoeksterend	CY	18
Julianastr.	AX	19
Kleine Kerkstr.	BY	21
Monnikemuurstr.	CY	22
Naauw	CZ	24
Nieuwe Kade	CY	25
Nieuwestad	BZ	
Over de Kelders	CYZ	27
Peperstr.	CZ	28
Pieter Stuyvesantweg	AX	30
Prins Hendrikstr.	BZ	31
Prof. M. Gerbrandweg	AV	33
Schoenmakersperk	BY	34
St. Jacobsstr.	CY	36
Sophialaan	BZ	37
Speelmansstr.	CY	39
Stephenson viaduct	AX	40
Tesselschadestr.	BZ	42
Torenstr.	BY	43
Tuinen	CY	44
Turfmarkt	CY	45
Tweebaksmarkt	CZ	46
Voorstreek	CY	
Waagplein	CZ	48
Westerplantage	BYZ	49
W. Lodewijkstr.	CZ	51
Wirdumerdijk	CZ	53

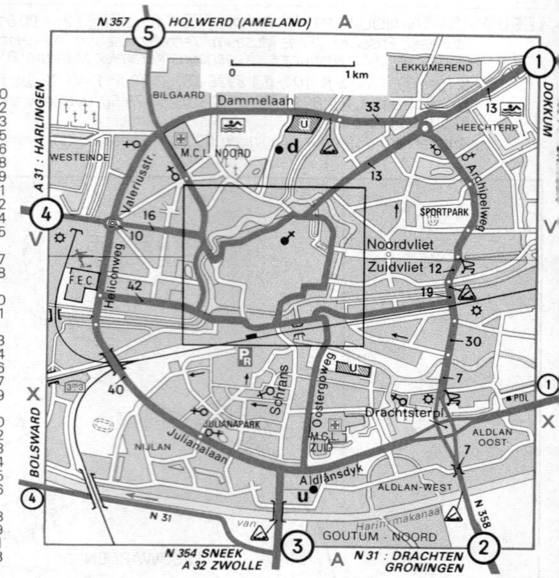

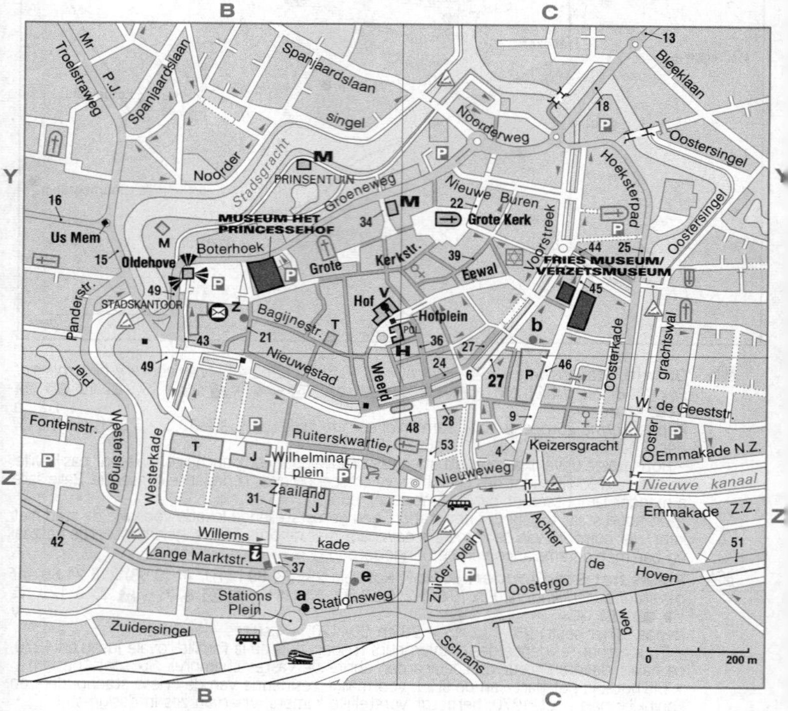

B C

Mr P.J. Troelstraweg
Spanjaardslaan
singel
Noorderweg
Bleeklaan
Oostersingel
Noorder
Stadsgracht
PRINSENTUIN
Groeneweg
MUSEUM HET PRINCESSEHOF
Nieuwe Buren
Grote Kerk
Hoeksterpad
Us Mem
Oldehove
Boterhoek
Grote
Kerkstr.
Eewal
Voorstreek
FRIES MUSEUM/ VERZETSMUSEUM
STADSKANTOOR
Bagijnestr.
Hof
Hofplein
Pier
Panderstr.
Nieuwestad
Weerd
Oosterkade
grachtswal
Fonteinstr.
Westersingel
Westerkade
Ruiterskwartier
Wilhelmina plein
Keizersgracht
W. de Geeststr.
Oostersingel
Emmakade N.Z.
Zaailand
Nieuweweg
Nieuwe kanaal
Willems kade
Achter de Hoven
Emmakade Z.Z.
Lange Marktstr.
Zuider plein
Oostergo weg
Stations Plein
Stationsweg
Zuidersingel
Schrans
0 200 m

B C

Wyswert (Établissement d'application hôtelière), Rengerslaan 8, ✉ 8917 DD, ☎ (0 58) 215 77 15, *hotel@chn.nl*, *Fax (0 58) 212 32 11*, – TV ♿ P – 🏛 25 à 250. AE ⓓ ⓜ VISA. AV d
fermé du 9 au 12 avril, 30 avril, 20, 21 et 30 mai, 12 juil.-23 août, sam. soir et dim. – **Repas** Lunch 15 – carte env. 28, ♀ – ☕ 10 – **28 ch** 80/90.
• Du "booking" des chambres à l'organisation de séminaires, les élèves de l'école hôtelière répondent partout présent. En réservant, dites "c'est de la part du Bibendum" ! Gourmande formule menu-carte au restaurant. Service assuré par les étudiants.
• Van kamers boeken tot seminars organiseren, de studenten van de hotelschool staan overal paraat. Als u reserveert, zeg dan "namens Bibendum" ! Menu en à la carte, het restaurant biedt beide. De bediening wordt door de studenten verzorgd.

Bastion, Legedijk 6, ✉ 8935 DG, ☎ (0 58) 289 01 12, *bastion@bastionhotel.nl*, *Fax (0 58) 289 05 12* – TV P. AE ⓓ ⓜ VISA. AX u
Repas (grillades, ouvert jusqu'à 23 h) carte env. 30 – ☕ 10 – **40 ch** 55.
• La grande ceinture entourant la ville passe près de cet hôtel de chaîne rafraîchi. Chambres pratiques. Salle de divertissement avec billard et jeu de fléchettes.
• De grote ring om de stad loopt vlak langs dit opgeknapte ketenhotel. Praktisch ingerichte kamers. Zaal voor ontspanning, met biljart en darts.

de Nieuwe Mulderij, Baljeestraat 19, ✉ 8911 AK, ☎ (0 58) 213 48 02, *info@denieuwemulderij.nl*, *Fax (0 58) 213 06 74* – ▤. AE ⓜ VISA BZ e
fermé 18 juil.-8 août, sam. midi et dim. – **Repas** 32/44, ♀.
• Il arrive parfois que le patron, sabots aux pieds, quitte ses fourneaux juste un instant, le temps de faire à la clientèle quelques suggestions s'ajoutant à son menu-carte.
• Soms komt de patron op zijn klompen even de keuken uit om zijn gasten wat suggesties te doen, een extraatje naast de menu's en de keuzes van de kaart.

Eindeloos, Korfmakersstraat 17, ✉ 8911 LA, ☎ (0 58) 213 08 35, *info@restauranteindeloos.nl*, *Fax (0 58) 216 11 07* – ⓜ VISA CY b
fermé 26 juil.-17 août, 2 prem. sem. janv., lundi et mardi – **Repas** (dîner seult) (menu unique) 32, ♀.
• Sages recettes de saison annoncées à l'ardoise, dans une salle à manger intime et chaleureuse, d'esprit bistrot. Vins du monde et jeune sommelier averti. Accueil avenant.
• In een intieme, gezellige eetzaal, type bistro, worden degelijke seizoengerechten op een lei aangekondigd. Wereldwijnen en jonge, deskundige sommelier. Vriendelijke ontvangst.

kostelijk, Kleine Kerkstraat 41, ✉ 8911 DL, ☎ (0 58) 216 52 52, *(0 58) 216 26 26* – ⓜ VISA BY z
fermé 30 juil.-16 août, 31 déc.-10 janv., dim. et lundi – **Repas** (déjeuner sur réservation) carte env. 40, ♀.
• Dans une ancienne demeure, restaurant sympathique concoctant une cuisine sobrement personnalisée. Salle à manger contemporaine de style scandinave. Le chef s'active à vue.
• In een voormalig herenhuis serveert dit sympathieke restaurant gerechten met een persoonlijk accent. Eigentijdse eetzaal in Scandinavische stijl. Open keuken.

à Aldtsjerk *(Oudkerk) par ① : 12 km* C *Tytsjerksteradiel 31 413 h :*

Landgoed De Klinze, Van Sminiaweg 32, ✉ 9064 KC, ☎ (0 58) 256 10 50, *info@klinze.nl*, *Fax (0 58) 256 10 60*, – ▤ rest, TV P – 🏛 25 à 250. AE ⓓ ⓜ VISA. rest
Repas 35/78 bc – ☕ 12 – **27 ch** 150/162 – ½ P 197/335.
• Une allée majestueuse conduit à cette opulente demeure du 17e s. et à son parc arboré. Grandes chambres, junior suites, salon cosy, beauty-center et tours en calèche. Cuisine aux influences méditerranéennes à savourer dans une élégante salle de restaurant.
• Een majestueuze laan leidt naar dit weelderige 17e-eeuwse verblijf met het boomrijke park. Grote kamers, junior suites, knusse lounge, beautycenter en ritjes in een calèche. Keuken met mediterrane invloeden en stijlvolle eetzaal.

LEGEMEER (LEGEMAR) *Fryslân* – *voir à Sint Nicolaasga.*

LEIDEN *Zuid-Holland* 532 L 10 et 715 E 5 – *117 170 h.*

Voir *La vieille ville et ses Musées*★★ – *Rapenburg*★ CZ.

Musées : *National d'Ethnologie*★★ *(Rijksmuseum voor Volkenkunde)* CY **M**4 – *Municipal (Stedelijk Museum) De Lakenhal*★★ DY **M**5 – *National des Antiquités*★★ *(Rijksmuseum van Oudheden)* CYZ **M**3 – *Boerhaave*★ DY **M**1 – *Naturalis*★★ AU.

Env. *par ⑥ : 10 km, Champs de fleurs*★★ – *par ③ à Alphen aan den Rijn : Archeon*★ *(parc à thèmes archéologiques).*

ℹ *Stationsweg 2d,* ✉ *2312 AV,* ☎ *0 900-222 23 33, leiden@hollandrijnland.nl, Fax (0 71) 516 12 27.*

Amsterdam 41 ⑤ – Rotterdam 36 ② – Den Haag 19 ② – Haarlem 32 ⑥

Holiday Inn, Haagse Schouwweg 10 (près A 44), ✉ 2332 KG, ☎ (0 71) 535 55 55, *hotel@holiday-inn-leiden.com, Fax (0 71) 535 55 53,* – 25 à 400. AE VISA JCB. rest
AU u
Repas carte 31 à 40 – 16 – **200 ch** 205 – ½ P 114/155.

◆ Établissement de chaîne élevé en 1968 à distance respectable du centre-ville, dans le proche voisinage de l'autoroute. Chambres distribuées autour d'un atrium central. Grande salle à manger agencée comme un jardin d'hiver. Buffets dressés à l'heure du lunch.

◆ Dit ketenhotel werd in 1968 op behoorlijke afstand van het centrum gebouwd, in de directe nabijheid van de snelweg. De kamers liggen gegroepeerd rond een centraal atrium. De grote eetzaal is als wintertuin opgezet. Lunchbuffetten.

Golden Tulip, Schipholweg 3, ✉ 2316 XB, ☎ (0 71) 522 11 21, *reservations@golden-tulip-leiden.nl, Fax (0 71) 522 66 75* – – 25 à 60. AE VISA JCB. rest
CX c
Repas *(fermé sam. et dim.)* 22/30 – **54 ch** 110/130.

◆ En quête d'une chambre confortable dans le secteur de la gare ? Cet immeuble à la façade miroir promet des nuits sans histoire, avec la garantie de ne pas manquer son train.

◆ Op zoek naar een comfortabele kamer in de buurt van het station ? Dit pand met spiegelende façade belooft een ongestoorde nachtrust en... de zekerheid dat u de trein niet mist !

Nieuw Minerva, Boommarkt 23, ✉ 2311 EA, ☎ (0 71) 512 63 58, *hotel@nieuwminerva.nl, Fax (0 71) 514 26 74* – – 25 à 80. AE VISA JCB.
DY p
fermé 24 déc.-4 janv. – **Repas** carte env. 22 – **39 ch** 75/125 – ½ P 66/91.

◆ À deux pas de l'effervescente Breestraat, hôtel familial surveillant un canal qu'enjambe un pont typique. Les meilleures chambres déclinent un thème décoratif différent. Restaurant affichant un petit air de café.

◆ Dit familiehotel op loopafstand van de bruisende Breestraat kijkt uit op een gracht met een karakteristieke brug. De beste kamers hebben elk een ander decoratief thema. Het restaurant heeft meer iets weg van een café.

De Doelen sans rest, Rapenburg 2, ✉ 2311 EV, ☎ (0 71) 512 05 27, *hotel@dedoelen.com, Fax (0 71) 512 84 53* – . AE VISA – *fermé 19 déc.-3 janv.* – 8 – **16 ch** 70/105.

◆ Bon point de chute pour découvrir Leiden, cette demeure historique abrite des chambres de divers formats et une belle salle de breakfast. Le canal d'en face est ravissant.

◆ Dit historische pand is een goede uitvalsbasis voor wie Leiden wil bezichtigen. De kamers variëren in grootte. Mooie ontbijtzaal. Het kanaal is net een plaatje.
CYZ k

Engelbertha Hoeve, Hoge Morsweg 140, ✉ 2332 HN, ☎ (0 71) 576 50 00, *Fax (0 71) 532 37 80,* – . AE VISA
AV s
fermé 27 déc.-4 janv., sam. midi, dim. midi et lundi – **Repas** Lunch 32 – carte 49 à 61.

◆ Au bord du Vieux Rhin, ferme du 18e s. transformée en maison de bouche agréable : délicieuse terrasse estivale dressée au jardin et carte aussi appétissante qu'élaborée.

◆ Deze 18e-eeuwse boerderij aan de Oude Rijn is tot een aangenaam restaurant verbouwd. Heerlijk zomerterras in de tuin en een even aantrekkelijke als verzorgde menukaart.

het Prentenkabinet, Kloksteeg 25, ✉ 2311 SK, ☎ (0 71) 512 66 66, *info@prentenkabinet.nl, Fax (0 71) 512 52 50,* – VISA.
DZ s
fermé 3 oct. et 30 déc.-1er janv. – **Repas** (dîner seult) carte 36 à 52.

◆ Restaurant occupant les murs d'une ancienne bibliothèque dont l'origine remonte au Siècle des lumières. La pièce où l'on mange servait jadis de cabinet des estampes.

◆ Restaurant in een voormalige bibliotheek waarvan de oorsprong teruggaat tot het tijdperk van de verlichting. De restaurantzaal was vroeger het prentenkabinet.

Fabers, Kloksteeg 13, ✉ 2311 SK, ☎ (0 71) 512 40 12, *restaurantfabers@hotmail.com, Fax (0 71) 513 11 20* – . AE VISA.
CDZ n
fermé dim. et lundi – **Repas** (dîner seult) 33/43 bc, ♀.

◆ À l'ombre de la gothique Pieterskerk, petite adresse auréolée d'une certaine reconnaissance locale. Salles de restaurant en enfilade. Cuisine française d'aujourd'hui.

◆ Dit adresje in de schaduw van de Pieterskerk geniet een zekere erkenning in de studentenstad. Restaurantzalen en suite. Eigentijdse Franse keuken.

In den Doofpot, Turfmarkt 9, ✉ 2312 CE, ☎ (0 71) 512 24 34, – AE VISA JCB.
CY a
fermé prem. sem. oct., 2 sem. après Noël et dim. – **Repas** (dîner seult) carte 36 à 73, ♀.

◆ Murs éclatants, chaises tressées, lustres rutilants, lames de parquet et lambris clairs composent un décor soigné. Terrasse estivale avec vue batelière. Carte à la page.

◆ Helwitte muren, fonkelende lampen, parketstroken en een lichtkleurige lambrisering bepalen het verzorgde decor. Terras met uitzicht op het water. Eigentijdse kaart.

La Cloche, Kloksteeg 3, ✉ 2311 SK, ☎ (0 71) 512 30 53, *info@laclocheleiden.nl, Fax (0 71) 514 60 51* – AE VISA JCB
CDZ m
fermé dim. et lundi – **Repas** (déjeuner sur réservation) 35/60 bc, ♀.

◆ Enseigne de circonstance pour "se taper la cloche" près de l'église St-Pierre. Pimpante façade fleurie en été, bar "sympa" et coquettes salles à manger étagées.

◆ Dat wordt smikkelen op dit adres vlak bij de Pieterskerk. Charmante voorgevel met bloemen in de zomer, sympathieke bar en gezellige eetzalen op verschillende verdiepingen.

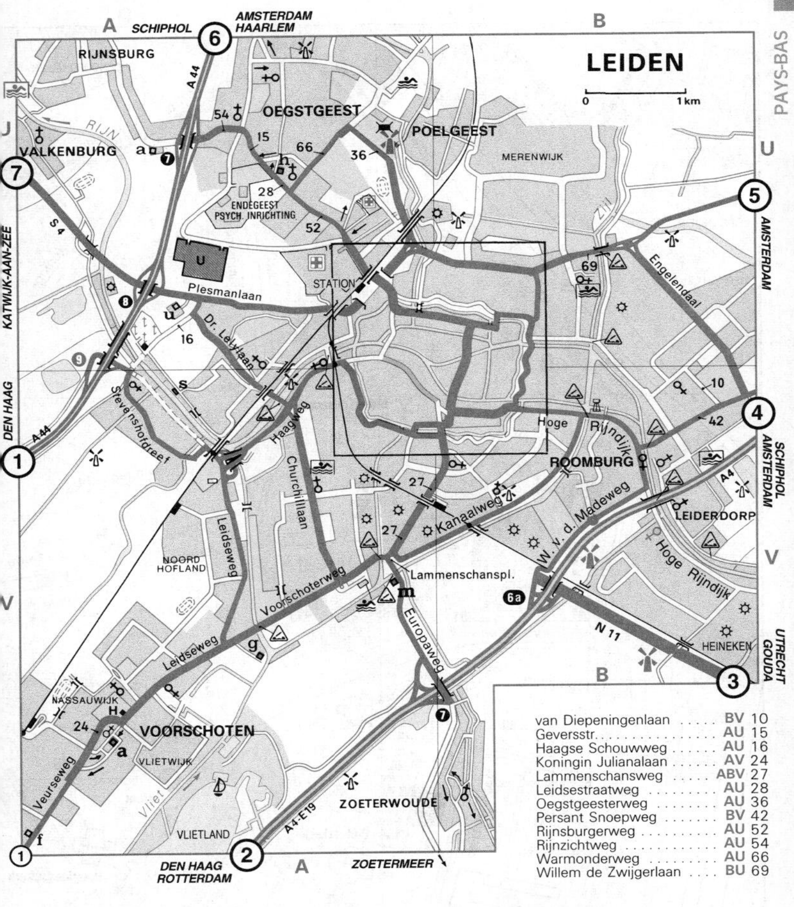

Cronesteyn, Vlietweg 2 (près A 4 - E 19, sortie ⑦), ✉ 2323 LB, ✆ (0 71) 576 69 30, *over devest46@zonnet.nl, Fax (0 71) 531 82 00,* – ▤ P. AE ⓓ ⓜ VISA JCB — AV m
fermé 25 août-15 sept. et lundi – **Repas** *Lunch 25* – 26/33.
◆ Élégante villa judicieusement mise à profit. Préparations au goût du jour servies dans deux salles à manger actuelles. L'été, le couvert est dressé en terrasse.
◆ Deze elegante villa wordt met visie geëxploiteerd als restaurant. Eigentijdse gerechten worden in twee moderne eetzalen geserveerd. 's Zomers wordt er op het terras gegeten.

Mangerie De Jonge Koekop, Lange Mare 60, ✉ 2312 GS, ✆ (0 71) 514 19 37, *info@koekop.nl* – ⓜ VISA — DY a
fermé dim. – **Repas** (déjeuner sur réservation) 30, ♀.
◆ Accueil gentil, service jeune et dynamique, intérieur actuel avec mezzanine et recettes à la page. En été, sur réservation, repas servi en bateau, au fil des canaux.
◆ Vriendelijke ontvangst, jonge en enthousiaste bediening, eigentijds interieur met vide, trendy gerechten. 's Zomers kunt u tijdens een rondvaart aan boord eten (reserveren).

Hèt Panacee, Rapenburg 97, ✉ 2311 GL, ✆ (0 71) 566 14 94, *info@hetpanacee.nl* – AE ⓓ ⓜ VISA. — CZ b
fermé 19 juil.-10 août, 31 déc.-4 janv., lundi et mardi – **Repas** (dîner seult) 28/35, ♀.
◆ N'espérez pas trouver la panacée dans cette ancienne droguerie habilement transformée en restaurant. Une carte actuelle vous y sera néanmoins soumise. Ambiance "bistrot".
◆ Verwacht niet in deze oude drogisterij een wondermiddel tegen uw kwalen te vinden. Op de eigentijdse menukaart vindt u wel de remedie tegen een gezonde trek. Ambiance bistro.

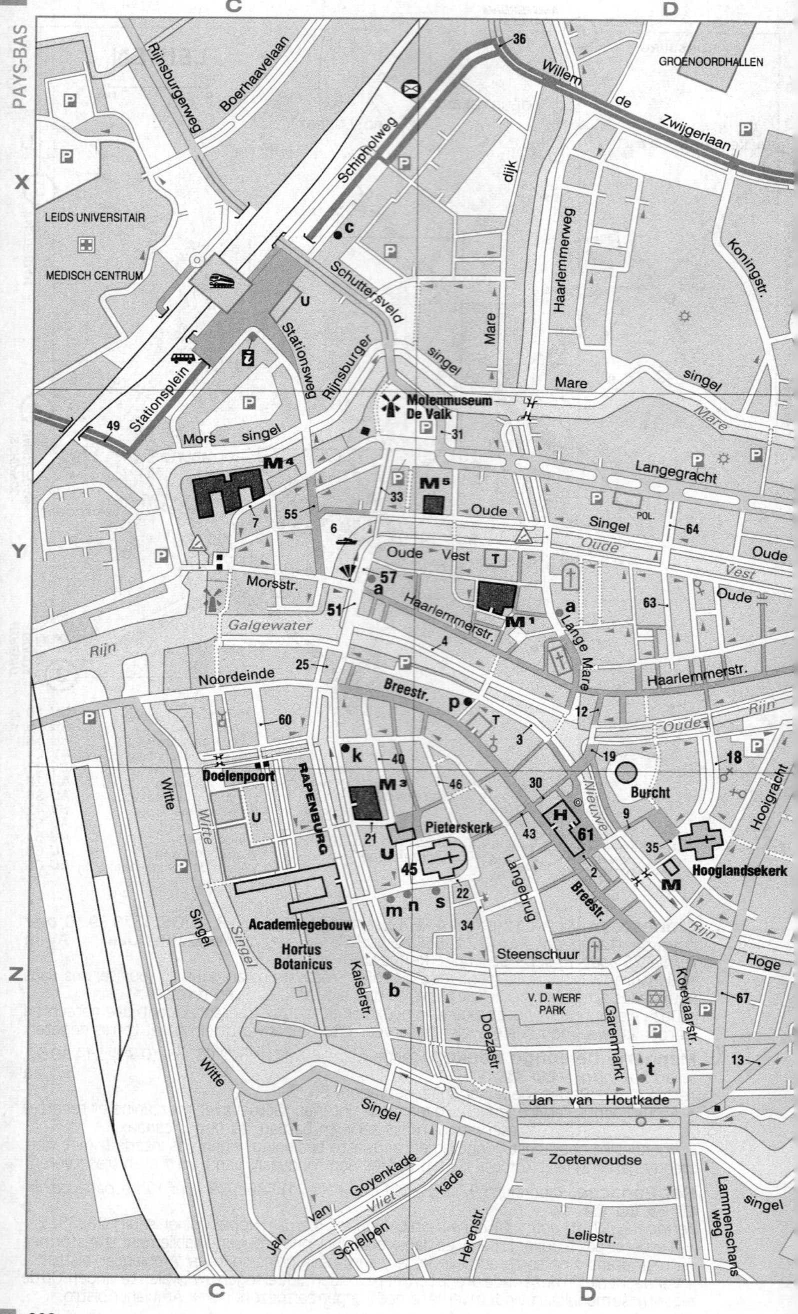
C
D
X
Y
Z
GROENOORDHALLEN
Willem de Zwijgerlaan
Rijnsburgerweg
Boerhaavelaan
Schipholweg
LEIDS UNIVERSITAIR MEDISCH CENTRUM
Schuttersveld
Stationsweg
Rijnsburger singel
Stationsplein
Mors singel
Molenmuseum De Valk
Haarlemmerweg
Koningstr.
Mare
dijk
singel
Langegracht
Oude Singel
Oude Vest
Morsstr.
Haarlemmerstr.
Lange Mare
Galgewater
Rijn
Noordeinde
Breestr.
Oude Rijn
Doelenpoort
RAPENBURG
Pieterskerk
Burcht
Hooglandsekerk
Hooigracht
Nieuwe
Langebrug
Academiegebouw
Hortus Botanicus
Kaiserstr.
Witte Singel
Steenschuur
Hoge
V. D. WERF PARK
Doezastr.
Garenmarkt
Korevaarstr.
Jan van Houtkade
Zoeterwoudse singel
Goyenkade
Vliet
Jan van Goyenkade
Schelpen kade
Herenstr.
Leliestr.
Lammenschans weg
POL.

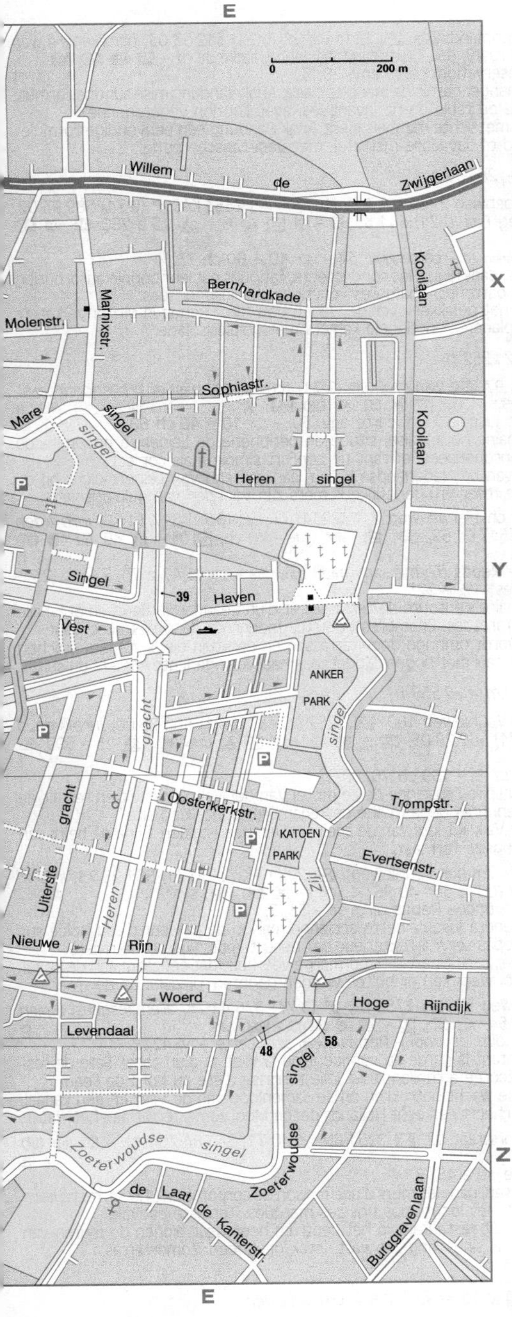

LEIDEN

Rue	Carré	N°
Aalmarkt	DY	3
Apothekersdijk	DY	4
Beestenmarkt	CY	6
Bernhardkade	EX	
Binnenvestgracht	CY	7
Boerhaavelaan	CX	
Breestraat	DYZ	
Burggravenlaan	EZ	
Burgsteeg	DZ	9
Doezastr.	DZ	
Donkersteeg	DY	12
Evertsenstr.	EZ	
Garenmarkt	DZ	
Geregracht	DZ	13
Haarlemmerstr.	DEY	
Haarlemmerweg	DX	
Haven	EY	
Herensingel	EY	
Herenstr.	DZ	
Hogerijndijk	EZ	
Hogewoerd	DEZ	
Hooglandse Kerkgracht	DYZ	18
Hoogstraat	DY	19
Hooigracht	DZ	
Houtstraat	CZ	21
Jan van Goyenkade	CZ	
Jan van Houtkade	DZ	
Kaiserstr.	CZ	
Kloksteeg	DZ	22
Koningstr.	DX	
Kooilaan	EXY	
Koornbrugsteeg	DZ	2
Korevaarstr.	DZ	
Kort Rapenburg	CY	25
de Laat de Kanterstr.	EZ	
Lammenschansweg	DZ	
Langebrug	DZ	
Langegracht	DY	
Langemare	DY	
Leiliestr.	DZ	
Levendaal	EZ	
Maarsmansteeg	CYZ	30
Maredijk	DX	
Maresingel	DEX	
Marnixstr.	EX	
Molenstr.	EX	
Molenwerf	CDY	31
Morssingel	CY	
Morsstr.	CY	
Nieuwe Beestenmarkt	CY	33
Nieuwerijn	EZ	
Nieuwsteeg	DZ	34
Nieuwstr.	DZ	
Noordeinde	CY	
Oegstgeesterweg	DX	36
Ooesterkerkstr.	EZ	
Oude Herengracht	EY	39
Oudesingel	DEY	
Oudevest	DEY	
Papengracht	CYZ	40
Pieterskerkchoorsteeg	DZ	43
Pieterskerkhof	CDZ	45
Pieterskerkstr.	DYZ	46
Plantagelaan	EZ	48
Plesmanlaan	CY	49
Prinsessekade	CY	51
Rapenburg	CZ	
Rijnsburgersingel	CDX	
Rijnsburgerweg	CX	
Schelpenkade	CZ	
Schipholweg	CX	
Schuttersveld	CX	
Sophiastr.	EX	
Stationsplein	CX	
Stationsweg	CX	
Steenschuur	DZ	
Steenstr.	CY	55
Trompstr.	EZ	
Turfmarkt	CY	57
Uiterstegracht	EZ	
Utrechtsebrug	EZ	58
Varkenmarkt	CY	60
Vismarkt	DZ	61
Vollersgracht	DY	63
Volmolengracht	DY	64
Watersteeg	DZ	67
Willem de Zwijgerlaan	DEX	
Wittesingel	CZ	
Zoeterwoudsesingel	DEZ	

PAYS-BAS

Anak Bandung, Garenmarkt 24a, ✉ 2311 PJ, ☏ (0 71) 512 53 03, *hans.kagie@wanadoo.nl, Fax (0 71) 512 10 49,* Cuisine indonésienne, table de riz – AE VISA
Repas (déjeuner sur réservation) carte env. 28, ♀. DZ t
◆ Dans sa sobre salle à manger garnie de meubles clairs, Anak Bandung mise sur une formule simple : grande assiette ou table de riz javanaises, avec l'option végétarienne.
◆ In zijn sobere eetzaal met lichte meubels biedt Anak Bandung een eenvoudige formule : een groot Javaans bord of Javaanse rijsttafel, met vegetarische optie.

à Leiderdorp *Sud-Est : 2 km – 26 709 h*

AC Hotel, Persant Snoepweg 2 (près A 4, sortie ⑥), ✉ 2353 KA, ☏ (0 71) 589 93 02, *leiderdorp@autogrill.net, Fax (0 71) 541 56 69* – 25 à 250. AE VISA JCB
Repas (avec buffets) *Lunch 10* – carte env. 34 – ☕ 10 – **60 ch** 73.
◆ Hôtel de chaîne récent, dans lequel les conducteurs, fatigués par leur périple autoroutier, pourront recharger les batteries. Chambres fonctionnelles insonorisées.
◆ Autobestuurders die het gejakker over de wegen beu zijn, kunnen in dit jonge ketenhotel hun accu weer opladen. Functionele kamers met geluidsisolatie.

à Oegstgeest *Nord : 3 km – 21 252 h*

Bastion, Rijnzichtweg 97, ✉ 2342 AX, ☏ (0 71) 515 38 41, *bastion@bastionhotel.nl, Fax (0 71) 515 49 81,* – AE VISA. AU a
Repas (grillades, ouvert jusqu'à 23 h) carte env. 30 – ☕ 10 – **40 ch** 60.
◆ Ixième unité de la chaîne hollandaise, située en périphérie de Leiden, à proximité de l'autoroute. Chambres insonorisées, offrant un confort simple mais correct.
◆ Het zoveelste hotel van de Nederlandse keten, aan de rand van Leiden, dicht bij de snelweg. De eenvoudige maar vrij gerieflijke kamers zijn voorzien van geluidsisolatie.

De Beukenhof avec ch, Terweeweg 2, ✉ 2341 CR, ☏ (0 71) 517 31 88, *info@debeukenhof.nl, Fax (0 71) 517 61 69,* – ch, – 40. AE VISA. AU h
fermé 29 déc.-2 janv. – **Repas** *(fermé sam. midi) Lunch 33* – carte 47 à 75, ♀ – ☕ 23 – **6 ch** 175/250, – 3 suites – ½ P 223.
◆ Cette auberge centenaire s'entoure de terrasses et d'un beau jardin fleuri en été. Salle de restaurant animée d'arcades. Chambres et suites modernes décorées avec goût.
◆ Deze oude herberg wordt omringd door terrassen en een tuin die 's zomers prachtig in bloei staat. Restaurantzaal met bogen. Moderne, smaakvol ingerichte kamers en suites.

à Voorschoten *Sud-Ouest : 5 km – 22 558 h*

De Gouden Leeuw, Veurseweg 180, ✉ 2252 AG, ☏ (0 71) 560 28 00, *info@goudenleeuw.valk.nl, Fax (0 71) 560 28 05,* – rest, – 25 à 300. AE VISA AV f
Repas carte env. 31 – ☕ 8 – **139 ch** 70/80.
◆ Le roi des animaux a inspiré l'enseigne de ce motel Van der Valk construit en retrait de la route Den Haag-Leiden. Près de la moitié des chambres sont "king size".
◆ Dit motel van Van der Valk ligt iets van de snelweg Den Haag-Leiden. Bijna de helft van de kamers heeft een kingsize formaat.

De Knip, Kniplaan 22 (4 km par Veurseweg), ✉ 2251 AK, ☏ (0 71) 561 25 73, *info@restaurantdeknip.nl, Fax (0 71) 561 40 96,* – VISA. AV
fermé sam. midi, dim. et lundi – **Repas** *Lunch 30* – 33, ♀.
◆ Un cul-de-sac vous mènera jusqu'à cette ancienne maison de passeur d'eau isolée sur les berges de la Vliet. Repas servi à l'extérieur par beau temps. Vue sur la rivière.
◆ Een doodlopend weggetje leidt naar dit voormalige veerhuis, dat eenzaam aan de oever van de Vliet ligt. Bij mooi weer kan er buiten worden gegeten. Uitzicht op de rivier.

Allemansgeest, Hofweg 55, ✉ 2251 LP, ☏ (0 71) 576 41 75, *allemansgeest@planet.nl, Fax (0 71) 531 55 54,* – AE VISA. AV g
fermé 23 déc.-1er janv., dim. et lundi – **Repas** *Lunch 37* – carte env. 42, ♀.
◆ Auberge familiale montant la garde au confluent de la Vliet et d'un canal. Salle de restaurant panoramique décorée à l'hollandaise. Jolie terrasse d'été au bord de l'eau.
◆ Dit restaurant heeft de wacht betrokken bij de samenloop van de Vliet en een kanaal. De panoramische eetzaal heeft een echt Hollands decor. Mooi zomerterras aan het water.

Gasterij Floris V, Voorstraat 12, ✉ 2251 BN, ☏ (0 71) 561 84 70, – AE VISA JCB. AV a
Repas (dîner seult) carte 30 à 45, ♀.
◆ Au centre de Voorschoten, dans les murs d'une maison de corporation (17e s.), restaurant où la clientèle locale a depuis longtemps pris ses marques. Terrasse estivale.
◆ De lokale clientèle van dit restaurant in het centrum heeft hier binnen de muren van een 17e-eeuws gildehuis al sinds lang zijn vaste stek gevonden. Zomerterras.

LEIDERDORP *Zuid-Holland* 532 M 10 *et* 715 E 5 – *voir à Leiden.*

LEIDSCHENDAM *Zuid-Holland* 532 L 10 *et* 715 E 5 *– voir à Den Haag, environs.*

LELYSTAD P *Flevoland* 531 R 7 *et* 715 H 4 *– 66 460 h.*

Parklaan 2a, ✉ 8241 BC, ✆ (0 320) 23 00 77, Fax (0 320) 23 09 32 – au Sud : 20 km à Zeewolde, Golflaan 1, ✉ 3896 LL, ✆ (0 36) 522 20 73, Fax (0 36) 522 41 00 et Pluvierenweg 7, ✉ 3898 LL, ✆ (0 320) 28 81 16, Fax (0 320) 28 80 09.

Stationsplein 186, ✉ 8232 VT, ✆ (0 320) 24 34 44, lelystad@vvvflevoland.nl, Fax (0 320) 28 02 18.

Amsterdam 57 – Amersfoort 55 – Arnhem 96 – Zwolle 49.

Mercure, Agoraweg 11, ✉ 8224 BZ, ✆ (0 320) 24 24 44, *h1657@accor-hotels.com, Fax (0 320) 22 75 69,* , – , ch, – 25 à 150. AE VISA. rest
Repas *(fermé vend. soir, sam. et dim.) Lunch 8* – carte 31 à 39, – **86 ch** 106/129 – ½ P 119/131.
◆ Cet hôtel de chaîne construit dans un secteur piétonnier du centre-ville est un point de chute valable pour l'homme d'affaires. Chambres assez spacieuses.
◆ Dit ketenhotel in een voetgangersgebied in het centrum is een interessante pleisterplaats voor de zakelijke gast. Vrij ruime kamers.

Raedtskelder, Maerlant 14 (Centre Commercial), ✉ 8224 AC, ✆ (0 320) 22 23 25 – AE VISA JCB
fermé 10 juil.-22 sept., sam. midi et dim. – **Repas** *Lunch 33* – 40, .
◆ Un petit restaurant intime qui vous accueille depuis plus de vingt-cinq ans. Décoration intérieure d'esprit bistrot. Parking public et centre commercial à deux pas.
◆ Een klein, intiem restaurant dat hier al 25 jaar klaarstaat voor zijn gasten. Interieur met bistroambiance. Openbare parking en winkelcentrum op loopafstand.

à Lelystad-Haven C *Lelystad* :

't Dijkhuysje, Oostvaardersdijk 57, ✉ 8244 PB, ✆ (0 320) 26 20 22, *Fax (0 320) 21 29 48,* ≤ Markermeer, , Taverne-rest, – . VISA.
Repas carte env. 39.
◆ Taverne-restaurant aménagée dans une construction en bois où l'on remisait jadis l'outillage d'entretien des digues. À l'étage, vue imprenable sur le Markermeer.
◆ Café-restaurant in een houten loods waarin vroeger het materieel voor het onderhoud van de dijk werd opgeborgen. Vanaf de verdieping vrij uitzicht op het Markermeer.

LEMMER (DE LEMMER) *Fryslân* C *Lemsterland 12 957 h.* 531 T 5 *et* 715 I 3.

Nieuwburen 1, ✉ 8531 EE, ✆ 0 900 540 00 01, info@friesekust.nl, Fax (0 514) 56 16 64.

Amsterdam 106 – Leeuwarden 49 – Zwolle 51.

De Connoisseur, Vuurtorenweg 15, ✉ 8531 HJ, ✆ (0 514) 56 55 59, *connoisseur@wanadoo.nl, Fax (0 514) 56 53 49,* , – P. AE VISA JCB
fermé 29 déc.-4 fév., lundi et mardi – **Repas** (dîner seult) carte env. 46.
◆ Préparations soignées à savourer dans une ambiance intime. Jolie terrasse d'été avec vue sur le port. À côté, un hangar à bateaux abrite une taverne-restaurant originale.
◆ In een intieme ambiance worden verzorgde gerechten geserveerd. Mooi zomerterras met uitzicht op de haven. In het botenhuis ernaast is een origineel Grand café ingericht.

LENGEL *Gelderland* 532 W 11 *– voir à Zeddam.*

LEUSDEN *Utrecht* 532 R 10 *et* 715 H 5 *– voir à Amersfoort.*

LEUVENUM *Gelderland* C *Ermelo 26 760 h.* 531 T 9, 532 T 9 *et* 715 I 5.

Amsterdam 80 – Arnhem 46 – Apeldoorn 24 – Zwolle 38.

Het Roode Koper , Jhr. Dr. J.C. Sandbergweg 82, ✉ 3852 PV Ermelo, ✆ (0 577) 40 73 93, *info@roodekoper.nl, Fax (0 577) 40 75 61,* , , , , – P – 25 à 60. AE VISA JCB. rest
Repas *Lunch 35* – carte 40 à 66 – **37 ch** 60/135 – ½ P 110/150.
◆ Cette belle villa retirée dans les bois dispose d'une aguichante terrasse s'ouvrant sur un parc agrémenté de magnifiques rhododendrons. Chambres douillettes et junior suites. Coquette salle à manger aux tons chauds. Cuisine actuelle.
◆ Deze mooie villa in de bossen heeft een verleidelijk terras dat uitkijkt op een park met prachtige rododendrons. Behaaglijke kamers en junior suites. Charmante eetzaal in warme tinten, waar eigentijdse gerechten worden geserveerd.

LHEE *Drenthe* 531 X 6 *et* 715 K 3 *– voir à Dwingeloo.*

LIES *Fryslân* 531 Q 2 *– voir à Waddeneilanden (Terschelling).*

LIMMEN *Noord-Holland* 531 N 7 *et* 715 F 4 – *voir à Heiloo.*

LINSCHOTEN *Utrecht* 532 O 10 *et* 715 F 5 – *voir à Montfoort.*

LISSE *Zuid-Holland* 532 M 9 *et* 715 E 5 – *22 051 h.*

Voir *Parc de Keukenhof*** *(fin mars à mi-mai), passerelle du moulin* ≤**.

Grachtweg 53, ✉ 2161 HM, ☎ (0 252) 41 42 62, vvv.lisse@hollandrijnland.nl, Fax (0 252) 41 86 39.

Amsterdam 36 – Den Haag 29 – Haarlem 16.

De Nachtegaal, Heereweg 10 (Nord : 2 km), ✉ 2161 AG, ☎ (0 252) 43 30 30, *info@nachtegaal.nl, Fax (0 252) 43 30 10,* – 25 à 700. AE VISA JCB

Repas *Lunch 18* – carte 33 à 46, ♀ – 13 – **148 ch** 125/165, – 2 suites – ½ P 75/115.

◆ Confortable hôtel situé dans une célèbre région floricole. Chambres actuelles et jardin reposant. De magnifiques tulipières vous invitent à papillonner durant tout l'été. Le couvert est dressé sous une véranda donnant sur la terrasse estivale.

◆ Comfortabel hotel in de beroemde bollenstreek. Eigentijdse kamers en rustige tuin. Met al die prachtige tulpenvelden zou je gewoon zin krijgen om hier de hele zomer te blijven. De tafels worden gedekt in de serre, waaraan het zomerterras ligt.

De Duif, Westerdreef 49, ✉ 2161 EN, ☎ (0 252) 41 00 76, *hotel_de_duif@planet.nl, Fax (0 252) 41 09 99,* – 50. AE VISA JCB. rest

Repas (dîner seult) carte 24 à 37, ♀ – 10 – **39 ch** 70/90, – 12 suites – ½ P 93/129.

◆ Ressource hôtelière proposant diverses catégories de chambres, dont douze suites. Aux beaux jours, courrez admirer le tout proche Keukenhof, un splendide jardin paysager.

◆ Dit hotel beschikt over verschillende categorieën kamers, waaronder twaalf suites. Bij mooi weer kunt u zo doorlopen naar de Keukenhof, een prachtige tuin in landschapsstijl.

De Vier Seizoenen, Heereweg 224, ✉ 2161 BR, ☎ (0 252) 41 80 23, *info@restaurantdevierseizoenen.nl, Fax (0 252) 53 15 14,* – AE VISA JCB.

fermé sem. carnaval, dern. sem. juil.-prem. sem. août et mardi – **Repas** *Lunch 26* – 25/52 bc, ♀.

◆ Cette table dédiée aux quatre saisons (vier seizoenen) surveille la place du village. À l'arrière, terrasse d'été verdoyante s'entourant de murs de facture ancienne.

◆ Dit restaurant aan het dorpsplein houdt gelijke tred met de vier jaargetijden. In de zomer heeft het aan de achterkant een groen terras dat wordt omgeven door oude muren.

Het Lisser Spijshuis, Heereweg 234, ✉ 2161 BR, ☎ (0 252) 41 16 65, *info@spijshuis.nl, Fax (0 252) 41 97 77,* – AE VISA JCB

fermé 31 déc.-1er janv., sam. midi, dim. midi et lundi – **Repas** *Lunch 30* – 32, ♀.

◆ La devanture de cette petite maison du cœur de Lisse rappelle un peu une boutique anglaise. Coquette salle à manger "terra cotta" et cuisine en phase avec l'époque.

◆ Aan de voorkant doet dit kleine huis in het hartje van de stad een beetje denken aan een Engels winkeltje. Charmante eetzaal in terracotta en eigentijdse keuken.

à Lisserbroek *Est : 1 km* C *Haarlemmermeer 118 553 h :*

Het Oude Dykhuys, Lisserdijk 567, ✉ 2165 AL, ☎ (0 252) 41 39 05, *dijkhuys@cistron.nl, Fax (0 252) 41 89 77,* – AE VISA JCB

fermé sam. midi, dim. midi et lundi – **Repas** *Lunch 33* – 30/48, ♀.

◆ Cheminée d'un rouge éclatant, poutres blanches laquées et tableaux d'une vive polychromie composent un décor bien dans le coup, assorti aux recettes qu'annonce la carte.

◆ Knalrode schouw, wit gelakte balken en schilderijen in levendige kleuren vormen een mooi decor dat in harmonie is met de gerechten op de kaart.

LISSERBROEK *Noord-Holland* 532 M 9 – *voir à Lisse.*

LOCHEM *Gelderland* 532 X 10 *et* 715 K 5 – *19 413 h.*

Tramstraat 4, ✉ 7241 CJ, ☎ (0 573) 25 18 98, vvv.lochem@planet.nl, Fax (0 573) 25 68 85.

Amsterdam 121 – Arnhem 49 – Apeldoorn 37 – Enschede 42.

De Scheperskamp , Paasberg 3 (Sud-Ouest : 1 km), ✉ 7241 JR, ☎ (0 573) 25 40 51, *reserveringen@scheperskamp.nl, Fax (0 573) 25 71 50,* – rest, – 25 à 150. AE VISA.

Repas *Lunch 25* – carte 36 à 48 – **50 ch** 58/150 – ½ P 74/99.

◆ Quiétude assurée dans cet hôtel environné de bois. Chambres amples et actuelles, souvent dotées d'un balconnet. Expo de sculptures au jardin, fleuri à la belle saison. Alternative brasserie ou restaurant.

◆ Rust verzekerd in dit hotel midden in de bossen. Ruime eigentijdse kamers, waarvan de meeste een balkonnetje hebben. Expositie van beeldhouwwerken in de tuin, die 's zomers prachtig in bloei staat. Keuze tussen brasserie en restaurant.

't Hof van Gelre, Nieuweweg 38, ✉ 7241 EW, ☏ (0 573) 25 33 51, *info@hofvangelre.nl, Fax (0 573) 25 42 45,* – 🅿 – 25 à 120. MC VISA.
fermé du 7 au 10 janv. – **Repas** carte 35 à 44, ♀ – **46 ch** 60/120 – ½ P 79/99.
◆ Au calme, affaire familiale mettant à votre disposition des chambres peu à peu rénovées et, pour le "farniente", un salon avec cheminée ainsi qu'un jardin meublé en été. La carte du restaurant combine terroir et goût du jour.
◆ De kamers in dit rustig gelegen familiehotel worden geleidelijk gerenoveerd. U kunt hier heerlijk bijkomen in de lounge met schouw of in de tuin, waar 's zomers zitjes staan. De menukaart combineert streekgerechten met eigentijdse culinaire verrassingen.

Tulip Inn, Paasberg 2 (Sud-Ouest : 1 km), ✉ 7241 JR, ☏ (0 573) 25 47 51, *info@ti-lochem.nl, Fax (0 573) 25 33 41,* – rest, 🅿 – 25 à 200. AE MC VISA JCB.
Repas *(fermé dim. de nov. à mars et après 20 h)* 26, ♀ – **36 ch** 90/120 – ½ P 67/78.
◆ Établissement très convenable pour les séjours en groupe ou en famille dans ce petit coin tranquille du Gelderland. Certaines chambres offrent la vue sur le Paasberg.
◆ Dit comfortabele hotel in een rustig stukje Gelderland is zowel geschikt voor groepen als voor een verblijf met het gezin. Sommige kamers bieden uitzicht op de Paasberg.

Kawop, Markt 23, ✉ 7241 AA, ☏ (0 573) 25 33 42, *info@kawop.nl, Fax (0 573) 25 88 60,* – AE MC VISA
fermé jeudi et dim. midi – **Repas** (dîner seult sauf en saison) *Lunch 20* – 32/36.
◆ Maison ancienne surveillant la pittoresque place du marché. Menu-carte parsemé de plats régionaux français. Accueil et service aussi aimable qu'élégant. Terrasses ombragées.
◆ Restaurant in een oud herenhuis aan het pittoreske marktplein. Kaart met tal van Franse streekgerechten. Vriendelijke ontvangst en charmante bediening. Lommerrijke terrassen.

à Barchem *Sud-Est : 4 km* C *Lochem :*

Bon'Aparte, Lochemseweg 37 (Nord-Ouest : 2,5 km), ✉ 7244 RR, ☏ (0 573) 25 71 96, *info@hotelbonaparte.nl, Fax (0 573) 25 62 38,* – 🅿 – 25 à 250. AE MC VISA
fermé du 10 au 14 janv. – **Repas** *Lunch 19* – 33, ♀ – **39 ch** 88/155 – ½ P 93.
◆ Un frère de Napoléon aurait séjourné en ces lieux, d'où l'enseigne ! Chambres et suites actuelles bien équipées, confortable salon et belle piscine complétée d'un sauna. Ample salle à manger où l'on vient faire des repas au goût du jour et assez élaborés.
◆ Een broer van Napoleon zou hier ooit hebben gelogeerd, vandaar de naam ! Moderne kamers en junior suites met goed comfort. Aangename lounge en een mooi zwembad met sauna. In de grote eetzaal kunt u genieten van een vrij verzorgde, eigentijdse maaltijd.

De Lochemse Berg, Lochemseweg 42 (Nord-Ouest : 2,5 km), ✉ 7244 RS, ☏ (0 573) 25 13 77, *info@delochemseberg.nl, Fax (0 573) 25 82 24,* – 🅿. MC VISA.
rest
6 avril-oct. et du 20 au 31 déc. – **Repas** (résidents seult) – **15 ch** 52.
◆ Jolie demeure bourgeoise du siècle dernier, agrémentée d'un reposant petit parc bordé de bois propices aux promenades. Chambres sans histoire. Accueil familial gentil.
◆ Dit fraaie herenhuis uit de vorige eeuw ligt in een rustig park aan de rand van het bos, waar u heerlijk kunt wandelen. Prima kamers. Vriendelijke, gastvrije ontvangst.

LOENEN *Gelderland* C *Apeldoorn 154 859 h.* 532 V 10 *et* 715 J 5.

Amsterdam 104 – Arnhem 25 – Apeldoorn 16 – Enschede 80.

De Loenermark, Eerbeekseweg 4, ✉ 7371 CG, ☏ (0 55) 505 13 28, *info@loenermark.nl, Fax (0 55) 505 11 59,* – 🅿. AE MC VISA. ch
Repas *(fermé 31 déc.-14 janv. et après 20 h 30) Lunch 11* – carte 27 à 40, ♀ – **9 ch** 45/65 – ½ P 44/60.
◆ Voici une adresse villageoise qui servira utilement de "case départ" aux randonneurs, cyclistes ou pédestres, désireux de rayonner dans la région. Chambres très convenables. Repas classico-traditionnel.
◆ Dit adres in het dorpje Loenen is een handige uitvalsbasis voor fietsers en wandelaars die de streek willen verkennen. De kamers zijn zeer behoorlijk. Er wordt een klassiek-traditionele maaltijd geserveerd.

LOENEN *Utrecht* 532 P 9 *et* 715 G 5 – *8 408 h.*

Amsterdam 22 – Utrecht 17 – Hilversum 14.

Tante Koosje, Kerkstraat 1, ✉ 3632 EL, ☏ (0 294) 23 32 01, *info@tante-koosje.nl, Fax (0 294) 23 46 13,* – AE MC VISA.
fermé 31 déc., merc., sam. midi et dim. midi – **Repas** *Lunch 34* – carte 49 à 63.
◆ Les fines fourchettes du cru se piquent d'avoir leur rond de serviette à cette table avoisinant le clocher. Nouveau décor intérieur produisant tout son effet. Mets soignés.
◆ De lokale fijnproevers gaan prat op hun vaste stek in dit restaurant vlakbij de klokkentoren. Verrassend nieuw decor. Verzorgde keuken.

De Proeverij, Kerkstraat 5a, ✉ 3632 EL, ℘ (0 294) 23 47 74, *info@deproeverij.nl, Fax (0 294) 23 08 30,* 🏖 – AE ⓓ ⓜ VISA. ✗
fermé 31 déc. et lundi – **Repas** (dîner seult) carte 39 à 48, ♀.
◆ Il règne une ambiance bon enfant dans cette maisonnette bâtie au pied de l'église. Petite salle de restaurant sagement rustique, éclairée par de nombreuses bougies.
◆ Er hangt een gemoedelijke sfeer in dit pandje, dat in de schaduw van de grote kerk staat. De kleine, ietwat rustieke eetzaal wordt met veel kaarsen verlicht.

LOPPERSUM *Groningen* 531 Z 3 *et* 715 L 2 – *11 049 h.*

Voir *Fresques★ dans l'église.*
Amsterdam 216 – Groningen 21 – Appingedam 8.

't Regthuys, Fromaweg 1 (Sud-Est : 3 km à Wirdum), ✉ 9917 PK, ℘ (0 596) 57 18 90, *regthuys@wxs.nl, Fax (0 596) 57 30 54,* 🏖 – P. AE ⓓ ⓜ VISA JCB. ✗
fermé 31 déc.-10 janv. et lundi – **Repas** (déjeuner sur réservation) carte 24 à 35.
◆ Cet établissement familial situé au cœur d'un pittoresque hameau accueille ses convives dans un décor chaleureux. Les banquets se tiennent à part, sous la véranda.
◆ Dit familierestaurant midden in een schilderachtig dorpje ontvangt zijn gasten in een warme ambiance. Voor partijen wordt de serre gebruikt.

LUNTEREN *Gelderland* C *Ede 103 708 h.* 532 S 10 *et* 715 H 5.

Amsterdam 69 – Arnhem 29 – Apeldoorn 43 – Utrecht 46.

Host. De Lunterse Boer 🐎, Boslaan 87, ✉ 6741 KD, ℘ (0 318) 48 36 57, *receptie@lunterseboer.nl, Fax (0 318) 48 55 21,* 🏖, 🌳, 🚲 – TV P – 🔬 25. AE ⓓ ⓜ VISA JCB
fermé 27 déc.-6 janv. – **Repas** carte env. 37 – **16 ch** ☕ 62/105 – ½ P 82.
◆ Dans un cadre paisible et boisé, près d'un grand bâtiment à toit de chaume où l'on retirera sa clé, hôtel abritant des chambres bien tenues, avec terrasse ou balcon. Une carte actuelle est proposée sous la belle charpente de l'ancienne grange.
◆ Dit hotel in een bosrijke omgeving staat vlak bij een gebouw met rieten dak, waar u de sleutel kunt halen. Goed onderhouden kamers met terras of balkon. Onder het kapgebint van de oude schuur is het sfeervol tafelen. De menukaart past bij de huidige trend.

De LUTTE *Overijssel* C *Losser 22 703 h.* 531 AA 9, 532 AA 9 *et* 715 L 5.

Plechelmusstraat 14, ✉ 7587 AM, ℘ 0 900 202 19 81, info@vvvdelutte.nl, Fax (0 541) 55 22 11.
Amsterdam 165 – Zwolle 78 – Enschede 15.

Landgoed de Wilmersberg 🐎, Rhododendronlaan 7, ✉ 7587 NL, ℘ (0 541) 58 55 55, *info@wilmersberg.nl, Fax (0 541) 58 55 65,* ≤, 🏖, ⊘, ≘s, ⛱, 🌳, 🎾, 🚲 – 🛗 ⚡ TV ♿ P – 🔬 25 à 200. AE ⓓ ⓜ VISA. ✗
Repas *(fermé dim. midi)* 38/82 bc, ♀ – ☕ 16 – **62 ch** 98/235, – 2 suites – ½ P 108.
◆ Domaine verdoyant, belles chambres tout confort, terrasses estivales panoramiques, jardin soigné, quiétude absolue : un capital séduction auquel on ne reste pas insensible. Salle de restaurant décorée à l'anglaise. Cuisine de notre temps.
◆ Landhuis in het groen, mooie kamers met alle comfort, panoramische zomerterrassen, verzorgde tuin en absolute rust. Wie kan de verleiding weerstaan ? Gerechten uit de eigentijdse keuken worden geserveerd in een restaurantzaal die in Engelse stijl is ingericht.

De Bloemenbeek 🐎, Beuningerstraat 6 (Nord-Est : 1 km), ✉ 7587 LD, ℘ (0 541) 55 12 24, *info@bloemenbeek.nl, Fax (0 541) 55 22 85,* 🏖, ⊘, 🏋, ≘s, ⛱, 🌳, 🎾, 🚲 – 🛗 ⚡ TV P – 🔬 25 à 250. AE ⓓ ⓜ VISA JCB. ✗ rest
fermé 29 déc.-5 janv. – **Repas** 35/58 – **55 ch** ☕ 130/160, – 5 suites – ½ P 110/135.
◆ Le Ruisseau Fleuri (Bloemenbeek) : l'enseigne traduit bien la situation agreste dont profite l'hôtel. Piscine relaxante et chaises longues pour paresser. Chambres amples. Tables dressées dans une atmosphère feutrée et, aux beaux jours, sur la pelouse ombragée.
◆ Een passende naam voor dit landelijk gelegen hotel. Zwembad voor een verkoelende duik en ligstoelen om lekker op weg te dromen. Ruime kamers. De tafels worden in een stemmige ambiance gedekt en, op zomerse dagen, op het lommerrijke gazon.

't Kruisselt, Kruisseltlaan 3, ✉ 7587 NM, ℘ (0 541) 55 15 67, *info@kruisselt.nl, Fax (0 541) 55 18 62,* ≤, 🏖, ≘s, ⛱, 🚲 – ⚡ TV – 🔬 25 à 100. ⓜ VISA. ✗ rest
fermé 30 déc.-7 janv. – **Repas** carte 28 à 54 – **43 ch** ☕ 75/110 – ½ P 73/80.
◆ Les Tiger Woods en herbe pourront enchaîner les coups sur le "green", un parcours en neuf trous, bordé d'arbres, visible de la terrasse d'été. Dix chambres plus récentes. Repas servi à ciel ouvert par météo clémente.
◆ De Tiger Woods in de dop kunnen hier hun slag slaan op de green, een baan van negen holes die door bomen wordt omzoomd en vanaf het zomerterras te zien is. Er zijn onlangs tien nieuwe kamers bij gekomen. Bij mooi weer worden de maaltijden buiten geserveerd.

XX **Berg en Dal** avec ch, Bentheimerstraat 34, ✉ 7587 NH, ☎ (0 541) 55 12 02, *info@bergendal.nl, Fax (0 541) 55 15 54,* – TV P AE MC VISA
Repas Lunch 25 – 37 – **12 ch** ☐ 57/80 – ½ P 57/74.
◆ Auberge typique postée au bord de la route. Salle à manger en deux parties que séparent des baies garnies de petits vitraux modernes. Chambres en annexe, côté jardin.
◆ Restaurant-hotel in een karakteristiek pand langs de weg. De eetzaal is in tweeën gedeeld door grote ramen met modern glas in lood bovenin. Kamers in de annexe, aan de tuin.

MAARSSEN *Utrecht* 532 P 10 *et* 715 G 5 – *40 134 h.*
Amsterdam 32 – Utrecht 9.

XX **Auguste,** Straatweg 144, ✉ 3603 CS, ☎ (0 346) 56 56 66, *info@auguste.nl, Fax (0 346) 56 56 66,* – P AE MC VISA
fermé du 1er au 19 août, 26 déc.-1er janv., sam. midi et dim. – **Repas** Lunch 30 – carte 42 à 67, ♀.
◆ Une auguste enseigne signale cette petite adresse où l'on vient pour une cuisine classique remise à la page. Fourneaux à vue, tout comme la cave, assez bien fournie.
◆ Fijnproevers komen hier genieten van klassieke gerechten in een eigentijds jasje, die in het zicht van de gasten worden bereid. Vrij goed gevulde, open wijnkelder.

XX **De Nonnerie,** Langegracht 51, ✉ 3601 AK, ☎ (0 346) 56 22 01, *restaurant@nonnerie.nl, Fax (0 346) 56 18 24,* – P – 25 à 110. AE MC VISA
fermé 27 déc.-1er janv., sam. midi et dim. midi – **Repas** Lunch 29 – carte 42 à 56, ♀.
◆ Ancienne habitation bourgeoise convertie en restaurant et "business center", De Nonnerie vous attable dans un décor de notre temps, à l'image des mets. Banquets fréquents.
◆ Dit oude herenhuis is verbouwd tot restaurant en businesscenter. U kunt hier tafelen in een decor dat net als de gerechten een eigentijds karakter heeft. Veel evenementen.

MAARTENSDIJK *Utrecht* C *De Bilt 42 309 h.* 532 Q 10 *et* 715 G 5.
Amsterdam 53 – Utrecht 19 – Apeldoorn 70.

X **Martinique,** Dorpsweg 153, ✉ 3738 CD, ☎ (0 346) 21 26 27, *restaurantmartinique@planet.nl, Fax (0 346) 21 26 27,* – P AE MC VISA
fermé lundi – **Repas** (déjeuner sur réservation) carte env. 37.
◆ Tout nouveau "look" pour cette petite affaire familiale redécorée dans les tons chocolat, sable et ivoire. Recettes au goût du moment et formule menu-carte.
◆ Een compleet nieuwe look voor dit familierestaurantje, in de kleuren chocolade, ivoor en zand. Er worden seizoengerechten geserveerd en à la carte menu.

à Hollandsche Rading *Nord : 3 km* C *De Bilt :*

XX **De Fazantenhof,** Karnemelkseweg 1, ✉ 3739 LA, ☎ (0 35) 577 14 64, *info@defazantenhof.nl, Fax (0 35) 577 12 28,* – P – 25 à 45. AE MC VISA
fermé 27 déc.-2 janv., lundi, mardi et merc. – **Repas** Lunch 25 – carte 32 à 43, ♀.
◆ Dans les bois, au croisement de pistes cyclables, vaste pavillon devancé d'une terrasse d'été. Registre culinaire en accord avec son temps. Sélection de vins bien montée.
◆ Groot paviljoen met een terras aan de voorzijde, bij een kruispunt van fietspaden in de bossen. Het culinaire repertoire volgt de smaak van het moment. Goede selectie wijnen.

MAASBRACHT *Limburg* 532 U 16 *et* 715 I 8 – *13 697 h.*
Amsterdam 176 – Maastricht 39 – Eindhoven 48 – Venlo 40.

XXX ✿ **Da Vinci** (Mme Reuten), Havenstraat 27 (au port des péniches), ✉ 6051 CS, ☎ (0 475) 46 59 79, *info@davinci-restaurant.nl, Fax (0 475) 46 66 11* – AE MC VISA.
fermé 1 sem. carnaval, 3 sem. vacances bâtiment, 1 sem. après Noël, lundi et mardi sauf jours fériés – **Repas** Lunch 38 – 55/118 bc, carte 52 à 85, ♀.
◆ Belle démonstration de cuisine classique actualisée, dans cette maison de bouche que dirige une sagace cuisinière. Intérieur résolument design, et pourtant fort chaleureux.
◆ Een vrouwelijke chef-kok zwaait de scepter in dit eethuis ; zij geeft er een fraai staaltje van klassieke kookkunst met een vleugje modern. Designinterieur met warme ambiance.
Spéc. Cannelloni d'artichauts, petits légumes et fromage de chèvre. Langoustines en salade de pommes de terre Rosevall et tapenade au caviar. Pigeon de Bresse au foie d'oie et ravioli à l'oignon

MAASDAM *Zuid-Holland* C *Binnenmaas 19 213 h.* 532 M 12 *et* 715 E 6.
Amsterdam 100 – Rotterdam 21 – Breda 35 – Dordrecht 14.

De Hoogt , Raadhuisstraat 3, ✉ 3299 AP, ☎ (0 78) 676 18 11, *hoteldehoogt@wxs.nl, Fax (0 78) 676 47 25,* – rest, TV P. AE ① MC VISA JCB
Repas *(fermé sam. midi et dim. midi)* 24/28 – **10 ch** ☕ 72/85 – ½ P 60/90.
◆ Distribuées à l'arrière pour plus de calme, les chambres de ce petit hôtel familial offrent un confort correct. La meilleure, avec whirlpool, profite d'une vue sur l'eau. Salle des repas décorée de marines, terrasse estivale sur le devant, plats traditionnels.
◆ De vrij gerieflijke kamers van dit familiehotelletje liggen aan de achterkant, waar het wat rustiger is. De beste kamer, met whirlpool, kijkt uit op het water. Eetzaal waar zeegezichten hangen, zomerterras aan de voorkant, traditionele gerechten.

MAASSLUIS *Zuid-Holland* 532 K 11 *et* 715 D 6 – *32 876 h.*
vers Rozenburg : Veer Maassluis, Burg. v.d. Lelykade 15 ☎ (0 10) 591 22 12, Fax (0 10) 592 85 55. Durée de la traversée : 10 min.
Amsterdam 81 – Rotterdam 17 – Den Haag 26.

XX **De Ridderhof,** Sportlaan 2, ✉ 3141 XN, ☎ (0 10) 591 12 11, *info@restaurantderidderhof.nl, Fax (0 10) 591 37 80,* – P. AE MC VISA JCB
fermé sam. midi, dim. midi et lundi – **Repas** Lunch 28 – carte 42 à 50, ♀.
◆ Ancienne ferme rustique fondée au temps de Rembrandt et Vermeer. Plats classiques et belle cave globe-trotter où s'épanouissent aussi vieux whiskies et portos. Terrasse d'été.
◆ Oude rustieke boerderij uit de tijd van Rembrandt en Vermeer. Klassieke schotels en mooie, kosmopolitische kelder waarin ook oude whisky's en port liggen te rijpen.

MAASTRICHT P *Limburg* 532 T 17 *et* 715 I 9 – *122 005 h.*
Voir *La vieille ville★ - Basilique St-Servais★★ (St. Servaasbasiliek) : Portail royal★, chœur★, chapiteaux★, trésor★★ (kerkschat)* CY **B** – *Basilique Notre-Dame★ (O. L. Vrouwebasiliek) : chœur★★* CZ **A** – *Remparts Sud★ (Walmuur)* CZ – *Carnaval★ – au Sud : 2 km, St. Pietersberg★* AX.
Musée : *des Bons Enfants★★ (Bonnefantenmuseum)* DZ **M¹**.
par ① : 11 km à Beek ☎ (0 43) 358 99 99, Fax (0 43) 358 99 88.
Kleine Staat 1, ✉ 6211 ED, ☎ (0 43) 321 78 78, info@vvvmaastricht.nl, Fax (0 43) 321 37 46.
Amsterdam 213 ① – Bruxelles 124 ⑤ – Liège 33 ⑤ – Aachen 36 ② – Mönchengladbach 81 ①

Plans pages suivantes

Quartiers du Centre :

Derlon sans rest, O.L.Vrouweplein 6, ✉ 6211 HD, ☎ (0 43) 321 67 70, *info@derlon.com, Fax (0 43) 325 19 33,* – TV – 25 à 50. AE ① MC VISA JCB. CZ e
☕ 19 – **42 ch** 225/299.
◆ Hôtel très confortable installé au pied du plus vieux monument de la ville, sur une jolie placette, effervescente les soirs d'étés. Vestiges romains exposés au sous-sol.
◆ Zeer comfortabel hotel aan de voet van het oudste monument van de stad, aan een leuk pleintje dat 's zomers verandert in een bruisend trefpunt. Romeinse resten in de kelder.

Botticelli sans rest, Papenstraat 11, ✉ 6211 LG, ☎ (0 43) 352 63 00, *reception@botticellihotel.nl, Fax (0 43) 352 63 36* – TV. AE ① MC VISA. CZ s
fermé carnaval, du 24 au 27 déc. et 31 déc.-1er janv. – ☕ 14 – **18 ch** 88/180.
◆ Charmante maison patricienne relookée façon "Renaissance italienne". Chambres actuelles et plaisantes. Terrasse close de murs, embellie d'une pièce d'eau et de statues.
◆ Charmant patriciërshuis met een nieuwe look in Italiaanse renaissancestijl. Aangename, eigentijdse kamers. Ommuurd terras met waterpartij en beelden.

de Pauwenhof sans rest, Boschstraat 70, ✉ 6211 AX, ☎ (0 43) 350 33 33, *info@pauwenhof.nl, Fax (0 43) 350 33 39* – TV P. AE ① MC VISA JCB. CY k
15 ch ☕ 117/155.
◆ Heureux mélange d'ancien et de moderne dans cette demeure bourgeoise du 19e s. Chambres de style contemporain et terrasse estivale intérieure, garnie de meubles design.
◆ Geslaagde melange van klassiek en modern in dit 19e-eeuwse herenhuis. Kamers in eigentijdse stijl. Zomerterras met designmeubels aan de tuinkant.

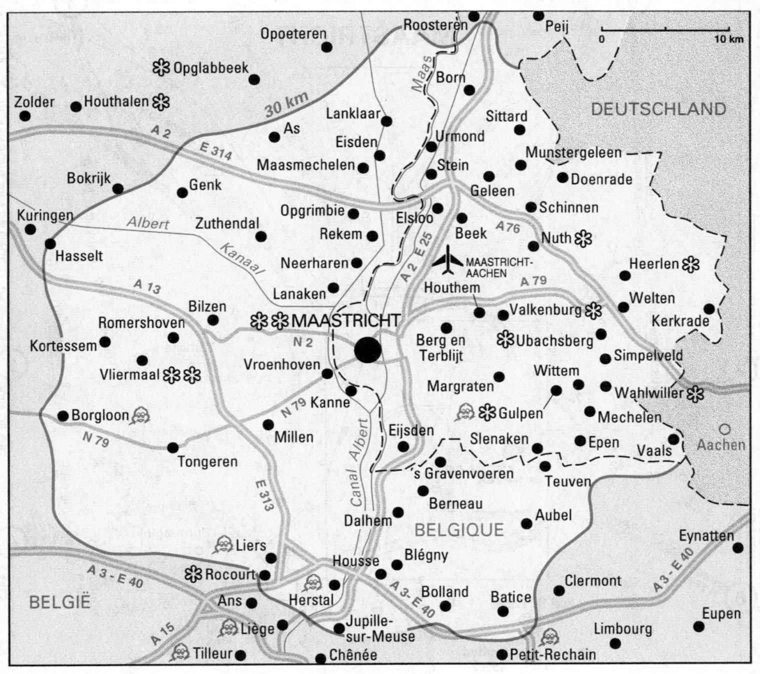

Mabi, Kleine Gracht 24, ✉ 6211 CB, ☎ (0 43) 351 44 44, *info@hotel-mabi.nl, Fax (0 43) 351 44 55* – |♦|, rest, TV P – 35. AE D MC VISA. CY q
Repas *(fermé sam. midi et dim. midi) Lunch 28* – carte 36 à 48 – ☕ 14 – **55 ch** 95/140 – ½ P 90.

◆ Avis aux cinéphiles : un ancien "bioscoop" (cinéma) sert de cadre à cet agréable hôtel. Intérieur moderne aux couleurs vives. Bel effort d'insonorisation dans les chambres. Salle de restaurant dans l'air du temps et registre culinaire à la page, lui aussi.

◆ Filmliefhebbers opgelet : een oude bioscoop vormt het decor van dit aangename hotel. Modern interieur in levendige kleuren. Kamers met goede geluidsisolatie. Restaurantzaal en culinair register hebben een eigentijds karakter.

d'Orangerie sans rest, Kleine Gracht 4, ✉ 6211 CB, ☎ (0 43) 326 11 11, *info@hotel-orangerie.nl, Fax (0 43) 326 12 87* – TV. AE D MC VISA CY d
☕ 12 – **22 ch** 70/97.

◆ Sympathique petit hôtel de caractère occupant une habitation patricienne du 18e s. Plusieurs catégories de chambres au décor "british", toutes assez cosy. Accueil aimable.

◆ Sympathiek, karaktervol hotelletje in een 18e-eeuws patriciërshuis. Verschillende categorieën kamers met Engels decor en vrij knusse ambiance. Vriendelijke ontvangst.

Bastion Centrum, Boschstraat 27, ✉ 6211 AS, ☎ (0 43) 321 22 22, *bastion@bastionhotel.nl, Fax (0 43) 321 34 32* – |♦| TV P – 25 à 120. AE D MC VISA. CY g
Repas (grillades, ouvert jusqu'à 23 h) carte env. 30, ♀ – ☕ 10 – **128 ch** 89/110.

◆ À distance respectable du centre animé, près d'une sortie du ring, immeuble de brique récent disposant de chambres bien calibrées et d'une poignée de junior suites.

◆ Dit recente bakstenen gebouw op respectabele afstand van het drukke centrum, nabij een afslag van de ringweg, herbergt behoorlijke kamers en een paar junior suites.

Les Charmes sans rest, Lenculenstraat 18, ✉ 6211 KR, ☎ (0 43) 321 74 00, *info@hotellescharmes.nl, Fax (0 43) 325 85 74* – TV. AE D MC VISA JCB. CZ t
☕ 11 – **11 ch** 100/130.

◆ D'agréables chambres personnalisées, dont plusieurs junior suites, se partagent ces deux maisons anciennes entretenant un peu la nostalgie de la Belle Époque.

◆ Aangename kamers met een eigen karakter, waaronder diverse junior suites, liggen verdeeld over twee oude panden, waarin een zekere nostalgie naar de belle époque voelbaar is.

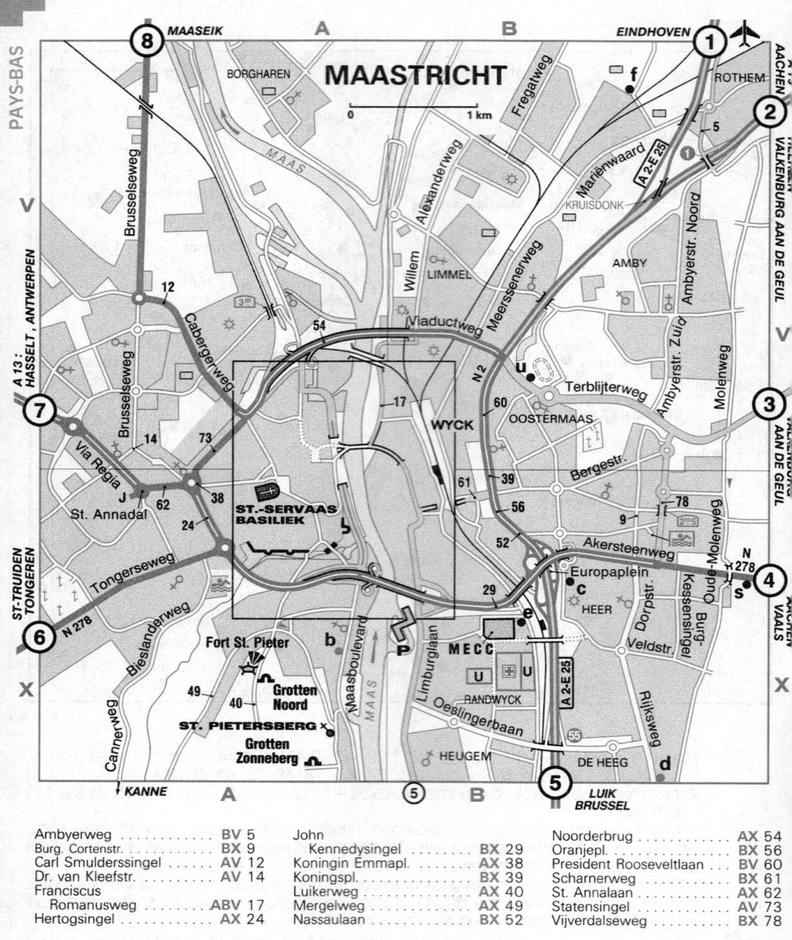

Ambyerweg BV 5	John Kennedysingel BX 29	Noorderbrug AX 54
Burg. Cortenstr. BX 9	Koningin Emmapl. AX 38	Oranjepl. BX 56
Carl Smulderssingel AV 12	Koningspl. BX 39	President Rooseveltlaan BV 60
Dr. van Kleefstr. AV 14	Luikerweg AX 40	Scharnerweg BX 61
Franciscus Romanusweg ABV 17	Mergelweg AX 49	St. Annalaan AX 62
Hertogsingel AX 24	Nassaulaan BX 52	Statensingel AV 73
		Vijverdalseweg BX 78

Du Casque sans rest, Helmstraat 14, ✉ 6211 TA, ☎ (0 43) 321 43 43, *info@ducasque.nl*, *Fax (0 43) 325 51 55* – 🛗 TV – 🏛 35. AE VISA JCB — CY m

☕ 14 – **41 ch** 110/138.

◆ Dans une rue voisine du Vrijthof et de la basilique St-Servais, ressource hôtelière idéale si l'on recherche la proximité immédiate du secteur commercial piétonnier.

◆ Dit hotel in een straat naast het Vrijthof en de St.-Servaasbasiliek is een ideale stek voor wie graag dicht bij de winkels in het voetgangerscentrum zit.

Bigarré sans rest, Van Hasseltkade 9, ✉ 6211 CC, ☎ (0 43) 310 03 10, *info@bigarre.nl*, *Fax (0 43) 310 02 40* – TV. AE VISA. — CY z

☕ 12 – **10 ch** 100.

◆ Un adorable point de chute pour partir à la découverte de Maastricht. Chambres de bon format, habillées de tissus coordonnés. Salle des petits-déjeuners très soignée.

◆ Een verrukkelijk hotelletje als u de stad wilt gaan verkennen. Kamers van goed formaat en smaakvol gestoffeerd. Zeer verzorgde ontbijtzaal.

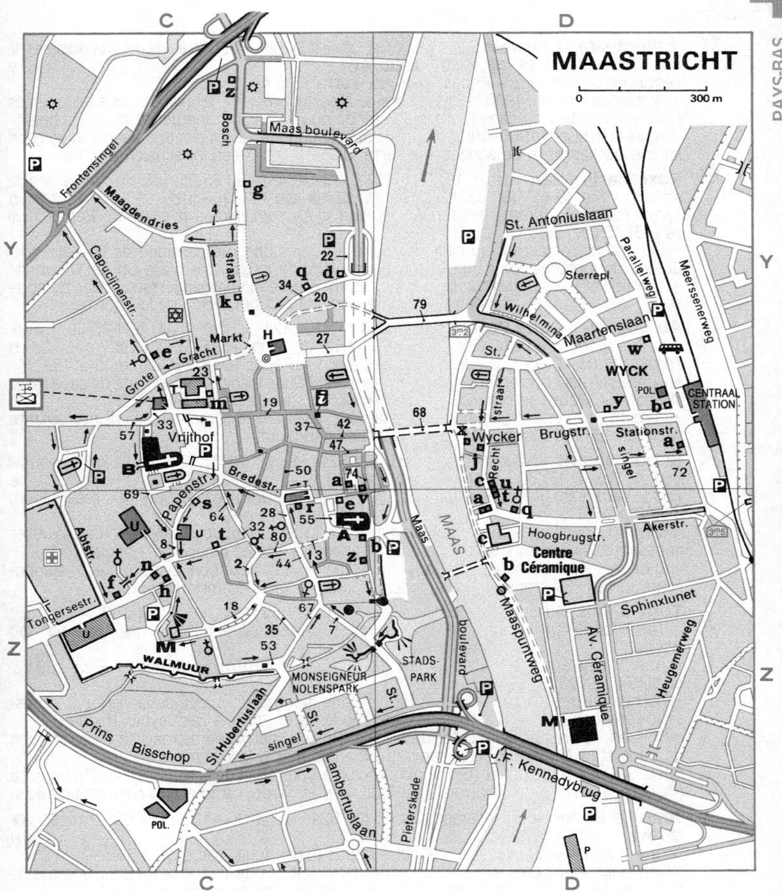

Achter de Molens	CZ 2	Hondstr.	CZ 28	Onze Lieve Vrouweplein	CZ 55
A. D. Barakken	CY 4	Kapoenstr.	CZ 32	Oude Tweebergenpoort	CY 57
Begijnenstr.	CZ 7	Keizer Karelpl.	CY 33	St. Jacobstr.	CY 64
Bouillonstr.	CZ 8	Kleine Gracht	CY 34	St. Pieterstr.	CZ 67
Cortenstr.	CZ 13	Kleine Looiersstr.	CZ 35	St. Servaasbrug	DY 68
Grote Looiersstr.	CZ 18	Kleine Staat	CY 37	St. Servaasklooster	CZ 69
Grote Staat	CY 19	Maastr. Brugstr.	CY 42	Spoorweglaan	DY 72
Gubbelstr.	CY 20	Maastr. Heidenstr.	CZ 44	Stokstr.	CY 74
van Hasseltkade	CY 22	Maastr. Smedenstr.	CY 47	Wilhelminabrug	DY 79
Helmstr.	CY 23	Mickelersstr.	CY 50	Witmakersstr.	CZ 80
Hoenderstr.	CY 27	Nieuwenhofstr.	CZ 53	Wycker Brugstr.	DY

XXX ✿ **Toine Hermsen,** St-Bernardusstraat 2, ✉ 6211 HL, ☎ (0 43) 325 84 00, *toine.hermsen@wxs.nl, Fax (0 43) 325 83 73* – ▤. AE ⓪ ⓂⒸ VISA JCB. ✗ CZ **b**
fermé sem. carnaval, 2 sem. vacances bâtiment, dern. sem. déc, sam. midi, dim., lundi midi et jours fériés – **Repas** *Lunch 25* – 79/105, carte 61 à 107, ♀.
◆ L'une des meilleures tables du Limbourg batave : belle cuisine classique actualisée, servie dans une salle aux tons ocre et terre de Sienne. Chic, mais pas du tout guindé.
◆ Een van de beste restaurants in Nederlands Limburg : mooie klassieke keuken met eigentijdse invulling. Eetzaal met oker- en terratinten, die chic maar beslist niet stijfjes is.
Spéc. Cuisses de grenouilles à la crème légère de cerfeuil et ail. Confit de pigeon de Bresse en salade de chou vert tiède. Perdreau sauvage rôti au naturel ou à l'ancienne (sept.-nov.)

XX **'t Plenkske,** Plankstraat 6, ✉ 6211 GA, ☎ (0 43) 321 84 56, *plenkske@wordlaccess.nl, Fax (0 43) 325 81 33,* – AE ⓓ MC VISA CYZ v
fermé fin déc. et dim. – **Repas** *Lunch 22* – carte 33 à 46, ♀.
◆ Ambiance "bistrot 1900" à cette adresse assez courue. Prenez place sur les banquettes rouges rebondies ou dans l'agréable véranda qui surplombe une petite place cachée.
◆ Ambiance bistro 1900-stijl in dit vrij favoriete adresje. Neem plaats op een van de rood knusse banken of in de aangename serre, die uitkijkt op een verscholen pleintje.

XX **Rozemarijn,** Havenstraat 19, ✉ 6211 GJ, ☎ (0 43) 450 65 05, *info@rozemarijnmaastricht.nl, Fax (0 43) 450 65 09,* – ▤. AE ⓓ MC VISA JCB. ✻ CYZ a
fermé carnaval, 2 prem. sem. sept., Noël, Nouvel An, sam. midi, dim. et lundi – **Repas** *Lunch 25* – 38/55 bc, ♀.
◆ Engageant restaurant au cadre actuel établi dans une rue piétonne de la vieille ville. Cuisine du moment. Fringante et lumineuse véranda jouxtant la place Op de Thermen.
◆ Aantrekkelijk restaurant met eigentijds interieur, in een voetgangersstraat van de oude stad. Actuele keuken. Genoegelijke, lichte veranda aan het plein Op de Thermen.

XX **Au Coin des Bons Enfants,** Ezelmarkt 4, ✉ 6211 LJ, ☎ (0 43) 321 23 59, *mail@aucoindesbonsenfants.nl, Fax (0 43) 325 82 52,* – ▤ – 30. AE ⓓ CZ h
fermé 26 juil.-10 août, 27 déc.-4 janv. et mardi – **Repas** *Lunch 30* – carte 49 à 75.
◆ L'enseigne est "bon enfant" ; l'atmosphère aussi. Plats traditionnels et livre de cave assez intéressant. Petite terrasse dressée à l'arrière lorsque le temps s'y prête.
◆ In naam en sfeer een goedmoedig restaurant. Traditionele gerechten en vrij interessante wijnkaart. Bij mooi weer klein terras aan de achterkant.

XX **le bon vivant,** Capucijnenstraat 91, ✉ 6211 RP, ☎ (0 43) 321 08 16, *info@lebonvivant.nl, Fax (0 43) 325 37 82* – ▤. AE MC VISA CY e
fermé sem. carnaval, mi-juil.-mi-août, dim. et lundi – **Repas** (déjeuner sur réservation) 34/60 bc, ♀.
◆ Garnie de meubles classiques, la salle à manger du bon vivant vous enrobe sous ses voûtes imposantes. Parements de brique nue, éclairage tamisé et ambiance "bougie".
◆ In de met klassiek meubilair ingerichte eetzaal omhult deze bon-vivant u met zijn imposante gewelf. Bakstenen muren, gedempt licht en kaarsjesambiance.

X ✿ **Tout à Fait** (Ausems), St-Bernardusstraat 16, ✉ 6211 HL, ☎ (0 43) 350 04 05, *tout.a.fait@planet.nl, Fax (0 43) 350 05 35,* Avec rôtisserie – ▤. AE ⓓ MC VISA. ✻ CZ z
fermé 21 fév.-3 mars, 25 déc.-2 janv., lundi, mardi et sam. midi – **Repas** *Lunch 35* – 88 bc, carte 54 à 90, ♀.
◆ Derrière les remparts, dans une rue piétonne marquant l'entrée de la vieille ville, brasserie-rôtisserie étagée sur trois niveaux, moderne et "tout à fait" sympathique.
◆ Brasserie-grillrestaurant achter de stadswal, in een voetgangersstraatje aan de rand van de oude stad. Modern, uiterst sympathiek adres met drie verdiepingen.
Spéc. Saumon fumé et rillettes de porc régional. Coq faisan de la rôtissoire en choucroute (mi-oct.-mi-janv.). Homard braisé à l'huile d'olives et citron, caramel au vinaigre balsamique

X **Jean La Brouche,** Tongersestraat 9, ✉ 6211 LL, ☎ (0 43) 321 46 09 – ▤. AE ⓓ MC VISA CZ n
fermé 2 dern. sem. juil., dim. et lundi – **Repas** (dîner seult) carte 37 à 56.
◆ Déjà vingt ans de présence pour ce petit restaurant de quartier où se mitonne une cuisine française aux accents bourgeois. Carte avec menu. Fonctionnement familial.
◆ Al twintig jaar bereidt dit buurtrestaurantje een Franse keuken met traditionele accenten. À la carte en menu. Familiebedrijf.

X **sagittarius,** Bredestraat 7, ✉ 6211 HA, ☎ (0 43) 321 14 92 – AE ⓓ MC VISA JCB
fermé dim., lundi, mardi et merc. midi – **Repas** carte 34 à 44. CZ r
◆ Amateurs de grillades et de produits de la mer, cette adresse connue de longue date autour de la basilique N.-D. n'attend que votre passage. Jardin d'hiver à toit ouvrant.
◆ Liefhebbers van grillgerechten en visschotels worden al jarenlang met open armen ontvangen op dit adres bij de O.-L.-Vrouwebasiliek. Serre met dak dat kan worden geopend.

X **'t Drifke,** Lage Kanaaldijk 22, ✉ 6212 AE, ☎ (0 43) 321 45 81, *Fax (0 43) 321 45 81* – MC VISA AX b
fermé carnaval et lundis et mardis non fériés – **Repas** (dîner seult) carte env. 33.
◆ Affaire familiale un peu rustique, située aux portes de la ville, dans le quartier St-Pieter. Travaillés à la mode d'aujourd'hui, les plats cultivent l'accent du Midi.
◆ Een ietwat rustiek familierestaurant aan de rand van de stad, in de wijk St.-Pieter. De gerechten worden op eigentijdse wijze bereid en hebben een Zuid-Frans accent.

X **Sukhothai,** Tongersestraat 54, ✉ 6211 LP, ☎ (0 43) 321 79 46, *sukhothai@home.nl, Fax (0 43) 325 89 59,* , Cuisine thaïlandaise – AE ⓓ MC VISA JCB CZ f
fermé lundi – **Repas** (dîner seult) 25/38.
◆ Cuisine thaïlandaise aussi typique que savoureuse. Un bel éventail de menus facilitera peut-être votre choix, vu l'ampleur de la carte. Cadre adapté. Terrasse intérieure.
◆ Karakteristieke, smaakvolle Thaise keuken. Zeer uitgebreide kaart. Bij zoveel aanbod maken de menu's uw keuze misschien wat gemakkelijker. Aangepast decor. Besloten terras.

Rive droite (Wyck - Station - MECC) :

Crowne Plaza, Ruiterij 1, ✉ 6221 EW, ☎ (0 43) 350 91 91, *cpmaastricht@bilderberg.nl, Fax (0 43) 350 91 92*, ≤, – 25 à 500. AE MC VISA. rest DZ c
Repas carte env. 47, ♀ – ☕ 21 – **139 ch** 198/288, – 2 suites – ½ P 123/210.
♦ Hôtel haut de gamme occupant un immeuble des années 1970 élevé le long de la Meuse. Chambres et suites "full equipment". Vue sur le trafic des péniches en terrasse. Repas à l'extérieur par beau temps. Carte d'inspiration méditerranéenne.
♦ Eersteklas hotel aan de Maas, in een pand uit de jaren zeventig. De kamers en suites zijn van alle faciliteiten voorzien. Terras met uitzicht op het scheepvaartverkeer. Bij mooi weer wordt er buiten geserveerd. Mediterraan geïnspireerde menukaart.

NH Maastricht, Forum 110, ✉ 6229 GV, ☎ (0 43) 383 82 81, *nhmaastricht@nh-hotels.nl, Fax (0 43) 361 58 62*, rest, – 25 à 300. AE MC VISA. BX e
Repas *Lunch 18* – carte 28 à 38, ♀ – ☕ 16 – **274 ch** 104/225, – 2 suites.
♦ Cet établissement très confortable avoisine le MECC, centre de congrès et d'exposition où se tient, début mars, un salon d'art et d'antiquités de réputation internationale. Salle à manger classiquement aménagée. Registre culinaire franco-italien.
♦ Dit zeer comfortabele etablissement staat naast het MECC, het Maastrichts Expositie en Congres Centrum, waar begin maart een kunst- en antiekbeurs van internationale allure wordt gehouden. Klassiek ingerichte eetzaal. Frans-Italiaanse keuken.

Gd H. de l'Empereur, Stationsstraat 2, ✉ 6221 BP, ☎ (0 43) 321 38 38, *empereur@bestwestern.nl, Fax (0 43) 321 68 19*, – 25 à 350. AE MC VISA JCB. DY b
Repas *(fermé sam. midi et dim. midi)* carte env. 48 – ☕ 15 – **149 ch** 131/155 – ½ P 172/266.
♦ Hostellerie 1900 flanquée d'une tourelle surveillant l'entrée de la gare. Chambres doubles ou simples, junior suites - dont trois duplex - et studios avec kitchenette. Ambiance nostalgique au restaurant, mais cuisine bien de notre temps.
♦ Hotelpand uit 1900, met een torentje dat uitkijkt op de ingang van het station. Een- en tweepersoonskamers, junior suites - waarvan drie split-level - en studio's met kitchenette. Restaurant met nostalgische ambiance, maar eigentijdse keuken.

Beaumont H. Résidence, Wycker Brugstraat 2, ✉ 6221 EC, ☎ (0 43) 325 44 33, *info@beaumont.nl, Fax (0 43) 325 36 55* – rest, – 25 à 75. AE MC VISA JCB. DY e
Repas *(fermé dim. midi)* (avec cuisine alsacienne) *Lunch 25* – carte 48 à 62, ♀ – ☕ 16 – **117 ch** 115/150.
♦ Une devanture néoclassique personnalise cet hôtel établi dans la rue commerçante reliant la gare au pont cyclo-piétonnier par lequel on rejoint le centre animé. Foie gras, choucroute, munster, gewürztraminer, riesling : à table, l'Alsace pavoise.
♦ Een neoklassieke façade geeft dit hotel een persoonlijk karakter. Het bevindt zich in de winkelstraat tussen het station en de brug naar het centrum. Ganzenlever, zuurkool, munster, gewürztraminer, riesling : de Elzas in volle glorie !

Apple Park sans rest, Pierre de Coubertinweg 3, ✉ 6225 XT, ☎ (0 43) 352 90 00, *info@applepark.nl, Fax (0 43) 352 02 24*, – 25 à 170. AE MC VISA JCB. BV u
☕ 17 – **166 ch** 167.
♦ Construit à proximité de l'autoroute, cet immeuble moderne renferme des chambres standard correctement équipées. Décor intérieur résolument contemporain.
♦ Dit moderne pand vlak bij de snelweg herbergt standaardkamers die van de nodige faciliteiten zijn voorzien. Zeer eigentijds interieur.

Maastricht, Nijverheidsweg 35, ✉ 6227 AL, ☎ (0 43) 387 35 00, *frontdesk@maastricht.valk.nl, Fax (0 43) 387 35 10*, – rest, – 25 à 250. AE MC VISA. BX c
Repas *Lunch 22* – 27/32, ♀ – ☕ 10 – **186 ch** 75/86, – 4 suites – ½ P 59/99.
♦ Aussi spacieuse que moderne, cette nouvelle unité de la chaîne hôtelière Van der Valk abrite des chambres pimpantes où l'on a ses aises. Terrasse estivale avec pièce d'eau.
♦ Dit nieuwe hotel van de Van der Valk-keten, dat even ruim als modern is, beschikt over prima kamers met het nodige comfort. Zomerterras met waterpartij.

la bergère sans rest, Stationsstraat 40, ✉ 6221 BR, ☎ (0 43) 328 25 25, *info@la-bergere.com, Fax (0 43) 328 25 26*, – . AE MC VISA JCB. DY y
☕ 18 – **76 ch** 160/165.
♦ Façade néoclassique pour cet établissement aménagé dans la note design, du hall aux chambres, en passant par la réception, le salon, le bar et la salle de breakfast.
♦ Dit etablissement met neoklassieke façade is geheel design ingericht, van lobby tot kamers, inclusief de receptie, de lounge, de bar en de ontbijtzaal.

PAYS-BAS

In den Hoof, Akersteenweg 218, ✉ 6227 AE, ✆ (0 43) 361 06 00, *info@indenhoof.nl, Fax (0 43) 361 80 40,* – 25. BX s
fermé du 24 au 26 déc. et 31 déc.-1er janv. – **Repas** *(fermé après 20 h 30)* 24/43 bc – **24 ch** 65/100 – ½ P 82/97.
◆ À l'entrée de la ville, ancien relais de poste devenu auberge familiale. Chambres d'ampleur satisfaisante distribuées sur deux étages. Préférez celles donnant à l'arrière. L'été, repas en terrasse. Carte étoffée de plusieurs menus et d'une formule lunch.
◆ Deze oude poststation aan de rand van de stad is nu een familiehotel. Redelijk ruime kamers op twee verdiepingen. Vragen naar een kamer aan de achterzijde. 's Zomers wordt er op het terras gegeten. Rijk gevulde kaart met diverse menu's en een lunchformule.

Kasteel Vaeshartelt, Weert 9, ✉ 6222 PG, ✆ (0 43) 369 02 00, *info@vaeshartelt.nl, Fax (0 43) 362 60 60,* – 25 à 200. BV f
Repas (dîner pour résidents seult) – **84 ch** 105/136 – ½ P 72/93.
◆ Ce château du 17e s s'entoure d'un grand parc à l'anglaise. Aménagement intérieur mêlant adroitement le moderne et l'ancien. Chambres réparties dans l'annexe récente.
◆ Dit 17e-eeuwse kasteel wordt omringd door een groot Engels park. In het interieur zijn oud en nieuw vakkundig gecombineerd. De kamers zijn ingericht in de nieuwe annexe.

Le Roi sans rest, St-Maartenslaan 1, ✉ 6221 AV, ✆ (0 43) 325 38 38, *info@hotelleroi.nl, Fax (0 43) 321 08 35,* – 30. DY w
11 – **42 ch** 100/104.
◆ Petit hôtel bien pratique lorsqu'on a un train à prendre, Le Roi dispose de chambres convenablement équipées, dont quatre sont des junior suites.
◆ Een praktisch hotelletje voor wie zijn trein beslist niet wil missen. Het beschikt over comfortabele kamers, waaronder vier junior suites.

Beluga (Van Wolde), Plein 1992 nr 12 (Centre Céramique), ✉ 6221 JP, ✆ (0 43) 321 33 64, *Fax (0 43) 326 03 56,* – 30. DZ b
fermé sam. midi, dim. et lundi – **Repas** Lunch 40 – 50/135 bc, carte 70 à 90, ♀.
◆ Déménagement réussi ! Espace, lumière, design élégant, vue sur les péniches et la vieille ville : tout cela ajoute encore au plaisir de l'assiette, personnalisée avec talent.
◆ Verhuizing geslaagd ! Ruimte, licht, elegant design, uitzicht op de Maas : dat betekent extra genieten van een keuken die talentvol van een persoonlijk accent wordt voorzien.
Spéc. Tajine de pigeon d'Anjou aux épices marocaines. Soufflé de langoustines et sauce curry vert. Rollmops de homard, thon rouge et truffes de saison

't Pakhoes, Waterpoort 4, ✉ 6221 GB, ✆ (0 43) 325 70 00, *pakhoes@yahoo.com, Fax (0 43) 325 59 61,* DZ a
fermé sem. carnaval et dim. – **Repas** (dîner seult) 38/72 bc, ♀.
◆ Une honorable maison de bouche s'est substituée à ce vieil entrepôt situé dans une ruelle piétonne accédant aux quais. Cuisine classique. Terrasse estivale tranquille.
◆ Dit achtenswaardige restaurant heeft in een voetgangersstraatje naar de kaden zijn intrek genomen in een oud pakhuis. Klassieke keuken. Rustig zomerterras.

Ca' del Biro, Hoogbrugstraat 66, ✉ 6221 CS, ✆ (0 43) 326 41 52, *info@biro.nl, Fax (0 43) 326 41 54,* Avec cuisine italienne – DZ q
fermé sem. carnaval, dern. sem. juin-prem. sem. juil., sam. midi et dim. – **Repas** Lunch 33 – carte 49 à 61.
◆ Cette table franco-transalpine assez plaisante vous accueille dans un décor moderne. Sur réservation, la jolie cave voûtée peut recevoir les petits groupes.
◆ In dit prettige Frans-Italiaanse restaurant wordt u in een modern decor ontvangen. Kleine groepen kunnen de fraaie gewelfde kelder reserveren.

Mediterraneo, Rechtstraat 73, ✉ 6221 EH, ✆ (0 43) 325 50 37, *Fax (0 43) 325 88 74,* Cuisine italienne – DY c
fermé 1 sem. carnaval, 2 sem. en juil. et dim. – **Repas** (dîner seult jusqu'à 23 h) 39/81 bc, ♀.
◆ Ambiance et service à l'italienne dans ce "ristorante" au cadre actuel. Mets venus en direct de la péninsule, avec un penchant pour la Toscane. Cave intéressante.
◆ Italiaanse ambiance en service in deze ristorante met modern decor. De gerechten komen rechtstreeks uit Italië, met een voorkeur voor Toscane. Interessante wijnkelder.

De eetkamer, Rechtstraat 83 (transfert prévu), ✉ 6221 EH, ✆ (0 43) 351 00 15, *deeetkamer@zonnet.nl, Fax (0 43) 351 00 15,* – DZ t
fermé 21 déc.-11 janv., dim. et lundi – **Repas** (dîner seult) 35/50, ♀.
◆ Près de la gare et du centre, nouvelle enseigne où se conçoit, sous la houlette d'un chef bardé de distinctions gastronomiques, une estimable cuisine au goût du jour.
◆ Een nieuwkomer vlak bij het station en het centrum. Onder leiding van een chef met tal van gastronomische onderscheidingen wordt een lofwaardige, eigentijdse keuken bereidt.

X **Fines Claires,** Cörversplein 9, ✉ 6221 EZ, ☎ (0 43) 325 25 25, *info@fines-claires.tm fweb.nl, Fax (0 43) 321 14 56,* – AE ⓓ MC VISA. DY x
fermé sem. carnaval, 2 sem. en août, 31 déc.-10 janv., dim. et lundi – **Repas** (dîner seult) carte 46 à 55, ♀.
◆ Les fines fourchettes du coin ont désormais leurs habitudes à cette bonne petite adresse jouxtant le pont cyclo-piétonnier. Registre culinaire élaboré, de base classique.
◆ Lokale fijnproevers weten inmiddels wel waar ze moeten zijn. Dit restaurantje bij de fiets- en voetgangersbrug heeft een verzorgd, culinair repertoire op klassieke basis.

X **Le Courage,** Rechtstraat 81, ✉ 6221 EH, ☎ (0 43) 321 17 27, *lecourage@zonnet.nl, Fax (0 43) 326 39 56,* – AE ⓓ MC VISA JCB DYZ u
fermé du 1er au 8 fév., du 8 au 22 août et dim. – **Repas** (dîner seult) 32/46.
◆ Du courage pour bien faire, ici, on n'en manque pas : accueil avenant, ambiance brasserie, menus et suggestions annoncées oralement, livre de cave concis mais bien conçu.
◆ Moed genoeg om er iets goeds van te maken : vriendelijk onthaal, ambiance brasserie, mondelinge aankondiging van menu's en dagsuggesties, kleine maar goede selectie wijnen.

X **Gadjah Mas,** Rechtstraat 42, ✉ 6221 EK, ☎ (0 43) 321 15 68, *info@gadjahmas.nl, Fax (0 43) 326 47 10,* Cuisine indonésienne – AE ⓓ MC VISA. DY j
Repas (dîner seult) 18/35.
◆ Les formules rijsttafel (table de riz) tiennent la vedette dans cet agréable restaurant indonésien posté à l'entrée de la Rechtstraat. Éclairage tamisé. Cadre exotique.
◆ De rijsttafels spannen de kroon in dit aangename Indonesische restaurant aan het begin van de Rechtstraat. Gedempt licht. Exotisch decor.

X **Tabkeaw,** Rechtstraat 102, ✉ 6221 EL, ☎ (0 43) 325 97 12, *Fax (0 43) 326 25 10,* , Cuisine thaïlandaise – ▤. AE MC VISA DZ a
fermé 3 sem. en fév., 2 dern. sem. juil.-prem. sem. août et merc. – **Repas** (dîner seult) carte env. 33.
◆ Initiation aux saveurs du Triangle d'or dans une salle à manger "siamoise". Très bon choix à la carte, qui énumère une cinquantaine de préparations assez authentiques.
◆ In het decor van een Siamese eetzaal wordt u "ondergedompeld" in de geuren en smaken van de Gouden Driehoek. Uitgebreide kaart met een vijftigtal vrij authentieke gerechten.

X **Wen-Chow,** Spoorweglaan 5, ✉ 6221 BS, ☎ (0 43) 321 45 40, *Fax (0 43) 310 09 37,* , Cuisine chinoise, ouvert jusqu'à 23 h – ▤. DY a
Repas Lunch 11 – carte 22 à 32.
◆ Restaurant chinois estimé de la diaspora asiatique. Trois cartes : touristique, cent pour cent cantonaise ou dans la langue de Confucius, pour les puristes. Bon menu-surprise.
◆ Dit door Aziaten gerespecteerde, Chinese restaurant heeft drie menukaarten : een toeristische, een 100 % Kantonese en een in de taal van Confucius. Heerlijk verrassingsmenu.

au Sud : *5 km par Bieslanderweg* :

XXX ✿ **Château Neercanne,** Cannerweg 800, ✉ 6213 ND, ☎ (0 43) 325 13 59, *info@neercanne.com, Fax (0 43) 321 34 06,* ≤, – P. AE ⓓ MC VISA
fermé lundi et sam. midi – **Repas** 65/77, carte 47 à 95.
◆ Petite "folie" du Siècle d'or dominant un admirable jardin étagé en terrasses : un lieu de rêve pour un grand moment de table. Jolie perspective sur la campagne environnante.
◆ Kasteeltje uit de Gouden Eeuw, met prachtige, in terrasvorm aangelegde tuinen : een droomdecor voor een gastronomisch moment. Mooi uitzicht op het omringende landschap.
Spéc. Tortellini à la compote d'aubergines et parmesan, sauce au céleri-rave. Rouget sauté, la mie de pain et légumes provençaux. Canette laquée aux échalotes, amandes fumées et salées

XX **Manjefiek,** Rijksweg 80, ✉ 6228 XZ, ☎ (0 43) 361 01 45, *w.rekko@manjefiek.nl, Fax (0 43) 361 64 86,* – P – 25 à 50. AE ⓓ MC VISA BX d
fermé 29 fév.-5 mars, mardi et sam. midi – **Repas** Lunch 33 – 43/53, ♀.
◆ Les fins gourmets entichés d'art contemporain applaudiront le concept de cette adresse. Cuisine d'aujourd'hui, galerie d'art, terrasse d'été et jardin avec pièce d'eau.
◆ Fijnproevers die verzot zijn op moderne kunst zullen het concept van dit adres toejuichen. Eigentijdse keuken, kunstgalerie, zomerterras en tuin met waterpartij.

X **L'Auberge,** Cannerweg 800 (cour intérieure du château), ✉ 6213 ND, ☎ (0 43) 325 13 59, *auberge@neercanne.com, Fax (0 43) 321 34 06,* – P. AE ⓓ MC VISA
fermé sam. – **Repas** (déjeuner seult) Lunch 53 bc – carte env. 42.
◆ Convertie en restaurant, l'ancienne chapelle du domaine seigneurial vous attable sous une imposante galerie de voûtes. Accès par la cour intérieure du château Neercanne.
◆ In de voormalige kapel van het kasteeldomein, die tot restaurant is verbouwd, gaat u aan tafel onder een imposant gewelf. Toegang via het binnenhof van Château Neercanne.

à Beek *par ① : 15 km – 17 120 h*

Mercure, Vliegveldweg 19 (Sud : 2,5 km à l'aéroport), ✉ 6191 SB, ☎ (0 43) 364 21 31, *H1243@accor-hotels.com, Fax (0 43) 364 46 68,* ≤, ☂, 🚲 – ✈, ▤ ch, TV P – 🎤 25 à 80. AE ① MO VISA
Repas Lunch 17 – 23 – ☕ 13 – **62 ch** 70/130 – ½ P 60/95.
◆ Cet établissement de chaîne ordonné à la façon d'un motel offre la meilleure possibilité de s'endormir sans risquer de rater son avion. Vue privilégiée sur les pistes.
◆ Dit ketenhotel is opgezet als een motel en is een ideaal adres om te overnachten zonder risico het vliegtuig te missen. Schitterend uitzicht op de landingsbanen.

De Bokkeriejer avec ch, Prins Mauritslaan 22, ✉ 6191 EG, ☎ (0 46) 437 13 19, *kempener.44@tiscali.nl, Fax (0 46) 437 47 47* – TV. AE ① MO VISA. ✗
fermé 2 sem. vacances bâtiment, lundi et sam. midi – **Repas** Lunch 29 – 34/52 bc – **5 ch** ☕ 53/83.
◆ Petite auberge connue de longue date, où l'on trouvera le gîte - une poignée de chambres fonctionnelles - et, moins accessoirement, le couvert. Accueil familial.
◆ Deze kleine herberg biedt al sinds jaar en dag logies - een paar functionele kamers - en, belangrijker nog, een maaltijd. Gastvrije ontvangst.

Pasta e Vino, Brugstraat 2, ✉ 6191 KC, ☎ (0 46) 437 99 94, *pastaevino@planet.nl, Fax (0 46) 436 03 79,* ☂, Cuisine italienne – ▤. MO VISA. ✗
fermé 2 sem. carnaval, 3 sem. en août, lundi et mardi – **Repas** (dîner seult) carte 45 à 59.
◆ L'enseigne annonce sans détour le programme qui vous attend ici : cuisine italienne sans concessions aux habitudes hollandaises, accompagnée de vins élevés dans la Botte.
◆ De naam vertelt u onomwonden welk programma u hier te wachten staat : Italiaanse keuken zonder concessies aan de Hollandse eetgewoonten, wijnen uit de Laars.

à Margraten *par ④ : 10 km – 13 678 h*

Groot Welsden ⛰, Groot Welsden 27, ✉ 6269 ET, ☎ (0 43) 458 13 94, *info@hotelgrootwelsden.nl, Fax (0 43) 458 23 55,* 🌳 – TV P. AE MO VISA JCB. ✗
fermé carnaval – **Repas** Lunch 12 – carte env. 36 – ☕ 10 – **14 ch** 64/80 – ½ P 59/72.
◆ Salon cossu, chambres coquettes, jardin avec pièce d'eau, accueil familial témoignant d'une courtoisie naturelle, et en prime, le calme absolu. Garnie de meubles de style et de toiles de petits maîtres, la salle de restaurant entretient une ambiance feutrée.
◆ Weelderige lounge, keurige kamers, tuin met waterpartij, een ontvangst die getuigt van natuurlijke hoffelijkheid, en vooral... absolute rust. Stemmige ambiance in de restaurantzaal, die is ingericht met stijlmeubilair en doeken van kleine meesters.

Wippelsdaal ⛰, Groot Welsden 13, ✉ 6269 ET, ☎ (0 43) 458 18 91, *info@wippelsdaal.nl, Fax (0 43) 458 27 15,* ≤ – TV P. MO VISA. ✗ rest
fermé 27 déc.-25 janv. – **Repas** (dîner pour résidents seult) – **14 ch** ☕ 47/74 – ½ P 50/51.
◆ Aménagée dans les dépendances d'une ancienne ferme, cette auberge tenue en famille dispose de grandes chambres fonctionnelles. Quiétude et environnement champêtre.
◆ Dit hotel is ingericht in de bijgebouwen van een voormalige boerderij en wordt in familiebeheer gerund. Grote, functionele kamers. Rust en landelijke omgeving.

MADE *Noord-Brabant* C *Drimmelen 26 772 h.* 532 N 12 *et* 715 F 6.
Amsterdam 94 – 's-Hertogenbosch 40 – Bergen op Zoom 45 – Breda 13 – Rotterdam 46.

De Korenbeurs, Kerkstraat 13, ✉ 4921 BA, ☎ (0 162) 68 21 50, *info@korenbeurs.nl, Fax (0 162) 68 46 47,* ☂, 🚲 – ♿ ✈ TV P – 🎤 25 à 350. AE ① MO VISA. ✗ rest
Repas *(fermé 24 déc. soir et 31 déc. soir)* Lunch 14 – carte 34 à 51, ♀ – ☕ 8 – **70 ch** 73/88 – ½ P 98/130.
◆ Au centre du village, établissement de conception récente renfermant des chambres correctement équipées ainsi qu'une infrastructure convenable pour la tenue de réunions. Restaurant avec terrasse d'été. Carte gravitant autour des standards culinaires bataves.
◆ Dit vrij nieuwe hotel in het centrum van het dorp herbergt comfortabele kamers en beschikt over een redelijke infrastructuur voor bijeenkomsten. Restaurant met zomerterras. De menukaart laat een duidelijke hang zien naar Nederlandse klassiekers.

MAKKUM *Fryslân* C *Wûnseradiel 11 972 h.* 531 R 4 *et* 715 H 2.
Amsterdam 112 – Leeuwarden 39 – Zwolle 114.

It Posthûs, Plein 15, ✉ 8754 ER, ☎ (0 515) 23 11 53, *info@itposthus.nl,* ☂ – MO VISA
mars-sept. ; fermé lundi – **Repas** (dîner seult) 33.
◆ Un chef irlandais bien inspiré s'active aux fourneaux de ce restaurant occupant l'ancienne poste de Makkum, port de pêche pittoresque également réputé pour sa faïence.
◆ Een zeer creatieve, Ierse chef-kok staat achter het fornuis in dit voormalige poststation van deze pittoreske vissersplaats, ook bekend om zijn aardewerk en keramiek.

MARGRATEN *Limburg* 532 T 18 *et* 715 I 9 – *voir à Maastricht.*

MARKELO *Overijssel* Ⓒ *Hof van Twente 35 041 h.* 531 X 9, 532 X 9 *et* 715 K 5.

Goorseweg 1, ✉ 7475 BB, ☎ (0 547) 36 15 55, info@vvvmarkelo.nl, Fax (0 547) 36 38 81.

Amsterdam 125 – Zwolle 50 – Apeldoorn 41 – Arnhem 59 – Enschede 34.

XX **In de Kop'ren Smorre** avec ch, Holterweg 20, ✉ 7475 AW, ☎ (0 547) 36 13 44, *markelo@koprensmorre.nl, Fax (0 547) 36 22 01,* – TV P. AE MC VISA.

fermé 31 déc.-1er janv., dim. midi et lundi – **Repas** Lunch 21 – 34/87 bc, ♀ – **4 ch** 63/78 – ½ P 75/84.

◆ Cuisine d'aujourd'hui servie dans une ancienne ferme au cadre immuable et typique : poutres massives, faïence de Delft, étains. Jardin paysager et chambres pratiques.

◆ Eigentijdse gerechten worden geserveerd in een oude boerderij met karakteristiek decor : massieve balken, Delfts aardewerk en tin. Tuin in landschapsstijl en praktische kamers.

MAURIK *Gelderland* Ⓒ *Buren 25 609 h.* 532 R 11 *et* 715 H 6.

Amsterdam 73 – Arnhem 49 – 's-Hertogenbosch 39 – Lelystad 96 – Utrecht 35.

X **Lodewijk XIII,** Dorpsplein 3a, ✉ 4021 EE, ☎ (0 344) 60 22 92, *Fax (0 344) 69 12 81,* MC VISA

fermé 3 sem. vacances bâtiment, 2 sem. après Noël, dim. et lundi – **Repas** (déjeuner sur réservation) (menu unique) 40, ♀.

◆ Petite table au goût du jour officiant devant l'église. Salles à manger étagées, terrasse d'été, ambiance à fois chic et décontractée et carte assez ramassée mais affriolante.

◆ Klein, trendy restaurant dicht bij de kerk. Eetzalen boven elkaar, zomerterras en een chique maar ongedwongen sfeer. Aanlokkelijke menukaart met een vrij beperkte keuze.

MECHELEN *Limburg* Ⓒ *Gulpen-Wittem 15 435 h.* 532 U 18 *et* 715 I 9.

Dalbissenweg 22, ✉ 6281 NC, ☎ (0 43) 455 13 97, Fax (0 43) 455 15 76.

Amsterdam 235 – Maastricht 21 – Aachen 14.

Brull, Hoofdstraat 26, ✉ 6281 BD, ☎ (0 43) 455 12 63, *Fax (0 43) 455 23 00,* – TV P. VISA. rest

fermé carnaval, Noël et Nouvel An – **Repas** (dîner pour résidents seult) – **26 ch** 51/108 – ½ P 72/80.

◆ Cette ferme convertie en hostellerie s'ordonne autour d'une jolie cour intérieure à colombages. Chambres sans reproche, vérandas, jardin-verger et animations culturelles.

◆ Deze hostellerie in een verbouwde boerderij ligt rond een fraai binnenhof met vakwerkdecoratie. Onberispelijke kamers, serre en boomgaard met tuin, culturele activiteiten.

MEDEMBLIK *Noord-Holland* 531 P 6 *et* 715 G 3 – *7 671 h.*

Voir *Oosterhaven*★.

Amsterdam 58 – Alkmaar 36 – Enkhuizen 21 – Hoorn 19.

Tulip Inn Het Wapen van Medemblik, Oosterhaven 1, ✉ 1671 AA, ☎ (0 227) 54 38 44, *post@tulipinnmedemblik.nl, Fax (0 227) 54 23 97,* – TV – 40 à 80. AE MC VISA JCB. ch

fermé 31 déc.-1er janv. – **Repas** 22/45, ♀ – **26 ch** 63/88 – ½ P 55.

◆ Dans une cité mignonne s'enorgueillant d'un passé hanséatique, hôtel aux chambres bien tenues, idéalement implanté le long d'un bassin bordé de jolies façades anciennes.

◆ Dit hotel met goed onderhouden kamers bevindt zich in het gezellige oude hanzestadje Medemblik, aan een havenbekken waarlangs fraaie oude gevels staan.

MEERKERK *Zuid-Holland* Ⓒ *Zederik 13 574 h.* 532 O 11 *et* 715 F 6.

Amsterdam 55 – Utrecht 24 – Den Haag 80 – Arnhem 76 – Breda 46 – Rotterdam 50.

AC Hotel, Energieweg 116 (près A 27, sortie ㉕), ✉ 4231 DJ, ☎ (0 183) 35 21 98, *meerkerk@autogrill.net, Fax (0 183) 35 22 99* – TV P – 25 à 250. AE MC VISA

Repas (avec buffets) carte 22 à 34 – 10 – **64 ch** 75.

◆ Proximité immédiate de l'autoroute, chambres et junior suites assez plaisantes, espaces de réunions, confort et qualité d'accueil propres à l'enseigne AC Hotel.

◆ Onmiddellijke nabijheid van de snelweg, vrij aangename kamers en junior suites, vergaderruimten, comfort, vriendelijke ontvangst : de gebruikelijke kenmerken van een AC Hotel.

De MEERN *Utrecht* 532 P 10 *et* 715 G 5 – *voir à Utrecht.*

MEGEN *Noord-Brabant* C *Oss 75 849 h.* 532 S 12 *et* 715 H 6.
Amsterdam (bac) 103 – Arnhem 45 – 's-Hertogenbosch 30 – Nijmegen 28.

XX **Den Uiver,** Torenstraat 3, ✉ 5366 BJ, ✆ (0 412) 46 25 48, *thonysuppers@planet.nl, Fax (0 412) 46 30 41,* – AE ⓓ ⓜ VISA.
fermé 20 fév.-1er mars, sam. midi, dim. midi et lundi – **Repas** 26/45 bc.
◆ Au cœur d'un village pittoresque, ancienne grange du 19e s. devenue un agréable restaurant taillé dans le rustique brabançon. Salon avec cheminée. Cuisine classique.
◆ Deze voormalige 19e-eeuwse schuur midden in het pittoreske dorp herbergt nu een aangenaam restaurant in rustieke, typisch Brabantse stijl. Salon met schouw. Klassieke keuken.

MEPPEL *Drenthe* 531 W 6 *et* 715 J 3 – *30 221 h.*
Kromme Elleboog 2, ✉ 7941 KC, ✆ (0 522) 25 28 88, vvv@boom.nl, Fax (0 522) 25 96 88.
Amsterdam 135 – Assen 55 – Groningen 82 – Leeuwarden 68 – Zwolle 25.

de reisiger sans rest, Dirk Jakobsstraat 6, ✉ 7941 KJ, ✆ (0 522) 25 66 49, *Fax (0 522) 25 55 14* – TV. ⓜ VISA
fermé fin déc. – **9 ch** ☕ 65/90.
◆ Maison bourgeoise un peu excentrée, située dans un quartier tranquille. Les chambres, équipées de bonnes salles de bains, offrent un confort avant tout fonctionnel.
◆ Dit hotel ligt in een rustige wijk even buiten het centrum. Alle kamers zijn voorzien van een goede badkamer en bieden vooral functioneel comfort.

à de Wijk *Est : 7,5 km* C *De Wolden 23 875 h :*

XXX **De Havixhorst** avec ch, Schiphorsterweg 34 (De Schiphorst), ✉ 7966 AC, ✆ (0 522) 44 14 87, *info@dehavixhorst.nl, Fax (0 522) 44 14 89,* – TV P – 25 à 150. AE ⓓ ⓜ VISA JCB.
Repas *(fermé 31 déc.-1er janv., dim. et lundi)* (déjeuner sur réservation) carte 46 à 60, ♀ – ☕ 12 – **8 ch** *(fermé 31 déc.-1er janv. et dim.)* 90/150 – ½ P 130/143.
◆ Devancée d'un parterre de buis, cette noble demeure du 18e s. donne sur un parc exquis. Repas-plaisir, avec tout l'agrément d'une bonne maison de bouche. Chambres cossues.
◆ Dit statige 18e-eeuwse landhuis staat in een schitterende tuin. De maaltijd is een lust voor het oog en biedt alle genoegens van een goed restaurant. Weelderige kamers.

MIDDELBURG P *Zeeland* 532 G 14 *et* 715 B 7 – *45 608 h.*
Voir *Hôtel de ville★ (Stadhuis)* AYZ **H** – *Abbaye★ (Abdij)* ABY.
Musée : *de Zélande★ (Zeeuws Museum)* AY **M**¹.
Nieuwe Burg 40, ✉ 4331 AH, ✆ (0 118) 65 99 44, vvvmid@zeelandnet.nl, Fax (0 118) 65 99 00.
Amsterdam 194 ① – Breda 98 ① – Rotterdam 106 ① – Antwerpen 91 ① – Brugge 83 ②

Plan page ci-contre

Arneville, Buitenruststraat 22 (par ①), ✉ 4337 EH, ✆ (0 118) 63 84 56, *info@hotelarneville.nl, Fax (0 118) 61 51 54,* – TV P – 25 à 250. AE ⓓ ⓜ VISA JCB. rest BZ
fermé 24 déc.-4 janv. – **Repas** Lunch 22 – carte 26 à 57 – ☕ 13 – **43 ch** 78/99 – ½ P 86/121.
◆ Hôtel-centre de congrès situé aux portes de la ville, le long d'une chaussée passante. Chambres standard et deux junior suites. Les meilleures se trouvent côté parking.
◆ Hotel-Congrescentrum aan de rand van de stad, aan een doorgaande weg. Standaardkamers en twee junior suites. De beste liggen aan de kant van de parking.

Gd H. Du Commerce, Loskade 1, ✉ 4331 HV, ✆ (0 118) 63 60 51, *info.du ommerce@fletcher.nl, Fax (0 118) 62 64 00,* – TV. AE ⓜ VISA. rest BZ x
Repas (dîner seult) carte 31 à 40 – **45 ch** ☕ 61/85 – ½ P 58/65.
◆ Une ribambelle de stores rouges attire l'œil sur cette ancienne hostellerie surveillant gare et pont à bascule. Chambres un peu menues. Jolie salle des petits-déjeuners. Miroirs profonds, grand comptoir, meubles de bistrot et ambiance brasserie au restaurant.
◆ Een hele rits rode markiezen vestigt de aandacht op dit oudste hotel van de stad, dat uitkijkt op het station en de basculebrug. Ietwat kleine kamers. Fraaie ontbijtzaal. Verzonken spiegels, grote toog, bistromeubels en brasseriesfeer in het restaurant.

XX **Het Groot Paradijs,** Damplein 13, ✉ 4331 GC, ✆ (0 118) 65 12 00, *fdolk@zeelandnet.nl, Fax (0 118) 65 12 21,* – AE ⓓ ⓜ VISA BY d
fermé 2 dern. sem. mars, 2 prem. sem. nov., dim. et lundi – **Repas** Lunch 43 – 60/85, ♀.
◆ Table gastronomique au cœur de Middelburg, la "perle de Walcheren". Salon-mezzanine, charmante salle à manger, fourneaux à vue, agréable restaurant d'été et service avenant.
◆ Gastronomisch restaurant in de "parel van Walcheren". Salon op de mezzanine, charmante eetzaal, open keuken, terras voor een zomerse maaltijd buiten en vriendelijke bediening.

MIDDELBURG

Achter de Houttuinen .... AZ 3
Bierkaai .... BZ 4
Damplein .... BY 6
Groenmarkt .... AYZ 7
Hoogstr. .... AZ 9
Houtkaai .... BZ 10
Koepoortstr. .... BY 12
Koestr. .... AZ 13
Koorkerkstr. .... BZ 15
Korte Burg .... AY 16
Korte Delft .... BYZ 18
Korte Noordstr. .... AY 19
Lange Delft .... ABZ
Lange Noordstr. .... AY 21
Langeviele .... AZ
Londensekaai .... BZ 22
Markt .... AZ
Nieuwe Burg .... AZ 24
Nieuwe Haven .... AZ 25
Nieuwe Vlissingseweg .... AZ 27
Nieuwstr. .... BZ 28
Plein 1940 .... AZ 30
Rotterdamsekaai .... BY 31
Segeerstr. .... BZ 33
Sint Pieterstr. .... BY 34
Stadhuisstr. .... AY 36
Vismarkt .... ABZ 37
Vlissingsestr. .... AZ 39
Volderijlaagte .... AY 40
Wagenaarstr. .... AY 42
Walensingel .... AYZ 43

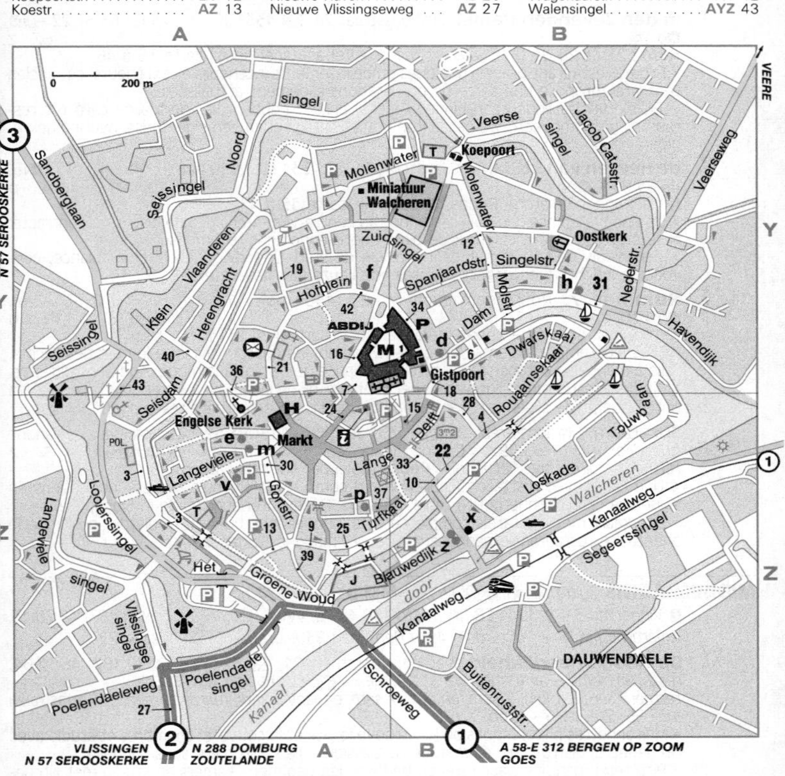

De Eetkamer, Wagenaarstraat 13, ✉ 4331 CX, ☎ (0 118) 63 56 76, *eetkamer@zeelandnet.nl* – MC VISA AY f
fermé dim. et lundi – **Repas** (déjeuner sur réservation) carte 46 à 64.

◆ Entre l'abbaye et le Miniatuur Walcheren, dans une ruelle calme, affaire familiale sympathique concoctant une cuisine de notre temps, à l'image du nouveau décor intérieur.

◆ Dit sympathieke familierestaurant in een rustig steegje tussen de abdij en Miniatuur Walcheren bereidt gerechten die, net als het nieuwe interieur, eigentijds zijn.

de Kluizenaar, Lammerensteeg 5, ✉ 4331 MB, ☎ (0 118) 62 52 87, *rdamme@zeelandnet.nl, Fax (0 118) 63 84 92,* – MC VISA AZ v
fermé mardi et sam. midi – **Repas** Lunch 27 – carte 33 à 45.

◆ Adorable petite adresse retranchée dans un mini-passage piétonnier. Salle à manger ornée de boiseries. Recettes travaillées à partir de produits du coin. Plusieurs menus.

◆ Verrukkelijk adresje in een minipassage. Eetzaal met lambrisering. De gerechten worden bereid van lokale producten. Verschillende menu's.

X **de Gespleten Arent,** Vlasmarkt 25, ✉ 4331 PC, ☎ (0 118) 63 61 22, *gespletenarent1@zeeland.nl, Fax (0 118) 61 80 35,* 🏠 – AE MC VISA AZ e
fermé 22 déc.-2 janv., mardi et merc. – **Repas** (dîner seult) 26.
◆ Assiettes au goût du jour, rehaussées, par-ci, par-là, de quelques notes asiatiques discrètes. Menu intéressant. Petite terrasse arrière dressée aux beaux jours.
◆ Eigentijdse gerechten worden met bescheiden Aziatische accenten in een creatief jasje gestoken. Interessant menu. Bij mooi weer klein terras aan de achterkant.

X **In den Zevenden Hemel,** Stationsstraat 24, ✉ 4331 JB, ☎ (0 118) 63 57 22 – MC VISA BZ z
fermé 25 et 26 déc., 1er janv. et mardi – **Repas** (dîner seult) carte 36 à 46.
◆ Promu restaurant grâce à quelques embellissements intérieurs et extérieurs, cet ancien "eetcafé" propose une carte de préparations sagement actualisées.
◆ Enkele verfraaiingen aan binnen- en buitenkant hebben dit voormalige café tot restaurant gepromoveerd. De gerechten op de kaart hebben een eigentijdse invulling gekregen.

X **de Heeren van St. Jan,** St. Janstraat 34, ✉ 4331 KD, ☎ (0 118) 63 45 34, *Fax (0 118) 46 85 29* – MC VISA AZ p
fermé lundi et mardi – **Repas** (dîner seult) carte 35 à 47.
◆ Une nouvelle enseigne qui "cartonne" au centre-ville. Ambiance de bistrot décontracté, mise en place simple et choix de plats quotidiennement recomposé.
◆ Een nieuw gezicht in het centrum van de stad. Ongedwongen bistroambiance, eenvoudige inrichting en dagelijks wisselende keuze aan gerechten.

X **Nummer 7,** Rotterdamsekaai 7, ✉ 4331 GM, ☎ (0 118) 62 70 77 – ▤. MC VISA BY h
fermé janv. et lundi – **Repas** (déjeuner sur réservation) 23, ♀.
◆ Très légèrement excentré, ce petit restaurant de quartier avoisine le port des yachts. Salle à manger aux tons "terracotta". Ambiance de bistrot à la mode. Additions digestes.
◆ Dit buurtrestaurantje ligt wat uit het centrum, bij de jachthaven. De eetzaal in terracotta tinten ademt de sfeer van een trendy bistro. Licht verteerbare rekeningen.

X **Surabaya,** Stationsstraat 20, ✉ 4331 JB, ☎ (0 118) 63 59 14, *surabaya@zeelandnet.net, Fax (0 118) 63 59 14,* Cuisine indonésienne, table de riz – AE MC VISA BZ z
fermé mardi en hiver et lundi – **Repas** (déjeuner sur réservation) 18.
◆ Une carte avec rijsttafels (tables de riz) complète la formule buffets indonésiens en vigueur à cette bonne petite table orientale. Décor intérieur "made in Singapore".
◆ Een kaart met rijsttafels completeert de Indonesische buffetformule die in dit goede oriëntaalse restaurantje gangbaar is. Decor "made in Singapore".

MIDDELHARNIS *Zuid-Holland* 532 J 12 *et* 715 D 6 – *17 224 h.*

Vingerling 3, ✉ 3241 EB, ☎ (0 187) 48 48 70, vvv@flakkee.net, Fax (0 187) 48 78 15.
Amsterdam 133 – Rotterdam 49 – Den Haag 83 – Breda 65 – Zierikzee 22.

XX **De Hooge Heerlijkheid** avec ch, Voorstraat 21, ✉ 3241 EE, ☎ (0 187) 48 32 64, *resthh@tref.nl, Fax (0 187) 48 53 29,* 🏠 – TV. AE MC VISA. ✂ ch
fermé 2 sem. en juin, 2 sem. en oct., 2 sem. en janv., lundi, mardi et merc. – **Repas** *Lunch 31* – 55, ♀ – ☕ 6 – **4 ch** 50/75.
◆ Maisonnettes pittoresques où l'on trouve le gîte et le couvert : chambres et studio avec kitchenette, bistrot chic et restaurant classique. Terrasse d'été sous tonnelle.
◆ Pittoreske pandjes waar tafel en bed worden geboden : kamers en studio met kitchenette, chique bistro en klassieke restaurant. Zomerterras onder een pergola.

X **Brasserie 't Vingerling,** Vingerling 23, ✉ 3241 EB, ☎ (0 187) 48 33 33, *wkern@tiscali.nl, Fax (0 187) 48 33 33,* ≤, 🏠, ⚓. VISA
fermé 2 sem. en fév., 2 sem. en oct., lundi et jeudi – Repas (déjeuner sur réservation) 25/33 bc.
◆ Cet entrepôt de pêcheurs élevé au 18e s abrite désormais une bonne petite table au "look" rustico-actuel. Menus courtisés. Vue sur les quais du port de plaisance.
◆ Dit 18e-eeuwse havenpakhuis biedt nu onderdak aan een goed restaurantje met een rustiek-eigentijdse look. Menu's. Uitzicht op de kaden van de jachthaven.

MIDDENBEEMSTER *Noord-Holland* 531 O 7 *et* 715 F 4 – *voir à Purmerend.*

MIDSLAND (MIDSLÂN) *Fryslân* 531 Q 2 *et* 715 G 1 – *voir à Waddeneilanden (Terschelling).*

Si vous êtes retardé sur la route, dès 18 h, confirmez votre réservation par téléphone, c'est plus sûr... et c'est l'usage.

MIERLO *Noord-Brabant* ⓒ *Geldrop-Mierlo 40 000 h.* 532 S 14 et 715 H 7.
Heiderschoor 26, ✉ 5731 RC, ☎ (0 492) 59 24 55, Fax (0 492) 66 76 73.
Amsterdam 129 – Eindhoven 16 – 's-Hertogenbosch 44 – Helmond 5.

Carlton De Brug, Arkweg 3, ✉ 5731 PD, ☎ (0 492) 67 89 11, *info@debrug.carlton.nl, Fax (0 492) 66 48 95,* – – rest, – 25 à 1000. AE VISA. rest
Repas *(fermé dim.) Lunch 17* – carte env. 42, ♀ – ☕ 14 – **145 ch** 96/128, – 3 suites – ½ P 80/199.
◆ Aux avant-postes de Mierlo, immeuble disposant de plusieurs types de chambres et d'une colossale infrastructure pour séminaires. Accès direct à un grand complexe sportif. À table, préparations classiques actualisées, formules lunch et menus.
◆ Dit hotel aan de rand van Mierlo beschikt over verschillende typen kamers en een kolossale infrastructuur voor bijeenkomsten en seminars. Directe toegang tot een groot sportcomplex. Klassieke gerechten in een eigentijds jasje, lunchformules en menu's.

De Cuijt, Burg. Termeerstraat 50 (Nord-Ouest : 1 km, direction Nuenen), ✉ 5731 SE, ☎ (0 492) 66 13 23, *decuijt@worldonline.nl, Fax (0 492) 66 57 41,* – P. VISA.
fermé du 21 au 28 fév., du 10 au 28 août, 24 déc.-3 janv., dim. et lundi – **Repas** *Lunch 25* – carte 29 à 50, ♀.
◆ Charmante auberge familiale assise au bord du canal. Salle à manger rustique, terrasse ombragée et jardin fleuri aux beaux jours. Repas classico-traditionnel.
◆ Charmant familierestaurant aan het kanaal. Rustieke eetzaal, lommerrijk terras en fleurige tuin in de zomer. Klassiek-traditionele gerechten.

MILL *Noord-Brabant* ⓒ *Mill en Sint Hubert 11 103 h.* 532 T 12 et 715 I 6.
Amsterdam 123 – 's-Hertogenbosch 41 – Eindhoven 48 – Nijmegen 25.

Aub. de Stoof, Kerkstraat 14, ✉ 5451 BM, ☎ (0 485) 45 11 37 – AE VISA
fermé merc. – **Repas** (déjeuner sur réservation) carte 22 à 45.
◆ Pour débusquer cette adresse où il fait bon s'attabler autour d'un repas au goût du jour, cherchez une façade rose au centre du village. Décor intérieur rustique soigné.
◆ Zoek naar een roze gevel in het centrum van het dorp, want daar kunt u aanschuiven voor een eigentijdse maaltijd. Verzorgd, rustiek interieur.

MILSBEEK *Limburg* ⓒ *Gennep 16 847 h.* 532 U 12 et 715 I 6.
Amsterdam 133 – Maastricht 126 – Arnhem 33 – 's-Hertogenbosch 60 – Utrecht 95.

Mangerie Milsbeek, Rijksweg 14 (N 271), ✉ 6596 AB, ☎ (0 485) 51 40 70, *angeliq ue.drogt@wolmail.nl, Fax (0 485) 51 40 70,* , Avec brasserie – P. VISA
fermé 31 déc.-5 janv., sam. midi, dim. midi et lundi – **Repas** *Lunch 23* – carte 43 à 54, ♀.
◆ Auberge de bonne renommée locale associant une petite brasserie à un restaurant rustique-contemporain. Accueil et service souriants et stylés, par la jeune patronne.
◆ Deze herberg geniet plaatselijk een goede reputatie en combineert een kleine brasserie met een rustiek-eigentijds restaurant. Vriendelijke, stijlvolle ontvangst en service.

MOLENRIJ *Groningen* ⓒ *De Marne 11 186 h.* 531 X 2.
Amsterdam 201 – Groningen 29 – Leeuwarden 59.

't Korensant, H. van Cappenbergweg 34, ✉ 9977 RW, ☎ (0 595) 48 11 34, *info@k orensant.nl, Fax (0 595) 48 11 05,* – VISA
fermé 2 prem. sem. vacances bâtiment, du 1er au 14 janv., lundi et mardi – **Repas** (déjeuner sur réservation) 30/45, ♀.
◆ Auberge villageoise devenue restaurant. Cuisine du moment et petite cave à vue où vous pourrez aller choisir votre vin préféré. Terrasse d'été dressée côté jardin.
◆ Deze dorpsherberg is tot restaurant gepromoveerd. Seizoengebonden keuken en kleine, open wijnkelder waar u zelf uw favoriete wijn kunt uitzoeken. Zomerterras aan de tuinkant.

MONNICKENDAM *Noord-Holland* ⓒ *Waterland 17 172 h.* 531 P 8 et 715 G 4.
Env. *à l'Est : 8 km, Marken★ : village★, costumes traditionnels★.*
Amsterdam 16 – Alkmaar 34 – Leeuwarden 122.

De Volle Maan, Galgeriet 5a, ✉ 1141 GA, ☎ (0 299) 65 46 41, *Fax (0 20) 403 84 65,* – P. AE VISA JCB
fermé 2 prem. sem. nov., lundi et mardi – **Repas** (déjeuner sur réservation) 25/38, ♀.
◆ Avant tout, il y a le charme des lieux : un petit port de plaisance sur le Gouwzee, enclave de l'IJsselmeer. Ensuite, il y a l'assiette, actuelle, fière des produits d'ici.
◆ Eerst is er de charmante lokatie : een kleine jachthaven aan de Gouwzee, een enclave in het IJsselmeer. Dan komt het "bord", eigentijds en trots op de producten van daarginder.

Four Seasons, Haringburgwal 3, ✉ 1141 AT, ✆ (0 299) 65 55 84, *Fax (0 299) 65 51 99*, Cuisine chinoise, – . AE ① ⓜ VISA JCB
fermé 31 déc. et lundi – **Repas** (dîner seult) carte 25 à 53.
• À l'entrée du port des yachts, honorable restaurant chinois offrant un peu plus de confort à ses convives depuis son récent déménagement. Plats présentés "à la française".
• Dit respectabele Chinese restaurant bij de ingang van de jachthaven biedt sinds de recente verhuizing iets meer comfort. De gerechten worden "à la française" gepresenteerd.

MONSTER *Zuid-Holland* *Westland 96 000 h.* 532 K 10 *et* 715 D 5.

Amsterdam 73 – Rotterdam 33 – Den Haag 13.

Elzenduin, Strandweg 18 (Nord : 1 km à Terheyde aan Zee), ✉ 2684 VT, ✆ (0 174) 21 42 00, *info@elzenduin.com, Fax (0 174) 21 42 04*, , – , rest, – 30. AE ① ⓜ VISA JCB
Repas carte 30 à 56, ♀ – **27 ch** 92/147.
• Derrière les dunes, à proximité immédiate de la plage, construction d'aujourd'hui distribuant ses chambres, assez tranquilles et bien calibrées, sur deux étages. Grande salle à manger au décor bourgeois, à l'image du choix de préparations.
• Dit eigentijdse hotelpand achter de duinen, in de onmiddellijke nabijheid van het strand, herbergt vrij rustige kamers die goed van formaat zijn en verdeeld liggen over twee verdiepingen. Grote eetzaal met klassiek decor, net als de keuze aan gerechten.

MONTFOORT *Utrecht* 532 O 10 *et* 715 F 5 – *13 298 h.*

Amsterdam 33 – Utrecht 15 – Den Haag 52 – Rotterdam 48.

Kasteel Montfoort 1er étage, Kasteelplein 1, ✉ 3417 JG, ✆ (0 348) 47 27 27, *info@kasteel-montfoort.nl, Fax (0 348) 47 27 28*, – – 25 à 80. AE ① ⓜ VISA JCB
fermé 26 juil.-8 août, 27 déc.-4 janv. et dim. – **Repas** Lunch 33 – carte 34 à 41.
• Un petit château dont l'origine remonte à l'époque médiévale sert de cadre à cette table de "grand seigneur". La carte, bien dans l'air du temps, associe lunch et menus.
• Een kasteeltje dat nog uit de Middeleeuwen dateert, vormt het decor van dit luxueuze restaurant. De zeer eigentijdse kaart combineert lunch en menu's.

de Schans, Willeskop 87 (Sud-Ouest : 4,5 km sur N 228), ✉ 3417 MC, ✆ (0 348) 56 23 09, *restdeschans@worldonline.nl, Fax (0 348) 56 27 03*, – . AE ① ⓜ VISA.
fermé dern. sem. août-prem. sem. sept., mardi et merc. – **Repas** Lunch 33 – carte 54 à 66, ♀.
• À distance respectable de Montfoort, au bord de la route nationale menant à Gouda, affaire familiale où se mitonne une cuisine classique gentiment actualisée.
• Dit familierestaurant op respectabele afstand van Montfoort, langs de binnenweg naar Gouda, bereidt een klassieke keuken met een subtiele eigentijdse invulling.

à Linschoten *Nord-Ouest : 3 km* *Montfoort :*

De Burgemeester, Raadhuisstraat 17, ✉ 3461 CW, ✆ (0 348) 41 40 40, *info@deburgemeester.nl, Fax (0 348) 43 25 95* – – 25 à 40. AE ① ⓜ VISA JCB
fermé dern. sem. juil.-prem. sem. août, 24 déc.-2 janv., dim. midi et lundi midi – **Repas** 30/55, ♀.
• Une agréable maison de bouche s'est substituée à l'ancienne mairie du village. Salle à manger contemporaine, cave à vue et recettes tournées vers la Méditerranée.
• Dit aangename restaurant heeft zijn intrek genomen in het voormalige raadhuis. Eigentijdse eetzaal, open wijnkelder en mediterraan georiënteerde gerechten.

MOOK *Limburg* *Mook en Middelaar 7 947 h.* 532 U 12 *et* 715 I 6.

Amsterdam 129 – Arnhem 30 – Maastricht 133 – 's-Hertogenbosch 48 – Nijmegen 12 – Venlo 54.

Jachtslot de Mookerheide, Heumensebaan 2 (Nord-Est : 2,5 km sur A 73, sortie ③), ✉ 6584 CL, ✆ (0 24) 358 30 35, *info@mookerheide.nl, Fax (0 24) 358 43 55*, , , – – 25 à 150. AE ① ⓜ VISA JCB.
Repas Lunch 33 – 40/60, ♀ – 14 – **17 ch** 100/140, – 6 suites – ½ P 95/125.
• Savourez l'atmosphère 1900 qui règne dans cette élégante demeure entourée d'un parc arboré. Chambres cossues, toutes nanties d'une baignoire à bulles. Belle salle de restaurant Jugendstil propice à un repas-plaisir. Cuisine française mi-classique mi-actuelle.
• In dit elegante buitenverblijf op een bosrijk landgoed kunt u zich koesteren in de sfeer van rond 1900. Luxueuze kamers met bubbelbad. Mooie eetzaal in Jugendstil voor een genoeglijke maaltijd in stijl. Franse, klassiek-eigentijdse keuken.

De Molenhoek, Rijksweg 1 (Nord : 1 km), ✉ 6584 AA, ✆ (0 24) 358 01 55, *info@motelmolenhoek.nl, Fax (0 24) 358 21 75,* – P – 25 à 150. AE VISA
Repas *Lunch 11* – carte 22 à 30, ♀ – ☐ 8 – **56 ch** 60.
◆ Ce confortable motel compte parmi les plus anciennes unités Van der Valk. Notez qu'il vous faudra traverser la route pour passer de la réception aux chambres.
◆ Dit comfortabele motel behoort tot de oudste hotelbedrijven van Van der Valk. Wel moet u hier eerst de weg oversteken om van de receptie bij uw kamer te komen.

MUGGENBEET *Overijssel* 531 U 6 – *voir à Blokzijl.*

MUIDEN *Noord-Holland* 531 P 9, 532 P 9 *et* 715 G 5 – *6 726 h.*
Voir *Château★ (Muiderslot).*
Amsterdam 18 – Hilversum 22.

De Doelen, Sluis 1, ✉ 1398 AR, ✆ (0 294) 26 32 00, *info@restaurantdedoelen.nl, Fax (0 294) 26 48 75,* ←, – P – 25 à 70. AE VISA.
fermé sam. midi et dim. midi – **Repas** carte 44 à 57.
◆ Salle à manger rustique parsemée de toiles modernes, terrasse estivale le long des écluses, vue sur le trafic plaisancier, mets classiques revisités et cave d'épicurien.
◆ Rustieke eetzaal met moderne doeken, zomerterras langs de sluizen, uitzicht op de plezierboten, klassieke gerechten in een modern jasje en goed gevulde wijnkelder.

à Muiderberg *Est : 4 km* C *Muiden :*

't Lagerhuys, Dorpsstraat 29, ✉ 1399 GT, ✆ (0 294) 26 29 80, *lagerhuys@hgm.nl, Fax (0 294) 26 29 81,* – P. VISA
fermé 31 déc.-2 janv. – **Repas** *Lunch 25* – 33, ♀.
◆ Bel hôtel de la fin du 19e s. adroitement réaffecté en restaurant. Cuisine actuelle servie dans un intérieur d'esprit "grand café" ou, aux beaux jours, sous les tonnelles.
◆ Dit mooie hotelpand uit 1882 is vakkundig tot restaurant verbouwd. Eigentijdse gerechten worden geserveerd in een ambiance grand café of, bij mooi weer, onder de pergola.

MUIDERBERG *Noord-Holland* 531 P 9, 532 P 9 *et* 715 G 5 – *voir à Muiden.*

MUNSTERGELEEN *Limburg* 532 U 17 – *voir à Sittard.*

NAALDWIJK *Zuid-Holland* C *Westland 96 000 h.* 532 K11 *et* 715 D 6.
Amsterdam 77 – Rotterdam 26 – Den Haag 13.

Carlton, Tiendweg 20, ✉ 2671 SB, ✆ (0 174) 27 26 25, *reservations@goldentulipcarlton.nl, Fax (0 174) 27 26 26,* – rest, P – 25 à 150. AE VISA JCB
Repas *(fermé sam. midi et dim.) Lunch 16* – 28 – **80 ch** ☐ 145/170 – ½ P 203.
◆ Établissement de chaîne situé aux portes de Naaldwijk, important centre horticole de la région maraîchère du Westland. Grandes chambres "full equipment". Room service. L'été, le couvert est dressé sur une terrasse agrémentée d'un étang.
◆ Dit ketenhotel ligt aan de rand van Naaldwijk, een belangrijk centrum in de tuinbouwstreek het Westland. De grote kamers zijn van alle faciliteiten voorzien. Roomservice. In de zomer worden de tafels gedekt op het terras naast de vijver.

NAARDEN *Noord-Holland* 531 P 9, 532 P 9 *et* 715 G 5 – *16 960 h.*
Voir *Fortifications★.*
Adriaan Dorstmanplein 1-B, ✉ 1411 RC, ✆ (0 35) 694 28 36, naarden@hollandsmidden.nl, Fax (0 35) 694 34 24.
Amsterdam 21 – Apeldoorn 66 – Utrecht 30.

NH Naarden, IJsselmeerweg 3 (près A 1, sortie ⑥ - Gooimeer), ✉ 1411 AA, ✆ (0 35) 695 15 14, *info@nhnaarden.nh-hotels.nl, Fax (0 35) 695 10 89,* rest, P – 25 à 150. AE VISA.
Repas *Lunch 16* – 33 – ☐ 15 – **107 ch** 150/180, – 21 suites.
◆ Aux avant-postes d'une jolie ville fortifiée, ressource hôtelière récente, dont les suites, en marge des chambres, se distribuent dans l'annexe voisine.
◆ Dit vrij nieuwe hotel staat aan de rand van een fraaie vestingstad. De suites zijn in de naburige annexe ingerecht, apart van de kamers.

XX **Het Arsenaal,** Kooltjesbuurt 1, ✉ 1411 RZ, ✆ (0 35) 694 91 48, *info@paulfagel.nl, Fax (0 35) 694 03 69,* 余 – ▤ P. AE ⓓ ⓜⓒ VISA. ⋟
fermé 25 déc.-2 janv., sam. midi et dim. midi – **Repas** 45/90 bc.
◆ Un point de repère dans le paysage gastronomique de Naarden. Cuisine française et décor intérieur contrasté : banquettes rouges, poutres claires, carrelage en damier.
◆ Een herkenningspunt in het gastronomische landschap van de stad. Franse keuken en interieur met contrastrijk decor : rode banken, lichte balken, ruitvormig gelegde plavuizen.

X **Chef's,** Cattenhagestraat 9, ✉ 1411 CR, ✆ (0 35) 694 88 03, *Fax (0 35) 694 88 03,* 余 – AE ⓓ ⓜⓒ VISA JCB
Repas 25.
◆ Cette maison de bouche sympathique s'est hissée parmi les valeurs sûres de la ville. Ambiance "bistrot". Terrasse d'été sur l'arrière, à l'ombre de la gothique Grote Kerk.
◆ Dit sympathieke eethuis behoort tot een van de trefzekere adressen van de stad. Bistroambiance. Zomerterras aan de achterkant, in de schaduw van de gotische Grote Kerk.

X **Mixit,** St-Annastraat 3 (Naarden-Vesting), ✆ (0 35) 694 66 05, *Fax (0 35) 694 66 05,* 余 – AE ⓓ ⓜⓒ VISA
fermé lundi – **Repas** 23/43.
◆ À côté de l'église, salles à manger "cosy" où l'on vient faire des repas au goût du jour dans une ambiance romantique. Une pergola fleurie tient lieu de restaurant d'été.
◆ Eethuis naast de kerk met gezellige zaaltjes waar in een romantische sfeer actuele maaltijden worden geserveerd. De pergola met bloemen dient als zomerrestaurant.

NECK *Noord-Holland* 531 O 7 – *voir à Purmerend.*

NEDERWEERT *Limburg* 532 T 15 *et* 715 I 8 – *voir à Weert.*

NEDERWETTEN *Noord-Brabant* 532 S 14 – *voir à Nuenen.*

NES *Fryslân* 531 T 2 *et* 715 I 1 – *voir à Waddeneilanden (Ameland).*

NIEUWEGEIN *Utrecht* 532 P 10 *et* 715 G 5 – *62 140 h.*
Amsterdam 50 – Utrecht 11 – Rotterdam 65.

Mercure, Buizerdlaan 10 (Ouest : 1 km), ✉ 3435 SB, ✆ (0 30) 604 48 44, *h1164@accor-hotels.com, Fax (0 30) 603 83 74,* ⅟₆, ≘s, ⊠, ⚲ – |♦| ⇔ ▤ TV ⇔ P – 🏟 25 à 450. AE ⓓ ⓜⓒ VISA
Repas *Lunch 20* – 26, ♀ – ⊏ 14 – **77 ch** 150/180.
◆ Hôtel de chaîne contemporain situé à quelques minutes d'Utrecht, dans le voisinage de l'autoroute Amsterdam-Eindhoven. Centre de congrès et chambres de bon gabarit.
◆ Eigentijds ketenhotel op een paar minuten van Utrecht, in de buurt van de snelweg Amsterdam-Eindhoven. Kamers van goed formaat en congrescentrum.

XX **De Bovenmeester,** Dorpsstraat 49 (Est : 1,5 km, Vreeswijk), ✉ 3433 CL, ✆ (0 30) 606 66 22, *Fax (0 30) 606 61 38,* 余 – ▤. AE ⓓ ⓜⓒ VISA. ⋟
fermé dern. sem. déc.-prem. sem. janv., sam. midi, dim. midi et lundi – **Repas** *Lunch 28* – carte 35 à 49.
◆ Gentille petite affaire familiale surveillant le pont à bascule qui dessert le port. Choix à la carte, lunch, menus et suggestions. Les beaux jours, repas au bord de l'eau.
◆ Dit vriendelijke familierestaurantje waakt over de ophaalbrug bij de haven. À la carte, lunch, menu's en dagsuggesties. Bij mooi weer kan aan het water worden gegeten.

NIEUWERKERK AAN DEN IJSSEL *Zuid-Holland* 532 M 11 *et* 715 E 6 – *22 131 h.*
⛳18 *Blaardorpseweg 1, ✉ 2911 BC, ✆ (0 180) 31 71 88, Fax (0 180) 39 02 12.*
Amsterdam 53 – Rotterdam 17 – Den Haag 42 – Gouda 12.

Nieuwerkerk a/d IJssel, Parallelweg Zuid 185 (près A 20, sortie ⑰), ✉ 2914 LE, ✆ (0 180) 32 11 03, *info@nieuwerkerk.valk.nl, Fax (0 180) 32 11 84,* 余 – |♦| ⇔ TV ♿ P – 🏟 25 à 150. AE ⓓ ⓜⓒ VISA. ⋟ ch
Repas *Lunch 13* – 25/30, ♀ – ⊏ 9 – **100 ch** 70, – 1 suite – ½ P 60/95.
◆ Le toucan de la chaîne hôtelière Van der Valk - dont le nom désigne pourtant un faucon (valk) - s'est perché sur cet immeuble de notre temps. Chambres confortables.
◆ De toekan van de bekende hotelketen - die een valk in zijn naam draagt - is geland op dit moderne gebouw. Comfortabele kamers.

NIEUW-VENNEP *Noord-Holland* ☐ *Haarlemmermeer 118 553 h.* 532 M 9 *et* 715 E 5.
Amsterdam 31 – Haarlem 17 – Den Haag 36.

De Rustende Jager, Venneperweg 471, ✉ 2153 AD, ℘ (0 252) 62 93 33, *rustend e_jager@planet.nl, Fax (0 252) 62 93 34,* – |‡|, rest, TV P – 25 à 300. AE MC VISA JCB.
Repas 29 – 10 – **42 ch** 80/100, – 2 suites – ½ P 72/99.
◆ Une grande verrière moderne dessert les deux ailes de cette construction récente toute proche de l'église. Chambres et junior suites assez coquettes. Accueil familial. Petite carte bistrotière présentée dans une ambiance "brasserie".
◆ Een grote moderne overkapping van glas verbindt de twee vleugels van dit eigentijdse pand vlak bij de kerk. Comfortabele kamers en junior suites. Hartelijke ontvangst. Kleine bistroachtige kaart, eetzaal met brasseriesfeer.

NIEUWVLIET *Zeeland* ☐ *Sluis 24 755 h.* 532 F 14 *et* 715 B 7.
Amsterdam 218 – Brugge 32 – Middelburg 61 – Den Haag 171 – Oostburg 7 – Sluis 11.

à Nieuwvliet-Bad *Nord-Ouest : 3 km* ☐ *Sluis :*

Nieuwvliet-Bad, Zouterik 2, ✉ 4504 RX, ℘ (0 117) 37 20 20, *info@nieuwvliet-bad.nl, Fax (0 117) 37 20 07,* – |‡| TV P – 25 à 200. AE MC VISA
Repas carte 26 à 44 – **35 ch** 75/115 – ½ P 94/134.
◆ Seul un petit cordon de dunes sépare cet hôtel de la plage. Chambres sobres et pratiques. Salons et belle infrastructure pour se distraire ou entretenir sa condition physique. Restaurant-véranda.
◆ Slechts een smalle strook duinen scheidt dit hotel van het strand. Eenvoudig ingerichte, praktische kamers. Zalen en diverse faciliteiten voor recreatie en ontspanning, zoals een sauna, fitness en beautysalon. Restaurant met serre.

NIJKERK *Gelderland* 532 R 9 *et* 715 H 5 – *37 327 h.*
Amsterdam 60 – Utrecht 34 – Apeldoorn 53 – Zwolle 57.

Ampt van Nijkerk, Berencamperweg 4, ✉ 3861 MC, ℘ (0 33) 247 16 16, *sales@amptvannykerk.nl, Fax (0 33) 247 16 00,* – |‡| TV P – 25 à 250. AE MC VISA. rest
Repas ***De Patio*** *Lunch 23* – 29/49 bc, ♀ – **107 ch** 190 – ½ P 75.
◆ Aux portes de Nijkerk, établissement cossu, complété d'une bonne infrastructure pour la tenue de banquets et séminaires. Chambres et junior suites joliment équipées. Brasserie actuelle maniant un répertoire culinaire bien dans le coup.
◆ Dit luxueuze hotel aan de rand van de stad heeft tevens een goede infrastructuur voor partijen en seminars. De kamers en junior suites zijn zeer comfortabel. Eigentijdse brasserie met een trendy culinair repertoire.

de Salentein, Putterstraatweg 7 (Nord-Est : 1,5 km), ✉ 3862 RA, ℘ (0 33) 245 41 14, *info@desalentein.nl, Fax (0 33) 246 20 18,* – P – 25 à 175. AE MC VISA
fermé sam. midi et dim. – **Repas** *Lunch 29* – 33/77 bc, ♀.
◆ Table élégante officiant au bord d'un canal, dans les dépendances (1826) d'un petit château de campagne. Cuisine au goût du jour. Ancienne grange séparée pour les banqueteurs.
◆ Een stijlvol restaurant aan een kanaal, in de dependances (1826) van een klein landhuis. Eigentijdse keuken. De voormalige schuur is bestemd voor feesten en partijen.

NIJMEGEN *Gelderland* 532 T 11 *et* 715 I 6 – *154 616 h – Casino* Y, *Waalkade 68,* ✉ *6511 XP,* ℘ *(0 24) 381 63 81, Fax (0 24) 381 62 09.*
Voir *Poids public★ (Waag)* BC – *Chapelle St-Nicolas★ (St. Nicolaaskapel)* C **R.**
Musée : *Nationaal Fietsmuseum Velorama★* C **M¹.**
18 *(2 parcours) au Sud-Est : 9 km à Groesbeek, Postweg 17,* ✉ *6561 KJ,* ℘ *(0 24) 397 66 44, Fax (0 24) 397 69 42* – 18 *au Sud-Ouest : 10 km à Wijchen, Weg door de Berendonck 40,* ✉ *6603 LP,* ℘ *(0 24) 642 00 39, Fax (0 24) 641 12 54.*
Keizer Karelplein 2, ✉ *6511 NC,* ℘ *0 900-112 23 44, Fax (0 24) 329 78 79.*
Amsterdam 119 ① *– Arnhem 19* ① *– Duisburg 114* ②

Plan page suivante

Mercure, Stationsplein 29, ✉ 6512 AB, ℘ (0 24) 323 88 88, *H1356@accor-hotels.com, Fax (0 24) 324 20 90,* – |‡|, ch, TV P – 25 à 100. AE MC VISA
Repas *(fermé 24 déc.-1ᵉʳ janv., sam. midi et dim. midi) Lunch 10* – carte 22 à 36, ♀ – 14 – **104 ch** 138/168. B r
◆ Hôtel de chaîne posté en face de la gare, à un kilomètre du centre animé. Chambres et "club rooms" de tailles respectables, réparties sur huit étages d'une tour polygonale.
◆ Ketenhotel tegenover het station, op loopafstand van het drukke centrum. Op de acht verdiepingen van de veelhoekige toren liggen kamers en club rooms van respectabel formaat.

NIJMEGEN

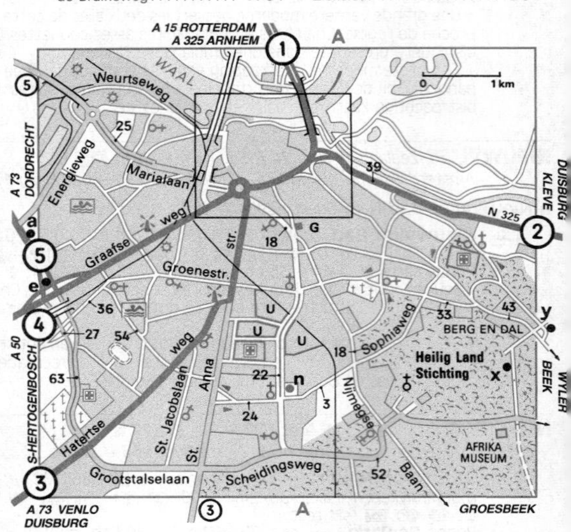

A 15 ROTTERDAM
A 325 ARNHEM
WAAL
Weurtseweg
A 73 DORDRECHT
Energieweg
Marialaan
Graafse weg
Groenestr.
St. Annastr.
St. Jacobslaan
Hatertse weg
Grootstalselaan
Scheidingsweg
Sophiaweg
Nijmegse Baan
N 325
DUISBURG KLEVE
BERG EN DAL
Heilig Land Stichting
AFRIKA MUSEUM
BEEK
WYLER
GROESBEEK
A 50 'S-HERTOGENBOSCH
A 73 VENLO DUISBURG
0 1 km

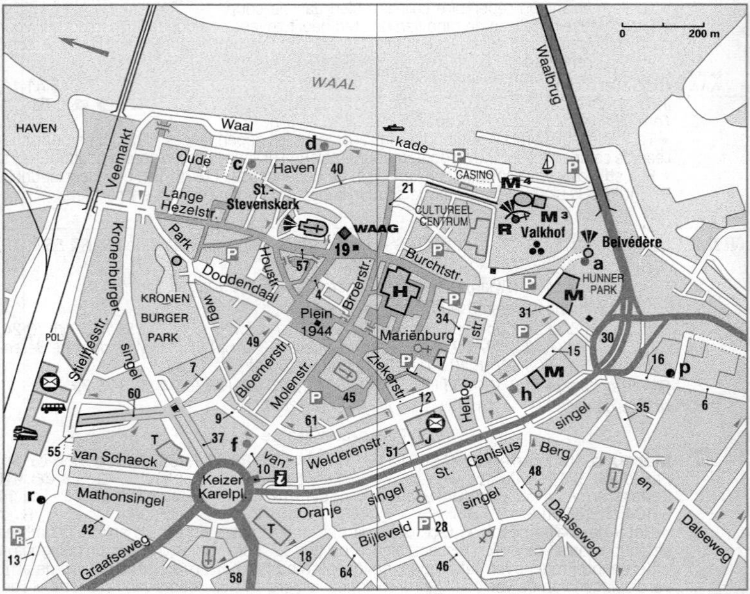

Belvoir, Graadt van Roggenstraat 101, ✉ 6522 AX, ✆ (0 24) 323 23 44, *info@belvoir.nl, Fax (0 24) 323 99 60,* – 25 à 350. AE VISA JCB. rest C p

Repas *(fermé 31 déc.)* carte 29 à 44 – 15 – **75 ch** 93 – ½ P 81/128.

◆ Junior suites et chambres assez spacieuses, salles de réunions, proximité de curiosités intéressantes, bref, un bon point de chute pour partir à la découverte de Nimègue.

◆ Junior suites en vrij ruime kamers, vergaderzalen, interessante bezienswaardigheden in de nabijheid. Kortom : een goede uitvalsbasis om Nijmegen te verkennen.

Het Slot van de Baron, Neerboscheweg 620, ✉ 6544 LL, ✆ (0 24) 379 15 00, *info@slotvandebaron.nl, Fax (0 24) 379 16 00,* – – 30. AE VISA A a

fermé 28 déc.-1er janv. – **Repas** *(fermé sam. midi et dim. midi)* *Lunch 29* – carte 40 à 64, ♀ – **6 ch** 145/169, – 2 suites – ½ P 124/149.

◆ À l'entrée de la ville, belle demeure ancienne où vous serez hébergé dans de vastes chambres "full equipment". Mention spéciale pour la junior suite et les deux vraies suites. Repas classique dans une salle bourgeoise habillée de lambris.

◆ Een mooi, oud landhuis aan de rand van de stad, met grote kamers die alle comfort bieden. Bijzondere vermelding verdienen de twee suites en de junior suite. In een deftige eetzaal met lambrisering kunt u genieten van een klassieke maaltijd.

Bastion, Neerbosscheweg 614, ✉ 6544 LL, ✆ (0 24) 373 01 00, *bastion@bastionhotel.nl, Fax (0 24) 373 03 73,* – AE VISA. A e

Repas (grillades, ouvert jusqu'à 23 h) carte env. 30 – 10 – **40 ch** 76.

◆ Pratique pour l'étape, et identique aux autres unités de la chaîne Bastion, cette ressource hôtelière proche de l'autoroute monte la garde à l'entrée de l'agglomération.

◆ Dit hotel dicht bij de snelweg houdt de wacht aan de rand van de agglomeratie. Een praktisch adres om de reis te onderbreken en identiek aan de andere Bastions.

Chalet Brakkestein, Driehuizerweg 285, ✉ 6525 PL, ✆ (0 24) 355 39 49, *info@chaletbrakkestein.nl, Fax (0 24) 356 46 19,* ←, – AE VISA A n

fermé 31 déc.-1er janv. – **Repas** (dîner seult) 38/68 bc, ♀.

◆ Demeure du 18e s. s'ouvrant sur parc public. Salle à manger cossue et véranda de style victorien avec vue sur un haras. Repas aux flambeaux en terrasse, les soirs d'été.

◆ Dit 18e-eeuwse landhuis in een park heeft een luxueuze eetzaal en een serre in Victoriaanse stijl met uitzicht op een stoeterij. 's Zomers diner bij fakkellicht.

Belvédère, Kelfkensbos 60, ✉ 6511 TB, ✆ (0 24) 322 68 61, *info@restaurantbelvedere.nl, Fax (0 24) 360 01 06,* ← rivière et ville, – AE VISA JCB. C a

fermé sam. midi et dim. – **Repas** *Lunch 29* – carte 43 à 58, ♀.

◆ Un escalier tournant dessert cette table recluse dans une tour de guet appartenant à l'ancienne enceinte de Nimègue. Vue plongeante sur la rivière, en salle comme en terrasse.

◆ Een wenteltrap leidt naar dit restaurant in een wachttoren, die vroeger deel uitmaakte van de stadsmuur. De eetzaal en het terras bieden uitzicht op de rivier.

De Schat, Lage Markt 79, ✉ 6511 VK, ✆ (0 24) 322 40 60, *Fax (0 24) 360 88 88,* , Ouvert jusqu'à 23 h – AE VISA JCB B d

fermé du 9 au 25 mars, du 4 au 12 août, 24 déc.-1er janv., merc., jeudi, sam. midi et dim. midi – **Repas** *Lunch 28* – carte 47 à 58, ♀.

◆ Petit restaurant pelotonné entre le rempart et le Waal. Décor intérieur mignon et mise en place soignée sur les tables. Repas dans l'air du temps. Mini-terrasse d'été.

◆ Klein restaurant tussen de stadswal en de Waal. Charmant interieur en een verzorgde mise en place op de tafels. Trendy gerechten. Miniterras in de zomer.

Het Heimwee, Oude Haven 76, ✉ 6511 XH, ✆ (0 24) 322 22 56, *info@heimwee.com, Fax (0 24) 350 54 45,* – AE VISA B c

fermé 31 déc.-1er janv. – **Repas** (dîner seult) carte 33 à 41, ♀.

◆ Nouveau "look" - toujours aussi moderne, mais un rien plus sobre - et confort amélioré, à cette adresse agréable où se concoctent des préparations actuelles de bon aloi.

◆ Nieuwe look - nog altijd even modern maar een tikje eenvoudiger - en verbeterd comfort op dit aangename adres, waar goede eigentijdse gerechten worden bereid.

Het Savarijn, Van der Brugghenstraat 14, ✉ 6511 SL, ✆ (0 24) 323 26 15, *post@savarijn.nl, Fax (0 24) 360 51 67,* – AE VISA JCB. C h

fermé 30 avril, Pâques, Pentecôte, 17 juil.-1er août, 31 déc.-1er janv., sam. midi et dim. – **Repas** *Lunch 25* – 29/48 bc, ♀.

◆ L'enseigne rend hommage à un célèbre gastronome française ; la cuisine, quant à elle, ne démérite pas. Carte saisonnière, menus bien vus, service efficace et souriant.

◆ De naam is een eerbetoon aan een beroemde Franse gastronoom, waartoe ook de keuken een steentje bijdraagt. Seizoengebonden gerechten, populaire menu's, vriendelijke bediening.

PAYS-BAS

Claudius, Bisschop Hamerstraat 12, ✉ 6511 NB, ✆ (0 24) 322 14 56, *restaurant.claudius @inter.nl.net, Fax (0 24) 322 14 56,* Grillades – AE Ⓓ MC VISA JCB. B f
fermé 2 sem. en juil. et lundi – **Repas** (dîner seult) carte 36 à 54, ♀.
◆ Déjà plus de 30 ans de présence pour cette rôtisserie sympathique où les grillades au feu de bois crépitent en salle. Terrasse d'été à l'arrière, garnie de meubles en teck.
◆ Dit sympathieke restaurant, al 30 jaar een vertrouwd adres in de stad, grilt zijn gerechten boven een houtskoolvuur in de eetzaal. Terras met teakmeubilair aan de achterkant.

à Berg en Dal C *Groesbeek 19 050 h :*

Val-Monte, Oude Holleweg 5, ✉ 6572 AA, ✆ (0 24) 684 20 00, *info@goldentulipvalmonte.nl, Fax (0 24) 684 33 53,* ← – 25 à 160. AE Ⓓ MC VISA. A y
Repas *Lunch 18* – carte 24 à 53, ♀ – 14 – **123 ch** 69/131, – 1 suite – ½ P 79/94.
◆ Sur une butte boisée dominant un secteur résidentiel, hôtel-centre de séminaires agrémenté d'un jardin où l'on pourra "décompresser". Plusieurs catégories de chambres. De la terrasse du restaurant, coup d'œil plongeant sur les alentours verdoyants.
◆ Dit hotel annex vergadercentrum ligt op een beboste heuvel aan de rand van een woonwijk. In de tuin kunt u in alle rust de druk weer van de ketel halen. Verschillende categorieën kamers. Het terras van het restaurant kijkt uit op de omringende bossen.

Erica, Molenbosweg 17, ✉ 6571 BA, ✆ (0 24) 684 35 14, *info@hotelerica.nl, Fax (0 24) 684 36 13,* – 25 à 250. AE Ⓓ MC VISA. rest A x
Repas *Lunch 18* – carte env. 37, ♀ – **59 ch** 120/158 – ½ P 120/180.
◆ Cet établissement enrobé de chlorophylle distribue ses chambres entre une ancienne villa et une aile récente hébergeant les meilleures d'entre elles. Séminaires fréquents. Repas classique à prix plancher.
◆ Dit etablissement midden in het groen beschikt over kamers in een oude villa en over een nieuwbouwvleugel, die de beste kamers herbergt. Er worden regelmatig seminars gehouden. Klassieke maaltijd voor een zachte prijs.

In Geuren en Kleuren, Oude Kleefsebaan 102 (par Berg en Dalseweg : 4 km), ✉ 6571 BJ, ✆ (0 24) 322 55 55, *info@ingeurenenkleuren.nl, Fax (0 24) 323 68 83,* – MC VISA
fermé sem. carnaval, 1 sem. en juil., mardi, sam. midi et dim. midi – **Repas** *Lunch 28* – carte env. 47, ♀.
◆ Un restaurant familial a pris ses quartiers dans cette maison rénovée dont la pimpante pergola affiche un petit air colonial. Carte élaborée. Service charmant par la patronne.
◆ Familierestaurant in een gerenoveerd pand, waarvan de elegante veranda iets koloniaals heeft. Verzorgde menukaart. Charmante bediening door de eigenaresse.

à Beuningen *par ⑤ : 7 km – 25 429 h*

De Croonprins, Van Heemstraweg 77, ✉ 6641 AB, ✆ (0 24) 677 12 17, *info@croonprins.nl, Fax (0 24) 677 81 26,* – P. AE Ⓓ MC VISA
fermé prem. sem. août, sam. midi, dim. midi et lundi – **Repas** 22/35, ♀.
◆ Belle villa de style normand où l'on vient faire de bons repas traditionnels sans trop bourse délier. Décor intérieur actuel, salon séparé et invitante terrasse sur l'arrière.
◆ Mooie villa in Normandische stijl, waar voor een zacht prijsje goede, traditionele gerechten worden bereid. Modern interieur, aparte salon en terras aan de achterkant.

à Groesbeek *Sud-Est : 9 km – 19 050 h*

De Wolfsberg, Mooksebaan 12, ✉ 6562 KB, ✆ (0 24) 397 13 27, *info@dewolfsberg.nl, Fax (0 24) 397 74 74,* ← – 25 à 80. AE MC VISA.
Repas *Lunch 28* – carte env. 36 – **17 ch** 75/100 – ½ P 105/115.
◆ Cette jolie demeure néo-classique élevée au 19e s. offre l'agrément d'un parc arboré et d'une vue apaisante sur la vallée. Confort fonctionnel dans les chambres. Restaurant prolongé d'une véranda.
◆ Dit fraaie neoklassieke pand uit de 19e eeuw is prachtig gelegen in een park aan de rand van uitgestrekte bossen en biedt een rustgevend uitzicht over het dal. Functioneel comfort in de kamers. Restaurant met serre.

à Ooij *par ② : 7,5 km* C *Ubbergen 9 261 h :*

De Haan, Koningin Julianalaan 32, ✉ 6576 AS, ✆ (0 24) 663 82 13, *Fax (0 24) 663 82 12,* – 25 à 120. AE MC VISA.
Repas carte 25 à 33 – **43 ch** 40/55 – ½ P 52/70.
◆ À 10 min de Nimègue, dans un village tranquille, hôtel familial aux grandes chambres d'une tenue exemplaire. Un bon hébergement pour partir à la découverte des rives du Waal. Restaurant d'été où les cyclotouristes ont leurs habitudes. Cuisine hollandaise.
◆ Dit familiehotel in een rustig dorp op 10 min. van Nijmegen heeft grote kamers die uitstekend worden onderhouden. Een goede pleisterplaats voor wie de oevers van de Waal wil gaan verkennen. Het zomerterras is erg in trek bij fietstoeristen. Hollandse keuken.

NOORDBEEMSTER *Noord-Holland* 531 O 7 – *voir à Purmerend.*

NOORDELOOS *Zuid-Holland* © *Giessenlanden 14 257 h.* 532 O 11 *et* 715 F 6.
Amsterdam 61 – Utrecht 30 – Den Haag 70 – Breda 45 – Rotterdam 43.

XXX **De Gieser Wildeman,** Botersloot 1, ✉ 4225 PR, ☎ (0 183) 58 25 01, *Fax (0 183) 58 29 44,* – AE VISA JCB
fermé 26 juil.-8 août, sam. midi et dim. – **Repas** Lunch 38 – carte 56 à 70.
• Promue maison de bouche grâce à un patron bien inspiré, cette ancienne ferme coiffée d'un toit de chaume vient de s'embellir d'une verrière s'ouvrant sur les terrasses.
• Deze voormalige boerderij met rieten dak is met de komst van een bezielde patron in een top-zaak veranderd. De grote nieuwe serre ziet uit op de terrassen.

NOORDEN *Zuid-Holland* © *Nieuwkoop 11 005 h.* 532 N 10 *et* 715 F 5.
Amsterdam 42 – Utrecht 50 – Den Haag 48 – Rotterdam 47.

XXX **De Watergeus** avec ch, Simon van Capelweg 10, ✉ 2431 AG, ☎ (0 172) 40 83 98, *info@dewatergeus.nl, Fax (0 172) 40 92 15,* ← étangs, – 25. AE VISA JCB
Repas *(fermé dim. et lundi)* Lunch 28 – 33/65 bc, ♀ – 8 – **7 ch** 50/87, – 1 suite – ½ P 64/79.
• Une "Lady chef of the year 2001" s'active aux fourneaux de ce restaurant privilégié par sa situation au bord de l'eau. Terrasse estivale invitante. Chambres de bon séjour.
• De Lady Chef van 2001 staat achter het fornuis van dit prachtig gelegen restaurant aan het water. Aanlokkelijk zomerterras. Comfortabele kamers.

NOORD-SCHARWOUDE *Noord-Holland* 531 N 6 – *voir à Alkmaar.*

NOORDWIJK AAN ZEE *Zuid-Holland* © *Noordwijk 24 601 h.* 532 L 9 *et* 715 E 5 – *Station balnéaire.*
Van Berckelweg 38, ✉ 2200 AA, ☎ (0 71) 364 65 43.
De Grent 8, ✉ 2202 EK, ☎ 0 900-202 04 04, noordwijk@hollandrijnland.nl, Fax (0 71) 361 69 45.
Amsterdam 42 ① – Den Haag 26 ① – Haarlem 28 ①

Plan page suivante

Gd H. Huis ter Duin , Koningin Astrid bd 5, ✉ 2202 BK, ☎ (0 71) 361 92 20 et 365 12 30 (rest), *info@huisterduin.com, Fax (0 71) 361 94 01,* ←, – ch, – 25 à 1050. AE VISA. AX a
Repas voir rest ***Latour*** ci-après – ***la Terrasse*** carte 32 à 47, ♀ – **232 ch** 300/340, – 22 suites.
• Perché sur sa dune, ce grand hôtel international scrute le front de mer. Sept catégories de chambres où rien ne manque. Centre de loisirs et importante capacité conférencière. Comme l'insinue l'enseigne de la brasserie, on mange à l'extérieur aux beaux jours.
• Vanaf de duin speurt dit grote internationale hotel de zee af. Zeven typen kamers waar werkelijk niets ontbreekt. Ontspanningscentrum en grote congrescapaciteit. Zoals de naam van het Grand Café al doet vermoeden, wordt er bij mooi weer buiten geserveerd.

Hotels van Oranje, Koningin Wilhelmina bd 20, ✉ 2202 GV, ☎ (0 71) 367 68 69, *info@hotelsvanoranje.nl, Fax (0 71) 367 68 00,* ←, – rest, – 25 à 900. AE VISA. rest AX d
Repas ***Romanoff*** *(fermé sam. sauf en juil.-août)* Lunch 40 – 45, ♀ – ***De Harmonie*** (grillades, dîner seult) carte 25 à 42 – **280 ch** 225/315, – 2 suites.
• Le long de la digue, hôtel haut de gamme aux chambres spacieuses et raffinées. Beauty-center, piscine à vagues et grande infrastructure pour se réunir. Repas gastronomique au Romanoff. Une collection d'instruments à vent égaye le steak-house De Harmonie.
• Eersteklas hotel aan de boulevard, met ruime, luxueuze kamers. Beauty center, golfslagbad, grote infrastructuur voor bijeenkomsten. Gastronomische maaltijd in de Romanoff. Een collectie blaasinstrumenten zorgt voor een vrolijke noot in steakhouse De Harmonie.

Palace , Picképlein 8, ✉ 2202 CL, ☎ (0 71) 365 30 00, *info@palacehotel.nl, Fax (0 71) 365 30 01,* – – 25 à 800. AE VISA JCB AX z
Repas Lunch 28 – carte env. 49 – **120 ch** 255/300 – ½ P 125/175.
• Palace flambant neuf que signale une imposante façade d'inspiration 1900. Communs modernes, chambres et junior suites "dernier cri" ; le tout, aménagé sans faute de goût. Élégante salle de restaurant où l'on vient faire des repas dans le tempo actuel.
• Een gloednieuw luxehotel met een imposante façade in 1900-stijl. Moderne gemeenschappelijke ruimten, kamers en junior suites met de nieuwste snufjes, alles smaakvol ingericht. Stijlvol restaurant waar de gasten de actuele keuken kunnen waarderen.

Bomstraat	AX	4
Bronckhorststraat	BZ	6
Douzastraat	BZ	7
Heilige Geestweg	BZ	10
Herenweg	BZ	12
Hoofdstraat	AX	
Kerkstraat	BZ	15
Kroonsplein (Jan)	AX	17
Limburg Stirumstraat (van)	BZ	19
Lindenhofstraat	BZ	21
Lindenplein	BZ	22
Palaceplein	AX	25
Royenstraat (Abraham van)	AX	27
Tappenbeckweg (Rudolf)	AX	29
Tramsteeg	BZ	31

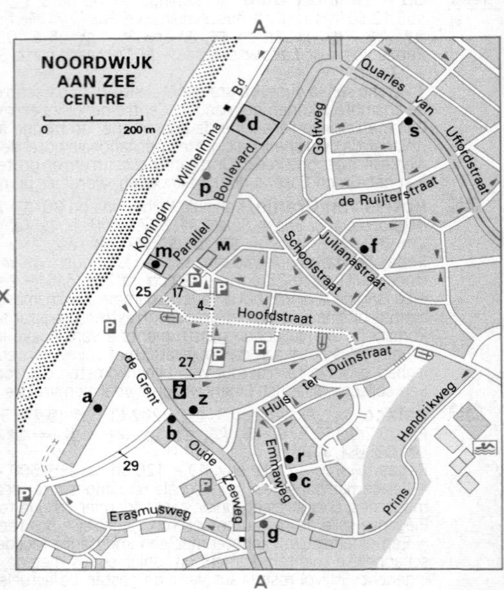

Aux Pays-Bas,
le petit déjeuner est
généralement inclus
dans le prix
de la chambre.

In Nederland
is het ontbijt
in het algemeen
bij de kamerprijs
inbegrepen.

Alexander, Oude Zeeweg 63, 2202 CJ, (0 71) 361 89 00, *info@alexanderhotel.nl, Fax (0 71) 361 78 82,* - rest, - 50 à 200. AX b
Repas *Lunch 15* - carte 33 à 50, - **62 ch** 105/135 - ½ P 88/98.
• À une encablure du bord de mer, construction contemporaine distribuant ses chambres, de tailles très respectables, sur trois étages. Chacune dispose de son balcon. Salle de restaurant garnie de meubles de style et rythmée par une rangée d'arcades.
• Eigentijds gebouw vlak aan zee, met ruime kamers die over drie verdiepingen verspreid liggen en alle zijn voorzien van een balkon. De restaurantzaal is tegen de achtergrond van een mooie arcaderij met stijlmeubilair ingericht.

De Witte Raaf, Duinweg 117 (Nord-Est : 4,5 km), 2204 AT, (0 252) 24 29 00, *info@hoteldewitteraaf.nl, Fax (0 252) 37 75 78,* - - 25 à 150. rest BY
fermé 27 déc.-3 janv. - **Repas** ***In de Tuin*** *Lunch 33* - 39/64 bc, - **39 ch** 140/177, - 2 suites - ½ P 102/125.
• Aux avant-postes de la mondaine Noordwijk aan Zee, paisible hôtel entouré de terrasses fleuries aux beaux jours. Bon équipement pour séjourner en famille ou en séminaire. Salle à manger lumineuse. Repas en plein air à la belle saison.
• Een rustig hotel aan de rand van het mondaine Noordwijk aan Zee, omringd door terrassen waar 's zomers volop bloemen staan. Goede voorzieningen, zowel voor een gezinsvakantie als voor seminars. Lichte eetzaal. Bij mooi weer wordt buiten geserveerd.

Marie Rose, Emmaweg 25, 2202 CP, (0 71) 361 73 00, *info@marierosehotel.nl, Fax (0 71) 361 73 01* - AX c
Repas (dîner pour résidents seult) - **32 ch** 70/100 - ½ P 60/68.
• Bonne petite adresse pour poser ses valises à l'écart de l'animation balnéaire. Chambres avec balconnet, salon-bibliothèque au coin du feu, gestion familiale dynamique.
• Een goed adresje om neer te strijken buiten de drukte van de badplaats. Kamers met balkonnetje, lounge met open haard, enthousiast familiemanagement.

Prominent Inn, Koningin Wilhelmina bd 4, 2202 GR, (0 71) 361 22 53, *info@prominentinn.nl, Fax (0 71) 361 13 65,* - - 25. AX m
Repas *Lunch 24* - carte 22 à 40 - **33 ch** 80/99 - ½ P 67/90.
• Aménagées fonctionnellement, la plupart des chambres de cet établissement reconstruit en bord de digue dans les années 1990 fixent l'horizon marin depuis leur balcon. L'été, on dresse le couvert sur une terrasse abritée offrant aussi la vue sur l'estran.
• Dit etablissement aan de boulevard dateert uit de jaren negentig van de vorige eeuw en beschikt over functioneel ingericht kamers met balkon, waarvan de meeste uitkijken op zee. In de zomer wordt geserveerd op een lommerrijk terras, eveneens met zeezicht.

Belvedere, Beethovenweg 5, 2202 AE, (0 71) 361 29 29, *hotbelv.@cistron.nl, Fax (0 71) 364 60 61* - - 35. rest AZ h
fermé 20 déc.-5 janv. - **Repas** (dîner pour résidents seult) - **31 ch** 75/120 - ½ P 120/140.
• Vaste bâtisse 1900 assise tel un belvédère au sommet d'une dune. Communs spacieux, salon garni de fauteuils moelleux et grandes chambres avec ou sans balcon.
• Dit grote pand uit rond 1900 staat als een belvédère op de top van de duin. Grote gemeenschappelijke ruimten, salon met heerlijke fauteuils, grote kamers met of zonder balkon.

Zonne, Rembrandtweg 17, 2202 AT, (0 71) 361 96 00, *Fax (0 71) 362 06 02,* - - 25 à 60. rest AZ n
fermé 20 déc.-4 janv. - **Repas** *(fermé après 20 h 30)* carte 22 à 64 - **27 ch** 68/105 - ½ P 70/95.
• Enseigne "solaire" pour cette résidence hôtelière implantée parmi les dunes, dans un quartier résidentiel proche de la plage. Chambres pratiques. Ambiance familiale. En période estivale, il est possible de prendre son repas autour de la piscine.
• Een zonnige naam voor dit hotel midden de duinen, in een woonwijk vlak bij het strand. De kamers zijn praktisch ingericht. Gezellige sfeer. In de zomer kan de maaltijd bij het zwembad worden genuttigd.

De Admiraal, Quarles van Uffordstraat 81, 2202 ND, (0 71) 361 24 60, *info@hoteladmiraal.nl, Fax (0 71) 361 68 14,* - ch AX s
fermé mi-déc.-mi-janv. - **Repas** *(fermé vend. de nov. à mars)* (dîner seult) 22 - **26 ch** 45/89 - ½ P 116/122.
• Point de chute recommandable avant de larguer les amarres : chambres claires et nettes, coin salon avec sa cheminée et ambiance "vieux loup de mer" au bar. Restaurant doté de meubles de style. Mets classico-bourgeois à la mode batave.
• Een rustplaats die aan te bevelen is alvorens de trossen los te gooien : lichte en keurige kamers, zithoek met schouw en intieme sfeer in de bar. Het restaurant is met stijlmeubilair ingericht. Klassiek-traditionele gerechten in Hollandse stijl.

Astoria, Emmaweg 13, 2202 CP, (0 71) 361 00 14, *info@hotelastoria.nl, Fax (0 71) 361 66 44,* – – 30. AX r
Repas (dîner pour résidents seult) – **34 ch** 55/90 – ½ P 45/55.
◆ Ressource hôtelière en léger retrait du centre animé. Chambres avant tout fonctionnelles ; celles du dernier étage, mansardées, sont en attente d'une rénovation.
◆ Hoteletablissement net buiten het drukke centrum. Kamers met het accent op functionaliteit ; de kamers op de dakverdieping staan op de nominatie om gerenoveerd te worden.

Fiankema, Julianastraat 32, 2202 KD, (0 71) 362 03 40, *info@hotelfiankema.nl, Fax (0 71) 362 03 70,* – . AX f
mars-oct. – **Repas** (résidents seult) – **29 ch** 65/90 – ½ P 50/60.
◆ Cette gentille petite affaire familiale située au centre de la localité balnéaire renferme des chambres certes un peu menues mais toutefois assez calmes.
◆ Dit vriendelijke hotelletje in het centrum van de badplaats heeft kamers die wat aan de krappe kant zijn, maar wel vrij rustig liggen.

Latour - H. Gd H. Huis ter Duin, 1er étage, Koningin Astrid bd 5, 2202 BK, (0 71) 365 12 39, *info@huisterduin.com, Fax (0 71) 361 94 01,* – . AX a
Repas (dîner seult) 58/75, ♀.
◆ Le restaurant gastronomique du Gd H. Huis ter Duin vous reçoit dans un cadre classique rajeuni. Pour apprécier la perspective marine, prenez place près des baies vitrées.
◆ In het gastronomische restaurant van Huis ter Duin wordt u ontvangen in een vernieuwd, klassiek decor. Voor een uitzicht op zee is een tafel bij het raam aan te bevelen.

Villa de Duinen avec ch, Oude Zeeweg 74, 2202 CE, (0 71) 364 89 32, *info@villadeduinen.nl, Fax (0 71) 364 71 49,* – – 25. AX g
fermé du 3 au 9 janv. – **Repas** *(fermé sam. midi) Lunch 29* – 34/52 – **9 ch** 135/175.
◆ Ce bel édifice centenaire évoquant une villa balnéaire normande a retrouvé l'éclat du neuf. Salle à manger moderne, cuisine d'aujourd'hui et pimpantes chambres contemporaines.
◆ Deze mooie villa uit het begin van de 20e eeuw is volledig gerenoveerd. Zowel de eetzaal als de fleurige kamers zijn modern ; in de keuken worden actuele gerechten bereid.

Petit Blanc, Koningin Wilhelmina bd 16a, 2202 GT, (0 71) 361 48 75, *Fax (0 71) 361 48 75,* – . AX p
fermé merc. – **Repas** (dîner seult) 33.
◆ Au rez-de-chaussée d'un immeuble sur digue, adresse familiale où l'on ressent le souci de faire bon avec des produits simples. Accueil d'une courtoisie toute naturelle.
◆ In dit restaurant op de benedenverdieping van een pand aan de boulevard wordt met zorg iets goeds bereid van eenvoudige producten. Hoffelijke, ongedwongen ontvangst.

à Noordwijk-Binnen C *Noordwijk* :

Het Hof van Holland, Voorstraat 79, 2201 HP, (0 71) 361 22 55, *hof@tref.nl, Fax (0 71) 362 06 01,* – rest, – 25 à 100. BZ a
fermé 27 déc.-5 janv. – **Repas** *(fermé dim. sauf Pâques et Pentecôte) Lunch 23* – carte 41 à 59 – **33 ch** 83/153, – 2 suites – ½ P 78/104.
◆ Tradition et romantisme dans cette auberge centenaire élevée au cœur d'un village de la Hollande méridionale. Les grandes chambres en annexe disposent d'une kitchenette. Salle de restaurant au décor typé. Préparations "couleur locale".
◆ Traditie en romantiek in dit honderd jaar oude restaurant midden in een dorpje in Zuid-Holland. De grote kamers in de annexe beschikken over een kitchenette. Restaurantzaal met karakteristiek decor. Streekgerechten.

Onder de Linde, Voorstraat 133, 2201 HS, (0 71) 362 31 97, *info@onderdelinde.com, Fax (0 71) 362 31 98* – . BZ z
fermé 26 juil.-11 août, 27 déc.-5 janv. et mardi – **Repas** (dîner seult) 33/68 bc.
◆ Sympathique affaire abritée sous les tilleuls (onder de linde). Les murs de la salle à manger sont habillés de gravures représentant la localité au début du 20e s.
◆ Sympathiek adresje in de schaduw van de lindeboom. Aan de wanden van de eetzaal hangen gravures van het plaatsje uit het begin van de vorige eeuw.

Hofstede Cleyburch, Herenweg 225 (Sud : 2 km), 2201 AG, (0 71) 364 84 48, *info@cleyburch.nl, Fax (0 71) 364 63 66,* – . BZ
fermé lundi – **Repas** (dîner seult) 35/65 bc, ♀.
◆ Un toit de chaume bien peigné encapuchonne cette ancienne fromagerie reconvertie en agréable maison de bouche. Intérieur mi-rustique, mi-classique. Cave bien montée.
◆ Een mooi rieten dak bekroont deze voormalige kaasmakerij, die verbouwd is tot een prettig restaurant. Rustiek-klassiek interieur. Goede wijnkaart.

à Noordwijkerhout *Nord-Est : 5 km – 15 253 h*

XX **Mangerie Zegers,** Herenweg 78 (Nord-Est : 1,5 km), ✉ 2211 CD, ☎ (0 252) 37 25 88, *info@mangeriezegers.com,* – ▤ P – 25 à 125. AE ① MO VISA.
Repas 33/40.
• Les bonnes fourchettes du coin ont leur rond de serviette à la Mangerie Zegers. Goûteuse cuisine de notre temps et salle de restaurant actuelle, en forme de demi-rotonde.
• Lokale liefhebbers van lekker eten weten de weg naar dit eethuis trouw te vinden. Smakelijke eigentijdse keuken en moderne, halfronde restaurantzaal.

NOORDWIJK-BINNEN *Zuid-Holland* 532 G 9 *et* 715 E 5 – *voir à Noordwijk aan Zee.*

NOORDWIJKERHOUT *Zuid-Holland* 532 L 9 *et* 715 E 5 – *voir à Noordwijk aan Zee.*

NORG *Drenthe* C *Noordenveld 31 565 h.* 531 X 4 *et* 715 K 2.
Amsterdam 176 – Groningen 21 – Assen 15 – Emmen 56.

Karsten, Brink 6, ✉ 9331 AA, ☎ (0 592) 61 34 84, *info@hotelkarsten.nl, Fax (0 592) 61 22 16,* – TV P – 40. AE ① MO VISA. rest
Repas *Lunch 21* – carte 28 à 41 – **21 ch** 51/80 – ½ P 53/64.
• Charmant hôtel familial surveillant le brink (place plantée de tilleuls) de Norg. Chambres rénovées, terrasse et salon où crépitent de bonnes flambées quand le froid sévit.
• Een charmant familiehotel dat waakt over de brink van Norg. Gerenoveerde kamers, terras en een gezellige lounge waar op koude dagen een behaaglijk haardvuur knappert.

à Westervelde *Sud : 1 km* C *Noordenveld :*

XX **De Jufferen Lunsingh** avec ch, Hoofdweg 13, ✉ 9337 PA, ☎ (0 592) 61 26 18, *de.jufferen.lunsingh@wxs.nl, Fax (0 592) 61 23 40,* – TV P – 25 à 50. VISA
fermé prem. sem. janv. – **Repas** *Lunch 23* – 32/41, ♀ – **8 ch** 55/90 – ½ P 68/135.
• Chaleur, tradition et saveurs locales dans une adorable demeure du 18e s. entourée de prés et de bois. Une véranda au charme "british" abrite la salle à manger.
• Hartelijkheid, traditie en lokale keuken in dit verrukkelijke pand uit de 18e eeuw, te midden van bos en weiden. De eetzaal is ingericht in een serre met Engelse ambiance.

NUENEN *Noord-Brabant* C *Nuenen, Gerwen en Nederwetten 23 645 h.* 532 S 14 *et* 715 H 7.
Amsterdam 125 – Eindhoven 7 – 's-Hertogenbosch 39.

de Collse Hoeve, Collse Hoefdijk 24 (à Eeneind, Sud : 3 km), ✉ 5674 VK, ☎ (0 40) 283 81 11, *Fax (0 40) 283 42 55,* – ▤ rest, TV P – 25 à 125. AE ① MO VISA.
fermé 24 et 31 déc. – **Repas** *(fermé sam. midi et dim. midi) Lunch 30* – 33/58, ♀ – **40 ch** 60/78 – ½ P 90/115.
• Près du bourg où Van Gogh s'initia à la peinture, ancienne ferme brabançonne habilement mise à profit. Les meilleures chambres, en rez-de-jardin, sont des junior suites. Derrière les fourneaux, le chef mise sur la tradition. Terrasse estivale ombragée.
• Hotel in een oude Brabantse boerderij, vlak bij het dorpje waar Van Gogh begon met schilderen. De beste kamers, op de begane grond aan de tuinkant, zijn junior suites. De chef-kok richt zich vooral op traditie. Lommerrijk zomerterras.

XX ✿ **De Lindehof** (Bahadoer), Beekstraat 1, ✉ 5671 CS, ☎ (0 40) 283 73 36, *lindehof@iae.nl, Fax (0 40) 284 01 16* – ▤. AE MO VISA
fermé 26 juil.-18 août, 28 déc.-5 janv., mardi et merc. – **Repas** (dîner seult) 44/73 bc, carte 42 à 54, ♀.
• Un point de repère dans le paysage gastronomique de la région : assiettes soignées et aménagement intérieur d'esprit contemporain, avec un curieux plafond "magique" !
• Een vast punt in het gastronomisch landschap van de streek : verzorgde gerechten en eigentijds interieur met een curieus "magisch" plafond.
Spéc. Carpaccio et croquette de viande au pecorino. Carré d'agneau façon Méditerranée. Crème brûlée et pomme rôtie

XX **de Zonnewende,** Park 63, ✉ 5671 GC, ☎ (0 40) 284 00 60, *info@dezonnewende.nl, Fax (0 40) 284 20 45,* – AE MO VISA
fermé carnaval, du 6 au 19 juil. et lundi – **Repas** (déjeuner sur réservation) carte env. 45, ♀.
• Ce restaurant de la place du marché concocte une cuisine bien en phase avec l'époque. L'été, quelques tables vous accueillent à l'arrière de l'établissement, côté jardin.
• Dit restaurant aan het marktplein bereidt een eigentijdse keuken. 's Zomers worden enkele tafeltjes gedekt op het terras in de tuin aan de achterkant.

à Nederwetten *Nord-Ouest : 3 km* *Nuenen, Gerwen en Nederwetten :*

XX **Heerendonck,** Hoekstraat 21, ✉ 5674 NN, ☎ (040) 283 39 27, *info@heerendonck.nl, Fax (0 40) 284 01 85,* – VISA
fermé 3 sem. en août, lundi, mardi et merc. – **Repas** (dîner seult) 30.
• Une terrasse d'été précède cette petite villa sur jardin postée à l'entrée d'un patelin typique. Plats classiques actualisés, à l'image de la salle à manger relookée.
• Kleine villa met tuin aan de rand van een karakteristiek dorpje. Zomerterras aan de voorkant. Klassieke gerechten in een modern jasje, net als de nieuwe look van de eetzaal.

NUTH *Limburg* 532 U 17 *et* 715 I 9 – *16 609 h.*
Amsterdam 207 – Maastricht 19 – Heerlen 8 – Aachen 24.

XX **In De'n Dillegaard** (Kagenaar), Dorpstraat 89, ✉ 6361 EK, ☎ (0 45) 524 55 94, *restaurant@dillegaard.nl, Fax (0 45) 567 08 44,* – P. VISA
fermé 27 déc.-4 janv., sam. midi, dim. midi, lundi et mardi – **Repas** *Lunch 34* – 38, carte 50 à 66, ♀.
• Table plaisante et actuelle contemplant l'église. Arcades et toiles modernes en salle. Menus prometteurs, sélection vineuse de même. Terrasse sous tonnelle dans la cour.
• Eigentijds restaurant tegenover de kerk. Eetzaal met bogen en moderne schilderijen. Veelbelovende menu's en dito wijnselectie. Terras onder de pergola op de binnenplaats.
Spéc. Ravioli de foie gras et asperges. Maquereau grillé à la plancha. Tout fraise

---

ODOORN *Drenthe* *Borger-Odoorn 26 333 h.* 531 AA 5 *et* 715 L 3.
Amsterdam 185 – Assen 32 – Emmen 8 – Groningen 49.

Lubbelinkhof ⛔, Hoofdstraat 19, ✉ 7873 TA, ☎ (0 591) 53 51 11, *info@hotel-lubbelinkhof.nl, Fax (0 591) 53 51 15,* , , – , – 25 à 100. VISA. rest
fermé 31 déc. – **Repas** *Lunch 30* – carte 42 à 55 – 14 – **32 ch** 95/146 – ½ P 104/146.
• Récemment agrandie d'une aile moderne où se distribuent plusieurs catégories de chambres "king size", cette ancienne exploitation agricole s'agrémente d'un parc ressourçant. Restaurant aménagé dans l'ex-corps de logis. Salon cossu et terrasse d'été.
• Deze voormalige boerderij is onlangs uitgebreid met een moderne vleugel waarin diverse categorieën kingsize kamers zijn ondergebracht. In het park kunt u nieuwe energie opdoen. Restaurant in het oude woongedeelte, luxueuze lounge en zomerterras.

De Stee, Hoofdstraat 24, ✉ 7873 BC, ☎ (0 591) 51 22 63, *Fax (0 591) 51 36 18,* – P. VISA. ch
Repas (résidents seult) – **12 ch** 50/73.
• Ressource hôtelière familiale installée au cœur de la localité. Salon agréable pour souffler un instant. Les chambres ne sont pas gigantesques, mais fonctionnelles.
• Dit familiehotel bevindt zich in hartje Odoorn. Aangename lounge om even uit te blazen. De kamers zijn niet geweldig groot, maar wel functioneel.

à Exloo *Nord : 4 km* *Borger-Odoorn :*

De Meulenhoek, Hoofdstraat 61, ✉ 7875 AB, ☎ (0 591) 54 91 88, *info@hotel-meulenhoek.nl, Fax (0 591) 54 96 49,* , – rest, . AE VISA JCB. ch
fermé du 1er au 15 janv. – **Repas** *(fermé après 20 h 30)* 28 – **14 ch** 55 – ½ P 50/60.
• Les balades sylvestres, ça fatigue ! Alors, voici une adresse utile pour dormir comme une souche. La plupart des chambres sont équipées d'un balcon ou d'une terrasse.
• Dit adres in een brinkdorp op de Hondsrug kan van pas komen. Na een fikse boswandeling zult u hier als een blok in slaap vallen. De meeste kamers hebben een balkon of terras.

à Valthe *Est : 3 km* *Borger-Odoorn :*

X **De Gaffel,** Odoornerweg 1, ✉ 7872 PA, ☎ (0 591) 51 35 36, *Fax (0 591) 51 31 85,* – P
fermé du 1er au 14 janv. et mardi – **Repas** *Lunch 26* – carte 32 à 42, ♀.
• Dans un hameau paisible et arboré, ancienne ferme saxonne à toit de chaume devancée d'une terrasse. Salle de restaurant à touche rustique. Préparations franco-hollandaises.
• Restaurant in een oude Saksische boerderij met rieten dak, in een rustig en boomrijk dorp. Terras aan de voorzijde en rustieke eetzaal. Hollandse keuken met een Frans tintje.

OEGSTGEEST *Zuid-Holland* 532 L 9 *et* 715 E 5 – *voir à Leiden.*

Si vous cherchez un hôtel tranquille,
consultez d'abord les cartes de l'introduction
ou repérez dans le texte les établissements indiqués avec le signe ⛔

OHÉ en LAAK *Limburg* C *Maasbracht 13 697 h.* 532 T 16 - U 16 *et* 715 I 8.
Amsterdam 182 – Maastricht 29 – Eindhoven 56 – Roermond 14.

Lakerhof, Walburgisstraat 3 (Laak), ✉ 6109 RE, ☎ (0 475) 55 16 54, *info@lakerhof.nl*, , – TV P. MC VISA.
fermé du 13 au 27 fév. – **Repas** *(fermé merc.)* (dîner seult) 27/30 – 6 – **8 ch** 39/58 – ½ P 65.
• Attention ! Ceux qui séjournent dans cette maison familiale s'exposent à une bonne humeur certainement contagieuse. Chambres plutôt vastes, pratiques et insonorisées.
• Pas op ! Wie verblijft in dit familiehotel loopt het risico met een goed humeur besmet te worden. De vrij grote en praktische kamers zijn voorzien van geluidsisolatie.

OIRSCHOT *Noord-Brabant* 532 Q 13 *et* 715 G 7 – *17 808 h.*
St-Odulphusstraat 11, ✉ 5688 BA, ☎ (0 499) 55 05 99, info@vvvoirschot.nl, Fax (0 499) 57 76 33.
Amsterdam 117 – Eindhoven 18 – 's-Hertogenbosch 28 – Tilburg 21.

de Moriaan sans rest, Moriaan 41a, ✉ 5688 ER, ☎ (0 499) 57 81 80, *info@hoteldemoriaan.nl, Fax (0 499) 57 81 33*, , – TV . AE MC VISA JCB.
fermé du 11 au 26 fév. – **2 ch** 90/125, – 8 suites.
• Au centre du bourg, hôtel de construction récente mettant à votre disposition des chambres spacieuses et confortables ainsi que plusieurs suites et un sauna. Parking commode.
• Dit vrij nieuwe hotel in het centrum van het plaatsje beschikt over ruime, comfortabele kamers alsmede enkele suites. Sauna. Parking.

De Kroon, Rijkesluisstraat 6, ✉ 5688 ED, ☎ (0 499) 57 10 95, *info@hoteldekroon.nl, Fax (0 499) 57 57 85*, , – TV. AE MC VISA. ch – *fermé dern. sem. déc.-prem. sem. janv.* – **Repas** *(fermé mardi)* Lunch 23 – 25/40, ♀ – **12 ch** 73/140 – ½ P 95.
• La puissante tour de la St.-Petruskerk vous servira de point de repère pour dénicher cet établissement familial avoisinant le Markt. Chambres plaisamment réaménagées.
• De stevige toren van de St.-Petruskerk helpt u de weg te vinden naar dit familiehotel bij de markt. Kamers met een nieuwe, aangename inrichting.

La Fleurie, Rijkesluisstraat 4, ✉ 5688 ED, ☎ (0 499) 57 41 36, *info@lafleurie.nl, Fax (0 499) 57 49 68*, – AE MC VISA
fermé lundi – **Repas** Lunch 23 – 31/46, ♀.
• Sur la place du marché, maison de bouche intime et chaleureuse où se conçoit une cuisine d'aujourd'hui. Salle de banquets dans la "tuinkamer" aux notes néo-baroques.
• In dit intieme, gezellige restaurant aan het marktplein wordt een eigentijdse keuken bereid. Zaal voor partijen in de tuinkamer met neobarokke accenten.

De Meulen, Korenaar 49, ✉ 5688 TS, ☎ (0 499) 57 51 92, *info@demeulen.nl, Fax (0 499) 57 50 22*, – P. AE MC VISA.
fermé 1 sem. carnaval, 2 sem. vacances bâtiment, sam. midi, dim. midi, lundi et mardi – **Repas** (déjeuner sur réservation) 30/42.
• Un vieux moulin à vent (19e s.) monté sur balustrade - et toujours en état de marche - jouxte la salle de restaurant. Terrasse d'été dressée au jardin, sur l'arrière.
• Een oude gaanderijmolen (19e eeuw) - die nog altijd in bedrijf is - staat naast dit restaurant. Zomerterras in de tuin, aan de achterkant.

De Zwaan, Markt 4, ✉ 5688 AJ, ☎ (0 499) 55 14 14, *info@dezwaan-oirschot.nl, Fax (0 499) 55 14 15*, – – 25 à 120. AE MC VISA
Repas Lunch 22 – 20/42 bc.
• A la fois brasserie et restaurant, De Zwaan ratisse large et présente une carte un peu "touche-à-tout" dans un décor assez cossu. Organisation de banquets.
• Dit restaurant annex brasserie krijgt een steeds breder publiek en voert een kaart waarop een beetje "van alles wat" staat. Interieur met vrij weelderig decor. Banqueting.

OISTERWIJK *Noord-Brabant* 532 Q 13 *et* 715 G 7 – *25 327 h.*
Voir *Site*★.
De Lind 57, ✉ 5061 HT, ☎ (0 13) 528 23 45, Fax (0 13) 528 52 17.
Amsterdam 106 – Eindhoven 38 – 's-Hertogenbosch 17 – Tilburg 10.

De Swaen, De Lind 47, ✉ 5061 HT, ☎ (0 13) 523 32 33, *info@hoteldeswaen.nl, Fax (0 13) 528 58 60*, , , – TV P. – 25 à 200. AE MC VISA.
Repas *(fermé sam. midi et dim. midi)* Lunch 28 – 38/78 bc, ♀ – 18 – **22 ch** *(fermé 31 déc.)* 160, – 2 suites.
• Vénérable auberge du centre récemment réaménagée dans un souci d'esthétique et de confort. Grandes chambres "full options" et superbe jardin anglais clos de murs. Salle à manger relookée, fine cuisine actuelle et cave d'épicurien. L'été, repas en plein air.
• Dit eerbiedwaardige pand is onlangs met zorg voor stijl en comfort opnieuw ingericht. Grote kamers met alle comfort. Mooie, ommuurde Engelse tuin. Eetzaal met een nieuwe look, verfijnde eigentijdse keuken, uitgelezen wijnkelder. 's Zomers kunt u buiten eten.

Landgoed De Rosep, Oirschotsebaan 15 (Sud-Est : 3 km), 5062 TE, (0 13) 523 21 00, *info@rosep.com, Fax (0 13) 523 21 99*, – rest, – 25 à 350.
Repas *(fermé 25 et 26 déc. et 1er janv.)* 33/45 – **73 ch** *(fermé 1er janv.)* 118/164 – ½ P 110/187.
• Tapis dans la verdure, le domaine De Rosep déploie ses trois ailes de chambres, calmes et bien calibrées, juste en face d'un étang. Centre sportif et petit parc ombragé. Terrasse prise d'assaut dès que la température grimpe. Recettes élaborées.
• Dit hotel in het groen heeft zijn drie vleugels met rustige en royale kamers uitgespreid tegenover een vijver. Sportfaciliteiten en klein lommerrijk park. Zodra de temperatuur stijgt, wordt het druk op het terras. Verfijnde keuken.

Bos en Ven, Klompven 26, 5062 AK, (0 13) 528 88 56, *info@bos-ven.nl, Fax (0 13) 528 68 10*, – rest, – 25 à 150.
fermé 27 déc.-1er janv. – **Repas** *Lunch 32* – 47, ♀ – **39 ch** 118/138 – ½ P 102/160.
• Demeure massive élevée en 1920 dans un quartier résidentiel. La terrasse et quelques chambres dévoilent une vue plaisante sur un jardin à la française et son mini plan d'eau. Restaurant d'été. Salon avec cheminée garnie de faïence de Delft.
• Dit monumentale pand werd in 1920 in een chique woonwijk opgetrokken. Schouw met Delfts blauwe tegeltjes in de lounge. Terras voor een zomerse maaltijd buiten. Het terras en enkele kamers kijken uit op een Franse tuin met miniwaterpartij.

Bosrand, Gemullehoekenweg 60, 5062 CE, (0 13) 521 90 15, *info@hotelbosrand.nl, Fax (0 13) 528 63 66*, – – 25 à 45. rest
fermé 28 déc.-6 janv. – **Repas** *(fermé après 20 h)* 22/28 – **25 ch** 85 – ½ P 59/63.
• L'enseigne dit vrai : cet établissement familial - aujourd'hui embelli et procurant plus d'agrément - est situé à la lisière des bois (bosrand). Chambres actuelles.
• De naam zegt al genoeg over de ligging van dit familiehotel. Het etablissement is opgeknapt en biedt nu meer comfort. Eigentijdse kamers.

De Blauwe Kei, Rosepdreef 4 (Sud-Est : 3 km), 5062 TB, (0 13) 528 23 14, *deblauwekei@yahoo.com, Fax (0 13) 528 22 21*, – .
fermé janv. et lundi, mardi et merc. de nov. à mars – **Repas** 22/45, ♀ – **11 ch** 48/81 – ½ P 54/61.
• Besoin d'une mise au vert ? Cette auberge retirée en forêt répond présent. Chambres menues. S'il fait beau, une grande terrasse est dressée. Table estimée des promeneurs pour son menu-carte bien pensé et sa sage politique de prix.
• Behoefte om te ontsnappen aan de hectiek van alledag ? Dit hotel in de bossen staat paraat. Kleine kamers. Bij warm weer wordt een groot terras uitgezet. Het restaurant is in trek bij wandelaars vanwege het doordachte à la carte menu en de vriendelijke prijzen.

Rasa Senang, Gemullehoekenweg 127, 5062 CC, (0 13) 528 60 86, *rasa.senang@tip.nl, Fax (0 13) 528 30 40*, Cuisine indonésienne –
fermé 24, 25 et 31 déc. et lundi de nov. à mars – **Repas** (dîner seult) 25/55 bc.
• Un petit coin d'Indonésie en plein Brabant septentrional : salle à manger où méditent quelques bouddhas de bronze et recettes écumant l'archipel, de Sumatra à Bali.
• Een stukje Indonesië in hartje Noord-Brabant. In de eetzaal zitten enkele bronzen boeddha's te mediteren. De gerechten schuimen de archipel af, van Sumatra tot Bali.

De Parel avec ch, Scheibaan 17 (Sud-Est : 4,5 km), 5062 TM, (0 13) 528 25 25, *info@pareloisterwijk.nl, Fax (0 13) 528 54 14*, – rest, – 25 à 50.
Repas *(fermé 24 et 31 déc.)* *Lunch 30* – 38 – **8 ch** 57/69 – ½ P 57.
• Peu enclin à la routine, le chef repense sa carte chaque mois, histoire de varier les plaisirs. Terrasse d'été dominant une pièce d'eau. Chambres menues et bon breakfast.
• Sleur is niets voor de chef-kok en verandering van spijs doet eten, dus maandelijks wisselende menukaart. Zomerterras met uitzicht op het water. Kleine kamers, goed ontbijt.

Het Geheim van de Smit, Gemullehoekenweg 13, 5061 MA, (0 13) 521 95 26, *info.geheimvandesmit@parelnet.nl, Fax (0 13) 528 75 49*, – .
fermé sem. carnaval, sam. midi et dim. midi – **Repas** *Lunch 30* – carte env. 39, ♀.
• Bistrot-restaurant rustique où un choix de préparations au goût du jour s'emploie à combler votre appétit. L'assiette est soignée. Repas en plein air par beau temps.
• Rustieke bistro waar een keur van eigentijdse gerechten het geheime wapen is om uw honger te stillen. Verzorgd opgemaakte borden. Bij mooi weer wordt buiten geserveerd.

OLDEBERKOOP (OLDEBERKEAP) *Fryslân* 🄲 *Ooststellingwerf 26 726 h.* 531 V 5 *et* 715 J 3.

Amsterdam 127 – Groningen 61 – Leeuwarden 50 – Assen 41 – Steenwijk 23.

XX **Lunia** avec ch, Molenhoek 2, ✉ 8421 PG, ✆ (0 516) 45 10 57, *lunia@hetnet.nl, Fax (0 516) 45 10 20,* – 30. AE VISA
fermé mardi soir en hiver – **Repas** *Lunch 13* – carte env. 44, ♀ – **18 ch** 58/70 – ½ P 60/73.
◆ À l'entrée du bourg, jolie demeure bourgeoise toujours prête à fournir le gîte et le couvert. Salle à manger classiquement aménagée, chambres basiques et jardin reposant.
◆ Mooi herenhuis aan de rand van het dorp, waar tafel en bed altijd voor u klaar staan. Klassiek ingerichte eetzaal, basic kamers en rustige tuin.

OLDENZAAL *Overijssel* 531 AA 9, 532 AA 9 *et* 715 L 5 – *31 180 h.*

St-Plechelmusplein 5, ✉ 7571 EG, ✆ 0 900 202 19 81, info@vvvanwboldenzaal.nl, Fax (0 541) 51 75 42.

Amsterdam 161 – Zwolle 74 – Enschede 11.

De Kroon, Steenstraat 17, ✉ 7571 BH, ✆ (0 541) 51 24 02, *dekroon@introweb.nl, Fax (0 541) 52 06 30,* – 30. AE VISA
fermé 30 déc.-2 janv. – **Repas** (dîner pour résidents seult) – **20 ch** 60/90 – ½ P 65/70.
◆ La quatrième génération a pris les commandes de cette sympathique auberge familiale. Chambres pour toutes les attentes, espace et agrément variables. Accueil gentil.
◆ De vierde generatie heeft het roer van dit sympathieke familiehotel overgenomen. Aan kamers is er voor elk wat wils, variërend in grootte en comfort. Vriendelijke ontvangst.

X **De oude Raadskelder,** Kerkstraat 18, ✉ 7571 EE, ✆ (0 541) 53 25 53, *info@oud eraadskelder.nl, Fax (0 541) 53 88 10* – . AE VISA JCB.
fermé 26 juil.-12 août, sam. midi, dim. midi et lundi – **Repas** (déjeuner sur réservation) 27/48, ♀.
◆ Agréable restaurant aménagé dans les caves voûtées de l'hôtel de ville d'Oldenzaal. Cuisine actuelle assez élaborée, salle à manger d'esprit rustique et ambiance bougie.
◆ Aangenaam restaurant in de gewelfde kelder van het stadhuis in Oldenzaal. Actuele en vrij verzorgde keuken, rustieke eetzaal en kaarslichtambiance.

OLTERTERP *Fryslân* 531 V 4 – *voir à Beetsterzwaag.*

OMMEN *Overijssel* 531 X 7 *et* 715 K 4 – *16 890 h.*

Kruisstraat 6, ✉ 7731 CR, ✆ (0 529) 45 16 38, info@vechtdalvvv.nl, Fax (0 529) 45 14 50.

Amsterdam 134 – Zwolle 24 – Assen 59 – Enschede 59.

Paping, Stationsweg 29, ✉ 7731 AX, ✆ (0 529) 45 19 45, *info@hotelpaping.nl, Fax (0 529) 45 47 82,* – 25 à 100. AE VISA
fermé 31 déc.-1er janv. – **Repas** *Lunch 25* – 28/38 – **38 ch** 53/108 – ½ P 60/71.
◆ Hôtel familial de situation centrale, tout proche de la gare. Chambres récemment refaites de neuf ; celles tournant le dos à la rue vous procureront un peu plus de quiétude. À table, cuisine en phase avec l'époque. On mange en terrasse aux beaux jours.
◆ Centraal gelegen familiehotel, vlak bij het station. De kamers zijn onlangs gerenoveerd. De kamers die de straat de rug toekeren, bieden wat meer rust. Eigentijdse keuken. Bij mooi weer wordt op het terras gegeten.

De Herbergier, Hammerweg 40, ✉ 7731 AK, ✆ (0 529) 45 15 92, *info@deherberg ier.nl, Fax (0 529) 45 51 92,* – 25 à 130. VISA
fermé 20 déc.-6 janv. – **Repas** carte 26 à 50 – **21 ch** 54/120 – ½ P 65/90.
◆ Aux abords du village, auberge de brique à laquelle vient de s'adjoindre une nouvelle aile de neuf chambres qui sont aussi les plus confortables. Piscine dans la verdure. Salle à manger rythmée d'arcades, donnant sur un petit parc arboré. Plats bourgeois.
◆ Dit bakstenen hotel aan de rand van het dorp heeft een nieuwe vleugel met negen kamers, die tevens de meest comfortabele zijn. Openluchtzwembad. Muurbogen geven de eetzaal een bijzonder charme. Klein park met bomen. Eenvoudige gerechten.

XXX **De Zon** avec ch, Voorbrug 1, ✉ 7731 BB, ✆ (0 529) 45 55 50, *info@hoteldezon.nl, Fax (0 529) 45 62 35,* rest, – 25 à 125. AE VISA. rest
Repas *Lunch 19* – 30/50 bc, ♀ – **35 ch** 80/130 – ½ P 70/85.
◆ Imposante hostellerie surveillant le cours de la Vecht. Rénovées, la salle à manger et les chambres affichent désormais un "look" contemporain. Terrasse au bord de l'eau.
◆ Imposant hotel-restaurant aan de oever van de Overijsselse Vecht. De eetzaal en kamers zijn gerenoveerd en hebben nu een eigentijdse look. Terras aan het water.

OOIJ *Gelderland* 532 U 11 *et* 715 I 6 – *voir à Nijmegen.*

OOSTBURG *Zeeland* C *Sluis 24 755 h.* 532 F 15 et 715 B 8.

Brugsevaart 10, ✉ 4501 NE, ☎ (0 117) 45 34 10, Fax (0 117) 45 55 11.

Amsterdam 216 – Brugge 27 – Middelburg 57 – Knokke-Heist 18.

XXX **De Eenhoorn** avec ch, Markt 1, ✉ 4501 CJ, ☎ (0 117) 45 27 28, *hreenhoorn@het net.nl, Fax (0 117) 45 33 94*, – – 25 à 60. AE MC VISA JCB. ch

Repas *(fermé carnaval, vend., sam. midi et après 20 h 30)* Lunch 35 – carte 27 à 57 – **5 ch** 70/100.

◆ Goûteuse cuisine archi-classique - avec spécialités de foie d'oie et de ris de veau - servie dans une salle de restaurant lambrissée. Chambres et petit appartement.

◆ Smaakvolle, superklassieke keuken - met specialiteiten als ganzenlever en kalfszwezerik - die wordt geserveerd in een gelambriseerde eetzaal. Kamers en klein appartement.

OOSTERBEEK *Gelderland* C *Renkum 32 250 h.* 532 U 11 et 715 I 6.

Amsterdam 97 – Arnhem 6.

De Bilderberg , Utrechtseweg 261, ✉ 6862 AK, ☎ (0 26) 339 63 33, *bilderberg @bilderberg.nl, Fax (0 26) 339 63 96*, , , , – – 25 à 200. AE MC VISA

fermé 27 déc.-2 janv. – **Repas** voir rest ***Trattoria Artusi*** ci-après – **145 ch** 162/192, – 1 suite – ½ P 90/110.

◆ Ce grand hôtel copieusement enrobé de chlorophylle met diverses catégories de chambres à votre disposition : suite, executives, studio, junior suites et standard.

◆ Dit grote hotel ligt in een bosrijke omgeving en beschikt over diverse categorieën kamers : suite, executives, studio, junior suites en standaardkamers.

X **Trattoria Artusi** - H. De Bilderberg, Utrechtseweg 261, ✉ 6862 AK, ☎ (0 26) 339 63 33, *bilderberg@bilderberg.nl, Fax (0 26) 339 63 96*, , Cuisine italienne – . AE MC VISA.

fermé 27 déc.-2 janv. et sam. midi – **Repas** Lunch 20 – 31/48, ♀.

◆ Aménagée dans un style italianisant, cette brasserie-véranda lumineuse et colorée partage ses murs avec l'hôtel De Bilderberg. Cuisine de la "Botte". Formule menu-carte.

◆ Dit lichte en kleurrijke serrerestaurant in Italiaanse stijl deelt zijn muren met hotel De Bilderberg. Keuken uit de Laars. À la carte menu.

X **De Kantine,** Valkenburglaan 1, ✉ 6861 AH, ☎ (0 26) 333 31 93, *Fax (0 26) 334 13 43*, – . AE MC VISA JCB

fermé 25 déc.-2 janv. et sam. midi – **Repas** Lunch 23 – 30/45, ♀.

◆ À l'orée des bois, agrégée à un manège, élégante salle de restaurant coiffée d'une mezzanine et complétée d'un superbe caveau où s'épanouissent d'excellents vins.

◆ Dit restaurant aan de rand van de bossen maakt deel uit van een ruitercentrum. Elegante eetzaal met mezzanine. In de prachtige kelders liggen uitstekende wijnen te rijpen.

OOSTEREND (AASTEREIN) *Fryslân* 531 R 2 et 715 H 1 – *voir à Waddeneilanden (Terschelling).*

OOSTEREND *Noord-Holland* 531 S 4 et 715 F 2 – *voir à Waddeneilanden (Texel).*

OOSTERHOUT *Noord-Brabant* 532 O 13 et 715 F 7 – *52 968 h.*

Dukaatstraat 21, ✉ 4903 RN, ☎ (0 162) 45 87 59, Fax (0 162) 43 32 85.

Bouwlingplein 1, ✉ 4901 KZ, ☎ 0 900-202 25 50, info@vvvoosterhout.nl, Fax (0 162) 43 10 48.

Amsterdam 92 – 's-Hertogenbosch 38 – Breda 8 – Rotterdam 58.

Golden Tulip, Waterlooplein 50, ✉ 4901 EN, ☎ (0 162) 45 20 03, *info@goldentulip .oosterhout.nl, Fax (0 162) 43 50 03*, , – – 25 à 70. AE MC VISA JCB

Repas Lunch 18 – 24/33 – **52 ch** 87/118, – 1 suite – ½ P 99/115.

◆ Hôtel-centre de congrès couplé à un espace culturel - appelé De Bussel - dont le théâtre peut accueillir 300 personnes. Chambres fonctionnelles.

◆ Dit hotel-congrescentrum is verbonden met cultureel centrum De Bussel, waarvan het theater plaats biedt aan driehonderd personen. Functionele kamers.

X **de Vrijheid,** Heuvel 11, ✉ 4901 KB, ☎ (0 162) 43 32 43, *colline@euronet.nl, Fax (0 162) 46 14 62*, , Taverne-rest – MC VISA.

fermé carnaval, du 20 au 25 août et 31 déc.-3 janv. – **Repas** 24.

◆ L'une des adresses en vogue au cœur d'Oosterhout. Cuisine bistrotière servie dans une ambiance décontractée. Dressée en été, la jolie terrasse donne sur un parc public.

◆ Een van de trendy adressen in het centrum. Gerechten uit een bistroachtige keuken worden in een ongedwongen ambiance geserveerd. Het fraaie zomerterras kijkt uit op een park.

OOSTERHOUT-Nijmegen *Gelderland* C *Overbetuwe 40 284 h.* 532 U 11 *et* 715 I 6.

Amsterdam 113 – Arnhem 22 – Nijmegen 8.

XX **De Altena,** Waaldijk 38, ✉ 6678 MC, ℘ (0 481) 48 21 96, *info@dealtena.nl, Fax (0 481) 45 00 29,* ≤, 帝 – ▤ P. AE MC VISA. ✈
fermé prem. sem. janv., sam. midi, dim. midi et lundi – **Repas** Lunch 33 – carte env. 45, ♀.
◆ Agréable restaurant posté au bord du Waal (bras du Rhin). L'été venu, réservez votre table près des baies ou en terrasse pour assister au va-et-vient des bateaux.
◆ Aangenaam restaurant aan de Waal. Reserveer in de zomer een tafeltje aan het raam of op het terras om tijdens het eten te kunnen kijken naar de voorbijvarende plezierboten.

OOSTERSCHELDEDAM, Stormvloedkering (Barrage de l'ESCAUT ORIENTAL) ★★★

Zeeland 532 H 3 *et* 715 C 7 *G. Hollande.*

OOSTERWOLDE (EASTERWÂLDE) *Fryslân* C *Ooststellingwerf 26 726 h.* 531 W 5 *et* 715 J 3.

Amsterdam 194 – Groningen 40 – Leeuwarden 46 – Assen 30.

De Zon, Stationsstraat 1, ✉ 8431 ET, ℘ (0 516) 51 24 30, *oosterwolde@hollandinn.nl, Fax (0 516) 51 30 68,* 🚲 – 🛗 TV P – 🎤 25 à 300. MC VISA. ✈ rest
Repas *(fermé après 19 h 30)* carte 24 à 32 – **31 ch** ☕ 75/85 – ½ P 46/49.
◆ Auberge fondée en 1870 au croisement d'un canal et de la principale rue commerçante. Les meilleures chambres se distribuent à l'arrière du parking. Petit théâtre d'époque.
◆ Deze herberg werd in 1870 geopend bij de kruising van een kanaal en de belangrijkste winkelstraat. De beste kamers liggen achter de parking. Klein, ouderwets theater.

OOSTKAPELLE *Zeeland* C *Veere 21 985 h.* 532 G 13 *et* 715 B 7.

Amsterdam 186 – Middelburg 12 – Rotterdam 107.

Villa Magnolia ⛺ sans rest, Oude Domburgseweg 20, ✉ 4356 CC, ℘ (0 118) 58 19 80, *info@villamagnolia.nl, Fax (0 118) 58 40 58,* 🪑, 🚲 – 🚭 TV P. MC VISA. ✈
25 ch ☕ 58/88.
◆ Cette jolie villa "1900", propre comme un sou neuf, s'embellit d'un jardin fleuri durant tout l'été. Chambres souvent dotées d'une terrasse ou d'un balcon.
◆ Deze mooie, kraakheldere villa van rond 1900 heeft een prachtige tuin die de hele zomer in bloei staat. De meeste kamers hebben een terras of balkon.

OOST-VLIELAND (EAST-FLYLÂN) *Fryslân* 531 P 3 *et* 715 G 2 – *voir à Waddeneilanden (Vlieland).*

OOSTVOORNE *Zuid-Holland* C *Westvoorne 14 195 h.* 532 J 11 *et* 715 D 6.

Amsterdam 106 – Rotterdam 37 – Den Haag 43 – Brielle 6.

XXX **Parkzicht,** Stationsweg 61, ✉ 3233 CS, ℘ (0 181) 48 22 84, *info@restaurantparkzicht.nl, Fax (0 181) 48 56 16* – MC VISA
fermé fin fév., fin juil., dim. et lundi – **Repas** Lunch 30 – carte env. 48, ♀.
◆ Dans une localité balnéaire connue pour sa réserve naturelle, maison de bouche concoctant une cuisine classique sagement actualisée. La carte annonce plusieurs menus.
◆ Dit restaurant in een badplaats die bekend is om zijn natuurreservaat, bereidt een klassieke keuken met een eigentijds accent. Op de kaart staan diverse menu's.

OOTMARSUM *Overijssel* C *Dinkelland 26 064 h.* 531 AA 8 *et* 715 L 4.

Voir *Village*★.

i *Markt 1, ✉ 7631 BW, ℘ 0 900 202 19 81, info@vvvootmarsum.nl, Fax (0 541) 29 18 84.*

Amsterdam 165 – Zwolle 67 – Enschede 28.

De Wiemsel ⛺, Winhofflaan 2 (Est : 1 km), ✉ 7631 HX, ℘ (0 541) 29 21 55, *info@wiemsel.nl, Fax (0 541) 29 32 95,* 帝, ⑦, ≘s, ⊠, 🪑, 🏸, 🚲 – TV ♿ P – 🎤 25 à 90. AE ⓓ MC VISA. ✈ rest
Repas voir rest ***De Wanne*** ci-après – **44 ch** ☕ 165/220, – 5 suites – ½ P 133/198.
◆ Hôtel de rêve pour un séjour "cocooning" : salon cossu, suites et junior suites très "cosy", terrasse d'été surplombant une piscine en forme de cœur et jardin exquis.
◆ Een droomhotel voor een verwenvakantie : luxueuze lounge, zeer knusse suites en junior suites, zomerterras, hartvormig zwembad en verrukkelijke tuin. De Wine and Dine is een prima alternatief voor het gastronomisch restaurant.

PAYS-BAS

Van der Maas, Grotestraat 7, ✉ 7631 BT, ☎ (0 541) 29 12 81, *info@vandermaas.nl, Fax (0 541) 29 34 62,* – rest, – 30 à 100. AE VISA.
fermé du 1er au 15 nov. – **Repas** *Lunch 8* – carte 22 à 38 – **20 ch** 50/70 – ½ P 50.
◆ Petit établissement familial situé au centre d'Ootmarsum, localité d'où l'on atteint la frontière allemande en quelques minutes. Les chambres offrent un bon confort. Grande salle à manger classiquement aménagée. L'assiette est au goût du jour.
◆ Dit kleine familiehotel bevindt zich in het centrum van Ootmarsum, een plaats die op enkele minuten van de Duitse grens ligt. De kamers zijn comfortabel. Grote, klassiek ingerichte eetzaal. Eigentijdse keuken.

de Landmarke, Rossummerstraat 5, ✉ 7636 PK, ☎ (0 541) 29 12 08, *info@landmarke.nl, Fax (0 541) 29 22 15,* – – 25 à 40. AE VISA. rest
fermé 30 déc.-10 janv. – **Repas** *Lunch 23* – carte env. 30 – **37 ch** 65/98 – ½ P 69/72.
◆ Cette hostellerie traditionnelle renfermant des chambres assez plaisantes occupe les avant-postes d'un bourg charmant bâti sur une butte autour d'une église gothique. Deux salles à manger, deux décorations : l'une d'esprit néo-rustique, l'autre plus actuelle.
◆ Dit traditionele hotel ligt net buiten het pittoreske plaatsje, dat op een heuvel rond een gotische kerk is gebouwd. Het heeft vrij aangename kamers en twee eetzalen, elk met een andere ambiance : de een neorustiek, de ander wat eigentijdser.

Résidence Wyllandrie , Tichelwerk 1, ✉ 7631 CJ, ☎ (0 541) 29 17 05, *info@wyllandrie.nl, Fax (0 541) 29 27 49,* – – 25 à 40. AE VISA. rest
Repas *Lunch 23* – 30, ♀ – **43 ch** 58/90 – ½ P 58/63.
◆ Estimée pour son calme et ses abords verdoyants, la Résidence Wyllandrie met à votre disposition des chambres de mise simple mais hospitalières et peu à peu rénovées. Agréable restaurant servant une cuisine de notre temps. Terrasse d'été "chlorophyllienne".
◆ Dit rustig gelegen hotel in een bosrijke omgeving beschikt over eenvoudige maar vriendelijke kamers die geleidelijk worden gerenoveerd. In het aangename restaurant wordt een eigentijdse keuken geserveerd. Zomerterras midden in het groen.

De Wanne - H. De Wiemsel, Winhofflaan 2 (Est : 1 km), ✉ 7631 HX, ☎ (0 541) 29 21 55, *info@wiemsel.nl, Fax (0 541) 29 32 95,* – AE VISA.
Repas (nombre de couverts limité - prévenir) *Lunch 48 bc* – 59/79, carte 70 à 80, ♀.
◆ Table gastronomique partageant ses installations avec un prestigieux hôtel. Salle à manger confortable, agréable restaurant d'été et beau jardin. Cuisine du moment.
◆ Gastronomisch tafelen tussen de muren van dit prestigieuze hotel. Comfortabele eetzaal en aangenaam zomerterras bij het zwembad in de tuin. Actuele keuken.
Spéc. Agnolotti de ris de veau fumé, sauce à la sauge. Pot-au-feu de coquillages et crustacés. Poussin à la truffe en croûte de sel et jus aux poireaux

à Lattrop *Nord-Est : 6 km* C *Dinkelland :*

De Holtweijde , Spiekweg 7, ✉ 7635 LP, ☎ (0 541) 22 92 34, *info@holtweijde.nl, Fax (0 541) 22 94 45,* – – 25 à 200. VISA.
Repas *Lunch 29* – carte env. 57, ♀ – **29 ch** 180/200, – 41 suites – ½ P 145/225.
◆ Étape revigorante où les meilleures chambres sont de douillettes "suites-bungalows" éparpillées dans un domaine bucolique. Salon anglais, superbe piscine et hydrothérapie. Une ferme saxonne joliment réaménagée donne un toit et beaucoup l'ampleur au restaurant.
◆ Een adres waar u weer energie kunt opdoen. De beste kamers zijn bungalowsuites die verspreid liggen over een idyllisch landgoed. Engelse lounge, schitterend zwembad en hydrotherapie. De fraaie Saksische boerderij biedt onderdak aan een groot restaurant.

ORANJEWOUD (ORANJEWÂLD) *Fryslân* 531 U 5 *et* 715 I 3 – *voir à Heerenveen.*

OSS *Noord-Brabant* 532 S 12 *et* 715 H 6 – *75 849 h.*

au Sud-Est : 7 km à Nistelrode, Slotenseweg 11, ✉ 5388 RC, ☎ (0 412) 61 19 92, Fax (0 412) 61 28 98.

Spoorlaan 24, ✉ 5348 KB, ☎ 0 900-112 23 34, info.vvvnob@planet.nl, Fax (0 412) 65 20 93.

Amsterdam 102 – Arnhem 49 – 's-Hertogenbosch 20 – Eindhoven 51 – Nijmegen 29.

De Weverij, Oostwal 175, ✉ 5341 KM, ☎ (0 412) 69 46 46, *info@deweverij.nl, Fax (0 412) 69 46 47* – – 25 à 150. AE VISA JCB
Repas voir rest ***Cordial*** ci-après – 15 – **45 ch** 99/135, – 3 suites – ½ P 99/165.
◆ Au centre-ville, hôtel très confortable dont l'enseigne - L'Atelier de Tissage - résume le passé. "Cousues de fil blanc", les chambres ne manquent évidemment pas d'étoffe !
◆ De naam van dit zeer comfortabele hotel in het centrum is een verwijzing naar het verleden : met de stoffering van de kamers zit het dus wel goed !

City, Raadhuislaan 43, ✉ 5341 GL, ☎ (0 412) 63 33 75, *info@cityhotel.nl, Fax (0 412) 62 26 55,* – ✈, rest, – 25 à 130. AE MC VISA JCB
Repas *(fermé 24 déc., 30 déc.-1er janv., sam. midi et dim. midi)* Lunch 33 – 38, ♀ – 8 – **45 ch** *(fermé 30 déc.-1er janv.)* 82/120 – ½ P 115.
◆ Établissement familial bien pratique pour les séjours d'affaires. Communs relookés et bonnes chambres munies d'un double vitrage atténuant la rumeur de l'avenue passante. Pimpante salle à manger de style design, due à l'architecte hollandais Jan des Bouvrie.
◆ Een praktisch etablissement voor een zakelijk verblijf. Gemeenschappelijke ruimten met een nieuwe look en goede kamers met dubbele beglazing waardoor het rumoer van de weg wordt getemperd. De piekfijne eetzaal in design is het werk van Jan des Bouvrie.

Cordial - H. De Weverij, Oostwal 175, ✉ 5341 KM, ☎ (0 412) 69 46 46, *info@deweverij.nl, Fax (0 412) 69 46 47* – AE MC VISA JCB
fermé 20 mai, du 1er au 15 août, 27 déc.-1er janv., sam. midi et dim. midi – **Repas** Lunch 30 – 50/85 bc, carte 58 à 76, ♀.
◆ Une savoureuse démonstration de cuisine au goût du jour vous sera faite dans cette ex-fabrique de tapis partageant ses murs avec l'hôtel De Weverij. Décor intérieur soigné.
◆ U krijgt een smakelijk staaltje van eigentijdse kookkunst voorgeschoteld in deze vroegere tapijtfabriek, die zijn muren deelt met hotel De Weverij. Verzorgd interieur.
Spéc. Ballottine de foie gras d'oie et de canard aux épices. Ris de veau glacé aux carottes et morilles. Homard canadien à la vanille et aux épinards

---

OSSENZIJL *Overijssel* C *Steenwijkerland 41 870 h.* 531 U 6 *et* 715 I 3.
Amsterdam 116 – Zwolle 57 – Leeuwarden 53.

Kolkzicht, Hoofdstraat 30, ✉ 8376 HG, ☎ (0 561) 47 72 52, *kolkzicht@planet.nl, Fax (0 561) 47 74 24,* ←, – MC VISA
fermé 24 déc.-9 janv., lundi et mardi de nov. à mars et merc. – **Repas** (déjeuner sur réservation de nov. à mars) Lunch 35 – 32/63 bc, ♀.
◆ Devant la terrasse ensoleillée, un pont mobile s'anime pour céder le passage aux bateaux. L'été, on cuisine aussi des plats de brasserie. Le charme d'un village pittoresque.
◆ Tegenover het zonnige terras gaat de brug voortdurend open om boten door te laten. In de zomer worden ook eenvoudiger spijzen bereid. De bekoring van een pittoresk dorp.

OTTERLO *Gelderland* C *Ede 103 708 h.* 532 T 10 *et* 715 I 5.
Voir *Parc National de la Haute Veluwe*** (Nationaal Park De Hoge Veluwe) : Musée Kröller-Müller*** – Parc à sculptures** (Beeldenpark).*
Amsterdam 79 – Arnhem 33 – Apeldoorn 22.

Sterrenberg, Houtkampweg 1, ✉ 6731 AV, ☎ (0 318) 59 12 28, *info@sterrenberg.nl, Fax (0 318) 59 16 93,* – rest, – 25 à 50. AE MC VISA.
Repas *(fermé après 20 h 30)* Lunch 15 – 26/39 bc, ♀ – **26 ch** 68/120 – ½ P 70/93.
◆ "Hôtel-cocooning" où vous séjournerez dans de fringantes chambres harmonieusement agencées, à l'image des communs, semés de touches artistiques évoquant la région. Belle salle de restaurant, à la fois tendance et couleur locale. L'été, repas en plein air.
◆ Comfortabel hotel met frisse, sfeervol ingerichte kamers. In de gemeenschappelijke ruimten hangen schilderijen met taferelen uit de streek. In de mooie restaurantzaal gaan trendy en couleur locale hand in hand. 's Zomers wordt buiten geserveerd.

't Witte Hoes, Dorpsstraat 35, ✉ 6731 AS, ☎ (0 318) 59 13 92, *wittehoes@hollandhotels.nl, Fax (0 318) 59 15 04,* – MC VISA JCB.
fermé déc.-janv. – **Repas** *(fermé après 19 h 30)* Lunch 25 – carte env. 35 – **10 ch** 70/100 – ½ P 63/75.
◆ Salon-bibliothèque flambant neuf, chambres agrandies, personnel accru, tenue irréprochable... La maison se démène afin que sa clientèle s'y sente mieux encore. Préparations franco-hollandaises servies dans une salle à manger classiquement aménagée.
◆ Spiksplinternieuwe lounge, vergrote kamers, extra personeel, onberispelijk onderhoud... Alles wordt hier uit de kast gehaald om de gasten te behagen. Gerechten uit de Frans-Nederlands georiënteerde keuken worden in een klassieke eetzaal geserveerd.

Kruller, Dorpsstraat 19, ✉ 6731 AS, ☎ (0 318) 59 12 31, *Fax (0 318) 59 20 34,* – – 25 à 40. AE MC VISA
Repas (taverne-rest) Lunch 12 – carte 26 à 35 – **14 ch** 70/85.
◆ Au cœur d'Otterlo, sympathique hôtel à taille humaine où vous séjournerez dans des chambres fonctionnelles disponibles en trois tailles. Redécoration intérieure complète. Taverne-restaurant actuelle fonctionnant en continu du matin jusqu'au soir.
◆ Dit sympathieke hotel op menselijke maat in hartje Otterloo beschikt over drie categorieën functionele kamers van verschillende afmeting. Geheel vernieuwd interieur. Eigentijds Grand café dat de hele dag geopend is.

Carnegie's Cottage, Onderlangs 35, ✉ 6731 BK, ☎ (0 318) 59 12 20, *info@carnegiecottage.nl, Fax (0 318) 59 20 93*, ←, – ⊁ TV P. ⊁
fermé 22 déc.-1er mars – **Repas** *(fermé après 19 h 30)* carte env. 40 – **13 ch** ☕ 93 – ½ P 67.
◆ Paisible auberge familiale voisine du Parc National de la Haute-Veluwe, site propice aux randonnées. Chambres mignonnes et junior suite aménagée dans un petit cottage. À table, menu-carte engageant et vue sur une nature omniprésente depuis la véranda.
◆ Rustig familiehotel aan de rand van het Nationaal Park de Hoge Veluwe, een prachtige wandelgebied. Charmante kamers alsmede een junior suite in een kleine cottage. Aantrekkelijk à la carte menu. De serre kijkt uit op de omringende natuur.

OUDERKERK AAN DE AMSTEL *Noord-Holland* 531 O 9, 532 O 9 *et* 715 F 5 – *voir à Amsterdam, environs.*

OUDESCHILD *Noord-Holland* 531 O 4 *et* 715 F 2 – *voir à Waddeneilanden (Texel).*

OUDEWATER *Utrecht* 532 O 10 *et* 715 F 5 – *9 699 h.*
Amsterdam 39 – Utrecht 21 – Den Haag 58 – Rotterdam 54.

Joia, Havenstraat 2, ✉ 3421 BS, ☎ (0 348) 56 71 50, *info@brasseriejoia.nl, Fax (0 348) 56 79 48*, Brasserie – MC VISA
fermé prem. sem. janv., mardi d'oct. à avril et lundi – **Repas** 25/33, ♀.
◆ Brasserie chaleureuse et "trendy" située au cœur d'une pittoresque localité célèbre pour sa "balance aux sorcières", visible dans le Poids public, à deux pas du Markt.
◆ Gezellige en trendy brasserie in het hart van het pittoreske plaatsje met de beroemde heksenwaag. Dit weegtoestel is te zien in de Waag, vlak bij de Markt.

OUDKERK *Fryslân – voir Aldtsjerk à Leeuwarden.*

OUD-LOOSDRECHT *Noord-Holland* C *Wijdemeren 9 339 h.* 532 P 9 *et* 715 G 5.
Voir *Étangs★★ (Loosdrechtse Plassen).*
Oud Loosdsrechtsedijk 198, ✉ *1231 NG,* ☎ *(0 35) 582 39 58, info@vvv-loosdrecht.nl, Fax (0 35) 582 72 04.*
Amsterdam 27 – Utrecht 23 – Hilversum 7.

Golden Tulip, Oud Loosdrechtsedijk 253, ✉ 1231 LZ, ☎ (0 35) 582 49 04, *reservations@gtloosdrecht.nl, Fax (0 35) 582 48 74*, ←, , – TV P. – 25 à 100. AE MC VISA JCB. ⊁ rest
Repas 25/47 bc – **68 ch** ☕ 160/195 – ½ P 85.
◆ Emplacement privilégié pour cet hôtel de chaîne dont un tiers des chambres - toutes avec balcon ou terrasse - profite d'une jolie vue sur le lac et les yachts. À la belle saison, on dresse le couvert sur une terrasse portuaire invitante.
◆ Prachtig gelegen ketenhotel aan de Loosdrechtse Plassen. Een derde van de kamers - allemaal met balkon of terras - biedt een fraai uitzicht op het water en de jachten. In de zomer wordt buiten geserveerd op een uitnodigend haventerras.

ZIN, Veendijk 1a (De Driesprong), ✉ 1231 PB, ☎ (0 35) 526 14 26, *Fax (0 35) 526 23 79*, ← lac, , – P. AE MC VISA
fermé 30 avril, 24 et 31 déc. et 1er janv. – **Repas** Lunch 38 – carte env. 57, ♀.
◆ Préparations classico-créatives servies dans une salle à manger moderne avec mezzanine. Terrasse balayant du regard le port de plaisance. Service dynamique et décontracté.
◆ Creatief-klassieke gerechten worden geserveerd in een moderne eetzaal met mezzanine. Terras met uitzicht op de jachthaven. Vlotte bediening in ongedwongen stijl.

Najade, Oud Loosdrechtsedijk 243, ✉ 1231 LX, ☎ (0 35) 582 27 05, *nimf@najade-loosdrecht.nl, Fax (0 35) 582 27 06*, , – P. AE MC VISA
fermé dim. et lundi – **Repas** (déjeuner sur réservation) carte 39 à 53, ♀.
◆ Ce relais de bouche alangui au bord de l'eau vous reçoit dans une jolie salle à manger "trendy" ou sur sa terrasse lacustre. Bon repas traditionnel. Hébergement en prévision.
◆ In deze culinaire pleisterplaats aan het water wordt u onthaald in een trendy eetzaal of op het terras. Goede, traditionele keuken. In de toekomst ook overnachting mogelijk.

à Breukeleveen *Sud : 11 km* C *Wijdemeren :*

De Veenhoeve, Herenweg 37, ✉ 3625 AB, ☎ (0 35) 582 43 99, *info@veenhoeve.nl, Fax (0 35) 582 32 80*, – AE MC VISA
fermé lundi et mardi de sept. à mai – **Repas** (déjeuner sur réservation) carte 29 à 48.
◆ Accueillante affaire familiale où l'on dîne dans une ambiance chaleureuse. Salle à manger avec cave à vue et cheminée. Véranda et terrasse d'été dressée au bord de l'eau.
◆ In dit vriendelijke familierestaurant wordt in een gemoedelijke ambiance getafeld. Eetzaal met open wijnkelder en schouw. Serre en zomerterras aan het water.

OUD-ZUILEN *Utrecht* 532 P 10 *et* 715 G 5 – *voir à Utrecht.*

OVERVEEN *Noord-Holland* 531 M 8, 532 M 8 *et* 715 E 4 – *voir à Haarlem.*

PAPENDRECHT *Zuid-Holland* 532 N 12 *et* 715 F 6 – *voir à Dordrecht.*

PEIJ *Limburg* 532 U 16 *et* 715 I 8 – *voir à Echt.*

PHILIPPINE *Zeeland* C *Terneuzen 55 478 h.* 532 H 15 *et* 715 C 8.
Amsterdam 196 – Middelburg 36 – Gent 35 – Sint-Niklaas 43.

au port, Waterpoortstraat 1, ✉ 4553 BG, ☎ (0 115) 49 18 55, *auport@zeelandnet.nl, Fax (0 115) 49 17 65,* – TV – 25 à 350. AE MC VISA
fermé fin mai-début juin et 28 déc.-15 janv. – **Repas** *(fermé mardi, merc. et sam. midi)* *Lunch 27* – 30, ♀ – **7 ch** 52/68 – ½ P 56/74.
◆ Au cœur d'un petit village zélandais tout proche de la frontière belge, établissement familial dont les quelques chambres fonctionnelles se distribuent à l'étage.
◆ Dit familiehotelletje staat in het centrum van een klein Zeeuws dorp vlak bij de Belgische grens. Op de verdieping liggen enkele kamers, die functioneel zijn ingericht.

Aub. des Moules, Visserslaan 3, ✉ 4553 BE, ☎ (0 115) 49 12 65, *Fax (0 115) 49 16 56,* , Produits de la mer – P. AE MC VISA
fermé du 8 au 29 juin, 21 déc.-4 janv. et lundi – **Repas** 28/43, ♀.
◆ L'enseigne est limpide : en saison, les moules sont "chez elles" dans cette auberge connue de longue date des amateurs du genre. Assiettes gorgées d'iode toute l'année.
◆ De naam is zo klaar als een klontje : in het seizoen voelen de mosselen zich thuis in deze herberg, die bij liefhebbers al jarenlang bekend is. Het hele jaar door volop vis.

Place du Marché, Havenstraat 12, ✉ 4553 AV, ☎ (0 115) 49 15 24, *pdm12@zeelandnet.nl, Fax (0 115) 49 21 12,* , Moules en saison – . AE MC VISA
fermé 2 sem. en fév. et mardi – **Repas** 29/41.
◆ Assez conséquent, le choix de recettes du grand large décliné à cette adresse inclut un menu du marché et un autre, d'orientation gastronomique, servi par table entière.
◆ Het spreekt voor zich dat er tussen de visgerechten op de kaart ook een "menu van de markt" staat. Een ander, gastronomisch menu kan alleen per tafel worden besteld.

De Fijnproever, Visserslaan 1, ✉ 4553 BE, ☎ (0 115) 49 13 13, Moules en saison – P. AE MC VISA
fermé 17 mai-28 juin, dern. sem. janv., merc. soir et jeudi – **Repas** *Lunch 28* – carte 23 à 49, ♀.
◆ La grande spécialité du coin, c'est assurément la moule, et Le Fin gourmet (De Fijnproever) n'y échappe pas, quoique l'anguille s'y trouve également bien à l'aise.
◆ De specialiteit bij uitstek in dit deel van het land is toch wel de mossel. Ook de Fijnproever ontkomt er niet aan, hoewel de paling zich hier eveneens op zijn gemak voelt.

PURMEREND *Noord-Holland* 531 O 7 *et* 715 F 4 – *73 476 h.*
18 (2 parcours) 9 Westerweg 60, ✉ 1445 AD, ☎ (0 299) 48 16 66, Fax (0 299) 64 70 81 - 9 au Sud-Ouest : 5 km à Wijdewormer (Wormerland), Zuiderweg 68, ✉ 1456 NH, ☎ (0 299) 47 91 23, Fax (0 299) 43 81 99.
Koestraat 11, ✉ 1441 CV, ☎ 0 900-400 40 40, info@amsterdamtourist.nl, Fax (0 20) 625 28 69.
Amsterdam 19 – Alkmaar 25 – Leeuwarden 117.

Hampshire Waterland , Westerweg 60 (Est : 3 km, direction Volendam), ✉ 1445 AD, ☎ (0 299) 48 16 66, *info@waterland.hampshire-hotels.com, Fax (0 299) 64 46 91,* – TV P – 25 à 200. AE MC VISA. rest
Repas 28 – 13 – **95 ch** 130/150 – ½ P 165/185.
◆ Proximité du green oblige, cet hôtel de chaîne est taillé sur mesure pour ceux qui aiment faire "swinguer" la petite balle blanche. Les chambres ont toutes été rafraîchies. Restaurant avec vue imprenable sur le parcours de golf.
◆ Hoe kan het ook anders met zo'n golfgreen voor de deur ? Dit ketenhotel is geheel afgestemd op liefhebbers die het witte balletje graag laten "swingen". De kamers hebben allemaal een opknapbeurt gehad. Restaurant met vrij uitzicht over de golfbaan.

Sichuan Food, Tramplein 9, ✉ 1441 GP, ☎ (0 299) 42 64 50, Cuisine chinoise – . AE MC VISA.
fermé 31 déc. – **Repas** (dîner seult) carte 25 à 36.
◆ L'enseigne pourrait difficilement être plus explicite : ici, les recettes du Sichuan, une région chinoise, sont autant de spécialités à consommer sur place, ou à emporter.
◆ Explicieter kan de naam niet zijn : hier kunnen specialiteiten uit Sichuan, een streek in China, worden genuttigd of afgehaald.

à Middenbeemster *Nord-Ouest : 5 km* *Beemster 8 583 h :*

Het Heerenhuis Beemster, Rijperweg 83, 1462 MD, (0 299) 68 20 10, *post@hetheerenhuis.nl, Fax (0 299) 68 20 20,* – – 25 à 150. AE MC VISA.
fermé 21 juil.-10 août et 28 déc.-6 janv. – **Repas** Lunch 25 – 28/47, ♀.
◆ L'ancienne mairie sert de cadre à cette affaire familiale. Salle à manger résolument contemporaine, attrayante carte à la page et cave bien montée. L'été, repas en terrasse.
◆ Het voormalige gemeentehuis vormt het decor van dit restaurant. Moderne eetzaal, aantrekkelijke eigentijdse kaart en goede selectie wijnen. 's Zomers maaltijd op het terras.

à Neck *Sud-Ouest : 2 km* *Wormerland 15 467 h :*

Mario Uva avec ch, Dorpstraat 15, 1456 AA, (0 299) 42 39 49, *Fax (0 299) 42 37 62,* – , rest, TV . AE MC VISA JCB.
fermé dim. et lundi – **Repas** *(fermé 23 déc.-5 janv.)* (déjeuner sur réservation, cuisine italienne, menu unique) – 45/118 bc, ♀ – **4 ch** 82/115.
◆ Un petit coin d'Italie perdu parmi les polders. Belle cuisine transalpine, menu dégustation et accords mets-vins parfaits. Collection de faïences décoratives exposée en salle.
◆ Een stukje Italië midden in de polder. De Italiaanse keuken in menu-vorm op zijn best ! Wijn en gerechten combineren uitstekend. Collectie decoratief aardewerk in de zaal.
Spéc. Mosaïque de poulpe aux tagliolini. Tortellinis à la piémontaise parfumé à la sauge. Cailles farcies dans un nid de tagliolini croquants

Trattoria Il Grappolo, Onderdijk 20, 1456 AA, (0299) 42 42 64, *Fax (0 299) 42 37 62,* , Cuisine italienne – . AE MC VISA JCB
fermé du 1er au 15 juin, 23 déc.-5 janv., lundi et mardi – **Repas** (déjeuner sur réservation) 35/60 bc.
◆ Alternative au "ristorante" d'à côté, cette sympathique trattoria vous concocte des plats simples mais goûteux. Jolie terrasse "al sole" et pergola mangée par la vigne.
◆ Een alternatief voor de ristorante ernaast. Deze sympathieke trattoria kokerelt eenvoudige, smakelijke gerechten. Leuk zomerterras met pergola die door wingerd is overwoekerd.

à Noordbeemster *Nord : 10 km direction Hoorn* *Beemster 8 583 h :*

De Beemster Hofstee, Middenweg 48, 1463 HC, (0 299) 69 05 22, *info@beemsterhofstee.nl, Fax (0 299) 69 05 04,* – . AE MC VISA JCB
fermé fin juil.-début août, sam. midi, dim. midi et lundi – **Repas** Lunch 33 – carte env. 45, ♀.
◆ Dans les polders, agréable restaurant occupant une ancienne ferme pimpante et typée, avec son toit de chaume et son alignement d'arbustes en façade. Terrasse estivale.
◆ Aangenaam restaurant in de polder, in een voormalige karakteristieke en charmante boerderij met rieten dak en een dichte haag langs de voorzijde. Zomerterras.

à Zuidoostbeemster *Nord : 2 km* *Beemster 8 583 h :*

Purmerend, Purmerenderweg 232, 1461 DN, (0 299) 43 68 58, *info@purmerend.valk.nl, Fax (0 299) 43 69 54,* , – , rest, TV – 25 à 80. AE MC VISA
Repas Lunch 18 – carte env. 38 – **38 ch** 81/90 – ½ P 99/117.
◆ Coquette devanture tapissée de lierre pour cet établissement à taille humaine sortant un peu des standards de la chaîne hôtelière au toucan. Chambres et junior suites. Couvert dressé sous la véranda. Carte franco-batave.
◆ Dit etablissement op menselijke maat heeft een leuke, met klimop begroeide gevel en valt enigszins buiten het keurslijf van de hotelketen Van der Valk. Kamers en junior suites. De maaltijden worden in de serre geserveerd. Frans-Hollandse kaart.

La Ciboulette, Kwadijkerweg 7 (dans l'ancienne forteresse), 1461 DW, (0 299) 68 35 85, *jacco.huitema@wxs.nl, Fax (0 299) 68 42 54,* – . AE MC VISA.
fermé lundi et mardi – **Repas** (dîner seult) carte 34 à 41, ♀.
◆ Petite table retranchée dans un site défensif. S'il fait beau, la terrasse, étagée sur plusieurs niveaux, regagne son poste au bord des douves entourant la forteresse.
◆ De kruitdampen van weleer zijn opgetrokken nu dit restaurant hier heeft post gevat. Bij mooi weer betrekt het terras de wacht aan de gracht rond het fort.

Les prix
Pour toutes précisions sur les prix indiqués dans ce guide, reportez-vous aux pages explicatives.

PUTTEN *Gelderland* 531 S 9, 532 S 9 et 715 H 5 – *23 161 h.*

Kerkplein 15, ✉ 3881 BH, ☎ (0 341) 35 17 77, info@vvvputten.nl, Fax (0 341) 35 30 40.

Amsterdam 66 – Arnhem 57 – Apeldoorn 41 – Utrecht 48 – Zwolle 49.

Mercure, Strandboulevard 3 (Ouest : 4 km sur A 28), ✉ 3882 RN, ☎ (0 341) 35 64 64, *h2111@accor-hotels.com, Fax (0 341) 35 85 16,* – rest, – 25 à 400. AE VISA JCB

Repas *Lunch 16* – 24/32 bc, ♀ – ☐ 14 – **84 ch** 115/125 – ½ P 58/78.

◆ Cet établissement proche de l'autoroute ne s'adresse pas qu'aux congressistes. Voisin des plages de l'IJsselmeer - visibles des chambres -, il attire pas mal de vacanciers. Restaurant procurant un coup d'œil sur l'étendue d'eau (réserve ornithologique).

◆ Dit etablissement vlak bij de snelweg is niet alleen voor congresgangers bedoeld. Ook vakantiegangers hebben de weg naar dit hotel aan de Randmeren gevonden. Vanuit de kamers ziet u de stranden liggen. Restaurant met uitzicht op het water (vogelreservaat).

RAALTE *Overijssel* 531 W 8, 532 W 8 et 715 J 4 – *36 632 h.*

Varkensmarkt 8, ✉ 8102 EG, ☎ (0 572) 35 24 06, info@vvv-raalte.nl, Fax (0 572) 35 23 43.

Amsterdam 124 – Zwolle 21 – Apeldoorn 35 – Enschede 50.

De Zwaan, Kerkstraat 2, ✉ 8102 EA, ☎ (0 572) 36 37 38, *dezwaan@euronet.nl, Fax (0 572) 36 37 39,* – – 25 à 60. AE VISA JCB. ch *fermé 27 déc.-5 janv.* – **Repas** carte 28 à 45, ♀ – **33 ch** ☐ 70/95 – ½ P 60/80.

◆ Au cœur de Raalte, bâtiment renfermant des chambres assez agréables ainsi qu'une petite infrastructure pour se détendre : bar, piscine, sauna, bain turc et bowling. Préparations classiques servies dans un décor néo-campagnard.

◆ In hartje Raalte herbergt dit hotel vrij aangename kamers en een kleine infrastructuur voor de broodnodige ontspanning : bar, zwembad, sauna, Turks bad en bowling. Klassieke gerechten worden geserveerd in een neorustiek decor.

RAVENSTEIN *Noord-Brabant* C *Oss 75 849 h.* 532 S 12 et 715 H 6.

Amsterdam 110 – Arnhem 36 – 's-Hertogenbosch 31 – Nijmegen 17.

Rôtiss. De Ravenshoeve, Mgr. Zwijsenstraat 5, ✉ 5371 BS, ☎ (0 486) 41 28 03, *deravenshoeve@hetnet.nl, Fax (0 486) 41 28 03,* – P. AE VISA

fermé carnaval, prem. sem. août et lundi – **Repas** (dîner seult) 30/49 bc.

◆ Repas au goût du jour, dans l'ambiance typique d'une vieille ferme villageoise. Bar et coin salon avec cheminée ont toutefois été actualisés. Terrasse d'été abritée.

◆ Eigentijdse gerechten worden geserveerd in de karakteristieke ambiance van een oude boerderij. De bar en zithoek met schouw zijn gemoderniseerd. Beschut zomerterras.

REEK *Noord-Brabant* C *Landerd 14 516 h.* 532 T 12 et 715 I 6.

Amsterdam 120 – Arnhem 34 – 's-Hertogenbosch 30 – Eindhoven 48 – Nijmegen 10.

In de Witte Molen, Rijksweg 76, ✉ 5375 KZ, ☎ (0 486) 47 62 66, *Fax (0 486) 47 63 09,* – P. VISA

fermé lundi et mardi – **Repas** (déjeuner sur réservation) carte env. 50, ♀.

◆ Un beau moulin à vent élevé vers 1830 prête ses murs à ce sympathique petit restaurant. L'été, avec la complicité du soleil, repas servi en plein air.

◆ Een mooie windmolen uit omstreeks 1830 verleent onderdak aan dit sympathieke restaurantje. Bij mooi weer wordt 's zomers de maaltijd buiten geserveerd.

REEUWIJK *Zuid-Holland* 532 N 10 et 715 F 5 – *voir à Gouda.*

RENESSE *Zeeland* C *Schouwen-Duiveland 34 503 h.* 532 H 12 et 715 C 6.

Zeeanemoonweg 4a, ✉ 4325 BZ, ☎ (0 111) 46 24 24, vvv@renesse.com, Fax (0 111) 46 14 36.

Amsterdam 140 – Middelburg 37 – Rotterdam 68.

De Zeeuwse Stromen, Duinwekken 5, ✉ 4325 GL, ☎ (0 111) 46 20 40, *info@zeeuwsestromen.nl, Fax (0 111) 46 20 65,* – – 25 à 400. AE VISA

Repas *Lunch 14* – carte 28 à 42, ♀ – **134 ch** ☐ 75/136 – ½ P 78/88.

◆ Complexe moderne à dénicher en lisière des dunes. Quelques pavillons éparpillés dans le parc abritent les chambres les plus paisibles. Au programme : détente et loisirs. À table, cuisine actuelle et ambiance décontractée.

◆ Modern complex aan de rand van de duinen. In het park rond het hoofdgebouw liggen enkele paviljoens die de rustigste kamers herbergen. Op het programma : ontspanning en recreatie. Aan tafel : actuele keuken in een ongedwongen ambiance.

Badhotel, Laône 2, ✉ 4325 EK, ☎ (0 111) 46 25 00, *info@badhotelrenesse.nl, Fax (0 111) 46 25 38,* – TV P – 30. AE VISA.
rest
Repas *(fermé dim. midi) Lunch 25* – 28/55 bc, ♀ – **36 ch** 72/136 – ½ P 79/89.
◆ Chambres sans reproche, accueillant bar façon " british library-pub", jardin intimiste, véranda et terrasse braquées sur la piscine. Not so "bad", cet hôtel, en définitive ! Restaurant confortablement installé. Carte mi-classique mi-actuelle.
◆ Onberispelijke kamers, gezellige Engelse pub annex lounge, sfeervolle tuin, serre en terras met uitzicht op het zwembad. Al met al een hotel dat er wezen mag ! De menukaart van het comfortabele restaurant laat een combinatie zien van klassiek en eigentijds.

Hampshire Inn, Hoogenboomlaan 5, ✉ 4325 DB, ☎ (0 111) 46 25 10, *info@hampshirehotels.nl, Fax (0 111) 46 25 69,* – TV P – 25 à 65. VISA
Repas *Lunch 12* – 25/35, ♀ – **48 ch** 53/100 – ½ P 77/127.
◆ À l'entrée du village, hôtel récent occupant une construction basse et longiligne. Pourvues d'une terrasse, les chambres de plain-pied sont les plus spacieuses. Une coupole évoquant le zénith coiffe la salle de restaurant. Carte au goût du jour.
◆ Deze nieuwkomer aan de rand van het dorp is gehuisvest in een laag en langwerpig gebouw. De ruimere kamers op de begane grond hebben een terras. Het restaurant is bekroond met een koepel die het zenit voorstelt. Eigentijdse menukaart.

RETRANCHEMENT *Zeeland* 532 F 14 et 715 B 7 – *voir à Sluis.*

REUSEL *Noord-Brabant* C *Reusel-De Mierden 12 429 h.* 532 P 14 et 715 G 7.

Amsterdam 135 – Eindhoven 30 – 's-Hertogenbosch 45 – Antwerpen 63.

XX **De Nieuwe Erven,** Mierdseweg 69, ✉ 5541 EP, ☎ (0 497) 64 33 76, *nieuwe.erven@wxs.nl, Fax (0 497) 64 54 08,* – P. AE VISA.
fermé lundi et mardi – **Repas** (dîner seult) 34, ♀.
◆ Aux abords de Reusel, villa blanche dont le jardin avec pièce d'eau, fleuri à la belle saison, procure un espace agréable à la terrasse. Confortable salle à manger-véranda.
◆ Restaurant in een witte villa aan de rand van het dorp. De tuin met waterpartij staat 's zomers volop in bloei en biedt ruimte voor een terras. Comfortabele eetzaal met serre.

RHEDEN *Gelderland* 532 V 10 et 715 J 5 – *44 831 h.*

Amsterdam 112 – Arnhem 11 – Lelystad 94 – Utrecht 75 – Zwolle 79.

XX **Bronckhorst,** Arnhemsestraatweg 251, ✉ 6991 JG, ☎ (0 26) 495 22 07, *Fax (0 26) 495 48 43,* – P. AE VISA
fermé merc. – **Repas** carte env. 45.
◆ Ancienne auberge rénovée, reconnaissable à ses murs jaunes et son toit de chaume. Salle à manger classique-actuelle, orientation culinaire de même. Terrasse ombragée.
◆ Deze oude, gerenoveerde herberg is te herkennen aan zijn gele muren en rieten dak. Klassiek-eigentijdse eetzaal en dito keuken. Schaduwrijk terras.

RHENEN *Utrecht* 532 S 11 et 715 H 6 – *17 529 h.*

Markt 20, ✉ 3911 LJ, ☎ (0 317) 61 23 33, vvv.rhenen@wxs.nl, Fax (0 317) 61 34 10.
Amsterdam 79 – Arnhem 26 – Utrecht 41 – Nijmegen 33.

't Paviljoen, Grebbeweg 103, ✉ 3911 AV, ☎ (0 317) 61 90 03, *info@paviljoen.nl, Fax (0 317) 61 72 13,* – rest, TV P – 25 à 80. AE VISA.
fermé 31 déc. soir-2 janv. – **Repas** (déjeuner sur réservation) carte env. 41, ♀ – 17 – **32 ch** 100/163 – ½ P 160/185.
◆ À l'entrée du bourg, auberge familiale renfermant des chambres récemment rééquipées. La proximité d'un jardin zoologique enchantera toute la famille. Plats de brasserie à midi et menu-carte au restaurant le soir.
◆ De kamers in dit familiehotel aan de rand van het dorp zijn onlangs met nieuwe voorzieningen uitgerust. Vlakbij bevindt zich een dierentuin. 's Middags kan in de brasserie worden gegeten, 's avonds biedt het restaurant een à la carte menu.

XX **'t Kalkoentje,** Utrechtsestraatweg 143 (Nord-Ouest : 2 km), ✉ 3911 TS, ☎ (0 317) 61 23 44, *info@kalkoentje.nl, Fax (0 317) 61 65 00,* – P. AE VISA
fermé 3 prem. sem. janv., sam. midi et dim. midi – **Repas** *Lunch 30* – 37/68 bc, ♀.
◆ Ancienne chaumière située aux portes de Rhenen. En été, quelques tables sont dressées sur une mignonne terrasse et dans le verger dégringolant la pente jusqu'au fleuve.
◆ Voormalig boerderijtje net buiten Rhenen. In de zomer worden enkele tafeltjes gedekt op een charmant terras en in de boomgaard op de uiterwaard langs de Rijn.

à Elst *Nord-Ouest : 6 km* Ⓒ *Rhenen :*

De Rotisserie, Veenendaalsestraatweg 50 (Nord : 3 km), ✉ 3921 EC, ☎ (0 318) 54 28 88, *info@residencerhenen.nl, Fax (0 318) 54 02 72,* ←, ☂, Rôtissoire en salle – P – 25 à 150. AE ⓓ MC VISA
Repas *Lunch 27* – carte 32 à 63, ♀.
◆ Alanguie dans un paysage boisé, cette élégante orangerie devancée d'un parc est l'endroit tout indiqué pour s'offrir un bon repas en plein air. Rôtissoire en salle.
◆ Deze prachtige oranjerie in een bosrijke omgeving, aan de rand van een park, is een uitgelezen plek voor een goede maaltijd in de buitenlucht. In de eetzaal wordt gegrilleerd.

RHOON *Zuid-Holland* 532 L 11 *et* 715 E 6 – *voir à Rotterdam, environs.*

RIIS *Fryslân – voir Rijs.*

RIJPERKERK *Fryslân – voir Ryptsjerk.*

RIJS (RIIS) *Fryslân* Ⓒ *Gaasterlân-Sleat 10 259 h.* 531 S 5 *et* 715 H 3.
Amsterdam 124 – Leeuwarden 50 – Lemmer 18 – Sneek 26.

Jans, Mientweg 1, ✉ 8572 WB, ☎ (0 514) 58 12 50, *info@hoteljans.nl, Fax (0 514) 58 16 41,* ☂, – TV P – 25 à 40. AE ⓓ MC VISA JCB
fermé 27 juin-13 juil. – **Repas** (dîner pour résidents seult) – **21 ch** 51/90 – ½ P 61/71.
◆ Auberge centenaire entourée de bois et de champs. Au fond du jardin, quelques chalets abritent les meilleures chambres. Terrasse verdoyante. Accueil gentil.
◆ Ruim honderd jaar oud logement omringd door bos en velden. Achter in de tuin staan enkele chalets die de beste kamers herbergen. Terras in het groen. Vriendelijke ontvangst.

RIJSOORD *Zuid-Holland* Ⓒ *Ridderkerk 46 196 h.* 532 M 11 *et* 715 E 6.
Amsterdam 90 – Rotterdam 14 – Den Haag 40 – Breda 39.

Hermitage (Klein), Rijksstraatweg 67 (par A 16 - E 19, sortie ㉓), ✉ 2988 BB, ☎ (0 180) 42 09 96, *hermitage@alliance.nl, Fax (0 180) 43 33 03,* ☂ Avec brasserie Corneille – P. AE ⓓ MC VISA.
fermé 24 juil.-12 août, 27 déc.-6 janv., sam. midi, dim., lundi midi et jours fériés – **Repas** *Lunch 48 bc* – 50/80, carte 50 à 70, ♀.
◆ Imposante auberge-relais postée au bord d'un canal pittoresque dont les flots défilent paisiblement le long d'une jolie terrasse estivale. Mets personnalisés.
◆ Restaurant in een imposant pand aan de oever van een pittoresk kanaal dat rustig voortkabbelt langs het fraaie zomerterras. Gerechten met een persoonlijke touch.
Spéc. Sandre poêlé farci de champignons et jambon de Bayonne (août-fév.). Bar mariné au poivre rose et citronnelle (avril-déc.). Tartare de filet de bœuf à l'œuf poché, salade de pommes de terre et huile d'herbes

RIJSSEN *Overijssel* Ⓒ *Rijssen-Holten 35 637 h.* 531 Y 9, 532 Y 9 *et* 715 K 5.
Oranjestraat 131, ✉ 7461 DK, ☎ (0 548) 52 00 11, vvvrijssen@introweb.nl, Fax (0 548) 52 14 29 – Amsterdam 131 – Zwolle 40 – Apeldoorn 45 – Enschede 36.

Rijsserberg, Burg. Knottenbeltlaan 77 (Sud : 2 km sur rte de Markelo), ✉ 7461 PA, ☎ (0 548) 51 69 00, *rijsserberg@bilderberg.nl, Fax (0 548) 52 02 30,* ☂, – TV P – 25 à 150. AE ⓓ MC VISA JCB. rest
Repas *Lunch 30* – carte env. 48 – 17 – **50 ch** 120/165, – 4 suites – ½ P 98/118.
◆ Confortable établissement retiré en pleine "Forêt Noire des Pays-Bas", une région revigorante, propice aux balades sylvestres. Chambres et junior suites de bon séjour. Ample salle à manger classiquement aménagée. Cuisine française d'aujourd'hui.
◆ Comfortabel etablissement midden in het "Zwarte Woud van Nederland", een streek waar u heerlijke boswandelingen kunt maken en nieuwe energie opdoen. Zeer comfortabele kamers en junior suites. Grote, klassiek ingerichte eetzaal. Eigentijdse, Franse keuken.

RIJSWIJK *Zuid-Holland* 532 K 10 *et* 715 D 5 – *voir à Den Haag, environs.*

RINSUMAGEEST (RINSUMAGEAST) *Fryslân* Ⓒ *Dantumadeel 19 765 h.* 531 U 3 *et* 715 I 2.
Amsterdam 157 – Leeuwarden 21 – Dokkum 5 – Groningen 59.

Het Rechthuis, Rechthuisstraat 1, ✉ 9105 KH, ☎ (0 511) 42 31 00, *info@hetrechthuis.nl, Fax (0 511) 42 50 15,* ☂ – MC VISA
fermé 26 juil.-18 août, lundi et mardi – **Repas** (dîner seult) 30/45.
◆ L'enseigne (La Maison de Justice) en témoigne : un magistrat rendait jadis ses verdicts dans ces murs. L'été, on dresse une terrasse donnant sur un jardinet bichonné.
◆ De naam is getuige ! Binnen deze muren werd vroeger rechtgesproken. In de zomer wordt er in het fraai aangelegde tuintje een terras ingericht.

ROCKANJE *Zuid-Holland* *Westvoorne 14 195 h.* 532 J 11 *et* 715 D 6.

Amsterdam 111 – Rotterdam 38 – Den Haag 48 – Hellevoetsluis 10.

Badhotel, Tweede Slag 1 (Ouest : 1 km), ✉ 3235 CR, ☎ (0 181) 40 17 55, *info@badhotel.nl, Fax (0 181) 40 39 33,* – – 25 à 110. AE VISA

Repas *(fermé 27 déc.-2 janv.)* *Lunch 15* – carte env. 30 – 14 – **63 ch** 68/86 – ½ P 50/79.

◆ Commode pour la clientèle active à l'Europoort, ce complexe hôtelier est établi dans un quartier résidentiel proche du littoral. Chambres pratiques et studios avec cuisinette.

◆ Dit hotelcomplex is praktisch gelegen voor wie in de Europoort werkt. Het staat in een woonwijk vlak bij de kust. Praktische kamers en studio's met kitchenette.

RODEN *Drenthe* *Noordenveld 31 565 h.* 531 X 4 *et* 715 K 2.

Oosteinde 7a, ✉ 9301 ZP, ☎ (0 50) 501 51 03, Fax (0 50) 501 36 85.

Amsterdam 205 – Groningen 14 – Leeuwarden 56 – Zwolle 94.

Langewold, Ceintuurbaan-Noord 1, ✉ 9301 NR, ☎ (0 50) 501 38 50, *info@langewoldhotel.nl, Fax (0 50) 501 38 18,* – – 25 à 150. AE VISA JCB.

Repas *(fermé 31 déc.-1er janv., sam. midi et dim. midi)* carte 24 à 37 – 10 – **30 ch** 83/115 – ½ P 65.

◆ Ce petit hôtel de chaîne bâti à la périphérie de Roden dispose de grandes chambres souvent dotées d'un balcon. Côté détente : sauna, whirlpool, bain turc, solarium et bowling. Alternative restaurant ou brasserie. Prix muselés.

◆ Dit moderne hotel aan de rand van Roden beschikt over grote kamers, waarvan de meeste met balkon. Ook aan ontspanning is gedacht : sauna, whirlpool, Turks bad, solarium en bowling. Restaurant en een brasserie. De prijzen rijzen niet uit de pan !

ROERMOND *Limburg* 532 V 15 *et* 715 I 8 – *45 332 h.*

au Sud-Est : 10 km à Herkenbosch, Stationsweg 100, ✉ 6075 CD, ☎ (0 475) 52 95 29, Fax (0 848) 33 82 69.

par ④ : 34 km à Beek ☎ (0 43) 358 99 99, Fax (0 43) 358 99 88.

Kraanpoort 1, ✉ 6041 EG, ☎ 0 900-202 55 88, vvv.roer@wxs.nl, Fax (0 475) 33 50 68.

Amsterdam 178 ⑤ – Maastricht 47 ④ – Eindhoven 50 ⑤ – Venlo 25 ① – Düsseldorf 65 ②

Plan page ci-contre

TheaterHotel De Oranjerie, Kloosterwandplein 12, ✉ 6041 JA, ☎ (0 475) 39 14 91, *info@oranjerie.valk.com, Fax (0 475) 31 71 88,* – – 25 à 800. AE VISA. rest Z b

Repas 30/40 – **98 ch** 78/86 – ½ P 97.

◆ L'un des fleurons du groupe hôtelier Van der Valk : communs soignés, splendide salle de spectacle (80 représentations par an), beauty-center complet et chambres luxueuses. Élégante table orientée cuisine au goût du jour.

◆ Een van de betere Van der Valk hotels. Verzorgde gemeenschappelijke ruimten, schitterend theater (80 voorstellingen per jaar), luxueuze kamers en beautycenter met alles erop en eraan. Elegante, eigentijds georiënteerde keuken.

Landhotel Cox, Maalbroek 102 (par ② sur N 68, à la frontière), ✉ 6042 KN, ☎ (0 475) 34 88 99, *gtcox@roermond.com, Fax (0 475) 32 51 42,* – , rest, – 25 à 80. AE VISA JCB. rest

fermé 27 déc.-2 janv. – **Repas** *(fermé sam. midi et dim. soir)* carte 24 à 54 – **53 ch** 85/115 – ½ P 90/105.

◆ Établissement approprié si vous souhaitez poser vos valises à deux pas de la frontière allemande. Chambres spacieuses, convenablement insonorisées. Au restaurant, carte classique assortie de plusieurs menus. Brunch dominical.

◆ Een prima hotel voor wie zich op een steenworp afstand van de Duitse grens in Morpheus armen wil nestelen. De ruime kamers zijn voorzien van goede geluidsisolatie. Het restaurant voert een klassieke kaart waarop ook enkele menu's staan. Brunch op zondag.

XXX ✿ **Onder de Boompjes in kasteeltje Hattem** (Brienen) avec ch, Maastrichterweg 25, ✉ 6041 NZ, ☎ (0 475) 31 92 22, *info@boompjes.nl, Fax (0 475) 31 92 92,* ←, – rest, – 25. AE VISA. rest Z a

fermé 2 sem. carnaval et 2 sem. en août – **Repas** *(fermé sam. midi, dim. et lundi)* (avec brasserie) *Lunch 35* – 60/128 bc, carte env. 74 – 18 – **7 ch** *(fermé lundi)* 165 – ½ P 265.

◆ Ce castel gourmand et ses dépendances aménagées en chambres "king size" s'ordonnent sur l'îlot d'un parc fleuri. Rotonde panoramique et belle terrasse d'été sous les arbres.

◆ Dit culinaire kasteeltje en de bijbehorende koetshuizen met kingsize kamers liggen in een prachtig park. Ronde, panoramische eetzaal en mooi zomerterras onder de bomen.

Spéc. Attelet de Saint-Jacques en trois préparations. Côte de porc régional truffe de saison. Langoustines gratinées

Les **cartes Michelin** sont constamment tenues à jour.

dielies, Roersingel 4, ✉ 6041 KX, ☎ (0 475) 42 06 62, *eyckholt@planet.nl, Fax (0 475) 42 06 65*, Avec taverne-rest – AE MC VISA JCB. ✂ YZ a
fermé dim. et lundi – **Repas** (dîner seult) 33/38, ♀.
◆ Derrière une belle façade ancienne, table vouée à la gastronomie du moment et café misant sur une carte simplifiée. Atmosphère tout à la fois nostalgique et "trendy".
◆ Achter een prachtige oude gevel gaat een restaurant schuil met een seizoengebonden keuken. Het eetcafé heeft een eenvoudiger kaart. De sfeer is trendy en nostalgisch tegelijk.

à Herkenbosch *6 km par Keulsebaan Z* C *Roerdalen 10 512 h* :

Kasteel Daelenbroeck ⓢ, Kasteellaan 2, ✉ 6075 EZ, ☎ (0 475) 53 24 65, *info@daelenbroeck.nl, Fax (0 475) 53 60 30*, ☀, ☀, 🚲 – TV P – 🏛 25 à 180. AE ⓓ MC VISA. ✂ rest – *fermé du 22 au 25 fév. et 1er janv.* – **Repas** (dîner seult) carte 41 à 59, ♀ – ☕ 15 – **16 ch** 90/120, – 2 suites – ½ P 70/164.
◆ Majestueuse ferme-château entourée de douves. L'une des dépendances, à environ 100 m de la réception, abrite de belles grandes chambres avec mezzanine et terrasse. Salle à manger cossue, garnie d'un mobilier inspiré des siècles passés. Cuisine à la page.
◆ Statige kasteelhoeve omringd door een slotgracht. Een van de dependances, op 100 m van de receptie, herbergt mooie, grote kamers met mezzanine en terras. Weelderig ingerichte eetzaal met meubilair dat is geïnspireerd op vervlogen tijden. Eigentijdse keuken.

à Horn *par ⑤ : 3 km* C *Haelen 10 105 h* :

De Abdij ⓢ, Kerkpad 5, ✉ 6085 BA, ☎ (0 475) 58 12 54, *de@abdij.etrade.nl, Fax (0 475) 58 31 31*, ☀, ☀, 🚲 – TV P – 🏛 25. AE ⓓ MC VISA. ✂
fermé 27 déc.-2 janv. – **Repas** (dîner seult) carte env. 27 **27 ch** ☕ 55/80.
◆ Dans les murs d'une ancienne abbaye, petit hôtel familial dont les chambres, d'ampleur restreinte mais de confort convenable, offrent un silence presque monastique. Beau jardin d'hiver où une carte de préparations méditerranéennes est présentée.
◆ Binnen de muren van een voormalige abdij biedt dit kleine familiehotel ietwat krappe maar vrij gerieflijke kamers, waar een bijna kloosterlijke stilte heerst. In de mooie serre kunt u genieten van mediterrane gerechten.

à Vlodrop *8 km par Keulsebaan Z* C *Roerdalen 10 512 h* :

Boshotel ⓢ, Boslaan 1 (près de la frontière), ✉ 6063 NN, ☎ (0 475) 53 49 59, *info@boshotel.nl, Fax (0 475) 53 45 80*, ☀, ⓔ, 🏋, ☕, 🏊, 🚲 – 🛗 ✂, ▤ rest, TV ♿ P – 🏛 25 à 250. AE ⓓ MC VISA JCB. ✂ rest
Repas carte 33 à 41, ♀ – **88 ch** ☕ 80/105 – ½ P 75/90.
◆ Cet établissement estimé pour sa tranquillité doit son enseigne au bois qui l'avoisine. Deux ailes se partagent salles de réunions et chambres où l'on dort comme une bûche. Restaurant au décor intérieur actuel. Recettes classico-bourgeoises.
◆ Een veelzeggende naam, want dit hotel is rustig gelegen midden in de bossen. De twee vleugels herbergen vergaderzalen en kamers waarin u als een blok in slaap zult vallen. Restaurant met eigentijds decor. Eenvoudige maar goede, klassieke keuken.

ROOSENDAAL *Noord-Brabant* 532 L 13 *et* 715 E 7 – *77 640 h.*

ℹ Markt 71, ✉ 4701 PC, ☎ (0 165) 55 44 00, vvv.roosendaal@tref.nl, Fax (0 165) 56 75 22.
– Amsterdam 127 – 's-Hertogenbosch 75 – Breda 25 – Rotterdam 56 – Antwerpen 44.

the Goderië, Stationsplein 5a, ✉ 4702 VX, ☎ (0 165) 55 54 00, *hotel@goderie.com, Fax (0 165) 56 06 60* – 🛗 ✂ TV – 🏛 25 à 80. AE ⓓ MC VISA JCB. ✂
Repas Lunch 19 – carte 40 à 49 – ☕ 14 – **49 ch** 75/115 – ½ P 64/100.
◆ Proche du ring et de la gare, adresse utile pour l'homme d'affaires de passage dans la région. Spacieuses le plus souvent, les chambres offrent un bon niveau de confort. Brasserie décontractée ou formule de restauration plus classique.
◆ Dit adres vlak bij de ringweg en het station is handig voor zakenlieden op doorreis. De kamers, waarvan de meeste ruim zijn, bieden een goed comfort. Er is de keuze tussen een brasserie met ongedwongen sfeer en een wat klassiekere formule.

Central, Stationsplein 9, ✉ 4702 VZ, ☎ (0 165) 53 56 57, *sistermans@hotelcentral.nl, Fax (0 165) 56 92 94*, ☀, 🚲 – 🛗, ▤ rest, TV – 🏛 40. AE ⓓ MC VISA JCB. ✂
Repas *(fermé 24 et 31 déc. et 1er janv.)* Lunch 23 – 35/56 bc, ♀ – **18 ch** *(fermé du 24 au 26 déc., 31 déc. et 1er janv.)* ☕ 79/95, – 3 suites – ½ P 71/102.
◆ Ceux qui gagnent Roosendaal par le rail seront avantagés car leur train s'arrêtera juste en face de cet hôtel familial. Chambres claires, fonctionnelles et insonorisées. Cuisine classique servie dans une accueillante salle de restaurant.
◆ Wie met de trein in Roosendaal aankomt, heeft geluk, want de trein stopt recht tegenover dit familiehotel. De lichte, functionele kamers zijn voorzien van geluidsisolatie. In de gezellige restaurantzaal wordt een klassieke keuken geserveerd.

XX **Vroenhout,** Vroenhoutseweg 21 (par A 17, sortie ⑲, direction Wouw), ✉ 4703 SG, ✆ (0 165) 53 26 32, *restaurant.vroenhout@home.nl, Fax (0 165) 53 52 31* – P. AE MC VISA
fermé prem. sem. janv., sam. midi, dim. midi et merc. – **Repas** Lunch 33 – 36/87 bc.
◆ En pleine campagne, ravissante ferme à toit de chaume construite au 18e s. Salle à manger rustique, salon avec cheminée et lit clos restituent l'âme paysanne des lieux.
◆ Een verrukkelijke 18e-eeuwse boerderij met rieten dak, midden op het platteland. Rustieke eetzaal, salon met schouw en bedstee die herinnert aan het boerenleven van weleer.

XX **van der Put,** Bloemenmarkt 9, ✉ 4701 JA, ✆ (0 165) 53 35 04, *Fax (0 165) 54 61 61,* – AE MC VISA JCB
fermé du 15 au 25 fév., 26 juil.-13 août, dim. midi et lundi – **Repas** 28/43, ♀.
◆ Sur le marché aux fleurs, près de l'église, affaire familiale où l'on s'attable en compagnie de clients fidèles. Cuisine traditionnelle batave déclinée en plusieurs menus.
◆ Dit gezellige restaurant aan de bloemenmarkt, vlak bij de kerk, heeft veel trouwe gasten. Traditionele Hollandse keuken die in verschillende menu's wordt gepresenteerd.

à Bosschenhoofd *Nord-Est : 4 km* C *Halderberge 29 625 h :*

De Reiskoffer, Pastoor van Breugelstraat 45, ✉ 4744 AA, ✆ (0 165) 31 63 10, *info@reiskoffer.nl, Fax (0 165) 31 82 00,* – TV P – 25 à 125. AE MC VISA.
fermé 26 et 31 déc. – **Repas** (ouvert jusqu'à 23 h) Lunch 24 – carte 26 à 36 – **53 ch** 115/146 – ½ P 69/72.
◆ Près d'une sortie d'autoroute, ancien couvent réaffecté en hôtel dont les chambres, munies d'un balcon ou d'une terrasse, sont rassemblées en annexe. La chapelle d'autrefois a été reconvertie en salle de restaurant.
◆ Dit voormalige klooster vlak bij een afrit van de snelweg is tot hotel verbouwd. De kamers, met balkon of terras, bevinden zich in de annexe. De voormalige kapel is tot restaurantzaal verbouwd.

ROOSTEREN *Limburg* C *Echt-Susteren 32 187 h.* 532 T 16 *et* 715 I 8.

Amsterdam 186 – Maastricht 33 – Eindhoven 57 – Roermond 18.

De Roosterhoeve, Hoekstraat 29, ✉ 6116 AW, ✆ (0 46) 449 31 31, *info@roosterhoeve.nl, Fax (0 46) 449 44 00,* – TV P – 25 à 150. AE MC VISA JCB.
Repas *(fermé sam. midi)* 35 – **60 ch** 60/80 – ½ P 63/73.
◆ Paisible hôtel familial plagiant l'architecture d'une ferme. Un conseil : réservez votre chambre à l'annexe (Maasburcht) située à l'arrière. Terrasse sur cour intérieure. Salle à manger-véranda où l'on vient faire des repas classiques à la mode hollandaise.
◆ Dit rustig gelegen hotel heeft wel wat weg van een oude hofstede. Een tip : reserveer uw kamer in de annexe aan de achterkant (Maasburcht). Terras op de binnenhof. In de eetzaal met serre kunt u genieten van klassieke maaltijden in Hollandse stijl.

XX **Kasteeltje Eyckholt,** Eyckholtstraat 13, ✉ 6116 BR, ✆ (0 46) 449 49 00, *Fax (0 46) 449 12 74* – P. AE MC VISA JCB
fermé 2 sem. carnaval, mi-juil.-mi-août, lundi, mardi et sam. midi – **Repas** Lunch 33 – carte 51 à 73, ♀.
◆ Agréable restaurant-véranda implanté dans une ferme-château vieille de plus de 350 ans. Bar rustique et possibilité de manger dans le jardin en été. Cuisine du moment.
◆ Plezierig restaurant met serre in een ruim 350 jaar oude kasteelhoeve. Rustieke bar. 's Zomers kunt u ook gezellig tafelen in de tuin. Seizoengebonden keuken.

ROSMALEN *Noord-Brabant* 532 Q 13 *et* 715 H 6 – *voir à 's-Hertogenbosch.*

ROSSUM *Gelderland* C *Maasdriel 23 576 h.* 532 R 12 *et* 715 H 6.

Amsterdam 80 – Utrecht 46 – Arnhem 62 – 's-Hertogenbosch 16

De Gouden Molen, Waaldijk 5, ✉ 5328 EZ, ✆ (0 418) 66 13 06, *info@de-gouden-molen.nl, Fax (0 418) 66 13 06,* – TV P – 25. AE MC VISA.
fermé 27 déc.-2 janv. – **Repas** Lunch 25 – carte 33 à 49, ♀ – **9 ch** 60/85 – ½ P 78.
◆ En contrebas de la digue, ancienne auberge réaménagée avec le souci de préserver son caractère typique. Confort actuel dans les chambres. Accueil familial sympathique. Aux beaux jours, le restaurant se complète d'une terrasse apéritive avec vue sur le Waal.
◆ Deze voormalige herberg onder aan de dijk is met zorg voor behoud van het specifieke karakter verbouwd. Eigentijds comfort in de kamers. Gastvrije, sympathieke ontvangst. Bij mooi weer kan op het terras een aperitiefje worden genomen, met uitzicht op de Waal.

ROTTERDAM

Zuid-Holland 532 L 11 *et* 715 E 6 – *598 660 h.*

Amsterdam 76 ① – *Den Haag 24* ① – *Antwerpen 103* ③ – *Bruxelles 148* ③ – *Utrecht 57* ②.

RENSEIGNEMENTS PRATIQUES

Coolsingel 67, ✉ *3012 AC,* ☎ *0 900-403 40 65, vvv.rotterdam@anwb.nl, Fax (010) 413 01 24.*

✈ *Zestienhoven* (BR) ☎ *(010) 446 34 44, Fax (010) 446 34 99.*

Europoort vers Hull : P and O North Sea Ferries ☎ *(0181) 25 55 00 (renseignements) et (0181) 25 55 55 (réservations), Fax (0181) 25 52 15.*

Casino JY, *Plaza-Complex, Weena 624,* ✉ *3012 CN,* ☎ *(010) 206 82 06, Fax (010) 206 85 00.*

Kralingseweg 200, ✉ *3062 CG* (DS), ☎ *(010) 452 22 83 – à Capelle aan den IJssel* (DR), *'s Gravenweg 311,* ✉ *2905 LB,* ☎ *(010) 442 21 09, Fax (010) 284 06 06 – à Rhoon* (AT), *Veerweg 2a,* ✉ *3161 EX,* ☎ *(010) 501 80 58, Fax (010) 501 56 04.*

CURIOSITÉS

Voir *Lijnbaan*★ JY – *Intérieur*★ *de l'Église St-Laurent (Grote of St-Laurenskerk)* KY – *Euromast*★ (★★, ≤★) JZ – *Le port*★★ *(Haven)* KZ – *Willemsbrug*★★ HV – *Erasmusbrug*★★ KZ – *Delftse Poort (bâtiment)*★ JY **C** – *World Trade Centre*★ KY **Y** – *Nederlands Architectuur Instituut*★ JZ **W** – *Boompjes*★ KZ – *Willemswerf (bâtiment)*★ KY.

Musées : *Historique (Historisch Museum) Het Schielandshuis*★ KY **M²** – *Boijmans Van Beuningen*★★★ JZ – *Historique « De Dubbelde Palmboom »*★ EV.

Env. *par* ③ : *7 km : Moulins de Kinderdijk*★★.

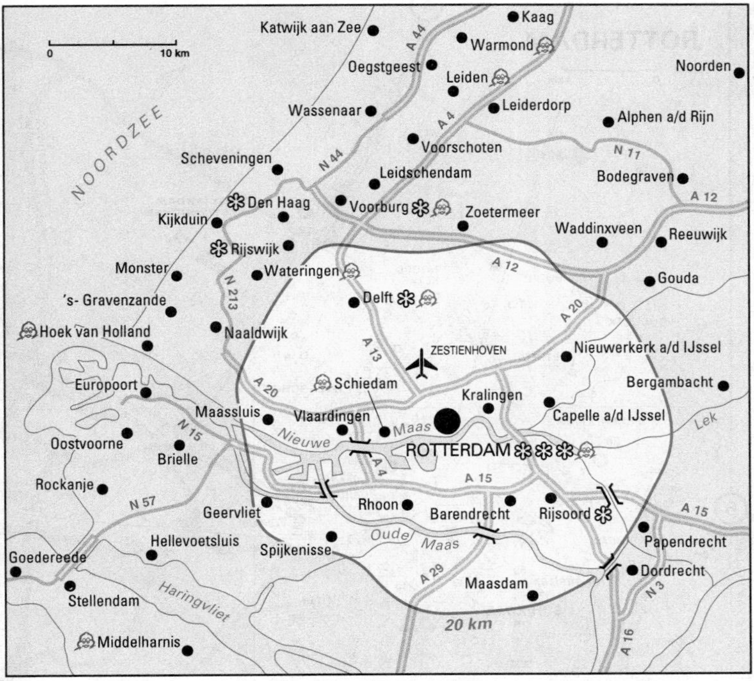

0 10 km
NOORDZEE
Katwijk aan Zee
Kaag
Warmond
Oegstgeest
Leiden
Noorden
Wassenaar
Leiderdorp
Alphen a/d Rijn
A 44
A 4
N 44
N 11
Voorschoten
Scheveningen
Leidschendam
Bodegraven
Den Haag
Voorburg
Zoetermeer
A 12
Kijkduin
Waddinxveen
Reeuwijk
Rijswijk
Monster
Wateringen
Gouda
N 213
's- Gravenzande
Delft
A 20
Hoek van Holland
Naaldwijk
A 13
ZESTIENHOVEN
Nieuwerkerk a/d IJssel
Europoort
Schiedam
Bergambacht
Kralingen
Maassluis
Vlaardingen
Capelle a/d IJssel
Lek
Oostvoorne
N 15
Nieuwe
Maas
ROTTERDAM
Brielle
A 4
A 15
Rockanje
N 57
Geervliet
Rhoon
Barendrecht
Rijsoord
Papendrecht
Hellevoetsluis
Oude
Maas
Spijkenisse
Goedereede
Dordrecht
N 3
A 29
Maasdam
Stellendam
Haringvliet
20 km
A 16
Middelharnis

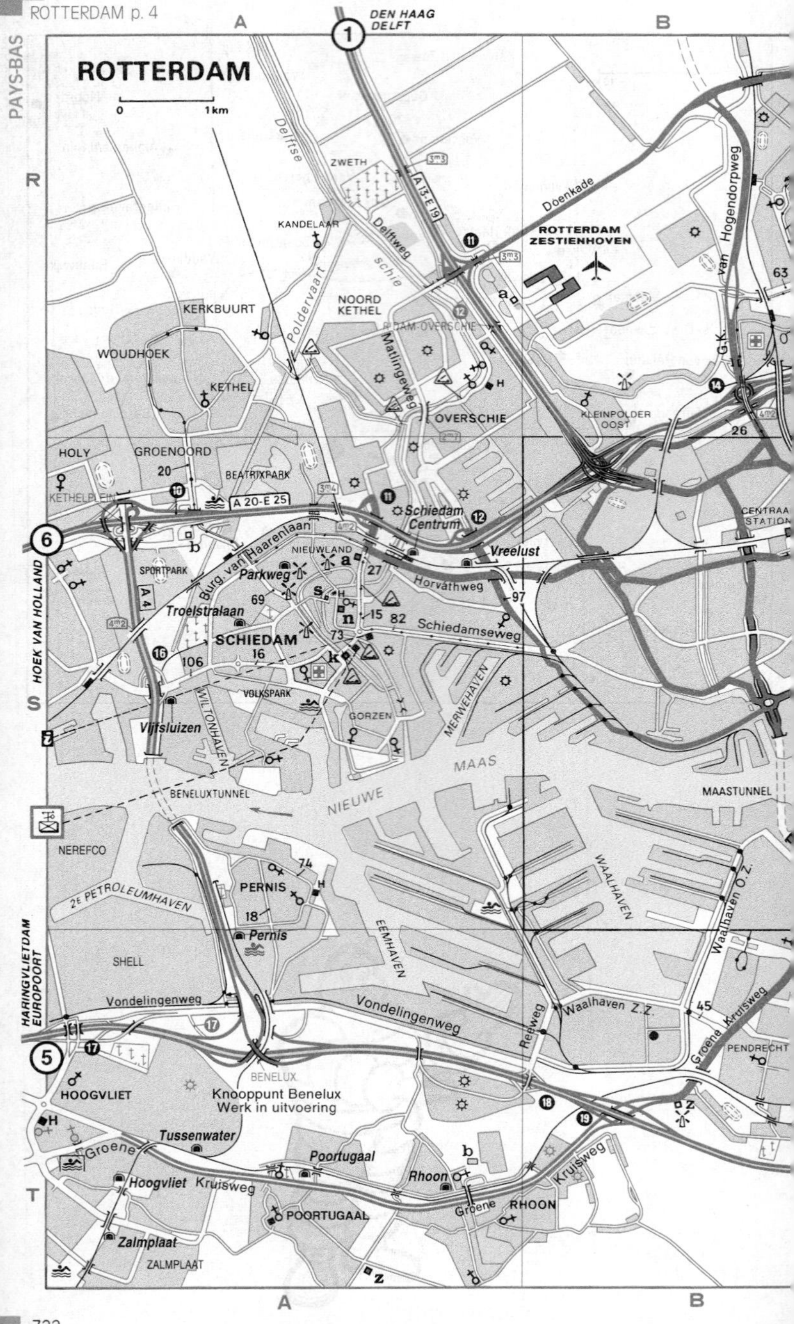
ROTTERDAM
0
1 km
DEN HAAG
DELFT
A
B
R
S
T
Delftse
ZWETH
A 13-E 19
KANDELAAR
Delftweg
schie
Doenkade
ROTTERDAM
ZESTIENHOVEN
van Hogendorpweg
Poldervaart
NOORD
KETHEL
KERKBUURT
WOUDHOEK
KETHEL
R'DAM-OVERSCHIE
Matlingeweg
OVERSCHIE
KLEINPOLDER
OOST
HOLY
GROENOORD
BEATRIXPARK
KETHELPLEIN
A 20-E 25
Schiedam
Centrum
Vreelust
CENTRAAL
STATION
Burg. van Haarenlaan
NIEUWLAND
SPORTPARK
Parkweg
Horvathweg
HOEK VAN HOLLAND
A 4
Troelstralaan
SCHIEDAM
Schiedamseweg
VOLKSPARK
GORZEN
MERWEHAVEN
WILTONHAVEN
Vijfsluizen
MAAS
NIEUWE
BENELUXTUNNEL
MAASTUNNEL
NEREFCO
WAALHAVEN
PERNIS
2E PETROLEUMHAVEN
Pernis
Waalhaven O.Z.
EEMHAVEN
HARINGVLIETDAM
EUROPOORT
SHELL
Vondelingenweg
Vondelingenweg
Waalhaven Z.Z.
Reeweg
Groene Kruisweg
PENDRECHT
BENELUX
HOOGVLIET
Knooppunt Benelux
Werk in uitvoering
Tussenwater
Groene
Hoogvliet
Kruisweg
Poortugaal
POORTUGAAL
Rhoon
Groene
RHOON
Kruisweg
Zalmplaat
ZALMPLAAT

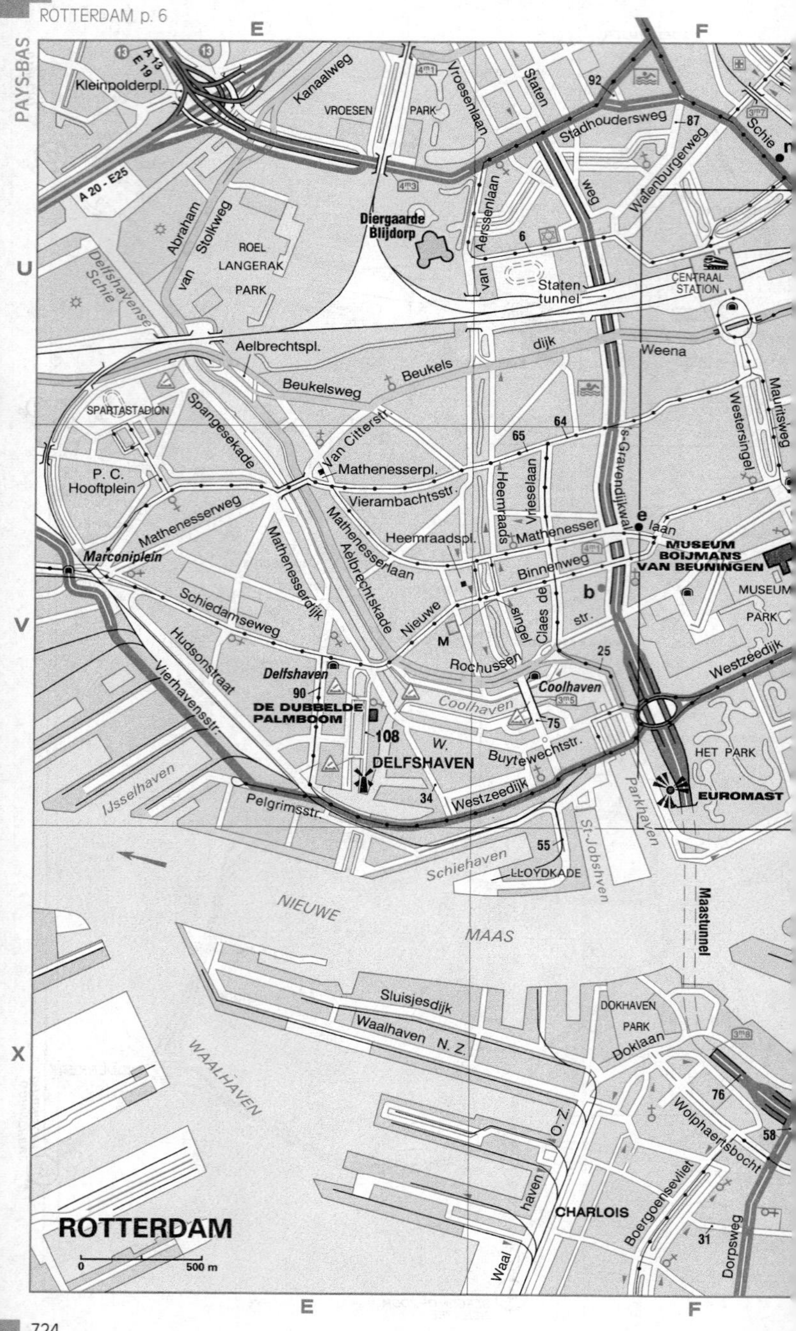
E
F
PAYS-BAS
U
V
X
Kleinpolderpl.
A 13
E 19
A 20 - E25
Kanaalweg
VROESEN
PARK
Vroesenlaan
Staten
92
Stadhoudersweg
87
Schie
Walenburgerweg
weg
Aerssenlaan
van
6
Diergaarde
Blijdorp
Abraham
van
Stolkweg
ROEL
LANGERAK
PARK
Delfshavense
Schie
Staten
tunnel
CENTRAAL
STATION
Aelbrechtspl.
dijk
Beukels
Beukelsweg
Weena
SPARTASTADION
Spangesekade
Van Citterstr.
65
64
Mauritsweg
Westersingel
's-Gravendijkwal
P. C.
Hooftplein
Mathenesserpl.
Vierambachtsstr.
Heemraads
Vrieselaan
Mathenesserweg
Mathenesserlaan
Heemraadspl.
Mathenesser
e
laan
Marconiplein
Mathenesserdijk
Aelbrechtskade
Binnenweg
MUSEUM
BOIJMANS
VAN BEUNINGEN
b
MUSEUM
PARK
Schiedamseweg
Nieuwe
singel
Claes de
str.
Hudsonstraat
M
Rochussen
25
Westzeedijk
Vierhavensstr.
Delfshaven
Coolhaven
90
DE DUBBELDE
PALMBOOM
Coolhaven
75
108
W.
Buytewechtstr.
DELFSHAVEN
HET PARK
IJsselhaven
Pelgrimsstr.
34
Westzeedijk
Parkhaven
EUROMAST
St-Jobshaven
55
Schiehaven
LLOYDKADE
NIEUWE
MAAS
Maastunnel
Sluisjesdijk
DOKHAVEN
PARK
Waalhaven N. Z.
Doklaan
WAALHAVEN
76
Wolphaertsbocht
58
O. Z.
Boergoensevliet
haven
CHARLOIS
Waal
31
Dorpsweg
ROTTERDAM
0
500 m

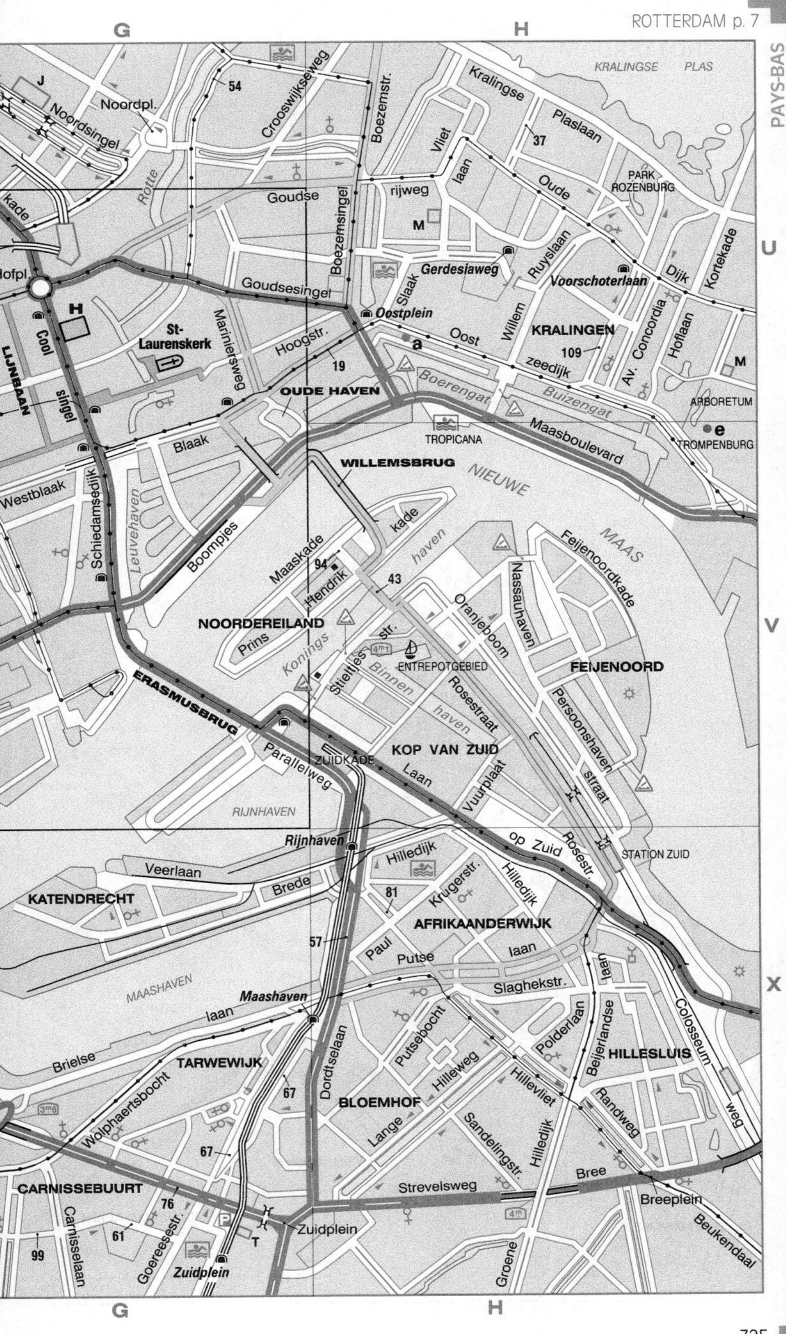

G
H
KRALINGSE PLAS
Kralingse
Plaslaan
Noordpl.
Noordsingel
Crooswijkseweg
Boezemstr.
Rotte
Goudse
rijweg
Vliet
laan
Oude
Dijk
Kortekade
PARK ROZENBURG
Boezemsingel
Goudsesingel
Gerdesiaweg
Ruyslaan
Voorschoterlaan
Hofpl.
Cool
LIJNBAAN
St-Laurenskerk
Mariniersweg
Hoogstr.
Ostplein
Slaak
Willem
KRALINGEN
Av. Concordia
Hoflaan
Oost
zeedijk
OUDE HAVEN
Boerengat
Buizengat
ARBORETUM
TRAMPENBURG
singel
Blaak
TROPICANA
Maasboulevard
WILLEMSBRUG
NIEUWE
MAAS
Westblaak
Schiedamsedijk
Leuvehaven
Boompjes
Maaskade
kade
haven
Feijenoordkade
Hendrik
Prins
NOORDEREILAND
Oranjeboom
Nassauhaven
Konings
str.
Stieltjes
Binnen
haven
ENTREPOTGEBIED
FEIJENOORD
ERASMUSBRUG
Rosestraat
Persoonshaven
straat
KOP VAN ZUID
ZUIDKADE
Parallelweg
Laan
Vuurplaat
RIJNHAVEN
op Zuid
Rosestr.
STATION ZUID
Rijnhaven
Hilledijk
Veerlaan
Brede
KATENDRECHT
Krugerstr.
AFRIKAANDERWIJK
Paul
Putse
laan
MAASHAVEN
Maashaven
Slaghekstr.
Brielse
laan
TARWEWIJK
Dordtselaan
Putsebocht
Polderlaan
Beijerlandse
HILLESLUIS
Colosseum
weg
Wolphaertsbocht
BLOEMHOF
Hilleweg
Hillevliet
Randweg
Lange
Sandelingstr.
Hilledijk
CARNISSEBUURT
Strevelsweg
Bree
Breeplein
Beukendaal
Carnisselaan
Goereesestr.
Zuidplein
Groene
U
V
X

PAYS-BAS

ROTTERDAM

RÉPERTOIRE DES RUES

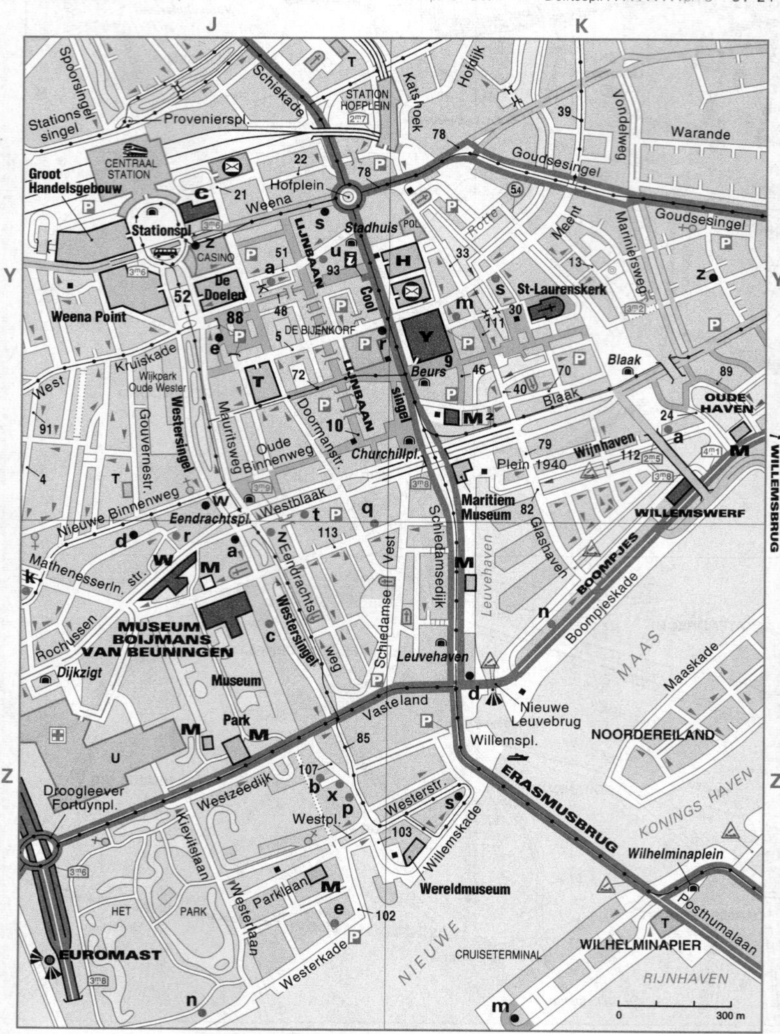

Sur la route :
la signalisation routière est rédigée
dans la langue de la zone linguistique traversée.

Dans ce guide,
les localités sont classées selon leur nom officiel :
Antwerpen pour Anvers, **Mechelen** pour Malines.

Quartiers du Centre - *plan p. 8 sauf indication spéciale :*

The Westin, Weena 686, ✉ 3012 CN, ☎ (0 10) 430 20 00, *rotterdam.westin@westin.com, Fax (0 10) 430 20 01,* ←, – 25 à 100. AE VISA. rest — JY z

Repas ***Lighthouse*** *(fermé dim.)* Lunch 19 – carte 39 à 49, ♀ – 21 – **227 ch** 300/330, – 4 suites.

◆ Posté devant la gare, ce nouveau gratte-ciel aux lignes futuristes abrite d'amples chambres avec tout le confort actuel. Salles de conférences et centre d'affaires. Cuisine d'aujourd'hui à savourer dans un décor d'esprit résolument contemporain.

◆ Deze nieuwe wolkenkrabber met zijn futuristische architectuur staat tegenover het station en beschikt over ruime kamers die van alle gemakken zijn voorzien. Congreszalen en business center. De hedendaagse keuken wordt geserveerd in een modern decor.

Parkhotel, Westersingel 70, ✉ 3015 LB, ☎ (0 10) 436 36 11, *parkhotel@bilderberg.nl, Fax (0 10) 436 42 12,* – 25 à 60. AE VISA — JZ a

Repas Lunch 21 – carte 36 à 50, ♀ – 20 – **187 ch** 115/295, – 2 suites.

◆ Six types de chambres équipées "dernier cri" garnissent cette tour d'un ton gris argenté dominant le quartier des musées. À deux pas, la commerçante Lijnbaan s'offre à vous. Élégante salle de restaurant actuelle et "bar-lounge".

◆ Zes typen kamers met up-to-date voorzieningen zijn ingericht in deze zilvergrijs getinte toren die uitkijkt over de museumwijk. Op een steenworp afstand ligt de Lijnbaan met zijn talloze winkels. Elegante, moderne restaurantzaal en lounge met bar.

Hilton, Weena 10, ✉ 3012 CM, ☎ (0 10) 710 80 00, *sales-rotterdam@hilton.com, Fax (0 10) 710 80 80,* – 25 à 250. AE VISA JCB — JY s

Repas (ouvert jusqu'à 23 h) carte 28 à 44, ♀ – 23 – **246 ch** 150/225, – 8 suites.

◆ Hôtel de chaîne haut de gamme occupant une construction récente proche du World Trade Center. Les chambres ne manquent ni d'allure, ni d'agrément. Petite restauration dans le lounge. Originale carte des vins façon "palette de peintre".

◆ Ketenhotel van prima kwaliteit, in een modern pand vlak bij het World Trade Center. Het ontbreekt de kamers beslist niet aan stijl en comfort. Klein restaurant in de lounge. Originele wijnkaart in de vorm van een schilderspalet.

NH Atlanta Rotterdam sans rest, Aert van Nesstraat 4, ✉ 3012 CA, ☎ (0 10) 206 78 00, *info@nhatlanta-rotterdam.nh-hotels.nl, Fax (0 10) 413 53 20* – – 25 à 325. AE VISA JCB — JY r

16 – **213 ch** 185, – 2 suites.

◆ Rénovations importantes dans cet hôtel-palace 1930 dont les espaces communs - hall, escalier, bar et salle de breakfast - préservent leur cachet Art déco.

◆ In dit luxehotel uit 1930 worden grootscheepse renovaties uitgevoerd. De art-decostijl van de gemeenschappelijke ruimten - lobby, trap, bar en ontbijtzaal - blijft behouden.

Holiday Inn City Centre, Schouwburgplein 1, ✉ 3012 CK, ☎ (0 10) 206 25 55, *hiccrotterdam@bilderberg.nl, Fax (0 10) 206 25 50* – – 25 à 300. AE VISA JCB. rest — JY e

Repas (ouvert jusqu'à 23 h) Lunch 25 – carte 34 à 44, ♀ – 18 – **100 ch** 190/268 – ½ P 133.

◆ Immeuble surplombant la place du Théâtre relookée par Adriaan Geuze. Mobilier actuel et double vitrage dans les chambres. Infrastructures conférencières.

◆ Hotelgebouw aan het Theaterplein, waar de hand van Adriaan Geuze een nieuwe look heeft gecreëerd. Modern meubilair en dubbele beglazing in de kamers. Congresinfrastructuur.

New York, Koninginnehoofd 1 (Wilhelminapier), ✉ 3072 AD, ☎ (0 10) 439 05 00, *info@hotelnewyork.nl, Fax (0 10) 484 27 01,* ←, – – 25 à 800. AE VISA JCB. rest — KZ m

Repas (ouvert jusqu'à minuit) carte 22 à 48, ♀ – 11 – **72 ch** 91/204.

◆ Cet ensemble de caractère fut le siège de la compagnie maritime Holland-America. Chambres originalement personnalisées offrant la vue sur le port, la ville ou le fleuve. Ample salle à manger garnie d'un mobilier de type brasserie.

◆ Dit karaktervolle complex was voorheen de zetel van de Holland-Amerika lijn. Kamers met een origineel en eigen karakter bieden uitzicht op de haven, de stad of de rivier. Ruime eetzaal met meubilair in Grand café stijl.

Inntel, Leuvehaven 80, ✉ 3011 EA, ☎ (0 10) 413 41 39, *info@hotelinntel.com, Fax (0 10) 413 32 22,* ←, – – 25 à 250. AE VISA JCB. rest — KZ d

Repas 23/55 – 19 – **148 ch** 130/230.

◆ Hôtel de chaîne élevé le long du bassin-musée portuaire, à une enjambée du majestueux pont Erasmusbrug. Piscine et bar panoramiques perchés au dernier étage.

◆ Ketenhotel aan de museumhaven, vlak bij de majestueuze Erasmusbrug. Zwembad en bar, beide met panoramisch uitzicht, bevinden zich op de bovenste verdieping.

Savoy sans rest, Hoogstraat 81, ✉ 3011 PJ, ☎ (0 10) 413 92 80, *info.savoy@edenhotelgroup.com, Fax (0 10) 404 57 12,* 🏋, 🚲 – 🛗 ⚹ ▤ 📺 – 🏛 25 à 60. AE ⓓ MC VISA JCB. ⚹ KY z
☕ 16 – **94 ch** 185/240.
◆ À deux pas des fameuses "maisons cubes" conçues par Blom, agréable hôtel distribuant ses chambres, actuelles et de bon confort, sur sept étages. Communs au décor nautique.
◆ Nabij de beroemde kubushuizen van Blom biedt dit aangename hotel moderne, comfortabele kamers verspreid over zeven verdiepingen. Gemeenschappelijke ruimten met nautisch decor.

Pax sans rest, Schiekade 658, ✉ 3032 AK, ☎ (0 10) 466 33 44, *pax@bestwestern.nl, Fax (0 10) 467 52 78* – 🛗 ⚹ ▤ 📺 ♿ 🚗 – 🏛 25 à 80. AE ⓓ MC VISA JCB. ⚹ plan p. 4 FU m
124 ch ☕ 125/165.
◆ En bordure d'un axe important, hôtel aussi pratique pour les automobilistes que pour les usagers du rail. Chambres plus ou moins spacieuses, au mobilier standard.
◆ Dit hotel aan een belangrijke verkeersader is handig voor automobilisten, maar ook voor treinreizigers. Vrij ruime kamers met standaardmeubilair.

Tulip Inn, Willemsplein 1, ✉ 3016 DN, ☎ (0 10) 413 47 90, *reservations@tulipinnrotterdam.nl, Fax (0 10) 412 78 90,* ≤ – 🛗 ⚹, ▤ rest, 📺 – 🏛 25 à 60. AE ⓓ MC VISA JCB. ⚹ KZ s
fermé 24 déc.-2 janv. – **Repas** carte env. 41, 🍷 – **108 ch** ☕ 109/119 – ½ P 131/191.
◆ Bonnes petites chambres fonctionnelles et assez confortables dans ce building construit au bord d'un quai de la Nieuwe Maas. L'Erasmusbrug se déploie juste devant vous.
◆ Aan een kade langs de Nieuwe Maas zijn in dit hotel goede, maar kleine kamers ingericht die functioneel zijn en vrij comfortabel. Vlak voor het pand ligt de Erasmusbrug.

Van Walsum, Mathenesserlaan 199, ✉ 3014 HC, ☎ (0 10) 436 32 75, *info@hotelvanwalsum.nl, Fax (0 10) 436 44 10* – 🛗 📺 🅿. AE ⓓ MC VISA JCB. ⚹ rest plan p. 6 FV e
fermé 24 déc.-2 janv. – **Repas** (résidents seult) – **29 ch** ☕ 78/110 – ½ P 90/96.
◆ Imposante demeure bourgeoise aux chambres d'ampleur différente, meublées à l'identique et munies du double vitrage. La salle des petits-déjeuners s'ouvre sur la terrasse.
◆ Imposant patriciërshuis met kamers die in grootte variëren, maar wel identiek zijn gemeubileerd en voorzien van dubbele beglazing. De ontbijtzaal kijkt uit op het terras.

Emma sans rest, Nieuwe Binnenweg 6, ✉ 3015 BA, ☎ (0 10) 436 55 33, *info@hotelemma.nl, Fax (0 10) 436 76 58* – 🛗 📺 🅿. AE ⓓ MC VISA JCB JY w
24 ch ☕ 85/105.
◆ Ce petit immeuble presque centenaire se partage entre un rez-de-chaussée commercial et trois étages de menues chambres fonctionnelles, convenablement équipées.
◆ Op de drie verdiepingen van dit bijna honderd jaar oude pandje liggen kleine, functionele kamers die vrij comfortabel zijn ingericht. Beneden is een winkel gevestigd.

Breitner, Breitnerstraat 23, ✉ 3015 XA, ☎ (0 10) 436 02 62, *info@hotelbreitner.nl, Fax (0 10) 436 40 91* – 🛗 📺 🚗 🅿. AE ⓓ MC VISA JCB. ⚹ rest JZ d
Repas (dîner pour résidents seult) – **36 ch** ☕ 75/105.
◆ Établissement familial occupant trois maisons d'habitation situées dans une rue calme, à mi-chemin du centre animé et du Museumpark. Chambres sobres et pratiques.
◆ Familiehotel dat gevestigd is in drie woonhuizen in een rustige straat, halverwege het drukke centrum en het Museumpark. Eenvoudige, praktische kamers.

XXXX ✿✿✿ **Parkheuvel** (Helder), Heuvellaan 21, ✉ 3016 GL, ☎ (0 10) 436 07 66, *Fax (0 10) 436 71 40,* ≤, 🏖 – 🅿. AE ⓓ MC VISA JCB JZ n
fermé 19 juil.-7 août, 27 déc.-8 janv., sam. midi et dim. – **Repas** Lunch 48 – 65/148 bc, carte 70 à 99, 🍷.
◆ Une cuisine ingénieuse et créative vous attend dans ce pavillon moderne en hémicycle. Prenez place côté terrasse pour profiter de la vue sur le trafic maritime. Un régal !
◆ In dit moderne, halfronde paviljoen wordt u onthaald op een vindingrijke, creatieve keuken. De tafels aan de terraskant bieden uitzicht op het scheepvaartverkeer. Een festijn !
Spéc. Turbot grillé, crème d'anchois et champignons au basilic. Risotto au parmesan et ballottine de langoustines aux cèpes. Pot-au-feu de filet de bœuf à la truffe et au foie d'oie (avril-sept.)

XXX **Old Dutch,** Rochussenstraat 20, ✉ 3015 EK, ☎ (0 10) 436 03 44, *avdstel@hotmail.com, Fax (0 10) 436 78 26,* 🏖 – 🅿. AE ⓓ MC VISA JZ r
fermé sam. soir en juil.-août, sam. midi, dim. et jours fériés – **Repas** Lunch 33 – 58, 🍷.
◆ Installé dans une auberge bâtie en 1932, le "Vieil Hollandais" est un agréable restaurant garni d'un mobilier bourgeois. Carte classique avec plusieurs menus. Vins du monde.
◆ Deze Oude Hollander runt in een herberg uit 1932 een aangenaam restaurant dat met traditioneel meubilair is ingericht. Klassieke kaart met menu's. Wereldwijnen.

PAYS-BAS

XXX **Radèn Mas** 1er étage, Kruiskade 72, ✉ 3012 EH, ☎ (0 10) 411 72 44, *Fax (0 10) 411 97 11*, Cuisine indonésienne – ▤. AE ⓓ ⓜ VISA JCB. ✈ JY a
Repas (dîner seult jusqu'à 23 h) carte 34 à 65.
• Au premier étage d'un immeuble commercial récent, établissement indonésien dont le choix, typique, comprend quelques menus et "tables de riz". Décor exotique contemporain.
• Op de eerste verdieping van een modern winkelcentrum worden in dit Indonesische restaurant diverse menu's en rijsttafels geserveerd. Modern, exotisch decor.

XX ✿ **La Vilette** (Mustert), Westblaak 160, ✉ 3012 KM, ☎ (0 10) 414 86 92, *Fax (0 10) 414 33 91* – ▤. AE ⓓ ⓜ VISA JCB. ✈ JY t
fermé 19 juil.-8 sept., 24 déc.-2 janv., sam. midi et dim. – **Repas** Lunch 29 – carte 39 à 52, ♀.
• Ambiance "brasserie sélecte" dans ce confortable restaurant où une appétissante petite carte au goût du jour vous sera soumise. Parking public aisé à proximité immédiate.
• Chique brasseriesfeer in dit comfortabele restaurant, waar een aantrekkelijke kleine kaart met trendy gerechten wordt gepresenteerd. Openbare parking in de directe nabijheid.
Spéc. Saint-Jacques au foie de canard. Turbot à la tomate. Eventail de chocolat et nougat

XX **De Harmonie,** Westersingel 95, ✉ 3015 LC, ☎ (0 10) 436 36 10, *Fax (0 10) 436 36 08*, 🏕 – 🅿 25 à 60. AE ⓓ ⓜ VISA JZ c
fermé 26 déc.-2 janv., sam. midi et dim. – **Repas** Lunch 32 – carte 44 à 55, ♀.
• Agréable restaurant jouxtant le Westersingel et le Museumpark. L'été venu, jardin et terrasse ne désavouent pas l'enseigne. Savoureuses préparations au goût du jour.
• Aangenaam restaurant dicht bij de Westersingel en het Museumpark. 's Zomers doen tuin en terras de naam van het etablissement alle eer aan. Smakelijke eigentijdse keuken.

XX **ZeeZout,** Westerkade 11b, ✉ 3016 CL, ☎ (0 10) 436 50 49, *Fax (0 10) 225 18 47*, 🏕, Produits de la mer – ▤. AE ⓓ ⓜ VISA JZ e
fermé 25 et 26 déc., 31 déc. soir, 1er janv. midi, sam. midi, dim. et lundi – **Repas** Lunch 28 – carte 44 à 61.
• Recettes tournées vers le grand large et terrasse orientée côté Nieuwe Maas font l'attrait de cette élégante brasserie dont le nom - "Sel de Mer "- annonce la couleur.
• What's in the name ! Gerechten die op de zee zijn geïnspireerd en het terras aan de Nieuwe Maas vormen de trekpleister van deze elegante brasserie.

XX **Brancatelli,** Boompjes 264, ✉ 3011 XD, ☎ (0 10) 411 41 51, *Fax (0 10) 404 57 34*, Cuisine italienne, ouvert jusqu'à 23 h – ▤. AE ⓓ ⓜ VISA KZ n
fermé sam. midi et dim. midi – **Repas** Lunch 32 – carte 35 à 56, ♀.
• Table italienne aménagée de façon actuelle, bordant un quai animé. Carte concise mais assez authentique, qu'accompagne une sélection de vins reçus en direct de la "Botte".
• Modern ingericht Italiaans restaurant aan een levendige kade. Kleine maar vrij authentieke kaart en keuze uit een selectie wijnen die rechtstreeks uit de Laars komen.

X **de Engel,** Eendrachtsweg 19, ✉ 3012 LB, ☎ (0 10) 413 82 56, *engel@engelgroep.com, Fax (0 10) 414 63 86* – ▤. AE ⓓ ⓜ VISA JCB JZ z
fermé 25, 26 et 31 déc. et dim. – **Repas** (dîner seult) carte env. 57, ♀.
• L'une des adresses en vogue à Rotterdam. Ambiance décontractée, salle à manger actuelle garnie de meubles de divers styles et soigneuse cuisine du marché.
• Een van de trendy adressen in de stad. Ongedwongen sfeer, eetzaal met meubilair in diverse stijlen en verzorgde keuken die wordt bereid van dagverse producten.

X **La Stanza,** Van Vollenhovenstraat 19, ✉ 3016 BE, ☎ (0 10) 277 14 14, *info@lastanza.nl, Fax (0 10) 277 14 10*, 🏕 – AE ⓓ ⓜ VISA JCB. ✈ JZ x
fermé 31 déc.-1er janv., sam. midi et dim. midi – **Repas** Lunch 28 – carte env. 42, ♀.
• Dans un quartier qui bouge, maison bourgeoise judicieusement mise à profit. Salle de restaurant sobrement décorée. Carte actuelle avouant un petit faible pour la Méditerranée.
• Dit patriciërshuis in een bruisende wijk is vakkundig tot restaurant verbouwd. Eetzaal met strak decor. De eigentijdse kaart toont een voorkeur voor de mediterrane keuken.

X **Foody's,** Nieuwe Binnenweg 151, ✉ 3014 GK, ☎ (0 10) 436 51 63, *Fax (0 10) 436 54 42*, 🏕 – ▤. AE ⓜ VISA. ✈ JZ k
fermé 25 et 26 déc. et lundi – **Repas** (dîner seult jusqu'à minuit) 34/45, ♀ 🍇.
• Brasserie d'aujourd'hui avec cuisines à vue où se concocte un choix de préparations actuelles très "nature", valorisant les produits de saison. Nombreux vins servis au verre.
• Modern restaurant met open keuken waar met seizoengebonden ingrediënten eigentijdse, eerlijke gerechten worden klaar gestoomd. Enorme keuze in wijnen per glas.

X **Lux,** 's-Gravendijkwal 133, ✉ 3021 EK, ☎ (0 10) 476 22 06, 🏕, Cuisine italienne – VISA plan p. 6 FV b
fermé 25, 26 et 31 déc. – **Repas** (dîner seult jusqu'à 23 h) carte env. 32, ♀.
• Salle de restaurant contemporaine jouant sur les contrastes, à dénicher derrière une belle façade recouverte de carrelages. Cuisine transalpine. Café animé l'après-midi.
• Eigentijdse eetzaal waar veel met contrasten wordt gespeeld. Achter een mooie, met tegels bedekte gevel worden Italiaanse gerechten geserveerd. Gezellig middagcafé.

Brasserie De Tijdgeest, Oost-Wijnstraat 14, ✉ 3011 TZ, ✆ (0 10) 233 13 11, *info@detijdgeest.nl, Fax (0 10) 413 94 21,* ☂, Taverne-rest – 35. AE ⓓ MC VISA JCB
fermé 24 déc. soir, sam. midi et dim. midi – **Repas** 25, ♀. KY a
◆ Taverne-restaurant à l'ambiance "trendy", occupant un ensemble historique au pied du plus ancien gratte-ciel batave et à une encablure du vieux port. Cuisine bistrotière.
◆ Trendy café-restaurant in een historisch pand aan de voet van de oudste wolkenkrabber in Nederland en vlak bij de oude haven. Bistroachtige keuken.

Kip, Van Vollenhovenstraat 25, ✉ 3016 BG, ✆ (0 10) 436 99 23, *info@kip-rotterdam.nl, Fax (0 10) 436 27 02,* ☂ – AE MC VISA JZ p
Repas (déjeuner sur réservation) 38, ♀.
◆ Détrompez-vous, on ne sert pas que du "Poulet" dans ce bistrot convivial dont la carte, assez contrastée, offre une belle variété de plats. Jolie terrasse fleurie en été.
◆ Geen nood, er wordt echt niet alleen kip geserveerd in deze gezellige bistro, waar de nogal contrastrijke kaart een ruime keuze aan gerechten biedt. Leuk terras in de zomer.

Rosso, Van Vollenhovenstraat 15 (accès par Westerlijk Handelsterrein), ✉ 3016 BE, ✆ (0 10) 225 07 05, *Fax (0 10) 436 95 04* – ▤. AE MC VISA. ✻ JZ b
fermé dim. et lundi – **Repas** (dîner seult jusqu'à 23 h) 33/40, ♀.
◆ Dans un ancien entrepôt du 19e s. habilement relooké, établissement dont la salle à manger voit la vie en rouge. Clientèle et ambiance "hype". En résumé : "the place to be".
◆ In een voormalig 19e-eeuws entrepot, dat handig is verbouwd, ziet de eetzaal het leven door een rode bril. Trendy gasten en ambiance. Kortom : the place to be !

Asian Glories, Leeuwenstraat 15, ✉ 3011 AL, ✆ (0 10) 411 71 07, *Fax (0 10) 280 91 78,* Cuisine chinoise, ouvert jusqu'à 23 h – AE ⓓ MC VISA KY m
fermé vacances bâtiment et merc. – **Repas** Lunch 22 – 23/35 bc, ♀.
◆ Petite affaire familiale installée dans un immeuble embrassant du regard la très moderne tour du World Trade Center. Éventail de préparations chinoises. Formule lunch.
◆ Gezellig restaurantje in een pand met zicht op de hypermoderne toren van het World Trade Center. Grote keuze aan Chinese gerechten. Lunchformule.

Oliva, Witte de Withstraat 15a, ✉ 3012 BK, ✆ (0 10) 412 14 13, *info@restaurantoliva.nl, Fax (0 10) 412 70 69,* ☂, Cuisine italienne – MC VISA
fermé sam. midi, dim. midi et lundi – **Repas** carte 26 à 42.
◆ Restaurant italien branché établi dans un ancien bâtiment industriel. Décor intérieur "loft", atmosphère vivante, carte sans prise de tête et suggestions du jour à l'ardoise.
◆ Trendy Italiaans restaurant in een naoorlogs gebouw. Het interieur doet denken aan een loft en het is er gezellig druk. Redelijke prijzen ; de dagsuggesties staan op een bord.

Kaat Mossel, Admiraliteitskade 85, ✉ 3063 EG, ✆ (0 10) 404 86 00, *Fax (0 10) 412 72 83,* ☂, Produits de la mer, moules en saison, ouvert jusqu'à 23 h – AE ⓓ MC VISA. ✻ – *fermé dim.* – **Repas** carte 27 à 55, ♀. plan p. 7 HU a
◆ Ancrée en face du port, table très populaire à Rotterdam notamment fréquentée par de grands sportifs du pays. Goûteuses recettes de la mer. Accueil et service affriolants.
◆ Dit zeer populaire visrestaurant ligt verankerd tegenover de haven en trekt met name ook bekende nationale sporters. Smakelijke keuken. Prettige ontvangst en service.

Anak Mas, Meent 72a, ✉ 3011 JN, ✆ (0 10) 414 84 87, *pturina@hotmail.com, Fax (0 10) 412 44 74,* Cuisine indonésienne – ▤. AE ⓓ MC VISA KY s
fermé juil. et dim. – **Repas** (dîner seult) 22/57 bc.
◆ Un aimable petit restaurant indonésien se cache derrière cette façade tristounette. Plats typiques sautés au "wok" et tables de riz. Décor intérieur de circonstance.
◆ Een vriendelijk Indonesisch restaurantje gaat schuil achter de ietwat mistroostige gevel. Karakteristieke wokgerechten en rijsttafels. Gelegenheidsdecor.

Fuji-Benkei en sous-sol, Kruiskade 26, ✉ 3012 EH, ✆ (0 10) 433 29 79, *Fax (0 10) 404 69 09,* Cuisine japonaise – ▤. AE ⓓ MC VISA JCB. ✻ JY u
fermé fin juil.-début août, dim. et lundi – **Repas** 35/50.
◆ Tous les types de restauration japonaise convergent vers le Fuji-Benkei : carte classique avec sa kyrielle de menus, formule Teppan-Yaki et bar à sushis. Service en kimono.
◆ Alle Japanse keukens komen samen in de Fuji-Benkei : klassieke kaart met een schat aan menu's, formule teppan-yaki en sushibar. Bediening in kimono.

Périphérie - *plans p. 4 et 5 sauf indication spéciale :*

à l'Aéroport :

Airport, Vliegveldweg 59, ✉ 3043 NT, ✆ (0 10) 462 55 66, *info@airporthotel.nl, Fax (0 10) 462 22 66,* ☂, 🚲 – 🛗 ⇎, ▤ rest, 📺 ♿ 🅿 – 25 à 425. AE ⓓ MC VISA JCB. ✻ – **Repas** carte 27 à 38 – ☕ 16 – **96 ch** 165/193, – 2 suites. AR a
◆ En face de l'aéroport (navette assurée), construction récente dont les chambres, coquettes et correctement équipées, viennent d'être rénovées. Bonne isolation phonique. Confortable salle à manger de notre temps. Choix de préparations traditionnelles.
◆ Dit moderne hotelgebouw staat tegenover de luchthaven (shuttleservice gegarandeerd) en beschikt over nette en gerieflijke kamers die onlangs zijn gerenoveerd. Goede geluidsisolatie. Comfortabele, moderne eetzaal. Traditionele gerechten.

à Kralingen C Rotterdam :

Novotel Brainpark, K.P. van der Mandelelaan 150 (près A 16), ✉ 3062 MB, ☎ (0 10) 253 25 32, *H1134@accor-hotels.com, Fax (0 10) 253 25 72,* – 🛗 – 25 à 400. AE VISA DS e

Repas carte 32 à 40 – ☕ 15 – **202 ch** 125/135 – ½ P 165.

◆ Immeuble contemporain installé dans un parc d'affaires, aux portes de la ville. Toutes les chambres ont été réaménagées selon les nouvelles normes Novotel. Brasserie-restaurant proposant des snacks et un choix varié à la carte.

◆ Hedendaags gebouw in een bedrijvenpark aan de rand van de stad. Alle kamers zijn opnieuw ingericht en voldoen aan de nieuwe standaardnormen van de hotelketen. Café-restaurant waar kleine hapjes verkrijgbaar zijn, maar ook à la carte kan worden gegeten.

In den Rustwat, Honingerdijk 96, ✉ 3062 NX, ☎ (0 10) 413 41 10, *info@indenrustwat.nl, Fax (0 10) 404 85 40,* – . AE VISA JCB plan p. 7 HV e

fermé dern. sem. juil.-2 prem. sem. août, fin déc.-début janv., sam. midi, dim. et lundi – **Repas** *Lunch 30* – carte 44 à 57, ♀.

◆ "1597", proclame le pignon. Bordant un arboretum, ravissante auberge à toit de chaume agrandie d'une aile récente. Carte inventive. Terrasse et jardin fleuri en été.

◆ "1597" staat er op de puntgevel van deze charmante herberg met rieten dak, die in een arboretum staat en pas is uitgebreid. Creatieve kaart. Terras en bloementuin in de zomer.

Zone Europoort *par ⑤ : 25 km :*

De Beer Europoort, Europaweg 210 (N 15), ✉ 3198 LD, ☎ (0 181) 26 23 77, *bienvenue@hoteldebeer.nl, Fax (0 181) 26 29 23,* ←, , , , – 🛗 – 25 à 180. AE VISA

Repas *Lunch 19* – 34 – **78 ch** ☕ 86/101 – ½ P 70/105.

◆ En retrait de l'effervescent Europoort, petit immeuble aux chambres fonctionnelles dont la moitié offrent la vue sur un canal. Installations sportives et pour séminaires. Depuis la salle à manger et la terrasse, échappée en direction du Hartelkanaal.

◆ Onder de rook van de bedrijvige Europoort bevindt zich dit kleine hotel met functionele kamers, waarvan de helft uitkijkt op een kanaal. Sportvoorzieningen en faciliteiten voor seminars. Eetzaal en terras bieden uitzicht op het Hartelkanaal.

Environs

à Barendrecht *- plan p. 5 – 33 894 h*

Bastion, Van der Waalsweg 27 (près A 15), ✉ 2991 XN, ☎ (0 10) 479 22 04, *bastion@bastionhotel.nl, Fax (0 10) 479 32 85* – . AE VISA. DT t

Repas (grillades, ouvert jusqu'à 23 h) carte env. 30 – ☕ 10 – **40 ch** 78.

◆ Proximité du ring, service "minimaliste", chambres standardisées avec coffre-fort, prise modem et double vitrage. Bref, un hôtel typique de cette chaîne hollandaise.

◆ Dit hotel in de nabijheid van de ringweg beschikt over standaardkamers met kluis, modem-aansluiting en dubbele beglazing. Beperkt servicepakket. Een getrouw hotel van de keten.

à Capelle aan den IJssel *- plan p. 5 – 65 226 h*

NH Capelle, Barbizonlaan 2 (près A 20), ✉ 2908 MA, ☎ (0 10) 456 44 55, *info@nhcapelle.nh-hotels.nl, Fax (0 10) 456 78 58,* ←, – 🛗 , ch, – 25 à 250. AE VISA JCB DR c

Repas *(fermé dim. midi) Lunch 19* – carte 34 à 43, ♀ – ☕ 16 – **100 ch** 190, – 1 suite.

◆ Building contemporain jouxtant une bretelle du périphérique par lequel vous gagnerez Rotterdam en 5 mn. Confort moderne dans les chambres, amples et refaites de neuf. L'été, on dresse le couvert sur la terrasse, en surplomb d'un étang.

◆ Dit eigentijdse gebouw staat vlak bij een afslag van de rondweg waarlangs het centrum van Rotterdam in 5 min. bereikbaar is. Modern comfort in de ruime, gerenoveerde kamers. 's Zomers wordt er geserveerd op het terras aan het water.

Bastion, Rhijnspoor 300, ✉ 2901 LC, ☎ (0 10) 202 01 04, *bastion@bastionhotel.nl, Fax (0 10) 202 02 47* – . AE VISA. DS a

Repas (grillades, ouvert jusqu'à 23 h) carte env. 30 – ☕ 10 – **40 ch** 78.

◆ Conçu de la même façon que tous les autres et posté juste en face d'un carrefour important, ce récent petit Bastion renferme des chambres fonctionnelles.

◆ Dit jonge Bastion is net zo opgezet als de andere hotels van de keten. Het bevindt zich tegenover een belangrijk kruispunt van wegen en herbergt functionele kamers.

Rivium Royale, Rivium Boulevard 188, ✉ 2909 LK, ☎ (0 10) 202 56 33, *reserveren@riviumroyale.nl, Fax (0 10) 202 65 37,* – . VISA DS z

fermé 19 juil.-9 août, 24 déc.-3 janv., sam. et dim. – **Repas** *Lunch 28* – carte 43 à 67, ♀.

◆ Sous un dôme contemporain entouré de "douves", belle salle de restaurant en rotonde que surmonte une mezzanine-salon. Agréable terrasse estivale avec vue sur l'eau.

◆ Dit restaurant onder een moderne koepel en omringd door een gracht heeft een fraaie ronde eetzaal met salon op de tussenverdieping. Aangenaam terras met uitzicht op het water.

XX **Johannahoeve,** 's Gravenweg 347, ✉ 2905 LB, ☎ (0 10) 450 38 00, *info@johannahoeve.nu, Fax (0 10) 442 07 34,* – MO VISA — DR g
fermé lundi et mardi en été, sam. midi et dim. midi – **Repas** 29.
◆ Dans un quartier résidentiel, jolie ferme du 17e s. coiffée d'un toit de chaume. Cuisine classique sobrement actualisée. Salle à manger rustique et terrasse sur jardin.
◆ Leuke 17e-eeuwse boerderij met rieten dak, in een woonwijk. Klassieke keuken met een licht modern accent. Rustieke eetzaal en terras aan de tuin.

à Rhoon - *plan p. 4 - C Albrandswaard 18 092 h :*

Bastion, Driemanssteenweg 5 (près A 15), ✉ 3084 CA, ☎ (0 10) 410 10 00, *bastion@bastionhotel.nl, Fax (0 10) 410 31 94* – TV P. AE MO VISA. — BT z
Repas (grillades, ouvert jusqu'à 23 h) carte env. 30 – ☐ 10 – **80 ch** 78.
◆ Chambres fonctionnelles et identiques, munies du double vitrage, dans cet hôtel de chaîne érigé à proximité d'un moulin et d'une bretelle d'autoroute.
◆ Functionele en identiek ingerichte kamers met dubbele beglazing. Dit ketenhotel staat vlak bij een molen en een afslag van de snelweg.

XXX **Het Kasteel van Rhoon,** Dorpsdijk 63, ✉ 3161 KD, ☎ (0 10) 501 88 96, *info@hetkasteelvanrhoon.nl, Fax (0 10) 506 72 59,* ←, – P – 25 à 100. AE MO VISA. — AT b
fermé sam. midi – **Repas** *Lunch 28* – carte env. 56, ♀.
◆ Confortable restaurant moderne occupant les dépendances d'un château cerné de douves. Cuisine assez élaborée, de base classique et choix de vins étoffé. Salles de banquets.
◆ Comfortabel, modern restaurant in de bijgebouwen van een kasteel met slotgracht. Verfijnde keuken op klassieke basis en een uitgebreide wijnkaart. Faciliteiten voor partijen.

X **Orangerie de Rhoonse Vrienden,** Albrandswaardsesijk 196 (Poortugaal, au port de plaisance), ✉ 3172 XB, ☎ (0 10) 501 15 00, *info@hetkasteelvanrhoon.nl, Fax (0 10) 501 15 02,* – P. AE MO VISA — AT z
fermé 1er janv., lundi, mardi et sam. midi – **Repas** *Lunch 17* – carte 22 à 37, ♀.
◆ Pavillon amarré juste en face du port des yachts. Lumineuse salle à manger contemporaine où l'on présente une carte actuelle sortant du lot. Terrasses enrobées de verdure.
◆ Dit paviljoen ligt pal tegenover de jachthaven. Eigentijdse lichte eetzaal, waar de kaart originele, actuele gerechten vermeldt. Terrassen in het groen.

à Schiedam - *plan p. 4 - 76 576 h.*

Buitenhavenweg 9, ✉ 3113 BC, ☎ (0 10) 473 30 00, vvv.schiedam@kabelfoon.nl, Fax (0 10) 473 66 95

Novotel, Hargalaan 2 (près A 20), ✉ 3118 JA, ☎ (0 10) 471 33 22, *H0517@accor-hotels.com, Fax (0 10) 470 06 56,* – TV P – 25 à 200. AE MO VISA. rest — AS b
Repas *Lunch 15* – carte 22 à 37 – ☐ 14 – **134 ch** 125/135.
◆ Sur un carrefour proche du ring, hôtel dont les chambres insonorisées ont été relookées dans le nouveau style de la chaîne. Terrasse au bord de la piscine. Jardin soigné.
◆ De kamers in dit hotel aan een kruispunt vlak bij de ringweg zijn opnieuw ingericht in de huisstijl van de keten. Geluidsisolatie. Terras aan het zwembad. Verzorgde tuin.

XX **Le Pêcheur,** Nieuwe Haven 97, ✉ 3116 AB, ☎ (0 10) 473 33 41, *email@le-pecheur.nl, Fax (0 10) 273 11 55,* – AE MO VISA — AS k
fermé mardi en juil.-août, sam. midi et dim. midi – **Repas** *Lunch 24* – carte 40 à 56.
◆ Cet ancien entrepôt d'une distillerie abrite un restaurant dont il faut nuancer l'enseigne car sa carte ne se limite pas au produit de la pêche. Ambiance rustique.
◆ Dit voormalige pakhuis van een distilleerderij herbergt een restaurant waarvan de naam misleidend kan zijn. Er wordt namelijk niet alleen vis geserveerd. Rustieke ambiance.

X **Bistrot Hosman Frères,** Korte Dam 10, ✉ 3111 BG, ☎ (0 10) 426 40 96, *Fax (0 10) 426 90 41* – AE MO VISA JCB — AS s
fermé 31 déc.-1er janv., sam. midi, dim. midi et lundi – **Repas** 26/52 bc, ♀.
◆ Sur un site pittoresque du quartier ancien, à deux pas de quatre vieux moulins, sympathique auberge où les amateurs de cuisine "bistrotière" trouvent leur bonheur.
◆ In dit sympathieke eethuis op een pittoreske lokatie in het historische centrum, vlak bij vier oude molens, kunnen liefhebbers van de bistro keuken hun hart ophalen.

X **Gauwigheid,** 's-Gravelandseweg 622, ✉ 3119 NA, ☎ (0 10) 273 22 00, *Fax (0 10) 273 28 00* – AE MO VISA — AS a
fermé fin déc., sam. midi, dim. midi et lundi – **Repas** 25/43.
◆ Une fresque représentant le vieux Schiedam et de massives tables vernies, éclairées de bougies le soir venu, confèrent à la salle de restaurant un charme particulier.
◆ Een fresco van oud Schiedam en massieve, gelakte tafels die 's avonds met kaarsen worden verlicht, geven de restaurantzaal een bijzondere charme.

Italia, Hoogstraat 118, ✉ 3111 HL, ☎ (0 10) 473 27 56, *info@italia.nu*, Cuisine italienne – ▤. AE ⓓ MC VISA AS n
fermé 25 juil.-9 août, 27 déc.-3 janv., lundi et mardi – **Repas** (dîner seult) 26/38, ♀.
◆ Préparations d'inspiration transalpine servies avec le sourire dans une intime salle à manger lambrissée où trône un beau petit poêle en fonte. Patron un peu "tchatcheur".
◆ Italiaans georiënteerde gerechten worden geserveerd in een intieme, gelambriseerde eetzaal waar een kleine smeedijzeren potkachel troont. De patron maakt graag een babbeltje.

ROTTEVALLE (ROTTEFALLE) *Fryslân* 531 V 4 – *voir à Drachten.*

ROZENDAAL *Gelderland* 532 U 10 *et* 715 I 5 – *voir à Arnhem.*

RUINEN *Drenthe* C *De Wolden 23 875 h.* 531 X 6 *et* 715 K 3.

Brink 3, ✉ *7963 AA,* ☎ *(0 522) 47 17 00, Fax (0 522) 47 30 45.*
Amsterdam 154 – Assen 36 – Emmen 51 – Zwolle 41.

De Stobbe, Westerstraat 84, ✉ 7963 BE, ☎ (0 522) 47 12 24, *info@stobbe.nl*, *Fax (0 522) 47 27 47*, , , , – , , ▤ rest, TV, ♿, P – 25 à 40. AE ⓓ MC VISA
Repas *(fermé après 20 h)* Lunch 16 – 22/48 bc – **24 ch** 55/85 – ½ P 52/60.
◆ Enracinée à l'entrée de Ruinen, De Stobbe (La Souche) dispose de chambres bien calibrées où vous dormirez "comme un bûcheron". Salon et bar anglais. Salle à manger au parquet luisant et meubles couleur merisier. Carte de préparations classiques.
◆ Deze stobbe heeft wortel geschoten aan de rand van het dorp en beschikt over kamers van goed formaat, waar u als een blok zult slapen. Engelse lounge en bar. Eetzaal met glanzend parket en meubels van kersenhout. Menukaart met klassieke gerechten.

RUURLO *Gelderland* 532 X 10 *et* 715 K 5 – *8 336 h.*

Amsterdam 134 – Arnhem 53 – Apeldoorn 45 – Doetinchem 21 – Enschede 39.

Avenarius, Dorpsstraat 2, ✉ 7261 AW, ☎ (0 573) 45 11 22, *info@avenarius.nl*, *Fax (0 573) 45 37 44*, , – , TV P – 25 à 200. AE ⓓ MC VISA JCB. ch
fermé 28 déc.-4 janv. – **Repas** carte 34 à 53, ♀ – **29 ch** 80/120 – ½ P 100.
◆ Cette hostellerie centenaire officiant à l'entrée du village s'est récemment agrandie d'une aile moderne dotée de belles chambres d'un style résolument contemporain. Salle de restaurant devancée d'une terrasse et d'une véranda.
◆ Dit ruim honderd jaar oude hotel aan de rand van het dorp is onlangs uitgebreid met een moderne vleugel. Hierin zijn prachtige kamers ondergebracht die in een uitgesproken eigentijdse stijl zijn ingericht. Restaurant met serre en terras.

De Tuinkamer en De Herberg avec ch, Hengeloseweg 1 (Sud-Ouest : 3 km), ✉ 7261 LV, ☎ (0 573) 45 21 47, *deherberg@hetnet.nl*, , , – TV. MC VISA. ch
fermé du 5 au 19 juil. et 29 déc.-24 janv. – **Repas** *(fermé lundi et mardi)* (dîner seult) 32/37, ♀ – **10 ch** *(fermé lundi et mardi sauf en saiosn)* 55/105 – ½ P 62/80.
◆ Cette jolie ferme-auberge propose une cuisine actuelle dans une agréable véranda s'ouvrant sur le jardin. Salon rustique et petites chambres aussi coquettes que paisibles.
◆ Deze fraaie boerderijherberg serveert eigentijdse gerechten in een aangename serre die uitziet op de tuin. Rustieke lounge en kleine kamers die even charmant als rustig zijn.

RYPTSJERK (RIJPERKERK) *Fryslân* C *Tytsjerksteradiel 31 413 h.* 531 U 3.

Amsterdam 148 – Leeuwarden 10 – Assen 64 – Groningen 60 – Lelystad 111.

Frouckje State, Binnendijk 74, ✉ 9256 HP, ☎ (0 511) 43 19 20, *info@froukjestate.nl*, *Fax (0 511) 43 14 66*, – P – 100
fermé 3 sem. vacances bâtiment et mardi – **Repas** (déjeuner sur réservation) carte 36 à 54, ♀.
◆ Aux abords du village, dans une ancienne ferme frisonne, table appréciée pour son chaleureux cadre contemporain, son environnement agreste et l'attrait de sa carte classique. Confortable salle de restaurant d'où vous balayerez la rivière du regard.
◆ Dit etablissement in een oude Friese boerderij buiten het dorp, is aanlokkelijk door de landelijke omgeving, het genoeglijke hedendaagse decor en de klassieke kaart. Comfortabele eetzaal met zicht op het water.

SANTPOORT *Noord-Holland* ⓒ *Velsen 67 407 h.* 407 M 8, 532 M 8 *et* 715 E 4.
Amsterdam 24 – Haarlem 7.

Landgoed Duin en Kruidberg, Duin en Kruidbergerweg 60 (Santpoort-Noord), ✉ 2071 LE, ☎ (0 23) 512 18 00, *info@duin-kruidberg.nl, Fax (0 23) 512 18 88*, ≤, ch, 25 à 225. AE VISA.
fermé 22 déc.-1er janv. – **Repas** ***De Vrienden van Jacob*** *(fermé dim.)* (dîner seult) 60/109 bc, ♀ – ☕ 17 – **73 ch** 195/335, – 2 suites – ½ P 171/269.
◆ Fastueuse demeure 1900 s'entourant d'un vaste parc avec étang. Belles chambres et communs parsemés d'objets d'art. Grande infrastructure pour séminaires. Salle à manger opulente procurant une vue sur le domaine. Cuisine créative. Terrasse estivale apéritive.
◆ Weelderige verblijf van begin 1900, in een groot park met vijver. Mooie kamers. De gemeenschappelijke ruimten zijn met kunstobjecten verfraaid. Groot conferentiecentrum. Luxueuze eetzaal met uitzicht op het landgoed. Creatieve keuken. Terras voor een aperitief.

De Weyman sans rest, Hoofdstraat 248, ✉ 2071 EP, ☎ (0 23) 537 04 36, *hotel@deweyman.nl, Fax (0 23) 537 06 53* – AE VISA JCB.
20 ch ☕ 78/86.
◆ Ressource hôtelière bien pratique comme point de chute aux alentours de Haarlem. Chambres d'ampleur respectable, avant tout fonctionnelles.
◆ Een heel praktisch hotel als uitvalsbasis voor wie Haarlem en omgeving wil verkennen. De kamers zijn respectabel van afmeting en vooral functioneel.

Bastion, Vlietweg 20, ✉ 2071 KW, ☎ (0 23) 538 74 74, *bastion@bastionhotel.nl, Fax (0 23) 538 43 34* – AE VISA.
Repas (grillades, ouvert jusqu'à 23 h) carte env. 30 – ☕ 10 – **40 ch** 69.
◆ Postée au carrefour des communes limitrophes de Santpoort, Velsen et Haarlem, cette unité Bastion ne diffère en rien de toutes celles partageant la même enseigne.
◆ Dit Bastion is te vinden nabij de omringende gemeenten van Santpoort, Velsen en Haarlem, en verschilt in niets van zijn soortgenoten die onder dezelfde naam actief zijn.

SAS VAN GENT *Zeeland* ⓒ *Terneuzen 55 478 h.* 532 H 15 *et* 715 C 8.
Amsterdam 214 – Gent 25 – Middelburg 42 – Antwerpen 49 – Brugge 46.

Royal (annexes), Gentsestraat 12, ✉ 4551 CC, ☎ (0 115) 45 18 53, *hotelroyal@zeelandnet.nl, Fax (0 115) 45 17 96*, – rest, AE VISA.
Repas *(fermé 26 déc.-4 janv. et sam.)* 34/40 – **48 ch** ☕ 69/115 – ½ P 73/100.
◆ Appartements avec kitchenette, junior suites, chambres doubles ou singles : chacun trouvera son compte dans l'une des proches annexes de cet établissement. Salle de restaurant affichant un petit air d'hostellerie traditionnelle.
◆ Appartementen met kitchenette, junior suites, een- of tweepersoonskamers : ieder vindt wel iets van zijn gading in een van de nabijgelegen dependances van dit etablissement. De restaurantzaal ademt de sfeer van een traditionele herberg.

SCHAGEN *Noord-Holland* 531 N 6 *et* 715 F 3 – *17 214 h.*
Amsterdam 64 – Alkmaar 19 – Den Helder 23 – Hoorn 29.

De Eetkamer, Molenstraat 21, ✉ 1741 GJ, ☎ (0 224) 21 58 17, *eetkamer@eetertainment.nl, Fax (0 224) 29 59 39*, – AE VISA JCB
fermé 2 sem. en juil., sam. midi, dim. midi et lundi – **Repas** Lunch 33 – 45/74 bc, ♀.
◆ Ambiance "brasserie contemporaine", mise en place d'une élégante sobriété et recettes de base classique présentées à la mode d'aujourd'hui. Au total, une adresse plaisante.
◆ Doe alsof u thuis bent ! Moderne, gezellige ambiance in een eenvoudig, smaakvol interieur en klassieke gerechten in een eigentijds jasje. Al met al, een prettig adres.

De Bourgondiër, Noord 8, ✉ 1741 BD, ☎ (0 224) 29 26 86, *Fax (0 224) 29 24 50* –
fermé lundi et mardi – **Repas** (dîner seult) 33, ♀.
◆ Axées sur les saveurs du moment, les préparations concoctées au Bourgondiër ont su s'attirer les faveurs de la clientèle locale. Atmosphère intime et service charmant.
◆ De gerechten die bij de Bourgondiër worden bereid, volgen de trends op de voet en zijn erg in trek bij lokale liefhebbers. Intieme sfeer en charmante bediening.

SCHAIJK *Noord-Brabant* ⓒ *Landerd 14 516 h.* 532 S 12 *et* 715 H 6.
Amsterdam 99 – Arnhem 44 – 's-Hertogenbosch 25 – Nijmegen 22.

De Peppelen, Schutsboomstraat 43, ✉ 5374 CB, ☎ (0 486) 46 35 48, *info@peppelen.nl*, – VISA
fermé mardi et merc. soir – **Repas** Lunch 23 – carte 34 à 46, ♀.
◆ Ancienne demeure de notaire renouant avec son passé festif. Salles bourgeoises, pergola "chlorophyllienne" meublée en teck et charmante terrasse rafraîchie d'une pièce d'eau.
◆ In dit oude notarishuis komt het verleden weer tot leven. Eetzalen in authentieke stijl, tuinterras met teakmeubilair onder een pergola en een tweede terras met waterpartij.

SCHERPENISSE *Zeeland* C *Tholen 23 884 h.* 532 J 13 *et* 715 D 7.
Amsterdam 141 – Bergen op Zoom 20 – Breda 57 – Rotterdam 68.

De Gouden Leeuw, Hoge Markt 8, ✉ 4694 CG, ✆ (0 166) 66 39 01, *degoudenleeuw1@hetnet.nl, Fax (0 166) 66 20 79,* – 25 à 50. AE VISA JCB. rest
Repas *(fermé fin déc.-prem. sem. janv., 2 dern. sem. août-prem. sem. sept. et dim.)* *Lunch 24* – 30/40, – 8 – **6 ch** 74/90 – ½ P 95/115.
• Quelques belles chambres modernes ont été aménagées à l'étage de cette petite auberge familiale "perdue" dans un village à l'écart des flux touristiques. On s'attable dans un intérieur bourgeois. Bonne cuisine actuelle et intéressante cave cosmopolite.
• Dit kleine familiehotel ligt "verscholen" in een dorp, op veilige afstand van het massatoerisme. Op de verdieping zijn enkele moderne kamers ingericht. Eetzaal met keurig interieur. Goede, eigentijdse keuken en interessante, kosmopolitische wijnkaart.

SCHERPENZEEL *Gelderland* 532 R 10 *et* 715 H 5 – *9 073 h.*
Amsterdam 64 – Utrecht 29 – Arnhem 34 – Amersfoort 13.

De Witte Holevoet, Holevoetplein 282, ✉ 3925 CA, ✆ (0 33) 277 91 11, *info@witteholevoet.nl, Fax (0 33) 277 26 13,* – 25 à 100. AE VISA JCB.
Repas *(fermé sam. midi et dim.)* *Lunch 28* – 27/38, – **22 ch** 80/105, – 1 suite.
• Grosse auberge villageoise où certains efforts viennent d'être consentis afin de mieux vous recevoir, notamment dans les chambres, amples et agréables à vivre. Salle des repas à touche "Art déco", agrandie d'une lumineuse véranda. Carte classique.
• In dit hotel-restaurant is nog niet zo lang geleden het nodige gedaan om de gasten optimaal te kunnen ontvangen, vooral in de kamers, die ruim en behaaglijk zijn. Eetzaal in art-decostijl en serre met veel licht. Klassieke kaart.

In deze gids
heeft eenzelfde letter of teken,
zwart of rood, dun of dik gedrukt
niet helemaal dezelfde betekenis.
Lees aandachtig de bladzijden met verklarende tekst.

SCHEVENINGEN *Zuid-Holland* 532 K 10 *et* 715 D 5 – *voir à Den Haag (Scheveningen).*

SCHIEDAM *Zuid-Holland* 532 L 11 *et* 715 E 6 – *voir à Rotterdam, environs.*

SCHIERMONNIKOOG (Ile de) *Fryslân* 531 W 2 *et* 715 J 1 – *voir à Waddeneilanden.*

SCHINNEN *Limburg* 532 U 17 *et* 715 I 9 – *13 680 h.*
Amsterdam 206 – Maastricht 20 – Aachen 25.

Aan Sjuuteeänjd, Dorpsstraat 74, ✉ 6365 BH, ✆ (0 46) 443 17 67, *info@sjuut.nl, Fax (0 46) 443 49 30,* – VISA.
fermé dern. sem. juin-prem. sem. juil., mardi et merc. – **Repas** *Lunch 29* – 33/68 bc.
• Si l'atmosphère d'une ferme rustique vous tente le temps d'un repas, retenez donc cette adresse située près de l'autoroute. La cour est en fleur à la belle saison.
• Zoekt u voor een etentje de sfeer van een rustieke boerderij ? Dan is dit adres vlak bij de snelweg geknipt voor u. 's Zomers staat de binnenhof in bloei.

SCHIPHOL *Noord-Holland* 531 N 9, 532 N 9 *et* 715 F 5 – *voir à Amsterdam, environs.*

SCHOONDIJKE *Zeeland* C *Sluis 24 755 h.* 532 G 14 *et* 715 B 7.
Amsterdam 212 – Brugge 34 – Middelburg 52 – Terneuzen 28.

de Zwaan, Prinses Beatrixstraat 1, ✉ 4507 AH, ✆ (0 117) 40 20 02, *ulijn@zeelandnet.nl, Fax (0 117) 40 12 12,* – rest, AE VISA
Repas carte 24 à 45 – **17 ch** 55/80 – ½ P 55/60.
• Auberge zélandaise connue sous la même enseigne depuis le début du 20e s. Chambres actuelles. Pour plus de tranquillité, préférez celles tournant le dos au carrefour.
• Dit hotel draagt sinds het begin van de 20e eeuw nog altijd dezelfde naam. Eigentijdse kamers. Zoekt u rust ? Vraag dan een kamer die het kruispunt de rug heeft toegekeerd.

SCHOONHOVEN *Zuid-Holland* 532 O 11 et 715 F 6 – *12 109 h.*

Voir *Collection d'horloges murales* dans le musée d'orfèvrerie et d'horlogerie (Nederlands Goud-, Zilver- en Klokkenmuseum) – route de digue de Gouda à Schoonhoven : parcours*.*

Stadhuisstraat 1, ✉ 2871 BR, ☎ (0 182) 38 50 09, Fax (0 182) 38 74 46.

Amsterdam 62 – Utrecht 32 – Den Haag 55 – Rotterdam 28.

Belvédère, Lekdijk West 4, ✉ 2871 MK, ☎ (0 182) 32 52 22, *info@hotelbelvedere.nl*, Fax (0 182) 32 52 29, ←, – 25 à 80. AE MC VISA

Repas *Lunch 23* – 25/43 bc – **12 ch** 65/95 – ½ P 65/80.

• Ancien "club house" sur digue, dans un bourg charmant. Six chambres ont vue sur la rivière, au même titre que la terrasse d'été dressée à l'ombre d'arbres centenaires. Salle des repas un rien mûrissante, avec le coup d'œil sur la Lek.

• Voormalig clubhuis op de dijk, in een charmant dorp. Zes kamers kijken uit op de rivier, net als het zomerterras in de schaduw van honderdjarige bomen. Ietwat verouderde restaurantzaal met uitzicht op de Lek.

de Hooiberg, Van Heuven Goedhartweg 1, ✉ 2871 AZ, ☎ (0 182) 38 36 01, *info@dehooiberg.nl*, – MC VISA

fermé lundi et mardi – **Repas** (dîner seult) 26/34.

• Restaurant aménagé dans une chaumière située aux portes de Schoonhoven, jolie localité perpétuant sa tradition de l'orfèvrerie et de l'horlogerie (musée, artisanat).

• Restaurant in een huis met rieten dak aan de rand van een charmant plaatsje, waar zilversmeden en klokkenmakers de traditie voortzetten (museum, ambachtskunst).

SCHOORL *Noord-Holland* C *Bergen 31 926 h.* 531 N 6 et 715 F 3.

Duinvoetweg 1, ✉ 1871 EA, ☎ (0 72) 581 31 00, info@vvvschoorl.nl, Fax (0 72) 509 49 28.

Amsterdam 49 – Alkmaar 10 – Den Helder 32.

Jan van Scorel, Heereweg 89, ✉ 1871 ED, ☎ (0 72) 509 44 44, *reserveringen@goldentulipjanvanscorel.nl*, Fax (0 72) 509 29 41, – 25 à 150. AE MC VISA. rest

Repas *Lunch 23* – carte env. 34 – **65 ch** 120/140, – 11 suites – ½ P 82.

• Junior suites, appartements et studios de diverses tailles : chacun trouvera un point de chute à sa mesure dans cette construction récente. Grand parking privé à deux pas. Ample salle à manger de notre temps.

• Junior suites, appartementen en studio's die in grootte variëren : voor eenieder is in dit vrij nieuwe pand wel een stekje op maat te vinden. Grote privéparking vlakbij. Ruime, eigentijdse eetzaal.

Merlet, Duinweg 15, ✉ 1871 AC, ☎ (0 72) 509 36 44, *merlet@worldonline.nl*, Fax (0 72) 509 14 06, ←, – 25 à 45. AE MC VISA JCB

fermé 31 déc.-14 janv. – **Repas** *(fermé sam. midi) Lunch 38* – carte env. 66 – **18 ch** 79/116 – ½ P 89/147.

• Un village entouré de polders boisés sert d'écrin à cette accueillante hôtellerie. Chambres personnalisées avec recherche, terrasse estivale champêtre et belle piscine. Table gastronomique agencée dans l'esprit "cottage" contemporain. Mets classico-inventifs.

• Een dorp te midden van beboste polders vormt het decor van dit gemoedelijke hotel. Smaakvol ingerichte kamers met een eigen karakter, zomerterras met landelijke entourage en mooi zwembad. Restaurant in cottagestijl. Klassieke en inventieve gerechten.

Spéc. Terrine de boudin noir et boudin de foie sauté, pommes caramélisées au Porto rouge (19 oct.-déc.). Langoustine gratinée au Parmesan et Saint-Jacques rissolées, sauce mousseuse de bouillabaise (17 juil.-19 oct.). Turbot braisé et tomates cerises confites au basilic (avril-déc.)

à Camperduin *Nord-Ouest : 6 km* C *Bergen :*

Strandhotel, Heereweg 395, ✉ 1871 GL, ☎ (0 72) 509 14 36, *info@strandhotel-camperduin.nl*, *Fax (0 72) 509 41 66*, – AE MC VISA. rest

Repas (dîner pour résidents seult) – **24 ch** 90/115 – ½ P 63/82.

• Petit hôtel balnéaire posté entre dunes et polders, à une encablure de la plage. Les chambres, munies d'un balcon ou d'une terrasse, promettent des nuitées récupératrices.

• Klein badhotel tussen duin en polder, dicht bij het strand. Kamers met balkon of terras, waar u weer helemaal tot rust zult komen.

SCHUDDEBEURS *Zeeland* 532 J 15 et 715 C 6 – *voir à Zierikzee.*

SEROOSKERKE *(Schouwen) Zeeland* C *Schouwen-Duiveland 34 503 h.* 532 H 12 *et* 715 C 6.
Amsterdam 137 – Middelburg 54 – Rotterdam 69.

XX **De Waag,** Dorpsplein 6, ✉ 4327 AG, ✆ (0 111) 67 15 70, *Fax (0 111) 67 29 08,* – P. AE MC VISA.
fermé 13 juin-1er juil., 27 déc.-5 janv., lundi et mardi – **Repas** (menu unique) *Lunch 40* – 60, ♀.
◆ Adresse villageoise dont l'enseigne ne laisse pas aisément deviner la couleur de l'assiette, volontiers inspirée par le pourtour méditerranéen. Menu annoncé de vive voix.
◆ Restaurant waarvan de naam niet bepaald kleur bekent. Dus verklappen wij maar wat u kunt verwachten : mediterraan georiënteerde keuken. Het menu wordt mondeling aangekondigd.

SIMPELVELD *Limburg* 532 U 17 *et* 715 I 9 – *11 418 h.*
Amsterdam 222 – Maastricht 29 – Heerlen 9 – Kerkrade 7 – Voerendaal 11.

XX **Bellevue** avec ch, Deus 1, ✉ 6369 GA, ✆ (0 45) 544 15 37, *info@hr-bellevue.nl, Fax (0 45) 544 68 80,* ≤ clochers environnants, , , – rest, TV P. AE MC VISA.
Repas *(fermé lundi, mardi et sam. midi) Lunch 27* – carte 43 à 61 – **10 ch** 51/78 – ½ P 57.
◆ Établissement familial perché tel un belvédère sur l'un des "sommets" des Pays-Bas. Le télescope installé devant le restaurant permet de viser 17 clochers à travers la plaine. Repas soigné dans une salle spacieuse et actuelle ou sur la terrasse panoramique.
◆ Dit familiehotel ligt als een belvédère boven op een van de "toppen" van Nederland. Door de telescoop voor het restaurant zijn in de vlakte beneden 17 klokkentorens te ontwaren. Verzorgde maaltijd in een ruime, eigentijdse eetzaal of op het panoramaterras.

SINT ANNA TER MUIDEN *Zeeland* 532 F 15 *et* 715 B 8 – *voir à Sluis.*

SINT NICOLAASGA (ST. NYK) *Fryslân* C *Skarsterlân 27 239 h.* 531 T 5 *et* 715 I 3.
18 *Legemeersterweg 16,* ✉ *8727 DS,* ✆ *(0 513) 49 94 66, Fax (0 513) 49 97 77.*
Amsterdam 117 – Groningen 74 – Leeuwarden 48 – Zwolle 64.

à Legemeer *(Legemar) Ouest : 4 km (direction Idskenhuizen (Jiskenhuzen)* C *Skarsterlân :*

Hampshire Inn sans rest, Legemeersterweg 1a (au golf), ✉ 8527 DS, ✆ (0 513) 43 29 99, *nicolaasga@hampshire-hotels.com, Fax (0 513) 43 47 94,* ≤, , , , , – TV P. AE MC VISA JCB
mars-nov. – **16 ch** 134.
◆ Une petite route de campagne dessert cette grosse villa jouxtant un terrain de golf. Chambres "king size" décorées à l'anglaise. Balcons avec vue sur les champs ou le green.
◆ Een buitenweggetje leidt naar deze robuuste villa naast een golfterrein. Kingsize kamers in Engelse stijl. De balkons kijken uit op de weidevelden of op de green.

SINT-OEDENRODE *Noord-Brabant* 532 R 13 *et* 715 H 7 – *17 113 h.*
9 *Schootsedijk 18,* ✉ *5491 TD,* ✆ *(0413) 47 92 56, Fax (0 413) 47 96 85.*
Amsterdam 107 – Eindhoven 17 – Nijmegen 48.

XXX ✿ **Wollerich,** Heuvel 23, ✉ 5492 AC, ✆ (0 413) 47 33 33, *wollerich@alliance.nl, Fax (0 413) 49 00 07,* – P. AE MC VISA.
fermé 24 déc., 31 déc.-13 janv., lundi, mardi du 26 juil. à fin août, sam. midi et dim. midi – **Repas** *Lunch 30* – 85 bc, carte 56 à 81, ♀.
◆ Au cœur du bourg, ancienne étude de notaire convertie en bonne maison de bouche. Salle à manger claire et spacieuse. Recettes au goût du jour teintées de touches créatives.
◆ Dit oude notariskantoor in het centrum is tot een goed restaurant verbouwd. Lichte en ruime eetzaal. Eigentijdse gerechten met een creatieve touch.
Spéc. Langoustines au four, coulis de homard et ail fumé. Foie d'oie aux pommes caramélisées et aigre-doux d'échalotes. Paupiettes de sole aux champignons des bois, sauce aux truffes

XX **de Rooise Boerderij,** Schijndelseweg 2, ✉ 5491 TB, ✆ (0 413) 47 49 01, *info@derooiseboerderij.nl, Fax (0 413) 47 65 65,* – P. AE MC VISA JCB.
fermé 26 juil.-17 août, fin déc.-1er janv., sam. midi, dim. midi et lundi – **Repas** *Lunch 27* – 34/83 bc.
◆ Ce confortable établissement met à profit une ferme brabançonne réaménagée dans l'esprit "rustico-actuel". Tea-room le dimanche après-midi. L'été, on ripaille en plein air.
◆ Dit comfortabele restaurant is gehuisvest in een Brabantse boerderij die in rustiek-eigentijdse stijl is verbouwd. Zondagnamiddag theesalon. 's Zomers wordt er buiten gegeten.

SINT WILLEBRORD *Noord-Brabant* C *Rucphen 22 601 h.* 532 M 13 *et* 715 E 7.
Amsterdam 122 – 's-Hertogenbosch 69 – Breda 17 – Rotterdam 59.

Nieuw Hong Kong, Dorpsstraat 138, ✉ 4711 EL, ℘ (0 165) 38 32 49, *Fax (0 165) 38 80 54,* , Cuisine asiatique – AE MC VISA.
fermé 2 prem. sem. juil. et lundi – **Repas** (déjeuner sur réservation) 27/35, ♀.
◆ Restaurant chinois à débusquer au centre d'une petite localité. La salle à manger, soigneusement agencée, s'anime de quelques statues. Service gentil et efficace.
◆ Chinees restaurant in het centrum van het plaatsje. De verzorgd ingerichte eetzaal is met enkele beelden opgeluisterd. Vriendelijke en efficiënte bediening.

SITTARD *Limburg* C *Sittard-Geleen 97 953 h.* 532 U 17 *et* 715 I 8.
au Sud : 8 km à Beek ℘ (0 43) 358 99 99, Fax (0 43) 358 99 88.
Rosmolenstraat 2, ✉ 6131 HX, ℘ (0 46) 631 06 20, info@b-toerisme.nl, Fax (0 46) 631 06 25.
Amsterdam 194 – Maastricht 29 – Eindhoven 66 – Roermond 27 – Aachen 36.

De Limbourg, Markt 22, ✉ 6131 EK, ℘ (0 46) 451 81 51, *hoteldelimbourg@hetnet.nl, Fax (0 46) 452 34 86,* – TV P – 25 à 60. AE D MC VISA JCB
Repas (taverne-rest) *Lunch 25* – carte 28 à 37, ♀ – **22 ch** 81/112.
◆ Sur le Markt d'une place forte jadis très disputée, hôtel familial dont toutes les chambres ont été rafraîchies. Les plus grandes occupent une annexe voisine. Restaurant avec terrasse d'été dressée devant le portail de la baroque St.-Michielskerk.
◆ In dit familiehotel op de Markt van een vroeger zeer betwiste vestingstad zijn alle kamers opgeknapt. De grootste zijn in de naburige dependance ingericht. Restaurant met zomerterras tegenover het portaal van de barokke St.-Michielskerk.

De Prins, Rijksweg Zuid 25, ✉ 6131 AL, ℘ (0 46) 451 50 41, *info@hoteldeprins.nl, Fax (0 46) 451 46 41,* – TV P – 25 à 60. AE D MC VISA JCB. rest
fermé 27 déc.-4 janv. – **Repas** *(fermé sam. et dim.) Lunch 10* – carte env. 36 – **23 ch** 62/98 – ½ P 72/93.
◆ Cette auberge évoquant vaguement un chalet monte la garde aux portes du centre-ville. Les chambres, de tailles respectables, offrent un confort fonctionnel. Salle des repas gentiment désuète. En saison, l'asperge est mise à l'honneur.
◆ Dit hotel aan de rand van het centrum heeft iets weg van een chalet. De kamers zijn respectabel van afmeting en bieden een functioneel comfort. Ietwat ouderwetse eetzaal, waar in het seizoen de asperge hoog in het prinselijk vaandel staat.

Silvester's, Paardestraat 25, ✉ 6131 HA, ℘ (0 46) 451 12 24, *genieten@silvesters.nl, Fax (0 46) 458 48 66,* – AE MC VISA.
fermé du 15 au 29 fév., du 1er au 15 août, sam. midi, dim. midi et lundi – **Repas** *Lunch 25* – 38, ♀.
◆ Accueil tout sourire, salle de restaurant intime et chaleureuse, carte actuelle assez ramassée mais appétissante et service avenant : quatre bonnes raisons de s'attabler ici !
◆ Hartelijke ontvangst, warme en gemoedelijke sfeer, vrij beperkte maar smaakvolle eigentijdse kaart en vriendelijke service : vier goede redenen om hier aan tafel te gaan !

à Doenrade *Sud : 6 km par N 276* C *Schinnen 13 680 h :*

Kasteel Doenrade , Limpensweg 20 (Klein-Doenrade), ✉ 6439 BE, ℘ (0 46) 442 41 41, *info@kasteeldoenrade.nl, Fax (0 46) 442 40 30,* , , , – TV P – 25 à 70. AE MC VISA. rest
Repas carte env. 49 – **24 ch** 135, – 1 suite – ½ P 118/243.
◆ En quête d'un point de chute tranquille à la campagne pour poser sa valise et décompresser ? Cette jolie ferme-château est alors toute indiquée. Chambres personnalisées. Agréable restaurant au goût du jour. D'avril à juin, spécialité d'asperges.
◆ Op zoek naar een rustig adres op het platteland om even aan de hectiek van alledag te ontsnappen ? Dan is deze mooie kasteelhoeve de aangewezen plek. Kamers met een eigen karakter. Comfortabel restaurant met een eigentijdse keuken. Van april tot juni : asperges !

à Munstergeleen *Sud : 3 km* C *Sittard-Geleen :*

Zelissen, Houbeneindstraat 4, ✉ 6151 CR, ℘ (0 46) 451 90 27, *nzelissen@vodafone.nl, Fax (0 46) 411 14 47* – AE MC VISA JCB
fermé 1 sem. carnaval, du 13 au 29 juil., 29 déc.-8 janv., mardi et merc. – **Repas** (déjeuner sur réservation) 24/30.
◆ Cette enseigne, connue depuis plus de trente ans à Munstergeleen, signale un restaurant familial animé par le souci de bien faire. Repas classique actualisé. Salle éclaircie.
◆ Een familierestaurant dat al ruim dertig jaar een vertrouwd adres is en waar men altijd klaarstaat voor zijn gasten. Klassieke borden in een modern jasje. Opgefriste eetzaal.

SLENAKEN *Limburg* C *Gulpen-Wittem 15 435 h.* 532 U 18 et 715 I 9.
Voir *Route de Epen* ≤★.
Amsterdam 230 – Maastricht 19 – Aachen 20.

Klein Zwitserland ⛵, Grensweg 11, ✉ 6277 NA, ☎ (0 43) 457 32 91, *info@kleinzwitserland.com, Fax (0 43) 457 32 94,* ≤ campagne, – |♦|, ≡ rest, TV P – 25. AE MC VISA.
fermé 31 déc.-19 fév. – **Repas** *(fermé après 20 h)* 30, ♀ – **26 ch** ⊒ 90/112, – 1 suite.
• Paisible hôtel posté à flanc de colline, la "Petite Suisse" offre une vue imprenable sur la campagne boisée. Chambres avec balcon, suite et junior suite de bon séjour. Ample salle à manger classiquement aménagée. Cuisine actualisée.
• Dit rustig gelegen hotel op een heuvel net buiten het dorp kijkt vrij uit over het bosrijke, glooiende landschap. Kamers met balkon, suite en junior suite voor een comfortabel verblijf. Grote, klassiek ingerichte eetzaal. Eigentijdse keuken.

Het Gulpdal, Dorpsstraat 40, ✉ 6277 NE, ☎ (0 43) 457 33 15, *info@gulpdal.nl, Fax (0 43) 457 33 16,* ≤, ≘s, , , , – |♦|, ≡ rest, TV P. AE ① MC VISA JCB. rest
fermé janv.-fév. – **Repas** (résidents seult) – **19 ch** ⊒ 95/130, – 5 suites – ½ P 72/99.
• Villa à l'anglaise agrémentée d'un adorable jardin paysager - idéal pour le farniente - procurant un panorama bucolique. Salon cossu, grandes chambres et junior suites.
• Villa in Engelse stijl met een verrukkelijke landschapstuin als idyllisch decor om lekker luierend in weg te dromen. Deftige lounge, grote kamers en junior suites.

Slenaker Vallei, Dorpsstraat 1, ✉ 6277 NC, ☎ (0 43) 457 35 41, *info@slenakervallei.nl, Fax (0 43) 457 26 28,* ≤, – |♦| TV P – 25 à 50. AE MC VISA. rest
fermé 31 déc.-1er janv. – **Repas** Lunch 27 – carte 36 à 69, ♀ – **20 ch** ⊒ 67/110 – ½ P 65/90.
• La majorité des chambres de cette hostellerie établie au centre de Slenaken profite d'un coup d'œil champêtre. Terrasse courtisée par les touristes sur le devant. Table au décor néo-rustique. Repas en plein air par beau temps.
• De meeste kamers van dit hotel in het centrum kijken uit op het prachtige Gulper landschap. Het terras aan de voorkant is bij toeristen erg in trek. Restaurant met neorustiek decor. Bij mooi weer wordt buiten geserveerd.

Slenaken, Heyenratherweg 4, ✉ 6276 PC, ☎ (0 43) 457 35 46, *slenaken@bestwestern.nl, Fax (0 43) 457 20 92,* – |♦| TV P. AE ① MC VISA. rest
Repas (résidents seult) – **37 ch** ⊒ 82/129 – ½ P 109/129.
• Hôtel de chaîne jouant la carte frontalière : l'Allemagne, et surtout la Belgique, sont rapidement accessibles. Chambres confortables et nombreuses junior suites.
• Ketenhotel dat zijn troeven uitspeelt in het grensgebied : Duitsland en vooral België zijn snel te bereiken. Comfortabele kamers en veel junior suites.

SLUIS *Zeeland* C *Sluis 24 755 h.* 532 F 15 et 715 B 8.
i *St-Annastraat 15,* ✉ *4524 JB,* ☎ *(0 117) 46 17 00, sluis@vvvzvl.nl, Fax (0 117) 46 26 84.*
Amsterdam 226 – Brugge 21 – Middelburg 67 – Knokke-Heist 9.

XXX ✿✿ **Oud Sluis** (Herman), Beestenmarkt 2, ✉ 4524 EA, ☎ (0 117) 46 12 69, *oudsluis@zeelandnet.nl, Fax (0 117) 46 30 05,* , Produits de la mer – AE ① MC VISA.
fermé prem. sem. avril, 2 sem. en juin, 2 sem. en oct., dern. sem. déc., lundi et mardi – **Repas** Lunch 45 – 63/85, carte env. 105, ♀.
• Sur une placette effervescente, typique petite auberge où se concocte une cuisine originale et raffinée, à base de produits de la mer. Service dans les règles de l'art.
• Kleine, karakteristieke herberg aan een bruisend pleintje, die met producten uit de zee een originele, geraffineerde keuken bereidt. Bediening volgens de regelen der kunst.
Spéc. 6 préparations d'huîtres de Zélande (sept.-avril). Langoustines de trois façons (mai-août). Filets de sole grillés et tempura d'anguilles régionales au jus de limon

X **Gasterij Balmoral,** Kaai 16, ✉ 4524 CK, ☎ (0 117) 46 14 98, *ha.rezouga@planet.nl, Fax (0 117) 46 18 07,* – AE ① MC VISA JCB
fermé dern. sem. janv.-2 prem. sem. fév. et vend. – **Repas** 19/31 bc.
• Ce restaurant conviant à sa table habitués et touristes de passage propose un choix de plats simples à prix plancher. L'après-midi, l'endroit se transforme en tea-room.
• Dit restaurant biedt vaste gasten en passanten een keur van eenvoudige gerechten voor een "bodemprijs". 's Namiddags verandert het in theesalon.

à Heille *Sud-Est : 5 km* C *Sluis :*

XX **De Schaapskooi,** Zuiderbruggeweg 23, ✉ 4524 KH, ☎ (0 117) 49 16 00, *info@deschaapskooi.nl, Fax (0 117) 49 22 19,* – P. AE MC VISA
fermé 2 prem. sem. fév., dern. sem. juin, 2 sem. en oct., lundi soir sauf en juil.-août et mardi – **Repas** carte 37 à 75.
• Maison aux abords champêtres dont l'enseigne (La Bergerie) résume le passé. Salle à manger rustique. Naturellement, les plats d'agneau participent au succès de la carte.
• De naam verwijst naar de vroegere bestemming van dit landelijk gelegen restaurant en verklaart de lamsgerechten op de succesvolle kaart. Rustiek ingerichte eetzaal.

à Retranchement *Nord : 6 km* 🄲 *Sluis :*

De Witte Koksmuts, Kanaalweg 8, ✉ 4525 NA, ✆ (0 117) 39 16 87, *Fax (0 117) 39 20 30*, ←, terrasse – P. AE MC
fermé 15 nov.-17 déc., merc. et jeudi – **Repas** carte 29 à 57.
◆ Polders, digue et canal procurent un environnement agréable à ce restaurant dont la carte "en pince" pour le tourteau. Préparations actuelles. Terrasse d'été.
◆ Polders, dijk en kanaal vormen een aangenaam decor voor dit restaurant, waar de kaart de krab behoorlijk in de tang heeft. Eigentijdse gerechten. Zomerterras.

à Sint Anna ter Muiden *Nord-Ouest : 2 km* 🄲 *Sluis :*

De Vijverhoeve, Greveningseweg 2, ✉ 4524 JK, ✆ (0 117) 46 13 94, *vijverhoeve@zeelandnet.nl*, terrasse – P. AE DC MC VISA JCB
fermé merc., jeudi et vend. midi – **Repas** 38/70, ♀.
◆ Fermette située dans un hameau agreste. Sur l'arrière, mini-terrasse d'été donnant sur un jardin avec tonnelle et étang. Foie gras, coquilles et homards règnent en cuisine.
◆ Boerderijtje in een landelijk dorp. Het miniterras aan de achterkant ligt aan een tuin met prieel en vijver. Ganzenlever, schelpdieren en kreeft voeren de boventoon.

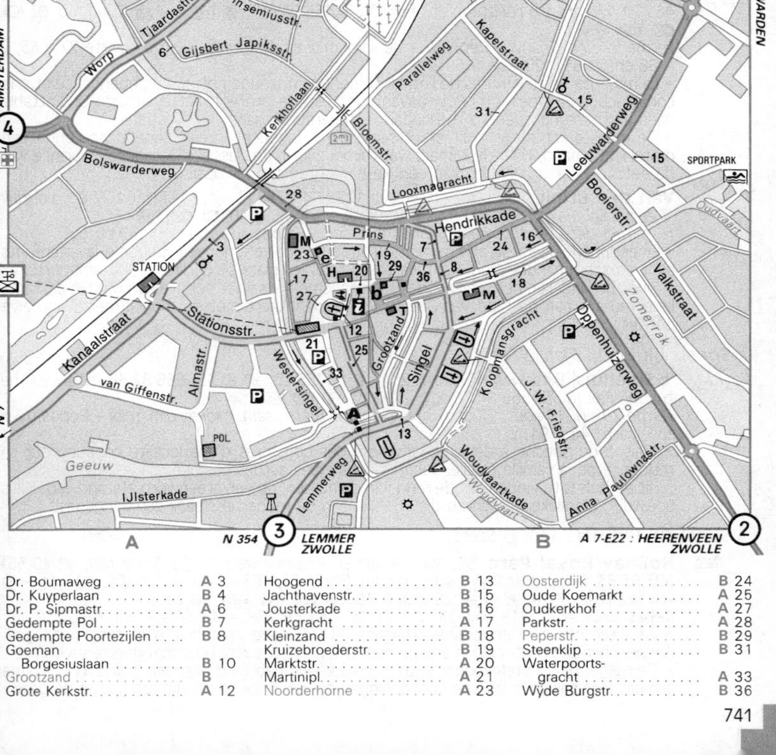

Dr. Boumaweg	A 3	Hoogend	B 13	Oosterdijk	B 24
Dr. Kuyperlaan	B 4	Jachthavenstr.	B 15	Oude Koemarkt	A 25
Dr. P. Sipmastr.	A 6	Jousterkade	B 16	Oudkerkhof	A 27
Gedempte Pol	B 7	Kerkgracht	A 17	Parkstr.	A 28
Gedempte Poortezijlen	B 8	Kleinzand	B 18	Peperstr.	B 29
Goeman Borgesiuslaan	B 10	Kruizebroederstr.	B 19	Steenklip	B 31
Grootzand	B	Marktstr.	A 20	Waterpoortsgracht	A 33
Grote Kerkstr.	A 12	Martinipl.	A 21	Wÿde Burgstr.	B 36
		Noorderhorne	A 23		

SNEEK (SNITS) *Fryslân* 531 T 4 *et* 715 I 2 – *32 504 h.*

Voir *Porte d'eau★ (Waterpoort)* A **A.**

Env. *par ③ à Sloten (Sleat)★ (ville fortifiée).*

Exc. *Circuit en Frise Méridionale★.*

Marktstraat 18, ✉ 8601 CV, ☎ (0 515) 41 40 96, Fax (0 58) 234 06 80.

Amsterdam 125 ④ – Leeuwarden 27 ① – Groningen 78 ② – Zwolle 74 ③

Plan page précédente

Hanenburg, Wijde Noorderhorne 2, ✉ 8601 EB, ☎ (0 515) 41 25 70, *info@hotelhanenburg.nl, Fax (0 515) 42 58 95,* – – 25 à 60. AE VISA. A e
Repas ***Piccolo*** *(fermé dim. midi)* *Lunch 33* – 42/59, ♀ – **19 ch** 55/105 – ½ P 55/75.
◆ Cet hôtel tenu en famille depuis quatre générations est implanté dans une rue commerçante du centre. Plusieurs chambres ont une salle de bains équipée d'un jacuzzi. Salle de restaurant éclairée par de grands lustres contemporains. Cuisine au goût du jour.
◆ Inmiddels staat de vierde generatie aan het roer van dit familiehotel, dat te vinden is in een winkelstraat in het centrum. Sommige kamers hebben een badkamer met jacuzzi. De eetzaal wordt verlicht door prachtige, moderne luchters. Eigentijdse keuken.

Onder de Linden, Marktstraat 30, ✉ 8601 CV, ☎ (0 515) 41 26 54, *info@restaurantonderdelinden.nl, Fax (0 515) 42 77 15,* , Taverne-rest – VISA B b
fermé 27 déc.-15 janv. et lundi – **Repas** *Lunch 18* – 21/24, ♀.
◆ Vénérable auberge rajeunie surveillant le Markt, où une terrasse d'été est dressée "sous les tilleuls" (onder de linden). Lunch régional et menu-choix à prix d'ami.
◆ Restaurant in een eerbiedwaardig, gerenoveerd pand aan de Markt, waar 's zomers onder de linden een terras wordt uitgezet. Regionale lunch en keuzemenu voor een vriendenprijs.

SOEST *Utrecht* 532 Q 9 *et* 715 G 5 – *44 705 h.*

Steenhoffstraat 9b, ✉ 3764 BH, ☎ (0 35) 601 20 75, info@vvv-soest.nl, Fax (0 35) 602 80 17.

Amsterdam 42 – Utrecht 18 – Amersfoort 7.

Het Witte Huis, Birkstraat 138 (Sud-Ouest : 3 km sur N 221), ✉ 3768 HN, ☎ (0 33) 461 71 47, *info@h-r-wittehuis.nl, Fax (0 33) 465 05 66* – – 25 à 160. AE VISA JCB
fermé 27 déc.-5 janv. – **Repas** *(fermé sam. midi et dim. midi)* *Lunch 20* – carte 27 à 43, ♀ – **68 ch** 83/120 – ½ P 60.
◆ La majorité des chambres de l'établissement se distribue entre une dépendance et une construction de type motel. Pour davantage d'espace, préférez cette dernière. On s'attable dans un cadre bourgeois à l'hollandaise. Préparations sans complications.
◆ De meeste kamers van dit etablissement zijn ingericht in een dependance en in een motelachtig pand, waar de kamers wat ruimer zijn. In de klassieke Hollandse ambiance van de eetzaal kunt u genieten van eerlijke gerechten zonder opsmuk.

Van den Brink, Soesterbergsestraat 122, ✉ 3768 EL, ☎ (0 35) 601 27 06, *vdbrink@eetvilla.nl, Fax (0 35) 601 97 18,* – – 25 à 40. AE VISA
fermé 31 déc.-12 janv., sam. midi et dim. soir – **Repas** *Lunch 29* – 34/69 bc, ♀.
◆ En périphérie de Soest, affaire familiale où souffle un vent nouveau depuis que les enfants sont aux commandes. Bon menu-carte où tous les plats se déclinent en demi portion.
◆ Sinds de kinderen het roer hebben overgenomen, waait er een nieuwe wind in dit familierestaurant aan de rand van Soest. Goede menukaart met de mogelijkheid van halve porties.

à Soestdijk *Nord : 3 km* C *Soest :*

't Spiehuis, Biltseweg 45 (sur N 234), ✉ 3763 LD, ☎ (0 35) 666 82 36, *spiehuis@hetnet.nl, Fax (0 35) 666 84 76,* – . AE VISA.
fermé 20 juil.-13 août, 27 déc.-8 janv., mardi, merc., sam. midi et dim. midi – **Repas** *Lunch 30* – carte 44 à 91, ♀.
◆ Maison de bouche à dénicher en lisière des bois, près d'une localité connue pour sa résidence de la famille royale. Recettes classiques actualisées avec sagesse.
◆ Dit eethuis is te vinden aan de rand van de bossen, op een steenworp afstand van Paleis Soestdijk. Klassieke gerechten die wijselijk aan de moderne smaak zijn aangepast.

à Soestduinen *Sud : 3 km* C *Soest :*

Holiday Royal Parc , Van Weerden Poelmanweg 4, ✉ 3788 MN, ☎ (0 35) 603 83 83, *info_soestduinen@hilton.com, Fax (0 35) 603 83 00,* , , , – , rest, – 25 à 500. AE VISA JCB. rest
Repas *Lunch 33* – carte env. 35, ♀ – 19 – **81 ch** 178, – 4 suites – ½ P 166/229.
◆ Architecture contemporaine profitant du voisinage immédiat d'un terrain de golf. Amples chambres avec balcon, équipements modernes et belle terrasse ouverte sur le green.
◆ Een eigentijds hotelgebouw in de onmiddellijke nabijheid van een golfterrein. Ruime kamers met balkon, moderne voorzieningen en een fraai terras dat uitkijkt op de green.

SOESTDIJK *Utrecht* 532 Q 9 *et* 715 G 5 – *voir à Soest.*

SOESTDUINEN *Utrecht* 532 Q 10 *et* 715 G 5 – *voir à Soest.*

SOMEREN *Noord-Brabant* 532 T 14 *et* 715 I 7 – *18 480 h.*
Amsterdam 151 – Eindhoven 26 – 's-Hertogenbosch 52 – Helmond 13 – Venlo 37.

XX **Gasterij De Zeuve Meeren** avec ch, Wilhelminaplein 14, ✉ 5711 EK, ☎ (0 493) 49 27 28, *info@gasterij-ezeuvemeeren.nl, Fax (0 493) 47 01 12,* – TV. AE ① MC VISA JCB. rest
fermé 2 sem. vacances bâtiment, 1 sem. en janv. et merc. – **Repas** (déjeuner sur réservation) 32/64 bc – **5 ch** 48/65 – ½ P 73.
◆ Cette adresse du centre-ville, située en léger retrait de la place du marché, a conquis de nombreuses papilles dans le secteur. Chambres de mise simple.
◆ Dit adres in het centrum, iets teruggetrokken van het marktplein, heeft heel wat smaakpapillen voor zich gewonnen. Eenvoudige kamers.

SON *Noord-Brabant* C *Son en Breugel 14 805 h.* 532 R 13 *et* 715 H 7.
Amsterdam 114 – Eindhoven 10 – Helmond 17 – Nijmegen 53.

la Sonnerie, Nieuwstraat 45, ✉ 5691 AB, ☎ (0 499) 46 02 22, *receptie@sonnerie.nl, Fax (0 499) 46 09 75,* – TV P – 25 à 100. AE ① MC VISA JCB.
Repas *(fermé carnaval et du 20 au 23 fév.)* Lunch 23 – 27/32 – 13 – **30 ch** 80/95 – ½ P 115/145.
◆ Cet ancien cloître adroitement converti en hôtel familial renferme diverses catégories de chambres. La chapelle a été réaffectée en salle de conférences et de banquets. Brasserie proposant une cuisine actuelle relevée d'un zeste d'originalité.
◆ Dit voormalige klooster is praktisch verbouwd tot familiehotel en herbergt verschillende categorieën kamers. De kapel doet nu dienst als zaal voor conferenties en partijen. De brasserie heeft een eigentijdse keuken met een snufje originaliteit.

SPAARNDAM *Noord-Holland* C *Haarlemmerliede en Spaarnwoude 5 547 h.* 532 N 8 *et* 715 F 4.
18 9 *au Nord : 8 km à Velsen-Zuid, Het Hoge Land 2,* ✉ *1981 LT, Recreatieoord Spaarnwoude* ☎ *(0 23) 538 27 08, Fax (0 23) 538 72 74.*
Amsterdam 18 – Haarlem 11 – Alkmaar 28.

X **Het Stille Water,** Oostkolk 19, ✉ 2063 JV, ☎ (0 23) 537 13 94, *stillewater@hetnet.nl, Fax (0 23) 539 59 64,* – AE ① MC VISA JCB
fermé fin déc. et mardi – **Repas** (dîner seult) carte env. 42, ♀.
◆ Maison du 18e s. alanguie près d'un pittoresque bassin d'écluse bordé de marronniers. Agencement intérieur contemporain et mise en place soignée. Plats de saison.
◆ Pand uit de 18e eeuw vlak bij een pittoreske sluis met kastanjebomen langs het water. Hedendaags interieur en verzorgde aankleding. Seizoengerechten.

SPAKENBURG *Utrecht* 532 R 9 *et* 715 H 5 – *voir à Bunschoten-Spakenburg.*

SPIER *Drenthe* 531 X 6 *et* 715 K 3 – *voir à Beilen.*

SPIJKENISSE *Zuid-Holland* 532 K 11 *et* 715 D 6 – *75 147 h.*
Amsterdam 92 – Rotterdam 16.

Carlton Oasis, Curieweg 1 (Sud : 1 km), ✉ 3208 KJ, ☎ (0 181) 62 52 22, *info@oasis.carlton.nl, Fax (0 181) 61 10 94,* – ch, TV P – 40 à 250. AE ① MC VISA
Repas (ouvert jusqu'à 23 h 30) Lunch 23 – carte 29 à 40 – 18 – **139 ch** 205/240.
◆ Point de chute prisé des hommes d'affaires, cet immeuble récent, assez proche de l'Europoort, est construit dans un secteur industriel. Chambres confortables et junior suites. Alternative restaurant ou brasserie.
◆ Dit nieuwe gebouw op een industrieterrein, aan de rand van Spijkenisse en op een steenworp afstand van de Europoort, is een ideaal logeeradres voor zakenmensen. Comfortabele kamers en junior suites. Restaurant en brasserie.

XX **'t Ganzengors,** Oostkade 4, ✉ 3201 AM, ☎ (0 181) 61 25 78, *info@ganzengors.nl, Fax (0 181) 61 77 32* – P. AE ① MC VISA JCB
fermé lundi – **Repas** (dîner seult) 30/68 bc, ♀.
◆ Affaire familiale gardant les portes d'un centre commercial au cœur de la localité. Salon de dégustation et wine-bar pour l'apéritif.
◆ Familierestaurant naast de ingang van een winkelcentrum in het hartje van de stad. Restaurantgedeelte en voor het aperitief een wijnbar.

STAPHORST *Overijssel* 531 W 7 *et* 715 J 4 – *15 438 h.*

Voir *Ville typique★ : fermes★, costume traditionnel★.*

Amsterdam 128 – Zwolle 18 – Groningen 83 – Leeuwarden 74.

Waanders, Rijksweg 12, ✉ 7951 DH, ✆ (0 522) 46 18 88, *hotel.waanders@tref.nl, Fax (0 522) 46 10 93,* – |‡|, ▤ rest, TV ♿ – 25 à 300. AE ◑ MC VISA JCB
Repas carte 32 à 48 – **24 ch** ☕ 67/95 – ½ P 72.
◆ Près de l'autoroute, établissement exploité de père en fils depuis 1901. Une aile plus récente regroupe de plain-pied la moitié des chambres, prévues pour deux personnes. À table, plats sagement traditionnels.
◆ Dit hotel vlak bij de snelweg gaat al sinds 1901 van vader op zoon over. In een nieuwere vleugel is de helft van de kamers (tweepersoons) ondergebracht, die allemaal op de begane grond liggen. In de eetzaal worden traditionele gerechten geserveerd.

Het Boerengerecht, Middenwolderweg 2, ✉ 7951 EC, ✆ (0 522) 46 19 67, *Fax (0 522) 46 11 66,* – P. AE MC VISA
fermé mi-juil.-mi-août, fin déc.-début janv. et dim. – **Repas** *Lunch 30* – carte 42 à 57, ♀.
◆ Carreaux de faïence, lit clos, poêles et poutres d'époque confèrent un cachet rustique, typiquement "staphortsien", à cette ferme du 17ᵉ s. Goûteuse cuisine d'aujourd'hui.
◆ Oude plavuizen, authentieke bedstee, originele kachels en balken geven deze typisch Staphorster boerderij uit de 17e eeuw een rustiek cachet. Smaakvolle, eigentijdse keuken.

De Molenmeester, Gemeenteweg 364 (Est : 3 km), ✉ 7951 PG, ✆ (0 522) 46 31 16, *demolenmeester@hetnet.nl, Fax (0 522) 46 09 34,* , Ouvert jusqu'à 23 h – P. AE MC VISA JCB
fermé sam. midi, dim. midi, lundi et mardi – **Repas** 28/38.
◆ Maison de brique située aux abords de Staphorst. Derrière le bâtiment, un moulin datant des années 1850 - toujours en activité - trône au jardin. Ambiance chaleureuse.
◆ Restaurant in een bakstenen huis aan de rand van het dorp. Aan de tuinkant staat een molen uit omstreeks 1850, die nog altijd in bedrijf is. Warme ambiance.

STEENWIJK *Overijssel* C *Steenwijkerland 41 870 h.* 531 V 6 *et* 715 J 3.

Markt 60, ✉ 8331 HK, ✆ 0 900-567 46 37, steenwijk@kopvanoverijssel.nl, Fax (0 521) 51 17 79.

Amsterdam 148 – Zwolle 38 – Assen 55 – Leeuwarden 54.

De "Eese" , Duivenslaagte 2 (Nord : 5,5 km, direction Frederiksoord à De Bult), ✉ 8346 KH, ✆ (0 521) 51 14 54, *info@eese.nl, Fax (0 521) 51 13 16,* , , , , – |‡| , ▤ rest, TV P – 80 à 180. AE ◑ MC VISA.
Repas *Lunch 15* – carte 30 à 59, ♀ – **56 ch** ☕ 70/125 – ½ P 63/75.
◆ Aux avant-postes de Steenwijk, paisible complexe hôtelier où vous séjournerez dans des chambres offrant un bon niveau de confort. Huit salles accueillent les séminaires. Carte actuelle avec lunch et menus. Recettes d'asperges en saison. Terrasse estivale.
◆ De kamers in dit rustig gelegen hotelcomplex aan de rand van Steenwijk bieden een goed comfort. Het etablissement beschikt over acht zalen voor seminars. Actuele kaart met lunch en menu's. Aspergegerechten in het seizoen. Zomerterras.

Hiddingerberg, Woldmeentherand 15 (près A 32, sortie ⑥), ✉ 8332 JE, ✆ (0 521) 51 23 11, *balie@hiddingerberg.nl, Fax (0 521) 51 20 64,* , – TV P – 25 à 500. AE MC VISA.
fermé 31 déc.-1ᵉʳ janv. – **Repas** carte env. 30 – **36 ch** ☕ 57/80 – ½ P 75/98.
◆ Ce petit hôtel d'étape proche de l'autoroute se double d'un grand centre de congrès. Les chambres, insonorisées et assez plaisantes à vivre, se distribuent de plain-pied. À l'heure des repas, snacks et choix de préparations plus traditionnelles.
◆ Dit kleine etappehotel vlak bij de snelweg runt tevens een groot zalencentrum. De vrij comfortabele kamers zijn voorzien van geluidsisolatie en liggen op de begane grond. Er worden zowel kleinere hapjes als een keur van traditionele gerechten geserveerd.

STEIN *Limburg* 532 T 17 *et* 715 I 9 – *26 520 h.*

Amsterdam 197 – Maastricht 21 – Roermond 30 – Aachen 36.

à Urmond *Nord : 3 km* C *Stein :*

Stein-Urmond, Mauritslaan 65 (près A 2), ✉ 6129 EL, ✆ (0 46) 433 85 73, *frontask@stein.valk.com, Fax (0 46) 433 86 86,* , , – |‡| TV ♿ P – 25 à 400. AE ◑ MC VISA
Repas (ouvert jusqu'à 23 h) *Lunch 13* – carte 22 à 33 – ☕ 8 – **162 ch** 63/75, – 1 suite – ½ P 57/79.
◆ Ce motel typique de la chaîne Van der Valk abrite des chambres à l'identique, une poignée de junior suites, ainsi qu'un appartement avec kitchenette.
◆ Dit motel is karakteristiek voor de Van der Valk-keten en herbergt identieke kamers, een handjevol junior suites en een appartement met kitchenette.

STELLENDAM *Zuid-Holland* © *Goedereede 11 363 h.* 532 J 12 *et* 715 D 6.
Amsterdam 115 – Rotterdam 43 – Den Haag 67 – Middelburg 60.

de Gard, Meester Iman Caustraat 4, ✉ 3251 AR, ✆ (0 187) 49 90 92, *info@degard.nl* – MC VISA JCB
fermé 11 juil.-10 août, lundi et mardi – **Repas** (déjeuner sur réservation) 55/80 bc, ♀.
◆ Agréable petit restaurant où l'on se sent directement entre de bonnes mains. La décoration intérieure, tendance design, est très réussie, et le menu du chef, fort demandé.
◆ Aangenaam restaurantje waar u direct voelt dat u in goede handen bent. Het interieur heeft een zeer geslaagd designdecor. Het menu van de chef is uitermate favoriet.

STEVENSWEERT *Limburg* © *Maasbracht 13 697 h.* 532 U 16 *et* 715 I 8.
Amsterdam 184 – Maastricht 37 – Eindhoven 58 – Venlo 39.

Herberg Stadt Stevenswaert, Veldstraat Oost 1, ✉ 6107 AS, ✆ (0 475) 55 23 76, *stadt-stevenswaert@hetnet.nl, Fax (0 475) 55 23 76,* – AE MC VISA
fermé 1 sem. en oct., 3 sem. en janv. et lundi – **Repas** *Lunch 30* – 40/70 bc, ♀.
◆ Sympathique auberge familiale montant la garde près du Markt, au centre de Stevensweert. Repas au goût du jour autour d'une vieille cheminée et son poêle en fonte.
◆ Deze sympathieke familieherberg staat in het centrum vlak bij de Markt. Bij de oude schouw met gietijzeren potkachel kunnen de gasten genieten van een eigentijdse maaltijd.

TEGELEN *Limburg* 532 V 14 *et* 715 J 7 – *voir à Venlo.*

TERBORG *Gelderland* © *Wisch 19 599 h.* 532 X 11 *et* 715 K 6.
Amsterdam 135 – Arnhem 37 – Enschede 58.

't Hoeckhuys, Stationsweg 16, ✉ 7061 CT, ✆ (0 315) 32 39 33, *info@hoeckhuys.nl, Fax (0 315) 33 04 97,* – P. AE ⓓ MC VISA
fermé 5 juil.-2 août et merc. – **Repas** (déjeuner sur réservation) 33/38.
◆ En face de la gare, maison de notable vous réservant un bon accueil familial. Salle à manger bien installée, cuisine classique-actuelle, jardins d'hiver et terrasse abritée.
◆ In dit statige herenhuis tegenover het station wacht u een hartelijk onthaal. Goed ingerichte eetzaal, klassiek-eigentijdse keuken, serres en beschut terras.

TERNEUZEN *Zeeland* 532 I 14 *et* 715 C 7 – *55 478 h.*
ℹ *Markt 11, ✉ 4531 EP, ✆ (0 115) 69 59 76, terneuzen@vvvzvl.nl, Fax (0 115) 64 87 70.*
Amsterdam 193 – Middelburg 33 – Antwerpen 56 – Brugge 58 – Gent 39.

L'Escaut, Scheldekade 65, ✉ 4531 EJ, ✆ (0 115) 69 48 55, *lescaut@zeelandnet.nl, Fax (0 115) 62 09 81,* – TV – 25 à 100. AE ⓓ MC VISA. rest
fermé 31 déc.-1er janv. – **Repas** *(fermé sam. midi et dim. midi)* carte 34 à 60 – 14 – **28 ch** 127/130 – ½ P 130/157.
◆ Ce petit immeuble actuel posté à proximité des bouches de l'Escaut - d'où l'enseigne - renferme des chambres de tailles très correctes mais assez sobrement équipées. Restaurant avec terrasse estivale. Carte au goût du jour.
◆ Dit kleine, actuele pand vlak bij de monding van de Schelde - vandaar de naam - herbergt kamers die goed van afmeting zijn maar een vrij eenvoudig comfort bieden. Restaurant met zomerterras. Eigentijdse kaart.

Churchill, Churchilllaan 700, ✉ 4532 JB, ✆ (0 115) 62 11 20, *info@hampshire-churchill.nl, Fax (0 115) 69 73 93,* – TV P – 25 à 125. AE ⓓ MC VISA.
Repas *Lunch 33* – carte 31 à 50 – 13 – **54 ch** 109/119 – ½ P 143/153.
◆ Établissement excentré, proche d'un carrefour important et d'un centre de loisirs avec piscine exotique. Chambres fonctionnelles distribuées sur trois étages.
◆ Dit etablissement ligt buiten het centrum, vlak bij een belangrijk kruispunt en een recreatiecentrum met exotisch zwembad. Functionele kamers op drie verdiepingen.

Triniteit sans rest, Kastanjelaan 2 (angle Axelsestraat), ✉ 4537 TR, ✆ (0 115) 61 41 50, *Fax (0 115) 61 44 69* – TV. AE ⓓ MC VISA JCB.
fermé week-end et jours fériés – **15 ch** 56/78.
◆ Dans un pavillon situé en retrait de la route reliant Zelzate à Terneuzen, chambres standard sans fioriture, dont dix singles. Aux beaux jours, petit-déjeuner en terrasse.
◆ Dit hotelpaviljoen ligt wat teruggetrokken van de weg Zelzate-Terneuzen. Standaardkamers zonder tierelantijnen, waarvan zes eenpersoons. Bij mooi weer ontbijt op het terras.

d'Ouwe Kercke, 1er étage, Noordstraat 77a (rue piétonne), ✉ 4531 GD, ✆ (0 115) 69 72 27, *Fax (0 115) 69 70 60* – AE ⓓ MC VISA.
fermé sam. midi et dim. midi – **Repas** *Lunch 34* – carte 53 à 58.
◆ Restaurant ample et agréable, aménagé au premier étage d'une église reconvertie en centre commercial. Recettes d'aujourd'hui, souvent basées sur des produits nobles.
◆ Prettig en ruim restaurant op de eerste verdieping van een kerk die tot winkelcentrum is verbouwd. Eigentijdse gerechten, veelal op basis van kwaliteitsproducten.

X **'t Arsenaal,** Nieuwstraat 27, ✉ 4531 CV, ☎ (0 115) 61 30 00, *info@hetarsenaal.com, Fax (0 115) 64 82 25,* – . MC VISA
fermé sam. midi et dim. – **Repas** Lunch 20 – 33/45 bc, ♀.
◆ Une ancienne forteresse élevée en 1840 au centre-ville abrite cette affaire familiale affichant un petit air de brasserie. Salle à manger coiffée de voûtes monumentales.
◆ In het centrum biedt een oude arsenaalkazerne uit 1840 onderdak aan dit familierestaurant, dat iets weg heeft van een brasserie. Monumentale gewelven overspannen de eetzaal.

TERSCHELLING (Ile de) *Fryslân* 531 R 2 *et* 715 H 1 – *voir à Waddeneilanden.*

TERWOLDE *Gelderland* C *Voorst 23 736 h.* 531 V 9, 532 V 9 *et* 715 J 5.
Amsterdam 112 – Apeldoorn 18 – Arnhem 48 – Deventer 9 – Zwolle 38.

XXX **'t Diekhuus,** Bandijk 2, ✉ 7396 NB, ☎ (0 571) 27 39 68, *info@diekhuus.nl, Fax (0 571) 27 04 07,* ≤, – P. AE MC VISA JCB
fermé 27 déc.-6 janv., lundi et sam. midi – **Repas** Lunch 30 – carte 36 à 52.
◆ Les fines fourchettes du coin ont leur rond de serviette dans cette belle auberge emmitouflée sous son toit de chaume. Registre culinaire actuel. Panorama sur l'IJssel.
◆ De lokale fijnproevers hebben hun vaste stekje wel gevonden in deze mooie herberg met rieten dak. Eigentijds culinair register. Uitzicht over de IJssel.

TEXEL (Ile de) *Noord-Holland* 531 N 4 *et* 715 F 2 – *voir à Waddeneilanden.*

THORN *Limburg* 532 U 16 *et* 715 I 8 – *2 584 h.*
Voir *Bourgade*★.
Wijngaard 14, ✉ *6017 AG,* ☎ *(0 475) 56 27 61, vvv.thorn@planet.nl, Fax (0 475) 56 37 99.*
Amsterdam 172 – Maastricht 44 – Eindhoven 44 – Venlo 35.

Host. La Ville Blanche, Hoogstraat 2, ✉ 6017 AR, ☎ (0 475) 56 23 41, *info@villeblanche.nl, Fax (0 475) 56 28 28,* – TV P – 25 à 90. MC VISA
fermé 30 déc.-5 janv. – **Repas** Lunch 24 – 28/45 – **23 ch** 48/65 – ½ P 68/78.
◆ Au centre d'une jolie bourgade aux briques roses souvent peintes en blanc, hostellerie proposant de sobres chambres bien calibrées. Terrasse d'été sur cour intérieure. Salle des repas classiquement aménagée. Cuisine d'aujourd'hui.
◆ Deze hostellerie bevindt zich in het centrum van een charmant stadje, waar de uit roze baksteen opgetrokken huizen wit zijn geverfd. Het hotel heeft eenvoudige kamers van goed formaat. Zomerterras aan de binnenhof. Klassieke eetzaal en eigentijdse keuken.

Host. Crasborn, Hoogstraat 6, ✉ 6017 AR, ☎ (0 475) 56 12 81, *crasborn@hollandhotels.nl, Fax (0 475) 56 22 33,* – TV. AE MC VISA JCB
fermé janv. et lundi d'oct. à avril – **Repas** *(fermé après 20 h d'oct. à mai)* (taverne-rest) Lunch 23 – carte 22 à 41 – **11 ch** 79 – ½ P 57/62.
◆ Postée dans le voisinage de l'église, au cœur d'un village "carte postale", cette ancienne auberge promue hostellerie familiale dispose de chambres correctement équipées. Taverne-restaurant complétée, en période estivale, d'une terrasse très touristique.
◆ Dit familiehotel heeft onderdak gevonden in een oude herberg in het centrum van een pittoresk stadje. Vrij comfortabele kamers. Het café-restaurant wordt 's zomers uitgebreid met een terras, waar de toeristen graag neerstrijken.

TIEL *Gelderland* 532 R 11 *et* 715 H 6 – *40 144 h.*
18 9 *au Nord-Ouest : 4 km à Zoelen, Oost Kanaalweg 1,* ✉ *4011 LA,* ☎ *(0 344) 62 43 70, Fax (0 344) 61 30 96.*
Amsterdam 80 – Utrecht 49 – Arnhem 44 – 's-Hertogenbosch 38 – Nijmegen 41 – Rotterdam 76.

Tiel, Laan van Westroyen 10 (près A 15, sortie ㉝), ✉ 4003 AZ, ☎ (0 344) 62 20 20, *Fax (0 344) 61 21 28,* – TV P – 30. AE MC VISA
Repas carte 22 à 32, ♀ – **125 ch** 77/97 – ½ P 61/66.
◆ Ce grand motel reconnaissable à ses toits pyramidaux monte la garde à l'entrée d'une ancienne ville hanséatique, près de l'autoroute. Infrastructure conférencière colossale.
◆ Dit grote motel vlak bij de snelweg, aan de rand van een oude hanzestad, is gemakkelijk te herkennen aan de piramidevormige daken. Kolossale vergaderinfrastructuur.

TILBURG *Noord-Brabant* 532 P 13 *et* 715 G 7 – *197 358 h.*

Voir *De Pont (Stichting voor Hedendaagse Kunst)*★★ V.

Musée : *Nederlands Textielmuseum*★ V **M**[1].

Env. *au Sud-Est : 4 km par ②, Domaine récréatif de Beekse Bergen*★.

Gilzerbaan 400, ✉ 5032 VC, ✆ (0 13) 462 82 00, Fax (0 13) 462 82 01 - Reeshofweg 55, ✉ 5044 VC, ✆ (0 13) 571 14 13, Fax (0 13) 572 04 94 - au Sud : 5 km à Goirle, Nieuwkerksedijk Zuid 50, ✉ 5051 DD, ✆ (0 13) 534 20 29, Fax (0 13) 534 53 60.

par ② : 32 km à Eindhoven-Welschap ✆ (0 40) 291 98 18, Fax (0 40) 291 98 20.

Spoorlaan 364, ✉ 5038 CD, ✆ 0 900-202 08 15, stadsvvv@tilburg.nl, Fax (0 13) 545 36 63.

Amsterdam 110 ① – Eindhoven 36 ② – Breda 22 ③ – 's-Hertogenbosch 23 ①

Plan page suivante

Aub. du Bonheur ⛓, Bredaseweg 441 (par ④ : 3 km), ✉ 5036 NA, ✆ (0 13) 468 69 42, *info@bonheurhorecagroep.nl, Fax (0 13) 590 09 59,* – – 25 à 80. AE ⓓ MC VISA

Repas *(fermé sam. midi et dim. midi)* Lunch 25 – 37/62, ♀ – **26 ch** ☐ 98/130 – ½ P 135.

◆ En quête d'un lieu douillet où passer la nuit ? Entourée de verdure et complétée d'une annexe moderne regroupant les chambres, cette auberge peut faire votre "bonheur". Restaurant confortable et chaleureux : mobilier de style, cheminée, briques apparentes.

◆ Wie op zoek is naar een behaaglijk onderkomen voor de nacht, kan in deze herberg in het groen zijn geluk beproeven. De kamers zijn ingericht in een moderne annexe. Comfortabel restaurant waar stijlmeubilair, schouw en baksteen bijdragen aan de warme ambiance.

De Postelse Hoeve, Dr. Deelenlaan 10, ✉ 5042 AD, ✆ (0 13) 463 63 35, *info@depostelsehoeve.nl, Fax (0 13) 463 93 90,* – , rest, – 25 à 400. AE ⓓ MC VISA. rest V v

Repas Lunch 22 – 32/42 bc, ♀ – **35 ch** ☐ 89/109 – ½ P 109/119.

◆ Immeuble longiligne construit dans les années 1960, De Postelse Hoeve distribue ses chambres, de confort fonctionnel et de format convenable, à l'étage. Salle de restaurant contemporaine.

◆ Dit hotel-restaurant is gehuisvest in een langwerpig pand uit omstreeks 1960 en beschikt over comfortabele kamers die redelijk van formaat zijn en op de verdieping liggen. Eigentijds ingerichte restaurantzaal.

Mercure, Heuvelpoort 300, ✉ 5038 DT, ✆ (0 13) 535 46 75, *mercure-tilburg@wxs.nl, Fax (0 13) 535 58 75,* – , rest, – 25 à 200. AE ⓓ MC VISA. rest Y b

Repas carte 22 à 38 – ☐ 15 – **61 ch** 103, – 2 suites – ½ P 135.

◆ Retrouvez, sur une place animée du centre de Tilburg, l'éventail habituel des prestations hôtelières de l'enseigne Mercure. Chambres pratiques pourvues du double vitrage. Salle des repas décorée sur le thème de Napoléon.

◆ Op een levendig pleintje in het centrum vindt u het gebruikelijke scala van hotelprestaties dat kenmerkend is voor de Mercure-keten. De praktische kamers zijn voorzien van dubbele beglazing. Het decor van de eetzaal staat in het teken van Napoleon.

de Lindeboom sans rest, Heuvelring 126, ✉ 5038 CL, ✆ (0 13) 535 13 55, *lindeboom@wxs.nl, Fax (0 13) 536 10 85* – . AE ⓓ MC VISA. Y c

18 ch ☐ 85/95.

◆ Enraciné à l'ombre des tours de l'église qui jouxte une place passante, Le Tilleul (De Lindeboom) est un établissement disposant de bonnes chambres insonorisées.

◆ Deze lindeboom heeft zich geworteld in de schaduw van de kerktorens bij een druk plein. Het hotel heeft goede kamers met geluidsisolatie.

Bastion, Kempenbaan 2, ✉ 5018 TK, ✆ (0 13) 544 19 99, *bastion@bastionhotel.nl, Fax (0 13) 543 89 10,* – . AE ⓓ MC VISA. X f

Repas (grillades, ouvert jusqu'à 23 h) carte env. 30 – ☐ 10 – **40 ch** 62.

◆ Un grand parc public avoisine ce petit hôtel de chaîne excentré dont l'accès ne pose aucun problème en raison de sa situation au bord du ring. Chambres de mise simple.

◆ Een groot openbaar park ligt naast dit kleine ketenhotel, dat aan de ringweg ligt en daardoor probleemloos te bereiken is. Eenvoudige kamers.

XX **Foyer Lucebert,** Schouwburgring, ✉ 5000 DA, ✆ (0 13) 543 25 15, *lucebert@theaterstilburg.nl, Fax (0 13) 543 09 57,* – 25 à 60. AE ⓓ MC VISA Z e

fermé du 2 au 29 août et lundi – **Repas** (dîner seult) 38/53 bc, ♀.

◆ Incorporé au théâtre municipal et agencé dans un style résolument contemporain, cet agréable restaurant vous concocte une cuisine au goût du jour. Service assez stylé.

◆ Dit aangename restaurant heeft onderdak gevonden in de stadsschouwburg en is in moderne stijl ingericht. Eigentijdse keuken en vrij stijlvolle bediening.

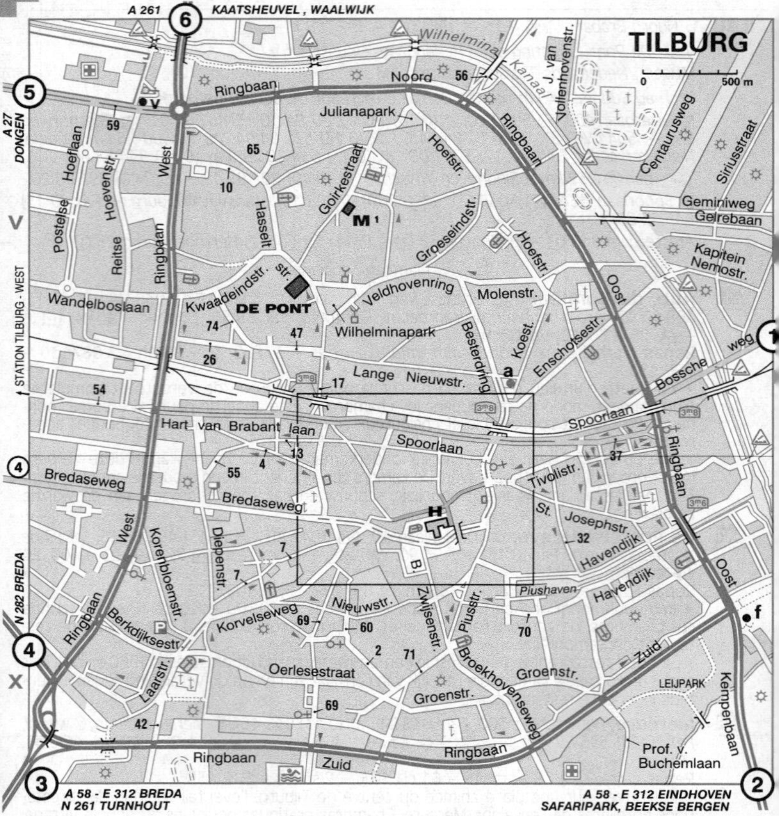

TILBURG

A 261 KAATSHEUVEL, WAALWIJK

A 27 DONGEN

STATION TILBURG - WEST

N 282 BREDA

A 58 - E 312 BREDA
N 261 TURNHOUT

A 58 - E 312 EINDHOVEN
SAFARIPARK, BEEKSE BERGEN

0 500 m

Wilhelmina Kanaal
Ringbaan Noord
Julianapark
Hoefstr.
Goirkestraat
M 1
Hasselt
Groeseindstr.
Veldhovenring
Molenstr.
Kwaadeindstr.
DE PONT
Wilhelminapark
Besterdring
Koest.
Enschotsestr.
Lange Nieuwstr.
Hart van Brabant laan
Spoorlaan
Bredaseweg
Tivolistr.
St. Josephstr.
Havendijk
Piushaven
Nieuwstr.
Korvelseweg
Zwijsenstr.
Piusstr.
Broekhovenseweg
Groenstr.
Oerlesestraat
Ringbaan Zuid
Ringbaan Oost
Ringbaan West
Kempenbaan
LEIJPARK
Prof. v. Buchemlaan
Bossche weg
J. van Vollenhovenstr.
Centaurusweg
Siriusstraat
Geminiweg
Gelrebaan
Kapitein Nemostr.
Postelse Hoeflaan
Hoevenstr.
Reitse
Wandelboslaan
Korenbloemstr.
Diepenstr.
Berkdijksestr.
Laarstr.

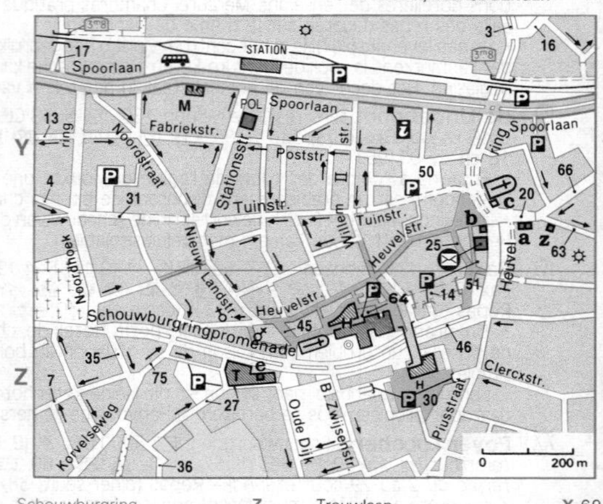

Abel Tasmanstr.	X	2
Besterdring	Y	3
Boomstr.	Y	4
Capucijnenstr.	Z	7
Dillenburglaan	V	10
Elzenstr.	VY	13
Emmapassage	Z	14
Enschotsestr.	Y	16
Gasthuisring	VY	17
Heuvel	Z	20
Heuvelstr.	Y	
Juliana van Stolbergstr.	Y	25
Keldermansstr.	V	26
Kloosterstr.	Z	27
Koningspl.	Z	30
Korte Schijfstr.	Y	31
Lanciersstr.	X	32
Lange Schijfstr.	Z	35
Nazarethstr.	Z	36
Nieuwe Bosscheweg	V	37
Oude Goirleseweg	X	42
Oude Markt	Z	45
Paleisring	Z	46
Philips Vingboonstr.	V	47
Pieter Vreedepl.	Y	50
Piuspl.	Z	51
Prof. Cobbenhagenlaan	V	54
Prunusstr.	VX	55
Quirijnstoklaan	V	56
Rueckertbaan	V	59
de Ruijterstr.	X	60
Schouwburgring	Z	
St. Josephstr.	Y	63
Stadhuisplein	Z	64
Textielpl.	V	65
Tivolistr.	Y	66
Trouwlaan	X	69
Vendeliersstr.	X	70
Voltstr.	X	71
Waterhoefstr.	V	74
Zomerstr.	Z	75

Sprakeloos, St. Josephstraat 138, ✉ 5017 GL, ☎ (0 13) 580 08 11, *info@sprakeloos.nl, Fax (0 13) 582 03 94,* – VISA. Y z
fermé lundis non fériés – **Repas** Lunch 31 – 33/64 bc, ♀.
♦ Belle salle à manger aménagée dans la note "bistrot". Attrayante carte actuelle qu'un sommelier averti escorte de bons crus. Bar-salon apéritif au rez-de-chaussée.
♦ Mooie eetzaal in bistrostijl. Aantrekkelijke eigentijdse menukaart met wijnsuggesties van een deskundig sommelier. Voor een aperitiefje is er de bar-salon op de begane grond.

L'Orangerie sur la butte, Heuvel 39, ✉ 5038 CS, ☎ (0 13) 543 11 32, *info@lorangerietilburg.nl, Fax (0 13) 542 54 65,* – . AE VISA. Y a
fermé merc. – **Repas** (déjeuner sur réservation) carte 36 à 50.
♦ Ne cherchez ni d'orangerie, ni de butte, mais une devanture jaune et blanche, avec des motifs de tournesols. Décoration intérieure moderne, dans la note méditerranéenne.
♦ Niet een oranjerie of heuvel, maar een geel-witte voorkant met zonnebloemmotieven is het aanzicht van dit pand. Interieur met modern decor in mediterrane stijl.

L'Olivo, Heuvel 41, ✉ 5038 CS, ☎ (0 13) 542 67 31, *info@lolivo.nl, Fax (0 13) 580 11 94,* , Avec cuisine italienne – VISA. Y a
fermé mardi – **Repas** (dîner seult) 35, ♀.
♦ Ce restaurant du centre-ville dont la façade évoque un chalet alpin vous attable dans un décor intérieur italianisant. Savoureuse cuisine de la Botte. Ambiance chaleureuse.
♦ Dit restaurant in het centrum heeft een voorgevel in chaletstijl en een interieur met Italiaans decor. Smakelijke keuken uit de Laars. Warme ambiance.

"Vissers"Geheim, NS Plein 32, ✉ 5014 DC, ☎ (0 13) 545 10 88, *info@vissersgeheim.nl, Fax (0 13) 545 10 89,* , Produits de la mer – P. AE VISA. V a
fermé dim. midi et lundi midi – **Repas** carte 36 à 46.
♦ Lumineuse salle de restaurant agencée dans l'esprit nautique et agréable terrasse abritée sur le devant. Cuisine gorgée d'iode. Beaux plateaux de fruits de mer.
♦ Klaar en helder interieur in nautische sfeer en met leuk overdekt terras aan de voorkant. Zeebanket en jodiumrijke visgerechten.

à Berkel-Enschot *par ① : 5 km* C *Tilburg :*

De Druiventros, Bosscheweg 11, ✉ 5056 PP, ☎ (0 13) 533 91 15, *info@druiventros.nl, Fax (0 13) 533 14 35,* , – TV P – 25 à 600. AE VISA JCB
fermé 31 déc.-1er janv. – **Repas** Lunch 13 – 22 – 10 – **56 ch** 80/190 – ½ P 110.
♦ Hôtel-centre conférencier proche de l'autoroute A 65 qui devient route nationale au-delà de la localité, vers 's-Hertogenbosch. Chambres de bon confort. Piste de bowling.
♦ Hotel-conferentiecentrum vlak bij de snelweg (A65), die voorbij het plaatsje in de hoofdweg (N65) richting Den Bosch overgaat. Kamers met goed comfort. Bowlingbaan.

à Goirle *Sud : 5 km – 22 517 h*

De Hovel, Tilburgseweg 37, ✉ 5051 AA, ☎ (0 13) 534 54 74, *info@hovel.nl, Fax (0 13) 534 03 54,* – – 40. VISA.
fermé dern. sem. déc., dim. midi et lundi – **Repas** carte 43 à 55.
♦ Au centre du bourg, ancienne demeure patricienne dont l'intérieur a été adroitement relooké dans un style design. Goûteuse cuisine à la page. Service prévenant.
♦ Dit oude patriciërshuis in het centrum van het plaatsje is verbouwd tot een restaurant met designinterieur. Smaakvolle, eigentijdse keuken. Voorkomende service.

De Eetkamer, Tilburgseweg 34, ✉ 5051 AH, ☎ (0 13) 534 49 00, *Fax (0 13) 534 11 58,* – P. VISA
Repas (dîner seult) carte 22 à 40, ♀.
♦ Une affaire très courtisée à Goirle : carte brasserie pour bonnes fourchettes, ambiance assortie et jolie terrasse d'été garnie de meubles en teck, ouverte sur le jardin.
♦ Een zeer favoriet adres in het plaatsje : brasseriekaart voor goede eters, bijpassende ambiance en in de tuin een fraai zomerterras met teakmeubilair.

TOLKAMER *Gelderland* C *Rijnwaarden 11 203 h.* 532 V 11 *et* 715 J 6.

Amsterdam 126 – Arnhem 26 – Emmerich 13.

de Tolkamer sans rest, Europakade 10, ✉ 6916 BG, ☎ (0 316) 54 75 25, *info@detolkamer.nl, Fax (0 316) 54 74 73,* <, , – TV P. AE VISA.
fermé 29 déc.-2 janv. – 10 – **18 ch** 49/82.
♦ Rien à déclarer ? Posez alors vos valises dans cet ancien poste de douane fluviale transformé en petit hôtel "sympa". Certaines chambres ont vue sur les quais du Rhin.
♦ Niets aan te geven ? Strijk dan neer in deze oude post van de rivierdouane, die tot een sympathiek hotelletje is verbouwd. Sommige kamers kijken uit op de kaden langs de Rijn.

X **Villa Copera,** Spijksedijk 2, ✉ 6917 AC, ☎ (0 316) 54 28 16, *info@copera.nl*, *Fax (0 316) 54 31 25*, ≤, 斋, ⚓ - P. MC VISA JCB. ✈
fermé du 3 au 24 fév., lundi midi, mardi et sam. midi – **Repas** *Lunch 35* – carte 34 à 52, ♀.
• Repas au goût du jour dans une maison de notable surveillant la digue. La salle à manger de l'étage profite d'une belle échappée "batelière". Sculptures modernes au jardin.
• Restaurant in een herenhuis dat een oogje houdt op de dijk. Eigentijdse maaltijden. De eetzaal op de eerste verdieping kijkt uit op de Rijn. Tuin met moderne sculpturen.

TRICHT *Gelderland* C *Geldermalsen 25 055 h.* 532 Q 11 *et* 715 G 6.
Amsterdam 68 – Utrecht 39 – Arnhem 59 – 's-Hertogenbosch 25 – Rotterdam 68.

XX **De Oude Betuwe,** Kerkstraat 19, ✉ 4196 AA, ☎ (0 345) 57 77 00, *deoudebetuwe@uwnet.nl*, *Fax (0 345) 57 06 70* – ▤ P. AE ⓓ MC VISA JCB
fermé fin déc., mardi, sam. midi et dim. midi – **Repas** *Lunch 30* – carte 46 à 85.
• Au centre de Tricht, table plaisante où l'on se sent en bonnes mains. Recettes de base classique, mais bien dans le coup, et mise en place également un peu "tendance".
• In dit prettige restaurant in het centrum zult u zich in goede handen voelen. Gerechten op klassieke basis maar in een zeer eigentijds jasje. Ook het interieur is wat trendy.

TUBBERGEN *Overijssel* 531 Z 8 *et* 715 L 4 – *20 161 h.*
ℹ *Eendracht 19, ✉ 7651 CZ, ☎ 0 900 202 19 81, info@vvvtubbergen.nl, Fax (0 546) 62 36 40.* – *Amsterdam 162 – Zwolle 65 – Enschede 28 – Nordhorn 28.*

Droste's, Uelserweg 95 (Nord-Est : 2 km), ✉ 7651 KV, ☎ (0 546) 62 12 64, *info@drostes.nl*, *Fax (0 546) 62 28 28*, 🚲 – ⇹, ▤ rest, TV P. AE ⓓ MC VISA. ✈ rest
fermé 27 déc.-10 janv. – **Repas** *(fermé sam. midi et dim. midi)* 28/45, ♀ – **24 ch** ☕ 65/109 – ½ P 70/95.
• Il règne une atmosphère un rien "trendy" dans cet agréable établissement familial excentré. Espaces communs d'un style contemporain, à l'image des bonnes petites chambres. Confortable restaurant aménagé dans l'esprit scandinave. Cuisine bien de notre temps.
• Er heerst een beetje trendy sfeer in dit aangename familiehotel buiten het centrum. Gemeenschappelijke ruimten met eigentijds decor, net als de kleine maar goede kamers. Comfortabel restaurant in Scandinavische stijl. De keuken is helemaal van deze tijd.

à Albergen *Est : 7 km* C *Tubbergen :*

't Elshuys 🐦, Gravendijk 6, ✉ 7665 SK, ☎ (0 546) 44 21 61, *info@elshuys.nl*, *Fax (0 546) 44 20 53*, 斋, ≘s, 🌳, 🚲 – ⇕ ⇹ TV ♿ P – 🏛 25 à 100. AE MC VISA. ✈ rest
Repas *(fermé 25 déc., 1er janv. et après 20 h) Lunch 13* – 22 – **27 ch** ☕ 55/75 – ½ P 55/65.
• Paisible hôtel de campagne agrémenté d'un jardin croquignolet, avec pièce d'eau. Les chambres, dont quelques-unes sont des duplex, se partagent deux ailes. Une carte traditionnelle batave s'emploie à combler votre appétit.
• Dit rustig gelegen hotel in een landelijke omgeving heeft een snoezige tuin met waterpartij. De kamers, waaronder enkele split-levels, liggen over twee vleugels verspreid. Een traditionele Nederlandse kaart wordt als wapen ingezet om uw honger te stillen.

TWELLO *Gelderland* C *Voorst 23 736 h.* 532 V 9 *et* 715 J 5.
Amsterdam 104 – Arnhem 40 – Apeldoorn 11 – Deventer 7 – Enschede 66.

XX **de Staten Hoed,** Dorpsstraat 12, ✉ 7391 DD, ☎ (0 571) 27 70 23, *info@destatenhoed.nl*, *Fax (0 571) 27 03 48*, 斋 – P. AE ⓓ MC VISA JCB
fermé dern. sem. juil.-prem. sem. août, sam. midi, dim. midi et lundi – **Repas** *Lunch 29* – carte 28 à 51, ♀.
• Près de l'église, relais de bouche prenant la relève d'une vénérable auberge. Salle prolongée d'une jolie véranda. Copieuse cuisine classique-actuelle. Terrasse exquise.
• Dit restaurant vlak bij de kerk heeft onderdak gevonden in een eerbiedwaardige herberg. Eetzaal met serre. Klassiek-eigentijdse keuken en een voortreffelijk terras.

UBACHSBERG *Limburg* C *Voerendaal 13 163 h.* 532 U 17 *et* 715 I 9.
Amsterdam 218 – Maastricht 31 – Eindhoven 88 – Aachen 16.

XXX ✿ **De Leuf** (van de Bunt), Dalstraat 2, ✉ 6367 JS, ☎ (0 45) 575 02 26, *info@deleuf.nl*, *Fax (0 45) 575 35 08*, 斋 – P. AE ⓓ MC VISA JCB
fermé sem. carnaval, du 1er au 21 août, sam. midi, dim. et lundi – **Repas** *Lunch 33* – 58/115 bc, carte 68 à 86, ♀.
• Une ferme restaurée avec habileté abrite cette grande table limbourgeoise. Cuisine savoureusement inventive, de base classique. Belle cave et cour intérieure délicieuse.
• Dit restaurant is gehuisvest in een vakkundig gerestaureerde boerderij. Smakelijke, inventieve keuken op klassieke basis. Mooie wijnkelder en heerlijke binnenplaats.
Spéc. Saint-Jacques au foie d'oie fondu et aux morilles (sept.-mars). Tempura de langoustines aux asperges régionales et coriandre (mi-avril-mi-juin). Palette de préparations de chocolat 70 % pur et orange

UDEN *Noord-Brabant* 532 S 13 *et* 715 H 7 – *40 014 h.*

Mondriaanplein 14a, ✉ 5401 HX, ☎ (0 413) 25 07 77, vvvuden@tref.nl, Fax (0 413) 25 52 02.

Amsterdam 113 – Eindhoven 32 – 's-Hertogenbosch 28 – Nijmegen 33.

Arrows sans rest, St. Janstraat 14, ✉ 5401 BB, ☎ (0 413) 26 85 55, *info@hotelarrows.com, Fax (0 413) 26 16 15,* – AE MC VISA JCB.
fermé 23 déc.-2 janv. – **38 ch** 98/118.
◆ Cet hôtel de situation centrale, toutefois assez tranquille, offre un bon niveau de confort. Les petits-déjeuners sont soignés, et l'accueil, individualisé.
◆ Dit vrij rustig gelegen hotel op loopafstand van het centrum biedt een goed comfort. Verzorgd ontbijt en persoonlijke ontvangst.

't Raadhuis, Markt 1a (dans la mairie), ✉ 5401 GN, ☎ (0 413) 25 70 00, *Fax (0 413) 25 67 22,* – AE MC VISA JCB
fermé dern. sem. fév., 2 sem. en juil., sam. midi et dim. midi – **Repas** *Lunch 25* – 35, ♀.
◆ On envie Monsieur le maire, qui n'a que quelques marches à descendre pour s'attabler au 't Raadhuis, adresse familiale occupant le rez-de-chaussée de la maison communale.
◆ Die burgemeester heeft geluk ! Hij hoeft maar een paar treetjes af om in zijn eigen raadhuis aan te schuiven in dit familierestaurant op de benedenverdieping.

UDENHOUT *Noord-Brabant* C *Tilburg 197 358 h.* 532 P 13 *et* 715 G 7.

Amsterdam 103 – Eindhoven 40 – 's-Hertogenbosch 18 – Tilburg 10.

L'Abeille, Kreitenmolenstraat 59, ✉ 5071 BB, ☎ (0 13) 511 36 12, *Fax (0 13) 511 00 65,* – P. AE MC VISA JCB.
fermé lundi et mardi – **Repas** (dîner seult) carte 32 à 43, ♀.
◆ Salle à manger mignonne et romantique, jouant la carte "tradition", avec des plats assez copieux. Les habitués se laissent volontiers surprendre par les menus surprise.
◆ Charmant, romantisch restaurant dat een traditionele kaart voert en vrij overvloedige maaltijden serveert. De stamgasten laten zich graag door de surprisemenu's verrassen.

UITHOORN *Noord-Holland* 532 N 9 *et* 715 F 5 – *26 423 h.*

Amsterdam 24 – Haarlem 23 – Den Haag 54 – Utrecht 31.

Het Rechthuis aan de Amstel , Schans 32, ✉ 1421 BB, ☎ (0 297) 56 13 80, *info@hetrechthuis.com, Fax (0 297) 53 04 11,* ←, – P– 25 à 80. AE MC VISA.
Repas *Lunch 28* – 30/63 – 14 – **12 ch** 119/145 – ½ P 150/200.
◆ Hôtel de caractère créé sur une rive de l'Amstel à partir d'un ancien tribunal de justice. Chambres nettes et convenablement équipées. Superbe terrasse au bord de l'eau. Confortable salle de restaurant d'où vous balayerez la rivière du regard.
◆ Karakteristiek hotel aan de Amstel in een voormalig gerechtsgebouw. Goed onderhouden, correct ingerichte kamers. Schitterend terras aan het water. Comfortabele eetzaal met zicht op de Amstel.

La Musette, Wilhelminakade 39h, ✉ 1421 AB, ☎ (0 297) 56 09 00, – AE MC VISA
fermé 3 sem. en juil., fin déc.-mi-janv., lundi et mardi – **Repas** (dîner seult) 24/53 bc, ♀.
◆ Affaire à débusquer sur un quai où accostent les plaisanciers. Au "piano", visible de tous, le chef adapte ses menus au tempo actuel. Jouez, hautbois, résonnez, musettes !
◆ Eethuis aan een kade waar plezierboten aanmeren. Aan het fornuis, in 't zicht van de gasten, bereidt de chef-kok zijn trendy menu's.

ULVENHOUT *Noord-Brabant* 532 N 13 – *voir à Breda.*

URK *Flevoland* 531 S 7 *et* 715 H 4 – *16 489 h.*

Voir *Site*★.

vers Enkhuizen : Rederij FRO FFF, Dormakade 4 ☎ (0 527) 68 34 07. Durée de la traversée : 1 h 30.

Amsterdam 84 – Emmeloord 12 – Zwolle 42.

Mes Amis 2e étage, Bootstraat 65 (face au port), ✉ 8321 EM, ☎ (0 527) 68 87 36, *info@mes-amis.nl, Fax (0 527) 68 08 01,* ← – AE MC VISA JCB.
fermé 2 prem. sem. mars, 2 prem. sem. oct. et dim. – **Repas** *Lunch 23* – 29/42, ♀.
◆ Une adresse qui se fait beaucoup d'amis : ravissante salle à manger bien dans l'air du temps, tables avec vue sur le port et belle carte illustrée de clichés nostalgiques.
◆ Een adres dat veel vrienden maakt : charmante eetzaal met trendy decor, tafels met uitzicht op de haven en een mooie menukaart die met nostalgische clichés is geïllustreerd.

URMOND *Limburg* 532 T 17 *et* 715 I 9 – *voir à Stein.*

USSELO *Overijssel* 532 Z 9 *et* 715 L 5 – *voir à Enschede.*

UTRECHT P 532 P 10 *et* 715 G 5 – *260 625 h – Casino* AY, *Overste den Oudenlaan 2,* ✉ *3527 KW,* ☎ *(0 30) 750 47 50, Fax (0 30) 750 47 00.*

Voir *La vieille ville*★★ – *Tour de la Cathédrale*★★ *(Domtoren)* ✲★★ BY – *Ancienne cathédrale*★ *(Domkerk)* BY **B** – *Vieux canal*★ *(Oudegracht) :* ≤★ ABXY – *Bas reliefs*★ *et crypte*★ *dans l'église St-Pierre (Pieterskerk)* BY – *Maison (Huis) Rietveld Schröder*★★ CY.

Musées : *Catharijneconvent*★★ BY – *Central*★★ *(Centraal Museum)* BZ – *Université*★ *(Universiteitsmuseum)* BZ **M**[5] – *Chemin de fer*★ *(Nederlands Spoorwegmuseum)* CY **M**[4].

Env. *par* ⑥ *: 10 km, Château de Haar : collections*★ *(mobilier, tapisseries, peinture).*

18 *par* ② *: 13 km à Bosch en Duin, Amersfoortseweg 1,* ✉ *3735 LJ,* ☎ *(0 30) 695 52 23, Fax (0 30) 696 37 69 -* 9 *à l'Ouest : 8 km à Vleuten, Parkweg 5,* ✉ *3451 RH,* ☎ *(0 30) 677 28 60, Fax (0 30) 677 39 03.*

✈ *par* ⑥ *: 37 km à Amsterdam-Schiphol* ☎ *0 900-72 44 74 65.*

🅘 *Vinkenburgstraat 19,* ✉ *3512 AA,* ☎ *0 900-128 87 32, info@vvvutrecht.nl, Fax (0 30) 236 00 37.*

Amsterdam 36 ⑥ *– Den Haag 61* ⑤ *– Rotterdam 57* ⑤

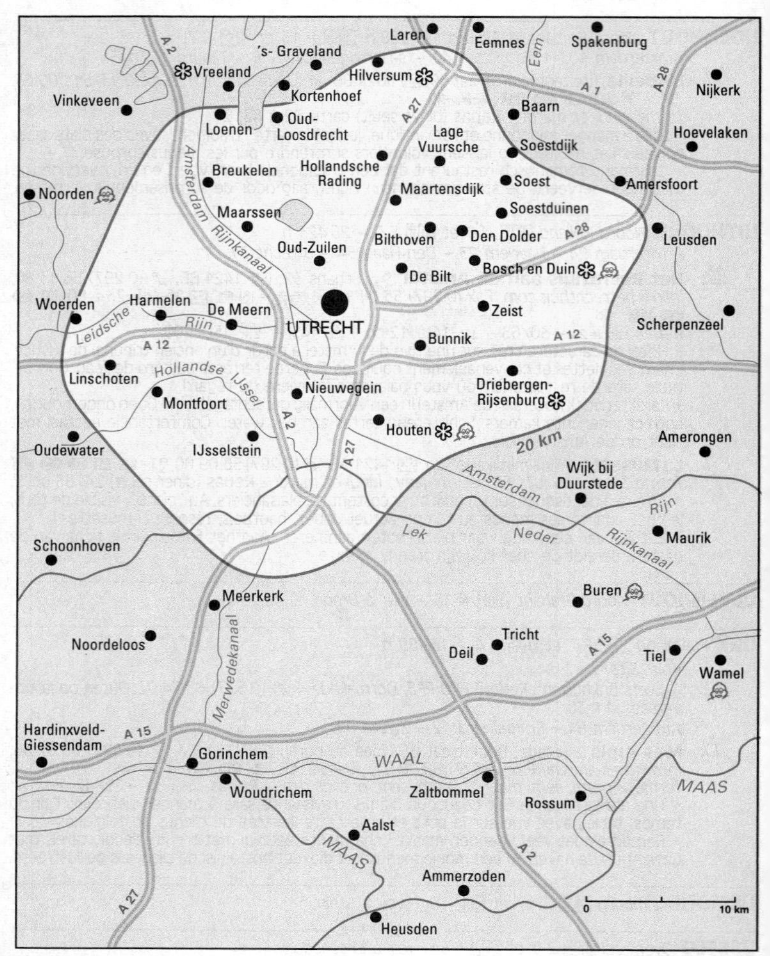

UTRECHT

Ahornstr. . . . . FU 7
Antonius Matthaeuslaan . . GU 9
Biltse Rading . . . . GU 13
Biltsestraatweg . . . . GU 15
Blauwkapelseweg . . . . GU 18
Brailledreef . . . . GU 24
Burg. van Tuyllkade . . . . . . FU 27
Carnegiedreef . . . . GU 28
Cartesiusweg . . . . FU 30
Damstr. . . . . FUV 34
Darwindreef . . . . GU 36
Ds. Martin Luther
Kinglaan . . . . FV 42
van Egmondkade . . . . FU 44
Einthovendreef . . . . GV 45
't Goy laan . . . . GV 46
Graadt van Roggenweg . . FV 47
Herculeslaan . . . . GV 48
van Hoornekade . . . . FU 51
J. M. de Muinck
Keizerlaan . . . . FU 52
Joseph Haydnlaan . . . . FV 58
Koningin Wilhelminalaan . FV 64
Laan van Chartroise . . . . . FU 72
Lessinglaan . . . . FV 81
Marnixlaan . . . . FU 85
Omloop . . . . GU 94
Oudenoord . . . . GU 96
Overste den Oudenlaan . . FV 99
Pieter Nieuwlandstr. . . . . . GU 102
Pijperlaan . . . . FV 105
Prins Bernhardlaan . . . . . . FU 109
Rio Brancodreef . . . . FU 112
Royaards van den
Hamkade . . . . FU 114
Sint Josephlaan . . . . FU 118
Socrateslaan . . . . GV 120
Spinozaweg . . . . FU 121
Sweder van Zuylenweg . . FU 125
Talmalaan . . . . GU 126
Thomas à Kempisweg . . . FU 127
Verlengde
Vleutenseweg . . . . FU 132
W. A. Vultostr. . . . . GV 136
Weg der Verenigde
Naties . . . . FV 138
Weg tot de Wetenschap . GV 139
Zamenhofdreef . . . . GU 147

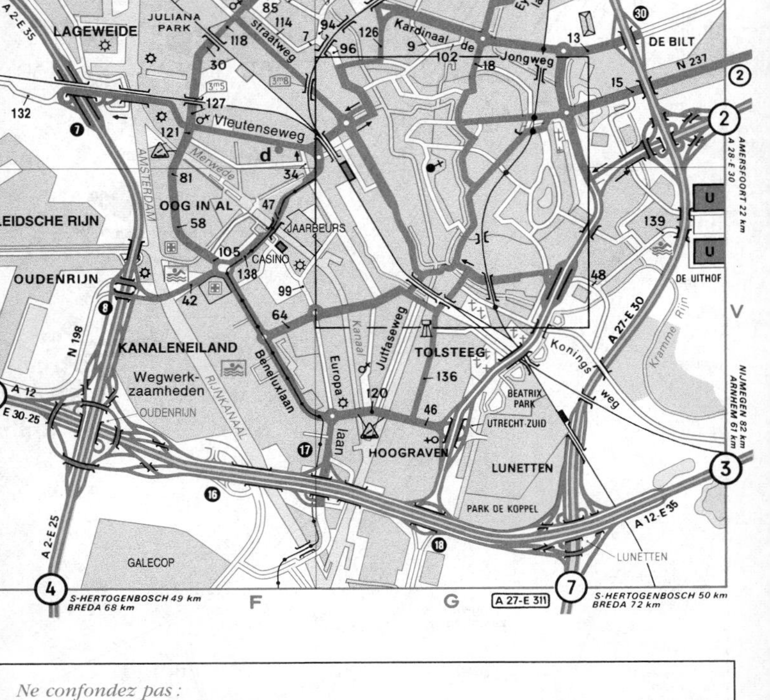

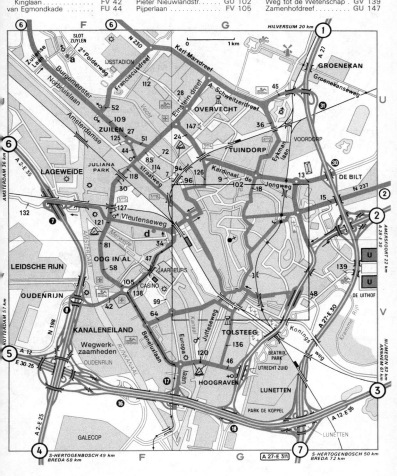

Ne confondez pas :

Confort des hôtels	: 🏨🏨🏨🏨🏨 ... 🏨
Confort des restaurants	: XXXXX ... X
Qualité de la table	: ✿✿✿, ✿✿, ✿, Repas

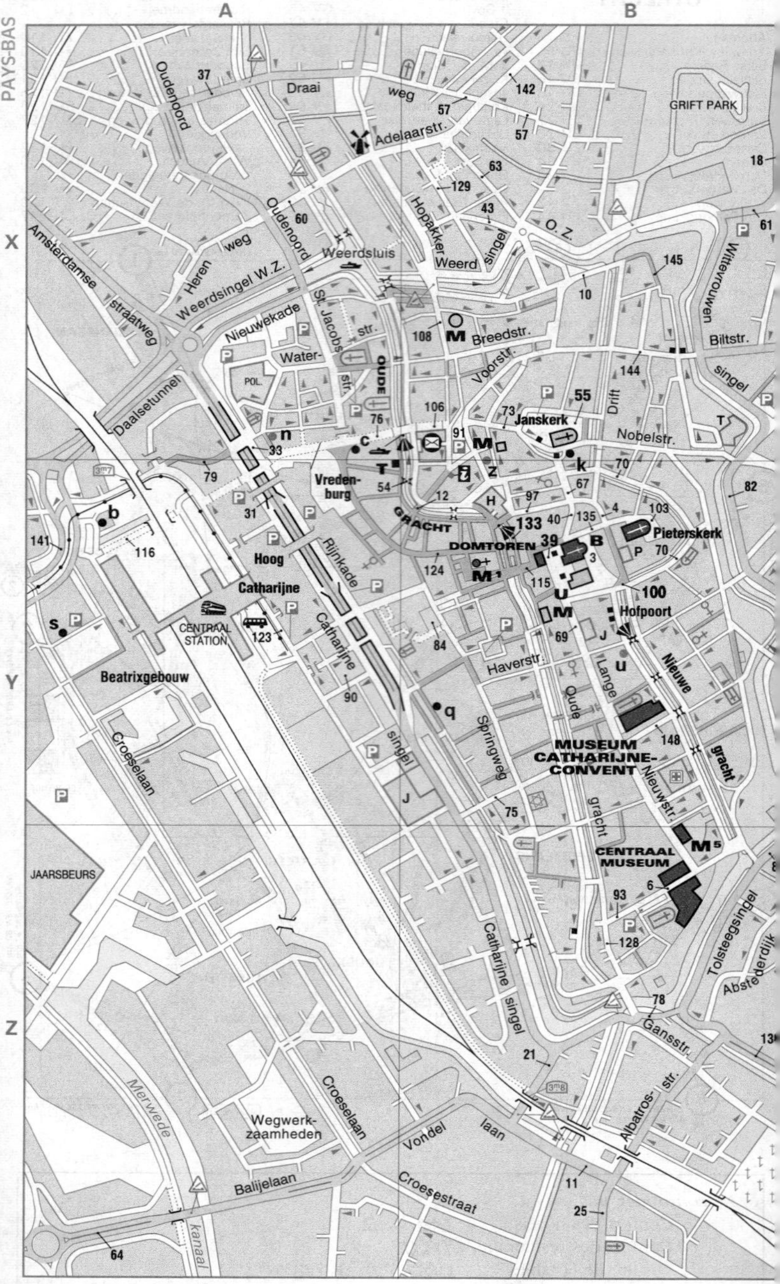

A B

Draai
weg
Adelaarstr.
Oudenoord
Hopakker
Weerd
singel
O. Z.
GRIFT PARK
Amsterdamse straatweg
Heren weg
Weerdsingel W.Z.
Weerdsluis
Wittevrouwen
Biltstr.
singel
Nieuwekade
St. Jacobs str.
Water- str.
POL.
OUDE
Breedstr.
Voorstr.
Drift
Janskerk
Nobelstr.
Daalsetunnel
Vredenburg
GRACHT
DOMTOREN
Pieterskerk
Hofpoort
Hoog Catharijne
Rijnkade
CENTRAAL STATION
Catharijne singel
Haverstr.
Oude gracht
Lange Nieuwstr.
Nieuwe gracht
Beatrixgebouw
Springweg
MUSEUM CATHARIJNE-CONVENT
CENTRAAL MUSEUM
Croeselaan
JAARSBEURS
Tolsteegsingel
Abstederdijk
Catharijne singel
Gansstr.
Albatros-str.
Merwede kanaal
Wegwerk-zaamheden
Croeselaan
Vondel laan
Balijelaan
Croesestraat

X
Y
Z

A B

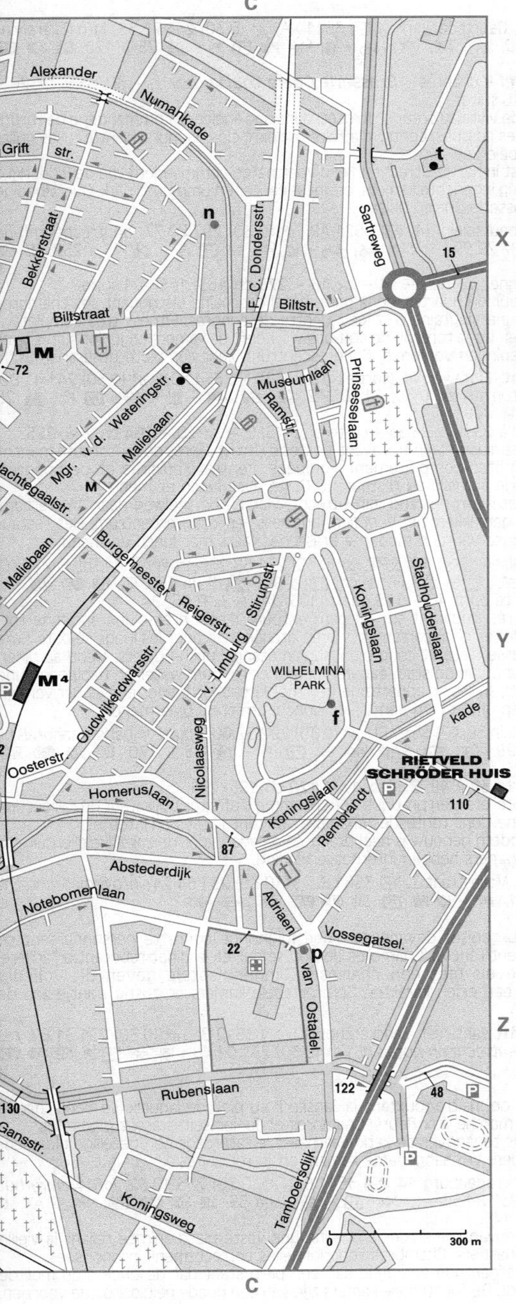

UTRECHT

Street	Grid	No.
Achter de Dom	BY	3
Achter St.-Pieter	BY	4
Agnietenstr.	BZ	6
van Asch van Wijckskade	BX	10
Badenpowellweg	BZ	11
Bakkerbrug	BY	12
Biltsestraatweg	CX	15
Blauwkapelseweg	BX	18
Bleekstr.	BZ	21
Bosboomstr.	CZ	22
Briljantlaan	BZ	25
Catharijnebaan	AY	31
Catharijnekade	AX	33
Dav. van Mollemstr.	AX	37
Domplein	BY	39
Domstr.	BY	40
Duifstr.	BX	43
Herculeslaan	CZ	48
Jansbrug	ABY	54
Janskerkhof	BX	55
Johannes de Bekastr.	BX	57
Kaatstr.	AX	60
Kleinesingel	BX	61
Koekoekstr.	BX	63
Koningin Wilhelminalaan	AZ	64
Korte Jansstr.	BY	67
Korte nieuwstr.	BY	69
Kromme Nieuwegracht	BY	70
Kruisstr.	CX	72
Lange Jansstr.	BX	73
Lange Smeestr.	BY	75
Lange Viestr.	AX	76
Ledig Erf	BZ	78
Leidseveer	AXY	79
Maliesingel	BCYZ	82
Mariaplaats	BY	84
Mecklenburglaan	CYZ	87
Moreelsepark	AY	90
Nachtegaalstr.	CY	
Neude	BXY	91
Nicolaasstr.	BZ	93
Oudegracht	BXYZ	
Oudkerkhof	BY	97
Pausdam	BY	100
Pieterskerkhof	BY	103
Potterstr.	BX	106
Predikherenkerkhof	BX	108
Prins Hendriklaan	CY	110
Servetstr.	BY	115
van Sijpesteijnkade	AY	116
Stadionlaan	CZ	122
Stationsplein	AY	123
Steenweg	ABY	124
Twijnstr.	BZ	128
Valkstr.	BX	129
Venuslaan	BCZ	130
Vismarkt	BY	133
Voetiusstr.	BY	135
Voorstr.	BX	
Vredenburg	AY	
Westplein	AY	141
Willem van Noortstr.	BX	142
Wittevrouwenstr.	BX	144
Wolvenplein	BX	145
Zuilenstr.	BY	148

PAYS-BAS

Gd H. Karel V, Geertebolwerk 1, ✉ 3511 XA, ☎ (0 30) 233 75 55, *info@karelv.nl, Fax (0 30) 233 75 00*, – 25 à 120. AE VISA JCB BY q
Repas voir rest ***Karel V*** ci-après – ***Brasserie Goeie Louisa*** *Lunch 25* – 30/35 – 20 – **75 ch** 220/265, – 16 suites.
◆ Tranquillité et art de vivre au cœur d'Utrecht, dans une ancienne commanderie de l'ordre Teutonique. Chambres cossues, centre d'affaires et parc clos de murs. Plantureuses grillades à la brasserie Goeie Louisa.
◆ Rust en levenskunst in hartje Utrecht, in een voormalige commanderij van de Ridderlijke Duitse Orde. Weelderig ingerichte kamers, business center en ommuurd park. Overvloedige grillgerechten in brasserie Goeie Louisa.

NH Utrecht, Jaarbeursplein 24, ✉ 3521 AR, ☎ (0 30) 297 79 77, *nhutrecht@nh-hotels.nl, Fax (0 30) 297 79 99*, – 25 à 250. AE VISA JCB. AY s
Repas (cuisine italienne) *Lunch 23* – 34 – 16 – **275 ch** 165/195, – 1 suite.
◆ Dans une haute tour du quartier de la gare, hôtel de chaîne distribuant ses chambres et junior suites sur une vingtaine d'étages. Centre de congrès. Fitness très complet.
◆ Dit ketenhotel in een hoge toren in de stationswijk heeft de kamers en junior suites over een twintigtal verdiepingen verspreid. Congrescentrum. Zeer complete fitnessruimte.

Carlton President, Floraweg 25 (sortie ⑥ sur A 2), ✉ 3542 DX, ☎ (0 30) 241 41 82, *info@president.carlton.nl, Fax (0 30) 241 05 42*, – 25 à 300. AE VISA JCB
Repas (ouvert jusqu'à 23 h) *Lunch 30* – carte env. 45, ♀ – 20 – **164 ch** 208/225.
◆ Hôtel de forme pyramidale élevé aux avant-postes d'Utrecht, près de l'autoroute menant à Amsterdam. Chambres complètement équipées, centre d'affaires et de congrès. Ambiance de brasserie actuelle au restaurant. Carte avec lunch et menu.
◆ Piramidevormig hotel aan de rand van Utrecht, vlak bij de snelweg naar Amsterdam. Kamers die van alle gemakken zijn voorzien, business- en congrescentrum. Het restaurant heeft de ambiance van een moderne brasserie. Kaart met lunch en menu.

Mitland, Ariënslaan 1, ✉ 3573 PT, ☎ (0 30) 271 58 24, *info@mitland.nl, Fax (0 30) 271 90 03*, ch, – 25 à 150. AE VISA.
Repas *Lunch 16* – carte 31 à 40 – **135 ch** 103/140 – ½ P 85/94. CX t
◆ Immeubles excentrés s'ouvrant sur un parc entouré d'eau, près d'une ancienne forteresse. Chambres, suites et appartements avec kitchenette, pour les longs séjours. Salle des repas avec terrasse d'été et coup d'œil sur un étang. Lunch-buffets. Menu au dîner.
◆ Dit hotel aan de rand van de stad, aan een park met rondom water en nabij een oude vesting, heeft kamers, suites en appartementen met kitchenette voor een langer verblijf. Eetzaal met terras en uitzicht op een vijver. Lunchbuffetten. Dinermenu.

Park Plaza, Westplein 50, ✉ 3531 BL, ☎ (0 30) 292 52 00, *ppures@parkplazahotels.nl, Fax (0 30) 292 51 99*, – 25 à 170. AE VISA JCB. AY b
Repas *Lunch 22* – carte 39 à 49, ♀ – 17 – **120 ch** 195/235.
◆ Cette ressource hôtelière bien pratique pour l'homme d'affaires utilisateur du rail occupe un immeuble moderne dont toutes les chambres offrent l'accès à l'Internet.
◆ Dit hotel in een modern gebouw is heel praktisch gelegen voor de zakelijke clientèle die per trein reist. Alle kamers hebben internetverbinding.

Malie sans rest, Maliestraat 2, ✉ 3581 SL, ☎ (0 30) 231 64 24, *info@maliehotel.nl, Fax (0 30) 234 06 61*, – . AE VISA JCB. CX e
45 ch 99/180.
◆ Deux façades bourgeoises devancées d'une mignonne courette personnalisent ce petit hôtel entièrement rénové. Chambres de bon séjour et jardinet reposant à l'arrière.
◆ Twee statige gevels met een charmant binnenplaatsje geven dit volledig gerenoveerde hotel een eigen karakter. Comfortabele kamers en rustig tuintje aan de achterkant.

NH Centre Utrecht sans rest, Janskerkhof 10, ✉ 3512 BL, ☎ (0 30) 231 31 69, *reservations@nhcentre-utrecht.nh-hotels.nl, Fax (0 30) 231 01 48* – . AE VISA. BX k
13 – **45 ch** 150.
◆ Imposante maison de maître jouxtant la Janskerk au pied de laquelle se tient chaque samedi un ravissant marché aux fleurs. Chambres et junior suites assez plaisantes.
◆ Imposant herenhuis tegenover de kerk waarnaast 's zaterdags een gezellige bloemenmarkt wordt gehouden. Vrij aangename kamers en junior suites.

Amrâth sans rest, Vredenburg 14, ✉ 3511 BA, ☎ (0 30) 233 12 32, *info@amrathutrecht.nl, Fax (0 30) 232 84 51* – – 25 à 55. AE VISA. AX c
14 – **86 ch** 138/148.
◆ Immeuble dont la devanture arrondie domine une vaste place animée reliant la vieille ville aux nouveaux quartiers. Chambres fonctionnelles correctement insonorisées.
◆ Pand waarvan de afgeronde voorzijde aan een plein staat dat de oude stad met de nieuwe wijken verbindt. De functionele kamers zijn van een goede geluidsisolatie voorzien.

XXX **Karel V** - H. Gd H. Karel V, Geertebolwerk 1, ✉ 3511 XA, ☎ (0 30) 233 75 55, *info@karelv.nl, Fax (0 30) 233 75 00,* ☂ - ▤ P. AE ⓓ MC VISA JCB BY q
fermé 18 juil.-8 août et dim. – **Repas** (dîner seult) 49/90 bc, ♀.
◆ Une table qui n'aurait probablement pas déplu à l'empereur éponyme Charles Quint : opulente salle à manger, fines recettes au goût du jour et service très attentionné.
◆ Karel V zou zich vast wel thuis hebben gevoeld in dit luxueuze restaurant : weelderige eetzaal, fijne eigentijdse keuken en zeer attente bediening.

XXX **Wilhelminapark,** Wilhelminapark 65, ✉ 3581 NP, ☎ (0 30) 251 06 93, *info@wilhelminapark.nl, Fax (0 30) 254 07 64,* ≤, ☂ - ▤ - 🏛 25. AE MC VISA CY f
fermé sam. midi et dim. – **Repas** *Lunch 36* – 48.
◆ Pavillon à toit de chaume élevé dans les années 1920 au milieu d'un parc proche de la maison Rietveld Schröder. Salle et terrasse ont vue sur l'eau. Belle cheminée Art déco.
◆ Vrijstaand huis met rieten dak uit circa 1920, midden in een park, vlak bij het Rietveld Schröder huis. Eetzaal en terras kijken uit op het water. Mooie schouw in art deco.

XX **Jean d'Hubert,** Vleutenseweg 228, ✉ 3532 HP, ☎ (0 30) 294 59 52, *jeandhubert@jeandhubert.nl, Fax (0 30) 296 48 35* – ▤. AE MC VISA FU d
fermé dern. sem. juil.-2 prem. sem. août, sam. midi et dim. – **Repas** *Lunch 30* – 48/100 bc.
◆ Cet agréable restaurant décoré à la mode d'aujourd'hui - lambris rouges, tables nues, sièges modernes et toiles contemporaines - propose une cuisine dans le tempo actuel.
◆ Dit aangename restaurant met eigentijds decor - rode lambrisering, kale tafels, moderne zittingen, hedendaagse schilderijen - bereidt gerechten die de huidige smaak volgen.

XX **Goesting,** Veeartsenijpad 150, ✉ 3572 DH, ☎ (0 30) 273 33 46, ☂ – AE MC VISA CX n
fermé 2 dern. sem. juil. et dim. – **Repas** (dîner seult) carte 43 à 63, ♀.
◆ Au fond d'une impasse, dans un parc, bonne table actuelle occupant un bâtiment en forme de chapelle. Apaisante salle animée d'arcades, jolies assiettes et belle terrasse.
◆ Goed, eigentijds restaurant in een parkje aan het einde van een steeg. Vanbuiten is het net een kapel. Eetzaal met arcaden, rustige sfeer en mooi opgemaakte borden. Terras.

XX **Bistro Chez Jacqueline,** Korte Koestraat 4, ✉ 3511 RP, ☎ (0 30) 231 10 89, *chezjacqueline@planet.nl, Fax (0 30) 232 18 55,* ☂ - AE ⓓ MC VISA AX n
fermé du 3 au 24 août, dim. et lundi – **Repas** (dîner seult) carte 33 à 46.
◆ Plusieurs maisons établies à l'angle d'une rue piétonne composent cette gentille petite affaire familiale où se mitonnent des plats sagement traditionnels. Parking difficile.
◆ Enkele huizen op de hoek van een winkelstraat vormen dit vriendelijke familierestaurantje, waar traditionele gerechten worden bereid. Een parkeerplek is hier lastig te vinden.

XX **het Grachtenhuys,** Nieuwegracht 33, ✉ 3512 LD, ☎ (0 30) 231 74 94, *grachtenhuys@zonnet.nl, Fax (0 30) 236 70 25* – ▤. AE ⓓ MC VISA BY u
Repas (déjeuner seur réservation) 32/70 bc.
◆ Maison de maître postée au bord d'un canal (gracht), comme le proclame son enseigne. Préparations classiques sobrement réactualisées et déclinées en plusieurs menus.
◆ Waarin zou dit restaurant zijn ondergebracht ? De naam zegt genoeg. Klassieke gerechten worden voorzichtig in een bescheiden eigentijds jasje gestoken en in menu's aangeboden.

X **Hoofje's,** Schoutenstraat 19, ✉ 3512 GA, ☎ (0 30) 240 00 96, *wxs@hoofjes.nl, Fax (0 20) 238 09 41,* ☂, Produits de la mer – AE MC VISA JCB BXY z
fermé 30 déc.-début janv. et lundi – **Repas** (dîner seult jusqu'à 23 h 30) carte env. 44, ♀.
◆ Cuisine littorale, mémorables plateaux de fruits de mer, coude à coude convivial et service aussi gentil que charmant, dans une salle sobre et moderne, savamment éclairée.
◆ Visrestaurant waar u gezellig zij aan zij zit in een eenvoudige, moderne zaal met ingenieuze verlichting. Mooie plateaus met fruits de mer. Vriendelijke, charmante bediening.

X **Kaatje's,** A. van Ostadelaan 67a, ✉ 3583 AC, ☎ (0 30) 251 11 82, *kaatje.valkenburg@12move.nl, Fax (0 30) 252 33 19* – ▤. MC CZ p
fermé dern. sem. juil.-prem. sem. août, sam. midi et dim. midi – **Repas** *Lunch 25* – 33, ♀.
◆ Grand comme un mouchoir, ce restaurant de quartier affiche un petit air de bistrot. Aux fourneaux, le souci de faire bien avec des produits simples. Clientèle d'habitués.
◆ Dit piepkleine buurtrestaurant heeft iets weg van een bistro. Achter het fornuis wordt met zorg van eenvoudige producten iets goeds bereid. Vaste klantenkring.

à De Meern *Ouest : 9 km* C *Utrecht :*

X **Castellum Novum,** Castellumlaan 1, ✉ 3454 VA, ☎ (0 30) 666 45 80, *demeern@castellumnovum.nl, Fax (0 30) 666 45 70,* ☂ – ▤ P – 🏛 25 à 90. AE MC VISA JCB
fermé sam. midi et dim. midi – **Repas** *Lunch 25* – 30.
◆ Grosse auberge couleur terre de Sienne nichée au centre du village. La carte, trimestrielle, honore tour à tour les pays d'Europe baignés par la Méditerranée. Ambiance "Sud".
◆ Robuust restaurant in terrakleur, in het dorpscentrum. Op de driemaandelijks wisselende kaart passeert telkens een ander mediterraan land de revue : zuidelijke ambiance dus !

à **Oud-Zuilen** C *Maarssen 40 134 h :*

X **Belle,** Dorpsstraat 12, ✉ 3611 AE, ℘ (0 30) 244 17 90, *restaurant.belle@12move.nl, Fax (0 30) 243 72 90,* – P. MC VISA
fermé 27 déc.-1er janv. – **Repas** *Lunch 32* – 35, ♀.
◆ Aux abords du château d'Oud-Zuilen, demeure du 18e s. dont les salles à manger entretiennent une plaisante atmosphère rustique. Carte parsemée d'intitulés amusants.
◆ Restaurant in een 18e-eeuws huis in de buurt van Slot Zuylen. In de eetkamers heerst nog altijd een prettige, rustieke ambiance. Op de kaart staan tal van amusante benamingen.

VAALS *Limburg* 532 V 18 *et* 715 J 9 – *10 732 h.*

Voir *au Sud : 1,5 km, Drielandenpunt★, ≤★, de la tour Baudouin ※★ (Boudewijntoren).*
ℹ *Maastrichterlaan 73a,* ✉ *6291 EL,* ℘ *0 900-97 98, info@vvvzuidlimburg.nl, Fax (0 43) 609 85 25.*
Amsterdam 229 – Maastricht 27 – Aachen 4.

Dolce Vaalsbroek ⛎, Vaalsbroek 1, ✉ 6291 NH, ℘ (0 43) 308 93 08, *info@vaalsbroek.nl, Fax (0 43) 308 93 33,* – rest, TV ♿ P – 25 à 220. AE ⓓ MC VISA. rest
Repas (dîner seult) 34, ♀ – 15 – **125 ch** 150/250, – 5 suites – ½ P 110/135.
◆ Hôtel de luxe renfermant de paisibles chambres tout confort ainsi qu'un centre de remise en forme bien équipé. Les congrès se tiennent à deux pas, dans un beau château. Un ancien moulin à eau prête ses murs au restaurant. Terrasse d'été au bord de l'étang.
◆ Luxehotel met rustige kamers die van alle gemakken zijn voorzien, en een goed uitgerust fitnesscentrum. Op een steenworp afstand worden in een mooi kasteel congressen gehouden. Een oude watermolen herbergt het restaurant. Zomerterras aan de vijver.

Kasteel Bloemendal ⛎, Bloemendalstraat 150, ✉ 6291 CM, ℘ (0 43) 365 98 00, *info@bloemendal.valk.nl, Fax (0 43) 306 66 12,* – TV P – 25 à 200. AE ⓓ MC VISA.
Repas *Lunch 28* – carte 35 à 51 – 11 – **74 ch** 85/125, – 3 suites – ½ P 99.
◆ Château du 18e s. devancé d'un parc et s'ouvrant sur un jardin en terrasses à l'arrière. Communs amples et cossus. Diverses catégories de chambres bien agencées. Confortable restaurant de style classique où l'on vient faire des repas au goût du jour.
◆ Een 18e-eeuws kasteel met een park aan de voorzijde en een terrasvormige tuin aan de achterkant. Luxueuze gemeenschappelijke ruimten. Goed ingedeelde kamers in diverse categorieën. Comfortabel restaurant met klassieke ambiance en een eigentijdse keuken.

X **Ambiente,** Lindenstraat 1, ✉ 6291 AE, ℘ (0 43) 306 59 39, *ambiente@vodafone.de,*
fermé merc. et jeudi – **Repas** (dîner seult) 30/42 bc, ♀.
◆ L'enseigne de cette maison bourgeoise est transalpine, mais l'Italie n'a pas l'exclusivité en cuisine. Préparations françaises et méditerranéennes.
◆ De naam van dit restaurant in een herenhuis mag dan Italiaans zijn, in de keuken heeft de Laars niet het alleenrecht. Franse en mediterrane gerechten.

VAASSEN *Gelderland* C *Epe 33 224 h.* 531 U 9, 532 U 9 *et* 715 I 5.

Amsterdam 98 – Arnhem 36 – Apeldoorn 10 – Zwolle 33.

XX ✿ **De Leest** (Boerma), Kerkweg 1, ✉ 8171 VT, ℘ (0 578) 57 13 82, *info@restaurantdeleest.nl, Fax (0 578) 57 74 88,* – AE MC VISA JCB.
fermé 2 dern. sem juil.-prem. sem. août, 31 déc.-2 janv., sam. midi et lundi – **Repas** *Lunch 33* – 53, carte 55 à 74, ♀.
◆ Agréable refuge gourmand établi au centre du village. Décor intérieur moderne ; cuisine du moment présentée avec esthétisme. Terrasse à l'abri des regards et parking public.
◆ Aangename culinaire pleisterplaats in het dorp. Modern intérieur. Zeer verzorgde, eigentijdse en subtiel opgemaakte gerechten. Discreet terras en openbare parkeergelegenheid.
Spéc. Langoustines poêlées, girolles, pomme verte et fondue d'avocat vinaigrette. Chevreuil aux épices et aigre-doux de betteraves rouges (en saison). Tartare d'ananas, glace verveine et crème de coriandre (été)

VALKENBURG *Limburg* C *Valkenburg aan de Geul 17 834 h.* 532 U 17 *et* 715 I 9 – *Station thermale – Casino* Y *, Kuurpark Cauberg 28,* ✉ *6301 BT,* ℘ *(0 43) 609 96 00, Fax (0 43) 609 96 99.*

Musée : *de la mine★ (Steenkolenmijn Valkenburg)* Z.

Exc. *Circuit Zuid-Limburg★ ((Limbourg Méridional).*

ℹ *Theodoor Dorrenplein 5,* ✉ *6301 DV,* ℘ *0 900-97 98, valkenburg@vvvzuidlimburg.nl, Fax (0 43) 609 85 08.*
Amsterdam 212 ① *– Maastricht 15* ① *– Liège 40* ③ *– Aachen 26* ①

VALKENBURG

Street	Square	No.
Berkelstr.	Z	3
Dr. Erensstr.	Y	4
Emmalaan	Y	6
Grendelpl.	Z	7
Grotestr.	Z	9
Halderstr.	Z	10
Hekerbeekstr.	Y	12
Jan Dekkerstr.	Y	13
Kerkstr.	Z	15
Kloosterweg	Y	16
Louis van der Maessenstr.	Y	18
Muntstr.	Z	19
Oranjelaan	Y	21
Palankastr.	Z	22
Plenkertstr.	YZ	
Poststr.	Y	24
Prinses Margrietlaan	Y	25
Sittarderweg	Y	27
Theodoor Dorrenpl.	Y	28
Walrampl.	Z	30
Walravenstr.	Z	31
Wilhelminalaan	YZ	

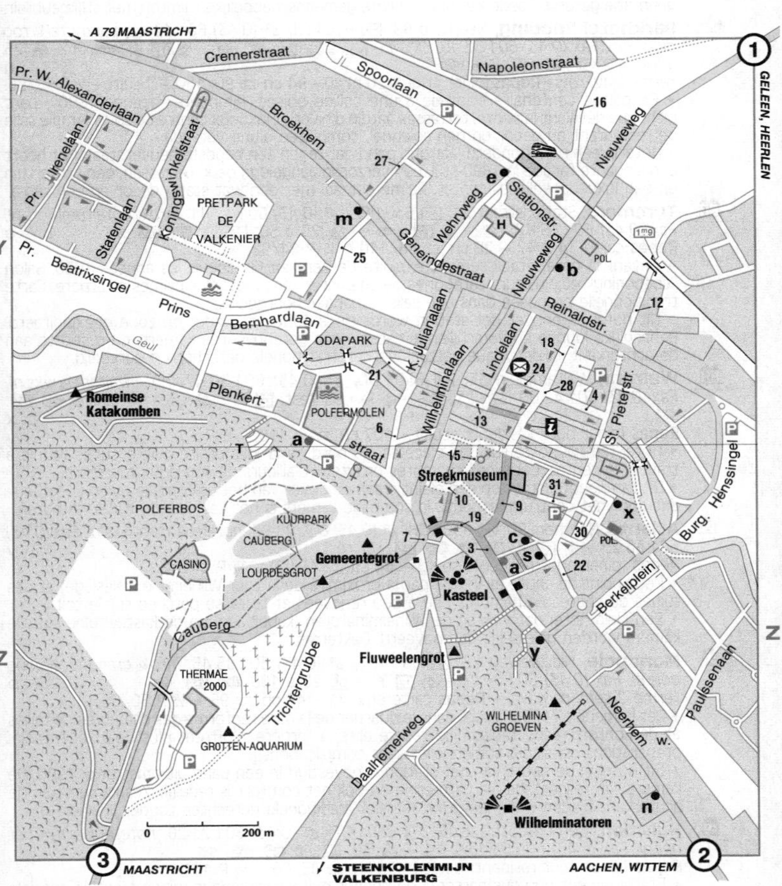

Prinses Juliana, Broekhem 11, ✉ 6301 HD, ☎ (0 43) 601 22 44, *info@juliana.nl*, *Fax (0 43) 601 44 05*, – TV P – 50. AE VISA Y m

fermé sem. carnaval, 25 juil.-10 août, du 1er au 15 janv. et lundi – **Repas** voir rest ***Juliana*** ci-après – 17 – **15 ch** 105/130 – ½ P 130/148.

◆ Charmante hostellerie agrémentée d'un jardin à l'anglaise. La plupart des chambres sont de fringantes junior suites au mobilier patiné. Très bons petits-déjeuners.

◆ Charmant hotel met een Engelse tuin. De meeste kamers zijn fleurige junior suites met gepatineerd meubilair. Uitstekend ontbijt.

Grand-Hotel, Walramplein 1, ✉ 6301 DC, ☎ (0 43) 601 28 41, *info@hotelvoncken.nl, Fax (0 43) 601 62 45* – 25 à 100. Z s
fermé 27 déc.-7 janv. – **Repas** voir rest **Voncken** ci-après – **37 ch** 85/140, – 2 suites – ½ P 85/100.
◆ Sur une place arborée, près des vestiges du château, "grand-hôtel" tenu en famille depuis cinq générations. Bonnes chambres et communs spacieux garnis de meubles de style.
◆ Dit familiehotel aan een plein, vlak bij de kasteelruïne, wordt inmiddels door de vijfde generatie gerund. Goede kamers en grote gemeenschappelijke ruimten met stijlmeubilair.

Parkhotel Rooding, Neerhem 68, ✉ 6301 CJ, ☎ (0 43) 601 32 41, *parkhotel@rooding.com, Fax (0 43) 601 32 40*, – 25 à 140. Z n
fermé janv.-fév. – **Repas** (dîner jusqu'à 20 h) 40 – **94 ch** 90/150, – 1 suite – ½ P 65/85.
◆ Ce palace centenaire s'adosse à une colline boisée. Pimpante façade "1890", parc bichonné dévalant la pente, terrasses, jardin d'hiver et luxueux centre de soins. Ample salle de restaurant au décor un rien solennel, complétée d'une véranda.
◆ Hotel in een ruim honderd jaar oud pand dat tegen een beboste heuvel staat. Het heeft een elegante façade in 1890-stijl, een verzorgd aangelegd park, terrassen, een wintertuin en een luxueus wellness center. Ruime eetzaal met een wat statig decor en een serre.

Tummers, Stationstraat 21, ✉ 6301 EZ, ☎ (0 43) 601 37 41, *info@hoteltummers.nl, Fax (0 43) 601 36 47*, – 25 à 50. Y e
Repas carte 34 à 47 – **28 ch** 86/110 – ½ P 64/98.
◆ Devant la gare, établissement exploité de père en fils depuis les années 1930. Salon "cocooning" et plusieurs catégories de chambres rénovées, plus calmes à l'arrière. Carte traditionnelle proposée dans une salle à manger bourgeoise.
◆ Dit hotel tegenover het station wordt sinds 1930 van vader op zoon geëxploiteerd. Behaaglijke lounge en verschillende categorieën gerenoveerde kamers, de rustigste aan de achterkant. In de chique eetzaal worden traditionele gerechten geserveerd.

Walram, Walramplein 37, ✉ 6301 DC, ☎ (0 43) 601 30 47, *hotelwalram@wxs.nl, Fax (0 43) 601 42 00*, rest, – 25 à 60. Z x
Repas (dîner pour résidents seult) – **107 ch** 60/99 – ½ P 55/75.
◆ Hôtel familial posté sur une placette, au bord de la jolie petite rivière qui se faufile à travers le centre. Certaines chambres profitent d'ailleurs de son doux murmure.
◆ Dit familiehotel staat op een pleintje aan de oever van het bekoorlijke riviertje de Geul, dat door het centrum stroomt. In sommige kamers is het kabbelende water te horen.

Atlanta, Neerhem 20, ✉ 6301 CH, ☎ (0 43) 601 21 93, *hotelatlanta@wxs.nl, Fax (0 43) 601 53 29* – rest Z y
Repas (dîner pour résidents seult) – **34 ch** 49/90 – ½ P 56/62.
◆ Petit point de chute avantagé par la proximité de la tour Wilhelmine (télésiège) et des ruines du château. Chambres peu à peu rénovées et terrasse perchée sur le toit.
◆ Een klein hotel dat vlak bij de Wilhelminatoren (kabelbaan) en de kasteelruïne ligt. De kamers worden geleidelijk gerenoveerd. Dakterras.

Monopole, Nieuweweg 22, ✉ 6301 ET, ☎ (0 43) 601 35 45, *info@grandhotelmonopole.nl, Fax (0 43) 601 47 11* – – 25 à 100. Y b
fermé 2 sem. carnaval – **Repas** carte env. 41 – **48 ch** 95 – ½ P 50/60.
◆ Cet immeuble "1900" établi dans le quartier de la gare renferme des chambres de tailles et de confort respectables. Six d'entre elles, à l'arrière, s'offrent plus de luxe. À table, préparations classico-traditionnelles sans complications.
◆ Dit hotel in de buurt van het station is gevestigd in een pand uit omstreeks 1900. De kamers zijn respectabel van afmeting en ook het comfort is redelijk. Zes kamers aan de achterkant bieden wat meer luxe. Klassiek-traditionele gerechten zonder liflafjes.

Hulsman, De Guascostraat 16, ✉ 6301 CT, ☎ (0 43) 601 23 26, *hotel.hulsman@hetnet.nl, Fax (0 43) 609 03 13* – – 30.
Repas (dîner pour résidents seult) – **24 ch** 45/66 – ½ P 101.
◆ Établissement où vous passerez de bonnes nuitées sans vous ruiner. Mention spéciale pour le menu demi pension servi au dîner, d'un rapport qualité-prix avantageux.
◆ Hier zult u van de rekening niet met hoofdpijn wakker worden. Een speciale vermelding verdient het halfpensionmenu ('s avonds) met zijn uitstekende prijs-kwaliteitverhouding.

Juliana - H. Prinses Juliana, Broekhem 11, ✉ 6301 HD, ☎ (0 43) 601 22 44, *info@juliana.nl, Fax (0 43) 601 44 05*, – Y m
fermé sem. carnaval, 25 juil.-10 août, du 1er au 15 janv., sam. midi et lundi – **Repas** Lunch 45 – 63/120 bc, carte 58 à 82, ♀.
◆ Cuisine actuelle raffinée servie avec style dans un décor aussi chaleureux qu'élégant. Un jardin paysager sert d'écrin à la superbe terrasse où l'on dresse le couvert en été.
◆ De geraffineerde, eigentijdse keuken wordt met stijl geserveerd in een warm en smaakvol decor. 's Zomers worden de tafels gedekt op het magnifieke terras in de Engelse tuin.
Spéc. Salade de homard canadien et saumon fumé, pommes de terre et crème truffée. Langoustines sautées, leurs raviolis et leurs jus. Canard rôti et tourte de ses cuisses, melon (printemps-été)

XXX **Voncken** - H. Grand-Hotel, Walramplein 1, ✉ 6301 DC, ✆ (0 43) 601 28 41, *info@hotelvoncken.nl, Fax (0 43) 601 62 45*, – P. AE ① MC VISA JCB. Z s
fermé du 22 au 25 fév., 27 déc.-7 janv., dim. soir d'oct. à avril, sam. midi et dim. midi – **Repas** *Lunch 30* – carte env. 57.
◆ Intégré au Grand-Hotel Voncken, ce restaurant gastronomique interprète un répertoire culinaire rigoureusement classique, assorti au style de la salle à manger.
◆ Dit gastronomische restaurant in Grand-Hotel Voncken heeft een uiterst klassiek culinair repertoire, dat in goede harmonie is met de stijl van de eetzaal.

XX **Hubert Haenen,** Plenkerstraat 47a, ✉ 6301 GL, ✆ (0 43) 601 27 97, *info@huberthaenen.nl* – P. AE MC VISA Y a
fermé dern. sem. juin, 3 prem. sem. janv., lundi, mardi et merc. – **Repas** (déjeuner sur réservation) 43/53, ♀.
◆ Un couple d'artistes tient cette table garnie de toiles modernes brossées "maison". Accueil avenant, petite carte actuelle, grillades au charbon de bois et vins à bon prix.
◆ Een artistiek echtpaar runt dit restaurant, dat wordt opgeluisterd met kleurrijke schilderijen "van het huis". Kleine eigentijdse kaart, houtoven en redelijk geprijsde wijnen.

XX **'t Mergelheukske** 1er étage, Berkelstraat 13a, ✉ 6301 CB, ✆ (0 43) 601 63 50, *Fax (0 43) 601 63 50*, – P. AE MC VISA. Z a
fermé 2 sem. carnaval, dern. sem. sept.-prem. sem. oct., lundi et mardi – **Repas** (déjeuner sur réservation) carte 24 à 40.
◆ Plaisante adresse du secteur piétonnier avoisinant les ruines du château. Salle de restaurant avec charpente apparente, mezzanine et terrasse d'été abritée à l'arrière.
◆ Plezierig adres in het voetgangersgebied bij de kasteelruïne. Restaurantzaal met balken, vide en een beschut zomerterras aan de achterkant.

à Berg en Terblijt *Ouest : 5 km* C *Valkenburg aan de Geul :*

Kasteel Geulzicht , Vogelzangweg 2, ✉ 6325 PN, ✆ (0 43) 604 04 32, *mail@kasteelgeulzicht.nl, Fax (0 43) 604 20 11*, ≤, , – |‡| TV P. AE ① MC VISA. rest
Repas (dîner pour résidents seult) – **9 ch** ☐ 106/186 – ½ P 94/120.
◆ Une atmosphère aristocratique flotte encore dans ce château surplombant la vallée. Splendides salons, restaurant d'été panoramique et quatre chambres avec bain romain.
◆ In dit kasteel boven het Geuldal hangt nog altijd een aristocratische sfeer. Schitterende salons, panoramisch zomerterras en vier kamers met Romeins bad.

Vue des Montagnes, Wolfsdriesweg 7, ✉ 6325 PM, ✆ (0 43) 604 06 52, *mail@vuedesmontagnes.nl, Fax (0 43) 604 25 25*, , – |‡| TV P – 25 à 70. AE ① MC VISA. rest
Repas (dîner seult) carte env. 35 – **38 ch** ☐ 80/94 – ½ P 65.
◆ Jadis maison de repos de mineurs, cet hôtel établi au pied de la "montagne" (il s'agit plus modestement d'une colline) avoisine aussi plusieurs entrées de grottes. Lumineuse salle de restaurant aux tables bien espacées, donnant sur un jardin. Repas classique.
◆ Dit hotel heeft onderdak gevonden in een voormalig rusthuis voor mijnwerkers, aan de voet van een heuvel en naast de ingang van enkele grotten. Heerlijk lichte eetzaal met veel ruimte tussen de tafels en uitzicht op de tuin. Klassieke maaltijden.

à Houthem *Ouest : 3,5 km* C *Valkenburg aan de Geul :*

Château St. Gerlach , Joseph Corneli Allée 1, ✉ 6301 KK, ✆ (0 43) 608 88 88, *reservations@stgerlach.chateauhotels.nl, Fax (0 43) 604 28 83*, ≤, , , , , , – |‡|, ch, TV P – 25 à 200. AE ① MC VISA JCB
Repas voir rest ***Les Trois Corbeaux*** ci-après – ***Bistrot de Liège*** *Lunch 36* – carte env. 40 – ☐ 21 – **58 ch** 180/230, – 39 suites – ½ P 168/185.
◆ Chambres et suites somptueuses, dans les dépendances (1759) d'un château néoclassique flanqué d'une église baroque. Parc séduisant. Vue sur la campagne boisée. Bistrot "sympa" mettant à profit l'ancienne cuisine du baron. Recettes traditionnelles.
◆ Luxueuze kamers en suites liggen verspreid over de dependances (1759) van een neoklassiek kasteel met barokkerk. Aanlokkelijk park en uitzicht op het boslandschap. De sympathieke bistro bereidt traditionele gerechten in de oude keuken van de baron.

XXX **Les Trois Corbeaux** - H. Château St. Gerlach, Joseph Corneli Allée 1, ✉ 6301 KK, ✆ (0 43) 608 88 88, *reservations@stgerlach.chateauhotels.nl, Fax (0 43) 604 28 83*, ≤, – P. AE ① MC VISA JCB.
Repas (dîner seult) – 60/117 bc.
◆ Meubles de styles, délicates boiseries et peintures murales "1900" composent l'opulent décor de cette table occupant le corps de logis du Château St. Gerlach. Parc admirable.
◆ Stijlmeubilair, lambrisering en wandschilderingen uit rond 1900 vormen het weelderige decor van dit restaurant in het hoofdgebouw van het Château St. Gerlach. Prachtig park.

VALKENSWAARD *Noord-Brabant 532 R 14 et 715 H 7 – 31 163 h.*

Oranje Nassaustraat 8a, ✉ 5554 AC, ☎ (0 40) 201 51 15, vvv-valkenswaard@acon.nl, Fax (0 40) 204 08 05.

Amsterdam 135 – Eindhoven 12 – 's-Hertogenbosch 46 – Venlo 58 – Turnhout 41.

XXX **Normandie,** Leenderweg 4, ✉ 5554 CL, ☎ (0 40) 201 88 80, *info@normandie.nl, Fax (0 40) 204 75 66,* – . AE VISA JCB.
fermé du 23 au 27 fév., du 1er au 14 août, 24 et 31 déc., 1er janv., sam. midi et dim. midi – **Repas** Lunch 27 – 45/50, ♀.
◆ Au centre-ville, avenante maison de bouche où vous vous sentirez dorlotés. Deux frères jumeaux y officient : l'un en salle, l'autre aux fourneaux. Terrasse d'été sur le toit.
◆ In dit aangename restaurant in het centrum wordt u echt een beetje vertroeteld. Tweelingbroers runnen de zaak : de een in de bediening, de ander achter het fornuis. Dakterras.

VALTHE *Drenthe 531 AA 5 et 715 L 3 – voir à Odoorn.*

VEENDAM *Groningen 531 AA 4 et 715 L 2 – 28 304 h.*

Ontspanningslaan 1, ☎ (0 598) 62 70 06, Fax (0 598) 63 43 85.

Amsterdam 213 – Groningen 35 – Assen 33.

Parkzicht, Winkler Prinsstraat 3, ✉ 9641 AD, ☎ (0 598) 62 64 64, *info@parkzicht.com, Fax (0 598) 61 90 37,* – – 25 à 500. AE VISA
Repas Lunch 14 – carte 28 à 39 – **50 ch** 58/91 – ½ P 37/46.
◆ Cet établissement tenu en famille depuis trois générations se partage entre une maison de coin et une récente construction communicante où se distribuent les chambres. Préparations simples servies dans une petite salle à manger précédée d'un bar.
◆ De derde generatie beheert nu dit familiehotel, dat een hoekhuis omvat en een daarmee in verbinding staand nieuw pand met de kamers. Eenvoudige gerechten worden geserveerd in een kleine eetzaal die voorbij de bar is ingericht.

VEENENDAAL *Utrecht 532 S 10 et 715 H 5 – 60 669 h.*

au Sud-Est : 10 km à Maarsbergen, Woudenbergseweg 13a, ✉ 3953 ME, ☎ (0 343) 43 19 11, Fax (0 343) 43 20 62.

Kerkewijk 10, ✉ 3901 EC, ☎ (0 318) 52 98 00, vvvanwb@vvvanwbveenendaal.nl, Fax (0 318) 55 31 33.

Amsterdam 74 – Arnhem 35 – Utrecht 36.

XX **De Vendel,** Vendelseweg 69, ✉ 3905 LC, ☎ (0 318) 52 55 06, *Fax (0 318) 52 25 02,* – – 40. AE VISA
fermé sam. midi et dim. – **Repas** Lunch 30 – carte 22 à 63.
◆ Ancienne ferme cachée dans un quartier résidentiel, près d'un vieux moulin. À midi, on s'attable dans une lumineuse véranda pyramidale, voire au jardin, si le temps s'y prête.
◆ Deze voormalige boerderij ligt verscholen in een woonwijk, vlak bij een oude molen. 's Middags kunt u aan tafel in een lichte, piramidale serre en bij mooi weer in de tuin.

X **'t Podium** De Sterke Arm 1, ✉ 3901 EK, ☎ (0 318) 50 80 90, *info@restaurantpodium.nl, Fax (0 318) 50 80 84,* – . AE VISA JCB
fermé dern. sem. juil.-2 prem. sem. août, 28 déc.-17 janv., dim. et lundi – **Repas** (déjeuner sur réservation) carte env. 35.
◆ Pavillon contemporain en verre et alluminium établi au bord d'un canal du centre. Grandes toiles et montages floraux modernes en salle. Terrasse sur l'eau. Cuisine du moment.
◆ Modern restaurant van glas en aluminium, aan een kanaal in het centrum. Interieur met grote schilderijen en moderne bloemstukken. Seizoengebonden keuken, terras aan het water.

VEERE *Zeeland 532 G 13 et 715 C 7 – 21 985 h.*

Voir *Maisons écossaises★ (Schotse Huizen)* **A** – *Ancien hôtel de ville★ (Oude stadhuis).*

Oudestraat 28, ✉ 4351 AV, ☎ 0 900 202 02 80, vvvveere@vvvwnb.nl, Fax (0 118) 50 17 92.

Amsterdam 181 ② – Middelburg 7 ① – Zierikzee 38 ②

Plan page ci-contre

XX **De Campveerse Toren** avec ch en annexe, Kaai 2, ✉ 4351 AA, ☎ (0 118) 50 12 91, *info@campveersetoren.nl, Fax (0 118) 50 16 95,* ←, – – 25. AE VISA JCB a
fermé du 3 au 30 janv. – **Repas** *(fermé lundi et mardi de nov. à mars)* Lunch 39 – 43/68 bc – **14 ch** 79/120 – ½ P 120/175.
◆ Retranché dans une tour-bastion (15e s.) surveillant le Veerse Meer, ce petit restaurant ne manque assurément pas de caractère. Décor rustique. Jolies chambres en annexe.
◆ Dit restaurantje heeft zich verschanst in een bastiontoren (15e eeuw) die waakt over het Veerse Meer. Aan karakter geen gebrek ! Rustiek decor. Mooie kamers in de annexe.

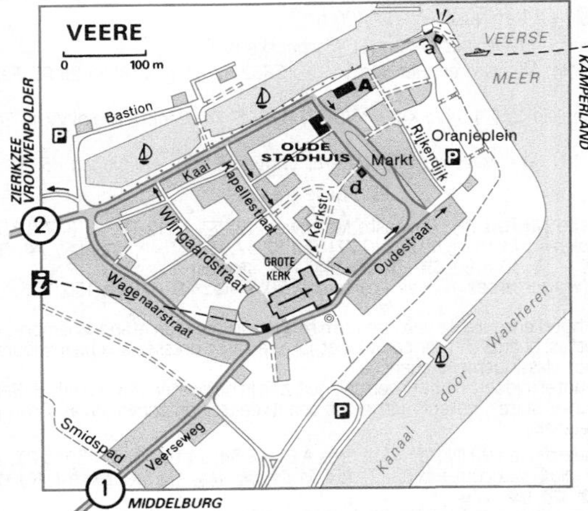

XX **'t Waepen van Veere** avec ch, Markt 23, ✉ 4351 AG, ☎ (0 118) 50 12 31, *info@waepen.nl*, *Fax (0 118) 50 60 09*, 🍴 – TV. AE MC VISA d
fermé du 31 déc.-12 fév. et lundi et mardi de nov. à mars – **Repas** 30/43 – **11 ch** ☕ 85 – ½ P 65.

◆ Sur le Markt, mignonne auberge familiale où se concocte une cuisine d'aujourd'hui. Des chambres de mise simple, toutefois très convenables, sont également proposées.

◆ In deze charmante familieherberg op de Markt wordt een eigentijdse keuken bereidt. Ook zijn er enkele eenvoudige, maar comfortabele kamers beschikbaar.

X **In den Struyskelder,** Kaai 25, ✉ 4351 AA, ☎ (0 118) 50 13 92, *info@struyskelder.nl*, *Fax (0 118) 50 16 95*, 🍴, Taverne-rest – AE MC VISA A
fermé janv.-mi-fév. et mardi, merc., jeudi et vend. d'oct. nov. à avril – **Repas** Lunch 18 – 22/27 bc.

◆ La cave voûtée d'un édifice gothique flamboyant procure un cadre original à cette table. Des fresques accentuent encore l'ambiance historique. Terrasse d'été close de murs.

◆ De gewelfde kelder van een laat-gotisch gebouw vormt het originele decor van dit restaurant. Fresco's accentueren de historische ambiance. Ommuurd zomerterras.

VELDHOVEN *Noord-Brabant* 532 R 14 *et* 715 H 7 – *42 718 h.*

Locht 140, ✉ 5504 RP, ☎ (0 40) 253 44 44, Fax (0 40) 254 97 47.
Amsterdam 129 – Eindhoven 8 – Venlo 67 – Turnhout 45.

XX **The Fisherman,** Kruisstraat 23, ✉ 5502 JA, ☎ (0 40) 254 58 38, *Fax (0 40) 254 58 57*, 🍴, Produits de la mer – P. AE D MC VISA JCB.
fermé 2 dern. sem. juil., dern. sem. déc., sam. midi et dim. midi – **Repas** Lunch 25 – carte 43 à 62.

◆ L'enseigne de cette imposante villa coiffée d'un toit de chaume n'autorise vraiment aucune équivoque : cuisine donnant toute sa mesure dans les produits de la mer.

◆ De naam van deze imposante villa met rieten dak geeft geen enkele aanleiding tot enig misverstand : de keuken staat geheel in het teken van de zee.

VELP *Gelderland* 532 U 10 *et* 715 I 6 – *voir à Arnhem.*

VELSEN *Noord-Holland* 531 N 8 *et* 715 E 4 – *voir à IJmuiden.*

Indien zich belangrijke stijgingen voordoen inzake kosten van levensonderhoud, mogen de door ons opgegeven prijzen verhoogd worden. Vraag bij het reserveren van een hotelkamer steeds naar de definitieve prijs.

VENLO *Limburg* 532 W 14 *et* 715 J 7 – *91 400 h.*

Voir *Mobilier★ de l'église St-Martin (St. Martinuskerk)* Y.

par ⑦ : 30 km à Geysteren, Het Spekt 2, ✉ 5862 AZ, ✆ (0 478) 53 25 92, Fax (0 478) 53 29 63.

Koninginneplein 2, ✉ 5911 KK, ✆ (0 77) 320 77 74, venlo@regiovvv.nl, Fax (0 77) 320 77 70.

Amsterdam 181 ⑥ – Maastricht 73 ④ – Eindhoven 51 ⑥ – Nijmegen 65 ⑧

Plan page suivante

De Bovenste Molen, Bovenste Molenweg 12, ✉ 5912 TV, ✆ (0 77) 359 14 14, *bovenste-molen@bilderberg.nl, Fax (0 77) 354 82 57*, – 30 à 80. AE VISA JCB. rest X v
Repas ***Het Zwanenmeer*** *Lunch 28* – carte env. 50, – 18 – **79 ch** 150/255, – 3 suites – ½ P 140.

◆ Ce paisible hôtel entouré de verdure se mire à la surface d'un étang. Chambres et junior suites douillettes, beauty-center complet et jolie terrasse dressée aux beaux jours. Grande salle à manger classiquement agencée.

◆ Dit rustige hotel midden in het groen spiegelt zich in het water van een vijver. Behaaglijke kamers en junior suites, volledig uitgerust beautycenter en zomerterras. Grote, klassiek ingerichte eetzaal.

Venlo, Nijmeegseweg 90 (Nord : 4 km près A 67 - E 34, sortie ㊵), ✉ 5916 PT, ✆ (0 77) 354 41 41, *venlo@valk.com, Fax (0 77) 354 31 33*, rest, – 25 à 220. AE VISA JCB V s
Repas (ouvert jusqu'à 23 h) carte 22 à 39, – **149 ch** 78/98.

◆ Récemment entré dans le giron de la chaîne hollandaise Van der Valk, cet établissement tout proche de l'autoroute vient de s'agrandir d'une soixantaine de chambres. Vaste restaurant misant sur de copieuses préparations régionales.

◆ Dit hotel dicht bij de snelweg maakt sinds kort deel uit van de Van der Valk-keten. Het heeft zijn capaciteit met een zestigtal kamers uitgebreid. Op de menukaart van het grote restaurant staan streekgerechten, die in royale porties worden geserveerd.

Wilhelmina, Kaldenkerkerweg 1, ✉ 5913 AB, ✆ (0 77) 351 62 51, *info@hotel-wilhelmina.nl, Fax (0 77) 351 22 52*, – , rest, – 25 à 125. AE VISA JCB Z a
Repas *(fermé sam. midi et dim. midi)* carte 33 à 56 – **43 ch** 68/85 – ½ P 53/70.

◆ Chambres fonctionnelles bien calibrées se partageant les deux étages d'une imposante maison de ville. Plus de calme à l'arrière. Situation avantageuse, point de vue mobilité. Restaurant soucieux de bien faire, avec de bons produits.

◆ Op de twee verdiepingen van dit imposante stadshuis liggen functionele kamers van goed formaat. Aan de achterkant heeft u wat meer rust. Het hotel is in alle opzichten goed bereikbaar. In het restaurant wordt met zorg iets goeds bereid van kwaliteitsproducten.

Puur sans rest, Parade 7a, ✉ 5911 CA, ✆ (0 77) 351 57 90, *info@hotelpuur.nl, Fax (0 77) 352 52 60*, – . AE VISA. YZ z
fermé du 25 au 28 déc. – **30 ch** 63/77 – ½ P 55/79.

◆ Estimable hôtel implanté dans une belle maison de notable proche des rues piétonnes commerçantes. Fringantes petites chambres de styles "tendance" ou vaguement nautique.

◆ Een verdienstelijk hotel in een mooi herenhuis, op loopafstand van de winkel- en wandelstraten. Kleine, fleurige kamers in trendy stijl of met een licht maritiem accent.

Campanile, Noorderpoort 5 (Nord : 4 km près A 67 - E 34, sortie ㊵), ✉ 5916 PJ, ✆ (0 77) 351 05 30, *venlo@campanile.nl, Fax (0 77) 354 80 57*, – – 30. AE VISA V d
Repas *(fermé sam. midi et dim. midi)* (avec buffets) carte 22 à 36 – 10 – **49 ch** 64/67 – ½ P 77/90.

◆ Établissement de chaîne dont l'accès aux sobres petites chambres insonorisées - conformes à l'esprit Campanile - se fait par un couloir extérieur. Grand parking à vue.

◆ In dit ketenhotel leidt een externe gang naar de kamers, die conform het Campanile-concept klein en eenvoudig zijn en voorzien van geluidsisolatie. Grote parking in het zicht.

XXX **Valuas** avec ch, St. Urbanusweg 11, ✉ 5914 CA, ✆ (0 77) 354 11 41, *valuas.hr@worldonline.nl, Fax (0 77) 354 70 22*, – – 25 à 125. AE VISA JCB. V r
fermé vacances bâtiment, fin déc., sam. midi et dim. – **Repas** (avec brasserie) *Lunch 38* – carte 59 à 80, – **18 ch** 65/90.

◆ Sur la route de Nimègue, hostellerie dissimulant une belle terrasse en bord de Meuse. Salle de restaurant animée d'arcades et de colonnes. Fine cuisine actuelle et bonne cave.

◆ Dit restaurant heeft een mooi terras aan de Maas. In de eetzaal vormen zuilen en arcaden een sfeervol decor. Verfijnde, eigentijdse keuken en een mooie wijnkelder.

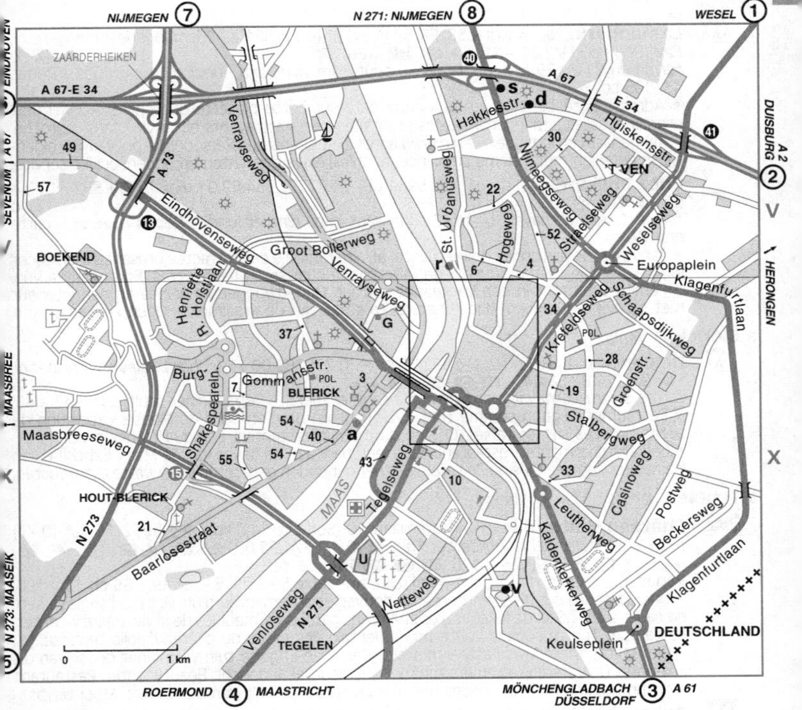

VENLO

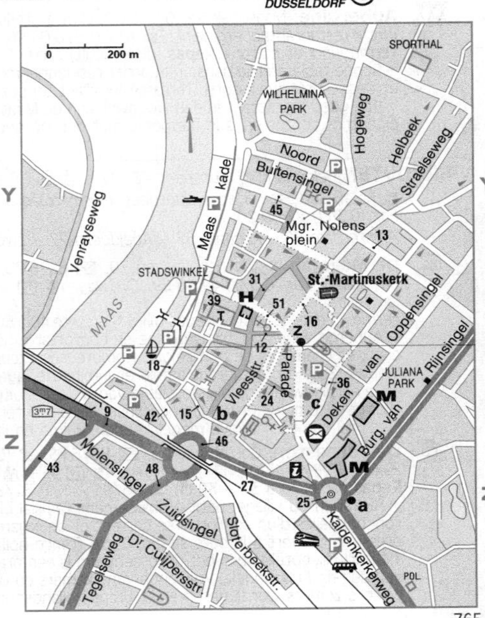

0
200 m
SPORTHAL
WILHELMINA PARK
Hogeweg
Helbeek
Straelseweg
Noord
Buitensingel
Maas kade
45
Mgr. Nolens plein
13
Venrayseweg
STADSWINKEL
31
St.-Martinuskerk
39
51
16
MAAS
12
Oppensingel
Rijnsingel
JULIANA PARK
18
Vleesstr.
Parade
36
van
Deken
24
42
15
Burg. van
46
43
Molensingel
48
27
25
Zuidsingel
Kaldenkerkerweg
Sloterbeekstr.
Dr. Cuijpersstr.
Tegelseweg
POL.

XXX **La Mangerie,** Nieuwstraat 58, ✉ 5911 JV, ☎ (0 77) 351 79 93, *mangerie@mangerie.nl, Fax (0 77) 351 72 61* – AE ⓓ ⓜ VISA JCB. ✕ Z b
fermé du 21 au 29 fév., du 1er au 30 août, sam. midi, dim., lundi et jours fériés – **Repas** 33/105 bc, ♀.
◆ Adresse agréable connue de longue date sur cette placette du centre. Accueil personnalisé, salles à manger actuelles et intimes, mets attrayants et service sans reproche.
◆ Aangenaam en inmiddels vertrouwd adres in het centrum. Persoonlijke ontvangst, eigentijdse eetzalen met intieme ambiance, aantrekkelijke gerechten en onberispelijke service.

X **Chez Philippe,** Parade 61, ✉ 5911 CB, ☎ (0 77) 354 89 01, *Fax (0 77) 352 31 77* – AE ⓓ ⓜ VISA Z c
fermé 1 sem. carnaval, 17 juil.-7 août, sam. midi, dim. et lundi – **Repas** Lunch 21 – carte env. 40.
◆ Dans une rue piétonne commerçante, affaire familiale décontractée présentant un décor intérieur sur le thème du manège. Alternative chaises ou banquettes. Fourneaux à vue.
◆ Familierestaurant in een voetgangersstraat. Ongedwongen ambiance en een interieur met stoelen en banken, dat in het teken staat van de draaimolen. Open keuken.

à Blerick © *Venlo :*

XX **De Cantharel,** Helling 2, ✉ 5921 GT, ☎ (0 77) 382 00 75, *richard.waleveld@planet.nl, Fax (0 77) 382 88 44* – AE ⓓ ⓜ VISA JCB X a
fermé 3 sem. carnaval, mardi de mai à sept. et merc. – **Repas** (dîner seult) carte 37 à 45.
◆ Restaurant mignon comme tout avoisinant un parc en bord de Meuse. Exposition de petits bronzes sur les tables. Cuisine du moment attentive à la qualité des produits.
◆ Een allercharmantst restaurant naast een park aan de oever van de Maas. Expositie van kleine bronzen beeldjes op de tafels. Seizoengebonden gerechten van kwaliteitsproducten.

à Tegelen *par ④ : 5 km* © *Venlo :*

Château Holtmühle ⛰, Kasteellaan 10 (Sud-Est : 1,5 km), ✉ 5932 AG, ☎ (0 77) 373 88 00, *holtmuehle@bilderberg.nl, Fax (0 77) 374 05 00,* ≤, ☂, ⓘ, ≘s, ⊡, ⚘, ✕, ⚲ – |‡| TV P – 🔬 25 à 120. AE ⓓ ⓜ VISA. ✕ rest
Repas *(fermé sam. midi et dim. midi)* Lunch 30 – carte 59 à 99, ♀ – ☐ 19 – **66 ch** 150/190.
◆ Une demeure du 14e s. entourée de douves et agrémentée d'un jardin à l'anglaise sert de cadre à cet hôtel de luxe. Vastes chambres garnies de meubles de style. Beauty-center. Restaurant feutré sous la voûte monumentale des caves du château. Jolie terrasse.
◆ Een statig 14e-eeuws kasteel met slotgracht en Engelse tuin vormt het decor van dit luxehotel. De vorstelijke kamers zijn met stijlmeubilair ingericht. Beautycenter. Restaurant met ingetogen ambiance onder het monumentale gewelf van de kelders. Mooi terras.

XXX **Aubergine,** Maashoek 2a (Ouest : 0,5 km à Steijl), ✉ 5935 BJ, ☎ (0 77) 326 03 90, *info@restaurantaubergine.nl, Fax (0 77) 326 03 90,* ☂ – AE ⓓ ⓜ VISA
fermé lundi et mardi – **Repas** (dîner seult) carte 39 à 62, ♀.
◆ Bonne table établie dans un quartier résidentiel mosan. Fine cuisine classique actualisée et décor intérieur assorti. Terrasse jouxtant un petit jardin d'herbes aromatiques.
◆ Een goed restaurant in een woonwijk aan de Maas. De fijne klassieke keuken heeft een eigentijds accent en is in harmonie met het interieur. Terras naast een kruidentuintje.

VIERHOUTEN *Gelderland* © *Nunspeet 26 317 h.* 532 T 9 *et* 715 I 4.

18 9 *au Sud-Est : 8 km à Nunspeet, Plesmanlaan 30,* ✉ *8072 PT,* ☎ *(0 341) 26 11 49, Fax (0 341) 27 09 20.*

Amsterdam 88 – Arnhem 53 – Apeldoorn 27 – Zwolle 34.

De Mallejan ⛰, Nunspeterweg 70, ✉ 8076 PD, ☎ (0 577) 41 12 41, *receptie@demallejan.nl, Fax (0 577) 41 16 29,* ☂, ⚲ – |‡| TV 🚗 P – 🔬 25 à 75. AE ⓓ ⓜ VISA. ✕ rest
fermé 23 déc.-10 janv. – **Repas** Lunch 30 – carte 40 à 50 – **38 ch** ☐ 125/150 – ½ P 85/115.
◆ Auberge vénérable transformée en confortable hôtel de notre temps. Communs spacieux et chambres de bon séjour. Nombreuses excursions possibles dans la région de la Veluwe. Salle de restaurant ample et lumineuse, agencée dans l'esprit "design".
◆ De eerbiedwaardige pleisterplaats van weleer is uitgegroeid tot een aangenaam, eigentijds hotelcomplex. Grote gemeenschappelijke ruimten en comfortabele kamers. De Veluwe biedt tal van recreatieve mogelijkheden. Ruime en lichte eetzaal met designdecor.

De Foreesten, Gortelseweg 8, ✉ 8076 PS, ☎ (0 577) 41 13 23, *info@foreesten.nl, Fax (0 577) 41 17 03,* ☂, ⚘, ⚲ – |‡| TV P – 🔬 25 à 80. AE ⓜ VISA JCB. ✕ rest
Repas carte 26 à 37 – **39 ch** ☐ 56/91 – ½ P 52/66.
◆ Au milieu du village, petit établissement familial bien pratique pour l'étape. Chambres fonctionnelles d'un confort très correct et deux jardinets. Terrasses ombragées où l'on dresse le couvert à la belle saison. Carte franco-hollandaise.
◆ Dit familiehotelletje in het dorpscentrum is een praktisch adres voor een onderbreking van de reis. Functionele, vrij aangename kamers en twee tuintjes. Lommerrijke terrassen waar 's zomers wordt geserveerd. Frans-Hollandse kaart.

VIERLINGSBEEK *Noord-Brabant* C *Boxmeer 29 282 h.* 532 V 13 *et* 715 J 7.
Amsterdam 149 – 's-Hertogenbosch 66 – Eindhoven 53 – Nijmegen 42.

XX **De Vier Linden,** Soetendaal 5 (face à la gare), ✉ 5821 BL, ☎ (0 478) 63 16 37, *Fax (0 478) 63 15 99,* – P – 25 à 140. MC VISA.
fermé 1 sem. carnaval, prem. sem. août, merc. midi, sam. midi et dim. midi – **Repas** carte 38 à 53.
◆ Adresse commode pour s'attabler au sortir de la gare. Chaleureux salon d'accueil, salle des repas actuelle et terrasse estivale abritée. Cuisine sobrement mise à la page.
◆ Een handig adres om vanuit het station aan tafel te gaan. Gezellige ontvangstsalon, eigentijdse eetzaal en beschut zomerterras. De keuken volgt voorzichtig de huidige trend.

VIJFHUIZEN *Noord-Holland* C *Haarlemmermeer 118 553 h.* 531 N 8, 532 I 8 *et* 715 F 4.
Spieringweg 745 (Cruquius), ✉ 2142 ED, ☎ (0 23) 558 90 01, Fax (0 23) 558 90 09.
Amsterdam 31 – Haarlem 5.

XXX **De Ouwe Meerpaal,** Vijfhuizerdijk 3, ✉ 2141 BA, ☎ (0 23) 558 12 89, *meerpaal@wxs.nl, Fax (0 23) 558 36 92,* – P. AE O MC VISA
fermé 27 déc.-13 janv. et lundi – **Repas** *Lunch 33* – 45/64 bc, ♀.
◆ Coquette auberge postée en bordure du canal, dans un beau paysage de polders. Salon cosy, salle à manger garnie de meubles de style et terrasse estivale invitante.
◆ Deze charmante herberg heeft post gevat aan een kanaal, in een mooi polderlandschap. Knusse salon, eetzaal met stijlmeubilair en uitnodigend zomerterras.

Onze hotelgidsen, toeristische gidsen en wegenkaarten vullen elkaar aan. Gebruik ze samen.

VINKEVEEN *Utrecht* C *De Ronde Venen 34 416 h.* 532 O 9 *et* 715 F 5.
au Sud-Ouest : 4 km à Wilnis, Bovendijk 16a, ✉ 3648 NM, ☎ (0 297) 28 11 43, Fax (0 297) 27 34 35.
Herenweg 144, ✉ 3645 DT, ☎ (0 297) 21 42 31, info@vvvderondevenen.nl, Fax (0 297) 21 42 35.
Amsterdam 23 – Utrecht 24 – Den Haag 61 – Haarlem 32.

Résidence Vinkeveen, Groenlandsekade 1 (Est : 3 km près A 2), ✉ 3645 BA, ☎ (0 294) 29 30 66, *vinkeveen@bilderberg.nl, Fax (0 294) 29 31 01,* ≤, – TV P – 25 à 120. AE O MC VISA
Repas voir rest ***Le Canard Sauvage*** ci-après – 18 – **65 ch** 189/222.
◆ À quelques brasses du port des yachts, motel haut de gamme distribuant ses chambres dans une ribambelle de pavillons mitoyens aux toits pentus. Jolie vue sur le lac.
◆ In dit kwaliteitsmotel op enkele schoolslagen van de jachthaven liggen de kamers verspreid over een aaneengesloten reeks paviljoens met puntdaken. Mooi uitzicht op de plassen.

XXX **Le Canard Sauvage** - H. Résidence Vinkeveen, Groenlandsekade 1 (Est : 3 km près A 2), ✉ 3645 BA, ☎ (0 294) 29 30 66, *vinkeveen@bilderberg.nl, Fax (0 294) 29 31 01,* ≤, – P. AE O MC VISA.
fermé sam. midi et dim. midi – **Repas** *Lunch 37* – carte 38 à 81, ♀.
◆ Table gastronomique de l'hôtel Résidence Vinkeveen. La salle à manger lambrissée offre une échappée lacustre, au même titre que la terrasse d'été dressée sur caillebotis.
◆ Gastronomisch restaurant van Résidence Vinkeveen. De gelambriseerde eetzaal kijkt uit op de Vinkeveense Plassen, net als het zomerterras dat op houten vlonders is ingericht.

XX **De Lokeend** avec ch, Groenlandsekade 61 (Est : 3 km près A 2), ✉ 3645 BB, ☎ (0 294) 29 15 44, *webmaster@delokeend.nl, Fax (0 294) 29 30 01,* – TV P. AE O MC VISA JCB
Repas *(fermé sam. midi, dim. midi et lundi) Lunch 38* – 29/48 – **7 ch** 80/103.
◆ Cette villa mignonne où l'on trouve le gîte et surtout le couvert donne, à l'arrière, sur le lac de Vinkeveen. Repas servi en terrasse par beau temps. Chambres duplex.
◆ Deze charmante villa met restaurant en enkele kamers kijkt aan de achterkant uit op de Vinkeveense Plassen. Bij mooi weer wordt op het terras geserveerd. Split-level kamers.

X **De Eetkamer van Vinkeveen,** Vinkenkade 2, ✉ 3645 AR, ☎ (0 294) 29 54 50, *Fax (0 294) 29 59 15,* – P. MC
fermé fin déc. et merc. – **Repas** *Lunch 30* – 45/60 bc.
◆ L'adresse à ne pas manquer pour manger simplement, et toutefois convenablement, dans une atmosphère décontractée. Jolie terrasse où l'on s'attable par météo clémente.
◆ Een must wanneer u eenvoudig maar goed wilt eten in een ongedwongen sfeer. Als het weer het toelaat, wordt op het fraaie terras geserveerd.

VLAARDINGEN *Zuid-Holland* 532 L 11 *et* 715 E 6 – *73 935 h.*
Westhavenkade 39, ✉ 3131 AD, ☎ (0 10) 426 26 54, info@vvv-vlaardingen.nl, Fax (0 10) 435 89 97.
Amsterdam 78 – Rotterdam 13 – Den Haag 28.

Delta, Maasboulevard 15, ✉ 3133 AK, ☎ (0 10) 434 54 77, *info@deltahotel.nl, Fax (0 10) 434 95 25,* ← Meuse (Maas), – 25 à 250.
Repas ***Nautique*** *(fermé sam. midi et dim. midi) Lunch 26* – 32/44 bc, – 16 – **78 ch** 120/213 – ½ P 122.
◆ Ce confortable hôtel occupe un immeuble contemporain profitant d'une vue imprenable sur le trafic fluvial mosan. Chambres actuelles de bonne ampleur. Room service. Salle de restaurant panoramique avec décor nautique bien dans le coup.
◆ Dit comfortabele hotel is gehuisvest in een modern pand dat vrij uitzicht biedt op de druk bevaren Maas. Eigentijdse kamers van goed formaat. Roomservice. Panoramisch restaurant met zeer eigentijds, nautisch decor.

Campanile, Kethelweg 220 (près A 20, sortie ⑩), ✉ 3135 GP, ☎ (0 10) 470 03 22, *vlaardingen@campanile.nl, Fax (0 10) 471 34 30,* – 30.
Repas (avec buffets) 22 – 10 – **48 ch** 70.
◆ Établissement de chaîne dont les menues chambres de mise simple, munies du double vitrage, se répartissent sur deux étages accessibles par un couloir extérieur.
◆ Ketenhotel met kleine, eenvoudige kamers die zijn voorzien van dubbele beglazing en verspreid liggen over twee verdiepingen. Deze zijn via een externe gaanderij bereikbaar.

VLIELAND (Ile de) *Fryslân* 531 O 3 *et* 715 F 2 – *voir à Waddeneilanden.*

VLIJMEN *Noord-Brabant* © *Heusden 43 138 h.* 532 Q 12 *et* 715 G 6.
Amsterdam 94 – 's-Hertogenbosch 8 – Breda 40.

Prinsen, Julianastraat 21, ✉ 5251 EC, ☎ (0 73) 511 91 31, *info-prinsen@fletcher.nl, Fax (0 73) 511 79 75,* – rest, – 25 à 200. rest
Repas *Lunch 33* – carte 33 à 65 – 10 – **27 ch** 64/115.
◆ Près de l'église, dans une rue assez tranquille, petit hôtel disposant de chambres sans fioriture, distribuées à l'arrière. Elles donnent toutes sur un jardin intérieur. Restaurant agrémenté d'une terrasse d'été.
◆ Dit kleine hotel in een rustig straatje vlak bij de kerk heeft kamers zonder tierelantijnen, die aan de achterkant liggen en uitkijken op de tuin. Restaurant met zomerterras.

VLISSINGEN *Zeeland* 532 G 14 *et* 715 B 7 – *45 416 h.*
vers Breskens : Prov. Stoombootdiensten Zeeland, Prins Hendrikweg 10 ☎ (0 118) 46 09 00, Fax (0 118) 46 80 96 (Pas de voitures !). Durée de la traversée : 20 min.
Oude Markt 3, ✉ 4381 ER, ☎ (0 118) 42 21 90, info@vvvvlissingen.nl, Fax (0 118) 58 35 45. – Amsterdam 205 – Middelburg 6 – Brugge 86 – Knokke-Heist 80.

Gd H. Arion, Boulevard Bankert 266, ✉ 4382 AC, ☎ (0 118) 41 05 02, *info@hotelarion.nl, Fax (0 118) 41 63 62,* ←, – 25 à 400. rest
Repas 30/70 bc – 14 – **64 ch** 96/188 – ½ P 162/227.
◆ Cet immeuble du front de mer renferme des chambres standard très fonctionnelles, mais munies d'un balcon. Côté façade, elles profitent d'une vue balnéaire plaisante. Salle à manger panoramique et terrasse dressée en période estivale. Plats au goût du jour.
◆ Dit hotel aan de boulevard heeft zeer functionele standaardkamers met balkon, aan de voorkant met uitzicht op het strand en de zee. Panoramische eetzaal en 's zomers een terras. Eigentijdse gerechten.

de Leugenaar, Boulevard Bankert 132, ✉ 4382 AC, ☎ (0 118) 41 25 00, *info@hoteldeleugenaar.nl, Fax (0 118) 41 25 58,* – . ch
Repas (taverne-rest) *Lunch 16* – carte 22 à 47 – **15 ch** 75/95 – ½ P 95/115.
◆ Des auvents rouges signalent ce petit établissement posté sur la digue. Chambres de taille et d'équipement corrects, réparties sur trois étages. Affluence touristique. Les repas se prennent dans un décor marin : cordages, gouvernails et peintures nautiques.
◆ Rode luifels markeren dit kleine hotel aan de boulevard. Vrij aangename kamers van goed formaat, op drie verdiepingen. Vooral toeristen als clientèle. U nuttigt uw maaltijd in een maritiem decor met scheepstouwen, roeren en nautische schilderingen.

De Bourgondiër, Boulevard Bankert 280, ✉ 4382 AC, ☎ (0 118) 41 38 91, *info@de-bourgondier.nl, Fax (0 118) 41 61 85,* ←, –
fermé merc. – **Repas** 30/65 bc.
◆ Au bord de la promenade, pavillon moderne et lumineux, avec ses grandes baies vitrées offrant une échappée vers le large. Terrasse estivale agréable. Cuisine de notre temps.
◆ Dit moderne paviljoen aan de boulevard baadt in het licht dat door de grote ramen naar binnen valt. Uitzicht op de zee. Aangenaam zomerterras. Eigentijdse keuken.

XX **Solskin,** Boulevard Bankert 58, ✉ 4382 AC, ℘ (0 118) 41 73 50, *solskin@tref.nl, Fax (0 118) 44 00 72,* ≤, – AE MC VISA JCB
fermé lundi – **Repas** *Lunch 25* – carte 30 à 57.
• Une carte classique surtout orientée "poisson" vous sera soumise à cette table littorale devancée d'une terrasse-pergola. La salle à manger décline le thème maritime.
• Dit boulevardrestaurant met terras en pergola voert een klassieke kaart die vooral in het teken van Neptunus staat. Eetzaal met maritiem decor.

X **Bleij,** Bellamypark 16, ✉ 4381 CJ, ℘ (0 118) 41 25 24, *bleij@proximedia.nl, Fax (0 118) 43 04 25,* , Taverne-rest – AE MC VISA JCB
Repas (déjeuner sur réservation) carte 35 à 43.
• Taverne-restaurant conviviale aménagée à la mode d'aujourd'hui sur la place centrale, devant le port et à deux pas du musée municipal ainsi que du jardin zoologique.
• Dit gezellige, modern ingerichte café-restaurant is te vinden aan het centrale plein tegenover de haven, op een steenworp afstand van het Stedelijk Museum en de reptielenzoo.

X **de Zeven Provinciën,** Smallekade 13 (Bellamypark), ✉ 4381 CE, ℘ (0 118) 41 71 62, *7provincien@zeelandnet.nl* – MC VISA
fermé 2 dern. sem. fév., 2 dern. sem.juil., mardi et merc. – **Repas** (dîner seult) carte 29 à 38.
• Sympathique petite affaire familiale installée à l'étage d'une vieille maisonnette du centre. On prend place sous les poutres massives d'une salle ornée de toiles modernes.
• Sympathiek familierestaurantje op de verdieping van een oud pand in het centrum. Er wordt getafeld onder de massieve balken van een eetzaal met moderne schilderijen.

à Koudekerke *Nord-Ouest : 3 km* C *Veere 21 985 h :*

Westduin, Westduin 1 (Dishoek), ✉ 4371 PE, ℘ (0 118) 55 25 10, *westduin@zeelandnet.nl, Fax (0 118) 55 27 76,* – – 25 à 1500. AE MC VISA.
Repas carte env. 31 – **111 ch** 83/155, – 1 suite – ½ P 65/160.
• Hôtel situé aux pieds des dunes, qu'il vous faudra traverser pour goûter les embruns et profiter des bains de mer. Petites chambres de bon séjour, avec terrasse ou balcon. Formule lunch dès midi et repas à la carte au dîner. L'été, on peut manger en plein air.
• Hotel onder aan een duin, die u nog even over moet om een duik te nemen in het zilte nat. Kleine, comfortabele kamers met terras of balkon. 's Middags lunchformule, 's avonds maaltijden à la carte. 's Zomers kan buiten worden gegeten.

VLODROP *Limburg* 532 V 16 *et* 715 J 8 – *voir à Roermond.*

VOGELENZANG *Noord-Holland* 531 M 9, 532 M 9 *et* 715 E 5 – *voir à Bennebroek.*

VOLENDAM *Noord-Holland* C *Edam-Volendam 27 833 h.* 531 P 8 *et* 715 G 4.

Voir *Costume traditionnel*★.
Zeestraat 37, ✉ 1131 ZD, ℘ (0 299) 36 37 47, info@vvv-volendam.nl, Fax (0 299) 36 84 84.
Amsterdam 23 – Alkmaar 33 – Leeuwarden 121.

Spaander, Haven 15, ✉ 1131 EP, ℘ (0 299) 36 35 95, *info@spaander.com, Fax (0 299) 36 96 15,* – , rest, – 25 à 70. AE MC VISA
Repas *Lunch 13* – carte 32 à 56 – 13 – **80 ch** 75/100 – ½ P 68/91.
• Complexe hôtelier né d'une vieille auberge dans un bourg portuaire touristique. Certaines chambres, avec balcon, ont vue sur la petite mer intérieure. Les toiles anciennes exposées au restaurant servirent de moyen de paiement aux peintres. Plats d'anguille.
• Hotelcomplex dat in dit toeristische havenplaatsje is voortgekomen uit een oude herberg. Sommige kamers, met balkon, kijken uit op het IJsselmeer. De oude doeken in het restaurant werden door de schilders als betaalmiddel gebruikt. Palinggerechten.

X **Van Den Hogen** avec ch, Haven 106, ✉ 1131 EV, ℘ (0 299) 36 37 75, *hotel@hogen.nl, Fax (0 299) 36 94 98,* ≤ – rest, . AE MC VISA. ch
Repas carte 27 à 50 – **5 ch** 80.
• Restaurant familial officiant sur la digue du port. Choix de préparations bourgeoises, dont quelques recettes "couleur locale". Trois petites chambres ont vue sur les yachts.
• Restaurant dat te vinden is op de havendijk. Traditionele keuken met enkele typische streekgerechten. Het heeft ook drie kleine kamers met zicht op de jachten.

VOLLENHOVE *Overijssel* Ⓒ *Steenwijkerland 41 870 h.* 531 U 6 *et* 715 I 3.
Amsterdam 103 – Zwolle 26 – Emmeloord 14.

XX **Seidel,** Kerkplein 3, ✉ 8325 BN, ☎ (0 527) 24 12 62, *info@seidel.nl, Fax (0 527) 24 42 72,* – AE ⓓ MC VISA JCB.
fermé fév. et lundi – **Repas** *Lunch* 35 – 38/60, ♀.
◆ Une étrange légende se rattache à ce restaurant familial établi dans l'ancien hôtel de ville (17e s.). Si le service n'est pas surmené, peut-être la laisserez-vous conter.
◆ Er bestaat een leuke legende over dit restaurant (17e eeuw), dat het oude gemeentehuis heeft betrokken. Als het niet zo druk is, krijgt u het verhaal wellicht te horen.

VOORBURG *Zuid-Holland* 532 L 10 *et* 715 E 5 – *voir à Den Haag, environs.*

VOORSCHOTEN *Zuid-Holland* 532 L 10 *et* 715 E 5 – *voir à Leiden.*

VORDEN *Gelderland* 532 W 10 *et* 715 J 5 – *8 535 h.*
au Sud : 6 km à Hengelo, Vierblokkenweg 1, ✉ 7255 MZ, ☎ (0 575) 46 75 33, Fax (0 575) 46 75 62.
Kerkstraat 1b, ✉ 7251 BC, ☎ (0 575) 55 32 22, info@vvvvorden.nl, Fax (0 575) 55 22 76.
Amsterdam 117 – Arnhem 41 – Apeldoorn 31 – Enschede 51.

Bakker (annexe), Dorpsstraat 24, ✉ 7251 BB, ☎ (0 575) 55 13 12, *info@bakkerinvorden.nl, Fax (0 575) 55 37 40,* – rest, – 25 à 200. AE MC VISA JCB
Repas *Lunch* 20 – carte 25 à 38, ♀ – **12 ch** 80 – ½ P 45/65.
◆ Au centre du village, auberge traditionnelle dont la pimpante devanture dissimule un jardin croquignolet avec une annexe récente regroupant des chambres de bon confort. Table franco-batave et terrasse d'été dressée près d'une pièce d'eau.
◆ Dit traditionele hotel-restaurant is te vinden in het dorpscentrum. Achter de charmante voorgevel gaat een vrij nieuwe annexe schuil met comfortabele kamers en een verzorgde tuin. Frans-Hollandse keuken en zomerterras bij een waterpartij.

Bloemendaal, Stationsweg 24, ✉ 7251 EM, ☎ (0 575) 55 12 27, *info@hotelbloemendaal.nl, Fax (0 575) 55 38 55,* – 35. MC VISA.
fermé déc.-janv. – **Repas** (dîner pour résidents seult) – **15 ch** 75.
◆ Cet établissement chaleureux, situé dans un quartier résidentiel, affiche un petit air de pension de famille. Chaque jour, un menu soigné est proposé aux seuls logeurs.
◆ Dit gemoedelijke hotel in een woonwijk heeft iets weg van een familiepension. Dagelijks wordt uitsluitend aan de hotelgasten een verzorgd menu geboden.

VREELAND *Utrecht* Ⓒ *Loenen 8 408 h.* 532 P 9 *et* 715 G 5.
Amsterdam 22 – Utrecht 24 – Hilversum 11.

XXX ✿ **De Nederlanden** avec ch, Duinkerken 3, ✉ 3633 EM, ☎ (0 294) 23 23 26, *denederlanden@hetnet.nl, Fax (0 294) 23 14 07,* ←, – rest, – 30. AE ⓓ MC VISA. rest
fermé 27 déc.-1er janv. – **Repas** (fermé sam. midi et dim. midi) *Lunch* 40 – 60/75, carte 59 à 78, ♀ – 18 – **9 ch** 225 – ½ P 175/195.
◆ Admirable relais gourmand regardant un typique pont à bascule jeté sur la Vecht. Intérieur chaleureux, de style "cottage" à la néerlandaise. Véranda. Fine cuisine inventive.
◆ Prachtig gastronomisch restaurant tegenover een ophaalbruggetje over de Vecht. Gezellig interieur met Hollandse karaktertrekjes. Veranda. Verfijnde, inventieve keuken.
Spéc. Marbré de joue de veau au foie d'oie. Joue de bœuf et ris de veau à la fondue d'oignons et céleri-rave. Pêche à la lavande au four

VROUWENPOLDER *Zeeland* Ⓒ *Veere 21 985 h.* 532 G 3 *et* 715 B 7.
Amsterdam 165 – Middelburg 12 – Rotterdam 96.

X **Vrouwe in den Polder,** Vrouwenpolderseweg 81, ✉ 4354 ND, ☎ (0 118) 59 19 00, *info@restaurantvrouwenpolder.nl, Fax (0 118) 59 19 65,* – MC VISA
fermé lundi sauf en juil.-août – **Repas** 24/40 bc.
◆ Ancré au pied de la digue séparant la mer du Nord du Veerse Meer, ce pavillon tout récemment rajeuni abrite une grande et lumineuse salle de restaurant. Plusieurs menus.
◆ Dit onlangs gerenoveerde paviljoen onder aan de dijk tussen de Noordzee en het Veerse Meer heeft een grote, heldere restaurantzaal. Diverse menu's.

VUGHT *Noord-Brabant* 532 Q 13 *et* 715 G 7 – *voir à 's-Hertogenbosch.*

De WAAL *Noord-Holland* 531 N 4 *et* 715 F 2 – *voir à Waddeneilanden (Texel).*

WAALRE *Noord-Brabant* 532 R 14 *et* 715 H 7 – *16 193 h.*
Amsterdam 128 – Eindhoven 9 – Venlo 56 – Turnhout 47.

XXX **De Treeswijkhoeve,** Valkenswaardseweg 14 (sur N 69), ✉ 5582 VB, ✆ (0 40) 221 55 93, *info@treeswijkhoeve.nl, Fax (0 40) 221 75 32,* – P. AE ⓓ ⓜⓒ VISA
fermé 24 fév., 9 avril, du 3 au 5 mai, 26 juil.-16 août, 27 déc.-10 janv., lundi et sam. midi – **Repas** 38/80 bc, ♀.
◆ Ravissante maison de bouche où s'attabler côté jardin, sous la tonnelle, est un pur plaisir dès que la température grimpe un peu. Appétissante carte teintée de modernité.
◆ Charmant restaurant waar het bij mooi weer een puur genot is om aan de tuinkant onder de pergola aan tafel te gaan. De aantrekkelijke menukaart is nieuwerwets getint.

WAALWIJK *Noord-Brabant* 532 P 12 *et* 715 G 6 – *45 453 h.*
Vredesplein 14, ✉ 5142 RA, ✆ (0 416) 33 22 28, Fax (0 416) 65 13 13.
Amsterdam 100 – 's-Hertogenbosch 18 – Breda 30 – Tilburg 17.

Waalwijk, Burg. van der Klokkenlaan 55, ✉ 5141 EG, ✆ (0 416) 33 60 45, *info@hotelwaalwijk.nl, Fax (0 416) 33 59 68,* – TV P – 25 à 300. AE ⓓ ⓜⓒ VISA.
Repas *(fermé sam. midi et dim. midi)* carte 22 à 34 – 9 – **62 ch** 85/103.
◆ Point de chute très convenable pour poser ses bagages et enfiler ses pantoufles dans la cité du cuir et du soulier. Chambres fonctionnelles bien tenues.
◆ Een aangenaam adres in deze leder- en schoenenstad om de koffers uit te pakken en de pantoffels aan te trekken. De functionele kamers zijn goed onderhouden.

XX **Het Heerenhuys,** Grotestraat 283, ✉ 5141 JT, ✆ (0 416) 65 03 15, *info@hetheerenhuys.nl, Fax (0 416) 65 16 91,* – AE ⓓ ⓜⓒ VISA
fermé jours fériés sauf Noël – **Repas** Lunch 29 – 30/58 bc, ♀.
◆ Cuisine actuelle servie dans une jolie maison bourgeoise de la commerçante Grotestraat. Une véranda donnant au jardin procure plus d'ampleur à la salle de restaurant.
◆ In dit mooie herenhuis in een winkelstraat wordt een eigentijdse keuken bereid. De eetzaal is uitgebreid met een serre die uitkijkt op de tuin.

X **De Gelegenheid,** Olympiaweg 8, ✉ 5143 NA, ✆ (0 416) 33 93 08, *Fax (0 416) 34 34 00,* – – 25 à 150. ⓜⓒ VISA
fermé merc., sam. midi et dim. midi – **Repas** Lunch 21 – 26/40.
◆ Une toute nouvelle équipe vient de "prendre pied" dans cet établissement situé à l'entrée de Waalwijk, pôle important de l'industrie de la chaussure aux Pays-Bas.
◆ Een heel nieuw team heeft de gelegenheid aangegrepen om vaste voet aan de grond te krijgen in dit restaurant aan de rand van het hart van de Nederlandse schoenenindustrie.

WADDENEILANDEN ILES DES WADDEN★★

210 - N 5 à X 1
908 - F 2 à J 1

● *Les îles des Wadden comprennent Texel (province de Hollande du Nord) et les îles Frisonnes (Vlieland, Terschelling, Ameland et Schiermonnikoog). Elles constituent une réserve naturelle exceptionnelle, peuplée de nombreux oiseaux. Sur Vlieland et Schiermonnikoog, les voitures ne sont pas admises.*

● *Texel (provincie Noord-Holland) en de Friese eilanden (Vlieland, Terschelling, Ameland en Schiermonnikoog) zijn de belangrijkste Nederlandse Waddeneilanden. Samen vormen zij een uitzonderlijk natuurreservaat met ontelbare vogels. Op Vlieland en Schiermonnikoog zijn geen auto's toegelaten.*

● *Die Westfriesischen Inseln mit Texel (Provinz Nordholland) und die Friesischen Inseln (Vlieland, Terschelling, Ameland und Schiermonnikoog) bilden ein außergewöhnliches Naturschutzgebiet, welches von zahlreichen Seevögeln bewohnt wird. Auf Vlieland und Schiermonnikoog sind Autos nicht zugelassen.*

● *The Wadden islands are made up of Texel (province of Northern Holland) and the Frisonnes islands (Vlieland, Terschelling, Ameland and Schiermonnikoog). These islands are areas of outstanding natural beauty, and are home to many different species of birds. Cars are not allowed on Vlieland or Schiermonnikoog.*

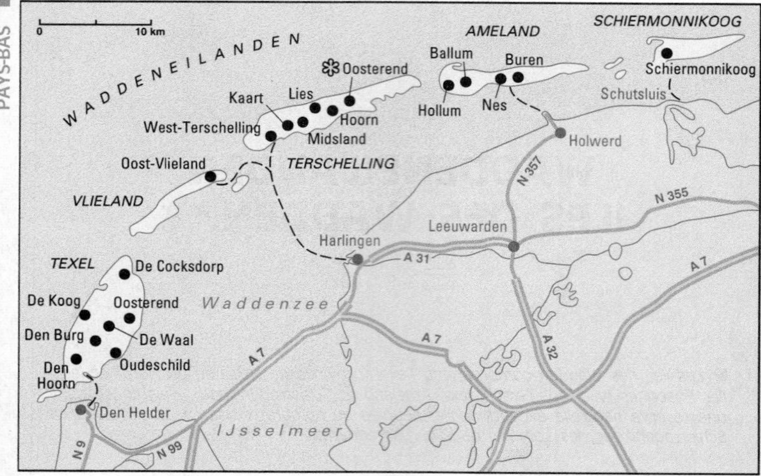

WADDENEILANDEN (ILES DES WADDEN) ★★ *Fryslân - Noord-Holland* 531 N 5 à X 1 *et* 715 F 2 à J 1 *G. Hollande.*

La plupart des hôteliers ne louent qu'à partir de 2 nuitées.

De meeste hotelhouders verhuren maar vanaf 2 overnachtingen.

AMELAND *Fryslân* 531 T 2 *et* 715 I 1 – *3 564 h.*

vers Holwerd : Rederij Wagenborg, Zeedijk 9 à Lauwersoog ✆ (0 519) 34 90 50. Durée de la traversée : 45 min.

Amsterdam (bac) 169 – Leeuwarden (bac) 30 – Dokkum (bac) 14.

Nes

Bureweg 2, ✉ 9163 KE, ✆ (0 519) 54 65 46, info@vvvameland.nl, Fax (0 519) 54 65 50.

Hofker sans rest, Johannes Hofkerweg 1, ✉ 9163 GW, ✆ (0 519) 54 20 02, *info@hotel-hofker.nl, Fax (0 519) 54 28 65,* – 25 à 50. VISA.
41 ch 49/95.

◆ Au cœur d'un petit village frison, hôtel familial discret abritant des chambres bien tenues. Quelques-unes ont été rénovées et remeublées. Abords un peu tristounets.

◆ Bescheiden familiehotel met goed onderhouden kamers, midden in een Fries dorp. Enkele zijn gerenoveerd en opnieuw gestoffeerd. Ietwat mistroostige omgeving.

Ameland, Strandweg 48 (Nord : 1 km), ✉ 9163 GN, ✆ (0 519) 54 21 50, *info@hotelameland.nl, Fax (0 519) 54 31 06,* – VISA.
21 fév.-nov. – **Repas** (dîner pour résidents seult) – **27 ch** 90 – ½ P 55/60.

◆ Cette enseigne empruntant le nom de l'île maintient le cap depuis plus de 40 ans. Pour marquer le coup, une série d'améliorations visent à rendre le séjour plus plaisant.

◆ Dit naar het eiland vernoemde hotel houdt al ruim 40 jaar vaste koers. Om deze mijlpaal te vieren, zijn verbeteringen gepland voor een nog aangenamer verblijf.

Nes sans rest, Strandweg 39 (Nord : 1 km), ✉ 9163 GL, ✆ (0 519) 54 21 83, *Fax (0 519) 54 35 44,* – VISA.
35 ch 99.

◆ Établissement légèrement excentré, situé en direction de la plage. Les chambres se partagent l'étage du bâtiment principal et l'annexe, qui dispose des meilleures.

◆ Dit etablissement ligt iets buiten het dorp richting strand. De kamers bevinden zich op de eerste verdieping van het hoofdgebouw, maar de beste zijn in de annexe ingericht.

De Klimop, Johannes Hofkerweg 2, ✉ 9163 GW, ✆ (0 519) 54 22 96, *Fax (0 519) 54 32 56,* – AE VISA
fermé 5 janv.-4 fév. et mardi – **Repas** Lunch 11 – 24/34.

◆ De Klimop a jeté l'ancre dans deux anciennes maisons de capitaine, rappelant l'époque où la chasse à la baleine était la spécialité d'Ameland. Taverne rustique.

◆ Deze klimop heeft zich vastgeklampt aan twee voormalige kapiteinshuizen, die herinneren aan de tijd dat Ameland van de walvisvaart leefde. Rustiek restaurant.

Ballum

XX **Nobel**, avec ch, Gerrit Kosterweg 16, ✉ 9162 EN, ✆ (0 519) 55 41 57, *Fax (0 519) 55 45 15*, – , rest, – 25. AE MC VISA.
Repas *Lunch 27* – 29/36 – **23 ch** 42/59 – ½ P 57/80.
◆ Cette auberge centenaire élevée dans un village pittoresque abrite l'une des meilleures tables de l'île. Carte élaborée, ambiance chaleureuse et chambres de bon séjour.
◆ In deze honderd jaar oude herberg in een pittoresk dorp vindt u een van de beste restaurants van het eiland. Verzorgde kaart, gemoedelijke ambiance en aangename kamers.

Buren (Bueren).

De Klok, Hoofdweg 11, ✉ 9164 KL, ✆ (0 519) 54 21 81, *Fax (0 519) 54 24 97*, – 80. AE MC VISA
Repas *Lunch 13* – carte env. 32 – **25 ch** 55/80 – ½ P 52/60.
◆ La même famille insulaire vous reçoit à cette enseigne depuis quatre générations. Douze chambres, désormais plus amples et lumineuses, viennent d'être rénovées. Salle de restaurant au décor évoquant la pêche. Repas traditionnel à l'hollandaise.
◆ De vierde generatie staat inmiddels aan het roer van dit hotel. De twaalf onlangs gerenoveerde kamers zijn ruimer en lichter geworden. In de eetzaal met visserijdecor worden traditionele Hollandse maaltijden geserveerd.

Hollum

Oosterhiemweg 20, ✉ 9161 CZ, ✆ (0 519) 55 42 19, Fax (0 519) 55 65 67.

d'Amelander Kaap, Oosterhiemweg 1, ✉ 9161 CZ, ✆ (0 519) 55 46 46, *info@amelander-kaap.nl, Fax (0 519) 55 48 09*, – 40 à 250. AE MC VISA.
Repas *Lunch 15* – carte 27 à 37 – **40 ch** 70/109 – ½ P 70/75.
◆ Au bout de l'île, à 5 mn de la plage, complexe hôtelier bien équipé pour les séjours en famille ou en séminaire. Chambres plaisantes, beauty-center et voisinage d'un golf. Salle à manger profitant de la clarté d'une véranda.
◆ Dit hotelcomplex op de punt van het eiland, op 5 min. van het strand, is zowel voor een zakelijk als een toeristisch verblijf geschikt. Aangename kamers, beautycenter en een golfterrein vlakbij. Eetzaal met veel licht dankzij de serre.

SCHIERMONNIKOOG *Fryslân* 531 W 2 *et* 715 J 1 – *1 025 h.*

Voir *Het Rif*★, ≤★.
vers Lauwersoog : Wagenborg Passagiersdiensten B.V., Zeedijk 9 à Lauwersoog ✆ (0 519) 34 90 50. Durée de la traversée : 45 min.
Amsterdam (bac) 181 – Groningen (bac) 44 – Leeuwarden (bac) 42.

Schiermonnikoog (Skiermûntseach).

Reeweg 5, ✉ 9166 PW, ✆ (0 519) 53 12 33, info@vvvschiermonnikoog.nl, Fax (0 519) 53 13 25.

Graaf Bernstorff avec appartements, Reeweg 1, ✉ 9166 PW, ✆ (0 519) 53 20 00, *hotel@bernstorff.nl, Fax (0 519) 53 20 50*, – 70. AE MC VISA JCB.
Repas (menu unique) 41 – **17 ch** 130/200 – ½ P 140/240.
◆ Hôtel agréable à vivre situé au centre du seul bourg que compte cette jolie petite île de la mer des Wadden. Superbes appartements et bonnes chambres agencées avec goût. Restaurant d'esprit "grand café". Le soir, menu-surprise unique. Terrasse abritée.
◆ Aangenaam hotel in het centrum van het enige dorp op dit mooie, kleine Waddeneiland. Schitterende appartementen en goede, smaakvol ingerichte kamers. Restaurant met de ambiance van een grand café. 's Avonds verrassingmenu. Beschut terras.

Duinzicht, Badweg 17, ✉ 9166 ND, ✆ (0 519) 53 12 18, *info@hotelduinzicht.nl, Fax (0 519) 53 14 25*, – 30. AE MC VISA JCB
Repas *Lunch 14* – carte 23 à 39 – **35 ch** 81 – ½ P 51/59.
◆ La mâchoire inférieure d'un cousin de Mobby Dick marque l'entrée de cet établissement posté au pied du phare. Chambres en annexe, aménagées autour d'une pelouse. À table, évocation de l'épopée des chasseurs de baleines qui ont lancé l'affaire voici 100 ans.
◆ De onderkaak van een neef van Moby Dick markeert de ingang van dit hotel aan de voet van de vuurtoren. Kamers in de annexe rond een gazon. Aan tafel wordt de gast herinnerd aan de heldhaftige walvisvaarders die het bedrijf 100 jaar geleden hebben opgezet.

Van der Werff, Reeweg 2, ✉ 9166 PX, ✆ (0 519) 53 12 03, *hotelvanderwerff@chello.nl, Fax (0 519) 53 17 48* – – 25. MC VISA. rest
Repas *Lunch 16* – carte 30 à 65 – **49 ch** 40/90 – ½ P 53/58.
◆ Issu d'un modeste "bruin café" fondé en 1726, cet édifice a connu le passé d'une villégiature cossue. C'est aujourd'hui un hôtel simple retraçant l'histoire locale. Ambiance nostalgique dans une salle des repas classiquement aménagée.
◆ Dit adres is ontstaan vanuit een klein bruin café uit 1726 en had in zijn glorietijd een deftige cliëntèle. Nu is het een eenvoudig maar zeer authentiek hotel. De klassiek ingerichte eetzaal druipt van de nostalgie.

TERSCHELLING *Fryslân* 531 R 2 *et* 715 H 1 – *4 769 h.*

Voir *Site*★★ – *De Boschplaat*★ *(réserve d'oiseaux).*

vers Harlingen : Rederij Doeksen, Willem Barentszkade 21 à West-Terschelling ✆ 0 900 363 57 36, Fax (0 562) 44 32 41. Durée de la traversée : 1 h 45. Il existe aussi un service rapide (pour passagers uniquement). Durée de la traversée : 50 min.
Amsterdam (bac) 115 – Leeuwarden (bac) 28 – (distances de West-Terschelling).

West-Terschelling (West-Skylge).

Willem Barentszkade 19a, ✉ 8881 BC, ✆ (0 562) 44 30 00, info@vvv.terschelling.org, Fax (0 562) 44 28 75.

Schylge, Burg. van Heusdenweg 37, ✉ 8881 ED, ✆ (0 562) 44 21 11, *schylge@westcadhotels.nl, Fax (0 562) 44 28 00,* ←, , , , – , rest, – 25 à 200. AE VISA.
Repas *Lunch 25* – carte env. 46 – **98 ch** 170 – ½ P 94/114.
◆ Hôtel récent - parmi les plus complets de l'île - dont toutes les chambres sont pourvues d'un balcon. Celles orientées côté littoral procurent davantage d'agrément. Restaurant-véranda dévoilant une vue plongeante sur la Waddenzee et le port de plaisance.
◆ Een vrij nieuw hotel - een van de meest complete op het eiland - waarvan alle kamers een balkon hebben. De kamers aan de zeezijde hebben wat meer charme. Het restaurant met serre biedt een prachtig uitzicht op de Waddenzee en de jachthaven.

Nap, Torenstraat 55, ✉ 8881 BH, ✆ (0 562) 44 32 10, *info@hotelnap.nl, Fax (0 562) 44 33 15,* , – . AE VISA JCB
Repas *(fermé après 20 h 30)* 23 – **32 ch** 67/111 – ½ P 66/76.
◆ Auberge familiale postée à l'ombre de la Brandaris, tour carrée élevée au 16e s. Six chambres sont des duplex et une annexe abrite un appartement avec kitchenette. Bistrot égayé d'une collection de toiles dédiée aux phares hollandais. Lunch à prix d'ami.
◆ Familiehotel in de schaduw van de 16e-eeuwse vuurtoren de Brandaris. Zes split-level kamers alsmede een appartement met kitchenette in de annexe. In het restaurant hangt een collectie doeken van Nederlandse vuurtorens. Lunch voor een vriendenprijs.

Oepkes, De Ruyterstraat 3, ✉ 8881 AM, ✆ (0 562) 44 20 05, *hotel@oepkes.nl, Fax (0 562) 44 33 45,* , – – 40. AE VISA JCB
fermé 5 janv.-20 fév. – **Repas** *(fermé après 20 h 30)* carte 22 à 33 – **19 ch** 58/92 – ½ P 62/77.
◆ Le bac assurant la liaison entre l'île et le continent accoste à quelques encablures de ce petit point de chute façon "pension de famille". Chambres actuelles proprettes. Formule lunch unique assez succincte, mais choix de préparations plus complet au dîner.
◆ Vlak bij dit adresje, dat veel weg heeft van een familiepension, meert de veerboot aan die de verbinding met het vasteland onderhoudt. Propere, eigentijdse kamers. Slechts één, vrij beknopte lunchformule, maar 's avonds een ruimere keuze aan gerechten.

Kaart

De Horper Wielen sans rest, Kaart 4, ✉ 8883 HD, ✆ (0 562) 44 82 00, *Fax (0 562) 44 82 45,* – .
avril-oct. – **12 ch** 66.
◆ Adresse à retenir si l'atmosphère intime d'une maison particulière vous tente, le temps d'un séjour insulaire. Chambres sans ampleur, mais tranquilles et bien tenues.
◆ Een adresje om te onthouden voor wie de intieme ambiance zoekt van een particulier huis. Kleine kamers, maar rustig en goed onderhouden.

Midsland (Midslân).

Claes Compaen sans rest, Heereweg 36 (Midsland-Noord), ✉ 8891 HT, ✆ (0 562) 44 80 10, *Fax (0 562) 44 94 49,* , – .
8 ch 84, – 2 suites.
◆ Établissement calme disposant de grandes chambres alignées de plain-pied, devant une pelouse. Breakfast personnalisé servi au saut du lit ou sur votre terrasse privative.
◆ Rustig etablissement met grote kamers die op de begane grond naast elkaar liggen, aan een grasveld. Het ontbijt wordt op uw kamer of uw eigen terras geserveerd.

Lies

De Walvisvaarder, Lies 23, ✉ 8895 KP, ✆ (0 562) 44 90 00, *info@walvisvaarder.nl, Fax (0 562) 44 82 78,* , , – .
fermé janv.-fév. – **Repas** (résidents seult) – **61 ch** 85 – ½ P 50/60.
◆ Au cœur d'un village marquant le centre de l'île, hôtel paisible dont les jolies chambres, souvent dotées d'un balcon ou d'une terrasse, occupent deux ailes côté jardin.
◆ Dit rustige hotel in een dorpje midden op het eiland beschikt over aangename kamers, de meeste met balkon of terras, die zijn ingericht in twee vleugels aan de tuinkant.

Oosterend (Aasterein).

De Grië (van Scheppingen), Hoofdstraat 43, ✉ 8897 HX, ☏ (0 562) 44 84 99, *Fax (0 562) 44 83 22*, – P. AE MC VISA
fermé 4 janv.-19 mars, merc. sauf vacances scolaires et mardi – **Repas** (dîner seult) 68 bc, carte env. 52, ♀.
◆ Digne écrin d'une gastronomie novatrice, cette ferme reconvertie vous reçoit sous une jolie charpente composée de vieux mâts. Feu ouvert, mezzanine et terrasse d'été fleurie.
◆ Een waardig bolwerk van vernieuwende gastronomie, deze karakteristieke boerderij. Eetzaal met fraai gebint van oude masten, open keuken en vide. Fleurig zomerterras.
Spéc. Soupe aux truffes d'été et pommes de terre. Bouillon de légumes safrané au rouget grillé à l'ail. Côte de bœuf fumée et rôtie, salade de légumes au fromage

TEXEL *Noord-Holland* 531 *N 4 et* 715 *F 2 – 13 728 h.*

Voir *Site★★ – Réserves d'oiseaux★ – De Slufter ≤★.*
vers Den Helder : Rederij Teso, Pontweg 1 à Den Hoorn ☏ (0 222) 36 96 00, Fax (0 222) 36 96 59. Durée de la traversée : 20 min.
Amsterdam (bac) 85 – Haarlem (bac) 78 – Leeuwarden (bac) 96 – (distances de Den Burg).

Den Burg

Emmalaan 66, ✉ 1791 AV, ☏ (0 222) 31 28 47, info@texel.net, Fax (0 222) 31 00 54.

Den Burg, Emmalaan 2, ✉ 1791 AV, ☏ (0 222) 31 21 06, *hoteldenburg@hetnet.nl, Fax (0 222) 32 20 53*, – TV P – 25 à 80. MC VISA
Repas (résidents seult) – **26 ch** 60/95 – ½ P 59/69.
◆ À l'entrée du centre de Den Burg, hôtel "sympa" affichant un petit air de pension familiale. Bon confort dans les diverses catégories de chambres, souvent très actuelles.
◆ Dit sympathieke hotel aan de rand van het centrum heeft iets weg van een familie-pension. Goed comfort in de diverse categorieën kamers, waarvan de meeste zeer eigentijds zijn.

De 14 Sterren, Smitsweg 4 (par Pontweg, sortie ⑪), ✉ 1791 PG, ☏ (0 222) 32 26 79, *14sterren@planet.nl, Fax (0 222) 32 26 81*, – TV P – 30. MC VISA.
fermé nov. et janv. – **Repas** voir rest ***De Worsteltent*** ci-après – 11 – **14 ch** 80/120 – ½ P 81/93.
◆ Cet agréable point de chute au cadre champêtre occupe une construction de type fermette. Chambres coquettes avec terrasses idéalement orientées pour un breakfast estival.
◆ Dit aangename, landelijk gelegen hotel heeft onderdak gevonden in een boerderijtje. Verzorgde kamers met een zomerterras, ideaal voor een zonnig ontbijtje.

Het Vierspan, Gravenstraat 3, ✉ 1791 CJ, ☏ (0 222) 31 31 76, *Fax (0 222) 31 39 55* – AE MC VISA
fermé lundi et mardi – **Repas** (dîner seult) carte 43 à 51, ♀.
◆ Une valeur sûre pour se restaurer au cœur de Den Burg. Accueil familial gentil, ambiance conviviale, recettes au goût du jour et buffet de fromages typiques de l'île.
◆ Een trefzeker adres voor een etentje in hartje Den Burg. Hartelijk onthaal, gemoedelijke sfeer, eigentijdse gerechten en buffet met kaassoorten van het eiland.

De Worsteltent - H. De 14 Sterren, Smitsweg 6 (par Pontweg, sortie ⑪), ✉ 1791 PG, ☏ (0 222) 31 02 88, *14sterren@planet.nl, Fax (0 222) 32 26 81*, , Avec cuisine italienne – P. MC VISA
fermé nov. et janv. – **Repas** carte 22 à 36, ♀.
◆ Cuisine d'esprit transalpin servie dans une ferme rénovée assise à la lisière des bois, devant une piste cyclable. Plaisante terrasse d'été. Animation musicale le dimanche.
◆ In deze gerenoveerde boerderij aan een fietspad langs de bosrand worden Italiaans georiënteerde gerechten geserveerd. Aangenaam zomerterras. Muzikale omlijsting op zondag.

De Cocksdorp

Roggeslootweg 3, ✉ 1795 JV, ☏ (0 222) 31 65 39, Fax (0 222) 31 60 19.

Molenbos, Postweg 224, ✉ 1795 JT, ☏ (0 222) 31 64 76, *info@molenbos.nl, Fax (0 222) 31 63 77*, ≤, – TV P. AE MC VISA
fermé 8 janv.-3 mars et 20 nov.-16 déc. – **Repas** *(fermé après 20 h 30)* Lunch 11 – carte 25 à 38 – **27 ch** 63/115 – ½ P 66/79.
◆ Paisible petit hôtel de notre temps posté en lisière d'une réserve naturelle, près de l'embouchure du canal. Chambres et junior suites. Accueil familial très "pro". Lumineuse salle des repas garnie d'un mobilier de bistrot.
◆ Rustig, eigentijds hotelletje aan de rand van een natuurreservaat en vlak bij de monding van het kanaal. Kamers en junior suites. Gastvrij en zeer professioneel onthaal. De lichte eetzaal is met bistromeubilair ingericht.

Nieuw Breda, Postweg 134 (Sud-Ouest : 4 km), ✉ 1795 JS, ☎ (0 222) 31 12 37, *info@hotelnieuwbreda.nl, Fax (0 222) 31 16 01,* – 25 à 100. AE MC VISA.
Repas (résidents seult) – **21 ch** 57/88.
◆ À la campagne, près de l'aéroport, chambres fonctionnelles réparties dans deux pavillons en forme de chalet. Distractions en rapport avec la nature environnante.
◆ Landelijk gelegen hotel vlak bij het vliegveld, met functionele kamers die verspreid liggen over twee paviljoens in chaletbouw. Recreatiemogelijkheden in de omringende natuur.

Den Hoorn

Bij Jef - Host. Keijser avec ch, Herenstraat 34, ✉ 1797 AJ, ☎ (0 222) 31 96 23, *info@bijjef.nl, Fax (0 222) 31 96 24,* – AE JCB VISA
fermé 6 janv.-3 fév. – **Repas** *(fermé mardi de nov. à Pâques)* (déjeuner sur réservation de nov. à Pâques) *Lunch 28* – carte 39 à 61, ♀ – **9 ch** 65/85 – ½ P 78/95.
◆ Une auberge rajeunie, mais six fois centenaire, abrite ce restaurant familial disposant aussi de chambres pratiques pour dépanner. Salle à manger moderne aux tons vifs.
◆ Een zes eeuwen oude, gerenoveerde herberg huisvest dit familierestaurant evenals enkele praktische kamers. Moderne eetzaal in heldere kleuren.

Het Kompas, Herenstraat 7, ✉ 1797 AE, ☎ (0 222) 31 93 60, *Fax (0 222) 31 93 56* – AE MC VISA.
fermé mi-janv.-mi-fév. et mardi – **Repas** (dîner seult) carte 39 à 51.
◆ Atmosphère "pub écossais" à cette enseigne du centre. Mets classiques, bon choix de vins, collection de whiskies et whiskeys et possibilité de choisir votre musique préférée.
◆ Restaurant in het centrum, met Schotse pubambiance. Klassieke gerechten, goede wijnselectie, Schotse en Ierse whisky's en de mogelijkheid een eigen muziekje uit te zoeken.

De Koog

Gd H. Opduin , Ruyslaan 22, ✉ 1796 AD, ☎ (0 222) 31 74 45, *info@opduin.nl, Fax (0 222) 31 77 77,* ≤, – rest, – 25 à 110. AE MC VISA JCB. rest
fermé 28 déc.-7 janv. – **Repas** *Lunch 22* – carte 27 à 54 – **92 ch** 116/232, – 3 suites – ½ P 114/150.
◆ En bordure des dunes et d'un bosquet, immeuble hôtelier d'aujourd'hui offrant le choix entre diverses sortes de chambres bien équipées, calmes et douillettes. De grandes baies vitrées inondent de clarté la salle de restaurant. Cuisine actuelle.
◆ Eigentijds hotelpand aan de rand van de duinen en een klein bos, met diverse typen rustige, behaaglijke kamers die van alle gemakken zijn voorzien. De restaurantzaal met de grote ramen baadt in een zee van licht. Eigentijdse keuken.

Boschrand, Bosrandweg 225, ✉ 1796 NA, ☎ (0 222) 31 72 81, *boschrand@tref.nl, Fax (0 222) 31 74 59,* – rest
Repas (dîner pour résidents seult) – **51 ch** 90 – ½ P 48/55.
◆ Construction récente située aux portes du village. Munies d'un balcon et distribuées sur deux étages, toutes les chambres offrent suffisamment d'espace et d'accessoires.
◆ Vrij nieuw pand aan de rand van het dorp. De kamers, die een balkon hebben en over twee verdiepingen verspreid liggen, zijn allemaal goed van formaat en voldoende uitgerust.

Strandh. Noordzee , Badweg 200, ✉ 1796 AA, ☎ (0 222) 31 73 65, *info@noordzee.nu, Fax (0 222) 31 75 77,* ≤, – rest, AE MC VISA JCB
Repas carte 28 à 46 – **10 ch** 90/125.
◆ Une passerelle dessert ce pavillon moderne posté au sommet des dunes, face à la plage. Chambres standard avec balcon panoramique. Quiétude et ambiance vacances assurées. Agréable salle à manger-véranda.
◆ Een loopbrug voert naar dit moderne paviljoen, dat bovenop de duinen aan zee ligt. Standaardkamers met panoramisch balkon. Rust en vakantiesfeer verzekerd. Aangename eetzaal met serre.

Zeerust, Boodtlaan 5, ✉ 1796 BD, ☎ (0 222) 31 72 61, *info@hotelzeerust.nl, Fax (0 222) 31 78 39,* – MC VISA.
21 fév.-15 nov. – **Repas** (dîner pour résidents seult) – **18 ch** 50/84 – ½ P 49/55.
◆ À 200 m du centre, près d'une étendue de dunes boisées, villa résidentielle convertie en petit hôtel évoquant une pension familiale. Confort fonctionnel dans les chambres.
◆ Deze villa op 200 m van beboste duinen is verbouwd tot een klein hotel met de sfeer van een familiepension. Functioneel comfort in de kamers.

Alpha sans rest, Boodtlaan 84, ✉ 1796 BC, ☎ (0 222) 31 76 77, *alpha@texel.to, Fax (0 222) 31 72 75* – AE MC VISA
mi-fév.-mi-nov. – **12 ch** 70/75.
◆ Parmi les meilleures adresses du patelin pour la clientèle touristique recherchant avant tout la tranquillité. Chambres standard de mise assez simple, mais sans reproche.
◆ Voor toeristen die hoofdzakelijk rust zoeken, is dit een van de beste adressen in De Koog. Vrij eenvoudige, maar onberispelijke standaardkamers.

Oosterend

Rôtiss.'t Kerckeplein, Oesterstraat 6, ✉ 1794 AR, ☎ (0 222) 31 89 50, *rotisserie@cistron.nl, Fax (0 222) 32 90 32* – P. AE Ⓓ MC VISA
fermé 15 janv.-15 fév., lundi et mardi – **Repas** (déjeuner sur réservation) carte 40 à 54, ♀.
◆ Cette maison typique, de style fermette, jouxte l'une des églises d'Oosterend. Repas où prime l'intention de bien faire, servi dans une ambiance rustique. Accueil avenant.
◆ Dit karakteristieke huis in boerderijstijl staat bij een van de kerken in Oosterend. De met zorg bereide maaltijd wordt geserveerd in een rustieke ambiance.

Oudeschild

't Pakhuus, Haven 8, ✉ 1792 AE, ☎ (0 222) 31 35 81, *info@pakhuus.nl, Fax (0 222) 31 04 04*, ≤, Taverne-rest, Produits de la mer – AE MC VISA JCB
Repas *Lunch 24* – carte 33 à 60.
◆ Taverne-restaurant sympathique aménagée dans un entrepôt du 17ᵉ s. préservant son cachet ancien. Salle à manger nostalgique, avec véranda. Préparations gorgées d'iode.
◆ Sympathiek café-restaurant in een 17e-eeuws pakhuis dat zijn oude karakter heeft behouden. Nostalgische eetzaal met serre. Visgerechten.

De Waal

Rebecca, Hogereind 39, ✉ 1793 AE, ☎ (0 222) 31 27 45, *hotel.rebecca@wxs.nl, Fax (0 222) 31 58 47*, 🌳, 🚲 – P. MC. ✱ rest
fermé nov. et janv. – **Repas** (résidents seult) – **18 ch** ☕ 55/110 – ½ P 55/60.
◆ Petit établissement familial où cyclistes et amis des oiseaux posent volontiers leurs valises. Jardin reposant, terrain de pétanque et chambres pratiques avant tout.
◆ Klein familiehotel waar fietsers en vogelliefhebbers graag toeven. Rustige tuin, jeu de boules banen en kamers die vooral functioneel zijn.

VLIELAND *Fryslân* 531 O 3 *et* 715 F 2 – *1 183 h.*

vers Harlingen : Rederij Doeksen, Willem Barentszkade 21 à West-Terschelling ☎ 0 900 363 57 36, Fax (0 562) 44 32 41. Durée de la traversée : 1 h 45. Il existe aussi un service rapide. Durée de la traversée : 50 min.
Havenweg 10, ✉ 8899 BB, ☎ (0 562) 45 11 11, info@vlieland.net, Fax (0 562) 45 13 61.
Amsterdam (bac) 115 – Leeuwarden (bac) 28.

Oost-Vlieland (East-Flylân).

Voir *Phare (Vuurtoren)* ≤★.

Strandhotel Seeduyn avec appartements, Badweg 3 (Nord : 2 km), ✉ 8899 BV, ☎ (0 562) 45 15 77, *seeduyn@westcordhotels.nl, Fax (0 562) 45 11 15*, ≤, 🌳, ⛭, 🏊, ✂ – 🛗 TV ♿ – 🎤 25 à 200. AE Ⓓ MC VISA. ✱ ch
fermé 14 janv.-20 fév. – **Repas** voir rest ***Entre deux Mers*** ci-après – ***De Brassery*** *(fermé du 18 au 25 janv.)* carte 27 à 41, ♀ – ***Strandpaviljoen 't Badhuys*** *(fermé lundi et mardi de nov. à mars)* carte 22 à 32, ♀ – **151 ch** ☕ 87/174 – ½ P 84/114.
◆ Le charme de l'hôtel tient surtout à son site, dominant le front de mer. Chambres et appartements avec balcon, brasserie-salon et beauty-center. "Pavillon de plage" très commode pour se restaurer agréablement sans quitter des yeux sa serviette de bain.
◆ Dit hotel heeft een prachtig uitzicht op de zee en de duinen, wat het een bijzondere charme geeft. Kamers en appartementen met balkon. Brasserie en beautycenter. Het strandpaviljoen is heel praktisch voor een hapje tussen het zonnen door.

Entre deux Mers - H. Strandhotel Seeduyn, Badweg 3 (Nord : 2 km), ✉ 8899 BV, ☎ (0 562) 45 15 77, *seeduyn@westcordhotels.nl, Fax (0 562) 45 11 15*, ≤, 🌳 – AE Ⓓ MC VISA. ✱
fermé du 18 au 25 janv. – **Repas** (déjeuner sur réservation) carte 33 à 50, ♀.
◆ Le restaurant gastronomique associé au Strandhotel Seeduyn sert une cuisine actuelle honorant les produits régionaux. Salle à manger d'esprit nautique. Vue littorale.
◆ Het gastronomische restaurant van Strandhotel Seeduyn bereidt een eigentijdse keuken op basis van regionale producten. Eetzaal met nautisch decor. Uitzicht op de kust.

De Wadden avec ch, Dorpsstraat 61, ✉ 8899 AD, ☎ (0 562) 45 26 26, *dewadden@westcordhotels.nl, Fax (0 562) 45 26 23*, 🌳, 🌳 – TV. AE Ⓓ MC VISA. ✱ ch
Repas *Lunch 18* – 22/31 bc – **23 ch** ☕ 76 – ½ P 60/99.
◆ Chaleureuse auberge où l'on s'attable dans un décor façon "grand café hollandais". Une annexe regroupant des chambres avec terrasse ou balcon se dissimule à l'arrière.
◆ In dit gemoedelijke restaurant gaat u aan tafel in het decor van een Hollands grand café. Aan de achterkant ligt een annexe waarin kamers met terras of balkon zijn ingericht.

WADDINXVEEN *Zuid-Holland* 532 M 10 *et* 715 E 5 – *26 884 h.*
Amsterdam 46 – Rotterdam 26 – Den Haag 29 – Utrecht 37.

XX **Bibelot,** Limaweg 54, ✉ 2743 CD, ☎ (0 182) 61 66 95, *info@bibelot.info, Fax (0 182) 63 09 55,* – ▤ 🅿 – 25 à 150. AE ⓓ MC VISA JCB
fermé sam. midi, dim. midi et lundi – **Repas** *Lunch 30* – 34/60 bc, ♀.
◆ Aménagé dans un pavillon semi-circulaire, ce confortable restaurant au goût du jour s'agrémente d'œuvres d'art contemporain. Bons accords mets-vins. Accueil et service "pro".
◆ In dit comfortabele, moderne restaurant in een halfrond paviljoen zijn hedendaagse kunstwerken te zien. Wijnen en gerechten zijn in goede harmonie. Prima ontvangst en service.

XX **Akkeroord,** Akkeroord 1 (Sud : 3 km direction Gouda), ✉ 2741 PZ, ☎ (0 182) 61 61 01, *akkeroord@zonnet.nl, Fax (0 182) 63 21 05,* – 🅿 AE ⓓ MC VISA JCB
fermé merc., sam. midi et dim. midi – **Repas** *Lunch 30* – carte 39 à 49.
◆ Pimpante devanture fleurie à la belle saison, jardin croquignolet, terrasse d'été ombragée, cuisine de bonne facture : l'Akkeroord ne manque pas d'atouts pour séduire.
◆ Elegante voorgevel met 's zomers veel bloemen, beeldige tuin, lommerrijk terras, goede keuken : de Akkeroord heeft heel wat in huis om de gasten te bekoren.

XX **'t Baarsje,** Zwarteweg 6 (Est : 2 km, direction Reeuwijk), ✉ 2741 LC, ☎ (0 182) 39 44 60, *info@baarsje.nl, Fax (0 182) 39 27 47,* – ▤ 🅿 AE ⓓ MC VISA JCB
fermé dern. sem. juil.-prem. sem. août, sam. midi, dim. et lundi – **Repas** *Lunch 31* – carte 49 à 58, ♀.
◆ Auberge mignonne et discrète retirée dans les polders. Son enseigne - une petite perche (baarsje) frétillante - résume le passé de l'établissement, naguère café de pêcheurs.
◆ Charmant restaurantje in de polder. Als de muren van dit vroegere visserscafé konden spreken, zouden er ongetwijfeld heel wat stoere hengelaarsverhalen loskomen.

XX **de Gouwe Dis,** Zuidkade 22 (près du pont), ✉ 2741 JB, ☎ (0 182) 61 20 26, *info@gouwedis.nl, Fax (0 182) 61 09 99* – AE ⓓ MC VISA
fermé 3 sem. en juil., sam. midi, dim. et lundi – **Repas** *Lunch 33* – carte env. 43.
◆ Face au canal, jolie maison dont la salle à manger restitue une ambiance nostalgique : parquet luisant, poutres, mobilier à l'épreuve du temps, poêle et cheminée carrelée.
◆ Het restaurant in dit charmante pand tegenover de rivier ademt een nostalgische sfeer : glimmend parket, balken, oude meubels, potkachel en schouw met tegeltjes.

WAGENINGEN *Gelderland* 532 S 11 *et* 715 I 6 – *33 987 h.*
Stadsbrink 1-C, ✉ 6707 AA, ☎ (0 317) 41 07 77, info@vvvwageningen.nl, Fax (0 317) 42 31 86.
Amsterdam 85 – Arnhem 19 – Utrecht 47.

Nol in't Bosch, Hartenseweg 60 (Nord-Est : 2 km), ✉ 6704 PA, ☎ (0 317) 31 91 01, *info@nolintbosch.nl, Fax (0 317) 31 36 11,* – 🅿 – 25 à 150. AE ⓓ MC VISA JCB. rest
Repas *Lunch 14* – carte env. 40 – **33 ch** 68/92 – ½ P 65.
◆ Il règne une attachante atmosphère de pension familiale dans cet hôtel à débusquer parmi les bois. Chambres de bonne ampleur, toutes dotées d'une terrasse ou d'un balcon. Salle à manger typiquement hollandaise et restaurant d'été estimé des cyclistes.
◆ In dit hotel in de bossen hangt de gemoedelijke sfeer van een familiepension. Kamers van goed formaat, alle met terras of balkon. De eetzaal heeft een typisch Hollandse ambiance en het terras is erg geliefd bij fietsers.

X **'t Gesprek,** Grintweg 247, ✉ 6704 AN, ☎ (0 317) 42 37 01, *ge.dierkens@wxs.nl, Fax (0 317) 42 58 26,* – ▤ 🅿 AE MC VISA
fermé sam. midi, dim. midi et lundi midi – **Repas** (dîner seult en juil.) *Lunch 27* – carte 35 à 49.
◆ Auberge engageante établie aux portes de Wageningen. Salle de restaurant agréable à vivre, terrasse d'été et répertoire culinaire néerlandais en phase avec l'époque.
◆ Vriendelijk restaurant aan de rand van de stad. Aangename eetzaal, zomerterras en een culinair repertoire dat goed aansluit bij de huidige trend.

WAHLWILLER *Limburg* 532 U 18 – *voir à Wittem.*

WAMEL *Gelderland* C *West Maas en Waal 18 241 h.* 532 R 11 *et* 715 H 6.
Amsterdam 94 – Utrecht 60 – Arnhem 48 – 's-Hertogenbosch 30 – Nijmegen 31.

X **d'Oude Weeghbrug,** Dorpsstraat 126, ✉ 6659 CH, ☎ (0 487) 50 12 73, *Fax (0 487) 50 15 26,* – 🅿 AE ⓓ MC VISA
fermé sem. carnaval, 2 prem. sem. janv. et mardi – Repas (dîner seult jusqu'à 20 h 30) 30/68 bc, ♀.
◆ Tout au bout de la Dorpsstraat, près de la digue du Waal, adorable auberge où un chef inspiré vous mitonne une goûteuse cuisine du marché. Ambiance typiquement batave.
◆ In deze charmante herberg bij de dijk langs de Waal bereidt een bevlogen chef-kok een smakelijke keuken met dagverse producten. Hollandse ambiance.

WANNEPERVEEN *Overijssel* 531 V 6 *et* 715 J 3 *– voir à Giethoorn.*

WANSSUM *Limburg* C *Meerlo-Wanssum 7 675 h.* 532 V 13 *et* 715 J 7.

au Nord-Est : 3 km à Geysteren, Het Spekt 2, ✉ 5862 AZ, ✆ (0 478) 53 25 92, Fax (0 478) 53 29 63.

Amsterdam 159 – Maastricht 104 – Eindhoven 51 – Nijmegen 48.

à Geysteren *Nord-Est : 3 km* C *Meerlo-Wanssum :*

Eethoeve de Boogaard, Wanssumseweg 1, ✉ 5862 AA, ✆ (0 478) 53 90 70, *Fax (0 478) 53 90 70,* – P. MC VISA
fermé 2 sem. carnaval, fin juil.-début août et lundis et mardis non fériés – **Repas** (dîner seult sauf dim.) carte 27 à 44.
◆ Restaurant de campagne occupant une ancienne ferme typiquement limbourgeoise. Salle à manger néo-rustique et cour intérieure carrée, abondamment fleurie aux beaux jours.
◆ Landelijk gelegen restaurant in een oude, karakteristieke Limburgse boerderij. Neorustieke eetzaal en vierkante binnenhof die 's zomers vol bloemen staat.

WARDER *Noord-Holland* C *Zeevang 6 330 h.* 531 P 7.

Amsterdam 38 – Haarlem 48 – Alkmaar 3.

't Tolhuus, IJsselmeerdijk 7a, ✉ 1473 PP, ✆ (0 299) 40 33 33, *tolhuus@hemhotels.nl, Fax (0 299) 40 33 39,* – P. – 25. MC VISA JCB. rest
Repas (avec buffets) *Lunch 18* – carte 22 à 32 – 10 – **39 ch** 90/120 – ½ P 80/150.
◆ Ressource hôtelière embusquée à l'écart d'un petit hameau des polders, entre Edam et Hoorn. Bonne isolation phonique dans les chambres, assez spacieuses. À l'heure du repas, choix de préparations traditionnelles. Formule buffets.
◆ Dit hotel ligt net buiten het dorp verscholen in de polder, tussen Edam en Hoorn. Goede geluidsisolatie in de vrij ruime kamers. In de eetzaal wordt een keur van traditionele gerechten geserveerd. Buffetformule.

WARKUM *Fryslân – voir Workum.*

WARMOND *Zuid-Holland* 532 M 9 *et* 715 E 5 – 5 058 h.

Veerpolder, ✉ 2360 AA, ✆ (0 71) 305 88 10.

Dorpsstraat 4a, ✉ 2361 BB, ✆ (0 71) 301 06 31, warmond@hollandrijnland.nl, Fax (0 71) 301 26 99.

Amsterdam 39 – Rotterdam 46 – Den Haag 20 – Haarlem 25.

De Moerbei, Dorpsstraat 5a, ✉ 2361 AK, ✆ (0 71) 515 68 98, *Fax (0 71) 515 68 98,* – P. MC VISA
fermé sam. midi et dim. – **Repas** *Lunch 29* – 32/52 bc, ♀.
◆ Au centre du village, derrière un écran végétal, restaurant aménagé dans une ancienne ferme à toit de chaume. Fringante salle à manger moderne. Mets classiques actualisés.
◆ Midden in het dorp staat, verscholen achter het groen, een oude boerderij met een rieten dak. Gezellige, moderne eetzaal. Geactualiseerde klassieke gerechten.

De Stad Rome, De Baan 4, ✉ 2361 GH, ✆ (0 71) 301 01 44, *informatie@stadrome.nl, Fax (0 71) 301 25 17,* , Grillades – P. AE MC VISA
fermé 2 sem. en fév., août et lundi – **Repas** (dîner seult jusqu'à minuit) 29/58 bc.
◆ Avis aux carnivores : voici une adresse familiale dont les plantureuses grillades font la réputation depuis plus de vingt ans. Terrasse estivale avec mini-cascade.
◆ Vleesliefhebbers opgelet ! Dit familierestaurant staat al ruim twintig jaar bekend om zijn overvloedige grillgerechten. Zomerterras met miniwaterval.

WASSENAAR *Zuid-Holland* 532 L 10 *et* 715 D 5 *– voir à Den Haag, environs.*

WATERINGEN *Zuid-Holland* C *Westland 96 000 h.* 532 K 10 *et* 715 D 5.

Amsterdam 65 – Rotterdam 24 – Den Haag 10.

't Raethuys, Plein 13g, ✉ 2291 CA, ✆ (0 174) 27 02 14, *Fax (0 174) 27 02 14,* – P. AE MC VISA
fermé dern. sem. juil.-prem. sem. août, sam. midi, dim. et lundi – **Repas** 25/50 bc, ♀.
◆ Sur la place de la localité, sympathique table ayant pris ses quartiers dans l'ancienne mairie (1936). Mets soignés au goût du jour. Petite terrasse d'été à l'avant.
◆ Dit sympathieke restaurant aan het Plein heeft zijn intrek genomen in het voormalige raadhuis (1936). Verzorgde, eigentijdse gerechten. Klein zomerterras aan de voorkant.

WEERT *Limburg 532 T 15 et 715 I 8 – 48 479 h.*

Laurabosweg 8, ✉ 6006 VR, ☎ (0 495) 51 84 38, Fax (0 475) 51 87 09.

Maasstraat 18, ✉ 6001 EC, ☎ (0 495) 53 68 00, weert@regiovvv.nl, Fax (0 495) 54 14 94. – Amsterdam 156 – Maastricht 57 – Eindhoven 28 – Roermond 21.

Golden Tulip, Driesveldlaan 99, ✉ 6001 KC, ☎ (0 495) 53 96 55, *info@goldentulipweert.nl, Fax (0 495) 54 08 07* – , rest, – 25 à 300. AE VISA JCB.
Repas (dîner seult) 25/73 bc – **60 ch** 115/135.
◆ Hôtel de chaîne avantagé par la proximité immédiate de la gare. Chambres souvent égayées de tissus écossais. Accès gratuit à la piscine tropicale située hors du centre. Nouveau restaurant de style et d'orientation culinaire contemporains.
◆ Dit hotel is gunstig gelegen, dicht bij het station. De meeste kamers hebben een stoffering met Schotse ruit. Gratis toegang tot het tropisch zwembad buiten het centrum. Nieuw restaurant met eigentijds interieur en dito keuken.

Host. Munten, Wilhelminasingel 276, ✉ 6001 GV, ☎ (0 495) 53 10 57, *info@hostelleriemunten.nl, Fax (0 495) 54 45 96*, – – 35. AE VISA JCB
fermé dim. non fériés et sam. midi – **Repas** (avec brasserie) Lunch 32 – 34/67 bc – **14 ch** 79/90 – ½ P 95/105.
◆ Réaménagée dans l'esprit actuel, cette hostellerie centenaire a encore de beaux jours devant elle. Chambres aux tissus coordonnés, salon cosy et jolie terrasse d'été. Une véranda moderne procure espace et clarté au restaurant. Repas estival en plein air.
◆ Deze honderd jaar oude hostellerie gaat met de eigentijdse inrichting nog een mooie toekomst tegemoet. Smaakvol gestoffeerde kamers, knusse lounge, fraai terras. De moderne serre geeft het restaurant licht en ruimte. 's Zomers wordt buiten gegeten.

De Brookhut, Heugterbroekdijk 2 (Nord : 3 km à Laar), ✉ 6003 RB, ☎ (0 495) 53 13 91, *Fax (0 495) 54 33 05*, – – 30. AE VISA.
Repas *(fermé sam. midi, dim. midi et lundi)* Lunch 25 – 33/53 – **8 ch** 61/87 – ½ P 86.
◆ Petite affaire familiale mettant à votre disposition des chambres claires et proprettes, pourvues d'un mobilier fonctionnel. Vous gagnerez Weert en 3 mn. Préparations classico-régionales servies dans une lumineuse salle à manger-véranda.
◆ Dit familiebedrijfje buiten de bebouwde kom ligt op nog geen 3 min. afstand van het plaatsje zelf. Het beschikt over lichte, propere kamers met functioneel meubilair. In een lichte eetzaal met serre kunt u genieten van streekgerechten met een klassiek tintje.

Les Deux Charmes, Bassin 4, ✉ 6001 GZ, ☎ (0 495) 54 32 82, *lesdeuxcharmes@planet.nl, Fax (0 495) 54 77 26*, – 25 à 40. AE VISA.
fermé 2 sem. carnaval, 2 dern. sem. sept., sam. midi, dim. midi, lundi et mardi – **Repas** Lunch 23 – 27/45.
◆ "Deux charmes", mais aussi un vieux canon, devancent la modeste façade de cette petite maison de bouche. Bons produits soigneusement travaillés dans le tempo actuel.
◆ Voor de bescheiden gevel van dit kleine restaurant staan twee "charmes" (haagbeuken) en een oud kanon. Kwaliteitsproducten worden hier met zorg in eigentijdse stijl bereid.

Bretelli, Hoogstraat 8, ✉ 6001 EV, ☎ (0 495) 45 20 28, *info@bretelli.nl, Fax (0 495) 45 20 38*, Ouvert jusqu'à 23 h – AE VISA
fermé carnaval, vacances bâtiment, fin déc., sam. midi, dim. et lundi – **Repas** Lunch 33 – 39/70, .
◆ Une table qui "cartonne" au cœur de Weert. Décor intérieur composite, carte inspirée par la Méditerranée, avec quelques recettes assez originales, et cave italo-ibérique.
◆ Een restaurantje in hartje Weert dat de wind in de zeilen heeft. Bont interieur, mediterraan getinte keuken met enkele originele gerechten en een Italiaanse wijnkaart.

à Nederweert *Nord-Est : 5 km – 16 136 h*

Kesselshof, Brugstraat 44, ✉ 6031 EG, ☎ (0 495) 62 50 00, *info@kesselshof.nl, Fax (0 495) 63 46 42*, – AE VISA JCB
fermé du 20 au 26 fév., du 16 au 31 août, 26 déc.-4 janv., lundis non fériés, sam. midi, dim. midi et lundi – **Repas** Lunch 25 – carte 47 à 53, .
◆ Pièces actuelles aux tons pastel, terrasse sous les frondaisons d'un peuplier pleureur, vaisselle provençale et cuisine aux accents du Sud, avec de bons menus "surprise".
◆ Eigentijdse eetzalen in pasteltinten, terras onder het bladerdak van een populier, Provençaals serviesgoed, keuken met zuidelijke accenten en heerlijke verrassingsmenu's.

WEESP *Noord-Holland 531 P 9, 532 P 9 et 715 G 5 – 17 958 h.*

Basisweg 2, ✉ 1383 NC, ☎ (0 294) 41 56 23, fax (0 294) 41 56 18.
Amsterdam 18 – Hilversum 17 – Utrecht 39.

Meyers CuliCafe, Nieuwstad 84, ✉ 1381 CD, ☎ (0 294) 41 54 63, *meyersculicafe@zonnet.nl, Fax (0 294) 41 54 63* – VISA
fermé lundi – **Repas** (dîner seult) 25/38.
◆ Au centre du village, bistrot alangui face au canal. Lambris, miroirs et vieux instruments de musique garnissent les murs de la salle de restaurant. Service tout sourire.
◆ Bistro in het centrum, tegenover de gracht. Eetzaal met lambrisering, spiegels en oude muziekinstrumenten. Zeer vriendelijke bediening.

Minevitus, Nieuwstad 32, ✉ 1381 CC, ☎ (0 294) 41 35 29, *info@minevitus.nl, Fax (0 294) 41 35 29,* – AE ⓓ MC VISA JCB.
fermé 2 sem. en sept., dern. sem. déc.-prem. sem. janv., lundi et sam. midi – **Repas** Lunch 25 – 34/45, ♀.
◆ Ravissant bistrot décoré d'objets d'hier, comme ces affiches vantant de fameux apéritifs français. Carte se référant à quelques coins de l'Hexagone. Terrasse au bord du canal.
◆ Bijzonder charmante bistro met decoratieve oude voorwerpen, zoals affiches van beroemde Franse aperitieven. Kaart met diverse Franse specialiteiten. Terras aan het water.

WEIDUM *Fryslân* C *Littenseradiel 10 821 h.* 531 T 4 *et* 715 I 2.
Amsterdam 142 – Leeuwarden 13 – Sneek 16 – Zwolle 91.

De Vijf Sinnen, Hegedijk 2, ✉ 9024 EA, ☎ (0 58) 251 92 17, *info@devijfsinnen.nl, Fax (0 58) 251 99 94,* – P. AE ⓓ MC VISA JCB
fermé 31 déc.-1er janv., dim. et lundi – **Repas** (dîner seult) 38/53, ♀.
◆ Restaurant auréolé d'une bonne réputation dans ce petit coin de Frise. Salle à manger façon Laura Ashley, ambiance bougie, cuisine au goût du jour et cave intéressante.
◆ Restaurant met een goede reputatie in dit stukje Friesland. Eetzaal in Laura Ashley stijl, kaarslichtambiance, eigentijdse keuken en interessante wijnkelder.

WELLERLOOI *Limburg* C *Bergen 13 539 h.* 532 V 13 *et* 715 J 7.
Amsterdam 160 – Maastricht 95 – Eindhoven 54 – Nijmegen 46 – Venlo 20.

Host. de Hamert avec ch, Hamert 2 (rte Nijmegen-Venlo), ✉ 5856 CL, ☎ (0 77) 473 12 60, *hamert@alliance.nl, Fax (0 77) 473 25 03,* ← trafic fluvial (Meuse-Maas) et campagne, , – |‡|, ▤ ch, TV P – 35. AE ⓓ MC VISA.
fermé 28 déc.-8 janv. et mardi et merc. de nov. à mars – **Repas** Lunch 45 – 63/100 bc, ♀ – **10 ch** 110/160.
◆ En saison, l'asperge est à l'honneur dans cette hostellerie cossue dominant la Maas. Jolie vue sur le trafic fluvial et la campagne, cave bien montée et chambres tout confort.
◆ Luxueuze hostellerie aan de Maas, met fraai uitzicht op het scheepvaartverkeer en het platteland. Goed voorziene wijnkelder, kamers met alle comfort, asperges in het seizoen.

WELTEN *Limburg* 532 U 17 – *voir à Heerlen.*

WESTERBORK *Drenthe* C *Midden-Drenthe 32 691 h.* 531 Y 5 *et* 715 K 3.
Amsterdam 173 – Assen 24 – Emmen 24 – Leeuwarden 77 – Zwolle 61.

Golden Tulip , Beilerstraat 24a, ✉ 9431 TA, ☎ (0 593) 33 14 44, *info@goldentulipwesterbork.nl, Fax (0 593) 33 28 88,* , – TV P – 25 à 150. AE ⓓ MC VISA. rest
Repas *Ruyghe Venne* Lunch 19 – 23/61 bc, ♀ – **34 ch** 60/97 – ½ P 79/108.
◆ En lisière de forêt, hôtel familial agrandi d'une aile récente regroupant des chambres bien équipées. Pendant la saison des frimas, flambées réconfortantes au salon. Salle à manger classiquement agencée. Terrasse estivale bénéficiant d'un environnement boisé.
◆ Dit familiehotel aan de rand van het bos heeft net een nieuwe vleugel gekregen met comfortabele kamers. Als het wat kouder wordt, knappert er in de lounge een behaaglijk vuurtje. Klassiek ingerichte eetzaal. Zomerterras in een bosrijk decor.

WESTERVELDE *Drenthe* 531 X 4 – *voir à Norg.*

WESTKAPELLE *Zeeland* C *Veere 21 985 h.* 532 F 13 *et* 715 B 7.
Amsterdam 219 – Middelburg 18.

Zuiderduin , De Bucksweg 2 (Sud : 3 km), ✉ 4361 SM, ☎ (0 118) 56 18 10, *info-zuiderduin@fletcher.nl, Fax (0 118) 56 22 61,* , , , , – ▤ rest, TV P – 25 à 240. AE MC VISA. rest
Repas carte 31 à 39 – **67 ch** 83/127 – ½ P 120/188.
◆ Toutes les chambres de cet établissement avoisinant les dunes sont dotées d'une terrasse ou d'un balcon. Certaines d'entre elles disposent également d'une kitchenette. Confortable brasserie.
◆ De kamers in dit etablissement bij de duinen hebben allemaal een terras of balkon. Sommige beschikken ook over een kitchenette. Comfortabele brasserie.

X **Badmotel,** Grindweg 2, ✉ 4361 JG, ☎ (0 118) 57 13 58, *info@badmotel.nl, Fax (0 118) 57 13 59,* ←, 🍴 – P. MC VISA
Pâques-oct. ; fermé lundi et mardi – **Repas** (dîner seult) carte 33 à 41.
◆ Cette table occupe un bungalow procurant une jolie vue sur le petit lac de la station balnéaire. Plats classico-bourgeois, grand bar et appartements pour longs séjours.
◆ Dit restaurant is gevestigd in een bungalow aan het meertje bij de badplaats. Eenvoudige maar goede klassieke keuken, grote bar en appartementen voor een langer verblijf.

X **De Westkaap,** Westkapelse Zeedijk 7, ✉ 4361 SJ, ☎ (0 118) 57 25 57, *info@westkaap.nl, Fax (0 118) 57 01 69,* ← trafic maritime, 🍴, Taverne-rest – P. MC VISA
fermé du 2 au 13 déc. – **Repas** 23, ♀.
◆ Ample taverne-restaurant installée au bord de la digue, dans un pavillon sur pilotis surveillant le va-et-vient des navires. Maquettes de bateaux exposées en salle.
◆ Dit Grand café aan de zeedijk is gehuisvest in een paviljoen op palen dat uitzicht biedt op de zee en de passerende schepen. Maquettes van boten in de eetzaal.

WEST-TERSCHELLING (WEST-SKYLGE) *Fryslân* 531 O 2 *et* 715 G 1 – *voir à Waddeneilanden (Terschelling).*

WIJDEWORMER *Noord-Holland* 531 O 8 – *voir à Zaandam.*

---

de WIJK *Drenthe* 531 W 6 *et* 715 J 3 – *voir à Meppel.*

WIJK AAN ZEE *Noord-Holland* © *Beverwijk 35 780 h.* 531 M 8 *et* 715 E 4.
Amsterdam 29 – Haarlem 18 – Alkmaar 27.

🏠 **Villa de Klughte** sans rest, Van Ogtropweg 2, ✉ 1949 BA, ☎ (0 251) 37 43 04, *hotel@hoteldeklughte.nl, Fax (0 251) 37 52 24,* 🌳, 🚲 – TV P. MC VISA JCB
11 ch ☕ 79/129.
◆ Belle villa sur jardin élevée au début du 20e s. en bordure des dunes. Chambres et junior suites au décor personnalisé, quelquefois pourvues d'un jacuzzi. Breakfast soigné.
◆ Deze mooie villa met tuin is begin vorige eeuw gebouwd aan de rand van de duinen. Kamers en junior suites met een eigen karakter, sommige met jacuzzi. Verzorgd ontbijt.

🏠 **Residentie Zeeduin** 🐚, Relweg 59, ✉ 1949 EC, ☎ (0 251) 37 61 61, *info@zeeduin.nl, Fax (0 251) 37 61 00,* 🍴, 🏋, ≘, 🚲 – 🛗 ⇄ TV P – 🏛 25 à 80. AE ⊙ MC VISA JCB
Repas *(fermé 25, 26 et 31 déc. soirs)* carte 32 à 40, ♀ – ☕ 11 – **60 ch** 92/115 – ½ P 88/122.
◆ Dans les dunes de la station balnéaire, immeuble récent dont les quatre étages renferment des chambres actuelles, assez grandes et complétées d'un coin cuisine.
◆ Dit nieuwe gebouw in de duinen, aan de rand van het dorp, telt vier verdiepingen met vrij grote, eigentijdse kamers die zijn voorzien van een kitchenette.

WIJK BIJ DUURSTEDE *Utrecht* 532 R 11 *et* 715 H 6 – *23 209 h.*
ℹ *Markt 24,* ✉ *3961 BC,* ☎ *(0 343) 57 59 95, vvvwbd@zonnet.nl, Fax (0 343) 57 10 67.*
Amsterdam 62 – Utrecht 24 – Arnhem 54 – 's-Hertogenbosch 48.

XX **Pippijn en H. de Oude Lantaarn** avec ch, Markt 2, ✉ 3961 BC, ☎ (0 343) 57 13 72, *info@pippijn.nl, Fax (0 343) 57 37 96* – TV. AE ⊙ MC VISA
Repas *(fermé lundi midi)* Lunch 29 – carte 43 à 53, ♀ – **18 ch** ☕ 68/94, – 2 suites – ½ P 98/110.
◆ Ancien relais de poste facilement repérable sur le Markt. Restaurant-véranda bien installé. Chambres douillettes réparties aux étages et dans les annexes voisines.
◆ Dit voormalige poststation aan de markt is gemakkelijk te vinden. Goed ingericht restaurant met serre. Behaaglijke kamers op de verdiepingen en in de aangrenzende dependances.

WILHELMINADORP *Zeeland* © *Goes 36 047 h.* 532 I 13 *et* 715 C 7.
Amsterdam 163 – Middelburg 27 – Goes 4.

XX **Katseveer,** Katseveerweg 2 (direction Roodewijk puis route parallèle à la N 256), ✉ 4475 PB, ☎ (0 113) 22 79 55, ← digue et plages, 🍴, ⚓ – P. AE ⊙ MC VISA
fermé sam. midi, dim. midi et lundi midi – **Repas** Lunch 35 – carte 45 à 72.
◆ Jolie vue sur le trafic de l'Oosterschelde depuis cet ancien pavillon d'où les voyageurs guettaient l'arrivée du bac. La cuisine travaille surtout les produits régionaux.
◆ Dit restaurant in het voormalige wachtlokaal van de veerpont biedt een mooi uitzicht op de Oosterschelde. In de keuken vormen streekproducten de hoofdingrediënten.

WINSCHOTEN *Groningen* 531 AB 4 *et* 715 M 2 *– 18 753 h.*

Stationsweg 21a, ✉ 9671 AL, ☎ (0 597) 41 22 55, vvvanwb.winschoten@planet.nl, Fax (0 597) 42 40 62.

Amsterdam 230 – Groningen 41 – Assen 49.

Royal York, Stationsweg 21, ✉ 9671 AL, ☎ (0 597) 41 43 00, *Fax (0 597) 42 32 24* – TV P – 25 à 60. AE VISA – *fermé 31 déc.-1er janv.* – **Repas** *(fermé sam. midi et dim. midi)* (grillades) carte 23 à 40 – **40 ch** ☐ 60/79 – ½ P 79.
◆ Situé à deux pas de la gare, cet hôtel du centre-ville dispose de chambres très convenables, avec un double vitrage adoucissant la rumeur de la rue passante. Chaleureuse salle à manger d'esprit "bistrot". Grillades saisies à la braise.
◆ Dit hotel in het centrum, op loopafstand van het station, beschikt over comfortabele kamers waar het rumoer van de straat wordt gedempt door de dubbele beglazing. Gezellige eetzaal in bistrostijl. Grillades van de houtskoolgrill.

In den Stallen avec ch, Oostereinde 10 (Nord-Est : 3 km, près A 7), ✉ 9672 TC, ☎ (0 597) 41 40 73, *info@indenstallen.nl, Fax (0 597) 42 26 53,* – TV P. AE VISA. ch – *fermé 31 déc.-1er janv.* – **Repas** 18/32 – ☐ 8 – **10 ch** 58 – ½ P 86.
◆ Aux avant-postes de Winschoten, près de l'autoroute, ancienne ferme où l'on mange à prix "plancher" dans un décor néo-rustique. Bowling et chambres de confort correct.
◆ In deze oude boerderij aan de rand van de stad, vlak bij de snelweg, kunt u voor een minimumprijs tafelen in een neorustiek decor. Bowling en kamers met redelijk comfort.

WINTERSWIJK *Gelderland* 532 Z 11 *et* 715 L 6 *– 28 750 h.*

Vredenseweg 150, ✉ 7113 AE, ☎ (0 543) 56 25 25.

Markt 17a, ✉ 7101 DA, ☎ (0 543) 51 23 02, vvvwinterswijk@tref.nl, Fax (0 543) 52 40 81.

Amsterdam 152 – Arnhem 67 – Apeldoorn 66 – Enschede 43.

De Frerikshof, Frerikshof 2 (Nord-Ouest : 2 km), ✉ 7103 CA, ☎ (0 543) 51 77 55, *hotel@frerikshof.nl, Fax (0 543) 52 20 35,* , , , – , rest, TV P – 25 à 200. AE VISA. rest
Repas Lunch 30 – 49/69 – ☐ 12 – **66 ch** 90/125 – ½ P 73/80.
◆ Complexe hôtelier implanté aux abords de la ville. Piscine, bowling, pimpantes chambres avec balcon et breakfast présenté sous forme de buffets dans une jolie véranda. Une coupole apporte espace et clarté au restaurant.
◆ Dit hotelcomplex aan de rand van de stad beschikt over een zwembad, een bowling en picobello kamers met balkon. 's Morgens staat er een ontbijtbuffet klaar in een fraaie serre. De koepel geeft licht en ruimte aan het restaurant.

Stad Munster, Markt 11, ✉ 7101 DA, ☎ (0 543) 51 21 21, *info@hotelstadmunster.nl, Fax (0 543) 52 24 15,* , – TV P. AE VISA. – *fermé 29 déc.-21 janv.* – **Repas** *(fermé dim. midi)* Lunch 26 – 32/60 bc – ☐ 12 – **20 ch** 55/105 – ½ P 70/90.
◆ Fondée au 17e s., reconstruite en 1911 dans l'esprit "Jugendstil", cette fière auberge familiale est un point de chute appréciable pour poser ses valises à Winterswijk. Repas au goût du jour. Asperge et gibier en saison. Belle terrasse d'été.
◆ Dit familiehotel-restaurant is in de 17e eeuw als herberg begonnen, werd in 1911 in Jugendstil herbouwd en is nu een vrij comfortabele pleisterplaats in Winterswijk. Eigentijdse keuken. Asperges en wild in het seizoen. Mooi zomerterras.

De Beukenhorst, Markt 27, ✉ 7101 DA, ☎ (0 543) 52 28 94, *info@debeukenhorst.com, Fax (0 543) 51 35 95,* – AE VISA. – *fermé 25 fév.-3 mars, du 4 au 11 août, 28 déc.-7 janv., lundi et mardi* – **Repas** Lunch 19 – 34/78 bc, ♀.
◆ Cuisine d'inspiration méditerranéenne servie dans une ancienne brûlerie de café postée sur le Markt. Coquette salle à manger avec charpente apparente et patio charmant.
◆ In deze voormalige koffiebranderij aan de Markt worden gerechten uit een mediterraan georiënteerde keuken geserveerd. Gezellige eetzaal met kapgebint en een charmante patio.

WITTEM *Limburg* C *Gulpen-Wittem 15 435 h.* 532 U 18 *et* 715 I 9.

au Sud : 2 km à Mechelen, Dalbissenweg 22, ✉ 6281 NC, ☎ (0 43) 455 13 97, Fax (0 43) 455 15 76.

Amsterdam 225 – Maastricht 19 – Aachen 13.

In den Roden Leeuw van Limburg, Wittemer Allee 28, ✉ 6286 AB, ☎ (0 43) 450 12 74, *info@indenrodenleeuw.nl, Fax (0 43) 450 23 62,* – TV P. VISA JCB.
Repas *(fermé lundi et après 20 h)* 28 – **9 ch** ☐ 28/63 – ½ P 47/75.
◆ Un lion rouge rugit sur la devanture de cette auberge familiale officiant depuis plus de 150 ans dans ce petit coin du Limbourg. Chambres de bonne ampleur. Une terrasse estivale et un café typé devancent le restaurant classiquement aménagé.
◆ Deze familieherberg met een brullende rode leeuw aan de voorgevel biedt reizigers in het uiterste zuiden van Limburg al ruim 150 jaar een slaapplaats. Aan de voorkant van het klassiek ingerichte restaurant liggen een karakteristiek café en een zomerterras.

XXX **Kasteel Wittem** avec ch, Wittemer Allee 3, ✉ 6286 AA, ☎ (0 43) 450 12 08, *wittem@alliance.nl, Fax (0 43) 450 12 60,* ≤, ⛱, - TV P - 🏛 30. AE ⊕ MC VISA JCB.
fermé 22 fév.-1er mars – **Repas** *(fermé lundi)* (dîner seult sauf dim.) 63/143 bc, ♀ – ☕ 17 – **10 ch** 145/190, – 2 suites – ½ P 158/170.
◆ Luxe, calme et art de vivre dans ce château du 15e s. entouré d'un parc avec douves. Salle à manger garnie de meubles de style. Chambres décorées sans fausse note.
◆ Luxe, rust en levenskunst in dit 15e-eeuwse kasteel met park en slotgracht. De eetzaal is met stijlmeubilair ingericht. Geen enkele wanklank verstoort het decor van de kamers.

à Wahlwiller *Est : 1,5 km* C *Gulpen-Wittem :*

XXX ✿ **Der Bloasbalg** (Waghemans), Botterweck 3, ✉ 6286 DA, ☎ (0 43) 451 13 64, *roger@derbloasbalg.nl, Fax (0 43) 451 25 15,* ⛱ – ▤ P. AE ⊕ MC VISA JCB
fermé 15 fév.-3 mars, du 13 au 29 sept., 24 déc., mardi, merc. et sam. midi – **Repas** Lunch 43 – 90 bc, carte 59 à 109.
◆ Bungalow posté en bordure d'un village typique, dans un cadre champêtre idéal pour un repas-plaisir. Mets classiques actualisés. Intérieur chaleureux. Terrasse estivale.
◆ Dat wordt een zeer genoeglijk uurtje tafelen in deze landelijke bungalow aan de rand van een pittoresk dorp. Klassieke keuken in een eigentijds jasje. Warme ambiance. Terras.
Spéc. Tartare de cabillaud et homard à la rémoulade. Rollmops de thon, crevettes grises et œuf poché au limon. Filet de bœuf au foie d'oie et aux truffes

XXX **'t Klauwes,** Oude Baan 1, ✉ 6286 BD, ☎ (0 43) 451 15 48, *info@klauwes.nl, Fax (0 43) 451 22 55,* ⛱ – P. AE ⊕ MC VISA
fermé carnaval, dern. sem. août, prem. sem. janv., lundi et sam. midi – **Repas** Lunch 35 – 43, ♀.
◆ Cette ferme du 18e s. a troqué cruches et bottes de foin contre spatules et casseroles. Les bonnes fourchettes ne s'en plaindront pas ! Vin blanc "maison". Ambiance rustique.
◆ Deze boerderij uit de 18e eeuw heeft kruiken en hooibalen verruild voor potten en pannen, tot grote tevredenheid van de lokale fijnproevers. Witte "huiswijn". Rustieke ambiance.

WOERDEN *Utrecht* 532 O 10 *et* 715 F 5 – *47 549 h.*

Molenstraat 40, ✉ 3441 BA, ☎ (0 348) 41 44 74, vvv-anwb@tiscali.nl, Fax (0 348) 41 78 43.
Amsterdam 52 – Utrecht 21 – Den Haag 46 – Rotterdam 41.

Woerden sans rest, Utrechtsestraatweg 25, ✉ 3445 AL, ☎ (0 348) 41 25 15, *bwwoerden@hetnet.nl, Fax (0 348) 42 18 53,* – TV P. AE ⊕ MC VISA
fermé 24 déc.-4 janv. – **62 ch** ☕ 85/112.
◆ Ressource hôtelière implantée à proximité de la gare et du centre de Woerden. Confort fonctionnel dans les chambres, conçues à l'identique et distribuées sur trois étages.
◆ Dit hotel dicht bij het station en het centrum heeft kamers met functioneel comfort die allemaal identiek zijn ingericht en verspreid liggen over drie verdiepingen.

X **Floyds,** Groenendaal 28, ✉ 3441 BD, ☎ (0 348) 41 53 00, *info@floyds.nl, Fax (0 348) 43 45 73,* ⛱ – ▤. MC VISA
fermé fin juil.-début août, fin déc.-début janv., dim. et jours fériés – **Repas** (dîner seult) 35/70 bc, ♀.
◆ Avec ses produits soigneusement choisis et ses jolis accords mets-vins, cette petite affaire familiale un peu "trendy" rencontre toutes les faveurs des gastronomes du coin.
◆ Met zijn zorgvuldig gekozen producten en mooie spijs-wijncombinaties heeft dit familierestaurantje de smulpapen uit de omgeving voor zich gewonnen. Vrij trendy interieur.

X **De Dukdalf,** Westdam 2, ✉ 3441 GA, ☎ (0 348) 43 07 85, *dedukdalf@zonnet.nl, Fax (0 348) 46 02 54,* ≤, ⛱, ⚓ – AE ⊕ MC VISA
fermé 24 déc.-3 janv., sam. midi et dim. – **Repas** Lunch 24 – carte 33 à 49.
◆ Kiosque sur pilotis émergeant du port de plaisance. Ambiance de bistrot décontracté, terrasse aquatique et choix de préparations actuelles recomposé toutes les six semaines.
◆ Een paviljoen op palen, aan de jachthaven. Ongedwongen bistrosfeer, terras aan het water en een menukaart met eigentijdse gerechten die elke zes weken wisselt.

X **bistro 't Pakhuis,** Havenstraat 15, ✉ 3441 BH, ☎ (0 348) 43 03 40, *pakhuis@zonnet.nl, Fax (0 348) 48 13 25* – ▤. AE MC VISA.
fermé du 6 au 17 mars, du 2 au 8 août et mardi – **Repas** (dîner seult) carte 33 à 43.
◆ Une façade mignonne signale cet ancien entrepôt à fromage situé dans une rue étroite du centre. Décor intérieur un peu chargé mais carte classico-traditionnelle bien conçue.
◆ Dit voormalige kaaspakhuis in een smalle straat is te herkennen aan de pittoreske voorgevel. Ietwat overdadig interieur, maar een evenwichtige klassiek-traditionele menukaart.

WOLDENDORP *Groningen* 531 AB 3 *et* 715 M 2 *– voir à Delfzijl.*

WOLFHEZE *Gelderland* C *Renkum 32 250 h.* 532 T 10 *et* 715 I 5.
Amsterdam 93 – Arnhem 10 – Amersfoort 41 – Utrecht 57.

De Buunderkamp , Buunderkamp 8, ✉ 6874 NC, ✆ (0 26) 482 11 66, *buunderkamp@bilderberg.nl, Fax (0 26) 482 18 98,* , , , , – , rest, – 25 à 150. AE VISA. rest
Repas Lunch 25 – 35/40 – 18 – **96 ch** 147/205, – 5 suites – ½ P 103.
• Hôtel très confortable retiré dans des bois. Toutes les chambres et parties communes ont retrouvé l'éclat du neuf et présentent une décoration uniformément moderne. Salle à manger pourvue de sièges en cuir et de tables bien espacées. Menu-carte classique.
• Zeer comfortabel hotel in de bossen. Alle kamers en gemeenschappelijke ruimten zijn gerenoveerd en hebben een moderne uitstraling gekregen. Eetzaal met leren stoelen en veel ruimte tusen de tafels. Klassieke menukaart.

Wolfheze , Wolfhezerweg 17, ✉ 6874 AA, ✆ (0 26) 333 78 52, *wolfheze@bilderberg.nl, Fax (0 26) 333 62 11,* , , , , , – , rest, – 25 à 85. AE VISA JCB.
Repas ***Brasserie de Paris*** (déjeuner sur réservation) 40 bc, ♀ – 19 – **69 ch** 115/165, – 1 suite – ½ P 85/107.
• Dans un environnement boisé, construction basse des années 1970 adoptant un plan en forme de U. Plusieurs catégories de chambres. Terrains de golf et de pétanque. Brasserie à l'accent très "parigot" : décoration intérieure, ambiance et recettes assorties.
• Een laag U-vormig gebouw uit de jaren zeventig herbergt dit hotel in een bosrijke omgeving. Diverse categorieën kamers. Golfterrein en jeu-de-boulesbaan. Brasserie met een echt Parijs accent, waar interieur, ambiance en gerechten uitstekend bij elkaar passen.

WOLPHAARTSDIJK *Zeeland* C *Goes 36 047 h.* 532 H 13 *et* 715 C 7.
Amsterdam 186 – Middelburg 26 – Goes 6.

XXX **'t Veerhuis,** Wolphaartsdijkseveer 1 (Nord : 2 km, au bord du Veerse Meer), ✉ 4471 ND, ✆ (0 113) 58 13 26, *veerhuiswolphaartsdijk@hetnet.nl, Fax (0 113) 58 10 92,* <, – , . AE VISA
fermé 20 déc.-23 janv., mardi sauf en juil.-août, merc. et sam. midi – **Repas** Lunch 32 – 55.
• À l'extrémité de la jetée, ancien logis de passeur d'eau surveillant le port des yachts. Salle de restaurant moderne décorée sur le thème nautique. Cuisine de notre temps.
• Dit restaurant in het veerhuis aan het einde van de pier kijkt uit over de jachthaven. Moderne restaurantzaal met nautisch decor. Eigentijdse keuken.

WORKUM (WARKUM) *Fryslân* C *Nijefurd 10 924 h.* 531 R 5 *et* 715 H 3.
Env. au Sud-Ouest : 6 km à Hindeloopen : Musée★ (Hidde Nijland Stichting).
Amsterdam 128 – Leeuwarden 40 – Zwolle 86.

X **Séburch,** Séburch 9, ✉ 8711 EE, ✆ (0 515) 54 13 74, *Fax (0 515) 54 17 53,* <, – AE VISA JCB
fermé fév., merc. d'oct. à avril et mardi – **Repas** (dîner seult) carte 28 à 36, ♀.
• À proximité d'un petit port, cuisine classique très féminine, et sagement actualisée, servie dans une ancienne auberge de pêcheurs datant du 19e s.
• In deze voormalige, 19e-eeuwse zeemansherberg vlak bij een haventje wordt met "vrouwelijke flair" een klassieke keuken met een eigentijds accent bereid.

WORMERVEER *Noord-Holland* 531 N 8 *et* 715 F 4 *– voir à Zaandam.*

WOUDRICHEM *Noord-Brabant* 532 P 12 *et* 715 G 6 *– 14 386 h.*
Amsterdam 79 – Utrecht 40 – 's-Hertogenbosch 32 – Breda 40 – Rotterdam 48.

XX **De Gevangenpoort,** Kerkstraat 3, ✉ 4285 BA, ✆ (0 183) 30 20 34 – . AE VISA JCB
fermé sam. midi, dim. midi et lundi – **Repas** Lunch 29 – 35/38.
• Cette table rustique occupe une imposante "porte-prison" (gevangenpoort) montant la garde depuis le 16e s. dans une ruelle proche du port et de l'ancien hôtel de ville.
• Dit rustieke restaurant heeft zich gevestigd in de imposante Gevangenpoort, die al sinds de 16e eeuw de wacht houdt in een straatje nabij de haven en het oude stadhuis.

Si le coût de la vie subit des variations importantes,
les prix que nous indiquons peuvent être majorés.
Lors de votre réservation à l'hôtel, faites-vous préciser le prix définitif.

YERSEKE *Zeeland* [C] *Reimerswaal 20 831 h.* 532 J 14 *et* 715 D 7.

Kerkplein 1, ✉ 4401 ED, ☎ 0 900-400 40 40, vvvyerseke@planet.nl, Fax (0 113) 57 43 74.

Amsterdam 173 – Middelburg 35 – Bergen op Zoom 35 – Goes 14.

XXX ✿ **Nolet-Het Reymerswale** 1er étage, Burg. Sinkelaan 5, ✉ 4401 AL, ☎ (0 113) 57 16 42, *nolet@alliance.nl, Fax (0 113) 57 25 05,* Produits de la mer et huîtres – P. AE ① MC VISA
fermé du 8 au 25 juin, 31 janv.-25 fév., mardi et merc. sauf jours fériés belges – **Repas** Lunch 45 – 63/73, carte 55 à 80.
◆ Belle cuisine de la mer servie au 1er étage d'une jolie maison bourgeoise avoisinant le port. Salle à manger classiquement aménagée. Vivier à homards et terrasse estivale.
◆ In dit restaurant op de eerste verdieping van een fraai herenhuis bij de haven worden heerlijke visgerechten geserveerd. Klassiek ingerichte eetzaal. Homarium en zomerterras.
Spéc. Homard de l'Oosterschelde (avril-juil.). Huîtres au Champagne (oct.-avril). Anguille fumée maison

X **Oesterbeurs,** Wijngaardstraat 2, ✉ 4401 CS, ☎ (0 113) 57 22 11, *Fax (0 113) 57 16 15,* Produits de la mer – MC VISA.
fermé 29 déc.-15 janv., lundi sauf en juil.-août et vend. midi – **Repas** carte 37 à 55.
◆ Au cœur de Yerseke, dans l'ancienne bourse où se déroulaient aussi les mariages, adresse assez plaisante, bien connue dans le secteur pour ses assiettes gorgées d'iode.
◆ Een vrij plezierig adres in hartje Yerseke, in de voormalige beurs waar ook trouwerijen plaatsvonden. Het restaurant staat lokaal goed bekend om de visgerechten.

X **Nolet,** Lepelstraat 7, ✉ 4401 EB, ☎ (0 113) 57 13 09, *Fax (0 113) 57 43 48,* Produits de la mer et huîtres – AE MC VISA JCB
fermé 2 dern. sem. juin-prem. sem. juil. et lundis non fériés – **Repas** carte 31 à 67.
◆ Avec le temps, ce café promu restaurant est devenu une sorte d'institution locale. Plats "neptuniens" et spécialité d'huîtres en saison. Ouvert en continu de 12 h à 21 h.
◆ Met de tijd is dit café gepromoveerd tot restaurant en een lokaal begrip geworden. Keuken in het teken van Neptunus, oesters in het seizoen. Doorlopend geopend 12-21 u.

X **Nolet's Vistro,** Burg. Sinkelaan 6, ✉ 4401 AL, ☎ (0 113) 57 21 01, *Fax (0 113) 57 25 05,* , Produits de la mer –
fermé 2 sem. en mai, janv. et lundi sauf en juil.-août – **Repas** Lunch 28 – 33/38.
◆ Près du port, maisonnette sympathique attenante à sa grande sœur, dont l'enseigne ne cache effectivement pas son petit air de famille. Menu de la mer bien balancé.
◆ Dit sympathieke eethuis bij de haven staat naast zijn grotere broer, wat ook aan de naam is af te lezen. Goed uitgebalanceerd zeemenu.

ZAANDAM *Noord-Holland* [C] *Zaanstad 137 669 h.* 531 N 8 *et* 715 F 4.

Voir *La région du Zaan★ (Zaanstreek) – La redoute Zanoise★ (De Zaanse Schans).*

au Nord : 5 km à Wijdewormer (Wormerland), Zuiderweg 68, ✉ 1456 NH, ☎ (0 299) 47 91 23, Fax (0 299) 43 81 99.

Gedempte Gracht 76, ✉ 1506 CJ, ☎ 0 900-400 40 40, info@amsterdamtoursit.nl, Fax (0 20) 625 28 69.

Amsterdam 9 – Haarlem 27 – Alkmaar 28.

Inntel, Provincialeweg 15, ✉ 1506 MA, ☎ (0 75) 631 17 11, *infozaandam@hotelinntel.com, Fax (0 75) 670 13 79,* – TV P. – 25 à 120. AE ① MC VISA. rest
Repas (dîner seult jusqu'à 23 h) carte 27 à 39 – 14 – **66 ch** 165/175 – ½ P 79/150.
◆ Hôtel de chaîne élevé dans les années 1980 en bordure du centre de Zaandam, à proximité de la gare. Chambres fonctionnelles insonorisées, réparties sur quatre étages.
◆ Ketenhotel uit de jaren tachtig van de vorige eeuw, aan de rand van het centrum van Zaandam en nabij het station. Functionele kamers met geluidsisolatie, op vier verdiepingen.

Bastion, Wibautstraat 278 (par A 8, sortie ①), ✉ 1505 HR, ☎ (0 75) 670 63 31, *bastion@bastionhotel.nl, Fax (0 75) 670 12 81* – TV P. AE ① MC VISA.
Repas (grillades, ouvert jusqu'à 23 h) carte env. 30 – 10 – **80 ch** 76/86.
◆ Cet hotel posté au bord d'un carrefour assez proche du ring d'Amsterdam fait partie des unités "haut de gamme" de la chaîne hollandaise Bastion.
◆ Dit hotel aan een kruispunt dicht bij de ringweg van Amsterdam behoort tot de betere etablissementen van de Nederlandse Bastion-keten.

XXXX **De Hoop Op d'Swarte Walvis,** Kalverringdijk 15 (Zaanse Schans), ✉ 1509 BT, ☎ (0 75) 616 56 29, *de.walvis@alliance.nl, Fax (0 75) 616 24 76,* ≤, , – P. AE ① MC VISA JCB
fermé 26 juil.-15 août, 26 déc.-2 janv., sam. midi et dim. – **Repas** Lunch 45 – 64, ♀.
◆ Dans un joli village-musée, ancien orphelinat du 18e s. transformé en bonne maison de bouche flirtant avec les saveurs d'aujourd'hui. Pergolas au bord de la digue.
◆ Dit 18e-eeuwse weeshuis in het museumdorp de Zaanse Schans is verbouwd tot een goed eethuis dat flirt met de eigentijdse keuken. Terras met pergola aan de dijk.

à Wijdewormer *Nord : 5 km* Ⓒ *Wormerland 15 467 h :*

X **'t Heerenhuis,** Zuiderweg 74b, ✉ 1456 NH, ☎ (0 75) 616 21 02, *Fax (0 75) 614 35 44,* – P. MC VISA
fermé 24 et 31 déc., 1er janv., sam. midi et dim. midi – **Repas** Lunch 26 – carte env. 40, ♀.
◆ Ambiance auberge de campagne dans ce petit restaurant sur digue avoisinant la très pittoresque redoute zanoise. Terrasse d'été garnie de meubles en teck.
◆ Dit restaurantje op de dijk vlak bij de pittoreske Zaanse Schans heeft de ambiance van een plattelandsherberg. Zomerterras met teakmeubilair.

à Wormerveer *Nord : 6 km* Ⓒ *Zaanstad :*

Huis te Zaanen, Zaanweg 93, ✉ 1521 DN, ☎ (0 75) 628 17 40, *info@huistezaanen.nl, Fax (0 75) 640 34 96,* – TV – 25 à 60. AE D MC VISA JCB
fermé 29 déc.-5 janv. – **Repas** *(fermé sam. midi et dim. midi)* Lunch 25 – 30/56 bc – ☕ 8 – **8 ch** 62.
◆ En face de la Zaan, ancienne hostellerie se signalant par une façade au charme suranné. Les chambres, récemment refaites de neuf, sont d'ampleur variable. Accueil avenant. Salle de restaurant typiquement hollandaise.
◆ De voorgevel van deze voormalige hostellerie straalt een ouderwetse charme uit, waardoor het hotel gemakkelijk te herkennen is. De onlangs gerenoveerde kamers variëren in grootte. Vriendelijke ontvangst. Typisch Hollandse restaurantzaal.

XX **De Rijcke Jonker,** Zaanweg 10, ✉ 1521 DH, ☎ (0 75) 628 55 88, *info@de-rijcke-jonker.nl, Fax (0 75) 621 19 78,* – AE MC VISA.
fermé 30 avril, 30 déc.-1er janv., sam. midi, dim. midi et lundi – **Repas** (déjeuner sur réservation) carte env. 42, ♀.
◆ Cette affaire familiale du centre de Wormerveer surveille le port et la Zaan. Longue salle à manger ornée de toiles et photos. Spécialités de poisson fumé et d'agneau de lait.
◆ Restaurant in het centrum van Wormerveer, met zicht op de haven en de Zaan. Schilderijen en foto's sieren de lange eetzaal. Specialiteiten van gerookte vis en zuiglam.

à Zaandijk *Nord-Ouest : 5 km* Ⓒ *Zaanstad :*

Sans Pareil, Lagedijk 32, ✉ 1544 BG, ☎ (0 75) 621 19 11, *info@sanspareil.nl, Fax (0 75) 621 85 61,* ←, – TV – 30. AE MC VISA
fermé 31 déc.-1er janv. – **Repas** *(fermé sam. midi et dim.)* Lunch 28 – carte 35 à 44 – ☕ 11 – **15 ch** 107/139.
◆ Agréable hôtel posté au bord de la Zaan, près du pont menant à la fameuse redoute. Bon confort dans les chambres. Terrasse à fleur d'eau. Salle de restaurant procurant une belle vue aquatique, avec de fiers moulins à l'arrière-plan.
◆ Aangenaam hotel aan de oever van de Zaan, vlak bij de brug naar de beroemde Zaanse Schans. Comfortabele kamers. Terras aan het water. De restaurantzaal biedt een mooi uitzicht over het water, waar op de achtergrond fier de molens draaien.

ZAANDIJK *Noord-Holland* 531 N 8 *et* 715 F 4 – *voir à Zaandam.*

ZALTBOMMEL *Gelderland* 532 Q 12 *et* 715 G 6 – *25 759 h.*

Amsterdam 73 – Utrecht 44 – Arnhem 64 – 's-Hertogenbosch 15.

XX **La Provence,** Gamersestraat 81, ✉ 5301 AR, ☎ (0 418) 51 40 70, *Fax (0 418) 54 10 77,* – P. AE D MC VISA JCB
fermé vacances bâtiment, fin déc., sam. midi, dim. et lundi – **Repas** Lunch 30 – 35/50.
◆ Ancienne maison de notable où l'on prend place en toute confiance sous un superbe lustre Belle Époque. Mets classiques et grands millésimes bordelais des années 1990.
◆ Zeer betrouwbaar restaurant in een herenhuis, waar een schitterende belle-époqueluchter de eetzaal siert. Klassieke gerechten en prachtige bordeaux uit topjaren.

X **De Eetgelegenheid,** Waterstraat 31, ✉ 5301 AH, ☎ (0 418) 51 50 18, *info@deeetgelegenheid.nl, Fax (0 418) 51 05 94,* – AE MC VISA
fermé 2 sem. carnaval, 3 sem. en sept., 24 déc. soir, 31 déc.-1er janv. et mardi – **Repas** Lunch 24 – 30.
◆ Au cœur de la ville fortifiée, maisonnette engageante renfermant trois petites salles de restaurant actuelles, disposées en enfilade. Préparations sages. Accueil familial.
◆ In het centrum van het versterkte plaatsje herbergt dit charmante huis drie kleine, eigentijdse restaurantzalen en suite. Degelijke keuken. Gastvrij onthaal.

Ecrivez-nous...
Vos louanges comme vos critiques seront examinées avec le plus grand soin.
Nous reverrons sur place les informations que vous nous signalez.
Par avance merci !

ZANDVOORT *Noord-Holland* 531 *M 8,* 532 *M 8 et* 715 *E 4 – 16 809 h – Station balnéaire★ –*
Casino AX*, Badhuisplein 7,* ✉ *2040 JB,* ✆ *(0 23) 574 05 74, Fax (0 23) 574 05 77.*
ℹ *Schoolplein 1,* ✉ *2042 VD,* ✆ *(0 23) 571 79 47, zvt@vvvzk.nl, Fax (0 23) 571 70 03.*
Amsterdam 29 ① – Haarlem 11 ① – Den Haag 49 ②

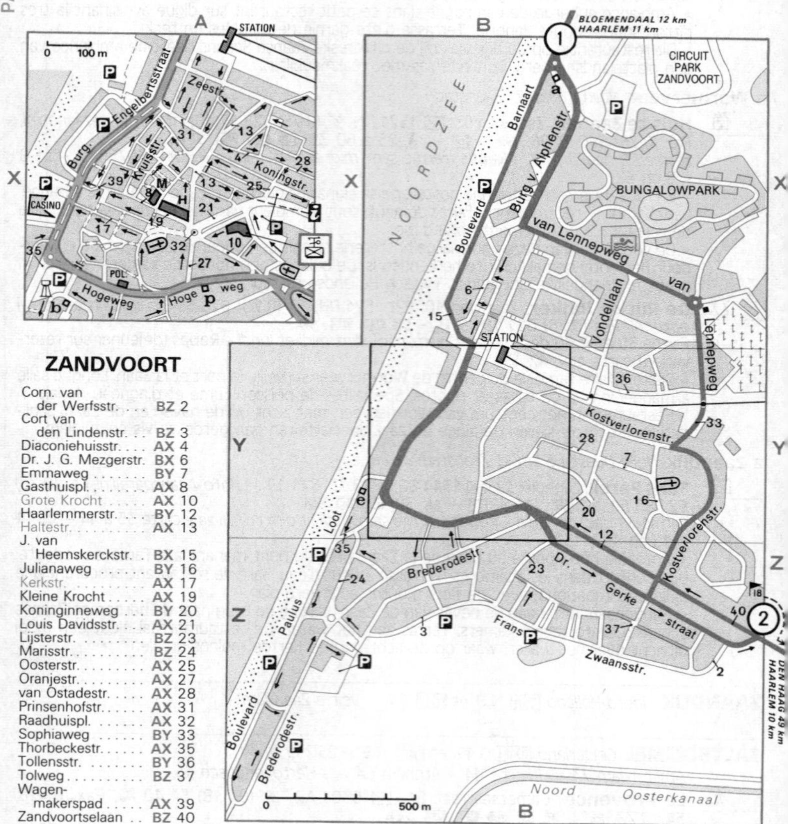

NH Zandvoort, Burg. van Alphenstraat 63, ✉ 2041 KG, ✆ (0 23) 576 07 60, *nhzandvoort@nh-hotels.nl, Fax (0 23) 571 90 94,* ←, ⛱, 🚲 – |‡| TV P – 🏠 25 à 180. AE ⓓ ⓜ VISA JCB. ⛌ rest BX a
Repas *Lunch 17* – carte 27 à 41 – ☕ 15 – **195 ch** 120/210, – 14 suites.
◆ Cet ensemble hôtelier contemporain dispose de chambres très fonctionnelles mais fort bien calibrées, d'où l'on ne perdra pas une miette du spectacle des bains de mer.
◆ Dit moderne hotelcomplex beschikt over zeer functionele maar bijzonder ruime kamers, die uitkijken op de zee en de gezellige drukte aan het strand.

Hoogland sans rest, Westerparkstraat 5, ✉ 2042 AV, ✆ (0 23) 571 55 41, *info@hotelhoogland.nl, Fax (0 23) 571 42 00* – TV. AE ⓓ ⓜ VISA AX b
30 ch ☕ 65/110.
◆ Petit hôtel familial posté à l'ombre de l'ancien château d'eau de Zandvoort, l'une des stations balnéaires les plus courues des Pays-Bas. Équipement hi-fi et vidéo en chambre.
◆ Klein familiehotel in de schaduw van de oude watertoren van een van de drukste badplaatsen van Nederland. Geluidsinstallatie en video op de kamers.

Zuiderbad, bd Paulus Loot 5, ✉ 2042 AD, ☎ (0 23) 571 26 13, *info@hotelzuiderbad.nl, Fax (0 23) 571 31 90,* ≤, – TV P. MC VISA BY e
fermé du 1er au 12 fév. et 22 nov.-27 déc. – **Repas** (dîner pour résidents seult) – **26 ch** 58/105 – ½ P 50/68.
◆ Affaire tenue en famille, située à un saut de la plage. Trois formats de chambres sobrement équipées, avec balcon panoramique au deuxième étage, côté front de mer.
◆ Familiebedrijf op een steenworp afstand van het strand. Drie formaten eenvoudig ingerichte kamers, op de tweede verdieping met panoramisch balkon aan de zeezijde.

Amare sans rest, Hogeweg 70, ✉ 2042 GJ, ☎ (0 23) 571 22 02, *hotel.amare@planet.nl, Fax (0 23) 571 43 74* – TV. AE MC VISA. AX p
15 ch 45/75.
◆ Un point de chute utile pour quelques jours de villégiature. Chambres de mise simple, toutefois convenables, offrant assez d'espace et donnant parfois sur un balconnet.
◆ Een handig adres voor een paar daagjes strand. Eenvoudige maar vrij aangename kamers die voldoende ruimte bieden. Sommige hebben een balkonnetje.

à Bentveld *par ② : 3 km* C *Zandvoort :*

Beaulieu, Zandvoortselaan 363, ✉ 2116 EN, ☎ (0 23) 524 00 29, *beaulieu@zonnet.nl, Fax (0 23) 524 74 01,* , Ouvert jusqu'à 23 h – P. AE DC MC VISA.
fermé lundi d'oct. à avril – **Repas** (déjeuner sur réservation) carte 43 à 59.
◆ Nouvelle enseigne pour cette auberge connue de longue date dans la région. Confortable salle à manger classiquement aménagée. Repas servi au jardin à la belle saison.
◆ Een nieuwe naam voor een zaak die in de regio al lang bekend is. Comfortabele, klassiek ingerichte eetzaal. In de zomer wordt buiten geserveerd.

ZEDDAM *Gelderland* C *Bergh 18 373 h.* 532 *W 11 et* 715 *J 6.*

Kilderseweg 1, ✉ 7038 BW, ☎ 0 900 666 31 31, vvvmontferland@hetnet.nl, Fax (0 314) 68 35 12.
Amsterdam 129 – Arnhem 29 – Doetinchem 8 – Emmerich 8.

Landgoed Montferland , Montferland 1, ✉ 7038 EB, ☎ (0 314) 65 14 44, *hzinger@hetnet.nl, Fax (0 314) 65 26 75,* , , – TV P – 25 à 75. AE MC VISA.
fermé 27 déc.-24 janv. – **Repas** *(fermé sam. midi et dim. midi)* carte 37 à 58, ♀ – **8 ch** 70/100 – ½ P 84/99.
◆ Cette grosse villa montant la garde sur les hauteurs d'une butte défensive boisée met quelques grandes chambres à votre disposition, ainsi qu'un jardin reposant. Terrasse où l'on dresse le couvert en été. Adorable "chambre de chasse" pour petits banquets.
◆ Deze grote villa heeft de wacht betrokken op een beboste verdedigingsheuvel en beschikt over enkele grote kamers. Rustgevende tuin en terras waar 's zomers wordt geserveerd. Charmante jachtkamer voor kleine banketten.

à Beek *Ouest : 5 km* C *Bergh :*

Mezzo, Arnhemseweg 11, ✉ 7037 CX, ☎ (0 316) 53 12 50, *info@mezzoweb.nl, Fax (0 316) 53 21 82,* , Cuisine italienne – P. MC VISA JCB
fermé 28 déc.-15 janv., lundi et mardi – **Repas** (dîner seult) 25/55 bc, ♀.
◆ Au centre de Beek, bungalow devancé d'un jardin et complété d'une terrasse à l'arrière. Salle contemporaine, carte italienne bien balancée et vins de là-bas à prix plancher.
◆ Bungalow in het centrum, met een tuin aan de voorkant en terras achter. Eigentijdse eetzaal, uitgebalanceerde Italiaanse kaart en wijnen van daarginder voor een zacht prijsje.

à Braamt *Nord : 3 km* C *Bergh :*

Host. Hettenheuvel, Hooglandseweg 6, ✉ 7047 CN, ☎ (0 314) 65 14 52, *hettenheuvel-hostellerie@planet.nl, Fax (0 314) 65 12 65,* , , – TV P. AE DC MC VISA JCB
fermé dern. sem. fév. – **Repas** (dîner pour résidents seult) – **8 ch** 85 – ½ P 58/68.
◆ Accueil et service personnalisés à cette sympathique petite adresse de campagne où règne une ambiance familiale. Douillettes chambres de style "cottage". Jardin croquignolet.
◆ Persoonlijke ontvangst en service in de gemoedelijke ambiance van dit sympathieke, landelijk gelegen hotelletje. Behaaglijke kamers in cottagestijl en een bekoorlijke tuin.

à Lengel *Sud : 2 km* C *Bergh :*

De Korenmolen, Drieheuvelenweg 1, ✉ 7044 AA, ☎ (0 314) 66 12 14, *alby.nawroth@compaqnet.nl, Fax (0 314) 66 60 28,* – P. AE DC MC VISA JCB
Repas Lunch 24 – 33/40, ♀.
◆ Cuisine traditionnelle mise à la page, avec quelques notes évoquant le Sud, à l'image des tons dont s'habille la salle de restaurant. Rotonde panoramique à l'arrière.
◆ Traditionele keuken in een modern jasje en, net als de kleuren van de eetzaal, met zuidelijke accenten. Panoramische rotonde aan de achterkant.

ZEEGSE *Drenthe* Ⓒ *Tynaarlo 31 865 h.* 531 Y 4 *et* 715 K 2.
Amsterdam 203 – Groningen 21 – Assen 16.

Golden Tulip, Schipborgerweg 8, ✉ 9483 TL, ☎ (0 592) 53 00 99, *info@goldentulipdrenthe.com, Fax (0 592) 53 00 88*, – 25 à 500. AE VISA
Repas ***La Lisière*** *Lunch 31* – carte 35 à 47 – 12 – **78 ch** 96/112, – 2 suites – ½ P 130.
◆ Construction basse située en lisière d'un parc parsemé de bois et bruyères. Chambres de bon confort, munies d'une terrasse ou d'un balcon. Nombreuses salles de séminaires. Le restaurant s'agrémente d'une terrasse estivale. Mets au goût du jour.
◆ Dit hotel is gehuisvest in een laag pand aan de rand van een natuurgebied met bossen en heidevelden. De comfortabele kamers hebben een terras of balkon. Groot aantal zalen voor bijeenkomsten en seminars. Restaurant met zomerterras. Eigentijdse gerechten.

ZEIST *Utrecht* 532 Q 10 *et* 715 G 5 – *59 682 h.*
18 *au Nord : 2 km à Bosch en Duin, Amersfoortseweg 1, ✉ 3735 LJ, ☎ (0 30) 695 52 23, Fax (0 30) 696 37 69.*
Slotlaan 24, ✉ 3701 GL, ☎ 0 900-109 10 13, vvvzeist@hetnet.nl, Fax (0 30) 692 00 17.
Amsterdam 55 – Utrecht 10 – Amersfoort 17 – Apeldoorn 66 – Arnhem 50.

Figi, Het Rond 2, ✉ 3701 HS, ☎ (0 30) 692 74 00, *info@figi.nl, Fax (0 30) 692 74 68*, – 25 à 500. AE VISA.
Repas ***Walkart Park*** *(fermé 31 déc. soir) Lunch 29* – carte env. 46, ♀ – 15 – **94 ch** 179/230, – 3 suites.
◆ Au centre de Zeist, hôtel contemporain complété d'un grand centre de congrès. Plusieurs catégories de chambres où l'on a ses aises. Jolie collection de vitraux Art déco. Ordonnée à la façon d'une brasserie, la salle à manger offre la vue sur l'hôtel de ville.
◆ Eigentijds hotel met een groot congrescentrum in het centrum van Zeist. Diverse categorieën kamers met veel comfort. Prachtige art-decoramen. De eetzaal heeft de ambiance van een brasserie en kijkt uit op het stadhuis.

Oud London, Woudenbergseweg 52 (Est : 3 km sur N 224), ✉ 3707 HX, ☎ (0 343) 49 12 45, *info@oudlondon.nl, Fax (0 343) 49 12 44*, – 25 à 350. AE VISA JCB.
Repas ***La Fine Bouche*** 39, ♀ – ***'t Voorhuys*** 28, ♀ – 15 – **88 ch** 125/173, – 1 suite.
◆ Un soldat de Napoléon est à l'origine de cette auberge dont l'enseigne "british" aurait probablement contrarié l'empereur. Chambres et communs de bonne ampleur. Restaurant avec cuisine actuelle goûtée des "fines bouches". Ambiance brasserie au 't Voorhuys.
◆ Een soldaat van Napoleon stichtte hier een herberg, die is uitgegroeid tot het huidige hotel-restaurant. Ruime kamers en gemeenschappelijke ruimten. Restaurant met een eigentijdse keuken die bij fijnproevers goed in de smaak valt. Brasserie in 't Voorhuys.

Kasteel 't Kerckebosch, Arnhemse Bovenweg 31 (Sud-Est : 1,5 km), ✉ 3708 AA, ☎ (0 30) 692 66 66, *kerckebosch@bilderberg.nl, Fax (0 30) 692 66 00*, – 25 à 135. AE VISA JCB. rest
fermé 27 déc.-3 janv. – **Repas** ***De kamer van Lintelo*** *(fermé sam. midi et dim.) Lunch 33* – carte 45 à 64, ♀ – 17 – **30 ch** 158/175 – ½ P 90/165.
◆ Élevée en 1904, cette opulente demeure de caractère s'entoure d'un parc reposant. Aménagement intérieur cossu, parsemé d'éléments décoratifs anciens. Chambres de bon séjour. Meubles de style, boiseries et cheminée donnent un certain cachet au restaurant.
◆ Dit weelderige, karaktervolle landhuis uit 1904 ligt in een rustig park. Luxueuze inrichting met ornamenten uit vroegere tijden. Zeer comfortabele kamers. Het stijlmeubilair, de lambrisering en de schouw geven het restaurant een zeker cachet.

Beyerick, Jagerlaan 1, ✉ 3701 XG, ☎ (0 30) 692 34 05, *beyerick@wanadoo.nl* – . AE VISA
fermé dern. sem. fév., 3 sem. en août, lundi et mardi – **Repas** (dîner seult) carte env. 49, ♀.
◆ Cette affaire familiale du centre de Zeist poursuit gentiment son petit bonhomme de chemin depuis plus de dix ans. Préparations bien balancées, dans le tempo actuel.
◆ Al ruim tien jaar gaat dit familierestaurant in het centrum rustig zijn gangetje. De goed uitgebalanceerde gerechten sluiten aan bij de huidige trend.

à Bosch en Duin *Nord : 2 km* Ⓒ *Zeist :*

de Hoefslag, Vossenlaan 28, ✉ 3735 KN, ☎ (0 30) 225 10 51, *info@hoefslag.nl, Fax (0 30) 228 58 21*, ch, – 25. AE VISA
Repas voir rest ***de Hoefslag*** ci-après – **Repas** ***Bistro de Ruif*** *(fermé 31 déc.-1er janv.)* (dîner seult jusqu'à 23 h) 28/38, ♀ – 20 – **26 ch** 190, – 4 suites.
◆ Agréable établissement environné de verdure, dans un quartier résidentiel assez chic. Accueil et service prévenants. Chambres douillettes au décor d'esprit "country club". Le Bistro de Ruif fournit une alternative à la formule gastronomique de la maison.
◆ Aangenaam etablissement in een boomrijke en vrij chique woonwijk. Vriendelijke ontvangst en attente service. De behaaglijke kamers ademen de sfeer van de Engelse countryside. Bistro De Ruif is een alternatief voor het gastronomische hotelrestaurant.

XXXX ✿ **de Hoefslag,** Vossenlaan 28, ✉ 3735 KN, ☎ (0 30) 225 10 51, *info@hoefslag.nl, Fax (0 30) 228 58 21,* ☂ - P. AE ◐ ◎ VISA
fermé 31 déc.-1er janv., sam. midi et dim. – **Repas** *Lunch 36* – 53/108 bc, carte 57 à 82, ♀.
◆ Belle cuisine classique actualisée, en parfaite osmose avec le style de la salle à manger. L'été venu, réservez votre table sur la délicieuse terrasse dressée "au vert".
◆ Uitstekende klassieke keuken in een eigentijds jasje, die perfect harmonieert met de inrichting van de eetzaal. 's Zomers wordt geserveerd op het terras in het groen.
Spéc. Queues de langoustines sautées aux witlof, marmelade d'oignons rouges et de pommes. Marbré de viande salée au confit de foie gras de canard (mai-sept.). Suprême de canard sauvage, foie gras d'oie sauté et pêche marinée au romarin (1 sept.-30 déc.)

à Den Dolder *Nord : 7 km* C *Zeist :*

XX **Anak Dèpok,** Dolderseweg 85, ✉ 3734 BD, ☎ (0 30) 229 29 15, *rimateillers@planet.nl, Fax (0 30) 228 11 26,* Cuisine indonésienne – ▤. AE ◐ ◎ VISA. ✂
fermé lundi et mardi – **Repas** (dîner seult) 24/36.
◆ Restaurant cent pour cent indonésien installé de longue date au milieu du patelin et auréolé d'une certaine reconnaissance locale. Formule "table de riz" intéressante.
◆ Een Indonesisch restaurant pur sang, dat al sinds lang een vertrouwd beeld is in het centrum van het stadje en lokaal een zeker aanzien geniet. Interessante rijsttafelformule.

XX **Sensa,** Dolderseweg 77, ✉ 3734 BD, ☎ (0 30) 225 20 00, *info@sensa.nl, Fax (0 30) 225 15 12,* ☂ – AE ◐ ◎ VISA
fermé 30 avril, sam. midi et dim. midi – **Repas** *Lunch 25* – carte 38 à 53.
◆ Établi au rez-de-chaussée d'un immeuble, ce beau restaurant décoré dans un style résolument design offre l'agrément d'une grande terrasse estivale dotée de meubles en teck.
◆ Op de benedenverdieping van een groot gebouw bevindt zich dit mooie restaurant, waarin design de boventoon voert. Groot zomerterras met teakhouten meubilair.

ZELHEM *Gelderland* 532 X 10 *et* 715 K 5 – *11 169 h.*
Amsterdam 139 – Arnhem 39 – Enschede 52.

XX **'t Wolfersveen,** Ruurloseweg 38 (Nord-Est : 4,5 km), ✉ 7021 HC, ☎ (0 314) 62 13 75, ☂ – P. AE ◐ ◎ VISA
fermé 2 prem. sem. janv. et lundi – **Repas** (dîner seult sauf dim.) 30/42.
◆ Connue comme le loup blanc dans ce petit coin du Gelderland, cette auberge familiale classiquement aménagée profite, côté jardin, d'une ample terrasse estivale ombragée.
◆ Dit klassiek ingerichte familierestaurant staat lokaal wel bekend en heeft aan de tuinkant een groot, lommerrijk zomerterras.

ZEVENAAR *Gelderland* 532 V 11 *et* 715 J 6 – *26 155 h.*
Amsterdam 114 – Arnhem 15 – Emmerich 21.

🏠 **Campanile,** Hunneveldweg 2a (près A 12 - E 35), ✉ 6903 ZM, ☎ (0 316) 52 81 11, *zevenaar@campanile.nl, Fax (0 316) 33 12 32,* ☂ – ⇔ TV P. AE ◐ ◎ VISA JCB
Repas (avec buffets) carte env. 33, ♀ – ☕ 10 – **52 ch** 72 – ½ P 38/50.
◆ Motel de chaîne situé à 15 mn de la ville d'Arnhem, que vous rejoindrez directement par l'autoroute A 12. Chambres fonctionnelles pourvues d'un double vitrage efficace.
◆ Dit ketenmotel ligt op 15 min. van Arnhem en is rechtstreeks via de A12 te bereiken. Functionele kamers met goede, dubbele beglazing.

ZEVENBERGEN *Noord-Brabant* C *Moerdijk 36 433 h.* 532 M 13 *et* 715 E 7.
Amsterdam 111 – Bergen op Zoom 30 – Breda 17 – Rotterdam 43.

XX **De 7 Bergsche Hoeve,** Schansdijk 3, ✉ 4761 RH, ☎ (0 168) 32 41 66, *zbhoeve@tip.nl, Fax (0 168) 32 38 72,* ☂ – P. AE ◐ ◎ VISA JCB
fermé sam. midi et dim. – **Repas** 35.
◆ Cuisine insensible aux modes servie dans une ancienne ferme reconstruite voici près de cinquante ans mais préservant son esprit rustique. Carte avec lunch et menus.
◆ Restaurant in een oude boerderij die zo'n vijftig jaar geleden met behoud van het rustieke karakter is herbouwd. De keuken is niet trendgevoelig. Kaart met lunch en menu's.

ZIERIKZEE *Zeeland* C *Schouwen-Duiveland 34 503 h.* 532 I 13 *et* 715 C 7.
Voir *Noordhavenpoort*★ Z **C.**
Env. *par* ③ *: Pont de Zélande*★ *(Zeelandbrug).*
⛳18 *à l'Est : 12 km à Bruinisse, Oudendijk 3, ✉ 4311 NA, ☎ (0 111) 48 26 50, Fax (0 111) 48 15 66.*
🅸 *Meelstraat 4, ✉ 4301 EC, ☎ (0 111) 45 05 24, vvv.schuwen-duiveland@edz.nl, Fax (0 111) 45 05 25.*
Amsterdam 149 ② – Middelburg 44 ③ – Breda 81 ② – Rotterdam 66 ②

PAYS-BAS

ZIERIKZEE

Appelmarkt . . . . Z 2
Basterstr. . . . . Z 3
Dam . . . . Z 5
Fonteine . . . . Z 7
Hoofdpoortstr. . . . . Z 12
Julianastr. . . . . Z 14
Karsteil . . . . Z 16
Kerkhof N.Z. . . . . Z 17
Kerkhof Z.Z. . . . . Z 18
Klokstr. . . . . Z 20
Korte Nobelstr. . . . . Y 22
Lange Nobelstr. . . . . Y 25
Lange St. Janstr. . . . . . . Z 26
Meelstr. . . . . Z
Melkmarkt . . . . Z 28
Minderbroederstr. . . . . . . Z 30
Oude Haven . . . . Z 32
P.D. de Vosstr. . . . . Y 34
Poststr. . . . . Z
Ravestr. . . . . Z 36
Schuithaven . . . . Z 38
Schuurbeque Boeyestr. . . . . Y 39
Verrenieuwstr. . . . . Y 42
Watermolen . . . . Y 44
Wevershoek . . . . Z 45
Zevengetijstr. . . . . Y 48
Zuidwellestr. . . . . Y 50

Les plans de villes sont orientés le Nord en haut.

De Drie Morianen, Kraanplein 14, 4301 CH, (0 111) 41 29 31, *j.kosters@wxs.nl, Fax (0 111) 41 79 36,* , Moules en saison – . AE VISA Z c
fermé du 5 au 23 janv. et mardi d'oct. à mars – **Repas** *Lunch 20* – carte 22 à 61.
• Très courtisée lorsque la saison des moules bat son plein, cette adresse compte parmi les valeurs sûres de Zierikzee. Recettes bourgeoises, assorties au décor intérieur.
• Dit restaurant is bijzonder favoriet in het mosselseizoen en behoort tot de trefzekere adressen van de stad. De eenvoudige maar goede keuken is in harmonie met het interieur.

à Schuddebeurs *Nord : 4 km* C *Schouwen-Duiveland :*

Host. Schuddebeurs , Donkereweg 35, 4317 NL, (0 111) 41 56 51, *hostellerie@schuddebeurs.nl, Fax (0 111) 41 31 03,* , , – – 25 à 40. VISA. rest – *fermé 22 déc.-15 janv.* – **Repas** *Lunch 28* – 32/56 – **19 ch** 122/141, – 3 suites – ½ P 100/130.
• À la campagne, hostellerie familiale dont on apprécie le calme et l'aspect "cosy" des chambres. Celles de l'annexe donnent sur un jardin agréable. Jolie salle de breakfast. À l'heure des repas, on prend place dans la véranda. Préparations au goût du jour.
• Dit familiebedrijf in het Zeeuwse landschap is geliefd vanwege de rustieke omgeving en de knusse ambiance van de kamers. Die in de annexe kijken uit op een aangename tuin. Mooie ontbijtzaal. De maaltijd wordt geserveerd in de serre. Eigentijdse gerechten.

ZOETERMEER *Zuid-Holland* 532 L 10 *et* 715 E 5 – *110 500 h.*

Heuvelweg 3, 2716 DZ, (0 79) 320 31 36, Fax (0 79) 352 13 35.
Amsterdam 64 – Rotterdam 24 – Den Haag 14.

NH Zoetermeer, Danny Kayelaan 20 (près A 12, wijk 19), 2719 EH, (0 79) 361 02 02, *nhzoetermeer@nh-hotels.nl, Fax (0 79) 362 24 65,* – – 25 à 250. AE VISA JCB. rest
Repas *(fermé sam. midi et dim. midi) Lunch 18* – carte 37 à 49 – 15 – **104 ch** 150/180 – ½ P 218/232.
• Immeuble moderne posté sur une esplanade aménagée à proximité de l'autoroute et de la gare. Confort fonctionnel dans les chambres, actuelles et bien calibrées. Hall design.
• Dit moderne hotelpand staat op een esplanade nabij de snelweg en het station. De eigentijdse kamers zijn goed van afmeting en bieden functioneel comfort. Lobby in designstijl.

Mercure, Boerhavelaan (près A 12, wijk 13), 2713 HB, (0 79) 321 92 28, *h5030@accor-hotels.com, Fax (0 79) 321 15 01,* , – – 25 à 250. AE VISA JCB. rest
Repas *(fermé sam. et dim.)* carte 25 à 45 – 14 – **60 ch** 140/160.
• Cet hôtel proche de la gare et d'une voie rapide (A12) met à votre disposition des chambres refaites de neuf en conformité avec les standards de la chaîne Mercure.
• Dit hotel vlak bij het station en de snelweg (A12) biedt kamers die zijn gerenoveerd naar de standaardmaatstaven van de Mercure-keten.

Bastion, Zilverstraat 6 (près A 12, sortie ⑦, wijk 18), ✉ 2718 RL, ☎ (0 79) 361 10 71, *bastion@bastionhotel.nl, Fax (0 79) 361 13 50,* – P. AE VISA.

Repas (grillades, ouvert jusqu'à 23 h) carte env. 30 – ☕ 10 – **40 ch** 72.

◆ À l'entrée d'un zoning industriel, près du chemin de fer et de l'autoroute, hôtel de chaîne disposant de petites chambres sobrement équipées, pratiques avant tout.

◆ Dit ketenmotel aan het begin van een industrieterrein, vlak bij het spoor en de snelweg, beschikt over kleine, eenvoudig uitgeruste kamers die vooral praktisch zijn.

Julius, Eerste Stationsstraat 39 (wijk 12), ✉ 2712 HB, ☎ (0 79) 316 61 62, *info@julius-restaurant.nl, Fax (0 79) 316 63 78,* – P. AE VISA

fermé sam. midi et dim. midi – **Repas** *Lunch 28* – 35/53 bc, ♀.

◆ Villa située au voisinage d'un auguste moulin (1897). Salle à manger bien en phase avec l'époque, tout comme la cuisine. Les beaux jours, repas servis en terrasse.

◆ Restaurant in een villa vlak bij een statige molen (1897). De eetzaal en de keuken hebben beide een eigentijds karakter. Bij mooi weer wordt op het terras geserveerd.

ZOUTELANDE *Zeeland* © *Veere 21 985 h.* 532 F 14 *et* 715 B 7.

Bosweg 2, ✉ 4374 EM, ☎ 0 900-202 02 80, vvvztld@vvv.wnb.nl, Fax (0 118) 56 12 38.

Amsterdam 213 – Middelburg 12 – Vlissingen 13.

Beach, Duinweg 97, ✉ 4374 EC, ☎ (0 118) 56 12 55, *beach@zeelandnet.nl, Fax (0 118) 56 12 69* – P – 25 à 50

Pâques-oct. et week-end – **Repas** (dîner seult) carte 22 à 40 – **43 ch** ☕ 50/92 – ½ P 41/61.

◆ Trois types de chambres, souvent munies d'un balcon ou d'une terrasse, se partagent cette villa et son annexe récente situées aux pieds des dunes. Ambiance familiale. On s'attable dans un décor un peu embourgeoisé.

◆ Dit hotel onder aan de duinen beschikt over drie typen kamers, de meeste met balkon of terras, die verspreid liggen over een villa en een nieuwe dependance. Huiselijke ambiance. Klassiek-traditionele eetzaal.

't Streefkerkse Huis avec ch, Duinweg 48, ✉ 4374 EG, ☎ (0 118) 56 15 21, *info@streefkerksehuis.nl, Fax (0 118) 56 32 12,* ← – P. VISA.

fermé janv. – **Repas** *(fermé lundi et mardi de nov. à mars)* (déjeuner sur réservation) 28/43 bc – **6 ch** ☕ 60/70.

◆ Adorable auberge à toit de chaume perchée au sommet d'une dune. Accueil familial gentil, salon avec cheminée, salle de restaurant rustique et chambres de mise simple.

◆ Charmante herberg met rieten dak op een duintop. Vriendelijk en gastvrij onthaal, lounge met schouw, rustieke restaurantzaal en eenvoudige kamers.

ZUIDBROEK *Groningen* © *Menterwolde 12 635 h.* 531 AA 3 *et* 715 L 2.

Amsterdam 200 – Groningen 24 – Assen 39.

Zuidbroek, Burg. Omtaweg 2, ✉ 9636 EM, ☎ (0 598) 45 37 87, *receptie@vanderwallehotelzuidbroek.nl, Fax (0 598) 45 39 32,* – P – 25 à 1200. AE VISA

Repas (ouvert jusqu'à 23 h) *Lunch 10* – carte 22 à 54 – **120 ch** ☕ 75/85.

◆ Infrastructure colossale pour les congrès, énorme complexe sportif, hall d'exposition gigantesque et chambres "king size" : Zuidbroek voit tout en grand !

◆ Kolossale infrastructuur voor congressen, enorm sportcomplex, gigantische expositiehal en kingsize kamers. Kortom, Zuidbroek is ruimdenkend !

ZUIDLAREN *Drenthe* © *Tynaarlo 31 865 h.* 531 Z 4 *et* 715 L 2.

Env. au Sud-Est : 13 km à Eexterhalte : Hunebed★ (dolmen).

au Nord-Ouest : 8 km à Glimmen (Haren), Pollselaan 5, ✉ 9756 CJ, ☎ (0 50) 406 20 04, Fax (0 50) 406 19 22.

Stationsweg 69, ✉ 9471 GL, ☎ (0 50) 409 23 33, vvv.tynaarlo@12move.nl, Fax (0 50) 402 95 50.

Amsterdam 207 – Groningen 20 – Assen 18 – Emmen 42.

Tulip Inn Brinkhotel, Brink O.Z. 6, ✉ 9471 AE, ☎ (0 50) 409 12 61, *info@tibrinkhotel.nl, Fax (0 50) 409 60 11,* – – 30 à 250. AE VISA JCB

Repas *Lunch 12* – carte 23 à 36 – **54 ch** ☕ 90/109 – ½ P 67/76.

◆ Au cœur de la localité, devant le marché aux chevaux, point de chute très convenable pour partir à la découverte du pays des hunebedden (dolmens). Chambres agrandies.

◆ Dit hotel tegenover de paardenmarkt in het centrum is een comfortabele uitvalsbasis om het land van de hunebedden te verkennen. De kamers zijn vergroot.

XXX **De Vlindertuin,** Stationsweg 41, ✉ 9471 GK, ✆ (0 50) 409 45 31, *cazemierbronda @hetnet.nl, Fax (0 50) 409 57 53,* – P. AE VISA JCB
fermé 27 juil.-14 août, dim. et lundi – **Repas** (dîner seult) 43/70 bc, ♀.
◆ Ancienne ferme à toit de chaume où se concocte un choix de préparations actuelles. Salle à manger de bon goût et jolie terrasse d'été surveillant le "brink" (place verte).
◆ In deze voormalige boerderij met rieten dak wordt een keur van eigentijdse gerechten bereid. Smaakvol ingerichte eetzaal en mooi zomerterras aan de typisch Drentse brink.

XX **Ni Hao Panorama,** Stationsweg 11, ✉ 9471 GJ, ✆ (0 50) 409 04 39, , Cuisine asiatique – . AE VISA.
Repas *Lunch 18* – 22/70 bc.
◆ Mobilier en bois de rose, scène de genre chinoise, terrasse avec fontaine et bambous : le décor ne manque pas d'exotisme. Saveurs sino-thaïlandaises et indonésiennes.
◆ Het rozenhouten meubilair, het Chinese tafereel, het terras met fontein en bamboe : hier staat alles in het teken van exotiek. Chinees-Thaise en Indonesische gerechten.

XX **Ni Hao Buitenpaviljoen,** Hondsrugstraat 14, ✉ 9471 GE, ✆ (0 50) 409 67 93, *info@nihaogroup.com, Fax (0 50) 409 67 81,* , Cuisine japonaise avec Teppan-Yaki – .
AE VISA.
Repas (dîner seult) 28/65.
◆ Un restaurant japonais aménagé dans une maison "1900" - l'association des genres est assez inattendue ! Recettes traditionnelles et, en spécialité, la formule Teppan-Yaki.
◆ Een Japans restaurant in een pand in 1900-stijl : een combinatie die niet echt voor de hand ligt ! Traditionele gerechten met als specialiteit de formule teppan yaki.

ZUIDOOSTBEEMSTER *Noord-Holland* 531 O 7 – *voir à Purmerend.*

ZUIDWOLDE *Drenthe* C *De Wolden 23 875 h.* 531 X 6 *et* 715 K 3.

Amsterdam 157 – Assen 38 – Emmen 38 – Zwolle 36.

XXX **In de Groene Lantaarn,** Hoogeveenseweg 17 (Nord : 2 km), ✉ 7921 PC, ✆ (0 528) 37 29 38, *indegroenelantaarn@indegroenelantaarn.nl, Fax (0 528) 37 20 47,* – P. VISA JCB
fermé du 2 au 18 août, 27 déc.-7 janv. lundi et mardi – **Repas** (déjeuner sur réservation) 30.
◆ Agréable restaurant aménagé dans une grosse ferme (18e s.) très typée. L'été venu, profitez du cadre reposant de la terrasse, embellie d'un jardin généreusement fleuri.
◆ Aangenaam restaurant in een grote, zeer karakteristieke boerderij uit de 18e eeuw. In de zomer kunt u genieten op het rustige terras in de prachtig bloeiende tuin.

ZUTPHEN *Gelderland* 532 W 10 *et* 715 J 5 – *36 179 h.*

Voir *La vieille ville★ – Bibliothèque★ (Librije) et lustre★ dans l'église Ste-Walburge (St. Walburgskerk) – Drogenapstoren★ – Martinetsingel ≤★.*
Stationsplein 39, ✉ 7201 MH, ✆ (0 900) 269 28 88, vvvzutphen@tref.nl, Fax (0 575) 51 79 28.
Amsterdam 112 – Arnhem 30 – Apeldoorn 21 – Enschede 58 – Zwolle 53.

Eden, 's Gravenhof 6, ✉ 7201 DN, ✆ (0 575) 54 61 11, *res.edenzutphen@edenhotel group.com, Fax (0 575) 54 59 99,* – – 35. AE VISA. rest
Repas *(fermé dim.)* (dîner seult) carte 39 à 46, ♀ – **74 ch** 94/145.
◆ Cet ancien orphelinat fondé au 16e s. a été transformé en un hôtel de bon confort. Ensemble de caractère et décoration intérieure composite, mêlant le moderne et l'ancien. Bar-restaurant installé dans une cave voûtée.
◆ Dit voormalige 16e-eeuwse weeshuis herbergt nu een karaktervol hotel met goed comfort. In het interieur gaan modern en antiek hand in hand. Bar-restaurant in de gewelfde kelder.

Golden Tulip Inntel, De Stoven 37 (Sud-Est : 2 km sur N 348), ✉ 7206 AZ, ✆ (0 575) 52 55 55, *infozutphen@hotelinntel.com, Fax (0 575) 52 96 76,* , , , , – , rest, P – 25 à 200. AE VISA. rest
Repas *Lunch 13* – carte env. 32 – 13 – **67 ch** 115 – ½ P 142.
◆ Cet hôtel légèrement excentré combine infrastructures sportives et de réunions. Une grande partie des chambres a été rénovée et un nouveau bowling est installé. Repas simple à prix "soft". Formule buffets.
◆ Dit hotel aan de rand van de stad combineert sportieve faciliteiten met een infrastructuur voor bijeenkomsten. De meeste kamers zijn gerenoveerd en er is een nieuw bowlingsysteem geïnstalleerd. Eenvoudige maaltijd voor een "zacht" prijsje. Buffetformule.

XX **Galantijn,** Stationsstraat 9, ✉ 7201 MC, ✆ (0 575) 51 72 86, *galantijn@compacnet.nl, Fax (0 575) 51 19 61* – AE VISA
fermé sam. midi, dim. et lundi – **Repas** *Lunch 23* – 33/68 bc.
◆ Une bonne réputation locale entoure cette petite adresse proche de la gare. Salle à manger garnie de meubles en merisier, exposition de tableaux et fourneaux à vue.
◆ Dit restaurantje vlak bij het station geniet lokaal een goede reputatie. Eetzaal met kersenhouten meubilair, schilderijenexpositie en open keuken.

't Schulten Hues sous-sol, Houtmarkt 79, ✉ 7201 KL, ☎ (0 575) 51 00 05, *info@schullenhues.nl, Fax (0 575) 51 27 06* – AE ⓓ MC VISA.
fermé prem sem. sept., fin déc.-mi-janv., sam. midi, dim. midi, lundi et mardi – **Repas** *Lunch 27* – 33/55, ♀.
◆ Maison du 17e s. dont la jolie cave voûtée vous accueille le temps d'un repas au goût du jour, aussi ambitieux qu'innovant. Formule "eetcafé" simplifiée au rez-de-chaussée.
◆ In de prachtige, gewelfde kelder van een 17e-eeuws pand wacht u een eigentijds diner dat even ambitieus als innovatief is. Eenvoudig eetcafé op de begane grond.

ZWARTSLUIS *Overijssel* Ⓒ *Zwartewaterland 22 178 h.* 531 V 7 *et* 715 J 4.
Amsterdam 123 – Zwolle 16 – Meppel 12.

Zwartewater, De Vlakte 20, ✉ 8064 PC, ☎ (0 38) 386 64 44, *info@hotel-zwartewater.nl, Fax (0 38) 386 62 75,* ←, ⛱, ≘s, ⊠, ✂, ⚓ – |♦|, ▤ rest, TV ♿ P – 🏋 25 à 2000. AE ⓓ MC VISA
Repas carte 22 à 40 – **51 ch** ☕ 46/88 – ½ P 65.
◆ Ce vaste complexe hôtelier dispose de bonnes installations sportives et d'un immense centre de congrès. Les meilleures chambres profitent d'un balcon avec vue sur l'eau. Par beau temps, on mange agréablement sur la terrasse dressée au bord du Zwartewater.
◆ Dit grote hotelcomplex beschikt over goede sportvoorzieningen en een immens congrescentrum. De beste kamers hebben een balkon met uitzicht op het Zwarte Water. Bij mooi weer kunt u op het terras aan de rivier van de maaltijd genieten.

ZWEELOO *Drenthe* Ⓒ *Coevorden 35 756 h.* 531 Z 6 *et* 715 L 3.
⛳ au Sud-Ouest : 1 km à Aalden, Aelderholt 4, ✉ 7854 TZ, ☎ (0 591) 37 24 50.
Amsterdam 184 – Assen 34 – Emmen 13 – Groningen 60.

Idylle (Zwiep), Kruisstraat 21, ✉ 7851 AE, ☎ (0 591) 37 18 57, *info@restaurantidylle.nl, Fax (0 591) 37 24 04,* ⛱ – P. AE ⓓ MC VISA JCB.
fermé 23 fév.-8 mars, 25 juil.-10 août, sam. midi et lundi – **Repas** *Lunch 33* – 70 bc, carte 50 à 68, ♀.
◆ Savourez l'ambiance rustique de cette ancienne ferme saxonne à dénicher dans un village pittoresque. Belle cuisine au goût du jour et service avenant. Jardin d'aromates.
◆ Geniet van de rustieke ambiance in deze oude Saksische boerderij in een pittoresk dorp. Mooie, eigentijdse keuken en vriendelijke bediening. Kruidentuin.
Spéc. Homard grillé, salade de pommes et fenouil. Foie d'oie sauté et soupe de figues. Filet de veau et ravioli de fromage de chèvre à la tomate séchée et romarin

à Aalden *Sud-Ouest : 1 km* Ⓒ *Coevorden :*

Adema, Aelderstraat 49, ✉ 7854 RP, ☎ (0 591) 37 14 54, *geert.adema@hetnet.nl, Fax (0 591) 37 25 59,* ⛱ – ▤.
fermé lundi – **Repas** (déjeuner sur réservation) 31/63 bc.
◆ Mignonne auberge bordant la grand-rue d'un patelin où abondent les fermes à toit de chaume. Menus appétissants, coquette décoration intérieure et exquise terrasse d'été.
◆ Bekoorlijke herberg aan de hoofdstraat van een gehucht dat tal van boerderijen met rieten dak telt. Aantrekkelijke menu's, gezellig interieur en een heerlijk zomerterras.

ZWOLLE Ⓟ *Overijssel* 531 V 7 *et* 715 J 4 – *109 000 h.*
Voir *Hôtel de ville (Stadhuis) sculptures★ du plafond dans la salle des Échevins (Schepenzaal)* BYZ **H** – *Sassenpoort★* CZ.
Musées : *Stedelijk Museum Zwolle★* BY **M**².
⛳ Zalnéweg 75, ✉ 8026 PZ, ☎ (0 38) 453 42 70.
ℹ Grote Kerkplein 14, ✉ 8011 PK, ☎ 0 900-112 23 75, info@vvvzwolle.nl, Fax (0 38) 422 26 79.
Amsterdam 111 ④ – Apeldoorn 44 ④ – Enschede 73 ② – Groningen 102 ① – Leeuwarden 94 ①

Plan page suivante

Gd H. Wientjes, Stationsweg 7, ✉ 8011 CZ, ☎ (0 38) 425 42 54, *wientjes@bilderberg.nl, Fax (0 38) 425 42 60,* ⛱, 🚲 – |♦| ⇔ TV ♿ P – 🏋 25 à 200. AE ⓓ MC VISA JCB. rest BZ **s**
fermé 27 déc.-2 janv. – **Repas** ***Bon Aparte*** *(fermé sam. midi et dim.)* 35/73 bc – ☕ 18 – **57 ch** 174.
◆ Commode pour les usagers du chemin de fer, cette hostellerie légèrement excentrée propose des chambres décorées avec goût. Espaces communs soignés. Plaisante salle à manger garnie de meubles de style. Mets classiques actualisés.
◆ Dit hotel ligt iets buiten het centrum maar pal tegenover het station en beschikt over diverse categorieën smaakvol ingerichte kamers. Verzorgde gemeenschappelijke ruimten. Aangename eetzaal met stijlmeubilair. Klassieke gerechten in een eigentijds jasje.

ZWOLLE

Achter de Broeren	BCY 3
Bagijnesingel	CY 6
Bisschop Willebrandlaan	AX 7
Buitenkant	BY 8
Deventerstraatweg	AX 9
Diezerpoortenplas	CY 10
Diezerstr.	CY
Grote Kerkplein	BY 12
Hanekamp	AX 13
Harm Smeengekade	BZ 15
Ittersumallee	AX 16
Kamperstr.	BY 18
Luttekestr.	BY 19
Meppelerstraatweg	AX 21
Middelweg	AX 22
Nieuwe Markt	CYZ 24
Oude Vismarkt	BY 25
Potgietersingel	BZ 27
Rhijnvis Feithlaan	AX 28
Roggenstr.	BY 30
Sassenstr.	BYZ 31
Spoolderbergweg	AX 33
Ter Pelkwijkstr.	CY 34
Thomas a Kempisstr.	CY 36
Veerallee	AX 37
Voorsterweg	AX 38
Voorstr.	BY 39
van Wevelinkhovenstr.	CY 40
Wipstrikkerallee	AX 42
Zuidbroek	AX 43

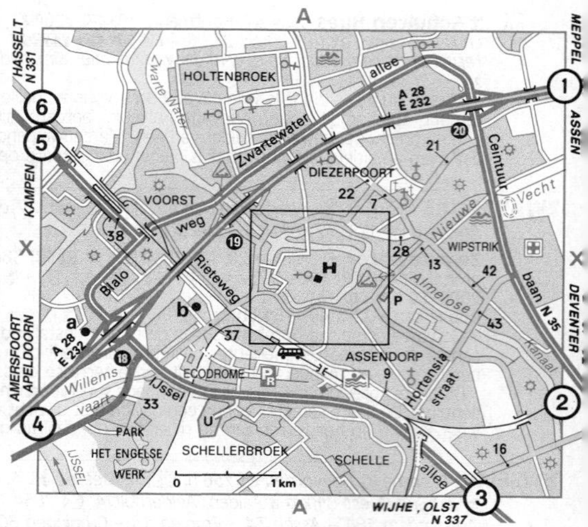

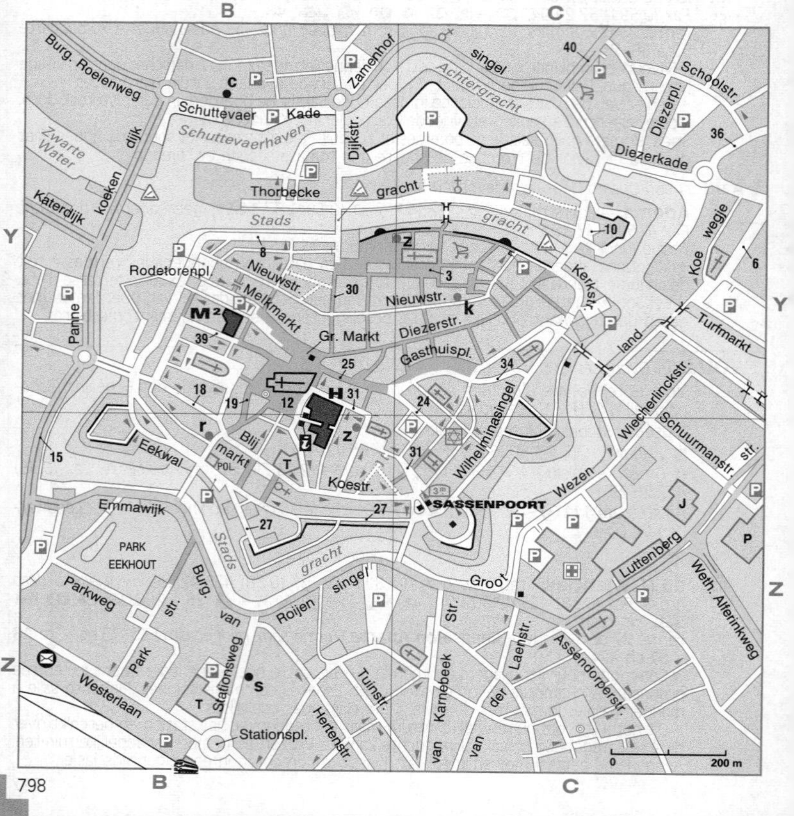

B C

Burg. Roelenweg
Schuttevaer Kade
Schuttevaerhaven
Zwarte Water
Zamenhof
singel
Achtergracht
Dijkstr.
Schoolstr.
Diezerpl.
Diezerkade
koeken dijk
Katerdijk
Thorbecke
gracht
Stads gracht
Koe wegje
Rodetorenpl.
Nieuwstr.
Melkmarkt
Kerkstr.
Turfmarkt
land
Panne
Gr. Markt
Diezerstr.
Gasthuispl.
Wiecherlinckstr.
Schuurmanstr.
Eekwal
Blij markt
POL
Koestr.
Wilhelminasingel
SASSENPOORT
Wezen
Luttenberg
Emmawijk
PARK EEKHOUT
Stads gracht
Groot
Weth. Alferinkweg
Parkweg
Park str.
Burg. van Roijen singel
Stationsweg
Str.
Karnebeek
van der Laenstr.
Assendorperstr.
Westerlaan
Tuinstr.
Hertenstr.
Stationspl.
0 200 m
B C

Mercure, Hertsenbergweg 1 (Sud-Ouest : 2 km), ✉ 8041 BA, ☎ (0 38) 421 60 31, *H2109@accor-hotels.com, Fax (0 38) 422 30 69,* – 🅿 – 25 à 450. AE ⓓ MC VISA AX a
Repas *Lunch 18* – carte 31 à 41, ♀ – ☕ 14 – **72 ch** 110/137 – ½ P 167/205.
• Aux avant-postes de l'ancienne ville hanséatique fortifiée, établissement de chaîne dont les chambres fonctionnelles se distribuent de plain-pied et sur deux étages.
• Dit ketenhotel aan de rand van de oude, versterkte hanzestad beschikt over functionele kamers op de begane grond en op twee verdiepingen.

Fidder sans rest, Koningin Wilhelminastraat 6, ✉ 8019 AM, ☎ (0 38) 421 83 95, *Fax (0 38) 423 02 98,* – TV. AE ⓓ MC VISA JCB. AX b
fermé 24 déc.-1er janv. – **22 ch** ☕ 100/150.
• Trois jolies maisons bourgeoises composent ce petit hôtel familial au charme nostalgique. Salons, bibliothèque, terrasse reposante et chambres pourvues de meubles anciens.
• Dit kleine familiehotel in drie mooie herenhuizen straalt een nostalgische charme uit. Lounges, bibliotheek, rustig terras en kamers met antieke meubels.

Campanile, Schuttevaerkade 40, ✉ 8021 DB, ☎ (0 38) 455 04 44, *zwolle@campanile.nl, Fax (0 38) 455 07 50,* – TV 🅿 – 25 à 70. AE ⓓ MC VISA BY c
Repas (avec buffets) 22, ♀ – ☕ 10 – **69 ch** 74/93.
• Toutes les chambres de cette unité de la chaîne hôtelière Campanile ont la particularité d'être accessibles par l'intérieur. Confort simple, mais convenable.
• Alle kamers in dit hotel van de Campanile-keten zijn van binnendoor bereikbaar, wat niet standaard is voor deze hotelgroep. Eenvoudig maar aangenaam comfort.

De Librije (Boer), Broerenkerkplein 13, ✉ 8011 TW, ☎ (0 38) 421 20 83, *librije@alliance.nl, Fax (0 38) 423 23 29* – 🅿. AE MC VISA. CY z
fermé 22 fév.-1er mars, 18 juil.-9 août, mardi midi, sam. midi, dim. et lundi – **Repas** *Lunch 50* – 85/95, carte 75 à 92, ♀.
• Une aile d'un ancien couvent remontant au 15e s. abrite cette grande table réaménagée à la mode d'aujourd'hui. Belle cuisine dans l'air du temps, personnalisée avec brio.
• Dit modern ingerichte restaurant is gehuisvest in een vleugel van een voormalig 15e-eeuws klooster. Mooie eigentijdse keuken met een professionele, persoonlijke noot.
Spéc. 4 façons de manger le maquereau (sept.-janv.). Collier d'agneau aux zestes de limon (avril-sept.). Dos de cabillaud à la pomme de terre aux truffes (oct.-fév.)

't Wolhuys, Bethlehemkerkplein 32, ✉ 8011 PH, ☎ (0 38) 344 75 81, *info@wolhuys.nl* – AE ⓓ MC VISA BY z
fermé 23 fév.-8 mars, 27 juil.-11 août, sam. midi, dim. et dim. – **Repas** (déjeuner sur réservation) 37/83 bc, ♀.
• Ce restaurant du centre-ville vous reçoit dans une jolie salle à manger résolument contemporaine, où dominent les tons rouge et beige. Cuisine assez inventive.
• In dit restaurant in het centrum wordt u onthaald in een zeer eigentijdse eetzaal rood en beige als hoofdtinten. Vrij inventieve keuken.

't Pestengasthuys, Weversgildeplein 1, ✉ 8011 XN, ☎ (0 38) 423 39 86, *restaurant@pestengasthuys.nl, Fax (0 38) 423 26 56,* – ▤. AE ⓓ MC VISA CY k
fermé sam. midi, dim. midi et lundi – Repas 28/63 bc, ♀.
• Repas plaisant servi dans une demeure historique élevée au 15e s. Salle de restaurant très haute de plafond, avec mezzanine. Menus actuels bien montés, donc fort courtisés.
• In dit historische pand uit de 15e eeuw wacht u een genoeglijke maaltijd. Restaurantzaal met zeer hoog plafond en vide. De doortimmerde, eigentijdse menu's zijn favoriet.

Poppe, Luttekestraat 66, ✉ 8011 LS, ☎ (0 38) 421 30 50, *Fax (0 38) 338 81 64,* Ouvert jusqu'à 23 h – ▤ – 30. AE ⓓ MC VISA BZ r
fermé prem. sem. janv. et lundi – **Repas** *Lunch 23* – carte 30 à 43, ♀.
• Affaire familiale installée dans une ancienne forge avoisinant la grand-place et les vestiges de plusieurs bastions défensifs. Décor intérieur rustique. Fourneaux à vue.
• Familierestaurant in een voormalige hoefsmederij vlak bij de Grote Markt en de enkele restanten van verdedigingswerken. Rustiek interieur. Open keuken.

Principales marques automobiles
Belangrijkste auto-importeurs
Wichtigste Automarken
Main car manufacturers

Belgique – België – Belgien Grand-Duché de Luxembourg

Audi
Porsche
Volkswagen
S.A. D'Ieteren N.V.
Rue du Mail, 50
Maliestraat, 50
1050 Bruxelles – Brussel
Tél. : 0 2 536 51 11

B.M.W.
S.A. B.M.W./
Lodderstraat, 16
2880 Bornem
Tél. : 0 38 90 97 11

Citroën
S.B.A. Citroën
Place de l'Yser, 7
Ijzerplein, 7
1000 Bruxelles – Brussel
Tél. : 0 2 206 06 11

Daewoo
Daewoo Motor
Belgium N.V.
Mechelsesteenweg, 309
1800 Vilvoorde
Tél. : 0 2 257 29 50

Daihatsu
N.V Autoproducts
Kipdorp, 57
2000 Antwerpen
Tél. : 0 3 206 02 02

Ferrari
Garage Francorchamps
Lozenberg, 13
1932 Sint Stevens Woluwe
Tél. : 0 2 725 67 60

Fiat
Lancia
Alfa-Romeo
S.A. Fiat Belgio N.V.
Rue de Genève 175
Genèvestraat 175
1140 Bruxelles – Brussel
Tél. : 0 2 702 65 11

Ford
Ford Motor CY
Groenenborgerlaan 16
2610 Wilrijk
Tél. : 0 3 821 20 00

Honda
S.A. Honda Belgium N.V.
Wijngaardveld, 1
9300 Aalst
Tél. : 0 53 72 51 11

Hyundai
S.A. Korean Motor CY N.V.
Pierstraat, 231
2550 Kontich
Tél. : 0 3 450 06 11

Jaguar
Jaguar Belgium
Sint Bernardsesteenweg, 534
2660 Antwerpen
Tél. : 0 3 830 18 80

Lada
S.A. Lada-Belux N.V.
Avenue Galilée 5
1300 Wavre
Tél. : 0 10 28 89 93

Mazda
Beherman European
Industrieweg, 3
2880 Bornem
Tél. : 0 3 890 91 11

Daimler-Chrysler
Daimler-Chrysler Belgium
Avenue du Péage, 68
Tollaan, 68
1200 Bruxelles – Brussel
Tél. : 0 2 724 12 11

Nissan
S.A. Nissan Belgium N.V.
Boomsesteenweg, 42
2630 Aartselaar
Tél. : 0 3 870 32 11

Opel *Opel Belgium N.V.*
Marketing Division
Prins Boudewijnlaan 30
2550 Kontich
Tél. : 0 3 450 63 11

Peugeot *S.A. Peugeot Talbot*
Belgique N.V.
Rue de l'Industrie, 22
1400 Nivelles
Tél. : 0 67 88 02 11

Renault *S.A. Renault Belgique*
Luxembourg N.V.
Avenue W.A. Mozart, 20
W.A.Mozartlaan, 20
1620 Drogenbos
Tél. : 0 2 334 76 11

Saab *Beherman European*
Distribution
Industrieweg 3
2880 Bornem
Tél. : 0 3 890 91 11

Seat *Seat Import*
Boulevard Industriel, 51
Industrielaan, 51
1070 Bruxelles – Brussel
Tél. : 0 2 556 35 11

Skoda *Skoda Import*
Avenue A. Giraud 29-35
A. Giraudlaan 29-35
1030 Bruxelles – Brussel
Tél. : 0 2 215 92 20

Ssangyong *Beherman European*
Industrieweg 3
2880 Bornem
Tél. : 0 3 890 91 11

Subaru *S.A. Subaru*
Belgium N.V.
Mechelsesteenweg, 588 d
1800 Vilvoorde
Tél. : 0 2 254 75 11

Suzuki *S.A. Suzuki*
Belgium N.V.
Satenrozen, 2
2550 Kontich
Tél. : 0 3 450 04 11

Toyota *S.A. Toyota*
Belgium N.V.
Avenue du Japon 51
1420 Braine-l'Alleud
Tél. : 0 2 386 72 11

Volvo *Volvo Cars Belgium*
Chaussée de Zellik, 30
Zelliksesteenweg, 30
1082 Bruxelles – Brussel
Tél. : 0 2 482 51 11

Nederland – Pays-Bas

BMW *BMW Nederland B.V.*
Einsteinlaan 5
2289 CC Rijswijk
Tél. : (070) 395 62 22

Citroën *Citroën Nederland B.V.*
Stadionplein 26-30
1076 CM Amsterdam
Tél. : (020) 570 19 11

Chrysler *Chrysler Holland Import B.V.*
Lange Dreef 12
4131 NH Vianen
Tél. (0347) 36 34 00

Daewoo *Daewoo Motor Benelux B.V.*
Jupiterstraat 210
2132 HJ Hoofddorp
Tél. : (023) 563 17 12

Daihatsu *Daihatsu Holland B.V.*
Witboom 2
4131 PL Vianen ZH
Tél. : (0347) 37 05 05

Ferrari *Kroymans B.V.*
Soestdijkerstr. wg. 64
1213 XE Hilversum
Tél. : (035) 685 51 51

Fiat
Lancia
Alfa-Romeo *Hullenbergweg 1-3*
1101 BW Amsterdam
Tél. : (020) 652 07 00

Ford *Ford Nederland B.V.*
Amsteldijk 217
1079 LK Amsterdam
Tél. : (020) 540 99 11

Honda *Honda Nederland B.V.*
Nikkelstraat 17
2984 AM Ridderkerk
Tél. : (0180) 45 73 33

Hyundai *Greenib Car B.V.*
H. v. Doorneweg 14
2171 KZ Sassenheim
Tél. : (0252) 21 33 94

Kia *Kia Motors*
Marconiweg 2
4131 PD Vianen
Tél. : (0347) 37 44 54

Mazda *Autopalace De Binckhorst B.V.*
Binckhorstlaan 312-334
2516 BL Den Haag
Tél. : (070) 348 94 00

Daimler-Chrysler *Daimler-Chrysler Nederland BV*
Reactorweg 25
3542 AD Utrecht
Tél. : (030) 247 19 11

Mitsubishi *Mitsubishi Motor Sales NL B.V.*
Diamantlaan 29
2132 WV Hoofddorp
Tél. : (023) 555 52 22

Nissan *Nissan Motor Nederland B.V.*
Hornweg 32
1044 AN Amsterdam
Tél. : (020) 516 31 11

Opel *Opel Nederland B.V.*
Lage Mosten 49-63
4822 NK Breda
Tél. : (078) 642 23 00

Peugeot *Peugeot Nederland N.V.*
Uraniumweg 25
3542 AK Utrecht
Tél. : (030) 247 54 75

Rover *Rover Nederland B.V.*
Sportlaan 1
4131 NN Vianen ZH
Tél. : (0347) 36 66 00

Renault *Renault Nederland N.V.*
Boeingavenue 235
1119 PD Schiphol-Rijk
Tél. : (020) 561 91 91

Saab *A.I.M. B.V.*
Jr. D.S. Tuynmanweg 7
4131 PN Vianen
Tél. : (0347) 37 26 04

Seat *Seat Importeur Pon Car B.V.*
Klepelhoek 2
3833 GZ Leusden
Tél. : (033) 495 15 50

Ssangyong *Ssangyoung Nederland cv*
Savannahweg 69C
3542 AW Utrecht
Tél. : (030) 241 40 42

Suzuki *Nimag B.V. – Reedijk 9*
3274 KE Heinenoord
Tél. : (0186) 60 79 11

Toyota *Louwman & Parqui*
Steurweg 8
4941 VR Raamsdonksveer
Tél. : (0162) 58 59 00

VW
Audi *Pon's Automobielhandel*
Zuiderinslag 2
3833 BP Leusden
Tél. : (033) 494 99 44

Volvo *Volvo Nederland B.V.*
Stationsweg 2
4153 RD Beesd
Tél. : (0345) 68 88 88

Jours fériés en 2004
Feestdagen in 2004
Feiertage im Jahre 2004
Bank Holidays in 2004

Belgique – België – Belgien

1er janvier	*Jour de l'An*
11 avril	*Pâques*
12 avril	*lundi de Pâques*
1er mai	*Fête du Travail*
20 mai	*Ascension*
30 mai	*Pentecôte*
31 mai	*lundi de Pentecôte*
21 juillet	*Fête Nationale*
15 août	*Assomption*
1er novembre	*Toussaint*
11 novembre	*Fête de l'Armistice*
25 décembre	*Noël*

Grand-Duché de Luxembourg

1er janvier	*Jour de l'An*
1er mars	*lundi de Carnaval*
11 avril	*Pâques*
12 avril	*lundi de Pâques*
1er mai	*Fête du Travail*
20 mai	*Ascension*
30 mai	*Pentecôte*
31 mai	*lundi de Pentecôte*
23 juin	*Fête Nationale*
15 août	*Assomption*
1er novembre	*Toussaint*
25 décembre	*Noël*
26 décembre	*Saint-Étienne*

Nederland – Pays-Bas

1er janvier	*Jour de l'An*
11 avril	*Pâques*
12 avril	*lundi de Pâques*
30 avril	*Jour de la Reine*
5 mai	*Jour de la Libération*
20 mai	*Ascension*
30 mai	*Pentecôte*
31 mai	*lundi de Pentecôte*
25 décembre	*Noël*
26 décembre	*2e jour de Noël*

Indicatifs Téléphoniques Internationaux

Internationale landnummers

de/van/ von/from \ vers/naar nach/to	A	B	CH	CZ	D	DK	E	FIN	F	GB	GR
A Austria		0032	0041	00420	0049	0045	0034	00358	0033	0044	0030
B Belgium	0043		0041	00420	0049	0045	0034	00358	0033	0044	0030
CH Switzerland	0043	0032		00420	0049	0045	0034	00358	0033	0044	0030
CZ Czech Republic	0043	0032	0041		0049	0045	0034	00358	0033	0044	0030
D Germany	0043	0032	0041	00420		0045	0034	00358	0033	0044	0030
DK Denmark	0043	0032	0041	00420	0049		0034	00358	0033	0044	0030
E Spain	0043	0032	0041	00420	0049	0045		00358	0033	0044	0030
FIN Finland	0043	0032	0041	00420	0049	0045	0034		0033	0044	0030
F France	0043	0032	0041	00420	0049	0045	0034	00358		0044	0030
GB United Kingdom	0043	0032	0041	00420	0049	0045	0034	00358	0033		0030
GR Greece	0043	0032	0041	00420	0049	0045	0034	00358	0033	0044	
H Hungary	0043	0032	0041	00420	0049	0045	0034	00358	0033	0044	0030
I Italy	0043	0032	0041	00420	0049	0045	0034	00358	0033	0044	0030
IRL Ireland	0043	0032	0041	00420	0049	0045	0034	00358	0033	0044	0030
J Japan	00143	00132	00141	001420	00149	00145	00134	001358	00133	00144	00130
L Luxembourg	0043	0032	0041	00420	0049	0045	0034	00358	0033	0044	0030
N Norway	0043	0032	0041	00420	0049	0045	0034	00358	0033	0044	0030
NL Netherlands	0043	0032	0041	00420	0049	0045	0034	00358	0033	0044	0030
PL Poland	0043	0032	0041	00420	0049	0045	0034	00358	0033	0044	0030
P Portugal	0043	0032	0041	00420	0049	0045	0034	00358	0033	0044	0030
RUS Russia	81043	81032	81041	810420	81049	81045	*	810358	81033	81044	*
S Sweden	0043	0032	0041	00420	0049	0045	0034	00358	0033	0044	0030
USA	01143	01132	01141	011420	01149	01145	01134	01358	01133	01144	01130

** Pas de sélection automatique*   ** Geen automatische selektie*

Important : pour les communications internationales, le zéro (0) initial de l'indicatif interurbain n'est pas à composer (excepté pour les appels vers l'Italie).
Aux Pays-Bas on n'utilise pas le préfixe dans la zone.
Appel d'urgence : Belgique : 100 ; Luxembourg : 112 ; Pays-Bas : 112

Belangrijk: bij internationale telefoongesprekken moet de eerste nul (0) van het netnummer worden weggelaten (behalve als u naar Italië opbelt). In Nederland moet men binnen eenzelfde zone geen kengetal draaien of intoetsen. Hulpdiensten : België : 100 ; Luxemburg : 112 ; Nederland : 112.

Internationale Telefon-Vorwahlnummern
International dialling codes

H	I	IRL	J	L	N	NL	PL	P	RUS	S	USA	
0036	0039	00353	0081	00352	0047	0031	0048	00351	007	0046	001	**Austria A**
0036	0039	00353	0081	00352	0047	0031	0048	00351	007	0046	001	**Belgium B**
0036	0039	00353	0081	00352	0047	0031	0048	00351	007	0046	001	**Switzerland CH**
0036	0039	00353	0081	00352	0047	0031	0048	00351	007	0046	001	**Czech Republic CZ**
0036	0039	00353	0081	00352	0047	0031	0048	00351	007	0046	001	**Germany D**
0036	0039	00353	0081	00352	0047	0031	0048	00351	007	0046	001	**Denmark DK**
0036	0039	00353	0081	00352	0047	0031	0048	00351	007	0046	001	**Spain E**
0036	0039	00353	0081	00352	0047	0031	0048	00351	007	0046	001	**Finland FIN**
0036	0039	00353	0081	00352	0047	0031	0048	00351	007	0046	001	**France F**
0036	0039	00353	0081	00352	0047	0031	0048	00351	007	0046	001	**United Kingdom GB**
0036	0039	00353	0081	00352	0047	0031	0048	00351	007	0046	001	**Greece GR**
	0039	00353	0081	00352	0047	0031	0048	00351	007	0046	001	**Hungary H**
0036		00353	0081	00352	0047	0031	0048	00351	*	0046	001	**Italy I**
0036	0039		0081	00352	0047	0031	0048	00351	007	0046	001	**Ireland IRL**
00136	00139	001353		001352	00147	00131	001480	001351	*	00146	0011	**Japan J**
0036	0039	00353	0081		0047	0031	0048	00351	007	0046	001	**Luxembourg L**
0036	0039	00353	0081	00352		0031	0048	00351	007	0046	001	**Norway N**
0036	0039	00353	0081	00352	0047		0048	00351	007	0046	001	**Netherlands NL**
0036	0039	00353	0081	00352	0047	0031		00351	007	0046	001	**Poland PL**
0036	0039	00353	0081	00352	0047	0031	0048		007	0046	001	**Portugal P**
81036	*	*	*	*	*	81031	81048	*		*	*	**Russia RUS**
0036	0039	00353	0081	00352	0047	0031	0048	00351	007		001	**Sweden S**
01136	01139	011353	01181	011352	01147	01131	01148	011351	*	01146		**USA**

* *Automatische Vorwahl nicht möglich* * *Direct dialling not possible*

Wichtig: bei Auslandsgesprächen darf die Null (0) der Ortsnetzkennzahl nicht gewählt werden (ausser bei Gesprächen nach Italien).
In den Niederlanden benötigt man keine Vorwahl innerhalb einer Zone.
Notruf : Belgien : 100 ; Luxembourg : 112 ; Niederlanden : 112.

Note: when making an international call, do not dial the first "0" of the city codes (except for calls to Italy).
The dialling code is not required for local calls in the Netherlands.
Emergency phone numbers : Belgium : 100 ; Luxembourg : 112 ; Netherlands : 112.

Distances

Quelques précisions

Au texte de chaque localité vous trouverez la distance de sa capitale d'état et des villes environnantes. Les distances intervilles du tableau les complètent.
La distance d'une localité à une autre n'est pas toujours répétée en sens inverse : voyez au texte de l'une ou de l'autre.
Utilisez aussi les distances portées en bordure des plans.
Les distances sont comptées à partir du centre-ville et par la route la plus pratique, c'est-à-dire celle qui offre les meilleures conditions de roulage, mais qui n'est pas nécessairement la plus courte.

Afstanden

Toelichting

In de tekst bij elke plaats vindt U de afstand tot de hoofdstad en tot de grotere steden in de omgeving. De afstandstabel dient ter aanvulling.
De afstand tussen twee plaatsen staat niet altijd onder beide plaatsen vermeld ; zie dan bij zowel de ene als de andere plaats.
Maak ook gebruik van de aangegeven afstanden rondom de plattegronden.
De afstanden zijn berekend vanaf het stadscentrum en via de gunstigste (niet altijd de kortste) route.

Entfernungen

Einige Erklärungen

Die Entfernungen zur Landeshauptstadt und zu den nächstgrößeren Städten in der Umgebung finden Sie in jedem Ortstext.
Die Kilometerangaben der Tabelle ergänzen somit die Angaben des Ortstextes.
Da die Entfernung von einer Stadt zu einer anderen nicht immer unter beiden Städten zugleich aufgeführt ist, sehen Sie bitte unter beiden entsprechenden Ortstexten nach. Eine weitere Hilfe sind auch die am Rande der Stadtpläne erwähnten Kilometerangaben.
Die Entfernungen gelten ab Stadmitte unter Berücksichtigung der güngstigsten (nicht immer kürzesten) Streckte.

Distances

Commentary

Each entry indicates how far the town or locality is from the capital and other nearby towns. The distances in the table complete those given under individual town headings for calculating total distances.
To avoid excessive repetition some distances have only been quoted once. You may, therefore, have to look under both town headings.
Note also that some distances appear in the margins of the town plans.
Distances are calculated from town centres and along the best roads from a motoring point of view – not necessarily the shortest.

Distances entre principales villes
Afstanden tussen de balangrijkste steden
Entfernungen zwischen den größeren Städten
Distances between major towns

Gent - Rotterdam: 153 km

	Amsterdam	Antwerpen	Apeldoorn	Arlon	Arnhem	Bastogne	Breda	Brugge	Bruxelles/Brussel	Charleroi	's-Gravenhage	Dinant	Eindhoven	Enschede	Gent	Groningen	Haarlem	Hasselt	's-Hertogenbosch	Kortrijk	Leeuwarden	Liège	Luxembourg	Maastricht	Mechelen	Middelburg	Mons	Namur	Nijmegen	Oostende	Rotterdam	Tilburg	Tournai	Turnhout	Utrecht
Antwerpen	159																																		
Apeldoorn	89	191																																	
Arlon	372	229	352																																
Arnhem	95	162	30	315																															
Bastogne	334	189	314	38	278																														
Breda	102	58	134	287	115	246																													
Brugge	267	105	299	294	270	254	166																												
Bruxelles/Brussel	205	45	237	188	208	147	104	101																											
Charleroi	266	106	297	172	268	132	165	156	62																										
's-Gravenhage	59	131	135	360	123	319	80	215	177	237																									
Dinant	294	135	314	111	277	78	193	202	93	55	266																								
Eindhoven	122	89	110	245	83	207	63	196	132	192	145	207																							
Enschede	161	256	74	380	98	342	206	366	302	362	208	361	178																						
Gent	220	58	251	253	222	212	118	50	57	111	191	159	146	317																					
Groningen	185	314	141	493	171	456	258	425	360	420	238	449	251	145	375																				
Haarlem	20	174	108	385	115	348	118	259	220	280	47	309	137	180	227	203																			
Hasselt	188	78	178	173	152	135	100	184	81	103	206	102	63	247	135	320	204																		
's-Hertogenbosch	86	100	92	283	66	245	49	210	145	205	109	234	33	160	160	234	101	100																	
Kortrijk	261	100	293	282	264	241	160	55	93	122	233	169	188	359	48	417	277	176	202																
Leeuwarden	139	286	134	486	164	449	230	396	332	392	192	421	244	170	347	66	140	313	210	389															
Liège	244	119	224	128	188	90	142	198	96	94	247	93	117	272	155	366	259	42	155	190	359														
Luxembourg	415	256	370	30	333	71	314	323	215	199	387	138	263	378	280	511	431	204	301	308	504	159													
Maastricht	216	109	196	160	160	122	151	216	113	123	234	122	89	239	167	338	231	32	127	208	331	33	178												
Mechelen	185	25	216	206	187	166	84	116	27	84	157	112	112	282	67	340	200	77	125	109	312	109	233	109											
Middelburg	174	85	232	314	213	273	101	86	131	181	127	220	164	304	62	355	171	160	152	111	327	201	340	191	111										
Mons	272	112	304	206	275	166	171	132	68	46	244	94	199	369	119	428	288	144	213	78	400	129	233	157	92	188									
Namur	264	105	284	131	248	91	163	172	64	39	236	29	177	332	129	420	280	72	205	148	392	64	158	92	83	190	75								
Nijmegen	121	142	47	298	18	260	95	252	188	248	145	260	64	116	203	189	137	133	46	244	182	171	316	142	168	197	258	230							
Oostende	285	124	317	313	288	272	184	31	117	171	257	218	212	383	66	441	301	200	226	71	413	215	339	232	133	107	149	189	268						
Rotterdam	74	101	125	330	112	290	51	185	147	207	27	236	116	197	153	248	71	176	79	204	207	218	357	205	127	107	217	204	114	228					
Tilburg	114	73	120	302	93	248	25	183	119	179	109	207	42	188	133	261	130	90	31	175	242	159	328	130	99	126	188	178	74	199	79				
Tournai	285	123	316	253	287	212	184	82	88	93	257	140	211	382	71	440	300	180	225	28	412	175	279	204	119	137	50	119	268	99	227	198			
Turnhout	133	47	158	233	132	196	39	154	89	150	118	178	49	226	104	300	148	61	56	146	260	103	265	93	69	129	159	149	112	170	88	29	170		
Utrecht	38	125	69	337	62	299	68	235	171	231	67	260	87	141	185	190	54	154	52	227	162	210	380	181	151	166	241	230	77	251	56	80	251	99	
Zwolle	113	215	41	393	71	355	158	325	261	321	159	349	151	74	275	102	132	220	133	317	95	266	411	237	240	256	330	320	89	341	149	161	341	199	93

Amsterdam	Antwerpen	Bruxelles/Brussel	Luxembourg	Rotterdam	
1505	1344	1310	1148	1447	***Barcelona***
708	589	548	335	690	***Basel***
663	724	767	766	698	***Berlin***
804	684	643	430	785	***Bern***
688	527	519	733	630	***Birmingham***
1086	925	892	926	1029	***Bordeaux***
2030	1911	1870	1656	2012	***Brindisi***
1544	1383	1349	1384	1486	***Burgos***
789	628	595	721	732	***Cherbourg***
928	767	733	604	870	***Clermont-Ferrand***
437	390	394	238	450	***FrankfurtamMain***
920	761	720	507	862	***Genève***
772	1000	992	1206	725	***Glasgow***
471	558	601	629	506	***Hamburg***
381	442	485	492	417	***Hannover***
783	870	913	942	819	***København***
289	128	114	310	231	***Lille***
2250	2089	2055	2090	2192	***Lisboa***
486	325	318	532	429	***London***
928	769	728	515	871	***Lyon***
1776	1615	1582	1616	1719	***Madrid***
2266	2105	2072	2101	2209	***Málaga***
1240	1080	1039	826	1182	***Marseille***
1045	925	884	671	1027	***Milano***
836	775	722	509	822	***München***
889	728	694	728	831	***Nantes***
1814	1694	1653	1440	1796	***Napoli***
1277	1364	1407	1436	1313	***Oslo***
1814	1695	1654	1441	1796	***Palermo***
505	344	310	355	447	***Paris***
2075	1915	1881	1915	2018	***Porto***
874	847	891	727	866	***Praha***
1617	1497	1456	1243	1599	***Roma***
1325	1164	1130	1164	1267	***SanSebastián***
1451	1538	1581	1610	1486	***Stockholm***
594	475	434	221	576	***Strasbourg***
1113	943	902	689	1045	***Torino***
1185	1024	990	1025	1127	***Toulouse***
1813	1652	1618	1490	1755	***Valencia***
1219	1177	1136	923	1279	***Venezia***
1153	1106	1110	932	1166	***Wien***
1341	1293	1297	1078	1353	***Zagreb***

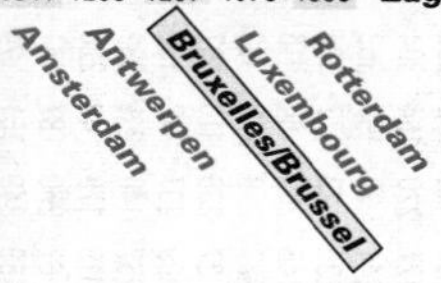

Bruxelles/Brussel-Madrid

1582 km

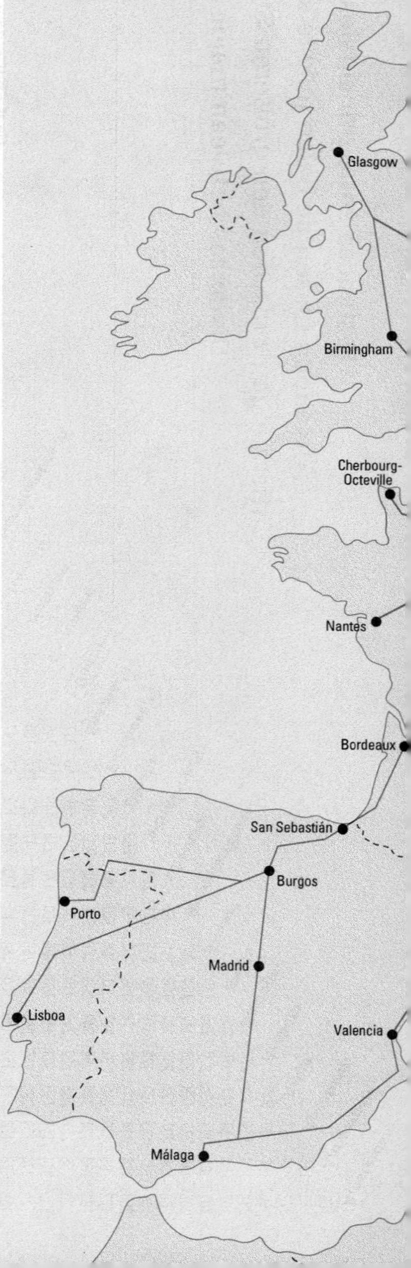

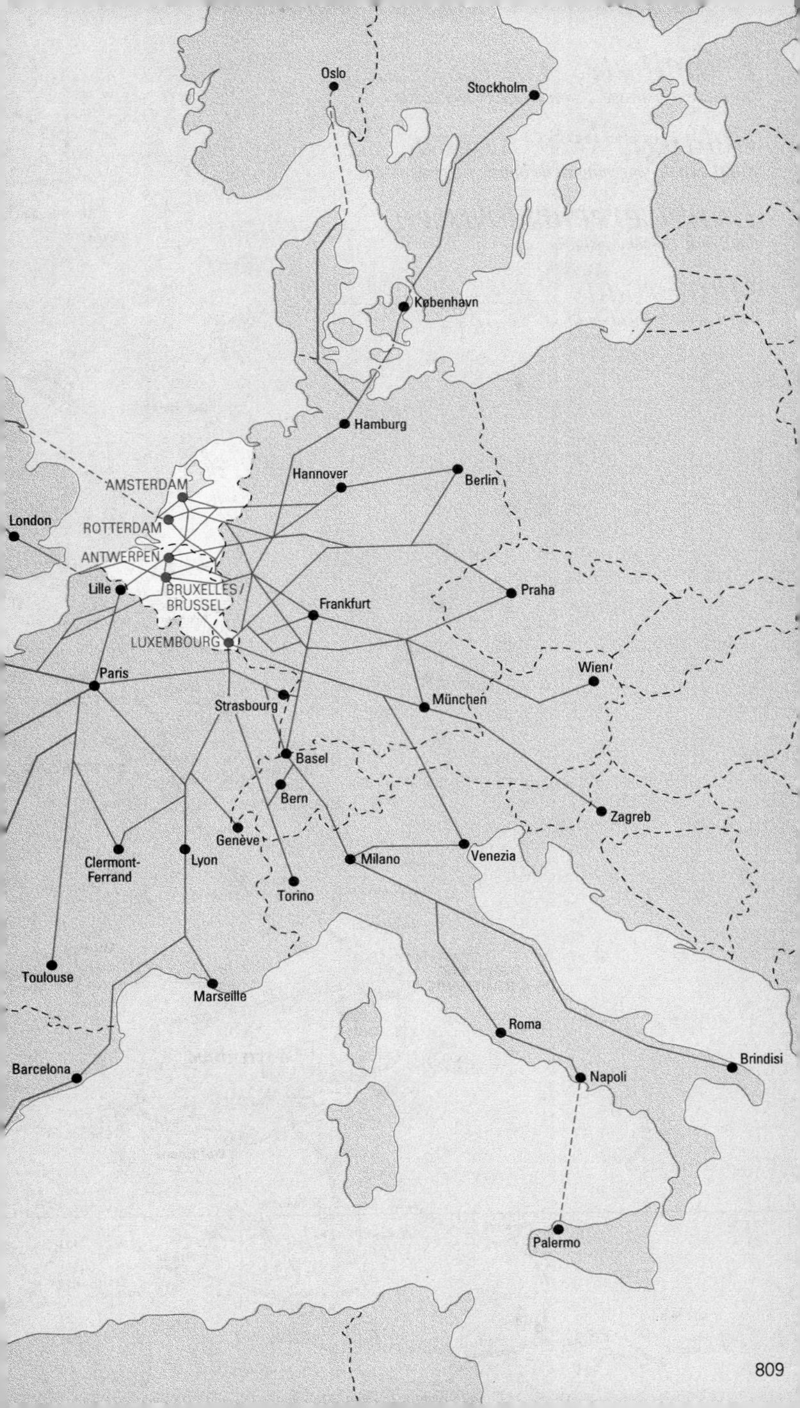
Oslo
Stockholm
København
Hamburg
Hannover
Berlin
AMSTERDAM
ROTTERDAM
London
ANTWERPEN
BRUXELLES/
BRUSSEL
Lille
Praha
Frankfurt
LUXEMBOURG
Paris
Wien
München
Strasbourg
Basel
Bern
Zagreb
Genève
Venezia
Milano
Clermont-
Ferrand
Lyon
Torino
Toulouse
Marseille
Roma
Brindisi
Barcelona
Napoli
Palermo

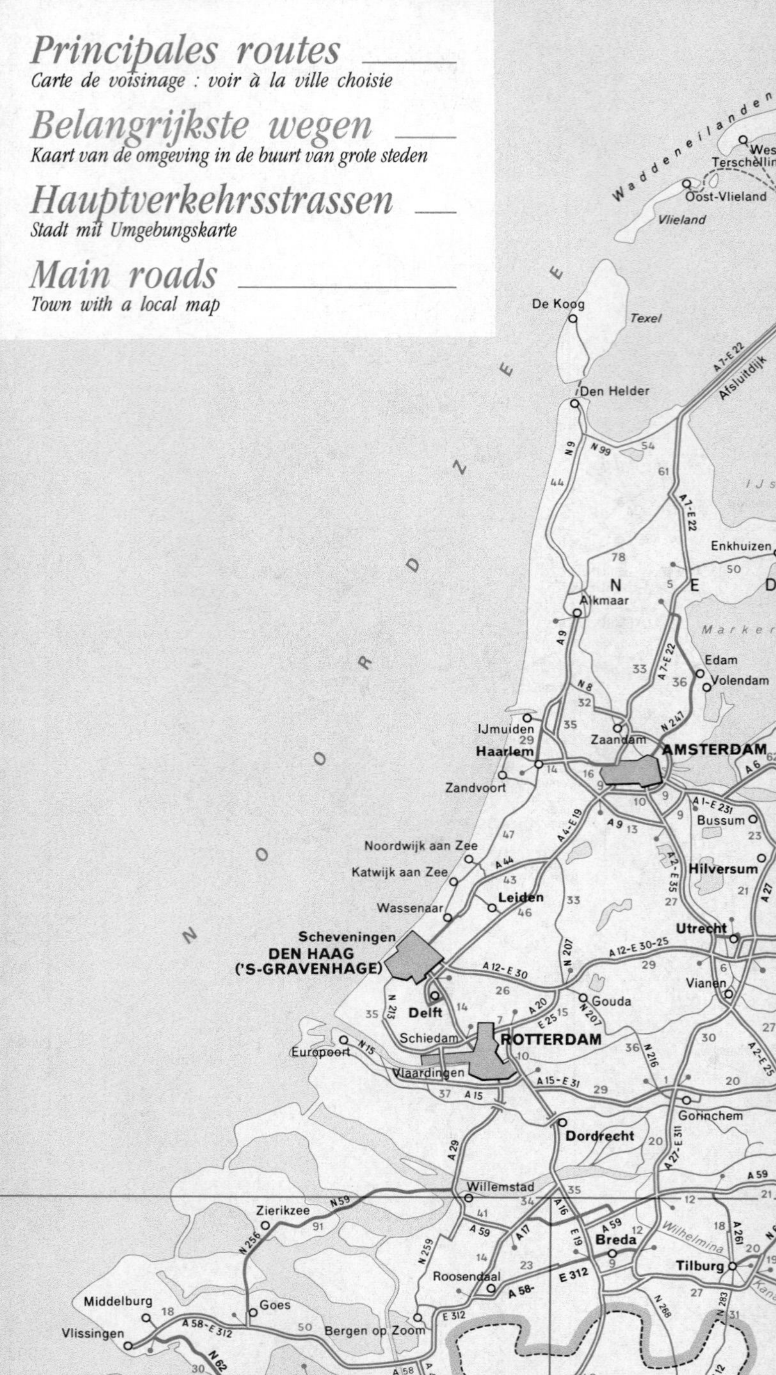

Principales routes
Carte de voisinage : voir à la ville choisie
Belangrijkste wegen
Kaart van de omgeving in de buurt van grote steden
Hauptverkehrsstrassen
Stadt mit Umgebungskarte
Main roads
Town with a local map
Waddeneilanden
West
Terschelling
Oost-Vlieland
Vlieland
De Koog
Texel
Den Helder
Afsluitdijk
A 7-E 22
N 9
N 99
Enkhuizen
Alkmaar
Marker
Edam
Volendam
N 8
IJmuiden
Zaandam
N 247
Haarlem
AMSTERDAM
A 6
Zandvoort
A 1-E 231
Bussum
A 9
A 4-E 19
Noordwijk aan Zee
A 44
Katwijk aan Zee
A 2-E 35
Hilversum
Leiden
A 27
Wassenaar
Utrecht
Scheveningen
DEN HAAG
('S-GRAVENHAGE)
A 12-E 30-25
N 207
A 12-E 30
Vianen
N 213
Delft
Gouda
A 20
E 25
Schiedam
ROTTERDAM
Europoort
N 15
N 216
Vlaardingen
A 2-E 25
A 15-E 31
A 15
Gorinchem
Dordrecht
A 29
A 27-E 311
A 59
Willemstad
A 16
Zierikzee
N 59
A 17
E 19
Breda
Wilhelmina
A 261
N 256
N 259
Tilburg
Roosendaal
E 312
A 58-
N 268
N 283
Middelburg
Goes
A 58-E 312
Vlissingen
Bergen op Zoom
N 62
A 58
N 12
N O O R D Z E E
N E D

Schiermonnikoog
Ameland
Nes
Eemshaven
Lauwersoog
Delfzijl
Holwerd
Dokkum
Groningen
Leeuwarden
Winschoten
Harlingen
Drachten
Bolsward
Sneek
Assen
Heerenvee
Ter Apel
Emmen
Steenwijk
Meppen
Emmeloord
Meppel
Hoogeveen
Kampen
Ommen
Zwolle
Lelystad
Almelo
Oldenzaal
Harderwijk
Epe
Hengelo
Deventer
Enschede
Apeldoorn
Amersfoort
Groenlo
Ede
Arnhem
Bocholt
Nijmegen
Gennep
Wesel
's-Hertogenbosch
Essen
Duisburg
Helmond
Eindhoven
Venlo
Wuppertal
Ems
Vecht
Berkel
Ijssel
WAAL
RHEIN
MAAS

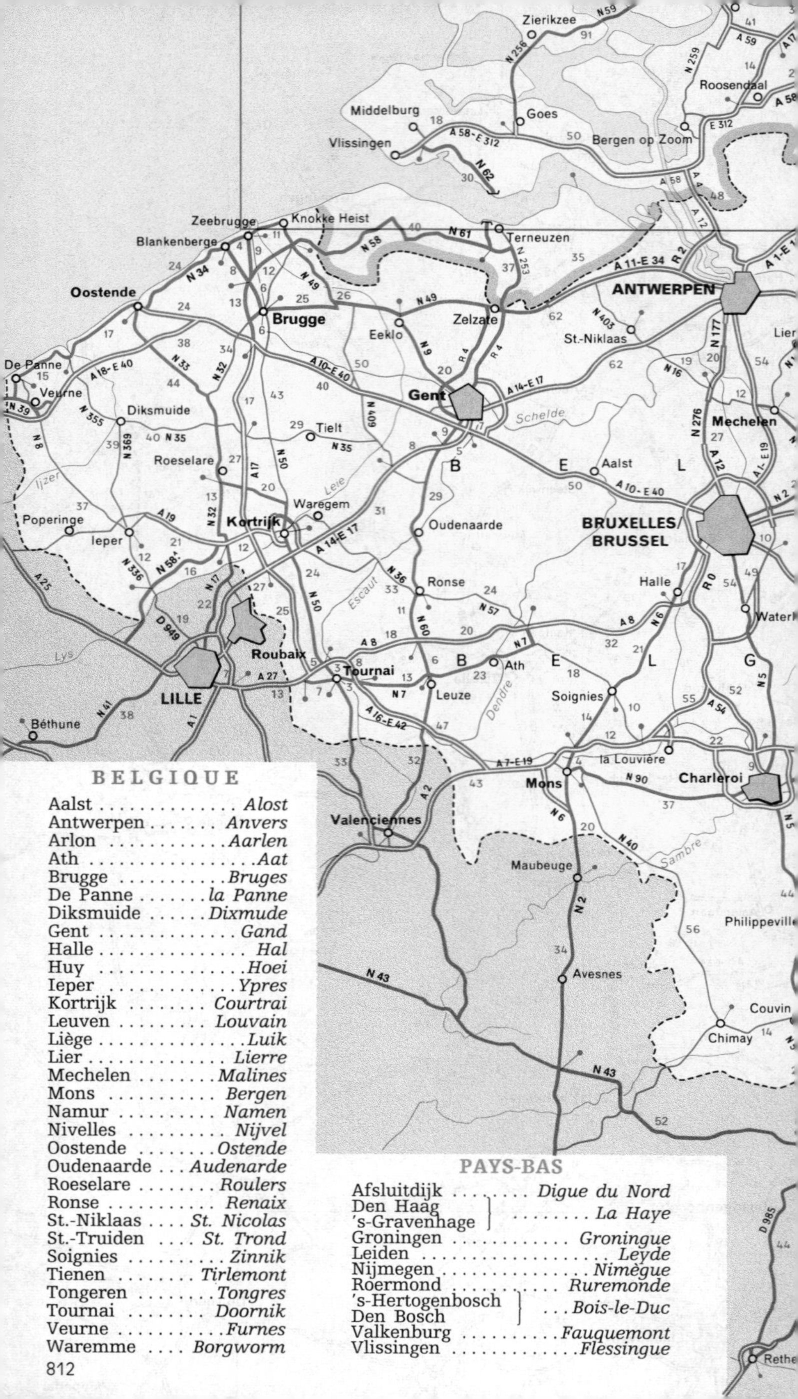

BELGIQUE

Aalst	*Alost*
Antwerpen	*Anvers*
Arlon	*Aarlen*
Ath	*Aat*
Brugge	*Bruges*
De Panne	*la Panne*
Diksmuide	*Dixmude*
Gent	*Gand*
Halle	*Hal*
Huy	*Hoei*
Ieper	*Ypres*
Kortrijk	*Courtrai*
Leuven	*Louvain*
Liège	*Luik*
Lier	*Lierre*
Mechelen	*Malines*
Mons	*Bergen*
Namur	*Namen*
Nivelles	*Nijvel*
Oostende	*Ostende*
Oudenaarde	*Audenarde*
Roeselare	*Roulers*
Ronse	*Renaix*
St.-Niklaas	*St. Nicolas*
St.-Truiden	*St. Trond*
Soignies	*Zinnik*
Tienen	*Tirlemont*
Tongeren	*Tongres*
Tournai	*Doornik*
Veurne	*Furnes*
Waremme	*Borgworm*

PAYS-BAS

Afsluitdijk	*Digue du Nord*
Den Haag / 's-Gravenhage	*La Haye*
Groningen	*Groningue*
Leiden	*Leyde*
Nijmegen	*Nimègue*
Roermond	*Ruremonde*
's-Hertogenbosch / Den Bosch	*Bois-le-Duc*
Valkenburg	*Fauquemont*
Vlissingen	*Flessingue*

Breda
Tilburg
Wilhelmina Kanaal
Eindhoven
Helmond
MAAS
Venlo
Turnhout
Weert
Roermond
Mönchengladbach
Albert Kanaal
Geel
Hechtel
Rur
BUNDESREPUBLIK
Aarschot
Demer
Diest
Genk
Hasselt
Heerlen
Leuven
Maastricht
Valkenburg
DEUTSCHLAND
St.-Truiden
Tienen
Tongeren
Aachen
Wavre
Hannut
Waremme
Liège
Eupen
Verviers
I Q U E
Huy
Meuse
Spa
Namur
Malmédy
Stavelot
Ourthe
Ciney
St.Vith
Dinant
Marche-en-Famenne
la Roche-en-A.
Prüm
Rochefort
Houffalize
Givet
Bre de Champlon
Wellin
Bastogne
Our
Esch
Semois
Diekirch
Ettelbrück
Echternach
Neufchâteau
Sûre
LUXEMBOURG
Bouillon
Charleville-Mézières
Arlon
Sedan
Longwy
Dudelange
Montmédy
Moselle
F R A N C E

Dans la même collection

In the same series

Deutschland
España & Portugal
Europe Main cities
France
Great Britain & Ireland
Ireland
Italia
London
Paris
Portugal
Suisse/Schweiz/Svizzera

Manufacture française des pneumatiques Michelin
Société en commandite par actions au capital de 304 000 000 EUR
Place des Carmes-Déchaux – 63 Clermont-Ferrand (France)
R.C.S. Clermont-Fd B 855 200 507

Michelin et Cie, propriétaires-éditeurs, 2004
Dépôt légal 02-2004 – ISBN 2-06-710243-5

Printed in Belgium : 12-2003/1

Compogravure : Maury Imprimeur S.A., Malesherbes.

Impression : Casterman à Tournai.

Reliure : S.I.R.C., Marigny-le-Châtel.

Illustrations : Introduction, Cécile Imbert/MICHELIN et Narratif Systèmes/Genclo.
Nomenclature, Rodolphe Corbel

SOLIDS (SPACE FIGURES):

L = Lateral Area; T (or S) = Total (Surface) Area; V = Volume

Parallelepiped (box):

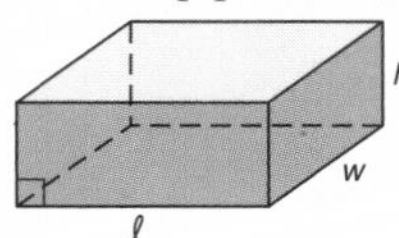

$T = 2\ell w + 2\ell h + 2wh$
$V = \ell wh$

Right Prism:

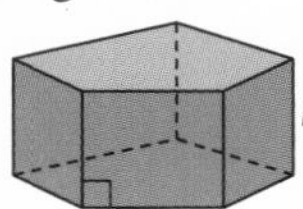

$L = hP$
$T = L + 2B$
$V = Bh$

Regular Pyramid:

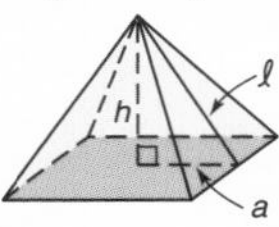

$L = \frac{1}{2}\ell P$
$\ell^2 = a^2 + h^2$
$T = L + B$
$V = \frac{1}{3}Bh$

Right Circular Cylinder:

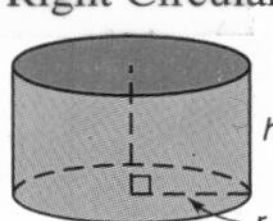

$L = 2\pi rh$
$T = 2\pi rh + 2\pi r^2$
$V = \pi r^2 h$

Right Circular Cone:

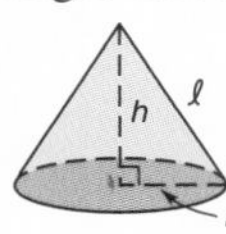

$L = \pi r\ell$
$\ell^2 = r^2 + h^2$
$T = \pi r\ell + \pi r^2$
$V = \frac{1}{3}\pi r^2 h$

Sphere:

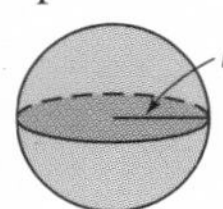

$S = 4\pi r^2$
$V = \frac{4}{3}\pi r^3$

Miscellaneous:
Euler's Equation: $V + F = E + 2$

dscproctor@smc.edu

ANALYTIC GEOMETRY:

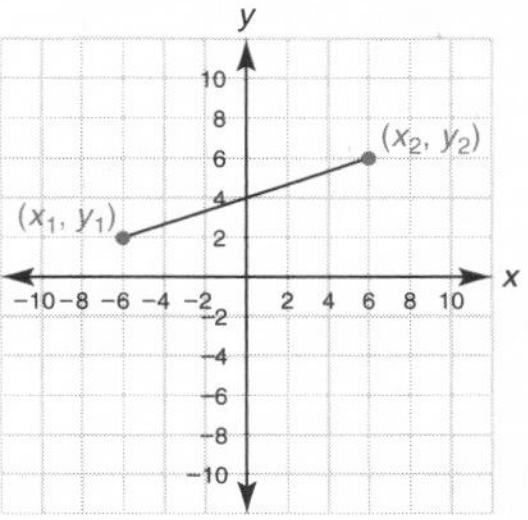

Distance:
$d = \sqrt{(x_2 - x_1)^2 + (y_2 - y_1)^2}$

Midpoint:
$M = \left(\frac{x_1 + x_2}{2}, \frac{y_1 + y_2}{2}\right)$

Slope: $m = \frac{y_2 - y_1}{x_2 - x_1}, x_1 \neq x_2$

Parallel Lines:
$\ell_1 \parallel \ell_2 \leftrightarrow m_1 = m_2$

Perpendicular Lines:
$\ell_1 \perp \ell_2 \leftrightarrow m_1 \cdot m_2 = -1$

Equations of a Line:
Slope-Intercept: $y = mx + b$
Point-Slope: $y - y_1 = m(x - x_1)$
General: $Ax + By = C$

TRIGONOMETRY:

Right Triangle:

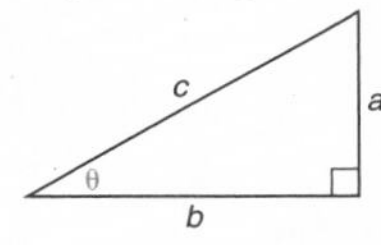

$\sin\theta = \frac{\text{opposite}}{\text{hypotenuse}} = \frac{a}{c}$

$\cos\theta = \frac{\text{adjacent}}{\text{hypotenuse}} = \frac{b}{c}$

$\tan\theta = \frac{\text{opposite}}{\text{adjacent}} = \frac{a}{b}$

$\sin^2\theta + \cos^2\theta = 1$

Triangle:

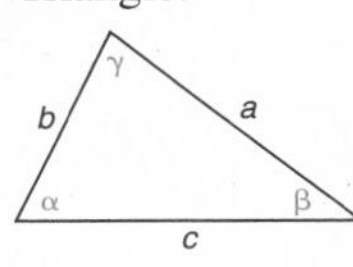

$A = \frac{1}{2}bc\sin\alpha$

$\frac{\sin\alpha}{a} = \frac{\sin\beta}{b} = \frac{\sin\gamma}{c}$

$c^2 = a^2 + b^2 - 2ab\cos\gamma$

or

$\cos\gamma = \frac{a^2 + b^2 - c^2}{2ab}$

Fifth Edition

Elementary Geometry for College Students

Daniel C. Alexander
Parkland College

Geralyn M. Koeberlein
Mahomet-Seymour High School

BROOKS/COLE
CENGAGE Learning™

Australia • Brazil • Japan • Korea • Mexico • Singapore • Spain • United Kingdom • United States

***Elementary Geometry for College Students,* Fifth Edition**
Daniel C. Alexander and Geralyn M. Koeberlein

Acquisitions Editor: Marc Bove
Assistant Editor: Shaun Williams
Editorial Assistant: Kyle O'Loughlin
Media Editor: Heleny Wong
Marketing Manager: Gordon Lee
Marketing Assistant: Erica O'Connell
Marketing Communications Manager: Katy Malatesta
Content Project Manager: Cheryll Linthicum
Creative Director: Rob Hugel
Art Director: Vernon Boes
Print Buyer: Linda Hsu
Rights Acquisitions Account Manager, Text: Tim Sisler
Rights Acquisitions Account Manager, Image: Don Schlotman
Production Service: Anne Seitz, Hearthside Publishing Services
Text Designer: Terri Wright
Art Editor: Leslie Lahr
Photo Researcher: Terri Wright
Copy Editor: Barbara Willette
Illustrator: Jade Myers, Matrix Art Services
Cover Designer: Terri Wright
Cover Image: Fancy Photography/Veer
Compositor: S4Carlisle Publishing Services

Library of Congress Control Number: 2009938196

Student Edition:

ISBN-13: 978-14390-4790-3

ISBN-10: 1-4390-4790-1

Brooks/Cole
20 Davis Drive
Belmont, CA 94002-3098
USA

Cengage Learning is a leading provider of customized learning solutions with office locations around the globe, including Singapore, the United Kingdom, Australia, Mexico, Brazil, and Japan. Locate your local office at **www.cengage.com/global**

Cengage Learning products are represented in Canada by Nelson Education, Ltd.

To learn more about Brooks/Cole visit **www.cengage.com/brookscole**

Purchase any of our products at your local college store or at our preferred online store **www.ichapters.com**

Printed in Canada
1 2 3 4 5 6 7 13 12 11 10 09

This edition is dedicated to our spouses, children, and grandchildren.
Dan Alexander and Geralyn Koeberlein

LETTER FROM THE AUTHOR

Through many years of teaching mathematics, particularly geometry, I found that geometry textbooks were lacking—lacking "whats, whys, and how tos." As I taught this subject, I amassed huge piles of notes that I used to supplement the text in class discussions and lectures. Because some explanations were so lacking in the textbooks, I found myself researching geometry to discover new and improved techniques, alternative approaches, and additional proofs and explanations. When unable to find what I sought, I often developed a more concise or more easily understood explanation of my own.

To contrast the presentation of geometry with a sportscast, geometry textbooks often appeared to me to provide the play-by-play without the color commentary. I found that entire topics might be missing and figures that would enable the student to "see" results intuitively were not always provided. The explanation of why a theorem must be true might be profoundly confusing, unnecessarily lengthy, or missing from the textbook altogether. Many geometry textbooks avoided proof and explanation as if they were a virus. Others would include proof, but not provide any suggestions or insights into the synthesis of proof.

During my years teaching at Parkland College, I was asked in the early 1980s to serve on the geometry textbook selection committee. Following the selection, I discovered serious flaws as I taught from the "best" textbook available. Really very shocking to me—I found that the textbook in use contained errors, including errors in logic that led to contradictions and even to more than one permissible answer for some problems.

At some point in the late 1980s, I began to envision a future for the compilation of my own notes and sample problems. There was, of course, the need for an outline of the textbook to be certain that it included all topics from elementary geometry. The textbook would have to be logical to provide a "stepping stone" approach for students. It would be developed so that it paved the way with explanation and proofs that could be read and understood and would provide enough guidance that a student could learn the vocabulary of geometry, recognize relationships visually, solve problems, and even create some proofs. Figures would be included if they provided an obvious relationship where an overly wordy statement of fact would be obscure. The textbook would have to provide many exercises, building blocks that in practice would transition the student from lower level to mid-range skills and also to more challenging problems.

In writing this textbook for college students, I have incorporated my philosophy for teaching geometry. With each edition, I have sought to improve upon an earlier form. I firmly believe that the student who is willing to study geometry as presented here will be well prepared for future study and will have developed skills of logic that are enduring and far-reaching.

Daniel C. Alexander

Contents

Preface

Elementary Geometry for College Students, Fifth Edition, was written in a style that was intended to teach students to explore principles of geometry, reason deductively, and perform geometric applications in the real world. This textbook has been written for many students: those who have never studied geometry, those who need a fresh approach, and those who need to look at geometry from a different perspective, including future teachers of geometry at many levels. Previous editions of this textbook have been well received and have been widely used in the geometry classroom.

Much as a classroom teacher would do, the authors (who have themselves been geometry teachers for many years) have written this textbook so that it introduces an idea with its relevant vocabulary, examines and explores the concept, develops a number of pertinent theories, verifies the theories deductively, and applies the concept in some real world situations. Throughout the textbook, our approach to geometry is largely visual, as it very well should be if the textbook is to be effective.

The concept of proof is rather sophisticated. It is our hope that students will grasp the significance of the role of proof in geometry, be able to understand the proofs that are provided, and even be able to generate some proofs themselves. The authors have provided proof in various formats: two-column, paragraph, and less formal "picture" proof. Because the creation of a proof requires logical sequencing of claims, it has far-reaching effects, expanding the student's ability to reason, to write a better paragraph or paper, and even to write better subroutines for a computer code.

The objectives of this textbook parallel the goals of many secondary level geometry programs. Content is heavily influenced by standards set by both the National Council of Teachers of Mathematics (NCTM) and the American Mathematical Association of Two-Year Colleges (AMATYC).

OUTCOMES FOR THE STUDENT

- Mastery of the essential concepts of geometry, for intellectual and vocational needs
- Preparation of the transfer student for further study of mathematics and geometry at the senior-level institution
- Understanding of the step-by-step reasoning necessary to fully develop a mathematical system such as geometry
- Enhancement of one's interest in geometry through discovery activities, features, and solutions to exercises

FEATURES NEW TO THE FIFTH EDITION

Use of a full-color format to aid in the development of concepts, solutions, and investigations through application of color to all figures and graphs. The author has overseen the introduction of color to all figures to insure that it is both accurate and instructionally meaningful.

Inclusion of approximately 150 new exercises, many of a challenging nature

Increased uniformity in the steps outlining construction techniques

Creation of a new Chapter 7 to isolate topics based upon locus and concurrence; this chapter can be treated as optional for a course with limited credit hours.

Inclusion of a new feature, *Strategy for Proof,* which provides insight into the development of proofs

Expanded coverage of regular polygons as found in Sections 7.3 and 8.3

TRUSTED FEATURES

Reminders found in the text margins provide a convenient recall mechanism.

Discover activities emphasize the importance of induction in the development of geometry.

Geometry in Nature and **Geometry in the Real World** illustrate geometry found in everyday life.

Tables found in chapter ending material organize important properties and other information from the chapter.

An **Index of Applications** calls attention to the practical applications of geometry.

A **Glossary of Terms** at the end of the textbook provides a quick reference of geometry terms.

Chapter opening photographs highlight subject matter for each chapter.

Warnings are provided so that students might avoid common pitfalls.

Chapter Summaries review the chapter, preview the chapter to follow, and provide a list of important concepts found in the current chapter.

Perspective on History boxes provide students with the context in which important theories of geometry were discovered.

Perspective on Application boxes explore classical applications and proofs.

Chapter Reviews provide numerous practice problems to help solidify student understanding of chapter concepts.

Chapter Tests provide students the opportunity to prepare for exams.

Formula pages at the front of the book list important formulas with relevant art to illustrate.

Reference pages at the back of the book summarize the important abbreviations and symbols used in the textbook.

STUDENT RESOURCES

Student Study Guide with Solutions Manual (1-439-04793-6) provides worked-out solutions to select odd-numbered problems from the text as well as new Interactive Exercise sets for additional review. Select solutions for the additional Interactive Exercise sets are provided within the study guide. Complete solutions are available on the instructors website.

Text-Specific DVDs (1-439-04795-2) hosted by Dana Mosely, provide professionally produced content that covers key topics of the text, offering a valuable resource to augment classroom instruction or independent study and review.

The Geometers Sketchpad CD-Rom (0-618-76840-8) helps you construct and measure geometric figures, explore properties and form conjectures, and create polished homework assignments and presentations. This CD-ROM is a must have resource for your classes.

STUDENT WEBSITE

Visit us on the web for access to a wealth of learning resources.

INSTRUCTOR RESOURCES

Instructor's Solutions Manual (0-538-73769-7) provides solutions to all the exercises in the book, alternatives for order of presentation of the topics included, transparency masters, and suggestions for teaching each topic.

PowerLecture with Examview (1-439-04797-9) This CD-ROM provides the instructor with dynamic media tools for teaching. Create, deliver, and customize tests (both print and online) in minutes with ExamView® Computerized Testing Featuring Algorithmic Equations. Easily build solution sets for homework or exams using Solution Builder's online solutions manual. Microsoft® PowerPoint® lecture slides, figures from the book, and Test Bank, in electronic format, are also included.

Text-Specific DVD's (1-439-04795-2) hosted by Dana Mosely, provide professionally produced content that covers key topics of the text, offering a valuable resource to augment classroom instruction or independent study and review.

The **Solution Builder** (1-439-04792-8) allows instructors to create customizable solutions that they can print out to distribute or post as needed. This is a convenient and expedient way to deliver solutions to specific homework sets.

The Geometer's Sketchpad CD-Rom (0-618-76840-8) helps users to construct and measure geometric figures, explore properties and form conjectures and create polished homework assignments and presentations. This CD-ROM is a must have resource for your classes.

INSTRUCTOR WEBSITE

Visit us on the web for access to a wealth of learning resources.

ACKNOWLEDGMENTS

We wish to thank Marc Bove, Acquisitions Editor; as well as these members of the team at Cengage Learning, Shaun Williams, Assistant Editor, Kyle O'Loughlin, Editorial Assistant, Maureen Ross, Senior Media Editor, Heleny Wong, Media Editor, Gordon Lee, Marketing Manager, Angela Kim, Marketing Assistant, and Mary Anne Payumo, Marketing Communications Manager. In addition, we would like to recognize and thank those who made earlier editions of this textbook possible: Beth Dahlke, Theresa Grutz, Florence Powers, Dawn Nuttall, Lynn Cox, Melissa Parkin, Noel Kamm, and Carol Merrigan.

We express our gratitude to reviewers of previous editions, including:

Paul Allen, *University of Alabama*
Jane C. Beatie, *University of South Carolina at Aiken*
Steven Blasberg, *West Valley College*
Barbara Brown, *Anoka Ramsey Community College*
Patricia Clark, *Indiana State University*
Joyce Cutler, *Framingham State College*
Walter Czarnec, *Framingham State College*
Darwin G. Dorn, *University of Wisconsin–Washington County*
William W. Durand, *Henderson State University*
Zoltan Fischer, *Minneapolis Community and Technical College*
Kathryn E. Godshalk, *Cypress College*
Chris Graham, *Mt. San Antonio Community College*

Sharon Gronberg, *Southwest Texas State University*
Geoff Hagopian, *College of the Desert*
Edith Hays, *Texas Woman's University*
Ben L. Hill, *Lane Community College*
George L. Holloway, *Los Angeles Valley College*
Tracy Hoy, *College of Lake County*
Josephine G. Lane, *Eastern Kentucky University*
John C. Longnecker, *University of Northern Iowa*
Erin C. Martin, *Parkland College*
Nicholas Martin, *Shepherd College*
Jill McKenney, *Lane Community College*
James R. McKinney, *Cal Poly at Pomona*
Iris C. McMurtry, *Motlow State Community College*
Michael Naylor, *Western Washington University*
Maurice Ngo, *Chabot College*
Ellen L. Rebold, *Brookdale Community College*
Lauri Semarne, *Los Angeles, California*
Patty Shovanec, *Texas Technical University*
Marvin Stick, *University of Massachusetts–Lowell*
Joseph F. Stokes, *Western Kentucky University*
Kay Stroope, *Phillips Community College–University of Arkansas*
Dr. John Stroyls, *Georgia Southwestern State University*
Karen R. Swick, *Palm Beach Atlantic College*
Steven L. Thomassin, *Ventura College*
Bettie A. Truitt, Ph.D., *Black Hawk College*
Jean A. Vrechek, *Sacramento City College*
Tom Zerger, *Saginaw Valley State University*

Foreword

In the Fifth Edition of *Elementary Geometry for College Students,* the topics that comprise a minimal course include most of Chapters 1–6 and Chapter 8. For a complete basic course, coverage of Chapters 1–8 is recommended. Some sections that can be treated as optional in formulating a course description include the following:

- Section 2.6 Symmetry and Transformations
- Section 3.4 Basic Constructions Justified
- Section 3.5 Inequalities in a Triangle
- Section 5.6 Segments Divided Proportionally
- Section 6.4 Some Constructions and Inequalities for the Circle
- Section 7.1 Locus of Points
- Section 7.2 Concurrence of Lines
- Section 7.3 More About Regular Polygons
- Section 8.5 More Area Relationships in the Circle

Given that this textbook is utilized for three-, four-, and five-hour courses, the following flowchart depicts possible orders in which the textbook can be used. As suggested by the preceding paragraph, it is possible to treat certain sections as optional.

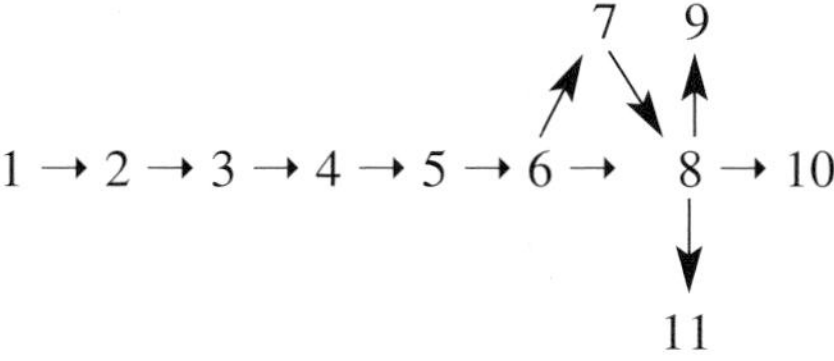

For students who need further review of related algebraic topics, consider these topics found in Appendix A:

A.1: Algebraic Expressions
A.2: Formulas and Equations
A.3: Inequalities
A.4: Quadratic Equations

Section A.4 includes these methods of solving quadratic equations: the factoring method, the square roots method, and the Quadratic Formula.

Logic appendices can be found at the textbook website. These include:

Logic Appendix 1: Truth Tables
Logic Appendix 2: Valid Arguments

Daniel C. Alexander and Geralyn M. Koeberlein

Index of Applications

Line and Angle Relationships

Chapter 1

CHAPTER OUTLINE

Additional Video explanation of concepts, sample problems, and applications are available on DVD. 

Magical! In geometry, figures can be devised so that an illusion is created. M. C. Escher (1898–1971), an artist known for his complicated optical illusions, created the "Waterfall" in 1961. Careful inspection of the figure draws attention to the perception that water can flow uphill. Even though the tower on the left is one story taller than the tower on the right, the two appear to have the same height. Escher's works often have the observer question his reasoning. This chapter opens with a discussion of statements and the types of reasoning used in geometry. Section 1.2 focuses upon the tools of geometry, such as the ruler and the protractor. The remainder of the chapter begins the formal and logical development of geometry by considering the relationships between lines and angles. For any student who needs an algebra refresher, selected topics can be found in the appendices of this textbook. Other techniques from algebra are reviewed or developed in conjunction with related topics of geometry. An introduction to logic can be found at our website.

1.1 Sets, Statements, and Reasoning

KEY CONCEPTS

Statement	Conclusion	Set
Variable	Intuition	Subset
Conjunction	Induction	Intersection
Disjunction	Deduction	Union
Negation	Argument (Valid and Invalid)	Venn Diagram
Implication (Conditional)	Law of Detachment	
Hypothesis		

A **set** is any collection of objects, all of which are known as the *elements* of the set. The statement $A = \{1, 2, 3\}$ is read, "A is the set of elements 1, 2, and 3." In geometry, geometric figures such as lines and angles are actually sets of points.

Where $A = \{1, 2, 3\}$ and $B = \{\text{counting numbers}\}$, A is a *subset* of B because each element in A is also in B; in symbols, $A \subseteq B$. In Chapter 2, we will discover that $T = \{\text{all triangles}\}$ is a subset of $P = \{\text{all polygons}\}$.

STATEMENTS

DEFINITION

A **statement** is a set of words and symbols that collectively make a claim that can be classified as true or false.

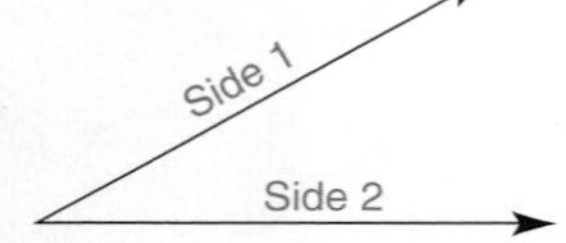

Figure 1.1

EXAMPLE 1

Classify each of the following as a true statement, a false statement, or neither.

1. $4 + 3 = 7$
2. An angle has two sides. (See Figure 1.1.)
3. Robert E. Lee played shortstop for the Yankees.
4. $7 < 3$ (This is read, "7 is less than 3.")
5. Look out!

Solution 1 and 2 are true statements; 3 and 4 are false statements; 5 is not a statement. ■

Some statements contain one or more *variables;* a **variable** is a letter that represents a number. The claim "$x + 5 = 6$" is called an *open sentence* or *open statement* because it can be classified as true or false, depending on the replacement value of x. For instance, $x + 5 = 6$ is true if $x = 1$; for x not equal to 1, $x + 5 = 6$ is false. Some statements containing variables are classified as true because they are true for all replacements. Consider the Commutative Property of Addition, usually stated in the form $a + b = b + a$. In words, this property states that the same result is obtained when two numbers are added in either order; for instance, when $a = 4$ and $b = 7$, it follows that $4 + 7 = 7 + 4$.

The **negation** of a given statement P makes a claim opposite that of the original statement. If the given statement is true, its negation is false, and vice versa. If P is a statement, we use $\sim P$ (which is read "not P") to indicate its negation.

EXAMPLE 2

Give the negation of each statement.

a) $4+3=7$ b) All fish can swim.

Solution

a) $4+3 \neq 7$ ($\neq$ means "is not equal to.")

b) Some fish cannot swim. (To negate "All fish can swim," we say that at least one fish cannot swim.)

TABLE 1.1
The Conjunction

P	*Q*	*P* and *Q*
T	T	T
T	F	F
F	T	F
F	F	F

A *compound* statement is formed by combining other statements used as "building blocks." In such cases, we may use letters such as P and Q to represent simple statements. For example, the letter P may refer to the statement "$4+3=7$," and the letter Q to the statement "Babe Ruth was a U.S. president." The statement "$4+3=7$ *and* Babe Ruth was a U.S. president" has the form P *and* Q and is known as the **conjunction** of P and Q. The statement "$4+3=7$ *or* Babe Ruth was a U.S. president" has the form P *or* Q and is known as the **disjunction** of P and Q. A conjunction is true only when P and Q are *both* true. A disjunction is false only when P and Q are *both* false. See Tables 1.1 and 1.2.

TABLE 1.2
The Disjunction

P	*Q*	*P* or *Q*
T	T	T
T	F	T
F	T	T
F	F	F

EXAMPLE 3

Assume that statements P and Q are true.

P: $4+3=7$
Q: An angle has two sides.

Classify the following statements as true or false.

1. $4+3 \neq 7$ and an angle has two sides.
2. $4+3 \neq 7$ or an angle has two sides.

Solution Statement 1 is false because the conjunction has the form "F and T." Statement 2 is true because the disjunction has the form "F or T."

The statement "If P, then Q," known as a **conditional statement** (or **implication**), is classified as true or false as a whole. A statement of this form can be written in equivalent forms; for instance, the conditional statement "If an angle is a right angle, then it measures 90 degrees" is equivalent to the statement "All right angles measure 90 degrees."

EXAMPLE 4

Classify each conditional statement as true or false.

1. If an animal is a fish, then it can swim. (States, "All fish can swim.")
2. If two sides of a triangle are equal in length, then two angles of the triangle are equal in measure. (See Figure 1.2 on page 4.)

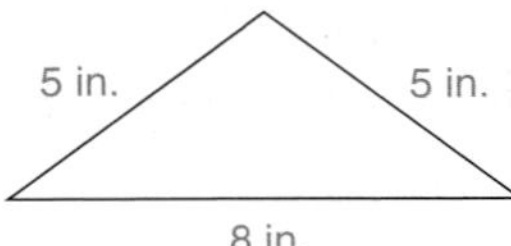

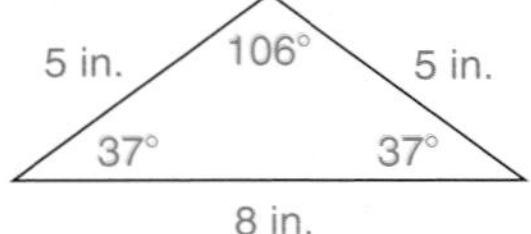

Figure 1.2

3. If Wendell studies, then he will receive an A on the test.

Solution Statements 1 and 2 are true. Statement 3 is false; Wendell may study yet not receive an A. ■

In the conditional statement "If P, then Q," P is the **hypothesis** and Q is the **conclusion.** In statement 2 of Example 4, we have

Hypothesis: Two sides of a triangle are equal in length.

Conclusion: Two angles of the triangle are equal in measure.

Exs. 1–7

For the true statement "If P, then Q," the hypothetical situation described in P implies the conclusion described in Q. This type of statement is often used in reasoning, so we turn our attention to this matter.

REASONING

Success in the study of geometry requires vocabulary development, attention to detail and order, supporting claims, and thinking. **Reasoning** is a process based on experience and principles that allow one to arrive at a conclusion. The following types of reasoning are used to develop mathematical principles.

1. Intuition	An inspiration leading to the statement of a theory
2. Induction	An organized effort to test and validate the theory
3. Deduction	A formal argument that proves the tested theory

▶ *Intuition*

We are often inspired to think and say, "It occurs to me that. . . ." With **intuition,** a sudden insight allows one to make a statement without applying any formal reasoning. When intuition is used, we sometimes err by "jumping" to conclusions. In a cartoon, the character having the "bright idea" (using intuition) is shown with a light bulb next to her or his head.

EXAMPLE 5

Figure 1.3 is called a *regular pentagon* because its five sides have equal lengths and its angles have equal measures. What do you suspect is true of the lengths of the dashed parts of lines from B to E and from B to D?

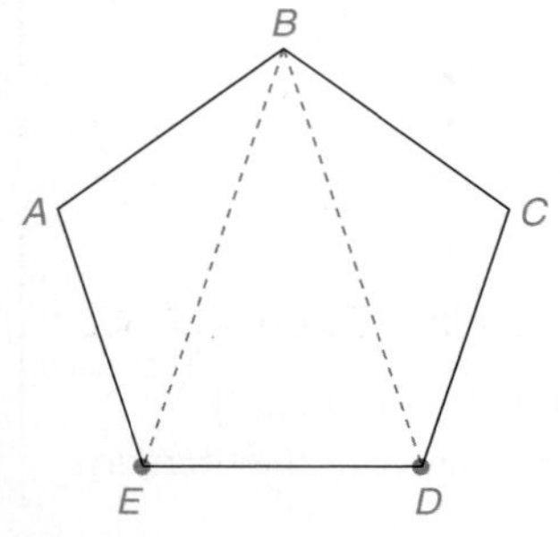

Figure 1.3

Solution Intuition suggests that the lengths of the dashed parts of lines (known as *diagonals* of the pentagon) are the same.

NOTE 1: A *ruler* can be used to verify that this claim is true. We will discuss measurement with the ruler in more detail in Section 1.2.

NOTE 2: Using methods found in Chapter 3, we could use deduction to prove that the two diagonals do indeed have the same length. ■

The role intuition plays in formulating mathematical thoughts is truly significant. But to have an idea is not enough! Testing a theory may lead to a revision of the theory or even to its total rejection. If a theory stands up to testing, it moves one step closer to becoming mathematical law.

▶ *Induction*

We often use specific observations and experiments to draw a general conclusion. This type of reasoning is called **induction.** As you would expect, the observation/experimentation process is common in laboratory and clinical settings. Chemists, physicists, doctors, psychologists, weather forecasters, and many others use collected data as a basis for drawing conclusions . . . and so will we!

EXAMPLE 6

While in a grocery store, you examine several 8-oz cartons of yogurt. Although the flavors and brands differ, each carton is priced at 75 cents. What do you conclude?

Conclusion Every 8-oz carton of yogurt in the store costs 75 cents. ■

As you may already know (see Figure 1.2), a figure with three straight sides is called a *triangle.*

EXAMPLE 7

In a geometry class, you have been asked to measure the three interior angles of each triangle in Figure 1.4. You discover that triangles I, II, and IV have two angles (as marked) that have equal measures. What may you conclude?

Conclusion The triangles that have two sides of equal length also have two angles of equal measure.

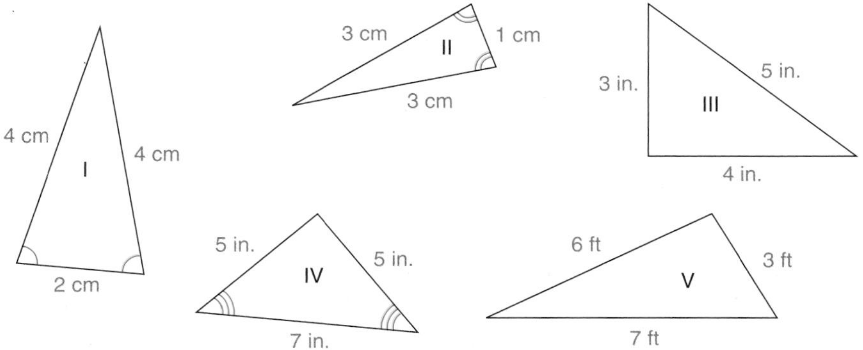

Figure 1.4

NOTE: A *protractor* can be used to support the conclusion found in Example 7. We will discuss the protractor in Section 1.2. ■

▶ *Deduction*

DEFINITION

Deduction is the type of reasoning in which the knowledge and acceptance of selected assumptions guarantee the truth of a particular conclusion.

In Example 8, we will illustrate the form of deductive reasoning used most frequently in the development of geometry. In this form, known as a **valid argument,** at least two statements are treated as facts; these assumptions are called the *premises* of the argument. On the basis of the premises, a particular *conclusion* must follow. This form of deduction is called the Law of Detachment.

EXAMPLE 8

If you accept the following statements 1 and 2 as true, what must you conclude?

1. If a student plays on the Rockville High School boys' varsity basketball team, then he is a talented athlete.
2. Todd plays on the Rockville High School boys' varsity basketball team.

Conclusion Todd is a talented athlete. ■

To more easily recognize this pattern for deductive reasoning, we use letters to represent statements in the following generalization.

LAW OF DETACHMENT

Let P and Q represent simple statements, and assume that statements 1 and 2 are true. Then a valid argument having conclusion C has the form

1. If P, then Q } premises
2. P

C. $\therefore Q$ } conclusion

NOTE: The symbol $\therefore$ means "therefore."

In the preceding form, the statement "If P, then Q" is often read "P implies Q." That is, when P is known to be true, Q must follow.

EXAMPLE 9

Is the following argument valid? Assume that premises 1 and 2 are true.

1. If it is raining, then Tim will stay in the house.
2. It is raining.

C. $\therefore$ Tim will stay in the house.

Conclusion The argument is valid because the form of the argument is

1. If P, then Q
2. P

C. $\therefore Q$

with P = "It is raining," and Q = "Tim will stay in the house." ■

EXAMPLE 10

Is the following argument valid? Assume that premises 1 and 2 are true.

1. If a man lives in London, then he lives in England.
2. William lives in England.

C. ∴ William lives in London.

Conclusion The argument is not valid. Here, P = "A man lives in London," and Q = "A man lives in England." Thus, the form of this argument is

1. If P, then Q
2. Q

C. $\therefore P$

But the Law of Detachment does not handle the question "If Q, then what?" Even though statement Q is true, it does not enable us to draw a valid conclusion about P. Of course, if William lives in England, he *might* live in London; but he might instead live in Liverpool, Manchester, Coventry, or any of countless other places in England. Each of these possibilities is a **counterexample** disproving the validity of the argument. Remember that deductive reasoning is concerned with reaching conclusions that *must be true,* given the truth of the premises. ■

Warning

In the box, the argument on the left is valid and patterned after Example 9. The argument on the right is invalid; this form was given in Example 10.

VALID ARGUMENT	INVALID ARGUMENT
1. If P, then Q	1. If P, then Q
2. P	2. Q
C. $\therefore Q$	C. $\therefore P$

We will use deductive reasoning throughout our work in geometry. For example, suppose that you know these two facts:

SSG *Exs. 8–12*

1. If an angle is a right angle, then it measures 90°.
2. Angle A is a right angle.

Then you may conclude

C. Angle A measures 90°.

VENN DIAGRAMS

Sets of objects are often represented by geometric figures known as *Venn Diagrams.* Their creator, John Venn, was an Englishman who lived from 1834 to 1923. In a Venn Diagram, each set is represented by a closed (bounded) figure such as a circle or rectangle. If statements P and Q of the conditional statement "If P, then Q" are represented by sets of objects P and Q, respectively, then the Law of Detachment can be justified

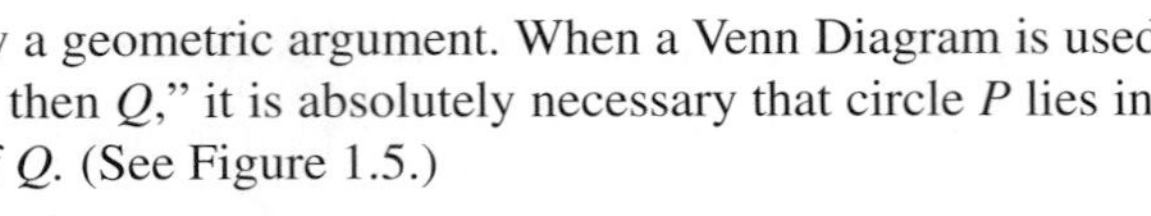

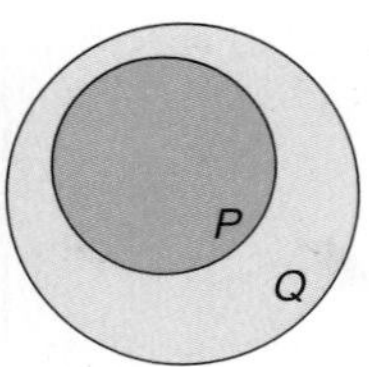

If P, then Q.

Figure 1.5

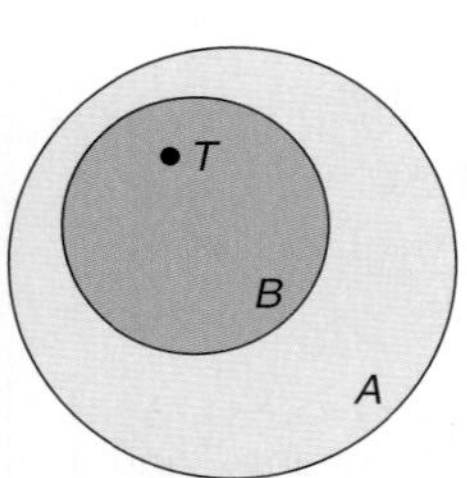

Figure 1.6

Discover

In the St. Louis area, an interview of 100 sports enthusiasts shows that 74 support the Cardinals baseball team and 58 support the Rams football team. All of those interviewed support one team or the other or both. How many support both teams?

ANSWER

32; 74 + 58 − 100

by a geometric argument. When a Venn Diagram is used to represent the statement "If P, then Q," it is absolutely necessary that circle P lies in circle Q; that is, P is a *subset* of Q. (See Figure 1.5.)

EXAMPLE 11

Use Venn Diagrams to verify Example 8.

Solution Let B = students on the Rockville High varsity boys' basketball team.

Let A = people who are talented athletes.
To represent the statement "If a basketball player (B), then a talented athlete (A)," we show B within A. In Figure 1.6 we use point T to represent Todd, a person on the basketball team (T in B). With point T also in circle A, we conclude that "Todd is a talented athlete." ■

The statement "If P, then Q" is sometimes expressed in the form "All P are Q." For instance, the conditional statement of Examples 8 and 11 can be written "All Rockville high school players are talented athletes." Venn Diagrams can also be used to demonstrate that the argument of Example 10 is not valid. To show the invalidity of the argument in Example 10, one must show that an object in Q may *not* lie in circle P. (See Figure 1.5.)

The compound statements known as the conjunction and the disjunction can also be related to the intersection and union of sets, relationships that can be illustrated by the use of Venn Diagrams. For the Venn Diagram, we assume that the sets P and Q may have elements in common. (See Figure 1.7.)

The elements common to P and Q form the **intersection** of P and Q, which is written $P \cap Q$. This set, $P \cap Q$, is the set of all elements in *both P* **and** Q. The elements that are in P, in Q, or in both form the **union** of P and Q, which is written $P \cup Q$. This set, $P \cup Q$, is the set of elements in P **or** Q.

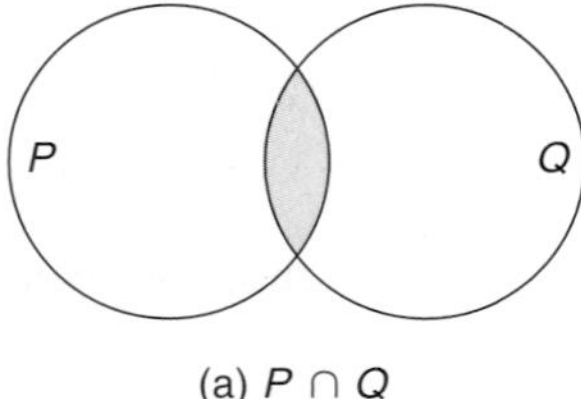

(a) $P \cap Q$

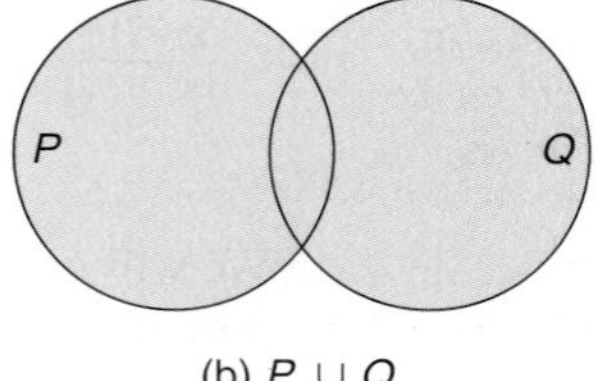

(b) $P \cup Q$

SSG *Exs. 13–15*

Figure 1.7

Exercises 1.1

In Exercises 1 and 2, which sentences are statements? If a sentence is a statement, classify it as true or false.

1. a) Where do you live?
b) $4 + 7 \neq 5$.
c) Washington was the first U.S. president.
d) $x + 3 = 7$ when $x = 5$.

2. a) Chicago is located in the state of Illinois.
b) Get out of here!
c) $x < 6$ (read as "x is less than 6") when $x = 10$.
d) Babe Ruth is remembered as a great football player.

In Exercises 3 and 4, give the negation of each statement.

3. a) Christopher Columbus crossed the Atlantic Ocean.
b) All jokes are funny.

4. a) No one likes me.
b) Angle 1 is a right angle.

In Exercises 5 to 10, classify each statement as simple, conditional, a conjunction, or a disjunction.

5. If Alice plays, the volleyball team will win.
6. Alice played and the team won.
7. The first-place trophy is beautiful.
8. An integer is odd or it is even.
9. Matthew is playing shortstop.
10. You will be in trouble if you don't change your ways.

In Exercises 11 to 18, state the hypothesis and the conclusion of each statement.

11. If you go to the game, then you will have a great time.
12. If two chords of a circle have equal lengths, then the arcs of the chords are congruent.
13. If the diagonals of a parallelogram are perpendicular, then the parallelogram is a rhombus.
14. If $\frac{a}{b} = \frac{c}{d}$, where $b \neq 0$ and $d \neq 0$, then $a \cdot d = b \cdot c$.
15. Corresponding angles are congruent if two parallel lines are cut by a transversal.
16. Vertical angles are congruent when two lines intersect.
17. All squares are rectangles.
18. Base angles of an isosceles triangle are congruent.

In Exercises 19 to 24, classify each statement as true or false.

19. If a number is divisible by 6, then it is divisible by 3.
20. Rain is wet and snow is cold.
21. Rain is wet or snow is cold.
22. If Jim lives in Idaho, then he lives in Boise.
23. Triangles are round or circles are square.
24. Triangles are square or circles are round.

In Exercises 25 to 32, name the type of reasoning (if any) used.

25. While participating in an Easter egg hunt, Sarah notices that each of the seven eggs she has found is numbered. Sarah concludes that all eggs used for the hunt are numbered.
26. You walk into your geometry class, look at the teacher, and conclude that you will have a quiz today.
27. Albert knows the rule "If a number is added to each side of an equation, then the new equation has the same solution set as the given equation." Given the equation $x - 5 = 7$, Albert concludes that $x = 12$.
28. You believe that "Anyone who plays major league baseball is a talented athlete." Knowing that Duane Gibson has just been called up to the major leagues, you conclude that Duane Gibson is a talented athlete.
29. As a handcuffed man is brought into the police station, you glance at him and say to your friend, "That fellow looks guilty to me."
30. While judging a science fair project, Mr. Cange finds that each of the first 5 projects is outstanding and concludes that all 10 will be outstanding.
31. You know the rule "If a person lives in the Santa Rosa Junior College district, then he or she will receive a tuition break at Santa Rosa." Candace tells you that she has received a tuition break. You conclude that she resides in the Santa Rosa Junior College district.
32. As Mrs. Gibson enters the doctor's waiting room, she concludes that it will be a long wait.

In Exercises 33 to 36, use intuition to state a conclusion.

33. You are told that the opposite angles formed when two lines cross are **vertical angles.** In the figure, angles 1 and 2 are vertical angles. Conclusion?

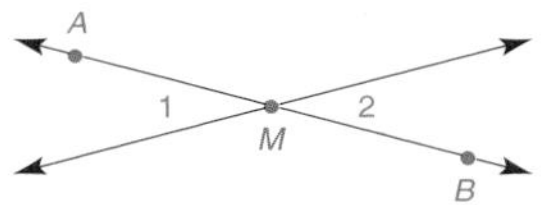

Exercises 33, 34

34. In the figure, point M is called the **midpoint** of line segment AB. Conclusion?
35. The two triangles shown are **similar** to each other. Conclusion?

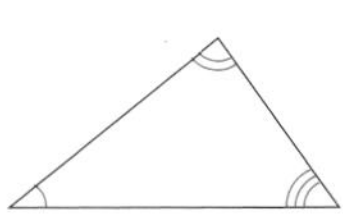
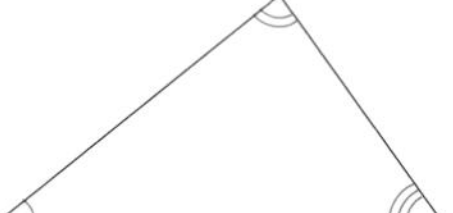

36. Observe (but do not measure) the following angles. Conclusion?

In Exercises 37 to 40, use induction to state a conclusion.

37. Several movies directed by Lawrence Garrison have won Academy Awards, and many others have received nominations. His latest work, *A Prisoner of Society,* is to be released next week. Conclusion?
38. On Monday, Matt says to you, "Andy hit his little sister at school today." On Tuesday, Matt informs you, "Andy threw his math book into the wastebasket during class." On Wednesday, Matt tells you, "Because Andy was throwing peas in the school cafeteria, he was sent to the principal's office." Conclusion?

39. While searching for a classroom, Tom stopped at an instructor's office to ask directions. On the office bookshelves are books titled *Intermediate Algebra, Calculus, Modern Geometry, Linear Algebra,* and *Differential Equations.* Conclusion?

40. At a friend's house, you see several food items, including apples, pears, grapes, oranges, and bananas. Conclusion?

In Exercises 41 to 50, use deduction to state a conclusion, if possible.

41. If the sum of the measures of two angles is 90°, then these angles are called "complementary." Angle 1 measures 27° and angle 2 measures 63°. Conclusion?

42. If a person attends college, then he or she will be a success in life. Kathy Jones attends Dade County Community College. Conclusion?

43. All mathematics teachers have a strange sense of humor. Alex is a mathematics teacher. Conclusion?

44. All mathematics teachers have a strange sense of humor. Alex has a strange sense of humor. Conclusion?

45. If Stewart Powers is elected president, then every family will have an automobile. Every family has an automobile. Conclusion?

46. If Tabby is meowing, then she is hungry. Tabby is hungry. Conclusion?

47. If a person is involved in politics, then that person will be in the public eye. June Jesse has been elected to the Missouri state senate. Conclusion?

48. If a student is enrolled in a literature course, then he or she will work very hard. Bram Spiegel digs ditches by hand 6 days a week. Conclusion?

49. If a person is rich and famous, then he or she is happy. Marilyn is wealthy and well-known. Conclusion?

50. If you study hard and hire a tutor, then you will make an A in this course. You make an A in this course. Conclusion?

In Exercises 51 to 54, use Venn Diagrams to determine whether the argument is valid or not valid.

51. (1) If an animal is a cat, then it makes a "meow" sound.
(2) Tipper is a cat.
(C) Then Tipper makes a "meow" sound.

52. (1) If an animal is a cat, then it makes a "meow" sound.
(2) Tipper makes a "meow" sound.
(C) Then Tipper is a cat.

53. (1) All Boy Scouts serve the United States of America.
(2) Sean serves the United States of America.
(C) Sean is a Boy Scout.

54. (1) All Boy Scouts serve the United States of America.
(2) Sean is a Boy Scout.
(C) Sean serves the United States of America.

55. Where $A = \{1,2,3\}$ and $B = \{2,4,6,8\}$, classify each of the following as true or false.
(a) $A \cap B = \{2\}$
(b) $A \cup B = \{1,2,3,4,6,8\}$
(c) $A \subseteq B$

1.2 Informal Geometry and Measurement

KEY CONCEPTS

Point	Midpoint	Perpendicular
Line	Congruence	Compass
Plane	Protractor	Constructions
Collinear Points	Parallel	Circle
Line Segment	Bisect	Arc
Betweenness of Points	Intersect	Radius

In geometry, the terms *point, line,* and *plane* are described but not defined. Other concepts that are accepted intuitively, but never defined, include the *straightness* of a line, the *flatness* of a plane, the notion that a point on a line lies *between* two other points on the line, and the notion that a point lies in the *interior* or *exterior* of an angle. Some of the terms found in this section are formally defined in later sections of Chapter 1. The following are descriptions of some of the undefined terms.

A **point,** which is represented by a dot, has location but not size; that is, a point has no dimensions. An uppercase italic letter is used to name a point. Figure 1.8 shows points *A, B,* and *C.* ("Point" may be abbreviated "pt." for convenience.)

A B C

Figure 1.8

The second undefined term is **line.** A line is an infinite set of points. Given any two points on a line, there is always a point that lies between them on that line. Lines have a quality of "straightness" that is not defined but assumed. Given several points on a

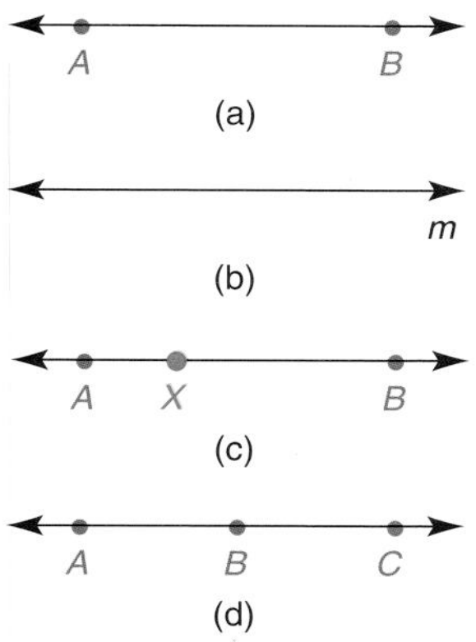

Figure 1.9

line, these points form a straight path. Whereas a point has no dimensions, a line is one-dimensional; that is, the distance between any two points on a given line can be measured. Line *AB*, represented symbolically by $\overleftrightarrow{AB}$, extends infinitely far in opposite directions, as suggested by the arrows on the line. A line may also be represented by a single lowercase letter. Figures 1.9(a) and (b) show the lines *AB* and *m*. When a lowercase letter is used to name a line, the line symbol is omitted; that is, $\overleftrightarrow{AB}$ and *m* can name the same line.

Note the position of point *X* on $\overleftrightarrow{AB}$ in Figure 1.9(c). When three points such as *A*, *X*, and *B* are on the same line, they are said to be **collinear.** In the order shown, which is symbolized *A*-*X*-*B* or *B*-*X*-*A*, point *X* is said to be *between* *A* and *B*.

When no drawing is provided, the notation *A*-*B*-*C* means that these points are collinear, with *B* *between* *A* and *C*. When a drawing is provided, we assume that all points in the drawing that appear to be collinear *are* collinear, *unless otherwise stated.* Figure 1.9(d) shows that *A*, *B*, and *C* are collinear, with *B* between *A* and *C*.

At this time, we informally introduce some terms that will be formally defined later. You have probably encountered the terms *angle, triangle,* and *rectangle* many times. An example of each is shown in Figure 1.10.

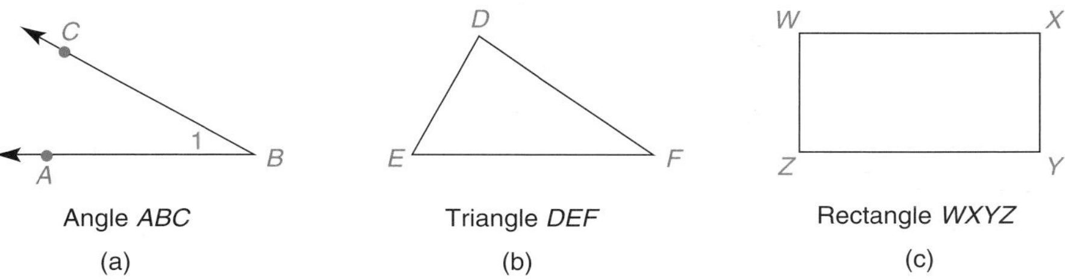

Figure 1.10

Using symbols and abbreviations, we refer to Figures 1.10(a), (b), and (c) as $\angle ABC$, $\triangle DEF$, and rect. *WXYZ*, respectively. Some caution must be used in naming figures; although the angle in Figure 1.10(a) can be called $\angle CBA$, it is incorrect to describe the angle as $\angle ACB$ because that order implies a path from point *A* to point *C* to point *B* . . . a different angle! In $\angle ABC$, the point *B* at which the sides meet is called the **vertex** of the angle. Because there is no confusion regarding the angle described, $\angle ABC$ is also known as $\angle B$ (using only the vertex) or as $\angle 1$. The points *D*, *E*, and *F* at which the sides of $\triangle DEF$ (also called $\triangle DFE$, $\triangle EFD$, etc.) meet are called the *vertices* (plural of *vertex*) of the triangle. Similarly, *W*, *X*, *Y*, and *Z* are the vertices of the rectangle.

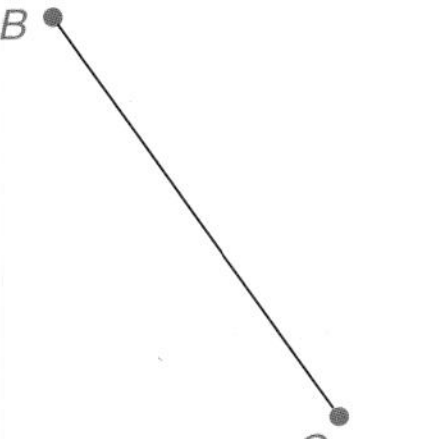

Figure 1.11

A **line segment** is part of a line. It consists of two distinct points on the line and all points between them. (See Figure 1.11.) Using symbols, we indicate the line segment by $\overline{BC}$; note that $\overline{BC}$ is a set of points but is not a number. We use *BC* (omitting the segment symbol) to indicate the *length* of this line segment; thus, *BC* is a number. The sides of a triangle or rectangle are line segments. The vertices of a rectangle are named in an order that traces its line segment sides in order.

EXAMPLE 1

Can the rectangle in Figure 1.10(c) be named a) *XYZW*? b) *WYXZ*?

Solution

a) Yes, because the points taken in this order trace the figure.
b) No; for example, $\overline{WY}$ is not a side of the rectangle. ■

In converting from U.S. units to the metric system, a known conversion is the fact that 1 inch ≈ 2.54 cm. What is the "cm" equivalent of 3.7 inches?

ANSWER

9.4 cm

MEASURING LINE SEGMENTS

The instrument used to measure a line segment is a scaled straightedge such as a *ruler,* a *yardstick,* or a *meter stick.* Generally, we place the "0 point" of the ruler at one end of the line segment and find the numerical length as the number at the other end. Line segment *RS* ($\overline{RS}$ in symbols) in Figure 1.12 measures 5 centimeters. Because we express the length of $\overline{RS}$ by *RS* (with no bar), we write $RS = 5$ cm.

Because manufactured measuring devices such as the ruler, yardstick, and meter stick may lack perfection or be misread, there is a margin of error each time one is used. In Figure 1.12, for instance, *RS* may actually measure 5.02 cm (and that could be rounded from 5.023 cm, etc.). Measurements are approximate, not perfect.

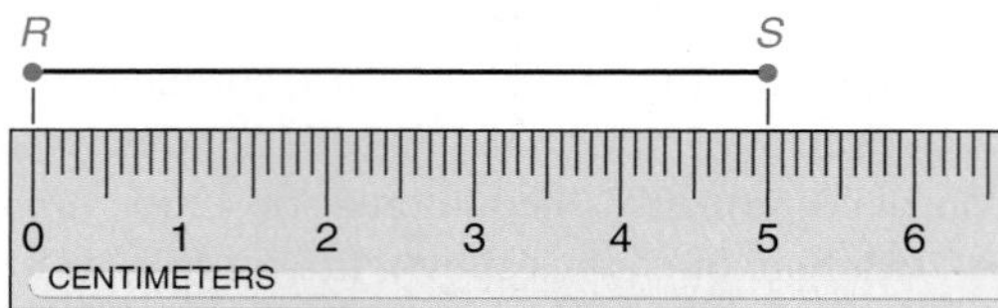

Figure 1.12

In Example 2, a ruler (not drawn to scale) is shown in Figure 1.13. In the drawing, the distance between consecutive marks on the ruler corresponds to 1 inch. The measure of a line segment is known as *linear measure.*

EXAMPLE 2

In rectangle *ABCD* of Figure 1.13, the line segments $\overline{AC}$ and $\overline{BD}$ shown are the diagonals of the rectangle. How do the lengths of the diagonals compare?

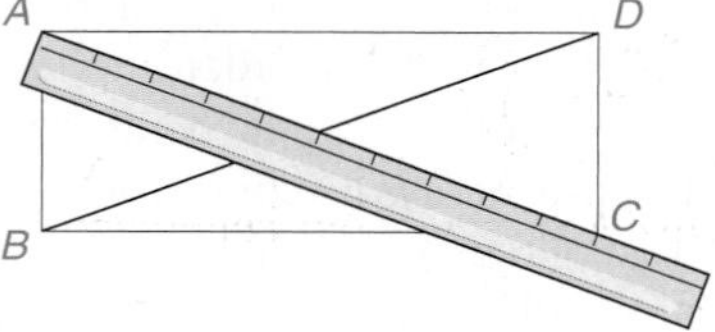

Figure 1.13

Solution As intuition suggests, the lengths of the diagonals are the same. As shown, $AC = 10''$ and $BD = 10''$.

NOTE: In linear measure, 10″ means 10 inches, and 10′ means 10 feet. ■

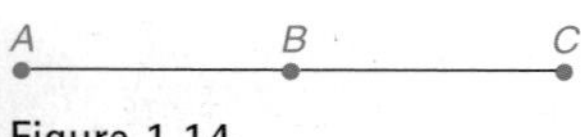

Figure 1.14

In Figure 1.14, point *B* lies between *A* and *C* on $\overline{AC}$. If $AB = BC$, then *B* is the **midpoint** of $\overline{AC}$. When $AB = BC$, the geometric figures $\overline{AB}$ and $\overline{BC}$ are said to be **congruent.** Numerical lengths may be equal, but the actual line segments (geometric figures) are congruent. The symbol for congruence is ≅; thus, $\overline{AB} \cong \overline{BC}$ if *B* is the midpoint of $\overline{AC}$. Example 3 emphasizes the relationship between $\overline{AB}$, $\overline{BC}$, and $\overline{AC}$ when *B* lies between *A* and *C*.

EXAMPLE 3

SSG *Exs. 1–8*

In Figure 1.15, the lengths of $\overline{AB}$ and $\overline{BC}$ are $AB = 4$ and $BC = 8$. What is AC, the length of $\overline{AC}$?

Figure 1.15

Solution As intuition suggests, the length of $\overline{AC}$ equals $AB + BC$. Thus, $AC = 4 + 8 = 12$. ■

MEASURING ANGLES

Although we formally define an angle in Section 1.4, we consider it intuitively at this time.

An angle's measure depends not on the lengths of its sides but on the amount of opening between its sides. In Figure 1.16, the arrows on the angles' sides suggest that the sides extend indefinitely.

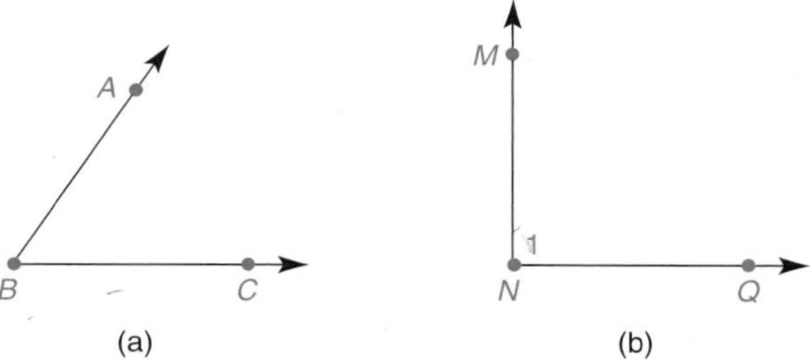

Figure 1.16

The instrument shown in Figure 1.17 (and used in the measurement of angles) is a **protractor.** For example, you would express the measure of $\angle RST$ by writing $m\angle RST = 50°$; this statement is read, "The measure of $\angle RST$ is 50 degrees." Measuring the angles in Figure 1.16 with a protractor, we find that $m\angle B = 55°$ and $m\angle 1 = 90°$. If the degree symbol is missing, the measure is understood to be in degrees; thus $m\angle 1 = 90$.

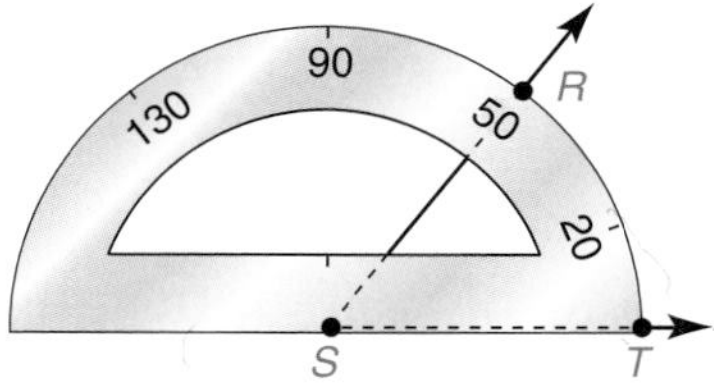

Figure 1.17

In practice, the protractor shown will measure an angle that is greater than 0° but less than or equal to 180°. To measure an angle with a protractor:

1. Place the notch of the protractor at the point where the sides of the angle meet (the vertex of the angle). See point S in Figure 1.18.
2. Place the edge of the protractor along a side of the angle so that the scale reads "0." See point T in Figure 1.18 where we use "0" on the outer scale.
3. Using the same (outer) scale, read the angle size by reading the degree measure that corresponds to the second side of the angle.

Warning

Many protractors have dual scales as shown in Figure 1.18.

EXAMPLE 4

For Figure 1.18, find the measure of $\angle RST$.

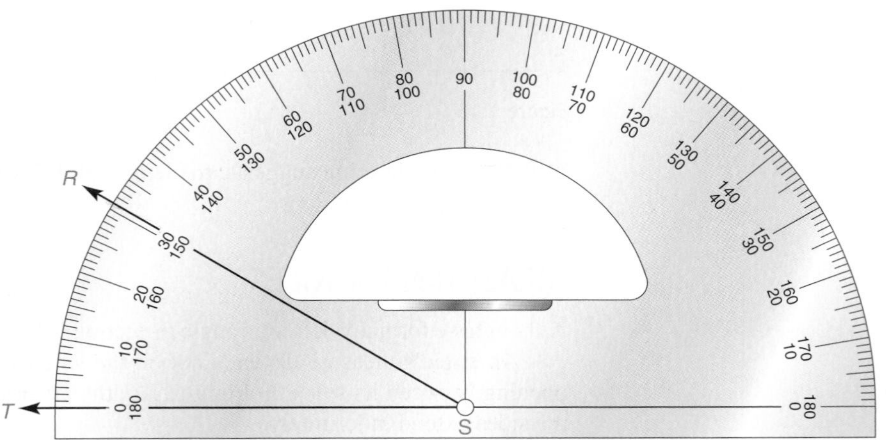

Figure 1.18

Solution Using the protractor, we find that the measure of angle RST is $31°$. (In symbols, $m\angle RST = 31°$ or $m\angle RST = 31$.) ■

Some protractors show a full 360° and are used to measure an angle whose measure is greater than 180°; this type of angle is known as a *reflex angle*.

Like measurement with a ruler, measurement with a protractor will not be perfect.

The lines on a sheet of paper in a notebook are *parallel*. Informally, **parallel** lines lie on the same page and won't cross over each other even if they are extended indefinitely. We say that lines ℓ and m in Figure 1.19(a) are parallel; note here the use of a lowercase letter to name a line. We say that line segments are parallel if they are parts of parallel lines; if $\overleftrightarrow{RS}$ is parallel to $\overleftrightarrow{MN}$, then $\overline{RS}$ is parallel to $\overline{MN}$ in Figure 1.19(b).

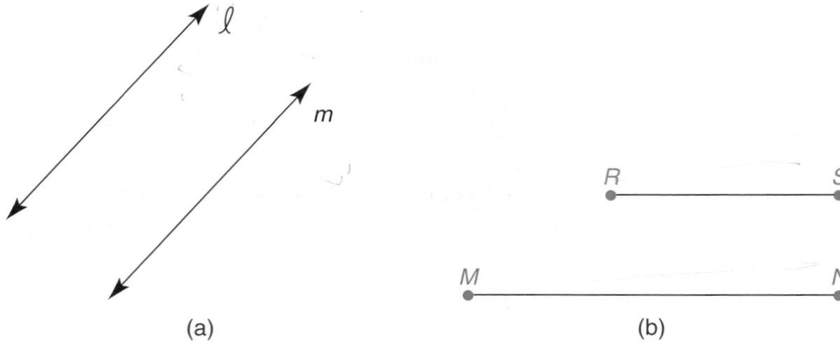

Figure 1.19

For $A = \{1, 2, 3\}$ and $B = \{6, 8, 10\}$, there are no common elements; for this reason, we say that the intersection of A and B is the **empty set** (symbol is $\emptyset$). Just as $A \cap B = \emptyset$, the parallel lines in Figure 1.19(a) are characterized by $\ell \cap m = \emptyset$.

EXAMPLE 5

In Figure 1.20 the sides of angles ABC and DEF are parallel ($\overline{AB}$ to $\overline{DE}$ and $\overline{BC}$ to $\overline{EF}$). Use a protractor to decide whether these angles have equal measures.

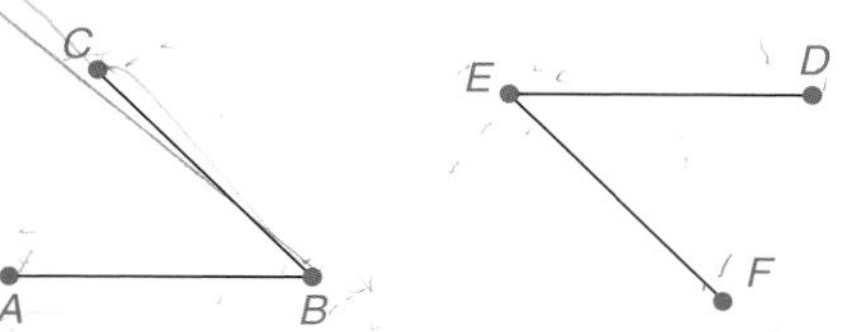

Figure 1.20

Solution The angles have equal measures. Both measure 44°. ■

Two angles with equal measures are said to be *congruent.* In Figure 1.20, we see that $\angle ABC \cong \angle DEF$. In Figure 1.21, $\angle ABC \cong \angle CBD$.

In Figure 1.21, angle ABD has been separated into smaller angles ABC and CBD; if the two smaller angles are congruent (have equal measures), then angle ABD has been *bisected.* In general, the word **bisect** means to separate into two parts of equal measure.

Any angle having a 180° measure is called a **straight angle,** an angle whose sides are in opposite directions. See straight angle RST in Figure 1.22(a). When a straight angle is bisected, as shown in Figure 1.22(b), the two angles formed are **right angles** (each measures 90°).

When two lines have a point in common, as in Figure 1.23, they are said to **intersect.** When two lines intersect and form congruent adjacent angles, they are said to be **perpendicular.**

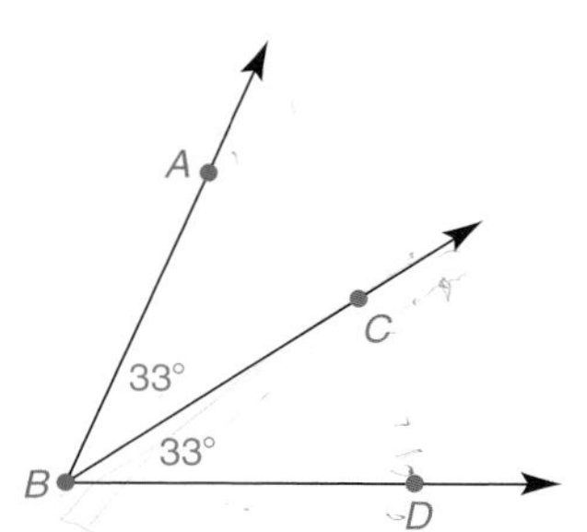

Figure 1.21

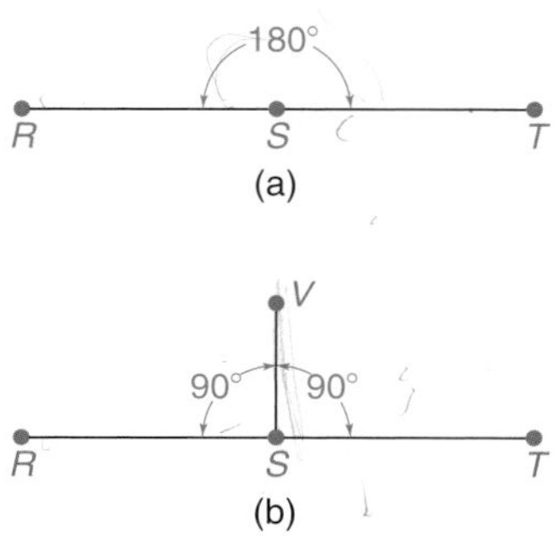

Figure 1.22

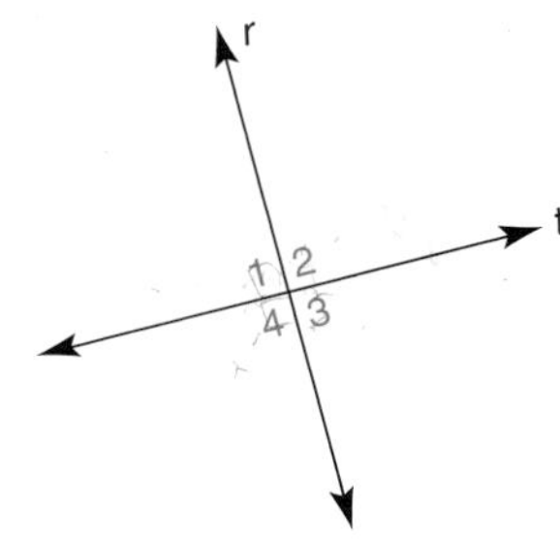

Figure 1.23

EXAMPLE 6

In Figure 1.23, suppose lines r and t are perpendicular. What is the measure of each of the angles formed?

SSG *Exs. 9–13*

Solution Each of the marked angles (numbered 1, 2, 3, and 4) is the result of bisecting a straight angle, so each angle is a right angle and measures 90°. ■

CONSTRUCTIONS

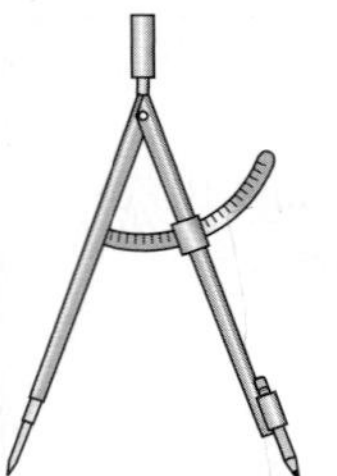
Figure 1.24

Another tool used in geometry is the **compass.** This instrument, shown in Figure 1.24, is used to construct circles and parts of circles known as *arcs*. The compass and circle are discussed in the following paragraphs.

The ancient Greeks insisted that only two tools (a compass and a straightedge) be used for geometric **constructions,** which were idealized drawings assuming perfection in the use of these tools. The compass was used to create "perfect" circles and for marking off segments of "equal" length. The straightedge could be used to pass a straight line through two designated points.

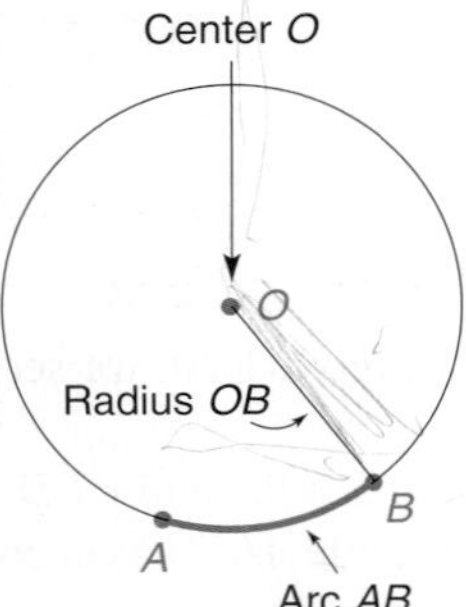

Figure 1.25

A **circle** is the set of all points in a plane that are at a given distance from a particular point (known as the "center" of the circle). The part of a circle between any two of its points is known as an **arc.** Any line segment joining the center to a point on the circle is a **radius** (plural: *radii*) of the circle. See Figure 1.25.

Construction 1, which follows, is quite basic and depends only on using arcs of the same radius length to construct line segments of the same length. The arcs are created by using a compass. Construction 2 is more difficult to perform and explain, so we will delay its explanation to a later chapter (see Section 3.4).

Construction 1 *To construct a segment congruent to a given segment.*

GIVEN: $\overline{AB}$ in Figure 1.26(a).

CONSTRUCT: $\overline{CD}$ on line m so that $\overline{CD} \cong \overline{AB}$ (or $CD = AB$)

CONSTRUCTION: With your compass open to the length of $\overline{AB}$, place the stationary point of the compass at C and mark off a length equal to AB at point D, as shown in Figure 1.26(b). Then $CD = AB$.

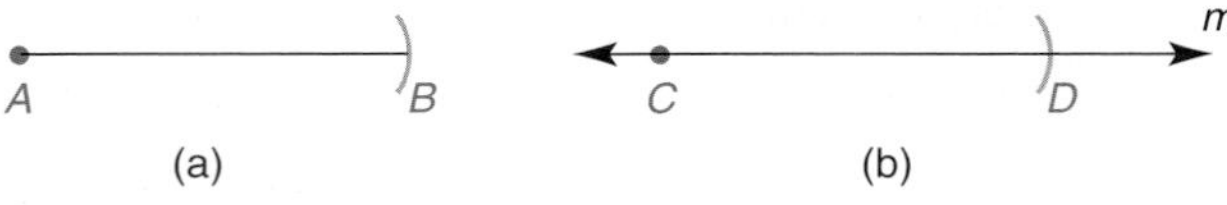

Figure 1.26

The following construction is shown step by step in Figure 1.27. Intuition suggests that point M in Figure 1.27(c) is the midpoint of $\overline{AB}$.

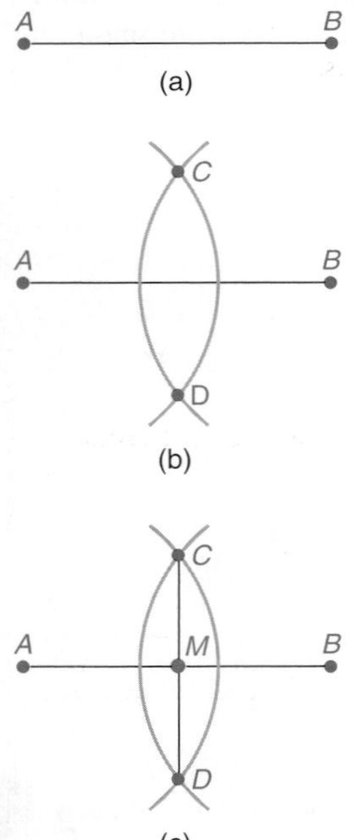

Figure 1.27

Construction 2 *To construct the midpoint M of a given line segment AB.*

GIVEN: $\overline{AB}$ in Figure 1.27(a)

CONSTRUCT: M on $\overline{AB}$ so that $AM = MB$

CONSTRUCTION: Figure 1.27(a): Open your compass to a length greater than one-half of $\overline{AB}$.

Figure 1.27(b): Using A as the center of the arc, mark off an arc that extends both above and below segment AB. With B as the center and keeping the same length of radius, mark off an arc that extends above and below $\overline{AB}$ so that two points (C and D) are determined where the arcs cross.

Figure 1.27(c): Now draw $\overline{CD}$. The point where $\overline{CD}$ crosses $\overline{AB}$ is the midpoint M.

SSG *Exs. 14–17*

EXAMPLE 7

In Figure 1.28, M is the midpoint of $\overline{AB}$.

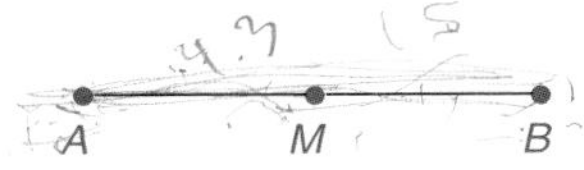

Figure 1.28

a) Find AM if $AB = 15$.
b) Find AB if $AM = 4.3$.
c) Find AB if $AM = 2x + 1$.

Solution

a) AM is one-half of AB, so $AM = 7\frac{1}{2}$.
b) AB is twice AM, so $AB = 2(4.3)$ or $AB = 8.6$.
c) AB is twice AM, so $AB = 2(2x + 1)$ or $AB = 4x + 2$.

The technique from algebra used in Example 8 and also needed for Exercises 47 and 48 of this section depends on the following properties of addition and subtraction.

If $a = b$ and $c = d$, then $a + c = b + d$.

Words: Equals added to equals provide equal sums.

Illustration: Since $0.5 = \frac{5}{10}$ and $0.2 = \frac{2}{10}$, it follows that $0.5 + 0.2 = \frac{5}{10} + \frac{2}{10}$; that is, $0.7 = \frac{7}{10}$.

If $a = b$ and $c = d$, then $a - c = b - d$.

Words: Equals subtracted from equals provide equal differences.

Illustration: Since $0.5 = \frac{5}{10}$ and $0.2 = \frac{2}{10}$, it follows that $0.5 - 0.2 = \frac{5}{10} - \frac{2}{10}$; that is, $0.3 = \frac{3}{10}$.

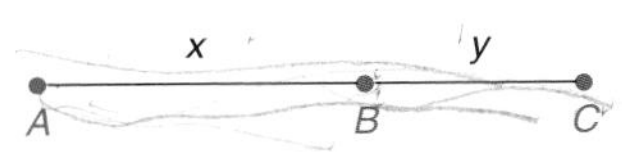

Figure 1.29

EXAMPLE 8

In Figure 1.29, point B lies on $\overline{AC}$ between A and C. If $AC = 10$ and AB is 2 units longer than BC, find the length x of $\overline{AB}$ and the length y of $\overline{BC}$.

Solution

Because $AB + BC = AC$, we have $x + y = 10$.
Because $AB - BC = 2$, we have $x - y = 2$.
Adding the left and right sides of these equations, we have

$$\begin{array}{rcl} x + y &=& 10 \\ x - y &=& 2 \\ \hline 2x &=& 12 \end{array} \qquad \text{so } x = 6.$$

If $x = 6$, then $x + y = 10$ becomes $6 + y = 10$ and $y = 4$.

SSG *Exs. 18, 19*

Thus, $AB = 6$ and $BC = 4$.

Exercises 1.2

1. If line segment AB and line segment CD are drawn to scale, what does intuition tell you about the lengths of these segments?

2. If angles ABC and DEF were measured with a protractor, what does intuition tell you about the degree measures of these angles?

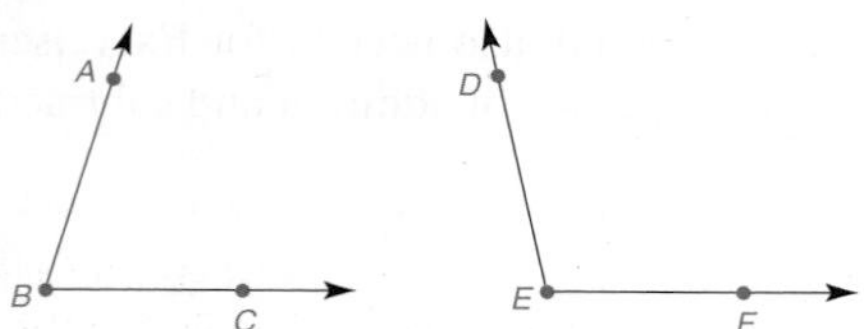

3. How many endpoints does a line segment have? How many midpoints does a line segment have?
4. Do the points A, B, and C appear to be collinear?

Exercises 4–6

5. How many lines can be drawn that contain both points A and B? How many lines can be drawn that contain points A, B, and C?
6. Consider noncollinear points A, B, and C. If each line must contain two of the points, what is the total number of lines that are determined by these points?
7. Name all the angles in the figure.

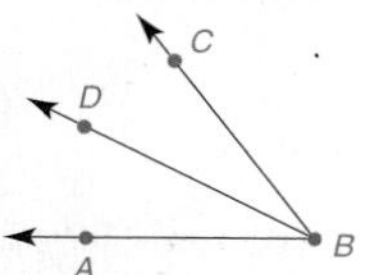

8. Which of the following measures can an angle have? 23°, 90°, 200°, 110.5°, −15°
9. Must two different points be collinear? Must three or more points be collinear? Can three or more points be collinear?
10. Which symbol(s) correctly expresses the order in which the points A, B, and X lie on the given line, A-X-B or A-B-X?

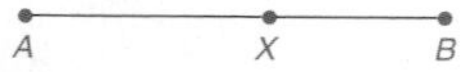

11. Which symbols correctly name the angle shown? $\angle ABC$, $\angle ACB$, $\angle CBA$

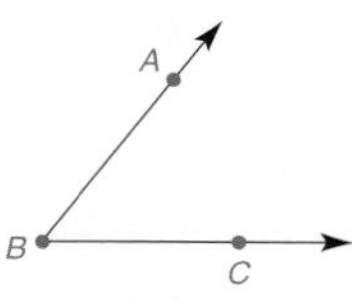

12. A triangle is named $\triangle ABC$. Can it also be named $\triangle ACB$? Can it be named $\triangle BAC$?
13. Consider rectangle $MNPQ$. Can it also be named rectangle $PQMN$? Can it be named rectangle $MNQP$?
14. Suppose $\angle ABC$ and $\angle DEF$ have the same measure. Which statements are expressed correctly?
    a) $m\angle ABC = m\angle DEF$ b) $\angle ABC = \angle DEF$
    c) $m\angle ABC \cong m\angle DEF$ d) $\angle ABC \cong \angle DEF$
15. Suppose $\overline{AB}$ and $\overline{CD}$ have the same length. Which statements are expressed correctly?
    a) $AB = CD$ b) $\overline{AB} = \overline{CD}$
    c) $AB \cong CD$ d) $\overline{AB} \cong \overline{CD}$
16. When two lines cross (intersect), they have exactly one point in common. In the drawing, what is the point of intersection? How do the measures of $\angle 1$ and $\angle 2$ compare?

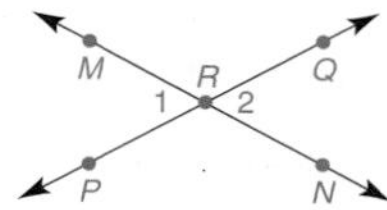

17. Judging from the ruler shown (not to scale), estimate the measure of each line segment.
    a) AB b) CD

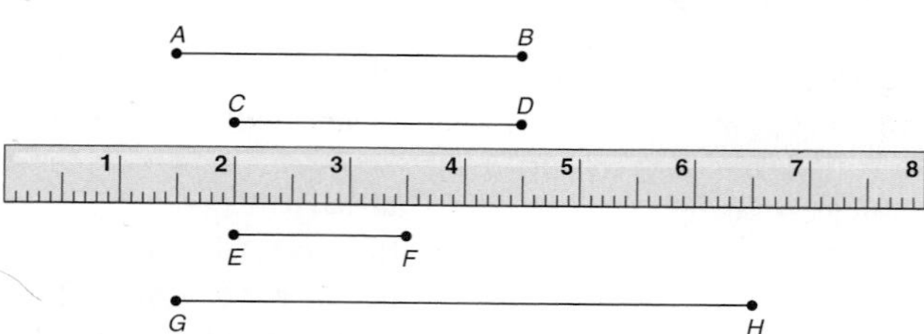

Exercises 17, 18

18. Judging from the ruler, estimate the measure of each line segment.
    a) EF b) GH

19. Judging from the protractor provided, estimate the measure of each angle to the nearest multiple of 5° (e.g., 20°, 25°, 30°, etc.).

a) m∠1 b) m∠2

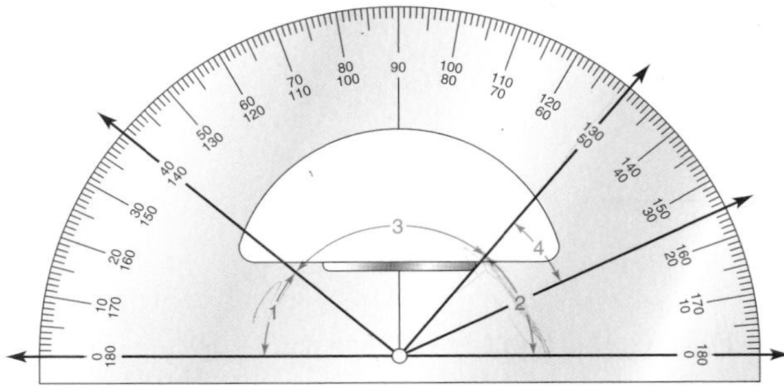

Exercises 19, 20

20. Judging from the protractor, estimate the measure of each angle to the nearest multiple of 5° (e.g., 20°, 25°, 30°, etc.).

a) m∠3 b) m∠4

21. Consider the square at the right, *RSTV*. It has four right angles and four sides of the same length. How are sides $\overline{RS}$ and $\overline{ST}$ related? How are sides $\overline{RS}$ and $\overline{VT}$ related?

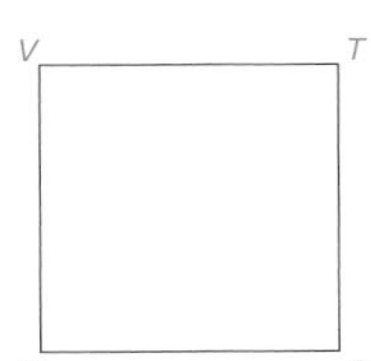

Exercises 21, 22

22. Square *RSTV* has diagonals $\overline{RT}$ and $\overline{SV}$ (not shown). If the diagonals are drawn, how will their lengths compare? Do the diagonals of a square appear to be perpendicular?

23. Use a compass to draw a circle. Draw a radius, a line segment that connects the center to a point on the circle. Measure the length of the radius. Draw other radii and find their lengths. How do the lengths of the radii compare?

24. Use a compass to draw a circle of radius 1 inch. Draw a chord, a line segment that joins two points on the circle. Draw other chords and measure their lengths. What is the largest possible length of a chord in this circle?

25. The sides of the pair of angles are parallel. Are ∠1 and ∠2 congruent?

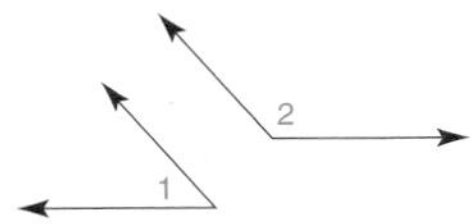

26. The sides of the pair of angles are parallel. Are ∠3 and ∠4 congruent?

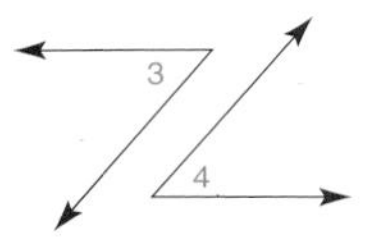

27. The sides of the pair of angles are perpendicular. Are ∠5 and ∠6 congruent?

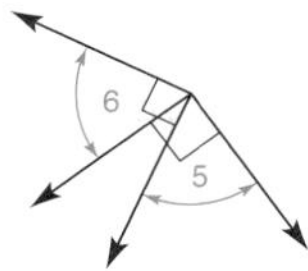

28. The sides of the pair of angles are perpendicular. Are ∠7 and ∠8 congruent?

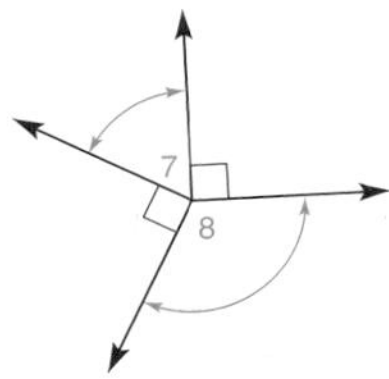

29. On a piece of paper, use your compass to construct a triangle that has two sides of the same length. Cut the triangle out of the paper and fold the triangle in half so that the congruent sides coincide (one lies over the other). What seems to be true of two angles of that triangle?

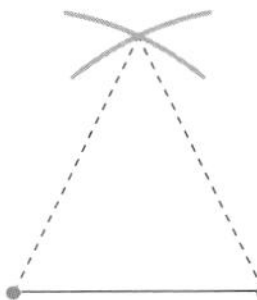

30. On a piece of paper, use your protractor to draw a triangle that has two angles of the same measure. Cut the triangle out of the paper and fold the triangle in half so that the angles of equal measure coincide (one lies over the other). What seems to be true of two of the sides of that triangle?

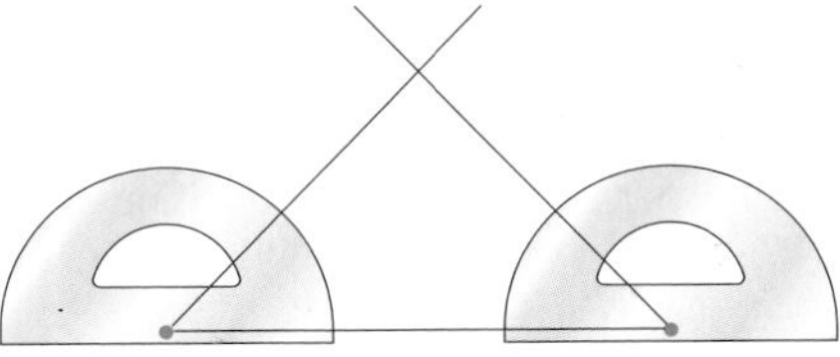

31. A trapezoid is a four-sided figure that contains one pair of parallel sides. Which sides of the trapezoid *MNPQ* appear to be parallel?

32. In the rectangle shown, what is true of the lengths of each pair of opposite sides?

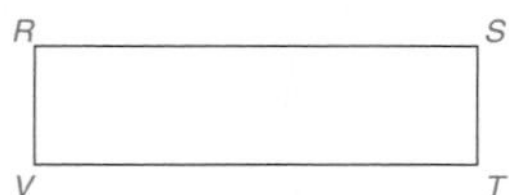

33. A line segment is bisected if its two parts have the same length. Which line segment, $\overline{AB}$ or $\overline{CD}$, is bisected at point X?

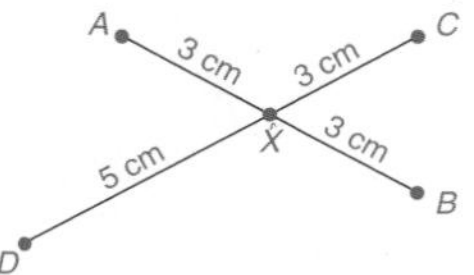

34. An angle is bisected if its two parts have the same measure. Use three letters to name the angle that is bisected.

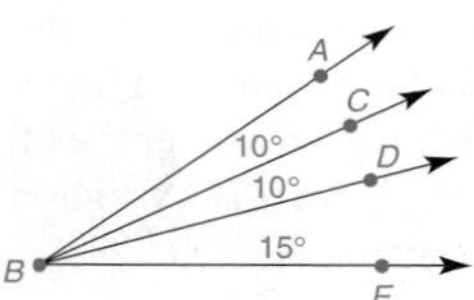

In Exercises 35 to 38, where A-B-C on $\overline{AC}$, it follows that AB + BC = AC.

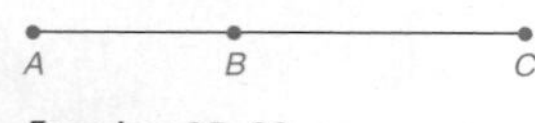

Exercises 35–38

35. Find AC if $AB = 9$ and $BC = 13$.

36. Find AB if $AC = 25$ and $BC = 11$.

37. Find x if $AB = x$, $BC = x + 3$, and $AC = 21$.

38. Find an expression for AC (the length of $\overline{AC}$) if $AB = x$ and $BC = y$.

39. $\angle ABC$ is a straight angle. Using your protractor, you can show that $m\angle 1 + m\angle 2 = 180°$. Find $m\angle 1$ if $m\angle 2 = 56°$.

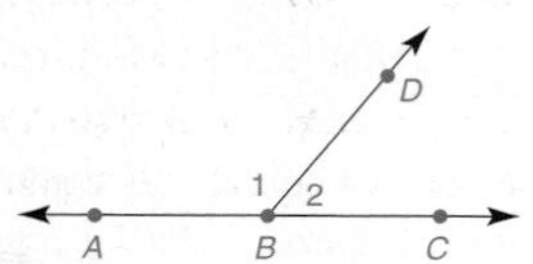

Exercises 39, 40

40. Find $m\angle 1$ if $m\angle 1 = 2x$ and $m\angle 2 = x$.

(HINT: See Exercise 39.)

In Exercises 41 to 44, $m\angle 1 + m\angle 2 = m\angle ABC$.

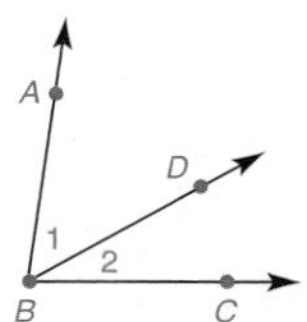

Exercises 41–44

41. Find $m\angle ABC$ if $m\angle 1 = 32°$ and $m\angle 2 = 39°$.

42. Find $m\angle 1$ if $m\angle ABC = 68°$ and $m\angle 1 = m\angle 2$.

43. Find x if $m\angle 1 = x$, $m\angle 2 = 2x + 3$, and $m\angle ABC = 72°$.

44. Find an expression for $m\angle ABC$ if $m\angle 1 = x$ and $m\angle 2 = y$.

45. A compass was used to mark off three congruent segments, $\overline{AB}$, $\overline{BC}$, and $\overline{CD}$. Thus, $\overline{AD}$ has been trisected at points B and C. If $AD = 32.7$, how long is $\overline{AB}$?

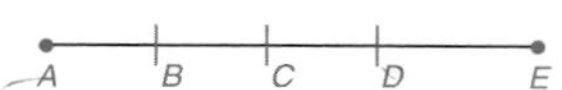

46. Use your compass and straightedge to bisect $\overline{EF}$.

E F

***47.** In the figure, $m\angle 1 = x$ and $m\angle 2 = y$. If $x - y = 24°$, find x and y.

(HINT: $m\angle 1 + m\angle 2 = 180°$.)

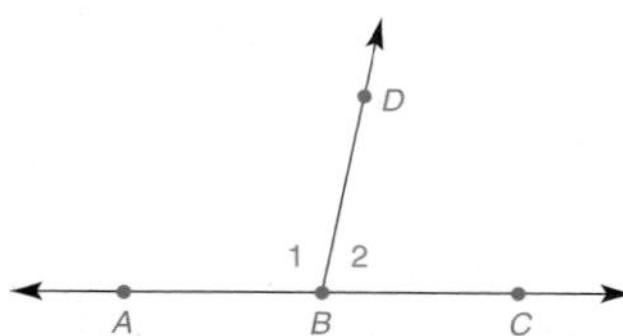

***48.** In the drawing, $m\angle 1 = x$ and $m\angle 2 = y$. If $m\angle RSV = 67°$ and $x - y = 17°$, find x and y.

(HINT: $m\angle 1 + m\angle 2 = m\angle RSV$.)

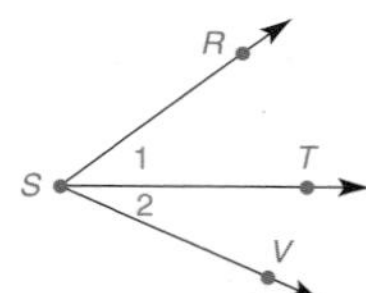

For Exercises 49 and 50, use the following information. Relative to its point of departure or some other point of reference, the angle that is used to locate the position of a ship or airplane is called its bearing. The bearing may also be used to describe the direction in which the airplane or ship is moving. By using an angle between 0° and 90°, a bearing is measured from the North-South line toward the East or West. In the diagram, airplane A (which is 250 miles from Chicago's O'Hare airport's control tower) has a bearing of S 53° W.

49. Find the bearing of airplane B relative to the control tower.

50. Find the bearing of airplane C relative to the control tower.

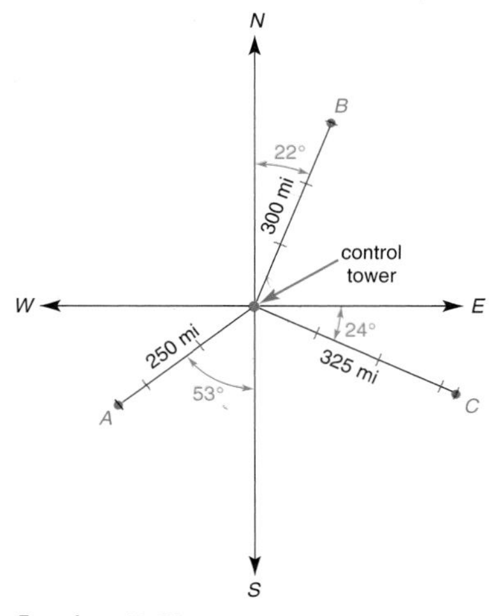

Exercises 49, 50

1.3 Early Definitions and Postulates

Mathematical System
Axiom or Postulate
Theorem
Ruler Postulate
Distance
Segment-Addition Postulate
Midpoint of a Line Segment
Ray
Opposite Rays
Intersection of Two Geometric Figures
Plane
Coplanar Points
Space

A MATHEMATICAL SYSTEM

Like algebra, the branch of mathematics called geometry is a **mathematical system.** Each system has its own vocabulary and properties. In the formal study of a mathematical system, we begin with undefined terms. Building on this foundation, we can then define additional terms. Once the terminology is sufficiently developed, certain properties (characteristics) of the system become apparent. These properties are known as **axioms** or **postulates** of the system; more generally, such statements are called **assumptions.** Once we have developed a vocabulary and accepted certain postulates, many principles follow logically when we apply deductive methods. These statements can be proved and are called **theorems.** The following box summarizes the components of a mathematical system (sometimes called a logical system or deductive system).

FOUR PARTS OF A MATHEMATICAL SYSTEM

1. Undefined terms } vocabulary
2. Defined terms }
3. Axioms or postulates } principles
4. Theorems }

CHARACTERISTICS OF A GOOD DEFINITION

Discover

Although we cannot actually define *line* and *plane*, we can compare them in the following analogy. Please complete: A _?_ is to *straight* as a _?_ is to *flat*.

ANSWERS
line; plane

Terms such as *point, line,* and *plane* are classified as undefined because they do not fit into any set or category that has been previously determined. Terms that *are* defined, however, should be described precisely. *But what is a good definition?* A good definition is like a mathematical equation written using words. A good definition must possess four characteristics. We illustrate this with a term that we will redefine at a later time.

DEFINITION

An **isosceles triangle** is a triangle that has two congruent sides.

In the definition, notice that: (1) The term being defined—*isosceles triangle*—is named. (2) The term being defined is placed into a larger category (a type of *triangle*). (3) The distinguishing quality (that two sides of the triangle are congruent) is included. (4) The *reversibility* of the definition is illustrated by these statements:

"If a triangle is isosceles, then it has two congruent sides."
"If a triangle has two congruent sides, then it is an isosceles triangle."

IN SUMMARY, A GOOD DEFINITION WILL POSSESS THESE QUALITIES

1. It names the term being defined.
2. It places the term into a set or category.
3. It distinguishes the defined term from other terms without providing unnecessary facts.
4. It is reversible.

In many textbooks, it is common to use the phrase "if and only if" in expressing the definition of a term. For instance, we could define *congruent angles* by saying that two angles are congruent if and only if these angles have equal measures. The "if and only if" statement has the following dual meaning:

"If two angles are congruent, then they have equal measures."
"If two angles have equal measures, then they are congruent."

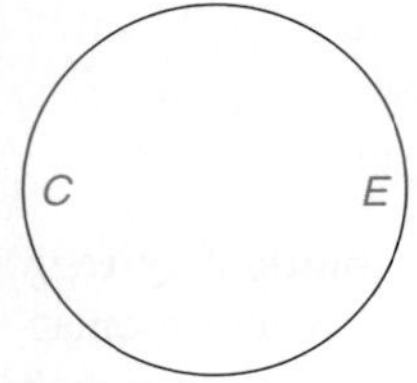

Figure 1.30

When represented by a Venn Diagram, this definition would relate set $C = \{$congruent angles$\}$ to set $E = \{$angles with equal measures$\}$ as shown in Figure 1.30. The sets C and E are identical and are known as **equivalent sets.**

Once undefined terms have been described, they become the building blocks for other terminology. In this textbook, primary terms are defined within boxes, whereas related terms are often boldfaced and defined within statements. Consider the following definition (see Figure 1.31).

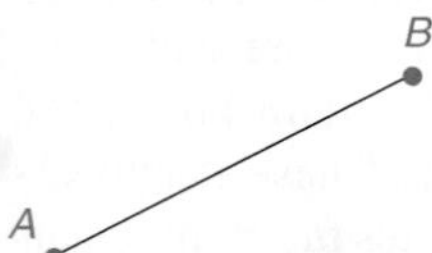

Figure 1.31

SSG *Exs. 1–4*

DEFINITION

A **line segment** is the part of a line that consists of two points, known as *endpoints,* and all points between them.

Considering this definition, we see that

1. The term being defined, *line segment*, is clearly present in the definition.
2. A line segment is defined as part of a line (a category).
3. The definition distinguishes the line segment as a specific part of a line.

Geometry in the Real World

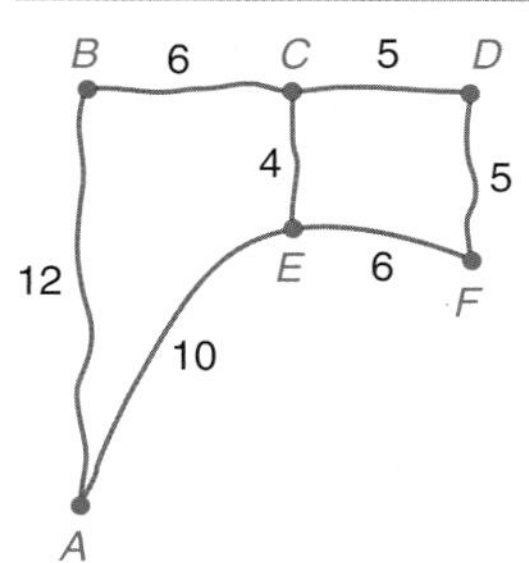

On the road map, driving distances between towns are shown. In traveling from town *A* to town *D*, which path traverses the least distance?

Solution *A* to *E*, *E* to *C*, *C* to *D*: $10 + 4 + 5 = 19$

4. The definition is reversible.
   i) A line segment is the part of a line between and including two points.
   ii) The part of a line between and including two points is a line segment.

INITIAL POSTULATES

Recall that a postulate is a statement that is assumed to be true.

POSTULATE 1

Through two distinct points, there is exactly one line.

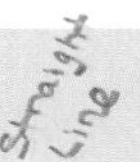

Postulate 1 is sometimes stated in the form "Two points determine a line." See Figure 1.32, in which points *C* and *D* determine exactly one line, namely, $\overleftrightarrow{CD}$. Of course, Postulate 1 also implies that there is a unique line segment determined by two distinct points used as endpoints. Recall Figure 1.31, in which points *A* and *B* determine $\overline{AB}$.

NOTE: In geometry, the reference numbers used with postulates (as in Postulate 1) need not be memorized.

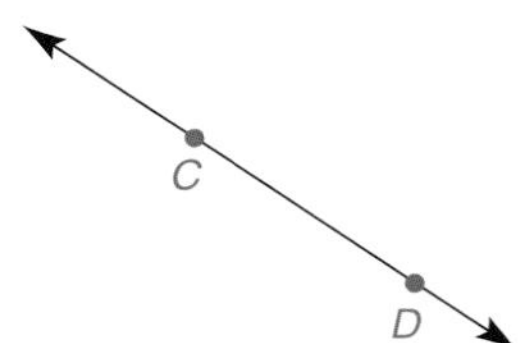

Figure 1.32

EXAMPLE 1

In Figure 1.33, how many distinct lines can be drawn through

a) point *A*?
b) both points *A* and *B* at the same time?
c) all points *A*, *B*, and *C* at the same time?

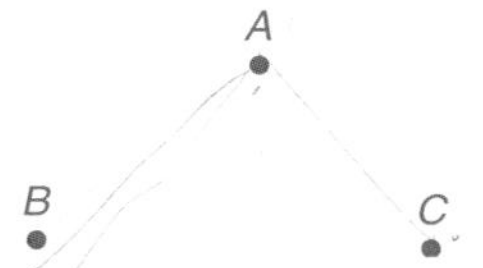

Figure 1.33

Solution

a) An infinite (countless) number
b) Exactly one
c) No line contains all three points.

Recall from Section 1.2 that the symbol for line segment *AB*, named by its endpoints, is $\overline{AB}$. Omission of the bar from $\overline{AB}$, as in *AB*, means that we are considering the *length* of the segment. These symbols are summarized in Table 1.3.

TABLE 1.3

Symbol	*Words for Symbol*	*Geometric Figure*
$\overleftrightarrow{AB}$	Line *AB*	A ←•———•→ B
$\overline{AB}$	Line segment *AB*	A •———• B
AB	Length of segment *AB*	A number

A ruler is used to measure the length of any line segment like $\overline{AB}$. This length may be represented by *AB* or *BA* (the order of *A* and *B* is not important). However, *AB* must be a positive number.

Geometry in the Real World

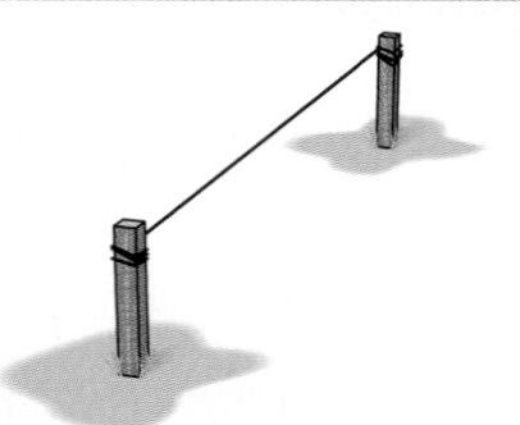

In construction, a string joins two stakes. The line determined is described in Postulate 1 on the previous page.

POSTULATE 2 ▶ (Ruler Postulate)

The measure of any line segment is a unique positive number.

We wish to call attention to the term *unique* and to the general notion of uniqueness. The Ruler Postulate implies the following:

1. There exists a number measure for each line segment.
2. Only *one* measure is permissible.

Characteristics 1 and 2 are both necessary for uniqueness! Other phrases that may replace the term *unique* include

One and only one

Exactly one

One and no more than one

A more accurate claim than the commonly heard statement "The shortest distance between two points is a straight line" is found in the following definition.

DEFINITION

The **distance** between two points A and B is the length of the line segment $\overline{AB}$ that joins the two points.

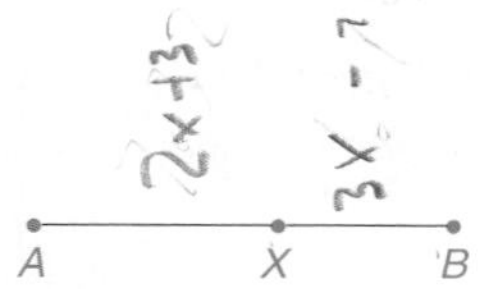

Figure 1.34

As we saw in Section 1.2, there is a relationship between the lengths of the line segments determined in Figure 1.34. This relationship is stated in the third postulate. It is the title and meaning of the postulate that are important!

POSTULATE 3 ▶ (Segment-Addition Postulate)

If X is a point of $\overline{AB}$ and A-X-B, then $AX + XB = AB$.

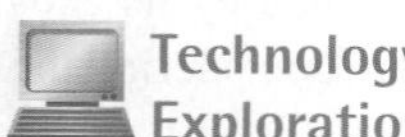

Technology Exploration

Use software if available.

1. Draw line segment $\overline{XY}$.
2. Choose point P on $\overline{XY}$.
3. Measure $\overline{XP}$, $\overline{PY}$, and $\overline{XY}$.
4. Show that $XP + PY = XY$.

EXAMPLE 2

In Figure 1.34, find AB if

a) $AX = 7.32$ and $XB = 6.19$. b) $AX = 2x + 3$ and $XB = 3x - 7$.

Solution

a) $AB = 7.32 + 6.19$, so $AB = 13.51$.
b) $AB = (2x + 3) + (3x - 7)$, so $AB = 5x - 4$. ■

DEFINITION

Congruent ($\cong$) line **segments** are two line segments that have the same length.

In general, geometric figures that can be made to coincide (fit perfectly one on top of the other) are said to be **congruent.** The symbol $\cong$ is a combination of the symbol ~,

Figure 1.35

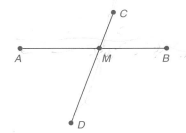

which means that the figures have the same shape, and $=$, which means that the corresponding parts of the figures have the same measure. In Figure 1.35, $\overline{AB} \cong \overline{CD}$, but $\overline{AB} \not\cong \overline{EF}$ (meaning that $\overline{AB}$ and $\overline{EF}$ are not congruent). Does it appear that $\overline{CD} \cong \overline{EF}$?

EXAMPLE 3

In the U.S. system of measures, 1 foot $=$ 12 inches. If $AB = 2.5$ feet and $CD = 2$ feet 6 inches, are $\overline{AB}$ and $\overline{CD}$ congruent?

Solution Yes, $\overline{AB} \cong \overline{CD}$ because 2.5 feet $=$ 2 feet $+$ 0.5 feet or 2 feet $+$ 0.5(12 inches) or 2 feet 6 inches. ■

DEFINITION

The **midpoint** of a line segment is the point that separates the line segment into two congruent parts.

Figure 1.36

In Figure 1.36, if A, M, and B are collinear and $\overline{AM} \cong \overline{MB}$, then M is the **midpoint** of $\overline{AB}$. Equivalently, M is the midpoint of $\overline{AB}$ if $AM = MB$. Also, if $\overline{AM} \cong \overline{MB}$, then $\overline{CD}$ is described as a **bisector** of $\overline{AB}$.

If M is the midpoint of $\overline{AB}$ in Figure 1.36, we can draw these conclusions:

$$AM = MB \qquad MB = \tfrac{1}{2}(AB) \qquad AB = 2\,(MB)$$
$$AM = \tfrac{1}{2}(AB) \qquad AB = 2\,(AM)$$

Discover

Assume that M is the midpoint of $\overline{AB}$ in Figure 1.36. Can you also conclude that M is the midpoint of $\overline{CD}$?

ANSWER
ON

EXAMPLE 4

GIVEN: M is the midpoint of $\overline{EF}$ (not shown). $EM = 3x + 9$ and $MF = x + 17$
FIND: x and EM

Solution Because M is the midpoint of $\overline{EF}$, $EM = MF$. Then

$$\begin{aligned} 3x + 9 &= x + 17 \\ 2x + 9 &= 17 \\ 2x &= 8 \\ x &= 4 \end{aligned}$$

By substitution, $EM = 3(4) + 9 = 12 + 9 = 21$. ■

In geometry, the word **union** is used to describe the joining or combining of two figures or sets of points.

DEFINITION

Ray AB, denoted by $\overrightarrow{AB}$, is the union of $\overline{AB}$ and all points X on $\overleftrightarrow{AB}$ such that B is between A and X.

In Figure 1.37, $\overleftrightarrow{AB}$, $\overrightarrow{AB}$, and $\overrightarrow{BA}$ are shown; note that $\overrightarrow{AB}$ and $\overrightarrow{BA}$ are not the same ray.

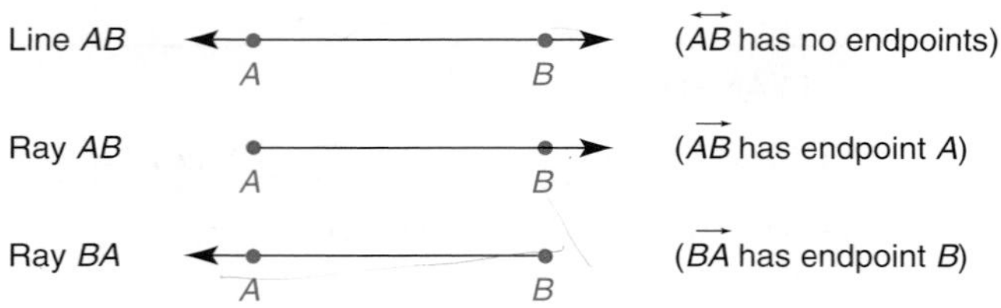

Figure 1.37

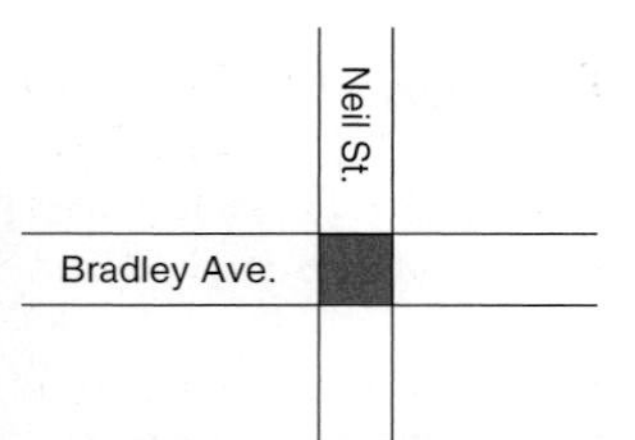

Figure 1.38

Opposite rays are two rays with a common endpoint; also, the union of opposite rays is a straight line. In Figure 1.39(a), $\overrightarrow{BA}$ and $\overrightarrow{BC}$ are opposite rays.

The **intersection** of two geometric figures is the set of points that the two figures have in common. In everyday life, the intersection of Bradley Avenue and Neil Street is the part of the roadway that the two roads have in common (Figure 1.38).

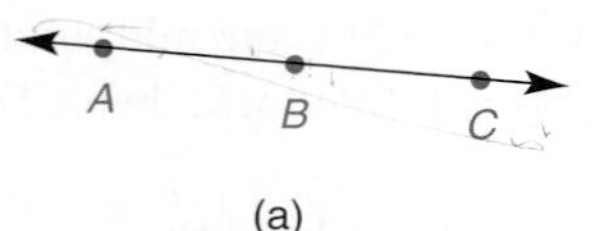

(a)

m ℓ P

(b)

Figure 1.39

POSTULATE 4

If two lines intersect, they intersect at a point.

When two lines share two (or more) points, the lines coincide; in this situation, we say there is only one line. In Figure 1.39(a), $\overleftrightarrow{AB}$ and $\overleftrightarrow{BC}$ are the same as $\overleftrightarrow{AC}$. In Figure 1.39(b), lines ℓ and m intersect at point P.

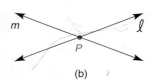

DEFINITION

Parallel lines are lines that lie in the same plane but do not intersect.

In Figure 1.40, ℓ and n are parallel; in symbols, $\ell \parallel n$ and $\ell \cap n = \emptyset$. However, ℓ and m intersect and are not parallel; so $\ell \cap m = A$ and $\ell \nparallel m$.

Exs. 5–12

EXAMPLE 5

In Figure 1.40, $\ell \parallel n$. What is the intersection of

a) lines ℓ and m?
b) line ℓ and line n?

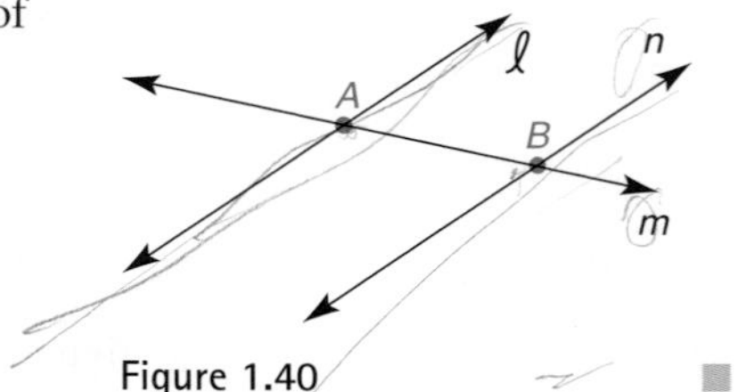

Figure 1.40

Solution

a) Point A
b) Parallel lines do not intersect. ■

Another undefined term in geometry is **plane.** A plane is two-dimensional; that is, it has infinite length and infinite width but no thickness. Except for its limited size, a flat surface such as the top of a table could be used as an example of a plane. An uppercase letter can be used to name a plane. Because a plane (like a line) is infinite, we can show only a portion of the plane or planes, as in Figure 1.41 on page 27.

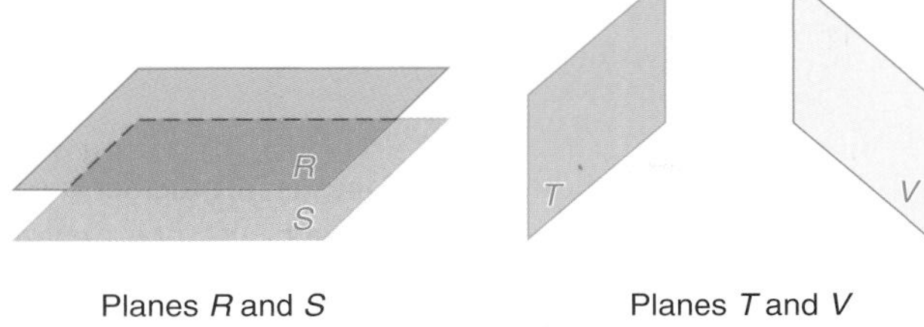

Figure 1.41

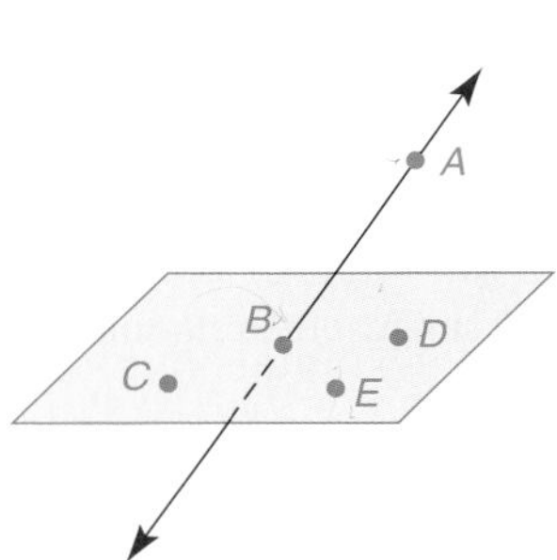

Figure 1.42

A plane is two-dimensional, consists of an infinite number of points, and contains an infinite number of lines. Two distinct points may determine (or "fix") a line; likewise, exactly three noncollinear points determine a plane. Just as collinear points lie on the same line, **coplanar points** lie in the same plane. In Figure 1.42, points *B*, *C*, *D*, and *E* are coplanar, whereas *A*, *B*, *C*, and *D* are noncoplanar.

In this book, points shown in figures are assumed to be coplanar unless otherwise stated. For instance, points *A*, *B*, *C*, *D*, and *E* are coplanar in Figure 1.43(a), as are points *F*, *G*, *H*, *J*, and *K* in Figure 1.43(b).

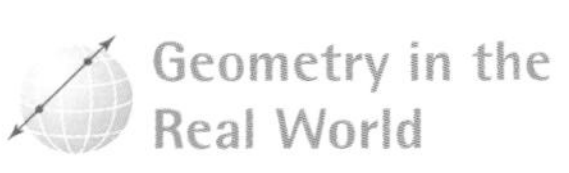

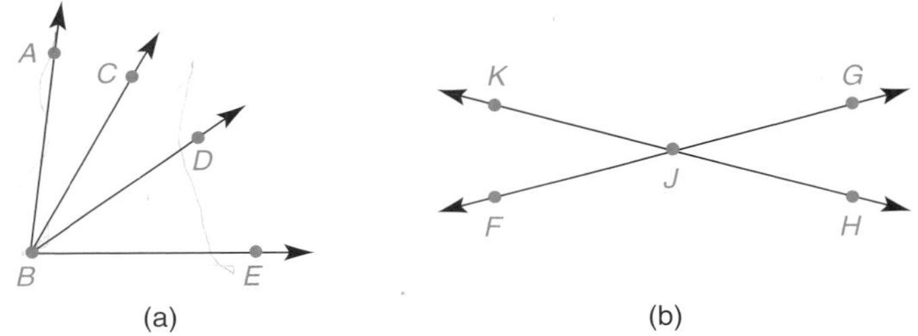

Figure 1.43

The tripod illustrates Postulate 5 in that the three points at the base enable the unit to sit level.

POSTULATE 5

Through three noncollinear points, there is exactly one plane.

On the basis of Postulate 5, we can see why a three-legged table sits evenly but a four-legged table would "wobble" if the legs were of unequal length.

Space is the set of all possible points. It is three-dimensional, having qualities of length, width, and depth. When two planes intersect in space, their intersection is a line. An opened greeting card suggests this relationship, as does Figure 1.44(a). This notion gives rise to our next postulate.

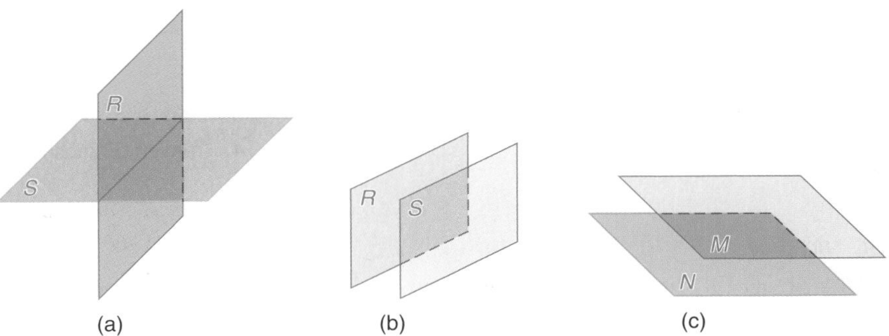

Figure 1.44

POSTULATE 6

If two distinct planes intersect, then their intersection is a line.

The intersection of two planes is infinite because it is a line. [See Figure 1.44(a) on page 27.] If two planes do not intersect, then they are **parallel.** The parallel **vertical** planes *R* and *S* in Figure 1.44(b) may remind you of the opposite walls of your classroom. The parallel horizontal planes *M* and *N* in Figure 1.44(c) suggest the relationship between ceiling and floor.

Imagine a plane and two points of that plane, say points *A* and *B*. Now think of the line containing the two points and the relationship of $\overleftrightarrow{AB}$ to the plane. Perhaps your conclusion can be summed up as follows.

POSTULATE 7

Given two distinct points in a plane, the line containing these points also lies in the plane.

Exs. 13–16

Because the uniqueness of the midpoint of a line segment can be justified, we call the following statement a theorem. The "proof" of the theorem is found in Section 2.2.

THEOREM 1.3.1

The midpoint of a line segment is unique.

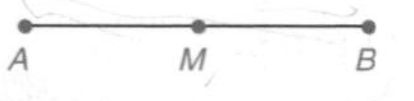

Figure 1.45

If *M* is the midpoint of $\overline{AB}$ in Figure 1.45, then no other point can separate $\overline{AB}$ into two congruent parts. The proof of this theorem is based on the Ruler Postulate. *M* is *the* point that is located $\frac{1}{2}(AB)$ units from *A* (and from *B*).

The numbering system used to identify Theorem 1.3.1 need not be memorized. However, this theorem number may be used in a later reference. The numbering system works as follows:

1	3	1
CHAPTER where found	SECTION where found	ORDER found in section

SSG *Exs. 17–20*

A summary of the theorems presented in this textbook appears at the end of the book.

▶▶▶ Exercises 1.3

In Exercises 1 and 2, complete the statement.

Exercises 1, 2

1. $AB + BC =$ __?__
2. If $AB = BC$, then *B* is the __?__ of $\overline{AC}$.

In Exercises 3 and 4, use the fact that 1 foot = 12 inches.

3. Convert 6.25 feet to a measure in inches.
4. Convert 52 inches to a measure in feet and inches.

In Exercises 5 and 6, use the fact that 1 meter ≈ 3.28 feet (measure is approximate).

5. Convert $\frac{1}{2}$ meter to feet.
6. Convert 16.4 feet to meters.

7. In the figure, the 15-mile road from A to C is under construction. A detour from A to B of 5 miles and then from B to C of 13 miles must be taken. How much farther is the "detour" from A to C than the road from A to C?

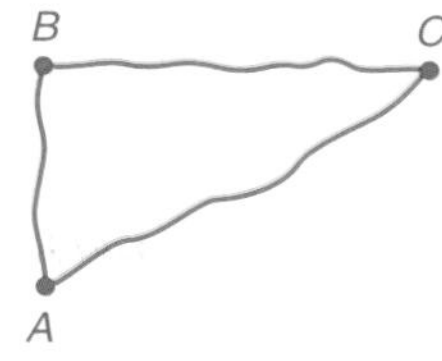

Exercises 7, 8

8. A cross-country runner jogs at a rate of 15 meters per second. If she runs 300 meters from A to B, 450 meters from B to C, and then 600 meters from C back to A, how long will it take her to return to point A?

(HINT: See figure for Exercise 7.)

In Exercises 9 to 28, use the drawings as needed to answer the following questions.

9. Name three points that appear to be
a) collinear. b) noncollinear.

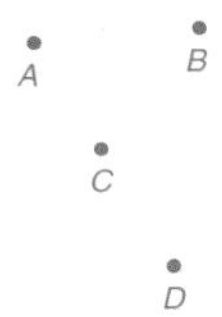

Exercises 9, 10

10. How many lines can be drawn through
a) point A?
b) points A and B?
c) points A, B, and C?
d) points A, B, and D?

11. Give the meanings of $\overleftrightarrow{CD}$, $\overline{CD}$, CD, and $\overrightarrow{CD}$.

12. Explain the difference, if any, between
a) $\overleftrightarrow{CD}$ and $\overleftrightarrow{DC}$.
b) $\overline{CD}$ and $\overline{DC}$.
c) CD and DC.
d) $\overrightarrow{CD}$ and $\overrightarrow{DC}$.

13. Name two lines that appear to be
a) parallel. b) nonparallel.

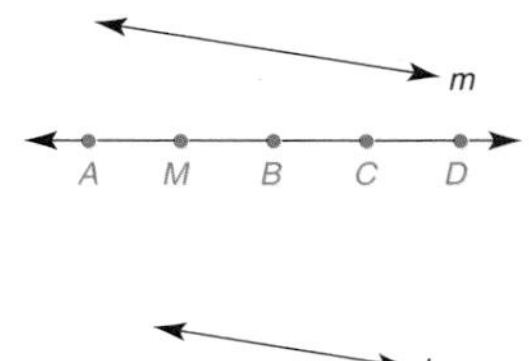

Exercises 13–17

14. Classify as true or false:
a) $AB + BC = AD$
b) $AD - CD = AB$
c) $AD - CD = AC$
d) $AB + BC + CD = AD$
e) $AB = BC$

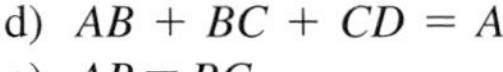
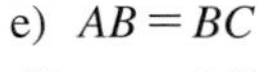

15. *Given:* M is the midpoint of $\overline{AB}$
$AM = 2x + 1$ and $MB = 3x - 2$
Find: x and AM

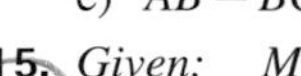

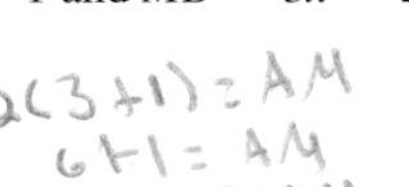

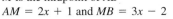

16. *Given:* M is the midpoint of $\overline{AB}$
$AM = 2(x + 1)$ and $MB = 3(x - 2)$
Find: x and AB

17. *Given:* $AM = 2x + 1$, $MB = 3x + 2$, and $AB = 6x - 4$
Find: x and AB

18. Can a segment bisect a line? a segment? Can a line bisect a segment? a line?

19. In the figure, name
a) two opposite rays.
b) two rays that are not opposite.

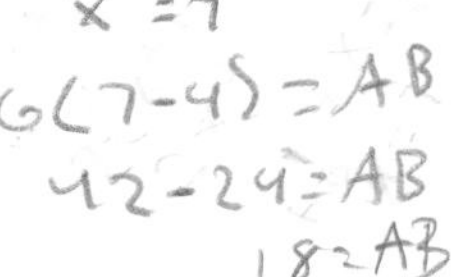

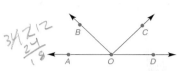

20. Suppose that (a) point C lies in plane X and (b) point D lies in plane X. What can you conclude regarding $\overleftrightarrow{CD}$?

21. Make a sketch of
a) two intersecting lines that are perpendicular.
b) two intersecting lines that are *not* perpendicular.
c) two parallel lines.

22. Make a sketch of
a) two intersecting planes.
b) two parallel planes.
c) two parallel planes intersected by a third plane that is not parallel to the first or the second plane.

23. Suppose that (a) planes M and N intersect, (b) point A lies in both planes M and N, and (c) point B lies in both planes M and N. What can you conclude regarding $\overleftrightarrow{AB}$?

24. Suppose that (a) points A, B, and C are collinear and (b) $AB > AC$. Which point can you conclude *cannot* lie between the other two?

25. Suppose that points A, R, and V are collinear. If $AR = 7$ and $RV = 5$, then which point cannot possibly lie between the other two?

26. Points A, B, C, and D are coplanar; B, C, and D are collinear; point E is not in plane M. How many planes contain
a) points A, B, and C?
b) points B, C, and D?
c) points A, B, C, and D?
d) points A, B, C, and E?

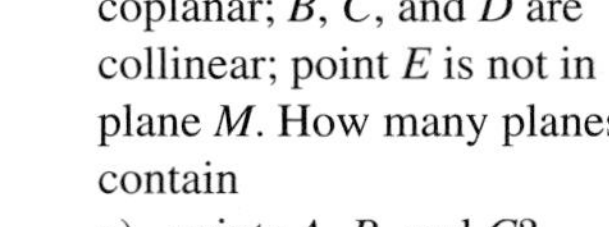

27. Using the number line provided, name the point that
a) is the midpoint of $\overline{AE}$.
b) is the endpoint of a segment of length 4, if the other endpoint is point G.
c) has a distance from B equal to $3(AC)$.

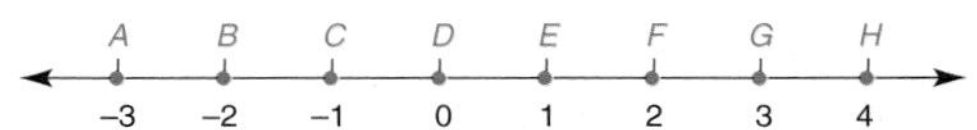

Exercises 27, 28

28. Consider the figure for Exercise 27. Given that B is the midpoint of $\overline{AC}$ and C is the midpoint of $\overline{BD}$, what can you conclude about the lengths of
a) $\overline{AB}$ and $\overline{CD}$?
b) $\overline{AC}$ and $\overline{BD}$?
c) $\overline{AC}$ and $\overline{CD}$?

In Exercises 29 to 32, use only a compass and a straightedge to complete each construction.

29. *Given:* $\overline{AB}$ and $\overline{CD}$ $(AB > CD)$
Construct: $\overline{MN}$ on line ℓ so that $MN = AB + CD$

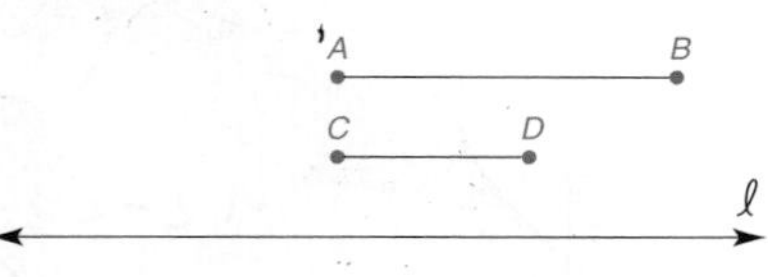

Exercises 29, 30

30. *Given:* $\overline{AB}$ and $\overline{CD}$ $(AB > CD)$
Construct: $\overline{EF}$ so that $EF = AB - CD$

31. *Given:* $\overline{AB}$ as shown in the figure
Construct: $\overline{PQ}$ on line n so that $PQ = 3(AB)$

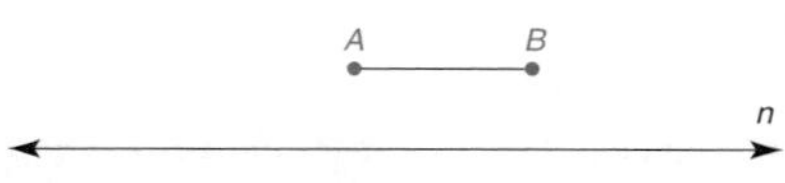

Exercises 31, 32

32. *Given:* $\overline{AB}$ as shown in the figure
Construct: $\overline{TV}$ on line n so that $TV = \frac{1}{2}(AB)$

33. Can you use the construction for the midpoint of a segment to divide a line segment into
a) three congruent parts?
b) four congruent parts?
c) six congruent parts?
d) eight congruent parts?

34. Generalize your findings in Exercise 33.

35. Consider points A, B, C, and D, no three of which are collinear. Using two points at a time (such as A and B), how many lines are determined by these points?

36. Consider noncoplanar points A, B, C, and D. Using three points at a time (such as A, B, and C), how many planes are determined by these points?

37. Line ℓ is parallel to plane P (that is, it will not intersect P even if extended). Line m intersects line ℓ. What can you conclude about m and P?

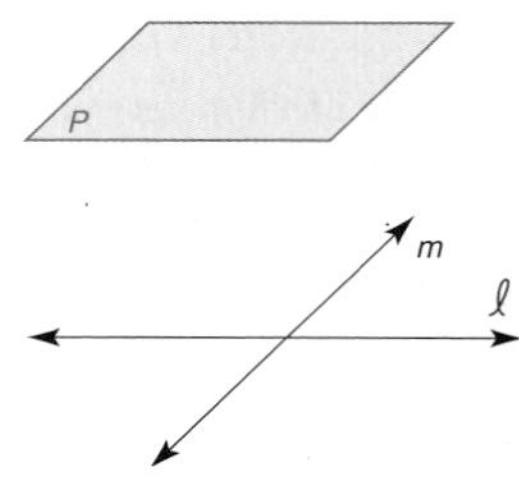

38. $\overleftrightarrow{AB}$ and $\overleftrightarrow{EF}$ are said to be **skew** lines because they neither intersect nor are parallel. How many planes are determined by
a) parallel lines AB and DC?
b) intersecting lines AB and BC?
c) skew lines AB and EF?
d) lines AB, BC, and DC?
e) points A, B, and F?
f) points A, C, and H?
g) points A, C, F, and H?

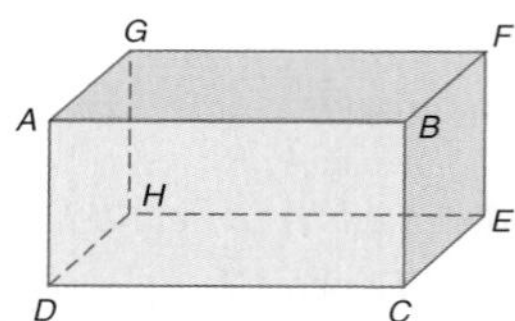

***39.** Let $AB = a$ and $BC = b$. Point M is the midpoint of $\overline{BC}$. If $AN = \frac{2}{3}(AB)$, find the length of $\overline{NM}$ in terms of a and b.

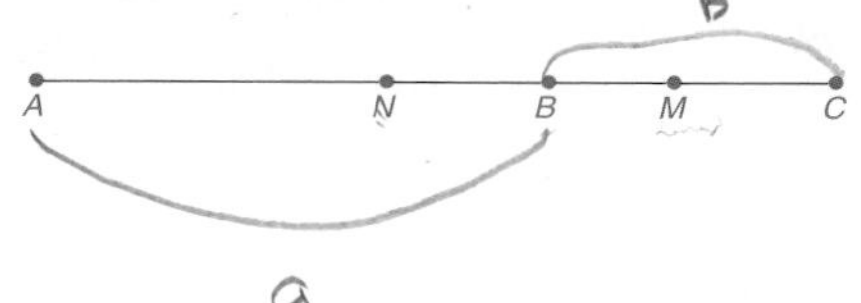

1.4 Angles and Their Relationships

KEY CONCEPTS

- Angle: Sides of Angle, Vertex of Angle
- Protractor Postulate
- Acute, Right, Obtuse, Straight, and Reflex Angles
- Angle-Addition Postulate
- Adjacent Angles
- Congruent Angles
- Bisector of an Angle
- Complementary Angles
- Supplementary Angles
- Vertical Angles

This section introduces you to the language of angles. Recall from Sections 1.1 and 1.3 that the word *union* means that two sets or figures are joined.

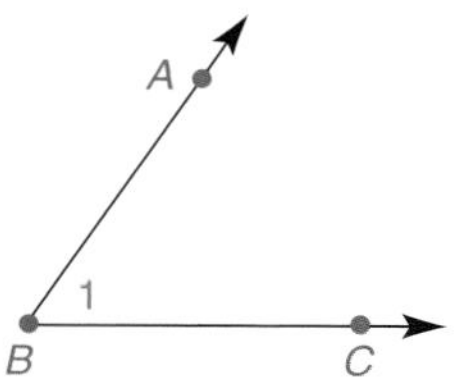

Figure 1.46

DEFINITION

An **angle** is the union of two rays that share a common endpoint.

In Figure 1.46, the angle is symbolized by $\angle ABC$ or $\angle CBA$. The rays BA and BC are known as the **sides** of the angle. B, the common endpoint of these rays, is known as the **vertex** of the angle. When three letters are used to name an angle, the vertex is always named in the middle. Recall that a single letter or numeral may be used to name the angle. The angle in Figure 1.46 may be described as $\angle B$ (the vertex of the angle) or as $\angle 1$. In set notation, $\angle B = \overrightarrow{BA} \cup \overrightarrow{BC}$.

POSTULATE 8 ▶ (Protractor Postulate)

The measure of an angle is a unique positive number.

NOTE: In Chapters 1 to 10, the measures of most angles will be between 0° and 180°, including 180°. Angles with measures between 180° and 360° are introduced in this section; these angles are not used often in our study of geometry.

TYPES OF ANGLES

An angle whose measure is less than 90° is an **acute angle.** If the angle's measure is exactly 90°, the angle is a **right angle.** If the angle's measure is between 90° and 180°, the angle is **obtuse.** An angle whose measure is exactly 180° is a **straight angle;** alternatively, a straight angle is one whose sides form opposite rays (a straight line). A **reflex angle** is one whose measure is between 180° and 360°. See Table 1.4 on page 32.

Figure 1.47

In Figure 1.47, $\angle ABC$ contains the noncollinear points A, B, and C. These three points, in turn, determine a plane. The plane containing $\angle ABC$ is separated into three subsets by the angle:

Points like D are said to be in the *interior* of $\angle ABC$.

Points like E are said to be *on* $\angle ABC$.

Points like F are said to be in the *exterior* of $\angle ABC$.

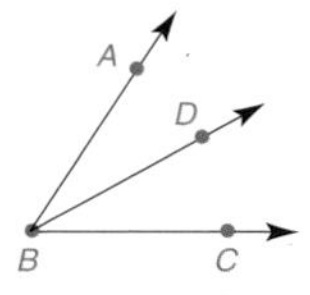

Figure 1.48

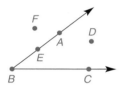

With this description, it is possible to state the counterpart of the Segment-Addition Postulate! Consider Figure 1.48 as you read Postulate 9.

POSTULATE 9 ▶ (Angle-Addition Postulate)

If a point D lies in the interior of an angle ABC, then $m\angle ABD + m\angle DBC = m\angle ABC$.

Technology Exploration

Use software if available.

1. Draw $\angle RST$.
2. Through point V in the interior of $\angle RST$, draw $\overrightarrow{SV}$.
3. Measure $\angle RST$, $\angle RSV$, and $\angle VST$.
4. Show that $m\angle RSV + m\angle VST = m\angle RST$.

TABLE 1.4
Angles

Angle	*Example*
Acute (1)	$m\angle 1 = 23°$
Right (2)	$m\angle 2 = 90°$
Obtuse (3)	$m\angle 3 = 112°$
Straight (4)	$m\angle 4 = 180°$
Reflex (5)	$m\angle 5 = 337°$

NOTE: An arc is necessary in indicating a reflex angle and can be used to indicate a straight angle as well.

Discover

When greater accuracy is needed in angle measurement, a degree can be divided into 60 minutes. In symbols, $1° = 60'$. Convert 22.5° to degrees and minutes.

ANSWER
22° 30′

EXAMPLE 1

Use Figure 1.48 on page 31 to find $m\angle ABC$ if:

a) $m\angle ABD = 27°$ and $m\angle DBC = 42°$
b) $m\angle ABD = x°$ and $m\angle DBC = (2x - 3)°$

Solution

a) Using the Angle-Addition Postulate, $m\angle ABC = m\angle ABD + m\angle DBC$. That is, $m\angle ABC = 27° + 42° = 69°$.
b) $m\angle ABC = m\angle ABD + m\angle DBC = x° + (2x - 3)° = (3x - 3)°$ ■

Discover

An index card can be used to categorize the types of angles displayed. In each sketch, an index card is placed over an angle. A dashed ray indicates that a side is hidden. What type of angle is shown in each figure? (Note the placement of the card in each figure.)

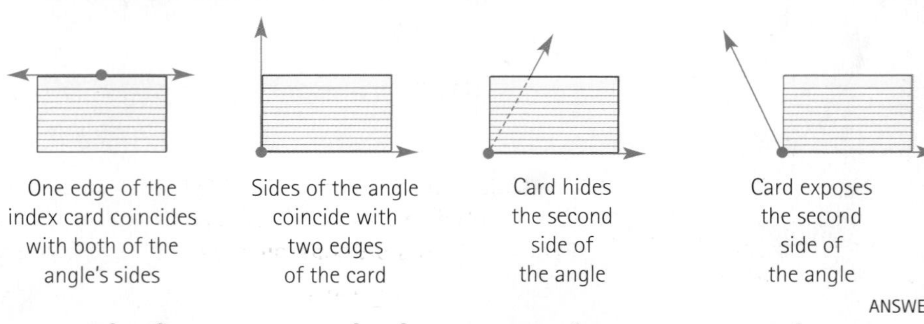

One edge of the index card coincides with both of the angle's sides

Sides of the angle coincide with two edges of the card

Card hides the second side of the angle

Card exposes the second side of the angle

SSG *Exs. 1–6*

ANSWERS
Straight angle Right angle Acute angle Obtuse angle

Figure 1.48

CLASSIFYING PAIRS OF ANGLES

Many angle relationships involve exactly two angles (a pair)—never more than two angles and never less than two angles!

In Figure 1.48, $\angle ABD$ and $\angle DBC$ are said to be *adjacent* angles. In this description, the term *adjacent* means that angles lie "next to" each other; in everyday life, one might say that the Subway sandwich shop is adjacent to the Baskin-Robbins ice cream shop. When two angles are adjacent, they have a common vertex and a common side between them. In Figure 1.48, $\angle ABC$ and $\angle ABD$ are not adjacent because they have interior points in common.

DEFINITION

Two angles are **adjacent** (adj. $\angle$s) if they have a common vertex and a common side between them.

We now recall the meaning of *congruent* angles.

DEFINITION

Congruent angles ($\cong\angle$**s**) are two angles with the same measure.

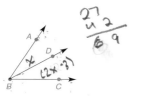

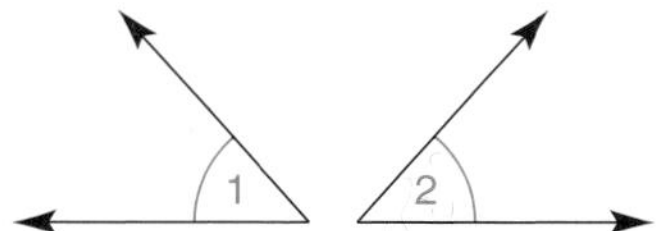

Figure 1.49

Congruent angles must coincide when one is placed over the other. (Do not consider that the sides appear to have different lengths; remember that rays are infinite in length!) In symbols, $\angle 1 \cong \angle 2$ if $m\angle 1 = m\angle 2$. In Figure 1.49, similar markings (arcs) indicate that $\angle 1 \cong \angle 2$.

EXAMPLE 2

GIVEN: $\angle 1 \cong \angle 2$
$m\angle 1 = 2x + 15$
$m\angle 2 = 3x - 2$

FIND: x

Solution $\angle 1 \cong \angle 2$ means $m\angle 1 = m\angle 2$. Therefore,

$$2x + 15 = 3x - 2$$
$$17 = x \qquad \text{or} \qquad x = 17$$

NOTE: $m\angle 1 = 2(17) + 15 = 49°$ and $m\angle 2 = 3(17) - 2 = 49°$. ■

DEFINITION

The **bisector** of an angle is the ray that separates the given angle into two congruent angles.

Figure 1.50

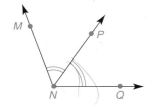

With P in the interior of $\angle MNQ$ so that $\angle MNP \cong \angle PNQ$, $\overrightarrow{NP}$ is said to **bisect** $\angle MNQ$. Equivalently, $\overrightarrow{NP}$ is the bisector or angle-bisector of $\angle MNQ$. On the basis of Figure 1.50, possible consequences of the definition of bisector of an angle are

$m\angle MNP = m\angle PNQ$ $\quad$ $m\angle MNQ = 2(m\angle PNQ)$ $\quad$ $m\angle MNQ = 2(m\angle MNP)$
$m\angle PNQ = \frac{1}{2}(m\angle MNQ)$ $\quad$ $m\angle MNP = \frac{1}{2}(m\angle MNQ)$

DEFINITION

Two angles are **complementary** if the sum of their measures is 90°. Each angle in the pair is known as the **complement** of the other angle.

Angles with measures of 37° and 53° are complementary. The 37° angle is the complement of the 53° angle, and vice versa. If the measures of two angles are x and y and it is known that $x + y = 90°$, then these two angles are complementary.

DEFINITION

Two angles are **supplementary** if the sum of their measures is 180°. Each angle in the pair is known as the **supplement** of the other angle.

EXAMPLE 3

Given that $m\angle 1 = 29°$, find:

a) the complement x b) the supplement y

Solution

a) $x + 29 = 90$, so $x = 61°$; complement $= 61°$
b) $y + 29 = 180$, so $y = 151°$; supplement $= 151°$ ■

EXAMPLE 4

GIVEN: $\angle P$ and $\angle Q$ are complementary, where

$$m\angle P = \frac{x}{2} \quad \text{and} \quad m\angle Q = \frac{x}{3}$$

FIND: x, $m\angle P$, and $m\angle Q$

Solution

$$m\angle P + m\angle Q = 90$$
$$\frac{x}{2} + \frac{x}{3} = 90$$

Multiplying by 6 (the least common denominator, or LCD, of 2 and 3), we have

$$6 \cdot \frac{x}{2} + 6 \cdot \frac{x}{3} = 6 \cdot 90$$
$$3x + 2x = 540$$
$$5x = 540$$
$$x = 108$$

$$m\angle P = \frac{x}{2} = \frac{108}{2} = 54°$$

$$m\angle Q = \frac{x}{3} = \frac{108}{3} = 36°$$

NOTE: $m\angle P = 54°$ and $m\angle Q = 36°$, so their sum is exactly 90°. ■

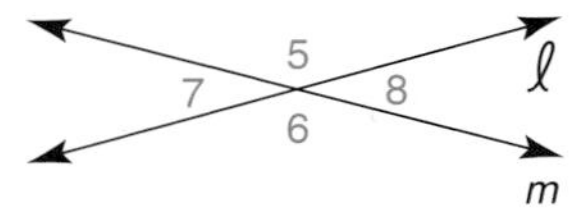

Figure 1.51

When two straight lines intersect, the pairs of nonadjacent angles in opposite positions are known as **vertical angles.** In Figure 1.51, $\angle 5$ and $\angle 6$ are vertical angles (as are $\angle 7$ and $\angle 8$). In addition, $\angle 5$ and $\angle 7$ can be described as adjacent and supplementary angles, as can $\angle 5$ and $\angle 8$. If $m\angle 7 = 30°$, what is $m\angle 5$ and what is $m\angle 8$? It is true in general that vertical angles are congruent, and we will prove this in Example 3 of Section 1.6. We apply this property in Example 5 of this section.

SSG *Exs. 7–12*

Recall the Addition and Subtraction Properties of Equality: If $a = b$ and $c = d$, then $a \pm c = b \pm d$. These principles can be used in solving a system of equations such as the following:

$$\begin{aligned} x + y &= 5 \\ 2x - y &= 7 \\ \hline 3x \quad &= 12 \qquad \text{(left and right sides are added)} \\ x &= 4 \end{aligned}$$

We can substitute 4 for x in either equation to solve for y:

$$\begin{aligned} x + y &= 5 \\ 4 + y &= 5 \qquad \text{(by substitution)} \\ y &= 1 \end{aligned}$$

If $x = 4$ and $y = 1$, then $x + y = 5$ *and* $2x - y = 7$.

When each term in an equation is multiplied by the same nonzero number, the solutions of the equation are not changed. For instance, the equations $2x - 3 = 7$ and $6x - 9 = 21$ (each term multiplied by 3) both have the solution $x = 5$. Likewise, the values of x and y that make the equation $4x + y = 180$ true also make the equation $16x + 4y = 720$ (each term multiplied by 4) true. We use this method in Example 5.

EXAMPLE 5

GIVEN: In Figure 1.51, ℓ and m intersect so that

$$\begin{aligned} m\angle 5 &= 2x + 2y \\ m\angle 8 &= 2x - y \\ m\angle 6 &= 4x - 2y \end{aligned}$$

FIND: x and y

Solution $\angle 5$ and $\angle 8$ are supplementary (adjacent and exterior sides form a straight angle). Therefore, $m\angle 5 + m\angle 8 = 180$. $\angle 5$ and $\angle 6$ are congruent (vertical). Therefore, $m\angle 5 = m\angle 6$. Consequently, we have

$$\begin{aligned} (2x + 2y) + (2x - y) &= 180 \qquad \text{(supplementary } \angle\text{s 5 and 8)} \\ 2x + 2y &= 4x - 2y \qquad (\cong \angle\text{s 5 and 6)} \end{aligned}$$

Simplifying,

$$\begin{aligned} 4x + y &= 180 \\ 2x - 4y &= 0 \end{aligned}$$

Using the Multiplication Property of Equality, we multiply the first equation by 4. Then the equivalent system allows us to eliminate variable y by addition.

$$\begin{aligned} 16x + 4y &= 720 \\ 2x - 4y &= 0 \\ \hline 18x &= 720 \qquad \text{(adding left, right sides)} \\ x &= 40 \end{aligned}$$

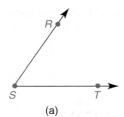

Using the equation $4x + y = 180$, it follows that

$$\begin{aligned} 4(40) + y &= 180 \\ 160 + y &= 180 \\ y &= 20 \end{aligned}$$

Summarizing, $x = 40$ and $y = 20$.

NOTE: $m\angle 5 = 120°$, $m\angle 8 = 60°$, and $m\angle 6 = 120°$. ■

CONSTRUCTIONS WITH ANGLES

In Section 1.2, we considered Constructions 1 and 2 with line segments. Now consider two constructions that involve angle concepts. In Section 3.4, it will become clear why these methods are valid. However, intuition suggests that the techniques are appropriate.

R S T

(a)

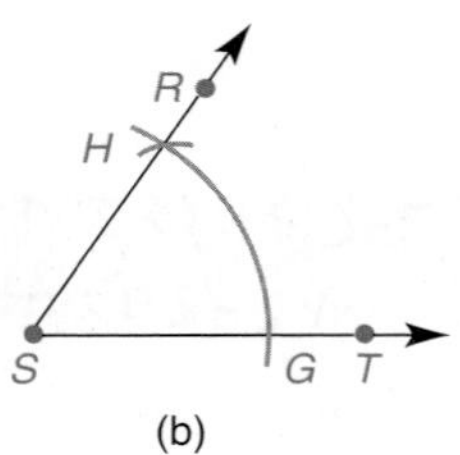

(b)

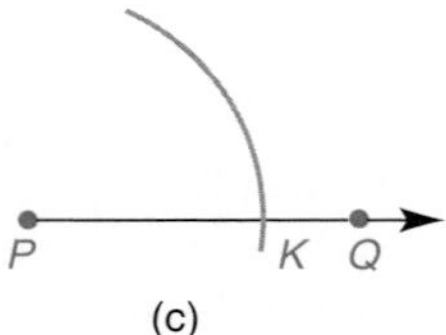

(c)

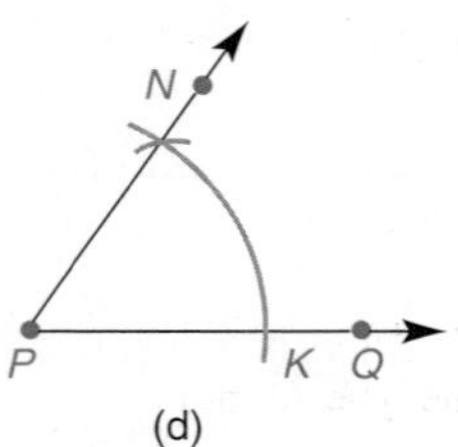

(d)

Figure 1.52

Construction 3 *To construct an angle congruent to a given angle.*

GIVEN: $\angle RST$ in Figure 1.52(a)

CONSTRUCT: With $\overrightarrow{PQ}$ as one side, $\angle NPQ \cong \angle RST$

CONSTRUCTION: Figure 1.52(b): With a compass, mark an arc to intersect both sides of $\angle RST$ (at points G and H, respectively).

Figure 1.52(c): Without changing the radius, mark an arc to intersect $\overrightarrow{PQ}$ at K and the "would-be" second side of $\angle NPQ$.

Figure 1.52(b): Now mark an arc to measure the distance from G to H.

Figure 1.52(d): Using the same radius, mark an arc with K as center to intersect the would-be second side of the desired angle. Now draw the ray from P through the point of intersection of the two arcs.

The resulting angle is the one desired, as we will prove in Section 3.4, Example 1.

Just as a line segment can be bisected, so can an angle. This takes us to a fourth construction method.

Construction 4 *To construct the angle bisector of a given angle.*

GIVEN: $\angle PRT$ in Figure 1.53(a)

CONSTRUCT: $\overrightarrow{RS}$ so that $\angle PRS \cong \angle SRT$

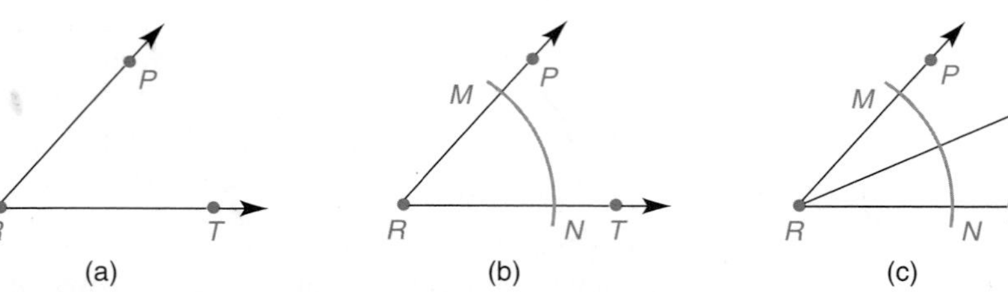

Figure 1.53

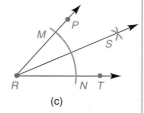

CONSTRUCTION: Figure 1.53(b): Using a compass, mark an arc to intersect the sides of $\angle PRT$ at points M and N.

Figure 1.53(c): Now, with M and N as centers, mark off two arcs with equal radii to intersect at point S in the interior of $\angle PRT$, as shown. Now draw ray RS, the desired angle bisector.

SSG *Exs. 13–20*

Reasoning from the definition of an angle bisector, the Angle-Addition Postulate, and the Protractor Postulate, we can justify the following theorem.

THEOREM 1.4.1

There is one and only one angle bisector for a given angle.

This theorem is often stated, “The angle bisector of an angle is unique.” This statement is proved in Example 5 of Section 2.2.

Exercises 1.4

1. What *type of angle* is each of the following?
a) 47° b) 90° c) 137.3°

2. What *type of angle* is each of the following?
a) 115° b) 180° c) 36°

3. What *relationship*, if any, exists between two angles:
a) with measures of 37° and 53°?
b) with measures of 37° and 143°?

4. What *relationship*, if any, exists between two angles:
a) with equal measures?
b) that have the same vertex and a common side between them?

In Exercises 5 to 8, describe in one word the relationship between the angles.

5. $\angle ABD$ and $\angle DBC$

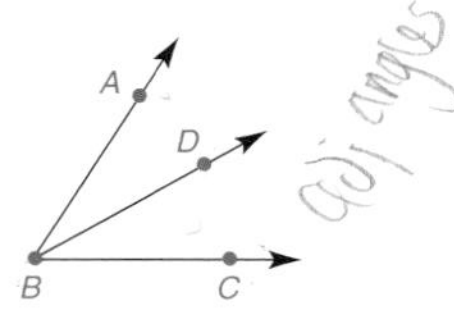

6. $\angle 7$ and $\angle 8$

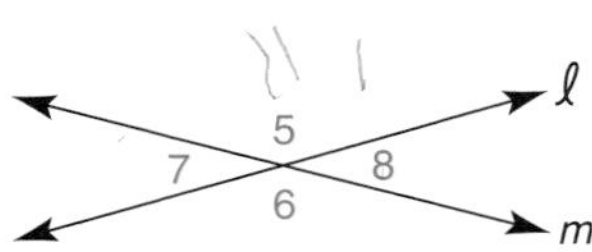

7. $\angle 1$ and $\angle 2$

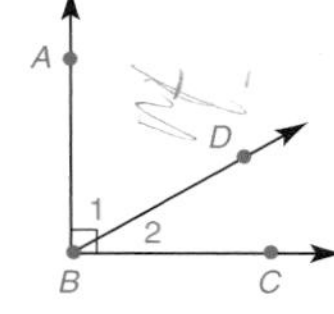

8. $\angle 3$ and $\angle 4$

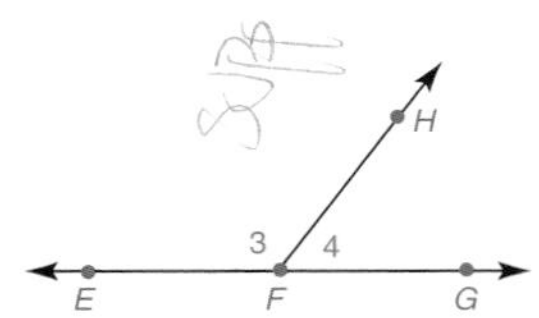

Use drawings as needed to answer each of the following questions.

9. Must two rays with a common endpoint be coplanar? Must three rays with a common endpoint be coplanar?

10. Suppose that $\overrightarrow{AB}$, $\overrightarrow{AC}$, $\overrightarrow{AD}$, $\overrightarrow{AE}$, and $\overrightarrow{AF}$ are coplanar.

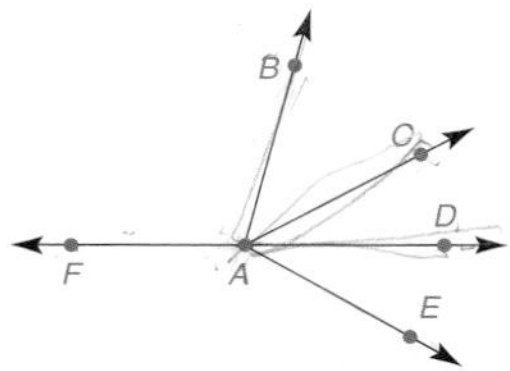

Exercises 10–13

Classify the following as true or false:
a) $m\angle BAC + m\angle CAD = m\angle BAD$
b) $\angle BAC \cong \angle CAD$
c) $m\angle BAE - m\angle DAE = m\angle BAC$
d) $\angle BAC$ and $\angle DAE$ are adjacent
e) $m\angle BAC + m\angle CAD + m\angle DAE = m\angle BAE$

11. Without using a protractor, name the type of angle represented by:
a) $\angle BAE$ b) $\angle FAD$ c) $\angle BAC$ d) $\angle FAE$

12. What, if anything, is wrong with the claim $m\angle FAB + m\angle BAE = m\angle FAE$?

13. $\angle FAC$ and $\angle CAD$ are adjacent and $\overrightarrow{AF}$ and $\overrightarrow{AD}$ are opposite rays. What can you conclude about $\angle FAC$ and $\angle CAD$?

For Exercises 14 and 15, let $m\angle 1 = x$ and $m\angle 2 = y$.

14. Using variables x and y, write an equation that expresses the fact that $\angle 1$ and $\angle 2$ are:
a) supplementary b) congruent

15. Using variables x and y, write an equation that expresses the fact that $\angle 1$ and $\angle 2$ are:
a) complementary b) vertical

For Exercises 16, 17, see figure on page 38.

16. *Given:* $m\angle RST = 39°$
$m\angle TSV = 23°$
Find: $m\angle RSV$

17. *Given:* $m\angle RSV = 59°$
$m\angle TSV = 17°$
Find: $m\angle RST$

18. *Given:* m∠$RST = 2x + 9$
m∠$TSV = 3x - 2$
m∠$RSV = 67°$
Find: x

19. *Given:* m∠$RST = 2x - 10$
m∠$TSV = x + 6$
m∠$RSV = 4(x - 6)$
Find: x and m∠RSV

20. *Given:* m∠$RST = 5(x + 1) - 3$
m∠$TSV = 4(x - 2) + 3$
m∠$RSV = 4(2x + 3) - 7$
Find: x and m∠RSV

21. *Given:* m∠$RST = \frac{x}{2}$
m∠$TSV = \frac{x}{4}$
m∠$RSV = 45°$
Find: x and m∠RST

22. *Given:* m∠$RST = \frac{2x}{3}$
m∠$TSV = \frac{x}{2}$
m∠$RSV = 49°$
Find: x and m∠TSV

23. *Given:* $\overrightarrow{ST}$ bisects ∠RSV
m∠$RST = x + y$
m∠$TSV = 2x - 2y$
m∠$RSV = 64°$
Find: x and y

24. *Given:* $\overrightarrow{ST}$ bisects ∠RSV
m∠$RST = 2x + 3y$
m∠$TSV = 3x - y + 2$
m∠$RSV = 80°$
Find: x and y

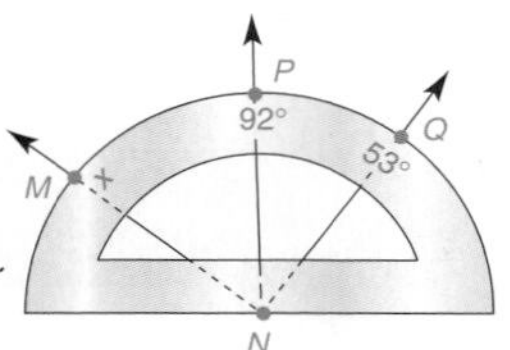

Exercises 16–24

25. *Given:* $\overleftrightarrow{AB}$ and $\overleftrightarrow{AC}$ in plane P as shown; $\overleftrightarrow{AD}$ intersects P at point A
∠CAB ≅ ∠DAC
∠DAC ≅ ∠DAB
What can you conclude?

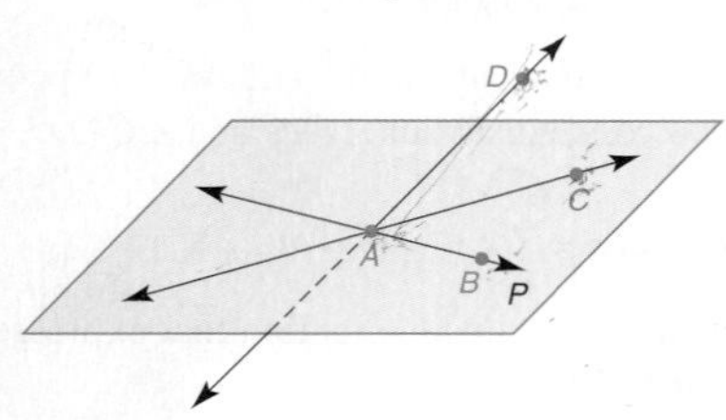

26. Two angles are complementary. One angle is 12° larger than the other. Using two variables x and y, find the size of each angle by solving a system of equations.

27. Two angles are supplementary. One angle is 24° more than twice the other. Using two variables x and y, find the measure of each angle.

28. For two complementary angles, find an expression for the measure of the second angle if the measure of the first is:
a) $x°$
b) $(3x - 12)°$
c) $(2x + 5y)°$

29. Suppose that two angles are supplementary. Find expressions for the supplements, using the expressions provided in Exercise 28, parts (a) to (c).

30. On the protractor shown, $\overrightarrow{NP}$ bisects ∠MNQ. Find x.

Exercises 30, 31

31. On the protractor shown for Exercise 30, ∠MNP and ∠PNQ are complementary. Find x.

32. Classify as true or false:
a) If points P and Q lie in the interior of ∠ABC, then $\overline{PQ}$ lies in the interior of ∠ABC.
b) If points P and Q lie in the interior of ∠ABC, then $\overleftrightarrow{PQ}$ lies in the interior of ∠ABC.
c) If points P and Q lie in the interior of ∠ABC, then $\overrightarrow{PQ}$ lies in the interior of ∠ABC.

In Exercises 33 to 40, use only a compass and a straightedge to perform the indicated constructions.

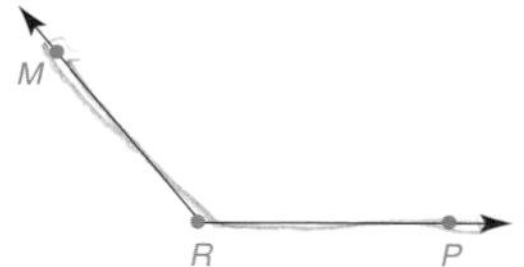

Exercises 33–35

33. *Given:* Obtuse ∠MRP
Construct: With $\overrightarrow{OA}$ as one side, an angle ≅ ∠MRP

34. *Given:* Obtuse ∠MRP
Construct: $\overrightarrow{RS}$, the angle bisector of ∠MRP

35. *Given:* Obtuse ∠MRP
Construct: Rays $\overrightarrow{RS}$, $\overrightarrow{RT}$, and $\overrightarrow{RU}$ so that ∠MRP is divided into four ≅ angles

36. *Given:* Straight ∠DEF
Construct: A right angle with vertex at E
(HINT: Use Construction 4.)

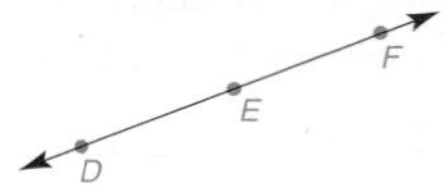

37. Draw a triangle with three acute angles. Construct angle bisectors for each of the three angles. On the basis of the appearance of your construction, what seems to be true?

38. *Given:* Acute $\angle 1$ and $\overline{AB}$
Construct: Triangle ABC with $\angle A \cong \angle 1$, $\angle B \cong \angle 1$, and side $\overline{AB}$

39. What seems to be true of two of the sides in the triangle you constructed in Exercise 38?

40. *Given:* Straight $\angle ABC$ and $\overrightarrow{BD}$
Construct: Bisectors of $\angle ABD$ and $\angle DBC$
What type of angle is formed by the bisectors of the two angles?

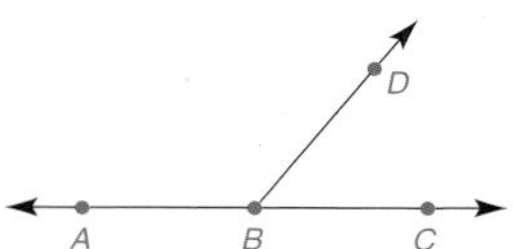

41. Refer to the circle with center O.
a) Use a protractor to find m$\angle B$.
b) Use a protractor to find m$\angle D$.
c) Compare results in parts (a) and (b).

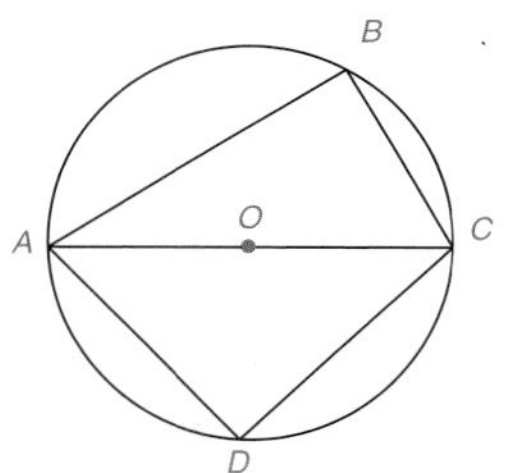

42. If m$\angle TSV = 38°$, m$\angle USW = 40°$, and m$\angle TSW = 61°$, find m$\angle USV$.

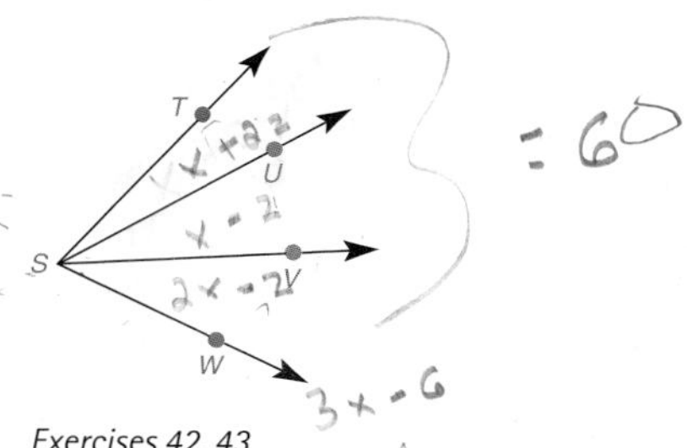

Exercises 42, 43

43. If m$\angle TSU = x + 2z$, m$\angle USV = x - z$, and m$\angle VSW = 2x - z$, find x if m$\angle TSW = 60$. Also, find z if m$\angle USW = 3x - 6$.

44. Refer to the circle with center P.
a) Use a protractor to find m$\angle 1$.
b) Use a protractor to find m$\angle 2$.
c) Compare results in parts (a) and (b).

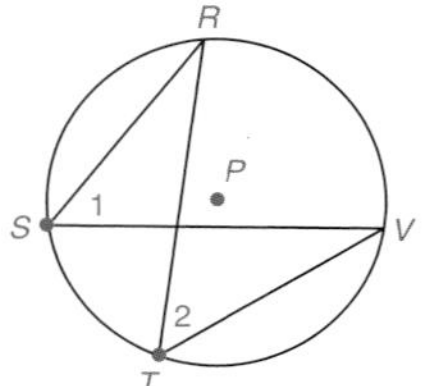

45. On the hanging sign, the three angles ($\angle ABD$, $\angle ABC$, and $\angle DBC$) at vertex B have the sum of measures 360°. If m$\angle DBC = 90°$ and $\overrightarrow{BA}$ bisects the indicated reflex angle, find m$\angle ABC$.

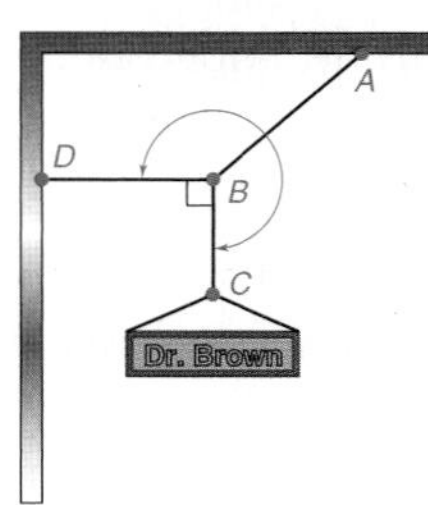

1.5 Introduction to Geometric Proof

KEY CONCEPTS

Proof	Given Problem and Prove Statement
Algebraic Properties	Sample Proofs

To believe certain geometric principles, it is necessary to have proof. This section introduces some guidelines for proving geometric properties. Several examples are offered to help you develop your own proofs. In the beginning, the form of proof will be a two-column proof, with statements in the left column and reasons in the right column. But where do the statements and reasons come from?

Reminder

Additional properties and techniques of algebra are found in Appendix A.

To deal with this question, you must ask "What" it is that is known (Given) and "Why" the conclusion (Prove) should follow from this information. Completing the proof often requires deducing several related conclusions and thus several intermediate "whys". In correctly piecing together a proof, you will usually scratch out several conclusions and reorder them. Each conclusion must be justified by citing the Given (hypothesis), a previously stated definition or postulate, or a theorem previously proved.

Selected properties from algebra are often used as reasons to justify statements. For instance, we use the Addition Property of Equality to justify adding the same number to each side of an equation. Reasons found in a proof often include the properties found in Tables 1.5 and 1.6.

TABLE 1.5
Properties of Equality (a, b, and c are real numbers)

Addition Property of Equality:	If $a = b$, then $a + c = b + c$.
Subtraction Property of Equality:	If $a = b$, then $a - c = b - c$.
Multiplication Property of Equality:	If $a = b$, then $a \cdot c = b \cdot c$.
Division Property of Equality:	If $a = b$ and $c \neq 0$, then $\frac{a}{c} = \frac{b}{c}$.

As we discover in Example 1, some properties can be used interchangably.

EXAMPLE 1

Which property of equality justifies each conclusion?

a) If $2x - 3 = 7$, then $2x = 10$. b) If $2x = 10$, then $x = 5$.

Solution

a) Addition Property of Equality; added 3 to each side of the equation.
b) Multiplication Property of Equality; multiplied each side of the equation by $\frac{1}{2}$. *OR* Division Property of Equality; divided each side of the equation by 2. ■

TABLE 1.6
Further Algebraic Properties of Equality (a, b, and c are real numbers)

Reflexive Property:	$a = a$.
Symmetric Property:	If $a = b$, then $b = a$.
Distributive Property:	$a(b + c) = a \cdot b + a \cdot c$.
Substitution Property:	If $a = b$, then a replaces b in any equation.
Transitive Property:	If $a = b$ and $b = c$, then $a = c$.

Before considering geometric proof, we study algebraic proof, in which each statement in a sequence of steps is supported by the reason *why* we can make that statement (claim). The first claim in the proof is the *Given* problem; and the sequence of steps must conclude with a final statement representing the claim to be proved (called the *Prove statement*).

SSG *Exs. 1–4*

Study Example 2. Then cover the reasons and provide the reason for each statement. With statements covered, find the statement corresponding to each reason.

EXAMPLE 2

GIVEN: $2(x-3)+4=10$
PROVE: $x=6$

PROOF

Statements	Reasons
1. $2(x-3)+4=10$	1. Given
2. $2x-6+4=10$	2. Distributive Property
3. $2x-2=10$	3. Substitution
4. $2x=12$	4. Addition Property of Equality
5. $x=6$	5. Division Property of Equality

NOTE 1: Alternatively, Step 5 could use the reason Multiplication Property of Equality (multiply by $\frac{1}{2}$). Division by 2 led to the same result.

SSG *Exs. 5–7*

NOTE 2: The fifth step is the final step because the Prove statement has been made and justified. ■

Discover

In the diagram, the wooden trim pieces are mitered (cut at an angle) to be equal and to form a right angle when placed together. Use the properties of algebra to explain why the measures of $\angle 1$ and $\angle 2$ are both 45°. What you have done is an informal "proof."

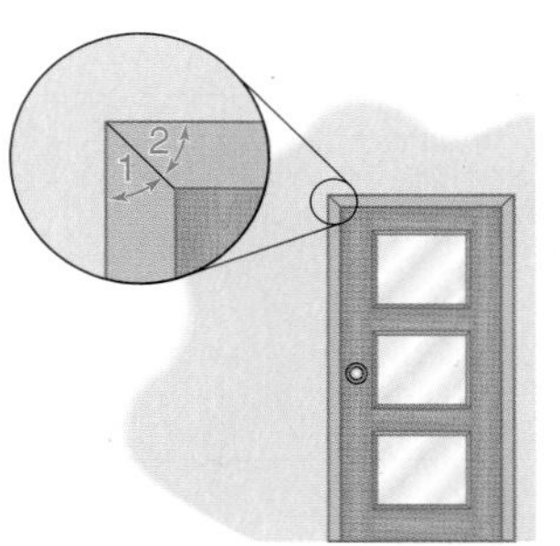

ANSWER

$m\angle 1 + m\angle 2 = 90°$. Because $m\angle 1 = m\angle 2$, we see that $m\angle 1 + m\angle 1 = 90°$. Thus, $2 \cdot m\angle 1 = 90°$, and, dividing by 2, we see that $m\angle 1 = 45°$. Then $m\angle 2 = 45°$ also.

The Discover activity at the left suggests that a formal geometric proof also exists. The typical format for a problem requiring geometric proof is

GIVEN: ________ [Drawing]

PROVE: ________

Consider this problem:

GIVEN: *A-P-B* on $\overline{AB}$ (Figure 1.54)

PROVE: $AP = AB - PB$

Figure 1.54

First consider the Drawing (Figure 1.54), and relate it to any additional information described by the Given. Then consider the Prove statement. Do you understand the claim, and does it seem reasonable? If it seems reasonable, the intermediate claims must be ordered and supported to form the contents of the proof. Because a proof must begin with the Given and conclude with the Prove, the proof of the preceding problem has this form:

PROOF

Statements	Reasons
1. *A-P-B* on $\overline{AB}$	1. Given
2. ?	2. ?
.	.
.	.
.	.
?. $AP = AB - PB$	?. ?

To construct the proof, you must glean from the Drawing and the Given that

$$AP + PB = AB$$

In turn, you deduce (through subtraction) that $AP = AB - PB$. The complete proof problem will have the appearance of Example 3, which follows the first of several "Strategy for Proof" features used in this textbook.

STRATEGY FOR PROOF ▶ The First Line of Proof

General Rule: The first *statement* of the proof includes the "Given" information; also, the first *reason* is Given.

Illustration: See the first line in the proof of Example 3.

EXAMPLE 3

Figure 1.55

GIVEN: A-P-B on $\overline{AB}$ (Figure 1.55)
PROVE: $AP = AB - PB$

PROOF

Statements	Reasons
1. A-P-B on $\overline{AB}$	1. Given
2. $AP + PB = AB$	2. Segment-Addition Postulate
3. $AP = AB - PB$	3. Subtraction Property of Equality

Exs. 8–10

Some of the properties of inequality that are used in Example 4 are found in Table 1.7. While the properties are stated for the "greater than" relation (>), they are valid also for the "less than" relation (<).

TABLE 1.7
Properties of Inequality (a, b, and c are real numbers)

Addition Property of Inequality:	If $a > b$, then $a + c > b + c$.
Subtraction Property of Inequality:	If $a > b$, then $a - c > b - c$.

SAMPLE PROOFS

Consider Figure 1.56 and this problem:

M N P Q

Figure 1.56

GIVEN: $MN > PQ$

PROVE: $MP > NQ$

To understand the situation, first study the Drawing (Figure 1.56) and the related Given. Then read the Prove with reference to the drawing. Constructing the proof requires that you begin with the Given and end with the Prove. What may be confusing here is that the Given involves MN and PQ, whereas the Prove involves MP and NQ. However, this is easily remedied through the addition of NP to each side of the inequality $MN > PQ$; see step 2 in the proof of Example 4.

M N P Q

Figure 1.57

EXAMPLE 4

GIVEN: $MN > PQ$ (Figure 1.57)

PROVE: $MP > NQ$

PROOF

Statements	Reasons
1. $MN > PQ$	1. Given
2. $MN + NP > NP + PQ$	2. Addition Property of Inequality
3. But $MN + NP = MP$ and $NP + PQ = NQ$	3. Segment-Addition Postulate
4. $MP > NQ$	4. Substitution

NOTE: The final reason may come as a surprise. However, the Substitution Axiom of Equality allows you to replace a quantity with its equal in *any* statement—including an inequality! See Appendix A.3 for more information.

STRATEGY FOR PROOF ▶ The last statement of the proof

General Rule: The final *statement* of the proof is the "Prove" statement.
Illustration: See the last statement in the proof of Example 5.

EXAMPLE 5

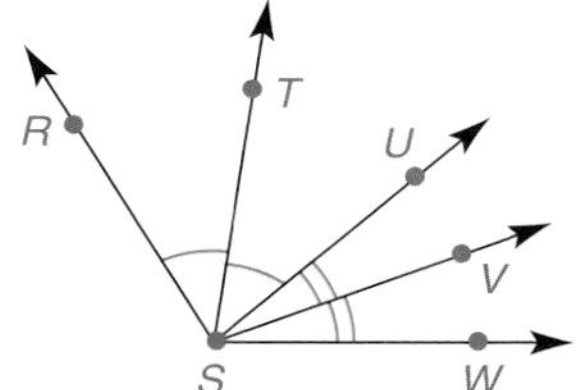

Figure 1.58

Study this proof, noting the order of the statements and reasons.

GIVEN: $\overrightarrow{ST}$ bisects $\angle RSU$
$\overrightarrow{SV}$ bisects $\angle USW$ (Figure 1.58)

PROVE: $m\angle RST + m\angle VSW = m\angle TSV$

PROOF

Statements	Reasons
1. $\overrightarrow{ST}$ bisects $\angle RSU$	1. Given
2. $m\angle RST = m\angle TSU$	2. If an angle is bisected, then the measures of the resulting angles are equal.
3. $\overrightarrow{SV}$ bisects $\angle USW$	3. Same as reason 1
4. $m\angle VSW = m\angle USV$	4. Same as reason 2
5. $m\angle RST + m\angle VSW = m\angle TSU + m\angle USV$	5. Addition Property of Equality (use the equations from statements 2 and 4)
6. $m\angle TSU + m\angle USV = m\angle TSV$	6. Angle-Addition Postulate
7. $m\angle RST + m\angle VSW = m\angle TSV$	7. Substitution

SSG *Exs. 11, 12*

Exercises 1.5

In Exercises 1 to 6, which property justifies the conclusion of the statement?

1. If $2x = 12$, then $x = 6$.

2. If $x + x = 12$, then $2x = 12$.

3. If $x + 5 = 12$, then $x = 7$.

4. If $x - 5 = 12$, then $x = 17$.

5. If $\frac{x}{5} = 3$, then $x = 15$.

6. If $3x - 2 = 13$, then $3x = 15$.

In Exercises 7 to 10, state the property or definition that justifies the conclusion (the "then" clause).

7. Given that ∠s 1 and 2 are supplementary, then $m\angle 1 + m\angle 2 = 180°$.

8. Given that $m\angle 3 + m\angle 4 = 180°$, then ∠s 3 and 4 are supplementary.

9. Given $\angle RSV$ and $\overrightarrow{ST}$ as shown, then $m\angle RST + m\angle TSV = m\angle RSV$.

10. Given that $m\angle RST = m\angle TSV$, then $\overrightarrow{ST}$ bisects $\angle RSV$.

R S T V

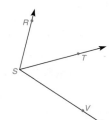

Exercises 9, 10

In Exercises 11 to 22, use the Given information to draw a conclusion based on the stated property or definition.

A M B

Exercises 11, 12

11. *Given:* A-M-B; Segment-Addition Postulate

12. *Given:* M is the midpoint of $\overline{AB}$; definition of midpoint

13. *Given:* $m\angle 1 = m\angle 2$; definition of angle bisector

14. *Given:* $\overrightarrow{EG}$ bisects $\angle DEF$; definition of angle bisector

15. *Given:* ∠s 1 and 2 are complementary; definition of complementary angles

D G 1 2 E F

Exercises 13–16

16. *Given:* $m\angle 1 + m\angle 2 = 90°$; definition of complementary angles

17. *Given:* $2x - 3 = 7$; Addition Property of Equality

18. *Given:* $3x = 21$; Division Property of Equality

19. *Given:* $7x + 5 - 3 = 30$; Substitution Property of Equality

20. *Given:* $\frac{1}{2} = 0.5$ and $0.5 = 50\%$; Transitive Property of Equality

21. *Given:* $3(2x - 1) = 27$; Distributive Property

22. *Given:* $\frac{x}{5} = -4$; Multiplication Property of Equality

In Exercises 23 and 24, fill in the missing reasons for the algebraic proof.

23. *Given:* $3(x - 5) = 21$
Prove: $x = 12$

PROOF

Statements	Reasons
1. $3(x - 5) = 21$	1. ?
2. $3x - 15 = 21$	2. ?
3. $3x = 36$	3. ?
4. $x = 12$	4. ?

24. *Given:* $2x + 9 = 3$
Prove: $x = -3$

PROOF

Statements	Reasons
1. $2x + 9 = 3$	1. ?
2. $2x = -6$	2. ?
3. $x = -3$	3. ?

In Exercises 25 and 26, fill in the missing statements for the algebraic proof.

25. *Given:* $2(x + 3) - 7 = 11$
Prove: $x = 6$

PROOF

Statements	Reasons
1. ?	1. Given
2. ?	2. Distributive Property
3. ?	3. Substitution (Addition)
4. ?	4. Addition Property of Equality
5. ?	5. Division Property of Equality

26. *Given:* $\frac{x}{5} + 3 = 9$
Prove: $x = 30$

PROOF

Statements	Reasons
1. ?	1. Given
2. ?	2. Subtraction Property of Equality
3. ?	3. Multiplication Property of Equality

In Exercises 27 to 30, fill in the missing reasons for each geometric proof.

D E F

Exercises 27, 28

27. *Given:* D-E-F on $\overleftrightarrow{DF}$
Prove: $DE = DF - EF$

PROOF

Statements	Reasons
1. D-E-F on $\overleftrightarrow{DF}$	1. ?
2. $DE + EF = DF$	2. ?
3. $DE = DF - EF$	3. ?

28. *Given:* E is the midpoint of $\overline{DF}$
Prove: $DE = \frac{1}{2}(DF)$

PROOF

Statements	Reasons
1. E is the midpoint of $\overline{DF}$	1. ?
2. $DE = EF$	2. ?
3. $DE + EF = DF$	3. ?
4. $DE + DE = DF$	4. ?
5. $2(DE) = DF$	5. ?
6. $DE = \frac{1}{2}(DF)$	6. ?

29. *Given:* $\overrightarrow{BD}$ bisects $\angle ABC$
Prove: $m\angle ABD = \frac{1}{2}(m\angle ABC)$

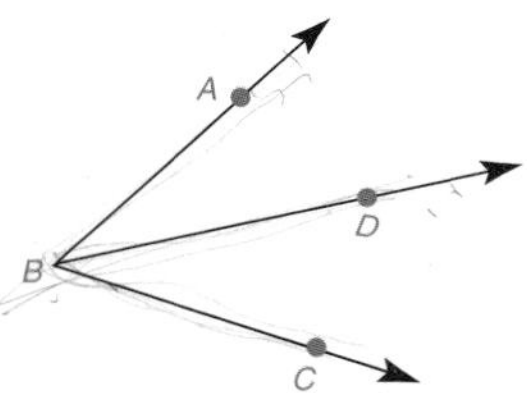

Exercises 29, 30

PROOF

Statements	Reasons
1. $\overrightarrow{BD}$ bisects $\angle ABC$	1. ?
2. $m\angle ABD = m\angle DBC$	2. ?
3. $m\angle ABD + m\angle DBC = m\angle ABC$	3. ?
4. $m\angle ABD + m\angle ABD = m\angle ABC$	4. ?
5. $2(m\angle ABD) = m\angle ABC$	5. ?
6. $m\angle ABD = \frac{1}{2}(m\angle ABC)$	6. ?

30. *Given:* $\angle ABC$ and $\overrightarrow{BD}$ (See figure for Exercise 29.)
Prove: $m\angle ABD = m\angle ABC - m\angle DBC$

PROOF

Statements	Reasons
1. $\angle ABC$ and $\overrightarrow{BD}$	1. ?
2. $m\angle ABD + m\angle DBC = m\angle ABC$	2. ?
3. $m\angle ABD = m\angle ABC - m\angle DBC$	3. ?

In Exercises 31 and 32, fill in the missing statements and reasons.

M N P Q

31. *Given:* M-N-P-Q on $\overline{MQ}$
Prove: $MN + NP + PQ = MQ$

PROOF

Statements	Reasons
1. ?	1. ?
2. $MN + NQ = MQ$	2. ?
3. $NP + PQ = NQ$	3. ?
4. ?	4. Substitution Property of Equality

32. *Given:* $\angle TSW$ with $\overrightarrow{SU}$ and $\overrightarrow{SV}$
Prove: $m\angle TSW = m\angle TSU + m\angle USV + m\angle VSW$

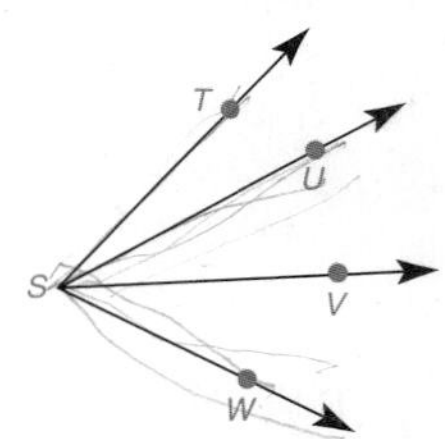

PROOF

Statements	Reasons
1. ? ∠TSW wit SU an SV	1. ? Given
2. $m\angle TSW = m\angle TSU + m\angle USW$	2. ? Angle Add
3. $m\angle USW = m\angle USV + m\angle VSW$	3. ? Angle
4. ? m∠USV = m∠VSW + m∠USW.	4. Substitution Property of Equality

33. When the Distributive Property is written in its *symmetric* form, it reads $a \cdot b + a \cdot c = a(b + c)$. Use this form to rewrite $5x + 5y$.

34. Another form of the Distributive Property (see Exercise 33) reads $b \cdot a + c \cdot a = (b + c)a$. Use this form to rewrite $5x + 7x$. Then simplify.

35. The Multiplication Property of Inequality requires that we *reverse* the inequality symbol when multiplying by a *negative* number. Given that $-7 < 5$, form the inequality that results when we multiply each side by -2.

36. The Division Property of Inequality requires that we *reverse* the inequality symbol when dividing by a *negative* number. Given that $12 > -4$, form the inequality that results when we divide each side by -4.

37. Provide reasons for this proof. "If $a = b$ and $c = d$, then $a + c = b + d$."

PROOF

Statements	Reasons
1. $a = b$	1. ?
2. $a + c = b + c$	2. ?
3. $c = d$	3. ?
4. $a + c = b + d$	4. ?

38. Write a proof for: "If $a = b$ and $c = d$, then $a - c = b - d$."

1.6 Relationships: Perpendicular Lines

Vertical Line(s)
Horizontal Line(s)
Perpendicular Lines
Relations: Reflexive, Symmetric, and Transitive Properties
Equivalence Relation
Perpendicular Bisector of a Line Segment

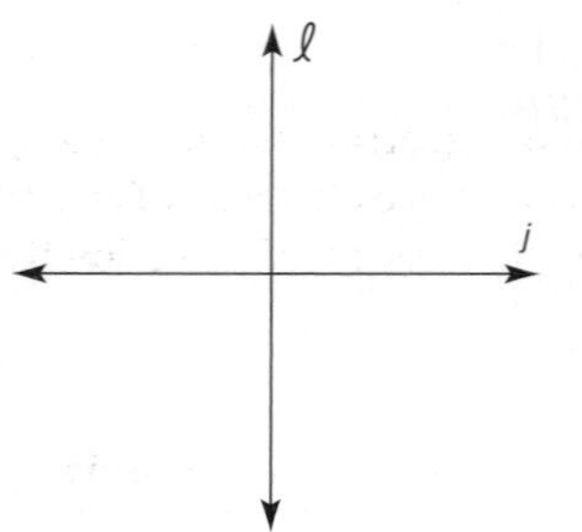

Figure 1.59

Informally, a **vertical** line is one that extends up and down, like a flagpole. On the other hand, a line that extends left to right is **horizontal.** In Figure 1.59, ℓ is vertical and j is horizontal. Where lines ℓ and j intersect, they appear to form angles of equal measure.

DEFINITION

Perpendicular lines are two lines that meet to form congruent adjacent angles.

Perpendicular lines do not have to be vertical and horizontal. In Figure 1.60, the slanted lines m and p are perpendicular ($m \perp p$). As we have seen, a small square is often placed in the opening of an angle formed by perpendicular lines to signify that the lines are perpendicular.

Example 1 provides a formal proof of the relationship between perpendicular lines and right angles. Study this proof, noting the order of the statements and reasons. The numbers in parentheses to the left of the statements refer to the earlier statement(s) upon which the new statement is based.

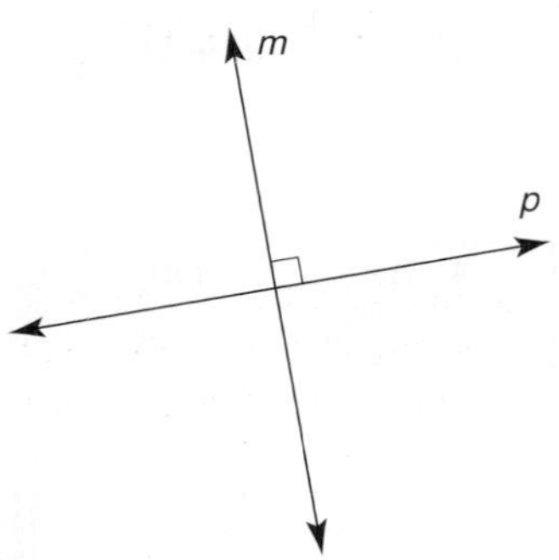

Figure 1.60

STRATEGY FOR PROOF ▶ The Drawing for the Proof

General Rule: Make a drawing that accurately characterizes the "Given" information.
Illustration: For the proof of Example 1, see Figure 1.61.

THEOREM 1.6.1

If two lines are perpendicular, then they meet to form right angles.

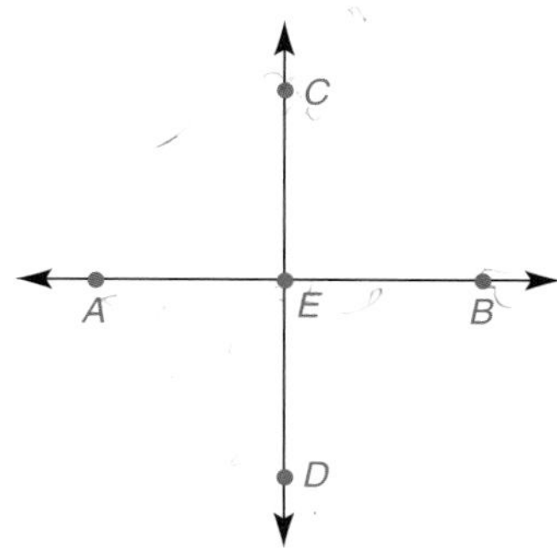

Figure 1.61

EXAMPLE 1

GIVEN: $\overleftrightarrow{AB} \perp \overleftrightarrow{CD}$, intersecting at E (See Figure 1.61)
PROVE: $\angle AEC$ is a right angle

PROOF

Statements	Reasons
1. $\overleftrightarrow{AB} \perp \overleftrightarrow{CD}$, intersecting at E	1. Given
(1) 2. $\angle AEC \cong \angle CEB$	2. Perpendicular lines meet to form congruent adjacent angles (Definition)
(2) 3. $m\angle AEC = m\angle CEB$	3. If two angles are congruent, their measures are equal
4. $\angle AEB$ is a straight angle and $m\angle AEB = 180°$	4. Measure of a straight angle equals 180°
5. $m\angle AEC + m\angle CEB = m\angle AEB$	5. Angle-Addition Postulate
(4), (5) 6. $m\angle AEC + m\angle CEB = 180°$	6. Substitution
(3), (6) 7. $m\angle AEC + m\angle AEC = 180°$ or $2 \cdot m\angle AEC = 180°$	7. Substitution
(7) 8. $m\angle AEC = 90°$	8. Division Property of Equality
(8) 9. $\angle AEC$ is a right angle	9. If the measure of an angle is 90°, then the angle is a right angle

■

RELATIONS

The relationship between perpendicular lines suggests the more general, but undefined, mathematical concept of **relation.** In general, a relation "connects" two elements of an associated set of objects. Table 1.8 provides several examples of the concept of a relation R.

SSG *Exs. 1, 2*

TABLE 1.8

Relation R	Objects Related	Example of Relationship
is equal to	numbers	$2 + 3 = 5$
is greater than	numbers	$7 > 5$
is perpendicular to	lines	$\ell \perp m$
is complementary to	angles	$\angle 1$ is comp. to $\angle 2$
is congruent to	line segments	$\overline{AB} \cong \overline{CD}$
is a brother of	people	Matt is a brother of Phil

Reminder

Numbers that measure may be **equal** ($AB = CD$ or $m\angle 1 = m\angle 2$) whereas geometric figures may be **congruent** ($\overline{AB} \cong \overline{CD}$ or $\angle 1 \cong \angle 2$).

There are three special properties that may exist for a given relation R. Where a, b, and c are objects associated with relation R, the properties consider one object (reflexive), two objects in either order (symmetric), or three objects (transitive). For the properties to exist, it is necessary that the statements be true for all objects selected from the associated set. These properties are generalized and given examples as follows:

Reflexive property: $a\text{R}a$ ($5 = 5$; equality of numbers has a reflexive property)

Symmetric property: If $a\text{R}b$, then $b\text{R}a$. (If $\ell \perp m$, then $m \perp \ell$; perpendicularity of lines has a symmetric property)

Transitive property: If $a\text{R}b$ and $b\text{R}c$, then $a\text{R}c$. (If $\angle 1 \cong \angle 2$ and $\angle 2 \cong \angle 3$, then $\angle 1 \cong \angle 3$; congruence of angles has a transitive property)

EXAMPLE 2

Does the relation "is less than" for numbers have a reflexive property? a symmetric property? a transitive property?

Solution Because "$2 < 2$" is false, there is *no* reflexive property.
"If $2 < 5$, then $5 < 2$" is also false; there is *no* symmetric property.
"If $2 < 5$ and $5 < 9$, then $2 < 9$" is true; there *is* a transitive property.

NOTE: The same results are obtained for choices other than 2, 5, and 9. ■

Congruence of angles (or of line segments) is closely tied to equality of angle measures (or line segment measures) by the definition of congruence. The following list gives some useful properties of the congruence of angles.

Reflexive: $\angle 1 \cong \angle 1$; an angle is congruent to itself.

Symmetric: If $\angle 1 \cong \angle 2$, then $\angle 2 \cong \angle 1$.

Transitive: If $\angle 1 \cong \angle 2$ and $\angle 2 \cong \angle 3$, then $\angle 1 \cong \angle 3$.

SSG *Exs. 3–9*

Any relation (such as congruence of angles) that has reflexive, symmetric, and transitive properties is known as an *equivalence relation*. In later chapters, we will see that congruence of triangles and similarity of triangles also have reflexive, symmetric, and transitive properties; these relations are also equivalence relations.

Returning to the formulation of a proof, the final example in this section is based on the fact that vertical angles are congruent when two lines intersect. See Figure 1.62. Because there are two pairs of congruent angles, the Prove could be stated

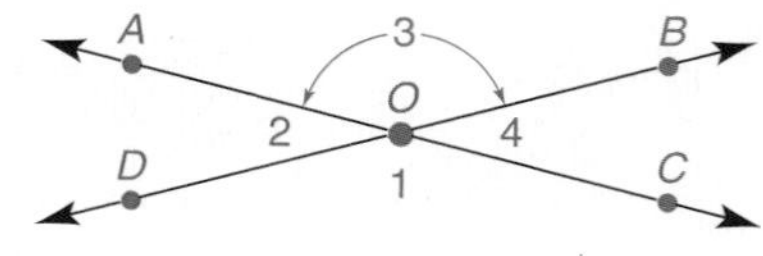

Figure 1.62

Prove: $\angle 1 \cong \angle 3$ and $\angle 2 \cong \angle 4$

Such a conclusion is a conjunction and would be proved if both congruences were established. For simplicity, the Prove of Example 3 is stated

Prove: $\angle 2 \cong \angle 4$

Study this proof of Theorem 1.6.2, noting the order of the statements and reasons.

Geometry in Nature

An icicle formed from freezing water assumes a vertical path.

THEOREM 1.6.2

If two lines intersect, then the vertical angles formed are congruent.

EXAMPLE 3

GIVEN: $\overleftrightarrow{AC}$ intersects $\overleftrightarrow{BD}$ at O (See Figure 1.62 on pge 48.)
PROVE: $\angle 2 \cong \angle 4$

PROOF

Statements	Reasons
1. $\overleftrightarrow{AC}$ intersects $\overleftrightarrow{BD}$ at O	1. Given
2. $\angle$s AOC and DOB are straight $\angle$s, with $m\angle AOC = 180$ and $m\angle DOB = 180$	2. The measure of a straight angle is 180°
3. $m\angle AOC = m\angle DOB$	3. Substitution
4. $m\angle 1 + m\angle 4 = m\angle DOB$ and $m\angle 1 + m\angle 2 = m\angle AOC$	4. Angle-Addition Postulate
5. $m\angle 1 + m\angle 4 = m\angle 1 + m\angle 2$	5. Substitution
6. $m\angle 4 = m\angle 2$	6. Subtraction Property of Equality
7. $\angle 4 \cong \angle 2$	7. If two angles are equal in measure, the angles are congruent
8. $\angle 2 \cong \angle 4$	8. Symmetric Property of Congruence of Angles

Technology Exploration

Use computer software if available.

1. Construct $\overleftrightarrow{AC}$ and $\overleftrightarrow{BD}$ to intersect at point O. (See Figure 1.62.)
2. Measure $\angle 1$, $\angle 2$, $\angle 3$, and $\angle 4$.
3. Show that $m\angle 1 = m\angle 3$ and $m\angle 2 = m\angle 4$.

In the preceding proof, there is no need to reorder the congruent angles from statement 7 to statement 8 because congruence of angles is symmetric; in the later work, statement 7 will be written to match the Prove statement even if the previous line does not have the same order. The same type of thinking applies to proving lines perpendicular or parallel: The order is simply not important!

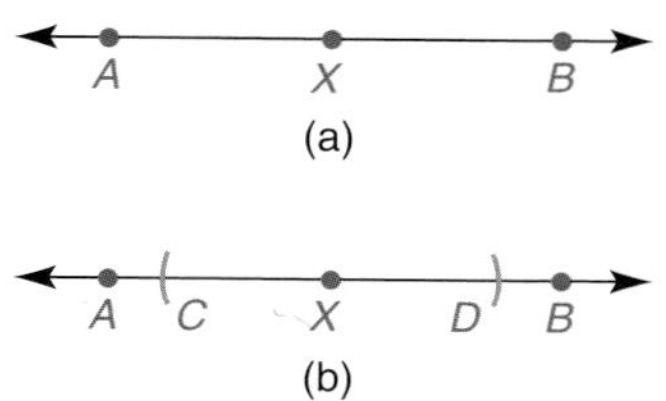

CONSTRUCTIONS LEADING TO PERPENDICULAR LINES

Construction 2 in Section 1.2 determined not only the midpoint of $\overline{AB}$ but also that of the **perpendicular bisector** of $\overline{AB}$. In many instances, we need the line perpendicular to another line at a point other than the midpoint of a segment.

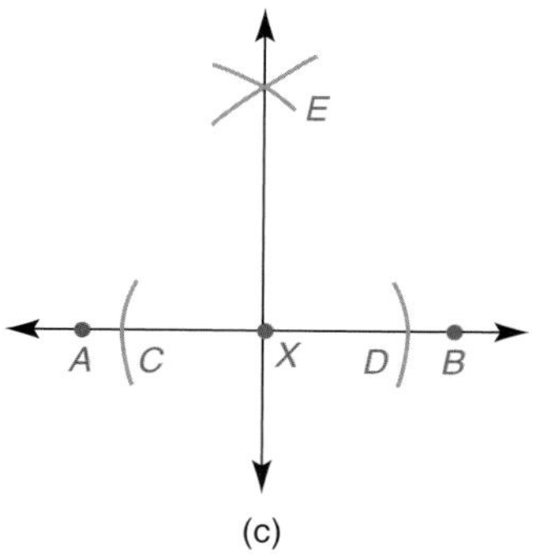

Figure 1.63

Construction 5 *To construct the line perpendicular to a given line at a specified point on the given line.*

GIVEN: $\overleftrightarrow{AB}$ with point X in Figure 1.63(a)

CONSTRUCT: A line $\overleftrightarrow{EX}$, so that $\overleftrightarrow{EX} \perp \overleftrightarrow{AB}$

CONSTRUCTION: Figure 1.63(b): Using X as the center, mark off arcs of equal radii on each side of X to intersect $\overleftrightarrow{AB}$ at C and D.

Figure 1.63(c): Now, using C and D as centers, mark off arcs of equal radii with a length greater than XD so that these arcs intersect either above (as shown) or below $\overleftrightarrow{AB}$.

Calling the point of intersection E, draw $\overleftrightarrow{EX}$, which is the desired line; that is, $\overleftrightarrow{EX} \perp \overleftrightarrow{AB}$.

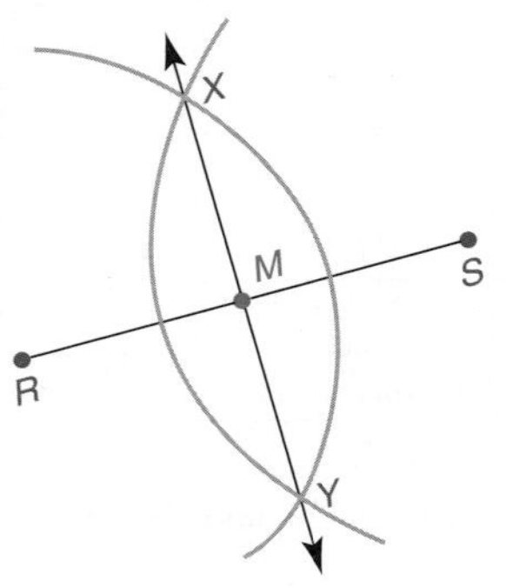

Figure 1.64

The theorem that Construction 5 is based on is a consequence of the Protractor Postulate, and we state it without proof.

THEOREM 1.6.3

In a plane, there is exactly one line perpendicular to a given line at any point on the line.

Construction 2, which was used to locate the midpoint of a line segment in Section 1.2, is also the method for constructing the perpendicular bisector of a line segment. In Figure 1.64, $\overleftrightarrow{XY}$ is the perpendicular bisector of $\overline{RS}$. The following theorem can be proved by methods developed later in this book.

THEOREM 1.6.4

The perpendicular bisector of a line segment is unique.

SSG *Exs. 10–14*

Exercises 1.6

In Exercises 1 and 2, supply reasons.

1. *Given:* $\angle 1 \cong \angle 3$
Prove: $\angle MOP \cong \angle NOQ$

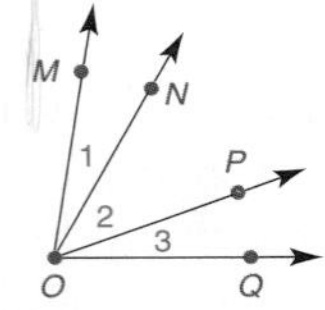

PROOF

Statements	Reasons
1. $\angle 1 \cong \angle 3$	1. ?
2. $m\angle 1 = m\angle 3$	2. ?
3. $m\angle 1 + m\angle 2 = m\angle MOP$ and $m\angle 2 + m\angle 3 = m\angle NOQ$	3. ?
4. $m\angle 1 + m\angle 2 = m\angle 2 + m\angle 3$	4. ?
5. $m\angle MOP = m\angle NOQ$	5. ?
6. $\angle MOP \cong \angle NOQ$	6. ?

2. *Given:* $\overleftrightarrow{AB}$ intersects $\overleftrightarrow{CD}$ at O so that $\angle 1$ is a right $\angle$ (Use the figure following Exercise 1.)
Prove: $\angle 2$ and $\angle 3$ are complementary

PROOF

Statements	Reasons
1. $\overleftrightarrow{AB}$ intersects $\overleftrightarrow{CD}$ at O	1. ?
2. $\angle AOB$ is a straight $\angle$, so $m\angle AOB = 180$	2. ?
3. $m\angle 1 + m\angle COB = m\angle AOB$	3. ?
4. $m\angle 1 + m\angle COB = 180$	4. ?
5. $\angle 1$ is a right angle	5. ?
6. $m\angle 1 = 90$	6. ?
7. $90 + m\angle COB = 180$	7. ?
8. $m\angle COB = 90$	8. ?
9. $m\angle 2 + m\angle 3 = m\angle COB$	9. ?
10. $m\angle 2 + m\angle 3 = 90$	10. ?
11. $\angle 2$ and $\angle 3$ are complementary	11. ?

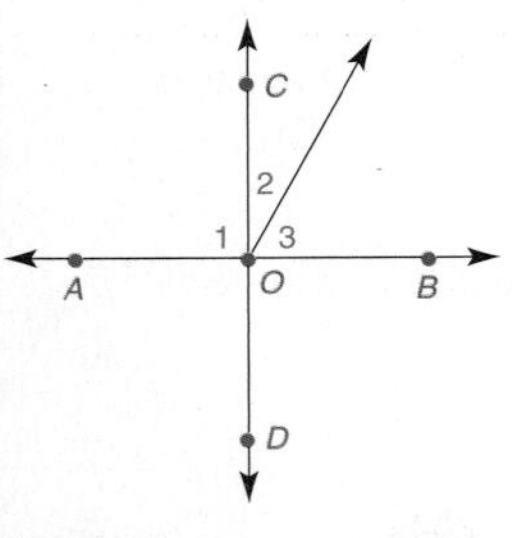

Exercise 2

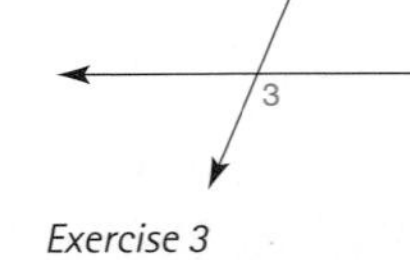

Exercise 3

In Exercises 3 and 4, supply statements.

3. *Given:* $\angle 1 \cong \angle 2$ and $\angle 2 \cong \angle 3$
Prove: $\angle 1 \cong \angle 3$
(Use the figure following Exercise 1.)

PROOF

Statements	Reasons
1. ?	1. Given
2. ?	2. Transitive Property of Congruence

4. *Given:* $m\angle AOB = m\angle 1$
$m\angle BOC = m\angle 1$
Prove: $\overrightarrow{OB}$ bisects $\angle AOC$

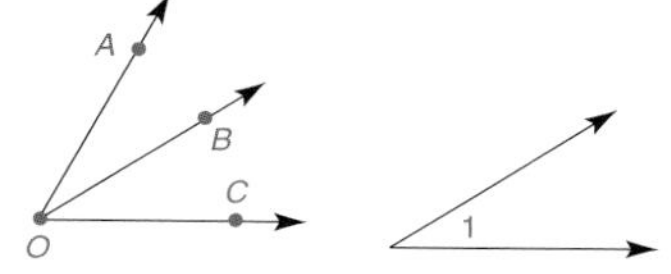

PROOF

Statements	Reasons
1. ?	1. Given
2. ?	2. Substitution
3. ?	3. Angles with equal measures are congruent
4. ?	4. If a ray divides an angle into two congruent angles, then the ray bisects the angle

In Exercises 5 to 9, use a compass and a straightedge to complete the constructions.

5. *Given:* Point N on line s
Construct: Line m through N so that $m \perp s$

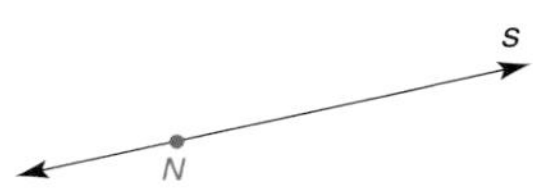

6. *Given:* $\overrightarrow{OA}$
Construct: Right angle BOA
(HINT: Use a straightedge to extend $\overrightarrow{OA}$ to the left.)

7. *Given:* Line ℓ containing point A
Construct: A 45° angle with vertex at A

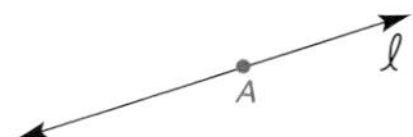

8. *Given:* $\overline{AB}$
Construct: The perpendicular bisector of $\overline{AB}$

9. *Given:* Triangle ABC
Construct: The perpendicular bisectors of sides $\overline{AB}$, $\overline{AC}$, and $\overline{BC}$

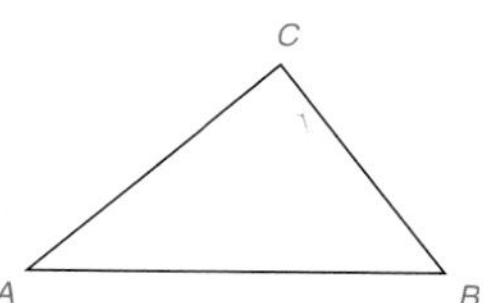

10. Draw a conclusion based on the results of Exercise 9.

In Exercises 11 and 12, provide the missing statements and reasons.

11. *Given:* $\angle$s 1 and 3 are complementary
$\angle$s 2 and 3 are complementary
Prove: $\angle 1 \cong \angle 2$

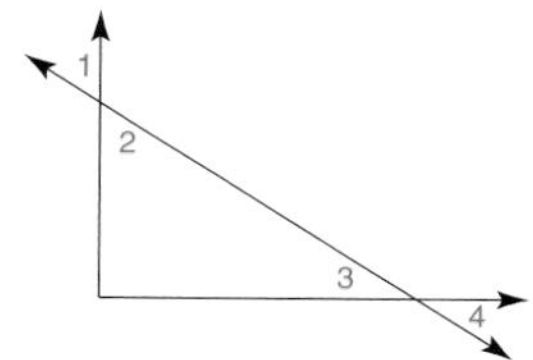

PROOF

Statements	Reasons
1. $\angle$s 1 and 3 are complementary; $\angle$s 2 and 3 are complementary	1. ?
2. $m\angle 1 + m\angle 3 = 90$; $m\angle 2 + m\angle 3 = 90$	2. The sum of the measures of complementary $\angle$s is 90
(2) 3. $m\angle 1 + m\angle 3 = m\angle 2 + m\angle 3$	3. ?
4. ?	4. Subtraction Property of Equality
(4) 5. ?	5. If two $\angle$s are = in measure, they are $\cong$

12. *Given:* $\angle 1 \cong \angle 2$; $\angle 3 \cong \angle 4$
$\angle$s 2 and 3 are complementary
Prove: $\angle$s 1 and 4 are complementary

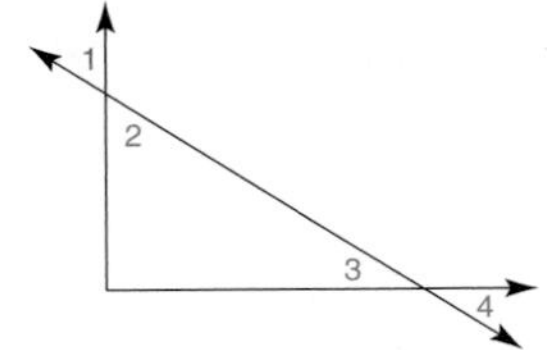

PROOF

	Statements	Reasons
	1. $\angle 1 \cong \angle 2$ and $\angle 3 \cong \angle 4$	1. ?
	2. ? and ?	2. If two $\angle$s are $\cong$, then their measures are equal
	3. $\angle$s 2 and 3 are complementary	3. ?
(3)	4. ?	4. The sum of the measures of complementary $\angle$s is 90
(2), (4)	5. $m\angle 1 + m\angle 4 = 90$	5. ?
	6. ?	6. If the sum of the measures of two angles is 90, then the angles are complementary

13. Does the relation "is perpendicular to" have a reflexive property (consider line ℓ)? a symmetric property (consider lines ℓ and m)? a transitive property (consider lines ℓ, m, and n)?

14. Does the relation "is greater than" have a reflexive property (consider real number a)? a symmetric property (consider real numbers a and b)? a transitive property (consider real numbers a, b, and c)?

15. Does the relation "is complementary to" for angles have a reflexive property (consider one angle)? a symmetric property (consider two angles)? a transitive property (consider three angles)?

16. Does the relation "is less than" for numbers have a reflexive property (consider one number)? a symmetric property (consider two numbers)? a transitive property (consider three numbers)?

17. Does the relation "is a brother of" have a reflexive property (consider one male)? a symmetric property (consider two males)? a transitive property (consider three males)?

18. Does the relation "is in love with" have a reflexive property (consider one person)? a symmetric property (consider two people)? a transitive property (consider three people)?

19. This textbook has used numerous symbols and abbreviations. In this exercise, indicate what word is represented or abbreviated by each of the following:
a) $\perp$ b) $\angle$s c) supp. d) rt. e) $m\angle 1$

20. This textbook has used numerous symbols and abbreviations. In this exercise, indicate what word is represented or abbreviated by each of the following:
a) post. b) $\cup$ c) $\varnothing$ d) $<$ e) pt.

21. This text book has used numerous symbols and abbreviations. In this exercise, indicate what word is represented or abbreviated by each of the following:
a) adj. b) comp. c) $\overrightarrow{AB}$ d) $\cong$ e) vert.

22. If there were no understood restriction to lines in a plane in Theorem 1.6.3, the theorem would be false. Explain why the following statement is false: "In space, there is exactly one line perpendicular to a given line at any point on the line."

23. Prove the Extended Segment Addition Property by using the Drawing, the Given, and the Prove that follow.
Given: M-N-P-Q on $\overline{MQ}$
Prove: $MN + NP + PQ = MQ$

24. The Segment-Addition Postulate can be generalized as follows: "The length of a line segment equals the sum of the lengths of its parts." State a general conclusion about AE based on the following figure.

25. Prove the Extended Angle Addition Property by using the Drawing, the Given, and the Prove that follow.
Given: $\angle TSW$ with $\overrightarrow{SU}$ and $\overrightarrow{SV}$
Prove: $m\angle TSW = m\angle TSU + m\angle USV + m\angle VSW$

26. The Angle-Addition Postulate can be generalized as follows: "The measure of an angle equals the sum of the measures of its parts." State a general conclusion about $m\angle GHK$ based on the figure shown.

27. If there were no understood restriction to lines in a plane in Theorem 1.6.4, the theorem would be false. Explain why the following statement is false: "In space, the perpendicular bisector of a line segment is unique."

*28. In the proof to the right, provide the missing reasons.

Given: $\angle 1$ and $\angle 2$ are complementary
$\angle 1$ is acute

Prove: $\angle 2$ is also acute

PROOF

Statements	Reasons
1. $\angle 1$ and $\angle 2$ are complementary	1. ?
(1) 2. $m\angle 1 + m\angle 2 = 90$	2. ?
3. $\angle 1$ is acute	3. ?
(3) 4. Where $m\angle 1 = x$, $0 < x < 90$	4. ?
(2) 5. $x + m\angle 2 = 90$	5. ?
(5) 6. $m\angle 2 = 90 - x$	6. ?
(4) 7. $-x < 0 < 90 - x$	7. ?
(7) 8. $90 - x < 90 < 180 - x$	8. ?
(7), (8) 9. $0 < 90 - x < 90$	9. ?
(6), (9) 10. $0 < m\angle 2 < 90$	10. ?
(10) 11. $\angle 2$ is acute	11. ?

1.7 The Formal Proof of a Theorem

KEY CONCEPTS: Formal Proof of a Theorem; Converse of a Theorem; Picture Proof (Informal) of a Theorem

Recall from Section 1.3 that statements that follow logically from known undefined terms, definitions, and postulates are called *theorems*. The formal proof of a theorem has several parts; to understand how these parts are related, consider carefully the terms *hypothesis* and *conclusion*. The hypothesis of a statement describes the given situation (Given), whereas the conclusion describes what you need to establish (Prove). When a statement has the form "If H, then C," the hypothesis is H and the conclusion is C. Some theorems must be reworded to fit into "If . . . , then . . ." form so that the hypothesis and conclusion are easy to recognize.

EXAMPLE 1

Give the hypothesis H and conclusion C for each of these statements.

a) If two lines intersect, then the vertical angles formed are congruent.
b) All right angles are congruent.
c) Parallel lines do not intersect.
d) Lines are perpendicular when they meet to form congruent adjacent angles.

Solution

a) As is H: Two lines intersect.
C: The vertical angles formed are congruent.

b) Reworded If two angles are right angles, then these angles are congruent.
H: Two angles are right angles.
C: The angles are congruent.

c) Reworded If two lines are parallel, then these lines do not intersect.
H: Two lines are parallel.
C: The lines do not intersect.

d) Reordered When (if) two lines meet to form congruent adjacent angles, these lines are perpendicular.
H: Two lines meet to form congruent adjacent angles.
C: The lines are perpendicular. ■

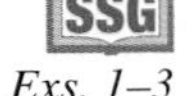
Exs. 1–3

Why do we need to distinguish between the hypothesis and the conclusion? For a theorem, the hypothesis determines the Drawing and the Given, providing a description of the Drawing's known characteristics. The conclusion determines the relationship (the Prove) that you wish to establish in the Drawing.

THE WRITTEN PARTS OF A FORMAL PROOF

The five necessary parts of a formal proof are listed in the accompanying box in the order in which they should be developed.

ESSENTIAL PARTS OF THE FORMAL PROOF OF A THEOREM

1. *Statement:* States the theorem to be proved.
2. *Drawing:* Represents the hypothesis of the theorem.
3. *Given:* Describes the Drawing according to the information found in the hypothesis of the theorem.
4. *Prove:* Describes the Drawing according to the claim made in the conclusion of the theorem.
5. *Proof:* Orders a list of claims (Statements) and justifications (Reasons), beginning with the Given and ending with the Prove; there must be a logical flow in this Proof.

The most difficult aspect of a formal proof is the thinking process that must take place between parts 4 and 5. This game plan or analysis involves deducing and ordering conclusions based on the given situation. One must be somewhat like a lawyer, selecting the claims that help prove the case while discarding those that are superfluous. In the process of ordering the statements, it may be beneficial to think in reverse order, like so:

The Prove statement would be true if what else were true?

The final proof must be arranged in an order that allows one to reason from an earlier statement to a later claim by using deduction (perhaps several times).

H: hypothesis ⟵ **statement of proof**
P: principle ⟵ **reason of proof**
∴ C: conclusion ⟵ **next statement in proof**

Consider the following theorem, which was proved in Example 1 of Section 1.6.

THEOREM 1.6.1

If two lines are perpendicular, then they meet to form right angles.

EXAMPLE 2

Write the parts of the formal proof of Theorem 1.6.1.

Solution

1. State the theorem.
   If two lines are perpendicular, then they meet to form right angles.
2. The hypothesis is H: Two lines are perpendicular.
   Make a Drawing to fit this description.
   (See Figure 1.65.)
3. Write the Given statement, using the Drawing and based on the hypothesis H: Two lines are $\perp$.
   Given: $\overleftrightarrow{AB} \perp \overleftrightarrow{CD}$ intersecting at E
4. Write the Prove statement, using the Drawing and based on the conclusion C: They meet to form right angles.
   Prove: $\angle AEC$ is a right angle.
5. Construct the Proof. This formal proof is found in Example 1, Section 1.6.

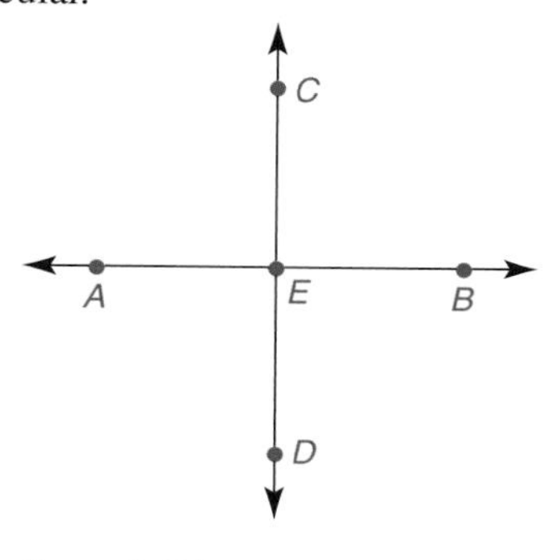

Figure 1.65

Exs. 4, 5

CONVERSE OF A STATEMENT

The converse of the statement "If *P*, then *Q*" is "If *Q*, then *P*." That is, the converse of a given statement interchanges its hypothesis and conclusion. Consider the following:

Statement: If a person lives in London, then that person lives in England.

Converse: If a person lives in England, then that person lives in London.

In this case, the given statement is true, whereas its converse is false. Sometimes the converse of a true statement is also true. In fact, Example 3 presents the formal proof of a theorem that is the converse of Theorem 1.6.1.

Once a theorem has been proved, it may be cited thereafter as a reason in future proofs. Thus, any theorem found in this section can be used for justification in proof problems found in later sections.

Warning

You should not make a drawing that embeds qualities beyond those described in the hypothesis; nor should your drawing indicate fewer qualities than the hypothesis prescribes!

The proof that follows is nearly complete! It is difficult to provide a complete formal proof that explains the "how to" and simultaneously presents the final polished form. Example 2 aims only at the "how to," whereas Example 3 illustrates the polished form. What you do not see in Example 3 are the thought process and the scratch paper needed to piece this puzzle together.

The proof of a theorem is not unique! For instance, students' Drawings need not match, even though the same relationships should be indicated. Certainly, different letters are likely to be chosen for the Drawing that illustrates the hypothesis.

THEOREM 1.7.1

If two lines meet to form a right angle, then these lines are perpendicular.

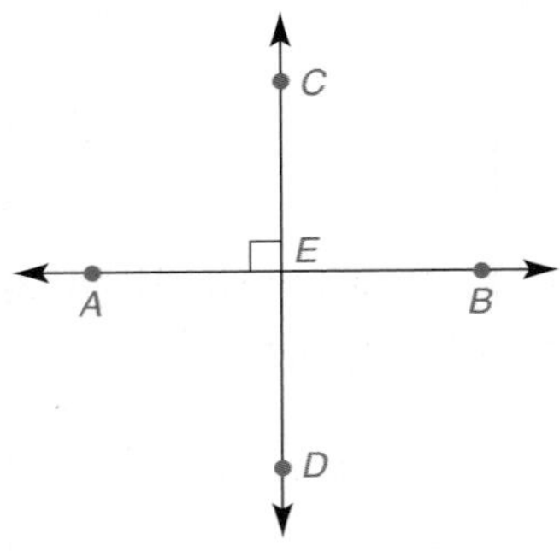

Figure 1.66

EXAMPLE 3

Give a formal proof for Theorem 1.7.1.

If two lines meet to form a right angle, then these lines are perpendicular.

Given: $\overleftrightarrow{AB}$ and $\overleftrightarrow{CD}$ intersect at E so that $\angle AEC$ is a right angle (Figure 1.66)
Prove: $\overleftrightarrow{AB} \perp \overleftrightarrow{CD}$

PROOF

	Statements	Reasons
	1. $\overleftrightarrow{AB}$ and $\overleftrightarrow{CD}$ intersect so that $\angle AEC$ is a right angle	1. Given
	2. $m\angle AEC = 90$	2. If an $\angle$ is a right $\angle$, its measure is 90
	3. $\angle AEB$ is a straight $\angle$, so $m\angle AEB = 180$	3. If an $\angle$ is a straight $\angle$, its measure is 180
	4. $m\angle AEC + m\angle CEB = m\angle AEB$	4. Angle-Addition Postulate
(2), (3), (4)	5. $90 + m\angle CEB = 180$	5. Substitution
(5)	6. $m\angle CEB = 90$	6. Subtraction Property of Equality
(2), (6)	7. $m\angle AEC = m\angle CEB$	7. Substitution
	8. $\angle AEC \cong \angle CEB$	8. If two $\angle$s have $=$ measures, the $\angle$s are $\cong$
	9. $\overleftrightarrow{AB} \perp \overleftrightarrow{CD}$	9. If two lines form $\cong$ adjacent $\angle$s, these lines are $\perp$

■

SSG *Exs. 6–8*

Several additional theorems are now stated, the proofs of which are left as exercises. This list contains theorems that are quite useful when cited as reasons in later proofs. A formal proof is provided only for Theorem 1.7.6.

THEOREM 1.7.2

If two angles are complementary to the same angle (or to congruent angles), then these angles are congruent.

See Exercise 25 for a drawing describing Theorem 1.7.2.

THEOREM 1.7.3

If two angles are supplementary to the same angle (or to congruent angles), then these angles are congruent.

See Exercise 26 for a drawing describing Theorem 1.7.3.

THEOREM 1.7.4

Any two right angles are congruent.

Use computer software if available.

1. Draw $\overleftrightarrow{EG}$ containing point F. Also draw $\overrightarrow{FH}$ as in Figure 1.68.
2. Measure $\angle 3$ and $\angle 4$.
3. Show that $m\angle 3 + m\angle 4 = 180°$. (Answer may not be perfect.)

THEOREM 1.7.5

If the exterior sides of two adjacent acute angles form perpendicular rays, then these angles are complementary.

For Theorem 1.7.5, we create an informal proof called a picture proof. Although such a proof is less detailed, the impact of the explanation is the same! This is the first of several "picture proofs" found in this textbook.

PICTURE PROOF OF THEOREM 1.7.5

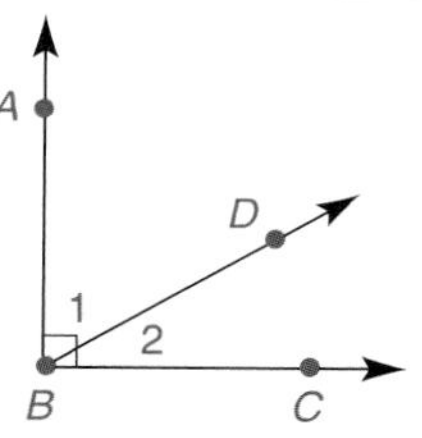

Figure 1.67

Given: $\overrightarrow{BA} \perp \overrightarrow{BC}$

Prove: $\angle 1$ and $\angle 2$ are complementary

Proof: We see that $\angle 1$ and $\angle 2$ are parts of a right angle.

Then $m\angle 1 + m\angle 2 = 90°$, so $\angle 1$ and $\angle 2$ are complementary.

STRATEGY FOR PROOF ▶ The Final Reason in the Proof

General Rule: The last reason explains why the last *statement* must be true. Never write "Prove" for any reason.

Illustration: The final reason in the proof of Theorem 1.7.6 is the definition of supplementary angles: If the sum of measures of 2 angles is 180°, the angles are supplementary.

EXAMPLE 4

Study the formal proof of Theorem 1.7.6.

THEOREM 1.7.6

If the exterior sides of two adjacent angles form a straight line, then these angles are supplementary.

Given: $\angle 3$ and $\angle 4$ and $\overleftrightarrow{EG}$ (Figure 1.68)
Prove: $\angle 3$ and $\angle 4$ are supplementary

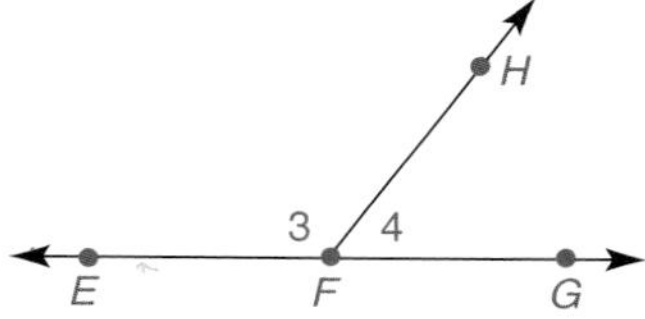

Figure 1.68

PROOF

Statements	Reasons
1. $\angle 3$ and $\angle 4$ and $\overleftrightarrow{EG}$	1. Given
2. $m\angle 3 + m\angle 4 = m\angle EFG$	2. Angle-Addition Postulate
3. $\angle EFG$ is a straight angle	3. If the sides of an $\angle$ are opposite rays, it is a straight $\angle$
4. $m\angle EFG = 180$	4. The measure of a straight $\angle$ is 180
5. $m\angle 3 + m\angle 4 = 180$	5. Substitution
6. $\angle 3$ and $\angle 4$ are supplementary	6. If the sum of the measures of two $\angle$s is 180, the $\angle$s are supplementary

SSG *Exs. 9–12*

The final two theorems in this section are stated for convenience. We suggest that the student make drawings to illustrate Theorem 1.7.7 and Theorem 1.7.8.

THEOREM 1.7.7

If two line segments are congruent, then their midpoints separate these segments into four congruent segments.

THEOREM 1.7.8

If two angles are congruent, then their bisectors separate these angles into four congruent angles.

SSG *Exs. 13, 14*

Exercises 1.7

In Exercises 1 to 6, state the hypothesis H and the conclusion C for each statement.

1. If a line segment is bisected, then each of the equal segments has half the length of the original segment.
2. If two sides of a triangle are congruent, then the triangle is isosceles.
3. All squares are quadrilaterals.
4. Every regular polygon has congruent interior angles.
5. Two angles are congruent if each is a right angle.
6. The lengths of corresponding sides of similar polygons are proportional.
7. Name, in order, the five parts of the formal proof of a theorem.
8. Which part (hypothesis or conclusion) of a theorem determines the
   a) Drawing?
   b) Given?
   c) Prove?
9. Which part (Given or Prove) of the proof depends upon the
   a) Hypothesis of Theorem?
   b) Conclusion of Theorem?
10. Which of the following can be cited as a reason in a proof?
    a) Given
    b) Prove
    c) Definition
    d) Postulate

For each theorem stated in Exercises 11 to 16, make a Drawing. On the basis of your Drawing, write a Given and a Prove for the theorem.

11. If two lines are perpendicular, then these lines meet to form a right angle.
12. If two lines meet to form a right angle, then these lines are perpendicular.
13. If two angles are complementary to the same angle, then these angles are congruent.
14. If two angles are supplementary to the same angle, then these angles are congruent.
15. If two lines intersect, then the vertical angles formed are congruent.
16. Any two right angles are congruent.

In Exercises 17 to 24, use the drawing at the right and apply the theorems of this section.

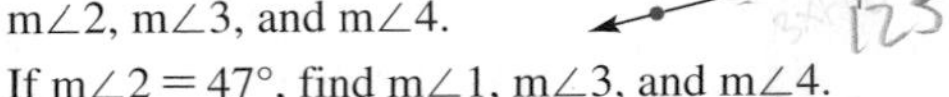

17. If $m\angle 1 = 125°$, find $m\angle 2$, $m\angle 3$, and $m\angle 4$.
18. If $m\angle 2 = 47°$, find $m\angle 1$, $m\angle 3$, and $m\angle 4$.
19. If $m\angle 1 = 3x + 10$ and $m\angle 3 = 4x - 30$, find x and $m\angle 1$.
20. If $m\angle 2 = 6x + 8$ and $m\angle 4 = 7x$, find x and $m\angle 2$.
21. If $m\angle 1 = 2x$ and $m\angle 2 = x$, find x and $m\angle 1$.
22. If $m\angle 2 = x + 15$ and $m\angle 3 = 2x$, find x and $m\angle 2$.
23. If $m\angle 2 = \frac{x}{2} - 10$ and $m\angle 3 = \frac{x}{3} + 40$, find x and $m\angle 2$.
24. If $m\angle 1 = x + 20$ and $m\angle 4 = \frac{x}{3}$, find x and $m\angle 4$.

In Exercises 25 to 33, complete the formal proof of each theorem.

25. If two angles are complementary to the same angle, then these angles are congruent.

    Given: $\angle 1$ is comp. to $\angle 3$
    $\angle 2$ is comp. to $\angle 3$

    Prove: $\angle 1 \cong \angle 2$

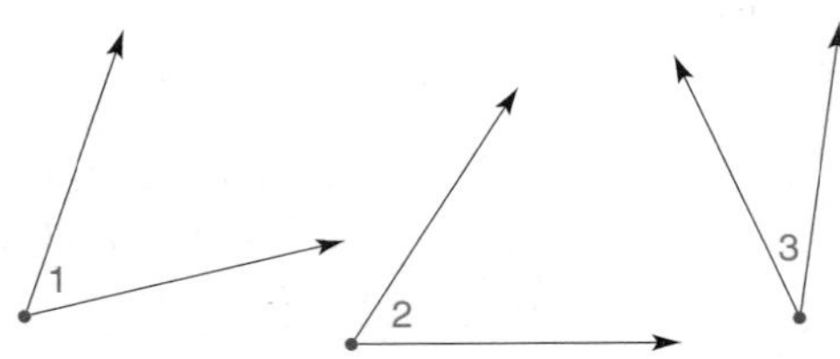

PROOF

Statements	Reasons
1. ∠1 is comp. to ∠3 ∠2 is comp. to ∠3	1. ?
2. m∠1 + m∠3 = 90 m∠2 + m∠3 = 90	2. ?
3. m∠1 + m∠3 = m∠2 + m∠3	3. ?
4. m∠1 = m∠2	4. ?
5. ∠1 ≅ ∠2	5. ?

26. If two angles are supplementary to the same angle, then these angles are congruent.

Given: ∠1 is supp. to ∠2
∠3 is supp. to ∠2

Prove: ∠1 ≅ ∠3

(HINT: See Exercise 25 for help.)

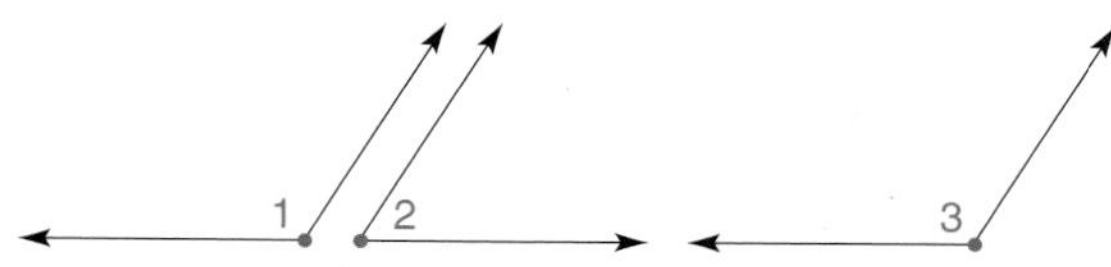

Exercise 26

27. If two lines intersect, the vertical angles formed are congruent.

28. Any two right angles are congruent.

29. If the exterior sides of two adjacent acute angles form perpendicular rays, then these angles are complementary.

Given: $\overrightarrow{BA} \perp \overrightarrow{BC}$

Prove: ∠1 is comp. to ∠2

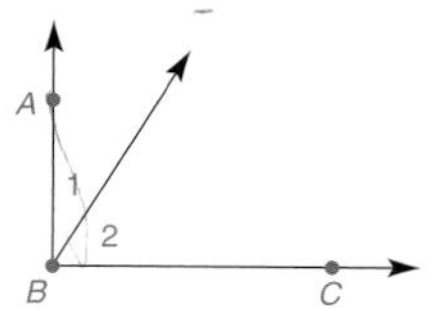

PROOF

Statements	Reasons
1. $\overrightarrow{BA} \perp \overrightarrow{BC}$	1. ?
2. ?	2. If two rays are ⊥, then they meet to form a rt. ∠
3. m∠*ABC* = 90	3. ?
4. m∠*ABC* = m∠1 + m∠2	4. ?
5. m∠1 + m∠2 = 90	5. Substitution
6. ?	6. If the sum of the measures of two angles is 90, then the angles are complementary

30. If two line segments are congruent, then their midpoints separate these segments into four congruent segments.

Given $\overline{AB} \cong \overline{DC}$
M is the midpoint of $\overline{AB}$
N is the midpoint of $\overline{DC}$

Prove: $\overline{AM} \cong \overline{MB} \cong \overline{DN} \cong \overline{NC}$

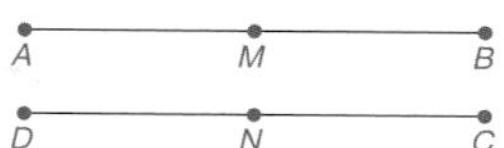

31. If two angles are congruent, then their bisectors separate these angles into four congruent angles.

Given: ∠*ABC* ≅ ∠*EFG*
$\overrightarrow{BD}$ bisects ∠*ABC*
$\overrightarrow{FH}$ bisects ∠*EFG*

Prove: ∠1 ≅ ∠2 ≅ ∠3 ≅ ∠4

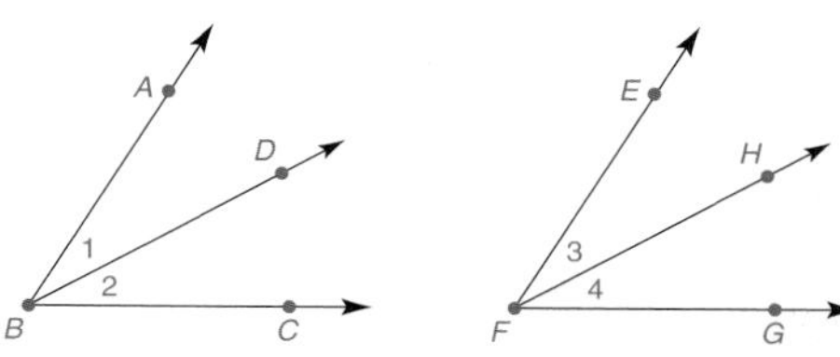

32. The bisectors of two adjacent supplementary angles form a right angle.

Given: ∠*ABC* is supp. to ∠*CBD*
$\overrightarrow{BE}$ bisects ∠*ABC*
$\overrightarrow{BF}$ bisects ∠*CBD*

Prove: ∠*EBF* is a right angle

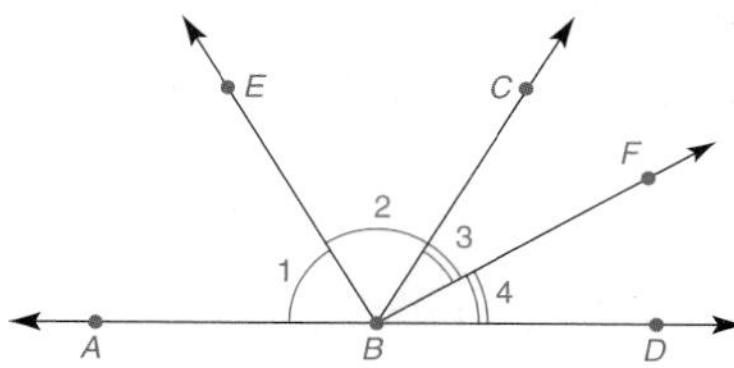

33. The supplement of an acute angle is an obtuse angle.

(HINT: Use Exercise 28 of Section 1.6 as a guide.)

PERSPECTIVE ON HISTORY

The Development of Geometry

One of the first written accounts of geometric knowledge appears in the Rhind papyrus, a collection of documents that date back to more than 1000 years before Christ. In this document, Ahmes (an Egyptian scribe) describes how north-south and east-west lines were redrawn following the overflow of the Nile River. Astronomy was used to lay out the north-south line. The rest was done by people known as "rope-fasteners." By tying knots in a rope, it was possible to separate the rope into segments with lengths that were in the ratio 3 to 4 to 5. The knots were fastened at stakes in such a way that a right triangle would be formed. In Figure 1.69, the right angle is formed so that one side (of length 4, as shown) lies in the north-south line, and the second side (of length 3, as shown) lies in the east-west line.

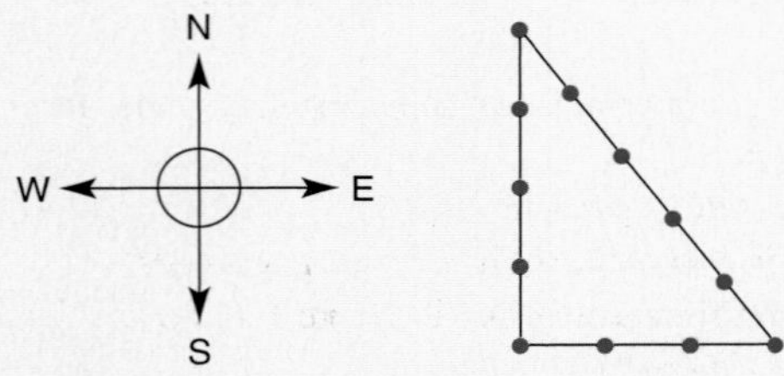

Figure 1.69

The principle that was used by the rope-fasteners is known as the Pythagorean Theorem. However, we also know that the ancient Chinese were aware of this relationship. That is, the Pythagorean Theorem was known and applied many centuries before the time of Pythagoras (the Greek mathematician for whom the theorem is named).

Ahmes describes other facts of geometry that were known to the Egyptians. Perhaps the most impressive of these facts was that their approximation of π was 3.1604. To four decimal places of accuracy, we know today that the correct value of π is 3.1416.

Like the Egyptians, the Chinese treated geometry in a very practical way. In their constructions and designs, the Chinese used the rule (ruler), the square, the compass, and the level. Unlike the Egyptians and the Chinese, the Greeks formalized and expanded the knowledge base of geometry by pursuing geometry as an intellectual endeavor.

According to the Greek scribe Proclus (about 50 B.C.), Thales (625–547 B.C.) first established deductive proofs for several of the known theorems of geometry. Proclus also notes that it was Euclid (330–275 B.C.) who collected, summarized, ordered, and verified the vast quantity of knowledge of geometry in his time. Euclid's work *Elements* was the first textbook of geometry. Much of what was found in *Elements* is the core knowledge of geometry and thus can be found in this textbook as well.

PERSPECTIVE ON APPLICATION

Patterns

In much of the study of mathematics, we seek patterns related to the set of counting numbers $N = \{1,2,3,4,5, \ldots\}$. Some of these patterns are geometric and are given special names that reflect the configuration of sets of points. For instance, the set of *square numbers* are shown geometrically in Figure 1.70 and, of course, correspond to the numbers 1, 4, 9, 16, ...

Figure 1.70

EXAMPLE 1

Find the fourth number in the pattern of triangular numbers shown in Figure 1.71(a).

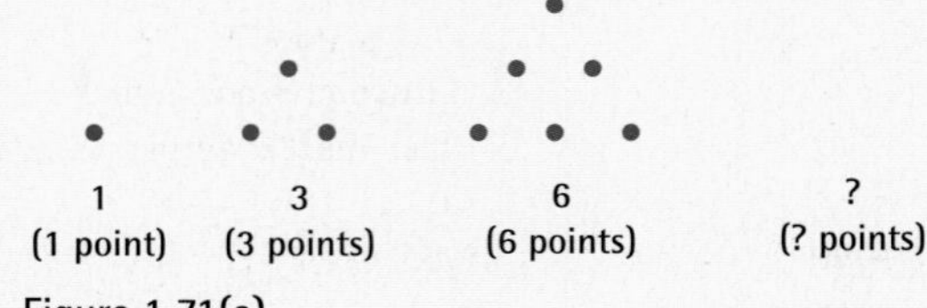

Figure 1.71(a)

Solution Adding a row of 4 points at the bottom, we have the diagram shown in Figure 1.71(b), which contains 10 points. The fourth triangular number is 10.

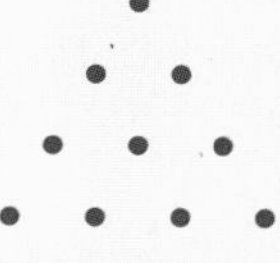

Figure 1.71(b)

Some patterns of geometry lead to principles known as postulates and theorems. One of the principles that we will explore in the next example is based on the total number of *diagonals* found in a polygon with a given number of sides. A diagonal of a polygon (many-sided figure) joins two nonconsecutive vertices of the polygon together. Of course, joining any two vertices of a triangle will determine a side; thus, a triangle has no diagonals. In Example 2, both the number of sides of the polygon and the number of diagonals are shown.

EXAMPLE 2

Find the total number of diagonals for a polygon of 6 sides.

3 sides
0 diagonals

4 sides
2 diagonals

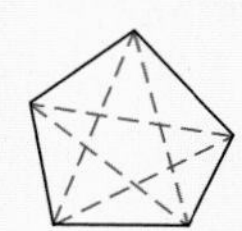

5 sides
5 diagonals

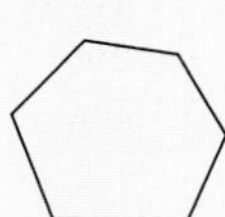

6 sides
? diagonals

Figure 1.72(a)

Solution By drawing all possible diagonals as shown in Figure 1.72(b) and counting them, we find that there are a total of 9 diagonals!

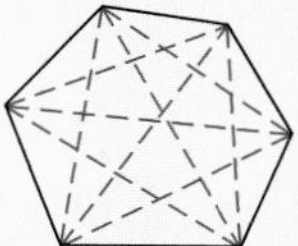

Figure 1.72(b)

Certain geometric patterns are used to test students, as in testing for intelligence (IQ) or on college admissions tests. A simple example might have you predict the next (fourth) figure in the pattern of squares shown in Figure 1.73(a).

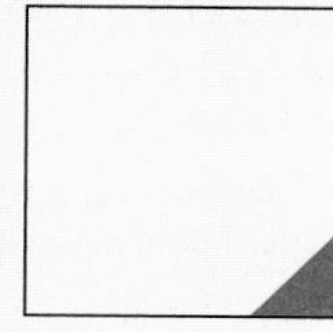

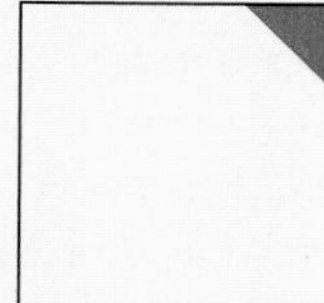

Figure 1.73(a)

We rotate the square once more to obtain the fourth figure as shown in Figure 1.73(b).

Figure 1.73(b)

EXAMPLE 3

Midpoints of the sides of a *square* are used to generate new figures in the sequence shown in Figure 1.74(a). Draw the fourth figure.

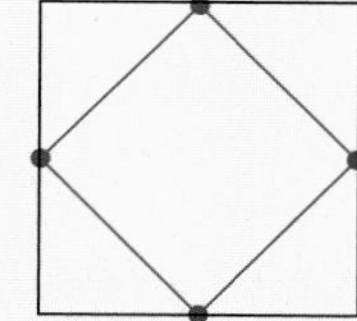

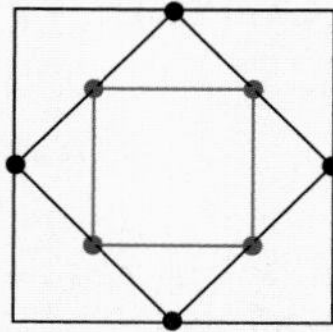

Figure 1.74(a)

Solution By continuing to add and join midpoints in the third figure, we form a figure like the one shown in Figure 1.74(b).

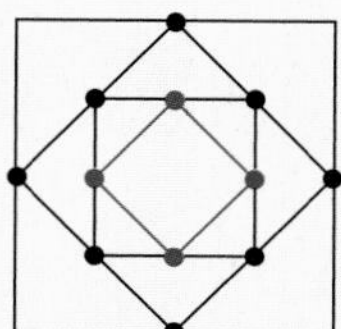

Figure 1.74(b)

Note that each new figure within the previous figure is also a square!

Summary

A LOOK BACK AT CHAPTER 1

Our goal in this chapter has been to introduce geometry. We discussed the types of reasoning that are used to develop geometric relationships. The use of the tools of measurement (ruler and protractor) was described. We encountered the four elements of a mathematical system: undefined terms, definitions, postulates, and theorems. The undefined terms were needed to lay the foundation for defining new terms. The postulates were needed to lay the foundation for the theorems we proved here and for the theorems that lie ahead. Constructions presented in this chapter included the bisector of an angle and the perpendicular to a line at a point on the line.

A LOOK AHEAD TO CHAPTER 2

The theorems we will prove in the next chapter are based on a postulate known as the Parallel Postulate. A new method of proof, called indirect proof, will be introduced; it will be used in later chapters. Although many of the theorems in Chapter 2 deal with parallel lines, several theorems in the chapter deal with the angles of a polygon. Symmetry and transformations will be discussed.

KEY CONCEPTS

1.1

Statement • Variable • Conjunction • Disjunction • Negation • Implication (Conditional) • Hypothesis • Conclusion • Intuition • Induction • Deduction • Argument (Valid and Invalid) • Law of Detachment • Set • Subets • Venn Diagram • Intersection • Union

1.2

Point • Line • Plane • Collinear Points • Vertex • Line Segment • Betweenness of Points • Midpoint • Congruent • Protractor • Parallel Lines • Bisect • Straight Angle • Right Angle • Intersect • Perpendicular • Compass • Constructions • Circle • Arc • Radius

1.3

Mathematical System • Axiom or Postulate • Assumption • Theorem • Ruler Postulate • Distance • Segment-Addition Postulate • Congruent Segments • Midpoint of a Line Segment • Bisector of a Line Segment • Union • Ray • Opposite Rays • Intersection of Two Geometric Figures • Parallel Lines • Plane • Coplanar Points • Space • Parallel, Vertical, Horizontal Planes

1.4

Angle • Sides of an Angle • Vertex of an Angle • Protractor Postulate • Acute, Right, Obtuse, Straight, and Reflex Angles • Angle-Addition Postulate • Adjacent Angles • Congruent Angles • Bisector of an Angle • Complementary Angles • Supplementary Angles • Vertical Angles

1.5

Algebraic Properties • Proof

1.6

Vertical Lines and Horizontal Lines • Perpendicular Lines • Relations • Reflexive, Symmetric, and Transitive Properties of Congruence • Equivalence Relation • Perpendicular Bisector of a Line Segment

1.7

Formal Proof of a Theorem • Converse of a Theorem

TABLE 1.9 An Overview of Chapter 1

▶ Line and Line Segment Relationships

FIGURE	RELATIONSHIP	SYMBOLS
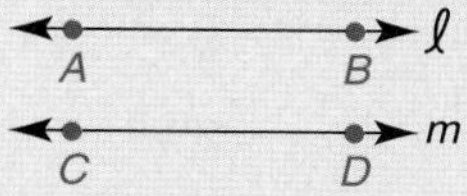 A, B on line ℓ; C, D on line m	Parallel lines (and segments)	$\ell \parallel m$ or $\overleftrightarrow{AB} \parallel \overleftrightarrow{CD}$; $\overline{AB} \parallel \overline{CD}$
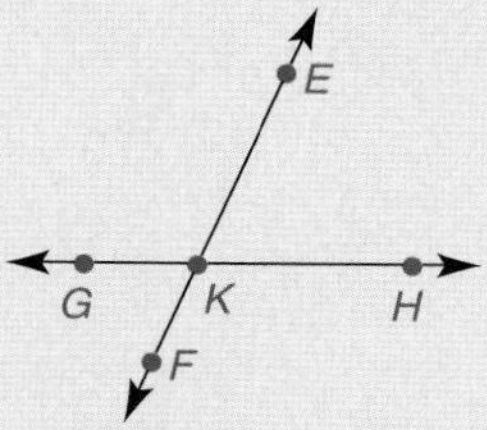 E, F, G, K, H	Intersecting lines	$\overrightarrow{EF} \cap \overleftrightarrow{GH} = K$
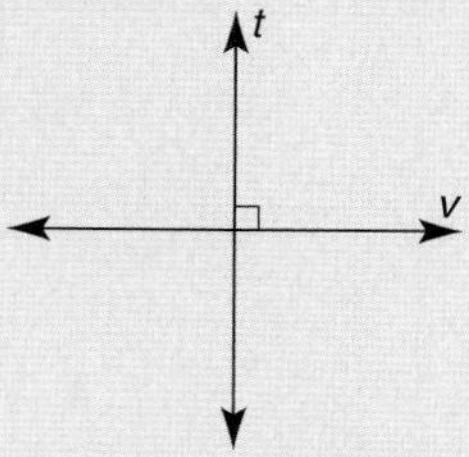 t, v	Perpendicular lines (*t* shown vertical, *v* shown horizontal)	$t \perp v$
 M, N; P, Q	Congruent line segments	$\overline{MN} \cong \overline{PQ}$; $MN = PQ$
 A, B, C	Point *B* between *A* and *C* on $\overline{AC}$	*A*-*B*-*C*; $AB + BC = AC$
 P, M, Q	Point *M* the midpoint of $\overline{PQ}$	$\overline{PM} \cong \overline{MQ}$; $PM = MQ$; $PM = \frac{1}{2}(PQ)$

▶ Angle Classification (One Angle)

FIGURE	TYPE	ANGLE MEASURE
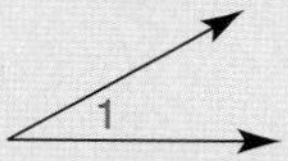 1	Acute angle	$0° < m\angle 1 < 90°$
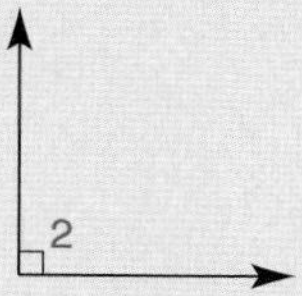 2	Right angle	$m\angle 2 = 90°$

continued

TABLE 1.9 *(continued)*

▶ Angle Classification (One Angle)

FIGURE	TYPE	ANGLE MEASURE
3	Obtuse angle	$90° < m\angle 3 < 180°$
4	Straight angle	$m\angle 4 = 180°$
5	Reflex angle	$180° < m\angle 5 < 360°$

▶ Angle Relationships (Two Angles)

FIGURE	RELATIONSHIP	SYMBOLS
1, 2	Congruent angles	$\angle 1 \cong \angle 2$; $m\angle 1 = m\angle 2$
A, D, 3, 4, B, C	Adjacent angles	$m\angle 3 + m\angle 4 = m\angle ABC$
G, K, 5, 6, H, J	Bisector of angle ($\overrightarrow{HK}$ bisects $\angle GHJ$)	$\angle 5 \cong \angle 6$; $m\angle 5 = m\angle 6$; $m\angle 5 = \frac{1}{2}(m\angle GHJ)$
7, 8	Complementary angles	$m\angle 7 + m\angle 8 = 90°$
9, 10	Supplementary angles	$m\angle 9 + m\angle 10 = 180°$
13, 11, 12, 14	Vertical angles ($\angle 11$ and $\angle 12$; $\angle 13$ and $\angle 14$)	$\angle 11 \cong \angle 12$; $\angle 13 \cong \angle 14$

▶▶▶ Chapter 1 REVIEW EXERCISES

1. Name the four components of a mathematical system.
2. Name three types of reasoning.
3. Name the four characteristics of a good definition.

In Review Exercises 4 to 6, name the type of reasoning illustrated.

4. While watching the pitcher warm up, Phillip thinks, "I'll be able to hit against him."
5. Laura is away at camp. On the first day, her mother brings her additional clothing. On the second day, her mother brings her another pair of shoes. On the third day, her mother brings her cookies. Laura concludes that her mother will bring her something on the fourth day.
6. Sarah knows the rule "A number (not 0) divided by itself equals 1." The teacher asks Sarah, "What is 5 divided by 5?" Sarah says, "The answer is 1."

In Review Exercises 7 and 8, state the hypothesis and conclusion for each statement.

7. If the diagonals of a trapezoid are equal in length, then the trapezoid is isosceles.
8. The diagonals of a parallelogram are congruent if the parallelogram is a rectangle.

In Review Exercises 9 to 11, draw a valid conclusion where possible.

9. 1. If a person has a good job, then that person has a college degree.
   2. Billy Fuller has a college degree.

   C. ∴ ?
10. 1. If a person has a good job, then that person has a college degree.
    2. Jody Smithers has a good job.

    C. ∴ ?
11. 1. If the measure of an angle is 90°, then that angle is a right angle.
    2. Angle A has a measure of 90°.

    C. ∴ ?
12. A, B, and C are three points on a line. $AC = 8$, $BC = 4$, and $AB = 12$. Which point must be between the other two points?
13. Use three letters to name the angle shown. Also use one letter to name the same angle. Decide whether the angle measure is less than 90°, equal to 90°, or greater than 90°.

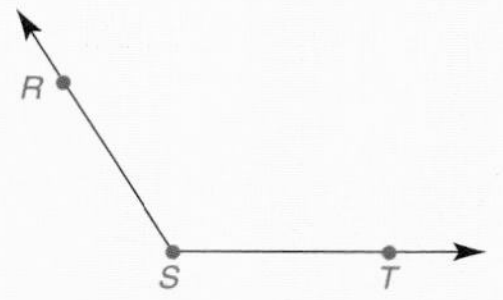

14. Figure $MNPQ$ is a rhombus. Draw diagonals $\overline{MP}$ and $\overline{QN}$ of the rhombus. How do $\overline{MP}$ and $\overline{QN}$ appear to be related?

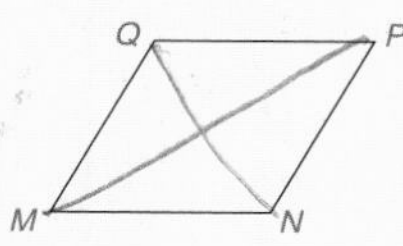

In Review Exercises 15 to 17, sketch and label the figures described.

15. Points A, B, C, and D are coplanar. A, B, and C are the only three of these points that are collinear.
16. Line ℓ intersects plane X at point P.
17. Plane M contains intersecting lines j and k.
18. On the basis of appearance, what *type of angle* is shown?

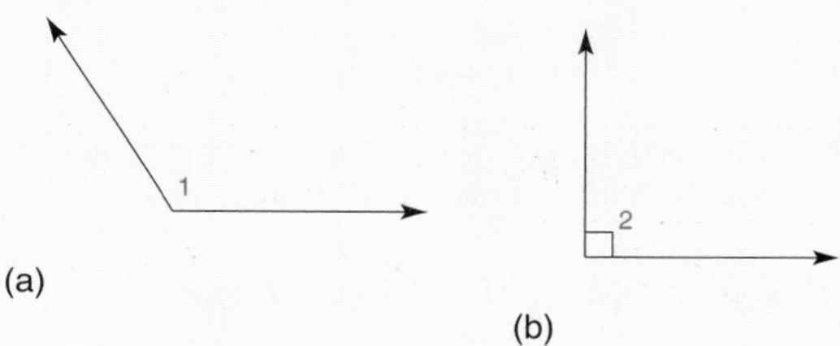

19. On the basis of appearance, what *type of angle* is shown?

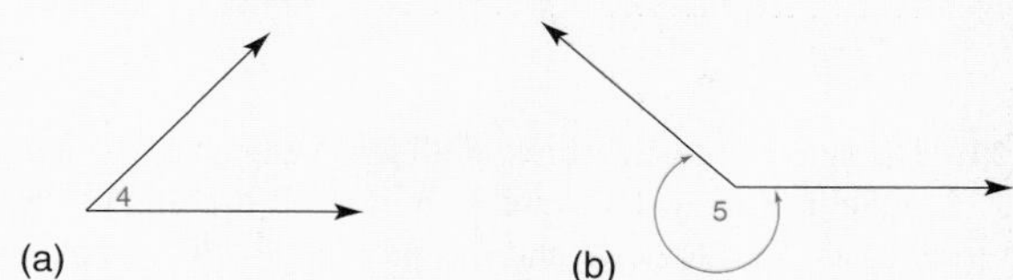

20. *Given:* $\overrightarrow{BD}$ bisects $\angle ABC$
    $m\angle ABD = 2x + 15$
    $m\angle DBC = 3x - 2$
    Find: $m\angle ABC$
21. *Given:* $m\angle ABD = 2x + 5$
    $m\angle DBC = 3x - 4$
    $m\angle ABC = 86°$
    Find: $m\angle DBC$

Exercises 20, 21

22. *Given:* $AM = 3x - 1$
    $MB = 4x - 5$
    M is the midpoint of $\overline{AB}$
    Find: AB
23. *Given:* $AM = 4x - 4$
    $MB = 5x + 2$
    $AB = 25$
    Find: MB

Exercises 22, 23

24. *Given:* D is the midpoint of $\overline{AC}$
    $\overline{AC} \cong \overline{BC}$
    $CD = 2x + 5$
    $BC = x + 28$
    Find: AC

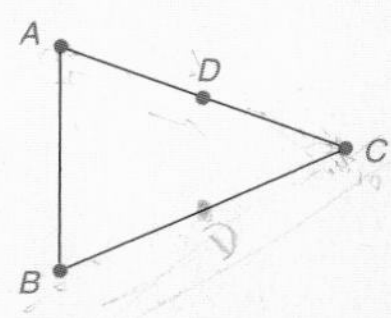

25. *Given:* $m\angle 3 = 7x - 21$
$m\angle 4 = 3x + 7$
Find: $m\angle FMH$

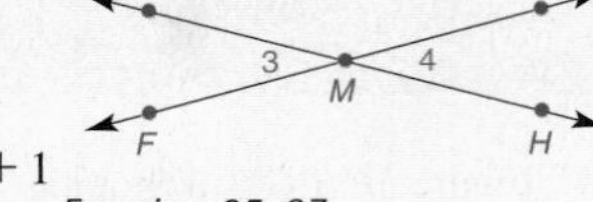

Exercises 25–27

26. *Given:* $m\angle FMH = 4x + 1$
$m\angle 4 = x + 4$
Find: $m\angle 4$

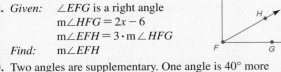

27. In the figure, find:
a) $\overleftrightarrow{KH} \cap \overleftrightarrow{FJ}$
b) $\overrightarrow{MJ} \cup \overrightarrow{MH}$
c) $\angle KMJ \cap \angle JMH$
d) $\overrightarrow{MK} \cup \overrightarrow{MH}$

28. *Given:* $\angle EFG$ is a right angle
$m\angle HFG = 2x - 6$
$m\angle EFH = 3 \cdot m\angle HFG$
Find: $m\angle EFH$

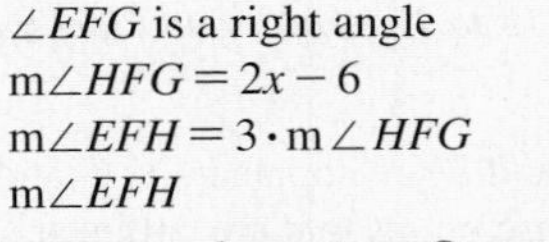

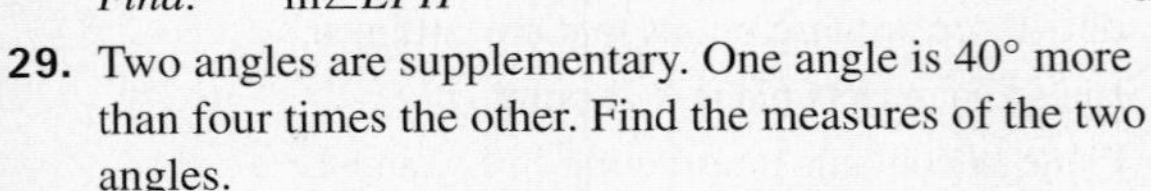

29. Two angles are supplementary. One angle is 40° more than four times the other. Find the measures of the two angles.

30. a) Write an expression for the perimeter of the triangle shown.

(HINT: Add the lengths of the sides.)

b) If the perimeter is 32 centimeters, find the value of x.
c) Find the length of each side of the triangle.

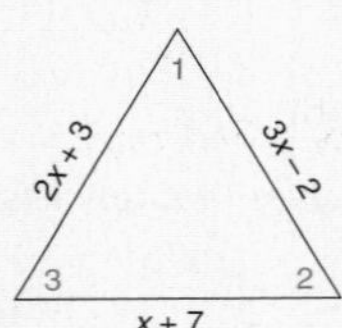

31. The sum of the measures of all three angles of the triangle in Review Exercise 30 is 180°. If the sum of the measures of angles 1 and 2 is more than 130°, what can you conclude about the measure of angle 3?

32. Susan wants to have a 4-ft board with some pegs on it. She wants to leave 6 in. on each end and 4 in. between pegs. How many pegs will fit on the board?

(HINT: If n represents the number of pegs, then (n - 1) represents the number of equal spaces.)

State whether the sentences in Review Exercises 33 to 37 are always true (A), sometimes true (S), or never true (N).

33. If $AM = MB$, then A, M, and B are collinear.
34. If two angles are congruent, then they are right angles.
35. The bisectors of vertical angles are opposite rays.
36. Complementary angles are congruent.
37. The supplement of an obtuse angle is another obtuse angle.

38. Fill in the missing statements or reasons.
Given: $\angle 1 \cong \angle P$
$\angle 4 \cong \angle P$
$\overrightarrow{VP}$ bisects $\angle RVO$
Prove: $\angle TVP \cong \angle MVP$

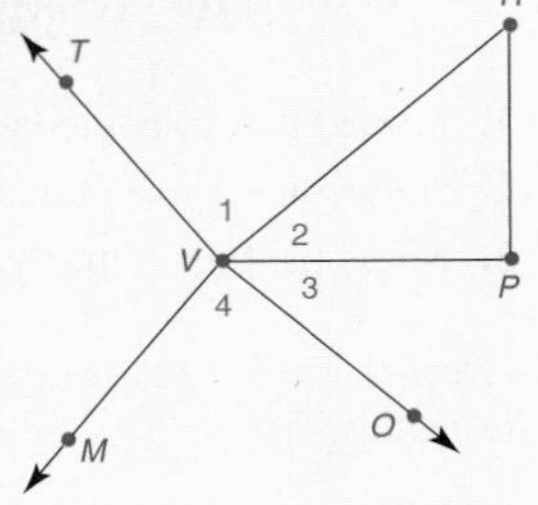

PROOF

	Statements	Reasons
	1. $\angle 1 \cong \angle P$	1. Given
	2. ?	2. Given
(1), (2)	3. ?	3. Transitive Prop. of $\cong$
(3)	4. $m\angle 1 = m\angle 4$	4. ?
	5. $\overrightarrow{VP}$ bisects $\angle RVO$	5. ?
	6. ?	6. If a ray bisects an $\angle$, it forms two $\angle$s of equal measure
(4), (6)	7. ?	7. Addition Prop. of Equality
	8. $m\angle 1 + m\angle 2 = m\angle TVP$; $m\angle 4 + m\angle 3 = m\angle MVP$	8. ?
(7), (8)	9. $m\angle TVP = m\angle MVP$	9. ?
	10. ?	10. If two $\angle$s are = in measure, then they are $\cong$

Write two-column proofs for Review Exercises 39 to 46.

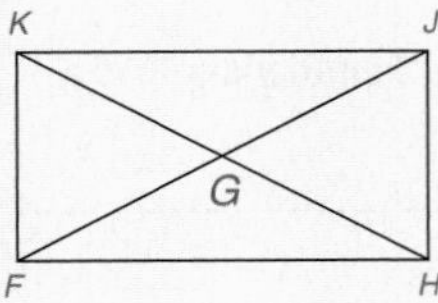

Exercises 39–41

39. *Given:* $\overline{KF} \perp \overline{FH}$
$\angle JHF$ is a right $\angle$
Prove: $\angle KFH \cong \angle JHF$

For Review Exercises 40 and 41, see the figure on page 66.

40. *Given:* $\overline{KH} \cong \overline{FJ}$
G is the midpoint of both $\overline{KH}$ and $\overline{FJ}$
Prove: $\overline{KG} \cong \overline{GJ}$

41. *Given:* $\overline{KF} \perp \overline{FH}$
Prove: $\angle KFJ$ is comp. to $\angle JFH$

42. *Given:* $\angle 1$ is comp. to $\angle M$
$\angle 2$ is comp. to $\angle M$
Prove: $\angle 1 \cong \angle 2$

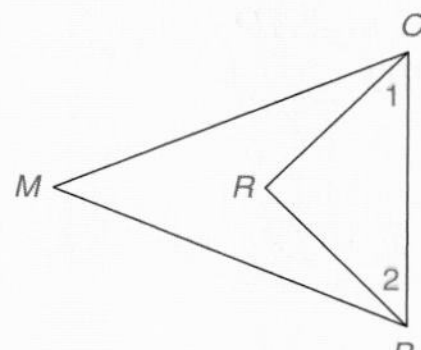

Exercises 42, 43

43. *Given:* $\angle MOP \cong \angle MPO$
$\overrightarrow{OR}$ bisects $\angle MOP$
$\overrightarrow{PR}$ bisects $\angle MPO$
Prove: $\angle 1 \cong \angle 2$

For Review Exercise 44, see the figure that follows Review Exercise 45.

44. *Given:* $\angle 4 \cong \angle 6$
Prove: $\angle 5 \cong \angle 6$

45. *Given:* Figure as shown
Prove: $\angle 4$ is supp. to $\angle 2$

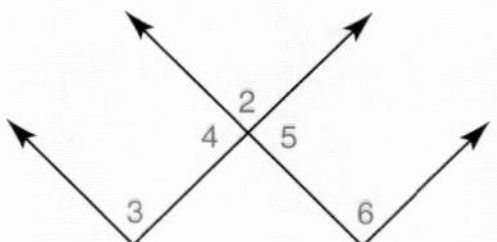

Exercises 44–46

46. *Given:* $\angle 3$ is supp. to $\angle 5$
$\angle 4$ is supp. to $\angle 6$
Prove: $\angle 3 \cong \angle 6$

47. *Given:* $\overline{VP}$
Construct: $\overline{VW}$ such that $VW = 4 \cdot VP$

V P

48. Construct a 135° angle.

49. *Given:* Triangle PQR
Construct: The three angle bisectors
What did you discover about the three angle bisectors of this triangle?

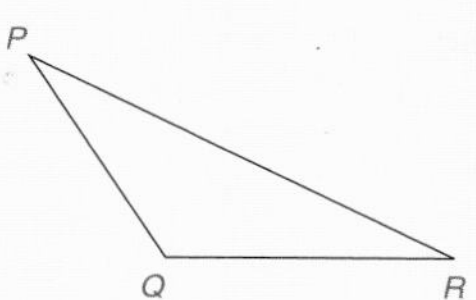

50. *Given:* $\overline{AB}$, $\overline{BC}$, and $\angle B$ as shown in Review Exercise 51.
Construct: Triangle ABC

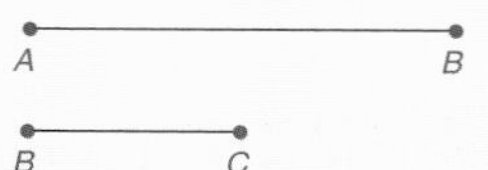

51. *Given:* $m\angle B = 50°$
Construct: An angle whose measure is 20°

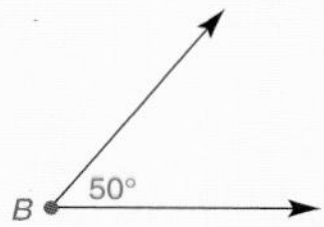

52. If $m\angle 1 = 90°$, find the measure of reflex angle 2.

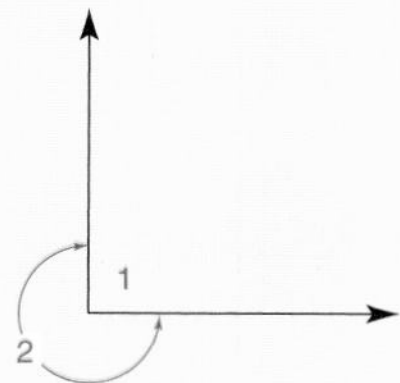

Chapter 1 TEST

1. Which type of reasoning is illustrated below? ________
   Because it has rained the previous four days, Annie concludes that it will rain again today.
2. Given $\angle ABC$ (as shown), provide a second correct method for naming this angle. ________

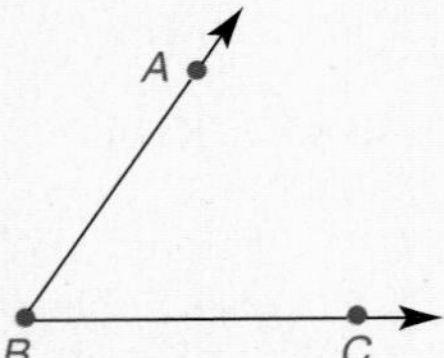

3. Using the Segment-Addition Postulate, state a conclusion regarding the accompanying figure. ________

4. Complete each postulate:
   a) If two lines intersect, they intersect in a ________
   b) If two planes intersect, they intersect in a ________
5. Given that x is the measure of an angle, name the type of angle when:
   a) $x = 90°$ ________ b) $90° < x < 180°$ ________
6. What word would describe two angles
   a) whose sum of measures is equal to 180°? ________
   b) that have equal measures? ________
7. Given that $\overrightarrow{NP}$ bisects $\angle MNQ$, state a conclusion involving $m\angle MNP$ and $m\angle PNQ$. ________________

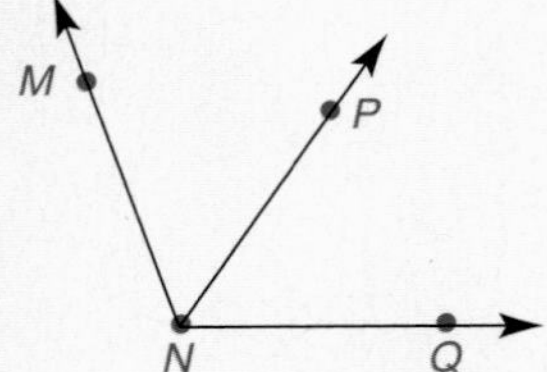

8. Complete each theorem:
   a) If two lines are perpendicular, they meet to form ________ angles.
   b) If the exterior sides of two adjacent angles form a straight line, these angles are ________
9. State the conclusion for the following deductive argument.
   (1) If you study geometry, then you will develop reasoning skills.
   (2) Kianna is studying geometry this semester.
   (C) ________________

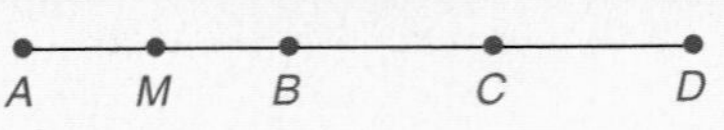

Questions 10, 11

10. In the figure, A-B-C-D and M is the midpoint of $\overline{AB}$. If $AB = 6.4$ inches and $BD = 7.2$ inches, find MD. ________
11. In the figure, $AB = x$, $BD = x + 5$, and $AD = 27$.
    Find: a) x ________ b) BD ________

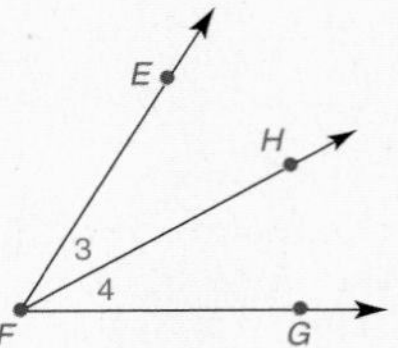

Questions 12, 13

12. In the figure, $m\angle EFG = 68°$ and $m\angle 3 = 33°$. Find $m\angle 4$. ________
13. In the figure, $m\angle 3 = x$ and $m\angle 4 = 2x - 3$. If $m\angle EFG = 69°$, find:
    a) x ______ b) $m\angle 4$ ______

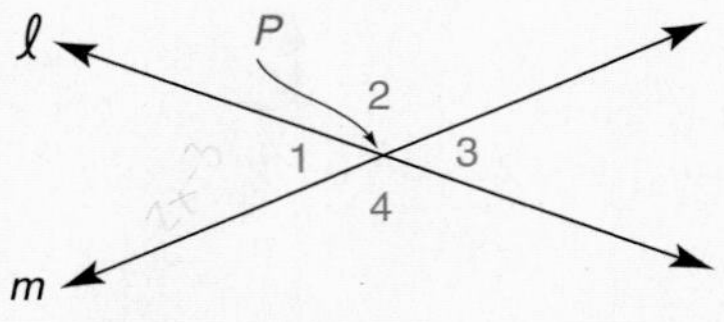

Questions 14–16

14. Lines ℓ and m intersect at point P. If $m\angle 1 = 43°$, find:
    a) $m\angle 2$ ________ b) $m\angle 3$ ________
15. If $m\angle 1 = 2x - 3$ and $m\angle 3 = 3x - 28$, find:
    a) x ________ b) $m\angle 1$ ________
16. If $m\angle 1 = 2x - 3$ and $m\angle 2 = 6x - 1$, find:
    a) x ________ b) $m\angle 2$ ________
17. $\angle$s 3 and 4 (not shown) are complementary. Where $m\angle 3 = x$ and $m\angle 4 = y$, write an equation using variables x and y. ________________
18. Construct the angle bisector of obtuse angle RST.

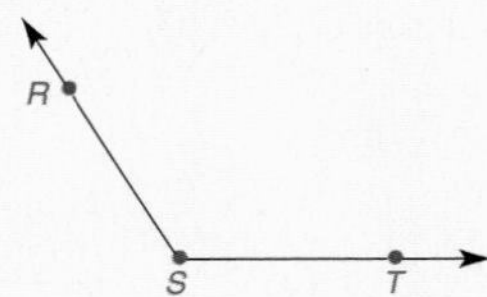

19. Construct the perpendicular bisector of $\overline{AB}$.

In Exercises 20 to 22, complete the missing statements/reasons for each proof.

20. *Given:* M-N-P-Q on $\overline{MQ}$
Prove: $MN + NP + PQ = MQ$

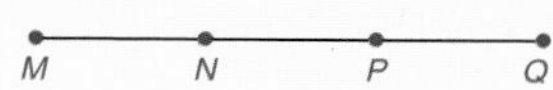

PROOF

Statements	Reasons
1. M-N-P-Q on $\overline{MQ}$	1. Given
2. $MN + NQ = MQ$	2. Seg Add pos
3. $NP + PQ = NQ$	3. Seg Add pos
4. $MN + NP + PQ = MQ$	4. [illegible]

21. *Given:* $2x - 3 = 17$
Prove: $x = 10$

PROOF

Statements	Reasons
1. $2x - 3 = 17$	1. Given
2. $2x = 20$	2. Addition Property of Equality
3. $x = 10$	3. Division Property of Equality

22. *Given:* $\angle ABC$ is a right angle; $\overrightarrow{BD}$ bisects $\angle ABC$
Prove: $m\angle 1 = 45°$

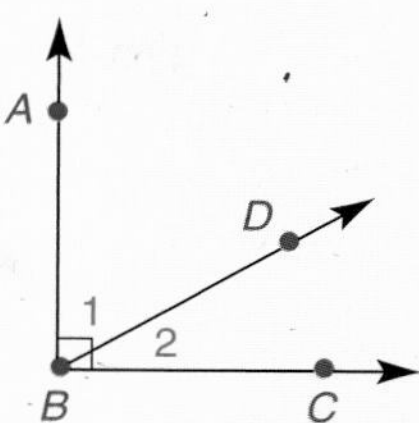

PROOF

Statements	Reasons
1. $\angle ABC$ is a right angle	1. Given
2. $m\angle ABC =$ 90'	2. Definition of a right angle
3. $m\angle 1 + m\angle 2 = m\angle ABC$	3. ______
4. $m\angle 1 + m\angle 2 =$ 90	4. Substitution Property of Equality
5. $\overrightarrow{BD}$ bisects $\angle ABC$	5. ______
6. $m\angle 1 = m\angle 2$	6. ______
7. $m\angle 1 + m\angle 1 = 90°$ or $2 \cdot m\angle 1 = 90°$	7. ______
8. ______	8. Division Property of Equality

23. Obtuse angle ABC is bisected by $\overrightarrow{BD}$ and is trisected by $\overrightarrow{BE}$ and $\overrightarrow{BF}$. If $m\angle EBD = 18°$, find $m\angle ABC$.

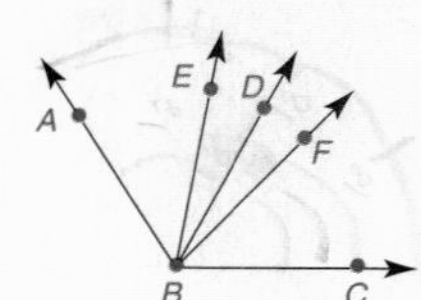

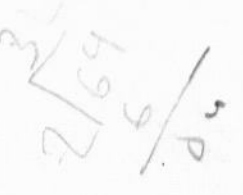

Parallel Lines

Chapter 2

© John Coletti/Getty Images

CHAPTER OUTLINE

Additional Video explanation of concepts, sample problems, and applications are available on DVD. 

Breathtaking! The widest cable-stayed bridge in the world, the Leonard P. Zakim Bridge (also known as the Bunker Hill Bridge) lies at the north end of Boston, Massachusetts. Lying above the Charles River, this modern design bridge was dedicated in 2002. Cables for the bridge are parallel or nearly parallel to each other. The vertical towers above the bridge are perpendicular to the bridge floor. In this chapter, we consider relationships among parallel and perpendicular lines. Thanks to the line relationships, we can establish a most important fact regarding angle measures for the triangle in Section 2.4. Another look at the Bunker Hill Bridge suggests the use of symmetry, a topic that is given considerable attention in Section 2.6.

2.1 The Parallel Postulate and Special Angles

KEY CONCEPTS

Perpendicular Lines
Perpendicular Planes
Parallel Lines
Parallel Planes
Parallel Postulate
Transversal
Interior Angles
Exterior Angles
Corresponding Angles
Alternate Interior Angles
Alternate Exterior Angles

PERPENDICULAR LINES

By definition, two lines (or segments or rays) are perpendicular if they meet to form congruent adjacent angles. Using this definition, we proved the theorem stating that "perpendicular lines meet to form right angles." We can also say that two rays or line segments are perpendicular if they are parts of perpendicular lines. We now consider a method for constructing a line perpendicular to a given line.

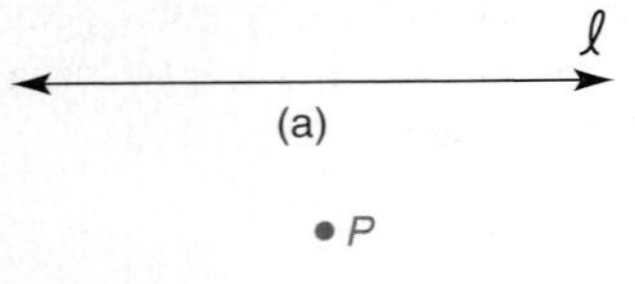

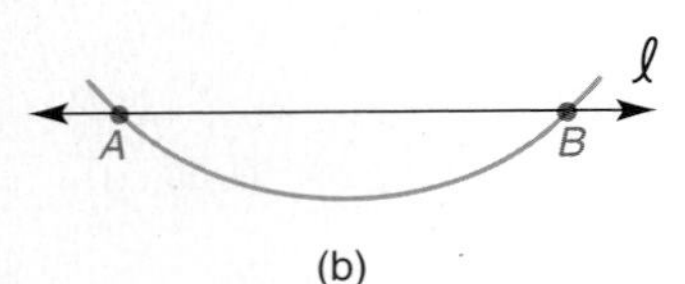

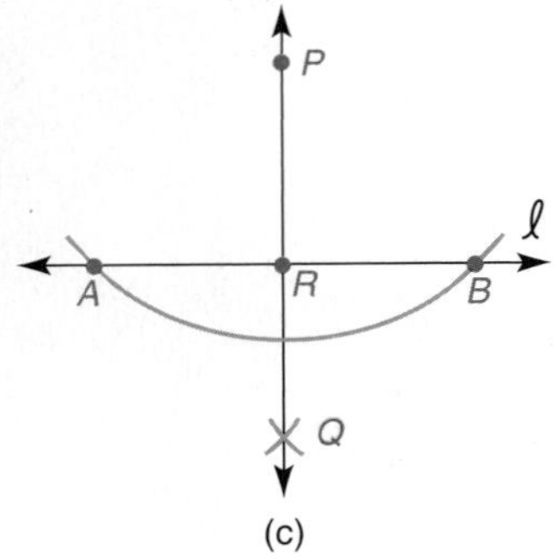

Figure 2.1

Construction 6 *To construct the line that is perpendicular to a given line from a point not on the given line.*

GIVEN: In Figure 2.1(a), line ℓ and point P not on ℓ

CONSTRUCT: $\overleftrightarrow{PQ} \perp \ell$

CONSTRUCTION: Figure 2.1(b): With P as the center, open the compass to a length great enough to intersect ℓ in two points A and B.

Figure 2.1(c): With A and B as centers, mark off arcs of equal radii (using the same compass opening) to intersect at a point Q, as shown. Draw $\overleftrightarrow{PQ}$ to complete the desired line.

In this construction, $\angle PRA$ and $\angle PRB$ are right angles. Greater accuracy is achieved if the arcs drawn from A and B intersect on the opposite side of line ℓ from point P.

Construction 6 suggests a uniqueness relationship that can be proved.

THEOREM 2.1.1

From a point not on a given line, there is exactly one line perpendicular to the given line.

The term *perpendicular* includes line-ray, line-plane, and plane-plane relationships. The drawings in Figure 2.2 on page 73 indicate two perpendicular lines, a line perpendicular to a plane, and two perpendicular planes. In Figure 2.1(c), $\overrightarrow{RP} \perp \ell$.

PARALLEL LINES

Just as the word *perpendicular* can relate lines and planes, the word *parallel* can also be used to describe relationships among lines and planes. However, parallel lines must lie in the same plane, as the following definition emphasizes.

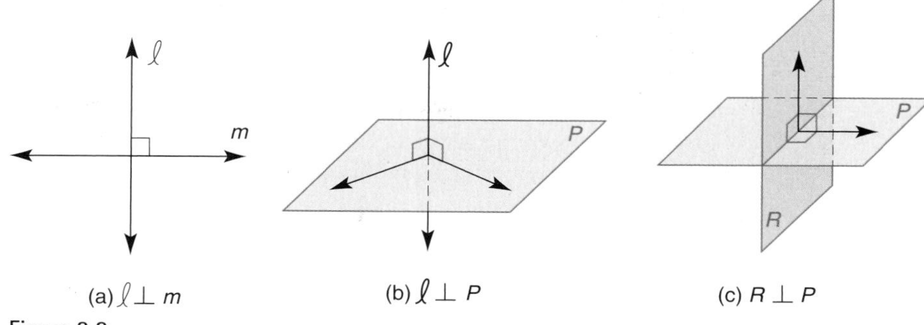

Figure 2.2

Discover

In the sketch below, lines ℓ and m lie in the same plane with line t and are perpendicular to line t. How are the lines ℓ and m related to each other?

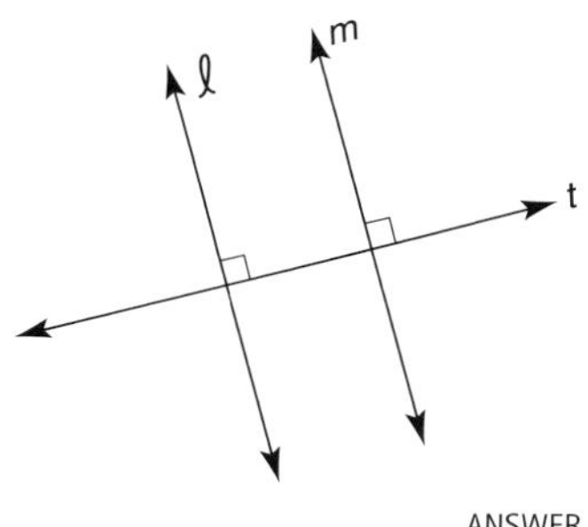

ANSWER

These lines are said to be *parallel*. They will not intersect.

© Angelo Gilardelli/Shutterstock

The rungs of a ladder are parallel line segments.

DEFINITION

Parallel lines are lines in the same plane that do not intersect.

More generally, two lines in a plane, a line and a plane, or two planes are parallel if they do not intersect (see Figure 2.3). Figure 2.3 illustrates possible applications of the word *parallel.* In Figure 2.4, two parallel planes M and N are both intersected by a third plane G. How must the lines of intersection, a and b, be related?

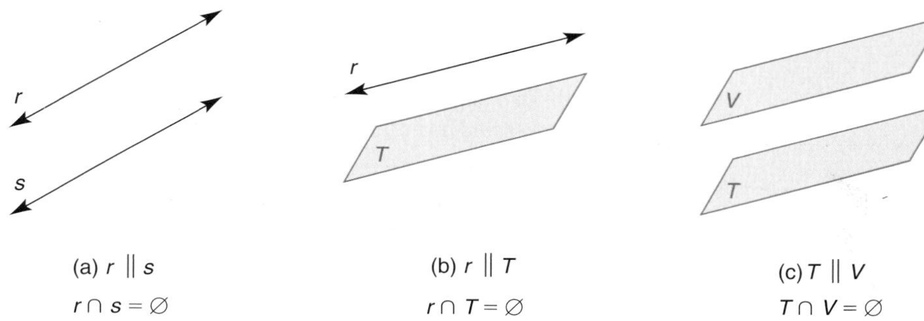

(a) $r \parallel s$ $r \cap s = \emptyset$

(b) $r \parallel T$ $r \cap T = \emptyset$

(c) $T \parallel V$ $T \cap V = \emptyset$

Figure 2.3

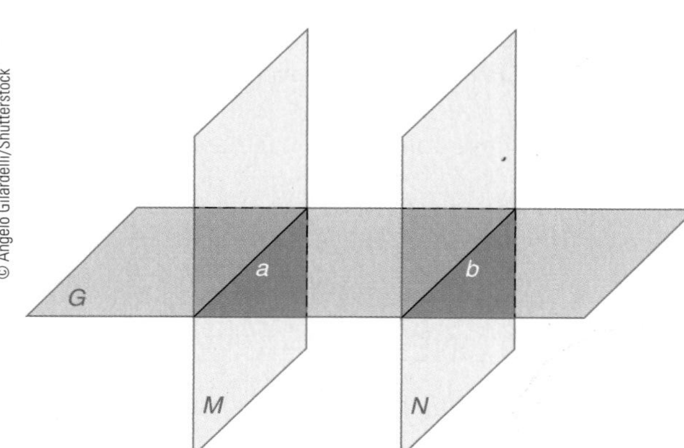

SSG *Exs. 1–3*

Figure 2.4

EUCLIDEAN GEOMETRY

The type of geometry found in this textbook is known as *Euclidean geometry*. In this geometry, a plane is a flat, two-dimensional surface in which the line segment joining any two points of the plane lies entirely within the plane. Whereas the postulate that follows characterizes Euclidean geometry, the Perspective on Application section near the end of this chapter discusses alternative geometries. Postulate 10, the Euclidean Parallel Postulate, is easy to accept because of the way we perceive a plane.

POSTULATE 10: (PARALLEL POSTULATE)

Through a point not on a line, exactly one line is parallel to the given line.

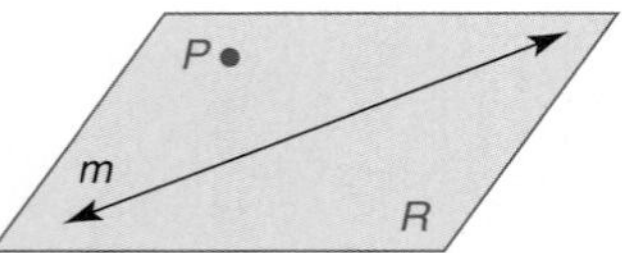

Figure 2.5

Consider Figure 2.5, in which line m and point P (with P not on m) both lie in plane R. It seems reasonable that exactly one line can be drawn through P parallel to line m. The method of construction for the unique line through P parallel to m is provided in Section 2.3.

A **transversal** is a line that intersects two (or more) other lines at distinct points; all of the lines lie in the same plane. In Figure 2.6, t is a transversal for lines r and s. Angles that are formed between r and s are **interior angles;** those outside r and s are **exterior angles.** Relative to Figure 2.6, we have

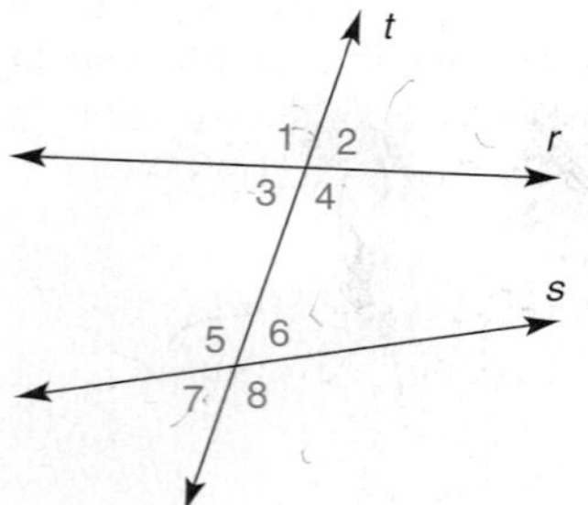

Figure 2.6

Interior angles: $\angle 3$, $\angle 4$, $\angle 5$, $\angle 6$

Exterior angles: $\angle 1$, $\angle 2$, $\angle 7$, $\angle 8$

Consider the angles in Figure 2.6 that are formed when lines are cut by a transversal. Two angles that lie in the same relative positions (such as *above* and *left*) are called **corresponding angles** for these lines. In Figure 2.6, $\angle 1$ and $\angle 5$ are corresponding angles; each angle is *above* the line and to the *left* of the transversal that together form the angle. As shown in Figure 2.6, we have

Corresponding angles:	$\angle 1$ and $\angle 5$	above left
(must be in pairs)	$\angle 3$ and $\angle 7$	below left
	$\angle 2$ and $\angle 6$	above right
	$\angle 4$ and $\angle 8$	below right

Two interior angles that have different vertices and lie on opposite sides of the transversal are **alternate interior angles.** Two exterior angles that have different vertices and lie on opposite sides of the transversal are **alternate exterior angles.** Both types of alternate angles must occur in pairs; in Figure 2.6, we have:

Alternate interior angles: $\angle 3$ and $\angle 6$
$\angle 4$ and $\angle 5$

Exs. 4–6

Alternate exterior angles: $\angle 1$ and $\angle 8$
$\angle 2$ and $\angle 7$

PARALLEL LINES AND CONGRUENT ANGLES

In Figure 2.7, *parallel* lines ℓ and m are cut by transversal v. If a protractor were used to measure $\angle 1$ and $\angle 5$, these corresponding angles would be found to have equal measures; that is, they are congruent. Similarly, any other pair of corresponding angles will be congruent as long as $\ell \parallel m$.

POSTULATE 11

If two parallel lines are cut by a transversal, then the corresponding angles are congruent.

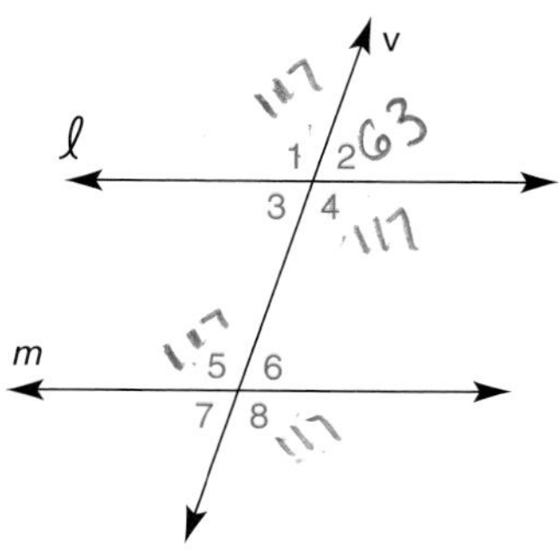

Figure 2.7

EXAMPLE 1

In Figure 2.7, $\ell \parallel m$ and $m\angle 1 = 117°$. Find:

a) $m\angle 2$ c) $m\angle 4$
b) $m\angle 5$ d) $m\angle 8$

Solution

a) $m\angle 2 = 63°$ supplementary to $\angle 1$
b) $m\angle 5 = 117°$ corresponding to $\angle 1$
c) $m\angle 4 = 117°$ vertical to $\angle 1$
d) $m\angle 8 = 117°$ corresponding to $\angle 4$ [found in part (c)]

Several theorems follow from Postulate 11; for some of these theorems, formal proofs are provided. Study the proofs and be able to state all the theorems. You can cite the theorems that have been proven as reasons in subsequent proofs.

THEOREM 2.1.2

If two parallel lines are cut by a transversal, then the alternate interior angles are congruent.

Technology Exploration

Use computer software if available.

1. Draw $\overleftrightarrow{AB} \parallel \overleftrightarrow{CD}$.
2. Draw transversal $\overleftrightarrow{EF}$.
3. By numbering the angles as in Figure 2.8, find the measures of all eight angles.
4. Show that pairs of corresponding angles are congruent.

GIVEN: $a \parallel b$ in Figure 2.8
Transversal k

PROVE: $\angle 3 \cong \angle 6$

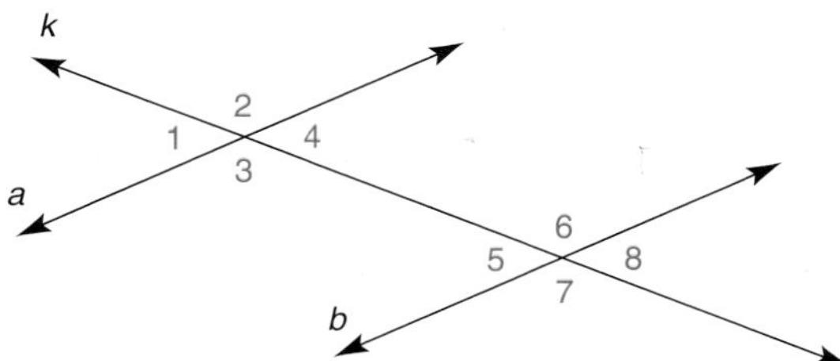

Figure 2.8

PROOF

Statements	Reasons
1. $a \parallel b$; transversal k	1. Given
2. $\angle 2 \cong \angle 6$	2. If two $\parallel$ lines are cut by a transversal, corresponding $\angle$s are $\cong$
3. $\angle 3 \cong \angle 2$	3. If two lines intersect, vertical $\angle$s formed are $\cong$
4. $\angle 3 \cong \angle 6$	4. Transitive (of $\cong$)

Although we did not establish that alternate interior angles 4 and 5 are congruent, it is easy to prove that these are congruent because they are supplements to $\angle 3$ and $\angle 6$. A theorem that is similar to Theorem 2.1.2 follows, but the proof is left as Exercise 28.

THEOREM 2.1.3

If two parallel lines are cut by a transversal, then the alternate exterior angles are congruent.

PARALLEL LINES AND SUPPLEMENTARY ANGLES

When two parallel lines are cut by a transversal, it can be shown that the two interior angles on the same side of the transversal are supplementary. A similar claim can be made for the pair of exterior angles on the same side of the transversal.

STRATEGY FOR PROOF ▶ Using Substitution in a Proof Statement

General Rule: In an equation, an expression can replace its equal.

Illustration: See statements 3, 6, and 7 in the proof of Theorem 2.1.4. Note that $m\angle 1$ (found in statement 3) is substituted for $m\angle 2$ in statement 6 to obtain statement 7.

THEOREM 2.1.4

If two parallel lines are cut by a transversal, then the interior angles on the same side of the transversal are supplementary.

GIVEN: In Figure 2.9, $\overleftrightarrow{TV} \parallel \overleftrightarrow{WY}$ with transversal $\overleftrightarrow{RS}$

PROVE: $\angle 1$ and $\angle 3$ are supplementary

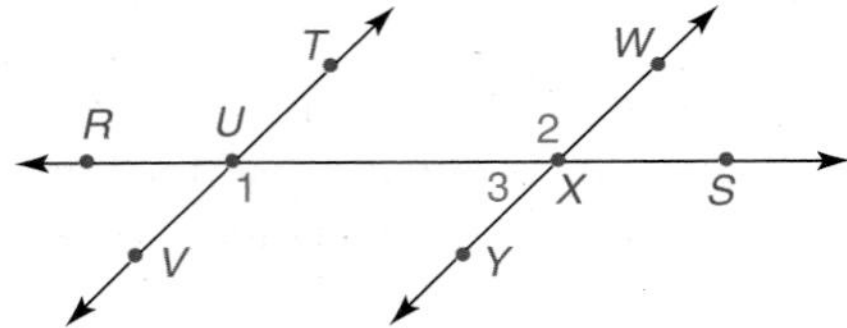

Figure 2.9

PROOF

Statements	Reasons
1. $\overleftrightarrow{TV} \parallel \overleftrightarrow{WY}$; transversal $\overleftrightarrow{RS}$	1. Given
2. $\angle 1 \cong \angle 2$	2. If two $\parallel$ lines are cut by a transversal, alternate interior $\angle$s are $\cong$
3. $m\angle 1 = m\angle 2$	3. If two $\angle$s are $\cong$, their measures are $=$
4. $\angle WXY$ is a straight $\angle$, so $m\angle WXY = 180°$	4. If an $\angle$ is a straight $\angle$, its measure is $180°$
5. $m\angle 2 + m\angle 3 = m\angle WXY$	5. Angle-Addition Postulate
6. $m\angle 2 + m\angle 3 = 180°$	6. Substitution
7. $m\angle 1 + m\angle 3 = 180°$	7. Substitution
8. $\angle 1$ and $\angle 3$ are supplementary	8. If the sum of measures of two $\angle$s is $180°$, the $\angle$s are supplementary

The proof of the following theorem is left as an exercise.

THEOREM 2.1.5

If two parallel lines are cut by a transversal, then the exterior angles on the same side of the transversal are supplementary.

SSG *Exs. 7–11*

The remaining examples in this section illustrate methods from algebra and deal with the angles formed when two parallel lines are cut by a transversal.

EXAMPLE 2

GIVEN: $\overleftrightarrow{TV} \parallel \overleftrightarrow{WY}$ with transversal $\overleftrightarrow{RS}$
$m\angle RUV = (x + 4)(x - 3)$
$m\angle WXS = x^2 - 3$

FIND: x

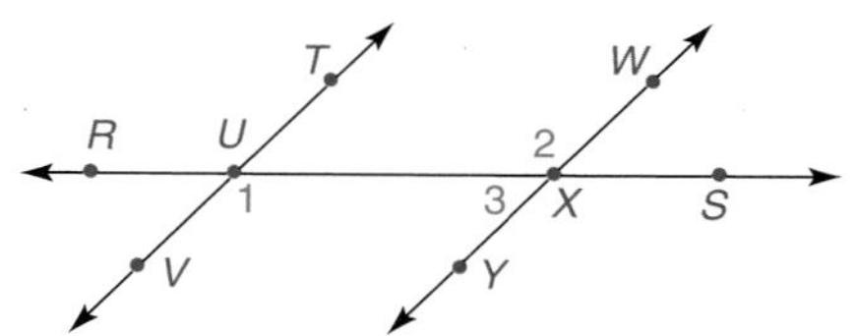

Solution $\angle RUV$ and $\angle WXS$ are alternate exterior angles, so they are congruent. Then $m\angle RUV = m\angle WXS$. Therefore,

$$(x + 4)(x - 3) = x^2 - 3$$
$$x^2 + x - 12 = x^2 - 3$$
$$x - 12 = -3$$
$$x = 9$$

NOTE: Both angles measure 78° when $x = 9$. ■

In Figure 2.10, lines r and s are known to be parallel; thus, $\angle 1 \cong \angle 5$, since these are corresponding angles.

For ℓ and m of Figure 2.10 to be parallel as well, name two angles that would have to be congruent. If we think of line s as a transversal, $\angle 5$ would have be congruent to $\angle 9$, since these are corresponding angles for ℓ and m cut by transversal s.

SSG *Exs. 12, 13*

For Example 3, recall that two equations are necessary to solve a problem in two variables.

EXAMPLE 3

GIVEN: In Figure 2.10, $r \parallel s$ and transversal ℓ

$m\angle 3 = 4x + y$
$m\angle 5 = 6x + 5y$
$m\angle 6 = 5x - 2y$

FIND: x and y

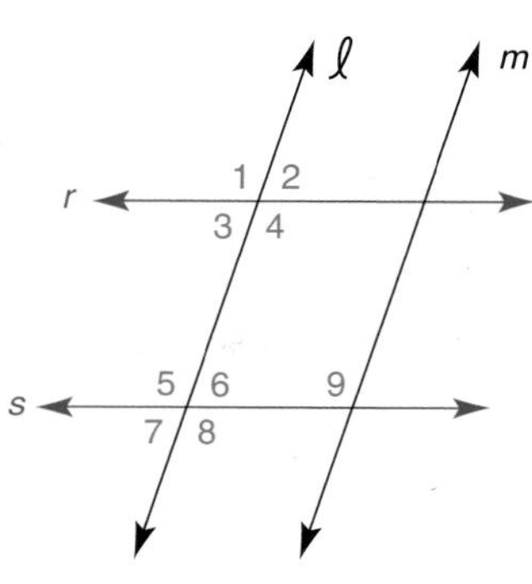

Figure 2.10

Solution $\angle 3$ and $\angle 6$ are congruent alternate interior angles; also, $\angle 3$ and $\angle 5$ are supplementary angles according to Theorem 2.1.4. These facts lead to the following system of equations:

$$4x + y = 5x - 2y$$
$$(4x + y) + (6x + 5y) = 180$$

These equations can be simplified to

$$x - 3y = 0$$
$$10x + 6y = 180$$

After we divide each term of the second equation by 2, the system becomes

$$\begin{aligned} x - 3y &= 0 \\ 5x + 3y &= 90 \end{aligned}$$

Addition leads to the equation $6x = 90$, so $x = 15$. Substituting 15 for x into the equation $x - 3y = 0$, we have

$$\begin{aligned} 15 - 3y &= 0 \\ -3y &= -15 \\ y &= 5 \end{aligned}$$

Our solution, $x = 15$ and $y = 5$, yields the following angle measures:

$$\begin{aligned} m\angle 3 &= 65^\circ \\ m\angle 5 &= 115^\circ \\ m\angle 6 &= 65^\circ \end{aligned}$$

NOTE: For an alternative solution, the equation $x - 3y = 0$ could be multiplied by 2 to obtain $2x - 6y = 0$. Then the equations $2x - 6y = 0$ and $10x + 6y = 180$ could be added. ■

Note that the angle measures determined in Example 3 are consistent with Figure 2.10 and the required relationships for the angles named. For instance, $m\angle 3 + m\angle 5 = 180^\circ$, and we see that interior angles on the same side of the transversal are indeed supplementary.

Exercises 2.1

For Exercises 1 to 4, $\ell \parallel m$ with transversal v.

1. If $m\angle 1 = 108^\circ$, find:
   a) $m\angle 5$ b) $m\angle 7$
2. If $m\angle 3 = 71^\circ$, find:
   a) $m\angle 5$ b) $m\angle 6$
3. If $m\angle 2 = 68.3^\circ$, find:
   a) $m\angle 3$ b) $m\angle 6$
4. If $m\angle 4 = 110.8^\circ$, find:
   a) $m\angle 5$ b) $m\angle 8$

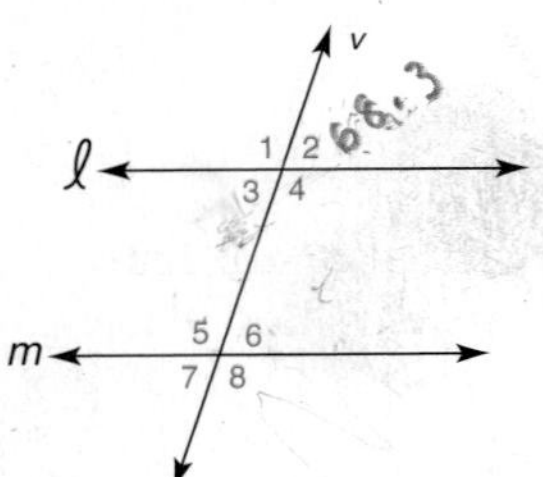

Use drawings, as needed, to answer each question.

5. Does the relation "is parallel to" have a
   a) reflexive property? (consider a line m)
   b) symmetric property? (consider lines m and n in a plane)
   c) transitive property? (consider coplanar lines m, n, and q)
6. In a plane, $\ell \perp m$ and $t \perp m$. By appearance, how are ℓ and t related?
7. Suppose that $r \parallel s$. Each interior angle on the right side of the transversal t has been bisected. Using intuition, what appears to be true of $\angle 9$ formed by the bisectors?

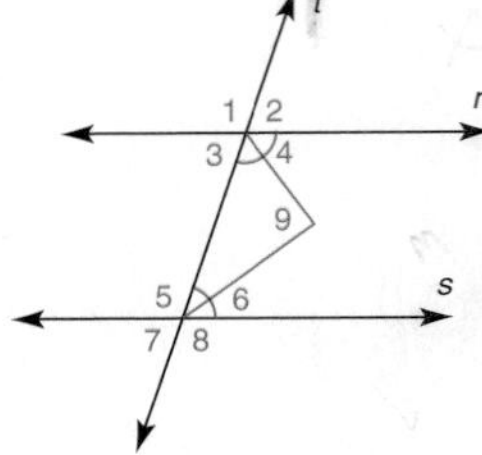

8. Make a sketch to represent two planes that are
   a) parallel.
   b) perpendicular.
9. Suppose that r is parallel to s and $m\angle 2 = 87^\circ$. Find:
   a) $m\angle 3$ c) $m\angle 1$
   b) $m\angle 6$ d) $m\angle 7$

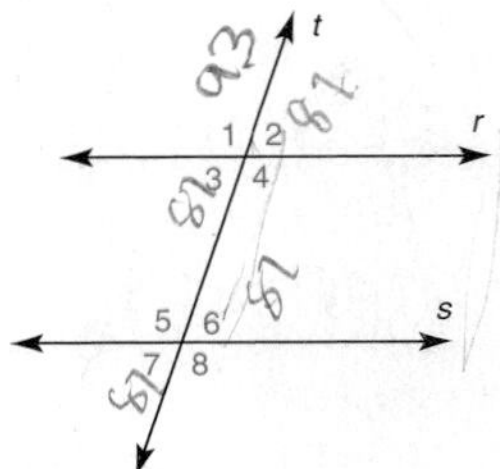

10. In Euclidean geometry, how many lines can be drawn through a point P not on a line ℓ that are
    a) parallel to line ℓ?
    b) perpendicular to line ℓ?

11. Lines r and s are cut by transversal t. Which angle
a) corresponds to $\angle 1$?
b) is the alternate interior $\angle$ for $\angle 4$?
c) is the alternate exterior $\angle$ for $\angle 1$?
d) is the other interior angle on the same side of transversal t as $\angle 3$?

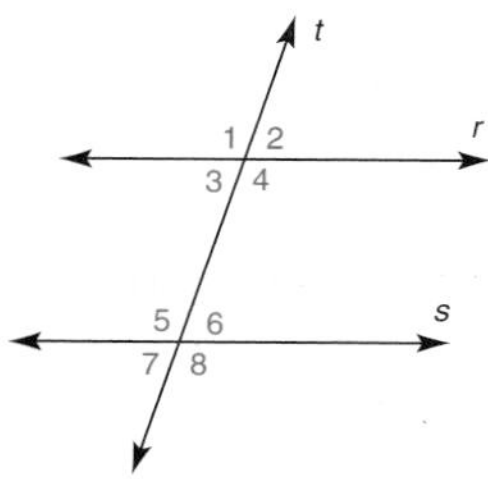

12. $\overline{AD} \parallel \overline{BC}$, $\overline{AB} \parallel \overline{DC}$, and $m\angle A = 92°$. Find:
a) $m\angle B$
b) $m\angle C$
c) $m\angle D$

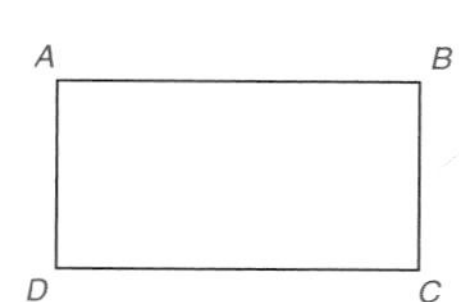

13. $\ell \parallel m$, with transversal t, and $\overrightarrow{OQ}$ bisects $\angle MON$.
If $m\angle 1 = 112°$, find the following:
a) $m\angle 2$
b) $m\angle 4$
c) $m\angle 5$
d) $m\angle MOQ$

14. *Given:* $\ell \parallel m$
Transversal t
$m\angle 1 = 4x + 2$
$m\angle 6 = 4x - 2$
Find: x and $m\angle 5$

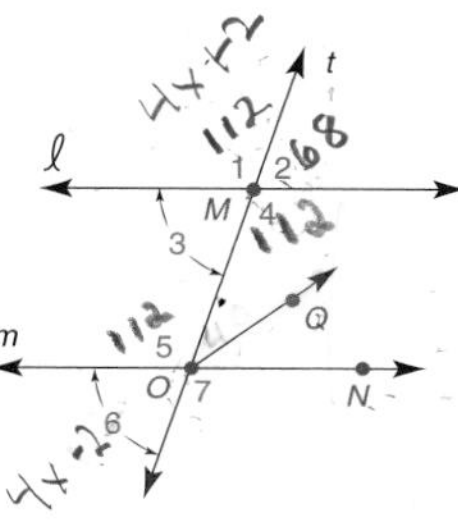
Exercises 13, 14

15. *Given:* $m \parallel n$
Transversal k
$m\angle 3 = x^2 - 3x$
$m\angle 6 = (x + 4)(x - 5)$
Find: x and $m\angle 4$

16. *Given:* $m \parallel n$
Transversal k
$m\angle 1 = 5x + y$
$m\angle 2 = 3x + y$
$m\angle 8 = 3x + 5y$
Find: x, y, and $m\angle 8$

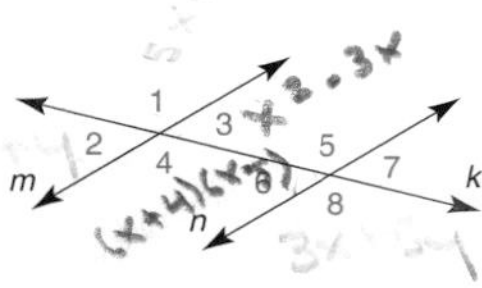
Exercises 15–17

17. *Given:* $m \parallel n$
Transversal k
$m\angle 3 = 6x + y$
$m\angle 5 = 8x + 2y$
$m\angle 6 = 4x + 7y$
Find: x, y, and $m\angle 7$

18. In the three-dimensional figure, $\overline{CA} \perp \overline{AB}$ and $\overline{BE} \perp \overline{AB}$. Are $\overleftrightarrow{CA}$ and $\overleftrightarrow{BE}$ parallel to each other? (Compare with Exercise 6.)

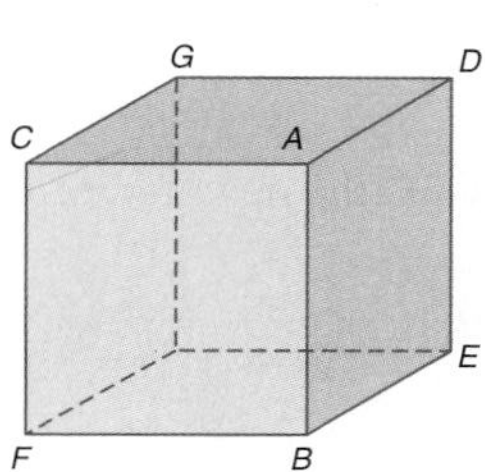

19. *Given:* $\ell \parallel m$ and $\angle 3 \cong \angle 4$
Prove: $\angle 1 \cong \angle 4$
(See figure in second column.)

PROOF

Statements	Reasons
1. $\ell \parallel m$	1. ?
2. $\angle 1 \cong \angle 2$	2. ?
3. $\angle 2 \cong \angle 3$	3. ?
4. ?	4. Given
5. ?	5. Transitive of $\cong$

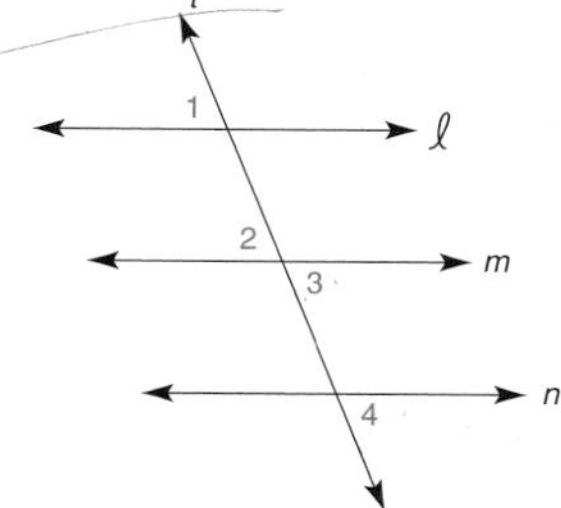

Exercises 19, 20

20. *Given:* $\ell \parallel m$ and $m \parallel n$
Prove: $\angle 1 \cong \angle 4$

PROOF

Statements	Reasons
1. $\ell \parallel m$	1. ?
2. $\angle 1 \cong \angle 2$	2. ?
3. $\angle 2 \cong \angle 3$	3. ?
4. ?	4. Given
5. $\angle 3 \cong \angle 4$	5. ?
6. ?	6. ?

21. *Given:* $\overleftrightarrow{CE} \parallel \overleftrightarrow{DF}$
Transversal $\overleftrightarrow{AB}$
$\overrightarrow{CX}$ bisects $\angle ACE$
$\overrightarrow{DE}$ bisects $\angle CDF$
Prove: $\angle 1 \cong \angle 3$

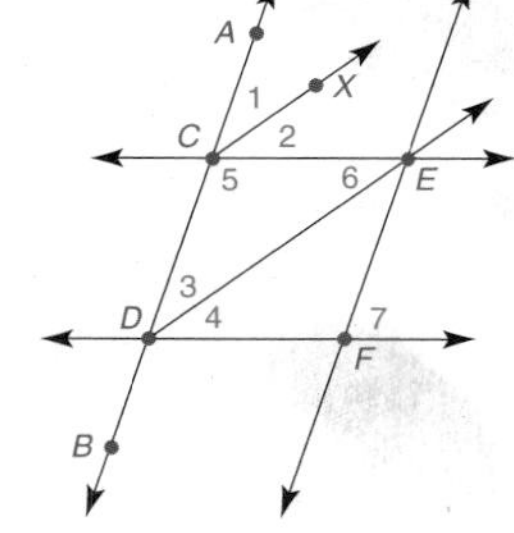

Exercises 21, 22

22. *Given:* $\overleftrightarrow{CE} \parallel \overleftrightarrow{DF}$
Transversal $\overleftrightarrow{AB}$
$\overrightarrow{DE}$ bisects $\angle CDF$
Prove: $\angle 3 \cong \angle 6$

23. *Given:* $r \parallel s$
Transversal t
$\angle 1$ is a right $\angle$
Prove: $\angle 2$ is a right $\angle$

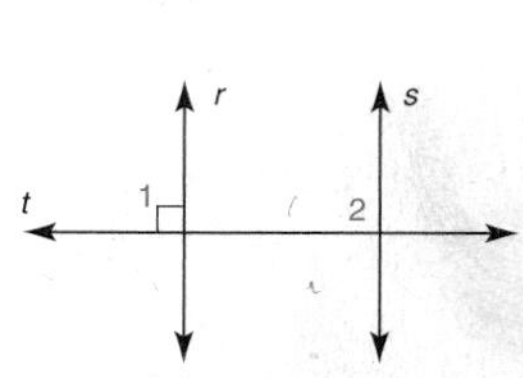

Exercises 23, 26

24. *Given:* $\overleftrightarrow{AB} \parallel \overleftrightarrow{DE}$,
$m\angle BAC = 42°$, and
$m\angle EDC = 54°$

Find: $m\angle ACD$

(HINT: There is a line through C parallel to both $\overleftrightarrow{AB}$ and $\overleftrightarrow{DE}$.)

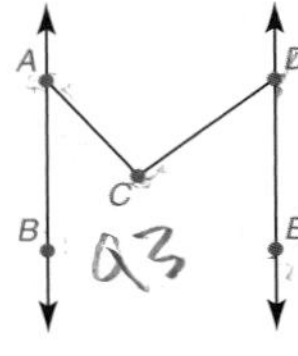

Exercises 24, 25

25. *Given:* $\overleftrightarrow{AB} \parallel \overleftrightarrow{DE}$ and
$m\angle BAC + m\angle CDE = 93°$

Find: $m\angle ACD$

(See "Hint" in Exercise 24.)

26. *Given:* $r \parallel s$, $r \perp t$ (See figure on page 79.)

Prove: $s \perp t$

27. In triangle ABC, line t is drawn through vertex A in such a way that $t \parallel \overline{BC}$.

a) Which pairs of $\angle$s are $\cong$?

b) What is the sum of $m\angle 1$, $m\angle 4$, and $m\angle 5$?

c) What is the sum of measures of the $\angle$s of $\triangle ABC$?

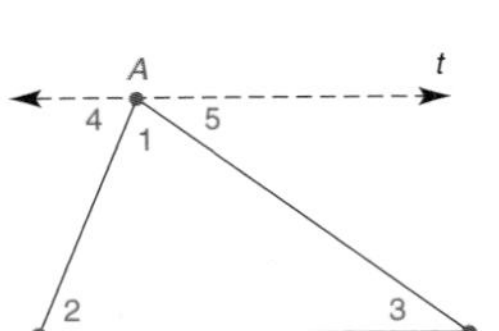

In Exercises 28 to 30, write a formal proof of each theorem.

28. If two parallel lines are cut by a transversal, then the alternate exterior angles are congruent.

29. If two parallel lines are cut by a transversal, then the exterior angles on the same side of the transversal are supplementary.

30. If a transversal is perpendicular to one of two parallel lines, then it is also perpendicular to the other line.

31. Suppose that two lines are cut by a transversal in such a way that corresponding angles are not congruent. Can those two lines be parallel?

32. *Given:* Line ℓ and point P not on ℓ

Construct: $\overleftrightarrow{PQ} \perp \ell$

33. *Given:* Triangle ABC with three acute angles

Construct: $\overline{BD} \perp \overline{AC}$

34. *Given:* Triangle MNQ with obtuse $\angle MNQ$

Construct: $\overline{NE} \perp \overline{MQ}$

35. *Given:* Triangle MNQ with obtuse $\angle MNQ$

Construct: $\overline{MR} \perp \overline{NQ}$

(HINT: Extend $\overline{NQ}$.)

Exercises 34, 35

36. *Given:* A line m and a point T not on m

Suppose that you do the following:

i) Construct a perpendicular line r from T to line m.

ii) Construct a line s perpendicular to line r at point T.

What is the relationship between lines s and m?

2.2 Indirect Proof

KEY CONCEPTS

Conditional	Inverse	Law of Negative Inference
Converse	Contrapositive	Indirect Proof

Let $P \rightarrow Q$ represent the statement "If P, then Q." The following statements are related to this conditional statement.

NOTE: Recall that $\sim P$ represents the negation of P.

Conditional (or Implication)	$P \rightarrow Q$	If P, then Q.
Converse of Conditional	$Q \rightarrow P$	If Q, then P.
Inverse of Conditional	$\sim P \rightarrow \sim Q$	If not P, then not Q.
Contrapositive of Conditional	$\sim Q \rightarrow \sim P$	If not Q, then not P.

For example, consider the following conditional statement.

If Tom lives in San Diego, then he lives in California.

This true statement has these related statements:

Converse: If Tom lives in California, then he lives in San Diego. (false)

Inverse: If Tom does not live in San Diego, then he does not live in California. (false)

Contrapositive: If Tom does not live in California, then he does not live in San Diego. (true)

In general, the conditional statement and its contrapositive are either both true or both false! Similarly, the converse and the inverse are also either both true or both false. See our textbook website for more information about the conditional and related statements.

EXAMPLE 1

For the conditional statement that follows, give the converse, the inverse, and the contrapositive. Then classify each as true or false.

If two angles are vertical angles, then they are congruent angles.

Solution

CONVERSE: If two angles are congruent angles, then they are vertical angles. (false)

INVERSE: If two angles are not vertical angles, then they are not congruent angles. (false)

CONTRAPOSITIVE: If two angles are not congruent angles, then they are not vertical angles. (true) ■

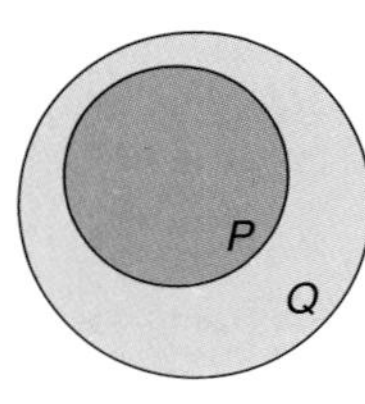

Figure 2.11

"If P, then Q" and "If not Q, then not P" are equivalent.

Venn Diagrams can be used to explain why the conditional statement $P \rightarrow Q$ and its contrapositive $\sim Q \rightarrow \sim P$ are equivalent. The relationship "If P, then Q" is represented in Figure 2.11. Note that if any point is selected outside of Q (that is, $\sim Q$), then it cannot possibly lie in set P.

THE LAW OF NEGATIVE INFERENCE (CONTRAPOSITION)

Exs. 1, 2

Consider the following circumstances, and accept each premise as true:

1. If Matt cleans his room, then he will go to the movie. ($P \rightarrow Q$)
2. Matt does not get to go to the movie. ($\sim Q$)

What can you conclude? You should have deduced that Matt did not clean his room; if he had, he would have gone to the movie. This "backdoor" reasoning is based on the fact that the truth of $P \rightarrow Q$ implies the truth of $\sim Q \rightarrow \sim P$.

LAW OF NEGATIVE INFERENCE (CONTRAPOSITION)

$$\begin{array}{r} P \rightarrow Q \\ \sim Q \\ \hline \therefore \sim P \end{array}$$

Like the Law of Detachment from Section 1.1, the Law of Negative Inference (Law of Contraposition) is a form of deduction. Whereas the Law of Detachment characterizes the method of "direct proof" found in preceding sections, the Law of Negative Inference characterizes the method of proof known as **indirect proof.**

INDIRECT PROOF

Exs. 3, 4

You will need to know when to use the indirect method of proof. Often the theorem to be proved has the form $P \rightarrow Q$, in which Q is a negation and denies some claim. For instance, an indirect proof might be best if Q reads in one of these ways:

c is *not* equal to d
ℓ is *not* perpendicular to m

However, we will see in Example 4 of this section that the indirect method can be used to prove that line ℓ is parallel to line m. Indirect proof is also used for proving existence and uniqueness theorems; see Example 5.

The method of indirect proof is illustrated in Example 2. All indirect proofs in this book are given in paragraph form (as are some of the direct proofs).

In any paragraph proof, each statement must still be justified. Because of the need to order your statements properly, writing this type of proof may have a positive impact on the essays you write for your other classes!

Geometry in the Real World

When the bubble displayed on the level is not centered, the board used in construction is neither vertical nor horizontal.

EXAMPLE 2

GIVEN: In Figure 2.12, $\overrightarrow{BA}$ is *not* perpendicular to $\overrightarrow{BD}$

PROVE: $\angle 1$ and $\angle 2$ are *not* complementary

PROOF: Suppose that $\angle 1$ and $\angle 2$ *are* complementary. Then $m\angle 1 + m\angle 2 = 90°$ because the sum of the measures of two complementary $\angle$s is 90. We also know that $m\angle 1 + m\angle 2 = m\angle ABD$, by the Angle-Addition Postulate. In turn, $m\angle ABD = 90°$ by substitution. Then $\angle ABD$ is a right angle. In turn, $\overrightarrow{BA} \perp \overrightarrow{BD}$. But this contradicts the given hypothesis; therefore, the supposition must be false, and it follows that $\angle 1$ and $\angle 2$ are not complementary. ■

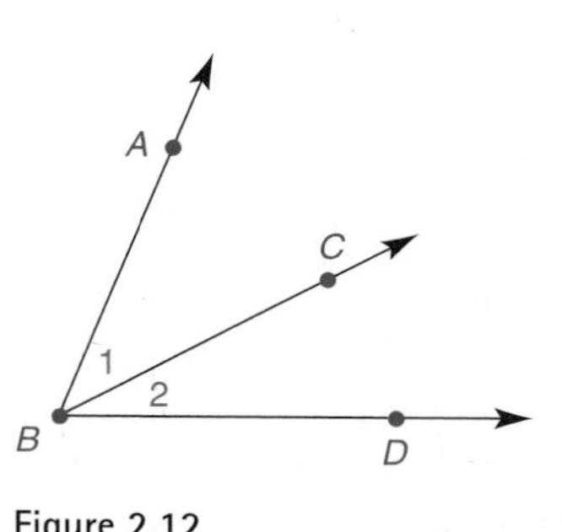

Figure 2.12

In Example 2 and in all indirect proofs, the first statement takes the form

"Suppose that . . ." or *"Assume that . . ."*

By its very nature, such a statement cannot be supported even though every other statement in the proof can be justified; thus, when a contradiction is reached, the finger of blame points to the supposition. Having reached a contradiction, we may say that the claim involving $\sim Q$ has failed and is false; thus, our only recourse is to conclude that Q is true. Following is an outline of this technique.

SSG *Exs. 5–7*

STRATEGY FOR PROOF ▶ Method of Indirect Proof

To prove the statement $P \rightarrow Q$ or to complete the proof problem of the form
Given: P
Prove: Q
by the indirect method, use the following steps:

1. Suppose that $\sim Q$ is true.
2. Reason from the supposition until you reach a contradiction.
3. Note that the supposition claiming that $\sim Q$ is true must be false and that Q must therefore be true.

Step 3 completes the proof.

The contradiction that is discovered in an indirect proof often has the form $\sim P$. Thus, the assumed statement $\sim Q$ has forced the conclusion $\sim P$, asserting that $\sim Q \rightarrow \sim P$ is true. Then the desired theorem $P \rightarrow Q$ (the contrapositive of $\sim Q \rightarrow \sim P$) is also true.

STRATEGY FOR PROOF ▶ The First Line of an Indirect Proof

General Rule: The first *statement* of an indirect proof is generally "Suppose/Assume the *opposite* of the Prove statement."
Illustration: See Example 3, which begins "Assume that $\ell \parallel m$."

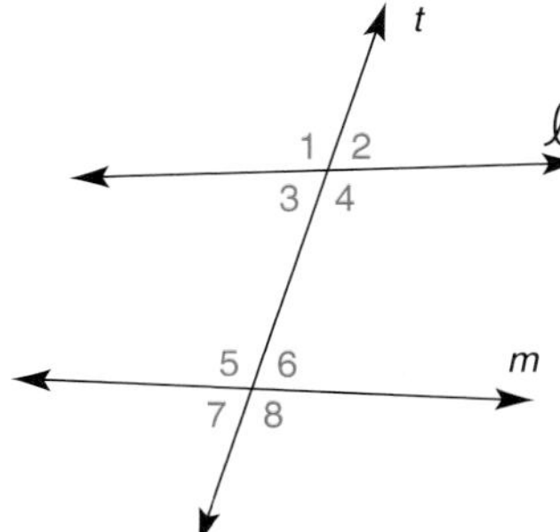

Figure 2.13

EXAMPLE 3

Complete a formal proof of the following theorem:

If two lines are cut by a transversal so that corresponding angles are not congruent, then the two lines are not parallel.

GIVEN: In Figure 2.13, ℓ and m are cut by transversal t
$\angle 1 \ncong \angle 5$

PROVE: $\ell \nparallel m$

PROOF: Assume that $\ell \parallel m$. When these lines are cut by transversal t, the corresponding angles (including $\angle 1$ and $\angle 5$) are congruent. But $\angle 1 \ncong \angle 5$ by hypothesis. Thus, the assumed statement, which claims that $\ell \parallel m$, must be false. It follows that $\ell \nparallel m$. ■

SSG *Exs. 8, 9*

The versatility of the indirect proof is shown in the final examples of this section. The indirect proofs preceding Example 4 contain a negation in the conclusion (Prove); the proofs in the final illustrations use the indirect method to arrive at a positive conclusion.

Figure 2.14

EXAMPLE 4

GIVEN: In Figure 2.14, plane T intersects parallel planes P and Q in lines ℓ and m, respectively

PROVE: $\ell \parallel m$

PROOF: Assume that ℓ is not parallel to m. Then ℓ and m intersect at some point A. But if so, point A must be on both planes P and Q, which means that planes P and Q intersect; but P and Q are parallel by hypothesis. Therefore, the assumption that ℓ and m are not parallel must be false, and it follows that $\ell \parallel m$. ■

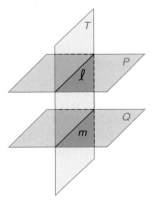

Indirect proofs are also used to establish uniqueness theorems, as Example 5 illustrates.

EXAMPLE 5

Prove the statement "The angle bisector of an angle is unique."

GIVEN: In Figure 2.15(a), $\overrightarrow{BD}$ bisects $\angle ABC$

PROVE: $\overrightarrow{BD}$ is the only angle bisector for $\angle ABC$

PROOF: $\overrightarrow{BD}$ bisects $\angle ABC$, so $m\angle ABD = \frac{1}{2}m\angle ABC$. Suppose that $\overrightarrow{BE}$ [as shown in Figure 2.15(b)] is also a bisector of $\angle ABC$ and that $m\angle ABE = \frac{1}{2}m\angle ABC$.

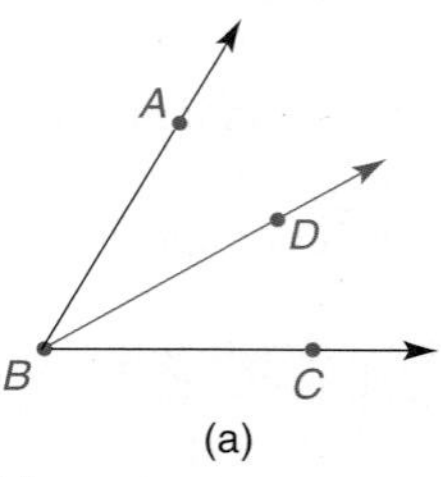

(a)

(b)

Figure 2.15

By the Angle-Addition Postulate, $m\angle ABD = m\angle ABE + m\angle EBD$. By substitution, $\frac{1}{2}m\angle ABC = \frac{1}{2}m\angle ABC + m\angle EBD$; but then $m\angle EBD = 0$ by subtraction. An angle with a measure of 0 contradicts the Protractor Postulate, which states that the measure of an angle is a unique positive number. Therefore, the assumed statement must be false, and it follows that the angle bisector of an angle is unique. ■

Ex. 10

Exercises 2.2

In Exercises 1 to 4, write the converse, the inverse, and the contrapositive of each statement. When possible, classify the statement as true or false.

1. If Juan wins the state lottery, then he will be rich.
2. If $x > 2$, then $x \neq 0$.
3. Two angles are complementary if the sum of their measures is 90°.
4. In a plane, if two lines are not perpendicular to the same line, then these lines are not parallel.

In Exercises 5 to 8, draw a conclusion where possible.

5. 1. If two triangles are congruent, then the triangles are similar.
   2. Triangles ABC and DEF are not congruent.

   C. ∴ ?
6. 1. If two triangles are congruent, then the triangles are similar.
   2. Triangles ABC and DEF are not similar.

   C. ∴ ?
7. 1. If $x > 3$, then $x = 5$.
   2. $x > 3$

   C. ∴ ?
8. 1. If $x > 3$, then $x = 5$.
   2. $x \neq 5$

   C. ∴ ?
9. Which of the following statements would you prove by the indirect method?
   a) In triangle ABC, if $m\angle A > m\angle B$, then $AC \neq BC$.
   b) If alternate exterior $\angle 1 \not\cong$ alternate exterior $\angle 8$, then ℓ is not parallel to m.
   c) If $(x + 2)\cdot(x - 3) = 0$, then $x = -2$ or $x = 3$.
   d) If two sides of a triangle are congruent, then the two angles opposite these sides are also congruent.
   e) The perpendicular bisector of a line segment is unique.
10. For each statement in Exercise 9 that can be proved by the indirect method, give the first statement in each proof.

For Exercises 11 to 14, the given statement is true. Write an equivalent (but more compact) statement that must be true.

11. If $\angle A$ and $\angle B$ are not congruent, then $\angle A$ and $\angle B$ are not vertical angles.

12. If lines ℓ and m are not perpendicular, then the angles formed by ℓ and m are not right angles.

13. If all sides of a triangle are not congruent, then the triangle is not an equilateral triangle.

14. If no two sides of a quadrilateral (figure with four sides) are parallel, then the quadrilateral is not a trapezoid.

In Exercises 15 and 16, state a conclusion for the argument. Statements 1 and 2 are true.

15. 1. If the areas of two triangles are not equal, then the two triangles are not congruent.
2. Triangle ABC is congruent to triangle DEF.

C. $\therefore$?

16. 1. If two triangles do not have the same shape, then the triangles are not similar.
2. Triangle RST is similar to triangle XYZ.

C. $\therefore$?

17. A periscope uses an indirect method of observation. This instrument allows one to see what would otherwise be obstructed. Mirrors are located (see $\overline{AB}$ and $\overline{CD}$ in the drawing) so that an image is reflected twice. How are $\overline{AB}$ and $\overline{CD}$ related to each other?

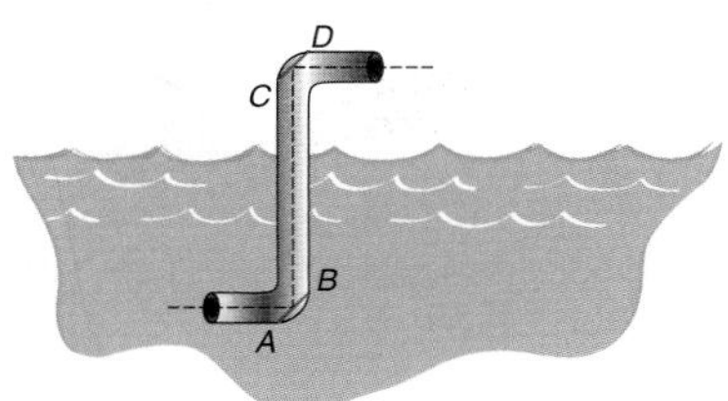

18. Some stores use an indirect method of observation. The purpose may be for safety (to avoid collisions) or to foil the attempts of would-be shoplifters. In this situation, a mirror (see $\overline{EF}$ in the drawing) is placed at the intersection of two aisles as shown. An observer at point P can then see any movement along the indicated aisle. In the sketch, what is the measure of $\angle GEF$?

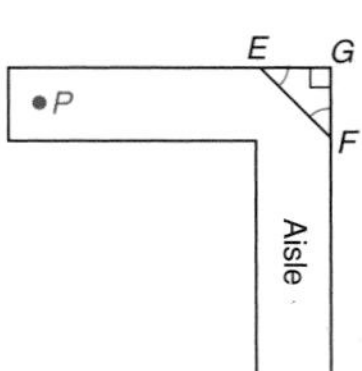

In Exercises 19 to 30, give the indirect proof for each problem or statement.

19. *Given:* $\angle 1 \not\cong \angle 5$
Prove: $r \nparallel s$

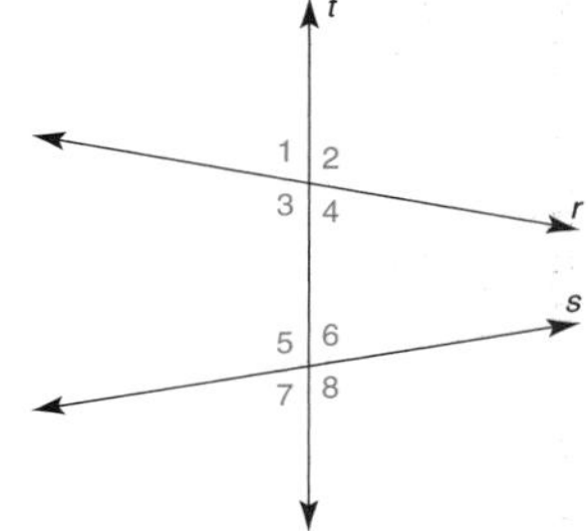

20. *Given:* $\angle ABD \not\cong \angle DBC$
Prove: $\overrightarrow{BD}$ does not bisect $\angle ABC$

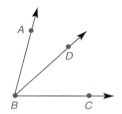

21. *Given:* $m\angle 3 > m\angle 4$
Prove: $\overrightarrow{FH}$ is not $\perp$ to $\overleftrightarrow{EG}$

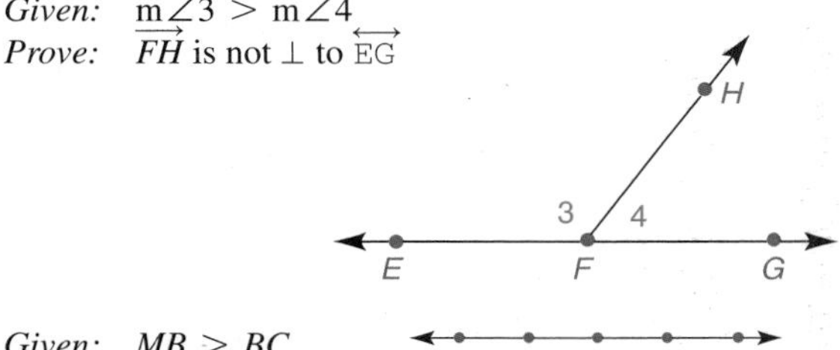

22. *Given:* $MB > BC$
$AM = CD$
Prove: B is not the midpoint of $\overline{AD}$

23. If two angles are not congruent, then these angles are not vertical angles.

24. If $x^2 \neq 25$, then $x \neq 5$.

25. If alternate interior angles are not congruent when two lines are cut by a transversal, then the lines are not parallel.

26. If a and b are positive numbers, then $\sqrt{a^2 + b^2} \neq a + b$.

27. The midpoint of a line segment is unique.

28. There is exactly one line perpendicular to a given line at a point on the line.

***29.** In a plane, if two lines are parallel to a third line, then the two lines are parallel to each other.

***30.** In a plane, if two lines are intersected by a transversal so that the corresponding angles are congruent, then the lines are parallel.

2.3 Proving Lines Parallel

KEY CONCEPTS Proving Lines Parallel

Here is a quick review of the relevant postulate and theorems from Section 2.1. Each has the hypothesis "If two parallel lines are cut by a transversal."

POSTULATE 11

If two parallel lines are cut by a transversal, then the corresponding angles are congruent.

THEOREM 2.1.2

If two parallel lines are cut by a transversal, then the alternate interior angles are congruent.

THEOREM 2.1.3

If two parallel lines are cut by a transversal, then the alternate exterior angles are congruent.

THEOREM 2.1.4

If two parallel lines are cut by a transversal, then the interior angles on the same side of the transversal are supplementary.

THEOREM 2.1.5

If two parallel lines are cut by a transversal, then the exterior angles on the same side of the transversal are supplementary.

Suppose that we wish to prove that two lines are parallel rather than to establish an angle relationship (as the previous statements do). Such a theorem would take the form "If . . . , then these lines are parallel." At present, the only method we have of proving lines parallel is based on the definition of parallel lines. Establishing the conditions of the definition (that coplanar lines do *not* intersect) is virtually impossible! Thus, we begin to develop methods for proving that lines in a plane are parallel by proving Theorem 2.3.1 by the indirect method. Counterparts of Theorems 2.1.2–2.1.5, namely, Theorems 2.3.2–2.3.5, are proved directly but depend on Theorem 2.3.1. Except for Theorem 2.3.6, the theorems of this section require coplanar lines.

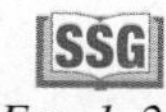

Exs. 1, 2

THEOREM 2.3.1

If two lines are cut by a transversal so that the corresponding angles are congruent, then these lines are parallel.

GIVEN: ℓ and m cut by transversal t

$\angle 1 \cong \angle 2$ (See Figure 2.16)

PROVE: $\ell \parallel m$

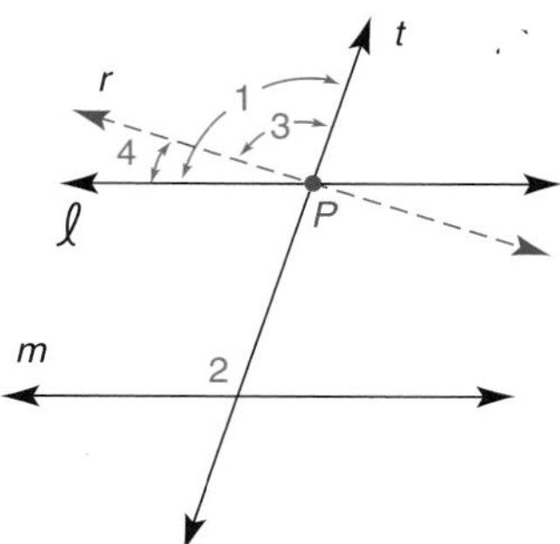

Figure 2.16

PROOF: Suppose that $\ell \nparallel m$. Then a line r can be drawn through point P that is parallel to m; this follows from the Parallel Postulate. If $r \parallel m$, then $\angle 3 \cong \angle 2$ because these angles correspond. But $\angle 1 \cong \angle 2$ by hypothesis. Now $\angle 3 \cong \angle 1$ by the Transitive Property of Congruence; therefore, $m\angle 3 = m\angle 1$. But $m\angle 3 + m\angle 4 = m\angle 1$. (See Figure 2.16.) Substitution of $m\angle 1$ for $m\angle 3$ leads to $m\angle 1 + m\angle 4 = m\angle 1$; and by subtraction, $m\angle 4 = 0$. This contradicts the Protractor Postulate, which states that the measure of any angle must be a positive number. Then r and ℓ must coincide, and it follows that $\ell \parallel m$. ■

Once proved, Theorem 2.3.1 opens the doors to a host of other methods for proving that lines are parallel. Each claim in Theorems 2.3.2–2.3.5 is the converse of its counterpart in Section 2.1.

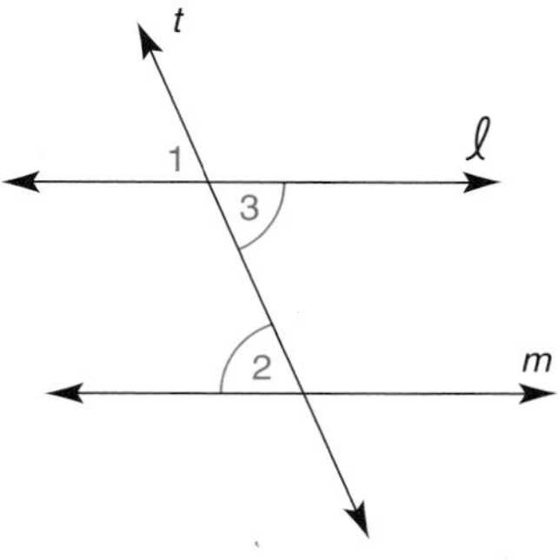

Figure 2.17

THEOREM 2.3.2

If two lines are cut by a transversal so that the alternate interior angles are congruent, then these lines are parallel.

GIVEN: Lines ℓ and m and transversal t
$\angle 2 \cong \angle 3$ (See Figure 2.17)

PROVE: $\ell \parallel m$

PLAN FOR THE PROOF: Show that $\angle 1 \cong \angle 2$ (corresponding angles). Then apply Theorem 2.3.1, in which $\cong$ corresponding $\angle$s imply parallel lines.

PROOF

Statements	Reasons
1. ℓ and m; trans. t; $\angle 2 \cong \angle 3$	1. Given
2. $\angle 1 \cong \angle 3$	2. If two lines intersect, vertical $\angle$s are $\cong$
3. $\angle 1 \cong \angle 2$	3. Transitive Property of Congruence
4. $\ell \parallel m$	4. If two lines are cut by a transversal so that corr. $\angle$s are $\cong$, then these lines are parallel

Discover

When a staircase is designed, "stringers" are cut for each side of the stairs as shown. How are angles 1 and 3 related? How are angles 1 and 2 related?

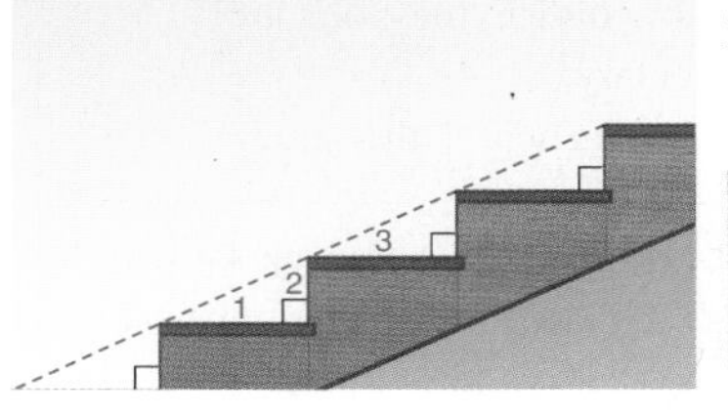

ANSWERS
Congruent, Complementary

The following theorem is proved in a manner much like the proof of Theorem 2.3.2. The proof is left as an exercise.

THEOREM 2.3.3

If two lines are cut by a transversal so that the alternate exterior angles are congruent, then these lines are parallel.

In a more involved drawing, it may be difficult to decide which lines are parallel because of congruent angles. Consider Figure 2.18 on page 88. Suppose that $\angle 1 \cong \angle 3$. Which lines must be parallel? The resulting confusion (it appears that a may be parallel to b and c may be parallel to d) can be overcome by asking, "Which lines help form $\angle 1$ and $\angle 3$?" In this case, $\angle 1$ and $\angle 3$ are formed by lines a and b with c as the transversal. Thus, $a \parallel b$.

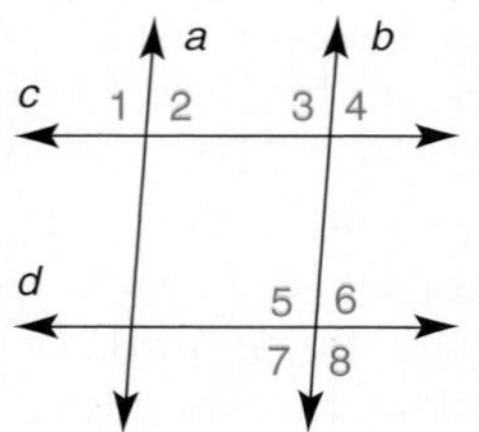

Figure 2.18

EXAMPLE 1

In Figure 2.18, which lines must be parallel if $\angle 3 \cong \angle 8$?

Solution $\angle 3$ and $\angle 8$ are the alternate exterior angles formed when lines c and d are cut by transversal b. Thus, $c \parallel d$. ■

EXAMPLE 2

In Figure 2.18, $m\angle 3 = 94°$. Find $m\angle 5$ such that $c \parallel d$.

Solution With b as a transversal for lines c and d, $\angle 3$ and $\angle 5$ are corresponding angles. Then c would be parallel to d if $\angle 3$ and $\angle 5$ were congruent. Thus, $m\angle 5 = 94°$. ■

Theorems 2.3.4 and 2.3.5 enable us to prove that lines are parallel when certain pairs of angles are supplementary.

THEOREM 2.3.4

If two lines are cut by a transversal so that the interior angles on the same side of the transversal are supplementary, then these lines are parallel.

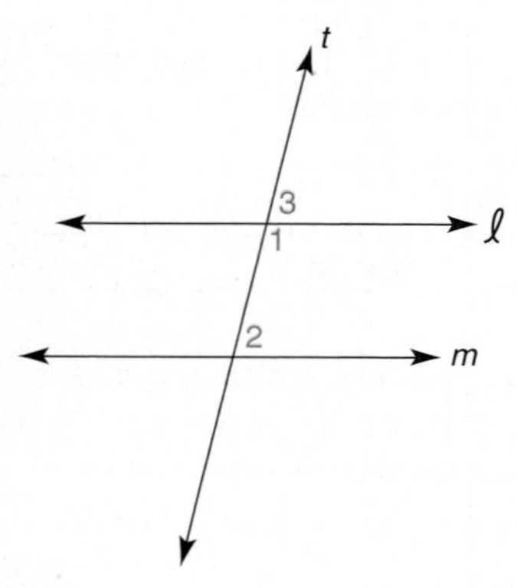

Figure 2.19

EXAMPLE 3

Prove Theorem 2.3.4. (See Figure 2.19.)

GIVEN: Lines ℓ and m; transversal t
$\angle 1$ is supplementary to $\angle 2$

PROVE: $\ell \parallel m$

PROOF

Statements	Reasons
1. ℓ and m; trans. t; $\angle 1$ is supp. to $\angle 2$	1. Given
2. $\angle 1$ is supp. to $\angle 3$	2. If the exterior sides of two adjacent $\angle$s form a straight line, these $\angle$s are supplementary
3. $\angle 2 \cong \angle 3$	3. If two $\angle$s are supp. to the same $\angle$, they are $\cong$
4. $\ell \parallel m$	4. If two lines are cut by a transversal so that corr. $\angle$s are $\cong$, then these lines are parallel

■

The proof of Theorem 2.3.5 is similar to that of Theorem 2.3.4. The proof is left as an exercise.

THEOREM 2.3.5

If two lines are cut by a transversal so that the exterior angles on the same side of the transversal are supplementary, then these lines are parallel.

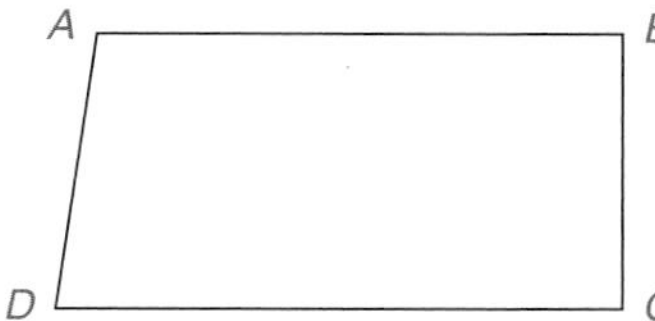

Figure 2.20

EXAMPLE 4

In Figure 2.20, which line segments must be parallel if $\angle B$ and $\angle C$ are supplementary?

Solution Again, the solution lies in the question "Which line segments form $\angle B$ and $\angle C$?" With $\overline{BC}$ as a transversal, $\angle B$ and $\angle C$ are formed by $\overline{AB}$ and $\overline{DC}$. Because $\angle$s B and C are supplementary, it follows that $\overline{AB} \parallel \overline{DC}$. ■

We include two final theorems that provide additional means of proving that lines are parallel. The proof of Theorem 2.3.6 (see Exercise 33) requires an auxiliary line (a transversal). Proof of Theorem 2.3.7 is found in Example 5.

THEOREM 2.3.6

If two lines are each parallel to a third line, then these lines are parallel to each other.

Theorem 2.3.6 is true even if the three lines described are not coplanar. In Theorem 2.3.7, the lines must be coplanar.

THEOREM 2.3.7

If two coplanar lines are each perpendicular to a third line, then these lines are parallel to each other.

STRATEGY FOR PROOF ▶ Proving That Lines are Parallel

General Rule: The proof of Theorem 2.3.7 depends upon establishing the condition found in one of the Theorems 2.3.1–2.3.6.

Illustration: In Example 5, we establish congruent corresponding angles in statement 3 so that lines are parallel by Theorem 2.3.1.

Exs. 3–8

EXAMPLE 5

GIVEN: $\overleftrightarrow{AC} \perp \overleftrightarrow{BE}$ and $\overleftrightarrow{DF} \perp \overleftrightarrow{BE}$ (See Figure 2.21)

PROVE: $\overleftrightarrow{AC} \perp \overleftrightarrow{DF}$

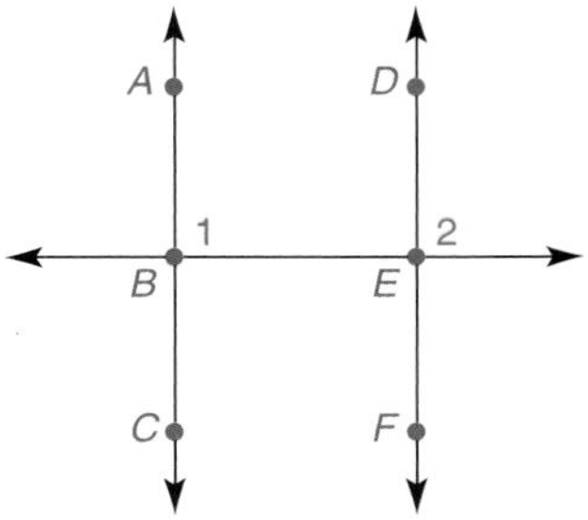

Figure 2.21

PROOF

Statements	Reasons
1. $\overleftrightarrow{AC} \perp \overleftrightarrow{BE}$ and $\overleftrightarrow{DF} \perp \overleftrightarrow{BE}$	1. Given
2. $\angle$s 1 and 2 are rt. $\angle$s	2. If two lines are perpendicular, they meet to form right $\angle$s
3. $\angle 1 \cong \angle 2$	3. All right angles are $\cong$
4. $\overleftrightarrow{AC} \parallel \overleftrightarrow{DF}$	4. If two lines are cut by a transversal so that corr. $\angle$s are $\cong$, then these lines are parallel

■

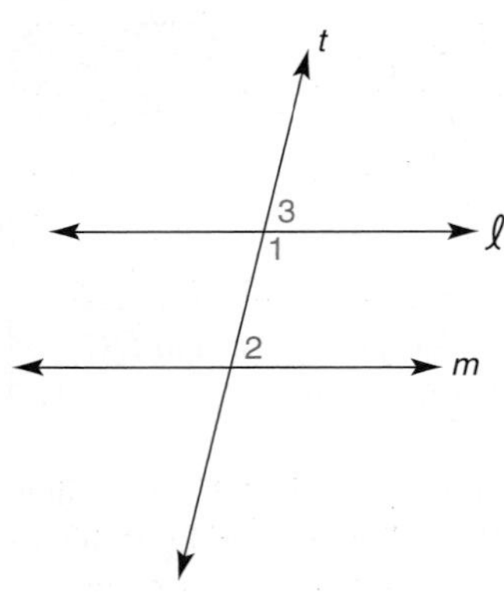

Figure 2.22

EXAMPLE 6

GIVEN: $m\angle 1 = 7x$ and $m\angle 2 = 5x$ (See Figure 2.22.)

FIND: x, so that ℓ will be parallel to m

Solution For ℓ to be parallel to m, $\angle$s 1 and 2 would have to be supplementary. This follows from Theorem 2.3.4 because $\angle$s 1 and 2 are interior angles on the same side of transversal t. Then

$$7x + 5x = 180$$
$$12x = 180$$
$$x = 15$$

NOTE: With $m\angle 1 = 105°$ and $m\angle 2 = 75°$, we see that $\angle 1$ and $\angle 2$ are supplementary. Then $\ell \parallel m$.

Construction 7 depends on Theorem 2.3.1, which is restated below.

THEOREM 2.3.1

If two lines are cut by a transversal so that corresponding angles are congruent, then these lines are parallel.

SSG *Exs. 9–16*

Construction 7 *To construct the line parallel to a given line from a point not on that line.*

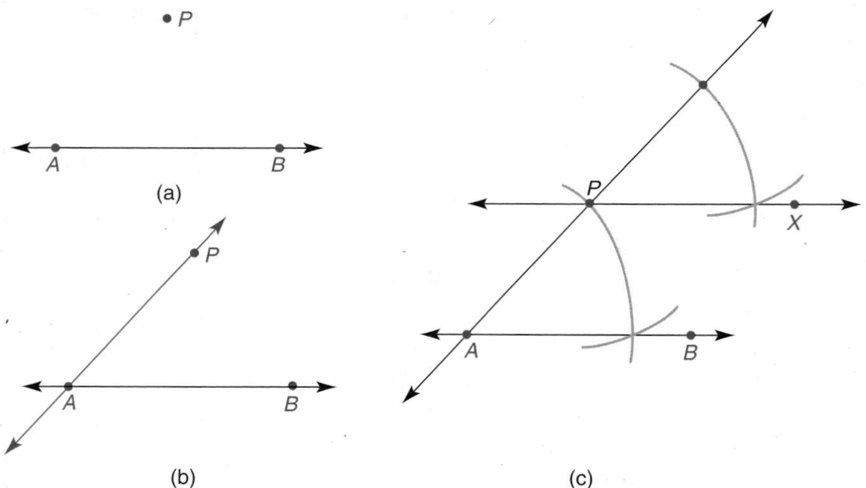

Figure 2.23

GIVEN: $\overleftrightarrow{AB}$ and point P not on $\overleftrightarrow{AB}$, as in Figure 2.23(a)

CONSTRUCT: The line through point P parallel to $\overleftrightarrow{AB}$

CONSTRUCTION: Figure 2.23(b): Draw a line (to become a transversal) through point P and some point on $\overleftrightarrow{AB}$. For convenience, we choose point A and draw $\overleftrightarrow{AP}$ as in Figure 2.23(c). Using P as the vertex, construct the angle that corresponds to $\angle PAB$ so that this angle is congruent to $\angle PAB$. It may be necessary to extend $\overleftrightarrow{AP}$ upward to accomplish this. $\overleftrightarrow{PX}$ is the desired line parallel to $\overleftrightarrow{AB}$.

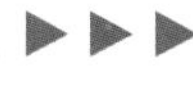

Exercises 2.3

In Exercises 1 to 6, ℓ and m are cut by transversal v. On the basis of the information given, determine whether ℓ must be parallel to m.

1. $m\angle 1 = 107°$ and $m\angle 5 = 107°$

2. $m\angle 2 = 65°$ and $m\angle 7 = 65°$

3. $m\angle 1 = 106°$ and $m\angle 7 = 76°$

4. $m\angle 1 = 106°$ and $m\angle 4 = 106°$

5. $m\angle 3 = 113.5°$ and $m\angle 5 = 67.5°$

6. $m\angle 6 = 71.4°$ and $m\angle 7 = 71.4°$

In Exercises 7 to 16, name the lines (if any) that must be parallel under the given conditions.

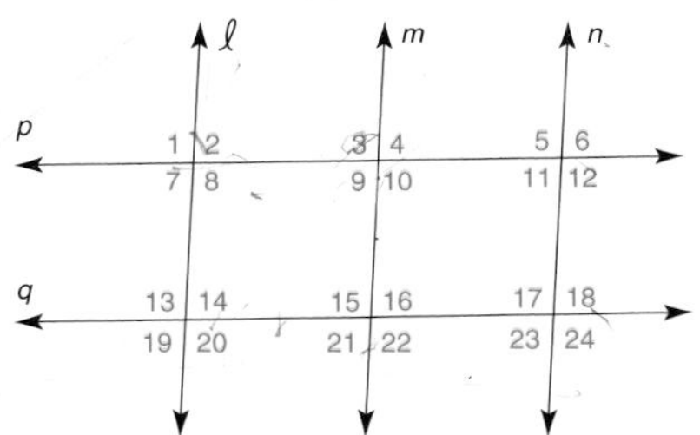

Exercises 7–16

7. $\angle 1 \cong \angle 20$

8. $\angle 3 \cong \angle 10$

9. $\angle 9 \cong \angle 14$

10. $\angle 7 \cong \angle 11$

11. $\ell \perp p$ and $n \perp p$

12. $\ell \parallel m$ and $m \parallel n$

13. $\ell \perp p$ and $m \perp q$

14. $\angle 8$ and $\angle 9$ are supplementary.

15. $m\angle 8 = 110°$, $p \parallel q$, and $m\angle 18 = 70°$

16. The bisectors of $\angle 9$ and $\angle 21$ are parallel.

In Exercises 17 and 18, complete each proof by filling in the missing statements and reasons.

17. *Given:* $\angle 1$ and $\angle 2$ are complementary
$\angle 3$ and $\angle 1$ are complementary
Prove: $\overline{BC} \parallel \overline{DE}$

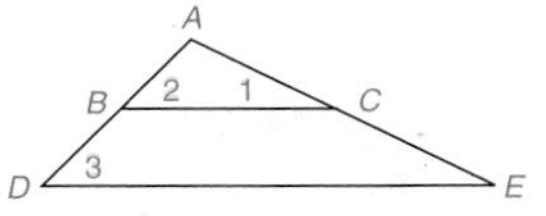

PROOF

Statements	Reasons
1. $\angle$s 1 and 2 are comp.; $\angle$s 3 and 1 are comp.	1. ?
2. $\angle 2 \cong \angle 3$	2. ?
3. ?	3. If two lines are cut by a transversal so that corr. $\angle$s are $\cong$, the lines are $\parallel$

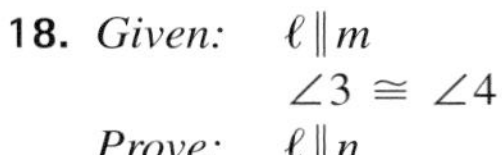

18. *Given:* $\ell \parallel m$
$\angle 3 \cong \angle 4$
Prove: $\ell \parallel n$

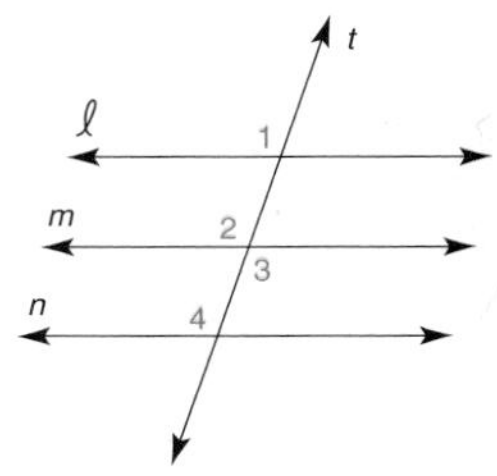

PROOF

Statements	Reasons
1. $\ell \parallel m$	1. ?
2. $\angle 1 \cong \angle 2$	2. ?
3. $\angle 2 \cong \angle 3$	3. If two lines intersect, the vertical $\angle$s formed are $\cong$
4. ?	4. Given
5. $\angle 1 \cong \angle 4$	5. Transitive Prop. of $\cong$
6. ?	6. ?

In Exercises 19 to 22, complete the proof.

19. *Given:* $\overline{AD} \perp \overline{DC}$
$\overline{BC} \perp \overline{DC}$
Prove: $\overline{AD} \parallel \overline{BC}$

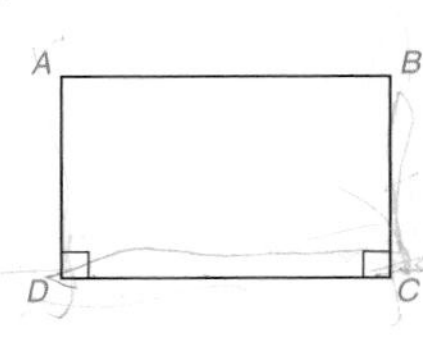

20. *Given:* $m\angle 2 + m\angle 3 = 90°$
$\overrightarrow{BE}$ bisects $\angle ABC$
$\overrightarrow{CE}$ bisects $\angle BCD$
Prove: $\ell \parallel n$

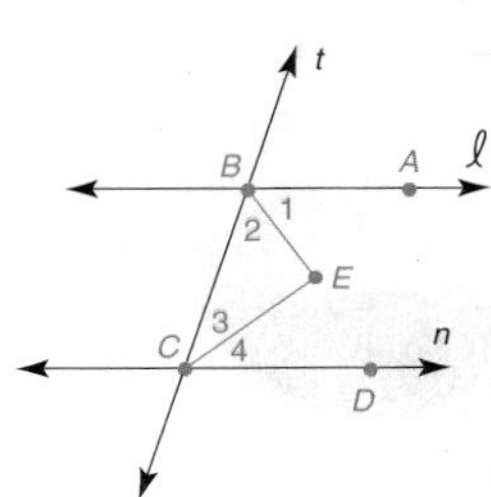

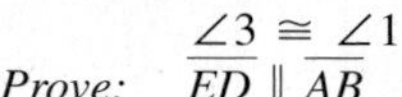

21. *Given:* $\overrightarrow{DE}$ bisects $\angle CDA$
$\angle 3 \cong \angle 1$
Prove: $\overline{ED} \parallel \overline{AB}$

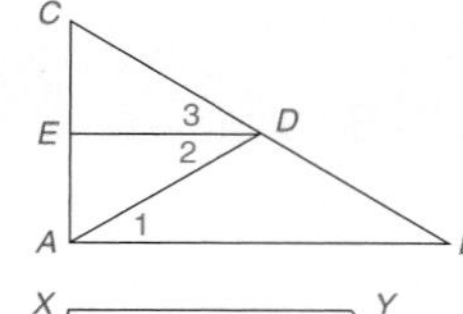

22. *Given:* $\overline{XY} \parallel \overline{WZ}$
$\angle 1 \cong \angle 2$
Prove: $\overline{MN} \parallel \overline{XY}$

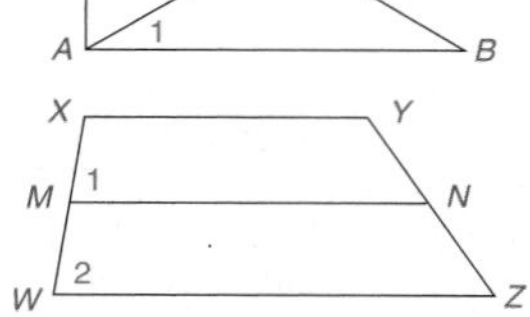

In Exercises 23 to 30, determine the value of x so that line ℓ will be parallel to line m.

23. $m\angle 4 = 5x$
$m\angle 5 = 4(x + 5)$
24. $m\angle 2 = 4x + 3$
$m\angle 7 = 5(x - 3)$
25. $m\angle 3 = \frac{x}{2}$
$m\angle 5 = x$
26. $m\angle 1 = \frac{x}{2} + 35$
$m\angle 5 = \frac{3x}{4}$

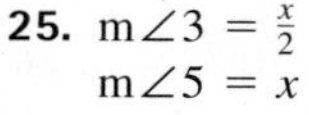

27. $m\angle 6 = x^2 - 9$
$m\angle 2 = x(x - 1)$
28. $m\angle 4 = 2x^2 - 3x + 6$
$m\angle 5 = 2x(x - 1) - 2$
29. $m\angle 3 = (x + 1)(x + 4)$
$m\angle 5 = 16(x + 3) - (x^2 - 2)$
30. $m\angle 2 = (x^2 - 1)(x + 1)$
$m\angle 8 = 185 - x^2(x + 1)$

Exercises 28–30

In Exercises 31 to 33, give a formal proof for each theorem.

31. If two lines are cut by a transversal so that the alternate exterior angles are congruent, then these lines are parallel.
32. If two lines are cut by a transversal so that the exterior angles on the same side of the transversal are supplementary, then these lines are parallel.
33. If two lines are parallel to the same line, then these lines are parallel to each other. (Assume three coplanar lines.)
34. Explain why the statement in Exercise 33 remains true even if the three lines are not coplanar.
35. Given that point P does *not* lie on line ℓ, construct the line through point P that is parallel to line ℓ.

36. Given that point Q does *not* lie on $\overline{AB}$, construct the line through point Q that is parallel to $\overline{AB}$.

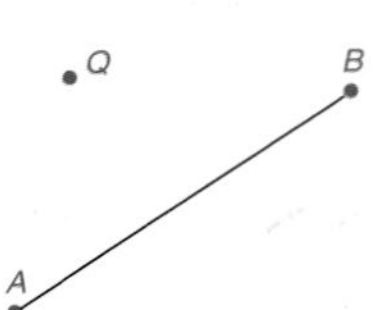

37. A carpenter drops a plumb line from point A to $\overline{BC}$. Assuming that $\overline{BC}$ is horizontal, the point D at which the plumb line intersects $\overline{BC}$ will determine the vertical line segment $\overline{AD}$. Use a construction to locate point D.

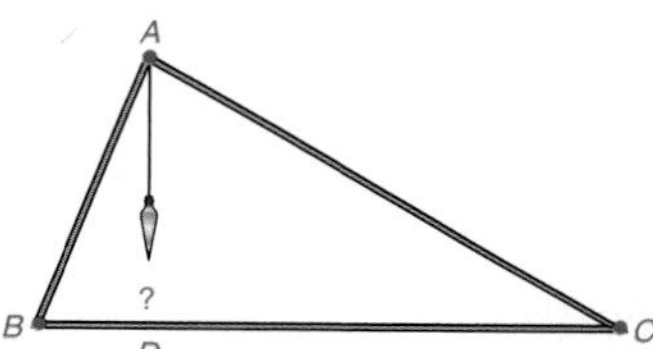

2.4 The Angles of a Triangle

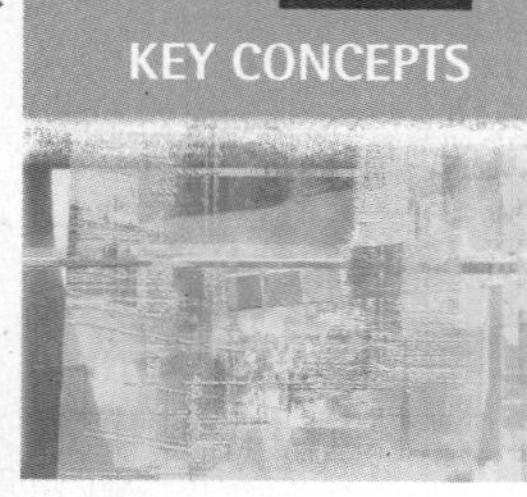

KEY CONCEPTS

- Triangles
- Vertices
- Sides of a Triangle
- Interior and Exterior of a Triangle
- Scalene Triangle
- Isosceles Triangle
- Equilateral Triangle
- Acute Triangle
- Obtuse Triangle
- Right Triangle
- Equiangular Triangle
- Auxiliary Line
- Determined
- Underdetermined
- Overdetermined
- Corollary
- Exterior Angle of a Triangle

In geometry, the word *union* means that figures are joined or combined.

DEFINITION

A **triangle** (symbol $\triangle$) is the union of three line segments that are determined by three noncollinear points.

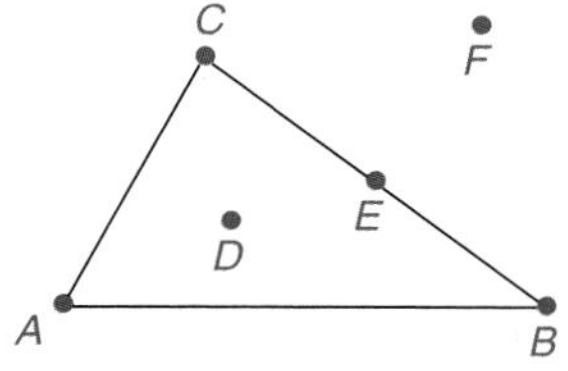

Figure 2.24

The triangle in Figure 2.24 is known as $\triangle ABC$, or $\triangle BCA$, etc. (order of letters A, B, and C being unimportant). Each point A, B, and C is a **vertex** of the triangle; collectively, these three points are the **vertices** of the triangle. $\overline{AB}$, $\overline{BC}$, and $\overline{AC}$ are the **sides** of the triangle. Point D is in the **interior** of the triangle; point E is on the triangle; and point F is in the **exterior** of the triangle.

Triangles may be categorized by the lengths of their sides. Table 2.1 presents each type of triangle, the relationship among its sides, and a drawing in which congruent sides are marked.

TABLE 2.1
Triangles Classified by Congruent Sides

Type		Number of Congruent Sides
Scalene		None
Isosceles		Two
Equilateral		Three

Triangles may also be classified according to their angles (See Table 2.2).

TABLE 2.2
Triangles Classified by Angles

Type		Angle(s)	Type		Angle(s)
Acute		All angles acute	Right		One right angle
Obtuse		One obtuse angle	Equiangular		All angles congruent

EXAMPLE 1

Exs. 1–7

In $\triangle HJK$ (not shown), $HJ = 4$, $JK = 4$, and $m\angle J = 90°$. Describe completely the type of triangle represented.

Solution $\triangle HJK$ is a right isosceles triangle, or $\triangle HJK$ is an isosceles right triangle. ■

Discover

From a paper triangle, cut the angles from the "corners." Now place the angles together at the same vertex as shown. What is the sum of the measures of the three angles?

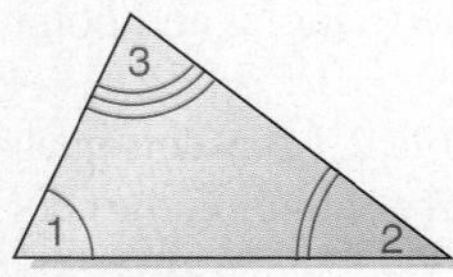

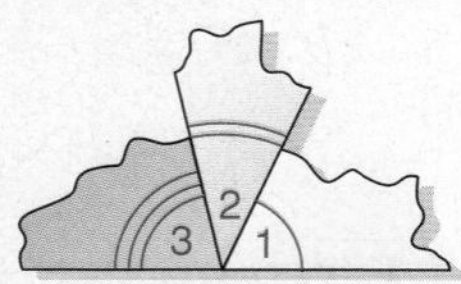

ANSWER
180°

In an earlier exercise, it was suggested that the sum of the measures of the three interior angles of a triangle is 180°. This is now stated as a theorem and proved through the use of an **auxiliary** (or helping) **line.** When an auxiliary line is added to the drawing for a proof, a justification must be given for the existence of that line. Justifications include statements such as

There is exactly one line through two distinct points.
An angle has exactly one bisector.
There is only one line perpendicular to another line at a point on that line.

When an auxiliary line is introduced into a proof, the original drawing is sometimes redrawn for the sake of clarity. Each auxiliary figure must be **determined,** but it must not be **underdetermined** or **overdetermined.** A figure is underdetermined when more than one possible figure is described. On the other extreme, a figure is overdetermined when it is impossible for *all* conditions described to be satisfied.

THEOREM 2.4.1

In a triangle, the sum of the measures of the interior angles is 180°.

The first statement in the following "picture proof" establishes the auxiliary line that is used. The auxiliary line is justified by the Parallel Postulate.

(a)

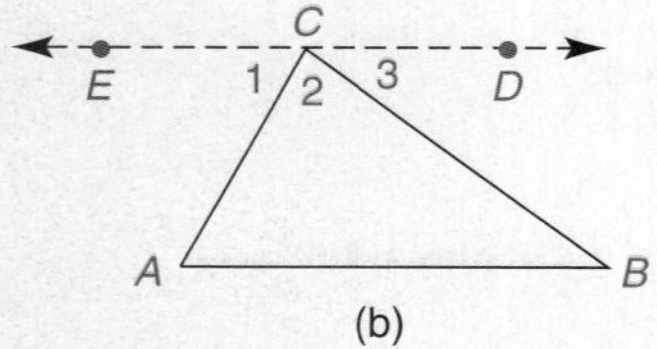

(b)

Figure 2.25

PICTURE PROOF OF THEOREM 2.4.1

GIVEN: $\triangle ABC$ in Figure 2.25(a)
PROVE: $m\angle A + m\angle B + m\angle C = 180°$
PROOF: Through C, draw $\overleftrightarrow{ED} \parallel \overline{AB}$.
We see that $m\angle 1 + m\angle 2 + m\angle 3 = 180°$. (See Figure 2.25(b)).
But $m\angle 1 = m\angle A$ and $m\angle 3 = m\angle B$ (alternate interior angles are congruent).
Then $m\angle A + m\angle B + m\angle C = 180°$ in Figure 2.25(a). ■

At times, we use the notions of the equality and congruence of angles interchangeably within a proof. See the preceding "picture proof."

EXAMPLE 2

In $\triangle RST$ (not shown), $m\angle R = 45°$ and $m\angle S = 64°$. Find $m\angle T$.

Solution In $\triangle RST$, $m\angle R + m\angle S + m\angle T = 180°$, so $45° + 64° + m\angle T = 180°$. Thus, $109° + m\angle T = 180°$ and $m\angle T = 71°$. ■

Technology Exploration

Use computer software, if available.

1. Draw $\triangle ABC$.
2. Measure $\angle A$, $\angle B$, and $\angle C$.
3. Show that $m\angle A + m\angle B + m\angle C = 180°$

(Answer may not be "perfect.")

A theorem that follows directly from a previous theorem is known as a **corollary** of that theorem. Corollaries, like theorems, must be proved before they can be used. These proofs are often brief, but they depend on the related theorem. Some corollaries of Theorem 2.4.1 are shown on page 95. We suggest that the student make a drawing to illustrate each corollary.

COROLLARY 2.4.2

Each angle of an equiangular triangle measures 60°.

Exs. 8–12

COROLLARY 2.4.3

The acute angles of a right triangle are complementary.

STRATEGY FOR PROOF ▶ Proving a Corollary

General Rule: The proof of a corollary is completed by using the theorem upon which the corollary depends.

Illustration: Using $\triangle NMQ$ of Example 3, the proof of Corollary 2.4.3 depends on the fact that $m\angle M + m\angle N + m\angle Q = 180°$. With $m\angle M = 90°$, it follows that $m\angle N + m\angle Q = 90°$.

EXAMPLE 3

GIVEN: $\angle M$ is a right angle in $\triangle NMQ$ (not shown); $m\angle N = 57°$

FIND: $m\angle Q$

Solution

Because the acute $\angle$s of a right triangle are complementary,

$$\begin{aligned} m\angle N + m\angle Q &= 90° \\ \therefore 57° + m\angle Q &= 90° \\ m\angle Q &= 33° \end{aligned}$$

■

COROLLARY 2.4.4

If two angles of one triangle are congruent to two angles of another triangle, then the third angles are also congruent.

The following example illustrates Corollary 2.4.4.

EXAMPLE 4

In $\triangle RST$ and $\triangle XYZ$ (triangles not shown), $m\angle R = m\angle X = 52°$. Also, $m\angle S = m\angle Y = 59°$.

a) Find $m\angle T$. b) Find $m\angle Z$. c) Is $\angle T \cong \angle Z$?

Solution

a)
$$\begin{aligned} m\angle R + m\angle S + m\angle T &= 180° \\ 52° + 59° + m\angle T &= 180° \\ 111° + m\angle T &= 180° \\ m\angle T &= 69° \end{aligned}$$

b) Using $m\angle X + m\angle Y + m\angle Z = 180°$, we repeat part (a) to find $m\angle Z = 69°$.

c) Yes, $\angle T \cong \angle Z$ (both measure 69°). ■

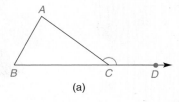

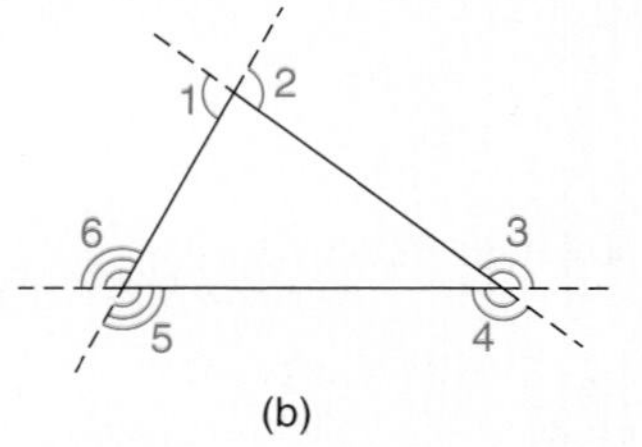

Figure 2.26

When the sides of a triangle are extended, each angle that is formed by a side and an extension of the adjacent side is an **exterior angle** of the triangle. With *B-C-D* in Figure 2.26(a), $\angle ACD$ is an exterior angle of $\triangle ABC$; for a triangle, there are a total of six exterior angles—two at each vertex. [See Figure 2.26(b).]

In Figure 2.26(a), $\angle A$ and $\angle B$ are the two *nonadjacent* interior angles for exterior $\angle ACD$. These angles (A and B) are sometimes called *remote* interior angles for exterior $\angle ACD$.

COROLLARY 2.4.5

The measure of an exterior angle of a triangle equals the sum of the measures of the two nonadjacent interior angles.

EXAMPLE 5

GIVEN: In Figure 2.27,

$$m\angle 1 = x^2 + 2x$$
$$m\angle S = x^2 - 2x$$
$$m\angle T = 3x + 10$$

FIND: x

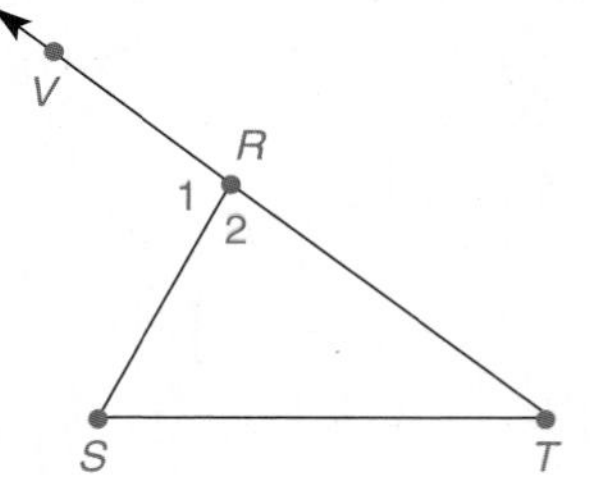

Figure 2.27

Solution By Corollary 2.4.5,

$$\begin{aligned} m\angle 1 &= m\angle S + m\angle T \\ x^2 + 2x &= (x^2 - 2x) + (3x + 10) \\ 2x &= x + 10 \\ x &= 10 \end{aligned}$$

SSG *Exs. 13–19*

Check: $m\angle 1 = 120°$, $m\angle S = 80°$, and $m\angle T = 40°$; so $120 = 80 + 40$, which satisfies the conditions of Corollary 2.4.5. ■

Exercises 2.4

In Exercises 1 to 4, refer to $\triangle ABC$. On the basis of the information given, determine the measure of the remaining angle(s) of the triangle.

1. $m\angle A = 63°$ and $m\angle B = 42°$
2. $m\angle B = 39°$ and $m\angle C = 82°$
3. $m\angle A = m\angle C = 67°$
4. $m\angle B = 42°$ and $m\angle A = m\angle C$
5. Describe the auxiliary line (segment) as determined, overdetermined, or underdetermined.
   a) Draw the line through vertex C of $\triangle ABC$.
   b) Through vertex C, draw the line parallel to $\overline{AB}$.
   c) With M the midpoint of $\overline{AB}$, draw $\overline{CM}$ perpendicular to $\overline{AB}$.

Exercises 1–6

6. Describe the auxiliary line (segment) as determined, overdetermined, or underdetermined.
   a) Through vertex B of $\triangle ABC$, draw $\overleftrightarrow{AB} \perp \overline{AC}$.
   b) Draw the line that contains A, B, and C.
   c) Draw the line that contains M, the midpoint of $\overline{AB}$.

In Exercises 7 and 8, classify the triangle (not shown) by considering the lengths of its sides.

7. a) All sides of $\triangle ABC$ are of the same length.
   b) In $\triangle DEF$, $DE = 6$, $EF = 6$, and $DF = 8$.

8. a) In $\triangle XYZ$, $\overline{XY} \cong \overline{YZ}$.
b) In $\triangle RST$, $RS = 6$, $ST = 7$, and $RT = 8$.

In Exercises 9 and 10, classify the triangle (not shown) by considering the measures of its angles.

9. a) All angles of $\triangle ABC$ measure 60°.
b) In $\triangle DEF$, $m\angle D = 40°$, $m\angle E = 50°$, and $m\angle F = 90°$.

10. a) In $\triangle XYZ$, $m\angle X = 123°$.
b) In $\triangle RST$, $m\angle R = 45°$, $m\angle S = 65°$, and $m\angle T = 70°$.

In Exercises 11 and 12, make drawings as needed.

11. Suppose that for $\triangle ABC$ and $\triangle MNQ$, you know that $\angle A \cong \angle M$ and $\angle B \cong \angle N$. Explain why $\angle C \cong \angle Q$.

12. Suppose that T is a point on side $\overline{PQ}$ of $\triangle PQR$. Also, $\overrightarrow{RT}$ bisects $\angle PRQ$, and $\angle P \cong \angle Q$. If $\angle 1$ and $\angle 2$ are the angles formed when $\overrightarrow{RT}$ intersects $\overline{PQ}$, explain why $\angle 1 \cong \angle 2$.

In Exercises 13 to 15, $j \parallel k$ and $\triangle ABC$.

13. *Given:* $m\angle 3 = 50°$
$m\angle 4 = 72°$
Find: $m\angle 1$, $m\angle 2$, and $m\angle 5$

14. *Given:* $m\angle 3 = 55°$
$m\angle 2 = 74°$
Find: $m\angle 1$, $m\angle 4$, and $m\angle 5$

Exercises 13–15

15. *Given:* $m\angle 1 = 122.3°$, $m\angle 5 = 41.5°$
Find: $m\angle 2$, $m\angle 3$, and $m\angle 4$

16. *Given:* $\overline{MN} \perp \overline{NQ}$ and $\angle$s as shown
Find: x, y, and z

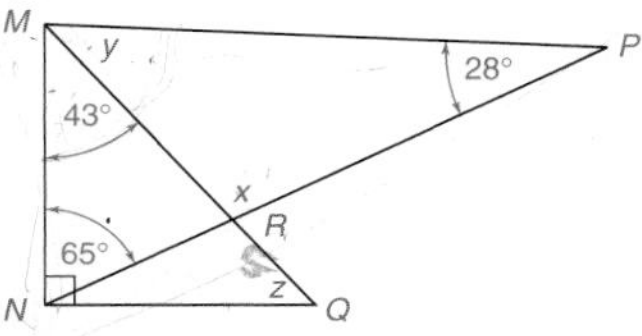

17. *Given:* $\overline{AB} \parallel \overline{DC}$
$\overrightarrow{DB}$ bisects $\angle ADC$
$m\angle A = 110°$
Find: $m\angle 3$

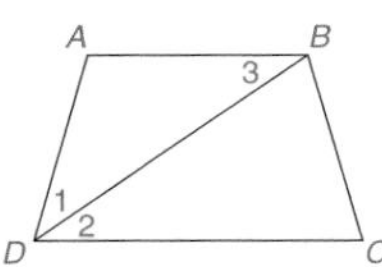

Exercises 17, 18

18. *Given:* $\overline{AB} \parallel \overline{DC}$
$\overrightarrow{DB}$ bisects $\angle ADC$
$m\angle 1 = 36°$
Find: $m\angle A$

19. *Given:* $\triangle ABC$ with B-D-E-C
$m\angle 3 = m\angle 4 = 30°$
$m\angle 1 = m\angle 2 = 70°$
Find: $m\angle B$

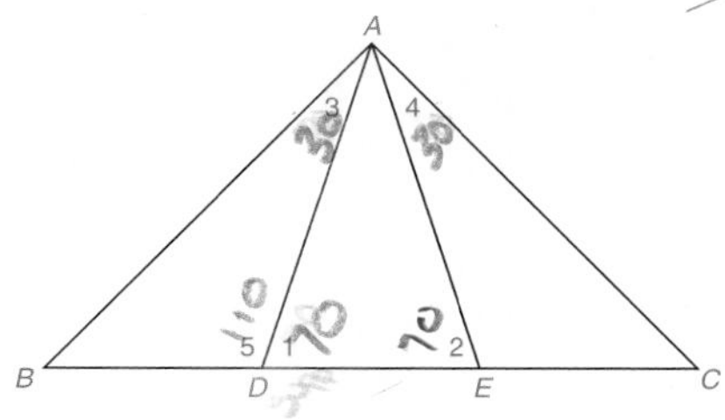

Exercises 19–22

20. *Given:* $\triangle ABC$ with B-D-E-C
$m\angle 1 = 2x$
$m\angle 3 = x$
Find: $m\angle B$ in terms of x

21. *Given:* $\triangle ADE$ with $m\angle 1 = m\angle 2 = x$ and $m\angle DAE = \frac{x}{2}$
Find: x, $m\angle 1$, and $m\angle DAE$

22. *Given:* $\triangle ABC$ with $m\angle B = m\angle C = \frac{x}{2}$ and $m\angle BAC = x$
Find: x, $m\angle BAC$, and $m\angle B$

23. Consider any triangle and one exterior angle at each vertex. What is the sum of the measures of the three exterior angles of the triangle?

24. *Given:* Right $\triangle ABC$ with right $\angle C$
$m\angle 1 = 7x + 4$
$m\angle 2 = 5x + 2$
Find: x

Exercises 24–27

25. *Given:* $m\angle 1 = x$
$m\angle 2 = y$
$m\angle 3 = 3x$
Find: x and y

26. *Given:* $m\angle 1 = x$, $m\angle 2 = \frac{x}{2}$
Find: x

27. *Given:* $m\angle 1 = \frac{x}{2}$ $m\angle 2 = \frac{x}{3}$
Find: x

28. *Given:* $m\angle 1 = 8(x + 2)$
$m\angle 3 = 5x - 3$
$m\angle 5 = 5(x + 1) - 2$
Find: x

29. *Given:* $m\angle 1 = x$
$m\angle 2 = 4y$
$m\angle 3 = 2y$
$m\angle 4 = 2x - y - 40$
Find: x, y, and $m\angle 5$

Exercises 28, 29

30. *Given:* Equiangular $\triangle RST$
$\overrightarrow{RV}$ bisects $\angle SRT$
Prove: $\triangle RVS$ is a right $\triangle$

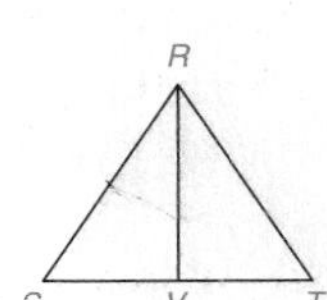

31. *Given:* $\overline{MN}$ and $\overline{PQ}$ intersect at K; $\angle M \cong \angle Q$
Prove: $\angle P \cong \angle N$

32. The sum of the measures of two angles of a triangle equals the measure of the third (largest) angle. What type of triangle is described?

33. Draw, if possible, an
a) isosceles obtuse triangle.
b) equilateral right triangle.

34. Draw, if possible, a
a) right scalene triangle.
b) triangle having both a right angle and an obtuse angle.

35. Along a straight shoreline, two houses are located at points H and M. The houses are 5000 feet apart. A small island lies in view of both houses, with angles as indicated. Find m$\angle I$.

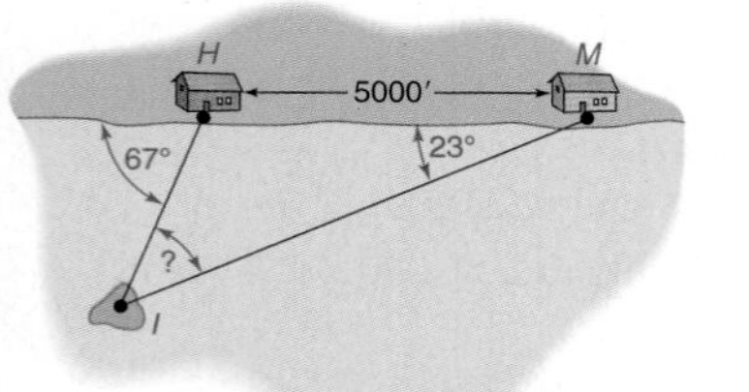

36. An airplane has leveled off (is flying horizontally) at an altitude of 12,000 feet. Its pilot can see each of two small towns at points R and T in front of the plane. With angle measures as indicated, find m$\angle R$.

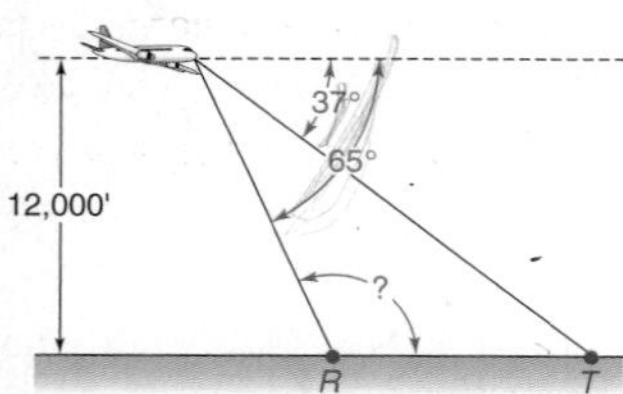

37. On a map, three Los Angeles suburbs are located at points N (Newport Beach), P (Pomona), and B (Burbank). With angle measures as indicated, determine m$\angle N$ and m$\angle P$.

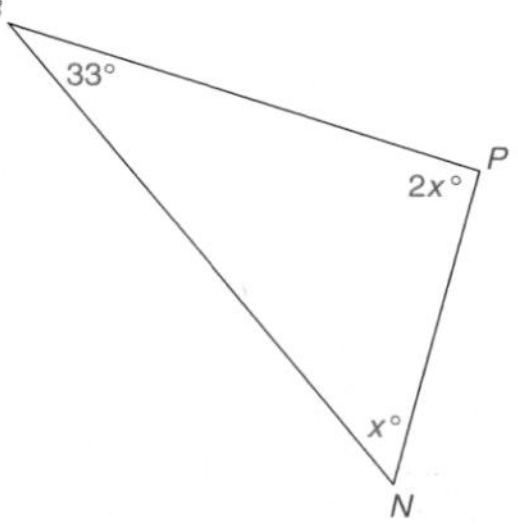

38. The roofline of a house shows the shape of right triangle ABC with m$\angle C = 90°$. If the measure of $\angle CAB$ is 24° larger than the measure of $\angle CBA$, then how large is each angle?

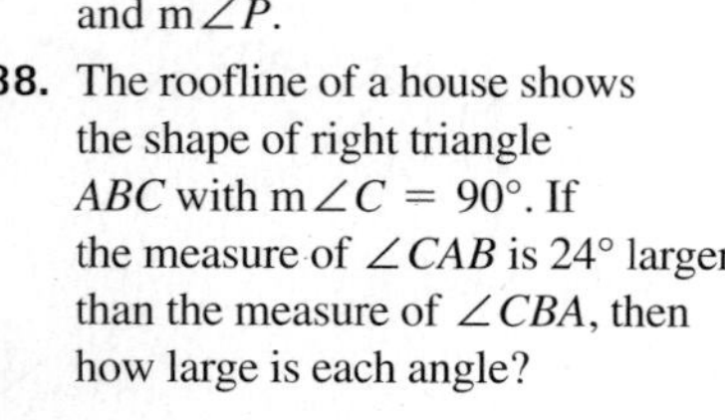

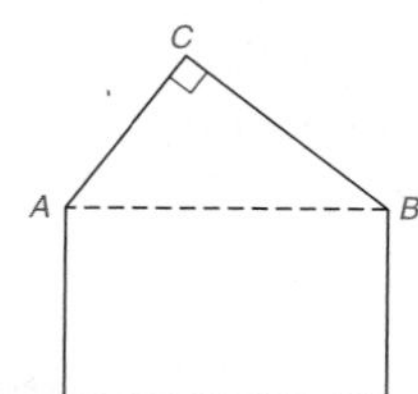

39. A lamppost has a design such that m$\angle C = 110°$ and $\angle A \cong \angle B$. Find m$\angle A$ and m$\angle B$.

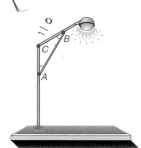

40. For the lamppost of Exercise 39, suppose that m$\angle A$ = m$\angle B$ and that m$\angle C$ = 3 (m$\angle A$). Find m$\angle A$, m$\angle B$, and m$\angle C$.

41. The triangular symbol on the "PLAY" button of a DVD has congruent angles at M and N. If m$\angle P = 30°$, what are the measures of angle M and angle N?

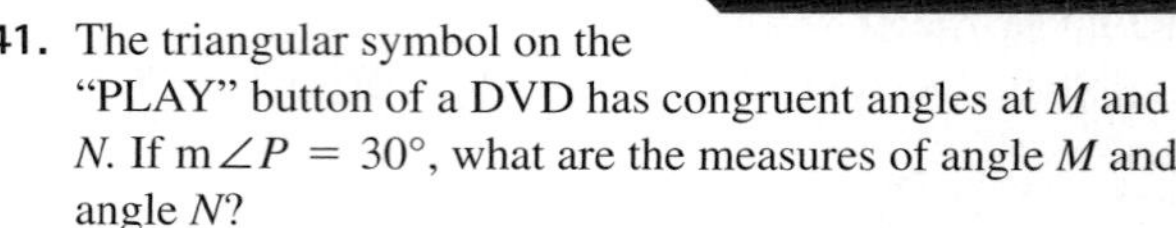

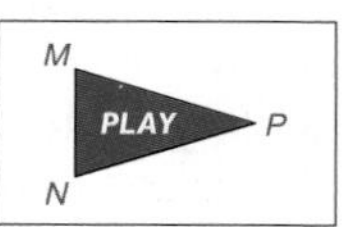

42. A polygon with four sides is called a *quadrilateral.* Consider the figure and the dashed auxiliary line. What is the sum of the measures of the four interior angles of this (or any other) quadrilateral?

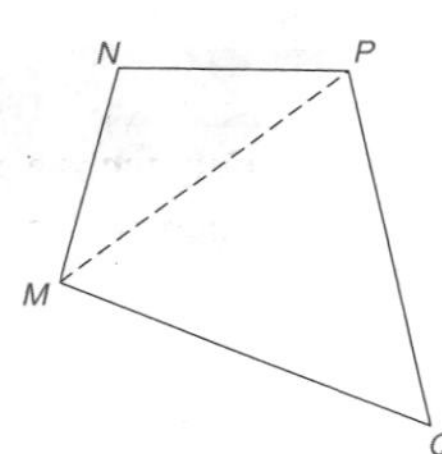

43. Explain why the following statement is true.
Each interior angle of an equiangular triangle measures 60°.

44. Explain why the following statement is true.
The acute angles of a right triangle are complementary.

In Exercises 45 to 47, write a formal proof for each corollary.

45. The measure of an exterior angle of a triangle equals the sum of the measures of the two nonadjacent interior angles.

46. If two angles of one triangle are congruent to two angles of another triangle, then the third angles are also congruent.

47. Use an indirect proof to establish the following theorem: A triangle cannot have more than one right angle.

48. *Given:* $\overleftrightarrow{AB}$, $\overleftrightarrow{DE}$, and $\overleftrightarrow{CF}$
$\overleftrightarrow{AB} \parallel \overleftrightarrow{DE}$
$\overrightarrow{CG}$ bisects $\angle BCF$
$\overrightarrow{FG}$ bisects $\angle CFE$
Prove: $\angle G$ is a right angle

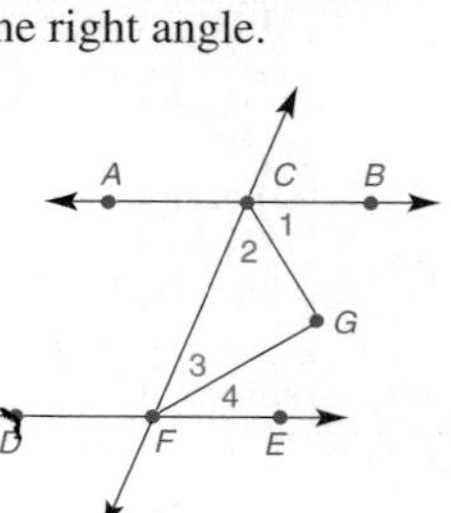

*49. *Given:* $\overrightarrow{NQ}$ bisects $\angle MNP$
$\overrightarrow{PQ}$ bisects $\angle MPR$
$m\angle Q = 42°$
Find: $m\angle M$

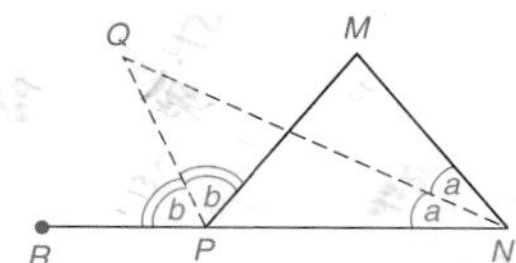

*50. *Given:* In rt. $\triangle ABC$, $\overline{AD}$ bisects $\angle CAB$ and $\overline{BF}$ bisects $\angle ABC$.
Find: $m\angle FED$

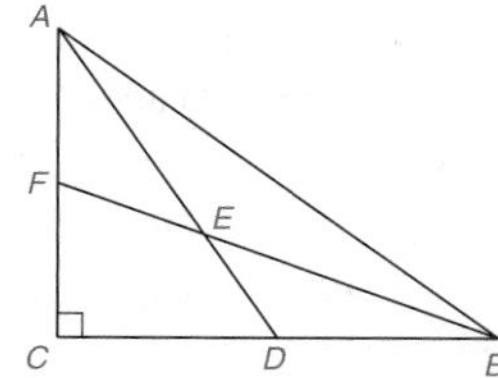

2.5 Convex Polygons

KEY CONCEPTS

- Convex Polygons (Triangle, Quadrilateral, Pentagon, Hexagon, Heptagon, Octagon, Nonagon, Decagon)
- Concave Polygon
- Diagonals of a Polygon
- Regular Polygon
- Equilateral Polygon
- Equiangular Polygon
- Polygram

DEFINITION

A **polygon** is a closed plane figure whose sides are line segments that intersect only at the endpoints.

The polygons we generally consider in this textbook are **convex;** the angle measures of convex polygons are between 0° and 180°. Convex polygons are shown in Figure 2.28; those in Figure 2.29 are **concave.** A line segment joining two points of a concave polygon can contain points in the exterior of the polygon. Thus, a concave polygon always has at least one reflex angle. Figure 2.30 shows some figures that aren't polygons at all!

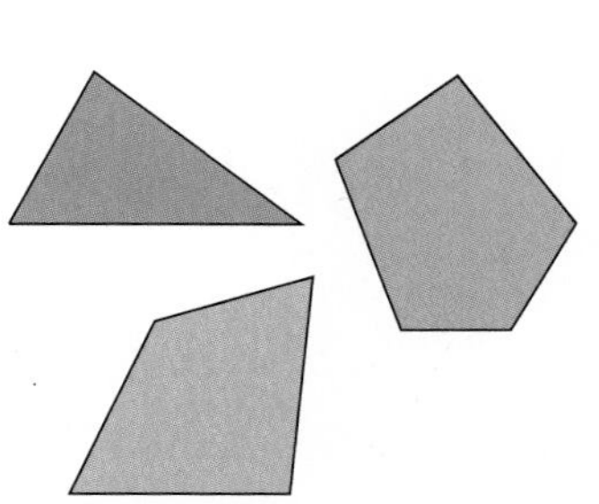

Convex Polygons

Figure 2.28

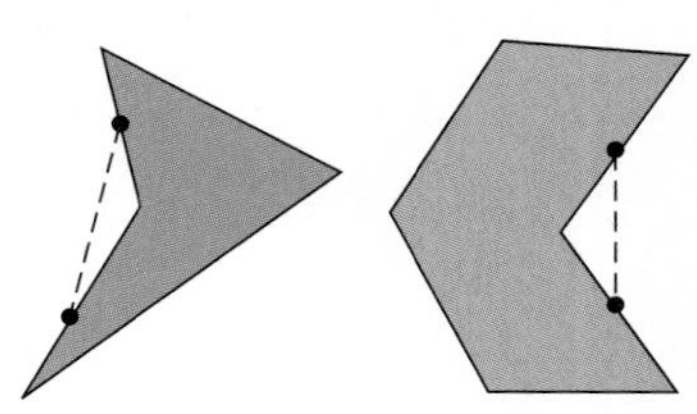

Concave Polygons

Figure 2.29

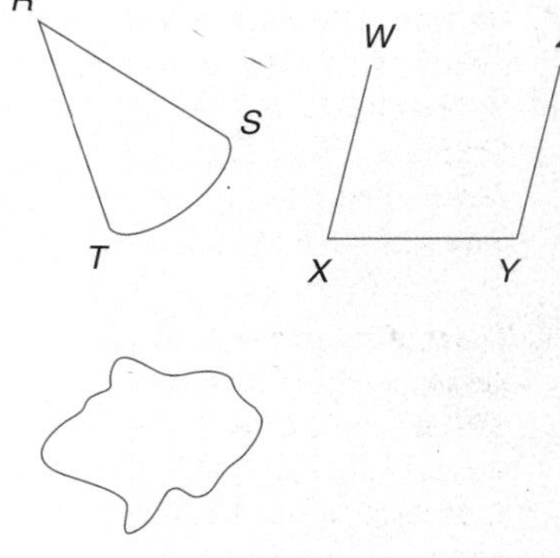

Not Polygons

Figure 2.30

A concave polygon can have more than one reflex angle.

Table 2.3 shows some special names for polygons with fixed numbers of sides.

TABLE 2.3

Polygon	Number of Sides	Polygon	Number of Sides
Triangle	3	Heptagon	7
Quadrilateral	4	Octagon	8
Pentagon	5	Nonagon	9
Hexagon	6	Decagon	10

With Venn Diagrams, the set of all objects under consideration is called the **universe.** If $P = \{\text{all polygons}\}$ is the universe, then we can describe sets $T = \{\text{triangles}\}$ and $Q = \{\text{quadrilaterals}\}$ as subsets that lie within universe P. Sets T and Q are described as **disjoint** because they have no elements in common. See Figure 2.31.

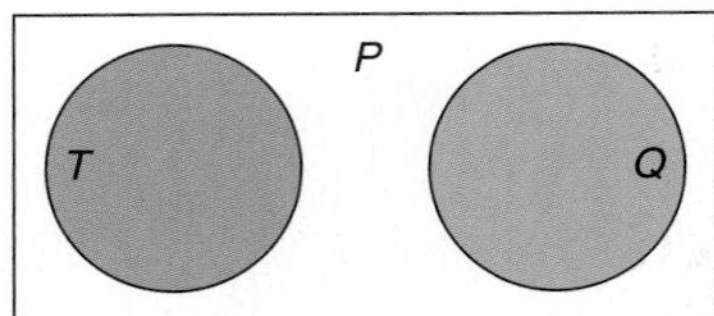

Figure 2.31

DIAGONALS OF A POLYGON

A **diagonal** of a polygon is a line segment that joins two nonconsecutive vertices.

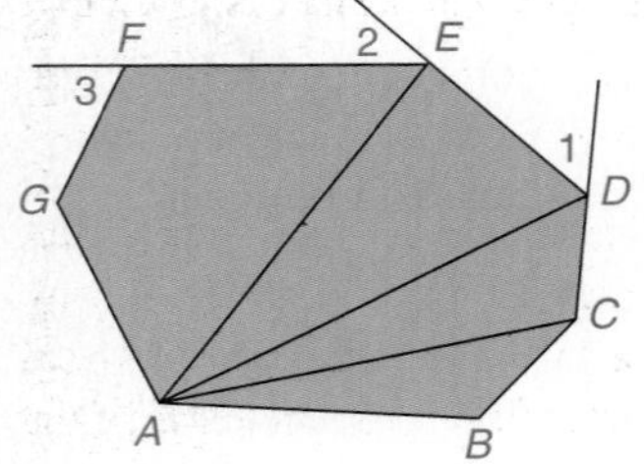

Figure 2.32

Figure 2.32 shows heptagon $ABCDEFG$ for which $\angle GAB$, $\angle B$, and $\angle BCD$ are some of the interior angles and $\angle 1$, $\angle 2$, and $\angle 3$ are some of the exterior angles. $\overline{AB}$, $\overline{BC}$, and $\overline{CD}$ are some of the sides of the heptagon, because these join consecutive vertices. Because a diagonal joins nonconsecutive vertices of $ABCDEFG$, $\overline{AC}$, $\overline{AD}$, and $\overline{AE}$ are among the many diagonals of the polygon.

Table 2.4 illustrates polygons by numbers of sides and the corresponding total number of diagonals for each type.

When the number of sides of a polygon is small, we can list all diagonals by name. For pentagon $ABCDE$ of Table 2.4, we see diagonals $\overline{AC}$, $\overline{AD}$, $\overline{BD}$, $\overline{BE}$, and $\overline{CE}$—a total of five. As the number of sides increases, it becomes more difficult to count all the

TABLE 2.4

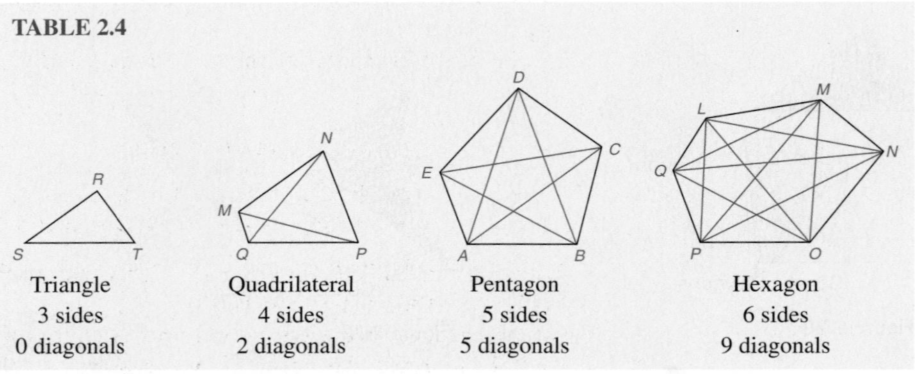

Triangle	Quadrilateral	Pentagon	Hexagon
3 sides	4 sides	5 sides	6 sides
0 diagonals	2 diagonals	5 diagonals	9 diagonals

diagonals. In such a case, the formula of Theorem 2.5.1 is most convenient to use. Although this theorem is given without proof, Exercise 39 of this section provides some insight for the proof.

THEOREM 2.5.1

The total number of diagonals D in a polygon of n sides is given by the formula $D = \frac{n(n-3)}{2}$.

Theorem 2.5.1 reaffirms the fact that a triangle has no diagonals; when $n = 3$, $D = \frac{3(3-3)}{2} = 0$.

EXAMPLE 1

Use Theorem 2.5.1 to find the number of diagonals for any pentagon.

SSG *Exs. 1–5*

Solution To use the formula of Theorem 2.5.1, we note that $n = 5$ in a pentagon.

Then $D = \frac{5(5-3)}{2} = \frac{5(2)}{2} = 5$. ■

SUM OF THE INTERIOR ANGLES OF A POLYGON

Reminder

The sum of the interior angles of a triangle is 180°.

The following theorem provides the formula for the sum of the interior angles of any polygon.

THEOREM 2.5.2

The sum S of the measures of the interior angles of a polygon with n sides is given by $S = (n-2) \cdot 180°$. Note that $n > 2$ for any polygon.

Let us consider an informal proof of Theorem 2.5.2 for the special case of a pentagon. The proof would change for a polygon of a different number of sides but only by the number of triangles into which the polygon can be separated. Although Theorem 2.5.2 is also true for concave polygons, we consider the proof only for the case of the convex polygon.

Proof

Consider the pentagon *ABCDE* in Figure 2.33 with auxiliary segments (diagonals from one vertex) as shown.

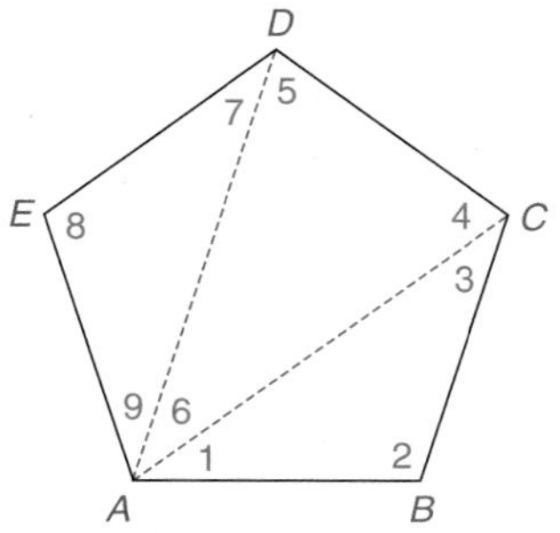

Figure 2.33

With angles marked as shown in triangles *ABC*, *ACD*, and *ADE*,

$$\begin{array}{r} m\angle 1 + m\angle 2 + m\angle 3 = 180° \\ m\angle 6 + m\angle 5 + m\angle 4 = 180° \\ m\angle 8 + m\angle 9 + m\angle 7 = 180° \\ \hline m\angle E + m\angle A + m\angle D + m\angle B + m\angle C = 540° \end{array} \quad \text{adding}$$

For pentagon *ABCDE*, in which $n = 5$, the sum of the measures of the interior angles is $(5-2) \cdot 180°$, which equals 540°.

When drawing diagonals from one vertex of a polygon of n sides, we always form $(n-2)$ triangles. The sum of the measures of the interior angles always equals $(n-2) \cdot 180°$. ■

EXAMPLE 2

Find the sum of the measures of the interior angles of a hexagon. Then find the measure of each interior angle of an equiangular hexagon.

Solution For the hexagon, $n = 6$, so the sum of the measures of the interior angles is $S = (6 - 2) \cdot 180°$ or $4(180°)$ or $720°$.

In an equiangular hexagon, each of the six interior angles measures $\frac{720°}{6}$, or $120°$. ■

EXAMPLE 3

Find the number of sides in a polygon whose sum of interior angles is 2160°.

Solution Here $S = 2160$ in the formula of Theorem 2.5.2. Because $(n - 2) \cdot 180 = 2160$, we have $180n - 360 = 2160$.

Then $180n = 2520$

$n = 14$

SSG *Exs. 6–9*

The polygon has 14 sides. ■

REGULAR POLYGONS

Figure 2.34 shows polygons that are, respectively, (a) **equilateral,** (b) **equiangular,** and (c) **regular** (both sides and angles are congruent). Note the dashes that indicate congruent sides and the arcs that indicate congruent angles.

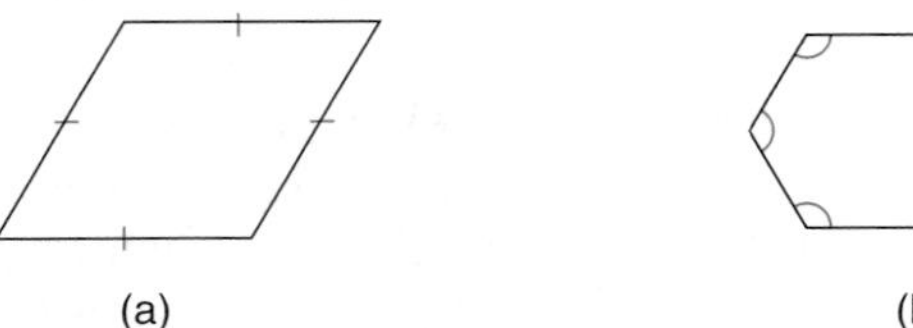
(a)

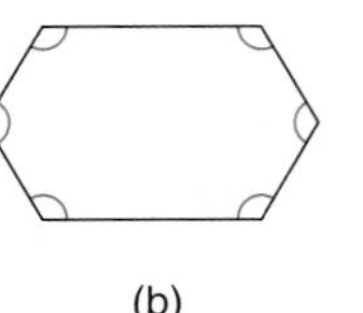
(b)

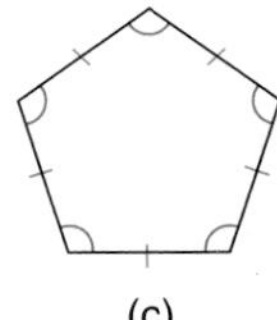
(c)

Figure 2.34

DEFINITION

A **regular polygon** is a polygon that is both equilateral and equiangular.

The polygon in Figure 2.34(c) is a *regular pentagon.* Other examples of regular polygons include the equilateral triangle and the square.

Based upon the formula $S = (n - 2) \cdot 180°$ from Theorem 2.5.2, there is also a formula for the measure of each interior angle of a regular polygon having n sides. It applies to equiangular polygons as well.

COROLLARY 2.5.3

The measure I of each interior angle of a regular polygon or equiangular polygon of n sides is $I = \frac{(n - 2) \cdot 180°}{n}$.

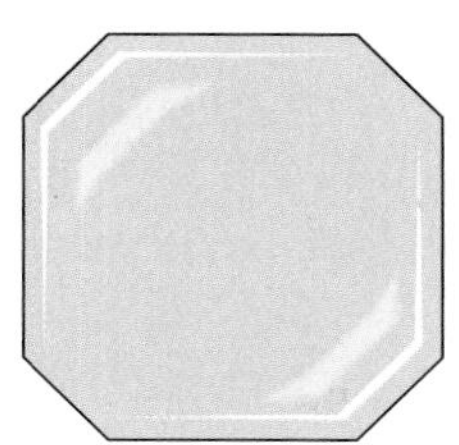

Figure 2.35

EXAMPLE 4

Find the measure of each interior angle of a ceramic floor tile in the shape of an equiangular octagon (Figure 2.35).

Solution For an octagon, $n = 8$.

Then
$$I = \frac{(8 - 2) \cdot 180}{8} = \frac{6 \cdot 180}{8} = \frac{1080}{8}, \quad \text{so} \quad I = 135^\circ$$

Each interior angle of the tile measures 135°.

NOTE: For the octagonal tiles of Example 4, small squares are used as "fillers" to cover the floor. The pattern, known as a tessellation, is found in Section 8.3. ■

EXAMPLE 5

Each interior angle of a certain regular polygon has a measure of 144°. Find its number of sides, and identify the type of polygon it is.

Solution Let n be the number of sides the polygon has. All n of the interior angles are equal in measure.

The measure of each interior angle is given by

$$I = \frac{(n - 2) \cdot 180}{n} \quad \text{where} \quad I = 144$$

SSG *Exs. 10–12*

Then
$$\frac{(n - 2) \cdot 180}{n} = 144$$
$$(n - 2) \cdot 180 = 144n \quad \textbf{(multiplying by } n\textbf{)}$$
$$180n - 360 = 144n$$
$$36n = 360$$
$$n = 10$$

With 10 sides, the polygon is a regular decagon. ■

Discover

From a paper quadrilateral, cut the angles from the "corners." Now place the angles so that they have the same vertex and do *not* overlap. What is the sum of measures of the four angles?

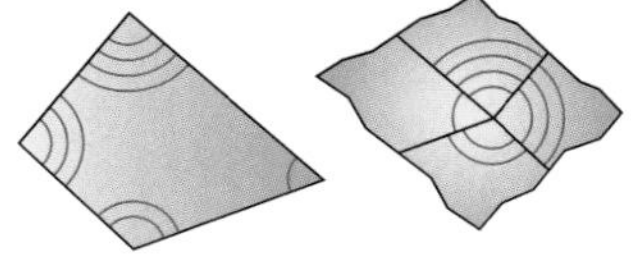

ANSWER
360°

A second corollary to Theorem 2.5.2 concerns the sum of the interior angles of any quadrilateral. For the proof, we simply let $n = 4$ in the formula $S = (n - 2) \cdot 180°$. Then $S = (4 - 2) \cdot 180° = 2 \cdot 180° = 360°$. Also, see the Discover at the left.

COROLLARY 2.5.4

The sum of the four interior angles of a quadrilateral is 360°.

On the basis of Corollary 2.5.4, it is clearly the case that each interior angle of a square or rectangle measures 90°.

The following interesting corollary to Theorem 2.5.2 can be established through algebra.

COROLLARY 2.5.5

The sum of the measures of the exterior angles of a polygon, one at each vertex, is 360°.

We now consider an algebraic proof for Corollary 2.5.5.

Proof

A polygon of n sides has n interior angles and n exterior angles, if one is considered at each vertex. As shown in Figure 2.36, these interior and exterior angles may be grouped into pairs of supplementary angles. Because there are n pairs of angles, the sum of the measures of all pairs is $180 \cdot n$ degrees.

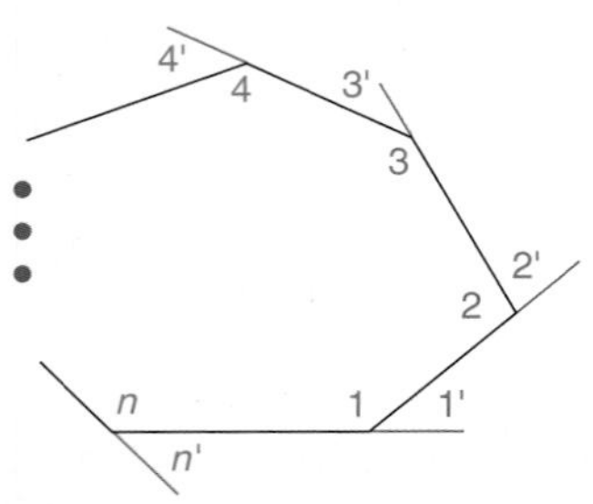

Figure 2.36

Of course, the sum of the measures of the interior angles is $(n - 2) \cdot 180°$.

In words, we have

$$\text{Sum of Measures of Interior Angles} + \text{Sum of Measures of Exterior Angles} = \text{Sum of Measures of All Supplementary Pairs}$$

Let S represent the sum of the measures of the exterior angles.

$$\begin{aligned}(n - 2) \cdot 180 + S &= 180n\\ 180n - 360 + S &= 180n\\ -360 + S &= 0\\ \therefore S &= 360\end{aligned}$$ ■

The next corollary follows from Corollary 2.5.5. The claim made in Corollary 2.5.6 is applied in Example 6.

COROLLARY 2.5.6

The measure E of each exterior angle of a regular polygon or equiangular polygon of n sides is $E = \frac{360°}{n}$.

EXAMPLE 6

Use Corollary 2.5.6 to find the number of sides of a regular polygon if each interior angle measures 144°. (Note that we are repeating Example 5.)

Solution If each interior angle measures 144°, then each exterior angle measures 36° (they are supplementary, because exterior sides of these adjacent angles form a straight line).

Now each of the n exterior angles has the measure

$$\frac{360°}{n}$$

In this case, $\frac{360}{n} = 36$, and it follows that $36n = 360$, so $n = 10$. The polygon (a decagon) has 10 sides. ■

POLYGRAMS

SSG *Exs. 13, 14*

A **polygram** is the star-shaped figure that results when the sides of convex polygons with five or more sides are extended. When the polygon is regular, the resulting polygram is also regular—that is, the interior acute angles are congruent, the interior reflex

Geometry in Nature

The starfish has the shape of a pentagram.

angles are congruent, and all sides are congruent. The names of polygrams come from the names of the polygons whose sides were extended. Figure 2.37 shows a pentagram, a hexagram, and an octagram. With congruent angles and sides indicated, these figures are **regular polygrams.**

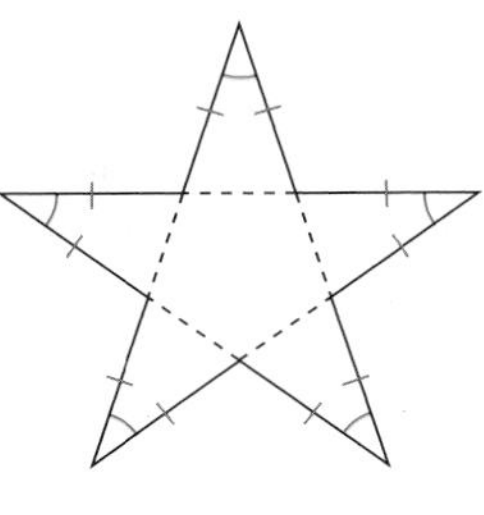

Pentagram

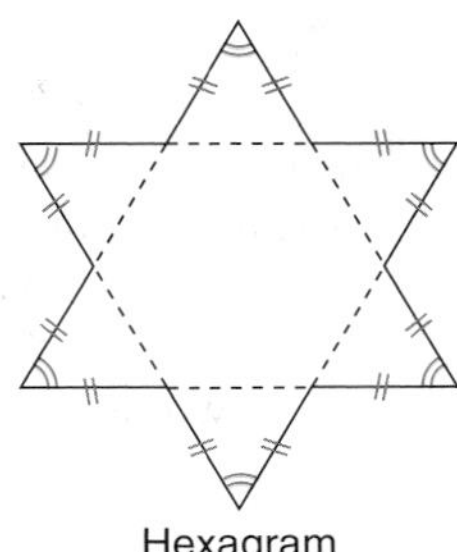

Hexagram

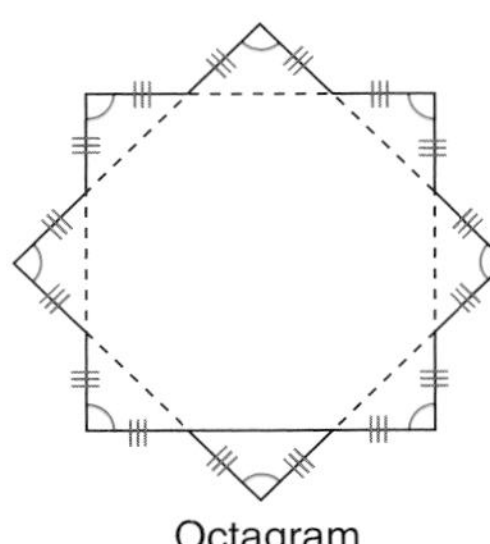

Octagram

SSG *Exs. 15, 16*

Figure 2.37

Exercises 2.5

1. As the number of sides of a regular polygon increases, does each interior angle increase or decrease in measure?
2. As the number of sides of a regular polygon increases, does each exterior angle increase or decrease in measure?
3. *Given:* $\overline{AB} \parallel \overline{DC}$, $\overline{AD} \parallel \overline{BC}$, $\overline{AE} \parallel \overline{FC}$, with angle measures as indicated
   Find: x, y, and z

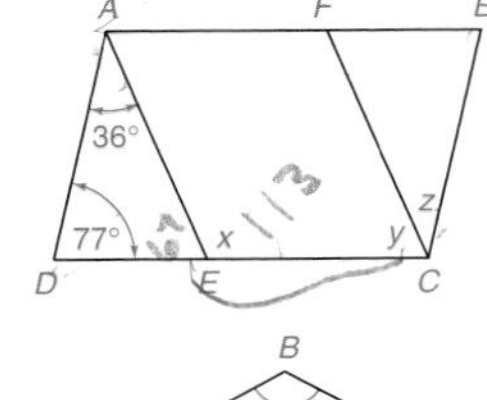

4. In pentagon $ABCDE$ with $\angle B \cong \angle D \cong \angle E$, find the measure of interior angle D.

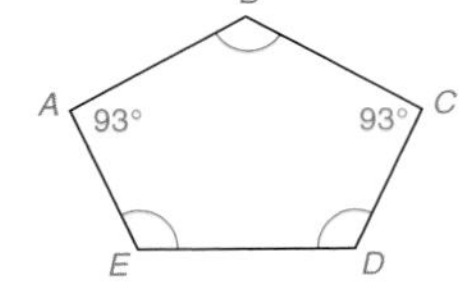

5. Find the total number of diagonals for a polygon of n sides if:
   a) $n = 5$ b) $n = 10$
6. Find the total number of diagonals for a polygon of n sides if:
   a) $n = 6$ b) $n = 8$
7. Find the sum of the measures of the interior angles of a polygon of n sides if:
   a) $n = 5$ b) $n = 10$
8. Find the sum of the measures of the interior angles of a polygon of n sides if:
   a) $n = 6$ b) $n = 8$
9. Find the measure of each interior angle of a regular polygon of n sides if:
   a) $n = 4$ b) $n = 12$
10. Find the measure of each interior angle of a regular polygon of n sides if:
    a) $n = 6$ b) $n = 10$
11. Find the measure of each exterior angle of a regular polygon of n sides if:
    a) $n = 4$ b) $n = 12$
12. Find the measure of each exterior angle of a regular polygon of n sides if:
    a) $n = 6$ b) $n = 10$
13. Find the number of sides that a polygon has if the sum of the measures of its interior angles is:
    a) 900° b) 1260°
14. Find the number of sides that a polygon has if the sum of the measures of its interior angles is:
    a) 1980° b) 2340°
15. Find the number of sides that a regular polygon has if the measure of each interior angle is:
    a) 108° b) 144°
16. Find the number of sides that a regular polygon has if the measure of each interior angle is:
    a) 150° b) 168°
17. Find the number of sides in a regular polygon whose exterior angles each measure:
    a) 24° b) 18°
18. Find the number of sides in a regular polygon whose exterior angles each measure:
    a) 45° b) 9°
19. What is the measure of each interior angle of a stop sign?

20. Lug bolts are equally spaced about the wheel to form the equal angles shown in the figure. What is the measure of each of the equal acute angles?

In Exercises 21 to 26, with P = {all polygons} as the universe, draw a Venn Diagram to represent the relationship between these sets. Describe a subset relationship, if one exists. Are the sets described disjoint or equivalent? Do the sets intersect?

21. $T = \{\text{triangles}\}$; $I = \{\text{isosceles triangles}\}$

22. $R = \{\text{right triangles}\}$; $S = \{\text{scalene triangles}\}$

23. $A = \{\text{acute triangles}\}$; $S = \{\text{scalene triangles}\}$

24. $Q = \{\text{quadrilaterals}\}$; $L = \{\text{equilateral polygons}\}$

25. $H = \{\text{hexagons}\}$; $O = \{\text{octagons}\}$

26. $T = \{\text{triangles}\}$; $Q = \{\text{quadrilaterals}\}$

27. *Given:* Quadrilateral *RSTQ* with exterior ∠s at *R* and *T*
Prove: $m\angle 1 + m\angle 2 = m\angle 3 + m\angle 4$

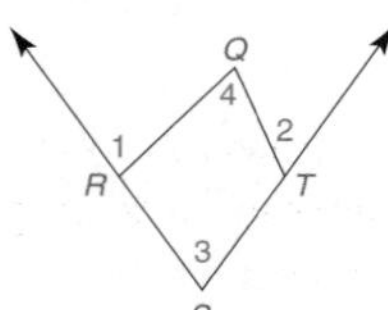

28. *Given:* Regular hexagon *ABCDEF* with diagonal $\overline{AC}$ and exterior ∠1
Prove: $m\angle 2 + m\angle 3 = m\angle 1$

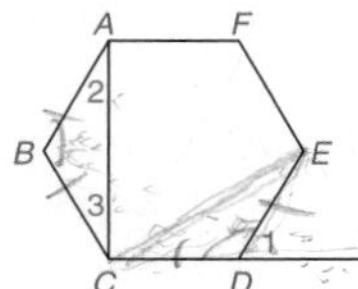

29. *Given:* Quadrilateral *RSTV* with diagonals $\overline{RT}$ and $\overline{SV}$ intersecting at *W*
Prove: $m\angle 1 + m\angle 2 = m\angle 3 + m\angle 4$

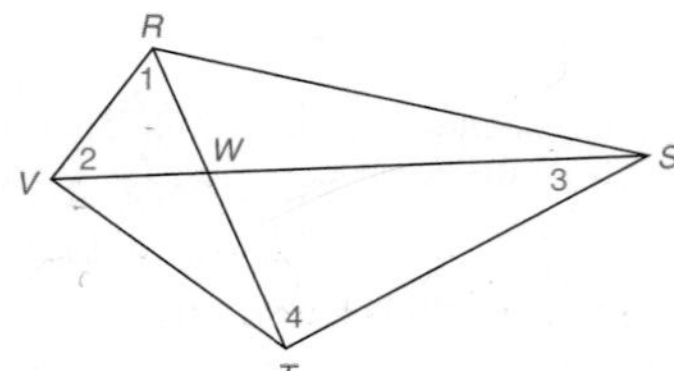

30. *Given:* Quadrilateral *ABCD* with $\overline{BA} \perp \overline{AD}$ and $\overline{BC} \perp \overline{DC}$
Prove: ∠s *B* and *D* are supplementary

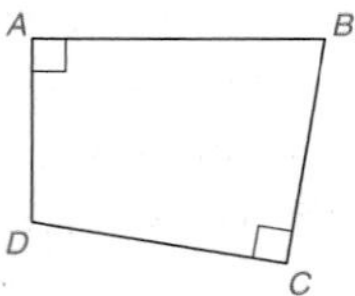

31. A father wishes to make a home plate for his son to use in practicing baseball. Find the size of each of the equal angles if the home plate is modeled on the one in (a) and if it is modeled on the one in (b).

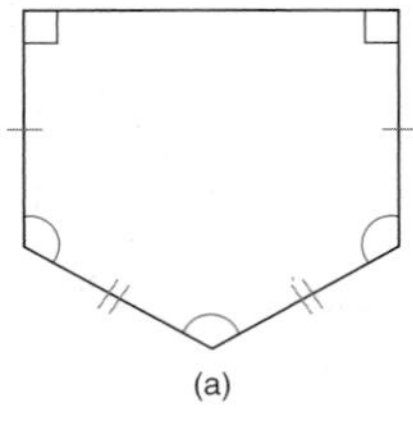
(a)

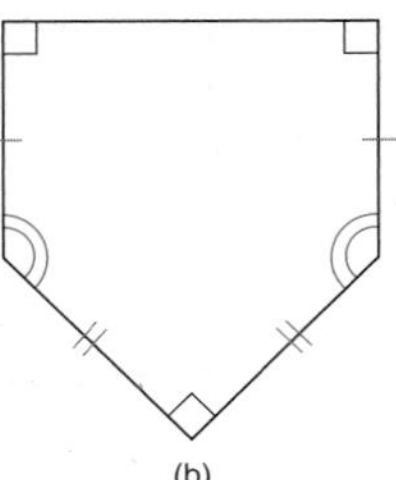
(b)

32. The adjacent interior and exterior angles of a certain polygon are supplementary, as indicated in the drawing. Assume that you know that the measure of each interior angle of a regular polygon is $\frac{(n-2)180}{n}$.

a) Express the measure of each exterior angle as the supplement of the interior angle.

b) Simplify the expression in part (a) to show that each exterior angle has a measure of $\frac{360}{n}$.

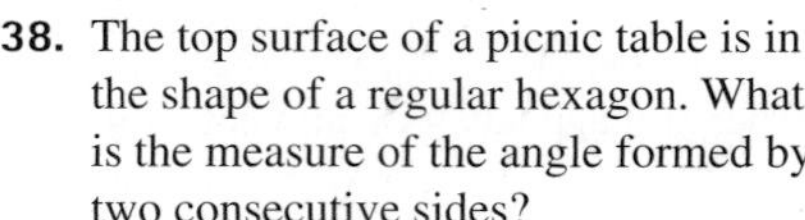

33. Find the measure of each acute interior angle of a regular pentagram.

34. Find the measure of each acute interior angle of a regular octagram.

35. Consider any regular polygon; find and join (in order) the midpoints of the sides. What does intuition tell you about the resulting polygon?

36. Consider a regular hexagon *RSTUVW*. What does intuition tell you about △*RTV*, the result of drawing diagonals $\overline{RT}$, $\overline{TV}$, and $\overline{VR}$?

37. The face of a clock has the shape of a regular polygon with 12 sides. What is the measure of the angle formed by two consecutive sides?

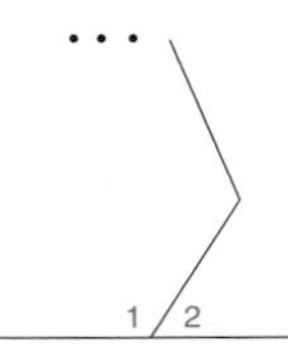

38. The top surface of a picnic table is in the shape of a regular hexagon. What is the measure of the angle formed by two consecutive sides?

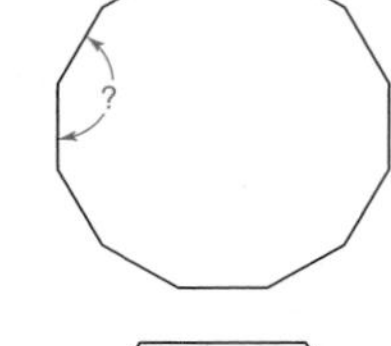

***39.** Consider a polygon of *n* sides determined by the *n* noncollinear vertics *A, B, C, D,* and so on.

a) Choose any vertex of the polygon. To how many of the remaining vertices of the polygon can the selected vertex be joined to form a diagonal?

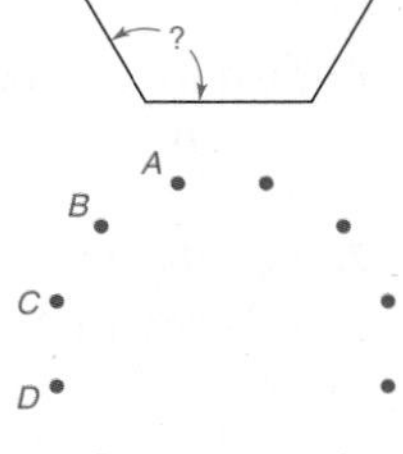

b) Considering that each of the *n* vertices in (a) can be joined to any one of the remaining $(n - 3)$ vertices to form diagonals, the product $n(n - 3)$ appears to represent the total number of diagonals possible. However, this number includes duplications, such as $\overline{AC}$ and $\overline{CA}$. What expression actually represents D, the total number of diagonals in a polygon of n sides?

40. For the concave quadrilateral $ABCD$, explain why the sum of the interior angles is 360°.

(HINT: Draw $\overline{BD}$.)

41. If $m\angle A = 20°$, $m\angle B = 88°$, and $m\angle C = 31°$, find the measure of the reflex angle at vertex D.

(HINT: See Exercise 40.)

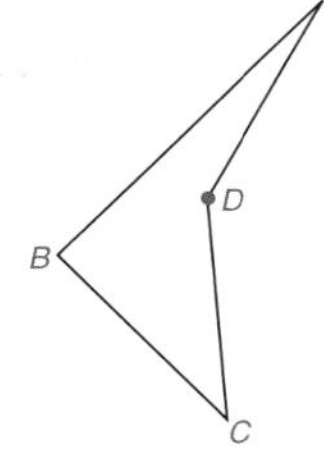

Exercises 40, 41

42. Is it possible for a polygon to have the following sum of measures for its interior angles?

a) 600°
b) 720°

43. Is it possible for a regular polygon to have the following measures for each interior angle?

a) 96°
b) 140°

2.6 Symmetry and Transformations

KEY CONCEPTS

Symmetry	Point Symmetry	Translations
Line of Symmetry	Transformations	Reflections
Axis of Symmetry	Slides	Rotations

LINE SYMMETRY

In the figure below, rectangle $ABCD$ is said to have *symmetry with respect to line* ℓ because each point to the left of the *line of symmetry* or *axis of symmetry* has a corresponding point to the right; for instance, X and Y are *corresponding points.*

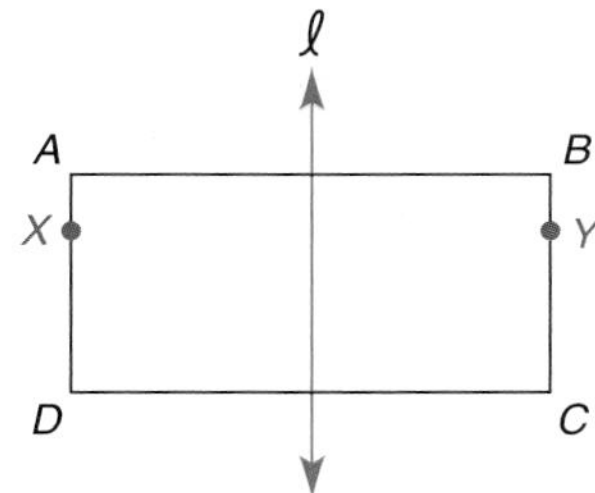

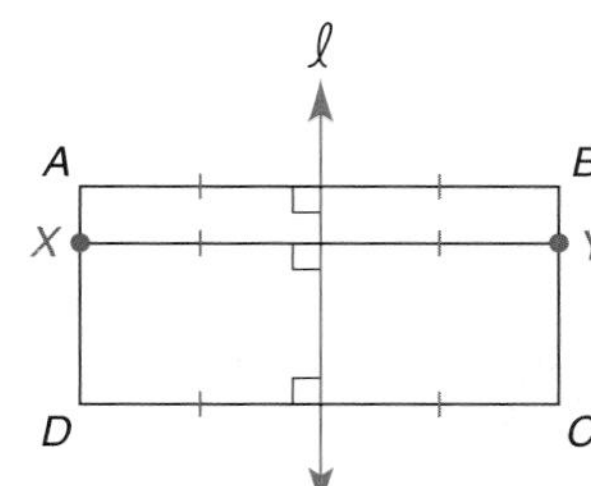

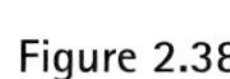
Figure 2.38

DEFINITION

A figure has *symmetry with respect to a line* ℓ if for every point A on the figure, there is a second point B on the figure for which ℓ is the perpendicular bisector of $\overline{AB}$.

In particular, $ABCD$ of Figure 2.38 has *horizontal symmetry* with respect to line ℓ. That is, a vertical axis of symmetry leads to a pairing of corresponding points on a horizontal line. In Example 1 on page 108, we see that a horizontal axis leads to *vertical* symmetry for points.

Geometry in Nature

Like many of nature's creations, the butterfly displays line symmetry.

EXAMPLE 1

Rectangle *ABCD* in Figure 2.38 on page 107 has a second line of symmetry. Draw this line (or axis) for which there is *vertical symmetry.*

Solution Line m (determined by the midpoints of $\overline{AD}$ and $\overline{BC}$) is the desired line of symmetry. As shown in Figure 2.39(b), R and S are located symmetrically with respect to line m.

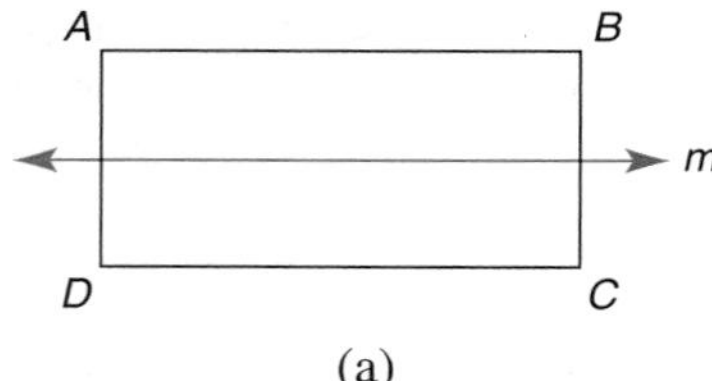

(a)

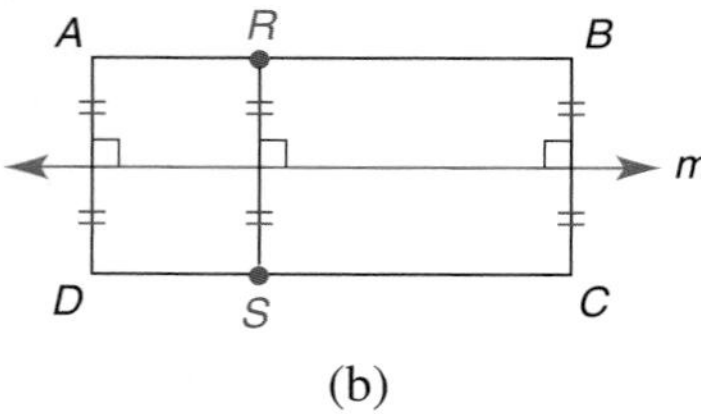

(b)

Figure 2.39

■

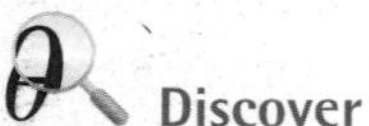

Discover

The uppercase block form of the letter A is shown below. Does it have symmetry with respect to a line?

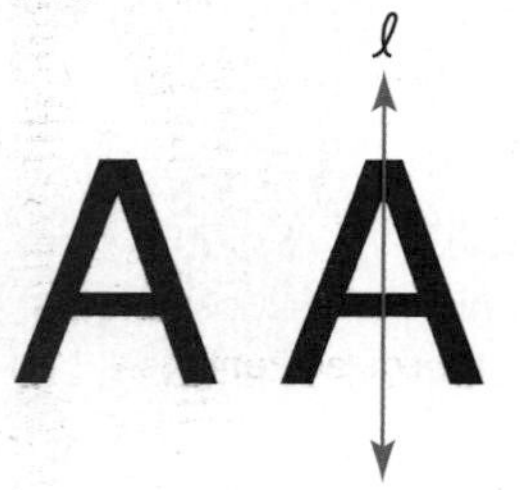

ANSWER

Yes, line ℓ as shown is a line of symmetry. This vertical line ℓ is the only line of symmetry for the uppercase A.

EXAMPLE 2

a) Which letter(s) shown below has (have) a line of symmetry?
b) Which letter(s) has (have) more than one line of symmetry?

B D F G H

Solution

a) B, D, and H as shown

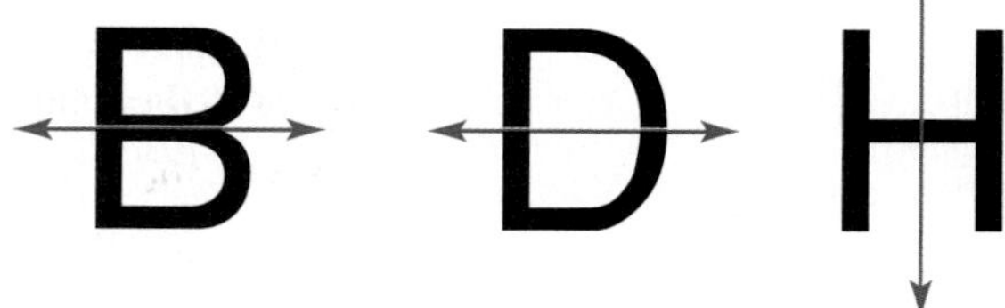

b) H as shown

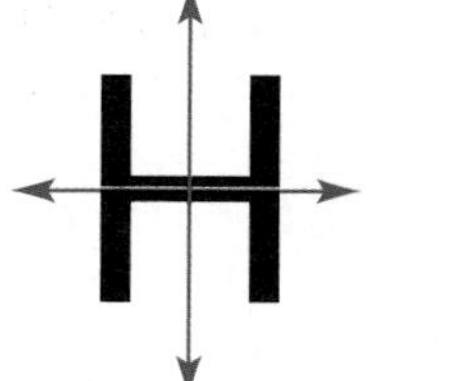

■

In Chapter 4, we will discover formal definitions of the types of quadrilaterals known as the parallelogram, square, rectangle, kite, rhombus, and rectangle. Some of these are included in Examples 3 and 5.

EXAMPLE 3

a) Which figures have at least one line of symmetry?
b) Which figures have more than one line of symmetry?

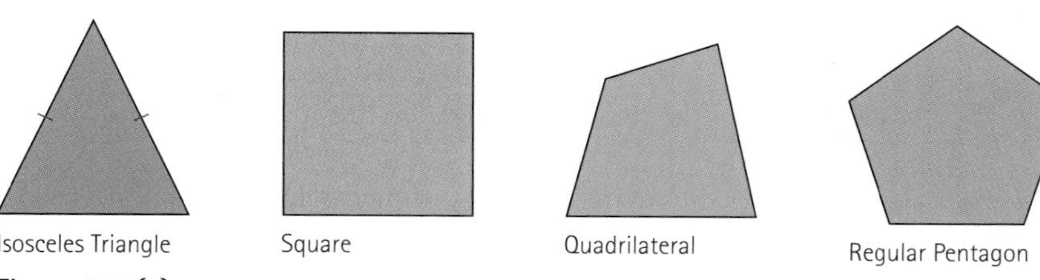

Figure 2.40(a)

Solution

a) The isosceles triangle, square, and the regular pentagon all have a line of symmetry.
b) The square and regular pentagon have more than one line of symmetry, so these figures are shown with two lines of symmetry. (There are actually more than two lines of symmetry.)

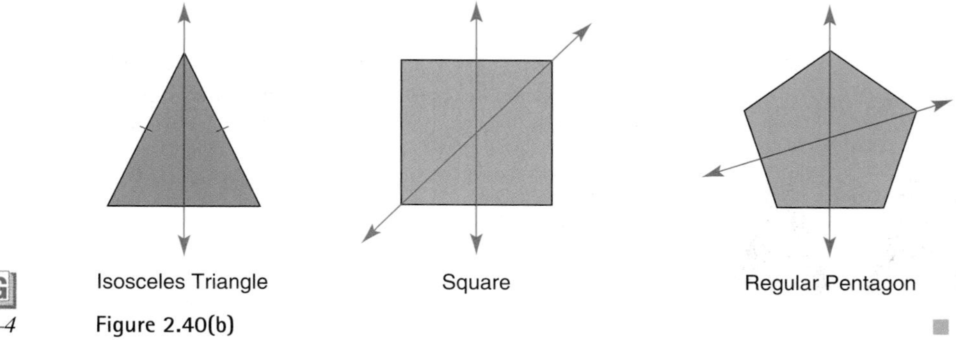

SSG *Exs. 1–4*

Figure 2.40(b)

POINT SYMMETRY

In Figure 2.41, rectangle *ABCD* is also said to have *symmetry with respect to a point.* As shown, point *P* is determined by the intersection of the diagonals of rectangle *ABCD*.

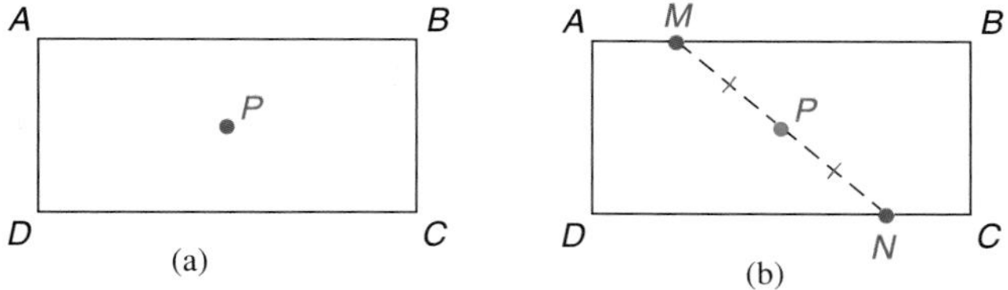

Figure 2.41

DEFINITION

A figure has **symmetry with respect to point *P*** if for every point *M* on the figure, there is a second point *N* on the figure for which point *P* is the midpoint of $\overline{MN}$.

Discover

The uppercase block form of the letter O is shown below. Does it have symmetry with respect to a point?

ANSWER

Yes, point *P* (centered) is the point of symmetry. This point *P* is the only point of symmetry for the uppercase O.

On the basis of this definition, each point on rectangle *ABCD* in Figure 2.41(a) has a corresponding point that is the same distance from *P* but lies in the opposite direction from *P*. In Figure 2.41(b), *M* and *N* are a pair of corresponding points. Even though a figure may have multiple lines of symmetry, a figure can have only one point of symmetry. Thus, the point of symmetry (when one exists) is unique.

EXAMPLE 4

Which letter(s) shown below have point symmetry?

M N P S X

Solution N, S, and X as shown all have point symmetry. ■

EXAMPLE 5

Which figures in Figure 2.42(a) have point symmetry?

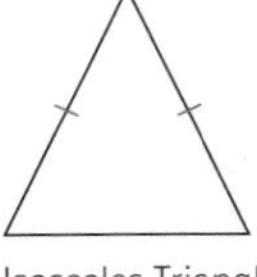
Isosceles Triangle

Square

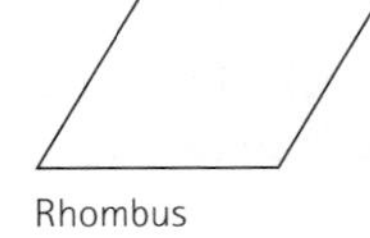
Rhombus

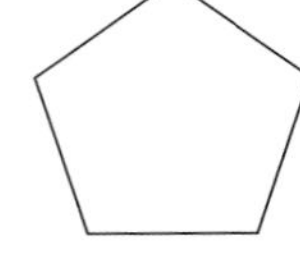
Regular Pentagon

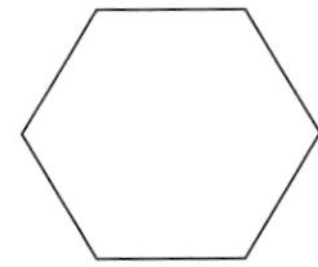
Regular Hexagon

Figure 2.42(a)

Solution Only the square, the rhombus, and the regular hexagon have point symmetry. In the regular pentagon, consider the "centrally" located point *P* and note that $AP \neq PM$.

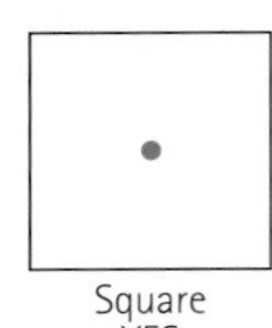
Square
YES

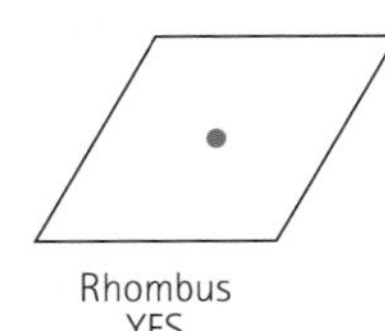
Rhombus
YES

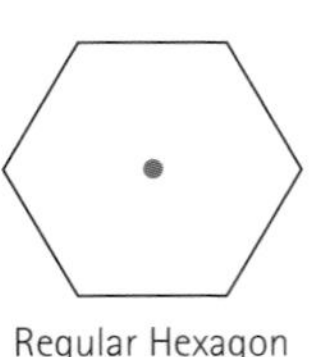
Regular Hexagon
YES

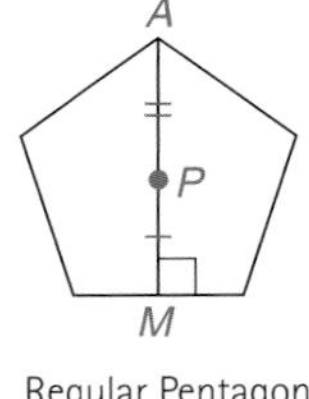

Regular Pentagon
NO

Figure 2.42(b) ■

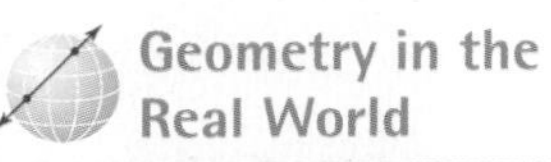

Geometry in the Real World

Taking a good look at the hexagonal shape used in the Hampton Inn logo reveals both point symmetry and line symmetry.

SSG *Exs. 5–8*

TRANSFORMATIONS

In the following material, we will generate new figures from old figures by association of points. In particular, the *transformations* included in this textbook will preserve the shape and size of the given figure; in other words, these transformations lead to a second figure that is *congruent* to the given figure. The types of transformations included are (1) the *slide* or *translation,* (2) the *reflection,* and (3) the *rotation.*

▶ *Slides (Translations)*

With this type of transformation, every point of the original figure is associated with a second point by locating it through a movement of a fixed length and direction. In Figure 2.43, $\triangle ABC$ is translated to the second triangle (its image $\triangle DEF$) by sliding each point through the distance and in the direction that takes point A to point D. The background grid is not necessary to demonstrate the slide, but it lends credibility to our claim that the same length and direction have been used to locate each point.

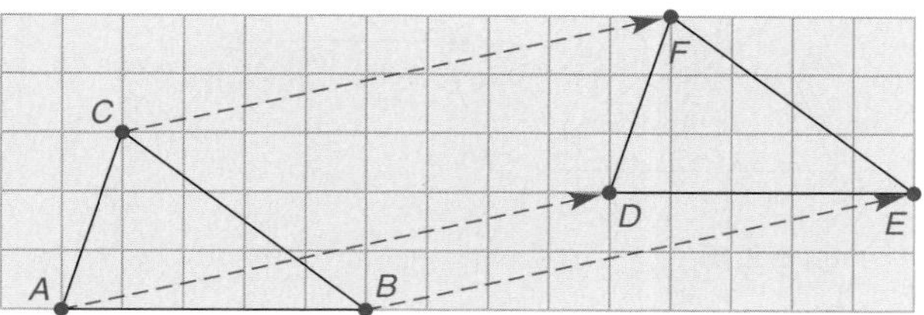

Figure 2.43

EXAMPLE 6

Slide $\triangle XYZ$ horizontally in Figure 2.44 to form $\triangle RST$. In this example, the distance (length of the slide) is XR.

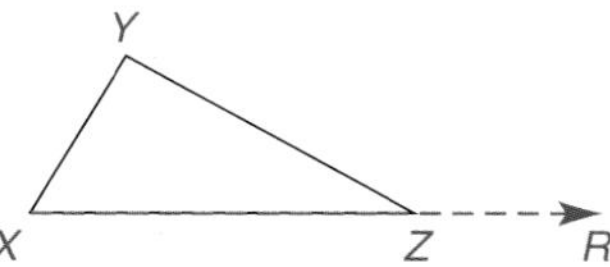

Solution

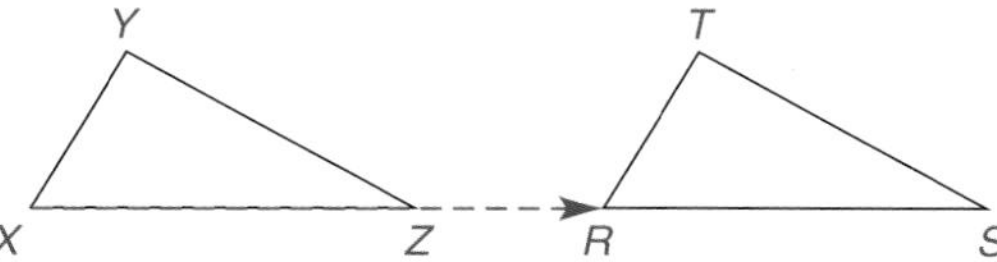

Figure 2.44

In Example 6, $\triangle XYZ \cong \triangle RTS$ and also $\triangle RTS \cong \triangle XYZ$. In every slide, the given figure and the produced figure (its *image*) are necessarily congruent. In Example 6, the correspondence of vertices is given by $X \leftrightarrow R$, $Y \leftrightarrow T$, and $Z \leftrightarrow S$.

EXAMPLE 7

Where $A \leftrightarrow E$, complete the slide of quadrilateral $ABCD$ to form quadrilateral $EFGH$. Indicate the correspondence among the remaining vertices.

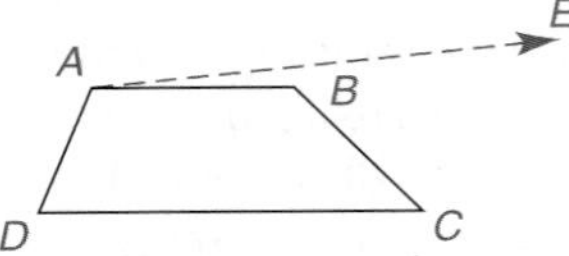

Solution

$B \leftrightarrow F$, $C \leftrightarrow G$, and $D \leftrightarrow H$ in Figure 2.45.

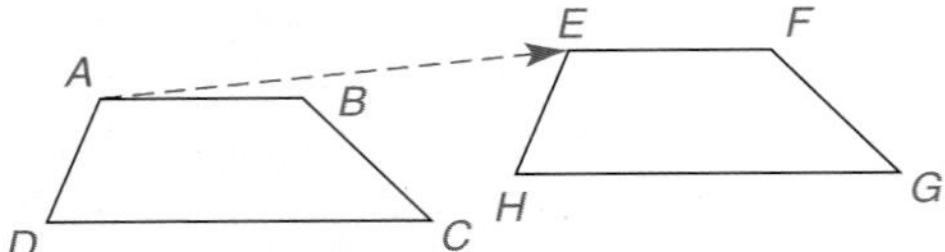

Figure 2.45

▶ *Reflections*

With the reflection, every point of the original figure is reflected across a line in such a way as to make the given line a line of symmetry. Each pair of corresponding points will lie on opposite sides of the line of reflection and at like distances. In Figure 2.46, obtuse triangle MNP is reflected across the vertical line $\overleftrightarrow{AB}$ to produce the image $\triangle GHK$. The vertex N of the given obtuse angle corresponds to the vertex H of the obtuse angle in the image triangle. It is possible for the line of reflection to be horizontal or oblique (slanted). With the vertical line as the axis of reflection, a drawing such as Figure 2.46 is sometimes called a *horizontal reflection*, since the image lies to the right of the given figure.

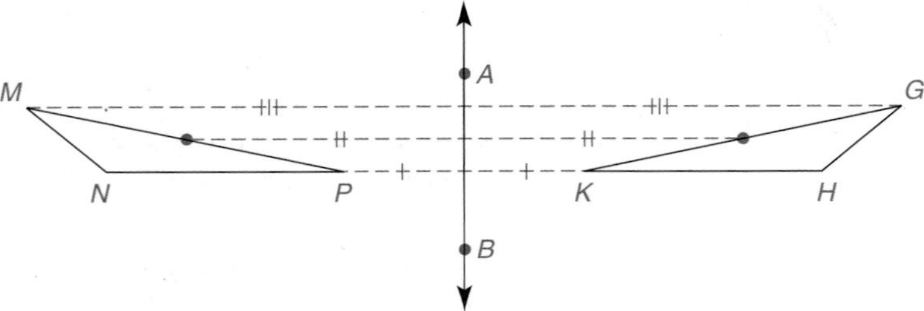

Figure 2.46

EXAMPLE 8

Draw the reflection of right $\triangle ABC$

a) across line ℓ to form $\triangle XYZ$.

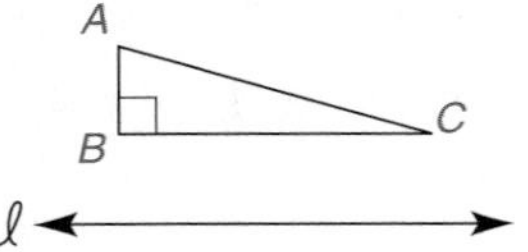

b) across line m to form $\triangle PQR$.

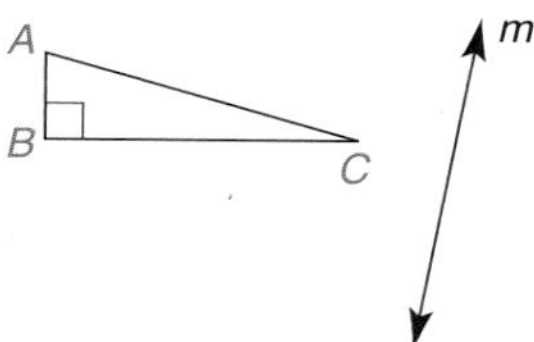

Solution As shown in Figure 2.47

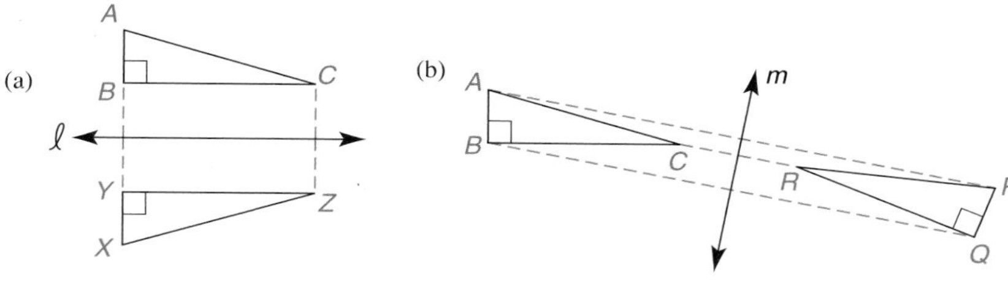

Figure 2.47

With the horizontal axis (line) of reflection, the reflection in Example 8(a) is often called a *vertical reflection.* In the vertical reflection of Figure 2.47(a), the image lies below the given figure. In Example 9, we use a side of the given figure as the line (line segment) of reflection. This reflection is neither horizontal nor vertical.

EXAMPLE 9

Draw the reflection of $\triangle ABC$ across side $\overline{BC}$ to form $\triangle DBC$ in Figure 2.48. How are $\triangle ABC$ and $\triangle DBC$ related?

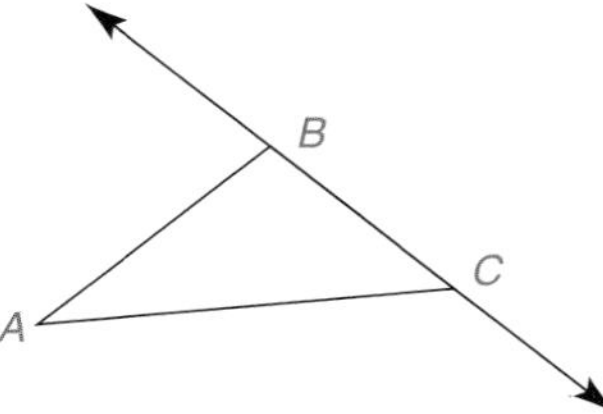

Solution

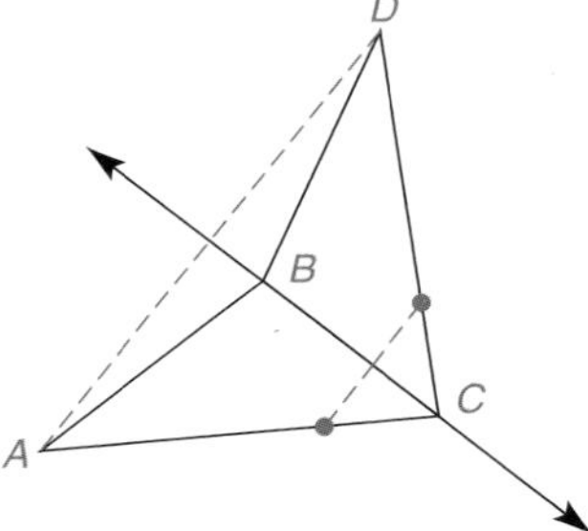

Figure 2.48

The triangles are congruent; also, notice that $D \leftrightarrow A$, $B \leftrightarrow B$, and $C \leftrightarrow C$.

EXAMPLE 10

Complete the figure produced by a reflection across the given line in Figure 2.49.

Solution

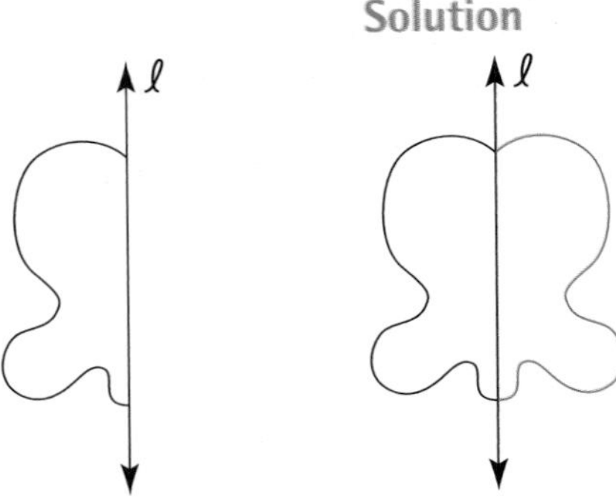

Figure 2.49

▶ *Rotations*

In this transformation, every point of the given figure leads to a point (its image) by rotation about a given point through a prescribed angle measure. In Figure 2.50, ray AB rotates about point A clockwise through an angle of 30° to produce the image ray AC. This has the same appearance as the second hand of a clock over a five-second period of time. In this figure, $A \leftrightarrow A$ and $B \leftrightarrow C$.

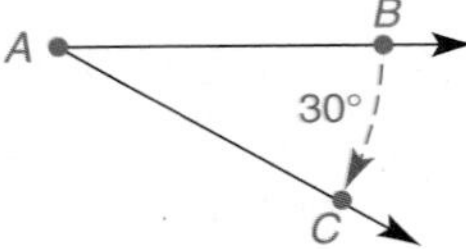

Figure 2.50

Geometry in the Real World

The logo that identifies the Health Alliance Corporation begins with a figure that consists of a rectangle and an adjacent square. The logo is completed by rotating this basic unit through angles of 90°.

EXAMPLE 11

In Figure 2.51, square $WXYZ$ has been rotated counterclockwise about its center (intersection of diagonals) through an angle of 45° to form congruent square $QMNP$. What is the name of the eight-pointed geometric figure that is formed by the two intersecting squares?

Solution

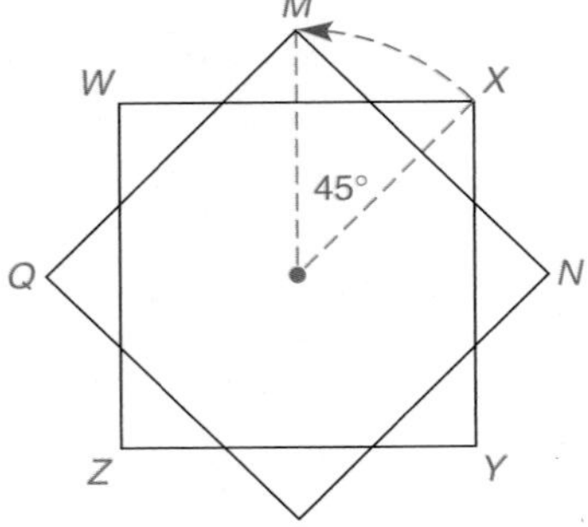

Figure 2.51

The eight-pointed figure formed is a regular octagram.

EXAMPLE 12

Shown in Figure 2.52 are the uppercase A, line ℓ, and point O. Which of the pairs of transformations produce the original figure?

a) The letter A is reflected across ℓ, and that image is reflected across ℓ again.
b) The letter A is reflected across ℓ, and that image is rotated clockwise 60° about point O.
c) The letter A is rotated 180° about O, followed by another 180° rotation about O.

Solution (a) and (c)

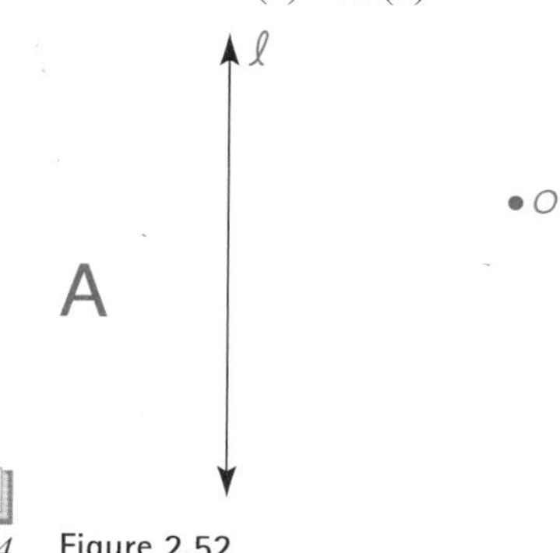

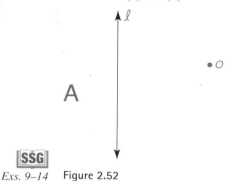

SSG *Exs. 9–14*

Figure 2.52

Exercises 2.6

1. Which letters have symmetry with respect to a line?
M N P T X
2. Which letters have symmetry with respect to a line?
I K S V Z
3. Which letters have symmetry with respect to a point?
M N P T X
4. Which letters have symmetry with respect to a point?
I K S V Z
5. Which geometric figures have symmetry with respect to at least one line?
a)  b) 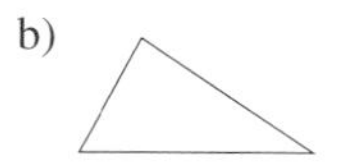 c) 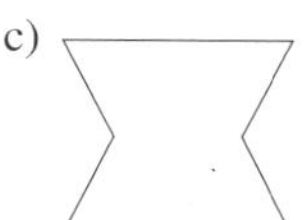
6. Which geometric figures have symmetry with respect to at least one line?
a) 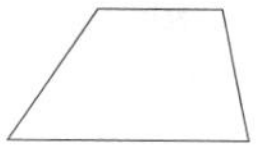  b)  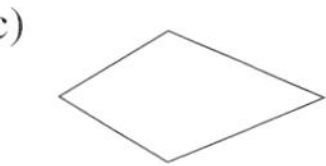 c)
7. Which geometric figures have symmetry with respect to a point?
a) 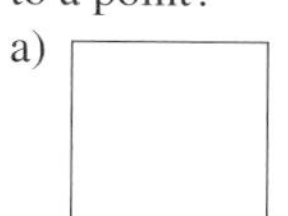 b) 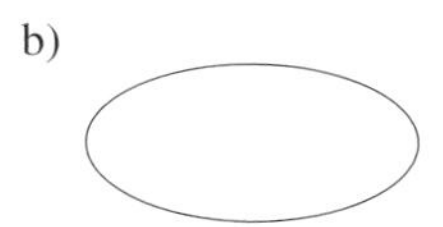 c) 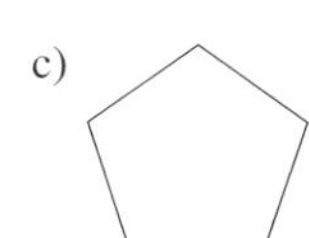
8. Which geometric figures have symmetry with respect to a point?
a) 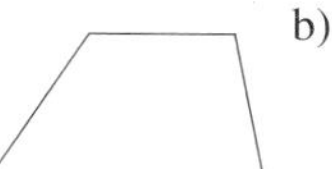 b)  c) 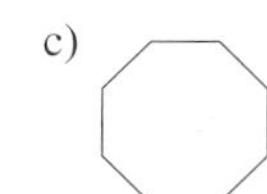
9. Which words have a vertical line of symmetry?
DAD MOM NUN EYE
10. Which words have a vertical line of symmetry?
WOW BUB MAM EVE
11. Complete each figure so that it has symmetry with respect to line ℓ.
a)  b) 

12. Complete each figure so that it has symmetry with respect to line m.

a) b)

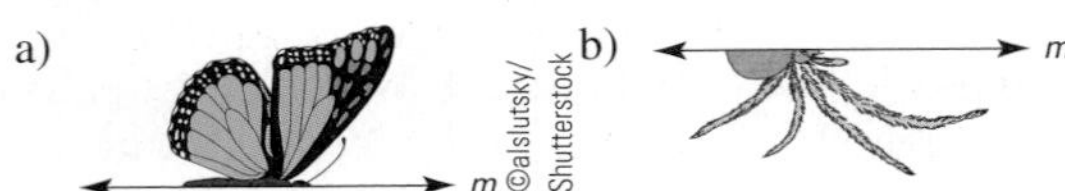

13. Complete each figure so that it reflects across line ℓ.

a) b)

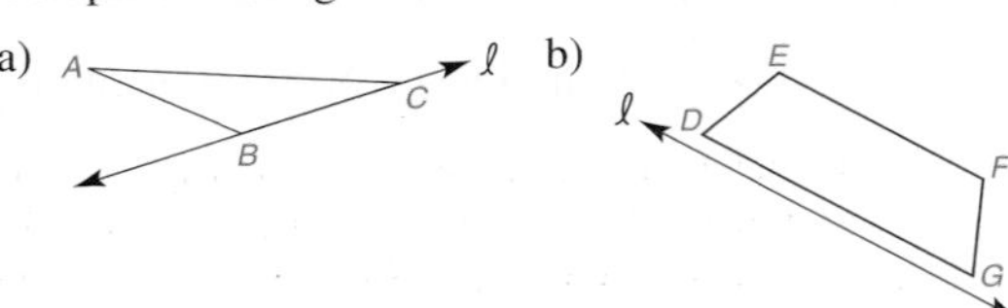

14. Complete each figure so that it reflects across line m.

a) b)

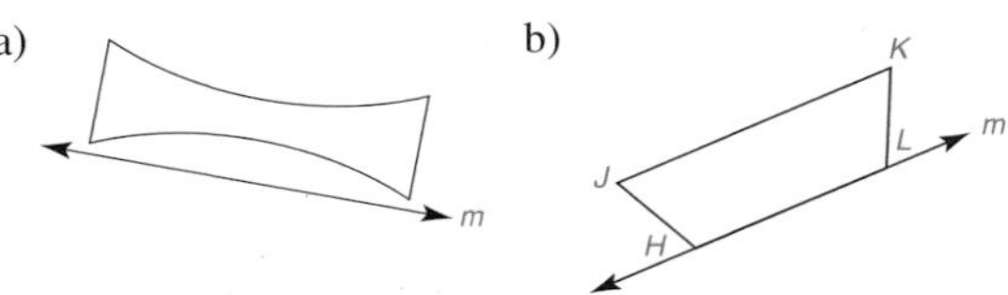

15. Suppose that $\triangle ABC$ slides to the right to the position of $\triangle DEF$.

a) If $m\angle A = 63°$, find $m\angle D$. b) Is $\overline{AC} \cong \overline{DF}$?
c) Is $\triangle ABC$ congruent to $\triangle DEF$?

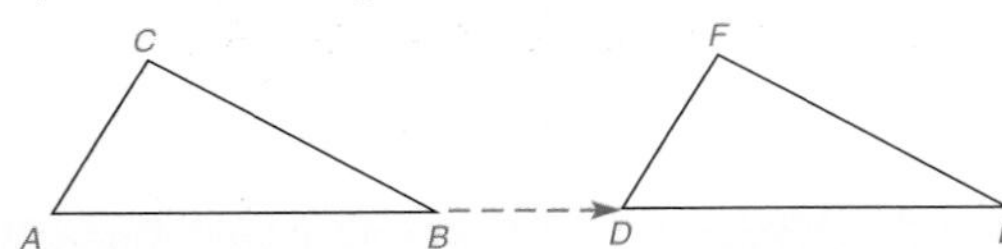

16. Suppose that square $RSTV$ slides point for point to form quadrilateral $WXYZ$.

a) Is $WXYZ$ a square? b) Is $RSTV \cong WXYZ$?
c) If $RS = 1.8\text{ cm}$, find WX.

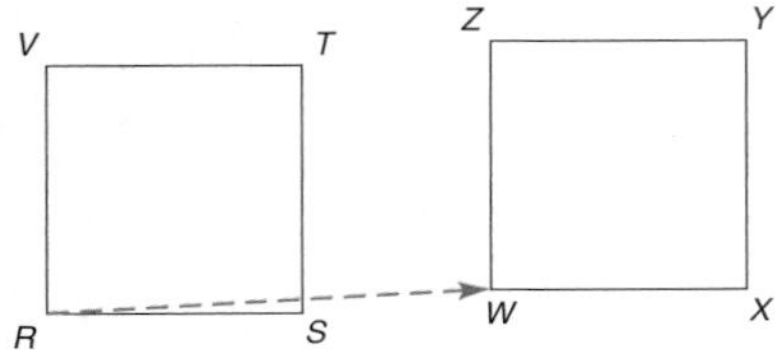

17. Given that the vertical line is a line of symmetry, complete each letter to discover the hidden word.

18. Given that the horizontal line is a line of symmetry, complete each letter to discover the hidden word.

19. Given that each letter has symmetry with respect to the indicated point, complete each letter to discover the hidden word.

SIX

20. What word is produced by a 180° rotation about the point?

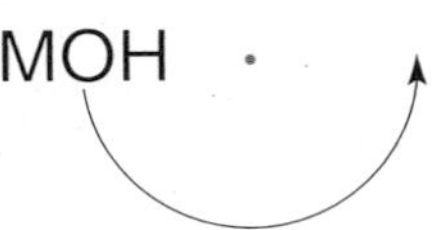

21. What word is produced by a 180° rotation about the point?

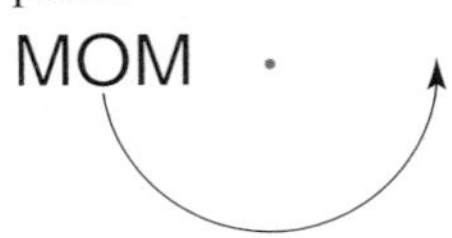

22. What word is produced by a 360° rotation about the point?

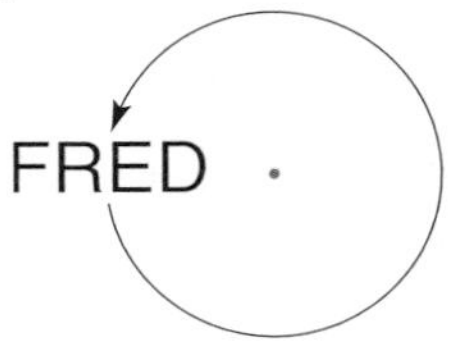

23. In which direction (clockwise or counterclockwise) will pulley 1 rotate if pulley 2 rotates in the clockwise direction?

a) b)

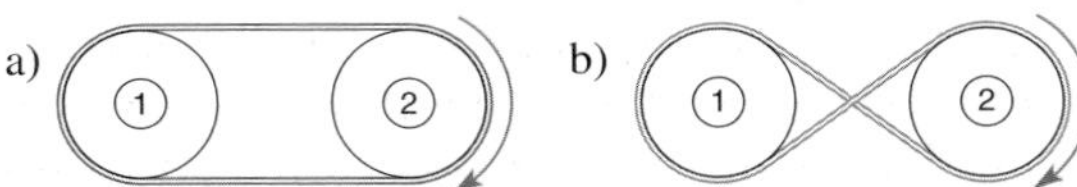

24. In which direction (clockwise or counterclockwise) will gear 1 rotate if gear 2 rotates in the clockwise direction?

a) b)

25. Considering that the consecutive dials on the electric meter rotate in opposite directions, what is the current reading in kilowatt hours of usage?

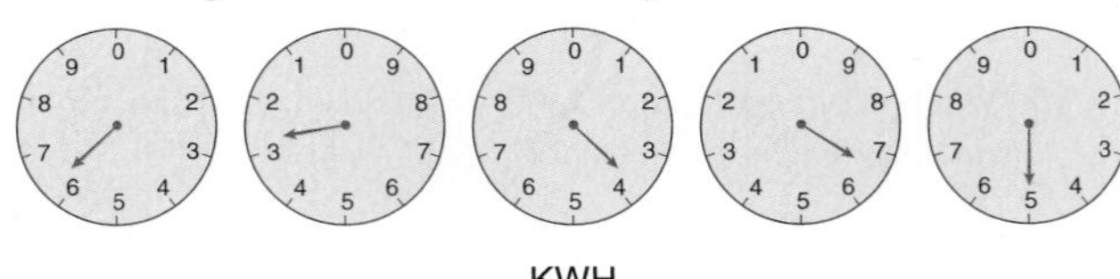

26. Considering that the consecutive dials on the natural gas meter rotate in opposite directions, what is the current reading in cubic feet of usage?

27. Describe the type(s) of symmetry displayed by each of these automobile logos.

a) Toyota

b) Mercury

c) Volkswagen

28. Describe the type(s) of symmetry displayed by each of these department store logos.

a) Kmart

b) Target

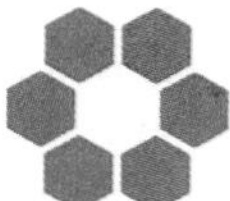
c) Bergner's

29. Given a figure, which of the following pairs of transformations leads to an image that repeats the original figure?

a) Figure slides 10 cm to the right *twice.*
b) Figure is reflected about a vertical line *twice.*
c) Figure is rotated clockwise about a point 180° *twice.*
d) Figure is rotated clockwise about a point 90° *twice.*

30. Given a figure, which of the following pairs of transformations leads to an image that repeats the original figure?

a) Figure slides 10 cm to the right, followed by slide of 10 cm to the left.
b) Figure is reflected about the same horizontal line *twice.*
c) Figure is rotated clockwise about a point 120° *twice.*
d) Figure is rotated clockwise about a point 360° *twice.*

31. A regular hexagon is rotated about a centrally located point (as shown). How many rotations are needed to repeat the given hexagon vertex for vertex if the angle of rotation is

a) 30°? b) 60°? c) 90°? d) 240°?

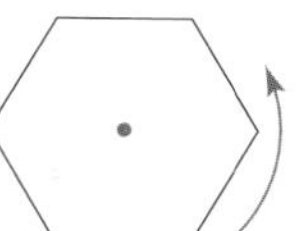

32. A regular octagon is rotated about a centrally located point (as shown). How many rotations are needed to repeat the given octagon vertex for vertex if the angle of rotation is

a) 10°? b) 45°? c) 90°? d) 120°?

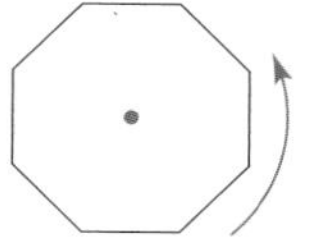

33. $\angle A'B'C'$ is the image of $\angle ABC$ following the reflection of $\angle ABC$ across line ℓ. If $m\angle A'B'C' = \frac{x}{5} + 20$ and $m\angle ABC = \frac{x}{2} + 5$, find x.

34. $\angle X'YZ'$ is the image of $\angle XYZ$ following a 100° counterclockwise rotation of $\angle XYZ$ about point Y. If $m\angle XYZ = \frac{5x}{6}$ and $m\angle X'YZ' = 130°$, find x.

PERSPECTIVE ON HISTORY

Sketch of Euclid

Names often associated with the early development of Greek mathematics, beginning in approximately 600 B.C., include Thales, Pythagoras, Archimedes, Appolonius, Diophantus, Eratosthenes, and Heron. However, the name most often associated with traditional geometry is that of Euclid, who lived around 300 B.C.

Euclid, himself a Greek, was asked to head the mathematics department at the University of Alexandria (in Egypt), which was the center of Greek learning. It is believed that Euclid told Ptolemy (the local ruler) that "There is no royal road to geometry," in response to Ptolemy's request for a quick and easy knowledge of the subject.

Euclid's best-known work is the *Elements,* a systematic treatment of geometry with some algebra and number theory. That work, which consists of 13 volumes, has dominated the study of geometry for more than 2000 years. Most secondary-level geometry courses, even today, are based on Euclid's *Elements* and in particular on these volumes:

Book I: Triangles and congruence, parallels, quadrilaterals, the Pythagorean theorem, and area relationships

Book III: Circles, chords, secants, tangents, and angle measurement

Book IV: Constructions and regular polygons

Book VI: Similar triangles, proportions, and the Angle Bisector theorem

Book XI: Lines and planes in space, and parallelepipeds

One of Euclid's theorems was a forerunner of the theorem of trigonometry known as the Law of Cosines. Although it is difficult to understand now, it will make sense to you later. As stated by Euclid, "In an obtuse-angled triangle, the square of the side opposite the obtuse angle equals the sum of the squares of the other two sides and the product of one side and the projection of the other upon it."

While it is believed that Euclid was a great teacher, he is also recognized as a great mathematician and as the first author of an elaborate textbook. In Chapter 2 of *this* textbook, Euclid's Parallel Postulate has been central to our study of plane geometry.

PERSPECTIVE ON APPLICATION

Non-Euclidean Geometries

The geometry we present in this book is often described as Euclidean geometry. A non-Euclidean geometry is a geometry characterized by the existence of at least one contradiction of a Euclidean geometry postulate. To appreciate this subject, you need to realize the importance of the word *plane* in the Parallel Postulate. Thus, the Parallel Postulate is now restated.

> PARALLEL POSTULATE
>
> *In a plane,* through a point not on a line, exactly one line is parallel to the given line.

The Parallel Postulate characterizes a course in plane geometry; it corresponds to the theory that "the earth is flat." On a small scale (most applications aren't global), the theory works well and serves the needs of carpenters, designers, and most engineers.

To begin the move to a different geometry, consider the surface of a **sphere** (like the earth). See Figure 2.53. By definition, a sphere is the set of all points in space that are at a fixed distance from a given point. If a line segment on the surface of the sphere is extended to form a line, it becomes a great circle (like the equator of the earth). Each line in this geometry, known as *spherical geometry,* is the intersection of a plane containing the center of the sphere with the sphere.

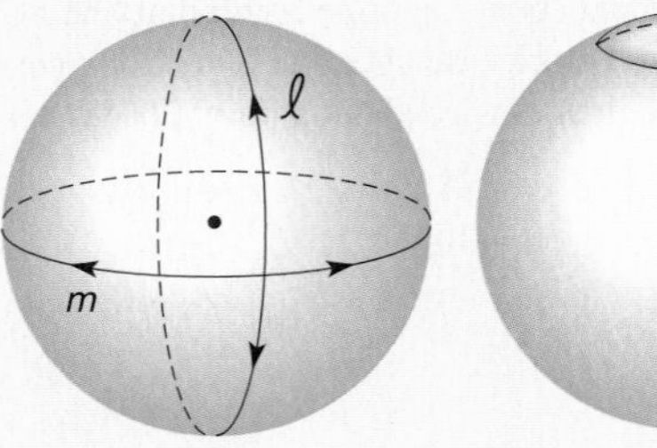

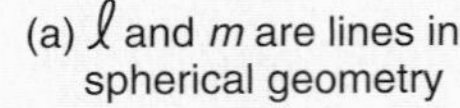
(a) ℓ and *m* are lines in spherical geometry

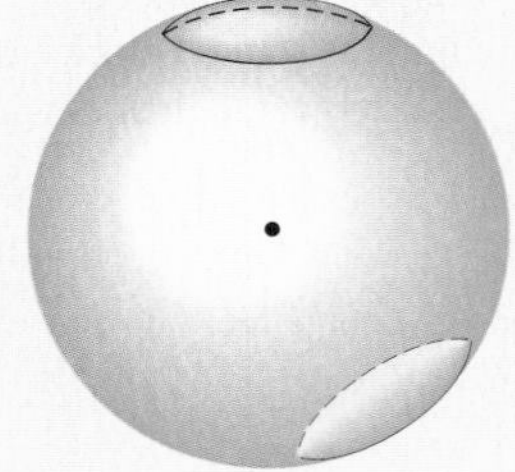
(b) These circles are *not* lines in spherical geometry

Figure 2.53

Spherical geometry (or elliptic geometry) is actually a model of Riemannian geometry, named in honor of Georg F. B. Riemann (1826–1866), the German mathematician responsible for the next postulate. The Reimannian Postulate is not numbered in this book, because it does not characterize Euclidean geometry.

> RIEMANNIAN POSTULATE
>
> Through a point not on a line, there are no lines parallel to the given line.

To understand the Reimannian Postulate, consider a sphere (Figure 2.54) containing line ℓ and point P not on ℓ. Any line drawn through point P must intersect ℓ in two points. To see this develop, follow the frames in Figure 2.55, which depict an attempt to draw a line parallel to ℓ through point P.

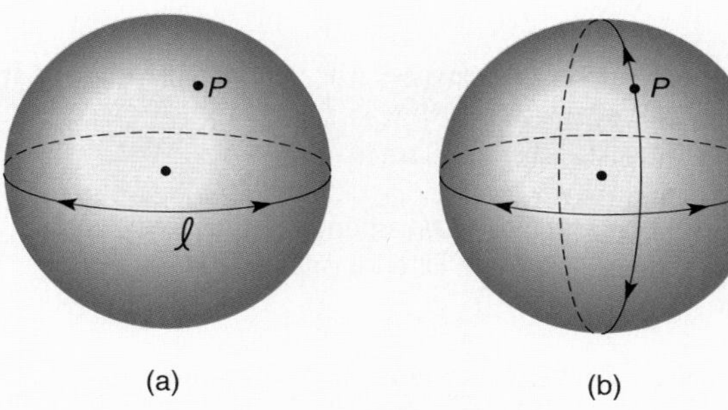

Figure 2.54

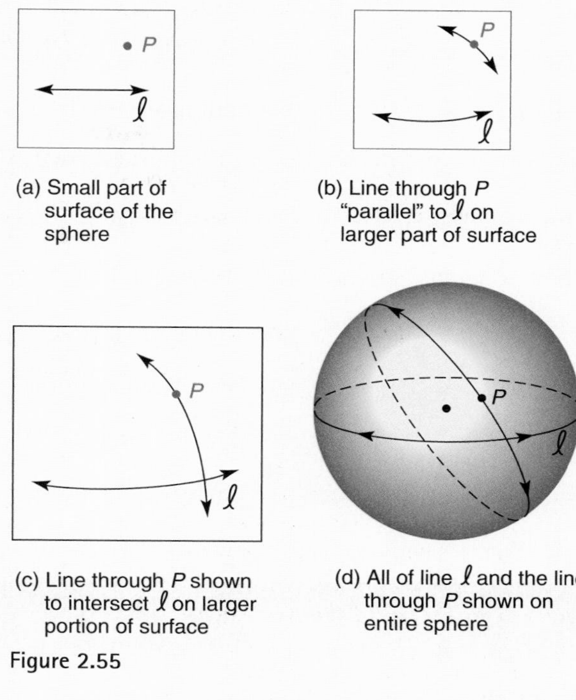

Figure 2.55

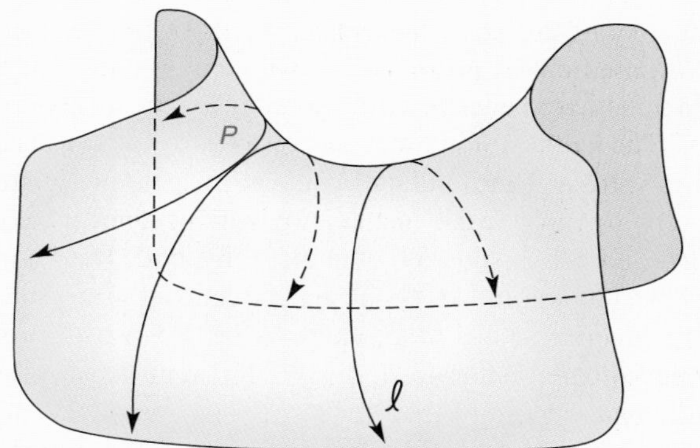

Figure 2.56

Consider the natural extension to Riemannian geometry of the claim that the shortest distance between two points is a straight line. For the sake of efficiency and common sense, a person traveling from New York City to London will follow the path of a line as it is known in spherical geometry. As you might guess, this concept is used to chart international flights between cities. In Euclidean geometry, the claim suggests that a person tunnel under the earth's surface from one city to the other.

A second type of non-Euclidean geometry is attributed to the works of a German, Karl F. Gauss (1777–1855), a Russian, Nikolai Lobachevski (1793–1856), and a Hungarian, Johann Bolyai (1802–1862). The postulate for this system of non-Euclidean geometry is as follows:

> LOBACHEVSKIAN POSTULATE
>
> Through a point not on line, there are infinitely many lines parallel to the given line.

This form of non-Euclidean geometry is termed *hyperbolic geometry.* Rather than using the plane or sphere as the surface for study, mathematicians use a saddle-like surface known as a **hyperbolic paraboloid.** (See Figure 2.56.) A line ℓ is the intersection of a plane with this surface. Clearly, more than one plane can intersect this surface to form a line containing P that does not intersect ℓ. In fact, an infinite number of planes intersect the surface in an infinite number of lines parallel to ℓ and containing P. Table 2.5 compares the three types of geometry.

TABLE 2.5
Comparison of Types of Geometry

Postulate	Model	Line	Number of Lines Through P Parallel to ℓ
Parallel (Euclidean)	Plane geometry	Intersection of two planes	One
Riemannian	Spherical geometry	Intersection of plane with sphere (plane contains center of sphere)	None
Lobachevskian	Hyperbolic geometry	Intersection of plane with hyperbolic paraboloid	Infinitely many

Summary

A LOOK BACK AT CHAPTER 2

One goal of this chapter has been to prove several theorems based on the postulate "If two parallel lines are cut by a transversal, then the corresponding angles are congruent." The method of indirect proof was introduced as a basis for proving lines parallel if the corresponding angles are congruent. Several methods of proving lines parallel were then demonstrated by the direct method. The Parallel Postulate was used to prove that the sum of the measures of the interior angles of a triangle is 180°. Several corollaries followed naturally from this theorem. A sum formula was then developed for the interior angles of any polygon. The chapter closed with a discussion of symmetry and transformations.

A LOOK AHEAD TO CHAPTER 3

In the next chapter, the concept of congruence will be extended to triangles, and several methods of proving triangles congruent will be developed. Several theorems dealing with the inequalities of a triangle will also be proved. The Pythagorean Theorem will be introduced.

KEY CONCEPTS

2.1
Perpendicular Lines • Perpendicular Planes • Parallel Lines • Parallel Planes • Parallel Postulate • Transversal • Interior Angles • Exterior Angles • Corresponding Angles • Alternate Interior Angles • Alternate Exterior Angles

2.2
Conditional • Converse • Inverse • Contrapositive • Law of Negative Inference • Indirect Proof

2.3
Proving Lines Parallel

2.4
Triangle • Vertices • Sides of a Triangle • Interior and Exterior of a Triangle • Scalene Triangle • Isosceles Triangle • Equilateral Triangle • Acute Triangle • Obtuse Triangle • Right Triangle • Equiangular Triangle • Auxiliary Line • Determined • Underdetermined • Overdetermined • Corollary • Exterior Angle of a Triangle

2.5
Convex Polygons (Triangle, Quadrilateral, Pentagon, Hexagon, Heptagon, Octagon, Nonagon, Decagon) • Concave Polygon • Diagonals of a Polygon • Regular Polygon • Equilateral Polygon • Equiangular Polygon • Polygram

2.6
Symmetry • Line of Symmetry • Axis of Symmetry • Point Symmetry • Transformations • Slides • Translations • Reflections • Rotations

TABLE 2.6 An Overview of Chapter 2

▶ Parallel Lines and Transversal

FIGURE	RELATIONSHIP	SYMBOLS
	$\ell \parallel m$	Corresponding ∠s ≅; ∠1 ≅ ∠5, ∠2 ≅ ∠6, etc. Alternate interior ∠s ≅; ∠3 ≅ ∠6 and ∠4 ≅ ∠5 Alternate exterior ∠s ≅; ∠1 ≅ ∠8 and ∠2 ≅ ∠7 Supplementary ∠s; m∠3 + m∠5 = 180°; m∠1 + m∠7 = 180°, etc.

▶ Triangles Classified by Sides

FIGURE	TYPE	NUMBER OF CONGRUENT SIDES
	Scalene	None
	Isosceles	Two
	Equilateral	Three

▶ Triangles Classified by Angles

FIGURE	TYPE	ANGLE(S)
	Acute	Three acute angles
	Right	One right angle
	Obtuse	One obtuse angle

continued

TABLE 2.6 *(continued)*

▶ Triangles Classified by Angles		
FIGURE	TYPE	ANGLE(S)
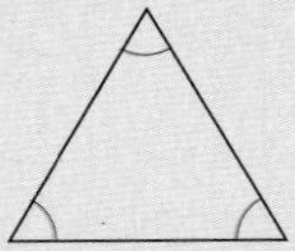	Equiangular	Three congruent angles

▶ Polygons: Sum S of All Interior Angles		
FIGURE	TYPE OF POLYGON	SUM OF INTERIOR ANGLES
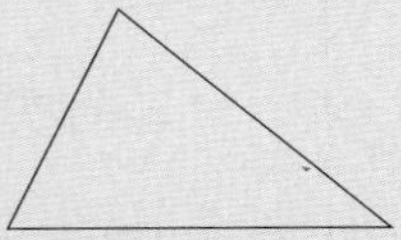	Triangle	$S = 180°$
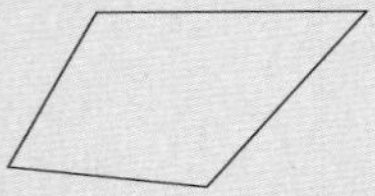	Quadrilateral	$S = 360°$
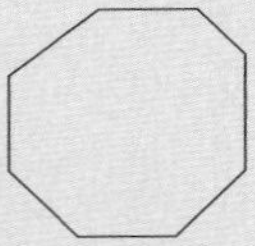	Polygon with n sides	$S = (n - 2) \cdot 180°$

▶ Polygons: Sum S of All Exterior Angles; D is the Total Number of Diagonals		
FIGURE	TYPE OF POLYGON	RELATIONSHIPS
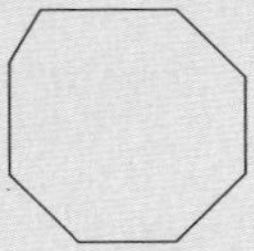	Polygon with n sides	$S = 360°$ $D = \frac{n(n-3)}{2}$

▶ Symmetry		
FIGURE	TYPE OF SYMMETRY	FIGURE REDRAWN TO DISPLAY SYMMETRY
Z	Point	 Z
D	Line	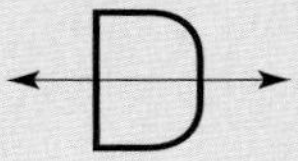 D

▶▶▶ Chapter 2 REVIEW EXERCISES

1. If m∠1 = m∠2, which lines are parallel?

(a)

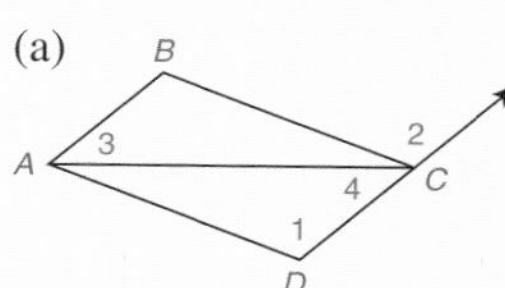

(b)

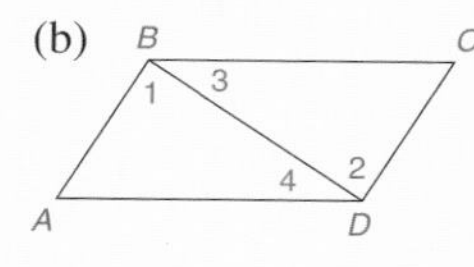

2. *Given:* m∠13 = 70°
Find: m∠3

3. *Given:* m∠9 = 2x + 17
m∠11 = 5x − 94
Find: x

4. *Given:* m∠B = 75°,
m∠DCE = 50°
Find: m∠D and m∠DEF

5. *Given:* m∠DCA = 130°
m∠BAC = 2x + y
m∠BCE = 150°
m∠DEC = 2x − y
Find: x and y

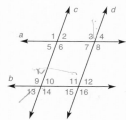

Exercises 2, 3

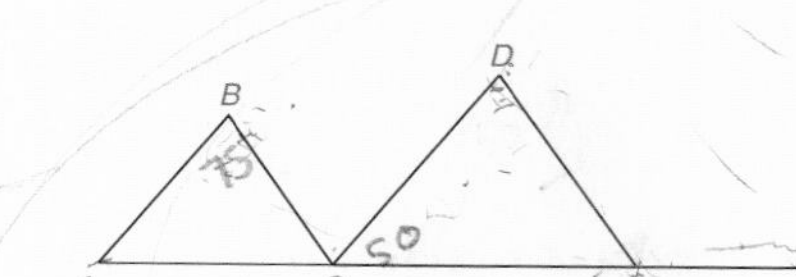

Exercises 4, 5

6. *Given:* In the drawing, $\overline{AB} \parallel \overline{CD}$ and $\overline{BC} \parallel \overline{DE}$,
$\overline{AC} \parallel \overline{DF}$
$\overline{AE} \parallel \overline{BF}$
m∠AEF = 3y
m∠BFE = x + 45
m∠FBC = 2x + 15
Find: x and y

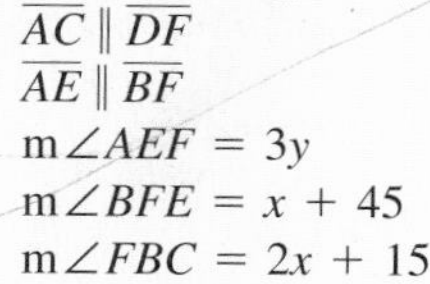

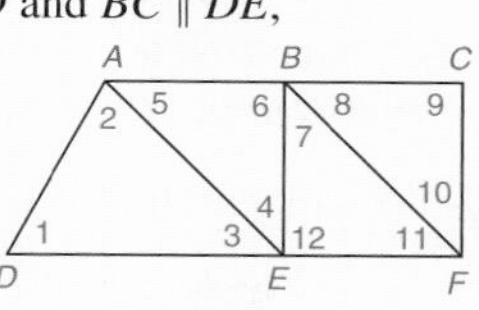

Exercises 6–11

For Review Exercises 7 to 11, use the given information to name the segments that must be parallel. If there are no such segments, write "none." Assume A-B-C and D-E-F. (Use the drawing from Exercise 6.)

7. ∠3 ≅ ∠11
8. ∠4 ≅ ∠5
9. ∠7 ≅ ∠10
10. ∠6 ≅ ∠9
11. ∠8 ≅ ∠5 ≅ ∠3

For Review Exercises 12 to 15, find the values of x and y.

12.

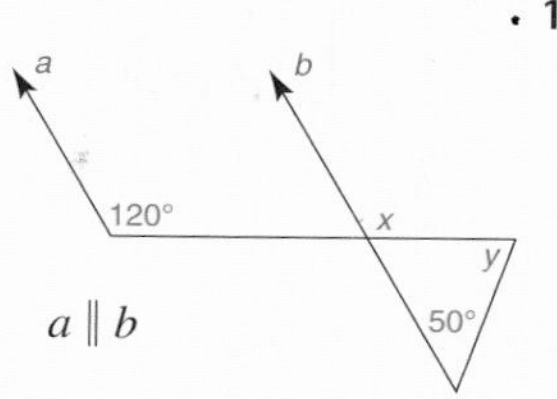

a ∥ b

13.

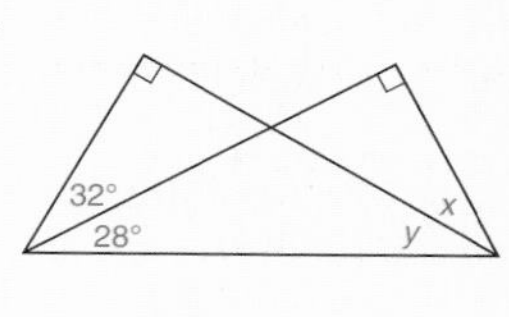

14.

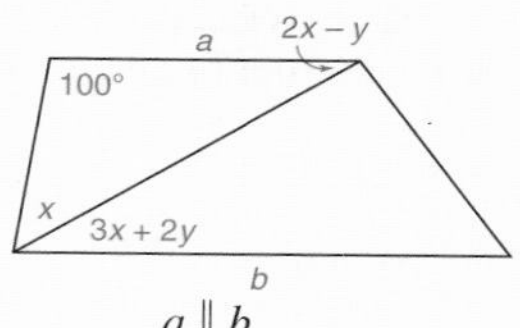

a ∥ b

15.

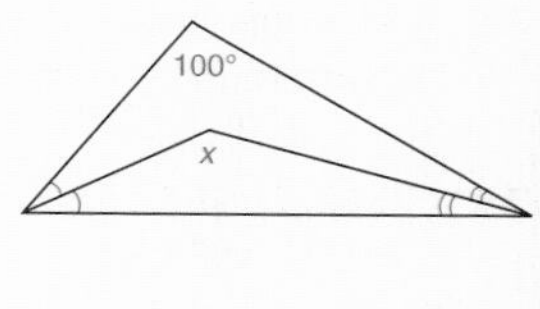

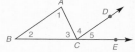

16. *Given:* m∠1 = $x^2 - 12$
m∠4 = $x(x - 2)$
Find: x so that $\overline{AB} \parallel \overrightarrow{CD}$

17. *Given:* $\overline{AB} \parallel \overrightarrow{CD}$
m∠2 = $x^2 - 3x + 4$
m∠1 = $17x - x^2 - 5$
m∠ACE = 111°
Find: m∠3, m∠4, and m∠5

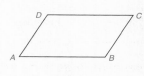

Exercises 16, 17

18. *Given:* $\overline{DC} \parallel \overline{AB}$
∠A ≅ ∠C
m∠A = 3x + y
m∠D = 5x + 10
m∠C = 5y + 20
Find: m∠B

For Review Exercises 19 to 24, decide whether the statements are always true (A), sometimes true (S), or never true (N).

19. An isosceles triangle is a right triangle.
20. An equilateral triangle is a right triangle.
21. A scalene triangle is an isosceles triangle.
22. An obtuse triangle is an isosceles triangle.
23. A right triangle has two congruent angles.
24. A right triangle has two complementary angles.
25. Complete the following table for regular polygons.

Number of sides	8	12	20				
Measure of each exterior ∠				24	36		
Measure of each interior ∠						157.5	178
Number of diagonals							

For Review Exercises 26 to 29, sketch, if possible, the polygon described.

26. A quadrilateral that is equiangular but not equilateral

27. A quadrilateral that is equilateral but not equiangular

28. A triangle that is equilateral but not equiangular

29. A hexagon that is equilateral but not equiangular

For Review Exercises 30 and 31, write the converse, inverse, and contrapositive of each statement.

30. If two angles are right angles, then the angles are congruent.

31. If it is not raining, then I am happy.

32. Which statement—the converse, the inverse, or the contrapositive—always has the same truth or falsity as a given implication?

33. *Given:* $\overline{AB} \parallel \overline{CF}$
$\angle 2 \cong \angle 3$
Prove: $\angle 1 \cong \angle 3$

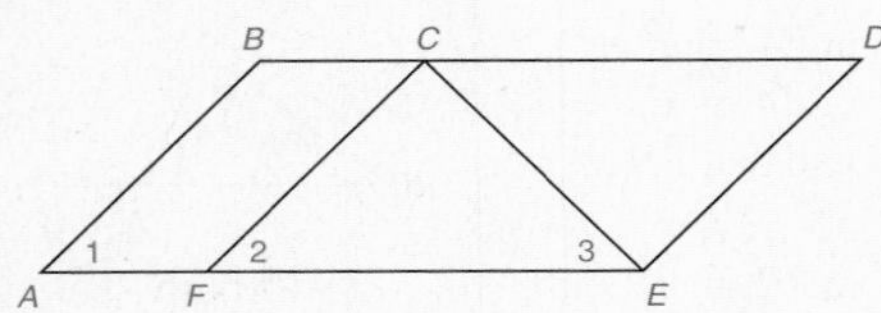

34. *Given:* $\angle 1$ is complementary to $\angle 2$; $\angle 2$ is complementary to $\angle 3$
Prove: $\overline{BD} \parallel \overline{AE}$

35. *Given:* $\overline{BE} \perp \overline{DA}$
$\overline{CD} \perp \overline{DA}$
Prove: $\angle 1 \cong \angle 2$

36. *Given:* $\angle A \cong \angle C$
$\overline{DC} \parallel \overrightarrow{AB}$
Prove: $\overline{DA} \parallel \overline{CB}$

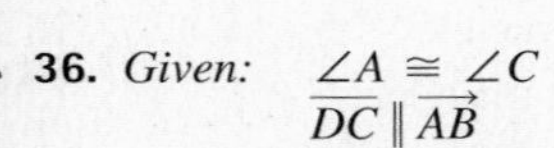

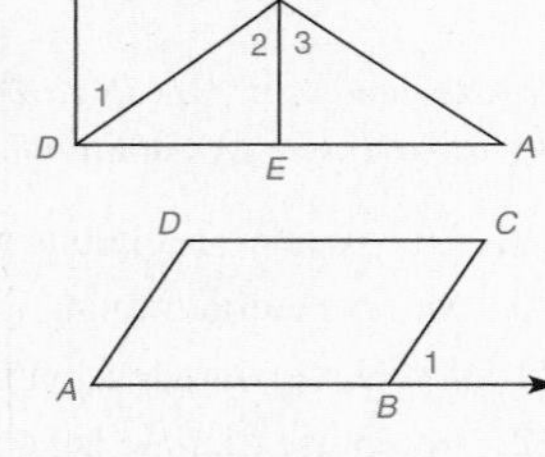

For Review Exercises 37 and 38, give the first statement for an indirect proof.

37. If $x^2 + 7x + 12 \neq 0$, then $x \neq -3$.

38. If two angles of a triangle are not congruent, then the sides opposite those angles are not congruent.

39. *Given:* $m \nparallel n$
Prove: $\angle 1 \not\cong \angle 2$

40. *Given:* $\angle 1 \not\cong \angle 3$
Prove: $m \nparallel n$

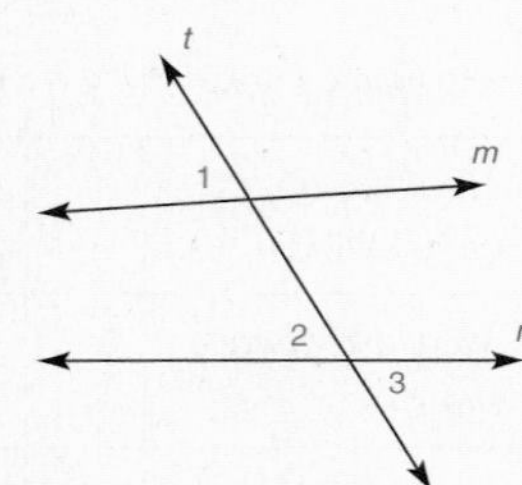

Exercises 39, 40

41. Construct the line through C parallel to $\overline{AB}$.

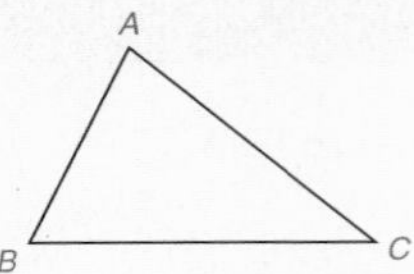

42. Construct an equilateral triangle ABC with side $\overline{AB}$.

43. Which block letters have

a) line symmetry (at least one axis)?
b) point symmetry?

B H J S W

44. Which figures have

a) line symmetry (at least one axis)?
b) point symmetry?

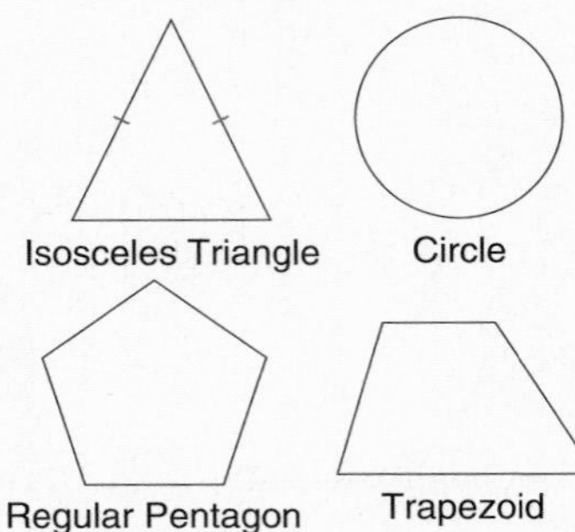

45. When $\triangle ABC$ slides to its image $\triangle DEF$, how are $\triangle ABC$ and $\triangle DEF$ related?

46. Complete the drawing so that the figure is reflected across

a) line ℓ. b) line m.

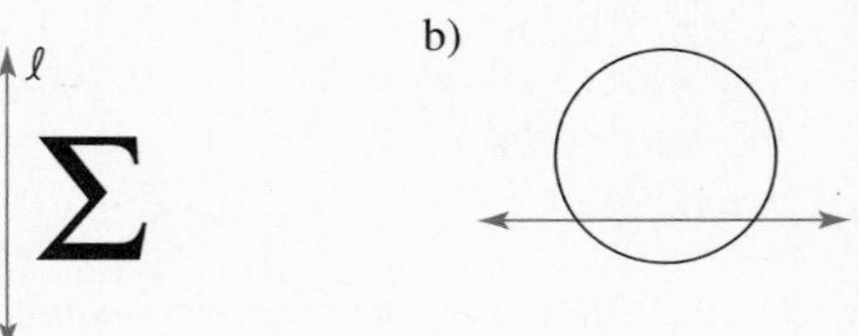

47. Through what approximate angle of rotation must a baseball pitcher turn when throwing to first base rather than home plate?

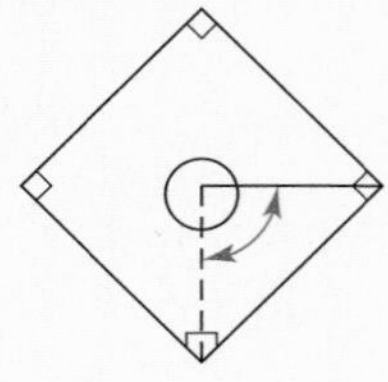

Chapter 2 TEST

1. Consider the figure shown at the right.
   a) Name the angle that corresponds to $\angle 1$.
   ____
   b) Name the alternate interior angle for $\angle 6$.
   ____

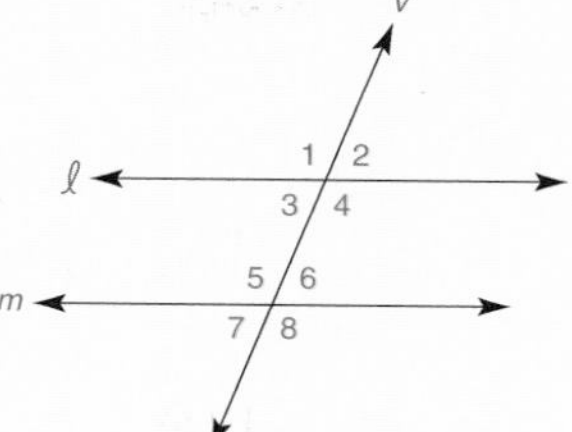

2. In the accompanying figure, $m\angle 2 = 68°$, $m\angle 8 = 112°$, and $m\angle 9 = 110°$.
   a) Which lines (r and s OR ℓ and m) must be parallel? ________
   b) Which pair of lines (r and s OR ℓ and m) cannot be parallel?
   ____

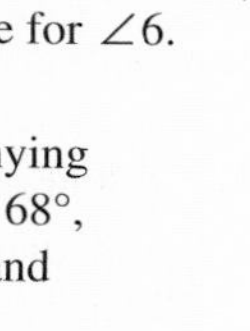

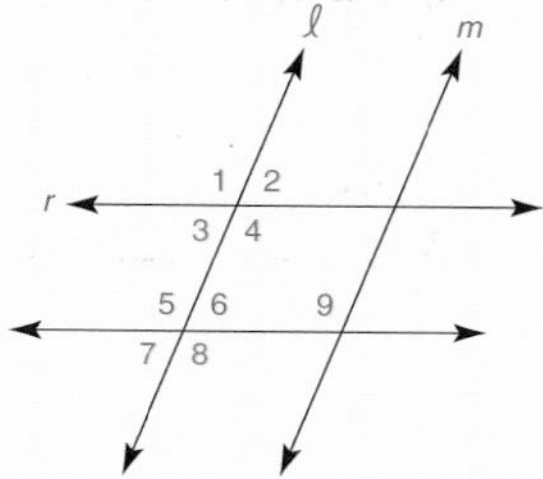

3. To prove a theorem of the form "If P, then Q" by the indirect method, the first line of the proof should read:
   Suppose that ________ is true.
4. Assuming that statements 1 and 2 are true, draw a valid conclusion if possible.
   1. If two angles are both right angles, then the angles are congruent.
   2. $\angle R$ and $\angle S$ are not congruent.

   C. ∴? ∠R and ∠S are not rt. angles
5. Let all of the lines named be coplanar. Make a drawing to reach a conclusion.
   a) If $r \parallel s$ and $s \parallel t$, then ________.
   b) If $a \perp b$ and $b \perp c$, then ________.
6. Through point A, construct the line that is perpendicular to line ℓ.

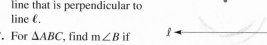

A

ℓ

7. For $\triangle ABC$, find $m\angle B$ if
   a) $m\angle A = 65°$ and $m\angle C = 79°$.

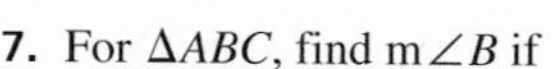

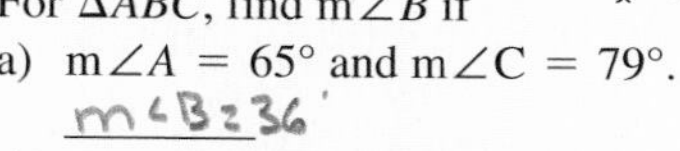

   b) $m\angle A = 2x$, $m\angle B = x$, and $m\angle C = 2x + 15$. ________

C
2x+15
2x
x
A
B

8. a) What word describes a polygon with five sides? ________
   b) How many diagonals does a polygon with five sides have? ________
9. a) Given that the polygon shown has six congruent angles, this polygon is known as a(n) ________ ________.
   b) What is the measure of each of the congruent interior angles? ________

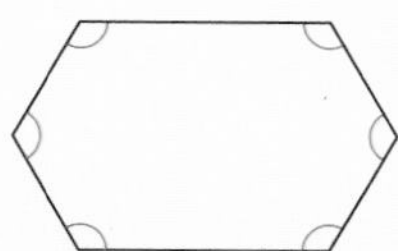

10. Consider the block letters A, D, N, O, and X.
    Which type of symmetry (line symmetry, point symmetry, both types, or neither type) is illustrated by each letter?
    A ________ D ________
    N ________ O ________
    X ________
11. Which type of transformation (slide, reflection, or rotation) is illustrated?
    a) ________ b) ________ c) ________

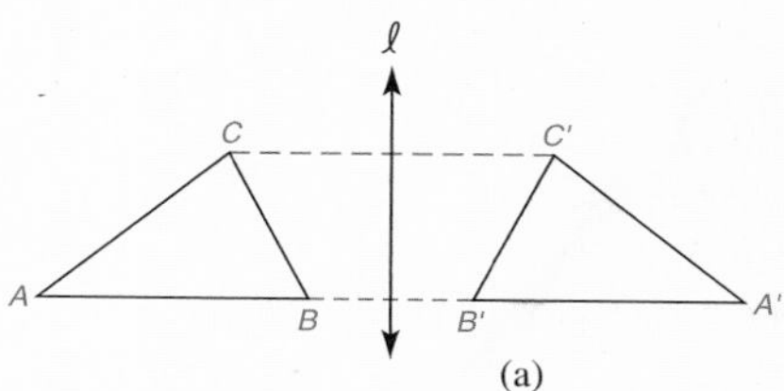

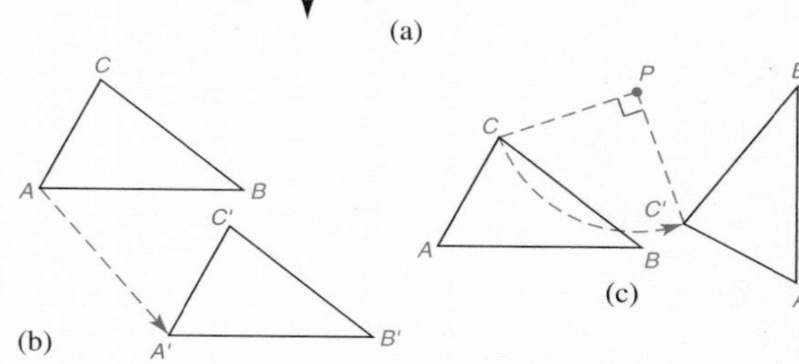

12. In the figure shown, suppose that $\overline{AB} \parallel \overline{DC}$ and $\overline{AD} \parallel \overline{BC}$. If $m\angle 1 = 82°$ and $m\angle 4 = 37°$, find $m\angle C$. ________

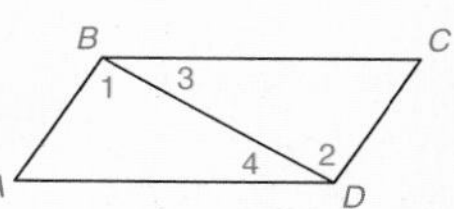

Exercises 12, 13

13. If $m\angle 1 = x + 28$ and $m\angle 2 = 2x - 26$, find the value x for which it follows that $\overline{AB} \parallel \overline{DC}$. ________
14. In the figure shown, suppose that ray CD bisects exterior angle $\angle ACE$ of $\triangle ABC$. If $m\angle 1 = 70°$ and $m\angle 2 = 30°$, find $m\angle 4$.
    ____

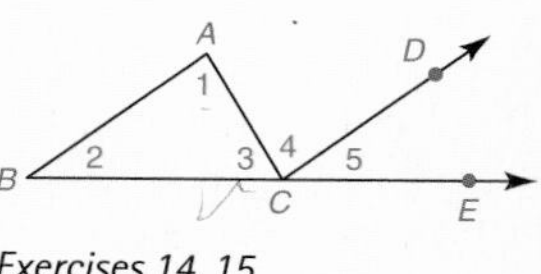

Exercises 14, 15

15. In the figure shown, $\angle ACE$ is an exterior angle of $\triangle ABC$. If $\overline{CD} \parallel \overline{BA}$, $m\angle 1 = 2(m\angle 2)$, and $m\angle ACE = 117°$, find the measure of $\angle 1$. ________

In Exercises 16 and 18, complete the missing statements or reasons for each proof.

16. *Given:* $\angle 1 \cong \angle 2$
    $\angle 3 \cong \angle 4$
    Prove: $\ell \parallel n$

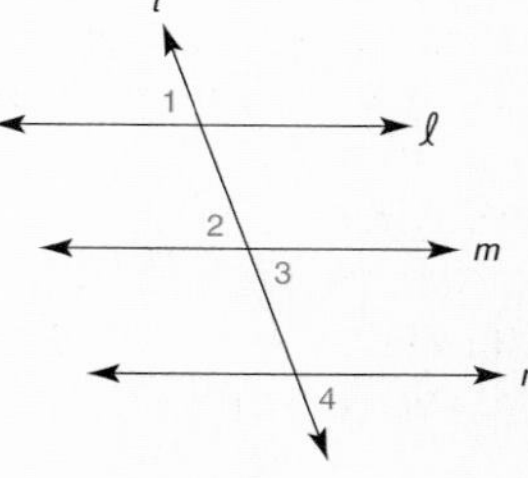

PROOF

Statements	Reasons
1. $\angle 1 \cong \angle 2$ and $\angle 3 \cong \angle 4$	1. Given
2. $\angle 1 \cong \angle 2$	2. If two lines intersect, the vertical $\angle$s are $\cong$
3. $\angle 1 \cong 4$	3. alt. ext $\angle$'s
4. $\angle 3 \cong \angle 4$	4. If two lines are cut by a transversal so that alternate exterior $\angle$s are $\cong$, the lines are $\parallel$

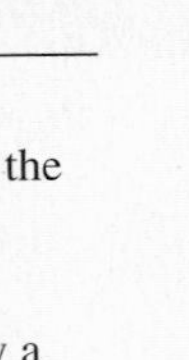

17. Use an indirect proof to complete the following proof.

Given: $\triangle MNQ$ with $m\angle N = 120°$

Prove: $\angle M$ and $\angle Q$ are not complementary

18. *Given:* In $\triangle ABC$, $m\angle C = 90°$

Prove: $\angle 1$ and $\angle 2$ are complementary

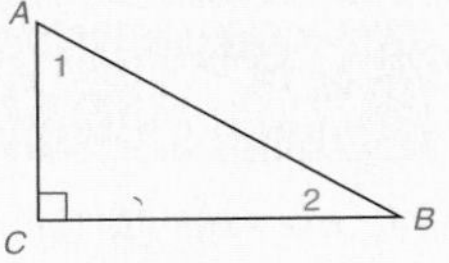

PROOF

Statements	Reasons
1. $\triangle ABC$, $m\angle C = 90°$	1. ________
2. $m\angle 1 + m\angle 2 + m\angle C =$ 180	2. The sum of $\angle$s of a $\triangle$ is 180°
3. m∠1 + m∠2 = 18	3. Substitution Prop. of Equality
4. $m\angle 1 + m\angle 2 =$ 90	4. Subtraction Prop. of Equality
5. ∠1 and ∠2 com	5. Def com

19. In $\triangle XYZ$, $\angle XYZ$ is trisected as indicated. With angle measures as shown, find $m\angle Z$. ________

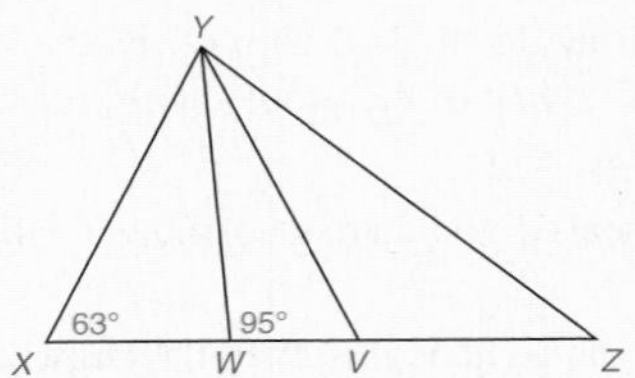

Chapter 3

Triangles

© IMAGEMORE Co, Ltd./Getty Images

CHAPTER OUTLINE

Additional Video explanation of concepts, sample problems, and applications are available on DVD. 

Majestic! In Statue Square of Hong Kong, the Bank of China (the structure shown at the left in the photograph above) rises 1209 feet above the square. Designed by I. M. Pei (who studied at the Massachusetts Institute of Technology and also graduated from the Harvard Graduate School of Design), the Bank of China displays many triangles of the same shape and size. Such triangles, known as congruent triangles, are also displayed in the Ferris wheel found in Exercise 41 of Section 3.3. While Chapter 3 is devoted to the study of triangle types and their characteristics, the properties of triangles developed herein also provide a much needed framework for the study of quadrilaterals found in Chapter 4.

3.1 Congruent Triangles

KEY CONCEPTS

Congruent Triangles
SSS
SAS
ASA
AAS
Included Side
Included Angle
Reflexive Property of Congruence (Identity)
Symmetric and Transitive Properties of Congruence

Two triangles are **congruent** if one coincides with (fits perfectly over) the other. In Figure 3.1, we say that $\triangle ABC \cong \triangle DEF$ if these congruences hold:

$$\angle A \cong \angle D,\ \angle B \cong \angle E,\ \angle C \cong \angle F,\ \overline{AB} \cong \overline{DE},\ \overline{BC} \cong \overline{EF},\text{ and } \overline{AC} \cong \overline{DF}$$

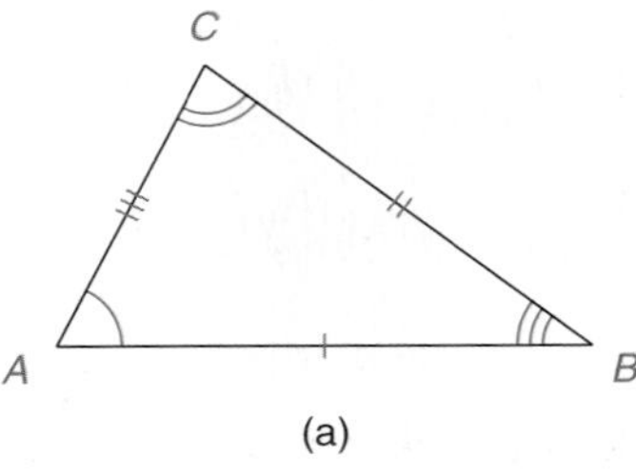

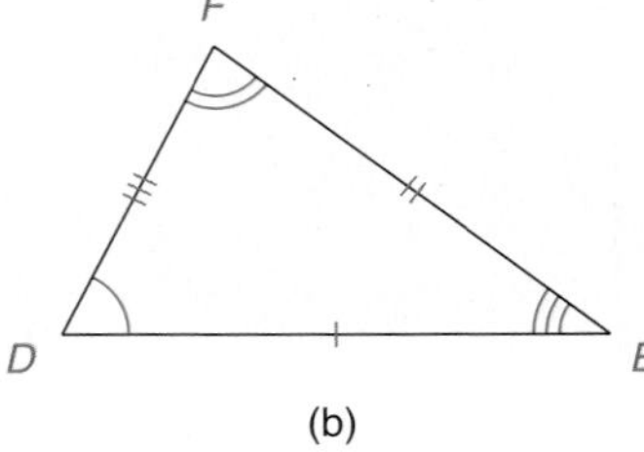

Figure 3.1

From the indicated congruences, we also say that vertex A corresponds to vertex D, as does B to E and C to F. In symbols, the correspondences are represented by

$$A \leftrightarrow D, \quad B \leftrightarrow E, \quad \text{and} \quad C \leftrightarrow F.$$

In Section 2.6, we used a slide transformation on $\triangle ABC$ to form its image $\triangle DEF$. The claim $\triangle MNQ \cong \triangle RST$ orders corresponding vertices of the triangles (not shown), so we can conclude from this statement that

$$M \leftrightarrow R, \quad N \leftrightarrow S, \quad \text{and} \quad Q \leftrightarrow T$$

This correspondence of vertices implies the congruence of corresponding parts such as $\angle M \cong \angle R$ and $\overline{NQ} \cong \overline{ST}$.

Conversely, if the correspondence of vertices of two congruent triangles is $M \leftrightarrow R$, $N \leftrightarrow S$, and $Q \leftrightarrow T$, we order vertices to make the claims $\triangle MNQ \cong \triangle RST$, $\triangle NQM \cong \triangle STR$, and so on.

EXAMPLE 1

For two congruent triangles, the correspondence of vertices is given by $A \leftrightarrow D$, $B \leftrightarrow E$, and $C \leftrightarrow F$. Complete each statement:

a) $\triangle BCA \cong ?$ b) $\triangle DEF \cong ?$

Solution With due attention to the order of corresponding vertices, we have

a) $\triangle BCA \cong \triangle EFD$ b) $\triangle DEF \cong \triangle ABC$ ■

DEFINITION

Two triangles are **congruent** if the six parts of the first triangle are congruent to the six corresponding parts of the second triangle.

Discover

Holding two sheets of construction paper together, use scissors to cut out two triangles. How do the triangles compare?

ANSWER

The triangles are congruent.

As always, any definition is reversible! If two triangles are known to be congruent, we may conclude that the corresponding parts are congruent. Moreover, if the six pairs of parts are known to be congruent, then so are the triangles! From the congruent parts indicated in Figure 3.2, we can conclude that $\triangle MNQ \cong \triangle RST$. Using the terminology introduced in Section 2.6 and Figure 3.2, $\triangle TSR$ is the reflection of $\triangle QNM$ across a vertical line (not shown) that lies midway between the two triangles.

Following Figure 3.2 are some of the properties of congruent triangles that are useful in later proofs and explanations.

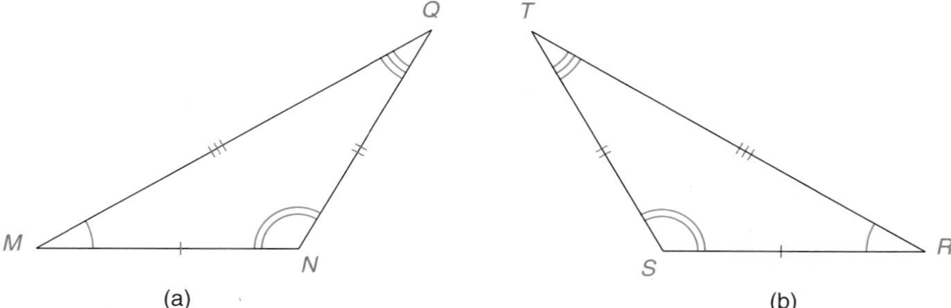

Figure 3.2

1. $\triangle ABC \cong \triangle ABC$ (Reflexive Property of Congruence)
2. If $\triangle ABC \cong \triangle DEF$, then $\triangle DEF \cong \triangle ABC$. (Symmetric Property of Congruence)
3. If $\triangle ABC \cong \triangle DEF$ and $\triangle DEF \cong \triangle GHI$, then $\triangle ABC \cong \triangle GHI$. (Transitive Property of Congruence)

SSG *Exs. 1, 2*

On the basis of the properties above, we see that the "congruence of triangles" is an equivalence relation.

It would be difficult to establish that triangles were congruent if six pairs of congruent parts had to first be verified. Fortunately, it is possible to prove triangles congruent by establishing fewer than six pairs of congruences. To suggest a first method, consider the construction in Example 2.

EXAMPLE 2

Construct a triangle whose sides have the lengths of the segments provided in Figure 3.3(a).

Solution Figure 3.3(b): Choose $\overline{AB}$ as the first side of the triangle (the choice of $\overline{AB}$ is arbitrary) and mark its length as shown.

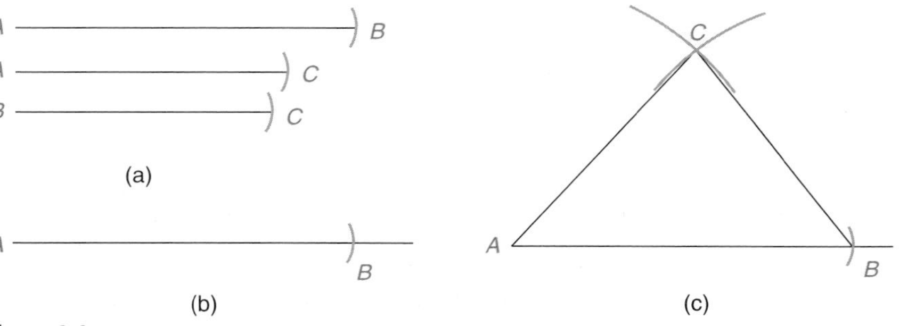

Figure 3.3

Figure 3.3(c): Using the left endpoint A, mark off an arc of length equal to that of $\overline{AC}$. Now mark off an arc the length of $\overline{BC}$ from the right endpoint B so that these arcs intersect at C, the third vertex of the triangle. Joining point C to A and then to B completes the desired triangle. ■

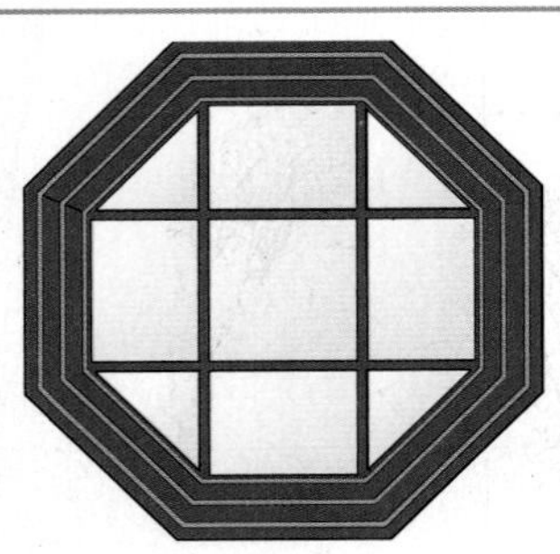

The four triangular panes in the octagonal window are congruent triangles.

Consider Example 2 once more. If a "different" triangle were constructed by choosing $\overline{AC}$ to be the first side, it would be congruent to the one shown. It might be necessary to flip or rotate it to have corresponding vertices match. The objective of Example 2 is that it provides a method for establishing the congruence of triangles by using only three pairs of parts. If corresponding angles are measured in the given triangle or in the constructed triangle with the same lengths for sides, these pairs of angles will also be congruent!

SSS (METHOD FOR PROVING TRIANGLES CONGRUENT)

POSTULATE 12

If the three sides of one triangle are congruent to the three sides of a second triangle, then the triangles are congruent (SSS).

The designation SSS will be cited as a reason in the proof that follows. The three S letters refer to the three *pairs* of congruent sides.

EXAMPLE 3

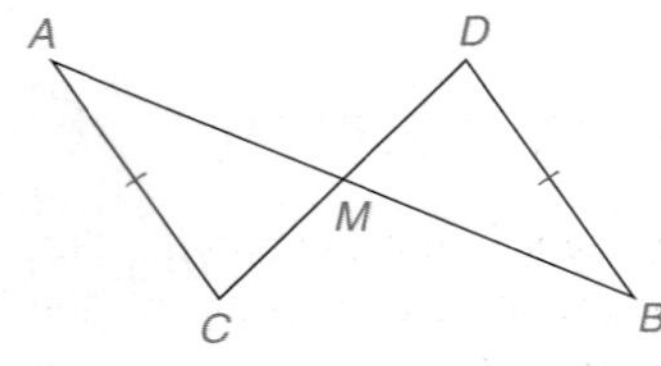

Figure 3.4

GIVEN: $\overline{AB}$ and $\overline{CD}$ bisect each other at M
$\overline{AC} \cong \overline{DB}$
(See Figure 3.4.)

PROVE: $\triangle AMC \cong \triangle BMD$

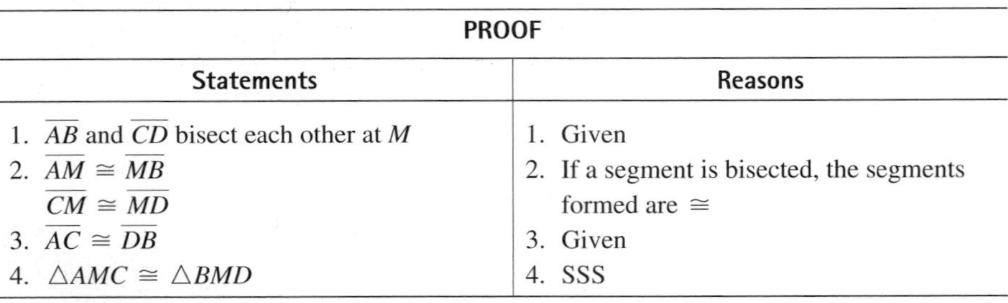

PROOF

Statements	Reasons
1. $\overline{AB}$ and $\overline{CD}$ bisect each other at M	1. Given
2. $\overline{AM} \cong \overline{MB}$ $\overline{CM} \cong \overline{MD}$	2. If a segment is bisected, the segments formed are $\cong$
3. $\overline{AC} \cong \overline{DB}$	3. Given
4. $\triangle AMC \cong \triangle BMD$	4. SSS

NOTE 1: In steps 2 and 3, the three pairs of sides were shown to be congruent; thus, SSS is cited as the reason that justifies why $\triangle AMC \cong \triangle BMD$.

NOTE 2: $\triangle BMD$ is the image determined by the rotation of $\triangle AMC$ about point M through a 180° angle. ■

The two sides that form an angle of a triangle are said to **include that angle** of the triangle. In $\triangle TUV$ in Figure 3.5(a), sides $\overline{TU}$ and $\overline{TV}$ form $\angle T$; therefore, $\overline{TU}$ and $\overline{TV}$ include $\angle T$. In turn, $\angle T$ is said to be the included angle for $\overline{TU}$ and $\overline{TV}$. Similarly, any two angles of a triangle must have a common side, and these two angles are said to **include that side.** In $\triangle TUV$, $\angle U$ and $\angle T$ share the common side $\overline{UT}$; therefore, $\angle U$ and $\angle T$ include the side $\overline{UT}$; equivalently, $\overline{UT}$ is the side included by $\angle U$ and $\angle T$.

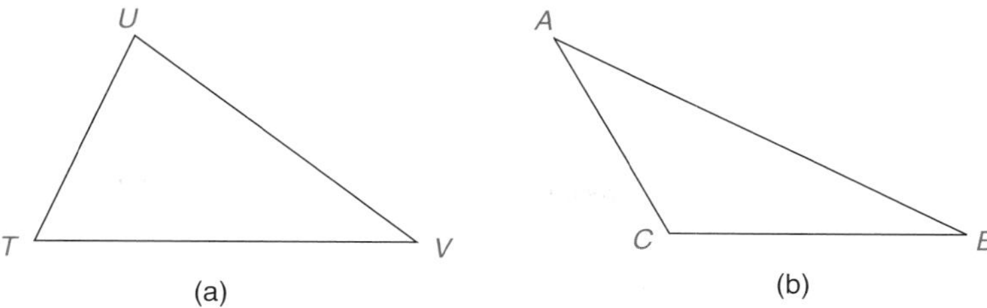

Figure 3.5

Informally, the term *include* names the part of a triangle that is "between" two other named parts.

EXAMPLE 4

In $\triangle ABC$ of Figure 3.5(b):

a) Which angle is included by $\overline{AC}$ and $\overline{CB}$?
b) Which sides include $\angle B$?
c) What is the included side for $\angle A$ and $\angle B$?
d) Which angles include $\overline{CB}$?

Solution

a) $\angle C$ (because it is formed by $\overline{AC}$ and $\overline{CB}$)
b) $\overline{AB}$ and $\overline{BC}$ (because these form $\angle B$)
c) $\overline{AB}$ (because it is the common side for $\angle A$ and $\angle B$)
d) $\angle C$ and $\angle B$ (because $\overline{CB}$ is a side of each angle) ■

SAS (METHOD FOR PROVING TRIANGLES CONGRUENT)

A second way of establishing that two triangles are congruent involves showing that two sides and the included angle of one triangle are congruent to two sides and the included angle of a second triangle. If two people each draw a triangle so that two of the sides measure 2 cm and 3 cm and their included angle measures 54°, then those triangles are congruent. (See Figure 3.6.)

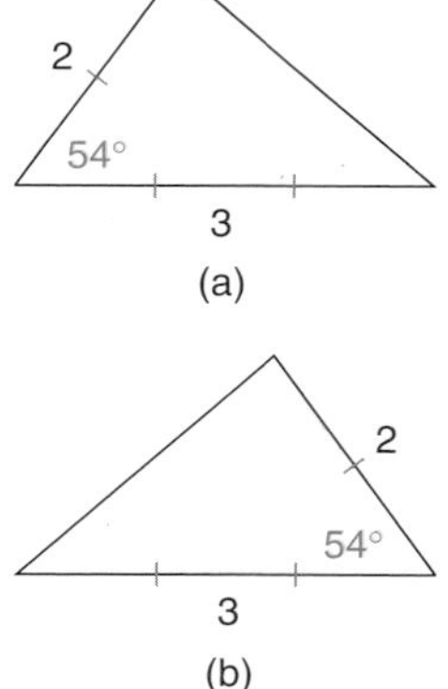

Figure 3.6

POSTULATE 13

If two sides and the included angle of one triangle are congruent to two sides and the included angle of a second triangle, then the triangles are congruent (SAS).

The order of the letters SAS in Postulate 13 helps us to remember that the two sides that are named have the angle "between" them. That is, in each triangle, the two sides form the angle.

In Example 5, which follows, the two triangles to be proved congruent share a common side; the statement $\overline{PN} \cong \overline{PN}$ is justified by the Reflexive Property of Congruence, which is conveniently expressed as **Identity.**

DEFINITION

In this context, **Identity** is the reason we cite when verifying that a line segment or an angle is congruent to itself; also known as the Reflexive Property of Congruence.

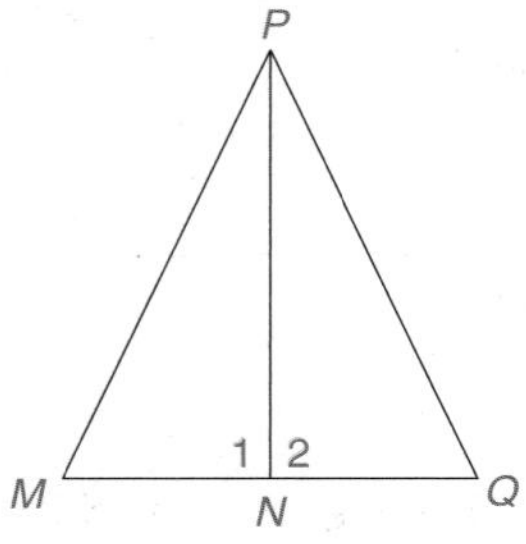

Figure 3.7

In Example 5, note the use of Identity and SAS as the final reasons.

EXAMPLE 5

GIVEN: $\overline{PN} \perp \overline{MQ}$
$\overline{MN} \cong \overline{NQ}$
(See Figure 3.7.)

PROVE: $\triangle PNM \cong \triangle PNQ$

PROOF

Statements	Reasons
1. $\overline{PN} \perp \overline{MQ}$	1. Given
2. $\angle 1 \cong \angle 2$	2. If two lines are $\perp$, they meet to form $\cong$ adjacent $\angle$s
3. $\overline{MN} \cong \overline{NQ}$	3. Given
4. $\overline{PN} \cong \overline{PN}$	4. Identity (or Reflexive)
5. $\triangle PNM \cong \triangle PNQ$	5. SAS

NOTE: In $\triangle PNM$, $\overline{MN}$ (step 3) and $\overline{PN}$ (step 4) include $\angle 1$; similarly, $\overline{NQ}$ and $\overline{PN}$ include $\angle 2$ in $\triangle PNQ$. Thus, SAS is used to verify that $\triangle PNM \cong \triangle PNQ$ in reason 5. ■

Exs. 3–6

ASA (METHOD FOR PROVING TRIANGLES CONGRUENT)

The next method for proving triangles congruent requires a combination of two angles and the included side. If two people each draw a triangle for which two of the angles measure 33° and 47° and the included side measures 5 centimeters, then those triangles are congruent. See the figure below.

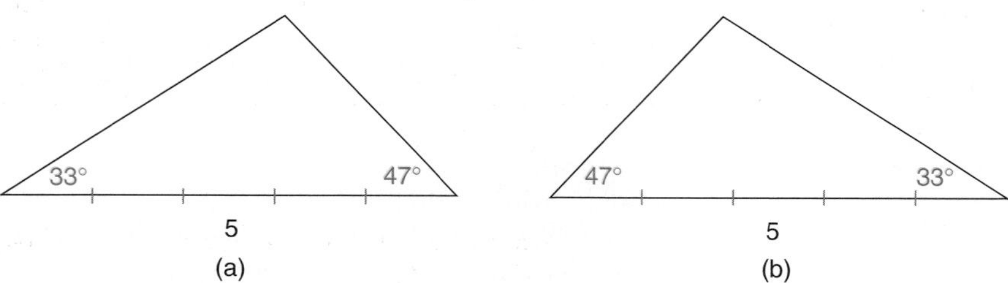

Figure 3.8

POSTULATE 14

If two angles and the included side of one triangle are congruent to two angles and the included side of a second triangle, then the triangles are congruent (ASA).

Although this method is written compactly as ASA, you must be careful as you write these abbreviations! For example, ASA refers to two angles and the included side, whereas SAS refers to two sides and the included angle. For us to apply any postulate, the specific conditions described in it must be satisfied.

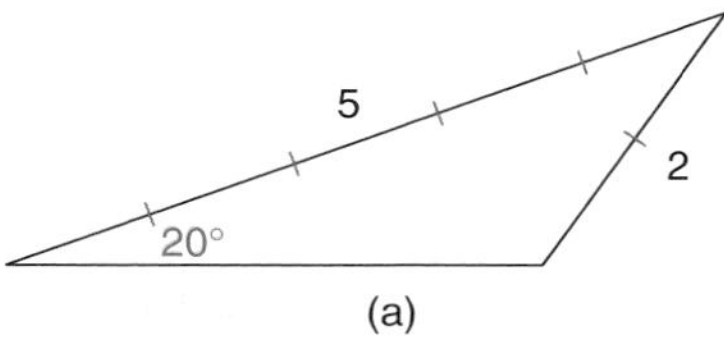

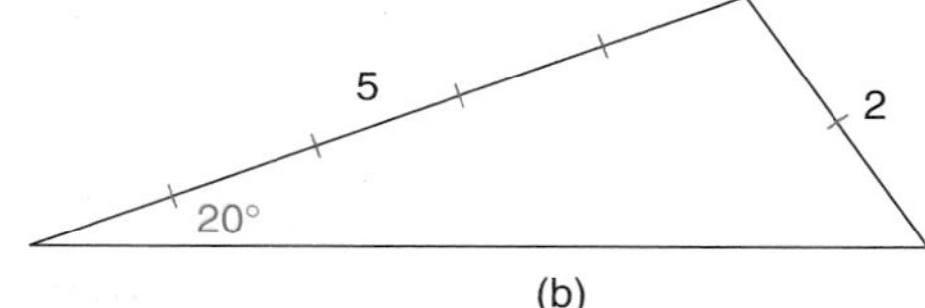

Figure 3.9

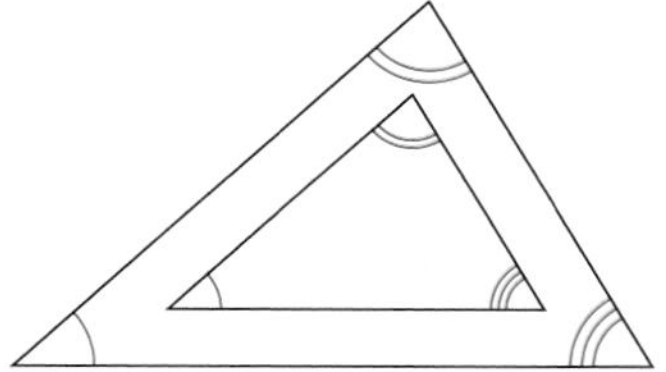

Figure 3.10

SSS, SAS, and ASA are all valid methods of proving triangles congruent, but SSA is *not* a method and *cannot* be used. In Figure 3.9, the two triangles are marked to show SSA, yet the two triangles are *not* congruent.

Another combination that cannot be used to prove triangles congruent is AAA. See Figure 3.10. Three congruent pairs of angles in two triangles do not guarantee congruent pairs of sides!

In Example 6, the triangles to be proved congruent overlap (see Figure 3.11). To clarify relationships, the triangles have been redrawn separately in Figure 3.12. Note that the parts indicated as congruent are established as congruent in the proof. For statement 3, Identity (or Reflexive) is also used to justify that an angle is congruent to itself.

SSG *Exs. 7–11*

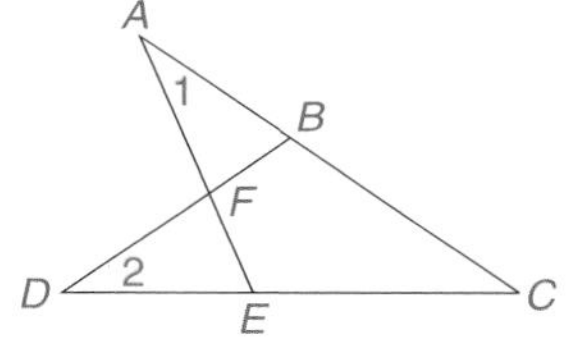

Figure 3.11

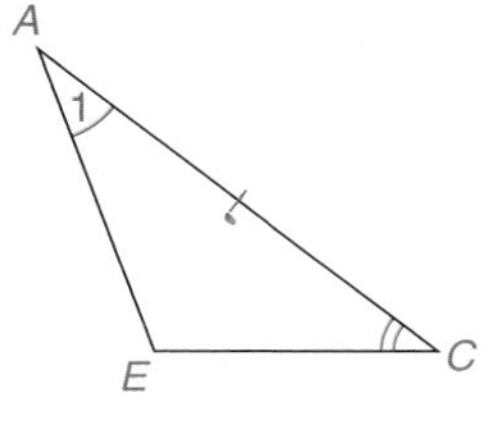

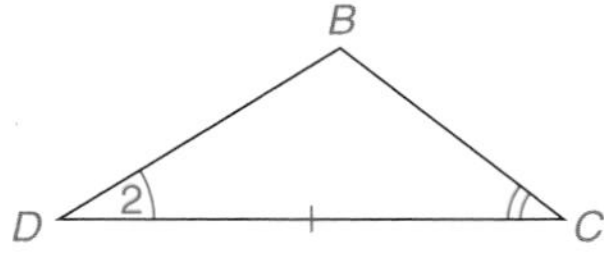

Figure 3.12

EXAMPLE 6

GIVEN: $\overline{AC} \cong \overline{DC}$
$\angle 1 \cong \angle 2$
(See Figure 3.11.)

PROVE: $\triangle ACE \cong \triangle DCB$

PROOF

Statements	Reasons
1. $\overline{AC} \cong \overline{DC}$ (See Figure 3.12.)	1. Given
2. $\angle 1 \cong \angle 2$	2. Given
3. $\angle C \cong \angle C$	3. Identity
4. $\triangle ACE \cong \triangle DCB$	4. ASA

■

Next we consider a theorem (proved by the ASA postulate) that is convenient as a reason in many proofs.

AAS (METHOD FOR PROVING TRIANGLES CONGRUENT)

THEOREM 3.1.1

If two angles and a nonincluded side of one triangle are congruent to two angles and a nonincluded side of a second triangle, then the triangles are congruent (AAS).

GIVEN: $\angle T \cong \angle K$, $\angle S \cong \angle J$, and $\overline{SR} \cong \overline{HJ}$ (See Figure 3.13 on page 134.)

PROVE: $\triangle TSR \cong \triangle KJH$

Warning

Do not use AAA or SSA, because they are simply not valid for proving triangles congruent; with AAA the triangles have the same shape but are not necessarily congruent.

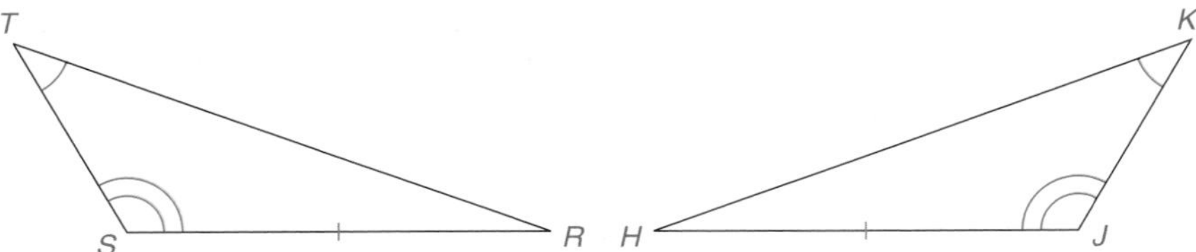

Figure 3.13

PROOF

Statements	Reasons
1. $\angle T \cong \angle K$ $\angle S \cong \angle J$	1. Given
2. $\angle R \cong \angle H$	2. If two $\angle$s of one $\triangle$ are $\cong$ to two $\angle$s of another $\triangle$, then the third $\angle$s are also congruent
3. $\overline{SR} \cong \overline{HJ}$	3. Given
4. $\triangle TSR \cong \triangle KJH$	4. ASA

SSG *Exs. 12–14*

STRATEGY FOR PROOF ▶ Proving That Two Triangles Are Congruent

General Rule: Methods of proof (possible final reasons) available in Section 3.1 are SSS, SAS, ASA, and AAS.

Illustration: See Exercises 9–12 of this section.

▶▶▶ Exercises 3.1

In Exercises 1 to 8, use the drawings provided to answer each question.

1. Name a common angle and a common side for $\triangle ABC$ and $\triangle ABD$. If $\overline{BC} \cong \overline{BD}$, can you conclude that $\triangle ABC$ and $\triangle ABD$ are congruent? Can SSA be used as a reason for proving triangles congruent?

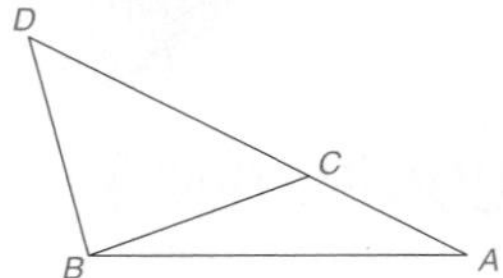

For Exercises 2 and 3, see the figure in the second column.

2. With corresponding angles indicated, the triangles are congruent. Find values for a, b, and c.

3. With corresponding angles indicated, find $m\angle A$ if $m\angle F = 72°$.

4. With corresponding angles indicated, find $m\angle E$ if $m\angle A = 57°$ and $m\angle C = 85°$.

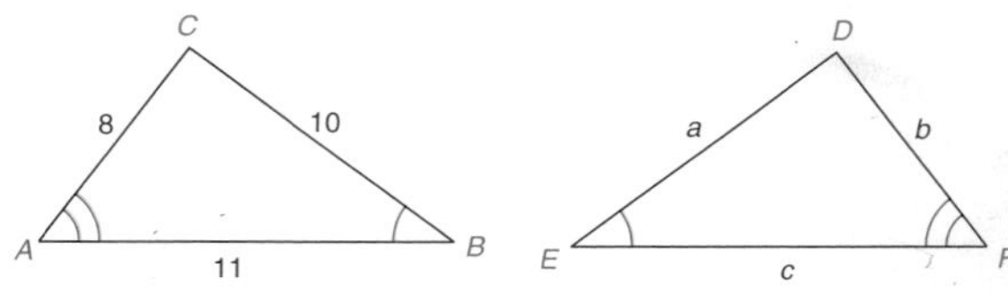

Exercises 2–4, 6

5. In a right triangle, the sides that form the right angle are the **legs;** the longest side (opposite the right angle) is the **hypotenuse.** Some textbooks say that when two right triangles have congruent pairs of legs, the right triangles are congruent by the reason LL. In our work, LL is just a special case of one of the postulates in this section. Which postulate is that?

6. In the figure for Exercise 2, write a statement that the triangles are congruent, paying due attention to the order of corresponding vertices.

7. In $\triangle ABC$, the midpoints of the sides are joined. What does intuition tell you about the relationship between $\triangle AED$ and $\triangle FDE$? (We will prove this relationship later.)

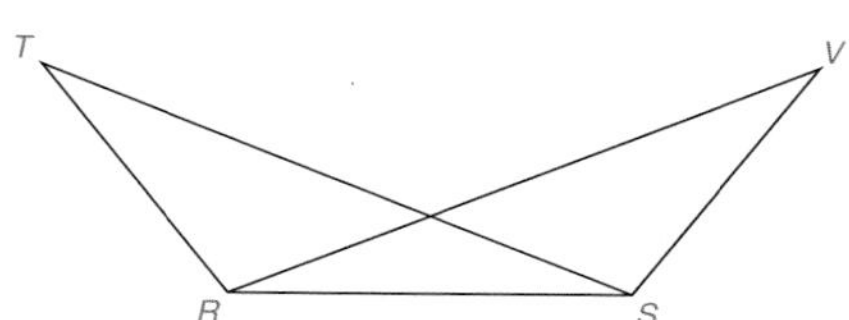

8. Suppose that you wish to prove that $\triangle RST \cong \triangle SRV$. Using the reason Identity, name one pair of corresponding parts that are congruent.

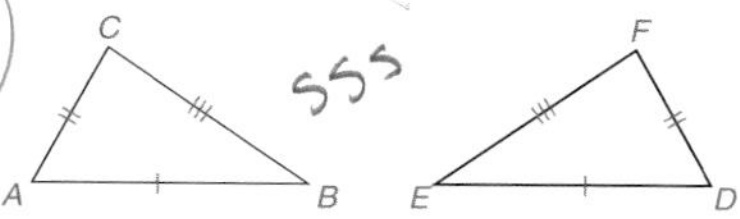

In Exercises 9 to 12, congruent parts are indicated by like dashes (sides) or arcs (angles). State which method (SSS, SAS, ASA, or AAS) would be used to prove the two triangles congruent.

9.

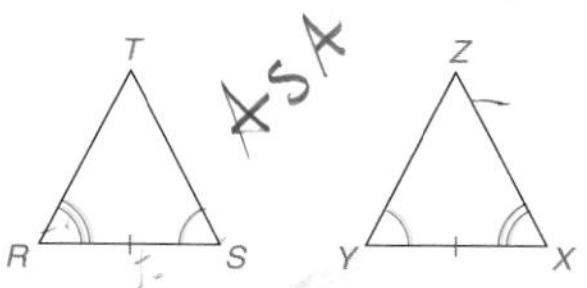

10.

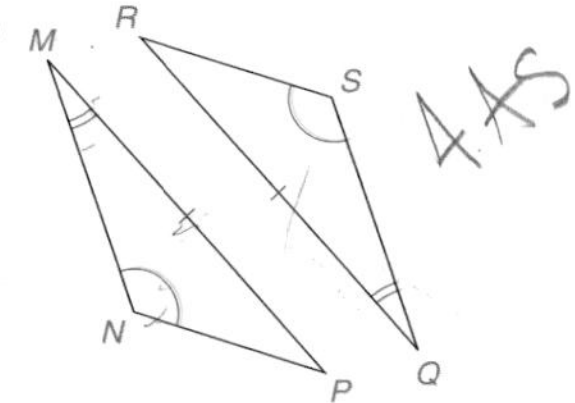

11.

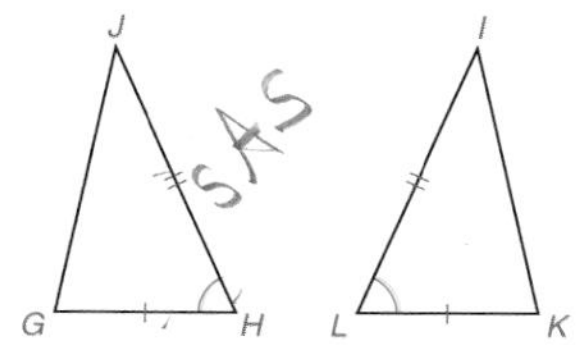

12.

In Exercises 13 to 18, use only the given information to state the reason why $\triangle ABC \cong \triangle DBC$. Redraw the figure and use marks like those used in Exercises 9 to 12.

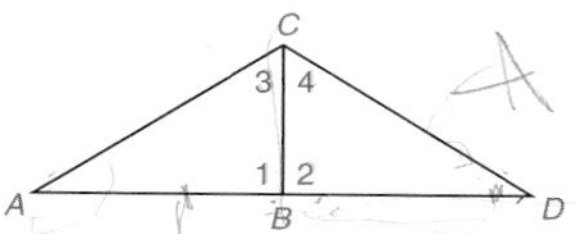

Exercises 13–18

13. $\angle A \cong \angle D$, $\overline{AB} \cong \overline{BD}$, and $\angle 1 \cong \angle 2$
14. $\angle A \cong \angle D$, $\overline{AC} \cong \overline{CD}$, and B is the midpoint of $\overline{AD}$
15. $\angle A \cong \angle D$, $\overline{AC} \cong \overline{CD}$, and $\overrightarrow{CB}$ bisects $\angle ACD$
16. $\angle A \cong \angle D$, $\overline{AC} \cong \overline{CD}$, and $\overline{AB} \cong \overline{BD}$
17. $\overline{AC} \cong \overline{CD}$, $\overline{AB} \cong \overline{BD}$, and $\overline{CB} \cong \overline{CB}$ (by Identity)
18. $\angle 1$ and $\angle 2$ are right $\angle$s, $\overline{AB} \cong \overline{BD}$, and $\angle A \cong \angle D$

In Exercises 19 and 20, the triangles to be proved congruent have been redrawn separately. Congruent parts are marked.

a) *Name an additional pair of parts that are congruent by Identity.*
b) *Considering the congruent parts, state the reason why the triangles must be congruent.*

19. $\triangle ABC \cong \triangle AED$

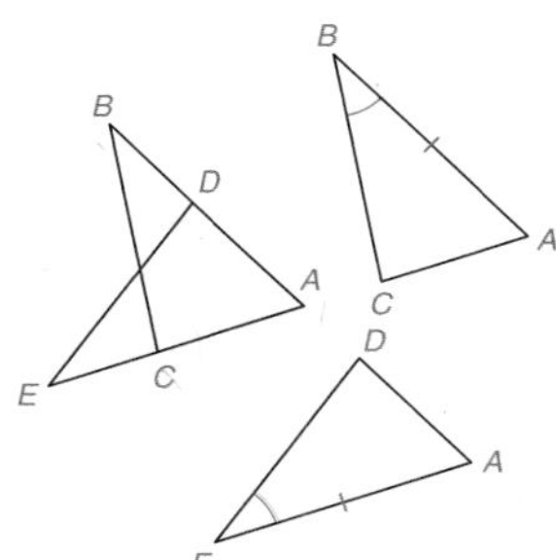

20. $\triangle MNP \cong \triangle MQP$

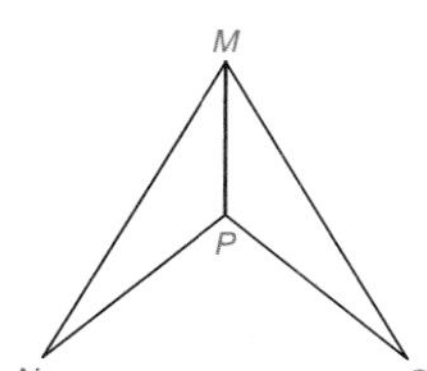

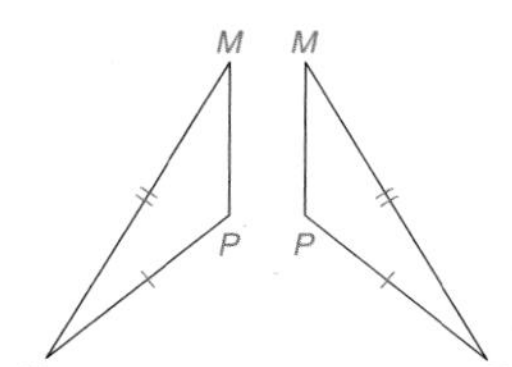

In Exercises 21 to 24, the triangles named can be proven congruent. Considering the congruent pairs marked, name the additional pair of parts that must be congruent for us to use the method named.

21. SAS

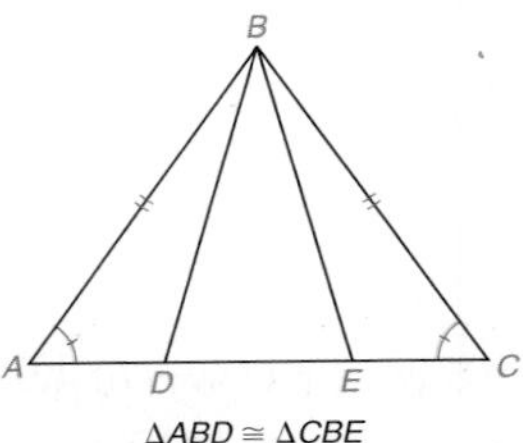

22. ASA

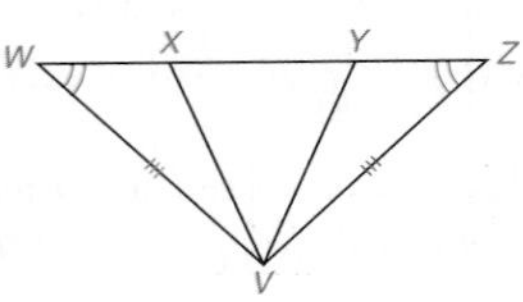

23. SSS

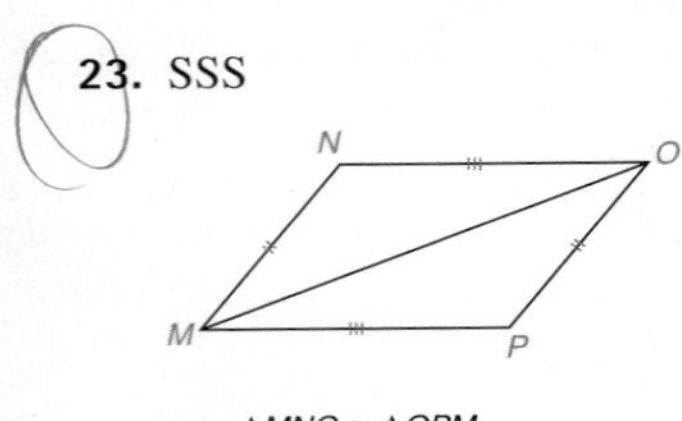

24. AAS

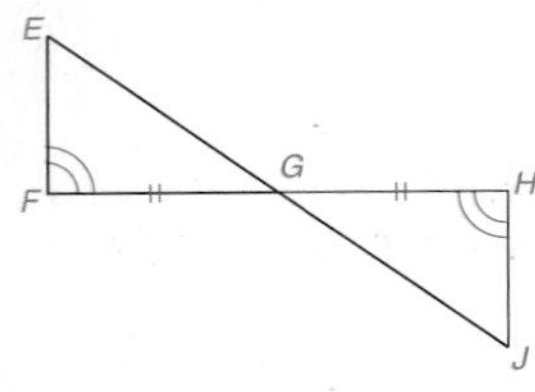

In Exercises 25 and 26, complete each proof. Use the figure at the top of the second column.

25. *Given:* $\overline{AB} \cong \overline{CD}$ and $\overline{AD} \cong \overline{CB}$
Prove: $\triangle ABC \cong \triangle CDA$

PROOF

Statements	Reasons
1. $\overline{AB} \cong \overline{CD}$ and $\overline{AD} \cong \overline{CB}$	1. ?
2. ?	2. Identity
3. $\triangle ABC \cong \triangle CDA$	3. ?

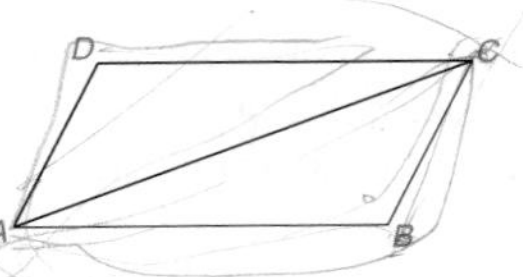

Exercises 25, 26

26. *Given:* $\overline{DC} \parallel \overline{AB}$ and $\overline{AD} \parallel \overline{BC}$
Prove: $\triangle ABC \cong \triangle CDA$

PROOF

Statements	Reasons
1. $\overline{DC} \parallel \overline{AB}$	1. ?
2. $\angle DCA \cong \angle BAC$	2. ?
3. ?	3. Given
4. ?	4. If two ∥ lines are cut by a transversal, alt. int. ∠s are ≅
5. $\overline{AC} \cong \overline{AC}$	5. ?
6. ?	6. ASA

In Exercises 27 to 32, use SSS, SAS, ASA, or AAS to prove that the triangles are congruent.

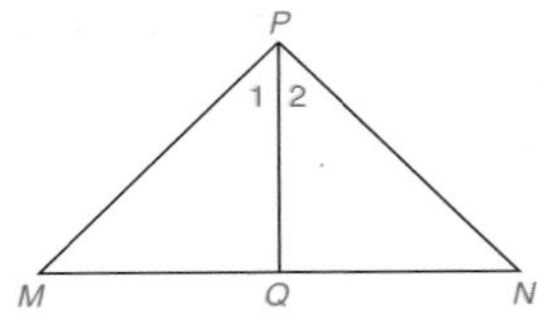

Exercises 27, 28

27. *Given:* $\overrightarrow{PQ}$ bisects $\angle MPN$
$\overline{MP} \cong \overline{NP}$
Prove: $\triangle MQP \cong \triangle NQP$

28. *Given:* $\overline{PQ} \perp \overline{MN}$ and $\angle 1 \cong \angle 2$
Prove: $\triangle MQP \cong \triangle NQP$

29. *Given:* $\overline{AB} \perp \overline{BC}$ and $\overline{AB} \perp \overline{BD}$
$\overline{BC} \cong \overline{BD}$
Prove: $\triangle ABC \cong \triangle ABD$

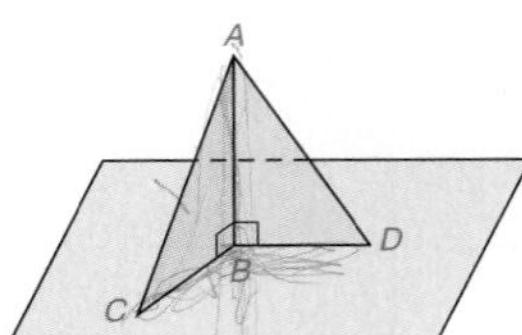

30. *Given:* $\overline{PN}$ bisects $\overline{MQ}$
$\angle M$ and $\angle Q$ are right angles
Prove: $\triangle PQR \cong \triangle NMR$

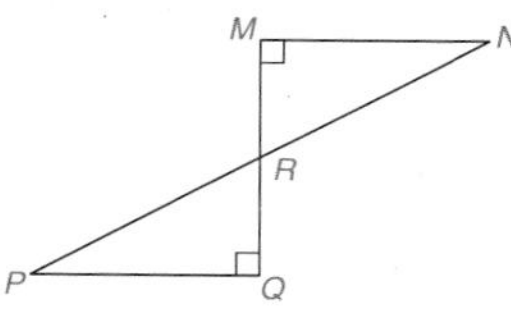

31. *Given:* $\angle VRS \cong \angle TSR$ and $\overline{RV} \cong \overline{TS}$
Prove: $\triangle RST \cong \triangle SRV$

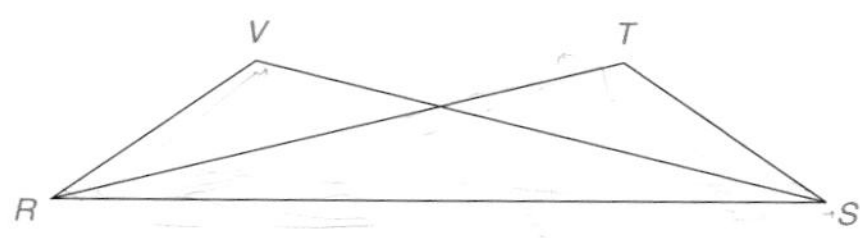

Exercises 31, 32

32. *Given:* $\overline{VS} \cong \overline{TR}$ and $\angle TRS \cong \angle VSR$
Prove: $\triangle RST \cong \triangle SRV$

In Exercises 33 to 36, the methods to be used are SSS, SAS, ASA, and AAS.

33. Given that $\triangle RST \cong \triangle RVU$, does it follow that $\triangle RSU$ is also congruent to $\triangle RVT$? Name the method, if any, used in arriving at this conclusion.

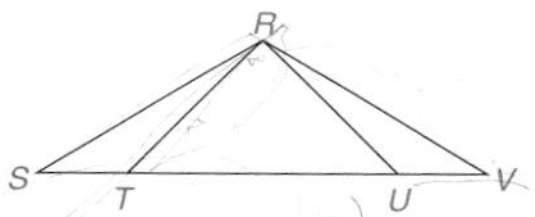

Exercises 33, 34

34. Given that $\angle S \cong \angle V$ and $\overline{ST} \cong \overline{UV}$, does it follow that $\triangle RST \cong \triangle RVU$? Which method, if any, did you use?

35. Given that $\angle A \cong \angle E$ and $\angle B \cong \angle D$, does it follow that $\triangle ABC \cong \triangle EDC$? If so, cite the method used in arriving at this conclusion.

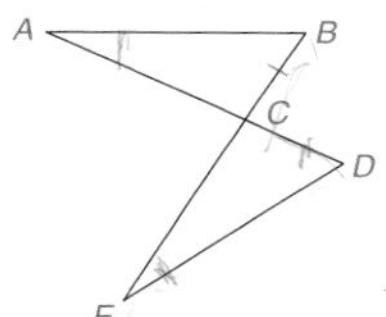

Exercises 35, 36

36. Given that $\angle A \cong \angle E$ and $\overline{BC} \cong \overline{DC}$, does it follow that $\triangle ABC \cong \triangle EDC$? Cite the method, if any, used in reaching this conclusion.

37. In quadrilateral $ABCD$, $\overline{AC}$ and $\overline{BD}$ are perpendicular bisectors of each other. Name all triangles that are congruent to:

a) $\triangle ABE$ b) $\triangle ABC$ c) $\triangle ABD$

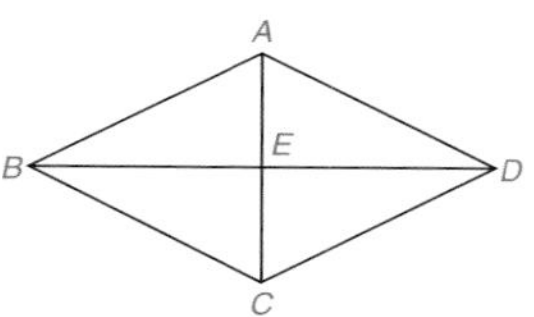

38. In $\triangle ABC$ and $\triangle DEF$, you know that $\angle A \cong \angle D$, $\angle C \cong \angle F$, and $\overline{AB} \cong \overline{DE}$. Before concluding that the triangles are congruent by ASA, you need to show that $\angle B \cong \angle E$. State the postulate or theorem that allows you to confirm this statement ($\angle B \cong \angle E$).

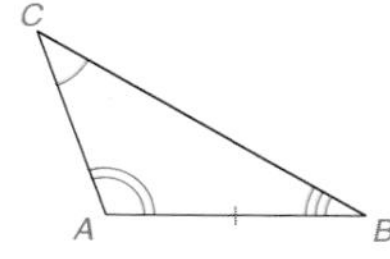

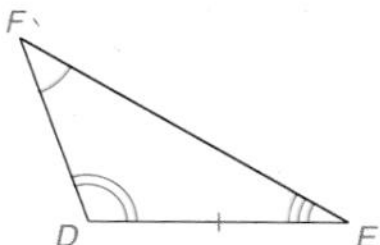

In Exercises 39 and 40, complete each proof.

39. *Given:* Plane M
C is the midpoint of $\overline{EB}$
$\overline{AD} \perp \overline{BE}$ and $\overline{AB} \parallel \overline{ED}$
Prove: $\triangle ABC \cong \triangle DEC$

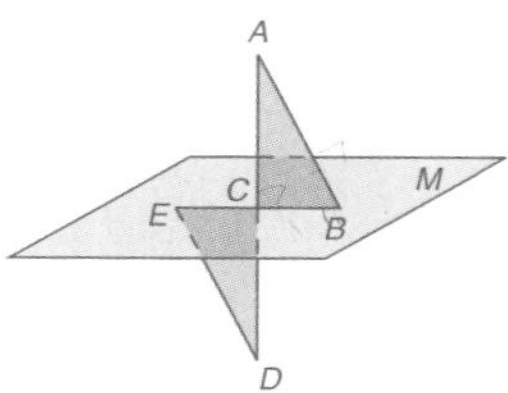

40. *Given:* $\overline{SP} \cong \overline{SQ}$ and $\overline{ST} \cong \overline{SV}$
Prove: $\triangle SPV \cong \triangle SQT$ and $\triangle TPQ \cong \triangle VQP$

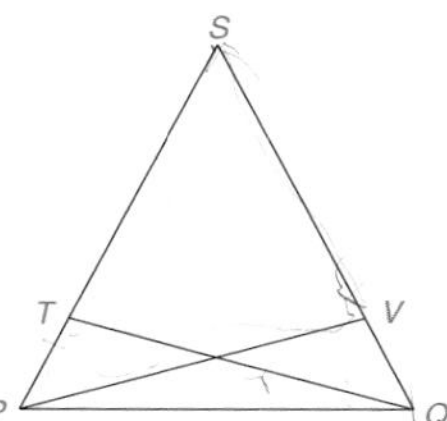

41. *Given:* $\angle ABC$; $\overline{RS}$ is the perpendicular bisector of $\overline{AB}$; $\overline{RT}$ is the perpendicular bisector of $\overline{BC}$.
Prove: $\overline{AR} \cong \overline{RC}$

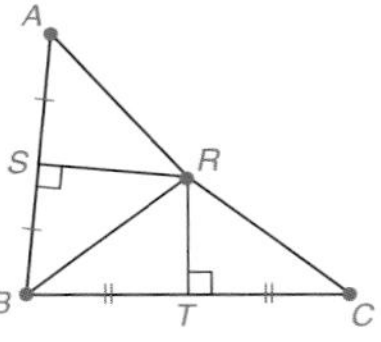

3.2 Corresponding Parts of Congruent Triangles

KEY CONCEPTS

CPCTC
Hypotenuse and Legs of a Right Triangle
HL
Pythagorean Theorem
Square Roots Property

Recall that the definition of congruent triangles states that *all* six parts (three sides and three angles) of one triangle are congruent respectively to the six corresponding parts of the second triangle. If we have proved that $\triangle ABC \cong \triangle DEF$ by SAS (the congruent parts are marked in Figure 3.14), then we can draw conclusions such as $\angle C \cong \angle F$ and $\overline{AC} \cong \overline{DF}$. The following reason (CPCTC) is often cited for drawing such conclusions and is based on the definition of congruent triangles.

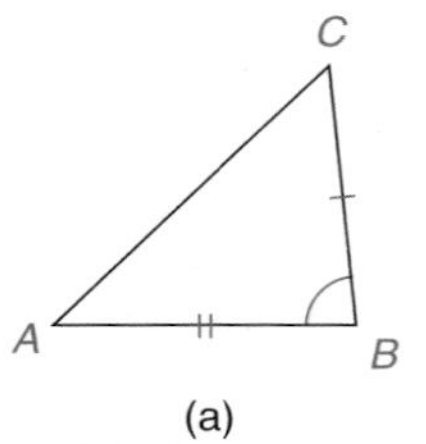

(a)

F
E
D

(b)

Figure 3.14

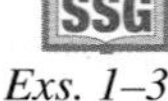

SSG *Exs. 1–3*

CPCTC: Corresponding parts of congruent triangles are congruent.

STRATEGY FOR PROOF ▶ Using CPCTC

General Rule: In a proof, two triangles must be proven congruent *before* CPCTC can be used to verify that another pair of sides or angles of these triangles are also congruent.

Illustration: In the proof of Example 1, statement 5 (triangles congruent) must be stated before we conclude that $\overline{TZ} \cong \overline{VZ}$ by CPCTC.

EXAMPLE 1

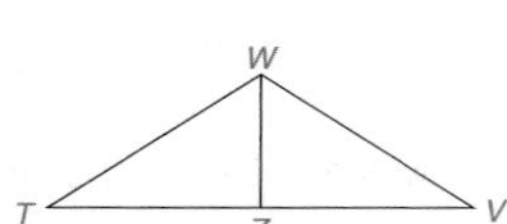

Figure 3.15

GIVEN: $\overrightarrow{WZ}$ bisects $\angle TWV$
$\overline{WT} \cong \overline{WV}$
(See Figure 3.15.)

PROVE: $\overline{TZ} \cong \overline{VZ}$

PROOF

Statements	Reasons
1. $\overrightarrow{WZ}$ bisects $\angle TWV$	1. Given
2. $\angle TWZ \cong \angle VWZ$	2. The bisector of an angle separates it into two $\cong \angle$s
3. $\overline{WT} \cong \overline{WV}$	3. Given
4. $\overline{WZ} \cong \overline{WZ}$	4. Identity
5. $\triangle TWZ \cong \triangle VWZ$	5. SAS
6. $\overline{TZ} \cong \overline{VZ}$	6. CPCTC

■

Reminder

CPCTC means "corresponding parts of congruent triangles are congruent."

In Example 1, we could just as easily have used CPCTC to prove that two angles are congruent. If we had been asked to prove that $\angle T \cong \angle V$, then the final statement would have read

6. $\angle T \cong \angle V$	6. CPCTC

We can take the proof in Example 1 a step further by proving triangles congruent and then using CPCTC to reach another conclusion, such as parallel or perpendicular lines. In Example 1, suppose we had been asked to prove that $\overline{WZ}$ bisects $\overline{TV}$. Then steps 1–6 would have remained as is, and a seventh step would have read

7. $\overline{WZ}$ bisects $\overline{TV}$	7. If a line segment is divided into two $\cong$ parts, then it has been bisected

STRATEGY FOR PROOF ▶ Proofs that Involve Congruent Triangles

In our study of triangles, we will establish three types of conclusions:

1. *Proving triangles congruent*, such as $\triangle TWZ \cong \triangle VWZ$
2. *Proving corresponding parts of congruent triangles congruent*, like $\overline{TZ} \cong \overline{VZ}$ (Note that two $\triangle$s have to be proved $\cong$ before CPCTC can be used.)
3. *Establishing a further relationship*, like $\overline{WZ}$ bisects $\overline{TV}$ (Note that we must establish that two $\triangle$s are $\cong$ and also apply CPCTC before this goal can be reached.)

Little is said in this book about a "plan for proof," but every geometry student and teacher must have a plan before a proof can be completed. Though we generally do not write the "plan," we demonstrate the technique in Example 2.

EXAMPLE 2

GIVEN: $\overline{ZW} \cong \overline{YX}$
$\overline{ZY} \cong \overline{WX}$
(See Figure 3.16.)

PROVE: $\overline{ZY} \parallel \overline{WX}$

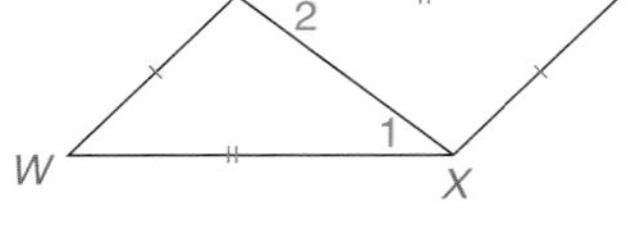

Figure 3.16

PLAN FOR PROOF: By showing that $\triangle ZWX \cong \triangle XYZ$, we can show that $\angle 1 \cong \angle 2$ by CPCTC. Then $\angle$s 1 and 2 are congruent alternate interior angles for $\overline{ZY}$ and $\overline{WX}$, which must be parallel.

PROOF

Statements	Reasons
1. $\overline{ZW} \cong \overline{YX}$; $\overline{ZY} \cong \overline{WX}$	1. Given
2. $\overline{ZX} \cong \overline{ZX}$	2. Identity
3. $\triangle ZWX \cong \triangle XYZ$	3. SSS
4. $\angle 1 \cong \angle 2$	4. CPCTC
5. $\overline{ZY} \parallel \overline{WX}$	5. If two lines are cut by a transversal so that the alt. int. $\angle$s are $\cong$, these lines are $\parallel$

SSG *Exs. 4–6*

SUGGESTIONS FOR PROVING TRIANGLES CONGRUENT

Because many proofs depend upon establishing congruent triangles, we offer the following suggestions.

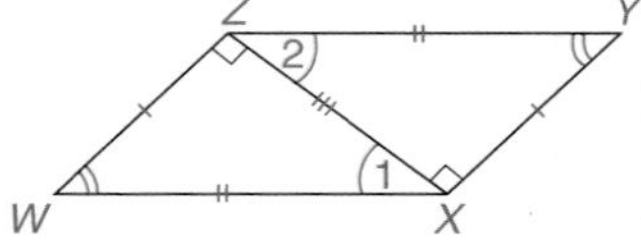

Figure 3.17

> **STRATEGY FOR PROOF ▶ Drawings Used to Prove Triangles Congruent**
>
> Suggestions for a proof that involves congruent triangles:
>
> 1. Mark the figures systematically, using:
>   a) A *square* in the opening of each right angle
>   b) The same number of *dashes* on congruent sides
>   c) The same number of *arcs* on congruent angles
> 2. Trace the triangles to be proved congruent in different colors.
> 3. If the triangles overlap, draw them separately.
>
> **NOTE:** In Figure 3.17, consider like markings.

Exs. 7–9

RIGHT TRIANGLES

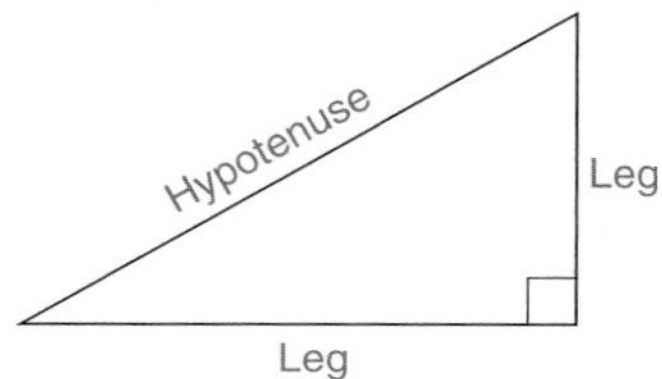

Figure 3.18

In a right triangle, the side opposite the right angle is the **hypotenuse** of the triangle, and the sides of the right angle are the **legs** of the triangle. These parts of a right triangle are illustrated in Figure 3.18.

Another method for proving triangles congruent is the HL method, which applies exclusively to right triangles. In HL, H refers to hypotenuse and L refers to leg. The proof of this method will be delayed until Section 5.4.

HL (METHOD FOR PROVING TRIANGLES CONGRUENT)

> **THEOREM 3.2.1**
>
> If the hypotenuse and a leg of one right triangle are congruent to the hypotenuse and a leg of a second right triangle, then the triangles are congruent (HL).

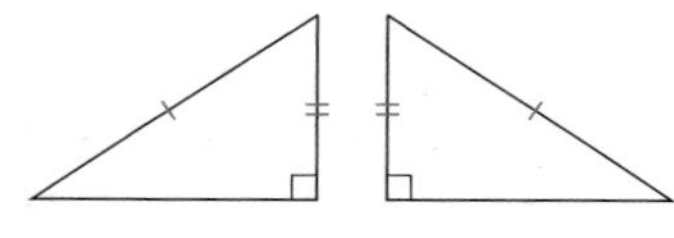

Figure 3.19

The relationship described in Theorem 3.2.1 (HL) is illustrated in Figure 3.19. In Example 3, the construction based upon HL leads to a unique right triangle.

EXAMPLE 3

GIVEN: $\overline{AB}$ and $\overline{CA}$ in Figure 3.20(a); note that $AB > CA$. (See page 141.)

CONSTRUCT: The right triangle with hypotenuse of length equal to AB and one leg of length equal to CA

Solution Figure 3.20(b): Construct $\overleftrightarrow{CQ}$ perpendicular to $\overleftrightarrow{EF}$ at point C.
Figure 3.20(c): Now mark off the length of $\overline{CA}$ on $\overleftrightarrow{CQ}$.

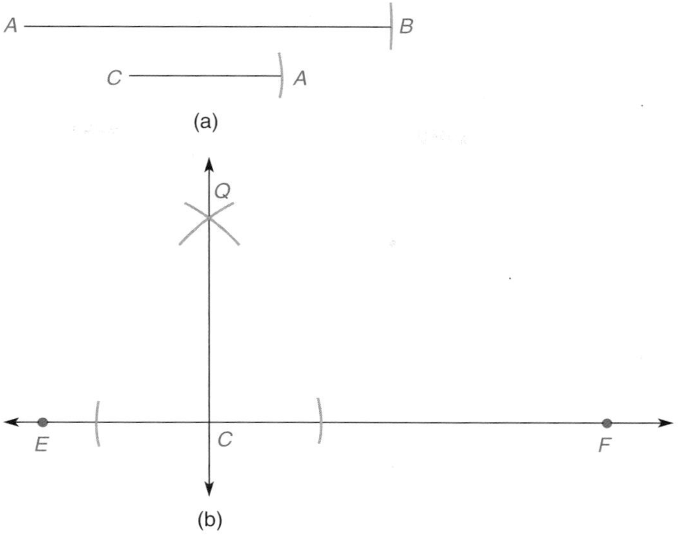

Geometry in the Real World

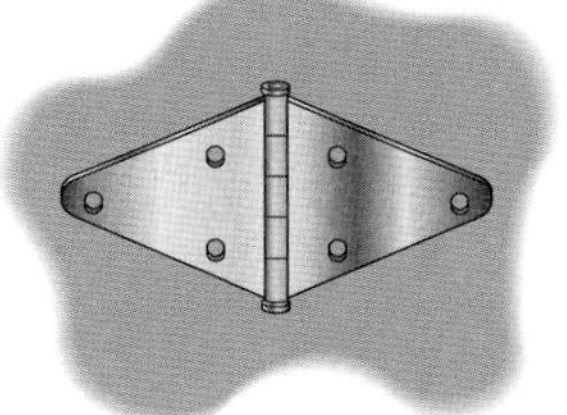

In the manufacturing process, the parts of many machines must be congruent. The two sides of the hinge shown are congruent.

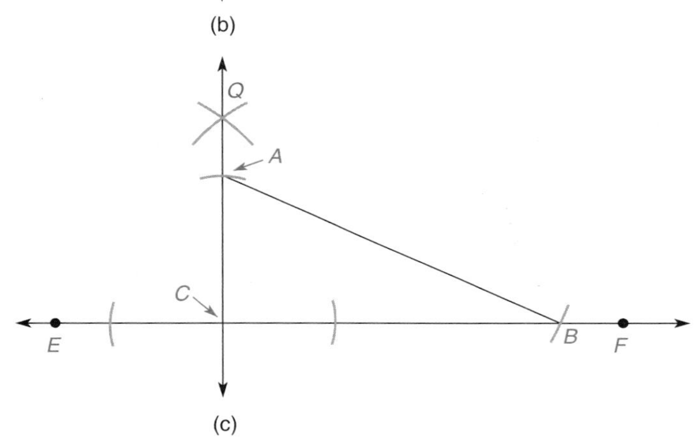

Figure 3.20

Finally, with point A as center, mark off a length equal to that of $\overline{AB}$ as shown. $\triangle ABC$ is the desired right $\triangle$. ■

EXAMPLE 4

Figure 3.21

Cite the reason why the right triangles $\triangle ABC$ and $\triangle ECD$ in Figure 3.21 are congruent if:

a) $\overline{AB} \cong \overline{EC}$ and $\overline{AC} \cong \overline{ED}$
b) $\angle A \cong \angle E$ and C is the midpoint of $\overline{BD}$
c) $\overline{BC} \cong \overline{CD}$ and $\angle 1 \cong \angle 2$
d) $\overline{AB} \cong \overline{EC}$ and $\overline{EC}$ bisects $\overline{BD}$

Solution

SSG *Exs. 10–11*

a) HL b) AAS c) ASA d) SAS ■

The following theorem can be applied only when a triangle is a right triangle (contains a right angle). Proof of the theorem is delayed until Section 5.4.

PYTHAGOREAN THEOREM

The square of the length (c) of the hypotenuse of a right triangle equals the sum of squares of the lengths (a and b) of the legs of the right triangle; that is, $c^2 = a^2 + b^2$.

Technology Exploration

Computer software and a calculator are needed.

1. Form a right $\triangle ABC$ with $m\angle C = 90°$.
2. Measure AB, AC, and BC.
3. Show that $(AC)^2 + (BC)^2 = (AB)^2$.

(Answer will probably not be "perfect.")

In applications of the Pythagorean Theorem, we often arrive at statements such as $c^2 = 25$. Using the following property, we see that $c = \sqrt{25}$ or $c = 5$.

SQUARE ROOTS PROPERTY

Let x represent the length of a line segment, and let p represent a positive number. If $x^2 = p$, then $x = \sqrt{p}$.

The *square root* of p, symbolized $\sqrt{p}$, represents the number that when multiplied times itself equals p. As we indicated earlier, $\sqrt{25} = 5$ because $5 \times 5 = 25$. When a square root is not exact, a calculator can be used to find its approximate value; where the symbol $\approx$ means "is equal to approximately," $\sqrt{22} \approx 4.69$ because $4.69 \times 4.69 = 21.9961 \approx 22$.

EXAMPLE 5

Find the length of the third side of the right triangle. See the figure below.

a) Find c if $a = 6$ and $b = 8$.
b) Find b if $a = 7$ and $c = 10$.

Solution

a) $c^2 = a^2 + b^2$, so $c^2 = 6^2 + 8^2$
or $c^2 = 36 + 64 = 100$.
Then $c = \sqrt{100} = 10$.

b) $c^2 = a^2 + b^2$, so $10^2 = 7^2 + b^2$
or $100 = 49 + b^2$. Subtracting yields
$b^2 = 51$, so $b = \sqrt{51} \approx 7.14$.

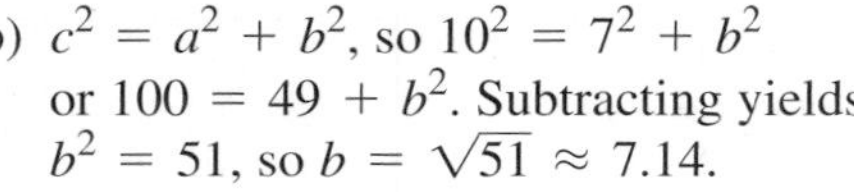

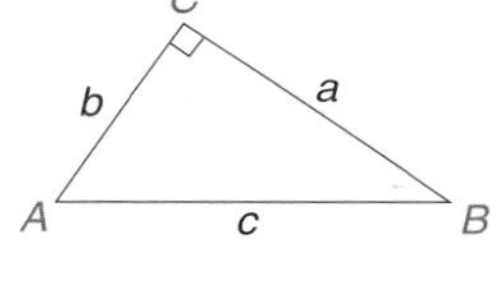

SSG *Exs. 12–14*

Exercises 3.2

In Exercises 1 to 8, plan and write the two-column proof for each problem.

1. *Given:* $\angle 1$ and $\angle 2$ are right $\angle$s
$\overline{CA} \cong \overline{DA}$
Prove: $\triangle ABC \cong \triangle ABD$

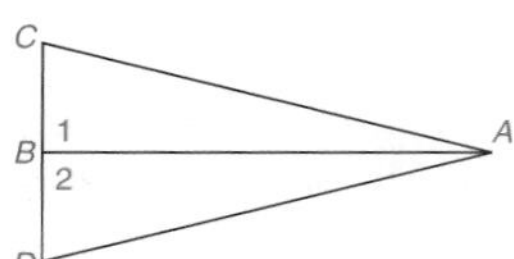

Exercises 1, 2

2. *Given:* $\angle 1$ and $\angle 2$ are right $\angle$s
$\overrightarrow{AB}$ bisects $\angle CAD$
Prove: $\triangle ABC \cong \triangle ABD$

3. *Given:* P is the midpoint of both $\overline{MR}$ and $\overline{NQ}$
Prove: $\triangle MNP \cong \triangle RQP$

4. *Given:* $\overline{MN} \parallel \overline{QR}$ and $\overline{MN} \cong \overline{QR}$
Prove: $\triangle MNP \cong \triangle RQP$

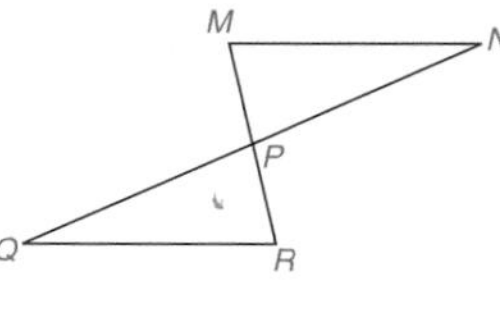

Exercises 3, 4

5. *Given:* $\angle R$ and $\angle V$ are right $\angle$s
$\angle 1 \cong \angle 2$
Prove: $\triangle RST \cong \triangle VST$

6. *Given:* $\angle 1 \cong \angle 2$ and $\angle 3 \cong \angle 4$
Prove: $\triangle RST \cong \triangle VST$

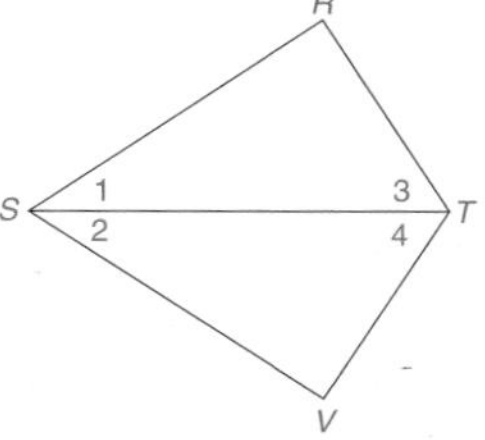

Exercises 5–8

Video exercises are available on DVD.

For Exercises 7 and 8, use the figure on page 142.

7. *Given:* $\overline{SR} \cong \overline{SV}$ and $\overline{RT} \cong \overline{VT}$
Prove: $\triangle RST \cong \triangle VST$

8. *Given:* $\angle R$ and $\angle V$ are right $\angle$s
$\overline{RT} \cong \overline{VT}$
Prove: $\triangle RST \cong \triangle VST$

9. *Given:* $\overline{UW} \parallel \overline{XZ}$, $\overline{VY} \perp \overline{UW}$, and $\overline{VY} \perp \overline{XZ}$
$m\angle 1 = m\angle 4 = 42°$
Find: $m\angle 2$, $m\angle 3$, $m\angle 5$, and $m\angle 6$

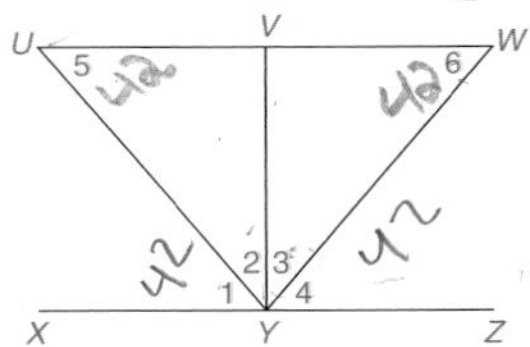

Exercises 9, 10

10. *Given:* $\overline{UW} \parallel \overline{XZ}$, $\overline{VY} \perp \overline{UW}$, and $\overline{VY} \perp \overline{XZ}$
$m\angle 1 = m\angle 4 = 4x + 3$
$m\angle 2 = 6x - 3$
Find: $m\angle 1$, $m\angle 2$, $m\angle 3$, $m\angle 4$, $m\angle 5$, and $m\angle 6$

In Exercises 11 and 12, complete each proof.

11. *Given:* $\overline{HJ} \perp \overline{KL}$ and $\overline{HK} \cong \overline{HL}$
Prove: $\overline{KJ} \cong \overline{JL}$

PROOF

Statements	Reasons
1. $\overline{HJ} \perp \overline{KL}$ and $\overline{HK} \cong \overline{HL}$	1. ?
2. $\angle$s HJK and HJL are rt. $\angle$s	2. ?
3. $\overline{HJ} \cong \overline{HJ}$	3. ?
4. ?	4. HL
5. ?	5. CPCTC

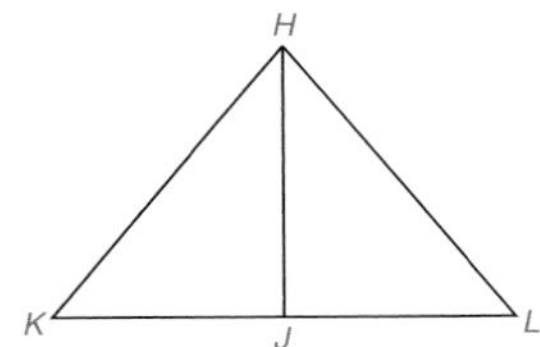

Exercises 11, 12

12. *Given:* $\overrightarrow{HJ}$ bisects $\angle KHL$
$\overline{HJ} \perp \overline{KL}$
Prove: $\angle K \cong \angle L$

PROOF

Statements	Reasons
1. ?	1. Given
2. $\angle JHK \cong \angle JHL$	2. ?
3. $\overline{HJ} \perp \overline{KL}$	3. ?
4. $\angle HJK \cong \angle HJL$	4. ?
5. ?	5. Identity
6. ?	6. ASA
7. $\angle K \cong \angle L$	7. ?

In Exercises 13 to 16, first prove that triangles are congruent, and then use CPCTC.

13. *Given:* $\angle P$ and $\angle R$ are right $\angle$s
M is the midpoint of $\overline{PR}$
Prove: $\angle N \cong \angle Q$

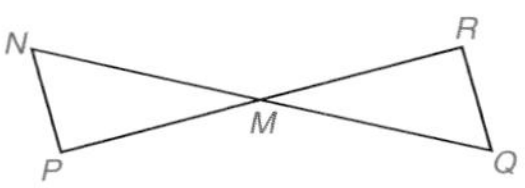

Exercises 13, 14

14. *Given:* M is the midpoint of $\overline{NQ}$
$\overline{NP} \parallel \overline{RQ}$ with transversals $\overline{PR}$ and $\overline{NQ}$
Prove: $\overline{NP} \cong \overline{QR}$

15. *Given:* $\angle 1$ and $\angle 2$ are right $\angle$s
H is the midpoint of $\overline{FK}$
$\overline{FG} \parallel \overline{HJ}$
Prove: $\overline{FG} \cong \overline{HJ}$

16. *Given:* $\overline{DE} \perp \overline{EF}$ and $\overline{CB} \perp \overline{AB}$
$\overline{AB} \parallel \overline{FE}$
$\overline{AC} \cong \overline{FD}$
Prove: $\overline{EF} \cong \overline{BA}$

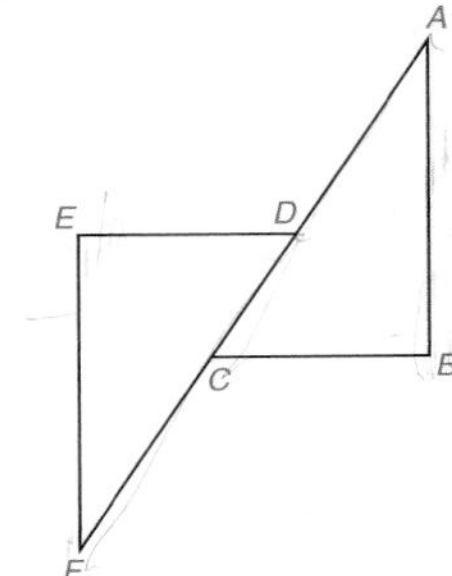

In Exercises 17 to 22, $\triangle ABC$ is a right triangle. Use the given information to find the length of the third side of the triangle.

17. $a = 4$ and $b = 3$

18. $a = 12$ and $b = 5$

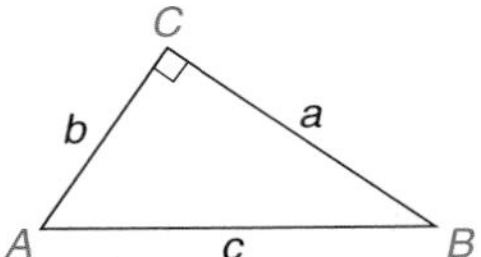

19. $a = 15$ and $c = 17$

20. $b = 6$ and $c = 10$

21. $a = 5$ and $b = 4$

22. $a = 7$ and $c = 8$

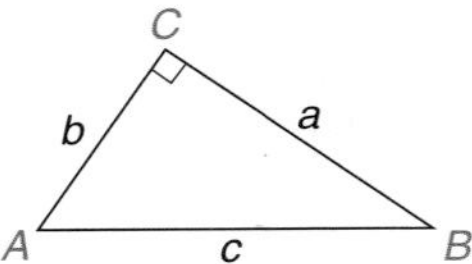

In Exercises 23 to 25, prove the indicated relationship.

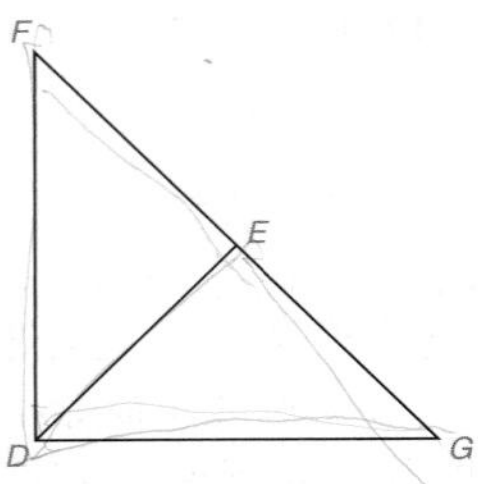

Exercises 23–25

23. *Given:* $\overline{DF} \cong \overline{DG}$ and $\overline{FE} \cong \overline{EG}$
Prove: $\overrightarrow{DE}$ bisects $\angle FDG$

24. *Given:* $\overrightarrow{DE}$ bisects $\angle FDG$
$\angle F \cong \angle G$
Prove: E is the midpoint of $\overline{FG}$

25. *Given:* E is the midpoint of $\overline{FG}$
$\overline{DF} \cong \overline{DG}$
Prove: $\overline{DE} \perp \overline{FG}$

In Exercises 26 to 28, draw the triangles that are to be shown congruent separately.

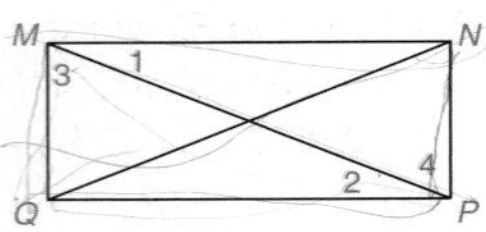

Exercises 26–28

26. *Given:* $\angle MQP$ and $\angle NPQ$ are rt. $\angle$s
$\overline{MQ} \cong \overline{NP}$
Prove: $\overline{MP} \cong \overline{NQ}$
(*HINT:* Show $\triangle MQP \cong \triangle NPQ$.)

27. *Given:* $\angle 1 \cong \angle 2$ and $\overline{MN} \cong \overline{QP}$
Prove: $\overline{MQ} \parallel \overline{NP}$
(*HINT:* Show $\triangle NMP \cong \triangle QPM$.)

28. *Given:* $\overline{MN} \parallel \overline{QP}$ and $\overline{MQ} \parallel \overline{NP}$
Prove: $\overline{MQ} \cong \overline{NP}$
(*HINT:* Show $\triangle MQP \cong \triangle PNM$.)

29. *Given:* $\overrightarrow{RW}$ bisects $\angle SRU$
$\overline{RS} \cong \overline{RU}$
Prove: $\triangle TRU \cong \triangle VRS$
(*HINT:* First show that $\triangle RSW \cong \triangle RUW$.)

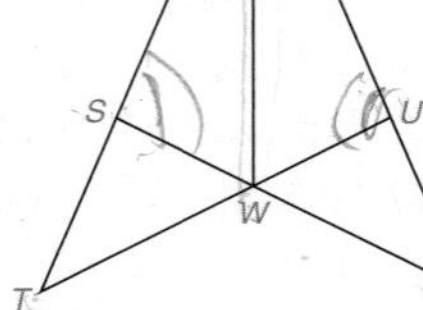

Exercise 29

30. *Given:* $\overline{DB} \perp \overline{BC}$ and $\overline{CE} \perp \overline{DE}$
$\overline{AB} \cong \overline{AE}$
Prove: $\triangle BDC \cong \triangle ECD$
(*HINT:* First show that $\triangle ACE \cong \triangle ADB$.)

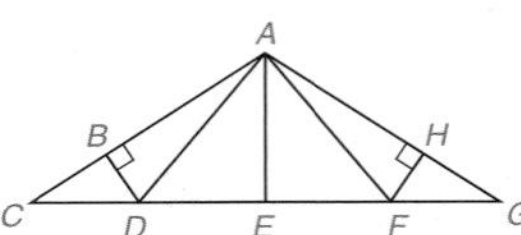

31. In the roof truss shown, $AB = 8$ and $m\angle HAF = 37°$. Find:
a) AH b) $m\angle BAD$ c) $m\angle ADB$

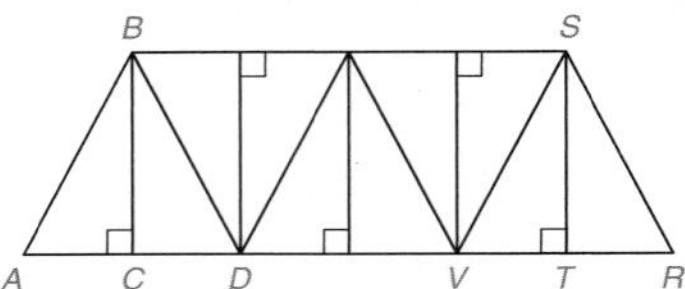

32. In the support system of the bridge shown, $AC = 6$ ft and $m\angle ABC = 28°$. Find:
a) $m\angle RST$ b) $m\angle ABD$ c) BS

33. As a car moves along the roadway in a mountain pass, it passes through a horizontal run of 750 feet and through a vertical rise of 45 feet. To the nearest foot, how far does the car move along the roadway?

34. Because of construction along the road from A to B, Alinna drives 5 miles from A to C and then 12 miles from C to B. How much farther did Alinna travel by using the alternative route from A to B?

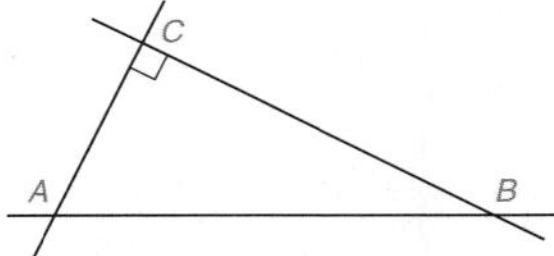

35. *Given:* Regular pentagon $ABCDE$ with diagonals $\overline{BE}$ and $\overline{BD}$
Prove: $\overline{BE} \cong \overline{BD}$
(*HINT:* First prove $\triangle ABE \cong \triangle CBD$.)

36. In the figure with regular pentagon $ABCDE$, do $\overrightarrow{BE}$ and $\overrightarrow{BD}$ trisect $\angle ABC$?
(*HINT:* $m\angle ABE = m\angle AEB$.)

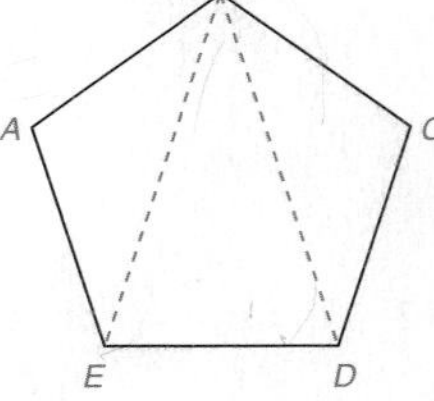

Exercises 35, 36

3.3 Isosceles Triangles

Isosceles Triangle	Median	Equilateral and Equiangular Triangles
Vertex, Legs, and Base of an Isosceles Triangle	Altitude	Perimeter
Base Angles	Perpendicular Bisector	
Vertex Angle	Auxiliary Line	
Angle Bisector	Determined, Overdetermined, Undetermined	

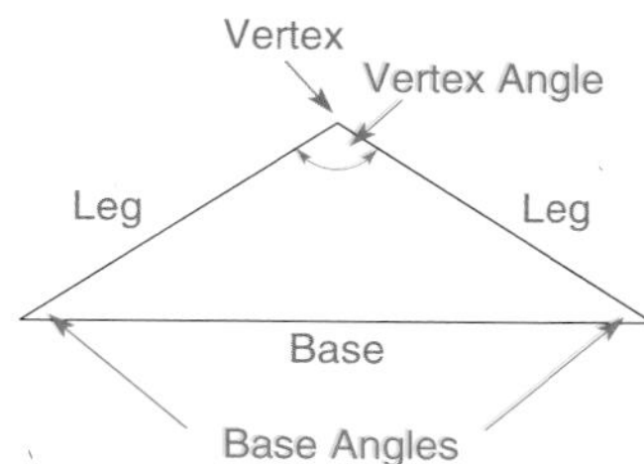

Figure 3.22

In an isosceles triangle, the two sides of equal length are **legs,** and the third side is the **base.** See Figure 3.22. The point at which the two legs meet is the **vertex** of the triangle, and the angle formed by the legs (and opposite the base) is the **vertex angle.** The two remaining angles are **base angles.** If $\overline{AC} \cong \overline{BC}$ in Figure 3.23, then $\triangle ABC$ is isosceles with legs $\overline{AC}$ and $\overline{BC}$, base $\overline{AB}$, vertex C, vertex angle C, and base angles at A and B. With $\overline{AC} \cong \overline{BC}$, we see that the base $\overline{AB}$ of this isosceles triangle is not necessarily the "bottom" side.

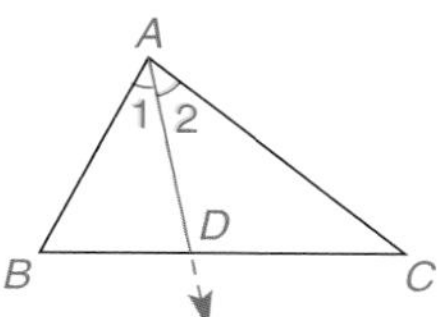

$\angle 1 \cong \angle 2$, so $\overrightarrow{AD}$ is the angle-bisector of $\angle BAC$ in $\triangle ABC$

(a)

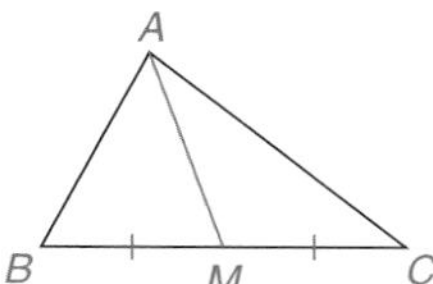

M is the midpoint of $\overline{BC}$, so $\overline{AM}$ is the median from A to $\overline{BC}$

(b)

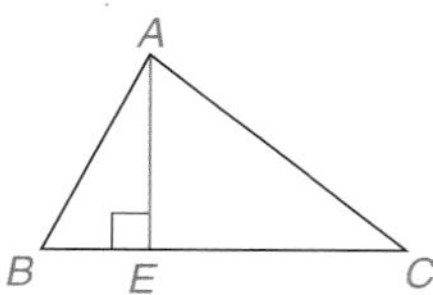

$\overline{AE} \perp \overline{BC}$, so $\overline{AE}$ is the altitude of $\triangle ABC$ from vertex A to $\overline{BC}$

(c)

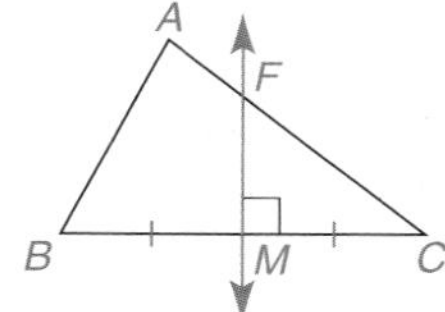

M is the midpoint of $\overline{BC}$ and $\overleftrightarrow{FM} \perp \overline{BC}$, so $\overleftrightarrow{FM}$ is the perpendicular bisector of side $\overline{BC}$ in $\triangle ABC$

(d)

Figure 3.23

Consider $\triangle ABC$ in Figure 3.23 once again. Each angle of a triangle has a unique **angle bisector,** and this may be indicated by a ray or segment from the vertex of the bisected angle. Just as an angle bisector begins at the vertex of an angle, the **median** also joins a vertex to the midpoint of the opposite side. Generally, the median from a vertex of a triangle is not the same as the angle bisector from that vertex. An **altitude** is a line segment drawn from a vertex to the opposite side such that it is perpendicular to the opposite side. Finally, the **perpendicular bisector** of a side of a triangle is shown as a line in Figure 3.23(d). A segment or ray could also perpendicularly bisect a side of the triangle. In Figure 3.24, $\overrightarrow{AD}$ is the bisector of $\angle BAC$; $\overline{AE}$ is the altitude from A to $\overline{BC}$; M is the midpoint of $\overline{BC}$; $\overline{AM}$ is the median from A to $\overline{BC}$; and $\overleftrightarrow{FM}$ is the perpendicular bisector of $\overline{BC}$.

An altitude can actually lie in the exterior of a triangle. In Figure 3.25 (on page 146), which shows obtuse triangle $\triangle RST$, the altitude from R must be drawn to an extension of side $\overline{ST}$. Later we will use the length h of the altitude $\overline{RH}$ and the length b of side $\overline{ST}$ in the following formula for the area of a triangle:

$$A = \frac{1}{2}bh$$

Any angle bisector and any median necessarily lie in the interior of the triangle.

Figure 3.24

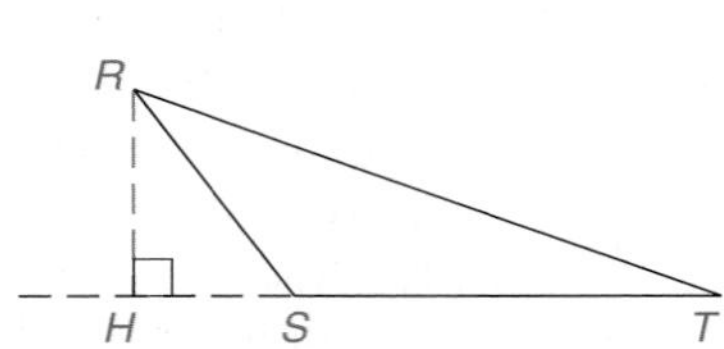

Figure 3.25

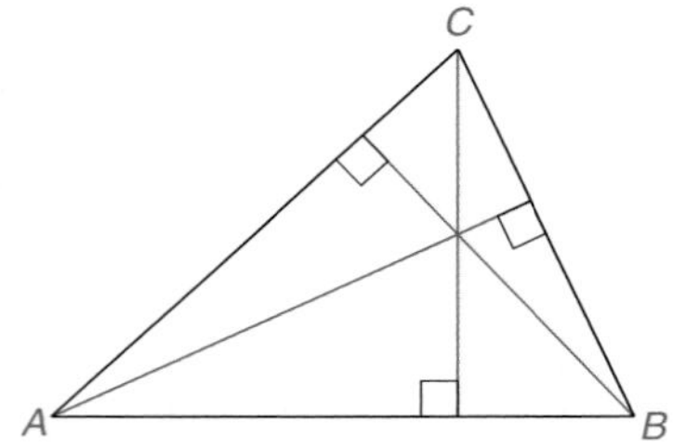

Figure 3.26

Each triangle has three altitudes—one from each vertex. As these are shown for $\triangle ABC$ in Figure 3.26, the three altitudes seem to meet at a common point.

We now consider the proof of a statement that involves the corresponding altitudes of congruent triangles; corresponding altitudes are those drawn to corresponding sides of the triangles.

THEOREM 3.3.1

Corresponding altitudes of congruent triangles are congruent.

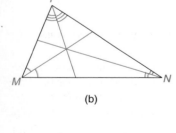

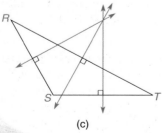

GIVEN: $\triangle ABC \cong \triangle RST$
Altitudes $\overline{CD}$ to $\overline{AB}$ and $\overline{TV}$ to $\overline{RS}$
(See Figure 3.27.)

PROVE: $\overline{CD} \cong \overline{TV}$

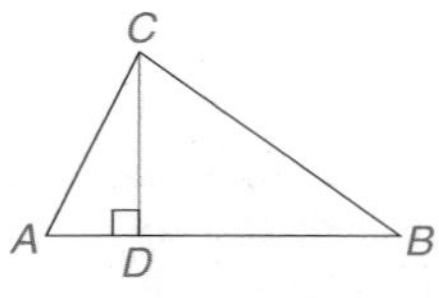

Figure 3.27

PROOF

Statements	Reasons
1. $\triangle ABC \cong \triangle RST$ Altitudes $\overline{CD}$ to $\overline{AB}$ and $\overline{TV}$ to $\overline{RS}$	1. Given
2. $\overline{CD} \perp \overline{AB}$ and $\overline{TV} \perp \overline{RS}$	2. An altitude of a $\triangle$ is the line segment from one vertex drawn $\perp$ to the opposite side
3. $\angle CDA$ and $\angle TVR$ are right $\angle$s	3. If two lines are $\perp$, they form right $\angle$s
4. $\angle CDA \cong \angle TVR$	4. All right angles are $\cong$
5. $\overline{AC} \cong \overline{RT}$ and $\angle A \cong \angle R$	5. CPCTC (from $\triangle ABC \cong \triangle RST$)
6. $\triangle CDA \cong \triangle TVR$	6. AAS
7. $\overline{CD} \cong \overline{TV}$	7. CPCTC

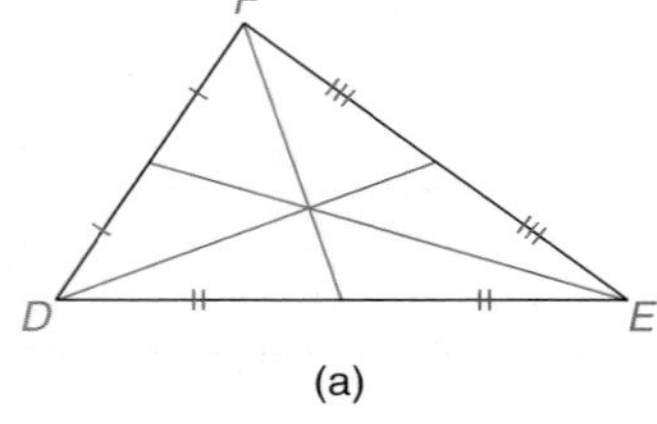

Figure 3.28

Each triangle has three medians—one from each vertex to the midpoint of the opposite side. As the medians are drawn for $\triangle DEF$ in Figure 3.28(a), it appears that the three medians intersect at a point.

Each triangle has three angle bisectors—one for each of the three angles. As these are shown for $\triangle MNP$ in Figure 3.28(b), it appears that the three angle bisectors have a point in common. See Figure 3.28 on page 146.

Each triangle has three perpendicular bisectors for its sides; these are shown for $\triangle RST$ in Figure 3.28(c). Like the altitudes, medians, and angle bisectors, the perpendicular bisectors of the sides also meet at a single point.

The angle bisectors (like the medians) of a triangle *always* meet in the interior of the triangle. However, the altitudes (like the perpendicular bisectors of the sides) can meet in the exterior of the triangle; see Figure 3.28(c). These points of intersection will be given greater attention in Chapter 7.

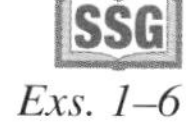

Exs. 1–6

The Discover activity at the left opens the doors to further discoveries.

In Figure 3.29, the bisector of the vertex angle of isosceles $\triangle ABC$ is a line (segment) of symmetry for $\triangle ABC$.

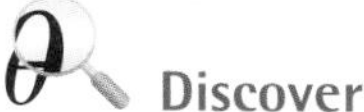

Discover

Using a sheet of construction paper, cut out an isosceles triangle. Now use your compass to bisect the vertex angle. Fold along the angle bisector to form two smaller triangles. How are the smaller triangles related?

ANSWER

They are congruent.

EXAMPLE 1

Give a formal proof of Theorem 3.3.2.

THEOREM 3.3.2

The bisector of the vertex angle of an isosceles triangle separates the triangle into two congruent triangles.

GIVEN: Isosceles $\triangle ABC$, with $\overline{AB} \cong \overline{BC}$
$\overrightarrow{BD}$ bisects $\angle ABC$
(See Figure 3.29.)

PROVE: $\triangle ABD \cong \triangle CBD$

PROOF

Statements	Reasons
1. Isosceles $\triangle ABC$ with $\overline{AB} \cong \overline{BC}$	1. Given
2. $\overrightarrow{BD}$ bisects $\angle ABC$	2. Given
3. $\angle 1 \cong \angle 2$	3. The bisector of an $\angle$ separates it into two $\cong$ $\angle$s
4. $\overline{BD} \cong \overline{BD}$	4. Identity
5. $\triangle ABD \cong \triangle CBD$	5. SAS

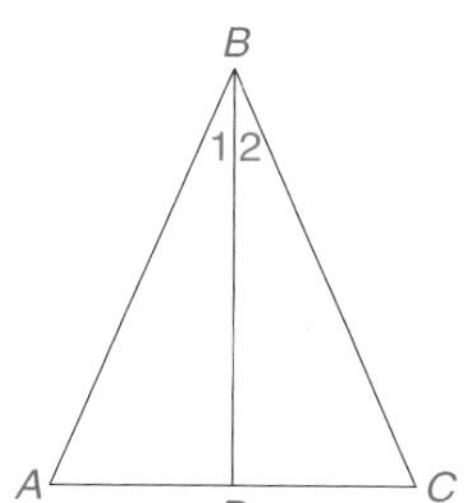

Figure 3.29

Recall from Section 2.4 that an auxiliary figure must be determined. Consider Figure 3.30 and the following three descriptions, which are coded **D** for determined, **U** for underdetermined, and **O** for overdetermined:

D: Draw a line segment from A perpendicular to $\overline{BC}$ so that the terminal point is on $\overline{BC}$. [*Determined* because the line from A perpendicular to $\overline{BC}$ is unique; see Figure 3.30(a).]

U: Draw a line segment from A to $\overline{BC}$ so that the terminal point is on $\overline{BC}$. [*Underdetermined* because many line segments are possible; see Figure 3.30(b).]

O: Draw a line segment from A perpendicular to $\overline{BC}$ so that it bisects $\overline{BC}$. [*Overdetermined* because the line segment from A drawn perpendicular to $\overline{BC}$ will not contain the midpoint M of $\overline{BC}$; see Figure 3.30(c).]

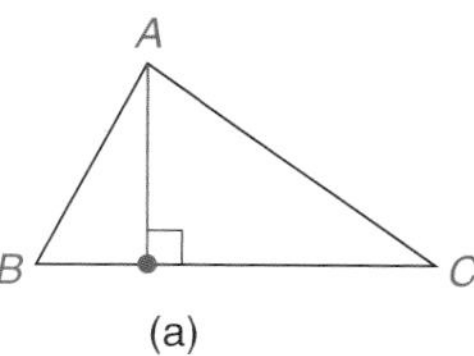

(a)

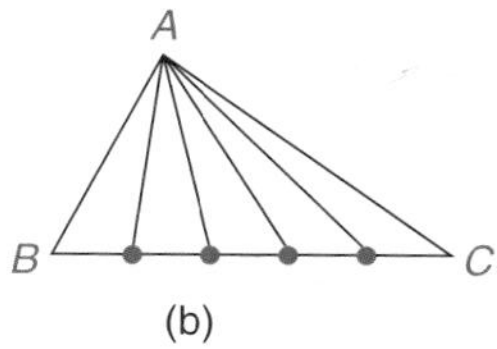

(b)

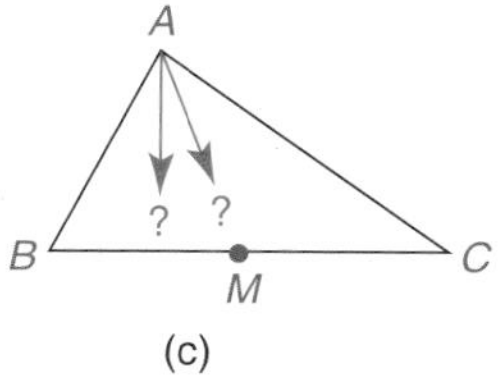

(c)

Figure 3.30

In Example 2, an auxiliary segment is needed. As you study the proof, note the uniqueness of the segment and its justification (reason 2) in the proof.

STRATEGY FOR PROOF ▶ Using an Auxiliary Line

General Rule: An early *statement* of the proof establishes the "helping line" as *the* altitude or *the* angle bisector or whatever else.

Illustration: See the second line in the proof of Example 2. The chosen angle bisector leads to congruent triangles, which enable us to complete the proof.

EXAMPLE 2

Give a formal proof of Theorem 3.3.3.

THEOREM 3.3.3

If two sides of a triangle are congruent, then the angles opposite these sides are also congruent.

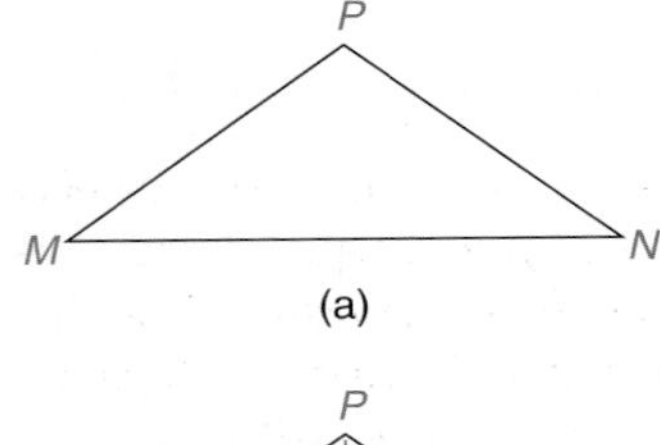

(a)

P
M
Q
N
(b)

Figure 3.31

GIVEN: Isosceles $\triangle MNP$ with $\overline{MP} \cong \overline{NP}$ [See Figure 3.31(a).]

PROVE: $\angle M \cong \angle N$

NOTE: Figure 3.31(b) shows the auxiliary segment.

PROOF

Statements	Reasons
1. Isosceles $\triangle MNP$ with $\overline{MP} \cong \overline{NP}$	1. Given
2. Draw $\angle$ bisector $\overrightarrow{PQ}$ from P to $\overline{MN}$	2. Every angle has one and only one bisector
3. $\triangle MPQ \cong \triangle NPQ$	3. The bisector of the vertex angle of an isosceles $\triangle$ separates it into two $\cong$ $\triangle$s
4. $\angle M \cong \angle N$	4. CPCTC

■

Theorem 3.3.3 is sometimes stated, "The base angles of an isosceles triangle are congruent." We apply this theorem in Example 3.

EXAMPLE 3

Find the size of each angle of the isosceles triangle shown in Figure 3.32 on page 149 if:

a) $m\angle 1 = 36°$

b) The measure of each base angle is 5° less than twice the measure of the vertex angle

Discover

Using construction paper and scissors, cut out an isosceles triangle MNP with $\overline{MP} \cong \overline{PN}$. Fold it so that $\angle M$ coincides with $\angle N$. What can you conclude?

ANSWER
$\angle M \cong \angle N$

Solution

a) $m\angle 1 + m\angle 2 + m\angle 3 = 180°$. Since $m\angle 1 = 36°$ and $\angle 2$ and $\angle 3$ are $\cong$, we have

$$\begin{aligned} 36 + 2(m\angle 2) &= 180 \\ 2(m\angle 2) &= 144 \\ m\angle 2 &= 72 \end{aligned}$$

Now $m\angle 1 = 36°$, and $m\angle 2 = m\angle 3 = 72°$.

b) Let the vertex angle measure be given by x. Then the size of each base angle is $2x - 5$. Because the sum of the measures is $180°$,

$$\begin{aligned} x + (2x - 5) + (2x - 5) &= 180 \\ 5x - 10 &= 180 \\ 5x &= 190 \\ x &= 38 \\ 2x - 5 = 2(38) - 5 = 76 - 5 &= 71 \end{aligned}$$

Therefore, $m\angle 1 = 38°$ and $m\angle 2 = m\angle 3 = 71°$. ■

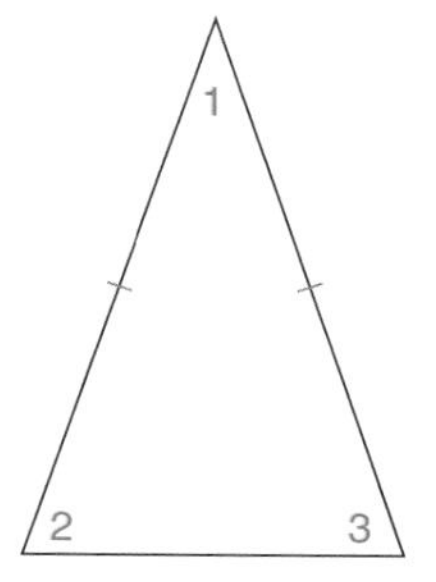

Figure 3.32

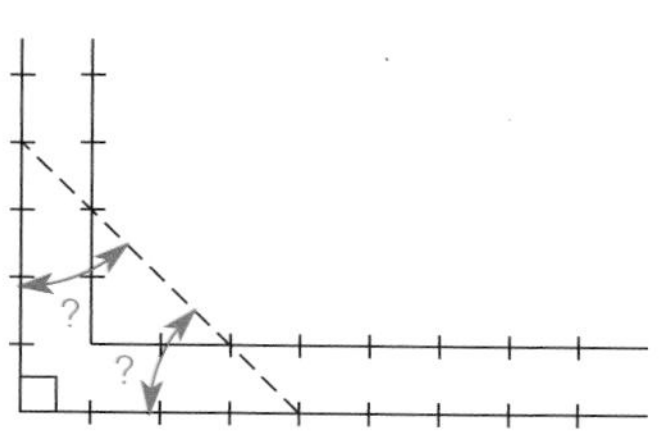

Figure 3.33

In some instances, a carpenter may want to get a quick, accurate measurement without having to go get his or her tools. Suppose that the carpenter's square shown in Figure 3.33 is handy but that a miter box is not nearby. If two marks are made at lengths of 4 inches from the corner of the square and these are then joined, what size angle is determined? You should see that each angle indicated by an arc measures 45°.

Example 4 shows us that the converse of the theorem "The base angles of an isosceles △ are congruent" is also true. However, see the accompanying Warning.

Warning

The converse of an "If, then" statement is not always true.

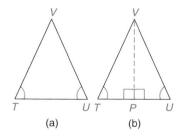

EXAMPLE 4

Study the picture proof of Theorem 3.3.4.

THEOREM 3.3.4

If two angles of a triangle are congruent, then the sides opposite these angles are also congruent.

V V
T U T P U
(a) (b)

Figure 3.34

PICTURE PROOF OF THEOREM 3.3.4

GIVEN: $\triangle TUV$ with $\angle T \cong \angle U$ [See Figure 3.34(a).]

PROVE: $\overline{VU} \cong \overline{VT}$

PROOF: Drawing $\overline{VP} \perp \overline{TU}$ [see Figure 3.34(b)], we see that $\triangle VPT \cong \triangle VPU$ (by AAS). Now $\overline{VU} \cong \overline{VT}$ (by CPCTC). ■

SSG *Exs. 7–17*

When all three sides of a triangle are congruent, the triangle is **equilateral.** If all three angles are congruent, then the triangle is **equiangular.** Theorems 3.3.3 and 3.3.4 can be used to prove that the sets {equilateral triangles} and {equiangular triangles} are equivalent.

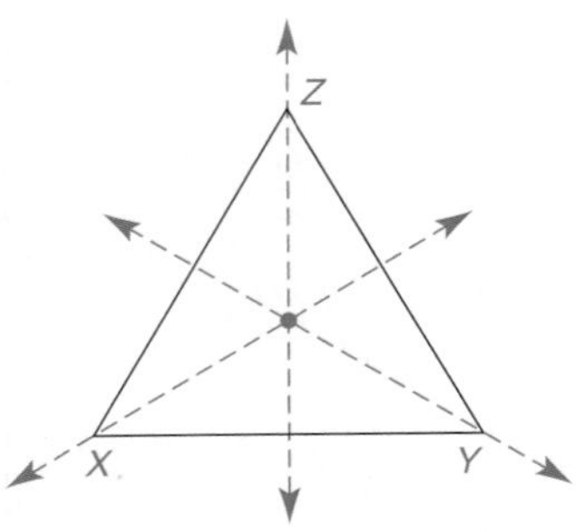

Figure 3.35

COROLLARY 3.3.5

An equilateral triangle is also equiangular.

COROLLARY 3.3.6

An equiangular triangle is also equilateral.

An equilateral (or equiangular) triangle has line symmetry with respect to each of the three axes shown in Figure 3.35.

DEFINITION

The **perimeter** of a triangle is the sum of the lengths of its sides. Thus, if a, b, and c are the lengths of the three sides, then the perimeter P is given by $P = a + b + c$. (See Figure 3.36.)

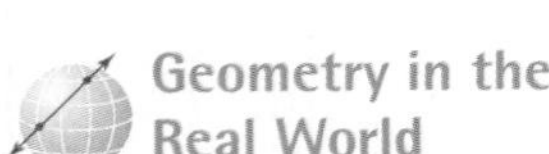

Geometry in the Real World

Braces that create triangles are used to provide stability for a bookcase. The triangle is called a rigid figure.

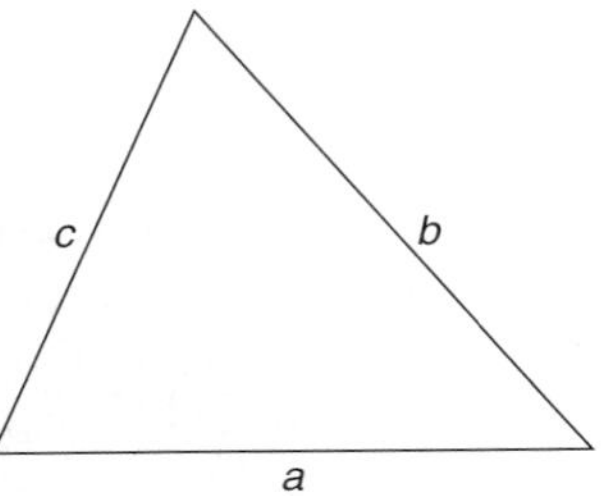

Figure 3.36

EXAMPLE 5

GIVEN: $\angle B \cong \angle C$
$AB = 5.3$ and $BC = 3.6$

FIND: The perimeter of $\triangle ABC$

Solution If $\angle B \cong \angle C$, then $AC = AB = 5.3$. Therefore,

$$P = a + b + c$$
$$P = 3.6 + 5.3 + 5.3$$
$$P = 14.2$$

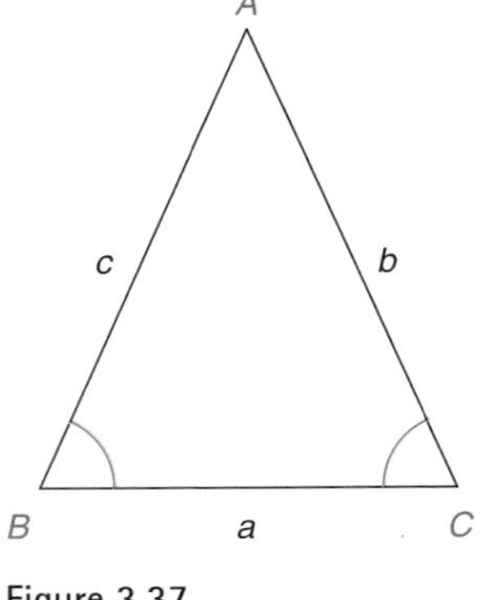

Figure 3.37

Exs. 18–22

Many of the properties of triangles that were investigated in earlier sections are summarized in Table 3.1.

TABLE 3.1
Selected Properties of Triangles

	Scalene	Isosceles	Equilateral (equiangular)	Acute	Right	Obtuse
Sides	No two are ≅	Exactly two are ≅	All three are ≅	Possibly two or three ≅ sides	Possibly two ≅ sides; $c^2 = a^2 + b^2$	Possibly two ≅ sides
Angles	Sum of ∠s is 180°	Sum of ∠s is 180°; two ∠s ≅	Sum of ∠s is 180°; three ≅ 60° ∠s	All ∠s acute; sum of ∠s is 180°; possibly two or three ≅ ∠s	One right ∠; sum of ∠s is 180°; possibly two ≅ 45° ∠s; acute ∠s are complementary	One obtuse ∠; sum of ∠s is 180°; possibly two ≅ acute ∠s

Exercises 3.3

For Exercises 1 to 8, use the accompanying drawing.

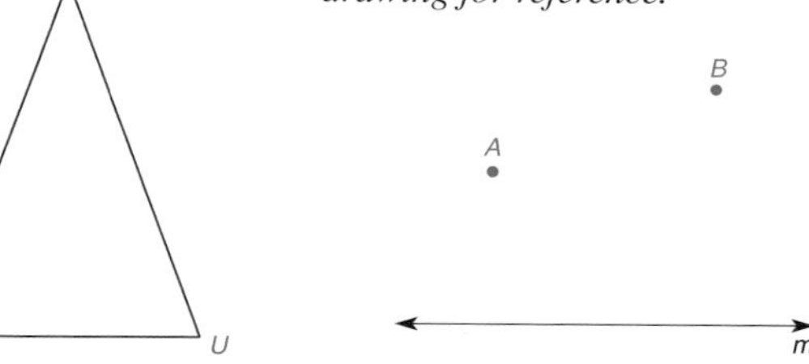

Exercises 1–8

1. If $\overline{VU} \cong \overline{VT}$, what type of triangle is $\triangle VTU$?
2. If $\overline{VU} \cong \overline{VT}$, which angles of $\triangle VTU$ are congruent?
3. If $\angle T \cong \angle U$, which sides of $\triangle VTU$ are congruent?
4. If $\overline{VU} \cong \overline{VT}$, $VU = 10$, and $TU = 8$, what is the perimeter of $\triangle VTU$?
5. If $\overline{VU} \cong \overline{VT}$ and $m\angle T = 69°$, find $m\angle U$.
6. If $\overline{VU} \cong \overline{VT}$ and $m\angle T = 69°$, find $m\angle V$.
7. If $\overline{VU} \cong \overline{VT}$ and $m\angle T = 72°$, find $m\angle V$.
8. If $\overline{VU} \cong \overline{VT}$ and $m\angle V = 40°$, find $m\angle T$.

In Exercises 9 to 12, determine whether the sets have a subset relationship. Are the two sets disjoint or equivalent? Do the sets intersect?

9. L = {equilateral triangles}; E = {equiangular triangles}
10. S = {triangles with two ≅ sides}; A = {triangles with two ≅ ∠s}
11. R = {right triangles}; O = {obtuse triangles}
12. I = {isosceles triangles}; R = {right triangles}

In Exercises 13 to 18, describe the segment as determined, underdetermined, or overdetermined. Use the accompanying drawing for reference.

Exercises 13–18

13. Draw a segment through point A.
14. Draw a segment with endpoints A and B.
15. Draw a segment $\overline{AB}$ parallel to line m.
16. Draw a segment $\overline{AB}$ perpendicular to m.
17. Draw a segment from A perpendicular to m.
18. Draw $\overline{AB}$ so that line m bisects $\overline{AB}$.
19. A surveyor knows that a lot has the shape of an isosceles triangle. If the vertex angle measures 70° and each equal side is 160 ft long, what measure does each of the base angles have?

20. In concave quadrilateral $ABCD$, the angle at A measures $40°$. $\triangle ABD$ is isosceles, $\overrightarrow{BC}$ bisects $\angle ABD$, and $\overrightarrow{DC}$ bisects $\angle ADB$. What are the measures of $\angle ABC$, $\angle ADC$, and $\angle 1$?

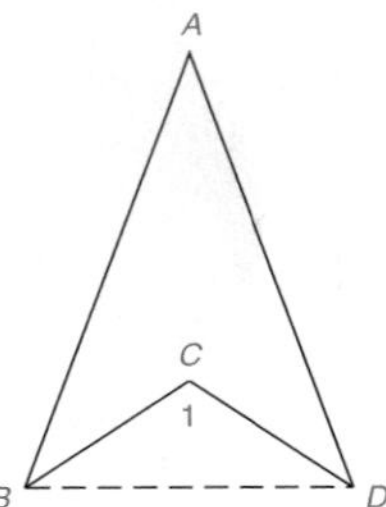

In Exercises 21 to 26, use arithmetic or algebra as needed to find the measures indicated. Note the use of dashes on equal sides of the given isosceles triangles.

21. Find $m\angle 1$ and $m\angle 2$ if $m\angle 3 = 68°$.

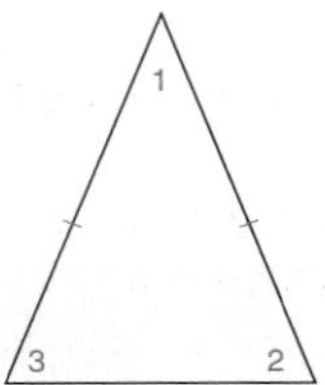

22. If $m\angle 3 = 68°$, find $m\angle 4$, the angle formed by the bisectors of $\angle 3$ and $\angle 2$.

23. Find the measure of $\angle 5$, which is formed by the bisectors of $\angle 1$ and $\angle 3$. Again let $m\angle 3 = 68°$.

24. Find an expression for the measure of $\angle 5$ if $m\angle 3 = 2x$ and the segments shown bisect the angles of the isosceles triangle.

25. In isosceles $\triangle ABC$ with vertex A (not shown), each base angle is $12°$ larger than the vertex angle. Find the measure of each angle.

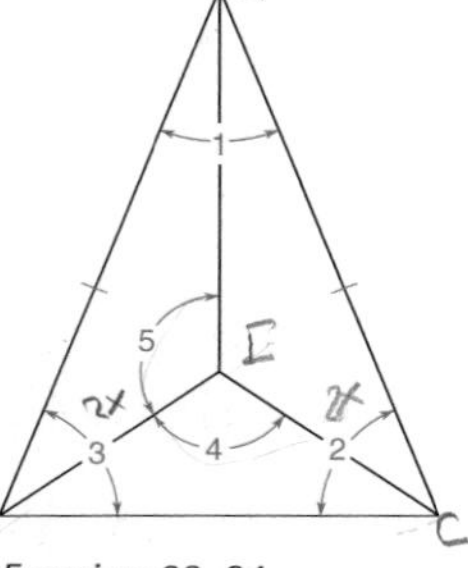

Exercises 22–24

26. In isosceles $\triangle ABC$ (not shown), vertex angle A is $5°$ more than one-half of base angle B. Find the size of each angle of the triangle.

In Exercises 27 to 30, suppose that $\overline{BC}$ is the base of isosceles $\triangle ABC$ (not shown).

27. Find the perimeter of $\triangle ABC$ if $AB = 8$ and $BC = 10$.

28. Find AB if the perimeter of $\triangle ABC$ is 36.4 and $BC = 14.6$.

29. Find x if the perimeter of $\triangle ABC$ is 40, $AB = x$, and $BC = x + 4$.

30. Find x if the perimeter of $\triangle ABC$ is 68, $AB = x$, and $BC = 1.4x$.

31. Suppose that $\triangle ABC \cong \triangle DEF$. Also, $\overline{AX}$ bisects $\angle CAB$ and $\overline{DY}$ bisects $\angle FDE$. Are the corresponding angle bisectors of congruent triangles congruent?

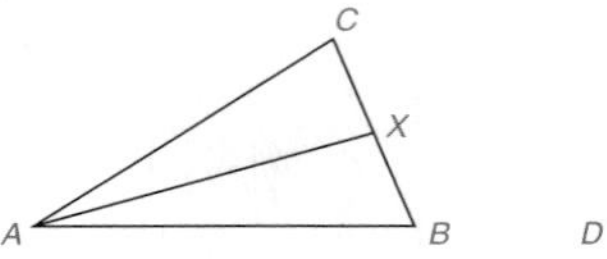

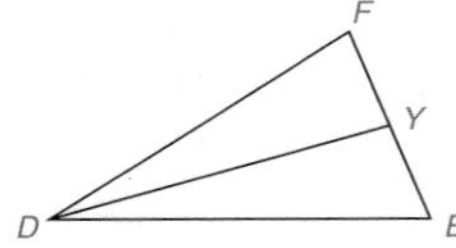

Exercises 31, 32

32. Suppose that $\triangle ABC \cong \triangle DEF$, $\overline{AX}$ is the median from A to $\overline{BC}$, and $\overline{DY}$ is the median from D to $\overline{EF}$. Are the corresponding medians of congruent triangles congruent?

In Exercises 33 and 34, complete each proof using the drawing below.

33. *Given:* $\angle 3 \cong \angle 1$
Prove: $\overline{AB} \cong \overline{AC}$

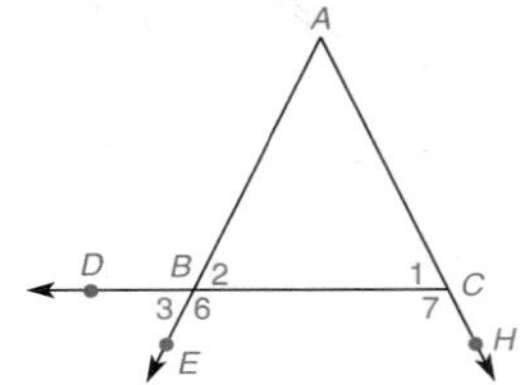

Exercises 33, 34

PROOF

Statements	Reasons
1. $\angle 3 \cong \angle 1$	1. ?
2. ?	2. If two lines intersect, the vertical $\angle$s formed are $\cong$
3. ?	3. Transitive Property of Congruence
4. $\overline{AB} \cong \overline{AC}$	4. ?

34. *Given:* $\overline{AB} \cong \overline{AC}$
Prove: $\angle 6 \cong \angle 7$

PROOF

Statements	Reasons
1. ?	1. Given
2. $\angle 2 \cong \angle 1$	2. ?
3. $\angle 2$ and $\angle 6$ are supplementary; $\angle 1$ and $\angle 7$ are supplementary	3. ?
4. ?	4. If two $\angle$s are supplementary to $\cong$ $\angle$s, they are $\cong$ to each other

In Exercises 35 to 37, complete each proof.

35. *Given:* $\angle 1 \cong \angle 3$
$\overline{RU} \cong \overline{VU}$
Prove: $\triangle STU$ is isosceles
(HINT: First show that $\triangle RUS \cong \triangle VUT$.)

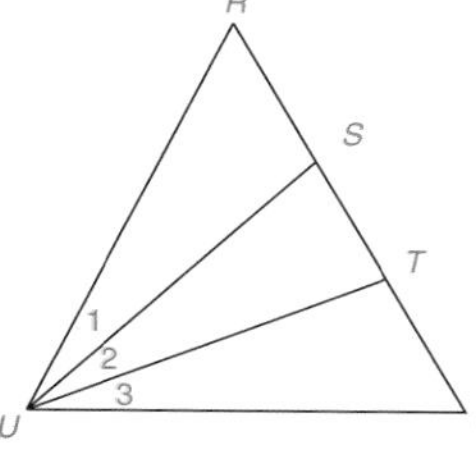

36. *Given:* $\overline{WY} \cong \overline{WZ}$
M is the midpoint of $\overline{YZ}$
$\overline{MX} \perp \overline{WY}$ and
$\overline{MT} \perp \overline{WZ}$
Prove: $\overline{MX} \cong \overline{MT}$

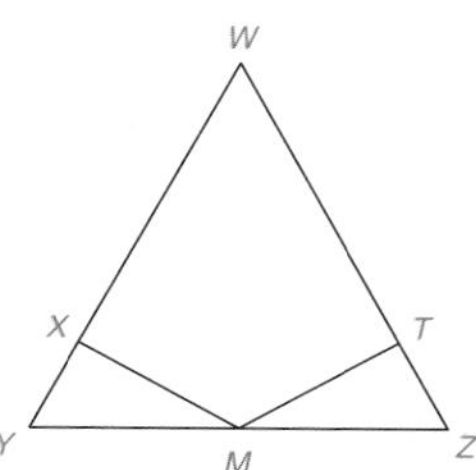

37. *Given:* Isosceles $\triangle MNP$ with vertex P
Isosceles $\triangle MNQ$ with vertex Q
Prove: $\triangle MQP \cong \triangle NQP$

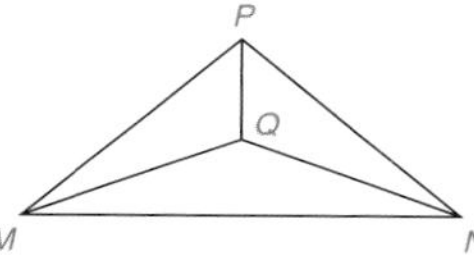

38. In isosceles triangle BAT, $\overline{AB} \cong \overline{AT}$. Also, $\overline{BR} \cong \overline{BT} \cong \overline{AR}$. If $AB = 12.3$ and $AR = 7.6$, find the perimeter of:
a) $\triangle BAT$
b) $\triangle ARB$
c) $\triangle RBT$

39. In $\triangle BAT$, $\overline{BR} \cong \overline{BT} \cong \overline{AR}$, and $m\angle RBT = 20°$. Find:
a) $m\angle T$
b) $m\angle ARB$
c) $m\angle A$

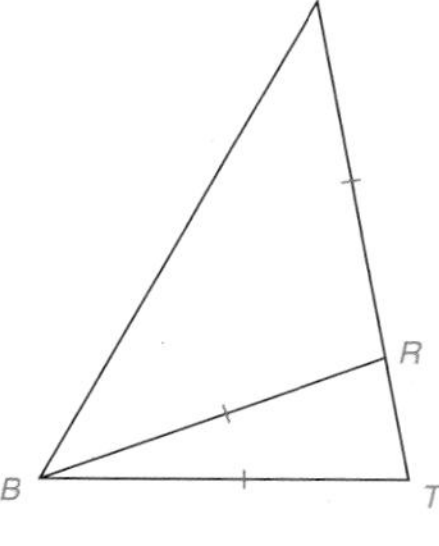

Exercises 38, 39

40. In $\triangle PMN$, $\overline{PM} \cong \overline{PN}$. $\overrightarrow{MB}$ bisects $\angle PMN$, and $\overrightarrow{NA}$ bisects $\angle PNM$. If $m\angle P = 36°$, name all isosceles triangles shown in the drawing.

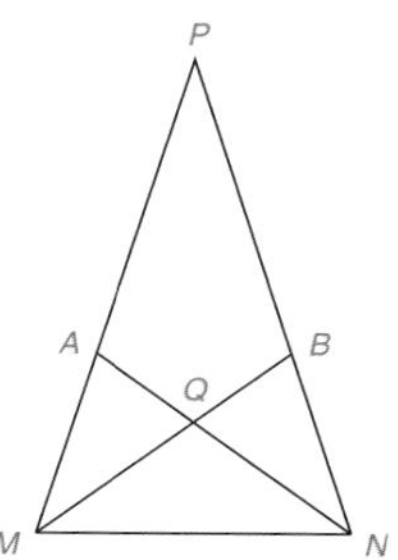

41. $\triangle ABC$ lies in the structural support system of the Ferris wheel. If $m\angle A = 30°$ and $AB = AC = 20$ ft, find the measures of $\angle B$ and $\angle C$.

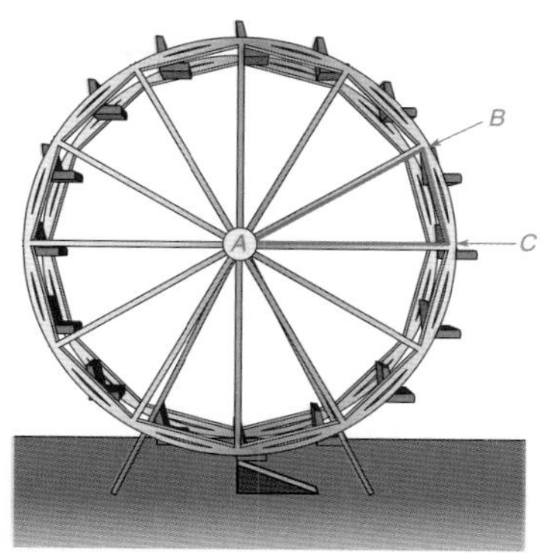

In Exercises 42 to 44, explain why each statement is true.

42. The altitude from the vertex of an isosceles triangle is also the median to the base of the triangle.

43. The bisector of the vertex angle of an isosceles triangle bisects the base.

44. The angle bisectors of the base angles of an isosceles triangle, together with the base, form an isosceles triangle.

***45.** *Given:* In the figure, $\overline{XZ} \cong \overline{YZ}$, and Z is the midpoint of $\overline{XW}$.

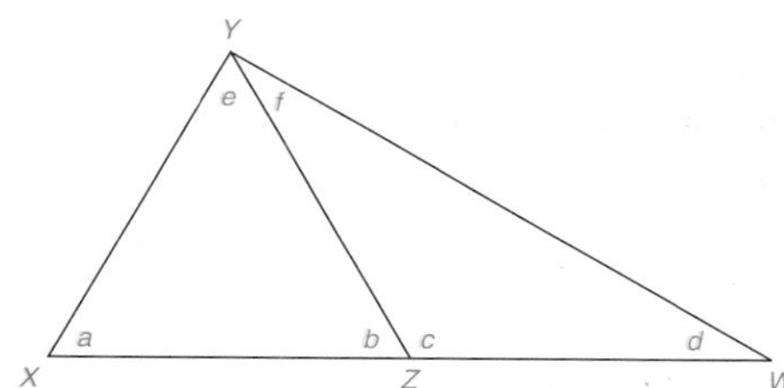

Prove: $\triangle XYW$ is a right triangle with $m\angle XYW = 90°$.
(HINT: Let $m\angle X = a$.)

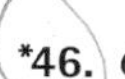

***46.** *Given:* In the figure, $a = e = 66°$. Also, $\overline{YZ} \cong \overline{ZW}$. If $YW = 14.3$ in. and $YZ = 7.8$ in., find the perimeter of $\triangle XYW$ to the nearest tenth of an inch.

3.4 Basic Constructions Justified

KEY CONCEPTS

Justifying Constructions

In earlier sections, construction methods were introduced that appeared to achieve their goals; however, the methods were presented intuitively. In this section, we justify the construction methods and apply them in further constructions. The justification of the method is a "proof" that demonstrates that the construction accomplished its purpose. See Example 1.

EXAMPLE 1

Justify the method for constructing an angle congruent to a given angle.

GIVEN: $\angle ABC$
$\overline{BD} \cong \overline{BE} \cong \overline{ST} \cong \overline{SR}$ (by construction)
$\overline{DE} \cong \overline{TR}$ (by construction)

PROVE: $\angle B \cong \angle S$

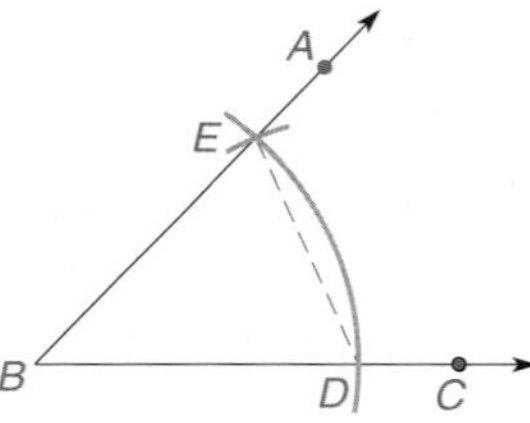

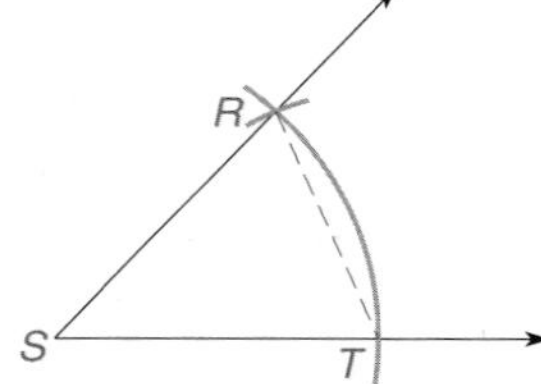

Figure 3.38

PROOF

Statements	Reasons
1. $\angle ABC$; $\overline{BD} \cong \overline{BE} \cong \overline{ST} \cong \overline{SR}$	1. Given
2. $\overline{DE} \cong \overline{TR}$	2. Given
3. $\triangle EBD \cong \triangle RST$	3. SSS
4. $\angle B \cong \angle S$	4. CPCTC

■

In Example 2, we will apply the construction method that was justified in Example 1. Our goal is to construct an isosceles triangle that contains an obtuse angle. It is necessary that the congruent sides include the obtuse angle.

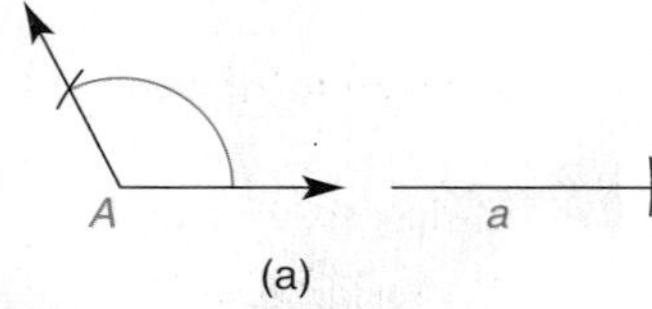

(a)

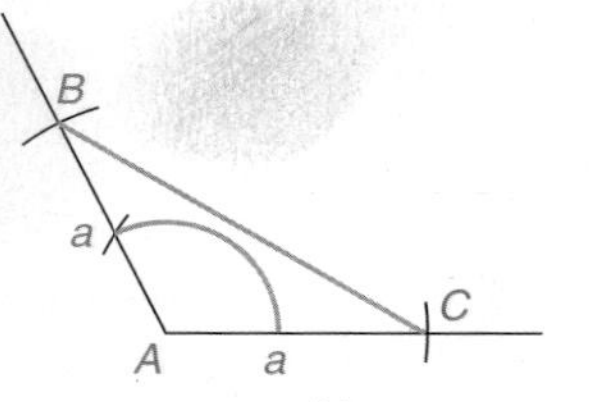

(b)

Figure 3.39

EXAMPLE 2

Construct an isosceles triangle in which obtuse $\angle A$ is included by two sides of length a [see Figure 3.39(a)].

Solution Construct an angle congruent to $\angle A$. From A, mark off arcs of length a at points B and C as shown in Figure 3.39(b). Join B to C to complete $\triangle ABC$. ■

Exs. 1–2

In Example 3, we recall the method of construction used to bisect an angle. Although the technique is illustrated, the objective here is to justify the method.

EXAMPLE 3

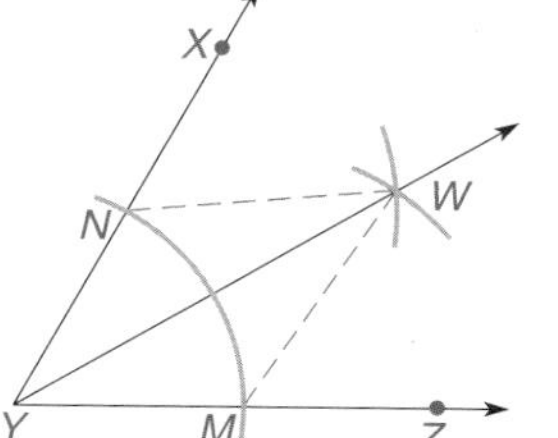

Figure 3.40

Justify the method for constructing the bisector of an angle. Provide the missing reasons in the proof.

GIVEN: $\angle XYZ$
$\overline{YM} \cong \overline{YN}$ (by construction)
$\overline{MW} \cong \overline{NW}$ (by construction)
(See Figure 3.40.)

PROVE: $\overrightarrow{YW}$ bisects $\angle XYZ$

PROOF

Statements	Reasons
1. $\angle XYZ$; $\overline{YM} \cong \overline{YN}$ and $\overline{MW} \cong \overline{NW}$	1. ?
2. $\overline{YW} \cong \overline{YW}$	2. ?
3. $\triangle YMW \cong \triangle YNW$	3. ?
4. $\angle MYW \cong \angle NYW$	4. ?
5. $\overrightarrow{YW}$ bisects $\angle XYZ$	5. ?

The angle bisector method can be used to construct angles of certain measures. For instance, if a right angle has been constructed, then an angle of measure 45° can be constructed by bisecting the 90° angle. In Example 4, we construct an angle of measure 30°.

EXAMPLE 4

Construct an angle that measures 30°.

Solution Figures 3.41(a) and (b): We begin by constructing an equilateral (and therefore equiangular) triangle. To accomplish this, mark off a line segment of length a. From the endpoints of this line segment, mark off arcs using the same radius length a. The point of intersection determines the third vertex of this triangle, whose angles measure 60° each.

Figure 3.41(c): By constructing the bisector of one angle, we determine an angle that measures 30°.

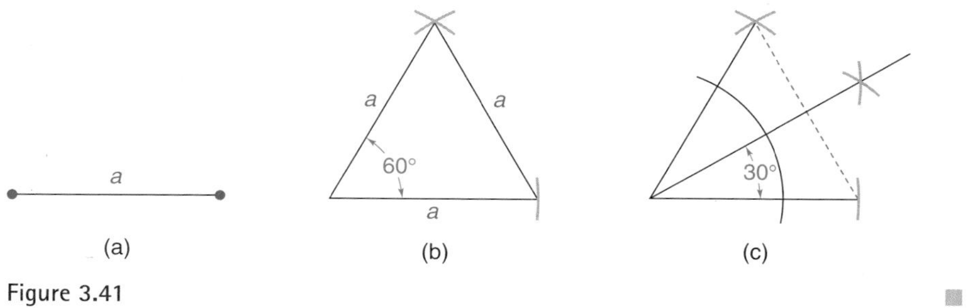

Figure 3.41

In Example 5, we justify the method for constructing a line perpendicular to a given line from a point not on that line. In the example, point P lies above line ℓ.

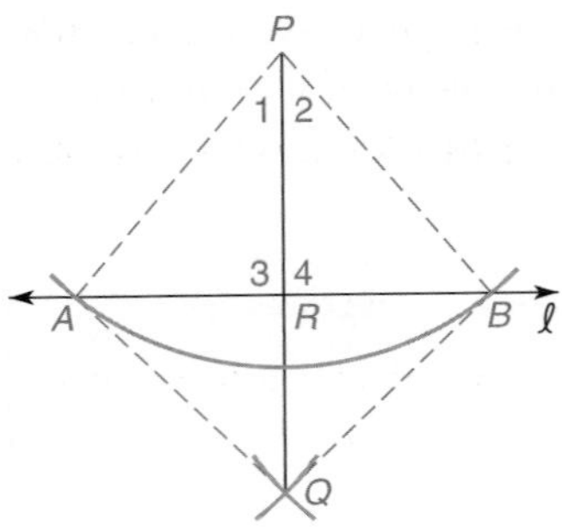

Figure 3.42

EXAMPLE 5

GIVEN: P not on ℓ
$\overline{PA} \cong \overline{PB}$ (by construction)
$\overline{AQ} \cong \overline{BQ}$ (by construction)
(See Figure 3.42.)

PROVE: $\overline{PQ} \perp \overline{AB}$

Provide the missing statements and reasons in the proof.

PROOF

Statements	Reasons
1. P not on ℓ $\overline{PA} \cong \overline{PB}$ and $\overline{AQ} \cong \overline{BQ}$	1. ?
2. $\overline{PQ} \cong \overline{PQ}$	2. ?
3. $\triangle PAQ \cong \triangle PBQ$	3. ?
4. $\angle 1 \cong \angle 2$	4. ?
5. $\overline{PR} \cong \overline{PR}$	5. ?
6. $\triangle PRA \cong \triangle PRB$	6. ?
7. $\angle 3 \cong \angle 4$	7. ?
8. ?	8. If two lines meet to form $\cong$ adjacent $\angle$s, these lines are $\perp$

In Example 6, we recall the method for constructing the line perpendicular to a given line at a point on the line. We illustrate the technique in the example and ask that the student justify the method in Exercise 29. In Example 6, we construct an angle that measures 45°.

EXAMPLE 6

Construct an angle that measures 45°.

Solution Figure 3.43(a): We begin by constructing a line segment perpendicular to line ℓ at point P.
Figure 3.43(b): Next we bisect one of the right angles that was determined. The bisector forms an angle whose measure is 45°.

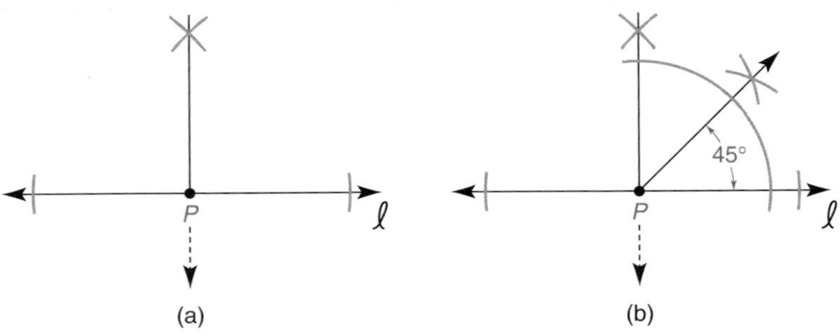

SSG *Exs. 3–5*

Figure 3.43

As we saw in Example 4, constructing an equilateral triangle is fairly simple. It is also possible to construct other regular polygons, such as a square or a regular hexagon. In the following box, we recall some facts that will help us to perform such constructions.

> To construct a regular polygon with n sides:
>
> 1. Each interior angle must measure $I = \frac{(n-2)180}{n}$ degrees; alternatively, each exterior angle must measure $E = \frac{360}{n}$ degrees.
> 2. All sides must be congruent.

EXAMPLE 7

Construct a regular hexagon having sides of length a.

Solution Figure 3.44(a): We begin by marking off a line segment of length a.

Figure 3.44(b): Each exterior angle of the hexagon ($n = 6$) must measure $E = \frac{360}{6} = 60°$; then each interior angle measures 120°. We construct an equilateral triangle (all sides measure a) so that a 60° exterior angle is formed.

Figure 3.44(c): Again marking off an arc of length a for the second side, we construct another exterior angle of measure 60°.

Figure 3.44(d): This procedure is continued until the regular hexagon $ABCDEF$ is determined.

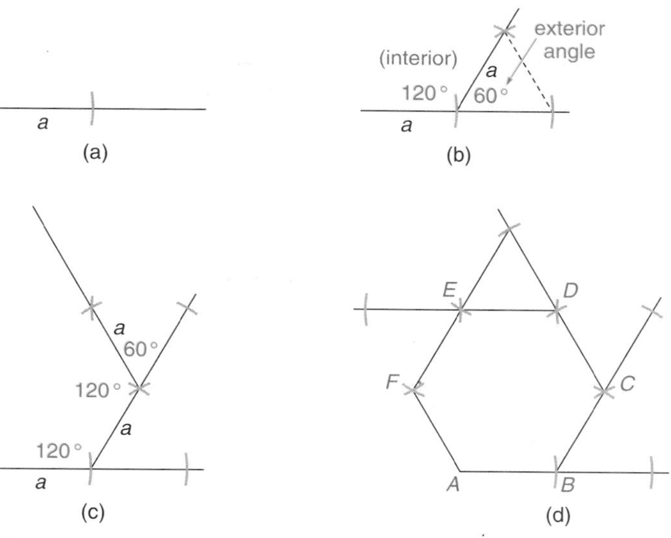

SSG
Exs. 6–7

Figure 3.44 ■

Exercises 3.4

In Exercises 1 to 6, use line segments of given lengths a, b, and c to perform the constructions.

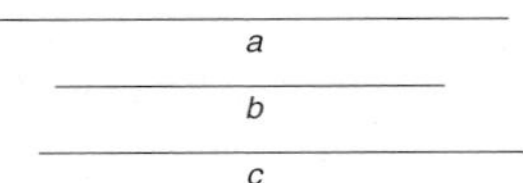

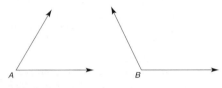

Exercises 1–6

1. Construct a line segment of length $2b$.
2. Construct a line segment of length $b + c$.
3. Construct a line segment of length $\frac{1}{2}c$.
4. Construct a line segment of length $a - b$.
5. Construct a triangle with sides of lengths a, b, and c.
6. Construct an isosceles triangle with a base of length b and legs of length a.

In Exercises 7 to 12, use the angles provided to perform the constructions.

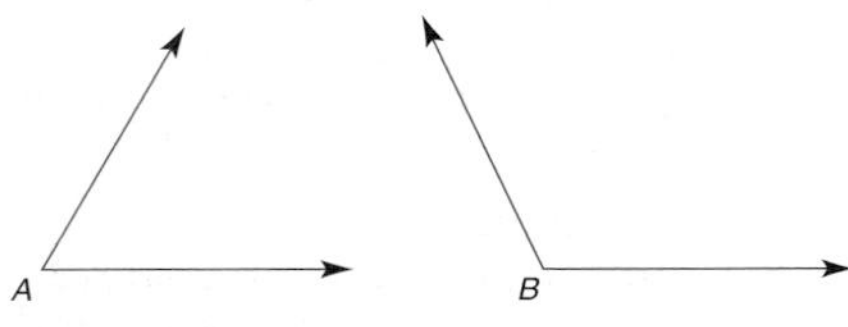

Exercises 7–12

7. Construct an angle that is congruent to acute $\angle A$.
8. Construct an angle that is congruent to obtuse $\angle B$.
9. Construct an angle that has one-half the measure of $\angle A$.
10. Construct an angle that has a measure equal to $m\angle B - m\angle A$.
11. Construct an angle that has twice the measure of $\angle A$.
12. Construct an angle whose measure averages the measures of $\angle A$ and $\angle B$.

In Exercises 13 and 14, use the angles and lengths of sides provided to construct the triangle described.

13. Construct the triangle that has sides of lengths r and t with included angle S.

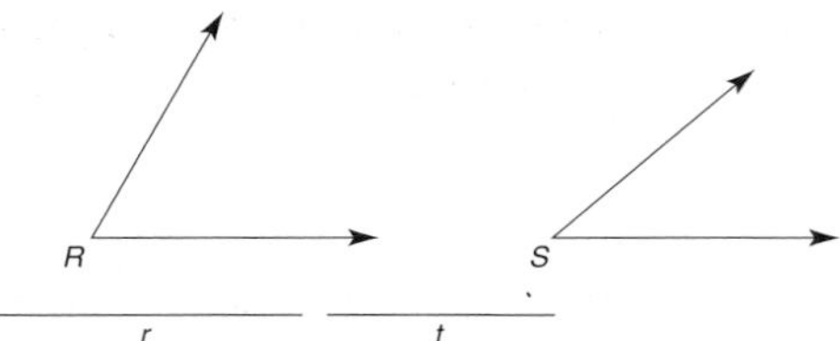

Exercises 13, 14

14. Construct the triangle that has a side of length t included by angles R and S.

Video exercises are available on DVD.

In Exercises 15 to 18, construct angles having the given measures.

15. 90° and then 45°
16. 60° and then 30°
17. 30° and then 15°
18. 45° and then 105°

    (HINT: $105° = 45° + 60°$)

19. Describe how you would construct an angle measuring 22.5°.
20. Describe how you would construct an angle measuring 75°.
21. Construct the complement of the acute angle shown.

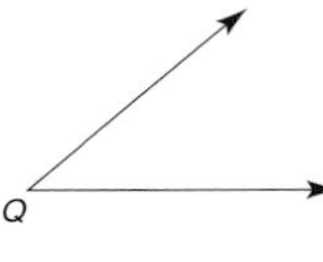

22. Construct the supplement of the obtuse angle shown.

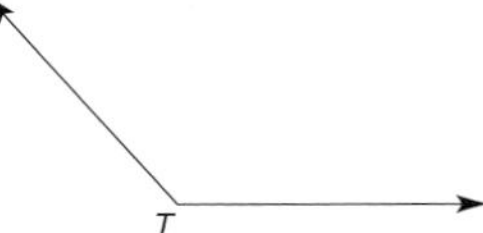

In Exercises 23 to 26, use line segments of lengths a and c as shown.

23. Construct the right triangle with hypotenuse of length c and a leg of length a.

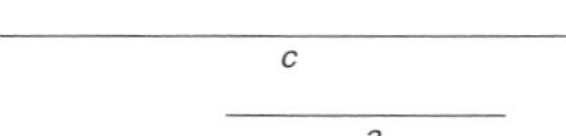

Exercises 23–26

24. Construct an isosceles triangle with base of length c and altitude of length a.

    (HINT: The altitude lies on the perpendicular bisector of the base.)

25. Construct an isosceles triangle with a vertex angle of 30° and each leg of length c.
26. Construct a right triangle with base angles of 45° and hypotenuse of length c.

In Exercises 27 and 28, use the given angle and the line segment of length b.

27. Construct the right triangle in which acute angle R has a side (one leg of the triangle) of length b.

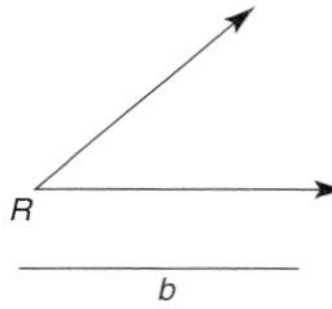

Exercises 27, 28

28. Construct an isosceles triangle with base of length b and congruent base angles having the measure of angle R. (See the figure for Exercise 27.)

29. Complete the justification of the construction of the line perpendicular to a given line at a point on that line.

Given: Line m, with point P on m
$\overline{PQ} \cong \overline{PR}$ (by construction)
$\overline{QS} \cong \overline{RS}$ (by construction)

Prove: $\overleftrightarrow{SP} \perp m$

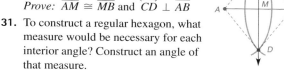

30. Complete the justification of the construction of the perpendicular bisector of a line segment.

Given: $\overline{AB}$ with $\overline{AC} \cong \overline{BC} \cong \overline{AD} \cong \overline{BD}$ (by construction)

Prove: $\overline{AM} \cong \overline{MB}$ and $\overleftrightarrow{CD} \perp \overline{AB}$

31. To construct a regular hexagon, what measure would be necessary for each interior angle? Construct an angle of that measure.

32. To construct a regular octagon, what measure would be necessary for each interior angle? Construct an angle of that measure.

33. To construct a regular dodecagon (12 sides), what measure would be necessary for each interior angle? Construct an angle of that measure.

34. Draw an acute triangle and construct the three medians of the triangle. Do the medians appear to meet at a common point?

35. Draw an obtuse triangle and construct the three altitudes of the triangle. Do the altitudes appear to meet at a common point?

(HINT: In the construction of two of the altitudes, sides need to be extended.)

36. Draw a right triangle and construct the angle bisectors of the triangle. Do the angle bisectors appear to meet at a common point?

37. Draw an obtuse triangle and construct the three perpendicular bisectors of its sides. Do the perpendicular bisectors of the three sides appear to meet at a common point?

38. Construct an equilateral triangle and its three altitudes. What does intuition tell you about the three medians, the three angle bisectors, and the three perpendicular bisectors of the sides of that triangle?

39. A carpenter has placed a square over an angle in such a manner that $\overline{AB} \cong \overline{AC}$ and $\overline{BD} \cong \overline{CD}$ (see drawing). What can you conclude about the location of point D?

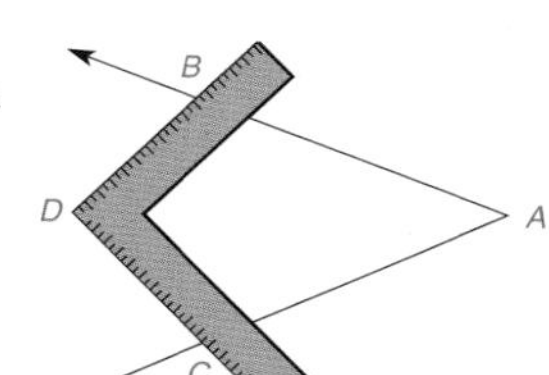

***40.** In right triangle ABC, $m\angle C = 90°$. Also, $BC = a$, $CA = b$, and $AB = c$. Construct the bisector of $\angle B$ so that it intersects $\overline{CA}$ at point D. Now construct $\overline{DE}$ perpendicular to $\overline{AB}$ and with E on $\overline{AB}$. In terms of a, b, and c, find the length of $\overline{EA}$.

3.5 Inequalities in a Triangle

KEY CONCEPTS: Lemma | Inequality of Sides and Angles in a Triangle | The Triangle Inequality

Important inequality relationships exist among the measured parts of a triangle. To establish some of these, we recall and apply some facts from both algebra and geometry. A more in-depth review of inequalities can be found in Appendix A, Section A.3.

DEFINITION

Let a and b be real numbers. $\mathbf{a} > \mathbf{b}$ (read "a is greater than b") if and only if there is a positive number p for which $a = b + p$.

SSG *Exs. 1–3*

For instance, $9 > 4$, because there is the positive number 5 for which $9 = 4 + 5$. Because $5 + 2 = 7$, we also know that $7 > 2$ and $7 > 5$. In geometry, let A-B-C on $\overline{AC}$ so that $AB + BC = AC$; then $AC > AB$, because BC is a positive number.

LEMMAS (HELPING THEOREMS)

We will use the following theorems to help us prove the theorems found later in this section. In their role as "helping" theorems, each of the five boxed statements that follow is called a **lemma.** We will prove the first four lemmas, because their content is geometric.

Figure 3.45

LEMMA 3.5.1

If B is between A and C on $\overline{AC}$, then $AC > AB$ and $AC > BC$. (The measure of a line segment is greater than the measure of any of its parts. See Figure 3.45.)

PROOF

By the Segment-Addition Postulate, $AC = AB + BC$. According to the Ruler Postulate, $BC > 0$ (meaning BC is positive); it follows that $AC > AB$. Similarly, $AC > BC$. These relationships follow directly from the definition of $a > b$.

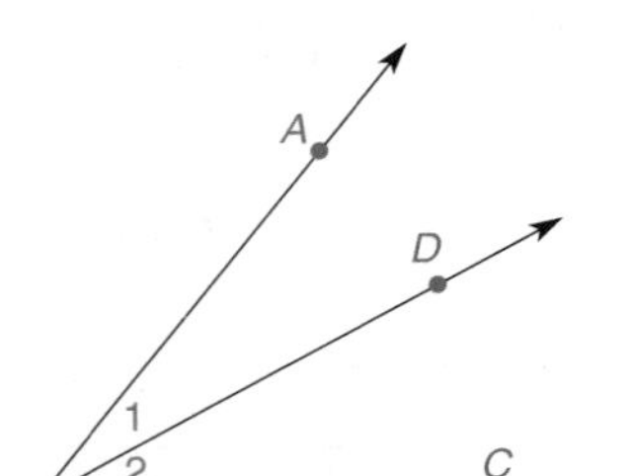

Figure 3.46

LEMMA 3.5.2

If $\overrightarrow{BD}$ separates $\angle ABC$ into two parts ($\angle 1$ and $\angle 2$), then $m\angle ABC > m\angle 1$ and $m\angle ABC > m\angle 2$. (The measure of an angle is greater than the measure of any of its parts. See Figure 3.46.)

PROOF

By the Angle-Addition Postulate, $m\angle ABC = m\angle 1 + m\angle 2$. Using the Protractor Postulate, $m\angle 2 > 0$; it follows that $m\angle ABC > m\angle 1$. Similarly, $m\angle ABC > m\angle 2$.

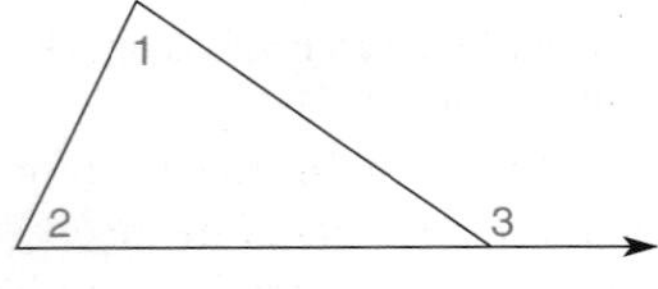

Figure 3.47

LEMMA 3.5.3

If $\angle 3$ is an exterior angle of a triangle and $\angle 1$ and $\angle 2$ are the nonadjacent interior angles, then $m\angle 3 > m\angle 1$ and $m\angle 3 > m\angle 2$. (The measure of an exterior angle of a triangle is greater than the measure of either nonadjacent interior angle. See Figure 3.47.)

PROOF

Because the measure of an exterior angle of a triangle equals the sum of measures of the two nonadjacent interior angles, $m\angle 3 = m\angle 1 + m\angle 2$. It follows that $m\angle 3 > m\angle 1$ and $m\angle 3 > m\angle 2$.

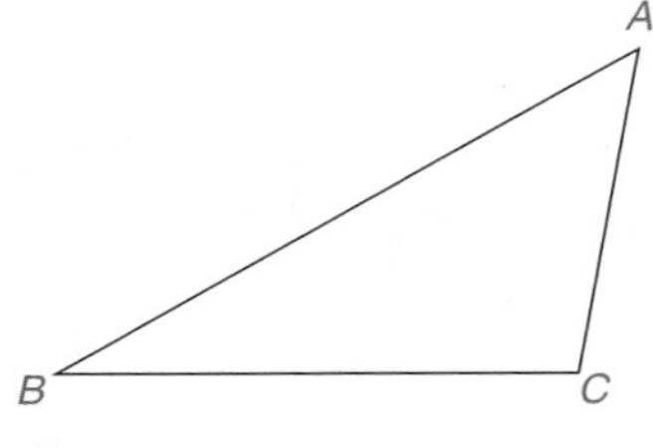

Figure 3.48

LEMMA 3.5.4

In $\triangle ABC$, if $\angle C$ is a right angle or an obtuse angle, then $m\angle C > m\angle A$ and $m\angle C > m\angle B$. (If a triangle contains a right or an obtuse angle, then the measure of this angle is greater than the measure of either of the remaining angles. See Figure 3.48.)

PROOF

In $\triangle ABC$, $m\angle A + m\angle B + m\angle C = 180°$. With $\angle C$ being a right angle or an obtuse angle, $m\angle C \geq 90°$; it follows that $m\angle A + m\angle B \leq 90°$. Then each angle ($\angle A$ and $\angle B$) must be acute. Thus, $m\angle C > m\angle A$ and $m\angle C > m\angle B$.

The following theorem (also a lemma) is used in Example 1. Its proof (not given) depends on the definition of "is greater than," which is found on the previous page.

LEMMA 3.5.5 (Addition Property of Inequality)

If $a > b$ and $c > d$, then $a + c > b + d$.

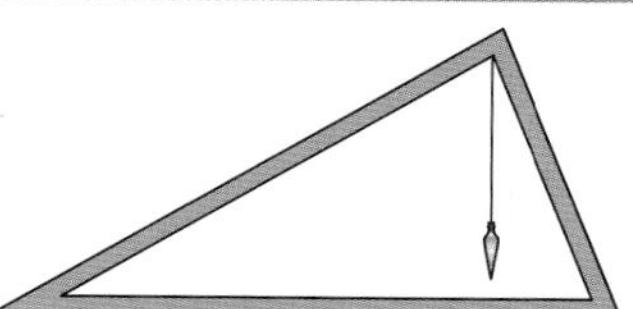

A carpenter's "plumb" determines the shortest distance to a horizontal line. A vertical brace provides structural support for the roof.

EXAMPLE 1

Give a paragraph proof for the following problem. See Figure 3.49.

GIVEN: $AB > CD$ and $BC > DE$

PROVE: $AC > CE$

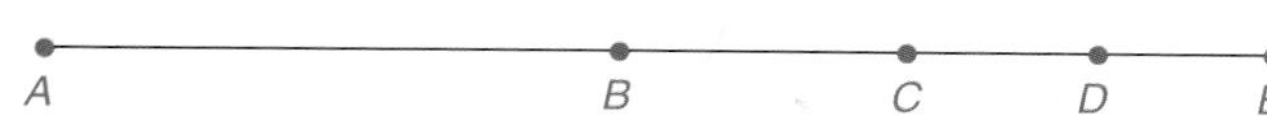

Figure 3.49

PROOF: If $AB > CD$ and $BC > DE$, then $AB + BC > CD + DE$ by Lemma 3.5.5. But $AB + BC = AC$ and $CD + DE = CE$ by the Segment-Addition Postulate. Using substitution, it follows that $AC > CE$. ■

The paragraph proof in Example 1 could have been written in this standard format.

PROOF

Statements	Reasons
1. $AB > CD$ and $BC > DE$	1. Given
2. $AB + BC > CD + DE$	2. Lemma 3.5.5
3. $AB + BC = AC$ and $CD + DE = CE$	3. Segment-Addition Postulate
4. $AC > CE$	4. Substitution

SSG *Exs. 4–8*

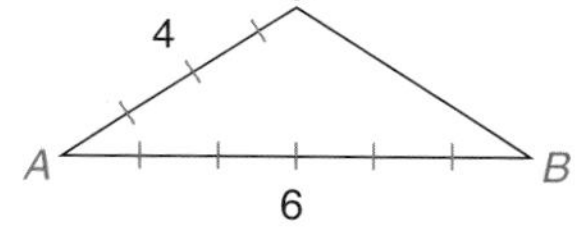

Figure 3.50

The paragraph proof and the two-column proof of Example 1 are equivalent. In either format, statements must be ordered and justified.

The remaining theorems are the "heart" of this section. Before studying the theorem and its proof, it is a good idea to visualize each theorem. Many statements of inequality are intuitive; that is, they are easy to believe even though they may not be easily proved.

Study Theorem 3.5.6 and consider Figure 3.50, in which it appears that $m\angle C > m\angle B$.

THEOREM 3.5.6

If one side of a triangle is longer than a second side, then the measure of the angle opposite the longer side is greater than the measure of the angle opposite the shorter side.

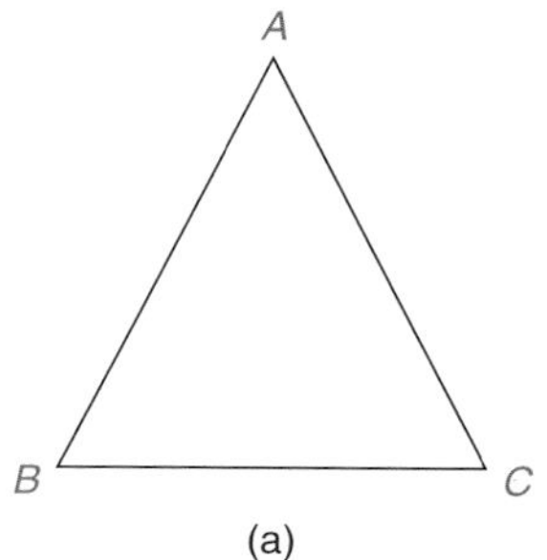

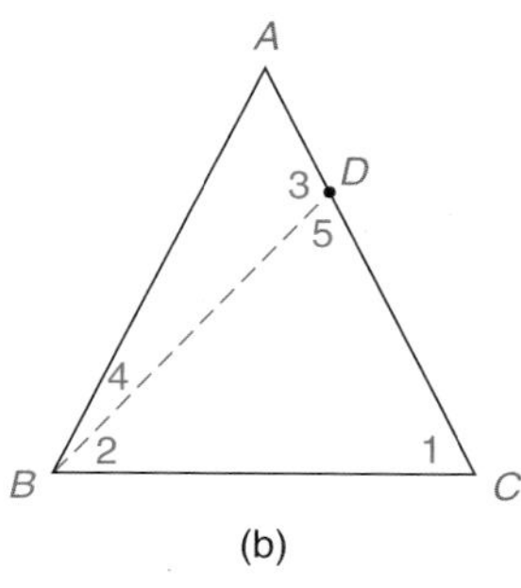

Figure 3.51

EXAMPLE 2

Provide a paragraph proof of Theorem 3.5.6.

GIVEN: $\triangle ABC$, with $AC > BC$ [See Figure 3.51(a).]

PROVE: $m\angle B > m\angle A$

PROOF: Given $\triangle ABC$ with $AC > BC$, we use the Ruler Postulate to locate point D on $\overline{AC}$ so that $\overline{CD} \cong \overline{BC}$ in Figure 3.51(b). Now $m\angle 2 = m\angle 5$ in the isosceles triangle BDC. By Lemma 3.5.2, $m\angle ABC > m\angle 2$; therefore, $m\angle ABC > m\angle 5$ (*) by substitution. By Lemma 3.5.3, $m\angle 5 > m\angle A$ (*) because $\angle 5$ is an exterior angle of $\triangle ADB$. Using the two starred statements, we can conclude by the Transitive Property of Inequality that $m\angle ABC > m\angle A$; that is, $m\angle B > m\angle A$ in Figure 3.51(a). ■

Technology Exploration

Use computer software if available.

1. Draw a $\triangle ABC$ with $\overline{AB}$ as the longest side.
2. Measure $\angle A$, $\angle B$, and $\angle C$.
3. Show that $\angle C$ has the greatest measure.

The relationship described in Theorem 3.5.6 extends, of course, to all sides and all angles of a triangle. That is, the largest of the three angles of a triangle is opposite the longest side, and the smallest angle is opposite the shortest side.

EXAMPLE 3

Given that the three sides of $\triangle ABC$ (not shown) are $AB = 4$, $BC = 5$, and $AC = 6$, arrange the angles by size.

Solution Because $AC > BC > AB$, the largest angle is $\angle B$, which lies opposite $\overline{AC}$. The angle intermediate in size is $\angle A$, which lies opposite $\overline{BC}$. The smallest angle is $\angle C$, which lies opposite the shortest side, $\overline{AB}$. Thus, the order of the angles by size is

$$m\angle B > m\angle A > m\angle C$$ ■

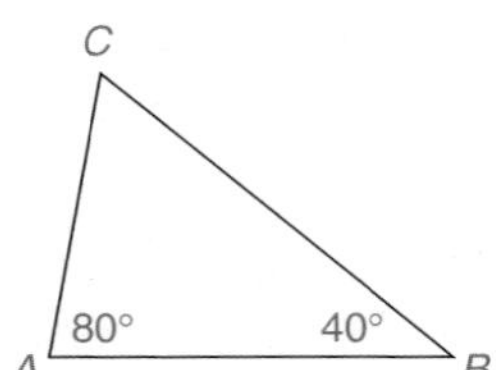

Figure 3.52

The converse of Theorem 3.5.6 is also true. It is necessary, however, to use an indirect proof to establish the converse. Recall that this method of proof begins by supposing the opposite of what we want to show. Because this assumption leads to a contradiction, the assumption must be false and the desired claim is therefore true.

Study Theorem 3.5.7 and consider Figure 3.52, in which $m\angle A = 80°$ and $m\angle B = 40°$. It appears that the longer side lies opposite the larger angle; that is, it appears that $BC > AC$.

Discover

Using construction paper and a protractor, draw $\triangle RST$ so that $m\angle R = 75°$, $m\angle S = 60°$, and $m\angle T = 45°$. Measure the length of each side.

a) Which side is longest?
b) Which side is shortest?

ANSWERS
(a) $\overline{ST}$ (b) $\overline{RS}$

THEOREM 3.5.7

If the measure of one angle of a triangle is greater than the measure of a second angle, then the side opposite the larger angle is longer than the side opposite the smaller angle.

The proof of Theorem 3.5.7 depends on this fact: Given real numbers a and b, only one of the following can be true.

$$a > b, \quad a = b, \quad \text{or} \quad a < b$$

EXAMPLE 4

Prove Theorem 3.5.7 by using an indirect approach.

GIVEN: $\triangle ABC$ with $m\angle B > m\angle A$ (See Figure 3.53.)

PROVE: $AC > BC$

PROOF: Given $\triangle ABC$ with $m\angle B > m\angle A$, assume that $AC \leq BC$. But if $AC = BC$, then $m\angle B = m\angle A$, which contradicts the hypothesis. Also, if $AC < BC$, then it follows by Theorem 3.5.6 that $m\angle B < m\angle A$, which also contradicts the hypothesis. Thus, the assumed statement must be false, and it follows that $AC > BC$. ■

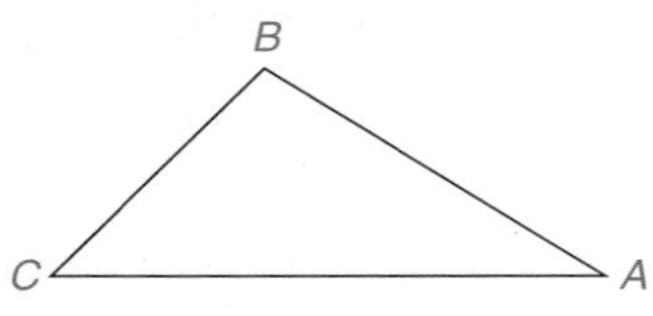

Figure 3.53

EXAMPLE 5

Given $\triangle RST$ (not shown) in which $m\angle R = 80°$ and $m\angle S = 55°$, write an extended inequality that compares the lengths of the three sides.

Solution Because the sum of angles of $\triangle RST$ is 180°, it follows that $m\angle T = 45°$. With $m\angle R > m\angle S > m\angle T$, it follows that the sides opposite these $\angle$s are unequal in the same order. That is,

$$ST > RT > SR$$ ■

SSG *Exs. 9–12*

The following corollary is a consequence of Theorem 3.5.7.

COROLLARY 3.5.8

The perpendicular line segment from a point to a line is the shortest line segment that can be drawn from the point to the line.

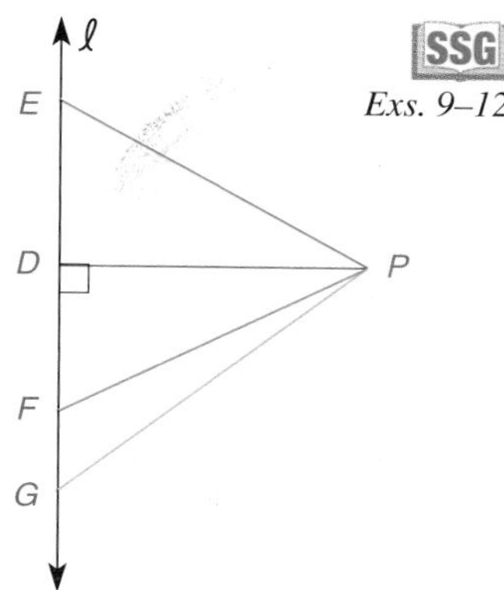

Figure 3.54

In Figure 3.54, $PD < PE$, $PD < PF$, and $PD < PG$. In every case, $\overline{PD}$ is opposite an acute angle of a triangle, whereas the second segment is always opposite a right angle (necessarily the largest angle of the triangle involved). With $\overline{PD} \perp \ell$, we say that PD is the *distance* from P to ℓ.

Corollary 3.5.8 can easily be extended to three dimensions.

COROLLARY 3.5.9

The perpendicular line segment from a point to a plane is the shortest line segment that can be drawn from the point to the plane.

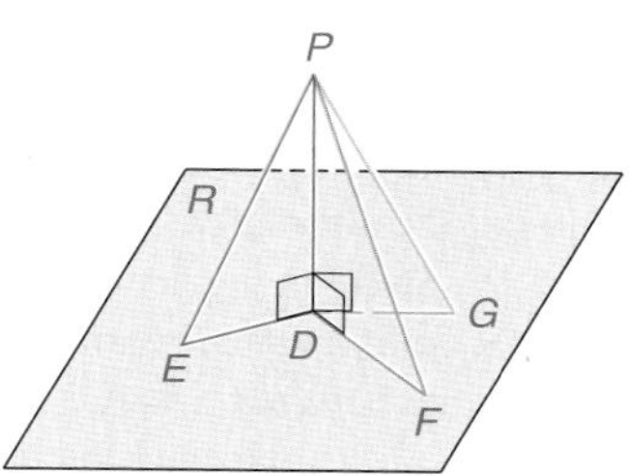

Figure 3.55

In Figure 3.55, $\overline{PD}$ is a leg of each right triangle shown. With $\overline{PE}$ the hypotenuse of $\triangle PDE$, $\overline{PF}$ the hypotenuse of $\triangle PDF$, and $\overline{PG}$ the hypotenuse of $\triangle PDG$, the length of $\overline{PD}$ is less than that of $\overline{PE}$, $\overline{PF}$, $\overline{PG}$, or any other line segment joining point P to a point in plane R. The length of $\overline{PD}$ is known as the *distance* from point P to plane R.

SSG *Exs. 13–14*

Our final theorem shows that no side of a triangle can have a length greater than or equal to the sum of the lengths of the other two sides. In the proof, the relationship is validated for only one of three possible inequalities. Theorem 3.5.10 is often called the Triangle Inequality. (See Figure 3.56.)

THEOREM 3.5.10 ▶ (Triangle Inequality)

The sum of the lengths of any two sides of a triangle is greater than the length of the third side.

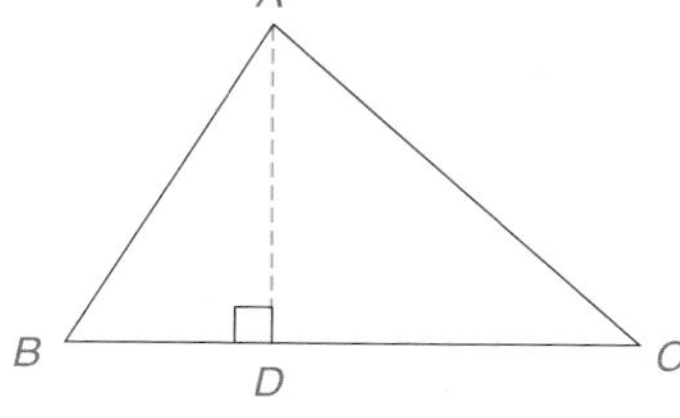

Figure 3.56

GIVEN: $\triangle ABC$

PROVE: $BA + CA > BC$

PROOF: Draw $\overline{AD} \perp \overline{BC}$. Because the shortest segment from a point to $\overline{AD}$ is the perpendicular segment, $BA > BD$ and $CA > CD$. Using Lemma 3.5.5, we add the inequalities; $BA + CA > BD + CD$. By the Segment-Addition Postulate, the sum $BD + CD$ can be replaced by BC to yield $BA + CA > BC$.

The following statement is an alternative and expanded form of Theorem 3.5.10. If a, b, and c are the lengths of the sides of a triangle and c is the length of any side, then $a - b < c < a + b$.

THEOREM 3.5.10 ▶ (Triangle Inequality)

The length of any side of a triangle must lie between the sum and difference of the lengths of the other two sides.

EXAMPLE 6

Can a triangle have sides of the following lengths?

a) 3, 4, and 5
b) 3, 4, and 7
c) 3, 4, and 8
d) 3, 4, and x

Solution

a) Yes, because no side has a length greater than or equal to the sum of the lengths of the other two sides (that is, $4 - 3 < 5 < 3 + 4$)
b) No, because $7 = 3 + 4$ (need $4 - 3 < 7 < 3 + 4$)
c) No, because $8 > 3 + 4$ (need $4 - 3 < 8 < 3 + 4$)
d) Yes, if $4 - 3 < x < 4 + 3$ ■

From Example 6, you can see that the length of one side cannot be greater than or equal to the sum of the lengths of the other two sides. Considering the alternative form of Theorem 3.5.10, we see that $4 - 3 < 5 < 4 + 3$ in part (a). When 5 [as in part (a)] is replaced by 7 [as in part (b)] or 8 [as in part (c)], this inequality becomes a false statement. Part (d) of Example 6 shows that the length of the third side must be between 1 and 7.

Our final example illustrates a practical application of inequality relationships in triangles.

EXAMPLE 7

On a map, firefighters are located at points A and B. A fire has broken out at point C. Which group of firefighters is nearer the location of the fire? (See Figure 3.57.)

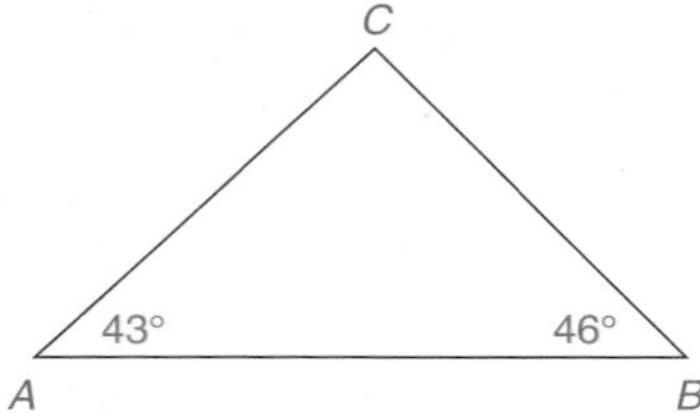

Figure 3.57

Solution With $m\angle A = 43°$ and $m\angle B = 46°$, the side opposite $\angle B$ has a greater length than the side opposite $\angle A$. It follows that $AC > BC$. Because the distance from B to C is less than the distance from A to C, the firefighters at site B should be dispatched to the fire located at C.

SSG *Exs. 15–18*

NOTE: In Example 7 we assume that highways from A and B (to C) are equally accessible. ■

Exercises 3.5

In Exercises 1 to 10, classify each statement as true or false.

1. $\overline{AB}$ is the longest side of $\triangle ABC$.

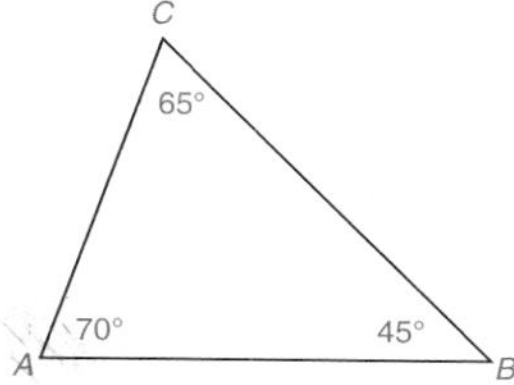

Exercises 1, 2

2. $AB < BC$
3. $DB > AB$

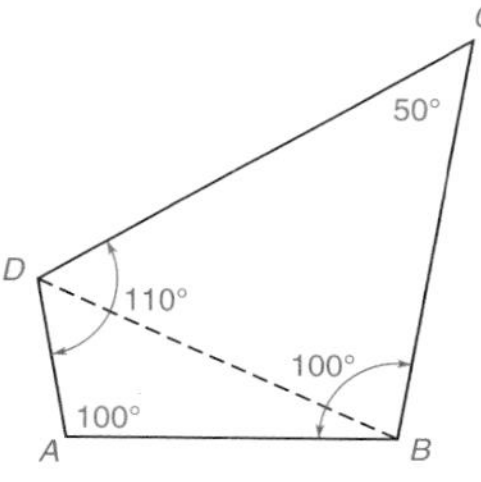

Exercises 3, 4

4. Because $m\angle A = m\angle B$, it follows that $DA = DC$.
5. $m\angle A + m\angle B = m\angle C$

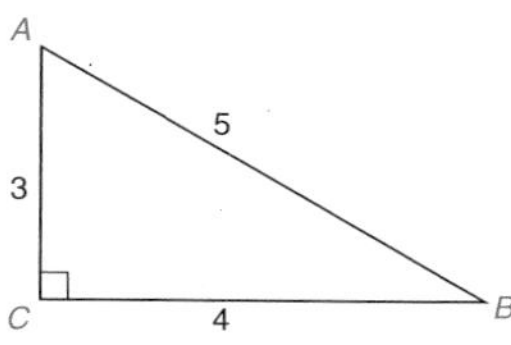

Exercises 5, 6

6. $m\angle A > m\angle B$
7. $DF > DE + EF$

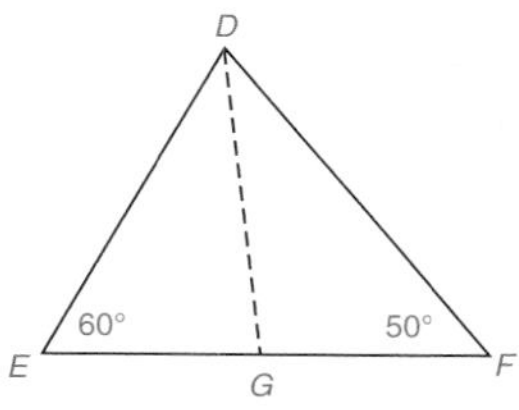

Exercises 7, 8

8. If $\overrightarrow{DG}$ is the bisector of $\angle EDF$, then $DG > DE$.
9. $DA > AC$

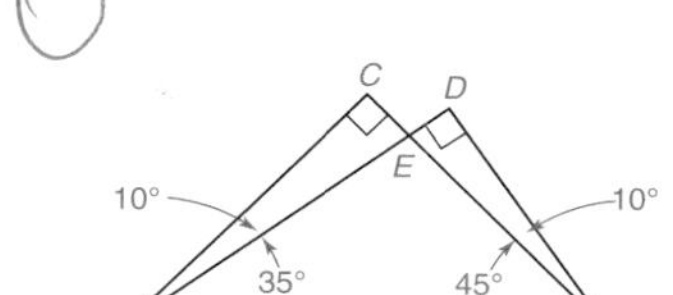

Exercises 9, 10

10. $CE = ED$
11. If possible, draw a triangle whose angles measure:
    a) 100°, 100°, and 60°
    b) 45°, 45°, and 90°
12. If possible, draw a triangle whose angles measure:
    a) 80°, 80°, and 50°
    b) 50°, 50°, and 80°
13. If possible, draw a triangle whose sides measure:
    a) 8, 9, and 10
    b) 8, 9, and 17
    c) 8, 9, and 18
14. If possible, draw a triangle whose sides measure:
    a) 7, 7, and 14
    b) 6, 7, and 14
    c) 6, 7, and 8

In Exercises 15 to 18, describe the triangle ($\triangle XYZ$, not shown) as scalene, isosceles, or equilateral. Also, is the triangle acute, right, or obtuse?

15. $m\angle X = 43°$ and $m\angle Y = 47°$
16. $m\angle X = 60°$ and $\angle Y \cong \angle Z$.
17. $m\angle X = m\angle Y = 40°$
18. $m\angle X = 70°$ and $m\angle Y = 40°$
19. Two of the sides of an isosceles triangle have lengths of 10 cm and 4 cm. Which length must be the length of the base?
20. The sides of a right triangle have lengths of 6 cm, 8 cm, and 10 cm. Which length is that of the hypotenuse?
21. A triangle is both isosceles *and* acute. If one angle of the triangle measures 36°, what is the measure of the largest angle(s) of the triangle? What is the measure of the smallest angle(s) of the triangle?
22. One of the angles of an isosceles triangle measures 96°. What is the measure of the largest angle(s) of the triangle? What is the measure of the smallest angle(s) of the triangle?

23. NASA in Huntsville, Alabama (at point H), has called a manufacturer for parts needed as soon as possible. NASA will, in fact, send a courier for the necessary equipment. The manufacturer has two distribution centers located in nearby Tennessee—one in Nashville (at point N) and the other in Jackson (at point J). Using the angle measurements indicated on the accompanying map, determine to which town the courier should be dispatched to obtain the needed parts.

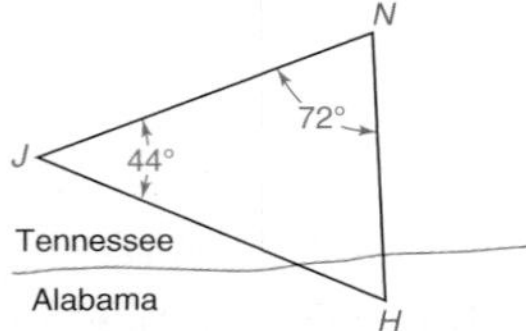

24. A tornado has just struck a small Kansas community at point T. There are Red Cross units stationed in both Salina (at point S) and Wichita (at point W). Using the angle measurements indicated on the accompanying map, determine which Red Cross unit would reach the victims first. (Assume that both units have the same mode of travel and accessible roadways available.)

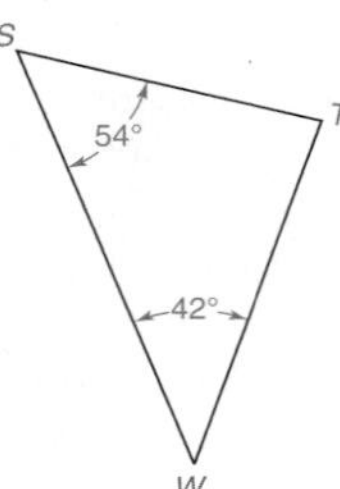

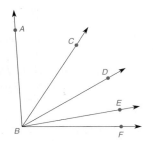

In Exercises 25 and 26, complete each proof.

25. *Given:* $m\angle ABC > m\angle DBE$
$m\angle CBD > m\angle EBF$
Prove: $m\angle ABD > m\angle DBF$

PROOF

Statements	Reasons
1. ?	1. Given
2. $m\angle ABC + m\angle CBD > m\angle DBE + m\angle EBF$	2. Addition Property of Inequality
3. $m\angle ABD = m\angle ABC + m\angle CBD$ and $m\angle DBF = m\angle DBE + m\angle EBF$	3. ?
4. ?	4. Substitution

26. *Given:* Equilateral $\triangle ABC$ and D-B-C
Prove: $DA > AC$

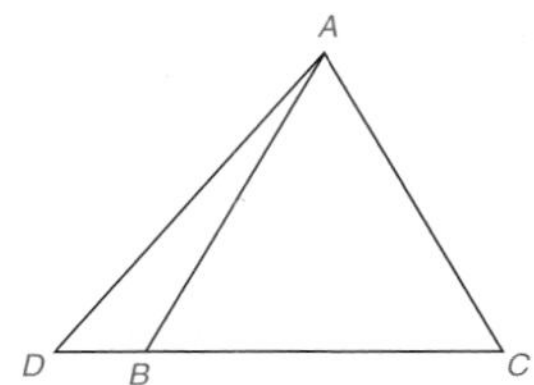

PROOF

Statements	Reasons
1. ?	1. Given
2. $\triangle ABC$ is equiangular, so $m\angle ABC = m\angle C$	2. ?
3. $m\angle ABC > m\angle D$ ($\angle D$ of $\triangle ABD$)	3. The measure of an ext. $\angle$ of a $\triangle$ is greater than the measure of either nonadjacent int. $\angle$
4. ?	4. Substitution
5. ?	5. ?

In Exercises 27 and 28, construct proofs.

27. *Given:* Quadrilateral $RSTU$ with diagonal $\overline{US}$
$\angle R$ and $\angle TUS$ are right $\angle$s
Prove: $TS > UR$

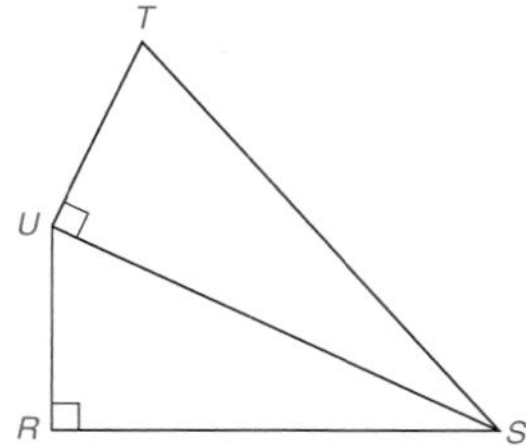

28. *Given:* Quadrilateral $ABCD$ with $\overline{AB} \cong \overline{DE}$
Prove: $DC > AB$

A B D E C

29. For $\triangle ABC$ and $\triangle DEF$ (not shown), suppose that $\overline{AC} \cong \overline{DF}$ and $\overline{AB} \cong \overline{DE}$ but that $m\angle A < m\angle D$. Draw a conclusion regarding the lengths of $\overline{BC}$ and $\overline{EF}$.

30. In $\triangle MNP$ (not shown), point Q lies on $\overline{NP}$ so that $\overrightarrow{MQ}$ bisects $\angle NMP$. If $MN < MP$, draw a conclusion about the relative lengths of $\overline{NQ}$ and $\overline{QP}$.

In Exercises 31 to 34, apply a form of Theorem 3.5.10.

31. The sides of a triangle have lengths of 4, 6, and x. Write an inequality that states the possible values of x.

32. The sides of a triangle have lengths of 7, 13, and x. As in Exercise 31, write an inequality that describes the possible values of x.

33. If the lengths of two sides of a triangle are represented by $2x + 5$ and $3x + 7$ (in which x is positive), describe in terms of x the possible lengths of the third side whose length is represented by y.

34. Prove by the indirect method: "The length of a diagonal of a square is not equal in length to the length of any of the sides of the square."

35. Prove by the indirect method:

Given: $\triangle MPN$ is not isosceles
Prove: $PM \neq PN$

36. Prove by the indirect method:

Given: Scalene $\triangle XYZ$ in which $\overline{ZW}$ bisects $\angle XYZ$ (point W lies on $\overline{XY}$).
Prove: $\overline{ZW}$ is not perpendicular to $\overline{XY}$.

In Exercises 37 and 38, prove each theorem.

37. The length of the median from the vertex of an isosceles triangle is less than the length of either of the legs.

38. The length of an altitude of an acute triangle is less than the length of either side containing the same vertex as the altitude.

35) Assume $PM = PN$

$\Rightarrow \triangle MPN$ is isosceles $\triangle$.

This contradicts to the hypothesis of $\triangle MPN$ is not isoceles $\triangle$

$\therefore PM \neq PN$

PERSPECTIVE ON HISTORY

Sketch of Archimedes

Whereas Euclid (see Perspective on History, Chapter 2) was a great teacher and wrote so that the majority might understand the principles of geometry, Archimedes wrote only for the very well educated mathematicians and scientists of his day. Archimedes (287–212 B.C.) wrote on such topics as the measure of the circle, the quadrature of the parabola, and spirals. In his works, Archimedes found a very good approximation of π. His other geometric works included investigations of conic sections and spirals, and he also wrote about physics. He was a great inventor and is probably remembered more for his inventions than for his writings.

Several historical events concerning the life of Archimedes have been substantiated, and one account involves his detection of a dishonest goldsmith. In that story, Archimedes was called upon to determine whether the crown that had been ordered by the king was constructed entirely of gold. By applying the principle of hydrostatics (which he had discovered), Archimedes established that the goldsmith had not constructed the crown entirely of gold. (The principle of hydrostatics states that an object placed in a fluid displaces an amount of fluid equal in weight to the amount of weight the object loses while submerged.)

One of his inventions is known as Archimedes' screw. This device allows water to flow from one level to a higher level so that, for example, holds of ships can be emptied of water. Archimedes' screw was used in Egypt to drain fields when the Nile River overflowed its banks.

When Syracuse (where Archimedes lived) came under siege by the Romans, Archimedes designed a long-range catapult that was so effective that Syracuse was able to fight off the powerful Roman army for three years before being overcome.

One report concerning the inventiveness of Archimedes has been treated as false, because his result has not been duplicated. It was said that he designed a wall of mirrors that could focus and reflect the sun's heat with such intensity as to set fire to Roman ships at sea. Because recent experiments with concave mirrors have failed to produce such intense heat, this account is difficult to believe.

Archimedes eventually died at the hands of a Roman soldier, even though the Roman army had been given orders not to harm him. After his death, the Romans honored his brilliance with a tremendous monument displaying the figure of a sphere inscribed in a right circular cylinder.

PERSPECTIVE ON APPLICATION

Pascal's Triangle

Blaise Pascal (1623–1662) was a French mathematician who contributed to several areas of mathematics, including conic sections, calculus, and the invention of a calculating machine. But Pascal's name is most often associated with the array of numbers known as Pascal's Triangle, which follows:

$$\begin{array}{c} 1 \\ 1 \quad 1 \\ 1 \quad 2 \quad 1 \\ 1 \quad 3 \quad 3 \quad 1 \\ 1 \quad 4 \quad 6 \quad 4 \quad 1 \end{array}$$

Each row of entries in Pascal's Triangle begins and ends with the number 1. Intermediate entries in each row are found by the addition of the upper-left and upper-right entries of the preceding row. The row following 1 4 6 4 1 has the form

$$\begin{array}{c} 1 \quad 4 \quad 6 \quad 4 \quad 1 \\ \downarrow\swarrow\downarrow\swarrow\downarrow\swarrow\downarrow\swarrow\downarrow \\ 1 \quad 5 \quad 10 \quad 10 \quad 5 \quad 1 \end{array}$$

Applications of Pascal's Triangle include the counting of subsets of a given set, which we will consider in the following paragraph. While we do not pursue this notion, Pascal's Triangle is also useful in the algebraic expansion of a binomial to a power such as $(a + b)^2$, which equals $a^2 + 2ab + b^2$. Notice that the multipliers in the product found with exponent 2 are 1 2 1, from a row of Pascal's Triangle. In fact, the expansion $(a + b)^3$ leads to $a^3 + 3a^2b + 3ab^2 + b^3$, in which the multipliers (also known as coefficients) take the form 1 3 3 1, a row of Pascal's Triangle.

Subsets of a Given Set

A subset of a given set is a set formed from choices of elements from the given set. Because a subset of a set with n elements can have from 0 to n elements, we find that Pascal's Triangle provides a count of the number of subsets containing a given counting number of elements.

Pascal's Triangle	Set	Number of Elements	Subsets of the Set	Number of Subsets
1	∅	0	∅	1
1 1	{a}	1	∅, {a} 1 + 1 subsets	2
1 2 1	{a, b}	2	∅, {a}, {b}, {a, b} 1 + 2 + 1 subsets	4
1 3 3 1	{a, b, c}	3	∅, {a}, {b}, {c}, {a, b}, {a, c}, {b, c}, {a, b, c} 1 + 3 + 3 + 1 subsets	8

1 subset of 0 elements, **3** subsets of 1 element each, **3** subsets of 2 elements each, **1** subset of 3 elements

In algebra, it is shown that $2^0 = 1$; not by coincidence, the set ∅, which has 0 elements, has 1 subset. Just as $2^1 = 2$, the set $\{a\}$ which has 1 element, has 2 subsets. The pattern continues so that a set with 2 elements has $2^2 = 4$ subsets and a set with 3 elements has $2^3 = 8$ subsets. A quick examination suggests this fact:

> The total number of subsets for a set with n elements is 2^n.

The entries of the fifth row of Pascal's Triangle correspond to the numbers of subsets of the four-element set $\{a, b, c, d\}$; of course, the subsets of $\{a, b, c, d\}$ must have 0 elements, 1 element each, 2 elements each, 3 elements each, or 4 elements each. Based upon the preceding principle, there will be a total of $2^4 = 16$ subsets for $\{a, b, c, d\}$.

EXAMPLE 1

List all 16 subsets of the set $\{a, b, c, d\}$ by considering the fifth row of Pascal's Triangle, namely 1 4 6 4 1. Notice also that 1 + 4 + 6 + 4 + 1 must equal 16.

Solution ∅, $\{a\}$, $\{b\}$, $\{c\}$, $\{d\}$, $\{a, b\}$, $\{a, c\}$, $\{a, d\}$, $\{b, c\}$, $\{b, d\}$, $\{c, d\}$, $\{a, b, c\}$, $\{a, b, d\}$, $\{a, c, d\}$, $\{b, c, d\}$, $\{a, b, c, d\}$. ■

EXAMPLE 2

Find the number of subsets for a set with six elements.

Solution The number of subsets is 2^6, or 64. ■

Looking back at Example 1, we notice that the number of subsets of the four-element set $\{a, b, c, d\}$ is $1 + 4 + 6 + 4 + 1$, which equals 16, or 2^4. The preceding principle can be restated in the following equivalent form:

> The sum of the entries in row n of Pascal's Triangle is 2^{n-1}.

EXAMPLE 3

The sixth row of Pascal's Triangle is 1 5 10 10 5 1. Use the principle above to find the sum of the entries of this row.

Solution With $n = 6$, it follows that $n - 1 = 5$. Then $1 + 5 + 10 + 10 + 5 + 1 = 2^5$, or 32. ■

NOTE: There are 32 subsets for a set containing five elements; consider $\{a, b, c, d, e\}$.

In closing, we note that only a few of the principles based upon Pascal's Triangle have been explored in this Perspective on Application!

Summary

A LOOK BACK AT CHAPTER 3

In this chapter, we considered several methods for proving triangles congruent. We explored properties of isosceles triangles and justified construction methods of earlier chapters. Inequality relationships for the sides and angles of a triangle were also investigated.

A LOOK AHEAD TO CHAPTER 4

In the next chapter, we use properties of triangles to develop the properties of quadrilaterals. We consider several special types of quadrilaterals, including the parallelogram, kite, rhombus, and trapezoid.

KEY CONCEPTS

3.1

Congruent Triangles • SSS, SAS, ASA, AAS • Included Angle, Included Side • Reflexive Property of Congruence (Identity) • Symmetric and Transitive Properties of Congruence

3.2

CPCTC • Hypotenuse and Legs of a Right Triangle • HL • Pythagorean Theorem • Square Roots Property

3.3

Isosceles Triangle • Vertex, Legs, and Base of an Isosceles Triangle • Base Angles • Vertex Angle • Angle Bisector • Median • Altitude • Perpendicular Bisector • Auxiliary Line • Determined, Underdetermined, Overdetermined • Equilateral and Equiangular Triangles • Perimeter

3.4

Justifying Constructions

3.5

Lemma • Inequality of Sides and Angles of a Triangle • The Triangle Inequality

TABLE 3.2 An Overview of Chapter 3

▶ Methods of Proving Triangles Congruent: $\triangle ABC \cong \triangle DEF$

FIGURE (NOTE MARKS)	METHOD	STEPS NEEDED IN PROOF
A, B, C; D, E, F	SSS	$\overline{AB} \cong \overline{DE}$, $\overline{AC} \cong \overline{DF}$, and $\overline{BC} \cong \overline{EF}$
A, B, C; D, E, F	SAS	$\overline{AB} \cong \overline{DE}$, $\angle A \cong \angle D$, and $\overline{AC} \cong \overline{DF}$
A, B, C; D, E, F	ASA	$\angle A \cong \angle D$, $\overline{AC} \cong \overline{DF}$, and $\angle C \cong \angle F$
A, B, C; D, E, F	AAS	$\angle A \cong \angle D$, $\angle C \cong \angle F$, and $\overline{BC} \cong \overline{EF}$
A, B, C; D, E, F	HL	$\angle A$ and $\angle D$ are rt. $\angle$s, $\overline{AC} \cong \overline{DF}$, and $\overline{BC} \cong \overline{EF}$

TABLE 3.2 *(continued)*

▶ Special Relationships

FIGURE	RELATIONSHIP	CONCLUSION
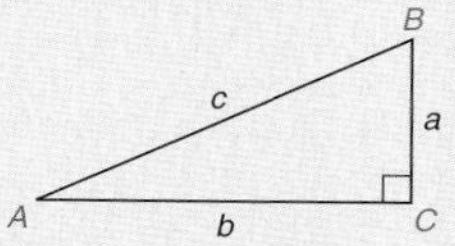	Pythagorean Theorem	$c^2 = a^2 + b^2$
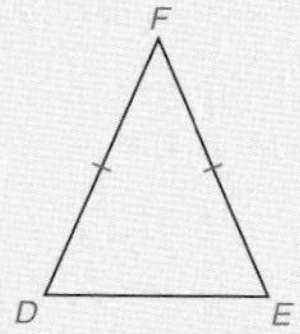	$\overline{DF} \cong \overline{EF}$ (two $\cong$ sides)	$\angle E \cong \angle D$ (opposite $\angle$s $\cong$)
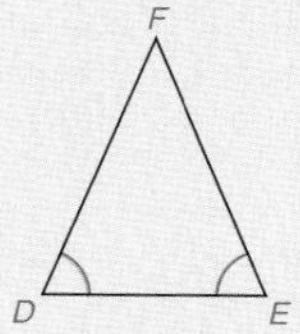	$\angle D \cong \angle E$ (two $\cong$ angles)	$\overline{EF} \cong \overline{DF}$ (opposite sides $\cong$)

▶ Inequality Relationships in a Triangle

FIGURE	RELATIONSHIP	CONCLUSION
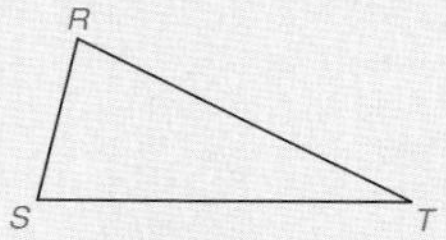	$ST > RS$	$m\angle R > m\angle T$ (opposite angles)
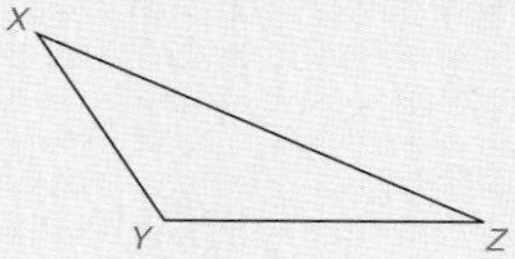	$m\angle Y > m\angle X$	$XZ > YZ$ (opposite sides)

Chapter 3 REVIEW EXERCISES

1. *Given:* $\angle AEB \cong \angle DEC$
$\overline{AE} \cong \overline{ED}$
Prove: $\triangle AEB \cong \triangle DEC$

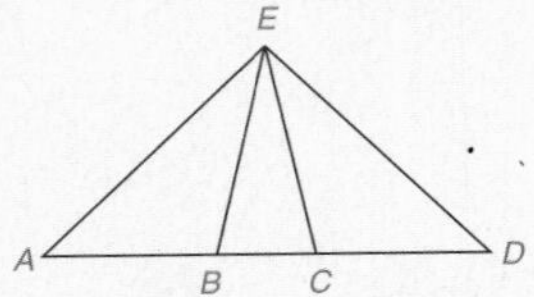

2. *Given:* $\overline{AB} \cong \overline{EF}$
$\overline{AC} \cong \overline{DF}$
$\angle 1 \cong \angle 2$
Prove: $\angle B \cong \angle E$

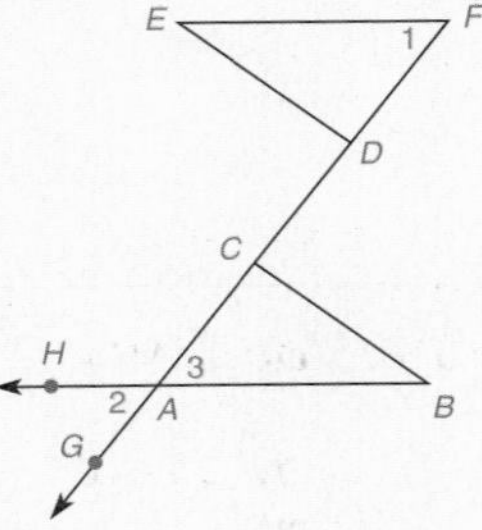

3. *Given:* $\overline{AD}$ bisects $\overline{BC}$
$\overline{AB} \perp \overline{BC}$
$\overline{DC} \perp \overline{BC}$
Prove: $\overline{AE} \cong \overline{ED}$

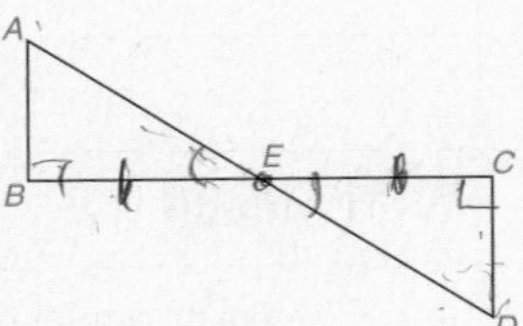

4. *Given:* $\overline{OA} \cong \overline{OB}$
$\overline{OC}$ is the median to $\overline{AB}$
Prove: $\overline{OC} \perp \overline{AB}$

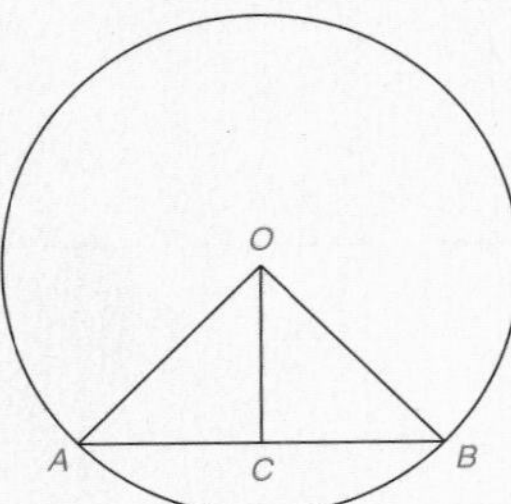

5. *Given:* $\overline{AB} \cong \overline{DE}$
$\overline{AB} \parallel \overline{DE}$
$\overline{AC} \cong \overline{DF}$
Prove: $\overline{BC} \parallel \overline{FE}$

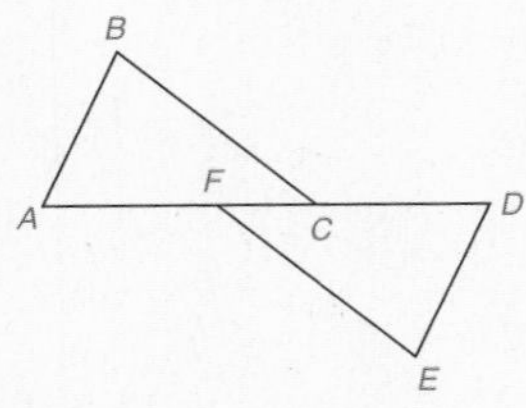

6. *Given:* B is the midpoint of $\overline{AC}$
$\overline{BD} \perp \overline{AC}$
Prove: $\triangle ADC$ is isosceles

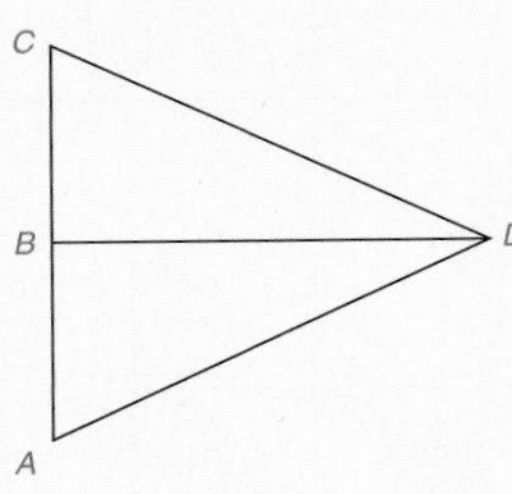

7. *Given:* $\overline{JM} \perp \overline{GM}$ and $\overline{GK} \perp \overline{KJ}$
$\overline{GH} \cong \overline{HJ}$
Prove: $\overline{GM} \cong \overline{JK}$

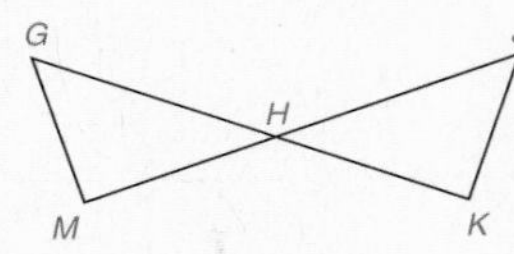

8. *Given:* $\overline{TN} \cong \overline{TR}$
$\overline{TO} \perp \overline{NP}$
$\overline{TS} \perp \overline{PR}$
$\overline{TO} \cong \overline{TS}$
Prove: $\angle N \cong \angle R$

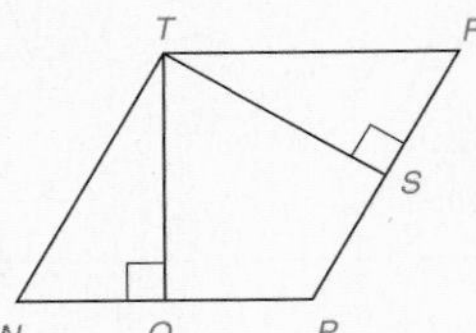

9. *Given:* $\overline{YZ}$ is the base of an isosceles triangle; $\overrightarrow{XA} \parallel \overline{YZ}$
Prove: $\angle 1 \cong \angle 2$

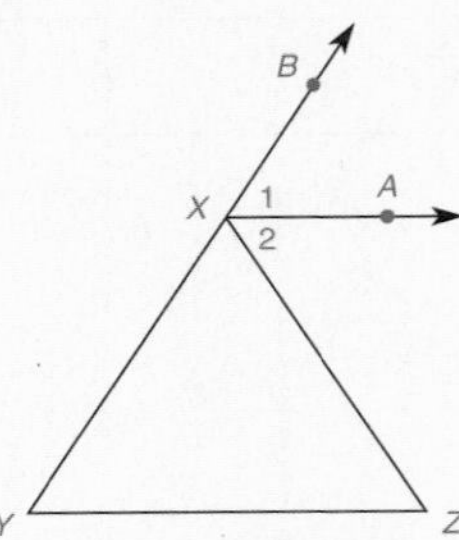

10. *Given:* $\overline{AB} \parallel \overline{DC}$
$\overline{AB} \cong \overline{DC}$
C is the midpoint of $\overline{BE}$
Prove: $\overline{AC} \parallel \overline{DE}$

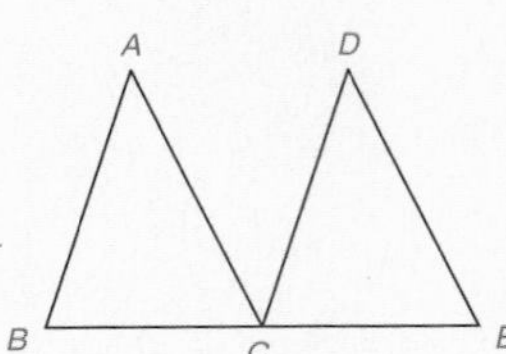

11. *Given:* $\angle BAD \cong \angle CDA$
$\overline{AB} \cong \overline{CD}$
Prove: $\overline{AE} \cong \overline{ED}$

(HINT: Prove $\triangle BAD \cong \triangle CDA$ first.)

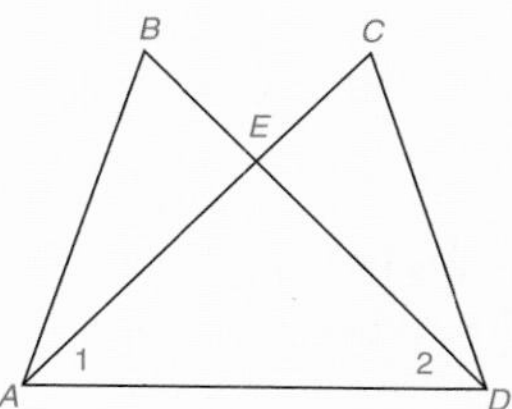

12. Given: $\overline{BE}$ is the altitude to $\overline{AC}$
$\overline{AD}$ is the altitude to $\overline{CE}$
$\overline{BC} \cong \overline{CD}$
Prove: $\overline{BE} \cong \overline{AD}$

(HINT: Prove $\triangle CBE \cong \triangle CDA$.)

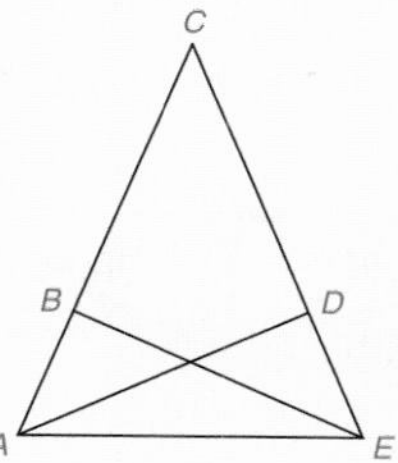

13. *Given:* $\overline{AB} \cong \overline{CD}$
$\angle BAD \cong \angle CDA$
Prove: $\triangle AED$ is isosceles

(HINT: Prove $\angle CAD \cong \angle BDA$ by CPCTC.)

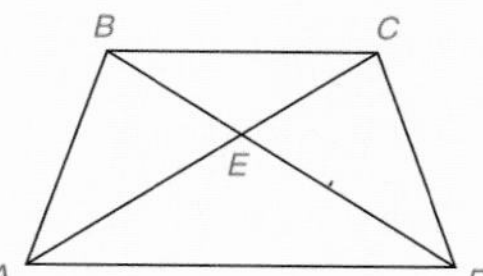

14. *Given:* $\overrightarrow{AC}$ bisects $\angle BAD$
Prove: $AD > CD$

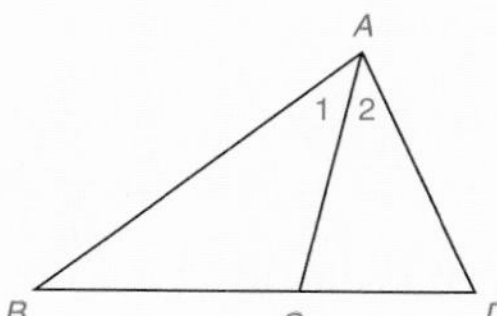

15. In $\triangle PQR$ (not shown), $m\angle P = 67°$ and $m\angle Q = 23°$.
a) Name the shortest side.
b) Name the longest side.

16. In $\triangle ABC$ (not shown), $m\angle A = 40°$ and $m\angle B = 65°$. List the sides in order of their lengths, starting with the smallest side.

17. In $\triangle PQR$ (not shown), $PQ = 1.5$, $PR = 2$, and $QR = 2.5$. List the angles in order of size, starting with the smallest angle.

18. Name the longest line segment shown in quadrilateral $ABCD$.

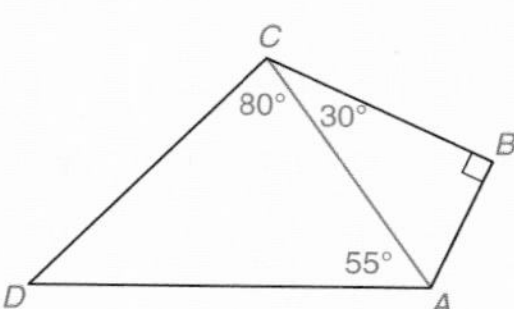

19. Which of the following can be the lengths of the sides of a triangle?
a) 3, 6, 9
b) 4, 5, 8
c) 2, 3, 8

20. Two sides of a triangle have lengths 15 and 20. The length of the third side can be any number between _?_ and _?_.

21. *Given:* $\overline{DB} \perp \overline{AC}$
$\overline{AD} \cong \overline{DC}$
$m\angle C = 70°$
Find: $m\angle ADB$

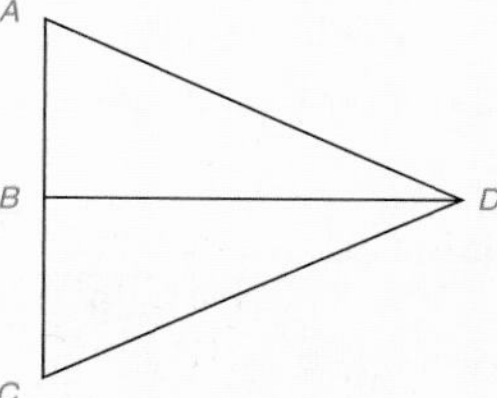

22. *Given:* $\overline{AB} \cong \overline{BC}$
$\angle DAC \cong \angle BCD$
$m\angle B = 50°$
Find: $m\angle ADC$

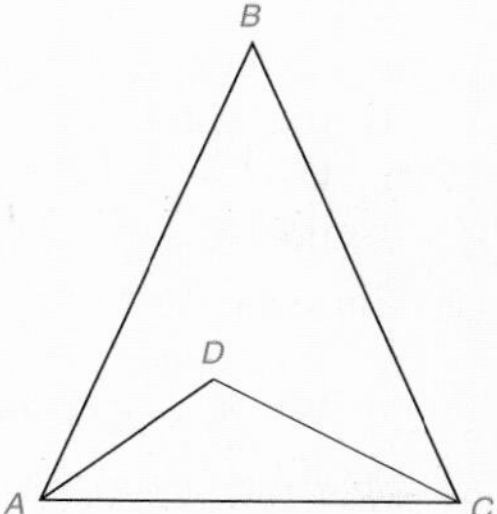

23. *Given:* $\triangle ABC$ is isosceles with base $\overline{AB}$
$m\angle 2 = 3x + 10$
$m\angle 4 = \frac{5}{2}x + 18$
Find: $m\angle C$

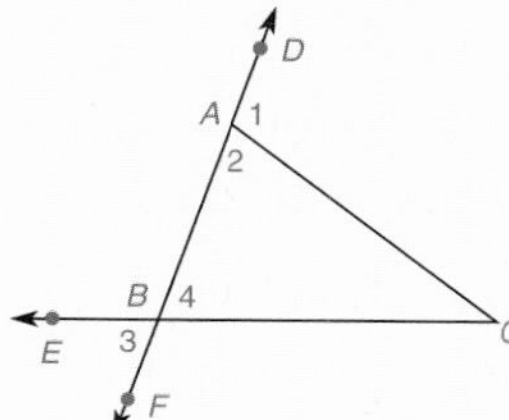

Exercises 23, 24

24. *Given:* $\triangle ABC$ with perimeter 40
$AB = 10$
$BC = x + 6$
$AC = 2x - 3$
Find: Whether $\triangle ABC$ is scalene, isosceles, or equilateral

25. *Given:* $\triangle ABC$ is isosceles with base $\overline{AB}$
$AB = y + 7$
$BC = 3y + 5$
$AC = 9 - y$
Find: Whether $\triangle ABC$ is also equilateral

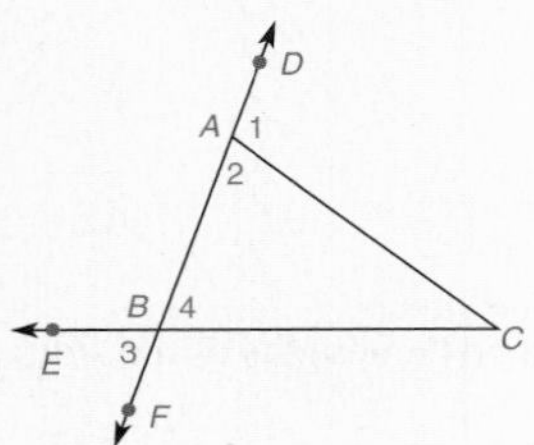

Exercises 25, 26

26. *Given:* $\overline{AC}$ and $\overline{BC}$ are the legs of isosceles $\triangle ABC$
$m\angle 1 = 5x$
$m\angle 3 = 2x + 12$
Find: $m\angle 2$

27. Construct an angle that measures 75°.

28. Construct a right triangle that has acute angle A and hypotenuse of length c.

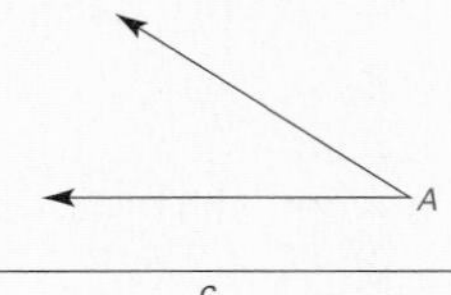

29. Construct a second isosceles triangle in which the base angles are half as large as the base angles of the given isosceles triangle.

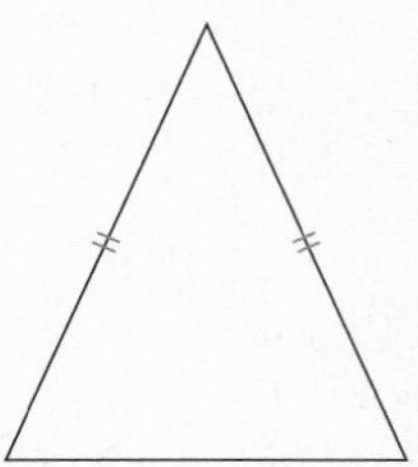

Chapter 3 TEST

1. It is given that $\triangle ABC \cong \triangle DEF$ (triangles not shown).
a) If $m\angle A = 37°$ and $m\angle E = 68°$, find $m\angle F$. _____
b) If $AB = 7.3$ cm, $BC = 4.7$ cm, and $AC = 6.3$ cm, find EF. _____

2. Consider $\triangle XYZ$ (not shown).
a) Which side is included by $\angle X$ and $\angle Y$? _____
b) Which angle is included by sides $\overline{XY}$ and $\overline{YZ}$? _____

3. State the reason (SSS, SAS, ASA, AAS, or HL) why the triangles are congruent. Note the marks that indicate congruent parts.

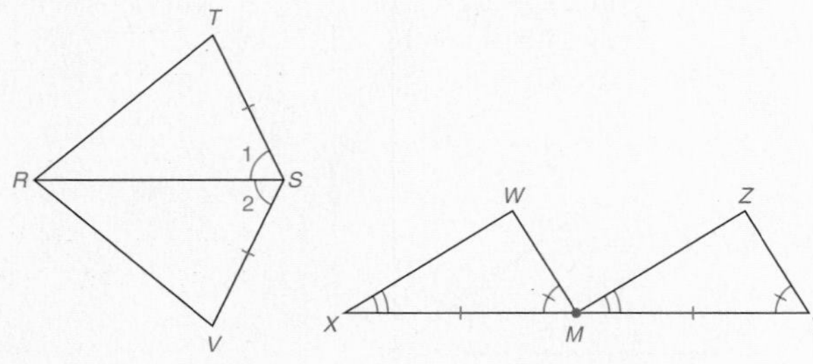

$\triangle RVS \cong \triangle RTS$ _____ $\triangle XMW \cong \triangle MYZ$ _____

4. Write the statement that is represented by the acronym CPCTC. __________

5. With congruent parts marked, are the two triangles congruent?
Answer YES or NO.
$\triangle ABC$ and $\triangle DAC$ _____
$\triangle RSM$ and $\triangle WVM$ _____

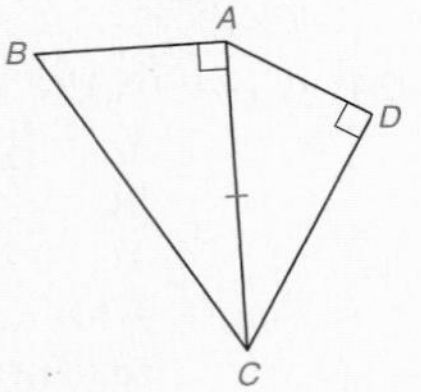

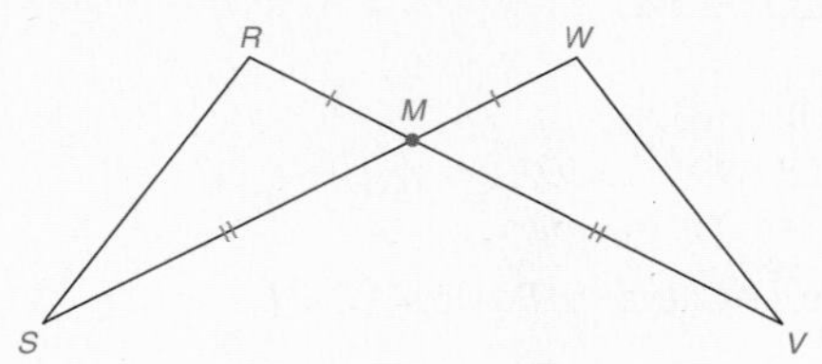

6. With $\triangle ABD \cong \triangle CBE$ and A-D-E-C, does it necessarily follow that $\triangle AEB$ and $\triangle CDB$ are congruent?
Answer YES or NO. _____

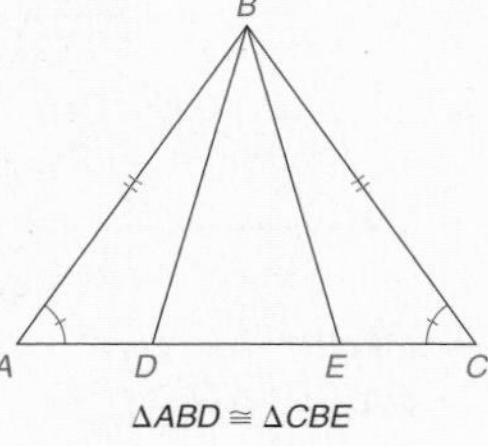

$\triangle ABD \cong \triangle CBE$

7. In $\triangle ABC$, $m\angle C = 90°$. Find:
a) c if $a = 8$ and $b = 6$ _____
b) b if $a = 6$ and $c = 8$ _____

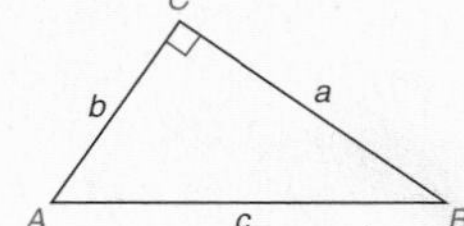

8. $\overline{CM}$ is the median for $\triangle ABC$ from vertex C to side $\overline{AB}$.
a) Name two line segments that must be congruent.

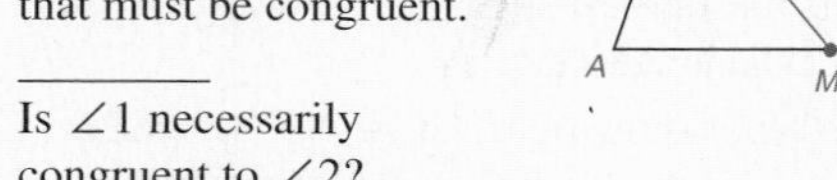

____
b) Is $\angle 1$ necessarily congruent to $\angle 2$? ________

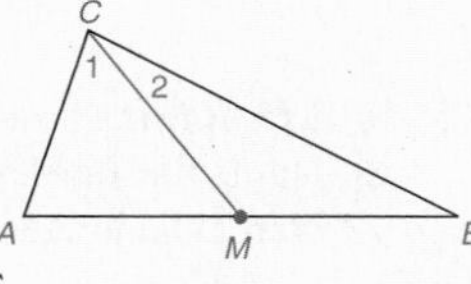

9. In $\triangle TUV$, $\overline{TV} \cong \overline{UV}$.
a) If $m\angle T = 71°$, find $m\angle V$.

____

b) If $m\angle T = 7x + 2$ and $m\angle U = 9(x - 2)$, find $m\angle V$.

____

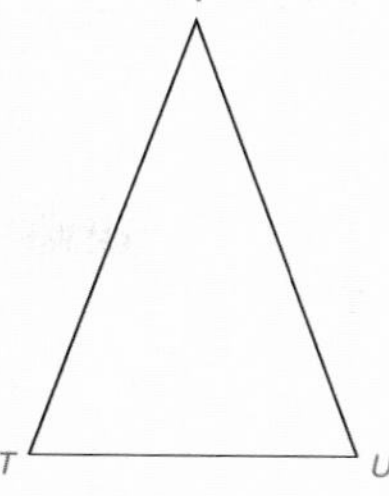

Exercises 9, 10

10. In $\triangle TUV$, $\angle T \cong \angle U$.
a) If $VT = 7.6$ inches and $TU = 4.3$ inches, find VU.

____

b) If $VT = 4x + 1$, $TU = 2x$ and $VU = 6x - 10$, find the perimeter of $\triangle TUV$. ________

(HINT: Find the value of x.)

11. Show all arcs in the following construction.
a) Construct an angle that measures 60°.
b) Using the result from part (a), construct an angle that measures 30°.

12. Show all arcs in the following construction. Construct an isoceles right triangle in which each leg has the length of line segment $\overline{AB}$.

13. In $\triangle ABC$, $m\angle C = 46°$, and $m\angle B = 93°$.
a) Name the shortest side of $\triangle ABC$.

____

b) Name the longest side of $\triangle ABC$. ________

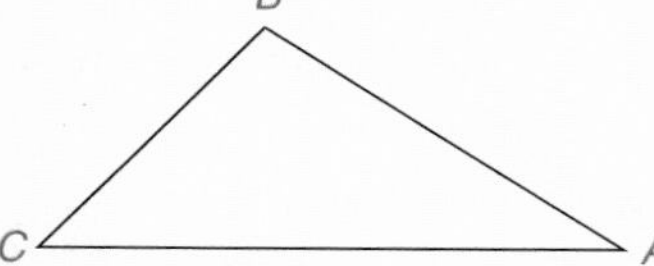

14. In $\triangle TUV$ (not shown), $TU > TV > VU$. Write a three-part inequality that compares the measures of the three angles of $\triangle TUV$. ________

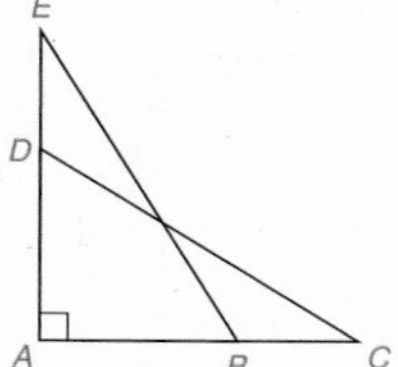

15. In the figure, $\angle A$ is a right angle, $AD = 4$, $DE = 3$, $AB = 5$, and $BC = 2$. Of the two line segments $\overline{DC}$ and $\overline{EB}$, which one is longer? ________

16. Given $\triangle ABC$, draw the triangle that results when $\triangle ABC$ is rotated clockwise 180° about M, the midpoint of $\overline{AC}$. Let D name the image of point B. In these congruent triangles, which side of $\triangle CDA$ corresponds to side $\overline{BC}$ of $\triangle ABC$? ________

17. Complete *all* statements and reasons for the following proof problem.

Given: $\angle R$ and $\angle V$ are right angles; $\angle 1 \cong \angle 2$
Prove: $\triangle RST \cong \triangle VST$

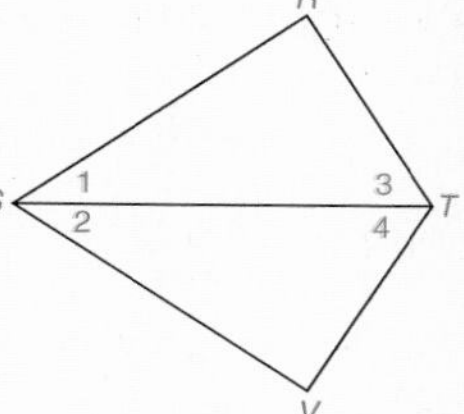

Statements	Reasons

18. Complete the missing statements and reasons in the following proof.

Given: $\triangle RUV$; $\angle R \cong \angle V$, and $\angle 1 \cong \angle 3$
Prove: $\triangle STU$ is an isosceles triangle

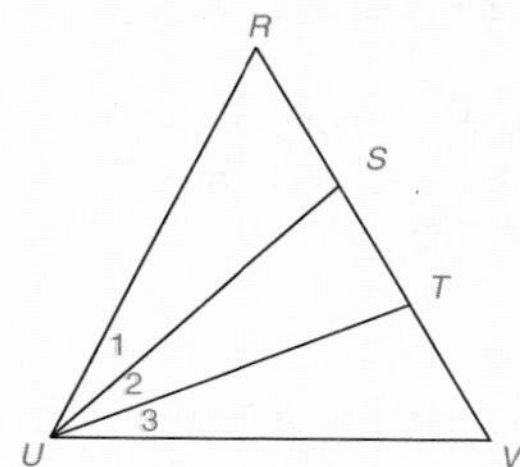

Statements	Reasons
1. $\triangle RUV$; $\angle R \cong \angle V$	1. ________
2. $\therefore \overline{UV} \cong \overline{UR}$	2. ________
3. ________	3. Given
4. $\triangle RSU \cong \triangle VTU$	4. ________
5. ________	5. CPCTC
6. ________	6. If 2 sides of a $\triangle$ are $\cong$, this triangle is an isosceles triangle.

19. The perimeter of an isosceles triangle is 32 cm. If the length of the altitude drawn to the base is 8 cm, how long is each leg of the isosceles triangle? ________

Chapter 4

Quadrilaterals

© Richard A. Cooke/CORBIS.

CHAPTER OUTLINE

Additional Video explanation of concepts, sample problems, and applications are available on DVD. 

Comforting! Designed by architect Frank Lloyd Wright (1867–1959), this private home is nestled among the trees in the Bear Run Nature Preserve of southwestern Pennsylvania. Known as Fallingwater, this house was constructed in the 1930s. The geometric figure that dominates the homes designed by Wright is the quadrilateral. In this chapter, we consider numerous types of quadrilaterals—among them the parallelogram, the rhombus, and the trapezoid. Also, the language and properties for each type of quadrilateral are developed. Although each quadrilateral has its own properties and applications, some of the applications for the trapezoid can be found in Exercises 37–40 of Section 4.4.

4.1 Properties of a Parallelogram

KEY CONCEPTS

- Quadrilateral
- Skew Quadrilateral
- Parallelogram
- Diagonals of a Parallelogram
- Altitudes of a Parallelogram

A **quadrilateral** is a polygon that has four sides. Unless otherwise stated, the term *quadrilateral* refers to a figure such as *ABCD* in Figure 4.1(a), in which the line segment sides lie within a single plane. When the sides of the quadrilateral are not coplanar, as with *MNPQ* in Figure 4.1(b), the quadrilateral is said to be **skew.** Thus, *MNPQ* is a skew quadrilateral. In this textbook, we generally consider quadrilaterals whose sides are coplanar.

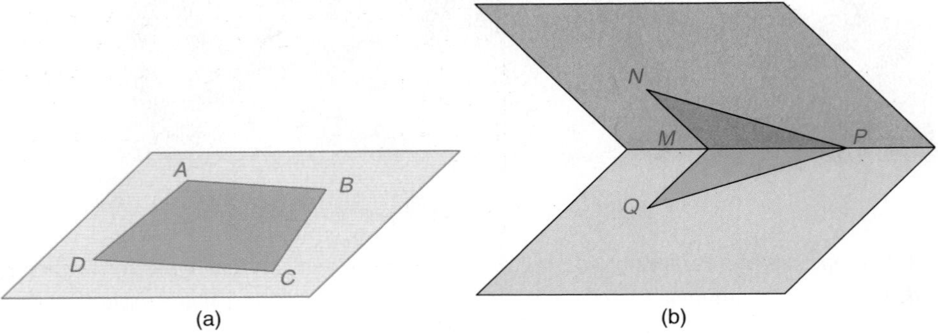

Figure 4.1

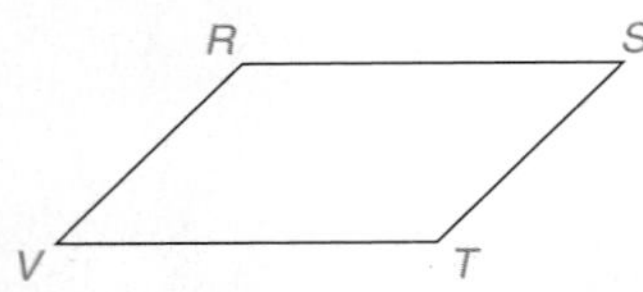

Figure 4.2

DEFINITION

A **parallelogram** is a quadrilateral in which both pairs of opposite sides are parallel. (See Figure 4.2.)

Because the symbol for parallelogram is ▱, the quadrilateral in Figure 4.2 is ▱*RSTV*. The set $P = \{\text{parallelograms}\}$ is a subset of $Q = \{\text{quadrilaterals}\}$.

The Discover activity at the left leads to many of the theorems of this section.

Discover

From a standard sheet of construction paper, cut out a parallelogram as shown. Then cut along one diagonal. How are the two triangles that are formed related?

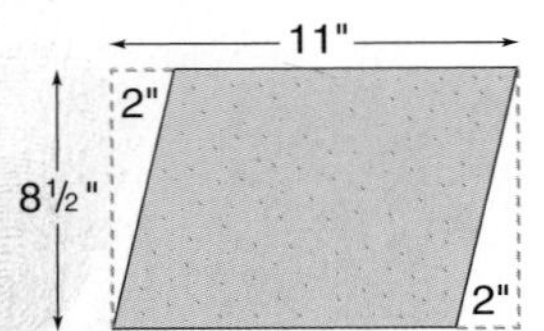

ANSWER

They are congruent.

EXAMPLE 1

Give a formal proof of Theorem 4.1.1.

THEOREM 4.1.1

A diagonal of a parallelogram separates it into two congruent triangles.

GIVEN: ▱*ABCD* with diagonal $\overline{AC}$ (See Figure 4.3 on page 179.)

PROVE: $\triangle ACD \cong \triangle CAB$

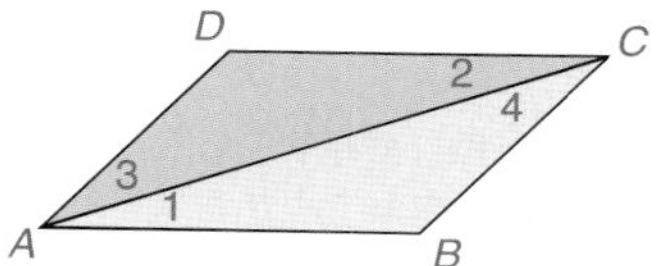

Figure 4.3

PROOF

Statements	Reasons
1. ▱$ABCD$	1. Given
2. $\overline{AB} \parallel \overline{CD}$	2. The opposite sides of a ▱ are $\parallel$ (definition)
3. $\angle 1 \cong \angle 2$	3. If two $\parallel$ lines are cut by a transversal, the alternate interior $\angle$s are congruent
4. $\overline{AD} \parallel \overline{BC}$	4. Same as reason 2
5. $\angle 3 \cong \angle 4$	5. Same as reason 3
6. $\overline{AC} \cong \overline{AC}$	6. Identity
7. $\triangle ACD \cong \triangle CAB$	7. ASA

Reminder

The sum of the measures of the interior angles of a quadrilateral is 360°.

STRATEGY FOR PROOF ▶ Using Congruent Triangles

General Rule: To prove that parts of a quadrilateral are congruent, we often use an auxiliary line to prove that triangles are congruent. Then we apply CPCTC.

Illustration: This strategy is used in the proof of Corollaries 4.1.2 and 4.1.3. In the proof of Corollary 4.1.4, we do not need the auxiliary line.

COROLLARY 4.1.2

The opposite angles of a parallelogram are congruent.

COROLLARY 4.1.3

The opposite sides of a parallelogram are congruent.

COROLLARY 4.1.4

The diagonals of a parallelogram bisect each other.

Recall Theorem 2.1.4: "If two parallel lines are cut by a transversal, then the interior angles on the same side of the transversal are supplementary." A corollary of that theorem is stated next.

SSG *Exs. 1–6*

COROLLARY 4.1.5

Two consecutive angles of a parallelogram are supplementary.

EXAMPLE 2

In ▱$RSTV$, m$\angle S$ = 42°, ST = 5.3 cm, and VT = 8.1 cm. Find:

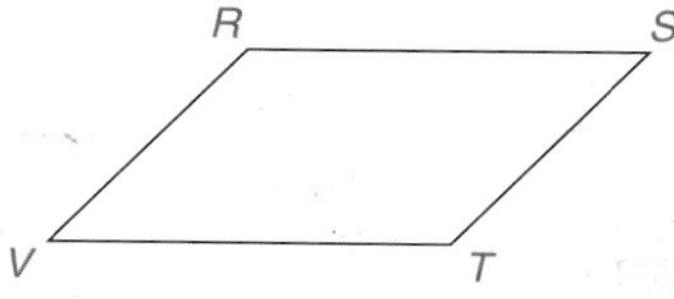

a) m$\angle V$ b) m$\angle T$ c) RV d) RS

Solution

a) m$\angle V$ = 42°; $\angle V \cong \angle S$ because these are opposite $\angle$s of ▱$RSTV$.

b) m$\angle T$ = 138°; $\angle T$ and $\angle S$ are supplementary because these angles are consecutive angles of ▱*RSTV*.
c) RV = 5.3 cm; $\overline{RV} \cong \overline{ST}$ because these are opposite sides of ▱*RSTV*.
d) RS = 8.1 cm; $\overline{RS} \cong \overline{VT}$, also a pair of opposite sides of ▱*RSTV*. ■

Example 3 illustrates Theorem 4.1.6, the fact that two parallel lines are everywhere equidistant. In general, the phrase *distance between two parallel lines* refers to the length of the perpendicular segment between the two parallel lines. These concepts will provide insight into the definition of altitude of a parallelogram.

STRATEGY FOR PROOF ▶ Separating the Given Information

General Rule: When only part of the "Given" information leads to an important conclusion, it may be separated (for emphasis) from other Given facts in the statements of the proof.

Illustration: See lines 1 and 2 in the proof of Example 3. Notice that the Given facts found in statement 2 lead to statement 3.

THEOREM 4.1.6

Two parallel lines are everywhere equidistant.

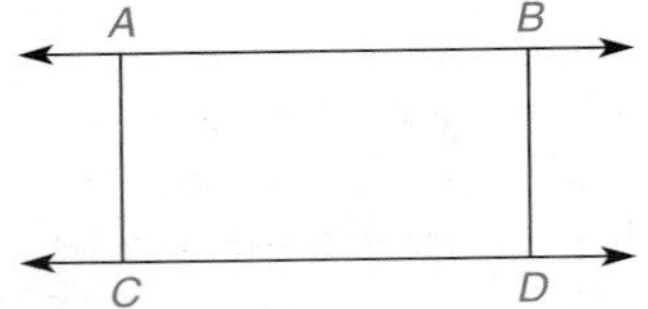

Figure 4.4

EXAMPLE 3

GIVEN: $\overleftrightarrow{AB} \parallel \overleftrightarrow{CD}$
$\overline{AC} \perp \overleftrightarrow{CD}$ and $\overline{BD} \perp \overleftrightarrow{CD}$
(See Figure 4.4.)

PROVE: $\overline{AC} \cong \overline{BD}$

PROOF

Statements	Reasons
1. $\overleftrightarrow{AB} \parallel \overleftrightarrow{CD}$	1. Given
2. $\overline{AC} \perp \overleftrightarrow{CD}$ and $\overline{BD} \perp \overleftrightarrow{CD}$	2. Given
3. $\overline{AC} \parallel \overline{BD}$	3. If two lines are ⊥ to the same line, they are parallel
4. *ABDC* is a ▱	4. If both pairs of opposite sides of a quadrilateral are ∥, the quadrilateral is a ▱
5. $\overline{AC} \cong \overline{BD}$	5. Opposite sides of a ▱ are congruent

■

Geometry in the Real World

The central brace for the gate shown is a parallelogram.

In Example 3, we used the definition of a parallelogram to prove that a particular quadrilateral was a parallelogram, but there are other ways of establishing that a given quadrilateral is a parallelogram. We will investigate those methods in Section 4.2.

DEFINITION

An **altitude** of a parallelogram is a line segment from one vertex that is perpendicular to a nonadjacent side (or to an extension of that side).

SSG
Exs. 7–11

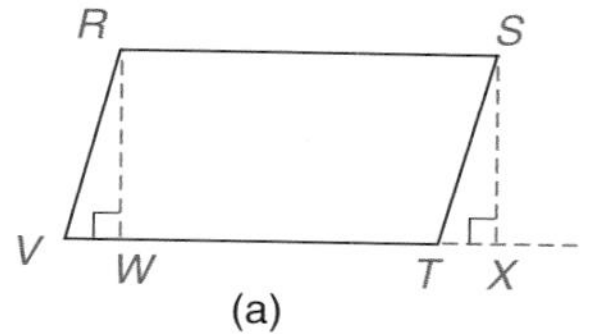

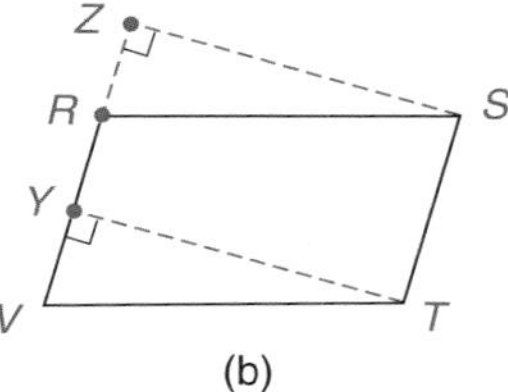

Figure 4.5

For $\square RSTV$, $\overline{RW}$ and $\overline{SX}$ are altitudes to side $\overline{VT}$ (or to side $\overline{RS}$), as shown in Figure 4.5(a). With respect to side $\overline{RS}$, sometimes called base $\overline{RS}$, the length RW (or SX) is the *height* of $RSTV$. Similarly, in Figure 4.5(b), $\overline{TY}$ and $\overline{SZ}$ are altitudes to side $\overline{RV}$ (or to side $\overline{ST}$). Also, the length TY (or ZS) is called the *height* of parallelogram $RSTV$ with respect to side $\overline{ST}$ (or $\overline{RV}$).

Next we consider an inequality relationship for the parallelogram. To develop this relationship, we need to investigate an inequality involving two triangles.

In $\triangle ABC$ and $\triangle DEF$ of Figure 4.6, $\overline{AB} \cong \overline{DE}$ and $\overline{BC} \cong \overline{EF}$. If $m\angle B > m\angle E$, then $AC > DF$.

We will use, but not prove, the following relationship found in Lemma 4.1.7.

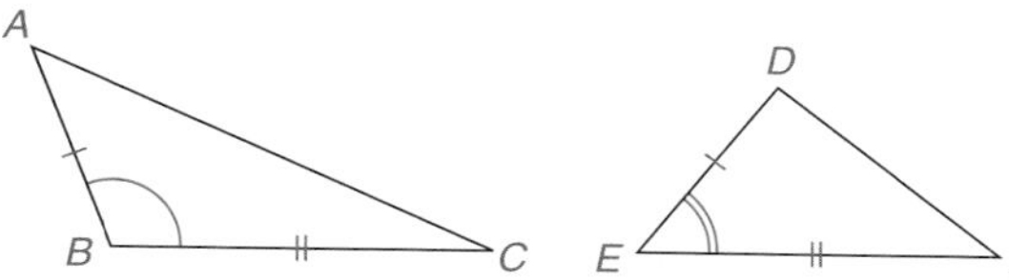

Figure 4.6

GIVEN: $\overline{AB} \cong \overline{DE}$ and $\overline{BC} \cong \overline{EF}$; $m\angle B > m\angle E$ (See Figure 4.6.)

PROVE: $AC > DF$

The corresponding lemma follows.

Discover

On one piece of paper, draw a triangle ($\triangle ABC$) so that $AB = 3$, $BC = 5$, and $m\angle B = 110°$. Then draw $\triangle DEF$, in which $DE = 3$, $EF = 5$, and $m\angle E = 50°$. Which is longer, $\overline{AC}$ or $\overline{DF}$?

ANSWER
$\overline{AC}$

LEMMA 4.1.7

If two sides of one triangle are congruent to two sides of a second triangle and the included angle of the first triangle is greater than the included angle of the second, then the length of the side opposite the included angle of the first triangle is greater than the length of the side opposite the included angle of the second.

Now we can compare the lengths of the diagonals of a parallelogram. For a parallelogram having no right angles, two consecutive angles are unequal but supplementary; thus, one angle of the parallelogram will be acute and the consecutive angle will be obtuse. In Figure 4.7(a), $\square ABCD$ has acute angle A and obtuse angle D. Note that the lengths of the two sides of the triangles that include $\angle A$ and $\angle D$ are congruent. In Figure 4.7(b), diagonal $\overline{AC}$ lies opposite the obtuse angle ADC in $\triangle ACD$, and diagonal $\overline{BD}$ lies opposite the acute angle DAB in $\triangle ABD$. In Figures 4.7(c) and (d), we have taken $\triangle ACD$ and $\triangle ABD$ from $\square ABCD$ of Figure 4.7(b). Note that $\overline{AC}$ (opposite obtuse $\angle D$) is longer than $\overline{DB}$ (opposite acute $\angle A$).

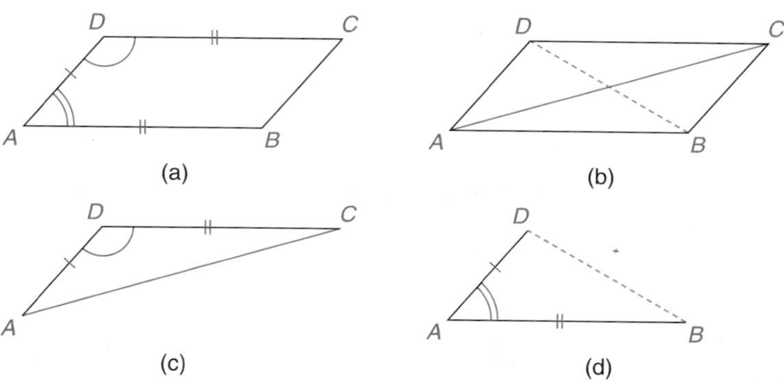

Figure 4.7

On the basis of Lemma 4.1.7 and the preceding discussion, we have the following theorem.

Discover

Draw $\square ABCD$ so that $m\angle A > m\angle B$. Which diagonal has the greater length?

ANSWER
BD

THEOREM 4.1.8

In a parallelogram with unequal pairs of consecutive angles, the longer diagonal lies opposite the obtuse angle.

EXAMPLE 4

In parallelogram *RSTV* (not shown), $m\angle R = 67°$.

a) Find the measure of $\angle S$.
b) Determine which diagonal ($\overline{RT}$ or $\overline{SV}$) has the greater length.

Solution
a) $m\angle S = 180° - 67° = 113°$ ($\angle R$ and $\angle S$ are supplementary.)
b) Because $\angle S$ is obtuse, the diagonal opposite this angle is longer; that is, $\overline{RT}$ is the longer diagonal. ■

We use an indirect approach to solve Example 5.

EXAMPLE 5

In parallelogram *ABCD* (not shown), $\overline{AC}$ and $\overline{BD}$ are diagonals, and $AC > BD$. Determine which angles of the parallelogram are obtuse and which angles are acute.

SSG *Exs. 12–15*

Solution Because the longer diagonal $\overline{AC}$ lies opposite angles *B* and *D*, these angles are obtuse. The remaining angles *A* and *C* are necessarily acute. ■

Our next example uses algebra to relate angle sizes and diagonal lengths.

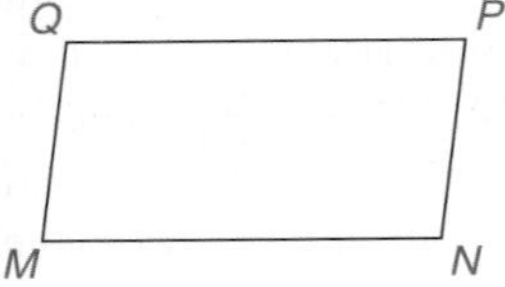

Figure 4.8

EXAMPLE 6

In $\square MNPQ$ in Figure 4.8, $m\angle M = 2(x + 10)$ and $m\angle Q = 3x - 10$. Determine which diagonal would be longer, $\overline{QN}$ or $\overline{MP}$.

Solution Consecutive angles *M* and *Q* are supplementary, so $m\angle M + m\angle Q = 180°$.

$$2(x + 10) + (3x - 10) = 180$$
$$2x + 20 + 3x - 10 = 180$$
$$5x + 10 = 180 \rightarrow 5x = 170 \rightarrow x = 34$$

Then $m\angle M = 2(34 + 10) = 88°$, whereas $m\angle Q = 3(34) - 10 = 92°$. Because $m\angle Q > m\angle M$, diagonal $\overline{MP}$ (opposite $\angle Q$) would be longer than $\overline{QN}$. ■

SPEED AND DIRECTION OF AIRCRAFT

For the application to follow in Example 7, we indicate the velocity of an airplane or of the wind by drawing a directed arrow. In each case, a scale is used on a grid in which a north-south line meets an east-west line at right angles. Consider the sketches in Figure 4.9 on page 183 and read their descriptions.

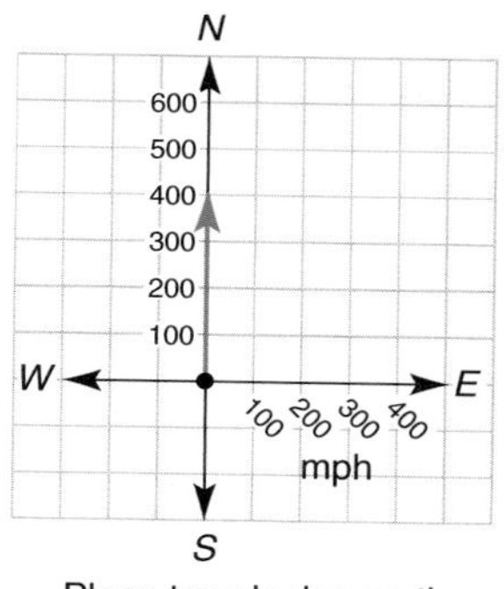

Plane travels due north at 400 mph

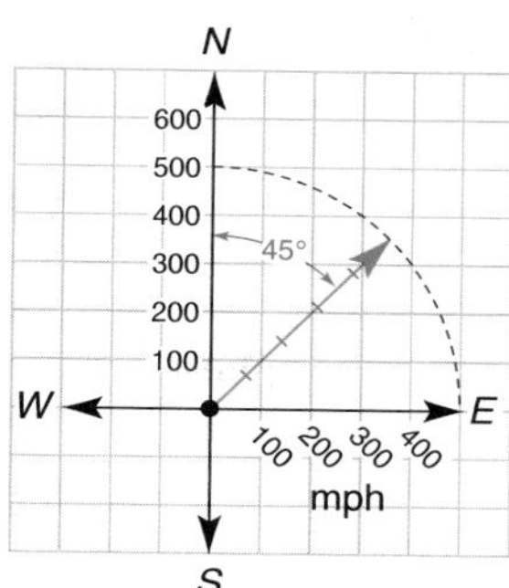

Plane travels at 500 mph in the direction N 45° E

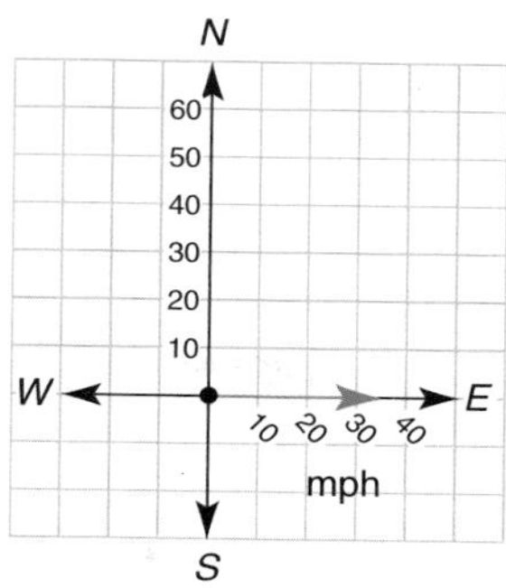

Wind blows at 30 mph in the direction west to east

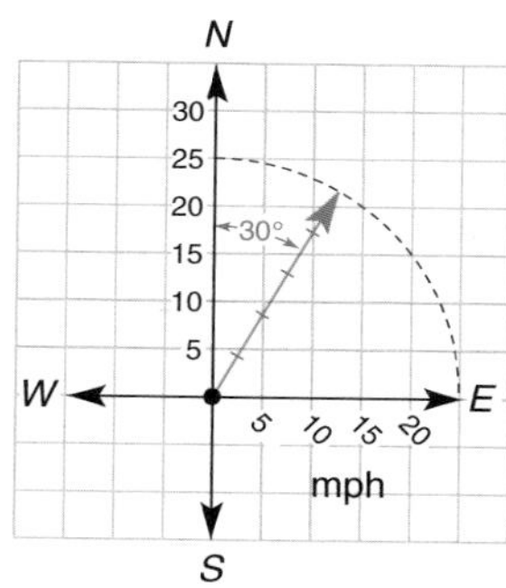

Wind blows at 25 mph in the direction N 30° E

Figure 4.9

In some scientific applications, such as Example 7, a parallelogram can be used to determine the solution to the problem. For instance, the Parallelogram Law enables us to determine the resulting speed and direction of an airplane when the velocity of the airplane and that of the wind are considered together. In Figure 4.10, the arrows representing the two velocities are placed head-to-tail from the point of origin. Because the order of the two velocities is reversible, the drawing leads to a parallelogram. In the parallelogram, it is the length and direction of the diagonal that solve the problem. In Example 7, accuracy is critical in scaling the drawing that represents the problem. Otherwise, the ruler and protractor will give poor results in your answer.

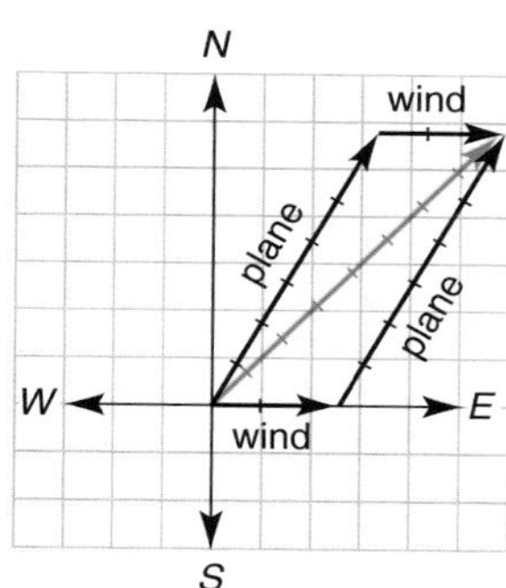

Figure 4.10

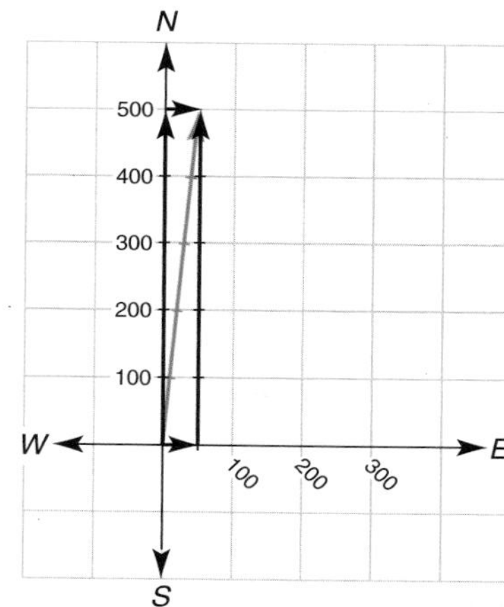

Figure 4.11

NOTE: In Example 7, kph means *kilometers per hour.*

EXAMPLE 7

An airplane travels due north at 500 kph. If the wind blows at 50 kph from west to east, what are the resulting speed and direction of the plane?

Solution Using a ruler to measure the diagonal of the parallelogram, we find that the length corresponds to a speed of approximately 505 kph. Using a protractor, we find that the direction is approximately N 6° E. (See Figure 4.11.)

SSG *Exs. 16–17*

NOTE: The actual speed is approximately 502.5 kph while the direction is N 5.7° E. ■

Exercises 4.1

1. $ABCD$ is a parallelogram.
   a) Using a ruler, compare the lengths of sides $\overline{AB}$ and $\overline{DC}$.
   b) Using a protractor, compare the measures of $\angle A$ and $\angle C$.

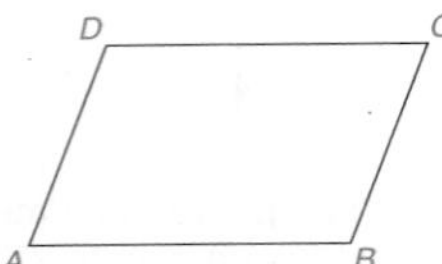

Exercises 1, 2

2. $ABCD$ is a parallelogram.
   a) Using a ruler, compare the lengths of $\overline{AD}$ and $\overline{BC}$.
   b) Using a protractor, compare the measures of $\angle B$ and $\angle D$.
3. $MNPQ$ is a parallelogram. Suppose that $MQ = 5$, $MN = 8$, and $m\angle M = 110°$. Find:
   a) QP
   b) NP
   c) $m\angle Q$
   d) $m\angle P$

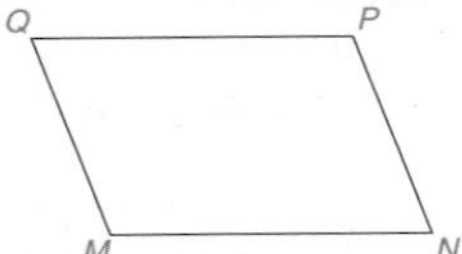

Exercises 3, 4

4. $MNPQ$ is a parallelogram. Suppose that $MQ = 12.7$, $MN = 17.9$, and $m\angle M = 122°$. Find:
   a) QP
   b) NP
   c) $m\angle Q$
   d) $m\angle P$
5. Given that $AB = 3x + 2$, $BC = 4x + 1$, and $CD = 5x - 2$, find the length of each side of $\square ABCD$.

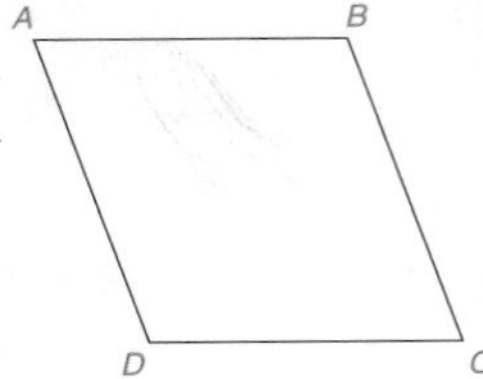

Exercises 5–12

6. Given that $m\angle A = 2x + 3$ and $m\angle C = 3x - 27$, find the measure of each angle of $\square ABCD$.
7. Given that $m\angle A = 2x + 3$ and $m\angle B = 3x - 23$, find the measure of each angle of $\square ABCD$.
8. Given that $m\angle A = \frac{2x}{5}$ and $m\angle B = \frac{x}{2}$, find the measure of each angle of $\square ABCD$.
9. Given that $m\angle A = \frac{2x}{3}$ and $m\angle C = \frac{x}{2} + 20$, find the measure of each angle of $\square ABCD$.
10. Given that $m\angle A = 2x + y$, $m\angle B = 2x + 3y - 20$, and $m\angle C = 3x - y + 16$, find the measure of each angle of $\square ABCD$.
11. Assuming that $m\angle B > m\angle A$ in $\square ABCD$, which diagonal ($\overline{AC}$ or $\overline{BD}$) would be longer?
12. Suppose that diagonals $\overline{AC}$ and $\overline{BD}$ of $\square ABCD$ are drawn and that $AC > BD$. Which angle ($\angle A$ or $\angle B$) would have the greater measure?

In Exercises 13 and 14, consider $\square RSTV$ with $\overline{VX} \perp \overline{RS}$ and $\overline{VY} \perp \overline{ST}$.

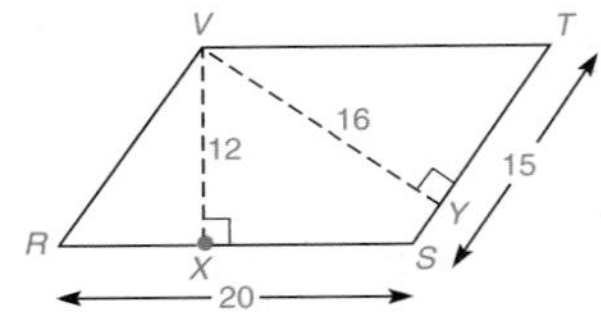

Exercises 13, 14

13. a) Which line segment is the altitude of $\square RSTV$ with respect to base $\overline{ST}$?
    b) Which number is the height of $\square RSTV$ with respect to base $\overline{ST}$?
14. a) Which line segment is the altitude of $\square RSTV$ with respect to base $\overline{RS}$?
    b) Which number is the height of $\square RSTV$ with respect to base $\overline{RS}$?

In Exercises 15 to 18, classify each statement as true or false. In Exercises 15 and 16, recall that the symbol $\subseteq$ means "is a subset of."

15. Where $Q = \{\text{quadrilaterals}\}$ and $P = \{\text{polygons}\}$, $Q \subseteq P$.
16. Where $Q = \{\text{quadrilaterals}\}$ and $P = \{\text{parallelograms}\}$, $Q \subseteq P$.
17. A parallelogram has point symmetry about the point where its two diagonals intersect.
18. A parallelogram has line symmetry and either diagonal is an axis of symmetry.
19. In quadrilateral $RSTV$, the midpoints of consecutive sides are joined in order. Try drawing other quadrilaterals and joining their midpoints. What can you conclude about the resulting quadrilateral in each case?

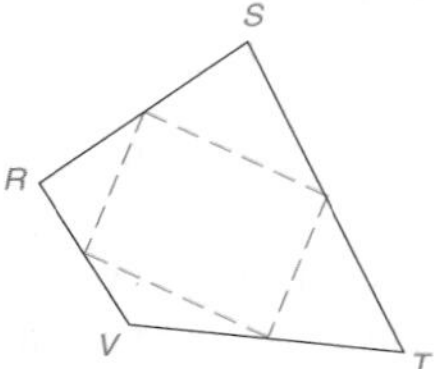

20. In quadrilateral $ABCD$, the midpoints of opposite sides are joined to form two intersecting segments. Try drawing other quadrilaterals and joining their opposite midpoints. What can you conclude about these segments in each case?

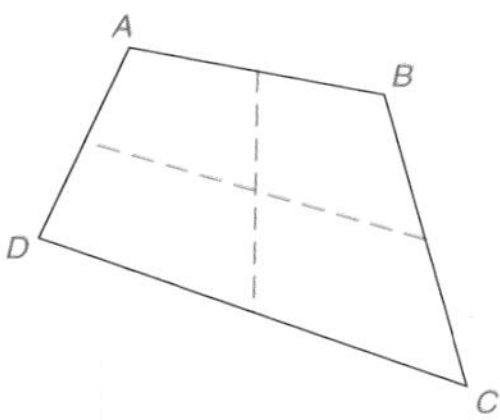

21. Quadrilateral $ABCD$ has $\overline{AB} \cong \overline{DC}$ and $\overline{AD} \cong \overline{BC}$. Using intuition, what type of quadrilateral is $ABCD$?

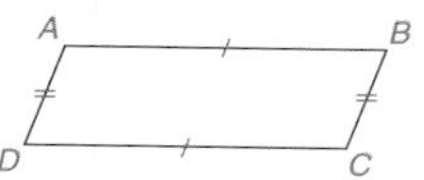

22. Quadrilateral $RSTV$ has $\overline{RS} \cong \overline{TV}$ and $\overline{RS} \parallel \overline{TV}$. Using intuition, what type of quadrilateral is $RSTV$?

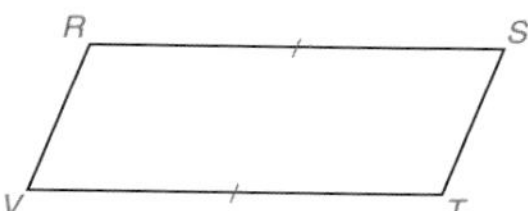

In Exercises 23 to 26, use the definition of parallelogram to complete each proof.

23. *Given:* $\overline{RS} \parallel \overline{VT}$, $\overline{RV} \perp \overline{VT}$, and $\overline{ST} \perp \overline{VT}$
Prove: $RSTV$ is a parallelogram

PROOF

Statements	Reasons
1. $\overline{RS} \parallel \overline{VT}$	1. ?
2. ?	2. Given
3. ?	3. If two lines are $\perp$ to the same line, they are $\parallel$ to each other
4. ?	4. If both pairs of opposite sides of a quadrilateral are $\parallel$, the quad. is a ▱

• **24.** *Given:* $\overline{WX} \parallel \overline{ZY}$ and $\angle$s Z and Y are supplementary
Prove: $WXYZ$ is a parallelogram

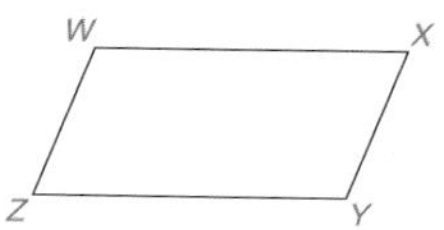

PROOF

Statements	Reasons
1. $\overline{WX} \parallel \overline{ZY}$	1. ?
2. ?	2. Given
3. ?	3. If two lines are cut by a transversal so that int. $\angle$s on the same side of the trans. are supplementary, these lines are $\parallel$
4. ?	4. If both pairs of opposite sides of a quadrilateral are $\parallel$, the quad. is a ▱

25. *Given:* Parallelogram $RSTV$; also $\overline{XY} \parallel \overline{VT}$
Prove: $\angle 1 \cong \angle S$
Plan: First show that $RSYX$ is a parallelogram.

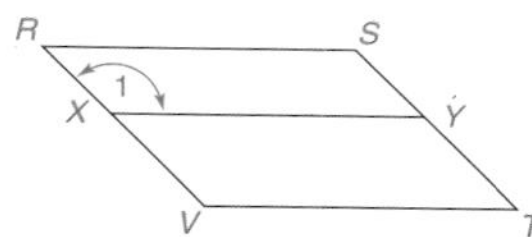

26. *Given:* Parallelogram $ABCD$ with $\overline{DE} \perp \overline{AB}$ and $\overline{FB} \perp \overline{AB}$
Prove: $\overline{DE} \cong \overline{FB}$
Plan: First show that $DEBF$ is a parallelogram.

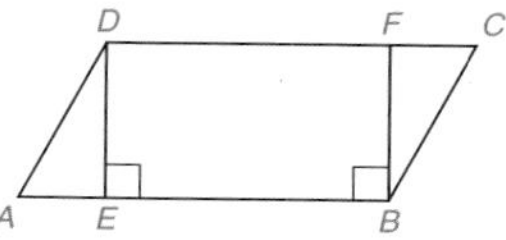

In Exercises 27 to 30, write a formal proof of each theorem or corollary.

27. The opposite angles of a parallelogram are congruent.

28. The opposite sides of a parallelogram are congruent.

29. The diagonals of a parallelogram bisect each other.

30. The consecutive angles of a parallelogram are supplementary.

31. The bisectors of two consecutive angles of $\square HJKL$ are shown. What can you conclude about $\angle P$?

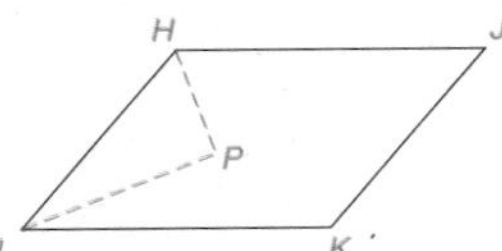

32. When the bisectors of two consecutive angles of a parallelogram meet at a point on the remaining side, what type of triangle is:
a) $\triangle DEC$? b) $\triangle ADE$? c) $\triangle BCE$?

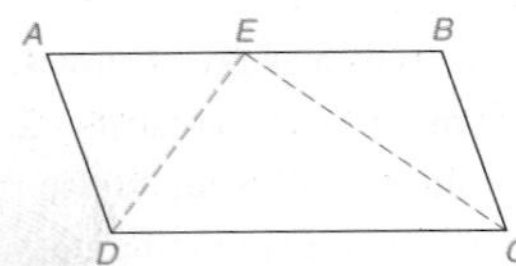

33. Draw parallelogram $RSTV$ with $m\angle R = 70°$ and $m\angle S = 110°$. Which diagonal of $\square RSTV$ has the greater length?

34. Draw parallelogram $RSTV$ so that the diagonals have the lengths $RT = 5$ and $SV = 4$. Which two angles of $\square RSTV$ have the greater measure?

35. The following problem is based on the Parallelogram Law. In the scaled drawing, each unit corresponds to 50 mph. A small airplane travels due east at 250 mph. The wind is blowing at 50 mph in the direction due north. Using the scale provided, determine the approximate length of the indicated diagonal and use it to determine the speed of the airplane in miles per hour.

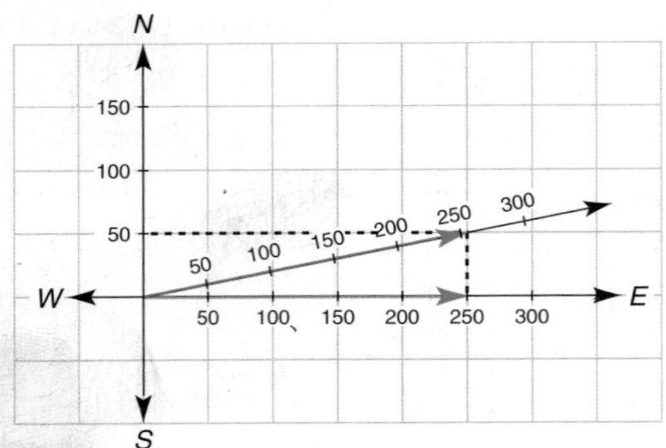

Exercises 35, 36

36. In the drawing for Exercise 35, the bearing (direction) in which the airplane travels is described as north $x°$ east, where x is the measure of the angle from the north axis toward the east axis. Using a protractor, find the approximate bearing of the airplane.

37. Two streets meet to form an obtuse angle at point B. On that corner, the newly poured foundation for a building takes the shape of a parallelogram. Which diagonal, $\overline{AC}$ or $\overline{BD}$, is longer?

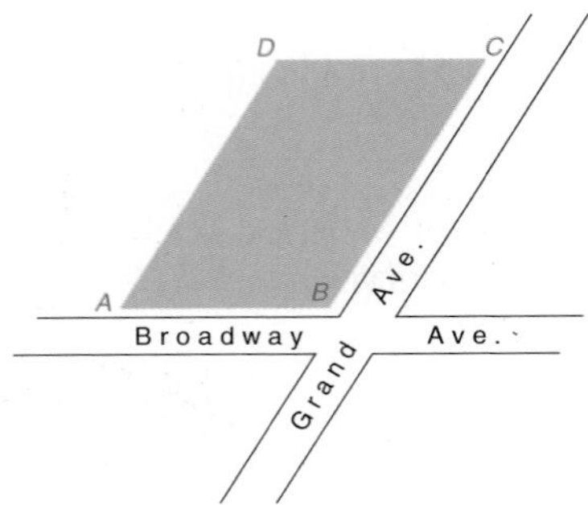

Exercises 37, 38

38. To test the accuracy of the foundation's measurements, lines (strings) are joined from opposite corners of the building's foundation. How should the strings that are represented by $\overline{AC}$ and $\overline{BD}$ be related?

39. For quadrilateral $ABCD$, the measures of its angles are $m\angle A = x + 16$, $m\angle B = 2(x + 1)$, $m\angle C = \frac{3}{2}x - 11$, and $m\angle D = \frac{7}{3}x - 16$. Determine the measure of each angle of $ABCD$ and whether $ABCD$ is a parallelogram.

***40.** *Prove:* In a parallelogram, the sum of squares of the lengths of its diagonals is equal to the sum of squares of the lengths of its sides.

4.2 The Parallelogram and Kite

KEY CONCEPTS

Quadrilaterals That Are Parallelograms

Rectangle

Kite

The quadrilaterals discussed in this section have two pairs of congruent sides.

THE PARALLELOGRAM

Because the hypothesis of each theorem in Section 4.1 included a given parallelogram, our goal was to develop the properties of parallelograms. In this section, Theorems 4.2.1 to 4.2.3 take the form "If . . ., then this quadrilateral is a parallelogram." In this section, we find that quadrilaterals having certain characteristics must be parallelograms.

STRATEGY FOR PROOF ▶ The "Bottom Up" Approach to Proof

General Rule: This method answers the question, "Why would the last statement be true?"
The answer often provides insight into the statement(s) preceding the last statement.

Illustration: In line 8 of Example 1, we state that $RSTV$ is a parallelogram by definition.
With $\overline{RS} \parallel \overline{VT}$ in line 1, we need to show that $\overline{RV} \parallel \overline{ST}$ as shown in line 7.

EXAMPLE 1

Give a formal proof of Theorem 4.2.1.

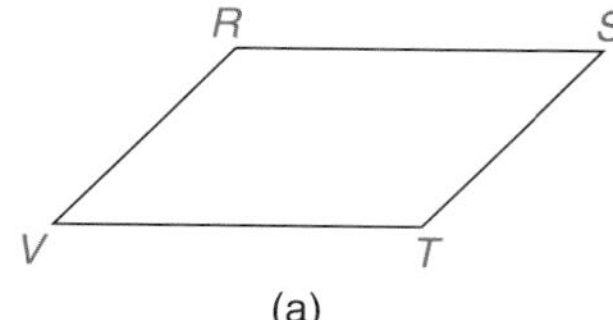

(a)

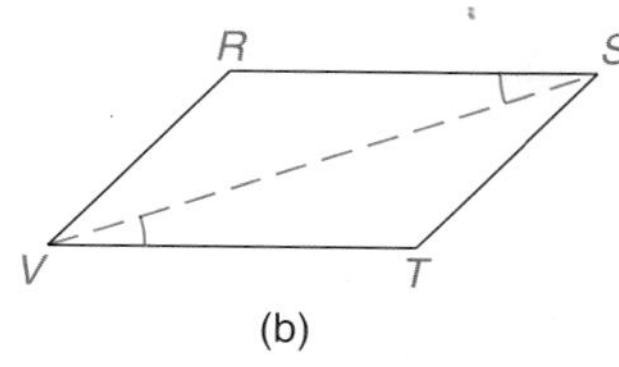

(b)

Figure 4.12

THEOREM 4.2.1

If two sides of a quadrilateral are both congruent and parallel, then the quadrilateral is a parallelogram.

GIVEN: In Figure 4.12(a), $\overline{RS} \parallel \overline{VT}$ and $\overline{RS} \cong \overline{VT}$

PROVE: $RSTV$ is a $\square$

PROOF

Statements	Reasons
1. $\overline{RS} \parallel \overline{VT}$ and $\overline{RS} \cong \overline{VT}$	1. Given
2. Draw diagonal $\overline{VS}$, as in Figure 4.12(b)	2. Exactly one line passes through two points
3. $\overline{VS} \cong \overline{VS}$	3. Identity
4. $\angle RSV \cong \angle SVT$	4. If two $\parallel$ lines are cut by a transversal, alternate interior $\angle$s are $\cong$
5. $\triangle RSV \cong \triangle TVS$	5. SAS
6. $\therefore \angle RVS \cong \angle VST$	6. CPCTC
7. $\overline{RV} \parallel \overline{ST}$	7. If two lines are cut by a transversal so that alternate interior $\angle$s are $\cong$, these lines are $\parallel$
8. $RSTV$ is a $\square$	8. If both pairs of opposite sides of a quadrilateral are $\parallel$, the quadrilateral is a parallelogram

Discover

Take two straws and cut each straw into two pieces so that the lengths of the pieces of one straw match those of the second. Now form a quadrilateral by placing the pieces end to end so that congruent sides lie in opposite positions. What type of quadrilateral is always formed?

ANSWER

A parallelogram

Consider the Discover activity at the left. Through it, we discover another type of quadrilateral that must be a parallelogram. This activity also leads to the following theorem; proof of the theorem is left to the student.

THEOREM 4.2.2

If both pairs of opposite sides of a quadrilateral are congruent, then the quadrilateral is a parallelogram.

Another quality of quadrilaterals that determines a parallelogram is stated in Theorem 4.2.3. Its proof is also left to the student. To clarify the meaning of Theorem 4.2.3, see the drawing for Exercise 3 on page 193.

THEOREM 4.2.3

If the diagonals of a quadrilateral bisect each other, then the quadrilateral is a parallelogram.

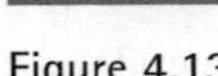

Figure 4.13

When a figure is drawn to represent the hypothesis of a theorem, we should not include more conditions than the hypothesis states. Relative to Theorem 4.2.3, if we drew two diagonals that not only bisected each other but also were equal in length, then the quadrilateral would be the special type of parallelogram known as a **rectangle.** We will deal with rectangles in the next section.

THE KITE

The next quadrilateral we consider is known as a *kite*. This quadrilateral gets its name from the child's toy pictured in Figure 4.13. In the construction of the kite, there are two pairs of congruent *adjacent* sides. See Figure 4.14(a) on page 189. This leads to the formal definition of a kite.

Exs. 1–4

DEFINITION

A **kite** is a quadrilateral with two distinct pairs of congruent adjacent sides.

The word *distinct* is used in this definition to clarify that the kite does not have four congruent sides.

Discover

Take two straws and cut them into pieces so the lengths match. Now form a quadrilateral by placing congruent pieces together. What type of quadrilateral is always formed?

ANSWER

Kite

THEOREM 4.2.4

In a kite, one pair of opposite angles are congruent.

In Example 2, we verify Theorem 4.2.4 by proving that $\angle B \cong \angle D$. With congruent sides as marked, $\angle A \not\cong \angle C$.

Discover

From a sheet of construction paper, cut out kite *ABCD* so that $AB = AD$ and $BC = DC$.

a) When you fold kite *ABCD* along the diagonal $\overline{AC}$, are two congruent triangles formed?

b) When you fold kite *ABCD* along diagonal $\overline{BD}$, are two congruent triangles formed?

ANSWERS

(a) Yes (b) No

EXAMPLE 2

Complete the proof of Theorem 4.2.4.

GIVEN: Kite *ABCD* with congruent sides as marked. [See Figure 4.14(a).]

PROVE: $\angle B \cong \angle D$

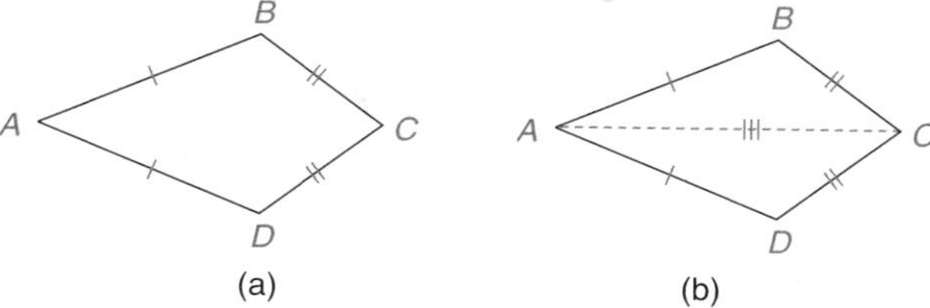

Figure 4.14

PROOF

Statements	Reasons
1. Kite *ABCD*	1. ?
2. $\overline{BC} \cong \overline{CD}$ and $\overline{AB} \cong \overline{AD}$	2. A kite has two pairs of ≅ adjacent sides
3. Draw $\overline{AC}$ [Figure 4.14(b)]	3. Through two points, there is exactly one line
4. $\overline{AC} \cong \overline{AC}$	4. ?
5. $\triangle ACD \cong \triangle ACB$	5. ?
6. ?	6. CPCTC

SSG *Exs. 5–10*

Two additional theorems involving the kite are found in Exercises 27 and 28 of this section.

When observing an old barn or shed, we often see that it has begun to lean. Unlike a triangle, which is rigid in shape [Figure 4.15(a)] and bends only when broken, a quadrilateral [Figure 4.15(b)] does *not* provide the same level of strength and stability. In the construction of a house, bridge, building, or swing set [Figure 4.15(c)], note the use of wooden or metal triangles as braces.

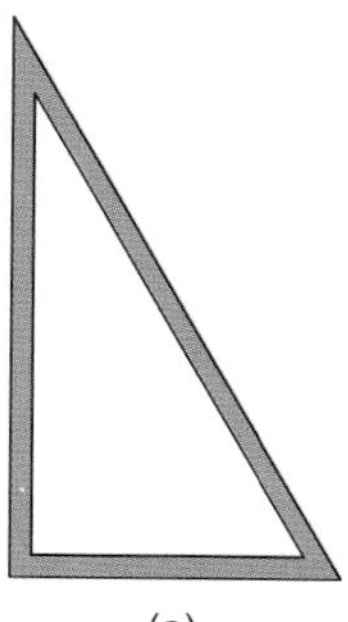

(a)

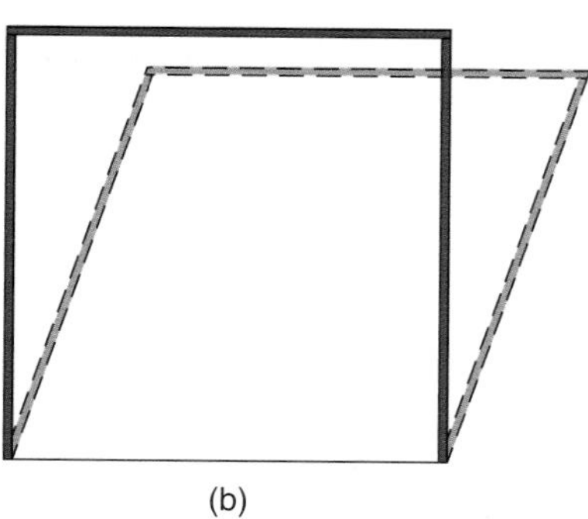

(b)

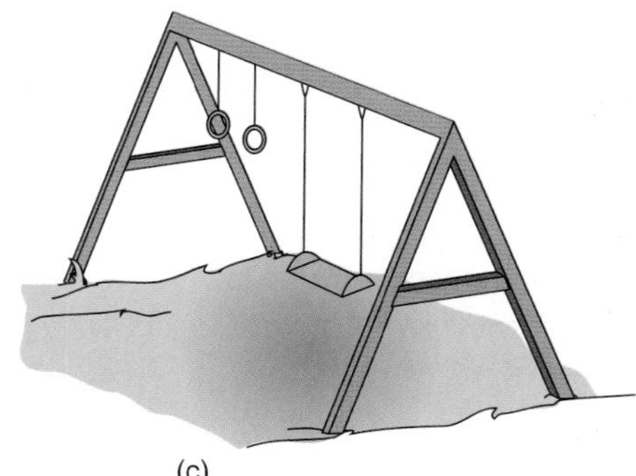

(c)

Figure 4.15

The brace in the swing set in Figure 4.15(c) suggests the following theorem.

THEOREM 4.2.5

The segment that joins the midpoints of two sides of a triangle is parallel to the third side and has a length equal to one-half the length of the third side.

Refer to Figure 4.16(a); Theorem 4.2.5 claims that $\overline{MN} \parallel \overline{BC}$ and $MN = \frac{1}{2}(BC)$. We will prove the first part of this theorem but leave the second part as an exercise.

> The line segment that joins the midpoints of two sides of a triangle is parallel to the third side of the triangle.

GIVEN: In Figure 4.16(a), $\triangle ABC$ with midpoints M and N of $\overline{AB}$ and $\overline{AC}$, respectively.

PROVE: $\overline{MN} \parallel \overline{BC}$

Discover

Sketch regular hexagon *ABCDEF*. Draw diagonals $\overline{AE}$ and $\overline{CE}$. What type of quadrilateral is *ABCE*?

ANSWER

Kite

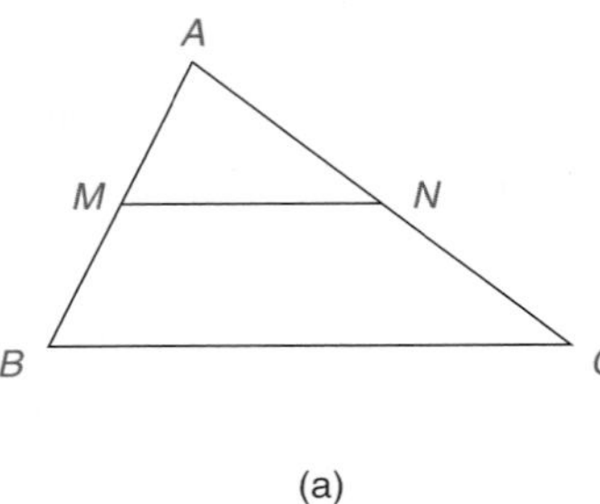

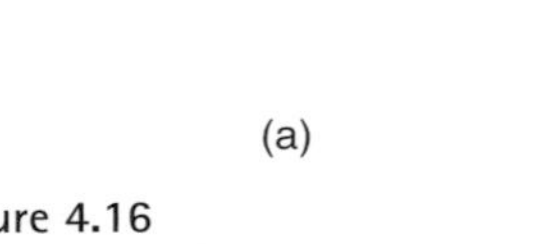

(a)

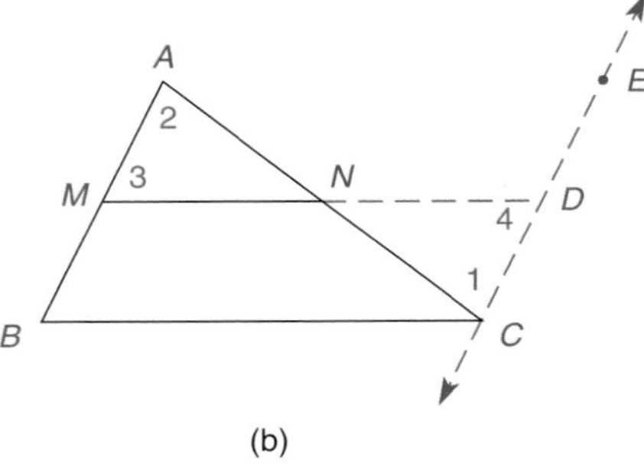

(b)

Figure 4.16

Technology Exploration

Use computer software if available.

1. Construct $\triangle ABC$ (any triangle).
2. Where M is the midpoint of $\overline{AB}$ and N is the midpoint of $\overline{AC}$, draw $\overline{MN}$.
3. Measure $\angle AMN$ and $\angle B$.
4. Show that $m\angle AMN = m\angle B$, which shows that $\overline{MN} \parallel \overline{BC}$.
5. Now measure $\overline{MN}$ and $\overline{BC}$.
6. Show that $MN = \frac{1}{2}(BC)$. (Measures may not be "perfect.")

PROOF

Statements	Reasons
1. $\triangle ABC$, with midpoints M and N of $\overline{AB}$ and $\overline{AC}$, respectively	1. Given
2. Through C, construct $\overleftrightarrow{CE} \parallel \overline{AB}$, as in Figure 4.16(b)	2. Parallel Postulate
3. Extend $\overline{MN}$ to meet $\overleftrightarrow{CE}$ at D, as in Figure 4.16(b)	3. Exactly one line passes through two points
4. $\overline{AM} \cong \overline{MB}$ and $\overline{AN} \cong \overline{NC}$	4. The midpoint of a segment divides it into ≅ segments
5. $\angle 1 \cong \angle 2$ and $\angle 4 \cong \angle 3$	5. If two ∥ lines are cut by a transversal, alternate interior ∠s are ≅
6. $\triangle ANM \cong \triangle CND$	6. AAS
7. $\overline{AM} \cong \overline{DC}$	7. CPCTC
8. $\overline{MB} \cong \overline{DC}$	8. Transitive (both are ≅ to $\overline{AM}$)
9. Quadrilateral $BMDC$ is a ▱	9. If two sides of a quadrilateral are both ≅ and ∥, the quadrilateral is a parallelogram
10. $\overline{MN} \parallel \overline{BC}$	10. Opposite sides of a ▱ are ∥

In the preceding proof, we needed to show that a quadrilateral having certain characteristics is a parallelogram.

STRATEGY FOR PROOF ▶ Proving That a Quadrilateral Is a Parallelogram

General Rule: Methods for proof include the definition of parallelogram as well as Theorems 4.2.1, 4.2.2, and 4.2.3.

Illustration: In the proof of Theorem 4.2.5, statements 2 and 8 allow the conclusion in statement 9 (used Theorem 4.2.1).

Theorem 4.2.5 also asserts the following:

> The line segment that joins the midpoints of two sides of a triangle has a length equal to one-half the length of the third side.

Discover

Draw a triangle $\triangle ABC$ with midpoints D of $\overline{CA}$ and E of $\overline{CB}$. Cut out $\triangle CDE$ and place it at the base $\overline{AB}$. By sliding $\overline{DE}$ along $\overline{AB}$, what do you find?

ANSWER

$DE = \frac{1}{2}(AB)$ or $AB = 2(DE)$

EXAMPLE 3

In $\triangle RST$ in Figure 4.17, M and N are the midpoints of $\overline{RS}$ and $\overline{RT}$, respectively.

a) If $ST = 12.7$, find MN.
b) If $MN = 15.8$, find ST.

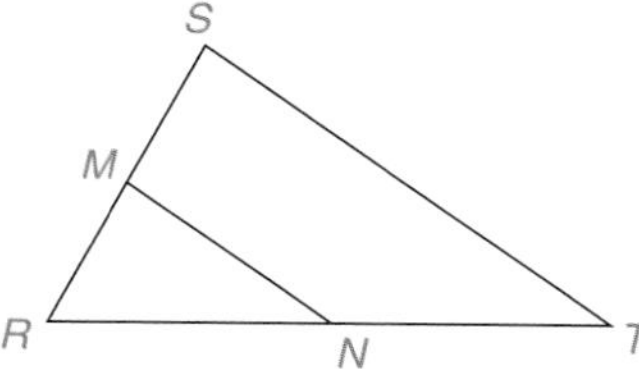

Figure 4.17

Solution

a) $MN = \frac{1}{2}(ST)$, so $MN = \frac{1}{2}(12.7) = 6.35$.
b) $MN = \frac{1}{2}(ST)$, so $15.8 = \frac{1}{2}(ST)$.
Multiplying by 2, we find that $ST = 31.6$. ■

EXAMPLE 4

GIVEN: $\triangle ABC$ in Figure 4.18, with D the midpoint of $\overline{AC}$ and E the midpoint of $\overline{BC}$; $DE = 2x + 1$; $AB = 5x - 1$

FIND: x, DE, and AB

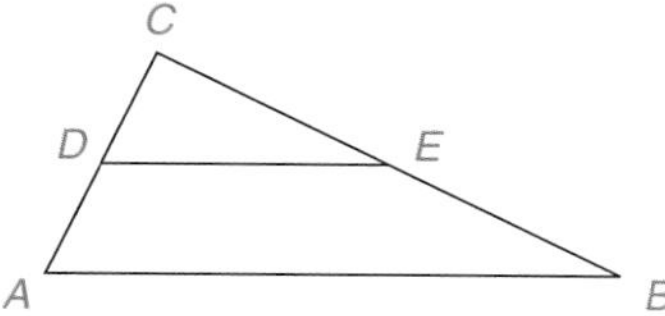

Figure 4.18

Solution By Theorem 4.2.5,

$$DE = \frac{1}{2}(AB)$$

so

$$2x + 1 = \frac{1}{2}(5x - 1)$$

Multiplying by 2, we have

$$4x + 2 = 5x - 1$$
$$3 = x$$

Therefore, $DE = 2 \cdot 3 + 1 = 7$. Similarly, $AB = 5 \cdot 3 - 1 = 14$.

SSG *Exs. 11–15*

NOTE: In Example 4, a check shows that $DE = \frac{1}{2}(AB)$. ■

In the final example of this section, we consider the design of a product. Also see related Exercises 17 and 18 of this section.

EXAMPLE 5

In a studio apartment, there is a bed that folds down from the wall. In the vertical position, the design shows drop-down legs of equal length; that is, $AB = CD$ [see Figure 4.19(a)]. Determine the type of quadrilateral $ABDC$, shown in Figure 4.19(b), that is formed when the bed is lowered to a horizontal position.

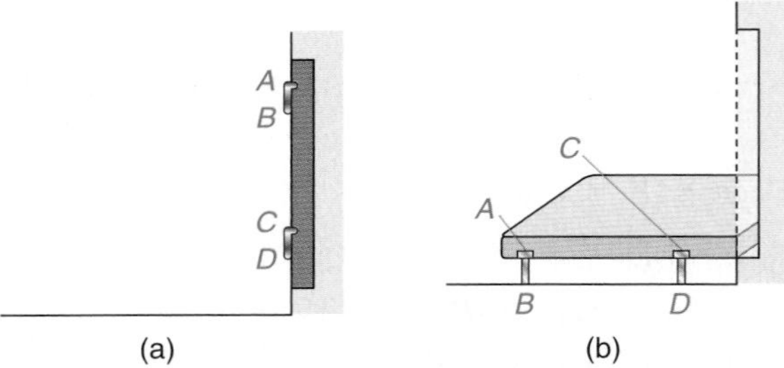

Figure 4.19

Solution See Figure 4.19(a). Because $AB = CD$, it follows that $AB + BC = BC + CD$; here, BC was added to each side of the equation. But $AB + BC = AC$ and $BC + CD = BD$. Thus, $AC = BD$ by substitution.

In Figure 4.19(b), we see that $AB = CD$ and $AC = BD$. Because both pairs of opposite sides of the quadrilateral are congruent, $ABDC$ is a parallelogram.

NOTE: In Section 4.3, we will also show that $ABDC$ of Figure 4.19(b) is a *rectangle* (a special type of parallelogram). ■

Exercises 4.2

1. a) As shown, must quadrilateral $ABCD$ be a parallelogram?
   b) Given the lengths of the sides as shown, is the measure of $\angle A$ unique?

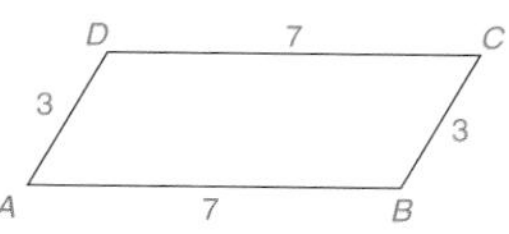

2. a) As shown, must $RSTV$ be a parallelogram?
   b) With measures as indicated, is it necessary that $RS = 8$?

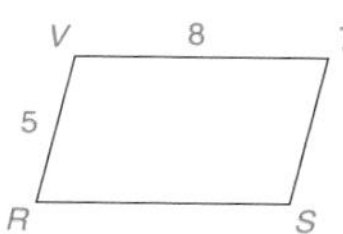

3. In the drawing, suppose that $\overline{WY}$ and $\overline{XZ}$ bisect each other. What type of quadrilateral is $WXYZ$?

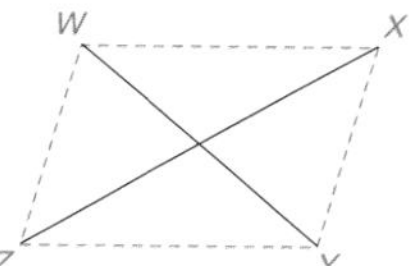

Exercises 3, 4

4. In the drawing, suppose that $\overline{ZX}$ is the perpendicular bisector of $\overline{WY}$. What type of quadrilateral is $WXYZ$?
5. A carpenter lays out boards of lengths 8 ft, 8 ft, 4 ft, and 4 ft by placing them end to end.
   a) If these are joined at the ends to form a quadrilateral that has the 8-ft pieces connected in order, what type of quadrilateral is formed?
   b) If these are joined at the ends to form a quadrilateral that has the 4-ft and 8-ft pieces alternating, what type of quadrilateral is formed?
6. A carpenter joins four boards of lengths 6 ft, 6 ft, 4 ft, and 4 ft, in that order, to form quadrilateral $ABCD$ as shown.
   a) What type of quadrilateral is formed?
   b) How are angles B and D related?

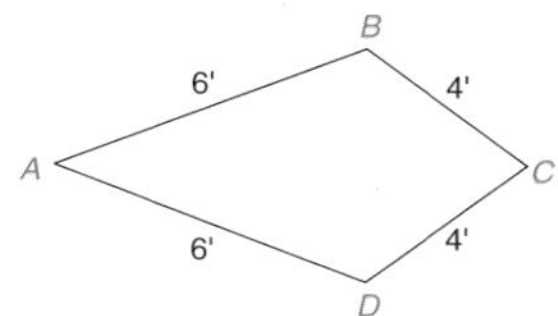

7. In parallelogram $ABCD$ (not shown), $AB = 8$, $m\angle B = 110°$, and $BC = 5$. Which diagonal has the greater length?

8. In kite $WXYZ$, the measures of selected angles are shown. Which diagonal of the kite has the greater length?

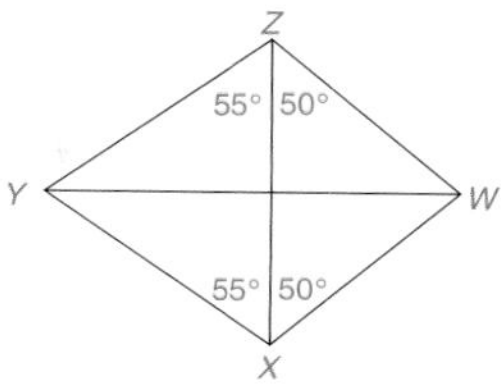

9. In $\triangle ABC$, M and N are midpoints of $\overline{AC}$ and $\overline{BC}$, respectively. If $AB = 12.36$, how long is $\overline{MN}$?

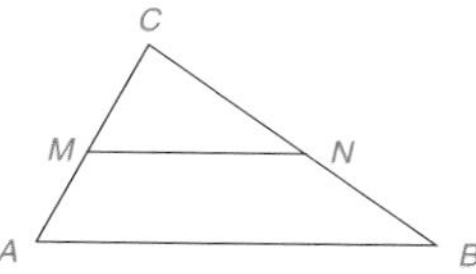

Exercises 9, 10

10. In $\triangle ABC$, M and N are midpoints of $\overline{AC}$ and $\overline{BC}$, respectively. If $MN = 7.65$, how long is $\overline{AB}$?

In Exercises 11 to 14, assume that X, Y, and Z are midpoints of the sides of $\triangle RST$.

11. If $RS = 12$, $ST = 14$, and $RT = 16$, find:
   a) XY b) XZ c) YZ

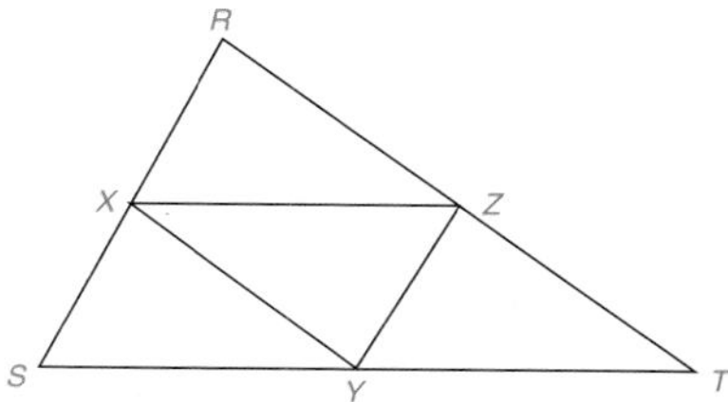

Exercises 11–14

12. If $XY = 6$, $YZ = 8$, and $XZ = 10$, find:
   a) RS b) ST c) RT
13. If the perimeter (sum of the lengths of all three sides) of $\triangle RST$ is 20, what is the perimeter of $\triangle XYZ$?
14. If the perimeter (sum of the lengths of all three sides) of $\triangle XYZ$ is 12.7, what is the perimeter of $\triangle RST$?
15. Consider any kite.
   a) Does it have line symmetry? If so, describe an axis of symmetry.
   b) Does it have point symmetry? If so, describe the point of symmetry.

16. Consider any parallelogram.
a) Does it have line symmetry? If so, describe an axis of symmetry.
b) Does it have point symmetry? If so, describe the point of symmetry.

17. For compactness, the drop-down wheels of a stretcher (or gurney) are folded under it as shown. In order for the board's upper surface to be parallel to the ground when the wheels are dropped, what relationship must exist between $\overline{AB}$ and $\overline{CD}$?

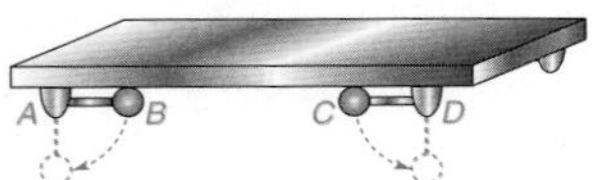

18. For compactness, the drop-down legs of an ironing board fold up under the board. A sliding mechanism at point A and the legs being connected at common midpoint M cause the board's upper surface to be parallel to the floor. How are $\overline{AB}$ and $\overline{CD}$ related?

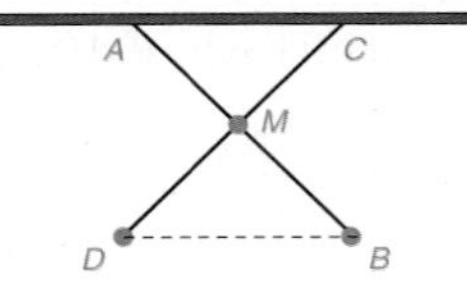

In Exercises 19 to 24, complete each proof.

19. *Given:* $\angle 1 \cong \angle 2$ and $\angle 3 \cong \angle 4$
Prove: $MNPQ$ is a kite

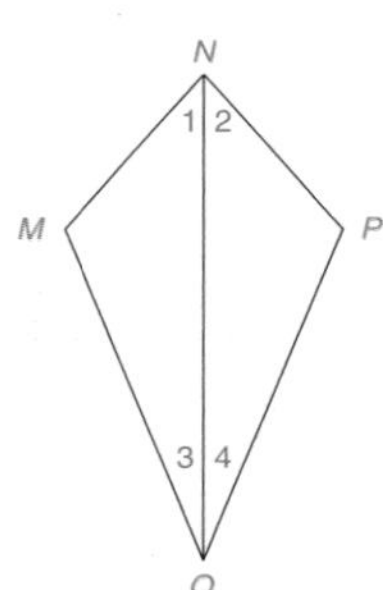

PROOF

Statements	Reasons
1. $\angle 1 \cong \angle 2$ and $\angle 3 \cong \angle 4$	1. ?
2. $\overline{NQ} \cong \overline{NQ}$	2. ?
3. ?	3. ASA
4. $\overline{MN} \cong \overline{PN}$ and $\overline{MQ} \cong \overline{PQ}$	4. ?
5. ?	5. If a quadrilateral has two pairs of $\cong$ adjacent sides, it is a kite

20. *Given:* Quadrilateral $ABCD$, with midpoints E, F, G, and H of the sides
Prove: $\overline{EF} \parallel \overline{HG}$

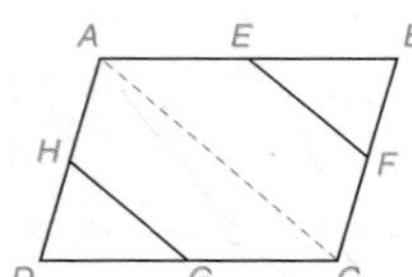

PROOF

Statements	Reasons
1. ?	1. Given
2. Draw $\overline{AC}$	2. Through two points, there is one line
3. In $\triangle ABC$, $\overline{EF} \parallel \overline{AC}$ and in $\triangle ADC$, $\overline{HG} \parallel \overline{AC}$	3. ?
4. ?	4. If two lines are $\parallel$ to the same line, these lines are $\parallel$ to each other

21. *Given:* M-Q-T and P-Q-R such that $MNPQ$ and $QRST$ are ▱s
Prove: $\angle N \cong \angle S$

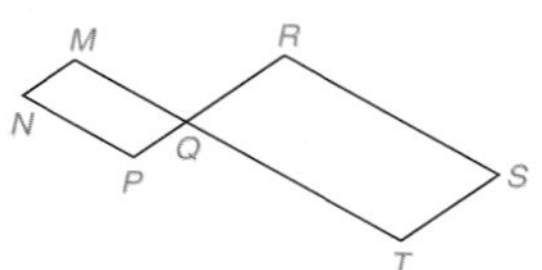

22. *Given:* ▱$WXYZ$ with diagonals $\overline{WY}$ and $\overline{XZ}$
Prove: $\triangle WMX \cong \triangle YMZ$

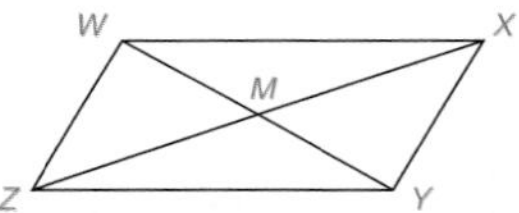

23. *Given:* Kite $HJKL$ with diagonal $\overline{HK}$
Prove: $\overrightarrow{HK}$ bisects $\angle LHJ$

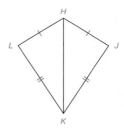

24. *Given:* ▱$MNPQ$, with T the midpoint of $\overline{MN}$ and S the midpoint of $\overline{QP}$
Prove: $\triangle QMS \cong \triangle NPT$, and $MSPT$ is a ▱

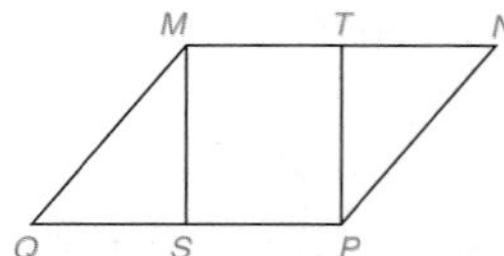

In Exercises 25 to 28, write a formal proof of each theorem or corollary.

25. If both pairs of opposite sides of a quadrilateral are congruent, then the quadrilateral is a parallelogram.

26. If the diagonals of a quadrilateral bisect each other, then the quadrilateral is a parallelogram.

27. In a kite, one diagonal is the perpendicular bisector of the other diagonal.

28. One diagonal of a kite bisects two of the angles of the kite.

In Exercises 29 to 31, $\triangle RST$ has M and N for midpoints of sides $\overline{RS}$ and $\overline{RT}$, respectively.

29. *Given:* $MN = 2y - 3$
$ST = 3y$
Find: y, MN, and ST

30. *Given:* $MN = x^2 + 5$
$ST = x(2x + 5)$
Find: x, MN, and ST

31. *Given:* $RM = RN = 2x + 1$
$ST = 5x - 3$
$m\angle R = 60°$
Find: x, RM, and ST

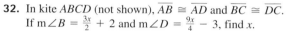

Exercises 29–31

32. In kite $ABCD$ (not shown), $\overline{AB} \cong \overline{AD}$ and $\overline{BC} \cong \overline{DC}$. If $m\angle B = \frac{3x}{2} + 2$ and $m\angle D = \frac{9x}{4} - 3$, find x.

33. In kite $ABCD$ of Exercise 32, $AB = \frac{x}{6} + 5$, $AD = \frac{x}{3} + 3$, and $BC = x - 2$. Find the perimeter (sum of lengths of all sides) of kite $ABCD$.

34. $RSTV$ is a kite, with $\overline{RS} \perp \overline{ST}$ and $\overline{RV} \perp \overline{VT}$. If $m\angle STV = 40°$, how large is the angle formed:
a) by the bisectors of $\angle RST$ and $\angle STV$?
b) by the bisectors of $\angle SRV$ and $\angle RST$?

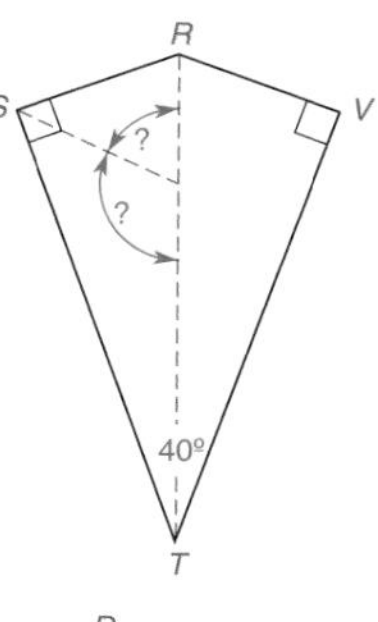

35. In concave kite $ABCD$, there is an interior angle at vertex B that is a reflex angle. Given that $m\angle A = m\angle C = m\angle D = 30°$, find the measure of the indicated reflex angle.

36. If the length of side $\overline{AB}$ (for kite $ABCD$) is 6 in., find the length of $\overline{AC}$ (not shown). Recall that $m\angle A = m\angle C = m\angle D = 30°$

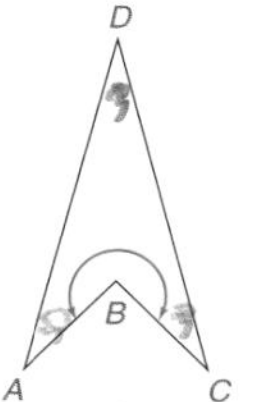

Exercises 35, 36

***37.** Prove that the segment that joins the midpoints of two sides of a triangle has a length equal to one-half the length of the third side.

(HINT: In the drawing, $\overline{MN}$ is extended to D, a point on $\overline{CD}$. Also, $\overline{CD}$ is parallel to $\overline{AB}$.)

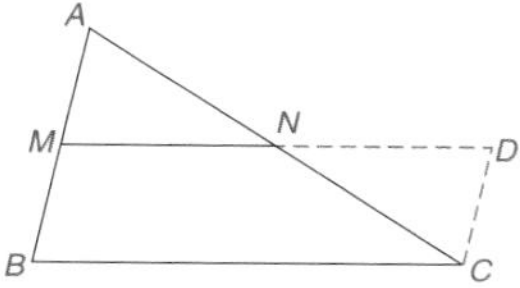

***38.** Prove that when the midpoints of consecutive sides of a quadrilateral are joined in order, the resulting quadrilateral is a parallelogram.

4.3 The Rectangle, Square, and Rhombus

KEY CONCEPTS

Rectangle
Square
Rhombus
Pythagorean Theorem

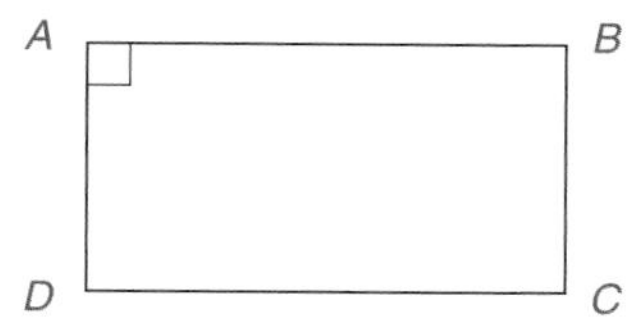

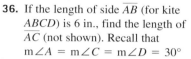

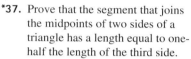

Figure 4.20

THE RECTANGLE

In this section, we investigate special parallelograms. The first of these is the rectangle (abbreviated "rect."), which is defined as follows:

DEFINITION

A **rectangle** is a parallelogram that has a right angle. (See Figure 4.20.)

Any reader who is familiar with the rectangle may be confused by the fact that the preceding definition calls for only one right angle. Because a rectangle is a parallelogram by definition, the fact that a rectangle has four right angles is easily proved by applying Corollaries 4.1.3 and 4.1.5. The proof of Corollary 4.3.1 is left to the student.

COROLLARY 4.3.1

All angles of a rectangle are right angles.

Reminder

A rectangle is a parallelogram. Thus, it has all the properties of a parallelogram plus some properties of its own.

The following theorem is true for rectangles but not for parallelograms in general.

THEOREM 4.3.2

The diagonals of a rectangle are congruent.

NOTE: To follow the flow of the proof in Example 1, it may be best to draw triangles *NMQ* and *PQM* of Figure 4.21 separately.

EXAMPLE 1

Complete a proof of Theorem 4.3.2.

GIVEN: Rectangle *MNPQ* with diagonals $\overline{MP}$ and $\overline{NQ}$ (See Figure 4.21.)

PROVE: $\overline{MP} \cong \overline{NQ}$

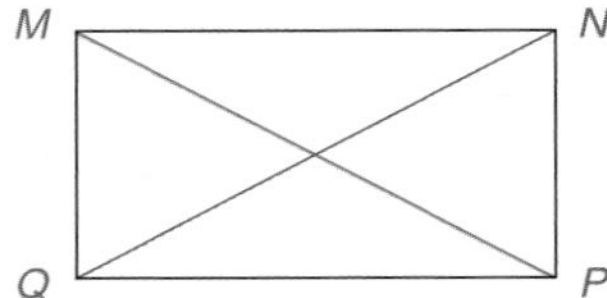

Figure 4.21

Discover

Given a rectangle *MNPQ* (like a sheet of paper), draw diagonals $\overline{MP}$ and $\overline{NQ}$. From a second sheet, cut out $\triangle MPQ$ (formed by two sides and a diagonal of *MNPQ*). Can you position $\triangle MPQ$ so that it coincides with $\triangle NQP$?

ANSWER

Yes

PROOF

Statements	Reasons
1. Rectangle *MNPQ* with diagonals $\overline{MP}$ and $\overline{NQ}$	1. Given
2. *MNPQ* is a ▱	2. By definition, a rectangle is a ▱ with a right angle
3. $\overline{MN} \cong \overline{QP}$	3. Opposite sides of a ▱ are ≅
4. $\overline{MQ} \cong \overline{MQ}$	4. Identity
5. $\angle NMQ$ and $\angle PQM$ are right ∠s	5. By Corollary 4.3.1, the four ∠s of a rectangle are right ∠s
6. $\angle NMQ \cong \angle PQM$	6. All right ∠s are ≅
7. $\triangle NMQ \cong \triangle PQM$	7. SAS
8. $\overline{MP} \cong \overline{NQ}$	8. CPCTC

Exs. 1–4

THE SQUARE

All rectangles are parallelograms; some parallelograms are rectangles; and some rectangles are *squares*.

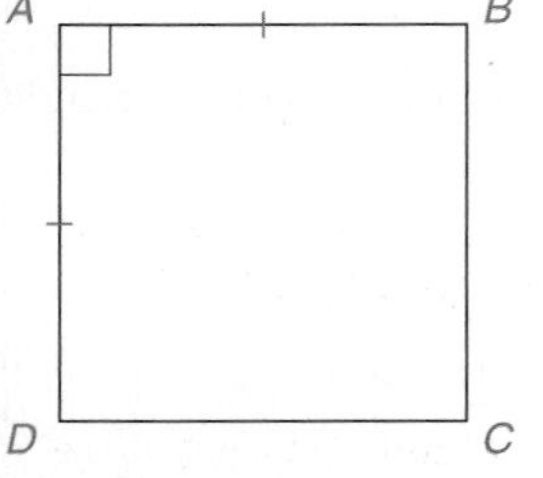

Square *ABCD*

Figure 4.22

DEFINITION

A **square** is a rectangle that has two congruent adjacent sides. (See Figure 4.22.)

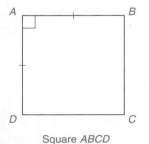

COROLLARY 4.3.3

All sides of a square are congruent.

SSG
Exs. 5–7

Because a square is a type of rectangle, it has four right angles and its diagonals are congruent. Because a square is also a parallelogram, its opposite sides are parallel. For any square, we can show that the diagonals are perpendicular.

In Chapter 8, we measure area in "square units."

THE RHOMBUS

The next type of quadrilateral we consider is the rhombus. The plural of the word *rhombus* is *rhombi* (pronounced rhŏm-bī).

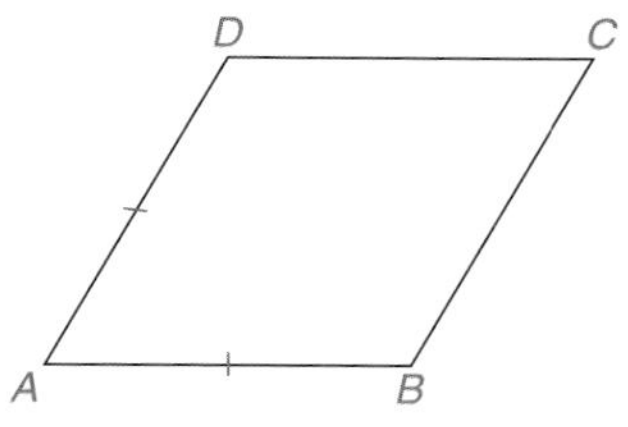

Figure 4.23

DEFINITION

A **rhombus** is a parallelogram with two congruent adjacent sides.

In Figure 4.23, the adjacent sides $\overline{AB}$ and $\overline{AD}$ of rhombus $ABCD$ are marked congruent. Because a rhombus is a type of parallelogram, it is also necessary that $\overline{AB} \cong \overline{DC}$ and $\overline{AD} \cong \overline{BC}$. Thus, we have Corollary 4.3.4.

COROLLARY 4.3.4

All sides of a rhombus are congruent.

We will use Corollary 4.3.4 in the proof of the following theorem.

THEOREM 4.3.5

The diagonals of a rhombus are perpendicular.

Geometry in the Real World

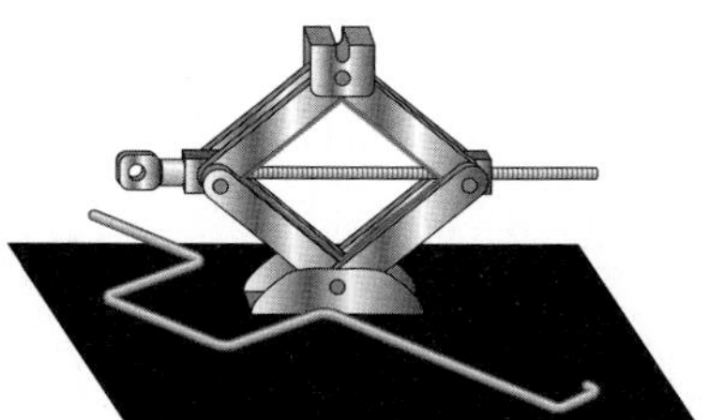

The jack used in changing an automobile tire illustrates the shape of a rhombus.

Discover

Sketch regular hexagon *RSTVWX*. Draw diagonals $\overline{RT}$ and $\overline{XV}$. What type of quadrilateral is *RTVX*?

ANSWER

Rectangle

EXAMPLE 2

Study the picture proof of Theorem 4.3.5. In the proof, pairs of triangles are congruent by the reason SSS.

PICTURE PROOF OF THEOREM 4.3.5

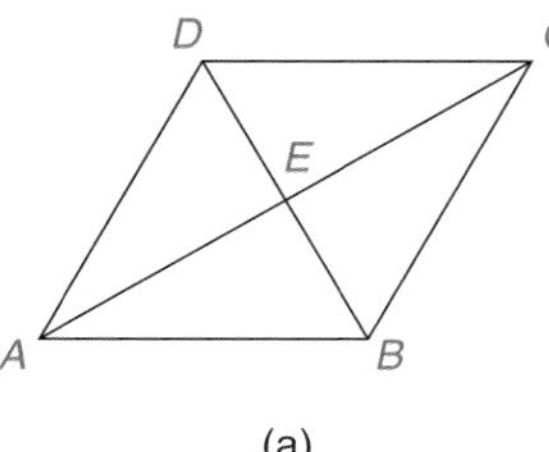

(a)

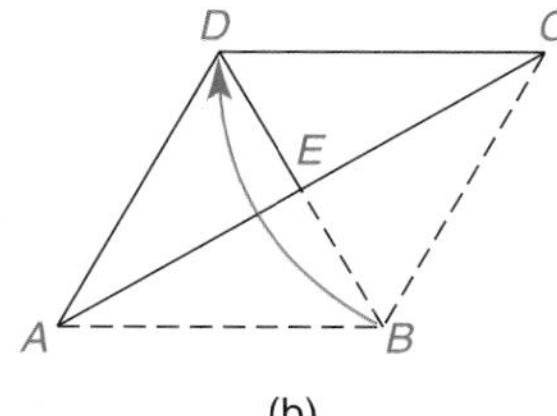

(b)

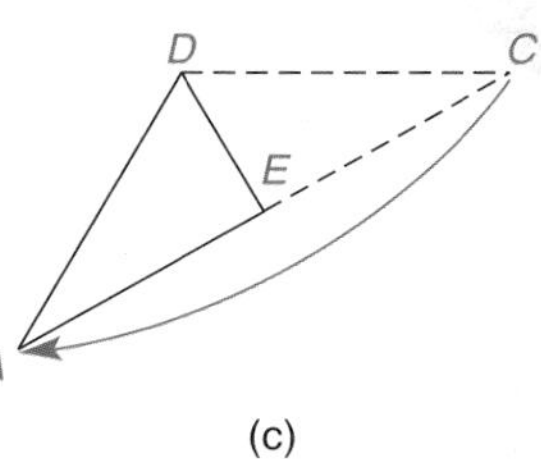

(c)

Figure 4.24

GIVEN: Rhombus $ABCD$, with diagonals $\overline{AC}$ and $\overline{DB}$ [See Figure 4.24(a)].

PROVE: $\overline{AC} \perp \overline{DB}$

PROOF: Fold $\triangle ABC$ across $\overline{AC}$ to coincide with $\triangle CED$ [see Figure 4.24(b)]. Now fold $\triangle CED$ across half-diagonal $\overline{DE}$ to coincide with $\triangle AED$ [see Figure 4.24(c)]. The four congruent triangles formed in Figure 4.24(c) can be unwrapped to return rhombus $ABCD$ of Figure 4.24(a). With four congruent right angles at vertex E, we see that $\overline{AC} \perp \overline{DB}$. ■

Exs. 8–11

An alternative definition of *square* is "A square is a rhombus whose adjacent sides form a right angle." Therefore, a further property of a square is that its diagonals are perpendicular.

The Pythagorean Theorem, which deals with right triangles, is also useful in applications involving quadrilaterals that have right angles. In antiquity, the theorem claimed that "the square upon the hypotenuse equals the sum of the squares upon the legs of the right triangle." See Figure 4.25(a). This interpretation involves the area concept, which we study in a later chapter. By counting squares in Figure 4.25(a), one sees that 25 "square units" is the sum of 9 and 16 square units. Our interpretation of the Pythagorean Theorem uses number (length) relationships.

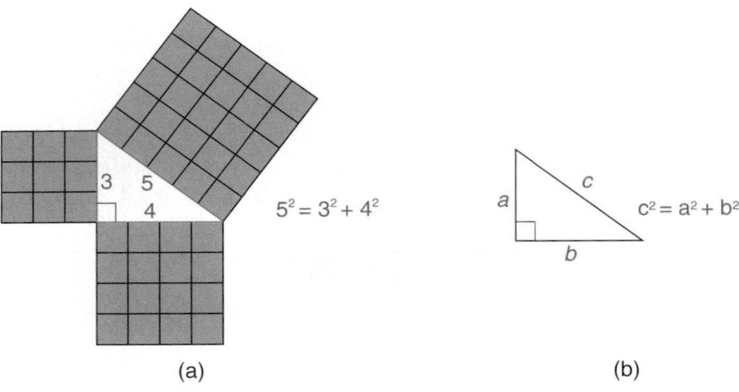

Figure 4.25

Discover

How many squares are shown?

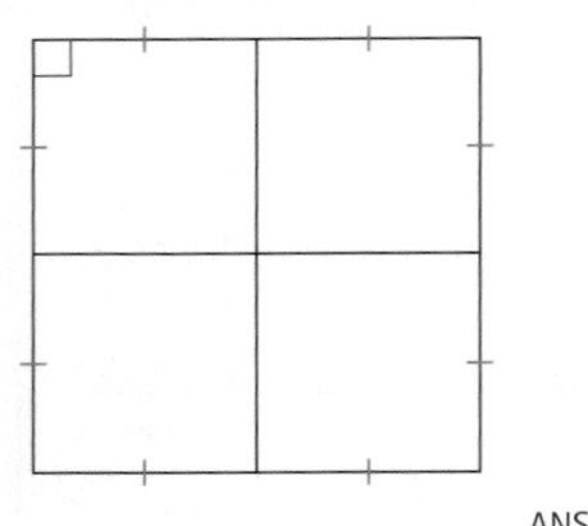

ANSWER

5 (four 1 by 1 and one 2 by 2)

THE PYTHAGOREAN THEOREM

The Pythagorean Theorem will be proved in Section 5.4. Although it was introduced in Section 3.2, we restate the Pythagorean Theorem here for convenience and then review its application to the *right* triangle in Example 3. When right angle relationships exist in quadrilaterals, we can often apply the "rule of Pythagoras" as well; see Examples 4, 5, and 6.

> **The Pythagorean Theorem** In a right triangle with hypotenuse of length c and legs of lengths a and b, it follows that $c^2 = a^2 + b^2$.

Provided that the lengths of two of the sides of a right triangle are known, the Pythagorean Theorem can be applied to determine the length of the third side. In Example 3, we seek the length of the hypotenuse in a right triangle whose lengths of legs are known. When we are using the Pythagorean Theorem, c must represent the length of the hypotenuse; however, either leg can be chosen for length a (or b).

EXAMPLE 3

What is the length of the hypotenuse of a right triangle whose legs measure 6 in. and 8 in.? (See Figure 4.26.)

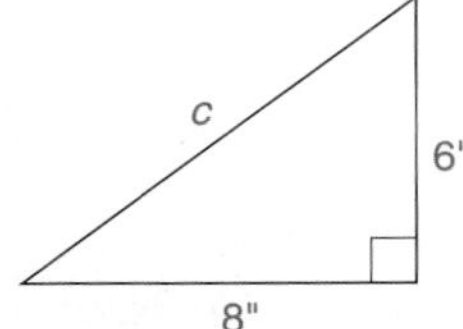

Figure 4.26

Solution

$$c^2 = a^2 + b^2$$
$$c^2 = 6^2 + 8^2$$
$$c^2 = 36 + 64 \rightarrow c^2 = 100 \rightarrow c = 10 \text{ in.}$$

■

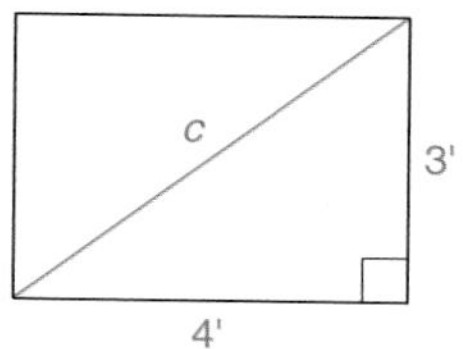

Figure 4.27

In the following example, the diagonal of a rectangle separates it into two right triangles. As shown in Figure 4.27, the diagonal of the rectangle is the hypotenuse of each right triangle formed by the diagonal.

EXAMPLE 4

What is the length of the diagonal in a rectangle whose sides measure 3 ft and 4 ft?

Solution For each triangle in Figure 4.27, $c^2 = a^2 + b^2$ becomes $c^2 = 3^2 + 4^2$ or $c^2 = 9 + 16$. Then $c^2 = 25$, so $c = 5$. The length of the diagonal is 5 ft. ■

In Example 5, we use the fact that a rhombus is a parallelogram to justify that its diagonals bisect each other. By Theorem 4.3.5, the diagonals of the rhombus are also perpendicular.

EXAMPLE 5

What is the length of each side of a rhombus whose diagonals measure 10 cm and 24 cm? (See Figure 4.28.)

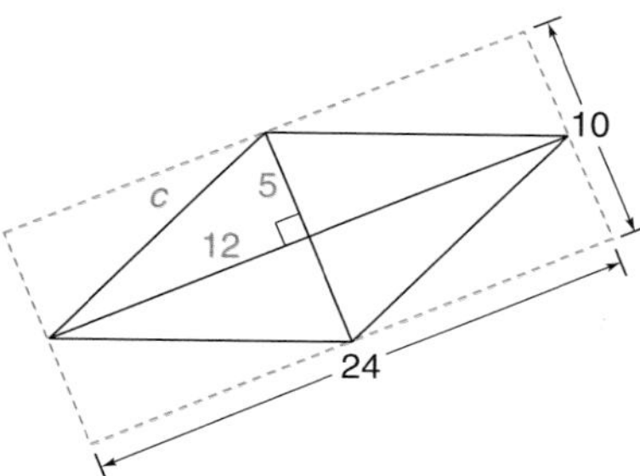

Figure 4.28

Solution The diagonals of a rhombus are perpendicular bisectors of each other. Thus, the diagonals separate the rhombus shown into four congruent right triangles with legs of lengths 5 cm and 12 cm. For each triangle, $c^2 = a^2 + b^2$ becomes $c^2 = 5^2 + 12^2$, or $c^2 = 25 + 144$. Then $c^2 = 169$, so $c = 13$. The length of each side is 13 cm. ■

EXAMPLE 6

On a softball diamond (actually a square), the distance along the base paths is 60 ft. Using the triangle in Figure 4.29, find the distance from home plate to second base.

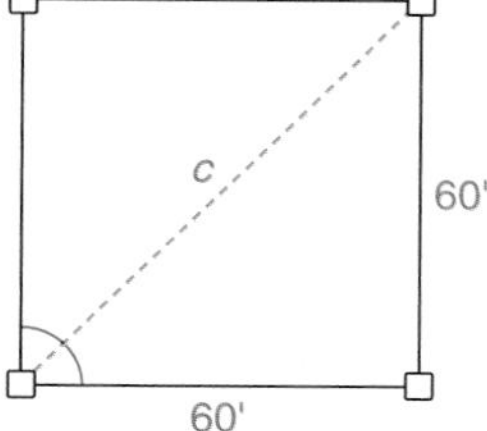

Figure 4.29

Solution Using $c^2 = a^2 + b^2$, we have

$$c^2 = 60^2 + 60^2$$
$$c^2 = 7200$$

Exs. 12–14

Then

$$c = \sqrt{7200} \qquad \text{or} \qquad c \approx 84.85 \text{ ft.}$$

■

Discover

A logo is a geometric symbol that represents a company. The very sight of the symbol serves as advertising for the company or corporation. Many logos are derived from common geometric shapes. Which company is represented by these symbols?

The sides of an equilateral triangle are trisected and then connected as shown, and finally the middle sections are erased.

The vertices of a regular pentagon are joined to the "center" of the polygon as shown.

A square is superimposed on and centered over a long and narrow parallelogram as shown. Interior line segments are then eliminated.

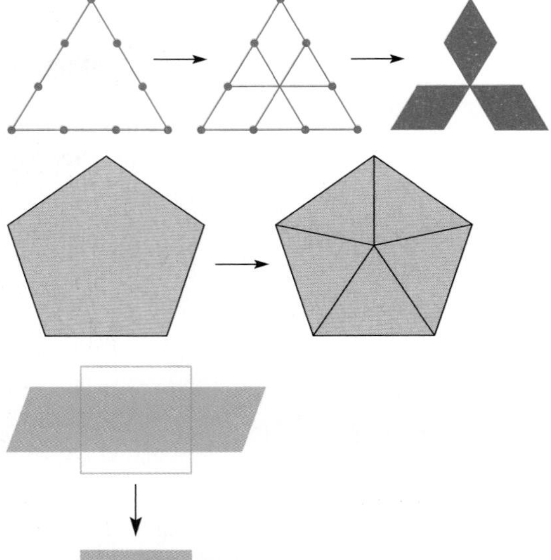

ANSWERS

Mitsubishi; Chrysler; Chevrolet

When all vertices of a quadrilateral lie on a circle, the quadrilateral is a *cyclic quadrilateral*. As it happens, all rectangles are cyclic quadrilaterals, but no rhombus is a cyclic quadrilateral. The key factor in determining whether a quadrilateral is cyclic lies in the fact that the diagonals must intersect at a point that is equidistant from all four vertices. In Figure 4.30(a), rectangle $ABCD$ is cyclic because A, B, C, and D all lie on the circle. However, rhombus $WXYZ$ in Figure 4.30(b) is *not* cyclic because X and Z cannot lie on the circle when W and Y do lie on the circle.

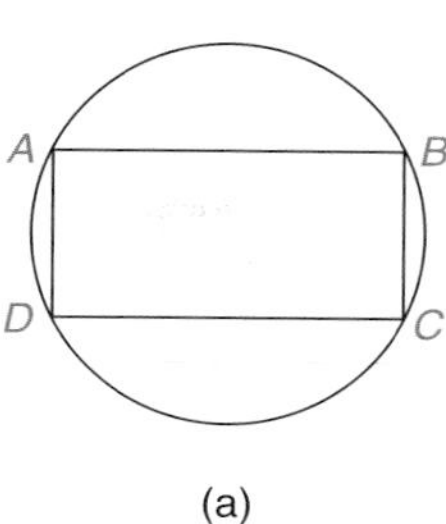

(a)

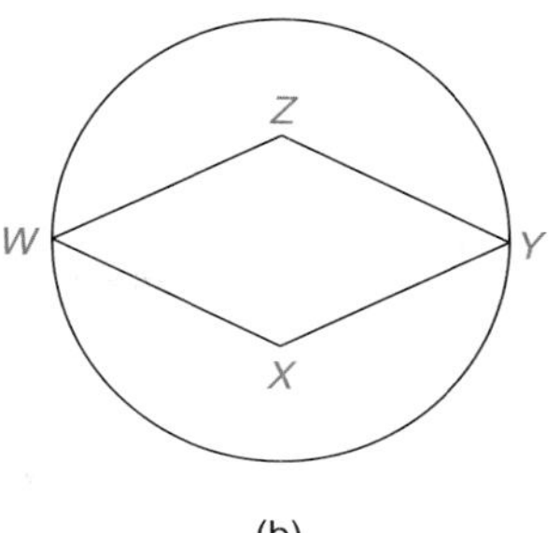

(b)

Figure 4.30

EXAMPLE 7

For cyclic rectangle $ABCD$, $AB = 8$. Diagonal $\overline{DB}$ of the rectangle is also a diameter of the circle and $DB = 10$. Find the perimeter of $ABCD$ shown in Figure 4.31.

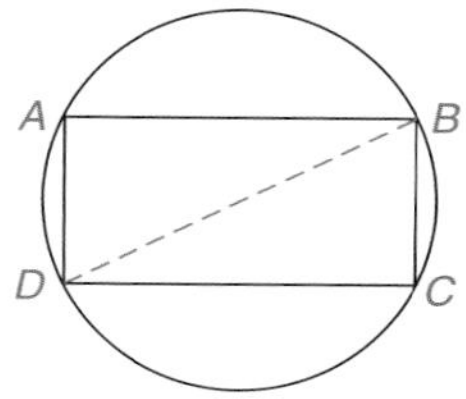

Figure 4.31

Solution $AB = DC = 8$. Let $AD = b$; applying the Pythagorean Theorem with right triangle ABD, we find that $10^2 = 8^2 + b^2$.

Then $100 = 64 + b^2$ and $b^2 = 36$, so $b = \sqrt{36}$ or 6.
In turn, $AD = BC = 6$. The perimeter of $ABCD$ is $2(8) + 2(6) = 16 + 12 = 28$. ■

Exercises 4.3

1. If diagonal $\overline{DB}$ is congruent to each side of rhombus $ABCD$, what is the measure of $\angle A$? Of $\angle ABC$?

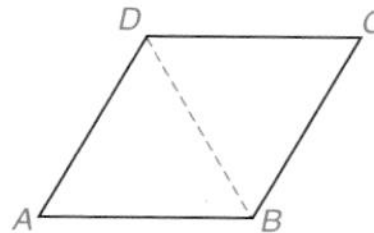

2. If the diagonals of a parallelogram are perpendicular, what can you conclude about the parallelogram?

   (HINT: Make a number of drawings in which you use only the information suggested.)

3. If the diagonals of a parallelogram are congruent, what can you conclude about the parallelogram?
4. If the diagonals of a parallelogram are perpendicular and congruent, what can you conclude about the parallelogram?
5. If the diagonals of a quadrilateral are perpendicular bisectors of each other (but not congruent), what can you conclude about the quadrilateral?
6. If the diagonals of a rhombus are congruent, what can you conclude about the rhombus?
7. A line segment joins the midpoints of two opposite sides of a rectangle as shown. What can you conclude about $\overline{MN}$ and MN?

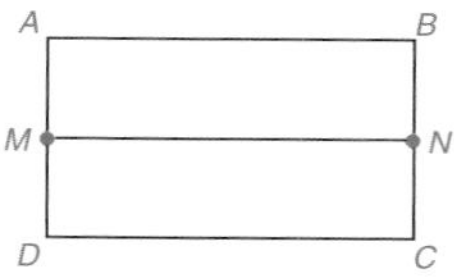

In Exercises 8 to 10, use the properties of rectangles to solve each problem. Rectangle ABCD is shown in the figure.

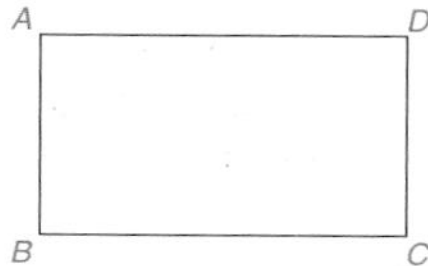

Exercises 8–10

8. *Given:* $AB = 5$ and $BC = 12$
   Find: CD, AD, and AC (not shown)
9. *Given:* $AB = 2x + 7$, $BC = 3x + 4$, and $CD = 3x + 2$
   Find: x and DA

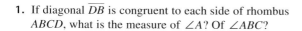

10. *Given:* $AB = x + y$, $BC = x + 2y$, $CD = 2x - y - 1$, and $DA = 3x - 3y + 1$
Find: x and y
(See figure for Exercise 8.)

In Exercises 11 to 14, consider rectangle MNPQ with diagonals $\overline{MP}$ and $\overline{NQ}$. When the answer is not a whole number, leave a square root answer.

11. If $MQ = 6$ and $MN = 8$, find NQ and MP.

12. If $QP = 9$ and $NP = 6$, find NQ and MP.

13. If $NP = 7$ and $MP = 11$, find QP and MN.

14. If $QP = 15$ and $MP = 17$, find MQ and NP.

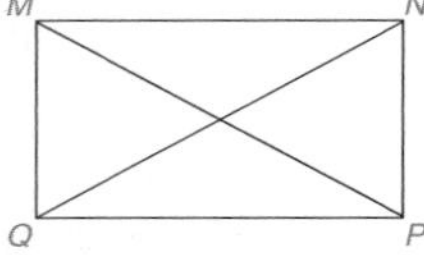

Exercises 11–14

In Exercises 15 to 18, consider rhombus ABCD with diagonals $\overline{AC}$ and $\overline{DB}$. When the answer is not a whole number, leave a square root answer.

15. If $AE = 5$ and $DE = 4$, find AD.

16. If $AE = 6$ and $EB = 5$, find AB.

17. If $AC = 10$ and $DB = 6$, find AD.

18. If $AC = 14$ and $DB = 10$, find BC.

Exercises 15–18

19. *Given:* Rectangle $ABCD$ (not shown) with $AB = 8$ and $BC = 6$; M and N are the midpoints of sides $\overline{AB}$ and $\overline{BC}$, respectively.
Find: MN

20. *Given:* Rhombus $RSTV$ (not shown) with diagonals $\overline{RT}$ and $\overline{SV}$ so that $RT = 8$ and $SV = 6$
Find: RS, the length of a side

For Exercises 21 and 22, let P = {parallelograms}, R = {rectangles}, and H = {rhombi}. Classify as true or false:

21. $H \subseteq P$ and $R \subseteq P$

22. $R \cup H = P$ and $R \cap H = \varnothing$

In Exercises 23 and 24, supply the missing statements and reasons.

23. *Given:* Quadrilateral $PQST$ with midpoints A, B, C, and D of the sides
Prove: $ABCD$ is a ▱

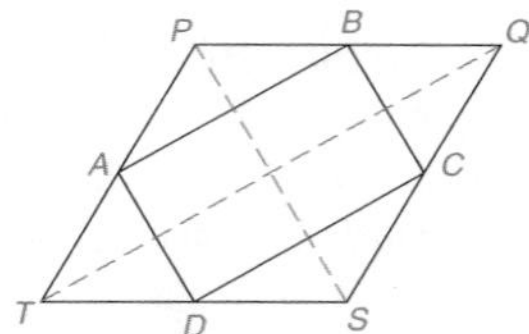

PROOF

Statements	Reasons
1. Quadrilateral $PQST$ with midpoints A, B, C, and D of the sides	1. ?
2. Draw $\overline{TQ}$	2. Through two points, there is one line
3. $\overline{AB} \parallel \overline{TQ}$ in $\triangle TPQ$	3. The line joining the midpoints of two sides of a triangle is $\parallel$ to the third side
4. $\overline{DC} \parallel \overline{TQ}$ in $\triangle TSQ$	4. ?
5. $\overline{AB} \parallel \overline{DC}$	5. ?
6. Draw $\overline{PS}$	6. ?
7. $\overline{AD} \parallel \overline{PS}$ in $\triangle TSP$	7. ?
8. $\overline{BC} \parallel \overline{PS}$ in $\triangle PSQ$	8. ?
9. $\overline{AD} \parallel \overline{BC}$	9. ?
10. ?	10. If both pairs of opposite sides of a quadrilateral are $\parallel$, the quad. is a ▱

24. *Given:* Rectangle $WXYZ$ with diagonals $\overline{WY}$ and $\overline{XZ}$
Prove: $\angle 1 \cong \angle 2$

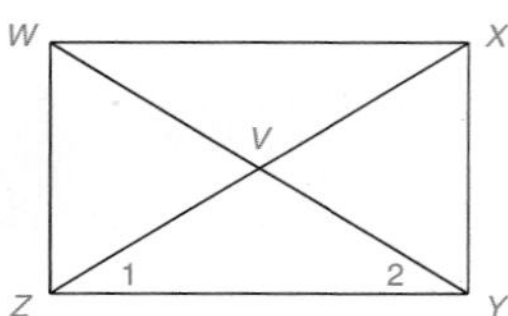

PROOF

Statements	Reasons
1. ?	1. Given
2. ?	2. The diagonals of a rectangle are $\cong$
3. $\overline{WZ} \cong \overline{XY}$	3. The opposite sides of a rectangle are $\cong$
4. $\overline{ZY} \cong \overline{ZY}$	4. ?
5. $\triangle XZY \cong \triangle WYZ$	5. ?
6. ?	6. ?

25. Which type(s) of quadrilateral(s) is(are) necessarily cyclic?
a) A square b) A parallelogram

26. Which type(s) of quadrilateral(s) is(are) necessarily cyclic?
a) A kite b) A rectangle

27. Find the perimeter of the cyclic quadrilateral shown.

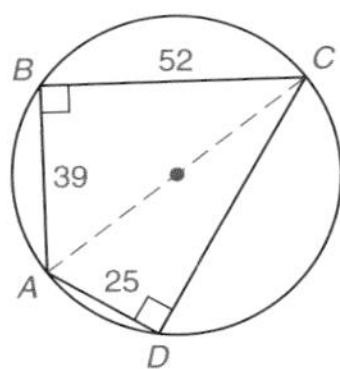

28. Find the perimeter of the square shown.

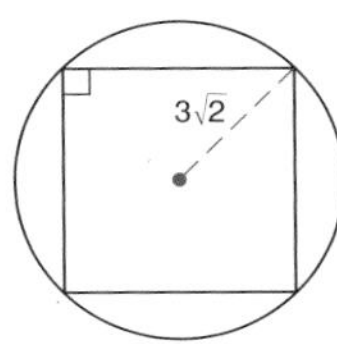

In Exercises 29 to 31, explain why each statement is true.

29. All angles of a rectangle are right angles.

30. All sides of a rhombus are congruent.

31. All sides of a square are congruent.

In Exercises 32 to 37, write a formal proof of each theorem.

32. The diagonals of a square are perpendicular.

33. A diagonal of a rhombus bisects two angles of the rhombus.

34. If the diagonals of a parallelogram are congruent, the parallelogram is a rectangle.

35. If the diagonals of a parallelogram are perpendicular, the parallelogram is a rhombus.

36. If the diagonals of a parallelogram are congruent and perpendicular, the parallelogram is a square.

37. If the midpoints of the sides of a rectangle are joined in order, the quadrilateral formed is a rhombus.

In Exercises 38 and 39, you will need to use the square root ($\sqrt{\ }$) function of your calculator.

38. A wall that is 12 ft long by 8 ft high has a triangular brace along the diagonal. Use a calculator to approximate the length of the brace to the nearest tenth of a foot.

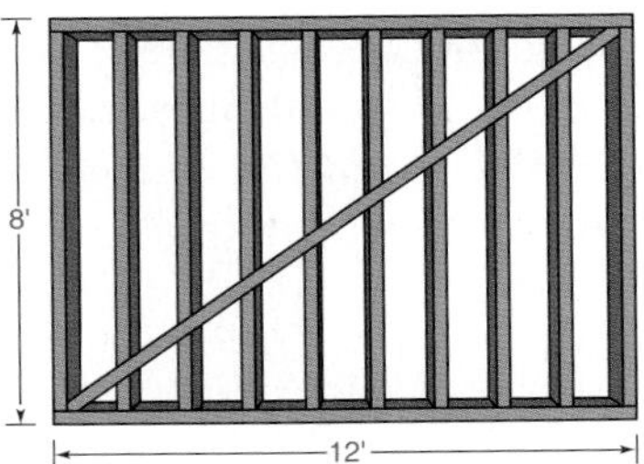

39. A walk-up ramp moves horizontally 20 ft while rising 4 ft. Use a calculator to approximate its length to the nearest tenth of a foot.

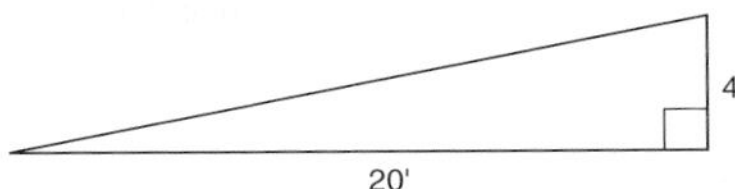

40. a) Argue that the midpoint of the hypotenuse of a right triangle is equidistant from the three vertices of the triangle. Use the fact that the congruent diagonals of a rectangle bisect each other. Be sure to provide a drawing.

b) Use the relationship from part (a) to find CM, the length of the median to the hypotenuse of right $\triangle ABC$, in which $m\angle C = 90°$, $AC = 6$, and $BC = 8$.

41. Two sets of rails (railroad tracks are equally spaced) intersect but not at right angles. Being as specific as possible, indicate what type of quadrilateral $WXYZ$ is formed.

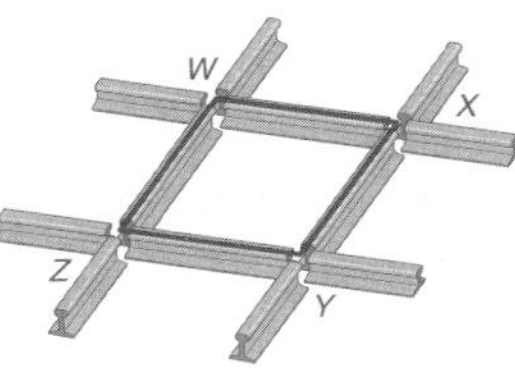

42. In square $ABCD$ (not shown), point E lies on side $\overline{DC}$. If $AB = 8$ and $AE = 10$, find BE.

43. In square $ABCD$ (not shown), point E lies in the interior of $ABCD$ in such a way that $\triangle ABE$ is an equilateral triangle. Find $m\angle DEC$.

4.4 The Trapezoid

KEY CONCEPTS

Trapezoid
Bases
Legs
Base Angles
Median
Isosceles Trapezoid

DEFINITION

A **trapezoid** is a quadrilateral with exactly two parallel sides.

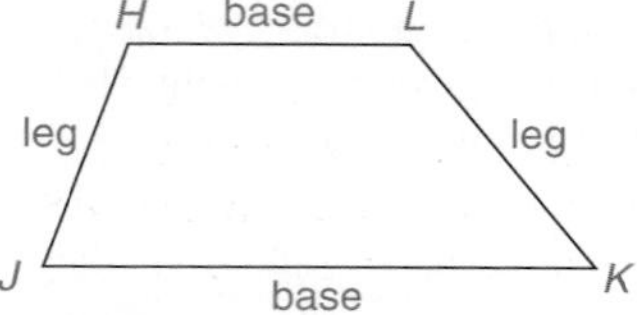

Figure 4.32

Figure 4.32 shows trapezoid $HJKL$, in which $\overline{HL} \parallel \overline{JK}$. The parallel sides $\overline{HL}$ and $\overline{JK}$ are **bases,** and the nonparallel sides $\overline{HJ}$ and $\overline{LK}$ are **legs.** Because $\angle J$ and $\angle K$ both have $\overline{JK}$ for a side, they are a pair of **base angles** of the trapezoid; $\angle H$ and $\angle L$ are also a pair of base angles because $\overline{HL}$ is a base.

When the midpoints of the two legs of a trapezoid are joined, the resulting line segment is known as the **median** of the trapezoid. Given that M and N are the midpoints of the legs $\overline{HJ}$ and $\overline{LK}$ in trapezoid $HJKL$, $\overline{MN}$ is the median of the trapezoid. [See Figure 4.33(a)].

If the two legs of a trapezoid are congruent, the trapezoid is known as an **isosceles trapezoid.** In Figure 4.33(b), $RSTV$ is an **isosceles trapezoid** because $\overline{RV} \cong \overline{ST}$ and $\overline{RS} \parallel \overline{VT}$.

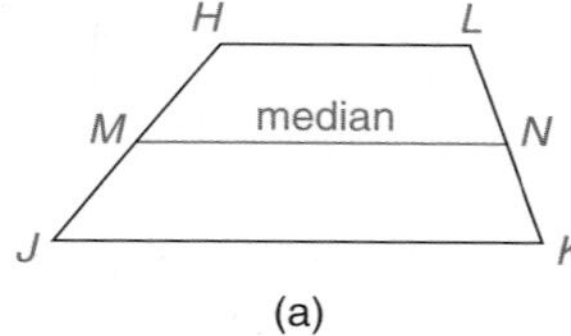

(a)

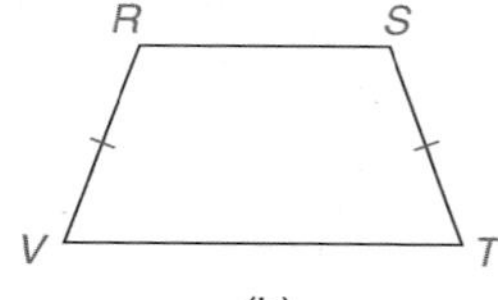

(b)

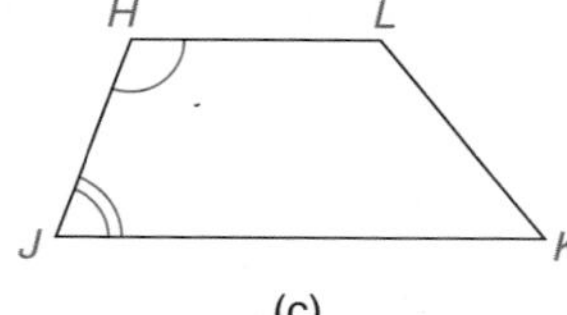

(c)

Figure 4.33

Reminder

If two parallel lines are cut by a transversal, then the interior angles on the same side of the transversal are supplementary.

Every trapezoid contains two pairs of consecutive interior angles that are supplementary. Each of these pairs of angles is formed when parallel lines are cut by a transversal. In Figure 4.33(c), angles H and J are supplementary, as are angles L and K. See the "Reminder" at the left.

EXAMPLE 1

In Figure 4.32, suppose that $m\angle H = 107°$ and $m\angle K = 58°$. Find $m\angle J$ and $m\angle L$.

Solution Because $\overline{HL} \parallel \overline{JK}$, $\angle$s H and J are supplementary angles, as are $\angle$s L and K. Then $m\angle H + m\angle J = 180$ and $m\angle L + m\angle K = 180$. Substitution leads to $107 + m\angle J = 180$ and $m\angle L + 58 = 180$, so $m\angle J = 73°$ and $m\angle L = 122°$. ■

DEFINITION

An **altitude** of a trapezoid is a line segment from one vertex of one base of the trapezoid perpendicular to the opposite base (or to an extension of that base).

In Figure 4.34, $\overline{HX}$, $\overline{LY}$, $\overline{JP}$, and $\overline{KQ}$ are altitudes of trapezoid $HJKL$. The length of any altitude of $HJKL$ is called the *height* of the trapezoid.

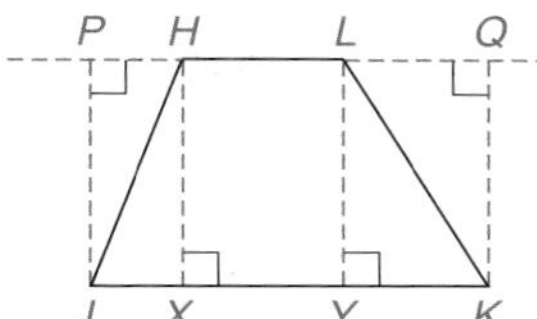

Figure 4.34

Exs. 1–6

Discover

Using construction paper, cut out two trapezoids that are copies of each other. To accomplish this, hold two pieces of paper together and cut once left and once right. Take the second trapezoid and turn it so that a pair of congruent legs coincide. What type of quadrilateral has been formed?

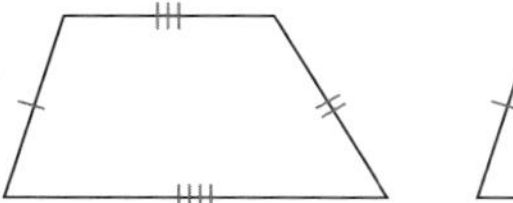

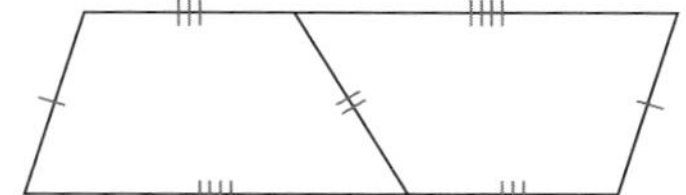

ANSWER
Parallelogram

The preceding activity may provide insight for a number of theorems involving the trapezoid.

THEOREM 4.4.1

The base angles of an isosceles trapezoid are congruent.

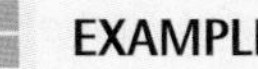

EXAMPLE 2

Study the picture proof of Theorem 4.4.1.

PICTURE PROOF OF THEOREM 4.4.1

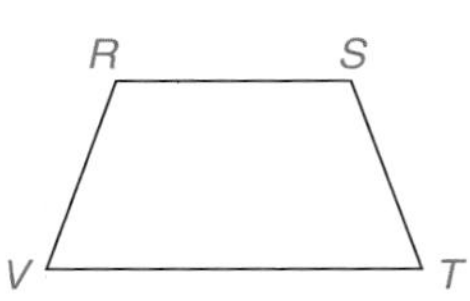

(a)

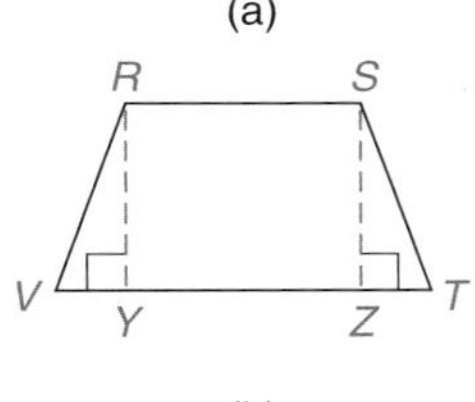

(b)

Figure 4.35

GIVEN: Trapezoid $RSTV$ with $\overline{RV} \cong \overline{ST}$ and $\overline{RS} \parallel \overline{VT}$ [See Figure 4.35(a)].

PROVE: $\angle V \cong \angle T$ and $\angle R \cong \angle S$

PROOF: By drawing $\overline{RY} \perp \overline{VT}$ and $\overline{SZ} \perp \overline{VT}$, we see that $\overline{RY} \cong \overline{SZ}$ (Theorem 4.1.6). By HL, $\triangle RYV \cong \triangle SZT$ so $\angle V \cong \angle T$ (CPCTC). $\angle R \cong \angle S$ in Figure 4.35(a) because these angles are supplementary to congruent angles ($\angle V$ and $\angle T$).

Geometry in the Real World

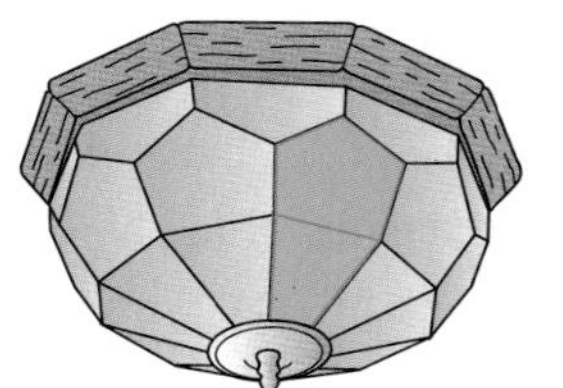

Some of the glass panels and trim pieces of the light fixture are isosceles trapezoids. Other glass panels are pentagons.

The following statement is a corollary of Theorem 4.4.1. Its proof is left to the student.

COROLLARY 4.4.2

The diagonals of an isosceles trapezoid are congruent.

If diagonals $\overline{AC}$ and $\overline{BD}$ were shown in Figure 4.36 (at the left), they would be congruent.

EXAMPLE 3

Given isosceles trapezoid $ABCD$ with $\overline{AB} \parallel \overline{DC}$ (see Figure 4.36):

a) Find the measures of the angles of $ABCD$ if $m\angle A = 12x + 30$ and $m\angle B = 10x + 46$.
b) Find the length of each diagonal (not shown) if it is known that $AC = 2y - 5$ and $BD = 19 - y$.

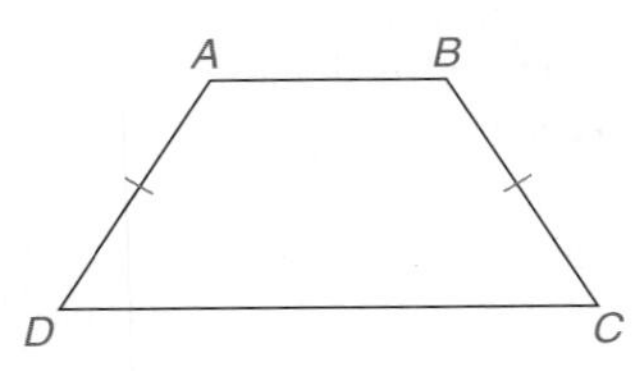

Figure 4.36

Solution

a) Because $m\angle A = m\angle B$, $12x + 30 = 10x + 46$, so $2x = 16$ and $x = 8$. Then $m\angle A = 12(8) + 30$ or $126°$, and $m\angle B = 10(8) + 46$ or $126°$. Subtracting $(180 - 126 = 54)$, we determine the supplements of $\angle$s A and B. That is, $m\angle C = m\angle D = 54°$.
b) By Corollary 4.4.2, $\overline{AC} \cong \overline{BD}$, so $2y - 5 = 19 - y$. Then $3y = 24$ and $y = 8$. Thus, $AC = 2(8) - 5 = 11$. Also $BD = 19 - 8 = 11$. ■

For completeness, we state two properties of the isosceles trapezoid.

1. An isosceles trapezoid has line symmetry; the axis of symmetry is the perpendicular-bisector of either base.
2. An isosceles trapezoid is cyclic; the center of the circle containing all four vertices of the trapezoid is the point of intersection of the perpendicular bisectors of any two consecutive sides (or of the two legs).

The proof of the following theorem is left as Exercise 33. We apply Theorem 4.4.3 in Examples 4 and 5.

THEOREM 4.4.3

The length of the median of a trapezoid equals one-half the sum of the lengths of the two bases.

NOTE: The length of the median of a trapezoid is the "average" of the lengths of the bases. Where m is the length of the median and b_1 and b_2 are the lengths of the bases, $m = \frac{1}{2}(b_1 + b_2)$.

EXAMPLE 4

In trapezoid $RSTV$ in Figure 4.37, $\overline{RS} \parallel \overline{VT}$ and M and N are the midpoints of $\overline{RV}$ and $\overline{TS}$, respectively. Find the length of median $\overline{MN}$ if $RS = 12$ and $VT = 18$.

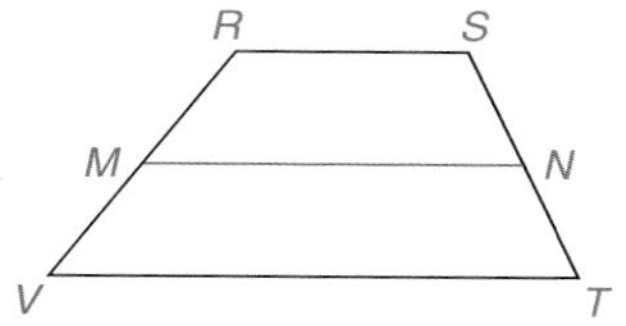

Figure 4.37

Solution Using Theorem 4.4.3, $MN = \frac{1}{2}(RS + VT)$, so $MN = \frac{1}{2}(12 + 18)$, or $MN = \frac{1}{2}(30)$. Thus, $MN = 15$. ■

EXAMPLE 5

In trapezoid $RSTV$, $\overline{RS} \parallel \overline{VT}$ and M and N are the midpoints of $\overline{RV}$ and $\overline{TS}$, respectively (see Figure 4.37). Find MN, RS, and VT if $RS = 2x$, $MN = 3x - 5$, and $VT = 2x + 10$.

Solution Using Theorem 4.4.3, we have $MN = \frac{1}{2}(RS + VT)$, so

$$3x - 5 = \tfrac{1}{2}[2x + (2x + 10)] \quad \text{or} \quad 3x - 5 = \tfrac{1}{2}(4x + 10)$$

Then $3x - 5 = 2x + 5$ and $x = 10$. Now $RS = 2x = 2(10)$, so $RS = 20$. Also, $MN = 3x - 5 = 3(10) - 5$; therefore, $MN = 25$. Finally, $VT = 2x + 10$; therefore, $VT = 2(10) + 10 = 30$.

NOTE: As a check, $MN = \frac{1}{2}(RS + VT)$ leads to the true statement $25 = \frac{1}{2}(20 + 30)$. ■

THEOREM 4.4.4

The median of a trapezoid is parallel to each base.

The proof of Theorem 4.4.4 is left as Exercise 28. In Figure 4.37, $\overline{MN} \parallel \overline{RS}$ and $\overline{MN} \parallel \overline{VT}$.

SSG *Exs. 7–12*

Theorems 4.4.5 and 4.4.6 enable us to show that a quadrilateral with certain characteristics is an isosceles trapezoid. We state these theorems as follows:

THEOREM 4.4.5

If two base angles of a trapezoid are congruent, the trapezoid is an isosceles trapezoid.

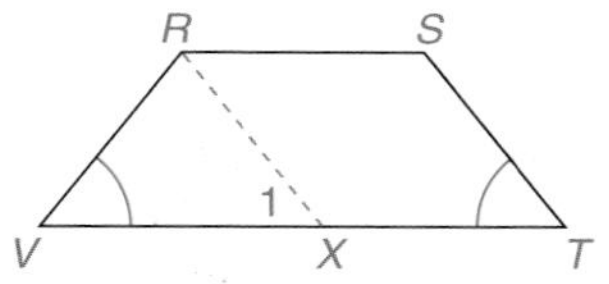

Figure 4.38

Consider the following plan for proving Theorem 4.4.5. See Figure 4.38.

GIVEN: Trapezoid $RSTV$ with $\overline{RS} \parallel \overline{VT}$ and $\angle V \cong \angle T$

PROVE: $RSTV$ is an isosceles trapezoid

PLAN: Draw auxiliary line $\overline{RX}$ parallel to $\overline{ST}$. Now show that $\angle V \cong \angle 1$, so $\overline{RV} \cong \overline{RX}$ in $\triangle RXV$. But $\overline{RX} \cong \overline{ST}$ in parallelogram $RXTS$, so $\overline{RV} \cong \overline{ST}$ and $RSTV$ is isosceles.

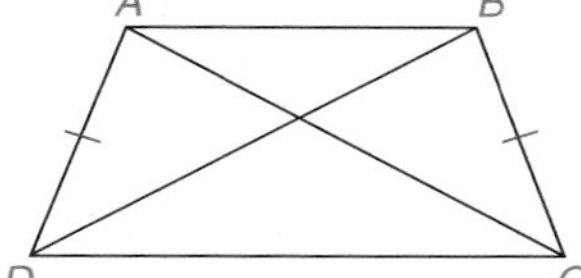

(a)

THEOREM 4.4.6

If the diagonals of a trapezoid are congruent, the trapezoid is an isosceles trapezoid.

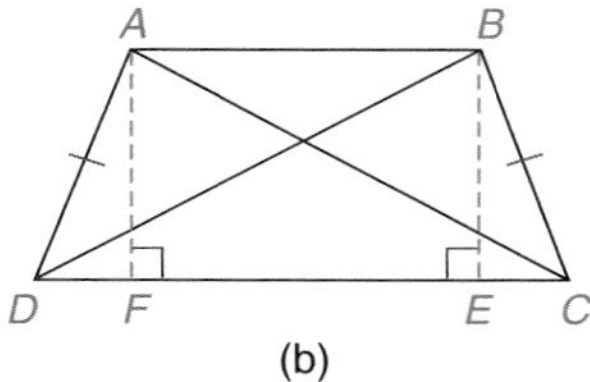

(b)

Figure 4.39

Theorem 4.4.6 has a lengthy proof, for which we have provided a sketch.

GIVEN: Trapezoid $ABCD$ with $\overline{AB} \parallel \overline{DC}$ and $\overline{AC} \cong \overline{DB}$ [See Figure 4.39(a) on page 208.]

PROVE: $ABCD$ is an isosceles trapezoid.

PLAN: Draw $\overline{AF} \perp \overline{DC}$ and $\overline{BE} \perp \overline{DC}$ in Figure 4.39(b). Now we can show that $ABEF$ is a rectangle. Because $\overline{AF} \cong \overline{BE}$, $\triangle AFC \cong \triangle BED$ by HL. Then

$\angle ACD \cong \angle BDC$ by CPCTC. With $\overline{DC} \cong \overline{DC}$ by Identity, $\triangle ACD \cong \triangle BDC$ by SAS. Now $\overline{AD} \cong \overline{BC}$ because these are corresponding parts of $\triangle ACD$ and $\triangle BDC$. Then trapezoid $ABCD$ is isosceles.

SSG *Exs. 13–15*

For several reasons, our final theorem is a challenge to prove. Looking at parallel lines a, b, and c in Figure 4.40, one sees trapezoids such as $ABED$ and $BCFE$. However, the proof (whose "plan" we provide) uses auxiliary lines, parallelograms, and congruent triangles.

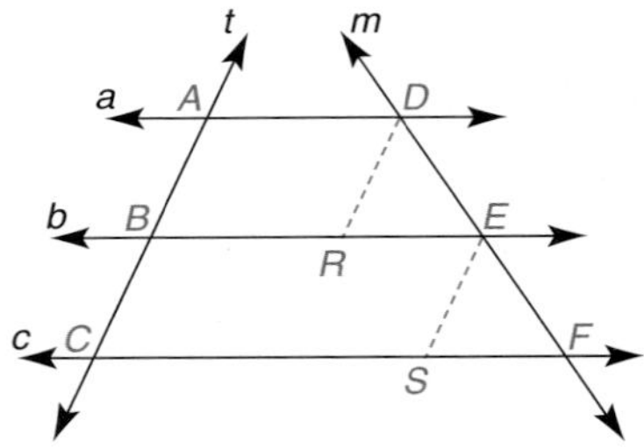

Figure 4.40

THEOREM 4.4.7

If three (or more) parallel lines intercept congruent line segments on one transversal, then they intercept congruent line segments on any transversal.

GIVEN: Parallel lines a, b, and c cut by transversal t so that $\overline{AB} \cong \overline{BC}$; also transversal m in Figure 4.40

PROVE: $\overline{DE} \cong \overline{EF}$

PLAN: Through D and E, draw $\overline{DR} \parallel \overline{AB}$ and $\overline{ES} \parallel \overline{AB}$. In each ▱ formed, $\overline{DR} \cong \overline{AB}$ and $\overline{ES} \cong \overline{BC}$. Given $\overline{AB} \cong \overline{BC}$, it follows that $\overline{DR} \cong \overline{ES}$. By AAS, we can show $\triangle DER \cong \triangle EFS$; then $\overline{DE} \cong \overline{EF}$ by CPCTC.

EXAMPLE 6

In Figure 4.40, $a \parallel b \parallel c$. If $AB = BC = 7.2$ and $DE = 8.4$, find EF.

SSG *Exs. 16, 17*

Solution Using Theorem 4.4.7, we find that $EF = 8.4$. ■

Exercises 4.4

1. Find the measures of the remaining angles of trapezoid $ABCD$ (not shown) if $\overline{AB} \parallel \overline{DC}$ and $m\angle A = 58°$ and $m\angle C = 125°$.
2. Find the measures of the remaining angles of trapezoid $ABCD$ (not shown) if $\overline{AB} \parallel \overline{DC}$ and $m\angle B = 63°$ and $m\angle D = 118°$.
3. If the diagonals of a trapezoid are congruent, what can you conclude about the trapezoid?
4. If two of the base angles of a trapezoid are congruent, what type of trapezoid is it?
5. What type of quadrilateral is formed when the midpoints of the sides of an isosceles trapezoid are joined in order?
6. In trapezoid $ABCD$, $\overline{MN}$ is the median. Without writing a formal proof, explain why $MN = \frac{1}{2}(AB + DC)$.

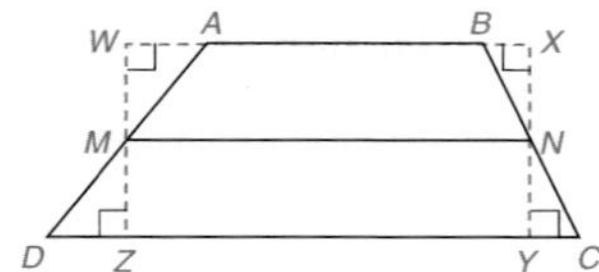

7. If $\angle H$ and $\angle J$ are supplementary, what type of quadrilateral is $HJKL$?

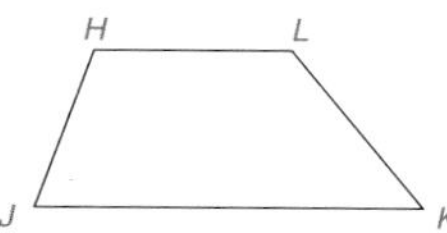

Exercises 7–8

8. If $\angle H$ and $\angle J$ are supplementary in $HJKL$, are $\angle K$ and $\angle L$ necessarily supplementary also?

For Exercises 9 and 10, consider isosceles trapezoid RSTV with $\overline{RS} \parallel \overline{VT}$ and midpoints M, N, P, and Q of the sides.

9. Would $RSTV$ have symmetry with respect to
a) $\overleftrightarrow{MP}$? b) $\overleftrightarrow{QN}$?

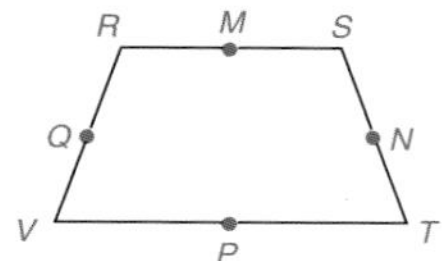

Exercises 9, 10

10. a) Does $QN = \frac{1}{2}(RS + VT)$?

b) Does $MP = \frac{1}{2}(RV + ST)$?

In Exercises 11 to 16, the drawing shows trapezoid ABCD with $\overline{AB} \parallel \overline{DC}$; also, M and N are midpoints of $\overline{AD}$ and $\overline{BC}$, respectively.

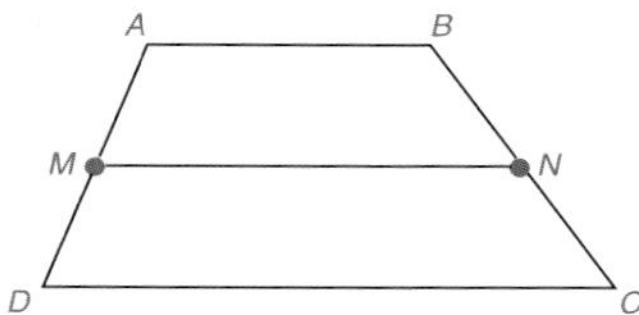

Exercises 11–16

11. *Given:* $AB = 7.3$ and $DC = 12.1$
Find: MN

12. *Given:* $MN = 6.3$ and $DC = 7.5$
Find: AB

13. *Given:* $AB = 8.2$ and $MN = 9.5$
Find: DC

14. *Given:* $AB = 7x + 5$, $DC = 4x - 2$, and $MN = 5x + 3$
Find: x

15. *Given:* $AB = 6x + 5$ and $DC = 8x - 1$
Find: MN, in terms of x

16. *Given:* $AB = x + 3y + 4$ and $DC = 3x + 5y - 2$
Find: MN, in terms of x and y

17. *Given:* $ABCD$ is an isosceles trapezoid (See figure for Exercise 18.)
Prove: $\triangle ABE$ is isosceles

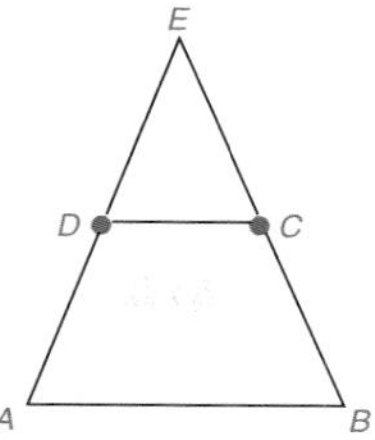

Exercises 17, 18

18. *Given:* Isosceles $\triangle ABE$ with $\overline{AE} \cong \overline{BE}$; also, D and C are midpoints of $\overline{AE}$ and $\overline{BE}$, respectively
Prove: $ABCD$ is an isosceles trapezoid

19. In isosceles trapezoid $WXYZ$ with bases $\overline{ZY}$ and $\overline{WX}$, $ZY = 8$, $YX = 10$, and $WX = 20$. Find height h (the length of $\overline{ZD}$ or $\overline{YE}$).

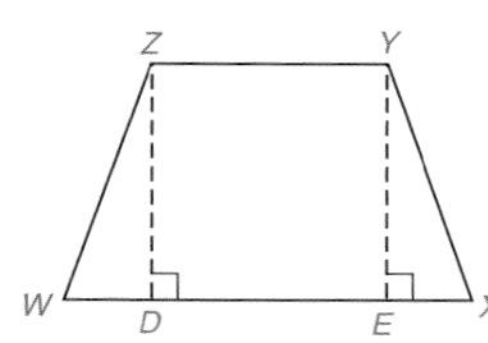

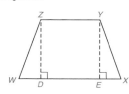

Exercises 19, 20

20. In trapezoid $WXYZ$ with bases $\overline{ZY}$ and $\overline{WX}$, $ZY = 12$, $YX = 10$, $WZ = 17$, and $ZD = 8$. Find the length of base $\overline{WX}$.

21. In isosceles trapezoid $MNPQ$ with $\overline{MN} \parallel \overline{QP}$, diagonal $\overline{MP} \perp \overline{MQ}$. If $PQ = 13$ and $NP = 5$, how long is diagonal $\overline{MP}$?

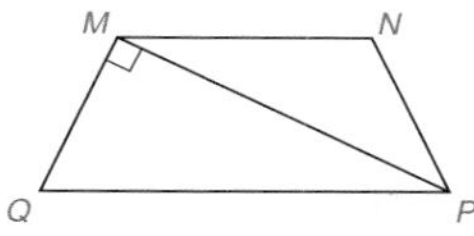

22. In trapezoid $RSTV$, $\overline{RV} \parallel \overline{ST}$, $m\angle SRV = 90°$, and M and N are midpoints of the nonparallel sides. If $ST = 13$, $RV = 17$, and $RS = 16$, how long is $\overline{RN}$?

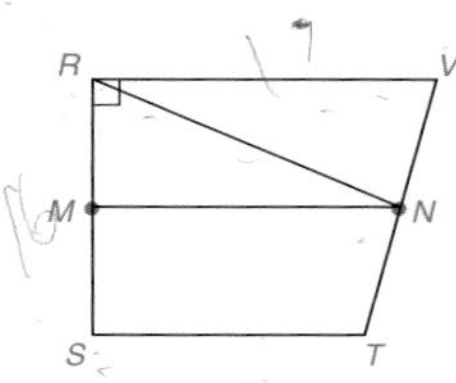

23. Each vertical section of a suspension bridge is in the shape of a trapezoid. For additional support, a vertical cable is placed midway as shown. If the two vertical columns shown have heights of 20 ft and 24 ft and the section is 10 ft wide, what will the height of the cable be?

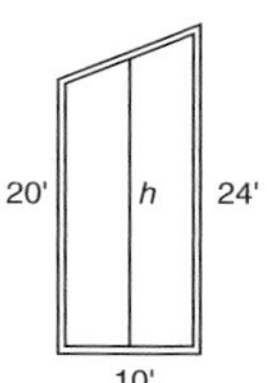

24. The state of Nevada approximates the shape of a trapezoid with these dimensions for boundaries: 340 miles on the north, 515 miles on the east, 435 miles on the south, and 225 miles on the west. If A and B are points located midway across the north and south boundaries, what is the approximate distance from A to B?

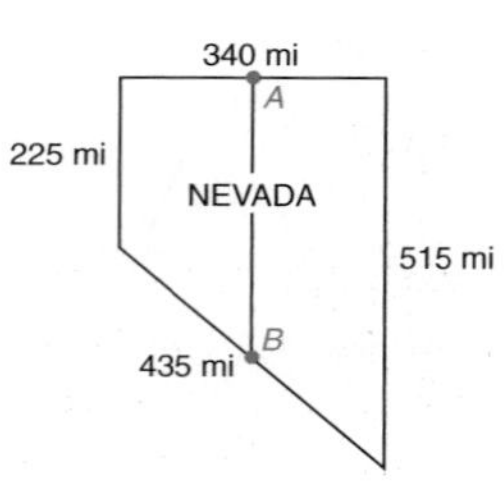

25. In the figure, $a \parallel b \parallel c$ and B is the midpoint of $\overline{AC}$. If $AB = 2x + 3$, $BC = x + 7$, and $DE = 3x + 2$, find the length of $\overline{EF}$.

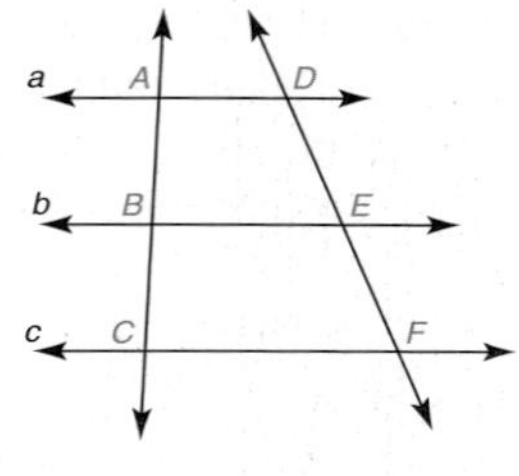

Exercises 25, 26

26. In the figure, $a \parallel b \parallel c$ and B is the midpoint of $\overline{AC}$. If $AB = 2x + 3y$, $BC = x + y + 7$, $DE = 2x + 3y + 3$, and $EF = 5x - y + 2$, find x and y.

In Exercises 27 to 33, complete a formal proof.

27. The diagonals of an isosceles trapezoid are congruent.

28. The median of a trapezoid is parallel to each base.

29. If two consecutive angles of a quadrilateral are supplementary, the quadrilateral is a trapezoid.

30. If two base angles of a trapezoid are congruent, the trapezoid is an isosceles trapezoid.

31. If three parallel lines intercept congruent segments on one transversal, then they intercept congruent segments on any transversal.

32. If the midpoints of the sides of an isosceles trapezoid are joined in order, then the quadrilateral formed is a rhombus.

33. *Given:* $\overline{EF}$ is the median of trapezoid $ABCD$
Prove: $EF = \frac{1}{2}(AB + DC)$

(HINT: Using Theorem 4.4.7, show that M is the midpoint of $\overline{AC}$. For $\triangle ADC$ and $\triangle CBA$, apply Theorem 4.2.5.)

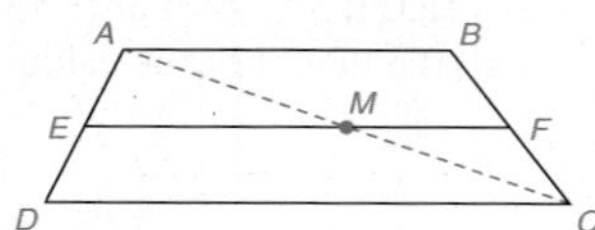

Exercises 33–35

For Exercises 34 and 35, $\overline{EF}$ is the median of trapezoid ABCD.

34. In the figure for Exercise 33, suppose that $AB = 12.8$ and $DC = 18.4$. Find:
a) MF c) EF
b) EM d) Whether $EF = \frac{1}{2}(AB + DC)$

35. In the figure for Exercise 33, suppose that $EM = 7.1$ and $MF = 3.5$. Find:
a) AB c) EF
b) DC d) Whether $EF = \frac{1}{2}(AB + DC)$

36. *Given:* $\overline{AB} \parallel \overline{DC}$
$m\angle A = m\angle B = 56°$
$\overline{CE} \parallel \overline{DA}$ and $\overrightarrow{CF}$ bisects $\angle DCB$
Find: $m\angle FCE$

37. In a gambrel style roof, the gable end of a barn has the shape of an isosceles trapezoid surmounted by an isosceles triangle. If $AE = 30$ ft and $BD = 24$ ft, find:
a) AS b) VD c) CD d) DE

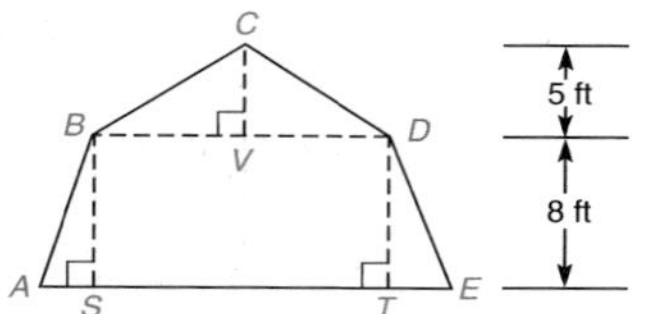

38. Successive steps on a ladder form isosceles trapezoids with the sides. $AH = 2$ ft and $BI = 2.125$ ft.
a) Find GN, the width of the bottom step
b) Which step is the median of the trapezoid with bases $\overline{AH}$ and $\overline{GN}$?

39. The vertical sidewall of an in-ground pool that is 24 ft in length has the shape of a trapezoid. What is the depth of the pool in the middle?

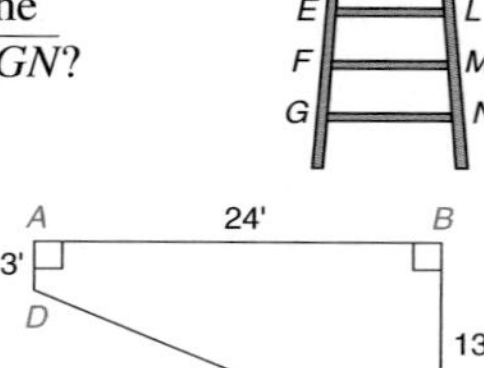

40. For the in-ground pool shown in Exercise 39, find the length of the sloped bottom from point D to point C.

***41.** In trapezoid $ABCD$ (not shown), $m\angle A = \frac{x}{2} + 10$, $m\angle B = \frac{x}{3} + 50$, and $m\angle C = \frac{x}{5} + 50$. Find all possible values of x.

***42.** In trapezoid $ABCD$, $\overline{BC} \perp \overline{AB}$ and $\overline{BC} \perp \overline{AC}$. If $DA = 17$, $AB = 6$, and $BC = 8$, find the perimeter of $\triangle DAC$.

PERSPECTIVE ON HISTORY

Sketch of Thales

One of the most significant contributors to the development of geometry was the Greek mathematician Thales of Miletus (625–547 B.C.). Thales is credited with being the "Father of Geometry" because he was the first person to organize geometric thought and utilize the deductive method as a means of verifying propositions (theorems). It is not surprising that Thales made original discoveries in geometry. Just as significant as his discoveries was Thales' persistence in verifying the claims of his predecessors. In this textbook, you will find that propositions such as these are only a portion of those that can be attributed to Thales:

Chapter 1: If two straight lines intersect, the opposite (vertical) angles formed are equal.
Chapter 3: The base angles of an isosceles triangle are equal.
Chapter 5: The sides of similar triangles are proportional.
Chapter 6: An angle inscribed in a semicircle is a right angle.

Thales' knowledge of geometry was matched by the wisdom that he displayed in everyday affairs. For example, he is known to have measured the height of the Great Pyramid of Egypt by comparing the lengths of the shadows cast by the pyramid and by his own staff. Thales also used his insights into geometry to measure the distances from the land to ships at sea.

Perhaps the most interesting story concerning Thales was one related by Aesop (famous for fables). It seems that Thales was on his way to market with his beasts of burden carrying saddlebags filled with salt. Quite by accident, one of the mules discovered that rolling in the stream where he was led to drink greatly reduced this load; of course, this was due to the dissolving of salt in the saddlebags. On subsequent trips, the same mule continued to lighten his load by rolling in the water. Thales soon realized the need to do something (anything!) to modify the mule's behavior. When preparing for the next trip, Thales filled the offensive mule's saddlebags with sponges. When the mule took his usual dive, he found that his load was heavier than ever. Soon the mule realized the need to keep the saddlebags out of the water. In this way, it is said that Thales discouraged the mule from allowing the precious salt to dissolve during later trips to market.

PERSPECTIVE ON APPLICATION

Square Numbers as Sums

In algebra, there is a principle that is generally "proved" by a quite sophisticated method known as mathematical induction. However, verification of the principle is much simpler when provided a geometric justification.

In the following paragraphs, we:

1. State the principle
2. Illustrate the principle
3. Provide the geometric justification for the principle

> Where n is a counting number, the sum of the first n positive odd counting numbers is n^2.

The principle stated above is illustrated for various choices of n.

Where $n = 1$, $1 = 1^2$.
Where $n = 2$, $1 + 3 = 2^2$, or 4.
Where $n = 3$, $1 + 3 + 5 = 3^2$, or 9.
Where $n = 4$, $1 + 3 + 5 + 7 = 4^2$, or 16.

The geometric explanation for this principle utilizes a *wrap-around* effect. Study the diagrams in Figure 4.41.

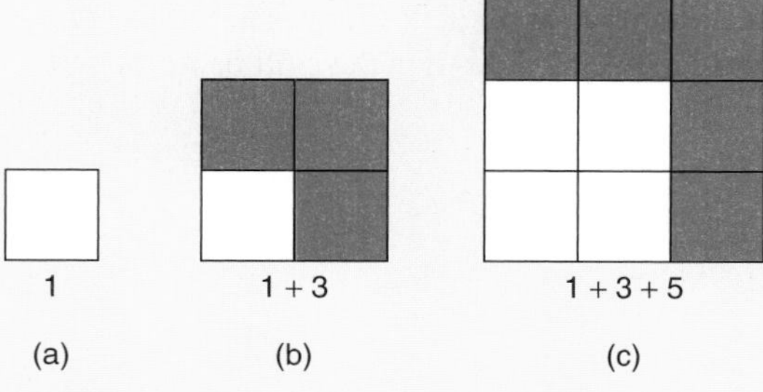

Figure 4.41

Given a unit square (one with sides of length 1), we build a second square by wrapping 3 unit squares around the first unit square; in Figure 4.41(b), the "wrap-around" is indicated by 3 shaded squares. Now for the second square (sides of length 2), we form the next square by wrapping 5 unit squares around this square; see Figure 4.41(c).

The next figure in the sequence of squares illustrates that

$$1 + 3 + 5 + 7 = 4^2, \text{ or } 16$$

In the "wrap-around," we emphasize that the next number in the sum is an odd number. The "wrap-around" approach adds $2 \times 3 + 1$, or 7 unit squares in Figure 4.42. When building each sequential square, we always add an odd number of unit squares as in Figure 4.42.

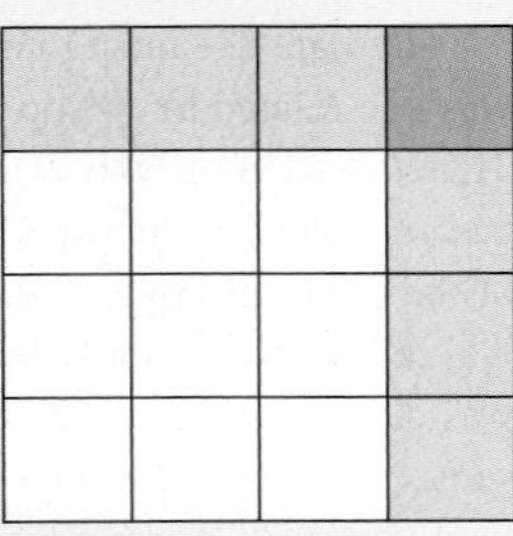

Figure 4.42

PROBLEM

Use the following principle to answer each question:

Where n is a counting number, the sum of the first n positive odd counting numbers is n^2.

a) Find the sum of the first five positive odd integers; that is, find $1 + 3 + 5 + 7 + 9$.
b) Find the sum of the first six positive odd integers.
c) How many positive odd integers were added to obtain the sum 81?

Solutions

a) 5^2, or 25 b) 6^2, or 36 c) 9, because $9^2 = 81$ ■

Summary

A LOOK BACK AT CHAPTER 4

The goal of this chapter has been to develop the properties of quadrilaterals, including special types of quadrilaterals such as the parallelogram, rectangle, and trapezoid. Table 4.1 on page 213 summarizes the properties of quadrilaterals.

A LOOK AHEAD TO CHAPTER 5

In the next chapter, similarity will be defined for all polygons, with an emphasis on triangles. The Pythagorean Theorem, which we applied in Chapter 4, will be proved in Chapter 5. Special right triangles will be discussed.

KEY CONCEPTS

4.1
Quadrilateral • Skew Quadrilateral • Parallelogram • Diagonals of a Parallelogram • Altitudes of a Parallelogram

4.2
Quadrilaterals That Are Parallelograms • Rectangle • Kite

4.3
Rectangle • Square • Rhombus • Pythagorean Theorem

4.4
Trapezoid (Bases, Legs, Base Angles, Median) • Isosceles Trapezoid

TABLE 4.1 An Overview of Chapter 4

Properties of Quadrilaterals

	PARALLELOGRAM	RECTANGLE	RHOMBUS	SQUARE	KITE	TRAPEZOID	ISOSCELES TRAPEZOID
Congruent sides	Both pairs of opposite sides	Both pairs of opposite sides	All four sides	All four sides	Both pairs of adjacent sides	Possible; also see isosceles trapezoid	Pair of legs
Parallel sides	Both pairs of opposite sides	Both pairs of opposite sides	Both pairs of opposite sides	Both pairs of opposite sides	Generally none	Pair of bases	Pair of bases
Perpendicular sides	If the parallelogram is a rectangle or square	Consecutive pairs	If rhombus is a square	Consecutive pairs	Possible	Possible	Generally none
Congruent angles	Both pairs of opposite angles	All four angles	Both pairs of opposite angles	All four angles	One pair of opposite angles	Possible; also see isosceles trapezoid	Each pair of base angles
Supplementary angles	All pairs of consecutive angles	Any two angles	All pairs of consecutive angles	Any two angles	Possibly two pairs	Each pair of leg angles	Each pair of leg angles
Diagonal relationships	Bisect each other	Congruent; bisect each other	Perpendicular; bisect each other and interior angles	Congruent; perpendicular; bisect each other and interior angles	Perpendicular; one bisects other and two interior angles	Intersect	Congruent

Chapter 4 REVIEW EXERCISES

State whether the statements in Review Exercises 1 to 12 are always true (A), sometimes true (S), or never true (N).

1. A square is a rectangle.
2. If two of the angles of a trapezoid are congruent, then the trapezoid is isosceles.
3. The diagonals of a trapezoid bisect each other.
4. The diagonals of a parallelogram are perpendicular.
5. A rectangle is a square.
6. The diagonals of a square are perpendicular.
7. Two consecutive angles of a parallelogram are supplementary.
8. Opposite angles of a rhombus are congruent.
9. The diagonals of a rectangle are congruent.
10. The four sides of a kite are congruent.
11. The diagonals of a parallelogram are congruent.
12. The diagonals of a kite are perpendicular bisectors of each other.

13. *Given:* ▱$ABCD$
$CD = 2x + 3$
$BC = 5x - 4$
Perimeter of ▱$ABCD = 96$ cm
Find: The lengths of the sides of ▱$ABCD$

Exercises 13, 14

14. *Given:* ▱$ABCD$
$m\angle A = 2x + 6$
$m\angle B = x + 24$
Find: $m\angle C$

15. The diagonals of ▱$ABCD$ (not shown) are perpendicular. If one diagonal has a length of 10 and the other diagonal has a length of 24, find the perimeter of the parallelogram.

16. *Given:* ▱$MNOP$
$m\angle M = 4x$
$m\angle O = 2x + 50$
Find: $m\angle M$ and $m\angle P$

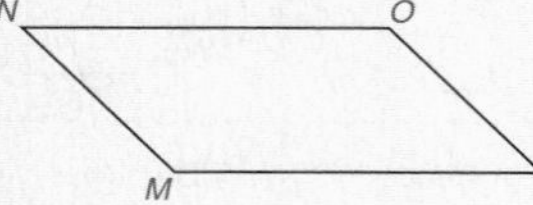

Exercises 16, 17

17. Using the information from Exercise 16, determine which diagonal ($\overline{MO}$ or $\overline{PN}$) would be longer.

18. In quadrilateral $ABCD$, M is the midpoint only of $\overline{BD}$ and $\overline{AC} \perp \overline{DB}$ at M. What special type of quadrilateral is $ABCD$?

19. In isosceles trapezoid $DEFG$, $\overline{DE} \parallel \overline{GF}$ and $m\angle D = 108°$. Find the measures of the other angles in the trapezoid.

20. One base of a trapezoid has a length of 12.3 cm and the length of the other base is 17.5 cm. Find the length of the median of the trapezoid.

21. In trapezoid $MNOP$, $\overline{MN} \parallel \overline{PO}$ and R and S are the midpoints of $\overline{MP}$ and $\overline{NO}$, respectively. Find the lengths of the bases if $RS = 15$, $MN = 3x + 2$, and $PO = 2x - 7$.

In Review Exercises 22 to 24, M and N are the midpoints of $\overline{FJ}$ and $\overline{FH}$, respectively.

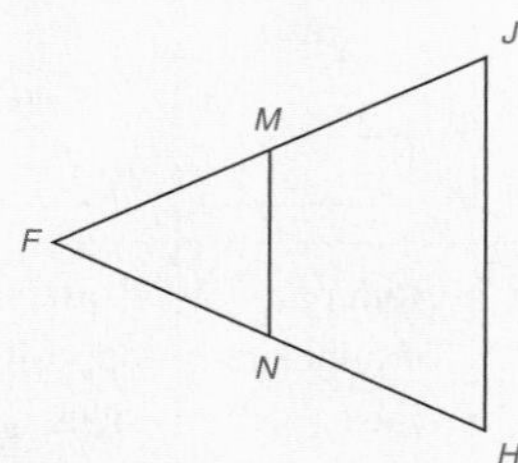

Exercises 22–24

22. *Given:* Isosceles $\triangle FJH$ with
$\overline{FJ} \cong \overline{FH}$
$FM = 2y + 3$
$NH = 5y - 9$
$JH = 2y$
Find: The perimeter of $\triangle FMN$

23. *Given:* $JH = 12$
$m\angle J = 80°$
$m\angle F = 60°$
Find: MN, $m\angle FMN$, $m\angle FNM$

24. *Given:* $MN = x^2 + 6$
$JH = 2x(x + 2)$
Find: x, MN, JH

25. *Given:* $ABCD$ is a ▱
$\overline{AF} \cong \overline{CE}$
Prove: $\overline{DF} \parallel \overline{EB}$

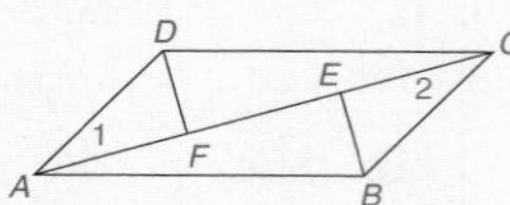

Exercise 25

26. *Given:* $ABEF$ is a rectangle
$BCDE$ is a rectangle
$\overline{FE} \cong \overline{ED}$
Prove: $\overline{AE} \cong \overline{BD}$ and $\overline{AE} \parallel \overline{BD}$

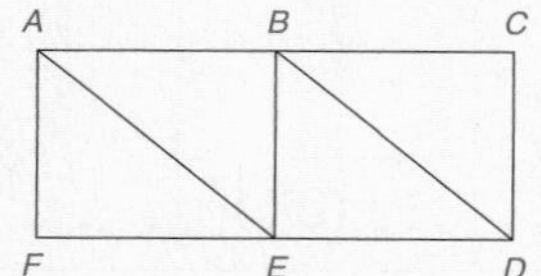

27. *Given:* $\overline{DE}$ is a median of $\triangle ADC$
$\overline{BE} \cong \overline{FD}$
$\overline{EF} \cong \overline{FD}$
Prove: $ABCF$ is a ▱

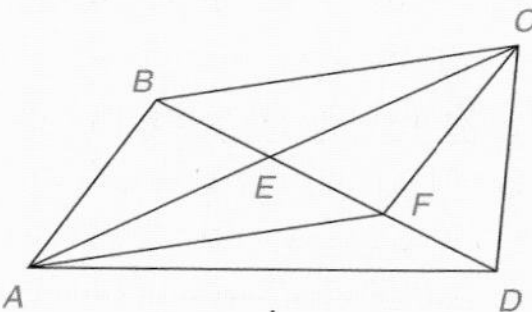

28. *Given:* $\triangle FAB \cong \triangle HCD$
$\triangle EAD \cong \triangle GCB$
Prove: $ABCD$ is a ▱

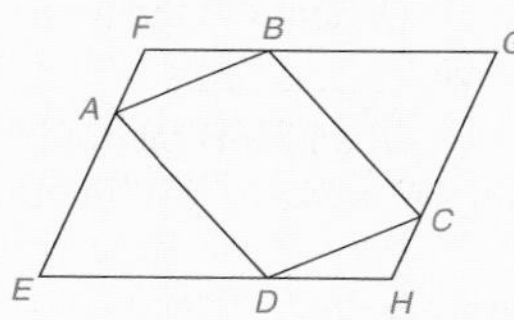

29. *Given:* $ABCD$ is a parallelogram
$\overline{DC} \cong \overline{BN}$
$\angle 3 \cong \angle 4$
Prove: $ABCD$ is a rhombus

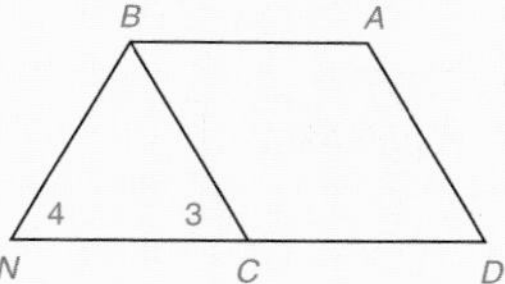

30. *Given:* $\triangle TWX$ is isosceles, with base $\overline{WX}$
$\overline{RY} \parallel \overline{WX}$
Prove: $RWXY$ is an isosceles trapezoid

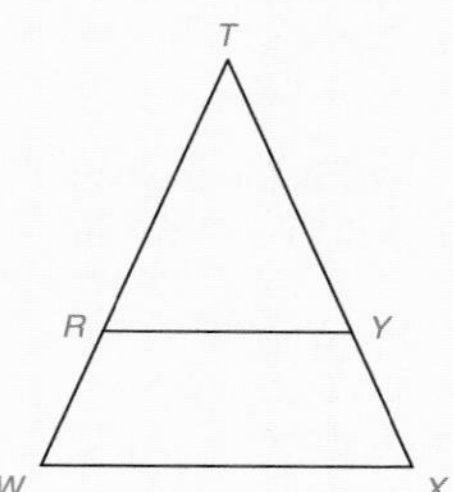

31. Construct a rhombus, given these lengths for the diagonals.

32. Draw rectangle $ABCD$ with $AB = 5$ and $BC = 12$. Include diagonals $\overline{AC}$ and $\overline{BD}$.
a) How are $\overline{AB}$ and $\overline{BC}$ related?
b) Find the length of diagonal $\overline{AC}$.

33. Draw rhombus $WXYZ$ with diagonals $\overline{WY}$ and $\overline{XZ}$. Let $\overline{WY}$ name the longer diagonal.
a) How are diagonals $\overline{WY}$ and $\overline{XZ}$ related?
b) If $WX = 17$ and $XZ = 16$, find the length of diagonal $\overline{WY}$.

34. Considering parallelograms, kites, rectangles, squares, rhombi, trapezoids, and isosceles trapezoids, which figures have
a) line symmetry?
b) point symmetry?

35. What type of quadrilateral is formed when the triangle is reflected across the indicated side?
a) Isosceles $\triangle ABC$ across $\overline{BC}$
b) Obtuse $\triangle XYZ$ across $\overline{XY}$

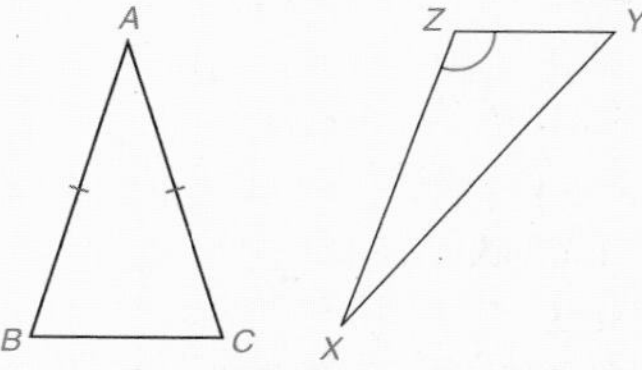

Chapter 4 TEST

1. Consider ▱$ABCD$ as shown.

a) How are $\angle A$ and $\angle C$ related? ____________

b) How are $\angle A$ and $\angle B$ related? ____________

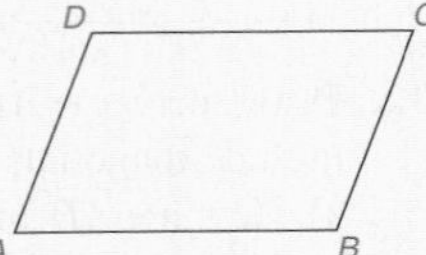

2. In ▱$RSTV$ (not shown), $RS = 5.3$ cm and $ST = 4.1$ cm. Find the perimeter of $RSTV$. ____________

3. In ▱$ABCD$, $AD = 5$ and $DC = 9$. If the altitude from vertex D to $\overline{AB}$ has length 4 (that is, $DE = 4$), find the length of $\overline{EB}$. ____________

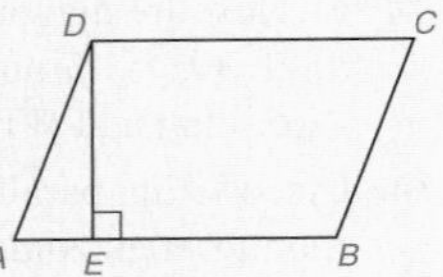

4. In ▱$RSTV$, $m\angle S = 57°$. Which diagonal ($\overline{VS}$ or $\overline{RT}$) would have the greater length? ____________

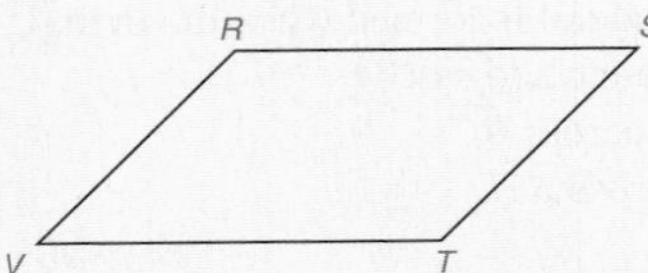

Exercises 4, 5

5. In ▱$RSTV$, $VT = 3x - 1$, $TS = 2x + 1$, and $RS = 4(x - 2)$. Find the value of x. ____________

6. Complete each statement:

a) If a quadrilateral has two pairs of congruent *adjacent* sides, then the quadrilateral is a(n) ____________.

b) If a quadrilateral has two pairs of congruent *opposite* sides, then the quadrilateral is a(n) ____________.

7. Complete each statement:

a) In ▱$RSTV$, $\overline{RW}$ is the ____________ from vertex R to base $\overline{VT}$.

b) If altitude $\overline{RW}$ of figure (a) is congruent to altitude $\overline{TY}$ of figure (b), then ▱$RSTV$ must also be a(n) ____________.

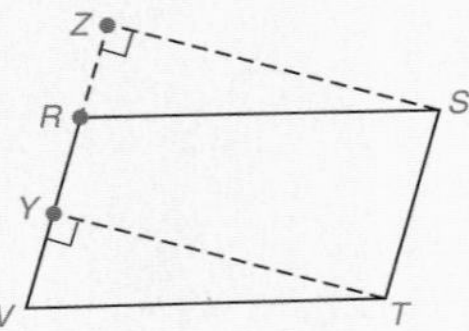

8. In $\triangle ABC$, M is the midpoint of $\overline{AB}$ and N is the midpoint of $\overline{AC}$.

a) How are line segments $\overline{MN}$ and $\overline{BC}$ related? ____________

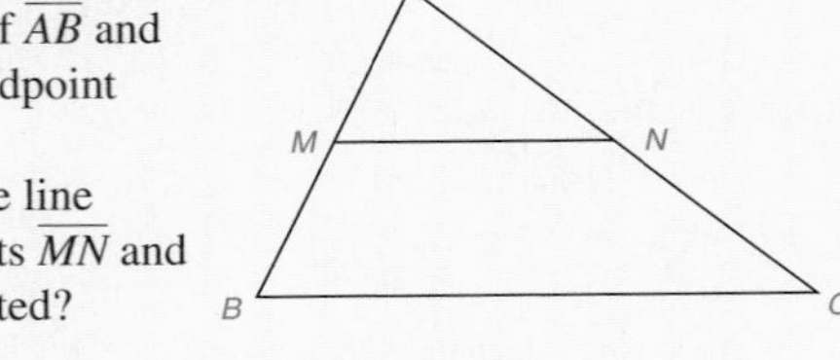

Exercises 8–10

b) Use an equation to state how the lengths MN and BC are related. ____________

9. In $\triangle ABC$, M is the midpoint of $\overline{AB}$ and N is the midpoint of $\overline{AC}$. If $MN = 7.6$ cm, find BC. ____________

10. In $\triangle ABC$, M is the midpoint of $\overline{AB}$ and N is the midpoint of $\overline{AC}$. If $MN = 3x - 11$ and $BC = 4x + 24$, find the value of x. ____________

11. In rectangle $ABCD$, $AD = 12$ and $DC = 5$. Find the length of diagonal $\overline{AC}$ (not shown). ____________

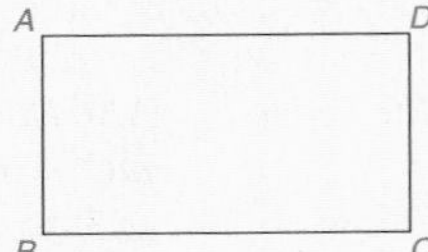

12. In trapezoid $RSTV$, $\overline{RS} \parallel \overline{VT}$.

a) Which sides are the legs of $RSTV$? ____________

b) Name two angles that are supplementary. ____________

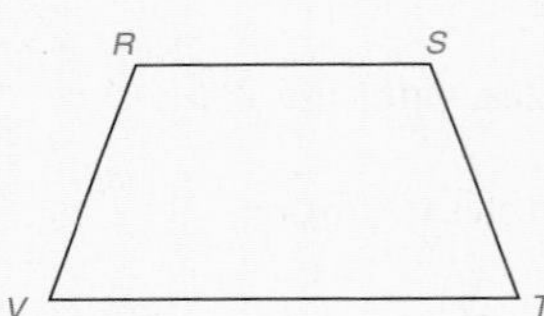

13. In trapezoid $RSTV$, $\overline{RS} \parallel \overline{VT}$ and $\overline{MN}$ is the median. Find the length MN if $RS = 12.4$ in. and $VT = 16.2$ in. ____________

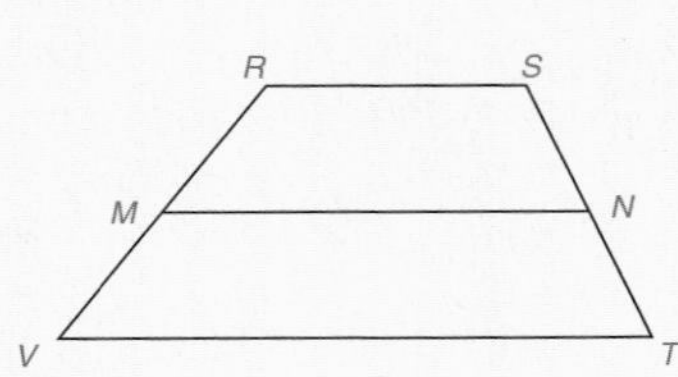

Exercises 13, 14

14. In trapezoid $RSTV$ of Exercise 13, $\overline{RS} \parallel \overline{VT}$ and $\overline{MN}$ is the median. Find x if $VT = 2x + 9$, $MN = 6x - 13$, and $RS = 15$. __________

15. Complete the proof of the following theorem:

"In a kite, one pair of opposite angles are congruent."

Given: Kite $ABCD$; $\overline{AB} \cong \overline{AD}$ and $\overline{BC} \cong \overline{DC}$

Prove: $\angle B \cong \angle D$

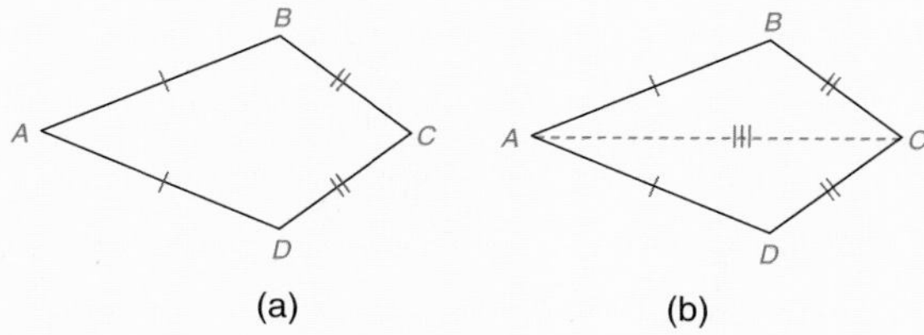

PROOF

Statements	Reasons
1. __________	1. __________
2. Draw $\overline{AC}$.	2. Through two points, there is exactly one line
3. __________	3. Identity
4. $\triangle ACD \cong \triangle ACB$	4. __________
5. __________	5. __________

16. Complete the proof of the following theorem:

"The diagonals of an isosceles trapezoid are congruent."

Given: Trapezoid $ABCD$ with $\overline{AB} \parallel \overline{DC}$ and $\overline{AD} \cong \overline{BC}$

Prove: $\overline{AC} \cong \overline{DB}$

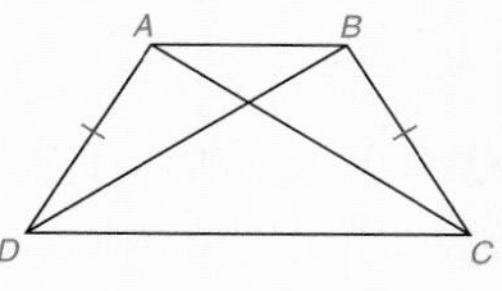

PROOF

Statements	Reasons
1. __________	1. __________
2. $\angle ADC \cong \angle BCD$	2. Base $\angle$s of an isosceles trapezoid are __________
3. $\overline{DC} \cong \overline{DC}$	3. __________
4. $\triangle ADC \cong \triangle BCD$	4. __________
5. __________	5. CPCTC

17. In kite $RSTV$, $RS = 2x - 4$, $ST = x - 1$, $TV = y - 3$, and $RV = y$. Find the perimeter of $RSTV$.

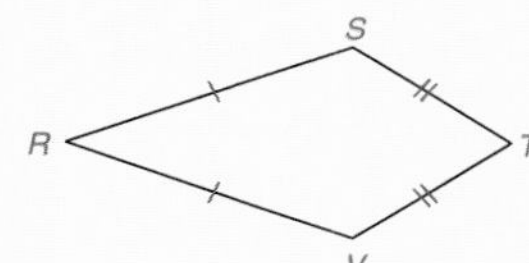

Chapter 5

Similar Triangles

© Gregor Schuster/Getty Images

CHAPTER OUTLINE

Additional Video explanation of concepts, sample problems, and applications are available on DVD. 

Talented! The handiwork of a skillful craftsman, these Russian nesting dolls have the same shape but different sizes. Because of their design, each doll can be placed within another so that they all nest together. Both the shells and the painted figures upon them are similar in shape. In nature, water lily pads have the same shape but different sizes. In the everyday world, cylindrical containers found on grocery store shelves may have the same shape but different sizes. In all these situations, one figure is merely an enlargement of the other. In geometry, we say that the two figures are *similar*. Further illustrations of both two- and three-dimensional similar figures can be found in Sections 5.2 and 5.3. The solutions for some applications in this and later chapters lead to quadratic equations. A review of the methods that are used to solve quadratic equations can be found in Appendix A.4 of this textbook.

5.1 Ratios, Rates, and Proportions

KEY CONCEPTS

Ratio	Extremes	Geometric Mean
Rate	Means	Extended Ratio
Proportion	Means-Extremes Property	Extended Proportion

The concepts and techniques discussed in Section 5.1 are often necessary for managing the geometry applications found throughout this chapter and beyond.

A **ratio** is the quotient $\frac{a}{b}$ (where $b \neq 0$) that provides a comparison between the numbers a and b. Because every fraction indicates a division, every fraction represents a ratio. Read "a to b," the ratio is sometimes written in the form $a{:}b$.

It is generally preferable to provide the ratio in simplest form, so the ratio 6 to 8 would be reduced (in fraction form) from $\frac{6}{8}$ to $\frac{3}{4}$. If units of measure are found in a ratio, these units must be **commensurable** (convertible to the same unit of measure). When simplifying the ratio of two quantities that are expressed in the same unit, we eliminate the common unit in the process. If two quantities cannot be compared because no common unit of measure is possible, the quantities are **incommensurable.**

Reminder

Units are neither needed nor desirable in a simplified ratio.

EXAMPLE 1

Find the best form of each ratio:

a) 12 to 20
b) 12 in. to 24 in.
c) 12 in. to 3 ft (NOTE: 1 ft = 12 in.)
d) 5 lb to 20 oz (NOTE: 1 lb = 16 oz)
e) 5 lb to 2 ft
f) 4 m to 30 cm (NOTE: 1 m = 100 cm)

Solution

a) $\frac{12}{20} = \frac{3}{5}$

b) $\frac{12\text{ in.}}{24\text{ in.}} = \frac{12}{24} = \frac{1}{2}$

c) $\frac{12\text{ in.}}{3\text{ ft}} = \frac{12\text{ in.}}{3(12\text{ in.})} = \frac{12\text{ in.}}{36\text{ in.}} = \frac{1}{3}$

d) $\frac{5\text{ lb}}{20\text{ oz}} = \frac{5(16\text{ oz})}{20\text{ oz}} = \frac{80\text{ oz}}{20\text{ oz}} = \frac{4}{1}$

e) $\frac{5\text{ lb}}{2\text{ ft}}$ is incommensurable!

f) $\frac{4\text{ m}}{30\text{ cm}} = \frac{4(100\text{ cm})}{30\text{ cm}} = \frac{400\text{ cm}}{30\text{ cm}} = \frac{40}{3}$ ■

Geometry in the Real World

At a grocery store, the cost per unit is a rate that allows the consumer to know which brand is more expensive.

A **rate** is a quotient that compares two quantities that are incommensurable. If an automobile can travel 300 miles along an interstate while consuming 10 gallons of gasoline, then its consumption *rate* is $\frac{300\text{ miles}}{10\text{ gallons}}$. In simplified form, the consumption rate is $\frac{30\text{ mi}}{\text{gal}}$, which is read as "30 miles per gallon" and is often abbreviated 30 mpg.

EXAMPLE 2

Simplify each rate. Units are necessary in each answer.

a) $\frac{120\text{ miles}}{5\text{ gallons}}$

b) $\frac{100\text{ meters}}{10\text{ seconds}}$

c) $\frac{12\text{ teaspoons}}{2\text{ quarts}}$

d) $\frac{\$8.45}{5\text{ gallons}}$

Solution

a) $\frac{120 \text{ mi}}{5 \text{ gal}} = \frac{24 \text{ mi}}{\text{gal}}$ (sometimes written 24 mpg)

b) $\frac{100 \text{ m}}{10 \text{ s}} = \frac{10 \text{ m}}{\text{s}}$

c) $\frac{12 \text{ teaspoons}}{2 \text{ quarts}} = \frac{6 \text{ teaspoons}}{\text{quart}}$

SSG *Exs. 1–2*

d) $\frac{\$8.45}{5 \text{ gal}} = \frac{\$1.69}{\text{gal}}$ ■

A **proportion** is a statement that two ratios or two rates are equal. Thus, $\frac{a}{b} = \frac{c}{d}$ is a proportion and may be read as "a is to b as c is to d." In the order read, a is the *first term* of the proportion, b is the *second term*, c is the *third term*, and d is the *fourth term*. The first and last terms (a and d) of the proportion are the **extremes,** whereas the second and third terms (b and c) are the **means.**

The following property is extremely convenient for solving proportions.

PROPERTY 1 ▶ (Means-Extremes Property)

In a proportion, the product of the means equals the product of the extremes; that is, if $\frac{a}{b} = \frac{c}{d}$ (where $b \neq 0$ and $d \neq 0$), then $a \cdot d = b \cdot c$.

A proportion, being a statement, can be true or false. In the false proportion $\frac{9}{12} = \frac{2}{3}$, it is obvious that $9 \cdot 3 \neq 12 \cdot 2$; on the other hand, the truth of the statement $\frac{9}{12} = \frac{3}{4}$ is evident from the fact that $9 \cdot 4 = 12 \cdot 3$. Henceforth, any proportion given in this text is intended to be a true proportion.

EXAMPLE 3

Use the Means-Extremes Property to solve each proportion for x.

a) $\frac{x}{8} = \frac{5}{12}$

b) $\frac{x+1}{9} = \frac{x-3}{3}$

c) $\frac{3}{x} = \frac{x}{2}$

d) $\frac{x+3}{3} = \frac{9}{x-3}$

e) $\frac{x+2}{5} = \frac{4}{x-1}$

Solution

a) $x \cdot 12 = 8 \cdot 5$ **(Means-Extremes Property)**

$12x = 40$

$x = \frac{40}{12} = \frac{10}{3}$

b) $3(x + 1) = 9(x - 3)$ **(Means-Extremes Property)**

$3x + 3 = 9x - 27$

$30 = 6x$

$x = 5$

c) $3 \cdot 2 = x \cdot x$ **(Means-Extremes Property)**

$x^2 = 6$

$x = \pm\sqrt{6} \approx \pm 2.45$

Warning

As you solve a proportion such as $\frac{x}{8} = \frac{5}{12}$, write $12x = 40$ on the next line. Do *not* write $\frac{x}{8} = \frac{5}{12} = 12x = 40$, which would imply that $\frac{5}{12} = 40$.

d) $(x + 3)(x - 3) = 3 \cdot 9$ **(Means-Extremes Property)**

$x^2 - 9 = 27$

$x^2 - 36 = 0$

$(x + 6)(x - 6) = 0$ **(using factoring)**

$x + 6 = 0$ or $x - 6 = 0$

$x = -6$ or $x = 6$

e) $(x + 2)(x - 1) = 5 \cdot 4$ **(Means-Extremes Property)**

$x^2 + x - 2 = 20$

$x^2 + x - 22 = 0$

$$x = \frac{-b \pm \sqrt{b^2 - 4ac}}{2a}$$ **(using Quadratic Formula; see Appendix A.4)**

$$= \frac{-1 \pm \sqrt{(1)^2 - 4(1)(-22)}}{2(1)}$$

$$= \frac{-1 \pm \sqrt{1 + 88}}{2}$$

$$= \frac{-1 \pm \sqrt{89}}{2}$$

≈ 4.22 or -5.22 ■

In application problems involving proportions, it is essential to order the related quantities in each ratio or rate. The first step in the solution of Example 4 illustrates the care that must be taken in forming the proportion for an application. Because of consistency, units may be eliminated in the actual proportion.

EXAMPLE 4

If an automobile can travel 90 mi on 4 gal of gasoline, how far can it travel on 6 gal of gasoline?

Geometry in the Real World

The automobile described in Example 4 has a consumption rate of 22.5 mpg (miles per gallon).

Solution By form,

$$\frac{\text{number miles first trip}}{\text{number gallons first trip}} = \frac{\text{number miles second trip}}{\text{number gallons second trip}}$$

Where x represents the number of miles traveled on the second trip, we have

$$\frac{90}{4} = \frac{x}{6}$$

$$4x = 540$$

$$x = 135$$

Thus, the car can travel 135 mi on 6 gal of gasoline. ■

In $\frac{a}{b} = \frac{b}{c}$, where the second and third terms of the proportion are identical, the value of b is known as the **geometric mean** of a and c. For example, 6 and -6 are the geometric means of 4 and 9 because $\frac{4}{6} = \frac{6}{9}$ and $\frac{4}{-6} = \frac{-6}{9}$. Because applications in geometry generally require positive solutions, we usually seek only the positive geometric mean of a and c.

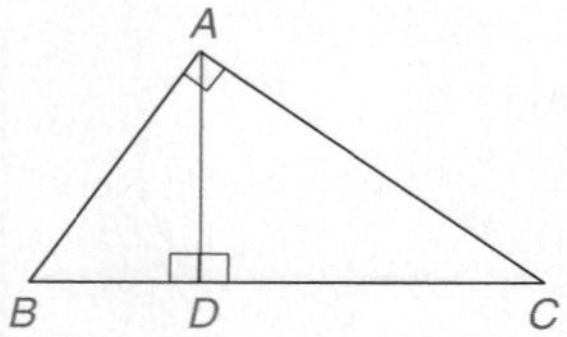

Figure 5.1

EXAMPLE 5

In Figure 5.1, AD is the geometric mean of BD and DC. If $BC = 10$ and $BD = 4$, determine AD.

Solution $\frac{BD}{AD} = \frac{AD}{DC}$. Because $DC = BC - BD$, we know that $DC = 10 - 4 = 6$. Therefore,

$$\frac{4}{x} = \frac{x}{6}$$

in which x is the length of $\overline{AD}$. Applying the Means-Extremes Property,

$$x^2 = 24$$
$$x = \pm\sqrt{24} = \pm\sqrt{4 \cdot 6} = \pm\sqrt{4} \cdot \sqrt{6} = \pm 2\sqrt{6}$$

SSG *Exs. 3–6*

To have a permissible length for $\overline{AD}$, the geometric mean is the positive solution. Thus, $AD = 2\sqrt{6}$ or $AD \approx 4.90$. ■

An **extended ratio** compares more than two quantities and must be expressed in a form such as *a:b:c* or *d:e:f:g*. If you know that the angles of a triangle are 90°, 60°, and 30°, then the ratio that compares these measures is 90:60:30, or 3:2:1 (because 90, 60, and 30 have the greatest common factor of 30).

PROPERTY OF RATIOS

Unknown quantities in the ratio $a : b : c : d$ should be represented by ax, bx, cx, and dx.

EXAMPLE 6

Suppose that the perimeter of a quadrilateral is 70 and the lengths of the sides are in the ratio 2:3:4:5. Find the measure of each side.

Solution Let the lengths of the sides be represented by $2x$, $3x$, $4x$, and $5x$. Then

$$2x + 3x + 4x + 5x = 70$$
$$14x = 70$$
$$x = 5$$

Because $2x = 10$, $3x = 15$, $4x = 20$, and $5x = 25$, the lengths of the sides are 10, 15, 20, and 25. ■

It is possible to solve certain problems in more ways than one, as is illustrated in the next example. However, the solution is unique and is not altered by the method chosen.

EXAMPLE 7

The measures of two complementary angles are in the ratio 2 to 3. Find the measure of each angle.

Solution Let the first of the complementary angles have measure x; then the second has measure $90 - x$. Thus, we have

$$\frac{x}{90 - x} = \frac{2}{3}$$

Using the Means-Extremes Property, we have

$$\begin{aligned} 3x &= 2(90 - x) \\ 3x &= 180 - 2x \\ 5x &= 180 \\ x &= 36 \\ 90 - x &= 54 \end{aligned}$$

The angles have measures of 36° and 54°.

Alternative Solution Because the measures of the angles are in the ratio 2:3, let their measures be $2x$ and $3x$. Because the angles are complementary,

$$\begin{aligned} 2x + 3x &= 90 \\ 5x &= 90 \\ x &= 18 \end{aligned}$$

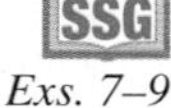

Exs. 7–9

Now $2x = 36$ and $3x = 54$, so the measures of the two angles are 36° and 54°. ■

The remaining properties of proportions are theorems. Because they are not cited as often as the Means-Extremes Property, they are not given titles. See Exercises 38 and 39.

STRATEGY FOR PROOF ▶ Proving Properties of Proportions

General Rule: To prove these theorems, apply the Means-Extremes Property as well as the Addition, Subtraction, Multiplication, and Division Properties of Equality.

Illustration: Proving the first part of Property 3 begins with the addition of 1 to each side of the proportion $\frac{a}{b} = \frac{c}{d}$.

PROPERTY 2

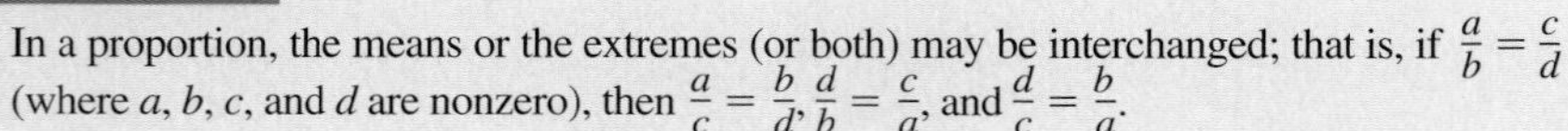

In a proportion, the means or the extremes (or both) may be interchanged; that is, if $\frac{a}{b} = \frac{c}{d}$ (where a, b, c, and d are nonzero), then $\frac{a}{c} = \frac{b}{d}$, $\frac{d}{b} = \frac{c}{a}$, and $\frac{d}{c} = \frac{b}{a}$.

When given the proportion $\frac{2}{3} = \frac{8}{12}$, Property 2 enables us to draw conclusions such as

1. $\frac{2}{8} = \frac{3}{12}$ (means interchanged)
2. $\frac{12}{3} = \frac{8}{2}$ (extremes interchanged)
3. $\frac{3}{2} = \frac{12}{8}$ (both sides inverted)

PROPERTY 3

If $\frac{a}{b} = \frac{c}{d}$ (where $b \neq 0$ and $d \neq 0$), then $\frac{a + b}{b} = \frac{c + d}{d}$ and $\frac{a - b}{b} = \frac{c - d}{d}$.

Given the proportion $\frac{2}{3} = \frac{8}{12}$, Property 3 enables us to draw conclusions such as

SSG
Exs. 10, 11

1. $\frac{2+3}{3} = \frac{8+12}{12}$ (**each side simplifies to $\frac{5}{3}$**)
2. $\frac{2-3}{3} = \frac{8-12}{12}$ (**each side simplifies to $-\frac{1}{3}$**)

Just as there are extended ratios, there are also **extended proportions,** such as

$$\frac{a}{b} = \frac{c}{d} = \frac{e}{f} = \cdots$$

Suggested by different numbers of servings of a particular recipe, the statement below is an extended proportion comparing numbers of eggs to numbers of cups of milk:

$$\frac{2\,\text{eggs}}{3\,\text{cups}} = \frac{4\,\text{eggs}}{6\,\text{cups}} = \frac{6\,\text{eggs}}{9\,\text{cups}}$$

EXAMPLE 8

In the triangles shown in Figure 5.2, $\frac{AB}{DE} = \frac{AC}{DF} = \frac{BC}{EF}$. Find the lengths of $\overline{DF}$ and $\overline{EF}$.

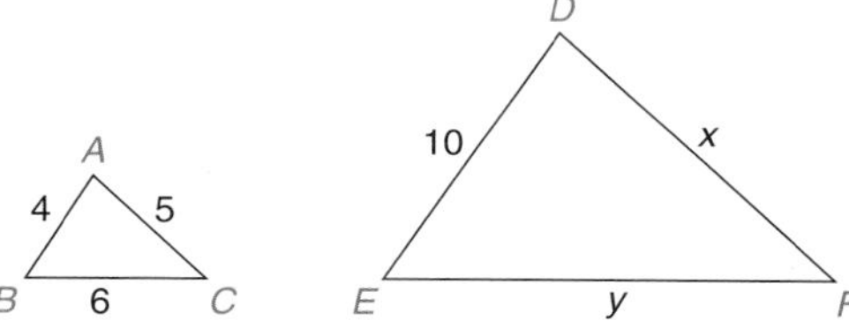

Figure 5.2

Solution Substituting into the proportion $\frac{AB}{DE} = \frac{AC}{DF} = \frac{BC}{EF}$, we have

$$\frac{4}{10} = \frac{5}{x} = \frac{6}{y}$$

From the equation

$$\frac{4}{10} = \frac{5}{x}$$

it follows that $4x = 50$ and that $x = DF = 12.5$. Using the equation

$$\frac{4}{10} = \frac{6}{y}$$

SSG
Exs. 12, 13

we find that $4y = 60$, so $y = EF = 15$. ■

Discover

THE GOLDEN RATIO

It is believed that the "ideal" rectangle is determined when a square can be removed in such a way as to leave a smaller rectangle with the same shape as the original rectangle. As we shall find, the rectangles are known as *similar* in shape. Upon removal of the square, the similarity in the shapes of the rectangles requires that $\frac{W}{L} = \frac{L - W}{W}$. To discover the relationship between L and W, we choose $W = 1$ and solve the equation $\frac{1}{L} = \frac{L - 1}{1}$ for L. The solution is $L = \frac{1 + \sqrt{5}}{2}$. The ratio comparing length to width is known as the *golden ratio*.

Because $L = \frac{1 + \sqrt{5}}{2}$ when $W = 1$ and $\frac{1 + \sqrt{5}}{2} \approx 1.62$, the *ideal* rectangle has a length that is approximately 1.62 times its width; that is, $L \approx 1.62W$.

Exercises 5.1

In Exercises 1 to 4, give the ratios in simplified form.

1. a) 12 to 15 b) 12 in. to 15 in. c) 1 ft to 18 in. d) 1 ft to 18 oz

2. a) 20 to 36 b) 24 oz to 52 oz c) 20 oz to 2 lb (1 lb = 16 oz) d) 2 lb to 20 oz

3. a) 15:24 b) 2 ft:2 yd (1 yd = 3 ft) c) 2 m:150 cm (1 m = 100 cm) d) 2 m:1 lb

4. a) 24:32 b) 12 in.:2 yd c) 150 cm:2 m d) 1 gal:24 mi

In Exercises 5 to 14, find the value of x in each proportion.

5. a) $\frac{x}{4} = \frac{9}{12}$ b) $\frac{7}{x} = \frac{21}{24}$

6. a) $\frac{x - 1}{10} = \frac{3}{5}$ b) $\frac{x + 1}{6} = \frac{10}{12}$

7. a) $\frac{x - 3}{8} = \frac{x + 3}{24}$ b) $\frac{x + 1}{6} = \frac{4x - 1}{18}$

8. a) $\frac{9}{x} = \frac{x}{16}$ b) $\frac{32}{x} = \frac{x}{2}$

9. a) $\frac{x}{4} = \frac{7}{x}$ b) $\frac{x}{6} = \frac{3}{x}$

10. a) $\frac{x + 1}{3} = \frac{10}{x + 2}$ b) $\frac{x - 2}{5} = \frac{12}{x + 2}$

11. a) $\frac{x + 1}{x} = \frac{10}{2x}$ b) $\frac{2x + 1}{x + 1} = \frac{14}{3x - 1}$

12. a) $\frac{x + 1}{2} = \frac{7}{x - 1}$ b) $\frac{x + 1}{3} = \frac{5}{x - 2}$

13. a) $\frac{x + 1}{x} = \frac{2x}{3}$ b) $\frac{x + 1}{x - 1} = \frac{2x}{5}$

14. a) $\frac{x + 1}{x} = \frac{x}{x - 1}$ b) $\frac{x + 2}{x} = \frac{2x}{x - 2}$

15. Sarah ran the 300-m hurdles in 47.7 sec. In meters per second, find the rate at which Sarah ran. Give the answer to the nearest tenth of a meter per second.

16. Fran has been hired to sew the dance troupe's dresses for the school musical. If $13\frac{1}{3}$ yd of material is needed for the four dresses, find the rate that describes the amount of material needed for each dress.

In Exercises 17 to 22, use proportions to solve each problem.

17. A recipe calls for 4 eggs and 3 cups of milk. To prepare for a larger number of guests, a cook uses 14 eggs. How many cups of milk are needed?

18. If a school secretary copies 168 worksheets for a class of 28 students, how many worksheets must be prepared for a class of 32 students?

19. An electrician installs 20 electrical outlets in a new six-room house. Assuming proportionality, how many outlets should be installed in a new construction having seven rooms? (Round up to an integer.)

20. The secretarial pool (15 secretaries in all) on one floor of a corporate complex has access to four copy machines. If there are 23 secretaries on a different floor, approximately what number of copy machines should be available? (Assume a proportionality.)

21. Assume that AD is the geometric mean of BD and DC in $\triangle ABC$ shown in the accompanying drawing.
a) Find AD if $BD = 6$ and $DC = 8$.
b) Find BD if $AD = 6$ and $DC = 8$.

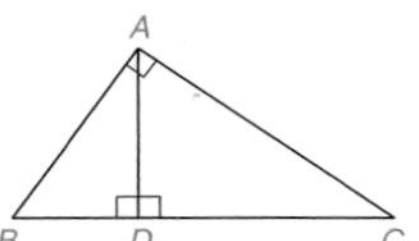

Exercises 21, 22

22. In the drawing for Exercise 21, assume that AB is the geometric mean of BD and BC.
   a) Find AB if $BD = 6$ and $DC = 10$.
   b) Find DC if $AB = 10$ and $BC = 15$.

23. The salaries of a secretary, a salesperson, and a vice president for a retail sales company are in the ratio 2:3:5. If their combined annual salaries amount to $124,500, what is the annual salary of each?

24. If the measures of the angles of a quadrilateral are in the ratio of 2:3:4:6, find the measure of each angle.

25. The measures of two complementary angles are in the ratio 4:5. Find the measure of each angle, using the two methods shown in Example 7.

26. The measures of two supplementary angles are in the ratio of 2:7. Find the measure of each angle, using the two methods of Example 7.

27. If 1 in. equals 2.54 cm, use a proportion to convert 12 in. to centimeters.
   (*HINT:* $\frac{2.54 \text{ cm}}{1 \text{ in.}} = \frac{x \text{ cm}}{12 \text{ in.}}$)

28. If 1 kg equals 2.2 lb, use a proportion to convert 12 pounds to kilograms.

29. For the quadrilaterals shown, $\frac{MN}{WX} = \frac{NP}{XY} = \frac{PQ}{YZ} = \frac{MQ}{WZ}$. If $MN = 7$, $WX = 3$, and $PQ = 6$, find YZ.

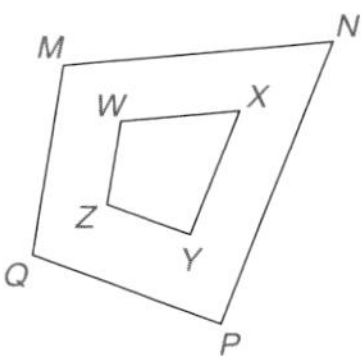

Exercises 29, 30

30. For this exercise, use the drawing and extended ratio of Exercise 29. If $NP = 2 \cdot XY$ and $WZ = 3\frac{1}{2}$, find MQ.

31. Two numbers a and b are in the ratio 3:4. If the first number is decreased by 2 and the second is decreased by 1, they are in the ratio 2:3. Find a and b.

32. Two numbers a and b are in the ratio 2:3. If both numbers are decreased by 2, the ratio of the resulting numbers becomes 3:5. Find a and b.

33. If the ratio of the measure of the complement of an angle to the measure of its supplement is 1:3, find the measure of the angle.

34. If the ratio of the measure of the complement of an angle to the measure of its supplement is 1:4, find the measure of the angle.

35. On a blueprint, a 1-in. scale corresponds to 3 ft. To show a room with actual dimensions 12 ft wide by 14 ft long, what dimensions should be shown on the blueprint?

36. To find the golden ratio (see the Discover activity on page 226), solve the equation $\frac{1}{L} = \frac{L-1}{1}$ for L.
   (*HINT: You will need the Quadratic Formula.*)

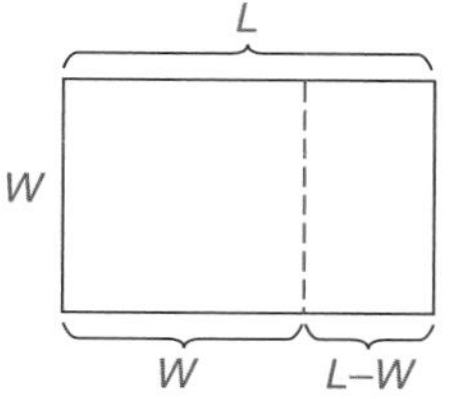

37. Find:
   a) The exact length of an ideal rectangle with width $W = 5$ by solving $\frac{5}{L} = \frac{L-5}{5}$
   b) The approximate length of an ideal rectangle with width $W = 5$ by using $L \approx 1.62W$

38. *Prove:* If $\frac{a}{b} = \frac{c}{d}$ (where a, b, c, and d are nonzero), then $\frac{a}{c} = \frac{b}{d}$.

39. *Prove:* If $\frac{a}{b} = \frac{c}{d}$ (where $b \neq 0$ and $d \neq 0$), then $\frac{a+b}{b} = \frac{c+d}{d}$.

5.2 Similar Polygons

KEY CONCEPTS

Similar Polygons
Congruent Polygons
Corresponding Vertices, Angles, and Sides

When two geometric figures have exactly the same shape, they are **similar;** the symbol for "is similar to" is $\sim$. When two figures have the same shape ($\sim$) and all corresponding parts have equal ($=$) measures, the two figures are **congruent** ($\cong$). Note that the symbol for congruence combines the symbols for similarity and equality. In fact, we include the following property for emphasis.

Two congruent polygons are also similar polygons.

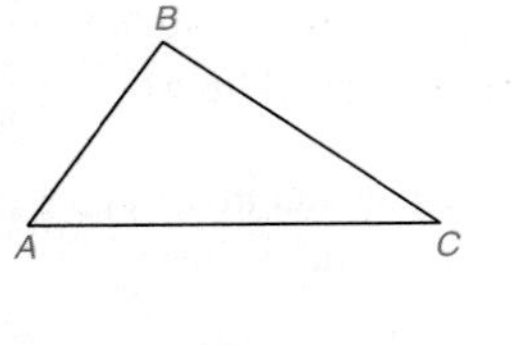

(a)

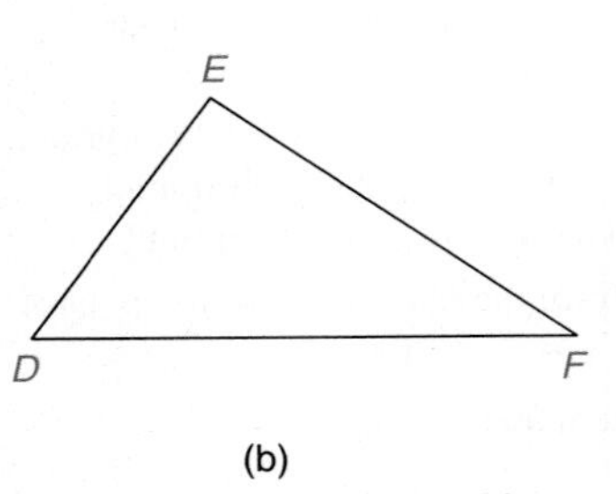

(b)

Figure 5.3

Two-dimensional figures such as $\triangle ABC$ and $\triangle DEF$ in Figure 5.3 can be similar, but it is also possible for three-dimensional figures to be similar. Similar orange juice containers are shown in Figures 5.4(a) and 5.4(b). Informally, two figures are "similar" if one is an enlargement of the other. Thus a tuna fish can and an orange juice can are *not* similar, even if both are right-circular cylinders [see Figures 5.4(b) and 5.4(c)]. We will consider cylinders in greater detail in Chapter 9.

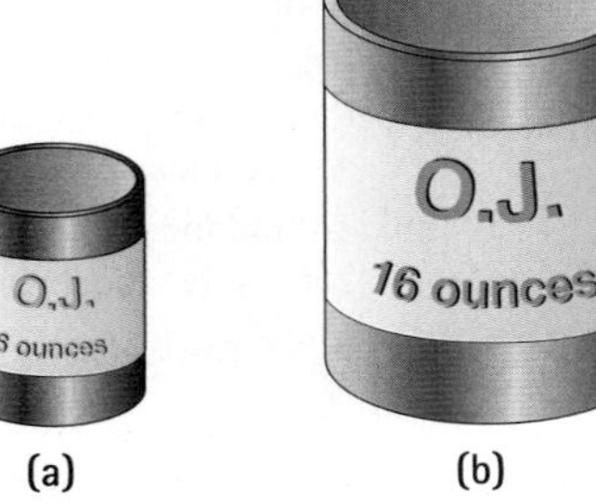

(a) (b) (c)

Figure 5.4

Our discussion of similarity will generally be limited to plane figures.

For two polygons to be similar, it is necessary that each angle of one polygon be congruent to the corresponding angle of the other. However, the congruence of angles is not sufficient to establish the similarity of polygons. The vertices of the congruent angles are **corresponding vertices** of the similar polygons. If $\angle A$ in one polygon is congruent to $\angle M$ in the second polygon, then vertex A corresponds to vertex M, and this is symbolized $A \leftrightarrow M$; we can indicate that $\angle A$ corresponds to $\angle M$ by writing $\angle A \leftrightarrow \angle M$. A pair of angles like $\angle A$ and $\angle M$ are **corresponding angles,** and the sides determined by consecutive and corresponding vertices are **corresponding sides** of the similar polygons. For instance, if $A \leftrightarrow M$ and $B \leftrightarrow N$, then $\overline{AB}$ corresponds to $\overline{MN}$.

Discover

When a transparency is projected onto a screen, the image created is similar to the projected figure.

EXAMPLE 1

Given similar quadrilaterals *ABCD* and *HJKL* with congruent angles as indicated in Figure 5.5, name the vertices, angles, and sides that correspond to each other.

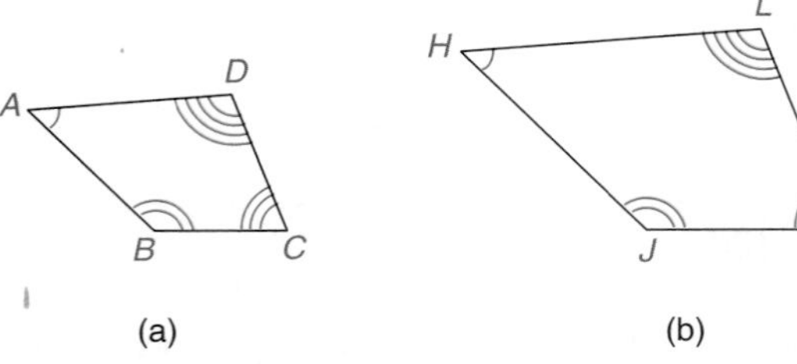

Figure 5.5

Solution Because $\angle A \cong \angle H$, it follows that

$$A \leftrightarrow H \quad \text{and} \quad \angle A \leftrightarrow \angle H$$

Similarly,

$$B \leftrightarrow J \quad \text{and} \quad \angle B \leftrightarrow \angle J$$
$$C \leftrightarrow K \quad \text{and} \quad \angle C \leftrightarrow \angle K$$
$$D \leftrightarrow L \quad \text{and} \quad \angle D \leftrightarrow \angle L$$

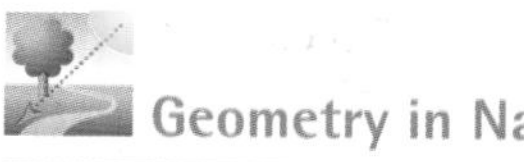

The segments of the chambered nautilus are similar (not congruent) in shape.

When pairs of consecutive and corresponding vertices are associated, the corresponding sides are included between the corresponding angles (or vertices).

$$\overline{AB} \leftrightarrow \overline{HJ}, \quad \overline{BC} \leftrightarrow \overline{JK}, \quad \overline{CD} \leftrightarrow \overline{KL}, \quad \text{and} \quad \overline{AD} \leftrightarrow \overline{HL}$$ ■

With an understanding of corresponding angles and corresponding sides, we can define similar polygons.

DEFINITION

Two polygons are **similar** if and only if two conditions are satisfied:

1. All pairs of corresponding angles are congruent.
2. All pairs of corresponding sides are proportional.

The second condition for similarity requires that the following extended proportion exists for the sides of the similar quadrilaterals of Example 1.

$$\frac{AB}{HJ} = \frac{BC}{JK} = \frac{CD}{KL} = \frac{AD}{HL}$$

Note that *both* conditions for similarity are necessary! Although condition 1 is satisfied for square *EFGH* and rectangle *RSTU* [see Figures 5.6(a) and (b)], the figures are not similar—that is, one is not an enlargement of the other—because the extended proportion is not true. On the other hand, condition 2 is satisfied for square *EFGH* and rhombus *WXYZ* [see Figures 5.6(a) and 5.6(c)], but the figures are not similar because the pairs of corresponding angles are not congruent.

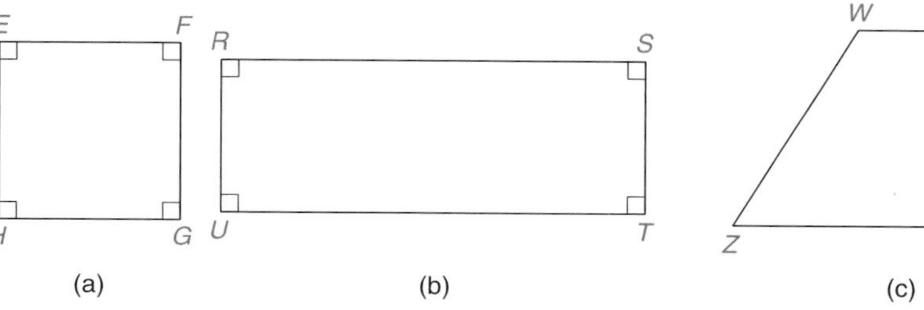

Figure 5.6

EXAMPLE 2

Which figures must be similar?

a) Any two isosceles triangles
b) Any two regular pentagons
c) Any two rectangles
d) Any two squares

Solution

a) No; ∠ pairs need not be ≅, nor do the pairs of sides need to be proportional.
b) Yes; all angles are congruent (measure 108° each), and all pairs of sides are proportional.
c) No; all angles measure 90°, but the pairs of sides are not necessarily proportional.
d) Yes; all angles measure 90°, and all pairs of sides are proportional. ■

SSG *Exs. 1–4*

It is common practice to name the corresponding vertices of similar polygons in the same order. For instance, if pentagon $ABCDE$ is similar to pentagon $MNPQR$, then we know that $A \leftrightarrow M$, $B \leftrightarrow N$, $C \leftrightarrow P$, $D \leftrightarrow Q$, $E \leftrightarrow R$, $\angle A \cong \angle M$, $\angle B \cong \angle N$, $\angle C \cong \angle P$, $\angle D \cong \angle Q$, and $\angle E \cong \angle R$. Because of the indicated correspondence of vertices, we also know that

$$\frac{AB}{MN} = \frac{BC}{NP} = \frac{CD}{PQ} = \frac{DE}{QR} = \frac{EA}{RM}$$

EXAMPLE 3

If $\triangle ABC \sim \triangle DEF$ in Figure 5.7, use the indicated measures to find the measures of the remaining parts of each of the triangles.

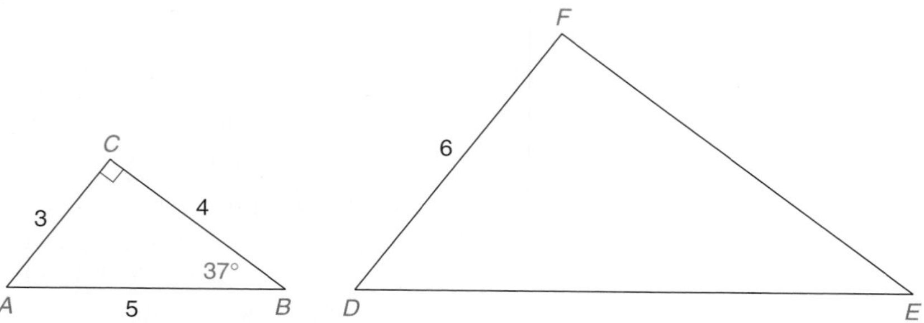

Figure 5.7

Solution Because the sum of the measures of the angles of a triangle is 180°,

$$m\angle A = 180 - (90 + 37) = 53°$$

And because of the similarity and the correspondence of vertices,

$$m\angle D = 53°, \quad m\angle E = 37°, \quad \text{and} \quad m\angle F = 90°$$

The proportion that relates the lengths of the sides is

$$\frac{AC}{DF} = \frac{CB}{FE} = \frac{AB}{DE} \quad \text{so} \quad \frac{3}{6} = \frac{4}{FE} = \frac{5}{DE}$$

From $\frac{3}{6} = \frac{4}{FE}$, we see that $3 \cdot FE = 6 \cdot 4$ so that $3 \cdot FE = 24$
$FE = 8$

From $\frac{3}{6} = \frac{5}{DE}$, we see that $3 \cdot DE = 6 \cdot 5$ so that $3 \cdot DE = 30$
$DE = 10$ ■

In a proportion, the ratios can all be inverted; thus, Example 3 could have been solved by using the proportion

$$\frac{DF}{AC} = \frac{FE}{CB} = \frac{DE}{AB}$$

In an extended proportion, the ratios must all be equal to the same constant value. By designating this number (which is often called the "constant of proportionality") by k, we see that

$$\frac{DF}{AC} = k, \quad \frac{FE}{CB} = k, \text{ and } \quad \frac{DE}{AB} = k$$

SSG Exs. 5–10

It follows that $DF = k \cdot AC$, $FE = k \cdot CB$, and $DE = k \cdot AB$. In Example 3, this constant of proportionality had the value $k = 2$, which means that the length of each side of the larger triangle was twice the length of the corresponding side of the smaller triangle.

If $k > 1$, the similarity leads to an enlargement, or *stretch*. If $0 < k < 1$, the similarity results in a *shrink*.

The constant of proportionality is also used to *scale* a map, a diagram, or a blueprint. As a consequence, scaling problems can be solved by using proportions.

EXAMPLE 4

On a map, a length of 1 in. represents a distance of 30 mi. On the map, how far apart should two cities appear if they are actually 140 mi apart along a straight line?

Solution Where $x =$ the map distance desired (in inches),

$$\frac{1}{30} = \frac{x}{140}$$

Then $30x = 140$ and $x = 4\frac{2}{3}$ in. ■

EXAMPLE 5

In Figure 5.8, $\triangle ABC \sim \triangle ADE$ with $\angle ADE \cong \angle B$. If $DE = 3$, $AC = 16$, and $EC = BC$, find the length BC.

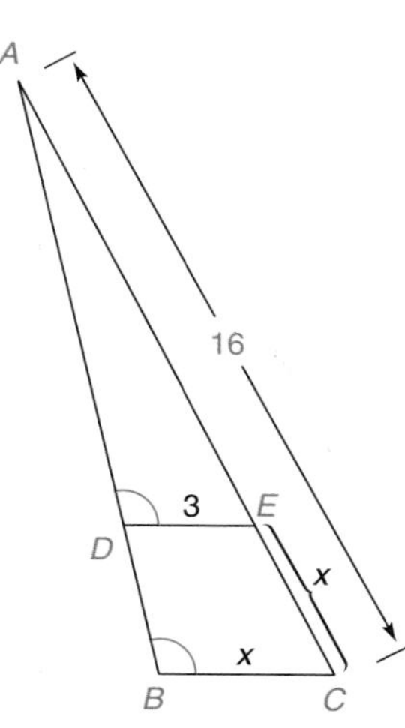

Figure 5.8

Solution From the similar triangles, we have $\frac{DE}{BC} = \frac{AE}{AC}$. With $AC = AE + EC$ and representing the lengths of the congruent segments ($\overline{EC}$ and $\overline{BC}$) by x, we have

$$16 = AE + x \quad \text{so} \quad AE = 16 - x$$

Substituting into the proportion, we have

$$\frac{3}{x} = \frac{16 - x}{16}$$

It follows that

$$\begin{aligned} x(16 - x) &= 3 \cdot 16 \\ 16x - x^2 &= 48 \\ x^2 - 16x + 48 &= 0 \\ (x - 4)(x - 12) &= 0 \end{aligned}$$

Now x (or BC) equals 4 or 12. Each length is acceptable, but the scaled drawings differ, as illustrated in Figure 5.9 on next page.

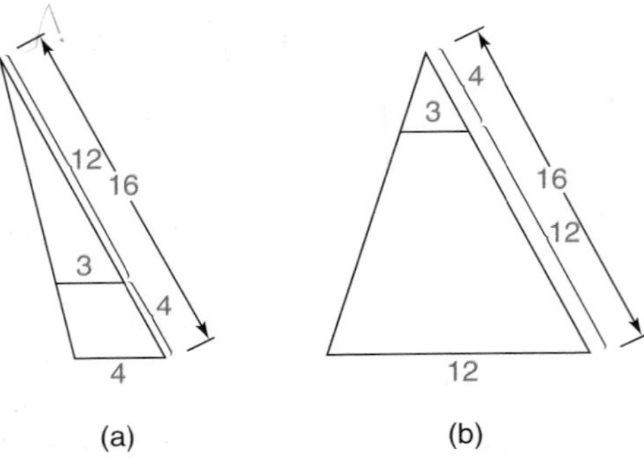

Figure 5.9

The following example uses a method called *shadow reckoning.* This method of calculating a length dates back more than 2500 years when it was used by the Greek mathematician, Thales, to estimate the height of the pyramids in Egypt. In Figure 5.10, the method assumes (correctly) that $\triangle ABC \sim \triangle DEF$. Note that $\angle A \cong \angle D$ and $\angle C \cong \angle F$.

EXAMPLE 6

Darnell is curious about the height of a flagpole that stands in front of his school. Darnell, who is 6 ft tall, casts a shadow that he paces off at 9 ft. He walks the length of the shadow of the flagpole, a distance of 30 ft. How tall is the flagpole?

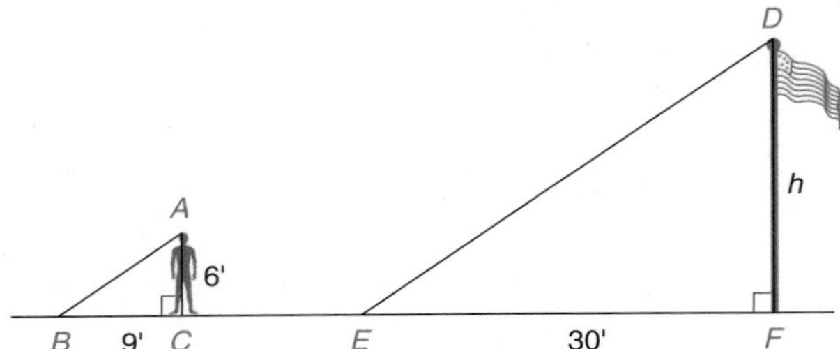

Figure 5.10

Solution In Figure 5.10, $\triangle ABC \sim \triangle DEF$. From similar triangles, we know that $\frac{AC}{DF} = \frac{BC}{EF}$ or $\frac{AC}{BC} = \frac{DF}{EF}$ by interchanging the means.

Where h is the height of the flagpole, substitution into the second proportion leads to

$$\frac{6}{9} = \frac{h}{30} \rightarrow 9h = 180 \rightarrow h = 20$$

SSG Exs. 11–13

The height of the flagpole is 20 ft. ■

Exercises 5.2

1. a) What is true of any pair of corresponding angles of two similar polygons?
   b) What is true of any pairs of corresponding sides of two similar polygons?
2. a) Are any two quadrilaterals similar?
   b) Are any two squares similar?
3. a) Are any two regular pentagons similar?
   b) Are any two equiangular pentagons similar?
4. a) Are any two equilateral hexagons similar?
   b) Are any two regular hexagons similar?

In Exercises 5 and 6, refer to the drawing.

5. a) Given that $A \leftrightarrow X$, $B \leftrightarrow T$, and $C \leftrightarrow N$, write a statement claiming that the triangles shown are similar.
b) Given that $A \leftrightarrow N$, $C \leftrightarrow X$, and $B \leftrightarrow T$, write a statement claiming that the triangles shown are similar.

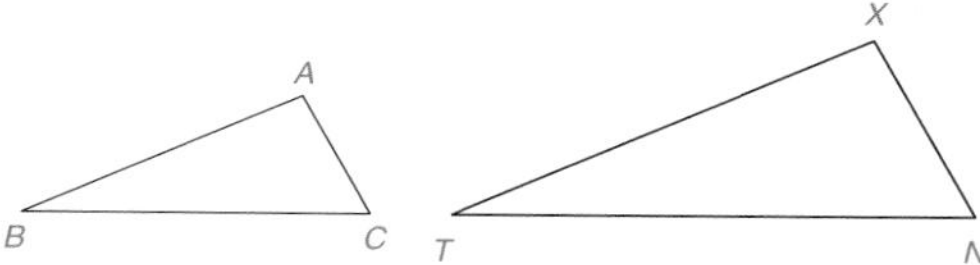

Exercises 5, 6

6. a) If $\triangle ABC \sim \triangle XTN$, which angle of $\triangle ABC$ corresponds to $\angle N$ of $\triangle XTN$?
b) If $\triangle ABC \sim \triangle XTN$, which side of $\triangle XTN$ corresponds to side $\overline{AC}$ of $\triangle ABC$?

7. A **sphere** is the three-dimensional surface that contains all points in space lying at a fixed distance from a point known as the center of the sphere. Consider the two spheres shown. Are these two spheres similar? Are any two spheres similar? Explain.

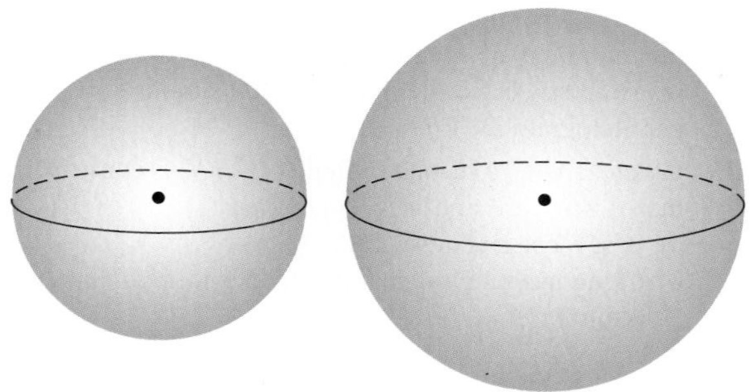

8. Given that rectangle $ABCE$ is similar to rectangle $MNPR$ and that $\triangle CDE \sim \triangle PQR$, what can you conclude regarding pentagon $ABCDE$ and pentagon $MNPQR$?

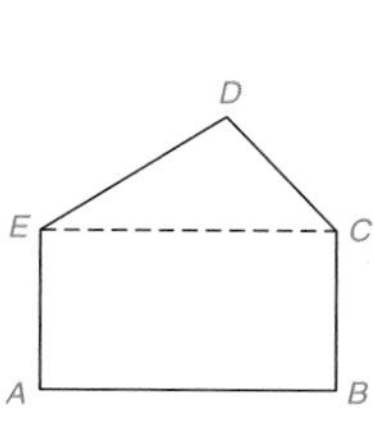

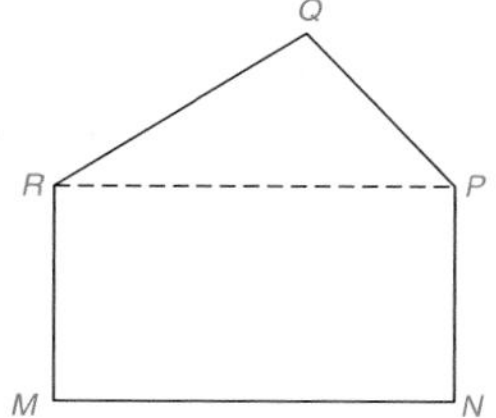

9. *Given:* $\triangle MNP \sim \triangle QRS$, $m\angle M = 56°$, $m\angle R = 82°$, $MN = 9$, $QR = 6$, $RS = 7$, $MP = 12$
Find: a) $m\angle N$ c) NP
b) $m\angle P$ d) QS

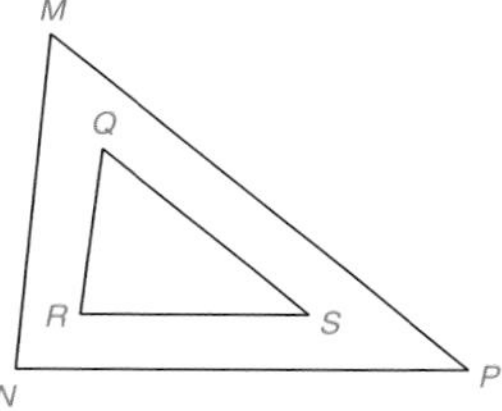

10. *Given:* $\triangle ABC \sim \triangle PRC$, $m\angle A = 67°$, $PC = 5$, $CR = 12$, $PR = 13$, $AB = 26$
Find: a) $m\angle B$
b) $m\angle RPC$
c) AC
d) CB

11. a) Does the similarity relationship have a **reflexive** property for triangles (and polygons in general)?
b) Is there a **symmetric** property for the similarity of triangles (and polygons)?
c) Is there a **transitive** property for the similarity of triangles (and polygons)?

12. Using the names of properties from Exercise 11, identify the property illustrated by each statement:
a) If $\triangle 1 \sim \triangle 2$, then $\triangle 2 \sim \triangle 1$.
b) If $\triangle 1 \sim \triangle 2$, $\triangle 2 \sim \triangle 3$, and $\triangle 3 \sim \triangle 4$, then $\triangle 1 \sim \triangle 4$.
c) $\triangle 1 \sim \triangle 1$

13. In the drawing, $\triangle HJK \sim \triangle FGK$. If $HK = 6$, $KF = 8$, and $HJ = 4$, find FG.

14. In the drawing, $\triangle HJK \sim \triangle FGK$. If $HK = 6$, $KF = 8$, and $FG = 5$, find HJ.

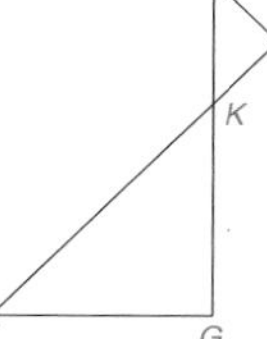

Exercises 13, 14

15. Quadrilateral $ABCD \sim$ quadrilateral $HJKL$. If $m\angle A = 55°$, $m\angle J = 128°$, and $m\angle D = 98°$, find $m\angle K$.

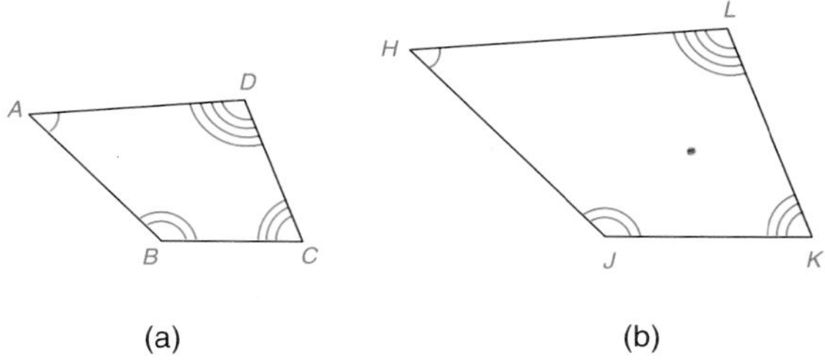

Exercises 15–20

16. Quadrilateral $ABCD \sim$ quadrilateral $HJKL$. If $m\angle A = x$, $m\angle J = x + 50$, $m\angle D = x + 35$, and $m\angle K = 2x - 45$, find x.

17. Quadrilateral $ABCD \sim$ quadrilateral $HJKL$. If $AB = 5$, $BC = n$, $HJ = 10$, and $JK = n + 3$, find n.

18. Quadrilateral $ABCD \sim$ quadrilateral $HJKL$. If $m\angle D = 90°$, $AD = 8$, $DC = 6$, and $HL = 12$, find the length of diagonal $\overline{HK}$ (not shown).

19. Quadrilateral $ABCD \sim$ quadrilateral $HJKL$. If $m\angle A = 2x + 4$, $m\angle H = 68°$, and $m\angle D = 3x - 6$, find $m\angle L$.

20. Quadrilateral $ABCD \sim$ quadrilateral $HJKL$. If $m\angle A = m\angle K = 70°$, and $m\angle B = 110°$, what types of quadrilaterals are $ABCD$ and $HJKL$?

In Exercises 21 to 24, $\triangle ADE \sim \triangle ABC$.

21. *Given:* $DE = 4, AE = 6, EC = BC$
Find: BC

22. *Given:* $DE = 5, AD = 8, DB = BC$
Find: AB

(HINT: Find DB first.)

23. *Given:* $DE = 4, AC = 20,$
$EC = BC$
Find: BC

24. *Given:* $AD = 4, AC = 18,$
$DB = AE$
Find: AE

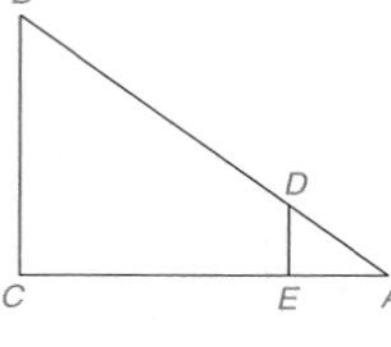

Exercises 21–24

25. Pentagon $ABCDE \sim$ pentagon $GHJKL$ (not shown), $AB = 6$, and $GH = 9$. If the perimeter of $ABCDE$ is 50, find the perimeter of $GHJKL$.

26. Quadrilateral $MNPQ \sim$ quadrilateral $WXYZ$ (not shown), $PQ = 5$, and $YZ = 7$. If the longest side of $MNPQ$ is of length 8, find the length of the longest side of $WXYZ$.

27. A blueprint represents the 72-ft length of a building by a line segment of length 6 in. What length on the blueprint would be used to represent the height of this 30-ft-tall building?

28. A technical drawing shows the $3\frac{1}{2}$-ft lengths of the legs of a baby's swing by line segments 3 in. long. If the diagram should indicate the legs are $2\frac{1}{2}$ ft apart at the base, what length represents this distance on the diagram?

In Exercises 29 to 32, use the fact that triangles are similar.

29. A person who is walking away from a 10-ft lamppost casts a shadow 6 ft long. If the person is at a distance of 10 ft from the lamppost at that moment, what is the person's height?

30. With 100 ft of string out, a kite is 64 ft above ground level. When the girl flying the kite pulls in 40 ft of string, the angle formed by the string and the ground does not change. What is the height of the kite above the ground after the 40 ft of string have been taken in?

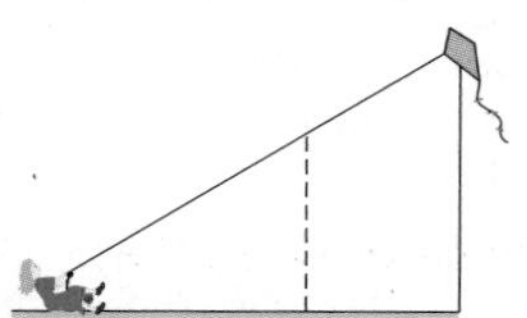

31. While admiring a rather tall tree, Fred notes that the shadow of his 6-ft frame has a length of 3 paces. On the level ground, he walks off the complete shadow of the tree in 37 paces. How tall is the tree?

32. As a garage door closes, light is cast 6 ft beyond the base of the door (as shown in the accompanying drawing) by a light fixture that is set in the garage ceiling 10 ft back from the door. If the ceiling of the garage is 10 ft above the floor, how far is the garage door above the floor at the time that light is cast 6 ft beyond the door?

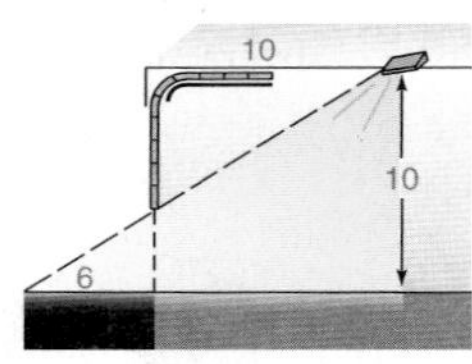

33. In the drawing, $\overleftrightarrow{AB} \parallel \overleftrightarrow{DC} \parallel \overleftrightarrow{EF}$ with transversals ℓ and m. If D and C are the midpoints of $\overline{AE}$ and $\overline{BF}$, respectively, then is trapezoid $ABCD$ similar to trapezoid $DCFE$?

34. In the drawing, $\overleftrightarrow{AB} \parallel \overleftrightarrow{DC} \parallel \overleftrightarrow{EF}$. Suppose that transversals ℓ and m are also parallel. D and C are the midpoints of $\overline{AE}$ and $\overline{BF}$, respectively. Is parallelogram $ABCD$ similar to parallelogram $DCFE$?

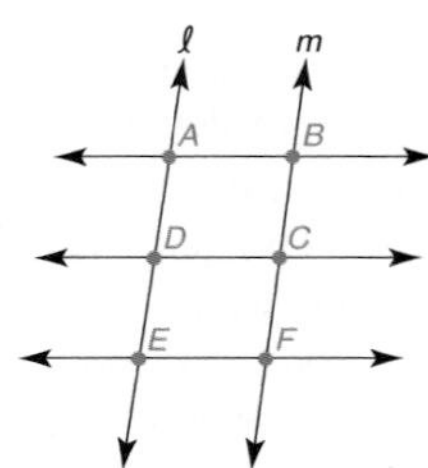

Exercises 33, 34

35. Given $\triangle ABC$, a second triangle ($\triangle XTN$) is constructed so that $\angle X \cong \angle A$ and $\angle N \cong \angle C$.
a) Is $\angle T$ congruent to $\angle B$?
b) Using intuition (appearance), does it seem that $\triangle XTN$ is similar to $\triangle ABC$?

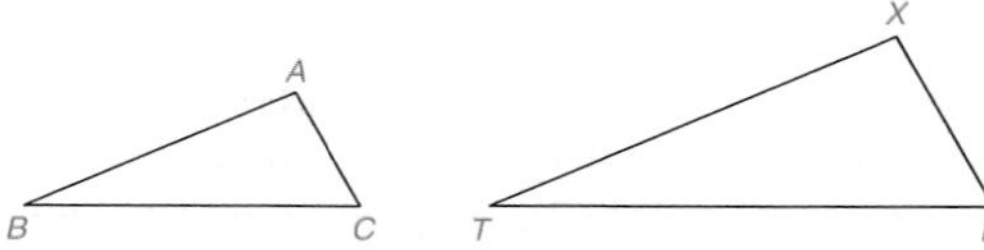

36. Given $\triangle RST$, a second triangle ($\triangle UVW$) is constructed so that $UV = 2(RS)$, $VW = 2(ST)$, and $WU = 2(RT)$.
a) What is the constant value of the ratios $\frac{UV}{RS}$, $\frac{VW}{ST}$, and $\frac{WU}{RT}$?
b) Using intuition (appearance), does it seem that $\triangle UVW$ is similar to $\triangle RST$?

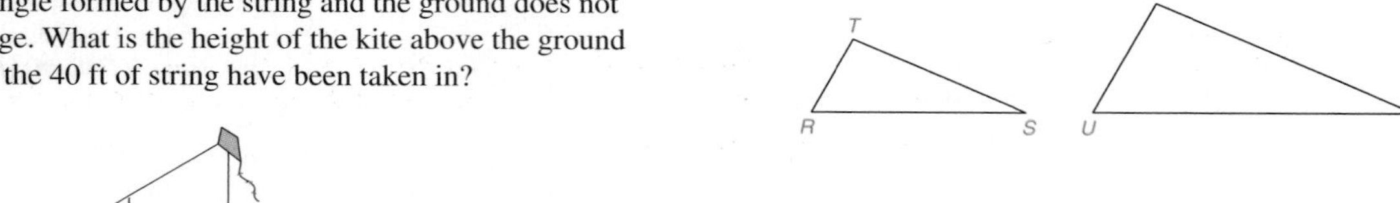

For Exercises 37 and 38, use intuition to form a proportion based on the drawing shown.

***37.** $\triangle ABC$ has an inscribed rhombus $ARST$. If $AB = 10$ and $AC = 6$, find the length x of each side of the rhombus.

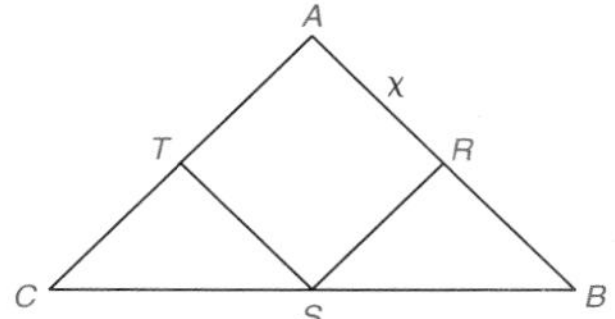

***38.** A square with sides of length 2 in. rests (as shown) on a square with sides of length 6 in. Find the perimeter of trapezoid $ABCD$.

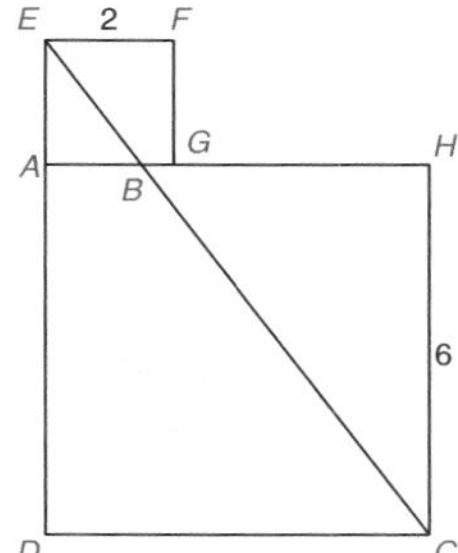

5.3 Proving Triangles Similar

▶▶▶ KEY CONCEPTS

AAA	CSSTP	SAS ~
AA	CASTC	SSS ~

Because of the difficulty of establishing proportional sides, our definition of similar polygons (and therefore of similar triangles) is almost impossible to use as a method of proof. Fortunately, some easier methods are available for proving triangles similar. If two triangles are carefully sketched or constructed so that their angles are congruent, they will appear to be similar, as shown in Figure 5.11.

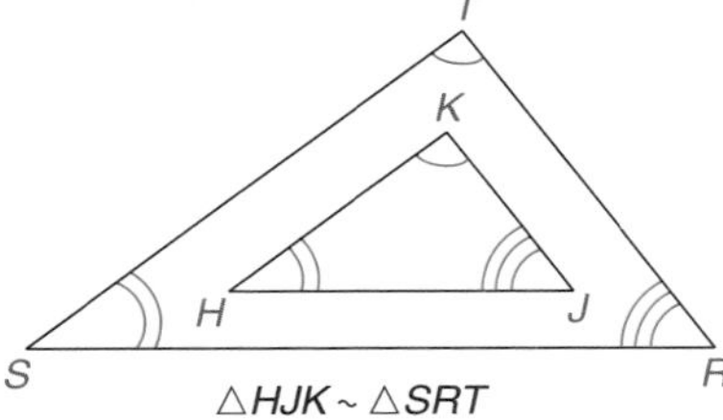

Figure 5.11

Technology Exploration

Use a calculator if available. On a sheet of paper, draw two similar triangles, $\triangle ABC$ and $\triangle DEF$. To accomplish this, use your protractor to form three pairs of congruent corresponding angles. Using a ruler, measure $\overline{AB}$, $\overline{BC}$, $\overline{AC}$, $\overline{DE}$, $\overline{EF}$, and $\overline{DF}$. Show that $\frac{AB}{DE} = \frac{BC}{EF} = \frac{AC}{DF}$.

NOTE: Answers are not "perfect."

POSTULATE 15

If the three angles of one triangle are congruent to the three angles of a second triangle, then the triangles are similar (AAA).

Corollary 5.3.1 of Postulate 15 follows from knowing that if two angles of one triangle are congruent to two angles of another triangle, then the third angles *must* also be congruent. See Corollary 2.4.4.

COROLLARY 5.3.1

If two angles of one triangle are congruent to two angles of another triangle, then the triangles are similar (AA).

Rather than use AAA to prove triangles similar, we will use AA instead because it requires fewer steps.

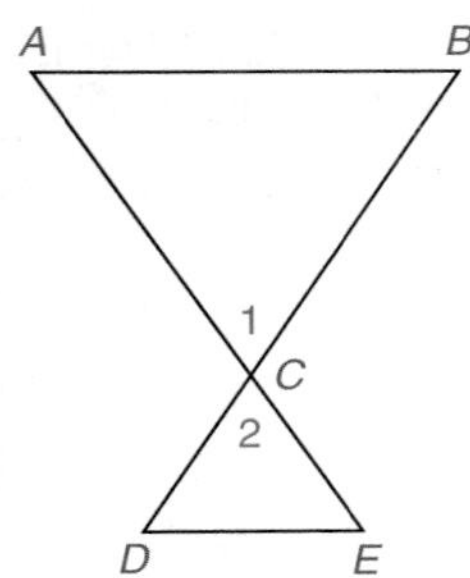

Figure 5.12

EXAMPLE 1

Provide a two-column proof of the following problem.

GIVEN: $\overline{AB} \parallel \overline{DE}$ in Figure 5.12

PROVE: $\triangle ABC \sim \triangle EDC$

PROOF

Statements	Reasons
1. $\overline{AB} \parallel \overline{DE}$	1. Given
2. $\angle A \cong \angle E$	2. If two $\parallel$ lines are cut by a transversal, the alternate interior angles are $\cong$
3. $\angle 1 \cong \angle 2$	3. Vertical angles are $\cong$
4. $\triangle ABC \sim \triangle EDC$	4. AA

■

STRATEGY FOR PROOF ▶ Proving That Two Triangles Are Similar

General Rule: Although there *will be* three methods of proof (AA, SAS~, and SSS~) for similar triangles, we use AA whenever possible. This leads to a more efficient proof.

Illustration: See lines 1 and 2 in the proof of Example 2. Notice that line 3 follows by the reason AA.

In some instances, we wish to prove a relationship that takes us beyond the similarity of triangles. The following consequences of the definition of similarity are often cited as reasons in a proof. The first fact, abbreviated CSSTP, is used in Example 2. Although the CSSTP statement involves triangles, the corresponding sides of *any* two similar polygons are proportional. That is, the ratio of any pair of corresponding sides equals the ratio of another pair of corresponding sides. The second fact, abbreviated CASTC, is used in Example 4.

Exs. 1–4

CSSTP

Corresponding sides of similar triangles are proportional.

CASTC

Corresponding angles of similar triangles are congruent.

STRATEGY FOR PROOF ▶ Proving a Proportion

General Rule: First prove that triangles are similar. Then apply CSSTP.

Illustration: See statements 3 and 4 of Example 2.

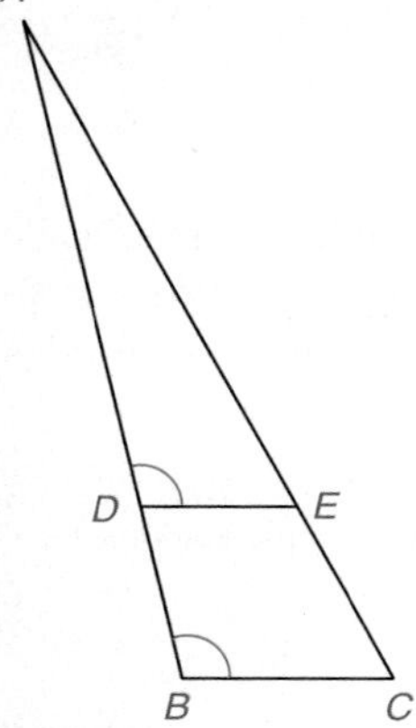

Figure 5.13

EXAMPLE 2

Complete the following two-column proof.

GIVEN: $\angle ADE \cong \angle B$ in Figure 5.13

PROVE: $\dfrac{DE}{BC} = \dfrac{AE}{AC}$

PROOF

Statements	Reasons
1. $\angle ADE \cong \angle B$	1. Given
2. $\angle A \cong \angle A$	2. Identity
3. $\triangle ADE \sim \triangle ABC$	3. AA
4. $\frac{DE}{BC} = \frac{AE}{AC}$	4. CSSTP

NOTE: In this proof, DE appears above BC because the sides with these names lie opposite $\angle A$ in the two similar triangles. AE and AC are the lengths of the sides opposite the congruent and corresponding angles $\angle ADE$ and $\angle B$. That is, corresponding sides of similar triangles always lie opposite corresponding angles. ■

THEOREM 5.3.2

The lengths of the corresponding altitudes of similar triangles have the same ratio as the lengths of any pair of corresponding sides.

The proof of this theorem is left to the student; see Exercise 33. Note that this proof also requires the use of CSSTP.

STRATEGY FOR PROOF ▶ Proving Products of Lengths Equal

General Rule: First prove that two triangles are similar. Then form a proportion involving the lengths of corresponding sides. Finally, apply the Means-Extremes Property.
Illustration: See the following proof and Example 3 (an alternative form of the proof).

The paragraph style of proof is generally used in upper-level mathematics classes. These paragraph proofs are no more than modified two-column proofs. Compare the following two-column proof to the paragraph proof found in Example 3.

GIVEN: $\angle M \cong \angle Q$ in Figure 5.14
PROVE: $NP \cdot QR = RP \cdot MN$

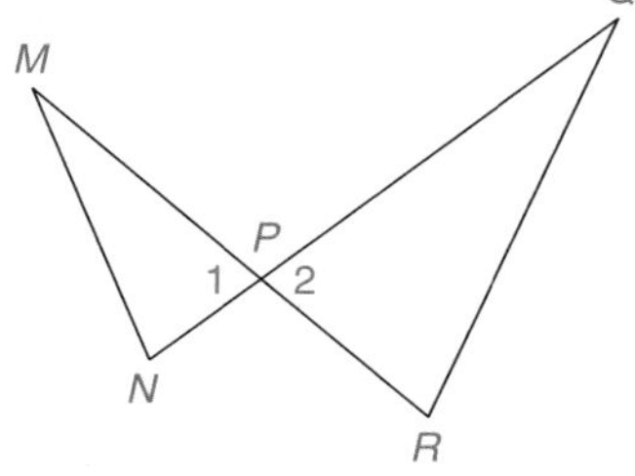

Figure 5.14

PROOF

Statements	Reasons
1. $\angle M \cong \angle Q$	1. Given (hypothesis)
2. $\angle 1 \cong \angle 2$	2. Vertical angles are $\cong$
3. $\triangle MPN \sim \triangle QPR$	3. AA
4. $\frac{NP}{RP} = \frac{MN}{QR}$	4. CSSTP
5. $NP \cdot QR = RP \cdot MN$	5. Means-Extremes Property

EXAMPLE 3

Use a paragraph proof to complete this problem.

GIVEN: $\angle M \cong \angle Q$ in Figure 5.14
PROVE: $NP \cdot QR = RP \cdot MN$

PROOF: By hypothesis, $\angle M \cong \angle Q$. Also, $\angle 1 \cong \angle 2$ by the fact that vertical angles are congruent. Now $\triangle MPN \sim \triangle QPR$ by AA. Using CSSTP, $\frac{NP}{RP} = \frac{MN}{QR}$. Then $NP \cdot QR = RP \cdot MN$ by the Means-Extremes Property.

Exs. 5–7

NOTE: In the proof, the sides selected for the proportion were carefully chosen. The statement to be proved suggested that we include *NP, QR, RP,* and *MN* in the proportion. ■

In addition to AA, there are other methods that can be used to establish similar triangles. To distinguish the following techniques for showing triangles similar from methods for proving triangles congruent, we use SAS~ and SSS~ to identify the similarity theorems. We prove SAS~ in Example 6 and prove SSS~ at our website.

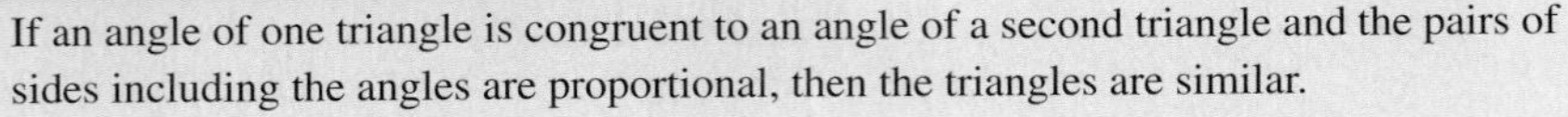

THEOREM 5.3.3 (SAS~)

If an angle of one triangle is congruent to an angle of a second triangle and the pairs of sides including the angles are proportional, then the triangles are similar.

Consider this application of Theorem 5.3.3.

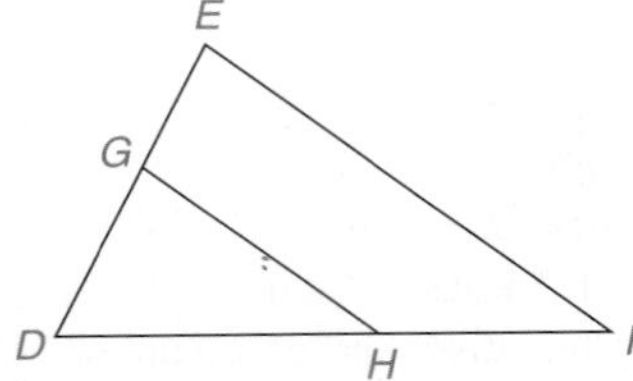

Figure 5.15

EXAMPLE 4

In Figure 5.15, $\frac{DG}{DE} = \frac{DH}{DF}$. Also, $m\angle E = x$, $m\angle D = x + 22$, and $m\angle DHG = x - 10$. Find the value of x and the measure of each angle.

Solution With $\angle D \cong \angle D$ (Identity) and $\frac{DG}{DE} = \frac{DH}{DF}$ (Given), $\triangle DGH \sim \triangle DEF$ by SAS~. By CASTC, $\angle F \cong \angle DHG$, so $m\angle F = x - 10$. The sum of angles in $\triangle DEF$ is $x + x + 22 + x - 10 = 180$, so $3x + 12 = 180$. Then $3x = 168$ and $x = 56$. In turn, $m\angle E = \angle DGH = 56°$, $m\angle F = m\angle DHG = 46°$, and $m\angle D = 78°$. ■

Warning

SSS and SAS prove that triangles are congruent. SSS~ and SAS~ prove that triangles are similar.

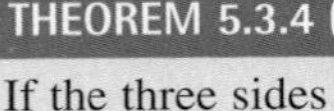

THEOREM 5.3.4 (SSS~)

If the three sides of one triangle are proportional to the three corresponding sides of a second triangle, then the triangles are similar.

Along with AA and SAS~, Theorem 5.3.4 (SSS~) provides the third (and final) method of establishing that triangles are similar.

EXAMPLE 5

Which method (AA, SAS~, or SSS~) establishes that $\triangle ABC \sim \triangle XTN$? See Figure 5.16.

a) $\angle A \cong \angle X$, $AC = 6$, $XN = 9$, $AB = 8$, and $XT = 12$
b) $AB = 6$, $AC = 4$, $BC = 8$, $XT = 9$, $XN = 6$, and $TN = 12$

Solution

a) SAS~; $\frac{AC}{XN} = \frac{AB}{XT}$

b) SSS~; $\frac{AB}{XT} = \frac{AC}{XN} = \frac{BC}{TN}$

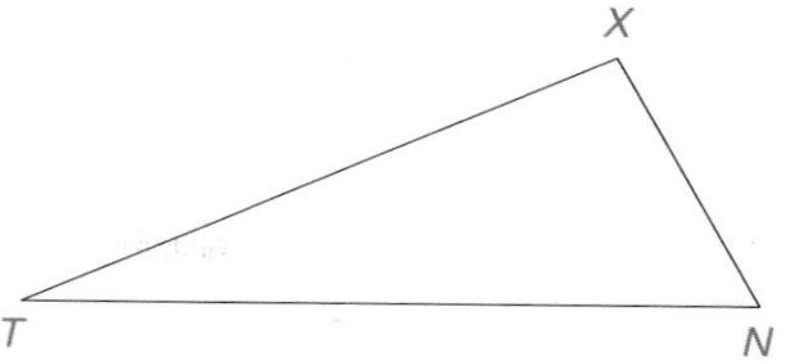

SSG Exs. 8–10

Figure 5.16 ■

We close this section by proving Theorem 5.3.3 (SAS~). To achieve this goal, we prove a helping theorem by the indirect method. In Figure 5.17, we say that sides $\overline{CA}$ and $\overline{CB}$ are divided proportionally by $\overline{DE}$ if $\frac{DA}{CD} = \frac{EB}{CE}$.

LEMMA 5.3.5

If a line segment divides two sides of a triangle proportionally, then this line segment is parallel to the third side of the triangle.

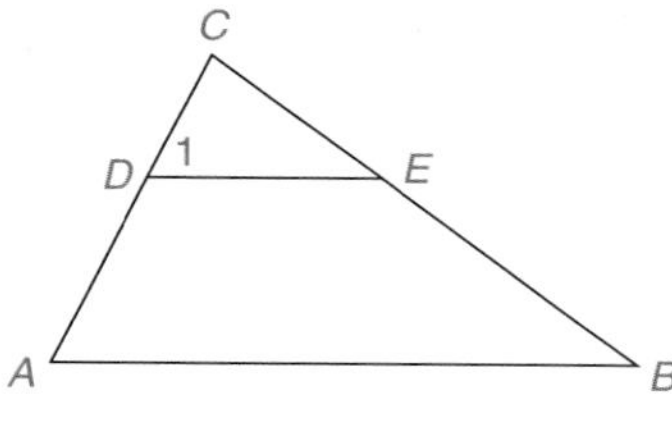

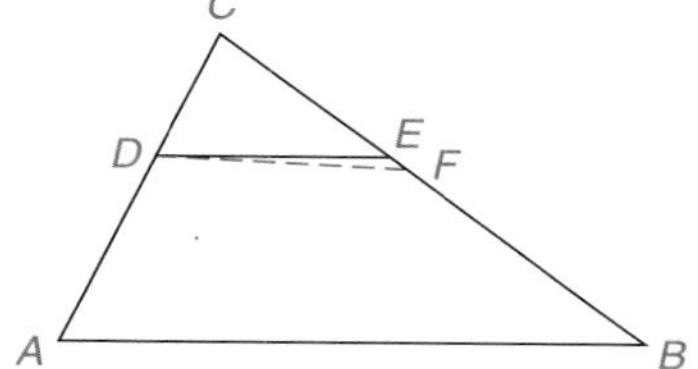

Figure 5.17

GIVEN: $\triangle ABC$ with $\frac{DA}{CD} = \frac{EB}{CE}$

PROVE: $\overline{DE} \parallel \overline{AB}$

PROOF: $\frac{DA}{CD} = \frac{EB}{CE}$ in $\triangle ABC$. Applying Property 3 of Section 5.1, we have $\frac{CD + DA}{CD} = \frac{CE + EB}{CE}$, so $\frac{CA}{CD} = \frac{CB}{CE}(*)$.

Now suppose that $\overline{DE}$ is not parallel to $\overline{AB}$. Through D, we draw $\overline{DF} \parallel \overline{AB}$. It follows that $\angle CDF \cong \angle A$. With $\angle C \cong \angle C$, it follows that $\triangle CDF \sim \triangle CAB$ by the reason AA. By CSSTP, $\frac{CA}{CD} = \frac{CB}{CF}(**)$. Using the starred statements and substitution, $\frac{CB}{CE} = \frac{CB}{CF}$ (both ratios are equal to $\frac{CA}{CD}$). Applying the Means-Extremes Property, $CB \cdot CF = CB \cdot CE$. Dividing each side of the last equation by CB, we find that $CF = CE$. That is, F must coincide with E; it follows that $\overline{DE} \parallel \overline{AB}$. ■

In Example 6, we use Lemma 5.3.5 to prove the SAS~ theorem.

EXAMPLE 6

GIVEN: $\triangle ABC$ and $\triangle DEC$; $\frac{CA}{CD} = \frac{CB}{CE}$

PROVE: $\triangle ABC \sim \triangle DEC$

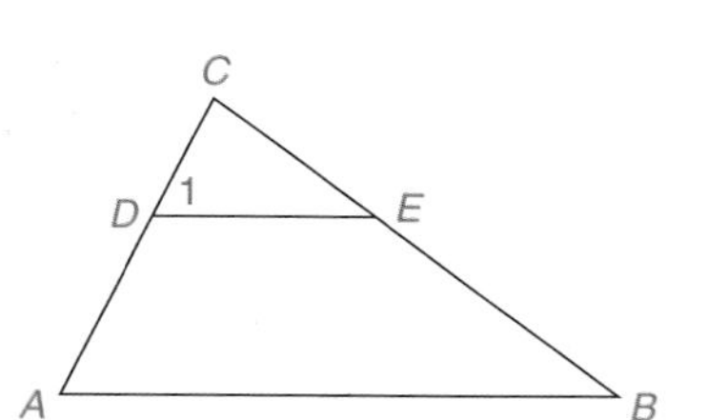

Statements	Reasons
1. $\triangle ABC$ and $\triangle DEC$; $\frac{CA}{CD} = \frac{CB}{CE}$	1. Given
2. $\frac{CA - CD}{CD} = \frac{CB - CE}{CE}$	2. Property 3 of Section 5.1
3. $\frac{DA}{CD} = \frac{EB}{CE}$	3. Substitution
4. $\therefore \overline{DE} \parallel \overline{AB}$	4. Lemma 5.3.5
5. $\angle 1 \cong \angle A$	5. If 2 $\parallel$ lines are cut by a trans., corr. $\angle$s are $\cong$
6. $\angle C \cong \angle C$	6. Identity
7. $\triangle ABC \sim \triangle DEC$	7. AA

Exs. 11, 12

Exercises 5.3

1. What is the acronym that is used to represent the statement "Corresponding angles of similar triangles are congruent?"
2. What is the acronym that is used to represent the statement "Corresponding sides of similar triangles are proportional?"
3. Classify as true or false:
   a) If the vertex angles of two isosceles triangles are congruent, the triangles are similar.
   b) Any two equilateral triangles are similar.
4. Classify as true or false:
   a) If the midpoints of two sides of a triangle are joined, the triangle formed is similar to the original triangle.
   b) Any two isosceles triangles are similar.

In Exercises 5 to 8, name the method (AA, SSS ~, or SAS ~) that is used to show that the triangles are similar.

5. $WU = \frac{3}{2} \cdot TR$, $WV = \frac{3}{2} \cdot TS$, and $UV = \frac{3}{2} \cdot RS$

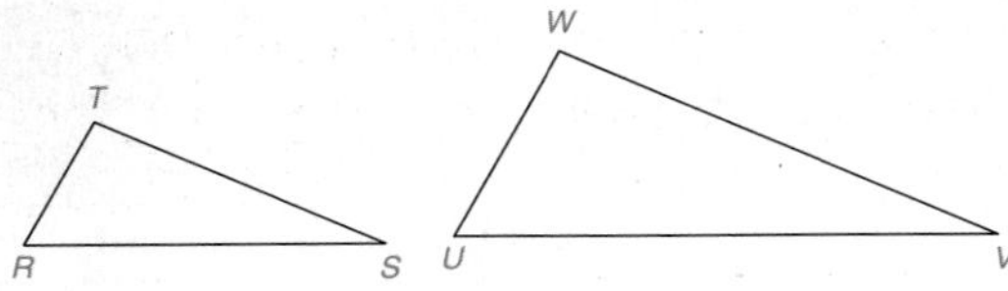

Exercises 5–8

6. $\angle T \cong \angle W$ and $\angle R \cong \angle U$
7. $\angle T \cong \angle W$ and $\frac{TR}{WU} = \frac{TS}{WV}$
8. $\frac{TR}{WU} = \frac{TS}{WV} = \frac{RS}{UV}$

In Exercises 9 and 10, name the method that explains why $\triangle DGH \sim \triangle DEF$.

9. $\frac{DG}{DE} = \frac{DH}{DF}$
10. $DE = 3 \cdot DG$ and $DF = 3 \cdot DH$

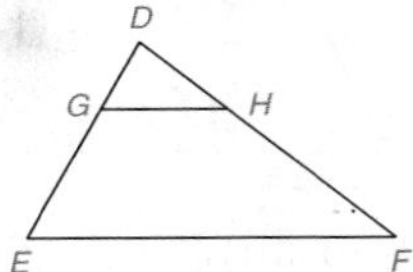

Exercises 9, 10

In Exercises 11 to 14, provide the missing reasons.

11. *Given:* $\square RSTV$; $\overline{VW} \perp \overline{RS}$; $\overline{VX} \perp \overline{TS}$
    Prove: $\triangle VWR \sim \triangle VXT$

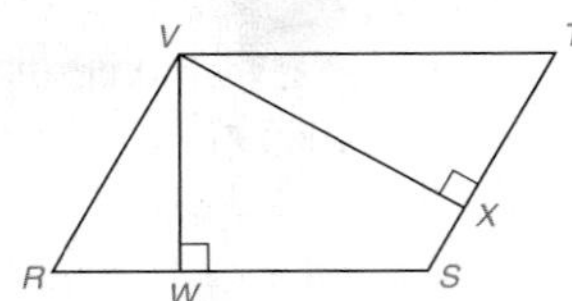

PROOF

Statements	Reasons
1. $\square RSTV$; $\overline{VW} \perp \overline{RS}$; $\overline{VX} \perp \overline{TS}$	1. ?
2. $\angle VWR$ and $\angle VXT$ are rt. $\angle$s	2. ?
3. $\angle VWR \cong \angle VXT$	3. ?
4. $\angle R \cong \angle T$	4. ?
5. $\triangle VWR \sim \triangle VXT$	5. ?

12. *Given:* $\triangle DET$ and $\square ABCD$
Prove: $\triangle ABE \sim \triangle CTB$

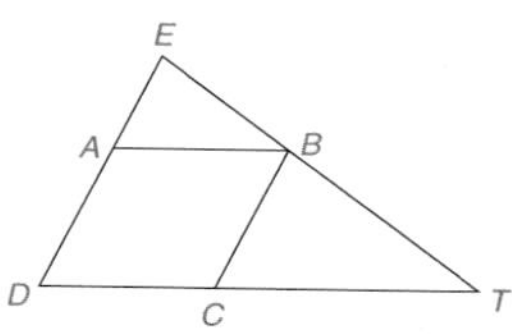

PROOF

Statements	Reasons
1. $\triangle DET$ and $\square ABCD$	1. ?
2. $\overline{AB} \parallel \overline{DT}$	2. Opposite sides of a $\square$ are $\parallel$
3. $\angle EBA \cong \angle T$	3. ?
4. $\overline{ED} \parallel \overline{CB}$	4. ?
5. $\angle E \cong \angle CBT$	5. ?
6. $\triangle ABE \sim \triangle CTB$	6. ?

13. *Given:* $\triangle ABC$; M and N are midpoints of $\overline{AB}$ and $\overline{AC}$, respectively
Prove: $\triangle AMN \sim \triangle ABC$

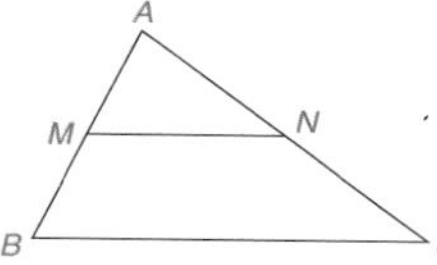

PROOF

Statements	Reasons
1. $\triangle ABC$; M and N are the midpoints of $\overline{AB}$ and $\overline{AC}$, respectively	1. ?
2. $AM = \frac{1}{2}(AB)$ and $AN = \frac{1}{2}(AC)$	2. ?
3. $MN = \frac{1}{2}(BC)$	3. ?
4. $\frac{AM}{AB} = \frac{1}{2}, \frac{AN}{AC} = \frac{1}{2}$, and $\frac{MN}{BC} = \frac{1}{2}$	4. ?
5. $\frac{AM}{AB} = \frac{AN}{AC} = \frac{MN}{BC}$	5. ?
6. $\triangle AMN \sim \triangle ABC$	6. ?

14. *Given:* $\triangle XYZ$ with $\overline{XY}$ trisected at P and Q and $\overline{YZ}$ trisected at R and S
Prove: $\triangle XYZ \sim \triangle PYR$

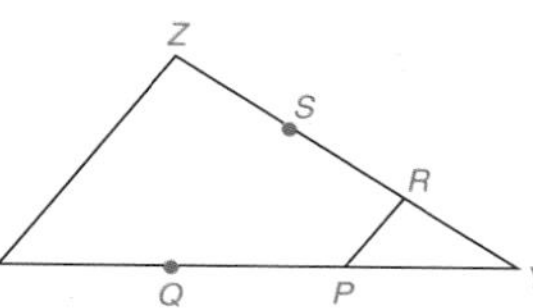

PROOF

Statements	Reasons
1. $\triangle XYZ$; $\overline{XY}$ trisected at P and Q; $\overline{YZ}$ trisected at R and S	1. ?
2. $\frac{YR}{YZ} = \frac{1}{3}$ and $\frac{YP}{YX} = \frac{1}{3}$	2. Definition of trisect
3. $\frac{YR}{YZ} = \frac{YP}{YX}$	3. ?
4. $\angle Y \cong \angle Y$	4. ?
5. $\triangle XYZ \sim \triangle PYR$	5. ?

In Exercises 15 to 22, complete each proof.

15. *Given:* $\overline{MN} \perp \overline{NP}$, $\overline{QR} \perp \overline{RP}$
Prove: $\triangle MNP \sim \triangle QRP$

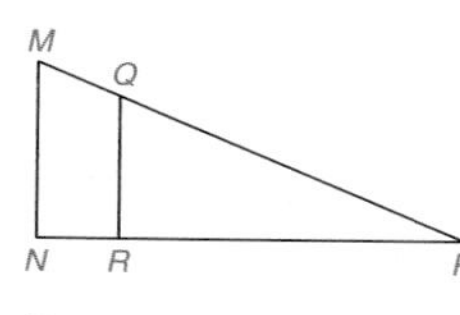

Exercises 15, 16

PROOF

Statements	Reasons
1. ?	1. Given
2. $\angle$s N and QRP are right $\angle$s	2. ?
3. ?	3. All right $\angle$s are $\cong$
4. $\angle P \cong \angle P$	4. ?
5. ?	5. ?

16. *Given:* $\overline{MN} \parallel \overline{QR}$ (See figure for Exercise 15.)
Prove: $\triangle MNP \sim \triangle QRP$

PROOF

Statements	Reasons
1. ?	1. Given
2. $\angle M \cong \angle RQP$	2. ?
3. ?	3. If two $\parallel$ lines are cut by a transversal, the corresponding $\angle$s are $\cong$
4. ?	4. ?

17. *Given:* $\angle H \cong \angle F$
Prove: $\triangle HJK \sim \triangle FGK$

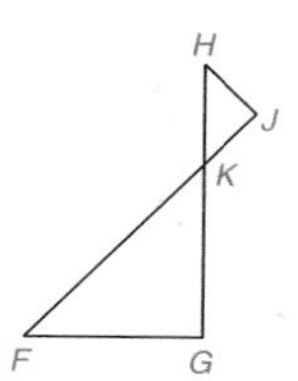

Exercises 17, 18

PROOF

Statements	Reasons
1. ?	1. Given
2. $\angle HKJ \cong \angle FKG$	2. ?
3. ?	3. ?

18. *Given:* $\overline{HJ} \perp \overline{JF}$, $\overline{HG} \perp \overline{FG}$ (See figure for Exercise 17.)
Prove: $\triangle HJK \sim \triangle FGK$

PROOF

Statements	Reasons
1. ?	1. Given
2. $\angle$s G and J are right $\angle$s	2. ?
3. $\angle G \cong \angle J$	3. ?
4. $\angle HKJ \cong \angle GKF$	4. ?
5. ?	5. ?

19. *Given:* $\frac{RQ}{NM} = \frac{RS}{NP} = \frac{QS}{MP}$
Prove: $\angle N \cong \angle R$

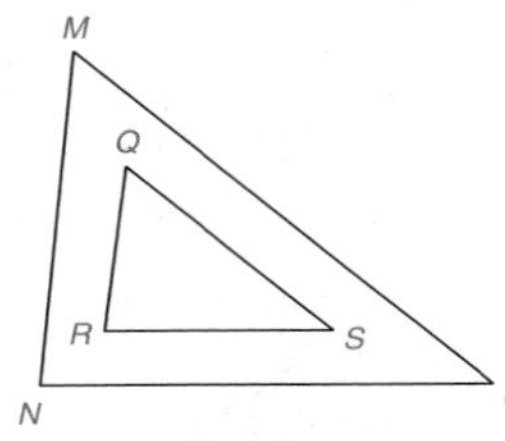

PROOF

Statements	Reasons
1. ?	1. Given
2. ?	2. SSS $\sim$
3. ?	3. CASTC

20. *Given:* $\frac{DG}{DE} = \frac{DH}{DF}$
Prove: $\angle DGH \cong \angle E$

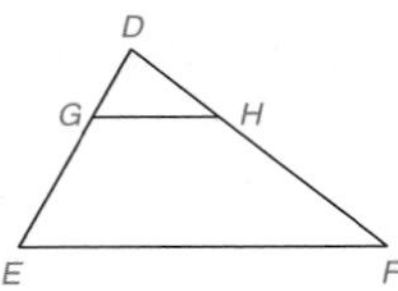

PROOF

Statements	Reasons
1. ?	1. ?
2. $\angle D \cong \angle D$	2. ?
3. $\triangle DGH \sim \triangle DEF$	3. ?
4. ?	4. ?

21. *Given:* $\overline{RS} \parallel \overline{UV}$
Prove: $\frac{RT}{VT} = \frac{RS}{VU}$

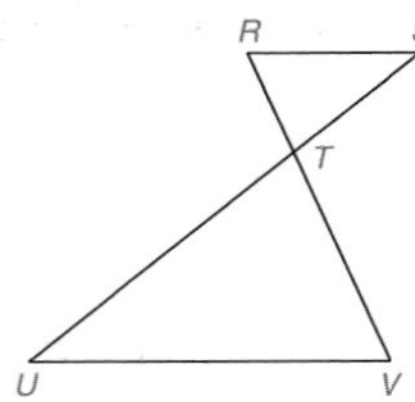

PROOF

Statements	Reasons
1. ?	1. ?
2. $\angle R \cong \angle V$ and $\angle S \cong \angle U$	2. ?
3. ?	3. AA
4. ?	4. ?

22. *Given:* $\overline{AB} \parallel \overline{DC}$, $\overline{AC} \parallel \overline{DE}$
Prove: $\frac{AB}{DC} = \frac{BC}{CE}$

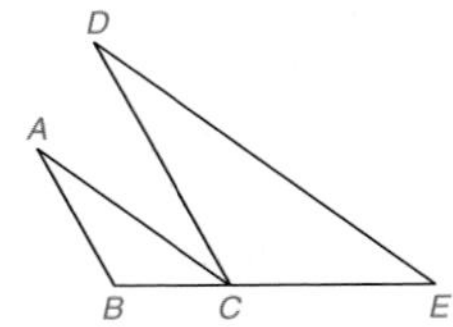

PROOF

Statements	Reasons
1. $\overline{AB} \parallel \overline{DC}$	1. ?
2. ?	2. If 2 $\parallel$ lines are cut by a trans. corr. $\angle$s are $\cong$
3. ?	3. Given
4. $\angle ACB \cong \angle E$	4. ?
5. $\triangle ACB \sim \triangle DEC$	5. ?
6. ?	6. ?

In Exercises 23 to 26, $\triangle ABC \sim \triangle DBE$.

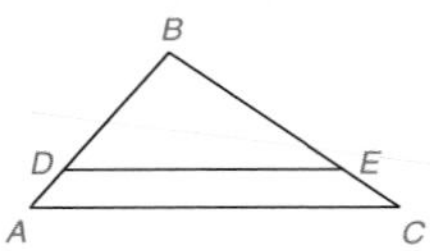

Exercises 23–26

23. *Given:* $AC = 8$, $DE = 6$, $CB = 6$
Find: EB
(*HINT: Let $EB = x$, and solve an equation.*)

24. *Given:* $AC = 10$, $CB = 12$
E is the midpoint of $\overline{CB}$
Find: DE

25. *Given:* $AC = 10$, $DE = 8$, $AD = 4$
Find: DB

26. *Given:* $CB = 12$, $CE = 4$, $AD = 5$
Find: DB

27. $\triangle CDE \sim \triangle CBA$ with $\angle CDE \cong \angle B$. If $CD = 10$, $DA = 8$, and $CE = 6$, find EB.

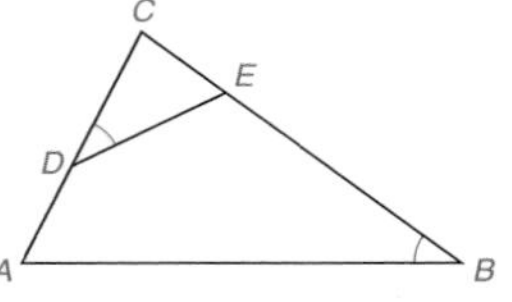

Exercises 27, 28

28. $\triangle CDE \sim \triangle CBA$ with $\angle CDE \cong \angle B$. If $CD = 10$, $CA = 16$, and $EB = 12$, find CE.

(see the figure for Exercise 27.)

29. $\triangle ABF \sim \triangle CBD$ with obtuse angles at vertices D and F as indicated. If $m\angle B = 45°$, $m\angle C = x$ and $m\angle AFB = 4x$, find x.

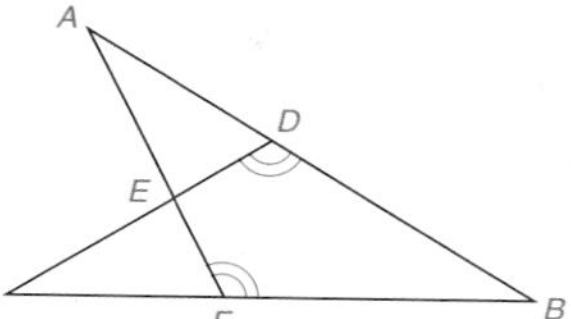

Exercises 29, 30

30. $\triangle ABF \sim \triangle CBD$ with obtuse angles at vertices D and F. If $m\angle B = 44°$ and $m\angle A : m\angle CDB = 1:3$, find $m\angle A$.

In Exercise 31, provide a two-column proof.

31. *Given:* $\overline{AB} \parallel \overline{DF}$, $\overline{BD} \parallel \overline{FG}$
Prove: $\triangle ABC \sim \triangle EFG$

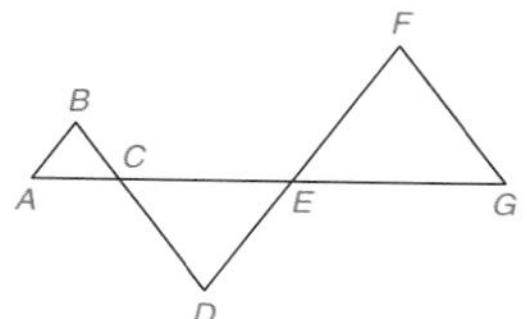

In Exercise 32, provide a paragraph proof.

32. *Given:* $\overline{RS} \perp \overline{AB}$, $\overline{CB} \perp \overline{AC}$
Prove: $\triangle BSR \sim \triangle BCA$

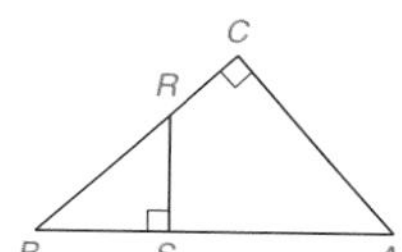

33. Use a two-column proof to prove the following theorem: "The lengths of the corresponding altitudes of similar triangles have the same ratio as the lengths of any pair of corresponding sides."

Given: $\triangle DEF \sim \triangle MNP$; $\overline{DG}$ and $\overline{MQ}$ are altitudes

Prove: $\dfrac{DG}{MQ} = \dfrac{DE}{MN}$

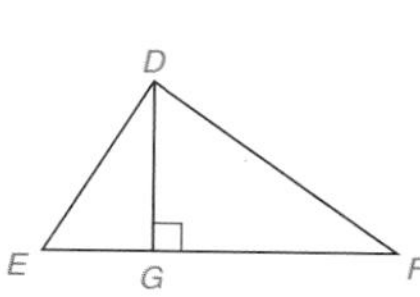

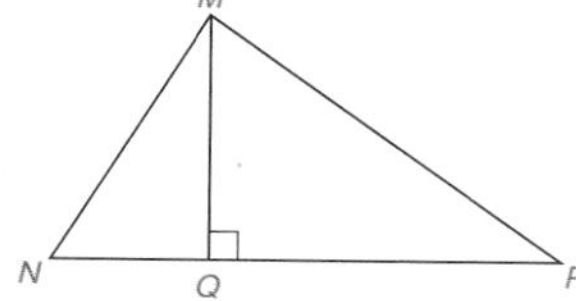

34. Provide a paragraph proof for the following problem.
Given: $\overline{RS} \parallel \overline{YZ}$, $\overline{RU} \parallel \overline{XZ}$
Prove: $RS \cdot ZX = ZY \cdot RT$

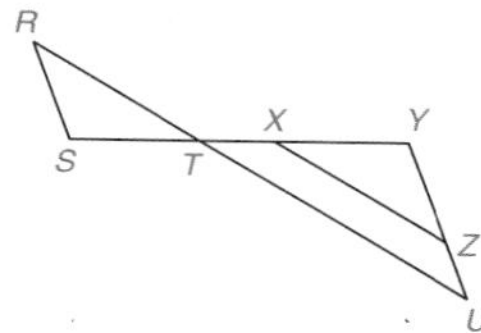

35. Use the result of Exercise 11 to do the following problem. In $\square MNPQ$, $QP = 12$ and $QM = 9$. The length of altitude $\overline{QR}$ (to side $\overline{MN}$) is 6. Find the length of altitude $\overline{QS}$ from Q to $\overline{PN}$.

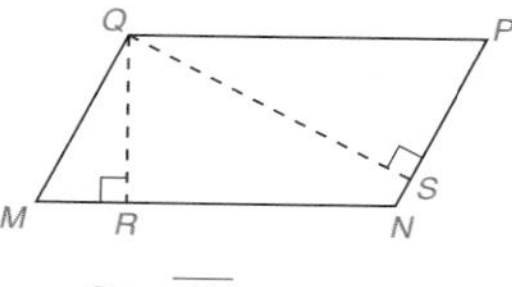

36. Use the result of Exercise 11 to do the following problem. In $\square ABCD$, $AB = 7$ and $BC = 12$. The length of altitude $\overline{AF}$ (to side $\overline{BC}$) is 5. Find the length of altitude $\overline{AE}$ from A to $\overline{DC}$.

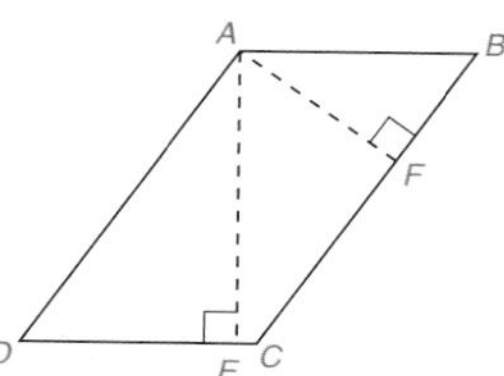

37. The distance across a pond is to be measured indirectly by using similar triangles. If $XY = 160$ ft, $YW = 40$ ft, $TY = 120$ ft, and $WZ = 50$ ft, find XT.

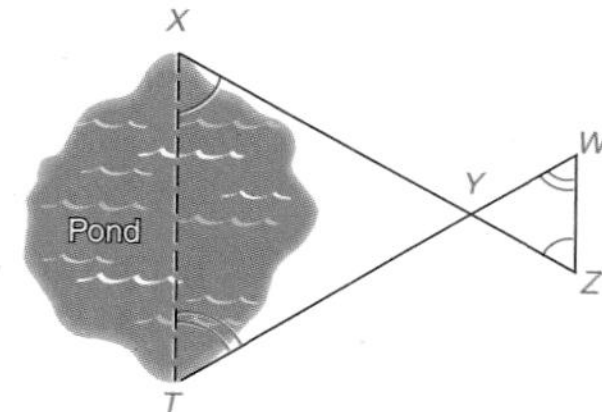

38. In the figure, $\angle ABC \cong \angle ADB$. Find AB if $AD = 2$ and $DC = 6$.

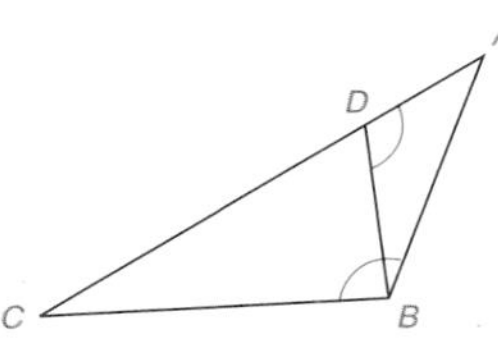

39. Prove that the altitude drawn to the hypotenuse of a right triangle separates the right triangle into two right triangles that are similar to each other and to the original right triangle.

40. Prove that the line segment joining the midpoints of two sides of a triangle determines a triangle that is similar to the original triangle.

5.4 The Pythagorean Theorem

KEY CONCEPTS

Pythagorean Theorem
Converse of Pythagorean Theorem
Pythagorean Triple

The following theorem, which was proved in Exercise 39 of Section 5.3, will enable us to prove the well-known Pythagorean Theorem.

THEOREM 5.4.1

The altitude drawn to the hypotenuse of a right triangle separates the right triangle into two right triangles that are similar to each other and to the original right triangle.

Theorem 5.4.1 is illustrated by Figure 5.18, in which the right triangle $\triangle ABC$ has its right angle at vertex C so that $\overline{CD}$ is the altitude to hypotenuse $\overline{AB}$. The smaller triangles are shown in Figures 5.18(b) and (c), and the original triangle is shown in Figure 5.18(d). Note the matching arcs indicating congruent angles.

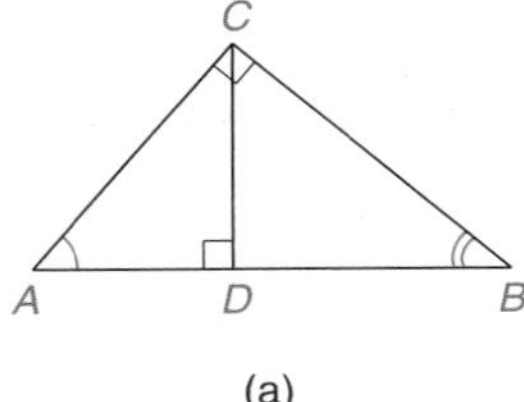

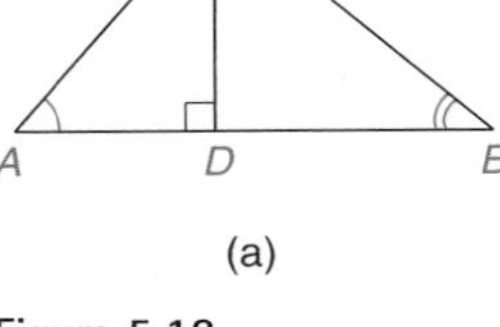

(a)

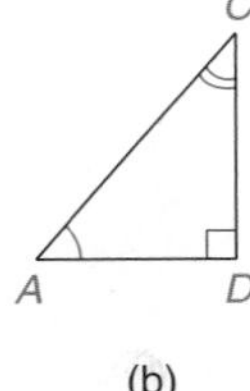

(b)

(c)

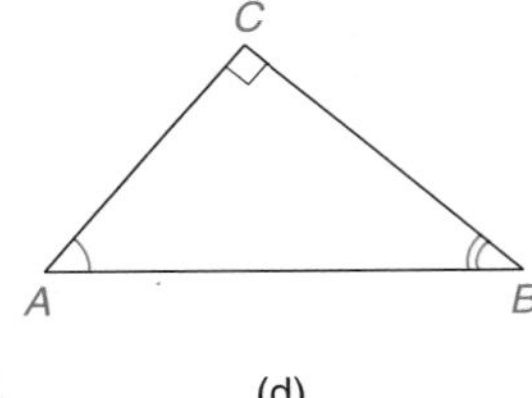

(d)

Figure 5.18

Reminder

CSSTP means "corresponding sides of similar triangles are proportional."

In Figure 5.18(a), $\overline{AD}$ and $\overline{DB}$ are known as *segments* (parts) of the hypotenuse $\overline{AB}$. Furthermore, $\overline{AD}$ is the segment of the hypotenuse *adjacent* to (next to) leg $\overline{AC}$, and $\overline{BD}$ is the segment of the hypotenuse *adjacent* to leg $\overline{BC}$. Proof of the following theorem is left as an exercise. Compare the statement of Theorem 5.4.2 to the "Prove" statement that follows it.

THEOREM 5.4.2

The length of the altitude to the hypotenuse of a right triangle is the geometric mean of the lengths of the segments of the hypotenuse.

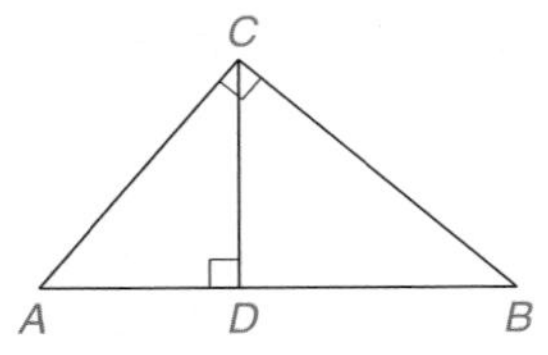

Figure 5.19

GIVEN: $\triangle ABC$ in Figure 5.19, with right $\angle ACB$; $\overline{CD} \perp \overline{AB}$

PROVE: $\dfrac{AD}{CD} = \dfrac{CD}{DB}$

PLAN FOR PROOF: Show that $\triangle ADC \sim \triangle CDB$. Then use CSSTP.

In the proportion $\frac{AD}{CD} = \frac{CD}{DB}$, recall that CD is a geometric mean because the second and the third terms are identical.

The proof of the following lemma is left as an exercise. Compare the statement of Lemma 5.4.3 to the "Prove" statement that follows it.

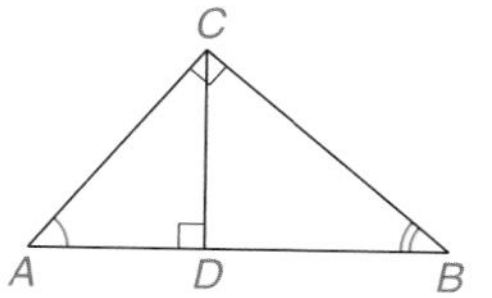

Figure 5.20

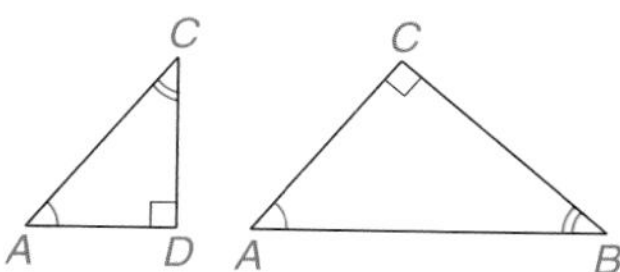

Figure 5.21

LEMMA 5.4.3

The length of each leg of a right triangle is the geometric mean of the length of the hypotenuse and the length of the segment of the hypotenuse adjacent to that leg.

GIVEN: $\triangle ABC$ with right $\angle ACB$; $\overline{CD} \perp \overline{AB}$ (See Figure 5.20.)

PROVE: $\dfrac{AB}{AC} = \dfrac{AC}{AD}$

PLAN: Show that $\triangle ADC \sim \triangle ACB$ in Figure 5.21. Then use CSSTP.

NOTE: Although $\overline{AD}$ and $\overline{DB}$ are both segments of the hypotenuse, $\overline{AD}$ is the segment adjacent to $\overline{AC}$.

SSG *Exs 1, 2*

Lemma 5.4.3 opens the doors to a proof of the famous Pythagorean Theorem, one of the most frequently applied relationships in geometry. Although the theorem's title gives credit to the Greek geometer Pythagoras, many other proofs are known, and the ancient Chinese were aware of the relationship before the time of Pythagoras.

THEOREM 5.4.4 ▶ (Pythagorean Theorem)

The square of the length of the hypotenuse of a right triangle is equal to the sum of the squares of the lengths of the legs.

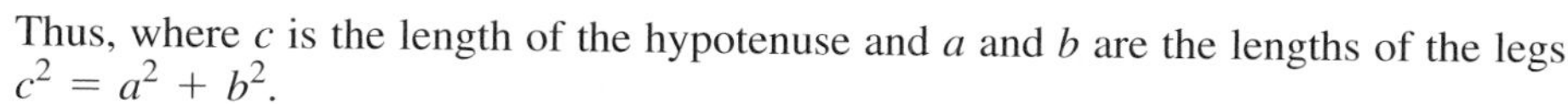
Thus, where c is the length of the hypotenuse and a and b are the lengths of the legs, $c^2 = a^2 + b^2$.

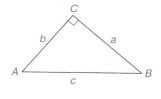

(a)

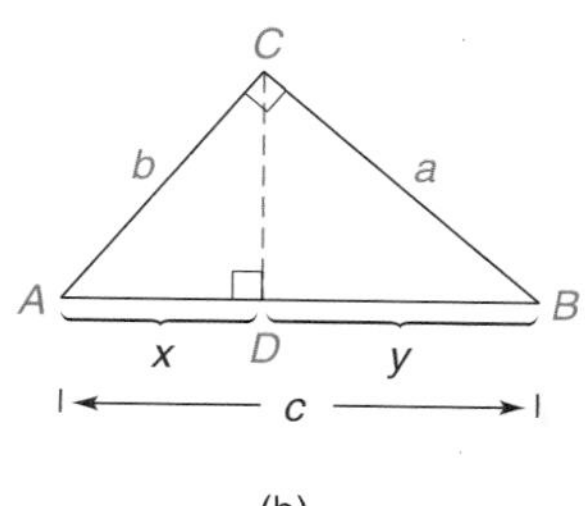

(b)

Figure 5.22

GIVEN: In Figure 5.22(a), $\triangle ABC$ with right $\angle C$

PROVE: $c^2 = a^2 + b^2$

PROOF: Draw $\overline{CD} \perp \overline{AB}$, as shown in Figure 5.22(b). Denote $AD = x$ and $DB = y$. By Lemma 5.4.3,

$$\frac{c}{b} = \frac{b}{x} \quad \text{and} \quad \frac{c}{a} = \frac{a}{y}$$

Therefore, $\quad b^2 = cx \quad$ and $\quad a^2 = cy$

Using the Addition Property of Equality, we have

$$a^2 + b^2 = cy + cx = c(y + x)$$

But $y + x = x + y = AD + DB = AB = c$. Thus, $a^2 + b^2 = c(c) = c^2$

Discover

A video entitled "The Rule of Pythagoras" is available through Project Mathematics at Cal Tech University in Pasadena, CA. It is well worth watching!

EXAMPLE 1

Given $\triangle RST$ with right $\angle S$ in Figure 5.23, find:

a) RT if $RS = 3$ and $ST = 4$
b) RT if $RS = 4$ and $ST = 6$
c) RS if $RT = 13$ and $ST = 12$
d) ST if $RS = 6$ and $RT = 9$

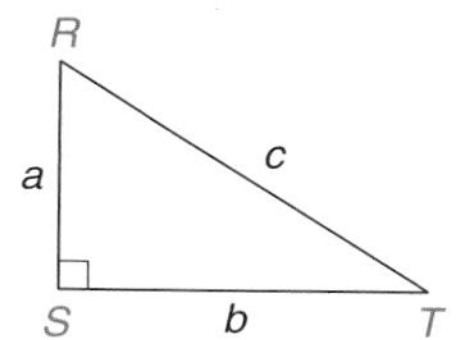

Figure 5.23

Solution With right $\angle S$, the hypotenuse is $\overline{RT}$. Then $RT = c$, $RS = a$, and $ST = b$.

a) $3^2 + 4^2 = c^2 \rightarrow 9 + 16 = c^2$
$c^2 = 25$
$c = 5; RT = 5$

b) $4^2 + 6^2 = c^2 \rightarrow 16 + 36 = c^2$
$c^2 = 52$
$c = \sqrt{52} = \sqrt{4 \cdot 13} = \sqrt{4} \cdot \sqrt{13} = 2\sqrt{13}$
$RT = 2\sqrt{13} \approx 7.21$

c) $a^2 + 12^2 = 13^2 \rightarrow a^2 + 144 = 169$
$a^2 = 25$
$a = 5; RS = 5$

d) $6^2 + b^2 = 9^2 \rightarrow 36 + b^2 = 81$
$b^2 = 45$
$b = \sqrt{45} = \sqrt{9 \cdot 5} = \sqrt{9} \cdot \sqrt{5} = 3\sqrt{5}$
$ST = 3\sqrt{5} \approx 6.71$ ■

SSG
Exs. 3, 4

The converse of the Pythagorean Theorem is also true.

THEOREM 5.4.5 ▶ (Converse of Pythagorean Theorem)

If a, b, and c are the lengths of the three sides of a triangle, with c the length of the longest side, and if $c^2 = a^2 + b^2$, then the triangle is a right triangle with the right angle opposite the side of length c.

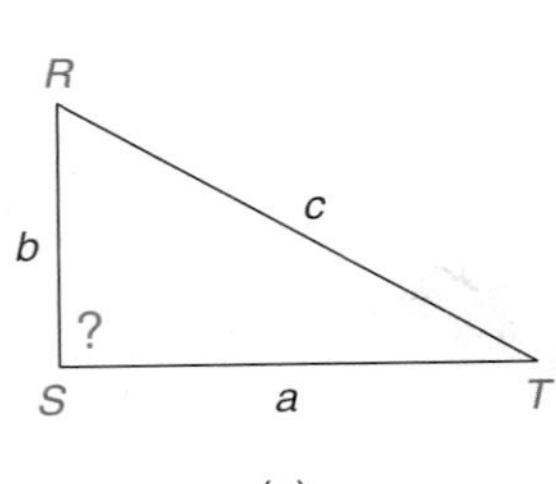

(a)

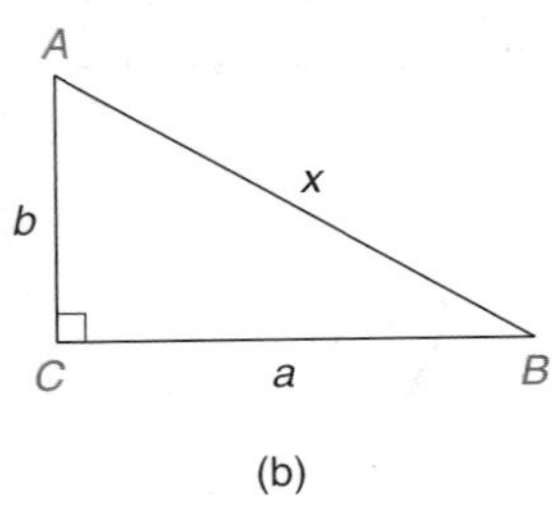

(b)

Figure 5.24

GIVEN: $\triangle RST$ [Figure 5.24(a)] with sides a, b, and c so that $c^2 = a^2 + b^2$

PROVE: $\triangle RST$ is a right triangle.

PROOF: We are given $\triangle RST$ for which $c^2 = a^2 + b^2$. Construct the right $\triangle ABC$, which has legs of lengths a and b and a hypotenuse of length x. [See Figure 5.24(b).] By the Pythagorean Theorem, $x^2 = a^2 + b^2$. By substitution, $x^2 = c^2$ and $x = c$. Thus, $\triangle RTS \cong \triangle ABC$ by SSS. Then $\angle S$ (opposite the side of length c) must be $\cong$ to $\angle C$, the right angle of $\triangle ABC$. Then $\angle S$ is a right angle, and $\triangle RST$ is a right triangle.

EXAMPLE 2

Do the following represent the lengths of the sides of a right triangle?

a) $a = 5, b = 12, c = 13$
b) $a = 15, b = 8, c = 17$
c) $a = 7, b = 9, c = 10$
d) $a = \sqrt{2}, b = \sqrt{3}, c = \sqrt{5}$

Solution

a) Yes. Because $5^2 + 12^2 = 13^2$ (that is, $25 + 144 = 169$), this triangle is a right triangle.
b) Yes. Because $15^2 + 8^2 = 17^2$ (that is, $225 + 64 = 289$), this triangle is a right triangle.
c) No. $7^2 + 9^2 = 49 + 81 = 130$, which is not 10^2 (that is, 100), so this triangle is not a right triangle.
d) Yes. Because $(\sqrt{2})^2 + (\sqrt{3})^2 = (\sqrt{5})^2$ leads to $2 + 3 = 5$, this triangle is a right triangle. ■

SSG
Exs. 5, 6

Discover

Construct a triangle with sides of lengths 3 in., 4 in., and 5 in. Measure the angles of the triangle. Is there a right angle?

ANSWER

Yes, opposite the 5-in. side.

EXAMPLE 3

A ladder 12 ft long is leaning against a wall so that its base is 4 ft from the wall at ground level (see Figure 5.25). How far up the wall does the ladder reach?

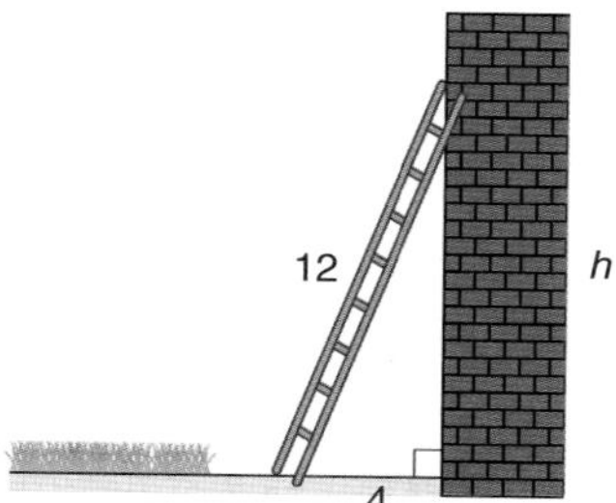

Figure 5.25

Solution The desired height is represented by h, so we have

$$\begin{aligned} 4^2 + h^2 &= 12^2 \\ 16 + h^2 &= 144 \\ h^2 &= 128 \\ h &= \sqrt{128} = \sqrt{64 \cdot 2} = \sqrt{64} \cdot \sqrt{2} = 8\sqrt{2} \end{aligned}$$

The height is exactly $h = 8\sqrt{2}$, which is approximately 11.31 ft. ■

Reminder

The diagonals of a rhombus are perpendicular bisectors of each other.

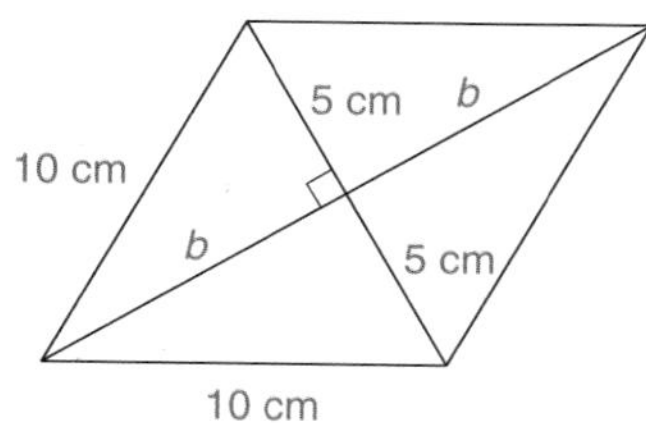

Figure 5.26

EXAMPLE 4

One diagonal of a rhombus has the same length, 10 cm, as each side (see Figure 5.26). How long is the other diagonal?

Solution Because the diagonals are perpendicular bisectors of each other, four right △s are formed. For each right △, a side of the rhombus is the hypotenuse. Half of the length of each diagonal is the length of a leg of each right triangle. Therefore,

$$\begin{aligned} 5^2 + b^2 &= 10^2 \\ 25 + b^2 &= 100 \\ b^2 &= 75 \\ b &= \sqrt{75} = \sqrt{25 \cdot 3} = \sqrt{25} \cdot \sqrt{3} = 5\sqrt{3} \end{aligned}$$

Thus, the length of the whole diagonal is $10\sqrt{3}$ cm ≈ 17.32 cm. ■

Example 5 also uses the Pythagorean Theorem, but it is considerably more complicated than Example 4. Indeed, it is one of those situations that may require some insight to solve. Note that the triangle described in Example 5 is *not* a right triangle because $4^2 + 5^2 \neq 6^2$.

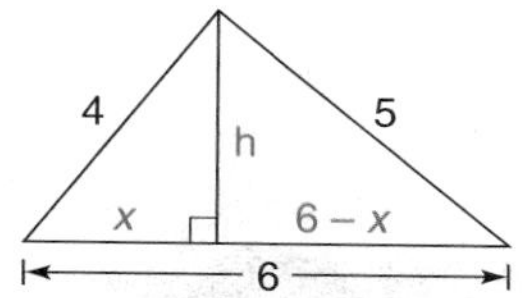

Figure 5.27

EXAMPLE 5

A triangle has sides of lengths 4, 5, and 6, as shown in Figure 5.27. Find the length of the altitude to the side of length 6.

Solution The altitude to the side of length 6 separates that side into two parts whose lengths are given by x and $6 - x$. Using the two right triangles formed, we apply the Pythagorean Theorem twice.

$$x^2 + h^2 = 4^2 \quad \text{and} \quad (6 - x)^2 + h^2 = 5^2$$

Subtracting the first equation from the second, we can calculate x.

$$\begin{array}{rl} 36 - 12x + x^2 + h^2 &= 25 \\ x^2 + h^2 &= 16 \\ \hline 36 - 12x \qquad\qquad &= 9 \qquad\qquad \textbf{(subtraction)} \\ -12x &= -27 \\ x &= \frac{27}{12} = \frac{9}{4} \end{array}$$

Now we use $x = \frac{9}{4}$ to find h.

$$\begin{aligned} x^2 + h^2 &= 4^2 \\ \left(\frac{9}{4}\right)^2 + h^2 &= 4^2 \\ \frac{81}{16} + h^2 &= 16 \\ \frac{81}{16} + h^2 &= \frac{256}{16} \\ h^2 &= \frac{175}{16} \\ h &= \frac{\sqrt{175}}{4} = \frac{\sqrt{25 \cdot 7}}{4} = \frac{\sqrt{25} \cdot \sqrt{7}}{4} = \frac{5\sqrt{7}}{4} \approx 3.31 \end{aligned}$$ ■

It is now possible to prove the HL method for proving the congruence of triangles, a method that was introduced in Section 3.2.

THEOREM 5.4.6

If the hypotenuse and a leg of one right triangle are congruent to the hypotenuse and a leg of a second right triangle, then the triangles are congruent (HL).

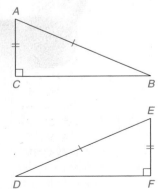

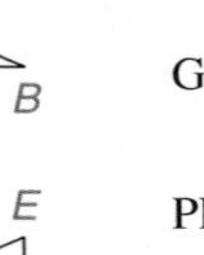

Figure 5.28

GIVEN: Right $\triangle ABC$ with right $\angle C$ and right $\triangle DEF$ with right $\angle F$ (see Figure 5.28); $\overline{AB} \cong \overline{DE}$ and $\overline{AC} \cong \overline{EF}$

PROVE: $\triangle ABC \cong \triangle EDF$

PROOF: With right $\angle C$, the hypotenuse of $\triangle ABC$ is $\overline{AB}$; similarly, $\overline{DE}$ is the hypotenuse of right $\triangle EDF$. Because $\overline{AB} \cong \overline{DE}$, we denote the common length by c; that is, $AB = DE = c$. Because $\overline{AC} \cong \overline{EF}$, we also have $AC = EF = a$. Then

$$a^2 + (BC)^2 = c^2 \quad \text{and} \quad a^2 + (DF)^2 = c^2 \text{ which leads to}$$
$$BC = \sqrt{c^2 - a^2} \quad \text{and} \quad DF = \sqrt{c^2 - a^2}$$

SSG *Exs. 7, 8*

Then $BC = DF$ so that $\overline{BC} \cong \overline{DF}$. Hence, $\triangle ABC \cong \triangle EDF$ by SSS. ■

Our work with the Pythagorean Theorem would be incomplete if we did not address two issues. The first, Pythagorean triples, involves natural (or counting) numbers as possible choices of a, b, and c. The second leads to the classification of triangles according to the lengths of their sides as found in Theorem 5.4.7 on page 250.

PYTHAGOREAN TRIPLES

DEFINITION

A **Pythagorean triple** is a set of three natural numbers (a, b, c) for which $a^2 + b^2 = c^2$.

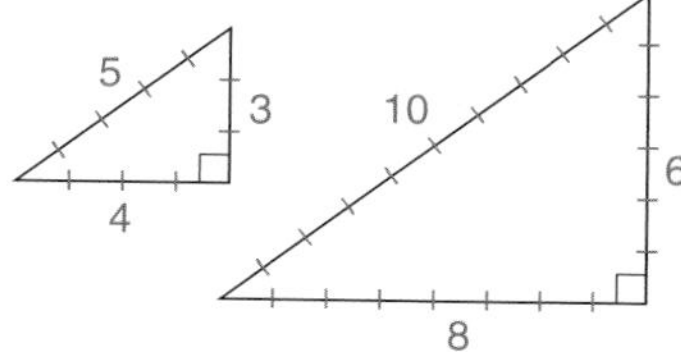

Figure 5.29

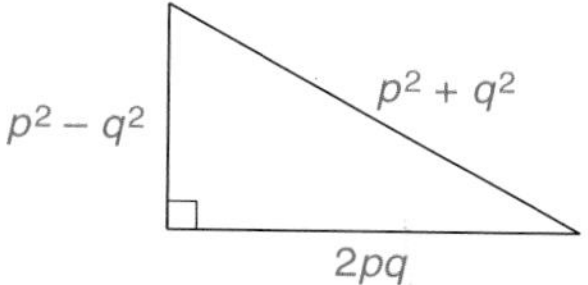

Figure 5.30

Three sets of Pythagorean triples encountered in this section are (3, 4, 5), (5, 12, 13), and (8, 15, 17). These numbers will always fit the sides of a right triangle.

Natural-number multiples of any of these triples will also constitute Pythagorean triples. For example, doubling (3, 4, 5) yields (6, 8, 10), which is also a Pythagorean triple. In Figure 5.29, the triangles are similar by SSS~.

The Pythagorean triple (3, 4, 5) also leads to (9, 12, 15), (12, 16, 20), and (15, 20, 25). The Pythagorean triple (5, 12, 13) leads to triples such as (10, 24, 26) and (15, 36, 39). Basic Pythagorean triples that are used less frequently include (7, 24, 25), (9, 40, 41), and (20, 21, 29).

Pythagorean triples can be generated by using select formulas. Where p and q are natural numbers and $p > q$, one formula uses $2pq$ for the length of one leg, $p^2 - q^2$ for the length of other leg, and $p^2 + q^2$ for the length of the hypotenuse (See Figure 5.30.).

Table 5.1 lists some Pythagorean triples corresponding to choices for p and q. The triples printed in boldface type are *basic triples*, also known as *primitive triples*. In application, knowledge of the primitive triples and their multiples will save you considerable time and effort. In the final column, the resulting triple is provided in the order from a (small) to c (large).

Exs. 9–11

TABLE 5.1
Pythagorean Triples

p	q	a (or b) $p^2 - q^2$	b (or a) $2pq$	c $p^2 + q^2$	(a, b, c)
2	1	3	4	5	**(3, 4, 5)**
3	1	8	6	10	(6, 8, 10)
3	2	5	12	13	**(5, 12, 13)**
4	1	15	8	17	**(8, 15, 17)**
4	3	7	24	25	**(7, 24, 25)**
5	1	24	10	26	(10, 24, 26)
5	2	21	20	29	**(20, 21, 29)**
5	3	16	30	34	(16, 30, 34)
5	4	9	40	41	**(9, 40, 41)**

THE CONVERSE OF THE PYTHAGOREAN THEOREM

The Converse of the Pythagorean Theorem allows us to recognize a right triangle by knowing the lengths of its sides. A variation on the converse allows us to determine whether a triangle is acute or obtuse. This theorem is stated without proof.

THEOREM 5.4.7

Let a, b, and c represent the lengths of the three sides of a triangle, with c the length of the longest side.

1. If $c^2 > a^2 + b^2$, then the triangle is obtuse and the obtuse angle lies opposite the side of length c.
2. If $c^2 < a^2 + b^2$, then the triangle is acute.

EXAMPLE 6

Determine the type of triangle represented if the lengths of its sides are as follows:

a) 4, 5, 7
b) 6, 7, 8
c) 9, 12, 15
d) 3, 4, 9

Solution

a) Choosing $c = 7$, we have $7^2 > 4^2 + 5^2$, or $49 > 16 + 25$; the triangle is obtuse.
b) Choosing $c = 8$, we have $8^2 < 6^2 + 7^2$, or $64 < 36 + 49$; the triangle is acute.
c) Choosing $c = 15$, we have $15^2 = 9^2 + 12^2$, or $225 = 81 + 144$; the triangle is a right triangle.
d) Because $9 > 3 + 4$, no triangle is possible. (Remember that the sum of the lengths of two sides of a triangle must be greater than the length of the third side.) ■

SSG Exs. 12, 13

Exercises 5.4

1. By naming the vertices in order, state three different triangles that are similar to each other.
2. Use Theorem 5.4.2 to form a proportion in which SV is a geometric mean.
   (HINT: $\triangle SVT \sim \triangle RVS$)
3. Use Lemma 5.4.3 to form a proportion in which RS is a geometric mean.
   (HINT: $\triangle RVS \sim \triangle RST$)

Exercises 1–6

4. Use Lemma 5.4.3 to form a proportion in which TS is a geometric mean.
   (HINT: $\triangle TVS \sim \triangle TSR$)
5. Use Theorem 5.4.2 to find RV if $SV = 6$ and $VT = 8$.
6. Use Lemma 5.4.3 to find RT if $RS = 6$ and $VR = 4$.
7. Find the length of $\overline{DF}$ if:
   a) $DE = 8$ and $EF = 6$
   b) $DE = 5$ and $EF = 3$
8. Find the length of $\overline{DE}$ if:
   a) $DF = 13$ and $EF = 5$
   b) $DF = 12$ and $EF = 6\sqrt{3}$

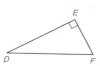

Exercises 7–10

9. Find EF if:
   a) $DF = 17$ and $DE = 15$
   b) $DF = 12$ and $DE = 8\sqrt{2}$
10. Find DF if:
    a) $DE = 12$ and $EF = 5$
    b) $DE = 12$ and $EF = 6$
11. Determine whether each triple (a, b, c) is a Pythagorean triple.
    a) (3, 4, 5)
    b) (4, 5, 6)
    c) (5, 12, 13)
    d) (6, 13, 15)
12. Determine whether each triple (a, b, c) is a Pythagorean triple.
    a) (8, 15, 17)
    b) (10, 13, 19)
    c) (6, 8, 10)
    d) (11, 17, 20)
13. Determine the type of triangle represented if the lengths of its sides are:
    a) $a = 4$, $b = 3$, and $c = 5$
    b) $a = 4$, $b = 5$, and $c = 6$
    c) $a = 2$, $b = \sqrt{3}$, and $c = \sqrt{7}$
    d) $a = 3$, $b = 8$, and $c = 15$

14. Determine the type of triangle represented if the lengths of its sides are:
a) $a = 1.5$, $b = 2$, and $c = 2.5$
b) $a = 20$, $b = 21$, and $c = 29$
c) $a = 10$, $b = 12$, and $c = 16$
d) $a = 5$, $b = 7$, and $c = 9$

15. A guy wire 25 ft long supports an antenna at a point that is 20 ft above the base of the antenna. How far from the base of the antenna is the guy wire secured?

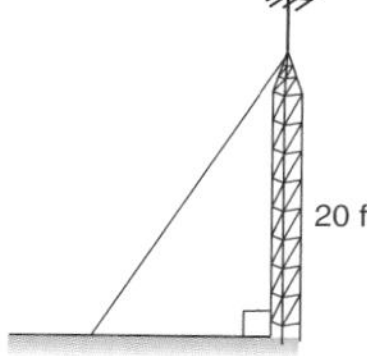

16. A strong wind holds a kite 30 ft above the earth in a position 40 ft across the ground. How much string does the girl have out (to the kite)?

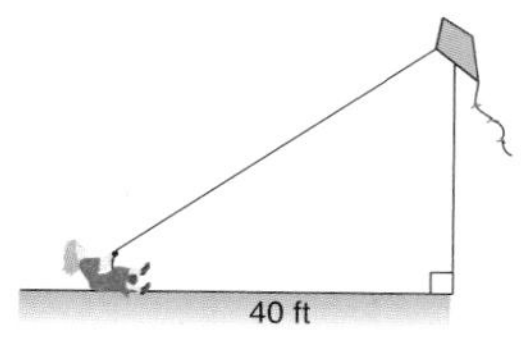

17. A boat is 6 m below the level of a pier and 12 m from the pier as measured across the water. How much rope is needed to reach the boat?

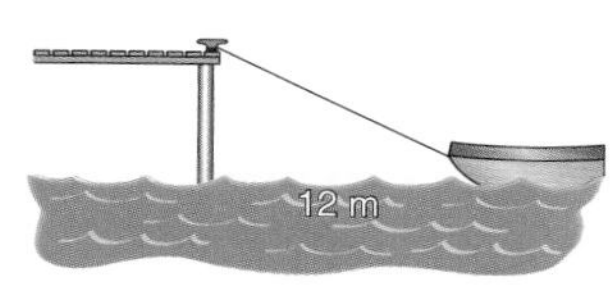

18. A hot-air balloon is held in place by the ground crew at a point that is 21 ft from a point directly beneath the basket of the balloon. If the rope is of length 29 ft, how far above ground level is the basket?

© Sonya Etchison/Shutterstock

19. A drawbridge that is 104 ft in length is raised at its midpoint so that the uppermost points are 8 ft apart. How far has each of the midsections been raised?

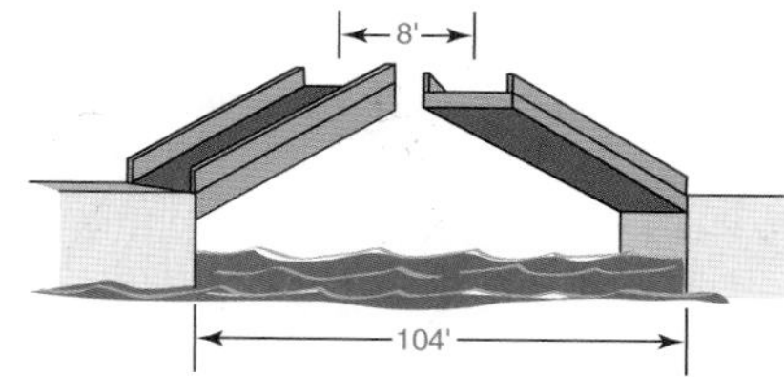

20. A drawbridge that is 136 ft in length is raised at its midpoint so that the uppermost points are 16 ft apart. How far has each of the midsections been raised?

(HINT: Consider the drawing for Exercise 19.)

21. A rectangle has a width of 16 cm and a diagonal of length 20 cm. How long is the rectangle?

22. A right triangle has legs of lengths x and $2x + 2$ and a hypotenuse of length $2x + 3$. What are the lengths of its sides?

23. A rectangle has base length $x + 3$, altitude length $x + 1$, and diagonals of length $2x$ each. What are the lengths of its base, altitude, and diagonals?

24. The diagonals of a rhombus measure 6 m and 8 m. How long are each of the congruent sides?

25. Each side of a rhombus measures 12 in. If one diagonal is 18 in. long, how long is the other diagonal?

26. An isosceles right triangle has a hypotenuse of length 10 cm. How long is each leg?

27. Each leg of an isosceles right triangle has a length of $6\sqrt{2}$ in. What is the length of the hypotenuse?

28. In right $\triangle ABC$ with right $\angle C$, $AB = 10$ and $BC = 8$. Find the length of $\overline{MB}$ if M is the midpoint of $\overline{AC}$.

29. In right $\triangle ABC$ with right $\angle C$, $AB = 17$ and $BC = 15$. Find the length of $\overline{MN}$ if M and N are the midpoints of $\overline{AB}$ and $\overline{BC}$, respectively.

30. Find the length of the altitude to the 10-in. side of a triangle whose sides are 6, 8, and 10 inches in length.

31. Find the length of the altitude to the 26-in. side of a triangle whose sides are 10, 24, and 26 inches in length.

32. In quadrilateral $ABCD$, $\overline{BC} \perp \overline{AB}$ and $\overline{DC} \perp$ diagonal $\overline{AC}$. If $AB = 4$, $BC = 3$, and $DC = 12$, determine DA.

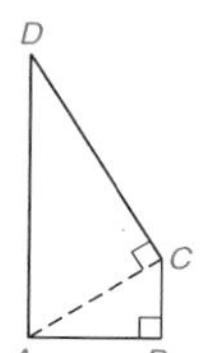

33. In quadrilateral $RSTU$, $\overline{RS} \perp \overline{ST}$ and $\overline{UT} \perp$ diagonal $\overline{RT}$. If $RS = 6$, $ST = 8$, and $RU = 15$, find UT.

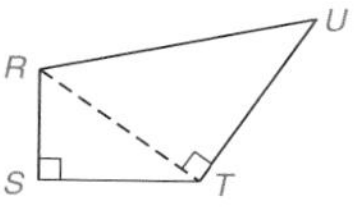

34. *Given:* $\triangle ABC$ is not a right $\triangle$
Prove: $a^2 + b^2 \neq c^2$
[NOTE: $AB = c$, $AC = b$, and $CB = a$.]

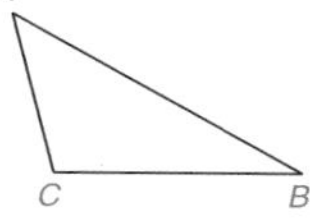

***35.** If $a = p^2 - q^2$, $b = 2pq$, and $c = p^2 + q^2$, show that $c^2 = a^2 + b^2$.

36. Given that the line segment shown has length 1, construct a line segment whose length is $\sqrt{2}$.

1

Exercises 36, 37

37. Using the line segment from Exercise 36, construct a line segment of length 2 and then a second line segment of length $\sqrt{5}$.

38. When the rectangle in the accompanying drawing (whose dimensions are 16 by 9) is cut into pieces and rearranged, a square can be formed. What is the perimeter of this square?

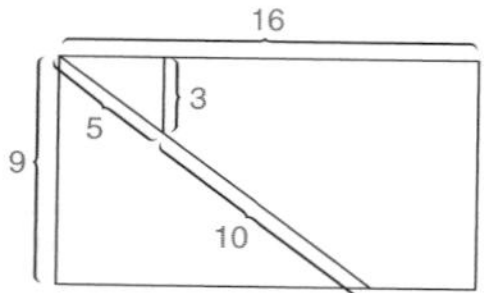

39. A, C, and F are three of the vertices of the cube shown in the accompanying figure. Given that each face of the cube is a square, what is the measure of angle ACF?

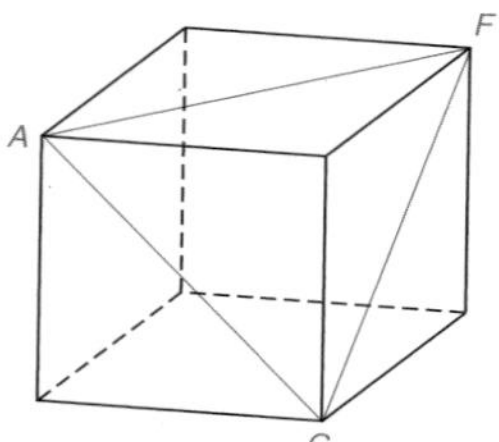

***40.** Find the length of the altitude to the 8-in. side of a triangle whose sides are 4, 6, and 8 in. long.

(HINT: See Example 5.)

41. In the figure, square $RSTV$ has its vertices on the sides of square $WXYZ$ as shown. If $ZT = 5$ and $TY = 12$, find TS. Also find RT.

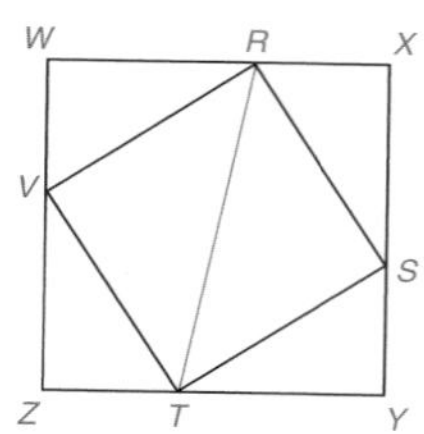

42. Prove that if (a, b, c) is a Pythagorean triple and n is a natural number, then (na, nb, nc) is also a Pythagorean triple.

43. Use Figure 5.19 to prove Theorem 5.4.2.

44. Use Figures 5.20 and 5.21 to prove Lemma 5.4.3.

5.5 Special Right Triangles

KEY CONCEPTS The 45°-45°-90° Triangle The 30°-60°-90° Triangle

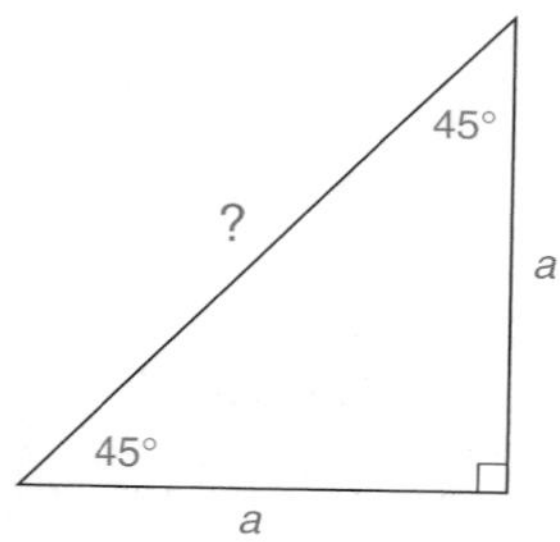

Figure 5.31

Many of the calculations that we do in this section involve square root radicals. To understand some of these calculations better, it may be necessary to review the Properties of Square Roots in Appendix A.4.

Certain right triangles occur so often that they deserve more attention than others. The two special right triangles that we consider in this section have angle measures of 45°, 45°, and 90° or of 30°, 60°, and 90°.

THE 45°-45°-90° RIGHT TRIANGLE

In the 45º-45º-90º triangle, the legs are opposite the congruent angles and are also congruent. Rather than using a and b to represent the lengths of the legs, we use a for both lengths, as shown in Figure 5.31. By the Pythagorean Theorem, it follows that

$$\begin{aligned} c^2 &= a^2 + a^2 \\ c^2 &= 2a^2 \\ c &= \sqrt{2a^2} \\ c &= \sqrt{2} \cdot \sqrt{a^2} \\ c &= a\sqrt{2} \end{aligned}$$

THEOREM 5.5.1 ▶ (45-45-90 Theorem)

In a triangle whose angles measure 45°, 45°, and 90°, the hypotenuse has a length equal to the product of $\sqrt{2}$ and the length of either leg.

SSG *Exs. 1–3*

It is better to memorize the sketch in Figure 5.32 than to repeat the steps of the "proof" that precedes the 45-45-90 Theorem.

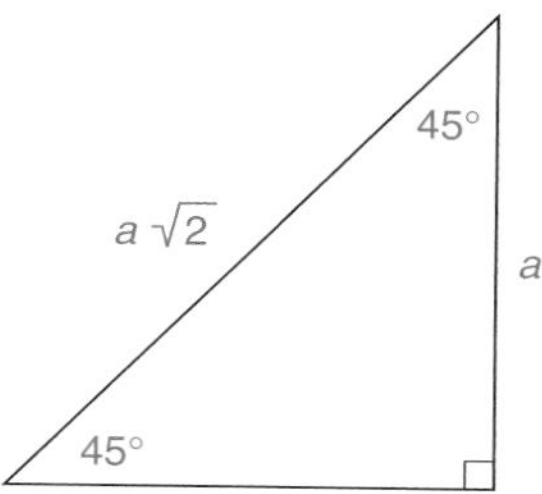

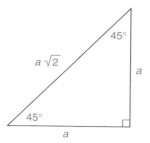

Figure 5.32

Reminder

If two angles of a triangle are congruent, then the sides opposite these angles are congruent.

EXAMPLE 1

Find the lengths of the missing sides in each triangle in Figure 5.33.

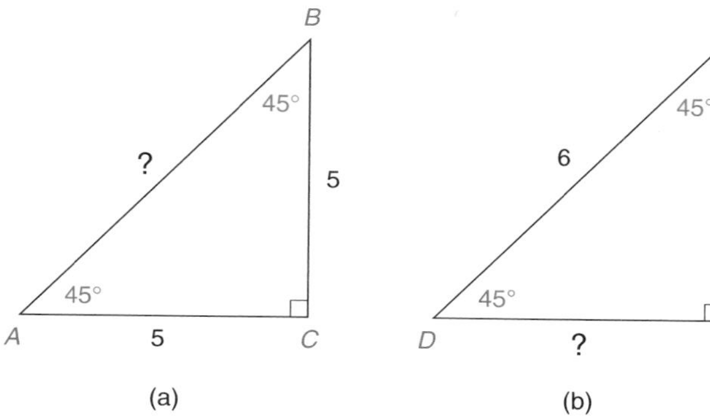

Figure 5.33

Solution

a) The length of hypotenuse $\overline{AB}$ is $5\sqrt{2}$, the product of $\sqrt{2}$ and the length of either of the equal legs.

b) Let a denote the length of $\overline{DE}$ and of $\overline{EF}$. The length of hypotenuse $\overline{DF}$ is $a\sqrt{2}$.

Then $a\sqrt{2} = 6$, so $a = \frac{6}{\sqrt{2}}$. Simplifying yields

$$\begin{aligned} a &= \frac{6}{\sqrt{2}} \cdot \frac{\sqrt{2}}{\sqrt{2}} \\ &= \frac{6\sqrt{2}}{2} \\ &= 3\sqrt{2} \end{aligned}$$

Therefore, $DE = EF = 3\sqrt{2} \approx 4.24$.

NOTE: If we use the Pythagorean Theorem to solve Example 1, the solution in part (a) can be found by solving the equation $5^2 + 5^2 = c^2$ and the solution in part (b) can be found by solving $a^2 + a^2 = 6^2$.

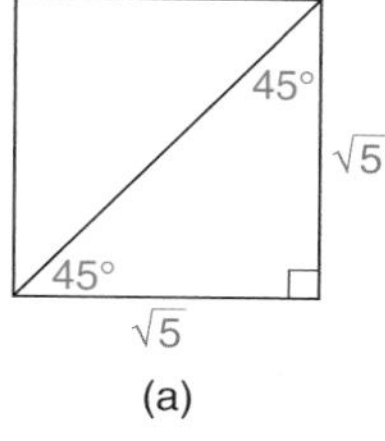

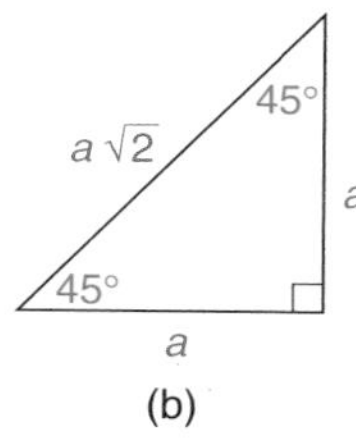

Figure 5.34

EXAMPLE 2

Each side of a square has a length of $\sqrt{5}$. Find the length of a diagonal.

Solution The square shown in Figure 5.34(a) is separated into two 45°-45°-90° triangles. With each of the congruent legs represented by a in Figure 5.34(b), we see that $a = \sqrt{5}$ and the diagonal (hypotenuse) length is $a \cdot \sqrt{2} = \sqrt{5} \cdot \sqrt{2}$, so $a = \sqrt{10} \approx 3.16$.

SSG *Exs. 4–7*

THE 30°-60°-90° RIGHT TRIANGLE

The second special triangle is the 30°-60°-90° triangle.

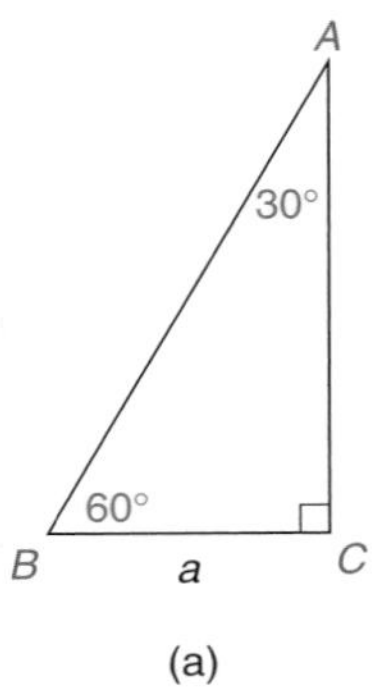

(a)

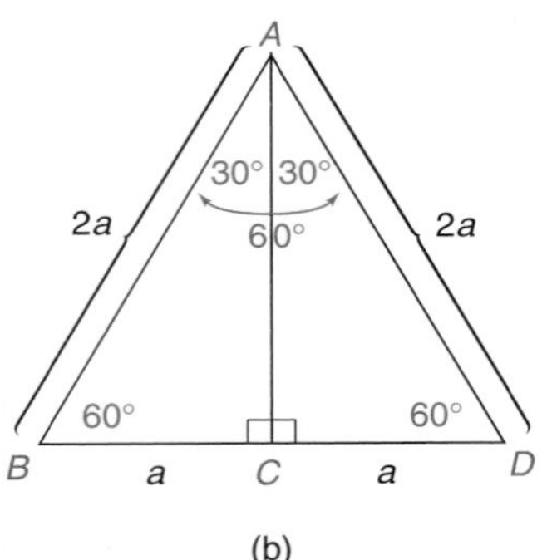

(b)

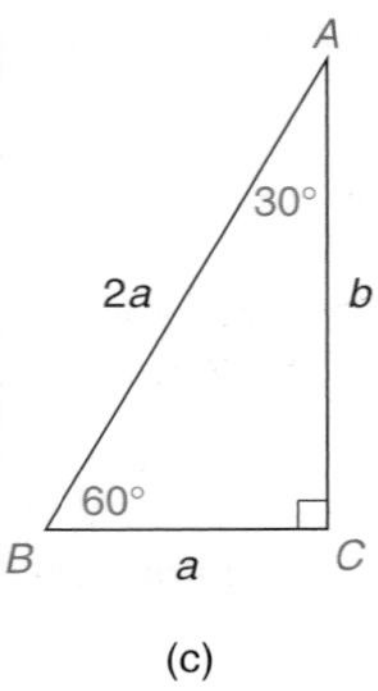

(c)

Figure 5.35

SSG *Exs. 8–10*

THEOREM 5.5.2 ▶ (30-60-90 Theorem)

In a triangle whose angles measure 30°, 60°, and 90°, the hypotenuse has a length equal to twice the length of the shorter leg, and the length of the longer leg is the product of $\sqrt{3}$ and the length of the shorter leg.

EXAMPLE 3

Study the picture proof of Theorem 5.5.2. See Figure 5.35(a).

PICTURE PROOF OF THEOREM 5.5.2

GIVEN: $\triangle ABC$ with $m\angle A = 30°$, $m\angle B = 60°$, $m\angle C = 90°$, and $BC = a$

PROVE: $AB = 2a$ and $AC = a\sqrt{3}$

PROOF: We reflect $\triangle ABC$ across $\overline{AC}$ to form an equiangular and therefore equilateral $\triangle ABD$. As shown in Figures 5.35(b) and 5.35(c), we have $AB = 2a$. To find b in Figure 5.35(c), we apply the Pythagorean Theorem.

$$c^2 = a^2 + b^2$$
$$(2a)^2 = a^2 + b^2$$
$$4a^2 = a^2 + b^2$$
$$3a^2 = b^2,$$

So

$$b^2 = 3a^2$$
$$b = \sqrt{3a^2}$$
$$b = \sqrt{3} \cdot \sqrt{a^2}$$
$$b = a\sqrt{3}$$

That is, $AC = a\sqrt{3}$. ■

It would be best to memorize the sketch in Figure 5.36. So that you will more easily recall which expression is used for each side, remember that the lengths of the sides follow the same order as the angles opposite them. Thus,

Opposite the 30°∠ (smallest angle) is a (length of shortest side).
Opposite the 60°∠ (middle angle) is $a\sqrt{3}$ (length of middle side).
Opposite the 90°∠ (largest angle) is $2a$ (length of longest side).

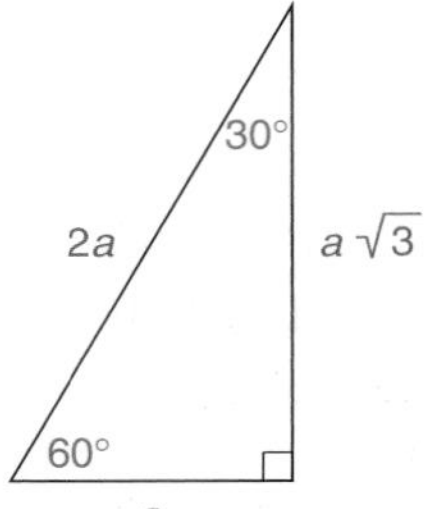

Figure 5.36

EXAMPLE 4

Find the lengths of the missing sides of each triangle in Figure 5.37.

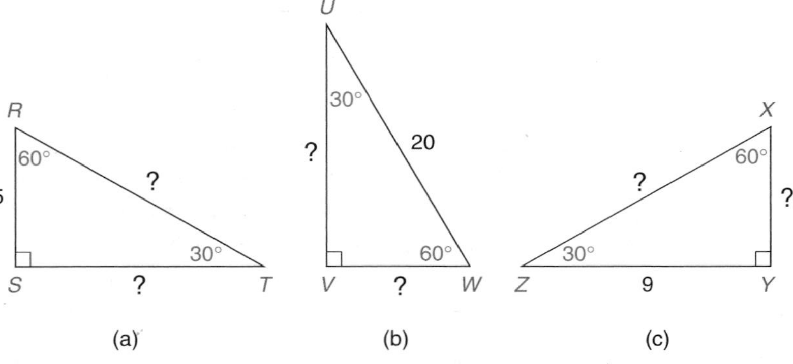

Figure 5.37

Solution

a) $RT = 2 \cdot RS = 2 \cdot 5 = 10$
$ST = RS\sqrt{3} = 5\sqrt{3} \approx 8.66$

b) $UW = 2 \cdot VW \rightarrow 20 = 2 \cdot VW \rightarrow VW = 10$
$UV = VW\sqrt{3} = 10\sqrt{3} \approx 17.32$

c) $ZY = XY\sqrt{3} \rightarrow 9 = XY \cdot \sqrt{3} \rightarrow XY = \frac{9}{\sqrt{3}} = \frac{9}{\sqrt{3}} \cdot \frac{\sqrt{3}}{\sqrt{3}}$
$= \frac{9\sqrt{3}}{3} = 3\sqrt{3} \approx 5.20$

$XZ = 2 \cdot XY = 2 \cdot 3\sqrt{3} = 6\sqrt{3} \approx 10.39$ ■

EXAMPLE 5

Each side of an equilateral triangle measures 6 in. Find the length of an altitude of the triangle.

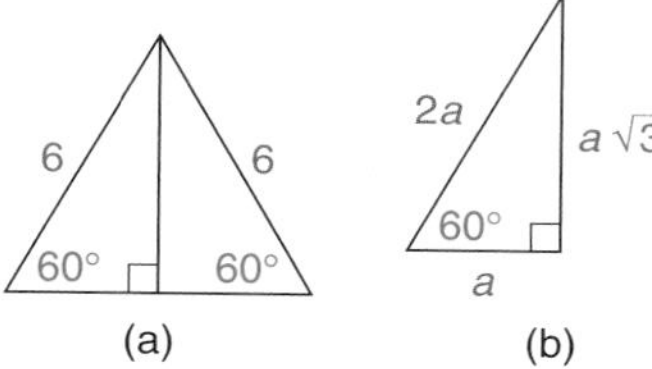

Figure 5.38

Solution The equilateral triangle shown in Figure 5.38(a) is separated into two 30°-60°-90° triangles by the altitude. In the 30°-60°-90° triangle in Figure 5.38(b), the side of the equilateral triangle becomes the hypotenuse, so $2a = 6$ and $a = 3$. The altitude lies opposite the 60° angle of the 30°-60°-90° triangle, so its length is $a\sqrt{3}$ or $3\sqrt{3}$ in. ≈ 5.20 in. ■

The converse of Theorem 5.5.1 is true and is described in the following theorem.

SSG
Exs. 11–13

THEOREM 5.5.3

If the length of the hypotenuse of a right triangle equals the product of $\sqrt{2}$ and the length of either leg, then the angles of the triangle measure 45°, 45°, and 90°.

GIVEN: The right triangle with lengths of sides a, a and $a\sqrt{2}$ (See Figure 5.39).

PROVE: The triangle is a 45°-45°-90° triangle

Proof

In Figure 5.39, the length of the hypotenuse is $a\sqrt{2}$, where a is the length of either leg. In a right triangle, the angles that lie opposite the congruent legs are also congruent. In a right triangle, the acute angles are complementary, so each of the congruent acute angles measures 45°.

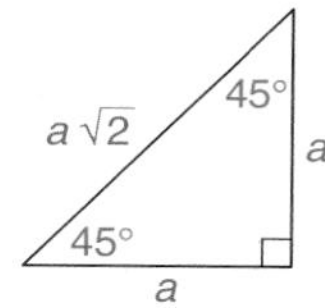

Figure 5.39 ■

EXAMPLE 6

In right $\triangle RST$, $RS = ST$. (See Figure 5.40.) What are the measures of the angles of the triangle? If $RT = 12\sqrt{2}$, what is the length of $\overline{RS}$ (or $\overline{ST}$)?

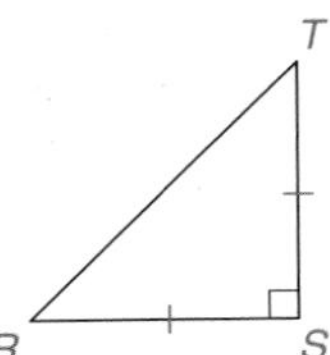

Figure 5.40

Solution The longest side is the hypotenuse $\overline{RT}$, so the right angle is $\angle S$ and $m\angle S = 90°$. Because $\overline{RS} \cong \overline{ST}$, the congruent acute angles are $\angle$s R and T and $m\angle R = m\angle T = 45°$. Because $RT = 12\sqrt{2}$, $RS = ST = 12$. ■

The converse of Theorem 5.5.2 is also true and can be proved by the indirect method. Rather than construct the proof, we state and apply this theorem. See Figure 5.41.

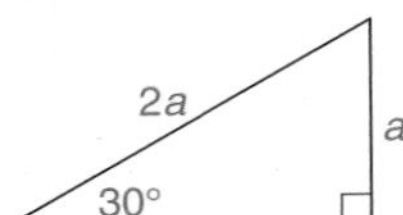

Figure 5.41

THEOREM 5.5.4

If the length of the hypotenuse of a right triangle is twice the length of one leg of the triangle, then the angle of the triangle opposite that leg measures 30°.

An equivalent form of this theorem is stated as follows:

If one leg of a right triangle has a length equal to one-half the length of the hypotenuse, then the angle of the triangle opposite that leg measures 30° (see Figure 5.42).

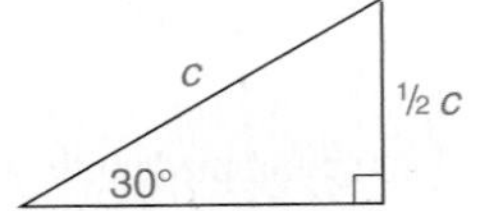

Figure 5.42

EXAMPLE 7

In right $\triangle ABC$ with right $\angle C$, $AB = 24.6$ and $BC = 12.3$ (see Figure 5.43). What are the measures of the angles of the triangle? Also, what is the length of $\overline{AC}$?

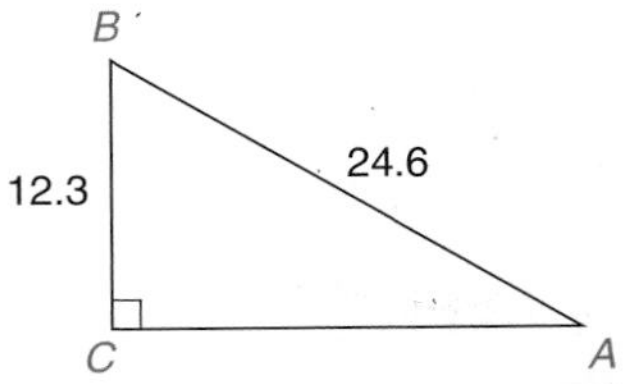

Figure 5.43

Solution Because $\angle C$ is a right angle, $m\angle C = 90°$ and $\overline{AB}$ is the hypotenuse. Because $BC = \frac{1}{2}(AB)$, the angle opposite $\overline{BC}$ measures 30°. Thus, $m\angle A = 30°$ and $m\angle B = 60°$.

Because $\overline{AC}$ lies opposite the 60° angle, $AC = (12.3)\sqrt{3} \approx 21.3$. ■

Exercises 5.5

1. For the 45°-45°-90° triangle shown, suppose that $AC = a$. Find:
 a) BC b) AB

2. For the 45°-45°-90° triangle shown, suppose that $AB = a\sqrt{2}$. Find:
 a) AC b) BC

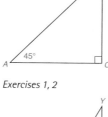

Exercises 1, 2

3. For the 30°-60°-90° triangle shown, suppose that $XZ = a$. Find:
 a) YZ b) XY

4. For the 30°-60°-90° triangle shown, suppose that $XY = 2a$. Find:
 a) XZ b) YZ

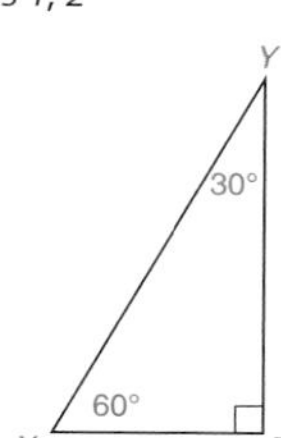

Exercises 3, 4

In Exercises 5 to 22, find the missing lengths. Give your answers in both simplest radical form and as approximations to two decimal places.

5. *Given:* Right $\triangle XYZ$ with $m\angle X = 45°$ and $XZ = 8$
 Find: YZ and XY

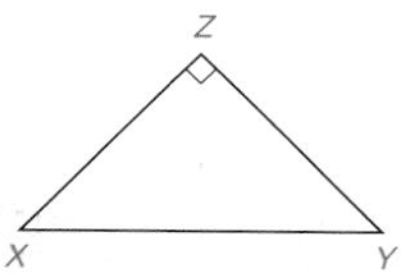

Exercises 5–8

6. *Given:* Right $\triangle XYZ$ with $\overline{XZ} \cong \overline{YZ}$ and $XY = 10$
 Find: XZ and YZ

7. *Given:* Right $\triangle XYZ$ with $\overline{XZ} \cong \overline{YZ}$ and $XY = 10\sqrt{2}$
 Find: XZ and YZ

8. *Given:* Right $\triangle XYZ$ with $m\angle X = 45°$ and $XY = 12\sqrt{2}$
 Find: XZ and YZ

9. *Given:* Right $\triangle DEF$ with $m\angle E = 60°$ and $DE = 5$
 Find: DF and FE

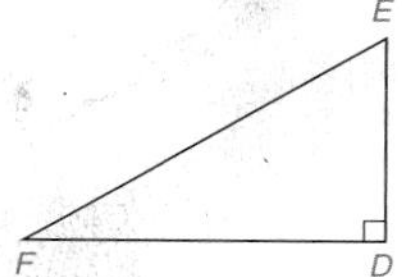

Exercises 9–12

10. *Given:* Right $\triangle DEF$ with $m\angle F = 30°$ and $FE = 12$
 Find: DF and DE

11. *Given:* Right $\triangle DEF$ with $m\angle E = 60°$ and $FD = 12\sqrt{3}$
 Find: DE and FE

12. *Given:* Right $\triangle DEF$ with $m\angle E = 2 \cdot m\angle F$ and $EF = 12\sqrt{3}$
 Find: DE and DF

13. *Given:* Rectangle $HJKL$ with diagonals $\overline{HK}$ and $\overline{JL}$; $m\angle HKL = 30°$
 Find: HL, HK, and MK

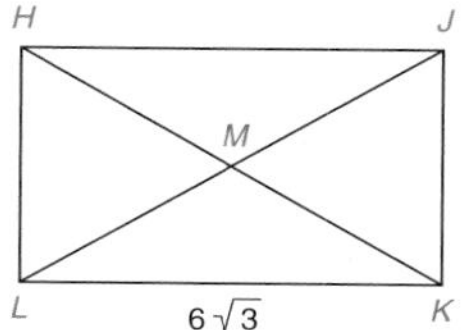

14. *Given:* Right $\triangle RST$ with $RT = 6\sqrt{2}$ and $m\angle STV = 150°$
 Find: RS and ST

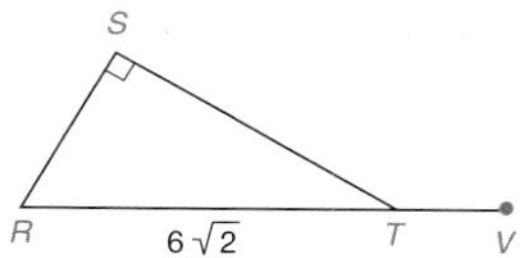

In Exercises 15–19, create drawings as needed.

15. *Given:* $\triangle ABC$ with $m\angle A = m\angle B = 45°$ and $BC = 6$
 Find: AC and AB

16. *Given:* Right $\triangle MNP$ with $MP = PN$ and $MN = 10\sqrt{2}$
 Find: PM and PN

17. *Given:* $\triangle RST$ with $m\angle T = 30°$, $m\angle S = 60°$, and $ST = 12$
 Find: RS and RT

18. *Given:* $\triangle XYZ$ with $\overline{XY} \cong \overline{XZ} \cong \overline{YZ}$; $\overline{ZW} \perp \overline{XY}$ with W on $\overline{XY}$; $YZ = 6$
 Find: ZW

19. *Given:* Square $ABCD$ with diagonals $\overline{DB}$ and $\overline{AC}$ intersecting at E; $DC = 5\sqrt{3}$
 Find: DB

20. *Given:* $\triangle NQM$ with angles as shown in the drawing; $\overline{MP} \perp \overline{NQ}$
 Find: NM, MP, MQ, PQ, and NQ

21. *Given:* $\triangle XYZ$ with angles as shown in the drawing
 Find: XY

(HINT: Compare this drawing to the one for Exercise 20.)

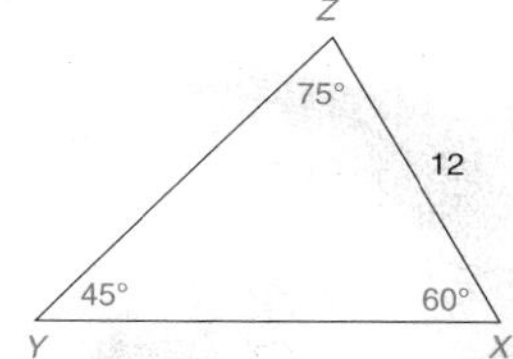

22. *Given:* Rhombus $ABCD$ in which diagonals $\overline{AC}$ and $\overline{DB}$ intersect at point E; $DB = AB = 8$
Find: AC

23. A carpenter is working with a board that is $3\frac{3}{4}$ in. wide. After marking off a point down the side of length $3\frac{3}{4}$ in., the carpenter makes a cut along $\overline{BC}$ with a saw. What is the measure of the angle ($\angle ACB$) that is formed?

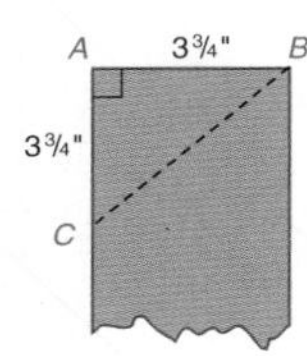

24. To unload groceries from a delivery truck at the Piggly Wiggly Market, an 8-ft ramp that rises 4 ft to the door of the trailer is used. What is the measure of the indicated angle ($\angle D$)?

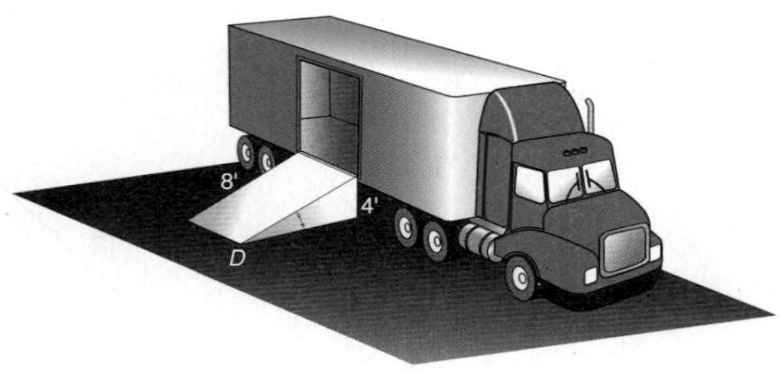

25. A jogger runs along two sides of an open rectangular lot. If the first side of the lot is 200 ft long and the diagonal distance across the lot is 400 ft, what is the measure of the angle formed by the 200-ft and 400-ft dimensions? To the nearest foot, how much farther does the jogger run by traveling the two sides of the block rather than the diagonal distance across the lot?

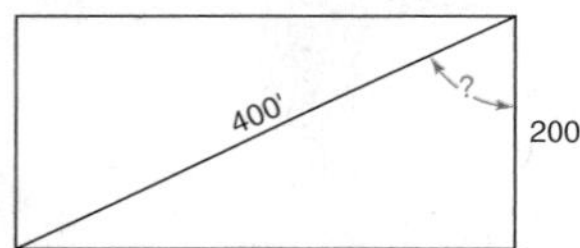

26. Mara's boat leaves the dock at the same time that Meg's boat leaves the dock. Mara's boat travels due east at 12 mph. Meg's boat travels at 24 mph in the direction N 30° E. To the nearest tenth of a mile, how far apart will the boats be in half an hour?

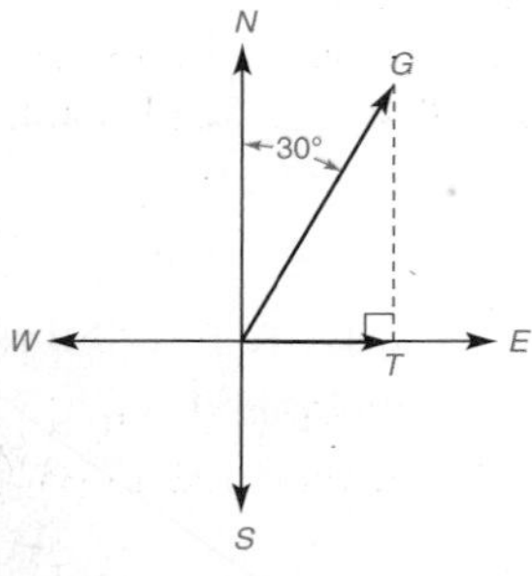

In Exercises 27 to 33, give both exact solutions and approximate solutions to two decimal places.

27. *Given:* In $\triangle ABC$, $\overrightarrow{AD}$ bisects $\angle BAC$
$m\angle B = 30°$ and $AB = 12$
Find: DC and DB

28. *Given:* In $\triangle ABC$, $\overrightarrow{AD}$ bisects $\angle BAC$
$AB = 20$ and $AC = 10$
Find: DC and DB

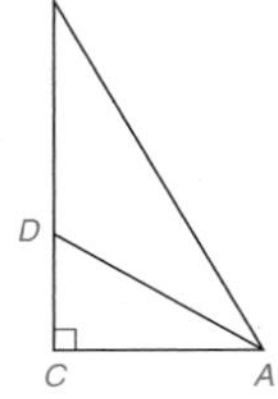

Exercises 27, 28

29. *Given:* $\triangle MNQ$ is equiangular and $NR = 6$
$\overrightarrow{NR}$ bisects $\angle MNQ$
$\overrightarrow{QR}$ bisects $\angle MQN$
Find: NQ

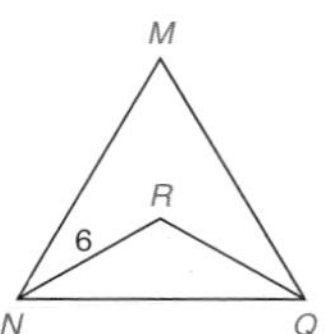

30. *Given:* $\triangle STV$ is an isosceles right triangle
M and N are midpoints of $\overline{ST}$ and $\overline{SV}$
Find: MN

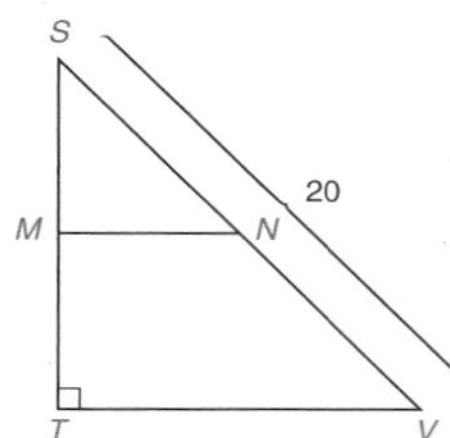

31. *Given:* Right $\triangle ABC$ with $m\angle C = 90°$ and $m\angle BAC = 60°$; point D on $\overline{BC}$; $\overrightarrow{AD}$ bisects $\angle BAC$ and $AB = 12$
Find: BD

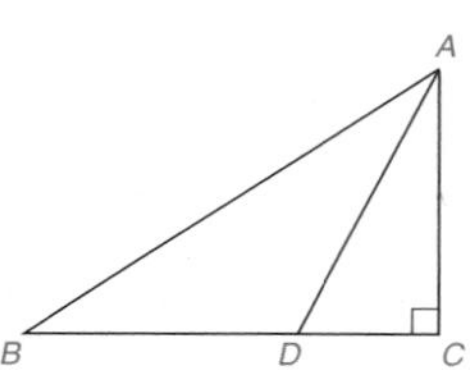

Exercises 31, 32

32. *Given:* Right $\triangle ABC$ with $m\angle C = 90°$ and $m\angle BAC = 60°$; point D on $\overline{BC}$; $\overrightarrow{AD}$ bisects $\angle BAC$ and $AC = 2\sqrt{3}$
Find: BD

33. *Given:* $\triangle ABC$ with $m\angle A = 45°$, $m\angle B = 30°$, and $BC = 12$
Find: AB

(*HINT: Use altitude $\overline{CD}$ from C to $\overline{AB}$ as an auxiliary line.*)

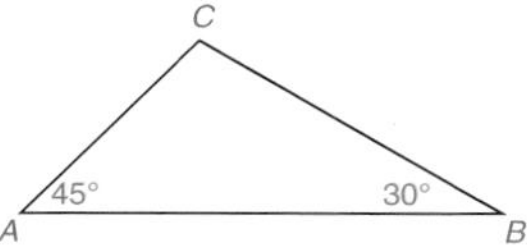

***34.** *Given:* Isosceles trapezoid $MNPQ$ with $QP = 12$ and $m\angle M = 120°$; the bisectors of $\angle$s MQP and NPQ meet at point T on $\overline{MN}$
Find: The perimeter of $MNPQ$

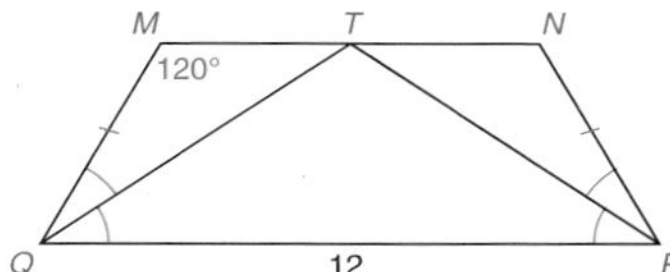

35. In regular hexagon $ABCDEF$, $AB = 6$ inches. Find the exact length of:
a) Diagonal $\overline{BF}$
b) Diagonal $\overline{CF}$

36. In regular hexagon $ABCDEF$, the length of AB is x centimeters. In terms of x, find the length of:
a) Diagonal $\overline{BF}$
b) Diagonal $\overline{CF}$

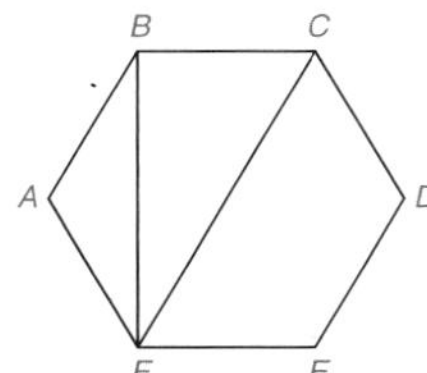

Exercises 35, 36

***37.** In right triangle XYZ, $XY = 3$ and $YZ = 4$. Where V is the midpoint of $\overline{YZ}$ and $m\angle VWZ = 90°$, find VW.

(*HINT: Draw $\overline{XV}$.*)

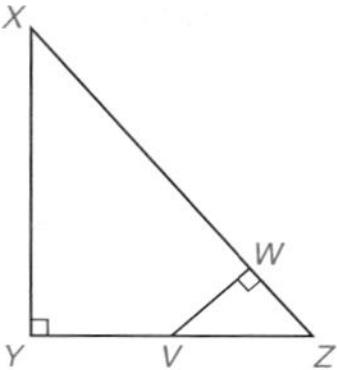

***38.** Diagonal $\overline{EC}$ separates pentagon $ABCDE$ into square $ABCE$ and isosceles triangle DEC. If $AB = 8$ and $DC = 5$, find the length of diagonal $\overline{DB}$.

(*HINT: Draw $\overline{DF} \perp \overline{AB}$.*)

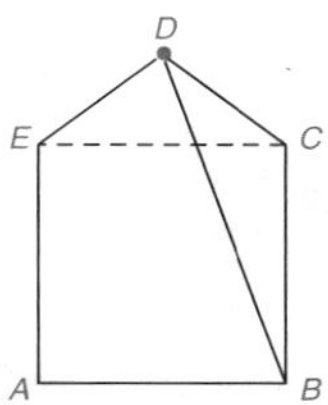

5.6 Segments Divided Proportionally

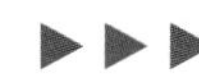

KEY CONCEPTS

- Segments Divided Proportionally
- The Angle-Bisector Theorem
- Ceva's Theorem

In this section, we begin with an informal description of the phrase *divided proportionally*. Suppose that three children have been provided with a joint savings account by their parents. Equal monthly deposits have been made to the account for each child since birth. If the ages of the children are 2, 4, and 6 (assume exactness of ages for simplicity) and the total in the account is \$7200, then the amount that each child should receive can be found by solving the equation

$$2x + 4x + 6x = 7200$$

Solving this equation leads to the solution \$1200 for the 2-year-old, \$2400 for the 4-year-old, and \$3600 for the 6-year-old. We say that the amount has been divided proportionally. Expressed as a proportion, this is

$$\frac{1200}{2} = \frac{2400}{4} = \frac{3600}{6}$$

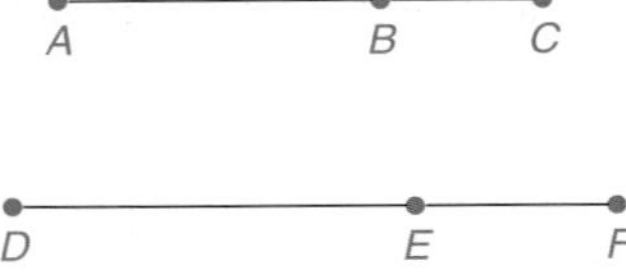

Figure 5.44

In Figure 5.44, $\overline{AC}$ and $\overline{DF}$ are divided proportionally at points B and E if

$$\frac{AB}{DE} = \frac{BC}{EF} \quad \text{or} \quad \frac{AB}{BC} = \frac{DE}{EF}$$

Of course, a pair of segments may be divided proportionally by several points, as shown in Figure 5.45. In this case, $\overline{RW}$ and $\overline{HM}$ are divided proportionally when

$$\frac{RS}{HJ} = \frac{ST}{JK} = \frac{TV}{KL} = \frac{VW}{LM} \quad \left(\text{notice that } \frac{6}{4} = \frac{12}{8} = \frac{15}{10} = \frac{9}{6}\right)$$

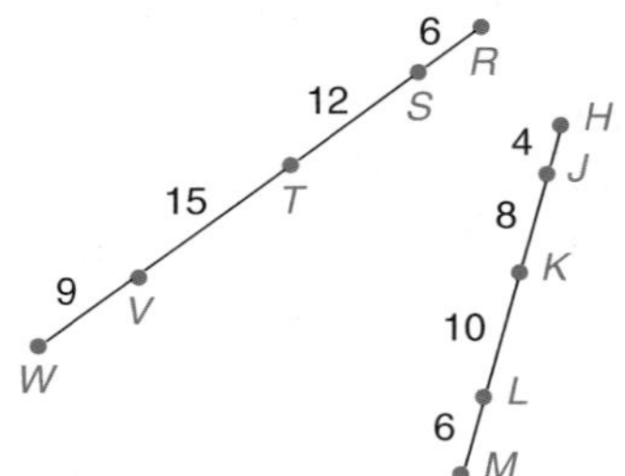

Figure 5.45

EXAMPLE 1

In Figure 5.46, points D and E divide $\overline{AB}$ and $\overline{AC}$ proportionally. If $AD = 4$, $DB = 7$, and $EC = 6$, find AE.

Solution $\frac{AD}{AE} = \frac{DB}{EC}$, so $\frac{4}{x} = \frac{7}{6}$, where $x = AE$. Then $7x = 24$, so $x = AE = \frac{24}{7} = 3\frac{3}{7}$. ■

A property that will be proved in Exercise 31 of this section is

$$\text{If } \frac{a}{b} = \frac{c}{d}, \text{ then } \frac{a + c}{b + d} = \frac{a}{b} = \frac{c}{d}$$

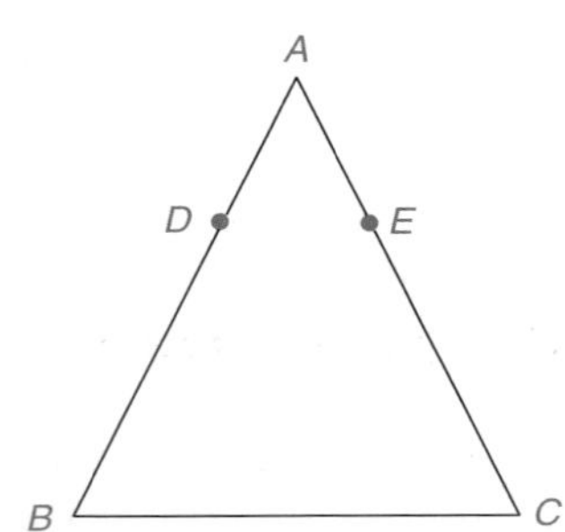

Figure 5.46

In words, we may restate this property as follows:

> The fraction whose numerator and denominator are determined, respectively, by adding numerators and denominators of equal fractions is equal to each of those equal fractions.

Here is a numerical example of this claim:

$$\text{If } \frac{2}{3} = \frac{4}{6}, \quad \text{then} \quad \frac{2 + 4}{3 + 6} = \frac{2}{3} = \frac{4}{6}$$

In Example 2, the preceding property is necessary as a reason.

EXAMPLE 2

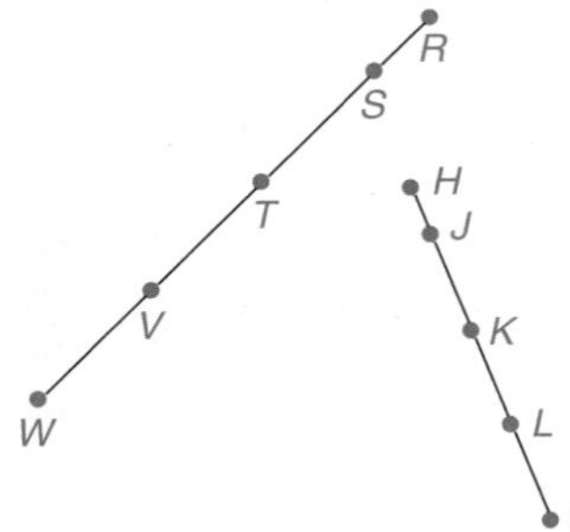

Figure 5.47

GIVEN: $\overline{RW}$ and $\overline{HM}$ are divided proportionally at the points shown in Figure 5.47.

PROVE: $\frac{RT}{HK} = \frac{TW}{KM}$

PROOF: $\overline{RW}$ and $\overline{HM}$ are divided proportionally so that

$$\frac{RS}{HJ} = \frac{ST}{JK} = \frac{TV}{KL} = \frac{VW}{LM}$$

Using the property that if $\frac{a}{b} = \frac{c}{d}$, then $\frac{a + c}{b + d} = \frac{a}{b} = \frac{c}{d}$, we have

$$\frac{RS}{HJ} = \frac{RS + ST}{HJ + JK} = \frac{TV + VW}{KL + LM} = \frac{TV}{KL}$$

Because $RS + ST = RT$, $HJ + JK = HK$, $TV + VW = TW$, and $KL + LM = KM$,

$$\frac{RT}{HK} = \frac{TW}{KM}$$

■

SSG *Exs. 1, 2*

Two properties that were introduced earlier (Property 3 of Section 5.1) are now recalled.

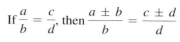

$$\text{If } \frac{a}{b} = \frac{c}{d}, \text{ then } \frac{a \pm b}{b} = \frac{c \pm d}{d}$$

The subtraction operation of the property is needed for the proof of Theorem 5.6.1.

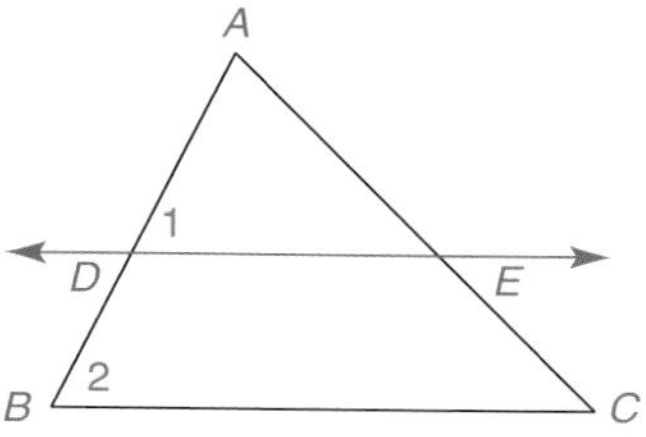

Figure 5.48

THEOREM 5.6.1

If a line is parallel to one side of a triangle and intersects the other two sides, then it divides these sides proportionally.

GIVEN: In Figure 5.48, $\triangle ABC$ with $\overleftrightarrow{DE} \parallel \overline{BC}$ and with $\overleftrightarrow{DE}$ intersecting $\overline{AB}$ at D and $\overline{AC}$ at E

PROVE: $\frac{AD}{DB} = \frac{AE}{EC}$

PROOF: Because $\overleftrightarrow{DE} \parallel \overline{BC}$, $\angle 1 \cong \angle 2$. With $\angle A$ as a common angle for $\triangle ADE$ and $\triangle ABC$, it follows by AA that these triangles are similar. Now

$$\frac{AB}{AD} = \frac{AC}{AE} \qquad \text{(by CSSTP)}$$

By Property 3 of Section 5.1,

$$\frac{AB - AD}{AD} = \frac{AC - AE}{AE}$$

Because $AB - AD = DB$ and $AC - AE = EC$, the proportion becomes

$$\frac{DB}{AD} = \frac{EC}{AE}$$

Using Property 2 of Section 5.1, we can invert both fractions to obtain the desired conclusion:

SSG
Exs. 3–6

$$\frac{AD}{DB} = \frac{AE}{EC}$$ ■

COROLLARY 5.6.2

When three (or more) parallel lines are cut by a pair of transversals, the transversals are divided proportionally by the parallel lines.

GIVEN: $p_1 \parallel p_2 \parallel p_3$ in Figure 5.49 on page 262

PROVE: $\frac{AB}{BC} = \frac{DE}{EF}$

PICTURE PROOF OF COROLLARY 5.6.2

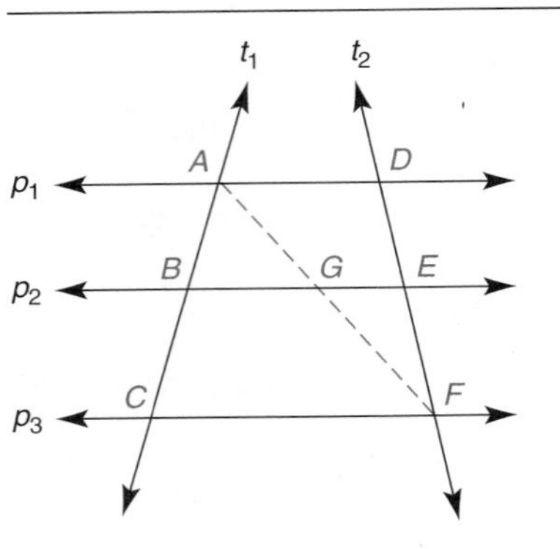

Figure 5.49

In Figure 5.49, draw $\overline{AF}$ as an auxiliary line segment.

On the basis of Theorem 5.6.1, we see that $\frac{AB}{BC} = \frac{AG}{GF}$ in $\triangle ACF$ and that $\frac{AG}{GF} = \frac{DE}{EF}$ in $\triangle ADF$.

By the Transitive Property of Equality, $\frac{AB}{BC} = \frac{DE}{EF}$.

NOTE: By interchanging the means, we can write the last proportion in the form $\frac{AB}{DE} = \frac{BC}{EF}$.

EXAMPLE 3

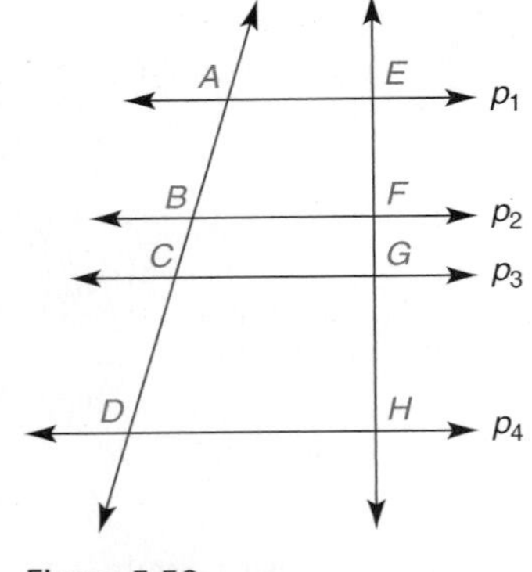

Figure 5.50

Given parallel lines p_1, p_2, p_3, and p_4 cut by t_1 and t_2 so that $AB = 4$, $EF = 3$, $BC = 2$, and $GH = 5$, find FG and CD. (See Figure 5.50.)

Solution Because the transversals are divided proportionally,

$$\frac{AB}{EF} = \frac{BC}{FG} = \frac{CD}{GH}$$

so

$$\frac{4}{3} = \frac{2}{FG} = \frac{CD}{5}$$

Then

$$4 \cdot FG = 6 \quad \text{and} \quad 3 \cdot CD = 20$$

$$FG = \frac{3}{2} = 1\tfrac{1}{2} \quad \text{and} \quad CD = \frac{20}{3} = 6\tfrac{2}{3}$$

Exs. 7, 8

The following activity leads us to the relationship described in Theorem 5.6.3.

Discover

On a piece of paper, draw or construct $\triangle ABC$ whose sides measure $AB = 4$, $BC = 6$, and $AC = 5$. Then construct the angle bisector $\overrightarrow{BD}$ of $\angle B$. How does $\frac{AB}{AD}$ compare to $\frac{BC}{DC}$?

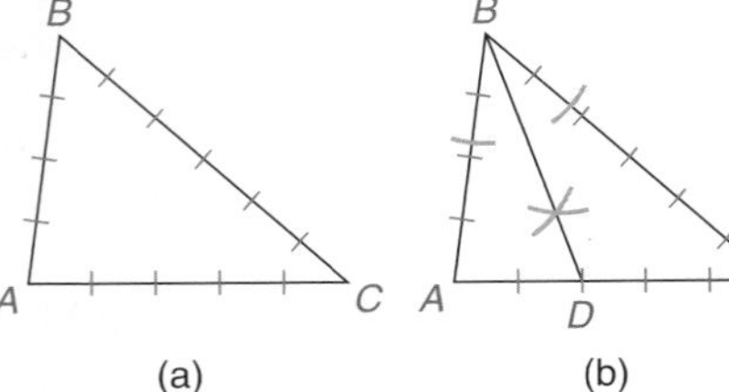

ANSWER

Though not by chance, it may come as a surprise that $\frac{AB}{AD} = \frac{BC}{DC}$ (that is, $\frac{4}{2} = \frac{6}{3}$) and $\frac{AB}{BC} = \frac{AD}{DC}$ $\left(\frac{4}{6} = \frac{2}{3}\right)$. It seems that the bisector of an angle included by two sides of a triangle separates the third side into segments whose lengths are proportional to the lengths of the two sides forming the angle.

The proof of Theorem 5.6.3 requires the use of Theorem 5.6.1.

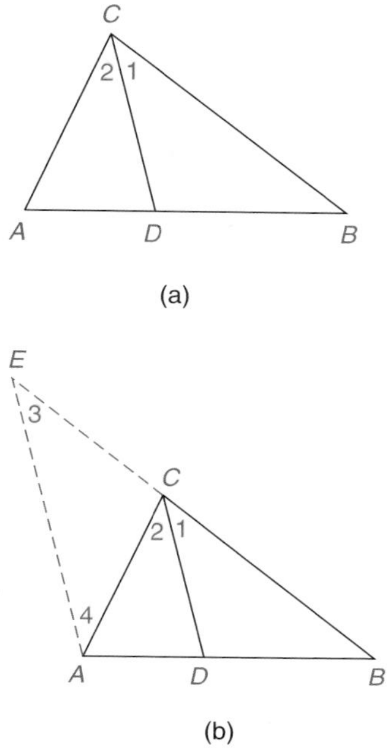

(a)

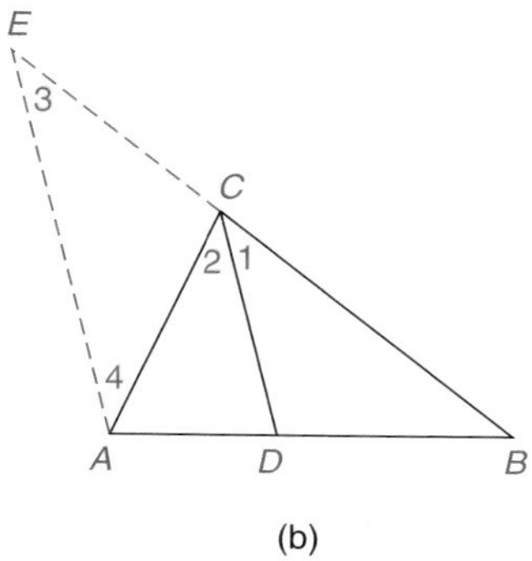

(b)

Figure 5.51

THEOREM 5.6.3 ▶ (The Angle-Bisector Theorem)

If a ray bisects one angle of a triangle, then it divides the opposite side into segments whose lengths are proportional to the lengths of the two sides that form the bisected angle.

GIVEN: $\triangle ABC$ in Figure 5.51(a), in which $\overrightarrow{CD}$ bisects $\angle ACB$

PROVE: $\frac{AD}{AC} = \frac{DB}{CB}$

PROOF: We begin by extending $\overline{BC}$ beyond C (there is only one line through B and C) to meet the line drawn through A parallel to $\overline{DC}$. [See Figure 5.51(b).] Let E be the point of intersection. (These lines must intersect; otherwise, $\overline{AE}$ would have two parallels, $\overline{BC}$ and $\overline{CD}$, through point C.)

Because $\overline{CD} \parallel \overline{EA}$, we have

$$\frac{EC}{AD} = \frac{CB}{DB} \ (*)$$

by Theorem 5.6.1. Now $\angle 1 \cong \angle 2$ because $\overrightarrow{CD}$ bisects $\angle ACB$, $\angle 1 \cong \angle 3$ (corresponding angles for parallel lines), and $\angle 2 \cong \angle 4$ (alternate interior angles for parallel lines). By the Transitive Property, $\angle 3 \cong \angle 4$, so $\triangle ACE$ is isosceles with $\overline{EC} \cong \overline{AC}$. Using substitution, the starred (*) proportion becomes

$$\frac{AC}{AD} = \frac{CB}{DB} \quad \text{or} \quad \frac{AD}{AC} = \frac{DB}{CB} \quad \textbf{(by inversion)}$$ ■

The "Prove statement" of the preceding theorem indicates that one form of the proportion described is given by comparing lengths as shown:

$$\frac{\text{segment at left}}{\text{side at left}} = \frac{\text{segment at right}}{\text{side at right}}$$

Equivalently, the proportion could compare lengths like this:

$$\frac{\text{segment at left}}{\text{segment at right}} = \frac{\text{side at left}}{\text{side at right}}$$

Other forms of the proportion are also possible!

EXAMPLE 4

For $\triangle XYZ$ in Figure 5.52, $XY = 3$ and $YZ = 5$. If $\overrightarrow{YW}$ bisects $\angle XYZ$ and $XW = 2$, find XZ.

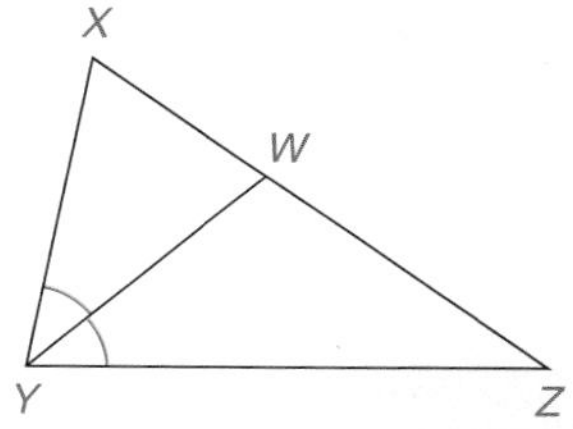

Solution Let $WZ = x$. We know that $\frac{YX}{XW} = \frac{YZ}{WZ}$, so $\frac{3}{2} = \frac{5}{x}$. Therefore,

$$3x = 10$$
$$x = \frac{10}{3} = 3\tfrac{1}{3}$$

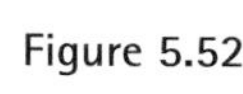

Figure 5.52

Then $WZ = 3\frac{1}{3}$.

SSG *Exs. 9–13*

Because $XZ = XW + WZ$, we have $XZ = 2 + 3\frac{1}{3} = 5\frac{1}{3}$. ■

EXAMPLE 5

In Figure 5.52 (shown in Example 6), suppose that $\triangle XYZ$ has sides of lengths $XY = 3$, $YZ = 4$, and $XZ = 5$. If $\overrightarrow{YW}$ bisects $\angle XYZ$, find XW and WZ.

Solution Let $XW = y$; then $WZ = 5 - y$, and $\frac{XY}{YZ} = \frac{XW}{WZ}$ becomes $\frac{3}{4} = \frac{y}{5-y}$. From this proportion, we can find y as follows.

$$\begin{aligned} 3(5 - y) &= 4y \\ 15 - 3y &= 4y \\ 15 &= 7y \\ y &= \frac{15}{7} \end{aligned}$$

Then $XW = \frac{15}{7} = 2\frac{1}{7}$ and $WZ = 5 - 2\frac{1}{7} = 2\frac{6}{7}$. ■

In the following example, we provide an alternative solution to a problem of the type found in Example 5.

EXAMPLE 6

In Figure 5.52, $\triangle XYZ$ is isosceles with $\overline{XZ} \cong \overline{YZ}$. If $XY = 3$ and $YZ = 6$, find XW and WZ.

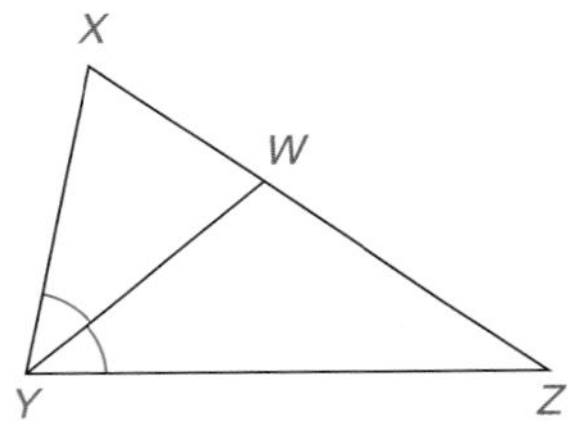

Solution Because the ratio $XY{:}YZ$ is 3:6, or 1:2, the ratio $XW{:}WZ$ is also 1:2. Thus, we can represent these lengths by

$$XW = a \qquad \text{and} \qquad WZ = 2a$$

With $XZ = 6$ in the isosceles triangle, the statement $XW + WZ = XZ$ becomes $a + 2a = 6$, so $3a = 6$, and $a = 2$. Now $XW = 2$ and $WZ = 4$. ■

Figure 5.52

You will find the proof of the following theorem in the Perspective on History section at the end of this chapter. In Ceva's Theorem, point D is *any* point in the interior of the triangle. See Figure 5.53(a). The auxiliary lines needed to complete the proof of Ceva's Theorem are shown in Figure 5.53(b). In the figure, line ℓ is drawn through vertex C so that it is parallel to $\overline{AB}$. Then $\overline{BE}$ and $\overline{AF}$ are extended to meet ℓ at R and S, respectively.

THEOREM 5.6.4 ▶ (Ceva's Theorem)

Let point D be any point in the interior of $\triangle ABC$, and let $\overline{BE}$, $\overline{AF}$, and $\overline{CG}$ be the line segments determined by D and vertices of $\triangle ABC$. Then the product of the ratios of the lengths of the segments of each of the three sides (taken in order from a given vertex of the triangle) equals 1; that is,

$$\frac{AG}{GB} \cdot \frac{BF}{FC} \cdot \frac{CE}{EA} = 1$$

(a) (b)

Figure 5.53

For Figure 5.53, Ceva's Theorem can be stated in many equivalent forms:

$$\frac{AE}{EC}\cdot\frac{CF}{FB}\cdot\frac{BG}{GA} = 1, \qquad \frac{CF}{FB}\cdot\frac{BG}{GA}\cdot\frac{AE}{EC} = 1, \qquad \text{etc.}$$

In each case, we select a vertex and form ratios of the lengths of segments of sides in a set order.

We will apply Ceva's Theorem in Example 7.

EXAMPLE 7

In $\triangle RST$ with interior point D, $RG = 6$, $GS = 4$, $SH = 4$, $HT = 3$, and $KR = 5$. Find TK. See Figure 5.54.

Solution Let $TK = a$. Applying Ceva's Theorem and following a counterclockwise path beginning at vertex R, we have $\frac{RG}{GS}\cdot\frac{SH}{HT}\cdot\frac{TK}{KR} = 1$. Then $\frac{6}{4}\cdot\frac{4}{3}\cdot\frac{a}{5} = 1$ and so $\frac{\cancel{6}^2}{\cancel{4}_1}\cdot\frac{\cancel{4}^1}{\cancel{3}_1}\cdot\frac{a}{5} = 1$ becomes $\frac{2a}{5} = 1$. Then $2a = 5$ and $a = 2.5$; thus, $TK = 2.5$.

SSG *Ex. 14*

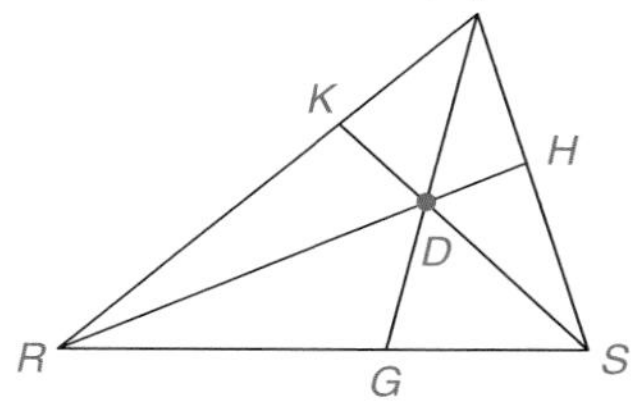

Figure 5.54

Exercises 5.6

1. In preparing a certain recipe, a chef uses 5 oz of ingredient A, 4 oz of ingredient B, and 6 oz of ingredient C. If 90 oz of this dish are needed, how many ounces of each ingredient should be used?

2. In a chemical mixture, 2 g of chemical A are used for each gram of chemical B, and 3 g of chemical C are needed for each gram of B. If 72 g of the mixture are prepared, what amount (in grams) of each chemical is needed?

3. Given that $\frac{AB}{EF} = \frac{BC}{FG} = \frac{CD}{GH}$, are the following proportions true?

   a) $\frac{AC}{EG} = \frac{CD}{GH}$

   b) $\frac{AB}{EF} = \frac{BD}{FH}$

4. Given that $\overleftrightarrow{XY} \parallel \overline{TS}$, are the following proportions true?

   a) $\frac{TX}{XR} = \frac{RY}{YS}$

   b) $\frac{TR}{XR} = \frac{SR}{YR}$

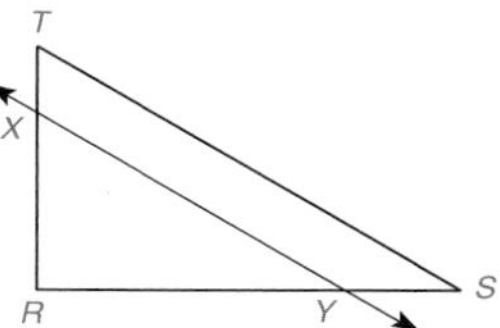

5. *Given:* $\ell_1 \parallel \ell_2 \parallel \ell_3 \parallel \ell_4$, $AB = 5$, $BC = 4$, $CD = 3$, $EH = 10$

   Find: EF, FG, GH

   (See the figure for Exercise 6).

6. *Given:* $\ell_1 \parallel \ell_2 \parallel \ell_3 \parallel \ell_4$, $AB = 7$, $BC = 5$, $CD = 4$, $EF = 6$
Find: FG, GH, EH

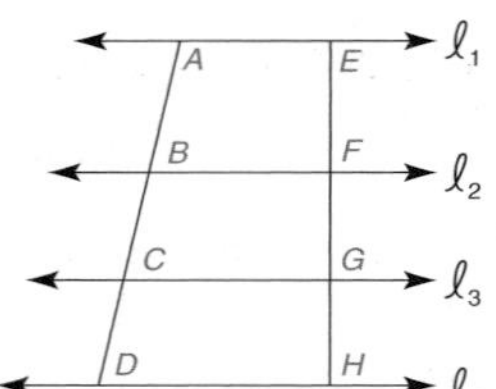

Exercises 5, 6

7. *Given:* $\ell_1 \parallel \ell_2 \parallel \ell_3$, $AB = 4$, $BC = 5$, $DE = x$, $EF = 12 - x$
Find: x, DE, EF

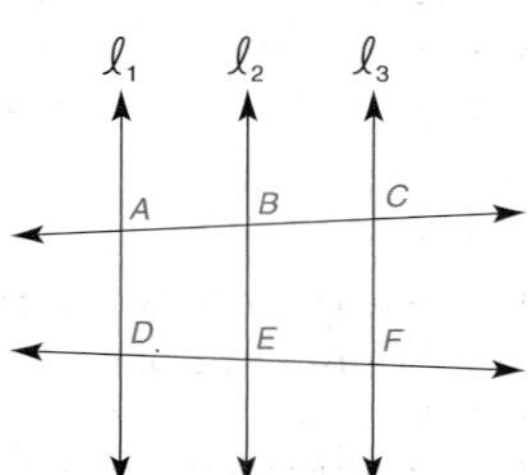

Exercises 7, 8

8. *Given:* $\ell_1 \parallel \ell_2 \parallel \ell_3$, $AB = 5$, $BC = x$, $DE = x - 2$, $EF = 7$
Find: x, BC, DE

9. *Given:* $\overleftrightarrow{DE} \parallel \overline{BC}$, $AD = 5$, $DB = 12$, $AE = 7$
Find: EC

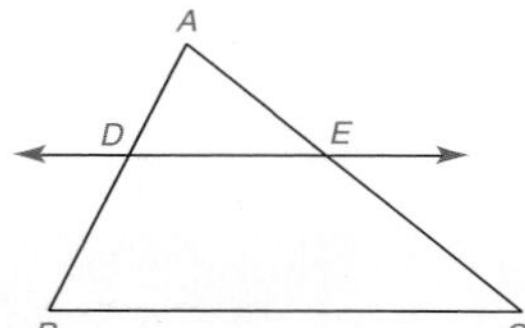

Exercises 9–12

10. *Given:* $\overleftrightarrow{DE} \parallel \overline{BC}$, $AD = 6$, $DB = 10$, $AC = 20$
Find: EC

11. *Given:* $\overleftrightarrow{DE} \parallel \overline{BC}$, $AD = a - 1$, $DB = 2a + 2$, $AE = a$, $EC = 4a - 5$
Find: a and AD

12. *Given:* $\overleftrightarrow{DE} \parallel \overline{BC}$, $AD = 5$, $DB = a + 3$, $AE = a + 1$, $EC = 3(a - 1)$
Find: a and EC

13. *Given:* $\overrightarrow{RW}$ bisects $\angle SRT$
Do the following equalities hold?
a) $SW = WT$
b) $\frac{RS}{RT} = \frac{SW}{WT}$

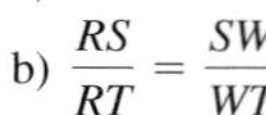

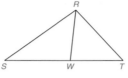

Exercises 13, 14

14. *Given:* $\overrightarrow{RW}$ bisects $\angle SRT$
Do the following equalities hold?
a) $\frac{RS}{SW} = \frac{RT}{WT}$
b) $m\angle S = m\angle T$

15. *Given:* $\overrightarrow{UT}$ bisects $\angle WUV$, $WU = 8$, $UV = 12$, $WT = 6$
Find: TV

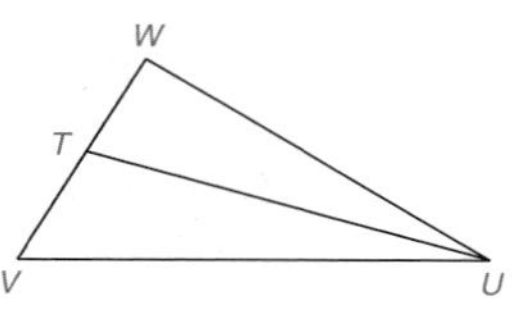

Exercises 15, 16

16. *Given:* $\overrightarrow{UT}$ bisects $\angle WUV$, $WU = 9$, $UV = 12$, $WV = 9$
Find: WT

17. *Given:* $\overrightarrow{NQ}$ bisects $\angle MNP$, $NP = MQ$, $QP = 8$, $MN = 12$
Find: NP

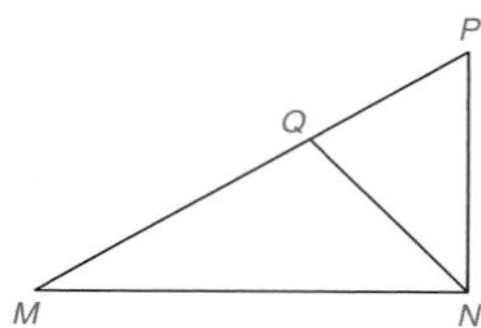

Exercises 17–19

Exercises 18 and 19 are based on a theorem (not stated) that is the converse of Theorem 5.6.3.

18. *Given:* $NP = 4$, $MN = 8$, $PQ = 3$, and $MQ = 6$; $m\angle P = 63°$ and $m\angle M = 27°$
Find: $m\angle PNQ$
(HINT: $\frac{NP}{MN} = \frac{PQ}{MQ}$.*)*

19. *Given:* $NP = 6$, $MN = 9$, $PQ = 4$, and $MQ = 6$; $m\angle P = 62°$ and $m\angle M = 36°$
Find: $m\angle QNM$
(HINT: $\frac{NP}{MN} = \frac{PQ}{MQ}$.*)*

20. *Given:* In $\triangle ABC$, $\overrightarrow{AD}$ bisects $\angle BAC$
$AB = 20$ and $AC = 16$
Find: DC and DB

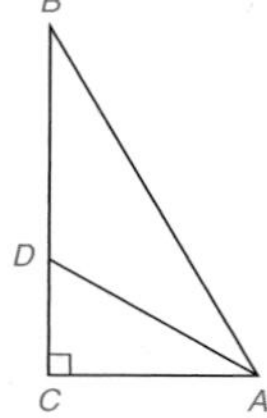

21. In $\triangle ABC$, $\angle ACB$ is trisected by $\overrightarrow{CD}$ and $\overrightarrow{CE}$ so that $\angle 1 \cong \angle 2 \cong \angle 3$. Write two different proportions that follow from this information.

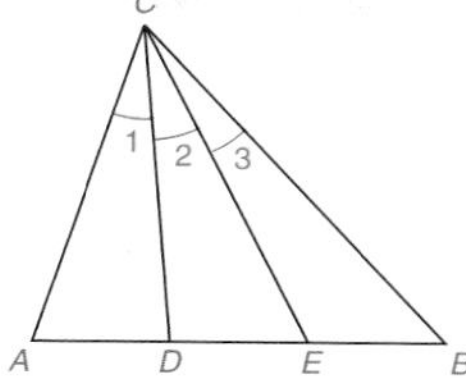

22. In $\triangle ABC$, $m\angle CAB = 80°$, $m\angle ACB = 60°$, and $m\angle ABC = 40°$. With the angle bisectors as shown, which line segment is longer?
a) $\overline{AE}$ or $\overline{EC}$? b) $\overline{CD}$ or $\overline{DB}$? c) $\overline{AF}$ or $\overline{FB}$?

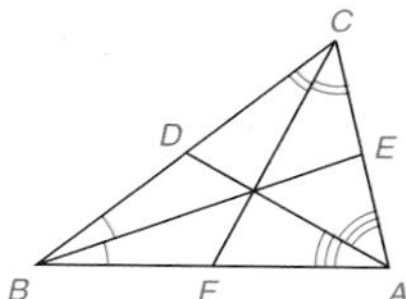

23. In right $\triangle RST$ (not shown) with right $\angle S$, $\overrightarrow{RV}$ bisects $\angle SRT$ so that V lies on side $\overline{ST}$. If $RS = 6$, $ST = 6\sqrt{3}$, and $RT = 12$, find SV and VT.

24. *Given:* AC is the geometric mean between AD and AB. $AD = 4$, and $DB = 6$
Find: AC

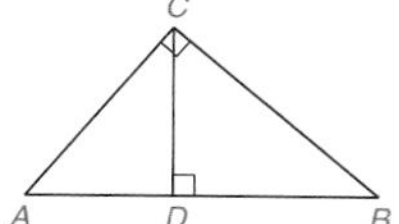

25. *Given:* $\overrightarrow{RV}$ bisects $\angle SRT$, $RS = x - 6$, $SV = 3$, $RT = 2 - x$, and $VT = x + 2$
Find: x
(HINT: You will need to apply the Quadratic Formula.)

26. *Given:* $\overrightarrow{MR}$ bisects $\angle NMP$, $MN = 2x$, $NR = x$, $RP = x + 1$, and $MP = 3x - 1$
Find: x

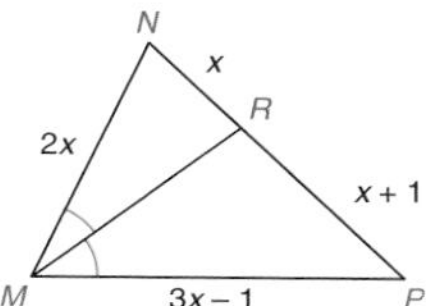

27. Given point D in the interior of $\triangle RST$, which statement(s) is (are) true?

a) $\frac{RK}{KT} \cdot \frac{TH}{HS} \cdot \frac{GS}{RG} = 1$

b) $\frac{TK}{KR} \cdot \frac{RG}{GS} \cdot \frac{SH}{HT} = 1$

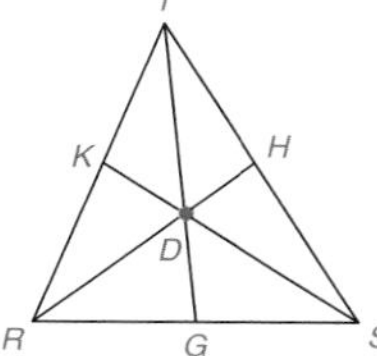

Exercises 27–30

28. In $\triangle RST$ shown in Exercise 27, suppose that $\overline{RH}$, $\overline{TG}$, and $\overline{SK}$ are medians. Find the value of:
a) $\frac{RK}{KT}$ b) $\frac{TH}{HS}$

29. Given point D in the interior of $\triangle RST$, suppose that $RG = 3$, $GS = 4$, $SH = 4$, $HT = 5$, and $KT = 3$. Find RK.

30. Given point D in the interior of $\triangle RST$, suppose that $RG = 2$, $GS = 3$, $SH = 3$, and $HT = 4$. Find $\frac{KT}{KR}$.

31. Complete the proof of this property:

If $\frac{a}{b} = \frac{c}{d}$, then $\frac{a+c}{b+d} = \frac{a}{b}$ and $\frac{a+c}{b+d} = \frac{c}{d}$

PROOF

Statements	Reasons
1. $\frac{a}{b} = \frac{c}{d}$	1. ?
2. $b \cdot c = a \cdot d$	2. ?
3. $ab + bc = ab + ad$	3. ?
4. $b(a + c) = a(b + d)$	4. ?
5. $\frac{a+c}{b+d} = \frac{a}{b}$	5. Means-Extremes Property (symmetric form)
6. $\frac{a+c}{b+d} = \frac{c}{d}$	6. ?

32. *Given:* $\triangle RST$, with $\overleftrightarrow{XY} \parallel \overline{RT}$, $\overleftrightarrow{YZ} \parallel \overline{RS}$
Prove: $\frac{RX}{XS} = \frac{ZT}{RZ}$

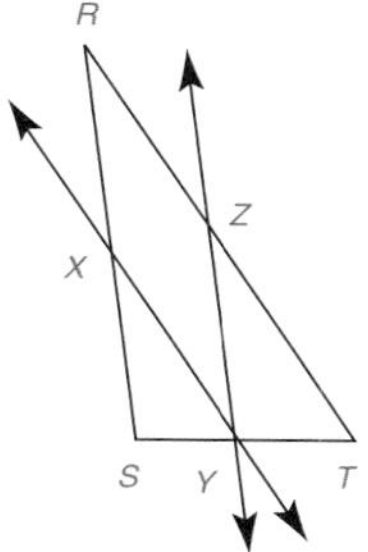

33. Use Theorem 5.6.1 and the drawing to complete the proof of this theorem: "If a line is parallel to one side of a triangle and passes through the midpoint of a second side, then it will pass through the midpoint of the third side."
Given: $\triangle RST$ with M the midpoint of $\overline{RS}$; $\overleftrightarrow{MN} \parallel \overline{ST}$
Prove: N is the midpoint of $\overline{RT}$

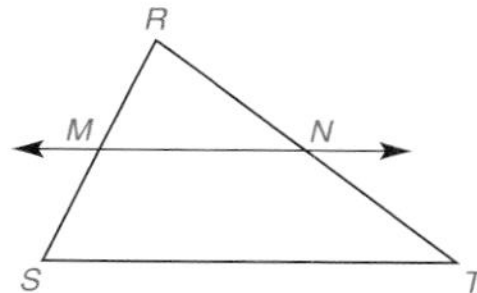

34. Use Exercise 33 and the following drawing to complete the proof of this theorem: "The length of the median of a trapezoid is one-half the sum of the lengths of the two bases."

Given: Trapezoid $ABCD$ with median $\overline{MN}$
Prove: $MN = \frac{1}{2}(AB + CD)$

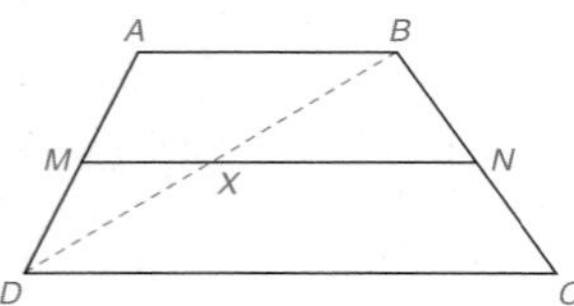

35. Use Theorem 5.6.3 to complete the proof of this theorem: "If the bisector of an angle of a triangle also bisects the opposite side, then the triangle is an isosceles triangle."

Given: $\triangle XYZ$; $\overrightarrow{YW}$ bisects $\angle XYZ$; $\overline{WX} \cong \overline{WZ}$
Prove: $\triangle XYZ$ is isosceles

(HINT: Use a proportion to show that $YX = YZ$.)

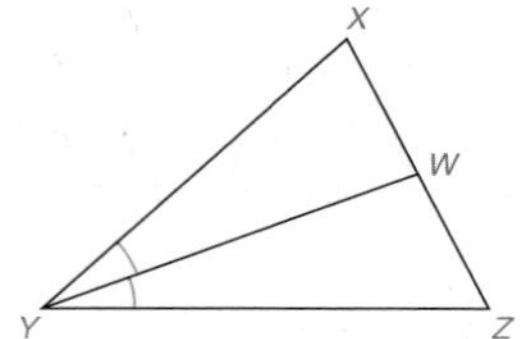

***36.** In right $\triangle ABC$ (not shown) with right $\angle C$, $\overrightarrow{AD}$ bisects $\angle BAC$ so that D lies on side $\overline{CB}$. If $AC = 6$ and $DC = 3$, find BD and AB.

(HINT: Let $BD = x$ and $AB = 2x$. Then use the Pythagorean Theorem.)

***37.** *Given:* $\triangle ABC$ (not shown) is isosceles with $m\angle ABC = m\angle C = 72°$; $\overrightarrow{BD}$ bisects $\angle ABC$ and $AB = 1$
Find: BC

***38.** *Given:* $\triangle RST$ with right $\angle RST$; $m\angle R = 30°$ and $ST = 6$; $\angle RST$ is trisected by $\overrightarrow{SM}$ and $\overrightarrow{SN}$
Find: TN, NM, and MR

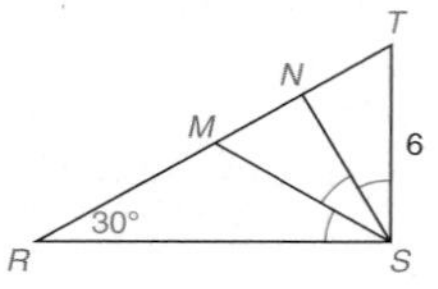

***39.** In the figure, the angle bisectors of $\triangle ABC$ intersect at a point in the interior of the triangle. If $BC = 5$, $BA = 6$, and $CA = 4$, find:

a) CD and DB
(HINT: Use Theorem 5.6.3.)
b) CE and EA
c) BF and FA
d) Use results from parts (a), (b), and (c) to show that $\frac{BD}{DC} \cdot \frac{CE}{EA} \cdot \frac{AF}{FB} = 1$.

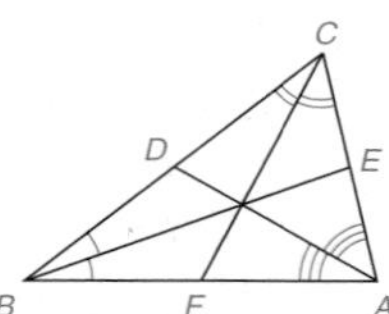

***40.** In $\triangle RST$, the altitudes of the triangle intersect at a point in the interior of the triangle. The lengths of the sides of $\triangle RST$ are $RS = 14$, $ST = 15$, and $TR = 13$.

a) If $TX = 12$, find RX and XS.
(HINT: Use the Pythagorean Theorem)
b) If $RY = \frac{168}{15}$, find TY and YS.
c) If $SZ = \frac{168}{13}$, find ZR and TZ.
d) Use results from parts (a), (b), and (c) to show that $\frac{RX}{XS} \cdot \frac{SY}{YT} \cdot \frac{TZ}{ZR} = 1$.

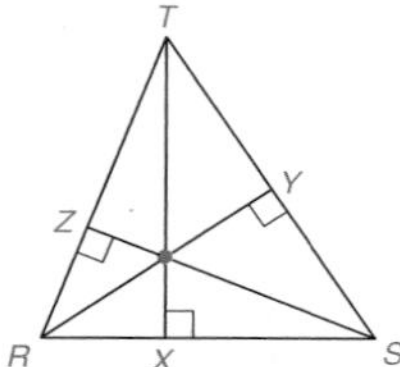

PERSPECTIVE ON HISTORY

Ceva's Proof

Giovanni Ceva (1647–1736) was the Italian mathematician for whom Ceva's Theorem is named. Although his theorem is difficult to believe, its proof is not lengthy. The proof follows.

THEOREM 5.6.4 ▶ (Ceva's Theorem)

Let point D be any point in the interior of $\triangle ABC$, and let $\overline{BE}$, $\overline{AF}$, and $\overline{CG}$ be the line segments determined by D and vertices of $\triangle ABC$. Then the product of the ratios of the segments of each of the three sides (taken in order from a given vertex of the triangle) equals 1; that is, $\frac{AG}{GB} \cdot \frac{BF}{FC} \cdot \frac{CE}{EA} = 1$.

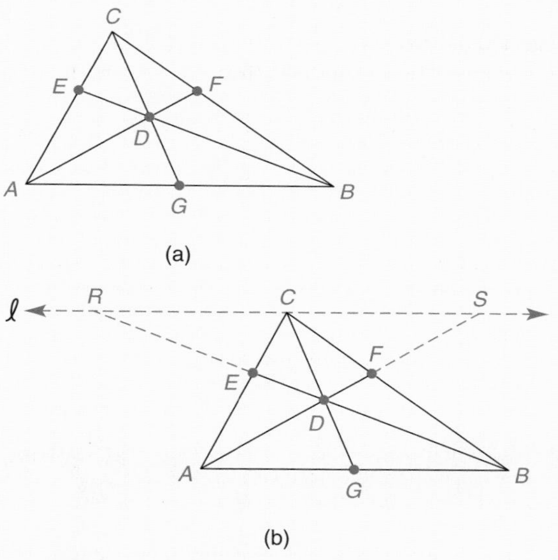

Figure 5.55

Proof

Given $\triangle ABC$ with interior point D [see Figure 5.55(a)], draw a line ℓ through point C that is parallel to $\overline{AB}$. Now extend $\overline{BE}$ to meet ℓ at point R. Likewise, extend $\overline{AF}$ to meet ℓ at point S. See Figure 5.55(b). With similar triangles, we will be able to substitute desired ratios into the obvious statement $\frac{CS}{CR} \cdot \frac{AB}{CS} \cdot \frac{CR}{AB} = 1(*)$, in which each numerator has a matching denominator. Because $\triangle AGD \sim \triangle SCD$ by AA, we have $\frac{AG}{CS} = \frac{GD}{CD}$. Also with $\triangle DGB \sim \triangle DCR$, we have $\frac{GD}{CD} = \frac{GB}{CR}$. By the Transitive Property of Equality, $\frac{AG}{CS} = \frac{GB}{CR}$, and by interchanging the means, we see that $\frac{AG}{BG} = \frac{CS}{CR}$. [The first ratio, $\frac{AG}{BG}$, of this proportion will replace the ratio $\frac{CS}{CR}$ in the starred (*) statement.]

From the fact that $\triangle CSF \sim \triangle BAF$, $\frac{AB}{SC} = \frac{BF}{FC}$. [The second ratio, $\frac{BF}{FC}$, of this proportion will replace the ratio $\frac{AB}{CS}$ in the starred (*) statement.]

With $\triangle RCE \sim \triangle BAE$, $\frac{CE}{EA} = \frac{CR}{AB}$. [The first ratio, $\frac{CE}{EA}$, of this proportion replaces $\frac{CR}{AB}$ in the starred (*) statement.] Making the indicated substitutions into the starred statement, we have

$$\frac{AG}{GB} \cdot \frac{BF}{FC} \cdot \frac{CE}{EA} = 1$$

PERSPECTIVE ON APPLICATION

An Unusual Application of Similar Triangles

The following problem is one that can be solved in many ways. If methods of calculus are applied, the solution is found through many complicated and tedious calculations. The simplest solution, which follows, utilizes geometry and similar triangles.

Problem: A hiker is at a location 450 ft downstream from his campsite. He is 200 ft away from the straight stream, and his tent is 100 ft away, as shown in Figure 5.56(a) on page 270. Across the flat field, he sees that a spark from his campfire has ignited the tent. Taking the empty bucket he is carrying, he runs to the river to get water and then on to the tent. To what point on the river should he run to minimize the distance he travels?

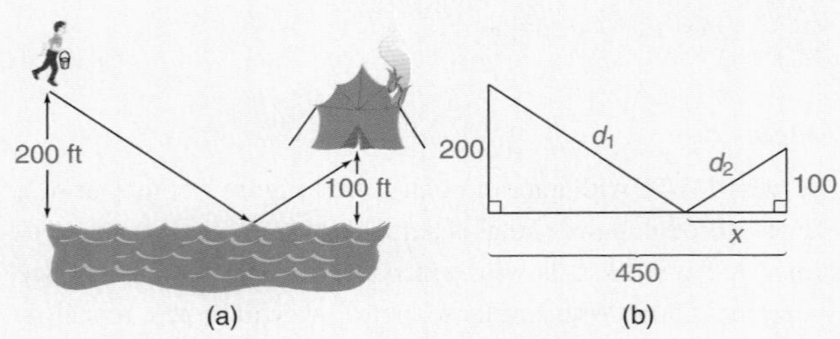

Figure 5.56

We wish to determine x in Figure 5.56(b) so that the total distance $D = d_1 + d_2$ is as small as possible. Consider three possible choices of this point on the river. These are suggested by dashed, dotted, and solid lines in Figure 5.57(a). Also consider the reflections of the triangles across the river. [See Figure 5.57(b).]

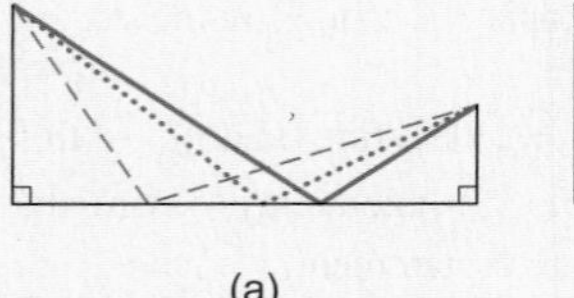

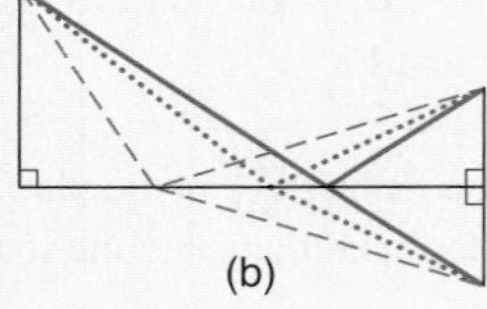

Figure 5.57

The minimum distance D occurs where the segments of lengths d_1 and d_2 form a straight line. That is, the configuration with the solid line segments minimizes the distance. In that case, the triangle at left and the reflected triangle at right are similar. See Figure 5.58.

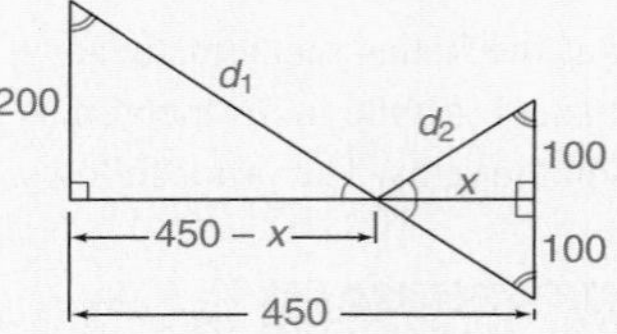

Figure 5.58

Thus
$$
\begin{aligned}
\frac{200}{100} &= \frac{450 - x}{x} \\
200x &= 100(450 - x) \\
200x &= 45{,}000 - 100x \\
300x &= 45{,}000 \\
x &= 150
\end{aligned}
$$

Accordingly, the desired point on the river is 300 ft (determined by $450 - x$) upstream from the hiker's location. ■

Summary

A LOOK BACK AT CHAPTER 5

One goal of this chapter has been to define similarity for two polygons. We postulated a method for proving triangles similar and showed that proportions are a consequence of similar triangles, a line parallel to one side of a triangle, and a ray bisecting one angle of a triangle. The Pythagorean Theorem and its converse were proved. We discussed the 30°-60°-90° triangle, the 45°-45°-90° triangle, and other special right triangles with sides forming Pythagorean triples. The final section developed the concept segments divided proportionally.

A LOOK AHEAD TO CHAPTER 6

In the next chapter, we will begin our work with the circle. Segments and lines of the circle will be defined, as will special angles in a circle. Several theorems dealing with the measurements of these angles and line segments will be proved. Our work with constructions will enable us to deal with the locus of points and the concurrence of lines that are found in Chapter 7.

KEY CONCEPTS

5.1

Ratio • Rate • Proportion • Extremes • Means • Means-Extremes Property • Geometric Mean • Extended Ratio • Extended Proportion

5.2

Similar Polygons • Congruent Polygons • Corresponding Vertices, Angles, and Sides

5.3
AAA • AA • CSSTP • CASTC • SAS~ and SSS~

5.4
Pythagorean Theorem • Converse of Pythagorean Theorem • Pythagorean Triple

5.5
The 45°-45°-90° Triangle • The 30°-60°-90° Triangle

5.6
Segments Divided Proportionally • The Angle-Bisector Theorem • Ceva's Theorem

TABLE 5.2 An Overview of Chapter 5

▶ Methods of Proving Triangles Similar ($\triangle ABC \sim \triangle DEF$)

FIGURE (NOTE MARKS.)	METHOD	STEPS NEEDED IN PROOF
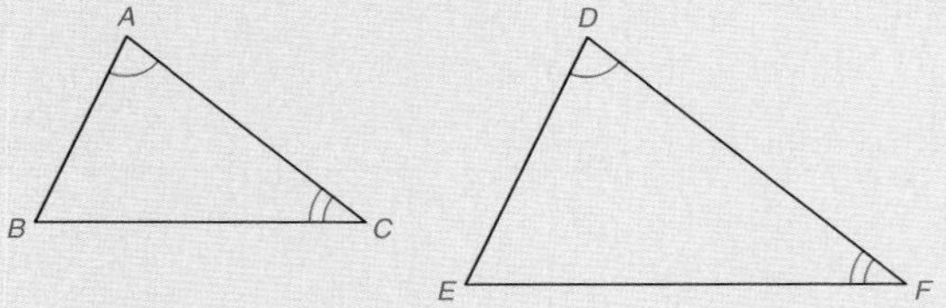	AA	$\angle A \cong \angle D$; $\angle C \cong \angle F$
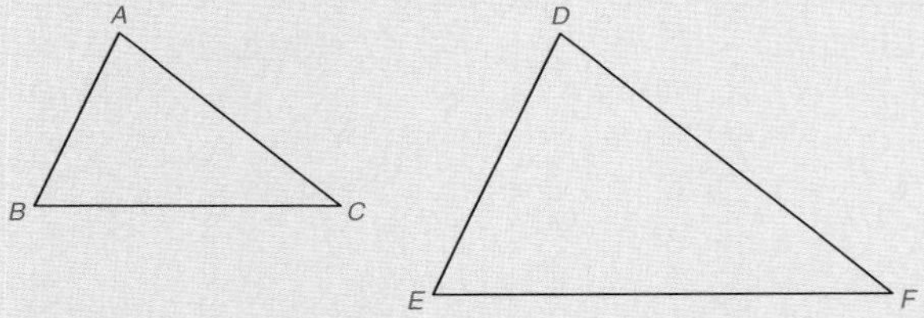	SSS~	$\frac{AB}{DE} = \frac{AC}{DF} = \frac{BC}{EF} = k$ (k is a constant.)
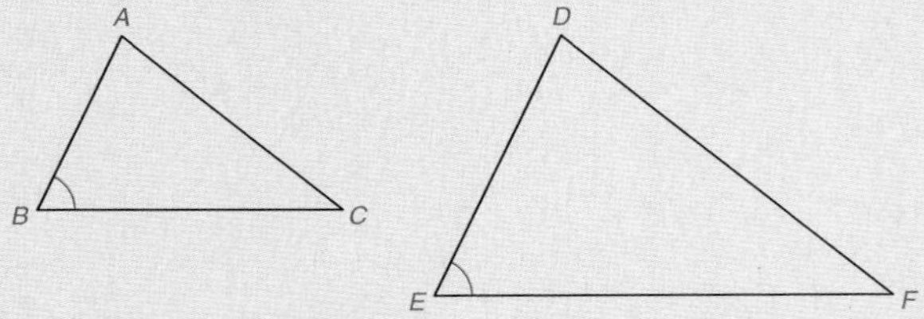	SAS~	$\frac{AB}{DE} = \frac{BC}{EF} = k$ $\angle B \cong \angle E$

(continued)

TABLE 5.2 *(continued)*

Special Relationships

FIGURE	RELATIONSHIP	CONCLUSION(S)
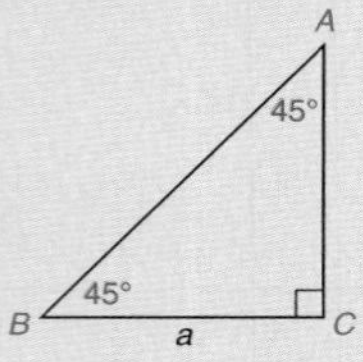	45°-45°-90° △ Note: $BC = a$	$AC = a$ $AB = a\sqrt{2}$
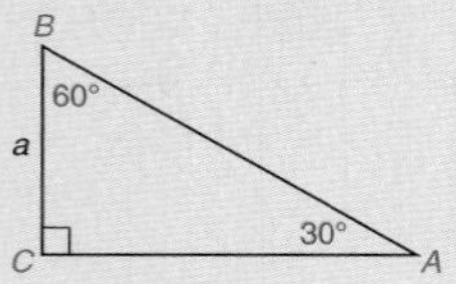	30°-60°-90° △ Note: $BC = a$	$AC = a\sqrt{3}$ $AB = 2a$

Segments Divided Proportionally

FIGURE	RELATIONSHIP	CONCLUSION
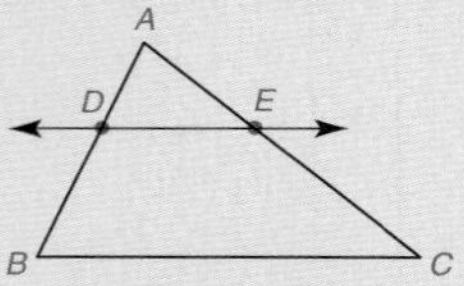	$\overleftrightarrow{DE} \parallel \overline{BC}$	$\frac{AD}{DB} = \frac{AE}{EC}$ or $\frac{AD}{AE} = \frac{DB}{EC}$
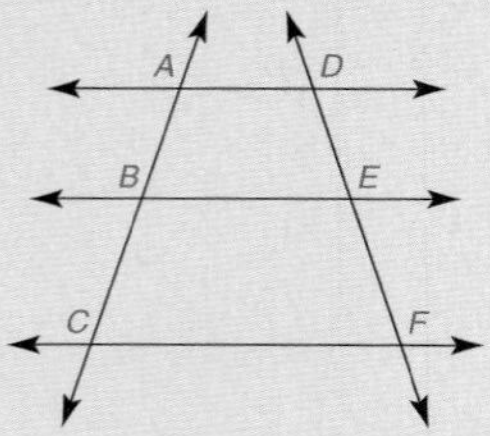	$\overleftrightarrow{AD} \parallel \overleftrightarrow{BE} \parallel \overleftrightarrow{CF}$	$\frac{AB}{BC} = \frac{DE}{EF}$ or $\frac{AB}{DE} = \frac{BC}{EF}$
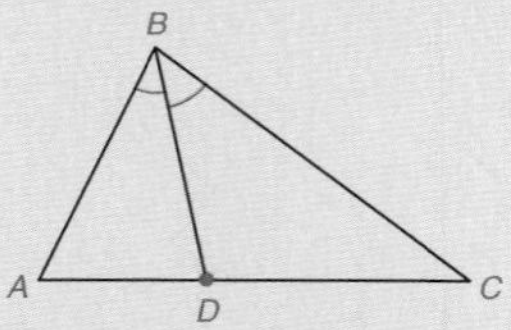	$\overrightarrow{BD}$ bisects $\angle ABC$	$\frac{AB}{BC} = \frac{AD}{DC}$ or $\frac{AB}{AD} = \frac{BC}{DC}$
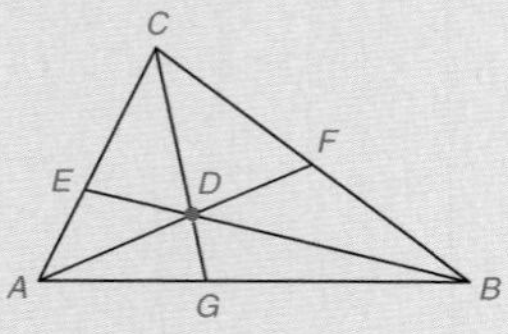	Ceva's Theorem (D is any point in the interior of $\triangle ABC$.)	$\frac{AG}{GB} \cdot \frac{BF}{FC} \cdot \frac{CE}{EA} = 1$ or equivalent

Chapter 5 REVIEW EXERCISES

Answer true or false for Review Exercises 1 to 7.

1. The ratio of 12 hr to 1 day is 2 to 1.
2. If the numerator and the denominator of a ratio are multiplied by 4, the new ratio equals the given ratio.
3. The value of a ratio must be less than 1.
4. The three numbers 6, 14, and 22 are in a ratio of 3:7:11.
5. To express a ratio correctly, the terms must have the same unit of measure.
6. The ratio 3:4 is the same as the ratio 4:3.
7. If the second and third terms of a proportion are equal, then either is the geometric mean of the first and fourth terms.
8. Find the value(s) of x in each proportion:

a) $\frac{x}{6} = \frac{3}{x}$

b) $\frac{x - 5}{3} = \frac{2x - 3}{7}$

c) $\frac{6}{x + 4} = \frac{2}{x + 2}$

d) $\frac{x + 3}{5} = \frac{x + 5}{7}$

e) $\frac{x - 2}{x - 5} = \frac{2x + 1}{x - 1}$

f) $\frac{x(x + 5)}{4x + 4} = \frac{9}{5}$

g) $\frac{x - 1}{x + 2} = \frac{10}{3x - 2}$

h) $\frac{x + 7}{2} = \frac{x + 2}{x - 2}$

Use proportions to solve Review Exercises 9 to 11.

9. Four containers of fruit juice cost \$2.52. How much do six containers cost?
10. Two packages of M&Ms cost 69¢. How many packages can you buy for \$2.25?
11. A rug measuring 20 square meters costs \$132. How much would a 12 square-meter rug of the same material cost?
12. The ratio of the measures of the sides of a quadrilateral is 2:3:5:7. If the perimeter is 68, find the length of each side.
13. The length and width of a rectangle are 18 and 12, respectively. A similar rectangle has length 27. What is its width?
14. The sides of a triangle are 6, 8, and 9. The shortest side of a similar triangle is 15. How long are its other sides?
15. The ratio of the measure of the supplement of an angle to that of the complement of the angle is 5:2. Find the measure of the supplement.
16. Name the method (AA, $SSS\sim$, or $SAS\sim$) that is used to show that the triangles are similar. Use the figure at the top of the second column.

a) $WU = 2 \cdot TR$, $WV = 2 \cdot TS$, and $UV = 2 \cdot RS$

b) $\angle T \cong \angle W$ and $\angle S \cong \angle V$

c) $\angle T \cong \angle W$ and $\frac{TR}{WU} = \frac{TS}{WV}$

d) $\frac{TR}{WU} = \frac{TS}{WV} = \frac{RS}{UV}$

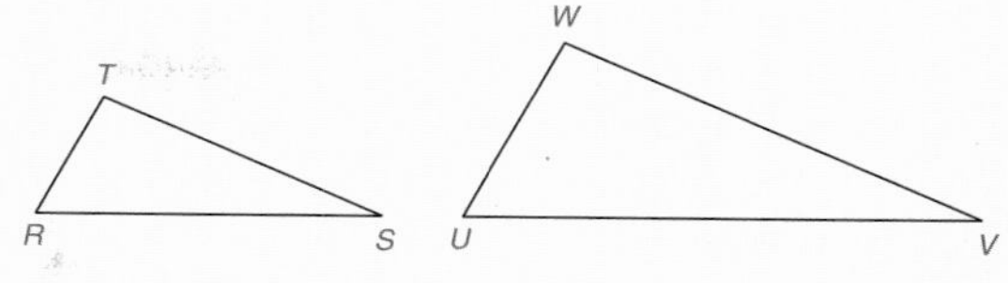

17. *Given:* $ABCD$ is a parallelogram; $\overline{DB}$ intersects $\overline{AE}$ at point F

Prove: $\frac{AF}{EF} = \frac{AB}{DE}$

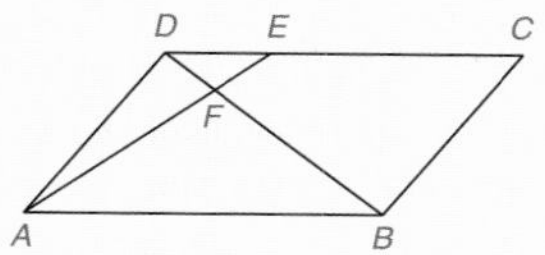

18. *Given:* $\angle 1 \cong \angle 2$

Prove: $\frac{AB}{AC} = \frac{BE}{CD}$

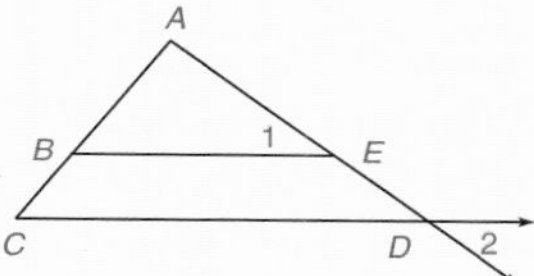

19. *Given:* $\triangle ABC \sim \triangle DEF$ (not shown); $m\angle A = 50°$, $m\angle E = 33°$; $m\angle D = 2x + 40$

Find: x, $m\angle F$

20. *Given:* In $\triangle ABC$ and $\triangle DEF$ (not shown); $\angle B \cong \angle F$ and $\angle C \cong \angle E$; $AC = 9$, $DE = 3$, $DF = 2$, $FE = 4$

Find: AB, BC

For Review Exercises 21 to 23, $\overline{DE} \parallel \overline{AC}$.

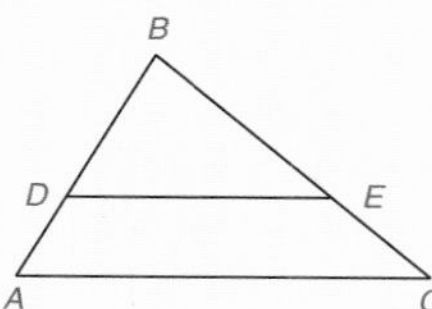

Exercises 21–23

21. $BD = 6$, $BE = 8$, $EC = 4$, $AD = ?$
22. $AD = 4$, $BD = 8$, $DE = 3$, $AC = ?$
23. $AD = 2$, $AB = 10$, $BE = 5$, $BC = ?$

For Review Exercises 24 to 26, $\overrightarrow{GJ}$ bisects $\angle FGH$.

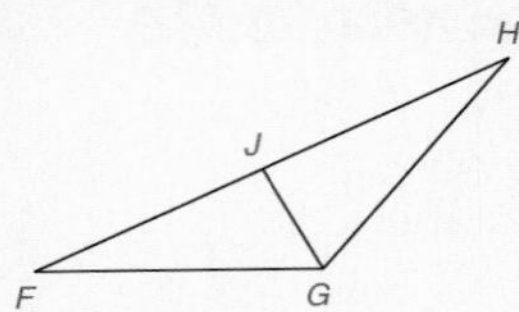

Exercises 24–26

24. *Given:* $FG = 10, GH = 8, FJ = 7$
Find: JH

25. *Given:* $GF:GH = 1:2, FJ = 5$
Find: JH

26. *Given:* $FG = 8, HG = 12, FH = 15$
Find: FJ

27. *Given:* $\overleftrightarrow{EF} \parallel \overleftrightarrow{GO} \parallel \overleftrightarrow{HM} \parallel \overleftrightarrow{JK}$, with transversals $\overline{FJ}$ and $\overline{EK}$
$FG = 2, GH = 8, HJ = 5, EM = 6$
Find: EO, EK

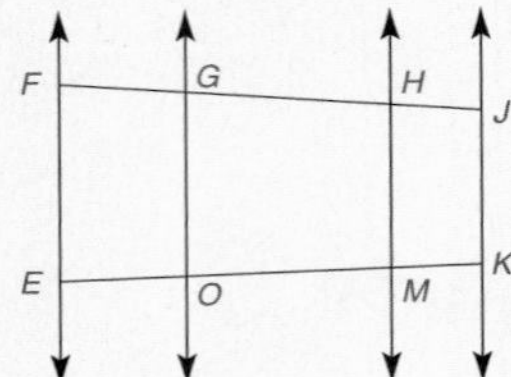

28. Prove that if a line bisects one side of a triangle and is parallel to a second side, then it bisects the third side.

29. Prove that the diagonals of a trapezoid divide themselves proportionally.

30. *Given:* $\triangle ABC$ with right $\angle BAC$
$\overline{AD} \perp \overline{BC}$

a) $BD = 3, AD = 5, DC = ?$
b) $AC = 10, DC = 4, BD = ?$
c) $BD = 2, BC = 6, BA = ?$
d) $BD = 3, AC = 3\sqrt{2}, DC = ?$

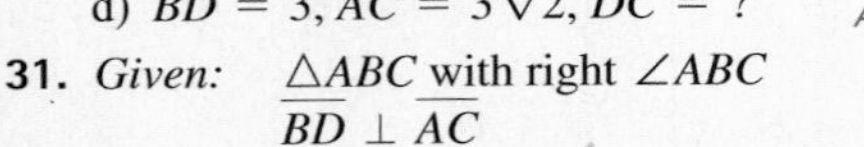

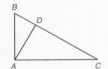

31. *Given:* $\triangle ABC$ with right $\angle ABC$
$\overline{BD} \perp \overline{AC}$

a) $BD = 12, AD = 9, DC = ?$
b) $DC = 5, BC = 15, AD = ?$
c) $AD = 2, DC = 8, AB = ?$
d) $AB = 2\sqrt{6}, DC = 2, AD = ?$

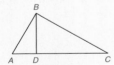

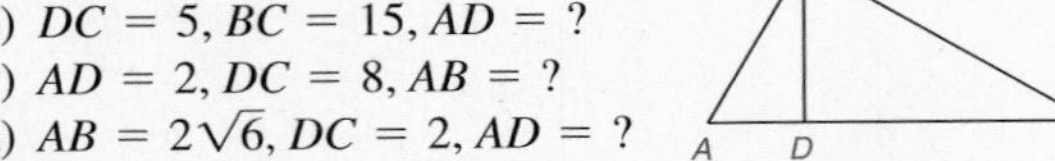

32. In the drawings shown, find x.

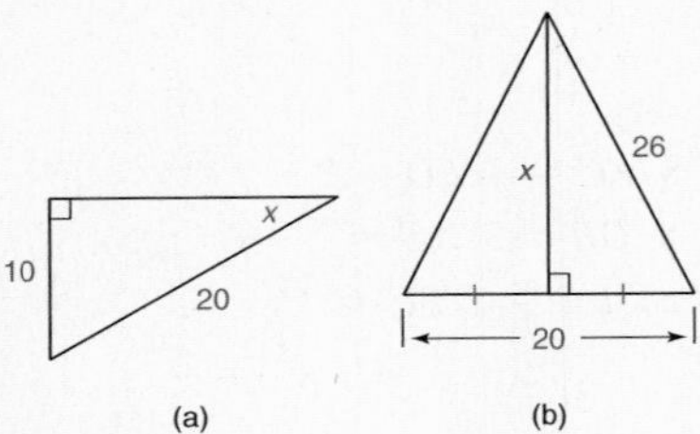

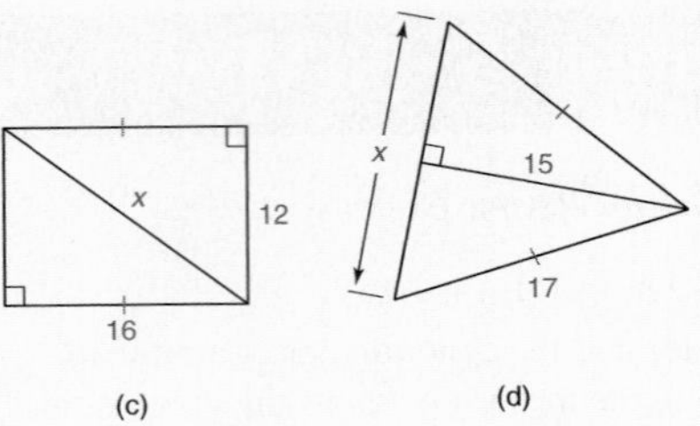

33. *Given:* $ABCD$ is a rectangle
E is the midpoint of $\overline{BC}$
$AB = 16, CF = 9, AD = 24$
Find: AE, EF, AF

34. Find the length of a diagonal of a square whose side is 4 in. long.

35. Find the length of a side of a square whose diagonal is 6 cm long.

36. Find the length of a side of a rhombus whose diagonals are 48 cm and 14 cm long.

37. Find the length of an altitude of an equilateral triangle if each side is 10 in. long.

38. Find the length of a side of an equilateral triangle if an altitude is 6 in. long.

39. The lengths of three sides of a triangle are 13 cm, 14 cm, and 15 cm. Find the length of the altitude to the 14-cm side.

40. In the drawings, find x and y.

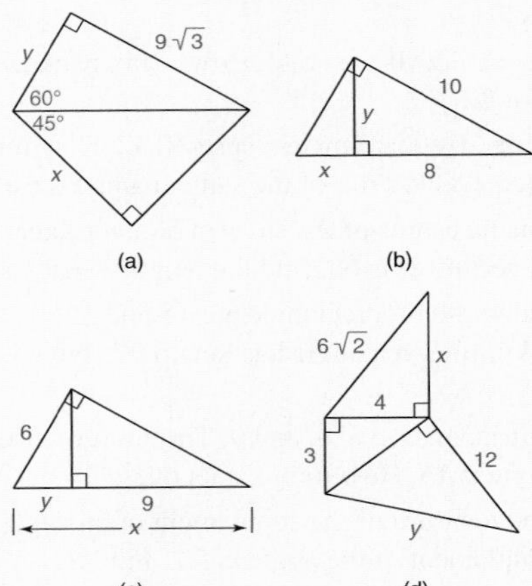

41. An observation aircraft flying at a height of 12 km has detected a Brazilian ship at a distance of 20 km from the aircraft and in line with an American ship that is 13 km from the aircraft. How far apart are the U.S. and Brazilian ships?

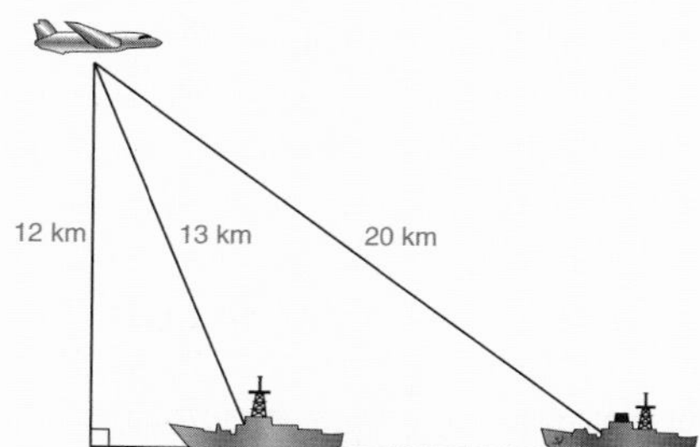

42. Tell whether each set of numbers represents the lengths of the sides of an acute triangle, of an obtuse triangle, of a right triangle, or of no triangle:

a) 12, 13, 14
b) 11, 5, 18
c) 9, 15, 18
d) 6, 8, 10
e) 8, 7, 16
f) 8, 7, 6
g) 9, 13, 8
h) 4, 2, 3

Chapter 5 TEST

1. Reduce to its simplest form:
   a) The ratio 12:20 ________
   b) The rate $\frac{200 \text{ miles}}{8 \text{ gallons}}$ ________
2. Solve each proportion for x. Show your work!
   a) $\frac{x}{5} = \frac{8}{13}$ ________ b) $\frac{x+1}{5} = \frac{16}{x-1}$ ________
3. The measures of two complementary angles are in the ratio 1:5. Find the measure of each angle.
   Smaller: ________;
   Larger: ________
4. $\triangle RTS \sim \triangle UWV$.
   a) Find $m\angle W$ if $m\angle R = 67°$ and $m\angle S = 21°$. ________
   b) Find WV if $RT = 4$, $UW = 6$, and $TS = 8$.
   ____

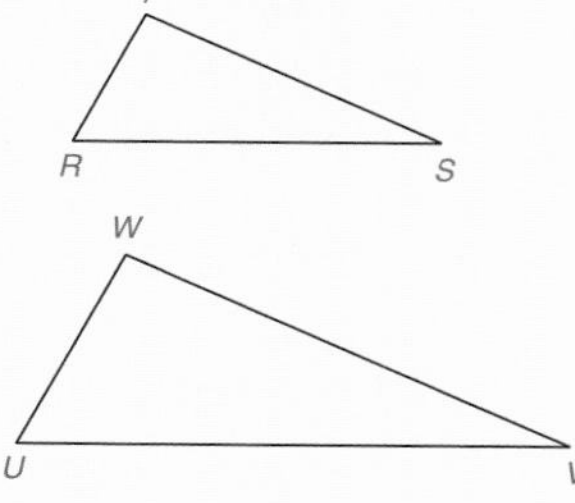

Exercises 4, 5

5. Give the reason (AA, SAS~, or SSS~) why $\triangle RTS \sim \triangle UTW$.
   a) $\angle R \cong \angle U$ and $\frac{TR}{WU} = \frac{RS}{UV}$
   ____
   b) $\angle S \cong \angle V$; $\angle T$ and $\angle W$ are right angles ________
6. In right triangle ABC, $\overline{CD}$ is the altitude from C to hypotenuse $\overline{AB}$. Name three triangles that are similar to each other. ________

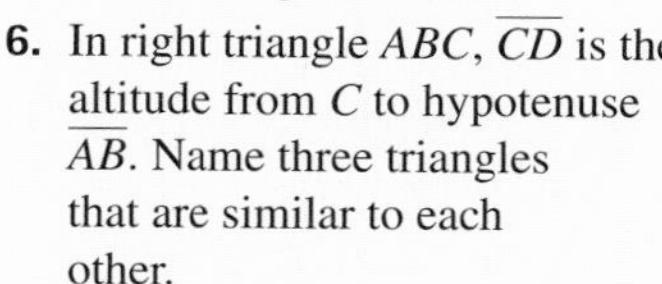

7. In $\triangle ABC$, $m\angle C = 90°$. Use a square root radical to represent:

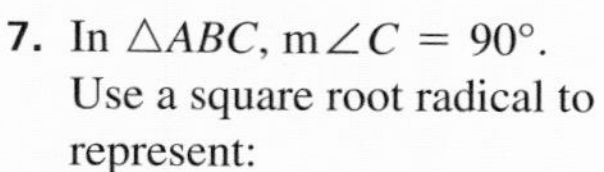

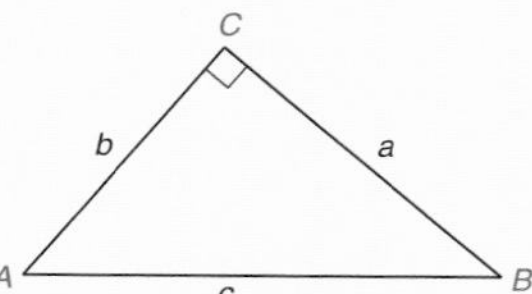

   a) c, if $a = 5$ and $b = 4$
   ____
   b) a, if $b = 6$ and $c = 8$
   ____

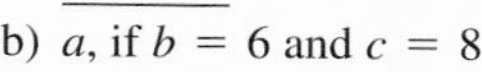

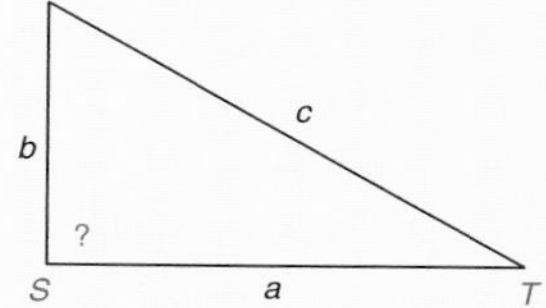

8. Given its lengths of sides, is $\triangle RST$ a right triangle?
   a) $a = 15$, $b = 8$, and $c = 17$ ________ (Yes or No)
   b) $a = 11$, $b = 8$, and $c = 15$ ________ (Yes or No)
9. Given quadrilateral $ABCD$ with diagonal $\overline{AC}$. If $\overline{BC} \perp \overline{AB}$ and $\overline{AC} \perp \overline{DC}$, find DA if $AB = 4$, $BC = 3$, and $DC = 8$. Express the answer as a square root radical. ________

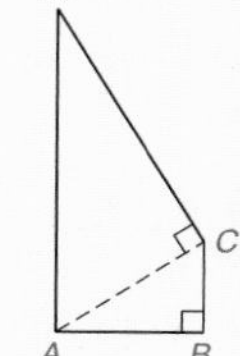

10. In $\triangle XYZ$, $\overline{XZ} \cong \overline{YZ}$ and $\angle Z$ is a right angle.
   a) Find XY if $XZ = 10$ in. ________
   b) Find XZ if $XY = 8\sqrt{2}$ cm.
   ____

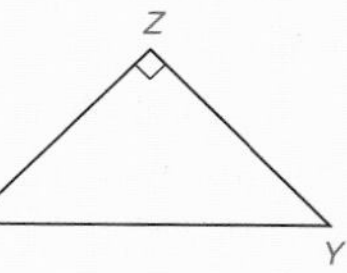

11. In $\triangle DEF$, $\angle D$ is a right angle and $m\angle F = 30°$.
   a) Find DE if $EF = 10$ m.
   ____
   b) Find EF if $DF = 6\sqrt{3}$ ft.
   ____

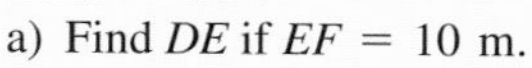

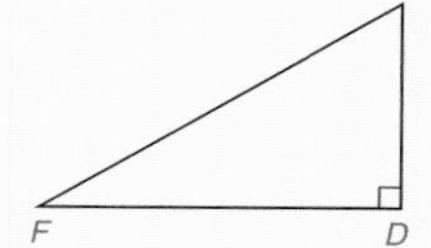

12. In $\triangle ABC$, $\overleftrightarrow{DE} \parallel \overline{BC}$. If $AD = 6$, $DB = 8$, and $AE = 9$, find EC. ________

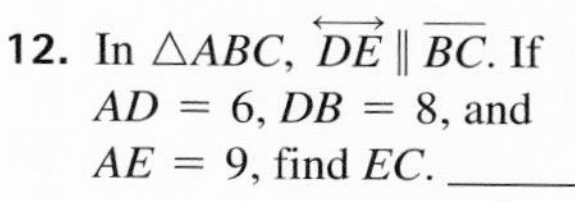

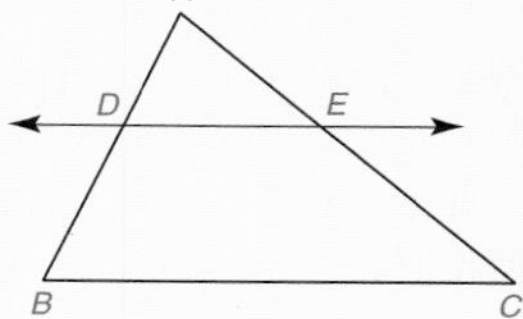

13. In $\triangle MNP$, $\overrightarrow{NQ}$ bisects $\angle MNP$. If $PN = 6$, $MN = 9$, and $MP = 10$, find PQ and QM.

$PQ =$ ______; $QM =$ ______

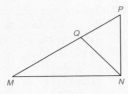

14. For $\triangle ABC$, the three angle bisectors are shown. Find the product $\frac{AE}{EC} \cdot \frac{CD}{DB} \cdot \frac{BF}{FA}$.

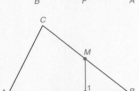

______

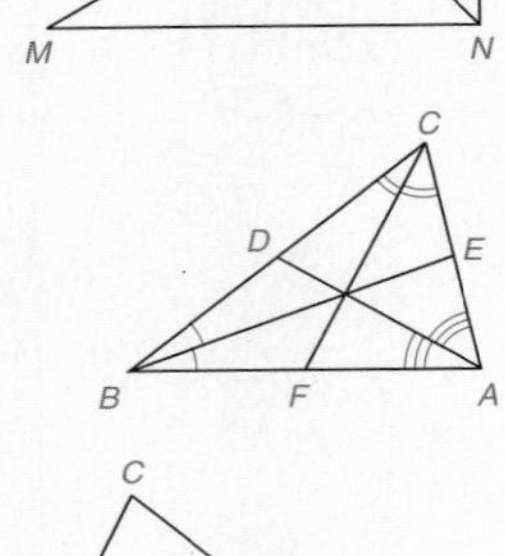

15. *Given:* $\angle 1 \cong \angle C$; M is the midpoint of $\overline{BC}$; $CM = MB = 6$ and $AD = 14$

Find: x, the length of $\overline{DB}$

In Exercises 16 and 17, complete the statements and reasons in each proof.

16. *Given:* $\overline{MN} \parallel \overline{QR}$

Prove: $\triangle MNP \sim \triangle QRP$

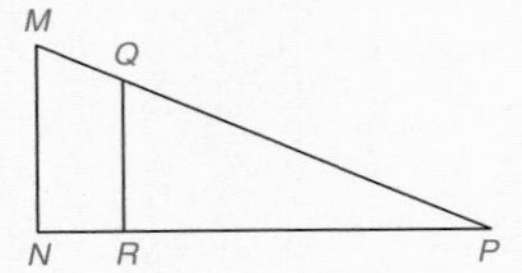

Statements	Reasons
1. ______	1. ______
2. $\angle N \cong \angle QRP$	2. If 2 ∥ lines are cut by a trans., ______
3. ______	3. Identity
4. $\triangle MNP \sim \triangle QRP$	4. ______

17. *Given:* In $\triangle ABC$, P is the midpoint of $\overline{AC}$, and R is the midpoint of $\overline{CB}$.

Prove: $\angle PRC \cong \angle B$

Statements	Reasons
1. $\triangle ABC$	1. ______
2. $\angle C \cong \angle C$	2. ______
3. P is the midpoint of $\overline{AC}$, and R is the midpoint of $\overline{CB}$	3. ______
4. $\frac{PC}{AC} = \frac{1}{2}$ and $\frac{CR}{CB} = \frac{1}{2}$	4. Definition of midpoint
5. $\frac{PC}{AC} = \frac{CR}{CB}$	5. ______
6. $\triangle CPR \sim \triangle CAB$	6. ______
7. ______	7. CASTC

Circles

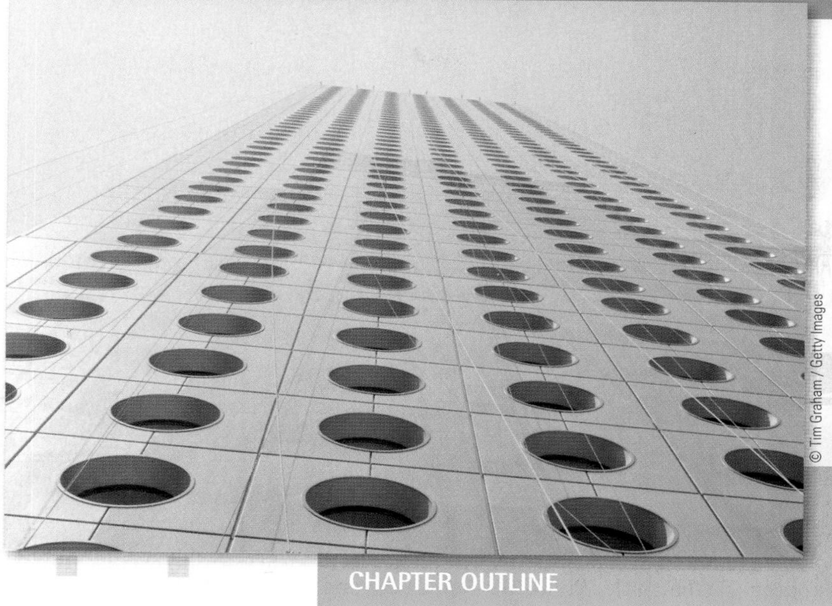
© Tim Graham / Getty Images

Chapter 6

CHAPTER OUTLINE

Additional Video explanation of concepts, sample problems, and applications are available on DVD. 

Towering! Displayed in the design of the Jardine House in Hong Kong are numerous windows that take the shape of circles. Circles appear everywhere in the real world, from the functional gear or pulley to the edible pancake. In this chapter, we will deal with the circle, related terminology, and properties. Based upon earlier principles, the theorems of this chapter follow logically from the properties found in previous chapters. For centuries, circular pulleys and gears have been used in mechanical applications. See Exercises 42 and 43 of Section 6.3 for applications of the gear. Another look at the Jardine House reveals that the circle has contemporary applications as well.

6.1 Circles and Related Segments and Angles

KEY CONCEPTS

Circle	Diameter	Minor Arc
Congruent Circles	Chord	Intercepted Arc
Concentric Circles	Semicircle	Congruent Arcs
Center	Arc	Central Angle
Radius	Major Arc	Inscribed Angle

In this chapter, we will expand the terminology related to the circle, some methods of measurement of arcs and angles, and many properties of the circle.

Warning

If the phrase "in a plane" is omitted from the definition of a circle, the result is the definition of a sphere.

DEFINITION

A **circle** is the set of all points in a plane that are at a fixed distance from a given point known as the *center* of the circle.

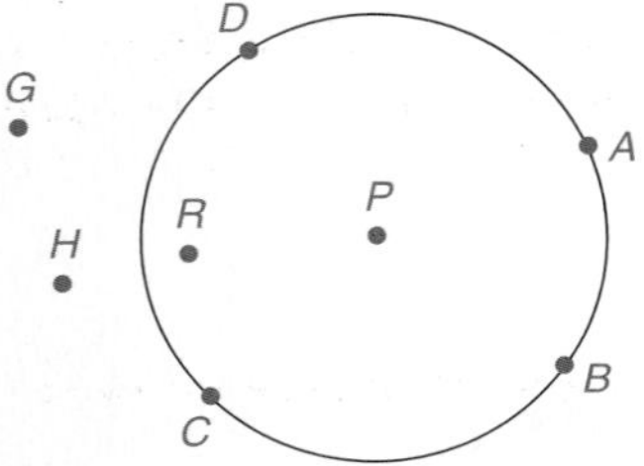

Figure 6.1

A circle is named by its center point. In Figure 6.1, point P is the center of the circle. The symbol for circle is $\odot$, so the circle in Figure 6.1 is $\odot P$. Points A, B, C, and D are points *of* (or *on*) the circle. Points P (the center) and R are in the *interior* of circle P; points G and H are in the *exterior* of the circle.

In $\odot Q$ of Figure 6.2, $\overline{SQ}$ is a radius of the circle. A **radius** is a segment that joins the center of the circle to a point on the circle. $\overline{SQ}$, $\overline{TQ}$, $\overline{VQ}$, and $\overline{WQ}$ are **radii** (plural of *radius*) of $\odot Q$. By definition, $SQ = TQ = VQ = WQ$.

The following statement is a consequence of the definition of a circle.

> All radii of a circle are congruent.

A line segment that joins two points of a circle (such as $\overline{SW}$ in Figure 6.2) is a **chord** of the circle. A **diameter** of a circle is a chord that contains the center of the circle; in Figure 6.2, $\overline{TW}$ is a diameter of $\odot Q$.

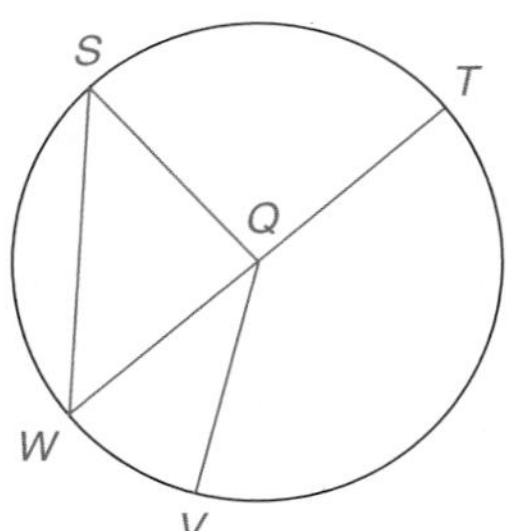

Figure 6.2

DEFINITION

Congruent circles are two or more circles that have congruent radii.

In Figure 6.3, circles P and Q are congruent because their radii have equal lengths. We can slide $\odot P$ to the right to coincide with $\odot Q$.

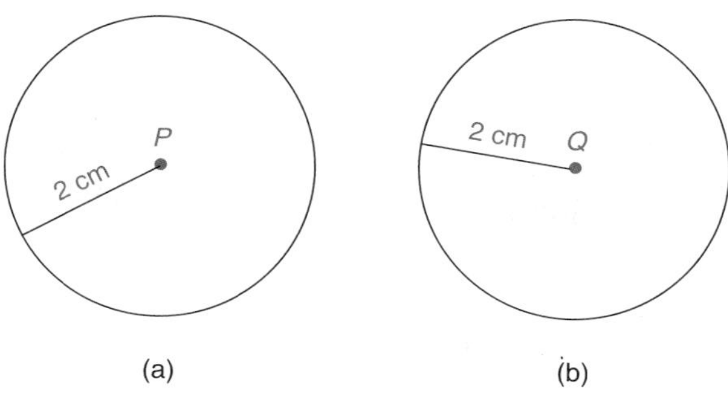

Figure 6.3

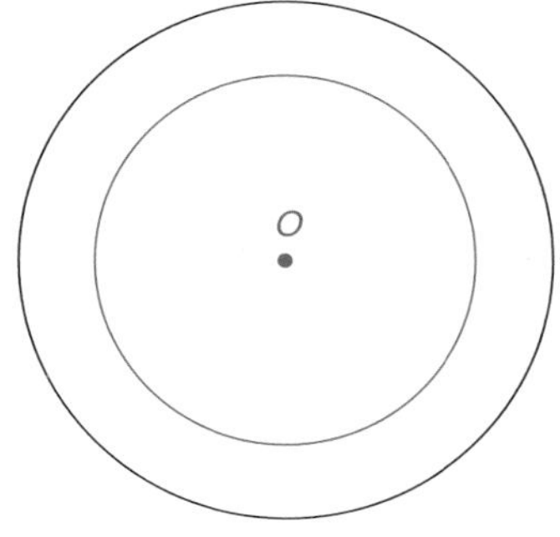

Figure 6.4

DEFINITION

Concentric circles are coplanar circles that have a common center.

The concentric circles in Figure 6.4 have the common center O.

In $\odot P$ of Figure 6.5, the part of the circle shown from point A to point B is **arc** AB, symbolized by $\overset{\frown}{AB}$. If $\overline{AC}$ is a diameter, then $\overset{\frown}{ABC}$ (three letters are used for clarity) is a **semicircle.** In Figure 6.5, a **minor arc** like $\overset{\frown}{AB}$ is part of a semicircle; a **major arc** such as $\overset{\frown}{ABCD}$ (also denoted by $\overset{\frown}{ABD}$ or $\overset{\frown}{ACD}$) is more than a semicircle but less than the entire circle.

SSG
Exs. 1–3

DEFINITION

A **central angle** of a circle is an angle whose vertex is the center of the circle and whose sides are radii of the circle.

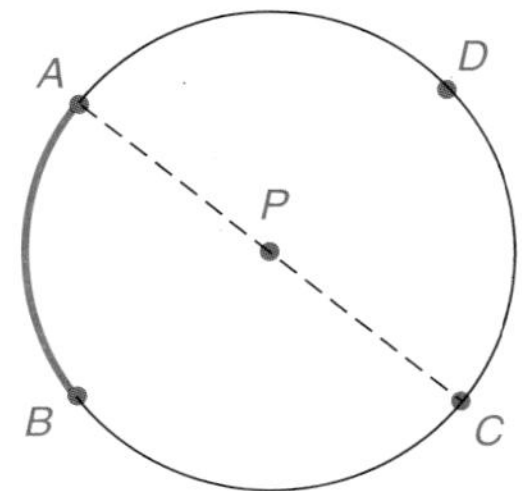

Figure 6.5

In Figure 6.6, $\angle NOP$ is a central angle of $\odot O$. The **intercepted arc** of $\angle NOP$ is $\overset{\frown}{NP}$. The intercepted arc of an angle is determined by the two points of intersection of the angle with the circle and all points of the arc in the interior of the angle.

In Example 1, we "check" the terminology just introduced.

EXAMPLE 1

In Figure 6.6, $\overline{MP}$ and $\overline{NQ}$ intersect at O, the center of the circle. Name:

a) All four radii (shown)
b) Both diameters (shown)
c) All four chords (shown)
d) One central angle
e) One minor arc
f) One semicircle
g) One major arc
h) Intercepted arc of $\angle MON$
i) Central angle that intercepts $\overset{\frown}{NP}$

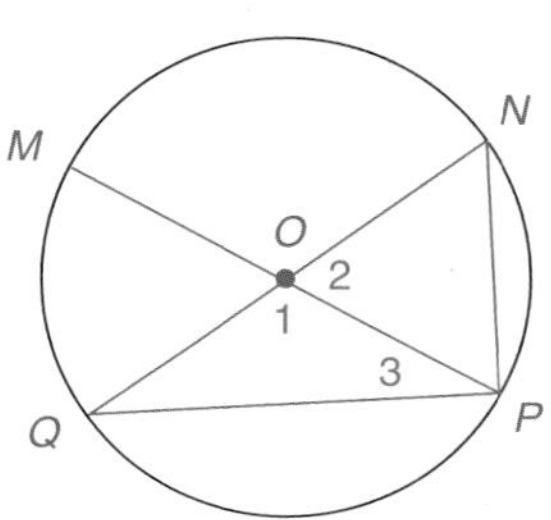

Figure 6.6

Solution

a) $\overline{OM}$, $\overline{OQ}$, $\overline{OP}$, and $\overline{ON}$
b) $\overline{MP}$ and $\overline{QN}$
c) $\overline{MP}$, $\overline{QN}$, $\overline{QP}$, and $\overline{NP}$
d) $\angle QOP$ (other answers are possible)
e) $\overset{\frown}{NP}$ (other answers are possible)
f) $\overset{\frown}{MQP}$ (other answers are possible)
g) $\overset{\frown}{MQN}$ (can be named $\overset{\frown}{MQPN}$; other answers are possible)
h) $\overset{\frown}{MN}$ (lies in the interior of $\angle MON$)
i) $\angle NOP$ (also called $\angle 2$) ■

The following statement is a consequence of the Segment-Addition Postulate.

In a circle, the length of a diameter is twice that of a radius.

EXAMPLE 2

$\overline{QN}$ is a diameter of $\odot O$ in Figure 6.6 and $PN = ON = 12$. Find the length of chord $\overline{QP}$.

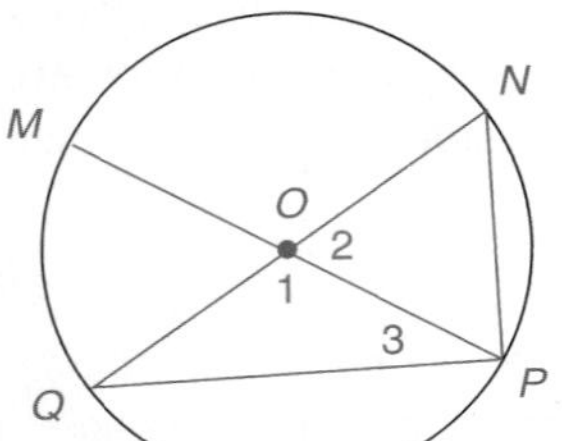
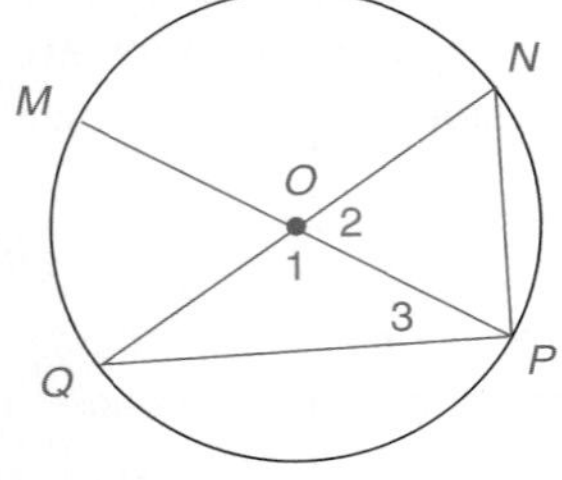

Figure 6.6

Solution Because $PN = ON$ and $ON = OP$, $\triangle NOP$ is equilateral. Then $m\angle 2 = m\angle N = m\angle NPO = 60°$. Also, $OP = OQ$; so $\triangle POQ$ is isosceles with $m\angle 1 = 120°$, because this angle is supplementary to $\angle 2$. Now $m\angle Q = m\angle 3 = 30°$ because the sum of the measures of the angles of $\triangle POQ$ is 180°. If $m\angle N = 60°$ and $m\angle Q = 30°$, then $\triangle NPQ$ is a right $\triangle$ whose angle measures are 30°, 60°, and 90°. It follows that $QP = PN \cdot \sqrt{3} = 12\sqrt{3}$. ■

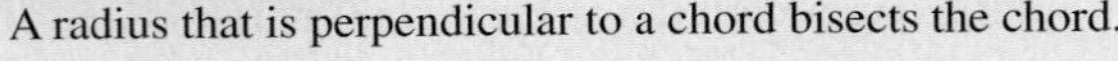

THEOREM 6.1.1

A radius that is perpendicular to a chord bisects the chord.

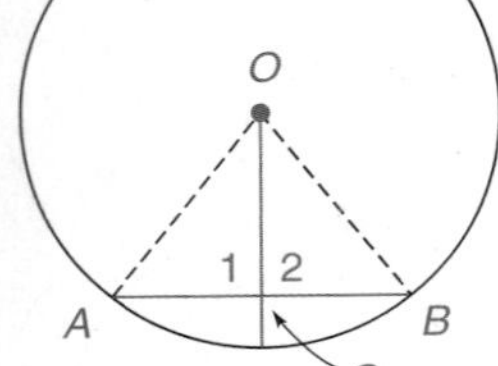

Figure 6.7

GIVEN: $\overline{OD} \perp \overline{AB}$ in $\odot O$ (See Figure 6.7.)

PROVE: $\overline{OD}$ bisects $\overline{AB}$

PROOF: $\overline{OD} \perp \overline{AB}$ in $\odot O$. Draw radii $\overline{OA}$ and $\overline{OB}$. Now $\overline{OA} \cong \overline{OB}$ because all radii of a circle are $\cong$. Because $\angle 1$ and $\angle 2$ are right $\angle$s and $\overline{OC} \cong \overline{OC}$, we see that $\triangle OCA \cong \triangle OCB$ by HL. Then $\overline{AC} \cong \overline{CB}$ by CPCTC, so $\overline{OD}$ bisects $\overline{AB}$. ■

Figure 6.8

ANGLE AND ARC RELATIONSHIPS IN THE CIRCLE

In Figure 6.8, the sum of the measures of the angles about point O (angles determined by perpendicular diameters $\overline{AC}$ and $\overline{BD}$) is 360°. Similarly, the circle can be separated into 360 equal arcs, *each of which measures 1° of arc measure;* that is, each arc would be intercepted by a central angle measuring 1°. Our description of arc measure leads to the following postulate.

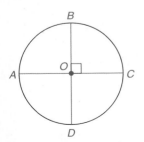

POSTULATE 16 ▶ (Central Angle Postulate)

In a circle, the degree measure of a central angle is equal to the degree measure of its intercepted arc.

If $m\overset{\frown}{AB} = 90°$ in Figure 6.8, then $m\angle AOB = 90°$. The reflex angle that intercepts $\overset{\frown}{BCA}$ and that is composed of three right angles measures 270°.

In Figure 6.8, $m\overset{\frown}{AB} = 90°$, $m\overset{\frown}{BCD} = 180°$, and $m\overset{\frown}{AD} = 90°$. It follows that $m\overset{\frown}{AB} + m\overset{\frown}{BCD} + m\overset{\frown}{AD} = 360°$. Consequently, we have the following generalization.

The sum of the measures of the consecutive arcs that form a circle is 360°.

In $\odot Y$ [Figure 6.9(a)], if $m\angle XYZ = 76°$, then $m\overset{\frown}{XZ} = 76°$ by the Central Angle Postulate. If two arcs have equal degree measures [Figures 6.9(b) and (c)] but are parts of two circles with unequal radii, then these arcs will not coincide. This observation leads to the following definition.

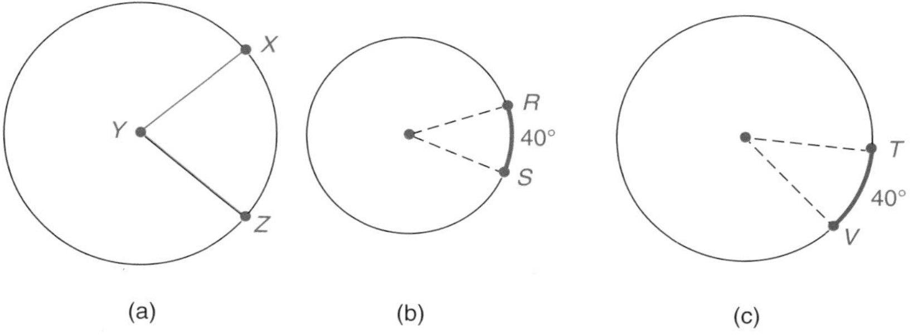

Figure 6.9

DEFINITION

In a circle or congruent circles, **congruent arcs** are arcs with equal measures.

SSG Exs. 4–10

To clarify the definition of congruent arcs, consider the concentric circles (having the same center) in Figure 6.10. Here the degree measure of $\angle AOB$ of the smaller circle is the same as the degree measure of $\angle COD$ of the larger circle. Even though $m\overset{\frown}{AB} = m\overset{\frown}{CD}$, $\overset{\frown}{AB} \ncong \overset{\frown}{CD}$ because the arcs would not coincide.

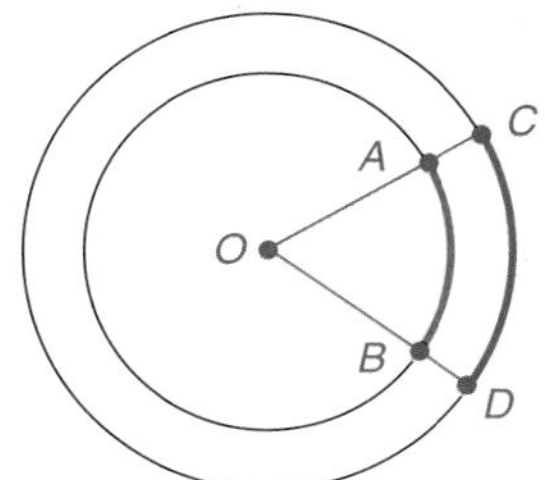

Figure 6.10

EXAMPLE 3

In $\odot O$ of Figure 6.11, $\overrightarrow{OE}$ bisects $\angle AOD$. Using the measures indicated, find:

a) $m\overset{\frown}{AB}$ b) $m\overset{\frown}{BC}$ c) $m\overset{\frown}{BD}$ d) $m\angle AOD$
e) $m\overset{\frown}{AE}$ f) $m\overset{\frown}{ACE}$ g) whether $\overset{\frown}{AE} \cong \overset{\frown}{ED}$
h) Measure of the reflex angle that intercepts $\overset{\frown}{ABCD}$

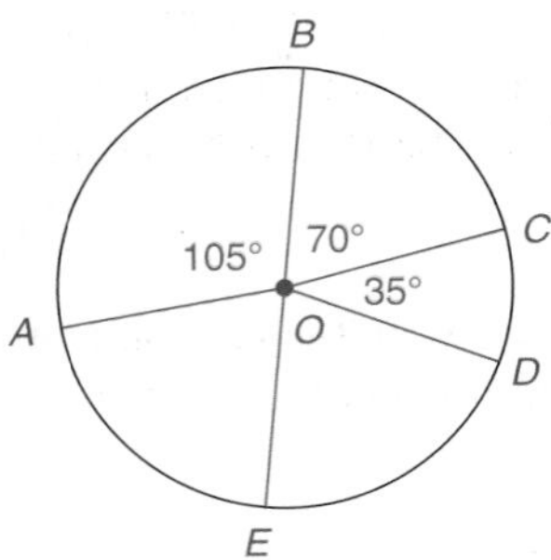

Figure 6.11

Solution a) 105° b) 70° c) 105° d) 150°, from 360 − (105 + 70 + 35) e) 75° because the corresponding central angle ($\angle AOE$) is the result of bisecting $\angle AOD$, which was found to be 150° f) 285° (from 360 − 75, the measure of $\overset{\frown}{AE}$) g) The arcs are congruent because both measure 75° and both are found in the same circle. h) 210° (from 105° + 70° + 35°) ■

In Figure 6.11, note that $m\overset{\frown}{BC} + m\overset{\frown}{CD} = m\overset{\frown}{BD}$ (or $m\overset{\frown}{BCD}$). Because the union of $\overset{\frown}{BD}$ and $\overset{\frown}{DA}$ is the major arc $\overset{\frown}{BDA}$, we also see that $m\overset{\frown}{BD} + m\overset{\frown}{DA} = m\overset{\frown}{BDA}$. With the understanding that $\overset{\frown}{AB}$ and $\overset{\frown}{BC}$ do not overlap, we generalize the relationship as follows.

POSTULATE 17 ▶ (Arc-Addition Postulate)

If $\overset{\frown}{AB}$ and $\overset{\frown}{BC}$ intersect only at point B, then $m\overset{\frown}{AB} + m\overset{\frown}{BC} = m\overset{\frown}{ABC}$.

The drawing in Figure 6.12(a) further supports the claim in Postulate 17.

Given points A, B, and C on $\odot O$ as shown in Figure 6.12(a), suppose that radii $\overline{OA}$, $\overline{OB}$, and $\overline{OC}$ are drawn. Because $m\angle AOB + m\angle BOC = m\angle AOC$

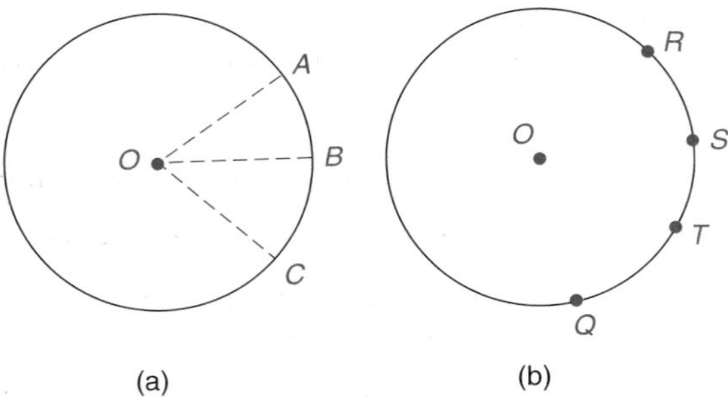

Figure 6.12

by the Angle-Addition Postulate, it follows that

$$m\overset{\frown}{AB} + m\overset{\frown}{BC} = m\overset{\frown}{ABC}$$

In the statement of the Arc-Addition Postulate, the reason for writing $\overset{\frown}{ABC}$ (rather than $\overset{\frown}{AC}$) is that the arc with endpoints at A and C *could be* a major arc. It is easy to show that $m\overset{\frown}{ABC} - m\overset{\frown}{BC} = m\overset{\frown}{AB}$.

The Arc-Addition Postulate can easily be extended to include more than two arcs. In Figure 6.12(b), $m\overset{\frown}{RS} + m\overset{\frown}{ST} + m\overset{\frown}{TQ} = m\overset{\frown}{RSTQ}$.

If $m\overset{\frown}{RS} = m\overset{\frown}{ST}$ in Figure 6.12(b), then point S is the **midpoint** of $\overset{\frown}{RT}$; alternately, $\overset{\frown}{RT}$ is **bisected** at point S.

In Example 4, we use the fact that the entire circle measures 360°.

© Austin Macrae

Figure 6.13

EXAMPLE 4

Determine the measure of the angle formed by the hands of a clock at 3:12 P.M. (See Figure 6.13.)

Solution The minute hand moves through 12 minutes, which is $\frac{12}{60}$ or $\frac{1}{5}$ of an hour. Thus, the minute hand points in a direction whose angle measure from the vertical is $\frac{1}{5}(360°)$ or 72°. At exactly 3 P.M., the hour hand would form an angle of 90° with the vertical. However, gears inside the clock also turn the hour hand through $\frac{1}{5}$ of the 30° arc from the 3 toward the 4; that is, the hour hand moves another $\frac{1}{5}(30°)$ or 6° to form an angle of 96° with the vertical. The angle between the hands must measure 96° − 72° or 24°. ■

Discover

In Figure 6.14, $\angle B$ is the inscribed angle whose sides are chords $\overline{BA}$ and $\overline{BC}$.

a. Use a protractor to find the measure of central $\angle AOC$.
b. Also find the measure of $\overset{\frown}{AC}$.
c. Finally, measure inscribed $\angle B$.
d. How is the measure of inscribed $\angle B$ related to the measure of its intercepted arc $\overset{\frown}{AC}$?

ANSWERS

a) 58° b) 58° c) 29° d) $m\angle B = \frac{1}{2}m\overset{\frown}{AC}$

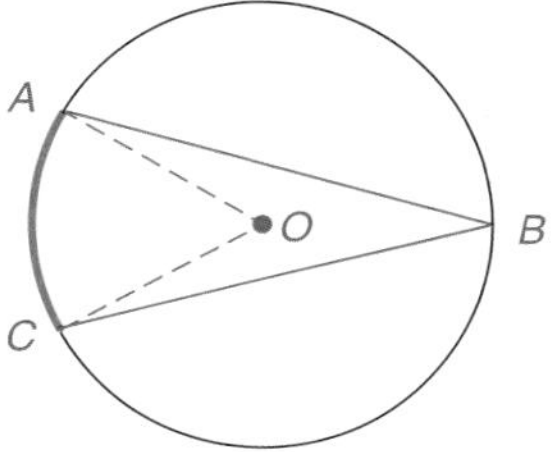

Figure 6.14

As we have seen, the measure of an arc can be used to measure the corresponding central angle. The measure of an arc can also be used to measure other types of angles related to the circle, including the inscribed angle.

DEFINITION

An **inscribed angle** of a circle is an angle whose vertex is a point on the circle and whose sides are chords of the circle.

The word *inscribed* is often linked to the word *inside*.

As suggested by the Discover activity at the left, the relationship between the measure of an inscribed angle and its intercepted arc is true in general.

THEOREM 6.1.2

The measure of an inscribed angle of a circle is one-half the measure of its intercepted arc.

The proof of Theorem 6.1.2 must be divided into three cases:

CASE 1. One side of the inscribed angle is a diameter. See Figure 6.16 on page 284.

CASE 2. The diameter to the vertex of the inscribed angle lies in the interior of the angle. See Figure 6.15(a).

CASE 3. The diameter to the vertex of the inscribed angle lies in the exterior of the angle. See Figure 6.15(b).

Reminder

The measure of an exterior angle of a triangle equals the sum of the measures of the two remote interior angles.

Technology Exploration

Use computer software if available:

1. Create circle O with inscribed angle RST.
2. Include radius $\overline{OR}$ in the figure. See Figure 6.16.
3. Measure $\overset{\frown}{RT}$, $\angle ROT$, and $\angle RST$.
4. Show that: $m\angle ROT = m\overset{\frown}{RT}$ and $m\angle RST = \frac{1}{2}m\overset{\frown}{RT}$

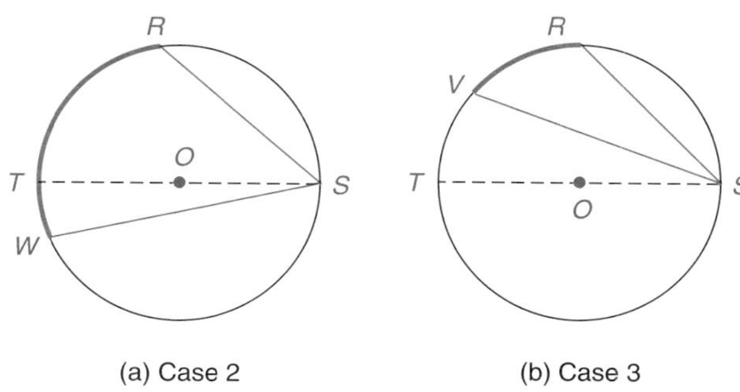

(a) Case 2 (b) Case 3

Figure 6.15

The proof of Case 1 follows, but proofs of the other cases are left as exercises.

GIVEN: $\odot O$ with inscribed $\angle RST$ and diameter $\overline{ST}$ (See Figure 6.16.)

PROVE: $m\angle S = \frac{1}{2}m\overset{\frown}{RT}$

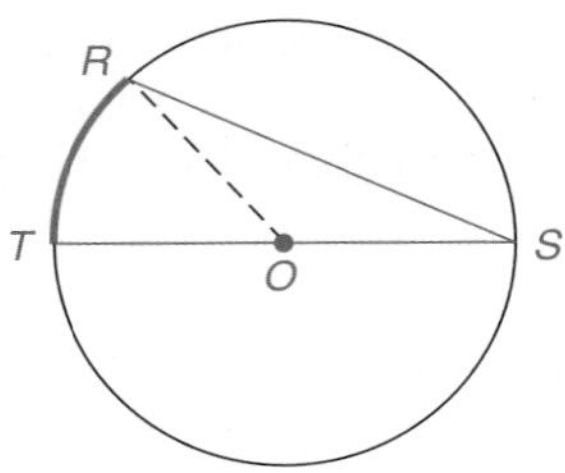

Figure 6.16

PROOF OF CASE 1: We begin by constructing radius $\overline{RO}$. Then $m\angle ROT = m\overset{\frown}{RT}$ because the central angle has a measure equal to the measure of its intercepted arc. With $\overline{OR} \cong \overline{OS}$, $\triangle ROS$ is isosceles and $m\angle R = m\angle S$. Now the exterior angle of the triangle is $\angle ROT$, so

$$m\angle ROT = m\angle R + m\angle S$$

Because $m\angle R = m\angle S$, $m\angle ROT = 2(m\angle S)$. Then $m\angle S = \frac{1}{2}m\angle ROT$. With $m\angle ROT = m\overset{\frown}{RT}$, we have $m\angle S = \frac{1}{2}m\overset{\frown}{RT}$ by substitution. ■

Exs. 11–15

Although proofs in this chapter generally take the less formal paragraph form, it remains necessary to justify each statement of the proof.

THEOREM 6.1.3

In a circle (or in congruent circles), congruent minor arcs have congruent central angles.

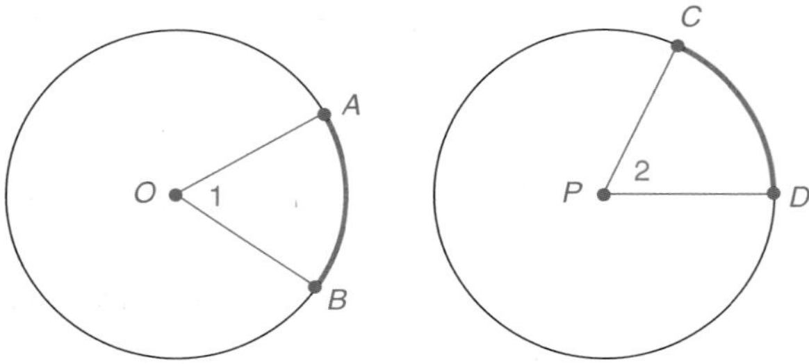

If $\overset{\frown}{AB} \cong \overset{\frown}{CD}$ in congruent circles O and P, then $\angle 1 \cong \angle 2$ by Theorem 6.1.3.

Figure 6.17

We suggest that the student make drawings to illustrate each of the next three theorems. Some of the proofs depend on auxiliary radii.

THEOREM 6.1.4

In a circle (or in congruent circles), congruent central angles have congruent arcs.

THEOREM 6.1.5

In a circle (or in congruent circles), congruent chords have congruent minor (major) arcs.

THEOREM 6.1.6

In a circle (or in congruent circles), congruent arcs have congruent chords.

On the basis of an earlier definition, we define the distance from the center of a circle to a chord to be the length of the perpendicular segment joining the center to that chord.

Congruent triangles are used to prove the next two theorems.

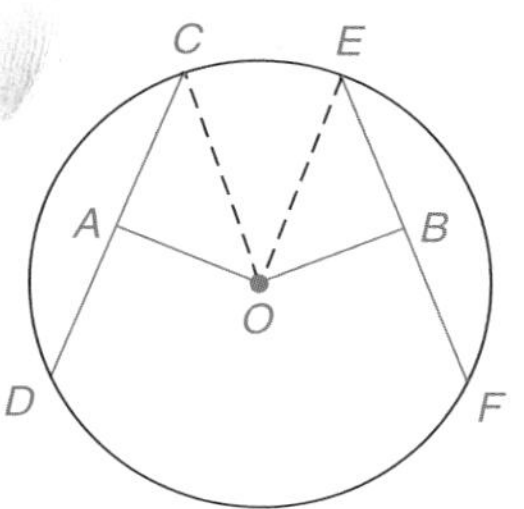

Figure 6.18

THEOREM 6.1.7

Chords that are at the same distance from the center of a circle are congruent.

GIVEN: $\overline{OA} \perp \overline{CD}$ and $\overline{OB} \perp \overline{EF}$ in $\odot O$ (See Figure 6.18.)
$\overline{OA} \cong \overline{OB}$

PROVE: $\overline{CD} \cong \overline{EF}$

PROOF: Draw radii $\overline{OC}$ and $\overline{OE}$. With $\overline{OA} \perp \overline{CD}$ and $\overline{OB} \perp \overline{EF}$, $\angle OAC$ and $\angle OBE$ are right $\angle$s. $\overline{OA} \cong \overline{OB}$ is given, and $\overline{OC} \cong \overline{OE}$ because all radii of a circle are congruent. $\triangle OAC$ and $\triangle OBE$ are right triangles. Thus, $\triangle OAC \cong \triangle OBE$ by HL.

By CPCTC, $\overline{CA} \cong \overline{BE}$ so $CA = BE$. Then $2(CA) = 2(BE)$. But $2(CA) = CD$ because A is the midpoint of chord $\overline{CD}$. ($\overline{OA}$ bisects chord $\overline{CD}$ because $\overline{OA}$ is part of a radius. See Theorem 6.1.1). Likewise, $2(BE) = EF$, and it follows that

$$CD = EF \quad \text{and} \quad \overline{CD} \cong \overline{EF}$$ ■

Proofs of the remaining theorems are left as exercises.

THEOREM 6.1.8

Congruent chords are located at the same distance from the center of a circle.

The student should make a drawing to illustrate Theorem 6.1.8.

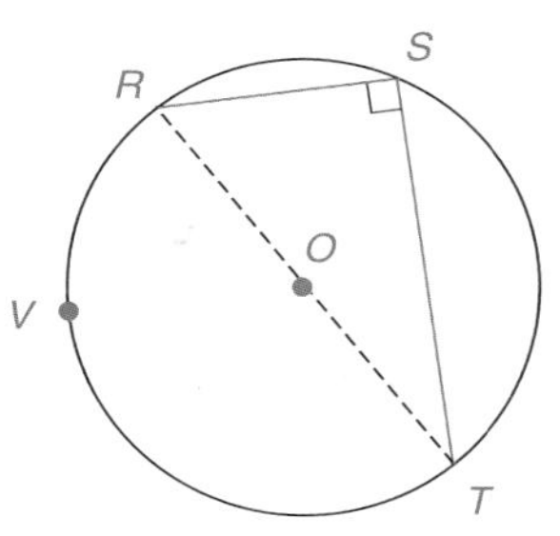

Figure 6.19

THEOREM 6.1.9

An angle inscribed in a semicircle is a right angle.

Theorem 6.1.9 is illustrated in Figure 6.19, where $\angle S$ is inscribed in the semicircle $\widehat{RST}$. Note that $\angle S$ also intercepts semicircle $\widehat{RVT}$.

THEOREM 6.1.10

If two inscribed angles intercept the same arc, then these angles are congruent.

SSG *Exs. 16, 17*

Theorem 6.1.10 is illustrated in Figure 6.20. Note that $\angle 1$ and $\angle 2$ both intercept $\widehat{XY}$. Because $m\angle 1 = \frac{1}{2}m\widehat{XY}$ and $m\angle 2 = \frac{1}{2}m\widehat{XY}$, $\angle 1 \cong \angle 2$.

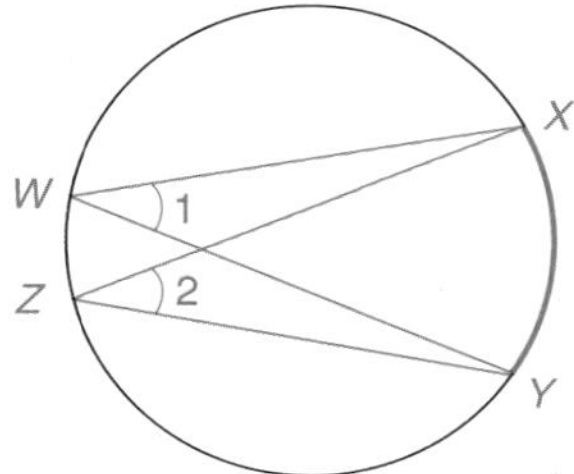

Figure 6.20

Exercises 6.1

For Exercises 1 to 8, use the figure provided.

1. If $m\overset{\frown}{AC} = 58°$, find $m\angle B$.

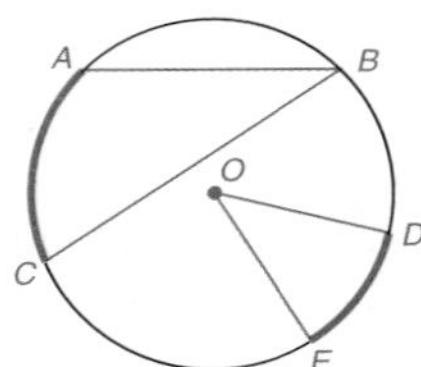

Exercises 1–8

2. If $m\overset{\frown}{DE} = 46°$, find $m\angle O$.
3. If $m\overset{\frown}{DE} = 47.6°$, find $m\angle O$.
4. If $m\overset{\frown}{AC} = 56.4°$, find $m\angle B$.
5. If $m\angle B = 28.3°$, find $m\overset{\frown}{AC}$.
6. If $m\angle O = 48.3°$, find $m\overset{\frown}{DE}$.
7. If $m\overset{\frown}{DE} = 47°$, find the measure of the reflex angle that intercepts $\overset{\frown}{DBACE}$.
8. If $m\overset{\frown}{ECABD} = 312°$, find $m\angle DOE$.
9. *Given:* $\overline{AO} \perp \overline{OB}$ and $\overline{OC}$ bisects $\overset{\frown}{ACB}$ in $\odot O$
   Find: a) $m\overset{\frown}{AB}$
   b) $m\overset{\frown}{ACB}$
   c) $m\overset{\frown}{BC}$
   d) $m\angle AOC$
10. *Given:* $ST = \frac{1}{2}(SR)$ in $\odot Q$
    $\overline{SR}$ is a diameter
    Find: a) $m\overset{\frown}{ST}$
    b) $m\overset{\frown}{TR}$
    c) $m\overset{\frown}{STR}$
    d) $m\angle S$
    (*HINT:* Draw $\overline{QT}$.)
11. *Given:* $\odot Q$ in which $m\overset{\frown}{AB}:m\overset{\frown}{BC}:m\overset{\frown}{CA} = 2:3:4$
    Find: a) $m\overset{\frown}{AB}$
    b) $m\overset{\frown}{BC}$
    c) $m\overset{\frown}{CA}$
    d) $m\angle 1$ ($\angle AQB$)
    e) $m\angle 2$ ($\angle CQB$)
    f) $m\angle 3$ ($\angle CQA$)
    g) $m\angle 4$ ($\angle CAQ$)
    h) $m\angle 5$ ($\angle QAB$)
    i) $m\angle 6$ ($\angle QBC$)
    (*HINT:* Let $m\overset{\frown}{AB} = 2x$, $m\overset{\frown}{BC} = 3x$, and $m\overset{\frown}{CA} = 4x$.)

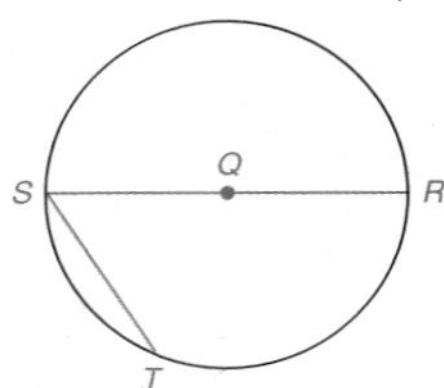

12. *Given:* $m\angle DOE = 76°$ and $m\angle EOG = 82°$ in $\odot O$
    $\overline{EF}$ is a diameter
    Find: a) $m\overset{\frown}{DE}$
    b) $m\overset{\frown}{DF}$
    c) $m\angle F$
    d) $m\angle DGE$
    e) $m\angle EHG$
    f) Whether $m\angle EHG = \frac{1}{2}(m\overset{\frown}{EG} + m\overset{\frown}{DF})$

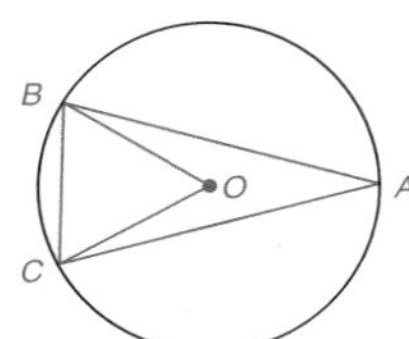

•13. *Given:* $\odot O$ with $\overline{AB} \cong \overline{AC}$ and $m\angle BOC = 72°$
    Find: a) $m\overset{\frown}{BC}$
    b) $m\overset{\frown}{AB}$
    c) $m\angle A$
    d) $m\angle ABC$
    e) $m\angle ABO$

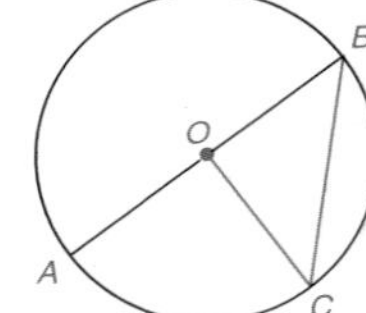

14. In $\odot O$ (not shown), $\overline{OA}$ is a radius, $\overline{AB}$ is a diameter, and $\overline{AC}$ is a chord.
    a) How does OA compare to AB?
    b) How does AC compare to AB?
    c) How does AC compare to OA?
15. *Given:* In $\odot O$, $\overline{OC} \perp \overline{AB}$ and $OC = 6$
    Find: a) AB
    b) BC

Exercise 15

16. *Given:* Concentric circles with center Q
    $SR = 3$ and $RQ = 4$
    $\overline{QS} \perp \overline{TV}$ at R
    Find: a) RV
    b) TV
17. *Given:* Concentric circles with center Q
    $TV = 8$ and $VW = 2$
    $\overline{RQ} \perp \overline{TV}$
    Find: RQ (*HINT:* Let $RQ = x$.)

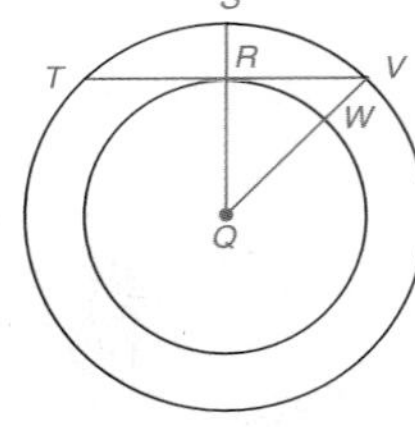

Exercises 16, 17

18. $\overline{AB}$ is the **common chord** of $\odot O$ and $\odot Q$. If $AB = 12$ and each circle has a radius of length 10, how long is $\overline{OQ}$?

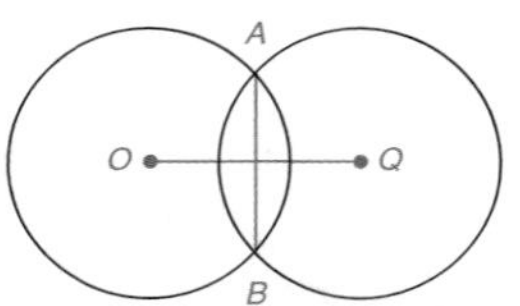

Exercises 18, 19

19. Circles O and Q have the common chord $\overline{AB}$. If $AB = 6$, $\odot O$ has a radius of length 4, and $\odot Q$ has a radius of length 6, how long is $\overline{OQ}$? See the figure for Exercise 18.

20. Suppose that a circle is divided into three congruent arcs by points A, B, and C. What is the measure of each arc? What type of figure results when A, B, and C are joined by line segments?

21. Suppose that a circle is divided by points A, B, C, and D into four congruent arcs. What is the measure of each arc? If these points are joined in order, what type of quadrilateral results?

22. Following the pattern of Exercises 20 and 21, what type of figure results from dividing the circle equally by five points and joining those points in order? What type of polygon is formed by joining consecutively the n points that separate the circle into n congruent arcs?

23. Consider a circle or congruent circles, and explain why each statement is true:

a) Congruent arcs have congruent central angles.
b) Congruent central angles have congruent arcs.
c) Congruent chords have congruent arcs.
d) Congruent arcs have congruent chords.
e) Congruent central angles have congruent chords.
f) Congruent chords have congruent central angles.

24. State the measure of the angle formed by the minute hand and the hour hand of a clock when the time is

a) 1:30 P.M. b) 2:20 A.M.

25. State the measure of the angle formed by the hands of the clock at

a) 6:30 P.M. b) 5:40 A.M.

26. Five points are equally spaced on a circle. A five-pointed star (pentagram) is formed by joining nonconsecutive points two at a time. What is the degree measure of an arc determined by two consecutive points?

27. A ceiling fan has five equally spaced blades. What is the measure of the angle formed by two consecutive blades?

28. Repeat Exercise 27, but with the ceiling fan having six equally spaced blades.

29. An amusement park ride (the "Octopus") has eight support arms that are equally spaced about a circle. What is the measure of the central angle formed by two consecutive arms?

In Exercises 30 and 31, complete each proof.

30. *Given:* Diameters $\overline{AB}$ and $\overline{CD}$ in $\odot E$
Prove: $\overset{\frown}{AC} \cong \overset{\frown}{DB}$

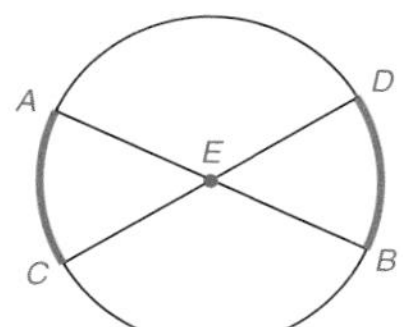

PROOF

Statements	Reasons
1. ?	1. Given
2. $\angle AEC \cong \angle DEB$	2. ?
3. $m\angle AEC = m\angle DEB$	3. ?
4. $m\angle AEC = m\overset{\frown}{AC}$ and $m\angle DEB = m\overset{\frown}{DB}$	4. ?
5. $m\overset{\frown}{AC} = m\overset{\frown}{DB}$	5. ?
6. ?	6. If two arcs of a circle have the same measure, they are $\cong$

31. *Given:* $\overline{MN} \parallel \overline{OP}$ in $\odot O$
Prove: $m\overset{\frown}{MQ} = 2(m\overset{\frown}{NP})$

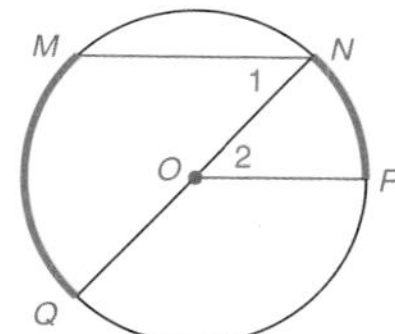

PROOF

Statements	Reasons
1. ?	1. Given
2. $\angle 1 \cong \angle 2$	2. ?
3. $m\angle 1 = m\angle 2$	3. ?
4. $m\angle 1 = \frac{1}{2}(m\overset{\frown}{MQ})$	4. ?
5. $m\angle 2 = m\overset{\frown}{NP}$	5. ?
6. $\frac{1}{2}(m\overset{\frown}{MQ}) = m\overset{\frown}{NP}$	6. ?
7. $m\overset{\frown}{MQ} = 2(m\overset{\frown}{NP})$	7. Multiplication Prop. of Equality

In Exercises 32 to 37, write a paragraph proof.

32. *Given:* $\overline{RS}$ and $\overline{TV}$ are diameters of $\odot W$

Prove: $\triangle RST \cong \triangle VTS$

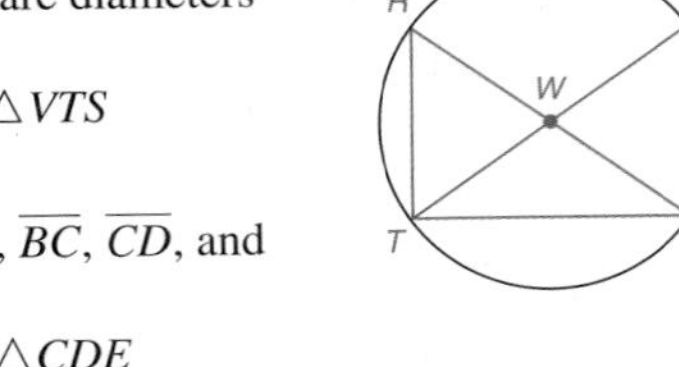

33. *Given:* Chords $\overline{AB}$, $\overline{BC}$, $\overline{CD}$, and $\overline{AD}$ in $\odot O$

Prove: $\triangle ABE \sim \triangle CDE$

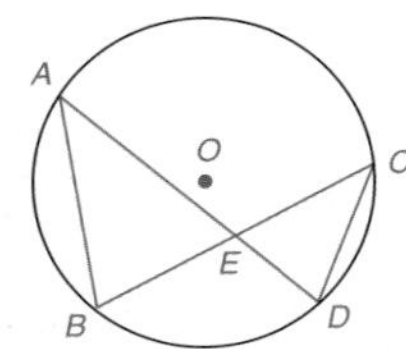

34. Congruent chords are located at the same distance from the center of a circle.

35. A radius perpendicular to a chord bisects the arc of that chord.

36. An angle inscribed in a semicircle is a right angle.

37. If two inscribed angles intercept the same arc, then these angles are congruent.

38. If $\overleftrightarrow{MN} \parallel \overleftrightarrow{PQ}$ in $\odot O$, explain why $MNPQ$ is an isosceles trapezoid.

(HINT: Draw a diagonal.)

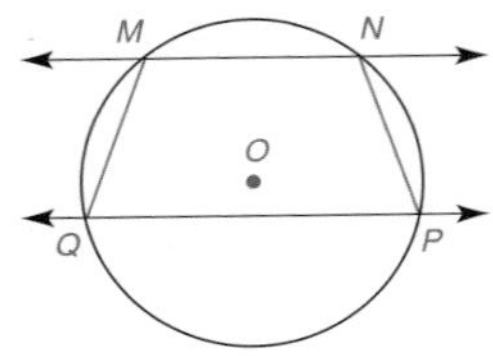

39. If $\overset{\frown}{ST} \cong \overset{\frown}{TV}$, explain why $\triangle STV$ is an isosceles triangle.

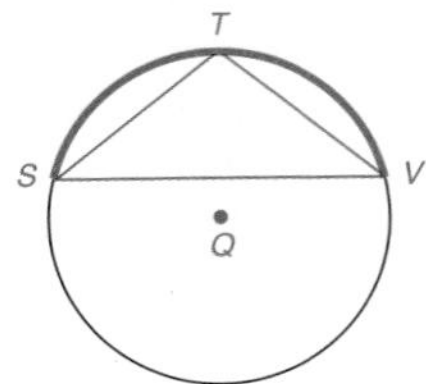

***40.** Use a paragraph proof to complete this exercise.

Given: $\odot O$ with chords $\overline{AB}$ and $\overline{BC}$, radii $\overline{AO}$ and $\overline{OC}$

Prove: $m\angle ABC < m\angle AOC$

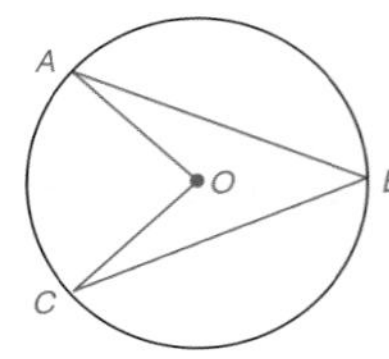

41. Prove Case 2 of Theorem 6.1.2.

42. Prove Case 3 of Theorem 6.1.2.

43. In $\odot O$, $OY = 5$ and $XZ = 6$. If $\overset{\frown}{XW} \cong \overset{\frown}{WY}$, find WZ.

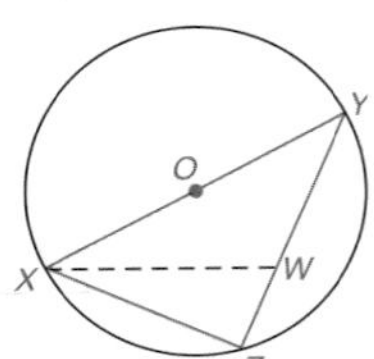

6.2 More Angle Measures in the Circle

KEY CONCEPTS

- Tangent
- Point of Tangency
- Secant
- Polygon Inscribed in a Circle
- Cyclic Polygon
- Circumscribed Circle
- Polygon Circumscribed about a Circle
- Inscribed Circle
- Interior and Exterior of a Circle

We begin this section by considering lines, rays, and segments that are related to the circle. We assume that the lines and circles are coplanar.

DEFINITION

A **tangent** is a line that intersects a circle at exactly one point; the point of intersection is the **point of contact,** or **point of tangency.**

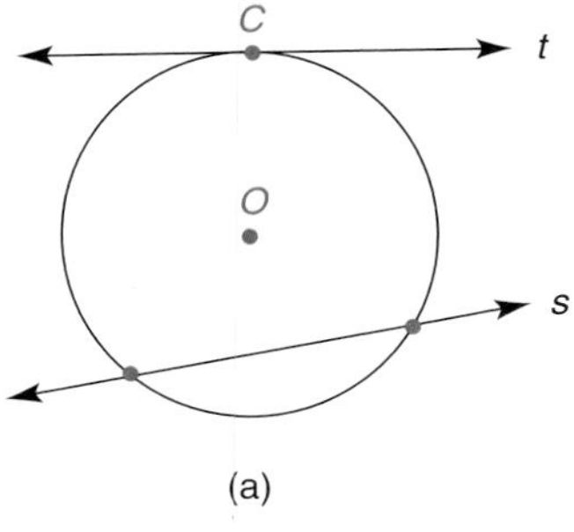

(a)

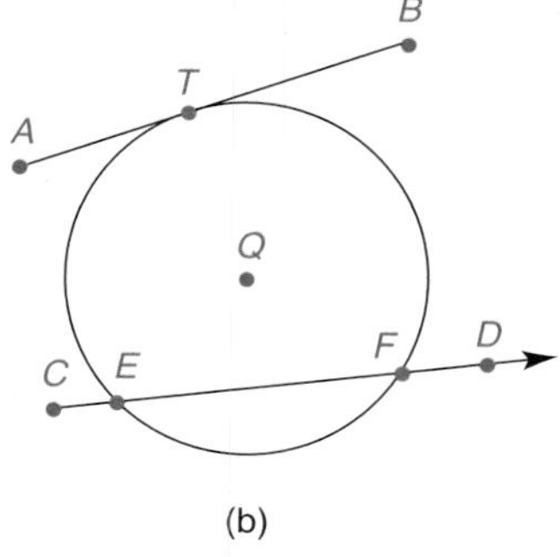

(b)

Figure 6.21

The term *tangent* also applies to a segment or ray that is part of a tangent line to a circle. In each case, the tangent touches the circle at one point.

DEFINITION

A **secant** is a line (or segment or ray) that intersects a circle at exactly two points.

In Figure 6.21(a), line s is a secant to $\odot O$; also, line t is a tangent to $\odot O$ and point C is its point of contact. In Figure 6.21(b), $\overline{AB}$ is a tangent to $\odot Q$ and point T is its point of tangency; $\overrightarrow{CD}$ is a secant with points of intersection at E and F.

DEFINITION

A polygon is **inscribed in a circle** if its vertices are points on the circle and its sides are chords of the circle. Equivalently, the circle is said to be **circumscribed about the polygon.** The polygon inscribed in a circle is further described as a **cyclic polygon.**

In Figure 6.22, $\triangle ABC$ is inscribed in $\odot O$ and quadrilateral $RSTV$ is inscribed in $\odot Q$. Conversely, $\odot O$ is circumscribed about $\triangle ABC$ and $\odot Q$ is circumscribed about quadrilateral $RSTV$. Note that $\overline{AB}$, $\overline{BC}$, and $\overline{AC}$ are chords of $\odot O$ and that $\overline{RS}$, $\overline{ST}$, $\overline{TV}$, and $\overline{RV}$ are chords of $\odot Q$. Quadrilateral $RSTV$ and $\triangle ABC$ are cyclic polygons.

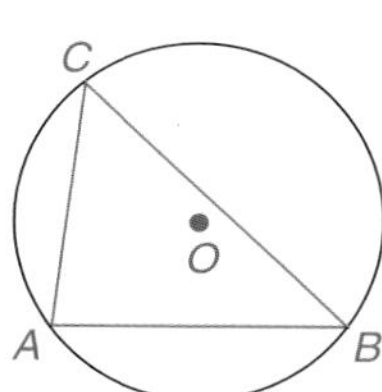

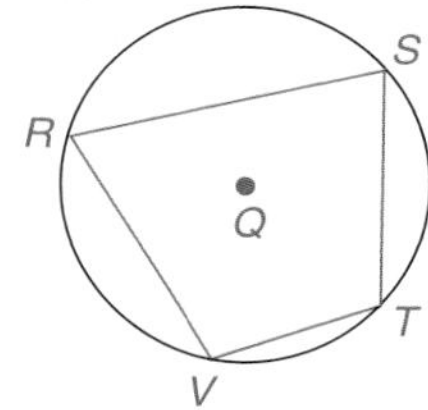

Figure 6.22

Discover

Draw any circle and call it $\odot O$. Now choose four points on $\odot O$ (in order, call these points A, B, C, and D). Join these points to form quadrilateral $ABCD$ inscribed in $\odot O$. Measure each of the inscribed angles ($\angle A$, $\angle B$, $\angle C$, and $\angle D$).

a. Find the sum $m\angle A + m\angle C$.

b. How are $\angle$s A and C related?

c. Find the sum $m\angle B + m\angle D$.

d. How are $\angle$s B and D related?

ANSWERS

a) 180° b) Supplementary c) 180° d) Supplementary

The preceding Discover activity prepares the way for the following theorem.

THEOREM 6.2.1

If a quadrilateral is inscribed in a circle, the opposite angles are supplementary.
Alternative Form: The opposite angles of a cyclic quadrilateral are supplementary.

The proof of Theorem 6.2.1 follows. In the proof, we show that $\angle R$ and $\angle T$ are supplementary. In a similar proof, we could also have shown that $\angle S$ and $\angle V$ are supplementary as well.

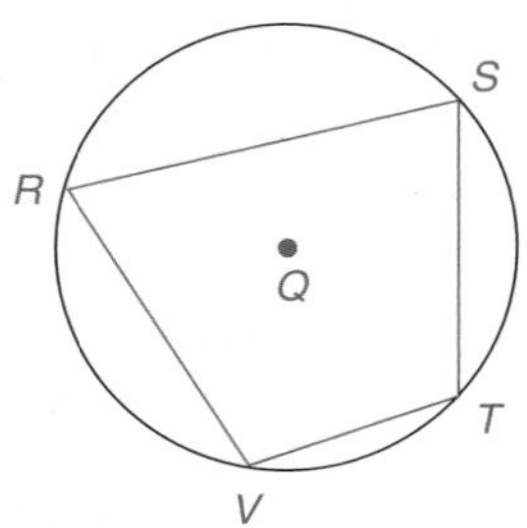

Figure 6.23

Reminder

A quadrilateral is said to be cyclic if its vertices lie on a circle.

GIVEN: $RSTV$ is inscribed in $\odot Q$ (See Figure 6.23.)

PROVE: $\angle R$ and $\angle T$ are supplementary

PROOF: From Section 6.1, an inscribed angle is equal in measure to one-half the measure of its intercepted arc. Because $m\angle R = \frac{1}{2}m\widehat{STV}$ and $m\angle T = \frac{1}{2}m\widehat{SRV}$, it follows that

$$\begin{aligned} m\angle R + m\angle T &= \frac{1}{2}m\widehat{STV} + \frac{1}{2}m\widehat{SRV} \\ &= \frac{1}{2}(m\widehat{STV} + m\widehat{SRV}) \end{aligned}$$

Because $\widehat{STV}$ and $\widehat{SRV}$ form the entire circle, $m\widehat{STV} + m\widehat{SRV} = 360°$. By substitution,

$$m\angle R + m\angle T = \frac{1}{2}(360°) = 180°$$

By definition, $\angle R$ and $\angle T$ are supplementary.

The proof of Theorem 6.2.1 shows that $m\angle R + m\angle T = 180°$. Because the sum of the interior angles of a quadrilateral is 360°, we know that

$$m\angle R + m\angle S + m\angle T + m\angle V = 360°$$

Using substitution, it is easy to show that $m\angle S + m\angle V = 180°$; that is, $\angle S$ and $\angle V$ are also supplementary. ■

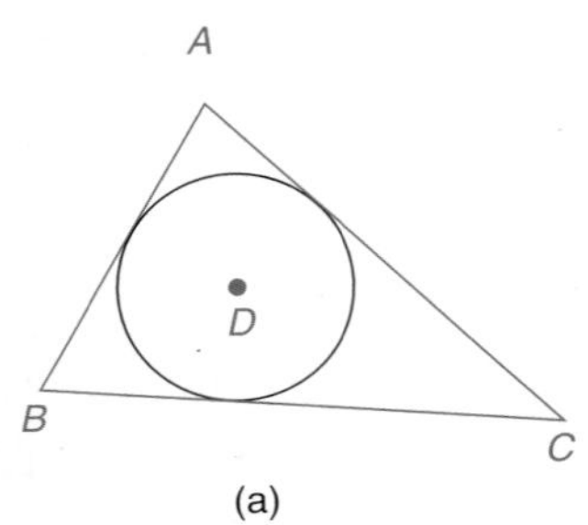

(a)

DEFINITION

A polygon is **circumscribed about a circle** if all sides of the polygon are line segments tangent to the circle; also, the circle is said to be **inscribed in the polygon.**

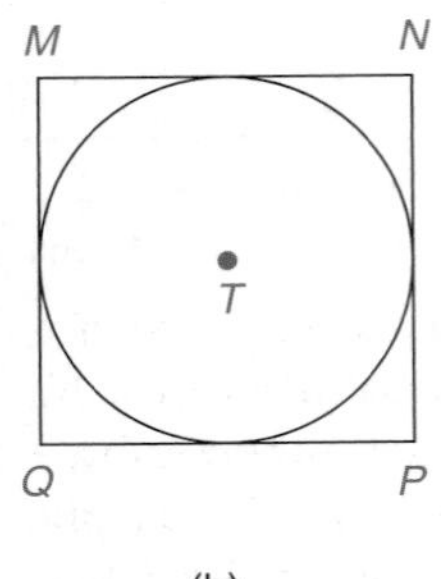

(b)

Figure 6.24

In Figure 6.24(a), $\triangle ABC$ is circumscribed about $\odot D$. In Figure 6.24(b), square $MNPQ$ is circumscribed about $\odot T$. Furthermore, $\odot D$ is inscribed in $\triangle ABC$, and $\odot T$ is inscribed in square $MNPQ$. Note that $\overline{AB}$, $\overline{AC}$, and $\overline{BC}$ are tangents to $\odot D$ and that $\overline{MN}$, $\overline{NP}$, $\overline{PQ}$, and $\overline{MQ}$ are tangents to $\odot T$.

We know that a central angle has a measure equal to the measure of its intercepted arc and that an inscribed angle has a measure equal to one-half the measure of its intercepted arc. Now we consider another type of angle in the circle.

THEOREM 6.2.2

The measure of an angle formed by two chords that intersect within a circle is one-half the sum of the measures of the arcs intercepted by the angle and its vertical angle.

SSG *Exs. 1–6*

In Figure 6.25(a) on page 291, $\angle 1$ intercepts $\widehat{DB}$ and $\angle AEC$ intercepts $\widehat{AC}$. According to Theorem 6.2.2,

$$m\angle 1 = \frac{1}{2}(m\widehat{AC} + m\widehat{DB})$$

To prove Theorem 6.2.2, we draw auxiliary line segment $\overline{CB}$ [See Figure 6.25(b)].

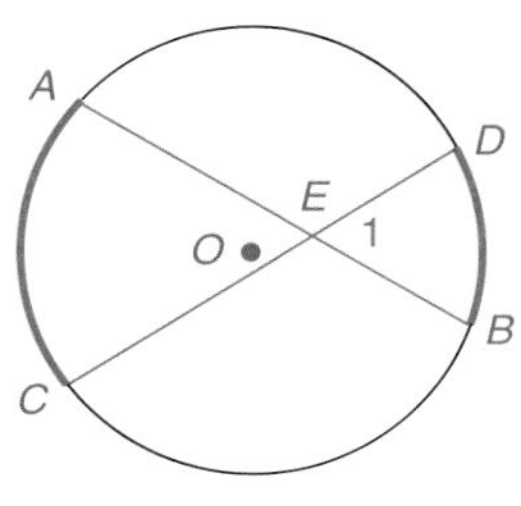

(a)

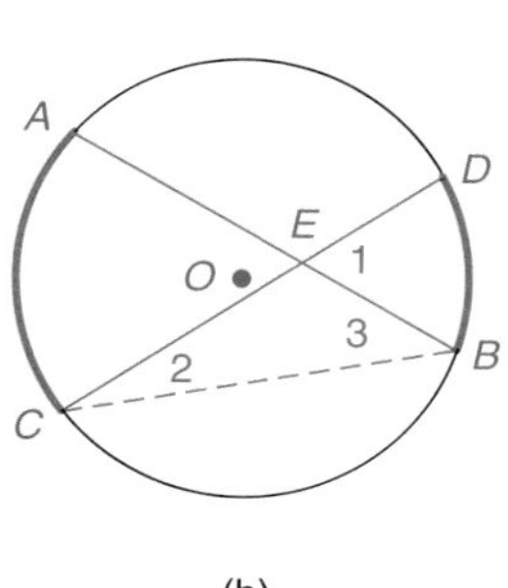

(b)

Figure 6.25

GIVEN: Chords $\overline{AB}$ and $\overline{CD}$ intersect at point E in $\odot O$

PROVE: $m\angle 1 = \frac{1}{2}(m\widehat{AC} + m\widehat{DB})$

PROOF

Draw $\overline{CB}$. Now $m\angle 1 = m\angle 2 + m\angle 3$ because $\angle 1$ is an exterior angle of $\triangle CBE$. Because $\angle 2$ and $\angle 3$ are inscribed angles of $\odot O$,

$$m\angle 2 = \frac{1}{2}m\widehat{DB} \quad \text{and} \quad m\angle 3 = \frac{1}{2}m\widehat{AC}$$

Substitution into the equation $m\angle 1 = m\angle 2 + m\angle 3$ leads to

$$m\angle 1 = \frac{1}{2}m\widehat{DB} + \frac{1}{2}m\widehat{AC}$$
$$= \frac{1}{2}(m\widehat{DB} + m\widehat{AC})$$

Equivalently,

$$m\angle 1 = \frac{1}{2}(m\widehat{AC} + m\widehat{DB})$$ ■

Next, we apply Theorem 6.2.2.

EXAMPLE 1

In Figure 6.25(a), $m\widehat{AC} = 84°$ and $m\widehat{DB} = 62°$. Find $m\angle 1$.

Solution By Theorem 6.2.2,

$$m\angle 1 = \frac{1}{2}(m\widehat{AC} + m\widehat{DB})$$
$$= \frac{1}{2}(84° + 62°)$$
$$= \frac{1}{2}(146°) = 73°$$ ■

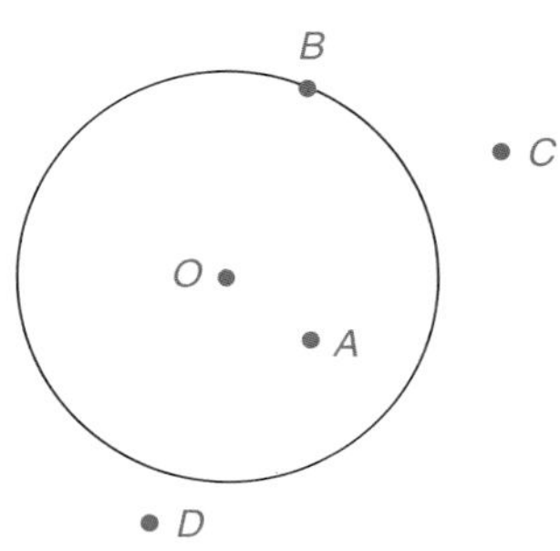

Figure 6.26

Recall that a circle separates points in the plane into three sets: points *in the interior* of the circle, points *on* the circle, and points *in the exterior* of the circle. In Figure 6.26, point A and center O are in the **interior** of $\odot O$ because their distances from center O are less than the length of the radius. Point B is on the circle, but points C and D are in the **exterior** of $\odot O$ because their distances from O are greater than the length of the radius. (See Exercise 46.) In the proof of Theorem 6.2.3, we use the fact that a tangent to a circle cannot contain an interior point of the circle.

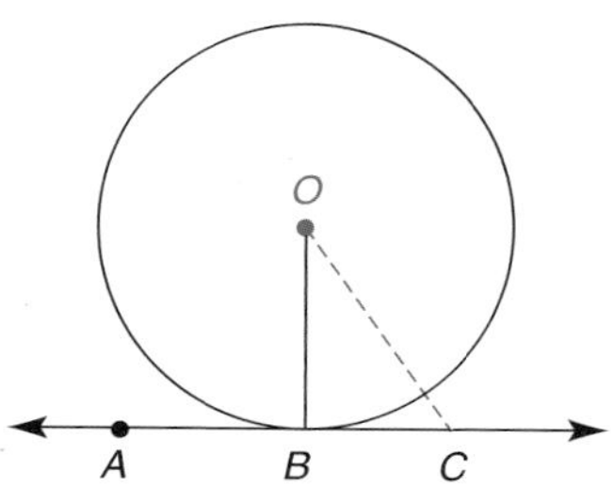

Figure 6.27

THEOREM 6.2.3

The radius (or any other line through the center of a circle) drawn to a tangent at the point of tangency is perpendicular to the tangent at that point.

GIVEN: $\odot O$ with tangent $\overleftrightarrow{AB}$; point B is the point of tangency (See Figure 6.27.)

PROVE: $\overline{OB} \perp \overleftrightarrow{AB}$

PROOF: $\odot O$ has tangent $\overleftrightarrow{AB}$ and radius $\overline{OB}$. Let C name any point on $\overleftrightarrow{AB}$ except B. Now $OC > OB$ because C lies in the exterior of the circle. It follows that $\overline{OB} \perp \overleftrightarrow{AB}$ because the shortest distance from a point to a line is determined by the perpendicular segment from that point to the line.

The following example illustrates an application of Theorem 6.2.3.

EXAMPLE 2

A shuttle going to the moon has reached a position that is 5 mi above its surface. If the radius of the moon is 1080 mi, how far to the horizon can the NASA crew members see? (See Figure 6.28.)

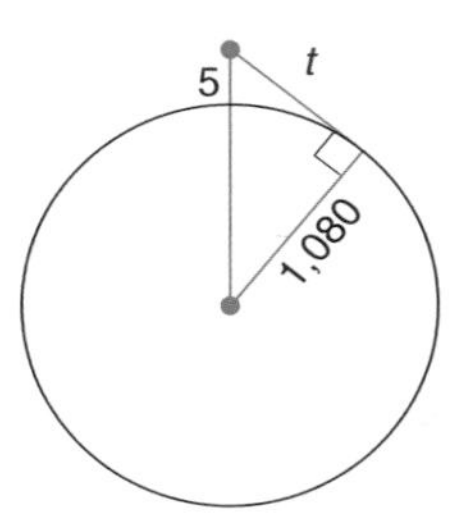

Figure 6.28

Solution According to Theorem 6.2.3, the tangent determining the line of sight and the radius of the moon form a right angle. In the right triangle determined, let t represent the desired distance. Using the Pythagorean Theorem,

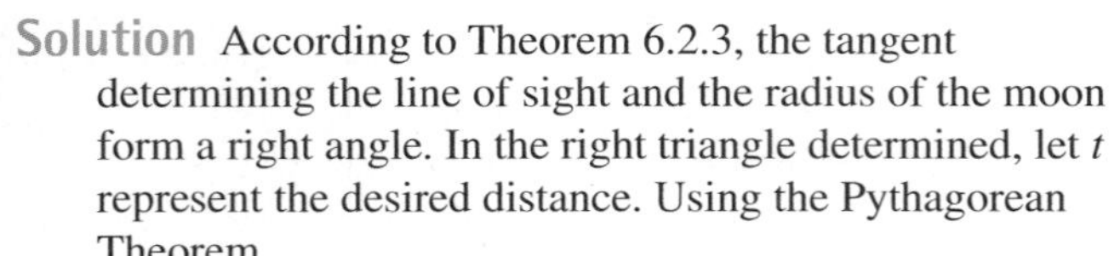

$$\begin{aligned} 1085^2 &= t^2 + 1080^2 \\ 1{,}177{,}225 &= t^2 + 1{,}166{,}400 \\ t^2 &= 10{,}825 \rightarrow t = \sqrt{10{,}825} \approx 104 \text{ mi} \end{aligned}$$ ■

SSG *Exs. 7–10*

A consequence of Theorem 6.2.3 is Corollary 6.2.4, which has three possible cases. Illustrated in Figure 6.29, only the first case is proved; the remaining two are left as exercises for the student. See Exercises 44 and 45.

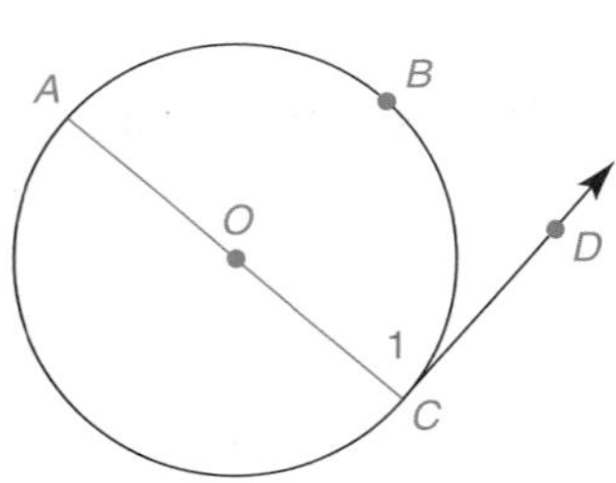

(a) Case 1
The chord is a diameter.

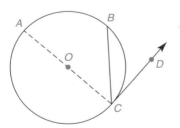

(b) Case 2
The diameter is in the exterior of the angle.

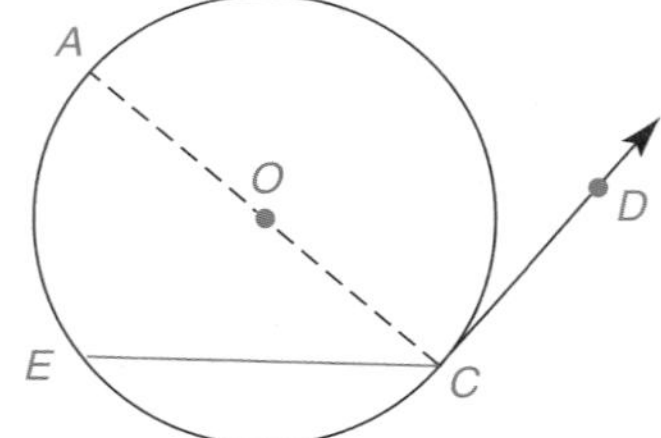

(c) Case 3
The diameter lies in the interior of the angle.

Figure 6.29

COROLLARY 6.2.4

The measure of an angle formed by a tangent and a chord drawn to the point of tangency is one-half the measure of the intercepted arc. (See Figure 6.29.)

GIVEN: Chord $\overline{CA}$ (which is a diameter) and tangent $\overrightarrow{CD}$ [See Figure 6.29(a).]

PROVE: $m\angle 1 = \frac{1}{2}m\widehat{ABC}$

PROOF: By Theorem 6.2.3, $\overline{AC} \perp \overrightarrow{CD}$. Then $\angle 1$ is a right angle and $m\angle 1 = 90°$. Because the intercepted arc $\widehat{ABC}$ is a semicircle, $m\widehat{ABC} = 180°$. Thus, it follows that $m\angle 1 = \frac{1}{2}m\widehat{ABC}$.

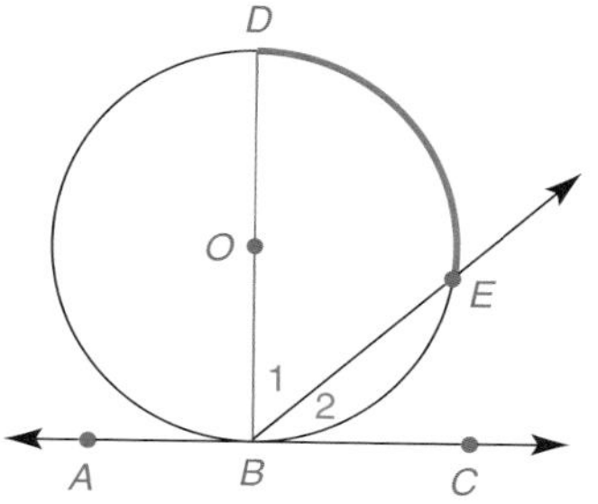

Figure 6.30

EXAMPLE 3

GIVEN: In Figure 6.30, $\odot O$ with diameter $\overline{DB}$, tangent $\overleftrightarrow{AC}$, and $m\widehat{DE} = 84°$

FIND: a) $m\angle 1$ c) $m\angle ABD$
b) $m\angle 2$ d) $m\angle ABE$

Solution

a) $\angle 1$ is an inscribed angle; $m\angle 1 = \frac{1}{2}m\widehat{DE} = 42°$
b) With $m\widehat{DE} = 84°$ and $\widehat{DEB}$ a semicircle, $m\widehat{BE} = 180° - 84° = 96°$. By Corollary 6.2.4, $m\angle 2 = \frac{1}{2}m\widehat{BE} = \frac{1}{2}(96°) = 48°$.
c) Because $\overline{DB}$ is perpendicular to $\overleftrightarrow{AB}$, $m\angle ABD = 90°$.
d) $m\angle ABE = m\angle ABD + m\angle 1 = 90° + 42° = 132°$ ■

STRATEGY FOR PROOF ▶ Proving Angle-Measure Theorems in the Circle

General Rule: With the help of an auxiliary line, Theorems 6.2.5, 6.2.6, and 6.2.7 can be proved by using Theorem 6.1.2 (measure of an inscribed angle).

Illustration: In the proof of Theorem 6.2.5, the auxiliary chord $\overline{BD}$ helps form $\angle 1$ as an exterior angle of $\triangle BCD$.

SSG *Exs. 11, 12*

THEOREM 6.2.5

The measure of an angle formed when two secants intersect at a point outside the circle is one-half the difference of the measures of the two intercepted arcs.

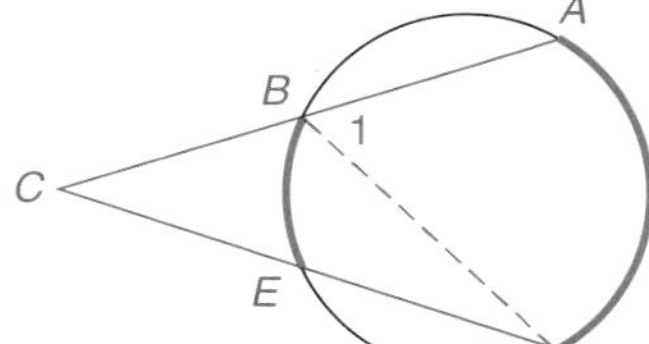

Figure 6.31

GIVEN: Secants $\overline{AC}$ and $\overline{DC}$ as shown in Figure 6.31

PROVE: $m\angle C = \frac{1}{2}(m\widehat{AD} - m\widehat{BE})$

PROOF: Draw $\overline{BD}$ to form $\triangle BCD$. Then the measure of the exterior angle of $\triangle BCD$ is given by

$$m\angle 1 = m\angle C + m\angle D$$

so

$$m\angle C = m\angle 1 - m\angle D$$

Because $\angle 1$ and $\angle D$ are inscribed angles, $m\angle 1 = \frac{1}{2}m\widehat{AD}$ and $m\angle D = \frac{1}{2}m\widehat{BE}$. Then

$$m\angle C = \frac{1}{2}m\widehat{AD} - \frac{1}{2}m\widehat{BE}$$

or

$$m\angle C = \frac{1}{2}(m\widehat{AD} - m\widehat{BE})$$

NOTE: In an application of Theorem 6.2.5, one subtracts the smaller arc measure from the larger arc measure. ■

Technology Exploration

Use computer software if available.

1. Form a circle containing points *A* and *D*.
2. From external point *C*, draw secants $\overline{CA}$ and $\overline{CD}$. Designate points of intersection as *B* and *E*. See Figure 6.31.
3. Measure $\widehat{AD}$, $\widehat{BE}$, and $\angle C$.
4. Show that $m\angle C = \frac{1}{2}(m\widehat{AD} - m\widehat{BE})$.

EXAMPLE 4

GIVEN: In $\odot O$ of Figure 6.32, $m\angle AOB = 136°$ and $m\angle DOC = 46°$

FIND: $m\angle E$

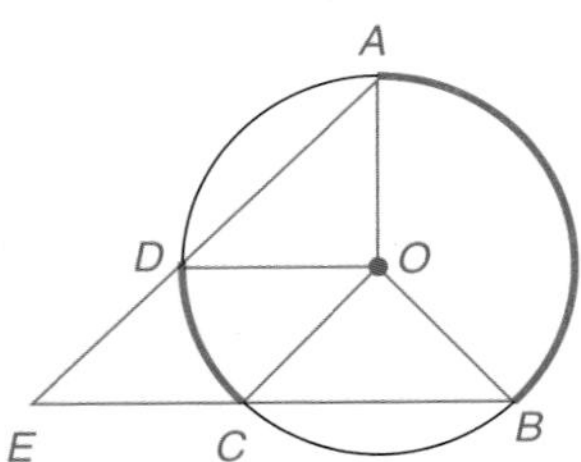

Figure 6.32

Solution If $m\angle AOB = 136°$, then $m\overset{\frown}{AB} = 136°$. If $m\angle DOC = 46°$, then $m\overset{\frown}{DC} = 46°$. By Theorem 6.2.5,

$$\begin{aligned} m\angle E &= \frac{1}{2}(m\overset{\frown}{AB} - m\overset{\frown}{DC}) \\ &= \frac{1}{2}(136° - 46°) \\ &= \frac{1}{2}(90°) = 45° \end{aligned}$$

■

Theorems 6.2.5–6.2.7 show that any angle formed by two lines that intersect *outside* a circle has a measure equal to one-half of the difference of the measures of the two intercepted arcs. The next two theorems are not proved, but the auxiliary lines shown in Figures 6.33 and 6.34(a) will help complete the proofs.

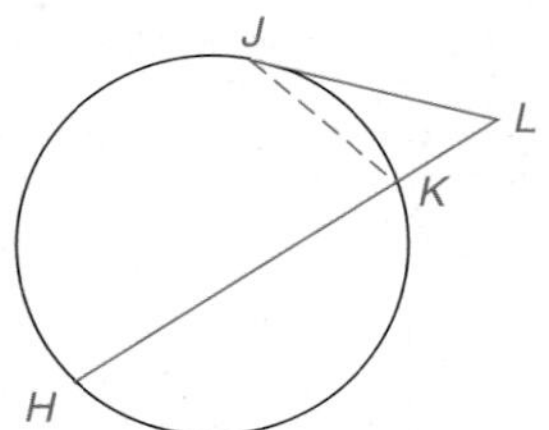

Figure 6.33

THEOREM 6.2.6

If an angle is formed by a secant and a tangent that intersect in the exterior of a circle, then the measure of the angle is one-half the difference of the measures of its intercepted arcs.

According to Theorem 6.2.6,

$$m\angle L = \frac{1}{2}(m\overset{\frown}{HJ} - m\overset{\frown}{JK})$$

in Figure 6.33. Again, we must subtract the measure of the smaller arc from the measure of the larger arc.

A quick study of the figures that illustrate Theorems 6.2.5–6.2.7 shows that the smaller arc is "nearer" the vertex of the angle and that the larger arc is "farther from" the vertex.

THEOREM 6.2.7

If an angle is formed by two intersecting tangents, then the measure of the angle is one-half the difference of the measures of the intercepted arcs.

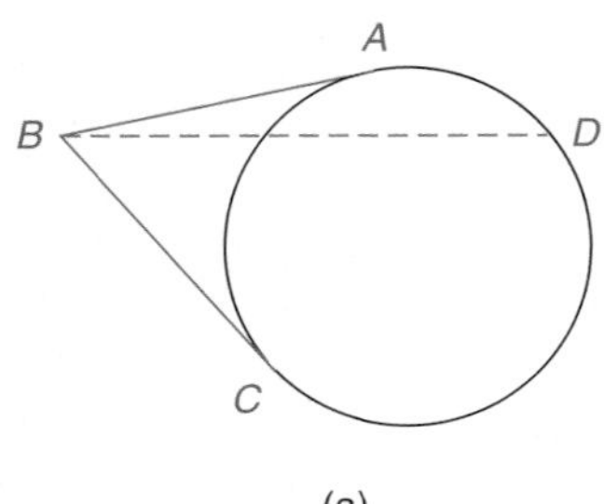

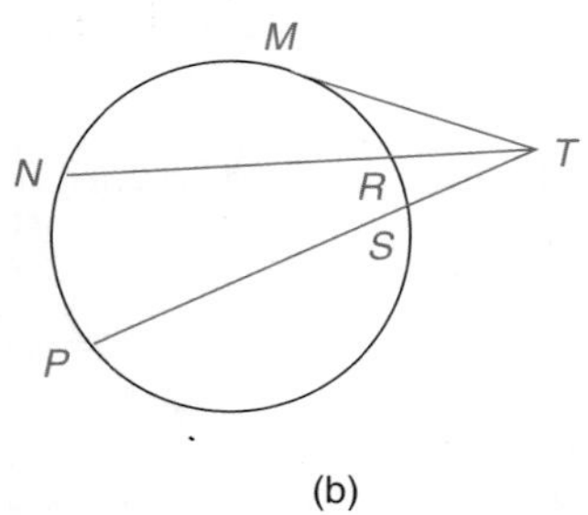

Figure 6.34

In Figure 6.34(a), $\angle ABC$ intercepts the two arcs determined by points A and C. The small arc is a minor arc ($\overset{\frown}{AC}$), and the large arc is a major arc ($\overset{\frown}{ADC}$). According to Theorem 6.2.7,

$$m\angle ABC = \frac{1}{2}(m\overset{\frown}{ADC} - m\overset{\frown}{AC}).$$

As always, we subtract the measure of the minor arc from the measure of the major arc.

EXAMPLE 5

GIVEN: In Figure 6.34(b), $m\overset{\frown}{MN} = 70°$, $m\overset{\frown}{NP} = 88°$, $m\overset{\frown}{MR} = 46°$, and $m\overset{\frown}{RS} = 26°$

FIND: a) $m\angle MTN$
b) $m\angle NTP$
c) $m\angle MTP$

Solution

a) $m\angle MTN = \frac{1}{2}(m\widehat{MN} - m\widehat{MR})$
$= \frac{1}{2}(70° - 46°)$
$= \frac{1}{2}(24°) = 12°$

b) $m\angle NTP = \frac{1}{2}(m\widehat{NP} - m\widehat{RS})$
$= \frac{1}{2}(88° - 26°)$
$= \frac{1}{2}(62°) = 31°$

c) $m\angle MTP = m\angle MTN + m\angle NTP$
Using results from (a) and (b), $m\angle MTP = 12° + 31° = 43°$ ■

Before considering our final example, let's review the methods used to measure the different types of angles related to a circle. These are summarized in Table 6.1.

TABLE 6.1
Methods for Measuring Angles Related to a Circle

Location of the Vertex of the Angle	Rule for Measuring the Angle
Center of the circle	The *measure* of the intercepted arc
In the *interior* of the circle	*One-half the sum* of the measures of the intercepted arcs
On the circle	*One-half the measure* of the intercepted arc
In the *exterior* of the circle	*One-half the difference* of the measures of the two intercepted arcs

SSG
Exs. 13–18

EXAMPLE 6

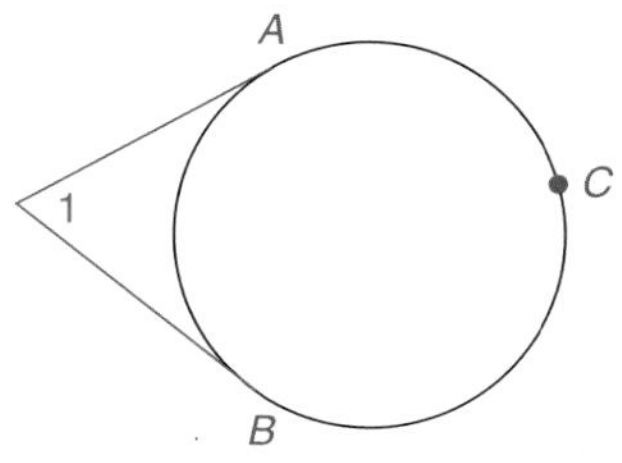

Figure 6.35

Given that $m\angle 1 = 46°$ in Figure 6.35, find the measures of $\widehat{AB}$ and $\widehat{ACB}$.

Solution Let $m\widehat{AB} = x$ and $m\widehat{ACB} = y$. Now

$$m\angle 1 = \frac{1}{2}(m\widehat{ACB} - m\widehat{AB})$$

so

$$46 = \frac{1}{2}(y - x)$$

Multiplying by 2, we have $92 = y - x$.

Also, $y + x = 360$ because these two arcs form the entire circle. We add these equations as shown.

$$\begin{aligned} y + x &= 360 \\ y - x &= 92 \\ \hline 2y &= 452 \\ y &= 226 \end{aligned}$$

Because $x + y = 360$, we know that $x + 226 = 360$ and $x = 134$. Then $m\widehat{AB} = 134°$ and $m\widehat{ACB} = 226°$. ■

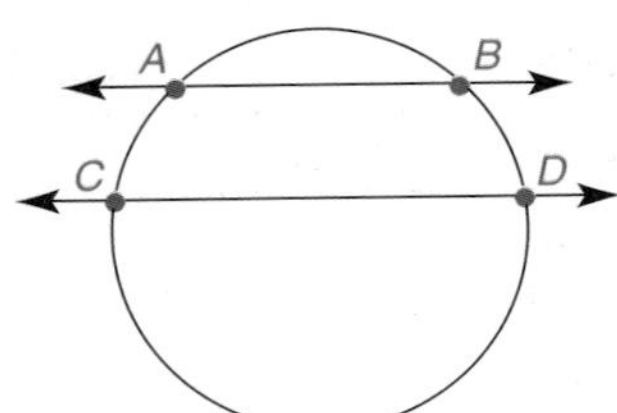

Figure 6.36

THEOREM 6.2.8

If two parallel lines intersect a circle, the intercepted arcs between these lines are congruent.

Where $\overleftrightarrow{AB} \parallel \overleftrightarrow{CD}$ in Figure 6.36, it follows that $\overset{\frown}{AC} \cong \overset{\frown}{BD}$. Equivalently, $m\overset{\frown}{AC} = m\overset{\frown}{BD}$. The proof of Theorem 6.2.8 is left as an exercise.

►►► Exercises 6.2

1. *Given:* $m\overset{\frown}{AB} = 92°$
   $m\overset{\frown}{DA} = 114°$
   $m\overset{\frown}{BC} = 138°$
   Find: a) $m\angle 1$ $(\angle DAC)$
   b) $m\angle 2$ $(\angle ADB)$
   c) $m\angle 3$ $(\angle AFB)$
   d) $m\angle 4$ $(\angle DEC)$
   e) $m\angle 5$ $(\angle CEB)$

Exercises 1, 2

2. *Given:* $m\overset{\frown}{DC} = 30°$ and $\overset{\frown}{DABC}$ is trisected at points A and B
   Find: a) $m\angle 1$ d) $m\angle 4$
   b) $m\angle 2$ e) $m\angle 5$
   c) $m\angle 3$
3. *Given:* Circle O with diameter $\overline{RS}$, tangent $\overrightarrow{SW}$, chord $\overline{TS}$, and $m\overset{\frown}{RT} = 26°$.
   Find: a) $m\angle WSR$
   b) $m\angle RST$
   c) $m\angle WST$

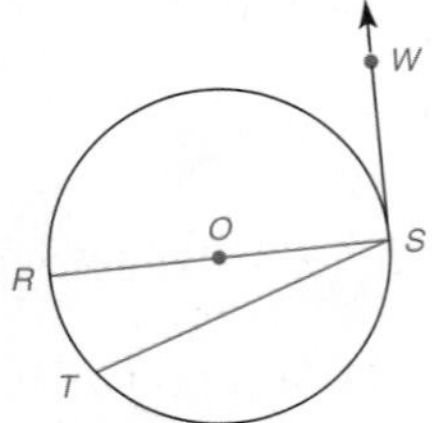

Exercises 3–5

4. Find $m\overset{\frown}{RT}$ if $m\angle RST{:}m\angle RSW = 1{:}5$.
5. Find $m\angle RST$ if $m\overset{\frown}{RT}{:}m\overset{\frown}{TS} = 1{:}4$.
6. Is it possible for
   a) a rectangle inscribed in a circle to have a diameter for a side? Explain.
   b) a rectangle circumscribed about a circle to be a square? Explain.
7. *Given:* In $\odot Q$, $\overline{PR}$ contains Q, $\overline{MR}$ is a tangent, $m\overset{\frown}{MP} = 112°$, $m\overset{\frown}{MN} = 60°$, and $m\overset{\frown}{MT} = 46°$
   Find: a) $m\angle MRP$
   b) $m\angle 1$
   c) $m\angle 2$

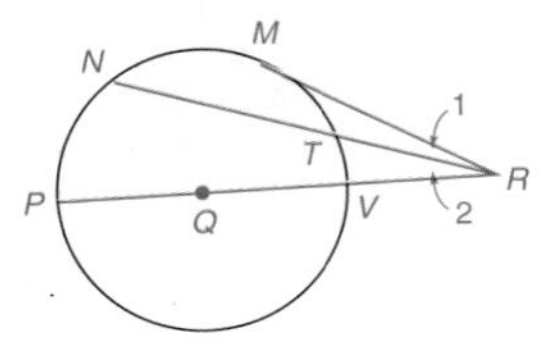

8. *Given:* $\overrightarrow{AB}$ and $\overrightarrow{AC}$ are tangent to $\odot O$, $m\overset{\frown}{BC} = 126°$
   Find: a) $m\angle A$
   b) $m\angle ABC$
   c) $m\angle ACB$
9. *Given:* Tangents $\overrightarrow{AB}$ and $\overrightarrow{AC}$ to $\odot O$
   $m\angle ACB = 68°$
   Find: a) $m\overset{\frown}{BC}$
   b) $m\overset{\frown}{BDC}$
   c) $m\angle ABC$
   d) $m\angle A$

Exercises 8, 9

10. *Given:* $m\angle 1 = 72°$, $m\overset{\frown}{DC} = 34°$
    Find: a) $m\overset{\frown}{AB}$
    b) $m\angle 2$
11. *Given:* $m\angle 2 = 36°$
    $m\overset{\frown}{AB} = 4 \cdot m\overset{\frown}{DC}$
    Find: a) $m\overset{\frown}{AB}$
    b) $m\angle 1$

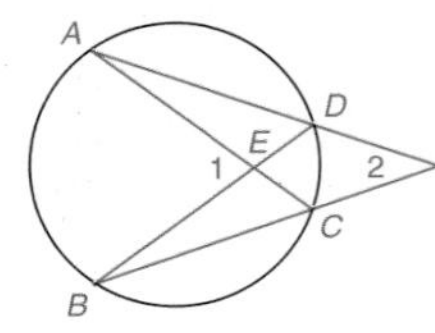

Exercises 10, 11

(HINT: Let $m\overset{\frown}{DC} = x$ and $m\overset{\frown}{AB} = 4x$.)

In Exercises 12 and 13, R and T are points of tangency.

12. *Given:* $m\angle 3 = 42^\circ$
Find: a) $m\overset{\frown}{RT}$
b) $m\overset{\frown}{RST}$

13. *Given:* $\overline{RS} \cong \overline{ST} \cong \overline{RT}$
Find: a) $m\overset{\frown}{RT}$
b) $m\overset{\frown}{RST}$
c) $m\angle 3$

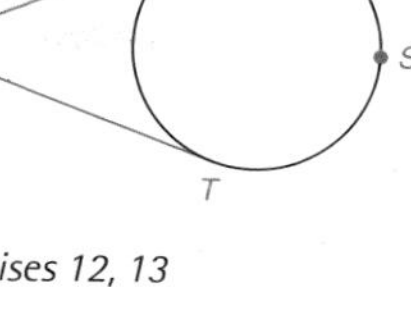

Exercises 12, 13

14. *Given:* $m\angle 1 = 63^\circ$
$m\overset{\frown}{RS} = 3x + 6$
$m\overset{\frown}{VT} = x$
Find: $m\overset{\frown}{RS}$

15. *Given:* $m\angle 2 = 124^\circ$
$m\overset{\frown}{TV} = x + 1$
$m\overset{\frown}{SR} = 3(x + 1)$
Find: $m\overset{\frown}{TV}$

Exercises 14, 15

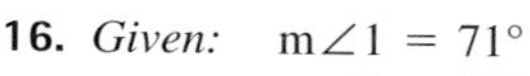

16. *Given:* $m\angle 1 = 71^\circ$
$m\angle 2 = 33^\circ$
Find: $m\overset{\frown}{CE}$ and $m\overset{\frown}{BD}$

17. *Given:* $m\angle 1 = 62^\circ$
$m\angle 2 = 26^\circ$
Find: $m\overset{\frown}{CE}$ and $m\overset{\frown}{BD}$

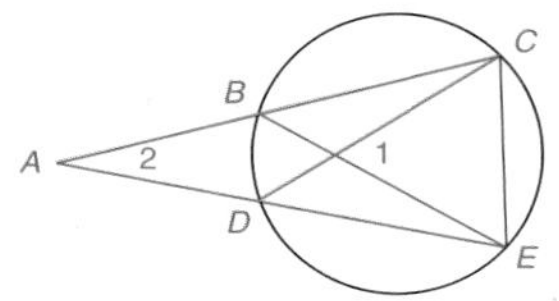

Exercises 16, 17

18. a) How are $\angle R$ and $\angle T$ related?
b) Find $m\angle R$ if $m\angle T = 112^\circ$.

19. a) How are $\angle S$ and $\angle V$ related?
b) Find $m\angle V$ if $m\angle S = 73^\circ$.

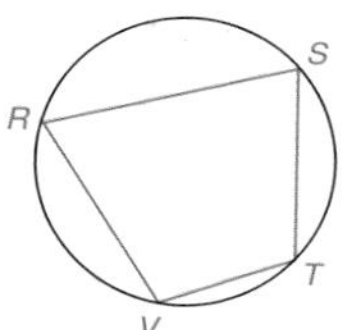

Exercises 18, 19

20. A quadrilateral *RSTV* is circumscribed about a circle so that its tangent sides are at the endpoints of two intersecting diameters.
a) What type of quadrilateral is *RSTV*?
b) If the diameters are also perpendicular, what type of quadrilateral is *RSTV*?

In Exercises 21 and 22, complete each proof.

21. *Given:* $\overline{AB}$ and $\overline{AC}$ are tangents to $\odot O$ from point *A*
Prove: $\triangle ABC$ is isosceles

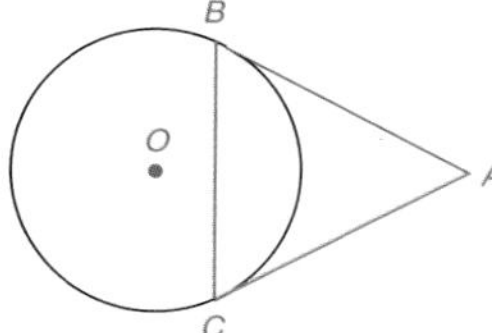

PROOF

Statements	Reasons
1. ?	1. Given
2. $m\angle B = \frac{1}{2}(m\overset{\frown}{BC})$ and $m\angle C = \frac{1}{2}(m\overset{\frown}{BC})$	2. ?
3. $m\angle B = m\angle C$	3. ?
4. $\angle B \cong \angle C$	4. ?
5. ?	5. If two $\angle$s of a $\triangle$ are $\cong$, the sides opposite the $\angle$s are $\cong$
6. ?	6. If two sides of a $\triangle$ are $\cong$, the $\triangle$ is isosceles

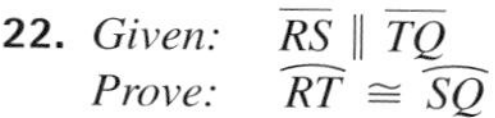

22. *Given:* $\overline{RS} \parallel \overline{TQ}$
Prove: $\overline{RT} \cong \overline{SQ}$

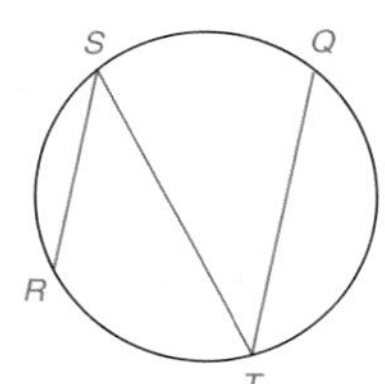

PROOF

Statements	Reasons
1. $\overline{RS} \parallel \overline{TQ}$	1. ?
2. $\angle S \cong \angle T$	2. ?
3. ?	3. If two $\angle$s are $\cong$, the $\angle$s are = in measure
4. $m\angle S = \frac{1}{2}(m\overset{\frown}{RT})$	4. ?
5. $m\angle T = \frac{1}{2}(m\overset{\frown}{SQ})$	5. ?
6. $\frac{1}{2}(m\overset{\frown}{RT}) = \frac{1}{2}(m\overset{\frown}{SQ})$	6. ?
7. $m\overset{\frown}{RT} = m\overset{\frown}{SQ}$	7. Multiplication Property of Equality
8. ?	8. If two arcs of a $\odot$ are = in measure, the arcs are $\cong$

In Exercises 23 to 25, complete a paragraph proof.

23. *Given:* Tangent $\overline{AB}$ to $\odot O$ at point *B*
$m\angle A = m\angle B$
Prove: $m\overset{\frown}{BD} = 2 \cdot m\overset{\frown}{BC}$

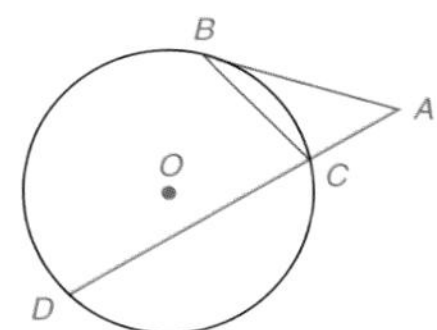

24. *Given:* Diameter $\overline{AB} \perp \overline{CE}$ at D
Prove: CD is the geometric mean of AD and DB

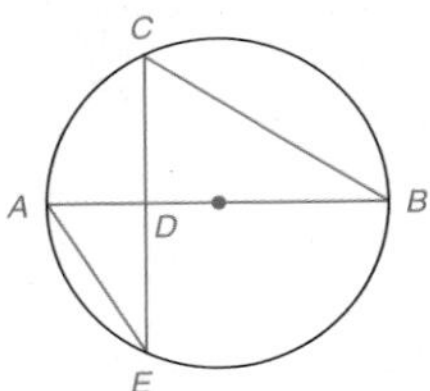

In Exercises 25 and 26, $\overline{CA}$ and $\overline{CB}$ are tangents.

25. *Given:* $m\widehat{AB} = x$
Prove: $m\angle 1 = 180° - x$

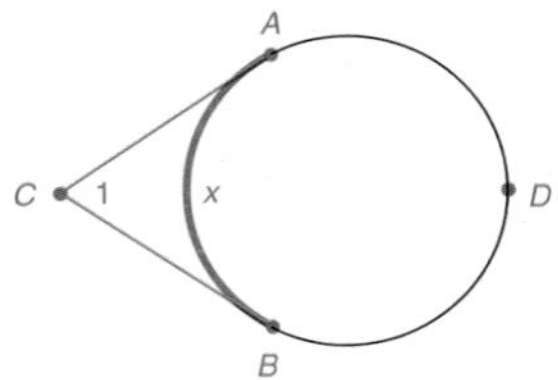

Exercises 25, 26

26. Use the result from Exercise 25 to find $m\angle 1$ if $m\widehat{AB} = 104°$.

27. An airplane reaches an altitude of 3 mi above the earth. Assuming a clear day and that a passenger has binoculars, how far can the passenger see?

(HINT: The radius of the earth is approximately 4000 mi.)

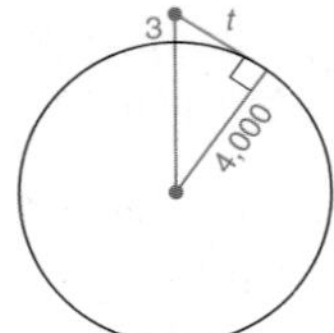

28. From the veranda of a beachfront hotel, Manny is searching the seascape through his binoculars. A ship suddenly appears on the horizon. If Manny is 80 ft above the earth, how far is the ship out at sea?

(HINT: See Exercise 27 and note that 1 mi = 5280 ft.*)*

29. For the five-pointed star (pentagram), inscribed in the circles, find the measures of $\angle 1$ and $\angle 2$.

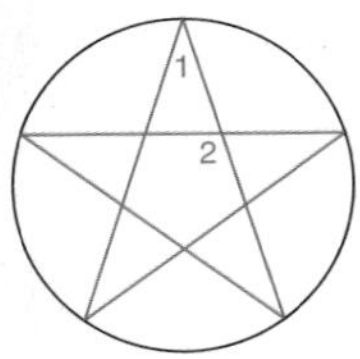

30. For the six-pointed star (hexagram) inscribed in the circle, find the measures of $\angle 1$ and $\angle 2$.

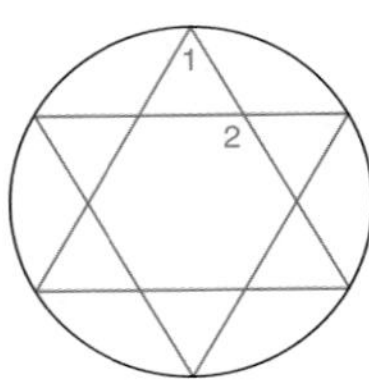

31. A satellite dish in the shape of a regular dodecagon (12 sides) is nearly "circular." Find:
a) $m\widehat{AB}$
b) $m\widehat{ABC}$
c) $m\angle ABC$ (inscribed angle)

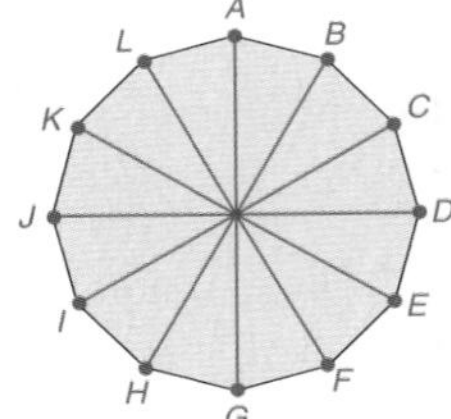

32. In the figure shown, $\triangle RST \sim \triangle WVT$ by the reason AA. Name two pairs of congruent angles in these similar triangles.

33. In the figure shown, $\triangle RXV \sim \triangle WXS$ by the reason AA. Name two pairs of congruent angles in these similar triangles.

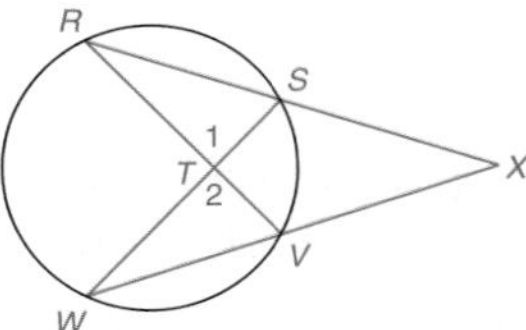

Exercises 32, 33

***34.** On a fitting for a hex wrench, the distance from the center O to a vertex is 5 mm. The length of radius $\overline{OB}$ of the circle is 10 mm. If $\overline{OC} \perp \overline{DE}$ at F, how long is $\overline{FC}$?

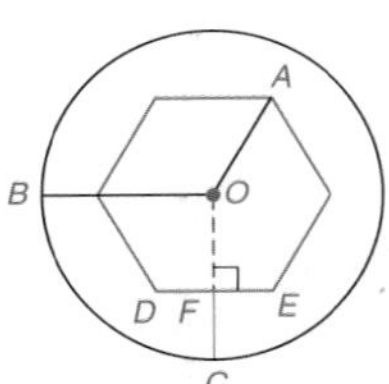

***35.** *Given:* $\overline{AB}$ is a diameter of $\odot O$
M is the midpoint of chord $\overline{AC}$
N is the midpoint of chord $\overline{CB}$
$MB = \sqrt{73}$, $AN = 2\sqrt{13}$
Find: The length of diameter $\overline{AB}$

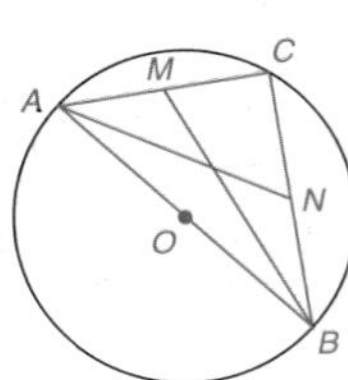

36. A surveyor sees a circular planetarium through a angle. If the surveyor is 45 ft from the door, what is the diameter of the planetarium?

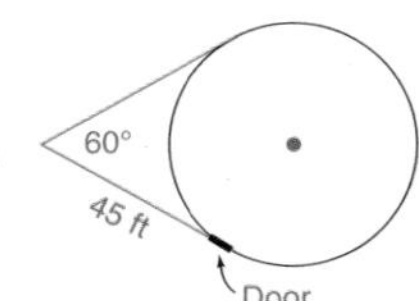

***37.** The larger circle is inscribed in a square with sides of length 4 cm. The smaller circle is tangent to the larger circle and to two sides of the square as shown. Find the radius of the smaller circle.

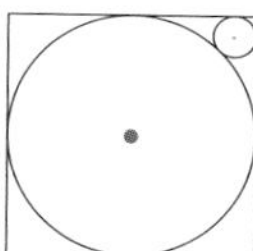

***38.** In $\odot R$, $QS = 2(PT)$. Also, $m\angle P = 23°$. Find $m\angle VRS$.

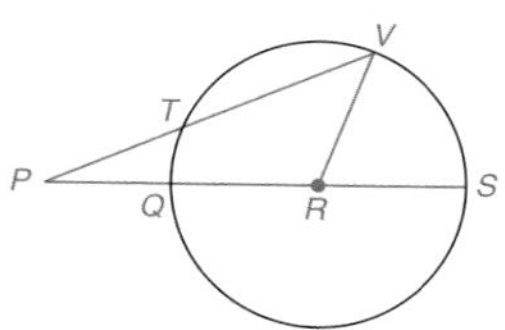

In Exercises 39 to 47, provide a paragraph proof. Be sure to provide a drawing, Given, and Prove where needed.

39. If two parallel lines intersect a circle, then the intercepted arcs between these lines are congruent.

(HINT: See Figure 6.36. Draw chord $\overline{AD}$.)

40. The line joining the centers of two circles that intersect at two points is the perpendicular bisector of the common chord.

41. If a trapezoid is inscribed in a circle, then it is an isosceles trapezoid.

42. If a parallelogram is inscribed in a circle, then it is a rectangle.

43. If one side of an inscribed triangle is a diameter, then the triangle is a right triangle.

44. Prove Case 2 of Corollary 6.2.4: The measure of an angle formed by a tangent and a chord drawn to the point of tangency is one-half the measure of the intercepted arc. (See Figure 6.29.)

45. Prove Case 3 of Corollary 6.2.4. (See Figure 6.29.)

46. *Given:* $\odot O$ with P in its exterior; O-Y-P

Prove: $OP > OY$

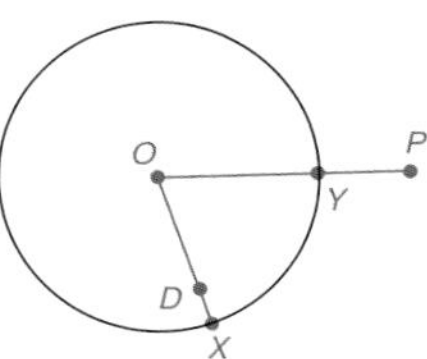

47. *Given:* Quadrilateral $RSTV$ inscribed in $\odot Q$

Prove: $m\angle R + m\angle T = m\angle V + m\angle S$

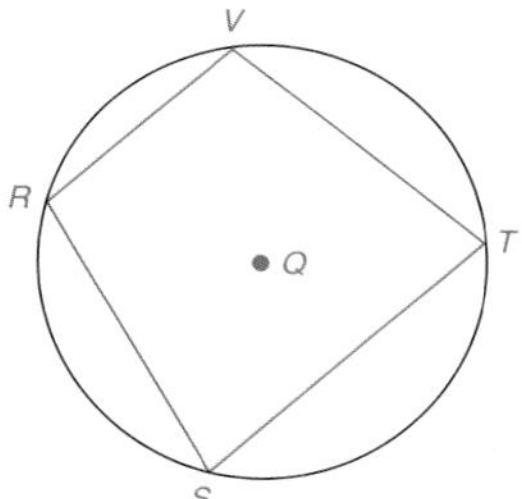

6.3 Line and Segment Relationships in the Circle

KEY CONCEPTS

- Tangent Circles
- Internally Tangent Circles
- Externally Tangent Circles
- Line of Centers
- Common Tangent
- Common External Tangents
- Common Internal Tangents

In this section, we consider further line and line segment relationships in the circle. Because some statements (such as Theorems 6.3.1–6.3.3) are so similar in wording, the student is strongly encouraged to make drawings and then compare the information that is given in each theorem to the conclusion of that theorem.

THEOREM 6.3.1

If a line is drawn through the center of a circle perpendicular to a chord, then it bisects the chord and its arc.

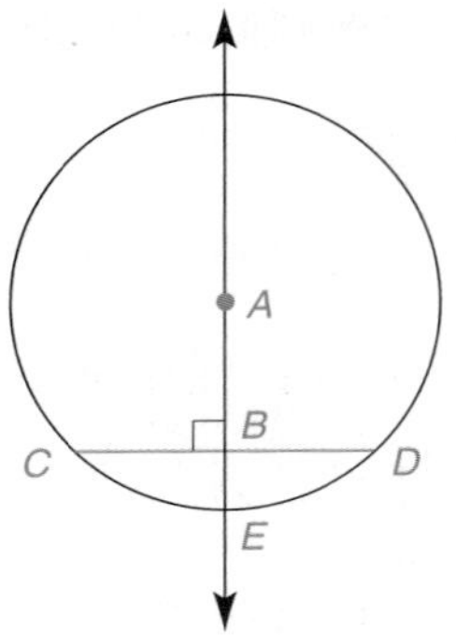

Figure 6.37

NOTE: Note that the term *arc* generally refers to the minor arc, even though the major arc is also bisected.

GIVEN: $\overleftrightarrow{AB} \perp$ chord $\overline{CD}$ in circle A (See Figure 6.37.)

PROVE: $\overline{CB} \cong \overline{BD}$ and $\overset{\frown}{CE} \cong \overset{\frown}{ED}$

The proof is left as an exercise for the student.

(HINT: Draw $\overline{AC}$ and $\overline{AD}$.)

Even though the Prove statement does not match the conclusion of Theorem 6.3.1, we know that $\overline{CD}$ is bisected by $\overleftrightarrow{AB}$ if $\overline{CB} \cong \overline{BD}$ and that $\overset{\frown}{CD}$ is bisected by $\overleftrightarrow{AE}$ if $\overset{\frown}{CE} \cong \overset{\frown}{ED}$.

THEOREM 6.3.2

If a line through the center of a circle bisects a chord other than a diameter, then it is perpendicular to the chord.

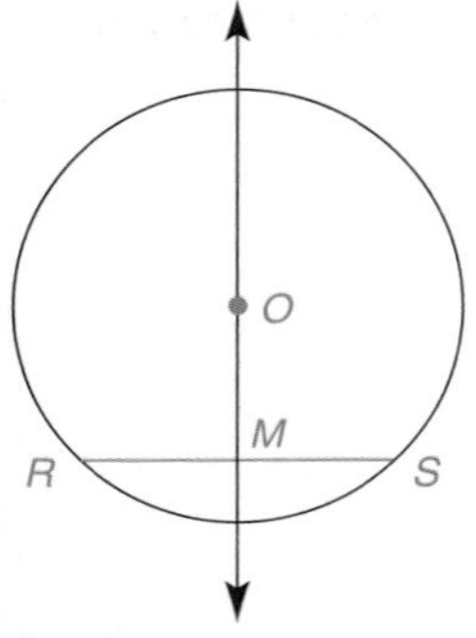

Figure 6.38

GIVEN: Circle O; $\overleftrightarrow{OM}$ is the bisector of chord $\overline{RS}$ (See Figure 6.38.)

PROVE: $\overleftrightarrow{OM} \perp \overline{RS}$

The proof is left as an exercise for the student.

(HINT: Draw radii $\overline{OR}$ and $\overline{OS}$.)

Figure 6.39(a) illustrates the following theorem. However, Figure 6.39(b) is used in the proof.

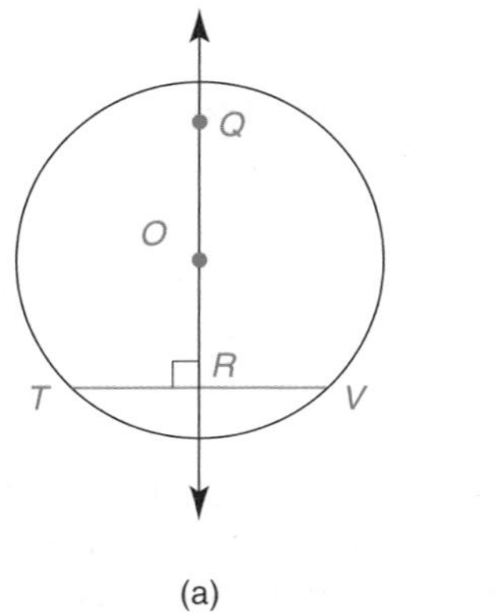

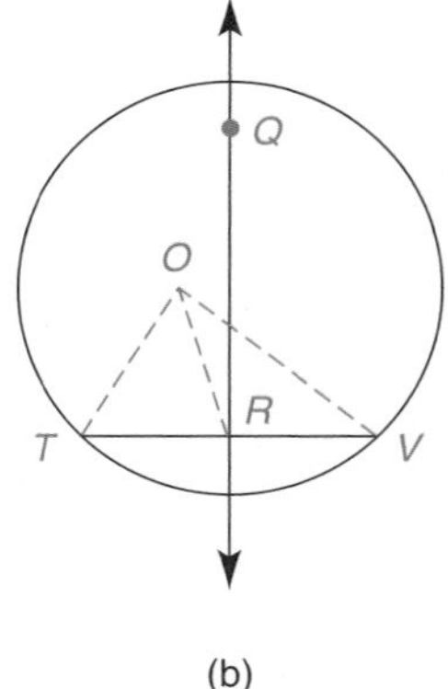

Figure 6.39

THEOREM 6.3.3

The perpendicular bisector of a chord contains the center of the circle.

GIVEN: In Figure 6.39(a), $\overleftrightarrow{QR}$ is the perpendicular bisector of chord $\overline{TV}$ in $\odot O$

PROVE: $\overleftrightarrow{QR}$ contains point O

PROOF (BY INDIRECT METHOD): Suppose that O is not on $\overleftrightarrow{QR}$. Draw $\overline{OR}$ and radii $\overline{OT}$ and $\overline{OV}$.
[See Figure 6.39(b).] Because $\overleftrightarrow{QR}$ is the perpendicular bisector of $\overline{TV}$, R must be the midpoint of $\overline{TV}$; then $\overline{TR} \cong \overline{RV}$. Also, $\overline{OT} \cong \overline{OV}$ (all radii of a $\odot$ are $\cong$). With $\overline{OR} \cong \overline{OR}$ by Identity, we have $\triangle ORT \cong \triangle ORV$ by SSS.

Now $\angle ORT \cong \angle ORV$ by CPCTC. It follows that $\overline{OR} \perp \overline{TV}$ because these line segments meet to form congruent adjacent angles.

Then $\overline{OR}$ is the perpendicular bisector of $\overline{TV}$. But $\overleftrightarrow{QR}$ is also the perpendicular bisector of $\overline{TV}$, which contradicts the uniqueness of the perpendicular bisector of a segment.

Thus, the supposition must be false, and it follows that center O is on $\overleftrightarrow{QR}$, the perpendicular bisector of chord $\overline{TV}$. ■

EXAMPLE 1

GIVEN: In Figure 6.40, $\odot O$ has a radius of length 5
$\overline{OE} \perp \overline{CD}$ at B and $OB = 3$

FIND: CD

Figure 6.40

Solution Draw radius $\overline{OC}$. By the Pythagorean Theorem,

$$\begin{aligned}(OC)^2 &= (OB)^2 + (BC)^2\\ 5^2 &= 3^2 + (BC)^2\\ 25 &= 9 + (BC)^2\\ (BC)^2 &= 16\\ BC &= 4\end{aligned}$$

According to Theorem 6.3.1, we know that $CD = 2 \cdot BC$; then it follows that $CD = 2 \cdot 4 = 8$. ■

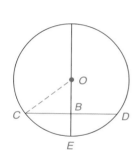

CIRCLES THAT ARE TANGENT

In this section, we assume that two circles are coplanar. Although concentric circles do not intersect, they do share a common center. For the concentric circles shown in Figure 6.41, the tangent of the smaller circle is a chord of the larger circle.

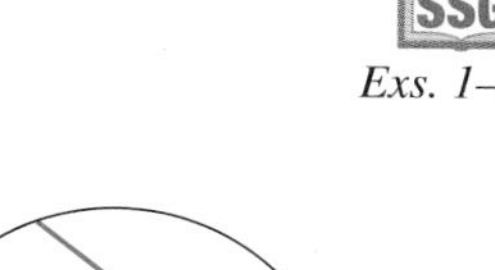

If two circles touch at one point, they are **tangent circles.** In Figure 6.42, circles P and Q are **internally tangent,** whereas circles O and R are **externally tangent.**

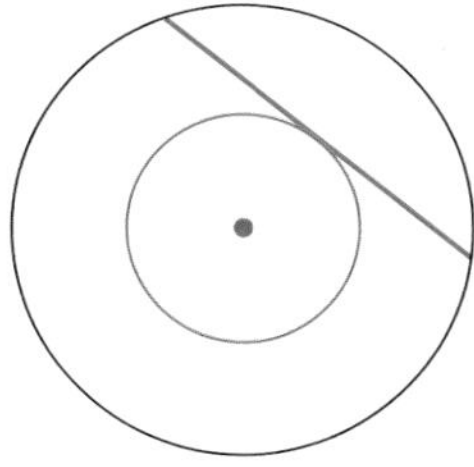

Figure 6.41

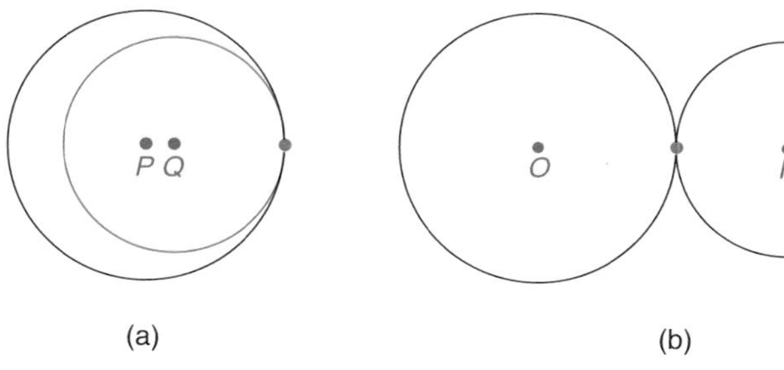

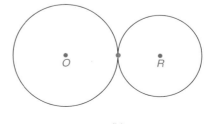

Figure 6.42

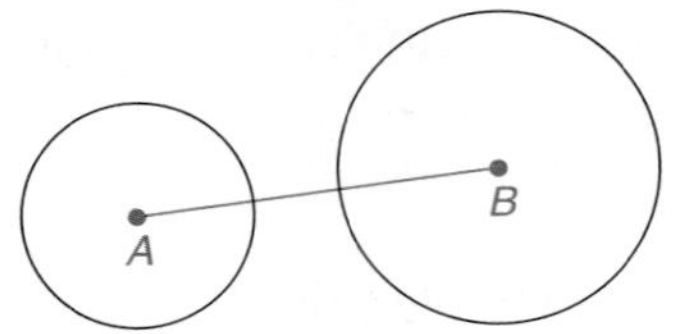

Figure 6.43

> **DEFINITION**
>
> For two circles with different centers, the **line of centers** is the line (or line segment) containing the centers of both circles.

As the definition suggests, the line segment joining the centers of two circles is also commonly called the line of centers of the two circles. In Figure 6.43, $\overleftrightarrow{AB}$ or $\overline{AB}$ is the line of centers for circles A and B.

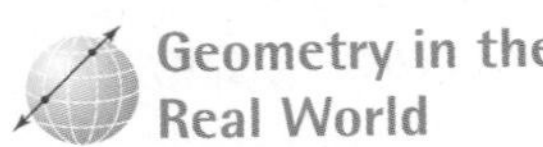

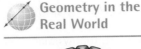

Geometry in the Real World

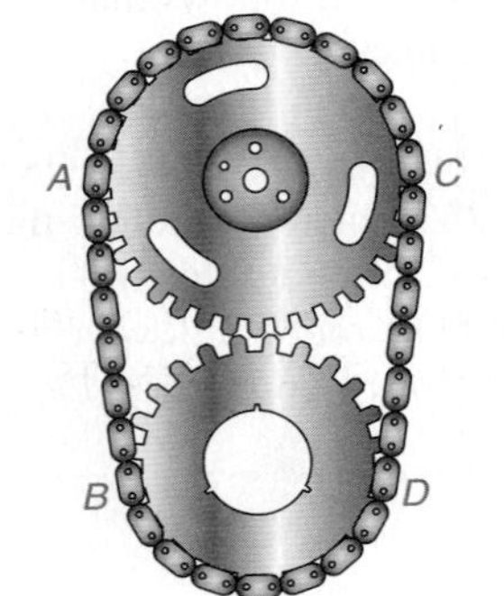

Parts $\overline{AB}$ and $\overline{CD}$ of the chain belt represent common external tangents to the circular gears.

COMMON TANGENT LINES TO CIRCLES

A line segment that is tangent to each of two circles is a **common tangent** for these circles. If the common tangent *does not* intersect the line of centers, it is a **common external tangent.** In Figure 6.44, circles P and Q have one common external tangent, $\overleftrightarrow{ST}$; circles A and B have two common external tangents, $\overleftrightarrow{WX}$ and $\overleftrightarrow{YZ}$.

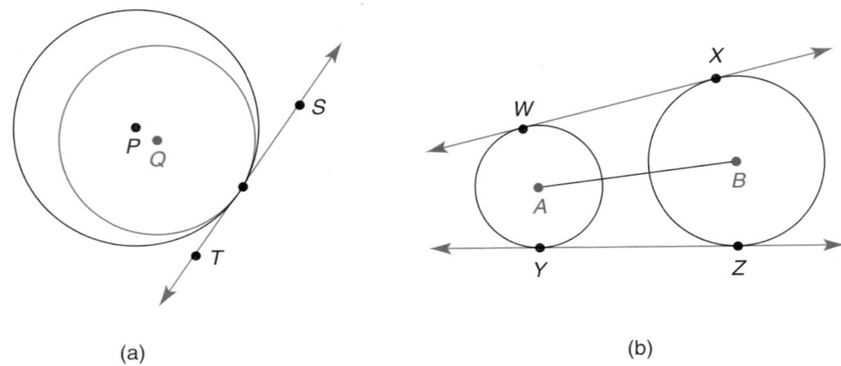

SSG *Exs. 5–6*

Figure 6.44

If the common tangent *does* intersect the line of centers for two circles, it is a **common internal tangent** for the two circles. In Figure 6.45, $\overleftrightarrow{DE}$ is a common internal tangent for externally tangent circles O and R; $\overleftrightarrow{AB}$ and $\overleftrightarrow{CD}$ are common internal tangents for $\odot M$ and $\odot N$.

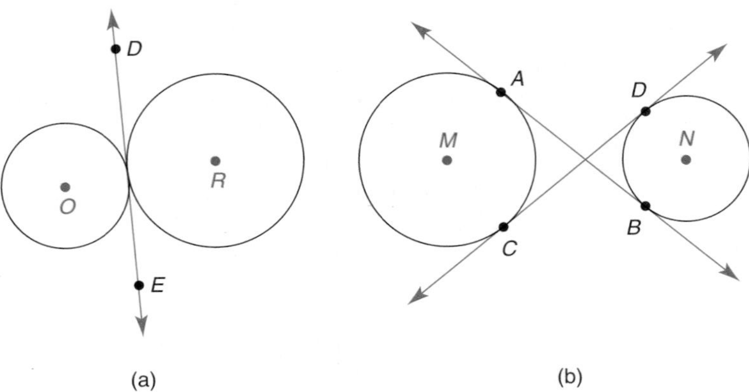

Figure 6.45

Discover

Measure the lengths of tangent segments $\overline{AB}$ and $\overline{AC}$ of Figure 6.46. How do AB and AC compare?

ANSWER

They are equal.

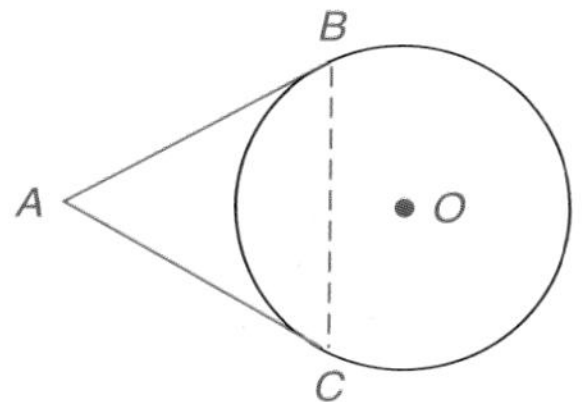

Figure 6.46

THEOREM 6.3.4

The tangent segments to a circle from an external point are congruent.

GIVEN: In Figure 6.46, $\overline{AB}$ and $\overline{AC}$ are tangents to $\odot O$ from point A

PROVE: $\overline{AB} \cong \overline{AC}$

PROOF: Draw $\overline{BC}$. Now $m\angle B = \frac{1}{2}m\widehat{BC}$ and $m\angle C = \frac{1}{2}m\widehat{BC}$. Then $\angle B \cong \angle C$ because these angles have equal measures. In turn, the sides opposite $\angle B$ and $\angle C$ of $\triangle ABC$ are congruent. That is, $\overline{AB} \cong \overline{AC}$. ■

We apply Theorem 6.3.4 in Examples 2 and 3.

EXAMPLE 2

A belt used in an automobile engine wraps around two pulleys with different lengths of radii. Explain why the straight pieces named $\overline{AB}$ and $\overline{CD}$ have the same length.

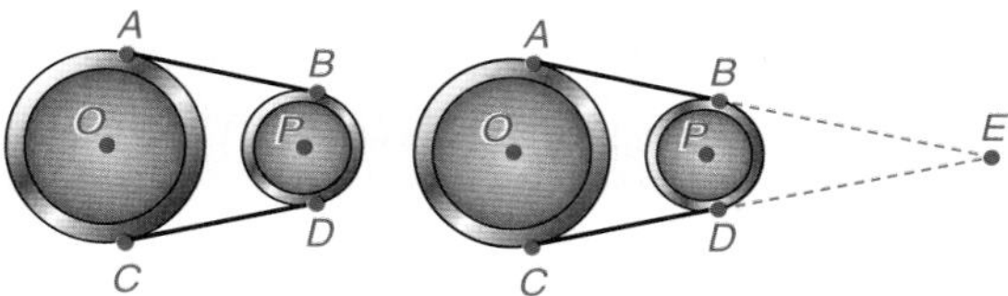

Figure 6.47

Discover

Place three coins of the same size together so that they all touch each other. What type of triangle is formed by joining their centers?

ANSWER

Equilateral or Equiangular

Solution Because the pulley centered at O has the larger radius length, we extend $\overline{AB}$ and $\overline{CD}$ to meet at point E. Because E is an external point to both $\odot O$ and $\odot P$, we know that $EB = ED$ and $EA = EC$ by Theorem 6.3.4. By subtracting equals from equals, $EA - EB = EC - ED$. Because $EA - EB = AB$ and $EC - ED = CD$, it follows that $AB = CD$. ■

EXAMPLE 3

The circle shown in Figure 6.48 is inscribed in $\triangle ABC$; $AB = 9$, $BC = 8$, and $AC = 7$. Find the lengths AM, MB, and NC.

Solution Because the tangent segments from an external point are $\cong$, we can let

$$AM = AP = x$$
$$BM = BN = y$$
$$NC = CP = z$$

Now

$$x + y = 9 \quad \text{(from } AB = 9\text{)}$$
$$y + z = 8 \quad \text{(from } BC = 8\text{)}$$
$$x + z = 7 \quad \text{(from } AC = 7\text{)}$$

Subtracting the second equation from the first, we have

$$\begin{array}{r} x + y = 9 \\ y + z = 8 \\ \hline x - z = 1 \end{array}$$

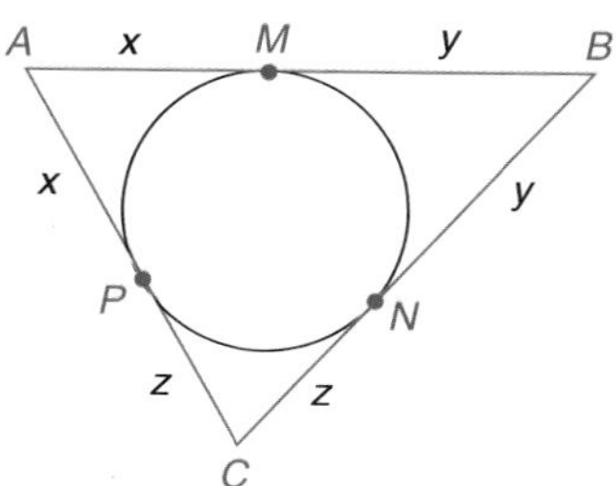

Figure 6.48

Now we use this new equation along with the third equation on the previous page and add:

$$\begin{array}{r} x - z = 1 \\ x + z = 7 \\ \hline 2x = 8 \rightarrow x = 4 \rightarrow AM = 4 \end{array}$$

SSG *Exs. 7–10*

Because $x = 4$ and $x + y = 9$, $y = 5$. Then $BM = 5$. Because $x = 4$ and $x + z = 7$, $z = 3$, so $NC = 3$. Summarizing, $AM = 4$, $BM = 5$, and $NC = 3$. ■

LENGTHS OF SEGMENTS IN A CIRCLE

To complete this section, we consider three relationships involving the lengths of chords, secants, or tangents. The first theorem is proved, but the proofs of the remaining theorems are left as exercises for the student.

Reminder

AA is the method used to prove triangles similar in this section.

STRATEGY FOR PROOF ▶ Proving Segment-Length Theorems in the Circle

General Rule: With the help of auxiliary lines, Theorems 6.3.5, 6.3.6, and 6.3.7 can be proved by establishing similar triangles, followed by use of CSSTP and the Means-Extremes Property.

Illustration: In the proof of Theorem 6.3.5, the auxiliary chords drawn lead to similar triangles *RTV* and *QSV*.

THEOREM 6.3.5

If two chords intersect within a circle, then the product of the lengths of the segments (parts) of one chord is equal to the product of the lengths of the segments of the other chord.

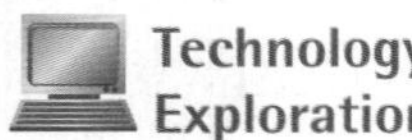

Technology Exploration

Use computer software if available.

1. Draw a circle with chords $\overline{HJ}$ and $\overline{LM}$ intersecting at point *P*. (See Figure 6.50.)
2. Measure $\overline{MP}$, $\overline{PL}$, $\overline{HP}$, and $\overline{PJ}$.
3. Show that $MP \cdot PL = HP \cdot PJ$. (Answers are not "perfect.")

GIVEN: Circle *O* with chords $\overline{RS}$ and $\overline{TQ}$ intersecting at point *V* (See Figure 6.49.)

PROVE: $RV \cdot VS = TV \cdot VQ$

PROOF: Draw $\overline{RT}$ and $\overline{QS}$. In $\triangle RTV$ and $\triangle QSV$, we have $\angle 1 \cong \angle 2$ (vertical $\angle$s). Also, $\angle R$ and $\angle Q$ are inscribed angles that intercept the same arc (namely $\overset{\frown}{TS}$), so $\angle R \cong \angle Q$. By AA, $\triangle RTV \sim \triangle QSV$. Using CSSTP, we have $\frac{RV}{VQ} = \frac{TV}{VS}$ and so $RV \cdot VS = TV \cdot VQ$.

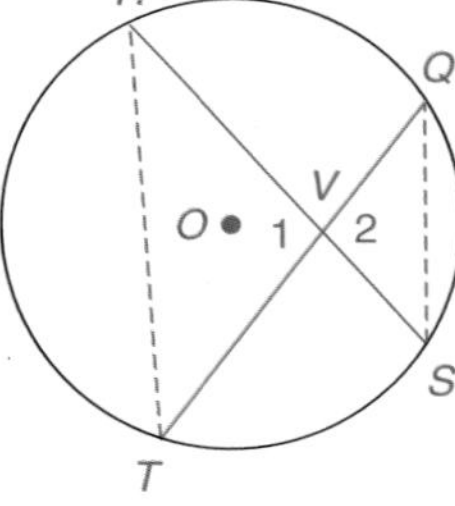

Figure 6.49 ■

EXAMPLE 4

In Figure 6.50, $HP = 4$, $PJ = 5$, and $LP = 8$. Find *PM*.

Solution Applying Theorem 6.3.5, we have $HP \cdot PJ = LP \cdot PM$. Then

$$\begin{aligned} 4 \cdot 5 &= 8 \cdot PM \\ 8 \cdot PM &= 20 \\ PM &= 2.5 \end{aligned}$$

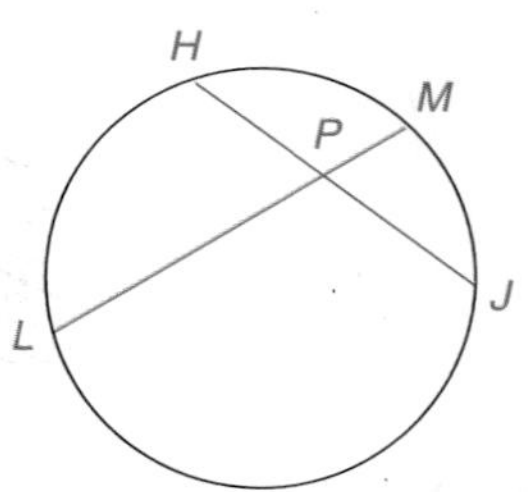

Figure 6.50 ■

EXAMPLE 5

In Figure 6.50 on page 304, $HP = 6$, $PJ = 4$, and $LM = 11$. Find LP and PM.

Solution Because $LP + PM = LM$, it follows that $PM = LM - LP$. If $LM = 11$ and $LP = x$, then $PM = 11 - x$. Now $HP \cdot PJ = LP \cdot PM$ becomes

$$\begin{aligned} 6 \cdot 4 &= x(11 - x) \\ 24 &= 11x - x^2 \\ x^2 - 11x + 24 &= 0 \\ (x - 3)(x - 8) &= 0, \text{ so } x - 3 = 0 \text{ or } x - 8 = 0 \\ x &= 3 \quad \text{or} \quad x = 8 \end{aligned}$$

Therefore, $LP = 3$ or $LP = 8$

SSG Exs. 11–13

If $LP = 3$, then $PM = 8$; conversely, if $LP = 8$, then $PM = 3$. That is, the segments of chord $\overline{LM}$ have lengths of 3 and 8. ■

In Figure 6.51, we say that secant $\overline{AB}$ has internal segment (part) $\overline{RB}$ and external segment (part) $\overline{AR}$.

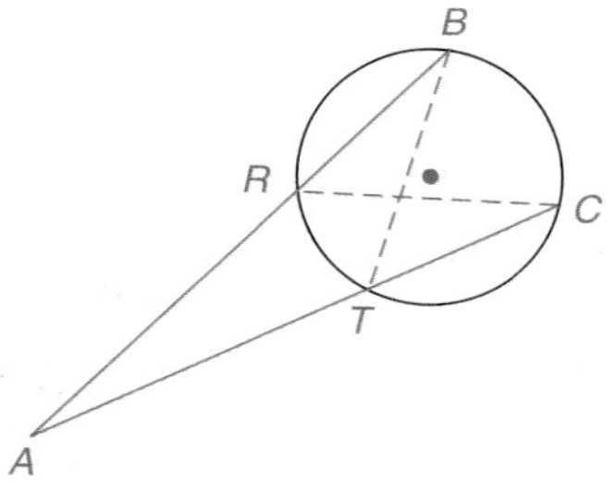

Figure 6.51

THEOREM 6.3.6

If two secant segments are drawn to a circle from an external point, then the products of the lengths of each secant with its external segment are equal.

GIVEN: Secants $\overline{AB}$ and $\overline{AC}$ for the circle in Figure 6.51

PROVE: $AB \cdot RA = AC \cdot TA$

The proof is left as Exercise 46 for the student.

(HINT: First use the auxiliary lines shown to prove that $\triangle ABT \sim \triangle ACR$.)

EXAMPLE 6

GIVEN: In Figure 6.51, $AB = 14$, $BR = 5$, and $TC = 5$

FIND: AC and TA

Solution Let $AC = x$. Because $AT + TC = AC$, we have $AT + 5 = x$, so $TA = x - 5$. If $AB = 14$ and $BR = 5$, then $AR = 9$. The statement $AB \cdot RA = AC \cdot TA$ becomes

$$\begin{aligned} 14 \cdot 9 &= x(x - 5) \\ 126 &= x^2 - 5x \\ x^2 - 5x - 126 &= 0 \\ (x - 14)(x + 9) &= 0, \text{ so } x - 14 = 0 \text{ or } x + 9 = 0 \\ x = 14 &\text{ or } x = -9 \end{aligned}$$

($x = -9$ is discarded because the length of $\overline{AC}$ cannot be negative.)

Thus, $AC = 14$, so $TA = 9$. ■

THEOREM 6.3.7

If a tangent segment and a secant segment are drawn to a circle from an external point, then the square of the length of the tangent equals the product of the length of the secant with the length of its external segment.

GIVEN: Tangent $\overline{TV}$ and secant $\overline{TW}$ in Figure 6.52

PROVE: $(TV)^2 = TW \cdot TX$

The proof is left as Exercise 47 for the student.

(HINT: Use the auxiliary lines shown to prove that $\triangle TVW \sim \triangle TXV$.)

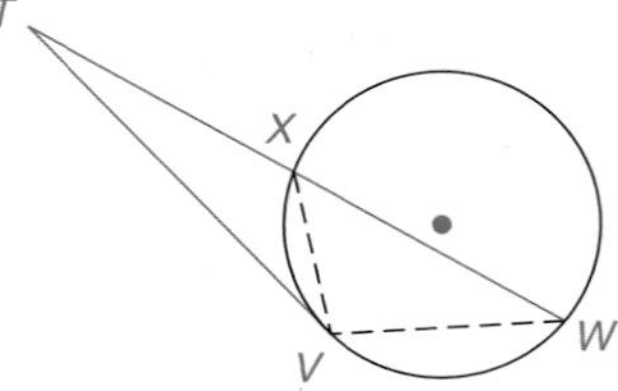

Figure 6.52

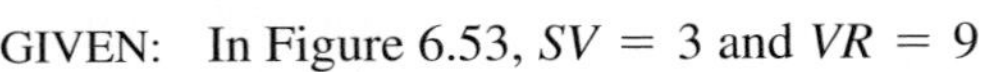

EXAMPLE 7

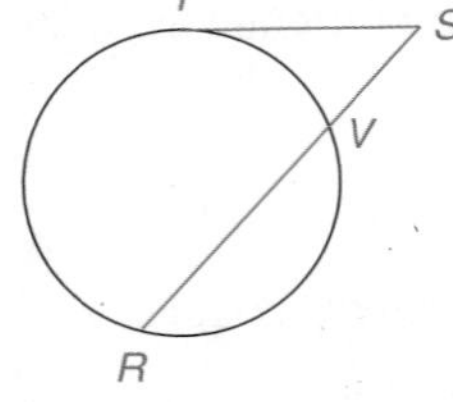

Figure 6.53

GIVEN: In Figure 6.53, $SV = 3$ and $VR = 9$

FIND: ST

Solution If $SV = 3$ and $VR = 9$, then $SR = 12$. Using Theorem 6.3.7, we find that

$$(ST)^2 = SR \cdot SV$$
$$(ST)^2 = 12 \cdot 3$$
$$(ST)^2 = 36$$
$$ST = 6 \text{ or } -6$$

SSG *Exs. 14–17*

Because ST cannot be negative, $ST = 6$. ■

Exercises 6.3

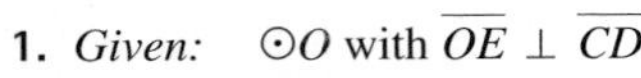

1. *Given:* $\odot O$ with $\overline{OE} \perp \overline{CD}$
   $CD = OC$
   Find: $m\overset{\frown}{CF}$
2. *Given:* $OC = 8$ and $OE = 6$
   $\overline{OE} \perp \overline{CD}$ in $\odot O$
   Find: CD
3. *Given:* $\overline{OV} \perp \overline{RS}$ in $\odot O$
   $OV = 9$ and $OT = 6$
   Find: RS

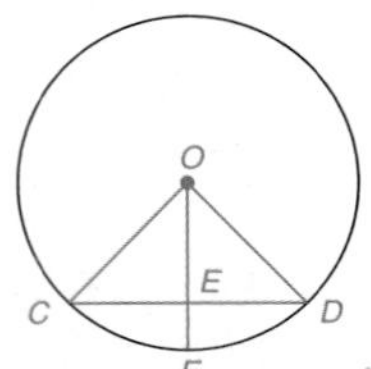

Exercises 1, 2

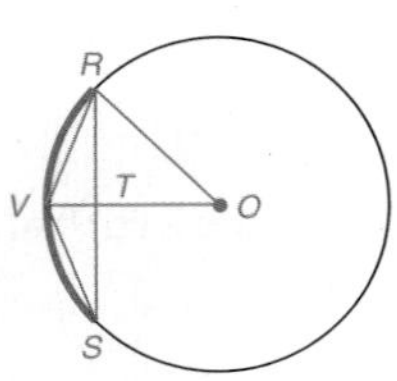

Exercises 3, 4

4. *Given:* V is the midpoint of $\overset{\frown}{RS}$ in $\odot O$
   $m\angle S = 15°$ and $OT = 6$
   Find: OR
5. Sketch two circles that have:
   a) No common tangents
   b) Exactly one common tangent
   c) Exactly two common tangents
   d) Exactly three common tangents
   e) Exactly four common tangents
6. Two congruent intersecting circles B and D (not shown) have a line (segment) of centers $\overline{BD}$ and a common chord $\overline{AC}$ that are congruent. Explain why quadrilateral $ABCD$ is a square.

In the figure for Exercises 7 to 16, O is the center of the circle. See Theorem 6.3.5.

7. *Given:* $AE = 6$, $EB = 4$, $DE = 8$
Find: EC

8. *Given:* $DE = 12$, $EC = 5$, $AE = 8$
Find: EB

9. *Given:* $AE = 8$, $EB = 6$, $DC = 16$
Find: DE and EC

10. *Given:* $AE = 7$, $EB = 5$, $DC = 12$
Find: DE and EC

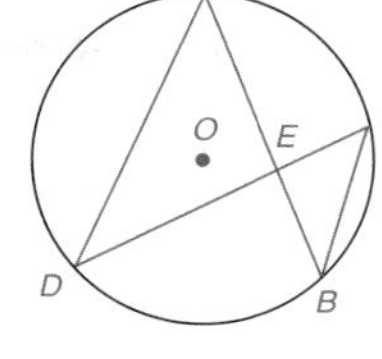

Exercises 7–16

11. *Given:* $AE = 6$, $EC = 3$, $AD = 8$
Find: CB

12. *Given:* $AD = 10$, $BC = 4$, $AE = 7$
Find: EC

13. *Given:* $AE = \frac{x}{2}$, $EB = 12$, $DE = \frac{x+6}{3}$, and $EC = 9$
Find: x and AE

14. *Given:* $AE = \frac{x}{2}$, $EB = \frac{x}{3}$, $DE = \frac{5x}{6}$, and $EC = 6$
Find: x and DE

15. *Given:* $AE = 9$ and $EB = 8$; $DE{:}EC = 2{:}1$
Find: DE and EC

16. *Given:* $AE = 6$ and $EB = 4$; $DE{:}EC = 3{:}1$
Find: DE and EC

For Exercises 17–20, see Theorem 6.3.6.

17. *Given:* $AB = 6$, $BC = 8$, $AE = 15$
Find: DE

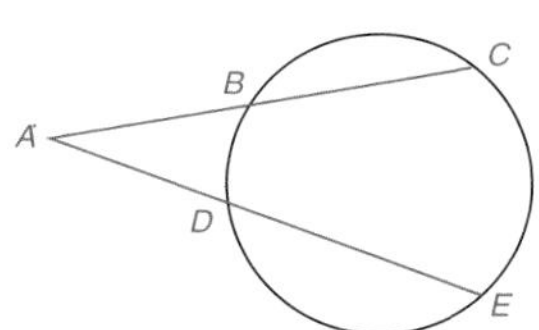

Exercises 17–20

18. *Given:* $AC = 12$, $AB = 6$, $AE = 14$
Find: AD

19. *Given:* $AB = 4$, $BC = 5$, $AD = 3$
Find: DE

20. *Given:* $AB = 5$, $BC = 6$, $AD = 6$
Find: AE

In the figure for Exercises 21 to 24, $\overline{RS}$ is tangent to the circle at S. See Theorem 6.3.7.

21. *Given:* $RS = 8$ and $RV = 12$
Find: RT

22. *Given:* $RT = 4$ and $TV = 6$
Find: RS

23. *Given:* $\overline{RS} \cong \overline{TV}$ and $RT = 6$
Find: RS

(HINT: Use the Quadratic Formula.)

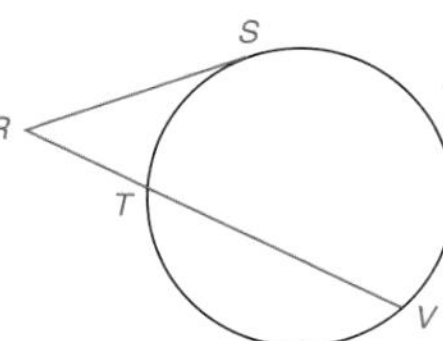

Exercises 21–24

24. *Given:* $RT = \frac{1}{2} \cdot RS$ and $TV = 9$
Find: RT

25. For the two circles in Figures (a), (b), and (c), find the total number of common tangents (internal and external).

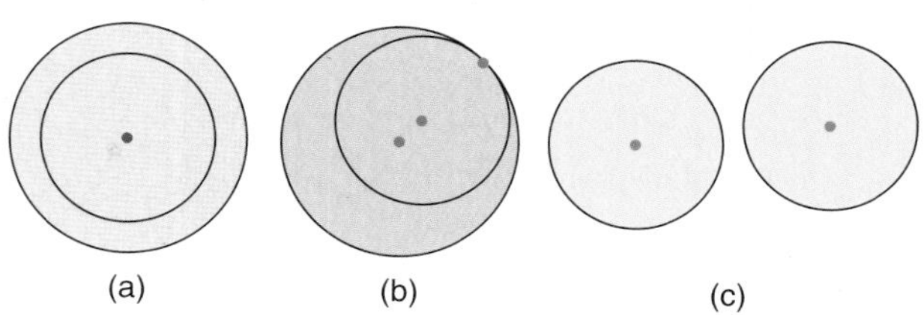

26. For the two circles in Figures (a), (b), and (c), find the total number of common tangents (internal and external).

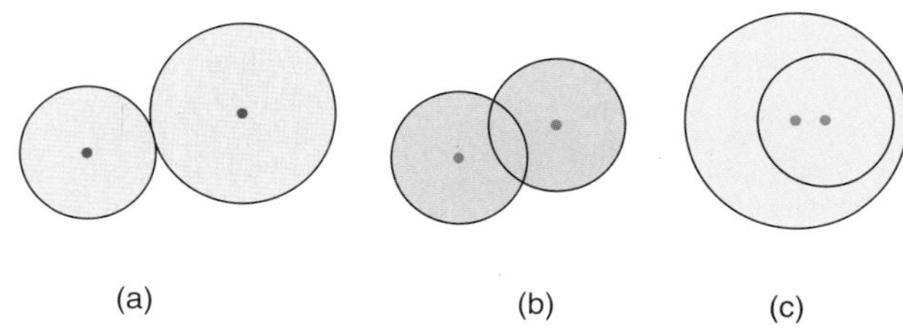

In Exercises 27 to 30, provide a paragraph proof.

27. *Given:* $\odot O$ and $\odot Q$ are tangent at point F
Secant $\overline{AC}$ to $\odot O$
Secant $\overline{AE}$ to $\odot Q$
Common internal tangent $\overline{AF}$
Prove: $AC \cdot AB = AE \cdot AD$

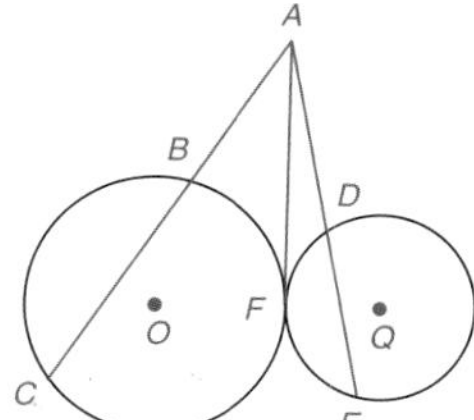

28. *Given:* $\odot O$ with $\overline{OM} \perp \overline{AB}$ and $\overline{ON} \perp \overline{BC}$
$\overline{OM} \cong \overline{ON}$
Prove: $\triangle ABC$ is isosceles

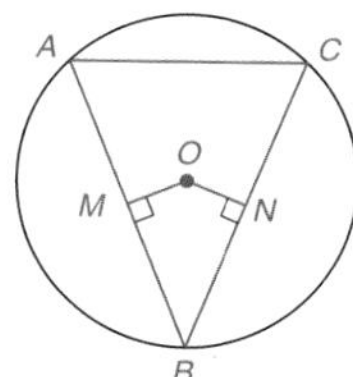

29. *Given:* Quadrilateral $ABCD$ is circumscribed about $\odot O$
Prove: $AB + CD = DA + BC$

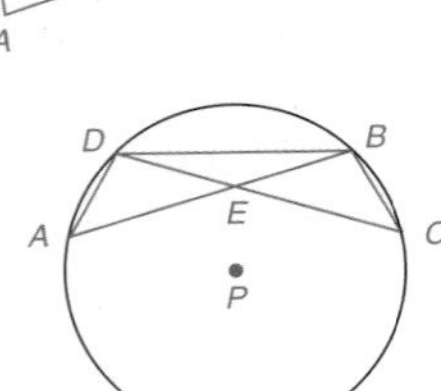

30. *Given:* $\overline{AB} \cong \overline{DC}$ in $\odot P$
Prove: $\triangle ABD \cong \triangle CDB$

31. Does it follow from Exercise 30 that $\triangle ADE$ is also congruent to $\triangle CBE$? What can you conclude about $\overline{AE}$ and $\overline{CE}$ in the drawing? What can you conclude about $\overline{DE}$ and $\overline{EB}$?

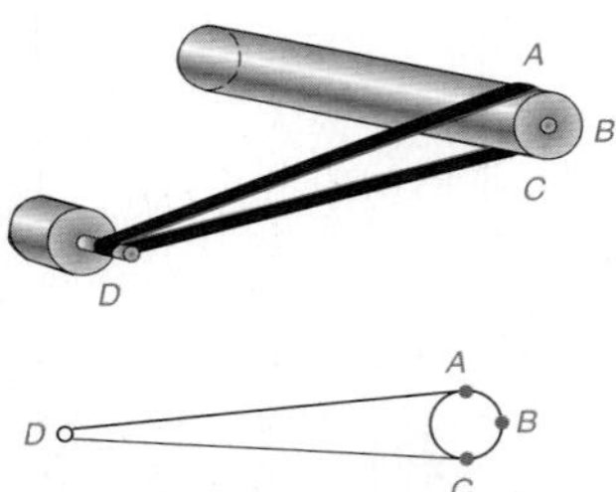

Exercises 30, 31

32. In $\odot O$ (not shown), $\overline{RS}$ is a diameter and T is the midpoint of semicircle $\widehat{RTS}$. What is the value of the ratio $\frac{RT}{RS}$? The ratio $\frac{RT}{RO}$?

33. The cylindrical brush on a vacuum cleaner is powered by an electric motor. In the figure, the drive shaft is at point D. If $m\widehat{AC} = 160°$, find the measure of the angle formed by the drive belt at point D; that is, find $m\angle D$.

Exercises 33, 34

34. The drive mechanism on a treadmill is powered by an electric motor. In the figure, find $m\angle D$ if $m\widehat{ABC}$ is 36° larger than $m\widehat{AC}$.

***35.** *Given:* Tangents $\overline{AB}$, $\overline{BC}$, and $\overline{AC}$ to $\odot O$ at points M, N, and P, respectively
$AB = 14$, $BC = 16$, $AC = 12$
Find: AM, PC, and BN

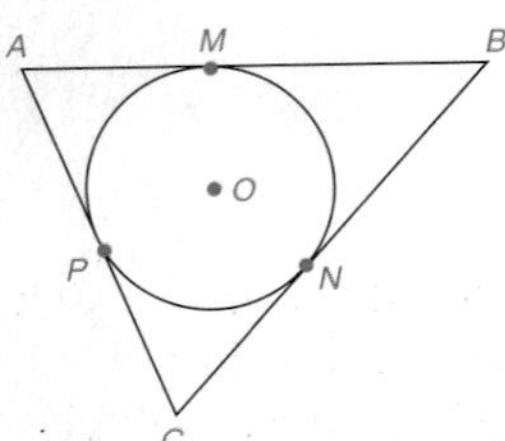

***36.** *Given:* $\odot Q$ is inscribed in isosceles right $\triangle RST$
The perimeter of $\triangle RST$ is $8 + 4\sqrt{2}$
Find: TM

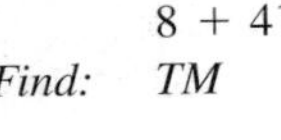

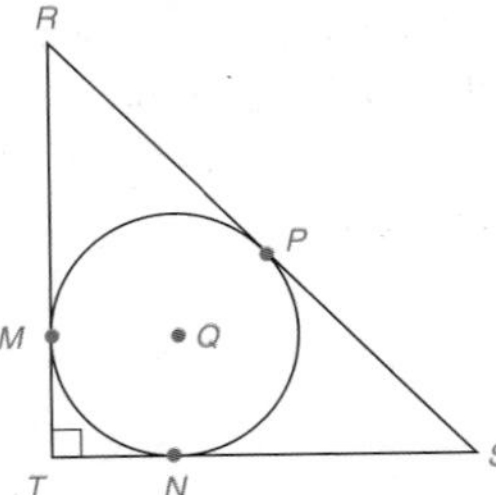

***37.** *Given:* $\overline{AB}$ is an external tangent to $\odot O$ and $\odot Q$ at points A and B; radii lengths for $\odot O$ and $\odot Q$ are 4 and 9, respectively
Find: AB

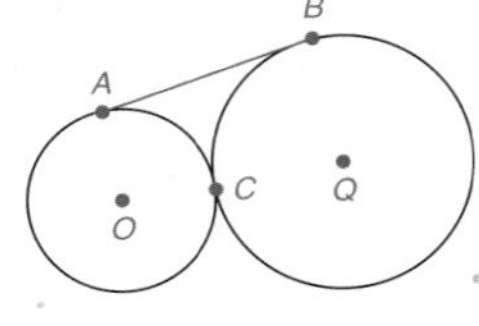

(HINT: The line of centers $\overline{OQ}$ contains point C, the point at which $\odot O$ and $\odot Q$ are tangent.)

38. The center of a circle of radius 3 inches is at a distance of 20 inches from the center of a circle of radius 9 inches. What is the exact length of common internal tangent $\overline{AB}$?

(HINT: Use similar triangles to find OD and DP. Then apply the Pythagorean Theorem twice.)

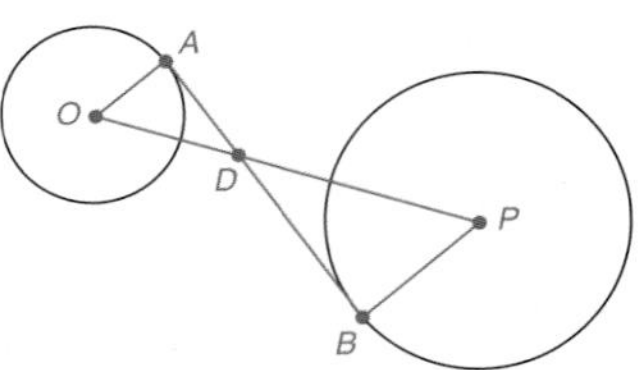

Exercises 38, 39

39. The center of a circle of radius 2 inches is at a distance of 10 inches from the center of a circle of radius length 3 inches. To the nearest tenth of an inch, what is the approximate length of a common internal tangent? Use the hint provided in Exercise 38.

40. Circles O, P, and Q are tangent (as shown) at points X, Y, and Z. Being as specific as possible, explain what type of triangle $\triangle PQO$ is if:
a) $OX = 2$, $PY = 3$, $QZ = 1$
b) $OX = 2$, $PY = 3$, $QZ = 2$

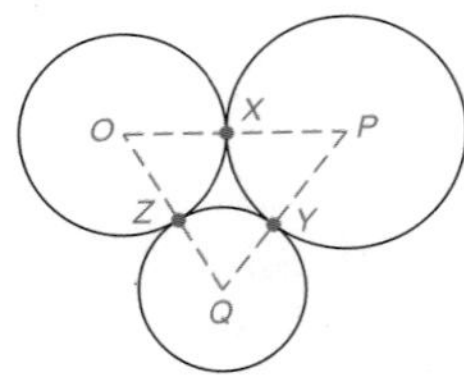

Exercises 40, 41

41. Circles O, P, and Q are tangent (as shown) at points X, Y, and Z. Being as specific as possible, explain what type of triangle $\triangle PQO$ is if:
a) $OX = 3$, $PY = 4$, $QZ = 1$
b) $OX = 2$, $PY = 2$, $QZ = 2$

***42.** If the larger gear has 30 teeth and the smaller gear has 18, then the gear ratio (larger to smaller) is 5:3. When the larger gear rotates through an angle of 60°, through what angle measure does the smaller gear rotate?

Exercises 42, 43

*43. For the drawing in Exercise 42, suppose that the larger gear has 20 teeth and the smaller gear has 10 (the gear ratio is 2:1). If the smaller gear rotates through an angle of 90°, through what angle measure does the larger gear rotate?

In Exercises 44 to 47, prove the stated theorem.

44. If a line is drawn through the center of a circle perpendicular to a chord, then it bisects the chord and its minor arc. See Figure 6.37.
(NOTE: The major arc is also bisected by the line.)

45. If a line is drawn through the center of a circle to the midpoint of a chord other than a diameter, then it is perpendicular to the chord. See Figure 6.38.

46. If two secant segments are drawn to a circle from an external point, then the products of the lengths of each secant with its external segment are equal. See Figure 6.51.

47. If a tangent segment and a secant segment are drawn to a circle from an external point, then the square of the length of the tangent equals the product of the length of the secant with the length of its external segment. See Figure 6.52.

6.4 Some Constructions and Inequalities for the Circle

Construction of Tangents to a Circle

Inequalities in the Circle

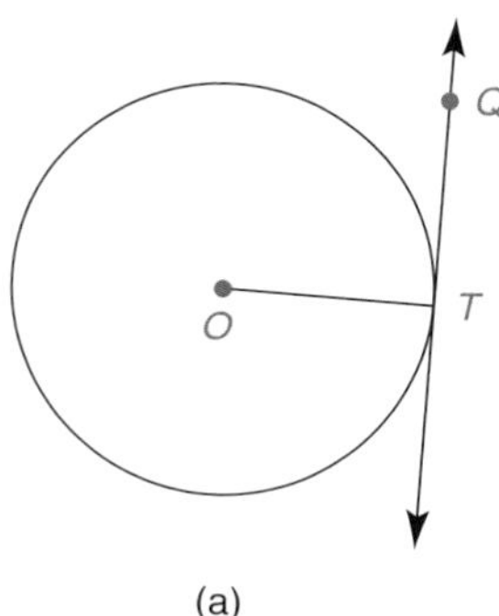

(a)

In Section 6.3, we proved that the radius drawn to a tangent at the point of contact is perpendicular to the tangent at that point. We now show, by using an indirect proof, that the converse of that theorem is also true. Recall that there is only one line perpendicular to a given line at a point on that line.

THEOREM 6.4.1

The line that is perpendicular to the radius of a circle at its endpoint on the circle is a tangent to the circle.

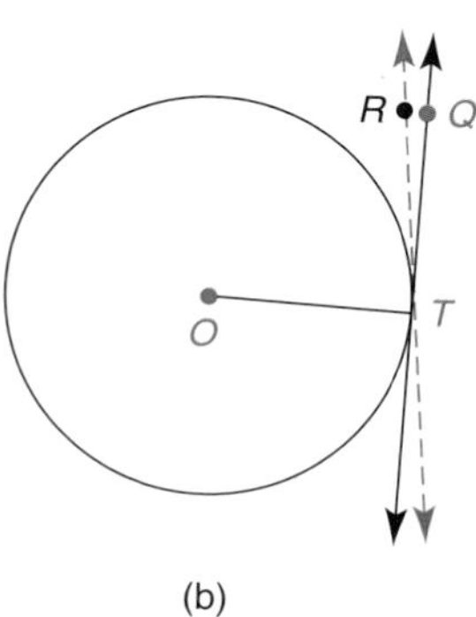

(b)

Figure 6.54

GIVEN: In Figure 6.54(a), $\odot O$ with radius $\overline{OT}$

$\overleftrightarrow{QT} \perp \overline{OT}$

PROVE: $\overleftrightarrow{QT}$ is a tangent to $\odot O$ at point T

PROOF: Suppose that $\overleftrightarrow{QT}$ is not a tangent to $\odot O$ at T. Then the tangent (call it $\overleftrightarrow{RT}$) can be drawn at T, the point of tangency. [See Figure 6.54(b).]

Now $\overline{OT}$ is the radius to tangent $\overleftrightarrow{RT}$ at T, and because a radius drawn to a tangent at the point of contact of the tangent is perpendicular to the tangent, $\overline{OT} \perp \overleftrightarrow{RT}$. But $\overline{OT} \perp \overleftrightarrow{QT}$ by hypothesis. Thus, two lines are perpendicular to $\overline{OT}$ at point T, contradicting the fact that there is only one line perpendicular to a line at a point on the line. Therefore, $\overleftrightarrow{QT}$ must be the tangent to $\odot O$ at point T.

CONSTRUCTIONS OF TANGENTS TO CIRCLES

Construction 8 *To construct a tangent to a circle at a point on the circle.*

PLAN: The strategy used in Construction 8 is based on Theorem 6.4.1. For Figure 6.55(a), we will draw a radius (extended beyond the circle). At the point on the circle (point X in Figure 6.55), we construct the line perpendicular to $\overline{PX}$. The constructed line [$\overleftrightarrow{WX}$ in Figure 6.55(c)] is tangent to circle P at point X.

GIVEN: $\odot P$ with point X on the circle [See Figure 6.55(a).]

CONSTRUCT: A tangent $\overleftrightarrow{XW}$ to $\odot P$ at point X

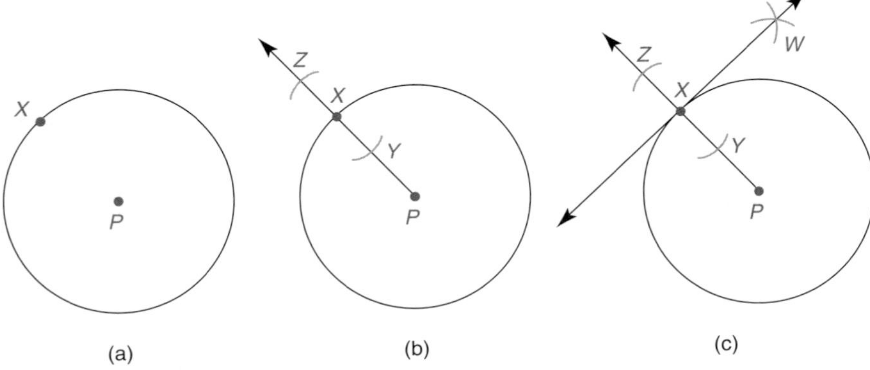

Figure 6.55

CONSTRUCTION: Figure 6.55(a): Consider $\odot P$ and point X on $\odot P$. Figure 6.55(b): Draw radius $\overline{PX}$ and extend it to form $\overrightarrow{PX}$. Using X as the center and any radius length less than XP, draw two arcs to intersect $\overleftrightarrow{PX}$ at points Y and Z.

Figure 6.55(c): Complete the construction of the perpendicular line to $\overrightarrow{PX}$ at point X. From Y and Z, mark arcs with equal radii of length greater than XY. Calling the point of intersection W, draw $\overleftrightarrow{XW}$, the desired tangent to $\odot P$ at point X.

EXAMPLE 1

Make a drawing so that points A, B, C, and D are on $\odot O$ in that order. If tangents are constructed at points A, B, C, and D, what type of quadrilateral will be formed by the tangent segments if

a) $m\overparen{AB} = m\overparen{CD}$ and $m\overparen{BC} = m\overparen{AD}$?
b) all arcs $\overparen{AB}$, $\overparen{BC}$, $\overparen{CD}$, and $\overparen{DA}$ are congruent?

Solution

a) A rhombus (all sides are congruent)
b) A square (all four $\angle$s are right $\angle$s; all sides $\cong$)

We now consider a more difficult construction. ■

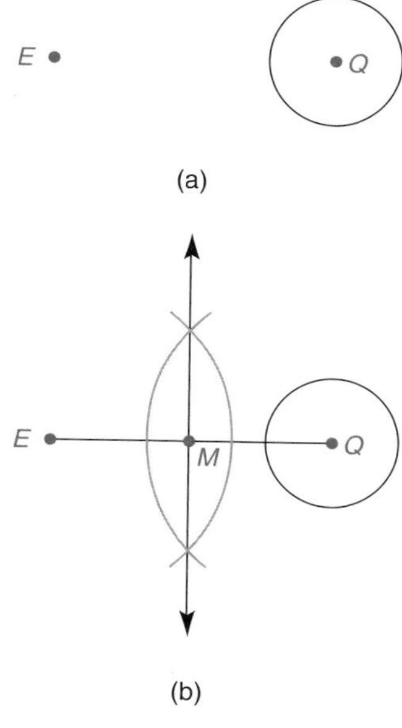

Figure 6.56

Construction 9 *To construct a tangent to a circle from an external point.*

GIVEN: $\odot Q$ and external point E [See Figure 6.56(a).]

CONSTRUCT: A tangent $\overline{ET}$ to $\odot Q$, with T as the point of tangency

CONSTRUCTION: Figure 6.56(a): Consider $\odot Q$ and external point E.
Figure 6.56(b): Draw $\overline{EQ}$. Construct the perpendicular bisector of $\overline{EQ}$, to intersect $\overline{EQ}$ at its midpoint M.

Figure 6.56(c): With M as center and MQ (or ME) as the length of radius, construct a circle. The points of intersection of circle M with circle Q are designated by T and V. Now draw $\overline{ET}$, the desired tangent.

NOTE: If drawn, $\overline{EV}$ would also be a tangent to $\odot Q$.

In the preceding construction, $\overline{QT}$ (not shown) is a radius of the smaller circle Q. In the larger circle M, $\angle ETQ$ is an inscribed angle that intercepts a semicircle. Thus, $\angle ETQ$ is a right angle and $\overline{ET} \perp \overline{TQ}$. Because the line drawn perpendicular to the radius of a circle at its endpoint on the circle is a tangent to the circle, $\overline{ET}$ is a tangent to circle Q.

INEQUALITIES IN THE CIRCLE

The remaining theorems in this section involve inequalities in the circle.

THEOREM 6.4.2

In a circle (or in congruent circles) containing two unequal central angles, the larger angle corresponds to the larger intercepted arc.

GIVEN: $\odot O$ with central angles $\angle 1$ and $\angle 2$ in Figure 6.57; $m\angle 1 > m\angle 2$

PROVE: $m\overset{\frown}{AB} > m\overset{\frown}{CD}$

PROOF: In $\odot O$, $m\angle 1 > m\angle 2$. By the Central Angle Postulate, $m\angle 1 = m\overset{\frown}{AB}$ and $m\angle 2 = m\overset{\frown}{CD}$. By substitution, $m\overset{\frown}{AB} > m\overset{\frown}{CD}$.

SSG *Exs. 1–3*

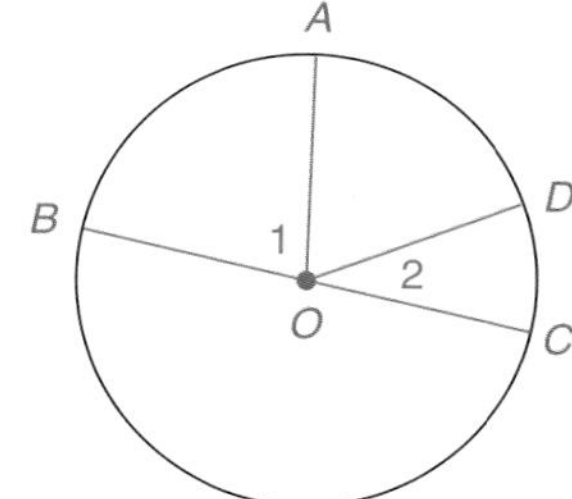

Figure 6.57

The converse of Theorem 6.4.2 follows, and it is also easily proved.

THEOREM 6.4.3

In a circle (or in congruent circles) containing two unequal arcs, the larger arc corresponds to the larger central angle.

GIVEN: In Figure 6.57, $\odot O$ with $\overset{\frown}{AB}$ and $\overset{\frown}{CD}$
$m\overset{\frown}{AB} > m\overset{\frown}{CD}$

PROVE: $m\angle 1 > m\angle 2$

The proof is left as Exercise 35 for the student.

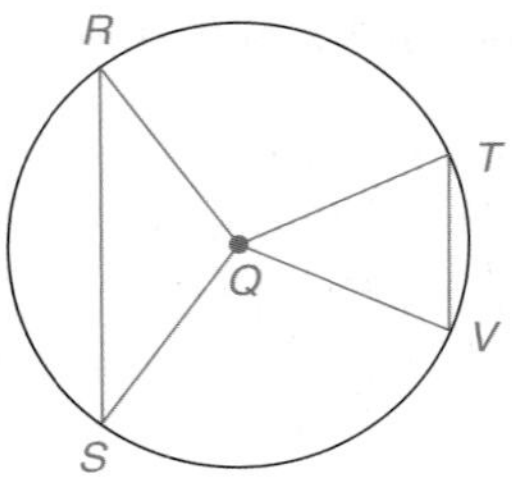

Figure 6.58

Discover

In Figure 6.59, $\overline{PT}$ measures the distance from center P to chord $\overline{EF}$. Likewise, $\overline{PR}$ measures the distance from P to chord $\overline{AB}$. Using a ruler, show that $PR > PT$. How do the lengths of chords $\overline{AB}$ and $\overline{EF}$ compare?

ANSWER

$AB < EF$

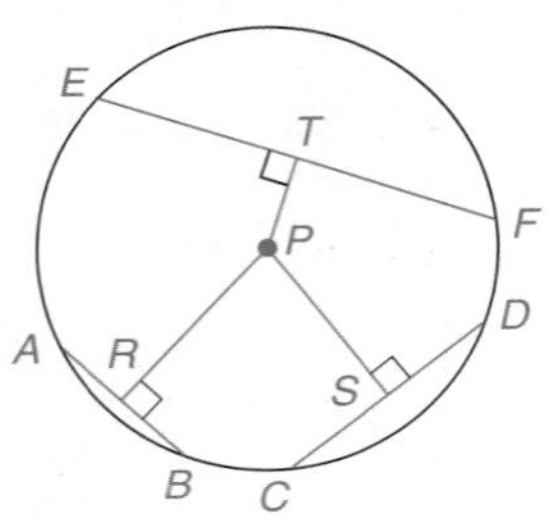

Figure 6.59

EXAMPLE 2

GIVEN: In Figure 6.58, $\odot Q$ with $m\widehat{RS} > m\widehat{TV}$.

a) Using Theorem 6.4.3, what conclusion can you draw regarding the measures of $\angle RQS$ and $\angle TQV$?

b) What does intuition suggest regarding RS and TV?

Solution

a) $m\angle RQS > m\angle TQV$

b) $RS > TV$ ■

Before we apply Theorem 6.4.4 and prove Theorem 6.4.5, consider the Discover activity at the left. The proof of Theorem 6.4.4 is not provided; however, the proof is similar to that of Theorem 6.4.5.

THEOREM 6.4.4

In a circle (or in congruent circles) containing two unequal chords, the shorter chord is at the greater distance from the center of the circle.

EXAMPLE 3

In circle P of Figure 6.59, any radius has a length of 6 cm, and the chords have lengths $AB = 4\,\text{cm}$, $DC = 6\,\text{cm}$, and $EF = 10\,\text{cm}$. Let $\overline{PR}$, $\overline{PS}$, and $\overline{PT}$ name perpendicular segments to these chords from center P.

a) Of $\overline{PR}$, $\overline{PS}$, and $\overline{PT}$, which is longest?

b) Of $\overline{PR}$, $\overline{PS}$, and $\overline{PT}$, which is shortest?

Solution

a) $\overline{PR}$ is longest, according to Theorem 6.4.4.

b) $\overline{PT}$ is shortest. ■

In the proof of Theorem 6.4.5, the positive numbers a and b represent the lengths of line segments. If $a < b$, then $a^2 < b^2$; the converse is also true.

THEOREM 6.4.5

In a circle (or in congruent circles) containing two unequal chords, the chord nearer the center of the circle has the greater length.

GIVEN: In Figure 6.60(a), $\odot Q$ with chords $\overline{AB}$ and $\overline{CD}$
$\overline{QM} \perp \overline{AB}$ and $\overline{QN} \perp \overline{CD}$
$QM < QN$

PROVE: $AB > CD$

PROOF: In Figure 6.60(b), we represent the lengths of $\overline{QM}$ and $\overline{QN}$ by a and c, respectively. Draw radii $\overline{QA}$, $\overline{QB}$, $\overline{QC}$, and $\overline{QD}$, and denote all lengths by r. $\overline{QM}$ is the perpendicular bisector of $\overline{AB}$, and $\overline{QN}$ is the perpendicular bisector of $\overline{CD}$, because a radius perpendicular to a chord bisects the chord and its arc. Let $MB = b$ and $NC = d$.

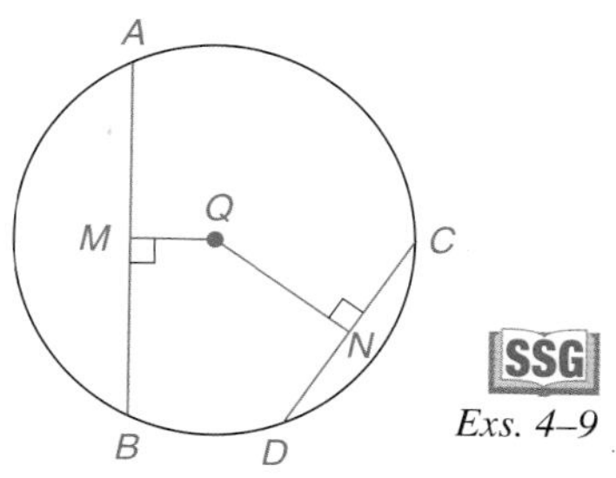

(a)

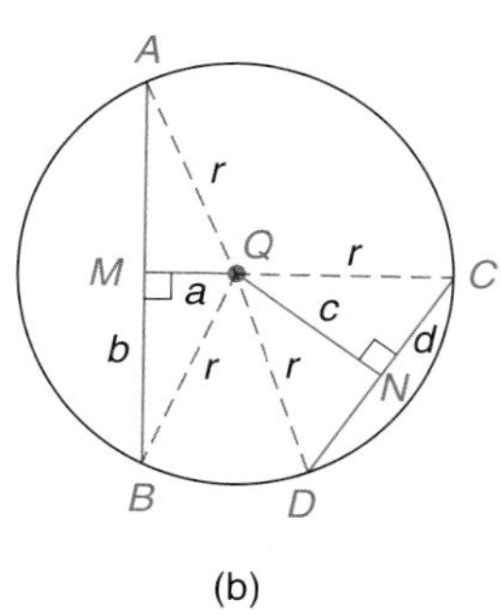

(b)

Figure 6.60

With right angles at M and N, we see that $\triangle QMB$ and $\triangle QNC$ are right triangles.

According to the Pythagorean Theorem, $r^2 = a^2 + b^2$ and $r^2 = c^2 + d^2$, so $b^2 = r^2 - a^2$ and $d^2 = r^2 - c^2$. If $QM < QN$, then $a < c$ and $a^2 < c^2$. Multiplication by -1 reverses the order of this inequality; therefore, $-a^2 > -c^2$. Adding r^2, we have $r^2 - a^2 > r^2 - c^2$ or $b^2 > d^2$, which implies that $b > d$. If $b > d$, then $2b > 2d$. But $AB = 2b$ and $CD = 2d$. Therefore, $AB > CD$. ■

SSG *Exs. 4–9*

It is important that the phrase *minor arc* be used in our final theorems. The proof of Theorem 6.4.6 is left to the student. For Theorem 6.4.7, the proof is provided because it is more involved. In each theorem, the chord and related minor arc share common endpoints.

THEOREM 6.4.6

In a circle (or in congruent circles) containing two unequal chords, the longer chord corresponds to the greater minor arc.

If $AB > CD$ in Figure 6.61, then $m\overset{\frown}{AB} > m\overset{\frown}{CD}$.

THEOREM 6.4.7

In a circle (or in congruent circles) containing two unequal minor arcs, the greater minor arc corresponds to the longer of the chords related to these arcs.

GIVEN: In Figure 6.61(a), $\odot O$ with $m\overset{\frown}{AB} > m\overset{\frown}{CD}$ and chords $\overline{AB}$ and $\overline{CD}$

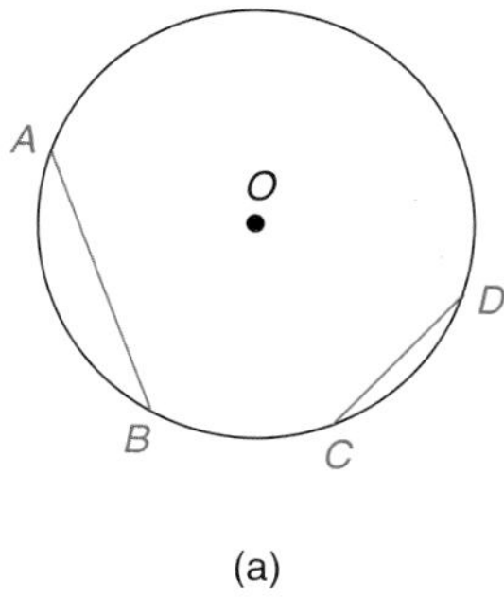

(a)

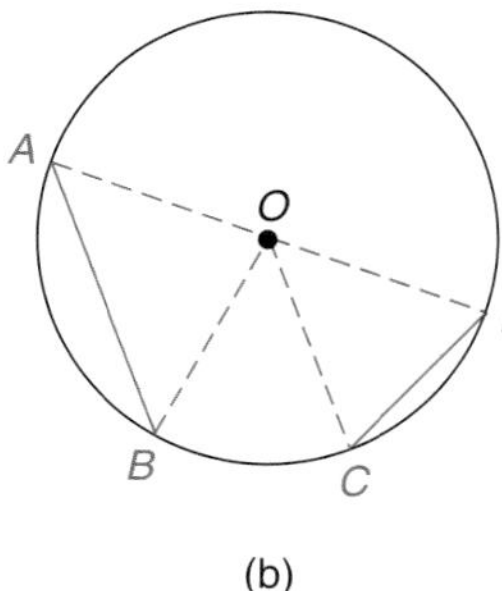

(b)

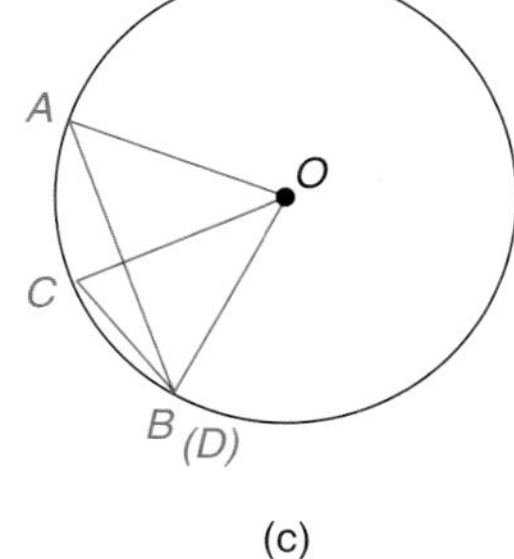

(c)

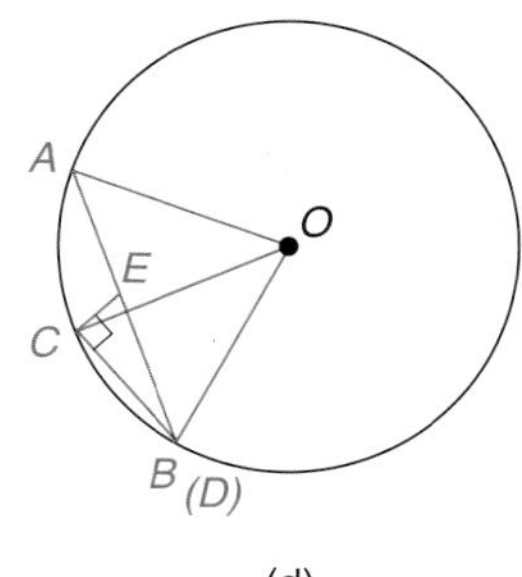

(d)

Figure 6.61

PROVE: $AB > CD$

PROOF: In circle O of Figure 6.61(b), draw radii $\overline{OA}$, $\overline{OB}$, $\overline{OC}$, and $\overline{OD}$. Because $m\overset{\frown}{AB} > m\overset{\frown}{CD}$, it follows that $m\angle AOB > m\angle COD$ because the larger arc in a circle corresponds to the larger central angle.

In Figure 6.61(c), we rotate $\triangle COD$ to the position on the circle for which D coincides with B. Because radii $\overline{OC}$ and $\overline{OB}$ are congruent, $\triangle COD$ is isosceles; also, $m\angle C = m\angle ODC$.

In $\triangle COD$, $m\angle COD + m\angle C + m\angle CDO = 180°$. Because $m\angle COD$ is positive, we have $m\angle C + m\angle CDO < 180°$ and $2 \cdot m\angle C < 180°$ by substitution. Therefore, $m\angle C < 90°$.

Now construct the perpendicular segment to $\overline{CD}$ at point C, as shown in Figure 6.61(d). Denote the intersection of the perpendicular segment and $\overline{AB}$ by point E. Because $\triangle DCE$ is a right $\triangle$ with hypotenuse $\overline{EB}$, $EB > CD$ (*). Because $AB = AE + EB$ and $AE > 0$, we have $AB > EB$ (*). By the Transitive Property, the starred (*) statements reveal that $AB > CD$.

SSG
Exs. 10–16

NOTE: In the preceding proof, $\overline{CE}$ must intersect $\overline{AB}$ at some point between A and B. If it were to intersect at A, the measure of inscribed $\angle BCA$ would have to be more than 90°; this follows from the facts that $\overset{\frown}{AB}$ is a minor arc and that the intercepted arc for $\angle BCA$ would have to be a major arc. ■

Exercises 6.4

In Exercises 1 to 8, use the figure provided.

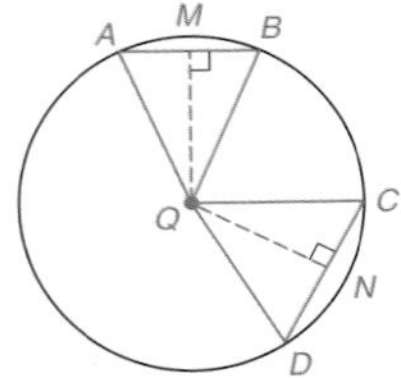

Exercises 1–8

1. If $m\overset{\frown}{CD} < m\overset{\frown}{AB}$, write an inequality that compares $m\angle CQD$ and $m\angle AQB$.
2. If $m\overset{\frown}{CD} < m\overset{\frown}{AB}$, write an inequality that compares CD and AB.
3. If $m\overset{\frown}{CD} < m\overset{\frown}{AB}$, write an inequality that compares QM and QN.
4. If $m\overset{\frown}{CD} < m\overset{\frown}{AB}$, write an inequality that compares $m\angle A$ and $m\angle C$.
5. If $m\angle CQD < m\angle AQB$, write an inequality that compares CD to AB.
6. If $m\angle CQD < m\angle AQB$, write an inequality that compares QM to QN.
7. If $m\overset{\frown}{CD}:m\overset{\frown}{AB} = 3:2$, write an inequality that compares QM to QN.
8. If $QN:QM = 5:6$, write an inequality that compares $m\overset{\frown}{AB}$ to $m\overset{\frown}{CD}$.
9. Construct a circle O and choose some point D on the circle. Now construct the tangent to circle O at point D.
10. Construct a circle P and choose three points R, S, and T on the circle. Construct the triangle that has its sides tangent to the circle at R, S, and T.
11. X, Y, and Z are on circle O such that $m\overset{\frown}{XY} = 120°$, $m\overset{\frown}{YZ} = 130°$, and $m\overset{\frown}{XZ} = 110°$. Suppose that triangle XYZ is drawn and that the triangle ABC is constructed with its sides tangent to circle O at X, Y, and Z. Are $\triangle XYZ$ and $\triangle ABC$ similar triangles?

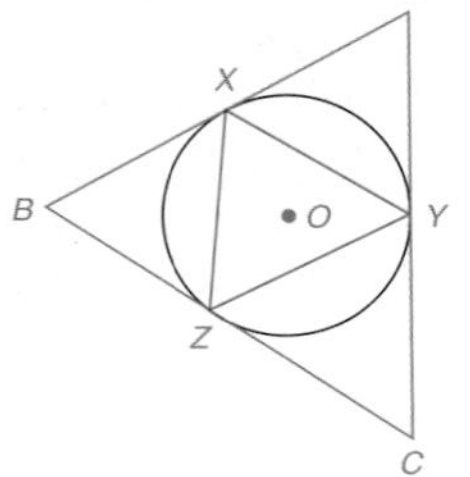

12. Construct the two tangent segments to circle P (not shown) from external point E.
13. Point V is in the exterior of circle Q (not shown) such that $\overline{VQ}$ is equal in length to the diameter of circle Q. Construct the two tangents to circle Q from point V. Then determine the measure of the angle that has vertex V and has the tangents as sides.
14. Given circle P and points R-P-T such that R and T are in the exterior of circle P, suppose that tangents are constructed from R and T to form a quadrilateral (as shown). Identify the type of quadrilateral formed
    a) when $RP > PT$.
    b) when $RP = PT$.
15. Given parallel chords $\overline{AB}$, $\overline{CD}$, $\overline{EF}$, and $\overline{GH}$ in circle O, which chord has the greatest length? Which has the least length? Why?

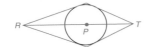

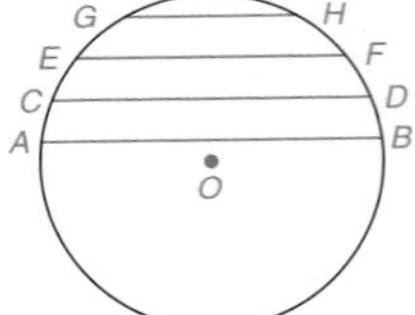

16. Given chords $\overline{MN}$, $\overline{RS}$, and $\overline{TV}$ in $\odot Q$ such that $QZ > QY > QX$, which chord has the greatest length? Which has the least length? Why?

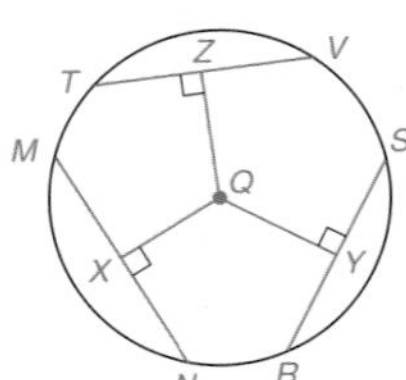

17. Given circle O with radius $\overline{OT}$, tangent $\overleftrightarrow{AD}$, and line segments $\overline{OA}$, $\overline{OB}$, $\overline{OC}$, and $\overline{OD}$:
    a) Which line segment drawn from O has the smallest length?
    b) If $m\angle 1 = 40°$, $m\angle 2 = 50°$, $m\angle 3 = 45°$, and $m\angle 4 = 30°$, which line segment from point O has the greatest length?

18. a) If $m\overset{\frown}{RS} > m\overset{\frown}{TV}$, write an inequality to compare $m\angle 1$ with $m\angle 2$.
b) If $m\angle 1 > m\angle 2$, write an inequality to compare $m\overset{\frown}{RS}$ with $m\overset{\frown}{TV}$.

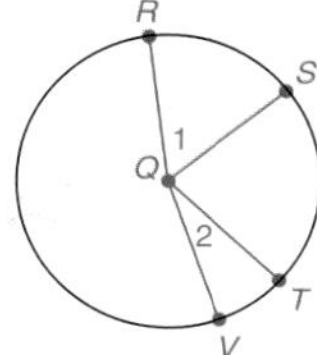

19. a) If $MN > PQ$, write an inequality to compare the measures of minor arcs $\overset{\frown}{MN}$ and $\overset{\frown}{PQ}$.
b) If $MN > PQ$, write an inequality to compare the measures of major arcs $\overset{\frown}{MPN}$ and $\overset{\frown}{PMQ}$.

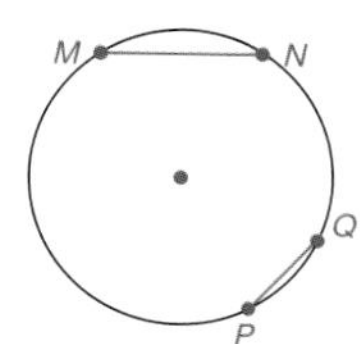

20. a) If $m\overset{\frown}{XY} > m\overset{\frown}{YZ}$, write an inequality to compare the measures of inscribed angles 1 and 2.
b) If $m\angle 1 < m\angle 2$, write an inequality to compare the measures of $\overset{\frown}{XY}$ and $\overset{\frown}{YZ}$.

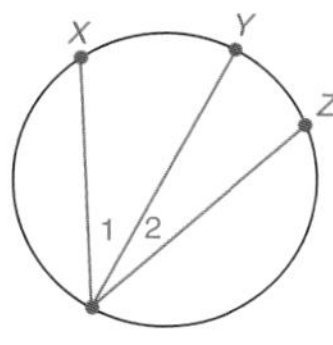

21. Quadrilateral $ABCD$ is inscribed in circle P (not shown). If $\angle A$ is an acute angle, what type of angle is $\angle C$?

22. Quadrilateral $RSTV$ is inscribed in circle Q (not shown). If arcs $\overset{\frown}{RS}$, $\overset{\frown}{ST}$, and $\overset{\frown}{TV}$ are all congruent, what type of quadrilateral is $RSTV$?

23. In circle O, points A, B, and C are on the circle such that $m\overset{\frown}{AB} = 60°$ and $m\overset{\frown}{BC} = 40°$.
a) How are $m\angle AOB$ and $m\angle BOC$ related?
b) How are AB and BC related?

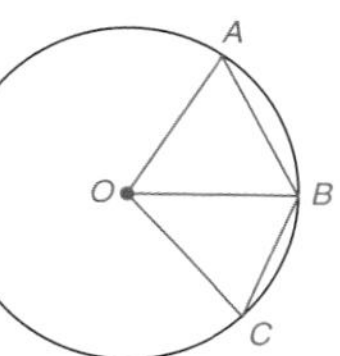

Exercises 23–25

24. In $\odot O$, $AB = 6$ cm and $BC = 4$ cm.
a) How are $m\angle AOB$ and $m\angle BOC$ related?
b) How are $m\overset{\frown}{AB}$ and $m\overset{\frown}{BC}$ related?

25. In $\odot O$, $m\angle AOB = 70°$ and $m\angle BOC = 30°$. See the figure above.
a) How are $m\overset{\frown}{AB}$ and $m\overset{\frown}{BC}$ related?
b) How are AB and BC related?

26. Triangle ABC is inscribed in circle O; $AB = 5$, $BC = 6$, and $AC = 7$.
a) Which is the largest minor arc of $\odot O$: $\overset{\frown}{AB}$, $\overset{\frown}{BC}$, or $\overset{\frown}{AC}$?
b) Which side of the triangle is nearest point O?

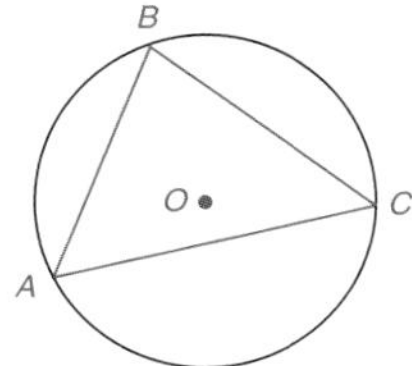

Exercises 26–29

27. Given circle O with $m\overset{\frown}{BC} = 120°$ and $m\overset{\frown}{AC} = 130°$:
a) Which angle of triangle ABC is smallest?
b) Which side of triangle ABC is nearest point O?

28. Given that $m\overset{\frown}{AC}$:$m\overset{\frown}{BC}$:$m\overset{\frown}{AB} = 4:3:2$ in circle O:
a) Which arc is largest?
b) Which chord is longest?

29. Given that $m\angle A$:$m\angle B$:$m\angle C = 2:4:3$ in circle O:
a) Which angle is largest?
b) Which chord is longest?

(Note: See the figure for Exercise 26.)

30. Circle O has a diameter of length 20 cm. Chord $\overline{AB}$ has length 12 cm, and chord $\overline{CD}$ has length 10 cm. How much closer is $\overline{AB}$ than $\overline{CD}$ to point O?

31. Circle P has a radius of length 8 in. Points A, B, C, and D lie on circle P in such a way that $m\angle APB = 90°$ and $m\angle CPD = 60°$. How much closer to point P is chord $\overline{AB}$ than $\overline{CD}$?

32. A tangent $\overline{ET}$ is constructed to circle Q from external point E. Which angle and which side of triangle QTE are largest? Which angle and which side are smallest?

33. Two congruent circles, $\odot O$ and $\odot P$, do not intersect. Construct a common external tangent for $\odot O$ and $\odot P$.

34. Explain why the following statement is incorrect:
"In a circle (or in congruent circles) containing two unequal chords, the longer chord corresponds to the greater major arc."

35. Prove: In a circle containing two unequal arcs, the larger arc corresponds to the larger central angle.

36. Prove: In a circle containing two unequal chords, the longer chord corresponds to the larger central angle.

(HINT: You may use any theorems stated in this section.)

***37.** In $\odot O$, chord $\overline{AB} \parallel$ chord $\overline{CD}$. Radius $\overline{OE}$ is perpendicular to $\overline{AB}$ and $\overline{CD}$ at points M and N, respectively. If $OE = 13$, $AB = 24$, and $CD = 10$, then the distance from O to $\overline{CD}$ is greater than the distance from O to $\overline{AB}$. Determine how much farther chord $\overline{CD}$ is from center O than chord $\overline{AB}$ is from center O; that is, find MN.

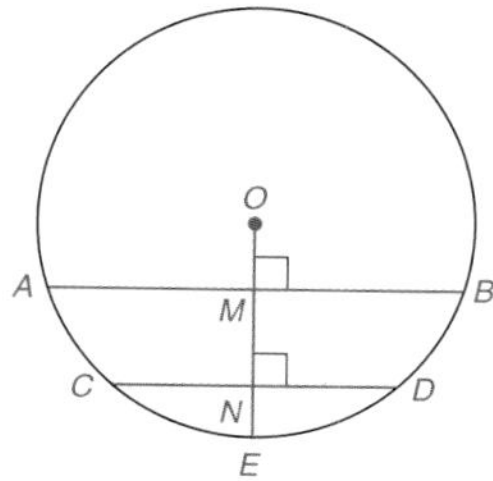

***38.** In $\odot P$, whose radius has length 8 in., $m\overset{\frown}{AB} = m\overset{\frown}{BC} = 60°$. Because $m\overset{\frown}{AC} = 120°$, chord $\overline{AC}$ is longer than either of the congruent chords $\overline{AB}$ and $\overline{BC}$. Determine how much longer $\overline{AC}$ is than $\overline{AB}$; that is, find the exact value and the approximate value of $AC - AB$.

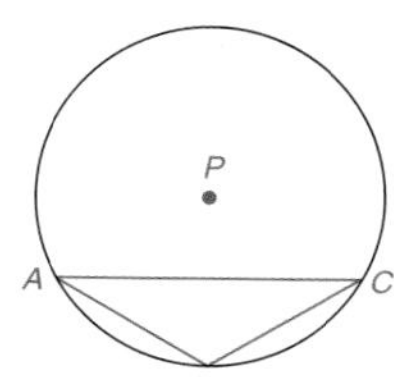

PERSPECTIVE ON HISTORY

Circumference of the Earth

By traveling around the earth at the equator, one would traverse the circumference of the earth. Early mathematicians attempted to discover the numerical circumference of the earth. But the best approximation of the circumference was due to the work of the Greek mathematician Eratosthenes (276–194 B.C.). In his day, Eratosthenes held the highly regarded post as the head of the museum at the university in Alexandria.

What Eratosthenes did to calculate the earth's circumference was based upon several assumptions. With the sun at a great distance from the earth, its rays would be parallel as they struck the earth. Because of parallel lines, the alternate interior angles shown in the diagram would have the same measure (indicated by the Greek letter α). In Eratosthenes' plan, an angle measurement in Alexandria would be determined when the sun was *directly* over the city of Syene. While the angle suggested at the center of the earth could not be measured, the angle (in Alexandria) formed by the vertical and the related shadow could be measured; in fact, the measure was $\alpha \approx 7.2°$.

Eratosthenes' solution to the problem was based upon this fact: The ratio comparing angle measures is equivalent to the ratio comparing land distances. The distance between Syene and Alexandria was approximately 5,000 stadia

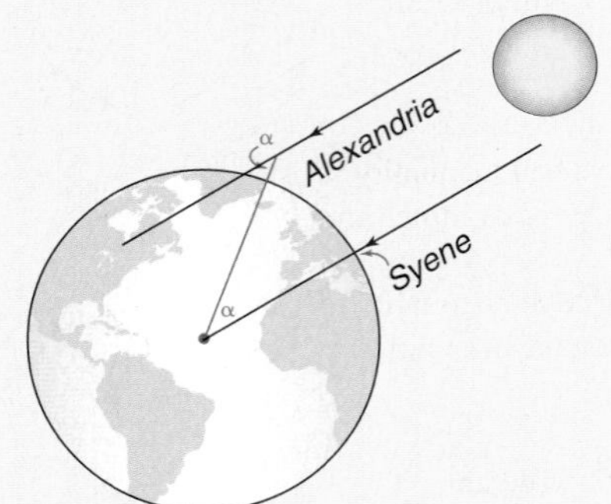

Figure 6.62

(1 stadium $\approx$ 516.73 ft). Where C is the circumference of the earth in stadia, this leads to the proportion

$$\frac{\alpha}{360°} = \frac{5000}{C} \text{ or } \frac{7.2}{360} = \frac{5000}{C}$$

Solving the proportion and converting to miles, Eratosthenes approximation of the earth's circumference was about 24,662 mi, which is about 245 mi less than the actual circumference.

Eratosthenes, a tireless student and teacher, lost his sight late in life. Unable to bear his loss of sight and lack of productivity, Eratosthenes committed suicide by refusing to eat.

PERSPECTIVE ON APPLICATIONS

Sum of Interior Angles of a Polygon

Suppose that we had studied the circle *before* studying polygons. Our methods of proof and justifications would be greatly affected. In particular, suppose that you do not know the sum of interior angles of a triangle but that you do know these facts:

1. The sum of the arc measures of a circle is 360°.
2. The measure of an inscribed angle of a circle is $\frac{1}{2}$ the measure of its intercepted arc.

Using these facts, we prove "The sum of the interior angles of a triangle is 180°."

Proof: In $\triangle ABC$, $m\angle A = \frac{1}{2}m\widehat{BC}$, $m\angle B = \frac{1}{2}m\widehat{AC}$, and $m\angle C = \frac{1}{2}m\widehat{AB}$. Then $m\angle A + m\angle B + m\angle C = \frac{1}{2}(m\widehat{BC} + m\widehat{AC} + m\widehat{AB}) = \frac{1}{2}(360°) = 180°$.

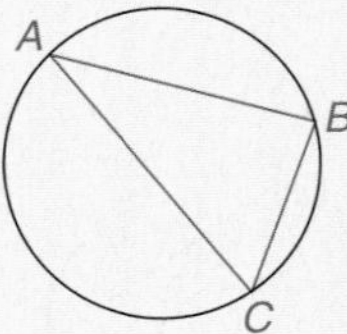

Figure 6.63

Using known facts 1 and 2, we can also show that "The sum of the interior angles of a quadrilateral is 360°." However, we would complete our proof by utilizing a cyclic quadrilateral. The strategic ordering and association of terms leads to the desired result.

Proof: For quadrilateral $HJKL$ in Figure 6.64,

$$m\angle H + m\angle J + m\angle K + m\angle L = \frac{1}{2}m\widehat{LKJ} + \frac{1}{2}m\widehat{HLK} + \frac{1}{2}m\widehat{LHJ} + \frac{1}{2}m\widehat{HJK}$$

or

$$\frac{1}{2}(m\widehat{LKJ} + m\widehat{LHJ}) + \frac{1}{2}(m\widehat{HLK} + m\widehat{HJK}) = \frac{1}{2}(360°) + \frac{1}{2}(360°)$$

In turn, we see that

$m\angle H + m\angle J + m\angle K + m\angle L =$
$180° + 180°$ or $360°$

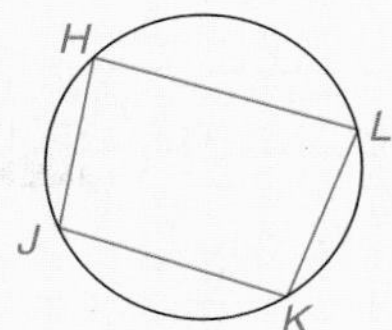

Figure 6.64

We could continue in this manner to show that the sum of the five interior angles of a pentagon (using a cyclic pentagon) is 540° and that the sum of the n interior angles of a cyclic polygon of n sides is $(n - 2)180°$.

Summary

A LOOK BACK AT CHAPTER 6

One goal in this chapter has been to classify angles inside, on, and outside the circle. Formulas for finding the measures of these angles were developed. Line and line segments related to a circle were defined, and some ways of finding the measures of these segments were described. Theorems involving inequalities in a circle were proved.

A LOOK AHEAD TO CHAPTER 7

One goal of Chapter 7 is the study of loci (plural of locus), which has to do with point location. In fact, a locus of points is often nothing more than the description of some well-known geometric figure. Knowledge of locus leads to the determination of whether certain lines must be concurrent (meet at a common point). Finally, we will extend the notion of concurrence to develop further properties and terminology for regular polygons.

KEY CONCEPTS

6.1

Circle • Congruent Circles • Concentric Circles • Center of the Circle • Radius • Diameter • Chord • Semicircle • Arc • Major Arc • Minor Arc • Intercepted Arc • Congruent Arcs • Central Angle • Inscribed Angle

6.2

Tangent • Point of Tangency • Secant • Polygon Inscribed in a Circle • Cyclic Polygon • Circumscribed Circle • Polygon Circumscribed about a Circle • Inscribed Circle • Interior and Exterior of a Circle

6.3

Tangent Circles • Internally Tangent Circles • Externally Tangent Circles • Line of Centers • Common Tangent • Common External Tangents • Common Internal Tangents

6.4

Constructions of Tangents to a Circle • Inequalities in the Circle

TABLE 6.2 An Overview of Chapter 6

▶ Selected Properties of Circles

FIGURE	ANGLE MEASURE	SEGMENT RELATIONSHIPS
Central angle 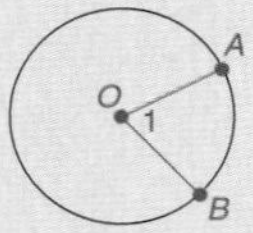	$m\angle 1 = m\widehat{AB}$	$OA = OB$
Inscribed angle 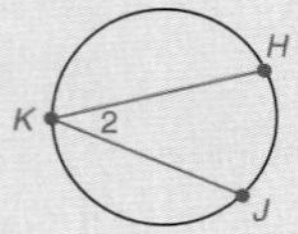	$m\angle 2 = \frac{1}{2}m\widehat{HJ}$	Generally, $HK \neq KJ$
Angle formed by intersecting chords 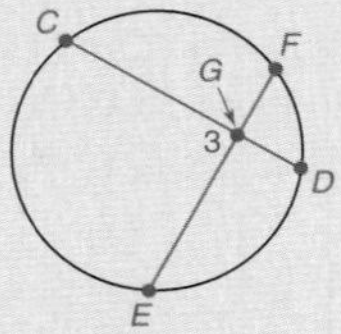	$m\angle 3 = \frac{1}{2}(m\widehat{CE} + m\widehat{FD})$	$CG \cdot GD = EG \cdot GF$
Angle formed by intersecting secants 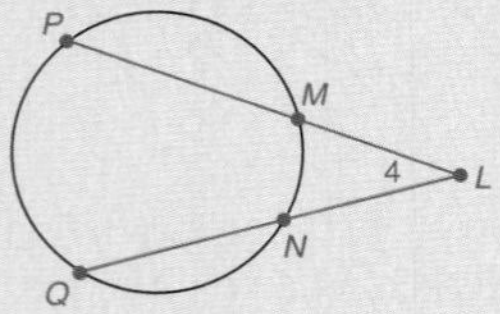	$m\angle 4 = \frac{1}{2}(m\widehat{PQ} - m\widehat{MN})$	$PL \cdot LM = QL \cdot LN$
Angle formed by intersecting tangents 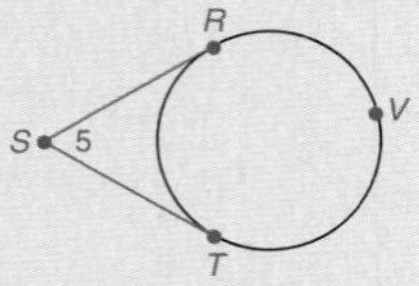	$m\angle 5 = \frac{1}{2}(m\widehat{RVT} - m\widehat{RT})$	$SR = ST$
Angle formed by radius drawn to tangent 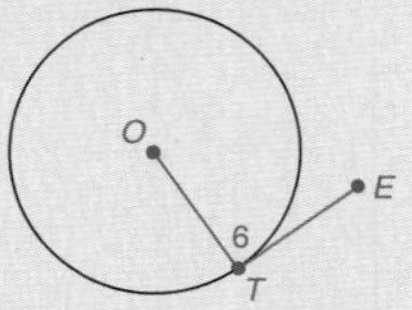	$m\angle 6 = 90°$	$\overline{OT} \perp \overline{TE}$

Chapter 6 REVIEW EXERCISES

1. The length of the radius of a circle is 15 mm. The length of a chord is 24 mm. Find the distance from the center of the circle to the chord.
2. Find the length of a chord that is 8 cm from the center of a circle that has a radius length of 17 cm.
3. Two circles intersect and have a common chord 10 in. long. The radius of one circle is 13 in. long and the centers of the circles are 16 in. apart. Find the radius of the other circle.
4. Two circles intersect and they have a common chord 12 cm long. The measure of the angles formed by the common chord and a radius of each circle to the points of intersection of the circles is 45°. Find the length of the radius of each circle.

In Review Exercises 5 to 10, $\overrightarrow{BA}$ is tangent to the circle at point A in the figure shown.

5. $m\angle B = 25°$, $m\widehat{AD} = 140°$, $m\widehat{DC} = ?$

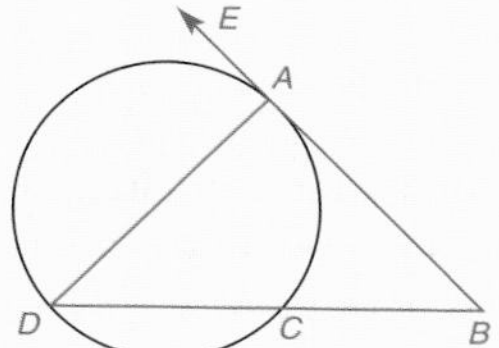

Exercises 5–10

6. $m\widehat{ADC} = 295°$, $m\widehat{AD} = 155°$, $m\angle B = ?$
7. $m\angle EAD = 70°$, $m\angle B = 30°$, $m\widehat{AC} = ?$
8. $m\angle D = 40°$, $m\widehat{DC} = 130°$, $m\angle B = ?$
9. *Given:* C is the midpoint of $\widehat{ACD}$ and $m\angle B = 40°$
   Find: $m\widehat{AD}$, $m\widehat{AC}$, $m\widehat{DC}$
10. *Given:* $m\angle B = 35°$ and $m\widehat{DC} = 70°$
    Find: $m\widehat{AD}$, $m\widehat{AC}$
11. *Given:* $\odot O$ with tangent ℓ and $m\angle 1 = 46°$
    Find: $m\angle 2$, $m\angle 3$, $m\angle 4$, $m\angle 5$

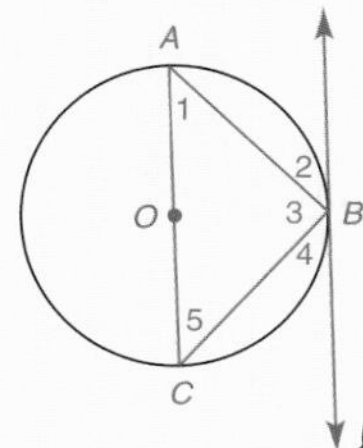

Exercises 11, 12

12. *Given:* $\odot O$ with tangent ℓ and $m\angle 5 = 40°$
    Find: $m\angle 1$, $m\angle 2$, $m\angle 3$, $m\angle 4$
13. Two circles are concentric. A chord of the larger circle is also tangent to the smaller circle. The lengths of the radii are 20 and 16, respectively. Find the length of the chord.
14. Two parallel chords of a circle each have length 16. The distance between these chords is 12. Find the length of the radius of the circle.

In Review Exercises 15 to 22, state whether the statements are always true (A), sometimes true (S), or never true (N).

15. In a circle, congruent chords are equidistant from the center.
16. If a triangle is inscribed in a circle and one of its sides is a diameter, then the triangle is an isosceles triangle.
17. If a central angle and an inscribed angle of a circle intercept the same arc, then they are congruent.
18. A trapezoid can be inscribed in a circle.
19. If a parallelogram is inscribed in a circle, then each of its diagonals must be a diameter.
20. If two chords of a circle are not congruent, then the shorter chord is nearer the center of the circle.
21. Tangents to a circle at the endpoints of a diameter are parallel.
22. Two concentric circles have at least one point in common.
23. a) $m\widehat{AB} = 80°$, $m\angle AEB = 75°$, $m\widehat{CD} = ?$
    b) $m\widehat{AC} = 62°$, $m\angle DEB = 45°$, $m\widehat{BD} = ?$
    c) $m\widehat{AB} = 88°$, $m\angle P = 24°$, $m\angle CED = ?$
    d) $m\angle CED = 41°$, $m\widehat{CD} = 20°$, $m\angle P = ?$
    e) $m\angle AEB = 65°$, $m\angle P = 25°$, $m\widehat{AB} = ?$, $m\widehat{CD} = ?$
    f) $m\angle CED = 50°$, $m\widehat{AC} + m\widehat{BD} = ?$

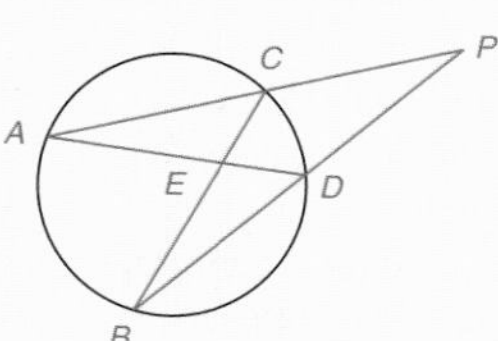

24. Given that $\overline{CF}$ is a tangent to the circle shown:
    a) $CF = 6$, $AC = 12$, $BC = ?$
    b) $AG = 3$, $BE = 10$, $BG = 4$, $DG = ?$
    c) $AC = 12$, $BC = 4$, $DC = 3$, $CE = ?$
    d) $AG = 8$, $GD = 5$, $BG = 10$, $GE = ?$
    e) $CF = 6$, $AB = 5$, $BC = ?$
    f) $EG = 4$, $GB = 2$, $AD = 9$, $GD = ?$
    g) $AC = 30$, $BC = 3$, $CD = ED$, $ED = ?$
    h) $AC = 9$, $BC = 5$, $ED = 12$, $CD = ?$
    i) $ED = 8$, $DC = 4$, $FC = ?$
    j) $FC = 6$, $ED = 9$, $CD = ?$

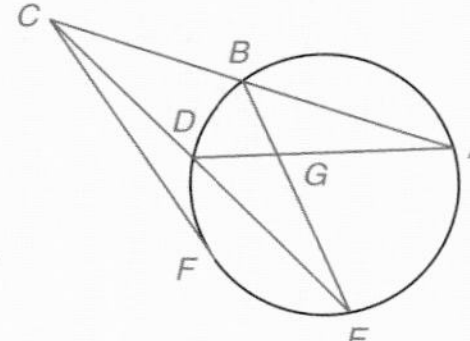

25. *Given:* $\overline{DF} \cong \overline{AC}$ in $\odot O$
$OE = 5x + 4$
$OB = 2x + 19$
Find: OE

26. *Given:* $\overline{OE} \cong \overline{OB}$ in $\odot O$
$DF = x(x - 2)$
$AC = x + 28$
Find: DE and AC

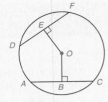

Exercises 25, 26

In Review Exercises 27 to 29, give a proof for each statement.

27. *Given:* $\overline{DC}$ is tangent to circles B and A at points D and C, respectively
Prove: $AC \cdot ED = CE \cdot BD$

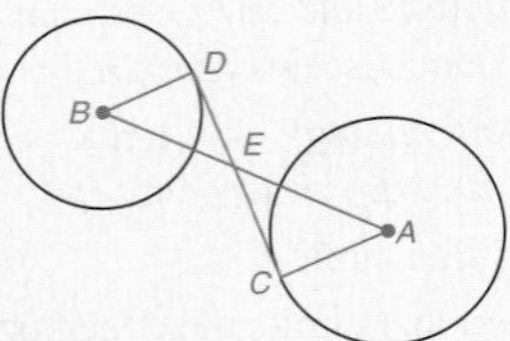

28. *Given:* $\odot O$ with $\overline{EO} \perp \overline{BC}$, $\overline{DO} \perp \overline{BA}$, $\overline{EO} \cong \overline{OD}$
Prove: $\widehat{BC} \cong \widehat{BA}$

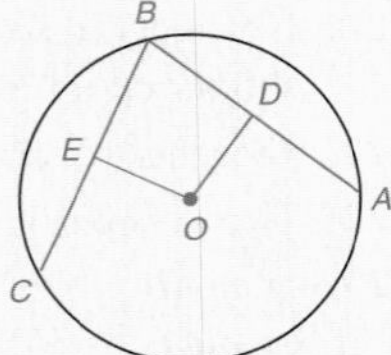

29. *Given:* $\overline{AP}$ and $\overline{BP}$ are tangent to $\odot Q$ at A and B
C is the midpoint of $\widehat{AB}$
Prove: $\overrightarrow{PC}$ bisects $\angle APB$

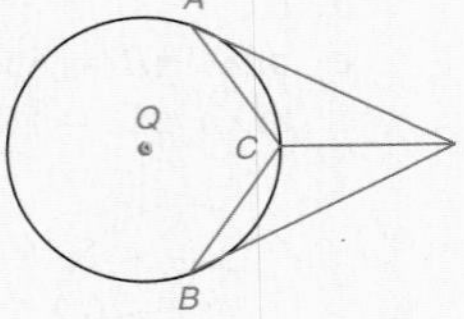

30. *Given:* $\odot O$ with diameter $\overline{AC}$ and tangent $\overleftrightarrow{DE}$
$m\widehat{AD} = 136°$ and $m\widehat{BC} = 50°$
Find: The measures of the angles, $\angle 1$ through $\angle 10$

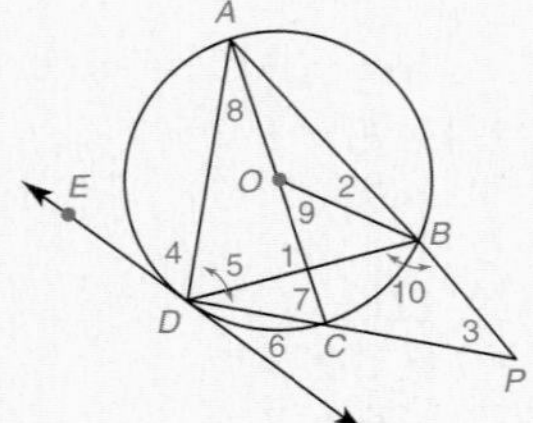

31. A square is inscribed in a circle with a radius of length 6 cm. Find the perimeter of the square.

32. A 30°-60°-90° triangle is inscribed in a circle with a radius of length 5 cm. Find the perimeter of the triangle.

33. A circle is inscribed in a right triangle. The length of the radius of the circle is 6 cm, and the length of the hypotenuse is 29 cm. Find the lengths of the two segments of the hypotenuse that are determined by the point of tangency.

34. *Given:* $\odot O$ is inscribed in $\triangle ABC$
$AB = 9$, $BC = 13$, $AC = 10$
Find: AD, BE, FC

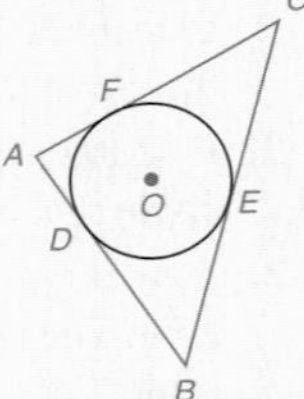

35. In $\odot Q$ with $\triangle ABQ$ and $\triangle CDQ$, $m\widehat{AB} > m\widehat{CD}$. Also, $\overline{QP} \perp \overline{AB}$ and $\overline{QR} \perp \overline{CD}$.
a) How are AB and CD related?
b) How are QP and QR related?
c) How are $\angle A$ and $\angle C$ related?

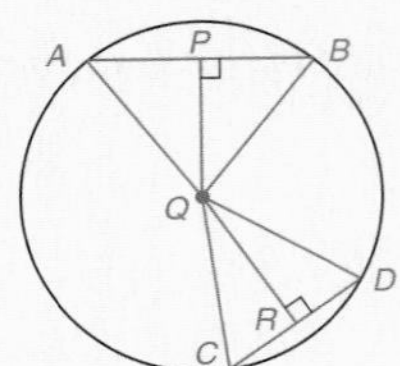

36. In $\odot O$ (not shown), secant $\overleftrightarrow{AB}$ intersects the circle at A and B; C is a point on $\overleftrightarrow{AB}$ in the exterior of the circle.
a) Construct the tangent to $\odot O$ at point B.
b) Construct the tangents to $\odot O$ from point C.

In Review Exercises 37 and 38, use the figures shown.

37. Construct a right triangle so that one leg has length AB and the other has length twice AB.

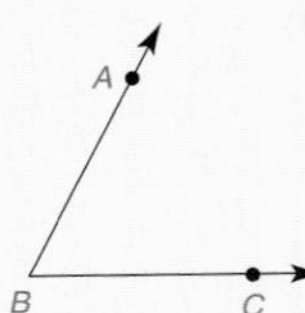

Exercises 37, 38

38. Construct a rhombus with side $\overline{AB}$ and $\angle ABC$.

Chapter 6 TEST

1. a) If $m\overset{\frown}{AB} = 88°$, then $m\overset{\frown}{ACB} = $ __________.
   b) If $m\overset{\frown}{AB} = 92°$ and C is the midpoint of major arc ACB, then $m\overset{\frown}{AC} = $ __________.

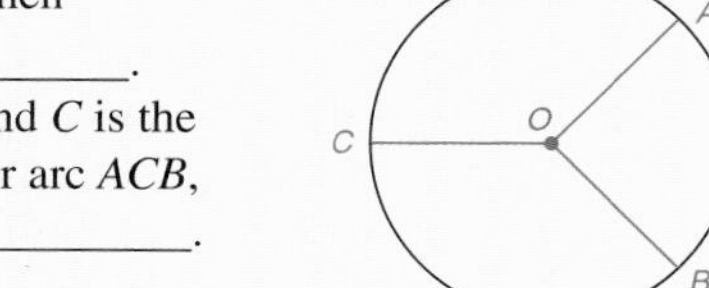

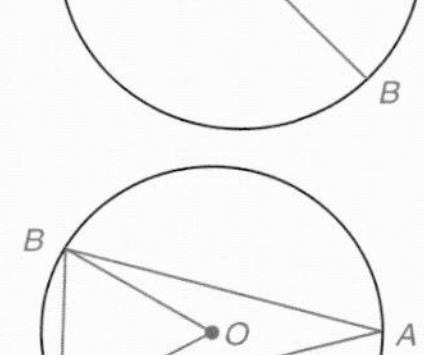

2. a) If $m\overset{\frown}{BC} = 69°$, then $m\angle BOC = $ __________.
   b) If $m\overset{\frown}{BC} = 64°$, then $m\angle BAC = $ __________.
3. a) If $m\angle BAC = 24°$, then $m\overset{\frown}{BC} = $ __________.
   b) If $\overline{AB} \cong \overline{AC}$, then $\triangle ABC$ is a(n) __________ triangle.

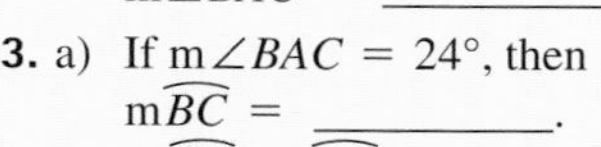

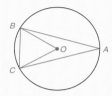

Exercises 2, 3

4. Complete each theorem:
   a) An angle inscribed in a semicircle is a(n) __________ angle.
   b) The two tangent segments drawn to a circle from an external point are __________.
5. Given that $m\overset{\frown}{AB} = 106°$ and $m\overset{\frown}{DC} = 32°$, find:
   a) $m\angle 1$ __________
   b) $m\angle 2$ __________

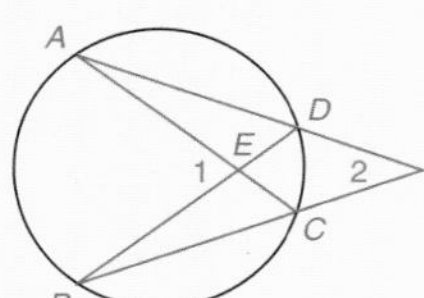

6. Given that $m\overset{\frown}{RT} = 146°$, find:
   a) $m\overset{\frown}{RST}$ __________
   b) $m\angle 3$ __________
7. Given that $m\angle 3 = 46°$, find:
   a) $m\overset{\frown}{RST}$ __________
   b) $m\overset{\frown}{RT}$ __________

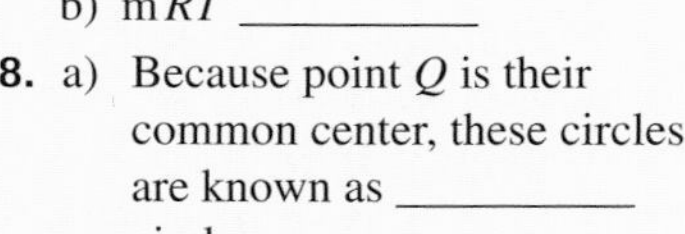

Exercises 6, 7

8. a) Because point Q is their common center, these circles are known as __________ circles.
   b) If $RQ = 3$ and $QV = 5$, find the length of chord $\overline{TV}$.

   ____

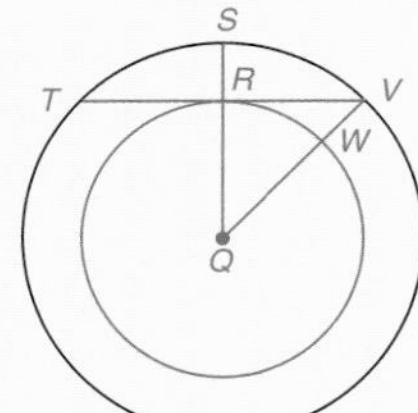

9. In $\odot O$, $OC = 5$ and $AB = 6$. If M is the midpoint of $\overline{BC}$, find AM.

   ____

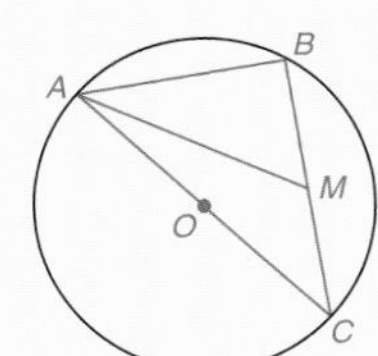

10. For the circles described and shown, how many common tangents do they possess?
    a) Internally tangent circles

    ____

    b) Circles that intersect in two points

    ____

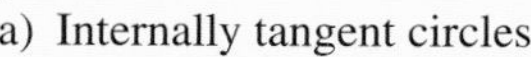

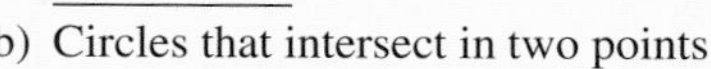

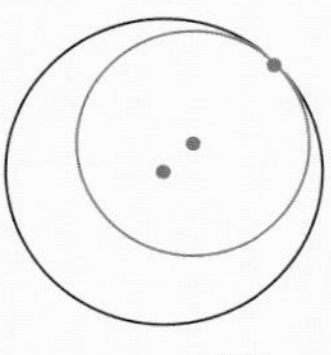

11. a) If $HP = 4$, $PJ = 5$, and $PM = 2$, find LP.

    ____

    b) If $HP = x + 1$, $PJ = x - 1$, $LP = 8$, and $PM = 3$, find x.

    ____

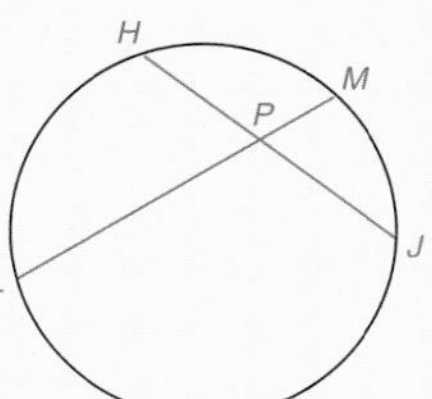

12. In the figure, $\triangle TVW \sim \triangle TXV$. Find TV if $TX = 3$ and $XW = 5$. __________

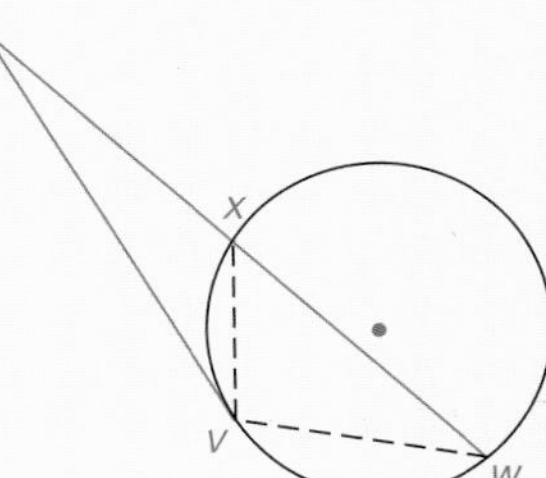

13. Construct the tangent line to $\odot P$ at point X.

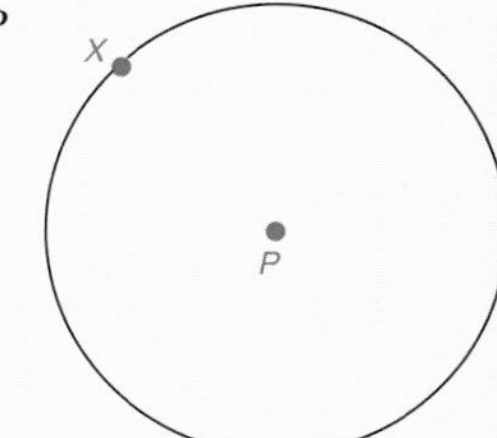

14. a) If $m\overset{\frown}{AB} > m\overset{\frown}{CD}$, write an inequality that compares $m\angle AQB$ and $m\angle CQD$.

    ____

    b) If $QR > QP$, write an inequality that compares AB and CD.

    ____

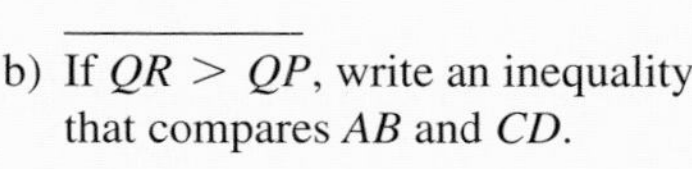

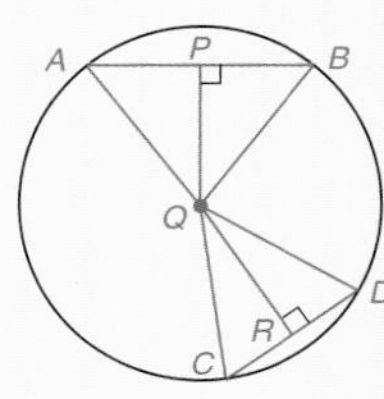

15. In $\odot P$ (not shown), the length of radius $\overline{PA}$ is 5. Also, chord $\overline{AB} \parallel$ chord $\overline{CD}$. If $AB = 8$ and $CD = 6$, find the distance between $\overline{AB}$ and $\overline{CD}$ if these chords:
a) lie on the same side of center P. ________
b) lie on opposite sides of center P. ________

16. Provide the missing statements and reasons in the following proof.

Given: In $\odot O$, chords $\overline{AD}$ and $\overline{BC}$ intersect at E.
Prove: $\frac{AE}{CE} = \frac{BE}{DE}$

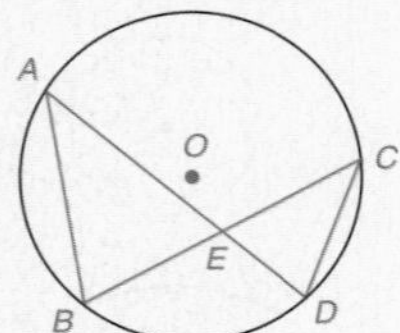

PROOF

Statements	Reasons
1. ________	1. ________
2. $\angle AEB \cong \angle DEC$	2. ________
3. $\angle B \cong \angle D$	3. If two inscribed angles intercept the same arc, these angles are congruent
4. $\triangle ABE \sim \triangle CDE$	4. ________
5. ________	5. CSSTP

Locus and Concurrence

Chapter 7

CHAPTER OUTLINE

Additional Video explanation of concepts, sample problems, and applications are available on DVD. 

Gorgeous! Not only are the gardens at the Chateau de Villandry in France beautiful, but the layout of the garden also demonstrates the importance of location in this design. At the core of this chapter is the notion of *locus*, a Latin term that means "location." In the symmetry of the garden, each flower or shrub has a counterpart located on the opposite side of (and at the same distance from) the central path. The notion of locus provides the background necessary to develop properties for the concurrence of lines as well as further properties of regular polygons.

7.1 Locus of Points

KEY CONCEPTS

Locus of Points in a Plane

Locus of Points in Space

At times, we need to describe a set of points that satisfy a given condition or set of conditions. The term used to describe the resulting geometric figure is *locus* (pronounced lō-kŭs), the plural of which is *loci* (pronounced lō-sī). The English word *location* is derived from the Latin word *locus*.

DEFINITION

A **locus** is the set of all points and only those points that satisfy a given condition (or set of conditions).

In this definition, the phrase "all points and only those points" has a dual meaning:

1. All points of the locus satisfy the given condition.
2. All points satisfying the given condition are included in the locus.

The set of points satisfying a given locus can be a well-known geometric figure such as a line or a circle. In Examples 1, 2, and 3, several points are located in a plane and then connected in order to form the locus.

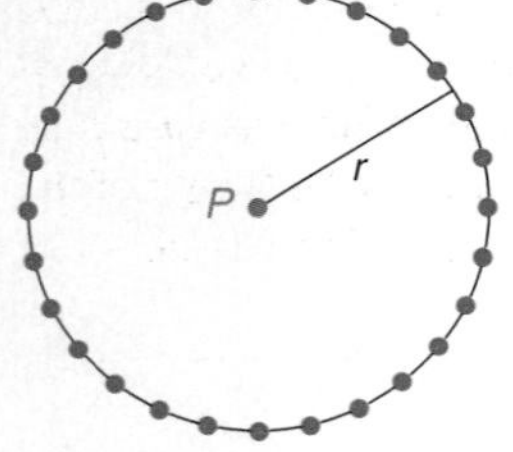

Figure 7.1

EXAMPLE 1

Describe the locus of points in a plane that are at a fixed distance (r) from a given point (P).

Solution The locus is the circle with center P and radius r. (See Figure 7.1.) ■

EXAMPLE 2

Describe the locus of points in a plane that are equidistant from two fixed points (P and Q).

Solution The locus is the line that is the perpendicular bisector of $\overline{PQ}$. In Figure 7.2, $PX = QX$ for any point X on line t.

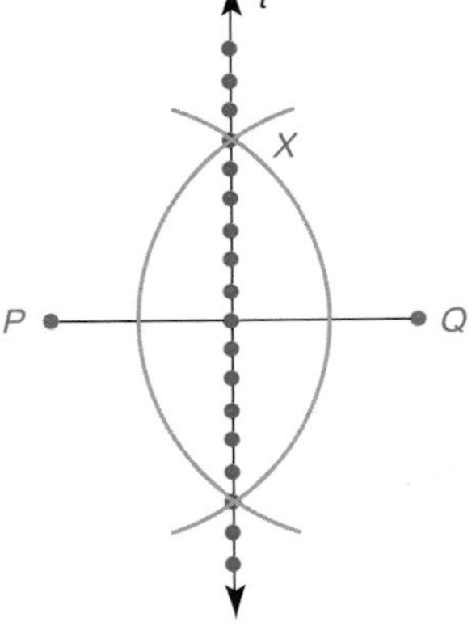

Figure 7.2

■

EXAMPLE 3

Describe the locus of points in a plane that are equidistant from the sides of an angle ($\angle ABC$) in that plane.

Solution The locus is the ray $\overrightarrow{BD}$ that bisects $\angle ABC$. (See Figure 7.3.)

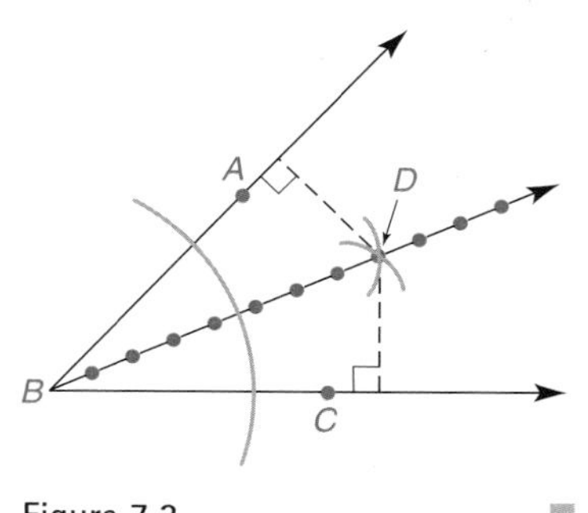

Figure 7.3

Some definitions are given in a locus format; for example, the following is an alternative definition of the term **circle**.

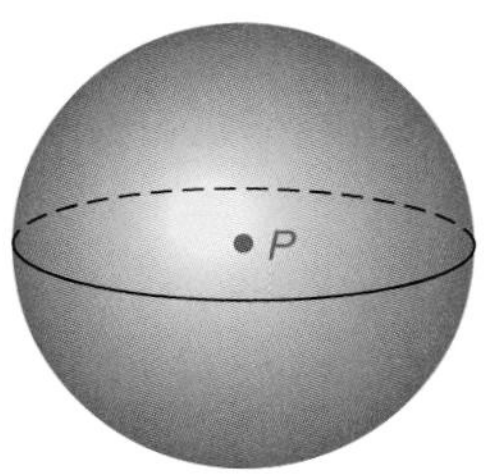

Figure 7.4

DEFINITION

A **circle** is the locus of points in a plane that are at a fixed distance from a given point.

Each of the preceding examples includes the phrase "in a plane." If that phrase is omitted, the locus is found "in space." For instance, the locus of points that are at a fixed distance from a given point is actually a *sphere* (the three-dimensional object in Figure 7.4); the sphere has the fixed point as center, and the fixed distance determines the length of the radius. Unless otherwise stated, we will consider the locus to be restricted to a plane.

SSG *Exs. 1–4*

EXAMPLE 4

Describe the locus of points *in space* that are equidistant from two parallel planes (P and Q).

Solution The locus is the plane parallel to each of the given planes and midway between them. (See Figure 7.5.)

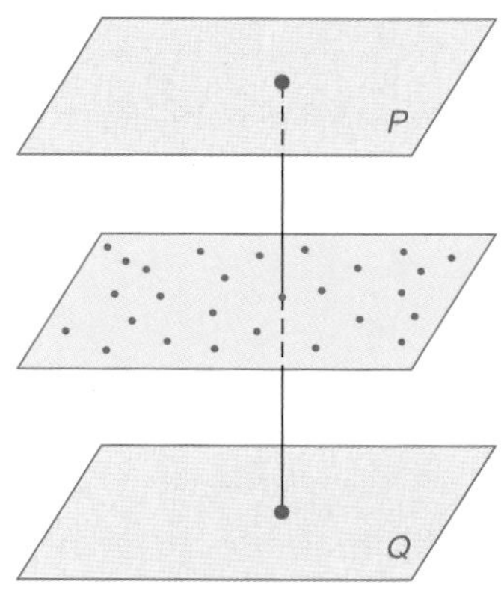

Figure 7.5

There are two very important theorems involving the locus concept. The results of these two theorems will be used in Section 7.2. When we verify the locus theorems, we *must* establish two results:

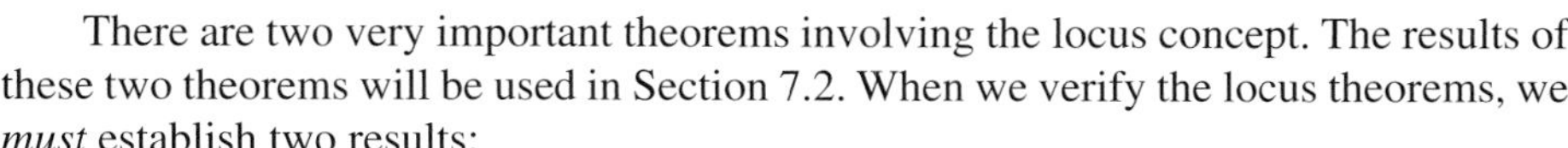

1. If a point is in the locus, then it satisfies the condition.
2. If a point satisfies the condition, then it is a point of the locus.

THEOREM 7.1.1

The locus of points in a plane and equidistant from the sides of an angle is the angle bisector.

PROOF

(Note that *both* parts i and ii are necessary.)

(a)

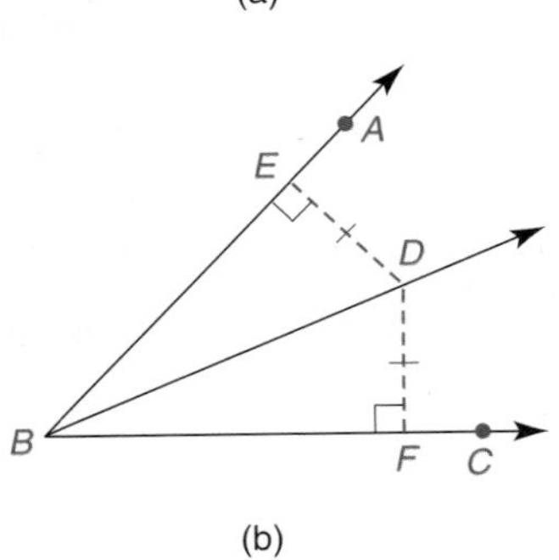

(b)

Figure 7.6

i) If a point is on the angle bisector, then it is equidistant from the sides of the angle.

GIVEN: $\overrightarrow{BD}$ bisects $\angle ABC$
$\overline{DE} \perp \overrightarrow{BA}$ and $\overline{DF} \perp \overrightarrow{BC}$

PROVE: $\overline{DE} \cong \overline{DF}$

PROOF: In Figure 7.6(a), $\overrightarrow{BD}$ bisects $\angle ABC$; thus, $\angle ABD \cong \angle CBD$. $\overline{DE} \perp \overrightarrow{BA}$ and $\overline{DF} \perp \overrightarrow{BC}$, so $\angle DEB$ and $\angle DFB$ are $\cong$ right $\angle$s. By Identity, $\overline{BD} \cong \overline{BD}$. By AAS, $\triangle DEB \cong \triangle DFB$. Then $\overline{DE} \cong \overline{DF}$ by CPCTC.

ii) If a point is equidistant from the sides of an angle, then it is on the angle bisector.

GIVEN: $\angle ABC$ such that $\overline{DE} \perp \overrightarrow{BA}$ and $\overline{DF} \perp \overrightarrow{BC}$
$\overline{DE} \cong \overline{DF}$

PROVE: $\overrightarrow{BD}$ bisects $\angle ABC$; that is, D is on the bisector of $\angle ABC$

PROOF: In Figure 7.6(b), $\overline{DE} \perp \overrightarrow{BA}$ and $\overline{DF} \perp \overrightarrow{BC}$, so $\angle DEB$ and $\angle DFB$ are right angles. $\overline{DE} \cong \overline{DF}$ by hypothesis. Also, $\overline{BD} \cong \overline{BD}$ by Identity. Then $\triangle DEB \cong \triangle DFB$ by HL. Then $\angle ABD \cong \angle CBD$ by CPCTC, so $\overrightarrow{BD}$ bisects $\angle ABC$ by definition. ■

In locus problems, we must remember to demonstrate two relationships in order to validate results.

A second important theorem regarding a locus of points follows.

THEOREM 7.1.2

The locus of points in a plane that are equidistant from the endpoints of a line segment is the perpendicular bisector of that line segment.

SSG *Exs. 5, 6*

PROOF

i) If a point is equidistant from the endpoints of a line segment, then it lies on the perpendicular bisector of the line segment.

GIVEN: $\overline{AB}$ and point X not on $\overline{AB}$, so that $AX = BX$ [See Figure 7.7(a).]

PROVE: X lies on the perpendicular bisector of $\overline{AB}$

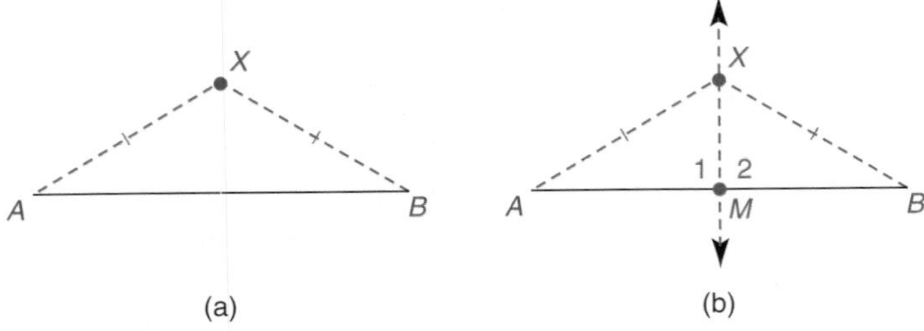

(a) (b)

Figure 7.7

PROOF: Let M represent the midpoint of $\overline{AB}$. Draw $\overleftrightarrow{MX}$ [See Figure 7.7(b).] Then $\overline{AM} \cong \overline{MB}$. Because $AX = BX$, we know that $\overline{AX} \cong \overline{BX}$. By Identity, $\overline{XM} \cong \overline{XM}$; thus, $\triangle AMX \cong \triangle BMX$ by SSS. By CPCTC, $\angle$s 1 and 2 are congruent and $\overleftrightarrow{MX} \perp \overline{AB}$. By definition, $\overleftrightarrow{MX}$ is the perpendicular bisector of $\overline{AB}$, so X lies on the perpendicular bisector of $\overline{AB}$.

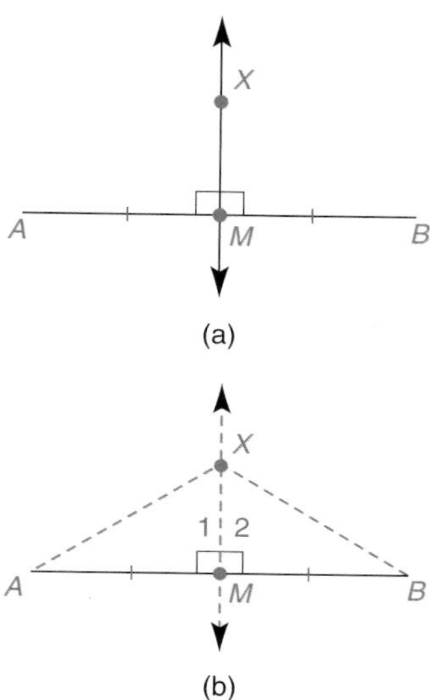

Figure 7.8

ii) If a point is on the perpendicular bisector of a line segment, then the point is equidistant from the endpoints of the line segment.

GIVEN: Point X lies on $\overleftrightarrow{MX}$, the perpendicular bisector of $\overline{AB}$ [See Figure 7.8(a).]

PROVE: X is equidistant from A and B ($AX = XB$) [See Figure 7.8(b).]

PROOF: X is on the perpendicular bisector of $\overline{AB}$, so $\angle$s 1 and 2 are congruent right angles and $\overline{AM} \cong \overline{MB}$. With $\overline{XM} \cong \overline{XM}$, $\triangle$s AMX and BMX are congruent by SAS; in turn, $\overline{XA} \cong \overline{XB}$ by CPCTC. Then $XA = XB$ and X is equidistant from A and B. ■

We now return to further considerations of a locus in a plane.

Suppose that a given line segment is to be used as the hypotenuse of a right triangle. How might you locate possible positions for the vertex of the right angle? One method might be to draw 30° and 60° angles at the endpoints so that the remaining angle formed must measure 90° [see Figure 7.9(a)]. This is only one possibility, but because of symmetry, it actually provides four permissible points, which are indicated in Figure 7.9(b). This problem is completed in Example 5.

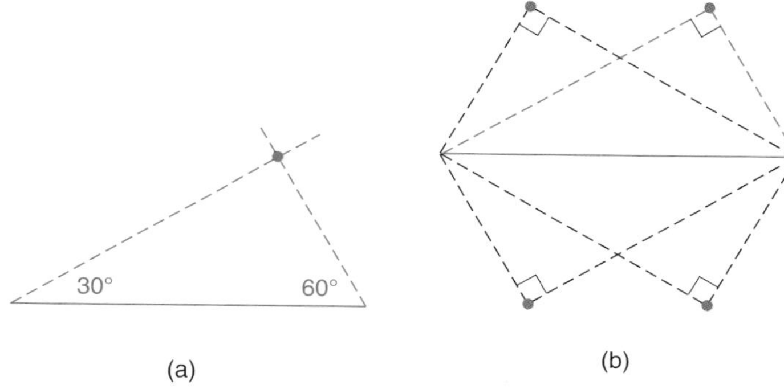

Figure 7.9

Exs. 7, 8

Reminder

An angle inscribed in a semicircle is a right angle.

EXAMPLE 5

Find the locus of the vertex of the right angle of a right triangle if the hypotenuse is $\overline{AB}$ in Figure 7.10(a).

Solution Rather than using a "hit or miss" approach for locating the possible vertices (as suggested in the paragraph preceding this example), recall that an angle inscribed in a semicircle is a right angle. Thus, we construct the circle whose center is the midpoint M of the hypotenuse and whose radius equals one-half the length of the hypotenuse.

Figure 7.10(b): First, the midpoint M of the hypotenuse $\overline{AB}$ is located.

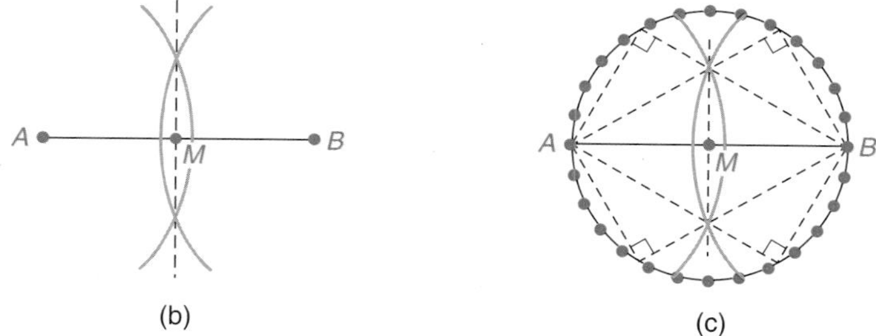

Figure 7.10

Figure 7.10(c): With the length of the radius of the circle equal to one-half the length of the hypotenuse (such as MB), the circle with center M is drawn.
The locus of the vertex of the right angle of a right triangle whose hypotenuse is given is the circle whose center is at the midpoint of the given segment and whose radius is equal in length to half the length of the given segment. Every point (except A and B) on $\odot M$ is the vertex of a right triangle with hypotenuse $\overline{AB}$; see Theorem 6.1.9. ■

In Example 5, the construction involves locating the midpoint M of $\overline{AB}$, and this is found by the construction of the perpendicular bisector. The compass is then opened to a radius whose length is MA or MB, and the circle is drawn. When a construction is performed, it falls into one of two categories:

1. A basic construction method
2. A compound construction problem that may require several steps and may involve several basic construction methods (as in Example 5)

The next example also falls into category 2.

Recall that the diagonals of a rhombus are perpendicular and also bisect each other. With this information, we can locate the vertices of the rhombus whose diagonals (lengths) are known.

EXAMPLE 6

Construct rhombus $ABCD$ given its diagonals $\overline{AC}$ and $\overline{BD}$. (See Figure 7.11.)

Solution Figure 7.11(a): To begin, we construct the perpendicular bisector of $\overline{AC}$; we know that the remaining vertices B and D must lie on this line. As shown, M is the midpoint of $\overline{AC}$.
Figure 7.11(b): To locate the midpoint of $\overline{BD}$, we construct its perpendicular bisector as well. The midpoint of $\overline{BD}$ is also called M.
Figure 7.11(c): Using an arc length equal to one-half the length of $\overline{BD}$ (such as MB), we mark off this distance both above and below $\overline{AC}$ on the perpendicular bisector determined in Figure 7.11(a).

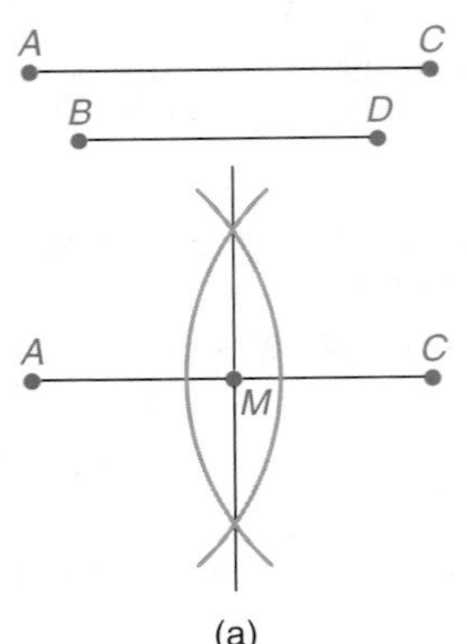

(a)

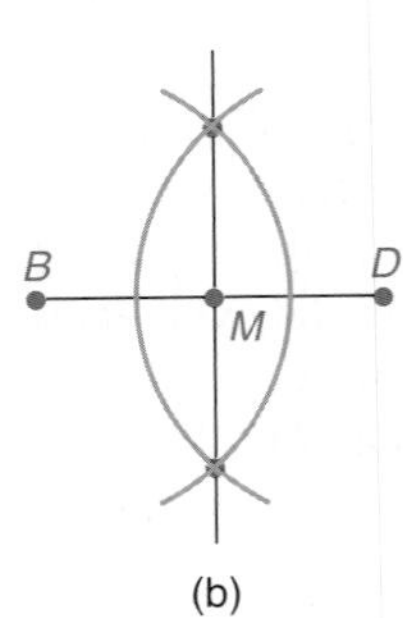

(b)

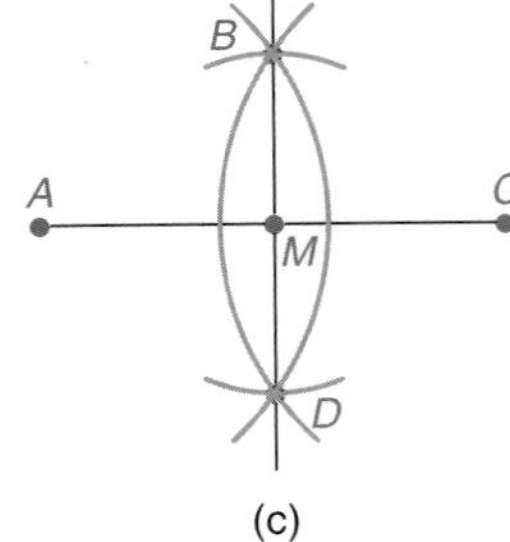

(c)

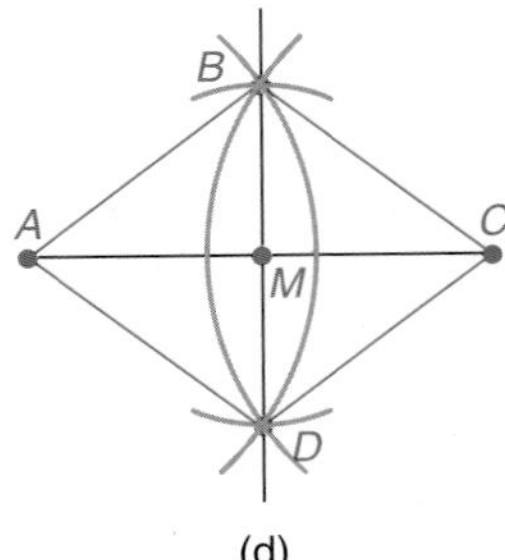

(d)

Figure 7.11

Figure 7.11(d): Using the marked arcs to locate (determine) points B and D, we join A to B, B to C, C to D, and D to A. The completed rhombus is $ABCD$ as shown. ■

SSG *Exs. 9, 10*

Exercises 7.1

1. In the figure, which of the points A, B, C, D, and E belong to "the locus of points in the plane that are at distance r from point P"?

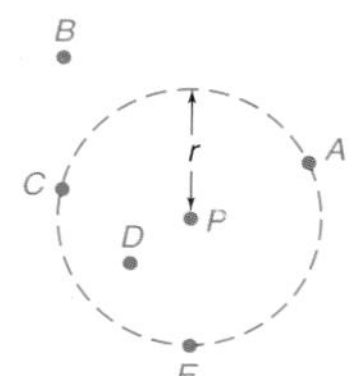

2. In the figure, which of the points F, G, H, J, and K belong to "the locus of points in the plane that are at distance r from line ℓ"?

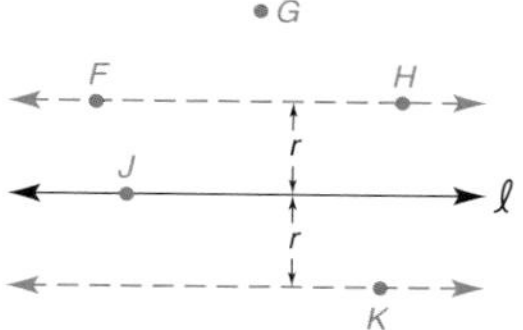

In Exercises 3 to 8, use the drawing provided.

3. *Given:* Obtuse $\triangle ABC$
   Construct: The bisector of $\angle ABC$

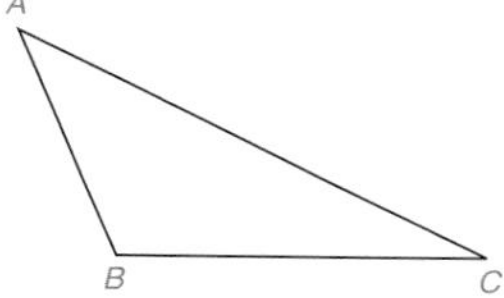

Exercises 3–8

4. *Given:* Obtuse $\triangle ABC$
   Construct: The bisector of $\angle BAC$
5. *Given:* Obtuse $\triangle ABC$
   Construct: The perpendicular bisector of $\overline{AB}$
6. *Given:* Obtuse $\triangle ABC$
   Construct: The perpendicular bisector of $\overline{AC}$
7. *Given:* Obtuse $\triangle ABC$
   Construct: The altitude from A to $\overline{BC}$
   (*HINT:* Extend $\overline{BC}$.)
8. *Given:* Obtuse $\triangle ABC$
   Construct: The altitude from B to $\overline{AC}$
9. *Given:* Right $\triangle RST$
   Construct: The median from S to $\overline{RT}$
10. *Given:* Right $\triangle RST$
    Construct: The median from R to $\overline{ST}$

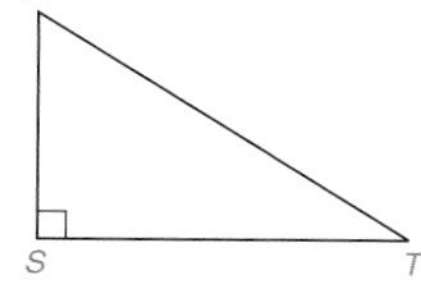

Exercises 9–10

In Exercises 11 to 22, sketch and describe each locus in the plane.

11. Find the locus of points that are at a given distance from a fixed line.
12. Find the locus of points that are equidistant from two given parallel lines.
13. Find the locus of points that are at a distance of 3 in. from a fixed point O.
14. Find the locus of points that are equidistant from two fixed points A and B.
15. Find the locus of points that are equidistant from three noncollinear points D, E, and F.
16. Find the locus of the midpoints of the radii of a circle O that has a radius of length 8 cm.
17. Find the locus of the midpoints of all chords of circle Q that are parallel to diameter $\overline{PR}$.
18. Find the locus of points in the interior of a right triangle with sides of 6 in., 8 in., and 10 in. and at a distance of 1 in. from the triangle.
19. Find the locus of points that are equidistant from two given intersecting lines.

*20. Find the locus of points that are equidistant from a fixed line and a point not on that line.
(**NOTE:** This figure is known as a *parabola*.)

21. Given that lines p and q intersect, find the locus of points that are at a distance of 1 cm from line p and also at a distance of 2 cm from line q.
22. Given that congruent circles O and P have radii of length 4 in. and that the line of centers has length 6 in., find the locus of points that are 1 in. from each circle.

In Exercises 23 to 30, sketch and describe the locus of points in space.

23. Find the locus of points that are at a given distance from a fixed line.
24. Find the locus of points that are equidistant from two fixed points.
25. Find the locus of points that are at a distance of 2 cm from a sphere whose radius is 5 cm.
26. Find the locus of points that are at a given distance from a given plane.
27. Find the locus of points that are the midpoints of the radii of a sphere whose center is point O and whose radius has a length of 5 m.

*28. Find the locus of points that are equidistant from three noncollinear points D, E, and F.

29. In a room, find the locus of points that are equidistant from the parallel ceiling and floor, which are 8 ft apart.

30. Find the locus of points that are equidistant from all points on the surface of a sphere with center point Q.

In Exercises 31 and 32, use the method of proof of Theorem 7.1.1 to justify each construction method.

31. The perpendicular bisector method.

32. The construction of a perpendicular to a line from a point outside the line.

In Exercises 33 to 36, refer to the line segments shown.

33. Construct an isosceles right triangle that has hypotenuse $\overline{AB}$.

Exercises 33–36

34. Construct a rhombus whose sides are equal in length to AB, and so that one diagonal of the rhombus has length CD.

35. Construct an isosceles triangle in which each leg has length CD and the altitude to the base has length AB.

36. Construct an equilateral triangle in which the altitude to any side has length AB.

37. Construct the three angle bisectors and then the inscribed circle for obtuse $\triangle RST$.

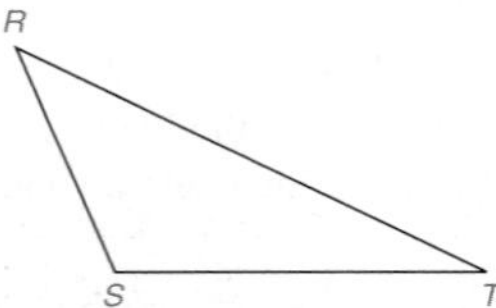

Exercises 37, 38

38. Construct the three perpendicular bisectors of sides and then the circumscribed circle for obtuse $\triangle RST$.

39. Use the following theorem to locate the center of the circle of which $\overset{\frown}{RT}$ is a part.

Theorem: The perpendicular bisector of a chord passes through the center of a circle.

***40.** Use the following theorem to construct the geometric mean of the numerical lengths of the segments $\overline{WX}$ and $\overline{YZ}$.

Theorem: The length of the altitude to the hypotenuse of a right triangle is the geometric mean between the lengths of the segments of the hypotenuse.

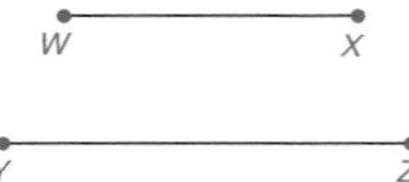

41. Use the following theorem to construct a triangle similar to the given triangle but with sides that are twice the length of those of the given triangle.

Theorem: If the three pairs of sides for two triangles are in proportion, then those triangles are similar (SSS ~).

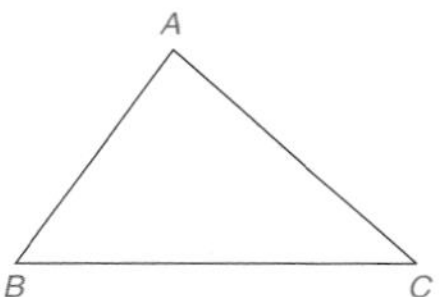

***42.** Verify this locus theorem:

The locus of points equidistant from two fixed points is the perpendicular bisector of the line segment joining those points.

7.2 Concurrence of Lines

KEY CONCEPTS

Concurrent Lines	Circumcenter	Orthocenter
Incenter	Circumcircle	Centroid
Incircle		

In this section, we consider lines that share a common point.

DEFINITION

A number of lines are **concurrent** if they have exactly one point in common.

Discover

A computer software program can be useful in demonstrating the concurrence of the lines described in each theorem in this section.

The three lines in Figure 7.12 are concurrent at point A. The three lines in Figure 7.13 are not concurrent even though any pair of lines (such as r and s) do intersect.

Parts of lines (rays or segments) are concurrent if they are parts of concurrent lines and the parts share a common point.

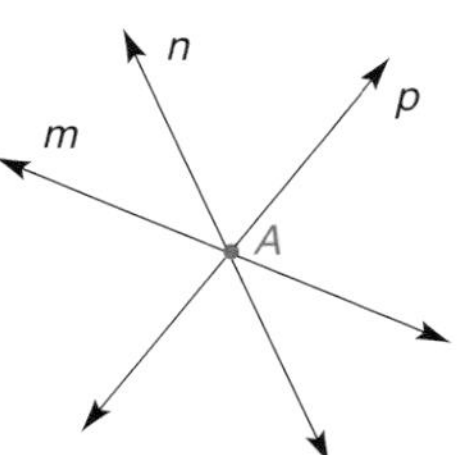

m, *n*, and *p* *are* concurrent

Figure 7.12

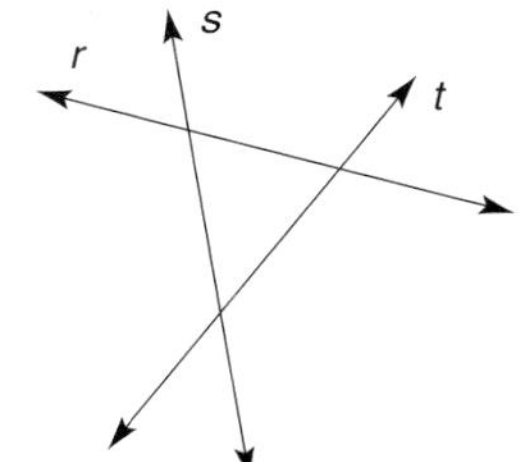

r, *s*, and *t* are *not* concurrent

Figure 7.13

Exs. 1, 2

THEOREM 7.2.1

The three angle bisectors of the angles of a triangle are concurrent.

For the informal proofs of this section, no Given or Prove is stated. In more advanced courses, these parts of the proof are understood.

EXAMPLE 1

Give an informal proof of Theorem 7.2.1.

Proof In Figure 7.14(a), the bisectors of $\angle BAC$ and $\angle ABC$ intersect at point E.

Because the bisector of $\angle BAC$ is the locus of points equidistant from the sides of $\angle BAC$, we know that $\overline{EM} \cong \overline{EN}$ in Figure 7.14(b). Similarly, $\overline{EM} \cong \overline{EP}$ because E is on the bisector of $\angle ABC$.

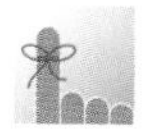

Reminder

A point on the bisector of an angle is equidistant from the sides of the angle.

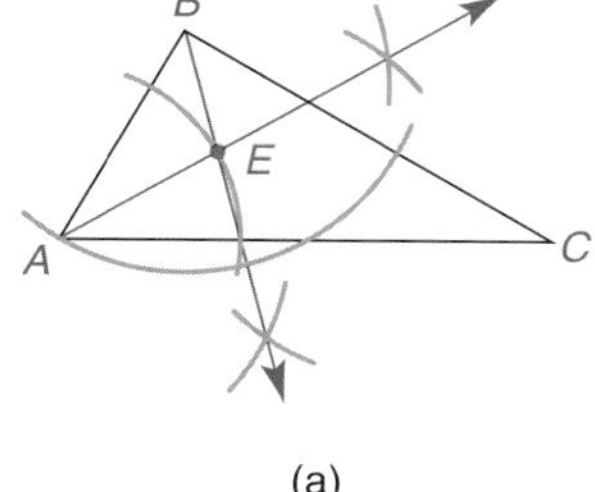

(a)

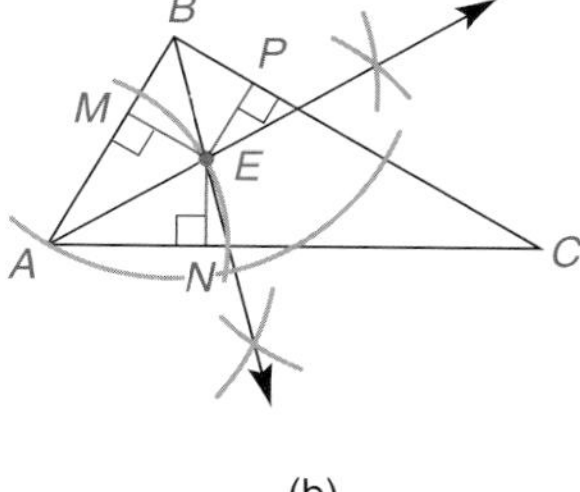

(b)

Figure 7.14

By the Transitive Property of Congruence, it follows that $\overline{EP} \cong \overline{EN}$.

Because the bisector of an angle is the locus of points equidistant from the sides of the angle, E is also on the bisector of the third angle, $\angle ACB$. Thus, the angle bisectors are concurrent at point E. ■

The point E at which the angle bisectors meet in Example 1 is the **incenter** of the triangle. As the following example shows, the term *incenter* is well deserved because this point is the *center* of the *in*scribed circle of the triangle.

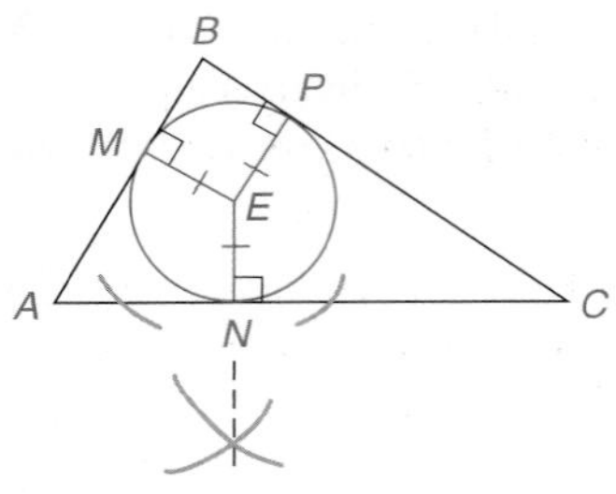

Figure 7.15

EXAMPLE 2

Complete the construction of the inscribed circle for $\triangle ABC$ in Figure 7.14(b).

Solution Having found the incenter E, we need the length of the radius. Because $\overline{EN} \perp \overline{AC}$ (as shown in Figure 7.15), the length of $\overline{EN}$ (or $\overline{EM}$ or $\overline{EP}$) is the desired radius; thus, the circle is completed.

NOTE: The sides of the triangle are tangents for the inscribed circle (or incircle) of the triangle. The *in*circle lies *in*side the triangle. ■

It is also possible to circumscribe a circle about a given triangle. The construction depends on the following theorem, the proof of which is sketched in Example 3.

Exs. 3–7

THEOREM 7.2.2

The three perpendicular bisectors of the sides of a triangle are concurrent.

EXAMPLE 3

Give an informal proof of Theorem 7.2.2. See $\triangle ABC$ in Figure 7.16.

Proof Let $\overline{FS}$ and $\overline{FR}$ name the perpendicular bisectors of sides $\overline{BC}$ and $\overline{AC}$, respectively. See Figure 7.16(a). Using Theorem 7.1.2, the point of concurrency F is equidistant from the endpoints of $\overline{BC}$; thus, $\overline{BF} \cong \overline{FC}$. In the same manner, $\overline{AF} \cong \overline{FC}$. By the Transitive Property, it follows that $\overline{AF} \cong \overline{BF}$; again citing Theorem 7.1.2, F must be on the perpendicular bisector of $\overline{AB}$ because this point is equidistant from the endpoints of $\overline{AB}$. Thus, F is the point of concurrence.

Reminder

A point on the perpendicular bisector of a line segment is equidistant from the endpoints of the line segment.

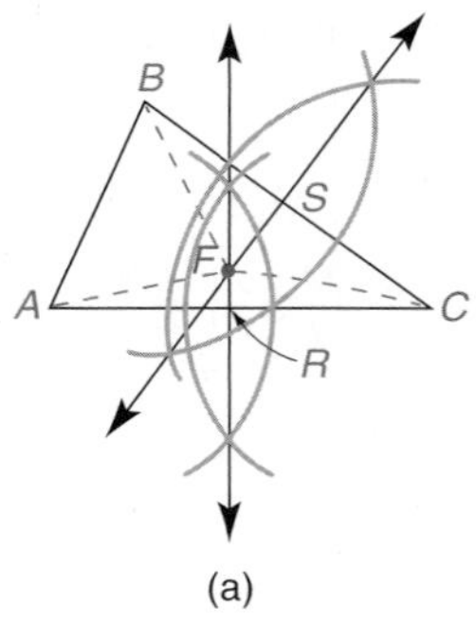

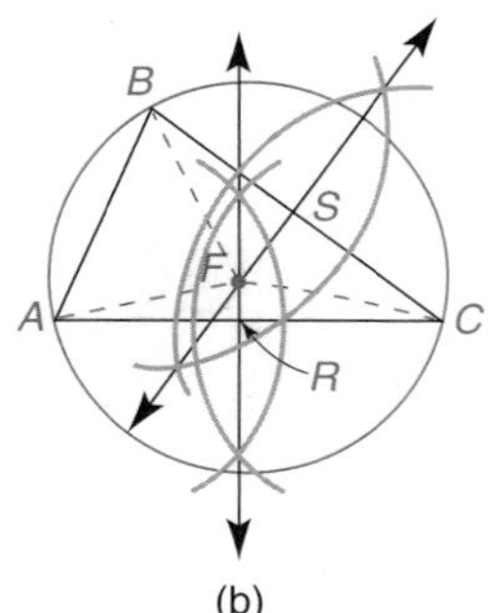

Figure 7.16 ■

The point at which the perpendicular bisectors of the sides of a triangle meet is the **circumcenter** of the triangle. The term *circumcenter* is easily remembered as the *center* of the *circum*scribed circle.

EXAMPLE 4

Complete the construction of the circumscribed circle for $\triangle ABC$ that was given in Figure 7.16(a).

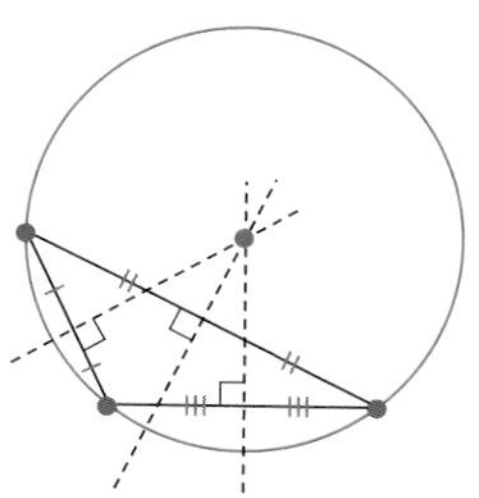

Figure 7.17

Solution We have already identified the center of the circle as point F. To complete the construction, we use F as the center and a radius of length equal to the distance from F to any one of the vertices A, B, or C. The circumscribed circle is shown in Figure 7.16(b).

NOTE: The sides of the inscribed triangle are chords of the circumscribed circle, which is called the **circumcircle** of the triangle. The circumcircle of a polygon lies outside the polygon except where it contains the vertices of the polygon. ■

The incenter and the circumcenter of a triangle are generally distinct points. However, it is possible for the two centers to coincide in a special type of triangle. Although the incenter of a triangle always lies in the interior of the triangle, the circumcenter of an obtuse triangle will lie in the exterior of the triangle. See Figure 7.17. The circumcenter of a right triangle is the midpoint of the hypotenuse.

SSG *Exs. 8–12*

To complete the discussion of concurrence, we include a theorem involving the altitudes of a triangle and a theorem involving the medians of a triangle.

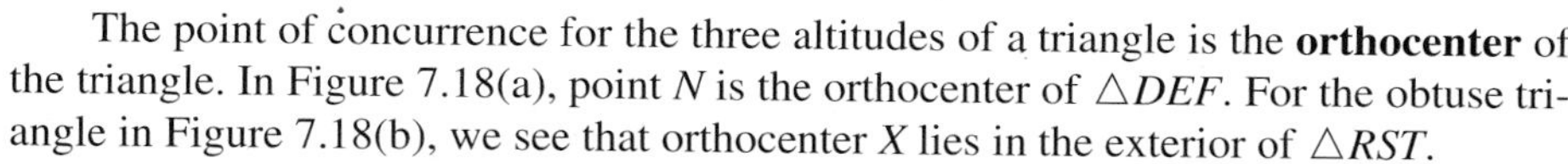

THEOREM 7.2.3

The three altitudes of a triangle are concurrent.

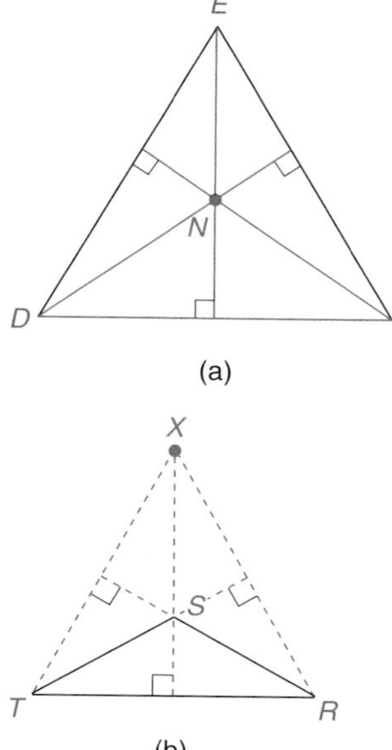

Figure 7.18

The point of concurrence for the three altitudes of a triangle is the **orthocenter** of the triangle. In Figure 7.18(a), point N is the orthocenter of $\triangle DEF$. For the obtuse triangle in Figure 7.18(b), we see that orthocenter X lies in the exterior of $\triangle RST$.

Rather than proving Theorem 7.2.3, we sketch a part of that proof. In Figure 7.19(a), $\triangle MNP$ is shown with its altitudes. To prove that the altitudes are concurrent requires

1. that we draw auxiliary lines through N parallel to $\overline{MP}$, through M parallel to $\overline{NP}$, and through P parallel to $\overline{NM}$. [See Figure 7.19(b).]
2. that we show that the altitudes of $\triangle MNP$ are perpendicular bisectors of the sides of the newly formed $\triangle RST$; thus altitudes $\overline{PX}$, $\overline{MY}$, and $\overline{NZ}$ are concurrent (a consequence of Theorem 7.2.2).

SKETCH OF PROOF THAT $\overline{PX}$ IS THE $\perp$ BISECTOR OF $\overline{RS}$:

Because $\overline{PX}$ is an altitude of $\triangle MNP$, $\overline{PX} \perp \overline{MN}$. But $\overline{RS} \parallel \overline{MN}$ by construction. Because a line perpendicular to one of two parallel lines must be perpendicular to the other, we have $\overline{PX} \perp \overline{RS}$. Now we need to show that $\overline{PX}$ bisects $\overline{RS}$. By construction, $\overline{MR} \parallel \overline{NP}$ and $\overline{RP} \parallel \overline{MN}$, so $MRPN$ is a parallelogram. Then $\overline{MN} \cong \overline{RP}$ because the opposite sides of a parallelogram are congruent. By construction, $MPSN$ is also a parallelogram and $\overline{MN} \cong \overline{PS}$. By the Transitive Property of Congruence, $\overline{RP} \cong \overline{PS}$. Thus, $\overline{RS}$ is bisected at point P, and $\overline{PX}$ is the $\perp$ bisector of $\overline{RS}$.

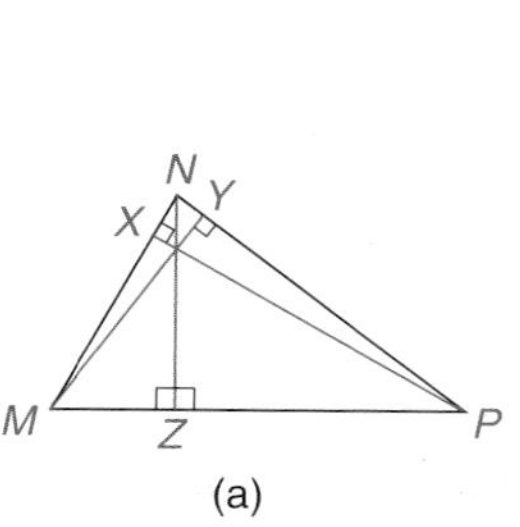
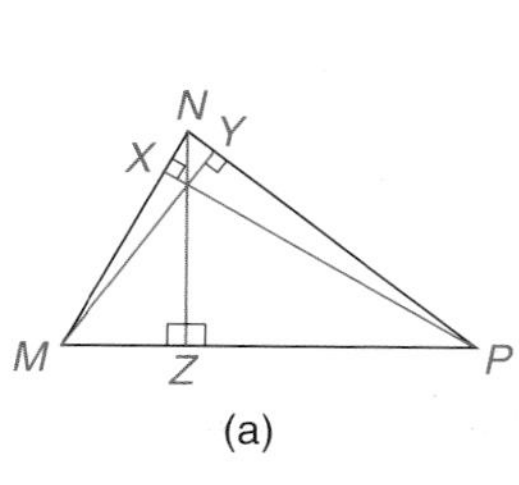

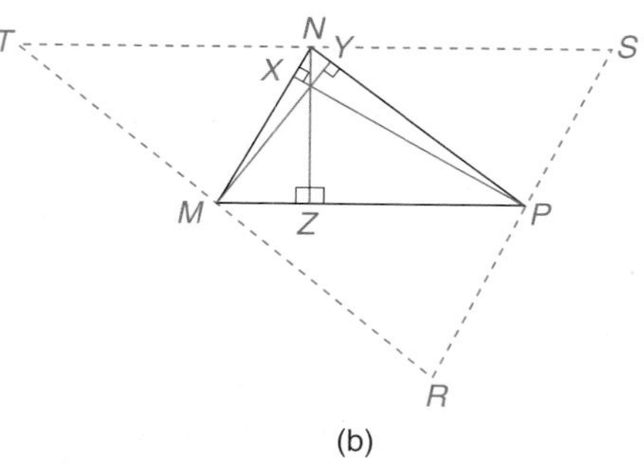

Figure 7.19

In Figure 7.19(b), similar arguments (leading to one long proof) could be used to show that $\overline{NZ}$ is the $\perp$ bisector of $\overline{TS}$ and also that $\overline{MY}$ is the $\perp$ bisector of $\overline{TR}$. Because the concurrent perpendicular bisectors of the sides of $\triangle RST$ are also the altitudes of $\triangle MNP$, these altitudes must be concurrent.

The intersection of any two altitudes determines the orthocenter of a triangle. We use this fact in Example 5. If the third altitude were constructed, it would contain the same point of intersection (the orthocenter).

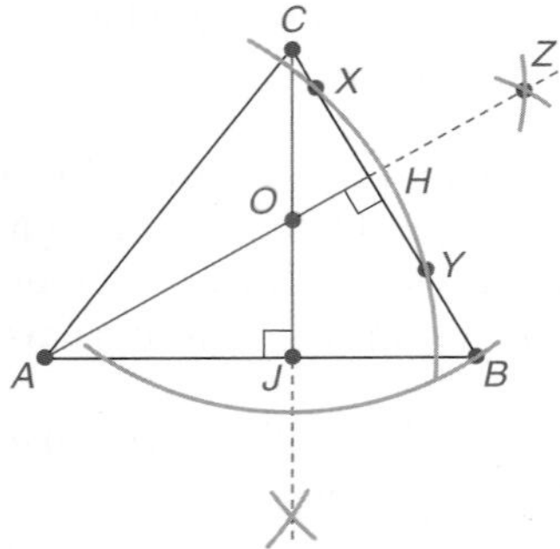

Figure 7.20

EXAMPLE 5

Construct the orthocenter of $\triangle ABC$ in Figure 7.20.

Solution First construct the altitude from A to $\overline{BC}$; here, we draw an arc from A to intersect $\overline{BC}$ at X and Y. Now draw equal arcs from X and Y to intersect at Z. $\overline{AH}$ is the desired altitude. Repeat the process to construct altitude $\overline{CJ}$ from vertex C to side $\overline{AB}$. The point of intersection O is the orthocenter of $\triangle ABC$. ■

SSG *Exs. 13–16*

Recall that a median of a triangle joins a vertex to the midpoint of the opposite side of the triangle. Through construction, we can show that the three medians of a triangle are concurrent. We will discuss the proof of the following theorem in Chapter 10.

THEOREM 7.2.4

The three medians of a triangle are concurrent at a point that is two-thirds the distance from any vertex to the midpoint of the opposite side.

Discover

On a piece of paper, draw a triangle and its medians. Label the figure the same as Figure 7.21.

a) Find the value of $\frac{RC}{RM}$.

b) Find the value of $\frac{SC}{CN}$.

ANSWERS

(a) $\frac{2}{3}$ (b) $\frac{2}{1}$ or 2

The point of concurrence for the three medians is the **centroid** of the triangle. In Figure 7.21, point C is the centroid of $\triangle RST$. According to Theorem 7.2.4, $RC = \frac{2}{3}(RM)$, $SC = \frac{2}{3}(SN)$, and $TC = \frac{2}{3}(TP)$.

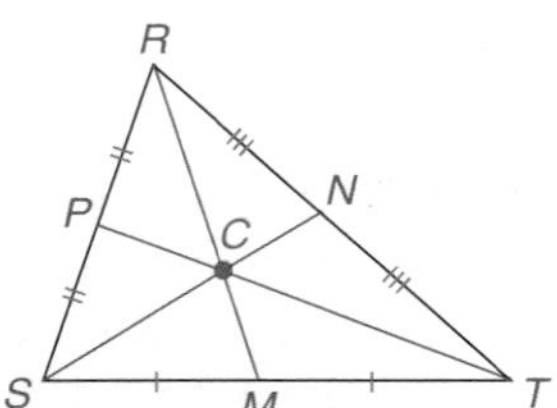

Figure 7.21

EXAMPLE 6

Suppose that the medians of $\triangle RST$ in Figure 7.21 have the lengths $RM = 12$, $SN = 15$, and $TP = 18$. The centroid of $\triangle RST$ is point C. Find the length of:

a) RC b) CM c) SC

Solution

a) $RC = \frac{2}{3}(RM)$, so $RC = \frac{2}{3}(12) = 8$.

b) $CM = RM - RC$, so $CM = 12 - 8 = 4$.

c) $SC = \frac{2}{3}(SN)$, so $SC = \frac{2}{3}(15) = 10$. ■

The following relationships are also implied by Theorem 7.2.4. In Figure 7.21, $RC = 2(CM)$, $SC = 2(CN)$, and $CT = 2(PC)$. Equivalently, $CM = \frac{1}{2}(RC)$, $CN = \frac{1}{2}(SC)$, and $PC = \frac{1}{2}(CT)$.

EXAMPLE 7

GIVEN: In Figure 7.22(a), isosceles $\triangle RST$ with $RS = RT = 15$, and $ST = 18$; medians $\overline{RZ}$, $\overline{TX}$, and $\overline{SY}$ meet at centroid Q.

FIND: RQ and QZ

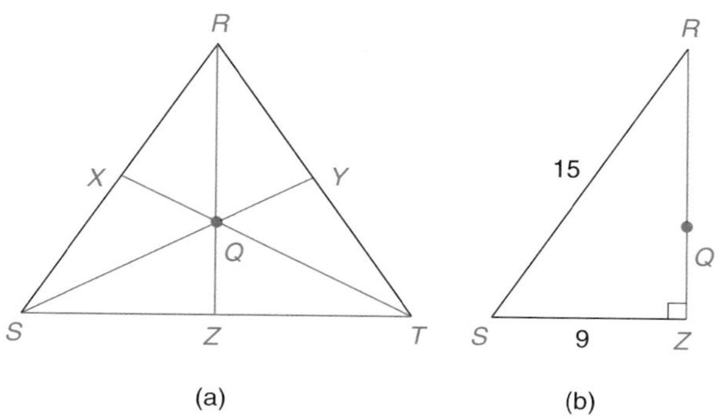

Figure 7.22

Solution Median $\overline{RZ}$ separates $\triangle RST$ into two congruent right triangles, $\triangle RZS$ and $\triangle RZT$; this follows from SSS. With Z the midpoint of $\overline{ST}$, $SZ = 9$.

Using the Pythagorean Theorem with $\triangle RZS$ in Figure 7.22(b), we have

$$\begin{aligned}(RS)^2 &= (RZ)^2 + (SZ)^2\\ 15^2 &= (RZ)^2 + 9^2\\ 225 &= (RZ)^2 + 81\\ (RZ)^2 &= 144\\ RZ &= 12\end{aligned}$$

SSG
Exs. 17–22

By Theorem 7.2.4, $RQ = \frac{2}{3}(RZ) = \frac{2}{3}(12) = 8$

Because $QZ = \frac{1}{2}(RQ)$, it follows that $QZ = 4$. ■

It is *possible* for the angle bisectors of certain quadrilaterals to be concurrent. Likewise, the perpendicular bisectors of the sides of a quadrilateral *can* be concurrent. Of course, there are four angle bisectors and four perpendicular bisectors of sides to consider. In Example 8, we explore this situation.

EXAMPLE 8

Use intuition and Figure 7.23 to decide which of the following are concurrent.

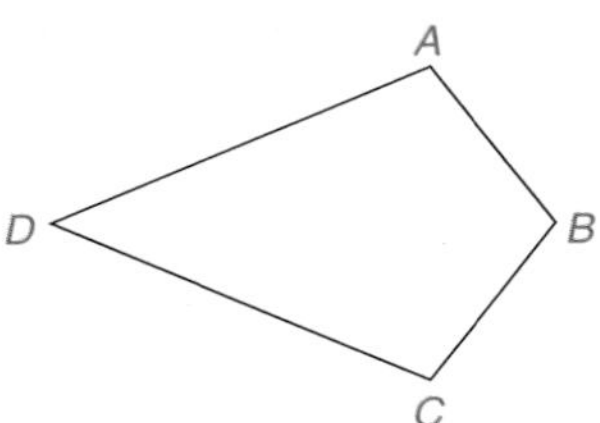

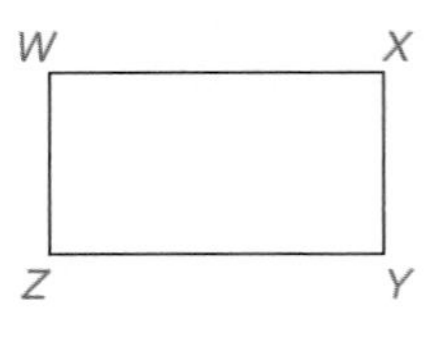

Figure 7.23

a) The angle bisectors of a kite
b) The perpendicular bisectors of the sides of a kite
c) The angle bisectors of a rectangle
d) The perpendicular bisectors of the sides of a rectangle

Solution

a) The angle bisectors of the kite are concurrent at a point (the incenter of the kite).
b) The $\perp$ bisectors of the sides of the kite are not concurrent (unless $\angle A$ and $\angle C$ are both right angles).
c) The angle bisectors of the rectangle are not concurrent (unless the rectangle is a square).
d) The $\perp$ bisectors of the sides of the rectangle are concurrent (the circumcenter of the rectangle is also the point of intersection of diagonals).

NOTE: The student should make drawings to verify the results in Example 8. ■

Discover

Take a piece of cardboard or heavy poster paper. Draw a triangle on the paper and cut out the triangular shape. Now use a ruler to mark the midpoints of each side and draw the medians to locate the centroid. Place the triangle on the point of a pen or pencil at the centroid and see how well you can balance the triangular region.

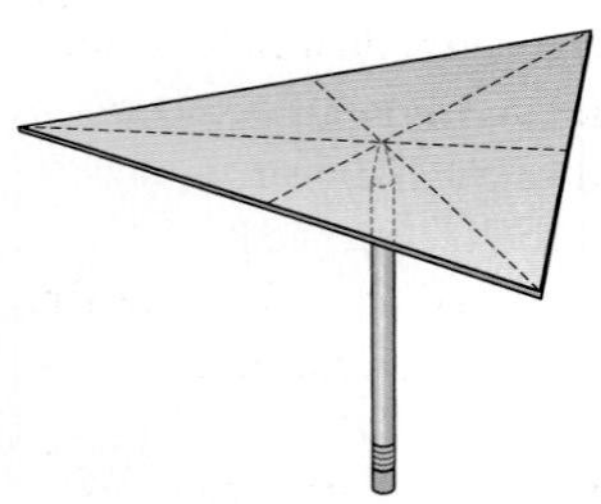

The centroid of a triangular region is sometimes called its *center of mass* or *center of gravity*. This is because the region of uniform thickness "balances" upon the point known as its centroid. Consider the Discover activity at the left.

Exercises 7.2

1. In the figure, are lines *m*, *n*, and *p* concurrent?
2. If one exists, name the point of concurrence for lines *m*, *n*, and *p*.

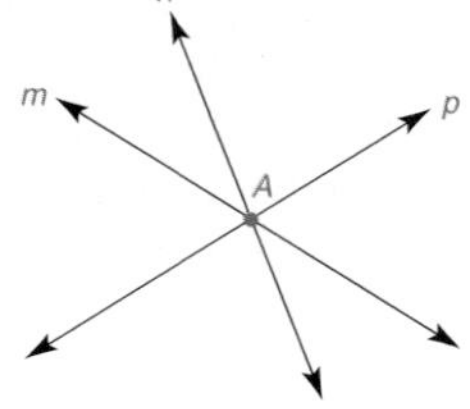

Exercises 1, 2

3. What is the general name of the point of concurrence for the three angle bisectors of a triangle?
4. What is the general name of the point of concurrence for the three altitudes of a triangle?
5. What is the general name of the point of concurrence for the three perpendicular bisectors of sides of a triangle?
6. What is the general name of the point of concurrence for the three medians of a triangle?
7. Which lines or line segments or rays must be drawn or constructed in a triangle to locate its
   a) incenter?
   b) circumcenter?
   c) orthocenter?
   d) centroid?
8. Is it really necessary to construct all three angle bisectors of the angles of a triangle to locate its incenter?
9. Is it really necessary to construct all three perpendicular bisectors of the sides of a triangle to locate its circumcenter?
10. To locate the orthocenter, is it necessary to construct all three altitudes of a right triangle?

11. For what type of triangle are the angle bisectors, the medians, the perpendicular bisectors of sides, and the altitudes all the same?
12. What point on a right triangle is the orthocenter of the right triangle?
13. What point on a right triangle is the circumcenter of the right triangle?
14. Must the centroid of an isosceles triangle lie on the altitude to the base?
15. Draw a triangle and, by construction, find its incenter.
16. Draw an acute triangle and, by construction, find its circumcenter.
17. Draw an obtuse triangle and, by construction, find its circumcenter.
18. Draw an acute triangle and, by construction, find its orthocenter.
19. Draw an obtuse triangle and, by construction, find its orthocenter.

    (HINT: You will have to extend the sides opposite the acute angles.)

20. Draw an acute triangle and, by construction, find the centroid of the triangle.

    (HINT: Begin by constructing the perpendicular bisectors of the sides.)

21. Draw an obtuse triangle and, by construction, find the centroid of the triangle.

    (HINT: Begin by constructing the perpendicular bisectors of the sides.)

22. Is the incenter always located in the interior of the triangle?
23. Is the circumcenter always located in the interior of the triangle?
24. Find the length of the radius of the inscribed circle for a right triangle whose legs measure 6 and 8.
25. Find the distance from the circumcenter to each vertex of an equilateral triangle whose sides have the length 10.
26. A triangle has angles measuring 30°, 30°, and 120°. If the congruent sides measure 6 units each, find the length of the radius of the circumscribed circle.
27. *Given:* Isosceles $\triangle RST$
    $RS = RT = 17$ and $ST = 16$
    Medians $\overline{RZ}$, $\overline{TX}$, and $\overline{SY}$ meet at centroid Q
    Find: RQ and SQ
28. *Given:* Isosceles $\triangle RST$
    $RS = RT = 10$ and $ST = 16$
    Medians $\overline{RZ}$, $\overline{TX}$, and $\overline{SY}$ meet at Q
    Find: RQ and QT

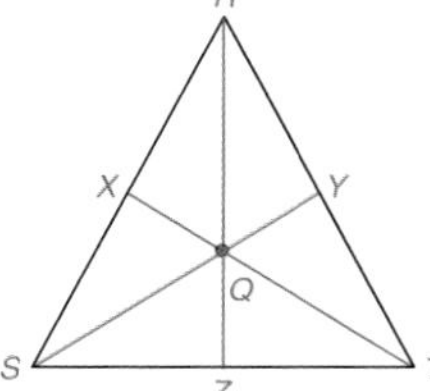

Exercises 27, 28

29. In $\triangle MNP$, medians $\overline{MB}$, $\overline{NA}$, and $\overline{PC}$ intersect at centroid Q.
    a) If $MQ = 8$, find QB.
    b) If $QC = 3$, find PQ.
    c) If $AQ = 3.5$, find AN.

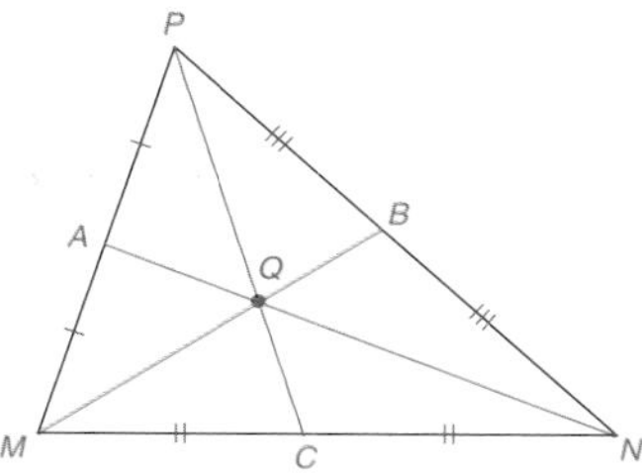

Exercises 29, 30

30. In $\triangle MNP$, medians $\overline{MB}$, $\overline{NA}$, and $\overline{PC}$ intersect at centroid Q.
    a) Find QB if $MQ = 8.2$.
    b) Find PQ if $QC = \frac{7}{2}$.
    c) Find AN if $AQ = 4.6$.
31. Draw a triangle. Construct its inscribed circle.
32. Draw a triangle. Construct its circumscribed circle.
33. For what type of triangle will the incenter and the circumcenter be the same?
34. Does a rectangle have (a) an incenter? (b) a circumcenter?
35. Does a square have (a) an incenter? (b) a circumcenter?
36. Does a regular pentagon have (a) an incenter? (b) a circumcenter?
37. Does a rhombus have (a) an incenter? (b) a circumcenter?
38. Does an isosceles trapezoid have (a) an incenter? (b) a circumcenter?
39. A distributing company plans an Illinois location that would be the same distance from each of its principal delivery sites at Chicago, St. Louis, and Indianapolis. Use a construction method to locate the approximate position of the distributing company.

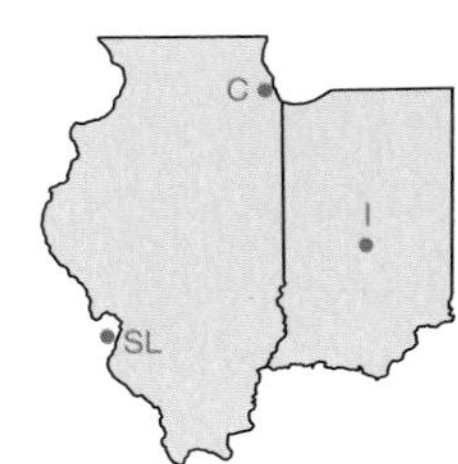

    (NOTE: Trace the outline of the two states on your own paper.)
40. There are plans to locate a disaster response agency in an area that is prone to tornadic activity. The agency is to be located at equal distances from Wichita, Tulsa, and Oklahoma City. Use a construction method to locate the approximate position of the agency.

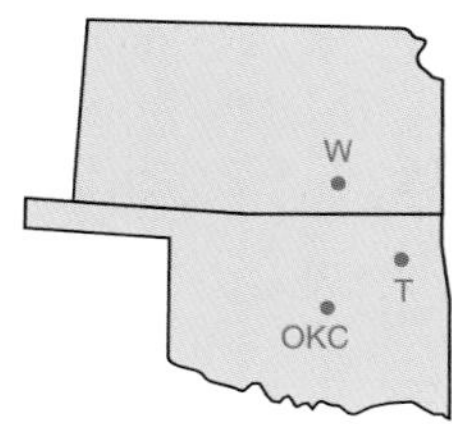

    (NOTE: Trace the outline of the two states on your own paper.)

*41. A circle is inscribed in an isosceles triangle with legs of length 10 in. and a base of length 12 in. Find the length of the radius for the circle.

7.3 More About Regular Polygons

KEY CONCEPTS Regular Polygon | Center and Central Angle of a Regular Polygon | Radius and Apothem of a Regular Polygon

Several interesting properties of regular polygons are developed in this section. For instance, every regular polygon has both an inscribed circle and a circumscribed circle; furthermore, these two circles are concentric. In Example 1, we use bisectors of the angles of a square to locate the center of the inscribed circle. The center, which is found by using the bisectors of any two consecutive angles, is equidistant from the sides of the square.

Reminder

A regular polygon is both equilateral and equiangular.

EXAMPLE 1

Given square $ABCD$ in Figure 7.24(a), construct inscribed $\odot O$.

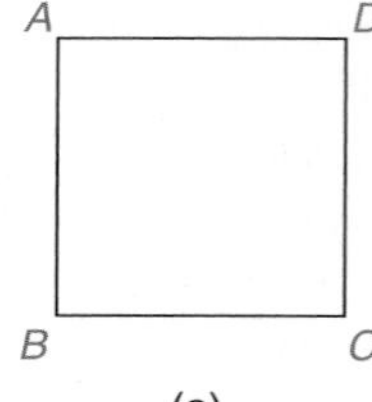

(a)

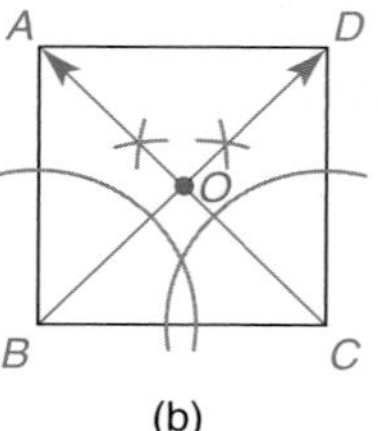

(b)

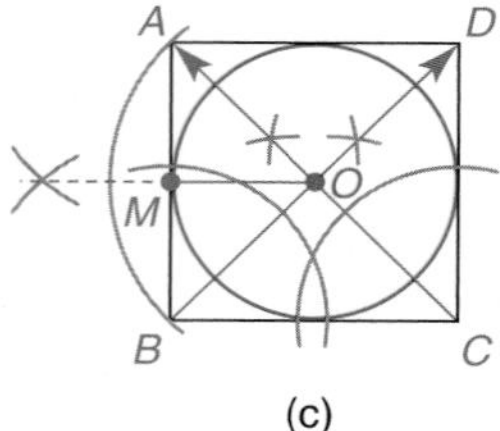

(c)

Figure 7.24

Solution Figure 7.24(b): The center of an inscribed circle must lie at the same distance from each side. Center O is the point of concurrency of the angle bisectors of the square. Thus, we construct the angle bisectors of $\angle B$ and $\angle C$ to identify point O.

Figure 7.24(c): Constructing $\overline{OM} \perp \overline{AB}$, OM is the distance from O to $\overline{AB}$ and the length of the radius of the inscribed circle. Finally we construct inscribed $\odot O$ with radius $\overline{OM}$ as shown. ■

In Example 2, we use the perpendicular bisectors of two consecutive sides of a regular hexagon to locate the center of the circumscribed circle. The center determines a point that is equidistant from the vertices of the hexagon.

EXAMPLE 2

Given regular hexagon $MNPQRS$ in Figure 7.25(a), construct circumscribed $\odot X$.

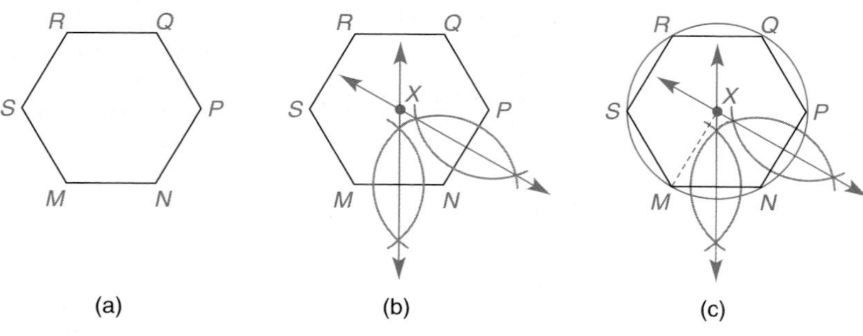

Figure 7.25

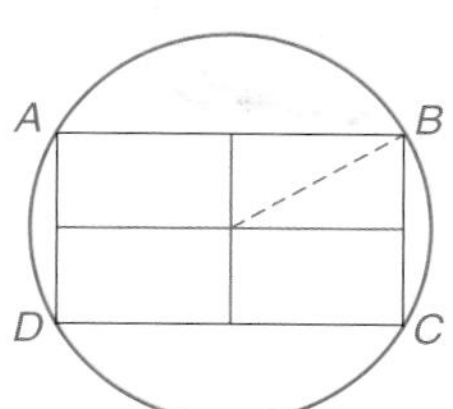

Figure 7.26

Solution Figure 7.25(b): The center of a circumscribed circle must lie at the same distance from each vertex of the hexagon. Center X is the point of concurrency of the perpendicular bisectors of two consecutive sides of the hexagon. In Figure 7.25(b), we construct the perpendicular bisectors of $\overline{MN}$ and $\overline{NP}$ to locate point X.

Figure 7.25(c): Where XM is the distance from X to vertex M, we use radius $\overline{XM}$ to construct circumscribed $\odot X$. ■

For a rectangle, which is not a regular polygon, we can only circumscribe the circle (see Figure 7.26). Why? For a rhombus (also not a regular polygon), we can only inscribe the circle (see Figure 7.27). Why?

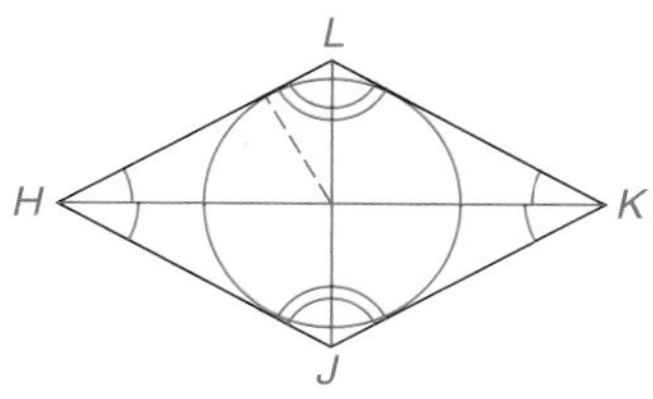

Figure 7.27

As we shall see, we can construct both inscribed and circumscribed circles for regular polygons because they are both equilateral and equiangular. A few of the regular polygons are shown in Figure 7.28.

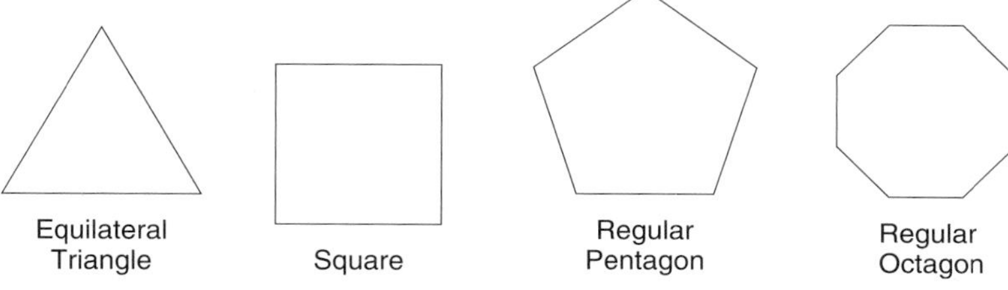

Figure 7.28

SSG *Exs. 1–6*

In Chapter 2, we saw that the sum of the measures of the interior angles of a polygon with n sides is given by $S = (n - 2)180$. In turn, the measure I of each interior angle of a regular polygon of n sides is given by $I = \frac{(n-2)180}{n}$. The sum of the measures of the exterior angles of any polygon is always 360°. Thus, the measure E of each exterior angle of a regular polygon of n sides is $E = \frac{360}{n}$.

EXAMPLE 3

a) Find the measure of each interior angle of a regular polygon with 15 sides.
b) Find the number of sides of a regular polygon if each interior angle measures 144°.

Solution

a) Because all of the n angles have equal measures, the formula for the measure of each interior angle,

$$I = \frac{(n - 2)180}{n}$$

becomes

$$I = \frac{(15 - 2)180}{15}$$

which simplifies to 156°.

b) Because $I = 144°$, we can determine the number of sides by solving the equation

$$\frac{(n-2)180}{n} = 144$$

Then

$$\begin{aligned}(n-2)180 &= 144n\\ 180n - 360 &= 144n\\ 36n &= 360\\ n &= 10\end{aligned}$$

NOTE: In Example 3(a), we could have found the measure of each exterior angle and then used the fact that the interior angle is its supplement. With $n = 15$, $E = \frac{360°}{n}$ leads to $E = 24°$. It follows that $I = 180° - 24°$ or $156°$. In Example 3(b), the fact that $I = 144°$ leads to $E = 36°$. In turn, $E = \frac{360°}{n}$ becomes $36° = \frac{360°}{n}$, which leads to $n = 10$. ■

SSG *Exs. 7, 8*

Regular polygons allow us to inscribe and to circumscribe a circle. The proof of the following theorem will establish the following relationships:

1. The centers of the inscribed and circumscribed circles of a regular polygon are the same.
2. The angle bisectors of two consecutive angles or the perpendicular bisectors of two consecutive sides can be used to locate the common center of the inscribed circle and the circumscribed circle.
3. The inscribed circle's radius is any line segment from the center drawn perpendicular to a side of the regular polygon; the radius of the circumscribed circle joins the center to any vertex of the regular polygon.

THEOREM 7.3.1

A circle can be circumscribed about (or inscribed in) any regular polygon.

GIVEN: Regular polygon *ABCDEF* [See Figure 7.29(a).]

PROVE: A circle *O* can be circumscribed about *ABCDEF* and a circle with center *O* can be inscribed in *ABCDEF*.

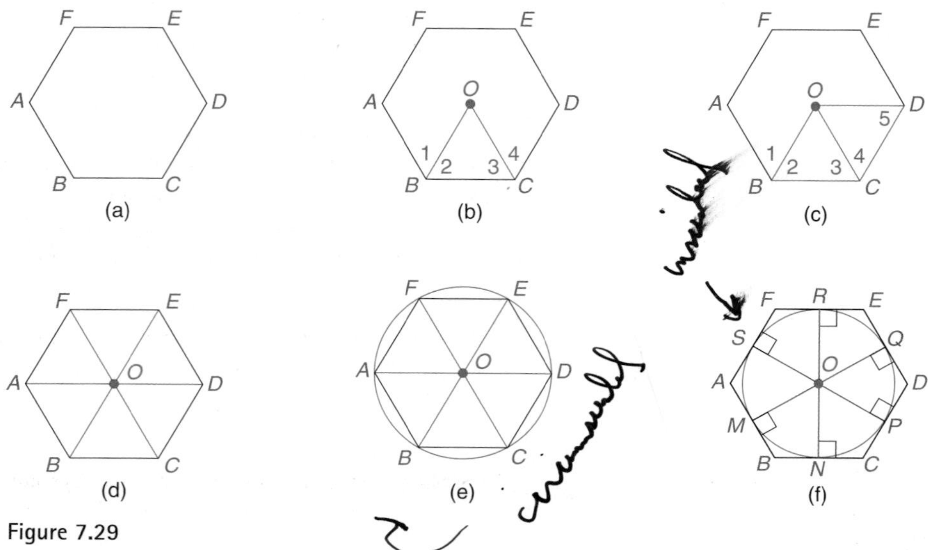

Figure 7.29

PROOF: Let point O be the point at which the angle bisectors for $\angle ABC$ and $\angle BCD$ meet. [See Figure 7.29(b) on page 340.] Then $\angle 1 \cong \angle 2$ and $\angle 3 \cong \angle 4$.

Because $\angle ABC \cong \angle BCD$ (by the definition of a regular polygon), it follows that

$$\frac{1}{2}\text{m}\angle ABC = \frac{1}{2}\text{m}\angle BCD$$

In turn, $\text{m}\angle 2 = \text{m}\angle 3$, so $\angle 2 \cong \angle 3$. Then $\overline{OB} \cong \overline{OC}$ (sides opposite $\cong$ $\angle$s of a $\triangle$ are also $\cong$).

From the facts that $\angle 3 \cong \angle 4$, $\overline{OC} \cong \overline{OC}$, and $\overline{BC} \cong \overline{CD}$, it follows that $\triangle OCB \cong \triangle OCD$ by SAS. [See Figure 7.29(c).] In turn, $\overline{OC} \cong \overline{OD}$ by CPCTC, so $\angle 4 \cong \angle 5$ because these lie opposite $\overline{OC}$ and $\overline{OD}$.

Because $\angle 5 \cong \angle 4$ and $\text{m}\angle 4 = \frac{1}{2}\text{m}\angle BCD$, it follows that $\text{m}\angle 5 = \frac{1}{2}\text{m}\angle BCD$. But $\angle BCD \cong \angle CDE$ because these are angles of a regular polygon. Thus, $\text{m}\angle 5 = \frac{1}{2}\text{m}\angle CDE$, and $\overline{OD}$ bisects $\angle CDE$.

By continuing this procedure, we can show that $\overline{OE}$ bisects $\angle DEF$, $\overline{OF}$ bisects $\angle EFA$, and $\overline{OA}$ bisects $\angle FAB$. The resulting triangles, $\triangle AOB$, $\triangle BOC$, $\triangle COD$, $\triangle DOE$, $\triangle EOF$, and $\triangle FOA$, are congruent by ASA. [See Figure 7.29(d).] By CPCTC, $\overline{OA} \cong \overline{OB} \cong \overline{OC} \cong \overline{OD} \cong \overline{OE} \cong \overline{OF}$. With O as center and $\overline{OA}$ as radius, circle O can be circumscribed about $ABCDEF$, as shown in Figure 7.29(e).

Because corresponding altitudes of $\cong$ $\triangle$s are also congruent, we see that $\overline{OM} \cong \overline{ON} \cong \overline{OP} \cong \overline{OQ} \cong \overline{OR} \cong \overline{OS}$, where these are the altitudes to the bases of the triangles.

Again with O as center, but now with a radius equal in length to OM, we complete the inscribed circle in $ABCDEF$. [See Figure 7.29(f).] ■

In the proof of Theorem 7.3.1, a regular hexagon was drawn. The method of proof would not change, regardless of the number of sides of the polygon chosen. In the proof, point O was the common center of the circumscribed and inscribed circles for $ABCDEF$.

Because any regular polygon can be inscribed in a circle, any regular polygon is cyclic.

DEFINITION

The **center of a regular polygon** is the common center for the inscribed and circumscribed circles of the polygon.

NOTE: The preceding definition does not tell us how to locate the center of a regular polygon. The center is the intersection of the angle bisectors of two consecutive angles; alternatively, the intersection of the perpendicular bisectors of two consecutive sides can be used to locate the center of the regular polygon. Note that a regular polygon has a center, whether or not either of the related circles is shown.

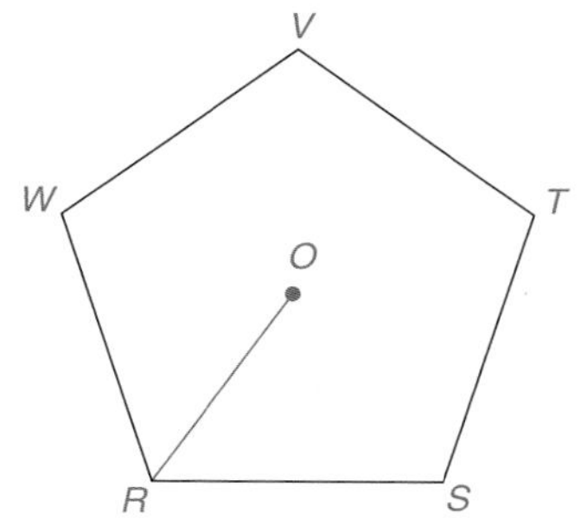

Figure 7.30

In Figure 7.30, point O is the center of the regular pentagon $RSTVW$. In this figure, $\overline{OR}$ is called a "radius" of the regular pentagon.

DEFINITION

A **radius of a regular polygon** is any line segment that joins the center of the regular polygon to one of its vertices.

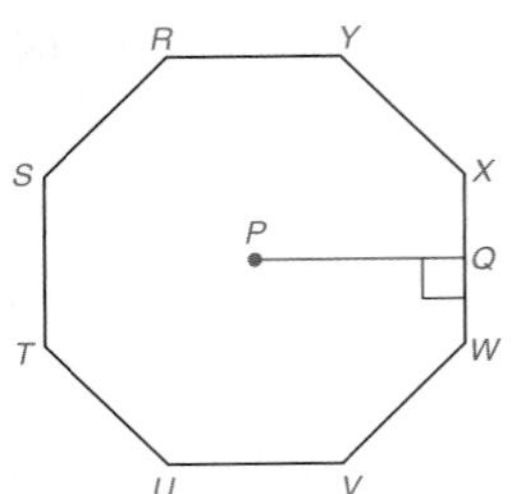

Figure 7.31

In the proof of Theorem 7.3.1, we saw that "All radii of a regular polygon are congruent."

DEFINITION

An **apothem** of a regular polygon is any line segment drawn from the center of that polygon perpendicular to one of the sides.

In regular octagon *RSTUVWXY* with center *P* (see Figure 7.31), the segment $\overline{PQ}$ is an apothem. Any regular polygon of *n* sides has *n* apothems and *n* radii. The proof of Theorem 7.3.1 establishes that "All apothems of a regular polygon are congruent."

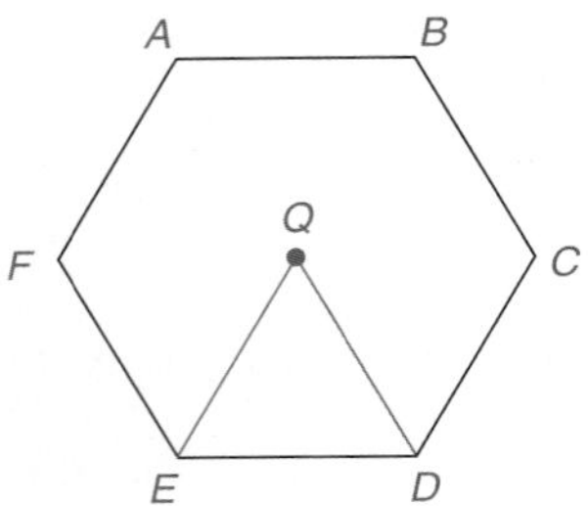

Figure 7.32

DEFINITION

A **central angle of a regular polygon** is an angle formed by two consecutive radii of the regular polygon.

In regular hexagon *ABCDEF* with center *Q* (see Figure 7.32), angle *EQD* is a central angle. Due to the congruences of the triangles in the proof of Theorem 7.3.1, we see that "All central angles of a regular polygon are congruent." This leads to Theorem 7.3.2.

THEOREM 7.3.2

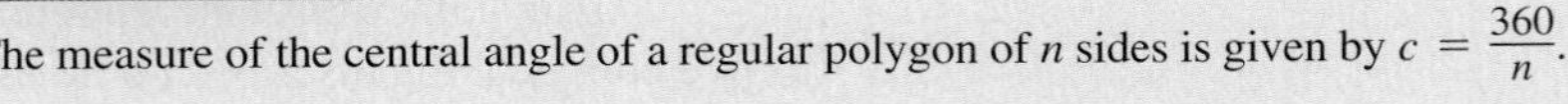

The measure of the central angle of a regular polygon of *n* sides is given by $c = \frac{360}{n}$.

We apply Theorem 7.3.2 in Example 4.

EXAMPLE 4

a) Find the measure of the central angle of a regular polygon of 9 sides.
b) Find the number of sides of a regular polygon whose central angle measures 72°.

Solution

a) $c = \frac{360}{9} = 40°$
b) $72 = \frac{360}{n} \rightarrow 72n = 360 \rightarrow n = 5$ sides ■

The next two theorems follow from the proof of Theorem 7.3.1.

THEOREM 7.3.3

Any radius of a regular polygon bisects the angle at the vertex to which it is drawn.

THEOREM 7.3.4

Any apothem of a regular polygon bisects the side of the polygon to which it is drawn.

EXAMPLE 5

Given that each side of regular hexagon $ABCDEF$ has the length 4 in., find the length of:

a) Radius $\overline{QE}$
b) Apothem $\overline{QG}$

A B F C Q E G D

Solution

a) By Theorem 7.3.2, the measure of $\angle EQD$ is $\frac{360°}{6}$, or 60°. With $\overline{QE} \cong \overline{QD}$, $\triangle QED$ is equiangular and equilateral. Then $QE = 4$ in.

b) With apothem $\overline{QG}$ as shown, $\triangle QEG$ is a 30°-60°-90° triangle in which $m\angle EQG = 30°$. By Theorem 7.3.4, $EG = 2$ in. With QG opposite the 60° angle of $\triangle QEG$, it follows that $QG = 2\sqrt{3}$ in. ■

Exs. 9–20

Exercises 7.3

1. Describe, if possible, how you would inscribe a circle within kite $ABCD$.

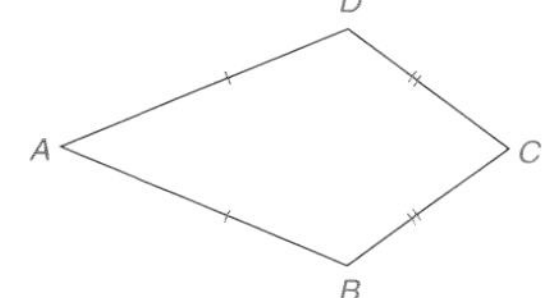

Exercises 1, 2

2. What condition must be satisfied for it to be possible to circumscribe a circle about kite $ABCD$?

3. Describe, if possible, how you would inscribe a circle in rhombus $JKLM$.

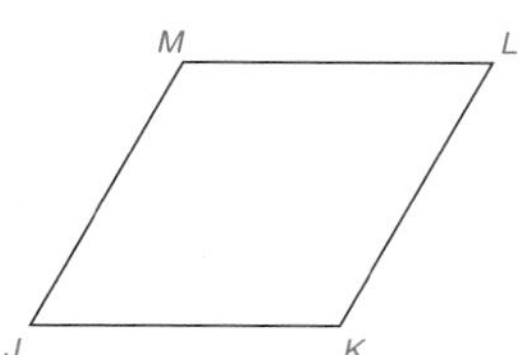

4. What condition must be satisfied for it to be possible to circumscribe a circle about trapezoid $RSTV$?

In Exercises 5 to 8, perform constructions.

5. Inscribe a regular octagon within a circle.
6. Inscribe an equilateral triangle within a circle.
7. Circumscribe a square about a circle.
8. Circumscribe an equilateral triangle about a circle.
9. Find the perimeter of a regular octagon if the length of each side is 3.4 in.
10. In a regular polygon with each side of length 6.5 cm, the perimeter is 130 cm. How many sides does the regular polygon have?
11. If the perimeter of a regular dodecagon (12 sides) is 99.6 cm, how long is each side?
12. If the apothem of a square measures 5 cm, find the perimeter of the square.
13. Find the lengths of the apothem and the radius of a square whose sides have length 10 in.
14. Find the lengths of the apothem and the radius of a regular hexagon whose sides have length 6 cm.
15. Find the lengths of the side and the radius of an equilateral triangle whose apothem's length is 8 ft.
16. Find the lengths of the side and the radius of a regular hexagon whose apothem's length is 10 m.
17. Find the measure of the central angle of a regular polygon of
    a) 3 sides. c) 5 sides.
    b) 4 sides. d) 6 sides.
18. Find the measure of the central angle of a regular polygon of
    a) 8 sides. c) 9 sides.
    b) 10 sides. d) 12 sides.
19. Find the number of sides of a regular polygon that has a central angle measuring
    a) 90°. c) 60°.
    b) 45°. d) 24°.
20. Find the number of sides of a regular polygon that has a central angle measuring
    a) 30°. c) 36°.
    b) 72°. d) 20°.

21. Find the measure of each interior angle of a regular polygon whose central angle measures

a) 40°.
b) 45°.
c) 60°.
d) 90°.

22. Find the measure of each exterior angle of a regular polygon whose central angle measures

a) 30°.
b) 40°.
c) 45°.
d) 120°.

23. Find the number of sides for a regular polygon in which the measure of each interior angle is 60° greater than the measure of each central angle.

24. Find the number of sides for a regular polygon in which the measure of each interior angle is 90° greater than the measure of each central angle.

25. Is there a regular polygon for which each central angle measures

a) 40°?
b) 50°?
c) 60°?
d) 70°?

26. Given regular hexagon $ABCDEF$ with each side of length 6, find the length of diagonal $\overline{AC}$.

(HINT: With G on $\overline{AC}$, draw $\overline{BG} \perp \overline{AC}$.)

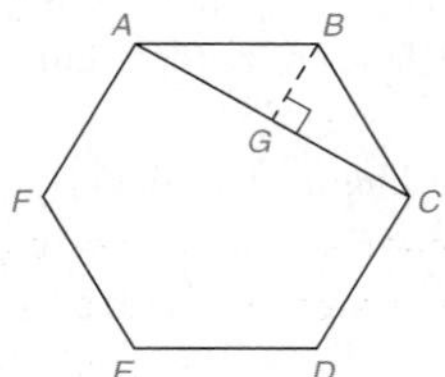

27. Given regular octagon $RSTUVWXY$ with each side of length 4, find the length of diagonal RU.

(HINT: Extended sides, as shown, form a square.)

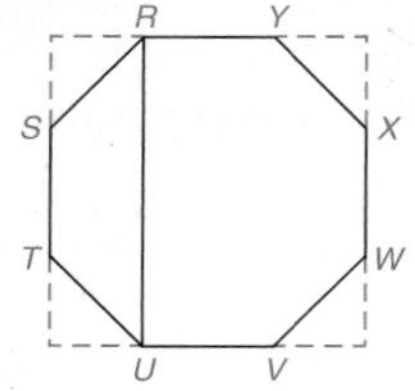

28. Given that $RSTVQ$ is a regular pentagon and $\triangle PQR$ is equilateral in the figure below, determine

a) the *type* of triangle represented by $\triangle VPQ$.
b) the *type* of quadrilateral represented by $TVPS$.

29. *Given:* Regular pentagon $RSTVQ$ with equilateral $\triangle PQR$

Find: $m\angle VPS$

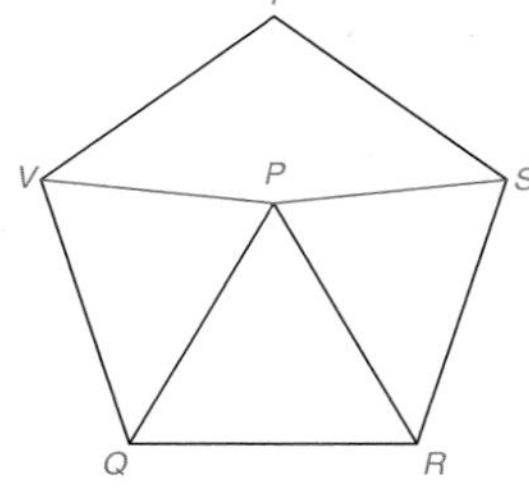

Exercises 28, 29

30. *Given:* Regular pentagon $JKLMN$ (not shown) with diagonals $\overline{LN}$ and $\overline{KN}$

Find: $m\angle LNK$

***31.** *Prove:* If a circle is divided into n congruent arcs ($n \geq 3$), the chords determined by joining consecutive endpoints of these arcs form a regular polygon.

***32.** *Prove:* If a circle is divided into n congruent arcs ($n \geq 3$), the tangents drawn at the endpoints of these arcs form a regular polygon.

▶▶▶ PERSPECTIVE ON HISTORY

The Value of π

In geometry, any two figures that have the same shape are described as similar. Because all circles have the same shape, we say that all circles are similar to each other. Just as a proportionality exists among the corresponding sides of similar triangles, we can demonstrate a proportionality among the circumferences (distances around) and diameters (distances across) of circles. By representing the circumferences of the circles in Figure 7.33 by C_1, C_2, and C_3 and their corresponding lengths of diameters by d_1, d_2, and d_3, we claim that

$$\frac{C_1}{d_1} = \frac{C_2}{d_2} = \frac{C_3}{d_3} = k$$

for some constant of proportionality k.

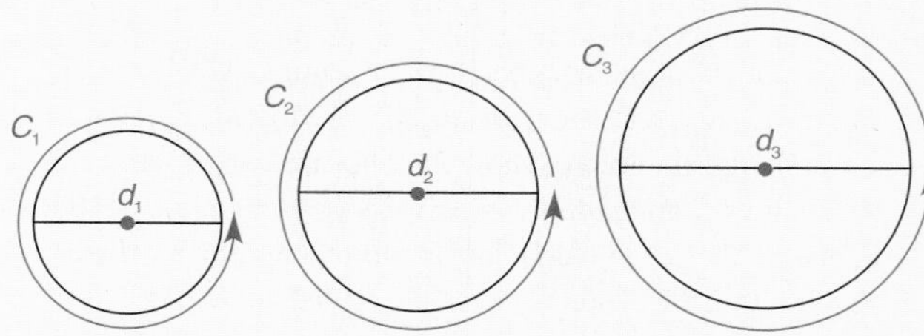

Figure 7.33

We denote the constant k described above by the Greek letter π. Thus, $\pi = \frac{C}{d}$ in any circle. It follows that $C = \pi d$ or $C = 2\pi r$ (because $d = 2r$ in any circle). In applying these formulas for the circumference of a circle, we often leave π in the answer so that the result is exact. When an approximation for the circumference (and later for the area) of a circle is needed, several common substitutions are used for π. Among these are $\pi \approx \frac{22}{7}$ and $\pi \approx 3.14$. A calculator may display the value $\pi \approx 3.1415926535$.

Because π is needed in many applications involving the circumference or area of a circle, its approximation is often necessary; but finding an accurate approximation of π was not quickly or easily done. The formula for circumference can be expressed as $C = 2\pi r$, but the formula for the area of the circle is $A = \pi r^2$. This and other area formulas will be given more attention in Chapter 8.

Several references to the value of π are made in literature. One of the earliest comes from the Bible; the passage from I Kings, Chapter 7, verse 23, describes the distance around a vat as three times the distance across the vat (which suggests that π equals 3, a very rough approximation). Perhaps no greater accuracy was needed in some applications of that time.

In the content of the Rhind papyrus (a document over 3000 years old), the Egyptian scribe Ahmes gives the formula for the area of a circle as $\left(d - \frac{1}{9}d\right)^2$. To determine the Egyptian approximation of π, we need to expand this expression as follows:

$$\left(d - \frac{1}{9}d\right)^2 = \left(\frac{8}{9}d\right)^2 = \left(\frac{8}{9}\cdot 2r\right)^2 = \left(\frac{16}{9}r\right)^2 = \frac{256}{81}r^2$$

In the formula for the area of the circle, the value of π is the multiplier (coefficient) of r^2. Because this coefficient is $\frac{256}{81}$ (which has the decimal equivalent of 3.1604), the Egyptians had a better approximation of π than was given in the book of I Kings.

Archimedes, the brilliant Greek geometer, knew that the formula for the area of a circle was $A = \frac{1}{2}Cr$ (with C the circumference and r the length of radius). His formula was equivalent to the one we use today and is developed as follows:

$$A = \frac{1}{2}Cr = \frac{1}{2}(2\pi r)r = \pi r^2$$

The second proposition of Archimedes' work *Measure of the Circle* develops a relationship between the area of a circle and the area of the square in which it is inscribed. (See Figure 7.34.) Specifically, Archimedes claimed that the ratio of the area of the circle to that of the square was 11:14. This leads to the following set of equations and to an approximation of the value of π.

$$\frac{\pi r^2}{(2r)^2} \approx \frac{11}{14}$$
$$\frac{\pi r^2}{4r^2} \approx \frac{11}{14}$$
$$\frac{\pi}{4} \approx \frac{11}{14}$$
$$\pi \approx 4\cdot\frac{11}{14} \approx \frac{22}{7}$$

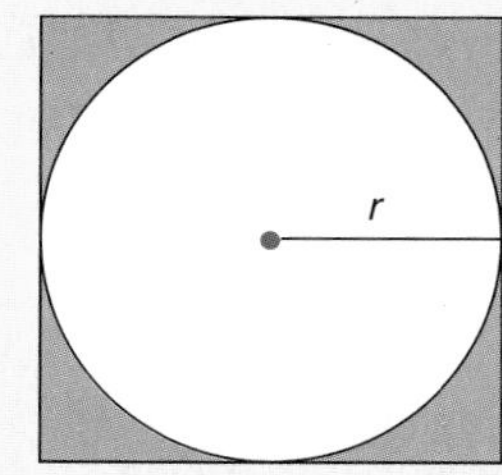

Figure 7.34

Archimedes later improved his approximation of π by showing that

$$3\frac{10}{71} < \pi < 3\frac{1}{7}$$

Today's calculators provide excellent approximations for the irrational number π. We should recall, however, that π is an irrational number that can be expressed as an exact value only by the symbol π.

PERSPECTIVE ON APPLICATION

The Nine-Point Circle

In the study of geometry, there is a curiosity known as the Nine-Point Circle—a curiosity because its practical value consists of the reasoning needed to verify its plausibility.

In $\triangle ABC$, in Figure 7.35 we locate these points:

> M, N, and P, the midpoints of the sides of $\triangle ABC$,
> D, E, and F, points on $\triangle ABC$ determined by its altitudes, and X, Y, and Z, the midpoints of the line segments determined by orthocenter O and the vertices of $\triangle ABC$.

Through these nine points, it is possible to draw or construct the circle shown in Figure 7.35.

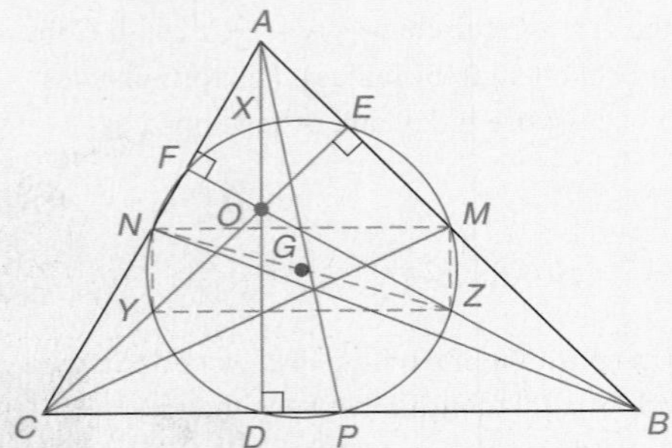

Figure 7.35

To understand why the nine-point circle can be drawn, we show that the quadrilateral $NMZY$ is both a parallelogram and a rectangle. Because $\overline{NM}$ joins the midpoints of $\overline{AC}$ and $\overline{AB}$, we know that $\overline{NM} \parallel \overline{CB}$ and $NM = \frac{1}{2}(CB)$. Likewise, Y and Z are midpoints of the sides of $\triangle OBC$, so $\overline{YZ} \parallel \overline{CB}$ and $YZ = \frac{1}{2}(CB)$. By Theorem 4.2.1, $NMZY$ is a parallelogram. Then $\overline{NY}$ must be parallel to $\overline{MZ}$. With $\overline{CB} \perp \overline{AD}$, it follows that $\overline{NM}$ must be perpendicular to $\overline{AD}$ as well. In turn, $\overline{MZ} \perp \overline{NM}$, and $NMZY$ is a rectangle in Figure 7.35. It is possible to circumscribe a circle about any rectangle; in fact, the length of the radius of the circumscribed circle is one-half the length of a diagonal of the rectangle, so we choose $r = \frac{1}{2}(NZ) = NG$. This circle certainly contains the points N, M, Z, and Y.

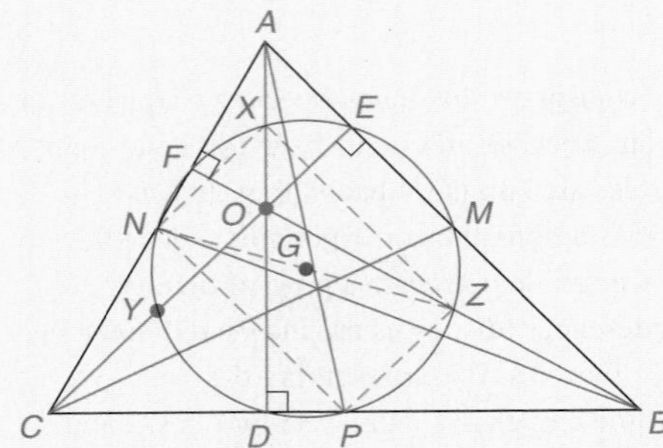

Figure 7.36

Although we do not provide the details, it can also be shown that quadrilateral $XZPN$ of Figure 7.36 is a rectangle as well. Further, $\overline{NZ}$ is also a diagonal of rectangle $XZPN$. Then we can choose the radius of the circumscribed circle for rectangle $XZPN$ to have the length $r = \frac{1}{2}(NZ) = NG$. Because it has the same center G and the same length of radius r as the circle that was circumscribed about rectangle $NMZY$, we see that the same circle must contain points N, X, M, Z, P, and Y.

Finally, we need to show that the circle in Figure 7.37 with center G and radius $r = \frac{1}{2}(NZ)$ will contain the points D, E, and F. This can be done by an indirect argument. If we suppose that these points do *not* lie on the circle, then we contradict the fact that an angle inscribed in a semicircle must be a right angle. Of course, $\overline{AD}$, $\overline{BF}$, and $\overline{CE}$ were altitudes of $\triangle ABC$, so inscribed angles at D, E, and F must measure 90°; in turn, these angles must lie inside semicircles. In Figure 7.35, $\angle NFZ$ intercepts an arc (a semicircle) determined by diameter $\overline{NZ}$. So D, E, and F are on the same circle that has center G and radius r. Thus, the circle described in the preceding paragraphs is the anticipated nine-point circle!

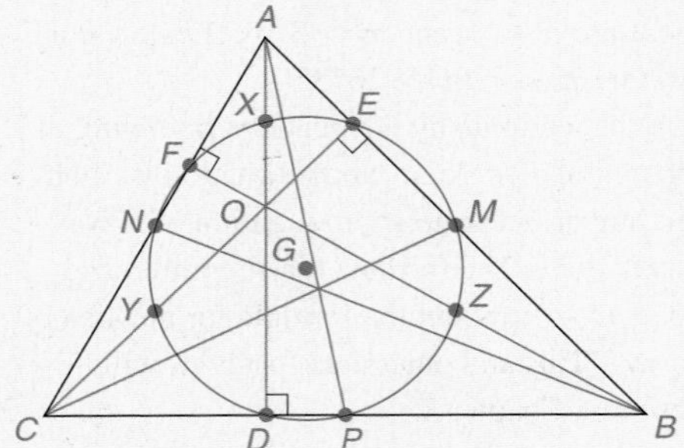

Figure 7.37

Summary

A LOOK BACK AT CHAPTER 7

In Chapter 7, we used the locus of points concept to establish concurrence of lines relationships in Section 7.2. In turn, these concepts of locus and concurrence allowed us to show that a regular polygon has both an inscribed and a circumscribed circle; in particular, these two circles have a common center.

A LOOK AHEAD TO CHAPTER 8

One goal of the next chapter is to deal with the areas of triangles, certain quadrilaterals, and regular polygons. We will consider perimeters of polygons and the circumference of a circle. The area of a circle and the area of a sector of a circle will be discussed. Special right triangles will play an important role in determining the areas of these plane figures.

KEY CONCEPTS

7.1
Locus of Points in a Plane • Locus of Points in Space

7.2
Concurrent Lines • Incenter • Incircle • Circumcenter • Circumcircle • Orthocenter • Centroid

7.3
Regular Polygon • Center and Central Angle • Radius • Apothem

TABLE 7.1

▶ Selected Locus Problems (in a plane)

LOCUS	FIGURE	DESCRIPTION
Locus of points that are at a fixed distance r from fixed point P	P	The circle with center P and radius r
Locus of points that are equidistant from the sides of an angle	A, D, B, C	The bisector $\overrightarrow{BD}$ of $\angle ABC$
Locus of points that are equidistant from the endpoints of a line segment	ℓ, R, S	The perpendicular bisector ℓ of $\overline{RS}$

continued

TABLE 7.1 *(continued)*

▶ Concurrence of Lines (in a triangle)

TYPE OF LINES	FIGURE	POINT OF CONCURRENCE
Angle bisectors	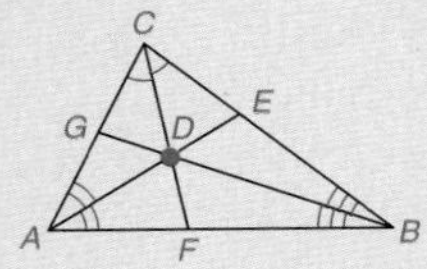 C, G, D, E, A, F, B	Incenter D of $\triangle ABC$
Perpendicular bisectors of the sides	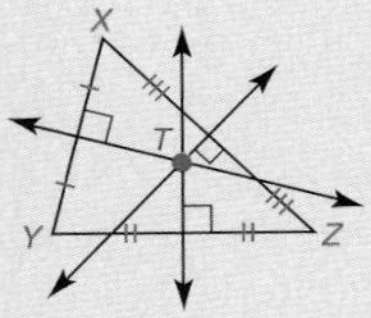 X, T, Y, Z	Circumcenter T of $\triangle XYZ$
Altitudes	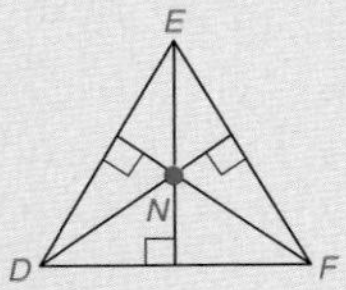 E, N, D, F	Orthocenter N of $\triangle DEF$
Medians	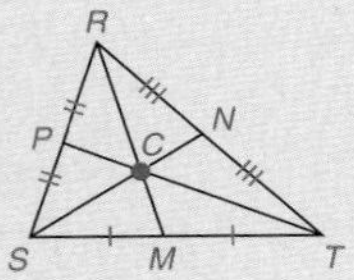 R, P, C, N, S, M, T	Centroid C of $\triangle RST$

▶ Properties of Regular Polygons

REGULAR POLYGON	FIGURE	DESCRIPTION
Point O is the center of regular pentagon $ABCDE$.	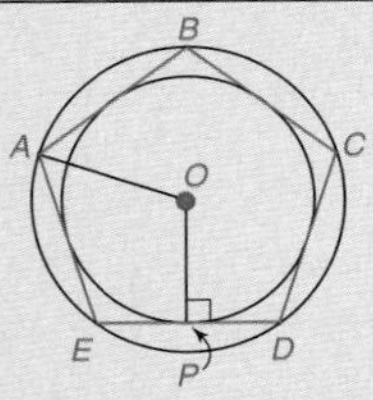 B, A, C, O, E, P, D	$\overline{OA}$ is a radius of $ABCDE$; $\overline{OA}$ bisects $\angle BAE$. $\overline{OP}$ is an apothem of $ABCDE$; $\overline{OP}$ is the perpendicular bisector of side $\overline{ED}$.

Chapter 7 REVIEW EXERCISES

In Review Exercises 1 to 6, use the figure shown.

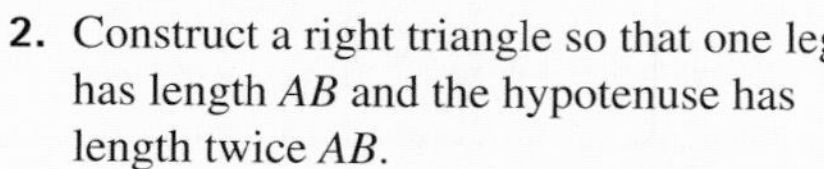

1. Construct a right triangle so that one leg has length AB and the other leg has length twice AB.
2. Construct a right triangle so that one leg has length AB and the hypotenuse has length twice AB.
3. Construct an isosceles triangle with vertex angle B and legs the length of $\overline{AB}$ (from the line segment shown).
4. Construct an isosceles triangle with vertex angle B and an altitude with the length of $\overline{AB}$ from vertex B to the base.
5. Construct a square with sides of length AB.
6. Construct a rhombus with side $\overline{AB}$ and $\angle ABC$.

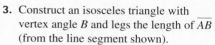

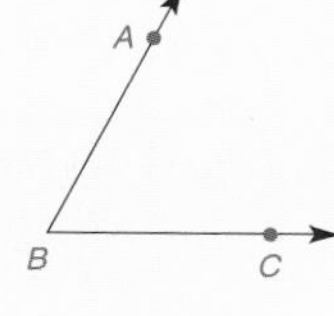

Exercises 1–6

In Review Exercises 7 to 13, sketch and describe the locus in a plane.

7. Find the locus of points equidistant from the sides of $\angle ABC$.
8. Find the locus of points that are 1 in. from a given point B.

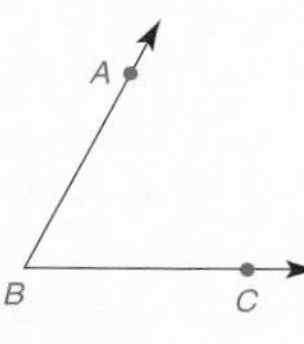

Exercises 7, 8

9. Find the locus of points equidistant from points D and E.
10. Find the locus of points that are $\frac{1}{2}$ in. from $\overleftrightarrow{DE}$.

Exercises 9, 10

11. Find the locus of the midpoints of the radii of a circle.
12. Find the locus of the centers of all circles passing through two given points.
13. What is the locus of the center of a penny that rolls around and remains tangent to a half-dollar?

In Exercises 14 to 17, sketch and describe the locus in space.

14. Find the locus of points 2 cm from a given point A.
15. Find the locus of points 1 cm from a given plane P.
16. Find the locus of points less than 3 units from a given point.
17. Find the locus of points equidistant from two parallel planes.

In Review Exercises 18 to 23, use construction methods with the accompanying figure.

18. *Given:* $\triangle ABC$
    Find: The incenter
19. *Given:* $\triangle ABC$
    Find: The circumcenter
20. *Given:* $\triangle ABC$
    Find: The orthocenter
21. *Given:* $\triangle ABC$
    Find: The centroid

Exercises 18–23

22. Use the result from Exercise 18 to inscribe a circle in $\triangle ABC$.
23. Use the result from Exercise 19 to circumscribe a circle about $\triangle ABC$.
24. *Given:* $\triangle ABC$ with medians $\overline{AE}$, $\overline{DC}$, $\overline{BF}$
    Find: a) BG if $BF = 18$
    b) GE if $AG = 4$
    c) DG if $CG = 4\sqrt{3}$

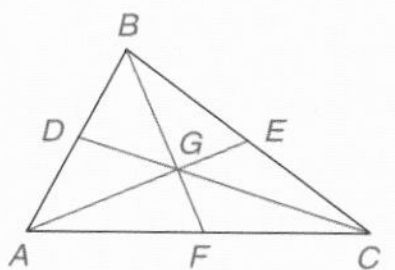

Exercises 24, 25

25. *Given:* $\triangle ABC$ with medians $\overline{AE}$, $\overline{DC}$, $\overline{BF}$
    $AG = 2x + 2y$, $GE = 2x - y$
    $BG = 3y + 1$, $GF = x$
    Find: BF and AE
26. For a regular pentagon, find the measure of each
    a) central angle.
    b) interior angle.
    c) exterior angle.
27. For a regular decagon (10 sides), find the measure of each
    a) central angle.
    b) interior angle.
    c) exterior angle.
28. In a regular polygon, each central angle measures 45°.
    a) How many sides does the regular polygon have?
    b) If each side measures 5 cm and each apothem is approximately 6 cm in length, what is the perimeter of the polygon?
29. In a regular polygon, the apothem measures 3 in. Each side of the same regular polygon measures 6 in.
    a) Find the perimeter of the regular polygon.
    b) Find the length of radius for this polygon.

30. Can a circle be circumscribed about each of the following figures?
 a) Parallelogram c) Rectangle
 b) Rhombus d) Square

31. Can a circle be inscribed in each of the following figures?
 a) Parallelogram c) Rectangle
 b) Rhombus d) Square

32. The length of the radius of a circle inscribed in an equilateral triangle is 7 in. Find the length of radius of the triangle.

33. The length of the radius of a circle inscribed in a regular hexagon is 10 cm. Find the perimeter of the hexagon.

Chapter 7 TEST

1. Draw and describe the locus of points in the plane that are equidistant from parallel lines ℓ and m.

 ____

 ____

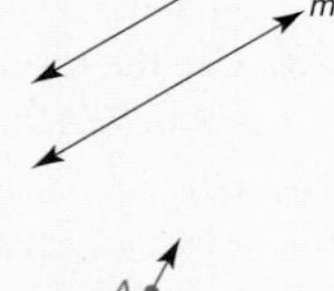

2. Draw and describe the locus of points in the plane that are equidistant from the sides of $\angle ABC$.

 ____

 ____

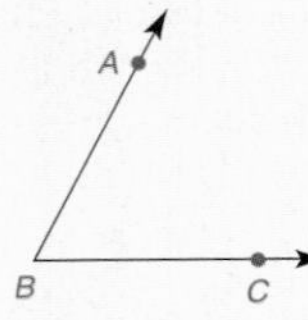

3. Draw and describe the locus of points in the plane that are equidistant from the endpoints of $\overline{DE}$.

 ____

 ____

4. Describe the locus of points in a plane that are at a distance of 3 cm from point P.

 ____

 ____

• P

Exercises 4, 5

5. Describe the locus of points *in space* that are at a distance of 3 cm from point P.

 ____

 ____

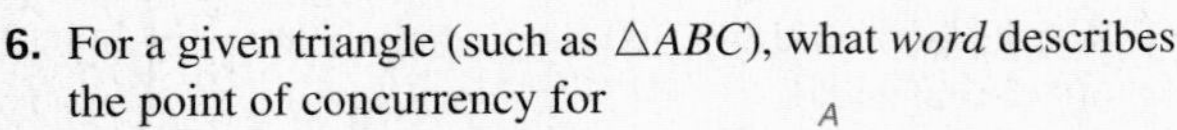

6. For a given triangle (such as $\triangle ABC$), what *word* describes the point of concurrency for
 a) the three angle bisectors? ____________________
 b) the three medians? ____________________

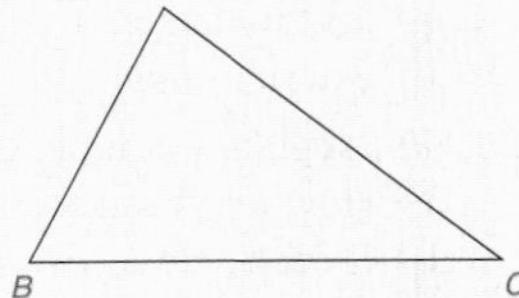

Exercises 6, 7

7. For a given triangle (such as $\triangle ABC$), what *word* describes the point of concurrency for
 a) the three perpendicular bisectors of sides? __________
 b) the three altitudes? ____________

8. In what type of triangle are the angle bisectors, perpendicular bisectors of sides, altitudes, and medians the same? ____________

9. Which of the following *must be* concurrent at an interior point of any triangle?
 angle bisectors perpendicular bisectors of sides
 altitudes medians ____________________

10. Classify as true/false:
 a) A circle can be inscribed in any regular polygon. ____________
 b) A regular polygon can be circumscribed about any circle. ____________
 c) A circle can be inscribed in any rectangle. ____________
 d) A circle can be circumscribed about any rhombus. ____________

11. An equilateral triangle has a radius of length 3 in. Find the length of
 a) an apothem. ____________
 b) a side. ____________

12. For a regular pentagon, find the measure of each
 a) central angle. ____________
 b) interior angle. ____________

13. The measure of each central angle of a regular polygon is 36°. How many sides does this regular polygon have? ____________

14. For a regular octagon, the length of the apothem is approximately 12 cm and the length of the radius is approximately 13 cm. To the nearest centimeter, find the perimeter of the regular octagon. ____________

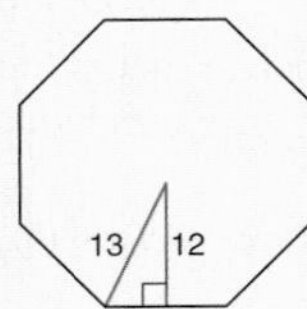

15. For regular hexagon $ABCDEF$, the length of side $\overline{AB}$ is 4 in. Find the exact length of
 a) diagonal $\overline{AC}$. ____________
 b) diagonal $\overline{AD}$. ____________

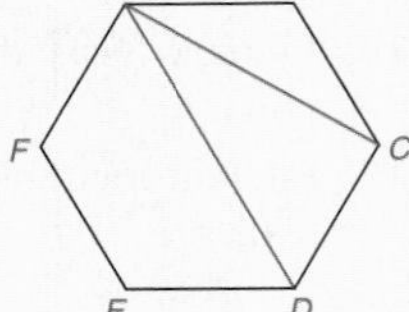

Areas of Polygons and Circles

Chapter 8

© Digital Vision/Getty Images

CHAPTER OUTLINE

Additional Video explanation of concepts, sample problems, and applications are available on DVD. 

Powerful! The unique shape and the massive size of the Pentagon in Washington, D.C., manifest the notion of strength. In this chapter, we introduce the concept of area. The area of an enclosed plane region is a measure of size that has applications in construction, farming, real estate, and more. Some of the units that are used to measure area include the square inch and the square centimeter. While the areas of square and rectangular regions are generally easily calculated, we will also develop formulas for the areas of less common polygonal regions. In particular, Section 8.3 is devoted to areas of regular polygons, such as the Pentagon shown in the photograph. Many real-world applications of the area concept are found in the exercise sets of this chapter.

8.1 Area and Initial Postulates

KEY CONCEPTS

- Plane Region
- Square Unit
- Area Postulates
- Area of Rectangle, Parallelogram, and Triangle
- Altitude and Base of a Parallelogram or Triangle

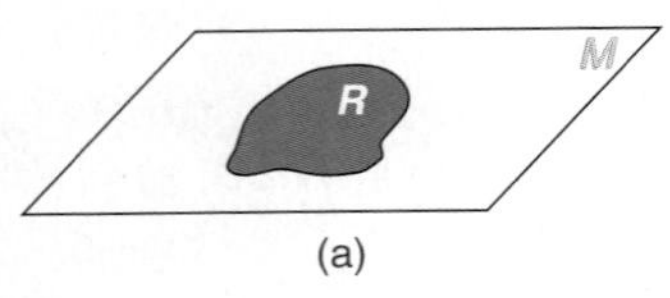

(a)

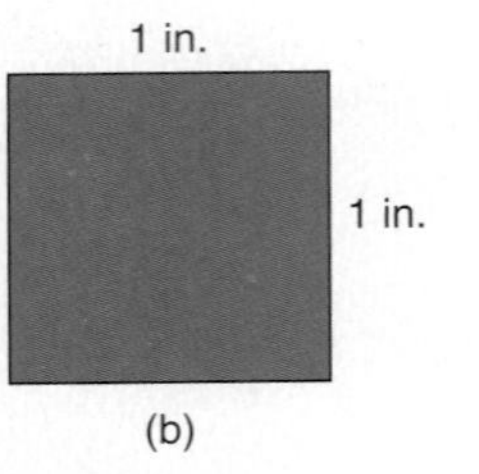

(b)

Figure 8.1

Because lines are *one-dimensional*, we consider only length when measuring a line segment. A line segment is measured in linear units such as inches, centimeters, or yards. When a line segment measures 5 centimeters, we write $AB = 5$ cm or simply $AB = 5$ (if the units are apparent or are not stated). The instrument of measure is the ruler.

A plane is an infinite *two-dimensional* surface. A closed or bounded portion of the plane is called a **region.** When a region such as R in plane M [see Figure 8.1(a)] is measured, we call this measure the "area of the plane region." The unit used to measure area is called a **square unit** because it is a square with each side of length 1 [see Figure 8.1(b)]. The measure of the area of region R is the number of non-overlapping square units that can be placed adjacent to each other in the region.

> Square units (not linear units) are used to measure area. Using an exponent, we write square inches as in^2. The unit represented by Figure 8.1(b) is 1 square inch or 1 in^2.

One application of area involves measuring the floor area to be covered by carpeting, which is often measured in square yards (yd^2). Another application of area involves calculating the number of squares of shingles needed to cover a roof; in this situation, a "square" is the number of shingles needed to cover a 100-ft^2 section of the roof.

In Figure 8.2, the regions have measurable areas and are bounded by figures encountered in earlier chapters. A region is **bounded** if we can distinguish between its interior and its exterior; in calculating area, we measure the interior of the region.

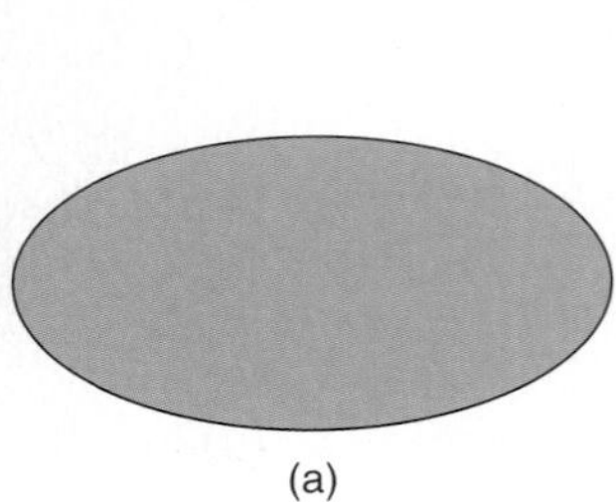

(a)

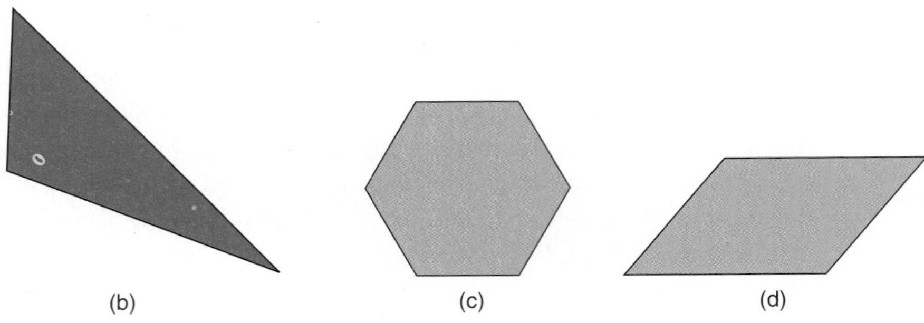

(b) (c) (d)

Figure 8.2

> We can measure the area of the region within a triangle [see Figure 8.2(b)]. However, we cannot actually measure the area of the triangle itself (three line segments do not have area). Nonetheless, the area of the region within a triangle is commonly referred to as the *area of the triangle*.

The preceding discussion does not formally define a region or its area. These are accepted as the undefined terms in the following postulate.

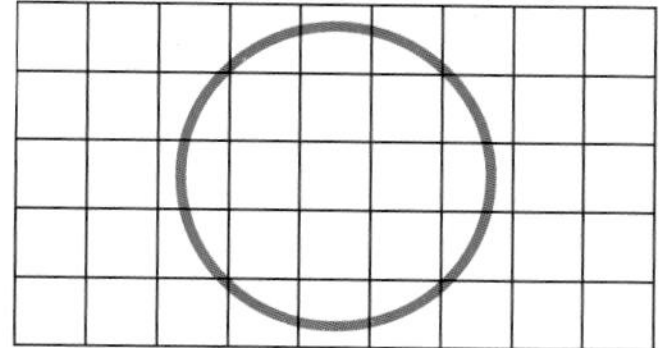

Figure 8.3

POSTULATE 18 ▶ (Area Postulate)

Corresponding to every bounded region is a unique positive number A, known as the area of that region.

One way to estimate the area of a region is to place it in a grid, as shown in Figure 8.3. Counting only the number of whole squares inside the region gives an approximation that is less than the actual area. On the other hand, counting squares that are inside or partially inside provides an approximation that is greater than the actual area. A fair estimate of the area of a region is often given by the average of the smaller and larger approximations just described. If the area of the circle shown in Figure 8.3 is between 9 and 21 square units, we might estimate its area to be $\frac{9 + 21}{2}$ or 15 square units.

To develop another property of area, we consider $\triangle ABC$ and $\triangle DEF$ (which are congruent) in Figure 8.4. One triangle can be placed over the other so that they coincide. How are the areas of the two triangles related? The answer is found in the following postulate.

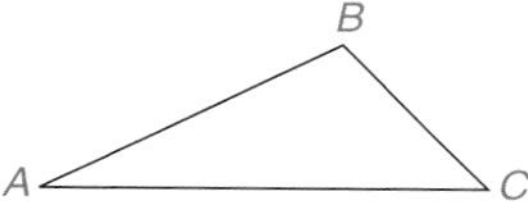

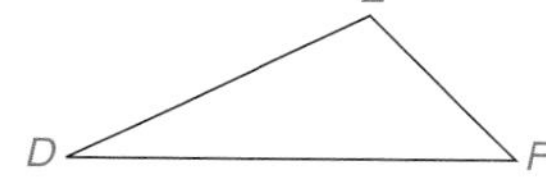

Figure 8.4

Discover

Complete this analogy: An inch is to the length of a line segment as a _?_ _?_ is to the area of a plane region.

ANSWER

Square inch

POSTULATE 19

If two closed plane figures are congruent, then their areas are equal.

EXAMPLE 1

In Figure 8.5, points B and C trisect $\overline{AD}$; $\overline{EC} \perp \overline{AD}$. Name two triangles with equal areas.

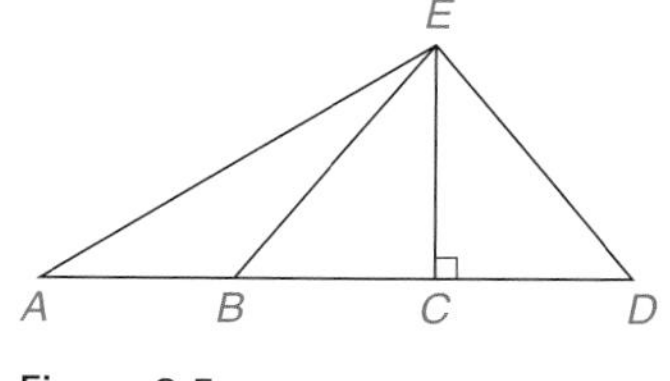

Figure 8.5

Solution $\triangle ECB \cong \triangle ECD$ by SAS. Then $\triangle ECB$ and $\triangle ECD$ have equal areas according to Postulate 19.

NOTE: $\triangle EBA$ is also equal in area to $\triangle ECB$ and $\triangle ECD$, but this relationship cannot be established until we consider Theorem 8.1.3. ■

Consider Figure 8.6. The entire region is bounded by a curve and then subdivided by a line segment into smaller regions R and S. These regions have a common boundary and do not overlap. Because a numerical area can be associated with each region R and S, the area of $R \cup S$ (read as "R union S" and meaning region R joined to region S) is equal to the sum of the areas of R and S. This leads to Postulate 20, in which A_R represents the "area of region R," A_S represents the "area of region S," and $A_{R \cup S}$ represents the "area of region $R \cup S$."

Figure 8.6

POSTULATE 20 ▶ (Area-Addition Postulate)

Let R and S be two enclosed regions that do not overlap. Then

$$A_{R \cup S} = A_R + A_S$$

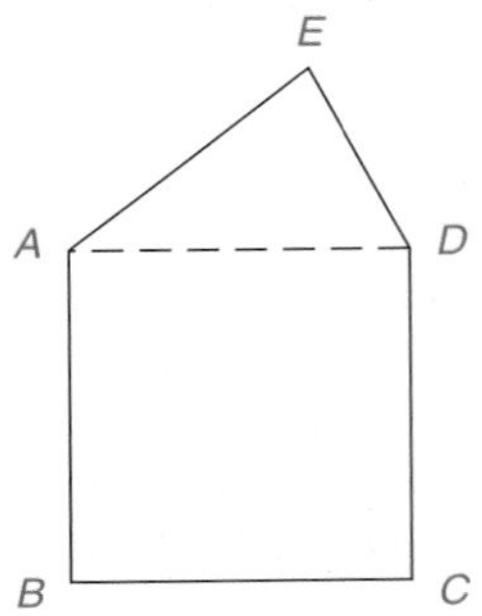

Figure 8.7

EXAMPLE 2

In Figure 8.7, the pentagon $ABCDE$ is composed of square $ABCD$ and $\triangle ADE$. If the area of the square is 36 in^2 and that of $\triangle ADE$ is 12 in^2, find the area of pentagon $ABCDE$.

Solution Square $ABCD$ and $\triangle ADE$ do not overlap and have a common boundary $\overline{AD}$. By the Area-Addition Postulate,

$$\text{Area (pentagon } ABCDE) = \text{area (square } ABCD) + \text{area } (\triangle ADE)$$
$$\text{Area (pentagon } ABCDE) = 36 \text{ in}^2 + 12 \text{ in}^2 = 48 \text{ in}^2$$ ■

It is convenient to provide a subscript for A (area) that names the figure whose area is indicated. The principle used in Example 2 is conveniently and compactly stated in the form

$$A_{ABCDE} = A_{ABCD} + A_{ADE}$$

Exs. 1–5

AREA OF A RECTANGLE

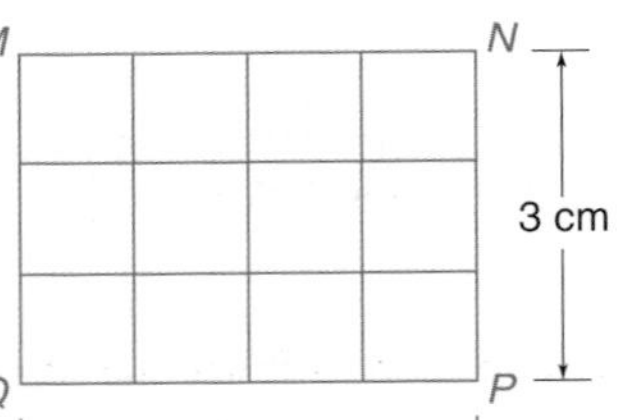

Figure 8.8

Discover

Study rectangle $MNPQ$ in Figure 8.8, and note that it has dimensions of 3 cm and 4 cm. The number of squares, 1 cm on a side, in the rectangle is 12. Rather than counting the number of squares in the figure, how can you calculate the area?

ANSWER

Multiply $3 \times 4 = 12$.

Warning

Although 1 ft = 12 in., 1 ft^2 = 144 in^2. See Figure 8.9.

In the preceding Discover activity, the unit of area is cm^2. Multiplication of dimensions is handled like algebraic multiplication. Compare

$$3x \cdot 4x = 12x^2 \qquad \text{and} \qquad 3 \text{ cm} \cdot 4 \text{ cm} = 12 \text{ cm}^2$$

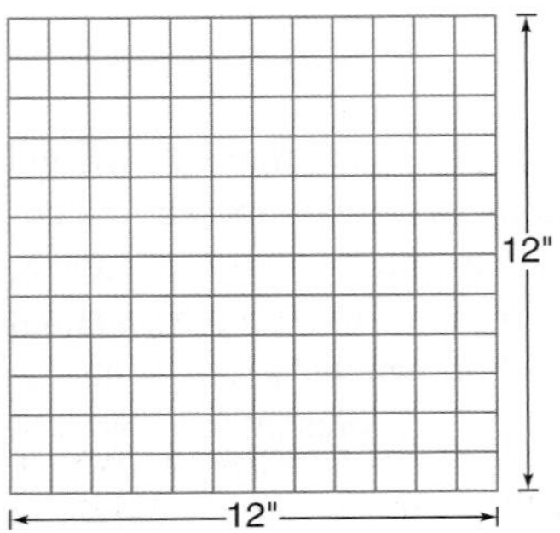

Figure 8.9

If the units used to measure the dimensions of a region are *not* the same, then they must be converted into like units in order to calculate area. For instance, if we need to multiply 2 ft by 6 in., we note that 2 ft $= 2(12 \text{ in.}) = 24$ in., so $A = 2 \text{ ft} \cdot 6 \text{ in.} = 24 \text{ in.} \cdot 6 \text{ in.}$, and $A = 144 \text{ in}^2$. Alternatively, 6 in $= 6(\frac{1}{12} \text{ ft}) = \frac{1}{2}$ ft, so $A = 2 \text{ ft} \cdot \frac{1}{2} \text{ ft} = 1 \text{ ft}^2$. Because the area is unique, we know that 1 ft^2 = 144 in^2. See Figure 8.9.

Recall that one side of a rectangle is called its *base* and that either side perpendicular to the base is called the *altitude* of the rectangle. In the statement of Postulate 21, we assume that b and h are measured in like units.

POSTULATE 21

The area A of a rectangle whose base has length b and whose altitude has length h is given by $A = bh$.

It is also common to describe the dimensions of a rectangle as its length ℓ and its width w. The area of the rectangle is then written $A = \ell w$.

Figure 8.10

EXAMPLE 3

Find the area of rectangle $ABCD$ in Figure 8.10 if $AB = 12$ cm and $AD = 7$ cm.

Solution Because it makes no difference which dimension is chosen as base b and which as altitude h, we arbitrarily choose $AB = b = 12$ cm and $AD = h = 7$ cm. Then

$$\begin{aligned} A &= bh \\ &= 12 \text{ cm} \cdot 7 \text{ cm} \\ &= 84 \text{ cm}^2 \end{aligned}$$

■

If units are not provided for the dimensions of a region, we assume that they are alike. In such a case, we simply give the area as a number of square units.

THEOREM 8.1.1

The area A of a square whose sides are each of length s is given by $A = s^2$.

Exs. 6–10

No proof is given for Theorem 8.1.1, which follows immediately from Postulate 21.

Discover

Because congruent squares "cover" a plane region, it is common to measure area in "square units." It is also possible to cover the region with congruent equilateral triangles; however, area is generally *not* measured in "triangular units." Is it possible to cover a plane region with

a) congruent regular pentagons?
b) congruent regular hexagons?

ANSWERS

(a) No (b) Yes

AREA OF A PARALLELOGRAM

A rectangle's altitude is one of its sides, but that is not true of a parallelogram. An **altitude** of a parallelogram is a perpendicular segment from one side to the opposite side, known as the **base.** A side may have to be extended in order to show this altitude-base relationship in a drawing. In Figure 8.11(a), if $\overline{RS}$ is designated as the base, then any of the segments $\overline{ZR}$, $\overline{VX}$, or $\overline{YS}$ is an altitude corresponding to that base (or, for that matter, to base $\overline{VT}$).

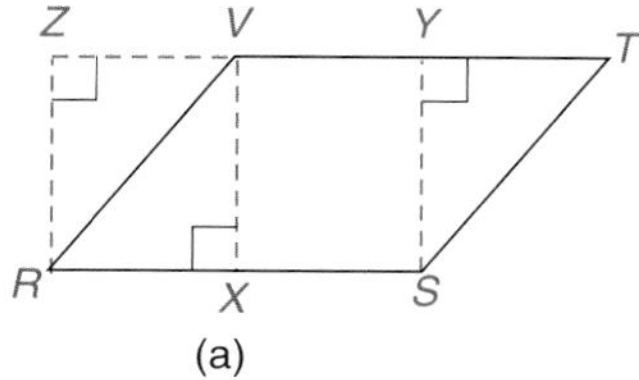

(a)

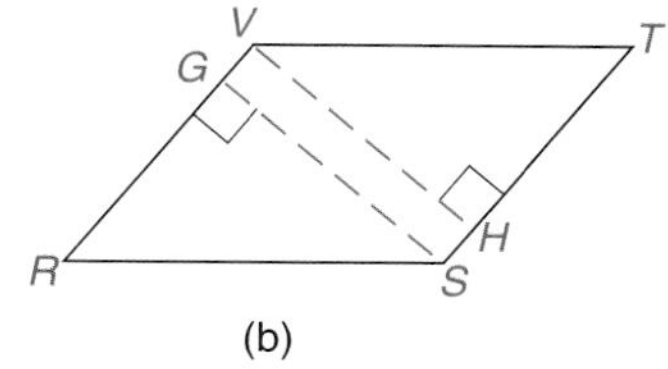

(b)

Figure 8.11

Another look at ▱$RSTV$ [in Figure 8.11(b)] shows that $\overline{ST}$ (or $\overline{VR}$) could just as well have been chosen as the base. Possible choices for the corresponding altitude in this case include $\overline{VH}$ and $\overline{GS}$. In the theorem that follows, it is necessary to select a base and an altitude drawn to that base!

THEOREM 8.1.2

The area A of a parallelogram with a base of length b and with corresponding altitude of length h is given by

$$A = bh$$

Discover

On a geoboard (or pegboard), a parallelogram is formed by a rubber band. With base $b = 6$ and altitude $h = 4$, count wholes and halves to find the area of the parallelogram.

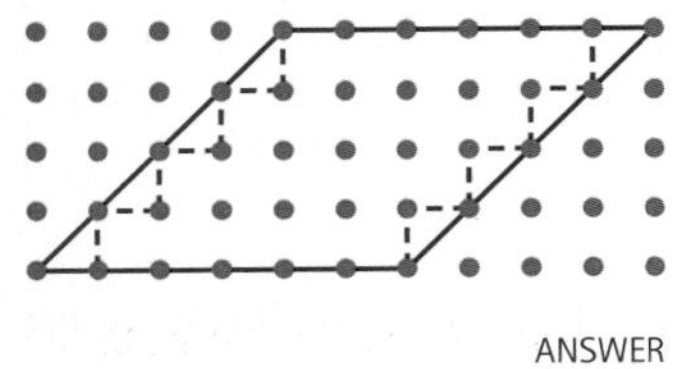

ANSWER

24 units²

GIVEN: In Figure 8.12(a), ▱$RSTV$ with $\overline{VX} \perp \overline{RS}$, $RS = b$, and $VX = h$

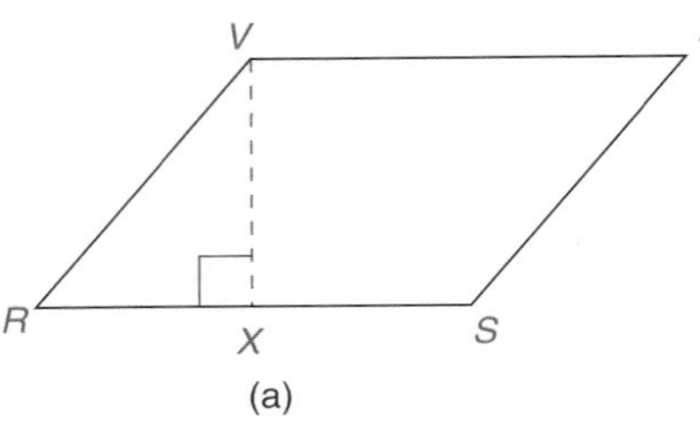

(a)

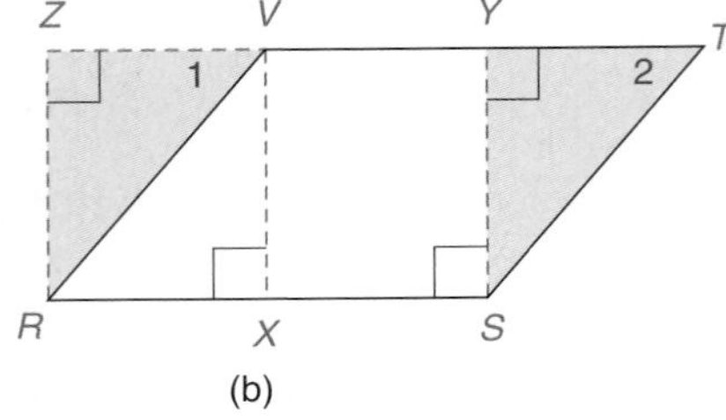

(b)

Figure 8.12

PROVE: $A_{RSTV} = bh$

PROOF: Construct $\overline{YS} \perp \overline{VT}$ and $\overline{RZ} \perp \overline{VT}$, in which Z lies on an extension of $\overline{VT}$, as shown in Figure 8.12(b). Right $\angle Z$ and right $\angle SYT$ are $\cong$. Also, $\overline{ZR} \cong \overline{SY}$ because parallel lines are everywhere equidistant.

Because $\angle 1$ and $\angle 2$ are $\cong$ corresponding angles for parallel segments $\overline{VR}$ and $\overline{TS}$, $\triangle RZV \cong \triangle SYT$ by AAS. Then $A_{RZV} = A_{SYT}$ because congruent $\triangle$s have equal areas.

Because $A_{RSTV} = A_{RSYV} + A_{SYT}$, it follows that $A_{RSTV} = A_{RSYV} + A_{RZV}$. But $RSYV \cup RZV$ is rectangle RSYZ, which has the area bh. Therefore, $A_{RSTV} = A_{RSYZ} = bh$. ■

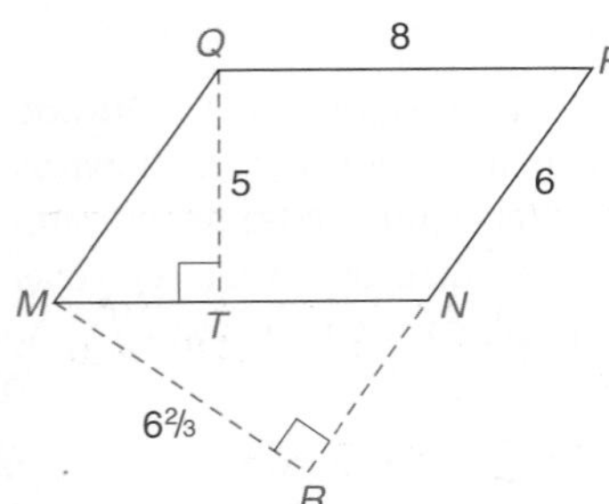

Figure 8.13

EXAMPLE 4

Given that all dimensions in Figure 8.13 are in inches, find the area of ▱$MNPQ$ by using base

a) MN. b) PN.

Solution

a) $MN = QP = b = 8$, and the corresponding altitude is of length $QT = h = 5$. Then

$$\begin{aligned} A &= 8 \text{ in.} \cdot 5 \text{ in.} \\ &= 40 \text{ in}^2 \end{aligned}$$

b) $PN = b = 6$, so the corresponding altitude length is $MR = h = 6\frac{2}{3}$. Then

$$\begin{aligned} A &= 6 \cdot 6\tfrac{2}{3} \\ &= 6 \cdot \tfrac{20}{3} \\ &= 40 \text{ in}^2 \end{aligned}$$ ■

In Example 4, the area of ▱$MNPQ$ was not changed when a different base and its corresponding altitude were used to calculate its area. See Postulate 18.

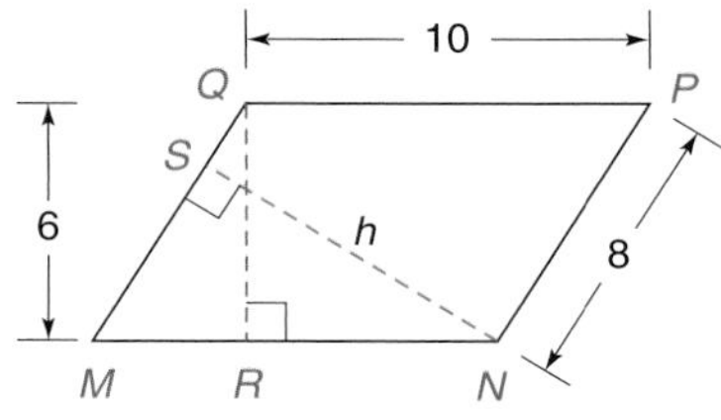

Figure 8.14

EXAMPLE 5

GIVEN: In Figure 8.14, ▱$MNPQ$ with $PN = 8$ and $QP = 10$
Altitude $\overline{QR}$ to base $\overline{MN}$ has length $QR = 6$

FIND: SN, the length of the altitude between $\overline{QM}$ and $\overline{PN}$

Solution Choosing $MN = b = 10$ and $QR = h = 6$, we see that

$$A = bh = 10 \cdot 6 = 60$$

Now we choose $PN = b = 8$ and $SN = h$, so $A = 8h$. Because the area of the parallelogram is unique, it follows that

$$8h = 60$$
$$h = \frac{60}{8} = 7.5$$

SSG *Exs. 11–14*

that is, $SN = 7.5$ ■

AREA OF A TRIANGLE

The formula used to calculate the area of a triangle follows easily from the formula for the area of a parallelogram. In the formula, any side of the triangle can be chosen as its base; however, we must use the length of the corresponding altitude for that base.

THEOREM 8.1.3

The area A of a triangle whose base has length b and whose corresponding altitude has length h is given by

$$A = \frac{1}{2}bh$$

Following is a picture proof of Theorem 8.1.3.

PICTURE PROOF OF THEOREM 8.1.3

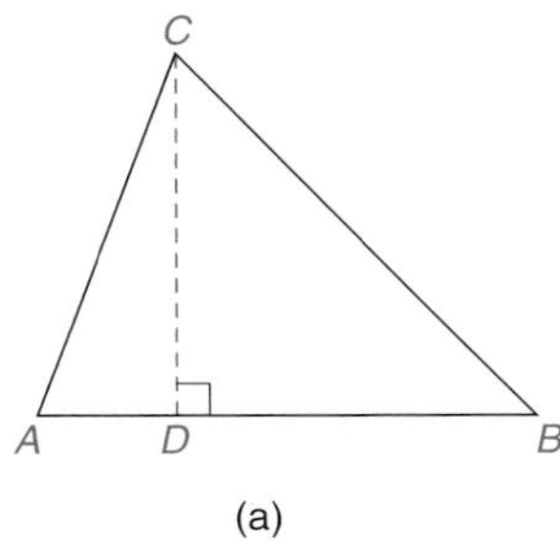

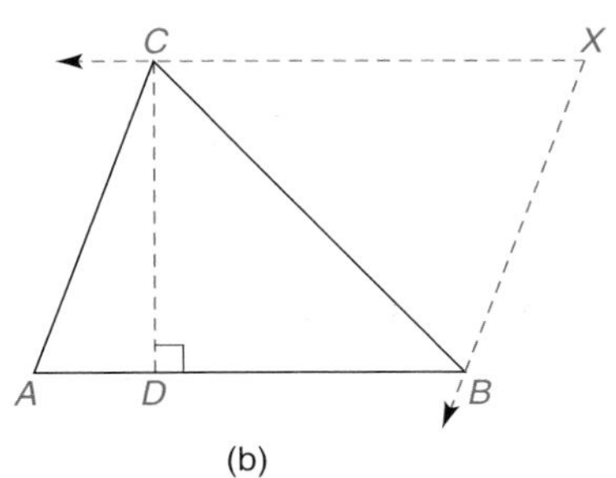

Figure 8.15

GIVEN: In Figure 8.15(a), $\triangle ABC$ with $\overline{CD} \perp \overline{AB}$
$AB = b$ and $CD = h$

PROVE: $A = \frac{1}{2}bh$

PROOF: Let lines through C parallel to $\overline{AB}$ and through B parallel to $\overline{AC}$ meet at point X [see Figure 8.15(b)]. With ▱$ABXC$ and congruent triangles ABC and XCB, we see that $A_{ABC} = \frac{1}{2} \cdot A_{ABXC} = \frac{1}{2}bh$.

EXAMPLE 6

In the figure, find the area of $\triangle ABC$ if $AB = 10$ cm and $CD = 7$ cm.

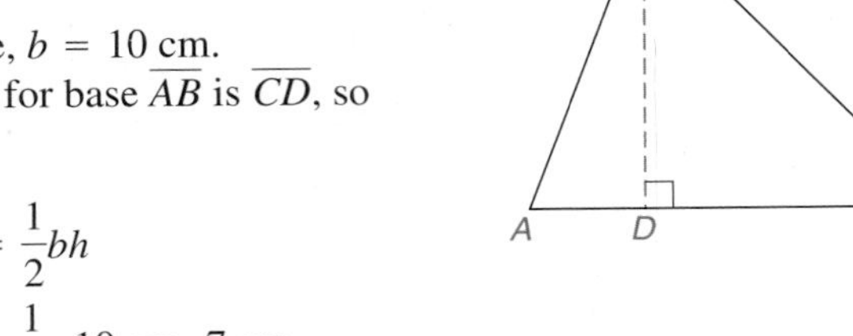

Solution With $\overline{AB}$ as base, $b = 10$ cm. The corresponding altitude for base $\overline{AB}$ is $\overline{CD}$, so $h = 7$ cm. Now

$$A = \frac{1}{2}bh$$

becomes

$$A = \frac{1}{2} \cdot 10 \text{ cm} \cdot 7 \text{ cm}$$

$$A = 35 \text{ cm}^2$$

The following theorem is a corollary of Theorem 8.1.3.

Warning

The phrase *area of a polygon* really means the area of the region enclosed by the polygon.

COROLLARY 8.1.4

The area of a right triangle with legs of lengths a and b is given by $A = \frac{1}{2}ab$.

In the proof of Corollary 8.1.4, the length of either leg can be chosen as the base; in turn, the length of the altitude to that base is the length of the remaining leg. This follows from the fact "The legs of a right triangle are perpendicular."

EXAMPLE 7

GIVEN: In Figure 8.16, right $\triangle MPN$ with $PN = 8$ and $MN = 17$

FIND: A_{MNP}

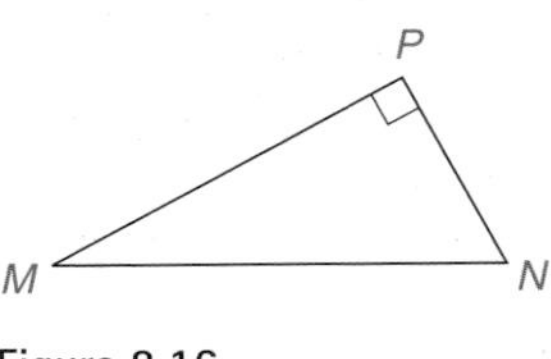

Figure 8.16

Solution With $\overline{PN}$ as one leg of $\triangle MPN$, we need the length of the second leg $\overline{PM}$. By the Pythagorean Theorem,

$$17^2 = (PM)^2 + 8^2$$
$$289 = (PM)^2 + 64$$

Then $(PM)^2 = 225$, so $PM = 15$.

With $PN = a = 8$ and $PM = b = 15$,

$$A = \frac{1}{2}ab$$

becomes

$$A = \frac{1}{2} \cdot 8 \cdot 15 = 60 \text{ units}^2$$

Exs. 15–20

Exercises 8.1

1. Suppose that two triangles have equal areas. Are the triangles congruent? Why or why not? Are two squares with equal areas necessarily congruent? Why or why not?
2. The area of the square is 12, and the area of the circle is 30. Does the area of the entire shaded region equal 42? Why or why not?

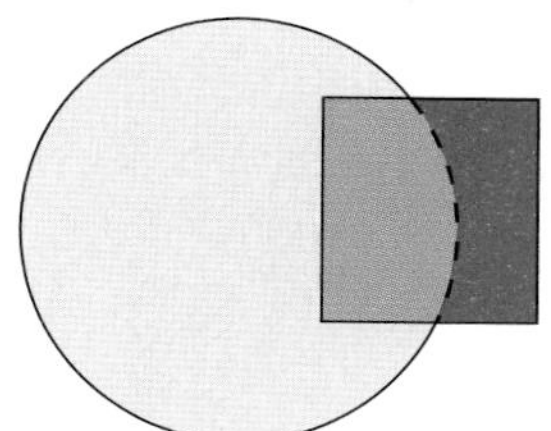

Exercises 2, 3

3. Consider the information in Exercise 2, but suppose you know that the area of the region defined by the intersection of the square and the circle measures 5. What is the area of the entire colored region?
4. If $MNPQ$ is a rhombus, which formula from this section should be used to calculate its area?

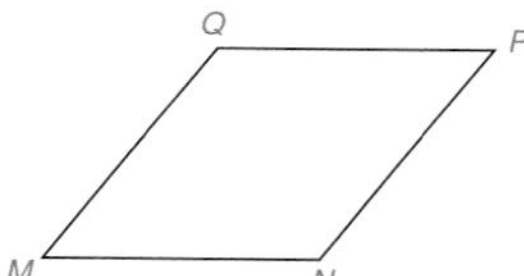

Exercises 4–6

5. In rhombus $MNPQ$, how does the length of the altitude from Q to $\overline{PN}$ compare to the length of the altitude from Q to $\overline{MN}$? Explain.
6. When the diagonals of rhombus $MNPQ$ are drawn, how do the areas of the four resulting smaller triangles compare to each other and to the area of the given rhombus?
7. $\triangle ABC$ is an obtuse triangle with obtuse angle A. $\triangle DEF$ is an acute triangle. How do the areas of $\triangle ABC$ and $\triangle DEF$ compare?

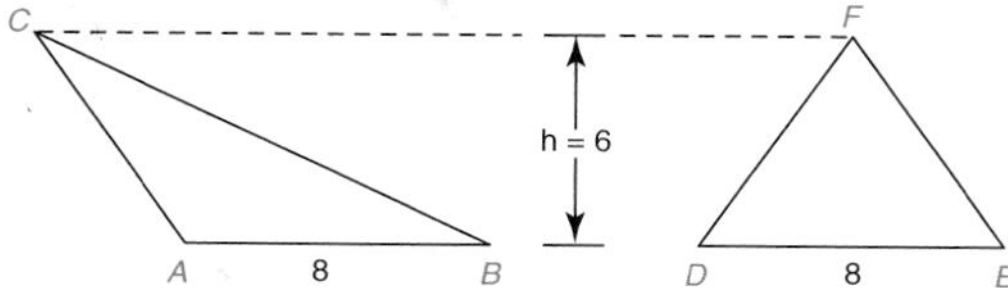

Exercises 7, 8

8. Are $\triangle ABC$ and $\triangle DEF$ congruent?

In Exercises 9 to 18, find the areas of the figures shown or described.

9. A rectangle's length is 6 cm, and its width is 9 cm.
10. A right triangle has one leg measuring 20 in. and a hypotenuse measuring 29 in.
11. A 45-45-90 triangle has a leg measuring 6 m.
12. A triangle's altitude to the 15-in. side measures 8 in.
13. 14.

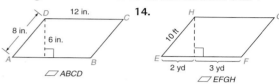

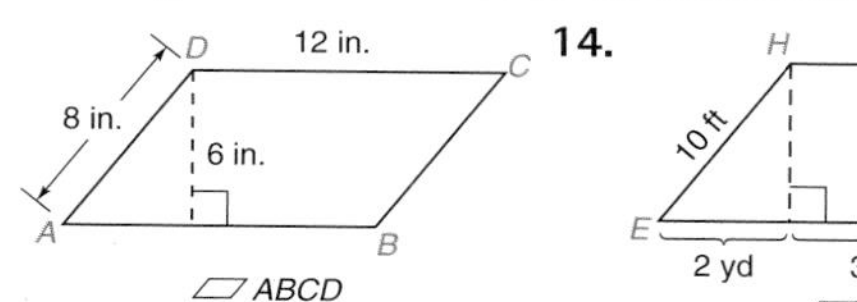

15. 16.

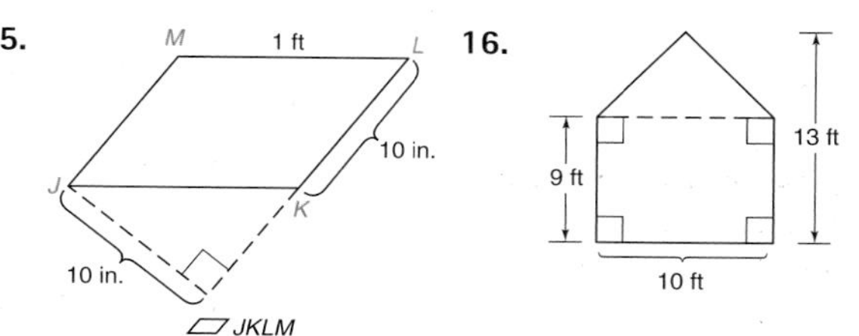

17.

18.

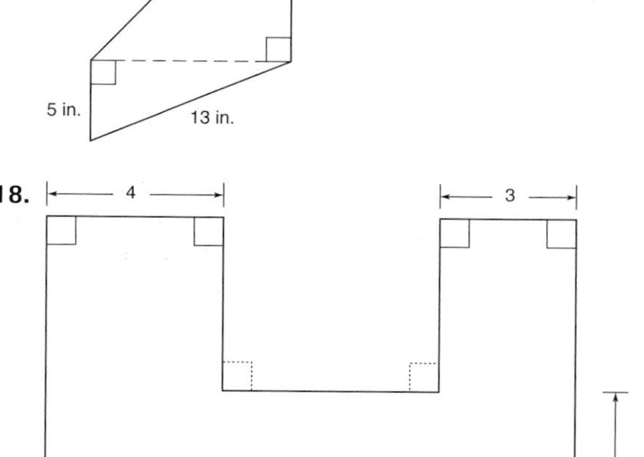

In Exercises 19 to 22, find the area of the shaded region.

19.

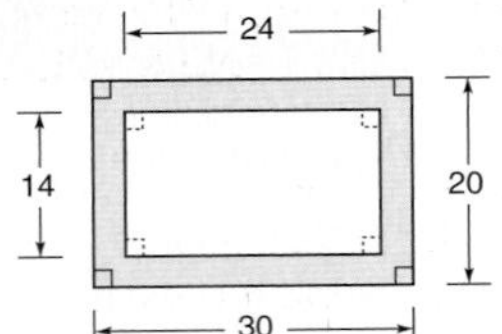

20.

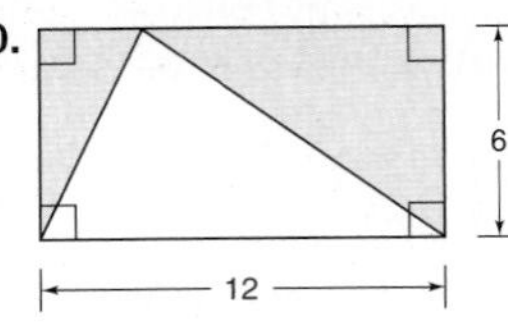

21.

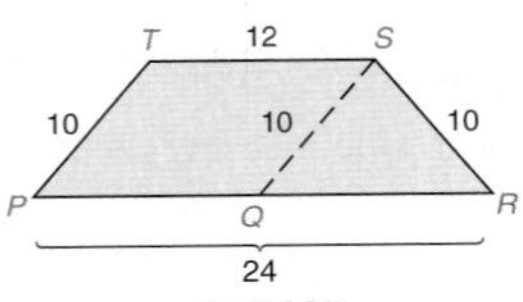

22.

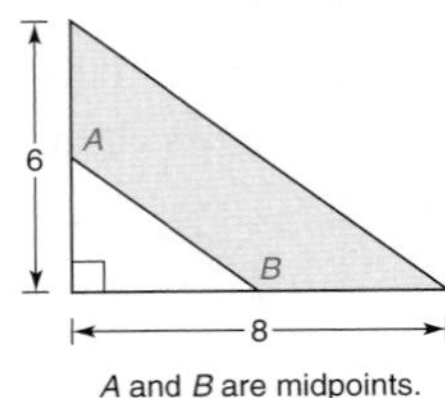

A and B are midpoints.

23. A triangular corner of a store has been roped off to be used as an area for displaying Christmas ornaments. Find the area of the display section.

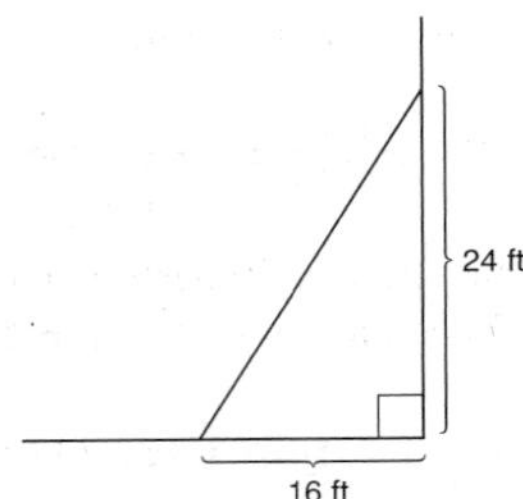

24. Carpeting is to be purchased for the family room and hallway shown. What is the area to be covered?

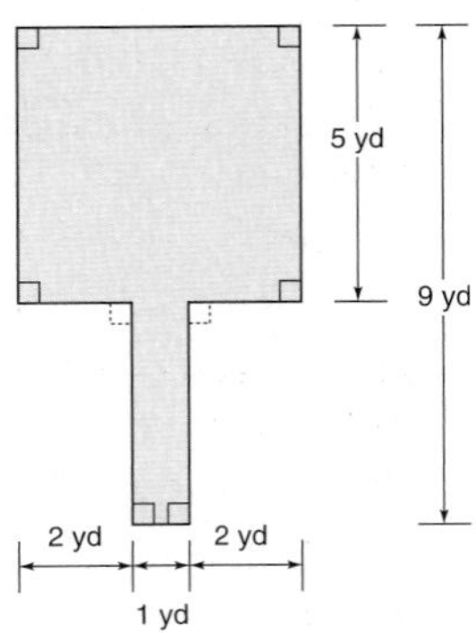

25. The exterior wall (the gabled end of the house shown) remains to be painted.

a) What is the area of the outside wall?

b) If each gallon of paint covers approximately 105 ft^2, how many gallons of paint must be purchased?

c) If each gallon of paint is on sale for \$15.50, what is the total cost of the paint?

15 ft
10 ft
24 ft

26. The roof of the house shown needs to be shingled.

a) Considering that the front and back sections of the roof have equal areas, find the total area to be shingled.

b) If roofing is sold in squares (each covering 100 ft^2), how many squares are needed to complete the work?

c) If each square costs \$22.50 and an extra square is allowed for trimming around vents, what is the total cost of the shingles?

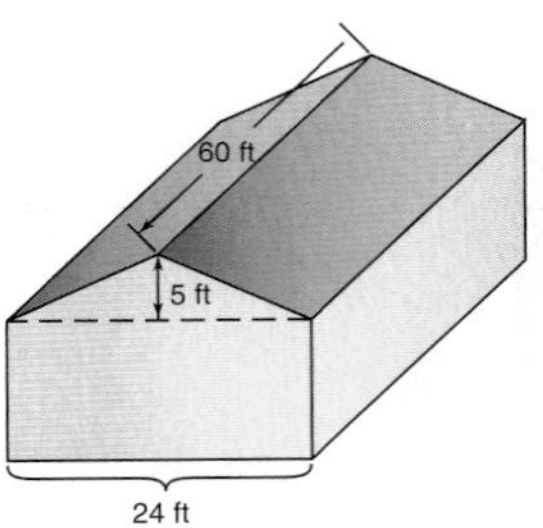

27. A beach tent is designed so that one side is open. Find the number of square feet of canvas needed to make the tent.

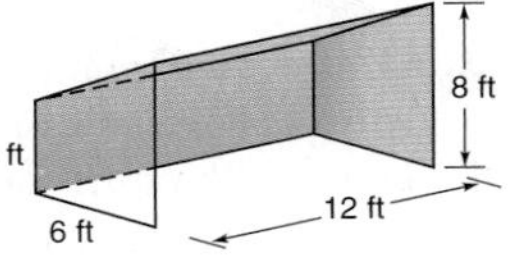

28. Gary and Carolyn plan to build the deck shown.

a) Find the total floor space (area) of the deck.

b) Find the approximate cost of building the deck if the estimated cost is \$3.20 per ft^2.

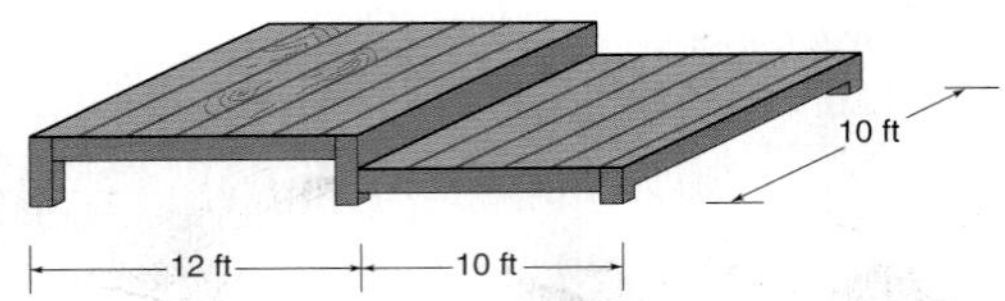

29. A *square yard* is a square with sides 1 yard in length.

a) How many *square feet* are in 1 square yard?

b) How many *square inches* are in 1 square yard?

30. The following problem is based on this theorem: "A median of a triangle separates it into two triangles of equal area."

a) Given $\triangle RST$ with median $\overline{RV}$, explain why $A_{RSV} = A_{RVT}$.

b) If $A_{RST} = 40.8$ cm^2, find A_{RSV}.

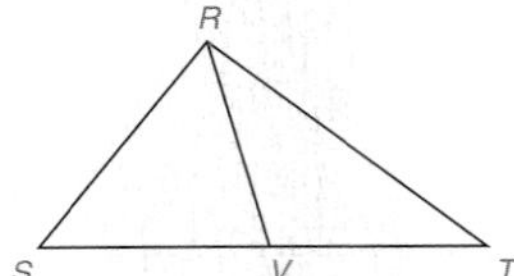

For Exercises 31 and 32, X is the midpoint of $\overline{VT}$ and Y is the midpoint of $\overline{TS}$.

31. If $A_{RSTV} = 48$ cm^2, find A_{RYTX}.

32. If $A_{RYTX} = 13.5$ in^2, find A_{RSTV}.

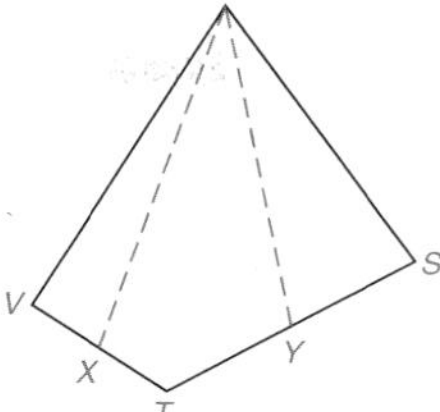

Exercises 31, 32

33. Given $\triangle ABC$ with midpoints M, N, and P of the sides, explain why $A_{ABC} = 4 \cdot A_{MNP}$.

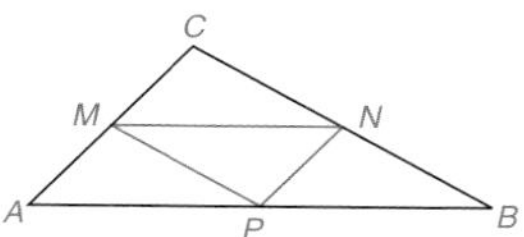

In Exercises 34 to 36, provide paragraph proofs.

34. *Given:* Right $\triangle ABC$

Prove: $h = \dfrac{ab}{c}$

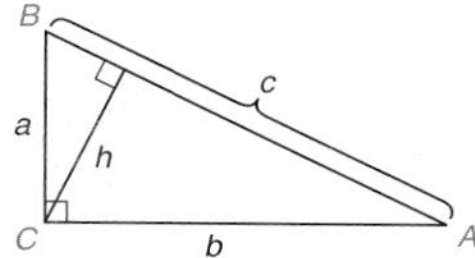

35. *Given:* Square $HJKL$ with $LJ = d$

Prove: $A_{HJKL} = \dfrac{d^2}{2}$

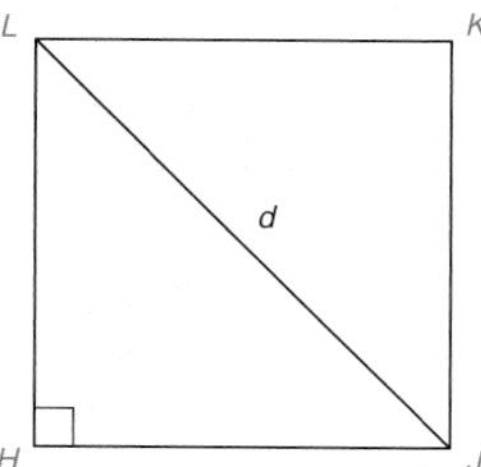

36. *Given:* ▱$RSTV$ with $\overline{VW} \cong \overline{VT}$

Prove: $A_{RSTV} = (RS)^2$

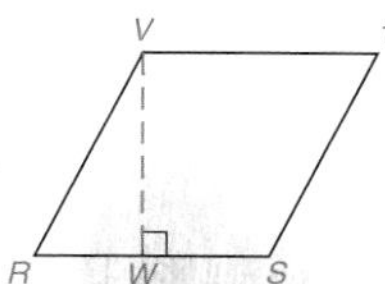

37. *Given:* The area of right $\triangle ABC$ (not shown) is 40 in^2.
$m\angle C = 90°$
$AC = x$
$BC = x + 2$

Find: x

38. The lengths of the legs of a right triangle are consecutive even integers. The numerical value of the area is three times that of the longer leg. Find the lengths of the legs of the triangle.

***39.** *Given:* $\triangle ABC$, whose sides are 13 in., 14 in., and 15 in.

Find: a) BD, the length of the altitude to the 14-in. side

(HINT: Use the Pythagorean Theorem twice.)

b) The area of $\triangle ABC$, using the result from part (a)

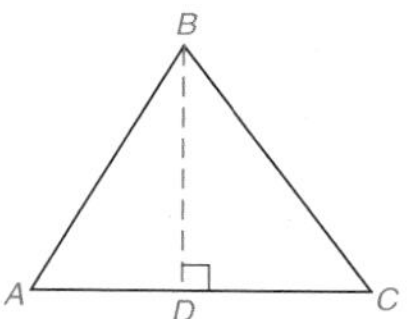

Exercises 39, 40

***40.** *Given:* $\triangle ABC$, whose sides are 10 cm, 17 cm, and 21 cm

Find: a) BD, the length of the altitude to the 21-cm side

b) The area of $\triangle ABC$, using the result from part (a)

41. If the base of a rectangle is increased by 20 percent and the altitude is increased by 30 percent, by what percentage is the area increased?

42. If the base of a rectangle is increased by 20 percent but the altitude is decreased by 30 percent, by what percentage is the area changed? Is this an increase or a decrease in area?

43. Given region $R \cup S$, explain why $A_{R \cup S} > A_R$.

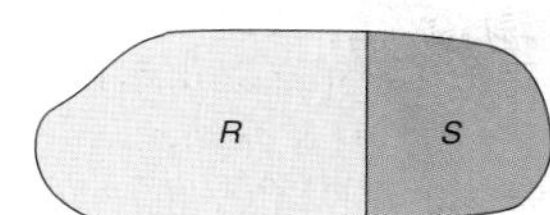

44. Given region $R \cup S \cup T$, explain why $A_{R \cup S \cup T} = A_R + A_S + A_T$.

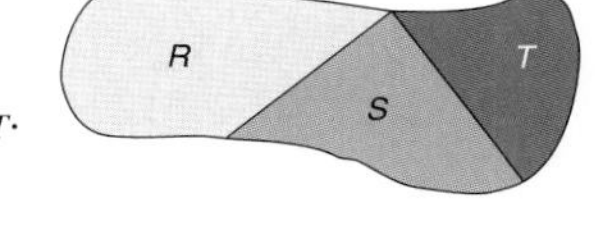

45. The algebra method of FOIL multiplication is illustrated geometrically in the drawing. Use the drawing with rectangular regions to complete the following rule:
$(a + b)(c + d) =$ ____________________

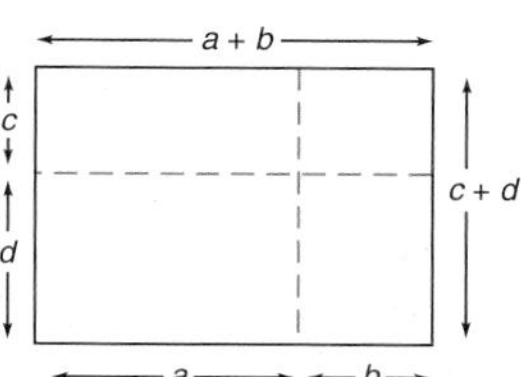

46. Use the square configuration to complete the following algebra rule: $(a + b)^2 =$ ______________________
(**NOTE:** Simplify where possible.)

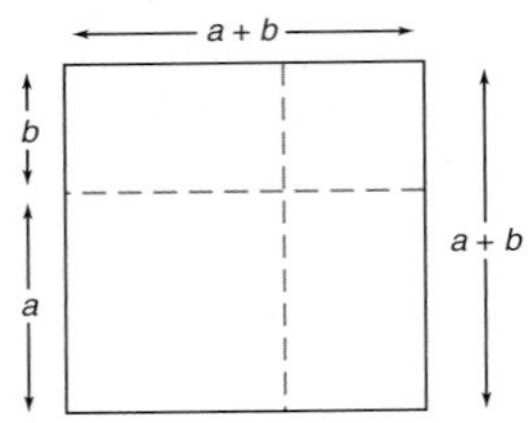

In Exercises 47 to 50, use the fact that the area of the polygon is unique.

47. In the right triangle, find the length of the altitude drawn to the hypotenuse.

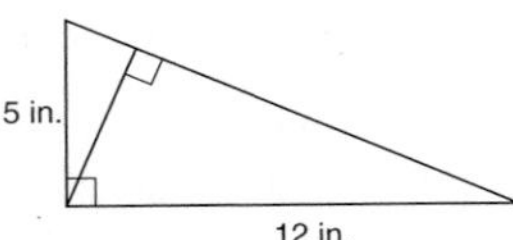

48. In the triangle whose sides are 13, 20, and 21 cm long, the length of the altitude drawn to the 21-cm side is 12 cm. Find the lengths of the remaining altitudes of the triangle.

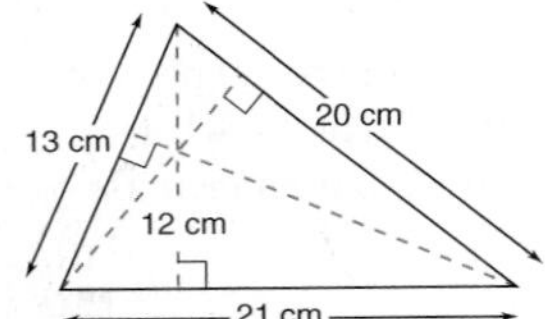

49. In ▱$MNPQ$, $QP = 12$ and $QM = 9$. The length of altitude $\overline{QR}$ (to side $\overline{MN}$) is 6. Find the length of altitude $\overline{QS}$ from Q to $\overline{PN}$.

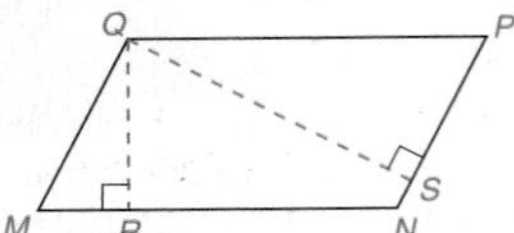

50. In ▱$ABCD$, $AB = 7$ and $BC = 12$. The length of altitude $\overline{AF}$ (to side $\overline{BC}$) is 5. Find the length of altitude $\overline{AE}$ from A to $\overline{DC}$.

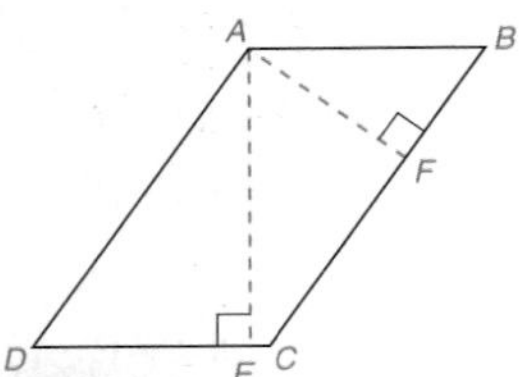

***51.** The area of a rectangle is 48 in^2. Where x is the width and y is the length, express the perimeter P of the rectangle in terms only of x.

***52.** The perimeter of a rectangle is 32 cm. Where x is the width and y is the length, express the area A of the rectangle in terms only of x.

***53.** Square $DEFG$ is inscribed in right $\triangle ABC$ as shown. If $AD = 6$ and $EB = 8$, find the area of square $DEFG$.

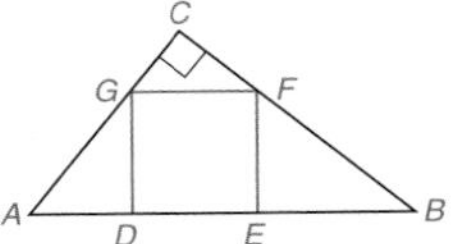

***54.** $\overline{TV}$ bisects $\angle STR$ of $\triangle STR$. $ST = 6$ and $TR = 9$. If the area of $\triangle RST$ is 25 m^2, find the area of $\triangle SVT$.

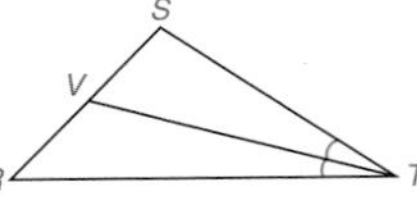

55. a) Find a lower estimate of the area of the figure by counting whole squares within the figure.
b) Find an upper estimate of the area of the figure by counting whole and partial squares within the figure.
c) Use the average of the results in parts (a) and (b) to provide a better estimate of the area of the figure.
d) Does intuition suggest that the area estimate of part (c) is the exact answer?

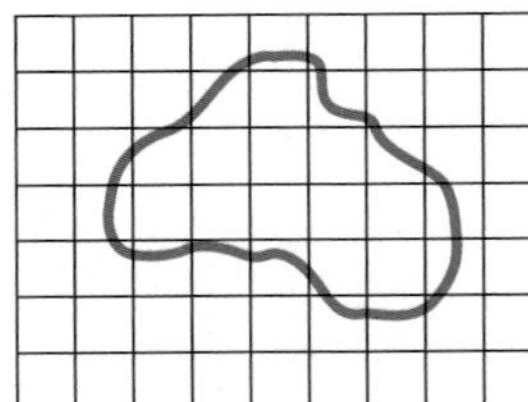

56. a) Find a lower estimate of the area of the figure by counting whole squares within the figure.
b) Find an upper estimate of the area of the figure by counting whole and partial squares within the figure.
c) Use the average of the results in parts (a) and (b) to provide a better estimate of the area of the figure.
d) Does intuition suggest that the area estimate of part (c) is the exact answer?

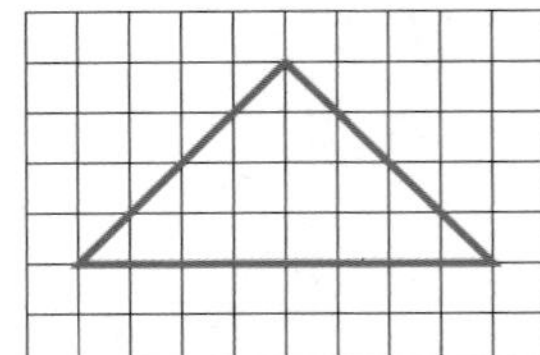

8.2 Perimeter and Area of Polygons

KEY CONCEPTS

Perimeter of a Polygon
Semiperimeter of a Triangle
Heron's Formula
Brahmagupta's Formula
Area of Trapezoid, Rhombus, and Kite
Areas of Similar Polygons

We begin this section with a reminder of the meaning of perimeter.

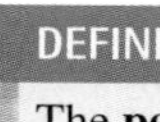

DEFINITION

The **perimeter** of a polygon is the sum of the lengths of all sides of the polygon.

Table 8.1 summarizes perimeter formulas for types of triangles, and Table 8.2 summarizes formulas for the perimeters of selected types of quadrilaterals. However, it is more important to understand the concept of perimeter than to memorize formulas. See whether you can explain each formula.

TABLE 8.1
Perimeter of a Triangle

Scalene Triangle	Isosceles Triangle	Equilateral Triangle
$P = a + b + c$	$P = b + 2s$	$P = 3s$

TABLE 8.2
Perimeter of a Quadrilateral

Quadrilateral	Rectangle	Square (or Rhombus)	Parallelogram
$P = a + b + c + d$	$P = 2b + 2h$ or $P = 2(b + h)$	$P = 4s$	$P = 2b + 2s$ or $P = 2(b + s)$

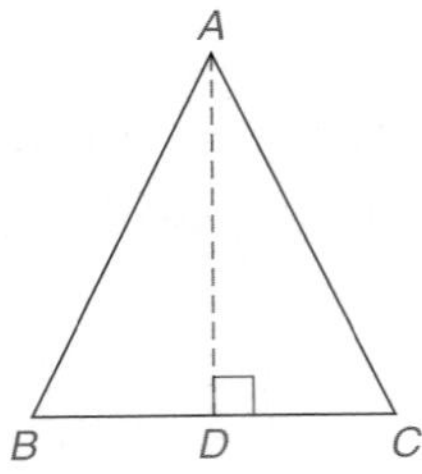

Figure 8.17

EXAMPLE 1

Find the perimeter of $\triangle ABC$ shown in Figure 8.17 if:

a) $AB = 5$ in., $AC = 6$ in., and $BC = 7$ in.
b) Altitude $AD = 8$ cm, $BC = 6$ cm, and $\overline{AB} \cong \overline{AC}$

Solution

a) $P_{ABC} = AB + AC + BC$
$= 5 + 6 + 7$
$= 18$ in.

b) With $\overline{AB} \cong \overline{AC}$, $\triangle ABC$ is isosceles. Then $\overline{AD}$ is the $\perp$ bisector of $\overline{BC}$. If $BC = 6$, it follows that $DC = 3$. Using the Pythagorean Theorem, we have

$$(AD)^2 + (DC)^2 = (AC)^2$$
$$8^2 + 3^2 = (AC)^2$$
$$64 + 9 = (AC)^2$$
$$AC = \sqrt{73}$$

Now $P_{ABC} = 6 + \sqrt{73} + \sqrt{73} = 6 + 2\sqrt{73} \approx 23.09$ cm.

NOTE: Because $x + x = 2x$, we have $\sqrt{73} + \sqrt{73} = 2\sqrt{73}$. ■

We apply the perimeter concept in a more general manner in Example 2.

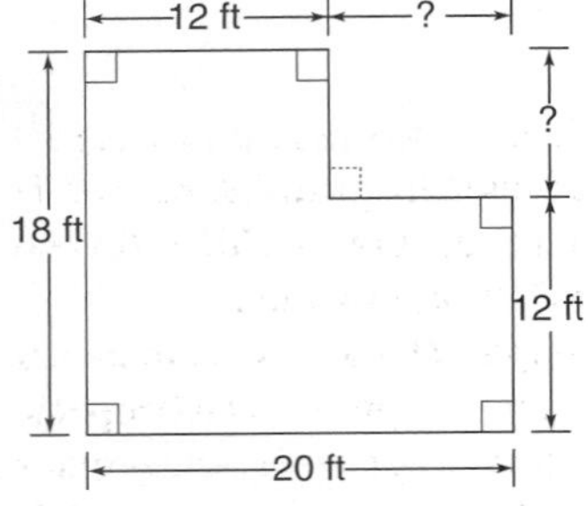

Figure 8.18

EXAMPLE 2

While remodeling, the Gibsons have decided to replace the old woodwork with Colonial-style oak woodwork.

a) Using the floor plan provided in Figure 8.18, find the amount of baseboard (in linear feet) needed for the room. Do *not* make any allowances for doors!
b) Find the cost of the baseboard if the price is \$1.32 per linear foot.

Solution

a) Dimensions not shown measure $20 - 12$ or 8 ft and $18 - 12$ or 6 ft. The perimeter, or "distance around," the room is

$$12 + 6 + 8 + 12 + 20 + 18 = 76 \text{ linear ft}$$

SSG *Exs. 1–4*

b) The cost is $76 \cdot \$1.32 = \$100.32$. ■

HERON'S FORMULA

If the lengths of the sides of a triangle are known, the formula generally used to calculate the area is **Heron's Formula** (named in honor of Heron of Alexandria, circa A.D. 75). One of the numbers found in this formula is the *semiperimeter* of a triangle, which is defined as one-half the perimeter. For the triangle that has sides of lengths a, b, and c, the semiperimeter is $s = \frac{1}{2}(a + b + c)$. We apply Heron's Formula in Example 3. The proof of Heron's Formula can be found at our website.

THEOREM 8.2.1 ▶ (Heron's Formula)

If the three sides of a triangle have lengths a, b, and c, then the area A of the triangle is given by

$$A = \sqrt{s(s-a)(s-b)(s-c)},$$

where the semiperimeter of the triangle is

$$s = \frac{1}{2}(a+b+c)$$

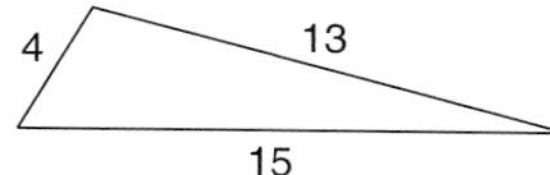

Figure 8.19

EXAMPLE 3

Find the area of a triangle which has sides of lengths 4, 13, and 15. (See Figure 8.19.)

Solution If we designate the sides as $a = 4$, $b = 13$, and $c = 15$, the semiperimeter of the triangle is given by $s = \frac{1}{2}(4 + 13 + 15) = \frac{1}{2}(32) = 16$. Therefore,

$$\begin{aligned} A &= \sqrt{s(s-a)(s-b)(s-c)} \\ &= \sqrt{16(16-4)(16-13)(16-15)} \\ &= \sqrt{16(12)(3)(1)} = \sqrt{576} = 24 \text{ units}^2 \end{aligned}$$

■

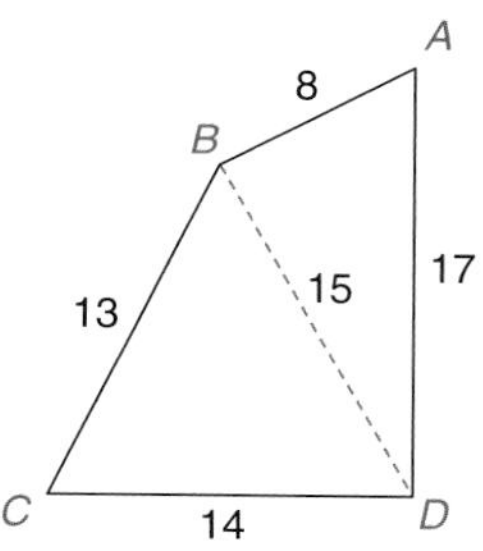

Figure 8.20

When the lengths of the sides of a quadrilateral are known, we can apply Heron's Formula to find the area if the length of a diagonal is also known. In quadrilateral $ABCD$ in Figure 8.20, Heron's Formula can be used to show that the area of $\triangle ABD$ is 60 and the area of $\triangle BCD$ is 84. Thus, the area of quadrilateral $ABCD$ is 144 units^2.

The following theorem is named in honor of Brahmagupta, a Hindu mathematician born in A.D. 598. We include the theorem without its rather lengthy proof. As it happens, Heron's Formula for the area of any triangle is actually a special case of Brahmagupta's Formula, which is used to determine the area of a cyclic quadrilateral. In Brahmagupta's Formula, as in Heron's Formula, the letter s represents the numerical value of the semiperimeter. The formula is applied in essentially the same manner as Heron's Formula. See Exercises 11, 12, 41, and 42 of this section.

THEOREM 8.2.2 ▶ (Brahmagupta's Formula)

For a cyclic quadrilateral with sides of lengths a, b, c, and d, the area is given by

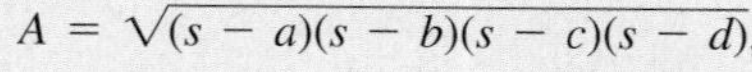

$$A = \sqrt{(s-a)(s-b)(s-c)(s-d)},$$

where $s = \frac{1}{2}(a+b+c+d)$

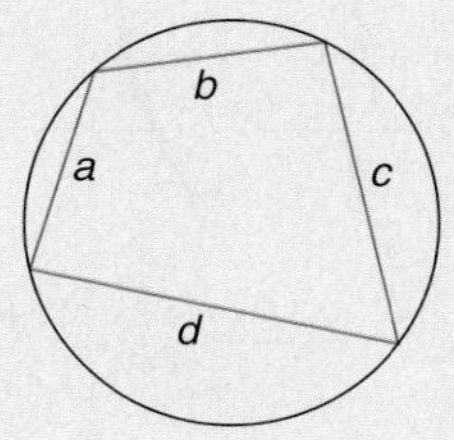

Brahmagupta's Formula becomes Heron's Formula when the length d of the fourth side shrinks (the length d approaches 0) so that the quadrilateral becomes a triangle with sides of lengths a, b, and c.

The remaining theorems of this section contain *numerical subscripts*. In practice, subscripts enable us to distinguish quantities. For instance, the lengths of the two unequal bases of a trapezoid are written b_1 (read "b sub 1") and b_2. In particular, b_1 represents the

SSG
Exs. 5–8

numerical length of the first base, and b_2 represents the length of the second base. The following chart illustrates the use of numerical subscripts.

Theorem	Subscripted Symbol	Meaning
Theorem 8.2.3	b_1	Length of *first* base of trapezoid
Corollary 8.2.5	d_2	Length of *second* diagonal of rhombus
Theorem 8.2.7	A_1	Area of *first* triangle

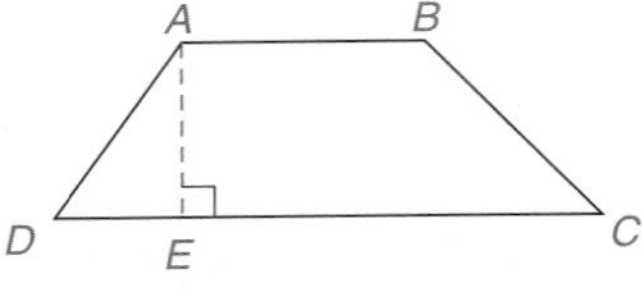

Figure 8.21

AREA OF A TRAPEZOID

Recall that the two parallel sides of a trapezoid are its *bases*. The *altitude* is any line segment that is drawn perpendicular from one base to the other. In Figure 8.21, $\overline{AB}$ and $\overline{DC}$ are bases and $\overline{AE}$ is an altitude for the trapezoid.

We use the more common formula for the area of a triangle (namely, $A = \frac{1}{2}bh$) to develop our remaining theorems. In Theorem 8.2.3, b_1 and b_2 represent the lengths of the bases of the trapezoid. (In some textbooks, b represents the length of the *shorter* base and B represents the length of the *longer* base.)

STRATEGY FOR PROOF ▶ Proving Area Relationships

General Rule: Many area relationships depend upon the use of the Area-Addition Postulate.

Illustration: In the proof of Theorem 8.2.3, the area of the trapezoid is developed as the sum of areas of two triangles.

THEOREM 8.2.3

The area A of a trapezoid whose bases have lengths b_1 and b_2 and whose altitude has length h is given by

$$A = \frac{1}{2}h(b_1 + b_2)$$

GIVEN: Trapezoid $ABCD$ with $\overline{AB} \parallel \overline{DC}$; $AB = b_1$ and $DC = b_2$.

PROVE: $A_{ABCD} = \frac{1}{2}h(b_1 + b_2)$

PROOF: Draw $\overline{AC}$ as shown in Figure 8.22(a). Now $\triangle ADC$ has an altitude of length h and a base of length b_2. As shown in Figure 8.22(b),

$$A_{ADC} = \frac{1}{2}hb_2$$

Also, $\triangle ABC$ has an altitude of length h and a base of length b_1. [See Figure 8.22(c).] Then

$$A_{ABC} = \frac{1}{2}hb_1$$

Thus,

$$\begin{aligned} A_{ABCD} &= A_{ABC} + A_{ADC} \\ &= \frac{1}{2}hb_1 + \frac{1}{2}hb_2 \\ &= \frac{1}{2}h(b_1 + b_2) \end{aligned}$$

■

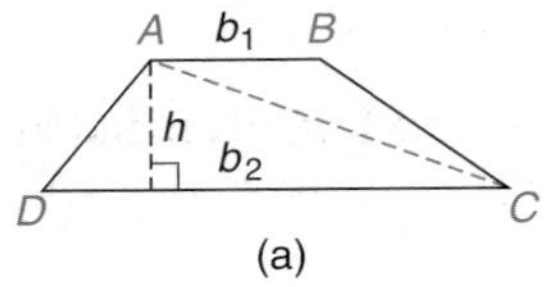

(a)

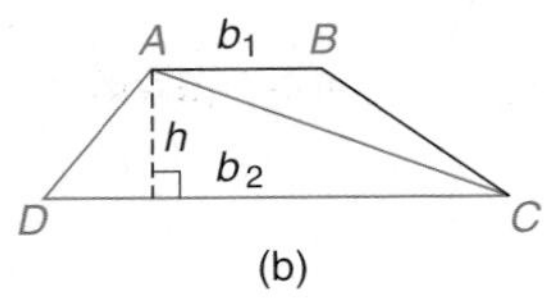

(b)

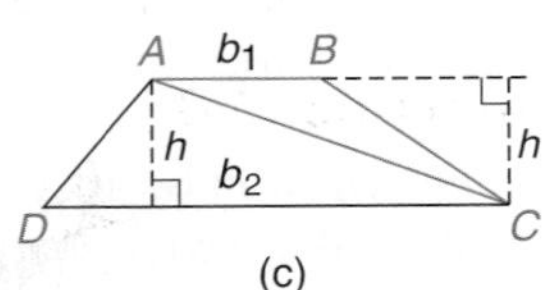

(c)

Figure 8.22

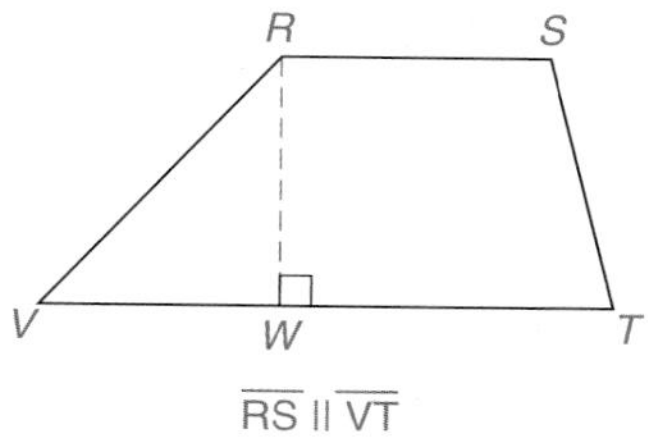

Figure 8.23

EXAMPLE 4

Given that $\overline{RS} \parallel \overline{VT}$, find the area of the trapezoid in Figure 8.23. Note that $RS = 5$, $TV = 13$, and $RW = 6$.

Solution Let $RS = 5 = b_1$ and $TV = 13 = b_2$. Also, $RW = h = 6$. Now,

$$A = \frac{1}{2}h(b_1 + b_2)$$

becomes

$$A = \frac{1}{2} \cdot 6(5 + 13)$$

$$= \frac{1}{2} \cdot 6 \cdot 18$$

$$= 3 \cdot 18 = 54 \text{ units}^2$$

The following activity reinforces the formula for the area of a trapezoid.

Discover

Cut out two trapezoids that are copies of each other and place one next to the other to form a parallelogram.

a) How long is the base of the parallelogram?
b) What is the area of the parallelogram?
c) What is the area of the trapezoid?

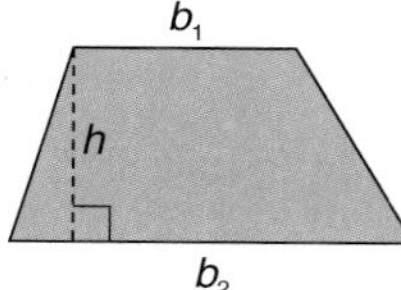

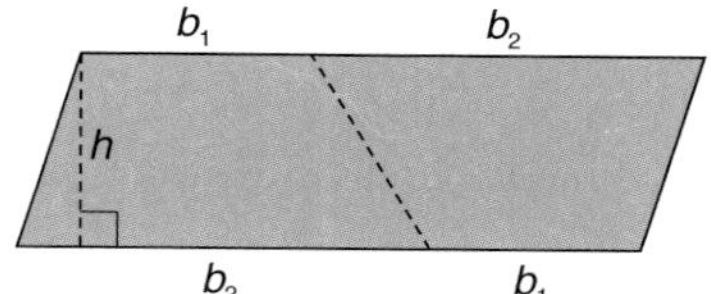

ANSWERS

a) $b_1 + b_2$ b) $h(b_1 + b_2)$ c) $\frac{1}{2}h(b_1 + b_2)$

SSG *Exs. 9–12*

QUADRILATERALS WITH PERPENDICULAR DIAGONALS

The following theorem leads to Corollaries 8.2.5 and 8.2.6, where the formula found in Theorem 8.2.4 is also used to find the area of a rhombus and kite.

THEOREM 8.2.4

The area of any quadrilateral with perpendicular diagonals of lengths d_1 and d_2 is given by

$$A = \frac{1}{2}d_1 d_2$$

GIVEN: Quadrilateral $ABCD$ with $\overline{AC} \perp \overline{BD}$ [see Figure 8.24(a) on page 368.]

PROVE: $A_{ABCD} = \frac{1}{2}d_1 d_2$

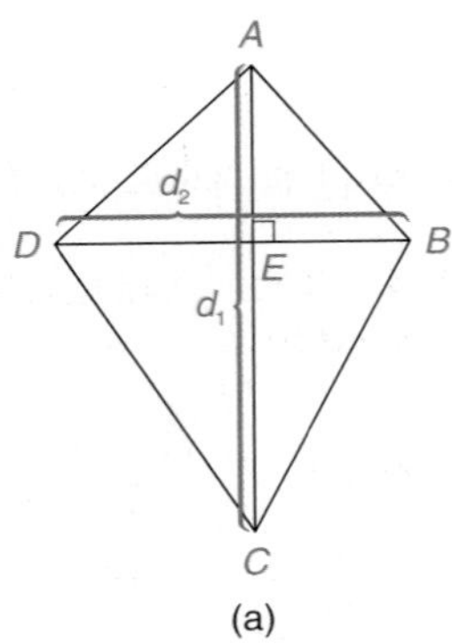

(a)

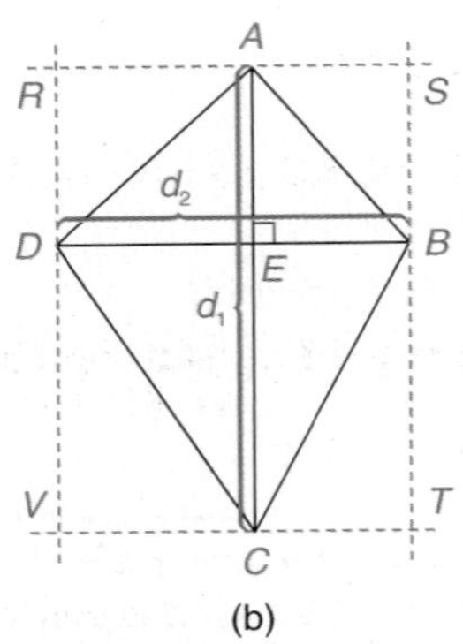

(b)

Figure 8.24

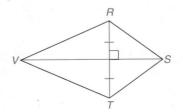

PROOF: Through points A and C, draw lines parallel to $\overline{DB}$. Likewise, draw lines parallel to $\overline{AC}$ through points B and D. Let the points of intersection of these lines be R, S, T, and V, as shown in Figure 8.24(b). Because each of the quadrilaterals $ARDE$, $ASBE$, $BECT$, and $CEDV$ is a parallelogram containing a right angle, each is a rectangle. Furthermore, $A_{\triangle ADE} = \frac{1}{2} \cdot A_{ARDE}$, $A_{\triangle ABE} = \frac{1}{2} \cdot A_{ASBE}$, $A_{\triangle BEC} = \frac{1}{2} \cdot A_{BECT}$, and $A_{\triangle DEC} = \frac{1}{2} \cdot A_{CEDV}$.

Then $A_{ABCD} = \frac{1}{2} \cdot A_{RSTV}$. But $RSTV$ is a rectangle, because it is a parallelogram containing a right angle. Because $RSTV$ has dimensions d_1 and d_2 [see Figure 8.24(b)], its area is $d_1 d_2$. By substitution, $A_{ABCD} = \frac{1}{2} d_1 d_2$. ■

AREA OF A RHOMBUS

Recall that a rhombus is a parallelogram with two congruent adjacent sides; in turn, we proved that all four sides were congruent. Because the diagonals of a rhombus are perpendicular, we have the following corollary of Theorem 8.2.4. See Figure 8.25.

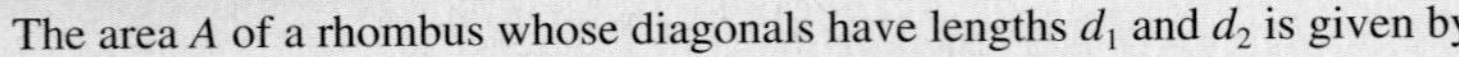

COROLLARY 8.2.5

The area A of a rhombus whose diagonals have lengths d_1 and d_2 is given by

$$A = \frac{1}{2} d_1 d_2$$

Corollary 8.2.5 and Corollary 8.2.6 are immediate consequences of Theorem 8.2.4. Example 5 illustrates Corollary 8.2.5.

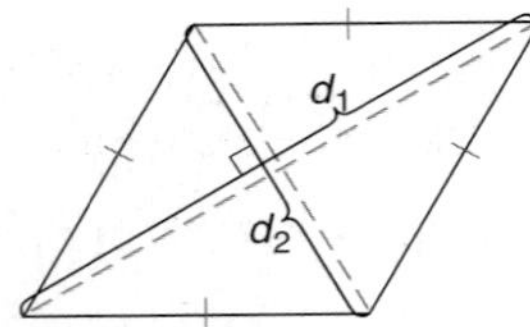

Figure 8.25

EXAMPLE 5

Find the area of the rhombus $MNPQ$ in Figure 8.26 if $MP = 12$ and $NQ = 16$.

Solution By Corollary 8.2.5,

$$A_{MNPQ} = \frac{1}{2} d_1 d_2 = \frac{1}{2} \cdot 12 \cdot 16 = 96 \text{ units}^2$$ ■

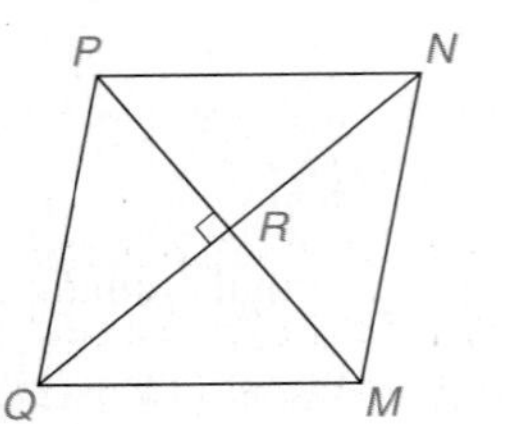

Figure 8.26

In problems involving the rhombus, we often utilize the fact that its diagonals are perpendicular. If the length of a side and the length of either diagonal are known, the length of the other diagonal can be found by applying the Pythagorean Theorem.

AREA OF A KITE

For a kite, we proved in Exercise 27 of Section 4.2 that one diagonal is the perpendicular bisector of the other. (See Figure 8.27.)

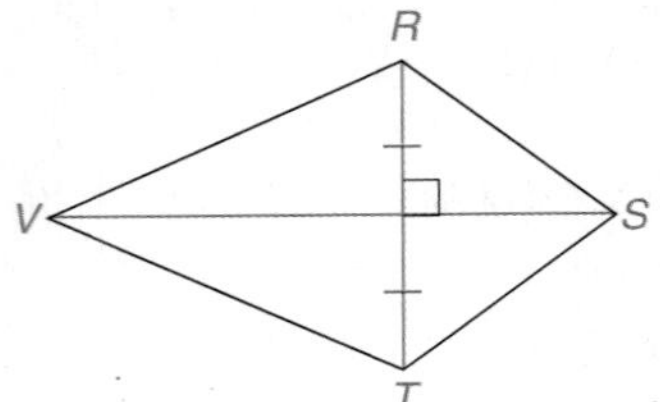

Figure 8.27

COROLLARY 8.2.6

The area A of a kite whose diagonals have lengths d_1 and d_2 is given by

$$A = \frac{1}{2} d_1 d_2$$

We apply Corollary 8.2.6 in Example 6.

EXAMPLE 6

Find the length of $\overline{RT}$ in Figure 8.28 if the area of the kite $RSTV$ is 360 in.^{2} and $SV = 30$ in.

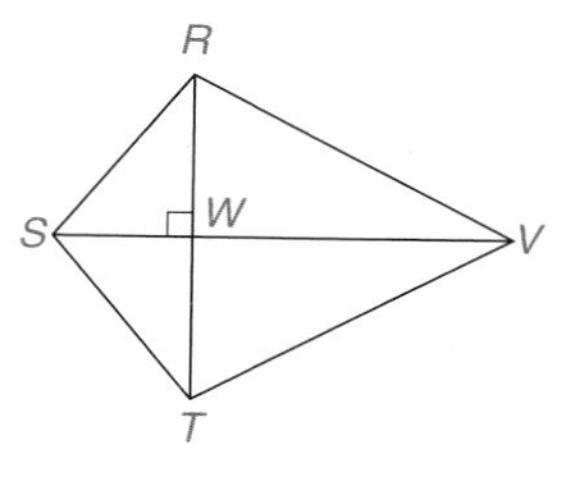

Figure 8.28

Solution $A = \frac{1}{2}d_1d_2$ becomes $360 = \frac{1}{2}(30)d$, in which d is the length of the remaining diagonal $\overline{RT}$. Then $360 = 15d$, which means that $d = 24$. Then $RT = 24$ in. ■

SSG *Exs. 13–17*

AREAS OF SIMILAR POLYGONS

Reminder

Corresponding altitudes of similar triangles have the same ratio as any pair of corresponding sides.

The following theorem compares the areas of similar triangles. In Figure 8.29, we refer to the areas of the similar triangles as A_1 and A_2. The triangle with area A_1 has sides of lengths a_1, b_1, and c_1, and the triangle with area A_2 has sides of lengths a_2, b_2, and c_2. Where a_1 corresponds to a_2, b_1 to b_2, and c_1 to c_2, Theorem 8.2.7 implies that

$$\frac{A_1}{A_2} = \left(\frac{a_1}{a_2}\right)^2 \quad \text{or} \quad \frac{A_1}{A_2} = \left(\frac{b_1}{b_2}\right)^2 \quad \text{or} \quad \frac{A_1}{A_2} = \left(\frac{c_1}{c_2}\right)^2$$

We prove only the first relationship; the other proofs are analogous.

THEOREM 8.2.7

The ratio of the areas of two similar triangles equals the square of the ratio of the lengths of any two corresponding sides; that is,

$$\frac{A_1}{A_2} = \left(\frac{a_1}{a_2}\right)^2$$

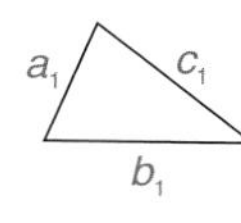

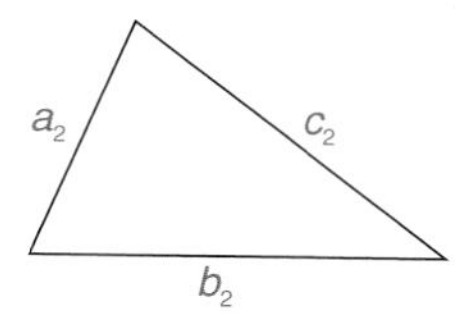

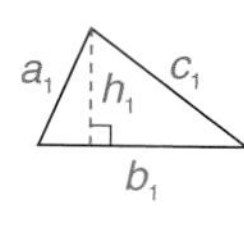

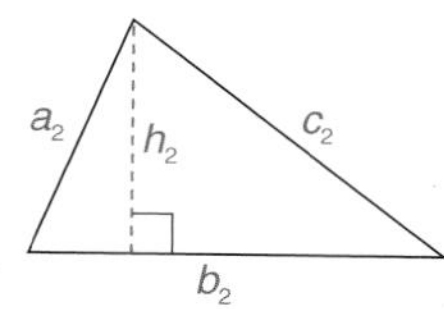

Figure 8.29

GIVEN: Similar triangles as shown in Figure 8.29

PROVE: $\frac{A_1}{A_2} = \left(\frac{a_1}{a_2}\right)^2$

PROOF: For the similar triangles, h_1 and h_2 are the respective lengths of altitudes to the corresponding sides of lengths b_1 and b_2. Now $A_1 = \frac{1}{2}b_1h_1$ and $A_2 = \frac{1}{2}b_2h_2$, so

$$\frac{A_1}{A_2} = \frac{\frac{1}{2}b_1h_1}{\frac{1}{2}b_2h_2} \quad \text{or} \quad \frac{A_1}{A_2} = \frac{\frac{1}{2}}{\frac{1}{2}} \cdot \frac{b_1}{b_2} \cdot \frac{h_1}{h_2}$$

Simplifying, we have

$$\frac{A_1}{A_2} = \frac{b_1}{b_2} \cdot \frac{h_1}{h_2}$$

Because the triangles are similar, we know that $\frac{b_1}{b_2} = \frac{a_1}{a_2}$. Because corresponding altitudes of similar triangles have the same ratio as a pair of corresponding sides (Theorem

5.3.2), we also know that $\frac{h_1}{h_2} = \frac{a_1}{a_2}$. Through substitution, $\frac{A_1}{A_2} = \frac{b_1}{b_2} \cdot \frac{h_1}{h_2}$ becomes $\frac{A_1}{A_2} = \frac{a_1}{a_2} \cdot \frac{a_1}{a_2}$. Then $\frac{A_1}{A_2} = \left(\frac{a_1}{a_2}\right)^2$. ■

Because Theorem 8.2.7 can be extended to any pair of similar polygons, we could also prove that the ratio of the areas of two squares equals the square of the ratio of the lengths of any two sides. We apply this relationship in Example 7.

EXAMPLE 7

Use the ratio $\frac{A_1}{A_2}$ to compare the areas of:

a) Two similar triangles in which the sides of the first triangle are $\frac{1}{2}$ as long as the sides of the second triangle
b) Two squares in which each side of the first square is 3 times as long as each side of the second square

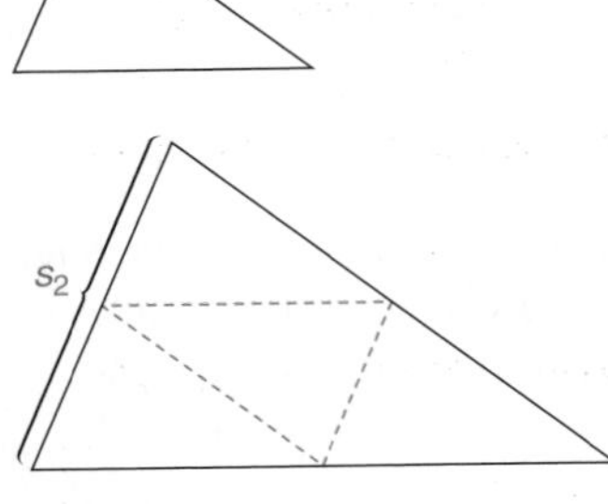

Figure 8.30

Solution

a) $s_1 = \frac{1}{2}s_2$, so $\frac{s_1}{s_2} = \frac{1}{2}$. (See Figure 8.30.)
Now $\frac{A_1}{A_2} = \left(\frac{s_1}{s_2}\right)^2$, so that $\frac{A_1}{A_2} = \left(\frac{1}{2}\right)^2$ or $\frac{A_1}{A_2} = \frac{1}{4}$. That is, the area of the first triangle is $\frac{1}{4}$ the area of the second triangle.

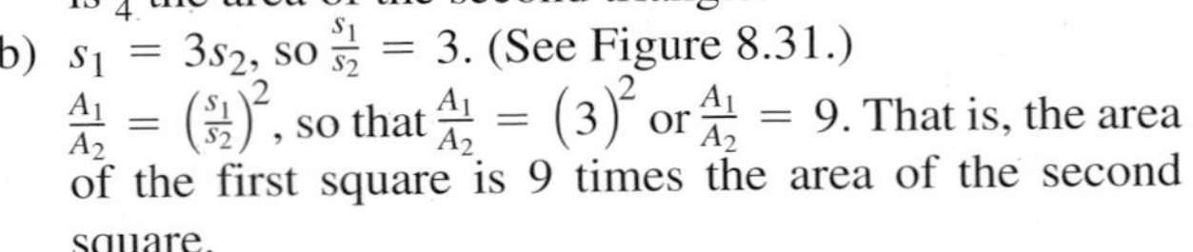

b) $s_1 = 3s_2$, so $\frac{s_1}{s_2} = 3$. (See Figure 8.31.)
$\frac{A_1}{A_2} = \left(\frac{s_1}{s_2}\right)^2$, so that $\frac{A_1}{A_2} = (3)^2$ or $\frac{A_1}{A_2} = 9$. That is, the area of the first square is 9 times the area of the second square.

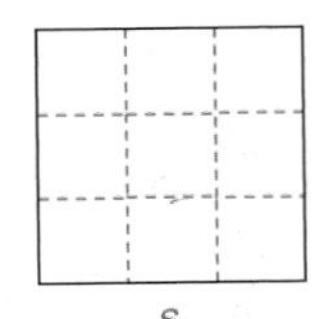

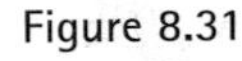
Figure 8.31

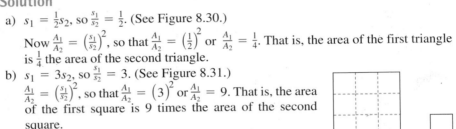

NOTE: For Example 7, Figures 8.30 and 8.31 provide visual evidence of the relationship described in Theorem 8.2.7. ■

SSG *Exs. 18–21*

Exercises 8.2

In Exercises 1 to 8, find the perimeter of each figure.

1\.

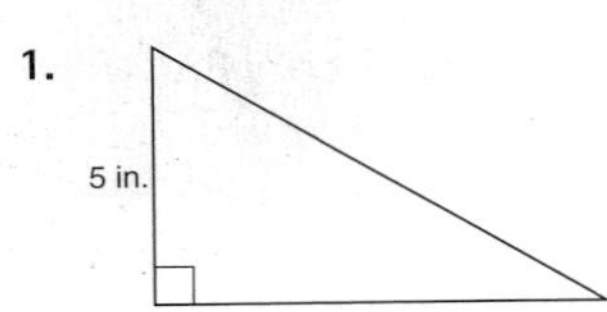

2\.

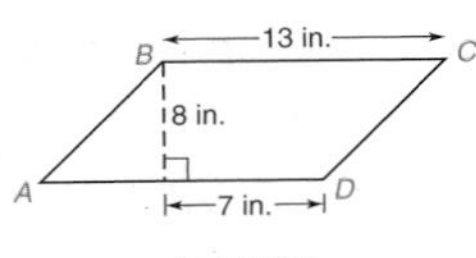

▱ ABCD

5\.

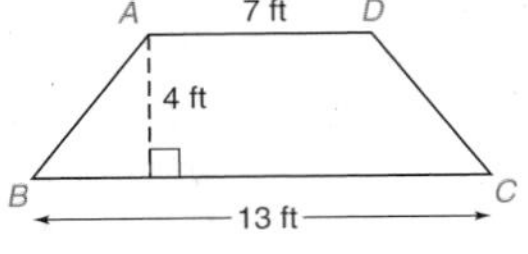

Trapezoid $ABCD$ with $\overline{AB} \cong \overline{DC}$

6\.

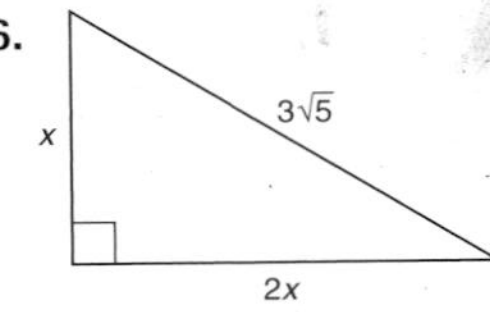

3\.

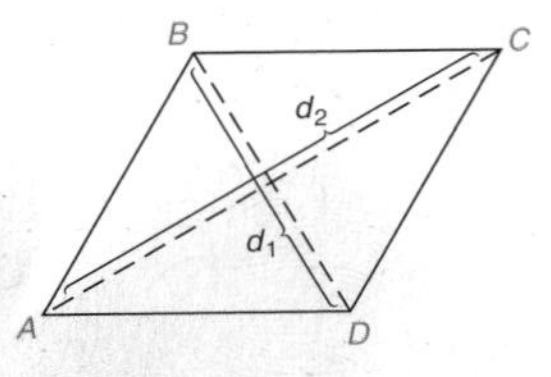

▱ $ABCD$ with $\overline{AB} \cong \overline{BC}$
$d_1 = 4$ m
$d_2 = 10$ m

4\.

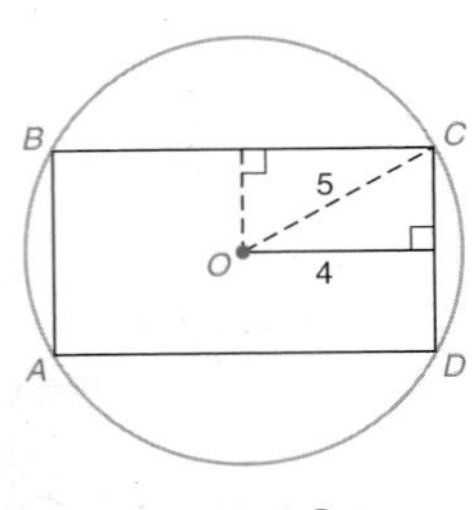

▱ $ABCD$ in ⊙O

7\.

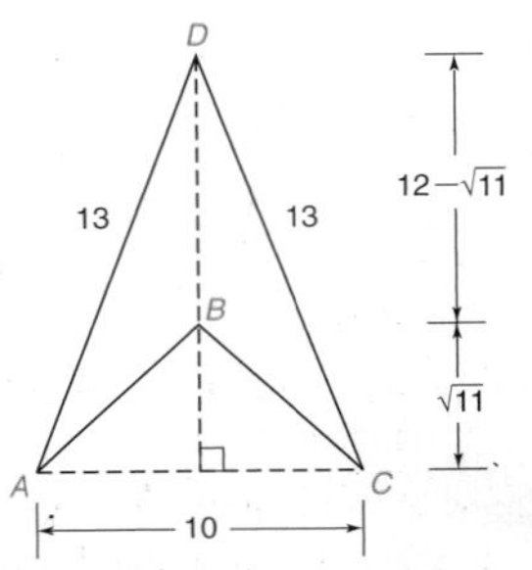

$\overline{AB} \cong \overline{BC}$ in concave quadrilateral $ABCD$

8\.

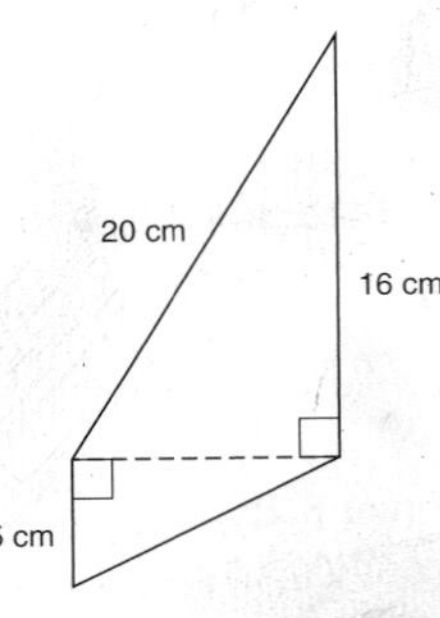

In Exercises 9 and 10, use Heron's Formula.

9. Find the area of a triangle whose sides measure 13 in., 14 in., and 15 in.

10. Find the area of a triangle whose sides measure 10 cm, 17 cm, and 21 cm.

For Exercises 11 and 12, use Brahmagupta's Formula.

11. For cyclic quadrilateral *ABCD*, find the area if $AB = 39$ mm, $BC = 52$ mm, $CD = 25$ mm, and $DA = 60$ mm.

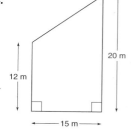

12. For cyclic quadrilateral *ABCD*, find the area if $AB = 6$ cm, $BC = 7$ cm, $CD = 2$ cm, and $DA = 9$ cm.

In Exercises 13 to 18, find the area of the given polygon.

13.

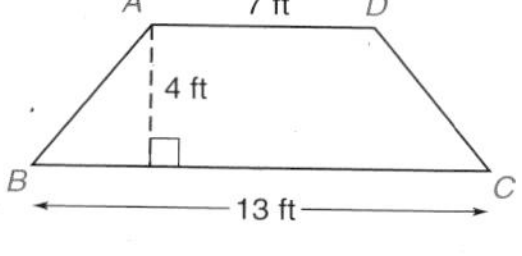

Trapezoid *ABCD* with $\overline{AB} \cong \overline{DC}$

14.

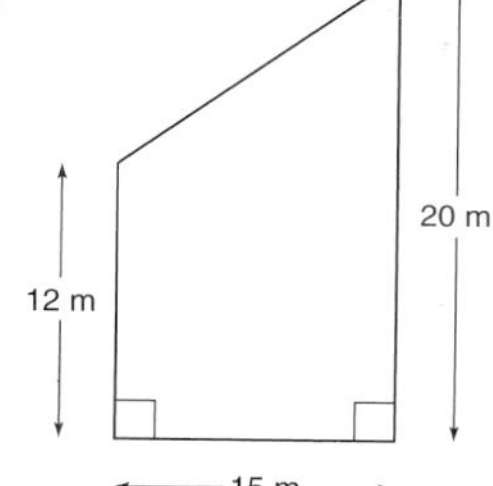

15.

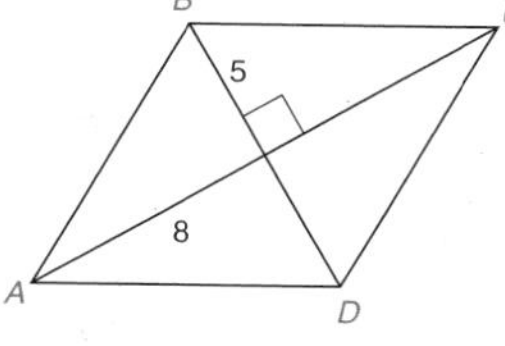

▱ *ABCD*

16.

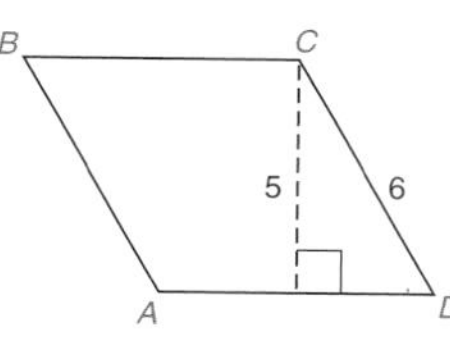

▱ *ABCD* with $\overline{BC} \cong \overline{CD}$

17.

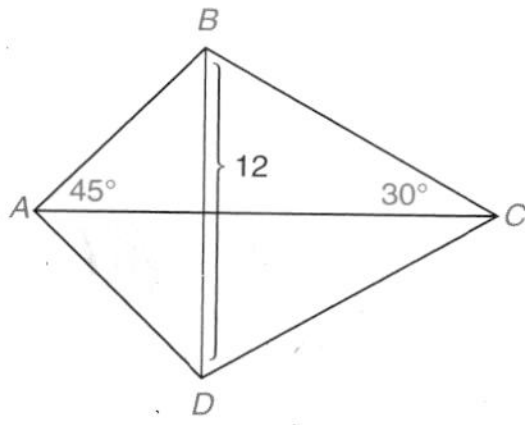

Kite *ABCD* with *BD* = 12
m∠*BAC* = 45°, m∠*BCA* = 30°

18.

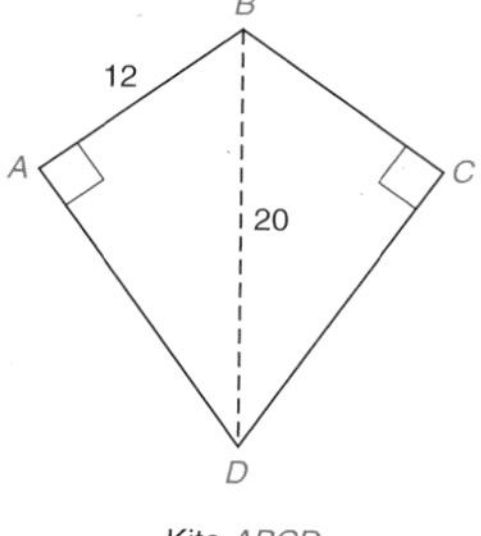

Kite *ABCD*

19. In a triangle of perimeter 76 in., the length of the first side is twice the length of the second side, and the length of the third side is 12 in. more than the length of the second side. Find the lengths of the three sides.

20. In a triangle whose area is 72 in^2, the base has a length of 8 in. Find the length of the corresponding altitude.

21. A trapezoid has an area of 96 cm^2. If the altitude has a length of 8 cm and one base has a length of 9 cm, find the length of the other base.

22. The numerical difference between the area of a square and the perimeter of that square is 32. Find the length of a side of the square.

23. Find the ratio $\frac{A_1}{A_2}$ of the areas of two similar triangles if:
a) The ratio of corresponding sides is $\frac{s_1}{s_2} = \frac{3}{2}$.
b) The lengths of the sides of the first triangle are 6, 8, and 10 in., and those of the second triangle are 3, 4, and 5 in.

24. Find the ratio $\frac{A_1}{A_2}$ of the areas of two similar rectangles if:
a) The ratio of corresponding sides is $\frac{s_1}{s_2} = \frac{2}{5}$.
b) The length of the first rectangle is 6 m, and the length of the second rectangle is 4 m.

In Exercises 25 and 26, give a paragraph form of proof. Provide drawings as needed.

25. *Given:* Equilateral $\triangle ABC$ with each side of length s
Prove: $A_{ABC} = \frac{s^2}{4}\sqrt{3}$
(HINT: Use Heron's Formula.)

26. *Given:* Isosceles $\triangle MNQ$ with $QM = QN = s$ and $MN = 2a$
Prove: $A_{MNQ} = a\sqrt{s^2 - a^2}$
(NOTE: $s > a$.)

In Exercises 27 to 30, find the area of the figure shown.

27. *Given:* In $\odot O$, $OA = 5$, $BC = 6$, and $CD = 4$
Find: A_{ABCD}

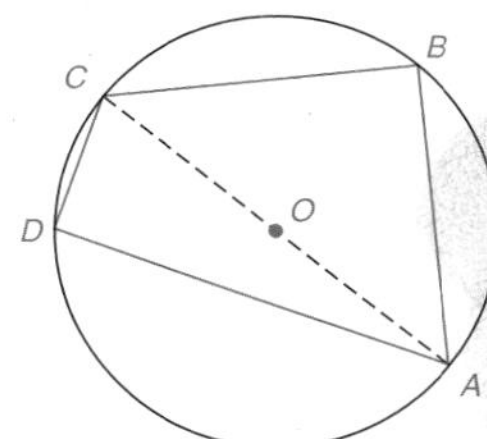

28. *Given:* Hexagon *RSTVWX* with $\overline{WV} \parallel \overline{XT} \parallel \overline{RS}$
$RS = 10$
$ST = 8$
$TV = 5$
$WV = 16$
$\overline{WX} \cong \overline{VT}$
Find: A_{RSTVWX}

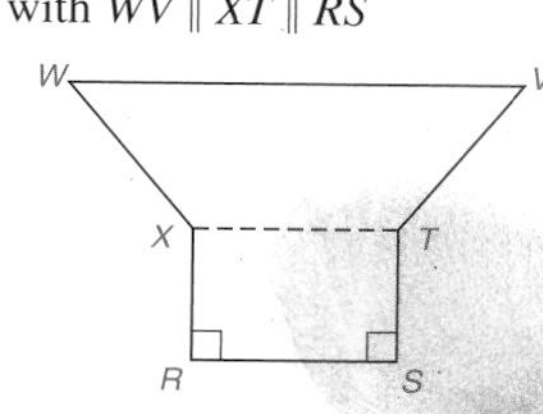

29. *Given:* Pentagon *ABCDE* with $\overline{DC} \cong \overline{DE}$
$AE = AB = 5$
$BC = 12$
Find: A_{ABCDE}

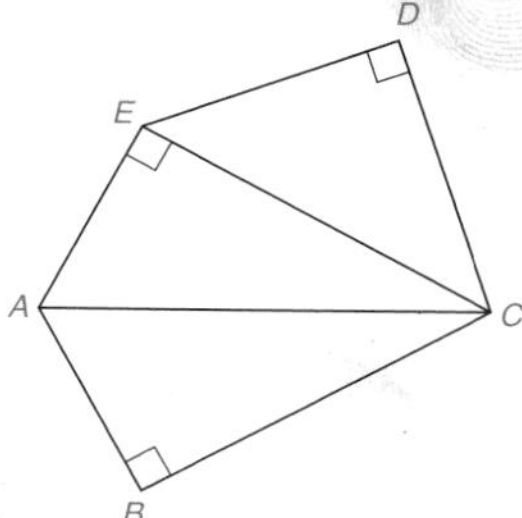

30. *Given:* Pentagon $RSTVW$ with $m\angle VRS = m\angle VSR = 60°$, $RS = 8\sqrt{2}$, and $\overline{RW} \cong \overline{WV} \cong \overline{VT} \cong \overline{TS}$

Find: A_{RSTVW}

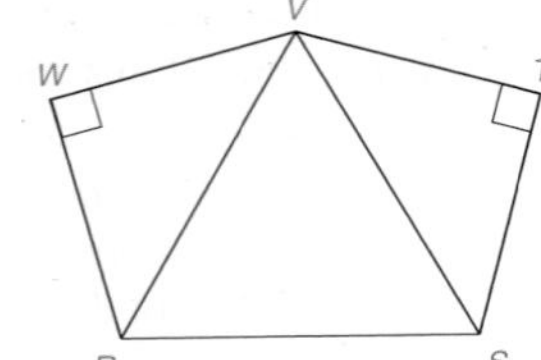

31. Mary Frances has a rectangular garden plot that encloses an area of 48 yd^2. If 28 yd of fencing are purchased to enclose the garden, what are the dimensions of the rectangular plot?

32. The perimeter of a right triangle is 12 m. If the hypotenuse has a length of 5 m, find the lengths of the two legs.

33. Farmer Watson wishes to fence a rectangular plot of ground measuring 245 ft by 140 ft.
   a) What amount of fencing is needed?
   b) What is the total cost of the fencing if it costs $0.59 per foot?

34. The farmer in Exercise 33 has decided to take the fencing purchased and use it to enclose the subdivided plots shown.
   a) What are the overall dimensions of the rectangular enclosure shown?
   b) What is the total area of the enclosures shown?

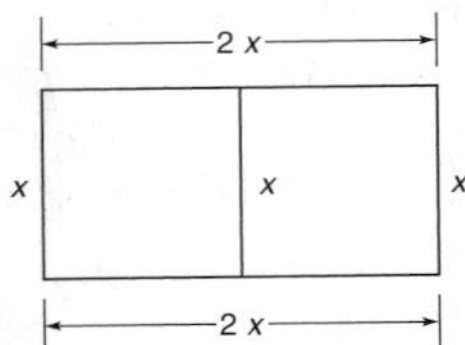

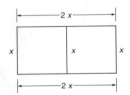

35. Find the area of the room whose floor plan is shown.

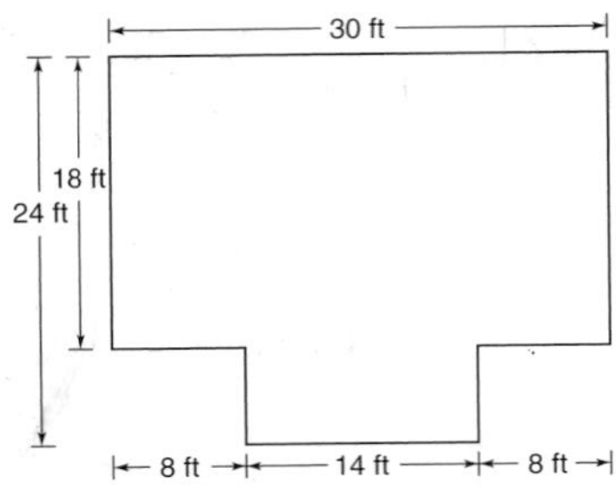

Exercises 35, 36

36. Find the perimeter of the room in Exercise 35.

37. Examine several rectangles, each with a perimeter of 40 in., and find the dimensions of the rectangle that has the largest area. What type of figure has the largest area?

38. Examine several rectangles, each with an area of 36 in^2, and find the dimensions of the rectangle that has the smallest perimeter. What type of figure has the smallest perimeter?

39. Square $RSTV$ is inscribed in square $WXYZ$ as shown. If $ZT = 5$ and $TY = 12$, find
   a) the perimeter of $RSTV$.
   b) the area of $RSTV$.

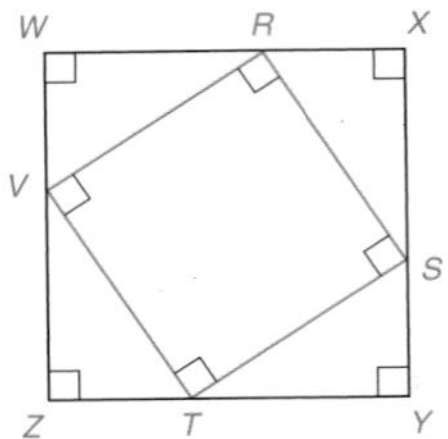

Exercises 39, 40

40. Square $RSTV$ is inscribed in square $WXYZ$ as shown. If $ZT = 8$ and $TY = 15$, find
   a) the perimeter of $RSTV$.
   b) the area of $RSTV$.

41. Although not all kites are cyclic, one with sides of lengths 5 in., 1 ft, 1 ft, and 5 in. would be cyclic. Find the area of this kite. Give the resulting area in *square inches*.

42. Although not all trapezoids are cyclic, one with bases of lengths 12 cm and 28 cm and both legs of length 10 cm would be cyclic. Find the area of this isosceles trapezoid.

For Exercises 43 and 44, use this information: Let a, b, and c be the integer lengths of the sides of a triangle. If the area of the triangle is also an integer, then (a, b, c) is known as a Heron triple.

43. Which of these are Heron triples?
   a) (5, 6, 7) b) (13, 14, 15)

44. Which of these are Heron triples?
   a) (9, 10, 17) b) (8, 10, 12)

45. Prove that the area of a trapezoid whose altitude has length h and whose median has length m is $A = hm$.

For Exercises 46 and 47, use the formula found in Exercise 45.

46. Find the area of a trapezoid with an altitude of length 4.2 m and a median of length 6.5 m.

47. Find the area of a trapezoid with an altitude of length $5\frac{1}{3}$ ft and a median of length $2\frac{1}{4}$ ft.

48. Prove that the area of a square whose diagonal length is d is $A = \frac{1}{2}d^2$.

For Exercises 49 and 50, use the formula found in Exercise 48.

49. Find the area of a square whose diagonal has length $\sqrt{10}$ in.

50. Find the area of a square whose diagonal has length 14.5 cm.

*51. The shaded region is that of a trapezoid. Determine the height of the trapezoid.

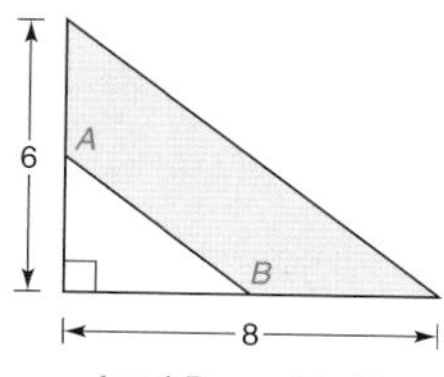

52. Trapezoid $ABCD$ (not shown) is inscribed in $\odot O$ so that side $\overline{DC}$ is a diameter of $\odot O$. If $DC = 10$ and $AB = 6$, find the exact area of trapezoid $ABCD$.

53. Each side of square $RSTV$ has length 8. Point W lies on $\overline{VR}$ and point Y lies on $\overline{TS}$ in such a way to form parallelogram $VWSY$, which has an area of 16 units^2. Find x, the length of $\overline{VW}$.

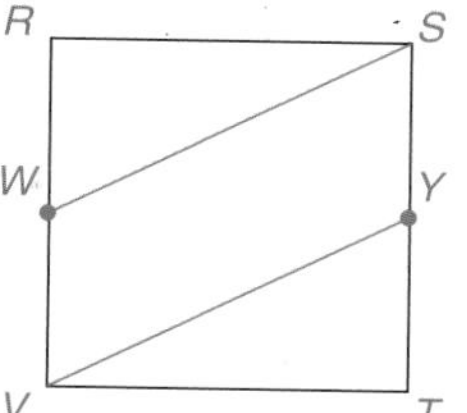

8.3 Regular Polygons and Area

KEY CONCEPTS

- Regular Polygon
- Center and Central Angle of a Regular Polygon
- Radius and Apothem of a Regular Polygon
- Area of a Regular Polygon

Regular polygons are, of course, both equilateral and equiangular. As we saw in Section 7.3, we can inscribe a circle within any regular polygon and we can circumscribe a circle about any regular polygon. For regular hexagon $ABCDEF$ shown in Figure 8.32, suppose that $\overline{QE}$ and $\overline{QD}$ bisect the interior angles of $ABCDEF$ as shown. In terms of hexagon $ABCDEF$, recall these terms and theorems.

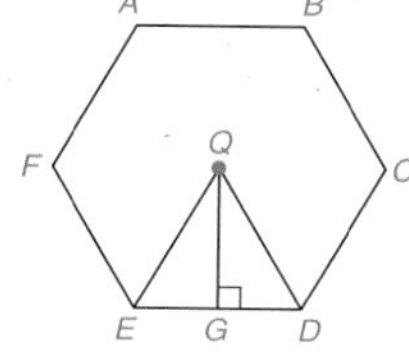

Figure 8.32

1. Point Q is the *center* of regular hexagon $ABCDEF$. This point Q is the common center of both the inscribed and circumscribed circles for regular hexagon $ABCDEF$.
2. $\overline{QE}$ is a *radius* of regular hexagon $ABCDEF$. A radius joins the center of the regular polygon to a vertex.
3. $\overline{QG}$ is an *apothem* of regular hexagon $ABCDEF$. An apothem is a line segment drawn from the center of a regular polygon so that it is perpendicular to a side of the polygon.
4. $\angle EQD$ is a *central angle* of regular hexagon $ABCDEF$. Center point Q is the vertex of a central angle, whose sides are consecutive radii of the polygon. The measure of a central angle of a regular polygon of n sides is $c = \frac{360°}{n}$.
5. Any radius of a regular polygon bisects the interior angle to which it is drawn.
6. Any apothem of a regular polygon bisects the side to which it is drawn.

Among regular polygons are the square and the equilateral triangle. As we saw in Section 8.1, the area of a square whose sides have length s is given by $A = s^2$.

EXAMPLE 1

Find the area of the square whose length of apothem is $a = 2$ in.

Solution The apothem is the distance from the center to a side. For the square, $s = 2a$; that is, $s = 4$ in. Then $A = s^2$ becomes $A = 4^2$ and $A = 16\text{ in}^2$.

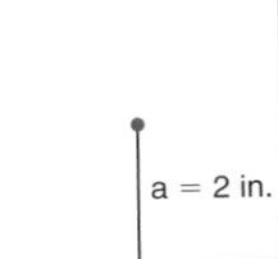

Figure 8.33 ■

SSG
Exs. 1–4

In Exercise 25 of Section 8.2, we showed that the area of an equilateral triangle whose sides are of length s is given by

$$A = \frac{s^2}{4}\sqrt{3}$$

Following is a picture proof of this area relationship.

PICTURE PROOF

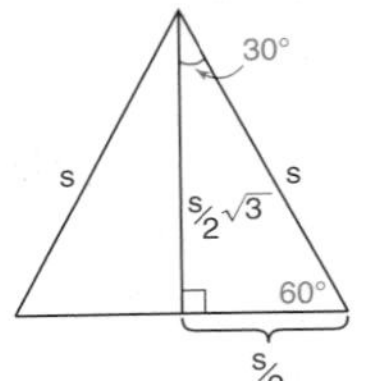

Figure 8.34

GIVEN: The equilateral triangle with sides of length s

PROVE: $A = \frac{s^2}{4}\sqrt{3}$

PROOF: Based upon the 30°-60°-90° triangle in Figure 8.34, $A = \frac{1}{2}bh$ becomes

$$A = \frac{1}{2}\cdot s\cdot\frac{s}{2}\sqrt{3}$$

so $A = \frac{s^2}{4}\sqrt{3}$.

EXAMPLE 2

Find the area of an equilateral triangle (not shown) in which each side measures 4 inches.

Solution $A = \frac{s^2}{4}\sqrt{3}$ becomes $A = \frac{4^2}{4}\sqrt{3}$ or $A = 4\sqrt{3}\text{ in}^2$. ■

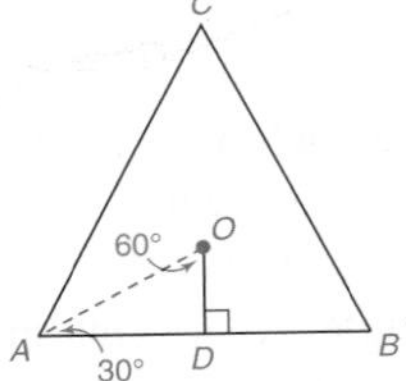

Figure 8.35

EXAMPLE 3

Find the area of equilateral triangle ABC in which apothem $\overline{OD}$ has a length of 6 cm.

Solution See Figure 8.35. If $OD = 6$ cm, then $AD = 6\sqrt{3}$ cm in the indicated 30°-60°-90° triangle AOD. In turn, $AB = 12\sqrt{3}$ cm. Now $A = \frac{s^2}{4}\sqrt{3}$ becomes

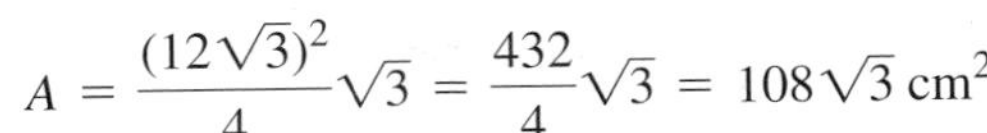

$$A = \frac{(12\sqrt{3})^2}{4}\sqrt{3} = \frac{432}{4}\sqrt{3} = 108\sqrt{3}\text{ cm}^2$$ ■

SSG
Exs. 5–8

We now seek a general formula for the area of any regular polygon.

AREA OF A REGULAR POLYGON

In Chapter 7 and Chapter 8, we have laid the groundwork for determining the area of a regular polygon. In the proof of Theorem 8.3.1, the figure chosen is a regular pentagon; however, the proof applies to a regular polygon of any number of sides.

It is also worth noting that the perimeter P of a regular polygon is the sum of its equal sides. If there are n sides and each has length s, the perimeter of the regular polygon is $P = ns$.

THEOREM 8.3.1

The area A of a regular polygon whose apothem has length a and whose perimeter is P is given by

$$A = \frac{1}{2}aP$$

SSG *Exs. 9–11*

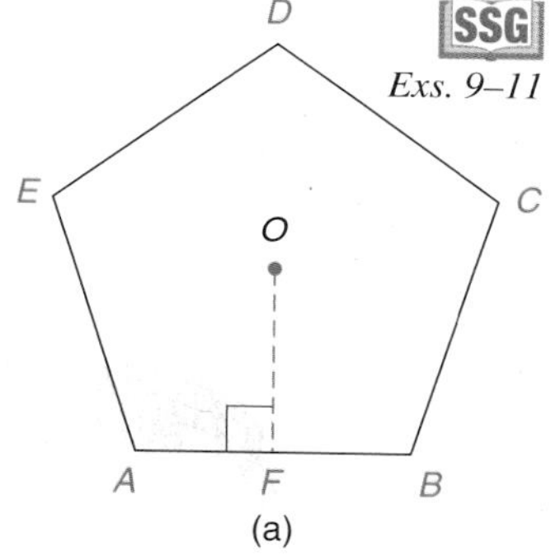

(a)

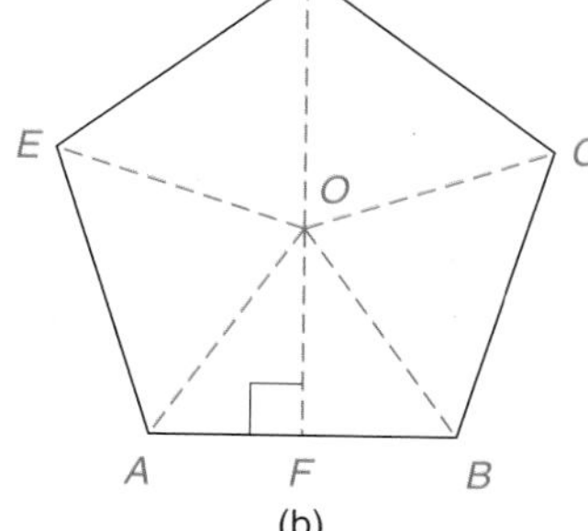

(b)

Figure 8.36

GIVEN: Regular polygon $ABCDE$ in Figure 8.36(a) such that $OF = a$ and the perimeter of $ABCDE$ is P

PROVE: $A_{ABCDE} = \frac{1}{2}aP$

PROOF: From center O, draw radii $\overline{OA}$, $\overline{OB}$, $\overline{OC}$, $\overline{OD}$, and $\overline{OE}$. [See Figure 8.36(b).] Now $\triangle AOB$, $\triangle BOC$, $\triangle COD$, $\triangle DOE$, and $\triangle EOA$ are all $\cong$ by SSS. Where s represents the length of each of the congruent sides of the regular polygon and a is the length of an apothem, the area of each triangle is $\frac{1}{2}sa$ (from $A = \frac{1}{2}bh$). Therefore, the area of the pentagon is

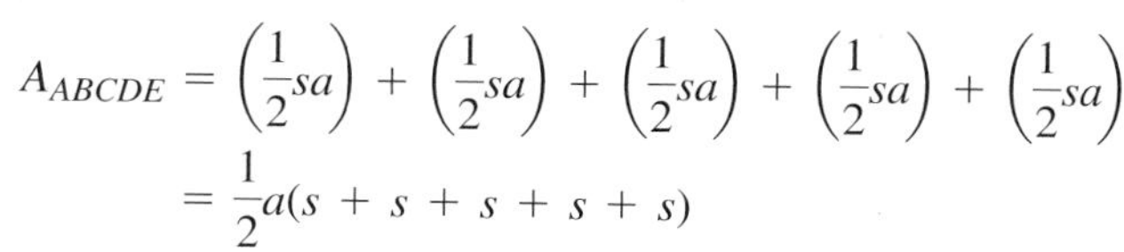

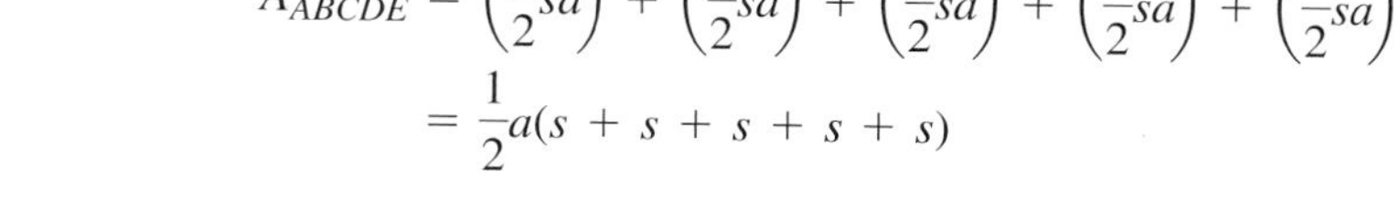

$$A_{ABCDE} = \left(\frac{1}{2}sa\right) + \left(\frac{1}{2}sa\right) + \left(\frac{1}{2}sa\right) + \left(\frac{1}{2}sa\right) + \left(\frac{1}{2}sa\right)$$
$$= \frac{1}{2}a(s + s + s + s + s)$$

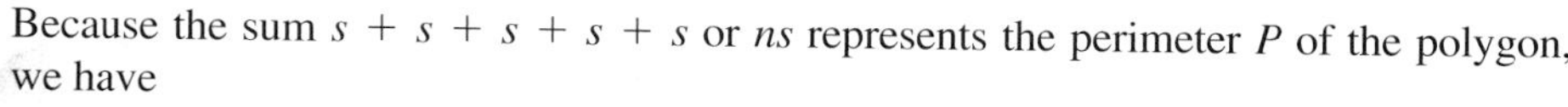

Because the sum $s + s + s + s + s$ or ns represents the perimeter P of the polygon, we have

$$A_{ABCDE} = \frac{1}{2}aP$$

■

EXAMPLE 4

Use $A = \frac{1}{2}aP$ to find the area of the square whose length of apothem is $a = 2$ in.

Solution For this repeat of Example 1, see Figure 8.33 as needed. When the length of apothem of a square is $a = 2$, the length of side is $s = 4$. In turn, the perimeter is $P = 16$ in.

Now $A = \frac{1}{2}aP$ becomes $A = \frac{1}{2} \cdot 2 \cdot 16$, so $A = 16 \text{ in}^2$.

NOTE: As expected, the answer from Example 1 is repeated in Example 4. ■

EXAMPLE 5

Use $A = \frac{1}{2}aP$ to find the area of the equilateral triangle whose apothem has the length 6 cm.

Solution For this repeat of Example 3, refer to Figure 8.35 on page 374. Because the length of apothem $\overline{OD}$ is 6 cm, the length of $\overline{AD}$ is $6\sqrt{3}$ cm. In turn, the length of side $\overline{AB}$ is $12\sqrt{3}$ cm. For the equilateral triangle, the perimeter is $P = 36\sqrt{3}$ cm.

Now $A = \frac{1}{2}aP$ becomes $A = \frac{1}{2}\cdot 6\cdot 36\sqrt{3}$, so $A = 108\sqrt{3}$ cm^2.

NOTE: As is necessary, the answer found in Example 3 is repeated in Example 5. ■

For Examples 6 and 7, the measures of the line segments that represent the length of the apothem, the radius, or the side of a regular polygon depend upon relationships that are developed in the study of trigonometry. The methods used to find related measures will be developed in Chapter 11 but are not given attention at this time. Many of the measures that are provided in the following examples and the exercise set for this section are actually only *good approximations.*

EXAMPLE 6

In Figure 8.36(a) on page 375, find the area of the regular pentagon *ABCDE* with center *O* if $OF = 4$ and $AB = 5.9$.

Solution $OF = a = 4$ and $AB = 5.9$. Therefore, $P = 5(5.9)$ or $P = 29.5$. Consequently,

$$A_{ABCDE} = \frac{1}{2}\cdot 4(29.5)$$
$$= 59 \text{ units}^2$$ ■

EXAMPLE 7

Find the area of the regular octagon shown in Figure 8.37. The center of *PQRSTUVW* is point *O*. The length of apothem $\overline{OX}$ is 12.1 cm, and the length of side $\overline{QR}$ is 10 cm.

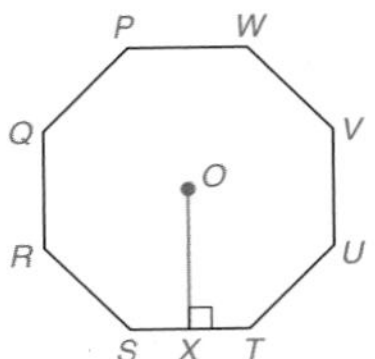

Figure 8.37

Solution If $QR = 10$ cm, then the perimeter of regular octagon *PQRSTUVW* is $8\cdot 10$ cm or 80 cm. With the length of apothem being $OX = 12.1$ cm, the area formula $A = \frac{1}{2}aP$ becomes $A = \frac{1}{2}\cdot 12.1\cdot 80$, so $A = 484$ cm^2. ■

Exs. 12–15

EXAMPLE 8

Find the exact area of equilateral triangle *ABC* in Figure 8.38 if each side measures 12 in. Use the formula $A = \frac{1}{2}aP$.

Solution In $\triangle ABC$, the perimeter is $P = 3 \cdot 12$ or 36 in.

To find the length a of an apothem, we draw the radius $\overline{OA}$ from center O to point A and the apothem $\overline{OM}$ from O to side $\overline{AB}$. Because the radius bisects $\angle BAC$, $m\angle OAB = 30°$. Because apothem $\overline{OM} \perp \overline{AB}$, $m\angle OMA = 90°$. $\overline{OM}$ also bisects $\overline{AB}$. Using the 30°-60°-90° relationship in $\triangle OMA$, we see that $a\sqrt{3} = 6$. Thus

$$a = \frac{6}{\sqrt{3}} = \frac{6}{\sqrt{3}} \cdot \frac{\sqrt{3}}{\sqrt{3}} = \frac{6\sqrt{3}}{3} = 2\sqrt{3}$$

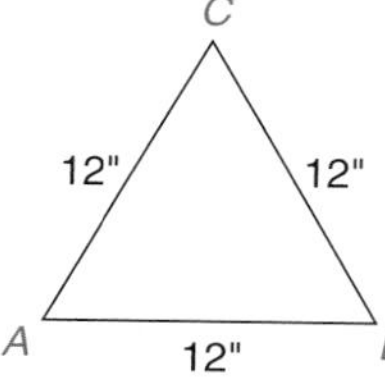

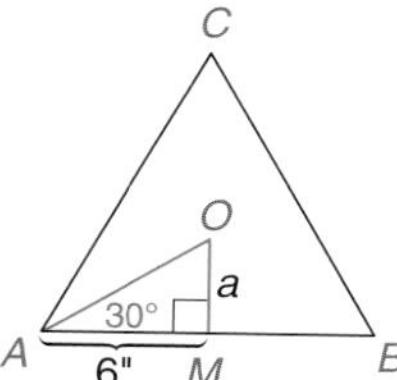

Figure 8.38

Now $A = \frac{1}{2}aP$ becomes $A = \frac{1}{2} \cdot 2\sqrt{3} \cdot 36 = 36\sqrt{3}$ in^2.

SSG Exs. 12–15 **NOTE:** Using the calculator's value for $\sqrt{3}$ leads to an approximation of the area rather than to an exact area. ■

Discover

TESSELLATIONS

Tessellations are patterns composed strictly of interlocking and non-overlapping regular polygons. All of the regular polygons of a given number of sides will be congruent. Tessellations are commonly used in design, but especially in flooring (tiles and vinyl sheets). A *pure tessellation* is one formed by using only one regular polygon in the pattern. An *impure tessellation* is one formed by using two different regular polygons.

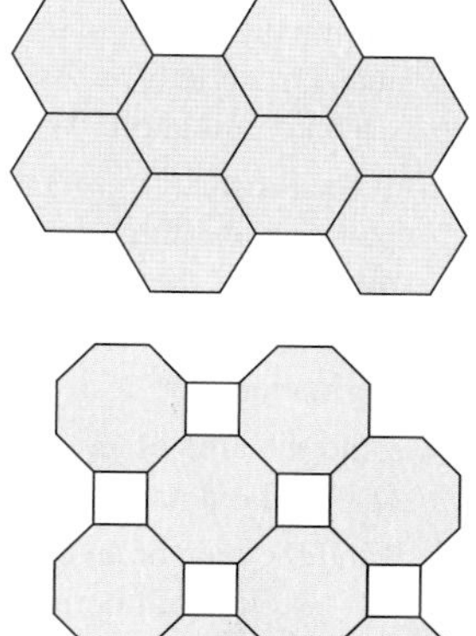

In the accompanying pure tessellation, only the regular hexagon appears. In nature, the beehive has compartments that are regular hexagons. Note that the adjacent angles' measures must sum to 360°; in this case, 120° + 120° + 120° = 360°. It would also be possible to form a pure tessellation of congruent squares because the sum of the adjacent angles' measures would be 90° + 90° + 90° + 90° = 360°.

In the impure tessellation shown, the regular octagon and the square are used. In Champaign-Urbana, sidewalks found on the University of Illinois campus use this tessellation pattern. Again it is necessary that the sum of the adjacent angles' measures be 360°; for this impure tessellation, 135° + 135° + 90° = 360°.

a) Can congruent equilateral triangles be used to form a pure tessellation?

b) Can two regular hexagons and a square be used to build an impure tessellation?

ANSWERS

a) Yes, because 6 × 60° = 360° b) No, because 120° + 120° + 90° ≠ 360°

Exercises 8.3

1. Find the area of a square with
   a) sides of length 3.5 cm each.
   b) apothem of length 4.7 in.
2. Find the area of a square with
   a) a perimeter of 14.8 cm.
   b) radius of length $4\sqrt{2}$ in.
3. Find the area of an equilateral triangle with
   a) sides of length 2.5 m each.
   b) apothem of length 3 in.
4. Find the area of an equiangular triangle with
   a) a perimeter of 24.6 cm.
   b) radius of length 4 in.
5. In a regular polygon, each central angle measures 30°. If each side of the regular polygon measures 5.7 in., find the perimeter of the polygon.
6. In a regular polygon, each interior angle measures 135°. If each side of the regular polygon measures 4.2 cm, find the perimeter of the polygon.
7. For a regular hexagon, the length of the apothem is 10 cm. Find the length of the radius for the circumscribed circle for this hexagon.
8. For a regular hexagon, the length of the radius is 12 in. Find the length of the radius for the inscribed circle for this hexagon.
9. In a particular type of regular polygon, the length of the radius is exactly the same as the length of a side of the polygon. What type of regular polygon is it?
10. In a particular type of regular polygon, the length of the apothem is exactly one-half the length of a side. What type of regular polygon is it?
11. In one type of regular polygon, the measure of each interior angle $\left(I = \frac{(n-2)180°}{n}\right)$ is equal to the measure of each central angle. What type of regular polygon is it?
12. If the area ($A = \frac{1}{2}aP$) and the perimeter of a regular polygon are numerically equal, find the length of the apothem of the regular polygon.
13. Find the area of a square with apothem a = 3.2 cm and perimeter P = 25.6 cm.
14. Find the area of an equilateral triangle with apothem a = 3.2 cm and perimeter $P = 19.2\sqrt{3}$ cm.
15. Find the area of an equiangular triangle with apothem a = 4.6 in. and perimeter $P = 27.6\sqrt{3}$ in.
16. Find the area of a square with apothem a = 8.2 ft and perimeter P = 65.6 ft.

In Exercises 17 to 30, use the formula $A = \frac{1}{2}aP$ to find the area of the regular polygon described.

17. Find the area of a regular pentagon with an apothem of length a = 5.2 cm and each side of length s = 7.5 cm.
18. Find the area of a regular pentagon with an apothem of length a = 6.5 in. and each side of length s = 9.4 in.
19. Find the area of a regular octagon with an apothem of length a = 9.8 in. and each side of length s = 8.1 in.
20. Find the area of a regular octagon with an apothem of length a = 7.9 ft and each side of length s = 6.5 ft.
21. Find the area of a regular hexagon whose sides have length 6 cm.
22. Find the area of a square whose apothem measures 5 cm.
23. Find the area of an equilateral triangle whose radius measures 10 in.
24. Find the approximate area of a regular pentagon whose apothem measures 6 in. and each of whose sides measures approximately 8.9 in.
25. In a regular octagon, the approximate ratio of the length of an apothem to the length of a side is 6:5. For a regular octagon with an apothem of length 15 cm, find the approximate area.
26. In a regular dodecagon (12 sides), the approximate ratio of the length of an apothem to the length of a side is 15:8. For a regular dodecagon with a side of length 12 ft, find the approximate area.
27. In a regular dodecagon (12 sides), the approximate ratio of the length of an apothem to the length of a side is 15:8. For a regular dodecagon with an apothem of length 12 ft, find the approximate area.
28. In a regular octagon, the approximate ratio of the length of an apothem to the length of a side is 6:5. For a regular octagon with a side of length 15 ft, find the approximate area.
29. In a regular polygon of 12 sides, the measure of each side is 2 in., and the measure of an apothem is exactly $(2 + \sqrt{3})$ in. Find the exact area of this regular polygon.
30. In a regular octagon, the measure of each apothem is 4 cm, and each side measures exactly $8(\sqrt{2} - 1)$ cm. Find the exact area of this regular polygon.
31. Find the ratio of the area of a square circumscribed about a circle to the area of a square inscribed in the circle.
*32. Given regular hexagon $ABCDEF$ with each side of length 6 and diagonal $\overline{AC}$, find the area of pentagon $ACDEF$.

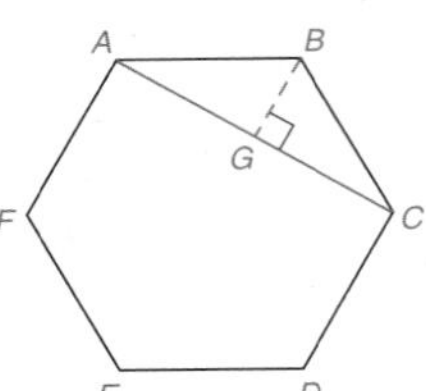

*33. Given regular octagon $RSTUVWXY$ with each side of length 4 and diagonal $\overline{RU}$, find the area of hexagon $RYXWVU$.

34. Regular octagon *ABCDEFGH* is inscribed in a circle whose radius is $\frac{7}{2}\sqrt{2}$ cm. Considering that the area of the octagon is less than the area of the circle and greater than the area of the square *ACEG*, find the two integers between which the area of the octagon must lie.
(NOTE: For the circle, use $A = \pi r^2$ with $\pi \approx \frac{22}{7}$.)

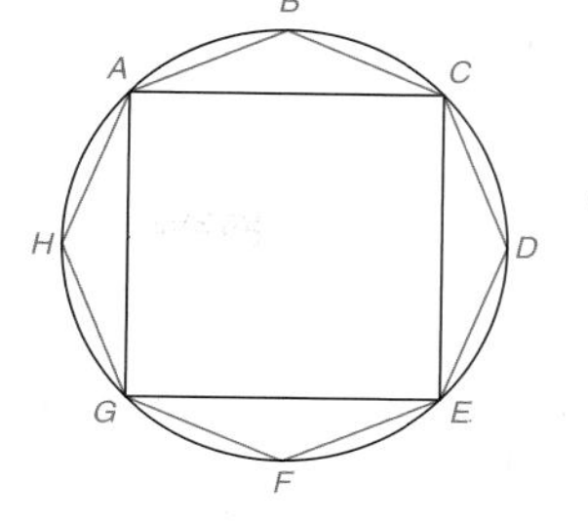

***35.** Given regular pentagon *RSTVQ* and equilateral triangle *PQR*, the length of an apothem (not shown) of *RSTVQ* is 12, while the length of each side of the equilateral triangle is 10. If $PV \approx 8.2$, find the approximate area of kite *VPST*.

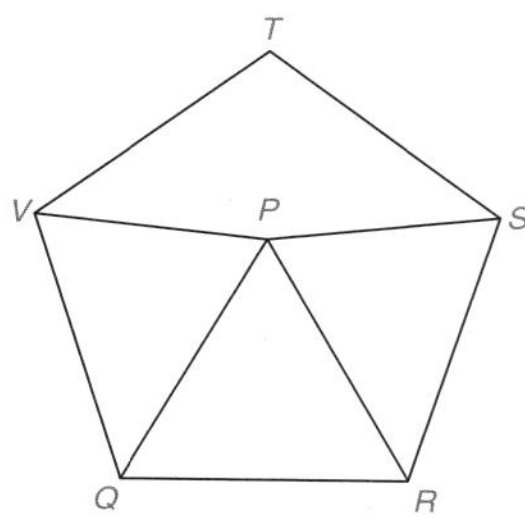

***36.** Consider regular pentagon *RSTVQ* (not shown). Given that diagonals $\overline{QT}$ and $\overline{VR}$ intersect at point *F*, show that $VF \cdot FR = TF \cdot FQ$.

***37.** Consider a regular hexagon *ABCDEF* (not shown). By joining midpoints of consecutive sides, a smaller regular hexagon *MNPQRS* is formed. Show that the ratio of areas is

$$\frac{A_{MNPQRS}}{A_{ABCDEF}} = \frac{3}{4}$$

8.4 Circumference and Area of a Circle

KEY CONCEPTS

Circumference of a Circle	Length of an Arc	Area of a Circle
π (Pi)	Limit	

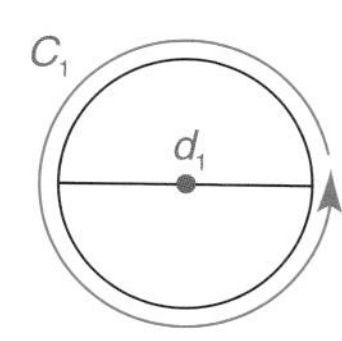

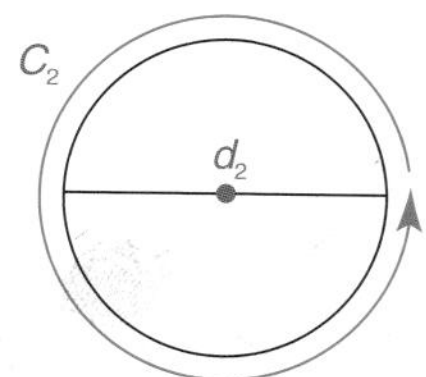

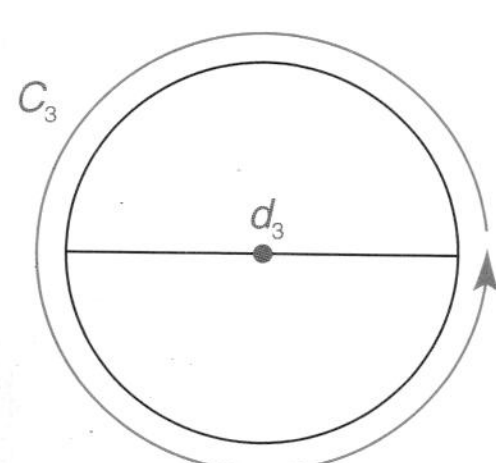

Figure 8.39

In geometry, any two figures that have the same shape are described as similar. For this reason, we say that all circles are similar to each other. Just as a proportionality exists among the sides of similar triangles, experimentation shows that there is a proportionality among the circumferences (distances around) and diameters (distances across) of circles; see the Discover activity on page 380. Representing the circumferences of the circles in Figure 8.39 by C_1, C_2, and C_3 and their respective lengths of diameters by d_1, d_2, and d_3, we claim that

$$\frac{C_1}{d_1} = \frac{C_2}{d_2} = \frac{C_3}{d_3} = k$$

where k is the constant of proportionality.

POSTULATE 22

The ratio of the circumference of a circle to the length of its diameter is a unique positive constant.

Discover

Find an object of circular shape, such as the lid of a jar. Using a flexible tape measure (such as a seamstress or carpenter might use), measure both the distance around (circumference) and the distance across (length of diameter) the circle. Now divide the circumference C by the diameter length d. What is your result?

ANSWER

The ratio should be slightly larger than 3.

The constant of proportionality k described in the opening paragraph of this section, in Postulate 22, and in the Discover activity is represented by the Greek letter π (*pi*).

DEFINITION

π is the ratio between the circumference C and the diameter length d of any circle; thus, $\pi = \frac{C}{d}$ in any circle.

In the following theorem, the lengths of the diameter and radius of the circle are represented by d and r respectively.

THEOREM 8.4.1

The circumference of a circle is given by the formula

$$C = \pi d \qquad \text{or} \qquad C = 2\pi r$$

GIVEN: Circle O with length of diameter d and length of radius r. (See Figure 8.40.)

PROVE: $C = 2\pi r$

PROOF: By Postulate 22, $\pi = \frac{C}{d}$. Multiplying each side of the equation by d, we have $C = \pi d$. Because $d = 2r$ (the diameter's length is twice that of the radius), the formula for the circumference can be written $C = \pi(2r)$, or $C = 2\pi r$. ■

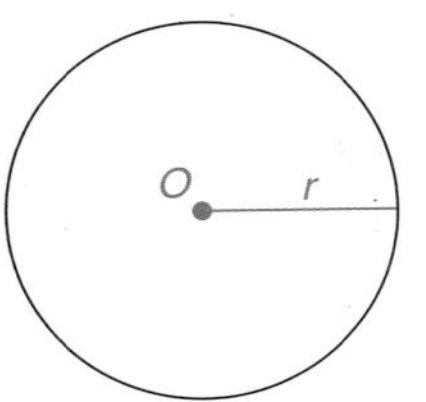

Figure 8.40

VALUE OF π

Exs. 1–2

In calculating the circumference of a circle, we generally leave the symbol π in the answer in order to state an *exact* result. However, the value of π is irrational and cannot be represented exactly by a common fraction or by a terminating decimal. When an approximation is needed for π, we use a calculator. Approximations of π that have been commonly used throughout history include $\pi \approx \frac{22}{7}$, $\pi \approx 3.14$, and $\pi \approx 3.1416$. Although these approximate values have been used for centuries, your calculator provides greater accuracy. A calculator will show that $\pi \approx 3.141592654$.

Technology Exploration

Use computer software if available.

1. Draw a circle with center O.
2. Through O, draw diameter $\overline{AB}$.
3. Measure the circumference C and length d of diameter $\overline{AB}$.
4. Show that $\frac{C}{d} \approx 3.14$.

EXAMPLE 1

In $\odot O$ in Figure 8.41, $OA = 7$ cm. Using $\pi \approx \frac{22}{7}$,

a) find the approximate circumference C of $\odot O$.
b) find the approximate length of the minor arc $\overset{\frown}{AB}$.

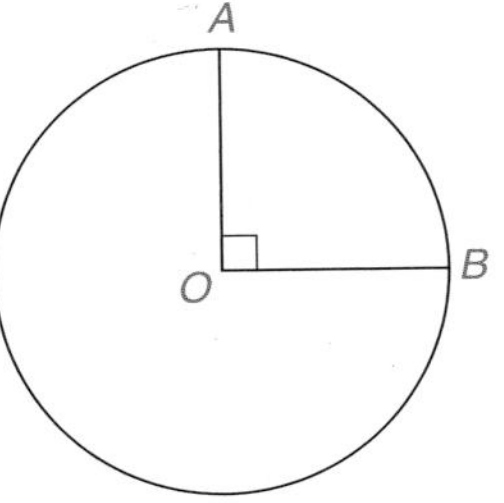

Figure 8.41

Solution

a) $C = 2\pi r$
$= 2 \cdot \frac{22}{\not 7} \cdot \not 7$
$= 44$ cm

b) Because the degree of measure of $\overset{\frown}{AB}$ is 90°, we have $\frac{90}{360}$ or $\frac{1}{4}$ of the circumference for the arc length. Then

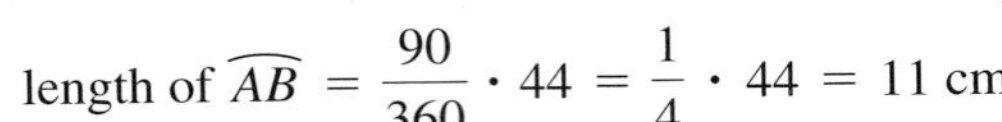

$$\text{length of } \overset{\frown}{AB} = \frac{90}{360} \cdot 44 = \frac{1}{4} \cdot 44 = 11 \text{ cm}$$ ■

Reminder

More background regarding the value of π can be found in the Perspective on History in Chapter 7.

EXAMPLE 2

The exact circumference of a circle is 17π in.

a) Find the length of the radius.
b) Find the length of the diameter.

Solution

a)
$$C = 2\pi r$$
$$17\pi = 2\pi r$$
$$\frac{17\pi}{2\pi} = \frac{2\pi r}{2\pi}$$
$$r = \frac{17}{2} = 8.5 \text{ in.}$$

b) Because $d = 2r$, $d = 2(8.5)$ or $d = 17$ in.

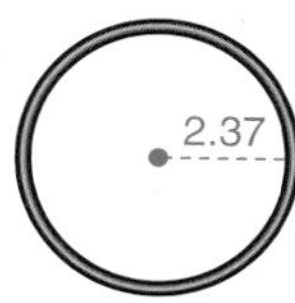

Figure 8.42

EXAMPLE 3

A thin circular rubber gasket is used as a seal to prevent oil from leaking from a tank (see Figure 8.42). If the gasket has a radius of 2.37 in., use the value of π provided by your calculator to find the circumference of the gasket to the nearest hundredth of an inch.

SSG *Exs. 3–5*

Solution Using the calculator with $C = 2\pi r$, we have $C = 2 \cdot \pi \cdot 2.37$ or $C \approx 14.89114918$. Rounding to the nearest hundredth of an inch, $C \approx 14.89$ in.

LENGTH OF AN ARC

In Example 1(b), we used the phrase *length of arc* without a definition. Informally, the length of an arc is the distance between the endpoints of the arc as though it were measured along a straight line. If we measured one-third of the circumference of the rubber gasket (a 120° arc) in Example 3, we would expect the length to be slightly less than 5 in. This measurement could be accomplished by holding that part of the gasket taut in a straight line, but not so tightly that it would be stretched.

Two further observations can be made with regard to the measurement of arc length.

1. The ratio of the degree measure m of the arc to 360 (the degree measure of the entire circle) is the same as the ratio of the length ℓ of the arc to the circumference; that is, $\frac{m}{360} = \frac{\ell}{C}$.
2. Just as $m\widehat{AB}$ denotes the degree measure of an arc, $\ell\widehat{AB}$ denotes the length of the arc. Whereas $m\widehat{AB}$ is measured in degrees, $\ell\widehat{AB}$ is measured in linear units such as inches, feet, or centimeters.

THEOREM 8.4.2

In a circle whose circumference is C, the length ℓ of an arc whose degree measure is m is given by

$$\ell = \frac{m}{360} \cdot C$$

NOTE: For arc AB, $\ell\widehat{AB} = \frac{m\widehat{AB}}{360} \cdot C$.

SSG *Exs. 6–8*

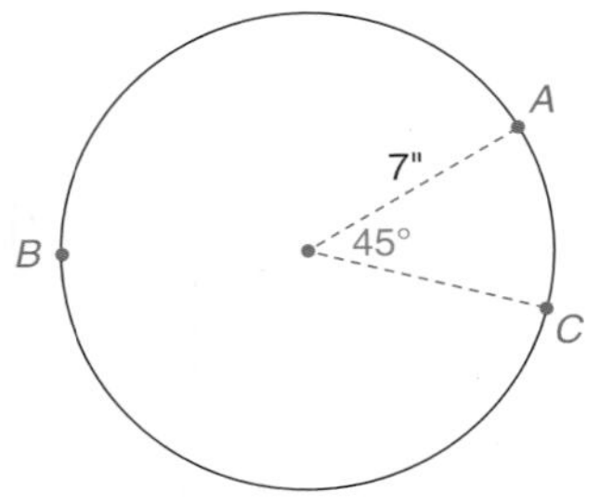

Figure 8.43

EXAMPLE 4

Find the approximate length of major arc ABC in a circle of radius 7 in. if $m\widehat{AC} = 45°$. See Figure 8.43. Use $\pi \approx \frac{22}{7}$.

Solution $m\widehat{ABC} = 360° - 45° = 315°$. Theorem 8.4.2 tells us that

$\ell\widehat{ABC} = \frac{m\widehat{ABC}}{360} \cdot C$, or $\ell\widehat{ABC} = \frac{315}{360} \cdot 2 \cdot \frac{22}{7} \cdot 7$, which can be simplified to

$\ell\widehat{ABC} = 38\frac{1}{2}$ in. ■

LIMITS

In the discussion that follows, we use the undefined term *limit;* in practice, a limit represents a numerical measure. In some situations, we seek an upper limit, a lower limit, or both. The following example illustrates this notion.

EXAMPLE 5

Find the upper limit (largest possible number) for the length of a chord in a circle whose length of radius is 5 cm.

Solution By considering several chords in the circle in Figure 8.44, we see that the greatest possible length of a chord is that of a diameter. Thus, the limit of the length of a chord is 10 cm.

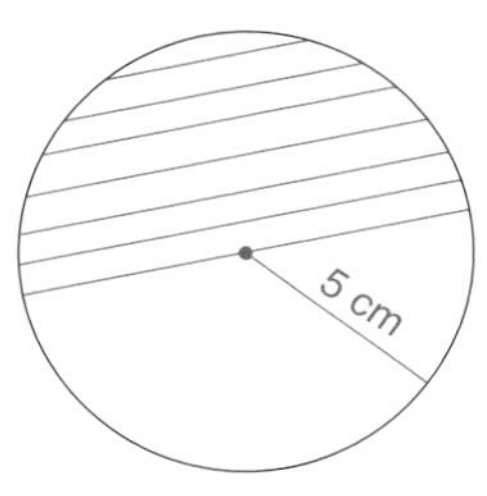

Figure 8.44

NOTE: In Example 5, the lower limit is 0. ■

SSG *Exs. 9–11*

Geometry in the Real World

A measuring wheel can be used by a police officer to find the length of skid marks or by a cross-country coach to determine the length of a running course.

AREA OF A CIRCLE

Now consider the problem of finding the area of a circle. To do so, let a regular polygon of n sides be inscribed in the circle. As we allow n to grow larger (often written as $n \to \infty$ and read "n approaches infinity"), two observations can be made:

1. The length of an apothem of the regular polygon approaches the length of a radius of the circle as its limit ($a \to r$).
2. The perimeter of the regular polygon approaches the circumference of the circle as its limit ($P \to C$).

In Figure 8.45, the area of an inscribed regular polygon with n sides approaches the area of the circle as its limit as n increases. Using observations 1 and 2, we make the following claim. Because the formula for the area of a regular polygon is

$$A = \frac{1}{2}aP$$

the area of the circumscribed circle is given by the limit

$$A = \frac{1}{2}rC$$

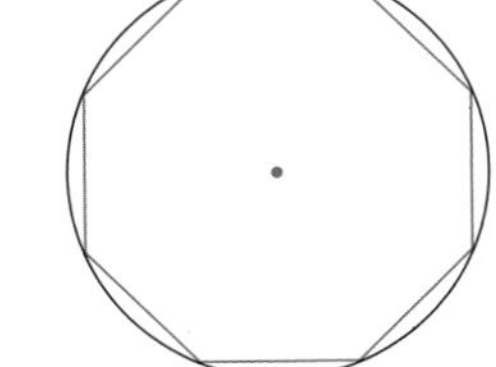

Figure 8.45

Because $C = 2\pi r$, this formula becomes

$$A = \frac{1}{\cancel{2}} r(\cancel{2}\pi r) \quad \text{or} \quad A = \pi r^2$$

Based upon the preceding discussion, we state Theorem 8.4.3.

THEOREM 8.4.3

The area A of a circle whose radius has length r is given by $A = \pi r^2$.

Another justification of the formula $A = \pi r^2$ is found in the following Discover activity.

Discover

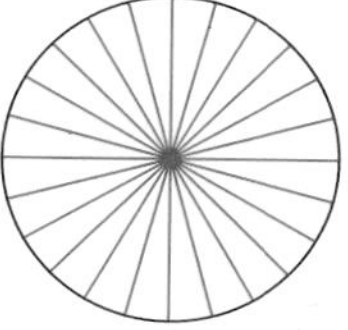

Area of a Circle

Use a protractor to divide a circle into several congruent "sectors." For instance, 15° central angles will divide the circle into $\frac{360}{15} = 24$ sectors. If these sectors are alternated as shown, the resulting figure approximates a parallelogram. With the parallelogram having a base of length πr (half the circumference of the circle) and an altitude of length r (radius of the circle), the area of the parallelogram (and of the circle) can be seen to be $A = (\pi r)r$, or $A = \pi r^2$.

EXAMPLE 6

Find the approximate area of a circle whose radius has a length of 10 in. (Use $\pi \approx 3.14$.)

Solution $A = \pi r^2$ becomes $A = 3.14(10)^2$. Then

$$A = 3.14(100) = 314 \text{ in}^2$$

EXAMPLE 7

The approximate area of a circle is 38.5 cm^2. Find the length of the radius of the circle. $\left(\text{Use } \pi \approx \frac{22}{7}.\right)$

Solution By substituting known values, the formula $A = \pi r^2$ becomes $38.5 = \frac{22}{7} \cdot r^2$, or $\frac{77}{2} = \frac{22}{7} \cdot r^2$. Multiplying each side of the equation by $\frac{7}{22}$, we have

$$\frac{7}{{}_2\cancel{22}} \cdot \frac{\cancel{77}^7}{2} = \frac{\cancel{7}}{\cancel{22}} \cdot \frac{\cancel{22}}{\cancel{7}} \cdot r^2$$

or

$$r^2 = \frac{49}{4}$$

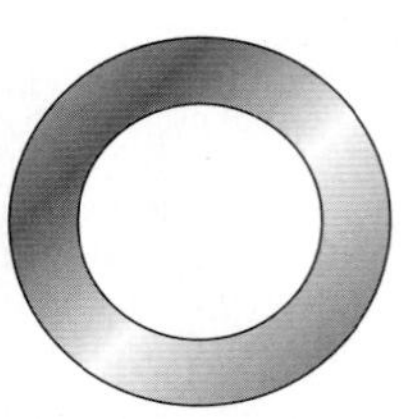

Figure 8.46

Taking the positive square root for the approximate length of radius,

$$r = \sqrt{\frac{49}{4}} = \frac{\sqrt{49}}{\sqrt{4}} = \frac{7}{2} = 3.5 \text{ cm}$$ ■

A plane figure bounded by concentric circles is known as a *ring* or *annulus* (see Figure 8.46). The piece of hardware known as a *washer* has the shape of an annulus.

SSG *Exs. 12–17*

EXAMPLE 8

A machine cuts washers from a flat piece of metal. The radius of the inside circular boundary of the washer is 0.3 in., and the radius of the outer circular boundary is 0.5 in. What is the area of the annulus? Give both an exact answer and an approximate answer rounded to tenths of a square inch. Using the approximate answer, determine the number of square inches of material used to produce 1000 washers. Figure 8.46 illustrates the shape of a washer.

Solution Where R is the larger radius and r is the smaller radius, $A = \pi R^2 - \pi r^2$. Then $A = \pi(0.5)^2 - \pi(0.3)^2$, or $A = 0.16\pi$. The exact number of square inches used in producing a washer is 0.16π in^2, or approximately 0.5 in^2. When 1000 washers are produced, approximately 500 in^2 of metal is used. ■

Many students have a difficult time remembering which expression ($2\pi r$ or πr^2) is used in the formula for the circumference or area of a circle. This is understandable because each expression contains a 2, a radius r, and the factor π. To remember that $C = 2\pi r$ gives the circumference and $A = \pi r^2$ gives the area, *think about the units involved.* Considering a circle of radius 3 in., $C = 2\pi r$ becomes $C = 2 \times 3.14 \times 3$ in., or Circumference equals 18.84 *inches.* (We measure the *distance around* a circle in *linear* units such as inches.) For the circle of radius 3 in., $A = \pi r^2$ becomes $A = 3.14 \times 3$ in. $\times$ 3 in., or Area equals 28.26 in^2. (We measure the area of a circular region in *square* units.)

Exercises 8.4

1. Find the exact circumference and area of a circle whose radius has length 8 cm.
2. Find the exact circumference and area of a circle whose diameter has length 10 in.
3. Find the approximate circumference and area of a circle whose radius has length $10\frac{1}{2}$ in. Use $\pi \approx \frac{22}{7}$.
4. Find the approximate circumference and area of a circle whose diameter is 20 cm. Use $\pi \approx 3.14$.
5. Find the exact lengths of a radius and a diameter of a circle whose circumference is:
   a) 44π in. b) 60π ft
6. Find the approximate lengths of a radius and a diameter of a circle whose circumference is:
   a) 88 in. (Use $\pi \approx \frac{22}{7}$.) b) 157 m (Use $\pi \approx 3.14$.)
7. Find the exact lengths of a radius and a diameter of a circle whose area is:
   a) 25π in^2 b) 2.25π cm^2
8. Find the exact length of a radius and the exact circumference of a circle whose area is:
   a) 36π m^2 b) 6.25π ft^2
9. Find the exact length $\ell\widehat{AB}$, where $\widehat{AB}$ refers to the minor arc of the circle.

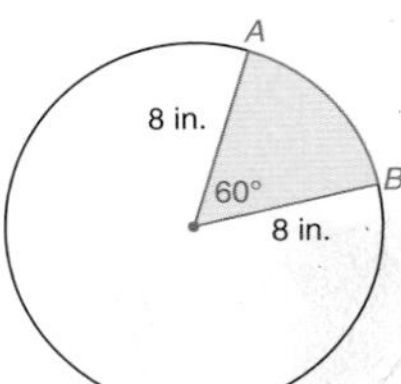

10. Find the exact length $\ell\widehat{CD}$ of the minor arc shown.

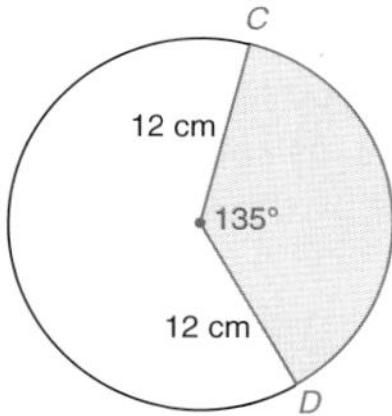

11. Use your calculator value of π to find the approximate circumference of a circle with radius 12.38 in.

12. Use your calculator value of π to find the approximate area of a circle with radius 12.38 in.

13. A metal circular disk whose area is 143 cm^2 is used as a knockout on an electrical service in a factory. Use your calculator value of π to find the radius of the disk to the nearest tenth of a centimeter.

14. A circular lock washer whose outside circumference measures 5.48 cm is used in an electric box to hold an electrical cable in place. Use your calculator value of π to find the outside radius to the nearest tenth of a centimeter.

15. The central angle corresponding to a circular brake shoe measures 60°. Approximately how long is the curved surface of the brake shoe if the length of radius is 7 in.?

16. Use your calculator to find the approximate lengths of the radius and the diameter of a circle with area 56.35 in^2.

17. A rectangle has a perimeter of 16 in. What is the limit (largest possible value) of the area of the rectangle?

18. Two sides of a triangle measure 5 in. and 7 in. What is the limit of the length of the third side?

19. Let N be any point on side $\overline{BC}$ of the right triangle ABC. Find the upper and lower limits for the length of $\overline{AN}$.

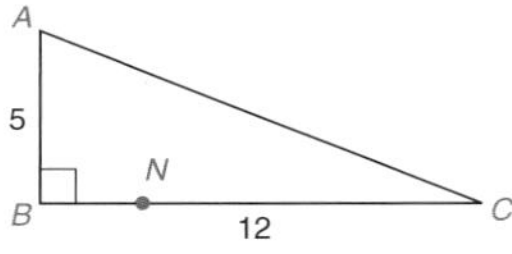

20. What is the limit of m$\angle RTS$ if T lies in the interior of the shaded region?

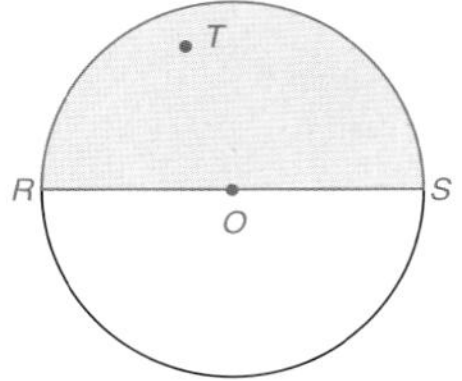

In Exercises 21 to 24, find the exact areas of the shaded regions.

21.

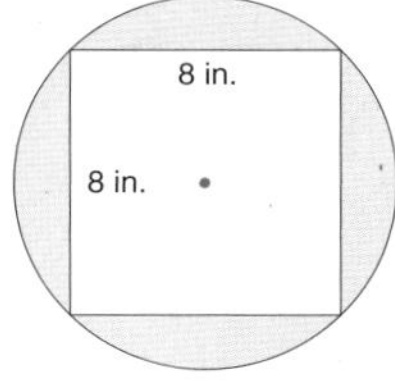

Square inscribed in a circle

22.

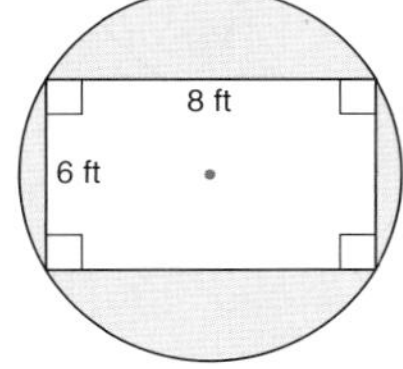

23.

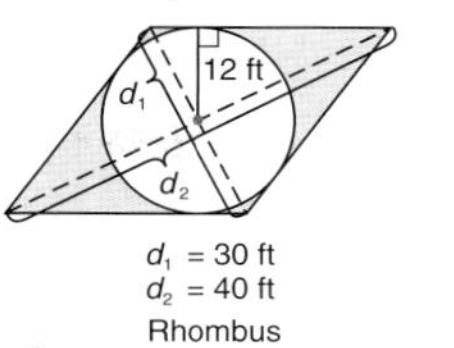

24.

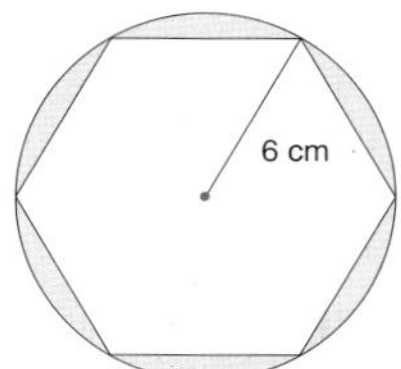

Regular hexagon inscribed in a circle

In Exercises 25 and 26, use your calculator value of π to solve each problem. Round answers to the nearest integer.

25. Find the length of the radius of a circle whose area is 154 cm^2.

26. Find the length of the diameter of a circle whose circumference is 157 in.

27. Assuming that a 90° arc has an exact length of 4π in., find the length of the radius of the circle.

28. The ratio of the circumferences of two circles is 2:1. What is the ratio of their areas?

29. Given concentric circles with radii of lengths R and r, where $R > r$, explain why $A_{\text{ring}} = \pi(R + r)(R - r)$.

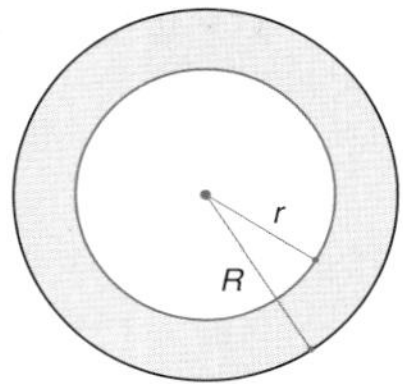

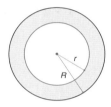

30. Given a circle with diameter of length d, explain why $A_{\text{circle}} = \frac{1}{4}\pi d^2$.

31. The radii of two concentric circles differ in length by exactly 1 in. If their areas differ by exactly 7π in^2, find the lengths of the radii of the two circles.

In Exercises 32 to 42, use your calculator value of π unless otherwise stated. Round answers to two decimal places.

32. The carpet in the circular entryway of a church needs to be replaced. The diameter of the circular region to be carpeted is 18 ft.

a) What length (in feet) of a metal protective strip is needed to bind the circumference of the carpet?

b) If the metal strips are sold in lengths of 6 ft, how many will be needed?

(**NOTE:** Assume that these can be bent to follow the circle and that they can be placed end to end.)

c) If the cost of the metal strip is $1.59 per linear foot, find the cost of the metal strips needed.

33. At center court on a gymnasium floor, a large circular emblem is to be painted. The circular design has a radius length of 8 ft.
a) What is the area to be painted?
b) If a pint of paint covers 70 ft^2, how many pints of paint are needed to complete the job?
c) If each pint of paint costs \$2.95, find the cost of the paint needed.

34. A track is to be constructed around the football field at a junior high school. If the straightaways are 100 yd in length, what length of radius is needed for each of the semicircles shown if the total length around the track is to be 440 yd?

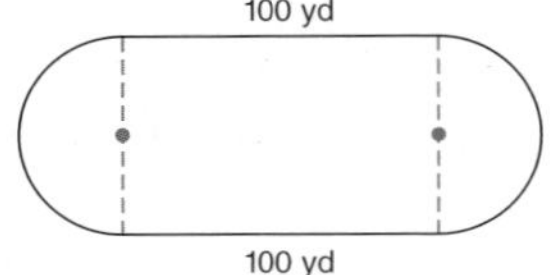

35. A circular grass courtyard at a shopping mall has a 40-ft diameter. This area needs to be reseeded.
a) What is the total area to be reseeded? (Use $\pi \approx 3.14$.)
b) If 1 lb of seed is to be used to cover a 60-ft^2 region, how many pounds of seed will be needed?
c) If the cost of 1 lb of seed is \$1.65, what is the total cost of the grass seed needed?

36. Find the approximate area of a regular polygon that has 20 sides if the length of its radius is 7 cm.

37. Find the approximate perimeter of a regular polygon that has 20 sides if the length of its radius is 7 cm.

38. In a two-pulley system, the centers of the pulleys are 20 in. apart. If the radius of each pulley measures 6 in., how long is the belt used in the pulley system?

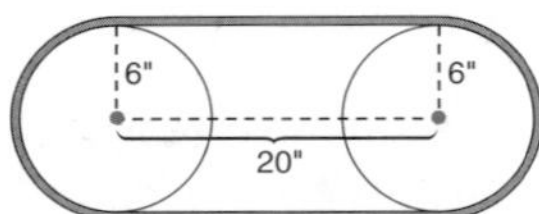

39. If two gears, each of radius 4 in., are used in a chain drive system with a chain of length 54 in., what is the distance between the centers of the gears?

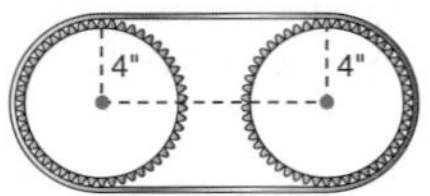

40. A pizza with a 12-in. diameter costs \$6.95. A 16-in. diameter pizza with the same ingredients costs \$9.95. Which pizza is the better buy?

41. A communications satellite forms a circular orbit 375 mi above the earth. If the earth's radius is approximately 4000 mi, what distance is traveled by the satellite in one complete orbit?

42. The radius of the Ferris wheel's circular path is 40 ft. If a "ride" of 12 revolutions is made in 3 minutes, at what rate in *feet per second* is the passenger in a cart moving during the ride?

43. The diameter of a carousel (merry-go-round) is 30 ft. At full speed, it makes a complete revolution in 6 s. At what rate, in *feet per second*, is a horse on the outer edge moving?

44. A tabletop is semicircular when its three congruent drop-leaves are used. By how much has the table's area increased when the drop-leaves are raised? Give the answer to the nearest *whole* percent.

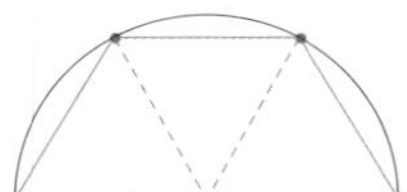

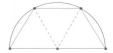

***45.** Given that the length of each side of a rhombus is 8 cm and that an interior angle (shown) measures 60°, find the area of the inscribed circle.

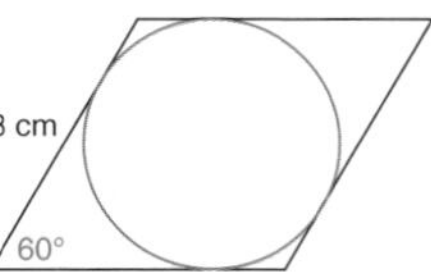

8.5 More Area Relationships in the Circle

Sector
Area and Perimeter of Sector

Segment of a Circle
Area and Perimeter of Segment

Area of Triangle with Inscribed Circle

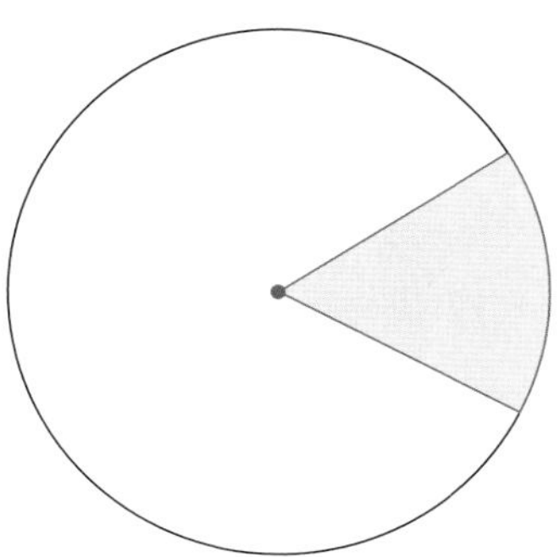
Figure 8.47

DEFINITION

A **sector** of a circle is a region bounded by two radii of the circle and an arc intercepted by those radii. (See Figure 8.47.)

A sector will generally be shaded to avoid confusion about whether the related arc is a major arc or a minor arc. In simple terms, the sector of a circle generally has the shape of a center-cut piece of pie.

AREA OF A SECTOR

Just as the length of an arc is part of the circle's circumference, the area of a sector is part of the area of this circle. When fractions are illustrated by using circles, $\frac{1}{4}$ is represented by shading a 90° sector, and $\frac{1}{3}$ is represented by shading a 120° sector (see Figure 8.48). Thus, we make the following assumption about the measure of the area of a sector.

90°　120°

$\frac{1}{4} = \frac{90°}{360°}$　$\frac{1}{3} = \frac{120°}{360°}$

Figure 8.48

POSTULATE 23

The ratio of the degree measure m of the arc (or central angle) of a sector to 360° is the same as the ratio of the area of the sector to the area of the circle; that is,

$$\frac{\text{area of sector}}{\text{area or circle}} = \frac{m}{360}.$$

THEOREM 8.5.1

In a circle of radius r, the area A of a sector whose arc has degree measure m is given by

$$A = \frac{m}{360}\pi r^2.$$

Theorem 8.5.1 follows directly from Postulate 23.

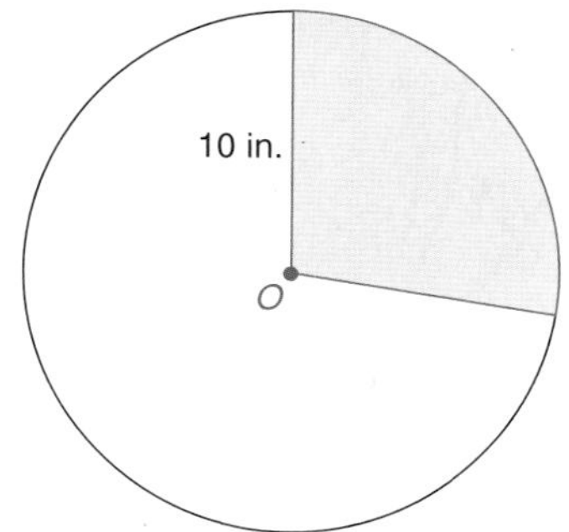

Figure 8.49

EXAMPLE 1

If $m\angle O = 100°$, find the area of the 100° sector shown in Figure 8.49. Use your calculator and round the answer to the nearest hundredth of a square inch.

Solution

$$A = \frac{m}{360}\pi r^2$$

becomes

$$A = \frac{100}{360} \cdot \pi \cdot 10^2 \approx 87.27 \text{ in}^2$$

■

In applications with circles, we often seek exact answers for circumference and area; in such cases, we simply leave π in the result. For instance, in a circle of radius length 5 in., the exact circumference is 10π in. and the exact area is expressed as 25π in^2.

Because a sector is bounded by two radii and an arc, the perimeter of a sector is the sum of the lengths of the two radii and the length of its arc. In Example 2, we apply this formula, $P_{\text{sector}} = 2r + \ell\widehat{AB}$.

EXAMPLE 2

Find the perimeter of the sector shown in Figure 8.49 on page 387. Use the calculator value of π and round your answer to the nearest hundredth of an inch.

Solution Because $r = 10$ and $m\angle O = 100°$, $\ell\widehat{AB} = \frac{100}{360} \cdot 2 \cdot \pi \cdot 10 \approx 17.45$ in. Now $P_{\text{sector}} = 2r + \ell\widehat{AB}$ becomes $P_{\text{sector}} = 2(10) + 17.45 \approx 37.45$ in. ■

Because a semicircle is one-half of a circle, a semicircular region corresponds to a central angle of 180°. As stated in the following corollary to Theorem 8.5.1, the area of the semicircle is $\frac{180}{360}$ (or one-half) the area of the entire circle.

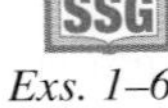

Exs. 1–6

COROLLARY 8.5.2

The area of a semicircular region of radius length r is $A = \frac{1}{2}\pi r^2$.

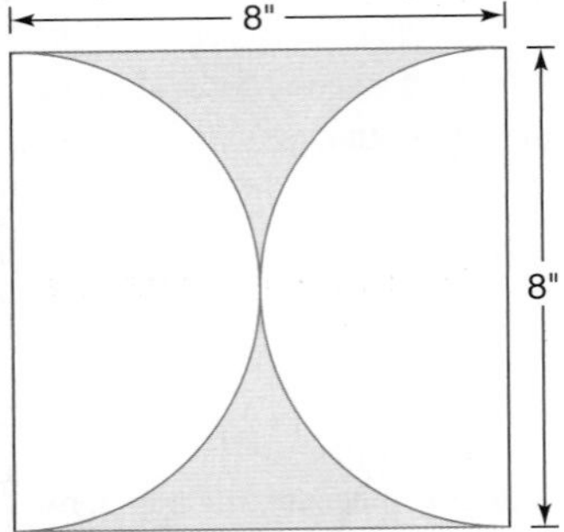

Figure 8.50

EXAMPLE 3

In Figure 8.50, a square of side 8 in. is shown with semicircles cut away. Find the exact shaded area by leaving π in the answer.

Solution To find the shaded area A, we see that $A + 2 \cdot A_{\text{semicircle}} = A_{\text{square}}$. It follows that $A = A_{\text{square}} - 2 \cdot A_{\text{semicircle}}$.

If the side of the square is 8 in., then the radius of each semicircle is 4 in. Now $A = 8^2 - 2\left(\frac{1}{2}\pi \cdot 4^2\right)$, or $A = 64 - 2(8\pi)$, so $A = (64 - 16\pi)$ in^2. ■

Discover

In statistics, a pie chart can be used to represent the breakdown of a budget. In the pie chart shown, a 90° sector (one-fourth the area of the circle) is shaded to show that 25% of a person's income (one-fourth of the income) is devoted to rent payment. What degree measure of sector must be shaded if a sector indicates that 20% of the person's income is used for a car payment?

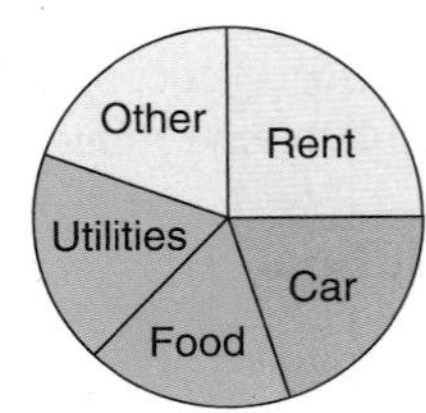

ANSWER

72° (from 20% of 360°)

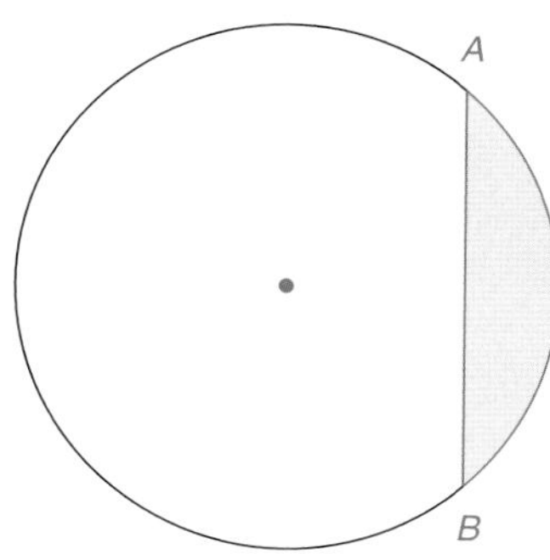

Figure 8.51

AREA OF A SEGMENT

DEFINITION

A **segment** of a circle is a region bounded by a chord and its minor (or major) arc.

In Figure 8.51, the segment is bounded by chord $\overline{AB}$ and its minor arc $\overset{\frown}{AB}$. Again, we avoid confusion by shading the segment whose area or perimeter we seek.

EXAMPLE 4

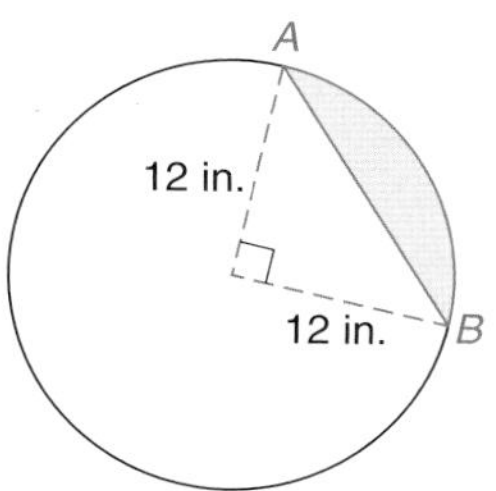

Figure 8.52

Find the exact area of the segment bounded by a chord and an arc whose measure is 90°. The radius has length 12 in., as shown in Figure 8.52.

Solution Let $A_\triangle$ represent the area of the triangle shown. Because $A_\triangle + A_{\text{segment}} = A_{\text{sector}}$,

$$\begin{aligned} A_{\text{segment}} &= A_{\text{sector}} - A_\triangle \\ &= \frac{90}{360} \cdot \pi \cdot 12^2 - \frac{1}{2} \cdot 12 \cdot 12 \\ &= (36\pi - 72) \text{ in}^2. \end{aligned}$$

In Example 4, the boundaries of the segment shown are chord $\overline{AB}$ and minor arc $\overset{\frown}{AB}$. Therefore, the perimeter of the segment is given by $P_{\text{segment}} = AB + \ell\overset{\frown}{AB}$. We use this formula in Example 5.

EXAMPLE 5

Find the exact perimeter of the segment shown in Figure 8.53. Then use your calculator to approximate this answer to the nearest hundredth of an inch.

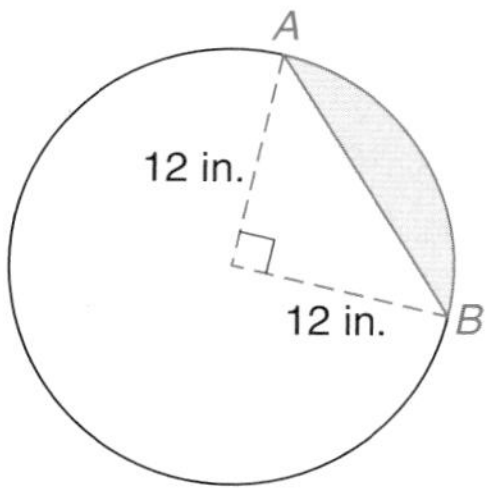

Figure 8.53

Solution Because $\ell\overset{\frown}{AB} = \frac{90}{360} \cdot 2 \cdot \pi \cdot r$, we have $\ell\overset{\frown}{AB} = \frac{1}{4} \cdot 2 \cdot \pi \cdot 12 = 6\pi$ in.

Using either the Pythagorean Theorem or the 45°-45°-90° relationship, $AB = 12\sqrt{2}$.

Now $P_{\text{segment}} = AB + \ell\overset{\frown}{AB}$ becomes $P_{\text{segment}} = (12\sqrt{2} + 6\pi)$ in. Using a calculator, we find that the approximate perimeter is 35.82 in.

SSG *Exs. 7–11*

AREA OF A TRIANGLE WITH AN INSCRIBED CIRCLE

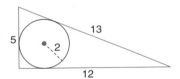

THEOREM 8.5.3

Where P represents the perimeter of a triangle and r represents the length of the radius of its inscribed circle, the area of the triangle is given by

$$A = \frac{1}{2}rP$$

PICTURE PROOF OF THEOREM 8.5.3

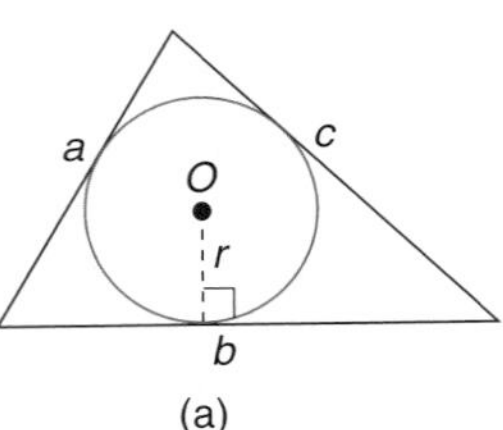

(a)

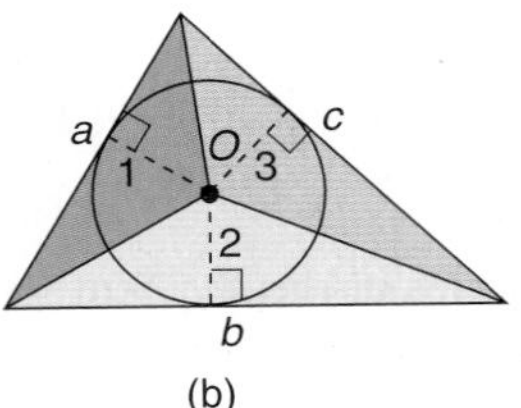

(b)

Figure 8.54

GIVEN: A triangle with perimeter P, whose sides measure a, b, and c; the radius of the inscribed circle measures r. See Figure 8.54(a).

PROVE: $A = \frac{1}{2}rP$

PROOF: In Figure 8.54(b), the triangle has been separated into three smaller triangles (each with altitude r). Hence

$$A = A_1 + A_2 + A_3$$
$$A = \tfrac{1}{2}r \cdot a + \tfrac{1}{2}r \cdot b + \tfrac{1}{2}r \cdot c$$
$$A = \tfrac{1}{2}r(a + b + c)$$
$$A = \tfrac{1}{2}rP$$

EXAMPLE 6

Find the area of a triangle whose sides measure 5 cm, 12 cm, and 13 cm if the radius of the inscribed circle is 2 cm. See Figure 8.55.

Figure 8.55

Solution With the given lengths of sides, the perimeter of the triangle is $P = 5 + 12 + 13 = 30$ cm. Using $A = \frac{1}{2}rP$, we have $A = \frac{1}{2} \cdot 2 \cdot 30$, or $A = 30 \text{ cm}^2$. ■

Because the triangle shown in Example 6 is a right triangle $(5^2 + 12^2 = 13^2)$, the area of the triangle could have been determined by using either $A = \frac{1}{2}ab$ or $A = \sqrt{s(s-a)(s-b)(s-c)}$. The advantage provided by Theorem 8.5.3 lies in applications where we need to determine the length of the radius of the inscribed circle of a triangle.

EXAMPLE 7

In an attic, wooden braces supporting the roof form a triangle whose sides measure 4 ft, 6 ft, and 6 ft; see Figure 8.56 on page 391. To the nearest inch, find the radius of the largest circular cold-air duct that can be run through the opening formed by the braces.

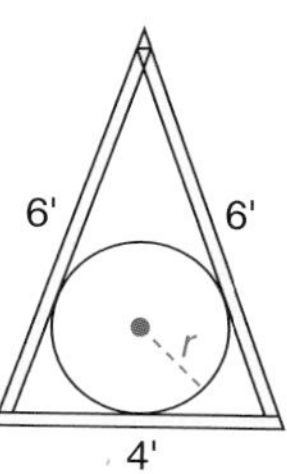

Figure 8.56

Solution Where s is the semiperimeter of the triangle, Heron's Formula states that $A = \sqrt{s(s-a)(s-b)(s-c)}$. Because $s = \frac{1}{2}(a+b+c) = \frac{1}{2}(4+6+6) = 8$, we have $A = \sqrt{8(8-4)(8-6)(8-6)} = \sqrt{8(4)(2)(2)} = \sqrt{128}$. We can simplify the area expression to $\sqrt{64} \cdot \sqrt{2}$, so $A = 8\sqrt{2}\text{ ft}^2$.

Recalling Theorem 8.5.3, we know that $A = \frac{1}{2}rP$. Substitution leads to $8\sqrt{2} = \frac{1}{2}r(4+6+6)$, or $8\sqrt{2} = 8r$. Then $r = \sqrt{2}$. Where $r \approx 1.414$ ft, it follows that $r \approx 1.414(12\text{ in.})$, or $r \approx 16.97\text{ in.} \approx 17\text{ in.}$

SSG *Exs. 11–15*

NOTE: If the ductwork is a flexible plastic tubing, the duct having radius 17 in. can probably be used. If the ductwork were a rigid metal or heavy plastic, the radius might need to be restricted to perhaps 16 in. ■

Exercises 8.5

1. In the circle, the radius length is 10 in. and the length of $\overset{\frown}{AB}$ is 14 in. What is the perimeter of the shaded sector?

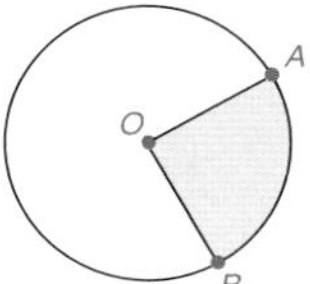

Exercises 1, 2

2. If the area of the circle is 360 in^2, what is the area of the sector if its central angle measures 90°?

3. If the area of the 120° sector is 50 cm^2, what is the area of the entire circle?

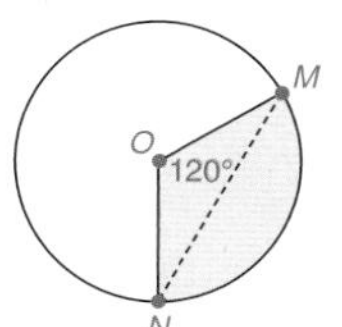

Exercises 3, 4

4. If the area of the 120° sector is 40 cm^2 and the area of $\triangle MON$ is 16 cm^2, what is the area of the segment bounded by chord $\overline{MN}$ and $\overset{\frown}{MN}$?

5. Suppose that a circle of radius r is inscribed in an equilateral triangle whose sides have length s. Find an expression for the area of the triangle in terms of r and s.
   (HINT: Use Theorem 8.5.3.)

6. Suppose that a circle of radius r is inscribed in a rhombus each of whose sides has length s. Find an expression for the area of the rhombus in terms of r and s.

7. Find the perimeter of a segment of a circle whose boundaries are a chord measuring 24 mm (millimeters) and an arc of length 30 mm.

8. A sector with perimeter 30 in. has a bounding arc of length 12 in. Find the length of the radius of the circle.

9. A circle is inscribed in a triangle having sides of lengths 6 in., 8 in., and 10 in. If the length of the radius of the inscribed circle is 2 in., find the area of the triangle.

10. A circle is inscribed in a triangle having sides of lengths 5 in., 12 in., and 13 in. If the length of the radius of the inscribed circle is 2 in., find the area of the triangle.

11. A triangle with sides of lengths 3 in., 4 in., and 5 in. has an area of 6 in^2. What is the length of the radius of the inscribed circle?

12. The approximate area of a triangle with sides of lengths 3 in., 5 in., and 6 in. is 7.48 in^2. What is the approximate length of the radius of the inscribed circle?

13. Find the exact perimeter and area of the sector shown.

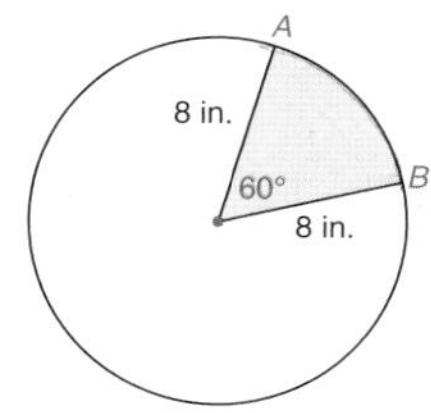

14. Find the exact perimeter and area of the sector shown.

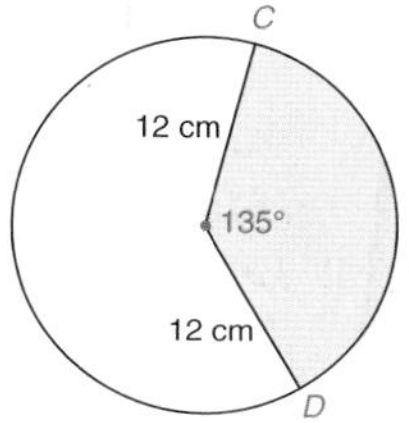

15. Find the approximate perimeter of the sector shown. Answer to the nearest hundredth of an inch.

16. Find the approximate area of the sector shown. Answer to the nearest hundredth of a square inch.

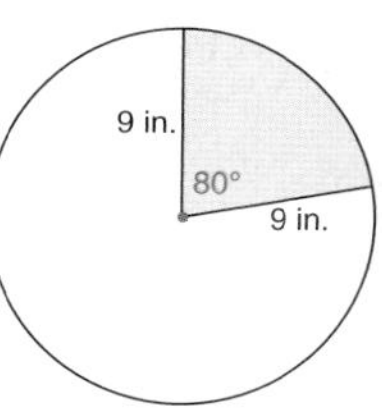

Exercises 15, 16

17. Find the exact perimeter and area of the segment shown, given that $m\angle O = 60°$ and $OA = 12$ in.

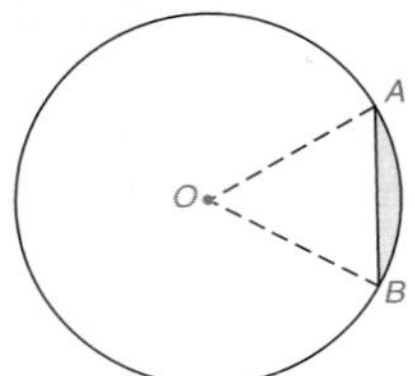

Exercises 17, 18

18. Find the exact perimeter and area of the segment shown, given that $m\angle O = 120°$ and $AB = 10$ in.

In Exercises 19 and 20, find the exact areas of the shaded regions.

19.

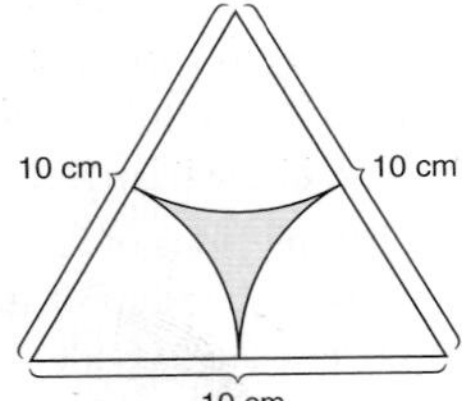

20.

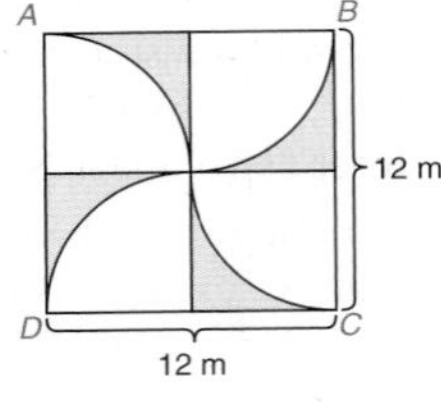

Square $ABCD$

21. Assuming that the exact area of a sector determined by a 40° arc is $\frac{9}{4}\pi$ cm^2, find the length of the radius of the circle.

22. For concentric circles with radii of lengths 3 in. and 6 in., find the area of the smaller segment determined by a chord of the larger circle that is also a tangent of the smaller circle.

*23. A circle can be inscribed in the trapezoid shown. Find the area of that circle.

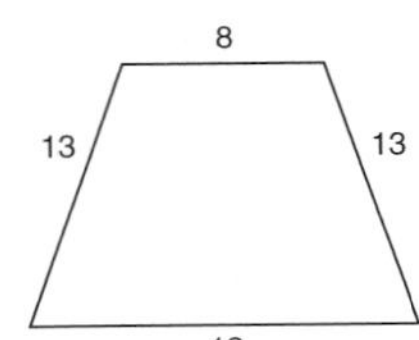

*24. A circle can be inscribed in an equilateral triangle each of whose sides has length 10 cm. Find the area of that circle.

25. In a circle whose radius has length 12 m, the length of an arc is 6π m. What is the degree measure of that arc?

26. At the Pizza Dude restaurant, a 12-in. pizza costs \$3.40 to make, and the manager wants to make at least \$2.20 from the sale of each pizza. If the pizza will be sold by the slice and each pizza is cut into 6 pieces, what is the minimum charge per slice?

27. At the Pizza Dude restaurant, pizza is sold by the slice. If the pizza is cut into 6 pieces, then the selling price is \$1.25 per slice. If the pizza is cut into 8 pieces, then each slice is sold for \$0.95. In which way will the Pizza Dude restaurant clear more money from sales?

28. Determine a formula for the area of the shaded region determined by the square and its inscribed circle.

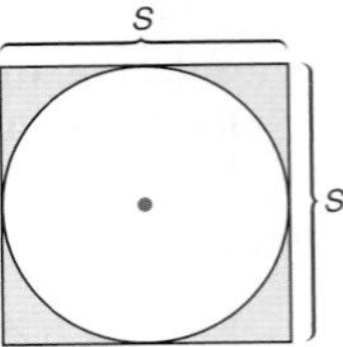

29. Determine a formula for the area of the shaded region determined by the circle and its inscribed square.

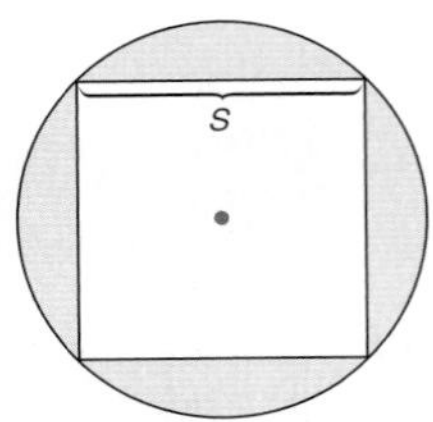

30. Find a formula for the area of the shaded region, which represents one-fourth of an annulus (ring).

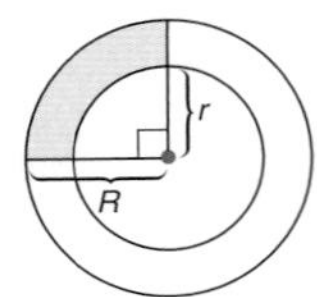

31. A company logo on the side of a building shows an isosceles triangle with an inscribed circle. If the sides of the triangle measure 10 ft, 13 ft, and 13 ft, find the length of the radius of the inscribed circle.

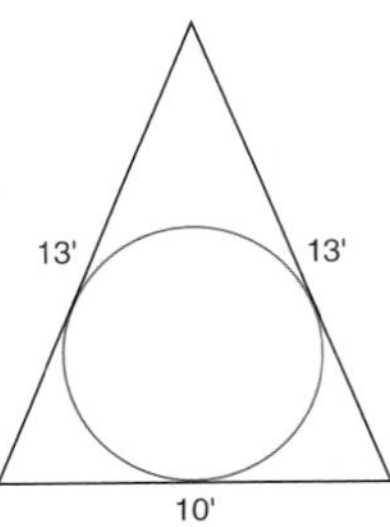

32. In a right triangle with sides of lengths a, b, and c (where c is the length of the hypotenuse), show that the length of the radius of the inscribed circle is $r = \frac{ab}{a + b + c}$.

33. In a triangle with sides of lengths a, b, and c and semiperimeter s, show that the length of the radius of the inscribed circle is

$$r = \frac{2\sqrt{s(s - a)(s - b)(s - c)}}{a + b + c}$$

34. Use the results from Exercises 32 and 33 to find the length of the radius of the inscribed circle for a triangle with sides of lengths

a) 8, 15, and 17. b) 7, 9, and 12.

35. Use the results from Exercises 32 and 33 to find the length of the radius of the inscribed circle for a triangle with sides of lengths
a) 7, 24, and 25. b) 9, 10, and 17.

36. Three pipes, each of radius 4 in., are stacked as shown. What is the height of the stack?

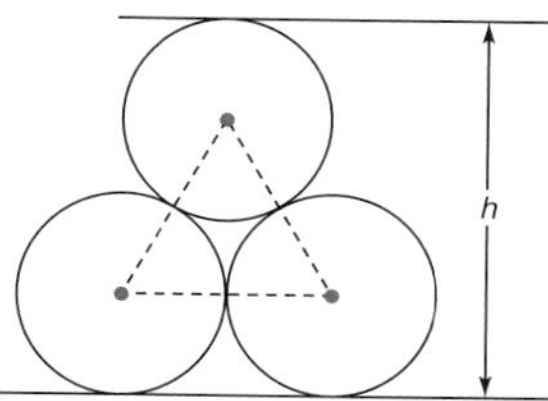

37. A windshield wiper rotates through a 120° angle as it cleans a windshield. From the point of rotation, the wiper blade begins at a distance of 4 in. and ends at a distance of 18 in. (The wiper blade is 14 inches in length.) Find the area cleaned by the wiper blade.

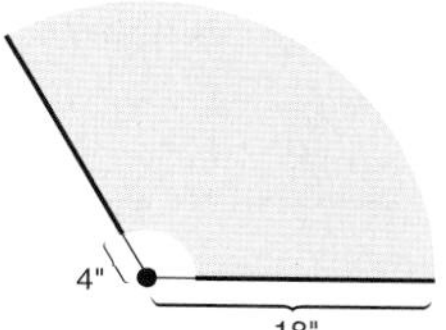

38. A goat is tethered to a barn by a 12-ft chain. If the chain is connected to the barn at a point 6 ft from one end of the barn, what is the area of the pasture that the goat is able to graze?

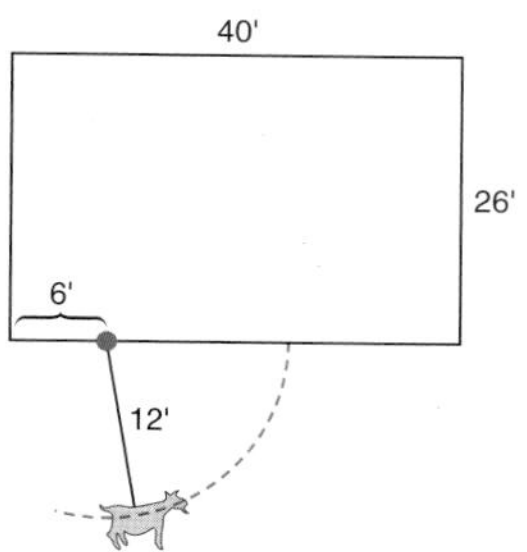

39. An exit ramp from one freeway onto another freeway forms a 90° arc of a circle. The ramp is scheduled for resurfacing. As shown, its inside radius is 370 ft, and its outside radius is 380 ft. What is the area of the ramp?

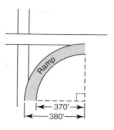

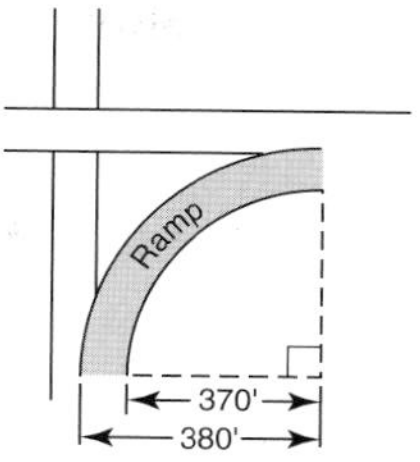

***40.** In $\triangle ABC$, $m\angle C = 90°$ and $m\angle B = 60°$. If $AB = 12$ in., find the radius of the inscribed circle. Give the answer to the nearest tenth of an inch.

***41.** A triangle has sides of lengths 6 cm, 8 cm, and 10 cm. Find the distance between the center of the inscribed circle and the center of the circumscribed circle for this triangle. Give the answer to the nearest tenth of a centimeter.

PERSPECTIVE ON HISTORY

Sketch of Pythagoras

Pythagoras (circa 580–500 B.C.) was a Greek philosopher and mathematician. Having studied under some of the great minds of the day, he formed his own school around 529 B.C. in Crotona, Italy.

Students of his school fell into two classes, the listeners and the elite Pythagoreans. Included in the Pythagoreans were brilliant students, including 28 women, and all were faithful followers of Pythagoras. The Pythagoreans, who adhered to a rigid set of beliefs, were guided by the principle "Knowledge is the greatest purification."

The apparent areas of study for the Pythagoreans included arithmetic, music, geometry, and astronomy, but underlying principles that led to a cult-like existence included self-discipline, temperance, purity, and obedience. The Pythagoreans recognized fellow members by using the pentagram (five-pointed star) as their symbol. With their focus on virtue, politics, and religion, the members of the group saw themselves as above others. Because of their belief in *transmigration* (movement of the soul after death to another human or animal), the Pythagoreans refused to eat meat or fish. On one occasion, it is said that Pythagoras came upon a person beating a dog. Approaching that person, Pythagoras said, "Stop beating the dog, for in this dog lives the soul of my friend; I recognize him by his voice."

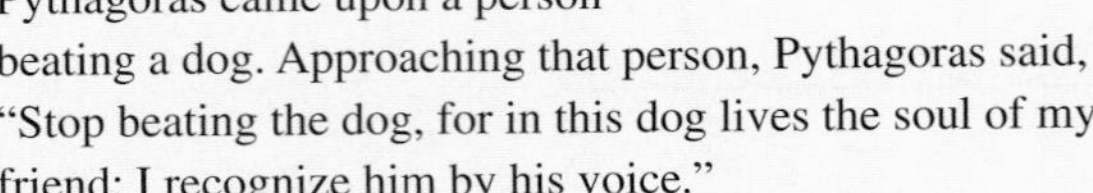

In time, the secrecy, clannishness, and supremacy of the Pythagoreans led to suspicion and fear on the part of other factions of society. Around 500 B.C., the revolution against the Pythagoreans led to the burning of their primary meeting house. Although many of the Pythagoreans died in the ensuing inferno, it is unclear whether Pythagoras himself died or escaped.

PERSPECTIVE ON APPLICATION

Another Look at the Pythagorean Theorem

Some of the many proofs of the Pythagorean Theorem depend on area relationships. One such proof was devised by President James A. Garfield (1831–1881), twentieth president of the United States.

In his proof, the right triangle with legs of lengths a and b and a hypotenuse of length c is introduced into a trapezoid. See Figures 8.57(a) and (b).

In Figure 8.57(b), the points A, B, and C are collinear. With $\angle 1$ and $\angle 2$ being complementary and the sum of the angles' measures about point B being 180°, it follows that $\angle 3$ is a right angle.

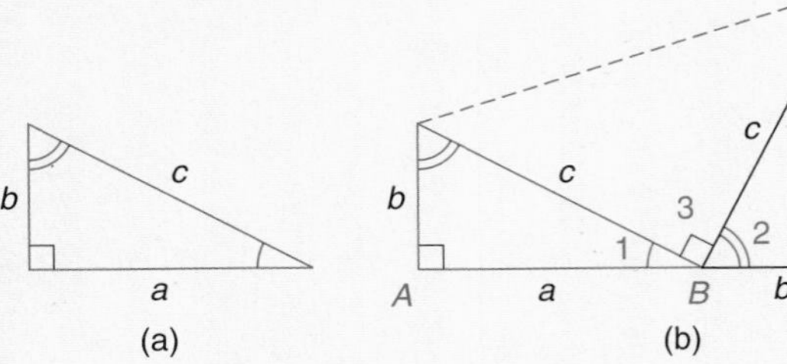

Figure 8.57

If the drawing is perceived as a trapezoid (as shown in Figure 8.58), the area is given by

$$\begin{aligned} A &= \frac{1}{2}h(b_1 + b_2) \\ &= \frac{1}{2}(a + b)(a + b) \\ &= \frac{1}{2}(a + b)^2 \\ &= \frac{1}{2}(a^2 + 2ab + b^2) \\ &= \frac{1}{2}a^2 + ab + \frac{1}{2}b^2 \end{aligned}$$

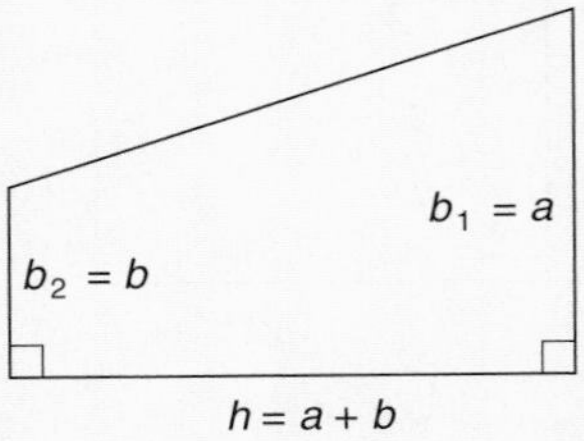

$b_1 = a$, $b_2 = b$, $h = a + b$

Figure 8.58

Now we treat the trapezoid as a composite of three triangles as shown in Figure 8.59.

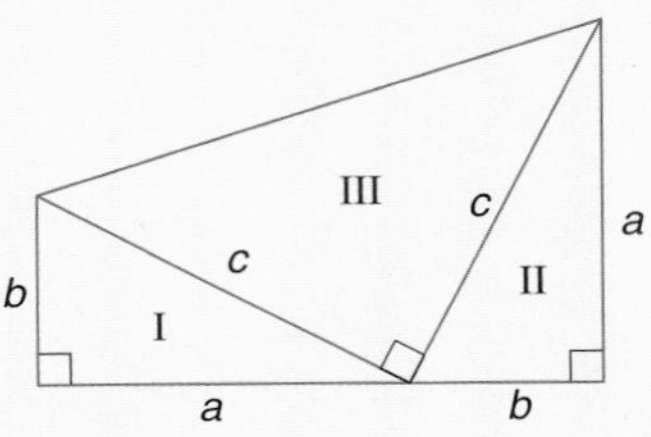

Figure 8.59

The total area of regions (triangles) I, II, and III is given by

$$
\begin{aligned}
A &= A_I + A_{II} + A_{III} \\
&= \frac{1}{2}ab + \frac{1}{2}ab + \left(\frac{1}{2}c \cdot c\right) \\
&= ab + \frac{1}{2}c^2
\end{aligned}
$$

Equating the areas of the trapezoid in Figure 8.58 and the composite in Figure 8.59, we find that

$$
\begin{aligned}
\frac{1}{2}a^2 + ab + \frac{1}{2}b^2 &= ab + \frac{1}{2}c^2 \\
\frac{1}{2}a^2 + \frac{1}{2}b^2 &= \frac{1}{2}c^2
\end{aligned}
$$

Multiplying by 2, we have

$$a^2 + b^2 = c^2$$

The earlier proof (over 2000 years earlier!) of this theorem by the Greek mathematician Pythagoras is found in many historical works on geometry. It is not difficult to see the relationship between the two proofs.

In the proof credited to Pythagoras, a right triangle with legs of lengths a and b and hypotenuse of length c is reproduced several times to form a square. Again, points A, B, C (and C, D, E; and so on) must be collinear. [See Figure 8.60(c).]

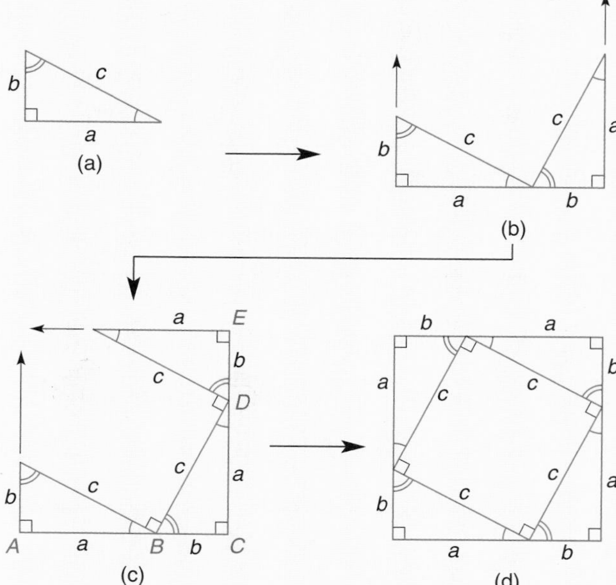

Figure 8.60

The area of the large square in Figure 8.61(a) is given by

$$
\begin{aligned}
A &= (a + b)^2 \\
&= a^2 + 2ab + b^2
\end{aligned}
$$

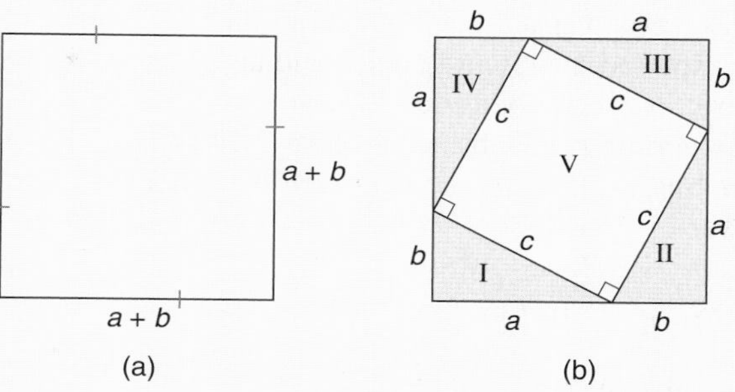

Figure 8.61

Considering the composite in Figure 8.61(b), we find that

$$
\begin{aligned}
A &= A_I + A_{II} + A_{III} + A_{IV} + A_V \\
&= 4 \cdot A_I + A_V
\end{aligned}
$$

because the four right triangles are congruent. Then

$$
\begin{aligned}
A &= 4\left(\frac{1}{2}ab\right) + c^2 \\
&= 2ab + c^2
\end{aligned}
$$

Again, because of the uniqueness of area, the results (area of square and area of composite) must be equal. Then

$$
\begin{aligned}
a^2 + 2ab + b^2 &= 2ab + c^2 \\
a^2 + b^2 &= c^2
\end{aligned}
$$

Another look at the proofs by President Garfield and by Pythagoras makes it clear that the results must be consistent. In Figure 8.62, observe that Garfield's trapezoid must have one-half the area of Pythagoras' square, while maintaining the relationship that

$$c^2 = a^2 + b^2$$

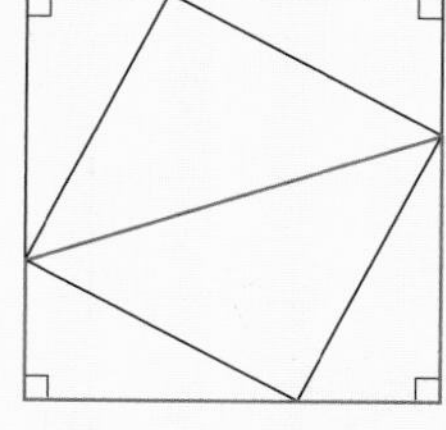

Figure 8.62

Summary

A LOOK BACK AT CHAPTER 8

One goal of this chapter was to determine the areas of triangles, certain quadrilaterals, and regular polygons. We also explored the circumference and area of a circle and the area of a sector of a circle. The area of a circle is sometimes approximated by using $\pi \approx 3.14$ or $\pi \approx \frac{22}{7}$. At other times, the exact area is given by leaving π in the answer.

A LOOK AHEAD TO CHAPTER 9

Our goal in the next chapter is to deal with a type of geometry known as solid geometry. We will find the surface areas of solids with polygonal or circular bases. We will also find the volumes of these solid figures. Select polyhedra will be discussed.

KEY CONCEPTS

8.1

Plane Region • Square Unit • Area Postulates • Area of a Rectangle, Parallelogram, and Triangle • Altitude and Base of a Parallelogram or Triangle

8.2

Perimeter of a Polygon • Semiperimeter of a Triangle • Heron's Formula • Brahmagupta's Formula • Area of a Trapezoid, Rhombus, and Kite • Areas of Similar Polygons

8.3

Regular Polygon • Center and Central Angle of a Regular Polygon • Radius and Apothem of a Regular Polygon • Area of a Regular Polygon

8.4

Circumference of a Circle • π (Pi) • Length of an Arc • Limit • Area of a Circle

8.5

Sector • Area and Perimeter of Sector • Segment of a Circle • Area and Perimeter of Segment • Area of Triangle with Inscribed Circle

TABLE 8.3 An Overview of Chapter 8

▶ Area and Perimeter Relationships

FIGURE	DRAWING	AREA	PERIMETER OR CIRCUMFERENCE
Rectangle	w, ℓ	$A = \ell w$ (or $A = bh$)	$P = 2\ell + 2w$ (or $P = 2b + 2h$)
Square	s	$A = s^2$	$P = 4s$
Parallelogram	s, h, b	$A = bh$	$P = 2b + 2s$
Triangle	a, h, c, b	$A = \frac{1}{2}bh$ $A = \sqrt{s(s-a)(s-b)(s-c)}$, where $s = \frac{1}{2}(a+b+c)$	$P = a + b + c$

TABLE 8.3 (continued)

Area and Perimeter Relationships

FIGURE	DRAWING	AREA	PERIMETER OR CIRCUMFERENCE
Right triangle	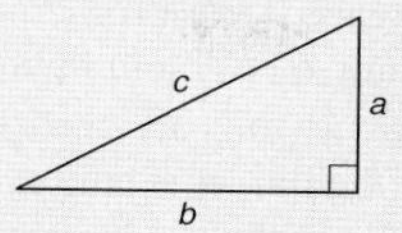	$A = \frac{1}{2}ab$	$P = a + b + c$
Trapezoid	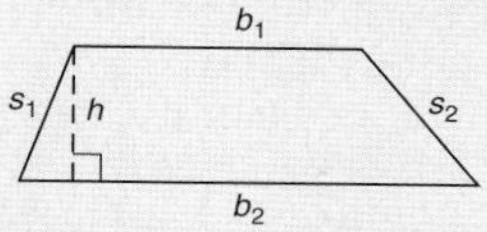	$A = \frac{1}{2}h(b_1 + b_2)$	$P = s_1 + s_2 + b_1 + b_2$
Rhombus (diagonals of lengths d_1 and d_2)	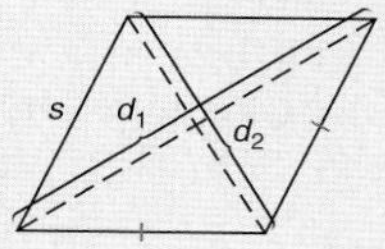	$A = \frac{1}{2}d_1d_2$	$P = 4s$
Kite (diagonals of lengths d_1 and d_2)	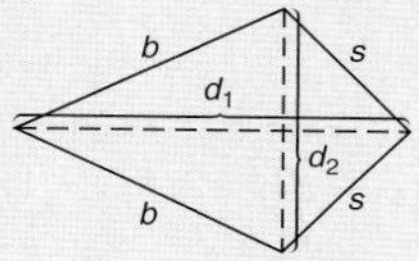	$A = \frac{1}{2}d_1d_2$	$P = 2b + 2s$
Regular polygon (n sides; s is length of side; a is length of apothem)	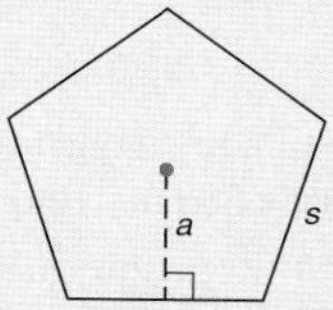	$A = \frac{1}{2}aP$ (P = perimeter)	$P = ns$
Circle	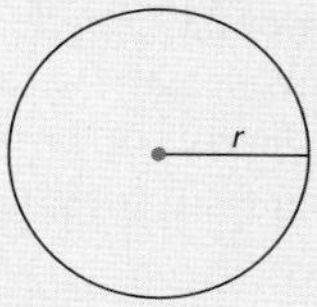	$A = \pi r^2$	$C = 2\pi r$
Sector (m$\widehat{AB}$ is degree measure of $\widehat{AB}$ and of central angle AOB)	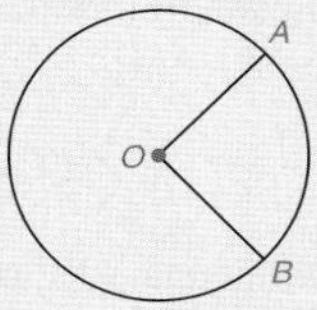	$A = \frac{m\widehat{AB}}{360}\pi r^2$	$P = 2r + \ell\widehat{AB}$, where $\ell\widehat{AB} = \frac{m\widehat{AB}}{360} \cdot 2\pi r$
Triangle with inscribed circle of radius r	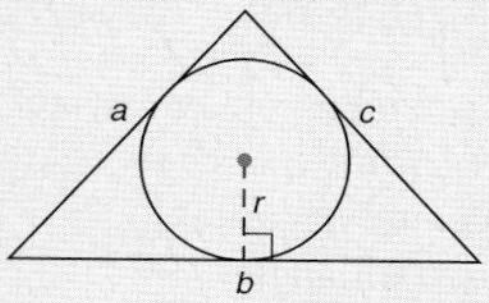	$A = \frac{1}{2}rP$ (P = perimeter)	$P = a + b + c$

Chapter 8 REVIEW EXERCISES

In Review Exercises 1 to 3, draw a figure that enables you to solve each problem.

1. *Given:* $\square ABCD$ with $BD = 34$ and $BC = 30$
$m\angle C = 90°$
Find: A_{ABCD}

2. *Given:* $\square ABCD$ with $AB = 8$ and $AD = 10$
Find: A_{ABCD} if:
a) $m\angle A = 30°$
b) $m\angle A = 60°$
c) $m\angle A = 45°$

3. *Given:* $\square ABCD$ with $\overline{AB} \cong \overline{BD}$ and $AD = 10$
$\overline{BD} \perp \overline{DC}$
Find: A_{ABCD}

In Review Exercises 4 and 5, draw $\triangle ABC$, if necessary, to solve each problem.

4. *Given:* $AB = 26$, $BC = 25$, and $AC = 17$
Find: A_{ABC}

5. *Given:* $AB = 30$, $BC = 26$, and $AC = 28$
Find: A_{ABC}

6. *Given:* Trapezoid $ABCD$, with $\overline{AB} \cong \overline{CD}$, $BC = 6$, $AD = 12$, and $AB = 5$
Find: A_{ABCD}

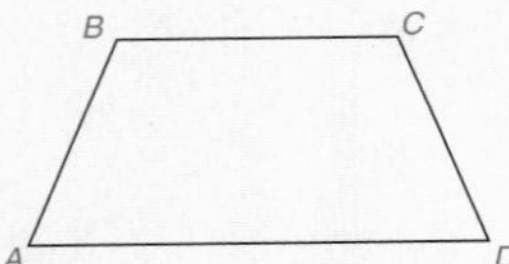

Exercises 6, 7

7. *Given:* Trapezoid $ABCD$, with $AB = 6$ and $BC = 8$,
$\overline{AB} \cong \overline{CD}$
Find: A_{ABCD} if:
a) $m\angle A = 45°$
b) $m\angle A = 30°$
c) $m\angle A = 60°$

8. Find the area and the perimeter of a rhombus whose diagonals have lengths 18 in. and 24 in.

9. Tom Morrow wants to buy some fertilizer for his yard. The lot size is 140 ft by 160 ft. The outside measurements of his house are 80 ft by 35 ft. The driveway measures 30 ft by 20 ft. All shapes are rectangular.
a) What is the square footage of his yard that needs to be fertilized?
b) If each bag of fertilizer covers 5000 ft^2, how many bags should Tom buy?
c) If the fertilizer costs $18 per bag, what is his total cost?

10. Alice's mother wants to wallpaper two adjacent walls in Alice's bedroom. She also wants to put a border along the top of all four walls. The bedroom is 9 ft by 12 ft by 8 ft high.
a) If each double roll covers approximately 60 ft^2 and the wallpaper is sold in double rolls only, how many double rolls are needed?
b) If the border is sold in rolls of 5 yd each, how many rolls of the border are needed?

11. *Given:* Isosceles trapezoid $ABCD$
Equilateral $\triangle FBC$
Right $\triangle AED$
$BC = 12$, $AB = 5$, and $ED = 16$
Find: a) A_{EAFD}
b) Perimeter of $EAFD$

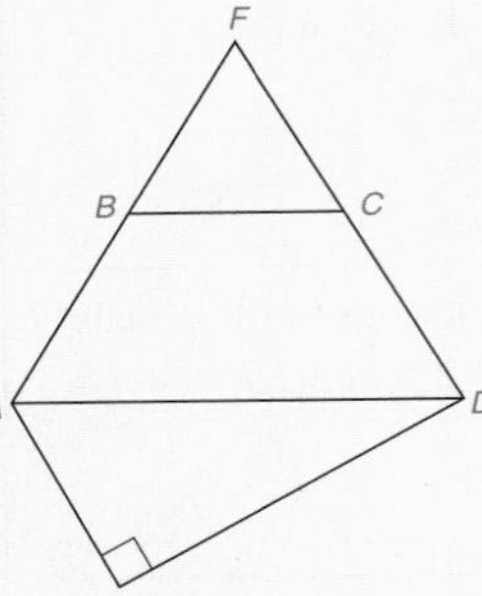

12. *Given:* Kite $ABCD$ with $AB = 10$, $BC = 17$, and $BD = 16$
Find: A_{ABCD}

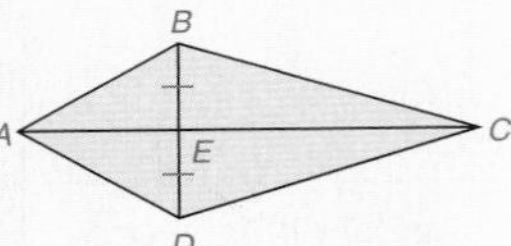

13. One side of a rectangle is 2 cm longer than a second side. If the area is 35 cm^2, find the dimensions of the rectangle.

14. One side of a triangle is 10 cm longer than a second side, and the third side is 5 cm longer than the second side. The perimeter of the triangle is 60 cm.
a) Find the lengths of the three sides.
b) Find the area of the triangle.

15. Find the area of $\triangle ABD$ as shown.

16. Find the area of an equilateral triangle if each of its sides has length 12 cm.

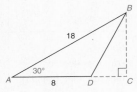

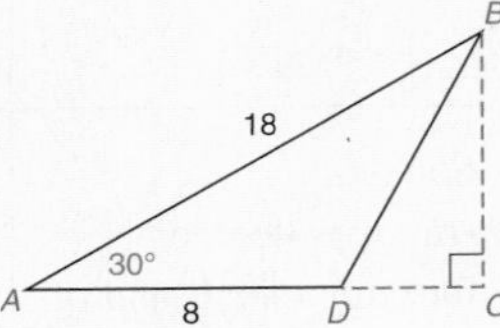

17. If $\overline{AC}$ is a diameter of $\odot O$, find the area of the shaded triangle.

18. For a regular pentagon, find the measure of each:
a) central angle
b) interior angle
c) exterior angle

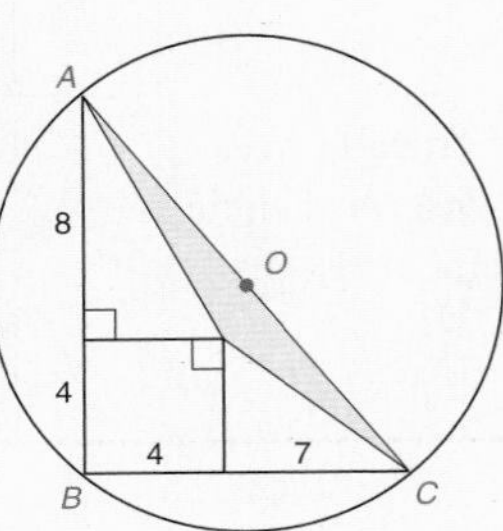

Exercise 17

19. Find the area of a regular hexagon each of whose sides has length 8 ft.

20. The area of an equilateral triangle is $108\sqrt{3}$ in^2. If the length of each side of the triangle is $12\sqrt{3}$ in, find the length of an apothem of the triangle.

21. Find the area of a regular hexagon whose apothem has length 9 in.

22. In a regular polygon, each central angle measures 45°.
   a) How many sides does the regular polygon have?
   b) If each side measures 5 cm and the length of each apothem is approximately 6 cm, what is the approximate area of the polygon?

23. Can a circle be circumscribed about each of the following figures? Why or why not?
   a) Parallelogram
   b) Rhombus
   c) Rectangle
   d) Square

24. Can a circle be inscribed in each of the following figures? Why or why not?
   a) Parallelogram
   b) Rhombus
   c) Rectangle
   d) Square

25. The length of the radius of a circle inscribed in an equilateral triangle is 7 in. Find the area of the triangle.

26. The Turners want to carpet the cement around their rectangular pool. The dimensions for the rectangular area formed by the pool and its cement walkway are 20 ft by 30 ft. The pool is 12 ft by 24 ft.
   a) How many square feet need to be covered?
   b) Carpet is sold only by the square yard. Approximately how many square yards does the area in part (a) represent?
   c) If the carpet costs $9.97 per square yard, what will be the total cost of the carpet?

Find the exact areas of the shaded regions in Exercises 27 to 31.

27.

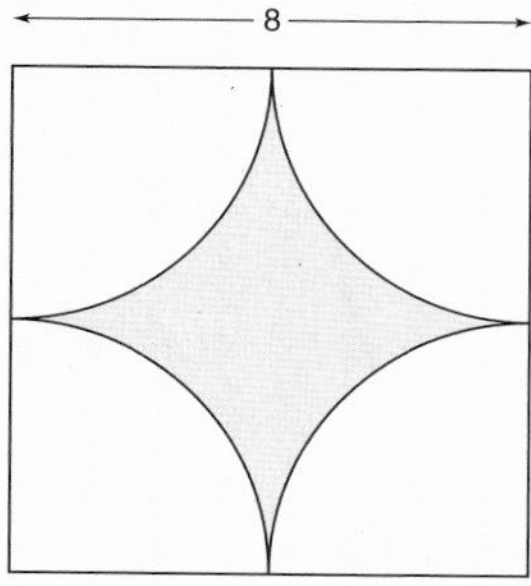

Square

28.

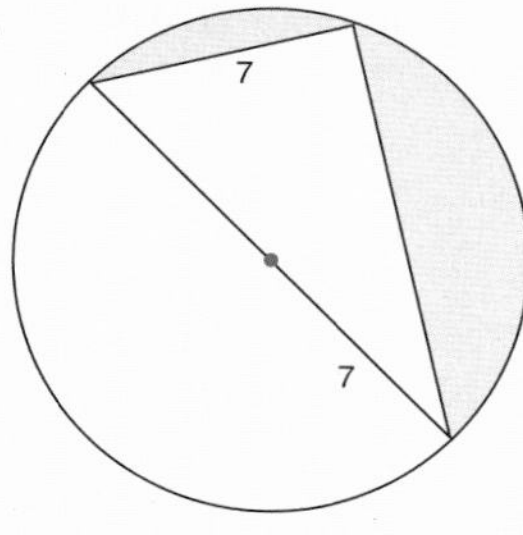

29.

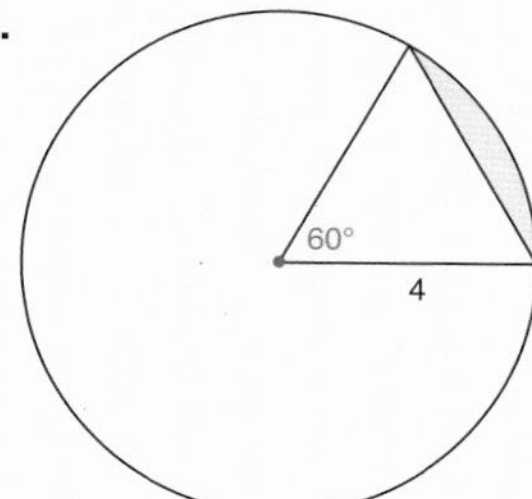

30.

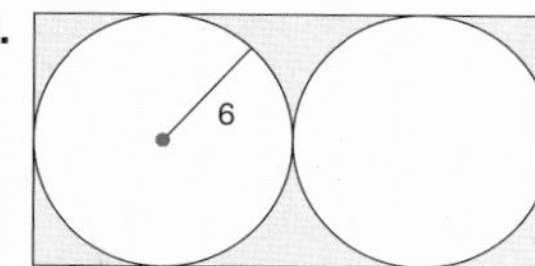

Two ≅ tangent circles, inscribed in a rectangle

31.

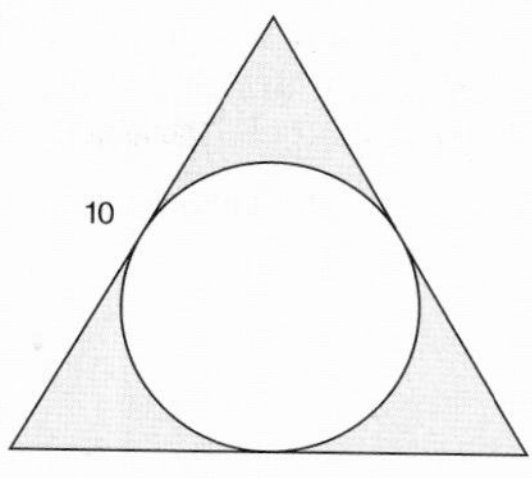

Equilateral triangle

32. The arc of a sector measures 40°. Find the exact length of the arc and the exact area of the sector if the radius measures $3\sqrt{5}$ cm.

33. The circumference of a circle is 66 ft.
   a) Find the diameter of the circle, using $\pi \approx \frac{22}{7}$.
   b) Find the area of the circle, using $\pi \approx \frac{22}{7}$.

34. A circle has an exact area of 27π ft^2.
   a) What is the area of a sector of this circle if the arc of the sector measures 80°?
   b) What is the exact perimeter of the sector in part (a)?

35. An isosceles right triangle is inscribed in a circle that has a diameter of 12 in. Find the exact area between one of the legs of the triangle and its corresponding arc.

36. *Given:* Concentric circles with radii of lengths R and r, with $R > r$

   Prove: $A_{\text{ring}} = \pi(BC)^2$

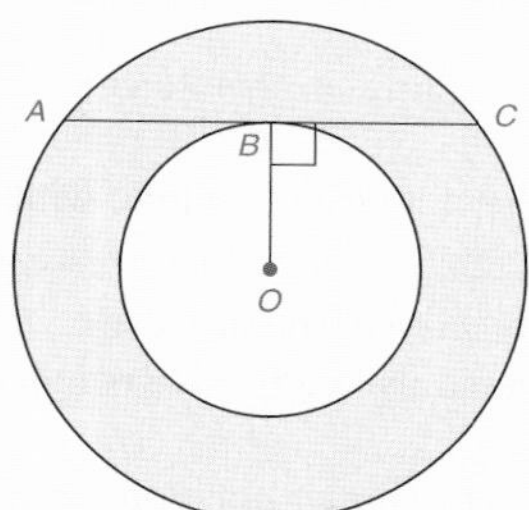

37. Prove that the area of a circle circumscribed about a square is twice the area of the circle inscribed within the square.

38. Prove that if semicircles are constructed on each of the sides of a right triangle, then the area of the semicircle on the hypotenuse is equal to the sum of the areas of the semicircles on the two legs.

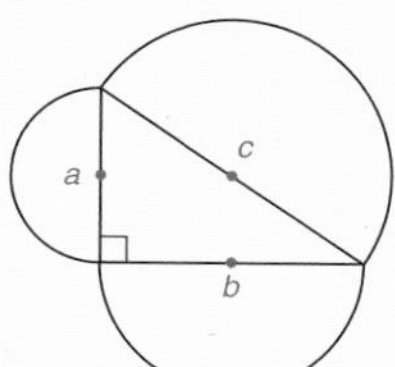

39. Jeff and Helen want to carpet their family room, except for the entranceway and the semicircle in front of the fireplace, both of which they want to tile.
a) How many square yards of carpeting are needed?
b) How many square feet are to be tiled?

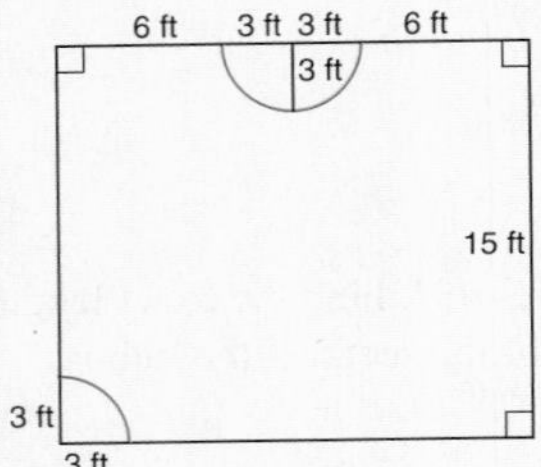

40. Sue and Dave's semicircular driveway is to be resealed, and then flowers are to be planted on either side.
a) What is the number of square feet to be resealed?
b) If the cost of resealing is \$0.18 per square foot, what is the total cost?
c) If individual flowers are to be planted 1 foot from the edge of the driveway at intervals of approximately 1 foot on both sides of the driveway, how many flowers are needed?

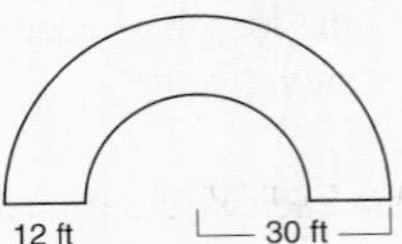

Chapter 8 TEST

1. Complete each statement.
a) Given that the length and the width of a rectangle are measured in inches, its area is measured in ________.
b) If two closed plane figures are congruent, then their areas are ________.

2. Give each formula.
a) The formula for the area of a square whose sides are of length s is ________.
b) The formula for the circumference of a circle with radius length r is ________.

3. Determine whether the statement is True or False.
a) The area of a circle with radius length r is given by $A = \pi r^2$. ________
b) With corresponding sides of similar polygons having the ratio $\frac{s_1}{s_2} = \frac{1}{2}$, the ratio of their areas is $\frac{A_1}{A_2} = \frac{1}{2}$. ________

4. If the area of rectangle $ABCD$ is 46 cm^2, find the area of $\triangle ABE$. ________

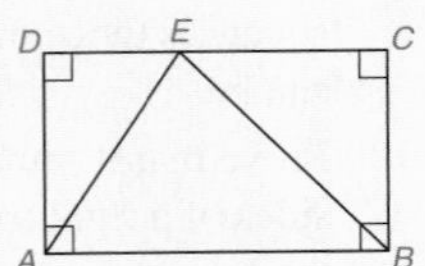

5. In *square feet*, find the area of ▱$EFGH$. ________

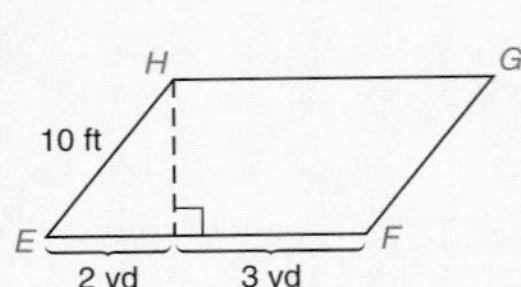

6. Find the area of rhombus $MNPQ$ given that $QN = 8$ ft and $PM = 6$ ft. ________

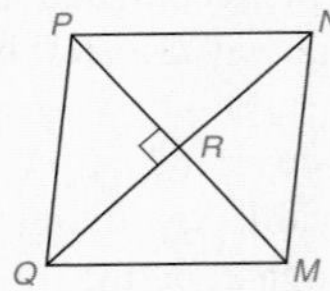

7. Use Heron's Formula, $A = \sqrt{s(s - a)(s - b)(s - c)}$, to find the exact area of a triangle that has lengths of sides 4 cm, 13 cm, and 15 cm. ________

8. In trapezoid $ABCD$, $AB = 7$ ft and $DC = 13$ ft. If the area of trapezoid $ABCD$ is 60 ft^2, find the length of altitude $\overline{AE}$. ________

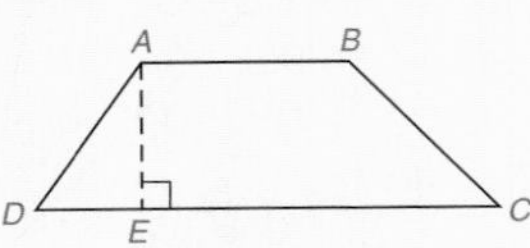

9. A regular pentagon has an apothem of length 4.0 in. and each side is of length $s = 5.8$ in. For the regular pentagon, find its:
a) Perimeter ________
b) Area ________

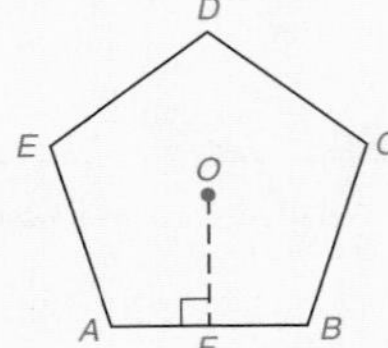

10. For the circle shown below, the length of the radius is $r = 5$ in. Find the exact:

a) Circumference ______________

b) Area ______________

(HINT: Leave π in the answer in order to achieve exactness.)

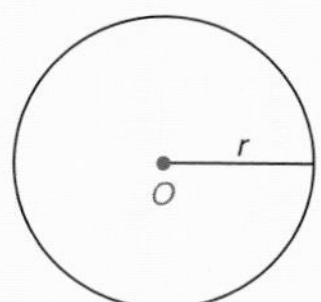

11. Where $\pi \approx \frac{22}{7}$, find the approximate length of $\overset{\frown}{AC}$.

$\ell\overset{\frown}{AC} \approx$ ______________

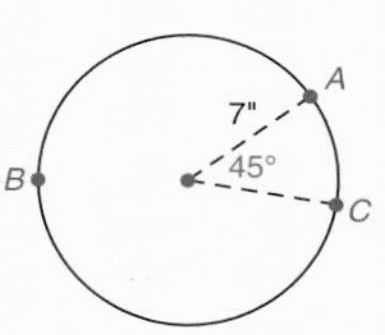

12. Where $\pi \approx 3.14$, find the approximate area of a circle (not shown) whose *diameter* measures 20 cm.

____

13. In the figure, a square is inscribed in a circle. If each side of the square measures $4\sqrt{2}$ in., find an expression for the exact area of the shaded region. ______________

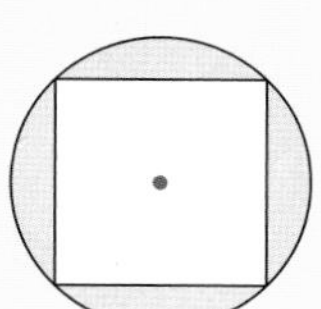

Square inscribed in a circle

14. Find the exact area of the 135° sector shown.

____

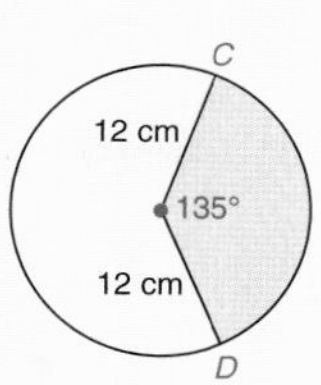

15. Find the exact area of the shaded segment.

____

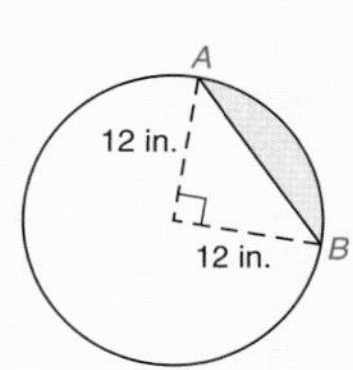

16. The area of a right triangle whose sides have lengths 5 in., 12 in., and 13 in. is exactly 30 in^2. Use the formula $A = \frac{1}{2}rP$ to find the length of the radius of the circle that can be inscribed in this triangle. ______________

Chapter 9

Surfaces and Solids

© Stephen Studd/Getty Images

CHAPTER OUTLINE

Additional Video explanation of concepts, sample problems, and applications are available on DVD. 

Colossal! Located near Cairo, Egypt, the Great Pyramids illustrate one of the types of solids that we study in Chapter 9. The architectural designs of buildings often illustrate other solid shapes that we study in this chapter. The real world is three-dimensional; that is, solids and space figures can be characterized by contrasting measures of length, width, and depth. Each solid determines a bounded region of space that has a measure known as *volume*. Some units that are used to measure volume include the cubic foot and the cubic meter. The same technique that is used to measure the volume of the pyramid in Example 5 of Section 9.2 could be used to measure the volumes of the Great Pyramids.

9.1 Prisms, Area, and Volume

KEY CONCEPTS

Prisms (Right and Oblique)
Bases
Altitude
Vertices
Edges
Faces
Lateral Area
Total (Surface) Area
Volume
Regular Prism
Cube
Cubic Unit

PRISMS

Suppose that two congruent polygons lie in parallel planes in such a way that their corresponding sides are parallel. If the corresponding vertices of these polygons [such as A and A' in Figure 9.1(a)] are joined by line segments, then the "solid" that results is a **prism**. The congruent figures that lie in the parallel planes are the **bases** of the prism. The parallel planes need not be shown in the drawings of prisms. Suggested by an empty box, the prism is like a shell that encloses a portion of space by the parts of planes that form the prism; thus, a prism does not contain interior points. In practice, it is sometimes convenient to call a prism such as a brick a *solid*; of course, this interpretation of prism would contain its interior points.

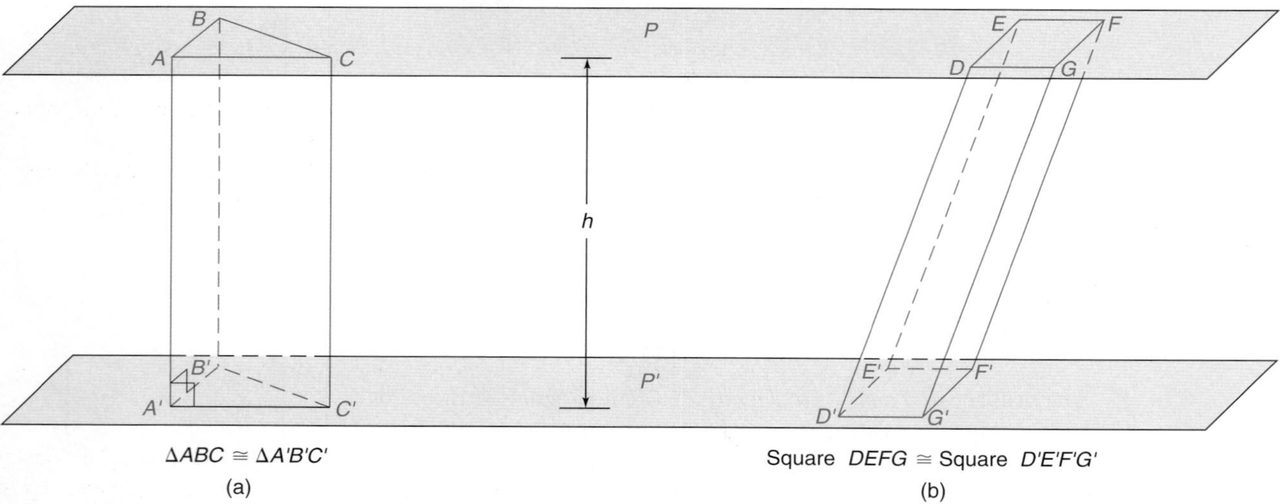

Figure 9.1

In Figure 9.1(a), $\overline{AB}$, $\overline{AC}$, $\overline{BC}$, $\overline{A'B'}$, $\overline{A'C'}$, and $\overline{B'C'}$ are **base edges**, and $\overline{AA'}$, $\overline{BB'}$, and $\overline{CC'}$ are **lateral edges** of the prism. Because the lateral edges of this prism are perpendicular to its base edges, the **lateral faces** (like quadrilateral $ACC'A'$) are rectangles. Points A, B, C, A', B', and C' are the **vertices** of the prism.

In Figure 9.1(b), the lateral edges of the prism are not perpendicular to its base edges; in this situation, the lateral edges are often described as **oblique** (slanted). For the oblique prism, the lateral faces are parallelograms. Considering the prisms in Figure 9.1, we are led to the following definitions.

DEFINITION

A **right prism** is a prism in which the lateral edges are perpendicular to the base edges at their points of intersection. An **oblique prism** is a prism in which the parallel lateral edges are oblique to the base edges at their points of intersection.

Part of the description used to classify a prism depends on its base. For instance, the prism in Figure 9.1(a) is a *right triangular prism*; in this case, the word *right* describes the prism, whereas the word *triangular* refers to the triangular base. Similarly, the prism in Figure 9.1(b) is an *oblique square prism*, if we assume that the bases are squares. Both prisms in Figure 9.1 have an **altitude** (a perpendicular segment joining italics on height the planes that contain the bases) of length h, also known as the *height* of the prism.

EXAMPLE 1

Name each type of prism in Figure 9.2.

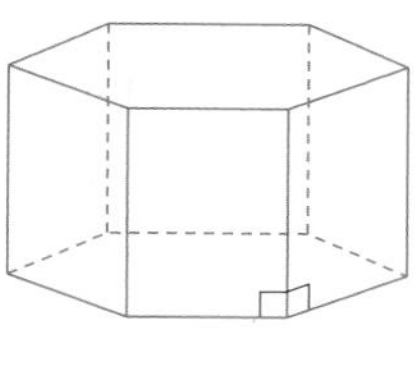

(a)

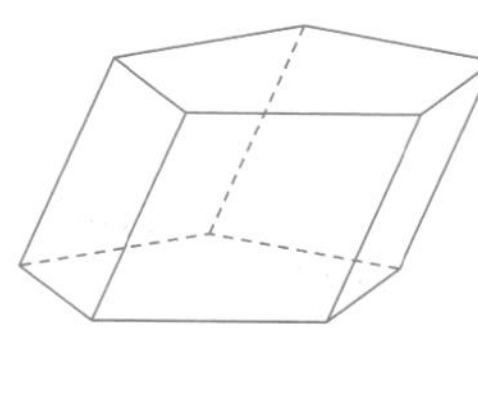

(b)

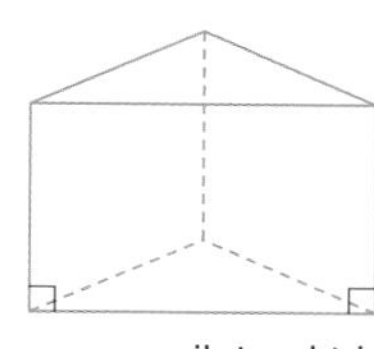

Bases are equilateral triangles

(c)

Figure 9.2

Solution

a) The lateral edges are perpendicular to the base edges of the hexagonal base. The prism is a *right hexagonal prism.*
b) The lateral edges are oblique to the base edges of the pentagonal base. The prism is an *oblique pentagonal prism.*
c) The lateral edges are perpendicular to the base edges of the triangular base. Because the base is equilateral, the prism is a *right equilateral triangular prism.* ■

SSG *Exs. 1, 2*

AREA OF A PRISM

DEFINITION

The **lateral area** L of a prism is the sum of the areas of all lateral faces.

Figure 9.3

In the right triangular prism of Figure 9.3, a, b, and c are the lengths of the sides of either base. These dimensions are used along with the length of the altitude (denoted by h) to calculate the lateral area, the sum of the areas of rectangles $ACC'A'$, $ABB'A'$, and $BCC'B'$. The lateral area L of the right triangular prism can be found as follows:

$$\begin{aligned} L &= ah + bh + ch \\ &= h(a + b + c) \\ &= hP \end{aligned}$$

where P is the perimeter of a base of the prism. This formula, $L = hP$, is valid for finding the lateral area of any *right* prism. Although lateral faces of an oblique prism are parallelograms, the formula $L = hP$ is also used to find its lateral area.

THEOREM 9.1.1

The lateral area L of any prism whose altitude has measure h and whose base has perimeter P is given by $L = hP$.

Many students (and teachers) find it easier to calculate the lateral area of a prism without using the formula $L = hP$. We illustrate this in Example 2.

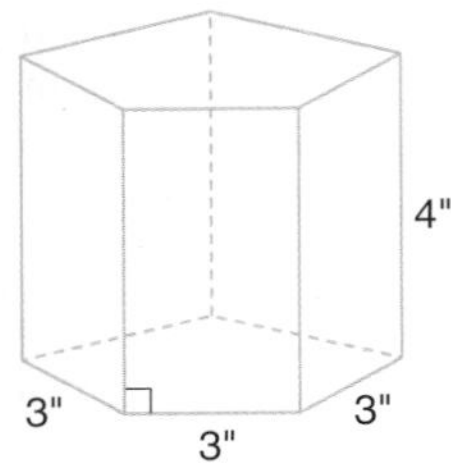

Figure 9.4

EXAMPLE 2

The bases of the right prism shown in Figure 9.4 are equilateral pentagons with sides of length 3 in. each. If the altitude measures 4 in., find the lateral area of the prism.

Solution Each lateral face is a rectangle with dimensions 3 in. by 4 in. The area of each rectangular face is 3 in. $\times$ 4 in. $=$ 12 in^2. Because there are five congruent lateral faces, the lateral area of the pentagonal prism is $5 \times 12 \text{ in.}^2 = 60 \text{ in}^2$.

NOTE: When applied in Example 2, the formula $L = hP$ leads to $L = 4 \text{ in.} \times 15 \text{ in.} = 60 \text{ in}^2$. ■

DEFINITION

For any prism, the **total area** T is the sum of the lateral area and the areas of the bases.

NOTE: The total area of the prism is also known as its surface area.

Both bases and lateral faces are known as *faces* of a prism. Thus, the total area T of the prism is the sum of the areas of all its faces.

Recalling Heron's Formula, we know that the base area B of the right triangular prism in Figure 9.3 can be found by the formula

$$B = \sqrt{s(s - a)(s - b)(s - c)}$$

in which s is the semiperimeter of the triangular base. We use Heron's Formula in Example 3.

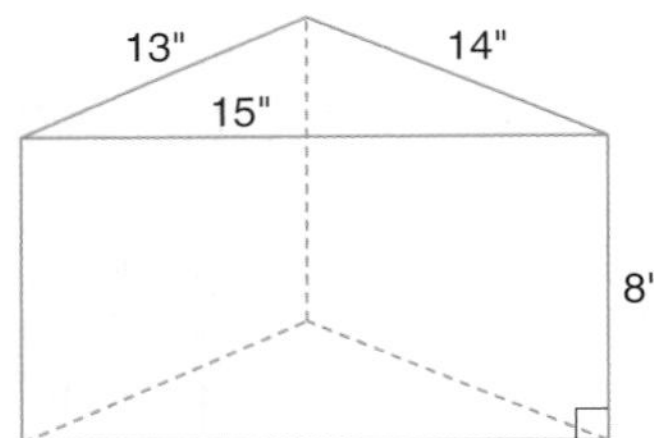

Figure 9.5

EXAMPLE 3

Find the total area of the right triangular prism with an altitude of length 8 in. if the sides of the triangular bases have lengths of 13 in., 14 in., and 15 in. See Figure 9.5.

Solution The lateral area is found by adding the areas of the three rectangular lateral faces. That is,

$$\begin{aligned} L &= 8 \text{ in.} \cdot 13 \text{ in.} + 8 \text{ in.} \cdot 14 \text{ in.} + 8 \text{ in.} \cdot 15 \text{ in.} \\ &= 104 \text{ in}^2 + 112 \text{ in}^2 + 120 \text{ in}^2 = 336 \text{ in}^2 \end{aligned}$$

We use Heron's Formula to find the area of each base. With $s = \frac{1}{2}(13 + 14 + 15)$, or $s = 21$, $B = \sqrt{21(21 - 13)(21 - 14)(21 - 15)} = \sqrt{21(8)(7)(6)} = \sqrt{7056} = 84$.

Calculating the total area (or surface area) of the triangular prism, we have

$$T = 336 + 2(84) \qquad \text{or} \qquad T = 504 \text{ in}^2$$ ■

The general formula for the total area of a prism follows.

THEOREM 9.1.2

The total area T of any prism with lateral area L and base area B is given by $T = L + 2B$.

PICTURE PROOF OF THEOREM 9.1.2

GIVEN: The pentagonal prism of Figure 9.6(a)

PROVE: $T = L + 2B$

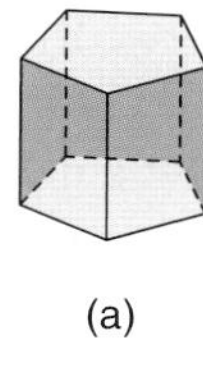
(a)

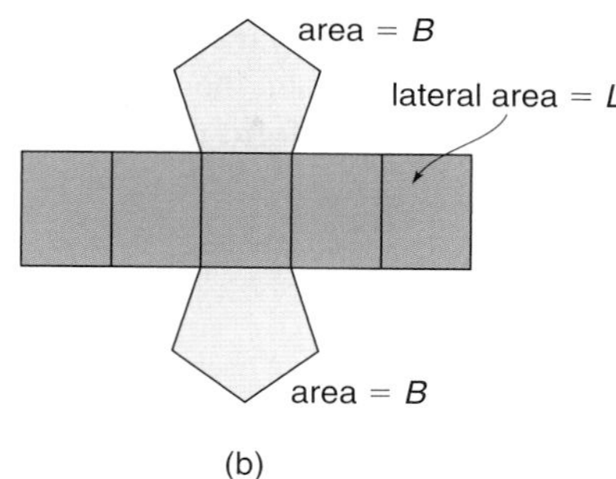

(b)

Figure 9.6

PROOF: When the prism is "taken apart" and laid flat, as shown in Figure 9.6(b), we see that the total area depends upon the lateral area (shaded darker) and the areas of the two bases; that is,

$$T = L + 2B$$

DEFINITION

A **regular prism** is a right prism whose bases are regular polygons.

Henceforth, the prism in Figure 9.2(c) on page 405 will be called a regular triangular prism.

In the following example, each base of the prism is a regular hexagon. Because the prism is a right prism, the lateral faces are congruent rectangles.

EXAMPLE 4

Find the lateral area L and the surface area T of the regular hexagonal prism in Figure 9.7(a).

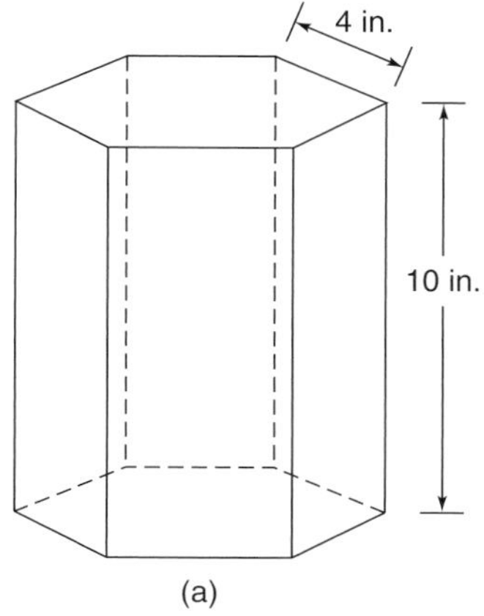

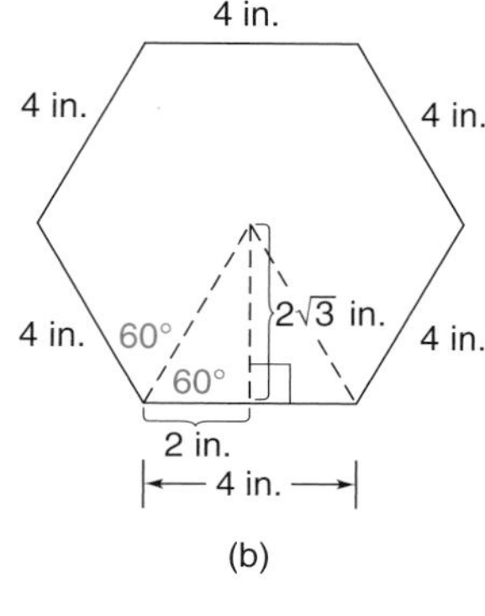

(b)

(a)

Figure 9.7

Solution In Figure 9.7(a) on page 407, there are six congruent lateral faces, each rectangular and with dimensions of 4 in. by 10 in. Then

$$\begin{aligned} L &= 6(4 \cdot 10) \\ &= 240 \text{ in}^2 \end{aligned}$$

For the regular hexagonal base [see Figure 9.7(b)], the apothem measures $a = 2\sqrt{3}$ in., and the perimeter is $P = 6 \cdot 4 = 24$ in. Then the area B of each base is given by the formula for the area of a regular polygon.

$$\begin{aligned} B &= \frac{1}{2}aP \\ &= \frac{1}{2} \cdot 2\sqrt{3} \cdot 24 \\ &= 24\sqrt{3} \text{ in}^2 \approx 41.57 \text{ in}^2 \end{aligned}$$

Now

$$\begin{aligned} T &= L + 2B \\ &= (240 + 48\sqrt{3}) \text{ in}^2 \approx 323.14 \text{ in}^2 \end{aligned}$$

■

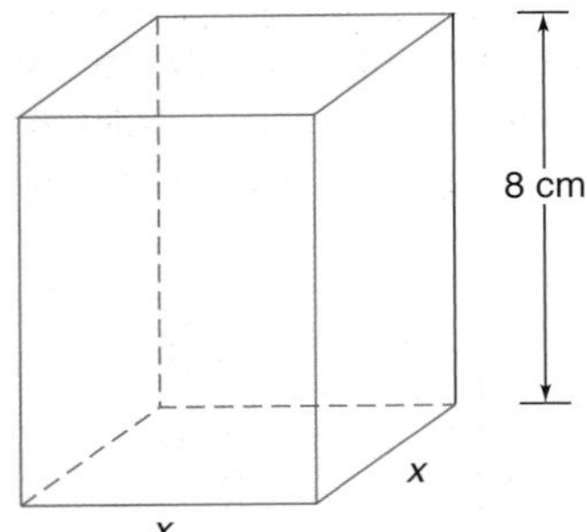

Figure 9.8

EXAMPLE 5

The total area of the right square prism in Figure 9.8 is 210 cm^2. Find the length of a side of the square base if the altitude of the prism is 8 cm.

Solution Let x be the length in cm of a side of the square. Then the area of the base is $B = x^2$ and the area of each of the four lateral faces is $8x$. Therefore,

$$\underbrace{2(x^2)}_{\textbf{2 bases}} + \underbrace{4(8x)}_{\textbf{4 lateral faces}} = 210$$

$$\begin{aligned} 2x^2 + 32x &= 210 \\ 2x^2 + 32x - 210 &= 0 \\ x^2 + 16x - 105 &= 0 \quad &\textbf{(dividing by 2)} \\ (x + 21)(x - 5) &= 0 \quad &\textbf{(factoring)} \\ x + 21 = 0 \quad \text{or} \quad x - 5 &= 0 \\ x = -21 \quad \text{or} \quad x &= 5 \quad &\textbf{(reject } \mathbf{-21} \textbf{ as a solution)} \end{aligned}$$

Then each side of the square base measures 5 cm. ■

Exs. 3–7

DEFINITION

A **cube** is a right square prism whose edges are congruent.

The cube is very important in determining the volume of a solid.

VOLUME OF A PRISM

To introduce the notion of *volume*, we realize that a prism encloses a portion of space. Without a formal definition, we say that **volume** is a number that measures the amount of enclosed space. To begin, we need a unit for measuring volume. Just as the meter can be used to measure length and the square yard can be used to measure area, a **cubic unit** is used to measure the amount of space enclosed within a bounded region of space. One such unit is described in the following paragraph.

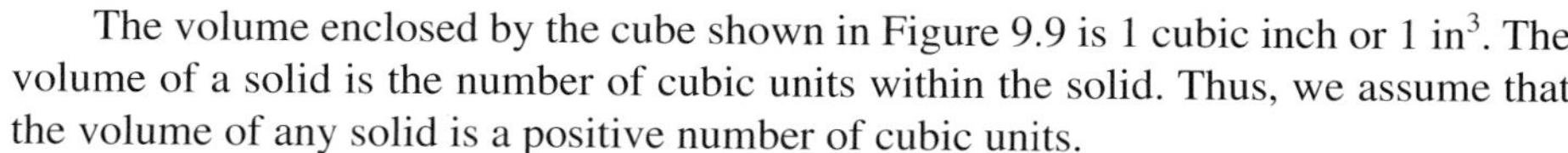

The volume enclosed by the cube shown in Figure 9.9 is 1 cubic inch or 1 in^3. The volume of a solid is the number of cubic units within the solid. Thus, we assume that the volume of any solid is a positive number of cubic units.

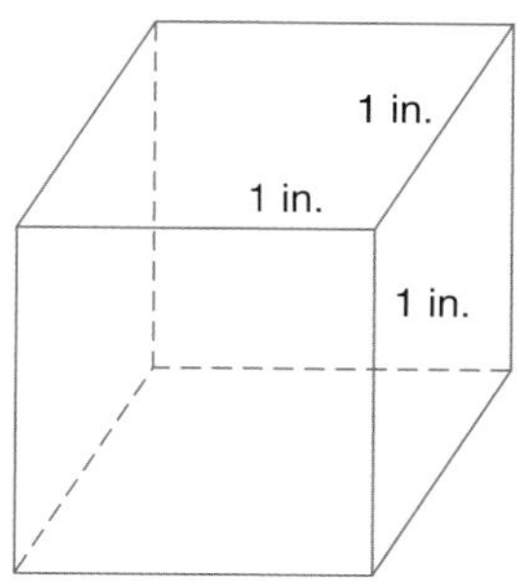

Figure 9.9

POSTULATE 24 ▶ (Volume Postulate)

Corresponding to every solid is a unique positive number V known as the volume of that solid.

The simplest figure for which we can determine volume is the **right rectangular prism**. Such a solid might be described as a **parallelpiped** or as a "box." Because boxes are used as containers for storage and shipping (such as a boxcar), it is important to calculate volume as a measure of capacity. A right rectangular prism is shown in Figure 9.10; its dimensions are length ℓ, width w, and height (or altitude) h.

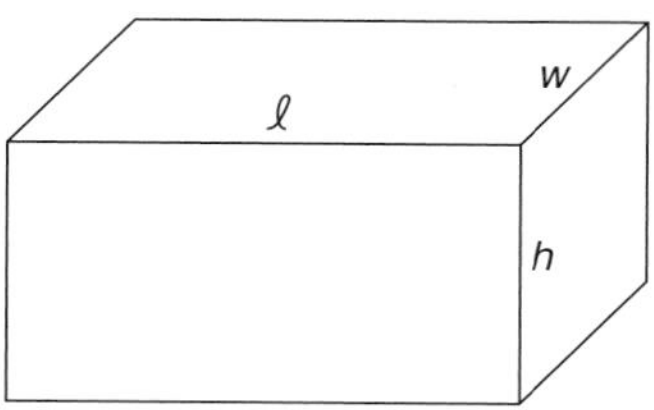

Figure 9.10

The volume of a right rectangular prism of length 4 in., width 3 in., and height 2 in. is easily shown to be 24 in^3. The volume is the product of the three dimensions of the given solid. We see not only that $4 \cdot 3 \cdot 2 = 24$ but also that the units of volume are $\text{in.} \cdot \text{in.} \cdot \text{in.} = \text{in}^3$. Figures 9.11(a) and (b) illustrate that the 4 by 3 by 2 box must have the volume 24 cubic units. We see that there are four layers of blocks, each of which is a 2 by 3 configuration of 6 units^3. Figure 9.11 provides the insight that leads us to our next postulate.

Geometry in the Real World

The frozen solids found in ice cube trays usually approximate the shapes of cubes.

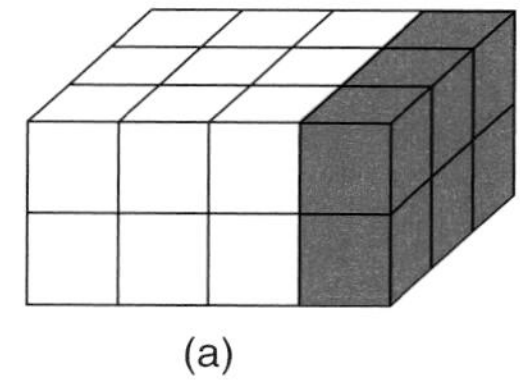

(a)

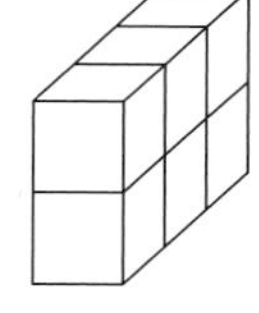

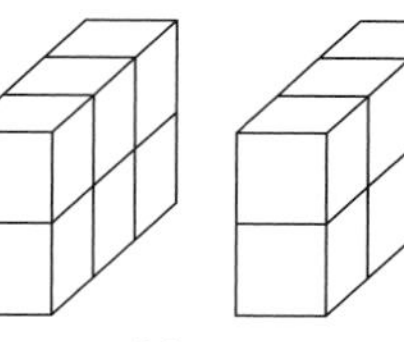

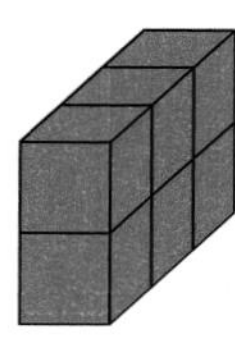

(b)

Figure 9.11

POSTULATE 25

The volume of a right rectangular prism is given by

$$V = \ell w h$$

where ℓ measures the length, w the width, and h the altitude of the prism.

In order to apply the formula found in Postulate 25, the units used for dimensions ℓ, w, and h must be alike.

EXAMPLE 6

Find the volume of a box whose dimensions are 1 ft, 8 in., and 10 in. (See Figure 9.12.)

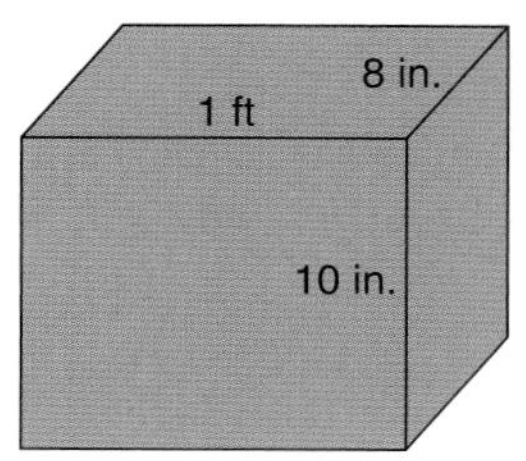

Figure 9.12

Solution Although it makes no difference which dimension is chosen for ℓ or w or h, it is most important that the units of measure be the same. Thus, 1 ft is replaced by 12 in. in the formula for volume:

$$\begin{aligned} V &= \ell w h \\ &= 12 \text{ in.} \cdot 8 \text{ in.} \cdot 10 \text{ in.} \\ &= 960 \text{ in}^3 \end{aligned}$$

■

Warning

The uppercase B found in formulas in this chapter represents the area of the base of a solid; because the base is a plane region, B is measured in square units.

Note that the formula for the volume of the right rectangular prism, $V = \ell wh$, could be replaced by the formula $V = Bh$, where B is the area of the base of the prism; that is, $B = \ell w$. As is stated in the next postulate, this volume relationship is true for right prisms in general.

POSTULATE 26

The volume of a right prism is given by

$$V = Bh$$

where B is the area of a base and h is the length of the altitude of the prism.

Exs. 9–13

In real-world applications, the formula $V = Bh$ is valid for calculating the volumes of oblique prisms as well as right prisms.

Technology Exploration

On your calculator, determine the method of "cubing." That is, find a value such as 2.1^3. On many calculators, we enter 2.1, a caret $\wedge$, and 3.

EXAMPLE 7

Find the volume of the right hexagonal prism in Figure 9.7 on page 407.

Solution In Example 4, we found that the area of the hexagonal base was $24\sqrt{3}\text{ in}^2$. Because the altitude of the hexagonal prism is 10 in., the volume is $V = Bh$, or $V = (24\sqrt{3}\text{ in.}^2)(10\text{ in.})$. Then $V = 240\sqrt{3}\text{ in.}^3 \approx 415.69\text{ in}^3$.

NOTE: Just as $x^2 \cdot x = x^3$, the units in Example 7 are $\text{in.}^2 \cdot \text{in.} = \text{in.}^3$ ■

In the final example of this section, we use the fact that $1\text{ yd}^3 = 27\text{ ft}^3$. In the cube shown in Figure 9.13, each dimension measures 1 yd, or 3 ft. The cube's volume is given by $1\text{ yd} \cdot 1\text{ yd} \cdot 1\text{ yd} = 1\text{ yd}^3$ or $3\text{ ft} \cdot 3\text{ ft} \cdot 3\text{ ft} = 27\text{ ft}^3$.

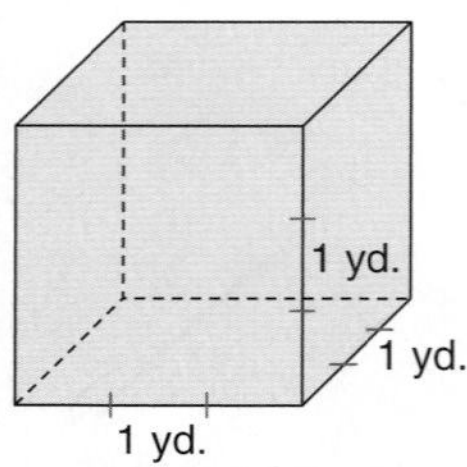

Figure 9.13

EXAMPLE 8

Sarah Balbuena is having a concrete driveway poured at her house. The section to be poured is rectangular, measuring 12 ft by 40 ft, and is 4 in. deep. How many cubic yards of concrete are needed?

Solution Using $V = \ell wh$, we must be consistent with units. Thus, $\ell = 12$ ft, $w = 40$ ft, and $h = \frac{1}{3}$ ft (from 4 in.). Now

$$V = 12\text{ ft} \cdot 40\text{ ft} \cdot \frac{1}{3}\text{ ft}$$
$$V = 160\text{ ft}^3$$

To change 160 ft^3 to cubic yards, we divide by 27 to obtain $5\frac{25}{27}\text{ yd}^3$.

SSG *Exs. 14, 15*

NOTE: Sarah will be charged for 6 yd^3 of concrete, the result of rounding upward. ■

Exercises 9.1

1. Consider the solid shown.
   a) Does it appear to be a prism?
   b) Is it right or oblique?
   c) What type of base(s) does the solid have?
   d) Name the type of solid.
   e) What type of figure is each lateral face?

Exercises 1, 3, 5, 7, 9

2. Consider the solid shown.
   a) Does it appear to be a prism?
   b) Is it right or oblique?
   c) What type of base(s) does the solid have?
   d) Name the type of solid.
   e) What type of figure is each lateral face?

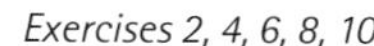

Exercises 2, 4, 6, 8, 10

3. Consider the hexagonal prism shown in Exercise 1.
   a) How many vertices does it have?
   b) How many edges (lateral edges plus base edges) does it have?
   c) How many faces (lateral faces plus bases) does it have?
4. Consider the triangular prism shown in Exercise 2.
   a) How many vertices does it have?
   b) How many edges (lateral edges plus base edges) does it have?
   c) How many faces (lateral faces plus bases) does it have?
5. If each edge of the hexagonal prism in Exercise 1 is measured in centimeters, what unit is used to measure its (a) surface area? (b) volume?
6. If each edge of the triangular prism in Exercise 2 is measured in inches, what unit is used to measure its (a) lateral area? (b) volume?
7. Suppose that each of the bases of the hexagonal prism in Exercise 1 has an area of 12 cm^2 and that each lateral face has an area of 18 cm^2. Find the total (surface) area of the prism.
8. Suppose that each of the bases of the triangular prism in Exercise 2 has an area of 3.4 in^2 and that each lateral face has an area of 4.6 in^2. Find the total (surface) area of the prism.
9. Suppose that each of the bases of the hexagonal prism in Exercise 1 has an area of 12 cm^2 and that the altitude of the prism measures 10 cm. Find the volume of the prism.
10. Suppose that each of the bases of the triangular prism in Exercise 2 has an area of 3.4 cm^2 and that the altitude of the prism measures 1.2 cm. Find the volume of the prism.
11. A solid is an octagonal prism.
    a) How many vertices does it have?
    b) How many lateral edges does it have?
    c) How many base edges are there in all?
12. A solid is a pentagonal prism.
    a) How many vertices does it have?
    b) How many lateral edges does it have?
    c) How many base edges are there in all?
13. Generalize the results found in Exercises 11 and 12 by answering each of the following questions. Assume that the number of sides in each base of the prism is n. For the prism, what is the
    a) number of vertices?
    b) number of lateral edges?
    c) number of base edges?
    d) total number of edges?
    e) number of lateral faces?
    f) number of bases?
    g) total number of faces?
14. In the accompanying regular pentagonal prism, suppose that each base edge measures 6 in. and that the apothem of the base measures 4.1 in. The altitude of the prism measures 10 in.
    a) Find the lateral area of the prism.
    b) Find the total area of the prism.
    c) Find the volume of the prism.

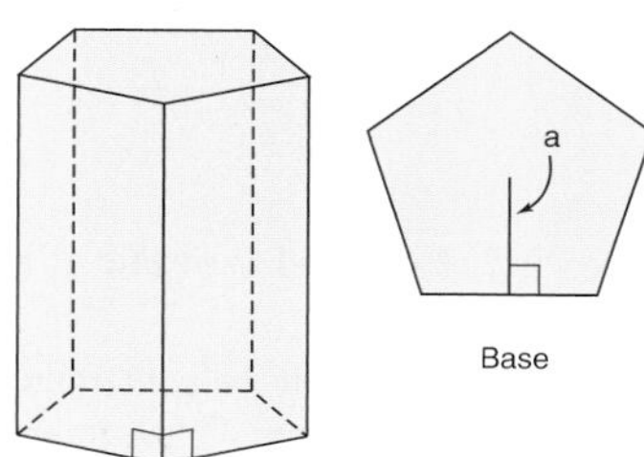

Exercises 14, 15

15. In the regular pentagonal prism shown above, suppose that each base edge measures 9.2 cm and that the apothem of the base measures 6.3 cm. The altitude of the prism measures 14.6 cm.
    a) Find the lateral area of the prism.
    b) Find the total area of the prism.
    c) Find the volume of the prism.
16. For the right triangular prism, suppose that the sides of the triangular base measure 4 m, 5 m, and 6 m. The altitude is 7 m.
    a) Find the lateral area of the prism.
    b) Find the total area of the prism.
    c) Find the volume of the prism.

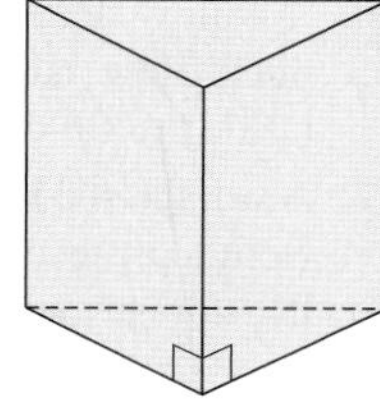

Exercises 16, 17

17. For the right triangular prism found in Exercise 16, suppose that the sides of the triangular base measure 3 ft, 4 ft, and 5 ft. The altitude is 6 ft in length.
   a) Find the lateral area of the prism.
   b) Find the total area of the prism.
   c) Find the volume of the prism.
18. Given that 100 cm = 1 m, find the number of cubic centimeters in 1 cubic meter.
19. Given that 12 in. = 1 ft, find the number of cubic inches in 1 cubic foot.
20. A cereal box measures 2 in. by 8 in. by 10 in. What is the volume of the box? How many square inches of cardboard make up its surface? (Disregard any hidden flaps.)
21. The measures of the sides of the square base of a box are twice the measure of the height of the box. If the volume of the box is 108 in^3, find the dimensions of the box.
22. For a given box, the height measures 4 m. If the length of the rectangular base is 2 m greater than the width of the base and the lateral area L is 96 m^2, find the dimensions of the box.
23. For the box shown, the total area is 94 cm^2. Determine the value of x.

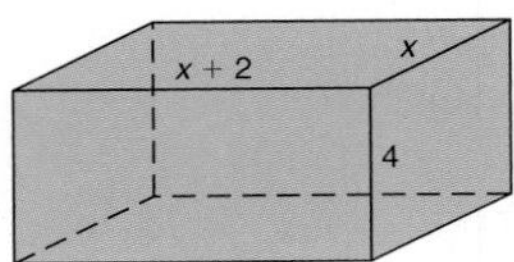

Exercises 23, 24

24. If the volume of the box is 252 in^3, find the value of x. (See the figure for Exercise 23.)
25. The box with dimensions indicated is to be constructed of materials that cost 1 cent per square inch for the lateral surface and 2 cents per square inch for the bases. What is the total cost of constructing the box?

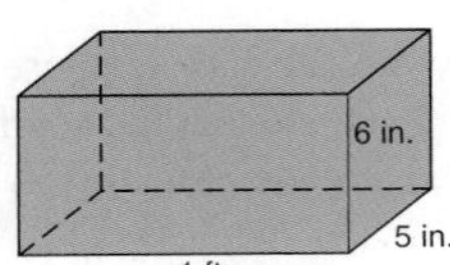

26. A hollow steel door is 32 in. wide by 80 in. tall by $1\frac{3}{8}$ in. thick. How many cubic inches of foam insulation are needed to fill the door?
27. A storage shed is in the shape of a pentagonal prism. The front represents one of its two pentagonal bases. What is the storage capacity (volume) of its interior?

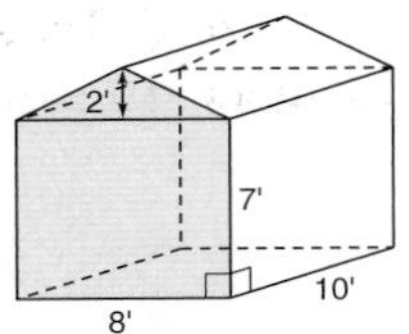

28. A storage shed is in the shape of a trapezoidal prism. Each trapezoid represents one of its bases. With dimensions as shown, what is the storage capacity (volume) of its interior?

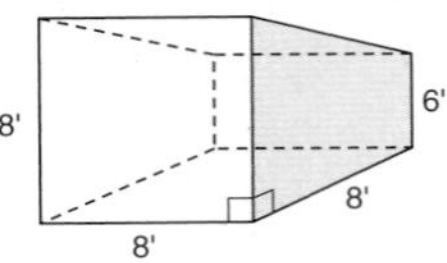

29. A cube is a right square prism in which all edges have the same length. For the cube with edge e,
   a) show that the total area is $T = 6e^2$.
   b) find the total area if $e = 4$ cm.
   c) show that the volume is $V = e^3$.
   d) find the volume if $e = 4$ cm.

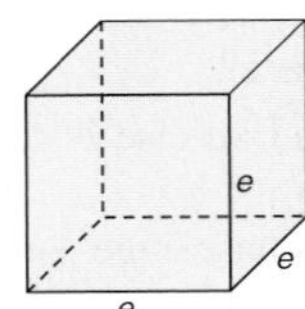

Exercises 29–31

30. Use the formulas and drawing in Exercise 29 to find (a) the total area T and (b) the volume V of a cube with edges of length 5.3 ft each.
31. When the length of each edge of a cube is increased by 1 cm, the volume is increased by 61 cm^3. What is the length of each edge of the original cube?
32. The numerical value of the volume of a cube equals the numerical value of its total surface area. What is the length of each edge of the cube?
*33. A diagonal of a cube joins two vertices so that the remaining points on the diagonal lie in the interior of the cube. Show that the diagonal of the cube having edges of length e is $e\sqrt{3}$ units long.
34. A concrete pad 4 in. thick is to have a length of 36 ft and a width of 30 ft. How many cubic yards of concrete must be poured?
   (HINT: 1 yd^3 = 27 ft^3.)
35. A raised flower bed is 2 ft high by 12 ft wide by 15 ft long. The mulch, soil, and peat mixture used to fill the raised bed costs $9.60 per cubic yard. What is the total cost of the ingredients used to fill the raised garden?
36. In excavating for a new house, a contractor digs a hole in the shape of a right rectangular prism. The dimensions of the hole are 54 ft long by 36 ft wide by 9 ft deep. How many cubic yards of dirt were removed?

37. An open box is formed by cutting congruent squares from the four corners of a square piece of cardboard that has a length of 24 in. per side. If the congruent squares that are removed have sides that measure 6 in. each, what is the volume of the box formed by folding and sealing the "flaps"?

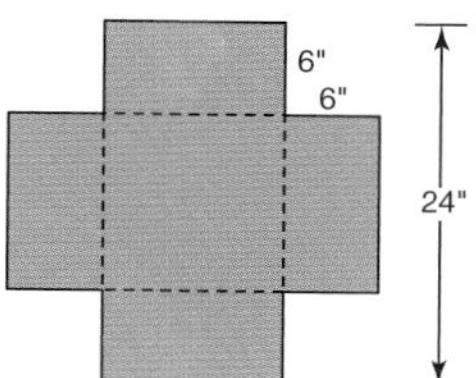

38. Repeat Exercise 37 (to find the volume), but with the four congruent squares with sides of length 6 in. being cut from the corners of a rectangular piece of poster board that is 20 in. wide by 30 in. long.

39. Kianna's aquarium is "box-shaped" with dimensions of 2 ft by 1 ft by 8 in. If 1 ft^3 corresponds to 7.5 gal of water, what is the water capacity of her aquarium in *gallons?*

40. The gasoline tank on an automobile is "box-shaped" with dimensions of 24 in. by 20 in. by 9 in. If 1 ft^3 corresponds to 7.5 gal of gasoline, what is the capacity of the automobile's fuel tank in *gallons?*

For Exercises 41–43, consider the oblique regular pentagonal prism shown. Each side of the base measures 12 cm, and the altitude measures 12 cm.

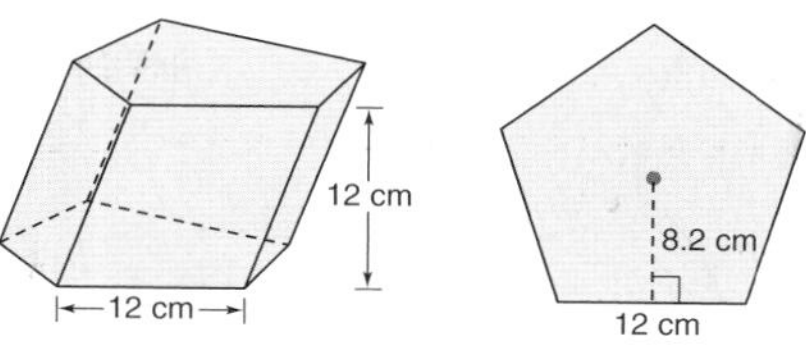

Exercises 41–43

41. Find the lateral area of the prism.

(HINT: Each lateral face is a parallelogram.)

42. Find the total area of the prism.

43. Find the volume of the prism.

44. It can be shown that the length of a diagonal of a right rectangular prism with dimensions ℓ, w, and h is given by $d = \sqrt{\ell^2 + w^2 + h^2}$. Use this formula to find the length of the diagonal when $\ell = 12$ in., $w = 4$ in., and $h = 3$ in.

9.2 Pyramids, Area, and Volume

KEY CONCEPTS

- Pyramid
- Base
- Altitude
- Vertices
- Edges
- Faces
- Vertex of a Pyramid
- Regular Pyramid
- Slant Height of a Regular Pyramid
- Lateral Area
- Total (Surface) Area
- Volume

The solids shown in Figure 9.14 on the following page are **pyramids**. In Figure 9.14(a), point A is noncoplanar with square $BCDE$. In Figure 9.14(b), F is noncoplanar with $\triangle GHJ$. In these pyramids, the noncoplanar point has been joined (by drawing line segments) to each vertex of the square and to each vertex of the triangle, respectively. Every pyramid has exactly one base. Square $BCDE$ is the base of the first pyramid, and $\triangle GHJ$ is the base of the second pyramid. Point A is known as the **vertex** of the **square pyramid**; likewise, point F is the vertex of the **triangular pyramid**.

The pyramid in Figure 9.15 is a **pentagonal pyramid**. It has vertex K, pentagon $LMNPQ$ for its **base**, and **lateral edges** $\overline{KL}$, $\overline{KM}$, $\overline{KN}$, $\overline{KP}$, and $\overline{KQ}$. Although K is called *the* **vertex of the pyramid**, there are actually six vertices: K, L, M, N, P, and Q. The sides of the base $\overline{LM}$, $\overline{MN}$, $\overline{NP}$, $\overline{PQ}$, and $\overline{QL}$ are **base edges**. All **lateral faces** of a pyramid

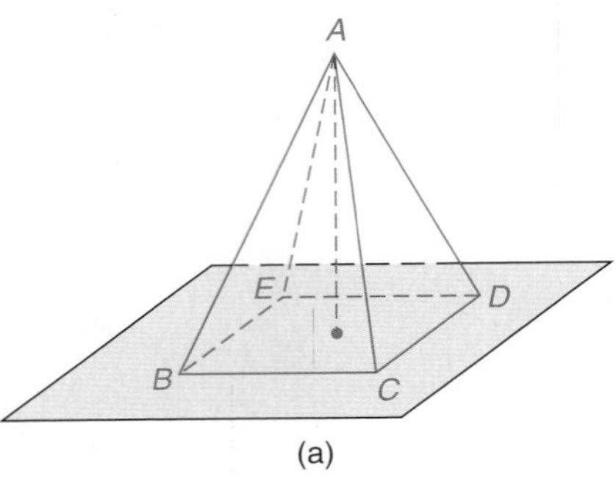

F
J
G
H
(b)

Figure 9.14

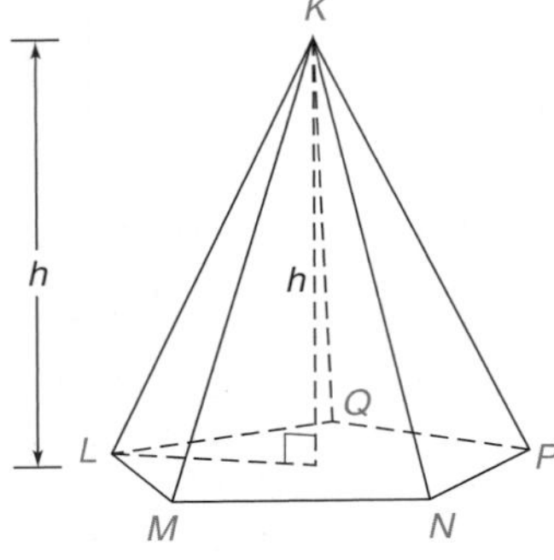

Figure 9.15

are triangles; $\triangle KLM$ is one of the five lateral faces of the pentagonal pyramid. Including base *LMNPQ*, this pyramid has a total of six faces. The **altitude** of the pyramid, of length *h*, is the line segment from the vertex *K* perpendicular to the plane of the base.

DEFINITION

A **regular pyramid** is a pyramid whose base is a regular polygon and whose lateral edges are all congruent.

Suppose that the pyramid in Figure 9.15 is a regular pentagonal pyramid. Then the lateral faces are necessarily congruent to each other; by SSS, $\triangle KLM \cong \triangle KMN \cong \triangle KNP \cong \triangle KPQ \cong \triangle KQL$. Each lateral face is an isosceles triangle. In a regular pyramid, the altitude joins the vertex of the pyramid to the center of the regular polygon that is the base of the pyramid. The length of the altitude is height *h*.

Exs. 1, 2

DEFINITION

The **slant height** of a regular pyramid is the altitude from the vertex of the pyramid to the base of any of the congruent lateral faces of the regular pyramid.

NOTE: Among pyramids, only a regular pyramid has a slant height.

In our formulas and explanations, we use ℓ to represent the length of the slant height of a regular pyramid. See Figure 9.16(c) on page 415.

EXAMPLE 1

For a regular square pyramid with height 4 in. and base edges of length 6 in. each, find the length of the slant height ℓ. (See Figure 9.16 on page 415.)

Solution In Figure 9.16, it can be shown that the apothem to any side has length 3 in. (one-half the length of the side of the square base). Also, the slant height is the hypotenuse of a right triangle with legs equal to the lengths of the altitude and the apothem. By the Pythagorean Theorem, we have

$$\ell^2 = a^2 + h^2$$
$$\ell^2 = 3^2 + 4^2$$
$$\ell^2 = 9 + 16$$
$$\ell^2 = 25$$
$$\ell = 5 \text{ in.}$$

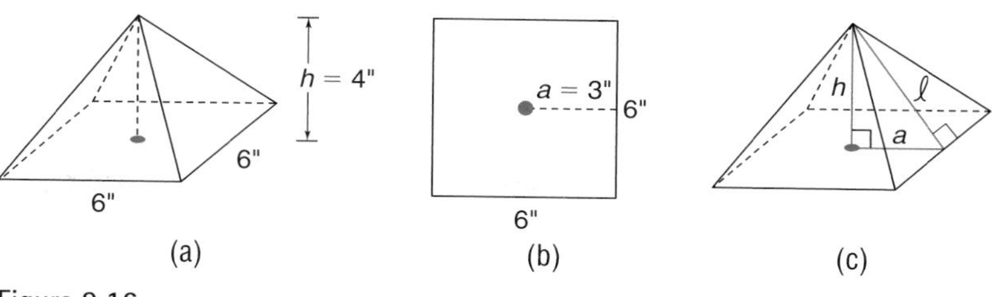

Figure 9.16

The following theorem was used in the solution of Example 1; see the pyramid in Figure 9.16(c). We accept Theorem 9.2.1 on the basis of the visual proof that Figure 9.16 provides.

SSG
Exs. 3, 4

THEOREM 9.2.1

In a regular pyramid, the length a of the apothem of the base, the altitude h, and the slant height ℓ satisfy the Pythagorean Theorem; that is, $\ell^2 = a^2 + h^2$ in every regular pyramid.

SURFACE AREA OF A PYRAMID

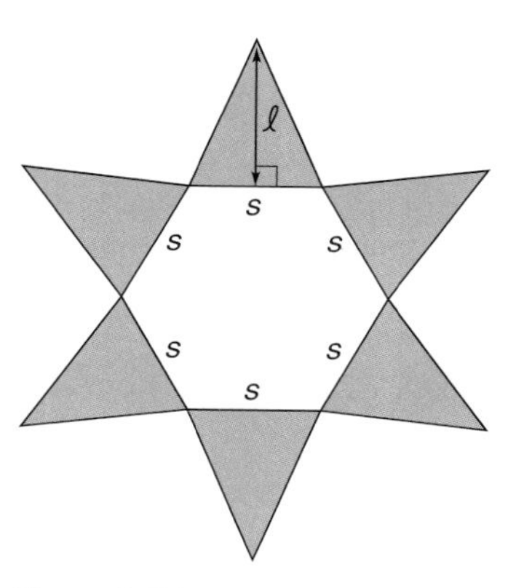

Figure 9.17

To lay the groundwork for the next theorem, we justify the result by "taking apart" one of the regular pyramids and laying it out flat. Although we use a regular hexagonal pyramid for this purpose, the argument is similar if the base is any regular polygon.

When the lateral faces of the regular pyramid are folded down into the plane, as shown in Figure 9.17, the shaded lateral area is the sum of the areas of the triangular lateral faces. Using $A = \frac{1}{2}bh$, we find that the area of each triangular face is $\frac{1}{2} \cdot s \cdot \ell$ (each side of the base of the pyramid has length s, and the slant height has length ℓ). The combined areas of the triangles give the lateral area. Because there are n triangles,

$$\begin{aligned} L &= n \cdot \frac{1}{2} \cdot s \cdot \ell \\ &= \frac{1}{2} \cdot \ell(n \cdot s) \\ &= \frac{1}{2}\ell P \end{aligned}$$

where P is the perimeter of the base.

THEOREM 9.2.2

The lateral area L of a regular pyramid with slant height of length ℓ and perimeter P of the base is given by

$$L = \frac{1}{2}\ell P$$

We will illustrate the use of Theorem 9.2.2 in Example 2.

EXAMPLE 2

Find the lateral area of a regular pentagonal pyramid if the sides of the base measure 8 cm and the lateral edges measure 10 cm each [see Figure 9.18(a) on page 416].

Solution For the triangular lateral face [see Figure 9.18(b)], the slant height bisects the base edge as indicated. Applying the Pythagorean Theorem, we have

$$4^2 + \ell^2 = 10^2, \text{ so } 16 + \ell^2 = 100$$
$$\ell^2 = 84$$
$$\ell = \sqrt{84} = \sqrt{4 \cdot 21} = \sqrt{4} \cdot \sqrt{21} = 2\sqrt{21}$$

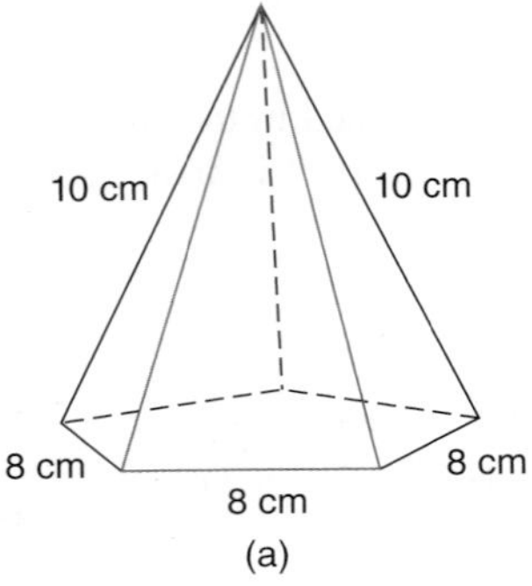

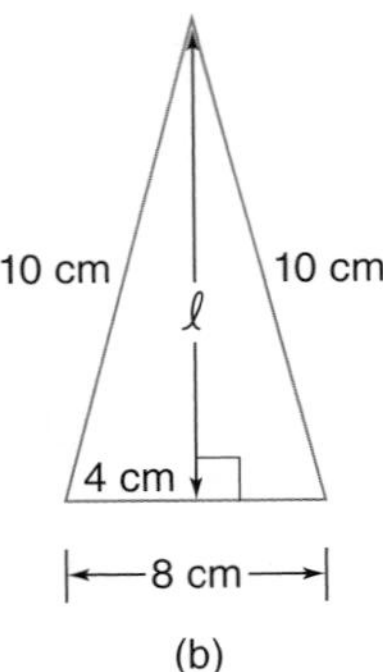

Figure 9.18

Now $L = \frac{1}{2}\ell P$ becomes $L = \frac{1}{2} \cdot 2\sqrt{21} \cdot (5 \cdot 8) = \frac{1}{2} \cdot 2\sqrt{21} \cdot 40 = 40\sqrt{21}$ cm$^2 \approx$ 183.30 cm^2. ■

It may be easier to find the lateral area of a regular pyramid without using the formula of Theorem 9.2.2; simply find the area of one lateral face and multiply by the number of faces. In Example 2, the area of each triangular face is $\frac{1}{2} \cdot 8 \cdot 2\sqrt{21}$ or $8\sqrt{21}$; thus, the lateral area of the regular pentagonal pyramid is $5 \cdot 8\sqrt{21} = 40\sqrt{21}$ cm^2.

THEOREM 9.2.3

The total area (surface area) T of a pyramid with lateral area L and base area B is given by $T = L + B$.

The formula for the total area T of the pyramid can be written $T = \frac{1}{2}\ell P + B$.

EXAMPLE 3

Find the total area of a regular square pyramid that has base edges of length 4 ft and lateral edges of length 6 ft. [See Figure 9.19(a).]

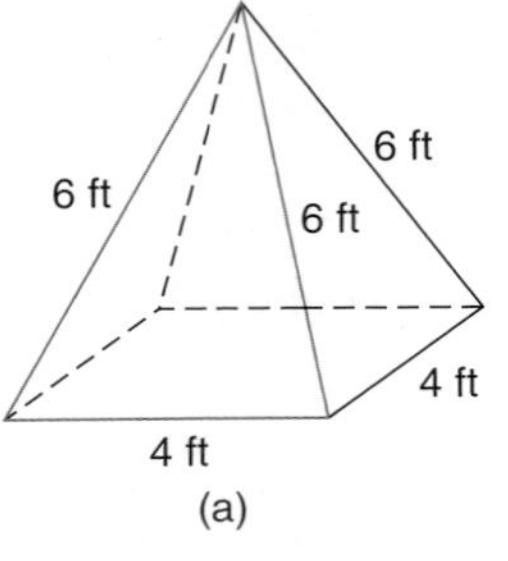

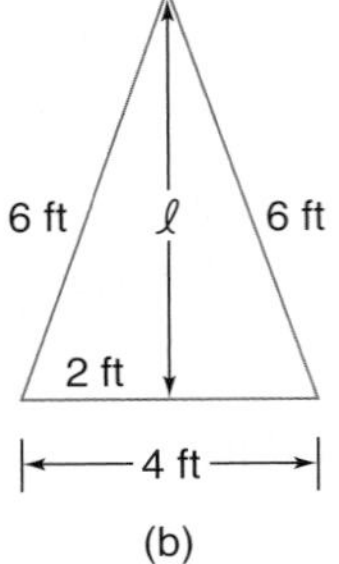

Figure 9.19

Solution To determine the lateral area, we need the length of the slant height. [See Figure 9.19(b) on the preceding page.]

$$\ell^2 + 2^2 = 6^2$$
$$\ell^2 + 4 = 36$$
$$\ell^2 = 32$$
$$\ell = \sqrt{32} = \sqrt{16 \cdot 2} = \sqrt{16} \cdot \sqrt{2} = 4\sqrt{2}$$

The lateral area is $L = \frac{1}{2}\ell P$. Therefore,

$$L = \frac{1}{2} \cdot 4\sqrt{2}(16) = 32\sqrt{2} \text{ ft}^2$$

Because the area of the square base is $B = 4^2$ or 16 ft^2, the total area is

SSG
Exs. 5–7

$$T = 16 + 32\sqrt{2} \approx 61.25 \text{ ft}^2$$ ■

The pyramid in Figure 9.20(a) is a regular square pyramid rather than just a square pyramid. It has congruent lateral edges and congruent faces. The pyramid shown in Figure 9.20(b) is oblique. It has neither congruent lateral edges nor congruent faces.

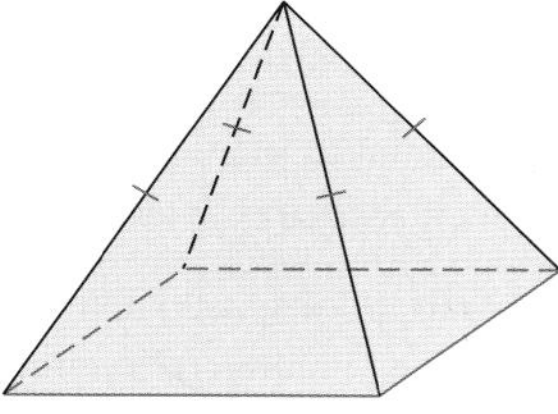

Regular square pyramid
(a)

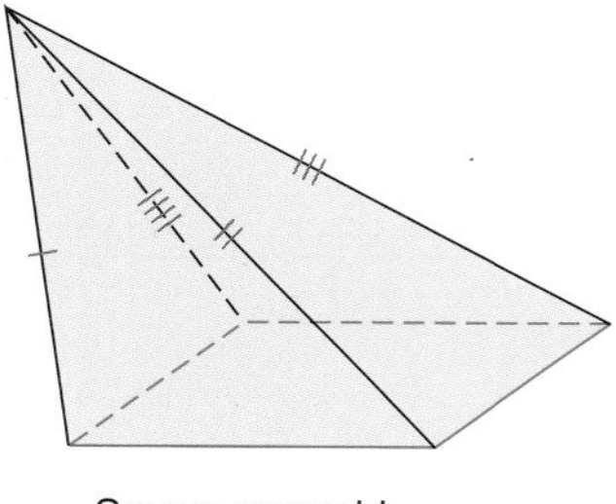

Square pyramid
(b)

Figure 9.20

Discover

There are kits that contain a hollow pyramid and a hollow prism that have congruent bases and the same altitude. Using a kit, fill the pyramid with water and then empty the water into the prism.

a) How many times did you have to empty the pyramid in order to fill the prism?
b) As a fraction, the volume of the pyramid is what part of the volume of the prism?

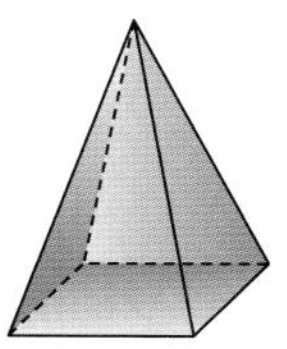

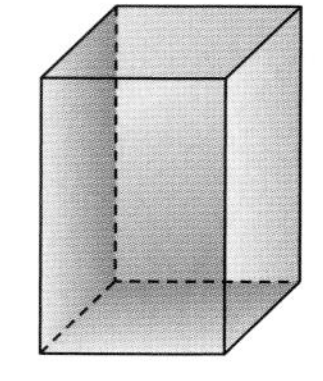

ANSWERS
(a) Three times (b) $\frac{1}{3}$

VOLUME OF A PYRAMID

The final theorem in this section is presented without any attempt to construct the proof. In an advanced course such as calculus, the statement can be proved. The factor "one-third" in the formula for the volume of a pyramid provides exact results. This formula can be applied to any pyramid, even one that is not regular; in Figure 9.20(b), the length of the altitude is the perpendicular distance from the vertex to the plane of the square base. Read the Discover activity in the margin at left before moving on to Theorem 9.2.4 and its applications.

THEOREM 9.2.4

The volume V of a pyramid having a base area B and an altitude of length h is given by

$$V = \frac{1}{3}Bh$$

EXAMPLE 4

Find the volume of the regular square pyramid with height $h = 4$ in. and base edges of length $s = 6$ in. (This was the pyramid in Example 1.)

Solution The area of the square base is $B = (6\text{ in.})^2$ or 36 in^2. Because $h = 4$ in., the formula $V = \frac{1}{3}Bh$ becomes

$$V = \frac{1}{3}(36\text{ in}^2)(4\text{ in.}) = 48\text{ in}^3$$

To find the volume of a pyramid, we use the formula $V = \frac{1}{3}Bh$. In many applications, it is necessary to determine B or h from other information that has been provided. In Example 5, calculating the length of the altitude h is a challenge! In Example 6, the difficulty lies in finding the area of the base. Before we consider either problem, Table 9.1 reminds us of the types of units necessary in different types of measure.

TABLE 9.1

Type of Measure	Geometric Measure	Type of Unit
Linear	Length of segment, such as length of slant height	in., cm, etc.
Area	Amount of plane region enclosed, such as area of lateral face	in^2, cm^2, etc.
Volume	Amount of space enclosed, such as volume of a pyramid	in^3, cm^3, etc.

In Example 5, we apply the following theorem. This application of the Pythagorean Theorem relates the lengths of the lateral edge, the radius of the base, and the altitude of a *regular* pyramid. Figure 9.21(c) provides a visual interpretation of the theorem.

THEOREM 9.2.5

In a regular pyramid, the lengths of altitude h, radius r of the base, and lateral edge e satisfy the Pythagorean Theorem; that is, $e^2 = h^2 + r^2$.

EXAMPLE 5

Find the volume of the regular square pyramid in Figure 9.21(a).

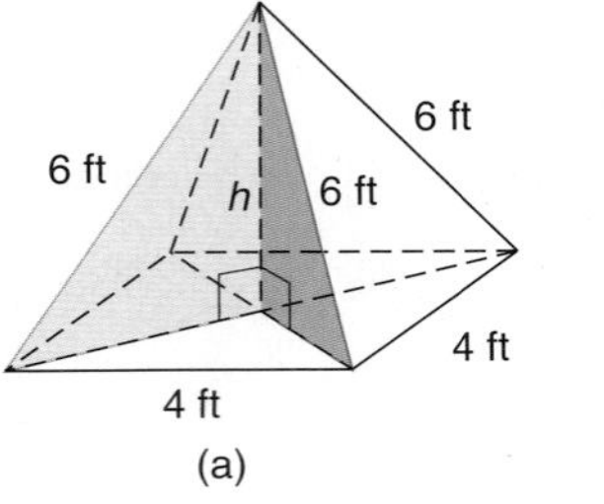

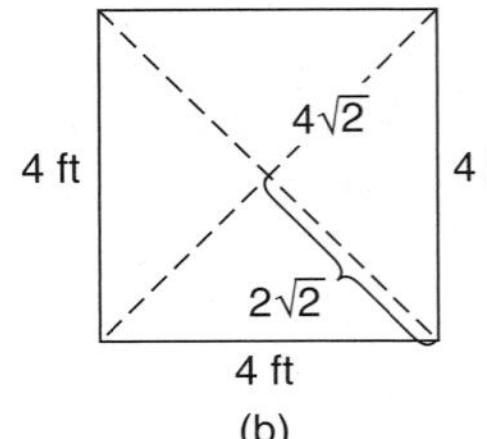

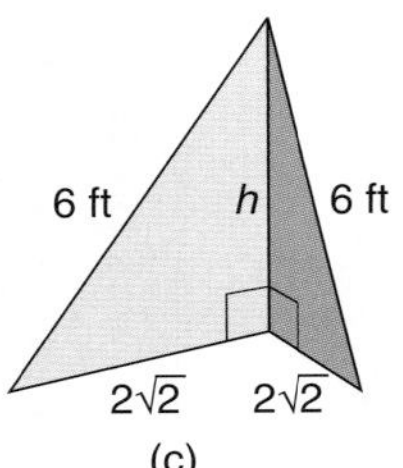

Figure 9.21

Solution The length of the altitude (of the pyramid) is represented by h, which is determined as follows.

The altitude meets the diagonals of the square base at their common midpoint [see Figure 9.21(b)]. Each diagonal of the base has the length $4\sqrt{2}$ ft by the 45°-45°-90° relationship. Thus, we have a right triangle whose legs are of lengths $2\sqrt{2}$ ft and h, and the hypotenuse has length 6 ft (the length of the lateral edge). See Figure 9.21(c), in which $r = 2\sqrt{2}$ and $e = 6$.

Applying Theorem 9.2.5 in Figure 9.21(c), we have

$$\begin{aligned} h^2 + (2\sqrt{2})^2 &= 6^2 \\ h^2 + 8 &= 36 \\ h^2 &= 28 \\ h &= \sqrt{28} = \sqrt{4 \cdot 7} = \sqrt{4} \cdot \sqrt{7} = 2\sqrt{7} \end{aligned}$$

The area of the square base is $B = 4^2$, or $B = 16$ ft^2. Now we have

$$\begin{aligned} V &= \frac{1}{3}Bh \\ &= \frac{1}{3}(16)(2\sqrt{7}) \\ &= \frac{32}{3}\sqrt{7} \text{ ft}^3 \approx 28.22 \text{ ft}^3 \end{aligned}$$

■

EXAMPLE 6

Find the volume of a regular hexagonal pyramid whose base edges have length 4 in. and whose altitude measures 12 in. [See Figure 9.22(a).]

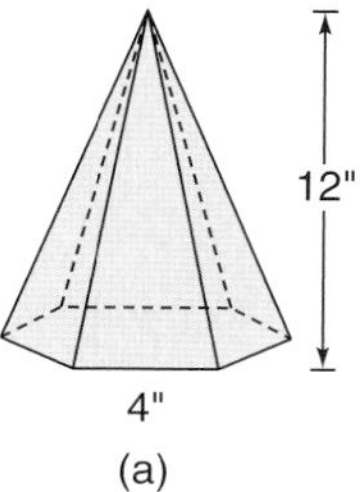

(a)

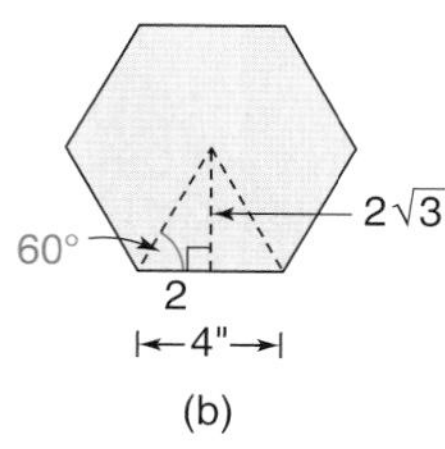

(b)

Figure 9.22

Solution In the formula $V = \frac{1}{3}Bh$, the altitude is $h = 12$. To find the area of the base, we use the formula $B = \frac{1}{2}aP$ (this was written $A = \frac{1}{2}aP$ in Chapter 8). In the 30°-60°-90° triangle formed by the apothem, radius, and side of the regular hexagon, we see that

$$a = 2\sqrt{3} \text{ in.} \qquad \text{[See Figure 9.22(b)]}$$

Now $B = \frac{1}{2} \cdot 2\sqrt{3} \cdot (6 \cdot 4)$, or $B = 24\sqrt{3}$ in^2.
In turn, $V = \frac{1}{3}Bh$ becomes $V = \frac{1}{3}(24\sqrt{3})(12)$, so $V = 96\sqrt{3}$ in^3. ■

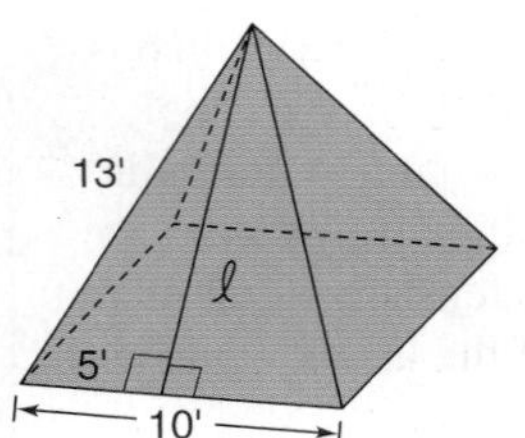

Figure 9.23

Reminder

It is sometimes easier to find the lateral area without memorizing and using another new formula.

Exs. 8–11

EXAMPLE 7

A church steeple has the shape of a regular square pyramid. Measurements taken show that the base edges measure 10 ft and that the length of a lateral edge is 13 ft. To determine the amount of roof needing to be reshingled, find the lateral area of the pyramid. (See Figure 9.23.)

Solution The slant height ℓ of each triangular face is determined by solving the equation

$$\begin{aligned} 5^2 + \ell^2 &= 13^2 \\ 25 + \ell^2 &= 169 \\ \ell^2 &= 144 \\ \ell &= 12 \end{aligned}$$

When we use the formula $A = \frac{1}{2}bh$, the area of a lateral face is $A = \frac{1}{2} \cdot 10 \cdot 12 = 60 \text{ ft}^2$. Considering the four lateral faces, the area to be reshingled measures

$$L = 4 \cdot 60 \text{ ft}^2 \qquad \text{or} \qquad L = 240 \text{ ft}^2$$

Plane and solid figures may have line symmetry and point symmetry. However, solid figures may also have **plane symmetry**. To have this type of symmetry, a plane can be drawn for which each point of the space figure has a corresponding point on the opposite side of the plane at the same distance.

Each solid in Figure 9.24 has more than one plane of symmetry. In Figure 9.24(a), the plane of symmetry shown is determined by the midpoints of the indicated edges of the "box." In Figure 9.24(b), the plane determined by the vertex and the midpoints of opposite sides of the square base leads to plane symmetry for the pyramid.

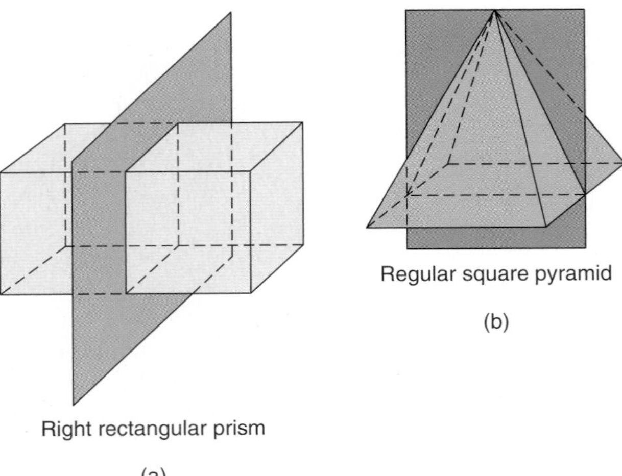

Figure 9.24

Exercises 9.2

In Exercises 1 to 4, name the solid that is shown. Answers are based on Sections 9.1 and 9.2.

1. a)

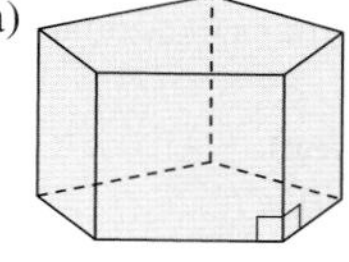

Bases are not regular.

b)

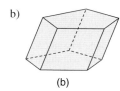

(b)

Bases are not regular.

2. a)

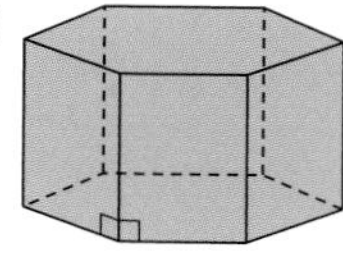

Bases are regular.

b)

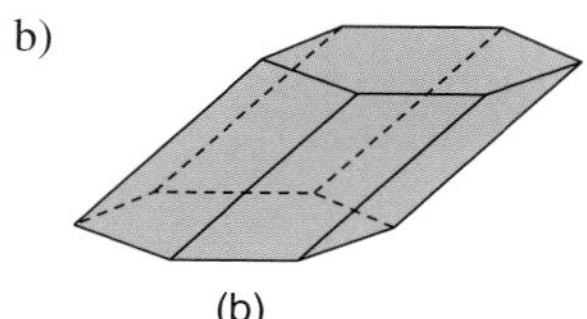

(b)

Bases are not regular.

3. a)

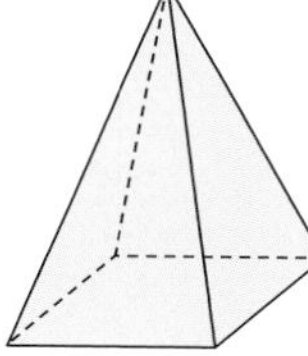

Lateral faces are congruent; base is a square.

b)

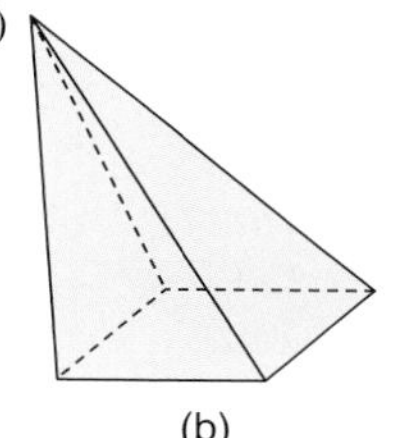

(b)

Base is a square.

4. a)

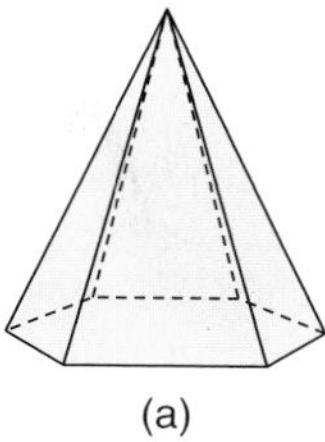

(a)

Lateral faces are congruent; base is a regular polygon.

b)

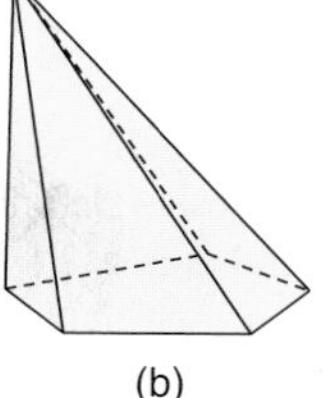

(b)

Lateral faces are not congruent.

5. In the solid shown, base $ABCD$ is a square.
 a) Is the solid a prism or a pyramid?
 b) Name the vertex of the pyramid.
 c) Name the lateral edges.
 d) Name the lateral faces.
 e) Is the solid a regular square pyramid?

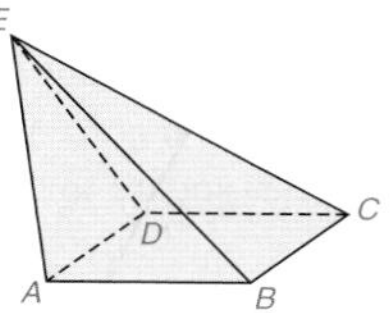

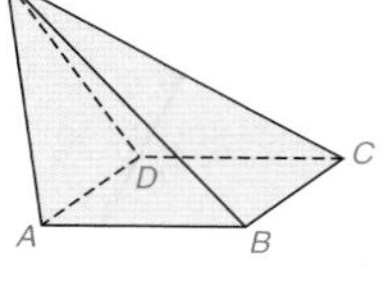

Exercises 5, 7, 9, 11

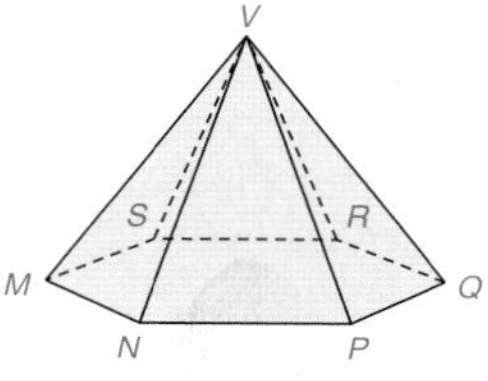

Exercises 6, 8, 10, 12

6. In the solid shown, the base is a regular hexagon.
 a) Name the vertex of the pyramid.
 b) Name the base edges of the pyramid.
 c) Assuming that lateral edges are congruent, are the lateral faces also congruent?
 d) Assuming that lateral edges are congruent, is the solid a regular hexagonal pyramid?

7. Consider the square pyramid in Exercise 5.
 a) How many vertices does it have?
 b) How many edges (lateral edges plus base edges) does it have?
 c) How many faces (lateral faces plus bases) does it have?

8. Consider the hexagonal pyramid in Exercise 6.
 a) How many vertices does it have?
 b) How many edges (lateral edges plus base edges) does it have?
 c) How many faces (lateral faces plus bases) does it have?

9. Suppose that the lateral faces of the pyramid in Exercise 5 have areas $A_{ABE} = 12 \text{ in}^2$, $A_{BCE} = 16 \text{ in}^2$, $A_{CED} = 12 \text{ in}^2$, and $A_{ADE} = 10 \text{ in}^2$. If each side of the square base measures 4 in., find the total surface area of the pyramid.

10. Suppose that the base of the hexagonal pyramid in Exercise 6 has an area of 41.6 cm^2 and that each lateral face has an area of 20 cm^2. Find the total (surface) area of the pyramid.

11. Suppose that the base of the square pyramid in Exercise 5 has an area of 16 cm^2 and that the altitude of the pyramid measures 6 cm. Find the volume of the square pyramid.

12. Suppose that the base of the hexagonal pyramid in Exercise 6 has an area of 41.6 cm^2 and that the altitude of the pyramid measures 3.7 cm. Find the volume of the hexagonal pyramid.

13. Assume that the number of sides in the base of a pyramid is n. Generalize the results found in earlier exercises by answering each of the following questions.
 a) What is the number of vertices?
 b) What is the number of lateral edges?
 c) What is the number of base edges?
 d) What is the total number of edges?
 e) What is the number of lateral faces?
 f) What is the total number of faces?
 (NOTE: Lateral faces and base = faces.)

14. Refer to the prisms of Exercises 1 and 2. Which of these have symmetry with respect to one (or more) plane(s)?

15. Refer to the pyramids of Exercises 3 and 4. Which of these have symmetry with respect to one (or more) plane(s)?

19 – 29 odd

16. Consider any regular pyramid. Indicate which line segment has the greater length:
    a) Slant height or altitude?
    b) Lateral edge or radius of the base?
17. Consider any regular pyramid. Indicate which line segment has the greater length:
    a) Slant height or apothem of base?
    b) Lateral edge or slant height?

In Exercises 18 and 19, use Theorem 9.2.1 in which the lengths of apothem a, altitude h, and slant height ℓ of a regular pyramid are related by the equation $\ell^2 = a^2 + h^2$.

18. In a regular square pyramid whose base edges measure 8 in., the apothem of the base measures 4 in. If the altitude of the pyramid is 8 in., find the length of its slant height.
19. In a regular hexagonal pyramid whose base edges measure $2\sqrt{3}$ in., the apothem of the base measures 3 in. If the slant height of the pyramid is 5 in., find the length of its altitude.
20. In the regular pentagonal pyramid, each lateral edge measures 8 in., and each base edge measures 6 in. The apothem of the base measures 4.1 in.
    a) Find the lateral area of the pyramid.
    b) Find the total area of the pyramid.

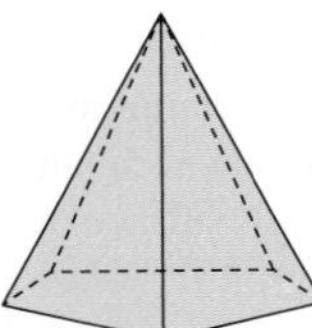

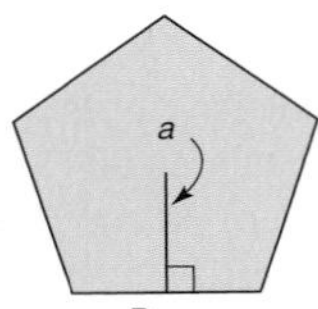

Exercises 20, 21

21. In the pentagonal pyramid, suppose that each base edge measures 9.2 cm and that the apothem of the base measures 6.3 cm. The altitude of the pyramid measures 14.6 cm.
    a) Find the base area of the pyramid.
    b) Find the volume of the pyramid.
22. For the regular square pyramid shown, suppose that the sides of the square base measure 10 m each and that the lateral edges measure 13 m each.
    a) Find the lateral area of the pyramid.
    b) Find the total area of the pyramid.
    c) Find the volume of the pyramid.

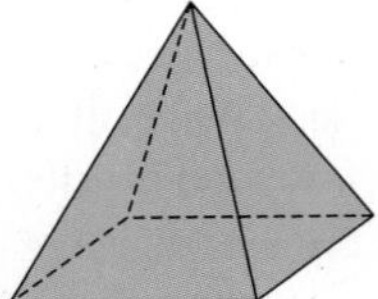

Exercises 22, 23

23. For the regular square pyramid shown in Exercise 22, suppose that the sides of the square base measure 6 ft each and that the altitude is 4 ft in length.
    a) Find the lateral area L of the pyramid.
    b) Find the total area T of the pyramid.
    c) Find the volume V of the pyramid.
24. a) Find the lateral area L of the regular hexagonal pyramid shown below.
    b) Find the total area T of the pyramid.
    c) Find the volume V of the pyramid.

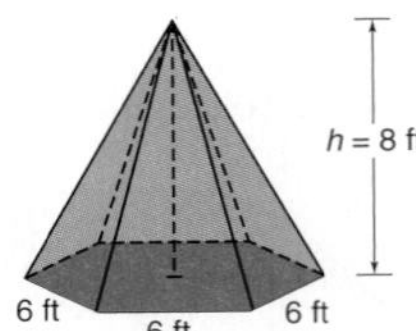

25. For a regular square pyramid, suppose that the altitude has a measure equal to that of the edges of the base. If the volume of the pyramid is 72 in^3, find the total area of the pyramid.

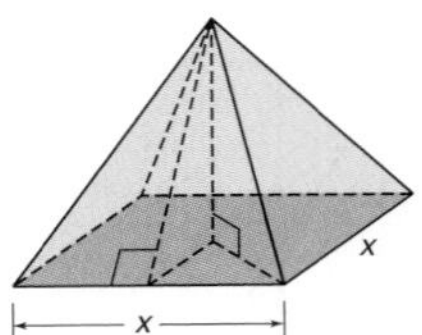

Exercises 25, 26

26. For a regular square pyramid, the slant height of each lateral face has a measure equal to that of each edge of the base. If the lateral area is 200 in^2, find the volume of the pyramid.
27. A church steeple in the shape of a regular square pyramid needs to be reshingled. The part to be covered corresponds to the lateral area of the square pyramid. If each lateral edge measures 17 ft and each base edge measures 16 ft, how many square feet of shingles need to be replaced?

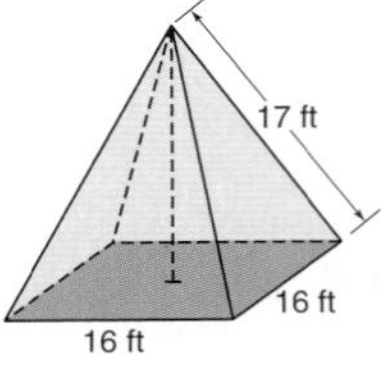

Exercises 27, 28

28. Before the shingles of the steeple (see Exercise 27) are replaced, an exhaust fan is to be installed in the steeple. To determine what size exhaust fan should be installed, it is necessary to know the volume of air in the attic (steeple). Find the volume of the regular square pyramid described in Exercise 27.

29. A teepee is constructed by using 12 poles. The construction leads to a regular pyramid with a dodecagon (12 sides) for the base. With the base as shown, and knowing that the altitude of the teepee is 15 ft, find its volume.

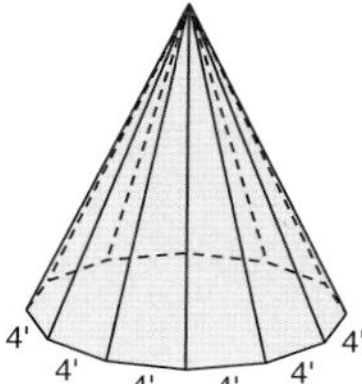

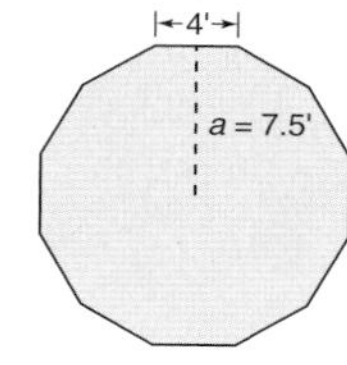

Exercises 29, 30

30. For its occupants to be protected from the elements, it was necessary that the teepee in Exercise 29 be enclosed. Find the amount of area to be covered; that is, determine the lateral area of the regular dodecagonal pyramid. Recall that its altitude measures 15 ft.

31. The street department's storage building, which is used to store the rock, gravel, and salt used on the city's roadways, is built in the shape of a regular hexagonal pyramid. The altitude of the pyramid has the same length as any side of the base. If the volume of the interior is 11,972 ft^3, find the length of the altitude and of each side of the base to the nearest foot.

32. The foyer planned as an addition to an existing church is designed as a regular octagonal pyramid. Each side of the octagonal floor has a length of 10 ft, and its apothem measures 12 ft. If 800 ft^2 of plywood is needed to cover the exterior of the foyer (that is, the lateral area of the pyramid is 800 ft^2), what is the height of the foyer?

33. The exhaust chute on a wood chipper has a shape like the part of a pyramid known as the *frustrum of the pyramid.* With dimensions as indicated, find the volume (capacity) of the chipper's exhaust chute.

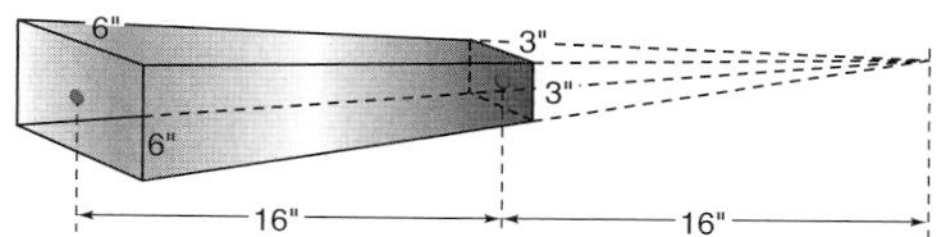

34. A popcorn container at a movie theater has the shape of a frustrum of a pyramid (see Exercise 33). With dimensions as indicated, find the volume (capacity) of the container.

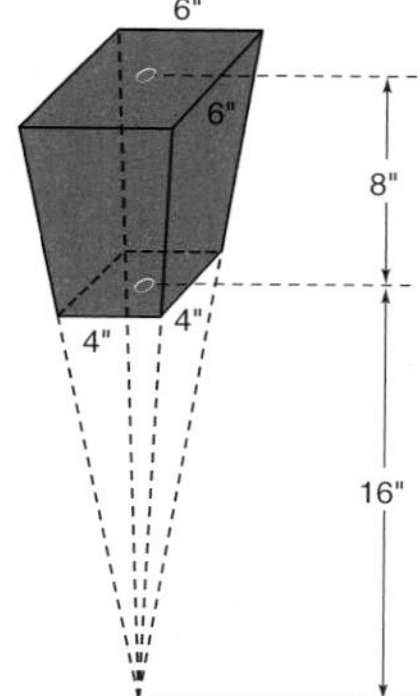

35. A regular tetrahedron is a regular triangular pyramid in which all faces (lateral faces and base) are congruent. If each edge has length e,

a) show that the area of each face is $A = \frac{e^2\sqrt{3}}{4}$.
b) show that the total area of the tetrahedron is $T = e^2\sqrt{3}$.
c) find the total area if each side measures $e = 4$ in.

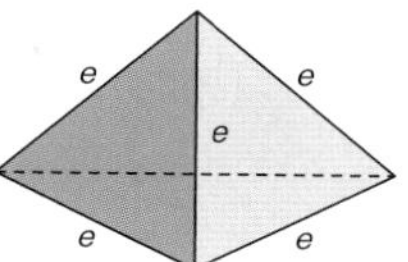

Exercises 35, 36

***36.** Each edge of a regular tetrahedron (see Exercise 35) has length e.

a) Show that the altitude of the tetrahedron measures $h = \frac{\sqrt{2}}{\sqrt{3}}e$.
b) Show that the volume of the tetrahedron is $V = \frac{\sqrt{2}}{12}e^3$.
c) Find the volume of the tetrahedron if each side measures $e = 4$ in.

37. Consider the accompanying figure. When the four congruent isosceles triangles are folded upward, a regular square pyramid is formed. What is the surface area (total area) of the pyramid?

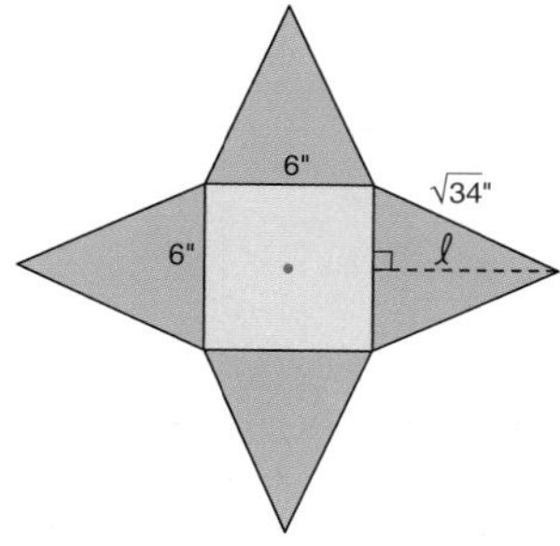

Exercises 37, 38

38. Find the volume of the regular square pyramid that was formed in Exercise 37.

39. Where e_1 and e_2 are the lengths of two corresponding edges (or altitudes) of similar prisms or pyramids, the ratio of their volumes is $\frac{V_1}{V_2} = \left(\frac{e_1}{e_2}\right)^3$. Write a ratio to compare volumes for two similar regular square pyramids in which $e_1 = 4$ in. and $e_2 = 2$ in.

40. Use the information from Exercise 39 to find the ratio of volumes $\frac{V_1}{V_2}$ for two cubes in which $e_1 = 2$ cm and $e_2 = 6$ cm.
(NOTE: $\frac{V_1}{V_2}$ can be found by determining the actual volumes of the cubes.)

41. A hexagonal pyramid (not regular) with base *ABCDEF* has plane symmetry with respect to a plane determined by vertex *G* and vertices *A* and *D* of its base. If the volume of the pyramid with vertex *G* and base *ABCD* is 19.7 in^3, find the volume of the given hexagonal pyramid.

9.3 Cylinders and Cones

KEY CONCEPTS

- Cylinders (Right and Oblique)
- Bases and Altitude of a Cylinder
- Axis of a Cylinder
- Cones (Right and Oblique)
- Base and Altitude of a Cone
- Vertex and Slant Height of a Cone
- Axis of a Cone
- Lateral Area
- Total Area
- Volume
- Solid of Revolution
- Axis of a Solid of Revolution

CYLINDERS

Consider the solids in Figure 9.25, in which congruent circles lie in parallel planes. For the circles on the left, suppose that centers O and O' are joined to form $\overline{OO'}$; similarly, suppose that $\overline{QQ'}$ joins the centers of the circles on the right. Let segments such as $\overline{XX'}$ join two points of the circles on the left, so that $\overline{XX'} \parallel \overline{OO'}$. If all such segments (like $\overline{XX'}$, $\overline{YY'}$, and $\overline{ZZ'}$) are parallel to each other, then a **cylinder** is generated. Because $\overline{OO'}$ is not perpendicular to planes P and P', the solid on the left is an **oblique circular cylinder**. With $\overline{QQ'}$ perpendicular to planes P and P', the solid on the right is a **right circular cylinder**. For both cylinders, the distance h between the planes P and P' is the length of the **altitude** of the cylinder; h is also called the *height* of the cylinder. The congruent circles are known as the **bases** of each cylinder.

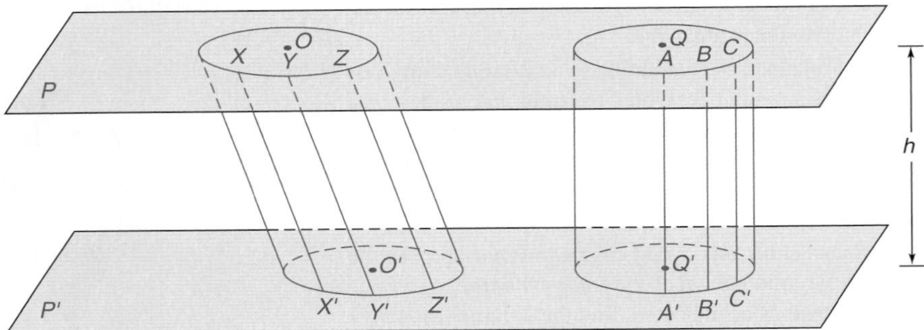

Figure 9.25

A right circular cylinder is shown in Figure 9.26; however, the parallel planes (such as P and P' in Figure 9.25) are not pictured. The line segment joining the centers of the two circular bases is known as the **axis** of the cylinder. For a right circular cylinder, it is necessary that the axis be perpendicular to the planes of the circular bases; in such a case, the length of the altitude h is the length of the axis.

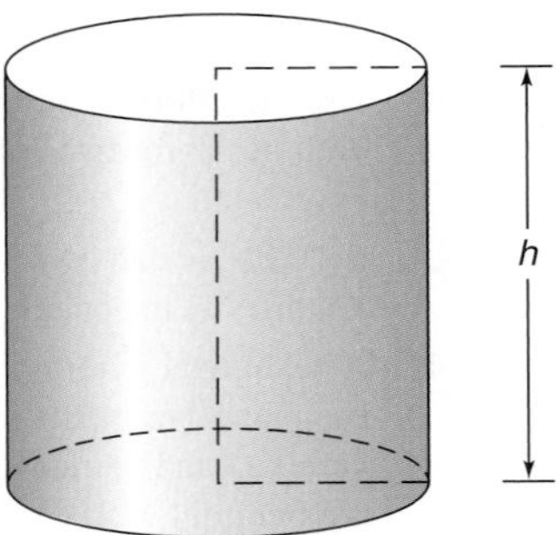

Figure 9.26

SURFACE AREA OF A CYLINDER

Discover

Think of the aluminum can pictured as a right circular cylinder. The cylinder's circular bases are the lid and bottom of the can, and the lateral surface is the "label" of the can. If the label were sliced downward by a perpendicular line between the planes, removed, and rolled out flat, it would be rectangular in shape. As shown below, that rectangle would have a length equal to the circumference of the circular base and a width equal to the height of the cylinder. Thus, the lateral area is given by $A = bh$, which becomes $L = Ch$, or $L = 2\pi rh$.

Exs. 1, 2

The formula for the lateral area of a right circular cylinder (found in the following theorem) should be compared to the formula $L = hP$, the lateral area of a right prism whose base has perimeter P.

THEOREM 9.3.1

The lateral area L of a right circular cylinder with altitude of length h and circumference C of the base is given by $L = hC$.
Alternative Form: The lateral area of the right circular cylinder can be expressed in the form $L = 2\pi rh$, where r is the length of the radius of the circular base.

Rather than constructing a formal proof of Theorem 9.3.1, consider the Discover activity shown at the top of this page.

THEOREM 9.3.2

The total area T of a right circular cylinder with base area B and lateral area L is given by $T = L + 2B$.
Alternative Form: Where r is the length of the radius of the base and h is the length of the altitude of the cylinder, the total area can be expressed in the form $T = 2\pi rh + 2\pi r^2$.

EXAMPLE 1

For the right circular cylinder shown in Figure 9.27, find the

a) exact lateral area L.
b) exact surface area T.

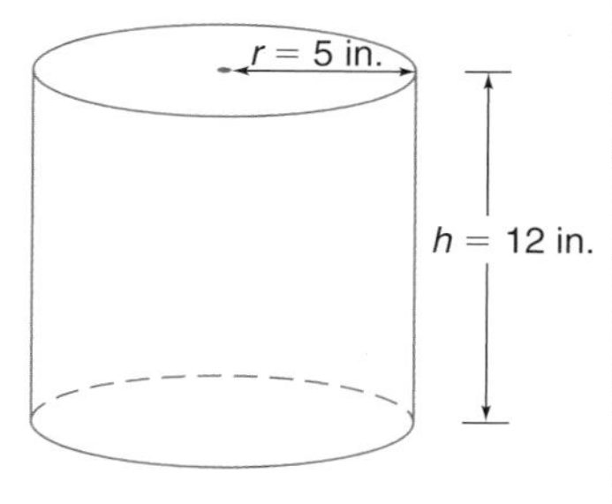

Figure 9.27

Solution

a) $L = 2\pi rh$
$= 2 \cdot \pi \cdot 5 \cdot 12$
$= 120\pi \text{ in}^2$

b) $T = L + 2B$
$= 2\pi rh + 2\pi r^2$
$= 2 \cdot \pi \cdot 5 \cdot 12 + 2 \cdot \pi \cdot 5^2$
$= 120\pi + 50\pi$
$= 170\pi \text{ in}^2$ ■

SSG *Exs. 3–5*

VOLUME OF A CYLINDER

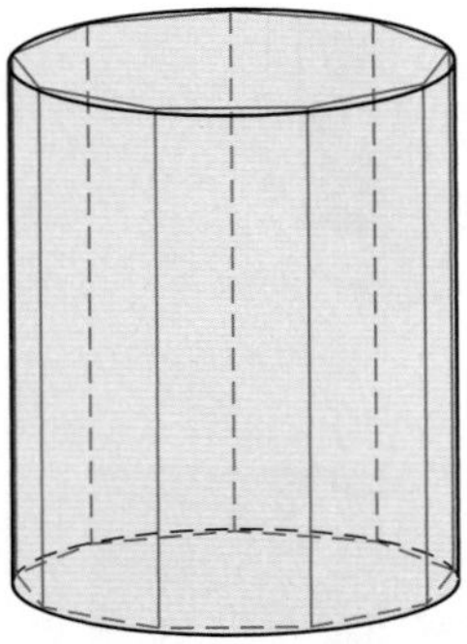

Figure 9.28

In considering the volume of a right circular cylinder, recall that the volume of a prism is given by $V = Bh$, where B is the area of the base. In Figure 9.28, we inscribe a prism in the cylinder as shown. Suppose that the prism is regular and that the number of sides in the inscribed polygon's base becomes larger and larger; thus, the base approaches a circle in this limiting process. The area of the polygonal base also approaches the area of the circle, and the volume of the prism approaches that of the right circular cylinder. Our conclusion is stated without proof in the following theorem.

THEOREM 9.3.3

The volume V of a right circular cylinder with base area B and altitude of length h is given by $V = Bh$.
Alternative Form: Where r is the length of the radius of the base, the volume for the right circular cylinder can be written $V = \pi r^2 h$.

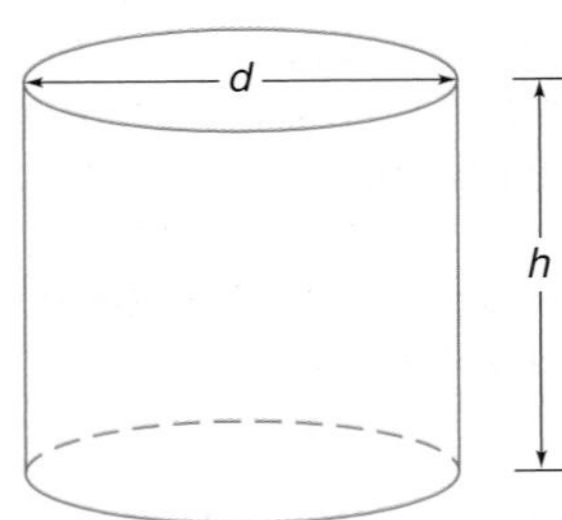

Figure 9.29

EXAMPLE 2

If $d = 4$ cm and $h = 3.5$ cm, use a calculator to find the approximate volume of the right circular cylinder shown in Figure 9.29. Give the answer correct to two decimal places.

Solution $d = 4$, so $r = 2$. Thus, $V = Bh$ or $V = \pi r^2 h$ becomes

$$V = \pi \cdot 2^2(3.5)$$
$$= \pi \cdot 4(3.5) = 14\pi \approx 43.98 \text{ cm}^3$$ ■

EXAMPLE 3

In the right circular cylinder shown in Figure 9.29, suppose that the height equals the diameter of the circular base. If the exact volume is 128π in^3, find the exact lateral area L of the cylinder.

Solution

$h = 2r$
so $V = \pi r^2 h$
becomes $V = \pi r^2(2r)$
$V = 2\pi r^3$

Thus, $2\pi r^3 = 128\pi$,
Dividing by 2π, $r^3 = 64$
$r = 4$
$h = 8$ **(from $h = 2r$)**

Now

$$\begin{aligned} L &= 2\pi rh \\ &= 2 \cdot \pi \cdot 4 \cdot 8 \\ &= 64\pi \text{ in}^2 \end{aligned}$$

■

Table 9.2 should help us recall and compare the area and volume formulas found in Sections 9.1 and 9.3.

Exs. 6, 7

TABLE 9.2

	Lateral Area	Total Area	Volume
Prism	$L = hP$	$T = L + 2B$	$V = Bh$
Cylinder	$L = hC$	$T = L + 2B$	$V = Bh$

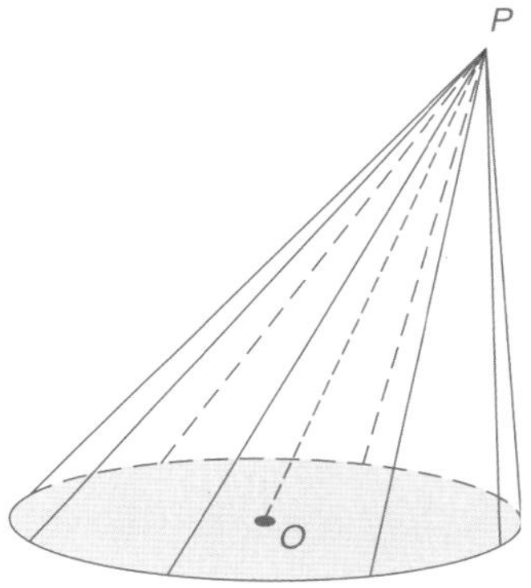

Figure 9.30

CONES

In Figure 9.30, consider point P, which lies outside the plane containing circle O. A surface known as a **cone** results when line segments are drawn from P to points on the circle. However, if P is joined to all possible points on the circle as well as to points in the interior of the circle, a solid is formed. If $\overline{PO}$ is not perpendicular to the plane of circle O in Figure 9.30, the cone is an **oblique circular cone**.

In Figures 9.30 and 9.31, point P is the **vertex** of the cone, and circle O is the **base**. The segment $\overline{PO}$, which joins the vertex to the center of the circular base, is the **axis** of the cone. If the axis is perpendicular to the plane containing the base, as in Figure 9.31, the cone is a **right circular cone**. In any cone, the perpendicular segment from the vertex to the plane of the base is the **altitude** of the cone. In a right circular cone, the length h of the altitude equals the length of the axis. For a right circular cone, and only for this type of cone, any line segment that joins the vertex to a point on the circle is a **slant height** of the cone; we will denote the length of the slant height by ℓ as shown in Figure 9.31.

Exs. 8, 9

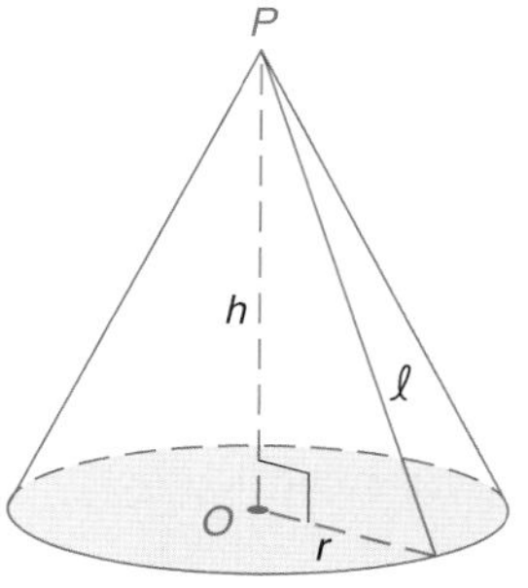

Figure 9.31

SURFACE AREA OF A CONE

Recall now that the lateral area for a regular pyramid is given by $L = \frac{1}{2}\ell P$. For a right circular cone, consider an inscribed regular pyramid as in Figure 9.32. As the number of sides of the inscribed polygon's base grows larger, the perimeter of the inscribed polygon approaches the circumference of the circle as a limit. In addition, the slant height of the congruent triangular faces approaches that of the slant height of the cone. Thus, the lateral area of the right circular cone can be compared to $L = \frac{1}{2}\ell P$; for the cone, we have

$$L = \frac{1}{2}\ell C$$

in which C is the circumference of the base. The fact that $C = 2\pi r$ leads to

$$L = \frac{1}{2}\ell(2\pi r)$$

so

$$L = \pi r\ell$$

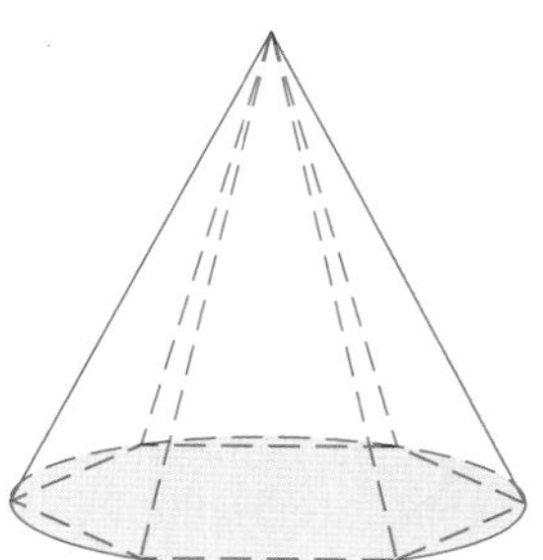

Figure 9.32

THEOREM 9.3.4

The lateral area L of a right circular cone with slant height of length ℓ and circumference C of the base is given by $L = \frac{1}{2}\ell C$.

Alternative Form: Where r is the length of the radius of the base, $L = \pi r\ell$.

The following theorem follows easily from Theorem 9.3.4 and is given without proof.

THEOREM 9.3.5

The total area T of a right circular cone with base area B and lateral area L is given by $T = B + L$.

Alternative Form: Where r is the length of the radius of the base and ℓ is the length of the slant height, $T = \pi r^2 + \pi r\ell$.

EXAMPLE 4

For the right circular cone in which $r = 3$ cm and $h = 6$ cm (see Figure 9.33), find the

a) exact and approximate lateral area L.
b) exact and approximate total area T.

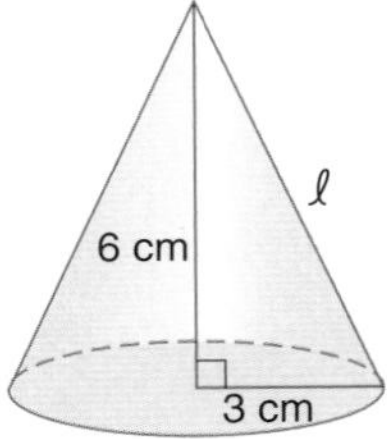

Figure 9.33

Solution

a) We need the length of the slant height ℓ for each problem part, so we apply the Pythagorean Theorem:

$$\begin{aligned} \ell^2 &= r^2 + h^2 \\ &= 3^2 + 6^2 \\ &= 9 + 36 = 45 \\ \ell &= \sqrt{45} = \sqrt{9 \cdot 5} \\ &= \sqrt{9} \cdot \sqrt{5} = 3\sqrt{5} \end{aligned}$$

Using $L = \pi r\ell$, we have

$$\begin{aligned} L &= \pi \cdot 3 \cdot 3\sqrt{5} \\ &= 9\pi\sqrt{5} \text{ cm}^2 \approx 63.22 \text{ cm}^2 \end{aligned}$$

b) We also have

$$\begin{aligned} T &= B + L \\ &= \pi r^2 + \pi r\ell \\ &= \pi \cdot 3^2 + \pi \cdot 3 \cdot 3\sqrt{5} \\ &= (9\pi + 9\pi\sqrt{5}) \text{ cm}^2 \approx 91.50 \text{ cm}^2 \end{aligned}$$

■

SSG *Exs. 10, 11*

The following theorem was demonstrated in the solution of Example 4.

THEOREM 9.3.6

In a right circular cone, the lengths of the radius r (of the base), the altitude h, and the slant height ℓ satisfy the Pythagorean Theorem; that is, $\ell^2 = r^2 + h^2$ in every right circular cone.

VOLUME OF A CONE

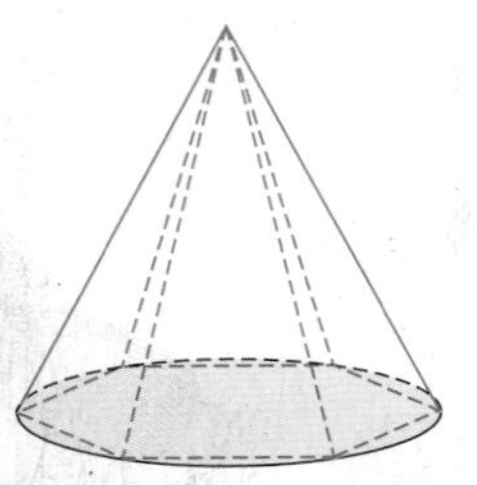
Figure 9.34

Recall that the volume of a pyramid is given by the formula $V = \frac{1}{3}Bh$. Consider a regular pyramid inscribed in a right circular cone. If its number of sides increases indefinitely, the volume of the pyramid approaches that of the right circular cone (see Figure 9.34).

Discover

Complete this analogy:
Prism is to Cylinder as Pyramid is to ____.

ANSWER

Cone

Then the volume of the right circular cone is $V = \frac{1}{3}Bh$. Because the area of the base of the cone is $B = \pi r^2$, an alternative formula for the volume of the cone is

$$V = \frac{1}{3}\pi r^2 h$$

We state this result as a theorem.

THEOREM 9.3.7

The volume V of a right circular cone with base area B and altitude of length h is given by $V = \frac{1}{3}Bh$.

Alternative Form: Where r is the length of the radius of the base, the formula for the volume of the cone is usually written $V = \frac{1}{3}\pi r^2 h$.

Table 9.3 should help us to recall and compare the area and volume formulas found in Sections 9.2 and 9.3.

TABLE 9.3

	Lateral Area	Total Area	Volume	Slant Height
Pyramid	$L = \frac{1}{2}\ell P$	$T = B + L$	$V = \frac{1}{3}Bh$	$\ell^2 = a^2 + h^2$
Cone	$L = \frac{1}{2}\ell C$	$T = B + L$	$V = \frac{1}{3}Bh$	$\ell^2 = r^2 + h^2$

NOTE: The formulas that contain the slant height ℓ are used only with the regular pyramid and the right circular cone.

SSG *Exs. 12, 13*

SOLIDS OF REVOLUTION

Suppose that part of the boundary for a plane region is a line segment. When the plane region is revolved about this line segment, the locus of points generated in space is called a **solid of revolution**. The complete 360° rotation moves the region about the edge until the region returns to its original position. The side (edge) used is called the **axis** of the resulting solid of revolution. Consider Example 5.

EXAMPLE 5

Describe the solid of revolution that results when

a) a rectangular region with dimensions 2 ft by 5 ft is revolved about the 5-ft side [see Figure 9.35(a)].
b) a semicircular region with radius of length 3 cm is revolved about the diameter shown in Figure 9.35(b).

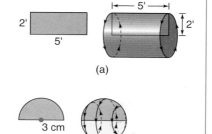

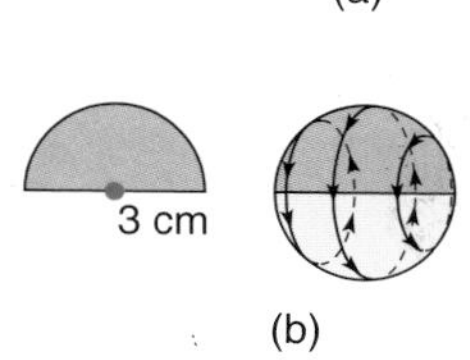

Figure 9.35

Solution

a) In Figure 9.35(a), the rectangle on the left is revolved about the 5-ft side to form the solid on the right. The solid of revolution generated is a right circular cylinder that has a base radius of 2 ft and an altitude of 5 ft.

b) In Figure 9.35(b) on page 429, the semicircle on the left is revolved about its diameter to form the solid on the right. The solid of revolution generated is a *sphere* with a radius of length 3 cm.

NOTE: We will study the sphere in greater detail in Section 9.4.

EXAMPLE 6

Determine the exact volume of the solid of revolution formed when the region bounded by a right triangle with legs of lengths 4 in. and 6 in. is revolved about the 6-in. side. The triangular region is shown in Figure 9.36(a).

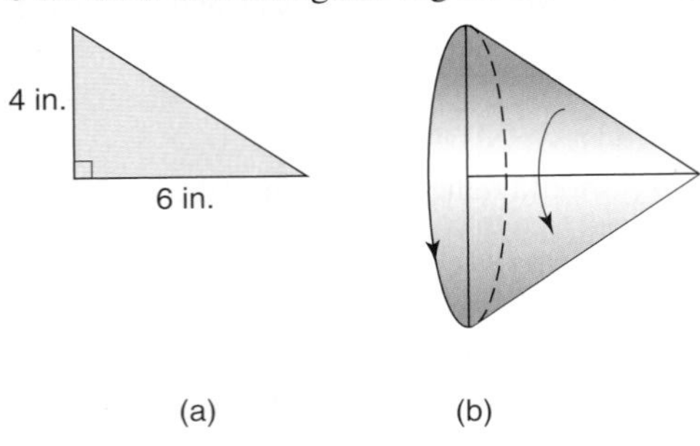

Figure 9.36

Solution As shown in Figure 9.36(b), the resulting solid is a cone whose altitude measures 6 in. and whose radius of the base measures 4 in.

Using $V = \frac{1}{3}Bh$, we have

$$V = \frac{1}{3}\pi r^2 h$$
$$= \frac{1}{3} \cdot \pi \cdot 4^2 \cdot 6 = 32\pi \text{ in}^3$$

Geometry in the Real World

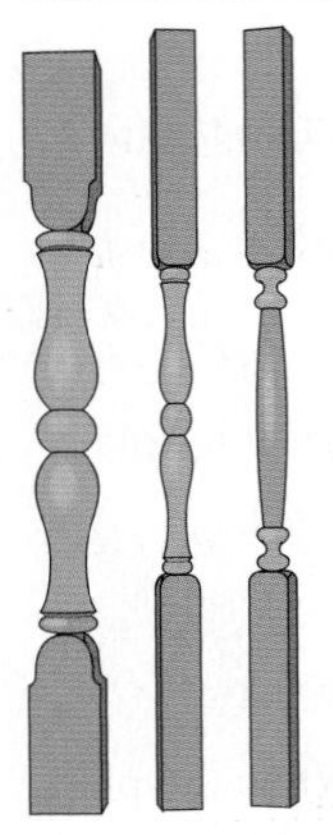

Spindles are examples of solids of revolution. As the piece of wood is rotated, the ornamental part of each spindle is shaped and smoothed by a machine (wood lathe).

It may come as a surprise that the formulas that are used to calculate the volumes of an oblique circular cylinder and a right circular cylinder are identical. To see why the formula $V = Bh$ or $V = \pi r^2 h$ can be used to calculate the volume of an oblique circular cylinder, consider the stacks of pancakes shown in Figures 9.37(a) and 9.37(b). With each stack h units high, the volume is the same regardless of whether the stack is vertical or oblique.

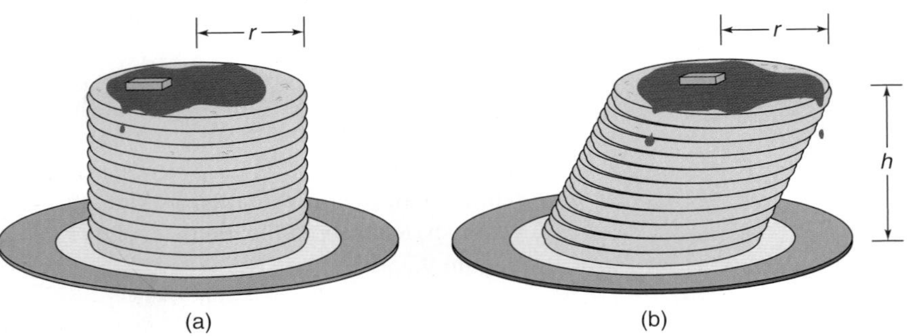

Figure 9.37

SSG
Exs. 14, 15

It is also true that the formula for the volume of an oblique circular cone is $V = \frac{1}{3}Bh$ or $V = \frac{1}{3}\pi r^2 h$. In fact, the motivating argument preceding Theorem 9.3.7 would be repeated, with the exception that the inscribed pyramid is oblique.

Exercises 9.3

1. Does a right circular cylinder such as an aluminum can have
a) symmetry with respect to at least one plane?
b) symmetry with respect to at least one line?
c) symmetry with respect to a point?

2. Does a right circular cone such as a wizard's cap have
a) symmetry with respect to at least one plane?
b) symmetry with respect to at least one line?
c) symmetry with respect to a point?

3. For the right circular cylinder, suppose that $r = 5$ in. and $h = 6$ in. Find the exact and approximate
a) lateral area.
b) total area.
c) volume.

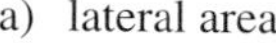

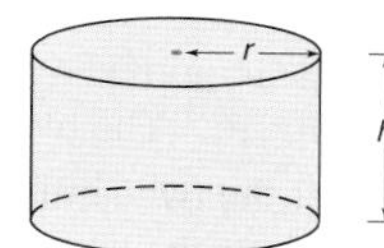

Exercises 3, 4

4. Suppose that $r = 12$ cm and $h = 15$ cm in the right circular cylinder. Find the exact and approximate
a) lateral area.
b) total area.
c) volume.

5. The tin can shown at the right has the indicated dimensions. Estimate the number of square inches of tin required for its construction.

(HINT: Include the lid and the base in the result.)

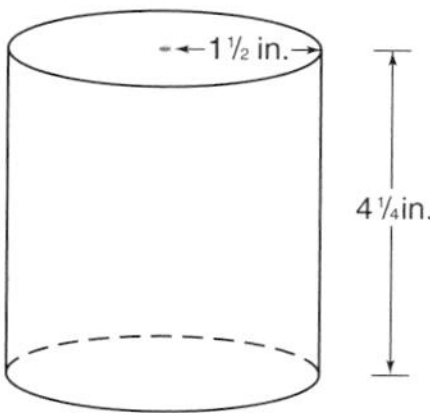

Exercises 5, 6

6. What is the volume of the tin can? If it contains 16 oz of green beans, what is the volume of the can used for 20 oz of green beans? Assume a proportionality between weight and volume.

7. If the exact volume of a right circular cylinder is 200π cm^3 and its altitude measures 8 cm, what is the measure of the radius of the circular base?

8. Suppose that the volume of an aluminum can is to be 9π in^3. Find the dimensions of the can if the diameter of the base is three-fourths the length of the altitude.

9. For an aluminum can, the lateral surface area is 12π in^2. If the length of the altitude is 1 in. greater than the length of the radius of the circular base, find the dimensions of the can.

10. Find the altitude of a storage tank in the shape of a right circular cylinder that has a circumference measuring 6π m and a volume measuring 81π m^3.

11. Find the volume of the oblique circular cylinder. The axis meets the plane of the base to form a 45° angle.

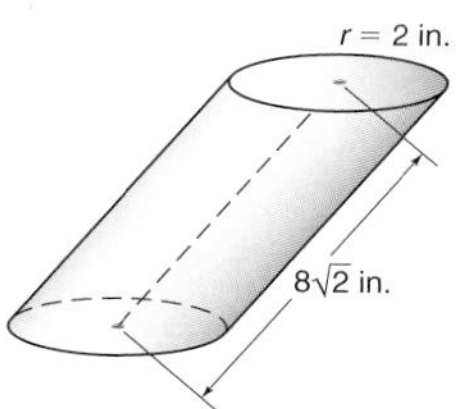

12. A cylindrical orange juice container has metal bases of radius 1 in. and a cardboard lateral surface 3 in. high. If the cost of the metal used is 0.5 cent per square inch and the cost of the cardboard is 0.2 cent per square inch, what is the approximate cost of constructing one container? Let $\pi \approx 3.14$.

In Exercises 13 to 18, use the fact that $r^2 + h^2 = \ell^2$ in a right circular cone (Theorem 9.3.6).

13. Find the length of the slant height ℓ of a right circular cone with $r = 4$ cm and $h = 6$ cm.

14. Find the length of the slant height ℓ of a right circular cone with $r = 5.2$ ft and $h = 3.9$ ft.

15. Find the height h of a right circular cone in which the diameter of the base measures $d = 9.6$ m and $\ell = 5.2$ m.

16. Find the length of the radius r of a right circular cone in which $h = 6$ yd and $\ell = 8$ yd.

17. Find the length of the slant height ℓ of a right circular cone with $r = 6$ in., length of altitude h, and $\ell = 2h$ in.

18. Find the length of the radius r of a right circular cone with $\ell = 12$ in. and $h = 3r$ in.

19. The oblique circular cone has an altitude and a diameter of base that are each of length 6 cm. The line segment joining the vertex to the center of the base is the axis of the cone. What is the length of the axis?

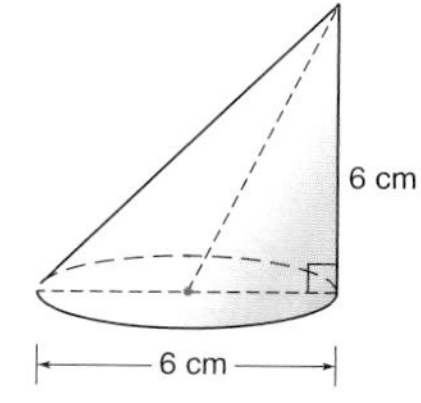

20. For the accompanying right circular cone, $h = 6$ m and $r = 4$ m. Find the exact and approximate
a) lateral area.
b) total area.
c) volume.

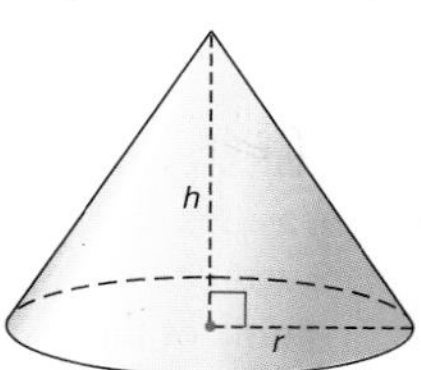

Exercises 20, 21

21. For the right circular cone shown in Exercise 20, suppose that $h = 7$ in. and $r = 6$ in. Find the exact and approximate
a) lateral area.
b) total area.
c) volume.

22. The teepee has a circular floor with a radius equal to 6 ft and a height of 15 ft. Find the volume of the enclosure.

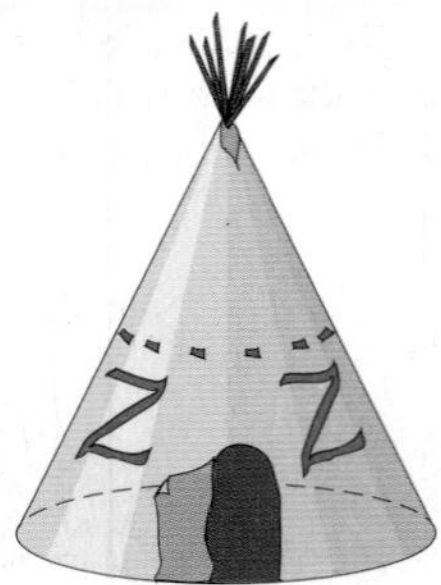

23. A rectangle has dimensions of 6 in. by 3 in. Find the exact volume of the solid of revolution formed when the rectangle is rotated about its 6-in. side.

24. A rectangle has dimensions of 6 in. by 3 in. Find the exact volume of the solid of revolution formed when the rectangle is rotated about its 3-in. side.

25. A triangle has sides that measure 15 cm, 20 cm, and 25 cm. Find the exact volume of the solid of revolution formed when the triangle is revolved about the side of length 15 cm.

26. A triangle has sides that measure 15 cm, 20 cm, and 25 cm. Find the exact volume of the solid of revolution formed when the triangle is revolved about the side of length 20 cm.

27. A triangle has sides that measure 15 cm, 20 cm, and 25 cm. Find the exact volume of the solid of revolution formed when the triangle is revolved about the side of length 25 cm.

(HINT: The altitude to the 25-cm side has length 12 cm.)

28. Where r is the length of the radius of a sphere, the volume of the sphere is given by $V = \frac{4}{3}\pi r^3$. Find the exact volume of the sphere that was formed in Example 5(b).

29. If a right circular cone has a circular base with a diameter of length 10 cm and a volume of 100π cm^3, find its lateral area.

30. A right circular cone has a slant height of 12 ft and a lateral area of 96π ft^2. Find its volume.

31. A solid is formed by cutting a conical section away from a right circular cylinder. If the radius measures 6 in. and the altitude measures 8 in., what is the volume of the resulting solid?

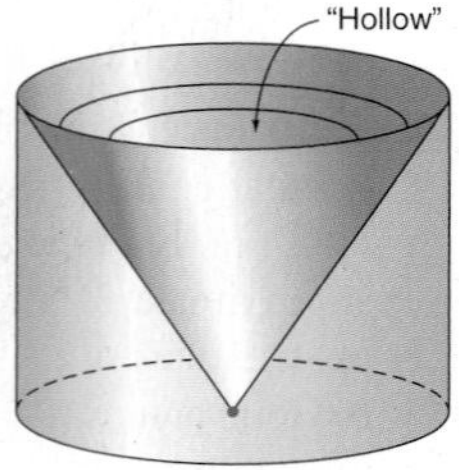

In Exercises 32 and 33, give a paragraph proof for each claim.

32. The total area T of a right circular cylinder whose altitude is of length h and whose circular base has a radius of length r is given by $T = 2\pi r(r + h)$.

33. The volume V of a washer that has an inside radius of length r, an outside radius of length R, and an altitude of measure h is given by $V = \pi h(R + r)(R - r)$.

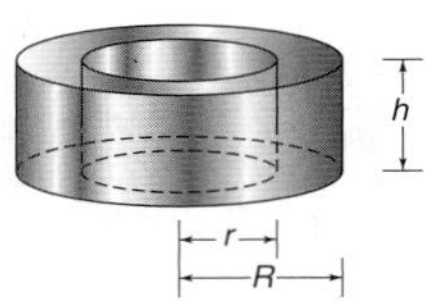

34. For a right circular cone, the slant height has a measure equal to twice that of the radius of the base. If the total area of the cone is 48π in^2, what are the dimensions of the cone?

35. For a right circular cone, the ratio of the slant height to the radius is 5:3. If the volume of the cone is 96π in^3, find the lateral area of the cone.

36. If the radius and height of a right circular cylinder are both doubled to form a larger cylinder, what is the ratio of the volume of the larger cylinder to the volume of the smaller cylinder?
(**NOTE:** The two cylinders are said to be "similar.")

37. For the two similar cylinders in Exercise 36, what is the ratio of the lateral area of the larger cylinder to that of the smaller cylinder?

38. For a right circular cone, the dimensions are $r = 6$ cm and $h = 8$ cm. If the radius is doubled while the height is made half as large in forming a new cone, will the volumes of the two cones be equal?

39. A cylindrical storage tank has a depth of 5 ft and a radius measuring 2 ft. If each cubic foot can hold 7.5 gal of gasoline, what is the total storage capacity of the tank (measured in gallons)?

40. If the tank in Exercise 39 needs to be painted and 1 pt of paint covers 50 ft^2, how many pints are needed to paint the exterior of the storage tank?

41. A frustrum of a cone is the portion of the cone bounded between the circular base and a plane parallel to the base. With dimensions as indicated, show that the volume of the frustrum of the cone is

$$V = \frac{1}{3}\pi R^2 H - \frac{1}{3}\pi r^2 h$$

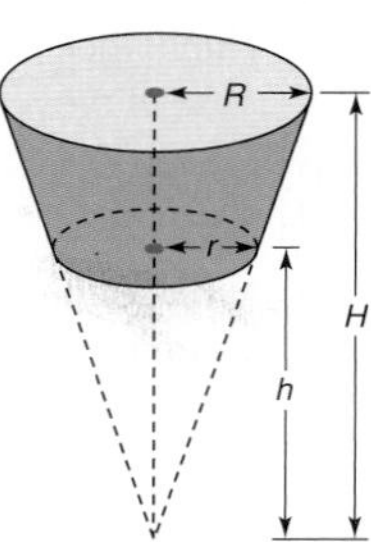

In Exercises 42 and 43, use the formula from Exercise 41. Similar triangles were used to find h and H.

42. A margarine tub has the shape of the frustrum of a cone. With the lower base having diameter 11 cm and the upper base having diameter 14 cm, the volume of such a container $6\frac{2}{3}$ cm tall can be determined by using $R = 7$ cm, $r = 5.5$ cm, $H = 32\frac{2}{3}$ cm, and $h = 26$ cm. Find its volume.

43. A container of yogurt has the shape of the frustrum of a cone. With the lower base having diameter 6 cm and the upper base having diameter 8 cm, the volume of such a container 7.5 cm tall can be determined by using $R = 4$ cm, $r = 3$ cm, $H = 30$ cm, and $h = 22.5$ cm. Find its volume. (See the formula in Exercise 41).

44. An oil refinery has storage tanks in the shape of right circular cylinders. Each tank has a height of 16 ft and a radius of 10 ft for its circular base. If 1 ft^3 of volume contains 7.5 gal of oil, what is the capacity of the fuel tank in *gallons?* Round the result to the nearest hundred (of gallons).

45. A farmer has a fuel tank in the shape of a right circular cylinder. The tank has a height of 6 ft and a radius of 1.5 ft for its circular base. If 1 ft^3 of volume contains 7.5 gal of gasoline, what is the capacity of the fuel tank in *gallons?*

46. When radii $\overline{OA}$ and $\overline{OB}$ are placed so that they coincide, a 240° sector of a circle is sealed to form a right circular cone. If the radius of the circle is 6.4 cm, what is the approximate lateral area of the cone that is formed? Use a calculator and round the answer to the nearest *tenth* of a square inch.

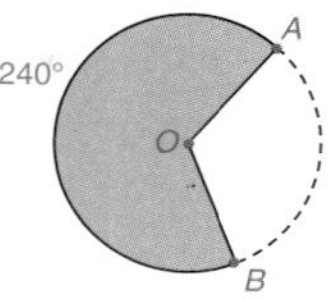

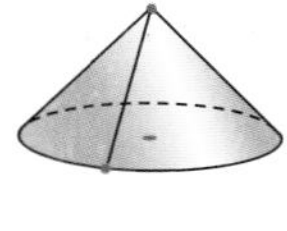

47. A lawn roller in the shape of a right circular cylinder has a radius of 18 in. and a length (height) of 4 ft. Find the area rolled during one complete revolution of the roller. Use the calculator value of π, and give the answer to the nearest square foot.

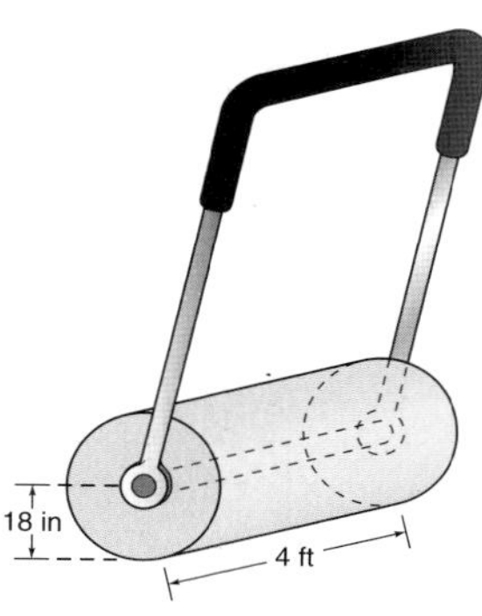

9.4 Polyhedrons and Spheres

- Dihedral Angle
- Polyhedron (Convex and Concave)
- Vertices
- Edges and Faces
- Euler's Equation
- Regular Polyhedrons (Tetrahedron, Hexahedron, Octahedron, Dodecahedron, Icosahedron)
- Sphere (Center, Radius, Diameter, Great Circle, Hemisphere)
- Surface Area and Volume of a Sphere

POLYHEDRONS

When two planes intersect, the angle formed by two half-planes with a common edge (the line of intersection) is a **dihedral angle**. The angle shown in Figure 9.38 is such an angle. In Figure 9.38, the measure of the dihedral angle is the same as that of the angle determined by two rays that

1. have a vertex (the common endpoint) on the edge.
2. lie in the planes so that they are perpendicular to the edge.

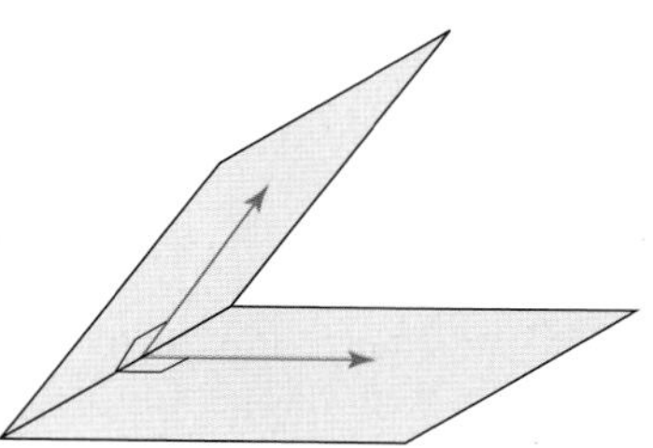

Figure 9.38

A **polyhedron** (plural *polyhedrons or polyhedra*) is a solid bounded by plane regions. Polygons form the **faces** of the solid, and the segments common to these polygons are the **edges** of the polyhedron. Endpoints of the edges are the **vertices** of the polyhedron. When a polyhedron is **convex**, each face determines a plane for which all remaining faces lie on the same side of that plane. Figure 9.39(a) illustrates a convex polyhedron, and Figure 9.39(b) illustrates a **concave** polyhedron; as shown in Figure 9.39(b), a line segment containing the two uppermost vertices lies in the exterior of the concave polyhedron.

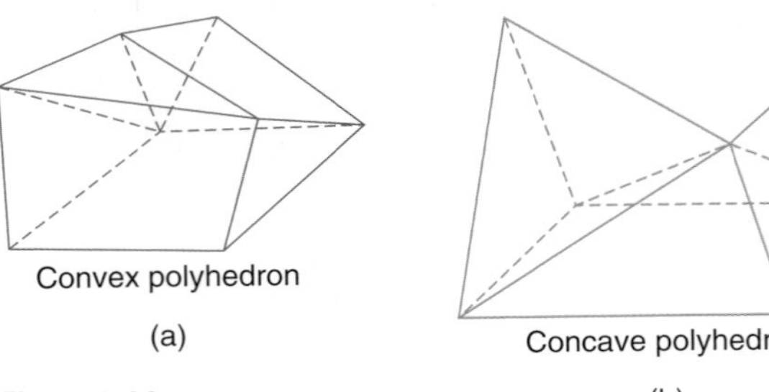

Convex polyhedron

(a)

Concave polyhedron

(b)

Figure 9.39

The prisms and pyramids discussed in Sections 9.1 and 9.2 were special types of polyhedrons. For instance, a pentagonal pyramid can be described as a hexahedron because it has six faces. Because some of their surfaces do not lie in planes, the cylinders and cones of Section 9.3 are not polyhedrons.

Leonhard Euler (Swiss, 1707–1763) found that the number of vertices, edges, and faces of any polyhedron are related by **Euler's equation**. This equation is given in the following theorem, which is stated without proof.

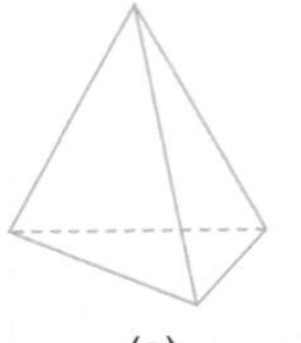

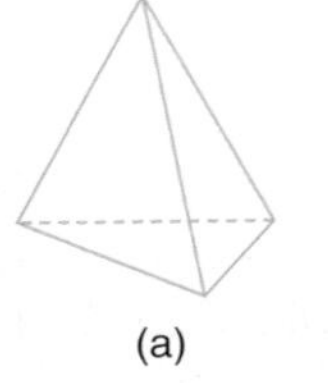

(a)

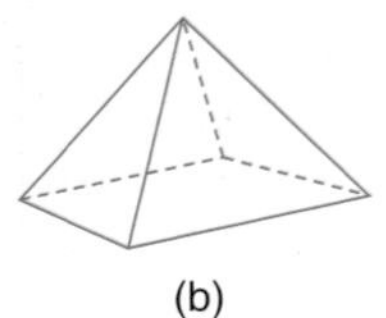

(b)

Figure 9.40

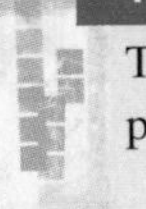

THEOREM 9.4.1 ▶ (Euler's Equation)

The number of vertices V, the number of edges E, and the number of faces F of a polyhedron are related by the equation

$$V + F = E + 2$$

EXAMPLE 1

Verify Euler's equation for the (a) tetrahedron and (b) square pyramid shown in Figure 9.40.

Solution

a) The tetrahedron has four vertices ($V = 4$), six edges ($E = 6$), and four faces ($F = 4$). So Euler's equation becomes $4 + 4 = 6 + 2$, which is true.

b) The pyramid has five vertices ("vertex" + vertices from the base), eight edges (4 base edges + 4 lateral edges), and five faces (4 triangular faces + 1 square base). Now $V + F = E + 2$ becomes $5 + 5 = 8 + 2$, which is also true. ■

SSG *Exs. 1–5*

REGULAR POLYHEDRONS

DEFINITION

A **regular polyhedron** is a convex polyhedron whose faces are congruent regular polygons arranged in such a way that adjacent faces form congruent dihedral angles.

There are exactly five regular polyhedrons, named as follows:

1. Regular **tetrahedron**, which has 4 faces (congruent equilateral triangles)
2. Regular **hexahedron** (or **cube**), which has 6 faces (congruent squares)
3. Regular **octahedron**, which has 8 faces (congruent equilateral triangles)
4. Regular **dodecahedron**, which has 12 faces (congruent regular pentagons)
5. Regular **icosahedron**, which has 20 faces (congruent equilateral triangles)

Four of the existing regular polyhedrons are shown in Figure 9.41.

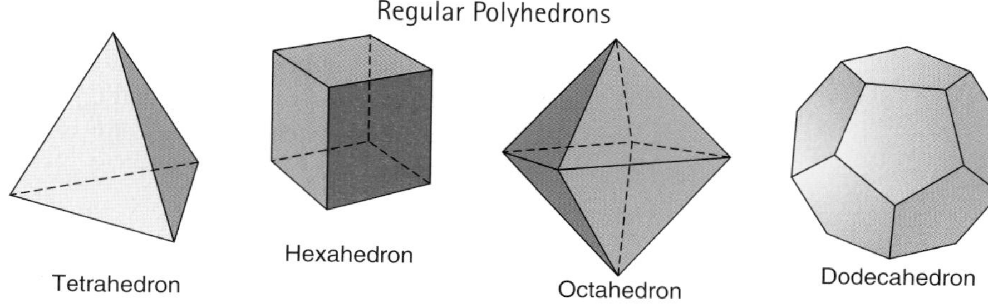

Figure 9.41

Geometry in the Real World

Polyhedra dice are used in numerous games.

Because each regular polyhedron has a central point, each solid is said to have a center. Except for the tetrahedron, these polyhedrons have *point symmetry* at the center. Each solid also has line symmetry and plane symmetry.

EXAMPLE 2

Consider a die that is a regular tetrahedron with faces numbered 1, 2, 3, and 4. Assuming that each face has an equal chance of being rolled, what is the likelihood (probability) that one roll produces (a) a "1"? (b) a result larger than "1"?

Solution

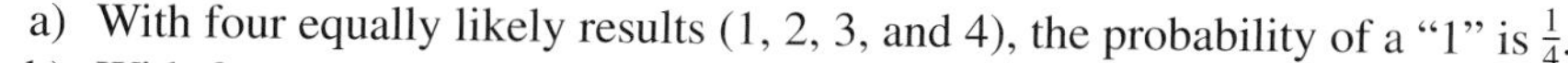

a) With four equally likely results (1, 2, 3, and 4), the probability of a "1" is $\frac{1}{4}$.

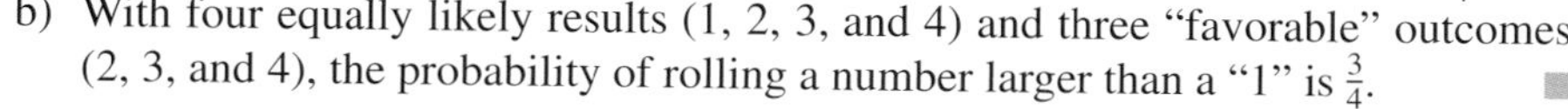

b) With four equally likely results (1, 2, 3, and 4) and three "favorable" outcomes (2, 3, and 4), the probability of rolling a number larger than a "1" is $\frac{3}{4}$. ■

Exs. 6, 7

SPHERES

Reminder

The sphere was defined as a locus of points in Chapter 7.

Another type of solid with which you are familiar is the sphere. Although the surface of a basketball correctly depicts the sphere, we often use the term *sphere* to refer to a solid like a baseball as well. The sphere has point symmetry about its center.

In space, the sphere is characterized in three ways:

1. A **sphere** is the locus of points at a fixed distance r from a given point O. Point O is known as the **center** of the sphere, even though it is not a part of the spherical surface.
2. A **sphere** is the surface determined when a circle (or semicircle) is rotated about any of its diameters.
3. A **sphere** is the surface that represents the theoretical limit of an "inscribed" regular polyhedron whose number of faces increases without limit.

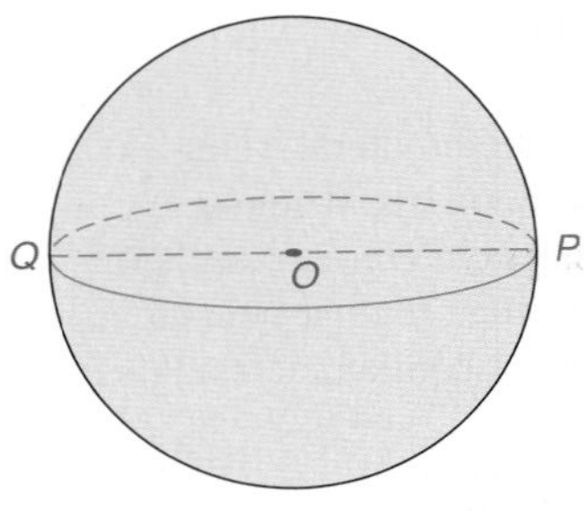

Figure 9.42

NOTE: In characterization 3, suppose that the number of faces of the regular polyhedron could grow without limit. In theory, the resulting regular polyhedra would appear more "spherical" as the number of faces increases without limit. In reality, a regular polyhedron can have no more than 20 faces (the regular icosahedron). It will be necessary to use this third characterization of the sphere when we determine the formula for its volume.

Each characterization of the sphere has its advantages.

▶ *Characterization 1*

In Figure 9.42, a sphere was generated as the locus of points in space at a distance r from point O. The line segment $\overline{OP}$ is a **radius** of sphere O, and $\overline{QP}$ is a **diameter** of the sphere. The intersection of a sphere and a plane that contains its center is a **great circle** of the sphere. For the earth, the equator is a great circle that separates the earth into two **hemispheres**.

Discover

Suppose that you use scissors to cut out each pattern. (You may want to copy and enlarge this page.) Then glue or tape the indicated tabs (shaded) to form regular polyhedra. Which regular polyhedron is formed in each pattern?

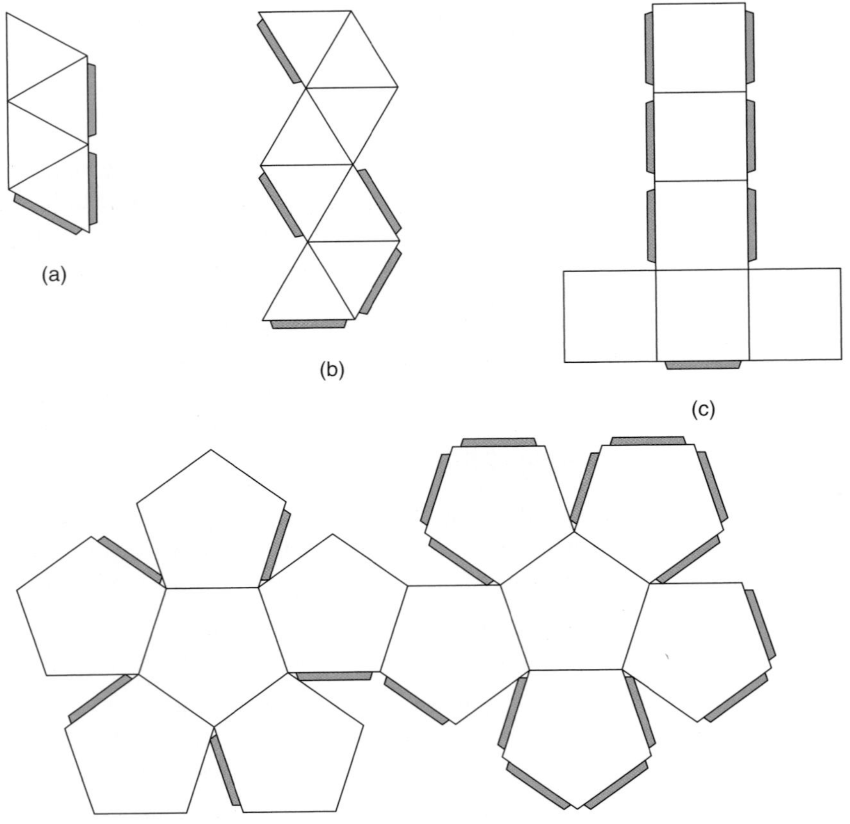

ANSWERS

(a) Tetrahedron (b) Octahedron (c) Hexahedron (cube) (d) Dodecahedron

SURFACE AREA OF A SPHERE

▶ *Characterization 2*

The following theorem claims that the surface area of a sphere equals four times the area of a great circle of that sphere. This theorem, which is proved in calculus, treats the sphere as a surface of revolution.

THEOREM 9.4.2

The surface area S of a sphere whose radius has length r is given by $S = 4\pi r^2$.

Fruits such as oranges have the shape of a sphere.

EXAMPLE 3

Find the surface area of a sphere whose radius is $r = 7$ in. Use your calculator to approximate the result.

Solution

$$S = 4\pi r^2 \rightarrow S = 4\pi \cdot 7^2 = 196\pi \text{ in}^2$$

Exs. 8–10

Then $S \approx 615.75$ in^2. ■

Although half of a circle is called a *semicircle*, remember that half of a sphere is generally called a *hemisphere*.

VOLUME OF A SPHERE

▶ *Characterization 3*

The third description of the sphere enables us to find its volume. To accomplish this, we treat the sphere as the theoretical limit of an inscribed regular polyhedron whose number of faces n increases without limit. The polyhedron can be separated into n pyramids; the center of the sphere is the vertex of each pyramid. As n increases, the altitude of each pyramid approaches the radius of the sphere in length. Next we find the sum of the volumes of these pyramids, the limit of which is the volume of the sphere.

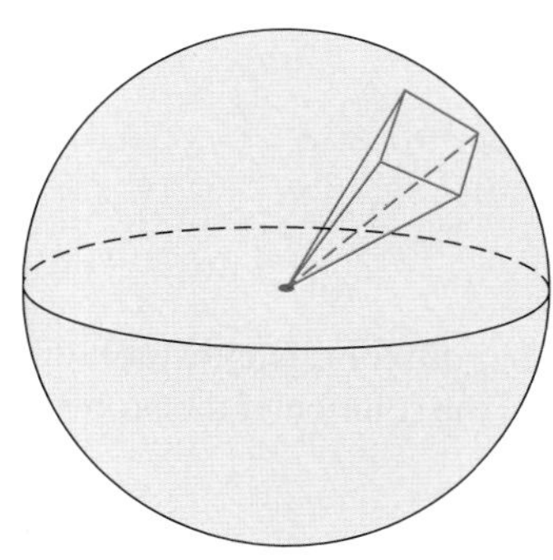

Figure 9.43

In Figure 9.43, one of the pyramids described in the preceding paragraph is shown. We designate the height of each and every pyramid by h. Where the areas of the bases of the pyramids are written B_1, B_2, B_3, and so on, the sum of the volumes of the n pyramids forming the polyhedron is

$$\frac{1}{3}B_1h + \frac{1}{3}B_2h + \frac{1}{3}B_3h + \cdots + \frac{1}{3}B_nh$$

Next we write the volume of the polyhedron in the form

$$\frac{1}{3}h(B_1 + B_2 + B_3 + \cdots + B_n)$$

As n increases, $h \rightarrow r$ and $B_1 + B_2 + B_3 + \cdots + B_n \rightarrow S$, the surface area of the sphere. Because the surface area of the sphere is $S = 4\pi r^2$, the sum approaches the following limit as the volume of the sphere:

$$\frac{1}{3}h(B_1 + B_2 + B_3 + \cdots + B_n) \rightarrow \frac{1}{3}rS \quad \text{or} \quad \frac{1}{3}r \cdot 4\pi r^2 = \frac{4}{3}\pi r^3$$

Discover

A farmer's silo is a composite shape. That is, it is actually composed of two solids. What are they?

ANSWER

Cylinder and hemisphere

The preceding discussion suggests the following theorem.

THEOREM 9.4.3

The volume V of a sphere with a radius of length r is given by $V = \frac{4}{3}\pi r^3$.

EXAMPLE 4

Find the exact volume of a sphere whose length of radius is 1.5 in.

Solution This calculation can be done more easily if we replace 1.5 by $\frac{3}{2}$.

$$\begin{aligned} V &= \frac{4}{3}\pi r^3 \\ &= \frac{\cancel{4}}{\cancel{3}} \cdot \pi \cdot \frac{\cancel{3}}{\cancel{2}} \cdot \frac{3}{\cancel{2}} \cdot \frac{3}{2} \\ &= \frac{9\pi}{2} \text{ in}^3 \end{aligned}$$

■

Technology Exploration

Determine the method of calculating "cube roots" on your calculator. Then show that $\sqrt[3]{27} = 3$.

EXAMPLE 5

A spherical propane gas storage tank has a volume of $\frac{792}{7}$ ft^3. Using $\pi \approx \frac{22}{7}$, find the radius of the sphere.

Solution $V = \frac{4}{3}\pi r^3$, which becomes $\frac{792}{7} = \frac{4}{3} \cdot \frac{22}{7} \cdot r^3$. Then $\frac{88}{21} r^3 = \frac{792}{7}$. In turn,

$$\frac{\cancel{21}}{\cancel{88}} \cdot \frac{\cancel{88}}{\cancel{21}} r^3 = \frac{\overset{3}{\cancel{21}}}{\underset{1}{\cancel{88}}} \cdot \frac{\overset{9}{\cancel{792}}}{\underset{1}{\cancel{7}}} \rightarrow r^3 = 27 \rightarrow r = \sqrt[3]{27} \rightarrow r = 3$$

The radius of the tank is 3 ft. ■

Just as two concentric circles have the same center but different lengths of radii, two spheres can also be concentric. This fact is the basis for the solution of the problem in the following example.

EXAMPLE 6

A child's hollow plastic ball has an inside diameter of 10 in. and is approximately $\frac{1}{8}$ in. thick (see the cross-section of the ball in Figure 9.44). Approximately how many cubic inches of plastic were needed to construct the ball?

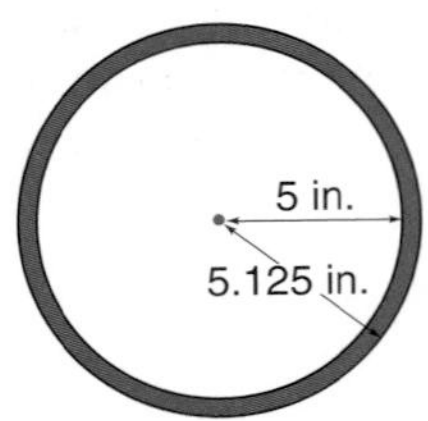

Figure 9.44

Solution The volume of plastic used is the difference between the outside volume and the inside volume. Where R denotes the length of the outside radius and r denotes the length of the inside radius, $R \approx 5.125$ and $r = 5$.

$$V = \frac{4}{3}\pi R^3 - \frac{4}{3}\pi r^3, \quad \text{so} \quad V = \frac{4}{3}\pi(5.125)^3 - \frac{4}{3}\pi \cdot 5^3$$

Then $$V \approx 563.86 - 523.60 \approx 40.26$$

The volume of plastic used was approximately 40.26 in^3. ■

Like circles, spheres may have tangent lines; however, spheres also have tangent planes. As is shown in Figure 9.45, it is also possible for spheres to be tangent to each other.

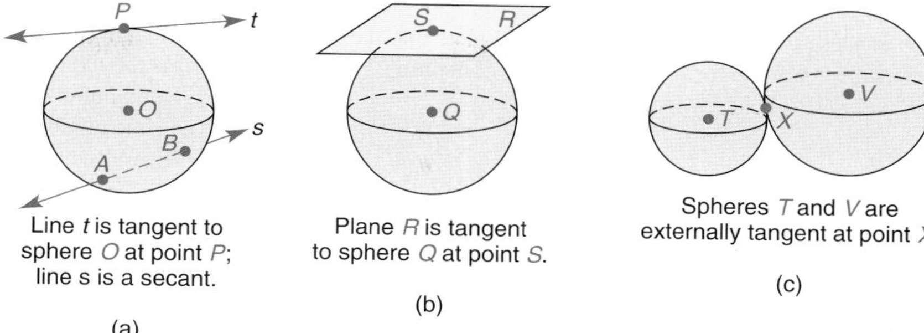
P
t
O
B
s
A
Line t is tangent to sphere O at point P; line s is a secant.
(a)
S
R
Q
Plane R is tangent to sphere Q at point S.
(b)
V
T
X
Spheres T and V are externally tangent at point X.
(c)

SSG *Exs. 11–13*

Figure 9.45

MORE SOLIDS OF REVOLUTION

In Section 9.3, each solid of revolution was generated by revolving a plane region about a horizontal line segment. It is also possible to form a solid of revolution by rotating a region about a vertical or oblique line segment.

EXAMPLE 7

Describe the solid of revolution that is formed when a semicircular region having a vertical diameter of length 12 cm [see Figure 9.46(a)] is revolved about that diameter. Then find the exact volume of the solid formed [see Figure 9.46(b)].

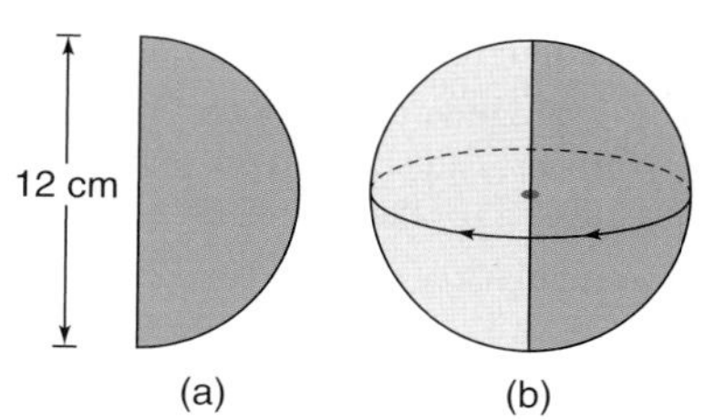
12 cm
(a)
(b)

Figure 9.46

Solution The solid that is formed is a sphere with length of radius $r = 6$ cm. The formula we use to find the volume is $V = \frac{4}{3}\pi r^3$. Then $V = \frac{4}{3}\pi \cdot 6^3$, which simplifies to $V = 288\pi \text{ cm}^3$. ■

When a circular region is revolved about a line in the circle's exterior, a doughnut-shaped solid results. The formal name of the resulting solid of revolution, shown in Figure 9.47, is the *torus*. Methods of calculus are necessary to calculate both the surface area and the volume of the torus.

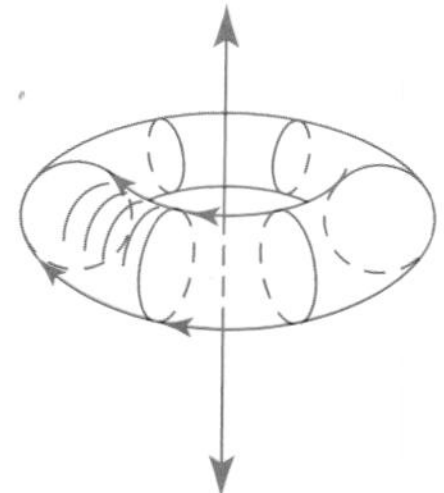

SSG *Exs. 14–16*

Figure 9.47

Exercises 9.4

1. Which of these two polyhedrons is concave? Note that the interior dihedral angle formed by the planes containing $\triangle EJF$ and $\triangle KJF$ is larger than 180°.

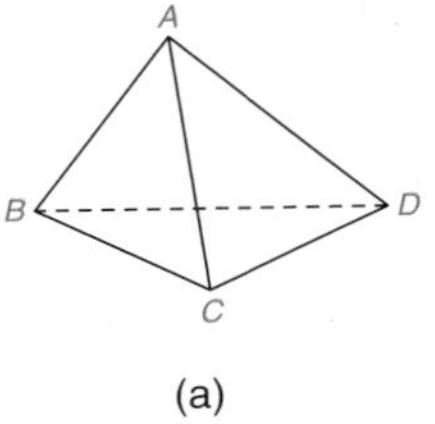

(a)

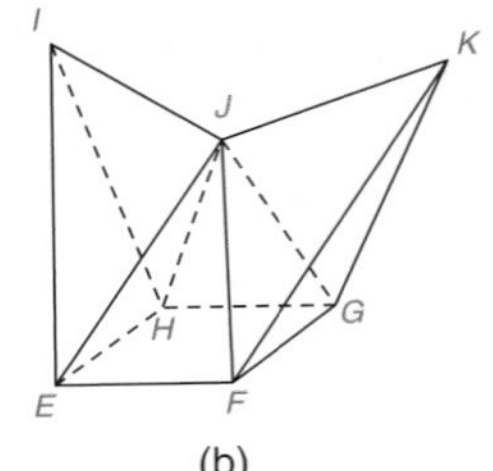

(b)

2. For Figure (a) of Exercise 1, find the number of faces, vertices, and edges in the polyhedron. Then verify Euler's equation for that polyhedron.
3. For Figure (b) of Exercise 1, find the number of faces, vertices, and edges in the polyhedron. Then verify Euler's equation for that polyhedron.
4. For a regular tetrahedron, find the number of faces, vertices, and edges in the polyhedron. Then verify Euler's equation for that polyhedron.
5. For a regular hexahedron, find the number of faces, vertices, and edges in the polyhedron. Then verify Euler's equation for that polyhedron.
6. A regular polyhedron has 12 edges and 8 vertices.
   a) Use Euler's equation to find the number of faces.
   b) Use the result from part (a) to name the regular polyhedron.
7. A regular polyhedron has 12 edges and 6 vertices.
   a) Use Euler's equation to find the number of faces.
   b) Use the result from part (a) to name the regular polyhedron.
8. A polyhedron (not regular) has 10 vertices and 7 faces. How many edges does it have?
9. A polyhedron (not regular) has 14 vertices and 21 edges. How many faces must it have?

In Exercises 10 to 12, the probability is the ratio $\frac{\text{number of favorable outcomes}}{\text{number of possible outcomes}}$. Use Example 2 of this section as a guide.

10. Assume that a die of the most common shape, a hexahedron, is rolled. What is the likelihood that
    a) a "2" results?
    b) an even number results?
    c) the result is larger than 2?
11. Assume that a die in the shape of a dodecahedron is rolled. What is the probability that
    a) an even number results?
    b) a prime number (2, 3, 5, 7, or 11) results?
    c) the result is larger than 2?
12. Assume that a die in the shape of an icosahedron is rolled. What is the likelihood that
    a) an odd number results?
    b) a prime number (2, 3, 5, 7, 11, 13, 17, or 19) results?
    c) the result is larger than 2?
13. In sphere O, the length of radius $\overline{OP}$ is 6 in. Find the length of the chord:
    a) $\overline{QR}$ if $m\angle QOR = 90°$
    b) $\overline{QS}$ if $m\angle SOP = 60°$

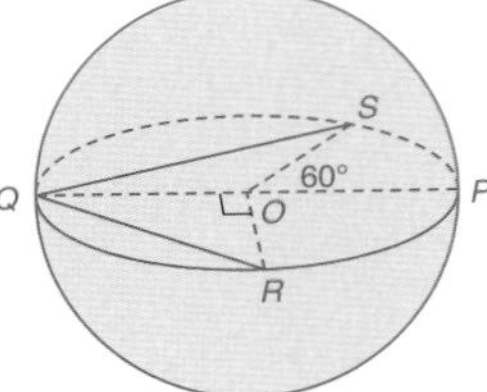

Exercises 13, 14

14. Find the approximate surface area and volume of the sphere if $OP = 6$ in. Use your calculator.
15. Find the total area (surface area) of a regular octahedron if the area of each face is 5.5 in^2.
16. Find the total area (surface area) of a regular dodecahedron (12 faces) if the area of each face is 6.4 cm^2.
17. Find the total area (surface area) of a regular hexahedron if each edge has a length of 4.2 cm.
18. Find the total area (surface area) of a regular tetrahedron if each edge has a length of 6 in.
19. The total area (surface area) of a regular hexahedron is 105.84 m^2. Find the
    a) area of each face.
    b) length of each edge.
20. The total area (surface area) of a regular octahedron is $32\sqrt{3}$ ft^2. Find the
    a) area of each face.
    b) length of each edge.
21. The surface of a soccer ball is composed of 12 regular pentagons and 20 regular hexagons. With each side of each regular polygon measuring 4.5 cm, the area of each regular pentagon is 34.9 cm^2 and the area of each regular hexagon is 52.5 cm^2.
    a) What is the surface area of the soccer ball?
    b) If the material used to construct the ball costs 0.6 cent per square centimeter, what is the cost of the materials used in construction?

22. A calendar is determined by using each of the 12 faces of a regular dodecahedron for one month of the year. With each side of the regular pentagonal face measuring 4 cm, the area of each face is approximately 27.5 cm^2.
    a) What is the total surface area of the calendar?
    b) If the material used to construct the calendar costs 0.8 cent per square centimeter, what is the cost of the materials used in construction?

23. A sphere is inscribed within a right circular cylinder whose altitude and diameter have equal measures.
    a) Find the ratio of the surface area of the cylinder to that of the sphere.
    b) Find the ratio of the volume of the cylinder to that of the sphere.

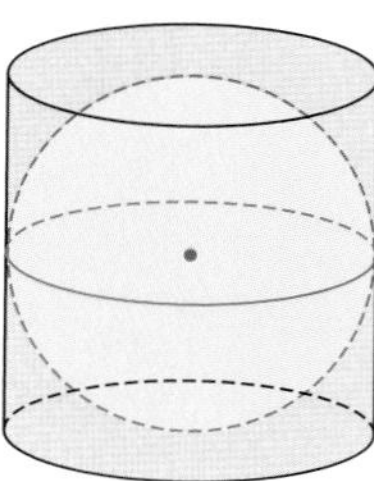

24. Given that a right circular cylinder is inscribed within a sphere, what is the least possible volume of the cylinder?
    (HINT: Consider various lengths for radius and altitude.)

25. In calculus, it can be shown that the largest possible volume for the inscribed right circular cylinder in Exercise 24 occurs when its altitude has a length equal to the diameter of the circular base. Find the length of the radius and the altitude of the cylinder of greatest volume if the radius of the sphere is 6 in.

26. Given that a *regular* polyhedron of n faces is inscribed in a sphere of radius 6 in., find the maximum (largest) possible volume for the polyhedron.

27. A right circular cone is inscribed in a sphere. If the slant height of the cone has a length equal to that of its diameter, find the length of the
    a) radius of the base of the cone.
    b) altitude of the cone.

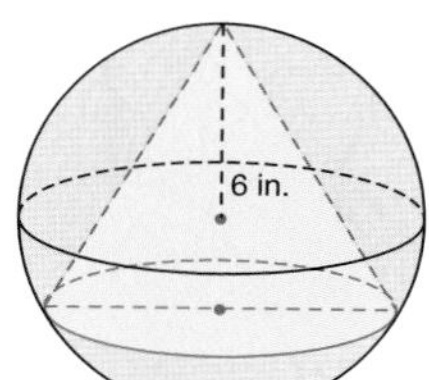

The radius of the sphere has a length of 6 in.

28. A sphere is inscribed in a right circular cone whose slant height has a length equal to the diameter of its base. What is the length of the radius of the sphere if the slant height and the diameter of the cone both measure 12 cm?

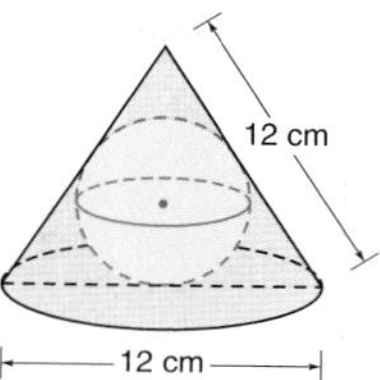

In Exercises 29 and 30, use the calculator value of π.

29. For a sphere whose radius has length 3 m, find the approximate
    a) surface area.
    b) volume.

30. For a sphere whose radius has length 7 cm, find the approximate
    a) surface area.
    b) volume.

31. A sphere has a volume equal to $\frac{99}{7}$ in^3. Determine the length of the radius of the sphere. $\left(\text{Let } \pi \approx \frac{22}{7}.\right)$

32. A sphere has a surface area equal to 154 in^2. Determine the length of the radius of the sphere. $\left(\text{Let } \pi \approx \frac{22}{7}.\right)$

33. The spherical storage tank described in Example 5 had a length of radius of 3 ft. Because the tank needs to be painted, we need to find its surface area. Also determine the number of pints of rust-proofing paint needed to paint the tank if 1 pt covers approximately 40 ft^2. Use your calculator.

34. An observatory has the shape of a right circular cylinder surmounted by a hemisphere. If the radius of the cylinder is 14 ft and its altitude measures 30 ft, what is the surface area of the observatory? If 1 gal of paint covers 300 ft^2, how many gallons are needed to paint the surface if it requires two coats? Use your calculator.

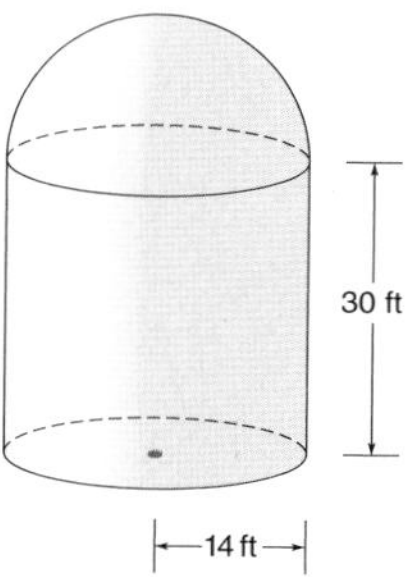

35. A leather soccer ball has an inside diameter of 8.5 in. and a thickness of 0.1 in. Find the volume of leather needed for its construction. Use your calculator.

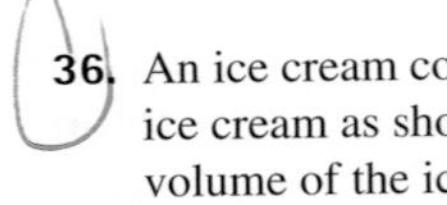

36. An ice cream cone is filled with ice cream as shown. What is the volume of the ice cream? Use your calculator.

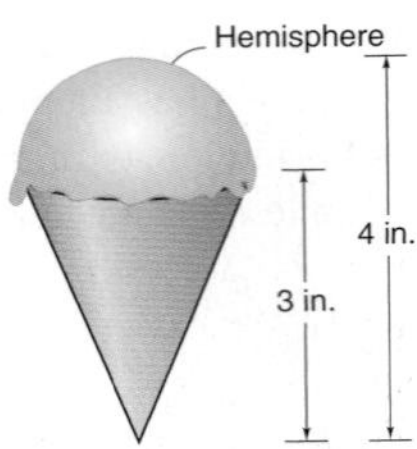

For Exercises 37 to 42, make drawings as needed.

37. Can two spheres
a) be internally tangent?
b) have no points in common?

38. If two spheres intersect at more than one point, what type of geometric figure is determined by their intersection?

39. Two planes are tangent to a sphere at the endpoints of a diameter. How are the planes related?

40. Plane R is tangent to sphere O at point T. How are radius $\overline{OT}$ and plane R related?

41. Two tangent segments are drawn to sphere Q from external point E. Where A and B are the points of tangency on sphere Q, how are $\overline{EA}$ and $\overline{EB}$ related?

42. How many common tangent planes do two externally tangent spheres have?

43. Suppose that a semicircular region with a vertical diameter of length 6 is rotated about that diameter. Determine the exact surface area and the exact volume of the resulting solid of revolution.

44. Suppose that a semicircular region with a vertical diameter of length 4 is rotated about that diameter. Determine the exact surface area and the exact volume of the resulting solid of revolution.

45. Sketch the torus that results when the given circle of radius 1 is revolved about the horizontal line that lies 4 units below the center of that circle.

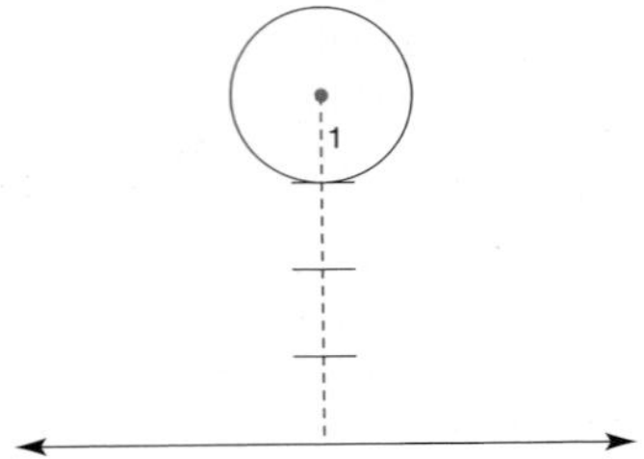

46. Sketch the solid that results when the given circle of radius 1 is revolved about the horizontal line that lies 1 unit below the center of that circle.

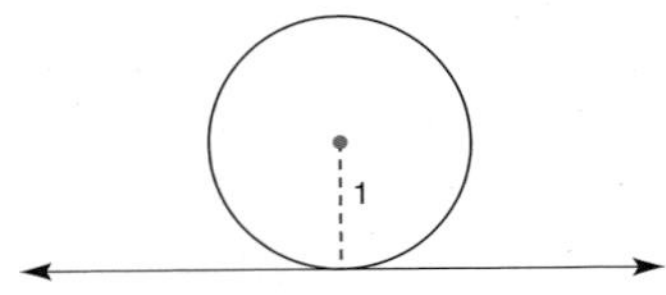

47. Explain how the following formula used in Example 6 was obtained:

$$V = \frac{4}{3}\pi R^3 - \frac{4}{3}\pi r^3$$

48. Derive a formula for the total surface area of the hollow-core sphere. (**NOTE:** Include both interior and exterior surface areas.)

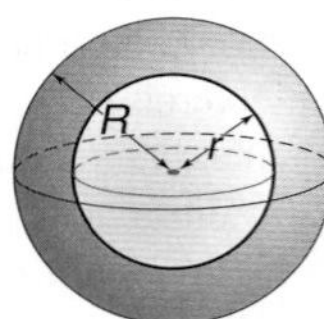

PERSPECTIVE ON HISTORY

Sketch of René Descartes

René Descartes was born in Tours, France, on March 31, 1596, and died in Stockholm, Sweden, on February 11, 1650. He was a contemporary of Galileo, the Italian scientist responsible for many discoveries in the science of dynamics. Descartes was also a friend of the French mathematicians Marin Mersenne (Mersenne Numbers) and Blaise Pascal (Pascal's Triangle).

As a small child, René Descartes was in poor health much of the time. Because he spent so much time reading in bed during his illnesses, he became a very well educated young man. When Descartes was older and stronger, he joined the French army. It was during his time as a soldier that Descartes had three dreams that vastly influenced his future. The dreams, dated to November 10, 1619, shaped his philosophy and laid the framework for his discoveries in mathematics.

Descartes resigned his commission with the army in 1621 so that he could devote his life to studying philosophy, science, and mathematics. In the ensuing years, Descartes came to be highly regarded as a philosopher and mathematician and was invited to the learning centers of France, Holland, and Sweden.

Descartes's work in mathematics, in which he used an oblique coordinate system as a means of representing points, led to the birth of analytical geometry. His convention for locating points was eventually replaced by a coordinate system with perpendicular axes. In this system, algebraic equations could be represented by geometric figures; subsequently, many conjectured properties of these figures could be established through algebraic (analytic) proof. The rectangular coordinate system (which is called the Cartesian system in honor of Descartes) can also be used to locate the points of intersection of geometric figures such as lines and circles. Much of the material in Chapter 10 depends on his work.

Generally, the phrase *conic sections* refers to four geometric figures: the **circle**, the **parabola**, the **ellipse**, and the **hyperbola**. These figures are shown in Figure 9.48 both individually and also in relation to the upper and lower nappes of a cone. The conic sections are formed when a plane intersects the nappe(s) of a cone.

Other mathematical works of Descartes were devoted to the study of tangent lines to curves. The notion of a tangent to a curve is illustrated in Figure 9.49; this concept is the basis for the branch of mathematics known as **differential calculus**.

Descartes's final contributions to mathematics involved his standardizing the use of many symbols. To mention a few of these, Descartes used (1) a^2 rather than aa and a^3 rather than aaa; (2) ab to indicate multiplication; and (3) a, b, and c as constants and x, y, and z as variables.

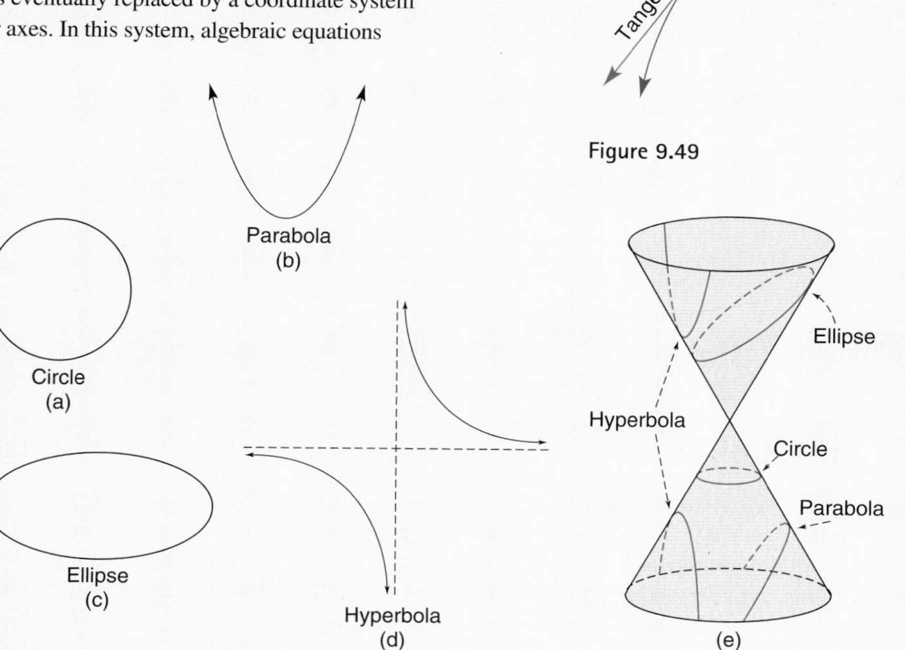

Figure 9.49

Figure 9.48

PERSPECTIVE ON APPLICATION

Birds in Flight

The following application of geometry is not so much practical as classical.

Two birds have been attracted to bird feeders that rest atop vertical poles. The bases of these poles where their perches are located are 20 ft apart. The poles are themselves 10 ft and 16 ft tall. See Figure 9.50. Each bird eyes birdseed that has fallen on the ground at the base of the other pole. Leaving their perches, the birds fly in a straight-line path toward their goal. Avoiding a collision in flight, the birds take paths that have them pass at a common point X. How far is the point above ground level?

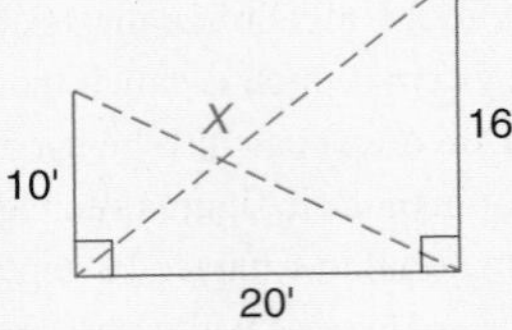

Figure 9.50

The solution to the problem follows. However, we redraw the figure to indicate that the 20-ft distance between poles is separated along the ground into line segments with lengths of a and $20 - a$ as shown. See Figures 9.51(a), 9.51(b), and 9.51(c).

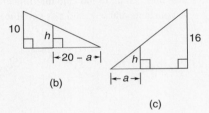

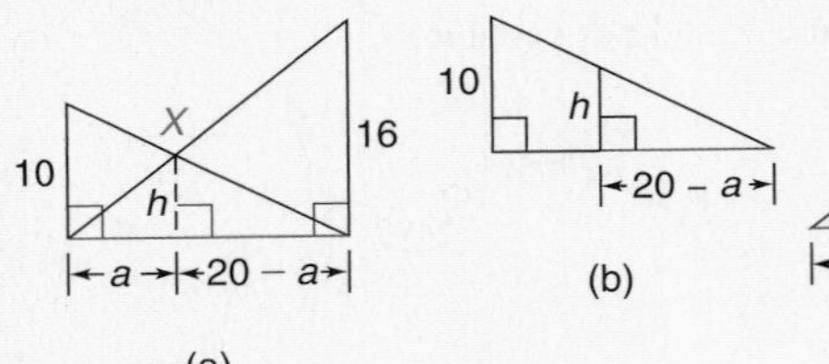

Figure 9.51

From Figures 9.51(b) and 9.51(c), we form the following equations based upon similarity of the right triangles:

$$\frac{10}{20} = \frac{h}{20 - a} \quad \text{and} \quad \frac{16}{20} = \frac{h}{a}$$

By the Means-Extremes Property of Proportions, $10(20 - a) = 20h$ and $16a = 20h$. By substitution,

$$\begin{aligned} 10(20 - a) &= 16a \\ 200 - 10a &= 16a \\ 26a &= 200 \end{aligned}$$

$$a = \frac{200}{26} \quad \text{or} \quad a = \frac{100}{13}$$

From the fact that $16a = 20h$, we see that

$$16 \cdot \frac{100}{13} = 20h$$

so $$h = \frac{1}{\cancel{20}_{1}} \cdot 16 \cdot \frac{\cancel{100}^{5}}{13} = \frac{80}{13} = 6\frac{2}{13} \text{ ft}$$

The point at which the birds flew past each other was $6\frac{2}{13}$ feet above the ground.

Summary

A LOOK BACK AT CHAPTER 9

Our goal in this chapter was to deal with a type of geometry known as solid geometry. We found formulas for the lateral area, the total area (surface area), and the volume of prisms, pyramids, cylinders, cones, and spheres. Some of the formulas used in this chapter were developed using the concept of "limit." Regular polyhedra were introduced.

A LOOK AHEAD TO CHAPTER 10

Our focus in the next chapter is analytic (or coordinate) geometry. This type of geometry relates algebra and geometry. Formulas for the midpoint of a line segment, the length of a line segment, and the slope of a line will be developed. We will not only graph the equations of lines but also determine equations for given lines. We will see that proofs of many geometric theorems can be completed by using analytic geometry.

KEY CONCEPTS

9.1

Prisms (Right and Oblique) • Bases • Altitude • Vertices • Edges • Faces • Lateral Area • Total (Surface) Area • Volume • Regular Prism • Cube • Cubic Unit

9.2

Pyramid • Base • Altitude • Vertices • Edges • Faces • Vertex of a Pyramid • Regular Pyramid • Slant Height of a Regular Pyramid • Lateral Area • Total (Surface) Area • Volume

9.3

Cylinders (Right and Oblique) • Bases and Altitude of a Cylinder • Axis of a Cylinder • Cones (Right and Oblique) • Base and Altitude of a Cone • Vertex and Slant Height of a Cone • Axis of a Cone • Lateral Area • Total Area • Volume • Solid of Revolution • Axis of a Solid of Revolution

9.4

Dihedral Angle • Polyhedron (Convex and Concave) • Vertices • Edges and Faces • Euler's Equation • Regular Polyhedrons (Tetrahedron, Hexahedron, Octahedron, Dodecahedron, and Icosahedron) • Sphere (Center, Radius, Diameter, Great Circle, Hemisphere) • Surface Area and Volume of a Sphere

TABLE 9.4 An Overview of Chapter 9

▶ Volume and Area Relationships for Solids

SOLID	FIGURE	VOLUME	AREA
Rectangular prism (box)	h, w, ℓ	$V = \ell wh$	$T = 2\ell w + 2\ell h + 2wh$
Cube	e, e, e	$V = e^3$	$T = 6e^2$
Prism (right prism shown)	h	$V = Bh$ (B = area of base)	$L = hP$ (P = perimeter of base) $T = L + 2B$
Regular pyramid (with slant height ℓ)	h, ℓ, a	$V = \frac{1}{3}Bh$ (B = area of base)	$L = \frac{1}{2}\ell P$ (P = perimeter of base) $T = L + B$ **NOTE:** $\ell^2 = a^2 + h^2$
Right circular cylinder	r, h	$V = Bh$ or $V = \pi r^2 h$	$L = 2\pi rh$ $T = L + 2B$ or $T = 2\pi rh + 2\pi r^2$

continued

TABLE 9.4 *(continued)*

Volume and Area Relationships for Solids

SOLID	FIGURE	VOLUME	AREA
Right circular cone (with slant height ℓ)		$V = \frac{1}{3}Bh$ or $V = \frac{1}{3}\pi r^2 h$	$L = \pi r\ell$; $T = L + B$ or $T = \pi r\ell + \pi r^2$ NOTE: $\ell^2 = r^2 + h^2$
Sphere		$V = \frac{4}{3}\pi r^3$	$S = 4\pi r^2$

Chapter 9 REVIEW EXERCISES

1. Each side of the base of a right octagonal prism is 7 in. long. The altitude of the prism measures 12 in. Find the lateral area.
2. The base of a right prism is a triangle whose sides measure 7 cm, 8 cm, and 12 cm. The altitude of the prism measures 11 cm. Calculate the lateral area of the right prism.
3. The height of a square box is 2 in. more than three times the length of a side of the base. If the lateral area is 480 in^2, find the dimensions of the box and the volume of the box.
4. The base of a right prism is a rectangle whose length is 3 cm more than its width. If the altitude of the prism is 12 cm and the lateral area is 360 cm^2, find the total area and the volume of the prism.
5. The base of a right prism is a triangle whose sides have lengths of 9 in., 15 in., and 12 in. The height of the prism is 10 in. Find the
   a) lateral area. b) total area. c) volume.
6. The base of a right prism is a regular hexagon whose sides are 8 cm in length. The altitude of the prism is 13 cm. Find the
   a) lateral area. b) total area. c) volume.
7. A regular square pyramid has a base whose sides are of length 10 cm each. The altitude of the pyramid measures 8 cm. Find the length of the slant height.
8. A regular hexagonal pyramid has a base whose sides are of length $6\sqrt{3}$ in. each. If the slant height is 12 in., find the length of the altitude of the pyramid.
9. The radius of the base of a right circular cone measures 5 in. If the altitude of the cone measures 7 in., what is the length of the slant height?
10. The diameter of the base of a right circular cone is equal in length to the slant height. If the altitude of the cone is 6 cm, find the length of the radius of the base.
11. The slant height of a regular square pyramid measures 15 in. One side of the base measures 18 in. Find the
    a) lateral area. b) total area. c) volume.
12. The base of a regular pyramid is an equilateral triangle each of whose sides is 12 cm. The altitude of the pyramid is 8 cm. Find the exact and approximate
    a) lateral area. b) total area. c) volume.
13. The radius of the base of a right circular cylinder is 6 in. The height of the cylinder is 10 in. Find the exact
    a) lateral area. b) total area. c) volume.
14. a) For the trough in the shape of a half-cylinder, find the volume of water it will hold. (Use $\pi \approx 3.14$ and disregard the thickness.)
    b) If the trough is to be painted inside and out, find the number of square feet to be painted. (Use $\pi \approx 3.14$.)

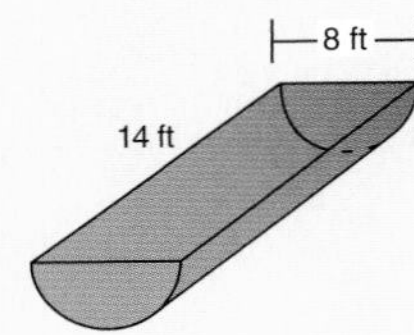

15. The slant height of a right circular cone is 12 cm. The angle formed by the slant height and the altitude is 30°. Find the exact and approximate

a) lateral area. b) total area. c) volume.

16. The volume of a right circular cone is 96π in^3. If the radius of the base is 6 in., find the length of the slant height.

17. Find the surface area of a sphere if the radius has the length 7 in. Use $\pi \approx \frac{22}{7}$.

18. Find the volume of a sphere if the diameter has the length 12 cm. Use $\pi \approx 3.14$.

19. The solid shown consists of a hemisphere (half of a sphere), a cylinder, and a cone. Find the exact volume of the solid.

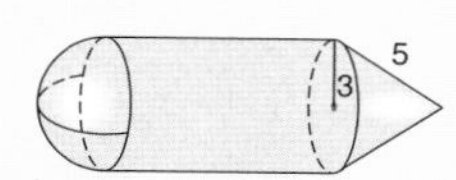

20. If the radius of one sphere is three times as long as the radius of another sphere, how do the surface areas of the spheres compare? How do the volumes compare?

21. Find the volume of the solid of revolution that results when a right triangle with legs of lengths 5 in. and 7 in. is rotated about the 7-in. leg. Use $\pi \approx \frac{22}{7}$.

22. Find the exact volume of the solid of revolution that results when a rectangular region with dimensions of 6 cm and 8 cm is rotated about a side of length 8 cm.

23. Find the exact volume of the solid of revolution that results when a semicircular region with diameter of length 4 in. is rotated about that diameter.

24. A plastic pipe is 3 ft long and has an inside radius of 4 in. and an outside radius of 5 in. How many cubic inches of plastic are in the pipe? (Use $\pi \approx 3.14$.)

25. A sphere with a diameter of 14 in. is inscribed in a hexahedron. Find the exact volume of the space inside the hexahedron but outside the sphere.

26. a) An octahedron has ________ faces that are ________.
b) A tetrahedron has ________ faces that are ________.
c) A dodecahedron has ________ faces that are ________.

27. A drug manufacturing company wants to manufacture a capsule that contains a spherical pill inside. The diameter of the pill is 4 mm, and the capsule is cylindrical with hemispheres on either end. The length of the capsule between the two hemispheres is 10 mm. What is the exact volume that the capsule will hold, excluding the volume of the pill?

28. For each of the following solids, verify Euler's equation by determining V, the number of vertices; E, the number of edges; and F, the number of faces.

a) Right octagonal prism
b) Tetrahedron
c) Octahedron

29. Find the volume of cement used in the block shown.

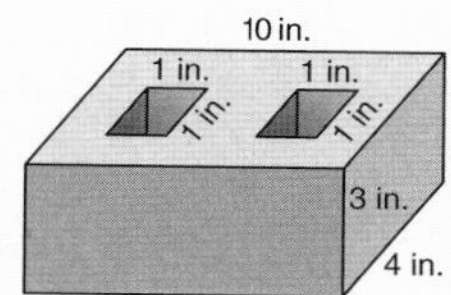

30. Given a die in the shape of a regular octahedron, find the probability that one roll produces

a) an even-number result.
b) a result of 4 or more.

31. Find the total surface area of

a) a regular dodecahedron with each face having an area of 6.5 in.^{2}
b) a regular tetrahedron with each edge measuring 4 cm.

32. Three spheres are tangent to each other in pairs. They have radii of 1 in., 2 in., and 3 in., respectively. What type of triangle is formed by the lines of center?

Chapter 9 TEST

1. For the regular pentagonal prism shown below, find the total number of

a) edges. ______ b) faces. ______

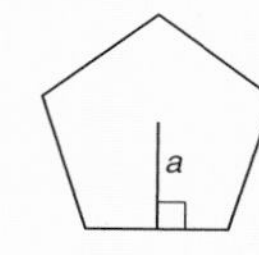

Exercises 1, 2

2. For the regular pentagonal base, each edge measures 3.2 cm and the apothem measures 2 cm.

a) Find the area of the base (use $A = \frac{1}{2}aP$). ______
b) Find the total area of the regular pentagonal prism if its altitude measures 5 cm. ______
c) Find the volume of the prism. ______

3. For the regular square pyramid shown, find the total number of

a) vertices. ______ b) lateral faces. ______

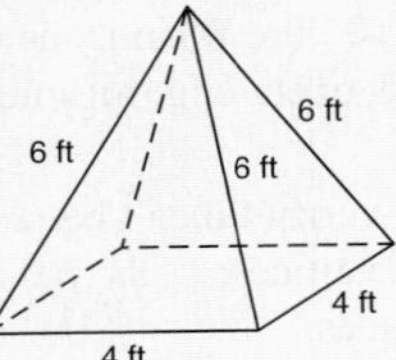

Exercises 3, 4

4. For the regular square pyramid shown above, find

a) the lateral area. ______

b) the total area. ______

5. For the regular square pyramid shown, find the length of the slant height. ______

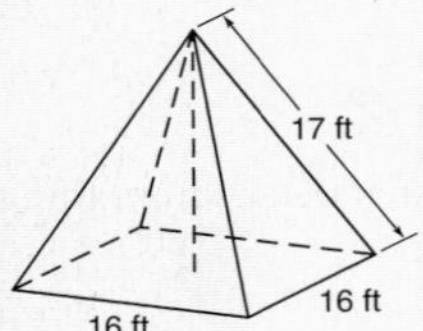

6. Find the altitude of a regular square pyramid (not shown) if each edge of the base measures 8 in. and the length of the slant height is 5 in. ______

7. Find the volume of the regular square pyramid shown if each edge of the base measures 5 ft and the altitude measures 6 ft. ______

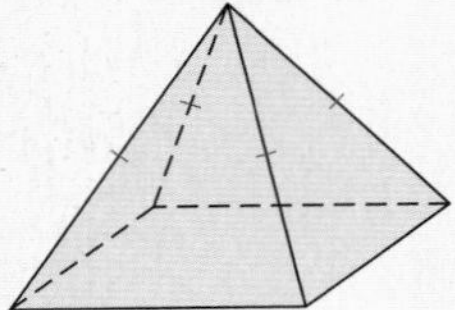

8. Determine whether the statement is true or false.

a) A right circular cone has exactly two bases. ______

b) The lateral area L of a right circular cylinder with radius of base r and altitude h is given by $L = 2\pi rh$. ______

9. Determine whether the statement is true or false.

a) The volume of a right circular cone is given by $V = \frac{1}{3}Bh$, which can also be expressed in the form $V = \frac{1}{3}\pi r^2 h$. ______

b) A regular dodecahedron has exactly 12 faces. ______

10. Recall Euler's Formula, $V + F = E + 2$. For a certain polyhedron, there are eight faces and six vertices. How many edges does it have? ______

11. Find the slant height of the right circular cone below. Leave the answer in simplified radical form. ______

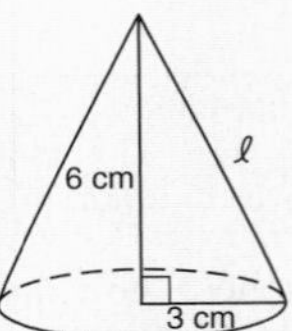

12. For the right circular cylinder shown, $r = 4$ cm and $h = 6$ cm. Find the exact

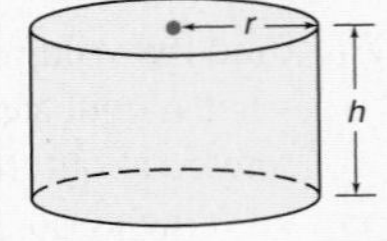

a) lateral area. ______

b) volume. ______

13. The exact volume of a right circular cone (not shown) is 32π in^3. If the length of the base radius is 4 in., find the length of the altitude of the cone. ______

14. Assume that a die used for gaming is in the shape of a regular octahedron. The faces are numbered 1, 2, 3, 4, . . ., and 8. When this die is rolled once, what is the probability that the roll produces

a) an even number result? ______

b) a result greater than or equal to 6? ______

15. A spherical storage tank filled with water has a radius of 10 ft. Use the calculator's stored value of π to find to nearest tenth of unit the approximate

a) surface area of the sphere. ______

b) volume of the sphere. ______

16. A pump moves water at a rate of 8π ft^3 per minute. How long will it take to empty the tank in Exercise 15? (Answer to the nearest whole minute.) ______

Analytic Geometry

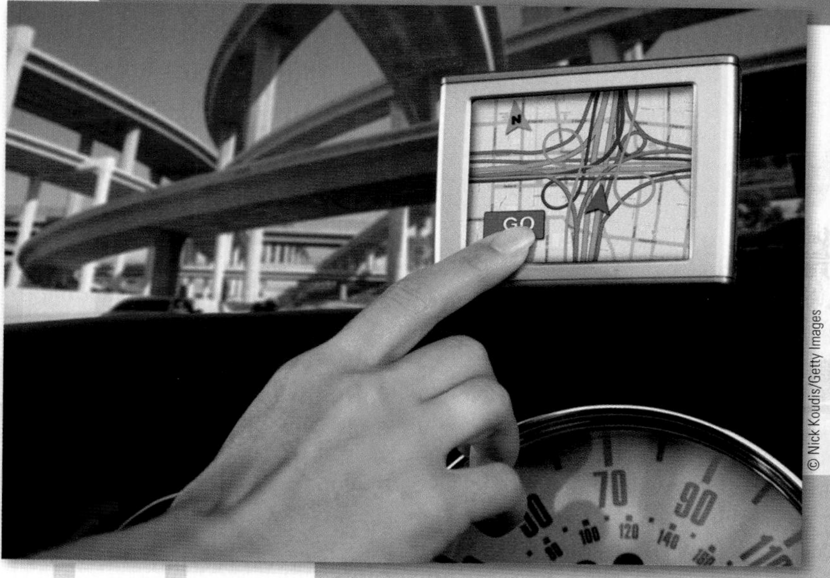

© Nick Koudis/Getty Images

Chapter 10

CHAPTER OUTLINE

Additional Video explanation of concepts, sample problems, and applications are available on DVD. 

Guidance! The French mathematician René Descartes is considered the father of analytic geometry. His inspiration relating algebra and geometry, the Cartesian coordinate system, was a major breakthrough in the development of much of mathematics. The photograph illustrates the use of a GPS (global positioning system). The system allows one to pinpoint locations such as that of a moving vehicle or that of a destination. On the map, locations identified by latitude and longitude are comparable to points whose *x* and *y* coordinates locate a position in the Cartesian coordinate system.

10.1 The Rectangular Coordinate System

KEY CONCEPTS

Analytic Geometry	Quadrants	Ordered Pair
Cartesian (Rectangular) Coordinate System	Origin	Distance Formula
x Axis	x Coordinate	Linear Equation
y Axis	y Coordinate	Midpoint Formula

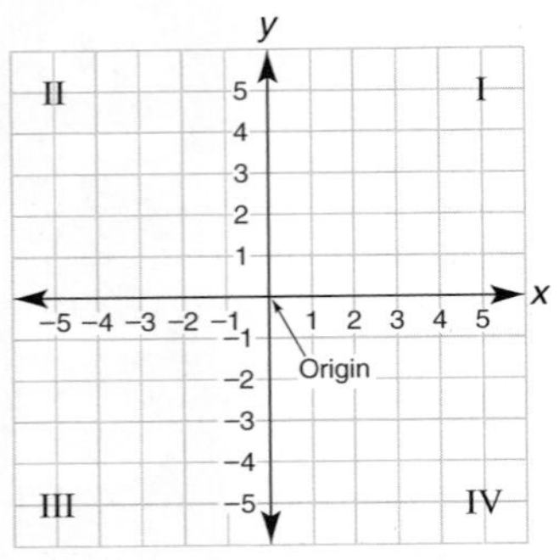

Figure 10.1

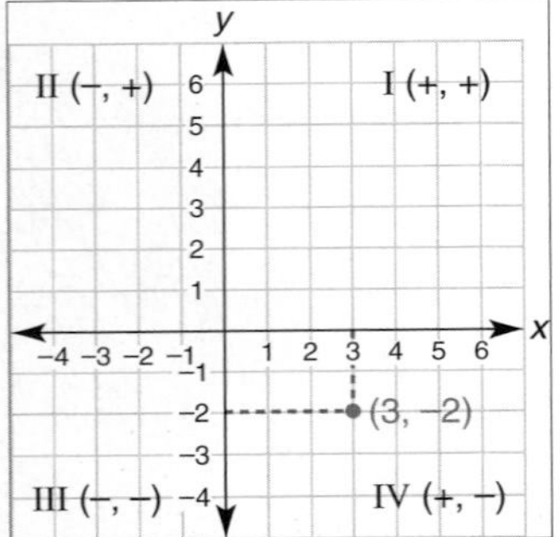

Figure 10.2

Graphing the solution sets for $3x - 2 = 7$ and $3x - 2 > 7$ required a single number line to indicate the value of x. (See Appendices A.2 and A.3 for further information.) In this chapter, we deal with equations containing two variables; to relate such algebraic statements to plane geometry, we will need two number lines.

The study of the relationships between number pairs and points is usually referred to as **analytic geometry.** The **Cartesian coordinate system** or **rectangular coordinate system** is the plane that results when two number lines intersect perpendicularly at the origin (the point corresponding to the number 0 of each line). The horizontal number line is known as the ***x* axis,** and its numerical coordinates increase from left to right. On the vertical number line, the ***y* axis,** values increase from bottom to top; see Figure 10.1. The two axes separate the plane into four **quadrants** which are numbered counterclockwise I, II, III, and IV, as shown. The point that marks the common origin of the two number lines is the **origin** of the rectangular coordinate system. It is convenient to identify the origin as (0, 0); this notation indicates that the ***x* coordinate** (listed first) is 0 and also that the ***y* coordinate** (listed second) is 0.

In the coordinate system in Figure 10.2, the point $(3, -2)$ is shown. For each point, we use the order (x, y); these pairs are called **ordered pairs** because x must precede y. To plot this point, we see that $x = 3$ and that $y = -2$; thus, the point is located by moving 3 units to the right of the origin and then 2 units down from the x axis. The dashed lines shown emphasize the reason why the grid is called the *rectangular coordinate system.* Note that this point $(3, -2)$ could also have been located by first moving down 2 units and then moving 3 units to the right of the y axis. This point is located in Quadrant IV. In Figure 10.2, ordered pairs of plus and minus signs characterize the signs of the coordinates of a point located in each quadrant.

EXAMPLE 1

Plot points $A\ (-3, 4)$ and $B\ (2, 4)$, and find the distance between them.

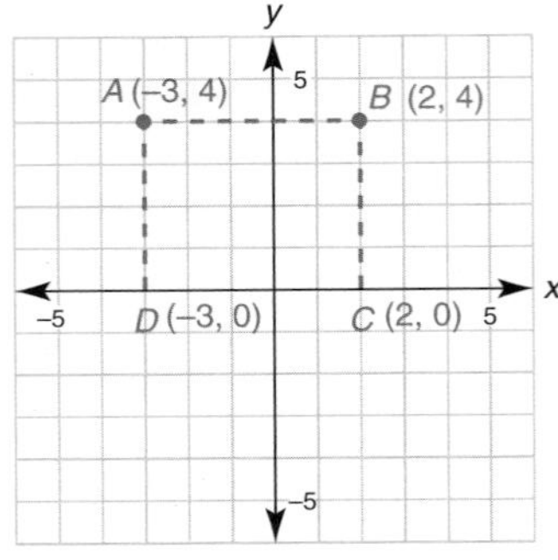

Figure 10.3

Solution Point A is located by moving 3 units to the left of the origin and then 4 units up from the x axis. Point B is located by moving 2 units to the right of the origin and then 4 units up from the x axis. In Figure 10.3, $\overline{AB}$ is a horizontal segment.

In the rectangular coordinate system, $ABCD$ is a rectangle in which $DC = 5$; $\overline{DC}$ is easily measured because it lies on the x axis. Because the opposite sides of a rectangle are congruent, it follows that $AB = 5$. ■

Exs. 1–4

In Example 1, the points $(-3, 4)$ and $(2, 4)$ have the same y coordinates. In this case, the distance between the points on a horizontal line is merely the positive difference in the x coordinates; thus, the distance between A and B is $2 - (-3)$, or 5. It is also easy to find the distance between two points on a vertical line. When the x coordinates are the same, the distance between points is the positive difference in the y coordinates. In Figure 10.3, where C is $(2, 0)$ and B is $(2, 4)$, the distance between the points is $4 - 0$ or 4.

DEFINITION

Given points $A(x_1, y_1)$ and $B(x_2, y_1)$ on a horizontal line segment $\overline{AB}$, the distance between these points is

$$AB = x_2 - x_1 \text{ if } x_2 > x_1 \quad \text{or} \quad AB = x_1 - x_2 \text{ if } x_1 > x_2$$

In the preceding definition, repeated y coordinates characterize a horizontal line segment. In the following definition, repeated x coordinates determine a vertical line segment. In each definition, the distance is found by subtracting the smaller from the larger of the two unequal coordinates.

DEFINITION

Given points $C(x_1, y_1)$ and $D(x_1, y_2)$ on a vertical line segment $\overline{CD}$, the distance between these points is

$$CD = y_2 - y_1 \text{ if } y_2 > y_1 \quad \text{or} \quad CD = y_1 - y_2 \text{ if } y_1 > y_2$$

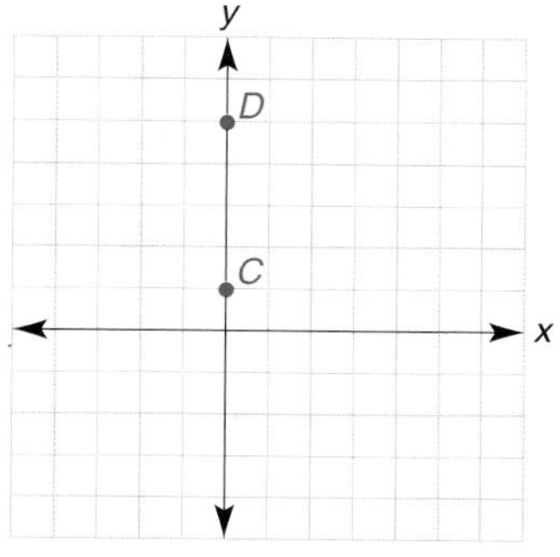

Figure 10.4

EXAMPLE 2

In Figure 10.4, name the coordinates of points C and D, and find the distance between them. The x coordinates of C and D are identical.

Solution C is the point $(0, 1)$ because C is 1 unit above the origin; similarly, D is the point $(0, 5)$. We designate the coordinates of point C by $x_1 = 0$ and $y_1 = 1$ and the coordinates of point D by $x_1 = 0$ and $y_2 = 5$. Using the preceding definition,

$$CD = y_2 - y_1 = 5 - 1 = 4$$

We now turn our attention to the more general problem of finding the distance between any two points.

Discover

Plot the points $A(0, 0)$ and $B(4, 3)$. Now find AB by using the Pythagorean Theorem. To accomplish this, you will need to form a path from A to B along horizontal and vertical line segments.

ANSWER
5

THE DISTANCE FORMULA

The following formula enables us to find the distance between two points that lie on a "slanted" line.

THEOREM 10.1.1 ▶ (Distance Formula)

The distance between two points (x_1, y_1) and (x_2, y_2) is given by the formula

$$d = \sqrt{(x_2 - x_1)^2 + (y_2 - y_1)^2}$$

PROOF

In the coordinate system in Figure 10.5 are points $P_1\ (x_1, y_1)$ and $P_2\ (x_2, y_2)$. In addition to drawing the segment joining these points, we draw an auxiliary horizontal segment through P_1 and an auxiliary vertical segment through P_2; these meet at point $C\ (x_2, y_1)$ in Figure 10.5(a). Using Figure 10.5(b) and the definitions for lengths of horizontal and vertical segments,

$$P_1C = x_2 - x_1 \quad \text{and} \quad P_2C = y_2 - y_1$$

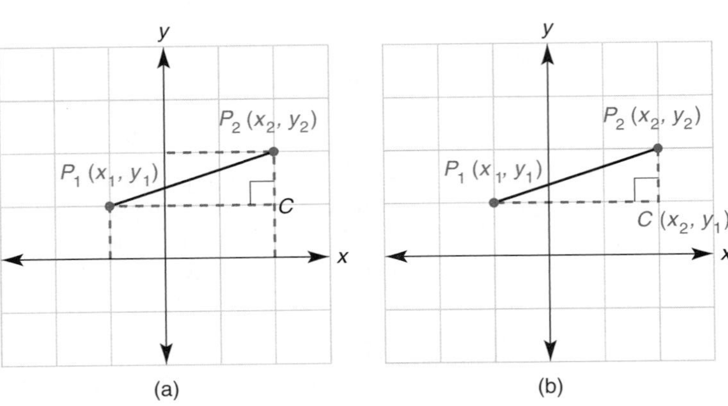

Figure 10.5

In right triangle P_1P_2C in Figure 10.5(b), let $d = P_1P_2$. By the Pythagorean Theorem,

$$d^2 = (x_2 - x_1)^2 + (y_2 - y_1)^2$$

Taking the positive square root for length d yields

$$d = \sqrt{(x_2 - x_1)^2 + (y_2 - y_1)^2}$$ ■

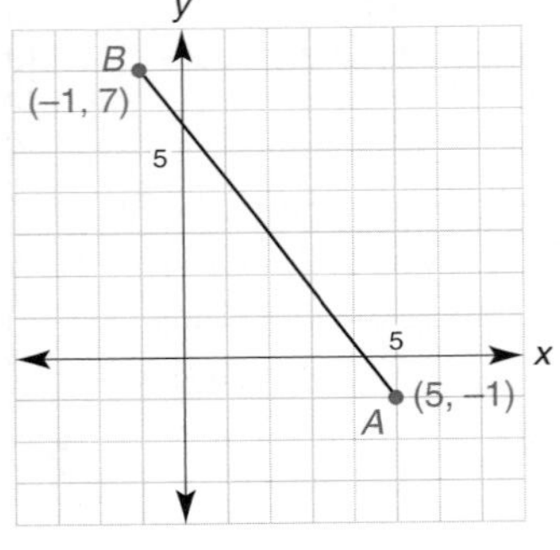

Figure 10.6

Figure 10.7

EXAMPLE 3

In Figure 10.6, find the distance between points $A(5, -1)$ and $B(-1, 7)$.

Solution Using the Distance Formula and choosing $x_1 = 5$ and $y_1 = -1$ (from point A) and $x_2 = -1$ and $y_2 = 7$ (from point B), we obtain

$$\begin{aligned} d &= \sqrt{(-1 - 5)^2 + [7 - (-1)]^2} \\ &= \sqrt{(-6)^2 + (8)^2} = \sqrt{36 + 64} \\ &= \sqrt{100} = 10 \end{aligned}$$

NOTE: If the coordinates of point A were designated as $x_2 = 5$ and $y_2 = -1$ and those of point B were designated as $x_1 = -1$ and $y_1 = 7$, the distance would remain the same. ■

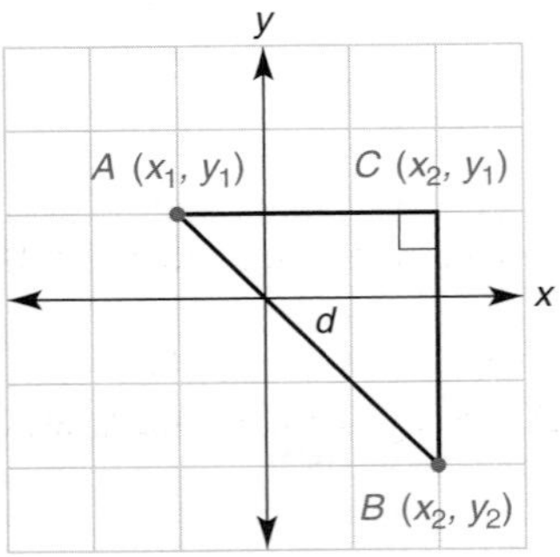

If we look back at the proof of the Distance Formula, Figure 10.5 shows only one of several possible placements of points. If the placement had been as shown in Figure 10.7, then we would have had $AC = x_2 - x_1$ because $x_2 > x_1$, and $BC = y_1 - y_2$ because $y_1 > y_2$. The Pythagorean Theorem leads to what looks like a different result:

$$d^2 = (x_2 - x_1)^2 + (y_1 - y_2)^2$$

But this can be converted to the earlier formula by using the fact that

$$(y_1 - y_2)^2 = (y_2 - y_1)^2$$

This follows from the fact that $(-a)^2 = a^2$ for any real number a.

The following example reminds us of the form of a **linear equation,** an equation whose graph is a straight line. In general, this form is $Ax + By = C$ for constants A, B, and C (where A and B do not both equal 0). We will consider the graphing of linear equations in Section 10.2.

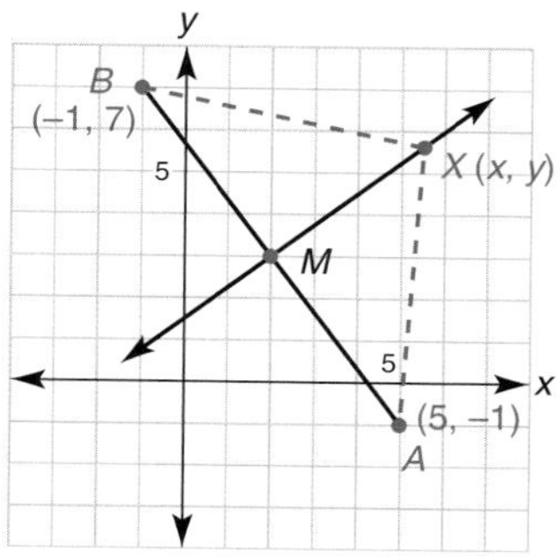

Figure 10.8

EXAMPLE 4

Find the equation that describes all points (x, y) that are equidistant from $A(5, -1)$ and $B(-1, 7)$. See Figure 10.8.

Solution In Chapter 7, we saw that the locus of points equidistant from two fixed points is a line. This line ($\overleftrightarrow{MX}$ in Figure 10.8) is the perpendicular bisector of $\overline{AB}$.

If X is on the locus, then $AX = BX$. By the Distance Formula, we have

$$\sqrt{(x-5)^2 + [y-(-1)]^2} = \sqrt{[x-(-1)]^2 + (y-7)^2}$$

or $$(x-5)^2 + (y+1)^2 = (x+1)^2 + (y-7)^2$$

after simplifying and squaring. Then

$$x^2 - 10x + 25 + y^2 + 2y + 1 = x^2 + 2x + 1 + y^2 - 14y + 49$$

Eliminating x^2 and y^2 terms by subtraction leads to the equation

$$-12x + 16y = 24$$

When we divide by 4, the equation of the line becomes

$$-3x + 4y = 6$$

If we divide the equation $-12x + 16y = 24$ by -4, an equivalent solution is

$$3x - 4y = -6$$ ■

SSG *Exs. 5–8*

Discover

On a number line, x_2 lies to the right of x_1. Then $x_2 > x_1$ and the distance between points is $(x_2 - x_1)$. To find the number a that is midway between x_1 and x_2, we add one-half the distance $(x_2 - x_1)$ to x_1. That is,

$$a = x_1 + \frac{1}{2}(x_2 - x_1).$$

Complete the simplification of a.

ANSWER

$a = \frac{1}{2}(x_1 + x_2)$ or $a = \frac{x_1 + x_2}{2}$

NOTE: The equations $-3x + 4y = 6$ and $3x - 4y = -6$ are said to be **equivalent** because their solutions are the same. For instance, $(-2, 0)$, $(2, 3)$, and $(6, 6)$ are all solutions for *both* equations.

THE MIDPOINT FORMULA

In Figure 10.8, point M is the midpoint of $\overline{AB}$. It will be shown in Example 5(a) that M is the point $(2, 3)$.

A generalized midpoint formula is given in Theorem 10.1.2. The result shows that the coordinates of the midpoint M of a line segment are the averages of the coordinates of the endpoints. See the Discover activity at the left.

THEOREM 10.1.2 ▶ (Midpoint Formula)

The midpoint M of the line segment joining $A(x_1, y_1)$ and $B(x_2, y_2)$ has coordinates x_M and y_M, where

$$(x_M, y_M) = \left(\frac{x_1 + x_2}{2}, \frac{y_1 + y_2}{2}\right)$$

that is,

$$M = \left(\frac{x_1 + x_2}{2}, \frac{y_1 + y_2}{2}\right)$$

To prove the Midpoint Formula, we need to establish two things:

1. $BM + MA = BA$, which establishes that the three points A, M, and B are collinear with A-M-B
2. $BM = MA$, which establishes that point M is midway between A and B

EXAMPLE 5

Use the Midpoint Formula to find the midpoint of the line segment joining:
a) $(5, -1)$ and $(-1, 7)$ b) (a, b) and (c, d)

Solution

a) Using the Midpoint Formula and setting $x_1 = 5$, $y_1 = -1$, $x_2 = -1$, and $y_2 = 7$, we have

$$M = \left(\frac{5 + (-1)}{2}, \frac{-1 + 7}{2}\right) = \left(\frac{4}{2}, \frac{6}{2}\right), \quad \text{so} \quad M = (2, 3)$$

b) Using the Midpoint Formula and setting $x_1 = a$, $y_1 = b$, $x_2 = c$, and $y_2 = d$, we have

$$M = \left(\frac{a + c}{2}, \frac{b + d}{2}\right)$$

■

For Example 5(a), the line segment described is shown in Figure 10.8; from appearances, the solution seems reasonable! In Example 5(b), we are generalizing the coordinates in preparation for the analytic geometry proofs that appear later in the chapter. In those sections, we will choose the x and y values of each point in such a way as to be as general as possible.

Exs. 9–12

PROOF OF THE MIDPOINT FORMULA (OPTIONAL)

For the segment joining P_1 and P_2, we name the midpoint M, as shown in Figure 10.9(a) on page 455. Let the coordinates of M be designated by (x_M, y_M). Now construct horizontal segments through P_1 and M and vertical segments through M and P_2 to intersect at points A and B, as shown in Figure 10.9(b). Because $\angle A$ and $\angle B$ are right angles, $\angle A \cong \angle B$.

Because $\overline{P_1A}$ and $\overline{MB}$ are both horizontal, these segments are parallel, as shown in Figure 10.9(c). Then $\angle 1 \cong \angle 2$ because these are corresponding angles. With $\overline{P_1M} \cong \overline{MP_2}$ by the definition of a midpoint, it follows that $\triangle P_1AM \cong \triangle MBP_2$ by AAS. Because A is the point (x_M, y_1), we have $P_1A = x_M - x_1$. Likewise, the coordinates

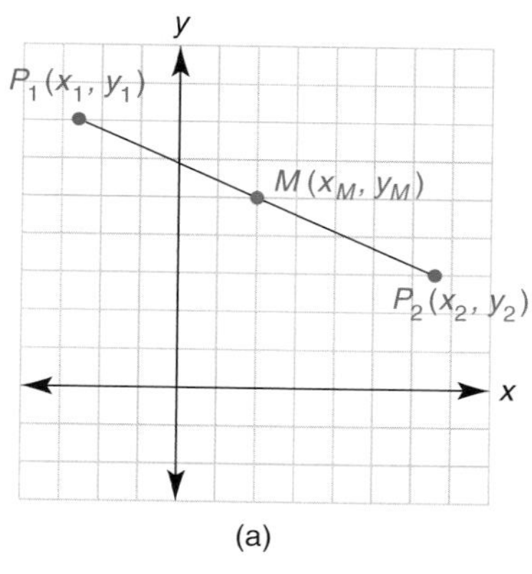

(a)

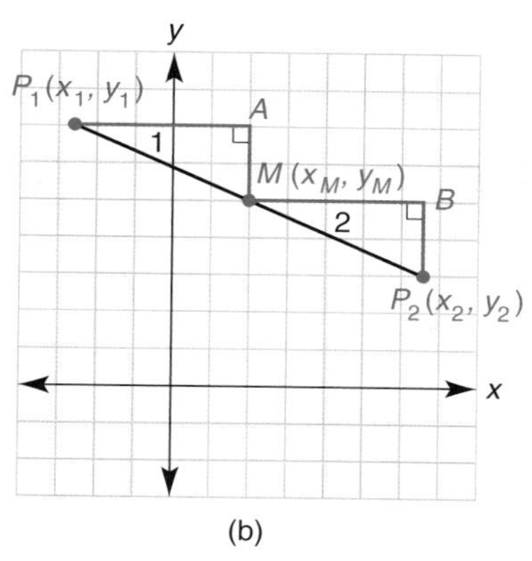

(b)

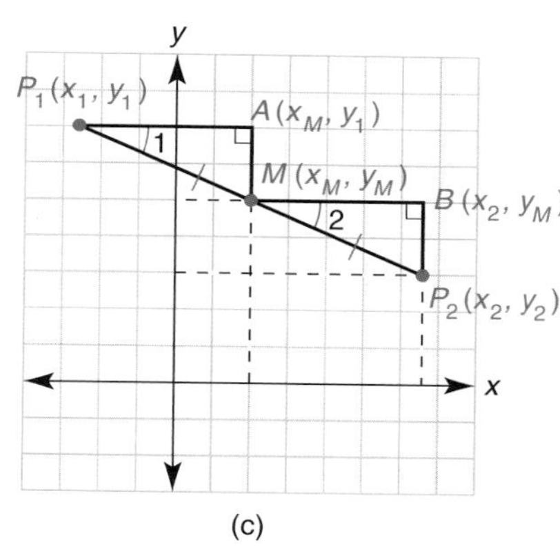

(c)

Figure 10.9

of B are (x_2, y_M), so $MB = x_2 - x_M$. Because $\overline{P_1A} \cong \overline{MB}$ by CPCTC, we represent the common length of the segments $\overline{P_1A}$ and $\overline{MB}$ by a. From the first equation, $x_M - x_1 = a$, so $x_M = x_1 + a$. From the second equation, $x_2 - x_M = a$, so $x_2 = x_M + a$. Substituting $x_1 + a$ for x_M into the second equation, we have

$$(x_1 + a) + a = x_2$$

Then

$$x_1 + 2a = x_2$$
$$2a = x_2 - x_1$$

so

$$a = \frac{x_2 - x_1}{2}$$

It follows that

$$\begin{aligned} x_M &= x_1 + a \\ &= x_1 + \frac{x_2 - x_1}{2} \\ &= \frac{2x_1}{2} + \frac{x_2 - x_1}{2} \\ &= \frac{x_1 + x_2}{2} \end{aligned}$$

Similarly, the y coordinate of the midpoint is $y_M = \frac{y_1 + y_2}{2}$. Then

$$M = \left(\frac{x_1 + x_2}{2}, \frac{y_1 + y_2}{2}\right)$$ ■

Discover

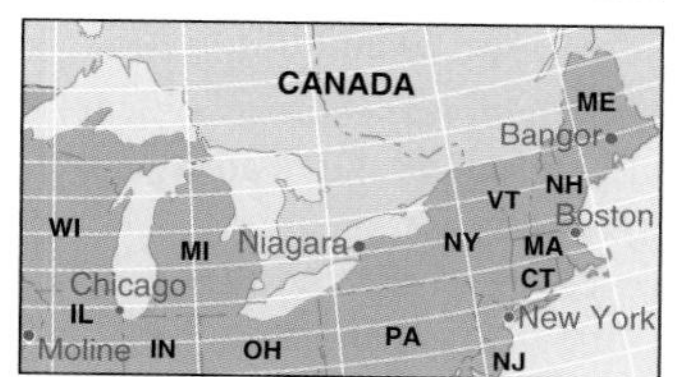

On a map, the approximate coordinates (latitude and longitude) of Bangor, Maine, are 45°N, 70°W and of Moline, Illinois, are 41°N, 90°W. If Niagara Falls has coordinates that are "midway" between those of Bangor and Moline, express its location in coordinates of latitude and longitude.

ANSWER
43°N, 80°W

The following example is based upon the definitions of symmetry with respect to a line and symmetry with respect to a point. Review Section 2.6 if necessary.

EXAMPLE 6

Consider a coordinate system containing the point $A(2, -3)$. Find point B if points A and B have symmetry with respect to:

a) The y axis b) The x axis c) The origin

SSG Exs. 13–15

Solution

a) $(-2, -3)$ b) $(2, 3)$ c) $(-2, 3)$ ■

Exercises 10.1

1. Plot and then label the points $A(0, -3)$, $B(3, -4)$, $C(5, 6)$, $D(-2, -5)$, and $E(-3, 5)$.

2. Give the coordinates of each point A, B, C, D, and E. Also name the quadrant in which each point lies.

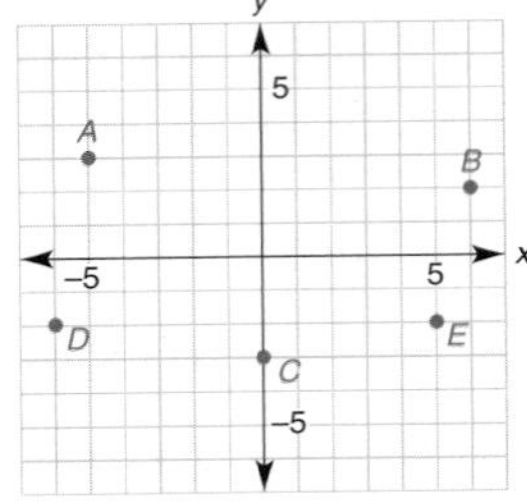

3. Find the distance between each pair of points:
   a) $(5, -3)$ and $(5, 1)$ c) $(0, 2)$ and $(0, -3)$
   b) $(-3, 4)$ and $(5, 4)$ d) $(-2, 0)$ and $(7, 0)$

4. If the distance between $(-2, 3)$ and $(-2, a)$ is 5 units, find all possible values of a.

5. If the distance between $(b, 3)$ and $(7, 3)$ is 3.5 units, find all possible values of b.

6. Find an expression for the distance between (a, b) and (a, c) if $b > c$.

7. Find the distance between each pair of points:
   a) $(0, -3)$ and $(4, 0)$ c) $(3, 2)$ and $(5, -2)$
   b) $(-2, 5)$ and $(4, -3)$ d) $(a, 0)$ and $(0, b)$

8. Find the distance between each pair of points:
   a) $(-3, -7)$ and $(2, 5)$ c) $(-a, -b)$ and (a, b)
   b) $(0, 0)$ and $(-2, 6)$ d) $(2a, 2b)$ and $(2c, 2d)$

9. Find the midpoint of the line segment that joins each pair of points:
   a) $(0, -3)$ and $(4, 0)$ c) $(3, 2)$ and $(5, -2)$
   b) $(-2, 5)$ and $(4, -3)$ d) $(a, 0)$ and $(0, b)$

10. Find the midpoint of the line segment that joins each pair of points:
    a) $(-3, -7)$ and $(2, 5)$ c) $(-a, -b)$ and (a, b)
    b) $(0, 0)$ and $(-2, 6)$ d) $(2a, 2b)$ and $(2c, 2d)$

11. Points A and B have *symmetry with respect to the origin O*. Find the coordinates of B if A is the point:
    a) $(3, -4)$ c) $(a, 0)$
    b) $(0, 2)$ d) (b, c)

12. Points A and B have *symmetry with respect to point* $C(2, 3)$. Find the coordinates of B if A is the point:
    a) $(3, -4)$ c) $(5, 0)$
    b) $(0, 2)$ d) (a, b)

13. Points A and B have *symmetry with respect to point C*. Find the coordinates of C given the points:
    a) $A(3, -4)$ and $B(5, -1)$ c) $A(5, -3)$ and $B(2, 1)$
    b) $A(0, 2)$ and $B(0, 6)$ d) $A(2a, 0)$ and $B(0, 2b)$

14. Points A and B have *symmetry with respect to* the x axis. Find the coordinates of B if A is the point:
    a) $(3, -4)$ c) $(0, a)$
    b) $(0, 2)$ d) (b, c)

15. Points A and B have *symmetry with respect to* the x axis. Find the coordinates of A if B is the point:
    a) $(5, 1)$ c) $(2, a)$
    b) $(0, 5)$ d) (b, c)

16. Points A and B have *symmetry with respect to the vertical line where* $x = 2$. Find the coordinates of A if B is the point:
    a) $(5, 1)$ c) $(-6, a)$
    b) $(0, 5)$ d) (b, c)

17. Points A and B have *symmetry with respect to* the y axis. Find the coordinates of A if B is the point:
    a) $(3, -4)$ c) $(a, 0)$
    b) $(2, 0)$ d) (b, c)

18. Points A and B have *symmetry with respect to* either the x axis or the y axis. Name the axis of symmetry for:
    a) $A(3, -4)$ and $B(3, 4)$ c) $A(3, -4)$ and $B(-3, -4)$
    b) $A(2, 0)$ and $B(-2, 0)$ d) $A(a, b)$ and $B(a, -b)$

19. Points A and B have *symmetry with respect to* a vertical line ($x = a$) or a horizontal line ($y = b$). Give an equation like $x = 3$ for the axis of symmetry for:
    a) $A(3, -4)$ and $B(5, -4)$ c) $A(7, -4)$ and $B(-3, -4)$
    b) $A(a, 0)$ and $B(a, 2b)$ d) $A(a, 7)$ and $B(a, -1)$

In Exercises 20 to 22, apply the Midpoint Formula.

20. $M(3, -4)$ is the midpoint of $\overline{AB}$, in which A is the point $(-5, 7)$. Find the coordinates of B.

21. $M(2.1, -5.7)$ is the midpoint of $\overline{AB}$, in which A is the point $(1.7, 2.3)$. Find the coordinates of B.

22. A circle has its center at the point $(-2, 3)$. If one endpoint of a diameter is at $(3, -5)$, find the other endpoint of the diameter.

23. A rectangle ABCD has three of its vertices at $A(2, -1)$, $B(6, -1)$, and $C(6, 3)$. Find the fourth vertex D and the area of rectangle ABCD.

24. A rectangle MNPQ has three of its vertices at $M(0, 0)$, $N(a, 0)$, and $Q(0, b)$. Find the fourth vertex P and the area of the rectangle MNPQ.

25. Use the Distance Formula to determine the type of triangle that has these vertices:
    a) $A(0, 0)$, $B(4, 0)$, and $C(2, 5)$
    b) $D(0, 0)$, $E(4, 0)$, and $F(2, 2\sqrt{3})$
    c) $G(-5, 2)$, $H(-2, 6)$, and $K(2, 3)$

26. Use the method of Example 4 to find the equation of the line that describes all points equidistant from the points $(-3, 4)$ and $(3, 2)$.

27. Use the method of Example 4 to find the equation of the line that describes all points equidistant from the points $(1, 2)$ and $(4, 5)$.

28. For coplanar points A, B, and C, suppose that you have used the Distance Formula to show that $AB = 5$, $BC = 10$, and $AC = 15$. What can you conclude regarding points A, B, and C?

29. If two vertices of an equilateral triangle are at (0, 0) and (2a, 0), what point is the third vertex?

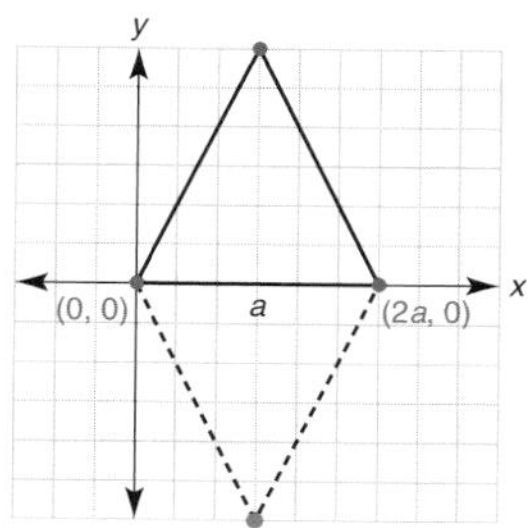

30. The rectangle whose vertices are $A(0, 0)$, $B(a, 0)$, $C(a, b)$, and $D(0, b)$ is shown. Use the Distance Formula to draw a conclusion concerning the lengths of the diagonals $\overline{AC}$ and $\overline{BD}$.

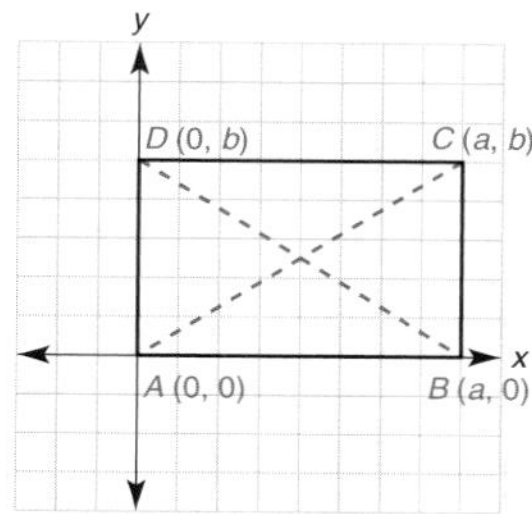

***31.** There are two points on the y axis that are located a distance of 6 units from the point (3, 1). Determine the coordinates of each point.

***32.** There are two points on the x axis that are located a distance of 6 units from the point (3, 1). Determine the coordinates of each point.

33. The triangle that has vertices at $M(-4, 0)$, $N(3, -1)$, and $Q(2, 4)$ has been boxed in as shown. Find the area of $\triangle MNQ$.

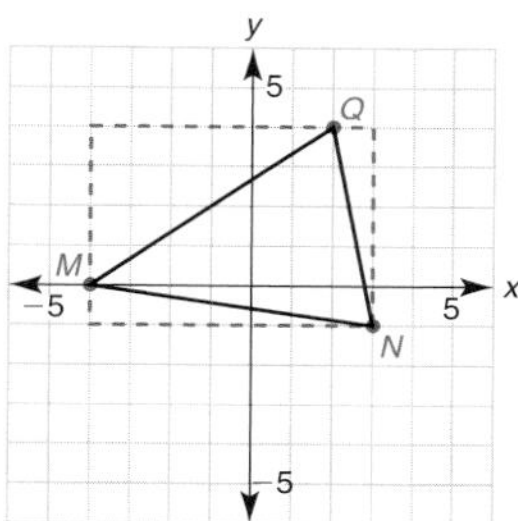

Exercises 33, 34

34. Use the method suggested in Exercise 33 to find the area of $\triangle RST$, with $R(-2, 4)$, $S(-1, -2)$, and $T(6, 5)$.

35. Determine the area of $\triangle ABC$ if $A = (2, 1)$, $B = (5, 3)$, and C is the reflection of B across the x axis.

36. Find the area of $\triangle ABC$ in Exercise 35, but assume that C is the reflection of B across the y axis.

For Exercises 37 to 42, refer to Examples 5 and 6 of Section 9.3.

37. Find the exact volume of the right circular cone that results when the triangular region with vertices at (0, 0), (5, 0), and (0, 9) is rotated about the
a) x axis. b) y axis.

38. Find the exact volume of the solid that results when the triangular region with vertices at (0, 0), (6, 0), and (6, 4) is rotated about the
a) x axis. b) y axis.

39. Find the exact volume of the solid formed when the rectangular region with vertices at (0, 0), (6, 0), (6, 4), and (0, 4) is revolved about the
a) x axis. b) y axis.

40. Find the exact volume of the solid formed when the region bounded in Quadrant I by the axes and the lines $x = 9$ and $y = 5$ is revolved about the
a) x axis. b) y axis.

41. Find the exact lateral area of each solid in Exercise 40.

***42.** Find the volume of the solid formed when the triangular region having vertices at (2, 0), (4, 0), and (2, 4) is rotated about the y axis.

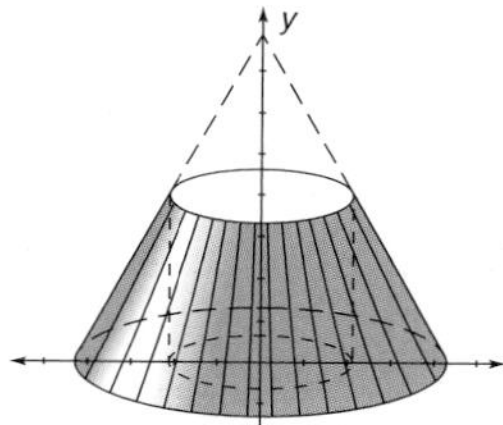

***43.** By definition, an *ellipse* is the locus of points whose sum of distances from two fixed points F_1 and F_2 (called foci) is constant. In the grid provided, find points whose sum of distances from points $F_1(3, 0)$ and $F_2(-3, 0)$ is 10. That is, locate some points for which $PF_1 + PF_2 = 10$; point $P(5, 0)$ is one such point. Then sketch the ellipse.

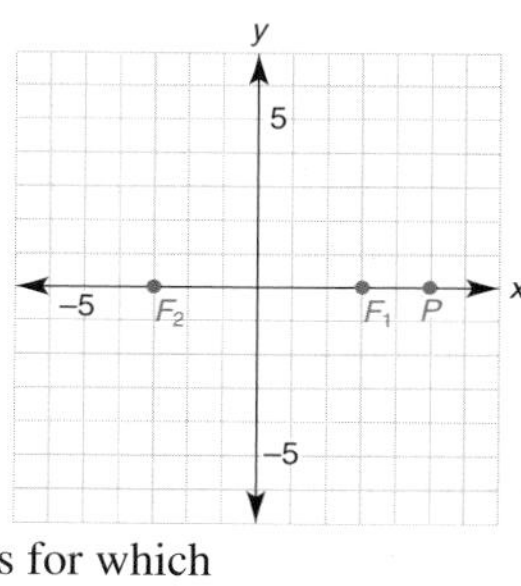

***44.** By definition, a *hyperbola* is the locus of points whose positive difference of distances from two fixed points F_1 and F_2 (called foci) is constant. In the grid provided, find points whose difference of distances from points $F_1(5, 0)$ and $F_2(-5, 0)$ is 6. That is, locate some points for which either $PF_1 - PF_2 = 6$ or $PF_2 - PF_1 = 6$; point $P(3, 0)$ is one such point, Then sketch the hyperbola.

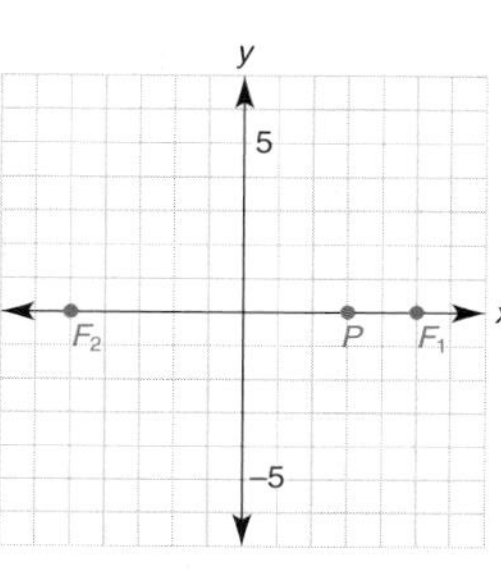

45. Following a 90° counterclockwise rotation about the origin, the image of $A(3, 1)$ is point $B(-1, 3)$. What is the image of point A following a counterclockwise rotation of
    a) 180° about the origin?
    b) 270° about the origin?
    c) 360° about the origin?

46. Consider the point $C(a, b)$. What is the image of C after a counterclockwise rotation of
    a) 90° about the origin?
    b) 180° about the origin?
    c) 360° about the origin?

47. Given the point $D(3, 2)$, find the image of D after a counterclockwise rotation of
    a) 90° about the point $E(3, 4)$.
    b) 180° about the point $F(4, 5)$.
    c) 360° about the point $G(a, b)$.

10.2 Graphs of Linear Equations and Slope

KEY CONCEPTS

Graphs of Equations	y Intercept	Slope Formula
x Intercept	Slope	Negative Reciprocal

In Section 10.1, we were reminded that the general form of the equation of a line is $Ax + By = C$ (where A and B do not both equal 0). Some examples of linear equations are $2x + 3y = 12$, $3x - 4y = 12$, and $3x = -6$; as we shall see, the graph of each of these equations is a line.

THE GRAPH OF AN EQUATION

DEFINITION

The **graph of an equation** is the set of all points (x, y) in the rectangular coordinate system whose ordered pairs satisfy the equation.

EXAMPLE 1

Draw the graph of the equation $2x + 3y = 12$.

Solution We begin by completing a table. It is convenient to use one point for which $x = 0$, a second point for which $y = 0$, and a third point as a check for collinearity.

$$x = 0 \rightarrow 2(0) + 3y = 12 \rightarrow y = 4$$
$$y = 0 \rightarrow 2x + 3(0) = 12 \rightarrow x = 6$$
$$x = 3 \rightarrow 2(3) + 3y = 12 \rightarrow y = 2$$

x	y	(x, y)
0	4	(0, 4)
6	0	(6, 0)
3	2	(3, 2)

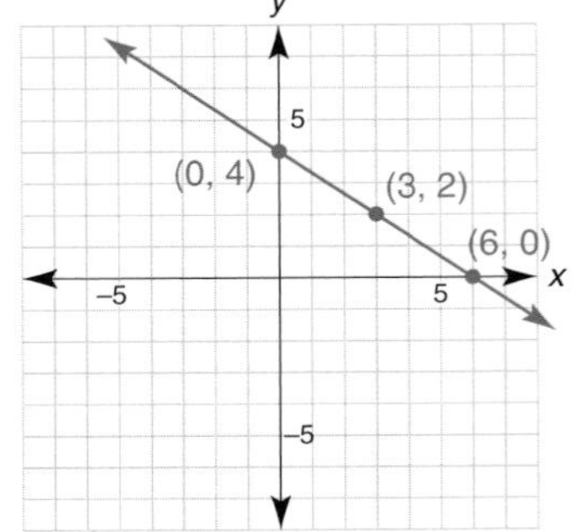

Figure 10.10

SSG *Exs. 1–3*

Upon plotting the third point, we see that the three points are collinear. The graph of a linear equation must be a straight line, as shown in Figure 10.10. ■

Technology Exploration

Use a graphing calculator if one is available.

1. To graph $2x + 3y = 12$, solve for y.
2. Enter your result from part (1) as the value of Y_1.

$$[Y_1 = -\left(\frac{2}{3}\right)x + 4]$$

3. Now GRAPH to see the line of Figure 10.10.

Because the graph in Example 1 is a locus, every point on the line must also satisfy the given equation. Notice that the point $(-3, 6)$ lies on the line shown in Figure 10.10. This ordered pair also satisfies the equation $2x + 3y = 12$; that is, $2(-3) + 3(6) = 12$ because $-6 + 18 = 12$.

For the equation in Example 1, the number 6 is known as the ***x* intercept** because $(6, 0)$ is the point at which the graph crosses the x axis; similarly, the number 4 is known as the ***y* intercept.** Most linear equations have two intercepts; these are generally represented by a (the x intercept) and b (the y intercept).

For the equation $Ax + By = C$, we determine the

a) x intercept by choosing $y = 0$. Solve the resulting equation for x.
b) y intercept by choosing $x = 0$. Solve the resulting equation for y.

EXAMPLE 2

Find the x and y intercepts of the equation $3x - 4y = -12$, and use them to graph the equation.

Solution The x intercept is found when $y = 0$; $3x - 4(0) = -12$, so $x = -4$. The x intercept is $a = -4$, so $(-4, 0)$ is on the graph. The y intercept results when $x = 0$; $3(0) - 4y = -12$, so $y = 3$. The y intercept is $b = 3$, so $(0, 3)$ is on the graph. Once the points $(-4, 0)$ and $(0, 3)$ have been plotted, the graph can be completed by drawing the line through these points. See Figure 10.11. ■

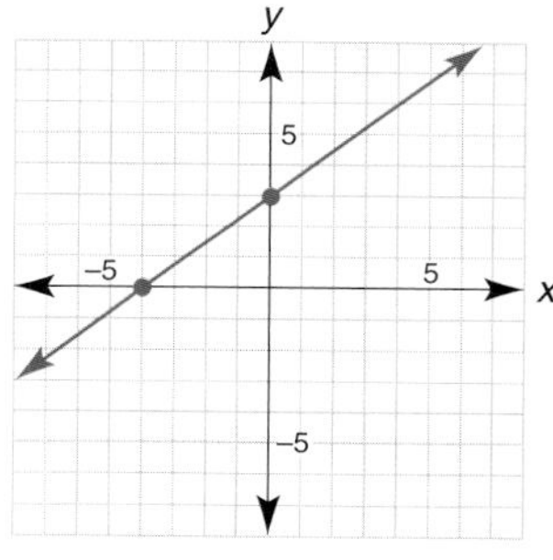

Figure 10.11

As we shall see in Example 3, a linear equation may have only one intercept. It is impossible for a linear equation to have no intercepts whatsoever.

EXAMPLE 3

Draw the graphs of the following equations:

a) $x = -2$ b) $y = 3$

Solution First note that each equation is a linear equation and can be written in the form $Ax + By = C$.

$x = -2$ is equivalent to $(1 \cdot x) + (0 \cdot y) = -2$
$y = 3$ is equivalent to $(0 \cdot x) + (1 \cdot y) = 3$

a) The equation $x = -2$ claims that the value of x is -2 regardless of the value of y; this leads to the following table:

x	y	$\rightarrow$	(x, y)
-2	-2	$\rightarrow$	$(-2, -2)$
-2	0	$\rightarrow$	$(-2, 0)$
-2	5	$\rightarrow$	$(-2, 5)$

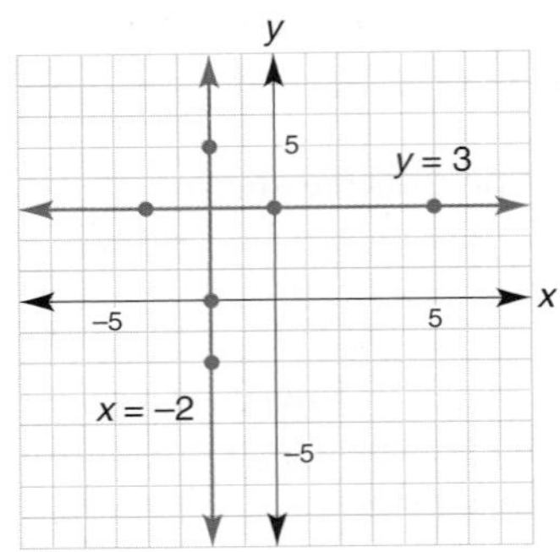

Figure 10.12

b) The equation $y = 3$ claims that the value of y is 3 regardless of the value of x; this leads to the following table:

x	y	→	(x, y)
−4	3	→	(−4, 3)
0	3	→	(0, 3)
5	3	→	(5, 3)

The graphs of the equations are shown in Figure 10.12. ■

NOTE: When an equation can be written in the form $x = a$ (for constant a), its graph is the vertical line containing the point $(a, 0)$. When an equation can be written in the form $y = b$ (for constant b), its graph is the horizontal line containing the point $(0, b)$.

Exs. 4–8

THE SLOPE OF A LINE

Most lines are oblique; that is, the line is neither horizontal nor vertical. Especially for oblique lines, it is convenient to describe the amount of "slant" by a number called the *slope* of the line.

DEFINITION ▶ (Slope Formula)

The slope of the line that contains the points (x_1, y_1) and (x_2, y_2) is given by

$$m = \frac{y_2 - y_1}{x_2 - x_1} \text{ for } x_1 \neq x_2$$

NOTE: When $x_1 = x_2$, the denominator of the Slope Formula becomes 0 and we say that the slope of the line is undefined.

Whereas the uppercase italic M means midpoint, we use the lowercase italic m for slope. Other terms that are used to describe the slope of a line include *pitch* and *grade.* A carpenter may say that a roofline has a $\frac{5}{12}$ pitch. [See Figure 10.13(a).] In constructing a stretch of roadway, an engineer may say that this part of the roadway has a grade of $\frac{3}{100}$, or 3 percent. [See Figure 10.13(b).]

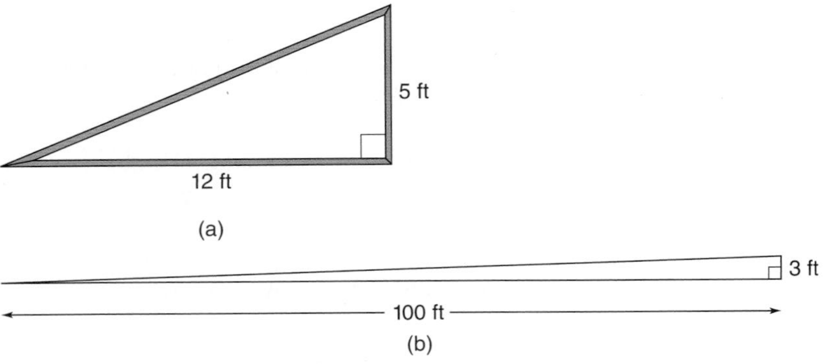

Figure 10.13

Whether in geometry, carpentry, or engineering, the **slope** of a line is a number. The slope of the line is the ratio of the change along the vertical to the change along the horizontal. For any two points on the line in question, a line that "rises" from left to right has a *positive* slope, and a line that "falls" from left to right has a *negative* slope. The lines shown in Figures 10.14(a) and (b) confirm these claims.

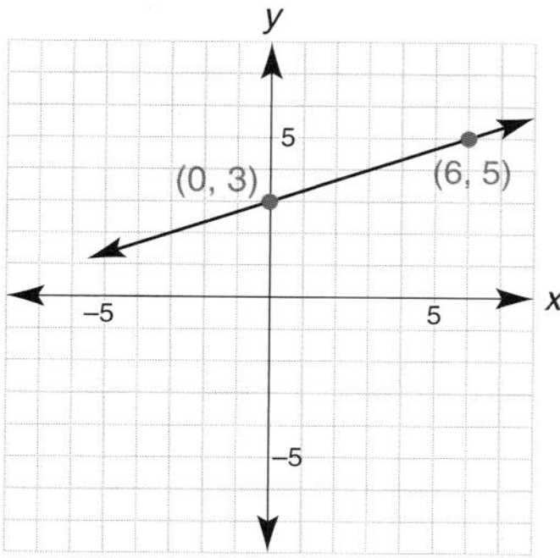

$$m = \frac{y_2 - y_1}{x_2 - x_1}$$

$$m = \frac{5 - 3}{6 - 0} = \frac{2}{6} = \frac{1}{3}$$

(a)

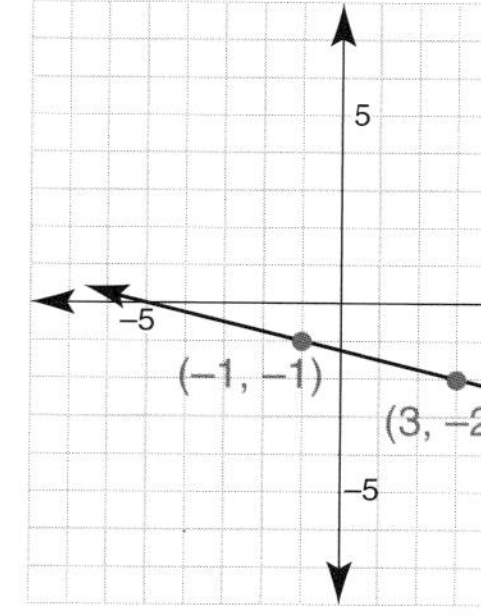

$$m = \frac{y_2 - y_1}{x_2 - x_1}$$

$$m = \frac{-2 - (-1)}{3 - (-1)} = -\frac{1}{4}$$

(b)

Figure 10.14

Any horizontal line has slope 0; any vertical line has an undefined slope. Figure 10.15 shows an example of each of these types of lines.

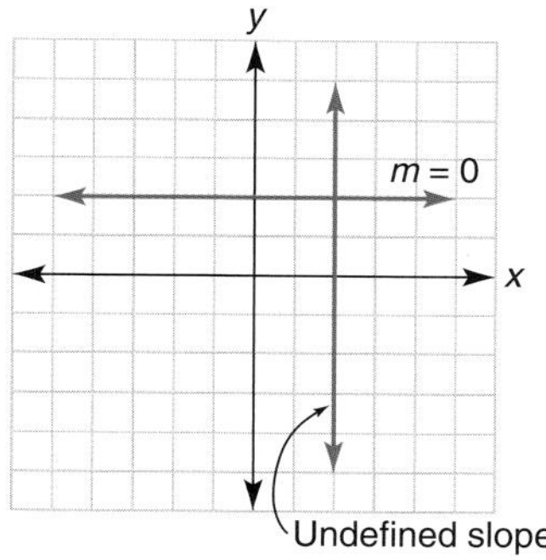

Figure 10.15

EXAMPLE 4

Without graphing, find the slope of the line that contains:

a) (2, 2) and (5, 3) b) (1, −1) and (1, 3)

Solution

a) Using the Slope Formula and choosing $x_1 = 2$, $y_1 = 2$, $x_2 = 5$, and $y_2 = 3$, we have

$$m = \frac{3 - 2}{5 - 2} = \frac{1}{3}$$

NOTE: If drawn, the line in part (a) will slant upward from left to right.

b) Let $x_1 = 1$, $y_1 = -1$, $x_2 = 1$, and $y_2 = 3$. Then we calculate

$$m = \frac{3 - (-1)}{1 - 1} = \frac{4}{0}$$

which is undefined.

NOTE: If drawn, the line in part (b) will be vertical because the x coordinates of the points are the same. ■

Reminder

In the Slope Formula, be sure to write the difference in values of y in the numerator; that is,

$$m = \frac{y_2 - y_1}{x_2 - x_1}$$

SSG *Exs. 9–12*

The slope of a line is unique; that is, the slope does not change when:

1. The order of the two points is reversed in the Slope Formula.
2. Different points on the line are selected.

The first situation is true because $\frac{-a}{-b} = \frac{a}{b}$. The second situation is more difficult to explain because it depends on similar triangles.

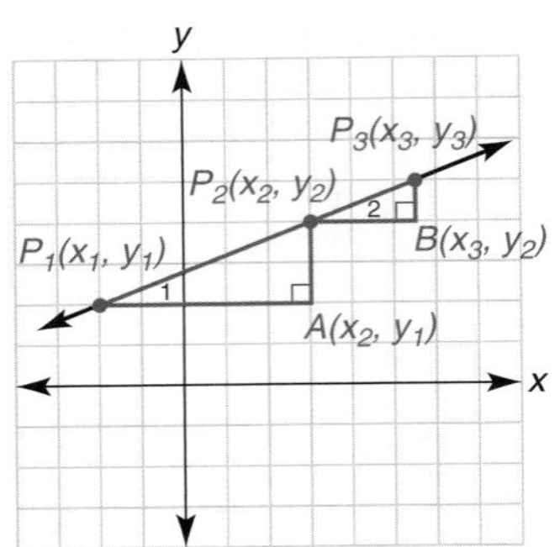

Figure 10.16

For an explanation of point 2, consider Figure 10.16, in which points P_1, P_2, and P_3 are collinear. We wish to show that the slope of the line is the same whether P_1 and P_2, or P_2 and P_3, are used in the Slope Formula. If horizontal and vertical segments are drawn as shown in Figure 10.16, we can show that triangles P_1P_2A and P_2P_3B are similar. The similarity follows from the facts that $\angle 1 \cong \angle 2$ (because $\overline{P_1A} \parallel \overline{P_2B}$) and that $\angle A$ and $\angle B$ are right angles. Then $\frac{P_2A}{P_3B} = \frac{P_1A}{P_2B}$ because these are corresponding sides of similar triangles. By interchanging the means, we have $\frac{P_2A}{P_1A} = \frac{P_3B}{P_2B}$. But

$$\frac{P_2A}{P_1A} = \frac{y_2 - y_1}{x_2 - x_1} \quad \text{and} \quad \frac{P_3B}{P_2B} = \frac{y_3 - y_2}{x_3 - x_2}$$

so

$$\frac{y_2 - y_1}{x_2 - x_1} = \frac{y_3 - y_2}{x_3 - x_2}$$

Thus, the slope of the line is not changed by our having used either pair of points. In summary, the slopes agree because of similar triangles.

If points P_1, P_2, and P_3 are collinear, then the slopes of $\overline{P_1P_2}$, $\overline{P_1P_3}$, and $\overline{P_2P_3}$ are the same. The converse of this statement is also true. If the slopes of $\overline{P_1P_2}$, $\overline{P_1P_3}$, and $\overline{P_2P_3}$ are equal, then P_1, P_2, and P_3 are collinear. See Example 5 for an application.

EXAMPLE 5

Are the points $A(2, -3)$, $B(5, 1)$, and $C(-4, -11)$ collinear?

Solution Let $m_{\overline{AB}}$ and $m_{\overline{BC}}$ represent the slopes of $\overline{AB}$ and $\overline{BC}$, respectively. By the Slope Formula, we have

$$m_{\overline{AB}} = \frac{1 - (-3)}{5 - 2} = \frac{4}{3} \quad \text{and} \quad m_{\overline{BC}} = \frac{-11 - 1}{-4 - 5} = \frac{-12}{-9} = \frac{4}{3}$$

Because $m_{\overline{AB}} = m_{\overline{BC}}$, it follows that A, B, and C are collinear. ■

As we trace a line from one point to a second point, the Slope Formula tells us that

$$m = \frac{\text{change in } y}{\text{change in } x} \quad \text{or} \quad m = \frac{\text{vertical change}}{\text{horizontal change}}$$

SSG *Exs. 13–15*

This interpretation of slope is used in Example 6.

EXAMPLE 6

Draw the line through $(-1, 5)$ with slope $m = -\frac{2}{3}$.

Solution First we plot the point $(-1, 5)$. The slope can be written as $m = \frac{-2}{3}$. Thus, we let the change in y from the first to the second point be -2 while the change in x is 3. From the first point $(-1, 5)$, we locate the second point by moving 2 units down and 3 units to the right. The line is then drawn as shown in Figure 10.17. ■

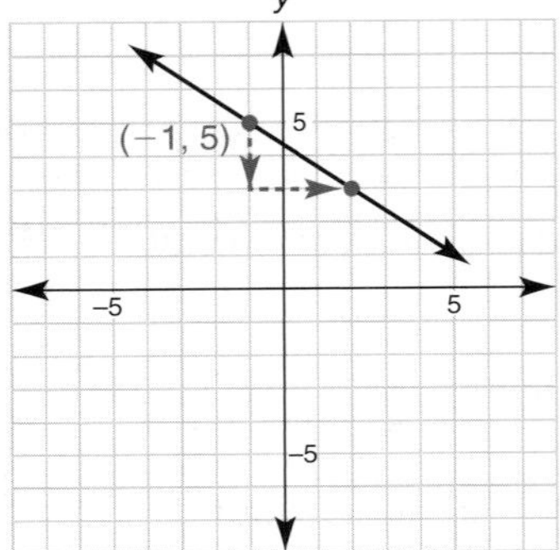

Figure 10.17

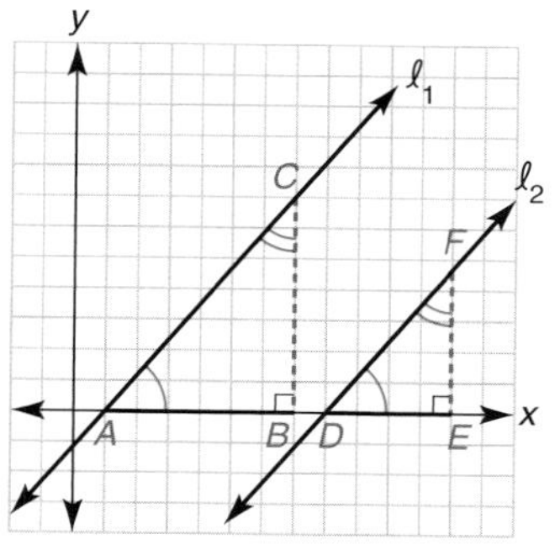

Figure 10.18

Two theorems are now stated without proof. However, drawings that can be used in the exercises following this section are provided. Each proof depends on similar triangles created through the use of the auxiliary segments found in the drawings.

THEOREM 10.2.1

If two nonvertical lines are parallel, then their slopes are equal.
Alternative Form: If $\ell_1 \parallel \ell_2$, then $m_1 = m_2$.

In Figure 10.18, note that $\overline{AC} \parallel \overline{DF}$. Also, $\overline{AB}$ and $\overline{DE}$ are horizontal, and $\overline{BC}$ and $\overline{EF}$ are auxiliary vertical segments. In the proof of Theorem 10.2.1, the goal is to show that $m_{\overline{AC}} = m_{\overline{DF}}$. The converse of Theorem 10.2.1 is also true; that is, if $m_1 = m_2$, then $\ell_1 \parallel \ell_2$.

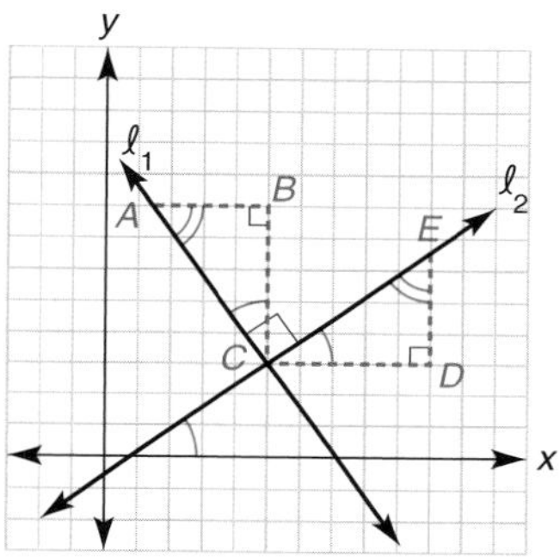

Figure 10.19

THEOREM 10.2.2

If two lines (neither horizontal nor vertical) are perpendicular, then the product of their slopes is -1.
Alternative Form: If $\ell_1 \perp \ell_2$, then $m_1 \cdot m_2 = -1$.

In Figure 10.19, auxiliary segments have been included. To prove Theorem 10.2.2, we need to show that $m_{\overline{AC}} \cdot m_{\overline{CE}} = -1$. Because the product of the slopes is -1, the slopes are **negative reciprocals.** In general, negative reciprocals take the forms $\frac{a}{b}$ and $\frac{-b}{a}$. The converse of Theorem 10.2.2 is also true; if $m_1 \cdot m_2 = -1$, then $\ell_1 \perp \ell_2$.

EXAMPLE 7

Given the points $A(-2, 3)$, $B(2, 1)$, $C(-1, 8)$, and $D(7, 3)$, are $\overline{AB}$ and $\overline{CD}$ parallel, perpendicular, or neither? (See Figure 10.20.)

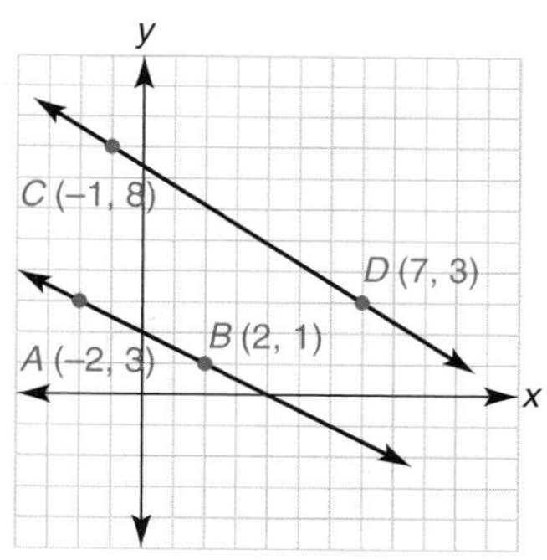

Figure 10.20

Solution

$$m_{\overline{AB}} = \frac{1 - 3}{2 - (-2)} = \frac{-2}{4} = -\frac{1}{2}$$
$$m_{\overline{CD}} = \frac{3 - 8}{7 - (-1)} = \frac{-5}{8} \text{ or } -\frac{5}{8}$$

Because $m_{\overline{AB}} \neq m_{\overline{CD}}$, $\overline{AB} \nparallel \overline{CD}$. The slopes are not negative reciprocals, so $\overline{AB}$ is not perpendicular to $\overline{CD}$. Neither relationship holds for $\overline{AB}$ and $\overline{CD}$. ■

SSG *Exs. 16–18*

In Example 7, it was worthwhile to sketch the lines described. It is apparent from Figure 10.20 that the lines are not perpendicular. A sketch may help to show that a relationship does *not* exist, but sketching is not a precise method for showing that lines are parallel or perpendicular.

EXAMPLE 8

Are the lines that are the graphs of $2x + 3y = 6$ and $3x - 2y = 12$ parallel, perpendicular, or neither?

Solution Because $2x + 3y = 6$ contains the points (3, 0) and (0, 2), its slope is $\frac{2-0}{0-3} = -\frac{2}{3}$. The line $3x - 2y = 12$ contains (0, −6) and (4, 0); thus, its slope is equal to $\frac{0-(-6)}{4-0} = \frac{6}{4}$ or $\frac{3}{2}$. Because the product of the slopes is $-\frac{2}{3} \cdot \frac{3}{2}$, or -1, the lines described are perpendicular. ■

EXAMPLE 9

Determine the value of a for which the line through (2, −3) and (5, a) is perpendicular to the line $3x + 4y = 12$.

Solution The line $3x + 4y = 12$ contains the points (4, 0) and (0, 3); this line has the slope

$$m = \frac{3-0}{0-4} = -\frac{3}{4}$$

For the two lines to be perpendicular, the second line must have slope $\frac{4}{3}$. Using the Slope Formula, we find that the second line has the slope

$$\frac{a-(-3)}{5-2}$$

so

$$\frac{a+3}{3} = \frac{4}{3}$$

Multiplying by 3, we obtain $a + 3 = 4$. It follows that $a = 1$. ■

EXAMPLE 10

In Figure 10.21, show that the quadrilateral with vertices $A(0, 0)$, $B(a, 0)$, $C(a, b)$, and $D(0, b)$ is a rectangle.

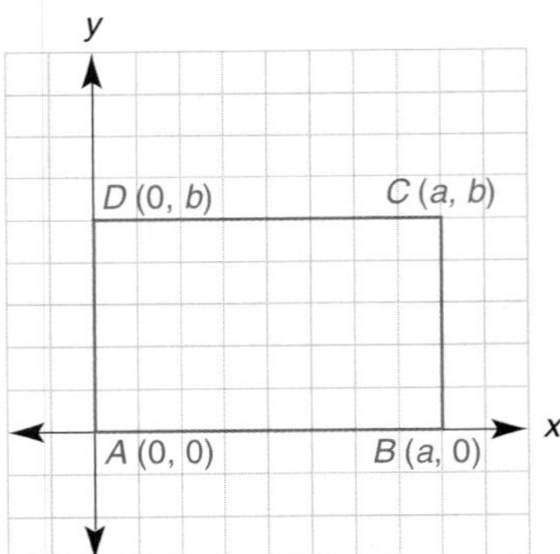

Figure 10.21

Solution By applying the Slope Formula, we see that

$$m_{\overline{AB}} = \frac{0-0}{a-0} = 0$$

and

$$m_{\overline{DC}} = \frac{b-b}{a-0} = 0$$

Then $\overline{AB}$ and $\overline{DC}$ are horizontal and therefore parallel to each other.

For $\overline{DA}$ and $\overline{CB}$, the slopes are undefined because the denominators in the Slope Formula both equal 0. Then $\overline{DA}$ and $\overline{CB}$ are both vertical and therefore parallel to each other.

SSG Ex. 19

Thus, $ABCD$ is a parallelogram. With $\overline{AB}$ being horizontal and $\overline{DA}$ vertical, it follows that $\overline{DA} \perp \overline{AB}$. Therefore, $ABCD$ is a rectangle by definition. ■

Exercises 10.2

In Exercises 1 to 8, draw the graph of each equation. Name any intercepts.

1. $3x + 4y = 12$
2. $3x + 5y = 15$
3. $x - 2y = 5$
4. $x - 3y = 4$
5. $2x + 6 = 0$
6. $3y - 9 = 0$
7. $\frac{1}{2}x + y = 3$
8. $\frac{2}{3}x - y = 1$
9. Find the slopes of the lines containing:
   a) $(2, -3)$ and $(4, 5)$
   b) $(3, -2)$ and $(3, 7)$
   c) $(1, -1)$ and $(2, -2)$
   d) $(-2.7, 5)$ and $(-1.3, 5)$
   e) (a, b) and (c, d)
   f) $(a, 0)$ and $(0, b)$
10. Find the slopes of the lines containing:
   a) $(3, -5)$ and $(-1, 2)$
   b) $(-2, -3)$ and $(-5, -7)$
   c) $(2\sqrt{2}, -3\sqrt{6})$ and $(3\sqrt{2}, 5\sqrt{6})$
   d) $(\sqrt{2}, \sqrt{7})$ and $(\sqrt{2}, \sqrt{3})$
   e) $(a, 0)$ and $(a + b, c)$
   f) (a, b) and $(-b, -a)$
11. Find x so that $\overline{AB}$ has slope m, where:
   a) A is $(2, -3)$, B is $(x, 5)$, and $m = 1$
   b) A is $(x, -1)$, B is $(3, 5)$, and $m = -0.5$
12. Find y so that $\overline{CD}$ has slope m, where:
   a) C is $(2, -3)$, D is $(4, y)$, and $m = \frac{3}{2}$
   b) C is $(-1, -4)$, D is $(3, y)$, and $m = -\frac{2}{3}$
13. Are these points collinear?
   a) $A(-2, 5)$, $B(0, 2)$, and $C(4, -4)$
   b) $D(-1, -1)$, $E(2, -2)$, and $F(5, -5)$
14. Are these points collinear?
   a) $A(-1, -2)$, $B(3, 2)$, and $C(5, 5)$
   b) $D(a, c - d)$, $E(b, c)$, and $F(2b - a, c + d)$
15. Parallel lines ℓ_1 and ℓ_2 have slopes m_1 and m_2, respectively. Find m_2 if m_1 equals:
   a) $\frac{3}{4}$ b) $-\frac{5}{3}$ c) -2 d) $\frac{a - b}{c}$
16. Parallel lines ℓ_1 and ℓ_2 have slopes m_1 and m_2, respectively. Find m_2 if m_1 equals:
   a) $\frac{4}{5}$ b) $-\frac{1}{5}$ c) 3 d) $\frac{f + g}{h + j}$
17. Perpendicular lines ℓ_1 and ℓ_2 have slopes m_1 and m_2, respectively. Find m_2 if m_1 equals:
   a) $-\frac{1}{2}$ b) $\frac{3}{4}$ c) 3 d) $\frac{f + g}{h + j}$
18. Perpendicular lines ℓ_1 and ℓ_2 have slopes m_1 and m_2, respectively. Find m_2 if m_1 equals:
   a) 5 b) $-\frac{5}{3}$ c) $-\frac{1}{2}$ d) $\frac{a - b}{c}$

In Exercises 19 to 22, state whether the lines are parallel, perpendicular, the same, or none of these.

19. $2x + 3y = 6$ and $2x - 3y = 12$
20. $2x + 3y = 6$ and $4x + 6y = -12$
21. $2x + 3y = 6$ and $3x - 2y = 12$
22. $2x + 3y = 6$ and $4x + 6y = 12$
23. Find x such that the points $A(x, 5)$, $B(2, 3)$, and $C(4, -5)$ are collinear.
24. Find a such that the points $A(1, 3)$, $B(4, 5)$, and $C(a, a)$ are collinear.
25. Find x such that the line through $(2, -3)$ and $(3, 2)$ is perpendicular to the line through $(-2, 4)$ and $(x, -1)$.
26. Find x such that the line through $(2, -3)$ and $(3, 2)$ is parallel to the line through $(-2, 4)$ and $(x, -1)$.

In Exercises 27 to 32, draw the line described.

27. Through $(3, -2)$ and with $m = 2$
28. Through $(-2, -5)$ and with $m = \frac{5}{7}$
29. With y intercept 5 and with $m = -\frac{3}{4}$
30. With x intercept -3 and with $m = 0.25$
31. Through $(-2, 1)$ and parallel to the line $2x - y = 6$
32. Through $(-2, 1)$ and perpendicular to the line that has intercepts $a = -2$ and $b = 3$
33. Use slopes to decide whether the triangle with vertices at $(6, 5)$, $(-3, 0)$, and $(4, -2)$ is a right triangle.
34. If $A(2, 2)$, $B(7, 3)$, and $C(4, x)$ are the vertices of a right triangle with right angle C, find the value of x.
*35. If $(2, 3)$, $(5, -2)$, and $(7, 2)$ are three vertices (not necessarily consecutive) of a parallelogram, find the possible locations of the fourth vertex.
36. Three vertices of rectangle $ABCD$ are $A(-5, 1)$, $B(-2, -3)$, and $C(6, y)$. Find the value of y and also the fourth vertex.
37. Show that quadrilateral $RSTV$ is an isosceles trapezoid.

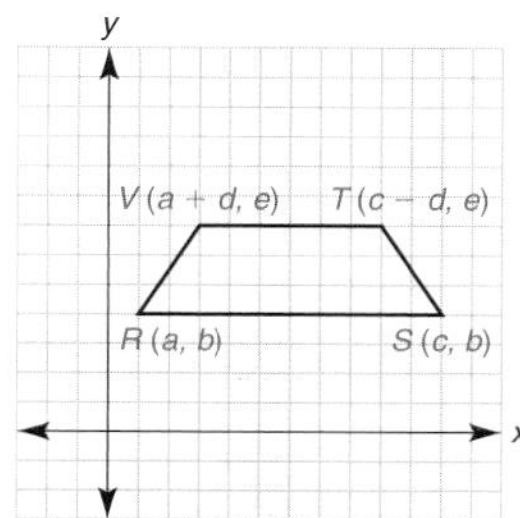

38. Show that quadrilateral $ABCD$ is a parallelogram.

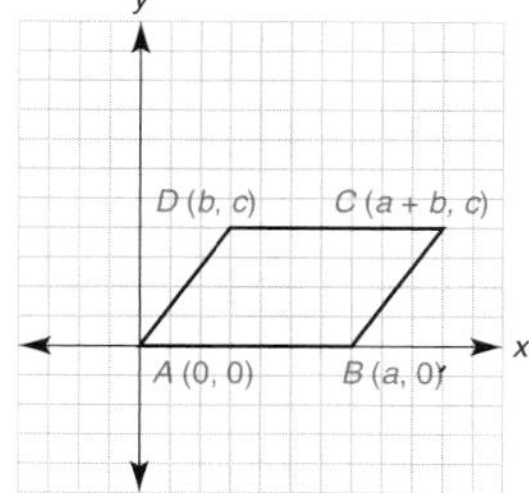

39. Quadrilateral *EFGH* has the vertices $E(0, 0)$, $F(a, 0)$, $G(a + b, c)$, and $H(2b, 2c)$. Verify that *EFGH* is a trapezoid by showing that the slopes of two sides are equal.

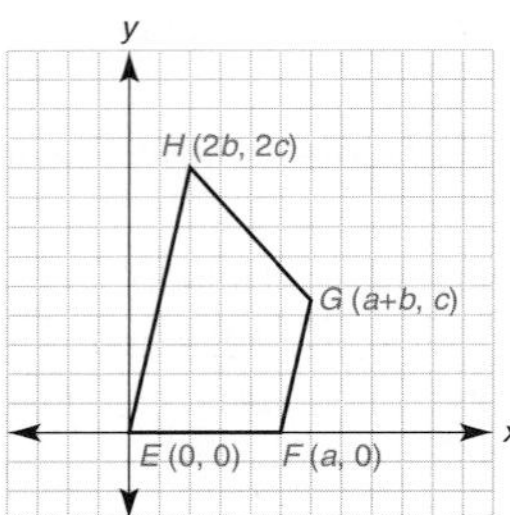

40. Find an equation involving *a, b, c, d,* and *e* if $\overleftrightarrow{AC} \perp \overleftrightarrow{BC}$.

(HINT: Use slopes.)

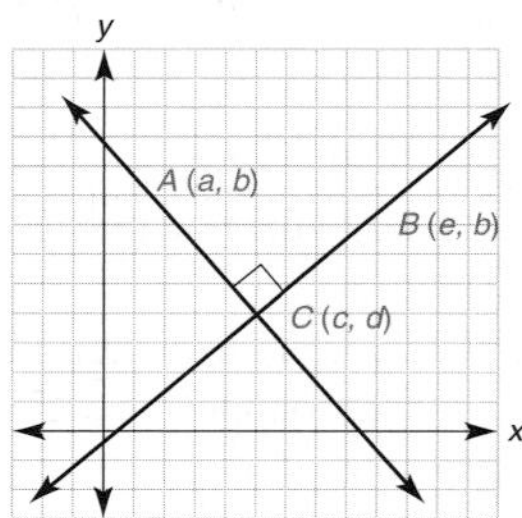

41. Prove that if two nonvertical lines are parallel, then their slopes are equal.

(HINT: See Figure 10.18.)

***42.** Prove that if two lines (neither horizontal nor vertical) are perpendicular, then the product of their slopes is -1.

(HINT: See Figure 10.19. You need to show and use the fact that $\triangle ABC \sim \triangle EDC$.)

***43.** Where $m < 0$ and $b > 0$, the graph of $y = mx + b$ (along with the *x* and *y* axes) determines a triangular region in Quadrant I. Find an expression for the area of the triangle in terms of *m* and *b*.

***44.** Where $m > 0$, $a > 0$, and $b > 0$, the graph of $y = mx + b$, the axes, and the vertical line through $(a, 0)$ determines a trapezoidal region in Quadrant I. Find an expression for the area of this trapezoid in terms of *a*, *b*, and *m*.

10.3 Preparing to Do Analytic Proofs

KEY CONCEPTS Formulas and Relationships Placement of Figure

In this section, we lay the groundwork for constructing analytic proofs of geometric theorems. An analytic proof requires the use of the coördinate system and the application of the formulas found in earlier sections of this chapter. Because of the need for these formulas, a summary follows. Be sure that you have these formulas memorized and know when and how to use them.

FORMULAS OF ANALYTIC GEOMETRY

Distance	$d = \sqrt{(x_2 - x_1)^2 + (y_2 - y_1)^2}$
Midpoint	$M = \left(\frac{x_1 + x_2}{2}, \frac{y_1 + y_2}{2}\right)$
Slope	$m = \frac{y_2 - y_1}{x_2 - x_1}$ where $x_1 \neq x_2$
Special relationships for lines	$\ell_1 \parallel \ell_2 \leftrightarrow m_1 = m_2$ $\ell_1 \perp \ell_2 \leftrightarrow m_1 \cdot m_2 = -1$

NOTE: Neither ℓ_1 nor ℓ_2 is a vertical line in the preceding claims.

SSG *Exs. 1–6*

To see how the preceding list might be used, consider the following examples.

EXAMPLE 1

Suppose that you are to prove the following relationships:
a) Two lines are parallel.
b) Two lines are perpendicular.
c) Two line segments are congruent.
Which formula(s) would you need to use? How would you complete your proof?

Solution
a) Use the Slope Formula to find the slope of each line. Then show that the slopes are equal.
b) Use the Slope Formula to find the slope of each line. Then show that $m_1 \cdot m_2 = -1$.
c) Use the Distance Formula to find the length of each line segment. Then show that the resulting lengths are equal. ■

The following example has a proof that is subtle. A drawing is provided to help you understand the concept.

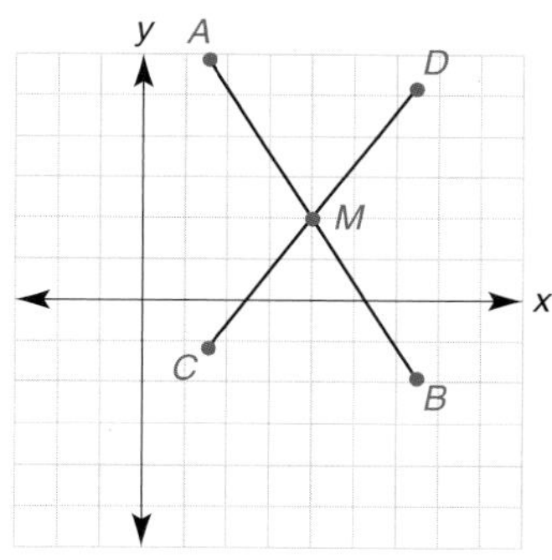

Figure 10.22

EXAMPLE 2

How can the Midpoint Formula be used to verify that the two line segments shown in Figure 10.22 bisect each other?

Solution If $\overline{AB}$ bisects $\overline{CD}$, and conversely, then M is the common midpoint of the two line segments. The Midpoint Formula is used to find the midpoint of each line segment, and the results are then shown to be the same point. This establishes that each line segment has been bisected at a point that is on the other line segment. ■

EXAMPLE 3

Suppose that line ℓ_1 has slope $\frac{c}{d}$. Use this fact to identify the slopes of the following lines:

a) ℓ_2 if $\ell_1 \parallel \ell_2$
b) ℓ_3 if $\ell_1 \perp \ell_3$

Solution
a) $m_2 = \frac{c}{d}$ ($m_1 = m_2$ when $\ell_1 \parallel \ell_2$.)
b) $m_3 = -\frac{d}{c}$ ($m_1 \cdot m_3 = -1$ when $\ell_1 \perp \ell_3$.) ■

EXAMPLE 4

What can you conclude if you know that the point (p, q) lies on the line $y = mx + b$?

Exs. 7–9

Solution Because (p, q) is on the line, it is also a solution for the equation $y = mx + b$. Therefore, $q = mp + b$. ■

To construct proofs of geometric theorems by using analytic methods, we must use the hypothesis to determine the drawing. Unlike the drawings in Chapters 1–9, the figure must be placed in the coordinate system. Making the drawing requires careful placement of the figure and proper naming of the vertices, using coordinates of the rectangular system. The following guidelines should prove helpful in positioning the figure and in naming its vertices.

STRATEGY FOR PROOF ▶ The Drawing for an Analytic Proof

Some considerations for preparing the drawing:

1. Coordinates of the vertices must be general; for instance, you may use (a, b) as a vertex, but do *not* use a specific point such as (2, 3).
2. Make the drawing satisfy the hypothesis without providing any additional qualities; if the theorem describes a rectangle, draw and label a rectangle but *not* a square.
3. For simplicity in your calculations, drop the figure into the rectangular coordinate system in such a manner that
   a) as many 0 coordinates as possible are used.
   b) the remaining coordinates represent positive numbers due to the positioning of the remaining vertices in Quadrant I.

NOTE: In some cases, it is convenient to place a figure so that it has symmetry with respect to the y axis, in which case some negative coordinates are present.

4. When possible, use horizontal and vertical line segments because you know their parallel and perpendicular relationships.
5. Use as few variable names in the coordinates as possible.

Discover

The geoboard (pegboard) creates a coordinate system of its own. Even though the coordinates of vertices are not named, describe the type of triangle represented by:

a) $\triangle ABC$ b) $\triangle DEF$

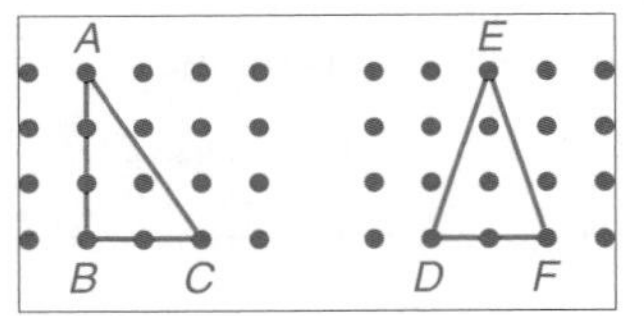

ANSWERS

a) Right b) Isosceles

Now consider Example 5, which clarifies the list of suggestions found in the "Strategy for Proof." As you observe the drawing in each part of the example, imagine that $\triangle ABC$ has been cut out of a piece of cardboard and dropped into the coordinate system in the position indicated. Because we have freedom of placement, we choose the positioning that allows the simplest solution for a proof or problem.

EXAMPLE 5

Suppose that you need to make a drawing for the following theorem, which is to be proved analytically: "The midpoint of the hypotenuse of a right triangle is equidistant from the three vertices of the triangle." Explain why the placement of right $\triangle ABC$ in each part of Figure 10.23 on page 469 could be improved.

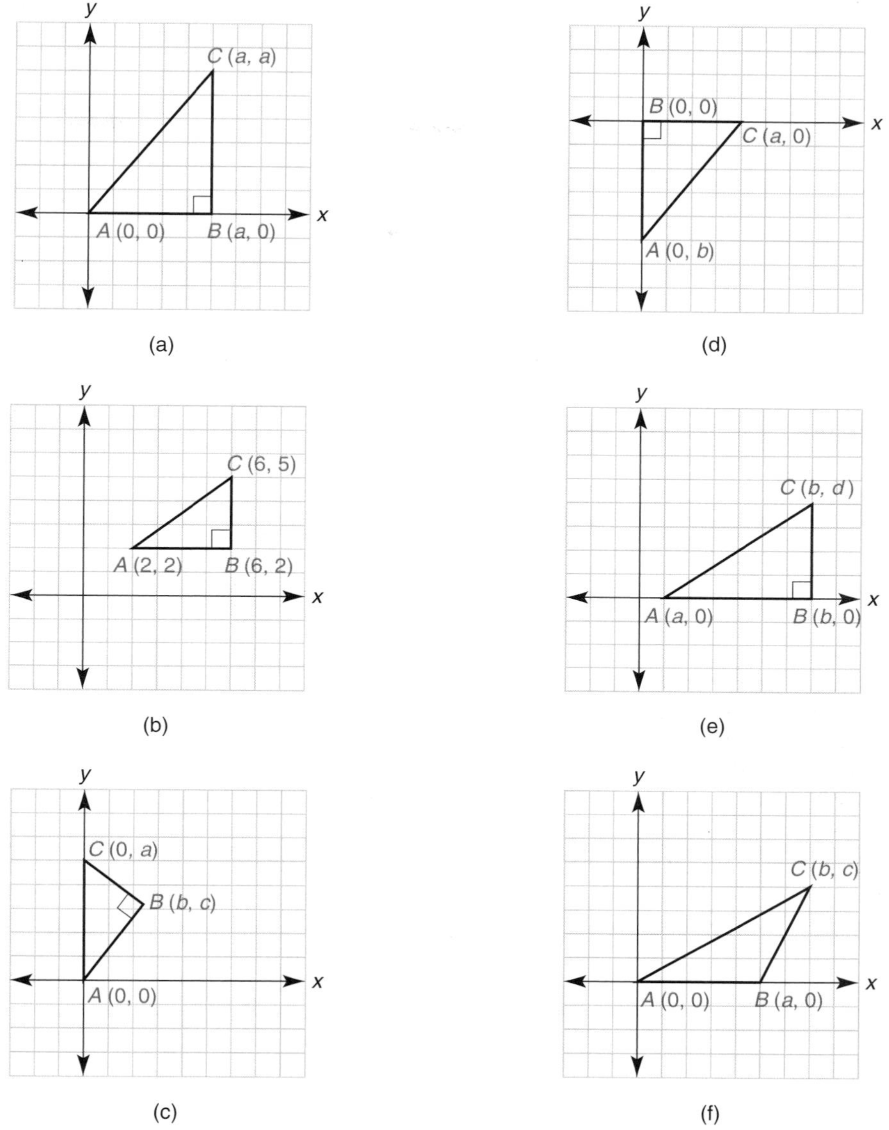

Figure 10.23

Solution Refer to Figure 10.23.

a) The choice of vertices causes $AB = BC$, so the triangle is also an isosceles triangle. This contradicts point 2 of the list of suggestions.
b) The coordinates are too specific! This contradicts point 1 of the list. A proof with these coordinates would *not* establish the general case.
c) The drawing does not make use of horizontal and vertical lines to obtain the right angle. This violates point 4 of the list.
d) This placement fails point 3 of the list, because b is a negative number. The length of $\overline{AB}$ would be $-b$, which could be confusing.
e) This placement fails point 3 because we have not used as many 0 coordinates as we could have used. As we shall see, it also fails point 5.
f) This placement fails point 2. The triangle is not a right triangle unless $a = b$. ■

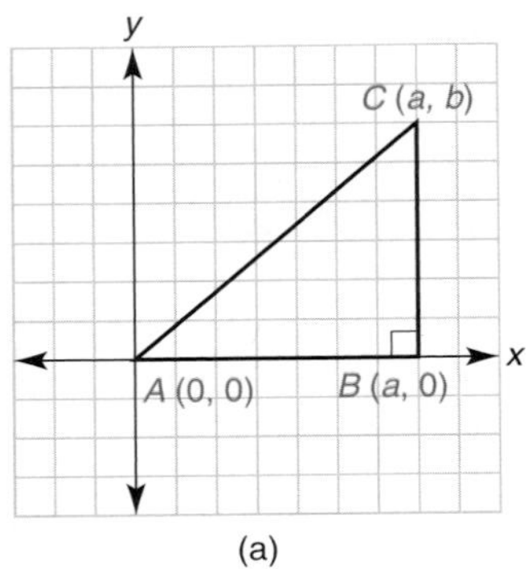

(a)

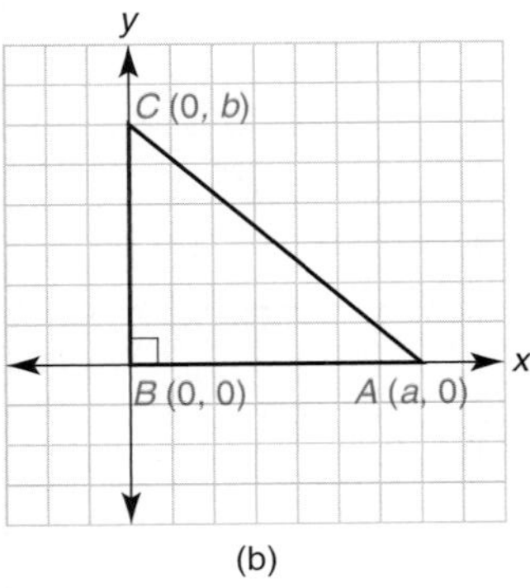

(b)

Figure 10.24

In Example 5, we wanted to place $\triangle ABC$ so that we met as many of the conditions listed on page 468 as possible. Two convenient placements are given in Figure 10.24. The triangle in Figure 10.24(b) is slightly better than the one in 10.24(a) in that it uses four 0 coordinates rather than three. Another advantage of Figure 10.24(b) is that the placement forces angle B to be a right angle, because the x and y axes are perpendicular.

We now turn our attention to the role of the conclusion of the theorem for the proof. A second list examines some considerations for proving statements analytically.

STRATEGY FOR PROOF ▶ The Conclusion for an Analytic Proof

Three considerations for using the conclusion as a guide:

1. If the conclusion is a conjunction "P and Q," be sure to verify both parts of the conclusion.
2. The following pairings indicate how to prove statements of the type shown in the left column.

To prove the conclusion:	*Use the:*
a) Segments are congruent or have equal lengths (like $AB = CD$).	Distance Formula
b) Segments are parallel (like $\overline{AB} \parallel \overline{CD}$).	Slope Formula (need $m_{\overline{AB}} = m_{\overline{CD}}$)
c) Segments are perpendicular (like $\overline{AB} \perp \overline{CD}$).	Slope Formula (need $m_{\overline{AB}} \cdot m_{\overline{CD}} = -1$)
d) A segment is bisected.	Distance Formula
e) Segments bisect each other.	Midpoint Formula

3. Anticipate the proof by thinking of the steps of the proof in reverse order; that is, reason backward from the conclusion.

SSG *Exs. 10–15*

EXAMPLE 6

a) Provide an ideal drawing for the following theorem: The midpoint of the hypotenuse of a right triangle is equidistant from the three vertices of the triangle.

b) By studying the theorem, name at least two of the formulas that will be used to complete the proof.

Solution

a) We improve Figure 10.24(b) by giving the value $2a$ to the x coordinate of A and the value $2b$ to the y coordinate of C. (A factor of 2 makes it easier to calculate and represent the midpoint M of $\overline{AC}$. See Figure 10.25.)

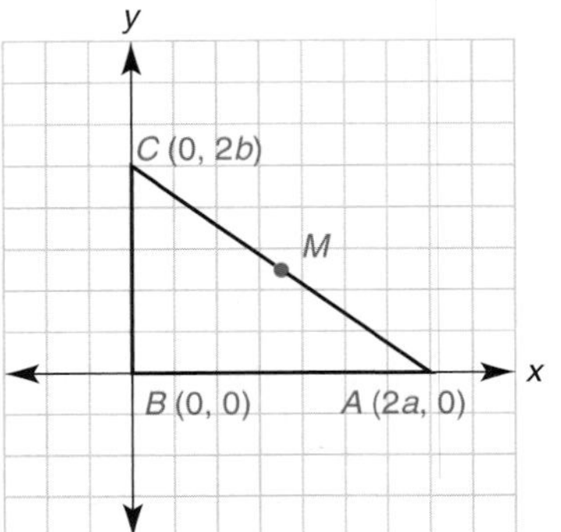

Figure 10.25

Discover

The geoboard (pegboard) creates a coordinate system of its own. Describe the type of quadrilateral represented by *ABCD*.

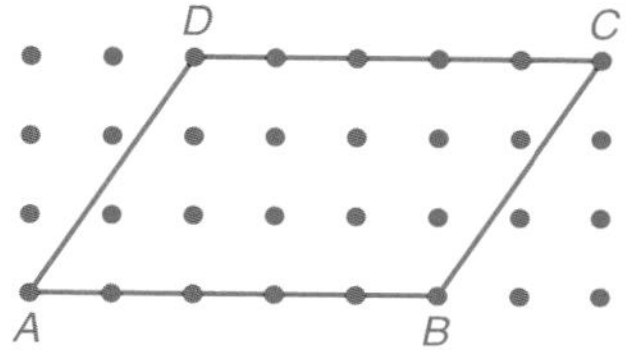

ANSWER

Parallelogram

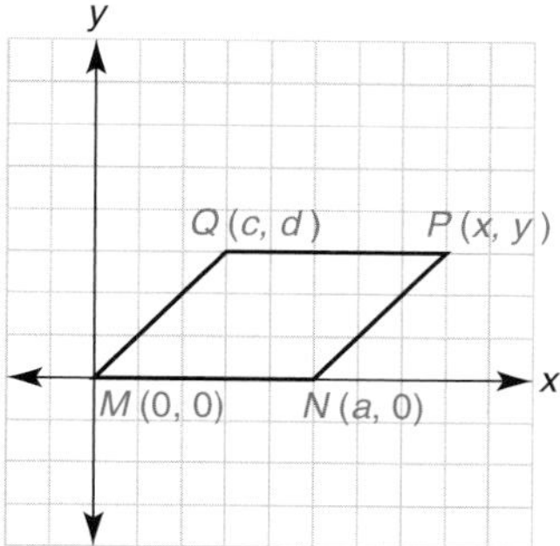

Figure 10.26

b) The Midpoint Formula is applied to describe the midpoint of $\overline{AC}$. Using the formula, we find that

$$M = \left(\frac{x_1 + x_2}{2}, \frac{y_1 + y_2}{2}\right) = \left(\frac{2a + 0}{2}, \frac{0 + 2b}{2}\right) = \left(\frac{2a}{2}, \frac{2b}{2}\right) = (a, b)$$

So the midpoint is (a, b). The Distance Formula will also be needed because the theorem states that the distances from M to A, from M to B, and from M to C should all be equal. ■

The purpose of our next example is to demonstrate efficiency in the labeling of vertices. Our goal is to use fewer variables in characterizing the vertices of the parallelogram found in Figure 10.26.

EXAMPLE 7

If $MNPQ$ is a parallelogram in Figure 10.26, find the coordinates of point P in terms of a, c, and d.

Solution Consider $\square MNPQ$ in which we refer to point P as (x, y).

Because $\overline{MN} \parallel \overline{QP}$, we have $m_{\overline{MN}} = m_{\overline{QP}}$. But $m_{\overline{MN}} = \frac{0 - 0}{a - 0} = 0$ and $m_{\overline{QP}} = \frac{y - d}{x - c}$, so we are led to the equation

$$\frac{y - d}{x - c} = 0 \rightarrow y - d = 0 \rightarrow y = d$$

Now P is described by (x, d). Because $\overline{MQ} \parallel \overline{NP}$, we are also led to equal slopes for these segments. But

$$m_{\overline{MQ}} = \frac{d - 0}{c - 0} = \frac{d}{c} \quad \text{and} \quad m_{\overline{NP}} = \frac{d - 0}{x - a} = \frac{d}{x - a}$$

Then

$$\frac{d}{c} = \frac{d}{x - a}$$

By using the Means-Extremes Property, we have

$$\begin{aligned} d(x - a) &= d \cdot c && \text{(with } d \neq 0\text{)} \\ x - a &= c && \text{(dividing by } d\text{)} \\ x &= a + c && \text{(adding } a\text{)} \end{aligned}$$

Therefore, P is the point $(a + c, d)$. ■

In retrospect, Example 7 shows that $\square MNPQ$ is characterized by vertices $M(0, 0)$, $N(a, 0)$, $P(a + c, d)$, and $Q(c, d)$. Because $\overline{MN}$ and $\overline{QP}$ are horizontal segments, it is obvious that $\overline{MN} \parallel \overline{QP}$. Both $\overline{MQ}$ (starting at M) and $\overline{NP}$ (starting at N) trace paths that move along each segment *c units to the right* and *d units upward.* Thus, the slopes of $\overline{MQ}$ and $\overline{NP}$ are both $\frac{d}{c}$, and it follows that $\overline{MQ} \parallel \overline{NP}$.

In Example 7, we named the coordinates of the vertices of a parallelogram with the fewest possible letters. We now extend our result in Example 7 to allow for a rhombus—a parallelogram with two congruent adjacent sides.

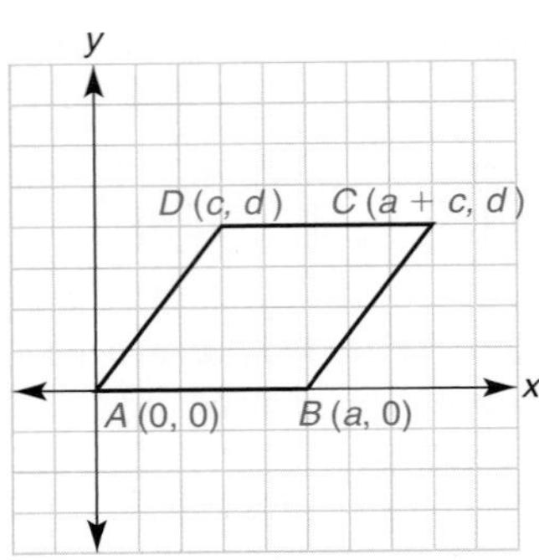

Figure 10.27

EXAMPLE 8

In Figure 10.27, find an equation that relates a, c, and d if $\square ABCD$ is a rhombus.

Solution As we saw in Example 7, the coordinates of the vertices of $ABCD$ define a parallelogram. For emphasis, we note that $\overline{AB} \parallel \overline{DC}$ and $\overline{AD} \parallel \overline{BC}$ because

$$m_{\overline{AB}} = m_{\overline{DC}} = 0 \qquad \text{and} \qquad m_{\overline{AD}} = m_{\overline{BC}} = \frac{d}{c}$$

For Figure 10.27 to represent a rhombus, it is necessary that $AB = AD$. Now $AB = a - 0 = a$ because $\overline{AB}$ is a horizontal segment. To find an expression for the length of $\overline{AD}$, we need to use the Distance Formula.

$$\begin{aligned} AD &= \sqrt{(x_2 - x_1)^2 + (y_2 - y_1)^2} \\ &= \sqrt{(c - 0)^2 + (d - 0)^2} \\ &= \sqrt{c^2 + d^2} \end{aligned}$$

SSG *Exs. 16–18*

Because $AB = AD$, we are led to $a = \sqrt{c^2 + d^2}$. Squaring, we have the desired relationship, $a^2 = c^2 + d^2$. ■

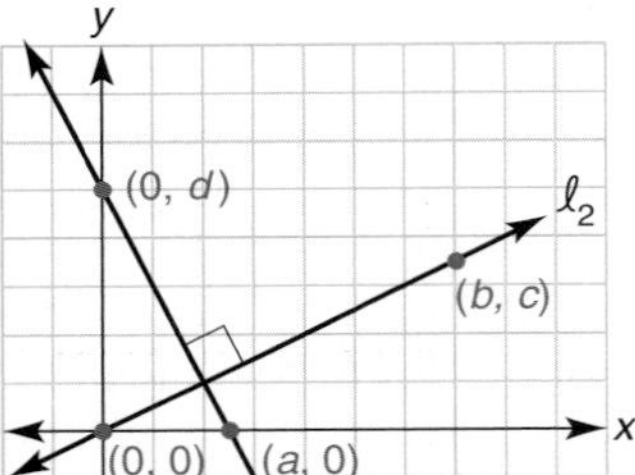

Figure 10.28

EXAMPLE 9

If $\ell_1 \perp \ell_2$ in Figure 10.28, find a relationship among the variables a, b, c, and d.

Solution First we find the slopes of lines ℓ_1 and ℓ_2. For ℓ_1, we have

$$m_1 = \frac{0 - d}{a - 0} = -\frac{d}{a}$$

For ℓ_2, we have

$$m_2 = \frac{c - 0}{b - 0} = \frac{c}{b}$$

With $\ell_1 \perp \ell_2$, it follows that $m_1 \cdot m_2 = -1$. Substituting the slopes found above into the equation $m_1 \cdot m_2 = -1$, we have

$$-\frac{d}{a} \cdot \frac{c}{b} = -1 \qquad \text{so} \qquad -\frac{dc}{ab} = -1$$

Equivalently, $\frac{dc}{ab} = 1$ and it follows that $dc = ab$. ■

▶▶▶ Exercises 10.3

1. Find an expression for:
   a) The distance between $(a, 0)$ and $(0, a)$
   b) The slope of the segment joining (a, b) and (c, d)
2. Find the coordinates of the midpoint of the segment that joins the points
   a) $(a, 0)$ and $(0, b)$ b) $(2a, 0)$ and $(0, 2b)$
3. Find the slope of the line containing the points
   a) $(a, 0)$ and $(0, a)$ b) $(a, 0)$ and $(0, b)$
4. Find the slope of the line that is:
   a) Parallel to the line containing $(a, 0)$ and $(0, b)$
   b) Perpendicular to the line through $(a, 0)$ and $(0, b)$

In Exercises 5 to 10, the real numbers a, b, c, and d are positive.

5. Consider the triangle with vertices at $A(0, 0)$, $B(a, 0)$, and $C(a, b)$. Explain why $\triangle ABC$ is a right triangle.

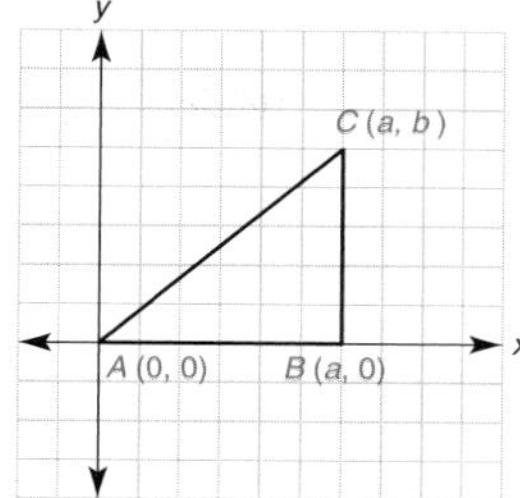

6. Consider the triangle with vertices at $R(-a, 0)$, $S(a, 0)$, and $T(0, b)$. Explain why $\triangle RST$ is an isosceles triangle.

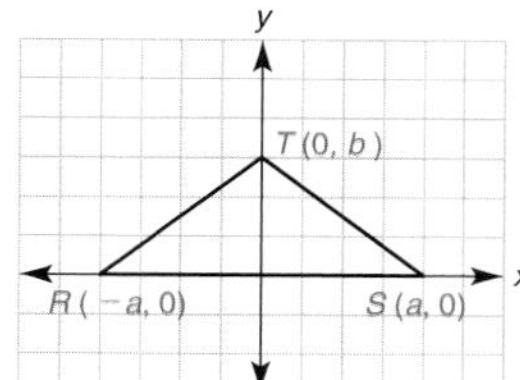

7. Consider the quadrilateral with vertices at $M(0, 0)$, $N(a, 0)$, $P(a + b, c)$, and $Q(b, c)$. Explain why $MNPQ$ is a parallelogram.

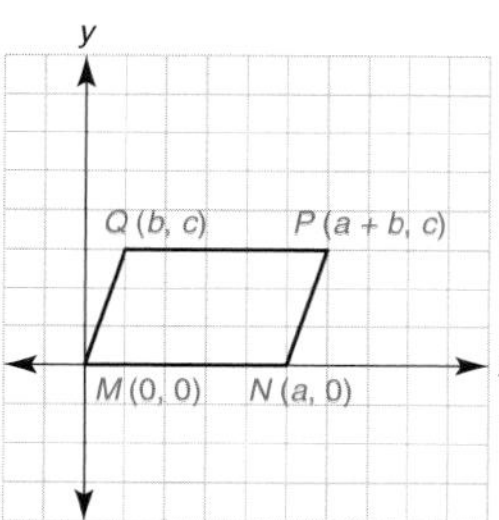

8. Consider the quadrilateral with vertices at $A(0, 0)$, $B(a, 0)$, $C(b, c)$, and $D(d, c)$. Explain why $ABCD$ is a trapezoid.

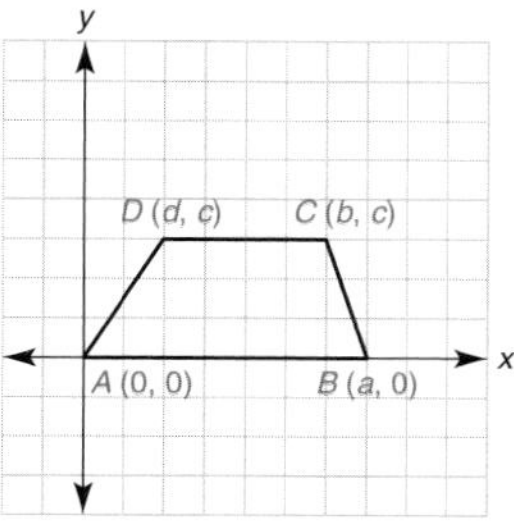

9. Consider the quadrilateral with vertices at $M(0, 0)$, $N(a, 0)$, $P(a, b)$, and $Q(0, b)$. Explain why $MNPQ$ is a rectangle.

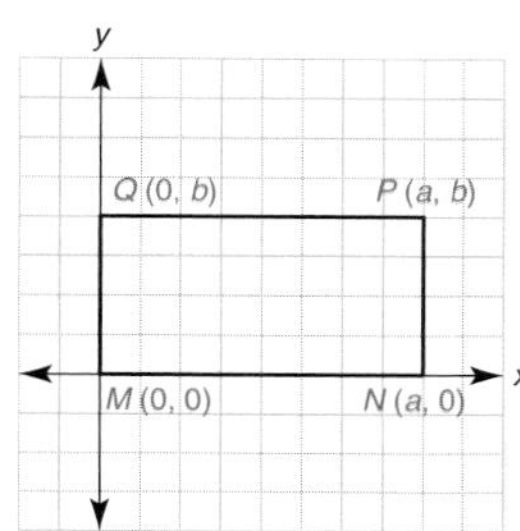

10. Consider the quadrilateral with vertices at $R(0, 0)$, $S(a, 0)$, $T(a, a)$, and $V(0, a)$. Explain why $RSTV$ is a square.

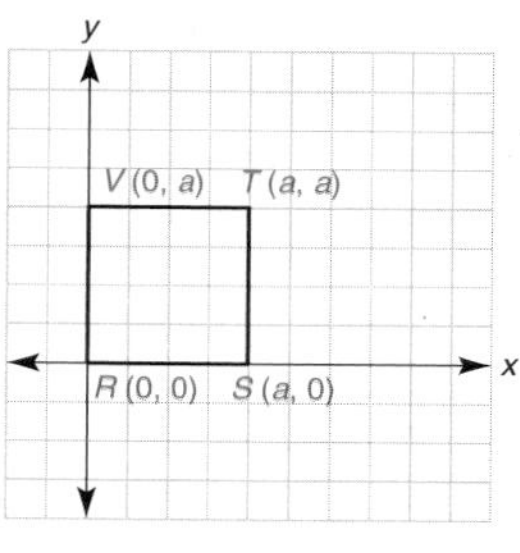

In Exercises 11 to 16, supply the missing coordinates for the vertices, using as few variables as possible.

11.

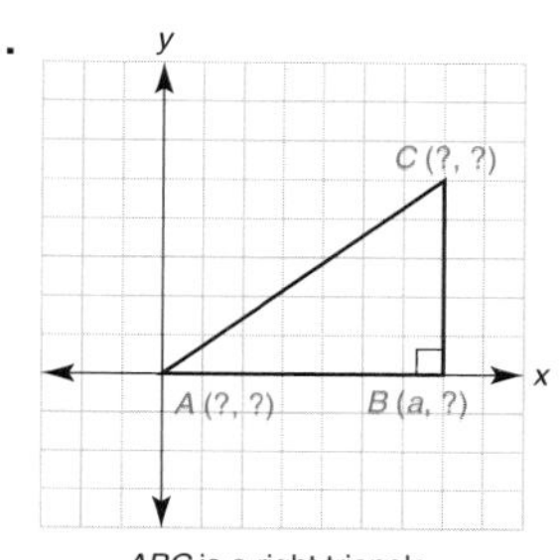

ABC is a right triangle.

12.

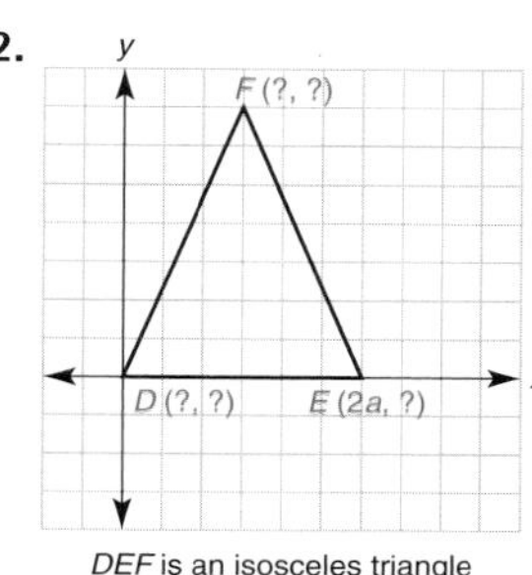

DEF is an isosceles triangle with $\overline{DF} \cong \overline{FE}$.

13.

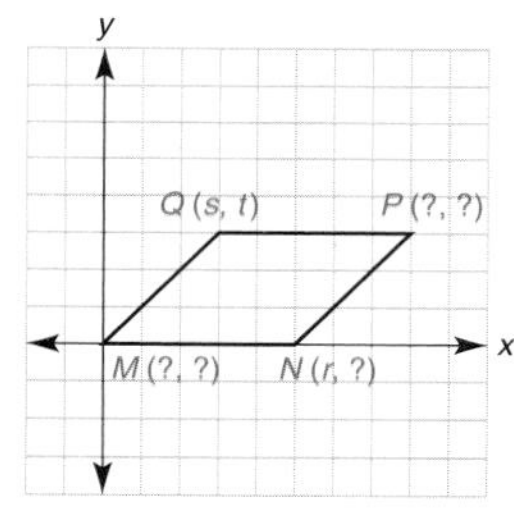

MNPQ is a parallelogram.

14.

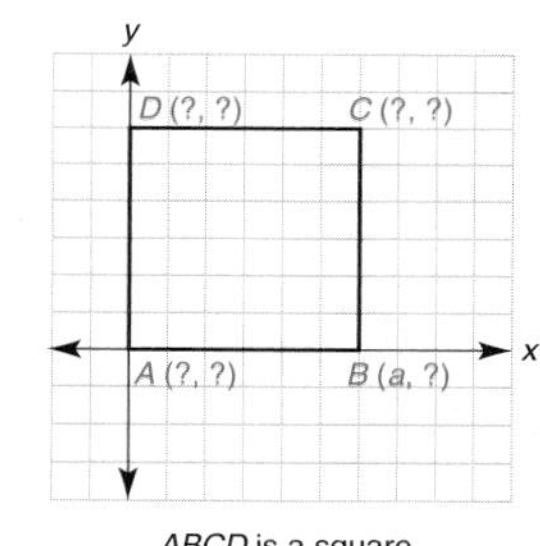

ABCD is a square.

15.

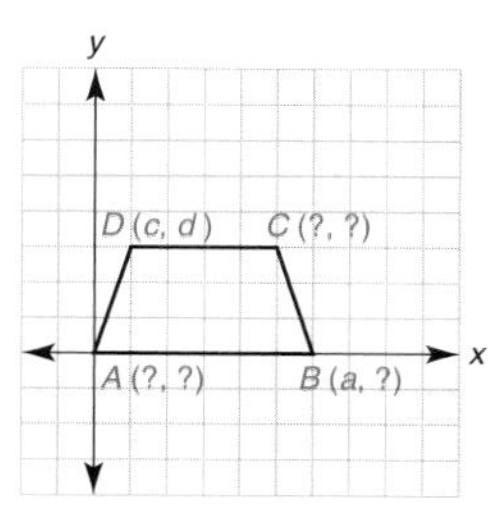

ABCD is an isosceles trapezoid; $\overline{AB} \parallel \overline{DC}$ and $\overline{AD} \cong \overline{BC}$.

16.

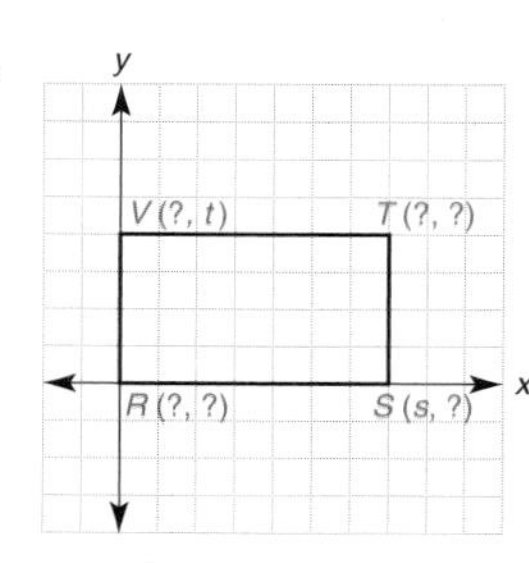

RSTV is a rectangle.

In Exercises 17 to 22, draw an ideally placed figure in the coordinate system; then name the coordinates of each vertex of the figure.

17. a) A square
b) A square (midpoints of sides are needed)

18. a) A rectangle
b) A rectangle (midpoints of sides are needed)

19. a) A parallelogram
b) A parallelogram (midpoints of sides are needed)

20. a) A triangle
b) A triangle (midpoints of sides are needed)

21. a) An isosceles triangle
b) An isosceles triangle (midpoints of sides are needed)

22. a) A trapezoid
b) A trapezoid (midpoints of sides are needed)

In Exercises 23 to 28, find the equation (relationship) requested. Then eliminate fractions and square root radicals from the equation.

23. If ▱$MNPQ$ is a rhombus, state an equation that relates r, s, and t.

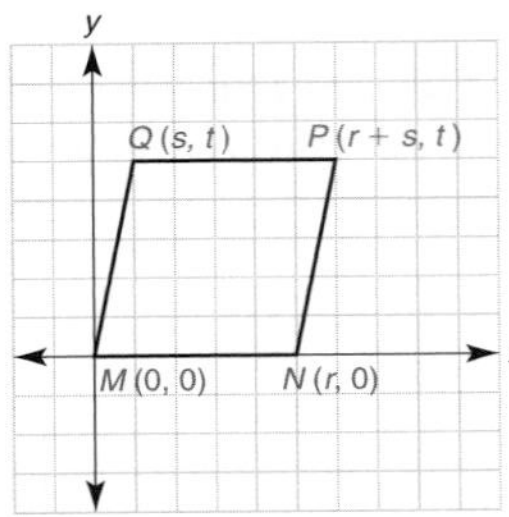

24. For ▱$RSTV$, suppose that $RT = VS$. State an equation that relates s, t, and v.

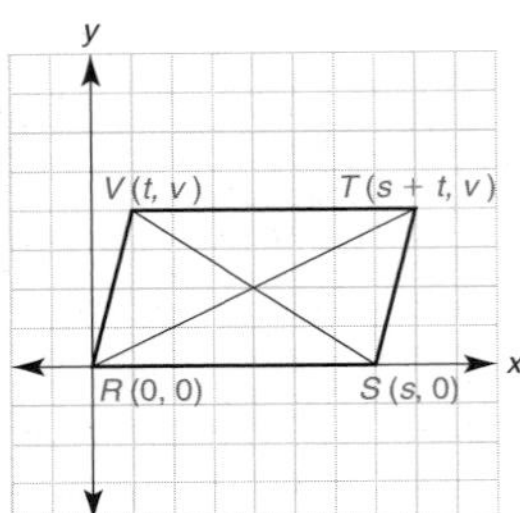

25. For ▱$ABCD$, suppose that diagonals $\overline{AC}$ and $\overline{DB}$ are perpendicular. State an equation that relates a, b, and c.

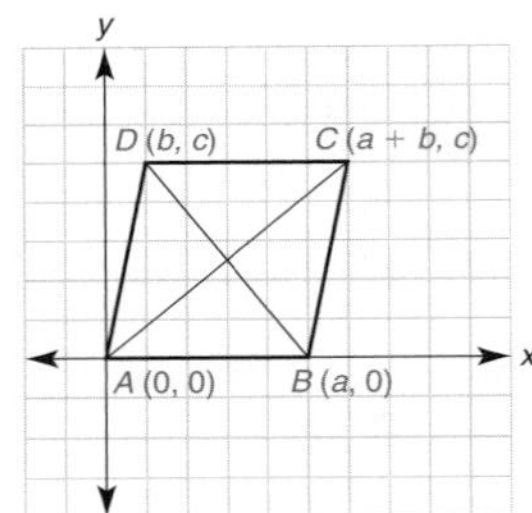

26. For quadrilateral $RSTV$, suppose that $\overline{RV} \parallel \overline{ST}$. State an equation that relates m, n, p, q, and r.

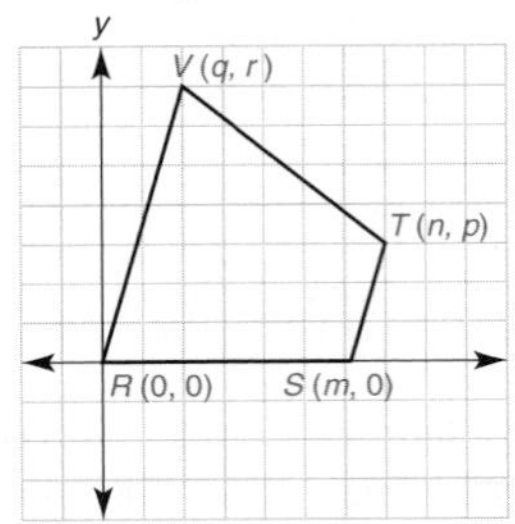

27. Suppose that $\triangle ABC$ is an equilateral triangle. State an equation that relates variables a and b.

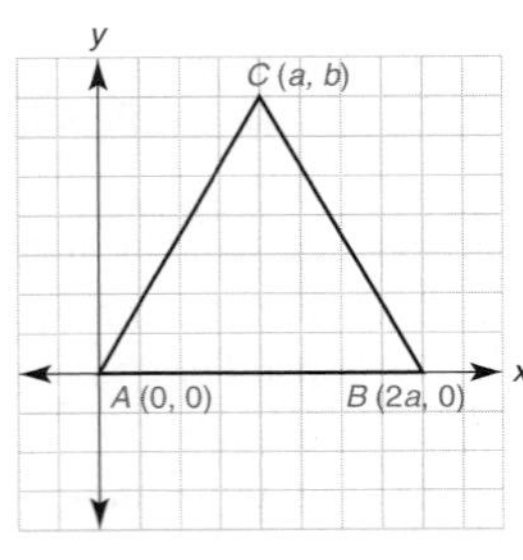

28. Suppose that $\triangle RST$ is an isosceles triangle, with $\overline{RS} \cong \overline{RT}$. State an equation that relates s, t, and v.

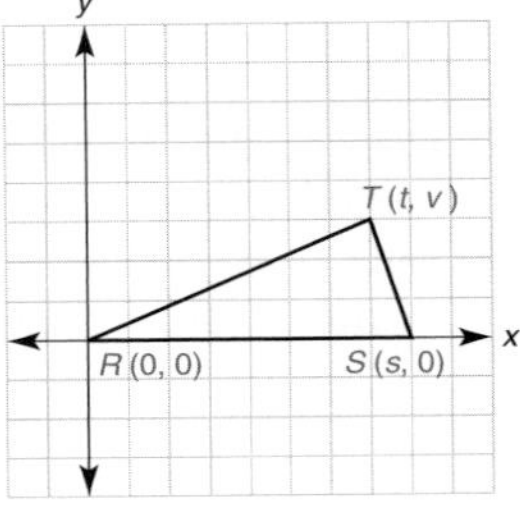

29. The drawing shows isosceles $\triangle ABC$ with $\overline{AC} \cong \overline{BC}$.
a) What type of number is a?
b) What type of number is $-a$?
c) Find an expression for the length of $\overline{AB}$.

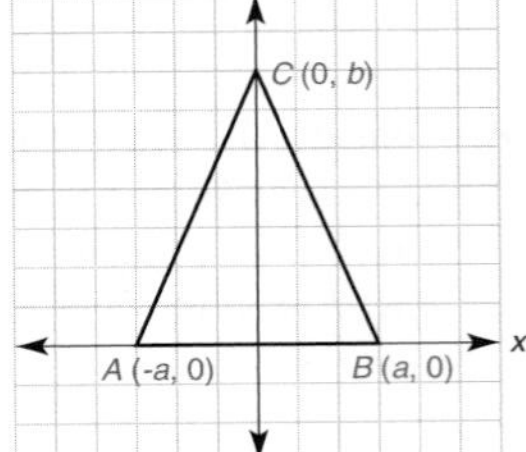

30. The drawing shows parallelogram $RSTV$.
a) What type of number is r?
b) Find an expression for RS.
c) Describe the coordinate t in terms of the other variables shown.

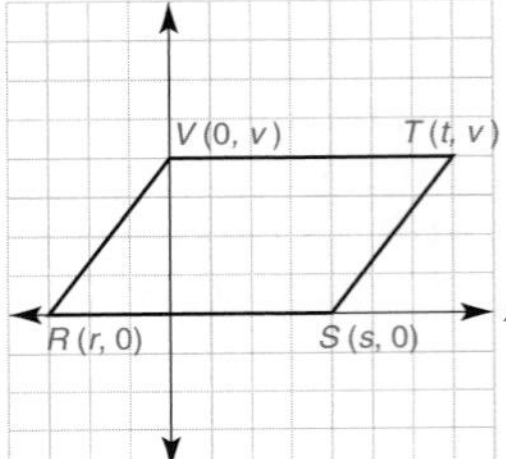

31. Which formula would you use to establish each of the following claims?
a) $\overline{AC} \perp \overline{DB}$
b) $AC = DB$
c) $\overline{DB}$ and $\overline{AC}$ bisect each other
d) $\overline{AD} \parallel \overline{BC}$

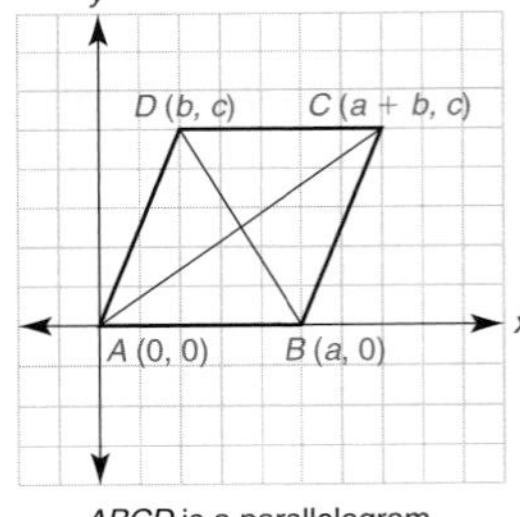

ABCD is a parallelogram.

32. Which formula would you use to establish each of the following claims?
a) The coordinates of X are (d, c).
b) $m_{\overline{VT}} = 0$
c) $\overline{VT} \parallel \overline{RS}$
d) The length of $\overline{RV}$ is $2\sqrt{d^2 + c^2}$.

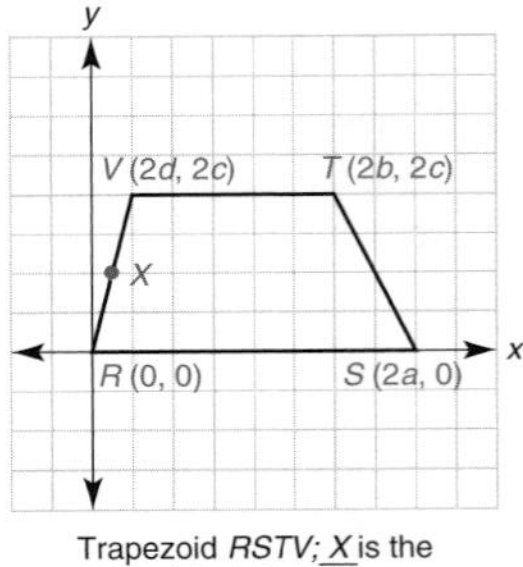

Trapezoid *RSTV*; *X* is the midpoint of $\overline{RV}$.

In Exercises 33 to 36, draw and label a well-placed figure in the coordinate system for each theorem. Do not attempt to prove the theorem!

33. The line segment joining the midpoints of the two nonparallel sides of a trapezoid is parallel to each base of the trapezoid.

34. If the midpoints of the sides of a quadrilateral are joined in order, the resulting quadrilateral is a parallelogram.
35. The diagonals of a rectangle are equal in length.
36. The diagonals of a rhombus are perpendicular to each other.

*37. In $\triangle RST$, $\overline{SV}$ bisects $\angle RST$. Find the coordinate of point T in terms of a.

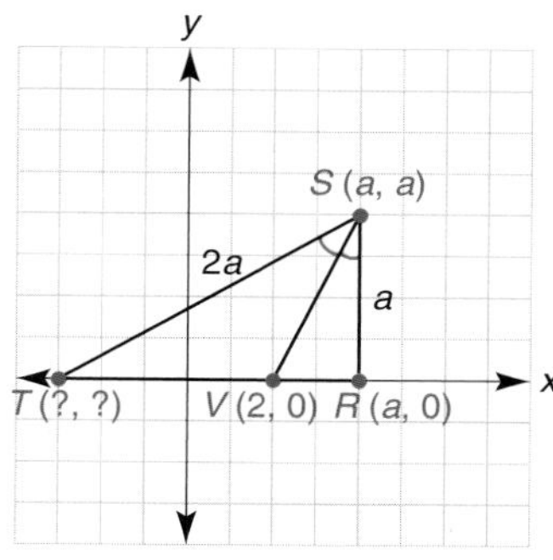

10.4 Analytic Proofs

KEY CONCEPTS Analytic Proof · Synthetic Proof

When we use algebra along with the rectangular coordinate system to prove a geometric theorem, the method of proof is **analytic.** The analytic (algebraic) approach relies heavily on the placement of the figure in the coordinate system and on the application of the Distance Formula, the Midpoint Formula, or the Slope Formula (at the appropriate time). In order to contrast analytic proof with **synthetic** proof (the two-column or paragraph proofs used in earlier chapters), we repeat in this section some earlier theorems and prove these analytically.

In Section 10.3, we saw how to place triangles having special qualities in the coordinate system. We review this information in Table 10.1; in Example 1, we consider the

TABLE 10.1
Analytic Proof: Suggestions for Placement of the Triangle

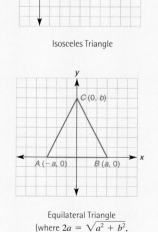

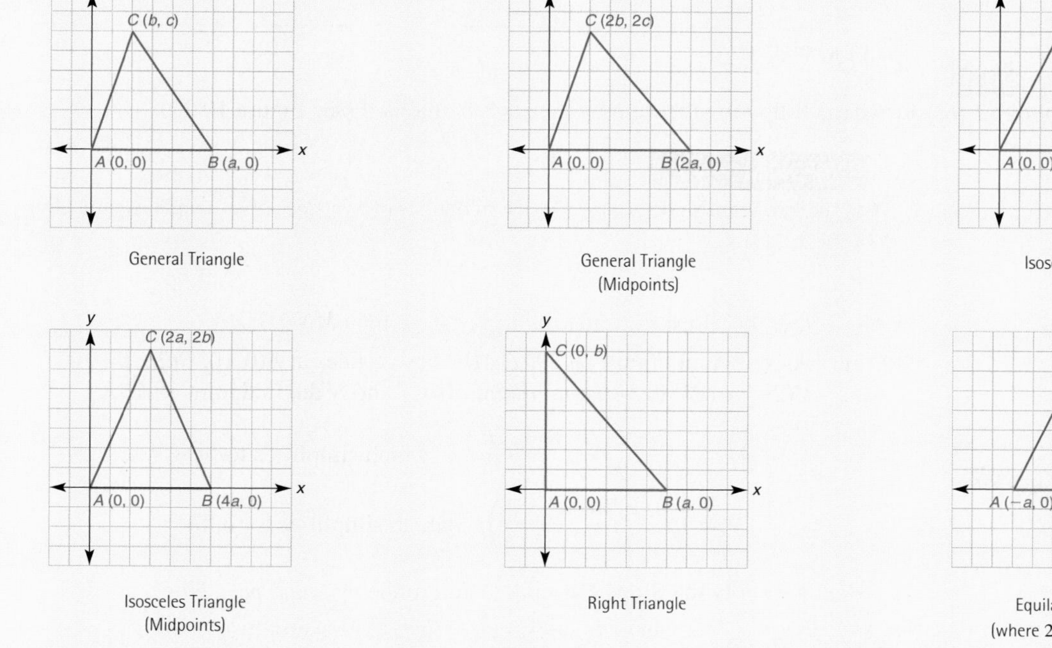

proof of a theorem involving triangles. In Table 10.1, you will find that the figure determined by any positive numerical choices of a, b, and c matches the type of triangle described. When midpoints are involved, we use coordinates such as $2a$ or $2b$.

In Table 10.2, we review convenient placements for types of quadrilaterals.

TABLE 10.2
Analytic Proof: Suggestions for Placement of the Quadrilateral

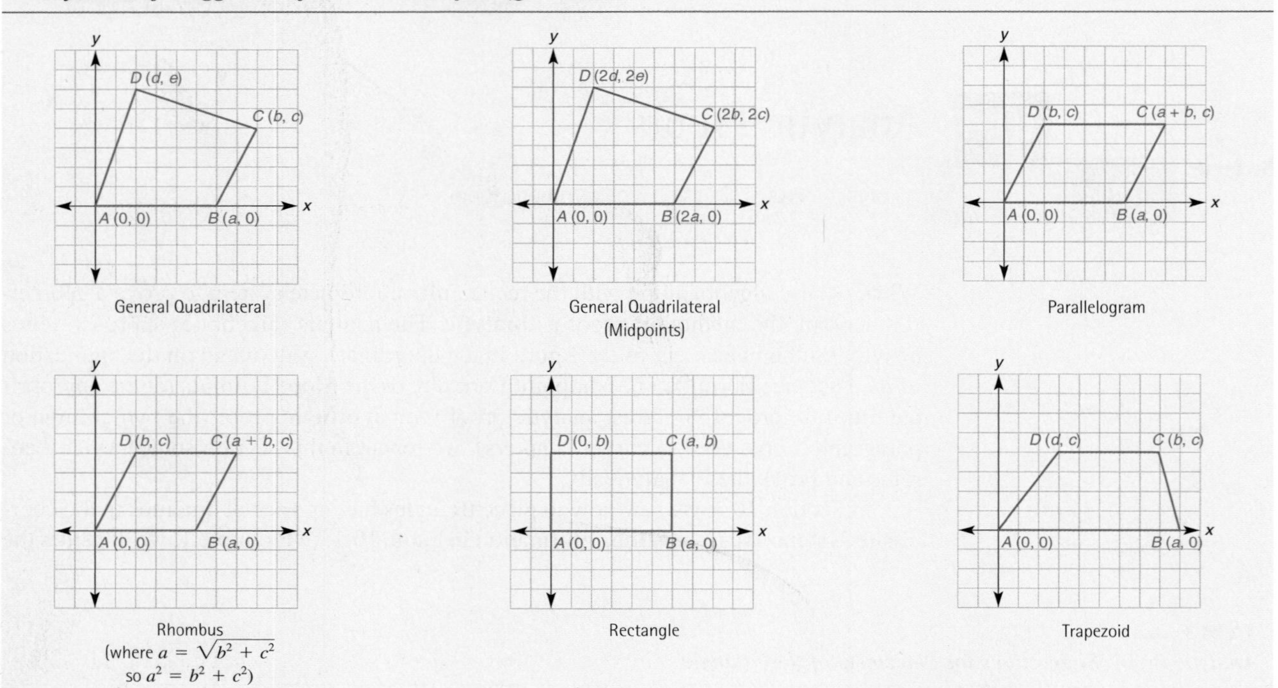

EXAMPLE 1

Exs. 1–4

Prove the following theorem by the analytic method (see Figure 10.29).

THEOREM 10.4.1

The line segment determined by the midpoints of two sides of a triangle is parallel to the third side.

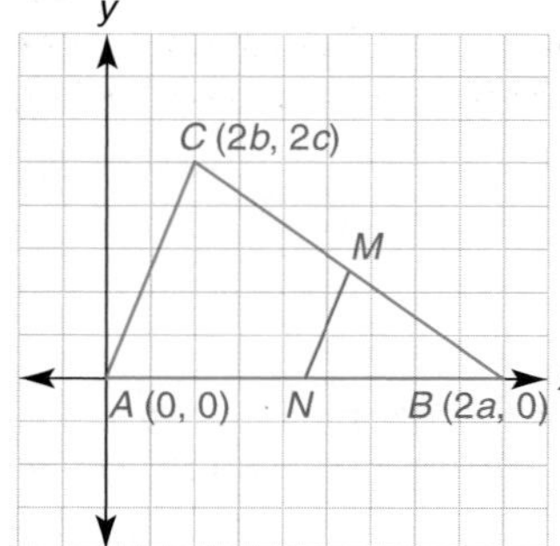

Figure 10.29

PLAN: Use the Slope Formula; if $m_{\overline{MN}} = m_{\overline{AC}}$, then $\overline{MN} \parallel \overline{AC}$.

PROOF: As shown in Figure 10.29, $\triangle ABC$ has vertices at $A(0, 0)$, $B(2a, 0)$, and $C(2b, 2c)$. With M the midpoint of $\overline{BC}$, and N the midpoint of $\overline{AB}$,

$$M = \left(\frac{2a + 2b}{2}, \frac{0 + 2c}{2}\right), \quad \text{which simplifies to } (a + b, c)$$

$$N = \left(\frac{0 + 2a}{2}, \frac{0 + 0}{2}\right), \quad \text{which simplifies to } (a, 0)$$

Next we apply the Slope Formula to determine $m_{\overline{MN}}$ and $m_{\overline{AC}}$. Now $m_{\overline{MN}} = \frac{c - 0}{(a + b) - a} = \frac{c}{b}$; also, $m_{\overline{AC}} = \frac{2c - 0}{2b - 0} = \frac{2c}{2b} = \frac{c}{b}$. Because $m_{\overline{MN}} = m_{\overline{AC}}$, we see that $\overline{MN} \parallel \overline{AC}$. ■

As we did in Example 1, we include a "plan" for Example 2. Although no plan is shown for Example 3 or Example 4, one is necessary before the proof can be written.

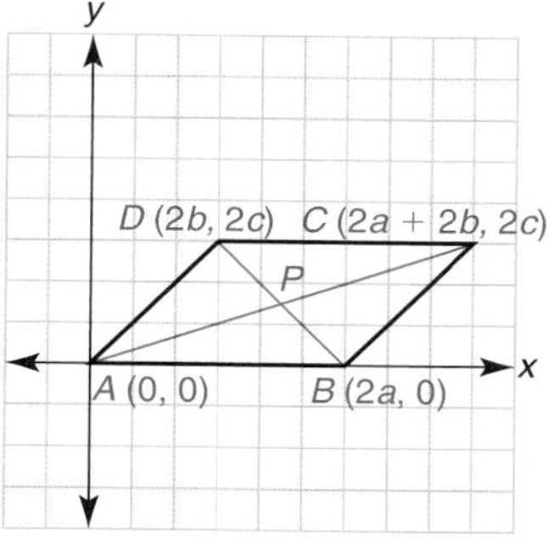

Figure 10.30

EXAMPLE 2

Prove the following theorem by the analytic method. See Figure 10.30.

THEOREM 10.4.2

The diagonals of a parallelogram bisect each other.

PLAN: Use the Midpoint Formula to show that the two diagonals have a common midpoint. Use a factor of 2 in the coordinates.

PROOF: With coordinates as shown in Figure 10.30, quadrilateral $ABCD$ is a parallelogram. The diagonals intersect at point P. By the Midpoint Formula, we have

$$M_{\overline{AC}} = \left(\frac{0 + (2a + 2b)}{2}, \frac{0 + 2c}{2}\right)$$
$$= (a + b, c)$$

Also, the midpoint of $\overline{DB}$ is

$$M_{\overline{DB}} = \left(\frac{2a + 2b}{2}, \frac{0 + 2c}{2}\right)$$
$$= (a + b, c)$$

Exs. 5–9

Thus, $(a + b, c)$ is the common midpoint of the two diagonals and must be the point of intersection of $\overline{AC}$ and $\overline{DB}$. Then $\overline{AC}$ and $\overline{DB}$ bisect each other at point P. ■

The proof of Theorem 10.4.2 is not unique! In Section 10.5, we could prove Theorem 10.4.2 by using a three-step proof:

1. Find the equations of the two lines.
2. Determine the point of intersection of these lines.
3. Show that this point of intersection is the common midpoint.

But the phrase *bisect each other* in Theorem 10.4.2 implied the use of the Midpoint Formula. Our approach to Example 2 was far easier and just as valid as the three steps described above. The use of the Midpoint Formula is generally the best approach when the phrase *bisect each other* appears in the statement of a theorem.

We now outline the method of analytic proof.

STRATEGY FOR PROOF ▶ Completing an Analytic Proof

1. Read the theorem carefully to distinguish the hypothesis and the conclusion. The hypothesis characterizes the figure to use.
2. Use the hypothesis (and nothing more) to determine a convenient placement of the figure in the rectangular coordinate system. Then label the figure. See Tables 10.1 and 10.2.

3. If any special quality is provided by the hypothesis, be sure to state this early in the proof. (For example, a rhombus should be described as a parallelogram that has two congruent adjacent sides.)
4. Study the conclusion, and devise a plan to prove this claim; this may involve reasoning backward from the conclusion step by step until the hypothesis is reached.
5. Write the proof, being careful to order the statements properly and to justify each statement.

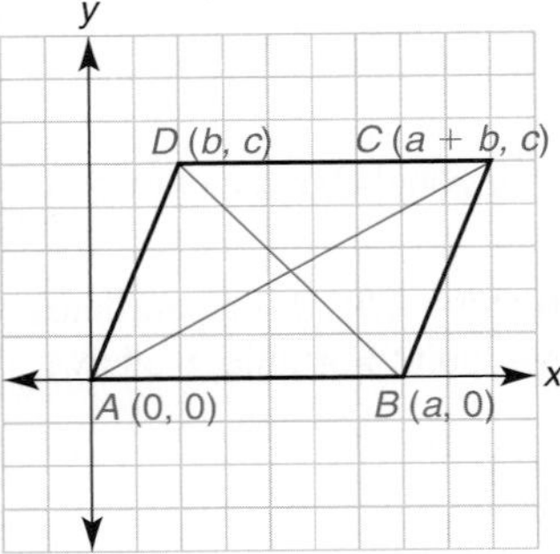

Figure 10.31

EXAMPLE 3

Prove Theorem 10.4.3 by the analytic method. (See Figure 10.31.)

THEOREM 10.4.3

The diagonals of a rhombus are perpendicular.

Solution In Figure 10.31, *ABCD* has the coordinates of a parallelogram. Because ▱*ABCD* is a rhombus, $AB = AD$. Then $a = \sqrt{b^2 + c^2}$ by the Distance Formula, and squaring gives $a^2 = b^2 + c^2$. The Slope Formula leads to

$$m_{\overline{AC}} = \frac{c - 0}{(a + b) - 0} \quad \text{and} \quad m_{\overline{DB}} = \frac{0 - c}{a - b}$$

so

$$m_{\overline{AC}} = \frac{c}{a + b} \quad \text{and} \quad m_{\overline{DB}} = \frac{-c}{a - b}$$

Then the product of the slopes of the diagonals is

$$\begin{aligned} m_{\overline{AC}} \cdot m_{\overline{DB}} &= \frac{c}{a + b} \cdot \frac{-c}{a - b} \\ &= \frac{-c^2}{a^2 - b^2} \\ &= \frac{-c^2}{(b^2 + c^2) - b^2} \quad \textbf{(replaced } a^2 \textbf{ by } b^2 + c^2\textbf{)} \\ &= \frac{-c^2}{c^2} = -1 \end{aligned}$$

Thus, $\overline{AC} \perp \overline{DB}$ because the product of their slopes equals -1. ■

Reminder

We prove that lines are perpendicular by showing that the product of their slopes is -1.

In Example 3, we had to use the condition that two adjacent sides of the rhombus were congruent to complete the proof. Had that condition been omitted, the product of slopes could not have been shown to equal -1. In general, the diagonals of a parallelogram are not perpendicular.

In our next example, we consider the proof of the converse of an earlier theorem. Although it is easy to complete an analytic proof of the statement "The diagonals of a rectangle are equal in length," the proof of the converse is not as straightforward.

SSG *Exs. 10, 11*

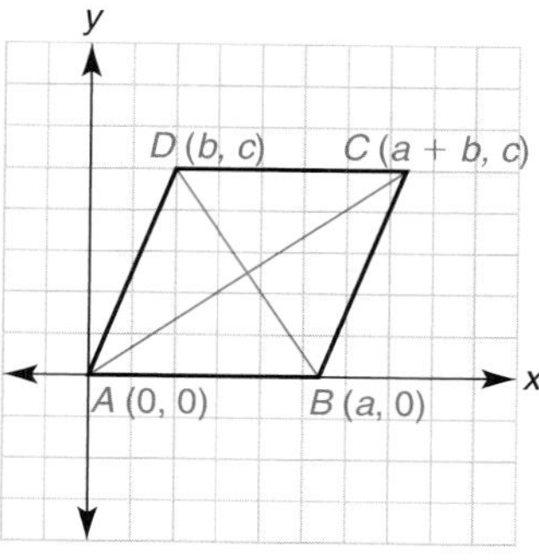

Figure 10.32

EXAMPLE 4

Prove Theorem 10.4.4 by the analytic method. See Figure 10.32.

THEOREM 10.4.4

If the diagonals of a parallelogram are equal in length, then the parallelogram is a rectangle.

Solution In parallelogram $ABCD$ in Figure 10.32, $AC = DB$. Applying the Distance Formula, we have

$$AC = \sqrt{[(a + b) - 0]^2 + (c - 0)^2}$$

and

$$DB = \sqrt{(a - b)^2 + (0 - c)^2}$$

Because the diagonals have the same length,

$$\begin{aligned} \sqrt{(a + b)^2 + c^2} &= \sqrt{(a - b)^2 + (-c)^2} \\ (a + b)^2 + c^2 &= (a - b)^2 + (-c)^2 && \textbf{(squaring)} \\ a^2 + 2ab + b^2 + c^2 &= a^2 - 2ab + b^2 + c^2 && \textbf{(simplifying)} \\ 4ab &= 0 \\ a \cdot b &= 0 && \textbf{(dividing by 4)} \end{aligned}$$

Thus, $a = 0$ or $b = 0$

Because $a \neq 0$ (otherwise, points A and B would coincide), it is necessary that $b = 0$, so point D is on the y axis. The resulting coordinates of the figure are $A(0, 0)$, $B(a, 0)$, $C(a, c)$, and $D(0, c)$. Because $\overline{AB}$ is horizontal and $\overline{AD}$ is vertical, $ABCD$ must be a rectangle with a right angle at A. ■

SSG *Exs. 12, 13*

Exercises 10.4

In Exercises 1 to 17, complete an analytic proof for each theorem.

1. The diagonals of a rectangle are equal in length.
2. The opposite sides of a parallelogram are equal in length.
3. The diagonals of a square are perpendicular bisectors of each other.
4. The diagonals of an isosceles trapezoid are equal in length.
5. The median from the vertex of an isosceles triangle to the base is perpendicular to the base.
6. The medians to the congruent sides of an isosceles triangle are equal in length.
7. The line segments that join the midpoints of the consecutive sides of a quadrilateral form a parallelogram.
8. The line segments that join the midpoints of the opposite sides of a quadrilateral bisect each other.
9. The line segments that join the midpoints of the consecutive sides of a rectangle form a rhombus.
10. The line segments that join the midpoints of the consecutive sides of a rhombus form a rectangle.
11. The midpoint of the hypotenuse of a right triangle is equidistant from the three vertices of the triangle.
12. The median of a trapezoid is parallel to the bases of the trapezoid and has a length equal to one-half the sum of the lengths of the two bases.
13. The line segment that joins the midpoints of two sides of a triangle is parallel to the third side and has a length equal to one-half the length of the third side.

14. The perpendicular bisector of the base of an isosceles triangle contains the vertex of the triangle.

15. If the midpoint of one side of a rectangle is joined to the endpoints of the opposite side, then an isosceles triangle is formed.

*16. If the median to one side of a triangle is also an altitude of the triangle, then the triangle is isosceles.

*17. If the diagonals of a parallelogram are perpendicular, then the parallelogram is a rhombus.

18. Use the analytic method to decide what type of quadrilateral is formed when the midpoints of the consecutive sides of a parallelogram are joined by line segments.

19. Use the analytic method to decide what type of triangle is formed when the midpoints of the sides of an isosceles triangle are joined by line segments.

20. Use slopes to verify that the graphs of the equations

$$Ax + By = C \quad \text{and} \quad Ax + By = D$$

are parallel.
(NOTE: $A \neq 0$, $B \neq 0$, and $C \neq D$.)

21. Use slopes to verify that the graphs of the equations

$$Ax + By = C \quad \text{and} \quad Bx - Ay = D$$

are perpendicular.
(NOTE: $A \neq 0$ and $B \neq 0$.)

22. Use the result in Exercise 20 to find the equation of the line that contains (4, 5) and is parallel to the graph of $2x + 3y = 6$.

23. Use the result in Exercise 21 to find the equation of the line that contains (4, 5) and is perpendicular to the graph of $2x + 3y = 6$.

24. Use the Distance Formula to show that the circle with center (0, 0) and radius length r has the equation $x^2 + y^2 = r^2$.

25. Use the result in Exercise 24 to find the equation of the circle with center (0, 0) and radius length $r = 3$.

26. Use the result in Exercise 24 to find the equation of the circle that has center (0, 0) and contains the point (3, 4).

27. Suppose that the circle with center (0, 0) and radius length r contains the point (a, b). Find the slope of the tangent line to the circle at the point (a, b).

28. Consider the circle with center (h, k) and radius length r. If the circle contains the point (c, d), find the slope of the tangent line to the circle at the point (c, d).

29. Would the theorem of Exercise 7 remain true for a concave quadrilateral like the one shown?

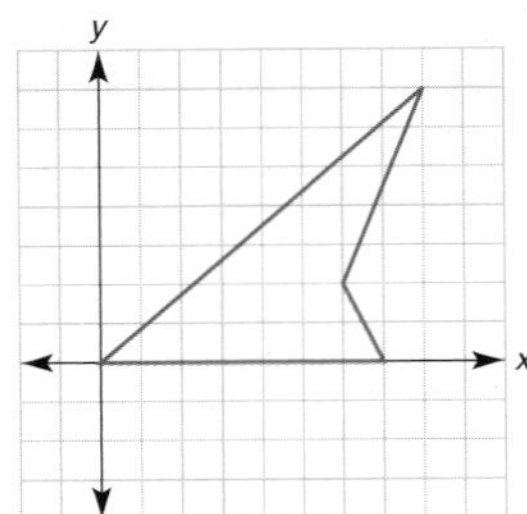

Exercise 29

*30. Complete an analytic proof of the following theorem: In a triangle that has sides of lengths a, b, and c, if $c^2 = a^2 + b^2$, then the triangle is a right triangle.

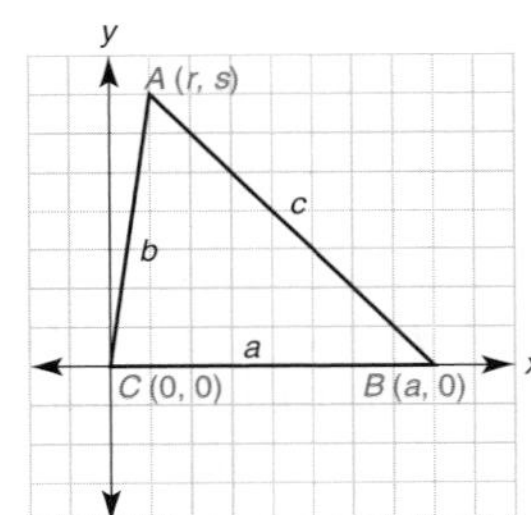

Exercise 30

10.5 Equations of Lines

KEY CONCEPTS: Slope-Intercept Form of a Line | Point-Slope Form of a Line | Systems of Equations

In Section 10.2, we saw that equations such as $2x + 3y = 6$ and $4x - 12y = 60$ have graphs that are lines. To graph an equation of the general form $Ax + By = C$, that equation is often replaced with an equivalent equation of the form $y = mx + b$. For instance, $2x + 3y = 6$ can be transformed into $y = -\frac{2}{3}x + 2$; equations such as these are known as *equivalent* because their ordered-pair solutions (and graphs) are identical. In particular, we must express a linear equation in the form $y = mx + b$ in order to plot it on a graphing calculator.

EXAMPLE 1

Write the equation $4x - 12y = 60$ in the form $y = mx + b$.

Solution Given $4x - 12y = 60$, we subtract $4x$ from each side of the equation to obtain $-12y = -4x + 60$. Dividing by -12,

$$\frac{-12y}{-12} = \frac{-4x}{-12} + \frac{60}{-12}$$

SSG *Exs. 1–3*

Then $y = \frac{1}{3}x - 5$. ■

SLOPE-INTERCEPT FORM OF A LINE

We now turn our attention to a method for finding the equation of a line. In the following technique, the equation can be found if the slope and the y intercept of the line are known. The form $y = mx + b$ is known as the Slope-Intercept Form of a line.

THEOREM 10.5.1 ▶ (Slope-intercept Form of a Line)

The line whose slope is m and whose y intercept is b has the equation $y = mx + b$.

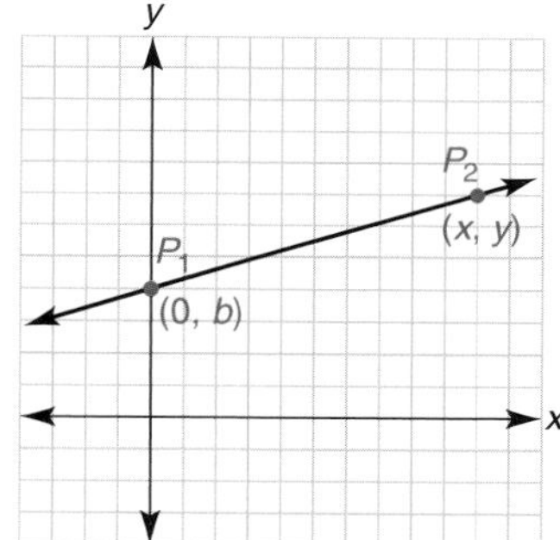

Figure 10.33

PROOF

Consider the line whose slope is m (see Figure 10.33). Using the Slope Formula

$$m = \frac{y_2 - y_1}{x_2 - x_1}$$

we designate (x, y) as P_2 and $(0, b)$ as P_1. Then

$$m = \frac{y - b}{x - 0} \quad \text{or} \quad m = \frac{y - b}{x}$$

Multiplying by x, we have $mx = y - b$. Then $mx + b = y$, or $y = mx + b$. ■

Discover

Use a graphing calculator to graph $Y_1 = x$, $Y_2 = x^2$, and $Y_3 = x^3$. Which of these is (are) a line(s)?

ANSWER
$Y_1 = x$

EXAMPLE 2

Find the general equation $Ax + By = C$ for the line with slope $m = -\frac{2}{3}$ and y intercept -2.

Solution With $y = mx + b$, we have

$$y = -\frac{2}{3}x - 2$$

Multiplying by 3, we obtain

$$3y = -2x - 6 \quad \text{so} \quad 2x + 3y = -6$$

NOTE: An equivalent and correct solution is $-2x - 3y = 6$. ■

It is often easier to graph an equation if it is in the form $y = mx + b$. When an equation has this form, we know that its graph is a line that has slope m and contains $(0, b)$.

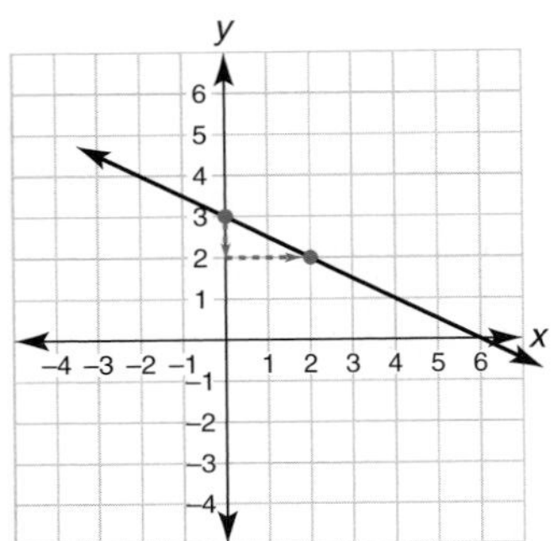

Figure 10.34

EXAMPLE 3

Draw the graph of $\frac{1}{2}x + y = 3$.

Solution Solving for y, we have $y = -\frac{1}{2}x + 3$. Then $m = -\frac{1}{2}$, and the y intercept is 3.

We first plot the point (0, 3). Because $m = -\frac{1}{2}$ or $\frac{-1}{2}$, the vertical change of -1 corresponds to a horizontal change of $+2$. Thus, the second point is located 1 unit down from and 2 units to the right of the first point. The line is drawn in Figure 10.34. ■

Another look at Figure 10.34 shows that the graph contains the points (2,2) and (6,0). Both ordered pairs are easily shown to be solutions for the equation $1/2x + y = 3$ of Example 3.

POINT-SLOPE FORM OF A LINE

SSG *Exs. 4–8*

If slope m and a point other than the y intercept of a line are known, we generally do not use the Slope-Intercept Form to find the equation of the line. Instead, the Point-Slope Form of the equation of a line is used. This form is also used when the coordinates of two points of the line are known; in that case, the value of m is found by the Slope Formula. The form $y - y_1 = m(x - x_1)$ is known as the Point-Slope Form of a line.

THEOREM 10.5.2 ▶ (Point-Slope Form of a Line)

The line that has slope m and contains the point (x_1, y_1) has the equation

$$y - y_1 = m(x - x_1)$$

PROOF

Let P_1 be the given point (x_1, y_1) on the line, and let P_2 be (x, y), which represents any other point on the line. (See Figure 10.35.) Using the Slope Formula, we have

$$m = \frac{y - y_1}{x - x_1}$$

Multiplying the equation by $(x - x_1)$ yields

$$m(x - x_1) = y - y_1$$

It follows that

$$y - y_1 = m(x - x_1)$$

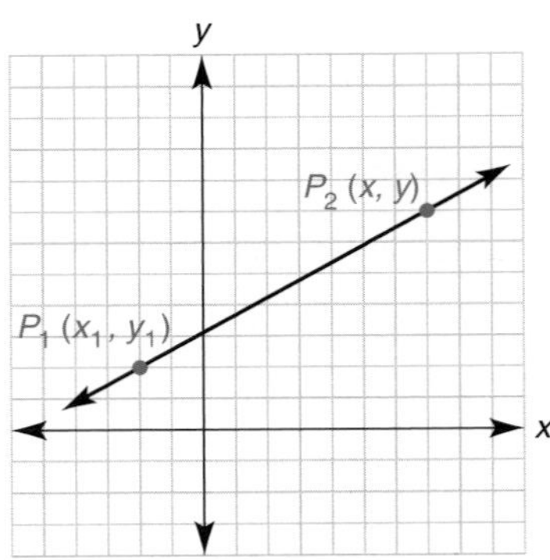

Figure 10.35

■

EXAMPLE 4

Find the general equation, $Ax + By = C$, for the line that has the slope $m = 2$ and contains the point $(-1, 3)$.

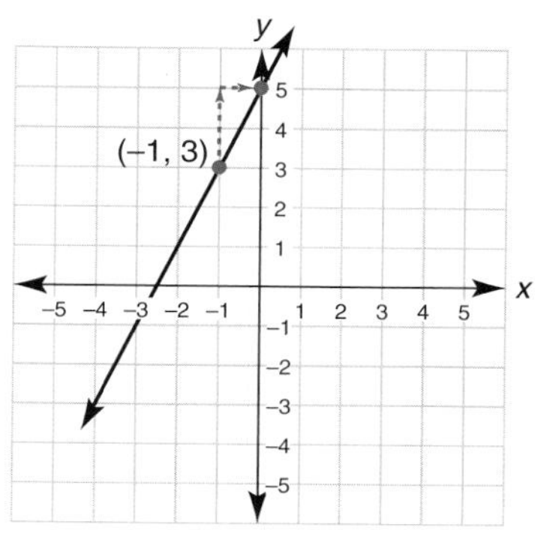

Figure 10.36

Solution We have $m = 2$, $x_1 = -1$, and $y_1 = 3$. Applying the Point-Slope Form, we find that the line in Figure 10.36 has the equation

$$\begin{aligned} y - 3 &= 2[x - (-1)] \\ y - 3 &= 2(x + 1) \\ y - 3 &= 2x + 2 \\ -2x + y &= 5 \end{aligned}$$

■

An equivalent answer for Example 4 is the equation $2x - y = -5$. The form $y = 2x + 5$ emphasizes that the slope is $m = 2$ and that the y intercept is $(0, 5)$. With $m = 2$, or $\frac{2}{1}$, the vertical change of 2 corresponds to a horizontal change of 1. See Figure 10.36.

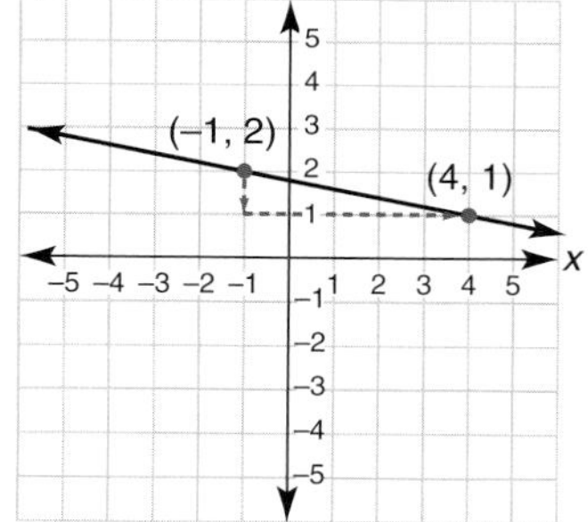

Figure 10.37

EXAMPLE 5

Find an equation for the line containing the points $(-1, 2)$ and $(4, 1)$.

Solution To use the Point-Slope Form, we need to know the slope of the line (see Figure 10.37). When we choose $P_1(-1, 2)$ and $P_2\ (4, 1)$, the Slope Formula reads

$$m = \frac{1 - 2}{4 - (-1)} = \frac{-1}{5} = -\frac{1}{5}$$

Therefore, $$y - 2 = -\frac{1}{5}[x - (-1)]$$

Then $$y - 2 = -\frac{1}{5}[x + 1]$$

and $$y - 2 = -\frac{1}{5}x - \frac{1}{5}$$

Multiplying the equation by 5, we obtain

$$5y - 10 = -1x - 1 \qquad \text{so} \qquad x + 5y = 9$$

NOTE: Other forms of the answer are $-x - 5y = -9$ and $y = -\frac{1}{5}x + \frac{9}{5}$. In any correct form, the given points P_1 and P_2 must satisfy the equation. ■

In Example 6, we use the Point-Slope Form to find an equation for a median of a triangle.

SSG *Exs. 9–12*

EXAMPLE 6

For $\triangle ABC$, the vertices are $A(0, 0)$, $B(2a, 0)$, and $C(2b, 2c)$. Find the equation of median $\overline{CM}$ in the form $y = mx + b$. See Figure 10.38 on page 484.

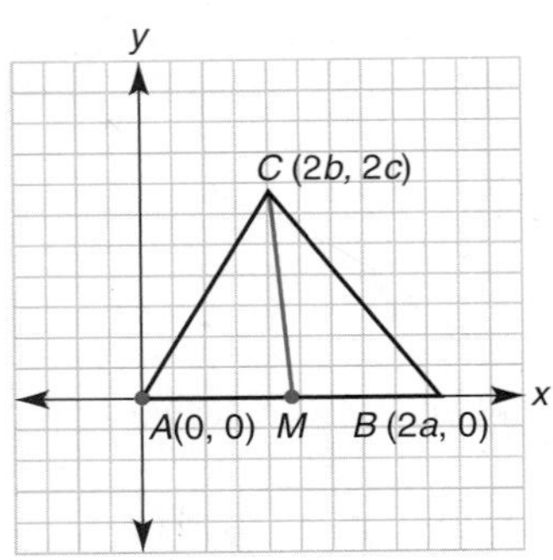

Figure 10.38

Solution For $\overline{CM}$ to be a median of $\triangle ABC$, M must be the midpoint of $\overline{AB}$. Then

$$M = \left(\frac{0 + 2a}{2}, \frac{0 + 0}{2}\right) = (a, 0)$$

To determine an equation for $\overline{CM}$, we also need to know its slope. With $M(a, 0)$ and $C(2b, 2c)$ on $\overline{CM}$, the slope is $m_{\overline{CM}} = \frac{2c - 0}{2b - a}$ or $\frac{2c}{2b - a}$. With $M = (a, 0)$ as the point on the line, $y - y_1 = m(x - x_1)$ becomes

$$y - 0 = \frac{2c}{2b - a}(x - a) \quad \text{or} \quad y = \frac{2c}{2b - a}x - \frac{2ac}{2b - a}$$

■

SOLVING SYSTEMS OF EQUATIONS

In earlier chapters, we solved systems of equations such as

$$\begin{aligned} x + 2y &= 6 \\ 2x - y &= 7 \end{aligned}$$

by using the Addition Property or the Subtraction Property of Equality. We review the method in Example 7. The solution for the system is an ordered pair; in fact, the solution is the point of intersection of the graphs of the given equations.

Technology Exploration

Use a graphing calculator if one is available.

1. Solve each equation of Example 7 for y.
2. Graph $Y_1 = -\left(\frac{1}{2}\right)x + 3$ and $Y_2 = 2x - 7$.
3. Use the Intersect feature to show that the solution for the system is (4, 1).

EXAMPLE 7

Solve the following system by using algebra:

$$\begin{cases} x + 2y = 6 \\ 2x - y = 7 \end{cases}$$

Solution When we multiply the second equation by 2, the system becomes

$$\begin{cases} x + 2y = 6 \\ 4x - 2y = 14 \end{cases}$$

Adding these equations yields $5x = 20$, so $x = 4$. Substituting $x = 4$ into the first equation, we get $4 + 2y = 6$, so $2y = 2$. Then $y = 1$. The solution is the ordered pair (4, 1). ■

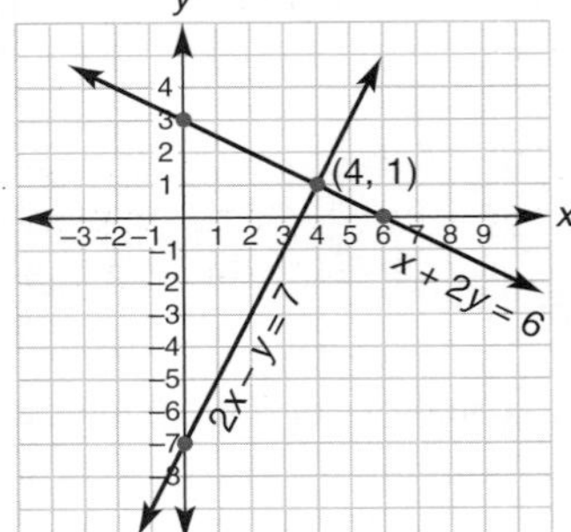

Figure 10.39

Another method for solving a system of equations is geometric and requires graphing. Solving by graphing amounts to finding the point of intersection of the linear graphs. That point is the ordered pair that is the common solution (when one exists) for the two equations. Notice that Example 8 repeats the system of Example 7. The graphs of the Technology Exploration should have the appearance of Figure 10.39.

EXAMPLE 8

Solve the following system by graphing:

$$\begin{cases} x + 2y = 6 \\ 2x - y = 7 \end{cases}$$

Solution Each equation is changed to the form $y = mx + b$ so that the slope and the y intercept are used in graphing:

$$x + 2y = 6 \rightarrow 2y = -1x + 6 \rightarrow y = -\frac{1}{2}x + 3$$
$$2x - y = 7 \rightarrow -y = -2x + 7 \rightarrow y = 2x - 7$$

The graph of $y = -\frac{1}{2}x + 3$ is a line with y intercept 3 and slope $m = -\frac{1}{2}$. The graph of $y = 2x - 7$ is a line with y intercept -7 and slope $m = 2$.

The graphs are drawn in the same coordinate system. See Figure 10.39. The point of intersection (4, 1) is the common solution for each of the given equations and thus is the solution of the system. ■

NOTE: To verify the result of Examples 7 and 8, we show that (4, 1) satisfies both of the given equations:

$$x + 2y = 6 \rightarrow 4 + 2(1) = 6 \text{ is } \textit{true}.$$
$$2x - y = 7 \rightarrow 2(4) - 1 = 7 \text{ is } \textit{true}.$$

The solution is verified in that both statements are true.

Advantages of the method of solving a system of equations by graphing include the following:

1. It is easy to understand why a system such as

$$\begin{cases} x + 2y = 6 \\ 2x - y = 7 \end{cases} \quad \text{can be replaced by} \quad \begin{cases} x + 2y = 6 \\ 4x - 2y = 14 \end{cases}$$

when we are solving by addition or subtraction. We know that the graphs of $2x - y = 7$ and $4x - 2y = 14$ are the same line because each can be changed to the form $y = 2x - 7$.

2. It is easy to understand why a system such as

$$\begin{cases} x + 2y = 6 \\ 2x + 4y = -4 \end{cases}$$

has no solution. In Figure 10.40, the graphs of these equations are parallel lines. The first equation is equivalent to $y = -\frac{1}{2}x + 3$, and the second equation can be changed to $y = -\frac{1}{2}x - 1$. Both lines have slope $m = -\frac{1}{2}$ but have different y intercepts. Therefore, the lines are parallel.

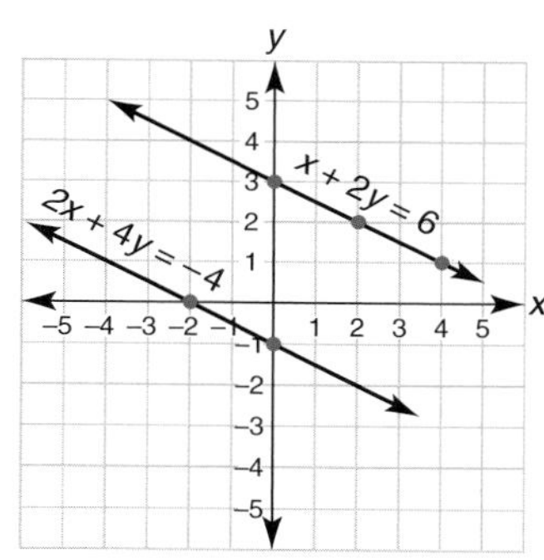

Figure 10.40

Algebraic substitution can also be used to solve a system of equations. In our approach, we write each equation in the form $y = mx + b$ and then equate the expressions for y. Once the x coordinate of the solution is known, we substitute this value of x into either equation to find the value of y.

EXAMPLE 9

Use substitution to solve $\begin{cases} x + 2y = 6 \\ 2x - y = 7 \end{cases}$

Solution Solving for y, we have

$$x + 2y = 6 \rightarrow 2y = -1x + 6 \rightarrow y = -\frac{1}{2}x + 3$$
$$2x - y = 7 \rightarrow -1y = -2x + 7 \rightarrow y = 2x - 7$$

Equating the expressions for y yields $-\frac{1}{2}x + 3 = 2x - 7$. Then $-2\frac{1}{2}x = -10$, or $-2.5x = -10$. Dividing by -2.5, we obtain $x = 4$. Substitution of 4 for x in the equation $y = 2x - 7$ leads to $y = 2(4) - 7$, so $y = 1$. The solution is the ordered pair (4, 1).

NOTE: Substitution of $x = 4$ into the equation $y = -\frac{1}{2}x + 3$ would lead to the same value of y, namely $y = 1$. Thus, one can substitute into either equation. ■

SSG *Exs. 13–16*

The method illustrated in Example 9 is also used in our final example. In the proof of Theorem 10.5.3, we use equations of lines to determine the centroid of a triangle.

EXAMPLE 10

Formulate a plan to complete the proof of Theorem 10.5.3. See Figure 10.41 on page 487.

THEOREM 10.5.3

The three medians of a triangle are concurrent at a point that is two-thirds the distance from any vertex to the midpoint of the opposite side.

Solution The proof can be completed as follows:

1. Find the coordinates of the two midpoints X and Y. See Figures 10.41(a) and 10.41(b). Note that

$$X = (a + b, c) \qquad \text{and} \qquad Y = (b, c)$$

2. Find the equations of the lines containing $\overline{AX}$ and $\overline{BY}$. The equations for $\overline{AX}$ and $\overline{BY}$ are $y = \frac{c}{a+b}x$ and $y = \frac{-c}{2a-b}x + \frac{2ac}{2a-b}$, respectively.

3. Find the point of intersection Z of $\overline{AX}$ and $\overline{BY}$, as shown in Figure 10.41(b). Solving the system provides the solution

$$Z = \left(\frac{2}{3}(a + b), \frac{2}{3}c\right)$$

4. It can now be shown that $AZ = \frac{2}{3} \cdot AX$ and $BZ = \frac{2}{3} \cdot BY$. See Figure 10.41(b), in which we can show that

$$AZ = \frac{2}{3}\sqrt{(a + b)^2 + c^2} \qquad \text{and} \qquad AX = \sqrt{(a + b)^2 + c^2}$$

5. It can also be shown that point Z lies on the third median $\overline{CW}$, whose equation is $y = \frac{2c}{2b - a}(x - a)$. See Figure 10.41(c).

6. We can also show that $CZ = \frac{2}{3} \cdot CW$, which would complete the proof. ■

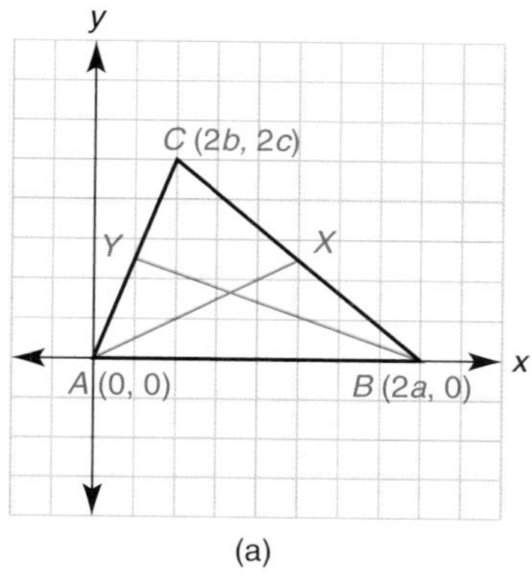

(a)

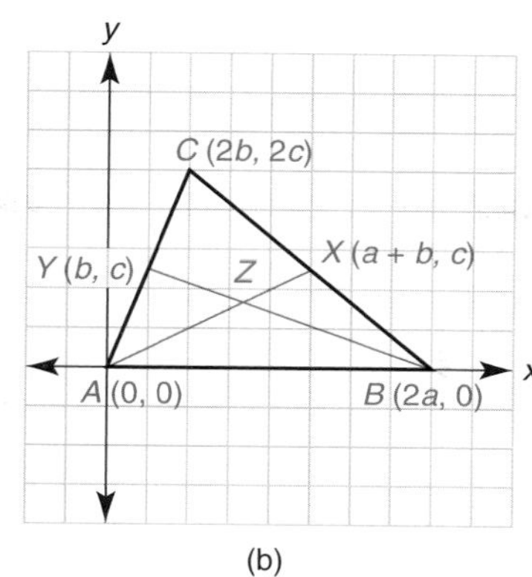

(b)

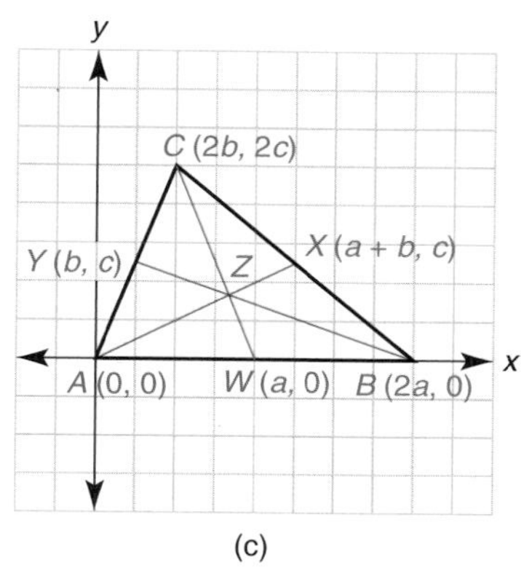

(c)

Figure 10.41

Exercises 10.5

In Exercises 1 to 4, use division to write an equation of the form $Ax + By = C$ that is equivalent to the one provided. Then write the given equation in the form $y = mx + b$.

1. $8x + 16y = 48$
2. $15x - 35y = 105$
3. $-6x + 18y = -240$
4. $27x - 36y = 108$

In Exercises 5 to 8, draw the graph of each equation by using the method of Example 3.

5. $y = 2x - 3$
6. $y = -2x + 5$
7. $\frac{2}{5}x + y = 6$
8. $3x - 2y = 12$

In Exercises 9 to 24, find the equation of the line described. Leave the solution in the form $Ax + By = C$.

9. The line has slope $m = -\frac{2}{3}$ and contains $(0, 5)$.
10. The line has slope $m = -3$ and contains $(0, -2)$.
11. The line contains $(2, 4)$ and $(0, 6)$.
12. The line contains $(-2, 5)$ and $(2, -1)$.
13. The line contains $(0, -1)$ and $(3, 1)$.
14. The line contains $(-2, 0)$ and $(4, 3)$.
15. The line contains $(0, b)$ and $(a, 0)$.
16. The line contains (b, c) and has slope d.
17. The line has intercepts $a = 2$ and $b = -2$.
18. The line has intercepts $a = -3$ and $b = 5$.
19. The line contains $(-1, 5)$ and is parallel to the line $5x + 2y = 10$.
20. The line contains $(0, 3)$ and is parallel to the line $3x + y = 7$.
21. The line contains $(0, -4)$ and is perpendicular to the line $y = \frac{3}{4}x - 5$.
22. The line contains $(2, -3)$ and is perpendicular to the line $2x - 3y = 6$.
23. The line is the perpendicular bisector of the line segment that joins $(3, 5)$ and $(5, -1)$.
24. The line is the perpendicular bisector of the line segment that joins $(-4, 5)$ and $(1, 1)$.

In Exercises 25 and 26, find the equation of the line in the form $y = mx + b$.

25. The line contains (g, h) and is *perpendicular* to the line $y = \frac{a}{b}x + c$.
26. The line contains (g, h) and is *parallel* to the line $y = \frac{a}{b}x + c$.

In Exercises 27 to 32, use graphing to find the point of intersection of the two lines. Use Example 8 as a guide.

27. $y = \frac{1}{2}x - 3$ and $y = \frac{1}{3}x - 2$
28. $y = 2x + 3$ and $y = 3x$
29. $2x + y = 6$ and $3x - y = 19$
30. $\frac{1}{2}x + y = -3$ and $\frac{3}{4}x - y = 8$
31. $4x + 3y = 18$ and $x - 2y = 10$
32. $2x + 3y = 3$ and $3x - 2y = 24$

In Exercises 33 to 38, use algebra to find the point of intersection of the two lines whose equations are provided. Use Example 7 as a guide.

33. $2x + y = 8$ and $3x - y = 7$
34. $2x + 3y = 7$ and $x + 3y = 2$
35. $2x + y = 11$ and $3x + 2y = 16$
36. $x + y = 1$ and $4x - 2y = 1$
37. $2x + 3y = 4$ and $3x - 4y = 23$
38. $5x - 2y = -13$ and $3x + 5y = 17$

In Exercises 39 to 42, use substitution to solve the system. Use Example 9 as a guide.

39. $y = \frac{1}{2}x - 3$ and $y = \frac{1}{3}x - 2$

40. $y = 2x + 3$ and $y = 3x$

41. $y = a$ and $y = bx + c$

42. $x = d$ and $y = fx + g$

43. For $\triangle ABC$, the vertices are $A(0, 0)$, $B(a, 0)$, and $C(b, c)$. In terms of a, b, and c, find the coordinates of the orthocenter of $\triangle ABC$. (The orthocenter is the point of concurrence for the altitudes of a triangle.)

44. For isosceles $\triangle PNQ$, the vertices are $P(-2a, 0)$, $N(2a, 0)$, and $Q(0, 2b)$. In terms of a and b, find the coordinates of the circumcenter of $\triangle PNQ$. (The circumcenter is the point of concurrence for the perpendicular bisectors of the sides of a triangle.)

In Exercises 45 and 46, complete an analytic proof for each theorem.

45. The altitudes of a triangle are concurrent.

46. The perpendicular bisectors of the sides of a triangle are concurrent.

47. Describe the steps of the procedure that enables us to find the distance from a point $P(a, b)$ to the line $Ax + By = C$.

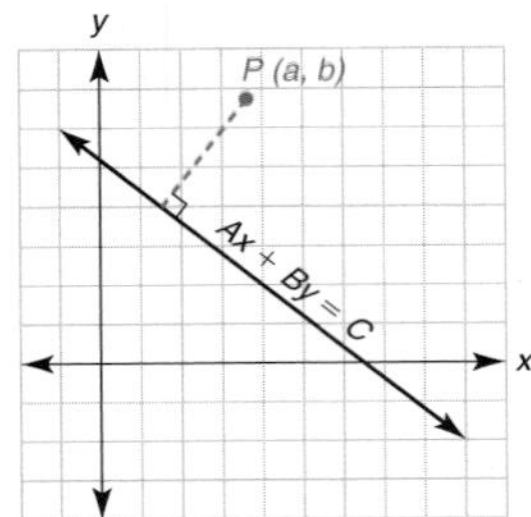

PERSPECTIVE ON HISTORY

The Banach-Tarski Paradox

In the 1920s, two Polish mathematicians proposed a mathematical dilemma to their colleagues. Known as the Banach-Tarski paradox, their proposal has puzzled students of geometry for decades. What was most baffling was that the proposal suggested that matter could be created through rearrangement of the pieces of a figure! The following steps outline the Banach-Tarski paradox.

First consider the square whose sides are each of length 8. [See Figure 10.42(a).] By counting squares or by applying a formula, it is clear that the 8-by-8 square must have an area of 64 square units. We now subdivide the square (as shown) to form two right triangles and two trapezoids. Note the dimensions indicated on each piece of the square in Figure 10.42(b).

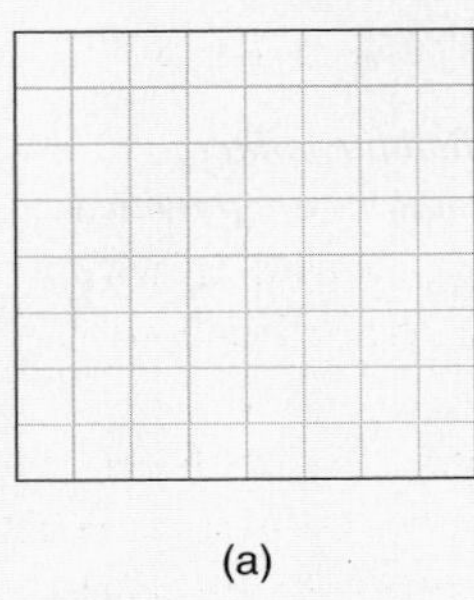

(a)

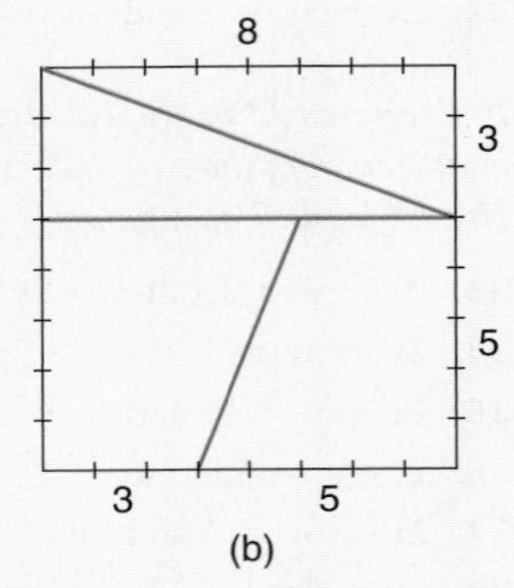

(b)

Figure 10.42

The parts of the square are now rearranged to form a rectangle (see Figure 10.43) whose dimensions are 13 and 5. This rectangle clearly has an area that measures 65 square units, 1 square unit more than the given square! How is it possible that the second figure has an area greater than that of the first?

The puzzle is real, but you may also sense that something is wrong. This paradox can be explained by considering the slopes of lines. The triangles, which have

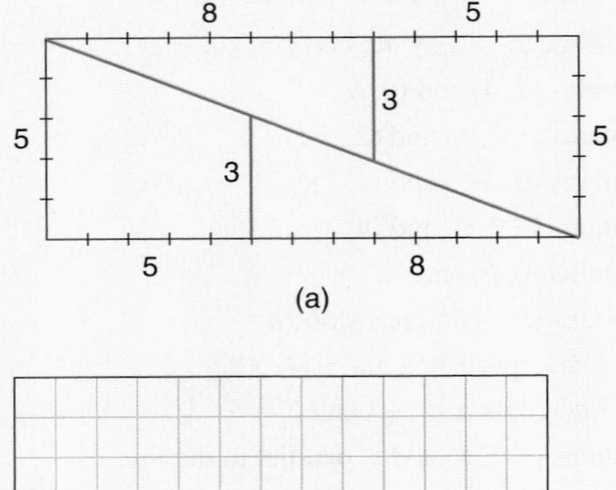

(a)

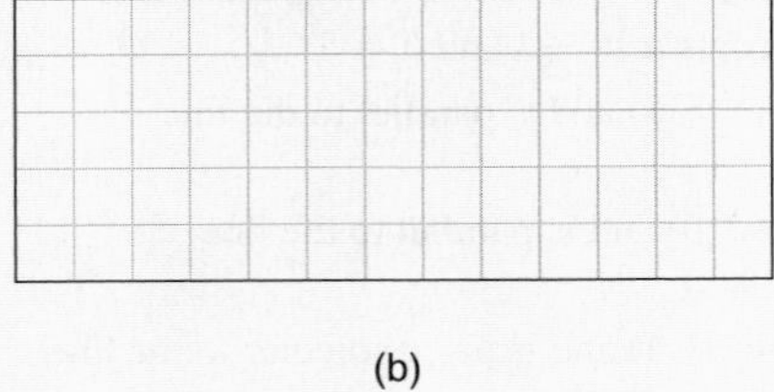

(b)

Figure 10.43

legs of lengths 3 and 8, determine a hypotenuse whose slope is $-\frac{3}{8}$. Although the side of the trapezoid appears to be collinear with the hypotenuse, it actually has a slope of $-\frac{2}{5}$. It was easy to accept that the segments were collinear because the slopes are nearly equal; in fact, $-\frac{3}{8} = -0.375$ and $\frac{2}{5} = -0.400$. In Figure 10.44 (which is somewhat exaggerated), a very thin parallelogram appears in the space between the original segments of the cut-up square. One may quickly conclude that the area of that parallelogram is 1 square unit, and the paradox has been resolved once more!

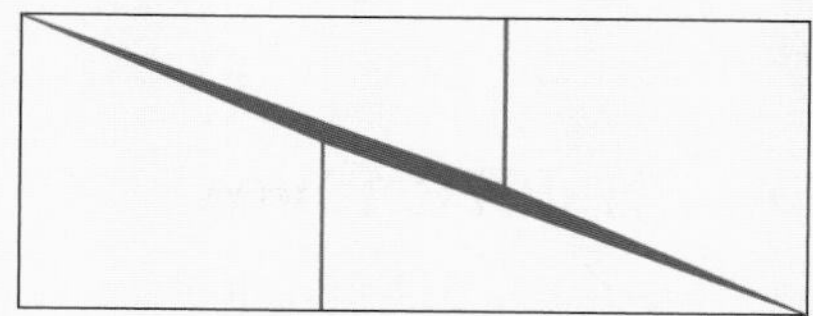

Figure 10.44

PERSPECTIVE ON APPLICATION

The Point-of-Division Formulas

The subject of this feature is a generalization of the formulas that led to the Midpoint Formula. Recall that the midpoint of the line segment that joins $A(x_1, y_1)$ to $B(x_2, y_2)$ is given by $M = \left(\frac{x_1 + x_2}{2}, \frac{y_1 + y_2}{2}\right)$, which is derived from the formulas $x = x_1 + \frac{1}{2}(x_2 - x_1)$ and $y = y_1 + \frac{1}{2}(y_2 - y_1)$. The formulas for a more general location of point between A and B follow; to better understand how these formulas can be applied, we note that r represents the fractional part of the distance from point A to point B on $\overline{AB}$; in the Midpoint Formula, $r = \frac{1}{2}$.

Point-of-Division Formulas: Let $A(x_1, y_1)$ and $B(x_2, y_2)$ represent the endpoints of $\overline{AB}$. Where r represents a common fraction $(0 < r < 1)$, the coordinates of the point P that lies this part r of the distance from A to B are given by

$$x = x_1 + r(x_2 - x_1) \quad \text{and} \quad y = y_1 + r(y_2 - y_1)$$

The following table clarifies the use of the formulas above.

TABLE 10.3

Value of r	Location of Point P on $\overline{AB}$
$\frac{1}{3}$	Point P lies $\frac{1}{3}$ of the distance from A to B.
$\frac{3}{4}$	Point P lies $\frac{3}{4}$ of the distance from A to B.

EXAMPLE 1

Find the point P on $\overline{AB}$ that is one-third of the distance from $A(-1, 2)$ to $B(8, 5)$.

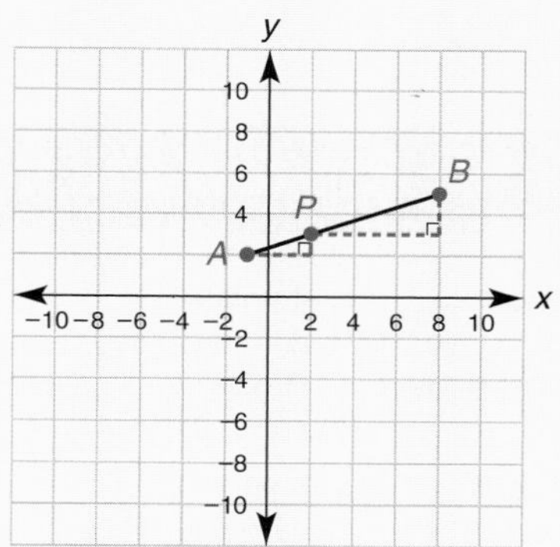

Solution

$x = -1 + \frac{1}{3}(8 - [-1])$ and $y = 2 + \frac{1}{3}(5 - 2)$

Then $x = -1 + \frac{1}{3}(9)$ so $x = -1 + 3$ or 2

Also, $y = 2 + \frac{1}{3}(3)$ so $y = 2 + 1$ or 3

The desired point is $P(2, 3)$.

NOTE: See the figure above, in which similar triangles can be used to explain why point P is the desired point. ■

In some higher-level courses, the value of r is not restricted to values between 0 and 1. For instance, we could choose $r = 2$ or $r = -1$. For such values of r, the point P produced by the Point-of-Division Formulas remains collinear with A and B. However, the point P that is produced does not lie between A and B.

Summary

A LOOK BACK AT CHAPTER 10

Our goal in this chapter was to relate algebra and geometry. This relationship is called *analytic geometry* or *coordinate geometry*. Formulas for the length of a line segment, the midpoint of a line segment, and the slope of a line were developed. We found the equation for a line and used it for graphing. Analytic proofs were provided for a number of theorems of geometry.

A LOOK AHEAD TO CHAPTER 11

In the next chapter, we will again deal with the right triangle. Three trigonometric ratios (sine, cosine, and tangent) will be defined for an acute angle of the right triangle in terms of its sides. An area formula for triangles will be derived using the sine ratio. We will also prove the Law of Sines and the Law of Cosines for acute triangles.

KEY CONCEPTS

10.1

Analytic Geometry • Cartesian Coordinate System • Rectangular Coordinate System • *x* Axis • *y* Axis • Quadrants • Origin • *x* Coordinate • *y* Coordinate • Ordered Pair • Distance Formula • Linear Equation • Midpoint Formula

10.2

Graphs of Equations • *x* Intercept • *y* Intercept • Slope • Slope Formula • Negative Reciprocal

10.3

Formulas and Relationships • Placement of Figure

10.4

Analytic Proof • Synthetic Proof

10.5

Slope-Intercept Form of a Line • Point-Slope Form of a Line • Systems of Equations

Chapter 10 REVIEW EXERCISES

1. Find the distance between each pair of points:
   a) $(6, 4)$ and $(6, -3)$
   b) $(1, 4)$ and $(-5, 4)$
   c) $(-5, 2)$ and $(7, -3)$
   d) $(x - 3, y + 2)$ and $(x, y - 2)$
2. Find the distance between each pair of points:
   a) $(2, -3)$ and $(2, 5)$
   b) $(3, -2)$ and $(-7, -2)$
   c) $(-4, 1)$ and $(4, 5)$
   d) $(x - 2, y - 3)$ and $(x + 4, y + 5)$
3. Find the midpoint of the line segment that joins each pair of points in Exercise 1.
4. Find the midpoint of the line segment that joins each pair of points in Exercise 2.
5. Find the slope of the line containing each pair of points in Exercise 1.
6. Find the slope of the line containing each pair of points in Exercise 2.
7. $(2, 1)$ is the midpoint of $\overline{AB}$, in which A has coordinates $(8, 10)$. Find the coordinates of B.
8. The y axis is the perpendicular bisector of $\overline{RS}$. Find the coordinates of R if S is the point $(-3, 7)$.
9. If A has coordinates $(2, 1)$ and B has coordinates $(x, 3)$, find x such that the slope of $\overleftrightarrow{AB}$ is -3.
10. If R has coordinates $(-5, 2)$ and S has coordinates $(2, y)$, find y such that the slope of $\overleftrightarrow{RS}$ is $\frac{-6}{7}$.
11. Without graphing, determine whether the pairs of lines are parallel, perpendicular, the same, or none of these:
    a) $x + 3y = 6$ and $3x - y = -7$
    b) $2x - y = -3$ and $y = 2x - 14$
    c) $y + 2 = -3(x - 5)$ and $2y = 6x + 11$
    d) $0.5x + y = 0$ and $2x - y = 10$
12. Determine whether the points $(-6, 5)$, $(1, 7)$, and $(16, 10)$ are collinear.
13. Find x such that $(-2, 3)$, $(x, 6)$, and $(8, 8)$ are collinear.
14. Draw the graph of $3x + 7y = 21$, and name the x intercept a and the y intercept b.
15. Draw the graph of $4x - 3y = 9$ by changing the equation to Slope-Intercept Form.
16. Draw the graph of $y + 2 = \frac{-2}{3}(x - 1)$.
17. Write the equation for:
    a) The line through $(2, 3)$ and $(-3, 6)$
    b) The line through $(-2, -1)$ and parallel to the line through $(6, -3)$ and $(8, -9)$
    c) The line through $(3, -2)$ and perpendicular to the line $x + 2y = 4$
    d) The line through $(-3, 5)$ and parallel to the x axis
18. Show that the triangle whose vertices are $A(-2, -3)$, $B(4, 5)$, and $C(-4, 1)$ is a right triangle.

19. Show that the triangle whose vertices are $A(3, 6)$, $B(-6, 4)$, and $C(1, -2)$ is an isosceles triangle.

20. Show that quadrilateral $RSTV$ with vertices $R(-5, -3)$, $S(1, -11)$, $T(7, -6)$, and $V(1, 2)$ is a parallelogram.

In Exercises 21 and 22, find the intersection of the graphs of the two equations by graphing.

21. $4x - 3y = -3$
$x + 2y = 13$

22. $y = x + 3$
$y = 4x$

In Exercises 23 and 24, solve the systems of equations in Exercises 21 and 22 by using algebraic methods.

23. Refer to Exercise 21.

24. Refer to Exercise 22.

25. Three of the four vertices of a parallelogram are $(0, -2)$, $(6, 8)$, and $(10, 1)$. Find the possibilities for the coordinates of the remaining vertex.

26. $A(3, 1)$, $B(5, 9)$, and $C(11, 3)$ are the vertices of $\triangle ABC$.
   a) Find the length of the median from B to $\overline{AC}$.
   b) Find the slope of the altitude from B to $\overline{AC}$.
   c) Find the slope of a line through B parallel to $\overline{AC}$.

In Exercises 27 to 30, supply the missing coordinates for the vertices, using as few variables as possible.

27.

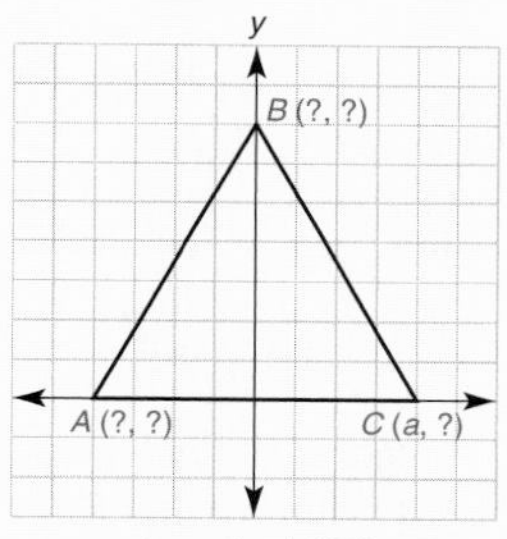

Isosceles $\triangle ABC$ with base $\overline{AC}$

28.

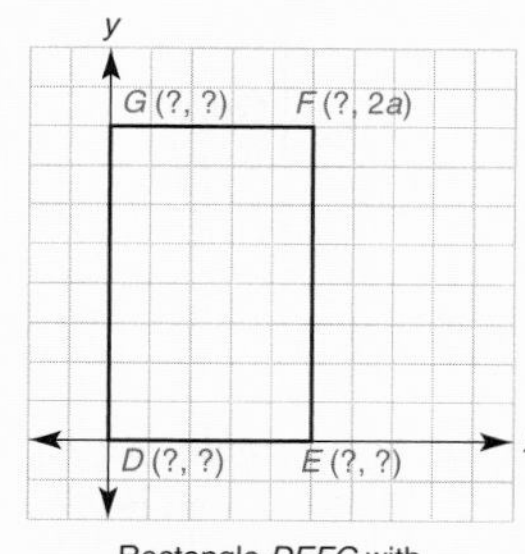

Rectangle $DEFG$ with $DG = 2 \cdot DE$

29.

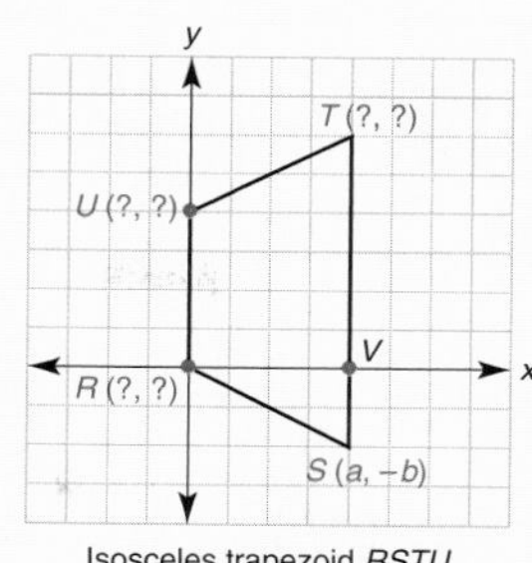

Isosceles trapezoid $RSTU$ with $\overline{RV} \cong \overline{RU}$

30.

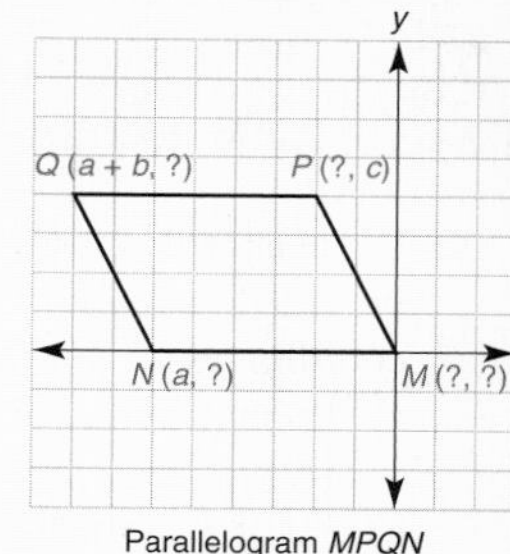

Parallelogram $MPQN$

31. $A(2a, 2b)$, $B(2c, 2d)$, and $C(0, 2e)$ are the vertices of $\triangle ABC$.
   a) Find the length of the median from C to $\overline{AB}$.
   b) Find the slope of the altitude from B to $\overline{AC}$.
   c) Find the equation of the altitude from B to $\overline{AC}$.

Prove the statements in Exercises 32 to 36 by using analytic geometry.

32. The line segments that join the midpoints of consecutive sides of a parallelogram form another parallelogram.

33. If the diagonals of a rectangle are perpendicular, then the rectangle is a square.

34. If the diagonals of a trapezoid are equal in length, then the trapezoid is an isosceles trapezoid.

35. If two medians of a triangle are equal in length, then the triangle is isosceles.

36. The line segments joining the midpoints of consecutive sides of an isosceles trapezoid form a rhombus.

Chapter 10 TEST

1. In the coordinate system provided, give the coordinates of:
   a) Point A in the form (x, y) ________
   b) Point B in the form (x, y) ________

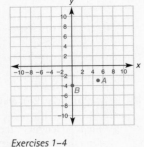

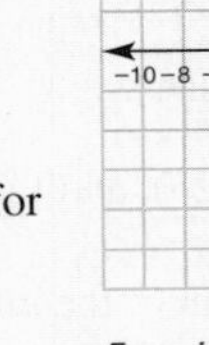

Exercises 1–4

2. In the coordinate system for Exercise 1, plot and label each point: $C(-6, 1)$ and $D(0, 9)$
3. Use $d = \sqrt{(x_2 - x_1)^2 + (y_2 - y_1)^2}$ to find the length of $\overline{CD}$ as described in Exercise 2. ________
4. In the form (x, y), determine the midpoint of $\overline{CD}$ as described in Exercise 2. ________
5. Complete the following table of x and y coordinates of points on the graph of the equation $2x + 3y = 12$.

x	0	3		9
y			4	

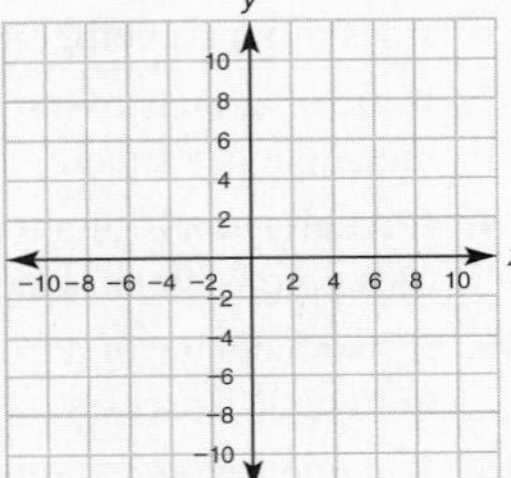

Exercises 5–6

6. Using the table from Exercise 5, sketch the graph of $2x + 3y = 12$.
7. Find the slope m of a line containing these points:
   a) $(-1, 3)$ and $(2, -6)$ ________
   b) (a, b) and (c, d) ________
8. Line ℓ has slope $m = \frac{2}{3}$. Find the slope of any line that is:
   a) Parallel to ℓ ________
   b) Perpendicular to ℓ ________
9. What type of quadrilateral $ABCD$ is represented if its vertices are $A(0, 0)$, $B(a, 0)$, $C(a + b, c)$, and $D(b, c)$?

   ____
10. For quadrilateral $ABCD$ of Exercise 9 to be a rhombus, it would be necessary that $AB = AD$. Using a, b, and c (as in Exercise 9), write the equation stating that $AB = AD$.

    ____
11. Being as specific as possible, describe the polygon shown in each figure.

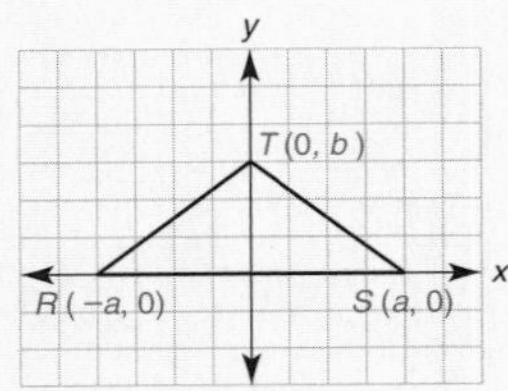

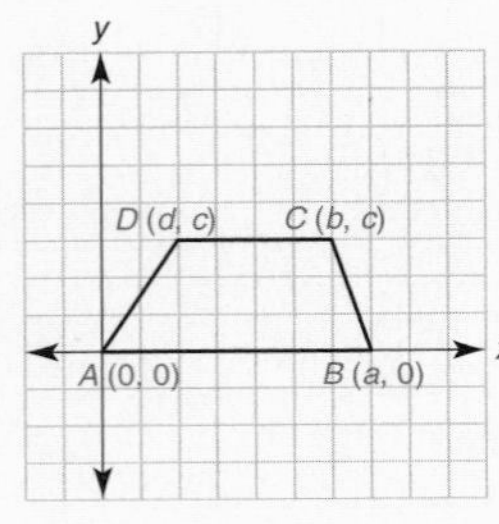

a) ________________ b) ________________

12. What formula (by name) is used to establish that
    a) two lines are parallel? ________
    b) two line segments are congruent? ________
13. Using as few variables as possible, state the coordinates of each point if $\triangle DEF$ is isosceles with $\overline{DF} \cong \overline{FE}$.

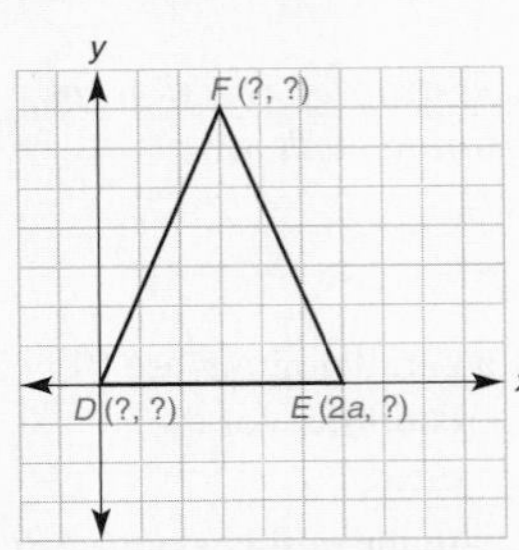

DEF is an isosceles triangle with $\overline{DF} \cong \overline{FE}$

D(__ , __), E ($2a$, __), F (__ , __).

14. For proving the theorem "The midpoint of the hypotenuse of a right triangle is equidistant from all three vertices," which drawing is best? ________

a) 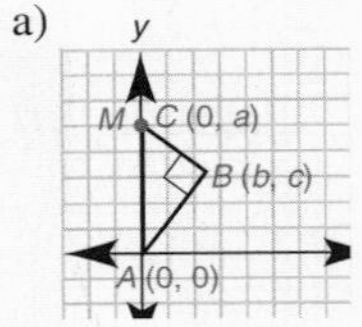

b) 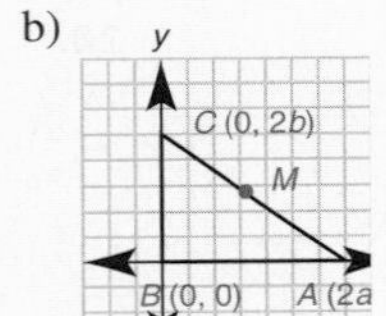

c) 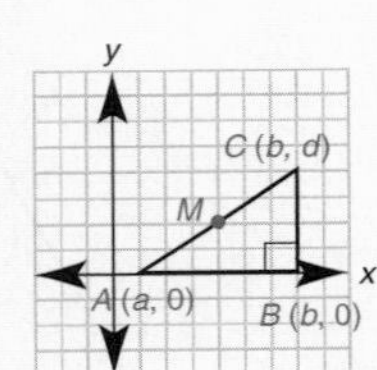

15. In the figure, we see that $m_{\overline{RS}} = m_{\overline{VT}} = 0$. Find the equation that relates r, s, and t if it is known that $RSTV$ is a parallelogram.

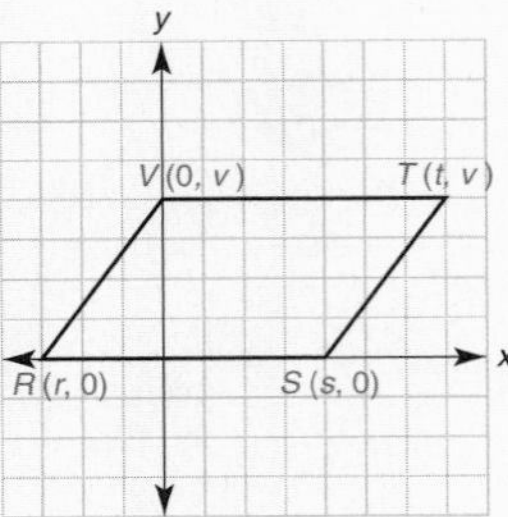

16. In the form $y = mx + b$, find the equation of the line that:
    a) Contains the points $(0, 4)$ and $(2, 6)$ ________
    b) Contains $(0, -3)$ and is parallel to the line $y = \frac{3}{4}x - 5$

    ____
17. Use $y - y_1 = m(x - x_1)$ to find the equation of the line that contains (a, b) and is perpendicular to the line $y = -\frac{1}{c}x + d$. Leave the answer (equation) in the form $y = mx + b$. ________

18. Use the graphs provided to solve the system consisting of the equations $x + 2y = 6$ and $2x - y = 7$. ________

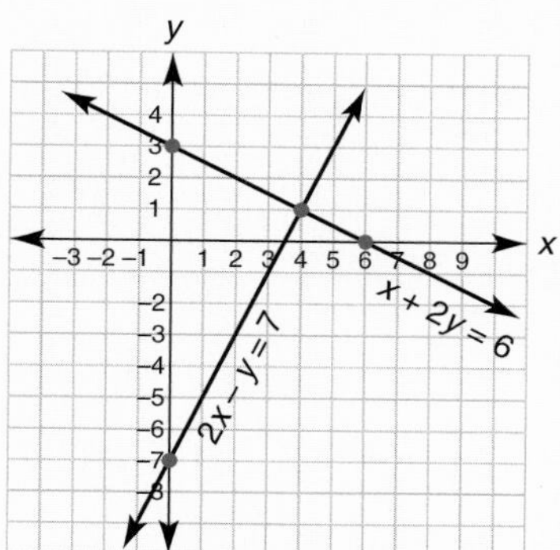

19. Use algebra to solve the system consisting of the equations $5x - 2y = -13$ and $3x + 5y = 17$.

____

20. Use the drawing provided to complete the proof of the theorem "The line segment that joins the midpoints of two sides of a triangle is parallel to the third side of the triangle."

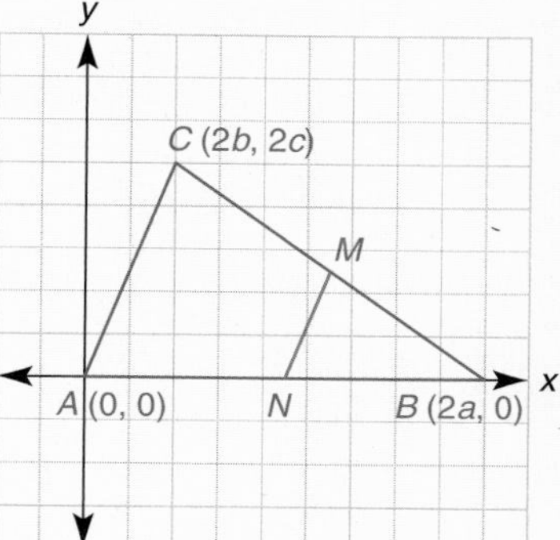

Proof: Given $\triangle ABC$ with vertices as shown, let M and N name the midpoints of sides $\overline{CB}$ and $\overline{AB}$, respectively. Then ________________

____

____

____

Introduction to Trigonometry

Chapter 11

© Travelpix Ltd/Getty Images

CHAPTER OUTLINE

Additional Video explanation of concepts, sample problems, and applications are available on DVD. 

Surreal! The Pontusval Lighthouse is located on the rugged shoreline of the Bretagne (Brittany) peninsula in northwest France. As with any lighthouse, it sends a "Welcome" message as well as a "Caution" message to the people on board an approaching vessel. Methods of trigonometry enable the ship captain to determine the distance from his or her ship to the rocky shoreline beneath the lighthouse. The word *trigonometry*, which means "the measure of a triangle," provides methods for the measurement of parts (sides and angles) of a triangle. Found in Chapter 11 are some techniques that enable you to find measures of one part of a right triangle when the measures of other parts are known. These methods can be expanded to include techniques for measuring parts of acute triangles as well.

For the applications of this chapter, you will find it necessary to use a scientific or graphing calculator.

11.1 The Sine Ratio and Applications

KEY CONCEPTS

Greek Letters: $\alpha, \beta, \gamma, \theta$
Opposite Side (Leg)
Hypotenuse

Sine Ratio:
$\sin \theta = \frac{\text{opposite}}{\text{hypotenuse}}$

Angle of Elevation
Angle of Depression

In this section, we will deal strictly with similar right triangles. In Figure 11.1, $\triangle ABC \sim \triangle DEF$ and $\angle C$ and $\angle F$ are right angles. Consider corresponding angles A and D; if we compare the length of the side opposite each angle to the length of the hypotenuse of each triangle, we obtain this result by the reason CSSTP:

$$\frac{BC}{AB} = \frac{EF}{DE} \quad \text{or} \quad \frac{3}{5} = \frac{6}{10}$$

In the two similar right triangles, the ratio of this pair of corresponding sides depends on the measure of acute $\angle A$ (or $\angle D$, because $m\angle A = m\angle D$); for this angle, the numerical value of the ratio

$$\frac{\text{length of side opposite the acute angle}}{\text{length of hypotenuse}}$$

is unique. This ratio becomes smaller for smaller measures of $\angle A$ and larger for larger measures of $\angle A$. This ratio is unique for each measure of an acute angle even though the lengths of the sides of the two similar right triangles containing the angle are different.

Geometry in the Real World

A surveyor uses trigonometry to find both angle measurements and distances.

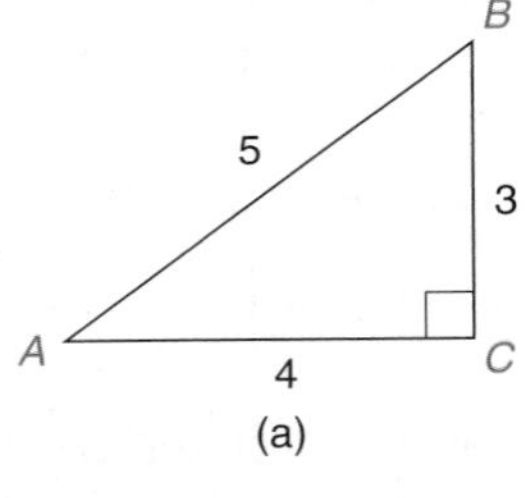

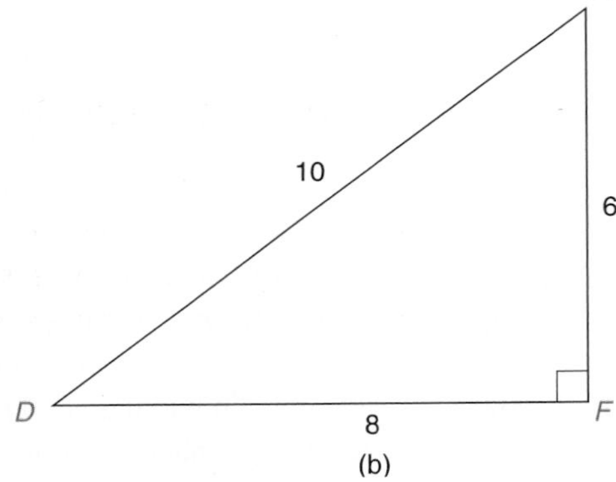

Figure 11.1

In Figure 11.2, we name the measures of the angles of the right triangle by the Greek letters α (alpha) at vertex A, β (beta) at vertex B, and γ (gamma) at vertex C. The lengths of the sides opposite vertices A, B, and C are a, b, and c, respectively. Relative to the acute angle, the lengths of the sides of the right triangle in the following definition are described as "opposite" and "hypotenuse." The word **opposite** is used to mean the length of the side opposite the angle named; the word **hypotenuse** is used to mean the length of the hypotenuse.

Figure 11.2

DEFINITION

In a right triangle, the **sine ratio** for an acute angle is the ratio $\frac{\text{opposite}}{\text{hypotenuse}}$.

NOTE: In right $\triangle ABC$ in Figure 11.2, we say that $\sin \alpha = \frac{a}{c}$ and $\sin \beta = \frac{b}{c}$, where "sin" is an abbreviation of the word *sine* (pronounced like *sign*). It is also correct to say that $\sin A = \frac{a}{c}$ and $\sin B = \frac{b}{c}$.

EXAMPLE 1

In Figure 11.3, find $\sin \alpha$ and $\sin \beta$ for right $\triangle ABC$.

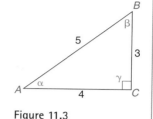

Solution $a = 3$, $b = 4$, and $c = 5$. Therefore,

$$\sin \alpha = \frac{a}{c} = \frac{3}{5}$$

and

$$\sin \beta = \frac{b}{c} = \frac{4}{5}$$

Figure 11.3

NOTE: In Example 1, it is correct to state that $\sin A = \frac{3}{5}$ and $\sin B = \frac{4}{5}$. ■

EXAMPLE 2

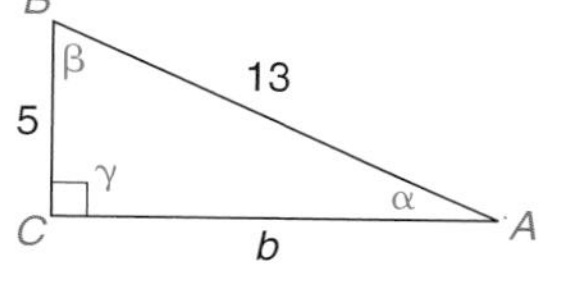

Figure 11.4

In Figure 11.4, find $\sin \alpha$ and $\sin \beta$ for right $\triangle ABC$.

Solution Where $a = 5$ and $c = 13$, we know that $b = 12$ because (5, 12, 13) is a Pythagorean triple. We verify this result using the Pythagorean Theorem.

$$\begin{aligned} c^2 &= a^2 + b^2 \\ 13^2 &= 5^2 + b^2 \\ 169 &= 25 + b^2 \\ b^2 &= 144 \\ b &= 12 \end{aligned}$$

Therefore, $\sin \alpha = \frac{a}{c} = \frac{5}{13}$ and $\sin \beta = \frac{b}{c} = \frac{12}{13}$ ■

Where α is the measure of an acute angle of a right triangle, the value of $\sin \alpha$ is unique. The following Discover activity is designed to give you a better understanding of the meaning of an expression such as sin 53° as well as its uniqueness.

Discover

Given that an acute angle of a right triangle measures 53°, find the approximate value of sin 53°. We can estimate the value of sin 53° as follows (refer to the triangle at the left).

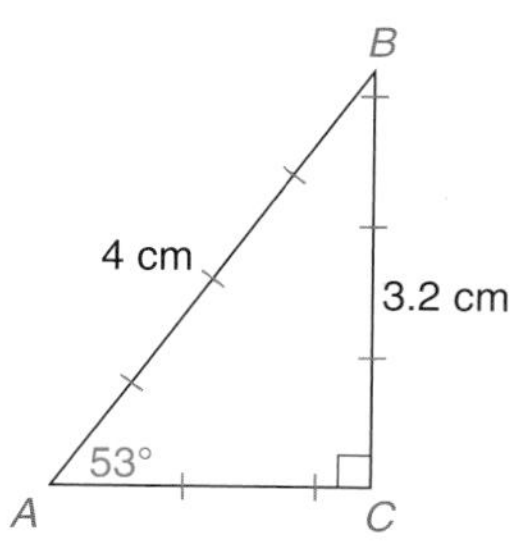

1. Draw right $\triangle ABC$ so that $\alpha = 53°$ and $\gamma = 90°$.
2. For convenience, mark off the length of the hypotenuse as 4 cm.
3. Using a ruler, measure the length of the leg opposite the angle measuring 53°. It is approximately 3.2 cm long.
4. Now divide $\frac{\text{opposite}}{\text{hypotenuse}}$ or $\frac{3.2}{4}$ to find that $\sin 53° \approx 0.8$.

NOTE: A calculator provides greater accuracy than the geometric approach found in the Discover activity; in particular, $\sin 53° \approx 0.7986$.

Exs. 1–5

Repeat the procedure in the preceding Discover activity and use it to find an approximation for sin 37°. You will need to use the Pythagorean Theorem to find AC. You should find that $\sin 37° \approx 0.6$.

Although the sine ratios for angle measures are readily available on a calculator, we can justify several of the calculator's results by using special triangles. For certain angles, we can find *exact* results whereas the calculator provides approximations.

Recall the 30-60-90 relationship, in which the side opposite the 30° angle has a length equal to one-half that of the hypotenuse; the remaining leg has a length equal to the product of the length of the shorter leg and $\sqrt{3}$. In Figure 11.5, we see that $\sin 30° = \frac{x}{2x} = \frac{1}{2}$, while $\sin 60° = \frac{x\sqrt{3}}{2x} = \frac{\sqrt{3}}{2}$. Although the exact value of sin 30° is 0.5 and the exact value of sin 60° is $\frac{\sqrt{3}}{2}$, a calculator would give an approximate value for sin 60° such as 0.8660254. If we round the ratio for sin 60° to four decimal places, then $\sin 60° \approx 0.8660$. Use your calculator to show that $\frac{\sqrt{3}}{2} \approx 0.8660$.

Warning

Be sure to write $\sin \alpha = \frac{5}{13}$ or $\sin 54° \approx 0.8090$. It is incorrect to write "sin" in a claim without naming the angle or its measure; for example, $\sin = \frac{5}{13}$ and $\sin \approx 0.8090$ are both absolutely meaningless.

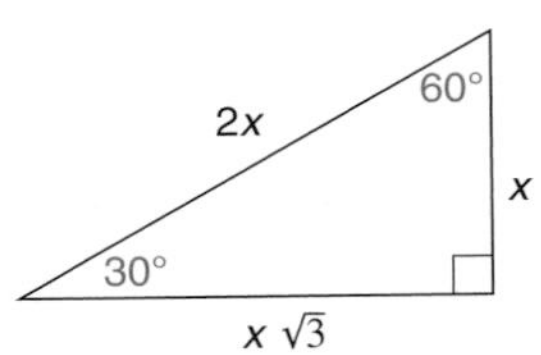

Figure 11.5

EXAMPLE 3

Find exact and approximate values for sin 45°.

Solution Using the 45°-45°-90° triangle in Figure 11.6, we see that $\sin 45° = \frac{x}{x\sqrt{2}} = \frac{1}{\sqrt{2}}$. Equivalently, $\sin 45° = \frac{\sqrt{2}}{2}$.

A calculator approximation is $\sin 45° \approx 0.7071$.

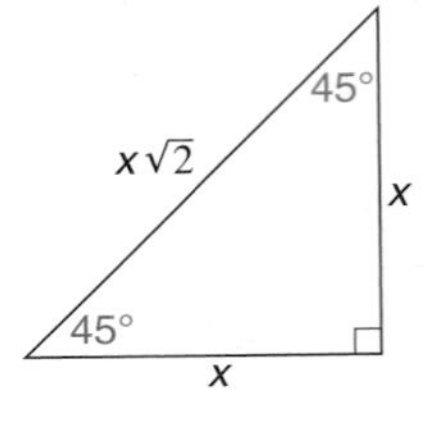

Figure 11.6 ■

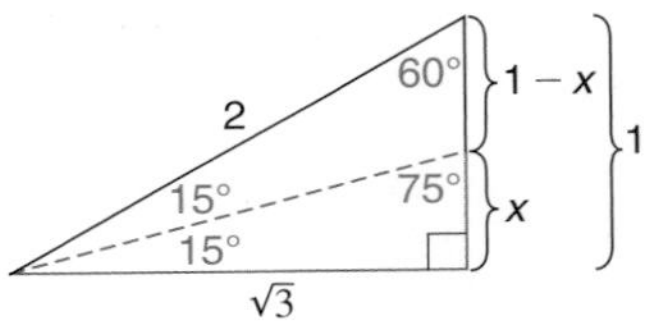

Figure 11.7

We will now use the Angle-Bisector Theorem (from Section 5.6) to determine the sine ratios for angles that measure 15° and 75°. Recall that an angle bisector of one angle of a triangle divides the opposite side into two segments that are proportional to the sides forming the bisected angle. Using this fact in the 30°-60°-90° triangle in Figure 11.7, we are led to the proportion

$$\frac{x}{1-x} = \frac{\sqrt{3}}{2}$$

Applying the Means-Extremes Property, we have

$$\begin{aligned} 2x &= \sqrt{3} - x\sqrt{3} \\ 2x + x\sqrt{3} &= \sqrt{3} \\ (2+\sqrt{3})x &= \sqrt{3} \\ x &= \frac{\sqrt{3}}{2+\sqrt{3}} \approx 0.4641 \end{aligned}$$

The number 0.4641 is the length of the side that is opposite the 15° angle of the 15°-75°-90° triangle (see Figure 11.8). Using the Pythagorean Theorem, we can show that the length of the hypotenuse is approximately 1.79315. In turn, $\sin 15° = \frac{0.46410}{1.79315} \approx 0.2588$. Using the same triangle, we get $\sin 75° = \frac{1.73205}{1.79315} \approx 0.9659$.

We now begin to formulate a small table of values of sine ratios. In Table 11.1, the Greek letter θ (theta) designates the angle measure in degrees. The second column has the heading $\sin \theta$ and provides the ratio for the corresponding angle; this ratio is generally given to four decimal places of accuracy. Note that the values of $\sin \theta$ increase as θ increases in measure.

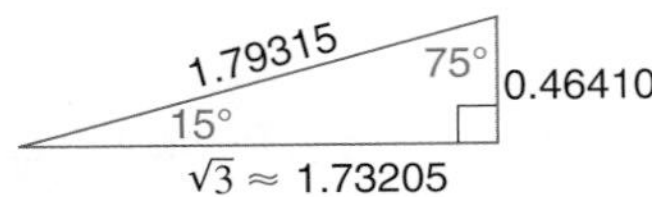

Figure 11.8

TABLE 11.1
Sine Ratios

θ	$\sin\theta$
15°	0.2588
30°	0.5000
45°	0.7071
60°	0.8660
75°	0.9659

Warning

Note that $\sin\left(\frac{1}{2}\theta\right) \neq \frac{1}{2}\sin\theta$ in Table 11.1. If $\theta = 60°$, $\sin 30° \neq \frac{1}{2}\sin 60°$ because $0.5000 \neq \frac{1}{2}(0.8660)$.

NOTE: Most values found in tables or provided by a calculator are approximations. Although we use the equality symbol (=) when reading values from a table (or calculator), the solutions to the problems that follow are generally approximations.

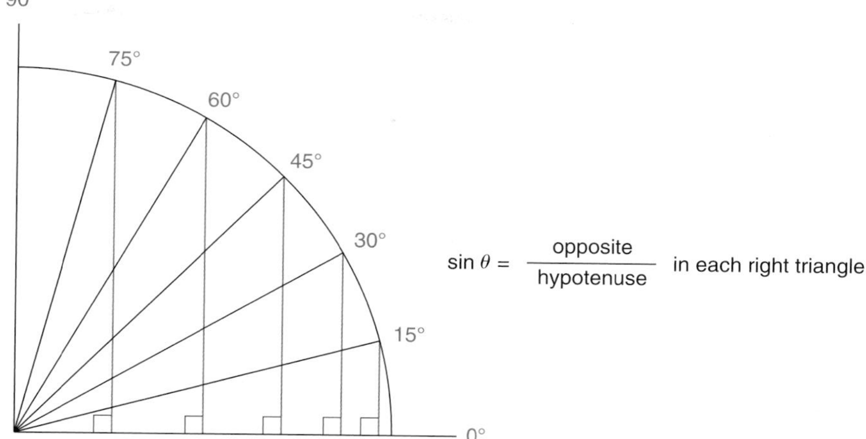

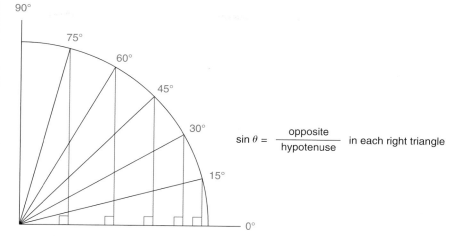

Figure 11.9

In Figure 11.9, let $\angle\theta$ be the acute angle whose measure increases as shown. In the figure, note that the length of the hypotenuse is constant—it is always equal to the length of the radius of the circle. However, the side opposite $\angle\theta$ gets larger as θ increases. In fact, as θ approaches 90° $(\theta \to 90°)$, the length of the leg opposite $\angle\theta$ approaches the length of the hypotenuse. As $\theta \to 90°$, $\sin\theta \to 1$. As θ decreases, $\sin\theta$ also decreases. As θ decreases $(\theta \to 0°)$, the length of the side opposite $\angle\theta$ approaches 0. As $\theta \to 0°$, $\sin\theta \to 0$. These observations lead to the following definition.

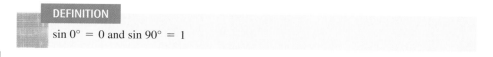

DEFINITION

$\sin 0° = 0$ and $\sin 90° = 1$

SSG *Exs. 6–10*

NOTE: Use your calculator to verify these results.

EXAMPLE 4

Using Table 11.1, find the length of a in Figure 11.10 to the nearest tenth of an inch.

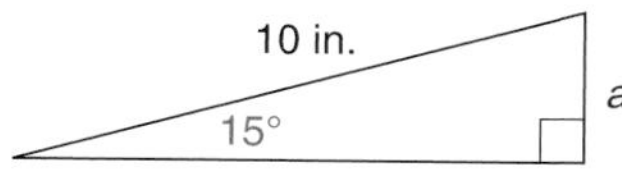

Figure 11.10

Solution

$$\sin 15° = \frac{\text{opposite}}{\text{hypotenuse}} = \frac{a}{10}$$

From the table, we have $\sin 15° = 0.2588$.

$$\frac{a}{10} = 0.2588 \qquad \textbf{(by substitution)}$$
$$a = 2.588$$

Therefore, $a \approx 2.6$ in. when rounded to tenths. ■

In an application problem, the sine ratio can be used to find the measure of either a side or an angle of a triangle. To find the sine ratio of the angle involved, you may use a table of ratios or a calculator. Table 11.2 provides ratios for many more angle measures than does Table 11.1. As with calculators, the sine ratios found in tables are only approximations.

Technology Exploration

If you have a graphing calculator, draw the graph of $y = \sin x$ subject to these conditions:

i. Calculator in degree mode.
ii. Window has $0 \leq x \leq 90$ and $0 \leq y \leq 1$.

Show by your graph that $y = \sin x$ increases as x increases.

TABLE 11.2
Sine Ratios

θ	$\sin \theta$	θ	$\sin \theta$	θ	$\sin \theta$	θ	$\sin \theta$
0°	0.0000	23°	0.3907	46°	0.7193	69°	0.9336
1°	0.0175	24°	0.4067	47°	0.7314	70°	0.9397
2°	0.0349	25°	0.4226	48°	0.7431	71°	0.9455
3°	0.0523	26°	0.4384	49°	0.7547	72°	0.9511
4°	0.0698	27°	0.4540	50°	0.7660	73°	0.9563
5°	0.0872	28°	0.4695	51°	0.7771	74°	0.9613
6°	0.1045	29°	0.4848	52°	0.7880	75°	0.9659
7°	0.1219	30°	0.5000	53°	0.7986	76°	0.9703
8°	0.1392	31°	0.5150	54°	0.8090	77°	0.9744
9°	0.1564	32°	0.5299	55°	0.8192	78°	0.9781
10°	0.1736	33°	0.5446	56°	0.8290	79°	0.9816
11°	0.1908	34°	0.5592	57°	0.8387	80°	0.9848
12°	0.2079	35°	0.5736	58°	0.8480	81°	0.9877
13°	0.2250	36°	0.5878	59°	0.8572	82°	0.9903
14°	0.2419	37°	0.6018	60°	0.8660	83°	0.9925
15°	0.2588	38°	0.6157	61°	0.8746	84°	0.9945
16°	0.2756	39°	0.6293	62°	0.8829	85°	0.9962
17°	0.2924	40°	0.6428	63°	0.8910	86°	0.9976
18°	0.3090	41°	0.6561	64°	0.8988	87°	0.9986
19°	0.3256	42°	0.6691	65°	0.9063	88°	0.9994
20°	0.3420	43°	0.6820	66°	0.9135	89°	0.9998
21°	0.3584	44°	0.6947	67°	0.9205	90°	1.0000
22°	0.3746	45°	0.7071	68°	0.9272		

NOTE: In later sections, we will use the calculator (rather than tables) to find values of trigonometric ratios such as sin 36°.

EXAMPLE 5

Find sin 36°, using

a) Table 11.2.
b) a scientific or graphing calculator.

Solution

a) Find 36° under the heading θ. Now read the number under the $\sin \theta$ heading: sin 36°= 0.5878
b) On a scientific calculator that is *in degree mode,* use the following key sequence:

[3] → [6] → [sin] → [**0.5878**]

The result is sin 36° = 0.5878, correct to four decimal places.

NOTE 1: The boldfaced number in the box represents the final answer.
NOTE 2: The key sequence for a graphing calculator follows. Here, the calculator is in degree mode and the answer is rounded to four decimal places.

[sin] → [3] → [6] → [Enter] → [**0.5878**]

The entry may require parentheses and have to be entered in the form sin (36). ■

The table or a calculator can also be used to find the measure of an angle. This is possible when the sine of the angle is known.

EXAMPLE 6

If $\sin\theta = 0.7986$, find θ to the nearest degree by using

a) Table 11.2.
b) a calculator.

Solution

a) Find 0.7986 under the heading $\sin\theta$. Now look to the left to find the degree measure of the angle in the θ column:

$$\sin\theta = 0.7986 \rightarrow \theta = 53°$$

b) On some scientific calculators, you can use the following key sequence (while in degree mode) to find θ:

[·] → [7] → [9] → [8] → [6] → [inv] → [sin] → [**53**]

The combination "inv" and "sin" yields the angle whose sine ratio is known, so $\theta = 53°$.

NOTE: On a graphing calculator that is in degree mode, use this sequence:

[$\sin^{-1}$] → [·] → [7] → [9] → [8] → [6] → [ENTER] → [**53**]

SSG
Exs. 11–15

This entry may require the form $\sin^{-1}(.7986)$. The expression $\sin^{-1}(.7986)$ means "the angle whose sine is 0.7986." The calculator function [$\sin^{-1}$] is found by pressing [2nd] followed by [sin]. ■

In most application problems, a drawing provides a good deal of information and affords some insight into the method of solution. For some drawings and applications, the phrases *angle of elevation* and *angle of depression* are used. These angles are measured from the horizontal as illustrated in Figures 11.11(a) and 11.11(b). In Figure 11.11(a), the angle α measured upward from the horizontal ray is the **angle of elevation.** In Figure 11.11(b), the angle β measured downward from the horizontal ray is the **angle of depression.**

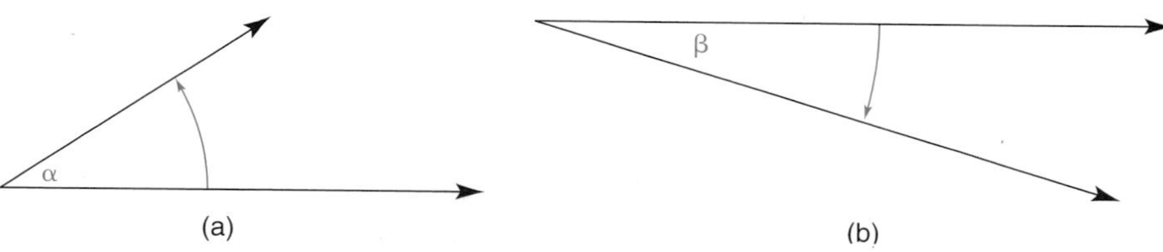

Figure 11.11

EXAMPLE 7

The tower for a radio station stands 200 ft tall. A guy wire 250 ft long supports the antenna, as shown in Figure 11.12. Find the measure of the angle of elevation α to the nearest degree.

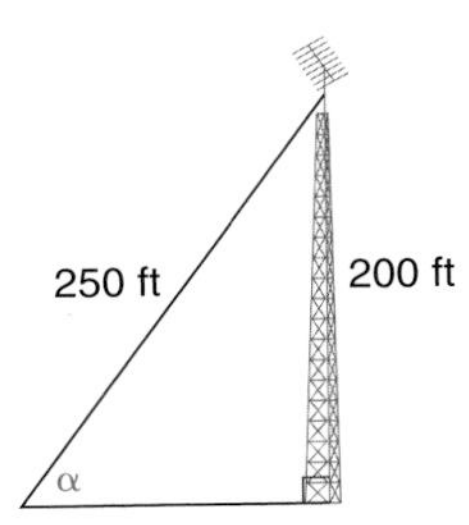

Figure 11.12

Solution

$$\sin \alpha = \frac{\text{opposite}}{\text{hypotenuse}} = \frac{200}{250} = 0.8$$

SSG *Exs. 16, 17*

From Table 11.2 (or from a calculator), we find that the angle whose sine ratio is 0.8 is $\alpha \approx 53°$. ■

Exercises 11.1

In Exercises 1 to 6, find sin α and sin β for the triangle shown.

1.

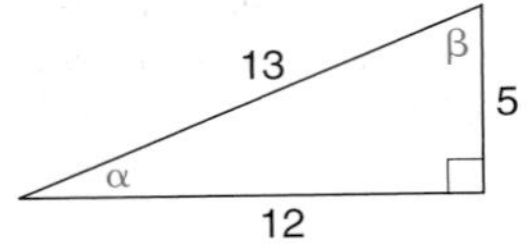

2.

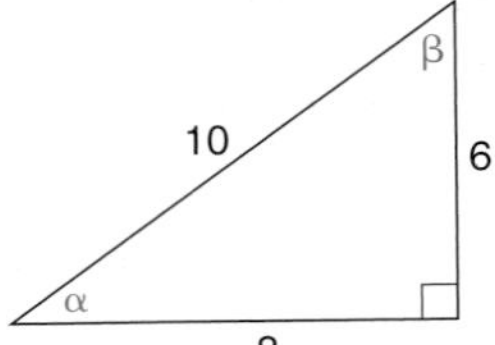

3.

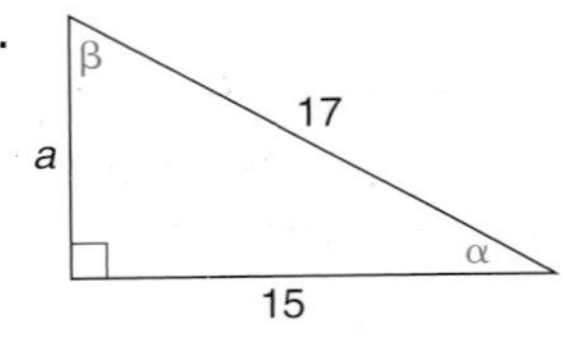

4.

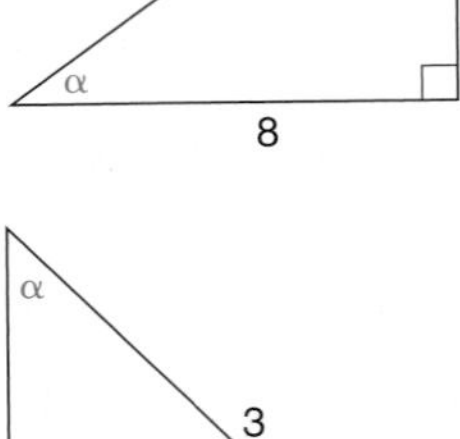

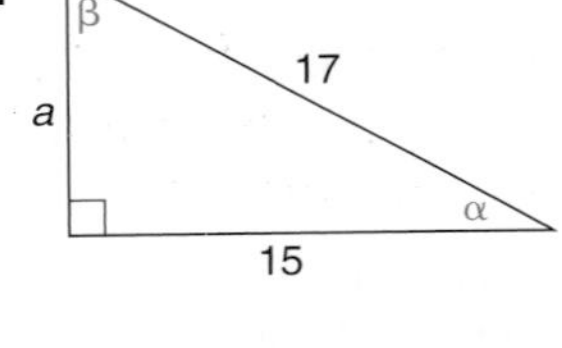

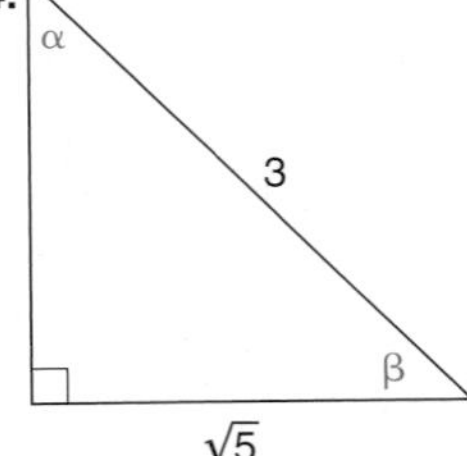

5.

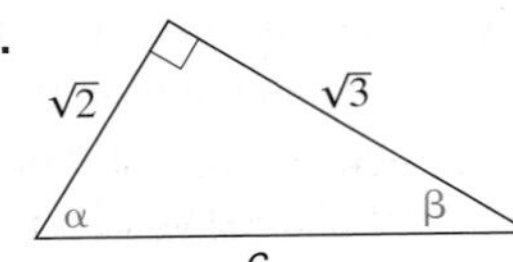

6.

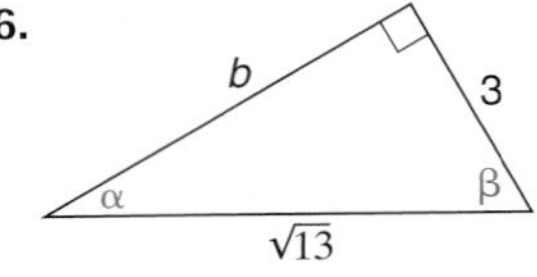

In Exercises 7 to 14, use either Table 11.2 or a calculator to find the sine of the indicated angle to four decimal places.

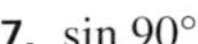

7. sin 90°
8. sin 0°
9. sin 17°
10. sin 23°
11. sin 82°
12. sin 46°
13. sin 72°
14. sin 57°

In Exercises 15 to 20, find the lengths of the sides indicated by the variables. Use either Table 11.2 or a calculator, and round answers to the nearest tenth of a unit.

15.

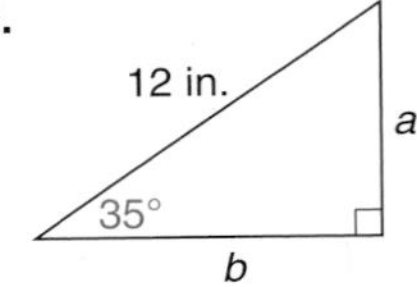

16.

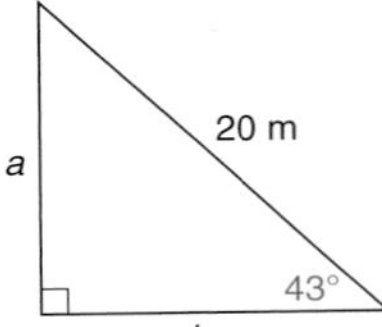

17.

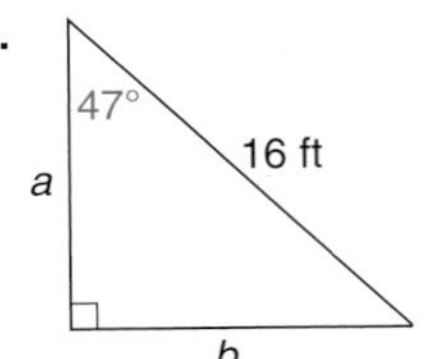

18.

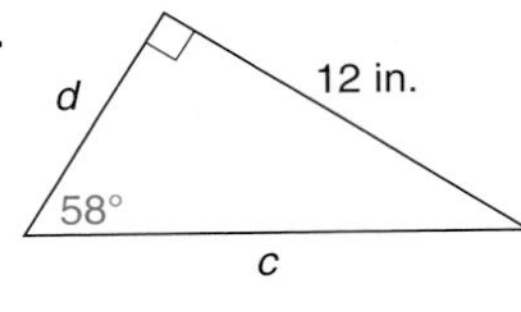

19.

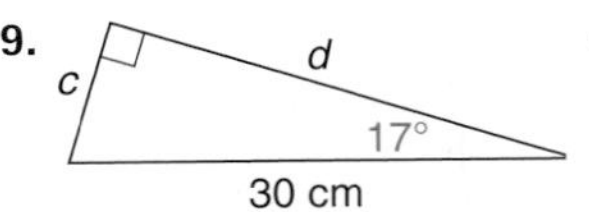

20.

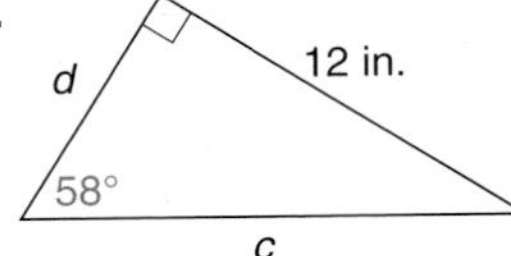

In Exercises 21 to 26, find the measures of the angles named to the nearest degree.

21.

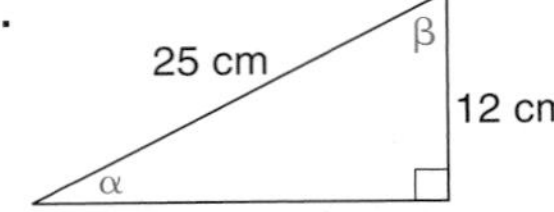

22.

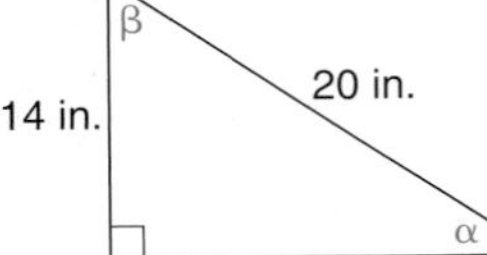

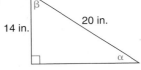

23. 

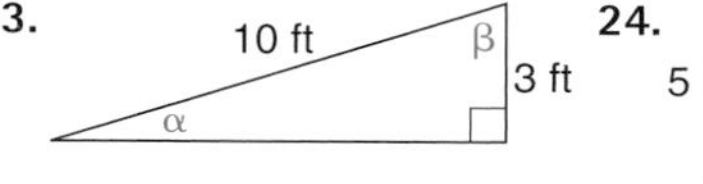

24.

25. 

26. 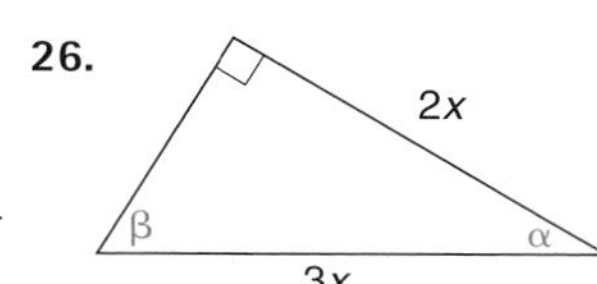

In Exercises 27 to 34, use the drawings where provided to solve each problem. Angle measures should be given to the nearest degree; distances should be given to the nearest tenth of a unit.

27. The pitch or slope of a roofline is 5 to 12. Find the measure of angle α.

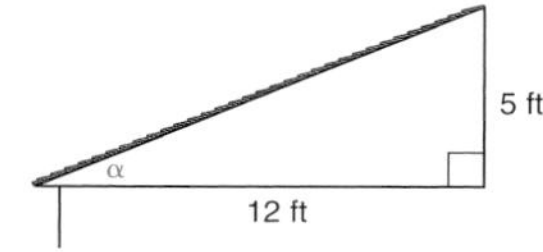

28. Zaidah is flying a kite at an angle of elevation of 67° from a point on the ground. If 100 ft of kite string is out, how far is the kite above the ground?

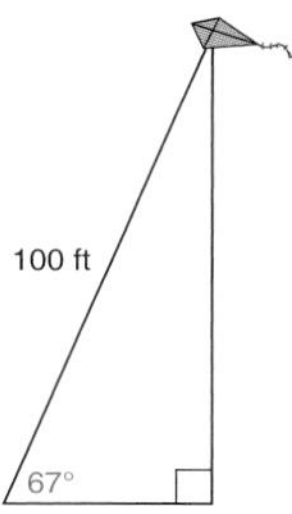

29. Danny sees a balloon that is 100 ft above the ground. If the angle of elevation from Danny to the balloon is 75°, how far from Danny is the balloon?

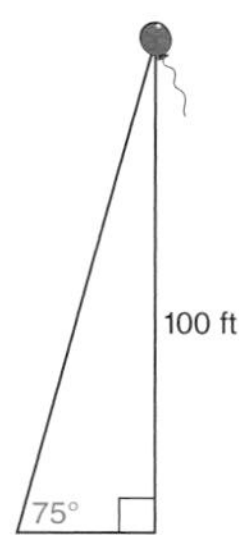

30. Over a 2000-ft span of highway through a hillside, there is a 100-ft rise in the roadway. What is the measure of the angle formed by the road and the horizontal?

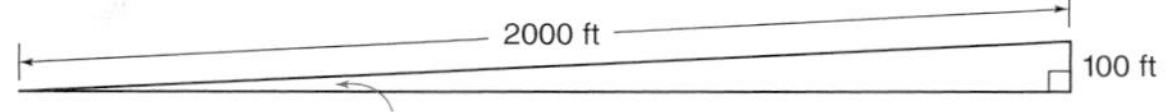

31. From a cliff, a person observes an automobile through an angle of depression of 23°. If the cliff is 50 ft high, how far is the automobile from the person?

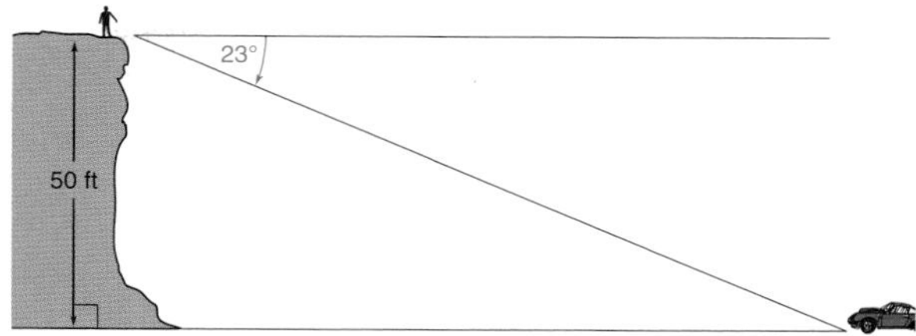

32. A 12-ft rope secures a rowboat to a pier that is 4 ft above the water. Assume that the lower end of the rope is at "water level." What is the angle formed by the rope and the water? Assume that the rope is taut.

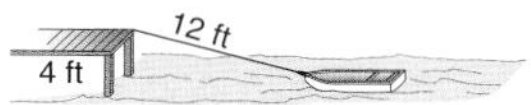

33. A 10-ft ladder is leaning against a vertical wall so that the bottom of the ladder is 4 ft away from the base of the wall. How large is the angle formed by the ladder and the wall?

34. An airplane flying at the rate of 350 feet per second begins to climb at an angle of 10°. What is the increase in altitude over the next 15 seconds?

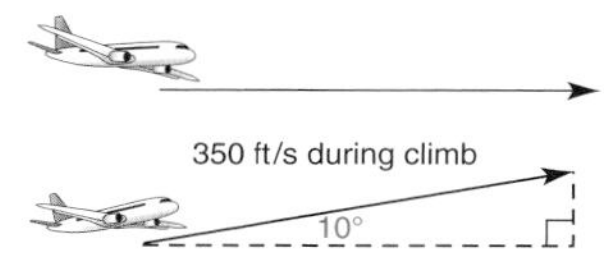

For Exercises 35 to 38, make drawings as needed.

35. In parallelogram $ABCD$, $AB = 6$ ft and $AD = 10$ ft. If $m\angle A = 65°$ and $\overline{BE}$ is the altitude to $\overline{AD}$, find:

a) BE correct to tenths

b) The area of $\square ABCD$

36. In right $\triangle ABC$, $\gamma = 90°$ and $\beta = 55°$. If $AB = 20$ in., find:

a) a (the length of $\overline{BC}$) correct to tenths

b) b (the length of $\overline{AC}$) correct to tenths

c) The area of right $\triangle ABC$

37. In a right circular cone, the slant height is 13 cm and the altitude is 10 cm. To the nearest degree, find the measure of the angle θ that is formed by the radius and slant height.

38. In a right circular cone, the slant height is 13 cm. Where θ is the angle formed by the radius and the slant height, $\theta = 48°$. Find the length of the altitude of the cone, correct to tenths.

***39.** In regular pentagon $ABCDE$, sides $\overline{AB}$ and $\overline{BC}$ along with diagonal $\overline{AC}$ form isosceles $\triangle ABC$. Let $AB = BC = s$. In terms of s, find an expression for

a) h, the length of the altitude of $\triangle ABC$ from vertex B to side $\overline{AC}$.

b) d, the length of diagonal $\overline{AC}$ of regular pentagon $ABCDE$.

11.2 The Cosine Ratio and Applications

KEY CONCEPTS

Adjacent Side (Leg)

Cosine Ratio: $\cos\theta = \frac{\text{adjacent}}{\text{hypotenuse}}$

Identity: $\sin^2\theta + \cos^2\theta = 1$

Again we deal strictly with similar right triangles, as shown in Figure 11.13. While $\overline{BC}$ is the leg opposite angle A, we say that $\overline{AC}$ is the leg **adjacent** to angle A. In the two triangles, the ratios of the form

$$\frac{\text{length of adjacent leg}}{\text{length of hypotenuse}}$$

are equal; that is,

$$\frac{AC}{AB} = \frac{DF}{DE} \quad \text{or} \quad \frac{4}{5} = \frac{8}{10}$$

This relationship follows from the fact that corresponding sides of similar triangles are proportional (CSSTP).

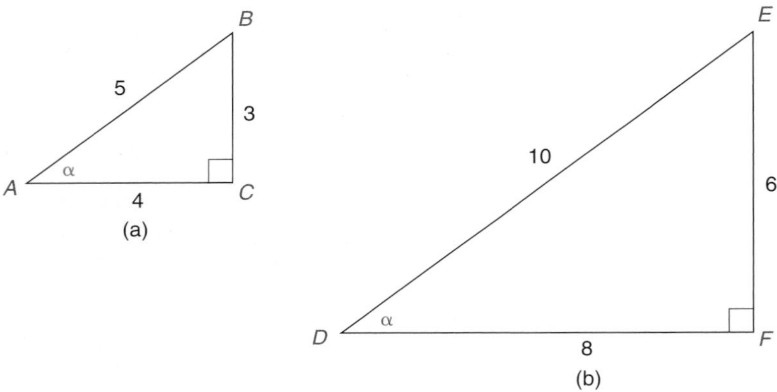

Figure 11.13

As with the sine ratio, the *cosine ratio* depends on the measure of acute angle A (or D) in Figure 11.13. In the following definition, the term *adjacent* refers to the length of the leg that is adjacent to the angle named.

DEFINITION

In a right triangle, the **cosine ratio** for an acute angle is the ratio $\frac{\text{adjacent}}{\text{hypotenuse}}$.

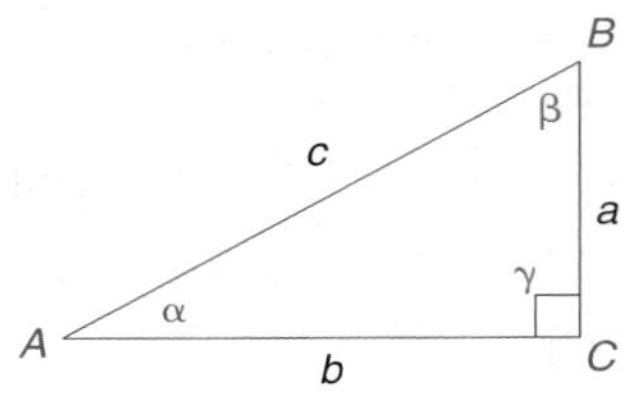

Figure 11.14

NOTE: For right $\triangle ABC$ in Figure 11.14, we have $\cos\alpha = \frac{b}{c}$ and $\cos\beta = \frac{a}{c}$; in each statement, "cos" is an abbreviated form of the word *cosine*. These claims can also be expressed in the forms $\cos A = \frac{b}{c}$ and $\cos B = \frac{a}{c}$.

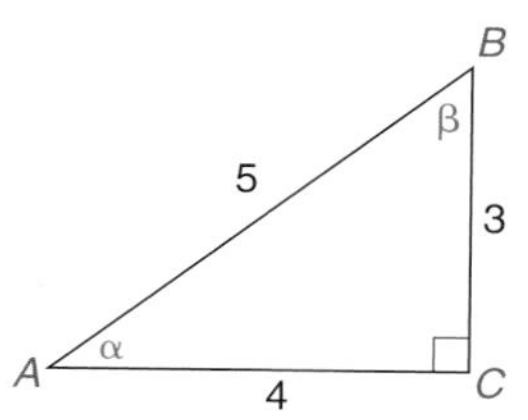

Figure 11.15

EXAMPLE 1

Find $\cos \alpha$ and $\cos \beta$ for right $\triangle ABC$ in Figure 11.15.

Solution $a = 3$, $b = 4$, and $c = 5$ for the triangle shown in Figure 11.15. Because b is the length of the leg adjacent to α and a is the length of the leg adjacent to β,

$$\cos \alpha = \frac{b}{c} = \frac{4}{5} \quad \text{and} \quad \cos \beta = \frac{a}{c} = \frac{3}{5}$$

EXAMPLE 2

Find $\cos \alpha$ and $\cos \beta$ for right $\triangle ABC$ in Figure 11.16.

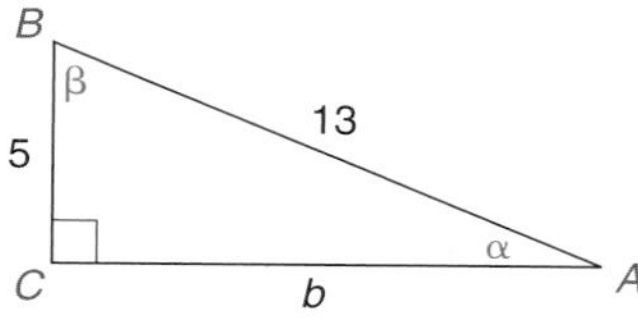

Figure 11.16

SSG *Exs. 1–5*

Solution $a = 5$ and $c = 13$. Then $b = 12$ from the Pythagorean triple (5, 12, 13). Consequently,

$$\cos \alpha = \frac{b}{c} = \frac{12}{13} \quad \text{and} \quad \cos \beta = \frac{a}{c} = \frac{5}{13}$$

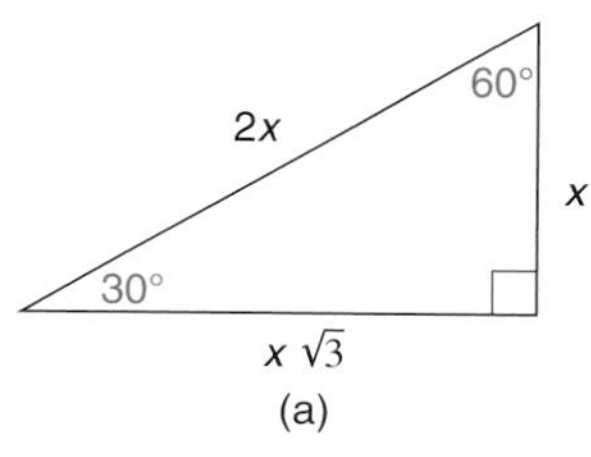

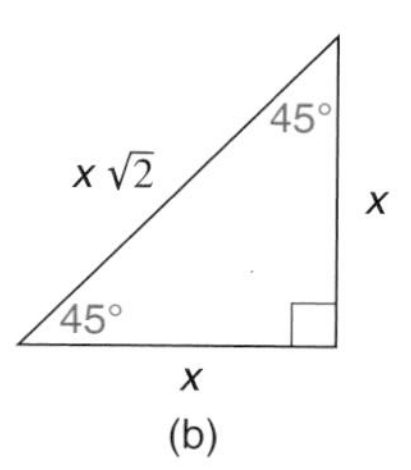

Figure 11.17

Just as the sine ratio of any angle is unique, the cosine ratio of any angle is also unique. Using the 30°-60°-90° and 45°-45°-90° triangles of Figure 11.17, we see that

$$\cos 30° = \frac{x\sqrt{3}}{2x} = \frac{\sqrt{3}}{2} \approx 0.8660$$

$$\cos 45° = \frac{x}{x\sqrt{2}} = \frac{1}{\sqrt{2}} = \frac{\sqrt{2}}{2} \approx 0.7071$$

$$\cos 60° = \frac{x}{2x} = \frac{1}{2} = 0.5$$

Now we use the 15°-75°-90° triangle shown in Figure 11.18 to find cos 75° and cos 15°. From Section 11.1, $\sin 15° = \frac{a}{c}$ and $\sin 15° = 0.2588$. But $\cos 75° = \frac{a}{c}$, so $\cos 75° = 0.2588$. Similarly, because $\sin 75° = \frac{b}{c} = 0.9659$, we see that $\cos 15° = \frac{b}{c} = 0.9659$.

In Figure 11.19 on page 506, the cosine ratios become larger as θ decreases and become smaller as θ increases. To understand why, consider the definition

$$\cos \theta = \frac{\text{length of adjacent leg}}{\text{length of hypotenuse}}$$

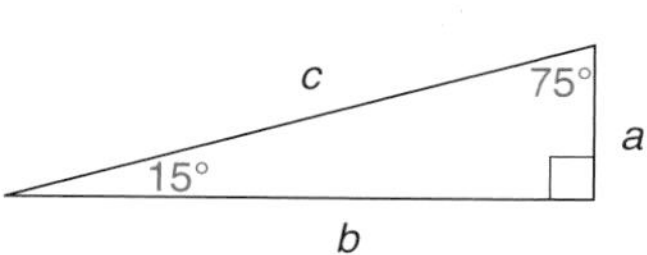

Figure 11.18

and Figure 11.19. Recall that the symbol $\rightarrow$ is read "approaches." As $\theta \rightarrow 0°$, length of adjacent leg $\rightarrow$ length of hypotenuse, and therefore $\cos 0° \rightarrow 1$. Similarly, $\cos 90° \rightarrow 0$ because the adjacent leg grows smaller as $\theta \rightarrow 90°$. Consequently, we have the following definition.

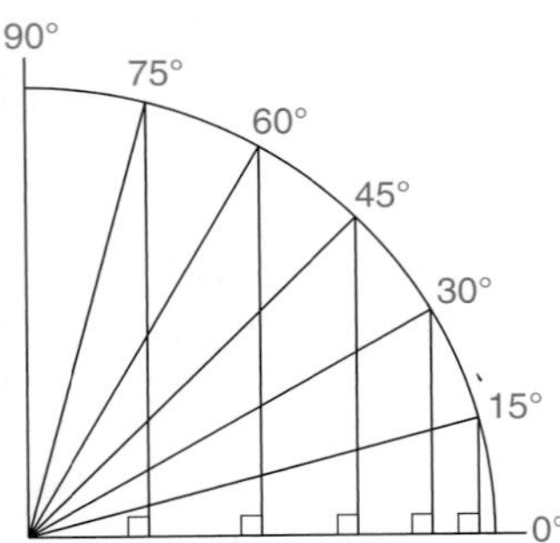

Figure 11.19

DEFINITION

$\cos 0° = 1$ and $\cos 90° = 0$.

NOTE: Use your calculator to verify the results found in this definition.

We summarize cosine ratios in Table 11.3.

TABLE 11.3
Cosine Ratios

θ	$\cos \theta$
0°	1.0000
15°	0.9659
30°	0.8660
45°	0.7071
60°	0.5000
75°	0.2588
90°	0.0000

Technology Exploration

If you have a graphing calculator, draw the graph of $y = \cos x$ subject to these conditions:

i. Calculator in degree mode.
ii. Window has $0 \leq x \leq 90$ and $0 \leq y \leq 1$.

Show by your graph that $y = \cos x$ decreases as x increases.

Some textbooks provide an expanded table of cosine ratios comparable to Table 11.2 for sine ratios. Although this text does not provide an expanded table of cosine ratios, we illustrate the application of such a table in Example 3.

Exs. 6–10

EXAMPLE 3

Using Table 11.3, find the length of b in Figure 11.20 correct to the nearest tenth.

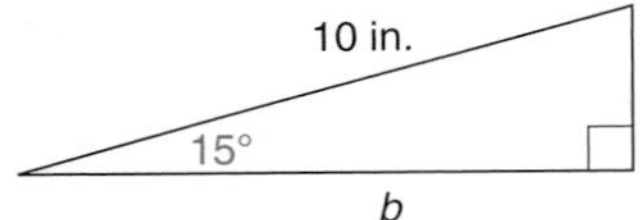

Figure 11.20

Solution $\cos 15° = \frac{\text{adjacent}}{\text{hypotenuse}} = \frac{b}{10}$ from the triangle. Also, $\cos 15° = 0.9659$ from the table. Then

$$\frac{b}{10} = 0.9659 \qquad \textbf{(because both equal } \cos 15°\textbf{)}$$

$$b = 9.659$$

Therefore, $b \approx 9.7$ in.

when rounded to the nearest tenth of an inch. ■

Reminder

$\sin \theta = \frac{\text{opposite}}{\text{hypotenuse}}$

$\cos \theta = \frac{\text{adjacent}}{\text{hypotenuse}}$

In a right triangle, the cosine ratio can often be used to find an unknown length or an unknown angle measure. Whereas the sine ratio requires that we use *opposite* and *hypotenuse,* the cosine ratio requires that we use *adjacent* and *hypotenuse.*

An equation of the form $\sin \alpha = \frac{a}{c}$ or $\cos \alpha = \frac{b}{c}$ contains three variables; for the equation $\cos \alpha = \frac{b}{c}$, the variables are α, b, and c. When the values of two of the variables are known, the value of the third variable can be determined. However, we must decide which trigonometric ratio is needed to solve the problem.

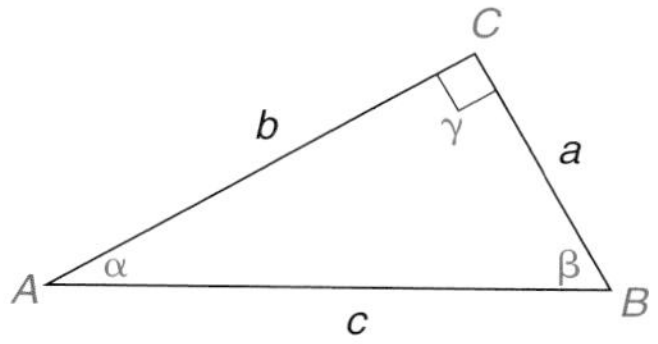

C
b γ a
A α β B
c

Figure 11.21

EXAMPLE 4

In Figure 11.21, which trigonometric ratio would you use to find

a) α, if a and c are known?
b) b, if α and c are known?
c) c, if a and α are known?
d) β, if a and c are known?

Solution

a) sine, because $\sin \alpha = \frac{a}{c}$ and a and c are known
b) cosine, because $\cos \alpha = \frac{b}{c}$ and α and c are known
c) sine, because $\sin \alpha = \frac{a}{c}$ and a and α are known
d) cosine, because $\cos \beta = \frac{a}{c}$ and a and c are know ■

To solve application problems, we generally use a calculator.

EXAMPLE 5

Find cos 67° correct to four decimal places by using a scientific calculator.

Solution On a scientific calculator that is in degree mode, use the following key sequence:

[6] → [7] → [cos] → **[0.3907]**

Using a graphing calculator (in degree mode), follow this key sequence:

[cos] → [6] → [7] → [ENTER] → **[0.3907]**

That is, $\cos 67° \approx 0.3907$. ■

EXAMPLE 6

Use a calculator to find the measure of angle θ to the nearest degree if $\cos \theta = 0.5878$.

Solution Using a scientific calculator (in degree mode), follow this key sequence:

[·] → [5] → [8] → [7] → [8] → [inv] → [cos] → **[54]**

Using a graphing calculator (in degree mode), follow this key sequence:

[$\cos^{-1}$] → [·] → [5] → [8] → [7] → [8] → [ENTER] → **[54]**

Thus, $\theta = 54°$.

SSG *Exs. 11–15*

NOTE: By pressing [2nd] and [cos] on a graphing calculator, you obtain [$\cos^{-1}$]. ■

EXAMPLE 7

For a regular pentagon, the length of the apothem is 12 in. Find the length of the pentagon's radius to the nearest tenth of an inch.

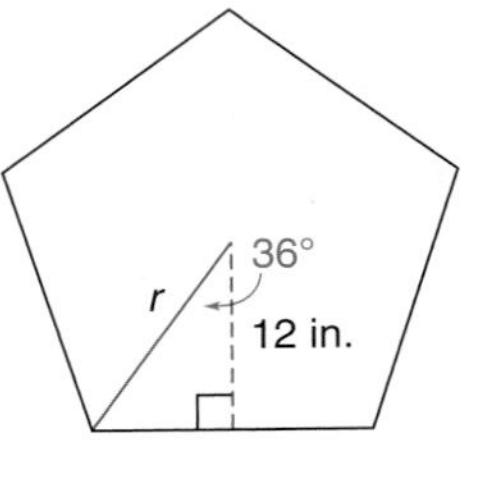

Figure 11.22

Solution The central angle of the regular pentagon measures $\frac{360}{5}$, or 72°. An apothem bisects this angle, so the angle formed by the apothem and the radius measures 36°. In Figure 11.22,

$$\cos 36° = \frac{\text{adjacent}}{\text{hypotenuse}} = \frac{12}{r}$$

Using a calculator, $\cos 36° = 0.8090$. Then $\frac{12}{r} = 0.8090$ and $0.8090r = 12$. By division, $r \approx 14.8$ in.

NOTE: The solution in Example 7 can be calculated as $r = \frac{12}{\cos 36°}$. ■

We now consider the proof of a statement that is called an **identity** because it is true for all angles; we refer to this statement as a theorem. As you will see, the proof of this statement is based entirely on the Pythagorean Theorem.

THEOREM 11.2.1

In any right triangle in which α is the measure of an acute angle,

$$\sin^2 \alpha + \cos^2 \alpha = 1$$

NOTE: $\sin^2 \alpha$ means $(\sin \alpha)^2$ and $\cos^2 \alpha$ means $(\cos \alpha)^2$.

PROOF

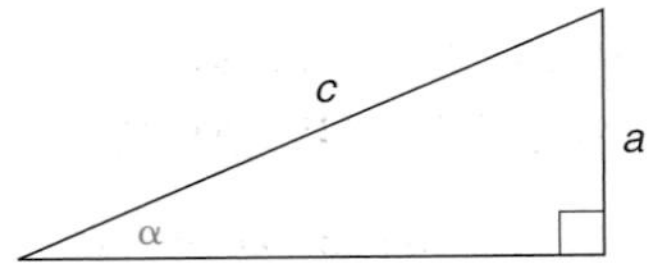

Figure 11.23

In Figure 11.23, $\sin \alpha = \frac{a}{c}$ and $\cos \alpha = \frac{b}{c}$. Then

$$\sin^2 \alpha + \cos^2 \alpha = \left(\frac{a}{c}\right)^2 + \left(\frac{b}{c}\right)^2 = \frac{a^2}{c^2} + \frac{b^2}{c^2} = \frac{a^2 + b^2}{c^2}$$

In the right triangle in Figure 11.23, $a^2 + b^2 = c^2$ by the Pythagorean Theorem. Substituting c^2 for $a^2 + b^2$, we have

$$\sin^2 \alpha + \cos^2 \alpha = \frac{c^2}{c^2} = 1$$

It follows that $\sin^2 \alpha + \cos^2 \alpha = 1$ for any angle α. ■

NOTE: Use your calculator to show that $(\sin 67°)^2 + (\cos 67°)^2 = 1$. Theorem 11.2.1 is also true for $\alpha = 0°$ and $\alpha = 90°$.

EXAMPLE 8

In right triangle ABC (not shown), $\sin \alpha = \frac{2}{3}$. Find $\cos \alpha$.

Solution

$$\sin^2 \alpha + \cos^2 \alpha = 1$$
$$\left(\frac{2}{3}\right)^2 + \cos^2 \alpha = 1$$
$$\frac{4}{9} + \cos^2 \alpha = 1$$
$$\cos^2 \alpha = \frac{5}{9}$$

SSG *Exs. 16, 17*

Therefore, $\cos \alpha = \sqrt{\frac{5}{9}} = \frac{\sqrt{5}}{\sqrt{9}} = \frac{\sqrt{5}}{3}$.

NOTE: Because $\cos \alpha > 0$, $\cos \alpha = \frac{\sqrt{5}}{3}$ rather than $-\frac{\sqrt{5}}{3}$.

Theorem 11.2.1 represents one of many trigonometric identities. In Section 11.3, we will encounter additional trigonometric identities embedded in Exercises 33–36 of that section.

Exercises 11.2

In Exercises 1 to 6, find $\cos \alpha$ and $\cos \beta$.

1. 13, 5, 12, α, β

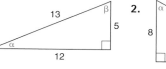

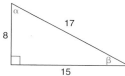

2. 17, 8, 15, α, β

3.

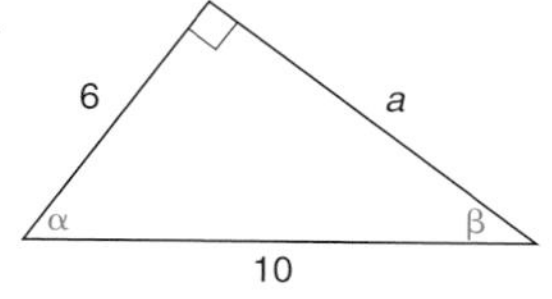

4.

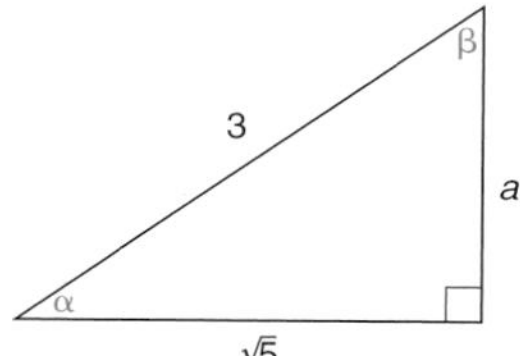

5.

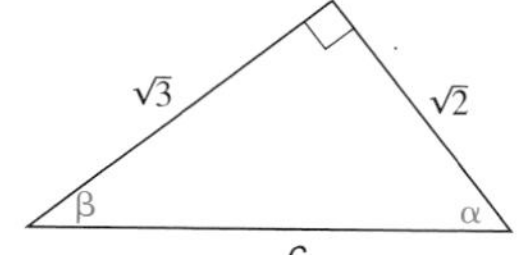

6.

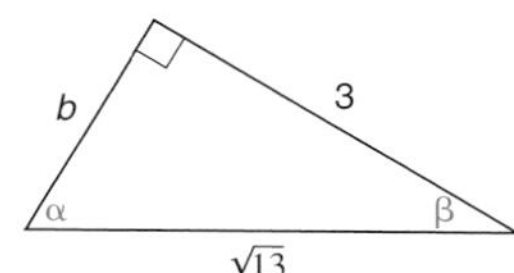

7. In Exercises 1 to 6:
a) Why does $\sin \alpha = \cos \beta$?
b) Why does $\cos \alpha = \sin \beta$?

8. Using the right triangle from Exercise 1, show that $\sin^2 \alpha + \cos^2 \alpha = 1$.

In Exercises 9 to 16, use a scientific calculator to find the indicated cosine ratio to four decimal places.

9. $\cos 23°$ **10.** $\cos 0°$ **11.** $\cos 17°$ **12.** $\cos 73°$
13. $\cos 90°$ **14.** $\cos 42°$ **15.** $\cos 82°$ **16.** $\cos 7°$

In Exercises 17 to 22, use either the sine ratio or the cosine ratio to find the lengths of the indicated sides of the triangle, correct to the nearest tenth of a unit.

17.

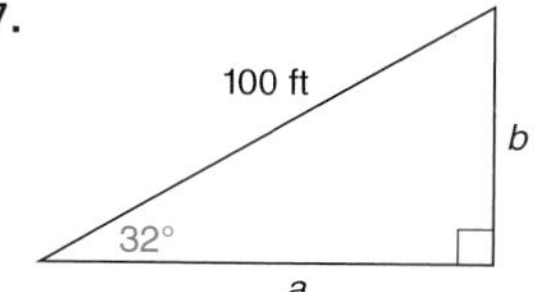

18.

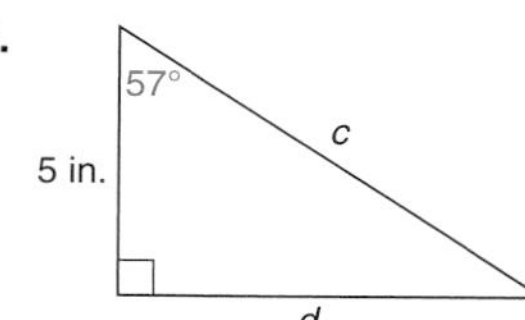

19.

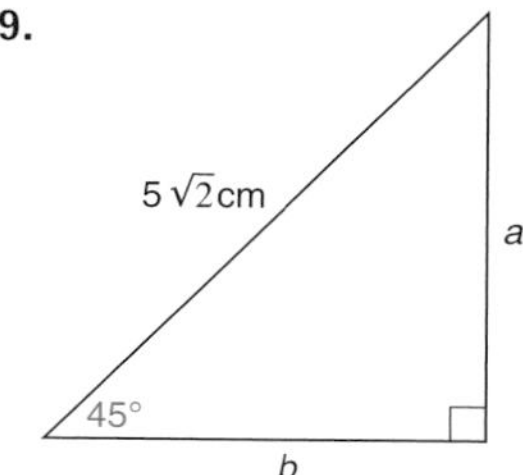

20.

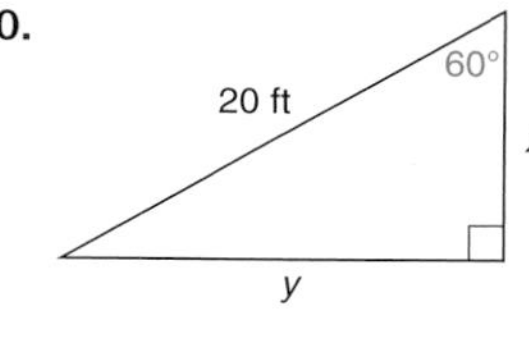

21.

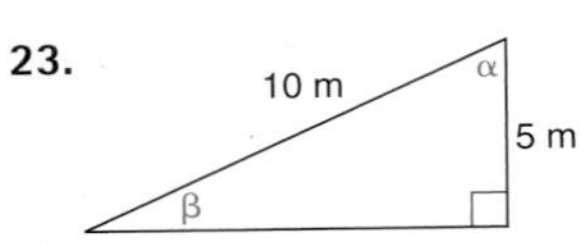

22.

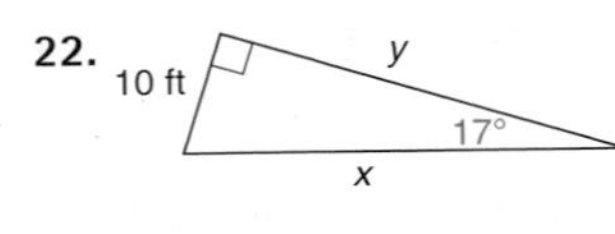

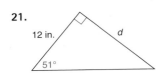

In Exercises 23 to 28, use the sine ratio or the cosine ratio as needed to find the measure of each indicated angle to the nearest degree.

23.

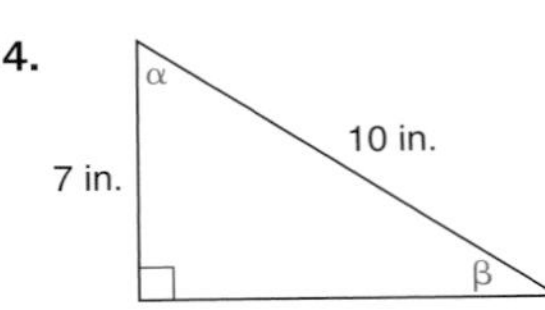

24.

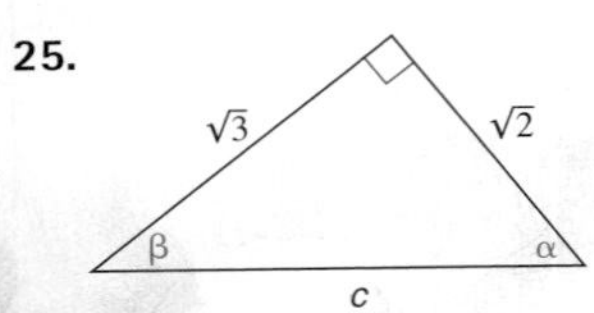

25.

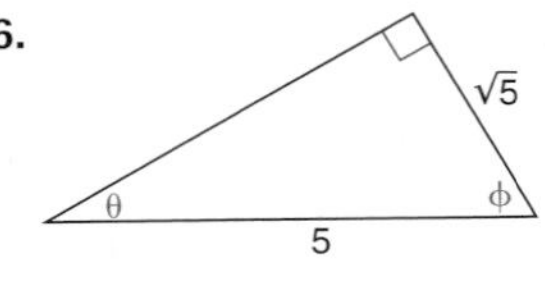

26.

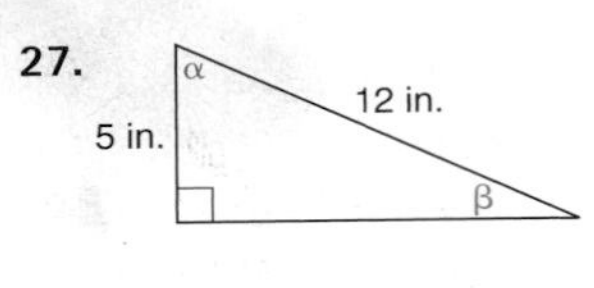

27.

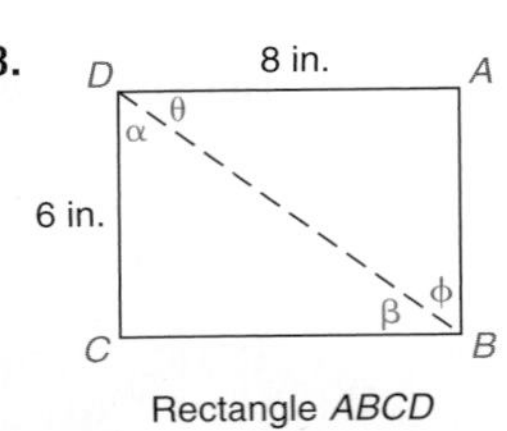

28.

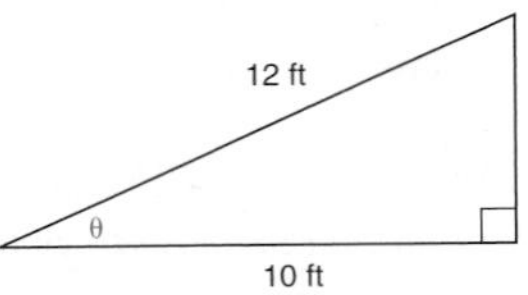

Rectangle $ABCD$

In Exercises 29 to 37, angle measures should be given to the nearest degree; distances should be given to the nearest tenth of a unit.

29. In building a garage onto his house, Gene wants to use a sloped 12-ft roof to cover an expanse that is 10 ft wide. Find the measure of angle θ.

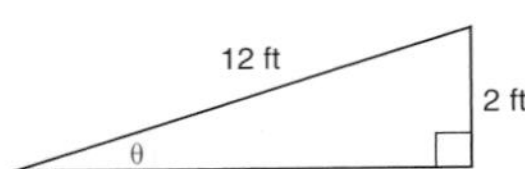

30. Gene redesigned the garage from Exercise 29 so that the 12-ft roof would rise 2 ft as shown. Find the measure of angle θ.

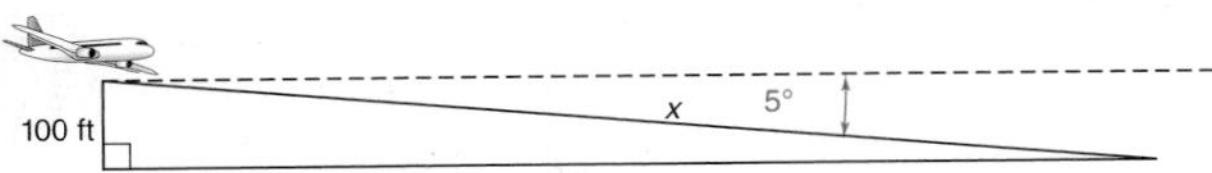

31. When an airplane is descending to land, the angle of depression is 5°. When the plane has a reading of 100 ft on the altimeter, what is its distance x from touchdown?

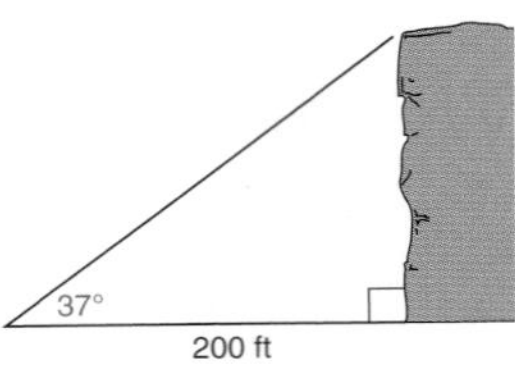

32. At a point 200 ft from the base of a cliff, Journey sees the top of the cliff through an angle of elevation of 37°. How tall is the cliff?

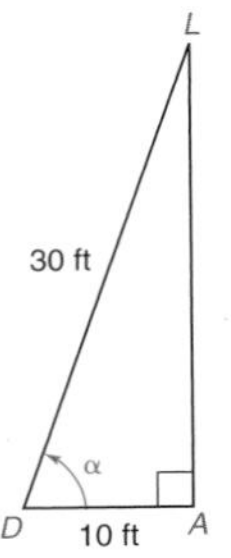

33. Find the length of each apothem in a regular pentagon whose radii measure 10 in. each.

34. Dale looks up to see his friend Lisa waving from her apartment window 30 ft from him. If Dale is standing 10 ft from the building, what is the angle of elevation as Dale looks up at Lisa?

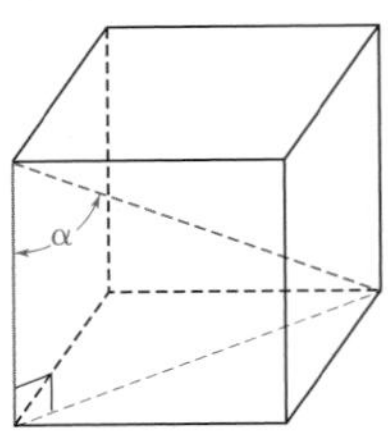

35. Find the length of the radius in a regular decagon for which each apothem has a length of 12.5 cm.

36. In searching for survivors of a boating accident, a helicopter moves horizontally across the ocean at an altitude of 200 ft above the water. If a man clinging to a life raft is seen through an angle of depression of 12°, what is the distance from the helicopter to the man in the water?

*37. What is the size of the angle α formed by a diagonal of a cube and one of its edges?

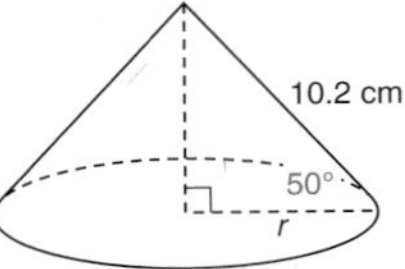

38. In the right circular cone,

a) find r correct to tenths.

b) use $L = \pi r \ell$ to find the lateral area of the cone.

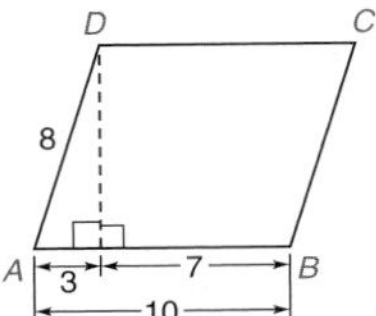

39. In parallelogram $ABCD$, find, to the nearest degree:

a) m$\angle A$ b) m$\angle B$

40. A ladder is carried horizontally through an L-shaped turn in a hallway. Show that the ladder has the length $L = \frac{6}{\sin\theta} + \frac{6}{\cos\theta}$.

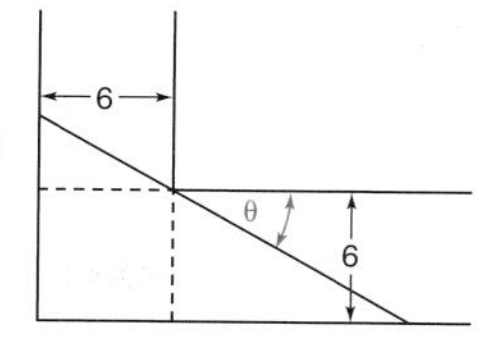

41. Use the drawing provided to show that the area of the isosceles triangle is $A = s^2 \sin\theta \cos\theta$.

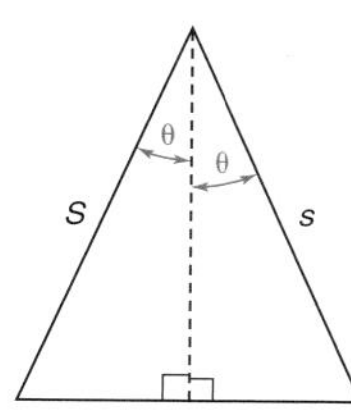

42. In regular pentagon *ABCDE*, each radius has length r. In terms of r, find an expression for the perimeter of *ABCDE*.

43. Consider regular pentagon *ABCDE* of Exercise 42. In terms of radius length r, find an expression for the area of *ABCDE*.

11.3 The Tangent Ratio and Other Ratios

KEY CONCEPTS

Tangent Ratio: $\tan\theta = \frac{\text{opposite}}{\text{adjacent}}$
Cotangent
Secant
Cosecant
Reciprocal Ratios

As in Sections 11.1 and 11.2, we deal strictly with right triangles in Section 11.3. The next trigonometric ratio that we consider is the **tangent** ratio, which is defined for an acute angle of the right triangle by

$$\frac{\text{length of leg } \textit{opposite} \text{ acute angle}}{\text{length of leg } \textit{adjacent} \text{ to acute angle}}$$

Like the sine ratio, the tangent ratio increases as the measure of the acute angle increases. Unlike the sine and cosine ratios, whose values range from 0 to 1, the value of the tangent ratio is from 0 upward; that is, there is no greatest value for the tangent.

Figure 11.24

DEFINITION

In a right triangle, the **tangent ratio** for an acute angle is the ratio $\frac{\text{opposite}}{\text{adjacent}}$.

NOTE: In right $\triangle ABC$ in Figure 11.24, $\tan\alpha = \frac{a}{b}$ and $\tan\beta = \frac{b}{a}$, in which "tan" is an abbreviated form of the word tangent.

Technology Exploration

If you have a graphing calculator, draw the graph of $y = \tan x$ subject to these conditions:

i. Calculator in degree mode.
ii. Window has $0 \leq x \leq 90$ and $0 \leq y \leq 4$

Show that $y = \tan x$ increases as x increases.

EXAMPLE 1

Find the values of $\tan\alpha$ and $\tan\beta$ for the triangle in Figure 11.25.

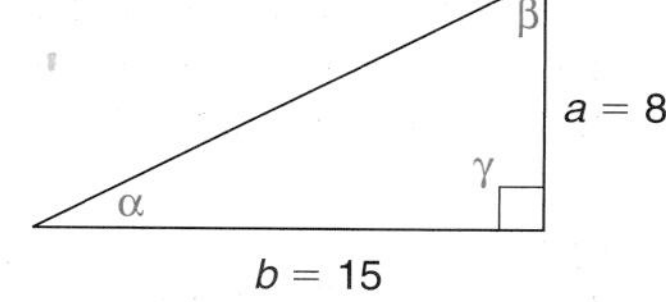

Figure 11.25

Solution Using the fact that the tangent ratio is $\frac{\text{opposite}}{\text{adjacent}}$, we find that

$$\tan\alpha = \frac{a}{b} = \frac{8}{15}$$

and

$$\tan\beta = \frac{b}{a} = \frac{15}{8}$$

■

Exs. 1–4

The value of $\tan\theta$ changes from 0 for a 0° angle to an immeasurably large value as the measure of the acute angle approaches 90°. That the tangent ratio $\frac{\text{opposite}}{\text{adjacent}}$ becomes infinitely large as $\theta \to 90°$ follows from the fact that the denominator becomes smaller and approaches 0 as the numerator increases.

Study Figure 11.26 to see why the value of the tangent of an angle grows immeasurably large as the angle approaches 90° in size. We often express this relationship by writing: As $\theta \to 90°$, $\tan\theta \to \infty$. The symbol ∞ is read "infinity" and implies that tan 90° is not measurable; thus, tan 90° is *undefined.*

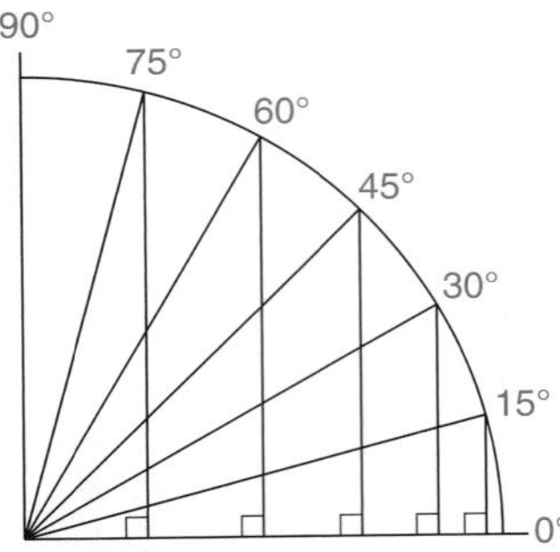

Figure 11.26

DEFINITION

tan 0° = 0 and tan 90° is undefined.

NOTE: Use your calculator to verify that tan 0° = 0. What happens when you use your calculator to find tan 90°?

Certain tangent ratios are found by using special right triangles. By observing the triangles in Figure 11.27 and using the fact that $\tan\theta = \frac{\text{opposite}}{\text{adjacent}}$, we have

$$\tan 30° = \frac{x}{x\sqrt{3}} = \frac{1}{\sqrt{3}} = \frac{\sqrt{3}}{3} \approx 0.5774$$

$$\tan 45° = \frac{x}{x} = 1$$

$$\tan 60° = \frac{x\sqrt{3}}{x} = \sqrt{3} \approx 1.7321$$

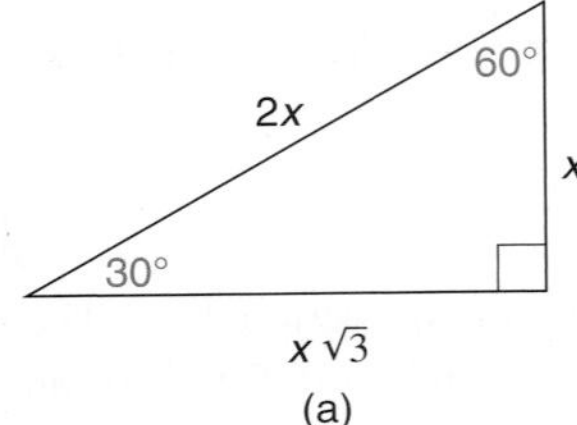

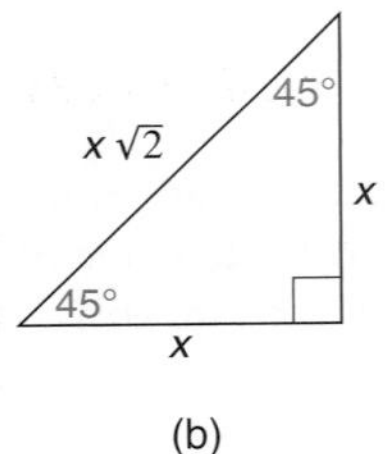

Figure 11.27

We apply the tangent ratio in Example 2.

EXAMPLE 2

A ski lift moves each chair through an angle of 25°, as shown in Figure 11.28. What vertical change (rise) accompanies a horizontal change (run) of 845 ft?

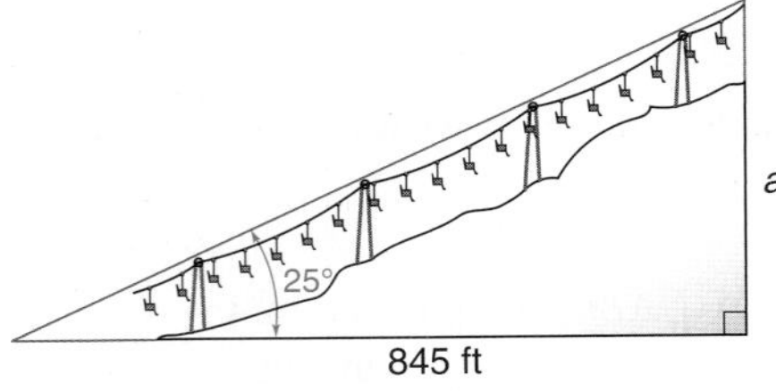

Figure 11.28

Exs. 5–8

Solution In the triangle, $\tan 25° = \frac{\text{opposite}}{\text{adjacent}} = \frac{a}{845}$. From $\tan 25° = \frac{a}{845}$, we multiply by 845 to obtain $a = 845 \cdot \tan 25°$. Using a calculator, we find that $a \approx 394$ ft. ■

The tangent ratio can also be used to find the measure of an angle if the lengths of the legs of a right triangle are known. This is illustrated in Example 3.

In the coordinate system shown, we see that the slope of the line is $m = \tan \alpha$.

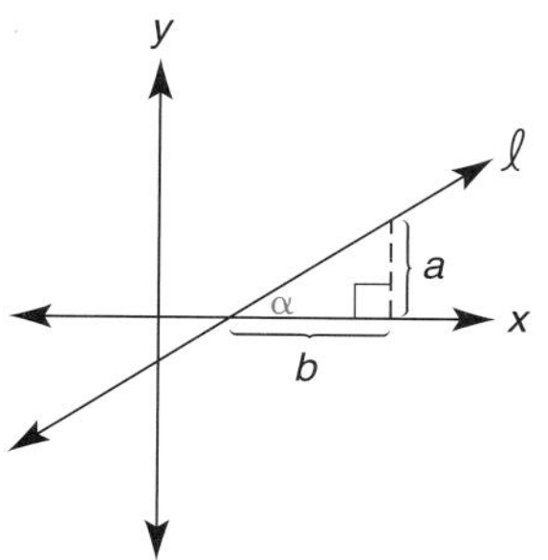

EXAMPLE 3

Mary Katherine sees an airplane flying over Mission Rock, which is 1 mi away. If Mission Rock is known to be 135 ft high and the airplane is 420 ft above it, then what is the angle of elevation through which Mary Katherine sees the plane?

Solution From Figure 11.29 and the fact that 1 mi = 5280 ft,

$$\tan \theta = \frac{\text{opposite}}{\text{adjacent}} = \frac{555}{5280}$$

Then $\tan \theta \approx 0.1051$, so $\theta = 6°$ to the nearest degree.

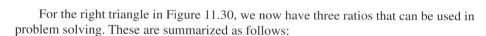

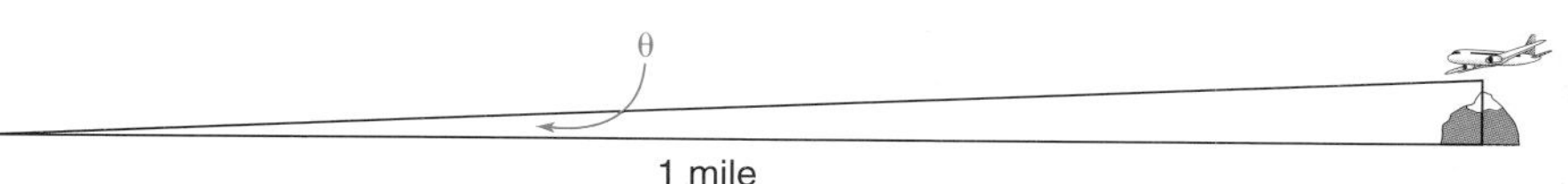

Figure 11.29

NOTE: The solution for Example 3 required the use of a calculator. When we use a scientific calculator in degree mode, the typical key sequence is

[·] → [1] → [0] → [5] → [1] → [inv] → [tan] → [6]

When we use a graphing calculator in degree mode, the typical key sequence is

[$\tan^{-1}$] → [·] → [1] → [0] → [5] → [1] → [ENTER] → [6]

For the right triangle in Figure 11.30, we now have three ratios that can be used in problem solving. These are summarized as follows:

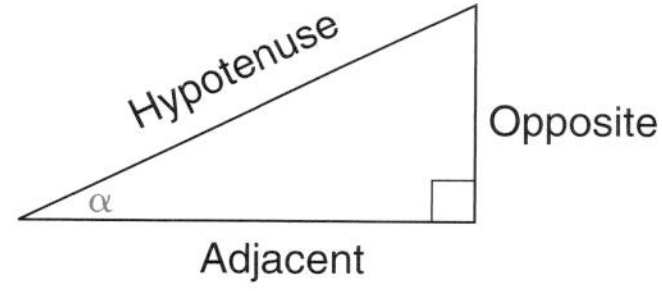

Figure 11.30

$$\sin \alpha = \frac{\text{opposite}}{\text{hypotenuse}}$$

$$\cos \alpha = \frac{\text{adjacent}}{\text{hypotenuse}}$$

$$\tan \alpha = \frac{\text{opposite}}{\text{adjacent}}$$

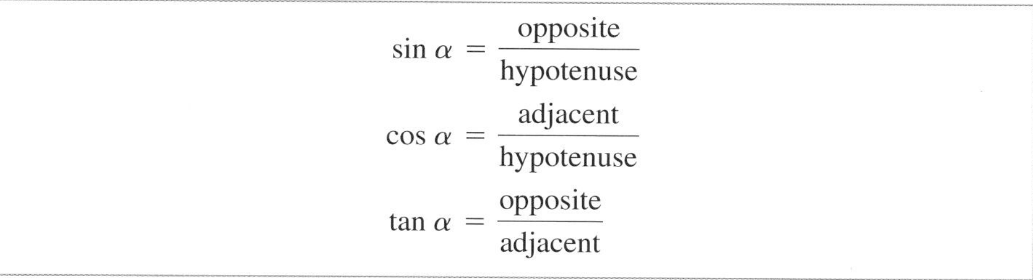

SSG *Exs. 9–11*

The equation $\tan \alpha = \frac{a}{b}$ contains three variables: α, a, and b. If the values of two of the variables are known, the value of the third variable can be found.

EXAMPLE 4

In Figure 11.31, name the ratio that should be used to find:

a) a, if α and c are known
b) α, if a and b are known
c) β, if a and c are known
d) b, if a and β are known

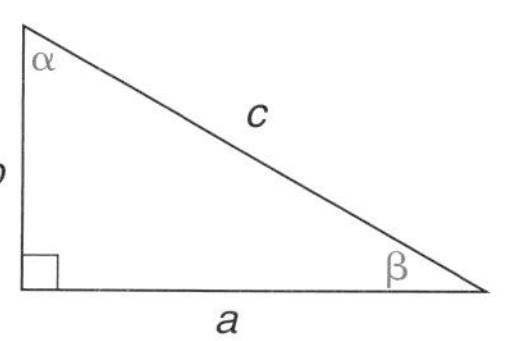

Figure 11.31

Solution

a) sine, because $\sin \alpha = \frac{a}{c}$
b) tangent, because $\tan \alpha = \frac{a}{b}$
c) cosine, because $\cos \beta = \frac{a}{c}$
d) tangent, because $\tan \beta = \frac{b}{a}$ ■

EXAMPLE 5

Two apartment buildings are 40 ft apart. From a window in her apartment, Izzi can see the top of the other apartment building through an angle of elevation of 47°. She can also see the base of the other building through an angle of depression of 33°. Approximately how tall is the other building?

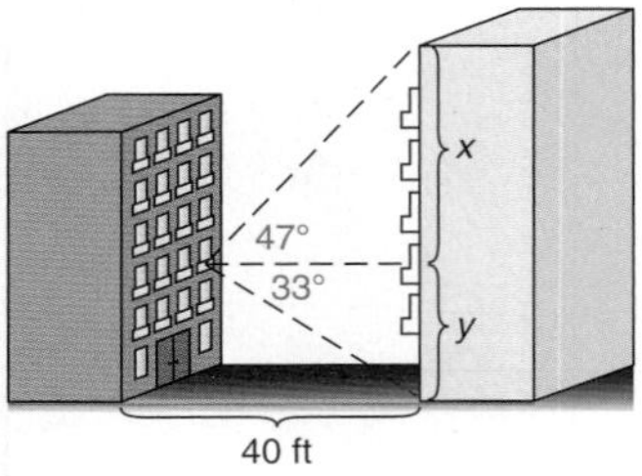

Figure 11.32

Solution In Figure 11.32, the height of the building is the sum $x + y$. Using the upper and lower right triangles, we have

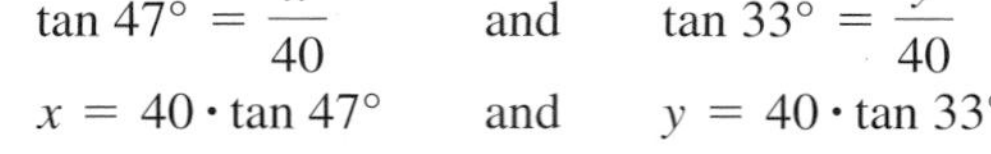

$$\tan 47° = \frac{x}{40} \quad \text{and} \quad \tan 33° = \frac{y}{40}$$

Now $$x = 40 \cdot \tan 47° \quad \text{and} \quad y = 40 \cdot \tan 33°$$

Then $x \approx 43$ and $y \approx 26$, so $x + y \approx 43 + 26 = 69$. The building is approximately 69 ft tall.

NOTE: In Example 5, you can determine the height of the building $(x + y)$ by entering the expression $40 \cdot \tan 47° + 40 \cdot \tan 33°$ on your calculator. ■

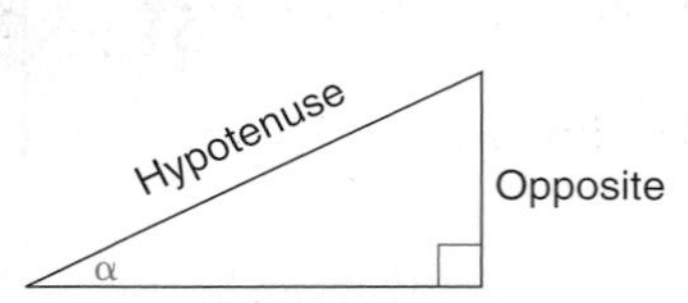

Figure 11.33

There are a total of six trigonometric ratios. We define the remaining ratios for completeness; however, we will be able to solve all application problems in this chapter by using only the sine, cosine, and tangent ratios. The remaining ratios are the **cotangent** (abbreviated "cot"), **secant** (abbreviated "sec"), and **cosecant** (abbreviated "csc"). These are defined in terms of the right triangle shown in Figure 11.33.

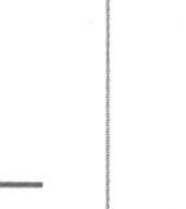

Technology Exploration

If you have a graphing calculator, show that tan 23° equals $\frac{\sin 23°}{\cos 23°}$. The identity $\tan \alpha = \frac{\sin \alpha}{\cos \alpha}$ is true as long as $\cos \alpha \neq 0$.

$$\cot \alpha = \frac{\text{adjacent}}{\text{opposite}}$$

$$\sec \alpha = \frac{\text{hypotenuse}}{\text{adjacent}}$$

$$\csc \alpha = \frac{\text{hypotenuse}}{\text{opposite}}$$

For the fraction $\frac{a}{b}$ (where $b \neq 0$), the reciprocal is $\frac{b}{a}$ $(a \neq 0)$. It is easy to see that $\cot \alpha$ is the reciprocal of $\tan \alpha$, $\sec \alpha$ is the reciprocal of $\cos \alpha$, and $\csc \alpha$ is the reciprocal of $\sin \alpha$. In the following chart, we invert the trigonometric ratio on the left to obtain the reciprocal ratio named to its right.

TRIGONOMETRIC RATIO	RECIPROCAL RATIO
$\text{sine } \alpha = \dfrac{\text{opposite}}{\text{hypotenuse}}$	$\text{cosecant } \alpha = \dfrac{\text{hypotenuse}}{\text{opposite}}$
$\text{cosine } \alpha = \dfrac{\text{adjacent}}{\text{hypotenuse}}$	$\text{secant } \alpha = \dfrac{\text{hypotenuse}}{\text{adjacent}}$
$\text{tangent } \alpha = \dfrac{\text{opposite}}{\text{adjacent}}$	$\text{cotangent } \alpha = \dfrac{\text{adjacent}}{\text{opposite}}$

Calculators display only the sine, cosine, and tangent ratios. By using the reciprocal key, [1/x] or [x^{-1}], you can obtain the values for the remaining ratios. See Example 6 for details.

EXAMPLE 6

Use a calculator to evaluate

a) csc 37° b) cot 51° c) sec 84°

Solution

a) First we use the calculator to find sin 37° ≈ 0.6081. Now use the [1/x] or [x^{-1}] key to show that csc 37° ≈ 1.6616.
b) First we use the calculator to find tan 51° ≈ 1.2349. Now use the [1/x] or [x^{-1}] key to show that cot 51° ≈ 0.8098.
c) First we use the calculator to find cos 84° ≈ 0.1045. Now use the [1/x] or [x^{-1}] key to show that sec 84° ≈ 9.5668

SSG *Exs. 12–16*

NOTE: In part (a), the value of csc 37° can be determined by using the following display on a graphing calculator: $(\sin 37)^{-1}$. Similar displays can be used in parts (b) and (c).

In Example 7, a calculator is not necessary for exact results.

EXAMPLE 7

For the triangle in Figure 11.34, find the exact values of all six trigonometric ratios for angle θ.

Solution We need the length c of the hypotenuse, which we find by the Pythagorean Theorem.

$$c^2 = 5^2 + 6^2$$
$$c^2 = 25 + 36$$
$$c^2 = 61$$
$$c = \sqrt{61}$$

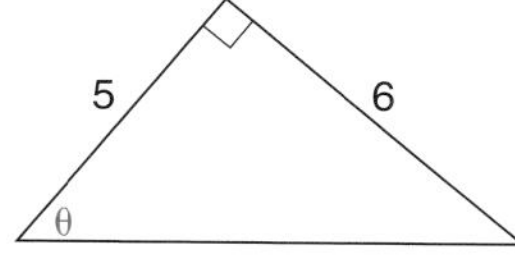

Figure 11.34

Reminder

The reciprocal of $\frac{a}{b}$ is $\frac{b}{a}$.

NOTE: $a \neq 0$, $b \neq 0$.

Therefore,

$$\sin\theta = \frac{\text{opposite}}{\text{hypotenuse}} = \frac{6}{\sqrt{61}} = \frac{6}{\sqrt{61}} \cdot \frac{\sqrt{61}}{\sqrt{61}} = \frac{6\sqrt{61}}{61}$$

$$\cos\theta = \frac{\text{adjacent}}{\text{hypotenuse}} = \frac{5}{\sqrt{61}} = \frac{5}{\sqrt{61}} \cdot \frac{\sqrt{61}}{\sqrt{61}} = \frac{5\sqrt{61}}{61}$$

$$\tan\theta = \frac{\text{opposite}}{\text{adjacent}} = \frac{6}{5}$$

$$\cot\theta = \frac{\text{adjacent}}{\text{opposite}} = \frac{5}{6}$$

$$\sec\theta = \frac{\text{hypotenuse}}{\text{adjacent}} = \frac{\sqrt{61}}{5}$$

$$\csc\theta = \frac{\text{hypotenuse}}{\text{opposite}} = \frac{\sqrt{61}}{6}$$

NOTE: The arrows in Example 7 indicate which pairs of ratios are reciprocals of each other. ■

EXAMPLE 8

Evaluate the ratio named by using the given ratio:

a) $\tan\theta$, if $\cot\theta = \frac{2}{3}$
b) $\sin\alpha$, if $\csc\alpha = 1.25$
c) $\sec\beta$, if $\cos\beta = \frac{\sqrt{3}}{2}$
d) $\csc\gamma$, if $\sin\gamma = 1$

Solution

a) If $\cot\theta = \frac{2}{3}$, then $\tan\theta = \frac{3}{2}$ (the reciprocal of $\cot\theta$).
b) If $\csc\alpha = 1.25$ or $\frac{5}{4}$, then $\sin\alpha = \frac{4}{5}$ (the reciprocal of $\csc\alpha$).
c) If $\cos\beta = \frac{\sqrt{3}}{2}$, then $\sec\beta = \frac{2}{\sqrt{3}}$ or $\frac{2\sqrt{3}}{3}$ (the reciprocal of $\cos\beta$).
d) If $\sin\gamma = 1$, then $\csc\gamma = 1$ (the reciprocal of $\sin\gamma$). ■

EXAMPLE 9

To the nearest degree, how large is θ in the triangle in Figure 11.35 if $\cot\theta = \frac{8}{5}$.

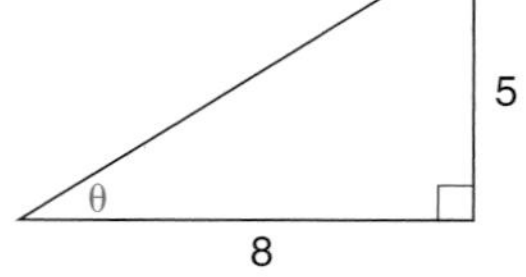

Figure 11.35

Solution Because the value of $\cot\theta$ is known, we can use its reciprocal to find θ. That is,

$$\tan\theta = \frac{5}{8}$$

With a scientific calculator, we determine θ by using the key sequence

[5] → [÷] → [8] → [=] → [inv] → [tan] → **[32]**

When we use a graphing calculator, the key sequence is

[$\tan^{-1}$] → [(] → [5] → [÷] → [8] → [)] → [ENTER] → **[32]**

Thus, $\theta \approx 32°$. ■

In the application exercises that follow this section, you will have to decide which trigonometric ratio enables you to solve the problem. The Pythagorean Theorem can be used as well.

EXAMPLE 10

As his fishing vessel moves into the bay, the captain notes that the angle of elevation to the top of the lighthouse is 11°. If the lighthouse is 200 ft tall, how far is the vessel from the lighthouse? See Figure 11.36.

Solution Again we use the tangent ratio; in Figure 11.36,

$$\begin{aligned} \tan 11^\circ &= \frac{200}{x} \\ x \cdot \tan 11^\circ &= 200 \\ x &= \frac{200}{\tan 11^\circ} \approx 1028.91 \end{aligned}$$

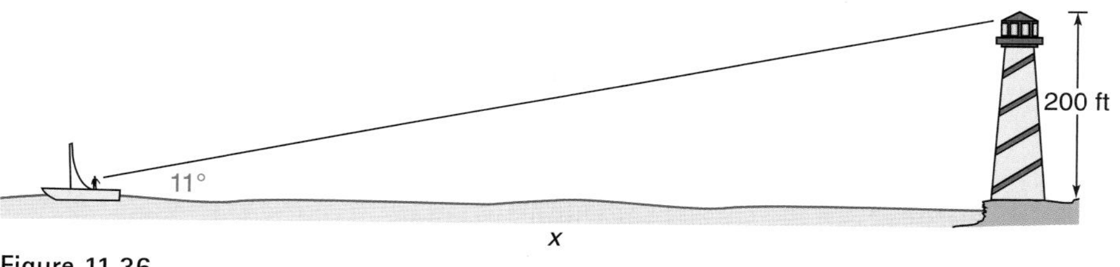

Figure 11.36

SSG Exs. 17, 18

The vessel is approximately 1029 ft from the lighthouse. ■

Exercises 11.3

In Exercises 1 to 4, find tan α and tan β for each triangle.

1.

2.

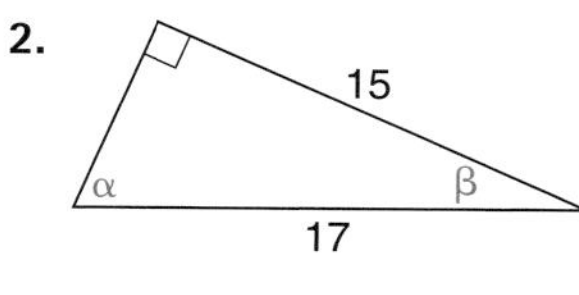

3.

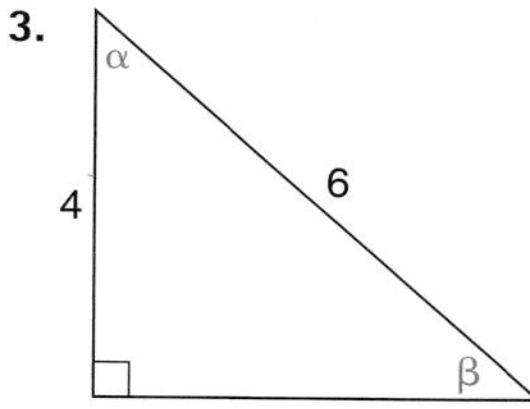

4.

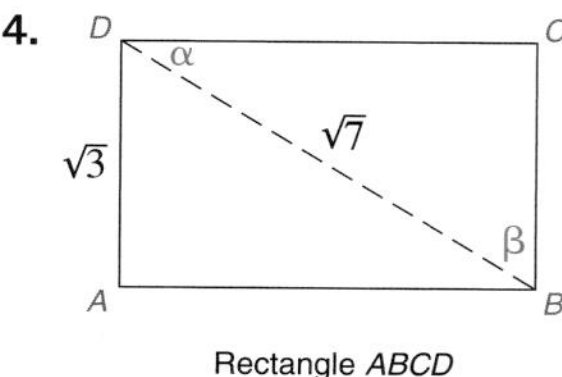

In Exercises 5 to 10, find the value (or expression) for each of the six trigonometric ratios of angle α. Use the Pythagorean Theorem as needed.

5.

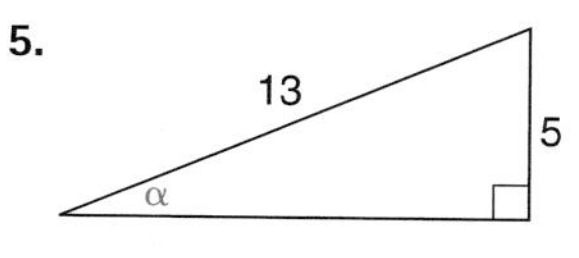

6.

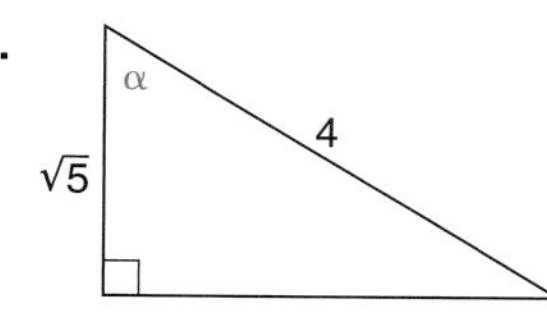

7.

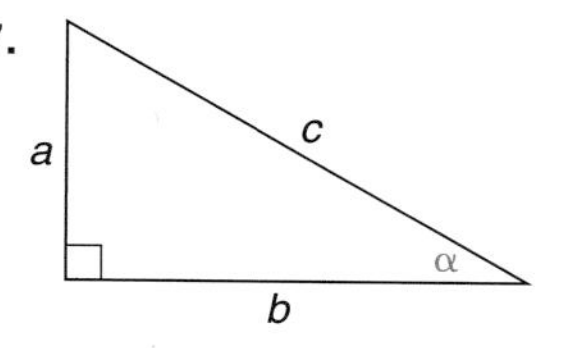

8.

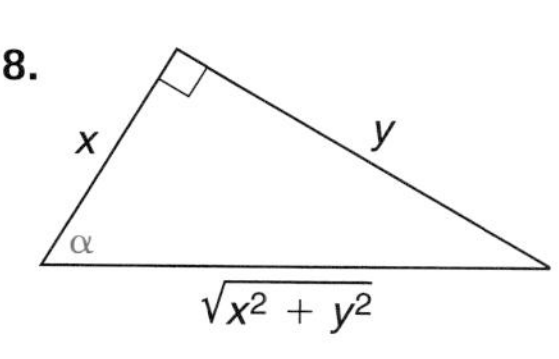

9.

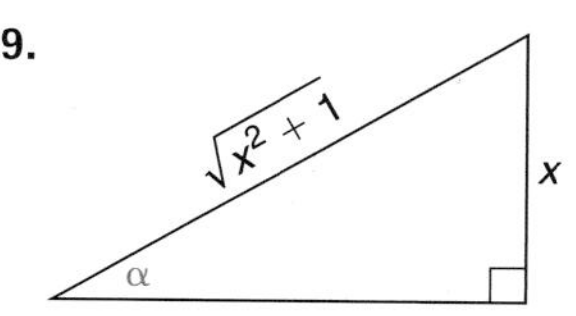

10.

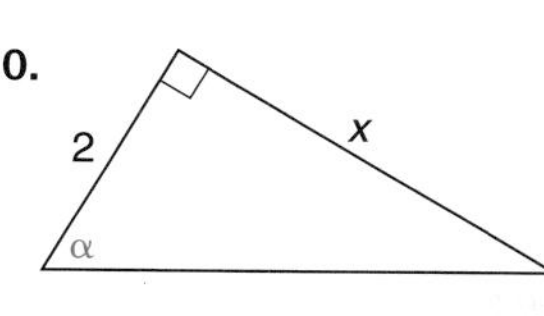

In Exercises 11 to 14, use a calculator to find the indicated tangent ratio correct to four decimal places.

11. tan 15° **12.** tan 45°

13. tan 57° **14.** tan 78°

In Exercises 15 to 20, use the sine, cosine, or tangent ratio to find the lengths of the indicated sides to the nearest tenth of a unit.

15.

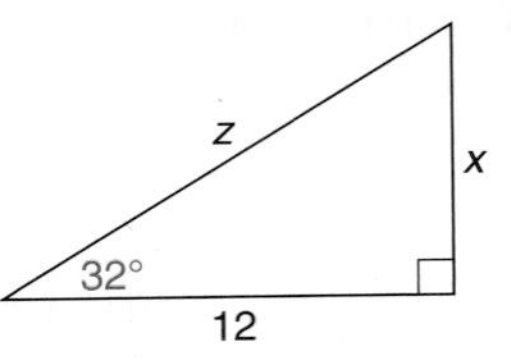

16.

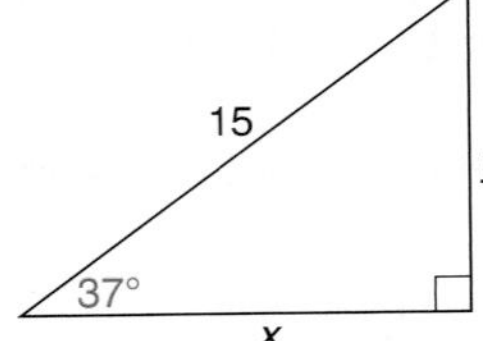

17.

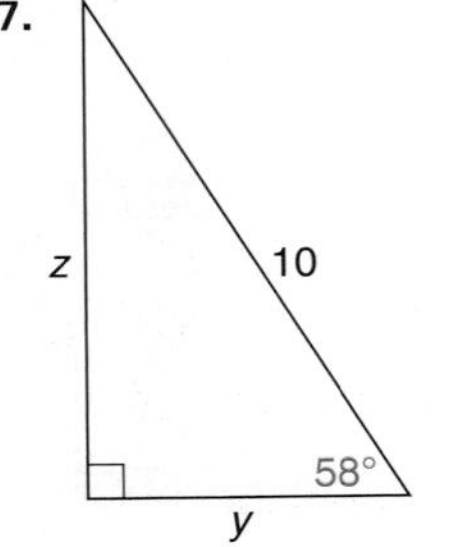

18.

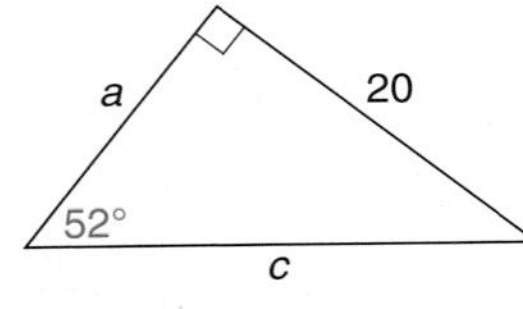

19.

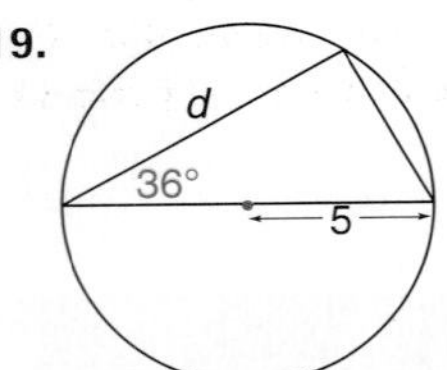

20.

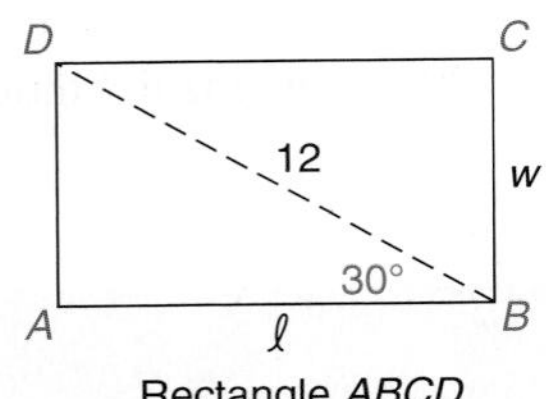

Rectangle *ABCD*

In Exercises 21 to 26, use the sine, cosine, or tangent ratio to find the indicated angle measures to the nearest degree.

21.

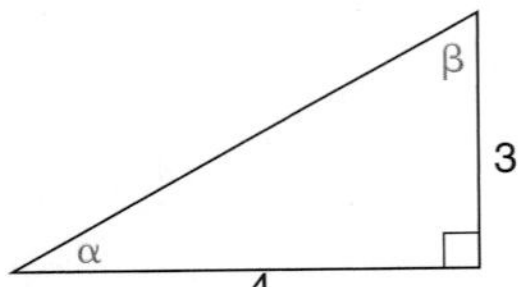

22.

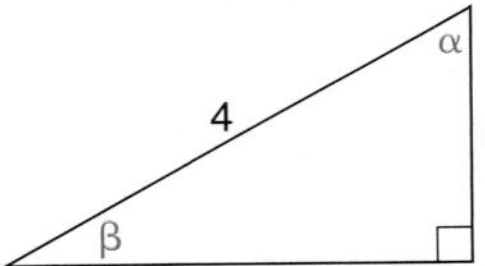

23.

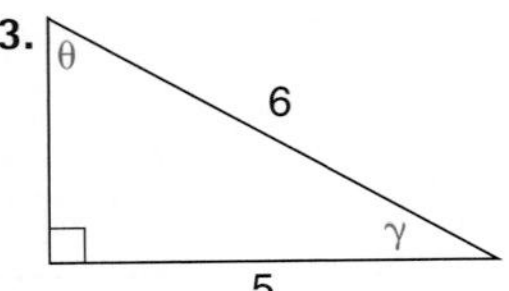

24.

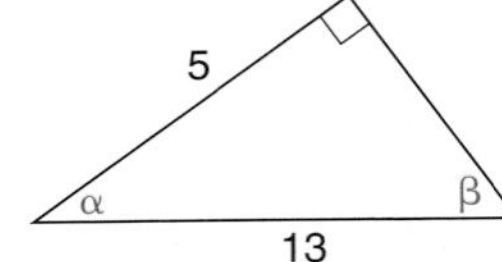

25.

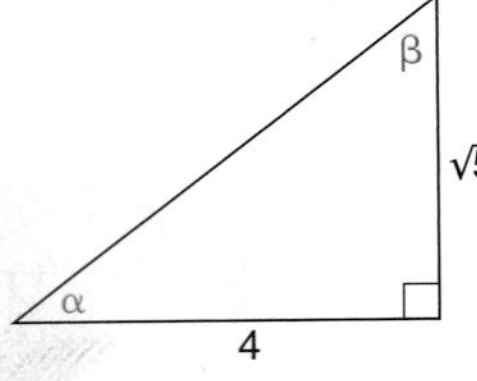

26.

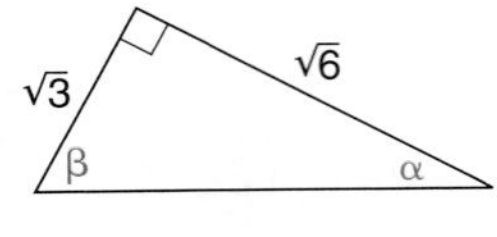

In Exercises 27 to 32, use a calculator and reciprocal relationships to find each ratio correct to four decimal places.

27. cot 34° **28.** sec 15°

29. csc 30° **30.** cot 67°

31. sec 42° **32.** csc 72°

In Exercises 33 to 36, we expand the list of trigonometric identities. As you may recall (see page 508), an identity is a statement that is true for all permissible choices of the variable.

33. a) For $\alpha \neq 90°$, prove the identity

$$\tan \alpha = \frac{\sin \alpha}{\cos \alpha}$$

(HINT: $\sin \alpha = \frac{a}{c}$ *and* $\cos \alpha = \frac{b}{c}$*.)*

b) Use your calculator to show that tan 23° and $\frac{\sin 23°}{\cos 23°}$ are equivalent.

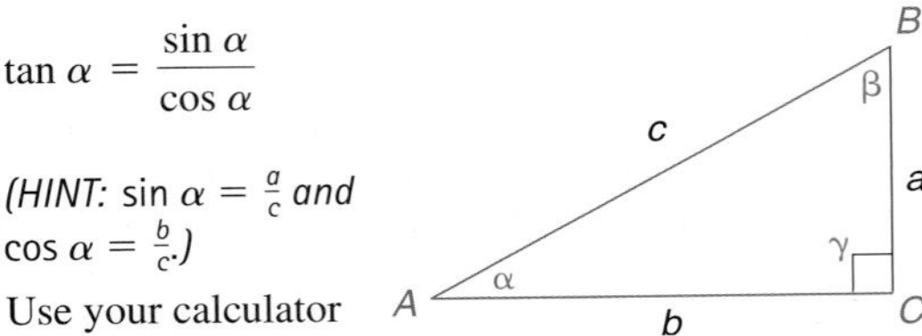

Exercises 33–36

34. a) For $\alpha \neq 0°$, prove the identity $\cot \alpha = \frac{\cos \alpha}{\sin \alpha}$.
b) Use your calculator to determine cot 57° by dividing cos 57° by sin 57°.

35. a) For $\alpha \neq 90°$, prove the identity $\sec \alpha = \frac{1}{\cos \alpha}$.
b) Use your calculator to determine sec 82°.

36. a) For $\alpha \neq 0°$, prove the identity $\csc \alpha = \frac{1}{\sin \alpha}$.
b) Use your calculator to determine csc 12.3°.

In Exercises 37 to 43, angle measures should be given to the nearest degree; distances should be given to the nearest tenth of a unit.

37. When her airplane is descending to land, the pilot notes an angle of depression of 5°. If the altimeter shows an altitude reading of 120 ft, what is the distance *x* from the plane to touchdown?

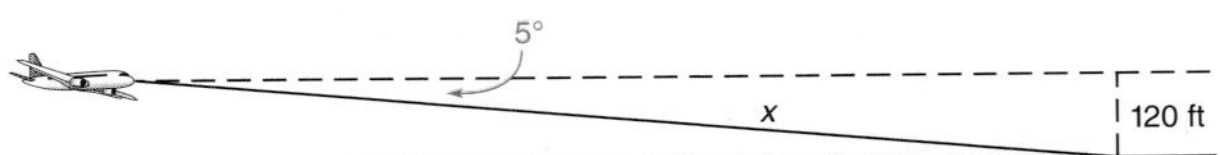

38. Raquel observes the top of a lookout tower from a point 270 ft from its base. If the angle of elevation is 37°, how tall is the tower?

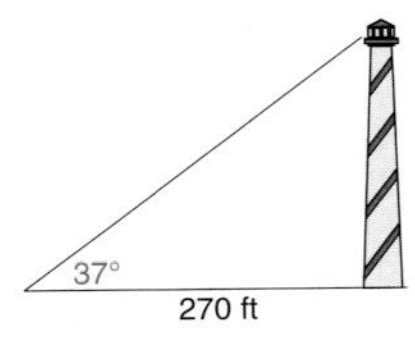

39. Find the length of the apothem to each of the 6-in. sides of a regular pentagon.

***40.** What is the measure of the angle between the diagonal of a cube and the diagonal of the face of the cube?

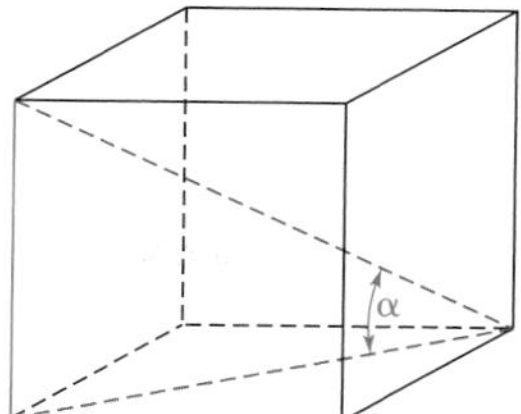

41. Upon approaching a house, Liz hears Lynette shout to her. Liz, who is standing 10 ft from the house, looks up to see Lynette in the third-story window approximately 32 ft away. What is the measure of the angle of elevation as Liz looks up at Lynette?

***42.** While a helicopter hovers 1000 ft above the water, its pilot spies a man in a lifeboat through an angle of depression of 28°. Along a straight line, a rescue boat can also be seen through an angle of depression of 14°. How far is the rescue boat from the lifeboat?

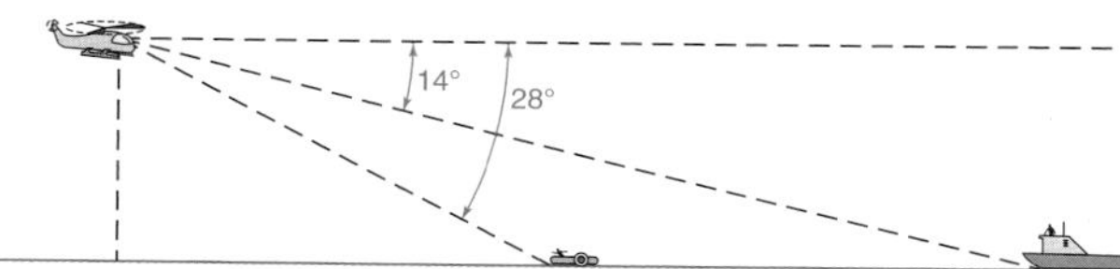

***43.** From atop a 200-ft lookout tower, a fire is spotted due north through an angle of depression of 12°. Firefighters located 1000 ft due east of the tower must work their way through heavy foliage to the fire. By their compasses, through what angle (measured from the north toward the west) must the firefighters travel?

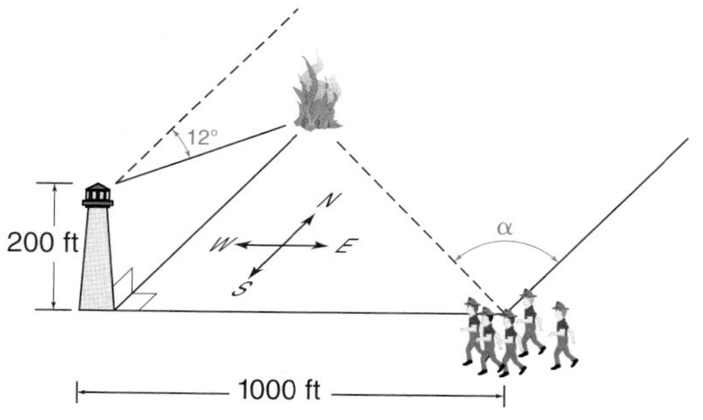

44. In the triangle shown, find each measure to the nearest tenth of a unit.

a) x b) y

c) A, the area of the triangle

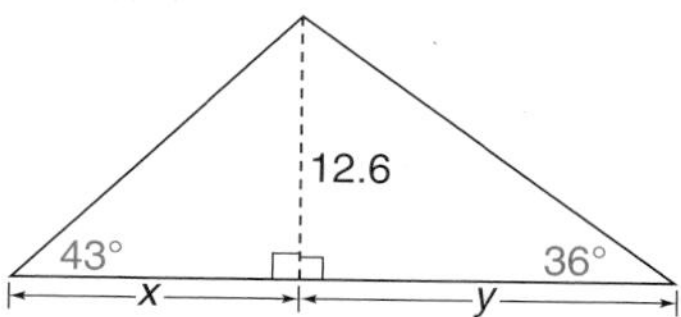

45. At an altitude of 12,000 ft, a pilot sees two towns through angles of depression of 37° and 48° as shown. To the nearest 10 ft, how far apart are the towns?

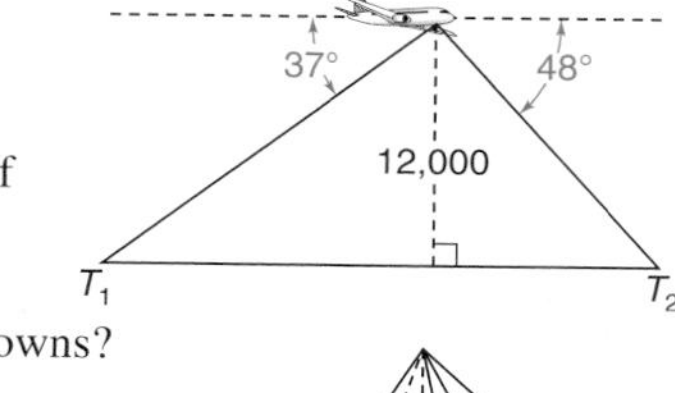

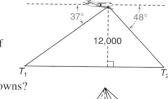

46. Consider the regular square pyramid shown.

a) Find the length of the slant height ℓ correct to tenths.

b) Use ℓ from part (a) to find the lateral area L of the pyramid.

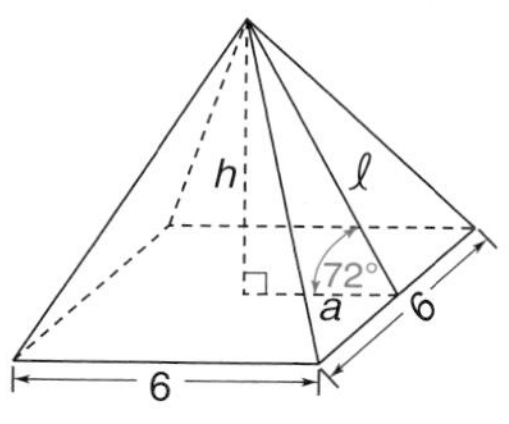

Exercises 46, 47

47. Consider the regular square pyramid shown.

a) Find the height h correct to the nearest tenth of a unit.

b) Use h from part (a) to find the volume of the pyramid.

11.4 Applications with Acute Triangles

KEY CONCEPTS

Area of a Triangle:

$A = \frac{1}{2}bc \sin \alpha$
$A = \frac{1}{2}ac \sin \beta$
$A = \frac{1}{2}ab \sin \gamma$

Law of Sines:

$$\frac{\sin \alpha}{a} = \frac{\sin \beta}{b} = \frac{\sin \gamma}{c}$$

Law of Cosines:

$c^2 = a^2 + b^2 - 2ab \cos \gamma$
$b^2 = a^2 + c^2 - 2ac \cos \beta$
$a^2 = b^2 + c^2 - 2bc \cos \alpha$

or

$\cos \alpha = \frac{b^2 + c^2 - a^2}{2bc}$
$\cos \beta = \frac{a^2 + c^2 - b^2}{2ac}$
$\cos \gamma = \frac{a^2 + b^2 - c^2}{2ab}$

In Sections 11.1 through 11.3, our focus was strictly on right triangles; thus, the sides of every triangle that we considered were two legs and a hypotenuse. We now turn our attention to some relationships that we will prove for, and apply with, *acute* triangles. The first relationship provides a formula for the area of a triangle in which α, β, and γ are all acute angles.

AREA OF A TRIANGLE

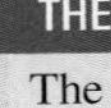

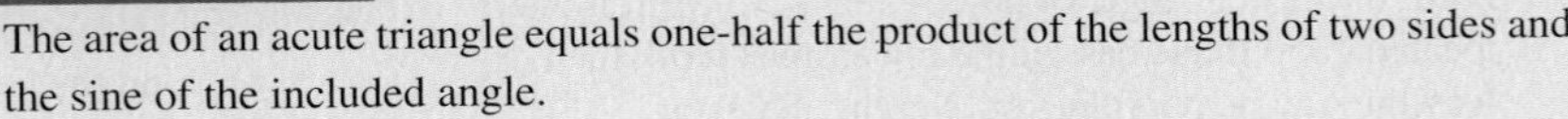

THEOREM 11.4.1

The area of an acute triangle equals one-half the product of the lengths of two sides and the sine of the included angle.

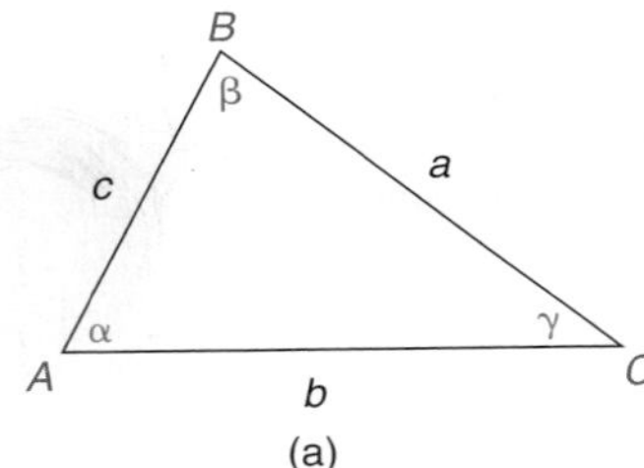

(a)

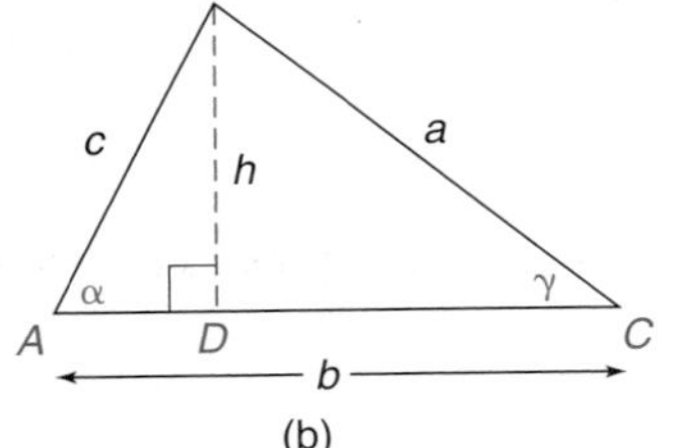

(b)

Figure 11.37

GIVEN: Acute $\triangle ABC$, as shown in Figure 11.37(a).

PROVE: $A = \frac{1}{2}bc \sin \alpha$

PROOF: The area of the triangle is given by $A = \frac{1}{2}bh$. With the altitude $\overline{BD}$ [see Figure 11.37(b)], we see that $\sin \alpha = \frac{h}{c}$ in right $\triangle ABD$. Then $h = c \sin \alpha$. Consequently, $A = \frac{1}{2}bh$ becomes

$$A = \frac{1}{2}b(c \sin \alpha), \quad \text{so} \quad A = \frac{1}{2}bc \sin \alpha$$ ■

Theorem 11.4.1 has three equivalent forms, as shown in the following box.

AREA OF A TRIANGLE

$$A = \frac{1}{2}bc \sin \alpha$$

Equivalently, we can prove that

$$A = \frac{1}{2}ac \sin \beta$$
$$A = \frac{1}{2}ab \sin \gamma$$

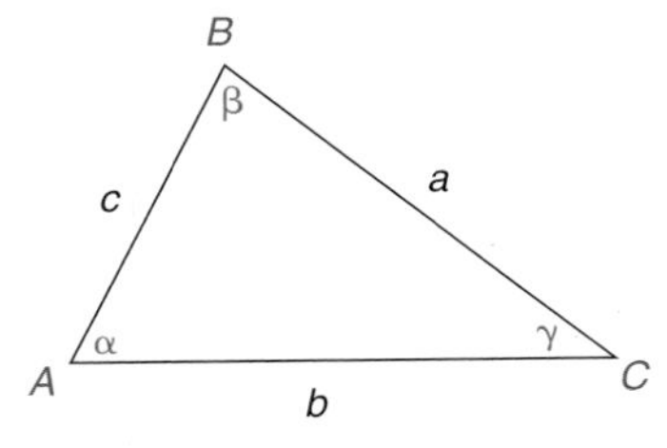

Technology Exploration

If you have a graphing calculator, you can evaluate many results rather easily. For Example 1, evaluate $\left(\frac{1}{2}\right)\cdot 6 \cdot 10 \cdot \sin(33)$. Use degree mode.

In the more advanced course called trigonometry, this area formula can also be proved for obtuse triangles. If the triangle is a right triangle with $\gamma = 90°$, then $A = \frac{1}{2}ab \sin \gamma$ becomes $A = \frac{1}{2}ab$ since $\sin \gamma = 1$. Recall Corollary 8.1.4.

EXAMPLE 1

In Figure 11.38, find the area of $\triangle ABC$.

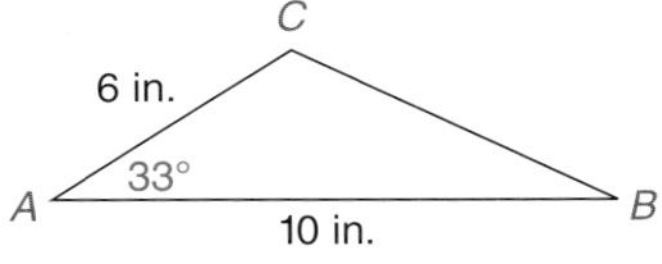

Figure 11.38

Solution We use $A = \frac{1}{2}bc \sin \alpha$, since α, b, and c are known.

$$\begin{aligned} A &= \frac{1}{2} \cdot 6 \cdot 10 \cdot \sin 33° \\ &= 30 \cdot \sin 33° \\ &\approx 16.3 \text{ in}^2 \end{aligned}$$

■

EXAMPLE 2

In $\triangle ABC$ (shown in Figure 11.39), $a = 7.6$ and $c = 10.2$. If the area of $\triangle ABC$ is approximately 38.3 square units, find β to the nearest degree. Note that $\angle B$ is acute.

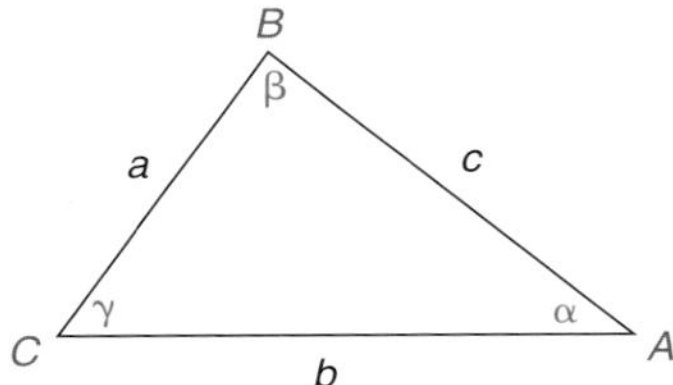

Figure 11.39

SSG *Exs. 1–4*

Solution Using the form $A = \frac{1}{2}ac \sin \beta$, we have $38.3 = (0.5)(7.6)(10.2) \sin \beta$, or $38.3 = 38.76 \sin \beta$. Thus, $\sin \beta = \frac{38.3}{38.76}$ so $\beta = \sin^{-1}\left(\frac{38.3}{38.76}\right)$. Then $\beta \approx 81°$ (rounded from 81.16). ■

LAW OF SINES

Because the area of a triangle is unique, we can equate the three area expressions characterized by Theorem 11.4.1 as follows:

$$\frac{1}{2}bc \sin \alpha = \frac{1}{2}ac \sin \beta = \frac{1}{2}ab \sin \gamma$$

Dividing each part of this equality by $\frac{1}{2}abc$, we find

$$\frac{\frac{1}{2}bc \sin \alpha}{\frac{1}{2}bca} = \frac{\frac{1}{2}ac \sin \beta}{\frac{1}{2}acb} = \frac{\frac{1}{2}ab \sin \gamma}{\frac{1}{2}abc}$$

So

$$\frac{\sin \alpha}{a} = \frac{\sin \beta}{b} = \frac{\sin \gamma}{c}$$

This relationship between the lengths of the sides of an acute triangle and the sines of their opposite angles is known as the Law of Sines. In trigonometry, it is shown that the Law of Sines is true for right triangles and obtuse triangles as well.

THEOREM 11.4.2 ▶ (Law of Sines)

In any acute triangle, the three ratios between the sines of the angles and the lengths of the opposite sides are equal. That is,

$$\frac{\sin \alpha}{a} = \frac{\sin \beta}{b} = \frac{\sin \gamma}{c} \quad \text{or} \quad \frac{a}{\sin \alpha} = \frac{b}{\sin \beta} = \frac{c}{\sin \gamma}$$

When solving a problem, we equate only two of the equal ratios described in Theorem 11.4.2. For instance, we can use

$$\frac{\sin \alpha}{a} = \frac{\sin \beta}{b} \quad \text{or} \quad \frac{\sin \alpha}{a} = \frac{\sin \gamma}{c} \quad \text{or} \quad \frac{\sin \beta}{b} = \frac{\sin \gamma}{c}$$

In each equation, the ratios used have the form

$$\frac{\text{sine of angle}}{\text{length of side opposite the angle}}$$

EXAMPLE 3

Use the Law of Sines to find the exact length ST in Figure 11.40.

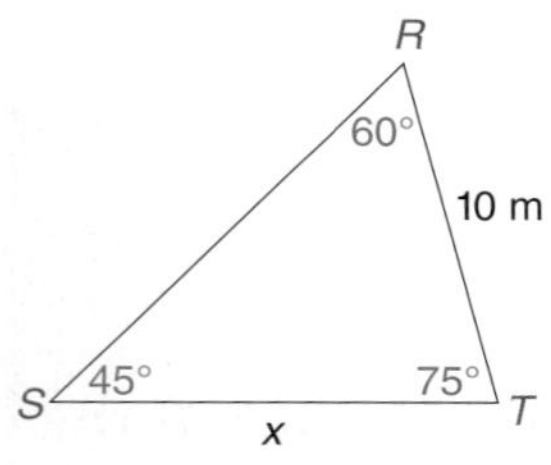

Figure 11.40

Solution Because we know RT and the measures of angles S and R, we use $\frac{\sin S}{RT} = \frac{\sin R}{ST}$. Substitution of known values leads to

$$\frac{\sin 45°}{10} = \frac{\sin 60°}{x}$$

Because $\sin 45° = \frac{\sqrt{2}}{2}$ and $\sin 60° = \frac{\sqrt{3}}{2}$, we have

$$\frac{\frac{\sqrt{2}}{2}}{10} = \frac{\frac{\sqrt{3}}{2}}{x}$$

By the Means-Extremes Property,

$$\frac{\sqrt{2}}{2} \cdot x = \frac{\sqrt{3}}{2} \cdot 10$$

Multiplying by $\frac{2}{\sqrt{2}}$, we have

$$\frac{\cancel{2}}{\cancel{\sqrt{2}}} \cdot \frac{\cancel{\sqrt{2}}}{\cancel{2}} \cdot x = \frac{\cancel{2}}{\sqrt{2}} \cdot \frac{\sqrt{3}}{\cancel{2}} \cdot 10$$

$$x = \frac{10\sqrt{3}}{\sqrt{2}} = \frac{10\sqrt{3}\sqrt{2}}{\sqrt{2}\sqrt{2}} = \frac{10\sqrt{6}}{2} = 5\sqrt{6}$$

Then $ST = 5\sqrt{6}$ m. ■

EXAMPLE 4

In $\triangle ABC$ (shown in Figure 11.41), $b = 12$, $c = 10$, and $\beta = 83°$.
Find γ to the nearest degree.

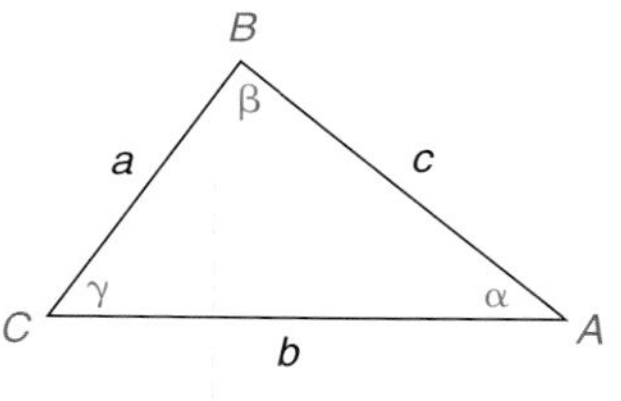

Figure 11.41

Solution Knowing values of b, c, and β, we use the following form of the Law of Sines to find γ:

$$\frac{\sin \beta}{b} = \frac{\sin \gamma}{c}.$$

$$\frac{\sin 83°}{12} = \frac{\sin \gamma}{10}, \quad \text{so} \quad 12 \sin \gamma = 10 \sin 83°$$

SSG
Exs. 5–7

Then $\sin \gamma = \frac{10 \sin 83°}{12} \approx 0.8271$, so $\gamma = \sin^{-1}(0.8271) \approx 56°$. ■

LAW OF COSINES

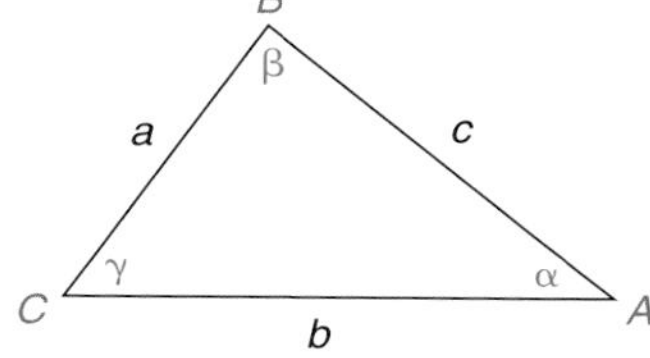

(a)

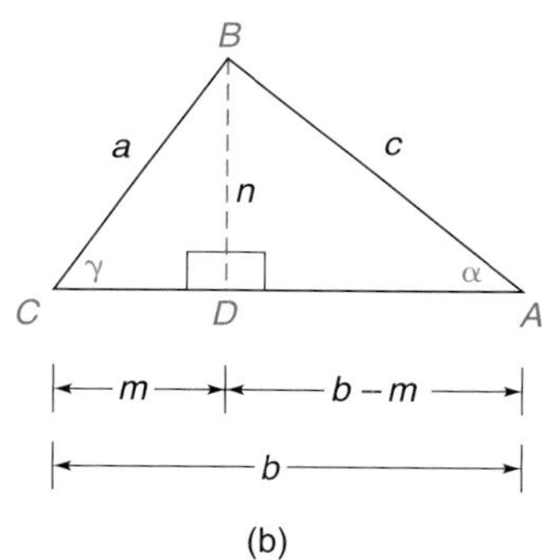

(b)

Figure 11.42

The final relationship that we consider is again proved only for an acute triangle. Like the Law of Sines, this relationship (known as the Law of Cosines) can be used to find unknown measures in a triangle. The Law of Cosines (which can also be established for obtuse triangles in a more advanced course) can be stated in words as "The square of one side of a triangle equals the sum of squares of the two remaining sides decreased by twice the product of those two sides and the cosine of their included angle." See Figure 11.42(a) as you read Theorem 11.4.3.

THEOREM 11.4.3 ▶ (Law of Cosines)

In acute $\triangle ABC$,

$$c^2 = a^2 + b^2 - 2ab \cos \gamma$$
$$b^2 = a^2 + c^2 - 2ac \cos \beta$$
$$a^2 = b^2 + c^2 - 2bc \cos \alpha$$

The proof of the first form of the Law of Cosines follows.

GIVEN: Acute $\triangle ABC$ in Figure 11.42(a)

PROVE: $c^2 = a^2 + b^2 - 2ab \cos \gamma$

PROOF: In Figure 11.42(a), draw the altitude $\overline{BD}$ from B to $\overline{AC}$. We designate lengths of the line segments as shown in Figure 11.42(b). Now

$$(b - m)^2 + n^2 = c^2 \quad \text{and} \quad m^2 + n^2 = a^2$$

by the Pythagorean Theorem.

The second equation is equivalent to $m^2 = a^2 - n^2$. After we expand $(b - m)^2$, the first equation becomes

$$b^2 - 2bm + m^2 + n^2 = c^2$$

Then we replace m^2 by $(a^2 - n^2)$ to obtain

$$b^2 - 2bm + (a^2 - n^2) + n^2 = c^2$$

Simplifying yields

$$c^2 = a^2 + b^2 - 2bm$$

In right $\triangle CDB$,

$$\cos \gamma = \frac{m}{a} \quad \text{so} \quad m = a \cos \gamma$$

Hence

$$\begin{aligned} c^2 &= a^2 + b^2 - 2bm \text{ becomes} \\ c^2 &= a^2 + b^2 - 2b(a \cos \gamma) \\ c^2 &= a^2 + b^2 - 2ab \cos \gamma \end{aligned}$$

■

Arguments similar to the preceding proof can be provided for both remaining forms of the Law of Cosines. Although the Law of Cosines holds true for right triangles, the statement $c^2 = a^2 + b^2 - 2ab \cos \gamma$ reduces to the Pythagorean Theorem when $\gamma = 90°$ because $\cos 90° = 0$.

EXAMPLE 5

Find the length of $\overline{AB}$ in the triangle in Figure 11.43.

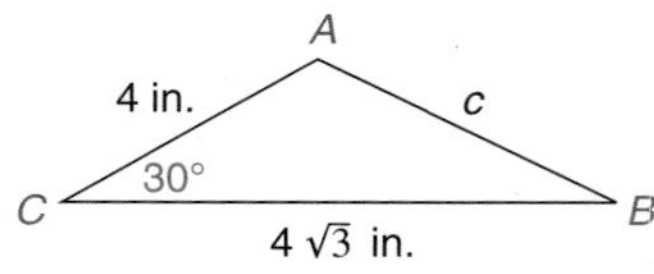

Figure 11.43

Solution Referring to the 30° angle as γ, we use the following form of the Law of Cosines:

$$\begin{aligned} c^2 &= a^2 + b^2 - 2ab \cos \gamma \\ c^2 &= (4\sqrt{3})^2 + 4^2 - 2 \cdot 4\sqrt{3} \cdot 4 \cdot \cos 30° \\ c^2 &= 48 + 16 - 2 \cdot 4\sqrt{3} \cdot 4 \cdot \frac{\sqrt{3}}{2} \\ c^2 &= 48 + 16 - 48 \\ c^2 &= 16 \\ c &= 4 \end{aligned}$$

Therefore, $AB = 4$ in.

NOTE: $\triangle ABC$ is isosceles because $\overline{AB} \cong \overline{AC}$. ■

The Law of Cosines can also be used to find the measure of an angle of a triangle when the lengths of its three sides are known. It is convenient to apply the alternative form of Theorem 11.4.3 in such applications. See Example 6 on page 525.

THEOREM 11.4.3 ▶ (Law of Cosines–Alternative Form)

In acute $\triangle ABC$,

$$\cos \alpha = \frac{b^2 + c^2 - a^2}{2bc}$$

$$\cos \beta = \frac{a^2 + c^2 - b^2}{2ac}$$

$$\cos \gamma = \frac{a^2 + b^2 - c^2}{2ab}$$

Proof of the third form

If $c^2 = a^2 + b^2 - 2ab\cos\gamma$, then

$$2ab\cos\gamma = a^2 + b^2 - c^2$$

Dividing each side of the equation by $2ab$, we have

$$\cos\gamma = \frac{a^2 + b^2 - c^2}{2ab}$$

■

Arguments for the remaining alternative forms are similar.

EXAMPLE 6

In acute $\triangle ABC$ in Figure 11.44, find β to the nearest degree.

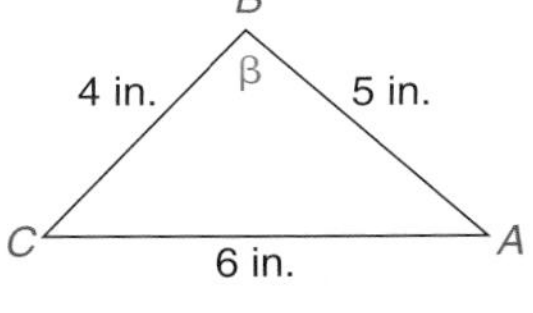

Figure 11.44

Solution The form of the Law of Cosines involving β is

$$\cos\beta = \frac{a^2 + c^2 - b^2}{2ac}$$

With $a = 4$, $b = 6$, and $c = 5$, we have

$$\cos\beta = \frac{4^2 + 5^2 - 6^2}{2 \cdot 4 \cdot 5}$$

so

$$\cos\beta = \frac{16 + 25 - 36}{40} = \frac{5}{40} = \frac{1}{8} = 0.1250$$

With $\beta = \cos^{-1}(0.1250)$, we use the calculator to show that $\beta \approx 83°$. ■

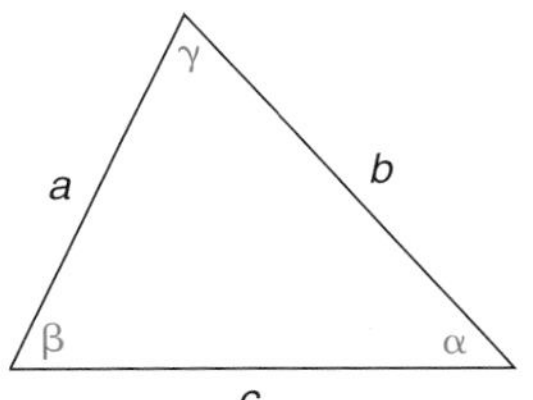

Figure 11.45

To find the measure of a side or an angle of an acute triangle, we often have to decide which form of the Law of Sines or of the Law of Cosines should be applied. Table 11.4 deals with that question and is based on the acute triangle shown in the accompanying drawing. Note that a, b, and c represent the lengths of the sides and that α, β, and γ represent the measures of the opposite angles, respectively (see Figure 11.45).

Warning

If we know *only* the measures of the three angles of the triangle, then no length of side can be determined.

TABLE 11.4
When to Use the Law of Sines/Law of Cosines

1. *Three sides are known:* Use the Law of Cosines to find *any* angle.
   Known measures: a, b, and c
   Desired measure: α

   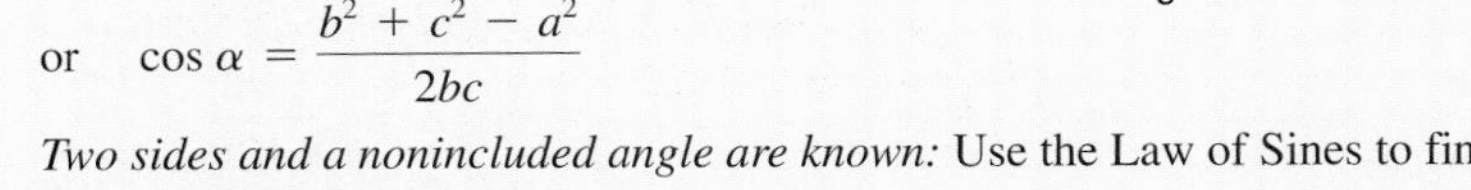

   $\therefore$ Use $a^2 = b^2 + c^2 - 2bc\cos\alpha$

   or $\cos\alpha = \dfrac{b^2 + c^2 - a^2}{2bc}$

2. *Two sides and a nonincluded angle are known:* Use the Law of Sines to find the remaining nonincluded angle.
   Known measures: a, b, and α
   Desired measure: β

   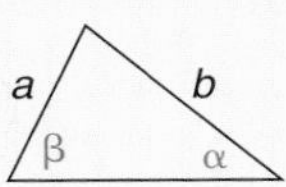

   $\therefore$ *Use* $\dfrac{\sin\alpha}{a} = \dfrac{\sin\beta}{b}$

continued

TABLE 11.4
Continued

3. *Two sides and an included angle are known:* Use the Law of Cosines to find the remaining side.
Known measures: a, b, and γ
Desired measure: c
$\therefore$ *Use* $c^2 = a^2 + b^2 - 2ab \cos \gamma$

4. *Two angles and a nonincluded side are known:* Use the Law of Sines to find the other nonincluded side.
Known measures: a, α, and β
Desired measure: b

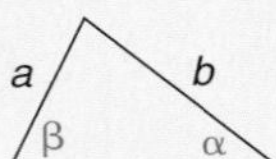

$\therefore$ *Use* $\dfrac{\sin \alpha}{a} = \dfrac{\sin \beta}{b}$

EXAMPLE 7

In the design of a child's swing set, each of the two metal posts that support the top bar measures 8 ft. At ground level, the posts are to be 6 ft apart (see Figure 11.46). At what angle should the two metal posts be secured? Give the answer to the nearest degree.

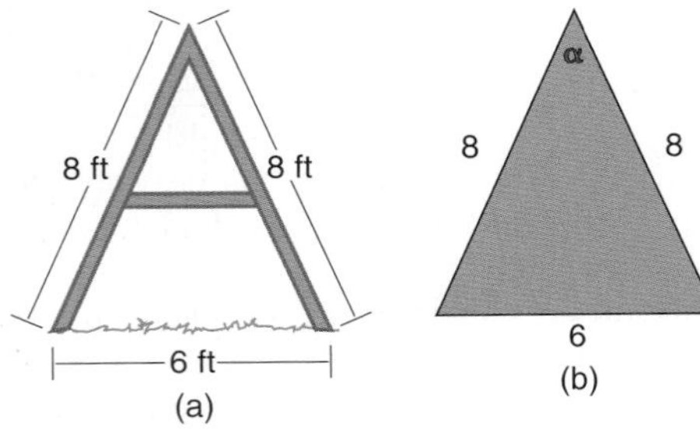

Figure 11.46

Solution Call the desired angle measure α. Because the three sides of the triangle are known, we use the Law of Cosines of the form $a^2 = b^2 + c^2 - 2bc \cos \alpha$. Because a represents the length of the side opposite the angle α, $a = 6$ while $b = 8$ and $c = 8$. Consequently, we have

$$
\begin{aligned}
6^2 &= 8^2 + 8^2 - 2 \cdot 8 \cdot 8 \cdot \cos \alpha \\
36 &= 64 + 64 - 128 \cos \alpha \\
36 &= 128 - 128 \cos \alpha \\
-92 &= -128 \cos \alpha \\
\cos \alpha &= \frac{-92}{-128} \\
\cos \alpha &\approx 0.7188
\end{aligned}
$$

Use of a calculator yields $\alpha \approx 44°$.

SSG *Exs. 8–10*

NOTE: The alternative form $\cos \alpha = \frac{b^2 + c^2 - a^2}{2bc}$ may be more easily applied in Example 7. ■

Exercises 11.4

In Exercises 1 and 2, use the given information to find an expression for the area of $\triangle ABC$. Give the answer in a form like $A = \frac{1}{2}(3)(4)\sin 32°$. See the figure for Exercises 1–8.

1. a) $a = 5, b = 6$, and $\gamma = 78°$
   b) $a = 5, b = 7, \alpha = 36°$, and $\beta = 88°$
2. a) $b = 7.3, c = 8.6$, and $\alpha = 38°$
   b) $a = 5.3, c = 8.4, \alpha = 36°$, and $\gamma = 87°$

In Exercises 3 and 4, state the form of the Law of Sines used to solve the problem. Give the answer in a form like $\frac{\sin 72°}{6.3} = \frac{\sin 55°}{a}$.

3. a) Find β if it is known that $a = 5$, $b = 8$, and $\alpha = 40°$.
   b) Find c if it is known that $a = 5.3, \alpha = 41°$, and $\gamma = 87°$.

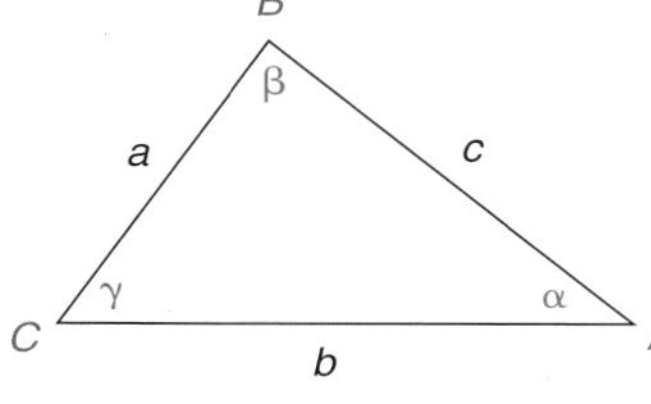

Exercises 1–8

4. a) Find β if it is known that $b = 8.1, c = 8.4$, and $\gamma = 86°$.
   b) Find c if it is known that $a = 5.3, \alpha = 40°$, and $\beta = 80°$.

In Exercises 5 and 6, state the form of the Law of Cosines used to solve the problem. Using the values provided, give the answer in a form like $a^2 = b^2 + c^2 - 2bc\cos\alpha$. See the figure for Exercises 1–8.

5. a) Find c if it is known that $a = 5.2, b = 7.9$, and $\gamma = 83°$.
   b) Find α if it is known that $a = 6, b = 9$, and $c = 10$.
6. a) Find b if it is known that $a = 5.7, c = 8.2$, and $\beta = 79°$.
   b) Find β if it is known that $a = 6, b = 8$, and $c = 9$.

In Exercises 7 and 8, state the form of the Law of Sines or the Law of Cosines that you would use to solve the problem. See the figure for Exercises 1–8.

7. a) Find α if you know the values of a, b, and β.
   b) Find α if you know the values of a, b, and c.
8. a) Find b if you know the values of a, c, and β.
   b) Find b if you know the values of a, α, and β.
9. For $\triangle ABC$ (not shown), suppose you know that $a = 3$, $b = 4$, and $c = 5$.
   a) Explain why you do *not* need to apply the Law of Sines or the Law of Cosines to find the measure of γ.
   b) Find γ.
10. For $\triangle ABC$ (not shown). suppose you know that $a = 3$, $\alpha = 57°$, and $\beta = 84°$.
    a) Explain why you do *not* need to apply the Law of Sines or the Law of Cosines to find the measure of γ.
    b) Find γ.

In Exercises 11 to 14, find the area of each triangle shown. Give the answer to the nearest tenth of a square unit.

11.

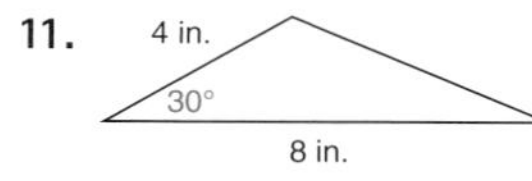

12.

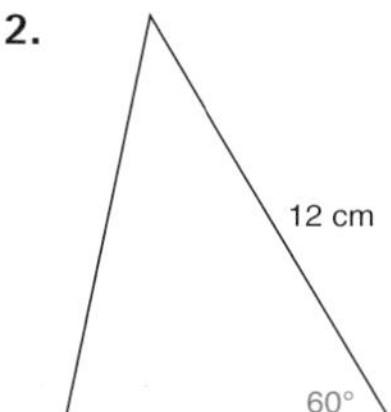

13.

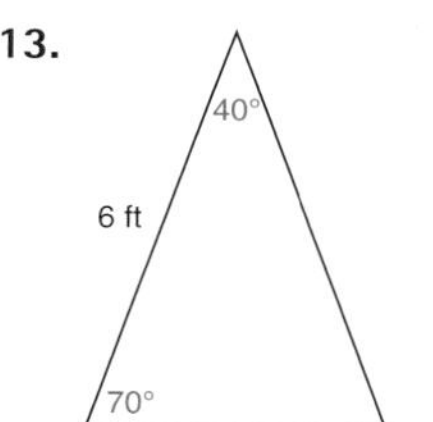

14.

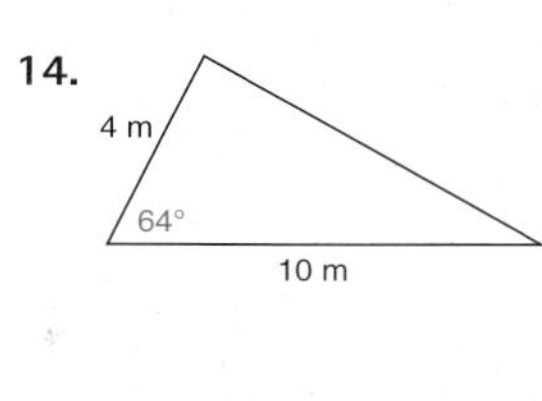

In Exercises 15 and 16, find the area of the given figure. Give the answer to the nearest tenth of a square unit.

15. 16.

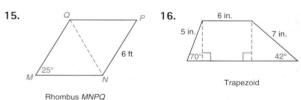

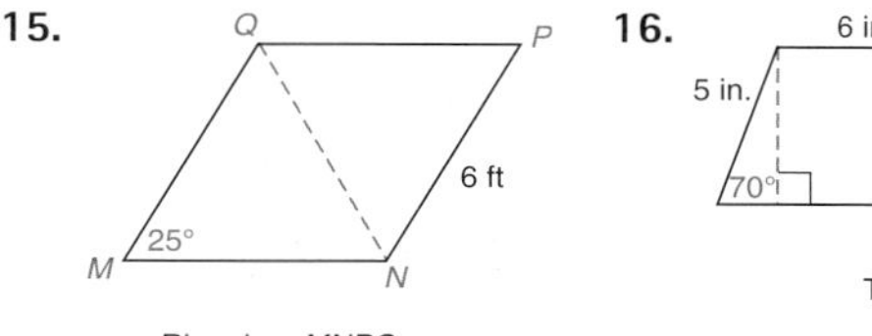

Rhombus $MNPQ$

Trapezoid

In Exercises 17 to 22, use a form of the Law of Sines to find the measure of the indicated side or angle. Angle measures should be found to the nearest degree and lengths of sides to the nearest tenth of a unit.

17. 18.

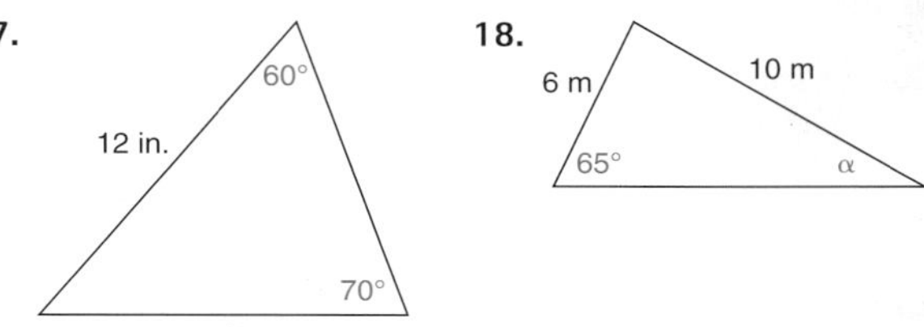

19.

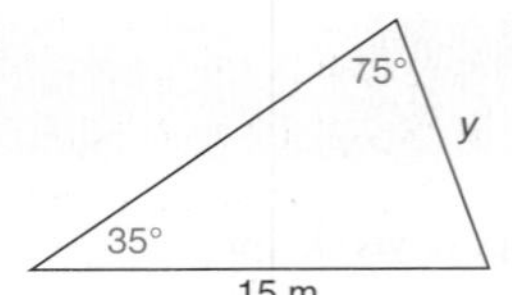

20.

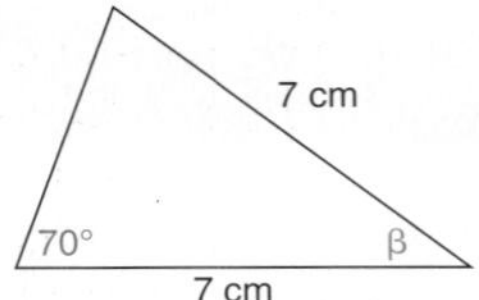

21.

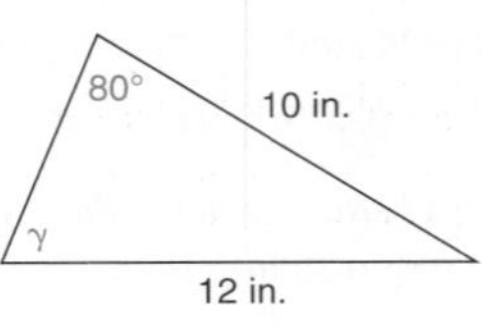

22.

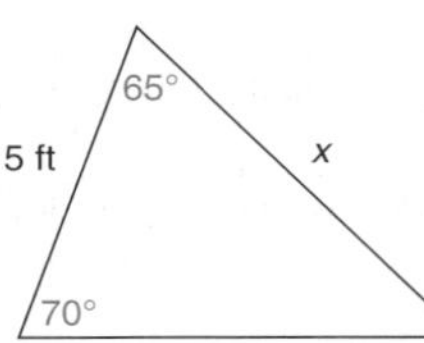

In Exercises 23 to 28, use a form of the Law of Cosines to find the measure of the indicated side or angle. Angle measures should be found to the nearest degree and lengths of sides to the nearest tenth of a unit.

23.

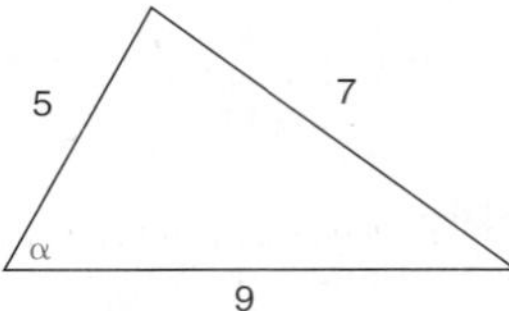

24.

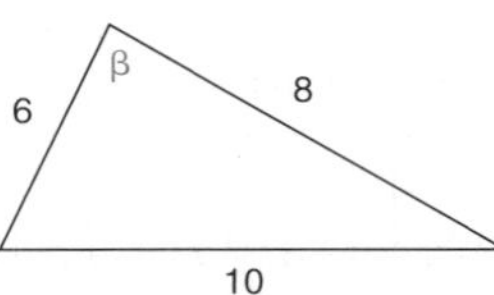

25.

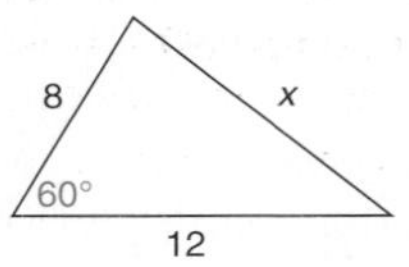

26.

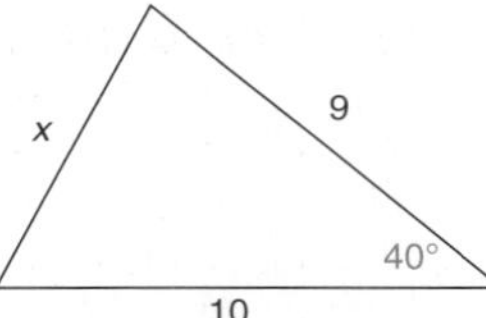

27.

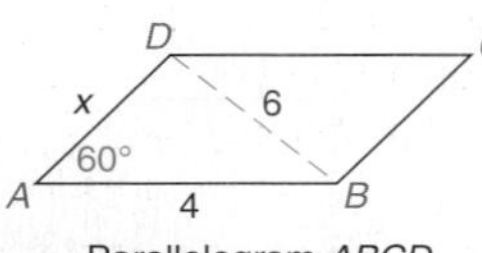

28.

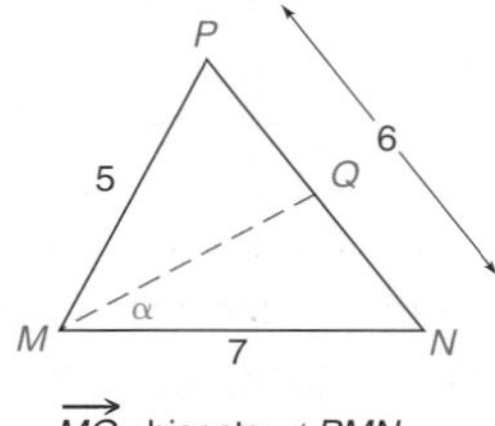

In Exercises 29 to 34, use the Law of Sines or the Law of Cosines to solve each problem. Angle measures should be found to the nearest degree and areas and distances to the nearest tenth of a unit.

29. A triangular lot has street dimensions of 150 ft and 180 ft and an included angle of 80° for these two sides.

a) Find the length of the remaining side of the lot.

b) Find the area of the lot in square feet.

30. Phil and Matt observe a balloon. They are 500 ft apart, and their angles of observation are 47° and 65°, as shown. Find the distance x from Matt to the balloon.

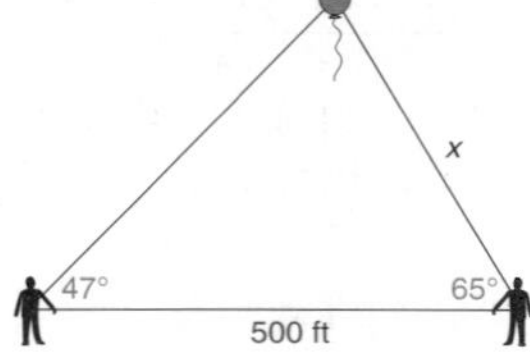

31. A surveillance aircraft at point C sights an ammunition warehouse at A and enemy headquarters at B through the angles indicated. If points A and B are 10,000 m apart, what is the distance from the aircraft to enemy headquarters?

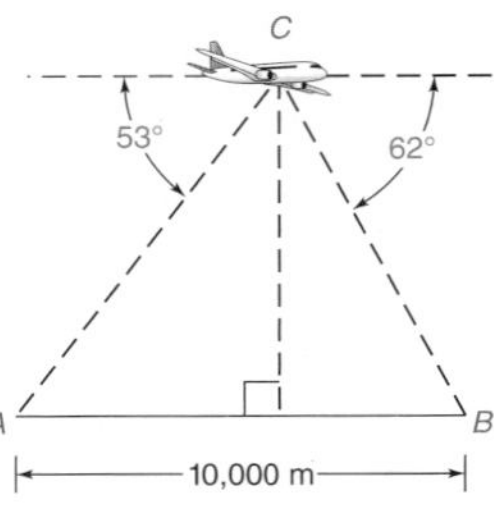

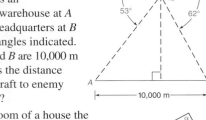

32. Above one room of a house the rafters meet as shown. What is the measure of the angle α at which they meet?

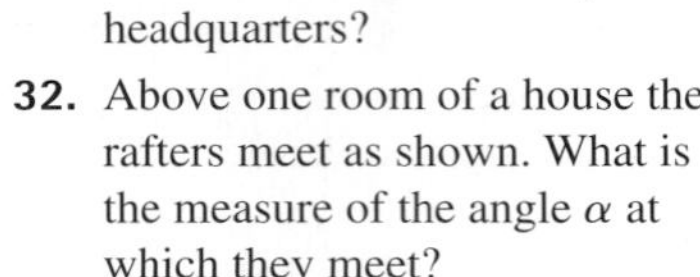

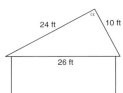

33. In an A-frame house, a bullet is found embedded at a point 8 ft up the sloped wall. If it was fired at a 30° angle with the horizontal, how far from the base of the wall was the gun fired?

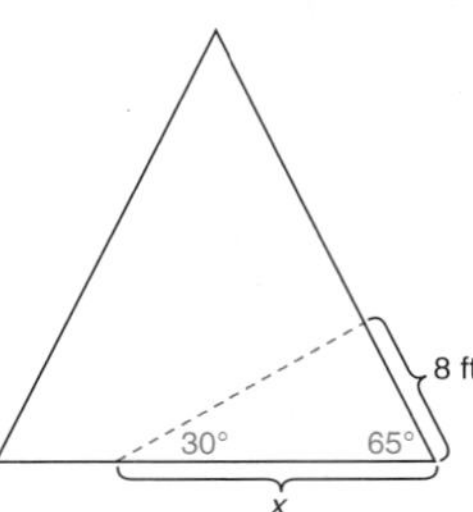

34. Clay pigeons are released at an angle of 30° with the horizontal. A sharpshooter hits one of the clay pigeons when shooting through an angle of elevation of 70°. If the point of release is 120 m from the sharpshooter, how far (x) is the sharpshooter from the target when it is hit?

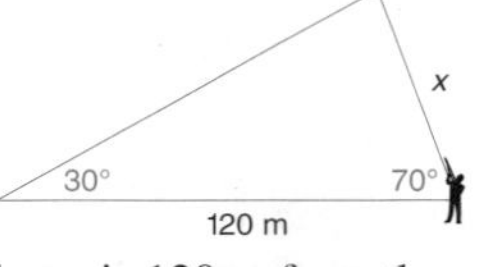

35. For the triangle shown, the area is exactly $18\sqrt{3}$ units². Determine the length x.

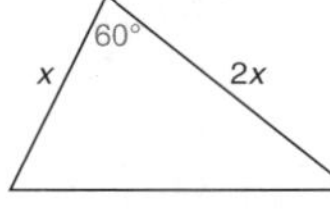

36. For the triangle shown, use the Law of Cosines to determine b.

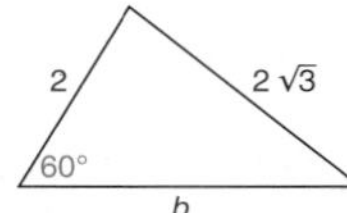

37. In the support structure for the Ferris wheel, $m\angle CAB = 30°$. If $AB = AC = 27$ ft, find BC.

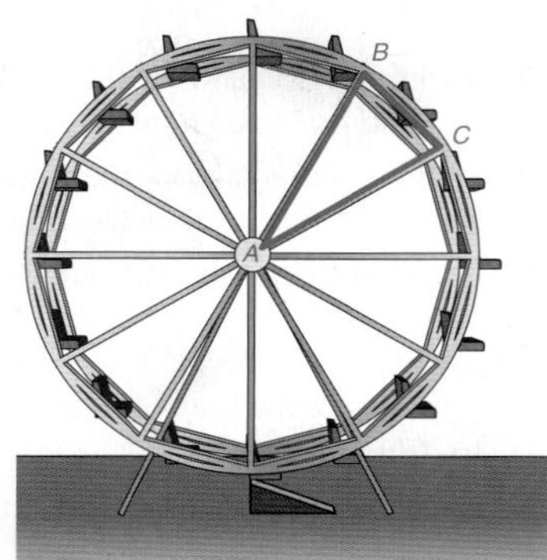

38. Show that the form of the Law of Cosines written $c^2 = a^2 + b^2 - 2ab \cos \gamma$ reduces to the Pythagorean Theorem when $\gamma = 90°$.

39. Explain why the area of the parallelogram shown is given by the formula $A = ab \sin \gamma$.

(HINT: You will need to use $\overline{QN}$.)

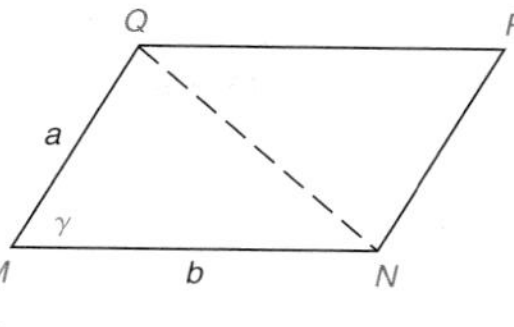

Exercises 39–42

40. Find the area of $\square MNPQ$ if $a = 8$ cm, $b = 12$ cm, and $\gamma = 70°$. Answer to the nearest tenth of a square centimeter. (See Exercise 39.)

41. Find the area of $\square MNPQ$ if $a = 6.3$ cm, $b = 8.9$ cm, and $\gamma = 67.5°$. Answer to the nearest *tenth* of a square centimeter. (See Exercise 39.)

42. The sides of a rhombus have length a. Two adjacent sides meet to form acute angle θ. Use the formula from Exercise 39 to show that the area of the rhombus is given by $A = a^2 \sin \theta$.

43. Two sides of a triangle have measures a inches and b inches, respectively. In terms of a and b, what is the largest (maximum) possible area for the triangle?

PERSPECTIVE ON HISTORY

Sketch of Plato

Plato (428–348 B.C.) was a Greek philosopher who studied under Socrates in Athens until the time of Socrates' death. Because his master had been forced to drink poison, Plato feared for his own life and left Greece to travel. His journey began around 400 B.C. and lasted for 12 years, taking Plato to Egypt, Sicily, and Italy, where he became familiar with the Pythagoreans (see page 394.)

Plato eventually returned to Athens where he formed his own school, the Academy. Though primarily a philosopher, Plato held that the study of mathematical reasoning provided the most perfect training for the mind. So insistent was Plato that his students have some background in geometry that he placed a sign above the door to the Academy that read, "Let no man ignorant of geometry enter here."

Plato was the first to insist that all constructions be performed by using only two instruments, the compass and the straightedge. Given a line segment of length 1, Plato constructed line segments of lengths $\sqrt{2}$, $\sqrt{3}$, and so on. Unlike Archimedes (see page 168), Plato had no interest in applied mathematics. In fact, Plato's methodology was quite strict and required accurate definitions, precise hypotheses, and logical reasoning. Without doubt, his methods paved the way for the compilation of geometric knowledge in the form of *The Elements* by Euclid (see page 118).

Commenting on the life of Plato, Proclus stated the Plato caused mathematics (and geometry in particular) to make great advances. At that time, many of the discoveries in mathematics were made by Plato's students and by those who studied at the Academy after the death of Plato. It is ironic that although Plato was not himself a truly great mathematician, yet he was largely responsible for its development in his time.

PERSPECTIVE ON APPLICATION

Radian Measure of Angles

In much of this textbook, we have considered angle measures from 0° to 180°. As you study mathematics, you will find that two things are true:

1. Angle measures used in applications do not have to be limited to measures from 0° to 180°.
2. The degree is not the only unit used in measuring angles.

We will address the first of these issues in Examples 1, 2, and 3.

EXAMPLE 1

As the time changes from 1 P.M. to 1:45 P.M., through what angle does the minute hand rotate? See Figure 11.47.

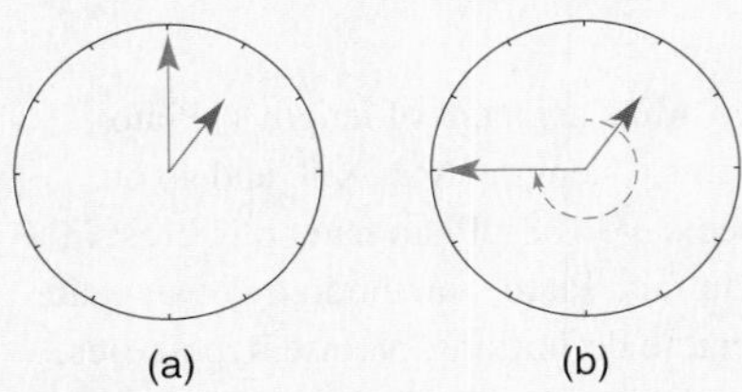

Figure 11.47

Solution Because the rotation is $\frac{3}{4}$ of a complete circle (360°), the result is $\frac{3}{4}$ (360°), or 270°.

EXAMPLE 2

An airplane pilot is instructed to circle the control tower twice during a holding pattern before receiving clearance to land. Through what angle does the airplane move? See Figure 11.48.

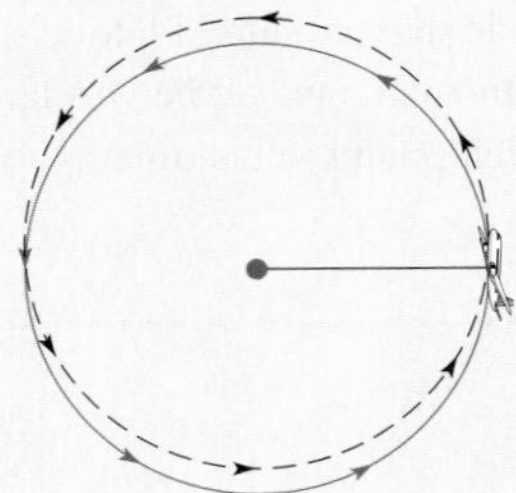

Figure 11.48

Solution Two circular rotations give 2(360°), or 720°.

In trigonometry, negative measures for angles are used to distinguish the direction of rotation. A counterclockwise rotation is measured as positive, a clockwise rotation as negative. The arcs with arrows in Figure 11.49 are used to indicate the direction of rotation.

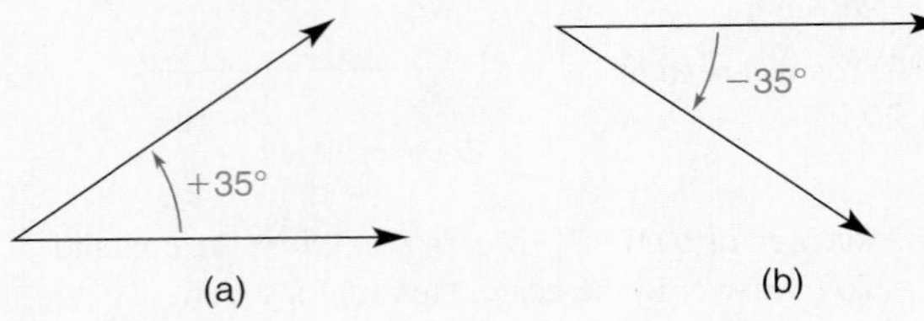

Figure 11.49

EXAMPLE 3

To tighten a hex bolt, a mechanic applies rotations of 60° several times. What is the measure of each rotation? See Figure 11.50.

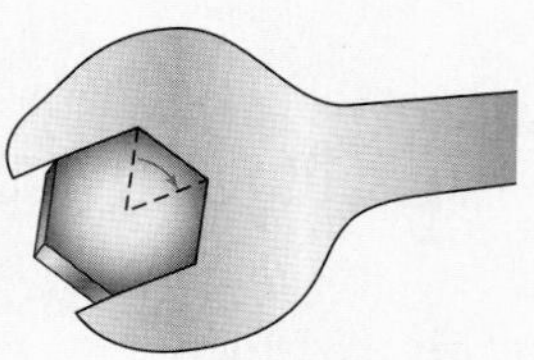

Figure 11.50

Solution Tightening occurs if the angle is −60°.

NOTE: If the angle of rotation is 60° (that is, +60°), the bolt is loosened.

Our second concern is with an alternative unit for measuring angles, a unit often used in the study of trigonometry and calculus.

DEFINITION

In a circle, a **radian** (rad) is the measure of a central angle that intercepts an arc whose length is equal to the radius of the circle.

In Figure 11.51, the length of each radius and the intercepted arc are all equal to r. Thus, the central angle shown measures 1 rad. A complete rotation about the circle corresponds to 360° and to $2\pi r$. Thus, the arc length of 1 radius corresponds to the central angle measure of 1 rad, and the circumference of 2π radii corresponds to the complete rotation of 2π rad.

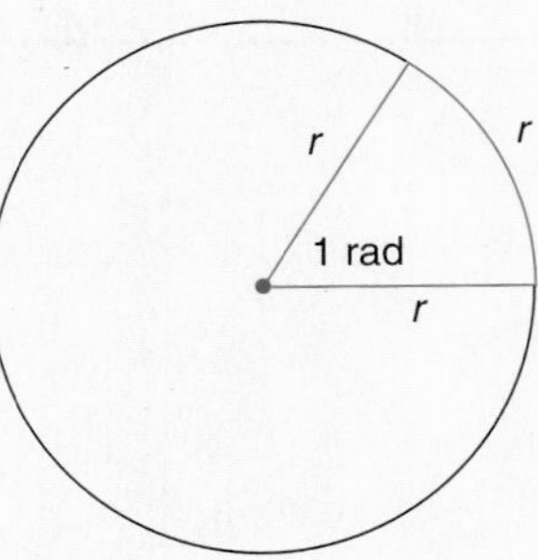

Figure 11.51

The angle relationship found in the preceding paragraph allows us to equate 360° and 2π radians. As suggested by Figure 11.52, there are approximately 6.28 rad (or exactly 2π radians) about the circle. The exact result leads to an important relationship.

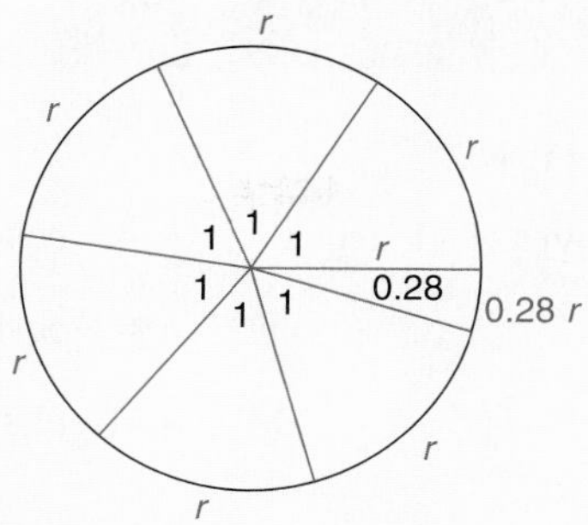

Figure 11.52

$$2\pi \text{ rad} = 360^\circ$$
or
$$360^\circ = 2\pi \text{ rad}$$

Through division by 2, the relationship is often restated as follows:

$$\pi \text{ rad} = 180^\circ$$
or
$$180^\circ = \pi \text{ rad}$$

With π rad = 180°, we divide each side of this equation by π to obtain the following relationship:

$$1 \text{ rad} = \frac{180^\circ}{\pi} \approx 57.3^\circ$$

To compare angle measures, we can also divide each side of the equation $180^\circ = \pi$ rad by 180 to get the following relationship:

$$1^\circ = \frac{\pi}{180} \text{ rad}$$

EXAMPLE 4

Using the fact that $1^\circ = \frac{\pi}{180}$ rad, find the radian equivalencies for:

a) 30° b) 45° c) 60° d) −90°

Solution

a) $30^\circ = 30(1^\circ) = 30\left(\frac{\pi}{180} \text{ rad}\right) = \frac{\pi}{6} \text{ rad}$

b) $45^\circ = 45(1^\circ) = 45\left(\frac{\pi}{180} \text{ rad}\right) = \frac{\pi}{4} \text{ rad}$

c) $60^\circ = 60(1^\circ) = 60\left(\frac{\pi}{180} \text{ rad}\right) = \frac{\pi}{3} \text{ rad}$

d) $-90^\circ = -90(1^\circ) = -90\left(\frac{\pi}{180}\right) \text{rad} = -\frac{\pi}{2} \text{ rad}$ ■

EXAMPLE 5

Using the fact that π rad = 180°, find the degree equivalencies for the following angles measured in radians:

a) $\frac{\pi}{6}$ b) $\frac{2\pi}{5}$ c) $\frac{-3\pi}{4}$ d) $\frac{\pi}{2}$

Solution

a) $\frac{\pi}{6} = \frac{180^\circ}{6} = 30^\circ$

b) $\frac{2\pi}{5} = \frac{2}{5} \cdot \pi = \frac{2}{5} \cdot 180^\circ = 72^\circ$

c) $\frac{-3\pi}{4} = \frac{-3}{4} \cdot \pi = \frac{-3}{4} \cdot 180^\circ = -135^\circ$

d) $\frac{\pi}{2} = \frac{180^\circ}{2} = 90^\circ$ ■

Although we did not use this method of measuring angles in the earlier part of this textbook, you may need to use this method of angle measurement in a more advanced course.

A LOOK BACK AT CHAPTER 11

One goal of this chapter was to define the sine, cosine, and tangent ratios in terms of the sides of a right triangle. We derived a formula for finding the area of a triangle, given two sides and the included angle. We also proved the Law of Sines and the Law of Cosines for acute triangles. Another unit, the radian, was introduced for the purpose of measuring angles.

KEY CONCEPTS

11.1

Greek Letters: $\alpha, \beta, \gamma, \theta$ • Opposite Side (Leg) • Hypotenuse • Sine Ratio: $\sin\theta = \frac{\text{opposite}}{\text{hypotenuse}}$ • Angle of Elevation • Angle of Depression

11.2

Adjacent Side (Leg) • Cosine Ratio: $\cos\theta = \frac{\text{adjacent}}{\text{hypotenuse}}$ • Identity: $\sin^2\theta + \cos^2\theta = 1$

11.3

Tangent Ratio: $\tan\theta = \frac{\text{opposite}}{\text{adjacent}}$ • Cotangent • Secant • Cosecant • Reciprocal Ratios

11.4

Area of a Triangle: $A = \frac{1}{2}bc\sin\alpha$

$A = \frac{1}{2}ac\sin\beta$

$A = \frac{1}{2}ab\sin\gamma$ •

Law of Sines: $\frac{\sin\alpha}{a} = \frac{\sin\beta}{b} = \frac{\sin\gamma}{c}$ •

Law of Cosines: $c^2 = a^2 + b^2 - 2ab\cos\gamma$

$b^2 = a^2 + c^2 - 2ac\cos\beta$

$a^2 = b^2 + c^2 - 2bc\cos\alpha$

or

$$\cos\alpha = \frac{b^2 + c^2 - a^2}{2bc}$$

$$\cos\beta = \frac{a^2 + c^2 - b^2}{2ac}$$

$$\cos\gamma = \frac{a^2 + b^2 - c^2}{2ab}$$

▶▶▶ Chapter 11 REVIEW EXERCISES

In Exercises 1 to 4, state the ratio needed, and use it to find the measure of the indicated line segment to the nearest tenth of a unit.

1.

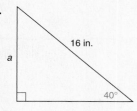

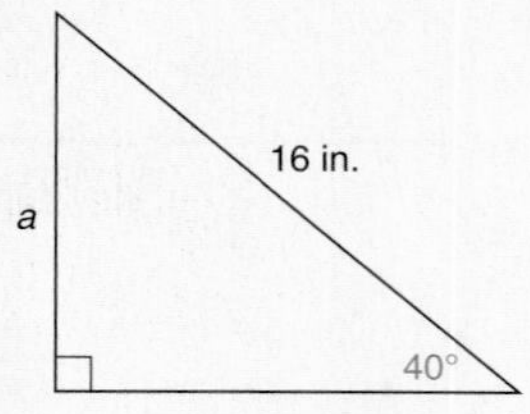

2.

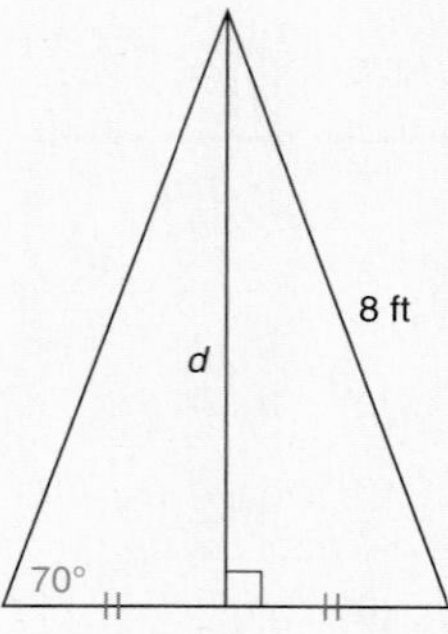

3.

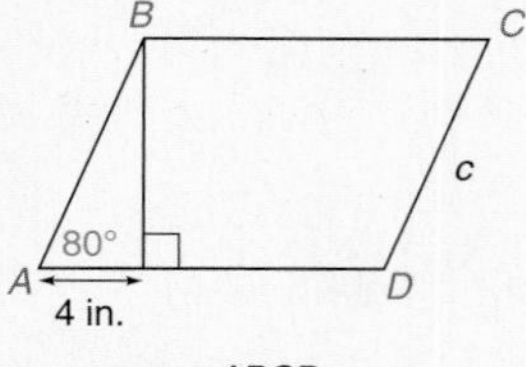

▱ABCD

4.

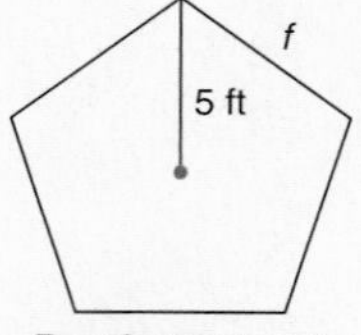

Regular pentagon with radius = 5 ft

In Exercises 5 to 8, state the ratio needed, and use it to find the measure of the indicated angle to the nearest degree.

5.

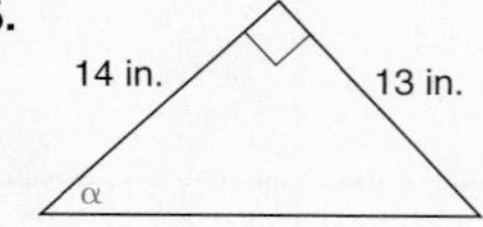

6.

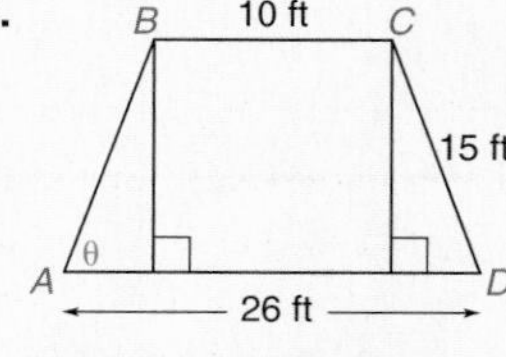

Isosceles trapezoid *ABCD*

7.

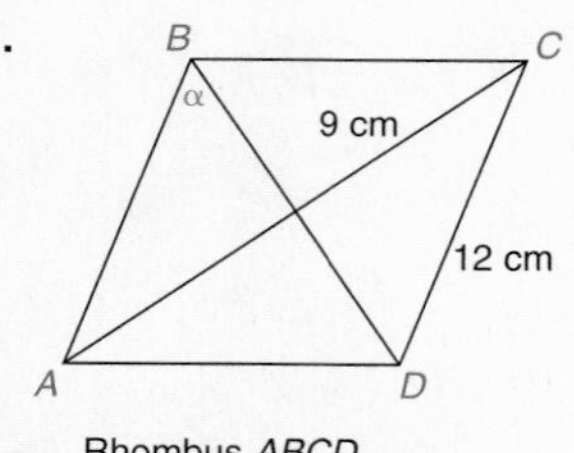

Rhombus *ABCD*

8.

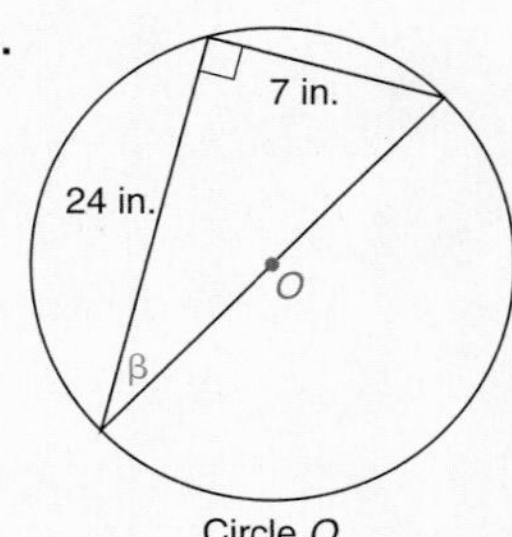

Circle *O*

In Exercises 9 to 12, use the Law of Sines or the Law of Cosines to solve each triangle for the indicated length of side or angle measure. Angle measures should be found to the nearest degree; distances should be found to the nearest tenth of a unit.

9.

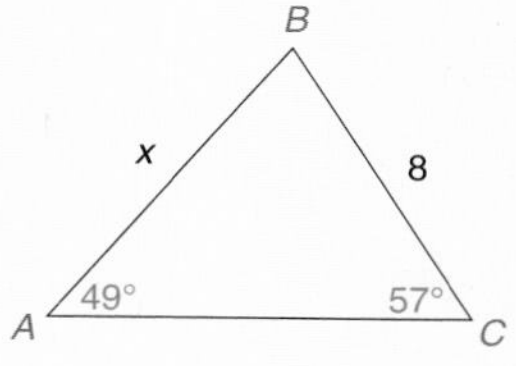

10.

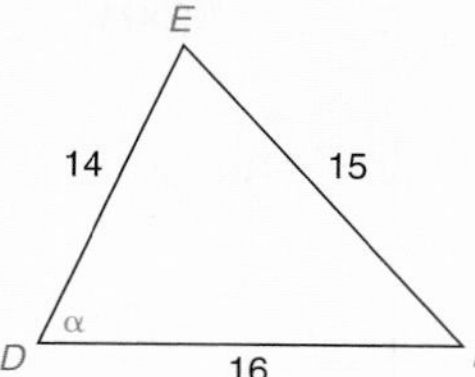

11.

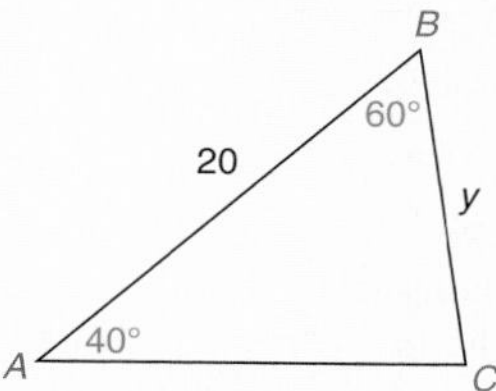

12.

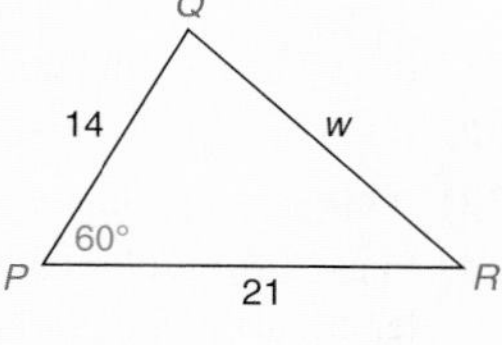

In Exercises 13 to 17, use the Law of Sines or the Law of Cosines to solve each problem. Angle measures should be found to the nearest degree; distances should be found to the nearest tenth of a unit.

13. A building 50 ft tall is on a hillside. A surveyor at a point on the hill observes that the angle of elevation to the top of the building measures 43° and the angle of depression to the base of the building measures 16°. How far is the surveyor from the base of the building?

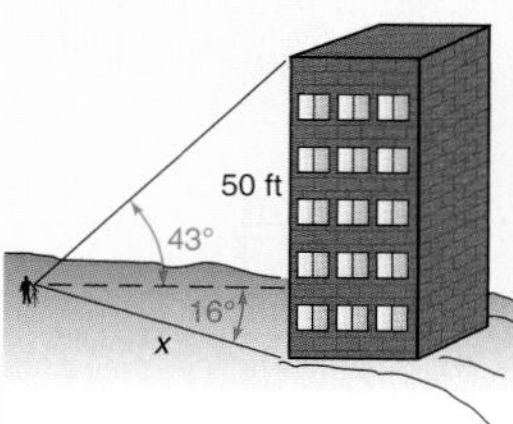

14. Two sides of a parallelogram are 50 cm and 70 cm long. Find the length of the shorter diagonal if a larger angle of the parallelogram measures 105°.

15. The sides of a rhombus are 6 in. each and the longer diagonal is 11 in. Find the measure of each of the acute angles of the rhombus.

16. The area of $\triangle ABC$ is 9.7 in^2. If $a = 6$ in. and $c = 4$ in., find the measure of angle B.

17. Find the area of the rhombus in Exercise 15.

In Exercises 18 to 20, prove each statement without using a table or a calculator. Draw an appropriate right triangle.

18. If $m\angle R = 45°$, then $\tan R = 1$.

19. If $m\angle S = 30°$, then $\sin S = \frac{1}{2}$.

20. If $m\angle T = 60°$, then $\sin T = \frac{\sqrt{3}}{2}$.

In Exercises 21 to 30, use the drawings where provided to solve each problem. Angle measures should be found to the nearest degree; lengths should be found to the nearest tenth of a unit.

21. In the evening, a tree that stands 12 ft tall casts a long shadow. If the angle of depression from the top of the tree to the tip of the shadow is 55°, what is the length of the shadow?

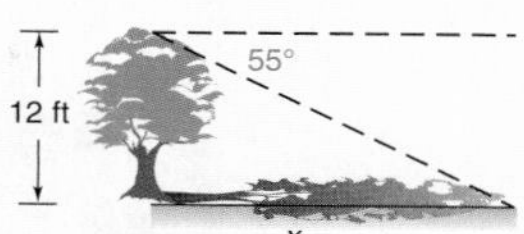

22. A rocket is shot into the air at an angle of 60°. If it is traveling at 200 ft per second, how high in the air is it after 5 seconds? (Ignoring gravity, assume that the path of the rocket is a straight line.)

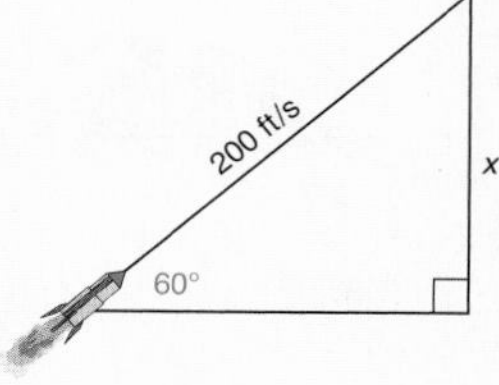

23. A 4-m beam is used to brace a wall. If the bottom of the beam is 3 m from the base of the wall, what is the angle of elevation to the top of the wall?

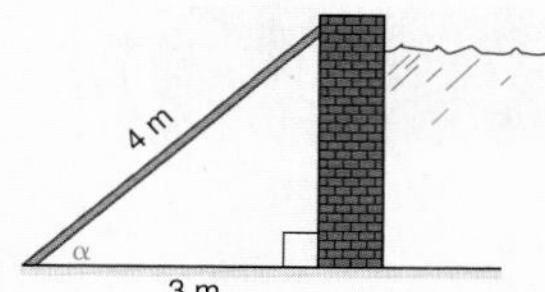

24. The basket of a hot-air balloon is 300 ft high. The pilot of the balloon observes a stadium 2200 ft away. What is the measure of the angle of depression?

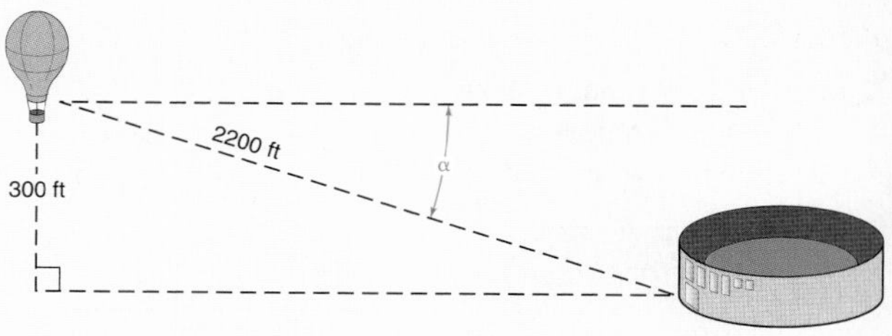

25. The apothem of a regular pentagon is approximately 3.44 cm. What is the approximate length of each side of the pentagon?

26. What is the approximate length of the radius of the pentagon in Exercise 25?

27. Each of the legs of an isosceles triangle is 40 cm in length. The base is 30 cm in length. Find the measure of a base angle.

28. The diagonals of a rhombus measure 12 in. and 16 in. Find the measure of the obtuse angle of the rhombus.

29. The unit used for measuring the steepness of a hill is the **grade.** A grade of a to b means the hill rises a vertical units for every b horizontal units. If, at some point, the hill is 3 ft above the horizontal and the angle of elevation to that point is 23°, what is the grade of this hill?

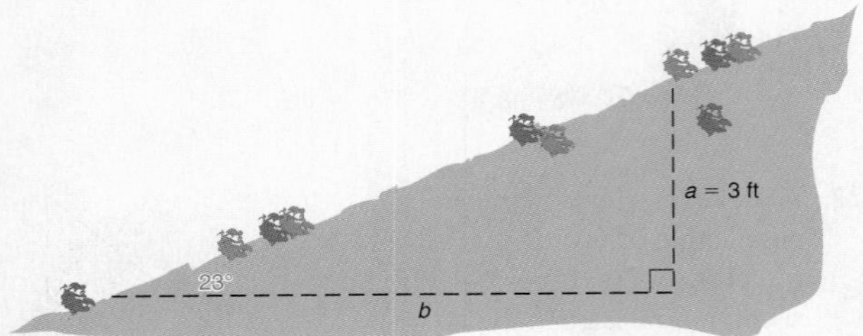

30. An observer in a plane 2500 m high sights two ships below. The angle of depression to one ship is 32°, and the angle of depression to the other ship is 44°. How far apart are the ships?

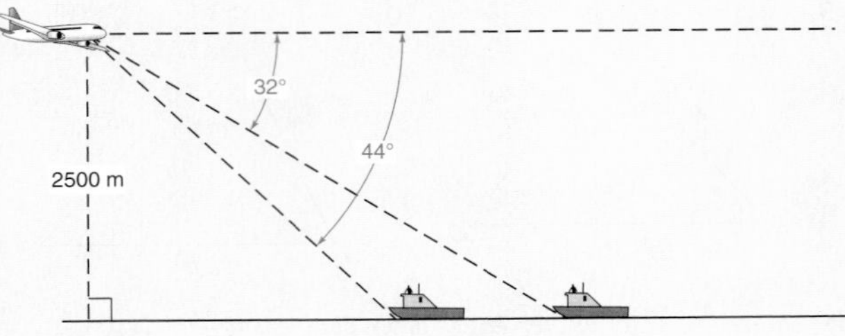

31. If $\sin \theta = \frac{7}{25}$, find $\cos \theta$ and $\sec \theta$.

32. If $\tan \theta = \frac{11}{60}$, find $\sec \theta$ and $\cot \theta$.

33. If $\cot \theta = \frac{21}{20}$, find $\csc \theta$ and $\sin \theta$.

34. In a right circular cone, the radius of the base is 3.2 ft in length and the angle formed by the radius and slant height measures $\theta = 65°$. To the nearest tenth of a foot, find the length of the altitude of the cone. Then use this length of altitude to find the volume of the cone to the nearest tenth of a cubic foot.

Chapter 11 TEST

1. For the right triangle shown, express each of the following in terms of a, b, and c:

a) $\sin \alpha$ ________

b) $\tan \beta$ ________

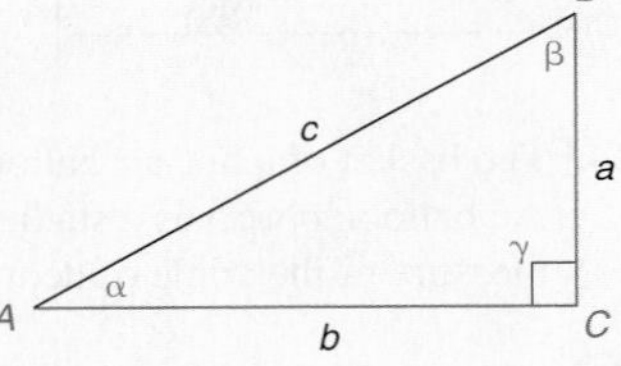

2. For the right triangle shown, express each ratio as a fraction in lowest terms:

a) $\cos \beta$ ________

b) $\sin \alpha$ ________

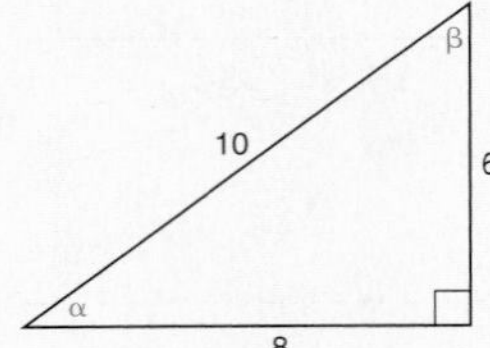

3. Without using a calculator, find the exact value of:

a) tan 45° ________ b) sin 60° ________

4. Use your calculator to find each number correct to four decimal places.

a) sin 23° ________ b) cos 79° ________

5. Using your calculator, find θ to the nearest degree if $\sin \theta = 0.6691$. ________

6. Without the calculator, determine which number is larger:

a) tan 25° or tan 26° ________

b) cos 47° or cos 48° ________

7. In the drawing provided, find the value of a to the nearest whole number. ________

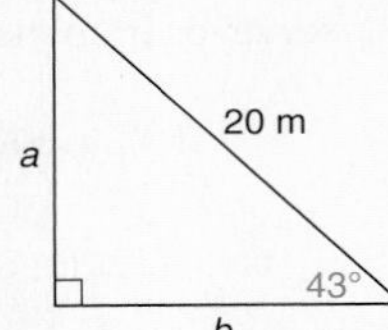

8. In the drawing provided, find the value of y to the nearest whole number.

____

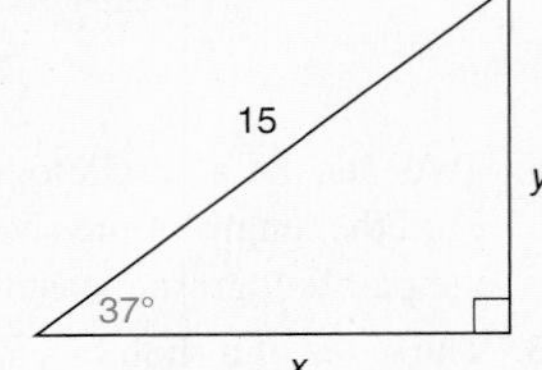

9. In the drawing provided, find the measure of θ to the nearest degree.________

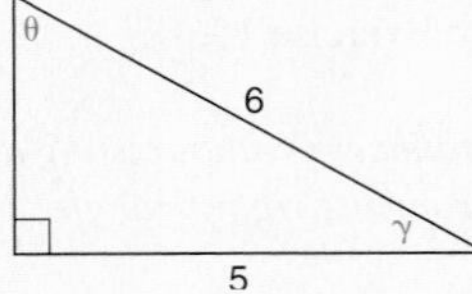

10. Using the drawing below, classify each statement as true or false:
a) $\cos \beta = \sin \alpha$ ________
b) $\sin^2 \alpha + \cos^2 \alpha = 1$ ________

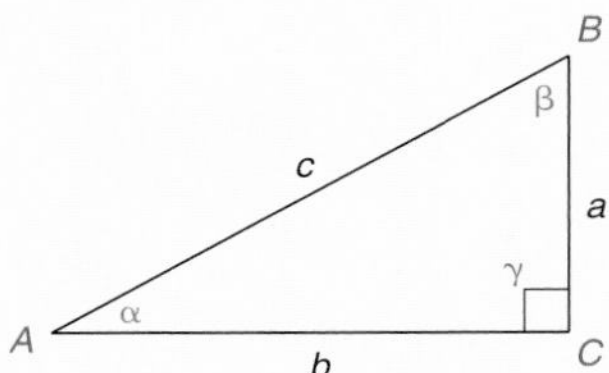

11. A kite is flying at an angle of elevation of 67° with the ground. If 100 feet of string have been paid out to the kite, how far is the kite above the ground? Answer to the nearest foot. ________

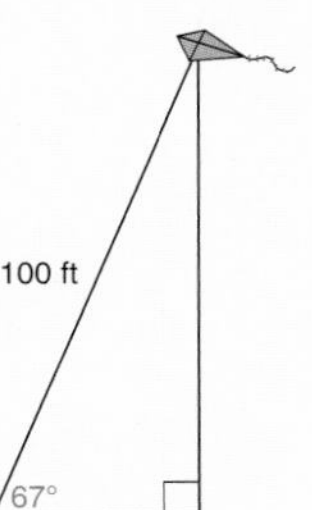

12. A roofline shows a span of 12 feet across a sloped roof and this span is accompanied by a 2 foot rise. To the nearest degree, find the measure of θ. ________

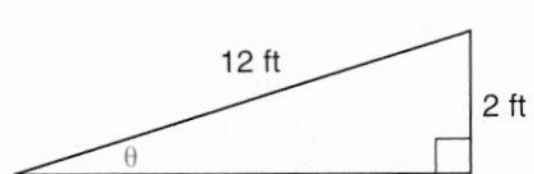

13. If $\sin \alpha = \frac{1}{2}$, find:
a) $\csc \alpha$ ________ b) α ________

14. In a right triangle with acute angles of measures α and β, $\cos \beta = \frac{a}{c}$. Find the following values in terms of the lengths of sides a, b, and c:
a) $\sin \alpha$ ________ b) $\sec \beta$ ________

15. Use one of the three forms for area (such as the form $A = \frac{1}{2}bc \sin \alpha$) to find the area of the triangle shown. Answer to the nearest whole number. ________

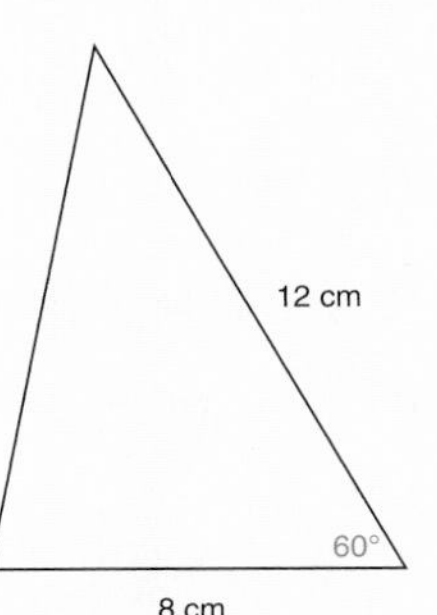

16. On the basis of the drawing provided, complete the Law of Sines.

$$\frac{\sin \alpha}{a} = \_\_\_\_\_\_\_\_ = \_\_\_\_\_\_\_\_$$

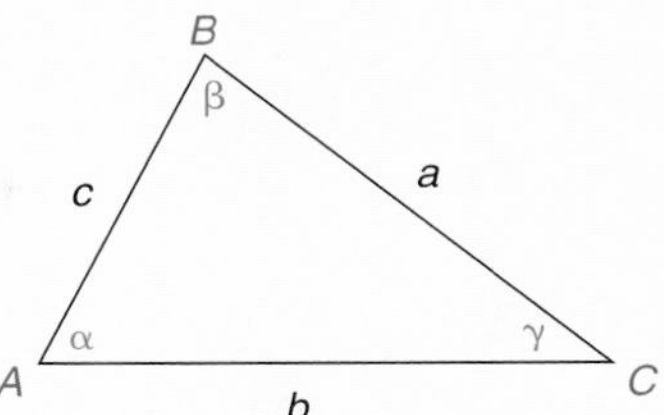

Exercises 16, 17

17. On the basis of the drawing provided, complete this form of the Law of Cosines.

$a^2 =$ ____________

18. Use the Law of Sines or the Law of Cosines to find α to the nearest degree. ________

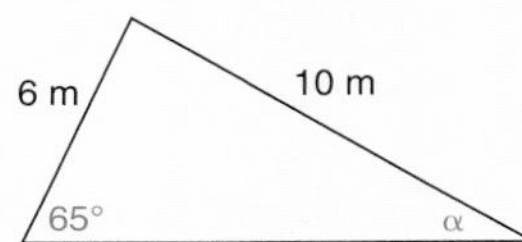

19. Use the Law of Sines or the Law of Cosines to find length x to the nearest whole number. ________

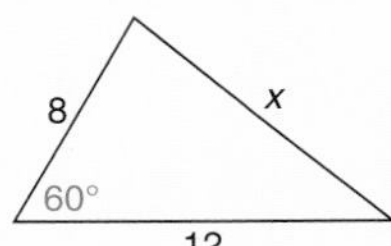

20. Each apothem of regular pentagon $ABCDE$ has length a. In terms of a, find an expression for the area A of pentagon $ABCDE$. ____________

Appendix A

Algebra Review

A.1 ALGEBRAIC EXPRESSIONS

In algebra, we do not define terms such as *addition, multiplication, number, positive,* and *equality.* For convenience, a *real number* is one that has a position on the number line, as shown in Figure A.1.

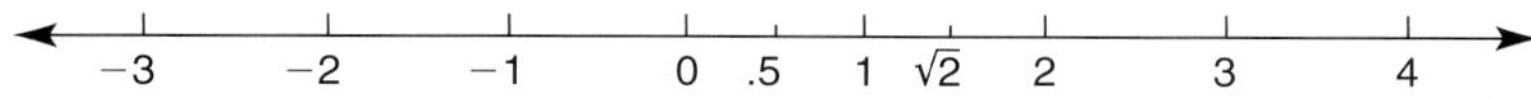

Figure A.1

Any real number positioned to the right of another real number is larger than that other number. For example, 4 is larger than -2; equivalently, -2 is less than 4 (smaller numbers are to the left). Numbers such as 3 and -3 are **opposites** or **additive inverses.** Two numerical expressions are **equal** if and only if they have the same value; for example, $2 + 3 = 5$. The axioms of equality are listed in the following box; they are also listed in Section 1.6.

> **AXIOMS OF EQUALITY**
>
> *Reflexive* ($a = a$): Any number equals itself.
>
> *Symmetric* (if $a = b$, then $b = a$): Two equal numbers are equal in either order.
>
> *Transitive* (if $a = b$ and $b = c$, then $a = c$): If a first number equals a second number and if the second number equals a third number, then the first number equals the third number.
>
> *Substitution:* If one numerical expression equals a second, then it may replace the second.

EXAMPLE 1

Name the axiom of equality illustrated in each case.

a) If AB is the numerical length of the line segment $\overline{AB}$, then $AB = AB$.
b) If $17 = 2x - 3$, then $2x - 3 = 17$.
c) Given that $2x + 3x = 5x$, the statement $2x + 3x = 30$ can be replaced by $5x = 30$.

Solution a) Reflexive b) Symmetric c) Substitution

To add two real numbers, think of the numbers as gains if positive and as losses if negative. For instance, $13 + (-5)$ represents the result of combining a gain of \$13 with a loss (or debt) of \$5. Therefore,

$$13 + (-5) = 8$$

The answer in addition is the **sum.** Three more examples of addition are

$$13 + 5 = 18 \qquad (-13) + 5 = -8 \quad \text{and} \quad (-13) + (-5) = -18$$

If you multiply two real numbers, the **product** (answer) will be positive if the two numbers have the same sign, negative if the two numbers have different signs, and 0 if either number is 0 or both numbers are 0.

EXAMPLE 2

Simplify each expression:

a) $5 + (-4)$ b) $5(-4)$ c) $(-7)(-6)$ d) $[5 + (-4)] + 8$

Solution

a) $5 + (-4) = 1$
b) $5(-4) = -20$
c) $(-7)(-6) = 42$
d) $[5 + (-4)] + 8 = 1 + 8 = 9$ ■

Just as $(-3) + 9 = 6$ and $9 + (-3) = 6$, two sums are equal when the order of the numbers added is reversed. This is often expressed by writing $a + b = b + a$, the property of real numbers known as the Commutative Axiom for Addition. There is also a Commutative Axiom for Multiplication, which is illustrated by the fact that $(6)(-4) = (-4)(6)$; both products are -24.

In a numerical expression, grouping symbols indicate which operation should be performed first. However, $[5 + (-4)] + 8$ equals $5 + [(-4) + 8]$ because $1 + 8$ equals $5 + 4$. In general, the fact that $(a + b) + c$ equals $a + (b + c)$ is known as the Associative Axiom for Addition. There is also an Associative Axiom for Multiplication, which is illustrated below:

$$\begin{aligned} (3 \cdot 5)(-2) &= 3[5(-2)] \\ (15)(-2) &= 3(-10) \\ -30 &= -30 \end{aligned}$$

SELECTED AXIOMS OF REAL NUMBERS

Commutative Axiom for Addition: $a + b = b + a$

Commutative Axiom for Multiplication: $a \cdot b = b \cdot a$

Associative Axiom for Addition: $a + (b + c) = (a + b) + c$

Associative Axiom for Multiplication: $a \cdot (b \cdot c) = (a \cdot b) \cdot c$

To subtract b from a (to find $a - b$), we change the subtraction problem to an addition problem. The answer in subtraction is the **difference** between a and b.

DEFINITION OF SUBTRACTION

$$a - b = a + (-b)$$

where $-b$ is the additive inverse (or opposite) of b.

For $b = 5$, we have $-b = -5$; and for $b = -2$, we have $-b = 2$. For the subtraction $a - (b + c)$, we use the additive inverse of $b + c$, which is $(-b) + (-c)$. That is,

$$a - (b + c) = a + [(-b) + (-c)]$$

EXAMPLE 3

Simplify each expression:

a) $5 - (-2)$ b) $(-7) - (-3)$ c) $12 - [3 + (-2)]$

Solution

a) $5 - (-2) = 5 + 2 = 7$
b) $(-7) - (-3) = (-7) + 3 = -4$
c) $12 - [3 + (-2)] = 12 + [(-3) + 2] = 12 + (-1) = 11$ ■

Division can be replaced by multiplication just as subtraction was replaced by addition. We cannot divide by 0! Two numbers whose product is 1 are called **multiplicative inverses** (or **reciprocals**); $-\frac{3}{4}$ and $-\frac{4}{3}$ are multiplicative inverses because $-\frac{3}{4} \cdot -\frac{4}{3} = 1$. The answer in division is the **quotient.**

DEFINITION OF DIVISION

For $b \neq 0$,

$$a \div b = a \cdot \frac{1}{b}$$

where $\frac{1}{b}$ is the multiplicative inverse of b.

NOTE: $a \div b$ is also indicated by a/b or $\frac{a}{b}$.

For $b = 5$ $\left(\text{that is, } b = \frac{5}{1}\right)$, we have $\frac{1}{b} = \frac{1}{5}$; and for $b = -\frac{2}{3}$, we have $\frac{1}{b} = -\frac{3}{2}$.

EXAMPLE 4

Simplify each expression:

a) $12 \div 2$ b) $(-5) \div \left(-\frac{2}{3}\right)$

Solution

a) $12 \div 2 = 12 \div \frac{2}{1}$

$= \frac{12}{1} \cdot \frac{1}{2}$ **(Product of two positive numbers is a positive number)**

$= 6$

b) $(-5) \div \left(-\frac{2}{3}\right) = \left(-\frac{5}{1}\right) \div \left(-\frac{2}{3}\right)$

$= \left(-\frac{5}{1}\right) \cdot \left(-\frac{3}{2}\right)$

$= \frac{15}{2}$ **(Product of two negative numbers is a positive number)** ■

EXAMPLE 5

Morgan works at the grocery store for 3 hours on Friday after school and for 8 hours on Saturday. If he is paid \$9 per hour, how much will he be paid in all?

Solution

Method I: Find the total number of hours worked and multiply by 9.

$$9(3 + 8) = 9 \cdot 11 = \$99$$

Method II: Figure the daily wages and add them.

$$\underbrace{(9 \cdot 3)}_{\text{Friday's wages}} + \underbrace{(9 \cdot 8)}_{\text{Saturday's wages}} = 27 + 72 = \$99$$

NOTE: We see that $9(3 + 8) = 9 \cdot 3 + 9 \cdot 8$, where the multiplications on the right are performed before the addition is completed. ■

The Distributive Axiom was illustrated in Example 5. Because multiplications are performed before additions, we write

$$a(b + c) = a \cdot b + a \cdot c$$
$$2(3 + 4) = 2 \cdot 3 + 2 \cdot 4$$
$$2(7) = 6 + 8$$

The "symmetric" form of the Distributive Axiom is

$$a \cdot b + a \cdot c = a(b + c)$$

This form can be used to combine *like terms* (expressions that contain the same variable factors). A **variable** is a letter that represents a number.

$4x + 5x = x \cdot 4 + x \cdot 5$ **(Commutative Axiom for Multiplication)**

$= x(4 + 5)$ **(Symmetric form of Distributive Axiom)**

$= x(9)$ **(Substitution)**

$= 9x$ **(Commutative Axiom for Multiplication)**

$\therefore 4x + 5x = 9x$

The Distributive Axiom also distributes multiplication over subtraction.

FORMS OF THE DISTRIBUTIVE AXIOM

$$a(b + c) = a \cdot b + a \cdot c$$
$$a \cdot b + a \cdot c = a(b + c)$$
$$a(b - c) = a \cdot b - a \cdot c$$
$$a \cdot b - a \cdot c = a(b - c)$$

EXAMPLE 6

Combine like terms:

a) $7x + 3x$ b) $7x - 3x$ c) $3x^2y + 4x^2y + 6x^2y$
d) $3x^2y + 4xy^2 + 6xy^2$ e) $7x + 5y$

Solution

a) $7x + 3x = 10x$
b) $7x - 3x = 4x$
c) $3x^2y + 4x^2y + 6x^2y = (3x^2y + 4x^2y) + 6x^2y = 7x^2y + 6x^2y = 13x^2y$
d) $3x^2y + 4xy^2 + 6xy^2 = 3x^2y + (4xy^2 + 6xy^2) = 3x^2y + 10xy^2$
e) $7x + 5y$; cannot combine unlike terms

NOTE: In part (d), $3x^2y$ and $10xy^2$ are not like terms because $x^2y \neq xy^2$. ■

The statement $4x + 5x = 9x$ says that "the sum of 4 times a number and 5 times the same number equals 9 times the same number." Because x can be any real number, we may also write

$$4\pi + 5\pi = 9\pi$$

in which π is the real number that equals approximately 3.14. Similarly,

$$4\sqrt{3} + 5\sqrt{3} = 9\sqrt{3}$$

in which $\sqrt{3}$ (read "the positive square root of 3") is equal to approximately 1.73.

You may recall the "order of operations" from a previous class; this order is used when simplifying more complicated expressions.

ORDER OF OPERATIONS

1. Simplify expressions within symbols such as parentheses ( ) or brackets [ ], beginning with the innermost symbols of inclusion.

NOTE: The presence of a fraction bar, ——, requires that you simplify a numerator or denominator before dividing.

2. Perform all calculations with exponents.
3. Perform all multiplications and/or divisions, in order, from left to right.
4. Last, perform all additions and/or subtractions, in order, from left to right.

EXAMPLE 7

Simplify each numerical expression:

a) $3^2 + 4^2$ b) $4 \cdot 7 \div 2$ c) $2 \cdot 3 \cdot 5^2$

d) $\dfrac{8 - 6 \div (-3)}{4 + 3(2 + 5)}$ e) $2 + [3 + 4(5 - 1)]$

Solution

a) $3^2 + 4^2 = 9 + 16 = 25$

b) $4 \cdot 7 \div 2 = 28 \div 2 = 14$

c) $2 \cdot 3 \cdot 5^2 = 2 \cdot 3 \cdot 25$
$= (2 \cdot 3) \cdot 25 = 6 \cdot 25 = 150$

d) $\dfrac{8 - [6 \div (-3)]}{4 + 3(2 + 5)} = \dfrac{8 - (-2)}{4 + 3(7)} = \dfrac{10}{4 + 21} = \dfrac{10}{25} = \dfrac{2}{5}$

e) $2 + [3 + 4(5 - 1)] = 2 + [3 + 4(4)] = 2 + (3 + 16) = 2 + 19 = 21$ ■

An expression such as $(2 + 5)(6 + 4)$ can be simplified by two different methods. By following the rules of order, we have (7)(10), or 70. An alternative method is described as the FOIL method: First, Outside, Inside, and Last terms are multiplied and then added. This is how it works:

$$\begin{aligned}(2 + 5)(6 + 4) &= 2 \cdot 6 + 2 \cdot 4 + 5 \cdot 6 + 5 \cdot 4 \\ &= 12 + 8 + 30 + 20 \\ &= 70\end{aligned}$$

FOIL is the Distributive Axiom in disguise. We would not generally use FOIL to find the product of $(2 + 5)$ and $(6 + 4)$, but we must use it to find the products in Example 8. Also see Example 2 in Section A.2.

EXAMPLE 8

Use the FOIL method to find the products.

a) $(3x + 4)(2x - 3)$ b) $(5x + 2y)(6x - 5y)$

Solution

a) $$\begin{aligned}(3x + 4)(2x - 3) &= 3x \cdot 2x + 3x(-3) + 4(2x) + 4(-3) \\ &= 6x^2 + (-9x) + 8x + (-12) \\ &= 6x^2 - 1x - 12 \\ &= 6x^2 - x - 12\end{aligned}$$

b) $$\begin{aligned}(5x + 2y)(6x - 5y) &= 5x \cdot 6x + 5x(-5y) + 2y(6x) + 2y(-5y) \\ &= 30x^2 + (-25xy) + 12xy + (-10y^2) \\ &= 30x^2 - 13xy - 10y^2\end{aligned}$$ ■

EXAMPLE 9

Use FOIL to express $ab + ac + db + dc$ in factored form as a product.

Solution

$$\begin{aligned}ab + ac + db + dc &= a(b + c) + d(b + c) \\ &= (b + c)(a + d)\end{aligned}$$ ■

Exercises A.1

1. Name the four parts of a mathematical system.
   (HINT: See Section 1.3.)
2. Name two examples of mathematical systems.
3. Which axiom of equality is illustrated in each of the following?
   a) $5 = 5$
   b) If $\frac{1}{2} = 0.5$ and $0.5 = 50\%$, then $\frac{1}{2} = 50\%$.
   c) Because $2 + 3 = 5$, we may replace $x + (2 + 3)$ by $x + 5$.
   d) If $7 = 2x - 3$, then $2x - 3 = 7$.
4. Give an example to illustrate each axiom of equality:
   a) Reflexive
   b) Symmetric
   c) Transitive
   d) Substitution
5. Find each sum:
   a) $5 + 7$
   b) $5 + (-7)$
   c) $(-5) + 7$
   d) $(-5) + (-7)$
6. Find each sum:
   a) $(-7) + 15$
   b) $7 + (-15)$
   c) $(-7) + (-15)$
   d) $(-7) + [(-7) + 15]$
7. Find each product:
   a) $5 \cdot 7$
   b) $5(-7)$
   c) $(-5)7$
   d) $(-5)(-7)$
8. Find each product:
   a) $(-7)(12)$
   b) $(-7)(-12)$
   c) $(-7)[(3)(4)]$
   d) $(-7)[(3)(-4)]$
9. The area (the number of squares) of the rectangle in the accompanying drawing can be determined by multiplying the measures of the two dimensions. Will the order of multiplication change the answer? Which axiom is illustrated?

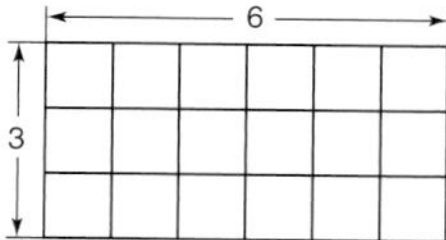

10. Identify the axiom of real numbers illustrated. Give a complete answer, such as Commutative Axiom for Multiplication.
    a) $7(5) = 5(7)$
    b) $(3 + 4) + 5 = 3 + (4 + 5)$
    c) $(-2) + 3 = 3 + (-2)$
    d) $(2 \cdot 3) \cdot 5 = 2 \cdot (3 \cdot 5)$
11. Perform each subtraction:
    a) $7 - (-2)$
    b) $(-7) - (+2)$
    c) $10 - 2$
    d) $(-10) - (-2)$
12. The temperature changes from $-3°$F at 2 A.M. to $7°$F at 7 A.M. Which expression represents the difference in temperatures from 2 A.M. to 7 A.M., $7 - (-3)$ or $(-3) - 7$?
13. Complete each division:
    a) $12 \div (-3)$
    b) $12 \div \left(-\frac{1}{3}\right)$
    c) $(-12) \div \left(-\frac{2}{3}\right)$
    d) $\left(-\frac{1}{12}\right) \div \left(\frac{1}{3}\right)$
14. Nine pegs are evenly spaced on a board so that the distance from each end to a peg equals the distance between any two pegs. If the board is 5 feet long, how far apart are the pegs?
15. The four owners of a shop realize a loss of \$240 in February. If the loss is shared equally, what number represents the profit for each owner for that month?
16. Bill works at a weekend convention by selling copies of a book. He receives a \$2 commission for each copy sold. If he sells 25 copies on Saturday and 30 copies on Sunday, what is Bill's total commission?
17. Use the Distributive Axiom to simplify each expression:
    a) $5(6 + 7)$
    b) $4(7 - 3)$
    c) $\frac{1}{2}(7 + 11)$
    d) $5x + 3x$
18. Use the Distributive Axiom to simplify each expression:
    a) $6(9 - 4)$
    b) $\left(\frac{1}{2}\right) \cdot 6(4 + 8)$
    c) $7y - 2y$
    d) $16x + 8x$
19. Simplify each expression:
    a) $6\pi + 4\pi$
    b) $8\sqrt{2} + 3\sqrt{2}$
    c) $16x^2y - 9x^2y$
    d) $9\sqrt{3} - 2\sqrt{3}$
20. Simplify each expression:
    a) $\pi r^2 + 2\pi r^2$
    b) $7xy + 3xy$
    c) $7x^2y + 3xy^2$
    d) $x + x + y$
21. Simplify each expression:
    a) $2 + 3 \cdot 4$
    b) $(2 + 3) \cdot 4$
    c) $2 + 3 \cdot 2^2$
    d) $2 + (3 \cdot 2)^2$
22. Simplify each expression:
    a) $3^2 + 4^2$
    b) $(3 + 4)^2$
    c) $3^2 + (8 - 2) \div 3$
    d) $[3^2 + (8 - 2)] \div 3$
23. Simplify each expression:
    a) $\dfrac{8 - 2}{2 - 8}$
    b) $\dfrac{8 - 2 \cdot 3}{(8 - 2) \cdot 3}$
    c) $\dfrac{5 \cdot 2 - 6 \cdot 3}{7 - (-2)}$
    d) $\dfrac{5 - 2 \cdot 6 + (-3)}{(-2)^2 + 4^2}$
24. Use the FOIL method to complete each multiplication:
    a) $(2 + 3)(4 + 5)$ b) $(7 - 2)(6 + 1)$
25. Use the FOIL method to complete each multiplication:
    a) $(3 - 1)(5 - 2)$ b) $(3x + 2)(4x - 5)$
26. Use the FOIL method to complete each multiplication:
    a) $(5x + 3)(2x - 7)$ b) $(2x + y)(3x - 5y)$
27. Using x and y, find an expression for the length of the pegged board shown in the accompanying figure.

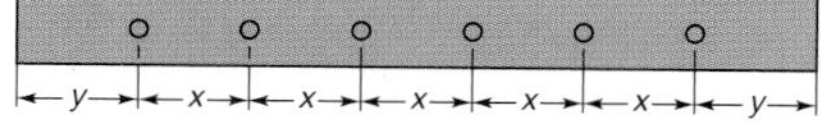

28. The cardboard used in the construction of the box shown in the accompanying figure has an area of $xy + yz + xz + xz + yz + xy$. Simplify this expression for the total area of the cardboard.

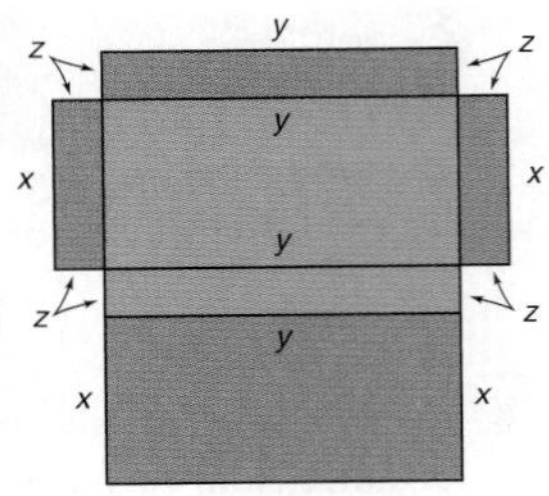

29. A large star is to be constructed, with lengths as shown in the accompanying figure. Give an expression for the total length of the wood strips used in the construction.

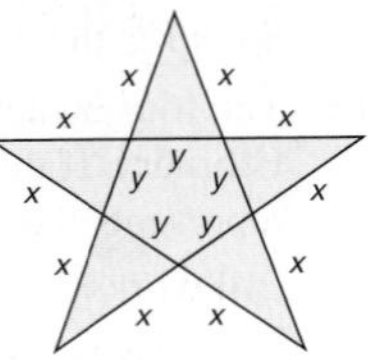

30. The area of an enclosed plot of ground that a farmer has subdivided can be found by multiplying $(x + y)$ times $(y + z)$. Use FOIL to complete the multiplication. How does this product compare with the total of the areas of the four smaller plots?

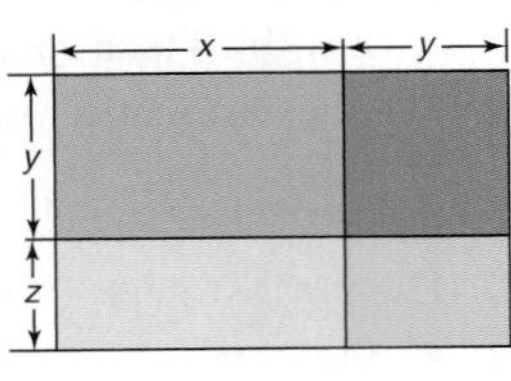

31. The degree measures of the angles of a triangle are $3x$, $5x$, and $2x$. Find an expression for the sum of the measures of these angles in terms of x.

32. The right circular cylinder shown in the accompanying figure has circular bases that have areas of 9π square units. The side has an area of 48π square units. Find an expression for the total surface area.

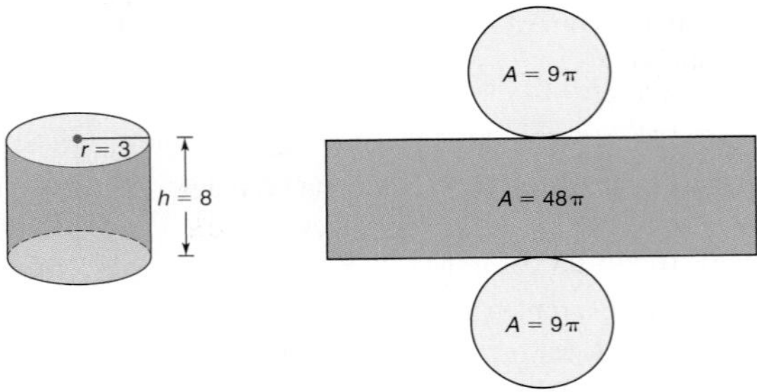

A.2 FORMULAS AND EQUATIONS

A **variable** is a letter used to represent an unknown number. However, the Greek letter π is known as a **constant** because it always equals the same number (approximately 3.14). Although we often use x, y, and z as variables, it is convenient to choose r for radius, h for height, b for base, and so on.

Figure A.2

EXAMPLE 1

For Figure A.2, combine like terms to find the perimeter P (sum of the lengths of all sides) of the figure.

Solution

$$\begin{aligned} P &= (x - 1) + (x + 2) + 2x + (2x + 1) \\ &= x + (-1) + x + 2 + 2x + 2x + 1 \\ &= 1x + 1x + 2x + 2x + (-1) + 2 + 1 \\ &= 6x + 2 \end{aligned}$$

When the FOIL method is used with variable expressions, we combine like terms in the simplification.

EXAMPLE 2

Find a simplified expression for the product $(x + 5)(x + 2)$.

Solution

$$(x + 5)(x + 2)$$
(F, O, I, L)

$$= x \cdot x + 2 \cdot x + 5 \cdot x + 10$$
$$= x^2 + 7x + 10$$

In Example 2, we multiplied by the FOIL method before adding like terms in accordance with rules of order. When evaluating a variable expression, we must also follow that order. For instance, the value of $a^2 + b^2$ when $a = 3$ and $b = 4$ is given by

$$3^2 + 4^2 \quad \text{or} \quad 9 + 16 \quad \text{or} \quad 25$$

because exponential expressions must be simplified before addition occurs.

EXAMPLE 3

Find the value of the following expressions.

a) $\pi r^2 h$, if $r = 3$ and $h = 4$ (leave π in the answer)
b) $\frac{1}{2}h(b + B)$, if $h = 10$, $b = 7$, and $B = 13$

Solution

a) $\pi r^2 h = \pi \cdot 3^2 \cdot 4$
$= \pi \cdot 9 \cdot 4 = \pi(36) = 36\pi$

b) $\frac{1}{2}h(b + B) = \frac{1}{2} \cdot 10(7 + 13)$
$= \frac{1}{2} \cdot 10(20)$
$= \frac{1}{2} \cdot 10 \cdot 20$
$= 5 \cdot 20 = 100$

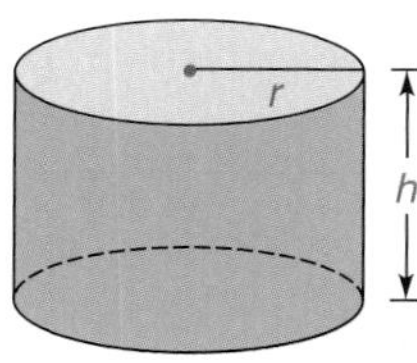

Figure A.3

Many variable expressions are found in formulas. A **formula** is an equation that expresses a rule. For example, $V = \pi r^2 h$ is a formula for the volume V of a right circular cylinder whose altitude has length h and for which the circular base has a radius of length r. (See Figure A.3.)

EXAMPLE 4

Given the formula $P = 2\ell + 2w$, find the value of P when $\ell = 7$ and $w = 3$.

Solution By substitution, $P = 2\ell + 2w$ becomes

$$P = (2 \cdot 7) + (2 \cdot 3)$$
$$= 14 + 6$$
$$= 20$$

An **equation** is a statement that two expressions are equal. Although formulas are special types of equations, most equations are not formulas. Consider the following four examples of equations:

$$x + (x + 1) = 7$$
$$2(x + 1) = 8 - 2x$$
$$x^2 - 6x + 8 = 0$$
$$P = 2\ell + 2w \qquad \textbf{(a formula)}$$

The phrase *solving an equation* means finding the values of the variable that make the equation true when the variable is replaced by those values. These values are known as **solutions** for the equation. For example, 3 is a solution (in fact, the only solution) for the equation $x + (x + 1) = 7$ because $3 + (3 + 1) = 7$ is true.

When each side of an equation is transformed (changed) without having its solutions changed, we say that an **equivalent equation** is produced. Some of the properties that are used for equation solving are listed in the following box.

Warning

We cannot multiply by 0 in solving an equation because the equation (say $2x - 1 = 7$) collapses to $0 = 0$. Division by 0 is likewise excluded.

PROPERTIES FOR EQUATION SOLVING

Addition Property of Equality (if $a = b$, then $a + c = b + c$): An equivalent equation results when the same number is added to each side of an equation.

Subtraction Property of Equality (if $a = b$, then $a - c = b - c$): An equivalent equation results when the same number is subtracted from each side of an equation.

Multiplication Property of Equality (if $a = b$, then $a \cdot c = b \cdot c$ for $c \neq 0$): An equivalent equation results when each side of an equation is multiplied by the same nonzero number.

Division Property of Equality $\left(\text{if } a = b, \text{ then } \frac{a}{c} = \frac{b}{c} \text{ for } c \neq 0\right)$: An equivalent equation results when each side of an equation is divided by the same nonzero number.

Addition and subtraction are **inverse operations,** as are multiplication and division. In problems that involve equation solving, we will utilize inverse operations.

Add	to eliminate	a subtraction.
Subtract	to eliminate	an addition.
Multiply	to eliminate	a division.
Divide	to eliminate	a multiplication.

EXAMPLE 5

Solve the equation $2x - 3 = 7$.

Solution First add 3 (to eliminate the subtraction of 3 from $2x$):

$$2x - 3 + 3 = 7 + 3$$
$$2x = 10 \qquad \textbf{(simplifying)}$$

Now divide by 2 (to eliminate the multiplication of 2 with x):

$$\frac{2x}{2} = \frac{10}{2}$$
$$x = 5 \qquad \textbf{(simplifying)}$$

■

In Example 5, the number 5 is the solution for the original equation. Replacing x with 5, we confirm this as shown:

$$\begin{aligned} 2x - 3 &= 7 \\ 2(5) - 3 &= 7 \\ 10 - 3 &= 7 \end{aligned}$$

An equation that can be written in the form $ax + b = c$ for constants a, b, and c is a **linear equation.** Our plan for solving such an equation involves getting variable terms together on one side of the equation and numerical terms together on the other side.

SOLVING A LINEAR EQUATION

1. Simplify each side of the equation; that is, combine like terms.
2. Eliminate additions and/or subtractions.
3. Eliminate multiplications and/or divisions.

EXAMPLE 6

Solve the equation $2(x - 3) + 5 = 13$.

Solution

$$\begin{aligned} 2(x - 3) + 5 &= 13 \\ 2x - 6 + 5 &= 13 && \text{(Distributive Axiom)} \\ 2x - 1 &= 13 && \text{(substitution)} \\ 2x &= 14 && \text{(addition)} \\ x &= 7 && \text{(division)} \end{aligned}$$

Some equations involve fractions. To avoid some of the difficulties that fractions bring, we often multiply each side of such equations by the **least common denominator (LCD)** of the fractions involved.

EXAMPLE 7

Solve the equation $\frac{x}{3} + \frac{x}{4} = 14$.

Solution For the denominators 3 and 4, the LCD is 12. We must therefore multiply each side of the equation by 12 and use the Distributive Axiom on the left side.

$$\begin{aligned} 12\left(\frac{x}{3} + \frac{x}{4}\right) &= 12 \cdot 14 \\ \frac{12}{1} \cdot \frac{x}{3} + \frac{12}{1} \cdot \frac{x}{4} &= 168 \\ 4x + 3x &= 168 \\ 7x &= 168 \\ x &= 24 \end{aligned}$$

To check this result, we have

$$\frac{24}{3} + \frac{24}{4} = 14$$
$$8 + 6 = 14$$

It may happen that the variable appears in the denominator of the only fraction in an equation. In such cases, our method does not change! See Example 8.

EXAMPLE 8

Solve the following equation for n:

$$\frac{360}{n} + 120 = 180$$

Solution Multiplying by n (the LCD), we have

$$n\left(\frac{360}{n} + 120\right) = 180 \cdot n$$
$$\frac{n}{1} \cdot \frac{360}{n} + 120 \cdot n = 180n$$
$$360 + 120n = 180n$$
$$360 = 60n$$
$$6 = n$$

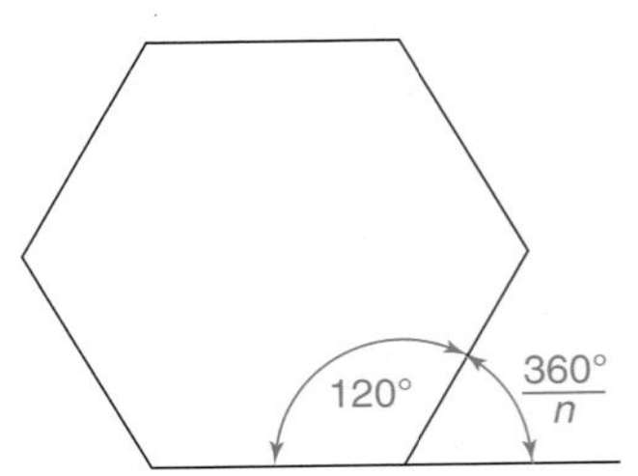

Figure A.4

NOTE: n represents the number of sides possessed by the polygon in Figure A.4; $\frac{360}{n}$ and 120 represent the measures of angles in the figure. ■

Our final example combines many of the ideas introduced in this section and the previous section. Example 9 is based on the formula for the area of a trapezoid.

EXAMPLE 9

See Figure A.5. For the formula $A = \frac{1}{2} \cdot h \cdot (b + B)$, suppose that $A = 77$, $b = 4$, and $B = 7$. Find the value of h.

Solution Substitution leads to the equation

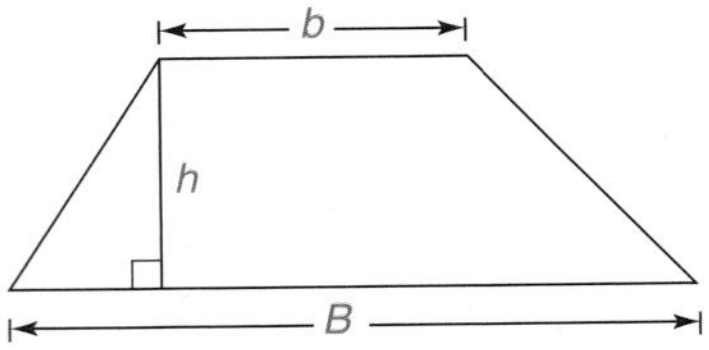

$$77 = \frac{1}{2} \cdot h \cdot (4 + 7)$$
$$77 = \frac{1}{2} \cdot h \cdot 11$$
$$2(77) = 2 \cdot \frac{1}{2} \cdot h \cdot 11 \quad \text{(multiplying by 2)}$$
$$154 = 11h \quad \text{(simplifying)}$$
$$14 = h \quad \text{(dividing by 11)}$$

Figure A.5

■

Exercises A.2

In Exercises 1 to 6, simplify by combining similar terms.

1. $(2x + 3) + (3x + 5)$
2. $(2x + 3) - (3x - 5)$
3. $x + (3x + 2) - (2x + 4)$
4. $(3x + 2) + (2x - 3) - (x + 1)$
5. $2(x + 1) + 3(x + 2)$

   (HINT: Multiply before adding.)
6. $3(2x + 5) - 2(3x - 1)$

In Exercises 7 to 12, simplify by using the FOIL method of multiplication.

7. $(x + 3)(x + 4)$
8. $(x - 5)(x - 7)$
9. $(2x + 5)(3x - 2)$
10. $(3x + 7)(2x + 3)$
11. $(a + b)^2 + (a - b)^2$
12. $(x + 2)^2 - (x - 2)^2$

In Exercises 13 to 16, evaluate each expression.

13. $\ell \cdot w \cdot h$, if $\ell = 4$, $w = 3$, and $h = 5$
14. $a^2 + b^2$, if $a = 5$ and $b = 7$
15. $2 \cdot \ell + 2 \cdot w$, if $\ell = 13$ and $w = 7$
16. $a \cdot b \div c$, if $a = 6$, $b = 16$, and $c = 4$

In Exercises 17 to 20, find the value of the variable named in each formula. Leave π in the answers for Exercises 19 and 20.

17. S, if $S = 2\ell w + 2wh + 2\ell h$, $\ell = 6$, $w = 4$, and $h = 5$
18. A, if $A = \frac{1}{2}a(b + c + d)$, $a = 2$, $b = 6$, $c = 8$, and $d = 10$
19. V, if $V = \frac{1}{3}\pi \cdot r^2 \cdot h$, $r = 3$, and $h = 4$
20. S, if $S = 4\pi r^2$ and $r = 2$

In Exercises 21 to 32, solve each equation.

21. $2x + 3 = 17$
22. $3x - 3 = -6$
23. $-\frac{y}{3} + 2 = 6$
24. $3y = -21 - 4y$
25. $a + (a + 2) = 26$
26. $b = 27 - \frac{b}{2}$
27. $2(x + 1) = 30 - 6(x - 2)$
28. $2(x + 1) + 3(x + 2) = 22 + 4(10 - x)$
29. $\frac{x}{3} - \frac{x}{2} = -5$
30. $\frac{x}{2} + \frac{x}{3} + \frac{x}{4} = 26$
31. $\frac{360}{n} + 135 = 180$
32. $\frac{(n - 2) \cdot 180}{n} = 150$

In Exercises 33 to 36, find the value of the indicated variable for each given formula.

33. w, if $S = 2\ell w + 2wh + 2\ell h$, $S = 148$, $\ell = 5$, and $h = 6$
34. b, if $A = \frac{1}{2} \cdot h \cdot (b + B)$, $A = 156$, $h = 12$, and $B = 11$
35. y, if $m = \frac{1}{2}(x - y)$, $m = 23$, and $x = 78$
36. Y, if $m = \frac{Y - y}{X - x}$, $m = \frac{-3}{2}$, $y = 1$, $X = 2$, and $x = -2$

A.3 INEQUALITIES

In geometry, we sometimes need to work with inequalities. **Inequalities** are statements that involve one of the following relationships:

$<$ means "is less than"
$>$ means "is greater than"
$\leq$ means "is less than or equal to"
$\geq$ means "is greater than or equal to"
$\neq$ means "is not equal to"

The statement $-4 < 7$ is true because negative 4 is less than positive 7. On a horizontal number line, the smaller number is always found to the left of the larger number. An equivalent claim is $7 > -4$, which means positive 7 is greater than negative 4. See the number line at the top of page 550.

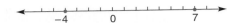

−4 0 7

Both statements $6 \leq 6$ and $4 \leq 6$ are true. The statement $6 \leq 6$ could also be expressed by the statement "$6 < 6$ or $6 = 6$," which is true because $6 = 6$ is true. Because $4 < 6$ is true, the statement $4 \leq 6$ is also true. A statement of the form *P or Q* is called a *disjunction*; see Section 1.1 for more information.

EXAMPLE 1

Give two true statements that involve the symbol $\geq$.

Solution

$5 \geq 5$	because	$5 = 5$ is true
$12 \geq 5$	because	$12 > 5$ is true

■

The symbol $\neq$ is used to join any two numerical expressions that do not have the same value; for example, $2 + 3 \neq 7$. The following definition is also found in Section 3.5.

DEFINITION

a is less than *b* (that is, $a < b$) if and only if there is a positive number *p* for which $a + p = b$; *a* is greater than *b* (that is, $a > b$) if and only if $b < a$.

EXAMPLE 2

Find, if possible, the following:

a) Any number *a* for which "$a < a$" is true.
b) Any numbers *a* and *b* for which "$a < b$ and $b < a$" is true.

Solution

a) There is no such number. If $a < a$, then $a + p = a$ for some positive number *p*. Subtracting *a* from each side of the equation gives $p = 0$. This statement ($p = 0$) contradicts the fact that *p* is positive.
b) There are no such numbers. If $a < b$, then *a* is to the left of *b* on the number line. Therefore, $b < a$ is false, because this statement claims that *b* is to the left of *a*. ■

EXAMPLE 3

What can you conclude regarding the numbers *y* and *z* if $x < y$ and $x > z$?

Solution $x < y$ means that *x* is to the left of *y*, as in Figure A.6. Similarly, $x > z$ (equivalently, $z < x$) means that *z* is to the left of *x*. With *z* to the left of *x*, which is itself to the left of *y*, we clearly have *z* to the left of *y*; thus $z < y$.

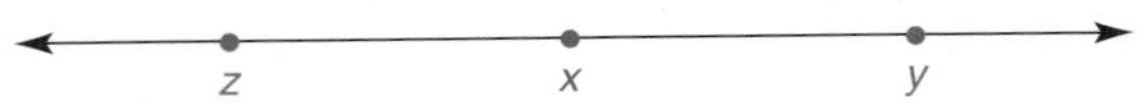

Figure A.6

■

Example 3 suggests a transitive relationship for the inequality "is less than," and this is stated in the following property. The Transitive Property of Inequality can also be stated using $>$, $\leq$, or $\geq$.

TRANSITIVE PROPERTY OF INEQUALITY

For numbers a, b, and c, if $a < b$ and $b < c$, then $a < c$.

This property can be proved as follows:

1. $a < b$ means that $a + p_1 = b$ for some positive number p_1.
2. $b < c$ means that $b + p_2 = c$ for some positive number p_2.
3. Substituting $a + p_1$ for b (from statement 1) into the statement $b + p_2 = c$, we have $(a + p_1) + p_2 = c$.
4. Now $a + (p_1 + p_2) = c$.
5. But the sum of two positive numbers is also positive; that is, $p_1 + p_2 = p$, so statement 4 becomes $a + p = c$.
6. If $a + p = c$, then $a < c$, by the definition of "is less than."

Therefore, $a < b$ and $b < c$ implies that $a < c$.

The Transitive Property of Inequality can be extended to a series of unequal expressions. When a first value is less than a second, the second is less than a third, and so on, then the first is less than the last.

EXAMPLE 4

Two angles are complementary if the sum of their measures is exactly 90°. If the measure of the first of two complementary angles is more than 27°, what must you conclude about the measure of the second angle?

Solution The second angle must measure less than 63°. ■

EXAMPLE 5

For the statement $-6 < 9$, determine the inequality that results when each side is changed as follows:

a) Has 4 added to it
b) Has 2 subtracted from it
c) Is multiplied by 3
d) Is divided by -3

Solution

a) $-6 + 4 ? 9 + 4$
$-2 ? 13 \rightarrow -2 < 13$

b) $-6 - 2 ? 9 - 2$
$-8 ? 7 \rightarrow -8 < 7$

c) $(-6)(3) ? 9(3)$
$-18 ? 27 \rightarrow -18 < 27$

d) $(-6) \div (-3) ? 9 \div (-3)$
$2 ? -3 \rightarrow 2 > -3$ ■

As Example 5 suggests, addition and subtraction preserve the inequality symbol. Multiplication and division by a *positive* number preserve the inequality symbol, but multiplication and division by a *negative* number reverse the inequality symbol.

PROPERTIES OF INEQUALITIES

Stated for $<$, these properties have counterparts involving $>$, $\leq$, and $\geq$.

Addition: If $a < b$, then $a + c < b + c$.

Subtraction: If $a < b$, then $a - c < b - c$.

Multiplication:
i) If $a < b$ and $c > 0$ (c is positive), then $a \cdot c < b \cdot c$.
ii) If $a < b$ and $c < 0$ (c is negative), then $a \cdot c > b \cdot c$.

Division:
i) If $a < b$ and $c > 0$ (c is positive), then $\frac{a}{c} < \frac{b}{c}$.
ii) If $a < b$ and $c < 0$ (c is negative), then $\frac{a}{c} > \frac{b}{c}$.

We now turn our attention to solving inequalities such as

$$x + (x + 1) < 7 \qquad \text{and} \qquad 2(x - 3) + 5 \geq 3$$

The method here is almost the same as the one used for equation solving, but there are some very important differences. See the following guidelines.

Warning

Be sure to reverse the inequality symbol upon multiplying or dividing by a *negative* number.

SOLVING AN INEQUALITY

1. Simplify each side of the inequality; that is, combine like terms.
2. Eliminate additions and subtractions.
3. Eliminate multiplications and divisions.

NOTE: For Step 3, see the "Warning at the left"

EXAMPLE 6

Solve $2x - 3 \leq 7$.

Solution

$$2x - 3 + 3 \leq 7 + 3 \quad \textbf{(adding 3 preserves} \leq\textbf{)}$$
$$2x \leq 10 \quad \textbf{(simplify)}$$
$$\frac{2x}{2} \leq \frac{10}{2} \quad \textbf{(division by 2 preserves} \leq\textbf{)}$$
$$x \leq 5 \quad \textbf{(simplify)}$$

The possible values of x are shown on a number line in Figure A.7; this picture is the **graph** of the solutions. Note that the point above the 5 is shown solid in order to indicate that 5 is included as a solution.

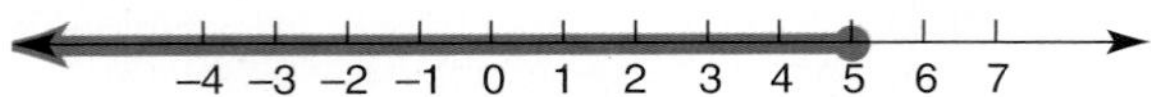

Figure A.7

EXAMPLE 7

Solve $x(x - 2) - (x + 1)(x + 3) < 9$.

Solution Using the Distributive Axiom and FOIL, we simplify the left side to get

$$(x^2 - 2x) - (x^2 + 4x + 3) < 9$$

Subtraction is performed by adding the additive inverse of each term in $(x^2 + 4x + 3)$.

$$\therefore (x^2 - 2x) + (-x^2 - 4x - 3) < 9$$

$$-6x - 3 < 9 \quad \text{(simplify)}$$

$$-6x < 12 \quad \text{(add 3)}$$

$$\frac{-6x}{-6} > \frac{12}{-6} \quad \text{(divide by } -6 \text{ and reverse the inequality symbol)}$$

$$x > -2 \quad \text{(simplify)}$$

The graph of the solution is shown in Figure A.8. Notice that the circle above the -2 is shown open in order to indicate that -2 is not included as a solution.

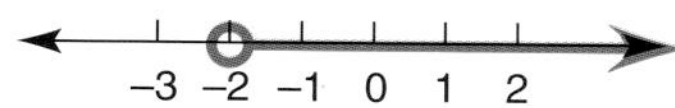

Figure A.8

Exercises A.3

1. If line segment AB and line segment CD in the accompanying drawing are drawn to scale, what does intuition tell you about the lengths of these segments?

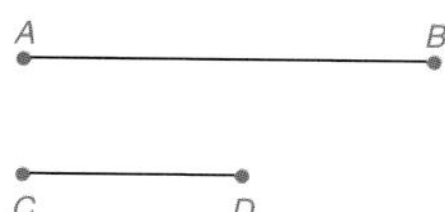

2. Using the number line shown, write two inequalities that relate the values of e and f.

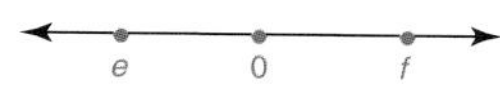

3. If angles ABC and DEF in the accompanying drawing were measured with a protractor, what does intuition tell you about the degree measures of these angles?

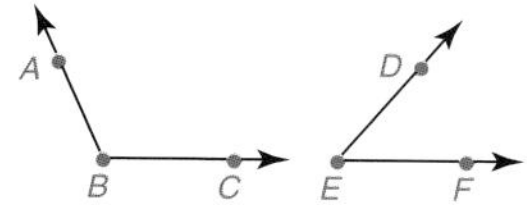

4. Consider the statement $x \geq 6$. Which of the following choices of x below will make this a true statement?

   $x = -3$ $\quad x = 0$ $\quad x = 6$ $\quad x = 9$ $\quad x = 12$

5. According to the definition of $a < b$, there is a positive number p for which $a + p = b$. Find the value of p for the statement given.
   a) $3 < 7$ b) $-3 < 7$

6. Does the Transitive Property of Inequality hold true for four real numbers a, b, c, and d? That is, is the following statement true?
   If $a < b$, $b < c$, and $c < d$, then $a < d$.

7. Of several line segments, $AB > CD$ (the length of segment AB is greater than that of segment CD), $CD > EF$, $EF > GH$, and $GH > IJ$. What conclusion does the Transitive Property of Inequality allow regarding IJ and AB?

8. Of several angles, the degree measures are related in this way: $m\angle JKL > m\angle GHI$ (the measure of angle JKL is greater than that of angle GHI), $m\angle GHI > m\angle DEF$, and $m\angle DEF > m\angle ABC$. What conclusion does the Transitive Property of Inequality allow regarding $m\angle ABC$ and $m\angle JKL$?

9. Classify as true or false.

a) $5 \leq 4$ c) $5 \leq 5$
b) $4 \leq 5$ d) $5 < 5$

10. Classify as true or false.

a) $-5 \leq 4$ c) $-5 \leq -5$
b) $5 \leq -4$ d) $5 \leq -5$

11. Two angles are supplementary if the sum of their measures is 180°. If the measure of the first of two supplementary angles is less than 32°, what must you conclude about the measure of the second angle?

12. Two trim boards need to be used together to cover a 12-ft length along one wall. If Jim recalls that one board is more than 7 ft long, what length must the second board be to span the 12-ft length?

13. Consider the inequality $-3 \leq 5$. Write the statement that results when

a) each side is multiplied by 4.
b) -7 is added to each side.
c) each side is multiplied by -6.
d) each side is divided by -1.

14. Consider the inequality $-6 > -9$. Write the statement that results when

a) 8 is added to each side.
b) each side is multiplied by -2.
c) each side is multiplied by 2.
d) each side is divided by -3.

15. Suppose that you are solving an inequality. Complete the chart in the next column by indicating whether the inequality symbol should be reversed or kept by writing "change" or "no change."

	Positive	*Negative*
Add		
Subtract		
Multiply		
Divide		

In Exercises 16 to 26, first solve each inequality. Then draw a number line graph of the solutions.

16. $5x - 1 \leq 29$

17. $2x + 3 \leq 17$

18. $5 + 4x > 25$

19. $5 - 4x > 25$

20. $5(2 - x) \leq 30$

21. $2x + 3x < 200 - 5x$

22. $5(x + 2) < 6(9 - x)$

23. $\frac{x}{3} - \frac{x}{2} \leq 4$

24. $\frac{2x - 3}{-5} > 7$

25. $x^2 + 4x \leq x(x - 5) - 18$

26. $x(x + 2) < x(2 - x) + 2x^2$

In Exercises 27 to 30, the claims made are not always true. Cite a counterexample to show why each claim fails.

27. If $a < b$, then $a \cdot c < b \cdot c$.

28. If $a < b$, then $a \cdot c \neq b \cdot c$.

29. If $a < b$, then $a^2 < b^2$.

30. If $a \neq b$ and $b \neq c$, then $a \neq c$.

A.4 QUADRATIC EQUATIONS

An equation that can be written in the form $ax^2 + bx + c = 0$ $(a \neq 0)$ is a **quadratic equation.** For example, $x^2 - 7x + 12 = 0$ and $6x^2 = 7x + 3$ are quadratic. Many quadratic equations can be solved by a factoring method that depends on the Zero Product Property.

ZERO PRODUCT PROPERTY

If $a \cdot b = 0$, then $a = 0$ or $b = 0$.

When this property is stated in words, it reads, "If the product of two expressions equals 0, then at least one of the factors must equal 0."

EXAMPLE 1

Solve $x^2 - 7x + 12 = 0$.

Solution First factor the polynomial by reversing the FOIL method of multiplication.

$$
\begin{aligned}
(x-3)(x-4) &= 0 && \text{(factoring)} \\
x-3=0 \quad \text{or} \quad x-4 &= 0 && \text{(Zero Product Property)} \\
x=3 \quad \text{or} \quad x &= 4 && \text{(Addition Property)}
\end{aligned}
$$

To check $x = 3$, substitute into the given equation:

$$3^2 - (7 \cdot 3) + 12 = 9 - 21 + 12 = 0$$

To check $x = 4$, substitute again:

$$4^2 - (7 \cdot 4) + 12 = 16 - 28 + 12 = 0$$

The solutions are usually expressed as the set $\{3, 4\}$. ■

If you were asked to use factoring to solve the quadratic equation

$$6x^2 = 7x + 3,$$

it would be necessary to change the equation so that one side would be equal to 0. The form $ax^2 + bx + c = 0$ is the **standard form** of a quadratic equation.

SOLVING A QUADRATIC EQUATION BY THE FACTORING METHOD

1. Be sure the equation is in standard form (one side = 0).
2. Factor the polynomial side of the equation.
3. Set each factor containing the variable equal to 0.
4. Solve each equation found in step 3.
5. Check solutions by substituting into the original equation.

Step 5, which was shown in Example 1, is omitted in Example 2.

EXAMPLE 2

Solve $6x^2 = 7x + 3$.

Solution First changing to standard form, we have

$$
\begin{aligned}
6x^2 - 7x - 3 &= 0 && \text{(standard form)} \\
(2x-3)(3x+1) &= 0 && \text{(factoring)} \\
2x-3=0 \quad \text{or} \quad 3x+1 &= 0 && \text{(Zero Product Property)} \\
2x=3 \quad \text{or} \quad 3x &= -1 && \text{(Addition-Subtraction Property)} \\
x=\frac{3}{2} \quad \text{or} \quad x &= \frac{-1}{3} && \text{(division)}
\end{aligned}
$$

Therefore, $\left\{\frac{3}{2}, -\frac{1}{3}\right\}$ is the solution set. ■

In some instances, a common factor can be extracted from each term in the factoring step. In the equation $2x^2 + 10x - 48 = 0$, the left side of the equation has the common factor 2. Factoring leads to $2(x^2 + 5x - 24) = 0$ and then to $2(x + 8)(x - 3) = 0$. Of course, only the factors containing variables can equal 0, so the solutions to this equation are -8 and 3.

Equations such as $4x^2 = 9$ and $4x^2 - 12x = 0$ are **incomplete quadratic equations** because one term is missing from the standard form. Either equation can be solved by factoring; in particular, the factoring is given by

$$4x^2 - 9 = (2x + 3)(2x - 3)$$

and

$$4x^2 - 12x = 4x(x - 3)$$

When solutions to $ax^2 + bx + c = 0$ cannot be found by factoring, they may be determined by the following formula, in which a is the number multiplied by x^2, b is the number multiplied by x, and c is the constant term. The $\pm$ symbol tells us that there are generally two solutions, one found by adding and one by subtracting. The symbol $\sqrt{a}$ is read "the square root of a."

QUADRATIC FORMULA

$$x = \frac{-b \pm \sqrt{b^2 - 4ac}}{2a}$$ are solutions for $ax^2 + bx + c = 0$, where $a \neq 0$.

Although the formula may provide two solutions for the equation, an application problem in geometry may have a single positive solution representing a segment (or angle) measure. Recall that for $a > 0$, $\sqrt{a}$ represents the principal square root of a.

DEFINITION

Where $a > 0$, the number $\sqrt{a}$ is the positive number for which $(\sqrt{a})^2 = a$.

EXAMPLE 3

a) Explain why $\sqrt{25}$ is equal to 5.
b) Without a calculator, find the value of $\sqrt{3} \cdot \sqrt{3}$.
c) Use a calculator to show that $\sqrt{5} \approx 2.236$.

Solution

a) We see that $\sqrt{25}$ must equal 5 because $5^2 = 25$.
b) By definition, $\sqrt{3}$ is the number for which $(\sqrt{3})^2 = 3$.
c) By using a calculator, we see that $2.236^2 \approx 5$. ■

EXAMPLE 4

Simplify each expression, if possible.

a) $\sqrt{16}$ b) $\sqrt{0}$ c) $\sqrt{7}$ d) $\sqrt{400}$ e) $\sqrt{-4}$

Solution

a) $\sqrt{16} = 4$ because $4^2 = 16$.
b) $\sqrt{0} = 0$ because $0^2 = 0$.

c) $\sqrt{7}$ cannot be simplified; however, $\sqrt{7} \approx 2.646$.
d) $\sqrt{400} = 20$ because $20^2 = 400$; a calculator can be used.
e) $\sqrt{-4}$ is not a real number; a calculator gives an "ERROR" message. ■

Whereas $\sqrt{25}$ represents the principal square root of 25 (namely, 5), the expression $-\sqrt{25}$ can be interpreted as "the negative number whose square is 25"; thus, $-\sqrt{25} = -5$ because $(-5)^2 = 25$. In expressions such as $\sqrt{9 + 16}$ and $\sqrt{4 + 9}$, we first simplify the **radicand** (the expression under the bar of the square root); thus $\sqrt{9 + 16} = \sqrt{25} = 5$ and $\sqrt{4 + 9} = \sqrt{13} \approx 3.606$.

Just as fractions are reduced to lower terms ($\frac{6}{8}$ is replaced by $\frac{3}{4}$), it is also customary to reduce the size of the radicand when possible. To accomplish this, we use the Product Property of Square Roots.

> **PRODUCT PROPERTY OF SQUARE ROOTS**
>
> For $a \geq 0$ and $b \geq 0$, $\sqrt{a \cdot b} = \sqrt{a} \cdot \sqrt{b}$.

When simplifying, we replace the radicand by a product in which the largest possible number from the list of perfect squares below is selected as one of the factors:

4, 9, 16, 25, 36, 49, 64, 81, 100, 121, . . .

For example,

$$\begin{aligned}\sqrt{45} &= \sqrt{9 \cdot 5}\\ &= \sqrt{9} \cdot \sqrt{5}\\ &= 3\sqrt{5}\end{aligned}$$

The radicand has now been reduced from 45 to 5. Using a calculator, we see that $\sqrt{45} \approx 6.708$. Also, $3\sqrt{5}$ means 3 times $\sqrt{5}$, and with the calculator we see that $3\sqrt{5} \approx 6.708$.

> Leave the smallest possible integer under the square root symbol.

EXAMPLE 5

Simplify the following radicals:

a) $\sqrt{27}$ b) $\sqrt{50}$

Solution

a) 9 is the largest perfect square factor of 27. Therefore,

$$\sqrt{27} = \sqrt{9 \cdot 3} = \sqrt{9} \cdot \sqrt{3} = 3\sqrt{3}$$

b) 25 is the largest perfect square factor of 50. Therefore,

$$\sqrt{50} = \sqrt{25 \cdot 2} = \sqrt{25} \cdot \sqrt{2} = 5\sqrt{2}$$

■

Warning

In Example 5(b), the correct solution is $5\sqrt{2}$, not $2\sqrt{5}$.

The Product Property of Square Roots has a symmetric form that reads $\sqrt{a} \cdot \sqrt{b} = \sqrt{ab}$; for example, $\sqrt{2} \cdot \sqrt{3} = \sqrt{6}$ and $\sqrt{5} \cdot \sqrt{5} = \sqrt{25} = 5$.

The expression $ax^2 + bx + c$ may be **prime** (meaning "not factorable"). Because $x^2 - 5x + 3$ is prime, we solve the equation $x^2 - 5x + 3 = 0$ by using the Quadratic Formula $x = \frac{-b \pm \sqrt{b^2 - 4ac}}{2a}$; see Example 6.

NOTE: When square root radicals are left in an answer, the answer is exact. Once we use the calculator, the solutions are only approximate.

EXAMPLE 6

Find exact solutions for $x^2 - 5x + 3 = 0$. Then use a calculator to approximate these solutions correct to two decimal places.

Solution With the equation in standard form, we see that $a = 1$, $b = -5$, and $c = 3$. So

$$x = \frac{-(-5) \pm \sqrt{(-5)^2 - 4(1)(3)}}{2(1)}$$

$$x = \frac{5 \pm \sqrt{25 - 12}}{2} \quad \text{or} \quad x = \frac{5 \pm \sqrt{13}}{2}$$

The exact solutions are $\frac{5 + \sqrt{13}}{2}$ and $\frac{5 - \sqrt{13}}{2}$. Using a calculator, we find that the approximate solutions are 4.30 and 0.70, respectively. ■

Using the Quadratic Formula to solve the equation $x^2 - 6x + 7 = 0$ yields $x = \frac{6 \pm \sqrt{8}}{2}$. In Example 7, we focus on the simplification of such an expression.

EXAMPLE 7

Simplify $\frac{6 \pm \sqrt{8}}{2}$.

Solution Because $\sqrt{8} = \sqrt{4} \cdot \sqrt{2}$ or $2\sqrt{2}$, we simplify the expression as follows:

$$\frac{6 \pm \sqrt{8}}{2} = \frac{6 \pm 2\sqrt{2}}{2} = \frac{\cancel{2}(3 \pm \sqrt{2})}{\cancel{2}} = 3 \pm \sqrt{2}$$

NOTE 1: The number 2 was a common factor for the numerator and the denominator. We then reduced the fraction to lowest terms.

NOTE 2: The approximate values of $3 \pm \sqrt{2}$ are 4.41 and 1.59, respectively. Use your calculator to show that these values are the approximate solutions of the equation $x^2 - 6x + 7 = 0$. ■

Our final method for solving quadratic equations is used if the equation has the form $ax^2 + c = 0$.

> **SQUARE ROOTS PROPERTY**
>
> If $x^2 = p$ where $p \geq 0$, then $x = \pm\sqrt{p}$.

According to the Square Roots Property, the equation $x^2 = 6$ has the solutions $\pm\sqrt{6}$.

EXAMPLE 8

Use the Square Roots Property to solve the equation $2x^2 - 56 = 0$.

Solution

$$2x^2 - 56 = 0 \rightarrow 2x^2 = 56 \rightarrow x^2 = 28$$

Then

$$x = \pm\sqrt{28} = \pm\sqrt{4}\cdot\sqrt{7} = \pm 2\sqrt{7}$$

The exact solutions are $2\sqrt{7}$ and $-2\sqrt{7}$; the approximate solutions are 5.29 and −5.29, respectively.

In Example 10, the solutions for the quadratic equation will involve fractions. For this reason, we consider the Quotient Property of Square Roots and Example 9. The Quotient Property enables us to replace the square root of a fraction by the square root of its numerator divided by the square root of its denominator.

QUOTIENT PROPERTY OF SQUARE ROOTS

For $a \geq 0$ and $b > 0$, $\sqrt{\frac{a}{b}} = \frac{\sqrt{a}}{\sqrt{b}}$.

EXAMPLE 9

Simplify the following square root expressions:

a) $\sqrt{\dfrac{16}{9}}$ b) $\sqrt{\dfrac{3}{4}}$

Solution

a) $\sqrt{\dfrac{16}{9}} = \dfrac{\sqrt{16}}{\sqrt{9}} = \dfrac{4}{3}$ b) $\sqrt{\dfrac{3}{4}} = \dfrac{\sqrt{3}}{\sqrt{4}} = \dfrac{\sqrt{3}}{2}$

EXAMPLE 10

Solve the equation $4x^2 - 9 = 0$.

Solution

$$4x^2 - 9 = 0 \rightarrow 4x^2 = 9 \rightarrow x^2 = \tfrac{9}{4}$$

Then

$$x = \pm\sqrt{\frac{9}{4}} = \pm\frac{\sqrt{9}}{\sqrt{4}} = \pm\tfrac{3}{2}$$

In summary, quadratic equations have the form $ax^2 + bx + c = 0$ and are solved by one of the following methods:

1. Factoring, when $ax^2 + bx + c$ is easily factored
2. The Quadratic Formula

$$x = \frac{-b \pm \sqrt{b^2 - 4ac}}{2a},$$

   when $ax^2 + bx + c$ is not easily factored or cannot be factored
3. The Square Roots Property, when the equation has the form $ax^2 + c = 0$.

Exercises A.4

1. Use your calculator to find the approximate value of each number, correct to two decimal places:
a) $\sqrt{13}$ b) $\sqrt{8}$ c) $-\sqrt{29}$ d) $\sqrt{\frac{3}{5}}$

2. Use your calculator to find the approximate value of each number, correct to two decimal places:
a) $\sqrt{17}$ b) $\sqrt{400}$ c) $-\sqrt{7}$ d) $\sqrt{1.6}$

3. Which equations are quadratic?
a) $2x^2 - 5x + 3 = 0$ d) $\frac{1}{2}x^2 - \frac{1}{4}x - \frac{1}{8} = 0$
b) $x^2 = x^2 + 4$ e) $\sqrt{2x - 1} = 3$
c) $x^2 = 4$ f) $(x + 1)(x - 1) = 15$

4. Which equations are incomplete quadratic equations?
a) $x^2 - 4 = 0$ d) $2x^2 - 4 = 2x^2 + 8x$
b) $x^2 - 4x = 0$ e) $x^2 = \frac{9}{4}$
c) $3x^2 = 2x$ f) $x^2 - 2x - 3 = 0$

5. Simplify each expression by using the Product Property of Square Roots:
a) $\sqrt{8}$ c) $\sqrt{900}$
b) $\sqrt{45}$ d) $(\sqrt{3})^2$

6. Simplify each expression by using the Product Property of Square Roots:
a) $\sqrt{28}$ c) $\sqrt{54}$
b) $\sqrt{32}$ d) $\sqrt{200}$

7. Simplify each expression by using the Quotient Property of Square Roots:
a) $\sqrt{\frac{9}{16}}$ c) $\sqrt{\frac{7}{16}}$
b) $\sqrt{\frac{25}{49}}$ d) $\sqrt{\frac{6}{9}}$

8. Simplify each expression by using the Quotient Property of Square Roots:
a) $\sqrt{\frac{1}{4}}$ c) $\sqrt{\frac{5}{36}}$
b) $\sqrt{\frac{16}{9}}$ d) $\sqrt{\frac{3}{16}}$

9. Use your calculator to verify that the following expressions are equivalent:
a) $\sqrt{54}$ and $3\sqrt{6}$
b) $\sqrt{\frac{5}{16}}$ and $\frac{\sqrt{5}}{4}$

10. Use your calculator to verify that the following expressions are equivalent:
a) $\sqrt{48}$ and $4\sqrt{3}$ b) $\sqrt{\frac{7}{9}}$ and $\frac{\sqrt{7}}{3}$

In Exercises 11 to 18, solve each quadratic equation by factoring.

11. $x^2 - 6x + 8 = 0$
12. $x^2 + 4x = 21$
13. $3x^2 - 51x + 180 = 0$

(HINT: There is a common factor.)

14. $2x^2 + x - 6 = 0$
15. $3x^2 = 10x + 8$
16. $8x^2 + 40x - 112 = 0$
17. $6x^2 = 5x - 1$
18. $12x^2 + 10x = 12$

In Exercises 19 to 26, solve each equation by using the Quadratic Formula. Give exact solutions in simplified form. When answers contain square roots, approximate the solutions rounded to two decimal places.

19. $x^2 - 7x + 10 = 0$
20. $x^2 + 7x + 12 = 0$
21. $x^2 + 9 = 7x$
22. $2x^2 + 3x = 6$
23. $x^2 - 4x - 8 = 0$
24. $x^2 - 6x - 2 = 0$
25. $5x^2 = 3x + 7$
26. $2x^2 = 8x - 1$

In Exercises 27 to 32, solve each incomplete quadratic equation. Use the Square Roots Property as needed.

27. $2x^2 = 14$

28. $2x^2 = 14x$

29. $4x^2 - 25 = 0$

30. $4x^2 - 25x = 0$

31. $ax^2 - bx = 0$

32. $ax^2 - b = 0$

33. The length of a rectangle is 3 more than its width. If the area of the rectangle is 40, the dimensions x and $x + 3$ can be found by solving the equation $x(x + 3) = 40$. Find these dimensions.

34. To find the length of $\overline{CP}$ (which is x), one must solve the equation

$$x \cdot (x + 5) = (x + 1) \cdot 4$$

Find the length of $\overline{CP}$.

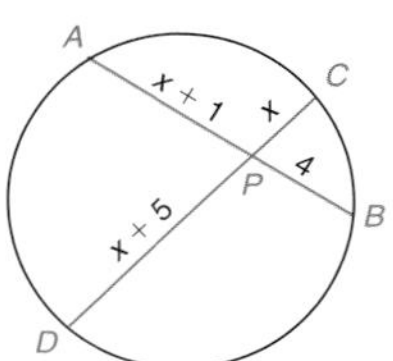

In Exercises 35 and 36, use Theorem 2.5.1 to solve the problem. According to this theorem, the number of diagonals in a polygon of n sides is given by $D = \frac{n(n-3)}{2}$.

35. Find the number of sides in a polygon that has 9 diagonals.

36. Find the number of sides in a polygon that has the same number of diagonals as it has sides.

37. In the right triangle, find c if $a = 3$ and $b = 4$.

(HINT: $c^2 = a^2 + b^2$)

38. In the right triangle, find b if $a = 6$ and $c = 10$.

(HINT: $c^2 = a^2 + b^2$)

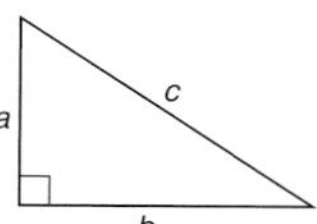

Exercises 37, 38

Appendix B

Summary of Constructions, Postulates, and Theorems and Corollaries

CONSTRUCTIONS

Section 1.2

1. To construct a segment congruent to a given segment.
2. To construct the midpoint M of a given line segment AB.

Section 1.4

3. To construct an angle congruent to a given angle.
4. To construct the angle bisector of a given angle.

Section 1.6

5. To construct the line perpendicular to a given line at a specified point on the given line.

Section 2.1

6. To construct the line that is perpendicular to a given line from a point not on the given line.

Section 2.3

7. To construct the line parallel to a given line from a point not on that line.

Section 6.4

8. To construct a tangent to a circle at a point on the circle.
9. To construct a tangent to a circle from an external point.

POSTULATES

Section 1.3

1. Through two distinct points, there is exactly one line.
2. (Ruler Postulate) The measure of any line segment is a unique positive number.
3. (Segment-Addition Postulate) If X is a point on $\overline{AB}$ and A-X-B, then $AX + XB = AB$.
4. If two lines intersect, they intersect at a point.
5. Through three noncollinear points, there is exactly one plane.
6. If two distinct planes intersect, then their intersection is a line.
7. Given two distinct points in a plane, the line containing these points also lies in the plane.

Section 1.4

8. (Protractor Postulate) The measure of an angle is a unique positive number.
9. (Angle-Addition Postulate) If a point D lies in the interior of angle ABC, then $m\angle ABD + m\angle DBC = m\angle ABC$.

Section 2.1

10. (Parallel Postulate) Through a point not on a line, exactly one line is parallel to the given line.
11. If two parallel lines are cut by a transversal, then the corresponding angles are congruent.

Section 3.1

12. If the three sides of one triangle are congruent to the three sides of a second triangle, then the triangles are congruent (SSS).
13. If two sides and the included angle of one triangle are congruent to two sides and the included angle of a second triangle, then the triangles are congruent (SAS).
14. If two angles and the included side of one triangle are congruent to two angles and the included side of a second triangle, then the triangles are congruent (ASA).

Section 5.2

15. If the three angles of one triangle are congruent to the three angles of a second triangle, then the triangles are similar (AAA).

Section 6.1

16. (Central Angle Postulate) In a circle, the degree measure of a central angle is equal to the degree measure of its intercepted arc.
17. (Arc-Addition Postulate) If $\overset{\frown}{AB}$ and $\overset{\frown}{BC}$ intersect only at point B, then $m\overset{\frown}{AB} + m\overset{\frown}{BC} = m\overset{\frown}{ABC}$.

Section 8.1

18. (Area Postulate) Corresponding to every bounded region is a unique positive number A, known as the area of that region.
19. If two closed plane figures are congruent, then their areas are equal.
20. (Area-Addition Postulate) Let R and S be two enclosed regions that do not overlap. Then $A_{R \cup S} = A_R + A_S$.
21. The area A of a rectangle whose base has length b and whose altitude has length h is given by $A = bh$.

Section 8.4

22. The ratio of the circumference of a circle to the length of its diameter is a unique positive constant.

Section 8.5

23. The ratio of the degree measure m of the arc (or central angle) of a sector to 360° is the same as the ratio of the area of the sector to the area of the circle; that is, $\frac{\text{area of sector}}{\text{area of circle}} = \frac{m}{360°}$.

Section 9.1

24. (Volume Postulate) Corresponding to every solid is a unique positive number V known as the volume of that solid.

25. The volume of a right rectangular prism is given by

$$V = \ell wh$$

where ℓ measures the length, w the width, and h the altitude of the prism.

26. The volume of a right prism is given by

$$V = Bh$$

where B is the area of a base and h is the length of the altitude of the prism.

THEOREMS AND COROLLARIES

1.3.1 The midpoint of a line segment is unique.

1.4.1 There is one and only one angle bisector for a given angle.

1.6.1 If two lines are perpendicular, then they meet to form right angles.

1.6.2 If two lines intersect, then the vertical angles formed are congruent.

1.6.3 In a plane, there is exactly one line perpendicular to a given line at any point on the line.

1.6.4 The perpendicular bisector of a line segment is unique.

1.7.1 If two lines meet to form a right angle, then these lines are perpendicular.

1.7.2 If two angles are complementary to the same angle (or to congruent angles), then these angles are congruent.

1.7.3 If two angles are supplementary to the same angle (or to congruent angles), then these angles are congruent.

1.7.4 Any two right angles are congruent.

1.7.5 If the exterior sides of two adjacent acute angles form perpendicular rays, then these angles are complementary.

1.7.6 If the exterior sides of two adjacent angles form a straight line, then these angles are supplementary.

1.7.7 If two line segments are congruent, then their midpoints separate these segments into four congruent segments.

1.7.8 If two angles are congruent, then their bisectors separate these angles into four congruent angles.

2.1.1 From a point not on a given line, there is exactly one line perpendicular to the given line.

2.1.2 If two parallel lines are cut by a transversal, then the alternate interior angles are congruent.

2.1.3 If two parallel lines are cut by a transversal, then the alternate exterior angles are congruent.

2.1.4 If two parallel lines are cut by a transversal, then the interior angles on the same side of the transversal are supplementary.

2.1.5 If two parallel lines are cut by a transversal, then the exterior angles on the same side of the transversal are supplementary.

2.3.1 If two lines are cut by a transversal so that the corresponding angles are congruent, then these lines are parallel.

2.3.2 If two lines are cut by a transversal so that the alternate interior angles are congruent, then these lines are parallel.

2.3.3 If two lines are cut by a transversal so that the alternate exterior angles are congruent, then these lines are parallel.

2.3.4 If two lines are cut by a transversal so that the interior angles on the same side of the transversal are supplementary, then these lines are parallel.

2.3.5 If two lines are cut by a transversal so that the exterior angles on the same side of the transversal are supplementary, then these lines are parallel.

2.3.6 If two lines are both parallel to a third line, then these lines are parallel to each other.

2.3.7 If two coplanar lines are both perpendicular to a third line, then these lines are parallel to each other.

2.4.1 In a triangle, the sum of the measures of the interior angles is 180°.

2.4.2 Each angle of an equiangular triangle measures 60°.

2.4.3 The acute angles of a right triangle are complementary.

2.4.4 If two angles of one triangle are congruent to two angles of another triangle, then the third angles are also congruent.

2.4.5 The measure of an exterior angle of a triangle equals the sum of the measures of the two nonadjacent interior angles.

2.5.1 The total number of diagonals D in a polygon of n sides is given by the formula $D = \frac{n(n-3)}{2}$.

2.5.2 The sum S of the measures of the interior angles of a polygon with n sides is given by $S = (n - 2) \cdot 180°$. Note that $n > 2$ for any polygon.

2.5.3 The measure I of each interior angle of a regular or equiangular polygon of n sides is $I = \frac{(n-2) \cdot 180°}{n}$.

2.5.4 The sum of the measures of the four interior angles of a quadrilateral is 360°.

2.5.5 The sum of the measures of the exterior angles, one at each vertex, of a polygon is 360°.

2.5.6 The measure E of each exterior angle of a regular or equiangular polygon of n sides is $E = \frac{360°}{n}$.

3.1.1 If two angles and a nonincluded side of one triangle are congruent to two angles and a nonincluded side of a second triangle, then the triangles are congruent (AAS).

3.2.1 If the hypotenuse and a leg of one right triangle are congruent to the hypotenuse and a leg of a second right triangle, then the triangles are congruent (HL).

3.3.1 Corresponding altitudes of congruent triangles are congruent.

3.3.2 The bisector of the vertex angle of an isosceles triangle separates the triangle into two congruent triangles.

3.3.3 If two sides of a triangle are congruent, then the angles opposite these sides are also congruent.

3.3.4 If two angles of a triangle are congruent, then the sides opposite these angles are also congruent.
3.3.5 An equilateral triangle is also equiangular.
3.3.6 An equiangular triangle is also equilateral.
3.5.1 The measure of a line segment is greater than the measure of any of its parts.
3.5.2 The measure of an angle is greater than the measure of any of its parts.
3.5.3 The measure of an exterior angle of a triangle is greater than the measure of either nonadjacent interior angle.
3.5.4 If a triangle contains a right or an obtuse angle, then the measure of this angle is greater than the measure of either of the remaining angles.
3.5.5 (Addition Property of Inequality): If $a > b$ and $c > d$, then $a + c > b + d$.
3.5.6 If one side of a triangle is longer than a second side, then the measure of the angle opposite the first side is greater than the measure of the angle opposite the second side.
3.5.7 If the measure of one angle of a triangle is greater than the measure of a second angle, then the side opposite the larger angle is longer than the side opposite the smaller angle.
3.5.8 The perpendicular line segment from a point to a line is the shortest line segment that can be drawn from the point to the line.
3.5.9 The perpendicular line segment from a point to a plane is the shortest line segment that can be drawn from the point to the plane.
3.5.10 (Triangle Inequality) The sum of the lengths of any two sides of a triangle is greater than the length of the third side.
3.5.10 *(Alternative)* The length of one side of a triangle must be between the sum and the difference of the lengths of the other two sides.
4.1.1 A diagonal of a parallelogram separates it into two congruent triangles.
4.1.2 The opposite angles of a parallelogram are congruent.
4.1.3 The opposite sides of a parallelogram are congruent.
4.1.4 The diagonals of a parallelogram bisect each other.
4.1.5 Two consecutive angles of a parallelogram are supplementary.
4.1.6 Two parallel lines are everywhere equidistant.
4.1.7 If two sides of one triangle are congruent to two sides of a second triangle and the included angle of the first triangle is greater than the included angle of the second, then the length of the side opposite the included angle of the first triangle is greater than the length of the side opposite the included angle of the second.
4.1.8 In a parallelogram with unequal pairs of consecutive angles, the longer diagonal lies opposite the obtuse angle.
4.2.1 If two sides of a quadrilateral are both congruent and parallel, then the quadrilateral is a parallelogram.
4.2.2 If both pairs of opposite sides of a quadrilateral are congruent, then the quadrilateral is a parallelogram.
4.2.3 If the diagonals of a quadrilateral bisect each other, then the quadrilateral is a parallelogram.
4.2.4 In a kite, one pair of opposite angles are congruent.
4.2.5 The segment that joins the midpoints of two sides of a triangle is parallel to the third side and has a length equal to one-half the length of the third side.
4.3.1 All angles of a rectangle are right angles.
4.3.2 The diagonals of a rectangle are congruent.
4.3.3 All sides of a square are congruent.
4.3.4 All sides of a rhombus are congruent.
4.3.5 The diagonals of a rhombus are perpendicular.
4.4.1 The base angles of an isosceles trapezoid are congruent.
4.4.2 The diagonals of an isosceles trapezoid are congruent.
4.4.3 The length of the median of a trapezoid equals one-half the sum of the lengths of the two bases.
4.4.4 The median of a trapezoid is parallel to each base.
4.4.5 If two base angles of a trapezoid are congruent, the trapezoid is an isosceles trapezoid.
4.4.6 If the diagonals of a trapezoid are congruent, the trapezoid is an isosceles trapezoid.
4.4.7 If three (or more) parallel lines intercept congruent segments on one transversal, then they intercept congruent segments on any transversal.
5.3.1 If two angles of one triangle are congruent to two angles of another triangle, then the triangles are similar (AA).
5.3.2 The lengths of the corresponding altitudes of similar triangles have the same ratio as the lengths of any pair of corresponding sides.
5.3.3 If an angle of one triangle is congruent to an angle of a second triangle and the pairs of sides including these angles are proportional (in length), then the triangles are similar (SAS~).
5.3.4 If the three sides of one triangle are proportional (in length) to the three corresponding sides of a second triangle, then the triangles are similar (SSS~).
5.3.5 If a line segment divides two sides of a triangle proportionally, then it is parallel to the third side.
5.4.1 The altitude drawn to the hypotenuse of a right triangle separates the right triangle into two right triangles that are similar to each other and to the original right triangle.
5.4.2 The length of the altitude to the hypotenuse of a right triangle is the geometric mean of the lengths of the segments of the hypotenuse.
5.4.3 The length of each leg of a right triangle is the geometric mean of the length of the hypotenuse and the length of the segment of the hypotenuse adjacent to that leg.
5.4.4 (Pythagorean Theorem) The square of the length of the hypotenuse of a right triangle is equal to the sum of the squares of the lengths of the legs.
5.4.5 (Converse of Pythagorean Theorem) If a, b, and c are the lengths of the three sides of a triangle, with c the

length of the longest side, and if $c^2 = a^2 + b^2$, then the triangle is a right triangle with the right angle opposite the side of length c.

5.4.6 If the hypotenuse and a leg of one right triangle are congruent to the hypotenuse and a leg of a second right triangle, then the triangles are congruent (HL).

5.4.7 Let a, b, and c represent the lengths of the three sides of a triangle, with c the length of the longest side.
1. If $c^2 > a^2 + b^2$, then the triangle is obtuse and the obtuse angle lies opposite the side of length c.
2. If $c^2 < a^2 + b^2$, then the triangle is acute.

5.5.1 (45-45-90 Theorem) In a triangle whose angles measure 45°, 45°, and 90°, the hypotenuse has a length equal to the product of $\sqrt{2}$ and the length of either leg.

5.5.2 (30-60-90 Theorem) In a triangle whose angles measure 30°, 60°, and 90°, the hypotenuse has a length equal to twice the length of the shorter leg, and the length of the longer leg is the product of $\sqrt{3}$ and the length of the shorter leg.

5.5.3 If the length of the hypotenuse of a right triangle equals the product of $\sqrt{2}$ and the length of either leg, then the angles of the triangle measure 45°, 45°, and 90°.

5.5.4 If the length of the hypotenuse of a right triangle is twice the length of one leg of the triangle, then the angle of the triangle opposite that leg measures 30°.

5.6.1 If a line is parallel to one side of a triangle and intersects the other two sides, then it divides these sides proportionally.

5.6.2 When three (or more) parallel lines are cut by a pair of transversals, the transversals are divided proportionally by the parallel lines.

5.6.3 (The Angle-Bisector Theorem) If a ray bisects one angle of a triangle, then it divides the opposite side into segments whose lengths are proportional to the two sides that form the bisected angle.

5.6.4 (Ceva's Theorem) Let D be any point in the interior of $\triangle ABC$ and let $\overline{BE}$, $\overline{AF}$, and $\overline{CG}$ be determined by D and the vertices of $\triangle ABC$. Then the product of the ratios of lengths of segments of the sides (taken in order) equals 1; that is, $\frac{AG}{GB} \cdot \frac{BF}{FC} \cdot \frac{CE}{EA} = 1$.

6.1.1 A radius that is perpendicular to a chord bisects the chord.

6.1.2 The measure of an inscribed angle of a circle is one-half the measure of its intercepted arc.

6.1.3 In a circle (or in congruent circles), congruent minor arcs have congruent central angles.

6.1.4 In a circle (or in congruent circles), congruent central angles have congruent arcs.

6.1.5 In a circle (or in congruent circles), congruent chords have congruent minor (major) arcs.

6.1.6 In a circle (or in congruent circles), congruent arcs have congruent chords.

6.1.7 Chords that are at the same distance from the center of a circle are congruent.

6.1.8 Congruent chords are located at the same distance from the center of a circle.

6.1.9 An angle inscribed in a semicircle is a right angle.

6.1.10 If two inscribed angles intercept the same arc, then these angles are congruent.

6.2.1 If a quadrilateral is inscribed in a circle, the opposite angles are supplementary.
(Alternative) The opposite angles of a cyclic quadrilateral are supplementary.

6.2.2 The measure of an angle formed by two chords that intersect within a circle is one-half the sum of the measures of the arcs intercepted by the angle and its vertical angle.

6.2.3 The radius (or any other line through the center of a circle) drawn to a tangent at the point of tangency is perpendicular to the tangent at that point.

6.2.4 The measure of an angle formed by a tangent and a chord drawn to the point of tangency is one-half the measure of the intercepted arc.

6.2.5 The measure of an angle formed when two secants intersect at a point outside the circle is one-half the difference of the measures of the two intercepted arcs.

6.2.6 If an angle is formed by a secant and tangent that intersect in the exterior of a circle, then the measure of the angle is one-half the difference of the measures of its intercepted arcs.

6.2.7 If an angle is formed by two intersecting tangents, then the measure of the angle is one-half the difference of the measures of the intercepted arcs.

6.2.8 If two parallel lines intersect a circle, the intercepted arcs between these lines are congruent.

6.3.1 If a line is drawn through the center of a circle perpendicular to a chord, then it bisects the chord and its arc.

6.3.2 If a line through the center of a circle bisects a chord other than a diameter, then it is perpendicular to the chord.

6.3.3 The perpendicular bisector of a chord contains the center of the circle.

6.3.4 The tangent segments to a circle from an external point are congruent.

6.3.5 If two chords intersect within a circle, then the product of the lengths of the segments (parts) of one chord is equal to the product of the lengths of the segments of the other chord.

6.3.6 If two secant segments are drawn to a circle from an external point, then the products of the lengths of each secant with its external segment are equal.

6.3.7 If a tangent segment and a secant segment are drawn to a circle from an external point, then the square of the length of the tangent equals the product of the length of the secant with the length of its external segment.

6.4.1 The line that is perpendicular to the radius of a circle at its endpoint on the circle is a tangent to the circle.

6.4.2 In a circle (or in congruent circles) containing two unequal central angles, the larger angle corresponds to the larger intercepted arc.

6.4.3 In a circle (or in congruent circles) containing two unequal arcs, the larger arc corresponds to the larger central angle.

6.4.4 In a circle (or in congruent circles) containing two unequal chords, the shorter chord is at the greater distance from the center of the circle.

6.4.5 In a circle (or in congruent circles) containing two unequal chords, the chord nearer the center of the circle has the greater length.

6.4.6 In a circle (or in congruent circles) containing two unequal chords, the longer chord corresponds to the greater minor arc.

6.4.7 In a circle (or in congruent circles) containing two unequal minor arcs, the greater minor arc corresponds to the longer of the chords related to these arcs.

7.1.1 The locus of points in a plane and equidistant from the sides of an angle is the angle bisector.

7.1.2 The locus of points in a plane that are equidistant from the endpoints of a line segment is the perpendicular bisector of that line segment.

7.2.1 The three angle bisectors of the angles of a triangle are concurrent.

7.2.2 The three perpendicular bisectors of the sides of a triangle are concurrent.

7.2.3 The three altitudes of a triangle are concurrent.

7.2.4 The three medians of a triangle are concurrent at a point that is two-thirds the distance from any vertex to the midpoint of the opposite side.

7.3.1 A circle can be circumscribed about (or inscribed in) any regular polygon.

7.3.2 The measure of the central angle of a regular polygon of n sides is given by $c = \frac{360}{n}$.

7.3.3 Any radius of a regular polygon bisects the angle at the vertex to which it is drawn.

7.3.4 Any apothem of a regular polygon bisects the side of the polygon to which it is drawn.

8.1.1 The area A of a square whose sides are each of length s is given by $A = s^2$.

8.1.2 The area A of a parallelogram with a base of length b and with corresponding altitude of length h is given by

$$A = bh$$

8.1.3 The area A of a triangle whose base has length b and whose corresponding altitude has length h is given by

$$A = \frac{1}{2}bh$$

8.1.4 The area A of a right triangle with legs of lengths a and b is given $A = \frac{1}{2}ab$.

8.2.1 (Heron's Formula) If the three sides of a triangle have lengths a, b, and c, then the area A of the triangle is given by

$$A = \sqrt{s(s - a)(s - b)(s - c)}$$

where the semiperimeter of the triangle is

$$s = \frac{1}{2}(a + b + c)$$

8.2.2 (Brahmagupta's Formula) For a cyclic quadrilateral with sides of lengths a, b, c, and d, the area A is given by

$$A = \sqrt{(s - a)(s - b)(s - c)(s - d)}$$

where the semiperimeter of the quadrilateral is

$$s = \frac{1}{2}(a + b + c + d)$$

8.2.3 The area A of a trapezoid whose bases have lengths b_1 and b_2 and whose altitude has length h is given by

$$A = \frac{1}{2}h(b_1 + b_2)$$

8.2.4 The area A of any quadrilateral with perpendicular diagonals of lengths d_1 and d_2 is given by

$$A = \frac{1}{2}d_1d_2$$

8.2.5 The area A of a rhombus whose diagonals have lengths d_1 and d_2 is given by

$$A = \frac{1}{2}d_1d_2$$

8.2.6 The area A of a kite whose diagonals have lengths d_1 and d_2 is given by

$$A = \frac{1}{2}d_1d_2$$

8.2.7 The ratio of the areas of two similar triangles equals the square of the ratio of the lengths of any two corresponding sides; that is,

$$\frac{A_1}{A_2} = \left(\frac{a_1}{a_2}\right)^2$$

8.3.1 The area A of a regular polygon whose apothem has length a and whose perimeter is P is given by

$$A = \frac{1}{2}aP$$

8.4.1 The circumference C of a circle is given by the formula

$$C = \pi d \quad \text{or} \quad C = 2\pi r$$

8.4.2 In a circle whose circumference is C, the length ℓ of an arc whose degree measure is m is given by

$$\ell = \frac{m}{360} \cdot C$$

8.4.3 The area A of a circle whose radius has length r is given by $A = \pi r^2$.

8.5.1 In a circle of radius length r, the area A of a sector whose arc has degree measure m is given by

$$A = \frac{m}{360} \pi r^2$$

8.5.2 The area of a semicircular region of radius length r is $A = \frac{1}{2}\pi r^2$.

8.5.3 Where P represents the perimeter of a triangle and r represents the length of the radius of its inscribed circle, the area A of the triangle is given by

$$A = \frac{1}{2} rP$$

9.1.1 The lateral area L of any prism whose altitude has measure h and whose base has perimeter P is given by $L = hP$.

9.1.2 The total area T of any prism with lateral area L and base area B is given by $T = L + 2B$.

9.2.1 In a regular pyramid, the length a of the apothem of the base, the altitude h, and the slant height ℓ satisfy the Pythagorean Theorem; that is, $\ell^2 = a^2 + h^2$ in every regular pyramid.

9.2.2 The lateral area L of a regular pyramid with slant height of length ℓ and perimeter P of the base is given by

$$L = \frac{1}{2} \ell P$$

9.2.3 The total area (surface area) T of a pyramid with lateral area L and base area B is given by $T = L + B$.

9.2.4 The volume V of a pyramid having a base area B and an altitude of length h is given by

$$V = \frac{1}{3} Bh$$

9.2.5 In a regular pyramid, the lengths of altitude h, radius r of the base, and lateral edge e satisfy the Pythagorean Theorem; that is, $e^2 = h^2 + r^2$.

9.3.1 The lateral area L of a right circular cylinder with altitude of length h and circumference C of the base is given by $L = hC$.
(Alternative) Where r is the length of the radius of the base, $L = 2\pi rh$.

9.3.2 The total area T of a right circular cylinder with base area B and lateral area L is given by $T = L + 2B$.
(Alternative) Where r is the length of the radius of the base and h is the length of the altitude, $T = 2\pi rh + 2\pi r^2$.

9.3.3 The volume V of a right circular cylinder with base area B and altitude of length h is given by $V = Bh$.
(Alternative) Where r is the length of the radius of the base, $V = \pi r^2 h$.

9.3.4 The lateral area L of a right circular cone with slant height of length ℓ and circumference C of the base is given by $L = \frac{1}{2}\ell C$.
(Alternative) Where r is the length of the radius of the base, $L = \pi r \ell$.

9.3.5 The total area T of a right circular cone with base area B and lateral area L is given by $T = B + L$.
(Alternative) Where r is the length of the radius of the base and ℓ is the length of the slant height, the total area is $T = \pi r^2 + \pi r \ell$.

9.3.6 In a right circular cone, the lengths of the radius r (of the base), the altitude h, and the slant height ℓ satisfy the Pythagorean Theorem; that is, $\ell^2 = r^2 + h^2$ in every right circular cone.

9.3.7 The volume V of a right circular cone with base area B and altitude of length h is given by $V = \frac{1}{3}Bh$.
(Alternative) Where r is the length of the radius of the base, $V = \frac{1}{3}\pi r^2 h$.

9.4.1 (Euler's Equation) The number of vertices V, the number of edges E, and the number of faces F of a polyhedron are related by the equation $V + F = E + 2$.

9.4.2 The surface area S of a sphere whose radius has length r is given by $S = 4\pi r^2$.

9.4.3 The volume V of a sphere with radius of length r is given by $V = \frac{4}{3}\pi r^3$.

10.1.1 (Distance Formula) The distance d between two points (x_1, y_1) and (x_2, y_2) is given by the formula

$$d = \sqrt{(x_2 - x_1)^2 + (y_2 - y_1)^2}$$

10.1.2 (Midpoint Formula) The midpoint M of the line segment joining (x_1, y_1) and (x_2, y_2) has coordinates x_M and y_M, where

$$(x_M, y_M) = \left(\frac{x_1 + x_2}{2}, \frac{y_1 + y_2}{2}\right)$$

That is, $M = \left(\frac{x_1 + x_2}{2}, \frac{y_1 + y_2}{2}\right)$

10.2.1 If two nonvertical lines are parallel, then their slopes are equal.
(Alternative) If $\ell_1 \parallel \ell_2$, then $m_1 = m_2$

10.2.2 If two lines (neither horizontal nor vertical) are perpendicular, then the product of their slopes is -1.
(Alternative) If $\ell_1 \perp \ell_2$, then $m_1 \cdot m_2 = -1$

10.4.1 The line segment determined by the midpoints of two sides of a triangle is parallel to the third side.

10.4.2 The diagonals of a parallelogram bisect each other.

10.4.3 The diagonals of a rhombus are perpendicular.

10.4.4 If the diagonals of a parallelogram are equal in length, then the parallelogram is a rectangle.

10.5.1 (Slope-Intercept Form of a Line) The line whose slope is m and whose y intercept is b has the equation $y = mx + b$.

10.5.2 (Point-Slope Form of a Line) The line that has slope m and contains the point (x_1, y_1) has the equation

$$y - y_1 = m(x - x_1)$$

10.5.3 The three medians of a triangle are concurrent at a point that is two-thirds the distance from any vertex to the midpoint of the opposite side.

11.2.1 In any right triangle in which α is the measure of an acute angle,

$$\sin^2\alpha + \cos^2\alpha = 1$$

11.4.1 The area of any acute triangle equals one-half the product of the lengths of two sides and the sine of the included angle. That is,

$$A = \tfrac{1}{2}ab \sin \gamma$$
$$A = \tfrac{1}{2}ac \sin \beta$$
$$A = \tfrac{1}{2}bc \sin \alpha$$

11.4.2 (Law of Sines) In any acute triangle, the three ratios between the sines of the angles and the lengths of the opposite sides are equal. That is,

$$\frac{\sin \alpha}{a} = \frac{\sin \beta}{b} = \frac{\sin \gamma}{c}$$

11.4.3 (Law of Cosines) In acute triangle ABC,

$$c^2 = a^2 + b^2 - 2ab \cos \gamma$$
$$b^2 = a^2 + c^2 - 2ac \cos \beta$$
$$a^2 = b^2 + c^2 - 2bc \cos \alpha$$

or

$$\cos \alpha = \frac{b^2 + c^2 - a^2}{2bc}$$
$$\cos \beta = \frac{a^2 + c^2 - b^2}{2ac}$$
$$\cos \gamma = \frac{a^2 + b^2 - c^2}{2ab}$$

Answers

Selected Exercises and Proofs

CHAPTER 1

1.1 Exercises

1. (a) Not a statement (b) Statement; true (c) Statement; true (d) Statement; false **3.** (a) Christopher Columbus did not cross the Atlantic Ocean. (b) Some jokes are not funny. **5.** Conditional **7.** Simple **9.** Simple **11.** H: You go to the game. C: You will have a great time. **13.** H: The diagonals of a parallelogram are perpendicular. C: The parallelogram is a rhombus. **15.** H: Two parallel lines are cut by a transversal. C: Corresponding angles are congruent. **17.** First write the statement in "If, then" form: If a figure is a square, then it is a rectangle. H: A figure is a square. C: It is a rectangle. **19.** True **21.** True **23.** False **25.** Induction **27.** Deduction **29.** Intuition **31.** None **33.** Angle 1 looks equal in measure to angle 2. **35.** The three angles in one triangle are equal in measure to the corresponding three angles in the other triangle. **37.** *A Prisoner of Society* might be nominated for an Academy Award. **39.** The instructor is a math teacher. **41.** Angles 1 and 2 are complementary. **43.** Alex has a strange sense of humor. **45.** None **47.** June Jesse will be in the public eye. **49.** Marilyn is a happy person. **51.** Valid **53.** Not valid **55.** (a) True (b) True (c) False

1.2 Exercises

1. $AB < CD$ **3.** Two; one **5.** One; none **7.** $\angle ABC$, $\angle ABD$, $\angle DBC$ **9.** Yes; no; yes **11.** $\angle ABC$, $\angle CBA$ **13.** Yes; no **15.** a, d **17.** (a) 3 (b) $2\frac{1}{2}$ **19.** (a) 40° (b) 50° **21.** Congruent; congruent **23.** Equal **25.** No **27.** Yes **29.** Congruent **31.** $\overline{MN}$ and $\overline{QP}$ **33.** $\overline{AB}$ **35.** 22 **37.** $x = 9$ **39.** 124° **41.** 71° **43.** $x = 23$ **45.** 10.9 **47.** $x = 102$; $y = 78$ **49.** N 22° E

1.3 Exercises

1. AC **3.** 75 in. **5.** 1.64 ft **7.** 3 mi **9.** (a) A-C-D (b) A, B, C or B, C, D or A, B, D **11.** $\overleftrightarrow{CD}$ means line CD; $\overline{CD}$ means segment CD; CD means the measure or length of $\overline{CD}$; $\overrightarrow{CD}$ means ray CD with endpoint C. **13.** (a) m and t (b) m and $\overleftrightarrow{AD}$ or $\overleftrightarrow{AD}$ and t **15.** $x = 3$; $AM = 7$ **17.** $x = 7$; $AB = 38$ **19.** (a) $\overrightarrow{OA}$ and $\overrightarrow{OD}$ (b) $\overrightarrow{OA}$ and $\overrightarrow{OB}$ (There are other possible answers.) **23.** Planes M and N intersect at $\overleftrightarrow{AB}$. **25.** A **27.** (a) C (b) C (c) H **33.** (a) No (b) Yes (c) No (d) Yes **35.** Six **37.** Nothing **39.** $\frac{1}{3}a + \frac{1}{2}b$ or $\frac{2a + 3b}{6}$

1.4 Exercises

1. (a) Acute (b) Right (c) Obtuse **3.** (a) Complementary (b) Supplementary **5.** Adjacent angles **7.** Complementary angles (also adjacent) **9.** Yes; no **11.** (a) Obtuse (b) Straight (c) Acute (d) Obtuse **13.** $m\angle FAC + m\angle CAD = 180$; $\angle FAC$ and $\angle CAD$ are supplementary. **15.** (a) $x + y = 90$ (b) $x = y$ **17.** 42° **19.** $x = 20$; $m\angle RSV = 56°$ **21.** $x = 60$; $m\angle RST = 30°$ **23.** $x = 24$; $y = 8$ **25.** $\angle CAB \cong \angle DAB$ **27.** Angles measure 128° and 52°. **29.** (a) $(180 - x)°$ (b) $(192 - 3x)°$ (c) $(180 - 2x - 5y)°$ **31.** $x = 143$ **37.** It appears that the angle bisectors meet at one point. **39.** It appears that the two sides opposite $\angle$s A and B are congruent. **41.** (a) 90° (b) 90° (c) Equal **43.** $x = 15$; $z = 3$ **45.** 135°

1.5 Exercises

1. Division (or Multiplication) Prop. of Equality **3.** Subtraction Prop. of Equality **5.** Multiplication Prop. of Equality **7.** If 2 $\angle$s are supp., the sum of their measures is 180°. **9.** Angle-Addition Postulate **11.** $AM + MB = AB$ **13.** $\overrightarrow{EG}$ bisects $\angle DEF$. **15.** $m\angle 1 + m\angle 2 = 90°$ **17.** $2x = 10$ **19.** $7x + 2 = 30$ **21.** $6x - 3 = 27$ **23.** 1. Given 2. Distributive Prop. 3. Addition Prop. of Equality 4. Division Prop. of Equality **25.** 1. $2(x + 3) - 7 = 11$ 2. $2x + 6 - 7 = 11$ 3. $2x - 1 = 11$ 4. $2x = 12$ 5. $x = 6$ **27.** 1. Given 2. Segment-Addition Postulate 3. Subtraction Prop. of Equality **29.** 1. Given 2. Definition of angle bisector 3. Angle-Addition Postulate 4. Substitution 5. Substitution (Distribution) 6. Multiplication Prop. of Equality **31.** S1. M-N-P-Q on $\overline{MQ}$ R1. Given 2. Segment-Addition Postulate 3. Segment-Addition Postulate 4. $MN + NP + PQ = MQ$ **33.** $5(x + y)$ **35.** $(-7)(-2) > 5(-2)$ or $14 > -10$ **37.** R1 Given R2 Add. Prop. of Eq. R3 Given R4 Substitution

1.6 Exercises

1. 1. Given 2. If two $\angle$s are $\cong$, then they are equal in measure. 3. Angle-Addition Postulate 4. Addition Property of Equality 5. Substitution 6. If two $\angle$s are equal in measure, then they are $\cong$. **3.** 1. $\angle 1 \cong \angle 2$ and $\angle 2 \cong \angle 3$ 2. $\angle 1 \cong \angle 3$ **11.** 1. Given 3. Substitution 4. $m\angle 1 = m\angle 2$ 5. $\angle 1 \cong \angle 2$ **13.** No; yes; no **15.** No; yes; no **17.** No; yes; yes **19.** (a) Perpendicular (b) Angles(c) Supplementary (d) Right (e) Measure of angle 1

21. (a) Adjacent (b) Complementary (c) Ray AB (d) Is congruent to (e) Vertical

23.

PROOF	
Statements	**Reasons**
1. M-N-P-Q on $\overline{MQ}$	1. Given
2. $MN + NQ = MQ$	2. Segment-Addition Postulate
3. $NP + PQ = NQ$	3. Segment-Addition Postulate
4. $MN + NP + PQ = MQ$	4. Substitution

25.

PROOF	
Statements	**Reasons**
1. $\angle TSW$ with $\overrightarrow{SU}$ and $\overrightarrow{SV}$	1. Given
2. $m\angle TSW = m\angle TSU + m\angle USW$	2. Angle-Addition Postulate
3. $m\angle USW = m\angle USV + m\angle VSW$	3. Angle-Addition Postulate
4. $m\angle TSW = m\angle TSU + m\angle USV + m\angle VSW$	4. Substitution

27. In space, there are an infinite number of lines that perpendicularly bisect a given line segment at its midpoint.

1.7 Exercises

1. H: A line segment is bisected. C: Each of the equal segments has half the length of the original segment.
3. First write the statement in "If, then" form. If a figure is a square, then it is a quadrilateral. H: A figure is a square. C: It is a quadrilateral. **5.** H: Each angle is a right angle. C: Two angles are congruent. **7.** Statement, Drawing, Given, Prove, Proof **9.** (a) Given (b) Prove

11. *Given:* $\overleftrightarrow{AB} \perp \overleftrightarrow{CD}$
Prove: $\angle AEC$ is a right angle

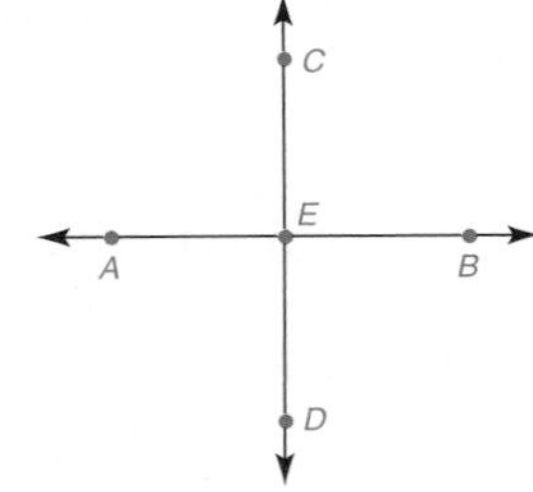

13. *Given:* $\angle 1$ is comp. to $\angle 3$; $\angle 2$ is comp. to $\angle 3$
Prove: $\angle 1 \cong \angle 2$

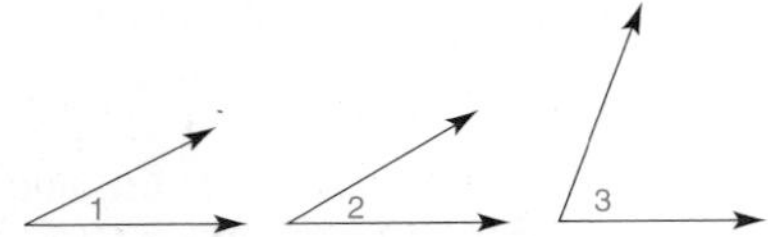

15. *Given:* Lines ℓ and m intersect as shown
Prove: $\angle 1 \cong \angle 2$ and $\angle 3 \cong \angle 4$

17. $m\angle 2 = 55°$; $m\angle 3 = 125°$; $m\angle 4 = 55°$ **19.** $x = 40$; $m\angle 1 = 130°$
21. $x = 60$; $m\angle 1 = 120°$ **23.** $x = 180$; $m\angle 2 = 80°$
25. 1. Given 2. If two $\angle$s are complementary, the sum of their measures is 90. 3. Substitution 4. Subtraction Property of Equality 5. If two $\angle$s are equal in measure, then they are $\cong$. **29.** 1. Given 2. $\angle ABC$ is a right $\angle$. 3. The measure of a rt. $\angle = 90$. 4. Angle-Addition Postulate 6. $\angle 1$ is comp. to $\angle 2$.

1.7 Selected Proof

31.

PROOF	
Statements	**Reasons**
1. $\angle ABC \cong \angle EFG$	1. Given
2. $m\angle ABC = m\angle EFG$	2. If two $\angle$s are $\cong$, their measures are $=$
3. $m\angle ABC = m\angle 1 + m\angle 2$ $m\angle EFG = m\angle 3 + m\angle 4$	3. Angle-Addition Postulate
4. $m\angle 1 + m\angle 2 = m\angle 3 + m\angle 4$	4. Substitution
5. $\overrightarrow{BD}$ bisects $\angle ABC$ $\overrightarrow{FH}$ bisects $\angle EFG$	5. Given
6. $m\angle 1 = m\angle 2$ and $m\angle 3 = m\angle 4$	6. If a ray bisects an $\angle$, then two $\angle$s of equal measure are formed
7. $m\angle 1 + m\angle 1 = m\angle 3 + m\angle 3$ or $2 \cdot m\angle 1 = 2 \cdot m\angle 3$	7. Substitution
8. $m\angle 1 = m\angle 3$	8. Division Prop. of Equality
9. $m\angle 1 = m\angle 2 = m\angle 3 = m\angle 4$	9. Substitution (or Transitive)
10. $\angle 1 \cong \angle 2 \cong \angle 3 \cong \angle 4$	10. If $\angle$s are $=$ in measure, then they are $\cong$

CHAPTER 1 REVIEW EXERCISES

1. Undefined terms, defined terms, axioms or postulates, theorems **2.** Induction, deduction, intuition **3.** 1. Names the term being defined 2. Places the term into a set or category 3. Distinguishes the term from other terms in the same category 4. Reversible **4.** Intuition **5.** Induction **6.** Deduction
7. H: The diagonals of a trapezoid are equal in length. C: The trapezoid is isosceles. **8.** H: The parallelogram is a rectangle. C: The diagonals of a parallelogram are congruent.

9. No conclusion **10.** Jody Smithers has a college degree. **11.** Angle A is a right angle. **12.** C **13.** $\angle RST$; $\angle S$; greater than 90° **14.** Perpendicular **18.** (a) Obtuse (b) Right **19.** (a) Acute (b) Reflex **20.** 98° **21.** 47° **22.** 22 **23.** 17 **24.** 34 **25.** 152° **26.** 39° **27.** (a) Point M (b) $\angle JMH$ (c) $\overrightarrow{MJ}$ (d) $\overleftrightarrow{KH}$ **28.** $67\frac{1}{2}°$ **29.** 28° and 152° **30.** (a) $6x + 8$ (b) $x = 4$ (c) 11; 10; 11 **31.** The measure of angle 3 is less than 50°. **32.** 10 pegs **33.** S **34.** S **35.** A **36.** S **37.** N **38.** 2. $\angle 4 \cong \angle P$ 3. $\angle 1 \cong \angle 4$ 4. If two $\angle$s are $\cong$, then their measures are =. 5. Given 6. $m\angle 2 = m\angle 3$ 7. $m\angle 1 + m\angle 2 = m\angle 4 + m\angle 3$ 8. Angle-Addition Postulate 9. Substitution 10. $\angle TVP \cong \angle MVP$ **52.** 270°

CHAPTER 1 REVIEW EXERCISES SELECTED PROOFS

39.

PROOF

Statements	Reasons
1. $\overline{KF} \perp \overline{FH}$	1. Given
2. $\angle KFH$ is a rt. $\angle$	2. If two segments are $\perp$, then they form a rt. $\angle$
3. $\angle JHF$ is a rt. $\angle$	3. Given
4. $\angle KFH \cong \angle JHF$	4. Any two rt. $\angle$s are $\cong$

40.

PROOF

Statements	Reasons
1. $\overline{KH} \cong \overline{FJ}$ G is the midpoint of both $\overline{KH}$ and $\overline{FJ}$	1. Given
2. $\overline{KG} \cong \overline{GJ}$	2. If two segments are $\cong$, then their midpoints separate these segments into four $\cong$ segments

41.

PROOF

Statements	Reasons
1. $\overline{KF} \perp \overline{FH}$	1. Given
2. $\angle KFJ$ is comp. to $\angle JFH$	2. If the exterior sides of two adjacent $\angle$s form $\perp$ rays, then these $\angle$s are comp.

42.

PROOF

Statements	Reasons
1. $\angle 1$ is comp. to $\angle M$	1. Given
2. $\angle 2$ is comp. to $\angle M$	2. Given
3. $\angle 1 \cong \angle 2$	3. If two $\angle$s are comp. to the same $\angle$, then these angles are $\cong$

43.

PROOF

Statements	Reasons
1. $\angle MOP \cong \angle MPO$	1. Given
2. $\overrightarrow{OR}$ bisects $\angle MOP$; $\overrightarrow{PR}$ bisects $\angle MPO$	2. Given
3. $\angle 1 \cong \angle 2$	3. If two $\angle$s are $\cong$, then their bisectors separate these $\angle$s into four $\cong$ $\angle$s

44.

PROOF

Statements	Reasons
1. $\angle 4 \cong \angle 6$	1. Given
2. $\angle 4 \cong \angle 5$	2. If two angles are vertical $\angle$s, then they are $\cong$
3. $\angle 5 \cong \angle 6$	3. Transitive Property

45.

PROOF

Statements	Reasons
1. Figure as shown	1. Given
2. $\angle 4$ is supp. to $\angle 2$	2. If the exterior sides of two adjacent $\angle$s form a line, then the $\angle$s are supp.

46.

PROOF

Statements	Reasons
1. $\angle 3$ is supp. to $\angle 5$ $\angle 4$ is supp. to $\angle 6$	1. Given
2. $\angle 4 \cong \angle 5$	2. If two lines intersect, the vertical angles formed are $\cong$
3. $\angle 3 \cong \angle 6$	3. If two $\angle$s are supp. to congruent angles, then these angles are $\cong$

Chapter 1 Test

1. Induction [1.1] **2.** $\angle CBA$ or $\angle B$ [1.4] **3.** $AP + PB = AB$ [1.3] **4.** (a) Point (b) Line [1.3] **5.** (a) Right (b) Obtuse [1.4] **6.** (a) Supplementary (b) Congruent [1.4] **7.** $m\angle MNP = m\angle PNQ$ [1.4] **8.** (a) Right (b) Supplementary [1.7] **9.** Kianna will develop reasoning skills. [1.1] **10.** 10.4 in. [1.2] **11.** (a) 11 (b) 16 [1.3] **12.** 35° [1.4] **13.** (a) 24° (b) 45° [1.4] **14.** (a) 137° (b) 43° [1.4] **15.** (a) 25° (b) 47° [1.7] **16.** (a) 23° (b) 137° [1.7] **17.** $x + y = 90$ [1.4] **20.** 1. Given 2. Segment-Addition Postulate 3. Segment-Addition Postulate 4. Substitution [1.5] **21.** 1. $2x - 3 = 17$ 2. $2x = 20$ 3. $x = 10$ [1.5] **22.** 1. Given 2. 90° 3. Angle-Addition Postulate 4. 90° 5. Given 6. Definition of Angle-Bisector 7. Substitution 8. $m\angle 1 = 45°$ [1.7] **23.** 108° [1.4]

CHAPTER 2

2.1 Exercises

1. (a) 108° (b) 72° **3.** (a) 68.3° (b) 68.3° **5.** (a) No (b) Yes (c) Yes **7.** Angle 9 appears to be a right angle. **9.** (a) $m\angle 3 = 87°$ (b) $m\angle 6 = 87°$ (c) $m\angle 1 = 93°$ (d) $m\angle 7 = 87°$ **11.** (a) $\angle 5$ (b) $\angle 5$ (c) $\angle 8$ (d) $\angle 5$ **13.** (a) $m\angle 2 = 68°$ (b) $m\angle 4 = 112°$ (c) $m\angle 5 = 112°$ (d) $m\angle MOQ = 34°$ **15.** $x = 10$; $m\angle 4 = 110°$ **17.** $x = 12$; $y = 4$; $m\angle 7 = 76°$ **19.** 1. Given 2. If two parallel lines are cut by a transversal, then the corresponding angles are ≅ 3. If two lines intersect, then the vertical angles are ≅ 4. $\angle 3 \cong \angle 4$ 5. $\angle 1 \cong \angle 4$ **25.** 93° **27.** (a) $\angle 4 \cong \angle 2$ and $\angle 5 \cong \angle 3$ (b) 180° (c) 180° **31.** No

2.1 Selected Proof

21.

PROOF

Statements	Reasons
1. $\overleftrightarrow{CE} \parallel \overleftrightarrow{DF}$; transversal $\overleftrightarrow{AB}$	1. Given
2. $\angle ACE \cong \angle ADF$	2. If two ∥ lines are cut by a transversal, then the corresponding ∠s are ≅
3. $\overrightarrow{CX}$ bisects $\angle ACE$ $\overrightarrow{DE}$ bisects $\angle CDF$	3. Given
4. $\angle 1 \cong \angle 3$	4. If two ∠s are ≅, then their bisectors separate these ∠s into four ≅ ∠s

2.2 Exercises

1. *Converse:* If Juan is rich, then he won the state lottery. FALSE.
Inverse: If Juan does not win the state lottery, then he will not be rich. FALSE.
Contrapositive: If Juan is not rich, then he did not win the state lottery. TRUE.

3. *Converse:* If two angles are complementary, then the sum of their measures is 90°. TRUE.
Inverse: If the sum of the measures of two angles is not 90°, then the two angles are not complementary. TRUE.
Contrapositive: If two angles are not complementary, then the sum of their measures is not 90°. TRUE.
5. No conclusion **7.** $x = 5$ **9.** (a), (b), and (e) **11.** If $\angle A$ and $\angle B$ are vertical angles, then $\angle A$ and $\angle B$ are congruent. **13.** If a triangle is equilateral, then all sides of the triangle are congruent. **15.** The areas of $\triangle ABC$ and $\triangle DEF$ are equal. **17.** Parallel

2.2 Selected Proofs

19. Assume that $r \parallel s$. Then $\angle 1 \cong \angle 5$ because they are corresponding angles. But it is given that $\angle 1 \not\cong \angle 5$, which leads to a contradiction. Thus, the assumption that $r \parallel s$ is false and it follows that $r \nparallel s$. **21.** Assume that $\overrightarrow{FH} \perp \overleftrightarrow{EG}$. Then $\angle 3 \cong \angle 4$ and $m\angle 3 = m\angle 4$. But it is given that $m\angle 3 > m\angle 4$, which leads to a contradiction. Then the assumption that $\overrightarrow{FH} \perp \overleftrightarrow{EG}$ must be false and it follows that $\overrightarrow{FH}$ is not perpendicular to $\overleftrightarrow{EG}$. **23.** Assume that the angles are vertical angles. If they are vertical angles, then they are congruent. But this contradicts the hypothesis that the two angles are not congruent. Hence, our assumption must be false, and the angles are not vertical angles.
27. If M is a midpoint of $\overline{AB}$, then $AM = \frac{1}{2}(AB)$. Assume that N is also a midpoint of $\overline{AB}$ so that $AN = \frac{1}{2}(AB)$. By substitution, $AM = AN$. By the Segment-Addition Postulate, $AM = AN + NM$. Using substitution again, $AN + NM = AN$. Subtracting gives $NM = 0$. But this contradicts the Ruler Postulate, which states that the measure of a line segment is a positive number. Therefore, our assumption is wrong and M is the only midpoint for $\overline{AB}$.

2.3 Exercises

1. $\ell \parallel m$ **3.** $\ell \nparallel m$ **5.** $\ell \nparallel m$ **7.** $p \parallel q$ **9.** None **11.** $\ell \parallel n$ **13.** None **15.** $\ell \parallel n$ **17.** 1. Given 2. If two ∠s are comp. to the same ∠, then they are ≅ 3. $\overline{BC} \parallel \overline{DE}$ **23.** $x = 20$ **25.** $x = 120$ **27.** $x = 9$ **29.** $x = 6$

2.3 Selected Proof

19.

PROOF

Statements	Reasons
1. $\overline{AD} \perp \overline{DC}$ and $\overline{BC} \perp \overline{DC}$	1. Given
2. $\overline{AD} \parallel \overline{BC}$	2. If two lines are each ⊥ to a third line, then these lines are ∥ to each other

2.4 Exercises

1. $m\angle C = 75°$ **3.** $m\angle B = 46°$ **5.** (a) Underdetermined (b) Determined (c) Overdetermined **7.** (a) Equilateral (b) Isosceles **9.** (a) Equiangular (b) Right **11.** If two ∠s of one triangle are ≅ to two ∠s of another triangle, then the third ∠s of the triangles are ≅.

13. $m\angle 1 = 122°$; $m\angle 2 = 58°$; $m\angle 5 = 72°$
15. $m\angle 2 = 57.7°$; $m\angle 3 = 80.8°$; $m\angle 4 = 41.5°$ **17.** 35°
19. 40° **21.** $x = 72$; $m\angle 1 = 72°$; $m\angle DAE = 36°$
23. 360° **25.** $x = 45°$; $y = 45°$ **27.** $x = 108$
29. $y = 20°$; $x = 100°$; $m\angle 5 = 60°$ **35.** 44°
37. $m\angle N = 49°$; $m\angle P = 98°$ **39.** 35° **41.** 75°
49. $m\angle M = 84°$

2.5 Exercises

1. Increase **3.** $x = 113°$; $y = 67°$; $z = 36°$ **5.** (a) 5 (b) 35 **7.** (a) 540° (b) 1440° **9.** (a) 90° (b) 150° **11.** (a) 90° (b) 30° **13.** (a) 7 (b) 9 **15.** (a) $n = 5$ (b) $n = 10$ **17.** (a) 15 (b) 20 **19.** 135°

21.

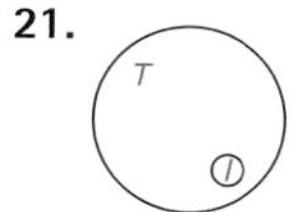

23.

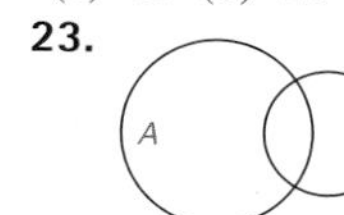

25.

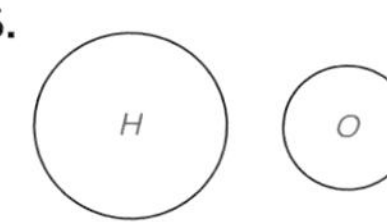

31. Figure (a): 90°, 90°, 120°, 120°, 120° Figure (b): 90°, 90°, 90°, 135°, 135° **33.** 36° **35.** The resulting polygon is also a regular polygon. **37.** 150° **39.** (a) $n - 3$ (b) $\frac{n(n-3)}{2}$
41. 221° **43.** (a) No (b) Yes

2.5 Selected Proof

29.

PROOF

Statements	Reasons
1. Quad. $RSTV$ with diagonals $\overline{RT}$ and $\overline{SV}$ intersecting at W	1. Given
2. $m\angle RWS = m\angle 1 + m\angle 2$	2. The measure of an exterior $\angle$ of a $\triangle$ equals the sum of the measures of the nonadjacent interior $\angle$s of the $\triangle$
3. $m\angle RWS = m\angle 3 + m\angle 4$	3. Same as 2
4. $m\angle 1 + m\angle 2 = m\angle 3 + m\angle 4$	4. Substitution

2.6 Exercises

1. M, T, X **3.** N, X **5.** (a), (c) **7.** (a), (b)
9. MOM **11.** (a)

(b)

13. (a)

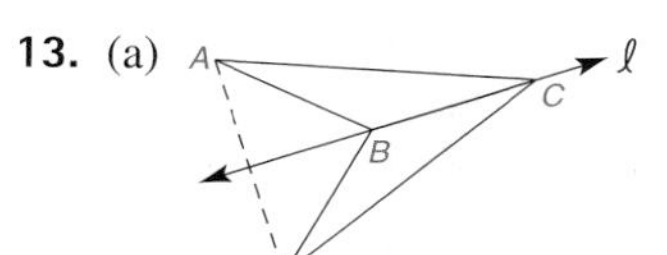

(b)

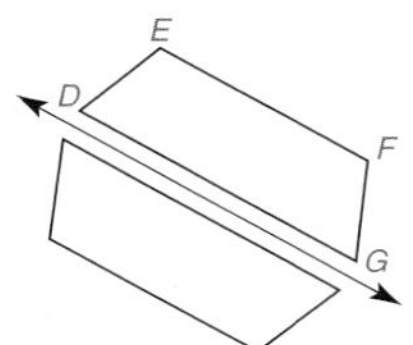

15. (a) 63° (b) Yes (c) Yes **17.** WHIM **19.** SIX
21. WOW **23.** (a) Clockwise (b) Counterclockwise
25 62,365 kilowatt-hours **27.** (a) Line (b) None (c) Line
29. (b), (c) **31.** (a) 12 (b) 6 (c) 4 (d) 3 **33.** $x = 50$

CHAPTER 2 REVIEW EXERCISES

1. (a) $\overline{BC} \parallel \overline{AD}$ (b) $\overline{AB} \parallel \overline{CD}$ **2.** 110° **3.** $x = 37$
4. $m\angle D = 75°$; $m\angle DEF = 125°$ **5.** $x = 20$; $y = 10$
6. $x = 30$; $y = 35$ **7.** $\overline{AE} \parallel \overline{BF}$ **8.** None **9.** $\overline{BE} \parallel \overline{CF}$
10. $\overline{BE} \parallel \overline{CF}$ **11.** $\overline{AC} \parallel \overline{DF}$ and $\overline{AE} \parallel \overline{BF}$ **12.** $x = 120°$; $y = 70°$ **13.** $x = 32°$; $y = 30°$ **14.** $y = -8$; $x = 24$
15. $x = 140°$ **16.** $x = 6$ **17.** $m\angle 3 = 69°$; $m\angle 4 = 67°$; $m\angle 5 = 44°$ **18.** 110° **19.** S **20.** N **21.** N **22.** S
23. S **24.** A
25.

Number of sides	8	12	20	15	10	16	180
Measure of each ext. $\angle$	45	30	18	24	36	22.5	2
Measure of each int. $\angle$	135	150	162	156	144	157.5	178
Number of diagonals	20	54	170	90	35	104	15,930

28. Not possible
30. *Statement:* If two angles are right angles, then the angles are congruent.
Converse: If two angles are congruent, then the angles are right angles.
Inverse: If two angles are not right angles, then the angles are not congruent.
Contrapositive: If two angles are not congruent, then the angles are not right angles.
31. *Statement:* If it is not raining, then I am happy.
Converse: If I am happy, then it is not raining.
Inverse: If it is raining, then I am not happy.
Contrapositive: If I am not happy, then it is raining.
32. *Contrapositive* **37.** Assume $x = -3$.
38. Assume the sides opposite these angles are $\cong$.
39. Assume that $\angle 1 \cong \angle 2$. Then $m \parallel n$ because congruent corresponding angles are formed. But this contradicts our hypothesis. Therefore, our assumption must be false, and it follows that $\angle 1 \not\cong \angle 2$. **40.** Assume that $m \parallel n$. Then $\angle 1 \cong \angle 3$ because alternate exterior angles are congruent when parallel lines are cut by a transversal. But this contradicts the given fact that $\angle 1 \not\cong \angle 3$. Therefore, our assumption must be false, and it follows that $m \nparallel n$. **43.** (a) B, H, W (b) H, S
44. (a) Isosceles triangle, Circle, Regular pentagon (b) Circle **45.** Congruent

46. (a) (b)

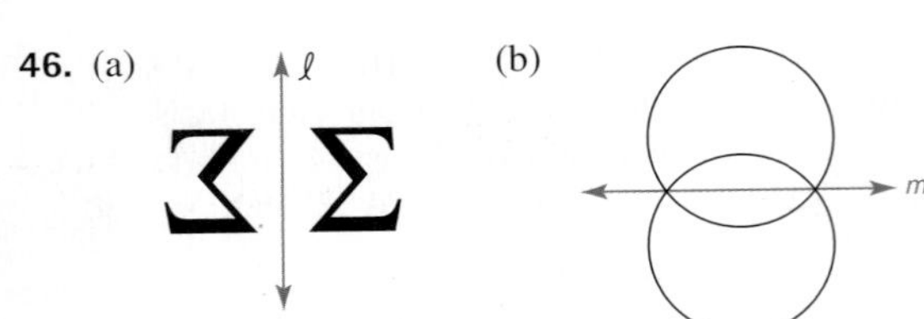

47. 90°

CHAPTER 2 REVIEW EXERCISES SELECTED PROOFS

33.

PROOF

Statements	Reasons
1. $\overline{AB} \parallel \overline{CF}$	1. Given
2. $\angle 1 \cong \angle 2$	2. If two $\parallel$ lines are cut by a transversal, then corresponding $\angle$s are $\cong$
3. $\angle 2 \cong \angle 3$	3. Given
4. $\angle 1 \cong \angle 3$	4. Transitive Prop. of Congruence

34.

PROOF

Statements	Reasons
1. $\angle 1$ is comp. to $\angle 2$ $\angle 2$ is comp. to $\angle 3$	1. Given
2. $\angle 1 \cong \angle 3$	2. If two $\angle$s are comp. to the same $\angle$, then these $\angle$s are $\cong$
3. $\overline{BD} \parallel \overline{AE}$	3. If two lines are cut by a transversal so that corresponding $\angle$s are $\cong$, then these lines are $\parallel$

35.

PROOF

Statements	Reasons
1. $\overline{BE} \perp \overline{DA}$ $\overline{CD} \perp \overline{DA}$	1. Given
2. $\overline{BE} \parallel \overline{CD}$	2. If two lines are each $\perp$ to a third line, then these lines are parallel to each other
3. $\angle 1 \cong \angle 2$	3. If two $\parallel$ lines are cut by a transversal, then the alternate interior $\angle$s are $\cong$

36.

PROOF

Statements	Reasons
1. $\angle A \cong \angle C$	1. Given
2. $\overline{DC} \parallel \overrightarrow{AB}$	2. Given
3. $\angle C \cong \angle 1$	3. If two $\parallel$ lines are cut by a transversal, the alt. int. $\angle$s are $\cong$
4. $\angle A \cong \angle 1$	4. Transitive Prop. of Congruence
5. $\overline{DA} \parallel \overline{CB}$	5. If two lines are cut by a transversal so that corr. $\angle$s are $\cong$, then these lines are $\parallel$

Chapter 2 Test

1. (a) $\angle 5$ (b) $\angle 3$ [2.1] **2.** (a) r and s (b) ℓ and m [2.3] **3.** "not Q" [2.2] **4.** $\angle R$ and $\angle S$ are not both right angles. [2.2] **5.** (a) $r \parallel t$ (b) $a \parallel c$ [2.3] **7.** (a) 36° (b) 33° [2.4] **8.** (a) Pentagon (b) Five [2.5] **9.** (a) Equiangular hexagon (b) 120° [2.5] **10.** A: line; D: line; N: point; O: both; X: both [2.6] **11.** (a) Reflection (b) Slide (c) Rotation [2.6] **12.** 61° [2.1] **13.** 54 [2.3] **14.** 50° [2.4] **15.** 78° [2.4] **16.** 1. Given 2. $\angle 2 \cong \angle 3$ 3. Transitive Prop. of Congruence 4. $\ell \parallel n$ [2.3] **17.** Assume that $\angle M$ and $\angle Q$ are complementary. By definition, $m\angle M + m\angle Q = 90°$. Also, $m\angle M + m\angle Q + m\angle N = 180°$ because these are the three angles of $\triangle MNQ$. By substitution, $90° + m\angle N = 180°$, so it follows that $m\angle N = 90°$. But this leads to a contradiction because it is given that $m\angle N = 120°$. The assumption must be false, and it follows that $\angle M$ and $\angle Q$ are *not* complementary. [2.2] **18.** 1. Given 2. 180° 3. $m\angle 1 + m\angle 2 + 90° = 180°$ 4. 90° S5. $\angle 1$ and $\angle 2$ are complementary. R5. Definition of complementary angles [2.4] **19.** 21° [2.4]

CHAPTER 3

3.1 Exercises

1. $\angle A$; $\overline{AB}$; No; No **3.** $m\angle A = 72°$ **5.** SAS **7.** $\triangle AED \cong \triangle FDE$ **9.** SSS **11.** AAS **13.** ASA **15.** ASA **17.** SSS **19.** (a) $\angle A \cong \angle A$ (b) ASA **21.** $\overline{AD} \cong \overline{EC}$ **23.** $\overline{MO} \cong \overline{MO}$ **25.** 1. Given 2. $\overline{AC} \cong \overline{AC}$ 3. SSS **33.** Yes; SAS or SSS **35.** No **37.** (a) $\triangle CBE$, $\triangle ADE$, $\triangle CDE$ (b) $\triangle ADC$ (c) $\triangle CBD$

3.1 Selected Proofs

27.

PROOF

Statements	Reasons
1. $\overrightarrow{PQ}$ bisects $\angle MPN$	1. Given
2. $\angle 1 \cong \angle 2$	2. If a ray bisects an $\angle$, it forms two $\cong$ $\angle$s
3. $\overline{MP} \cong \overline{NP}$	3. Given
4. $\overline{PQ} \cong \overline{PQ}$	4. Identity
5. $\triangle MQP \cong \triangle NQP$	5. SAS

31.

PROOF

Statements	Reasons
1. $\angle VRS \cong \angle TSR$ and $\overline{RV} \cong \overline{TS}$	1. Given
2. $\overline{RS} \cong \overline{RS}$	2. Identity
3. $\triangle RST \cong \triangle SRV$	3. SAS

3.2 Exercises

9. $m\angle 2 = 48°$; $m\angle 3 = 48°$; $m\angle 5 = 42°$; $m\angle 6 = 42°$
11. 1. Given 2. If two lines are $\perp$, then they form right $\angle$s 3. Identity 4. $\triangle HJK \cong \triangle HJL$ 5. $\overline{KJ} \cong \overline{JL}$
17. $c = 5$ **19.** $b = 8$ **21.** $c = \sqrt{41}$
31. (a) 8 (b) 37° (c) 53° **33.** 751 feet

3.2 Selected Proofs

1.

PROOF

Statements	Reasons
1. $\angle 1$ and $\angle 2$ are right $\angle$s $\overline{CA} \cong \overline{DA}$	1. Given
2. $\overline{AB} \cong \overline{AB}$	2. Identity
3. $\triangle ABC \cong \triangle ABD$	3. HL

5.

PROOF

Statements	Reasons
1. $\angle R$ and $\angle V$ are right $\angle$s $\angle 1 \cong \angle 2$	1. Given
2. $\angle R \cong \angle V$	2. All right $\angle$s are $\cong$
3. $\overline{ST} \cong \overline{ST}$	3. Identity
4. $\triangle RST \cong \triangle VST$	4. AAS

13.

PROOF

Statements	Reasons
1. $\angle$s P and R are right $\angle$s	1. Given
2. $\angle P \cong \angle R$	2. All right $\angle$s are $\cong$
3. M is the midpoint of $\overline{PR}$	3. Given
4. $\overline{PM} \cong \overline{MR}$	4. The midpoint of a segment forms two $\cong$ segments
5. $\angle NMP \cong \angle QMR$	5. If two lines intersect, the vertical angles formed are $\cong$
6. $\triangle NPM \cong \triangle QRM$	6. ASA
7. $\angle N \cong \angle Q$	7. CPCTC

23.

PROOF

Statements	Reasons
1. $\overline{DF} \cong \overline{DG}$ and $\overline{FE} \cong \overline{EG}$	1. Given
2. $\overline{DE} \cong \overline{DE}$	2. Identity
3. $\triangle FDE \cong \triangle GDE$	3. SSS
4. $\angle FDE \cong \angle GDE$	4. CPCTC
5. $\overrightarrow{DE}$ bisects $\angle FDG$	5. If a ray divides an $\angle$ into two $\cong$ $\angle$s, then the ray bisects the angle

27.

PROOF

Statements	Reasons
1. $\angle 1 \cong \angle 2$ and $\overline{MN} \cong \overline{QP}$	1. Given
2. $\overline{MP} \cong \overline{MP}$	2. Identity
3. $\triangle NMP \cong \triangle QPM$	3. SAS
4. $\angle 3 \cong \angle 4$	4. CPCTC
5. $\overline{MQ} \parallel \overline{NP}$	5. If two lines are cut by a transversal so that the alt. int. $\angle$s are $\cong$, then the lines are $\parallel$

3.3 Exercises

1. Isosceles **3.** $\overline{VT} \cong \overline{VU}$ **5.** $m\angle U = 69°$
7. $m\angle V = 36°$ **9.** $L = E$ (equivalent) **11.** R and S are disjoint; so $R \cap S = \emptyset$. **13.** Underdetermined
15. Overdetermined **17.** Determined **19.** 55°
21. $m\angle 2 = 68°$; $m\angle 1 = 44°$ **23.** $m\angle 5 = 124°$
25. $m\angle A = 52°$; $m\angle B = 64°$; $m\angle C = 64°$
27. 26 **29.** 12 **31.** Yes **33.** 1. Given 2. $\angle 3 \cong \angle 2$ 3. $\angle 1 \cong \angle 2$ 4. If two $\angle$s of a $\triangle$ are $\cong$, then the opposite sides are $\cong$ **39.** (a) 80° (b) 100° (c) 40° **41.** 75° each

3.3 Selected Proof

35.

Statements	Reasons
1. $\angle 1 \cong \angle 3$	1. Given
2. $\overline{RU} \cong \overline{VU}$	2. Given
3. $\angle R \cong \angle V$	3. If two sides of a △ are ≅, then the ∠s opposite these sides are also ≅
4. $\triangle RUS \cong \triangle VUT$	4. ASA
5. $\overline{SU} \cong \overline{TU}$	5. CPCTC
6. $\triangle STU$ is isosceles	6. If a △ has two ≅ sides, it is an isosceles △

3.4 Exercises

19. Construct a 90° angle; bisect it to form two 45° ∠s. Bisect one of the 45° angles to get a 22.5° ∠. **31.** 120° **33.** 150° **39.** D is on the bisector of $\angle A$.

3.5 Exercises

1. False **3.** True **5.** True **7.** False **9.** True **11.** (a) Not possible $(100° + 100° + 60° \neq 180°)$ (b) Possible $(45° + 45° + 90° = 180°)$ **13.** (a) Possible (b) Not possible $(8 + 9 = 17)$ (c) Not possible $(8 + 9 < 18)$ **15.** Scalene right triangle $(m\angle Z = 90°)$ **17.** Isosceles obtuse triangle $(m\angle Z = 100°)$ **19.** 4 cm **21.** 72° (two such angles); 36° (one angle only) **23.** Nashville **25.** 1. $m\angle ABC > m\angle DBE$ and $m\angle CBD > m\angle EBF$ 3. Angle-Addition Postulate 4. $m\angle ABD > m\angle DBF$ **29.** $BC < EF$ **31.** $2 < x < 10$ **33.** $x + 2 < y < 5x + 12$ **35.** Proof: Assume that $PM = PN$. Then $\triangle MPN$ is isosceles. But that contradicts the hypothesis; thus, our assumption must be wrong, and $PM \neq PN$.

3.5 Selected Proof

27.

Statements	Reasons
1. Quad. $RSTU$ with diagonal $\overline{US}$; $\angle R$ and $\angle TUS$ are right ∠s	1. Given
2. $TS > US$	2. The shortest distance from a point to a line is the ⊥ distance
3. $US > UR$	3. Same as (2)
4. $TS > UR$	4. Transitive Prop. of Inequality

CHAPTER 3 REVIEW EXERCISES

15. (a) $\overline{PR}$ (b) $\overline{PQ}$ **16.** $\overline{BC}, \overline{AC}, \overline{AB}$ **17.** $\angle R, \angle Q, \angle P$ **18.** $\overline{DA}$ **19.** (b) **20.** 5, 35 **21.** 20° **22.** 115° **23.** $m\angle C = 64°$ **24.** Isosceles **25.** The triangle is also equilateral. **26.** 60°

CHAPTER 3 REVIEW EXERCISES SELECTED PROOFS

1.

Statements	Reasons
1. $\angle AEB \cong \angle DEC$	1. Given
2. $\overline{AE} \cong \overline{ED}$	2. Given
3. $\angle A \cong \angle D$	3. If two sides of a △ are ≅, then the ∠s opposite these sides are also ≅
4. $\triangle AEB \cong \triangle DEC$	4. ASA

5.

Statements	Reasons
1. $\overline{AB} \cong \overline{DE}$ and $\overline{AB} \parallel \overline{DE}$	1. Given
2. $\angle A \cong \angle D$	2. If two ∥ lines are cut by a transversal, then the alt. int. ∠s are ≅
3. $\overline{AC} \cong \overline{DF}$	3. Given
4. $\triangle BAC \cong \triangle EDF$	4. SAS
5. $\angle BCA \cong \angle EFD$	5. CPCTC
6. $\overline{BC} \parallel \overline{FE}$	6. If two lines are cut by a transversal so that alt. int. ∠s are ≅, then the lines are ∥

9.

Statements	Reasons
1. $\overline{YZ}$ is the base of an isosceles triangle	1. Given
2. $\angle Y \cong \angle Z$	2. Base ∠s of an isosceles △ are ≅
3. $\overrightarrow{XA} \parallel \overline{YZ}$	3. Given
4. $\angle 1 \cong \angle Y$	4. If two ∥ lines are cut by a transversal, then the corresponding ∠s are ≅
5. $\angle 2 \cong \angle Z$	5. If two ∥ lines are cut by a transversal, then the alt. int. ∠s are ≅
6. $\angle 1 \cong \angle 2$	6. Transitive Prop. for Congruence

13.

PROOF

Statements	Reasons
1. $\overline{AB} \cong \overline{CD}$	1. Given
2. $\angle BAD \cong \angle CDA$	2. Given
3. $\overline{AD} \cong \overline{AD}$	3. Identity
4. $\triangle BAD \cong \triangle CDA$	4. SAS
5. $\angle CAD \cong \angle BDA$	5. CPCTC
6. $\overline{AE} \cong \overline{ED}$	6. If two $\angle$s of a $\triangle$ are $\cong$, then the sides opposite these $\angle$s are also $\cong$
7. $\triangle AED$ is isosceles	7. If a $\triangle$ has two $\cong$ sides, then it is an isosceles $\triangle$

Chapter 3 Test

1. (a) 75° (b) 4.7 cm [3.1] **2.** (a) $\overline{XY}$ (b) $\angle Y$ [3.1] **3.** (a) SAS (b) ASA [3.1] **4.** Corresponding parts of congruent triangles are congruent. [3.2] **5.** (a) No (b) Yes [3.2] **6.** Yes [3.2] **7.** (a) $c = 10$ (b) $\sqrt{28}$ (or $2\sqrt{7}$) [3.2] **8.** (a) $\overline{AM} \cong \overline{MB}$ (b) No [3.3] **9.** (a) 38° (b) 36° [3.3] **10.** (a) 7.6 inches (b) 57 [3.3] **13.** (a) $\overline{BC}$ (b) $\overline{CA}$ [3.5] **14.** $m\angle V > m\angle U > m\angle T$ [3.5] **15.** $EB > DC$ since $EB = \sqrt{74}$ and $DC = \sqrt{65}$ [3.2] **16.** $\overline{DA}$ [3.1] **17.**

Statements	Reasons
1. $\angle R$ and $\angle V$ are rt $\angle$s	1. Given
2. $\angle R \cong \angle V$	2. All rt $\angle$s are $\cong$
3. $\angle 1 \cong \angle 2$	3. Given
4. $\overline{ST} \cong \overline{ST}$	4. Identity
5. $\triangle RST \cong \triangle VST$	5. AAS [3.1]

18. R1. Given R2. If 2 $\angle$s of a $\triangle$ are $\cong$, the opposite sides are $\cong$ S3. $\angle 1 \cong \angle 3$ R4. ASA S5. $\overline{US} \cong \overline{UT}$ S6. $\triangle STU$ is an isosceles triangle [3.3] **19.** $a = 10$ cm [3.3]

CHAPTER 4

4.1 Exercises

1. (a) $AB = DC$ (b) $AD = BC$ **3.** (a) 8 (b) 5 (c) 70° (d) 110° **5.** $AB = DC = 8$; $BC = AD = 9$ **7.** $m\angle A = m\angle C = 83°$; $m\angle B = m\angle D = 97°$ **9.** $m\angle A = m\angle C = 80°$; $m\angle B = m\angle D = 100°$ **11.** $\overline{AC}$ **13.** (a) $\overline{VY}$ (b) 16 **15.** True **17.** True **19.** Parallelogram **21.** Parallelogram **23.** 1. Given 2. $\overline{RV} \perp \overline{VT}$ and $\overline{ST} \perp \overline{VT}$ 3. $\overline{RV} \parallel \overline{ST}$ 4. $RSTV$ is a parallelogram **31.** $\angle P$ is a right angle **33.** $\overline{RT}$ **35.** 255 mph **37.** $\overline{AC}$ **39.** $m\angle A = m\angle C = 70°$; $m\angle B = m\angle D = 110°$; $ABCD$ is a parallelogram

4.1 Selected Proof

25.

PROOF

Statements	Reasons
1. Parallelogram $RSTV$	1. Given
2. $\overline{RS} \parallel \overline{VT}$	2. Opposite sides of a parallelogram are $\parallel$
3. $\overline{XY} \parallel \overline{VT}$	3. Given
4. $\overline{RS} \parallel \overline{XY}$	4. If two lines are each $\parallel$ to a third line, then the lines are $\parallel$
5. $RSYX$ is a parallelogram	5. If a quadrilateral has opposite sides $\parallel$, then the quadrilateral is a parallelogram
6. $\angle 1 \cong \angle S$	6. Opposite angles of a parallelogram are $\cong$

4.2 Exercises

1. (a) Yes (b) No **3.** Parallelogram **5.** (a) Kite (b) Parallelogram **7.** $\overline{AC}$ **9.** 6.18 **11.** (a) 8 (b) 7 (c) 6 **13.** 10 **15.** (a) Yes; diagonal separating kite into 2 $\cong$ $\triangle$s (b) No **17.** Congruent **19.** 1. Given 2. Identity 3. $\triangle NMQ \cong \triangle NPQ$ 4. CPCTC 5. $MNPQ$ is a kite **29.** $y = 6$; $MN = 9$; $ST = 18$ **31.** $x = 5$; $RM = 11$; $ST = 22$ **33.** $P = 34$ **35.** 270°

4.2 Selected Proofs

21.

PROOF

Statements	Reasons
1. M-Q-T and P-Q-R so that $MNPQ$ and $QRST$ are parallelograms	1. Given
2. $\angle N \cong \angle MQP$	2. Opposite $\angle$s in a parallelogram are $\cong$
3. $\angle MQP \cong \angle RQT$	3. If two lines intersect, the vertical $\angle$s formed are $\cong$
4. $\angle RQT \cong \angle S$	4. Same as (2)
5. $\angle N \cong \angle S$	5. Transitive Prop. for Congruence

23.

PROOF

Statements	Reasons
1. Kite *HJKL* with diagonal $\overline{HK}$	1. Given
2. $\overline{LH} \cong \overline{HJ}$ and $\overline{LK} \cong \overline{JK}$	2. A kite is a quadrilateral with two distinct pairs of ≅ adjacent sides
3. $\overline{HK} \cong \overline{HK}$	3. Identity
4. $\triangle LHK \cong \triangle JHK$	4. SSS
5. $\angle LHK \cong \angle JHK$	5. CPCTC
6. $\overrightarrow{HK}$ bisects $\angle LHJ$	6. If a ray divides an ∠ into two ≅ ∠s, then the ray bisects the ∠

4.3 Exercises

1. $m\angle A = 60°$; $m\angle ABC = 120°$ **3.** The parallelogram is a rectangle. **5.** The quadrilateral is a rhombus. **7.** $\overline{MN} \parallel$ to both $\overline{AB}$ and $\overline{DC}$; $MN = AB = DC$ **9.** $x = 5$; $DA = 19$ **11.** $NQ = 10$; $MP = 10$ **13.** $QP = \sqrt{72}$ or $6\sqrt{2}$; $MN = \sqrt{72}$ or $6\sqrt{2}$ **15.** $\sqrt{41}$ **17.** $\sqrt{34}$ **19.** 5 **21.** True **23.** 1. Given 4. Same as (3) 5. If two lines are each ∥ to a third line, then the two lines are ∥ 6. Same as (2) 7. Same as (3) 8. Same as (3) 9. Same as (5) 10. *ABCD* is a parallelogram **25.** (a) **27.** 176 **39.** 20.4 ft **41.** Rhombus **43.** 150°

4.4 Exercises

1. $m\angle D = 122°$; $m\angle B = 55°$ **3.** The trapezoid is an isosceles trapezoid. **5.** The quadrilateral is a rhombus. **7.** Trapezoid **9.** (a) Yes (b) No **11.** 9.7 **13.** 10.8 **15.** $7x + 2$ **19.** $h = 8$ **21.** 12 **23.** 22 ft **25.** 14 **35.** (a) 7.0 (b) 14.2 (c) 10.6 (d) Yes **37.** (a) 3 ft (b) 12 ft (c) 13 ft (d) $\sqrt{73}$ ft **39.** 8 ft **41.** $x = 144°$ or $x = 150°$

CHAPTER 4 REVIEW EXERCISES

1. A **2.** S **3.** N **4.** S **5.** S **6.** A **7.** A **8.** A **9.** A **10.** N **11.** S **12.** N **13.** $AB = DC = 17$; $AD = BC = 31$ **14.** 106° **15.** 52 **16.** $m\angle M = 100°$; $m\angle P = 80°$ **17.** $\overline{PN}$ **18.** Kite **19.** $m\angle G = m\angle F = 72°$; $m\angle E = 108°$ **20.** 14.9 cm **21.** $MN = 23$; $PO = 7$ **22.** 26 **23.** $MN = 6$; $m\angle FMN = 80°$; $m\angle FNM = 40°$ **24.** $x = 3$; $MN = 15$; $JH = 30$ **32.** (a) Perpendicular (b) 13 **33.** (a) Perpendicular (b) 30 **34.** (a) Kites, rectangles, squares, rhombi, isosceles trapezoids (b) Parallelograms, rectangles, squares, rhombi **35.** (a) Rhombus (b) Kite

CHAPTER 4 REVIEW EXERCISES SELECTED PROOFS

25.

PROOF

Statements	Reasons
1. *ABCD* is a parallelogram	1. Given
2. $\overline{AD} \cong \overline{CB}$	2. Opposite sides of a parallelogram are ≅
3. $\overline{AD} \parallel \overline{CB}$	3. Opposite sides of a parallelogram are ∥
4. $\angle 1 \cong \angle 2$	4. If two ∥ lines are cut by a transversal, then the alt. int. ∠s are ≅
5. $\overline{AF} \cong \overline{CE}$	5. Given
6. $\triangle DAF \cong \triangle BCE$	6. SAS
7. $\angle DFA \cong \angle BEC$	7. CPCTC
8. $\overline{DF} \parallel \overline{EB}$	8. If two lines are cut by a transversal so that alt. ext. ∠s are ≅, then the lines are ∥

26.

PROOF

Statements	Reasons
1. *ABEF* is a rectangle	1. Given
2. *ABEF* is a parallelogram	2. A rectangle is a parallelogram with a rt. ∠
3. $\overline{AF} \cong \overline{BE}$	3. Opposite sides of a parallelogram are ≅
4. *BCDE* is a rectangle	4. Given
5. ∠*F* and ∠*BED* are rt. ∠s	5. All angles of a rectangle are rt. ∠s
6. $\angle F \cong \angle BED$	6. Any two rt. ∠s are ≅
7. $\overline{FE} \cong \overline{ED}$	7. Given
8. $\triangle AFE \cong \triangle BED$	8. SAS
9. $\overline{AE} \cong \overline{BD}$	9. CPCTC
10. $\angle AEF \cong \angle BDE$	10. CPCTC
11. $\overline{AE} \parallel \overline{BD}$	11. If lines are cut by a transversal so that the corresponding ∠s are ≅, then the lines are ∥

27.

PROOF

Statements	Reasons
1. $\overline{DE}$ is a median of $\triangle ADC$	1. Given
2. E is the midpoint of $\overline{AC}$	2. A median of a $\triangle$ is a line segment drawn from a vertex to the midpoint of the opposite side
3. $\overline{AE} \cong \overline{EC}$	3. Midpoint of a segment forms two $\cong$ segments
4. $\overline{BE} \cong \overline{FD}$ and $\overline{EF} \cong \overline{FD}$	4. Given
5. $\overline{BE} \cong \overline{EF}$	5. Transitive Prop. for Congruence
6. $ABCF$ is a parallelogram	6. If the diagonals of a quadrilateral bisect each other, then the quad. is a parallelogram

28.

PROOF

Statements	Reasons
1. $\triangle FAB \cong \triangle HCD$	1. Given
2. $\overline{AB} \cong \overline{DC}$	2. CPCTC
3. $\triangle EAD \cong \triangle GCB$	3. Given
4. $\overline{AD} \cong \overline{BC}$	4. CPCTC
5. $ABCD$ is a parallelogram	5. If a quadrilateral has both pairs of opposite sides $\cong$, then the quad. is a parallelogram

29.

PROOF

Statements	Reasons
1. $ABCD$ is a parallelogram	1. Given
2. $\overline{DC} \cong \overline{BN}$	2. Given
3. $\angle 3 \cong \angle 4$	3. Given
4. $\overline{BN} \cong \overline{BC}$	4. If two $\angle$s of a $\triangle$ are $\cong$, then the sides opposite these $\angle$s are also $\cong$
5. $\overline{DC} \cong \overline{BC}$	5. Transitive Prop. for Congruence
6. $ABCD$ is a rhombus	6. If a parallelogram has two $\cong$ adjacent sides, then the parallelogram is a rhombus

30.

PROOF

Statements	Reasons
1. $\triangle TWX$ is isosceles with base $\overline{WX}$	1. Given
2. $\angle W \cong \angle X$	2. Base $\angle$s of an isosceles $\triangle$ are $\cong$
3. $\overline{RY} \parallel \overline{WX}$	3. Given
4. $\angle TRY \cong \angle W$ and $\angle TYR \cong \angle X$	4. If two $\parallel$ lines are cut by a transversal, then the corr. $\angle$s are $\cong$
5. $\angle TRY \cong \angle TYR$	5. Transitive Prop. for Congruence
6. $\overline{TR} \cong \overline{TY}$	6. If two $\angle$s of a $\triangle$ are $\cong$, then the sides opposite these $\angle$s are also $\cong$
7. $\overline{TW} \cong \overline{TX}$	7. An isosceles $\triangle$ has two $\cong$ sides
8. $TR = TY$ and $TW = TX$	8. If two segments are $\cong$, then they are equal in length
9. $TW = TR + RW$ and $TX = TY + YX$	9. Segment-Addition Postulate
10. $TR + RW = TY + YX$	10. Substitution
11. $RW = YX$	11. Subtraction Prop. of Equality
12. $\overline{RW} \cong \overline{YX}$	12. If segments are $=$ in length, then they are $\cong$
13. $RWXY$ is an isosceles trapezoid	13. If a quadrilateral has one pair of $\parallel$ sides and the nonparallel sides are $\cong$, then the quad. is an isosceles trapezoid

Chapter 4 Test

1. (a) Congruent (b) Supplementary [4.1] **2.** 18.8 cm [4.1] **3.** $EB = 6$ [4.1] **4.** $\overline{VS}$ [4.1] **5.** $x = 7$ [4.1] **6.** (a) Kite (b) Parallelogram [4.2] **7.** (a) Altitude (b) Rhombus [4.1] **8.** (a) The line segments are parallel. (b) $MN = \frac{1}{2}(BC)$ [4.2] **9.** 15.2 cm [4.2] **10.** $x = 23$ [4.2] **11.** $AC = 13$ [4.3] **12.** (a) $\overline{RV}, \overline{ST}$ (b) $\angle R$ and $\angle V$ (or $\angle S$ and $\angle T$) [4.4] **13.** $MN = 14.3$ in. [4.4] **14.** $x = 5$ [4.4] **15.** S1. Kite $ABCD$; $\overline{AB} \cong \overline{AD}$ and $\overline{BC} \cong \overline{DC}$ R1. Given S3. $\overline{AC} \cong \overline{AC}$ R4. SSS S5. $\angle B \cong \angle D$ R5. CPCTC [4.3] **16.** S1. Trap. $ABCD$ with $\overline{AB} \parallel \overline{DC}$ and $\overline{AD} \cong \overline{BC}$ R1. Given R2. Congruent R3. Identity R4. SAS S5. $\overline{AC} \cong \overline{DB}$ [4.4] **17.** $P = 26$ [4.4]

CHAPTER 5

5.1 Exercises

1. (a) $\frac{4}{5}$ (b) $\frac{4}{5}$ (c) $\frac{2}{3}$ (d) Incommensurable **3.** (a) $\frac{5}{8}$ (b) $\frac{1}{3}$ (c) $\frac{4}{3}$ (d) Incommensurable **5.** (a) 3 (b) 8 **7.** (a) 6 (b) 4 **9.** (a) $\pm 2\sqrt{7} \approx \pm 5.29$ (b) $\pm 3\sqrt{2} \approx \pm 4.24$ **11.** (a) 4 (b) $-\frac{5}{6}$ or 3 **13.** (a) $\frac{3 \pm \sqrt{33}}{4} \approx 2.19$ or -0.69 (b) $\frac{7 \pm \sqrt{89}}{4} \approx 4.11$ or -0.61 **15.** 6.3 m/sec **17.** $10\frac{1}{2}$ **19.** $\approx$ 24 outlets **21.** (a) $4\sqrt{3} \approx 6.93$ (b) $4\frac{1}{2}$ **23.** Secretary's salary is \$24,900; salesperson's salary is \$37,350; vice-president's salary is \$62,250. **25.** 40° and 50° **27.** 30.48 cm **29.** $2\frac{4}{7} \approx 2.57$ **31.** $a = 12$; $b = 16$ **33.** 45° **35.** 4 in. by $4\frac{2}{3}$ in. **37.** (a) $\frac{5 + 5\sqrt{5}}{2}$ (b) 8.1

5.2 Exercises

1. (a) Congruent (b) Proportional **3.** (a) Yes (b) No **5.** (a) $\triangle ABC \sim \triangle XTN$ (b) $\triangle ACB \sim \triangle NXT$ **7.** Yes; Yes; Spheres have the same shape; one is an enlargement of the other unless they are congruent. **9.** (a) 82° (b) 42° (c) $10\frac{1}{2}$ (d) 8 **11** (a) Yes (b) Yes (c) Yes **13.** $5\frac{1}{3}$ **15.** 79° **17.** $n = 3$ **19.** 90° **21.** 12 **23.** $10 + 2\sqrt{5}$ or $10 - 2\sqrt{5}$; ≈ 14.47 or 5.53 **25.** 75 **27.** 2.5 in. **29.** 3 ft, 9 in. **31.** 74 ft **33.** No **35.** (a) Yes (b) Yes **37.** 3.75

5.3 Exercises

1. CASTC **3.** (a) True (b) True **5.** SSS~ **7.** SAS~ **9.** SAS~ **11.** 1. Given 2. If 2 lines are ⊥, they form right angles. 3. All right angles are ≅. 4. Opposite ∠s of a ▱ are ≅ 5. AA **13.** 1. Given 2. Definition of midpoint 3. If a line segment joins the midpoints of two sides of a △, its length is $\frac{1}{2}$ the length of the third side 4. Division Prop. of Eq. 5. Substitution 6. SSS~ **15.** 1. $\overline{MN} \perp \overline{NP}$ and $\overline{QR} \perp \overline{RP}$ 2. If two lines are ⊥, then they form a rt. ∠3. $\angle N \cong \angle QRP$ 4. Identity S5. $\triangle MNP \sim \triangle QRP$ R5. AA **17.** 1. $\angle H \cong \angle F$ 2. If two ∠s are vertical ∠s, then they are ≅ S3. $\triangle HJK \sim \triangle FGK$ R3. AA **19.** 1. $\frac{RQ}{NM} = \frac{RS}{NP} = \frac{QS}{MP}$ 2. $\triangle RQS \sim \triangle NMP$ 3. $\angle N \cong \angle R$ **21.** S1. $\overline{RS} \parallel \overline{UV}$ R1. Given 2. If 2 ∥ lines are cut by a transversal, alternate interior ∠s are ≅ 3. $\triangle RST \sim \triangle VUT$ S4. $\frac{RT}{VT} = \frac{RS}{VU}$ R4. CSSTP **23.** $4\frac{1}{2}$ **25.** 16 **27.** $EB = 24$ **29.** 27° **35.** $QS = 8$ **37.** 150 ft

5.3 Selected Proofs

31.

PROOF

Statements	Reasons
1. $\overline{AB} \parallel \overline{DF}$ and $\overline{BD} \parallel \overline{FG}$	1. Given
2. $\angle A \cong \angle FEG$ and $\angle BCA \cong \angle G$	2. If two ∥ lines are cut by a transversal, then the corresponding ∠s are ≅
3. $\triangle ABC \sim \triangle EFG$	3. AA

33.

PROOF

Statements	Reasons
1. $\triangle DEF \sim \triangle MNP$ $\overline{DG}$ and $\overline{MQ}$ are altitudes	1. Given
2. $\overline{DG} \perp \overline{EF}$ and $\overline{MQ} \perp \overline{NP}$	2. An altitude is a segment drawn from a vertex ⊥ to the opposite side
3. $\angle DGE$ and $\angle MQN$ are rt. ∠s	3. ⊥ lines form a rt. ∠
4. $\angle DGE \cong \angle MQN$	4. Right ∠s are ≅
5. $\angle E \cong \angle N$	5. If two △s are ~ then the corresponding ∠s are ≅ (CASTC)
6. $\triangle DGE \sim \triangle MQN$	6. AA
7. $\frac{DG}{MQ} = \frac{DE}{MN}$	7. Corresponding sides of ~ △s are proportional (CSSTP)

5.4 Exercises

1. $\triangle RST \sim \triangle RVS \sim \triangle SVT$ **3.** $\frac{RT}{RS} = \frac{RS}{RV}$ or $\frac{RV}{RS} = \frac{RS}{RT}$ **5.** 4.5 **7.** (a) 10 (b) $\sqrt{34} \approx 5.83$ **9.** (a) 8 (b) 4 **11.** (a) Yes (b) No (c) Yes (d) No **13.** (a) Right (b) Acute (c) Right (d) No △ **15.** 15 ft **17.** $6\sqrt{5} \approx 13.4$ m **19.** 20 ft **21.** 12 cm **23.** The base is 8; the altitude is 6; the diagonals are 10. **25.** $6\sqrt{7} \approx 15.87$ in **27.** 12 in **29.** 4 **31.** $9\frac{3}{13}$ in **33.** $5\sqrt{5} \approx 11.18$ **39.** 60° **41.** $TS = 13$; $RT = 13\sqrt{2} \approx 18.38$

5.5 Exercises

1. (a) a (b) $a\sqrt{2}$ **3.** (a) $a\sqrt{3}$ (b) $2a$ **5.** $YZ = 8$; $XY = 8\sqrt{2} \approx 11.31$ **7.** $XZ = 10$; $YZ = 10$ **9.** $DF = 5\sqrt{3} \approx 8.66$; $FE = 10$ **11.** $DE = 12$; $FE = 24$ **13.** $HL = 6$; $HK = 12$; $MK = 6$ **15.** $AC = 6$; $AB = 6\sqrt{2} \approx 8.49$ **17.** $RS = 6$; $RT = 6\sqrt{3} \approx 10.39$ **19.** $DB = 5\sqrt{6} \approx 12.25$ **21.** $6\sqrt{3} + 6 \approx 16.39$ **23.** 45° **25.** 60°; 146 ft further **27.** $DC = 2\sqrt{3} \approx 3.46$; $DB = 4\sqrt{3} \approx 6.93$ **29.** $6\sqrt{3} \approx 10.39$ **31.** $4\sqrt{3} \approx 6.93$ **33.** $6 + 6\sqrt{3} \approx 16.39$ **35.** (a) $6\sqrt{3}$ inches (b) 12 inches **37.** $VW = 1.2$

5.6 Exercises

1. 30 oz of ingredient A; 24 oz of ingredient B; 36 oz of ingredient C **3.** (a) Yes (b) Yes **5.** $EF = 4\frac{1}{6}$, $FG = 3\frac{1}{3}$, $GH = 2\frac{1}{2}$ **7.** $x = 5\frac{1}{3}$, $DE = 5\frac{1}{3}$, $EF = 6\frac{2}{3}$ **9.** $EC = 16\frac{4}{5}$ **11.** $a = 5$; $AD = 4$ **13.** (a) No (b) Yes **15.** 9 **17.** $4\sqrt{6} \approx 9.80$ **19.** 41° **21.** $\frac{AC}{CE} = \frac{AD}{DE}$; $\frac{DC}{CB} = \frac{DE}{EB}$ **23.** $SV = 2\sqrt{3} \approx 3.46$; $VT = 4\sqrt{3} \approx 6.93$ **25.** $x = \frac{1 + \sqrt{73}}{2}$ or $x = \frac{1 - \sqrt{73}}{2}$; reject both because each will give a negative number for the length of a side. **27.** (a) True (b) True **29.** $RK = 1.8$ **31.** 1. Given 2. Means-Extremes Property 3. Addition Property of Equality 4. Distributive Property 6. Substitution

37. $\frac{-1+\sqrt{5}}{2} \approx 0.62$ **39.** (a) $CD = 2$; $DB = 3$ (b) $CE = \frac{20}{11}$; $EA = \frac{24}{11}$ (c) $BF = \frac{10}{3}$; $FA = \frac{8}{3}$ (d) $\frac{3}{2}\cdot\frac{5}{6}\cdot\frac{4}{5} = 1$

5.6 Selected Proof

33.

PROOF

Statements	Reasons
1. $\triangle RST$ with M the midpoint of $\overline{RS}$; $\overleftrightarrow{MN} \parallel \overline{ST}$	1. Given
2. $RM = MS$	2. The midpoint of a segment divides the segment into two segments of equal measure
3. $\frac{RM}{MS} = \frac{RN}{NT}$	3. If a line is $\parallel$ to one side of a $\triangle$ and intersects the other two sides, then it divides these sides proportionally
4. $\frac{MS}{MS} = 1 = \frac{RN}{NT}$	4. Substitution
5. $RN = NT$	5. Means-Extremes Property
6. N is the midpoint of $\overline{RT}$	6. If a point divides a segment into two segments of equal measure, then the point is a midpoint

CHAPTER 5 REVIEW EXERCISES

1. False **2.** True **3.** False **4.** True **5.** True **6.** False **7.** True **8.** (a) $\pm 3\sqrt{2} \approx \pm 4.24$ (b) 26 (c) -1 (d) 2 (e) 7 or -1 (f) $-\frac{9}{5}$ or 4 (g) 6 or -1 (h) -6 or 3 **9.** \$3.78 **10.** Six packages **11.** \$79.20 **12.** The lengths of the sides are 8, 12, 20, and 28. **13.** 18 **14.** 20 and $22\frac{1}{2}$ **15.** 150° **16.** (a) SSS~ (b) AA (c) SAS~ (d) SSS~ **19.** $x = 5$; $m\angle F = 97°$ **20.** $AB = 6$; $BC = 12$ **21.** 3 **22.** $4\frac{1}{2}$ **23.** $6\frac{1}{4}$ **24.** $5\frac{3}{5}$ **25.** 10 **26.** 6 **27.** $EO = 1\frac{1}{5}$; $EK = 9$ **30.** (a) $8\frac{1}{3}$ (b) 21 (c) $2\sqrt{3} \approx 3.46$ (d) 3 **31.** (a) 16 (b) 40 (c) $2\sqrt{5} \approx 4.47$ (d) 4 **32.** (a) 30° (b) 24 (c) 20 (d) 16 **33.** $AE = 20$; $EF = 15$; $AF = 25$ **34.** $4\sqrt{2} \approx 5.66$ in. **35.** $3\sqrt{2} \approx 4.24$ cm **36.** 25 cm **37.** $5\sqrt{3} \approx 8.66$ in. **38.** $4\sqrt{3} \approx 6.93$ in. **39.** 12 cm **40.** (a) $x = 9\sqrt{2} \approx 12.73$; $y = 9$ (b) $x = 4\frac{1}{2}$; $y = 6$ (c) $x = 12$; $y = 3$ (d) $x = 2\sqrt{14} \approx 7.48$; $y = 13$ **41.** 11 km **42.** (a) Acute (b) No $\triangle$ (c) Obtuse (d) Right (e) No $\triangle$ (f) Acute (g) Obtuse (h) Obtuse

CHAPTER 5 REVIEW EXERCISES SELECTED PROOFS

17.

PROOF

Statements	Reasons
1. $ABCD$ is a parallelogram; $\overline{DB}$ intersects $\overline{AE}$ at point F	1. Given
2. $\overline{DC} \parallel \overline{AB}$	2. Opposite sides of a parallelogram are $\parallel$
3. $\angle CDB \cong \angle ABD$	3. If two $\parallel$ lines are cut by a transversal, then the alt. int. $\angle$s are $\cong$
4. $\angle DEF \cong \angle BAF$	4. Same as (3)
5. $\triangle DFE \sim \triangle BFA$	5. AA
6. $\frac{AF}{EF} = \frac{AB}{DE}$	6. CSSTP

18.

PROOF

Statements	Reasons
1. $\angle 1 \cong \angle 2$	1. Given
2. $\angle ADC \cong \angle 2$	2. If two lines intersect, then the vertical $\angle$s formed are $\cong$
3. $\angle ADC \cong \angle 1$	3. Transitive Prop. for Congruence
4. $\angle A \cong \angle A$	4. Identity
5. $\triangle BAE \sim \triangle CAD$	5. AA
6. $\frac{AB}{AC} = \frac{BE}{CD}$	6. CSSTP

Chapter 5 Test

1. (a) 3:5 $\left(\text{or } \frac{3}{5}\right)$ (b) $\frac{25 \text{ mi}}{\text{gal}}$ [5.1] **2.** (a) $\frac{40}{13}$ (b) 9, -9 [5.1] **3.** 15°; 75° [5.1] **4.** (a) 92° (b) 12 [5.2] **5.** (a) SAS ~ (b) AA [5.3] **6.** $\triangle ABC \sim \triangle ACD \sim \triangle CBD$ [5.4] **7.** (a) $c = \sqrt{41}$ (b) $a = \sqrt{28} = 2\sqrt{7}$ [5.4] **8.** (a) Yes (b) No [5.4] **9.** $DA = \sqrt{89}$ [5.4] **10.** (a) $10\sqrt{2}$ in. (b) 8 cm [5.5] **11.** (a) 5 m (b) 12 ft [5.5] **12.** $EC = 12$ [5.6] **13.** $PQ = 4$; $QM = 6$ [5.6] **14.** 1 [5.6] **15.** $DB = 4$ [5.2] **16.** S1. $\overline{MN} \parallel \overline{QR}$ R1. Given 2. Corresponding $\angle$s are $\cong$ 3. $\angle P \cong \angle P$ 4. AA [5.3] **17.** 1. Given 2. Identity 3. Given 5. Substitution 6. SAS ~ 7. $\angle PRC \cong \angle B$ [5.3]

CHAPTER 6

6.1 Exercises

1. 29° **3.** 47.6° **5.** 56.6° **7.** 313° **9.** (a) 90° (b) 270° (c) 135° (d) 135° **11.** (a) 80° (b) 120° (c) 160° (d) 80° (e) 120° (f) 160° (g) 10° (h) 50° (i) 30° **13.** (a) 72° (b) 144° (c) 36° (d) 72° (e) 18° **15.** (a) 12 (b) $6\sqrt{2}$ **17.** 3 **19.** $\sqrt{7} + 3\sqrt{3}$ **21.** 90°; square **23.** (a) The measure of an arc equals the measure of its corresponding central angle. Therefore, congruent arcs have congruent central angles. (b) The measure of a central angle equals the measure of its intercepted arc. Therefore, congruent central angles have congruent arcs. (c) Draw the radii to the endpoints of the congruent chords. The two triangles formed are congruent by SSS. The central angles of each triangle are congruent by CPCTC. Therefore, the arcs corresponding to the central angles are also congruent. Hence, congruent chords have congruent arcs. (d) Draw the four radii to the endpoints of the congruent arcs. Also draw the chords corresponding to the congruent arcs. The central angles corresponding to the congruent arcs are also congruent. Therefore, the triangles are congruent by SAS. The chords are congruent by CPCTC. Hence, congruent arcs have congruent chords. (e) Congruent central angles have congruent arcs (from b). Congruent arcs have congruent chords (from d). Hence, congruent central angles have congruent chords. (f) Congruent chords have congruent arcs (from c). Congruent arcs have congruent central angles (from a). Therefore, congruent chords have congruent central angles. **25.** (a) 15° (b) 70° **27.** 72° **29.** 45° **31.** 1. $\overline{MN} \parallel \overline{OP}$ in $\odot O$ 2. If two $\parallel$ lines are cut by a transversal, then the alt. int. $\angle$s are $\cong$ 3. If two $\angle$s are $\cong$, then their measures are = 4. The measure of an inscribed $\angle$ equals $\frac{1}{2}$ the measure of its intercepted arc 5. The measure of a central $\angle$ equals the measure of its arc 6. Substitution **39.** If $\widehat{ST} \cong \widehat{TV}$, then $\overline{ST} \cong \overline{TV}$ ($\cong$ arcs in a circle have $\cong$ chords). $\triangle STV$ is an isosceles $\triangle$ because it has two $\cong$ sides. **43.** $WZ = 1.75$

6.1 Selected Proof

33. *Proof:* Using the chords $\overline{AB}$, $\overline{BC}$, $\overline{CD}$, and $\overline{AD}$ in $\odot O$ as sides of inscribed angles, $\angle B \cong \angle D$ and $\angle A \cong \angle C$ because they are inscribed angles intercepting the same arc. $\triangle ABE \sim \triangle CDE$ by AA.

6.2 Exercises

1. (a) 8° (b) 46° (c) 38° (d) 54° (e) 126° **3.** (a) 90° (b) 13° (c) 103° **5.** 18° **7.** (a) 22° (b) 7° (c) 15° **9.** (a) 136° (b) 224° (c) 68° (d) 44° **11.** (a) 96° (b) 60° **13.** (a) 120° (b) 240° (c) 60° **15.** 28° **17.** $m\widehat{CE} = 88°$; $m\widehat{BD} = 36°$ **19.** (a) Supplementary (b) 107° **21.** 1. $\overline{AB}$ and $\overline{AC}$ are tangents to $\odot O$ from A 2. The measure of an $\angle$ formed by a tangent and a chord equals $\frac{1}{2}$ the arc measure 3. Substitution 4. If two $\angle$s are = in measure, they are $\cong$ 5. $\overline{AB} \cong \overline{AC}$ 6. $\triangle ABC$ is isosceles **27.** ≈ 154.95 mi **29.** $m\angle 1 = 36°$; $m\angle 2 = 108°$ **31.** (a) 30° (b) 60° (c) 150° **33.** $\angle X \cong \angle X$; $\angle R \cong \angle W$; also, $\angle RVX \cong \angle WSX$ **35.** 10 **37.** $(\sqrt{2} - 1)$ cm

6.2 Selected Proof

23. *Given:* Tangent $\overline{AB}$ to $\odot O$ at point B; $m\angle A = m\angle B$

Prove: $m\widehat{BD} = 2 \cdot m\widehat{BC}$

Proof: $m\angle BCD = m\angle A + m\angle B$; but because $m\angle A = m\angle B$, $m\angle BCD = m\angle B + m\angle B$ or $m\angle BCD = 2 \cdot m\angle B$. $m\angle BCD$ also equals $\frac{1}{2}m\widehat{BD}$ because it is an inscribed $\angle$. Therefore, $\frac{1}{2}m\widehat{BD} = 2 \cdot m\angle B$ or $m\widehat{BD} = 4 \cdot m\angle B$. But if $\overline{AB}$ is a tangent to $\odot O$ at B, then $m\angle B = \frac{1}{2}m\widehat{BC}$. By substitution, $m\widehat{BD} = 4(\frac{1}{2}m\widehat{BC})$ or $m\widehat{BD} = 2 \cdot m\widehat{BC}$.

6.3 Exercises

1. 30° **3.** $6\sqrt{5}$ **7.** 3 **9.** $DE = 4$ and $EC = 12$ or $DE = 12$ and $EC = 4$ **11.** 4 **13.** $x = 6$; $AE = 3$ **15.** $DE = 12$; $EC = 6$ **17.** $9\frac{2}{5}$ **19.** 9 **21.** $5\frac{1}{3}$ **23.** $3 + 3\sqrt{5}$ **25.** (a) None (b) One (c) 4 **31.** Yes; $\overline{AE} \cong \overline{CE}$; $\overline{DE} \cong \overline{EB}$ **33.** 20° **35.** $AM = 5$; $PC = 7$; $BN = 9$ **37.** 12 **39.** 8.7 inches **41.** (a) Obtuse (b) Equilateral **43.** 45°

6.3 Selected Proofs

27. If $\overline{AF}$ is a tangent to $\odot O$ and $\overline{AC}$ is a secant to $\odot O$, then $(AF)^2 = AC \cdot AB$. If $\overline{AF}$ is a tangent to $\odot Q$ and $\overline{AE}$ is a secant to $\odot Q$, then $(AF)^2 = AE \cdot AD$. By substitution, $AC \cdot AB = AE \cdot AD$.

29. *Proof:* Let M, N, P, and Q be the points of tangency for $\overline{DC}$, $\overline{DA}$, $\overline{AB}$, and $\overline{BC}$, respectively. Because the tangent segments from an external point are congruent, $AP = AN$, $PB = BQ$, $CM = CQ$, and $MD = DN$. Thus $AP + PB + CM + MD = AN + BQ + CQ + DN$. Reordering and associating, $(AP + PB) + (CM + MD) = (AN + DN) + (BQ + CQ)$ or $AB + CD = DA + BC$.

45. *Given:* $\overleftrightarrow{AB}$ contains O, the center of the circle, and $\overleftrightarrow{AB}$ contains M, the midpoint of $\overline{RS}$ (See Figure 6.38.)

Prove: $\overleftrightarrow{AB} \perp \overline{RS}$

Proof: If M is the midpoint of $\overline{RS}$ in $\odot O$, then $\overline{RM} \cong \overline{MS}$. Draw $\overline{RO}$ and $\overline{OS}$, which are $\cong$ because they are radii in the same circle. Using $\overline{OM} \cong \overline{OM}$, $\triangle ROM \cong \triangle SOM$ by SSS. By CPCTC, $\angle OMS \cong \angle OMR$, and hence $\overleftrightarrow{AB} \perp \overline{RS}$.

6.4 Exercises

1. $m\angle CQD < m\angle AQB$ **3.** $QM < QN$ **5.** $CD < AB$ **7.** $QM > QN$ **11.** No; angles are not congruent. **15.** $\overline{AB}$; $\overline{GH}$; for a circle containing unequal chords, the chord nearest the center has the greatest length and the chord at the greatest distance from the center has the least length. **17.** (a) $\overline{OT}$ (b) $\overline{OD}$ **19.** (a) $m\widehat{MN} > m\widehat{QP}$ (b) $m\widehat{MPN} < m\widehat{PMQ}$ **21.** Obtuse **23.** (a) $m\angle AOB > m\angle BOC$ (b) $AB > BC$ **25.** (a) $m\widehat{AB} > m\widehat{BC}$ (b) $AB > BC$

27. (a) $\angle C$ (b) $\overline{AC}$ **29.** (a) $\angle B$ (b) $\overline{AC}$
31. $\overline{AB}$ is $(4\sqrt{3} - 4\sqrt{2})$ closer than $\overline{CD}$. **37.** 7

CHAPTER 6 REVIEW EXERCISES

1. 9 mm **2.** 30 cm **3.** $\sqrt{41}$ in. **4.** $6\sqrt{2}$ cm
5. 130° **6.** 45° **7.** 80° **8.** 35°
9. $m\widehat{AC} = m\widehat{DC} = 93\frac{1}{3}°$; $m\widehat{AD} = 173\frac{1}{3}°$
10. $m\widehat{AC} = 110°$ and $m\widehat{AD} = 180°$
11. $m\angle 2 = 44°$; $m\angle 3 = 90°$; $m\angle 4 = 46°$; $m\angle 5 = 44°$
12. $m\angle 1 = 50°$; $m\angle 2 = 40°$; $m\angle 3 = 90°$; $m\angle 4 = 50°$
13. 24 **14.** 10 **15.** A **16.** S **17.** N **18.** S **19.** A
20. N **21.** A **22.** N **23.** (a) 70° (b) 28° (c) 64°
(d) $m\angle P = 21°$ (e) $m\widehat{AB} = 90°$; $m\widehat{CD} = 40°$ (f) 260°
24. (a) 3 (b) 8 (c) 16 (d) 4 (e) 4 (f) 8 or 1 (g) $3\sqrt{5}$
(h) 3 (i) $4\sqrt{3}$ (j) 3 **25.** 29 **26.** If $x = 7$, then $AC = 35$; $DE = 17\frac{1}{2}$. If $x = -4$, then $AC = 24$; $DE = 12$.
30. $m\angle 1 = 93°$; $m\angle 2 = 25°$; $m\angle 3 = 43°$; $m\angle 4 = 68°$; $m\angle 5 = 90°$; $m\angle 6 = 22°$; $m\angle 7 = 68°$; $m\angle 8 = 22°$; $m\angle 9 = 50°$; $m\angle 10 = 112°$ **31.** $24\sqrt{2}$ cm
32. $15 + 5\sqrt{3}$ cm **33.** 14 cm and 15 cm **34.** $AD = 3$; $BE = 6$; $FC = 7$ **35.** (a) $AB > CD$ (b) $QP < QR$
(c) $m\angle A < m\angle C$

CHAPTER 6 REVIEW EXERCISES SELECTED PROOFS

27. *Proof:* If $\overline{DC}$ is tangent to circles B and A at points D and C, then $\overline{BD} \perp \overline{DC}$ and $\overline{AC} \perp \overline{DC}$. $\angle$s D and C are congruent because they are right angles. $\angle DEB \cong \angle CEA$ because of vertical angles. $\triangle BDE \sim \triangle ACE$ by AA. It follows that $\frac{AC}{CE} = \frac{BD}{ED}$ because corresponding sides are proportional. Hence, $AC \cdot ED = CE \cdot BD$.

28. *Proof:* In $\odot O$, if $\overline{EO} \perp \overline{BC}$, $\overline{DO} \perp \overline{BA}$, and $\overline{EO} \cong \overline{OD}$, $\overline{BC} \cong \overline{BA}$. (Chords equidistant from the center of the circle are congruent.) It follows that $\widehat{BC} \cong \widehat{BA}$.

29. *Proof:* If $\overline{AP}$ and $\overline{BP}$ are tangent to $\odot Q$ at A and B, then $\overline{AP} \cong \overline{BP}$. $\widehat{AC} \cong \widehat{BC}$ because C is the midpoint of $\widehat{AB}$. It follows that $\overline{AC} \cong \overline{BC}$ and, using $\overline{CP} \cong \overline{CP}$, we have $\triangle ACP \cong \triangle BCP$ by SSS. $\angle APC \cong \angle BPC$ by CPCTC and hence $\overrightarrow{PC}$ bisects $\angle APB$.

Chapter 6 Test

1. (a) 272° (b) 134° [6.1] **2.** (a) 69° (b) 32° [6.1]
3. (a) 48° (b) Isosceles [6.1] **4.** (a) Right (b) Congruent [6.2] **5.** (a) 69° (b) 37° [6.2] **6.** (a) 214° (b) 34° [6.2]
7. (a) 226° (b) 134° [6.2] **8.** (a) Concentric (b) 8 [6.1]
9. $2\sqrt{13}$ [6.1] **10.** (a) 1 (b) 2 [6.3] **11.** (a) 10 (b) 5 [6.3] **12.** $2\sqrt{6}$ [6.3] **14.** (a) $m\angle AQB > m\angle CQD$
(b) $AB > CD$ [6.4] **15.** (a) 1 (b) 7 [6.2]
16. S1. In $\odot O$, chords $\overline{AD}$ and $\overline{BC}$ intersect at E R1. Given 2. Vertical angles are congruent 4. AA 5. $\frac{AE}{CE} = \frac{BE}{DE}$ [6.3]

CHAPTER 7

7.1 Exercises

1. A, C, E **11.** The locus of points at a given distance from a fixed line is two parallel lines on either side of the fixed line at the same (given) distance from the fixed line. **13.** The locus of points at a distance of 3 in. from point O is a circle with center O and radius 3 in. **15.** The locus of points equidistant from points D, E, and F is the point G for which $DG = EG = FG$. **17.** The locus of the midpoints of the chords in $\odot Q$ parallel to diameter $\overline{PR}$ is the perpendicular bisector of $\overline{PR}$. **19.** The locus of points equidistant from two given intersecting lines is two perpendicular lines that bisect the angles formed by the two intersecting lines.
25. The locus of points at a distance of 2 cm from a sphere whose radius is 5 cm is two concentric spheres with the same center. The radius of one sphere is 3 cm, and the radius of the other sphere is 7 cm. **27.** The locus is another sphere with the same center and a radius of length 2.5 m. **29.** The locus of points equidistant from an 8-ft ceiling and the floor is a plane parallel to the ceiling and the floor and midway between them.

7.2 Exercises

1. Yes **3.** Incenter **5.** Circumcenter **7.** (a) Angle bisectors (b) Perpendicular bisectors of sides (c) Altitudes (d) Medians **9.** No (need 2) **11.** Equilateral triangle
13. Midpoint of the hypotenuse **23.** No **25.** $\frac{10\sqrt{3}}{3}$
27. $RQ = 10$; $SQ = \sqrt{89}$ **29.** (a) 4 (b) 6
(c) 10.5 **33.** Equilateral **35.** (a) Yes (b) Yes
37. (a) Yes (b) No **41.** 3 in.

7.3 Exercises

1. First, construct the angle bisectors of two consecutive angles, say A and B. The point of intersection, O, is the center of the inscribed circle.
Second, construct the line segment $\overline{OM}$ perpendicular to $\overline{AB}$. Then, using the radius length $r = OM$, construct the inscribed circle with center O.
3. Draw the diagonals (angle bisectors) $\overline{JL}$ and $\overline{MK}$. These determine center O of the inscribed circle. Now construct the line segment $\overline{OR} \perp \overline{MJ}$. Use OR as the length of the radius of the inscribed circle. **9.** 27.2 in. **11.** 8.3 cm
13. $a = 5$ in.; $r = 5\sqrt{2}$ in. **15.** $16\sqrt{3}$ ft; 16 ft
17. (a) 120° (b) 90° (c) 72° (d) 60° **19.** (a) 4 (b) 8 (c) 6 (d) 15 **21.** (a) 140° (b) 135° (c) 120° (d) 90°
23. 6 **25.** (a) Yes (b) No (c) Yes (d) No
27. $4 + 4\sqrt{2}$ **29.** 168°

CHAPTER 7 REVIEW EXERCISES

7. The locus of points equidistant from the sides of $\angle ABC$ is the bisector of $\angle ABC$. **8.** The locus of points 1 in. from point B is the circle with center B and radius length 1 in.
9. The locus of points equidistant from D and E is the perpendicular bisector of $\overline{DE}$. **10.** The locus of points $\frac{1}{2}$ inch from $\overleftrightarrow{DE}$ are two lines parallel to each other and $\overleftrightarrow{DE}$, each line $\frac{1}{2}$ inch from $\overleftrightarrow{DE}$ and on opposite sides of $\overleftrightarrow{DE}$.

11. The locus of the midpoints of the radii of a circle is a concentric circle with radius half the length of the given radius. **12.** The locus of the centers of all circles passing through two given points is the perpendicular bisector of the line segment joining the two given points. **13.** The locus of the center of a penny that rolls around a half-dollar is a circle.
14. The locus of points in space 2 cm from point A is the sphere with center A and radius 2 cm. **15.** The locus of points 1 cm from plane P is the two planes parallel to each other and plane P, each plane 1 cm from P and on opposite sides of P. **16.** The locus of points in space less than 3 units from a given point is the interior of a sphere. **17.** The locus of points equidistant from two parallel planes is a parallel plane midway between the two planes. **24.** (a) 12 (b) 2 (c) $2\sqrt{3}$ **25.** $BF = 6; AE = 9$ **26.** (a) 72° (b) 108° (c) 72° **27.** (a) 36° (b) 144° (c) 36° **28.** (a) 8 (b) 40 cm **29.** (a) 24 in. (b) $3\sqrt{2}$ in. **30.** (a) No (b) No (c) Yes (d) Yes **31.** (a) No (b) Yes (c) No (d) Yes **32.** 14 in. **33.** $40\sqrt{3}$ cm

Chapter 7 Test

1. The locus of points equidistant from parallel lines l and m is the line parallel to both l and m and midway between them. [7.1] **2.** The locus of points equidistant from the sides of $\angle ABC$ is the bisector of $\angle ABC$. [7.1] **3.** The locus of points equidistant from D and E is the perpendicular bisector of $\overline{DE}$ [7.1] **4.** The locus of points 3 cm from point P is the circle with center P and radius length 3 cm. [7.1]
5. The locus of points in space 3 cm from point P is the sphere with center P and radius length 3 cm. [7.1]
6. (a) Incenter (b) Centroid [7.2] **7.** (a) Circumcenter (b) Orthocenter [7.2] **8.** Equilateral triangle or equiangular triangle [7.2] **9.** Angle bisectors and medians [7.2]
10. (a) T (b) T (c) F (d) F [7.3] **11.** (a) 1.5 in. (b) $3\sqrt{3}$ in. [7.3] **12.** (a) 72° (b) 108° [7.3]
13. 10 sides [7.3] **14.** 80 cm [7.3]
15. (a) $4\sqrt{3}$ in. (b) 8 in. [7.3]

CHAPTER 8

8.1 Exercises

1. Two triangles with equal areas are not necessarily congruent. Two squares with equal areas must be congruent because the sides are congruent. **3.** 37 units^2
5. The altitudes to $\overline{PN}$ and to $\overline{MN}$ are congruent. This is because $\triangle$s QMN and QPN are congruent; corresponding altitudes of $\cong$ $\triangle$s are $\cong$. **7.** Equal **9.** 54 cm^2 **11.** 18 m^2 **13.** 72 in^2 **15.** 100 in^2 **17.** 126 in^2 **19.** 264 units^2 **21.** 144 units^2 **23.** 192 ft^2 **25.** (a) 300 ft^2 (b) 3 gallons (c) \$46.50 **27.** $156 + 24\sqrt{10}$ ft^2 **29.** (a) 9 sq ft = 1 sq yd (b) 1296 sq in. = 1 sq yd **31.** 24 cm^2 **33.** $\overline{MN}$ joins the midpoints of $\overline{CA}$ and $\overline{CB}$, so $MN = \frac{1}{2}(AB)$. Therefore, $\overline{AP} \cong \overline{PB} \cong \overline{MN}$. $\overline{PN}$ joins the midpoints of $\overline{CB}$ and $\overline{AB}$, so $PN = \frac{1}{2}(AC)$. Therefore $\overline{AM} \cong \overline{MC} \cong \overline{PN}$. $\overline{MP}$ joins the midpoints of $\overline{AB}$ and $\overline{AC}$, so $MP = \frac{1}{2}(BC)$. Therefore $\overline{CN} \cong \overline{NB} \cong \overline{MP}$. The four triangles are all $\cong$ by SSS. Therefore, the areas of all these triangles are the same. Hence, the area of the big triangle is equal to four times the area of one of the smaller triangles. **37.** 8 in. **39.** (a) 12 in. (b) 84 in^2 **41.** 56 percent **43.** By the Area-Addition Postulate, $A_{R \cup S} = A_R + A_S$. Now $A_{R \cup S}$, A_R, and A_S are all positive numbers. Let p represent the area of region S, so that $A_{R \cup S} = A_R + p$. By the definition of inequality, $A_R < A_{R \cup S}$, or $A_{R \cup S} > A_R$. **45.** $(a + b)(c + d) = ac + ad + bc + bd$ **47.** $4\frac{8}{13}$ in. **49.** 8 **51.** $P = 2x + \frac{96}{x}$ **53.** 48 units^2
55. (a) 10 (b) 26 (c) 18 (d) No

8.1 Selected Proof

35. *Proof:* $A = (LH)(HJ) = s^2$. By the Pythagorean Theorem, $s^2 + s^2 = d^2$.

$$2s^2 = d^2$$
$$s^2 = \frac{d^2}{2}$$

Thus, $$A = \frac{d^2}{2}$$

8.2 Exercises

1. 30 in. **3.** $4\sqrt{29}$ m **5.** 30 ft **7.** 38 **9.** 84 in^2
11. 1764 mm^2 **13.** 40 ft^2 **15.** 80 units^2
17. $36 + 36\sqrt{3}$ units^2 **19.** 16 in., 32 in., and 28 in.
21. 15 cm **23.** (a) $\frac{9}{4}$ (b) $\frac{4}{1}$ **27.** $24 + 4\sqrt{21}$ units^2
29. 96 units^2 **31.** 6 yd by 8 yd **33.** (a) 770 ft (b) \$454.30
35. 624 ft^2 **37.** Square with sides of length 10 in.
39. (a) 52 units (b) 169 units^2 **41.** 60 in^2
43. (a) No (b) Yes **47.** 12 ft^2 **49.** 5 in^2
51. $h = 2.4$ **53.** 2 units

8.2 Selected Proofs

25. Using Heron's Formula, the semiperimeter is $\frac{1}{2}(3s)$, or $\frac{3s}{2}$. Then

$$A = \sqrt{\frac{3s}{2}\left(\frac{3s}{2} - s\right)\left(\frac{3s}{2} - s\right)\left(\frac{3s}{2} - s\right)}$$
$$A = \sqrt{\frac{3s}{2}\left(\frac{s}{2}\right)\left(\frac{s}{2}\right)\left(\frac{s}{2}\right)}$$
$$A = \sqrt{\frac{3s^4}{16}} = \frac{\sqrt{3}\cdot\sqrt{s^4}}{\sqrt{16}}$$
$$A = \frac{s^2\sqrt{3}}{4}$$

45. The area of a trapezoid $= \frac{1}{2}h(b_1 + b_2) = h \cdot \frac{1}{2}(b_1 + b_2)$. The length of the median of a trapezoid is $m = \frac{1}{2}(b_1 + b_2)$. By substitution, the area of a trapezoid is $A = hm$.

Section 8.3

1. (a) 12.25 cm^2 (b) 88.36 in^2
3. (a) $1.5625\sqrt{3}$ m^2 (b) $27\sqrt{3}$ in^2
5. $P = 68.4$ in. **7.** $r = \frac{20}{3}\sqrt{3}$ cm
9. Regular hexagon **11.** Square

13. 40.96 cm^2 **15.** $63.48\sqrt{3}$ in^2
17. 97.5 cm^2 **19.** 317.52 in^2
21. $54\sqrt{3}$ cm^2 **23.** $75\sqrt{3}$ in^2
25. 750 cm^2 **27.** 460.8 ft^2
29. $(24 + 12\sqrt{3})$ in^2 **31.** $\frac{2}{1}$ or 2:1
33. $(24 + 24\sqrt{2})$ $units^2$
35. $\approx$ 182 $units^2$ **37.** $\frac{3}{4}$ or 3:4

8.4 Exercises

1. $C = 16\pi$ cm; $A = 64\pi$ cm^2 **3.** $C = 66$ in.; $A = 346\frac{1}{2}$ in^2
5. (a) $r = 22$ in.; $d = 44$ in. (b) $r = 30$ ft; $d = 60$ ft
7. (a) $r = 5$ in.; $d = 10$ in. (b) $r = 1.5$ cm; $d = 3.0$ cm
9. $\frac{8}{3}\pi$ in. **11.** $C \approx 77.79$ in. **13.** $r \approx 6.7$ cm
15. $\ell \approx 7.33$ in. **17.** 16 in^2 **19.** $5 < AN < 13$
21. $(32\pi - 64)$ $in.^2$ **23.** $(600 - 144\pi)$ ft^2
25. $\approx$ 7 cm **27.** 8 in.
29. $A = A_{\text{LARGER CIRCLE}} - A_{\text{SMALLER CIRCLE}}$
$A = \pi R^2 - \pi r^2$
$A = \pi(R^2 - r^2)$
But $R^2 - r^2$ is a difference of two squares, so
$A = \pi(R + r)(R - r)$.
31. 3 in. and 4 in. **33.** (a) $\approx$ 201.06 ft^2 (b) 2.87 pints. Thus, 3 pints must be purchased. (c) \$8.85
35. (a) $\approx$ 1256 ft^2 (b) 20.93. Thus 21 lb of seed is needed. (c) \$34.65 **37.** $\approx$ 43.98 cm
39. $\approx$ 14.43 in. **41.** $\approx$ 27,488.94 mi **43.** 15.7 ft/s
45. 12π cm^2

8.5 Exercises

1. 34 in. **3.** 150 cm^2 **5.** $\frac{3}{2}rs$ **7.** 54 mm **9.** 24 in^2
11. 1 in. **13.** $P = \left(16 + \frac{8}{3}\pi\right)$in. and $A = \frac{32}{3}\pi$ in^2
15. $\approx$ 30.57 in. **17.** $P = (12 + 4\pi)$ in.; $A = (24\pi - 36\sqrt{3})$ in^2 **19.** $\left(25\sqrt{3} - \frac{25}{2}\pi\right)$$cm^2$
21. $\frac{9}{2}$ cm **23.** 36π **25.** 90° **27.** Cut the pizza into 8 slices.
29. $A = \left(\frac{\pi}{2}\right)s^2 - s^2$ **31.** $r = 3\frac{1}{3}$ ft or 3 ft, 4 in.
35. (a) 3 (b) 2 **37.** $\frac{308\pi}{3} \approx 322.54$ in^2
39. $1875\pi \approx 5890$ ft^2 **41.** $\sqrt{5}$ cm $\approx$ 2.2 cm

CHAPTER 8 REVIEW EXERCISES

1. 480 **2.** (a) 40 (b) $40\sqrt{3}$ (c) $40\sqrt{2}$ **3.** 50
4. 204 **5.** 336 **6.** 36 **7.** (a) $24\sqrt{2} + 18$ (b) $24 + 9\sqrt{3}$ (c) $33\sqrt{3}$ **8.** $A = 216$ in^2; $P = 60$ in.
9. (a) 19,000 ft^2 (b) 4 bags (c) \$72
10. (a) 3 double rolls (b) 3 rolls
11. (a) $\frac{289}{4}\sqrt{3} + 8\sqrt{33}$ (b) $50 + \sqrt{33}$ **12.** 168
13. 5 cm by 7 cm **14.** (a) 15 cm, 25 cm, and 20 cm (b) 150 cm^2 **15.** 36 **16.** $36\sqrt{3}$ cm^2 **17.** 20
18. (a) 72° (b) 108° (c) 72° **19.** $96\sqrt{3}$ ft^2
20. 6 in. **21.** $162\sqrt{3}$ in^2 **22.** (a) 8 (b) $\approx$ 120 cm^2
23. (a) No. ⊥ bisectors of sides of a parallelogram are not necessarily concurrent. (b) No. ⊥ bisectors of sides of a rhombus are not necessarily concurrent. (c) Yes. ⊥ bisectors of sides of a rectangle are concurrent. (d) Yes. ⊥ bisectors of sides of a square are concurrent.
24. (a) No. ∠ bisectors of a parallelogram are not necessarily concurrent. (b) Yes. ∠ bisectors of a rhombus are concurrent. (c) No. ∠ bisectors of a rectangle are not necessarily concurrent. (d) Yes. ∠ bisectors of a square are concurrent.
25. $147\sqrt{3} \approx 254.61$ in^2
26. (a) 312 ft^2 (b) 35 yd^2 (c) \$348.95
27. $64 - 16\pi$ **28.** $\frac{49}{2}\pi - \frac{49}{2}\sqrt{3}$ **29.** $\frac{8}{3}\pi - 4\sqrt{3}$
30. $288 - 72\pi$ **31.** $25\sqrt{3} - \frac{25}{3}\pi$ **32.** $\ell = \frac{2\pi\sqrt{5}}{3}$ cm; $A = 5\pi$ cm^2 **33.** (a) 21 ft (b) $\approx 346\frac{1}{2}$ ft^2
34. (a) 6π ft^2 (b) $(6\sqrt{3} + \frac{4\pi}{3}\sqrt{3})$ ft **35.** $(9\pi - 18)$ in^2
39. (a) $\approx$ 28 yd^2 (b) $\approx$ 21.2 ft^2 **40.** (a) $\approx$ 905 ft^2 (b) \$162.90 (c) Approximately 151 flowers

CHAPTER 8 REVIEW EXERCISES SELECTED PROOF

36. *Proof:* By an earlier theorem,

$$A_{\text{RING}} = \pi R^2 - \pi r^2 = \pi(OC)^2 - \pi(OB)^2 = \pi[(OC)^2 - (OB)^2]$$

In rt. $\triangle OBC$,

$$(OB)^2 + (BC)^2 = (OC)^2$$

Thus, $(OC)^2 - (OB)^2 = (BC)^2$

In turn, $A_{\text{RING}} = \pi(BC)^2$.

Chapter 8 Test

1. (a) Square inches (b) Equal [8.1] **2.** (a) $A = s^2$ (b) $C = 2\pi r$ [8.4] **3.** (a) True (b) False [8.2]
4. 23 cm^2 [8.1] **5.** 120 ft^2 [8.1] **6.** 24 ft^2 [8.2]
7. 24 cm^2 [8.2] **8.** 6 ft [8.2] **9.** (a) 29 in. (b) 58 in^2 [8.3]
10. (a) 10π in. (b) 25π in^2 [8.4] **11.** $\approx 5\frac{1}{2}$ in. [8.4]
12. 314 cm^2 [8.4] **13.** $(16\pi - 32)$ in^2 [8.5]
14. 54π cm^2 [8.5] **15.** $(36\pi - 72)$ in^2 [8.5]
16. $r = 2$ in. [8.3]

CHAPTER 9

9.1 Exercises

1. (a) Yes (b) Oblique (c) Hexagon (d) Oblique hexagonal prism (e) Parallelogram
3. (a) 12 (b) 18 (c) 8
5. (a) cm^2 (b) cm^3
7. 132 cm^2 **9.** 120 cm^3 **11.** (a) 16 (b) 8 (c) 16
13. (a) $2n$ (b) n (c) $2n$ (d) $3n$ (e) n (f) 2 (g) $n + 2$
15. (a) 671.6 cm^2 (b) 961.4 cm^2 (c) 2115.54 cm^3
17. (a) 72 ft^2 (b) 84 ft^2 (c) 36 ft^3
19. 1728 in^3 **21.** 6 in. by 6 in. by 3 in.
23. $x = 3$ **25.** \$4.44 **27.** 640 ft^3
29. (a) $T = L + 2B$, $T = hP + 2(e \cdot e)$, $T = e(4e) + 2e^2$, $T = 4e^2 + 2e^2$, $T = 6e^2$ (b) 96 cm^2 (c) $V = Bh$, $V = e^2 \cdot e$, $V = e^3$ (d) 64 cm^3

31. 4 cm **35.** \$128
37. 864 in^3 **39.** 10 gal **41.** 720 cm^2 **43.** 2952 cm^3

9.2 Exercises

1. (a) Right pentagonal prism (b) Oblique pentagonal prism
3. (a) Regular square pyramid (b) Oblique square pyramid
5. (a) Pyramid (b) E (c) $\overline{EA}, \overline{EB}, \overline{EC}, \overline{ED}$
(d) $\triangle EAB, \triangle EBC, \triangle ECD, \triangle EAD$ (e) No **7.** (a) 5 (b) 8
(c) 5 **9.** 66 in^2 **11.** 32 cm^3 **13.** (a) $n + 1$ (b) n (c) n
(d) $2n$ (e) n (f) $n + 1$ **15.** 3a, 4a
17. (a) Slant height (b) Lateral edge **19.** 4 in.
21. (a) 144.9 cm^2 (b) 705.18 cm^3 **23.** (a) 60 ft^2
(b) 96 ft^2 (c) 48 ft^3 **25.** $36\sqrt{5} + 36 \approx 116.5$ in^2
27. 480 ft^2 **29.** 900 ft^3 **31.** $\approx$ 24 ft **33.** 336 in^3
37. 96 in^2 **39.** $\frac{8}{1}$ or 8:1 **41.** 39.4 in^3

9.3 Exercises

1. (a) Yes (b) Yes (c) Yes **3.** (a) $60\pi \approx 188.50$ in^2
(b) $110\pi \approx 345.58$ in^2 (c) $150\pi \approx 471.24$ in^3
5. ≈ 54.19 in^2 **7.** 5 cm **9.** The radius has a length of 2 in., and the altitude has a length of 3 in.
11. $32\pi \approx 100.53$ in^3 **13.** $2\sqrt{13} \approx 7.21$ cm **15.** 2 m
17. $4\sqrt{3} \approx 6.93$ in. **19.** $3\sqrt{5} \approx 6.71$ cm
21. (a) $6\pi\sqrt{85} \approx 173.78$ in^2
(b) $6\pi\sqrt{85} + 36\pi \approx 286.88$ in^2 (c) $84\pi \approx 263.89$ in^3
23. 54π in^3 **25.** 2000π cm^3
27. 1200π cm^3 **29.** $65\pi \approx 204.2$ cm^2
31. $192\pi \approx 603.19$ in^3 **35.** $60\pi \approx 188.5$ in^2
37. $\frac{4}{1}$ or 4:1 **39.** $\approx$ 471.24 gal **43.** ≈ 290.60 cm^3
45. $\approx$ 318 gal **47.** $\approx$ 38 ft^2

9.4 Exercises

1. Polyhedron *EFGHIJK* is concave.
3. Polyhedron *EFGHIJK* has nine faces (F), seven vertices (V), and 14 edges (E). $V + F = E + 2$ becomes
$$7 + 9 = 14 + 2$$
5. A regular hexahedron has six faces (F), eight vertices (V), and 12 edges (E). $V + F = E + 2$ becomes
$$8 + 6 = 12 + 2$$
7. (a) 8 faces (b) Regular octahedron **9.** 9 faces
11. (a) $\frac{1}{2}$ (b) $\frac{5}{12}$ (c) $\frac{5}{6}$ **13.** (a) $6\sqrt{2} \approx 8.49$ in.
(b) $6\sqrt{3} \approx 10.39$ in. **15.** 44 in^2 **17.** 105.84 cm^2
19. (a) 17.64 m^2 (b) 4.2 m **21.** (a) 1468.8 cm^2 (b) \$8.81
23. (a) $\frac{3}{2}$ or 3:2 (b) $\frac{3}{2}$ or 3:2
25. $r = 3\sqrt{2} \approx 4.24$ in.; $h = 6\sqrt{2} \approx 8.49$ in.
27. (a) $3\sqrt{3} \approx 5.20$ in. (b) 9 in.
29. (a) $36\pi \approx 113.1$ m^2 (b) $36\pi \approx 113.1$ m^3 **31.** 1.5 in.
33. 113.1 ft^2; $\approx$ 3 pints **35.** $7.4\pi \approx 23.24$ in^3
37. (a) Yes (b) Yes **39.** Parallel **41.** Congruent
43. $S = 36\pi$ $units^2$; $V = 36\pi$ $units^3$

CHAPTER 9 REVIEW EXERCISES

1. 672 in^2 **2.** 297 cm^2
3. Dimensions are 6 in. by 6 in. by 20 in.; $V = 720$ in^3
4. $T = 468$ cm^2; $V = 648$ cm^3 **5.** (a) 360 in^2 (b) 468 in^2
(c) 540 in^3
6. (a) 624 cm^2 (b) $624 + 192\sqrt{3} \approx 956.55$ cm^2
(c) $1248\sqrt{3} \approx 2161.6$ cm^3
7. $\sqrt{89} \approx 9.43$ cm **8.** $3\sqrt{7} \approx 7.94$ in.
9. $\sqrt{74} \approx 8.60$ in. **10.** $2\sqrt{3} \approx 3.46$ cm **11.** (a) 540 in^2
(b) 864 in^2 (c) 1296 in^3 **12.** (a) $36\sqrt{19} \approx 156.92$ cm^2
(b) $36\sqrt{19} + 36\sqrt{3} \approx 219.27$ cm^2 (c) $96\sqrt{3} \approx 166.28$ cm^3
13. (a) 120π in^2 (b) 192π in^2 (c) 360π in^3
14. (a) ≈ 351.68 ft^3 (b) ≈ 452.16 ft^2
15. (a) $72\pi \approx 226.19$ cm^2 (b) $108\pi \approx 339.29$ cm^2
(c) $72\pi\sqrt{3} \approx 391.78$ cm^3 **16.** $\ell = 10$ in. **17.** ≈ 616 in^2
18. ≈ 904.32 cm^3 **19.** 120π $units^3$
20. $\frac{\text{surface area of smaller}}{\text{surface area of larger}} = \frac{1}{9}$; $\frac{\text{volume of smaller}}{\text{volume of larger}} = \frac{1}{27}$
21. $\approx 183\frac{1}{3}$ in^3 **22.** 288π cm^3 **23.** $\frac{32\pi}{3}$ in^3
24. ≈ 1017.36 in^3 **25.** $(2744 - \frac{1372}{3}\pi)$ in^3
26. (a) 8 (b) 4 (c) 12 **27.** 40π mm^3
28. (a) $V = 16, E = 24, F = 10$, so $V + F = E + 2$ becomes $16 + 10 = 24 + 2$
(b) $V = 4, E = 6, F = 4$, so $V + F = E + 2$ becomes $4 + 4 = 6 + 2$
(c) $V = 6, E = 12, F = 8$, so $V + F = E + 2$ becomes $6 + 8 = 12 + 2$
29. 114 in^3 **30.** (a) $\frac{1}{2}$ (b) $\frac{5}{8}$
31. (a) 78 in^2 (b) $16\sqrt{3}$ cm^2 **32.** Right triangle (3,4,5)

Chapter 9 Test

1. (a) 15 (b) 7 [9.1] **2.** (a) 16 cm^2 (b) 112 cm^2
(c) 80 cm^3 [9.1] **3.** (a) 5 (b) 4 [9.2]
4. (a) $32\sqrt{2}$ ft^2 (b) $(16 + 32\sqrt{2})$ ft^2 [9.2]
5. 15 ft [9.2] **6.** 3 in. [9.2] **7.** 50 ft^3 [9.2]
8. (a) False (b) True [9.3] **9.** (a) True (b) True [9.3, 9.4]
10. 12 [9.4]
11. $3\sqrt{5}$ cm [9.3] **12.** (a) 48π cm^2 (b) 96π cm^3 [9.3]
13. $h = 6$ in. [9.3]
14. (a) $\frac{1}{2}$ (b) $\frac{3}{8}$ [9.4] **15.** (a) 1256.6 ft^2 (b) 4188.8 ft^3 [9.4]
16. 2 hours and 47 minutes [9.4]

CHAPTER 10

10.1 Exercises

3. (a) 4 (b) 8 (c) 5 (d) 9 **5.** $b = 3.5$ or $b = 10.5$
7. (a) 5 (b) 10 (c) $2\sqrt{5}$ (d) $\sqrt{a^2 + b^2}$
9. (a) $\left(2, \frac{-3}{2}\right)$ (b) (1, 1) (c) (4, 0) (d) $\left(\frac{a}{2}, \frac{b}{2}\right)$
11. (a) $(-3, 4)$ (b) $(0, -2)$ (c) $(-a, 0)$ (d) $(-b, -c)$
13. (a) $\left(4, -\frac{5}{2}\right)$ (b) (0, 4) (c) $\left(\frac{7}{2}, -1\right)$ (d) (a, b)
15. (a) $(5, -1)$ (b) $(0, -5)$ (c) $(2, -a)$ (d) $(b, -c)$
17. (a) $(-3, -4)$ (b) $(-2, 0)$ (c) $(-a, 0)$ (d) $(-b, c)$
19. (a) $x = 4$ (b) $y = b$ (c) $x = 2$ (d) $y = 3$
21. $(2.5, -13.7)$ **23.** (2, 3); 16 **25.** (a) Isosceles
(b) Equilateral (c) Isosceles right triangle
27. $x + y = 6$ **29.** $(a, a\sqrt{3})$ or $(a, -a\sqrt{3})$
31. $(0, 1 + 3\sqrt{3})$ and $(0, 1 - 3\sqrt{3})$ **33.** 17 **35.** 9
37. (a) 135π $units^3$ (b) 75π $units^3$
39. (a) 96π $units^3$ (b) 144π $units^3$

41. (a) 90π units^2 (b) 9π units^2

43.

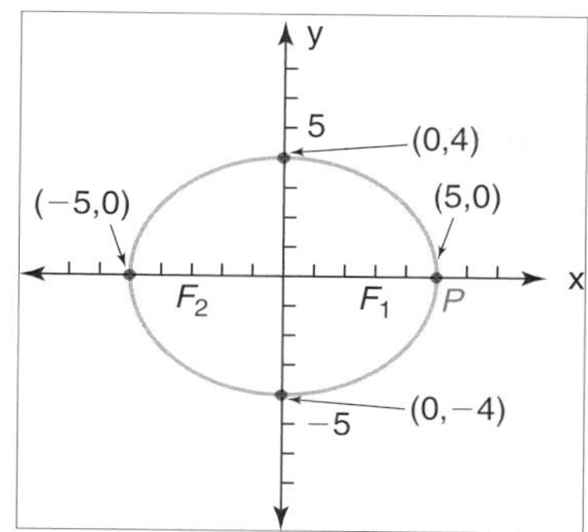

45. (a) $(-3, -1)$ (b) $(1, -3)$ (c) $(3, 1)$

47. (a) $(5, 4)$ (b) $(5, 8)$ (c) $(3, 2)$

10.2 Exercises

1. $(4, 0)$ and $(0, 3)$ **3.** $(5, 0)$ and $\left(0, -\frac{5}{2}\right)$ **5.** $(-3, 0)$ **7.** $(6, 0)$ and $(0, 3)$ **9.** (a) 4 (b) Undefined (c) -1 (d) 0 (e) $\frac{d-b}{c-a}$ (f) $-\frac{b}{a}$ **11.** (a) 10 (b) 15 **13.** (a) Collinear (b) Noncollinear **15.** (a) $\frac{3}{4}$ (b) $-\frac{5}{3}$ (c) -2 (d) $\frac{a-b}{c}$ **17.** (a) 2 (b) $-\frac{4}{3}$ (c) $-\frac{1}{3}$ (d) $-\frac{h+j}{f+g}$ **19.** None of these **21.** Perpendicular **23.** $\frac{3}{2}$ **25.** 23 **33.** Right triangle **35.** $(4, 7)$; $(0, -1)$; $(10, -3)$

39. $m_{\overline{EH}} = \frac{2c-0}{2b-0} = \frac{2c}{2b} = \frac{c}{b}$

$m_{\overline{FG}} = \frac{c-0}{(a+b)-a} = \frac{c}{b}$

Because of equal slopes, $\overline{EH} \parallel \overline{FG}$. Thus $EFGH$ is a trapezoid.

43. $-\frac{b^2}{2m}$

10.2 Selected Proof

37. $m_{\overline{VT}} = \dfrac{e-e}{(c-d)-(a+d)} = \dfrac{0}{c-a-2d} = 0$

$m_{\overline{RS}} = \dfrac{b-b}{c-a} = \dfrac{0}{c-a} = 0$

$\therefore \overline{VT} \parallel \overline{RS}$

$RV = \sqrt{[(a+d)-a]^2 + (e-b)^2}$
$= \sqrt{d^2 + (e-b)^2} = \sqrt{d^2 + e^2 - 2be + b^2}$

$ST = \sqrt{[c-(c-d)]^2 + (b-e)^2}$
$= \sqrt{(d)^2 + (b-e)^2}$
$= \sqrt{d^2 + b^2 - 2be + e^2}$

$\therefore RV = ST$

$RSTV$ is an isosceles trapezoid.

10.3 Exercises

1. (a) $a\sqrt{2}$ if $a > 0$ (b) $\frac{d-b}{c-a}$ **3.** (a) -1 (b) $-\frac{b}{a}$

5. $\overline{AB}$ is horizontal and $\overline{BC}$ is vertical; $\therefore \overline{AB} \perp \overline{BC}$. Hence, $\angle B$ is a right $\angle$ and $\triangle ABC$ is a right triangle.

7. $m_{\overline{QM}} = \frac{c-0}{b-0} = \frac{c}{b}$

$m_{\overline{PN}} = \frac{c-0}{(a+b)-a} = \frac{c}{b}$

$\therefore \overline{QM} \parallel \overline{PN}$

$m_{\overline{QP}} = \frac{c-c}{(a+b)-b} = \frac{0}{a} = 0$

$m_{\overline{MN}} = \frac{0-0}{a-0} = \frac{0}{a} = 0$

$\therefore \overline{QP} \parallel \overline{MN}$

Because both pairs of opposite sides are parallel, $MNPQ$ is a parallelogram.

9. $m_{\overline{MN}} = 0$ and $m_{\overline{QP}} = 0$; $\therefore \overline{MN} \parallel \overline{QP}$. $\overline{QM}$ and $\overline{PN}$ are both vertical; $\therefore \overline{QM} \parallel \overline{PN}$. Hence, $MQPN$ is a parallelogram. Because $\overline{QM}$ is vertical and $\overline{MN}$ is horizontal, $\angle QMN$ is a right angle. Because parallelogram $MQPN$ has a right $\angle$, it is also a rectangle.

11. $A = (0, 0)$; $B = (a, 0)$; $C = (a, b)$

13. $M = (0, 0)$; $N = (r, 0)$; $P = (r + s, t)$

15. $A = (0, 0)$; $B = (a, 0)$; $C = (a - c, d)$

17. (a) Square
$A = (0, 0)$; $B = (a, 0)$; $C = (a, a)$; $D = (0, a)$
(b) Square (with midpoints of sides)
$A = (0, 0)$; $B = (2a, 0)$; $C = (2a, 2a)$; $D = (0, 2a)$

19. (a) Parallelogram
$A = (0, 0)$; $B = (a, 0)$; $C = (a + b, c)$; $D = (b, c)$
(NOTE: D chosen before C)
(b) Parallelogram (with midpoints of sides)
$A = (0, 0)$; $B = (2a, 0)$; $C = (2a + 2b, 2c)$; $D = (2b, 2c)$

21. (a) Isosceles triangle
$R = (0, 0)$; $S = (2a, 0)$; $T = (a, b)$
(b) Isosceles triangle (with midpoints of sides)
$R = (0, 0)$; $S = (4a, 0)$; $T = (2a, 2b)$

23. $r^2 = s^2 + t^2$ **25.** $c^2 = a^2 - b^2$ **27.** $b^2 = 3a^2$

29. (a) Positive (b) Negative (c) $2a$

31. (a) Slope Formula (b) Distance Formula (c) Midpoint Formula (d) Slope Formula

37. $(6 - 2a, 0)$

10.4 Exercises

21. $m_1 = -\frac{A}{B}$; $m_2 = \frac{B}{A}$; $m_1 \cdot m_2 = -1$, so $\ell_1 \perp \ell_2$.

23. $3x - 2y = 2$ **25.** $x^2 + y^2 = 9$ **27.** $m = -\frac{a}{b}$

29. True. The quadrilateral that results is a parallelogram.

10.4 Selected Proofs

3. The diagonals of a square are perpendicular bisectors of each other.

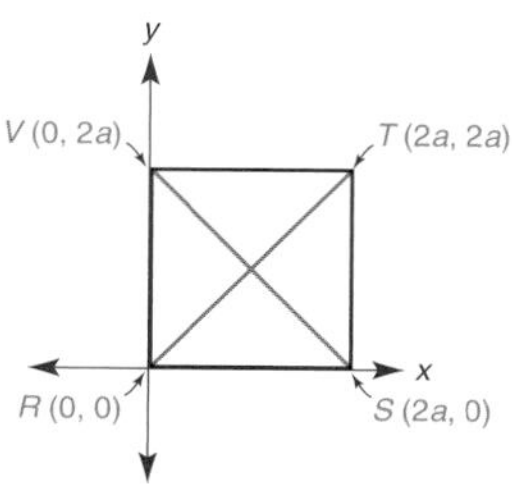

Proof: Let square $RSTV$ have the vertices shown. Then the midpoints of the diagonals are $M_{\overline{RT}} = (a, a)$ and $M_{\overline{VS}} = (a, a)$. Also, $m_{\overline{RT}} = 1$ and $m_{\overline{VS}} = -1$. Because the two diagonals share the midpoint (a, a) and the product of their slopes is -1, they are perpendicular bisectors of each other.

7. The segments that join the midpoints of the consecutive sides of a quadrilateral form a parallelogram.

Proof: The midpoints, as shown, of the sides of quadrilateral *ABCD* are

$$R = \left(\frac{0 + 2a}{2}, \frac{0 + 0}{2}\right) = (a, 0)$$
$$S = \left(\frac{2a + 2b}{2}, \frac{0 + 2c}{2}\right) = (a + b, c)$$
$$T = \left(\frac{2d + 2b}{2}, \frac{2e + 2c}{2}\right) = (d + b, e + c)$$
$$V = \left(\frac{0 + 2d}{2}, \frac{0 + 2e}{2}\right) = (d, e)$$

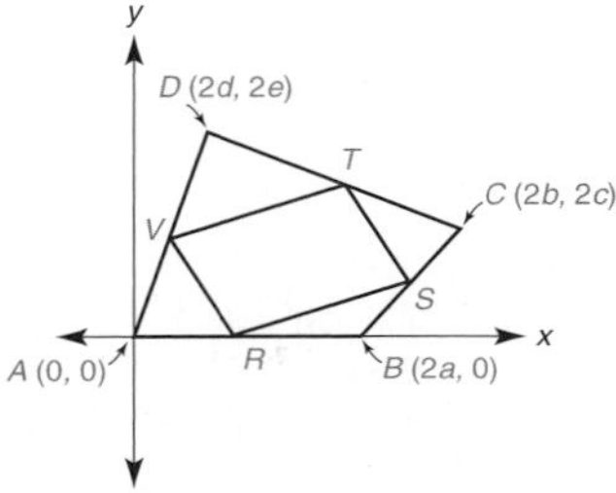

Now we determine slopes as follows:

$$m_{\overline{RS}} = \frac{c - 0}{(a + b) - a} = \frac{c}{b}$$
$$m_{\overline{ST}} = \frac{(e + c) - c}{(d + b) - (a + b)} = \frac{e}{d - a}$$
$$m_{\overline{TV}} = \frac{(e + c) - e}{(d + b) - d} = \frac{c}{b}$$
$$m_{\overline{VR}} = \frac{e - 0}{d - a} = \frac{e}{d - a}$$

Because $m_{\overline{RS}} = m_{\overline{TV}}$, $\overline{RS} \parallel \overline{TV}$. Also $m_{\overline{ST}} = m_{\overline{VR}}$, so $\overline{ST} \parallel \overline{VR}$. Then *RSTV* is a parallelogram.

11. The midpoint of the hypotenuse of a right triangle is equidistant from the three vertices of the triangle.

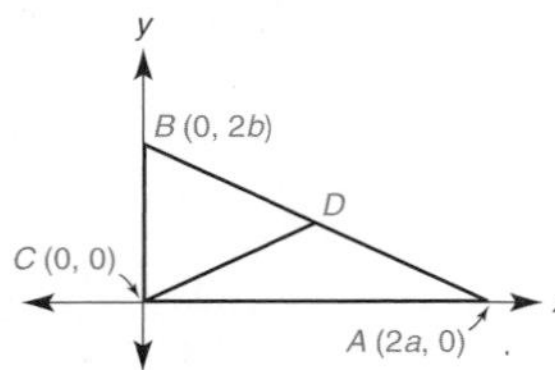

Proof: Let rt. $\triangle ABC$ have vertices as shown. Then *D*, the midpoint of the hypotenuse, is given by

$$D = \left(\frac{0 + 2a}{2}, \frac{2b + 0}{2}\right) = (a, b)$$

Now $\quad BD = DA = \sqrt{(2a - a)^2 + (0 - b)^2}$
$\quad = \sqrt{a^2 + (-b)^2} = \sqrt{a^2 + b^2}$

Also, $\quad CD = \sqrt{(a - 0)^2 + (b - 0)^2}$
$\quad = \sqrt{a^2 + b^2}$

Then *D* is equidistant from *A, B,* and *C*.

15. If the midpoint of one side of a rectangle is joined to the endpoints of the opposite side, an isosceles triangle is formed.

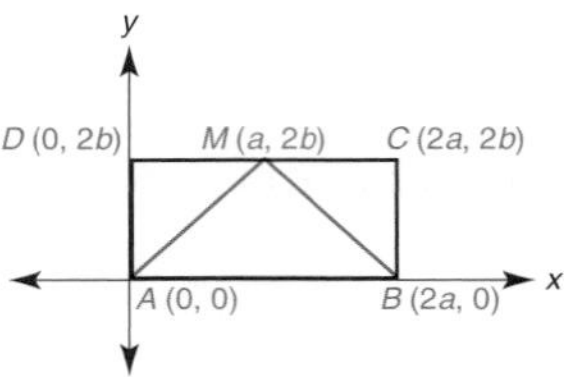

Proof: Let rectangle *ABCD* have endpoints as shown above. With *M* the midpoint of $\overline{DC}$,

$$M = \left(\frac{0 + 2a}{2}, \frac{2b + 2b}{2}\right) = (a, 2b)$$
$$MA = \sqrt{(a - 0)^2 + (2b - 0)^2}$$
$$MA = \sqrt{a^2 + 4b^2}$$
$$MB = \sqrt{(a - 2a)^2 + (2b - 0)^2}$$
$$MB = \sqrt{a^2 + 4b^2}$$

Because $MA = MB$, $\triangle AMB$ is isosceles.

10.5 Exercises

1. $x + 2y = 6$; $y = -\frac{1}{2}x + 3$
3. $-x + 3y = -40$; $y = \frac{1}{3}x - \frac{40}{3}$ **9.** $2x + 3y = 15$
11. $x + y = 6$ **13.** $-2x + 3y = -3$ **15.** $bx + ay = ab$
17. $-x + y = -2$ **19.** $5x + 2y = 5$
21. $4x + 3y = -12$ **23.** $-x + 3y = 2$
25. $y = -\frac{b}{a}x + \frac{bg + ha}{a}$ **27.** $(6, 0)$ **29.** $(5, -4)$
31. $(6, -2)$ **33.** $(3, 2)$ **35.** $(6, -1)$ **37.** $(5, -2)$
39. $(6, 0)$ **41.** $\left(\frac{a - c}{b}, a\right)$ **43.** $\left(b, \frac{ab - b^2}{c}\right)$

10.5 Selected Proofs

45. The altitudes of a triangle are concurrent.

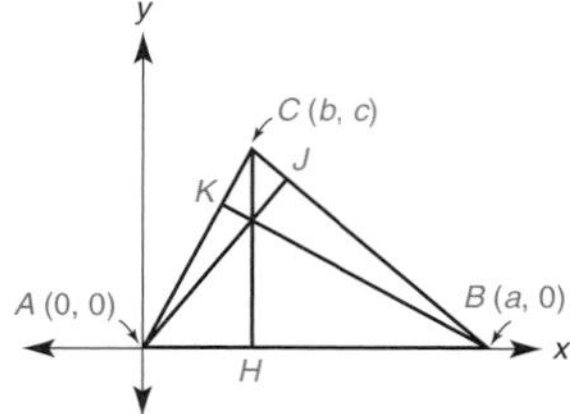

Proof: For $\triangle ABC$, let $\overline{CH}$, $\overline{AJ}$, and $\overline{BK}$ name the altitudes. Because $\overline{AB}$ is horizontal ($m_{\overline{AB}} = 0$), $\overline{CH}$ is vertical and has the equation $x = b$.

Because $m_{\overline{BC}} = \frac{c - 0}{b - a} = \frac{c}{b - a}$, the slope of altitude $\overline{AJ}$ is $m_{\overline{AJ}} = -\frac{b - a}{c} = \frac{a - b}{c}$. Since $\overline{AJ}$ contains (0, 0), its equation is $y = \frac{a - b}{c}x$.

The intersection of altitudes $\overline{CH}(x = b)$ and $\overline{AJ}$ $\left(y = \frac{a - b}{c}x\right)$ is at $x = b$, so $y = \frac{a - b}{c} \cdot b = \frac{b(a - b)}{c} = \frac{ab - b^2}{c}$. That is, $\overline{CH}$ and $\overline{AJ}$ intersect at $\left(b, \frac{ab - b^2}{c}\right)$. The remaining altitude is $\overline{BK}$. Since $m_{\overline{AC}} = \frac{c - 0}{b - 0} = \frac{c}{b}$, $m_{\overline{BK}} = -\frac{b}{c}$. Because $\overline{BK}$ contains (a, 0), its equation is $y - 0 = -\frac{b}{c}(x - a)$ or $y = \frac{-b}{c}(x - a)$.

For the three altitudes to be concurrent, $\left(b, \frac{ab - b^2}{c}\right)$ must lie on the line $y = \frac{-b}{c}(x - a)$. Substitution leads to

$$\begin{aligned}\frac{ab - b^2}{c} &= \frac{-b}{c}(b - a)\\ &= \frac{-b(b - a)}{c}\\ &= \frac{-b^2 + ab}{c}\end{aligned}$$

which is true. Then the three altitudes are concurrent.

47. First, find the equation of the line through P that is perpendicular to $Ax + By = C$. Second, find the point of intersection D of the two lines. Finally, use the Distance Formula to find the length of $\overline{PD}$.

CHAPTER 10 REVIEW EXERCISES

1. (a) 7 (b) 6 (c) 13 (d) 5
2. (a) 8 (b) 10 (c) $4\sqrt{5}$ (d) 10
3. (a) $\left(6, \frac{1}{2}\right)$ (b) $(-2, 4)$ (c) $\left(1, -\frac{1}{2}\right)$ (d) $\left(\frac{2x - 3}{2}, y\right)$
4. (a) $(2, 1)$ (b) $(-2, -2)$ (c) $(0, 3)$ (d) $(x + 1, y + 1)$
5. (a) Undefined (b) 0 (c) $-\frac{5}{12}$ (d) $-\frac{4}{3}$
6. (a) Undefined (b) 0 (c) $\frac{1}{2}$ (d) $\frac{4}{3}$
7. $(-4, -8)$ **8.** $(3, 7)$ **9.** $x = \frac{4}{3}$ **10.** $y = -4$
11. (a) Perpendicular (b) Parallel (c) Neither (d) Perpendicular **12.** Noncollinear
13. $x = 4$ **14.** $(7, 0)$ and $(0, 3)$
17. (a) $3x + 5y = 21$ (b) $3x + y = -7$ (c) $-2x + y = -8$ (d) $y = 5$
18. $m_{\overline{AB}} = \frac{4}{3}$; $m_{\overline{BC}} = \frac{1}{2}$; $m_{\overline{AC}} = -2$. Because $m_{\overline{AC}} \cdot m_{\overline{BC}} = -1$, $\overline{AC} \perp \overline{BC}$ and $\angle C$ is a rt. $\angle$; the triangle is a rt. $\triangle$.
19. $AB = \sqrt{85}$; $BC = \sqrt{85}$. Because $AB = BC$, the triangle is isosceles.
20. $m_{\overline{RS}} = \frac{-4}{3}$; $m_{\overline{ST}} = \frac{5}{6}$; $m_{\overline{TV}} = \frac{-4}{3}$; $m_{\overline{RV}} = \frac{5}{6}$. Therefore, $\overline{RS} \parallel \overline{VT}$ and $\overline{RV} \parallel \overline{ST}$ and $RSTV$ is a parallelogram.
21. $(3, 5)$ **22.** $(1, 4)$ **23.** $(3, 5)$
24. $(1, 4)$ **25.** $(16, 11)$, $(4, -9)$, $(-4, 5)$
26. (a) $\sqrt{53}$ (b) -4 (c) $\frac{1}{4}$
27. $A = (-a, 0)$; $B = (0, b)$; $C = (a, 0)$
28. $D = (0, 0)$; $E = (a, 0)$; $F = (a, 2a)$; $G = (0, 2a)$
29. $R = (0, 0)$; $U = (0, a)$; $T = (a, a + b)$
30. $M = (0, 0)$; $N = (a, 0)$; $Q = (a + b, c)$; $P = (b, c)$
31. (a) $\sqrt{(a + c)^2 + (b + d - 2e)^2}$ (b) $-\frac{a}{b - e}$ or $\frac{a}{e - b}$ (c) $y - 2d = \frac{a}{e - b}(x - 2c)$

Chapter 10 Test

1. (a) $(5, -3)$ (b) $(0, -4)$ [10.1] **3.** $CD = 10$ [10.1]
4. $(-3, 5)$ [10.1]
5.

x	0	3	**0**	9
y	**4**	**2**	4	**−2**

[10.2]

6. [10.2]

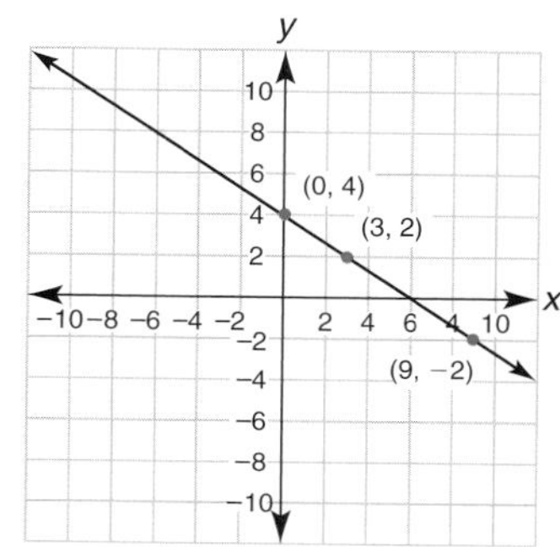

7. (a) -3 (b) $\frac{d - b}{c - a}$ [10.2]
8. (a) $\frac{2}{3}$ (b) $-\frac{3}{2}$ [10.2]
9. Parallelogram [10.3]
10. $a = \sqrt{b^2 + c^2}$ or $a^2 = b^2 + c^2$ [10.3]
11. (a) Isosceles triangle (b) Trapezoid [10.3]
12. (a) Slope Formula (b) Distance Formula [10.3]
13. $D(0, 0)$, $E(2a, 0)$, $F(a, b)$ [10.3] **14.** (b) [10.4]
15. $m_{\overline{VR}} = m_{\overline{TS}}$ so $-\frac{v}{r} = \frac{v}{t - s}$. Possible answers: $r = s - t$ or $s = r + t$ or equivalent [10.4]
16. (a) $y = x + 4$ (b) $y = \frac{3}{4}x - 3$ [10.5]
17. $y = cx + (b - ac)$ [10.5] **18.** $(4, 1)$ [10.5]
19. $(-1, 4)$ [10.5] **20.** $M = (a + b, c)$ and $N = (a, 0)$. Then $m_{\overline{AC}} = \frac{2c - 0}{2b - 0} = \frac{c}{b}$ and $m_{\overline{MN}} = \frac{c - 0}{a + b - a} = \frac{c}{b}$. With $m_{\overline{AC}} = m_{\overline{MN}}$, it follows that $\overline{AC} \parallel \overline{MN}$. [10.4]

CHAPTER 11

11.1 Exercises

1. $\sin\alpha = \frac{5}{13}$; $\sin\beta = \frac{12}{13}$ **3.** $\sin\alpha = \frac{8}{17}$; $\sin\beta = \frac{15}{17}$
5. $\sin\alpha = \frac{\sqrt{15}}{5}$; $\sin\beta = \frac{\sqrt{10}}{5}$ **7.** 1 **9.** 0.2924
11. 0.9903 **13.** 0.9511 **15.** $a \approx 6.9$ in.; $b \approx 9.8$ in.
17. $a \approx 10.9$ ft; $b \approx 11.7$ ft **19.** $c \approx 8.8$ cm; $d \approx 28.7$ cm
21. $\alpha \approx 29°$; $\beta \approx 61°$ **23.** $\alpha \approx 17°$; $\beta \approx 73°$
25. $\alpha \approx 19°$; $\beta \approx 71°$ **27.** $\alpha \approx 23°$ **29.** $d \approx 103.5$ ft
31. $d \approx 128.0$ ft **33.** $\alpha \approx 24°$
35. (a) ≈ 5.4 ft (b) ≈ 54 ft^2 **37.** $\theta \approx 50°$
39. (a) $h = s \cdot \sin 36°$; (b) $d = 2s \cdot \sin 54°$

11.2 Exercises

1. $\cos\alpha = \frac{12}{13}$; $\cos\beta = \frac{5}{13}$ **3.** $\cos\alpha = \frac{3}{5}$; $\cos\beta = \frac{4}{5}$
5. $\cos\alpha = \frac{\sqrt{10}}{5}$; $\cos\beta = \frac{\sqrt{15}}{5}$ **7.** (a) $\sin\alpha = \frac{a}{c}$; $\cos\beta = \frac{a}{c}$. Thus, $\sin\alpha = \cos\beta$. (b) $\cos\alpha = \frac{b}{c}$; $\sin\beta = \frac{b}{c}$. Thus, $\cos\alpha = \sin\beta$. **9.** 0.9205 **11.** 0.9563
13. 0 **15.** 0.1392 **17.** $a \approx 84.8$ ft; $b \approx 53.0$ ft
19. $a = b = 5$ cm **21.** $c \approx 19.1$ in.; $d \approx 14.8$ in.
23. $\alpha = 60°$; $\beta = 30°$ **25.** $\alpha \approx 51°$; $\beta \approx 39°$
27. $\alpha \approx 65°$; $\beta \approx 25°$ **29.** $\theta \approx 34°$ **31.** $x \approx 1147.4$ ft
33. ≈ 8.1 in. **35.** ≈ 13.1 cm **37.** $\alpha \approx 55°$
39. (a) $m\angle A = 68°$ (b) $m\angle B = 112°$
43. $5r^2 \sin 54° \cos 54°$.

11.3 Exercises

1. $\tan\alpha = \frac{3}{4}$; $\tan\beta = \frac{4}{3}$ **3.** $\tan\alpha = \frac{\sqrt{5}}{2}$; $\tan\beta = \frac{2\sqrt{5}}{5}$
5. $\sin\alpha = \frac{5}{13}$; $\cos\alpha = \frac{12}{13}$; $\tan\alpha = \frac{5}{12}$; $\cot\alpha = \frac{12}{5}$; $\sec\alpha = \frac{13}{12}$; $\csc\alpha = \frac{13}{5}$ **7.** $\sin\alpha = \frac{a}{c}$; $\cos\alpha = \frac{b}{c}$; $\tan\alpha = \frac{a}{b}$; $\cot\alpha = \frac{b}{a}$; $\sec\alpha = \frac{c}{b}$; $\csc\alpha = \frac{c}{a}$
9. $\sin\alpha = \frac{x\sqrt{x^2+1}}{x^2+1}$; $\cos\alpha = \frac{\sqrt{x^2+1}}{x^2+1}$; $\tan\alpha = \frac{x}{1}$; $\cot\alpha = \frac{1}{x}$; $\sec\alpha = \sqrt{x^2+1}$; $\csc\alpha = \frac{\sqrt{x^2+1}}{x}$ **11.** 0.2679
13. 1.5399 **15.** $x \approx 7.5$; $z \approx 14.2$
17. $y \approx 5.3$; $z \approx 8.5$ **19.** $d \approx 8.1$
21. $\alpha \approx 37°$; $\beta \approx 53°$ **23.** $\theta \approx 56°$; $\gamma \approx 34°$
25. $\alpha \approx 29°$; $\beta \approx 61°$ **27.** 1.4826 **29.** 2.0000
31. 1.3456 **33.** (b) ≈ 0.4245 **35.** (b) ≈ 7.1853
37. $\approx$ 1376.8 ft **39.** $\approx$ 4.1 in. **41.** $\approx 72°$
43. $\alpha \approx 47°$. The heading may be described as N 47° W.
45. $\approx$ 26,730 ft
47. (a) $h \approx 9.2$ ft (b) $V \approx 110.4\text{ ft}^3$

11.4 Exercises

1. (a) $\frac{1}{2}\cdot 5\cdot 6\cdot \sin 78°$ (b) $\frac{1}{2}\cdot 5\cdot 7\cdot \sin 56°$
3. (a) $\frac{\sin 40°}{5} = \frac{\sin\beta}{8}$ (b) $\frac{\sin 41°}{5.3} = \frac{\sin 87°}{c}$
5. (a) $c^2 = 5.2^2 + 7.9^2 - 2(5.2)(7.9)\cos 83°$ (b) $6^2 = 9^2 + 10^2 - 2\cdot 9\cdot 10\cdot\cos\alpha$
7. (a) $\frac{\sin\alpha}{a} = \frac{\sin\beta}{b}$ (b) $a^2 = b^2 + c^2 - 2bc\cos\alpha$
9. (a) (3, 4, 5) is a Pythagorean Triple; γ lies opposite the longest side and must be a right angle. (b) 90°
11. 8 in^2 **13.** $\approx$ 11.6 ft^2 **15.** $\approx$ 15.2 ft^2
17. $\approx$ 11.1 in. **19.** $\approx$ 8.9 m **21.** $\approx 55°$
23. $\approx 51°$ **25.** $\approx$ 10.6 **27.** $\approx$ 6.9
29. (a) $\approx$ 213.4 ft (b) $\approx$ 13,294.9 ft^2 **31.** $\approx$ 8812 m
33. $\approx$ 15.9 ft **35.** 6 **37.** $\approx$ 14.0 ft **41.** 51.8 cm^2
43. $\frac{1}{2}ab$

CHAPTER 11 REVIEW EXERCISES

1. sine; $\approx$ 10.3 in. **2.** sine; $\approx$ 7.5 ft
3. cosine; $\approx$ 23.0 in. **4.** sine; $\approx$ 5.9 ft
5. tangent; $\approx 43°$ **6.** cosine; $\approx 58°$ **7.** sine; $\approx 49°$
8. tangent; $\approx 16°$ **9.** $\approx$ 8.9 units **10.** $\approx 60°$
11. $\approx$ 13.1 units **12.** $\approx$ 18.5 units **13.** $\approx$ 42.7 ft
14. $\approx$ 74.8 cm **15.** $\approx 47°$ **16.** $\approx 54°$
17. $\approx$ 26.3 in^2 **19.** If $m\angle S = 30°$ and $m\angle Q = 90°$, then the sides of $\triangle RQS$ can be represented by $RQ = x$, $RS = 2x$, and $SQ = x\sqrt{3}$. $\sin S = \sin 30° = \frac{x}{2x} = \frac{1}{2}$. **21.** $\approx$ 8.4 ft
22. $\approx$ 866 ft **23.** $\approx 41°$ **24.** $\approx 8°$ **25.** $\approx$ 5.0 cm
26. $\approx$ 4.3 cm **27.** $\approx 68°$ **28.** $\approx 106°$
29. 3 to 7 (or 3:7) **30.** $\approx$ 1412.0 m
31. $\cos\theta = \frac{24}{25}$; $\sec\theta = \frac{25}{24}$ **32.** $\sec\theta = \frac{61}{60}$; $\cot\theta = \frac{60}{11}$
33. $\csc\theta = \frac{29}{20}$; $\sin\theta = \frac{20}{29}$ **34.** $h \approx 6.9$ ft; $V \approx 74.0\text{ ft}^3$

Chapter 11 Test

1. (a) $\frac{a}{c}$ (b) $\frac{b}{a}$ [11.1, 11.3] **2.** (a) $\frac{3}{5}$ (b) $\frac{3}{5}$ [11.1, 11.2]
3. (a) 1 (b) $\frac{\sqrt{3}}{2}$ [11.1, 11.3]
4. (a) 0.3907 (b) 0.1908 [11.1, 11.2]
5. $\theta \approx 42°$ [11.1] **6.** (a) tan 26° (b) cos 47° [11.2, 11.3]
7. $a \approx 14$ [11.1]
8. $y \approx 9$ [11.1] **9.** $\theta \approx 56°$ [11.1]
10. (a) True (b) True [11.2] **11.** 92 ft [11.1]
12. 10° [11.1] **13.** (a) $\csc\alpha = 2$ (b) $\alpha = 30°$ [11.1, 11.3]
14. (a) $\frac{a}{c}$ (b) $\frac{c}{a}$ [11.3]
15. $\approx$ 42 cm^2 [11.4] **16.** $\frac{\sin\alpha}{a} = \frac{\sin\beta}{b} = \frac{\sin\gamma}{c}$ [11.4]
17. $a^2 = b^2 + c^2 - 2bc\cos\alpha$ [11.4]
18. $\alpha \approx 33°$ [11.4] **19.** $x \approx 11$ [11.4]
20. $5a^2\tan 54°$ [11.3]

APPENDIX A

A.1 ALGEBRAIC EXPRESSIONS

1. Undefined terms, definitions, axioms or postulates, and theorems **3.** (a) Reflexive (b) Transitive (c) Substitution (d) Symmetric **5.** (a) 12 (b) −2 (c) 2 (d) −12
7. (a) 35 (b) −35 (c) −35 (d) 35 **9.** No; Commutative Axiom for Multiplication **11.** (a) 9 (b) −9 (c) 8 (d) −8
13. (a) −4 (b) −36 (c) 18 (d) $-\frac{1}{4}$ **15.** −$60
17. (a) 65 (b) 16 (c) 9 (d) $8x$ **19.** (a) 10π (b) $11\sqrt{2}$ (c) $7x^2y$ (d) $7\sqrt{3}$ **21.** (a) 14 (b) 20 (c) 14 (d) 38
23. (a) −1 (b) $\frac{1}{9}$ (c) $-\frac{8}{9}$ (d) $-\frac{1}{2}$ **25.** (a) 6 (b) $12x^2 - 7x - 10$ **27.** $5x + 2y$ **29.** $10x + 5y$ **31.** $10x$

A.2 FORMULAS AND EQUATIONS

1. $5x + 8$ **3.** $2x - 2$ **5.** $5x + 8$ **7.** $x^2 + 7x + 12$
9. $6x^2 + 11x - 10$ **11.** $2a^2 + 2b^2$ **13.** 60
15. 40 **17.** 148 **19.** 12π **21.** 7 **23.** −12
25. 12 **27.** 5 **29.** 30 **31.** 8 **33.** 4 **35.** 32

A.3 INEQUALITIES

1. The length of $\overline{AB}$ is greater than the length of $\overline{CD}$.
3. The measure of angle ABC is greater than the measure of angle DEF. **5.** (a) 4 (b) 10 **7.** $IJ < AB$
9. (a) False (b) True (c) True (d) False
11. The measure of the second angle must be greater than 148° and less than 180°. **13.** (a) $-12 \le 20$ (b) $-10 \le -2$ (c) $18 \ge -30$ (d) $3 \ge -5$

15.

No change	No change
No change	No change
No change	Change
No change	Change

17. $x \le 7$ **19.** $x < -5$ **21.** $x < 20$
23. $x \ge -24$ **25.** $x \le -2$ **27.** Not true if $c < 0$
29. Not true if $a = -3$ and $b = -2$

A.4 QUADRATIC EQUATIONS

1. (a) 3.61 (b) 2.83 (c) −5.39 (d) 0.77
3. a, c, d, f **5.** (a) $2\sqrt{2}$ (b) $3\sqrt{5}$ (c) 30 (d) 3
7. (a) $\frac{3}{4}$ (b) $\frac{5}{7}$ (c) $\frac{\sqrt{7}}{4}$ (d) $\frac{\sqrt{6}}{3}$
9. (a) $\sqrt{54} \approx 7.35$ and $3\sqrt{6} \approx 7.35$
(b) $\sqrt{\frac{5}{16}} \approx 0.56$ and $\frac{\sqrt{5}}{4} \approx 0.56$
11. $x = 4$ or $x = 2$ **13.** $x = 12$ or $x = 5$
15. $x = -\frac{2}{3}$ or $x = 4$ **17.** $x = \frac{1}{3}$ or $x = \frac{1}{2}$
19. $x = 5$ or $x = 2$ **21.** $x = \frac{7 \pm \sqrt{13}}{2} \approx 5.30$ or 1.70
23. $x = 2 \pm 2\sqrt{3} \approx 5.46$ or -1.46
25. $x = \frac{3 \pm \sqrt{149}}{10} \approx 1.52$ or -0.92
27. $x = \pm\sqrt{7} \approx \pm 2.65$ **29.** $x = \pm\frac{5}{2}$ **31.** $x = 0$ or $x = \frac{b}{a}$
33. 5 by 8 **35.** $n = 6$ **37.** $c = 5$

Glossary

acute angle an angle whose measure is between 0° and 90°

acute triangle a triangle whose three interior angles are all acute

adjacent angles two angles that have a common vertex and a common side between them

altitude of cone (pyramid) the line segment from the vertex of the cone perpendicular to the plane of the base

altitude of cylinder (prism) a line segment between and perpendicular to each of the two bases

altitude of parallelogram a line segment drawn perpendicularly from a vertex to a nonadjacent side (known as the related base) of the parallelogram

altitude of trapezoid a line segment drawn perpendicularly from a vertex to the remaining parallel side

altitude of triangle a line segment drawn perpendicularly from a vertex of the triangle to the opposite side of the triangle; the length of the altitude is the height of the triangle

angle the plane figure formed by two rays that share a common endpoint

angle bisector *see* bisector of angle

angle of depression (elevation) acute angle formed by a horizontal ray and a ray determined by a downward (an upward) rotation

apothem of regular polygon any line segment drawn from the center of the regular polygon perpendicular to one of its sides

arc the segment (part) of a circle determined by two points on the circle and all points between them

area the measurement, in square units, of the amount of region within an enclosed plane figure

auxiliary line a line (or part of a line) added to a drawing to help complete a proof or solve a problem

axiom *see* postulate

base a side (of a plane figure) or face (of a solid figure) to which an altitude is drawn

base angles of isosceles triangle the two congruent angles of the isosceles triangle

base of isosceles triangle the side of the triangle whose length is unique; the side opposite the vertex

bases of trapezoid the two parallel sides of the trapezoid

bisector of angle a ray that separates the given angle into two smaller, congruent angles

center of circle the interior point of the circle whose distance from all points on the circle is the same

center of regular polygon the common center of the inscribed and circumscribed circles of the regular polygon

center of sphere the interior point of the sphere whose distance from all points on the sphere is the same

central angle of circle an angle whose vertex is at the center of the circle and whose sides are radii of the circle

central angle of regular polygon an angle whose vertex is at the center of the regular polygon and whose sides are two consecutive radii of the polygon

centroid of triangle the point of concurrence for the three medians of the triangle

chord of circle any line segment that joins two points on the circle

circle the set of points in a plane that are at a fixed distance from a given point (the center of the circle) in the plane

circumcenter of triangle the center of the circumscribed circle of a triangle; the point of concurrence for the perpendicular bisectors of the three sides of the triangle

circumference the linear measure of the distance around a circle

circumscribed circle a circle that contains all vertices of a polygon whose sides are chords of the circle

circumscribed polygon a polygon whose sides are all tangent to a circle in the interior of the polygon

collinear points points that lie on the same line

common tangent a line (or segment) that is tangent to more than one circle; can be a common external tangent or a common internal tangent

complementary angles two angles whose sum of measures is 90°

concave polygon a polygon in which at least one diagonal lies in the exterior of the polygon

concentric circles (spheres) two or more circles (spheres) that have the same center

conclusion the "then" clause of an "If, then" statement; the part of a theorem indicating the claim to be proved

concurrent lines three or more lines that contain the same point

congruent refers to figures (such as angles) that can be made to coincide

converse relative to the statement "If *P*, then *Q*," this statement has the form "If *Q*, then *P*"

convex polygon a polygon in which all diagonals lie in the interior of the polygon

coplanar points points that lie in the same plane

corollary a theorem that follows from another theorem as a "by-product"; a theorem that is easily proved as the consequence of another theorem

cosecant in a right triangle, the ratio $\frac{\text{hypotenuse}}{\text{opposite}}$

cosine in a right triangle, the ratio $\frac{\text{adjacent}}{\text{hypotenuse}}$

cotangent in a right triangle, the ratio $\frac{\text{adjacent}}{\text{opposite}}$

cube a right square prism whose edges are congruent

cyclic polygon a polygon that can be inscribed in a circle

cylinder (circular) the solid generated by all line segments parallel to the axis of the cylinder and which contain corresponding endpoints on the two congruent circular bases

decagon a polygon with exactly 10 sides

deduction a form of reasoning in which specific conclusions are reached through the use of established principles

degree the unit of measure that corresponds to $\frac{1}{360}$ of a complete revolution; used with angles and arcs

diagonal of polygon a line segment that joins two nonconsecutive vertices of a polygon

diameter any line segment that joins two points on a circle (or sphere) and that also contains the center of the circle (or sphere)

dodecagon a polygon that has exactly 12 sides

dodecahedron (regular) a polyhedron that has exactly 12 faces that are congruent regular pentagons

edge of polyhedron any line segment that joins two consecutive vertices of the polyhedron (includes prisms and pyramids)

equiangular polygon a type of polygon whose angles are congruent (equal)

equilateral polygon a type of polygon whose sides are congruent (equal)

equivalent equations equations for which the solutions are the same

extended proportion a proportion that has three or more members, such as $\frac{a}{b} = \frac{c}{d} = \frac{e}{f}$

extended ratio a ratio that compares three or more numbers, such as $a{:}b{:}c$

exterior refers to all points that lie outside an enclosed (bounded) plane or solid figure

exterior angle of polygon an angle formed by one side of the polygon and an extension of a second side that has a common endpoint with the first side

extremes of a proportion the first and last terms of a proportion; in $\frac{a}{b} = \frac{c}{d}$, *a* and *d* are the extremes

face of polyhedron any one of the polygons that lies in a plane determined by the vertices of the polyhedron; includes base(s) and lateral faces of prisms and pyramids

geometric mean the repeated second and third terms of certain proportions; in $\frac{a}{b} = \frac{b}{c}$, *b* is the geometric mean of *a* and *c*

height the length of the altitude of a geometric figure

heptagon a polygon that has exactly seven sides

hexagon a polygon that has exactly six sides

hexahedron (regular) a polyhedron that has six congruent square faces; also called a cube

hypotenuse of right triangle the side of a right triangle that lies opposite the right angle

hypothesis the "if" clause of an "If, then" statement; the part of a theorem providing the given information

icosahedron (regular) a polyhedron with 20 congruent faces that are equilateral triangles

incenter of triangle the center of the inscribed circle of a triangle; the point of concurrence for the three angle bisectors of the angles of the triangle

induction a form of reasoning in which a number of specific observations are used to draw a general conclusion

inscribed angle of circle an angle whose vertex is on a circle and whose sides are chords of the circle

inscribed circle a circle that lies inside a polygon in such a way that the sides of the polygon are tangents of the circle

inscribed polygon a polygon whose vertices all lie on a circle in such a way that the sides of the polygon are chords of the circle

intercepted arc the arc (an arc) of a circle that is cut off in the interior of an angle (or related angle)

intercepts the points at which the graph of an equation intersects the axes

interior refers to all points that lie inside an enclosed (bounded) plane or solid figure

interior angle of polygon any angle formed by two consecutive sides of the polygon in such a way that the angle lies in the interior of the polygon

intersection the points that two geometric figures share

intuition drawing a conclusion through insight

inverse relative to the statement "If P, then Q," this statement has the form "If not P, then not Q"

isosceles trapezoid a trapezoid that has two congruent legs (its nonparallel sides)

isosceles triangle a triangle that has two congruent sides

kite a quadrilateral that has two distinct pairs of congruent adjacent sides

lateral area the sum of areas of the lateral faces of a solid or the area of the curved lateral surface, excluding the base area(s) (as in prisms, pyramids, cylinders, and cones)

legs of isosceles triangle the two congruent sides of the triangle

legs of right triangle the two sides that form the right angle of the triangle

legs of trapezoid the two nonparallel sides of the trapezoid

lemma a theorem that is introduced and proved so that a later theorem can be proved

line of centers the line (or line segment) that joins the centers of two circles

line segment the part of a line determined by two points and all points on the line that lie between those two points

locus the set of all points that satisfy a given condition or conditions

major arc an arc whose measure is between 180° and 360°

mean proportional *see* geometric mean

means of a proportion the second and third terms of a proportion; in $\frac{a}{b} = \frac{c}{d}$, b and c are the means

median of trapezoid the line segment that joins the midpoints of the two legs (nonparallel sides) of the trapezoid

median of triangle the line segment joining a vertex of the triangle to the midpoint of the opposite side

midpoint the point on a line segment (or arc) that separates the line segment (arc) into two congruent parts

minor arc an arc whose measure is between 0° and 180°

nonagon a polygon that has exactly nine sides

noncollinear points three or more points that do not lie on the same line

noncoplanar points four or more points that do not lie in the same plane

obtuse angle an angle whose measure is between 90° and 180°

obtuse triangle a triangle that has exactly one interior angle that is obtuse

octagon a polygon that has exactly eight sides

octahedron (regular) a polyhedron with eight congruent faces that are equilateral triangles

opposite rays two rays having a common endpoint and which together form a line

orthocenter of triangle the point of concurrence for the three altitudes of the triangle

parallel lines (planes) two lines in a plane (or two planes) that do not intersect

parallelogram a quadrilateral that has two pairs of parallel sides

parallelepiped a right rectangular prism; a box

pentagon a polygon that has exactly five sides

perimeter of polygon the sum of the lengths of the sides of the polygon

perpendicular bisector of line segment a line (or part of a line) that is both perpendicular to a given line segment and bisects that line segment

perpendicular lines two lines that intersect to form congruent adjacent angles

pi (π) the constant ratio of the circumference C of a circle to the length of its diameter, this ratio is commonly approximated by the fraction $\frac{22}{7}$ or the decimal 3.1416

point of tangency (contact) the point at which a tangent to a circle touches the circle

polygon a plane figure whose sides are line segments that intersect only at their endpoints

polyhedron a solid figure whose faces are polygons that intersect other faces along common sides of the polygons

postulate a statement that is assumed to be true

Quadratic Formula the formula $x = \frac{-b \pm \sqrt{b^2 - 4ac}}{2a}$, which provides solutions for the equation $ax^2 + bx + c = 0$, where a, b, and c are real numbers and $a \neq 0$

quadrilateral a polygon that has exactly four sides

radian the measure of a central angle of a circle whose intercepted arc has a length equal to the radius of the circle

radius the line segment that joins the center of a circle (or sphere) to any point on the circle (or sphere)

ratio a comparison between two quantities a and b, generally written $\frac{a}{b}$ or a:b

ray the part of a line that begins at a point and extends infinitely far in one direction

rectangle a parallelogram that contains a right angle

reflex angle an angle whose measure is between 180° and 360°

regular polygon a polygon whose sides are congruent and whose interior angles are congruent

regular polyhedron a polyhedron whose edges are congruent and whose faces are congruent

regular prism a right prism whose bases are regular polygons

regular pyramid a pyramid whose base is a regular polygon and whose lateral faces are congruent isosceles triangles

rhombus a parallelogram with two congruent adjacent sides

right angle an angle whose measure is exactly 90°

right circular cone a cone in which the line segment joining the vertex of the cone to the center of the circular base is perpendicular to the base

right circular cylinder a cylinder in which the line segment joining the centers of the circular bases is perpendicular to the plane of each base

right prism a prism in which lateral edges are perpendicular to the base edges that they intersect

right triangle a triangle in which exactly one interior angle is a right angle

scalene triangle a triangle in which no two sides are congruent

secant in a right triangle, the ratio $\frac{\text{hypotenuse}}{\text{adjacent}}$

secant of circle a line (or part of a line) that intersects a circle at two points

sector of circle the plane region bounded by two radii of the circle and the arc that is intercepted by the central angle formed by those radii

segment of circle the plane region bounded by a chord and a minor arc (major arc) that has the same endpoints as that chord

semicircle the arc of a circle determined by a diameter; an arc of a circle whose measure is exactly 180°

set any collection of objects, numbers, or points

similar polygons polygons that have the same shape

sine in a right triangle, the ratio $\frac{\text{opposite}}{\text{hypotenuse}}$

skew quadrilateral a quadrilateral whose sides do not all lie in one plane

slant height of cone any line segment joining the vertex of the cone to a point on the circular base

slant height of regular pyramid a line segment joining the vertex of the pyramid to the midpoint of a base edge of the pyramid

slope a measure of the steepness of a line; in the rectangular coordinate system, the slope m of the line through (x_1, y_1) and (x_2, y_2) is $m = \frac{y_2 - y_1}{x_2 - x_1}$ where $x_1 \neq x_2$

sphere the set of points in space that are at a fixed distance from a given point (the center of the sphere)

straight angle an angle whose measure is exactly 180°; an angle whose sides are opposite rays

straightedge an idealized instrument used to construct parts of lines

supplementary angles two angles whose sum of measures is 180°

surface area the measure of the total area of a solid; the sum of the lateral area and base area in many solid figures.

symmetry with respect to a line (ℓ) figure for which every point A has a second point B on the figure for which ℓ is the perpendicular bisector of $\overline{AB}$

symmetry with respect to a point (*P*) figure for which every point A has a second point C on the figure for which P is the midpoint of $\overline{AC}$.

tangent in a right triangle, the ratio $\frac{\text{opposite}}{\text{adjacent}}$

tangent circles two circles that have one point in common; the circles may be externally tangent or internally tangent

tangent line of circle a line (or part of a line) that touches a circle at only one point

tetrahedron (regular) a four-faced solid in which the faces are congruent equilateral triangles

theorem a statement that follows logically from previous definitions and principles; a statement that can be proved

torus a three-dimensional solid that has a "doughnut" shape

transversal a line that intersects two or more lines, intersecting each at one point

trapezoid a quadrilateral having exactly two parallel sides

triangle a polygon that has exactly three sides

triangle inequality a statement that the sum of the lengths of two sides of a triangle cannot be greater than the length of the third side

union the joining together of any two sets, such as geometric figures

valid argument an argument in which the conclusion follows logically from previously stated (and accepted) premises or assumptions

vertex angle of isosceles triangle the angle formed by the two congruent sides of the triangle

vertex of angle the point at which the two sides of the angle meet

vertex of isosceles triangle the point at which the two congruent sides of the triangle meet

vertex of polygon any point at which two sides of the polygon meet

vertex of polyhedron any point at which three edges of the polyhedron meet

vertical angles a pair of angles that lie in opposite positions when formed by two intersecting lines

volume the measurement, in cubic units, of the amount of space within a bounded region of space

Index

Abbreviations

AA	angle-angle (proves △s similar)
ASA	angle-side-angle (proves △s congruent)
AAS	angle-angle-side (proves △s congruent)
add.	addition
adj.	adjacent
alt.	altitude, alternate
ax.	axiom
CASTC	Corresponding angles of similar triangles are congruent.
cm	centimeters
cm^2	square centimeters
cm^3	cubic centimeters
comp.	complementary
corr.	corresponding
cos	cosine
cot	cotangent
CPCTC	Corresponding parts of congruent triangles are congruent.
csc	cosecant
CSSTP	Corresponding sides of similar triangles are proportional.
diag.	diagonal
eq.	equality
exs.	exercises
ext.	exterior
ft	foot (or feet)
gal	gallon
HL	hypotenuse-leg (proves △s congruent)
hr	hour
in.	inch (or inches)
ineq.	inequality
int.	interior
isos.	isosceles
km	kilometers
m	meters
mi	miles
mm	millimeters
n-gon	polygon of n sides
opp.	opposite
pent.	pentagon
post.	postulate
prop.	property
pt.	point
quad.	quadrilateral
rect.	rectangle
rt.	right
SAS	side-angle-side (proves △s congruent)
SAS~	side-angle-side (proves △s similar)
sec, sec.	secant, section
sin	sine
SSS	side-side-side (proves △s congruent)
SSS~	side-side-side (proves △s similar)
st.	straight
supp.	supplementary
tan	tangent
trans.	transversal
trap.	trapezoid
vert.	vertical (angle or line)
yd	yards